textile arts index
1950-1987

SELECTED **Weaving, Spinning, Dyeing, Knitting, Fiber** PERIODICALS

Sadye Tune Wilson
Ruth Davidson Jackson

Tunstede
Nashville, Tennessee

Library of Congress Catalogue Number: 88-72005
ISBN Number: 0-9616526-2-4

Manufactured in the United States of America

First Edition

Tunstede
212 Vaughn's Gap Road
Nashville, Tennessee 37205

To

Else Regensteiner---noted designer and teacher who was instrumental in helping to establish handweaving as an art.

CONTENTS

Key to Index...*x*

Subject Index...*1*

Author Index *813*

Acknowledgments

The publisher wishes to express appreciation to the publishers and editors of the selected journals for their allowing the indexing of the following publications in TEXTILE ARTS INDEX 1950-1987: Ralph Stanton and Janet Hoskins, <u>Ars Textrina</u>; Eleanor Best, <u>Complex Weavers</u>; Rob Pulleyn, <u>Fiberarts</u>; Linda C. Ligon, <u>Handwoven</u>, <u>Spin-Off</u>, and <u>Interweave</u>; Alexis Yiorgos Xenakis, <u>Knitters</u>, and <u>Prairie Wool Companion</u> (now <u>Weavers</u>); Robert Leclerc, <u>Master Weaver Library</u>; Jim and Lee Anderst, <u>Shuttle Craft Guild Monographs</u> and <u>Threads in Action Monographs</u>; Handweavers Guild of America, <u>Shuttle</u>, <u>Spindle</u>, & <u>Dyepot</u>; Patricia L. Fiske and Delores E. Fairbanks, <u>The Textile Museum Journal</u>; Paul Roman and John Kelsey, <u>Threads Magazine</u>; and, Karen Searle and Suzanne Baizerman, <u>Weaver's Journal</u>.

Sincere appreciation goes to family members, John Urban Wilson, William Howard Jackson, Nancy Tune Fitzgerald, and Leno E. Fitzgerald, for their unselfish help in the preparation of this index.

INDEX KEY

topics

subject

subject--assigned from article contents

title

title--recorded from article inside journal

author

author--name recorded from article inside journal

il

illustrations--include photographs, sketches, weave drafts, graphics

inst

instructions---
√ *used to indicate verbal instructions, graphic instructions, and weave drafts for four, or less, shafts*
>4 *used to indicate verbal instructions, graphic instructions, and weave drafts for more than four shafts*

jour

Journal---

AT	*Ars Textrina*
C W	*Complex Weavers*
Fa	*Fiberarts*
H&C	*Handweaver & Craftsman*
Hw	*Handwoven*
Iw	*Interweave*
Kn	*Knitters*
MWL	*Master Weaver Library*
PWC	*Prairie Wool Companion*
SCGM	*Shuttle Craft Guild Monograph*
S-O	*Spin-Off*
SS&D	*Shuttle, Spindle & Dyepot*
TIAM	*Threads In Action Monograph*
TM	*Threads Magazine*
TMJ	*The Textile Museum Journal*
W J	*Weaver's Journal*

vol

Volume---number

no

Number---within-year journal number

iss

Issue---number

date

Date---

Month	_Season_	_Bimonthly_
Ja---January	Sp---Spring	J/F---Jan/Feb
Fe---February	Su---Summer	M/A---March/April
Mr---March	Fa---Fall	M/J---May/June
Ap---April	Wi---Winter	J/A---July/Aug
My---May		S/O---Sept/Oct
Ju---June	S-S---Spring-Summer	N/D---Nov/Dec
Jy---July	S-F---Summer-Fall	D/J---Dec/Jan
Au---August	F-W---Fall-Winter	
Se---September	W-S---Winter-Spring	
Oc---October		
No---November		
De---December		

page

Page---
Number refers to _first_ page of article; number in
extremely long articles and in monographs refers to
subdivisions of total article or monograph

EXCLUSIONS------Events, Calendars, Directories, Exhibit Schedules,
Products and Equipment Reviews, News Items

subject index

SUBJECT	TITLE	AUTHOR	IL	INST	JOUR	VOL	NO	ISS	DATE	PAGE
Aaklae	Aaklae Weaving	Mundal, Maria	√	√	H&C	5	1		Wi 53	20
Aaklae	Rugs by an Architect		√	√	H&C	13	4		Fa 62	6
Abaca	Learning the Ropes: Abaca	Coffman, Charlotte	√	√	S-O	7	4		Wi 83	40
Abaca	Plant Fibers		√	√	WJ	8	2	30	Fa 83	67
Abaca	Survey of Leaf and Stem Fibers, A	Buchanan, Rita	√		S-O	10	3		Fa 86	24
Abbey of Regina Laudis	Abbey of Regina Laudis, O.S.B. from Notes of the Abbey Community		√		SS&D	16	3	63	Su 85	42
Aboriginal Textiles	String Bags	Nunn, Robin; Alan West	√	√	SS&D	14	2	54	Sp 83	10
Abstract Art/Textiles	Textiles and the Art of Kandinsky	Parks, Betty	√		Fa	9	4		J/A 82	11
Acadian Weaving	L'Amour de Maman: The Acadian Textile Heritage	Rossetter, Tabitha Wilson	√		Fa	8	3		M/J 81	29
Accession Records	Analysis and Documentation of Coverlets (error-corrected AT v3 85 p269)	Ulasewicz, Connie; Clarita Anderson; Steven M. Spivak	√	>4	AT	2			De 84	113
Accession Records	Table of Accession and Catalogue Numbers	Trilling, James			TMJ	21			82	110
Accessories and Novelties	Accessories: Bags and Slippers		√	√	WJ	5	3	19	Wi 81	42
Accessories and Novelties	Bags	Meiling, Nancy	√	√	WJ	6	3	23	Wi 81	40
Accessories and Novelties	Braided Twill Purse Organizer and Card Case (Sharon Alderman)		√	>4	Hw	5	1		J/F 84	49, 94
Accessories and Novelties	Calendar in Guatemalan Belt Weave (Evelyn Christensen)		√	√	Hw	7	2		M/A 86	69, I-14
Accessories and Novelties	Dress up Your Fall Wardrobe with These Two Autumn Accents		√		Hw	6	4		S/O 85	58
Accessories and Novelties	Evening Accents		√	√	Hw	8	4		S/O 87	54
Accessories and Novelties	Gift Needlebook		√	√	H&C	17	1		Wi 66	46
Accessories and Novelties	Idea Notebook: The Ultimate Brown Bag		√		Hw	7	4		S/O 86	36
Accessories and Novelties	Lee's Surrender — to Sachets	Xenakis, Alexis Yiorgos	√	√	Hw	1	2		S-S 80	18
Accessories and Novelties	Marketable Weed Holders	Lindbergh, Susie	√	√	SS&D	4	2	14	Sp 73	16
Accessories and Novelties	Needlework Tool Case	Reese, Sharron	√	√	S-O	10	3		Fa 86	21
Accessories and Novelties	Next to the Skin		√		SS&D	15	4	60	Fa 84	42
Accessories and Novelties	No More Hot Hands—A Handwoven Skillet Holder!		√	√	Hw	8	3		M/J 87	23
Accessories and Novelties	Noils Using Handspun Yarns	Conover, Jean	√		SS&D	12	1	45	Wi 80	63
Accessories and Novelties	Petit Point Glasses Case (Janice Jones)		√	√	Hw	7	1		J/F 86	66, I-12
Accessories and Novelties	Project by Guild Members		√	√	WJ	5	3	19	Wi 81	17
Accessories and Novelties	Scarf in Dornik Twill		√		Hw	6	5		N/D 85	42
Accessories and Novelties	Spindlemuff is a Mythical Beast, The	Seifert, Walter	√	√	H&C	24	2		M/A 73	36
Accessories and Novelties	Stylish No-Sew Hat	Anderson, Barbara	√	√	WJ	6	3	23	Wi 81	39
Accessories and Novelties	Uplifting, Creative, Expansive, Comfortable Baths		√	√	Hw	3	2		Mr 82	50
Accessories: Knitting	And a Necklace, Too	Upitis, Lizbeth	√	√	Kn	2	2	4	S-S 86	48
Accidental Drafts	Exploring the Textures: Accidental Weaves	Zielinski, S. A.; Robert Leclerc, ed.	√	>4	MWL	11			'51–'73	79
Acknowledgments	Two-Harness Textiles, The Open Work Weaves: Acknowledgments and Sources for Tools	Tidball, Harriet			SCGM		21		67	24
Addresses	Talk with Jack Lenor Larsen, A		√		SS&D	12	2	46	Sp 81	11
Adhesives: Textile, Use and Selection	Principles of Textile Conservation Science No. 12. Adhesives for Textile Conservation	Rice, James W.	√	√	TMJ	2	4		De 69	34
Adinkra Cloth	Adinkra: Weft African Textile of Pride	Rex, Chris	√		Fa	9	6		N/D 82	36
Adire Cloth	Learning to See Pattern	Morrison, Skye	√	√	TM			2	D/J 85	44
Adire Cloth	Wealth of Fiber: Nigeria's Adire Cloth , A	Ulrich, George	√		Fa	13	5		S/O 86	39
Advertising	Sales Brochures	LaLena, Constance	√	√	Hw	6	5		N/D 85	80

SUBJECT	TITLE	AUTHOR	IL	INST	JOUR	VOL	NO	ISS	DATE	PAGE
Afghanistan	Afghan Carpet Weavers		√		H&C	24	3		M/J 73	27
Afghanistan	Afghan Carpets	Spooner, Brian	√		SS&D	5	2	18	Sp 74	41
Afghanistan	Aid to Artisans	Cox-Chapman, Mally	√		TM			13	O/N 87	14
Afghanistan	Turkoman Yurt, The		√	√	SS&D	10	1	37	Wi 78	24
Afghans, Blankets, Throws	Afghan and Pillow Set	D'Ambrosio, Gina	√	√	S-O	11	2		Su 87	14
Afghans, Blankets, Throws	Afghans: Things to Consider and Finishes	Xenakis, Athanasios David	√	√	PWC	3	1	7		10
Afghans, Blankets, Throws	Baby Blanket		√	√	H&C	10	4		Fa 59	20
Afghans, Blankets, Throws	Baby Blanket	Ingebretsen, Cathy	√	√	PWC	3	1	7		6
Afghans, Blankets, Throws	Baby Blanket (Dian Stanley)		√	√	Hw	7	3		M/J 86	74, 91
Afghans, Blankets, Throws	Baby Blanket (Louise Bradley)		√	√	Hw	7	1		J/F 86	43, I-6
Afghans, Blankets, Throws	Baby Blanket (Margaretha Essén-Hedin)		√	> 4	Hw	8	2		M/A 87	45, I-7
Afghans, Blankets, Throws	Baby Blanket (Susan Ashley)		√	√	Hw	7	3		M/J 86	75
Afghans, Blankets, Throws	Baby Blanket with Light Blue Arrowpoint (Cat Brysch)		√	> 4	Hw	5	3		Su 84	50, 96
Afghans, Blankets, Throws	Baby Blanket with Pink Pattern Weave (Cat Brysch)		√	> 4	Hw	5	3		Su 84	50, 97
Afghans, Blankets, Throws	Baby's First Hang-Up	Gilbert, Donna Lee	√	√	SS&D	11	4	44	Fa 80	26
Afghans, Blankets, Throws	"Baltique Plaid" Throw (Morris Percelay)		√	√	Hw	4	5		N/D 83	53, 106
Afghans, Blankets, Throws	Beechwood Throw (Judy Steinkoenig)		√	√	Hw	5	2		M/A 84	58, 97
Afghans, Blankets, Throws	Blankets and Afghans on a Narrow Loom	Davenport, Betty	√	√	PWC	3	1	7		14
Afghans, Blankets, Throws	Blankets of New Mexico	Kozikowski, Janusz	√		SS&D	10	1	37	Wi 78	60
Afghans, Blankets, Throws	Bradbury Hit-and-Miss System	Bradbury, Mary Louise	√	√	SS&D	3	2	10	Sp 72	27
Afghans, Blankets, Throws	Bronson Lace Afghan (Judith Drumm)		√	√	Hw	3	2		Mr 82	59, 88
Afghans, Blankets, Throws	Brushed Mohair Throw (Halcyon)		√	√	Hw	4	4		S/O 83	59, 102
Afghans, Blankets, Throws	Canadian Weavers Design a Child's Cutter Rug		√	√	H&C	12	3		Su 61	15
Afghans, Blankets, Throws	Chilkat Blanket: It Soon May Be No More, The	Eggleston, Phyllis	√	√	SS&D	7	1	25	Wi 75	44
Afghans, Blankets, Throws	Chilkat Dancing Blanket, The	Samuel, Cheryl	√		SS&D	13	4	52	Fa 82	58
Afghans, Blankets, Throws	Chimayó—A Town of Weavers	Trujillo, Lisa Rockwood	√		WJ	11	1	41	Su 86	60
Afghans, Blankets, Throws	Christening Blanket	Nathans, Barbara	√	√	S-O	4		80		60
Afghans, Blankets, Throws	Chule: Freedom to Weave		√		Iw	4	4		Fa 79	47
Afghans, Blankets, Throws	Chule's Wool Creations	Carter, Dianne	√		SS&D	17	4	68	Fa 86	30
Afghans, Blankets, Throws	Cloud and Sky Brushed Afghan (Jean Scorgie)		√	√	Hw	7	1		J/F 86	I-7
Afghans, Blankets, Throws	Contemporary Overshot Afghan (Lee-lee Schlegel)		√	√	Hw	3	3		My 82	29, 89
Afghans, Blankets, Throws	Cotton Lap Robe (Janice Jones)		√	> 4	Hw	7	1		J/F 86	42, I-5
Afghans, Blankets, Throws	Country Casual Afghan (Morris Percelay)		√	√	Hw	3	3		My 82	29, 88
Afghans, Blankets, Throws	Cozy Afghan, A	Beetem, Debra	√	√	S-O	10	4		Wi 86	13
Afghans, Blankets, Throws	Crib Cover with Diamonds and X's (Cat Brysch)		√	> 4	Hw	5	3		Su 84	50, 96
Afghans, Blankets, Throws	Dhabla Weaving in India	De Bone, Mary	√	√	SS&D	8	3	31	Su 77	9
Afghans, Blankets, Throws	Double Corduroy	Lyon, Linda	√	√	PWC	3	1	7		51
Afghans, Blankets, Throws	Double Tartan	Xenakis, Athanasios David	√	> 4	PWC	3	1	7		42
Afghans, Blankets, Throws	Double Weave: Plain and Patterned: A Double-fold Blanket Weave by Mary Atwater, The	Tidball, Harriet	√	√	SCGM		1		60	26
Afghans, Blankets, Throws	Double Weave: Plain and Patterned: An Unusual Double Weave Blanket, The	Tidball, Harriet	√	> 4	SCGM		1		60	32
Afghans, Blankets, Throws	Doup Leno (error-corrected WJ v3 n2 78 insert p38a)		√	√	WJ	3	2	10	Oc 78	32
Afghans, Blankets, Throws	Each One Picked a Color—4th and 5th Graders Weave a Blanket	Hanna, Linda	√		WJ	9	1	33	Su 84	34
Afghans, Blankets, Throws	Easy Striped Knits	Walker, Barbara G.	√	√	TM			4	A/M 86	54

SUBJECT	TITLE	AUTHOR	IL	INST	JOUR	VOL	NO	ISS	DATE	PAGE
Afghans, Blankets, Throws	Fantastic Finnweave, Part 3	Xenakis, Athanasios David	√	>4	PWC			4	Ja 83	12
Afghans, Blankets, Throws	Fiesta Plaid	Xenakis, Athanasios David	√	√	PWC	3	1	7		39
Afghans, Blankets, Throws	Fireside Throw and Pillow (Betty Davenport)		√	√	Hw	8	1		J/F 87	72, I-13
Afghans, Blankets, Throws	Folk Textiles of Latin America	Kelemen, Pál	√		TMJ	1	4		De 65	2
Afghans, Blankets, Throws	Four-Block Double Weave on Four Shafts	Barrett, Clotilde	√	√	WJ	8	1	29	Su 83	72
Afghans, Blankets, Throws	Fullus: Ikat Blankets of Tarabuco, Bolivia	Meisch, Lynn A.	√	√	WJ	10	1	37	Su 85	54
Afghans, Blankets, Throws	Green Plaid Blanket or Scarf (Diane Tramba)		√	>4	Hw	2	1		F-W 80	27, 64
Afghans, Blankets, Throws	Guatemala Visited	Atwater, Mary Meigs	√	√	SCGM		15		65	24
Afghans, Blankets, Throws	Guatemala Visited	Atwater, Mary Meigs	√	√	SCGM		15		65	14
Afghans, Blankets, Throws	Halfghan	Xenakis, Athanasios David	√	√	PWC	3	1	7		34
Afghans, Blankets, Throws	Handspun Ikat	Bradley, Louise	√	√	Hw	2	4		Se 81	65
Afghans, Blankets, Throws	Home Weaving: A Happy Plaid (Halcyon)		√	√	Hw	1	1		F-W 79	40
Afghans, Blankets, Throws	Incredible Five-Color, Two-Tie Afghan for a Super Kid, The	Xenakis, Athanasios David	√	√	PWC	1	1		No 81	35
Afghans, Blankets, Throws	Keep Warm! Woolen Throw	Barrett, Clotilde	√	>4	WJ	5	2	18	Fa 80	14
Afghans, Blankets, Throws	Killarney	Xenakis, Athanasios David	√	>4	PWC	3	1	7		25
Afghans, Blankets, Throws	Lavender Luxury Afghan (Halcyon Schomp)		√	√	Hw	6	1		J/F 85	Cover, I-4
Afghans, Blankets, Throws	Loom Controlled Quilted Fabrics	Bardwell, Kathryn	√	√	WJ	7	1	25	Su 82	39
Afghans, Blankets, Throws	MacCallum Tartan Afghan (Jane Merryman)		√	√	Hw	4	5		N/D 83	Cover, 96
Afghans, Blankets, Throws	Macro Plaid, Macro Twill	Xenakis, Athanasios David	√	>4	PWC	3	1	7		55
Afghans, Blankets, Throws	Magnified Twill Throw (Sharon Alderman)		√	√	Hw	6	5		N/D 85	53, I-12
Afghans, Blankets, Throws	Man-Made Fibers: Baby Blankets		√	√	WJ	5	2	18	Fa 80	43
Afghans, Blankets, Throws	Michigan Weaving, Third Conference at Hartland Shows Wide Variety		√	√	H&C	13	1		Wi 62	18
Afghans, Blankets, Throws	Mohair Afghan/Great Shawl	Chastant, Kathryn Ross	√	√	S-O	6	4		82	57
Afghans, Blankets, Throws	Monk's Belt Lap Robe (Louise Bradley)		√	√	Hw	8	5		N/D 87	56, I-14
Afghans, Blankets, Throws	More About Fabrics: Practical Projects for Basket and Twill	Zielinski, S. A.; Robert Leclerc, ed.	√	√	MWL	20			'51–'73	38
Afghans, Blankets, Throws	National Spinning & Weaving Week, 1982: "A Blanket of Joy"		√		Hw	3	3		My 82	28
Afghans, Blankets, Throws	Natural Colors Wool Throw (Sharon Alderman)		√	√	Hw	2	1		F-W 80	Cover, 65
Afghans, Blankets, Throws	Navajo: Textiles, Blankets, Rugs, Tapestries	Morrow, Mable	√	√	SS&D	1	4	4	Se 70	3
Afghans, Blankets, Throws	Navajo: Textiles, Blankets, Rugs, Tapestries	Morrow, Mable	√	√	SS&D	2	1	5	De 70	5
Afghans, Blankets, Throws	New England Weavers' Seminar		√		H&C	18	4		Fa 67	14
Afghans, Blankets, Throws	New Look At Crochet, A	Lep, Annette	√		TM			9	F/M 87	86
Afghans, Blankets, Throws	Nineteenth Century Miniatures	Erf, Mary Elva Congleton	√		SS&D	16	1	61	Wi 84	60
Afghans, Blankets, Throws	Norse Kjøkken	Rowley, Elaine	√	√	PWC	3	1	7		16
Afghans, Blankets, Throws	Notebook: Baby Blankets and Afghans	Myers, Ruth Nordquist, ed.	√	>4	SS&D	12	4	48	Fa 81	50
Afghans, Blankets, Throws	Notebook:"Someday" File, The (Jeanean Middlebrooks)	Myers, Ruth Nordquist, ed.	√	>4	SS&D	15	3	59	Su 84	66
Afghans, Blankets, Throws	Pastel Throw and Pillow (Halcyon Schomp)		√	√	Hw	8	1		J/F 87	74, I-15
Afghans, Blankets, Throws	Patchwork Designs in Summer and Winter	Davenport, Betty	√	√	PWC	1	1		No 81	27
Afghans, Blankets, Throws	Peaches and Cream Bouclé Throw (Halcyon)		√	√	Hw	4	4		S/O 83	62, 108
Afghans, Blankets, Throws	Plaid Afghan (Lynette Theodore)		√	√	Hw	6	5		N/D 85	58

SUBJECT	TITLE	AUTHOR	IL	INST	JOUR	VOL	NO	ISS	DATE	PAGE
Afghans, Blankets, Throws	Plaid Blanket and Pillow (Margaretha Essén-Hedin)		√	>4	Hw	8	1		J/F 87	71, I-14
Afghans, Blankets, Throws	Plaid Blanket (Linda Ligon)		√	√	Hw	3	5		N/D 82	54, 96
Afghans, Blankets, Throws	Prism Pleasure Blanket (Hector Jaeger)		√	√	Hw	6	3		Su 85	58, I-13
Afghans, Blankets, Throws	Quilted Double Woven Baby Blanket, A		√	>4	H&C	10	1		Wi 59	13
Afghans, Blankets, Throws	Ramah Navajo Weavers, The	D'Andrea, Pat	√		WJ	12	1	45	Su 87	44
Afghans, Blankets, Throws	Red and Blue Canvas Weave Afghan	Xenakis, Athanasios David	√	√	PWC	3	1	7		22
Afghans, Blankets, Throws	Ribbon Afghan and Bed Cape (Chris Switzer)		√	√	Hw	1	2		S-S 80	37, 59
Afghans, Blankets, Throws	Rustic Roundel	Lyon, Linda; Athanasios David Xenakis	√	>4	PWC	3	1	7		36
Afghans, Blankets, Throws	S&W Wrapper	Sullivan, Donna	√	√	SS&D	15	1	57	Wi 83	24
Afghans, Blankets, Throws	Salish Weaving	Boxberger, Daniel L.	√		SS&D	13	4	52	Fa 82	30
Afghans, Blankets, Throws	Shades of Fall Lap Robe (Leslie Voiers)		√	√	Hw	5	4		S/O 84	71, 106
Afghans, Blankets, Throws	Sherbet Throw (Kay Hatthorn)		√	√	Hw	2	4		Se 81	52
Afghans, Blankets, Throws	Shimmering Pastel Blanket (Leslie Voiers)		√	√	Hw	7	1		J/F 86	41, I-4
Afghans, Blankets, Throws	Soft Cotton Baby Blanket	Wendler, Maxine	√	√	WJ	7	4	28	Sp 83	80
Afghans, Blankets, Throws	Soft & Cozy: Cotton Receiving Blankets	White, Jamie Leigh	√	√	WJ	11	2	42	Fa 86	34
Afghans, Blankets, Throws	Soft Pink Throw, A	Keeler, Betty	√	√	S-O	8	4		Wi 84	31
Afghans, Blankets, Throws	Spring Blanket (Halcyon)		√	√	Hw	1	2		S-S 80	37, 57
Afghans, Blankets, Throws	Sunny Skies Picnic Blanket (Halcyon Schomp and Hector Jaeger)		√	√	Hw	5	3		Su 84	69, 106
Afghans, Blankets, Throws	Three-Toned Blocks: Further Explorations with Long-Eyed Heddles	Broughton, Eve T.	√	>4	WJ	9	4	36	Sp 85	72
Afghans, Blankets, Throws	Traditional Berber Weaving in Central Morocco	Forelli, Sally; Jeanette Harries	√		TMJ	4	4		77	41
Afghans, Blankets, Throws	twill ^ 2 = Double Width Afghans	Guy, Sallie T.	√	>4	SS&D	15	1	57	Wi 83	34
Afghans, Blankets, Throws	Two Blankets: A Blanket for Baby Gregory	Smith, Kenneth Loyal	√		S-O	10	1		Sp 86	22
Afghans, Blankets, Throws	Two Blankets: Feather and Fan	Irwin, Marjorie	√		S-O	10	1		Sp 86	22
Afghans, Blankets, Throws	Two Pastel Throws (Sharon Alderman)		√	√	Hw	3	4		Se 82	34, 82
Afghans, Blankets, Throws	Using Unplanned Yarn in a Planned Project	Chandler, Deborah	√		Hw	8	2		M/A 87	24
Afghans, Blankets, Throws	Versatility of Four-shaft Twill, The		√	√	WJ	8	3	31	Wi 83	82
Afghans, Blankets, Throws	Vertical Loom (continued) Part 2, The Two-Beam Loom, The		√	√	WJ	2	1	5	Jy 77	8
Afghans, Blankets, Throws	Victorian Garden (error-corrected PWC i8 p66)	Xenakis, Athanasios David	√	√	PWC	3	1	7		31
Afghans, Blankets, Throws	Waffle Weave Throw (Hector Jaeger)		√	√	Hw	6	5		N/D 85	54, I-13
Afghans, Blankets, Throws	Weaving Primer	Parks, Deborah	√	√	PWC	4	2	12		36
Afghans, Blankets, Throws	White Crib Blanket (Linda Ligon)		√	√	Hw	3	5		N/D 82	47, 86
Afghans, Blankets, Throws	Window Pane Delivery Blanket	Mueller, Cynthia	√	√	PWC	3	1	7		8
Afghans, Blankets, Throws	Winter Warmer	Winther, Doris Aino B.	√	√	SS&D	15	1	57	Wi 83	27
Afghans, Blankets, Throws	Winter Wrap-Ups Revisited	Deschaines, Sybil	√	>4	SS&D	16	1	61	Wi 84	26
Afghans, Blankets, Throws	Wool and Mohair Throw (Pat Sheret)		√	√	Hw	6	5		N/D 85	59
Afghans, Blankets, Throws	Wool Blanket	Goony, Elaine	√	√	S-O	6	4		82	62
Afghans, Blankets, Throws	Wool from the Welsh Valleys	Rowe, Dilys	√		H&C	10	2		Sp 59	30
Afghans, Blankets, Throws	Wooly Afghan in Summer and Winter Pile Techniques	Champion, Ellen	√	√	WJ	4	4	16	Ap 80	14
Afghans, Blankets, Throws	Wooly Wrap-Up Throw (Susan Snover)		√	√	Hw	6	1		J/F 85	63, I-3
Afghans, Blankets, Throws	Wrap Up Your Warp	Voiers, Leslie	√	>4	SS&D	18	1	69	Wi 86	49
Africa	Adinkra: Weft African Textile of Pride	Rex, Chris	√		Fa	9	6		N/D 82	36
Africa	Africa Inspires A Weaver	Gawne, Arlene	√		SS&D	16	3	63	Su 85	46
Africa	African American Thread Fare	White, Marcia	√		Fa	9	6		N/D 82	56
Africa	African Artist in a Dying Trade, An	Kessler, Cristina	√	√	Fa	11	6		N/D 84	51

SUBJECT	TITLE	AUTHOR	IL	INST	JOUR	VOL	NO	ISS	DATE	PAGE
Africa	African Motifs, Interpreted by Jack Lenore Larsen in His Newest Fabrics		√		H&C	14	2		Sp 63	6
Africa	African Textiles	Hempel, Toby Anne	√		SS&D	15	1	57	Wi 83	12
Africa	African Textiles	Sieber, Roy	√		H&C	23	6		N/D 72	9
Africa	American Sojourn of African Textiles, An	Lonier, Terri	√		Fa	11	1		J/F 84	66
Africa	Ancient Awakenings		√		Hw	5	4		S/O 84	51
Africa	"Art of African Masquerade, The" (Exhibit)	Dyer, Carolyn Price	√		Fa	13	3		M/J 86	56
Africa	"Arts of Ghana" (Exhibit)	Dyer, Carolyn	√		Fa	5	1		J/F 78	19
Africa	Bit of Rope Turns Cloth Into a Dancer's Costume, A	Grace, Leslie	√		TM			10	A/M 87	20
Africa	Easily Constructed Loom from Africa, An	Kren, Margo	√	√	SS&D	7	3	27	Su 76	19
Africa	High-Status Caps of the Kongo and Mbundu Peoples	Gibson, Gordon D.; Cecilia R. McGurk	√		TMJ	4	4		77	71
Africa	Jacket Inspired by West African Narrow Strip Weaving	Bradley, Louise	√	√	WJ	5	3	19	Wi 81	31
Africa	Kente on Four Harnesses	McCarthy, Catherine L.	√	√	SS&D	16	3	63	Su 85	6
Africa	Kente: The Status Cloth of Ghana	Conklin, Sharon L.	√	√	SS&D	8	1	29	WI 76	18
Africa	Learning to See Pattern	Morrison, Skye	√	√	TM			2	D/J 85	44
Africa	My African Shirt	Linder, Harry	√		Iw	1	4		Su 76	8
Africa	Pelete Bite: Kalabari Cut-Thread Cloth	Thieme, Otto Charles	√		Fa	10	5		S/O 83	46
Africa	Wealth of Fiber: Nigeria's Adire Cloth, A	Ulrich, George	√		Fa	13	5		S/O 86	39
Africa	Wearable Coils: Nigerian Hair Sculpture	Rosen, Norma	√		Fa	12	4		J/A 85	33
Africa	Weaving in Africa	Cragholm, Lynn	√		H&C	23	1		J/F 72	18
Africa	Zamani Soweto Sisters: A Patchwork of Lives		√		Fa	10	2		M/A 83	48
Africa	Zulu Baskets		√		Fa	9	3		M/J 82	21
Africa, South	Spinning Mohair in Lesotho	Snieckus, Mary Ann	√		TM			8	D/J 86	66
Africa, West	Medieval Textiles from the Tellem Caves in Central Mali, West Africa	Bedaux, Rogier M. A.; Rita Bolland	√		TMJ	19 20			80,81	65
Agave	Plant Fibers		√	√	WJ	8	2	30	Fa 83	67
Agave	Survey of Leaf and Stem Fibers, A	Buchanan, Rita	√		S-O	10	3		Fa 86	24
Aid Programs: Aid to Artisans	Aid to Artisans	Cox-Chapman, Mally	√		TM			13	O/N 87	14
Aid Programs: Save the Children	Aid to Artisans	Cox-Chapman, Mally	√		TM			13	O/N 87	14
Airbrush	Jeff Glenn: Software for a High-Tech World	Poon, Vivian	√		Fa	12	4		J/A 85	9
Airbrush	Just Playing in Space: Ann McKenzie Nickolson's Textile Artwork	Koplos, Janet	√		Fa	8	2		M/A 81	34
Airbrush	Wear an Original Painting: Melody Weiler's Airbrushed Shirtscapes	Speight, Jerry	√	√	Fa	8	1		J/F 81	13
Airbrush Technique	Funeral	Knauer, Katherine	√		Fa	13	6		N/D 86	30
Akwete	Art and Tradition of Akwete Weaving, The	Lambrecht, Dora J.	√		SS&D	9	2	34	Sp 78	33
Alaga (Variegated)	Original Fabrics of Kaftan, The	El-Homossani, M. M.	√	> 4	AT	1			De 83	263
Alaska	Arctic Adventures with Qiviut	Hudson, Marjorie; Kathy Sparks	√	√	S-O	11	3		Fa 87	47
Alaska	Fishperson's Earflap Hat	Sherrodd, Kristie	√	√	S-O	11	3		Fa 87	53
Alaska	"Innerskins/Outerskins: Gut and Fishskin" (Exhibit)		√		TM			14	D/J 87	20
Alaska	Keeping Warm in Alaska		√		Fa	9	6		N/D 82	22
Alaska	Patricia Bulitt: Gutsongs and Other Dances	Scarborough, Jessica	√		Fa	11	5		S/O 84	50
Alaska	Spinning in a Special Climate	Allen, Marian			S-O	11	3		Fa 87	50
Alaska	Weaving in Alaska	Fohn-Hansen, Lydia	√		H&C	4	3		Su 53	27
Alkanet Root	Alkanet	Gerber, Frederick		√	Iw	5	3		Su 80	66
Alpaca	Alpaca in the Raw	Asman, Ann	√		S-O	9	2		Su 85	24
Alpaca	Classic Alpaca Sweater, A (error-corrected S-O v9 n2 85 p61)	Reynolds, Donna	√	√	S-O	9	1		Sp 85	24

SUBJECT	TITLE	AUTHOR	IL	INST	JOUR	VOL	NO	ISS	DATE	PAGE
Alpaca	Closer Look at Alpacas, A	Zorn, Elayne; Juan Cutipa Colque	√		S-O	9	2		Su 85	21
Alpaca	Fiber Foray: Spinning Combed Alpaca	Quinn, Celia	√	√	S-O	9	1		Sp 85	26
Alpaca	Indian Textiles from Ecuador		√		H&C	10	1		Wi 59	19
Alpaca	Spinners of Chijnaya, Alpaca Yarns from Peruvian Village	Cloney, Gordon	√		H&C	16	4		Fa 65	15
Alpaca	Weaving with Handspun Alpaca	Anderson, J.	√		H&C	17	2		Sp 66	20
Alphabets: Woven	Alphabet Soup	Chandler, Deborah	√	>4	Hw	8	5		N/D 87	90
Althorp Coat	Ravensthorpe: A Festival of Wool	Walker, Pauline; Carol Taylor	√		S-O	7	2		Su 83	17
American Craft Council	Art/Culture/Future: American Craft '86	Giles, Lynne	√		Hw	7	5		N/D 86	91
American Craft Council	Look at the American Crafts Council, A		√		Hw	8	2		M/A 87	79
Amish	Quilting Bee Among the Amish, A	Fox, Judy Kellar	√		TM			4	A/M 86	12
Amish Clothing	Costume of a Plain People, The	Schiess, Kate	√	√	TM			5	J/J 86	65
Amplification, Sound	Judit Kele: The Sound of the Way It Feels	Colton, Sarah	√		Fa	14	3		M/J 87	42
Analysis: Cloth	Drafting 101: Literacy in Weaving, Part 2	Redding, Debbie	√	√	Hw	4	1		J/F 83	24
Analysis, Comparative: Basketry/Weaving	Technology of Basketry: North American Roots and Relations to Cloth, The	Turnbaugh, Sarah Peabody	√	√	SS&D	8	1	29	WI 76	32
Analysis, Comparative: Batik and Ikat	Additions to the Indonesian Collection	Gittinger, Mattiebelle S.	√		TMJ	4	3		76	43
Analysis, Comparative: Coptic Textiles	Coptic Tapestry of Byzantine Style, A	Berliner, Rudolf	√		TMJ	1	1		No 62	3
Analysis, Comparative: Figured Silks	Newly Excavated Caftan from the Northern Caucasus, A	Riboud, Krishna	√		TMJ	4	3		76	21
Analysis, Comparative: Openwork, Weft-Wrapped, Mexico	Weft-Wrap Openwork Techniques in Archaeological and Contemporary Textiles of Mexico	Johnson, Irmgard Weitlaner	√	√	TMJ	4	3		76	63
Analysis, Comparative: Ottoman and Kashan Carpets	Gifts from Kashan to Cairo	Ellis, Charles Grant	√		TMJ	1	1		No 62	33
Analysis Comparative: Star and Diamond Drafts	Analysis of Star and Diamond Weave Structures, An (error-corrected SS&D v10 n1 78 p101)	Anderson, Clarita; Judith Gordon; Naomi Whiting Towner	√	>4	SS&D	9	4	36	Fa 78	71
Analysis, Comparative: Tapestry Roundels, Coptic	Horsemen in Tapestry Roundels Found in Egypt	Berliner, Rudolf	√		TMJ	1	2		De 63	39
Analysis, Comparative: Weaving, Mexico/Guatemala	Textiles and Looms from Guatemala & Mexico	Grossman, Ellin F.	√		H&C	7	1		Wi 55	6
Analysis, Comparative: Work Practices	Identifying Hands at Work on a Paracas Mantle	Paul, Anne; Susan A. Niles	√		TMJ	23			84	5
Analysis, Comparative: Worker Skills	Identifying Hands at Work on a Paracas Mantle	Paul, Anne; Susan A. Niles	√		TMJ	23			84	5
Analysis: Counterpane Fabrics and Construction	Anatomy of a Quilted Counterpane (page revised WJ v9 n1 84 p70)	Adrosko, Rita J.	√		WJ	8	4	32	Sp 84	42
Analysis: Coverlets, Technique	Analysis and Documentation of Coverlets (error-corrected AT v3 85 p269)	Ulasewicz, Connie; Clarita Anderson; Steven M. Spivak	√	>4	AT	2			De 84	113
Analysis, Cross Section: Two-Warp Fabrics	Double Weaves: Two-Warp Fabrics	Zielinski, S. A.; Robert Leclerc, ed.	√	√	MWL	15			'51–'73	16
Analysis, Cross Section: Two-Warp Weaves	Double Weaves: Two-Warp Weaves	Zielinski, S. A.; Robert Leclerc, ed.	√	√	MWL	15			'51–'73	17
Analysis: Design, Computer-Aided	Computer-Aided Design Analysis	Poague, Susan	√		WJ	11	4	44	Sp 87	8
Analysis: Fabric	Analysis Based on Warp Threads	Howard, Margaret	√	√	SS&D	3	2	10	Sp 72	15
Analysis, Fabric	Blocks and Profiles	Carey, Joyce Marquess	√	√	WJ	7	2	26	Fa 82	33
Analysis: Fabric	Chinese Drawloom: A Study in Weave Structure, The	Sellin, Helen	√	>4	WJ	9	2	34	Fa 84	6
Analysis: Fabric	Cloth Analysis — The Draft from the Fabric	Frey, Berta	√	√	H&C	2	4		Fa 51	11
Analysis: Fabric	Creative Drafting and Analysis: Analysis of Fabrics	Zielinski, S. A.; Robert Leclerc, ed.	√	√	MWL	3			'51–'73	81
Analysis: Fabric	Creative Weave Drafting, Scandinavian Style	Snow, Jean Brooker	√	>4	SS&D	17	4	68	Fa 86	61
Analysis: Fabric	Custom Fabrics for a Classic Cadillac	Kelly, Jacquie	√	>4	WJ	10	4	40	Sp 86	54

SUBJECT	TITLE	AUTHOR	IL	INST	JOUR	VOL	NO	ISS	DATE	PAGE
Analysis: Fabric	Discerning the Pattern	Keasby, Doramay	√	√	SS&D	7	2	26	Sp 76	84
Analysis: Fabric	Fabric Analysis	Hausner, Walter	√		H&C	23	1		J/F 72	12
Analysis: Fabric	Fabric Analysis	Strickler, Carol	√		Hw	6	5		N/D 85	83
Analysis: Fabric	Huckaback Lace, A Study of Fabric Structure	Needham, Bertha B.	√	>4	H&C	12	3		Su 61	26
Analysis: Fabric	Pattern Analysis	Gallagher, Constance D.	√	√	H&C	19	4		Fa 68	6
Analysis: Fabric	Qotny & Alaga: Traditional Striped Fabrics for the Middle Eastern Kaftan	El-Homossani, M. M.	√	>4	WJ	10	1	37	Su 85	33
Analysis: Fabric	Summer and Winter and Other Two-Tie Unit Weaves: Taking a Draft from a Textile	Tidball, Harriet	√	>4	SCGM		19		66	15
Analysis: Fabric	Textile Structure and Analysis, A Home Study Course in Twelve Lessons: Lessons in Weave Structure, 12. Analysis, Fabric	Tidball, Harriet	√		SCGM		18		66	30
Analysis: Fabric	Very Basics of Weaving Drafting: Two and Three Shafts, The	Carey, Joyce Marquess	√	√	WJ	6	2	22	Fa 81	50
Analysis: Fabric	Weave Analysis	Carey, Joyce Marquess	√	>4	WJ	7	1	25	Su 82	45
Analysis: Fabric	What is Fabric Analysis?	Kessenich, Loraine	√	√	H&C	18	1		Wi 67	15
Analysis: Fabric, Commercial	On Analyzing Commercial Fabrics	Gordon, Judith	√	√	Hw	6	2		M/A 85	89
Analysis: Fabric, Computer-Aided	Fabric Analysis	Strickler, Carol	√		Hw	6	5		N/D 85	83
Analysis: Fabric, Computerized	Computerized Fabric Analysis (error-corrected SS&D v14 n2 83 p4)	Hoskins, Janet A.	√	√	SS&D	14	1	53	Wi 82	26
Analysis: Fabric, Draw-Down	Creative Drafting and Analysis: Analysis Developed - 1	Zielinski, S. A.; Robert Leclerc, ed.	√	√	MWL	3			'51–'73	97
Analysis: Fabric, European Shawls	Woven Structures of European Shawls in The Textile Museum Collection, The	Rowe, Ann Pollard			TMJ	24			85	55
Analysis: Fabric, Importance	Textile Structure and Analysis, A Home Study Course in Twelve Lessons: Textile Structure and Analysis	Tidball, Harriet			SCGM		18		66	1
Analysis: Fabric, Kashmir Shawls	Catalogue of Kashmir Shawls in The Textile Museum	Mikosch, Elisabeth	√		TMJ	24			85	23
Analysis: Fabric, Overshot	Creative Drafting and Analysis: Analysis of Overshot	Zielinski, S. A.; Robert Leclerc, ed.	√	√	MWL	3			'51–'73	116
Analysis: Fabric, Profile Pattern	Creative Drafting and Analysis: Analysis Developed - 4	Zielinski, S. A.; Robert Leclerc, ed.	√	√	MWL	3			'51–'73	107
Analysis: Fabric, Technique	Textile Structure and Analysis, A Home Study Course in Twelve Lessons: Textile Analysis	Tidball, Harriet	√	>4	SCGM		18		66	18
Analysis: Fabric, Threading	Creative Drafting and Analysis: Analysis Developed - 2	Zielinski, S. A.; Robert Leclerc, ed.	√	√	MWL	3			'51–'73	101
Analysis: Fabric, Threading Rearranging	Creative Drafting and Analysis: Analysis Developed - 3	Zielinski, S. A.; Robert Leclerc, ed.	√	√	MWL	3			'51–'73	104
Analysis: Fabric, Tie-Up	Creative Drafting and Analysis: Analysis Developed - 2	Zielinski, S. A.; Robert Leclerc, ed.	√	√	MWL	3			'51–'73	103
Analysis: Fabric, Treadling	Creative Drafting and Analysis: Analysis Developed - 2	Zielinski, S. A.; Robert Leclerc, ed.	√	√	MWL	3			'51–'73	102
Analysis: Fabric, Treadling, Rearranging	Creative Drafting and Analysis: Analysis Developed - 3	Zielinski, S. A.; Robert Leclerc, ed.	√	√	MWL	3			'51–'73	104
Analysis: Fabric, Twill, Diamond	Fascination of Twills (Fourshafts): Diamond Twill Analysis	Zielinski, S. A.; Robert Leclerc, ed.	√	√	MWL	9			'51–'73	99
Analysis: Fabric, Twill Patterns	Creative Drafting and Analysis: Analysis of Pattern Twills - 1	Zielinski, S. A.; Robert Leclerc, ed.	√	>4	MWL	3			'51–'73	110
Analysis: Fabric, Twill Patterns, Complex Diagonals	Creative Drafting and Analysis: Analysis of Pattern Twills - 2	Zielinski, S. A.; Robert Leclerc, ed.	√	>4	MWL	3			'51–'73	113
Analysis, Fiber: Microanalysis	Fiber Analysis: The Thread of Fate	Porter, John	√		Fa	9	4		J/A 82	49
Analysis: Pattern	Treasury for Beginners: Analysis of Patterns	Zielinski, S. A.; Robert Leclerc, ed.	√	√	MWL	1			'51–'73	56
Analysis: Pattern, Bronson	Treasury for Beginners: Analysis of Patterns	Zielinski, S. A.; Robert Leclerc, ed.	√	√	MWL	1			'51–'73	61
Analysis: Pattern, Overshot	Treasury for Beginners: Analysis of Patterns	Zielinski, S. A.; Robert Leclerc, ed.	√	√	MWL	1			'51–'73	59
Analysis: Pattern, Twill, Diamond	Treasury for Beginners: Analysis of Patterns	Zielinski, S. A.; Robert Leclerc, ed.	√	√	MWL	1			'51–'73	57

SUBJECT	TITLE	AUTHOR	IL	INST	JOUR	VOL	NO	ISS	DATE	PAGE
Analysis: Pattern Weaves	Creative Drafting and Analysis: Analysis of Patterns	Zielinski, S. A.; Robert Leclerc, ed.	√	> 4	MWL	3			'51–'73	85
Analysis: Pigment, X-Ray Fluoroscent Analyzer	Where Did All the Silver Go? Identifying Eighteenth-Century Chinese Painted and Printed Silks	Lee-Whitman, Leanna; Maruta Skelton	√		TMJ	22			83	33
Analysis: Potsherds, Fabric Impressions	Prehistoric Textiles Revealed by Potsherds	Kuttruff, Jenna Tedrick	√		SS&D	11	3	43	Su 80	40
Analysis: Public Fiber	Fabric Analysis "On the Road"	Drooker, P. B.	√		CW	5	2	14	Ja 84	6
Analysis: Twill, Patterned	Fascination of Twills (Multishafts): Analysis of Pattern Twills	Zielinski, S. A.; Robert Leclerc, ed.	√	> 4	MWL	10			'51–'73	84
Analysis: Yarn	Creative Drafting and Analysis: Analysis of Yarns	Zielinski, S. A.; Robert Leclerc, ed.		√	MWL	3			'51–'73	92
Analysis: Yarn	Fabric Analysis	Hausner, Walter	√		H&C	23	1		J/F 72	12
Analysis: Yarn	Yarns and Fibers: Analysis of Yarns	Zielinski, S. A.; Robert Leclerc, ed.		√	MWL	4			'51–'73	109
Anatolia	Carpet-Makers of Western Anatolia, 1750–1914, The	Quataert, Donald			TMJ	25			86	25
Anatolia	"Flowers of the Yayla: Yoruk Weaving of the Toros Mountains" (Exhibit)	Bloom, Mary Jane	√		Fa	11	3		M/J 84	76
Anatolia	Some Weft-Float Brocaded Rugs of the Bergama-Ezine Region	Beattie, May H.	√		TMJ	3	2		De 71	20
Ancient Baskets	Ring Basket of the Anasazi, The	Turnbaugh, Sarah Peabody	√		SS&D	9	1	33	Wi 77	101
Ancient Records: Handbook, Silk Trade, Roman Empire	Some Early Silk Finds in Northwest Europe	Wild, John-Peter	√		TMJ	23			84	17
Ancient Textiles	Problem of Twist, A	Gordon, Judith	√	√	SS&D	12	4	48	Fa 81	28
Ancient Textiles: Basketry	Basketry Techniques: A Sampler (from 1902 Book)	Mason, Otis Tufton	√		Iw	4	1		Wi 78	26
Ancient Textiles: Bronze Age	Textiles from an Ancient Danish Tomb	Zethraus, Kamma	√		H&C	6	2		Sp 55	46
Ancient Textiles: Chinese Silks	Ancient Textiles, a Fascinating Study		√		H&C	9	2		Sp 58	23
Ancient Textiles: Figured Silks	Designs in Ancient Figured Silks	Blumenau, Lili	√		H&C	2	1		Wi 50	5
Ancient Textiles: Figured Silks	Weaves in Figured Silks	Blumenau, Lili	√	√	H&C	2	2		Sp 51	25
Ancient Textiles: Fragments, Greek	Classical Greek Textiles from Nymphaeum	Wild, John Peter	√		TMJ	4	4		77	33
Ancient Textiles: Kashmir Shawls, India	Scent of Flowers, Kishmir Shawls in the Collection of The Textile Museum, The	Mikosch, Elisabeth	√		TMJ	24			85	7
Ancient Textiles: Mexico	Weft-Wrap Openwork Techniques in Archaeological and Contemporary Textiles of Mexico	Johnson, Irmgard Weitlaner	√	√	TMJ	4	3		76	63
Ancient Textiles: Middle Horizon, Tapestry Shirt, Peru	Technical Features of a Middle Horizon Tapestry Shirt from Peru, The	Bird, Junius B.; Milica Dimitrijevic Skinner	√		TMJ	4	1		De 74	5
Ancient Textiles: North American	Fragment, Pre-Columbian Cloth Found in Utah	Turner, Alta R.	√	√	H&C	22	1		Wi 71	20
Ancient Textiles: Paracas Mantles	Re-Establishing Provenience of Two Paracas Mantles	Paul, Anne			TMJ	19 20			80,81	35
Ancient Textiles: Peru	Ancient Peruvian Weaver	Clement, Doris W.	√		H&C	18	4		Fa 67	21
Ancient Textiles: Peru	Before Heddles Were Invented	Bird, Junius B.	√		H&C	3	3		Su 52	5
Ancient Textiles: Peru	Brief History of the Study of Ancient Peruvian Textiles, A	King, Mary Elizabeth	√		TMJ	2	1		De 66	39
Ancient Textiles: Peru	Identifying Hands at Work on a Paracas Mantle	Paul, Anne; Susan A. Niles	√		TMJ	23			84	5
Ancient Textiles: Peru	Interlocking Warp and Weft in the Nasca 2 Style	Rowe, Ann Pollard	√		TMJ	3	3		De 72	67
Ancient Textiles: Peru	Paracas Needle Technique, A	Hoskins, Nancy	√	√	Iw	5	4		Fa 80	34
Ancient Textiles: Peru	Pre-Incan Weavers of Peru, The	Blumenau, Lili	√		H&C	3	3		Su 52	12
Ancient Textiles: Peru	Rare Peruvian Textiles		√		H&C	9	2		Sp 58	18
Ancient Textiles: Peru	Spaced-Weft Twining of Ancient Peru: A Contemporary Interpretation	Rogers, Nora	√	√	Iw	5	4		Fa 80	42
Ancient Textiles: Peru, Early Horizon	Chavin Textiles and the Origins of Peruvian Weaving	Conklin, William J	√		TMJ	3	2		De 71	13
Ancient Textiles: Roman, Late Antique	Roman Heritage, The	Angelil, Muriel	√		SS&D	13	3	51	Su 82	69

SUBJECT	TITLE	AUTHOR	IL	INST	JOUR	VOL	NO	ISS	DATE	PAGE
Ancient Textiles: Silk and Silk Damask, Europe, Northwest	Some Early Silk Finds in Northwest Europe	Wild, John-Peter	√		TMJ	23			84	17
Ancient Textiles: Tapestries, Peru	Shaped Tapestry Bags from the Nazca-Ica Area of Peru	Bird, Junius B.	√		TMJ	1	3		De 64	2
Ancient Textiles: Tapestry Tunics, Inca	Technical Features of Inca Tapestry Tunics	Rowe, Ann Pollard	√		TMJ	17			78	5
Ancient Textiles: Tiahuanaco Tapestries	Tiahuanaco Tapestry Design	Sawyer, Alan R.	√		TMJ	1	2		De 63	27
Andean Tubular Trim	Special Andean Tubular Trim—Woven Without Heddles, A	Cahlander, Adele; Ed Franquemont; Barbara Bergman	√	√	WJ	6	3	23	Wi 81	54
Andes	Andean Crossed-Warp Techniques for Decorative Trims, Part 1 — Flat Bands	Cahlander, Adele	√	√	WJ	2	4	8	Ap 78	10
Andes	Andean Crossed-Warp Techniques for Decorative Trims, Part 2 — Tubular Bands (error-corrected WJ v3 n1 insert for vol. 2)	Cahlander, Adele	√	√	WJ	3	1	9	Jy 78	38
Andes	Andean Spinning	Franquemont, Ed	√		S-O	9	1		Sp 85	54
Andes	Andes Tradition, An	McConnell, Kathleen	√	√	SS&D	18	2	70	Sp 87	29
Andes	Color and Design in Andean Warp-Faced Fabrics	Femenias, Blenda	√		WJ	12	2	46	Fa 87	44
Andes	Peruvian Slings: Their Uses and Regional Variations	Noble, Carol Rasmussen	√		WJ	6	4	24	Sp 82	53
Andes	Special Andean Tubular Trim—Woven Without Heddles, A	Cahlander, Adele; Ed Franquemont; Barbara Bergman	√	√	WJ	6	3	23	Wi 81	54
Andes	Understanding Some Complex Structures from Simple Andean Looms: Steps in Analysis and Reproduction	Cahlander, Adele	√	√	AT	1			De 83	181
Andes	Warp-Faced Double Cloth: Adaptation of an Andean Technique for the Treadle Loom	Cahlander, Adele	√	√	WJ	10	4	40	Sp 86	72
Angled Weaving: Turned Warps	Peter Collingwood, His Weaves and Weaving: A Sleeved Jacket Made in Two Pieces	Collingwood, Peter; Harriet Tidball, ed.	√	√	SCGM		8		63	34
Angora also see Mohair										
Angora: Goats	Angora Goats and Mohair	Chastant, Kathryn Ross	√	√	S-O	7	3		Fa 83	29
Angora: Goats	Angoras for the Spinner's Flock	Russell, Barbara	√		S-O	7	3		Fa 83	45
Angora: Goats	Australian Spinner Raises Profitable Flock of Goats	Berger, Charles	√		H&C	17	3		Su 66	11
Angora: Goats	Mohair: A Multimillion Dollar Industry for Australia	Gray, Isabel			S-O	8	4		Wi 84	47
Angora: Goats	Mo's Have It, The	Pinchin, Bryn	√	√	S-O	7	3		Fa 83	23
Angora: Goats	Raising Angora Goats in Texas	Franklin, Sue			TM			8	D/J 86	12
Angora: Goats	Spinning Mohair in Lesotho	Snieckus, Mary Ann	√		TM			8	D/J 86	66
Angora: Rabbits	Angora: A Spinner's Delight	Howard, Miranda	√	√	S-O	6	4		82	43
Angora: Rabbits	Angora Fiber Spinning	Betts, Diane		√	S-O	9	4		Wi 85	35
Angora: Rabbits	Angora: Frivolous Fluff or Fantistic Fiber?	Rowe, Erica	√	√	S-O	8	2		Su 84	13
Angora: Rabbits	Angora: Producing Your Own Fibers	Rowe, Erica	√	√	S-O	8	2		Su 84	17
Angora: Rabbits	Hand-Dyed Angora Bunny Scarf	Hart, Jacque	√	√	S-O	11	4		Wi 87	26
Angora: Rabbits	Handspun Angora Mittens	Rowe, Erica	√	√	S-O	8	1		Sp 84	51
Angora: Rabbits	Herbs for a Healthy Angora	McConnell, Kathleen	√		S-O	8	1		Sp 84	38
Angora: Rabbits	"Ice in Shadow" Sweater	Kluth, Liz	√	√	S-O	9	4		Wi 85	15
Angora: Rabbits	Jean Newsted's Angora Scarf		√		S-O	9	3		Fa 85	13
Angora: Rabbits	More About Angora			√	TM			7	O/N 86	4
Angora: Rabbits	Plucking Angora Rabbits	Byers, Patricia	√		TM			5	J/J 86	18
Angora: Rabbits	Report on the ARBA Convention	Almond, Bonnie H.			S-O	8	2		Su 84	21
Animal Trappings	"Turkmen: Tribal Carpets and Traditions" (Exhibit)	Dyer, Carol	√		Fa	8	3		M/J 81	70
Animal X	Body as Canvas, The	Koda, Harold	√		TM			8	D/J 86	56
Animals	Andrea V. Uravitch, "Wild and Domestic" (Exhibit)	Stevens, Rebecca A. T.	√		Fa	10	2		M/A 83	71

SUBJECT	TITLE	AUTHOR	IL	INST	JOUR	VOL	NO	ISS	DATE	PAGE
Animals	"Linda Maxwell and Caroline Dahl: Terror Sampler and Other Dogs" (Exhibit)	Poon, Vivian	√		Fa	11	6		N/D 84	79
Animals	Lynn DiNino	Greer, Tyson	√		Fa	13	2		M/A 86	14
Animals	Visual Language of Bella Feldman, The	Scarborough, Jessica	√		Fa	11	4		J/A 84	30
Animals, Cows	Cows in Fiber	Timmons, Chris	√		Fa	11	4		J/A 84	55
Animals: Fiber	Kari Lønning		√		Fa	4	4		J/A 77	49
Animals, Fiber	Whose Zoo? Julietta Thornton's Incredible Fiber Sculptures	Kennett, Don	√		Fa	8	5		S/O 81	20
Animals, Sculpture	Camrose Ducote's Menagerie: An Empathy with Animals	Redmond, Cheryl	√		Fa	10	3		M/J 83	27
Anthrax	Anthrax Reported				SS&D	9	4	36	Fa 78	32
Anthrax	Anthrax Sterilization Methods and Their Effects on Fibers	Towner, Naomi Whiting; Helen Cushman		√	SS&D	7	3	27	Su 76	94
Anthrax	Contaminated Yarn				SS&D	7	2	26	Sp 76	39
Anxiety, Weaving	Fear of Weaving	Fanning, Robbie	√		Hw	1	1		F-W 79	10
Appalachia	Appalachian Basketry	Overcast, Roy	√		Fa	4	1		J/F 77	20
Appalachia	Quicksand Craft Center: A New Way of Life for Kentucky Mountain Women	Guy, Sallie T.	√		Hw	2	4		Se 81	16
Apparel, Clothing, Costume	Air Robe	Dedekam, Phyllis	√	√	SS&D	18	3	71	Su 87	47
Apparel, Clothing, Costume	Albertje Koopman		√		Hw	4	1		J/F 83	56
Apparel, Clothing, Costume	Applying the Pulled Warp Technique to Loom-Shaped Clothing	Evans, Kerry	√	√	WJ	9	3	35	Wi 85	34
Apparel, Clothing, Costume	Art and Romance of Peasant Clothes, The		√		SS&D	9	2	34	Sp 78	76
Apparel, Clothing, Costume	Art As Clothing: Clothing As Art		√		SS&D	12	1	45	Wi 80	85
Apparel, Clothing, Costume	Barbara Knollenberg, Fashion Designer, A Personal Story		√		WJ	6	3	23	Wi 81	10
Apparel, Clothing, Costume	Batwings and Butterflies	West, Virginia	√		Hw	6	2		M/A 85	41
Apparel, Clothing, Costume	Beginning with Bands: Tablet Woven Garments and Accessories	Holtzer, Marilyn Emerson	√	√	WJ	9	3	35	Wi 85	28
Apparel, Clothing, Costume	Bias Striped Skirt, A	Alderman, Sharon D.	√	√	Hw	5	1		J/F 84	45
Apparel, Clothing, Costume	Body as Canvas, The	Koda, Harold	√		TM			8	D/J 86	56
Apparel, Clothing, Costume	Bouquet of Simple Summer Tops, A		√		Hw	1	2		S-S 80	45
Apparel, Clothing, Costume	Bright, Breezy Stripes	Leethem, Kaino	√		Hw	5	3		Su 84	60
Apparel, Clothing, Costume	California Rags	Saulson, Sarah F.	√	√	SS&D	18	1	69	Wi 86	44
Apparel, Clothing, Costume	Canadian Classic, A	Baker, William R. M.	√		SS&D	18	3	71	Su 87	52
Apparel, Clothing, Costume	City Couture		√		Hw	6	1		J/F 85	40
Apparel, Clothing, Costume	Clothing	Todd, Louise	√	√	H&C	24	4		Au 73	28
Apparel, Clothing, Costume	Clothing from Rectangles	Liebler, Barbara	√	√	Iw	5	4		Fa 80	52
Apparel, Clothing, Costume	Coat Couture	West, Virginia	√	> 4	SS&D	14	2	54	Sp 83	48
Apparel, Clothing, Costume	Collection, The		√		WJ	3	3	11	Ja 79	30
Apparel, Clothing, Costume	Contemporary Costume, Strictly Handwoven	Tidball, Harriet	√	√	SCGM		24		68	1-44
Apparel, Clothing, Costume	Contemporary Costume, Strictly Handwoven: A Winter Costume	Tidball, Harriet	√	√	SCGM		24		68	38
Apparel, Clothing, Costume	Contemporary Needle Lacers		√		TM			13	O/N 87	44
Apparel, Clothing, Costume	Convergence '86 Fashions	Dean, Ankaret	√		SS&D	18	1	69	Wi 86	16
Apparel, Clothing, Costume	Cool, Casual Cottons		√		Hw	5	3		Su 84	55
Apparel, Clothing, Costume	Costume of a Plain People, The	Schiess, Kate	√	√	TM			5	J/J 86	65
Apparel, Clothing, Costume	Costumes of Royal India	Levine, Betsy	√		TM			7	O/N 86	64
Apparel, Clothing, Costume	Coudre a Main: Costumes by Hand	Tacker, Sylvia	√		Fa	12	2		M/A 85	49
Apparel, Clothing, Costume	Country Casuals		√		Hw	6	4		S/O 85	52
Apparel, Clothing, Costume	Cozy Wrap-up for All Occasions, A		√		Hw	6	4		S/O 85	55
Apparel, Clothing, Costume	Crane Day Designs	Colton, Mary Rawcliffe	√		SS&D	18	2	70	Sp 87	48
Apparel, Clothing, Costume	Creative Clothing: Surface Embellishment	Mayer, Anita Luvera	√	√	WJ	11	3	43	Wi 87	30
Apparel, Clothing, Costume	Cylaine Handwoven Designs: Arlene Wohl and Lucy Matzger		√		WJ	7	3	27	Wi 82	8

10

SUBJECT	TITLE	AUTHOR	IL	INST	JOUR	VOL	NO	ISS	DATE	PAGE
Apparel, Clothing, Costume	Dazzling Designs	Eagle, Elsie	√	√	SS&D	15	1	57	Wi 83	19
Apparel, Clothing, Costume	Decorative Techniques of the Sarakatsani	Smith, Joyce	√	√	WJ	9	1	33	Su 84	14
Apparel, Clothing, Costume	Design Placement for Garments	Liebler, Barbara	√	√	Hw	7	5		N/D 86	26
Apparel, Clothing, Costume	Design Portfolio		√		Hw	2	2		Mr 81	53
Apparel, Clothing, Costume	Designing Handwoven Clothing	Thomason, Roger	√		SS&D	10	1	37	Wi 78	88
Apparel, Clothing, Costume	Designing Your Handwoven Garments	Scorgie, Jean	√	√	Hw	7	5		N/D 86	40
Apparel, Clothing, Costume	Double Two-Tie Twills and Basket Weave	Barrett, Clotilde	√	> 4	WJ	7	3	27	Wi 82	38
Apparel, Clothing, Costume	Dream Weaver: Joan Renne		√		WJ	12	1	45	Su 87	40
Apparel, Clothing, Costume	"Elegant Art: Fantasy and Fashion in the Eighteenth Century, An" (Exhibit)	Dyer, Carolyn Price	√		Fa	10	4		J/A 83	66
Apparel, Clothing, Costume	Fall Wrap Up — Weaves and Fabrics for Classic Garments		√	√	Hw	8	4		S/O 87	40
Apparel, Clothing, Costume	Family Warp, The		√		Hw	5	4		S/0 84	41
Apparel, Clothing, Costume	Fashion Show of Handwoven Garments		√	> 4	WJ	3	3	11	Ja 79	5
Apparel, Clothing, Costume	Fashion Trends		√		WJ	9	3	35	Wi 85	24
Apparel, Clothing, Costume	Fashion Trends	Hick, Susan	√		WJ	9	1	33	Su 84	12
Apparel, Clothing, Costume	Fashion Trends	Hick, Susan	√		WJ	9	2	34	Fa 84	10
Apparel, Clothing, Costume	Fashion Trends	Hick, Susan	√		WJ	7	2	26	Fa 82	16
Apparel, Clothing, Costume	Fashion Trends	Hick, Susan	√		WJ	7	3	27	Wi 82	16
Apparel, Clothing, Costume	Fashion Trends	Hick, Susan	√		WJ	7	4	28	Sp 83	40
Apparel, Clothing, Costume	Fashion Trends	Hick, Susan	√		WJ	8	2	30	Fa 83	28
Apparel, Clothing, Costume	Fashion Trends	Hick, Susan	√		WJ	8	3	31	Wi 83	26
Apparel, Clothing, Costume	Fashion Trends	Hick, Susan	√		WJ	8	4	32	Sp 84	56
Apparel, Clothing, Costume	Fashion Trends	Nelipovitch, Kate; Susan Hick	√		WJ	6	3	23	Wi 81	6
Apparel, Clothing, Costume	Fashion Trends: Fall	Hick, Susan	√		WJ	10	1	37	Su 85	20
Apparel, Clothing, Costume	Fashion Trends: Fall	Hick, Susan	√		WJ	11	1	41	Su 86	54
Apparel, Clothing, Costume	Fashion Trends: Spring	Hick, Susan	√		WJ	10	3	39	Wi 86	38
Apparel, Clothing, Costume	Fashion Trends: Summer	Hick, Susan	√		WJ	9	4	36	Sp 85	20
Apparel, Clothing, Costume	Fashion Trends: Summer	Hick, Susan	√		WJ	10	4	40	Sp 86	52
Apparel, Clothing, Costume	Fashion Trends: Winter	Hick, Susan	√		WJ	10	2	38	Fa 85	24
Apparel, Clothing, Costume	Fashionable Threads		√		SS&D	8	4	32	Fa 77	70
Apparel, Clothing, Costume	Few Observations on "Remains", A	Stanton, R. G.	√		AT	4			De 85	9
Apparel, Clothing, Costume	Five Fibre Pieces	Dean, Ankaret	√	√	SS&D	18	2	70	Sp 87	8
Apparel, Clothing, Costume	For Anneliese Ammann, Simplicity is Key to Woven Garments	Kaspar, Patricia	√		WJ	7	3	27	Wi 82	70
Apparel, Clothing, Costume	From Elegance to Rag Weaving	Mick, Catherine	√	√	WJ	7	3	27	Wi 82	64
Apparel, Clothing, Costume	Gala Raincoat	Moes, Dini	√	√	WJ	6	3	23	Wi 81	12
Apparel, Clothing, Costume	Garments from Narrow Fabrics	Davenport, Betty	√	√	Hw	6	2		M/A 85	18
Apparel, Clothing, Costume	Glad Rags	Wroten, Barbara	√	√	SS&D	15	4	60	Fa 84	28
Apparel, Clothing, Costume	Grace Marvin, Her Ideas on Making Clothing from Handwoven Fabrics		√	√	H&C	13	3		Su 62	14
Apparel, Clothing, Costume	Greek Chemises: Cut and Construction	Welters, Linda	√	√	WJ	10	1	37	Su 85	40
Apparel, Clothing, Costume	Guatemala Visited	Atwater, Mary Meigs	√	√	SCGM		15		65	15
Apparel, Clothing, Costume	Handwoven Clothing Today: The Couturier Touch	West, Virginia	√		Fa	8	1		J/F 81	39
Apparel, Clothing, Costume	Harmony of Pinks, A		√		Hw	5	3		Su 84	58
Apparel, Clothing, Costume	How Madame Grès Sculpts with Fabric	Cooper, Arlene	√	√	TM			10	A/M 87	50
Apparel, Clothing, Costume	Jhane Barnes: A Convergence '88 Chicago Preview		√		SS&D	18	4	72	Fa 87	12
Apparel, Clothing, Costume	Kathy Woell Original, A	Sitko, Jane Bradley	√		SS&D	19	1	73	Wi 87	36
Apparel, Clothing, Costume	Keeping Tradition Alive	Wilcox, Don	√		Fa	14	1		J/F 87	44
Apparel, Clothing, Costume	Knitted Palette of Brenda French, The	Pierce, Judith	√		Fa	13	2		M/A 86	43
Apparel, Clothing, Costume	Levi Strauss & Co.	Scarborough, Jessica	√		Fa	13	5		S/O 86	17

SUBJECT	TITLE	AUTHOR	IL	INST	JOUR	VOL	NO	ISS	DATE	PAGE
Apparel, Clothing, Costume	Long Sweeping Evening Cape	Roth, Bettie G.	√	>4	WJ	6	3	23	Wi 81	26
Apparel, Clothing, Costume	Loom Shaped—3 Ways (error-corrected Hw v4 n3 83 p79)		√	√	Hw	3	2		Mr 82	44
Apparel, Clothing, Costume	Loom-Shaped Garment, A	Haynes, Albertje Koopman (see also Koopman)	√	√	SS&D	9	1	33	Wi 77	83
Apparel, Clothing, Costume	Make it with Wool		√		Hw	6	2		M/A 85	10
Apparel, Clothing, Costume	Mary Crovatt Hambidge	Schaller, Karin	√		Fa	11	5		S/O 84	24
Apparel, Clothing, Costume	MidAtlantic Fiber Association	Van Artsdalen, Martha	√		SS&D	17	2	66	Sp 86	10
Apparel, Clothing, Costume	Modern Interpretations of Ethnic Garments	Dickey, Enola	√	√	SS&D	9	2	34	Sp 78	28
Apparel, Clothing, Costume	Modular Clothing	Mayer, Anita	√	√	Hw	7	3		M/J 86	58
Apparel, Clothing, Costume	Moorman Inspired Clothing	Durston, Linda Moore	√	√	SS&D	14	1	53	Wi 82	35
Apparel, Clothing, Costume	Naomi W. Towner: Hangings & Coverings		√		SS&D	5	2	18	Sp 74	92
Apparel, Clothing, Costume	Next to the Skin		√		SS&D	15	4	60	Fa 84	42
Apparel, Clothing, Costume	Nine-to-Five		√		Hw	5	1		J/F 84	43
Apparel, Clothing, Costume	Obi: The Textile Art of Nishijin	Donaldson, R. Alan	√		AT	1			De 83	115
Apparel, Clothing, Costume	One Warp, One Pattern, Five Garments	Bradley, Louise	√		Hw	3	3		My 82	34
Apparel, Clothing, Costume	Opera Elegance	Sylvan, Katherine	√	√	SS&D	15	4	60	Fa 84	24
Apparel, Clothing, Costume	Passion for Elegance: Master Dyer Marian Clayden Creates Clothing by Listening to the Fabric, A	Levine, Betsy	√	√	TM			14	D/J 87	36
Apparel, Clothing, Costume	Pat White: The "Small Things" Are Her Signature	Park, Betty	√	√	SS&D	13	3	51	Su 82	58
Apparel, Clothing, Costume	Production Weaving: From Nature-Inspired Warps to Linsey-Woolsey	Ligon, Linda	√		Iw	1	2		Wi 76	6
Apparel, Clothing, Costume	Qotny & Alaga: Traditional Striped Fabrics for the Middle Eastern Kaftan	El-Homossani, M. M.	√	>4	WJ	10	1	37	Su 85	33
Apparel, Clothing, Costume	Rabari Lodi: Creating a Fabric Through Social Alliance, The	Frater, Judy	√	√	WJ	10	1	37	Su 85	28
Apparel, Clothing, Costume	Recent Gifts of Chinese and Japanese Textiles	Hays, Mary V.	√		TMJ	4	2		75	4
Apparel, Clothing, Costume	Santa Fe Weaver Re-Creates Past	Ligon, Linda	√		Iw	1	1		Fa 75	4
Apparel, Clothing, Costume	Seattle Guild Garment Designs, Part 4: Edges, Closures, Capes and Dresses		√	√	SS&D	11	2	42	Sp 80	39
Apparel, Clothing, Costume	Simply-Styled Jumper for Autumn Afternoons, A		√		Hw	6	4		S/O 85	53
Apparel, Clothing, Costume	Suited to Silk	Turner, Kathryn M.	√	√	SS&D	18	2	70	Sp 87	68
Apparel, Clothing, Costume	Summer and Winter Garments (Melinda Raber Johnson)		√	√	WJ	11	3	43	Wi 87	44
Apparel, Clothing, Costume	Summer Sand & Sea		√		Hw	4	3		M/J 83	48
Apparel, Clothing, Costume	Textured Cottons	Henrikson, Sue	√	>4	WJ	6	3	23	Wi 81	20
Apparel, Clothing, Costume	That Wild & Wooly Weft		√		Hw	3	2		Mr 82	48
Apparel, Clothing, Costume	Two Spring Ensembles		√		Hw	6	2		M/A 85	56
Apparel, Clothing, Costume	Under Wraps		√		Fa	12	3		M/J 85	26
Apparel, Clothing, Costume	Veridian Green Cape	Barrett, Clotilde	√	>4	WJ	4	3	15	Ja 80	11
Apparel, Clothing, Costume	Warm and Wooly: Bright and Soft		√		Hw	1	1		F-W 79	28
Apparel, Clothing, Costume	Warm and Wooly: For Him, For Her		√		Hw	1	1		F-W 79	22
Apparel, Clothing, Costume	Warm and Wooly: In the Country, In the City!		√		Hw	1	1		F-W 79	20
Apparel, Clothing, Costume	Wearable Paintings	Auger, Shirley Venit	√	√	H&C	24	4		Au 73	34
Apparel, Clothing, Costume	Wearing Handwovens with Style	Mayer, Anita	√	√	WJ	10	3	39	Wi 86	22
Apparel, Clothing, Costume	Weavers Notebook: Simple Garments to Weave & Sew, A		√		Hw	8	1		J/F 87	43
Apparel, Clothing, Costume	Weaving a Lifestyle: Malin Selander	West, Virginia	√		Iw	5	2		Sp 80	30
Apparel, Clothing, Costume	Weaving & Felting	Berdinka, Regine	√	√	SS&D	15	2	58	Sp 84	10
Apparel, Clothing, Costume	Weaving for Ethnic Clothing	Marston, Ena	√	√	SS&D	10	1	37	Wi 78	42
Apparel, Clothing, Costume	Weaving in Quebec: Devotion to Garments	Barrett, Clotilde	√	√	WJ	6	4	24	Sp 82	18

SUBJECT	TITLE	AUTHOR	IL	INST	JOUR	VOL	NO	ISS	DATE	PAGE
Apparel, Clothing, Costume	Weavings of the Guatemalan Highland Maya	Marks, Copeland H.	√	√	SS&D	7	4	28	Fa 76	88
Apparel, Clothing, Costume	Where's the Sport in Sportswear?	McComb, Richard	√		TM			2	D/J 85	36
Apparel, Clothing, Costume	White Circular Wrap	Richards, Iris	√	√	WJ	4	3	15	Ja 80	7
Apparel, Clothing, Costume	Wooly Woolens	Thilenius, Carol; Marion Simpson	√	√	Hw	3	4		Se 82	44
Apparel, Clothing, Costume	Wrap It Up		√		Hw	4	4		S/O 83	41
Apparel, Clothing, Costume: Loom-Shaped	Anita Mayer	Wilson, Jean	√		Hw	2	2		Mr 81	28
Apparel, Clothing, Costume: Miniatures	Nativity Scene	Vargo, Bessie Mae	√	√	WJ	6	2	22	Fa 81	8
Appliqué	Applique Art of Nell Booker Sonnemann, The	Malarcher, Patricia	√		Fa	7	3		M/J 80	24
Appliqué	Building on Experience: Virginia Jacobs' Fabric Constructions	Rowland, Amy Zaffarano	√		Fa	7	4		J/A 80	39
Appliqué	Dazzling with Sequins	Kelsey, Barbara Shomer	√	√	TM			1	O/N 85	60
Appliqué	Easy Striped Knits	Walker, Barbara G.	√	√	TM			4	A/M 86	54
Appliqué	Fiber and Architecture: Rebecca Rogers Witsell		√		Fa	3	3		M/J 76	23
Appliqué	"Flexible Medium: Art Fabric from the Museum Collection, The" (Exhibit)	Goodman, Deborah Lerme	√		Fa	11	5		S/O 84	71
Appliqué	Fondness for Rabbits: Nancy Erickson's Quilts Deliver a Serious Message in a Soft Medium, A		√		Fa	8	6		N/D 81	17
Appliqué	From Paint to Fiber	Siewert-Miller, Elisabet	√		SS&D	3	2	10	Sp 72	18
Appliqué	Hawaiian Quilt, The	White-Hansen, Sue Ellen	√	√	TM			13	O/N 87	22
Appliqué	Helen Bitar	Park, Betty	√		Fa	5	2		M/A 78	44
Appliqué	Illuminated Tapestries of Amy Zerner, The	Daniels, Richard	√		Fa	9	3		M/J 82	22
Appliqué	"Jean Ray Laury — Exhibit of Stitchery" (Exhibit)	Gutcheon, Beth	√		Fa	6	2		M/A 79	66
Appliqué	Jo Diggs: An Interview with a Very Talented Woman		√		Fa	3	5		S/O 76	24
Appliqué	Just Playing in Space: Ann McKenzie Nickolson's Textile Artwork	Koplos, Janet	√		Fa	8	2		M/A 81	34
Appliqué	Keeping Culture Alive with Needle and Thread	White, Virginia L.	√		Fa	9	3		M/J 82	40
Appliqué	Keeping Warm in Alaska		√		Fa	9	6		N/D 82	22
Appliqué	Lamé	Boyce, Ann	√		TM			8	D/J 86	32
Appliqué	Lucinda Sheets: A Quiltmaker's Mural is a Poem in Fabric	Richerson, Suzanne	√		Fa	10	2		M/A 83	15
Appliqué	Margot Strand Jensen: Soft Painting	Singletary, Suzanne M.	√		Fa	11	1		J/F 84	18
Appliqué	Nancy Smeltzer	Smeltzer, Nancy	√		Fa	13	5		S/O 86	19
Appliqué	Night Stories	White, Virginia	√		TM			11	J/J 87	82
Appliqué	Obi: The Textile Art of Nishijin	Donaldson, R. Alan	√		AT	1			De 83	115
Appliqué	"Patchwork Garden, A" (Exhibit)	Hetzler, Patricia	√		Fa	8	5		S/O 81	73
Appliqué	Revival of Stitchery, Appliqué, and Collage	Belfer, Nancy	√		H&C	18	1		Wi 67	21
Appliqué	Salmon Run: The Work of Northwest Artists Peggy Vanbianchi and Emily Standley	Hirschi, Ron	√		Fa	10	2		M/A 83	16
Appliqué	"Silken Threads and Silent Needles" (Exhibit)	Dunnewold, Jane	√		Fa	11	6		N/D 84	78
Appliqué	Soft Boxes: Ritual for Our Common Life	McElroy, Jane	√		Fa	10	2		M/A 83	21
Appliqué	Songs in Fabric: Quiltmaker Nancy Herman Is an Unusual Musician	Rowland, Amy Zaffarano	√		Fa	9	4		J/A 82	22
Appliqué	Tree of Life	Renee, Paula	√		SS&D	17	2	66	Sp 86	80
Appliqué	Weaving, Applique and Stitchery	Belfer, Nancy	√		Iw	5	3		Su 80	41
Appliqué	Working with the Wall ... A Community Garden		√		SS&D	10	4	40	Fa 79	8
Appliqué, Contemporary	Deborah J. Felix	Bard, Elizabeth	√		Fa	12	2		M/A 85	34

SUBJECT	TITLE	AUTHOR	IL	INST	JOUR	VOL	NO	ISS	DATE	PAGE
Appliqué: Handwoven	Handwoven Applique on Handwoven Fabrics Used by Hortense Amram in Ecclesiastical Design		√	√	H&C	13	2		Sp 62	20
Appliqué, Reverse	Art to Wear — Three Innovators: Cate Fitt, Emma Vesey, Dina Schwartz Knapp		√		Fa	8	1		J/F 81	67
Appliqué, Reverse	Ethnic Textile Art at U.C.L.A. — "Yer Dailege: Kuna Women's Art" (Exhibit)	Dyer, Carolyn	√		Fa	8	2		M/A 81	59
Appliqué, Reverse	Flourishing Art: USA Hmong Women Show How to Stitch Pa ndau, Their Flowery Cloth, A	Porter-Francis, Wendy	√	√	TM			9	F/M 87	33
Appliqué, Reverse	Making Molas: Four Basic Techniques	Patera, Charlotte	√		Fa	8	5		S/O 81	38
Appliqué: Techniques	Mastering the Art of Hand Appliqué	Wolff, Colette	√	√	TM			4	A/M 86	49
Apprentices	Apprenticeship Conference				SS&D	9	4	36	Fa 78	98
Apprentices	Linda Gilbert	Gilbert, Linda	√		Fa	5	5		S/O 78	16
Apprentices	Scheuer Tapestry Studio: Applying Old Techniques to New Ideas, The	Scheuer, Ruth Tannenbaum	√		Fa	10	3		M/J 83	39
Apprentices	Shinnosuke Seino: Innovator with Wool	Schreiber, Lavonne	√		WJ	12	2	46	Fa 87	34
Apprentices: Fiber Arts	Give and Take of Apprenticeship: An Apprentice's Version, The	Molnar, Gail	√		Fa	8	4		J/A 81	25
Apprentices: Fiber Arts	Give and Take of Apprenticeship in the Fiber Arts: A Master's View, The (error-noted but uncorrected Fa v8 n5 81 p6)	Hall, Carolyn Vosburg			Fa	8	4		J/A 81	24
Apprentices: Tapestry	Bringing Tapestry into the 20th Century	Mattera, Joanne	√		TM			1	O/N 85	48
Apprentices: Textile	Textile Apprenticeship in Northern California	Montgomery, Larry			TM			9	F/M 87	20
Apprentices: Textile Conservation	Apprenticeship Program in Textile Conservation, The		√		TMJ	1	3		De 64	50
Apprentices: Weaving	Learning to Weave in Japan	Schrieber, LaVonne	√		WJ	8	1	29	Su 83	79
Apprentices: Weaving	Living the Craftsman's Gospel	Horton, Susan			H&C	24	2		M/A 73	46
Apprentices: Weaving	Thoughts on Apprenticeships		√		SS&D	5	4	20	Fa 74	15
Apprenticeship	Livin' and Workin' on the Land: Fiber Art Outside the Mainstream	Talley, Charles S.	√		Fa	8	6		N/D 81	38
Aprons	Alice's Apron	Meltzer, Bonnie	√		SS&D	5	2	18	Sp 74	29
Aprons	Apron and Kitchen Towels		√	√	Hw	1	2		S-S 80	26, 53
Aprons	Child's Apron (Sue Ellison)		√	√	Hw	1	2		S-S 80	35, 63
Aprons	Guatemala Visited	Atwater, Mary Meigs	√	√	SCGM		15		65	37
Aprons	Lacy Apron (Linda Ligon)		√	√	Hw	4	1		J/F 83	41, 81
Aprons	Lacy Apron, My	Ligon, Linda	√		Hw	4	1		J/F 83	40
Aprons	Practical Apron with M's and O's Border		√	√	WJ	7	2	26	Fa 82	29
Aprons	Suggestions for Christmas Gifts	Frey, Berta	√	> 4	H&C	16	4		Fa 65	18
Aprons	Wear Your Best Apron	MacNutt, Dawn	√	√	SS&D	8	4	32	Fa 77	65
Aprons	Weave for Your Kitchen	Frey, Berta	√		H&C	1	2		Su 50	19
Aprons	Weaver's Work Apron: A Project in Double Weave		√	√	WJ	7	2	26	Fa 82	27
Aprons, Spinner's	Perfect Spinner's Apron, The			√	TM			9	F/M 87	10
Aran Islands	Aran Knitting	Starmore, Alice	√	√	TM			14	D/J 87	50
Aran Islands	Arans: A Saga in Wool (error-corrected S-O V4 80 p4)	Schlegel, Lee-lee	√	√	S-O	3			79	56
Arashi Shibori	New Twist on Resist	Wada, Yoshiko Iwamoto; Shelley Karpilow	√	√	TM			8	D/J 86	20
Arashi Shibori	Textural Approach to Arashi Shibori, A	Beytebiere, D'Arcie	√	√	TM			8	D/J 86	24
Arashi Shibori	Working Method for the Home, A	Karpilow, Shelley	√	√	TM			8	D/J 86	22
Archeological Artifacts: Peru	Peru, Textiles Unlimited: Ancient Textiles and Artifacts	Tidball, Harriet	√		SCGM		25		68	2
Archeological Looms: Peruvian	Three Ancient Peruvian Gauze Looms	Rowe, Ann Pollard; Junius B. Bird	√		TMJ	19 20			80,81	27
Archeological Textile Artifacts: Bag	Prehistoric Twined Bag from Big Bone Cave, Tennessee: Manufacture, Repair, and Use, A	Kuttruff, Jenna Tedrick	√		AT	8			De 87	125

SUBJECT	TITLE	AUTHOR	IL	INST	JOUR	VOL	NO	ISS	DATE	PAGE
Archeological Textile Artifacts: Egypt	Textile Remains from a Late Temple in Egyptian Nubia	Adams, Nettie K.	√		AT	8			De 87	85
Archeological Textiles	Ancient Peruvian Weaver	Clement, Doris W.	√		H&C	18	4		Fa 67	21
Archeological Textiles	Five Thousand Fabrics: A Profile of the Kelsey Museum of Archeology		√		SS&D	11	4	44	Fa 80	33
Archeological Textiles: Africa	Medieval Textiles from the Tellem Caves in Central Mali, West Africa	Bedaux, Rogier M. A.; Rita Bolland	√		TMJ	19 20			80,81	65
Archeological Textiles: Caucasus	Newly Excavated Caftan from the Northern Caucasus, A	Riboud, Krishna	√		TMJ	4	3		76	21
Archeological Textiles, China	China and the Complexities of Weaving Technologies	Vollmer, John E.			AT	5			Ju 86	65
Archeological Textiles: Chinese Silks	Ancient Textiles, a Fascinating Study		√		H&C	9	2		Sp 58	23
Archeological Textiles: Denmark	Textiles from an Ancient Danish Tomb	Zethraus, Kamma	√		H&C	6	2		Sp 55	46
Archeological Textiles: Egypt, Sixth Century (likely)	Tapestry Roundel with Nilotic Scenes, A	Abdel-Malek, Laila	√		TMJ	25			86	33
Archeological Textiles: England	Roman Textiles from Vindolanda, Hexham, England	Wild, John Peter	√		TMJ	18			79	19
Archeological Textiles: England, Colchester Finds	Some Early Silk Finds in Northwest Europe	Wild, John-Peter	√		TMJ	23			84	17
Archeological Textiles: Europe, Halstatt Finds	Some Early Silk Finds in Northwest Europe	Wild, John-Peter	√		TMJ	23			84	17
Archeological Textiles: Grand Gulch, Utah	Fragment, Pre-Columbian Cloth Found in Utah	Turner, Alta R.	√	√	H&C	22	1		Wi 71	20
Archeological Textiles: Greek	Classical Greek Textiles from Nymphaeum	Wild, John Peter	√		TMJ	4	4		77	33
Archeological Textiles: Mexico	Weft-Wrap Openwork Techniques in Archaeological and Contemporary Textiles of Mexico	Johnson, Irmgard Weitlaner	√	√	TMJ	4	3		76	63
Archeological Textiles: Paracas Mantles	Re-Establishing Provenience of Two Paracas Mantles	Paul, Anne			TMJ	19 20			80,81	35
Archeological Textiles: Peru	Archeological Rags	Hickman, Pat	√		Fa	9	1		J/F 82	70
Archeological Textiles: Peru	Before Heddles were Invented	Bird, Junius B.	√		H&C	3	3		Su 52	5
Archeological Textiles: Peru	Peru, Textiles Unlimited: Ancient Textiles and Artifacts	Tidball, Harriet	√		SCGM		25		68	2
Archeological Textiles: Peru	Peru, Textiles Unlimited: Textile Collections	Tidball, Harriet	√		SCGM		25		68	14
Archeological Textiles: Peru	Pre-Incan Weavers of Peru, The	Blumenau, Lili	√		H&C	3	3		Su 52	12
Archeological Textiles: Peru	Rare Peruvian Textiles		√		H&C	9	2		Sp 58	18
Archeological Textiles: Peru	Shaped Tapestry Bags from the Nazca-Ica Area of Peru	Bird, Junius B.	√		TMJ	1	3		De 64	2
Archeological Textiles: Peru	Technical Features of a Middle Horizon Tapestry Shirt from Peru, The	Bird, Junius B.; Milica Dimitrijevic Skinner	√		TMJ	4	1		De 74	5
Archeological Textiles: Peru	Technical Features of Inca Tapestry Tunics	Rowe, Ann Pollard	√		TMJ	17			78	5
Archeological Textiles: Peru	Textile Evidence for Huari Music	Rowe, Ann Pollard	√		TMJ	18			79	5
Archeological Textiles: Peru, Paracas Mantle	Identifying Hands at Work on a Paracas Mantle	Paul, Anne; Susan A. Niles	√		TMJ	23			84	5
Archeological Textiles: Peru, Tunics, Musician	Textile Evidence for Huari Music	Rowe, Ann Pollard	√		TMJ	18			79	5
Archeological Textiles: Southeastern United States	Prehistoric Textiles Revealed by Potsherds	Kuttruff, Jenna Tedrick	√		SS&D	11	3	43	Su 80	40
Archeological Textiles: Tiahuanaco Tapestry Shirts, Peru	Tiahuanaco Tapestry Design	Sawyer, Alan R.	√		TMJ	1	2		De 63	27
Architectural Textiles	Architect-Weaver and His Workaday World: Bruce Bierman's Business is Good Design, An	Malarcher, Patricia	√		Fa	7	6		N/D 80	60
Architectural Textiles	At the Studio of Lenore Tawney		√		H&C	16	2		Sp 65	35
Architectural Textiles	Barn Raising Experience, A	Bujnowski, Donald	√	√	SS&D	8	4	32	Fa 77	100
Architectural Textiles	Commercial Establishment Discovers Fiber Arts, The	Jacopetti, Alexandra	√	√	SS&D	8	2	30	Sp 77	4

SUBJECT	TITLE	AUTHOR	IL	INST	JOUR	VOL	NO	ISS	DATE	PAGE
Architectural Textiles	Concrete and Grace, Fiber Allusions (error-corrected SS&D v6 n2 75 p44)	Kliot, Jules; Kaethe Kliot; Jenifer Kaufman	√		SS&D	6	1	21	Wi 74	33
Architectural Textiles	Conversing with Gerhardt Knodel	Park, Betty	√		Fa	12	1		J/F 85	27
Architectural Textiles	Corporate Commission, The	Creager, Clara	√	√	SS&D	16	1	61	Wi 84	38
Architectural Textiles	"Dolly Curtis Textile Graphics" (Exhibit)	Reed, Irene C.	√		Fa	6	2		M/A 79	70
Architectural Textiles	Dorothy Liebes Designs Fabrics for U.S. Theatre at the Brussels World's Fair		√		H&C	9	2		Sp 58	26
Architectural Textiles	Emphasis on Handwoven Fabrics in the Architect's Design		√		H&C	6	1		Wi 54	20
Architectural Textiles	Fiber and Architecture	Stanford, Shirley	√		Fa	3	3		M/J 76	14
Architectural Textiles	Fiber and Architecture: Amy Jo Lind and Maggie Nicholson		√		Fa	3	3		M/J 76	16
Architectural Textiles	Fiber and Architecture: Dennis Jenkins		√		Fa	3	3		M/J 76	35
Architectural Textiles	Fiber and Architecture: Gwenyth Mabry		√		Fa	3	3		M/J 76	24
Architectural Textiles	Fiber and Architecture: Janusz and Nancy Kozikowski		√		Fa	3	3		M/J 76	28
Architectural Textiles	Fiber and Architecture: John Ellis		√		Fa	3	3		M/J 76	17
Architectural Textiles	Fiber and Architecture: Marge Walters		√		Fa	3	3		M/J 76	33
Architectural Textiles	Fiber and Architecture: Rebecca Rogers Witsell		√		Fa	3	3		M/J 76	23
Architectural Textiles	Fiber and Architecture: Richard Worthen		√		Fa	3	3		M/J 76	32
Architectural Textiles	Fiber and Architecture: Wilcke Smith		√		Fa	3	3		M/J 76	18
Architectural Textiles	Fiber in Minnesota: "Traditions/Transitions II" and "Art in Architecture" (Exhibit)	Stack, Lotus	√		Fa	11	3		M/J 84	80
Architectural Textiles	Gerhardt Knodel	Olendorf, Donna	√		Fa	5	6		N/D 78	44
Architectural Textiles	"Gerhardt Knodel—Makes Places to Be" (Exhibit)	Livingstone, Joan	√		Fa	10	3		M/J 83	71
Architectural Textiles	Joyce Crain: Walls of Light	Malarcher, Patricia	√		Fa	12	5		S/O 85	55
Architectural Textiles	Keynote in Chicago: Knodel	Livingstone, Joan	√		SS&D	18	3	71	Su 87	37
Architectural Textiles	Knoll Textiles		√		H&C	9	3		Su 58	12
Architectural Textiles	Lever House Presents a Solution to a Unique Problem in Interior Design		√		H&C	4	3		Su 53	32
Architectural Textiles	Marianne Strengell, Textile Consultant to Architects	Bemis, Marion Holden	√		H&C	8	1		Wi 56	6
Architectural Textiles	Nantucket Looms and Sam Kasten	Erickson, Johanna	√		SS&D	17	3	67	Su 86	70
Architectural Textiles	"Patricia Campbell: The Modular Form" (Exhibit)	Itter, Diane	√		Fa	11	3		M/J 84	75
Architectural Textiles	Plastics in Fiber: A Persistent Presence	Malarcher, Patricia	√		Fa	12	1		J/F 85	56
Architectural Textiles	Profile: Robert L. Kidd	Fleming, Ray Frost	√		H&C	23	5		S/O 72	9
Architectural Textiles	Rancocas Fabrics		√		H&C	8	2		Sp 57	41
Architectural Textiles	Rosalie Seeks: Cascading Dream Garden	Richerson, Suzanne	√		Fa	12	1		J/F 85	21
Architectural Textiles	Sheila Hicks: An Affinity for Architecture	Koenigsberg, Nancy	√		Fa	12	5		S/O 85	60
Architectural Textiles	Sheila O'Hara: Wry Humor and Virtuoso Weaving	Park, Betty	√		Fa	10	1		J/F 83	64
Architectural Textiles	Sky Curtain (Jeanne Leffingwell)		√		TM			2	D/J 85	88
Architectural Textiles	Spatial Transitions	Gilbert, James	√		SS&D	9	3	35	Su 78	12
Architectural Textiles	Textiles in the United Nations Buildings	Blumenau, Lili	√		H&C	4	1		Wi 52	10
Architectural Textiles	"Trees and Other Things" (Exhibit)	Hillis, Anne	√		Fa	5	4		J/A 78	17
Architectural Textiles	Victoria Rivers: Sculpting in Fiber and Neon	Scarborough, Jessica	√		Fa	12	1		J/F 85	22
Architectural Textiles	Wall Hangings of Judith Content, The	Scarborough, Jessica	√		Fa	13	2		M/A 86	10
Architectural Textiles	Weaver's Commission Workshop	Meany, Janet	√		SS&D	10	3	39	Su 79	40
Architectural Textiles	Weaving, 'riting, and 'rithmetic	Tate, Blair	√		AT	6			De 86	57
Architectural Textiles	Working with the Wall ... A Community Garden		√		SS&D	10	4	40	Fa 79	8
Architectural Textiles	You Are Now Weaving Oakland	O'Hara, Sheila	√	> 4	AT	6			De 86	9

SUBJECT	TITLE	AUTHOR	IL	INST	JOUR	VOL	NO	ISS	DATE	PAGE
Architecture: Textile-Inspired	Textile-Inspired Architecture	Smeltzer, Nancy	√		Fa	14	4		S/O 87	5
Arctic North America	Qiviut from the Musk Ox		√		H&C	18	3		Su 67	5
Ardabil Carpets: Research Update	Ardabil Puzzle, The	Weaver, Martin E.	√		TMJ	23			84	43
Ardebil Carpets	Little Gems of Ardebil, The	Ellis, Charles Grant	√		TMJ	1	3		De 64	18
Argyle	Argyle: The Transformation of a Classical Pattern Through the Design Process	Faust, Regine	√		Fa	9	4		J/A 82	24
Argyle	Demystifying Complex Weaves: A Step-by-Step Exploration from Four to Sixteen Harnesses	Piroch, Sigrid	√	> 4	WJ	10	3	39	Wi 86	8
Armature	Wire Your Wall Hangings	Adams, Carol; Patricia L. Magee	√	√	SS&D	15	1	57	Wi 83	100
Armenia	Behind the Scenes: A "Missing" Tradition	Goodman, Deborah Lerme	√		Fa	13	3		M/J 86	46
Armor	Basketry Armor	Austin, Carole	√		Fa	14	1		J/F 87	28
Arrowcraft Shop	Arrowcraft: Tennessee Cottage Industry	Pilsk, Adele	√		Fa	5	5		S/O 78	20
Art	Thoughts on Money, Art, and Spinning	Chelsey, Randy			S-O	11	1		Sp 87	14
Art	When is Fiber Art "Art"?	Koplos, Janet	√		Fa	13	2		M/A 86	34
Art Bank: Public Programs	Canada Council Art Bank, The	Kirby, William	√		AT	7			Ju 87	75
Art Bank: Purchase Program	Canada Council Art Bank, The	Kirby, William	√		AT	7			Ju 87	75
Art Bank: Rental Program	Canada Council Art Bank, The	Kirby, William	√		AT	7			Ju 87	75
Art: Business Aspect	Thinking About the Business of Art	Dunwell, Anna			Fa	11	2		M/A 84	57
Art Criticism/Fiber	Critical Eye: Art Criticism and Fiber, The	Nelson, Leslee Corpier	√		Fa	14	1		J/F 87	13
Art Education	Art Education in the United States Today	Blumenau, Lili	√		H&C	2	3		Su 51	30
Art Fabric	Ed Rossbach: Embracing the Fabric of Art	West, Virginia	√		Fa	9	1		J/F 82	31
Art Fabric	"Flexible Medium: 20th Cnetury American Art Fabric, The" (Seminar)	Levine, Betsy			TM			1	O/N 85	12
Art Fabric, Mainstream	Conversation with Mildred Constantine	Park, Betty	√		Fa	8	6		N/D 81	14
Art Fabric, Non-Mainstream	Livin' and Workin' on the Land: Fiber Art Outside the Mainstream	Talley, Charles S.	√		Fa	8	6		N/D 81	38
Art Fiber	Conversation with Lillian Elliott, A	Janeiro, Jan	√		Fa	9	2		M/A 82	66
Art Fiber	"Fiber from the Marietta College Crafts National" (Exhibit)	Murray, Megan	√		Fa	11	2		M/A 84	76
Art Myths	Thinking About the Business of Art	Dunwell, Anna			Fa	11	2		M/A 84	57
Art: Site-Specific	Design Concepts and Aesthetic Concerns of Corporate Art Collections	Rutherford, Karen Jenson			AT	8			De 87	193
Art: Textile Patterns	Influence from the East: Textiles and Textile Patterns in Western Art	Park, Betty	√		Fa	12	2		M/A 85	22
Art Textiles	"Art Fabric: Mainstream, The" (Exhibit)	Janeiro, Jan	√		Fa	8	5		S/O 81	70
Art Textiles	Chinese Brushwork Converted Into Classical Embroidery	Stickler, John C.	√		H&C	22	2		Sp 71	11
Art Textiles	Conversation with Claire Zeisler, A	Koplos, Janet	√		Fa	10	4		J/A 83	25
Art Textiles	Cynthia Laymon: Pleated Interplay	Michaels-Paque, Joan	√		Fa	12	5		S/O 85	12
Art Textiles	"Deborah Warner's Visual Journal" (Exhibit)	Poon, Vivian	√		Fa	10	6		N/D 83	76
Art Textiles	Dora Jung: The Artist and the Person	Talley, Charles	√		Fa	12	1		J/F 85	39
Art Textiles	"Fiber in Focus" (Exhibit)	Skudera, Gail	√		Fa	10	6		N/D 83	82
Art Textiles	"Flexible Medium: Art Fabric from the Museum Collection, The" (Exhibit)	Goodman, Deborah Lerme	√		Fa	11	5		S/O 84	71
Art Textiles	Gyöngy Laky: Experimental Thinking in Textiles	Scarborough, Jessica	√		Fa	11	1		J/F 84	21
Art Textiles	Industrial Fabric & the Woven Form	Zausner, Judith	√		H&C	23	6		N/D 72	43
Art Textiles	Kate Woolstenhulme: A Sense of Place	Walters, Roberta	√		Fa	10	2		M/A 83	56
Art Textiles	Laura Militzer Bryant: Thought Process	Bryant, Laura Militzer	√		Fa	10	4		J/A 83	52
Art Textiles	"Michael Olszewski: Pleated and Stitched Silk" (Exhibit)	Poon, Vivian	√		Fa	11	3		M/J 84	78
Art Textiles	Missy Stevens: Connecting Art and Fabric	Mallinckrodt, Casey	√		Fa	14	4		S/O 87	20
Art Textiles	Olga de Amarol: Toward a Language of Freedom	Scarborough, Jessica	√		Fa	12	4		J/A 85	51

SUBJECT	TITLE	AUTHOR	IL	INST	JOUR	VOL	NO	ISS	DATE	PAGE
Art Textiles	Rena Thompson: Echoes of Intuitive Truths	Park, Betty	√		Fa	13	2		M/A 86	46
Art Textiles	Shigeki and Shihoko Fukumoto: Balancing Art and Function	Lancaster, Zöe Woodruff	√		Fa	13	6		N/D 86	5
Art Textiles	"Unsettled Images: Peggy Vanbianchi & Emily Standley" (Exhibit)	Rowlands-Tarbox, Jean L.	√		Fa	12	5		S/O 85	71
Art Textiles: Hanging	Point of View (Renie Breskin Adams)		√		TM		7		O/N 86	92
Art Textiles: Quilts	"Art Quilt, The" (Exhibit)	McMorris, Penny; Kile, Michael	√		TM		7		O/N 86	30
Art Textiles: Wearables	Lamé	Boyce, Ann	√		TM		8		D/J 86	32
Art Wearables	Art As Clothing: Clothing As Art		√		SS&D	12	1	45	Wi 80	85
Art Wearables	Artwear '87				TM		10		A/M 87	22
Art Wearables	Artwear/ACE Expo		√		WJ	12	1	45	Su 87	35
Art Wearables	Body as Canvas, The	Koda, Harold	√		TM		8		D/J 86	56
Art Wearables	Girls Who Wear Cactus	Akamine, Estelle	√		TM		4		A/M 86	66
Art Wearables	Pins and Needles				TM		13		O/N 87	4
Art Wearables	Safety-Pin Jacket (Mark Mahall)		√		TM		9		F/M 87	88
Art Wearables	Wearable Paintings	Auger, Shirley Venit	√	√	H&C	24	4		Au 73	34
Art Wearables	Why Be Needed by Pins?				TM		14		D/J 87	4
Art Wearables: Shoes	Shoemaker's Art, The	Bowen, Gaza	√	√	TM		5		J/J 86	56
Art Wearables: Tapestry	Dream Weaver: Joan Renne		√		WJ	12	1	45	Su 87	40
Art/Architecture	Art and Architecture	Janeiro, Jan	√		Fa	9	3		M/J 82	52
Art/Craft	Interview with Jack Lenor Larsen, An		√		WJ	7	1	25	Su 82	10
Art/Craft	Of Means and Ends				Fa	5	5		S/O 78	10
Art/Craft	Privilege of Craft, The	Van Winckle, Nance			Hw	8	5		N/D 87	30
Art/Craft	Why Sew Those Lines? An Interview with Giorgio Furioso and Carolyn Thomas	Paca, Al	√		Fa	7	4		J/A 80	25
Art/Craft Alliance	Exhibition by Larsen and Riegger Indicates Broadening Field of Craft Cooperation		√		H&C	2	2		Sp 51	32
Art/Culture/Future	Art/Culture/Future	Scarborough, Jessica	√		Fa	13	5		S/O 86	52
Art/Design/Business	Design Concepts and Aesthetic Concerns of Corporate Art Collections	Rutherford, Karen Jenson			AT	8			De 87	193
Art/Fashion	"Issey Miyake: Fashion Without Taboos" (Exhibit)	Mathews, Cleve	√		Fa	12	3		M/J 85	70
Art/Language	Words in Fiber	Rowley, Kathleen	√		Fa	11	2		M/A 84	66
Art/Truth	Elizabeth MacDonald: Finding the Ties That Bind Truth and Art	Reuter, Laurel	√		Fa	14	4		S/O 87	31
Artifacts: Potsherds, Textile Impressions	Prehistoric Textiles Revealed by Potsherds	Kuttruff, Jenna Tedrick	√		SS&D	11	3	43	Su 80	40
Artist/Industry: Finland	Artist and Industry — A Cooperative Effort		√		Hw	8	3		M/J 87	71
Artists-in-Residence	Fiber At Artpark	MacDonald, Claudia	√		Fa	10	6		N/D 83	47
Artpark	Fiber At Artpark	MacDonald, Claudia	√		Fa	10	6		N/D 83	47
Artpark	What Is Artpark?		√		Fa	9	3		M/J 82	20
Artpark	Yurt in Artpark, The	Brennan, Joan	√		Fa	9	3		M/J 82	19
Arts and Crafts Shows	Southern Tier Arts & Crafts Shows		√		H&C	23	2		M/A 72	28
Arts Center	Arizona Arts Center at Sedona Offers Program Year Around	Warren, Hamilton	√		H&C	13	1		Wi 62	16
Arts Center	Arizona Arts Center at Sedona Offers Program Year Around	Warren, Hamilton	√		H&C	13	1		Wi 62	16
Arvada Project	Arvada Project, The	Heath, Jennifer	√		Fa	5	4		J/A 78	45
As-Drawn-In, also see Treadling										
Asia	Dorothy Meredith in Asia	Stamsta, Jean			H&C	16	3		Su 65	29
Asia	Flat-Woven Structures Found in Nomadic and Village Weavings from the Near East and Central Asia	Wertime, John T.	√		TMJ	18			79	33
Asia	Highland Weavers in Asia	Hatch, David P.	√	√	H&C	11	1		Wi 60	6

SUBJECT	TITLE	AUTHOR	IL	INST	JOUR	VOL	NO	ISS	DATE	PAGE
Asia	Ritual Fiber: Weaving Hope for the Future Into the Fabric of Life	Wilcox, Don	√		Fa	13	6		N/D 86	7
Asia	Shelters and Symbols	Gordon, Beverly	√	√	SS&D	11	1	41	Wi 79	53
Asia	Some Contemporary Textiles in Southern Asia	Hatch, David P.	√	√	H&C	11	3		Su 60	23
Asia	Weaving in Southeast Asia (addition SS&D v7 n4 76 p27)	Marston, Ena			SS&D	7	2	26	Sp 76	30
Asia, Southeast	Dress and Design in Highland Southeast Asia: The Hmong (Miao) and the Yao	Adams, Monni	√		TMJ	4	1		De 74	51
Assemblage	Abigail Jurist Levy: Dyed Paper and Silk Assemblages	Goodman, Deborah Lerme	√		Fa	12	4		J/A 85	16
Assemblage	"Web of Kentucky Thread, A" (Exhibit)	Meloy, Margaret	√		Fa	12	5		S/O 85	72
Assemblage, Mixed Media	"Ceremonial Works" (Exhibit)		√		Fa	13	2		M/A 86	56
Associations: The Natural Colored Wool Growers Association	Villa de Cordero Negro: "Country Home of the Black Lamb"	Pepin, Yvonne	√		SS&D	17	3	67	Su 86	30
Atelier: Dovecot Studios	Edinburgh Tapestry Company: A Thriving Anachronism in Scotland, The	Soroka, Joanne	√		Fa	10	3		M/J 83	59
Atelier: Gobelins Royal Tapestry Works	Gobelins Royal Tapestry Works: Tradition and Change in France	Rex, Chris	√		Fa	10	3		M/J 83	58
Atelier: Handarbetets vanner	Handarbetets vanner: Artists and Craftsmakers Collaborate in Sweden	Talley, Charles	√		Fa	10	3		M/J 83	56
Atelier: The San Francisco Tapestry Workshop	San Francisco Tapestry Workshop: A European-Style Atelier in the United States, The	Rowley, Kathleen	√		Fa	10	3		M/J 83	60
Atelier: Victorian Tapestry Workshop	Victorian Tapestry Workshop: A New Tradition in Australia, The	Newman, Rochelle	√		Fa	10	3		M/J 83	38
Athens Tapestry Works	Athens Tapestry Works	Many, Paul	√		Fa	5	4		J/A 78	51
Attu Island	Attu Basketry	McIver, Lucy	√	√	H&C	24	1		J/F 73	35
Atwater-Bronson Weave	Celtic Knot Box Cushion	Xenakis, Athanasios David	√	√	PWC	3	4	10		60
Atwater-Bronson Weave	Simple Damask-Like Effects Using Element Diameter Differential and Element Tension Differential	Xenakis, Athanasios David	√	> 4	AT	1			De 83	317
Auction Houses: Textiles	Inspiration from the Past: Textile Treasures in the World of New York City Auctions	Sider, Sandra	√		Fa	11	6		N/D 84	62
Auctioning	Auctioning Rugs Among the Navajos	Marcus, Ruth-Claire	√		TM			6	A/S 86	16
Australia	Aussie Augments	George, Barbara	√	√	Kn	4	1	9	Wi 87	62
Australia	Australian Cashmere and Cashgora	Feldman-Wood, Florence	√		S-O	9	1		Sp 85	42
Australia	Australian Spinner Raises Profitable Flock of Goats	Berger, Charles	√		H&C	17	3		Su 66	11
Australia	Basketmaker's Year "Down Under", A	Malarcher, Patricia	√		Fa	8	4		J/A 81	47
Australia	Comminicating Through Craft	de Mar, Lola	√		Fa	14	1		J/F 87	38
Australia	Contemporary Fabrics from an Australia Handweaving Mill	Daniel, Robert	√		H&C	16	1		Wi 65	18
Australia	Dyepot in Australia	Taggart, Barbara	√	√	SS&D	5	4	20	Fa 74	56
Australia	Excellence of Spinning, Vitality of Dyes Impress Visitor to 'Down Under'	Barker, Mary	√		SS&D	4	4	16	Fa 73	46
Australia	Labor Banners of Australia	Mancini, Anne	√		Fa	14	5		N/D 87	36
Australia	Locker Hooking	Rough, Joan Z.	√	√	SS&D	16	1	61	Wi 84	54
Australia	Mohair: A Multimillion Dollar Industry for Australia	Gray, Isabel			S-O	8	4		Wi 84	47
Australia	Sheep Shearing Robots	Sector, Bob			S-O	8	1		Sp 84	16
Australia	Spinning—Australia	DeBoer, Janet			S-O	11	3		Fa 87	35
Australia	Spinning Down Under: What Are You Going to Do with the Yarn?	De Boer, Janet	√		S-O	1			77	23
Australia	String Bags	Nunn, Robin; Alan West	√	√	SS&D	14	2	54	Sp 83	10
Australia	Victorian Tapestry Workshop: A New Tradition in Australia, The	Newman, Rochelle	√		Fa	10	3		M/J 83	38
Australia	Weaving Down Under	McKay, Isabel	√		H&C	15	3		Su 64	20

19

SUBJECT	TITLE	AUTHOR	IL	INST	JOUR	VOL	NO	ISS	DATE	PAGE
Austria	Weaving in the Austrian Tyrol		√		H&C	7	1		Wi 55	28
Automatic Loom Weaving	Note on the Diffusion of the Automatic Loom Within the British Cotton Industry, A	Pourdeyhimi, B.; K. C. Jackson	√		AT	6			De 86	101
Automatic Looms: History	Development of Weaving Using Automatic Looms, The	Pourdeyhimi, B.; K. C. Jackson; K. Hepworth			AT	4			De 85	107
Automobile Upholstery	Handloom in the Automobile Industry, The	Clement, Doris	√		H&C	10	3		Su 59	61
Awards	Awards for "Sharpen Your Quills"				SS&D	4	3	15	Su 73	39
Awards	Dina Barzel Wins At Seattle		√		SS&D	4	2	14	Sp 73	26
Awards	Garments Win At 1974 Midwest Conference		√	√	SS&D	6	2	22	Sp 75	92
Awards	Handwoven Tapestries Chosen As Governor's Awards in the Arts		√		SS&D	2	2	6	Sp 71	13
Awards	Hot Lips Houlihan Loves to Stitch		√		Fa	l3	4		J/A 86	ll
Awards	'lectric Ikat Wins WHFL Award		√	√	SS&D	5	3	19	Su 74	92
Awards	Louvered Divider Wins Head Award		√		SS&D	1	4	4	Se 70	19
Awards	Marilyn Grisham Wins HGA Award		√		SS&D	3	4	12	Fa 72	14
Awards	Patty Curran Wins HGA Award at Northern California				SS&D	3	3	11	Su 72	44
Awards	Weaver's Journal Shared Traditions Award, The		√		WJ	12	2	46	Fa 87	21
Awards: A. I. D., Upholstery Fabric	Design Award to Isabel Scott Fabrics for Exclusive Sardinian Import		√		H&C	13	2		Sp 62	16
Awards: Therapy/Rehabilitation	Service Award to Mrs. Talmage				H&C	13	4		Fa 62	36
Baby Accessories	Baby's First Hang-Up	Gilbert, Donna Lee	√	√	SS&D	11	4	44	Fa 80	26
Back Strap Weaving	Keeping Tradition Alive	Wilcox, Don	√		Fa	14	1		J/F 87	44
Backed Weaves	Backed Weaves: Part 1	Marston, Ena	√	> 4	SS&D	8	3	31	Su 77	64
Backed Weaves	Backed Weaves, Part 2	Marston, Ena	√	> 4	SS&D	8	4	32	Fa 77	50
Backed Weaves	Double Weaves: Between the Single and the Double Fabrics	Zielinski, S. A.; Robert Leclerc, ed.			MWL	15			'51–'73	24
Backed Weaves	Pick-Up Piqué (error-corrected SS&D v19 n1 87 p33)	Fletcher, Joyce	√	√	SS&D	18	4	72	Fa 87	60
Backed Weaves	Pile Weaves, Rugs and Tapestry: Handwoven Furcoat	Zielinski, S. A.; Robert Leclerc, ed.	√	> 4	MWL	14			'51–'73	21
Backed Weaves	Pique (A Brief Synopsis)	Schneider, Mary	√	> 4	CW	7	2	20	Ja 86	22
Backed Weaves	Polly Yori (error-corrected H&C v21 n3 70 p45)	Marston, Ena	√	> 4	H&C	21	1		Wi 70	19
Backed Weaves	Ribbed Piqué	Sullivan, Donna	√	√	SS&D	18	3	71	Su 87	30
Backed Weaves	Stitching Traditional Coverlet Weaves	Sellin, Helen G.	√	> 4	AT	1			De 83	289
Backed Weaves, Basket	Double Weaves: Backing-2	Zielinski, S. A.; Robert Leclerc, ed.	√	√	MWL	15			'51–'73	29
Backed Weaves, Linton, Surface Interest	Surface Interest — Textiles of Today: Surface Interest Designs with Drafts, Group 5, Backed-Fabric Designs	Tidball, Harriet	√	> 4	SCGM		2		61	18
Backed Weaves, Twill	Double Weaves: Backing-1	Zielinski, S. A.; Robert Leclerc, ed.	√	√	MWL	15			'51–'73	25
Backing in Warp	Double Weaves: Backing in Warp	Zielinski, S. A.; Robert Leclerc, ed.	√	√	MWL	15			'51–'73	35
Backstrap Weaving	Art of Ixchel: Learning to Weave in Guatemala and Rhode Island, The	Schevill, Margot	√	√	WJ	8	1	29	Su 83	57
Backstrap Weaving	Back Strap Weaving in Zacualpan Mexico	Cooper, Jane	√	√	SS&D	5	3	19	Su 74	13
Backstrap Weaving	Backstrap Weaving for Penance and Profit	Coffman, Charlotte	√	√	WJ	7	1	25	Su 82	60
Backstrap Weaving	Backstrap Weaving in the Philippines	Ng, Mary	√		SS&D	9	1	33	Wi 77	18
Backstrap Weaving	Before Heddles Were Invented	Bird, Junius B.	√		H&C	3	3		Su 52	5
Backstrap Weaving	Complementary-Warp Weave (error-corrected WJ v7 n4 83 p4)	Coffman, Charlotte	√	√	WJ	7	3	27	Wi 82	53
Backstrap Weaving	Gifts from Ancient Peru	Nass, Ulla	√	√	WJ	8	1	29	Su 83	32
Backstrap Weaving	Guatemala Weaver, The	Marks, Copeland A.	√		H&C	26	5		Oc 75	2

SUBJECT	TITLE	AUTHOR	IL	INST	JOUR	VOL	NO	ISS	DATE	PAGE
Backstrap Weaving	Guatemala: Weaving, People	Frost, Gordon	√		lw	5	4		Fa 80	30
Backstrap Weaving	Handspun Yarn Production Rates in the Cuzco Region of Peru	Bird, Junius B.	√		TMJ	2	3		De 68	9
Backstrap Weaving	Mexican Travelogue, A	Hewitt, T. H.	√		H&C	3	3		Su 52	22
Backstrap Weaving	Noble Tradition Preserved: An Ecuadorian Weaving Co-op, A	Llewellyn, Charles; Deborah Llewellyn	√		SS&D	11	3	43	Su 80	12
Backstrap Weaving	Projects for a Six-Dent Rigid Heddle Backstrap Loom	Swanson, Karen	√	√	H&C	21	4		Fa 70	9
Backstrap Weaving	Selected Batak Textiles: Technique and Function	Gittinger, Mattiebelle S.	√		TMJ	4	2		75	13
Backstrap Weaving	Shaped Tapestry Bags from the Nazca-Ica Area of Peru	Bird, Junius B.	√		TMJ	1	3		De 64	2
Backstrap Weaving	Sumbanese Ikat	Hannon, Farrell	√	√	WJ	8	1	29	Su 83	38
Backstrap Weaving	Three Faces of the Eight-Pointed Star Motif (error-corrected SS&D v14 n4 83 p4)	Coffman, Charlotte	√	√	SS&D	14	3	55	Su 83	56
Backstrap Weaving	Work of A Huave Indian Weaver In Oaxaca, Mexico: Complex Weave Structures Utilizing One Warp Set and Two Complementary Weft Sets, The	Connolly, Loris	√		AT	3			My 85	7
Backstrap Weaving: Mexico	Mexican Motifs: Mexico, Land of Contrasts	Tidball, Harriet	√		SCGM		6		62	1
Backstrap Weaving: Multiple Heddle Rods	Warping and Weaving Mitla Cloth on the Backstrap Loom	Knottenbelt, Maaike	√	√	TMJ	22			83	53
Backstrap Weaving: Technique	Backstrap Weaving in MesoAmerica	Baizerman, Suzanne; Karen Searle	√	√	lw	5	4		Fa 80	38
Backstrap Weaving: Technique	Double-Woven Treasures from Old Peru	Cahlander, Adele	√	√	PWC			4	Ja 83	36
Bags, Purses, Totes	Accessories: Bags and Slippers		√	√	WJ	5	3	19	Wi 81	42
Bags, Purses, Totes	Accessories: Double Woven Bag		√	√	WJ	2	4	8	Ap 78	7
Bags, Purses, Totes	Accessories: Drawstring Bag		√	√	WJ	2	4	8	Ap 78	5
Bags, Purses, Totes	Accessories: Large Bags Made from Narrow Strips		√	√	WJ	2	4	8	Ap 78	6
Bags, Purses, Totes	Albuquerque Group Proves: Co-Ops Can Work	Ligon, Linda	√		lw	1	1		Fa 75	8
Bags, Purses, Totes	Another Loom Another Tote Bag, Rug Sampler Project for Beginners	Krasnoff, Julienne	√	√	H&C	22	1		Wi 71	32
Bags, Purses, Totes	Antique Stripe Evening Bag (Sigrid Piroch)		√	> 4	Hw	6	1		J/F 85	36, I-10
Bags, Purses, Totes	Aurora Borealis Evening Clutch Bag (Sigrid Piroch)		√	> 4	Hw	6	1		J/F 85	37, I-10
Bags, Purses, Totes	Bag for all Seasons (Barbara Grace), A		√	√	Hw	3	2		Mr 82	67
Bags, Purses, Totes	Bag, Hat and Quesquemitl	Thorne, Sylvia; June Segermark	√	√	SS&D	3	1	9	Wi 71	18
Bags, Purses, Totes	Bags	Meiling, Nancy	√	√	WJ	6	3	23	Wi 81	40
Bags, Purses, Totes	Bags with Strong Handles	Foeley, Cora V.	√		H&C	16	2		Sp 65	33
Bags, Purses, Totes	Band Bag (Jane Patrick) (error-corrected Hw v4 n3 83 p79)		√	√	Hw	4	2		M/A 83	Cover, 51, 89
Bags, Purses, Totes	Beach Bag (Sharon Alderman)		√	√	Hw	4	3		M/J 83	43, 80
Bags, Purses, Totes	Beading on Leather	Ellsworth, Wendy	√	√	TM			7	O/N 86	50
Bags, Purses, Totes	Beginning with Bands: Tablet Woven Garments and Accessories	Holtzer, Marilyn Emerson	√	√	WJ	9	3	35	Wi 85	28
Bags, Purses, Totes	Carpet Bag Briefcase (Linda Ligon)		√	√	Hw	5	1		J/F 84	49, 91
Bags, Purses, Totes	Checker Board (Julia Hanan)		√	√	Hw	2	1		F-W 80	55, 69
Bags, Purses, Totes	Diaper Bag (Eve Bostic)		√	√	Hw	8	2		M/A 87	46, I-6
Bags, Purses, Totes	Double Woven Bag Inspired by a South American Bag, A	Barrett, Clotilde	√	√	WJ	1	2	2	Oc 76	29
Bags, Purses, Totes	Double-Woven Treasures from Old Peru	Cahlander, Adele	√	√	PWC			4	Ja 83	36
Bags, Purses, Totes	Doubleweave Bag (Pam Bolesta)		√	√	Hw	1	1		F-W 79	20, 53
Bags, Purses, Totes	Envelope Purse		√	√	H&C	18	3		Su 67	41
Bags, Purses, Totes	Evening Bags that Shine with Flash & Glitter	Piroch, Sigrid	√	√	Hw	6	1		J/F 85	36

SUBJECT	TITLE	AUTHOR	IL	INST	JOUR	VOL	NO	ISS	DATE	PAGE
Bags, Purses, Totes	Fashion Show of Handwoven Garments		√	> 4	WJ	3	3	11	Ja 79	5
Bags, Purses, Totes	Florodora Bag	Upitis, Lizbeth	√	√	Kn	2	2	4	S-S 86	47
Bags, Purses, Totes	Folk Textiles of Latin America	Kelemen, Pál	√		TMJ	1	4		De 65	2
Bags, Purses, Totes	Four Projects from Mrs. Elsie H. Gubser	Gubser, Elsie H.	√	√	H&C	6	3		Su 55	49
Bags, Purses, Totes	Freestyle Embroidery: New Images with Traditional Stitches	Dahl, Caroline	√	√	TM		1		O/N 85	22
Bags, Purses, Totes	Go Adventuring with Your Pick-Up Stick (error-corrected H&C v2 n4 51 p64)	Roberts, Elizabeth	√	√	H&C	2	2		Sp 51	28
Bags, Purses, Totes	Hair of the Dog, The	Adams, Brucie	√	√	Hw	3	2		Mr 82	62
Bags, Purses, Totes	Hand Woven Garments	Piper, Aris	√	> 4	WJ	5	3	19	Wi 81	24
Bags, Purses, Totes	Handbag by Muriel Barnes (error-corrected H&C v14 n1 63 p46)		√	> 4	H&C	13	4		Fa 62	42
Bags, Purses, Totes	Handbag in Finnweave		√	√	H&C	16	1		Wi 65	33
Bags, Purses, Totes	Handbags and a Hat	Phelps, Marie	√	√	H&C	1	3		Fa 50	29
Bags, Purses, Totes	Handbags of Leather and Fabric	Emerson, Trudy	√	√	H&C	17	2		Sp 66	22
Bags, Purses, Totes	Handwoven Flight Bags	Dickey, Helen F.	√	√	H&C	11	3		Su 60	46
Bags, Purses, Totes	It Still Can Be Beautiful: Although Utilitarian	Rutkovsky, Fran Cutrell	√	√	SS&D	7	3	27	Su 76	57
Bags, Purses, Totes	Janet Markarian: From Baskets to Bags, Containers Transformed	Koplos, Janet	√		Fa	11	1		J/F 84	16
Bags, Purses, Totes	Japanese Tote—The Furoshiki, A	Griffin, Gertrude	√	√	SS&D	6	1	21	Wi 74	78
Bags, Purses, Totes	Journey in Thread, A	Rees, Linda	√		Hw	5	5		N/D 84	99
Bags, Purses, Totes	Knitted Trifle Bag	Xenakis, Alexis Yiorgos	√	√	PWC	1	1		No 81	52
Bags, Purses, Totes	Kohl Bags	Austin, Carole	√		Fa	11	4		J/A 84	48
Bags, Purses, Totes	Leamington Bags	Steedsman, Nell	√	√	SS&D	2	4	8	Fa 71	28
Bags, Purses, Totes	Mable Morrow—Collector, Scholar of Indian Arts, Part 2	Maxcy, Mabel E.	√		SS&D	5	2	18	Sp 74	33
Bags, Purses, Totes	Magazine Tote (Jean Anstine)		√	√	Hw	7	3		M/J 86	41, I-8
Bags, Purses, Totes	Make a Soumak Sampler Into a Tote Bag		√	√	WJ	2	2	6	Oc 77	28
Bags, Purses, Totes	Maurine Fair	Ligon, Linda	√	> 4	Iw	2	2		Wi 77	20
Bags, Purses, Totes	Michigan Weaving, Third Conference at Hartland Shows Wide Variety		√	> 4	H&C	13	1		Wi 62	18
Bags, Purses, Totes	Modern Twined Bags for Weaving Without a Loom	Spencer, Elsie H.	√	√	H&C	21	1		Wi 70	12
Bags, Purses, Totes	Nez Percé Indian Art and Craft Revival	Connette, Ann	√	√	H&C	21	4		Fa 70	5
Bags, Purses, Totes	Petit Point Evening Purse (Doramay Keasbey)		√	√	Hw	7	1		J/F 86	66, I-15
Bags, Purses, Totes	Plaited Twill Projects: Notes of a Pattern Weaver	Alvic, Philis	√	> 4	WJ	11	4	44	Sp 87	55
Bags, Purses, Totes	Plastic Tote Bag	Speckert, Gene K., OTR	√	√	SS&D	4	2	14	Sp 73	57
Bags, Purses, Totes	"Poppana" Shopping Bag (Riitta Mäkinen)		√	√	Hw	8	3		M/J 87	74, I-16
Bags, Purses, Totes	Prehistoric Twined Bag from Big Bone Cave, Tennessee: Manufacture, Repair, and Use, A	Kuttruff, Jenna Tedrick	√		AT	8			De 87	125
Bags, Purses, Totes	Projects At Chautauqua Summer School	Snyder, Mary E.	√	√	H&C	23	3		M/J 72	14
Bags, Purses, Totes	Projects for a Six-Dent Rigid Heddle Backstrap Loom	Swanson, Karen	√	√	H&C	21	4		Fa 70	9
Bags, Purses, Totes	Rag Bag (Connie Farnbach)		√	√	Hw	2	3		My 81	50, 79
Bags, Purses, Totes	Reviving the Lost Art of Woodland Indian Bag Weaving	King, Rod	√		Fa	13	2		M/A 86	27
Bags, Purses, Totes	Rita Buchanan's Knotted Net Onion Bag		√		S-O	9	3		Fa 85	15
Bags, Purses, Totes	Satin Weave Evening Bag	Lodge, Jean	√	> 4	WJ	10	1	37	Su 85	39
Bags, Purses, Totes	Shadow Weave Purse (Jane Patrick)		√	√	Hw	6	5		N/D 85	50, I-9
Bags, Purses, Totes	Shaped Tapestry Bags from the Nazca-Ica Area of Peru	Bird, Junius B.	√		TMJ	1	3		De 64	2
Bags, Purses, Totes	Silk Purse (Sharon Alderman)		√	√	Hw	4	1		J/F 83	43, 83
Bags, Purses, Totes	Simplest of all Tapestry Techniques Used in a Carrying Bag, The		√	√	WJ	7	3	27	Wi 82	37

SUBJECT	TITLE	AUTHOR	IL	INST	JOUR	VOL	NO	ISS	DATE	PAGE
Bags, Purses, Totes	Sprang and Frame Plaiting for Garments		√	√	WJ	3	3	11	Ja 79	26
Bags, Purses, Totes	String Bags	Nunn, Robin; Alan West	√	√	SS&D	14	2	54	Sp 83	10
Bags, Purses, Totes	Summer and Winter — Part 1		√	>4	WJ	2	4	8	Ap 78	28
Bags, Purses, Totes	Summertime!	Coifman, Lucienne	√	√	SS&D	15	3	59	Su 84	74
Bags, Purses, Totes	Tagari: A Greek Saddlebag of Handspun Wools, The	Koster, Joan Boura	√	√	WJ	6	2	22	Fa 81	24
Bags, Purses, Totes	Tale of a Talis, A	Sylvan, Katherine	√	√	WJ	6	1	21	Su 81	42
Bags, Purses, Totes	Tapestry Backpack		√	√	WJ	2	2	6	Oc 77	9
Bags, Purses, Totes	Tote Bags with a Difference		√	>4	H&C	17	3		Su 66	20
Bags, Purses, Totes	Trifles: Silk Purse, About the Size of a Sow's Ear (Linda Ligon)		√	√	Hw	1	1		F-W 79	47
Bags, Purses, Totes	Twined Bag, A		√	√	WJ	1	3	3	Ja 77	27
Bags, Purses, Totes	Twined Bags and Pouches of the Eastern Woodlands	White, John Kennardh	√	√	H&C	20	3		Su 69	8
Bags, Purses, Totes	Two Prize-winning Canadian Projects		√	√	H&C	13	3		Su 62	32
Bags, Purses, Totes	Two Tote Bags (Betty Davenport)		√	√	Hw	6	5		N/D 85	12, I-4
Bags, Purses, Totes	Ultimate Brown Bag, The (Barbara Smith Eychaner)		√	√	Hw	7	4		S/O 86	36, I-6
Bags, Purses, Totes	Unique Technique for a Braided Strap from Colombia	Cahlander, Adele	√	√	WJ	7	1	25	Su 82	56
Bags, Purses, Totes	Weavers Baby Bag		√	√	SS&D	5	2	18	Sp 74	19
Bags, Purses, Totes	Weavers Bag — From Many Lands to Convergence '74, The	West, Virginia	√	√	SS&D	5	1	17	Wi 73	38
Bags, Purses, Totes	Weavers Bag — From Montana to Convergence '74, The	Burlew, Margaret	√	√	SS&D	5	1	17	Wi 73	39
Bags, Purses, Totes	Weaving a Cotton Saddlebag on the Santa Elena Peninsula of Ecuador	Hagino, Jane Parker; Karen E. Stothert	√	√	TMJ	22			83	19
Bags, Purses, Totes	Weaving in Donegal (error-corrected H&C v23 n3 72 p11)	McNeill, Mary	√	√	H&C	23	2		M/A 72	35
Bags, Purses, Totes	Weaving with Fur for a Bag	Keeler, Betty	√	√	H&C	26	1		J/F 75	22
Bags, Purses, Totes	Weft Twining	Smith, Joyce Ronald	√	√	TM			2	D/J 85	69
Bags, Purses, Totes	Why Spin Cotton?	Baker, Ella	√	√	S-O	9	2		Su 85	31
Bags, Purses, Totes	Woven Leather Purse (Eileen Ternullo)		√	√	Hw	5	1		J/F 84	53, 102
Bags, Purses, Totes	Woven Leather Shoulder Bag (Eileen Ternullo)		√	√	Hw	5	1		J/F 84	53, 102
Baize	Green Baize for Independence Hall from Penland Looms	Ford, Howard C.	√		H&C	7	2		Sp 56	14
Balanced Weave	Summer and Winter and Other Two-Tie Unit Weaves: Balance and Yarns	Tidball, Harriet	√	√	SCGM		19		66	14
Balenciaga: Wedding Gown	Sunbonnet Sue				TM			13	O/N 87	4
Bali	Balinese Ikat	Hannon, Farrell	√	√	WJ	5	1	17	Su 80	49
Bali	Weavers of Bali	Hannon, Farrell	√		SS&D	18	4	72	Fa 87	46
Ballad Singing	Four Posts of Poverty, The	Xenaxis, Alexis Yiorgos	√		PWC	5	1	15		6
Balloons	Ballooning Art Form: The Making of a Hot Air Balloon Basket, A		√		SS&D	11	4	44	Fa 80	8
Balloons	Château de Balleroy Balloon, The		√		TM			4	A/M 86	88
Balloons	Hot-Air Balloons	Theil, Linda	√		TM			4	A/M 86	20
Balloons: Handwoven	Up, Up and Away in my Handwoven Balloon	Potter, Katie Forderhase	√	√	Hw	3	2		Mr 82	40
Balls, String	Temari: Threads to the Past	Beall, Karen F.	√		Fa	14	2		M/A 87	7
Bamboo	Shokansai Iizuka: Bamboo Craftsman and Living National Treasure of Japan	Adachi, Barbara Curtis	√		Fa	11	1		J/F 84	59
Banana Fiber	Banana, Ramie, and Hemp In Okinawa (error-corrected Fa v14 n3 87 p4)	Miller, Dorothy	√		Fa	14	2		M/A 87	46
Band Weaving: Backstrap	Ancient Peruvian Loom, An	Grossman, Ellin	√		H&C	9	2		Sp 58	20
Band Weaving: Backstrap	Backstrap Looms	Conrad, Elvira	√		H&C	14	3		Su 63	17
Band Weaving: Backstrap	Backstrap Weaving for Penance and Profit	Coffman, Charlotte	√	√	WJ	7	1	25	Su 82	60

SUBJECT	TITLE	AUTHOR	IL	INST	JOUR	VOL	NO	ISS	DATE	PAGE
Band Weaving: Backstrap	Camera Strap in Double-Weave Pick-Up	Gaston-Voûte, Suzanne	√	√	PWC			2	Ap 82	10
Band Weaving: Backstrap	Guatemala Weaver, The	Marks, Copeland A.	√		H&C	26	5		Oc 75	2
Band Weaving: Backstrap	Latvian Folk Costume Braids	Gulbis, Elina	√	√	SS&D	4	3	15	Su 73	46
Band Weaving: Backstrap	Mexican Motifs: Mexico, Land of Contrasts	Tidball, Harriet	√		SCGM		6		62	1
Band Weaving: Backstrap	Mexican Motifs: The Oaxaca Belts	Tidball, Harriet	√	√	SCGM		6		62	19
Band Weaving: Card	Beginning with Bands: Tablet Woven Garments and Accessories	Holtzer, Marilyn Emerson	√	√	WJ	9	3	35	Wi 85	28
Band Weaving: Card	Blouse of Cards	Holtzer, Marilyn Emerson	√		SS&D	16	3	63	Su 85	20
Band Weaving: Card	Card Weaving	Frey, Berta	√	√	H&C	18	3		Su 67	8
Band Weaving: Card	Card Weaving, A New Approach by a Chicago Weaver	Regensteiner, Else	√		H&C	16	3		Su 65	19
Band Weaving: Card	Card Weaving, Patterns Translated to a Handloom	Priest, Alice R.	√	√	H&C	12	2		Sp 61	15
Band Weaving: Card	Card Woven Fringe: The ABCD's for the Beginner	Searle, Karen	√	√	WJ	10	2	38	Fa 85	21
Band Weaving: Card	Card Woven Log Carrier		√	√	Hw	1	1		F-W 79	46, 61
Band Weaving: Card	Cardwoven Belt (Mary Pendergrass)		√	√	Hw	1	2		S-S 80	34, 54
Band Weaving: Card	Christmas Project, A	Richards, Iris	√	√	WJ	1	2	2	Oc 76	12
Band Weaving: Card	Considering Cardweaving	Crockett, Candace	√		H&C	22	3		Su 71	13
Band Weaving: Card	Diagonal Triple-turn Cardweaving	Holtzer, Marilyn	√	√	SS&D	11	2	42	Sp 80	100
Band Weaving: Card	Double-and Double-Faced Cloth on Six-Hole Cards	Holtzer, Marilyn F.	√	√	Iw	5	2		Sp 80	66
Band Weaving: Card	How to Warp and Weave Cards		√	√	Hw	7	3		M/J 86	45
Band Weaving: Card	It's in the Cards	Thorpe, Heather G.	√	√	H&C	3	4		Fa 52	17
Band Weaving: Card	Jacket with Card Woven Trim (Louise Bradley)		√	√	Hw	7	3		M/J 86	41, I-7
Band Weaving: Card	Magazine Tote (Jean Anstine)		√	√	Hw	7	3		M/J 86	41, I-8
Band Weaving: Card	Modern Loom from Medieval Sources, A	Cesari, Andrea	√	√	WJ	10	2	38	Fa 85	18
Band Weaving: Card	Needlepoint with Cardweaving	Porcella, Yvonne	√	√	SS&D	4	2	14	Sp 73	13
Band Weaving: Card	New Approaches to Cardweaving	Crockett, Candace	√		SS&D	4	4	16	Fa 73	72
Band Weaving: Card	Nineteen Forty-eight Cardwoven Belt Still in Frequent Use	Jenkins, Evelyn L.		√	SS&D	5	1	17	Wi 73	74
Band Weaving: Card	On the Edge		√	√	Hw	4	4		S/O 83	34
Band Weaving: Card	Portable Weaving: A Band of Ideas for Bands	Bradley, Louise; Jean Anstine	√	√	Hw	7	3		M/J 86	40
Band Weaving: Card	Preppy Look is in the Cards, The	Xenakis, Athanasios David	√	√	PWC	1	1		No 81	6
Band Weaving: Card	Reversible Cardwoven Hanging	Bradshaw, Susan	√		S-O	10	4		Wi 86	16
Band Weaving: Card	Simplified Warping for Cardweaving	Bradbury, Katherine	√	√	SS&D	5	1	17	Wi 73	84
Band Weaving: Card	Trifles: Christmas Ornaments (Pam Bolesta)		√	√	Hw	1	1		F-W 79	46
Band Weaving: Card	Weaving the Girdle of Rameses on Nine Harnesses	Parkinson, Alberta	√	> 4	CW	3	2	8	Ja 82	1
Band Weaving: Card, Floor Loom	Bands to Broadloom: Converting Card Weaving Designs to a Four-Harness Loom	De Peaux, Barbara; Mary Tyler	√	√	SS&D	8	1	29	WI 76	86
Band Weaving: Card, Floor Loom	Card Woven Belt of East Telemark—An Adaptation of a Traditional Norwegian Technique	Nelson, Lila	√	√	WJ	9	1	33	Su 84	30
Band Weaving: Card, Floor Loom	Cardweaving Patterns on a 4-Shaft Loom	Ohman, Polly	√	√	WJ	6	4	24	Sp 82	36
Band Weaving: Card, Floor Loom	Cardwoven Double Weave, Part 2	Gray, Herbi	√	√	SS&D	15	1	57	Wi 83	92
Band Weaving: Card, Floor Loom	Cardwoven Gauze	Gray, Herbi	√	√	PWC			6	Su 83	57
Band Weaving: Card, Floor Loom	Cardwoven Selvedge for Weft-Faced Rugs, A	Stanley, Martha	√	√	WJ	7	1	25	Su 82	48
Band Weaving: Card, Floor Loom	Technique Sources Sparse—So Weaver Innovates	Carlson, Estelle	√	√	SS&D	7	1	25	Wi 75	89
Band Weaving: Card, On-loom	Cardwoven Mattor (Part 1)	Gray, Herbi	√	√	SS&D	14	4	56	Fa 83	64
Band Weaving: Crossed-Warp	Peruvian Crossed-Warp Weave, A	Castle, Nancy	√	√	TMJ	4	4		77	61

SUBJECT	TITLE	AUTHOR	IL	INST	JOUR	VOL	NO	ISS	DATE	PAGE
Band Weaving: Crossed-Warp	Understanding Some Complex Structures from Simple Andean Looms: Steps in Analysis and Reproduction	Cahlander, Adele	√	√	AT	1			De 83	181
Band Weaving: Finger Manipulated	Andean Crossed-Warp Techniques for Decorative Trims, Part 1 — Flat Bands	Cahlander, Adele	√	√	WJ	2	4	8	Ap 78	10
Band Weaving: Finger Manipulated	Andean Crossed-Warp Techniques for Decorative Trims, Part 2 — Tubular Bands (error-corrected WJ v3 n1 insert for vol. 2)	Cahlander, Adele	√	√	WJ	3	1	9	Jy 78	38
Band Weaving: Finger Weaving	Cardweaving Without Cards	Tacker, Sylvia	√	√	SS&D	13	2	50	Sp 82	42
Band Weaving: Finger Weaving	Finger Weaving Being Revived by Cherokees (error-corrected SS&D v5 n4 74 p69)	Coulter, Doris	√	√	SS&D	5	3	19	Su 74	55
Band Weaving: Finger Weaving, Technique	Fingerweaving: Two Perspectives, The Practical Lesson	Lee, Pamela	√	√	SS&D	6	4	24	Fa 75	44
Band Weaving Handspun	Reversible Cardwoven Hanging	Bradshaw, Susan	√		S-O	10	4		Wi 86	16
Band Weaving: Inkle	Bag for all Seasons (Barbara Grace), A		√	√	Hw	3	2		Mr 82	67
Band Weaving: Inkle	Bags with Strong Handles	Foeley, Cora V.	√		H&C	16	2		Sp 65	33
Band Weaving: Inkle	Bands and Beads	Pettigrew, Dale	√	√	Hw	4	1		J/F 83	72
Band Weaving: Inkle	Designing Inkle Bands	Davenport, Betty	√	√	PWC			4	Ja 83	56
Band Weaving: Inkle	Four Projects from Mrs. Elsie H. Gubser	Gubser, Elsie H.	√	√	H&C	6	3		Su 55	49
Band Weaving: Inkle	How to Warp and Weave on an Inkle Loom		√	√	Hw	7	3		M/J 86	43
Band Weaving: Inkle	Inkle Bands as Finishing Details on Garments	Brones, Britta	√	√	WJ	7	3	27	Wi 82	35
Band Weaving: Inkle	Inkle Pattern for Belts and Neckties		√	√	WJ	4	4	16	Ap 80	21
Band Weaving: Inkle	Inkle Rug (Robin Wilton)		√	√	Hw	1	1		F-W 79	31, 58
Band Weaving: Inkle	Inkle Weaving, Fun and Challenge	Anderson, Marcile	√	√	SS&D	5	4	20	Fa 74	29
Band Weaving: Inkle	Lace Up in Style, Handwoven Shoelaces (Kathy Rug)		√	√	Hw	8	2		M/A 87	17
Band Weaving: Inkle	Magazine Tote (Jean Anstine)		√	√	Hw	7	3		M/J 86	41, I-8
Band Weaving: Inkle	New, Functional Inkle Loom, A	Spencer, Edith L.	√	√	H&C	6	2		Sp 55	42
Band Weaving: Inkle	Notebook: Dusting Off the Inkle Loom	Myers, Ruth Nordquist, ed.	√	√	SS&D	14	1	53	Wi 82	44
Band Weaving: Inkle	Portable Weaving: A Band of Ideas for Bands	Bradley, Louise; Jean Anstine	√	√	Hw	7	3		M/J 86	40
Band Weaving: Inkle	Shepherd's Dancing Coat	Fleischer, Helen	√	√	S-O	11	1		Sp 87	17
Band Weaving: Inkle	Summer Take-Along Project, A	Luebbers, Karen	√	√	Hw	6	2		M/A 85	92
Band Weaving: Inkle	Tetrahedron (Carol Strickler)		√	√	Hw	6	4		S/O 85	64, I-15
Band Weaving: Inkle	Tool Kit From Inkle Bands, A	Hinson, Dolores M.	√	√	WJ	6	4	24	Sp 82	46
Band Weaving: Inkle	Trifles: Christmas Ornaments (Pam Bolesta)		√	√	Hw	1	1		F-W 79	46
Band Weaving: Inkle	Two Unusual Multishaft Curtains	Xenakis, Athanasios David	√	> 4	PWC	4	1	11		40
Band Weaving: Inkle	Weaving Inkle Bands	Tidball, Harriet			SCGM		27		69	1-40
Band Weaving: Inkle	Weaving Inkle Bands: Preparing the Board Loom and Weaving, Weaving	Tidball, Harriet	√	√	SCGM		27		69	11
Band Weaving: Inkle	Weaving on a Diamond Grid: Bedouin Style	Race, Mary E.	√	√	SS&D	12	1	45	Wi 80	20
Band Weaving: Inkle	What and Why of "Inkle"	Atwater, Mary Meigs	√	√	H&C	3	2		Sp 52	18
Band Weaving, Inkle: Embellishments	Weaving Inkle Bands: Variations, Embellishments, Finishes, Adding Decorative Items	Tidball, Harriet		√	SCGM		27		69	29
Band Weaving: Inkle, Floor Loom	Adapting Inkle Patterns to Wider Widths	Carlson, Estelle	√	√	SS&D	8	1	29	WI 76	87
Band Weaving, Inkle, Kasuri	Resist Dyeing, Curiosities and Inventions: Kasuri on Inkle Loom	Zielinski, S. A.; Robert Leclerc, ed.	√	√	MWL	17			'51–'73	38
Band Weaving: Inkle, Pick-Up	Inkle Belt (Miranda Howard)		√	√	Hw	2	5		No 81	36, 90
Band Weaving, Inkle, Pick-Up	Little Known Weaves Worth Knowing Better: Pick-Up on Inkle	Zielinski, S. A.; Robert Leclerc, ed.	√	√	MWL	16			'51–'73	120
Band Weaving: Inkle, Pick-Up, Brocade	Weaving Inkle Bands: The Pick-Up Pattern Techniques, Brocade Patterns	Tidball, Harriet	√	√	SCGM		27		69	35

SUBJECT	TITLE	AUTHOR	IL	INST	JOUR	VOL	NO	ISS	DATE	PAGE
Band Weaving: Inkle, Pick-Up, Cross-Barred	Weaving Inkle Bands: The Pick-Up Pattern Techniques, Cross-Barred Pick-Up	Tidball, Harriet	√	√	SCGM		27		69	31
Band Weaving: Inkle, Pick-Up, Diamond Background	Weaving Inkle Bands: The Pick-Up Pattern Techniques, Diamond Background Pick-Up	Tidball, Harriet	√	√	SCGM		27		69	32
Band Weaving: Inkle, Pick-Up, Geometric	Weaving Inkle Bands: The Pick-Up Pattern Techniques, Geometric Style Pick-Up	Tidball, Harriet	√	√	SCGM		27		69	34
Band Weaving: Inkle, Slits	Weaving Inkle Bands: Variations, Embellishments, Finishes, Slits and Divisions	Tidball, Harriet	√	√	SCGM		27		69	29
Band Weaving: Inkle, Supplementary Warp Patterning	Weaving Inkle Bands: The Pick-Up Pattern Techniques, Supplementary Warp Patterning	Tidball, Harriet	√	√	SCGM		27		69	36
Band Weaving: Inkle, Technique	Designing Inkle Bands	Davenport, Betty	√	√	PWC			4	Ja 83	56
Band Weaving: Inkle, Tubular	Weaving Inkle Bands: Variations, Embellishments, Finishes, Tubular Inkles	Tidball, Harriet	√	√	SCGM		27		69	29
Band Weaving: Inkle, Weft Variations	Weaving Inkle Bands: Weft Variations	Tidball, Harriet	√	√	SCGM		27		69	26
Band Weaving: Inkle, Width Variations	Weaving Inkle Bands: Variations, Embellishments, Finishes, Widening and Narrowing Bands	Tidball, Harriet		√	SCGM		27		69	30
Band Weaving: Loom	Belts are Interesting Projects	Fitch, Marjorie	√	√	H&C	4	4		Fa 53	14
Band Weaving: Loom	Chevron Twill Belt (Gay Jensen)		√	√	Hw	3	4		Se 82	50, 85
Band Weaving: Loom	Guatemala Visited	Atwater, Mary Meigs	√	√	SCGM		15		65	17
Band Weaving: Loom	Guatemalan Belt Weave	Christensen, Evelyn	√	√	Hw	7	2		M/A 86	68
Band Weaving: Loom	Hat Band (Barbara Elkins)		√	√	Hw	2	1		F-W 80	35, 69
Band Weaving: Loom	Inkle Tape for Vest (Betty Davenport)		√	√	Hw	4	2		M/A 83	56, 93
Band Weaving: Loom	On the Edge		√	√	Hw	4	4		S/O 83	34
Band Weaving: Loom	Warp-Faced Double Cloth: Adaptation of an Andean Technique for the Treadle Loom	Cahlander, Adele	√	√	WJ	10	4	40	Sp 86	72
Band Weaving: Loom	Weaving the Girdle of Rameses	Hilts, Patricia	√	> 4	WJ	9	1	33	Su 84	22
Band Weaving: Loom	Woven Tape for Coat (Carol Thilenius)		√	√	Hw	3	4		Se 82	45, 86
Band Weaving: On-Loom	Weaving the Girdle of Rameses on Nine Harnesses	Parkinson, Alberta	√	> 4	CW	3	2	8	Ja 82	1
Band Weaving: Peruvian Pebble Weave	Jacquetta Nisbet to Give Workshop on Peruvian Pebble Weave (error-corrected SS&D v5 n1 73 p93)	Black, Mary	√		SS&D	4	4	16	Fa 73	76
Band Weaving: Rigid-Heddle	Belt for Guatemalan Shirt (Betty Davenport)		√	√	Hw	2	2		Mr 81	54, 74
Band Weaving: Rigid-Heddle	Double Woven Mailbag with Name Tags	Verlinden, Lieve	√	√	WJ	7	1	25	Su 82	34
Band Weaving: Tablet	New Way to Draft Double-Twist/Double-Turn Tablet Weaving, A	Doleman, Paul	√	√	SS&D	11	4	44	Fa 80	42
Band Weaving: Tablet	Problem of Twist, A	Gordon, Judith	√	√	SS&D	12	4	48	Fa 81	28
Band Weaving: Tablet, Technique	Double-Faced 3/1 Broken Twill Woven on Tablets	Collingwood, Peter	√	√	AT	1			De 83	91
Band Weaving: Tablet, Techniques	Too Late for the Book	Collingwood, Peter	√	√	PWC	3	4	10		29
Band Weaving: Tablet, Three-Dimensional Techniques	Too Late for the Book	Collingwood, Peter	√	√	PWC	3	4	10		29
Band Weaving: Tape Looms	Tape Loom — Then and Now, The	Chesley, Mariam Dolloff	√		Hw	3	5		N/D 82	56
Band Weaving: Tubular	Special Andean Tubular Trim—Woven Without Heddles, A	Cahlander, Adele; Ed Franquemont; Barbara Bergman	√	√	WJ	6	3	23	Wi 81	54
Band Weaving: Tubular, Crossed-Warp	Understanding Some Complex Structures from Simple Andean Looms: Steps in Analysis and Reproduction	Cahlander, Adele	√	√	AT	1			De 83	181
Band Weaving: Twining	Band Loom Offers New Approach to Weft Twining	Tacker, Sylvia; Harold Tacker	√	√	SS&D	6	2	22	Sp 75	38
Band Weaving: Twining	Hungarian Weaving	Allen, Jane Ingram	√	√	SS&D	10	3	39	Su 79	93

SUBJECT	TITLE	AUTHOR	IL	INST	JOUR	VOL	NO	ISS	DATE	PAGE
Band Weaving: Warp Manipulated	Verkkonauhaa	Tacker, Sylvia	√	√	SS&D	11	4	44	Fa 80	12
Bandanna	Highlights in Bandanna History		√		Fa	12	3		M/J 85	45
Bandhani (Tie Dye)	Bandhani (Tie Dye)	Westfall, Carol D.; Dipti Desai	√		AT	8			De 87	19
Bands, Belts, Sashes	A. Meder Inspired Belt (Louise Bradley)		√	√	Hw	5	5		N/D 84	52, I-4
Bands, Belts, Sashes	Andean Crossed-Warp Techniques for Decorative Trims, Part 1 — Flat Bands	Cahlander, Adele	√	√	WJ	2	4	8	Ap 78	10
Bands, Belts, Sashes	Andean Crossed-Warp Techniques for Decorative Trims, Part 2 — Tubular Bands (error-corrected WJ v3 n1 insert for vol. 2)	Cahlander, Adele	√	√	WJ	3	1	9	Jy 78	38
Bands, Belts, Sashes	Assomption Sash, A Long Tradition in French Canada	Whitelaw, Adrienne	√	√	H&C	21	3		Su 70	12
Bands, Belts, Sashes	Backstrap Weaving for Penance and Profit	Coffman, Charlotte	√	√	WJ	7	1	25	Su 82	60
Bands, Belts, Sashes	Bands and Beads	Pettigrew, Dale	√	√	Hw	4	1		J/F 83	72
Bands, Belts, Sashes	Belt for Guatemalan Shirt (Betty Davenport)		√	√	Hw	2	2		Mr 81	54, 74
Bands, Belts, Sashes	Belts are Interesting Projects	Fitch, Marjorie	√	√	H&C	4	4		Fa 53	14
Bands, Belts, Sashes	Bevy of Belts, A	Karjala, Beth	√	√	Hw	8	1		J/F 87	46
Bands, Belts, Sashes	Bobbin Lace, Part 4; A Belt	Southard, Doris	√	√	SS&D	6	2	22	Sp 75	66
Bands, Belts, Sashes	Braiding on a Frame		√	√	WJ	2	4	8	Ap 78	22
Bands, Belts, Sashes	"Camel Belts from the Great Indian Desert" (Exhibit)	Janeiro, Jan	√		Fa	10	6		N/D 83	75
Bands, Belts, Sashes	Card Woven Belt of East Telemark—An Adaptation of a Traditional Norwegian Technique	Nelson, Lila	√	√	WJ	9	1	33	Su 84	30
Bands, Belts, Sashes	Cardwoven Belt (Mary Pendergrass)		√	√	Hw	1	2		S-S 80	34, 54
Bands, Belts, Sashes	Chevron Twill Belt (Gay Jensen)		√	√	Hw	3	4		Se 82	50, 85
Bands, Belts, Sashes	Children's Corner — A Woven Strap or Belt		√	√	WJ	3	4	12	Ap 79	38
Bands, Belts, Sashes	Complementary-Warp Weave (error-corrected WJ v7 n4 83 p4)	Coffman, Charlotte	√	√	WJ	7	3	27	Wi 82	53
Bands, Belts, Sashes	Costume and Weaving in Saraguro, Ecuador	Meisch, Lynn Ann	√		TMJ	19 20			80,81	55
Bands, Belts, Sashes	Creative Sashes		√	√	Hw	6	1		J/F 85	11
Bands, Belts, Sashes	Custom Fabrics for a Classic Cadillac	Kelly, Jacquie	√	> 4	WJ	10	4	40	Sp 86	54
Bands, Belts, Sashes	Designing for Warp-face	Sullivan, Donna	√	√	SS&D	19	1	73	Wi 87	15
Bands, Belts, Sashes	Designing Inkle Bands	Davenport, Betty	√	√	PWC			4	Ja 83	56
Bands, Belts, Sashes	Detective Story: Unravelling the Mystery of a 7-Loop Braid, A	Cahlander, Adele	√	√	WJ	10	1	37	Su 85	12
Bands, Belts, Sashes	Double Woven Mailbag with Name Tags	Verlinden, Lieve	√	√	WJ	7	1	25	Su 82	34
Bands, Belts, Sashes	Double-Woven Treasures from Old Peru	Cahlander, Adele	√	√	PWC			4	Ja 83	36
Bands, Belts, Sashes	Embellishments on the Rain Sash	Baizerman, Suzanne	√	√	WJ	11	2	42	Fa 86	22
Bands, Belts, Sashes	Fashion Focus: Sashes, Belts & Buckles	Snover, Susan	√	√	Hw	6	1		J/F 85	10
Bands, Belts, Sashes	Finger Weaving	Cooper, Karen Coody	√	√	TM			12	A/S 87	46
Bands, Belts, Sashes	Guatemala Visited	Atwater, Mary Meigs	√	√	SCGM		15		65	17
Bands, Belts, Sashes	Guatemala Weaver, The	Marks, Copeland A.	√		H&C	26	5		Oc 75	2
Bands, Belts, Sashes	Guatemalan Belt Weave	Christensen, Evelyn	√	√	Hw	7	2		M/A 86	68
Bands, Belts, Sashes	Handspun/Handwoven Ramie Blouse	Champion, Ellen	√	> 4	WJ	9	2	34	Fa 84	52
Bands, Belts, Sashes	Idea Notebook: A Workshop Necklace	Sheppard, Margaret	√	√	Hw	7	5		N/D 86	25
Bands, Belts, Sashes	Indian Fingerweaving, Traditional Use for Ceremonial Sashes	White, John	√	√	H&C	19	3		Su 68	4
Bands, Belts, Sashes	Inkle Bands as Finishing Details on Garments	Brones, Britta	√	√	WJ	7	3	27	Wi 82	35
Bands, Belts, Sashes	Inkle Belt (Miranda Howard)		√	√	Hw	2	5		No 81	36, 90
Bands, Belts, Sashes	Inkle Pattern for Belts and Neckties		√	√	WJ	4	4	16	Ap 80	21
Bands, Belts, Sashes	Jacket with Card Woven Trim (Louise Bradley)		√	√	Hw	7	3		M/J 86	41, I-7

SUBJECT	TITLE	AUTHOR	IL	INST	JOUR	VOL	NO	ISS	DATE	PAGE
Bands, Belts, Sashes	Magazine Tote (Jean Anstine)		√	√	Hw	7	3		M/J 86	41, I-8
Bands, Belts, Sashes	Mexican Motifs: The Oaxaca Belts	Tidball, Harriet	√	√	SCGM		6		62	19
Bands, Belts, Sashes	On the Edge		√	√	Hw	4	4		S/O 83	34
Bands, Belts, Sashes	Peruvian Crossed-Warp Weave, A	Castle, Nancy	√	√	TMJ	4	4		77	61
Bands, Belts, Sashes	Portable Weaving: A Band of Ideas for Bands	Bradley, Louise; Jean Anstine	√	√	Hw	7	3		M/J 86	40
Bands, Belts, Sashes	Rainbow Jacket (Sara Lamb)		√	>4	Hw	4	1		J/F 83	45, 84
Bands, Belts, Sashes	Ribbon Striped Belts (Judie Tenn)		√	√	Hw	7	4		S/O 86	35, I-5
Bands, Belts, Sashes	Roggeband	Blinks, Anne	√	√	Iw	3	3		Sp 78	16
Bands, Belts, Sashes	Shaped Silk Sheath	Xenakis, Athanasios David; Alexis Yiorgos Xenakis	√	√	PWC			6	Su 83	39
Bands, Belts, Sashes	Sheaf of Shawls, Sashes and Scarves, A (Susan Snover)		√	√	Hw	6	2		M/A 85	52, I-9
Bands, Belts, Sashes	Special Andean Tubular Trim—Woven Without Heddles, A	Cahlander, Adele; Ed Franquemont; Barbara Bergman	√	√	WJ	6	3	23	Wi 81	54
Bands, Belts, Sashes	Summer Take-Along Project, A	Luebbers, Karen	√	√	Hw	6	2		M/A 85	92
Bands, Belts, Sashes	Supplementary Warp Patterning: A Sash from Chiapas	Tidball, Harriet	√	√	SCGM		17		66	17
Bands, Belts, Sashes	Tape Loom — Then and Now, The	Chesley, Mariam Dolloff	√		Hw	3	5		N/D 82	56
Bands, Belts, Sashes	Type of Mughal Sash, A	Sonday, Milton; Nobuko Kajitani	√		TMJ	3	1		De 70	45
Bands, Belts, Sashes	Unique Technique for a Braided Strap from Colombia	Cahlander, Adele	√	√	WJ	7	1	25	Su 82	56
Bands, Belts, Sashes	Warp-Faced Double Cloth: Adaptation of an Andean Technique for the Treadle Loom	Cahlander, Adele	√	√	WJ	10	4	40	Sp 86	72
Bands, Belts, Sashes	Weaving in Quebec: Traditional Quebecois Weaving	Barrett, Clotilde	√	√	WJ	6	4	24	Sp 82	10
Bands, Belts, Sashes	Weaving Processes in the Cuzco Area of Peru	Rowe, Ann Pollard	√	√	TMJ	4	2		75	30
Bands, Belts, Sashes	Weaving the Girdle of Rameses	Hilts, Patricia	√	>4	WJ	9	1	33	Su 84	22
Bands, Belts, Sashes	Windowpane Scarf/Belt (Louise Bradley)		√	√	Hw	8	4		S/O 87	54, I-11
Bands, Weft-Patterned	Peru, Textiles Unlimited, Part 2: A Structural Weft Pattern	Tidball, Harriet	√	√	SCGM		26		69	11
Bands, Weft-Patterned	Peru, Textiles Unlimited, Part 2: Modern Weft-Pattern Bands	Tidball, Harriet	√	√	SCGM		26		69	12
Bands, Weft-Patterned	Peru, Textiles Unlimited, Part 2: Structural Weft-Band Patterns	Tidball, Harriet	√	√	SCGM		26		69	10
Banner Traditions: Islamic	Group of Silk Islamic Banners, A	Denny, Walter B.	√		TMJ	4	1		De 74	67
Banners/Flags	Banners		√	√	SS&D	11	4	44	Fa 80	47
Banners/Flags	Banners for Peace	Adels, Jill	√		Fa	12	4		J/A 85	36
Banners/Flags	Bannerworks	Strosnider, Ann	√		Fa	10	5		S/O 83	66
Banners/Flags	Flying Colors		√		Fa	12	5		S/O 85	65
Banners/Flags	Haitian Voodoo Banners: Dazzling Invitations to the Spirits	Lorenzo, Lauri	√		Fa	13	6		N/D 86	11
Banners/Flags	Hi-Tech Banner Sculptures	Polster, Nancy; Elsa Sreenivasam	√		Fa	12	3		M/J 85	42
Banners/Flags	Joellen Benjamin-Fay: Public Artist, Private Businesswoman	Strosnider, Ann	√	√	Fa	6	5		S/O 79	64
Banners/Flags	"Joyce Kozloff" An Interior Decorated (Exhibit)	Greenberg, Blue	√		Fa	8	1		J/F 81	89
Banners/Flags	Margot Carter Blair		√	√	Fa	4	3		M/J 77	28
Banners/Flags	Personal Flags of Everyday Life	Fraas, Gayle; Duncan Slade	√		Fa	10	1		J/F 83	99
Banners/Flags	Ribbon: A Celebration of Life, The	Pettigrew, Dale	√		Hw	6	5		N/D 85	70
Banners/Flags	Ribbon Project: Miles of Banners for Peace, The		√		Fa	12	5		S/O 85	49
Banners/Flags	"Space Sails: American Banners" (Exhibit)	Deyo, Diane	√		Fa	9	5		S/O 82	82

SUBJECT	TITLE	AUTHOR	IL	INST	JOUR	VOL	NO	ISS	DATE	PAGE
Banners/Flags	"Space Sails" Soar (Exhibit)	Reid, Eve	√		Fa	13	4		J/A 86	51
Banners/Flags	Special Piece—A Special Place, A	Harvey, Nancy	√		WJ	8	1	29	Su 83	67
Banners/Flags	Star Spangled Banner, The	West, Virginia M.	√		H&C	15	2		Sp 64	13
Banners/Flags	Unicorn	Bogdan, Janet	√		SS&D	6	2	22	Sp 75	97
Banners/Flags	Vexillology? Call the ABC Flag Company	Kleinberg, Eliot	√		Fa	12	4		J/A 85	41
Banners/Flags	Woven Banner: For the Class of '76, A	Thomen, Lydia	√	√	SS&D	7	2	26	Sp 76	7
Banners/Flags: Cigar Silks	Silken Dreams of Faraway Lands	Rudich, Sally	√		Fa	12	4		J/A 85	80
Banners/Flags: Civil War	Civil War History Preserved: The Pennsylvania Flag Project	Ashton, Mary	√		Fa	14	5		N/D 87	10
Banners/Flags: Labor	Labor Banners of Australia	Mancini, Anne	√		Fa	14	5		N/D 87	36
Bark, Cedar	Cedar Bark, A Versatile Natural Weaving Material	Wilson, Patricia	√	√	H&C	20	3		Su 69	7
Bark Cloth	"Patterns of Paradise: Tapa Cloth" (Exhibit)	Dyer, Carolyn	√		Fa	10	3		M/J 83	73
Bark, Painted	Bark Papermakers of San Pablito, The	Wilcox, Don	√	√	Fa	12	4		J/A 85	22
Barley Corn	Baby Camel Down and Tussah Scarf		√	√	Hw	7	4		S/O 86	67, I-13
Barley Corn	Spot Weaves — Old and New: Barley Corn	Zielinski, S. A.; Robert Leclerc, ed.	√	> 4	MWL	12			'51–'73	35
Barley Corn	Whig Rose Study (continued)	Morgenstern, Marvin M.	√	√	WJ	7	3	27	Wi 82	23
Basket	Roman Textiles from Vindolanda, Hexham, England	Wild, John Peter	√		TMJ	18			79	19
Basket Weave	Alpaca Stripe Scarf (Chris Switzer) (error-corrected Hw v2 n2 81 p68)		√	√	Hw	2	1		F-W 80	55, 80
Basket Weave	Basket Squares (Virginia West)		√	√	Hw	5	2		M/A 84	74, 94
Basket Weave	Cotton-Linen Garment in Basket Weave		√	√	WJ	7	3	27	Wi 82	32
Basket Weave	Grouped Warp Threads	Davison, Marguerite Porter	√	√	H&C	26	3		M/J 75	24
Basket Weave	Loom Shaped—3 Ways (error-corrected Hw v4 n3 83 p79)		√	√	Hw	3	2		Mr 82	44
Basket Weave	Man-Made Fibers: Baby Blankets		√	√	WJ	5	2	18	Fa 80	43
Basket Weave	Mattweave Upholstery (Sharon D. Alderman)		√	√	Hw	5	2		M/A 84	68, 105
Basket Weave	More About Fabrics: Practical Projects for Basket and Twill	Zielinski, S. A.; Robert Leclerc, ed.	√	√	MWL	20			'51–'73	35
Basket Weave	Silk Weskit (Louise Bradley)		√	√	Hw	5	1		J/F 84	44, 110
Basket Weave	Skirt (Sharon Alderman)		√	√	Hw	4	2		M/A 83	58, 91
Basket Weave	Swatch #1, Basket Weave (Diana Sanderson)		√	√	Hw	7	5		N/D 86	46, I-4
Basket Weave	Swatch #2, Basket Weave (Diana Sanderson)		√	√	Hw	7	5		N/D 86	46, I-4
Basket Weave	Traditional Texture Weaves: Basket	Zielinski, S. A.; Robert Leclerc, ed.	√	√	MWL	11			'51–'73	36
Basket Weave	Treasury for Beginners: Basic Weaves	Zielinski, S. A.; Robert Leclerc, ed.	√	√	MWL	1			'51–'73	98
Basket Weave	Two-Harness Textiles, The Loom-Controlled Weaves: Basket Weave	Tidball, Harriet	√	√	SCGM		20		67	28
Basket Weave	Vadmal Jacket (Janice Jones)		√	√	Hw	8	4		S/O 87	45, I-7
Basket Weave, Backed	Tisket, a Tasket, A	Gordon, Judith	√	> 4	Hw	5	5		N/D 84	34
Basket Weave, Double Two-Tie Twill	Double Two-Tie Twills and Basket Weave	Barrett, Clotilde	√	> 4	WJ	7	3	27	Wi 82	38
Basket Weave, Multiple-Unit Warps	Two-Harness Textiles, The Loom-Controlled Weaves: Multiple-Unit Warps	Tidball, Harriet	√	√	SCGM		20		67	28
Basket Weave, Stitched	Traditional Texture Weaves: Stitched Basket	Zielinski, S. A.; Robert Leclerc, ed.	√	√	MWL	11			'51–'73	39
Basket Weave, Surface Interest	Surface Interest — Textiles of Today: Surface Interest Designs with Drafts, Group 2, Reinforced Designs	Tidball, Harriet	√	> 4	SCGM		2		61	10
Basket Weave, Tied	Checked Towels (Margaretha Essén-Hedin)		√	√	Hw	8	5		N/D 87	55, I-13

SUBJECT	TITLE	AUTHOR	IL	INST	JOUR	VOL	NO	ISS	DATE	PAGE
Basket Weave, Variation	Accent Fabric (Constance LaLena)		√	√	Hw	4	1		J/F 83	66, 91
Basket Weave/Plain Weave	Curtain, Fabric #5 (Constance LaLena)		√	√	Hw	8	4		S/O 87	36, I-4
Basket Weavers: Cherokee	Doubleweave Basketry of the Cherokees	Ligon, Linda	√		Iw	4	1		Wi 78	28
Basket Weaves	Textile Remains from a Late Temple in Egyptian Nubia	Adams, Nettie K.	√		AT	8			De 87	85
Basketry	Theme Issue		√		Fa	4	1		J/F 77	
Basketry	Theme Issue		√		Fa	11	1		J/F 84	
Basketry Traditions: China	Exploring Basketry in China Today	La Pierre, Sharon	√		Fa	12	4		J/A 85	54
Basketry Traditions: Native Americans	Basketry Techniques: A Sampler (from 1902 Book)	Mason, Otis Tufton	√		Iw	4	1		Wi 78	26
Basketry Traditions: Shaker	Shaker Baskets Today	Wetherbee, Martha	√		SS&D	19	1	73	Wi 87	60
Baskets and Basketry	Abundance of Baskets, An	Davis, Michael	√		SS&D	17	1	65	Wi 85	6
Baskets and Basketry	Afro-American Sweetgrass Basketry	Johnson, Beth	√		Fa	9	5		S/O 82	23
Baskets and Basketry	Almost Roman Glass	Elliott, Lillian	√		Fa	10	6		N/D 83	20
Baskets and Basketry	"Art of Basketry, The" (Exhibit)	Park, Betty	√		Fa	4	2		M/A 77	9
Baskets and Basketry	Art That Functions	Lønning, Kari	√		Fa	8	3		M/J 81	40
Baskets and Basketry	Ballooning Art Form: The Making of a Hot Air Balloon Basket, A		√		SS&D	11	4	44	Fa 80	8
Baskets and Basketry	"Basket and Paper Invitational Show" (Exhibit)	Howe, Cathe	√		Fa	12	3		M/J 85	71
Baskets and Basketry	Basket Inside Out: The Spiral Sculptures of Ellen Fanger Dickson, A	Dickson, Ellen Fanger	√		Fa	7	1		J/F 80	26
Baskets and Basketry	Basket Willow: Cultivating and Gathering the Withy	Hart, Carol	√	√	TM			3	F/M 86	63
Baskets and Basketry	"Basket-Maker's Art, The" (Exhibit)	Grover, Donald	√		Fa	6	6		N/D 79	73
Baskets and Basketry	Basketmakers of Nova Scotia, The	Gordon, Joleen	√		SS&D	17	4	68	Fa 86	44
Baskets and Basketry	Basketmaker's Year "Down Under", A	Malarcher, Patricia	√		Fa	8	4		J/A 81	47
Baskets and Basketry	Basketry Armor	Austin, Carole	√		Fa	14	1		J/F 87	28
Baskets and Basketry	Basketry Drop Spindle	Coutts, Lucele	√		SS&D	11	4	44	Fa 80	49
Baskets and Basketry	Basketry Technics, Part 2	Harvey, Virginia	√		SS&D	6	3	23	Su 75	30
Baskets and Basketry	"Basketry Today: And Quilts from the Collection of Phyllis Haders" (Exhibits)	von Weise, Wenda	√		Fa	9	4		J/A 82	75
Baskets and Basketry	"Basketry: Tradition in New Form" (Exhibit)	Scarborough, Jessica	√		Fa	9	3		M/J 82	83
Baskets and Basketry	Basketry Traditions of Nova Scotia, The	Gordon, Joleen	√		SS&D	17	2	66	Sp 86	52
Baskets and Basketry	Basketry Workshop & Show at the Fairtree Gallery, A	Hansen, Debby; Betty Morris	√	√	H&C	24	3		M/J 73	43
Baskets and Basketry	Baskets and Curls	LaPlantz, Shereen	√	√	SS&D	13	1	49	Wi 81	38
Baskets and Basketry	"Baskets in La Jolla" (Exhibit)	Blaylock, Mary P.	√		Fa	11	1		J/F 84	79
Baskets and Basketry	"Baskets of Akwesasne" (Exhibit)	Doyle, Claire	√		Fa	11	1		J/F 84	77
Baskets and Basketry	Baskets of Doug Elliot: Connecting with the Natural World, The	McMillan, Sue	√		Fa	11	1		J/F 84	71
Baskets and Basketry	Baskets of John Garrett: A Mesh of Ideas and Materials, The	Garrett, John	√		Fa	11	1		J/F 84	26
Baskets and Basketry	"Basketworks": Visit to an Exhibition (Exhibit)		√		Fa	9	1		J/F 82	17
Baskets and Basketry	Brookfield Basketry Institute, The	Smith, Sue M.	√		Fa	12	2		M/A 85	46
Baskets and Basketry	Char TerBeest: Basket Builder	TerBeest, Char	√		Fa	9	4		J/A 82	17
Baskets and Basketry	Coiled Hexagonal Plaiting	LaPlantz, Shereen	√	√	SS&D	18	2	70	Sp 87	17
Baskets and Basketry	Color in the Woven Basket	Hoppe, Flo	√	√	SS&D	16	3	63	Su 85	22
Baskets and Basketry	Common Sense Care of Baskets	Turnbaugh, Sarah P.	√	√	SS&D	9	3	35	Su 78	90
Baskets and Basketry	Confetti Basketry	Brown, Sally	√	√	SS&D	18	3	71	Su 87	9
Baskets and Basketry	Contemporary Archeology: The Baskets of Lissa Hunter	Scarborough, Jessica	√		Fa	9	5		S/O 82	25
Baskets and Basketry	Contemporary Basketry		√		Fa	8	3		M/J 81	39
Baskets and Basketry	Conversation with Lillian Elliott, A	Janeiro, Jan	√		Fa	9	2		M/A 82	66
Baskets and Basketry	Cornucopia (Horn of Plenty)	Graser, Marie E.	√	√	WJ	7	2	26	Fa 82	52

SUBJECT	TITLE	AUTHOR	IL	INST	JOUR	VOL	NO	ISS	DATE	PAGE
Baskets and Basketry	Day in the Life of a Basketmaker: The Very Personal Approach of Shereen LaPlantz, A	LaPlantz, Shereen	√		Fa	6	6		N/D 79	6
Baskets and Basketry	"Distilling the Essence of Basketry" (Exhibit)	Anderson, Ann Stewart	√		Fa	13	2		M/A 86	52
Baskets and Basketry	Dorothy Gill Barnes: Baskets from a Gathered Harvest	Fedders, Pat	√		Fa	11	1		J/F 84	24
Baskets and Basketry	Ed Rossbach: Embracing the Fabric of Art	West, Virginia	√		Fa	9	1		J/F 82	31
Baskets and Basketry	Exploring Basketry in China Today	La Pierre, Sharon	√		Fa	12	4		J/A 85	54
Baskets and Basketry	Family Album of Pomo Baskets, A	Metzler, Sandra	√		Fa	11	1		J/F 84	63
Baskets and Basketry	Ferne Jacobs: A Study in 3-Dimensional Order	Brown, Arleen Emery	√		SS&D	11	4	44	Fa 80	80
Baskets and Basketry	"Ferne Jacobs: New Works" (Exhibit)	Park, Betty	√		Fa	6	1		J/F 79	84
Baskets and Basketry	Fine Art of Collecting Baskets, The (error-corrected TM i14 '87 p4)	Bowers, Sandra W.		√	TM			13	O/N 87	16
Baskets and Basketry	Fran Kraynek-Prince and Neil Prince	Scarborough, Jessica	√		Fa	12	5		S/O 85	19
Baskets and Basketry	Fundamentals of Basketry	Rippy, Rachel	√	√	H&C	22	3		Su 71	25
Baskets and Basketry	Gammy Miller: Coiled Poems	Miller, Gammy	√		Fa	11	6		N/D 84	16
Baskets and Basketry	Gary Trentham's Objets d'Art: An Interview	West, Virginia	√		SS&D	11	3	43	Su 80	70
Baskets and Basketry	Giving Your Baskets a Long, Healthy Life: A Basic Guide to Basketry Conservation	Odegaard, Nancy; Dale Kronkright	√		Fa	11	1		J/F 84	43
Baskets and Basketry	"Grass" (Exhibit)	Dyer, Carolyn	√		Fa	4	1		J/F 77	5
Baskets and Basketry	Gyöngy Laky: Experimental Thinking in Textiles	Scarborough, Jessica	√		Fa	11	1		J/F 84	21
Baskets and Basketry	Hisako Sekijima, Basketmaker	Koplos, Janet	√		Fa	13	5		S/O 86	14
Baskets and Basketry	"Infrastructure" (Exhibit)	Malarcher, Patricia	√		Fa	11	4		J/A 84	76
Baskets and Basketry	Inspiration — Does it Come Before or After?	LaPlantz, Shereen	√		WJ	8	1	29	Su 83	54
Baskets and Basketry	Inspired by Fiber: Textile Sensibility in Other Media	Malarcher, Patricia	√		Fa	10	6		N/D 83	33
Baskets and Basketry	It's Really Only an Inverted Basket	Hoelter, Jane	√	√	SS&D	9	4	36	Fa 78	26
Baskets and Basketry	Jan Yatsko's Bird's Nest Baskets		√		Fa	11	1		J/F 84	57
Baskets and Basketry	Janet Markarian: From Baskets to Bags, Containers Transformed	Koplos, Janet	√		Fa	11	1		J/F 84	16
Baskets and Basketry	"Joanne Brandford: Recent Nets" (Exhibit)	Park, Betty	√		Fa	11	6		N/D 84	77
Baskets and Basketry	John McQueen: An Interview	Park, Betty	√		Fa	6	1		J/F 79	21
Baskets and Basketry	"John McQueen" (Exhibit)		√		Fa	4	4		J/A 77	14
Baskets and Basketry	Joyce Chown's "Fabricated Structure: Weir"	Weir, Jean; Joyce Chown	√		Fa	11	4		J/A 84	39
Baskets and Basketry	Kari Lønning: Exploring Color and Form in Rattan	Lønning, Kari	√	√	Fa	11	1		J/F 84	12
Baskets and Basketry	"Kari Lønning — Mary Billingsley" (Exhibit)	Beede, Beth	√		Fa	6	6		N/D 79	69
Baskets and Basketry	Knotted Sculpture of Jane Sauer, The	Falconer, Crisa Meahl	√		Fa	13	3		M/J 86	31
Baskets and Basketry	Louise Robbins	Vander Lee, Jana	√		Fa	3	2		M/A 76	26
Baskets and Basketry	Mable Morrow—Collector, Scholar of Indian Arts, Part 2	Maxcy, Mabel E.	√		SS&D	5	2	18	Sp 74	33
Baskets and Basketry	Margrit Schmidtke: An Evolving Artist	Schmidtke, Sheila	√		Fa	13	5		S/O 86	42
Baskets and Basketry	Michael Davis	Davis, Michael	√		Fa	13	4		J/A 86	26
Baskets and Basketry	"Nancy Moore Bess: Baskets" (Exhibit)	Waller, Elsa	√		Fa	7	5		S/O 80	74
Baskets and Basketry	Nantucket Lightship Baskets: A Sailor's Pastime Revisited	Lucas, Eleanor L.	√		Fa	5	5		S/O 78	52
Baskets and Basketry	Native American Basketry	Bernstein, Bruce	√		Fa	11	1		J/F 84	50
Baskets and Basketry	Natural Fiber Basketry	Smith, Sue M.	√		SS&D	15	3	59	Su 84	23
Baskets and Basketry	Nature's Baskets	Smith, Sue	√	√	Iw	2	4		Su 77	26
Baskets and Basketry	New Direction for the Art of Basketry, A	La Pierre, Sharon	√		WJ	8	3	31	Wi 83	54
Baskets and Basketry	Non-Native American Basketry	Frye, Melinda Young	√		Fa	11	1		J/F 84	51

SUBJECT	TITLE	AUTHOR	IL	INST	JOUR	VOL	NO	ISS	DATE	PAGE
Baskets and Basketry	Old Ways for the New	Gordon, Joleen	√		SS&D	17	4	68	Fa 86	48
Baskets and Basketry	Onion Basket	Graser, Marie E.	√	√	WJ	8	2	30	Fa 83	48
Baskets and Basketry	"Other Baskets" An Invitational Show in St. Louis (Exhibit)	Degener, Patricia	√		Fa	10	1		J/F 83	76
Baskets and Basketry	Other Ethnological Collections	Bernstein, Bruce			Fa	11	1		J/F 84	50
Baskets and Basketry	Paper Vessels of Sylvia Seventy, The	Stofflet, Mary	√		Fa	11	2		M/A 84	70
Baskets and Basketry	Pine Needle Basketry	Washington, Misti	√	√	SS&D	16	4	64	Fa 85	46
Baskets and Basketry	Plaited Basket, The	LaPlantz, Shereen	√	√	Hw	7	3		M/J 86	76
Baskets and Basketry	Pope of Lightship Baskets, The	Hoppe, Flo	√		SS&D	18	1	69	Wi 86	30
Baskets and Basketry	Portfolio of Contemporary Fiber Sculpture, A		√		Fa	11	4		J/A 84	34
Baskets and Basketry	Revival of Cherokee Arts and Crafts, The	Parris, John	√		H&C	4	2		Sp 53	9
Baskets and Basketry	Ring Basket of the Anasazi, The	Turnbaugh, Sarah Peabody	√		SS&D	9	1	33	Wi 77	101
Baskets and Basketry	Rites of Passage: Carol Shaw-Sutton's Twig and Thread Constructions	Park, Betty	√		Fa	7	6		N/D 80	49
Baskets and Basketry	Shaker Baskets Today	Wetherbee, Martha	√		SS&D	19	1	73	Wi 87	60
Baskets and Basketry	Shaker Technique: Part 1, Weaving with Wood, The	Gordon, Beverly	√		SS&D	7	4	28	Fa 76	32
Baskets and Basketry	Shokansai Iizuka: Bamboo Craftsman and Living National Treasure of Japan	Adachi, Barbara Curtis	√		Fa	11	1		J/F 84	59
Baskets and Basketry	Silver and Gold	Bramhall, Pat; Butch Bramhall	√	√	SS&D	19	1	73	Wi 87	40
Baskets and Basketry	Southwest Indian Twill Tapestry	Atwood, Betty	√		WJ	8	1	29	Su 83	35
Baskets and Basketry	Sunrise Handspun Basket	Burditt, Larry	√	√	S-O	11	1		Sp 87	18
Baskets and Basketry	Technology of Basketry: North American Roots and Relations to Cloth, The	Turnbaugh, Sarah Peabody	√	√	SS&D	8	1	29	WI 76	32
Baskets and Basketry	Thinking About Historical Baskets	Rossbach, Ed	√		Fa	11	1		J/F 84	32
Baskets and Basketry	Thoughts on the New Basketry	Goldin, Susan	√		Iw	3	3		Sp 78	11
Baskets and Basketry	Triaxial Weaves and Weaving: An Exploration for Hand Weavers	Mooney, David R.	√	√	AT	2			De 84	9
Baskets and Basketry	Twining with Leaves and Corn Husks (error-corrected SS&D v14 n4 83 p4)	Jensen, Elizabeth Jane	√	√	SS&D	14	3	55	Su 83	10
Baskets and Basketry	Variations on a Landes Theme	Coutts, Lucele	√	√	WJ	8	4	32	Sp 84	24
Baskets and Basketry	Wandering with My Hands	LaPlantz, Shereen	√		WJ	3	4	12	Ap 79	23
Baskets and Basketry	Weaving with the Maoris of New Zealand	Giacchina, Polly Jacobs	√	√	Fa	11	3		M/J 84	48
Baskets and Basketry	What Makes a Basket a Basket?	Malarcher, Patricia	√		Fa	11	1		J/F 84	34
Baskets and Basketry	Wickerwork Basket Weaving in Four-Strand Designs (error-corrected SS&D v14 n1 82 p6)	Jensen, Elizabeth Jane	√	√	SS&D	13	4	52	Fa 82	20
Baskets and Basketry	Words in Fiber	Rowley, Kathleen	√		Fa	11	2		M/A 84	66
Baskets and Basketry	Zulu Baskets		√		Fa	9	3		M/J 82	21
Baskets and Basketry: Attu	Attu Basketry	McIver, Lucy	√	√	H&C	24	1		J/F 73	35
Baskets and Basketry: Balloon	Hot-Air Balloons	Theil, Linda	√		TM			4	A/M 86	20
Baskets and Basketry: Cherokee	Doubleweave Basketry of the Cherokees	Ligon, Linda	√		Iw	4	1		Wi 78	28
Baskets and Basketry: Clay	Rina Peleg: Plaiting in Clay	Peleg, Rina	√		Fa	10	6		N/D 83	16
Baskets and Basketry: Coiled	Basketry Technics, Part 1	Harvey, Virginia	√	√	SS&D	6	2	22	Sp 75	12
Baskets and Basketry: Coiled	Easter Fun!		√	√	Hw	1	2		S-S 80	39
Baskets and Basketry: Coiled	Ellen Jones		√		Fa	4	1		J/F 77	38
Baskets and Basketry: Coiled	Ferne Jacobs		√		Fa	4	1		J/F 77	24
Baskets and Basketry: Coiled	Furniture in Coiled Basketry Technique		√	√	WJ	3	1	9	Jy 78	22
Baskets and Basketry: Coiled	Interview with Marge Bardacke, Basketmaker, An		√		Fa	4	1		J/F 77	34
Baskets and Basketry: Coiled	Lynn Haney		√		Fa	4	1		J/F 77	38
Baskets and Basketry: Coiled	Thrum Basketry	Coutts, Lucele	√	√	SS&D	8	3	31	Su 77	43
Baskets and Basketry: Coiled, Gourd-Base	Sharon La Pierre		√		Fa	4	1		J/F 77	28

SUBJECT	TITLE	AUTHOR	IL	INST	JOUR	VOL	NO	ISS	DATE	PAGE
Baskets and Basketry: Coiling	Technology of Basketry: North American Roots and Relations to Cloth, The	Turnbaugh, Sarah Peabody	√	√	SS&D	8	1	29	WI 76	32
Baskets and Basketry: Coiling Handspun	Sunrise Handspun Basket	Burditt, Larry	√	√	S-O	11	1		Sp 87	18
Baskets and Basketry: Crochet	Three Color Basket in Single Crochet	Klessen, Romy	√	√	PWC			4	Ja 83	60
Baskets and Basketry: Loom-Woven	Loom Woven Baskets	Bowman, Gloria	√	√	WJ	10	4	40	Sp 86	37
Baskets and Basketry: Oak Splits	Appalachian Basketry	Overcast, Roy	√		Fa	4	1		J/F 77	20
Baskets and Basketry: Pine Needles	Arlan Oftedahl: Pine Needle Basket Maker		√		Fa	4	1		J/F 77	31
Baskets and Basketry: Rattan Reed	Kari Lønning		√		Fa	4	4		J/A 77	49
Baskets and Basketry: Techniques	Appalachian Twin Bottomed Egg Basket	Dougherty, Robin Taylor	√	√	Hw	5	1		J/F 84	69
Baskets and Basketry: Techniques	Basketry Techniques: A Sampler (from 1902 Book)	Mason, Otis Tufton	√		Iw	4	1		Wi 78	26
Baskets and Basketry: Techniques	Double Handled Melon Basket (error-corrected WJ v7 n1 82 p36b)	Graser, Marie E.	√	√	WJ	6	4	24	Sp 82	42
Baskets and Basketry: Techniques	Heart Basket, The	Daugherty, Robin Taylor	√	√	Hw	8	1		J/F 87	62
Baskets and Basketry: Techniques	Pine Needle Basketry	Clark, June	√	√	WJ	5	1	17	Su 80	10
Baskets and Basketry: Techniques	Project Shared by Guild Members: Day Lily Basket		√	√	WJ	5	2	18	Fa 80	48
Baskets and Basketry: Techniques	Twill Woven Market Basket	Daugherty, Robin Taylor	√	√	Hw	6	1		J/F 85	80
Baskets and Basketry: Techniques, Coiling	Basketry...A New Approach to an Old Art Form	Meilach, Dona	√	√	Fa	4	1		J/F 77	16
Baskets and Basketry: Twined	Interview with Marge Bardacke, Basketmaker, An		√		Fa	4	1		J/F 77	34
Baskets and Basketry: Twined	Twine a Basket! (Mary Pendergrass)		√	√	Hw	1	1		F-W 79	34
Baskets and Basketry: Twining	Basketry Technics, Part 1	Harvey, Virginia	√	√	SS&D	6	2	22	Sp 75	12
Baskets and Basketry: Twining	Making an Open-Weave Willow Basket	Hart, Carol	√	√	TM			4	A/M 86	24
Basque Sheepmen	Amazing Basques and Their Sheep, The	Dayton, Rita	√		S-O	3			79	19
Bast Fibers	History of Bast Fibers, A	Mattera, Joanne	√		SS&D	8	4	32	Fa 77	27
Bast Fibers	History of Linen, A	Mattera, Joanne	√	√	SS&D	8	3	31	Su 77	16
Bast Fibers	Ramie	Cobb, Lorie	√		S-O	10	3		Fa 86	40
Bast Fibers	Survey of Leaf and Stem Fibers, A	Buchanan, Rita	√		S-O	10	3		Fa 86	24
Bast Fibers	Tree-Bast Fiber Textiles of Japan	Dusenbury, Mary	√	√	S-O	10	3		Fa 86	35
Bast Fibers	Yarns and Fibers: Coarse Fibers of the Linen Family	Zielinski, S. A.; Robert Leclerc, ed.			MWL	4			'51–'73	74
Bateman Blend System	Handloom Weaves: The Classification of Handloom Weaves, The Structural Group, Unit Class, Bateman Blend System	Tidball, Harriet	√	>4	SCGM		33		57	25
Bateman Blend Weaves	Bateman Blend Weaves Extended Beyond Eight Harnesses, Part 1	Harvey, Virginia I.	√	>4	CW	4	3	12	Ap 83	9
Bateman Blend Weaves	Bateman Blend Weaves Extended Beyond Eight Harnesses, Part 2	Harvey, Virginia I.	√	>4	CW	5	1	13	Se 83	3
Bateman Blend Weaves	Bateman Legacy, The	Harvey, Virginia	√	>4	PWC	4	4	14		50
Bateman Blend Weaves	Dr. Bateman and the Bateman Blend	Marston, Ena	√	>4	SS&D	5	2	18	Sp 74	37
Bateman Blend Weaves	Notes from a Beginning Complex Weaver	McKee, Marguerite	√	>4	CW		25		Se 87	3
Bateman Blend Weaves: Basic Blocks	Bateman Blend Weaves: The Structures of the Bateman Blend System	Bateman, Dr. William G.; Virginia I. Harvey, ed.	√	>4	SCGM		36		82	14
Bateman Blend Weaves, Division A: Unit Structure, 2-Tie, 6-Thread Blocks	Bateman Blend Weaves: Division A — Six-Thread Blocks	Bateman, Dr. William G.; Virginia I. Harvey, ed.	√	>4	SCGM		36		82	21
Bateman Blend Weaves, Division B: Unit Structure, 2-Tie, 8-Thread Blocks	Bateman Blend Weaves: Division B — Eight-Thread Blocks	Bateman, Dr. William G.; Virginia I. Harvey, ed.	√	>4	SCGM		36		82	51

SUBJECT	TITLE	AUTHOR	IL	INST	JOUR	VOL	NO	ISS	DATE	PAGE
Bateman Blend Weaves, Division C: Unit Structure, 2-Tie, 10-Thread Blocks	Bateman Blend Weaves: Division C — Ten-Thread Blocks	Bateman, Dr. William G.; Virginia I. Harvey, ed.	√	>4	SCGM		36		82	72
Bateman Blend Weaves, Division D: Unit Structure, 2-Tie, 12-Thread Blocks	Bateman Blend Weaves: Division D — Twelve-Thread Blocks	Bateman, Dr. William G.; Virginia I. Harvey, ed.	√	>4	SCGM		36		82	109
Bateman Blend Weaves: Introduction	Bateman Blend Weaves: The Bateman Blend System	Bateman, Dr. William G.; Virginia I. Harvey, ed.		>4	SCGM		36		82	12
Bateman Blend Weaves: Unit Structure, 3-Tie Block	Bateman Blend Weaves: Three-Tie and Four-Tie Blocks	Bateman, Dr. William G.; Virginia I. Harvey, ed.	√	>4	SCGM		36		82	120
Bateman Blend Weaves: Unit Structure, 4-Tie Blocks	Bateman Blend Weaves: Three-Tie and Four-Tie Blocks	Bateman, Dr. William G.; Virginia I. Harvey, ed.	√	>4	SCGM		36		82	120
Bateman Blend Weaves: Variations A, B, C Blocks	Bateman Blend Weaves: Variations of A, B, and C Blocks	Bateman, Dr. William G.; Virginia I. Harvey, ed.	√	>4	SCGM		36		82	112
Bateman Blend Weaves: Weaving Terms	Bateman Blend Weaves: Based on Dr. William G. Bateman's Manuscript	Bateman, Dr. William G.; Virginia I. Harvey, ed.	√	>4	SCGM		36		82	1-137
Bateman Boulevard Weaves	Bateman Legacy, The	Harvey, Virginia	√	>4	PWC	4	4	14		50
Bateman Boulevard Weaves	Boulevard, Chevron, and Combination Weaves: Based on Dr. William G. Bateman's Manuscript	Bateman, Dr. William G.; Virginia I. Harvey, ed.	√	>4	SCGM		38		87	1-93
Bateman Boulevard Weaves: Structures	Bateman Boulevard, Chevron, and Combination Weaves: Boulevard Structures	Bateman, Dr. William G.; Virginia I. Harvey, ed.	√	>4	SCGM		38		87	16
Bateman Chevron Weaves	Bateman Boulevard, Chevron, and Combination Weaves: Chevron Structures, Division 1	Bateman, Dr. William G.; Virginia I. Harvey, ed.	√	>4	SCGM		38		87	59
Bateman Chevron Weaves	Bateman Boulevard, Chevron, and Combination Weaves: Chevron Structures, Division 2	Bateman, Dr. William G.; Virginia I. Harvey, ed.	√	>4	SCGM		38		87	62
Bateman Chevron Weaves	Bateman Boulevard, Chevron, and Combination Weaves: Chevron Structures, Division 3	Bateman, Dr. William G.; Virginia I. Harvey, ed.	√	>4	SCGM		38		87	69
Bateman Chevron Weaves	Bateman Boulevard, Chevron, and Combination Weaves: Chevron Structures, Division 4	Bateman, Dr. William G.; Virginia I. Harvey, ed.	√	>4	SCGM		38		87	72
Bateman Chevron Weaves	Bateman Boulevard, Chevron, and Combination Weaves: Chevron Structures, Division 5	Bateman, Dr. William G.; Virginia I. Harvey, ed.	√	>4	SCGM		38		87	80
Bateman Chevron Weaves	Bateman Legacy, The	Harvey, Virginia	√	>4	PWC	4	4	14		50
Bateman Chevron Weaves	Boulevard, Chevron, and Combination Weaves: Based on Dr. William G. Bateman's Manuscript	Bateman, Dr. William G.; Virginia I. Harvey, ed.	√	>4	SCGM		38		87	1-93
Bateman Chevron Weaves: Structures	Bateman Boulevard, Chevron, and Combination Weaves: Structures of Chevron Weaves	Bateman, Dr. William G.; Virginia I. Harvey, ed.	√	>4	SCGM		38		87	57
Bateman Combination Weaves	Boulevard, Chevron, and Combination Weaves: Based on Dr. William G. Bateman's Manuscript	Bateman, Dr. William G.; Virginia I. Harvey, ed.	√	>4	SCGM		38		87	1-93
Bateman Combination Weaves: Structures	Bateman Boulevard, Chevron, and Combination Weaves: Structures of Combination Weaves	Bateman, Dr. William G.; Virginia I. Harvey, ed.	√	>4	SCGM		38		87	82
Bateman Multiple Tabby Weaves	Bateman Legacy, The	Harvey, Virginia	√	>4	PWC	4	4	14		50
Bateman Multiple Tabby Weaves	Extending Dr. William G. Bateman's Multiple Tabby Weaves Beyond Eight Harnesses (error-corrected CW v4 n3 83 p12)	Harvey, Virginia I.	√	>4	CW	4	2	11	Ja 83	4
Bateman Multiple Tabby Weaves: 6-Shaft	Multiple Tabby Weaves: Six-Harness Multiple Tabby Weaves	Bateman, Dr. William G.; Virginia I. Harvey, ed.	√	>4	SCGM		35		81	59
Bateman Multiple Tabby Weaves, Basic Blocks	Multiple Tabby Weaves: The Basic Blocks	Bateman, Dr. William G.; Virginia I. Harvey, ed.	√	√	SCGM		35		81	20
Bateman Multiple Tabby Weaves, Eight-Shaft	Multiple Tabby Weaves: Eight-Harness Multiple Tabby Weaves	Bateman, Dr. William G.; Virginia I. Harvey, ed.	√	>4	SCGM		35		81	70
Bateman Multiple Tabby Weaves, Expanding Blocks	Multiple Tabby Weaves: Expanding the Blocks	Bateman, Dr. William G.; Virginia I. Harvey, ed.	√	√	SCGM		35		81	46
Bateman Multiple Tabby Weaves: Introduction	Multiple Tabby Weaves: Multiple Tabby Weaves, Dr. Bateman's Introduction	Bateman, Dr. William G.; Virginia I. Harvey, ed.		√	SCGM		35		81	19

SUBJECT	TITLE	AUTHOR	IL	INST	JOUR	VOL	NO	ISS	DATE	PAGE
Bateman Multiple Tabby Weaves: Rearranging Block Threading	Multiple Tabby Weaves: Rearranging the Threading Within the Blocks	Bateman, Dr. William G.; Virginia I. Harvey, ed.	√	√	SCGM		35		81	26
Bateman Park Weaves	Bateman Legacy, The	Harvey, Virginia	√	>4	PWC	4	4	14		50
Bateman Park Weaves	Extending Dr. Bateman's Park Weaves	Harvey, Virginia I.	√	>4	CW	6	3	18	My 85	3
Bateman Park Weaves	Park Weaves: Bases on Dr. William G. Bateman's Manuscript	Bateman, Dr. William G.; Virginia I. Harvey, ed.	√	>4	SCGM		37		84	1-95
Bateman Park Weaves: Basic Blocks, Rules	Bateman Park Weaves: Park Weave Rules	Bateman, Dr. William G.; Virginia I. Harvey, ed.	√	>4	SCGM		37		84	18
Bateman Park Weaves, Division I: 7-Shaft Blocks, Tag Weave (Tag Treadling)	Bateman Park Weaves: Division I — Seven-Harness Blocks, Tag Weave or Tag Treadling	Bateman, Dr. William G.; Virginia I. Harvey, ed.	√	>4	SCGM		37		84	27
Bateman Park Weaves, Division I, Unit Structure, 1-Tie, 7-Shaft Blocks	Bateman Park Weaves: Division I — Seven-Harness Blocks	Bateman, Dr. William G.; Virginia I. Harvey, ed.	√	>4	SCGM		37		84	19
Bateman Park Weaves, Division II: Unit Structure, 1-Tie, 10-Thread Blocks, 8-Shaft	Bateman Park Weaves: Division II — Eight-Harness Blocks, Ten-Thread Blocks	Bateman, Dr. William G.; Virginia I. Harvey, ed.	√	>4	SCGM		37		84	79
Bateman Park Weaves, Division II: Unit Structure, 1-Tie, 12-Thread Blocks, 8-Shaft	Bateman Park Weaves: Division II — Eight-Harness Blocks, Twelve-Thread Blocks	Bateman, Dr. William G.; Virginia I. Harvey, ed.	√	>4	SCGM		37		84	83
Bateman Park Weaves, Division II: Unit Structure, 1-Tie, 4-Thread Blocks, 8-Shaft	Bateman Park Weaves: Division II — Eight-Harness Blocks	Bateman, Dr. William G.; Virginia I. Harvey, ed.	√	>4	SCGM		37		84	48
Bateman Park Weaves, Division II: Unit Structure, 1-Tie, 6-Thread Blocks, 8-Shaft	Bateman Park Weaves: Division II — Eight-Harness Blocks, Six-Thread Blocks	Bateman, Dr. William G.; Virginia I. Harvey, ed.	√	>4	SCGM		37		84	60
Bateman Park Weaves, Division II: Unit Structure, 1-Tie, 8-Thread Blocks 8-Shaft	Bateman Park Weaves: Division II — Eight-Harness Blocks, Eight-Thread Blocks	Bateman, Dr. William G.; Virginia I. Harvey, ed.	√	>4	SCGM		37		84	74
Bateman Park Weaves, Division II: Unit Structure, 1-Tie, Variable Thread Blocks, 8-Shaft	Bateman Park Weaves: Division II — Blocks of Varying Sizes Combined in a Draft	Bateman, Dr. William G.; Virginia I. Harvey, ed.	√	>4	SCGM		37		84	88
Bateman Park Weaves: Original Text Notation	Bateman Park Weaves: Dr. Bateman's Text	Bateman, Dr. William G.; Virginia I. Harvey, ed.		>4	SCGM		37		84	15
Bateman Weaves: Relationship of Park, Boulevard, Chevron and Weaves	Bateman Park Weaves: The Relationship of Park, Boulevard and Chevron Weaves	Bateman, Dr. William G.; Virginia I. Harvey, ed.	√	>4	SCGM		37		84	94
Batik also see Dyes and Dyeing: Resist										
Batik	Additions to the Indonesian Collection	Gittinger, Mattiebelle S.	√		TMJ	4	3		76	43
Batik	Alice McClelland	Heath, Jennifer	√		Fa	5	4		J/A 78	50
Batik	Angela Manno	Manno, Angela	√		Fa	12	5		S/O 85	18
Batik	Batik Making and the Royal Javanese Cemetery at Imogiri	Joseph, Rebecca M.	√		TMJ	24			85	83
Batik	Batik Plus Handweaving	D'Angelo, Anne A.; Margaret B. Windeknecht	√		SS&D	4	3	15	Su 73	57
Batik	Betsy Benjamin-Murray	Patton, Patti	√		Fa	4	3		M/J 77	43
Batik	Carol Westfall: Adapting Dye Transfer Methods	Park, Betty	√		Fa	5	1		J/F 78	64
Batik	Conversations with a Batik Master	Gittinger, Mattiebelle S.	√		TMJ	18			79	25
Batik	Dianne E. Soule: Batik Portraits	Bard, Elizabeth A.	√		Fa	12	6		N/D 85	11
Batik	"Dorte Christjansen" (Exhibit)	Dyer, Carolyn	√		Fa	6	2		M/A 79	62
Batik	Earth Batik: Jessica Scarborough Buries Her Art in the Earth	Scarborough, Jessica	√		Fa	7	6		N/D 80	41
Batik	Enza Quargnali: Batiker		√		Fa	4	2		M/A 77	34
Batik	"Fabled Cloth: Batik from Java's North Coast" (Exhibit)	Goodman, Deborah Lerme	√		Fa	12	4		J/A 85	58
Batik	Fiber and Architecture: Gwenyth Mabry		√		Fa	3	3		M/J 76	24
Batik	Flowers, Beautiful Flowers: Ronna Riebman, Batik: Mary Lynn O'Shea, Tapestry		√		Fa	8	3		M/J 81	35
Batik	Jeff Service		√		Fa	3	6		N/D 76	22

SUBJECT	TITLE	AUTHOR	IL	INST	JOUR	VOL	NO	ISS	DATE	PAGE
Batik	"New Works in Batik by Laura Adasko" (Exhibit)	Gutcheon, Beth	√		Fa	5	3		M/J 78	12
Batik	"Pat Rutledge: Batiks" (Exhibit)	Ellis, Betty	√		Fa	9	1		J/F 82	77
Batik	Phan Nguyen Barker	Rulli, Linda	√		Fa	13	5		S/O 86	18
Batik	Rebecca Munro: But It Turned Out All Right	Erler, Mary	√		Fa	6	6		N/D 79	28
Batik	Resist Dyeing, Curiosities and Inventions: Batik 1	Zielinski, S. A.; Robert Leclerc, ed.	√	√	MWL	17			'51–'73	21
Batik	Resist Dyeing, Curiosities and Inventions: Crackle in Batik	Zielinski, S. A.; Robert Leclerc, ed.		√	MWL	17			'51–'73	36
Batik	Symbolic Scenes in Javanese Batik	Adams, Monni	√		TMJ	3	1		De 70	25
Batik	Textile Arts of India	Bernier, Ronald M.	√		WJ	2	1	5	Jy 77	31
Batik	Van Zuylen Batik, Pekalongan, Central Java (1890-1946)	de Raadt-Apell, M. J.	√	√	TMJ	19 20			80,81	75
Batik	Verbena Collection, The (error-corrected Fa v11 n1 84 p11)		√		Fa	10	5		S/O 83	64
Batik	Wearable Paintings	Auger, Shirley Venit	√	√	H&C	24	4		Au 73	34
Batik Technique	Resisting Dyes: Three Ways to Put Color in Its Place	Northup, Wendy	√	√	TM			1	O/N 85	30
Batik Technique	Stretching Fabric in Small Spaces	Levy, Julie	√	√	TM			3	F/M 86	34
Batiste	Battenberg Lace: Making Lace with Woven Tape and a Needle	Kliot, Jules; Kaethe Kliot	√	√	TM			10	A/M 87	30
Batting: Soviet and American Fleeces	Spinning Fleece for Peace				TM			11	J/J 87	18
Batts	Carded Rainbow Batts	Amos, Alden	√	√	S-O	9	1		Sp 85	19
Batts: Color-Blended	Spinner's Specialty: Heathered Yarns, A	Searle, Karen	√	√	WJ	9	2	34	Fa 84	56
Batts: Wool	Wool Quilt Batting		√	√	TM			8	D/J 86	7
Bauhaus	Anni Albers — Innovator in Textile Design		√		H&C	10	4		Fa 59	6
Bauhaus	Chicago Weaving: Development and Impact	Regensteiner, Else	√		SS&D	12	1	45	Wi 80	9
Bauhaus	Marli Ehrman		√		H&C	11	2		Sp 60	25
Bauhaus	Marli-Weavers of Chicago, The	Uhlman, Ilse Etta	√		H&C	4	1		Wi 52	9
Bauhaus	Visit with Anni Albers, A	Margetts, Martina	√		TM			2	D/J 85	24
Bauhaus Weaving	Bauhaus Weaving	Dodge, Dorothy	√		H&C	22	4		Fa 71	17
Beachwear	Blanket Weave, The	Robitaille, Annette	√	> 4	WJ	8	4	32	Sp 84	62
Beachwear	Caftan (Sharon Alderman)		√	√	Hw	1	2		S-S 80	46, 65
Beachwear	Three in One	Moes, Dini	√	√	SS&D	18	2	70	Sp 87	74
Beading Techniques	Beading on Leather	Ellsworth, Wendy	√	√	TM			7	O/N 86	50
Beads and Beading	Bands and Beads	Pettigrew, Dale	√	√	Hw	4	1		J/F 83	72
Beads and Beading	Beaded Fish (Christine Olsen Reis)		√		TM			11	J/J 87	84
Beads and Beading	Beading on Leather	Ellsworth, Wendy	√	√	TM			7	O/N 86	50
Beads and Beading	Beads, Buttons & Findings	Green, Marilyn	√		Hw	7	5		N/D 86	84
Beads and Beading	Cid Suntrader: Weaving with Glass	Suntrader, Cid	√		Fa	14	4		S/O 87	5
Beads and Beading	Contemporary Appliqued Beadwork	Woodsmall, Annabel Whitney	√		TIAM		2		79	1-40
Beads and Beading	Haitian Voodoo Banners: Dazzling Invitations to the Spirits	Lorenzo, Lauri	√		Fa	13	6		N/D 86	11
Beads and Beading	Jerry Stefl: Fantasy, Beads, and Fiber	Matthews, Marianne R.	√		Fa	11	2		M/A 84	24
Beads and Beading	"Silken Threads and Silent Needles" (Exhibit)	Dunnewold, Jane	√		Fa	11	6		N/D 84	78
Beads and Beading	Sky Curtain (Jeanne Leffingwell)		√		TM			2	D/J 85	88
Beads and Beading	Stringing Beads			√	TM			6	A/S 86	10
Beads and Beading	Trimming the Southwestern Look	Chaudet, Annette	√	√	WJ	11	1	41	Su 86	35
Beads and Beading: Application Process	Contemporary Appliqued Beadwork: The Application Process	Woodsmall, Annabel Whitney	√	√	TIAM		2		79	12
Beads and Beading: Appliqued, Introduction	Contemporary Appliqued Beadwork: Introduction	Woodsmall, Annabel Whitney	√		TIAM		2		79	5

SUBJECT	TITLE	AUTHOR	IL	INST	JOUR	VOL	NO	ISS	DATE	PAGE
Beads and Beading: Bead Chart	Contemporary Appliqued Beadwork: Bead Chart	Woodsmall, Annabel Whitney	√		TIAM		2		79	6
Beads and Beading: Knitting	And a Necklace, Too	Upitis, Lizbeth	√	√	Kn	2	2	4	S-S 86	48
Beads and Beading: Knitting	Bead Basics		√	√	Kn	2	2	4	S-S 86	51
Beads and Beading: Knitting	Beaded Sweater	Drysdale, Rosemary; Gail Diven	√	√	Kn	2	2	4	S-S 86	50
Beads and Beading: Knitting	Florodora Bag	Upitis, Lizbeth	√	√	Kn	2	2	4	S-S 86	47
Beads and Beading: Knitting	Return of the Reticule	Upitis, Lizbeth	√		Kn	2	2	4	S-S 86	44
Beads and Beading: Materials	Contemporary Appliqued Beadwork: Materials	Woodsmall, Annabel Whitney	√	√	TIAM		2		79	7
Beads and Beading: Paper	Paper Clothing: West	Koplos, Janet	√		Fa	11	2		M/A 84	39
Beads and Beading: Retrieving	Retrieving Spilled Beads			√	TM			10	A/M 87	10
Beads and Beading: Suppliers	Contemporary Appliqued Beadwork: List of Suppliers	Woodsmall, Annabel Whitney			TIAM		2		79	39
Beads and Beading: Weaving	Ways to Weave Overshot: Part 2	Marston, Ena	√	√	SS&D	12	1	45	Wi 80	36
Beads and Beadwork	Meaning of Folk Art in Rabari Life: A Closer Look at Mirrored Embroidery, The	Frater, Judy	√		TMJ	4	2		75	47
Beaming, Double	More About Fabrics: Two-Warp Weaves	Zielinski, S. A.; Robert Leclerc, ed.	√	√	MWL	20			'51–'73	55
Beams: Back, Double	Supplementary Warp Patterning: Two Back Beams	Tidball, Harriet	√	√	SCGM		17		66	8
Bed Coverings: Bed Rugs, Sweden	From Mexico to Rumania to Sweden	Landreau, Anthony N.	√		TMJ	2	4		De 69	37
Bed Coverings: Bedspread	Charles Talley: A Candid Account of a Passionate Weaver and How He Got That Way	Talley, Charles	√		Fa	6	2		M/A 79	25
Bed Coverings: Bedspreads	Bedspread and Pillow (Beatrice E. Reeve)		√	√	H&C	12	3		Su 61	55
Bed Coverings: Bedspreads	Bedspread (Linda Ligon)		√	√	Hw	1	1		F-W 79	36, 59
Bed Coverings: Bedspreads	Bedspread (Marilyn Dillard)		√	√	Hw	4	4		S/O 83	60, 105
Bed Coverings: Bedspreads	Bedspreads	Phelps, Marie	√	√	H&C	2	3		Su 51	46
Bed Coverings: Bedspreads	Coverlets and Bedspreads: Variety in Early American Design	Saulpaugh, Dassah	√		H&C	17	4		Fa 66	8
Bed Coverings: Bedspreads	Crochet Pattern for Pinwheel Spread	Cannarella, Deborah	√	√	TM			7	O/N 86	18
Bed Coverings: Bedspreads	Designing Bedspreads for Use in Modern Interiors	Frey, Berta	√		H&C	13	3		Su 62	9
Bed Coverings: Bedspreads	English Bedspread		√		H&C	10	3		Su 59	50
Bed Coverings: Bedspreads	Handwoven Bedspread, A		√		Hw	3	2		Mr 82	56
Bed Coverings: Bedspreads	Inspired Bedspread (Anne-Mette Holm)		√	√	Hw	8	3		M/J 87	49, I-7, Cover
Bed Coverings: Bedspreads	King Size Bound Bouclé Blanket (Halcyon)		√	√	Hw	4	4		S/O 83	62, 106
Bed Coverings: Bedspreads	Loom Quilted Double Weave Bedspread (Wendy McKay)		√	> 4	Hw	8	4		S/O 87	88, I-15
Bed Coverings: Bedspreads	Michigan Weaving, Third Conference at Hartland Shows Wide Variety		√	√	H&C	13	1		Wi 62	18
Bed Coverings: Bedspreads	Monk's Belt Bedspread (Anne Bliss)		√	√	Hw	3	2		Mr 82	56, 87
Bed Coverings: Bedspreads	My Computer Designs a Bedspread	Salsbury, Nate	√	√	Hw	3	3		My 82	80
Bed Coverings: Bedspreads	Projects from a Connecticut Weaver	Krasnoff, Julienne	√	> 4	H&C	21	1		Wi 70	16
Bed Coverings: Bedspreads	Quilted Bedspread		√	> 4	H&C	16	3		Su 65	16, 46
Bed Coverings: Bedspreads	Roman Shades and Bedspread		√	√	WJ	3	1	9	Jy 78	32
Bed Coverings: Bedspreads	Ten Years and Ten Pounds of Crochet	Cannarella, Deborah	√		TM			1	O/N 85	80
Bed Coverings: Bedspreads	Weaving a Bedspread — A Case Study	McKay, Wendy	√	√	Hw	8	4		S/O 87	89
Bed Coverings: Bedspreads	Weaving in Quebec	Barrett, Clotilde	√	√	WJ	6	4	24	Sp 82	8
Bed Coverings: Counterpane, Quilted	Anatomy of a Quilted Counterpane (page revised WJ v9 n1 84 p70)	Adrosko, Rita J.	√		WJ	8	4	32	Sp 84	42
Bed Coverings: Coverlet (Quilt Lining)	Anatomy of a Quilted Counterpane (page revised WJ v9 n1 84 p70)	Adrosko, Rita J.	√		WJ	8	4	32	Sp 84	42
Bed Coverings: Coverlets	Aklae: Norwegian Tapestry	Irlbeck, Sonja	√	√	WJ	8	1	29	Su 83	27
Bed Coverings: Coverlets	Alling Museum, The	Rose, Kathy	√		Hw	3	5		N/D 82	33

SUBJECT	TITLE	AUTHOR	IL	INST	JOUR	VOL	NO	ISS	DATE	PAGE
Bed Coverings: Coverlets	Analysis and Documentation of Coverlets (error-corrected AT v3 85 p269)	Ulasewicz, Connie; Clarita Anderson; Steven M. Spivak	√	>4	AT	2			De 84	113
Bed Coverings: Coverlets	Analysis of Star and Diamond Weave Structures, An (error-corrected SS&D v10 n1 78 p101)	Anderson, Clarita; Judith Gordon; Naomi Whiting Towner	√	>4	SS&D	9	4	36	Fa 78	71
Bed Coverings: Coverlets	Arabesque	Herring, Connie	√	√	PWC	3	1	7		47
Bed Coverings: Coverlets	Art of Indiana Coverlets, The	Gilfoy, Peggy S.	√		AT	2			De 84	69
Bed Coverings: Coverlets	Artifacts Don't "Lie"	Anderson, Clarita	√		AT	7			Ju 87	9
Bed Coverings: Coverlets	Boundweave: Learning from the Past	Waggoner, Phyllis	√	√	WJ	10	4	40	Sp 86	44
Bed Coverings: Coverlets	Building on a Tradition	Alvic, Philis	√		Iw	4	3		Su 79	45
Bed Coverings: Coverlets	Colonial Coverlets, Part 3: Summer and Winter	Liebler, Barbara	√	√	Iw	1	4		Su 76	24
Bed Coverings: Coverlets	Colonial Coverlets, Part 4: Doubleweave	Liebler, Barbara	√	√	Iw	2	1		Fa 76	29
Bed Coverings: Coverlets	Contemporary Coverlet (Kathryn Wertenberger)		√	√	Hw	2	1		F-W 80	47, 70
Bed Coverings: Coverlets	Coverlet Bibliography	Anderson, Clarita			AT	2			De 84	203
Bed Coverings: Coverlets	Coverlet Care	Strickler, Carol	√	√	Hw	6	4		S/O 85	61
Bed Coverings: Coverlets	Coverlet for Convergence 1988, A		√	√	SS&D	19	1	73	Wi 87	46
Bed Coverings: Coverlets	Coverlet from Museum Collection	Clement, Doris	√	√	H&C	15	1		Wi 64	36
Bed Coverings: Coverlets	Coverlet from Start to Finish, A	van der Hoogt, Madelyn	√	√	PWC	5	1	15		20
Bed Coverings: Coverlets	Coverlet Homeconing '86	Thoeming, Bette; Kay Hulquist	√	√	Hw	8	5		N/D 87	70
Bed Coverings: Coverlets	Coverlet Information Sheet	Strickler, Carol	√	√	Iw	6	1		Wi 80	55
Bed Coverings: Coverlets	Coverlet Information Sheets, Nos. 1-4	Strickler, Carol	√	>4	Iw	3	1		Fa 77	38
Bed Coverings: Coverlets	Coverlet Information Sheets, Nos. 2.1—2.2	Strickler, Carol	√	√	Iw	3	4		Su 78	41
Bed Coverings: Coverlets	Coverlet Information Sheets, Nos. 2.3—2.4	Strickler, Carol	√	√	Iw	4	1		Wi 78	51
Bed Coverings: Coverlets	Coverlet Information Sheets, Nos. 2.5—2.6	Strickler, Carol	√	√	Iw	4	2		Sp 79	57
Bed Coverings: Coverlets	Coverlet Information Sheets, Nos. 3.1	Strickler, Carol	√	√	Iw	4	4		Fa 79	52
Bed Coverings: Coverlets	Coverlet Information Sheets, Nos. 5—6	Strickler, Carol	√	>4	Iw	3	2		Wi 78	36
Bed Coverings: Coverlets	Coverlet: Make Someday Today, Start a Coverlet, A	van der Hoogt, Madelyn	√	√	PWC	5	1	15		24
Bed Coverings: Coverlets	Coverlet Tradition in Kentucky, The	Guy, Sallie T.	√		Iw	4	3		Su 79	35
Bed Coverings: Coverlets	Coverlet Weaves Using Two Ties	Barrett, Clotilde	√	>4	WJ	3	4	12	Ap 79	26
Bed Coverings: Coverlets	Coverlet Weaving	Williams, Ann	√	√	SS&D	14	4	56	Fa 83	32
Bed Coverings: Coverlets	Coverlet: Weaving and Finishing Hints, A	van der Hoogt, Madelyn	√	√	PWC	5	1	15		34
Bed Coverings: Coverlets	Coverlets	Wilson, Sadye Tune; Doris Finch Kennedy	√		SS&D	14	4	56	Fa 83	34
Bed Coverings: Coverlets	"Coverlets: An American Tradition" (Exhibit)	Lowell-LaRoque, Jane	√		Fa	7	1		J/F 80	71
Bed Coverings: Coverlets	Coverlets and Bedspreads: Variety in Early American Design	Saulpaugh, Dassah	√		H&C	17	4		Fa 66	8
Bed Coverings: Coverlets	Designs for Today from Great-Grandmother's Drafts	Riswold, Margaret	√	√	H&C	3	3		Su 52	20
Bed Coverings: Coverlets	Doublecloth Coverlets	Shermeta, Margo	√		Fa	13	5		S/O 86	6
Bed Coverings: Coverlets	Doubleweave: A Popular Technique of the 19th Century Coverlet Weaver	Colwell, Ken	√	>4	PWC			2	Ap 82	53
Bed Coverings: Coverlets	Early American Coverlet of the Summer and Winter Type		√	>4	WJ	3	4	12	Ap 79	35
Bed Coverings: Coverlets	Fancy Coverlet Fringes	McGeary, Gay	√	√	Hw	2	5		No 81	38
Bed Coverings: Coverlets	Fifty Years As a Coverlet Weaver	Bright, Harriett H.	√	√	WJ	6	2	22	Fa 81	54
Bed Coverings: Coverlets	From Canada to China and Back Again (Edna Blackburn)	Blackburn, Edna	√	√	S-O	6	4		82	31
Bed Coverings: Coverlets	From Spinner to Weaver	Kluge, Gini	√		S-O	8	1		Sp 84	43
Bed Coverings: Coverlets	Gift to My Country: Lincoln Bedroom Coverlet, A	Jarvis, Helen N.	√	√	SS&D	9	4	36	Fa 78	17

SUBJECT	TITLE	AUTHOR	IL	INST	JOUR	VOL	NO	ISS	DATE	PAGE
Bed Coverings: Coverlets	Granny's Coverlet (or how do you tell if your coverlet's real?)	Strickler, Carol		√	S-O	6	4		82	26
Bed Coverings: Coverlets	Handwoven American Coverlets of the Overshot Type	Carey, Joyce Marquess	√	> 4	PWC	3	3	9		24
Bed Coverings: Coverlets	Happy Birthday, U.S.A. — Weavers Salute Bicentennial (Suzie Henzie)		√		SS&D	7	4	28	Fa 76	53
Bed Coverings: Coverlets	Heirlooms Don't Just Happen	Staines, Barbara			S-O	6	4		82	35
Bed Coverings: Coverlets	Historic Coverlets		√		H&C	7	3		Su 56	18
Bed Coverings: Coverlets	Historical American Weaving in Miniature	Strickler, Carol; Barbara Taggart	√	√	Iw	4	3		Su 79	48
Bed Coverings: Coverlets	History Lives on at Bishop Hill	Rohrer, Marge	√		Iw	4	3		Su 79	43
Bed Coverings: Coverlets	Huguenot Coverlets	Strickler, Carol	√	> 4	WJ	1	2	2	Oc 76	8
Bed Coverings: Coverlets	Jane Cox: Her Draft for Counterpins	Pinchin, C. B.	√	√	Iw	4	3		Su 79	31
Bed Coverings: Coverlets	Keep Warm! Colonial Comfort	Commings, Nancy	√	√	WJ	5	2	18	Fa 80	8
Bed Coverings: Coverlets	Ken Colwell on Collecting	Colwell, Ken	√		PWC	4	4	14		5
Bed Coverings: Coverlets	Ken Colwell on Coverlets	Colwell, Ken	√		PWC	3	3	9		56
Bed Coverings: Coverlets	"Lee's Surrender"	Ashwell, Eleanor V.	√	√	SS&D	6	2	22	Sp 75	85
Bed Coverings: Coverlets	Lee's Surrender — to Sachets	Xenakis, Alexis Yiorgos	√	√	Hw	1	2		S-S 80	18
Bed Coverings: Coverlets	Lining the Overshot	Moes, Dini	√	√	SS&D	13	4	52	Fa 82	64
Bed Coverings: Coverlets	Making Weaving History	Xenakis, Alexis Yiorgos	√		PWC	4	3	13		6
Bed Coverings: Coverlets	Mountain Heritage, A (Exhibit)		√		Fa	13	4		J/A 86	58
Bed Coverings: Coverlets	Multishaft Overshot on Opposites	van der Hoogt, Madelyn	√	> 4	WJ	8	3	31	Wi 83	76
Bed Coverings: Coverlets	New HGA Name Draft: Miniature Coverlet in Overshot, A	Marston, Ena	√	√	SS&D	12	3	47	Su 81	12
Bed Coverings: Coverlets	Nineteenth Century Miniatures	Erf, Mary Elva Congleton	√		SS&D	16	1	61	Wi 84	60
Bed Coverings: Coverlets	Nineteenth Century Miniatures	Erf, Mary Elva Congleton	√		SS&D	16	1	61	Wi 84	60
Bed Coverings: Coverlets	Notebook: Adapting Large Overshot Patterns	Meyers, Ruth Nordquist ed.	√	> 4	SS&D	14	4	56	Fa 83	16
Bed Coverings: Coverlets	Ohio's Woven Coverlets: Textile Industry in a Rural Economy	Cunningham, Patricia A.	√		AT	2			De 84	165
Bed Coverings: Coverlets	One-Woman Publishing Show, A	Xenakis, Alexis Yiorgos	√		PWC	5	2	16		6
Bed Coverings: Coverlets	Overshot Sampler Bedspread for a Narrow Loom, An	Keasbey, Doramay	√	√	PWC	5	1	15		42
Bed Coverings: Coverlets	PWC Coverlet Hall of Fame		√		PWC	5	1	15		26
Bed Coverings: Coverlets	Rummaging for Treasures	Strickler, Carol	√		SS&D	3	4	12	Fa 72	20
Bed Coverings: Coverlets	Sixteen-Harness Beiderwand Coverlet	Hoskinson, Marian K.	√	> 4	SS&D	14	4	56	Fa 83	19
Bed Coverings: Coverlets	Stars, Diamonds, Tables, and Sunrise: Motifs and Structures of Woven Coverlets	Cabeen, Lou	√	√	TM			14	D/J 87	32
Bed Coverings: Coverlets	Stitching Traditional Coverlet Weaves	Sellin, Helen G.	√	> 4	AT	1			De 83	289
Bed Coverings: Coverlets	Sturbridge Coverlet, A	Jarvis, Helen	√		PWC	5	2	16		20
Bed Coverings: Coverlets	Table Dressing and Bedcovers		√		Fa	8	3		M/J 81	43
Bed Coverings: Coverlets	Textile Resources in Brooklyn Museum		√		H&C	11	4		Fa 60	21
Bed Coverings: Coverlets	"Theme Show in Utah, A" (Exhibit)	Alderman, Sharon D.	√		Fa	8	3		M/J 81	68
Bed Coverings: Coverlets	Three-R's of Coverlets: Revival, Restoration, Research	Sellin, Helen; Peggy Hoyt			PWC	5	2	16		33
Bed Coverings: Coverlets	Time Warp on the Coldstream	McIntyre, Walter	√		SS&D	15	4	60	Fa 84	50
Bed Coverings: Coverlets	Traditional Coverlet (Marge Rohrer) (error-corrected Hw v2 n2 81 p68)		√	√	Hw	2	1		F-W 80	46, 73
Bed Coverings: Coverlets	Tromping Through the Ages	Dunwell, Anna	√		Fa	9	2		M/A 82	26
Bed Coverings: Coverlets	Twenty-Harness Madness	Moore, Gen	√	> 4	SS&D	12	4	48	Fa 81	46
Bed Coverings: Coverlets	Uncovering the Life and Weaving of John E. Schneider	Thieme, Otto Charles	√		SS&D	9	2	34	Sp 78	80
Bed Coverings: Coverlets	Weavers' Friendship Coverlet	Best, Eleanor	√	√	Hw	3	5		N/D 82	68
Bed Coverings: Coverlets	Weaving a Coverlet	Rohrer, Marge	√	√	S-O	6	4		82	28
Bed Coverings: Coverlets	Weaving in Quebec: Traditional Quebecois Weaving	Barrett, Clotilde	√	√	WJ	6	4	24	Sp 82	10
Bed Coverings: Coverlets	Wet-Cleaning Coverlets	McHugh, Maureen Collins	√	√	SS&D	1	3	3	Ju 70	6

SUBJECT	TITLE	AUTHOR	IL	INST	JOUR	VOL	NO	ISS	DATE	PAGE
Bed Coverings: Coverlets	White Coverlet (Carol Strickler)		√	√	Hw	3	5		N/D 82	49, 93
Bed Coverings: Coverlets	Wool from the Welsh Valleys	Rowe, Dilys	√		H&C	10	2		Sp 59	30
Bed Coverings: Coverlets, 19th Century	The Use of Eagles as a Decorative and Symbolic Motif in 19th Century American Coverlets	Anderson, Clarita; Jo B. Paoletti	√		AT	3			My 85	173
Bed Coverings: Coverlets (Kouverta)	Windows: Kouverta	Xenaxis, Alexis Yiorgos	√	√	PWC	5	1	15		14
Bed Coverings: Coverlets, Linsey-Woolsey, Quilted	Linsey-Woolseys at the Sheburne Museum, The (error-corrected SS&D v16 n3 85 p90)	Noordaa, Titia Vander	√		SS&D	16	2	62	Sp 85	59
Bed Coverings: Coverlets, Linsey-Woolsey, Quilted	Linsey-Woolseys at the Sheburne Museum, The (error-corrected SS&D v16 n3 85 p90)	Noordaa, Titia Vander	√		SS&D	16	2	62	Sp 85	59
Bed Coverings: Coverlets, Miniature	Christmas Miniatures, Part 1: Summer and Winter Coverlets	Lyon, Linda	√	√	PWC			3	Oc 82	50
Bed Coverings: Coverlets, Miniature	Home Weaving: It's the Little Things that Count		√	√	Hw	1	1		F-W 79	38
Bed Coverings: Coverlets, Miniature	Woven and Other Textile Miniatures (error-corrected WJ v2 n1 77 insert for vol. 1)		√	√	WJ	1	4	4	Ap 77	16
Bed Coverings: Coverlets, Miniature	Woven Miniatures		√	√	WJ	3	4	12	Ap 79	15
Bed Coverings: Quilts	American Quilt Study Group	Sears, Victoria	√		Fa	9	3		M/J 82	53
Bed Coverings: Quilts	"American Quilts: A Handmade Legacy" (Exhibit)	Janeiro, Jan	√		Fa	8	4		J/A 81	72
Bed Coverings: Quilts	"Baltimore Album Quilts" (Exhibit)	Park, Betty	√		Fa	8	6		N/D 81	69
Bed Coverings: Quilts	"Basketry Today: And Quilts from the Collection of Phyllis Haders" (Exhibits)	von Weise, Wenda	√		Fa	9	4		J/A 82	75
Bed Coverings: Quilts	Franklin Whitham	King, Bucky	√		Iw	2	2		Wi 77	13
Bed Coverings: Quilts	Group of Quilters Fit Ideas to Theme of Gift	Barnett, Linda Lowman	√		TM			7	O/N 86	33
Bed Coverings: Quilts	Guilding the Lily: Embroidery Stitches in Victorian Crazy Quilts	Horton, Margaret	√	√	TM			10	A/M 87	48
Bed Coverings: Quilts	Hawaiian Quilt, The	White-Hansen, Sue Ellen	√	√	TM			13	O/N 87	22
Bed Coverings: Quilts	Hawaiian Quilting: Tradition Through Change	Akana, Elizabeth A.	√		Fa	9	3		M/J 82	62
Bed Coverings: Quilts	"Hawaiian Quilts: Treasures of an Island Folk Art" (Exhibit)	Alonso, Harriet	√		Fa	6	6		N/D 79	77
Bed Coverings: Quilts	Ins and Outs of Hand Quilting, The	Giganti, Maria; Carol Clyne	√	√	TM			2	D/J 85	64
Bed Coverings: Quilts	Julie Silber: Exploring the Art and History of Quilts	Scarborough, Jessica	√		Fa	12	6		N/D 85	14
Bed Coverings: Quilts	Kantha Cloths of Bengal: The Sari Transformed	Gupta, Asha	√		Fa	9	6		N/D 82	19
Bed Coverings: Quilts	"Kentucky Quilt Project: 1800–1900, The" (Exhibit)		√		Fa	10	2		M/A 83	51
Bed Coverings: Quilts	Mastering the Art of Hand Appliqué	Wolff, Colette	√	√	TM			4	A/M 86	49
Bed Coverings: Quilts	Medallion Quilting	Miller, Kristin	√	√	TM			14	D/J 87	60
Bed Coverings: Quilts	Quilt Resource Sampler		√		Fa	8	3		M/J 81	10
Bed Coverings: Quilts	Quilting Bee Among the Amish, A	Fox, Judy Kellar	√		TM			4	A/M 86	12
Bed Coverings: Quilts	"Quilts: A Tradition of Variations" (Exhibit)	Rowley, Kathleen	√		Fa	10	2		M/A 83	68
Bed Coverings: Quilts	Quilts in Women's Lives	Mattera, Joanne	√		Fa	9	3		M/J 82	54
Bed Coverings: Quilts	Textile Resources of Brooklyn Museum		√		H&C	11	4		Fa 60	21
Bed Coverings: Quilts	Wailani Johansen, Quiltmaker: Sharing the Tradition of the Hawaiian Quilt	Rex, Chris	√		Fa	9	3		M/J 82	60
Bed Coverings: Quilts	When You See This Remember Me		√		Fa	9	5		S/O 82	100
Bed Coverings: Quilts	Zamani Soweto Sisters: A Patchwork of Lives		√		Fa	10	2		M/A 83	48
Bed Coverings: Quilts, Baby	Handing Down More Than Just a Quilt	Hamilton, Carolyn	√		TM			12	A/S 87	86
Bed Coverings: Quilts, Miniature	Small Endearments: 19th Century Quilts for Children and Dolls	Dyer, Carolyn	√		Fa	8	3		M/J 81	18

SUBJECT	TITLE	AUTHOR	IL	INST	JOUR	VOL	NO	ISS	DATE	PAGE
Bed Coverings: Quilts, Slave	Slave Quilts: Threads of History	Grabiner, Dana M.	√		Fa	13	5		S/O 86	22
Bed Coverings: Rugs	Handwoven Flocati of Epirus, The	Gans, Naomi Beth; Catherine Haywood	√	√	SS&D	12	3	47	Su 81	35
Bed Coverings: Sheet	Greek Dower Sheet (Alexis Yiorgos Xenakis)		√	> 4	Hw	1	2		S-S 80	36, 62
Bed Coverings: Sheets	Linen Bed Sheets		√		TM			4	A/M 86	86
Bedford Cord	#2: Vest Fabric (Sharon Alderman)		√	> 4	Hw	8	4		S/O 87	52, I-8
Bedford Cord	Bedford Cord Upholstery (Kathryn Wertenberger)		√	√	Hw	5	2		M/A 84	66, 104
Bedford Cord	Bedford Cord Vests (Sharon Alderman)		√	√	Hw	6	1		J/F 85	27, I-4
Bedford Cord	Secret of a Corrugated Surface: Bedford Cord, The (error-corrected Hw v6 n3 85 p I-2)	Alderman, Sharon	√	> 4	Hw	6	1		J/F 85	27
Bedford Cord	Verticals	O'Shaughnessy, Marjorie	√	> 4	SS&D	15	1	57	Wi 83	8
Bedford Cord Piqué	Bedford Cord Piqué	Xenakis, Athanasios David; Madelyn van der Hoogt	√	> 4	PWC	4	3	13		42
Bedspreads see Bed Coverings										
Beginnings: Knitting	Beginnings...	Rowley, Elaine	√	√	Kn	4	1	9	Wi 87	25
Beiderwand	Beiderwand Made Easy: An Old Weave Adapts to Four-Harness (revision SS&D v7 n4 76 p27)	Gordon, Judith	√	√	SS&D	7	3	27	Su 76	68
Beiderwand	But What's the Tie-Up?	van der Hoogt, Madelyn	√	> 4	PWC	5	1	15		36
Beiderwand	Coverlet Weaves Using Two Ties	Barrett, Clotilde	√	> 4	WJ	3	4	12	Ap 79	26
Beiderwand	Drafting: A Personal Approach, Part 2	Alvic, Philis	√	> 4	SS&D	13	2	50	Sp 82	46
Beiderwand	Gang: Technical and Conceptual Applications to Loom Controlled Weave Structures	Towner, Naomi Whiting	√	> 4	AT	5			Ju 86	91
Beiderwand	Introduction to Tied Unit Weaves, An	Kelly, Jacquie	√	> 4	PWC	4	4	14		40
Beiderwand	New HGA Textile Kits on Review		√		SS&D	12	3	47	Su 81	56
Beiderwand	Notes of a Pattern Weaver	Alvic, Philis	√		SS&D	13	4	52	Fa 82	76
Beiderwand	Ohio's Woven Coverlets: Textile Industry in a Rural Economy	Cunningham, Patricia A.	√		AT	2			De 84	165
Beiderwand	One-of-a-kind Garment in Beiderwand, A	Alvic, Philis	√		WJ	9	1	33	Su 84	51
Beiderwand	Sixteen-Harness Beiderwand Coverlet	Hoskinson, Marian K.	√	> 4	SS&D	14	4	56	Fa 83	19
Beiderwand, 2:1	Beiderwand	Gordon, Judith	√	> 4	CW	1	2	2	Fe 80	1
Beiderwand 4:1	Choosing a Loom, One Weaver's Experience with a Countermarch	Hoyt, Peggy	√	> 4	CW	4	1	10	Se 82	14
Beiderwand, Experimental	Beiderwand Revisited	Raymond, Nish		> 4	CW		24		My 87	20
Beiderwand Ground	Introduction to Tied Unit Weaves, An	Kelly, Jacquie	√	> 4	PWC	4	4	14		40
Beiderwand, Miniature	Miniature World, A	Piroch, Sigrid	√	> 4	PWC	5	2	16		26
Beiderwand, Tied	Rags Unlimited	Evans, Jane A.	√	> 4	Hw	2	3		My 81	44
Beiderwand, Tied, Turned	Turned Drafts in Double Two-Tie Unit Weave	van der Hoogt, Madelyn	√	> 4	WJ	9	2	34	Fa 84	13
Bell Pulls	Woven Bell Pulls	Bryan, Dorothy	√	√	H&C	11	1		Wi 60	46
Bellpulls (Miniature)	Christmas Miniatures, Part 2: Krokbragd Bellpulls (error-corrected PWC i4 83 p76)	Xenakis, Athanasios David	√	> 4	PWC			3	Oc 82	52
Belts see Bands, Belts, Sashes										
Berea College Fireside Industries	Berea College Fireside Industries Now Employ Sixty Weavers	Stahl, Sam	√		H&C	19	2		Sp 68	5
Bergman System	Handloom Weaves: The Classification of Handloom Weaves, The Structural Group, Unit Class, Bergman System	Tidball, Harriet	√	> 4	SCGM		33		57	24
Bergman Weaves	Bergman	Alvic, Philis	√	> 4	CW	2	1	4	Oc 80	10
Bergman Weaves	Bergman: Notes of a Pattern Weaver	Alvic, Philis	√	> 4	WJ	10	1	37	Su 85	64
Bergman Weaves	Drafting: A Personal Approach, Part 2	Alvic, Philis	√	> 4	SS&D	13	2	50	Sp 82	46
Bergman Weaves	Leonora Meek, Nebraska Weaver and Teacher		√	> 4	H&C	15	2		Sp 64	23
Bergman Weaves	Tablecloth in Bergman Weave	Morrison, Ruth	√	> 4	PWC	4	4	14		38

SUBJECT	TITLE	AUTHOR	IL	INST	JOUR	VOL	NO	ISS	DATE	PAGE
Bermuda	Back-Strap Looms in Bermuda		√		SS&D	4	2	14	Sp 73	22
Bias	How Madame Grès Sculpts with Fabric	Cooper, Arlene	√	√	TM			10	A/M 87	50
Bias	Working with the Bias	West, Virginia	√	> 4	WJ	12	1	45	Su 87	9
Bias Binding	Easy Way to Make a Bias Tube, An		√	√	TM			3	F/M 86	8
Bias Binding: Technique	Little Bit of Bias, A (error-corrected Hw v4 n5 83 p94)	Raymond, Nish	√		Hw	4	4		S/O 83	37
Bias Binding: Technique	Pillows		√	√	Hw	5	2		M/A 84	59
Bias Binding: Woven	Biased Toward Bias	Bradley, Louise	√	√	Hw	6	3		Su 85	24
Bias Strips	Cutting Bias Strips		√	√	TM			9	F/M 87	10
Bias Welt Casing	Making A Bias Welt Facing		√	√	Hw	5	2		M/A 84	61
Bibical Quotations	Persis Grayson, Weaver & Spinner	Amos, Mary Alice	√		H&C	19	1		Wi 68	10
Biblical Quotations	Spinning Wheels	Rizner, Constance	√		SS&D	14	3	55	Su 83	16
Biblical Quotations: Apparel	Nativity Scene	Vargo, Bessie Mae	√	√	WJ	6	2	22	Fa 81	8
Biblical Quotations: Color and Dyeing	Purple in Antiquity	Davidson, Mary Frances			SS&D	2	1	5	De 70	26
Biblical Quotations: Linen	Linen Lore	Goodman, Deborah Lerme	√		Fa	14	2		M/A 87	16
Biblical Quotations: Selvage	Flaunt It		√	√	Hw	6	1		J/F 85	65
Biblical Quotations: Thistles	Thistles	Bliss, Anne	√	√	Hw	7	1		J/F 86	84
Biblical Quotations: Yarn Colors	Tyrian Purple	Robinson, John P., Jr.	√		H&C	24	1		J/F 73	30
Bibliography: Basketry	Giving Your Baskets a Long, Healthy Life: A Basic Guide to Basketry Conservation	Odegaard, Nancy; Dale Kronkright	√		Fa	11	1		J/F 84	43
Bibliography: Beads and Beading	Contemporary Appliqued Beadwork: References	Woodsmall, Annabel Whitney			TIAM		2		79	40
Bibliography: Books, Articles by Clotilde Barrett	Clotilde Barrett: A Biographical Sketch		√		WJ	10	4	40	Sp 86	6
Bibliography: Children's Textile Literature	Bibliography of Children's Textile Literature, A	Grant, Susan			Iw	4	4		Fa 79	66
Bibliography: Color and Dyeing	Color and Dyeing, Lesson 1	Siminoff			SS&D	1	4	4	Se 70	20
Bibliography: Computer-Aided Design for Handweaving	Computer-Aided Design for Handweaving: Bibliography	Windeknecht, Margaret B.; Thomas G. Windeknecht			CW	2	1	4	Oc 80	9
Bibliography: Coverlet	Coverlet Bibliography	Anderson, Clarita			AT	2			De 84	203
Bibliography: Coverlets, Annotated	Annotated Coverlet Bibliography: Books and Magazines				PWC	5	2	16		48
Bibliography: Creative Process	Probing the Creative Process: A Book List to Begin With	Austin, Carole	√		Fa	11	6		N/D 84	53
Bibliography: Damask and Weft Compound Weaves	Damask and Weft Compound Weaves, Bibliography	Sellin, Helen			CW	4	2	11	Ja 83	12
Bibliography: Double Weave	Double Weave: Plain and Patterned: Bibliography, The	Tidball, Harriet	√	> 4	SCGM		1		60	34
Bibliography: Dyes and Dyeing	Dyer's Library, A	Taggart, Barbara			SS&D	4	2	14	Sp 73	51
Bibliography: Dyes and Dyeing	Dyer's Bookshelf, A				Fa	5	1		J/F 78	33
Bibliography: Fiber Students	Provocative Book List: Recommended Reading for Fiber Students, A	Towner, Naomi Whiting			Fa	8	4		J/A 81	16
Bibliography: Finishes and Finishing	Bibliography of Books on Finishes and Finishing, A				Hw	2	5		No 81	93
Bibliography: Four-Shaft Weaving	If You Have Four Harnesses	Hagarty, Harriet May			H&C	23	6		N/D 72	32
Bibliography: Grant References	Brief Bibliography of Grant References, A	Polster, Joanne			Fa	11	4		J/A 84	50
Bibliography: Indigo	Indigo Miscellany, An		√		Fa	13	5		S/O 86	25
Bibliography: Knitting	Books on Guernseys	Swansen, Meg			Kn	1	1	1	F-W 84 CI	71 54
Bibliography: Leno, Doup	Doup Leno: Bibliography	Skowronski, Hella; Sylvia Tacker			SCGM		32		80	46
Bibliography: Monk's Belt	Creative Monk's Belt: Bibliography	Windeknecht, Margaret B.			SCGM		30		76	40
Bibliography: Overshot	Books on Overshot: A Bibliography	Colwell, Ken	√		PWC	3	2	8		43
Bibliography: Overshot	Creative Overshot: Bibliography	Windeknecht, Margaret B.			SCGM		31		78	57

SUBJECT	TITLE	AUTHOR	IL	INST	JOUR	VOL	NO	ISS	DATE	PAGE
Bibliography: Papermaking	Bibliography: Where to Fine More Information on Papermaking and Its Possibilities				Fa	6	4		J/A 79	38
Bibliography: Peruvian Textiles	Peru, Textiles Unlimited: Bibliography	Tidball, Harriet			SCGM		25		68	34
Bibliography: Satin	Contemporary Satins: References on Satin	Tidball, Harriet			SCGM		7		62	33
Bibliography: Selected, Peruvian Textiles	Brief History of the Study of Ancient Peruvian Textiles, A	King, Mary Elizabeth	√		TMJ	2	1		De 66	39
Bibliography: Spinning	Bibliography				S-O	1			77	54
Bibliography: Spinning	Selected Bibliography for Handspinners, A				S-O	5			81	6
Bibliography: Spinning	Selected Bibliography for Handspinners, A	Lacey, Sue			S-O	8	3		Fa 84	11
Bibliography: Spinning	Selected Bibliography for Handspinners, A	Lacey, Sue			S-O	9	2		Su 85	49
Bibliography: Tartans, Scottish	Weaver's Book of Scottish Tartans: References and Bibliography of Sources, The	Tidball, Harriet			SCGM		5		62	29
Bibliography: Textile Art	Bibliography: Late Roman, Early Byzantine Textile Art	Trilling, James			TMJ	21			82	111
Bibliography: Twining, Weft	Weft Twining: Bibliography	Harvey, Virginia I.; Harriet Tidball			SCGM		28		69	38
Bibliography: Warps and Warping	Bibliography				Hw	3	3		My 82	71
Bibliography: Wearables	Who, How, What, and When of Wearables, The	Grover, Donald	√		Fa	6	3		M/J 79	66
Bibliography: Weaving Books	How to use A Weaving Book				H&C	26	2		Ap 75	22
Bibliography: Weaving Books, German	List of Early Published German Weaving Books (1677–1840)	Hilts, Patricia			AT	5			Ju 86	192
Bibliography: Weaving, Multiharness	Multi-Harness Book List				CW	1	1	1	De 79	3
Bibs	Baby Bib (Margaretha Essén-Hedin)		√	√	Hw	8	2		M/A 87	44, I-7
Bibs	Crocheted Baby Bib, A	Linder, Harry P.	√	√	S-O	10	1		Sp 86	32
Bicentennial, USA	Happy Birthday, U.S.A. — Weavers Salute Bicentennial		√		SS&D	7	4	28	Fa 76	53
Biennale, Lausanne	8th International Biennial of Tapestry: Three Perspectives, The	Marston, Ena; Shirley E. Held; Esther Dendel	√		SS&D	9	1	33	Wi 77	4
Biennale, Lausanne	Biennale, The	Taylor, Dianne; Elmer Taylor	√		SS&D	12	4	48	Fa 81	54
Biennale, Lausanne	Biennale, The	Waller, Irene	√		SS&D	14	4	56	Fa 83	20
Biennale, Lausanne	Biennale/Another View, The	Coifman, Lucienne	√		SS&D	15	1	57	Wi 83	76
Biennale, Lausanne	Brief History of the International Biennial of Tapestry or "Watch Out for Women Who Knit", A	Taylor, Dianne	√		Fa	10	5		S/O 83	43
Biennale, Lausanne	But Is It Tapestry?	Meltzer, Marilyn	√		SS&D	5	3	19	Su 74	39
Biennale, Lausanne	Eleventh International Biennial of Tapestry, The	Taylor, Elmer; Dianne Taylor	√		Fa	10	5		S/O 83	33
Biennale, Lausanne	Fifth International Tapestry Exhibit	Wick, Susan	√		H&C	22	4		Fa 71	16
Biennale, Lausanne	Lausanne Biennale: The Scene of an Adventure, The	Ritschard, Mlle. Claude	√		Iw	4	2		Sp 79	19
Biennale, Lausanne	Lausanne Notebook: Our Special Report on the 8th Lausanne Biennial of Tapestry, A	Mathews, Rich	√		Fa	4	5		S/O 77	30
Biennale, Lausanne	Ninth International Biennial of Tapestry: A Prime Reflector, The	West, Virginia	√		SS&D	11	1	41	Wi 79	96
Biennale, Lausanne	"Ninth International Biennial of Tapestry" (Exhibit)	Pulleyn, Rob	√		Fa	6	4		J/A 79	62
Biennale, Lausanne	Seventh Lausanne Biennial, The		√		SS&D	7	2	26	Sp 76	41
Biennale, Lausanne	"Tenth International Biennial of Tapestry: Four Views" (Exhibit)	Shawcroft, Barbara	√		Fa	8	6		N/D 81	52
Biennale, Lausanne	Thirteenth Biennale, The				SS&D	17	2	66	Sp 86	47

SUBJECT	TITLE	AUTHOR	IL	INST	JOUR	VOL	NO	ISS	DATE	PAGE
Biennale, Lausanne	To the Walls: The 13th Lausanne Biennial (Exhibit)	Zepeda, Susan G.	√		Fa	14	4		S/O 87	41
Biennale, Lausanne	Twelfth International Biennial of Tapestry	Taylor, Dianne; Elmer Taylor	√		Fa	12	6		N/D 85	50
Biennale: Lausanne	Twelfth International Tapestry Biennale, The	Coifman, Lucienne	√		SS&D	17	2	66	Sp 86	45
Biennale: Lausanne	Twelfth International Tapestry Biennale, The	Waller, Irene	√		SS&D	17	2	66	Sp 86	42
Biennale, Lausanne: Critique	"Tenth International Biennial of Tapestry: A Critic" (Exhibit)	Zoppetti, Patti	√		Fa	8	6		N/D 81	54
Biennale, Lausanne: Jurying	"Tenth International Biennial of Tapestry: A Juror" (Exhibit)	Berger, René	√		Fa	8	6		N/D 81	55
Biennale, Laussane	Entries from the 1973 Lausanne Biennale				H&C	24	3		M/J 73	39
Billedvev	Nineteenth Century Tapestry in Billedvev, A	Nelson, Lila	√		WJ	10	2	38	Fa 85	26
Binding Warps: Twill, Right-Hand	Chinese Drawloom: A Study in Weave Structure, The	Sellin, Helen	√	> 4	WJ	9	2	34	Fa 84	6
Biographical see People										
Birds, Woven	Whitewater Birds At Wisconsin Show		√	√	SS&D	2	2	6	Sp 71	10
Birth Project, The	"Birth Project, The" First Showing of Judy Chicago's New Work (Exhibit)	von Kreisler-Bomben, Kristin	√		Fa	10	1		J/F 83	81
Black Oak	Why Bother with Natural Dyeing?	Bulbach, Stanley	√	√	TM			5	J/J 86	32
Blanket see Afghans, Blankets, Throws										
Blanket Weave	Blanket Weave, The	Robitaille, Annette	√	> 4	WJ	8	4	32	Sp 84	62
Blanket Weave System	Handloom Weaves: The Classification of Handloom Weaves, The Structural Group, The Rhythmic Weave Class, Blanket Weave System	Tidball, Harriet	√	√	SCGM		33		57	35
Bleaching: Fibers	Color and Dyeing: Bleaching Fibers and Yarns	Tidball, Harriet	√	√	SCGM		16		65	33
Bleaching: Flax	Chemical Dyeing of Linen	Gwynne, Elaine	√	√	WJ	7	2	26	Fa 82	23
Bleaching: Techniques	Principles of Textile Conservation Science, No.15. The Control of Oxidation in Textile Conservation	Rice, James W.	√	√	TMJ	3	1		De 70	55
Blended Weave Structures	Anyone Can Blend	Kessenich, Loraine	√	√	H&C	7	1		Wi 55	22
Blended Weave Structures: Overshot and Twill	"Sand Dunes and Dune Grass": Two Garments from a Blended Draft (Ardis Dobrovolny)		√	√	Hw	6	2		M/A 85	57, I-14
Blending Colors	Technical Information for Cape Fabric (Sharon Alderman)		√	√	Hw	5	5		N/D 84	60, I-14
Blending Colors: Fiber	Spinner's Specialty: Heathered Yarns, A	Searle, Karen	√	√	WJ	9	2	34	Fa 84	56
Blending Colors: Swedish Woolens	Woolens and Tweeds: Designing Woolen Fabrics: Swedish Woolens	Tidball, Harriet		√	SCGM		4		61	26
Blending Fibers	Barbara's Blends		√		S-O	7	3		Fa 83	47
Blending Fibers	Blending Mohair with Other Fibers	Bliss, Anne	√	√	S-O	7	3		Fa 83	43
Blending Fibers	Carded Rainbow Batts	Amos, Alden	√	√	S-O	9	1		Sp 85	19
Blending Fibers	Closer Look at Cashgora, A	Presser, Fran	√	√	S-O	10	4		Wi 86	49
Blending Fibers	Exotic Fiber Blends	Royce, Beverly	√	√	S-O	9	4		Wi 85	43
Blending Fibers	Fiber Foray: Color Exercises for the Beginner	Quinn, Celia	√	√	S-O	9	3		Fa 85	36
Blending Fibers	Heathering	O'Connor, Marcie Archer	√	√	Kn	2	1	3	F-W 85	54
Blending Fibers	Six of One, Half a Dozen of the Other (a roundtable discussion with six spinners)		√		S-O	5			81	51
Blending Fibers	Spinning for an Ombré Project	Adams, Brucie	√	√	Hw	4	2		M/A 83	78
Blending Fibers	Spinning with Down and Knitting with Feathers	von Ammon, Helen	√		S-O	10	4		Wi 86	15
Blending Fibers	Using Your Mistakes	Martin, Jill			S-O	8	1		Sp 84	52
Blind see Disabled and Theraphy/Rehabilitation										

SUBJECT	TITLE	AUTHOR	IL	INST	JOUR	VOL	NO	ISS	DATE	PAGE
Blinds and Screens	Anemone Garden Transparency (Bobbie Irwin)		√	√	Hw	7	2		M/A 86	45, I-6
Blinds and Screens	Easy Weaving for Easy Living		√	√	Hw	1	2		S-S 80	48
Blinds and Screens	Michigan Guild Project: A Four-Panel Folding Screen	James, Esther	√	√	SS&D	9	1	33	Wi 77	114
Blinds and Screens	Robert D. Sailors		√		H&C	16	4		Fa 65	6
Blinds and Screens	Screen for All Seasons, A	Ridgeway, Terese	√	√	SS&D	16	4	64	Fa 85	52
Blinds and Screens	Textured Room Divider		√	√	H&C	13	1		Wi 62	33
Blinds and Screens	Woven Wood, Speciality of Robert Webb		√		H&C	16	2		Sp 65	19
Blinds and Screens	Yarns and Fibers: Unusual Yarns - Partitions	Zielinski, S. A.; Robert Leclerc, ed.		√	MWL	4			'51–'73	89
Blinds and Screens: Handwoven	Colorful Blinds and Fabrics from Texas		√		H&C	6	4		Fa 55	14
Blinds and Screens: Handwoven	Design in Handwoven Screens, Part 1	Rossbach, Ed	√	√	H&C	6	1		Wi 54	16
Blinds and Screens: Handwoven	Design in Handwoven Screens, Part 2	Rossbach, Ed	√		H&C	6	3		Su 55	16
Block Patterns: Motifs, Pine Tree	Roses and Snowballs: The Development of Block Patterns in the German Linen-Weaving Tradition	Hilts, Patricia	√	>4	AT	5			Ju 86	167
Block Patterns: Motifs, Rose	Roses and Snowballs: The Development of Block Patterns in the German Linen-Weaving Tradition	Hilts, Patricia	√	>4	AT	5			Ju 86	167
Block Patterns: Motifs, Snowball	Roses and Snowballs: The Development of Block Patterns in the German Linen-Weaving Tradition	Hilts, Patricia	√	>4	AT	5			Ju 86	167
Block Patterns: Motifs, Star	Roses and Snowballs: The Development of Block Patterns in the German Linen-Weaving Tradition	Hilts, Patricia	√	>4	AT	5			Ju 86	167
Block Printing	Stretching Fabric in Small Spaces	Levy, Julie	√	√	TM			3	F/M 86	34
Block Weaves	Anatomy of a Quilted Counterpane (page revised WJ v9 n1 84 p70)	Adrosko, Rita J.	√		WJ	8	4	32	Sp 84	42
Block Weaves	Bateman Blend Weaves: Division A — Six-Thread Blocks	Bateman, Dr. William G.; Virginia I. Harvey, ed.	√	>4	SCGM		36		82	21
Block Weaves	Bateman Blend Weaves: Division B — Eight-Thread Blocks	Bateman, Dr. William G.; Virginia I. Harvey, ed.	√	>4	SCGM		36		82	51
Block Weaves	Bateman Blend Weaves: Division C — Ten-Thread Blocks	Bateman, Dr. William G.; Virginia I. Harvey, ed.	√	>4	SCGM		36		82	72
Block Weaves	Bateman Blend Weaves: Division D — Twelve-Thread Blocks	Bateman, Dr. William G.; Virginia I. Harvey, ed.	√	>4	SCGM		36		82	109
Block Weaves	Bateman Blend Weaves: The Structures of the Bateman Blend System	Bateman, Dr. William G.; Virginia I. Harvey, ed.	√	>4	SCGM		36		82	14
Block Weaves	Bateman Blend Weaves: Three-Tie and Four-Tie Blocks	Bateman, Dr. William G.; Virginia I. Harvey, ed.	√	>4	SCGM		36		82	120
Block Weaves	Bateman Blend Weaves: Variations of A, B, and C Blocks	Bateman, Dr. William G.; Virginia I. Harvey, ed.	√	>4	SCGM		36		82	112
Block Weaves	Blanket Weave, The	Robitaille, Annette	√	>4	WJ	8	4	32	Sp 84	62
Block Weaves	Block: An Exploration of Weaves, The	Strickler, Carol	√		Hw	8	5		N/D 87	41
Block Weaves	Block Weaves as Color and Texture Effects	Znamierowski, Nell	√	√	Hw	8	5		N/D 87	48
Block Weaves	Blocks and Warp-Faced Weaving			√	Hw	8	5		N/D 87	61
Block Weaves	Blocks in Production	LaLena, Constance	√	√	Hw	8	5		N/D 87	22
Block Weaves	Computer as a Design Tool, The	Strickler, Carol	√	√	Hw	8	5		N/D 87	66
Block Weaves	Designing Rugs for Harness-Controlled Weaving		√	>4	WJ	4	4	16	Ap 80	27
Block Weaves	Diversified Plain Weave	Wertenberger, Kathryn	√	>4	Hw	8	5		N/D 87	62
Block Weaves	Double Weave Blocks on Eight	Howard, Miranda	√	>4	Hw	6	3		Su 85	36
Block Weaves	Doubleweave: A Popular Technique of the 19th Century Coverlet Weaver	Colwell, Ken	√	>4	PWC			2	Ap 82	53
Block Weaves	Early American Coverlet of the Summer and Winter Type		√	>4	WJ	3	4	12	Ap 79	35
Block Weaves	Even-Tied Overshot	Xenakis, Athanasios David	√	>4	PWC	3	3	9		40
Block Weaves	Four-Block Double Weave on Four Shafts	Barrett, Clotilde	√	√	WJ	8	1	29	Su 83	72

SUBJECT	TITLE	AUTHOR	IL	INST	JOUR	VOL	NO	ISS	DATE	PAGE
Block Weaves	Four-End Block Draft or Summer and Winter	McClanathan, Barbara	√	√	WJ	8	4	32	Sp 84	22
Block Weaves	Four-Shaft Double Weave with Color and Weave Effects	Scorgie, Jean; Gloria Martin	√	√	Hw	6	3		Su 85	38
Block Weaves	Lithuanian Pervarai: Producing a Twenty Shaft Pattern on a Twelve Shaft Loom	Meek, M. Kati	√	>4	AT	1			De 83	159
Block Weaves	Loom Controlled Designs		√	>4	WJ	3	3	11	Ja 79	18
Block Weaves	Metamorphosis: Two-Tie Weaves and the Changeable Image	Carey, Joyce Marquess	√	>4	AT	1			De 83	243
Block Weaves	Modification of the AVL Dobby Loom for Execution of Multi-Shaft Two-Tie Block Weaves	Gustafson, Susan L.	√	√	AT	1			De 83	235
Block Weaves	Monk's Belt and Ways to Think of Blocks		√	>4	Hw	8	5		N/D 87	57
Block Weaves	Multiple Tabby Weaves: Eight-Harness Multiple Tabby Weaves	Bateman, Dr. William G.; Virginia I. Harvey, ed.	√	>4	SCGM		35		81	70
Block Weaves	Multiple Tabby Weaves: Rearranging the Threading Within the Blocks	Bateman, Dr. William G.; Virginia I. Harvey, ed.	√	√	SCGM		35		81	26
Block Weaves	Multiple Tabby Weaves: The Basic Blocks	Bateman, Dr. William G.; Virginia I. Harvey, ed.	√	√	SCGM		35		81	20
Block Weaves	Notebook: Warmables (Nancy Britton)	Meyers, Ruth Nordquist, ed.	√	√	SS&D	15	1	57	Wi 83	80
Block Weaves	Rugs on a Three-End Block Draft	Kindahl, Connie	√	√	WJ	8	4	32	Sp 84	19
Block Weaves	Shadow Weave		√	√	Hw	8	5		N/D 87	51
Block Weaves	Simple Damask-Like Effects Using Element Diameter Differential and Element Tension Differential	Xenakis, Athanasios David	√	>4	AT	1			De 83	317
Block Weaves	Single-Tied Unit Weave		√	>4	Hw	8	5		N/D 87	54
Block Weaves	Spot Weave Rug	Hanley, Janet	√	√	WJ	3	4	12	Ap 79	40
Block Weaves	Summer and Winter: A Rug for All Seasons (Falene E. Hamilton)		√	√	Hw	7	4		S/O 86	42
Block Weaves	Summer and Winter for Four Shafts	Allen, Debbie	√	√	Hw	8	5		N/D 87	86
Block Weaves	Summer and Winter — Part 1		√	>4	WJ	2	4	8	Ap 78	28
Block Weaves	Twill and Plain Weave Blocks with Long-Eyed Heddles	Broughton, Eve T.	√	>4	WJ	8	4	32	Sp 84	58
Block Weaves	Two Block Rug in Boundweave	Waggoner, Phyllis	√	√	WJ	12	1	45	Su 87	26
Block Weaves	Warp Color Changes in Double and Multilayer Weaves	O'Connor, Paul	√	>4	WJ	12	2	46	Fa 87	55
Block Weaves	Weaving Block Twills		√	>4	Hw	8	5		N/D 87	52
Block Weaves	Weft-Faced Weaving of Block Weaves		√	√	Hw	8	5		N/D 87	59
Block Weaves: Bateman Park Weaves	Bateman Park Weaves: Division I — Seven-Harness Blocks, Tag Weave or Tag Treadling	Bateman, Dr. William G.; Virginia I. Harvey, ed.	√	>4	SCGM		37		84	27
Block Weaves: Bateman Park Weaves	Bateman Park Weaves: Division II — Blocks of Varying Sizes Combined in a Draft	Bateman, Dr. William G.; Virginia I. Harvey, ed.	√	>4	SCGM		37		84	88
Block Weaves: Bateman Park Weaves	Bateman Park Weaves: Division II — Eight-Harness Blocks	Bateman, Dr. William G.; Virginia I. Harvey, ed.	√	>4	SCGM		37		84	48
Block Weaves: Bateman Park Weaves	Bateman Park Weaves: Division II — Eight-Harness Blocks, Eight-Thread Blocks	Bateman, Dr. William G.; Virginia I. Harvey, ed.	√	>4	SCGM		37		84	74
Block Weaves: Bateman Park Weaves	Bateman Park Weaves: Division II — Eight-Harness Blocks, Six-Thread Blocks	Bateman, Dr. William G.; Virginia I. Harvey, ed.	√	>4	SCGM		37		84	60
Block Weaves: Bateman Park Weaves	Bateman Park Weaves: Division II — Eight-Harness Blocks, Ten-Thread Blocks	Bateman, Dr. William G.; Virginia I. Harvey, ed.	√	>4	SCGM		37		84	79
Block Weaves: Bateman Park Weaves	Bateman Park Weaves: Division II — Eight-Harness Blocks, Twelve-Thread Blocks	Bateman, Dr. William G.; Virginia I. Harvey, ed.	√	>4	SCGM		37		84	83
Block Weaves: Bateman Park Weaves	Bateman Park Weaves: Park Weave Rules	Bateman, Dr. William G.; Virginia I. Harvey, ed.	√	>4	SCGM		37		84	18
Block Weaves: Expanded	Multiple Tabby Weaves: Expanding the Blocks	Bateman, Dr. William G.; Virginia I. Harvey, ed.	√	√	SCGM		35		81	46

SUBJECT	TITLE	AUTHOR	IL	INST	JOUR	VOL	NO	ISS	DATE	PAGE
Block Weaves: Multiple Shaft	Multiple Tabby Weaves: Six-Harness Multiple Tabby Weaves	Bateman, Dr. William G.; Virginia I. Harvey, ed.	√	>4	SCGM		35		81	59
Block Weaves: Profile Designs	Composition and Designing Part 2: Variations of Four Block Patterns	Zielinski, S. A.; Robert Leclerc, ed.	√	√	MWL	19			'51–'73	20
Block-Printing Fabric	Classroom Block Printing Project, A	Green, Julie	√	√	Fa	14	1		J/F 87	41
Blouses, Shirts, Tops	African Inspiration, An (Louise Bradley)		√	√	Hw	5	4		S/O 84	51, 94
Blouses, Shirts, Tops	African Strip-Cloth Shirt Without Strips, An	O'Connor, Eileen	√	√	WJ	6	3	23	Wi 81	33
Blouses, Shirts, Tops	Alpaca "Jerga" (Pam Bolesta)		√	√	Hw	1	1		F-W 79	22, 55
Blouses, Shirts, Tops	Batwing Sleeved Blouse (Virginia West) (error-corrected Hw v7 n2 86 p I-3)		√	>4	Hw	7	1		J/F 86	52, I-7
Blouses, Shirts, Tops	Batwings and Butterflies (Virginia West)		√	√	Hw	6	2		M/A 85	41, I-4
Blouses, Shirts, Tops	Beautiful Fabric Is Not Enough	Lommen, Sandy	√	√	SS&D	15	2	58	Sp 84	40
Blouses, Shirts, Tops	Beginner's Tops	Legerski, Victoria	√	>4	WJ	8	3	31	Wi 83	14
Blouses, Shirts, Tops	Beyond Rags: Fabric Strip Design	Larson-Fleming, Susan	√	√	WJ	9	4	36	Sp 85	47
Blouses, Shirts, Tops	Blouse for Her — A Shirt for Him, A		√	√	WJ	4	3	15	Ja 80	4
Blouses, Shirts, Tops	Blouse of Cards	Holtzer, Marilyn Emerson	√		SS&D	16	3	63	Su 85	20
Blouses, Shirts, Tops	Blue Banded Shirt (Miranda Howard)		√	>4	Hw	3	4		Se 82	66, 89
Blouses, Shirts, Tops	Box-Pleated Blouse (Maury Young)		√	√	Hw	8	2		M/A 87	62, I-14
Blouses, Shirts, Tops	Bright Blouse	Lewis, Susanna	√	√	Kn	3	2	6	Sp 87	36
Blouses, Shirts, Tops	California Holiday Delight (Mary Kay Stoehr)		√	√	Hw	6	3		Su 85	41, I-6
Blouses, Shirts, Tops	Camisole (Lou Cabeen)		√	√	Hw	4	3		M/J 83	45, 93
Blouses, Shirts, Tops	Carla's Zebra Top	Fauske, Carla	√	√	PWC			2	Ap 82	88
Blouses, Shirts, Tops	Chenille Polo	Xenakis, Alexis Yiorgos	√	√	PWC			6	Su 83	34
Blouses, Shirts, Tops	"Chiola" India Top (Betty Davenport)		√	√	Hw	2	2		Mr 81	54, 74
Blouses, Shirts, Tops	Color Blanket Shawl & Top (Priscilla Plate)		√	√	Hw	2	4		Se 81	50, 89
Blouses, Shirts, Tops	Combine Techniques? Why not?	Derr, Mary L.	√		WJ	7	3	27	Wi 82	19
Blouses, Shirts, Tops	Cotton Shirts	Barnett-Westfall, Lynn	√	√	WJ	4	3	15	Ja 80	22
Blouses, Shirts, Tops	Cotton Skirt and Blouse	Gant, Helen Mosely	√	√	S-O	6	4		82	63
Blouses, Shirts, Tops	Cotton Top (Betty Davenport)		√	>4	Hw	7	3		M/J 86	68, I-16
Blouses, Shirts, Tops	Cotton-Linen Garment in Basket Weave		√	√	WJ	7	3	27	Wi 82	32
Blouses, Shirts, Tops	Country Silk Top (Betty Davenport)		√	√	Hw	5	3		Su 84	59, 102
Blouses, Shirts, Tops	Creative Clothing: Surface Embellishment	Mayer, Anita Luvera	√	√	WJ	11	3	43	Wi 87	30
Blouses, Shirts, Tops	Croatian Shirt, A	Gaustad, Stephenie	√	√	S-O	9	2		Su 85	28
Blouses, Shirts, Tops	Crochet—A Great Technique for Finishing Handwovens		√	>4	WJ	7	3	27	Wi 82	18
Blouses, Shirts, Tops	Designed for Narrow Looms: A Summer Shirt Inspired by the Macedonian Chemise	Temple, Mary	√	√	WJ	10	1	37	Su 85	46
Blouses, Shirts, Tops	Dolman Top (Elaine Rowley)		√	√	Hw	1	2		S-S 80	45, 67
Blouses, Shirts, Tops	Dolman Top (Sharon Alderman)		√	√	Hw	6	2		M/A 85	47, I-7
Blouses, Shirts, Tops	Don't Cry...Dye	Bliss, Anne	√	√	Hw	2	2		Mr 81	50
Blouses, Shirts, Tops	Double Two-Tie Twills and Basket Weave	Barrett, Clotilde	√	>4	WJ	7	3	27	Wi 82	38
Blouses, Shirts, Tops	Drafter, The Draper, The Flat Patternmaker, The	Nebesar, Rebecca Lanxner	√	√	TM			11	J/J 87	33
Blouses, Shirts, Tops	Draping a Blouse	Sperry, Ellen	√	√	TM			3	F/M 86	46
Blouses, Shirts, Tops	Egyptian Shirt (Kathryn Wertenberger)		√	√	Hw	2	2		Mr 81	54, 70
Blouses, Shirts, Tops	Elaine's Knitted Top	Rowley, Elaine D.	√	√	PWC			2	Ap 82	89
Blouses, Shirts, Tops	Embroidery for the Goddess	Kelly, Mary B.	√		TM			11	J/J 87	26
Blouses, Shirts, Tops	Evening Cocoon		√	√	S-O	5			81	56
Blouses, Shirts, Tops	Fashion Show of Handwoven Garments		√	>4	WJ	3	3	11	Ja 79	5
Blouses, Shirts, Tops	Fiesta Choli (Anita Luvera Mayer)		√	√	Hw	6	3		Su 85	54, I-12
Blouses, Shirts, Tops	Five Crackle Weave Projects	Macomber, Dorothea	√	√	H&C	9	3		Su 58	42
Blouses, Shirts, Tops	Folk Textiles of Latin America	Kelemen, Pál	√		TMJ	1	4		De 65	2
Blouses, Shirts, Tops	From Elegance to Rag Weaving	Mick, Catherine	√	√	WJ	7	3	27	Wi 82	64

SUBJECT	TITLE	AUTHOR	IL	INST	JOUR	VOL	NO	ISS	DATE	PAGE
Blouses, Shirts, Tops	From Ramie Top to Ramie Top	Knishern, Edna Maki	√	√	SS&D	9	2	34	Sp 78	78
Blouses, Shirts, Tops	Greek Chemises: Cut and Construction	Welters, Linda	√	√	WJ	10	1	37	Su 85	40
Blouses, Shirts, Tops	Guatemalan Blouse (Betty Davenport)		√	√	Hw	4	2		M/A 83	55, 94
Blouses, Shirts, Tops	Guatemalan Shirt (Betty Davenport)		√	√	Hw	2	2		Mr 81	54, 72
Blouses, Shirts, Tops	Hand Woven Garments	Piper, Aris	√	>4	WJ	5	3	19	Wi 81	24
Blouses, Shirts, Tops	Handspun/Handwoven Ramie Blouse	Champion, Ellen	√	>4	WJ	9	2	34	Fa 84	52
Blouses, Shirts, Tops	Handwoven Silk Garments: Ikat Shirt	Utzinger, Karen	√	√	WJ	3	2	10	Oc 78	29
Blouses, Shirts, Tops	Huck Blouse (Jean Scorgie)		√	√	Hw	8	4		S/O 87	43, I-6
Blouses, Shirts, Tops	Ice Blue Blouse (Jean Scorgie)		√	>4	Hw	7	5		N/D 86	42, I-3
Blouses, Shirts, Tops	Inlaid Blouse and Scarf (Jean Scorgie)		√	>4	Hw	8	2		M/A 87	58, I-12
Blouses, Shirts, Tops	Inside an Expensive Outfit	Galpin, Mary	√	√	TM			1	O/N 85	40
Blouses, Shirts, Tops	Instructions for Weaving a Bog Shirt	Kinahan, Barbara	√	√	WJ	3	1	9	Jy 78	26
Blouses, Shirts, Tops	Jacket and Camisole with Ikat Stripes (Ronnine Bohannan)		√	√	Hw	5	3		Su 84	56, 100
Blouses, Shirts, Tops	Jelly Bean Blouse (Louise Bradley)		√	√	Hw	6	3		Su 85	50, I-11
Blouses, Shirts, Tops	Lace Weave Skirt with Jacket and Top (Louise Bradley)		√	>4	Hw	5	3		Su 84	58, 104
Blouses, Shirts, Tops	Lace-Weave Pullover Top (Elaine Rowley)		√	√	Hw	1	1		F-W 79	21, 56
Blouses, Shirts, Tops	Lavender Top (Nancy Nelson)		√	√	Hw	8	1		J/F 87	54, I-8
Blouses, Shirts, Tops	Linbogarn Shirt	Scorgie, Jean	√	√	WJ	7	1	25	Su 82	53
Blouses, Shirts, Tops	Linen Lace Blouse (Sharon Alderman)		√	√	Hw	1	2		S-S 80	45, 66
Blouses, Shirts, Tops	Linsey-Woolsey Shirt (Nancy Kawabara)		√	√	Hw	3	5		N/D 82	53, 88
Blouses, Shirts, Tops	Loom Shaped Top with Dukagång Inlay	Searle, Karen	√	√	WJ	11	3	43	Wi 87	8
Blouses, Shirts, Tops	Lumber Jack Shirt (Jean Scorgie)		√	√	Hw	3	5		N/D 82	52, 89
Blouses, Shirts, Tops	Macedonian Shirt Design	Hoffman, Jenet	√	√	SS&D	8	2	30	Sp 77	97
Blouses, Shirts, Tops	Making a Great Shirt Collar	Coffin, David Page	√	√	TM			4	A/M 86	42
Blouses, Shirts, Tops	Man's Shirt		√	√	S-O	5			81	58
Blouses, Shirts, Tops	Man's Shirt in Peruvian Inlay	Linder, Harry	√	>4	WJ	4	2	14	Oc 79	8
Blouses, Shirts, Tops	Man's Shirt (Sue Hendrikson)		√	√	Hw	3	2		Mr 82	49, 83
Blouses, Shirts, Tops	Marimekko Farmer's Shirt (Miranda Howard)		√	√	Hw	2	3		My 81	35, 76
Blouses, Shirts, Tops	Marvelous Mistake, A	Cramer, Pauline E.	√	√	SS&D	17	1	65	Wi 85	34
Blouses, Shirts, Tops	Mexican Shirt (Anita Mayer)		√	√	Hw	2	2		Mr 81	29, 78
Blouses, Shirts, Tops	Molas	La Pierre, Sharon	√		TM			14	D/J 87	48
Blouses, Shirts, Tops	Musk Ox Projects		√	√	S-O	7	1		Sp 83	23
Blouses, Shirts, Tops	My African Shirt	Linder, Harry	√		Iw	1	4		Su 76	8
Blouses, Shirts, Tops	M's and O's Blouse (Mary Kay Stoehr)		√	√	Hw	5	3		Su 84	65, 112
Blouses, Shirts, Tops	Peruvian Accented Mexican Blouse: Analyze—Then Improvise	Lawrence, Margaret	√	√	SS&D	7	1	25	Wi 75	40
Blouses, Shirts, Tops	Picot Trimmed Top (Eileen O'Connor)		√	√	Hw	6	1		J/F 85	65, I-16
Blouses, Shirts, Tops	Plaid Silk Noils Shirt (Sharon Alderman)		√	√	Hw	7	1		J/F 86	56, I-11
Blouses, Shirts, Tops	Projects with Cotton		√	√	WJ	4	2	14	Oc 79	28
Blouses, Shirts, Tops	Proportions of the Bog Shirt	Klessen, Romy	√	√	PWC			3	Oc 82	34
Blouses, Shirts, Tops	Rainbow Blouse (Ruth Lantz)		√	>4	Hw	4	1		J/F 83	45, 86
Blouses, Shirts, Tops	Ribbon Blouse (Grace Hirsch)		√	√	Hw	4	1		J/F 83	44, 88
Blouses, Shirts, Tops	Romy's One-Shouldered Bodice	Klessen, Romy	√	√	PWC			2	Ap 82	87
Blouses, Shirts, Tops	Ruched Blouse	Bruzelius, Margaret	√	√	Kn	2	2	4	S-S 86	40
Blouses, Shirts, Tops	Russian Peasant Shirt Adaptation	Hendricks, Carolyn	√	√	SS&D	8	2	30	Sp 77	96
Blouses, Shirts, Tops	"Sand Dunes and Dune Grass": Two Garments from a Blended Draft (Ardis Dobrovolny)		√	√	Hw	6	2		M/A 85	57, I-14
Blouses, Shirts, Tops	Scaffold Weaving: A Contemporary Garment Inspired by an Ancient Technique	Searle, Karen	√	√	WJ	10	2	38	Fa 85	65
Blouses, Shirts, Tops	Seattle Guild Garment Designs, Part 1	Noble, Judy	√	√	SS&D	10	3	39	Su 79	26

SUBJECT	TITLE	AUTHOR	IL	INST	JOUR	VOL	NO	ISS	DATE	PAGE
Blouses, Shirts, Tops	Seattle Guild Garment Designs, Part 2: Completing the Top		√	√	SS&D	10	4	40	Fa 79	71
Blouses, Shirts, Tops	Seton Overblouse (Linda Ligon)		√	√	Hw	4	5		N/D 83	52, 99
Blouses, Shirts, Tops	Shirt for a Fellow Spinner, A	Gaustad, Stephenie	√	√	Hw	7	4		S/O 86	76
Blouses, Shirts, Tops	Shirt with Marbled Inset (Anne Bliss)		√	√	Hw	4	3		M/J 83	49, 82
Blouses, Shirts, Tops:	Shirts That Wander			√	TM			12	A/S 87	6
Blouses, Shirts, Tops	Silk	Lawrence, Mary Jo	√	√	WJ	7	3	27	Wi 82	74
Blouses, Shirts, Tops	Silk and Cotton Shirt, A	Daugherty, Robin	√	√	S-O	6	4		82	60
Blouses, Shirts, Tops	Silk Blouse and Skirt (Jean Sullivan)		√	√	Hw	7	3		M/J 86	52, I-14
Blouses, Shirts, Tops	Silk Blouse with Scarf (Sylvia Slater Berkowitz)		√	√	Hw	8	5		N/D 87	32, I-4
Blouses, Shirts, Tops	Silk Top		√	√	S-O	5			81	59
Blouses, Shirts, Tops	Silk Weskit (Louise Bradley)		√	√	Hw	5	1		J/F 84	44, 110
Blouses, Shirts, Tops	Silk/Cotton Smock (Leslie Burgess)		√	√	Hw	4	3		M/J 83	27, 86
Blouses, Shirts, Tops	Simple and Silk	Gibson-Roberts, Priscilla A.	√	√	Kn	2	2	4	S-S 86	54
Blouses, Shirts, Tops	Skirt for the Wall, A		√	√	WJ	3	4	12	Ap 79	19
Blouses, Shirts, Tops	Slave Shirt Woven for Booker T. Washington Museum		√		H&C	19	3		Su 68	21
Blouses, Shirts, Tops	Smocked Blouse (Melba Ellis Short)		√	√	Hw	5	3		Su 84	66, 114
Blouses, Shirts, Tops	Southwest Reflections: Fiber Artists Inspired by the New Mexico Landscape	Colton, Mary Rawcliffe	√		WJ	11	1	41	Su 86	20
Blouses, Shirts, Tops	Southwest Sunrise Top (Ardis Dobrovolny)		√	√	Hw	6	3		Su 85	42, I-7
Blouses, Shirts, Tops	Space-dyed Stripes Ensemble (Kathryn Wertenberger)		√	√	Hw	6	3		Su 85	44, I-8
Blouses, Shirts, Tops	Spring Celebration Top (Jean Scorgie)		√	√	Hw	6	3		Su 85	53, I-12
Blouses, Shirts, Tops	Spring Ensemble (Ronnine Bohannan)		√	√	Hw	6	2		M/A 85	56, I-13
Blouses, Shirts, Tops	Start with a Square	Shaw, Winifred	√		SS&D	16	3	63	Su 85	50
Blouses, Shirts, Tops	Strips & Stripes	Lewis, Lois	√	> 4	SS&D	14	2	54	Sp 83	60
Blouses, Shirts, Tops	Summer Blouse in Summer and Winter, A	Sullivan, Donna	√	√	PWC	4	4	14		18
Blouses, Shirts, Tops	Supplementary Warp Top (Betty Davenport)		√	√	Hw	6	1		J/F 85	34, I-8
Blouses, Shirts, Tops	Textured Cottons	Henrikson, Sue	√	> 4	WJ	6	3	23	Wi 81	20
Blouses, Shirts, Tops	Textured Cottons: Seamless, No-Sweat Shirt	Rasmussen, Peg	√	√	WJ	6	3	23	Wi 81	25
Blouses, Shirts, Tops	Textured Weave—An Alternative	Tanner, Virginia Leigh	√	√	WJ	7	3	27	Wi 82	58
Blouses, Shirts, Tops	Tiahuanaco Tapestry Design	Sawyer, Alan R.	√		TMJ	1	2		De 63	27
Blouses, Shirts, Tops	Tulip Blouse (Betty Davenport)		√	√	Hw	8	2		M/A 87	61, I-14
Blouses, Shirts, Tops	Turned Overshot	Rowley, Elaine; Alexis Yiorgos Xenakis	√	> 4	PWC	3	2	8		53
Blouses, Shirts, Tops	Tussah Silk Top (Debbie Buchele)		√	√	Hw	8	3		M/J 87	91, I-16
Blouses, Shirts, Tops	Twill Striped Blouse (Mary Kay Stoehr)		√	√	Hw	5	3		Su 84	64, 113
Blouses, Shirts, Tops	Two Silk Blouses (Amy Preckshot) (error-corrected Hw v7 n4 86 p I-16)		√	> 4	Hw	7	1		J/F 86	54, I-9
Blouses, Shirts, Tops	Ultimate T-Shirt, The	Xenakis, Alexis Yiorgos	√	√	PWC			6	Su 83	29
Blouses, Shirts, Tops	V-Neck Top with Lace Bands (Betty Davenport)		√	√	Hw	3	2		Mr 82	44, 80
Blouses, Shirts, Tops	Variation of the Macedonian Shirt	West, Virginia	√	√	WJ	7	2	26	Fa 82	50
Blouses, Shirts, Tops	Waffle Weave Wool Top (Betty Davenport)		√	√	Hw	1	1		F-W 79	21, 55
Blouses, Shirts, Tops	Wandering Shirts			√	TM			14	D/J 87	4
Blouses, Shirts, Tops	Wearing Heirloom Linens		√	√	TM			9	F/M 87	10
Blouses, Shirts, Tops	Weaving for Ethnic Clothing	Marston, Ena	√	√	SS&D	10	1	37	Wi 78	42
Blouses, Shirts, Tops	Weaving the Family Tartan	Buchanan, Rita	√	√	S-O	10	2		Su 86	36
Blouses, Shirts, Tops	Weaving with Ramie		√	> 4	WJ	8	2	30	Fa 83	80
Blouses, Shirts, Tops	Wedding Shirt (Sharon Alderman)		√	√	Hw	1	2		S-S 80	34, 61

SUBJECT	TITLE	AUTHOR	IL	INST	JOUR	VOL	NO	ISS	DATE	PAGE
Blouses, Shirts, Tops	Western Shirt (Louise Bradley)		√	√	Hw	3	2		Mr 82	48, 84
Blouses, Shirts, Tops	Winter Birches: The Blouse	Upitis, Lizbeth	√	√	Kn	1	2	2	S-S 85	46, 72B
Blouses, Shirts, Tops	Woman's Top (Lou Cabeen)		√	√	Hw	5	4		S/O 84	43, 92
Blouses, Shirts, Tops	Woven Garments	Henzie, Susie	√	√	WJ	3	4	12	Ap 79	44
Blouses, Shirts, Tops	Wrap Around Top (Betty Davenport)		√	√	Hw	6	2		M/A 85	18, I-3
Blouses, Shirts, Tops	Wrist-to-Wrist Garment, The	Allen, Rose Mary	√	√	WJ	9	3	35	Wi 85	19
Blouses, Shirts, Tops: Commercial	Shirtmaker from a Small Planet	Coffin, David Page			TM			9	F/M 87	16
Blouses, Shirts, Tops: Knitted	Circular T	Upitis, Lizbeth	√	√	Kn	3	3	7	Su 87	15
Blouses, Shirts, Tops: Knitted	Comfortable Cotton T's	Upitis, Lizbeth	√	√	Kn	3	3	7	Su 87	12
Blouses, Shirts, Tops: Knitted	Fit to a T		√	√	Kn	3	3	7	Su 87	22
Blouses, Shirts, Tops: Knitted	Four-Corner T-Shirt	Swansen, Meg	√	√	Kn	3	3	7	Su 87	28
Blouses, Shirts, Tops: Knitted	Lapsang Souchong	Upitis, Lizbeth	√	√	Kn	3	3	7	Su 87	16
Blouses, Shirts, Tops: Knitted	Over the Shoulder T	Upitis, Lizbeth	√	√	Kn	3	3	7	Su 87	14
Blouses, Shirts, Tops: Knitted	Sans Serif T	Rowley, Elaine	√	√	Kn	3	3	7	Su 87	22
Blouses, Shirts, Tops: Knitted	Soft Sleeveless Blouse	Upitis, Lizbeth	√	√	Kn	3	4	8	Fa 87	37
Blouses, Shirts, Tops: Knitted	Standard T.	Upitis, Lizbeth	√	√	Kn	3	3	7	Su 87	14
Blouses, Shirts, Tops: Knitted	T in a Basket		√	√	Kn	3	3	7	Su 87	19
Blouses, Shirts, Tops: Knitted	Tons of T's	Upitis, Lizbeth	√		Kn	3	3	7	Su 87	8
Board-Loom Weaving	Weaving on a Board	Kappler, Erda	√	√	Hw	4	4		S/O 83	46
Bobbin Lace	Bawdry History of a Precious Commodity, The	McIlvain, Myra Hargrave	√		Fa	13	3		M/J 86	14
Bobbin Lace	Bobbin Lace	Tod, Osma Gallinger	√	√	SS&D	2	1	5	De 70	28
Bobbin Lace	Bobbin Lace: An Exquisite Labor of Love	McIlvain, Myra Hargrave	√		Fa	13	3		M/J 86	14
Bobbin Lace	Bobbin Lace — Just Twist, Cross, and Throw	Southard, Doris	√	√	SS&D	5	3	19	Su 74	77
Bobbin Lace	Bobbin Lace, Part 4; A Belt	Southard, Doris	√	√	SS&D	6	2	22	Sp 75	66
Bobbin Lace	Brooks Lace and Weaving	Tod, Osma Gallinger	√		H&C	20	1		Wi 69	29
Bobbin Lace	Fringes from Warp Ends	Brooks, Marguerite G.	√	√	H&C	6	1		Wi 54	46
Bobbin Lace	Georgia Dille Abbott	Pauw, Alice Abbott			H&C	15	1		Wi 64	40
Bobbin Lace	Handspun into Lace	Fournier, Jane	√	√	SS&D	17	4	68	Fa 86	70
Bobbin Lace	Lace Flower	VanGelder, Lydia	√	√	SS&D	2	4	8	Fa 71	26
Bobbin Lace	Lace Maker of Holland, Henk van der Zanden		√		H&C	17	2		Sp 66	15
Bobbin Lace	Lace Weed	van Gelder, Lydia	√	√	SS&D	2	2	6	Sp 71	27
Bobbin Lace	Picture Lace	Larson-Fleming, Susan	√		WJ	9	4	36	Sp 85	42
Bobbin Lace	"Show-Off" Bobbin Lace	Harris, Pat	√		SS&D	6	3	23	Su 75	21
Bobbin Lace	"Spiders" on the Wall		√		SS&D	1	1	1	De 69	17
Bobbin Lace	Triaxial Weaves and Weaving: An Exploration for Hand Weavers	Mooney, David R.	√	√	AT	2			De 84	9
Bobbin Lace	What the Well-Dressed Baby Will Wear This Season	Davis, Judy Green	√	√	S-O	10	4		Wi 86	14
Bobbin Lace: Bookmark	Bobbin Lace, Part 6, A Bookmark	Southard, Doris	√	√	SS&D	6	4	24	Fa 75	76
Bobbin Lace, Contemporary	Bobbin Lace on a Grand Scale: When the Pillow Is a 12-ft. Pegboard	Lewis, Robin S.	√	√	TM			9	F/M 87	54
Bobbin Lace: Edging	Bobbin Lace, Part 7: A Simple Edging & Corner Pattern	Southard, Doris	√	√	SS&D	7	1	25	Wi 75	79
Bobbin Lace: Fringe	Bobbin Lace, Part 5, A Fringe	Southard, Doris	√	√	SS&D	6	3	23	Su 75	60
Bobbin Lace, Large Scale	Big Bobbin Lace	Scanlin, Tommye McClure	√		Fa	13	2		M/A 86	32
Bobbin Lace: Technique	Bobbin Lace & the Linen Stitch	Kliot, Jules; Kaethe Kliot	√	√	H&C	24	2		M/A 73	39
Bobbin Lace: Techniques	Bobbin Lace, A Simple Beginners' Pattern, Part 2	Southard, Doris	√	√	SS&D	5	4	20	Fa 74	81
Bobbin Lace: Techniques	Bobbin Lace, Part 3	Southard, Doris	√	√	SS&D	6	1	21	Wi 74	74
Bobbin Lace: Torchon	Bobbin Lace, Part 8: Torchon in Technicolor	Southard, Doris	√	√	SS&D	7	2	26	Sp 76	80
Bobbin Lace: Torchon	Bobbin Lace: Part 9, Spiders	Southard, Doris	√	√	SS&D	7	3	27	Su 76	90

SUBJECT	TITLE	AUTHOR	IL	INST	JOUR	VOL	NO	ISS	DATE	PAGE
Bobbin Winder	Making a Bobbin Winder	Mitchell, Peter J.; George A. McFadden	√	√	H&C	24	2		M/A 73	22
Bobbin Winding	Handweaver's Instruction Manual: Additional Equipment, Winding a Bobbin	Tidball, Harriet C. nee Douglas	√	√	SCGM		34		49	6
Bobbin Winding	Makeshift Weaving Bobbins		√	√	TM			3	F/M 86	8
Bobbin Winding	Techniques for Better Weaving (error-corrected TM i9 D/J 86 p4)	Osterkamp, Peggy	√	√	TM			7	O/N 86	42
Bobbin Winding	Technology of Handweaving: Shuttles, Bobbins, Quills	Zielinski, S. A.; Robert Leclerc, ed.	√	√	MWL	6			'51–'73	10
Bobbin Winding	To Wind Bobbins Use Your Spinning Wheel	Stowell, Robert F.	√	√	H&C	7	4		Fa 56	17
Bobbin Winding	Treasury for Beginners: Selvedges	Zielinski, S. A.; Robert Leclerc, ed.	√	√	MWL	1			'51–'73	88
Bobbin Winding	Wind It		√	√	Hw	6	1		J/F 85	66
Bobbin Winding	Winding a Bobbin	Brostoff, Laya	√	√	SS&D	8	1	29	WI 76	39
Bobbin Winding	Winding Bobbins on the Spinning Wheel		√	√	TM			10	A/M 87	12
Bobbins, Knitting Yarn	Homemade Yarn Bobbins		√	√	TM			11	J/J 87	8
Bobbins, Sewing Machine	Multipurpose Bobbin Thread			√	TM			11	J/J 87	8
Body Coverings	Through the Camera's Eye: Howard Munson's Body Coverings	Akamine, Estelle	√		Fa	14	3		M/J 87	44
Bog	Glad Rags: The Designs of Rose Jurisich		√	√	Hw	2	3		My 81	46
Bog	Ikat Spun Bog Jacket (Louise Bradley)	Bradley, Louise	√	√	Hw	2	4		Se 81	67
Bogs	Bog Affair, A	Homme, Audrey	√	√	PWC			3	Oc 82	44
Bogs	Bog Jacket, Basic Shaping	Davidsohn, Marty	√	√	PWC			3	Oc 82	35
Bogs	Bogs	Fauske, Clara	√	√	PWC			3	Oc 82	39
Bogs	Instructions for Weaving a Bog Shirt	Kinahan, Barbara	√	√	WJ	3	1	9	Jy 78	26
Bogs	Mind Boggling Bogs	Herring, Connie	√	√	PWC			3	Oc 82	36
Bogs	Mind Boggling Bogs	Klessen, Romy	√	√	PWC			3	Oc 82	40
Bogs	Mossy Bog, A	Rowley, Elaine	√	√	PWC			3	Oc 82	43
Bogs	Proportions of the Bog Shirt	Klessen, Romy	√	√	PWC			3	Oc 82	34
Bohus Knitting	Bogus Bohus	Bush, Nancy	√	√	Kn	2	1	3	F-W 85	49
Bohus Stickning Knitting	Exploring a Knitted Pattern	Bruzelius, Margaret	√	√	TM			6	A/S 86	35
Boleros	Twice Woven Bolero	Richards, Iris	√	√	WJ	4	3	15	Ja 80	24
Bolivia	Bolivian Highland Weaving, Part 1	Cason, Marjorie; Adele Cahlander	√		SS&D	6	2	22	Sp 75	4
Bolivia	Bolivian Highland Weaving, Part 2	Cason, Marjorie; Adele Cahlander	√	√	SS&D	6	3	23	Su 75	65
Bolivia	Color and Design in Andean Warp-Faced Fabrics	Femenias, Blenda	√		WJ	12	2	46	Fa 87	44
Bolivia	"Fabled Fabrics: Bolivian Fabrics from the Hill Collection" (Exhibit)	Dyer, Carolyn	√		Fa	9	6		N/D 82	84
Bolivia	Fullus: Ikat Blankets of Tarabuco, Bolivia	Meisch, Lynn A.	√	√	WJ	10	1	37	Su 85	54
Bolivia	Spinning in Bolivia	Meisch, Lynn A.	√	√	S-O	10	1		Sp 86	25
Bolivia	Tubular Edge-Binding from Bolivia, A	Cahlander, Adele; Marjorie Cason	√	√	WJ	1	4	4	Ap 77	13
Bolivia	Warp-Faced Double Cloth: Adaptation of an Andean Technique for the Treadle Loom	Cahlander, Adele	√	√	WJ	10	4	40	Sp 86	72
Bolivia	Weaving Tradition in the Andes, A	Adelson, Laurie; Bruce Takami	√		Fa	6	4		J/A 79	22
Bolivian Highland Weaving	Bolivian Highland Weaving, Part 1	Cason, Marjorie; Adele Cahlander	√		SS&D	6	2	22	Sp 75	4
Bolivian Highland Weaving	Bolivian Highland Weaving, Part 2	Cason, Marjorie; Adele Cahlander	√	√	SS&D	6	3	23	Su 75	65
Book Binding	Bind Your Weaving Records with Weaving	Minster, Marjorie	√	√	SS&D	9	3	35	Su 78	66
Book Binding: Technique	Book That's Bound to Please, A	Ligon, Linda	√	√	Hw	4	4		S/O 83	67
Book Covers	Woven Telephone Book Covers	Bryan, Dorothy	√	√	H&C	8	3		Su 57	26
Book List: Complex Weaves	Book List				CW	3	3	9	Ap 82	11

SUBJECT	TITLE	AUTHOR	IL	INST	JOUR	VOL	NO	ISS	DATE	PAGE
Book of Kells	Ballinskelligs Tapestry Works: Ancient Art/Modern Spirit, The	Burkhauser, Jude	√		Hw	3	1		Ja 82	55
Book Preview	Book Preview: Handwoven Fabric by Sharon Alderman and Kathryn Wertenberger		√		Hw	3	2		Mr 82	30
Book Sculpture	Get Into a Good Book: Public Art for Kids	Covel, John	√		Fa	6	5		S/O 79	33
Bookmaking	Wendy Shah: Subtle Rhythms	Mattera, Joanne	√		Fa	7	5		S/O 80	21
Bookmarks	Bobbin Lace, Part 6, A Bookmark	Southard, Doris	√	√	SS&D	6	4	24	Fa 75	76
Bookmarks	Bookmarks: A Family Tradition	Isleib, Carol M.	√		Hw	3	4		Se 82	54
Bookmarks	Fish Provide the Ideas for a Series of Colorful Bookmarks	Allan, G. Ernestine	√	√	H&C	16	4		Fa 65	17
Bookmarks	Flax	Miller, Suzanne	√	√	WJ	7	2	26	Fa 82	12
Bookmarks	Inspired Double Weave		√		Hw	7	2		M/A 86	58
Bookmarks	Psychedelic Bookworm	Marston, Ena		√	SS&D	1	1	1	De 69	17
Bookmarks: Jacquard, Pictorial	Jacquard and Woven Silk Pictures, The	Adrosko, Rita J.	√		AT	1			De 83	9
Books and Reviews	1983 Index to How To Do It Information	Lathrop, Nornan M.			Hw	7	5		N/D 86	14
Books and Reviews	1985 Home Index, Re Publications, The				Hw	7	5		N/D 86	14
Books and Reviews	Adventures in Fleece	Tramutola, Buhnne			SS&D	18	2	70	Sp 87	38
Books and Reviews	Adventures in Knitting	Aytes, Barbara			TM			9	F/M 87	76
Books and Reviews	Adventures in Weaving	Greer, Gertrude G.	√		H&C	2	1		Wi 50	60
Books and Reviews	Adventures in Weaving	Greer, Gertrude G.			H&C	2	3		Su 51	61
Books and Reviews	Adventures in Weaving on a 2 Harness Loom	Cripps, Alice K.			H&C	1	3		Fa 50	62
Books and Reviews	African Crafts and Craftsmen	Gandi, Rene			SS&D	3	3	11	Su 72	13
Books and Reviews	African Crafts & Craftsmen	Gardi, René			H&C	22	2		Sp 71	44
Books and Reviews	African Dress II	Eircher, Joanne B., et. al.	√		WJ	11	3	43	Wi 87	64
Books and Reviews	African Fabric Crafts, Sources of African Design and Technique	Dendel, Esther Warner			H&C	26	3		M/J 75	30
Books and Reviews	African Textiles and Decorative Arts	Sieber, Roy			SS&D	4	1	13	Wi 72	35
Books and Reviews	African Textiles and Decorative Arts	Sieber, Roy			TMJ	3	4		De 73	47
Books and Reviews	African Textiles: Loom, Weaving and Design	Picton, John; John Mack Picton			WJ	8	3	31	Wi 83	64
Books and Reviews	Afro-American Art & Craft	Chase, Judith Wragg			SS&D	4	1	13	Wi 72	34
Books and Reviews	Aftican Fabric Crafts	Dendel, Esther Warner			SS&D	6	3	23	Su 75	50
Books and Reviews	Ajrakh: Traditions of Textile Printing in Kutch	Varadarajan, Lotika			TM			11	J/J 87	72
Books and Reviews	Alive with Color	Eisman, Leatrice			Kn	2	1	3	F-W 85	73
Books and Reviews	All About Weaving	Creager, Clara			Hw	6	1		J/F 85	17
Books and Reviews	All Sweaters in Every Gauge	Goldstein, Barbara			Kn	1	1	1	F-W 84	15
Books and Reviews	Alphabet of Weaving, The	Mundal, Maria			H&C	11	3		Su 60	59
Books and Reviews	Alte Seidenstoffe	Schmidt, Heinrich J.			H&C	9	2		Sp 58	59
Books and Reviews	America's Printed & Painted Fabrics	Pettit, Florence			H&C	22	1		Wi 71	41
Books and Reviews	American Coverlets	Elvehjem Art Center, University Of Wisconsin			SS&D	6	2	22	Sp 75	63
Books and Reviews	American Crafts: A Source Book for the Home	Pearson, Katherine			Fa	11	4		J/A 84	54
Books and Reviews	American Fabrics and Fashions Magazine	Hicks, Shelia, ed.			Hw	2	4		Se 81	79
Books and Reviews	American Fiber Art: A New Definition	Sarah Campbell Bluffer Gallery (Catalogue)			Hw	2	2		Mr 81	21
Books and Reviews	American Furniture, Queen Anne and Chippendale Periods in the Henry Francis du Pont Winterthur Museum	Downs, Joseph, ed.			H&C	3	3		Su 52	61
Books and Reviews	American Handbook of Synthetic Textiles	Mauersberger, Hubert R.			H&C	4	1		Wi 52	59
Books and Reviews	American Indian Arts	Seton, Julia M.			H&C	13	4		Fa 62	44
Books and Reviews	American River College Textile Collection Bibliography	American River College			Hw	7	1		J/F 86	21

SUBJECT	TITLE	AUTHOR	IL	INST	JOUR	VOL	NO	ISS	DATE	PAGE
Books and Reviews	American Rugs and Carpets from the Seventeenth Century to Modern Times	Von Rosenstiel, Helene			SS&D	10	4	40	Fa 79	65
Books and Reviews	American Rugs and Carpets: From the Seventeenth Century to Modern Times	Von Rosenstiel, Helene			Iw	4	2		Sp 79	65
Books and Reviews	American Woven Coverlets	Strickler, Carol	√		PWC	5	2	16		53
Books and Reviews	America's Indigo Blues	Pettit, Florence H.			SS&D	6	4	24	Fa 75	29
Books and Reviews	America's Indigo Blues: Resist-printed and Dyed Textiles of the Eighteenth Century	Pettit, Florence H.			TMJ	4	2		75	81
Books and Reviews	America's Quilts and Coverlets	Safford, Carleton L.; Robert Bishop			TMJ	3	4		De 73	47
Books and Reviews	America's Sheep Trails	Wentworth, Edward			H&C	20	3		Su 69	42
Books and Reviews	Amish Crib Quilts	Pellman, Rachel; Kenneth Pellman			TM			3	F/M 86	78
Books and Reviews	Amish Doll Quilts, Dolls, and Other Playthings	Pellman, Rachel; Kenneth Pellman			TM			11	J/J 87	73
Books and Reviews	Ancient Arts of the Andes	Bennett, Wendell C.			H&C	5	3		Su 54	57
Books and Reviews	Ancient Danish Textiles from Bogs and Burials, A Comparative Study of Costume and Iron Age Textiles	Hald, Margrethe			SS&D	13	2	50	Sp 82	62
Books and Reviews	Ancient Danish Textiles from Bogs and Burials—A Comparative Study of Costume and Iron Age Textiles	Hald, Margrethe			WJ	6	4	24	Sp 82	58
Books and Reviews	Ancient Dyes for Modern Weavers	Weigle, Palmy			SS&D	6	2	22	Sp 75	63
Books and Reviews	Ancient People and Places — Peru	Bushnell, G. H. S.			H&C	9	1		Wi 57	60
Books and Reviews	Angel Threads: Creating Lovable Clothes for Little Ones	Martin, Karen Ericsson			SS&D	18	2	70	Sp 87	38
Books and Reviews	Angora Handbook	Fisher, Judy, ed.	√		S-O	11	2		Su 87	12
Books and Reviews	Animals: 1419 Copyrightfree Illustrations	Harter, Jim, selector			Fa	7	4		J/A 80	22
Books and Reviews	Anni Albers: On Design	Albers, Anni			H&C	13	3		Su 62	43
Books and Reviews	Anni Albers: On Designing	Albers, Anni			H&C	11	2		Sp 60	60
Books and Reviews	Anni Albers: On Weaving	Albers, Anni			H&C	16	4		Fa 65	43
Books and Reviews	Annie and the Old One	Miles, Miska			Iw	2	1		Fa 76	33
Books and Reviews	Annotated Directory of Self-Published Textile Books	Sommer, Elyse			Iw	3	3		Sp 78	50
Books and Reviews	Annotated Directory of Self-Published Textile Books	Sommer, Elyse, ed.			WJ	3	1	9	Jy 78	36
Books and Reviews	Antique Chinese Rugs	Tiffany Studios			H&C	21	2		Sp 70	43
Books and Reviews	Antique Rugs from the Near East	van Bode, Wilhelm; Ernst Kuhnel			H&C	10	1		Wi 59	60
Books and Reviews	Anyone Can Build a Spinning Wheel	West, W. C.			SS&D	7	1	25	Wi 75	35
Books and Reviews	Applied Basic Textiles: Raw Materials, Construction, Color and Finish	Linton, George E.			H&C	18	2		Sp 67	43
Books and Reviews	Applied Textiles — Raw Materials to Finished Fabrics	Linton, George			H&C	13	3		Su 62	44
Books and Reviews	Applied Textiles — Raw Materials to Finished Fabrics	Linton, George E.			H&C	13	1		Wi 62	44
Books and Reviews	Applying the Pulled Warp Technique to Loom-Shaped Clothing	Evans, Kerry	√		WJ	9	2	34	Fa 84	79
Books and Reviews	Applying the Pulled Warp Technique to Loom-Shaped Clothing	Evans, Kerry			Hw	7	1		J/F 86	21
Books and Reviews	Apprenons a Tisser	Grünig, Erika Deletaz			WJ	9	1	33	Su 84	59
Books and Reviews	Apprenticeship in Craft	Williams, Gerry, ed.			SS&D	14	1	53	Wi 82	64
Books and Reviews	Apprenticeship in Craft	Williams, Gerry, ed.			Hw	3	3		My 82	19
Books and Reviews	Approaching Design Through Nature: The Quiet Joy	Martin, Grace O.			SS&D	9	2	34	Sp 78	50
Books and Reviews	Approaching Design Through Nature — The Quiet Joy	Martin, Grace O.	√		Fa	4	5		S/O 77	48
Books and Reviews	Arans: A Saga in Wool	Schlegel, Lee-lee			S-O	4			80	15
Books and Reviews	Architectural Crafts: A Handbook and Catalog	McCarthy, Bridget Beattie	√		Fa	10	4		J/A 83	49

SUBJECT	TITLE	AUTHOR	IL	INST	JOUR	VOL	NO	ISS	DATE	PAGE
Books and Reviews	Architectural Crafts, A Handbook and Catalog	McCarthy, Bridget Beattie			WJ	7	2	26	Fa 82	58
Books and Reviews	Arco Encyclopedia of Embroidery Stitches, The	Butler, Anne			Iw	5	4		Fa 80	77
Books and Reviews	Arp	Soby, James Thrall			H&C	10	1		Wi 59	59
Books and Reviews	Art and Craft Catalyst 1983	Henry Niles, publ.			WJ	8	2	30	Fa 83	65
Books and Reviews	Art and Craft of Handmade Paper, The	Studley, Vance	√		Fa	5	2		M/A 78	58
Books and Reviews	Art & Craft Periodicals 85: A Guide to Art, Craft, Needlecraft, Crafts, Marketing, Home Business & Related Magazines, Newspapers & Newsletters	Dee, Anne Patterson, ed.			Hw	7	5		N/D 86	14
Books and Reviews	Art Fabric: Mainstream, The	Constantine, Mildred; Jack Lenor Larsen			WJ	12	2	46	Fa 87	66
Books and Reviews	Art Fabric: Mainstream, The	Constantine, Mildred; Jack Lenor Larsen	√		Fa	8	6		N/D 81	62
Books and Reviews	Art Fabric: Mainstream, The	Constantine, Mildred; Jack Lenor Larsen			WJ	7	2	26	Fa 82	59
Books and Reviews	Art Fabric: Mainstream, The	Constantine, Mildred; Jack Lenor Larsen			Hw	2	4		Se 81	79
Books and Reviews	Art Fabric: Mainstream, The	Constantine, Mildred; Jack Lenor Larsen			Hw	7	5		N/D 86	14
Books and Reviews	Art of Ancient Peru, The	Obbelohde-Doering, Heinrich			H&C	3	4		Fa 52	62
Books and Reviews	Art of Arabian Costume: A Saudi Arabian Profile, The	Ross, Heather Colyer	√		Fa	10	1		J/F 83	57
Books and Reviews	Art of Arabian Costume: A Saudi Arabian Profile, The	Ross, Heather Colyer			WJ	8	3	31	Wi 83	64
Books and Reviews	Art of Bolivian Highland Weaving, The	Cason, Marjorie; Adele Cahlander			WJ	1	4	4	Ap 77	25
Books and Reviews	Art of Bolivian Highland Weaving, The	Cason, Marjorie; Adele Cahlander	√		Fa	4	4		J/A 77	62
Books and Reviews	Art of Bolivian Highland Weaving, The	Cason, Marjorie; Adele Cahlander	√	√	Iw	2	2		Wi 77	32
Books and Reviews	Art of Bolivian Highland Weaving: Unique, Traditional Techniques for the Modern Weaver, The	Cason, Marjorie; Adele Cahlander			SS&D	8	3	31	Su 77	61
Books and Reviews	Art of Knot Tying, The	Macfarlan, A. & P.			H&C	18	3		Su 67	46
Books and Reviews	Art of Oriental Embroidery: History, Aesthetics, and Technique, The	Chung, Young Y.			Fa	7	4		J/A 80	75
Books and Reviews	Art of Paisley, The	Rossbach, Ed			Fa	8	4		J/A 81	34
Books and Reviews	Art of Paisley, The	Rossbach, Ed			WJ	6	3	23	Wi 81	59
Books and Reviews	Art of Paisley, The	Rossbach, Ed	√		Iw	6	1		Wi 80	72
Books and Reviews	Art of Papermaking, The	Toale, Bernard	√		Fa	11	2		M/A 84	58
Books and Reviews	Art of Papermaking, The	Toale, Bernard			Hw	7	3		M/J 86	12
Books and Reviews	Art of Piupiu Making, The	Hopa, Ngapara			SS&D	4	1	13	Wi 72	34
Books and Reviews	Art of Shetland Lace, The	Don, Sarah	√		Kn	1	2	2	S-S 85	78
Books and Reviews	Art of Simple Batik, The	Glaser, Liana J.			WJ	5	3	19	Wi 81	52
Books and Reviews	Art of Spinning in the Grease, The Pioneer Way, The	Bieck, Doris Spath			WJ	8	2	30	Fa 83	62
Books and Reviews	Art of Taaniko Weaving, The	Mead, S. M.			SS&D	4	1	13	Wi 72	34
Books and Reviews	Art of the Ancient Weaver: Textiles from Egypt (4th-12th century, A. D.), The	Kelsey Museum of Archaeology			SS&D	11	4	44	Fa 80	66
Books and Reviews	Art of the Embroiderer	de Saint-Aubin, Charles Germain			Fa	10	6		N/D 83	58
Books and Reviews	Art of the Felt Maker, The	Burkett, M. E.			WJ	6	3	23	Wi 81	59
Books and Reviews	Art of Weaving, Second Edition, The	Regensteiner, Else			Fa	9	4		J/A 82	53
Books and Reviews	Art of Weaving, The	Regensteiner, Else			SS&D	2	1	5	De 70	30
Books and Reviews	Art of Weaving, The	Regensteiner, Else			SS&D	14	1	53	Wi 82	64
Books and Reviews	Art of Weaving, The	Regensteiner, Else			H&C	21	4		Fa 70	43
Books and Reviews	Art of Weaving, The, Second Edition	Regensteiner, Else			WJ	7	1	25	Su 82	64

SUBJECT	TITLE	AUTHOR	IL	INST	JOUR	VOL	NO	ISS	DATE	PAGE
Books and Reviews	Art to Wear	Dale, Julie Schafler			TM			9	F/M 87	74
Books and Reviews	Artisans of the Appalachians	DuPuy, Edward L.			H&C	19	1		Wi 68	43
Books and Reviews	Artist & The Quilt, The	Robinson, Charlotte, ed.			Fa	10	5		S/O 83	57
Books and Reviews	Arts and Crafts Market, 1978 (error-corrected WJ v2 n4 78 insert for sheet vol. 2)	Lapin, Lynne; Betsy Wanes, eds.			WJ	2	3	7	Ja 78	34
Books and Reviews	Arts & Crafts of Japan — Textiles	Yamanobe, Tomoyuki			H&C	8	4		Fa 57	60
Books and Reviews	Ashford Book of Spinning, The	Field, Anne	√		WJ	12	2	46	Fa 87	65
Books and Reviews	Ashford Book of Spinning, The	Field, Anne			SS&D	18	4	72	Fa 87	56
Books and Reviews	Ashford Book of Spinning, The	Field, Anne	√		Hw	8	3		M/J 87	15
Books and Reviews	Ashley Book of Knots, The	Ashley, Clifford			H&C	21	3		Su 70	39
Books and Reviews	Atlas de 4000 Armures de Tissage et Elements d'Ornementation Pour Articles d'Aille	Serrure, Louis			WJ	6	4	24	Sp 82	59
Books and Reviews	Aymara Weavings: Ceremonial Textiles of Colonial and 19th Century Bolivia	Adelson, Laurie; Arthur Tracht	√		WJ	10	1	37	Su 85	84
Books and Reviews	Bachicoltura Moderna	Glauco, Reali; Adelchi Meneghini; Mario Trevisan			Hw	7	1		J/F 86	18
Books and Reviews	Back to Basics: How to Learn and Enjoy Traditional American Skills	Reader's Digest Association			WJ	6	2	22	Fa 81	40
Books and Reviews	Backstrap Weaving	Taber, Barbara; Marilyn Anderson			SS&D	7	1	25	Wi 75	34
Books and Reviews	Backstrap Weaving	Taber, Barbara; Marilyn Anderson			WJ	8	1	29	Su 83	52
Books and Reviews	Backstrap Weaving Of Northern Ecuador	Redwood			WJ	4	1	13	Jy 79	42
Books and Reviews	Backstrap Weaving of Northern Ecuador	Redwood			SS&D	5	3	19	Su 74	62
Books and Reviews	Bags and Purses	Foster, Vanda			WJ	9	1	33	Su 84	61
Books and Reviews	Band	Liv			H&C	10	1		Wi 59	60
Books and Reviews	Band Weaving	Tacker, Harold; Sylvia Tacker			SS&D	6	2	22	Sp 75	64
Books and Reviews	Band Weaving, The Techniques, Looms, and Uses for Woven Bands	Tacker, Harold; Sylvia Tacker			H&C	26	3		M/J 75	31
Books and Reviews	Banners and Hangings — Design and Construction	Laliberte, Norman			H&C	17	3		Su 66	43
Books and Reviews	Barbara 'n Me on Lichening and Learning	Merrill, Ruth R.; Barbara M. Haight			SS&D	7	2	26	Sp 76	34
Books and Reviews	Basic Approach to Designing and Drafting Original Overshot Patterns, A	Pocock, Sylvia Domingo			SS&D	7	2	26	Sp 76	34
Books and Reviews	Basic Basketry	Mataraso, Ann			Hw	7	2		M/A 86	89
Books and Reviews	Basic Book of Machine Knitting, The	Holbourne, David			SS&D	11	3	43	Su 80	75
Books and Reviews	Basic Book of Twining, The	Dendel, Esther Warner			SS&D	10	2	38	Sp 79	72
Books and Reviews	Basic Book of Twining, The	Dendel, Esther Warner			Iw	4	1		Wi 78	54
Books and Reviews	Basic Chemistry of Textile Colouring & Finishing	Crockett, S. R.; K. A. Hilton			H&C	7	4		Fa 56	60
Books and Reviews	Basic Chemistry of Textile Preparation	Crockett, S. R.; K. A. Hilton			H&C	7	4		Fa 56	59
Books and Reviews	Basic Tailoring: The Art of Sewing Series	Time-Life Books			TM			7	O/N 86	72
Books and Reviews	Basic Textile Book, A	Seagroatt, Margaret			SS&D	7	2	26	Sp 76	34
Books and Reviews	Basic Woven Fabric	Howard, Margaret F.			SS&D	5	3	19	Su 74	63
Books and Reviews	Basket Pioneering, A Complete Study of Round Basketry Materials, Revised Edition	Gallinger, Osma Couch			H&C	7	2		Sp 56	59
Books and Reviews	Basket Weavers of Arizona, The	Robinson, Bert			H&C	6	2		Sp 55	61
Books and Reviews	Basketmaker's Art: Contemporary Baskets and Their Makers, The	Pulleyn, Rob, ed.			TM			11	J/J 87	72
Books and Reviews	Basketry of the Appalachian Mountains	Stephenson, Sue H.			SS&D	9	3	35	Su 78	94
Books and Reviews	Basketry of the Applachian Mountains	Stephenson, Sue H.			Iw	2	4		Su 77	35
Books and Reviews	Basketry Today with Materials from Nature	Meilach, Dona; Dee Menagh			WJ	4	4	16	Ap 80	26

SUBJECT	TITLE	AUTHOR	IL	INST	JOUR	VOL	NO	ISS	DATE	PAGE
Books and Reviews	Basketry Today, With Materials from Nature	Meilach, Dona; Dee Menagh			Fa	7	2		M/A 80	22
Books and Reviews	Baskets and Basket Makers in Southern Appalachia	Irwin, John Rice			SS&D	14	4	56	Fa 83	75
Books and Reviews	Baskets and Beyond	Coutts, Lucele			SS&D	9	3	35	Su 78	96
Books and Reviews	Baskets and Beyond	Coutts, Lucele			Fa	5	4		J/A 78	59
Books and Reviews	Baskets and Beyond	Coutts, Lucele			Iw	3	2		Wi 78	42
Books and Reviews	Baskets as Textile Art	Rossbach, Ed			TMJ	4	2		75	81
Books and Reviews	Bateman Blend Weaves	Harvey, Virginia I., ed.	√		PWC	3	1	7		62
Books and Reviews	Bateman Blend Weaves. Based on Dr. William Bateman's Manuscript	Harvey, Virginia I., ed.			WJ	7	2	26	Fa 82	59
Books and Reviews	Bateman Blend Weaves: Based on Dr. William G. Bateman's Manuscript	Harvey, Virginia I., ed.	√		Hw	4	1		J/F 83	18
Books and Reviews	Bateman Blend Weaves, based on Dr. William G. Bateman's Unpublished Manuscript, Papers, Samples	Harvey, Virginia I., ed.			SS&D	14	4	56	Fa 83	74
Books and Reviews	Batik	Keller, Ila			SS&D	4	4	16	Fa 73	63
Books and Reviews	Batik — Art and Craft	Krevitsky, Nik			H&C	15	3		Su 64	45
Books and Reviews	Batik for Beginners	Martin, Beryl			SS&D	4	2	14	Sp 73	44
Books and Reviews	Batik Handbook: A Color Guide to Procion Dyes	D'Angelo, Anne A.; Margaret B. Windeknecht			SS&D	4	2	14	Sp 73	44
Books and Reviews	Batik in Many Forms	Adasko, Laura; Alice Huberman			SS&D	7	1	25	Wi 75	34
Books and Reviews	Batik, The Art and Craft	Keller, Ila			WJ	8	2	30	Fa 83	65
Books and Reviews	Batik: The Art & Craft	Keller, Ika			H&C	18	1		Wi 67	45
Books and Reviews	Battenberg and Point Lace Techniques, Stitches and Designs from Victorian Needlework	Kliot, Jules; Kaethe Kliot, eds.			WJ	3	1	9	Jy 78	35
Books and Reviews	Battenberg and Point Lace — Techniques, Stitches and Designs from Victorian Needlework	Kliot, Jules; Kaethe Kliot, eds.			SS&D	10	3	39	Su 79	36
Books and Reviews	Bauerliches Stricken	Fanderl, Liesl	√		Kn	1	2	2	S-S 85	79
Books and Reviews	Bäuerliches Stricken 1	Fanderl, Lisl			TM			9	F/M 87	76
Books and Reviews	Bäuerliches Stricken 2	Fanderl, Lisl			TM			9	F/M 87	76
Books and Reviews	Bäuerliches Stricken 3	Fanderl, Lisl			TM			9	F/M 87	76
Books and Reviews	Bauhaus 1919 — 1928	Bayer, Herbert; Walter Gropius; Ise Gropius, eds.			H&C	3	3		Su 52	64
Books and Reviews	Bauhaus Catalog				H&C	20	4		Fa 69	42
Books and Reviews	Beautiful Rugs	Aarnio, Rauha			H&C	11	2		Sp 60	60
Books and Reviews	Beauty Behind Barbed Wire	Eaton, Allen			H&C	3	2		Sp 52	62
Books and Reviews	Bed Rugs 1722 — 1833	Warren, William L.; J. Herbert Callister			TMJ	3	4		De 73	47
Books and Reviews	Beginner's Guide to Weaving	Ponting, Ken			WJ	8	4	32	Sp 84	67
Books and Reviews	Beginning Spinning	Cox, Truda			SS&D	4	1	13	Wi 72	34
Books and Reviews	Beyond Boundaries: Highland Maya Dress at the Museum of International Folk Art	Fisher, Nora; Malinda Elliott, eds.	√		WJ	9	2	34	Fa 84	78
Books and Reviews	Beyond Craft: The Art Fabric	Constantine, Mildred; Jack Lenor Larsen			WJ	12	2	46	Fa 87	66
Books and Reviews	Beyond Craft: The Art Fabric	Constantine, Mildred; Jack Lenor Larsen			SS&D	6	4	24	Fa 75	29
Books and Reviews	Beyond Craft: The Art Fabric	Constantine, Mildred; Jack Lenor Larsen			Hw	7	5		N/D 86	14
Books and Reviews	Beyond Craft: The Art Fabric	Constantine, Mildred; Jack Lenor Larsen			TMJ	4	2		75	79
Books and Reviews	Beyond Weaving	Chamberlain, Marcia; Candace Crockett			SS&D	6	3	23	Su 75	49
Books and Reviews	Bibliography: Basic Books				Hw	1	1		F-W 79	14
Books and Reviews	Binding and Repairing Books by Hand	Muir, David			Fa	6	4		J/A 79	16

SUBJECT	TITLE	AUTHOR	IL	INST	JOUR	VOL	NO	ISS	DATE	PAGE
Books and Reviews	Bizarre Designs in Silk — Trade and Traditions	Solmann, Vilhelm			H&C	5	3		Su 54	57
Books and Reviews	Black Sheep Newsletter Companion: Writings for the Shepherd and Handspinner, Vol. 1	Jones, Sachiye, ed.			SS&D	17	2	66	Sp 86	86
Books and Reviews	Blouses, Shirts and Tops	Musgrave, Belinda			Hw	8	2		M/A 87	14
Books and Reviews	Bobbin and Needle Laces: Identification And Care	Earnshaw, Pat			SS&D	17	1	65	Wi 85	90
Books and Reviews	Bobbin Lace	Gubser, Elsie H.			H&C	17	4		Fa 66	45
Books and Reviews	Bobbin Lace, A Contemporary Approach	Fuhrmann, Brigitta			SS&D	8	3	31	Su 77	62
Books and Reviews	Bobbin Lace: Designs and Instructions	Lawrence, Ellen			SS&D	11	1	41	Wi 79	32
Books and Reviews	Bobbin Lacemaking	Southard, Doris			SS&D	9	3	35	Su 78	95
Books and Reviews	Bobbin Lacemaking for Beginners	Dawson, Amy			SS&D	10	1	37	Wi 78	78
Books and Reviews	Body and Clothes: An Illustrated History of Costume	Broby-Johansen, R.			H&C	20	2		Sp 69	43
Books and Reviews	Bolivian Indian Textiles: Traditional Designs and Contumes	Wasserman, Tamara E.; Jonathan S. Hill	√		Fa	9	6		N/D 82	58
Books and Reviews	Bolivian Indian Textiles—Traditional Designs and Costumes	Wasserman, Tamara E.; Johathan Hill			WJ	6	3	23	Wi 81	60
Books and Reviews	Bolivian Indian Textiles: Traditional Designs and Costumes	Wasserman, Tamara E.; Jonathan S. Hill			Hw	3	2		Mr 82	22
Books and Reviews	Bolivian Tubular Edging and Crossed-Warp Techniques	Cahlander, Adele			Iw	3	4		Su 78	46
Books and Reviews	Book of Batik, The	Mühling, Ernst			H&C	18	4		Fa 67	45
Books and Reviews	Book of Carpets, The	Hubel, Reinhard G.			TMJ	3	2		De 71	44
Books and Reviews	Book of Costume, The	Countess of Wilton			TM			11	J/J 87	72
Books and Reviews	Book of Giving, The	Ontario Handweavers and Spinners Guild			Iw	5	1		Wi 79	65
Books and Reviews	Book of Hand-Woven Coverlets, A	Hall, Eliza Calvert			H&C	18	1		Wi 67	43
Books and Reviews	Book of Kimono: The Complete Guide to Style and Wear, The	Yamanaka, Norio	√		Fa	10	3		M/J 83	53
Books and Reviews	Book of Knitting, The	Nava, Marinella			TM			9	F/M 87	76
Books and Reviews	Book of Knots and Ropework, The	Fry, Eric C.			WJ	8	1	29	Su 83	52
Books and Reviews	Book of Knots and Ropework, The (Practical and Decorative)	Fry, Eric C.	√		Hw	4	4		S/O 83	24
Books and Reviews	Book of Looms: A History of the Handloom from Ancient Times to the Present, The	Broudy, Eric			SS&D	11	1	41	Wi 79	32
Books and Reviews	Book of Looms: A History of the Handloom from Ancient Times to the Present, The	Broudy, Eric	√		Iw	4	4		Fa 79	70
Books and Reviews	Book of Looms, The	Broudy, Eric			WJ	5	4	20	Sp 81	44
Books and Reviews	Book of Machine Knitting, The	Holbourne, David			TM			5	J/J 86	12
Books and Reviews	Book of Patterns for Handweaving, A	Landes, John			WJ	3	1	9	Jy 78	36
Books and Reviews	Book of Tapestry—History and Technique, The	Verlet, Pierre, et al.			SS&D	10	2	38	Sp 79	73
Books and Reviews	Book of Tapestry, The	Verlet, Pierre, et al.			Iw	4	4		Fa 79	72
Books and Reviews	Boundweave	Barrett, Clotilde			SS&D	15	3	59	Su 84	35
Books and Reviews	Boundweave	Barrett, Clotilde			WJ	7	4	28	Sp 83	49
Books and Reviews	Boundweave	Barrett, Clotilde			Hw	4	2		M/A 83	15
Books and Reviews	Boutonne D'Hier Et D'Aujourdhui	Les Tisserands-Créateurs de Québec			WJ	8	3	31	Wi 83	66
Books and Reviews	Braided Rug Book	Carter, Fern			H&C	4	3		Su 53	63
Books and Reviews	Braided Rugs for Fun and Profit	Ickis, Marguerite			H&C	2	4		Fa 51	62
Books and Reviews	Braiding and Knotting for Amateurs	Belash, Constantine A.			H&C	3	4		Fa 52	62
Books and Reviews	Brocade, Shuttle Craft Guild Monograph Twenty-Two, 1968	Tidball, Harriet			H&C	19	3		Su 68	42
Books and Reviews	Build or Buy A Loom, Part 1; Patterns for Pick-Ups, Part 2. Shuttle Craft Guild Monograph Twenty-Three, 1968	Tidball, Harriet			H&C	19	3		Su 68	42

SUBJECT	TITLE	AUTHOR	IL	INST	JOUR	VOL	NO	ISS	DATE	PAGE
Books and Reviews	Build Your Own Floor Loom	Lones, Steve; Darlene Lones			SS&D	6	4	24	Fa 75	31
Books and Reviews	Bulletin of the Needle and Bobbin Club, The	Needle and Bobbin Club			WJ	8	2	30	Fa 83	66
Books and Reviews	Business Forms and Contracts (In Plain English) for Craftspeople	DuBoff, Leonard D.	√		WJ	11	4	44	Sp 87	74
Books and Reviews	Business Forms and Contracts (in Plain English) for Craftspeople	DuBoff, Leonard D.			Hw	8	4		S/O 87	14
Books and Reviews	Business of Art, The	Caplin, Lee Evan, ed.			WJ	8	3	31	Wi 83	66
Books and Reviews	Business of Art, The	Caplin, Lee Evan, ed.			Hw	5	3		Su 84	16
Books and Reviews	Byways in Handweaving	Atwater, Mary Meigs			H&C	5	1		Wi 53	59
Books and Reviews	Cairene Rugs, 15 C. — 17 C. Technical Analysis by Louisa Bellinger	Kuhnel, Ernst			H&C	9	2		Sp 58	59
Books and Reviews	California Indian Basketry: An Artistic Overview	Silva, Arthur M.			Fa	4	1		J/F 77	40
Books and Reviews	Canadian Centennial Book 1967	Ontario Handweavers and Spinners			H&C	19	1		Wi 68	46
Books and Reviews	Caner's Handbook, The	Miller, Bruce W.; Jim Widess			Fa	11	4		J/A 84	54
Books and Reviews	Caner's Handbook,The	Miller, Bruce W.; Jim Widess			Hw	6	5		N/D 85	20
Books and Reviews	Card Weaving	Crockett, Candace			SS&D	5	3	19	Su 74	62
Books and Reviews	Card Weaving	Katz, Ruth			WJ	2	1	5	Jy 77	30
Books and Reviews	Card Weaving or Tablet Weaving	Groff, Russell E.			SS&D	3	4	12	Fa 72	47
Books and Reviews	Card Weaving or Tablet Weaving	Groff, Russell E.			H&C	12	2		Sp 61	59
Books and Reviews	Carding, Spinning, Dyeing	Hoppe, Elizabeth; Ragnar Edberg			Iw	2	1		Fa 76	33
Books and Reviews	Carding, Spinning, Dyeing, An Introduction to the Traditional Wool and Flax Crafts	Hoppe, Elisabeth; Ragnar Edberg			SS&D	7	3	27	Su 76	34
Books and Reviews	Care & Preservation of Textiles, The	Finch, Karen; Greta Putnam			Hw	7	3		M/J 86	14
Books and Reviews	Career Opportunities in Crafts	Sommer, Elyse			Iw	2	4		Su 77	34
Books and Reviews	Career Opportunities in Crafts: The First Complete Guide for Success as a Crafts Professional	Sommer, Elyse			SS&D	9	1	33	Wi 77	41
Books and Reviews	Careers in the Arts: A Resource Guide	Jevnikar, Jana			Fa	10	3		M/J 83	54
Books and Reviews	Caring for Textiles	Finch, Karen, O.B.E.; Greta Putman			SS&D	9	2	34	Sp 78	49
Books and Reviews	Carpets and Floor Coverings of India	Chattapadhyaya, Kamaladevi			H&C	22	3		Su 71	44
Books and Reviews	Carpets from the Orient	Con, J. M.			H&C	18	2		Sp 67	43
Books and Reviews	Carpets of Central Asia	Bogolyubov, Andrei Andreyevich			TMJ	4	1		De 74	85
Books and Reviews	Cataloging Your Needlework Library	Green, Marilyn			Hw	5	5		N/D 84	14
Books and Reviews	Catalogue of Spanish Rugs	Kuhnel, Ernest; Louisa Bellinger			H&C	4	4		Fa 53	59
Books and Reviews	Caucasian Carpets	Gans-Ruedin, E.			TM			11	J/J 87	72
Books and Reviews	Century of Change in Guatemalan Textiles, A	Rowe, Ann Pollard			WJ	7	2	26	Fa 82	57
Books and Reviews	Chair Seat Weaving for Antique Chairs	Sober, Marion Burr			SS&D	4	2	14	Sp 73	44
Books and Reviews	Chair Seat Weaving for Antique Chairs	Sober, Marion Burr			H&C	16	1		Wi 65	44
Books and Reviews	Changing Church, Its Architecture, Art and Decoration, The	McClinton, Katherine M.			H&C	9	3		Su 58	62
Books and Reviews	Charles Needs a Cloak	de Paola, Tomie			Iw	2	1		Fa 76	32
Books and Reviews	Charted Knitting Designs	Walker, Barbara			Kn	1	2	2	S-S 85	79
Books and Reviews	Charted Knitting Designs: A Third Treasury of Knitting Patterns	Walker, Barbara			TM			9	F/M 87	74
Books and Reviews	Checklist of American Coverlet Weavers, A	Heisey, John W.			SS&D	10	1	37	Wi 78	77

SUBJECT	TITLE	AUTHOR	IL	INST	JOUR	VOL	NO	ISS	DATE	PAGE
Books and Reviews	Checklist of American Coverlet Weavers, A	Heisey, John W. (Compiler)			Iw	4	3		Su 79	66
Books and Reviews	Chilkat Dancing Blanket, The	Samuel, Cheryl			SS&D	13	4	52	Fa 82	66
Books and Reviews	Chilkat Dancing Blanket, The	Samuel, Cheryl			WJ	7	2	26	Fa 82	57
Books and Reviews	Chilkat Dancing Blanket, The	Samuel, Cheryl	√		PWC			3	Oc 82	63
Books and Reviews	Chinese and Exotic Rugs	Eiland, Murray			Hw	3	5		N/D 82	14
Books and Reviews	Chinese Knotting	Chen, Lydia; Editors of Echo Books			WJ	8	1	29	Su 83	53
Books and Reviews	Choice Hooked Rugs	Rex, Stella Hay			H&C	5	4		Fa 54	57
Books and Reviews	Choice Hooked Rugs	Rex, Stella Hay			H&C	6	2		Sp 55	63
Books and Reviews	Classic Designs		√		Kn	2	2	4	S-S 86	79
Books and Reviews	Classic Knitted Cotton Edgings	Hewitt, Furze; Billie Daley	√		Kn	4	1	9	Wi 87	61
Books and Reviews	Classic Tailoring Techniques: A Construction Guide for Men's Wear	Cabrera, Roberto; Patricia Flaherty			TM			7	O/N 86	72
Books and Reviews	Classic Tailoring Techniques: A Construction Guide for Women' Wear	Cabrera, Roberto; Patricia Flaherty Meyers			TM			7	O/N 86	72
Books and Reviews	Cloth As a Metaphor: Nigerian Textiles from the Museum of Cultural History	Borgatti, Jean			WJ	8	3	31	Wi 83	68
Books and Reviews	Clothing: A Handwoven Approach	Hamaker, Barbara			WJ	4	3	15	Ja 80	45
Books and Reviews	Clothing, A Handwoven Approach	Hamaker, Barbara			SS&D	10	3	39	Su 79	35
Books and Reviews	Clothing: A Handwoven Approach	Hamaker, Barbara			Hw	1	2		S-S 80	14
Books and Reviews	Clothing: A Handwoven Approach	Hamaker, Barbara			Iw	4	2		Sp 79	62
Books and Reviews	Clothing from the Hands That Weave	Mayer, Anita Luvera	√		WJ	9	3	35	Wi 85	85
Books and Reviews	Clothing from the Hands That Weave	Mayer, Anita Luvera			TM			6	A/S 86	86
Books and Reviews	Cochineal and the Insect Dyes	Gerber, Fred			Iw	3	4		Su 78	46
Books and Reviews	Cochineal and the Insect Dyes	Gerber, Frederick H.			WJ	3	2	10	Oc 78	46
Books and Reviews	Cochineal and the Insect Dyes	Gerber, Frederick H.			SS&D	10	1	37	Wi 78	78
Books and Reviews	Coconut Palm Frond Weaving	Goodloe, William H.			WJ	8	2	30	Fa 83	65
Books and Reviews	Coconut Palm Frond Weaving	Goodloe, William H.			H&C	23	6		N/D 72	41
Books and Reviews	Coconut Palm Weaving	Goodloe, William H.			SS&D	4	1	13	Wi 72	35
Books and Reviews	Code of the Quipu	Ascher, Marcia; Robert Ascher			Fa	9	2		M/A 82	58
Books and Reviews	Colonial Craftsman, The	Bridenbaugh, Carl			H&C	1	3		Fa 50	60
Books and Reviews	Color: A Complete Guide for Artists	Fabri, Ralph			H&C	18	4		Fa 67	45
Books and Reviews	Color and Design in Macrame	Harvey, Virginia			SS&D	3	2	10	Sp 72	38
Books and Reviews	Color and Design in Macrame	Harvey, Virginia I.			H&C	22	4		Fa 71	26
Books and Reviews	Color and Design, Shuttle Craft Guild Monograph Sixteen, 1965	Tidball, Harriet			H&C	17	2		Sp 66	47
Books and Reviews	Color and Fiber	Lambert, Patricia; Barbara Staepelaere; Mary G. Fry	√		WJ	12	1	45	Su 87	69
Books and Reviews	Color and Fiber	Lambert, Patricia; Barbara Staepelaere; Mary G. Fry			TM			13	O/N 87	76
Books and Reviews	Color and Fiber	Lambert, Patricia; Barbara Staepelaere; Mary G. Fry	√		PWC	4	4	14		53
Books and Reviews	Color and Weave	Windeknecht, Margaret; Thomas Windeknecht			WJ	6	2	22	Fa 81	39
Books and Reviews	Color and Weave Effects for Four-Harness Twills	Ball, Margaret			SS&D	8	1	29	WI 76	71
Books and Reviews	Color Crazed	Rasband, Judith			Kn	2	1	3	F-W 85	73
Books and Reviews	Color Exercises for the Weaver	Weigle, Palmy			SS&D	8	2	30	Sp 77	37
Books and Reviews	Color Exercises for the Weaver	Weigle, Palmy			Fa	3	4		J/A 76	42
Books and Reviews	Color Exercises for the Weaver	Weigle, Palmy			Iw	1	4		Su 76	29
Books and Reviews	Color from Plants	Soderburg, Betty			SS&D	4	4	16	Fa 73	63

SUBJECT	TITLE	AUTHOR	IL	INST	JOUR	VOL	NO	ISS	DATE	PAGE
Books and Reviews	Color Guide for Handweavers	Chown, M. Joyce; Mary E. Black			H&C	11	4		Fa 60	59
Books and Reviews	Color: Order and Harmony. A Color Theory for Artists and Craftsmen	Renner, Paul			H&C	17	1		Wi 66	43
Books and Reviews	Color Related Decorating Textiles — Rugs, Draperies, Upholstery; Shuttle Craft Monograph Fourteen, 1965	Rhodes, Tonya Stalons; Harriet Tidball, ed.			H&C	16	3		Su 65	44
Books and Reviews	Color Trends	Wipplinger, Michele, ed.	√		WJ	10	1	37	Su 85	86
Books and Reviews	Color Trends: A Color Service for Fiberists	Wipplinger, Michele, ed.			SS&D	17	3	67	Su 86	86
Books and Reviews	Color-And-Weave	Windeknecht, Margaret; Thomas Windeknecht			SS&D	12	4	48	Fa 81	62
Books and Reviews	Color-and-Weave	Windeknecht, Margaret; Thomas Windeknecht			Fa	9	4		J/A 82	52
Books and Reviews	Color-and-Weave	Windeknecht, Margaret; Thomas Windeknecht			Hw	2	4		Se 81	78
Books and Reviews	Color-and-Weave	Windeknecht, Margaret; Thomas Windeknecht	√		PWC	3	1	7		60
Books and Reviews	Color-and-Weave Design, A Practical Reference Book	Sutton, Ann			Hw	8	4		S/O 87	13
Books and Reviews	Colour-and-Weave Design: A Practical Reference Book	Sutton, Ann			SS&D	18	1	69	Wi 86	38
Books and Reviews	Comalapa: Native Dress and Its Significance	de Barrios, Linda Asturias; et. al.	√		WJ	11	3	43	Wi 87	65
Books and Reviews	Comfort Clothes	Rex, Chris			Hw	2	4		Se 81	79
Books and Reviews	Comfort Clothes	Rose, Chris			WJ	7	1	25	Su 82	64
Books and Reviews	Comfortable Arts, The	Burnham, Dorothy K.			WJ	7	1	25	Su 82	63
Books and Reviews	Complete Book of Basketry, The	Wright, Dorothy			Iw	3	4		Su 78	45
Books and Reviews	Complete Book of Crazy Patchwork, The	Conroy, Mary	√		Fa	14	2		M/A 87	61
Books and Reviews	Complete Book of Furniture Repair and Refinishing, The	Kinney, Ralph Parsons			H&C	2	1		Wi 50	62
Books and Reviews	Complete Book of Handcrafts	Zechlin, Ruth			H&C	19	2		Sp 68	44
Books and Reviews	Complete Book of Handicrafts, The	Zechlin, Ruth			H&C	10	3		Su 59	59
Books and Reviews	Complete Book of Knitting, The	Abbey, Barbara			TM			9	F/M 87	76
Books and Reviews	Complete Book of Knitting, The	Abbey, Barbara			Kn	1	2	2	S-S 85	79
Books and Reviews	Complete Book of Rug Braiding, The	Feeley, Helen			H&C	9	2		Sp 58	53
Books and Reviews	Complete Book of Smocking	Durand, Dianne			Hw	4	1		J/F 83	18
Books and Reviews	Complete Book of Stuffed Work, The	Scott, Toni			Iw	3	4		Su 78	45
Books and Reviews	Complete Book of Stuffedwork, The	Scott, Toni			Fa	7	1		J/F 80	14
Books and Reviews	Complete Book of Traditional Aran Knitting, The	Hollingworth, Shelagh			TM			6	A/S 86	84
Books and Reviews	Complete Book of Traditional Fair Isle Knitting, The	McGregor, Sheila			TM			9	F/M 87	74
Books and Reviews	Complete Book of Traditional Fair Isle Knitting, The	McGregor, Sheila	√		Kn	2	1	3	F-W 85	78
Books and Reviews	Complete Book of Traditional Knitting, The	Compton, Rae			Kn	1	2	2	S-S 85	79
Books and Reviews	Complete Book of Traditional Knitting, The	Compton, Rae			Kn	2	1	3	F-W 85	78
Books and Reviews	Complete Book of Traditional Scandinavian Knitting, The	McGregor, Sheila	√		Kn	3	1	5	F-W 86	70
Books and Reviews	Complete Encyclopedia of Needlework, The	de Dillmont, Therese			WJ	7	1	25	Su 82	63
Books and Reviews	Complete International Book of Embroidery, The	Gostelow, Mary			SS&D	10	1	37	Wi 78	78
Books and Reviews	Complete Spinning Book, The	Crockett, Candace			SS&D	9	3	35	Su 78	97
Books and Reviews	Complete Spinning Book, The	Crockett, Candace			Fa	5	4		J/A 78	59
Books and Reviews	Complete Spinning Book, The	Crockett, Candace			WJ	8	2	30	Fa 83	62
Books and Reviews	Complete Spinning Book, The	Crockett, Candace			Iw	3	2		Wi 78	40
Books and Reviews	Computers & Crafts: A Practical Guide	Goldring, Marc; Pat Doran; Thomas Wolf			Hw	6	4		S/O 85	20

SUBJECT	TITLE	AUTHOR	IL	INST	JOUR	VOL	NO	ISS	DATE	PAGE
Books and Reviews	Concise Chemical and Technical Dictionary	Bennett, H., ed.			H&C	14	2		Sp 63	44
Books and Reviews	Considerations for the Care of Textiles and Costumes — A Handbook for the Non-Specialist	Mailand, Harold			SS&D	11	2	42	Sp 80	81
Books and Reviews	Considerations for the Care of Textiles And Costumes, A Handbook for the Non-Specialist	Mailand, Harold F.			SS&D	13	1	49	Wi 81	90
Books and Reviews	Considerations for the Care of Textiles and Costumes — A Handbook for the Non-Specialist	Mailand, Harold F.			WJ	6	2	22	Fa 81	40
Books and Reviews	Considerations for the Care of Textiles and Costumes: A Handbook for the Non-Specialist	Mailand, Harold F.			Hw	3	5		N/D 82	12
Books and Reviews	Constructive Design	Osburn, Dr. Burl			H&C	1	3		Fa 50	64
Books and Reviews	Container Book, The	Newman, Thelma R.; Jay Hartley Newman	√		Fa	4	5		S/O 77	48
Books and Reviews	Contemporary African Arts and Crafts	Newman, Thelma R.			H&C	26	1		J/F 75	30
Books and Reviews	Contemporary African Arts and Crafts: On-Site Working with Art Forms and Processes	Newman, Thelma R.			Fa	3	4		J/A 76	42
Books and Reviews	Contemporary Appliqued Beadwork	Woodsmall, Annabel Withney			Iw	5	3		Su 80	71
Books and Reviews	Contemporary Basketry	Robinson, Sharon			WJ	3	3	11	Ja 79	43
Books and Reviews	Contemporary Basketry	Robinson, Sharon			SS&D	10	1	37	Wi 78	77
Books and Reviews	Contemporary Basketry	Robinson, Sharon			Hw	7	1		J/F 86	19
Books and Reviews	Contemporary Costume: Strictly Handwoven, Shuttle Craft Guild Monograph Twenty-Four 1968	Tidball, Harriet			H&C	20	1		Wi 69	42
Books and Reviews	Contemporary Crafts of the Americas	Getty, Nilda C. Fernandez			Iw	1	1		Fa 75	20
Books and Reviews	Contemporary Handweaving	Overman, Ruth; Lula Smith			H&C	7	1		Wi 55	59
Books and Reviews	Contemporary Quilt: New American Quilts and Fabric Art, The	Chase, Patti; with Mimi Dolbier			Iw	4	2		Sp 79	63
Books and Reviews	Contemporary Quilting	Robinson, Sharon			Fa	10	1		J/F 83	58
Books and Reviews	Contemporary Satins, Shuttle Craft Monograph Seven 1962	Tidball, Harriet			H&C	14	1		Wi 63	44
Books and Reviews	Contemporary Tapestries from Czechoslovakia	Kybalova, Ludmilla			H&C	17	1		Wi 66	43
Books and Reviews	Contemporary Tapestry	Tidball, Harriet			H&C	15	3		Su 64	44
Books and Reviews	Contemporary Textile Art: Scandinavia	Talley, Charles S.			SS&D	14	1	53	Wi 82	65
Books and Reviews	Contemporary Textile Art—Scandinavia	Talley, Charles S.			WJ	7	3	27	Wi 82	52
Books and Reviews	Contemporary Textile Art: Scandinavia	Talley, Charles S.	√		Hw	4	3		M/J 83	12
Books and Reviews	Contemporary Textile Art: Scandinavia	Talley, Charles S.	√		PWC			4	Ja 83	68
Books and Reviews	Cookbook Weaving I	Aspell, Amy			SS&D	9	4	36	Fa 78	81
Books and Reviews	Coptic Art	Wessel, Klaus			H&C	17	1		Wi 66	44
Books and Reviews	Coptic Weaves	Seagroatt, Margaret			H&C	19	4		Fa 68	42
Books and Reviews	Cornish Guernseys & Knit-frocks	Wright, Mary	√		Kn	1	1	1	F-W 84	71
Books and Reviews	Cornish Guernseys & Knitfrocks	Wright, Mary	√		Fa	11	1		J/F 84	58
Books and Reviews	Costumes of Chios. Their Development from the XVth to the XXth Century, The	Argente, Philip P.			H&C	4	3		Su 53	61
Books and Reviews	Costumes of Mexico	Sayer, Chloe	√		WJ	10	3	39	Wi 86	72
Books and Reviews	Costumes of Mexico	Sayer, Chloe			TM			6	A/S 86	86
Books and Reviews	Costumes of the Greeks and Romans	Hope, Thomas	√		WJ	4	3	15	Ja 80	45
Books and Reviews	Cottage Crafts & Fibers; A Reference Book	Holtz-Carter, Nancy Merle	√		WJ	9	4	36	Sp 85	78
Books and Reviews	Cotton and Silk Making in Manchu China	du Halde, Pere Jean-Baptiste			Iw	6	1		Wi 80	70
Books and Reviews	Couture: The Great Designers	Milbank, Caroline Rennolds			TM			8	D/J 86	72
Books and Reviews	Covered Things	Haroutunian, Judith			WJ	8	1	29	Su 83	53

SUBJECT	TITLE	AUTHOR	IL	INST	JOUR	VOL	NO	ISS	DATE	PAGE
Books and Reviews	Coverlets	Davison, Mildred; Christa C. Mayer-Thurman			TMJ	3	4		De 73	46
Books and Reviews	Crackle Weave	Snyder, Mary E., ed.			H&C	13	2		Sp 62	43
Books and Reviews	Crackle Weave, The	Snyder, Mary E.			SS&D	4	4	16	Fa 73	63
Books and Reviews	Crackle Weave, The	Snyder, Mary E.			Fa	3	1		J/F 76	4
Books and Reviews	Craft International	Craft and Folk Art Museum, Los Angles, CA			PWC			5	Sp 83	68
Books and Reviews	Craft of Hand Spinning, The	Chadwick, Eileen			Iw	5	3		Su 80	70
Books and Reviews	Craft of Handspinning, The	Chadwick, Eileen			SS&D	12	1	45	Wi 80	82
Books and Reviews	Craft of Handweaving, The	Plath, Iona			SS&D	4	2	14	Sp 73	44
Books and Reviews	Craft of Hawaiian Lauhala Weaving, The	Bird, Adren J.; Steven Goldsberry; J. Puninani Kaneloa Bird			WJ	8	2	30	Fa 83	63
Books and Reviews	Craft of the Dyer: Colour from Plants and Lichens of the Northeast	Casselman, Karen Leigh			SS&D	12	2	46	Sp 81	70
Books and Reviews	Craft of the Dyer: Colour from Plants and Lichens of the Northeast	Casselman, Karen Leigh			Hw	2	4		Se 81	80
Books and Reviews	Craft of the Dyer: Colour from Plants and Lichens of the Northeast	Casselman, Karen Leight			WJ	5	3	19	Wi 81	51
Books and Reviews	Craft of the Weaver, a Practical Guide To Spinning, Dyeing and Weaving, The	Sutton, Ann; Peter Collingwood; Geraldine St. Aubyn Hubbard			Hw	8	2		M/A 87	15
Books and Reviews	Craft of Weaving, The	Waller, Irene			SS&D	8	1	29	WI 76	70
Books and Reviews	Craft Worker's Market, 1980	Lapin, Lynne, ed.			WJ	4	3	15	Ja 80	46
Books and Reviews	Craft Worker's Market, I980	Writer's Digest Books			Iw	5	1		Wi 79	65
Books and Reviews	Crafts Business Encyclopedia, The	Scott, Michael			Iw	2	4		Su 77	34
Books and Reviews	Crafts Business Encylopedia, The	Scott, Michael			SS&D	9	1	33	Wi 77	40
Books and Reviews	Crafts for the Aging — A Working Manual for Directors of Handcraft Programs for Older People	Lyon, Mary, ed.			H&C	14	2		Sp 63	43
Books and Reviews	Crafts from North American Indian Arts	Stribling, Mary Lou			Iw	1	2		Wi 76	28
Books and Reviews	Crafts from North American Indian Arts: Techniques, Designs and Contemporary Applications	Stribling, Mary Lou			SS&D	8	1	29	WI 76	70
Books and Reviews	Crafts of China	Carter, Michael			SS&D	9	4	36	Fa 78	82
Books and Reviews	Crafts of Israel	Dayan, Ruth; Wilburt Feinberg			SS&D	6	2	22	Sp 75	63
Books and Reviews	Crafts of Mexico	Sayer, Chloe			SS&D	9	4	36	Fa 78	82
Books and Reviews	Crafts of the Modern World	Slivka, Rose, ed.			H&C	19	4		Fa 68	45
Books and Reviews	Crafts of the Wiemar Bauhaus	Scheidig, Walter			H&C	18	3		Su 67	43
Books and Reviews	Craftsman in Textiles, The	Clarke, Leslie			H&C	19	4		Fa 68	44
Books and Reviews	Craftsman's Way, Canadian Expressions, The	Flanders, John			Hw	3	4		Se 82	16
Books and Reviews	Craftsman's Survival Manual	Wettlaufer, George; Nancy Wettlaufer			SS&D	6	2	22	Sp 75	63
Books and Reviews	Craftsworker's Market, 1979	Lapin, Lynne, ed.			WJ	3	4	12	Ap 79	46
Books and Reviews	Craftworker's Market, I979	Lapin, Lynne, ed.			Iw	4	2		Sp 79	62
Books and Reviews	Craftworker's Marketing Directory	Heller, K. J.			Hw	7	5		N/D 86	14
Books and Reviews	Crazy Quilts	McMorris, Penny	√		Fa	12	4		J/A 85	48
Books and Reviews	Create Your Own Natural Dyes	Schultz, Kathleen			SS&D	7	2	26	Sp 76	34
Books and Reviews	Creating Art from Fibers and Fabrics	Meilach, Dona Z.			SS&D	4	2	14	Sp 73	44
Books and Reviews	Creating Art from Fibers and Fabrics	Meilach, Dona Z.			H&C	24	2		M/A 73	5
Books and Reviews	Creating Hooked Rugs	Underhill, Vera Bisbee; Arthur J. Burks			H&C	3	1		Wi 51	61
Books and Reviews	Creating with Card Weaving	Specht, Sally; Sandra Rawlings			SS&D	5	2	18	Sp 74	68
Books and Reviews	Creative and Conceptual Analysis of Textiles, A	Michaels-Paque, Joan			SS&D	12	2	46	Sp 81	74

SUBJECT	TITLE	AUTHOR	IL	INST	JOUR	VOL	NO	ISS	DATE	PAGE
Books and Reviews	Creative Body Coverings	Laury, Jean Ray; Joyce Aiken			SS&D	6	4	24	Fa 75	30
Books and Reviews	Creative Bookbinding	Johnson, Pauline			Fa	6	4		J/A 79	15
Books and Reviews	Creative Cash	Brabec, Barbara	√		Iw	5	1		Wi 79	65
Books and Reviews	Creative Cash — How to Sell Your Crafts, Needlework, Designs and Know-How	Brabec, Barbara			WJ	4	3	15	Ja 80	46
Books and Reviews	Creative Crafts with Wool and Flax	Duncan, Molly			SS&D	3	1	9	Wi 71	38
Books and Reviews	Creative Crochet	Edson, Nicki Hitz; Arlene Stimmel	√		Fa	5	3		M/J 78	59
Books and Reviews	Creative Crochet	Edson, Nicki Hitz; Arlene Stimmel			TM			4	A/M 86	74
Books and Reviews	Creative Design in Wall Hangings	Blumenau, Lili			H&C	19	1		Wi 68	43
Books and Reviews	Creative Hands	Cox, Doris; Barbara Warren			H&C	2	4		Fa 51	62
Books and Reviews	Creative Handweaving	Parker, Xenia Ley			SS&D	7	4	28	Fa 76	66
Books and Reviews	Creative Knitting	Phillips, Mary Walker			TM			9	F/M 87	76
Books and Reviews	Creative Knitting, A New Art Form	Philips, Mary Walker			SS&D	3	2	10	Sp 72	38
Books and Reviews	Creative Monk's Belt	Windeknecht, Margaret B.			SS&D	9	1	33	Wi 77	40
Books and Reviews	Creative Overshot	Windeknecht, Margaret B.			WJ	3	4	12	Ap 79	46
Books and Reviews	Creative Overshot	Windeknecht, Margaret B.			SS&D	10	3	39	Su 79	35
Books and Reviews	Creative Overshot: Shuttle Craft Guild Monograph No. 31	Windeknecht, Margaret			Iw	4	2		Sp 79	60
Books and Reviews	Creative Spinning, Weaving and Plant Dyeing	Anderson, Beryl			H&C	24	3		M/J 73	6
Books and Reviews	Creative Textile Design—Color and Texture	Hartung, Rolf			SS&D	3	4	12	Fa 72	47
Books and Reviews	Creative Textile Design—Thread and Fabric	Hartung, Rolf			SS&D	3	4	12	Fa 72	47
Books and Reviews	Creative Textile Design — Thread and Fabric	Hartung, Rolf			H&C	16	1		Wi 65	43
Books and Reviews	Creative Woman's Getting-It-All-Together At Home Handbook, The	Laury, Jean Ray			Fa	5	5		S/O 78	62
Books and Reviews	Creative Woman's Getting-It-All-Together (At Home) Handbook, The	Laury, Jean Ray			Iw	3	2		Wi 78	40
Books and Reviews	Crochet Sweater Book, The	Cosh, Sylvia			TM			11	J/J 87	73
Books and Reviews	Crochet: Techniques and Projects	Sunset Books			TM			4	A/M 86	74
Books and Reviews	Crochet Workshop	Walters, James			TM			4	A/M 86	74
Books and Reviews	Cross Stitch Patterns	Abrahamsson, Greta			H&C	3	3		Su 52	64
Books and Reviews	Cultivation and Weaving of Cotton in the Prehistoric Southwest United States, The	Kent, Kate Peck			H&C	9	1		Wi 57	63
Books and Reviews	Custon Touch, Creative Sewing Techniques, The	Wealington, Mary J.			WJ	8	1	29	Su 83	51
Books and Reviews	Cut My Cote	Burnham, Dorothy K.			Fa	6	3		M/J 79	16
Books and Reviews	Cut My Cote	Burnham, Dorothy K.	√		SS&D	5	1	17	Wi 73	77
Books and Reviews	Damask and Opphamta, with Weaving Sword of Drawloom	Johansson, Lillemor			Hw	5	4		S/O 84	13
Books and Reviews	Damask and Opphamta with Weaving Sword or Drawloom	Johansson, Lillemor			WJ	9	3	35	Wi 85	84
Books and Reviews	Damask and Opphamta with Weaving Sword or Drawloom	Johansson, Lillemor			SS&D	16	1	61	Wi 84	22
Books and Reviews	Damask and Opphamta with Weaving Sword or Drawloom	Johansson, Lillemor	√		PWC	3	3	9		66
Books and Reviews	Danish Patterns for Handlooms	Poulsen, Grethe Poul			H&C	10	2		Sp 59	60
Books and Reviews	Danzig 1939: Treasures of a Destroyed Community	The Jewish Museum, New York			SS&D	11	4	44	Fa 80	67
Books and Reviews	Dated Tiraz Fabrics	Kuhnel, Ernst			H&C	4	1		Wi 52	60
Books and Reviews	Decorating with Fabric, Rev. Ed.	Lindahl, Judy			WJ	7	3	27	Wi 82	50
Books and Reviews	Decorating with Fabric/An Idea Book	Lindahl, Judy			WJ	7	3	27	Wi 82	50

SUBJECT	TITLE	AUTHOR	IL	INST	JOUR	VOL	NO	ISS	DATE	PAGE
Books and Reviews	Decorative Art and Modern Interiors 1977, Vol. 66	Schofield, Maria, ed.			SS&D	9	1	33	Wi 77	41
Books and Reviews	Decorative Art in Modern Interiors 1963/64	Moody, Ella, ed.			H&C	15	1		Wi 64	43
Books and Reviews	Decorative Art of Victoria's Era	Lichten, Frances			H&C	1	3		Fa 50	64
Books and Reviews	Decorative Arts of Sweden, The	Plath, Iona			H&C	17	3		Su 66	43
Books and Reviews	Decorative Braiding and Weaving	Baker, June			H&C	24	3		M/J 73	6
Books and Reviews	Decorative Wall Hangings — Art with Fabric	Van Dommelen, David			H&C	14	1		Wi 63	43
Books and Reviews	Den Stroa Vavboken	Block, Mary			H&C	3	4		Fa 52	61
Books and Reviews	Design and Form — The Basic Course at the Bauhaus	Itten, Johannes			H&C	15	3		Su 64	44
Books and Reviews	Design and the Handweaver, Shuttle Craft Guild Monograph No. 3	Atwater, Mary Meigs			H&C	12	3		Su 61	60
Books and Reviews	Design for Weaving: A Study Guide for Drafting, Design and Color	Kurtz, Carol S.	√		Hw	3	3		My 82	14
Books and Reviews	Design in Nature	Guyler, Vivian Varney			SS&D	3	2	10	Sp 72	38
Books and Reviews	Design in Sweden	Stavenow, Ake; Ake Huldt			H&C	14	1		Wi 63	44
Books and Reviews	Design Motifs of Ancient Mexico	Enciso, Jorge			H&C	5	1		Wi 53	61
Books and Reviews	Design on Fabrics	Johnson, Meda; Glen Kaufman			H&C	18	4		Fa 67	39
Books and Reviews	Design on Fabrics, 2nd ed.	Kaufman, Glen; Meda Parker Johnson			Fa	8	6		N/D 81	73
Books and Reviews	Design Principles and Fiber Techniques	Paque, Joan Michaels			SS&D	5	1	17	Wi 73	77
Books and Reviews	Design & Sew It Yourself, A Work Book for Creative Clothing	Ericson, Lois; Diane Ericson Frode			WJ	8	3	31	Wi 83	68
Books and Reviews	Design Sources for the Fiber Artist	Waller, Irene			Iw	4	3		Su 79	65
Books and Reviews	Designer's Drawloom	Hindson, Alice			H&C	9	3		Su 58	59
Books and Reviews	Designer's Guide to Color 3	Allen, Jeanne			SS&D	18	3	71	Su 87	73
Books and Reviews	Designer's Guide to Color, and Designer's Guide to Color 2	Stockton, James			Hw	6	5		N/D 85	18
Books and Reviews	Designing and Drafting for Handweavers	Frey, Berta			SS&D	7	1	25	Wi 75	35
Books and Reviews	Designing and Drafting for Handweavers	Frey, Berta			H&C	26	5		Oc 75	12
Books and Reviews	Designing and Drafting for Handweavers, Basic Principles of Cloth Construction	Frey, Berta			H&C	9	3		Su 58	60
Books and Reviews	Designing for Printed Textiles: A Guide to Studio and Free-lance Work	Joyce, Carol			Fa	10	3		M/J 83	52
Books and Reviews	Designing for Weaving: A Study Guide for Drafting, Design and Color	Kurtz, Carol S.	√		WJ	11	4	44	Sp 87	74
Books and Reviews	Designing for Weaving: A Study Guide for Drafting, Design and Color	Kurtz, Carol S.			SS&D	13	4	52	Fa 82	66
Books and Reviews	Designing for Weaving: A Study Guide for Drafting, Design and Color	Kurtz, Carol S.	√		Fa	9	3		M/J 82	58
Books and Reviews	Designing for Weaving: A Study Guide for Drafting, Design and Color	Kurtz, Carol S.			WJ	6	4	24	Sp 82	60
Books and Reviews	Designing from Nature	Dendel, Esther			WJ	4	2	14	Oc 79	38
Books and Reviews	Designing in Batik and Tie Dye	Belfer, Nancy			H&C	23	4		J/A 72	26
Books and Reviews	Designing on the Loom	Kirby, Mary			SS&D	5	2	18	Sp 74	68
Books and Reviews	Designing on the Loom	Kirby, Mary			Fa	3	1		J/F 76	4
Books and Reviews	Designing on the Loom	Kirby, Mary			H&C	6	4		Fa 55	59
Books and Reviews	Designing Tapestry	Lurçat, Jean			H&C	4	2		Sp 53	61
Books and Reviews	Designing with the Wool	Bennett, Noël			Iw	4	3		Su 79	66
Books and Reviews	Designing with Thread: From Fibre to Fabric	Waller, Irene			SS&D	5	1	17	Wi 73	77
Books and Reviews	Designs and Patterns from North African Carpets & Textiles	Revault, Jacques			SS&D	6	4	24	Fa 75	30
Books and Reviews	Deutsche Textilkunst	Jaques, Renate			H&C	5	1		Wi 53	59
Books and Reviews	Dictionary of Costume, The	Wilcox, R. Turner			H&C	21	2		Sp 70	42

SUBJECT	TITLE	AUTHOR	IL	INST	JOUR	VOL	NO	ISS	DATE	PAGE
Books and Reviews	Dictionary of Oriental Rugs	Neff, Ivan C,; Carol V. Maggs			Fa	7	6		N/D 80	34
Books and Reviews	Diderot Pictorial Encyclopedia of Trades and Industry, A	Gillispie, Charles, ed.			H&C	10	3		Su 59	59
Books and Reviews	Directions 1970	Myers, Virginia D., ed.			SS&D	2	3	7	Su 71	26
Books and Reviews	Discovering Design	Downer, Marion			H&C	4	2		Sp 53	62
Books and Reviews	Discovering Textile History and Design	Ponting, K. G.			WJ	7	3	27	Wi 82	50
Books and Reviews	Documents Sur Micro-Informatique Et Creation Textile	Thomas, Michel; Remy Prin			WJ	8	4	32	Sp 84	67
Books and Reviews	Domestic American Textiles; A Bibliographic Sourcebook	Gordon, Beverly	√		WJ	9	2	34	Fa 84	79
Books and Reviews	Domestic American Textiles: A Bibliographic Sourcebook	Gordon, Beverly			SS&D	10	2	38	Sp 79	73
Books and Reviews	Domestic American Textiles: "A Bibliographic Sourcebook"	Gordon, Beverly			Hw	5	4		S/O 84	15
Books and Reviews	Domestic Manufacturer's Assistant, The	Bronson, J.; R. Bronson			H&C	1	1		Ap 50	49
Books and Reviews	Double Cloth (on four-shaft looms) Monograph 2	Halsey, Mark			SS&D	11	1	41	Wi 79	34
Books and Reviews	Double Two-Tie Unit Weave	Barrett, Clotilde; Eunice Smith			Hw	5	5		N/D 84	12
Books and Reviews	Double Weave	Weigle, Palmy			WJ	4	1	13	Jy 79	42
Books and Reviews	Double Weave	Weigle, Palmy			SS&D	10	3	39	Su 79	35
Books and Reviews	Double Weave	Weigle, Palmy			Iw	4	2		Sp 79	60
Books and Reviews	Double Weave — Plain and Patterned, The	Tidball, Harriet			H&C	12	1		Wi 61	59
Books and Reviews	Double-Woven Treasures from Old Peru	Cahlander, Adele; Suzanne Baizerman	√		Hw	8	4		S/O 87	12
Books and Reviews	Double-Woven Treasures from Old Peru	Cahlander, Adele; Suzanne Baizerman	√		PWC	4	2	12		51
Books and Reviews	Doup Leno—A Quick and Simple System for Weaving Loom-Controlled Leno	Skowronski, Hella; Sylvia Tacker			WJ	5	3	19	Wi 81	52
Books and Reviews	Doup Leno: A Quick and Simple System for Weaving Loom-Controlled Leno	Skowronski, Hella; Sylvia Tacker			Hw	2	3		My 81	72
Books and Reviews	Drafting Primer	Guagliumi, Susan			WJ	5	2	18	Fa 80	33
Books and Reviews	Drafting Primer	Guagliumi, Susan			Hw	2	3		My 81	70
Books and Reviews	Drafts and Designs, A Guide for 5-12 Harness Weaves	Robin and Russ Handweavers			SS&D	3	3	11	Su 72	14
Books and Reviews	Dressing the Loom	Dean, Ida			H&C	4	4		Fa 53	59
Books and Reviews	Dressmaker's Dictionary, The	Ladbury, Ann			Fa	10	1		J/F 83	58
Books and Reviews	Dye Plants and Dyeing — A Handbook	Brooklyn Botanic Garden			Fa	5	1		J/F 78	40
Books and Reviews	Dye Plants and Dyeing — A Handbook	Brooklyn Botanic Gardens			H&C	16	1		Wi 65	44
Books and Reviews	Dye-Craft				SS&D	4	1	13	Wi 72	34
Books and Reviews	Dye-Pot, The	Davidson, Mary Frances			SS&D	6	1	21	Wi 74	32
Books and Reviews	Dye-Pot, The	Davidson, Mary Frances			H&C	1	3		Fa 50	64
Books and Reviews	Dyeing for Beginners	Freeborn, Mary-Eleanor			SS&D	3	2	10	Sp 72	39
Books and Reviews	Dyeing for Fibers and Fabrics	DeBoer, Janet, ed.			Hw	6	3		Su 85	20
Books and Reviews	Dyeing for Fibres and Fabrics	DeBoer, Janet, ed.	√		WJ	10	2	38	Fa 85	82
Books and Reviews	Dyeing with Lichens	Windt, Hal			Hw	3	1		Ja 82	20
Books and Reviews	Dyeing with Natural Materials	Las Aranas Spinners and Weavers Guild			SS&D	4	3	15	Su 73	53
Books and Reviews	Dyer's Art, Ikat, Batik, Plangi, The	Larsen, Jack Lenor, et. al.			SS&D	8	4	32	Fa 77	72
Books and Reviews	Dyer's Art: Ikat, Batik, Plangi, The	Larsen, Jack Lenor with Alfred Buhler, Bronwen Solyom, Garrett Solyom			Fa	5	1		J/F 78	40
Books and Reviews	Dyer's Companion, The	Bemis, Elijah			SS&D	6	1	21	Wi 74	32
Books and Reviews	Dyer's Manual, A	Goodwin, Jill			WJ	8	3	31	Wi 83	66
Books and Reviews	Dyer's Manual, A	Goodwin, Jill	√		PWC	3	1	7		61
Books and Reviews	Dyes and Dyeing	Simmons, Max			SS&D	10	4	40	Fa 79	65

SUBJECT	TITLE	AUTHOR	IL	INST	JOUR	VOL	NO	ISS	DATE	PAGE
Books and Reviews	Dyes and Dyeing	Simmons, Max			Iw	4	2		Sp 79	61
Books and Reviews	Dyes and Dyeing	Worst, Edward F.			SS&D	2	2	6	Sp 71	34
Books and Reviews	Dyes and Fabrics	Storey, Joyce			TM			8	D/J 86	72
Books and Reviews	Dyes from Lichens and Plants	McGrath, Judy Waldner			SS&D	9	4	36	Fa 78	81
Books and Reviews	Dyes from Lichens and Plants	McGrath, Judy Waldner			Fa	5	4		J/A 78	59
Books and Reviews	Dyes from Lichens and Plants	McGrath, Judy Waldner			Iw	3	2		Wi 78	41
Books and Reviews	Dyes from Natural Sources	Dyer, Anne			SS&D	8	3	31	Su 77	63
Books and Reviews	Dyes from Plants	Robertson, Seonaid			SS&D	5	3	19	Su 74	63
Books and Reviews	Dyes from Plants: An Annotated List of References	Zanoni, Thomas A.; Eileen K. Schofield			Hw	6	5		N/D 85	20
Books and Reviews	Dyes from Plants of Australia and New Zealand	Lloyd, Joyce			SS&D	4	1	13	Wi 72	34
Books and Reviews	Dyes from Plants of Australia and New Zealand	Lloyd, Joyce			SS&D	8	2	30	Sp 77	38
Books and Reviews	Dyes from Plants of Australia & New Zealand	Lloyd, Joyce			SS&D	3	3	11	Su 72	13
Books and Reviews	Early American Crafts & Hobbies	Yates, Raymond; Margurite Yates			H&C	5	4		Fa 54	59
Books and Reviews	Early American Design Motifs	Chapman, Suzanne E.			SS&D	6	4	24	Fa 75	30
Books and Reviews	Early American Design Motifs	Chapman, Suzanne E.			H&C	4	1		Wi 52	60
Books and Reviews	Early American Weaving and Dyeing	Bronson, J.; R. Bronson			SS&D	9	3	35	Su 78	96
Books and Reviews	Early American Weaving and Dyeing — The Domestic Manufacturer's Assistant and Family Directory In the Arts of Weaving and Dyeing	Bronson, J.; R. Bronson			WJ	3	1	9	Jy 78	37
Books and Reviews	Early Christian and Byzantine Art	Walters Art Gallery			H&C	4	1		Wi 52	62
Books and Reviews	Easy Dyeing	Mustard, Frances E.			Iw	3	2		Wi 78	43
Books and Reviews	Easy to Weave Wall Decorations	Craft Course Publishers			WJ	3	3	11	Ja 79	43
Books and Reviews	Easy Weaving	Lightbody, Donna M.			SS&D	6	2	22	Sp 75	63
Books and Reviews	Ecclesiastical Crafts	King, Bucky; Jude Martin			SS&D	10	4	40	Fa 79	63
Books and Reviews	Ecclesiastical Embroidery	Dean, Beryl			H&C	10	1		Wi 59	59
Books and Reviews	Eight Harness Patterned Double Weave Clothing	Boyd, Doris			Iw	5	3		Su 80	71
Books and Reviews	Elements of Design	Anderson, Donald			H&C	21	3		Su 70	39
Books and Reviews	Elements of Dynamic Symmetry, The	Hambidge, Jay			H&C	19	3		Su 68	42
Books and Reviews	Elements of Weaving	Thorpe, Azalea Stuart; Jack Lenor Larsen			H&C	18	4		Fa 67	39
Books and Reviews	Elements of Weaving (revised edition)	Thorpe, Azalea Stuart; Jack Lenor Larsen	√		Iw	3	4		Su 78	44
Books and Reviews	Elle Knitting Book: 50 Exclusive Designs from France, The	Carr, Sandy, ed.			TM			2	D/J 85	76
Books and Reviews	Elle Knitting Book, The		√		Kn	2	2	4	S-S 86	78
Books and Reviews	Embroidered Samplers in the Collection of the Cooper-Hewitt Muesum	Moss, Gillian	√		WJ	9	1	33	Su 84	60
Books and Reviews	Embroidering Our Heritage: The Dinner Party Needlework	Chicago, Judy; Susan Hill	√		Fa	9	3		M/J 82	58
Books and Reviews	Embroidering with the Loom	Drooker, Penelope B.			SS&D	11	2	42	Sp 80	83
Books and Reviews	Embroidering with the Loom: Creative Combinations of Weaving and Stitchery	Drooker, Penelope B.			Iw	4	3		Su 79	65
Books and Reviews	Embroidery: A Complete Course in Embroidery Design and Technique	Brown, Pauline, ed.			TM			13	O/N 87	76
Books and Reviews	Embroidery and Color	Howard, Constance	√		Fa	4	3		M/J 77	54
Books and Reviews	Embroidery of All of Russia	Gostelow, Mary			Fa	5	5		S/O 78	62
Books and Reviews	Encyclopaedia of Hand-Weaving	Zielinski, S. A.			H&C	10	4		Fa 59	59
Books and Reviews	Encyclopedia of Batik Designs	Donahue, Leo O.	√		Fa	10	4		J/A 83	50
Books and Reviews	Encyclopedia of Crafts, The	Torbet, Laura, ed.			SS&D	12	2	46	Sp 81	74
Books and Reviews	Encyclopedia of Hand-Weaving	Zielinski, S. A.			H&C	1	3		Fa 50	63

SUBJECT	TITLE	AUTHOR	IL	INST	JOUR	VOL	NO	ISS	DATE	PAGE
Books and Reviews	Encyclopedia of Hand-Weaving	Zielinski, Stanislaw A.			WJ	2	1	5	Jy 77	29
Books and Reviews	Encyclopedia of Handweaving	Zielinski, Stanislaw A.			SS&D	8	3	31	Su 77	62
Books and Reviews	Encyclopedia of Knitting and Crochet Stitch Patterns, The	Mariano, Linda			SS&D	8	4	32	Fa 77	72
Books and Reviews	Encyclopedia of Knitting Techniques, The	Robinson, Debby	√		Kn	3	4	8	Fa 87	62
Books and Reviews	Encyclopedia of Textiles	Editors of American Fabrics Magazine			H&C	12	2		Sp 61	59
Books and Reviews	Encyclopedia of Textiles	Jaques, Renate; Ernst Flemming			H&C	9	3		Su 58	60
Books and Reviews	English and Oriental Carpets at Williamsburg	Lanier, Mildred B.			TMJ	4	2		75	80
Books and Reviews	English Crewel Designs, Sixteenth to Eighteenth Centuries	Bradbury, Francis M.			WJ	8	3	31	Wi 83	67
Books and Reviews	English Embroidery in the Royal Ontario Museum	Brett, Katherine B.			TMJ	3	4		De 73	46
Books and Reviews	Essential Handbook of Weaving, The	Murray, Rosemary			WJ	7	4	28	Sp 83	48
Books and Reviews	Essential Handbook of Weaving, The	Murray, Rosemary			Hw	3	1		Ja 82	20
Books and Reviews	Essentials of Handspinning, The	Ross, Mabel			SS&D	15	3	59	Su 84	35
Books and Reviews	Essentials of Handspinning, The	Ross, Mabel			S-O	8	2		Su 84	51
Books and Reviews	Essentials of Handspinning, The	Ross, Mable			Hw	2	3		My 81	73
Books and Reviews	Essentials of Yarn Design for Handspinners, The	Ross, Mabel			SS&D	15	3	59	Su 84	35
Books and Reviews	Essentials of Yarn Design for the Handspinners, The	Ross, Mabel			S-O	8	2		Su 84	51
Books and Reviews	Everybody's Weaving Book	Lewis, Alfred Allan: Julienne Krasnoff			SS&D	7	4	28	Fa 76	65
Books and Reviews	Evolution in Textile Design from the Highlands of Guatemala	Schevill, Margot Blum	√		WJ	12	2	46	Fa 87	66
Books and Reviews	Experimental Embroidery	John, Edith	√		Fa	4	3		M/J 77	54
Books and Reviews	Experimental Stitchery and Other Fiber Techniques	Morrison, Arline K.	√		Fa	4	3		M/J 77	53
Books and Reviews	Fabric Book, The	Harrisville Designs			Iw	6	1		Wi 80	69
Books and Reviews	Fabric Collage	Ballarian, Anna			WJ	3	1	9	Jy 78	37
Books and Reviews	Fabric Printing by Hand	Russ, Stephen			H&C	16	2		Sp 65	43
Books and Reviews	Fabric Structures—Basic Weave Design	Goutmann, Marylyn			WJ	5	3	19	Wi 81	51
Books and Reviews	Fabrics. Eight Edition	Denny, Grace			H&C	14	2		Sp 63	43
Books and Reviews	Fabrics for Interiors	Larsen, Jack Lenor; Jeanne Weeks			SS&D	7	3	27	Su 76	34
Books and Reviews	Fabrics For Interiors: A Guide for Architects, Designers, and Consumers	Larsen, Jack Lenore; Jeanne Weeks			Fa	3	5		S/O 76	39
Books and Reviews	Fabrics in Celebration: From the Collection of the Indianapolis Museum of Art	Gilfoy, Peggy Stoltz			SS&D	16	3	63	Su 85	8
Books and Reviews	Fabrics, Seventh Revised Edition	Denny, Grace			H&C	4	3		Su 53	61
Books and Reviews	Fair Isle Knitting	Don, Sarah	√		Kn	2	1	3	F-W 85	78
Books and Reviews	Fans in Fashion	Bennett, Anna G.; Ruth Berson	√		Fa	9	4		J/A 82	53
Books and Reviews	Fashionable Mind, The	Fraser, Kennedy			Fa	10	5		S/O 83	57
Books and Reviews	Felt Making for the Artist	Green, Louise			WJ	3	1	9	Jy 78	36
Books and Reviews	Felt Making for the Fiber Artist	Green, Louise			SS&D	10	1	37	Wi 78	78
Books and Reviews	Felt Making for the Fiber Artist	Green, Louise			Iw	3	3		Sp 78	50
Books and Reviews	Feltmaking—Traditions, Techniques, and Contemporary Explorations	Gordon, Beverly			WJ	5	3	19	Wi 81	52
Books and Reviews	Fiber Expressions: Knotting and Looping	Rainey, Sarita			WJ	4	2	14	Oc 79	39
Books and Reviews	Fiber R/Evolution	Goldstein, Rosalie, ed.			Hw	8	2		M/A 87	12
Books and Reviews	Fiber Structures				SS&D	7	4	28	Fa 76	65
Books and Reviews	Fiberarts Design Book II, The	Hutchins, Jeane, ed.			WJ	8	4	32	Sp 84	65
Books and Reviews	Fiberarts Design Book II, The	Staff of Fiberarts Magazine	√		Hw	5	3		Su 84	18

SUBJECT	TITLE	AUTHOR	IL	INST	JOUR	VOL	NO	ISS	DATE	PAGE
Books and Reviews	Fiberarts Design Book, The	DeBoy, Kathleen, ed.			Hw	2	2		Mr 81	67
Books and Reviews	Fiberarts Design Book, The	Editors of Fiberarts Magazine			WJ	6	2	22	Fa 81	40
Books and Reviews	Fibers to Fabrics	Clark, Hazel			SS&D	17	3	67	Su 86	86
Books and Reviews	Fibre Facts	Hochberg, Bette			Fa	9	1		J/F 82	58
Books and Reviews	Fibre Facts	Hochberg, Bette			WJ	6	4	24	Sp 82	60
Books and Reviews	Fibres to Fabrics: Techniques and Projects for Handspinners	Clark, Hazel			TM			13	O/N 87	76
Books and Reviews	Fifty Masterpieces of Textiles: Victoria and Albert Museum, London				H&C	18	4		Fa 67	40
Books and Reviews	Final Step. Traditional Methods and Contemporary Applications for Finishing Cloth by Hand, The	Gordon, Beverly			WJ	7	2	26	Fa 82	57
Books and Reviews	Final Steps: Traditional Methods and Contemporary Applications for Finishing Cloth by Hand, The	Gordon, Beverly			Fa	10	1		J/F 83	57
Books and Reviews	Fine-Art Weaving	Waller, Irene			WJ	4	2	14	Oc 79	38
Books and Reviews	Finger Weaving: Indian Braiding	Turner, Alta R.	√		SS&D	4	4	16	Fa 73	63
Books and Reviews	Finger Weaving: Indian Braiding	Turner, Alta R.			H&C	24	3		M/J 73	6
Books and Reviews	Finishes in the Ethnic Tradition	Baizerman, Suzanne; Karen Searle			WJ	3	3	11	Ja 79	42
Books and Reviews	Finishes in the Ethnic Tradition	Baizerman, Suzanne; Karen Searle			SS&D	10	2	38	Sp 79	74
Books and Reviews	Finishes in the Ethnic Tradition	Baizerman, Suzanne; Karen Searle			Fa	8	4		J/A 81	34
Books and Reviews	Finishes in the Ethnic Tradition	Baizerman, Suzanne; Karen Searle			Iw	3	4		Su 78	45
Books and Reviews	Finishing Touches: A Study of Finishing Details for Handwoven Articles	West, Virginia W.			H&C	19	1		Wi 68	45
Books and Reviews	Finishing Touches for the Handweaver	West, Virginia M.			SS&D	1	3	3	Ju 70	22
Books and Reviews	Finnish Lace Weaves	Wahe, Matilda			H&C	10	2		Sp 59	56
Books and Reviews	Finnweave is Fun! The Way it is Woven in Finland	Ringler, Aina			H&C	6	1		Wi 54	62
Books and Reviews	First Book of Modern Lace Knitting, The	Kinzel, Marianne	√		Kn	1	2	2	S-S 85	78
Books and Reviews	Fisher-Gansey Patterns of N. E. England	Pearson, Michael			Kn	1	1	1	F-W 84	71
Books and Reviews	Fisher-Gansey Patterns of Scotland and the Scottish Fleet	Pearson, Michael			Kn	1	1	1	F-W 84	71
Books and Reviews	Five Block Diamond in Hand Weaving, Part V–Doubles, Eight Harness, The	Newman, Margaret			SS&D	5	4	20	Fa 74	66
Books and Reviews	Five Block Diamond in Handweaving	Newman, Margaret			SS&D	3	1	9	Wi 71	38
Books and Reviews	Five Centuries of Tapestry	Bennet, Anna G.			SS&D	8	3	31	Su 77	62
Books and Reviews	Flamskvävnad	Ingers, Gertrud			H&C	20	3		Su 69	43
Books and Reviews	Flamskvavnad — Flemish Weaving	Fischer, Ernst; Gertrud Ingers			H&C	12	3		Su 61	61
Books and Reviews	Flat-Woven Rugs of the World	Justin, Valerie Sharaf			Fa	7	6		N/D 80	34
Books and Reviews	Fleece Directory	Natural Colored Wool Growers Association			S-O	3			79	10
Books and Reviews	Fleece in Your Hands	Horne, Beverley			S-O	3			79	11
Books and Reviews	Fleece in Your Hands	Horne, Beverley			Iw	2	3		Sp 77	32
Books and Reviews	Flemish Weaving	Ingers, Gertrud			H&C	23	4		J/A 72	26
Books and Reviews	Flemish Weaving, A Guide to Tapestry Technique	Ingers, Gertrud			SS&D	3	3	11	Su 72	13
Books and Reviews	Flying Geese & Partidge Feet, More Mittens from Up North and Down East	Hansen, Robin; Janetta Dexter	√		Kn	3	1	5	F-W 86	69
Books and Reviews	Folk Art of Europe	Bossert, Helmuth			H&C	5	1		Wi 53	60
Books and Reviews	Folk Art of Rural Pennsylvania	Lichten, Frances			H&C	14	4		Fa 63	44
Books and Reviews	Folk Arts and Crafts	Ickis, Marguerite			H&C	9	2		Sp 58	59
Books and Reviews	Folk Arts and Crafts of New England, The	Lord, P. S.; D. J. Foley			H&C	22	1		Wi 71	41

SUBJECT	TITLE	AUTHOR	IL	INST	JOUR	VOL	NO	ISS	DATE	PAGE
Books and Reviews	Folk Arts of Norway, The	Stewart, Janice S.			H&C	23	6		N/D 72	41
Books and Reviews	Folk Designs from the Caucasus for Weaving and Needlework	Kerimov, Lyatif			SS&D	6	4	24	Fa 75	31
Books and Reviews	Folklore and Symbolism of Flowers, Plants and Trees	Lehner, Ernst; Johanna Lehner			H&C	12	3		Su 61	61
Books and Reviews	Footwear, Shoes & Socks You Can Make Yourself	Katz, Ruth			SS&D	11	2	42	Sp 80	83
Books and Reviews	For the Floor: An International Exhibition of Contemporary Handmade Rugs	American Craft Museum Catalogue	√		WJ	9	4	36	Sp 85	78
Books and Reviews	Foroysk Bindingarmynster Bundnaturriklaedid				Kn	4	1	9	Wi 87	60
Books and Reviews	Foundations for Handweavers	Tidball, Harriet			H&C	6	4		Fa 55	60
Books and Reviews	Foundations of Weaving	Halsy, Mike; Lore Youngmark	√		Fa	3	2		M/A 76	25
Books and Reviews	Four Harness Weaving	Frey, Berta			SS&D	3	4	12	Fa 72	47
Books and Reviews	Four-Harness Huck	Neher, Evelyn			H&C	4	4		Fa 53	60
Books and Reviews	Four-Harness Weaving	Bowen, Kernochan			Iw	3	4		Su 78	44
Books and Reviews	Four-Harness Weaving, The Complete Guide to Warping and Weaving on a Four-Harness Loom	Bowen, Kernochan			SS&D	10	1	37	Wi 78	77
Books and Reviews	Fox & Geese & Fences	Hansen, Robin	√		Kn	3	1	5	F-W 86	69
Books and Reviews	Frame Loom Weaving	Redman, Jane			SS&D	8	1	29	WI 76	70
Books and Reviews	Frame Loom Weaving	Redman, Jane			Fa	3	5		S/O 76	39
Books and Reviews	Frame-Loom Weaving	Redman, Jane			Iw	2	1		Fa 76	33
Books and Reviews	Free and Easy Speed Weaving	Green, Louise			WJ	3	1	9	Jy 78	36
Books and Reviews	Free and Easy Speed Weaving	Green, Louise			Iw	3	3		Sp 78	50
Books and Reviews	Free Weaving	Gilby, Myriam			SS&D	7	4	28	Fa 76	66
Books and Reviews	Free Weaving on Frame and Loom	Hoppe, E.; E. Ostlund; L. Melen			SS&D	6	3	23	Su 75	49
Books and Reviews	Free Weaving on Frame and Loom	Hoppe, Ostlund, Melen			H&C	26	3		M/J 75	30
Books and Reviews	French Hand Sewing	Stone, Sarah Howard			Hw	6	4		S/O 85	22
Books and Reviews	French Textiles from the Middle Ages Through the Second Empire	Carlano, Marianne; Larry Salmon, eds.	√		Hw	8	5		N/D 87	13
Books and Reviews	French-English Weaving Glossary	April-Proulx, Bibiane			WJ	8	4	32	Sp 84	67
Books and Reviews	From Craft to Industry: The Ethnography of Proto-Industrial Cloth Production	Goody, Esther N. ed.			WJ	9	3	35	Wi 85	85
Books and Reviews	From Fibers to Fabrics	Gale, Elizabeth			SS&D	4	1	13	Wi 72	34
Books and Reviews	From Fibres to Fabrics	Gale, Elizabeth			H&C	23	6		N/D 72	41
Books and Reviews	From Seed to Dye	Miller, Dorothy			Iw	4	1		Wi 78	55
Books and Reviews	From Swatches to Sweater: A Simple Method of Sweater Design (2 vols.)	Carpenter, Marie; Anne Wallace			TM			12	A/S 87	76
Books and Reviews	From Swatches to Sweaters	Carpenter, Marie; Anne Wallace	√		Kn	3	4	8	Fa 87	63
Books and Reviews	From the Bosporus to Samarkand: Flat-Woven Rugs	Landreau, Anthony; W. R. Pickering			H&C	20	3		Su 69	43
Books and Reviews	Fun with Felt	Feldman, Annette			WJ	6	2	22	Fa 81	40
Books and Reviews	Fun with String	Leeming, Joseph			SS&D	6	4	24	Fa 75	30
Books and Reviews	Fun with Weaving	Gilbreath, Alice			SS&D	8	4	32	Fa 77	72
Books and Reviews	Functional Overshot — Basic Sources for Modern Fabric Design	Blum, Grace D.			H&C	11	2		Sp 60	59
Books and Reviews	Furniture and Decoration	Aronson, Joseph			H&C	4	2		Sp 53	62
Books and Reviews	Gallery of Amish Quilts, Design Diversity from a Plain People, A	Bishop, Robert; Elizabeth Safanda			Fa	7	1		J/F 80	15
Books and Reviews	Geometric Design in Weaving	Regensteiner, Else	√		WJ	11	4	44	Sp 87	73
Books and Reviews	Geometric Design in Weaving	Regensteiner, Else			SS&D	18	4	72	Fa 87	55
Books and Reviews	Geometric Design in Weaving	Regensteiner, Else			Hw	8	5		N/D 87	15
Books and Reviews	Geometric Design in Weaving	Regensteiner, Else	√		PWC	4	4	14		53

SUBJECT	TITLE	AUTHOR	IL	INST	JOUR	VOL	NO	ISS	DATE	PAGE
Books and Reviews	Geometric Designs for Artists and Craftsmen	Lang, John			H&C	10	3		Su 59	60
Books and Reviews	George Walter Vincent and Belle Townsley Smith Collection of Islamic Rugs	McMullan, Joseph V.; Donald O. Reichert			TMJ	3	2		De 71	43
Books and Reviews	Gerhardt Knodel Makes Places to Be	Cranbrook Academy of Art Museum			WJ	7	4	28	Sp 83	49
Books and Reviews	German Weaver's Pattern Book 1784-1810, A	Galvin, Nellie L., ed.			H&C	12	4		Fa 61	43
Books and Reviews	Gift from A Sheep	Eisema, Alberta; Nicole Eisema			Iw	5	1		Wi 79	65
Books and Reviews	Gift from a Sheep: The Story of How Wool Is Made	Eiseman, Alberta; Nicole Eiseman			SS&D	12	1	45	Wi 80	83
Books and Reviews	Gift from the Hills	Blythe, LeGetta			H&C	9	3		Su 58	59
Books and Reviews	Girl Who Cried Flowers and Other Tales, The	Yolen, Jane			Iw	2	1		Fa 76	33
Books and Reviews	Glorious Knits	Fassett, Kaffe			Hw	7	2		M/A 86	88
Books and Reviews	Glorious Knits	Fassett, Kaffe	√		Kn	2	2	4	S-S 86	78
Books and Reviews	Glorious Knits: Thirty-Five Designs for Sweaters, Dresses, Vests, And Shawls	Fassett, Kaffe			SS&D	17	3	67	Su 86	85
Books and Reviews	Golden Age of Homespun, The	van Wagenen, Jared, Jr.			H&C	4	4		Fa 53	61
Books and Reviews	Goodfellow Catalog of Wonderful Things No. 3, The	Weills, Christopher; Sarah Satterlee			SS&D	14	1	53	Wi 82	64
Books and Reviews	Goodfellow Catalog of Wonderful Things. Number Three, The					Hw	3	3		My 82	18
Books and Reviews	Goodfellow Catalog of Wonderful Things, The	Weills, Christopher	√		Iw	3	2		Wi 78	40
Books and Reviews	Goodfellow Catalogues				Hw	6	4		S/O 85	24
Books and Reviews	Graded Lession in Macrame Knotting and Netting	Walker, Louisa			H&C	23	3		M/J 72	24
Books and Reviews	Grain d'Orge (French)	Association des Tisserands d'Ici, Quebec	√		WJ	11	3	43	Wi 87	64
Books and Reviews	Great Tapestries: The Web of History from the 12th to the 20th Century	Jobé, Joseph, ed.			H&C	19	2		Sp 68	43
Books and Reviews	Greek Islands Embroideries	MacMillan, Susan L.			TMJ	4	2		75	80
Books and Reviews	Groot Plantaardig Verfboek	van de Vrande, Let			WJ	8	2	30	Fa 83	66
Books and Reviews	Growing Herbs and Plants for Dyeing	Jacobs, Betty E. M.			WJ	3	1	9	Jy 78	36
Books and Reviews	Growing Herbs and Plants for Dyeing	Jacobs, Betty E. M.			Iw	3	1		Fa 77	44
Books and Reviews	Growing Herbs and Plants for Dyeing	Jacobs, E. M.			SS&D	9	4	36	Fa 78	81
Books and Reviews	Guatemala Visited, Shuttle Craft Bulletin #15, Reprint	Atwater, Mary M.			H&C	16	3		Su 65	45
Books and Reviews	Guatemalan Backstrap Weaving	Sperlich, Norbert; Elizabeth Katz Sperlich			Iw	5	4		Fa 80	74
Books and Reviews	Guatemalan Textiles Today	Anderson, Marilyn			WJ	8	1	29	Su 83	52
Books and Reviews	Guatemalan Textiles Today	Anderson, Marilyn			Iw	3	4		Su 78	45
Books and Reviews	Guide to Successful Tapestry Weaving, The	Harvey, Nancy	√		WJ	12	1	45	Su 87	69
Books and Reviews	Guide to Successful Tapestry Weaving, The	Harvey, Nancy			WJ	6	2	22	Fa 81	39
Books and Reviews	Guide to Successful Tapestry Weaving, The	Harvey, Nancy	√		PWC			3	Oc 82	63
Books and Reviews	Guide to Using Cushing Dyes	Kampert, Carol; Susan Henrickson			Hw	2	4		Se 81	79
Books and Reviews	Guidebook to Man-made Textile Fibers	Dembeck, Adeline			H&C	21	1		Wi 70	43
Books and Reviews	Guild: A Sourcebook of American Craft Artists, The	Sikes, Kraus			Hw	7	5		N/D 86	14
Books and Reviews	Gypsies, The	Yoors, Jan			H&C	18	2		Sp 67	45
Books and Reviews	Half for You	Azaad, Meyer			Iw	2	1		Fa 76	32
Books and Reviews	Hammock Making Techniques	Drooker, Penelope			WJ	6	4	24	Sp 82	60
Books and Reviews	Hammock Making Techniques	Drooker, Penelope			Hw	3	5		N/D 82	12

SUBJECT	TITLE	AUTHOR	IL	INST	JOUR	VOL	NO	ISS	DATE	PAGE
Books and Reviews	Hand Decoration of Fabrics, The	Kafka, Francis			H&C	10	2		Sp 59	54
Books and Reviews	Hand Knotted Rug Weaving	Paternayan Brothers			H&C	8	2		Sp 57	62
Books and Reviews	Hand Loom Weaving	Christopher, F. J.			H&C	7	2		Sp 56	64
Books and Reviews	Hand Loom Weaving for Amateurs	Van Cleve, Kate			H&C	2	2		Sp 51	63
Books and Reviews	Hand Spinning Cotton	Linder, Olive; Harry Linder			SS&D	9	4	36	Fa 78	82
Books and Reviews	Hand Spinning Cotton	Linder, Olive; Harry Linder			Iw	3	2		Wi 78	42
Books and Reviews	Hand Stitches for the Fine Custom Tailored Garment	Hostek, Stanley			TM			7	O/N 86	72
Books and Reviews	Hand Weaving	Duchemin, Mad			Iw	1	2		Wi 76	28
Books and Reviews	Hand Weaving: An Introduction to Weaving on 2, 3 And 4 Harnesses	Duchemin, Mad			SS&D	7	4	28	Fa 76	66
Books and Reviews	Hand Weaving and Education	Mairet, Ethel			H&C	3	1		Wi 51	62
Books and Reviews	Hand Weaving for Pleasure and Profit	Brown, Harriette J.			H&C	3	3		Su 52	61
Books and Reviews	Hand Weaving Patterns from Finland	Pyysalo, Helvi; Viivi Merisalo			SS&D	2	2	6	Sp 71	34
Books and Reviews	Hand Weaving with Reeds and Fibers	Gallinger, Osma Couch; Oscar H. Benson			H&C	2	1		Wi 50	59
Books and Reviews	Hand Woolcombing and Spinning: A Guide to Worsteds from the Spinning-Wheel	Teal, Peter			SS&D	10	2	38	Sp 79	72
Books and Reviews	Hand Woven Place Mats	Heartz, Robert F.			H&C	6	1		Wi 54	61
Books and Reviews	Hand-Loom Weaving	Hooper, Luther			WJ	5	1	17	Su 80	47
Books and Reviews	Hand-Loom Weaving	Hooper, Luther			H&C	2	4		Fa 51	61
Books and Reviews	Handbook of American Crewel Embroidery, A	Baker, Muriel L.			WJ	8	1	29	Su 83	53
Books and Reviews	Handbook of Designs and Devices	Hornung, Clarence P.			H&C	3	4		Fa 52	62
Books and Reviews	Handbook of Dyes from Natural Materials, A	Bliss, Anne			SS&D	13	2	50	Sp 82	63
Books and Reviews	Handbook of Dyes from Natural Materials, A	Bliss, Anne			Fa	9	4		J/A 82	52
Books and Reviews	Handbook of Dyes from Natural Materials, A	Bliss, Anne			Hw	2	4		Se 81	79
Books and Reviews	Handbook of Early American Decoration	Cramer, Edith			H&C	2	2		Sp 51	60
Books and Reviews	Handbook of Time Saving Tables for Weavers Spinners and Dyers	Roth, Bettie G.; Chris Schulz			WJ	8	1	29	Su 83	51
Books and Reviews	Handbook of Timesaving Tables for Weavers, Spinners and Dyers	Roth, Bettie G.; Chris Shulz			Hw	5	4		S/O 84	14
Books and Reviews	Handbook of Weaves	Oelsner, G. H.			H&C	2	2		Sp 51	60
Books and Reviews	Handbook of Weaves, A	Oelsner, E. H.			Fa	3	1		J/F 76	4
Books and Reviews	Handbook of Weaves, A	Oelsner, G. H.			SS&D	7	1	25	Wi 75	34
Books and Reviews	Handbook of Weaves, A	Oelsner, G. H.			H&C	13	3		Su 62	44
Books and Reviews	Handbook of Weaves, A	Oelsner, G. H.			Iw	2	4		Su 77	35
Books and Reviews	Handcraft Simplified	Amon, Martha; Ruth Rawson			H&C	12	3		Su 61	61
Books and Reviews	Handicrafts in Italy	Matteini, Cesare, ed.			H&C	20	3		Su 69	42
Books and Reviews	Handicrafts of New England	Eaton, Allen H.			H&C	1	1		Ap 50	52
Books and Reviews	Handknitter's Handbook, The	Stanley, Montse	√		Kn	3	2	6	Sp 87	50
Books and Reviews	Handknitter's Handbook, The	Stanley, Montse			TM			14	D/J 87	76
Books and Reviews	Handloom Construction: A Practical Guide for the Non-Expert	Koster, Joan			Iw	5	3		Su 80	71
Books and Reviews	Handloom Weaves, Enlarged Edition, The	Tidball, Harriet; Virginia I. Harvey (Additions)	√		PWC	4	1	11		54
Books and Reviews	Handloom Weaves, The	Tidball, Harriet	√		WJ	9	4	36	Sp 85	78
Books and Reviews	Handloom Weaves, The	Tidball, Harriet			Hw	6	3		Su 85	20
Books and Reviews	Handloom Weaves, The	Tidball, Harriet			H&C	9	2		Sp 58	59
Books and Reviews	Handloom Weaving	Orman, P.			H&C	6	1		Wi 54	61

SUBJECT	TITLE	AUTHOR	IL	INST	JOUR	VOL	NO	ISS	DATE	PAGE
Books and Reviews	Handloom Weaving Technology	Fannin, Allen A.			Fa	7	6		N/D 80	65
Books and Reviews	Handloom Weaving Technology	Fannin, Allen A.			WJ	5	4	20	Sp 81	44
Books and Reviews	Handloom Weaving Technology	Fannin, Allen A.			Iw	5	1		Wi 79	58
Books and Reviews	Handmade Felt	Ekert, Marianne	√		WJ	10	2	38	Fa 85	82
Books and Reviews	Handmade Felt	Ekert, Marianne			Hw	6	3		Su 85	20
Books and Reviews	Handmade Rugs	Aller, Doris			H&C	5	2		Sp 54	15
Books and Reviews	Handmade Rugs	Marmoff, Kathryn Andrews			H&C	9	2		Sp 58	60
Books and Reviews	Hands on Rigid Heddle Weaving	Davenport, Betty	√		PWC	5	1	15		55
Books and Reviews	Hands on Weaving	Liebler, Barbara			TM			11	J/J 87	72
Books and Reviews	Handspindles	Hochberg, Bette			WJ	1	4	4	Ap 77	26
Books and Reviews	Handspindles	Hochberg, Bette			WJ	5	2	18	Fa 80	32
Books and Reviews	Handspindles	Hochberg, Bette			SS&D	9	1	33	Wi 77	41
Books and Reviews	Handspindles	Hochberg, Bette			S-O	4			80	15
Books and Reviews	Handspindles	Hockberg, Bette			Iw	2	3		Sp 77	32
Books and Reviews	Handspinners Guide to Selling, The	Simmons, Paula			S-O	3			79	11
Books and Reviews	Handspinners Handbook	Hochberg, Bette	√		Fa	4	2		M/A 77	41
Books and Reviews	Handspinner's Guide to Selling, The	Simmons, Paula			SS&D	11	3	43	Su 80	74
Books and Reviews	Handspinner's Handbook	Hochberg, Bette			SS&D	8	2	30	Sp 77	38
Books and Reviews	Handspinner's Handbook	Hockberg, Bette			Iw	2	3		Sp 77	32
Books and Reviews	Handspinning	Leadbeater, Eliza			SS&D	7	4	28	Fa 76	65
Books and Reviews	Handspinning	Leadbeater, Eliza			Iw	2	3		Sp 77	32
Books and Reviews	Handspinning: Art and Technique	Fannin, Allen			SS&D	2	2	6	Sp 71	34
Books and Reviews	Handspinning: Art and Technique	Fannin, Allen			H&C	23	6		N/D 72	41
Books and Reviews	Handspinning—Art and Technique	Fannin, Allen			Iw	2	3		Sp 77	31
Books and Reviews	Handspinning: Art & Technique	Fannin, Allen			WJ	6	4	24	Sp 82	59
Books and Reviews	Handspinning: Art & Technique	Fannin, Allen			H&C	22	2		Sp 71	45
Books and Reviews	Handspinning Cotton	Linder, Olive: Harry Linder			WJ	2	4	8	Ap 78	39
Books and Reviews	Handspinning Cotton	Linder, Olive; Harry Linder			S-O	3			79	10
Books and Reviews	Handspinning Flax	Linder, Olive; Harry Linder	√		WJ	12	1	45	Su 87	70
Books and Reviews	Handspinning Flax	Linder, Olive; Harry Linder			Hw	7	5		N/D 86	14
Books and Reviews	Handspinning Flax	Linder, Olive; Harry Linder			S-O	10	3		Fa 86	48
Books and Reviews	Handspun Crochet Book, The	Millard, Nancy			S-O	8	4		Wi 84	11
Books and Reviews	Handspun Project Book, The	Kahn, Deborah, ed.			Iw	4	2		Sp 79	61
Books and Reviews	Handspun Project Book, The	Kahn, Debra, ed.			S-O	8	4		Wi 84	11
Books and Reviews	Handweavers' Instruction Manual	Tidball, Harriet Douglas			H&C	4	4		Fa 53	60
Books and Reviews	Handweaver's Pattern Book, A	Davison, Marguerite P.			Fa	3	1		J/F 76	4
Books and Reviews	Handweaver's Pattern Book, The	Plath, Iona			WJ	8	1	29	Su 83	53
Books and Reviews	Handweaver's Source Book, A	Davison, Marguerite Porter, ed.			H&C	5	1		Wi 53	60
Books and Reviews	Handweaver's Workbook	Thorpe, Heather G.			SS&D	6	2	22	Sp 75	63
Books and Reviews	Handweaver's Workbook, A	Thorpe, Heather G.			H&C	7	3		Su 56	59
Books and Reviews	Handweaver's Workbook, A	Thorpe, Heather G.			H&C	17	4		Fa 66	43
Books and Reviews	Handweaving	Plath, Iona			H&C	16	1		Wi 65	43
Books and Reviews	Handweaving	Schluter, Lis			SS&D	4	4	16	Fa 73	63
Books and Reviews	Handweaving, An Introduction to Weaving on 2, 3, 4 Harnesses	Duchemin, Mad			Fa	3	1		J/F 76	6
Books and Reviews	Handweaving and Cloth Design	Straub, Marianne			SS&D	9	2	34	Sp 78	47
Books and Reviews	Handweaving and Cloth Design	Straub, Marianne			Iw	2	4		Su 77	36
Books and Reviews	Handweaving: Designs and Instructions	Becher, Lotte			H&C	6	2		Sp 55	61
Books and Reviews	Handweaving in Cape Berton	Mackley, M. Florence			H&C	24	3		M/J 73	6

SUBJECT	TITLE	AUTHOR	IL	INST	JOUR	VOL	NO	ISS	DATE	PAGE
Books and Reviews	Handweaving Notes for Teachers	Mairet, Ethel			H&C	3	1		Wi 51	62
Books and Reviews	Handwoven	Guagliumi, Susan			WJ	1	3	3	Ja 77	32
Books and Reviews	Handwoven	Guagliumi, Susan			SS&D	8	2	30	Sp 77	38
Books and Reviews	Handwoven Embroidery Weaves	Beck, Dorothy; Hazel Chase			SS&D	2	1	5	De 70	31
Books and Reviews	Handwoven Embroidery Weaves	Beck, Dorothy; Hazel Chase			H&C	16	3		Su 65	43
Books and Reviews	Handwoven, Tailormade	Alderman, Sharon D.; Kathryn Wertenberger			Fa	10	1		J/F 83	58
Books and Reviews	Handwoven, Tailormade, A Tandem Guide to Fabric Designing, Weaving, Sewing and Tailoring	Alderman, Sharon D.; Kathryn Wertenberger			WJ	7	3	27	Wi 82	49
Books and Reviews	Handwoven Textiles of Early New England: The Legacy of a Rural People 1640-1880	Bogdonoff, Nancy Dick			SS&D	7	1	25	Wi 75	34
Books and Reviews	Hard Crochet	Dittrick, Mark	√		Fa	5	3		M/J 78	59
Books and Reviews	Harmony Guide To Knitting Stitches, The	Lyric Books			TM			9	F/M 87	74
Books and Reviews	Harness Lace	Nass, Ulla			SS&D	9	4	36	Fa 78	80
Books and Reviews	Harness Lace	Nass, Ulla			WJ	7	3	27	Wi 82	48
Books and Reviews	Harness-Lace	Nass, Ulla			Iw	3	3		Sp 78	50
Books and Reviews	Havasupai Baskets and Their Makers: 1930-1940	McKee, Barbara; Edwin McKee; Joyce Herold			TMJ	4	2		75	80
Books and Reviews	Hawaii Dye Plants and Dye Recipes	Krohn, Val Frieling	√		Fa	9	4		J/A 82	52
Books and Reviews	Hawaii Dye Plants and Dye Recipes	Krohn, Val Frieling			WJ	8	2	30	Fa 83	65
Books and Reviews	Hawaiian Shirt: Its Art and Its History, The	Steele, Tommy	√		Fa	12	3		M/J 85	54
Books and Reviews	Heirlooms from Old Looms — A Catalog of Coverlets Owned by the Colonial Coverlet Guild of America & its Members	Swygert, Mrs. Luther M., ed.			H&C	7	1		Wi 55	60
Books and Reviews	Heritage Linens Interpreted in Profile	Young, Helen D.			H&C	10	4		Fa 59	59
Books and Reviews	Heritage Linens with Modern Ideas	Young, Helen D			H&C	10	4		Fa 59	59
Books and Reviews	Hidden Language of Symbols in Oriental Rugs, The	Raphaelian, H. M.			H&C	5	1		Wi 53	61
Books and Reviews	Hierba, Montaña y El Arbol de la Vida en San Pedro Sacatepequez, Guatemala	Barrios, Lina E.			WJ	9	2	34	Fa 84	78
Books and Reviews	Highland Maya: Patterns of Life and Clothing in Indian Guatemala, The	Bunch, Roland; Roger Bunch			SS&D	9	3	35	Su 78	96
Books and Reviews	Hispanic Costume 1450-1530	Anderson, Ruth Matilda			WJ	8	3	31	Wi 83	64
Books and Reviews	History of Dyed Textiles, A	Robinson, Stuart			H&C	21	3		Su 70	39
Books and Reviews	History of Technology, A	Singer, Charles, ed., et al.			H&C	8	2		Sp 57	59
Books and Reviews	History of Textile Art, A	Geijer, Agnes			WJ	7	1	25	Su 82	63
Books and Reviews	History of Textiles, A	Wilson, Kax			WJ	4	4	16	Ap 80	26
Books and Reviews	History of Textiles, A	Wilson, Kax			Fa	8	6		N/D 81	73
Books and Reviews	History of Textiles, A	Wilson, Kax			Iw	5	1		Wi 79	64
Books and Reviews	Hobby Book of Stenciling and Brush-Stroke Painting, The	Yates, Raymond F.			H&C	3	1		Wi 51	63
Books and Reviews	Home Dyeing with Natural Dyes	Furry, Margaret S.; Bess M. Viemont			SS&D	5	2	18	Sp 74	68
Books and Reviews	Homemade Money	Brabec, Barbara	√		Hw	6	2		M/A 85	72
Books and Reviews	Homespun to Factory Made: Woolen Textiles in America, 1776–1876	Merrimack Valley Textile Museum			SS&D	10	1	37	Wi 78	77
Books and Reviews	Hooked Rugs and Ryas	Parker, Xenia Ley			H&C	24	3		M/J 73	6
Books and Reviews	Hooked Rugs & Ryas	Parker, Zenia Ley			SS&D	4	3	15	Su 73	53
Books and Reviews	House and Garden Complete Guide to Interior Decoration, Fifth Edition	Editors of House and Garden			H&C	5	1		Wi 53	59
Books and Reviews	How to Create Your Own Designs	Meilach, Dona Z.; Jay Hinz; Bill Hinz			SS&D	6	4	24	Fa 75	31
Books and Reviews	How to Enter and Win Fabric and Fiber Crafts Contests	Gadney, Alan			Fa	10	4		J/A 83	49

SUBJECT	TITLE	AUTHOR	IL	INST	JOUR	VOL	NO	ISS	DATE	PAGE
Books and Reviews	How to Identify Persian Rugs and Other Oriental Rugs	May, C. J. Delabere			H&C	5	4		Fa 54	58
Books and Reviews	How to Know Oriental Carpets & Rugs	Jacoby, Heinrich			H&C	5	4		Fa 54	59
Books and Reviews	How to Know the Wild Flowers	Dana, Mrs. William Starr			H&C	22	3		Su 71	43
Books and Reviews	How to Make Braided Rugs	Altpeter, Dorothy; Corinne Anderson; Margaret Thostesen			H&C	2	1		Wi 50	62
Books and Reviews	How to Make Draperies and Slipcovers	Brostrom, Ethel; Harry Marinsky			H&C	2	3		Su 51	63
Books and Reviews	How to Make Gloves	Close, Eunice			H&C	2	1		Wi 50	62
Books and Reviews	How to Make Money with Your Crafts	Clark, Leta W.			SS&D	5	2	18	Sp 74	68
Books and Reviews	How to Make More Money from Your Crafts	Dowd, Merle			Iw	1	4		Su 76	29
Books and Reviews	How to Make Sewing Patterns	McCunn, Donald H.			TM			3	F/M 86	76
Books and Reviews	How to Sell Your Art and Crafts	Holz, Loretta			Iw	2	4		Su 77	34
Books and Reviews	How to Sell Your Arts and Crafts: A Marketing Guide for Creative People	Holz, Loretta			SS&D	9	2	34	Sp 78	49
Books and Reviews	How to Sell Your Handicraft	Hart, Robert G.			H&C	5	1		Wi 53	59
Books and Reviews	How to Start Your Own Craft Business	Genfan, Herb; Lyn Taetzsch			H&C	26	1		J/F 75	28
Books and Reviews	How to Survive & Prosper as an Artist	Michels, Caroll	√		Hw	6	2		M/A 85	71
Books and Reviews	How to Weave	Clack Handcrafts			H&C	3	1		Wi 51	61
Books and Reviews	How to Weave Fine Cloth	Scarlett, James D.			WJ	10	2	38	Fa 85	81
Books and Reviews	How to Weave Fine Cloth	Scarlett, James D.			SS&D	13	2	50	Sp 82	62
Books and Reviews	How to Weave Fine Cloth	Scarlett, James D.			WJ	7	1	25	Su 82	63
Books and Reviews	How to Weave Fine Cloth	Scarlett, James D.			Hw	2	3		My 81	72
Books and Reviews	How to Weave Linens	Worst, Edward F.			H&C	4	2		Sp 53	61
Books and Reviews	Hundred and One Questions for Spinners, A	Amos, Alden, et al.			Iw	4	1		Wi 78	54
Books and Reviews	Hundred and One Questions for Spinners, A	Straw Into Gold			WJ	3	2	10	Oc 78	46
Books and Reviews	I Can Spin a Different Thread	Milner, Ann			Iw	5	3		Su 80	70
Books and Reviews	Ideas for Fabric Printing and Dyeing	Gooch, Peter H.			SS&D	7	1	25	Wi 75	35
Books and Reviews	Identification of Textile Fibres — Qualitative and Quantiative Analysis of Fibre Blends, The	Luniak, Bruno			H&C	5	3		Su 54	58
Books and Reviews	Identification of Vegetable Fibres	Catling, Dorothy; John Grayson			WJ	8	3	31	Wi 83	67
Books and Reviews	Ikat	Van Gelder, Lydia			SS&D	13	2	50	Sp 82	62
Books and Reviews	Ikat	Van Gelder, Lydia			Fa	8	3		M/J 81	50
Books and Reviews	Ikat: An Introduction Japanese Ikat—Warp—Weft—Figure	Ritch, Diane; Yoshiko Wada			SS&D	7	1	25	Wi 75	34
Books and Reviews	Ikat Technique	Battenfield, Jackie			Fa	5	5		S/O 78	82
Books and Reviews	Ikat Technique	Battenfield, Jackie			SS&D	10	2	38	Sp 79	72
Books and Reviews	Illustrated Guide to Making Oriental Rugs, An	Scott, Gordon W.	√		WJ	10	4	40	Sp 86	82
Books and Reviews	Illustrated Guide to Making Oriental Rugs, An	Scott, Gordon W.	√		Fa	12	6		N/D 85	46
Books and Reviews	Illustrated Guide to Making Oriental Rugs, An	Scott, Gordon W.			Hw	8	1		J/F 87	16
Books and Reviews	Illustrated Guide to Making Oriental Rugs, An	Scott, Gordon W.			TM			2	D/J 85	78
Books and Reviews	Illustrated Guide to Making Oriental Rugs, An	Scott, Gordon W.	√		PWC	4	1	11		53
Books and Reviews	In Celebration of the Curious Mind	Rogers, Nora; Martha Stanley, eds.			Hw	4	3		M/J 83	13
Books and Reviews	In Celebration of the Curious Mind—A Festschrift to Honor Anne Blinks on Her 80th Birthday	Rogers, Nora; Martha Stanley, eds.			WJ	8	1	29	Su 83	52
Books and Reviews	In Praise of Hands	Paz, Octavio			SS&D	6	4	24	Fa 75	31

SUBJECT	TITLE	AUTHOR	IL	INST	JOUR	VOL	NO	ISS	DATE	PAGE
Books and Reviews	In the Heart of Pennsylvania	Lasansky, Jeannette, ed.			TM			3	F/M 86	78
Books and Reviews	Incredible Secret Money Machine, The	Lancaster, Don			Iw	4	1		Wi 78	54
Books and Reviews	Index of American Design, The	Christensen, Erwin O.	√		H&C	2	1		Wi 50	59
Books and Reviews	Index of American Design, The	Christensen, Erwin O.			H&C	10	2		Sp 59	60
Books and Reviews	Index to Handweaver & Craftsman: 1950 — 1965	Potomac Craftsmen of Washington, D. C., ed.			H&C	18	2		Sp 67	44
Books and Reviews	Index to How to Do It Information 1981	Norman Lathrop Enterprises, publ			WJ	7	3	27	Wi 82	51
Books and Reviews	Indian and Eskimo Artifacts of North America	Miles, Charles			H&C	14	3		Su 63	43
Books and Reviews	Indian Art of the Americas	Appleton, LeRoy H.			H&C	1	3		Fa 50	60
Books and Reviews	Indian Basket Weaving	Navajo School of Indian Basketry			H&C	23	3		M/J 72	24
Books and Reviews	Indian Basket Weaving: How to Weave Pomo, Yurok, Pima and Navajo Baskets	Newman, Sandra Corrie	√		Fa	4	1		J/F 77	40
Books and Reviews	Indian Basket Weaving: How to Weave Pomo, Yurok, Pima and Navajo Baskets	Newman, Sandra Corrie			Iw	1	1		Fa 75	20
Books and Reviews	Indian Blankets and Their Makers: The Navaho	James, George Wharton			SS&D	6	2	22	Sp 75	64
Books and Reviews	Indian Clothing Before Cortes	Anawalt, Patricia Rieff			Fa	9	6		N/D 82	58
Books and Reviews	Indian Costumes from Guatemala	Deuss, Krystyna	√		WJ	9	2	34	Fa 84	78
Books and Reviews	Indian Crafts of Guatemala & El Salvador	Osborne, Lily			H&C	17	2		Sp 66	43
Books and Reviews	Indian Embroideries, Vol.II	Irwin, John; Margaret Hall			TMJ	4	2		75	80
Books and Reviews	Indian Life Crafts	Norbeck, Oscar E.			H&C	9	2		Sp 58	61
Books and Reviews	Indian Painted and Printed Fabrics	Irwin, John; Margaret Hall			TMJ	3	4		De 73	46
Books and Reviews	Indiana Coverlet Weavers and Their Coverlets	Montgomery, Pauline			SS&D	7	1	25	Wi 75	34
Books and Reviews	Indiana Coverlet Weavers and Their Coverlets	Montgomery, Pauline			TMJ	4	2		75	81
Books and Reviews	Indigo and the Antiquity of Dyeing	Gerber, Frederick H.			WJ	2	2	6	Oc 77	34
Books and Reviews	Indigo and the Antiquity of Dyeing	Gerber, Frederick H.			SS&D	9	1	33	Wi 77	40
Books and Reviews	Indigo and the Antiquity of Dyeing	Gerber, Frederick H.			Iw	3	2		Wi 78	43
Books and Reviews	Indigo, From Seed to Dye	Miller, Dorothy			WJ	7	2	26	Fa 82	58
Books and Reviews	Indigo from Seed to Dye	Miller, Dorothy			Hw	3	4		Se 82	16
Books and Reviews	Indigo: From Seed to Dye	Miller, Dorothy			TM			2	D/J 85	76
Books and Reviews	Indigo: From Seed to Dye	Miller, Dorothy	√		PWC	3	3	9		68
Books and Reviews	Influence of Ottoman Turkish Textiles and Costume in Eastern Europe, The	Gervers, Veronika			Fa	10	5		S/O 83	57
Books and Reviews	Influence of Ottoman Turkish Textiles and Costumes in Eastern Europe, The	Gervers, Veronika			WJ	8	2	30	Fa 83	65
Books and Reviews	Initiation A La Creation Dentelliere (French)	Van Steyvoort, Colette			WJ	8	4	32	Sp 84	67
Books and Reviews	Inkle Loom Weaving	Holland, Nina			SS&D	5	2	18	Sp 74	68
Books and Reviews	Inkle Path to Weaving, The	Folts, Teresa			WJ	2	3	7	Ja 78	34
Books and Reviews	Inkle Path to Weaving, The	Folts, Teressa			SS&D	9	3	35	Su 78	94
Books and Reviews	Inkle Weaving	Bradley, Lavinia			WJ	8	3	31	Wi 83	67
Books and Reviews	Inkle Weaving	Bradley, Lavinia	√		Hw	4	4		S/O 83	24
Books and Reviews	Inkle Weaving	Bradley, Lavinia	√		PWC			4	Ja 83	69
Books and Reviews	Inkle Weaving	Bress, Helene			SS&D	7	2	26	Sp 76	34
Books and Reviews	Inkle Weaving	Bress, Helene			H&C	26	5		Oc 75	14
Books and Reviews	Interior Decorating the Handloom Way	Tidball, Harriet			H&C	9	3		Su 58	59
Books and Reviews	Interlacing: The Elemental Fabric	Larsen, Jack Lenor; Betty Freudenheim	√		WJ	12	2	46	Fa 87	66
Books and Reviews	International Basketry for Weavers and Collectors	Will, Christoph			TM			10	A/M 87	76

SUBJECT	TITLE	AUTHOR	IL	INST	JOUR	VOL	NO	ISS	DATE	PAGE
Books and Reviews	International Handspinning Directory and Handbook 1971	Chapin, Doloria, ed.			SS&D	2	2	6	Sp 71	34
Books and Reviews	International Needlework Designs	Silverstein, Mira			Fa	5	6		N/D 78	74
Books and Reviews	Into Indigo: African Textiles and Dyeing Techniques	Polakoff, Claire			WJ	5	1	17	Su 80	48
Books and Reviews	Introducing Dyeing and Printing	Ash, Beryl; Anthony Dyson			SS&D	5	1	17	Wi 73	77
Books and Reviews	Introducing Rushcraft	Whitbourn, K.			H&C	21	1		Wi 70	42
Books and Reviews	Introducing Weaving	Shillinglaw, Phyl			SS&D	5	1	17	Wi 73	77
Books and Reviews	Introducing Weaving	Shillinglaw, Phyl			H&C	23	5		S/O 72	35
Books and Reviews	Introduction to Natural Dyeing, An	Thresh, Robert; Christine Thresh			SS&D	4	3	15	Su 73	53
Books and Reviews	Introduction to the Eucalypts: Substantive Dyes, An	Walsh, Joan Lea			WJ	3	2	10	Oc 78	47
Books and Reviews	Investigative Method of Natural Dyeing, The	Gerber, Fred			Iw	3	4		Su 78	45
Books and Reviews	Investigative Method of Natural Dyeing, The	Gerber, Frederick H.			WJ	3	3	11	Ja 79	42
Books and Reviews	Irish Crocheted Lace	Kliot, Jules; Kaethe Kliot, eds.			WJ	5	1	17	Su 80	47
Books and Reviews	Irish Spinning, Dyeing and Weaving: An Anthology	Mitchell, Lillias			SS&D	18	3	71	Su 87	73
Books and Reviews	Islamic Carpets from the Joseph V. McMullan Collection	Arts Council of Great Britain			TMJ	3	4		De 73	46
Books and Reviews	Itchiku Kubota: Kimono in the Tsujigahana Tradition (catalogue)	Barton, Jane; et al.			Hw	6	3		Su 85	14
Books and Reviews	Jacob Angstadt Designs Drawn from His Weavers Patron Book	Holroyd, Ruth N., ed			SS&D	7	4	28	Fa 76	65
Books and Reviews	Jacob Angstadt—His Weavers Patron Book	Holroyd, Ruth N., ed			SS&D	7	4	28	Fa 76	65
Books and Reviews	Jahrbuch Textil 85/86	Sterk, Beatrijs; Dietmar Laue, eds.			Hw	7	4		S/O 86	10
Books and Reviews	Japanese Costume and Textile Arts	Noma, Seiroku			Hw	6	3		Su 85	14
Books and Reviews	Japanese Costume and Textile Arts	Noma, Seiroku			TMJ	4	2		75	81
Books and Reviews	Japanese Country Weaving	Maxson, Mary Lou			WJ	3	3	11	Ja 79	43
Books and Reviews	Japanese Ikat Weaving	Tomita, Jun; Noriko Tomita	√		Fa	10	3		M/J 83	54
Books and Reviews	Japanese Ikat Weaving	Tomita, Jun; Noriko Tomita			WJ	8	2	30	Fa 83	64
Books and Reviews	Japanese Ikat Weaving	Tomita, Jun; Noriko Tomita			Hw	4	5		N/D 83	14
Books and Reviews	Japanese Ikat Weaving	Tomita, Jun; Noriko Tomita			Hw	6	3		Su 85	14
Books and Reviews	Japanese Papermaking: Traditions, Tools and Techniques	Barrett, Timothy			Fa	13	1		J/F 86	45
Books and Reviews	Japanese Stencil Designs	Tuer, Andrew W.	√		Fa	10	1		J/F 83	58
Books and Reviews	Japanese Stencil Dyeing—Paste Resist Techniques	Nakano, Eisha; Barbara B. Stephan			WJ	8	1	29	Su 83	51
Books and Reviews	Japanese Stencil Dyeing: Paste Resist Techniques	Nakano, Eisha; Barbara B. Stephan			Hw	6	3		Su 85	14
Books and Reviews	Japanese Stencil Dyeing: Paste-Resist Techniques	Nakano, Eisha; Barbara B. Stephan	√		Fa	10	3		M/J 83	53
Books and Reviews	Javanese Batiks	Arensberg, Susan MacMillan			WJ	8	2	30	Fa 83	65
Books and Reviews	Jean Wilson's Soumak Workbook	Wilson, Jean			SS&D	14	1	53	Wi 82	65
Books and Reviews	Jigging...100% Hand Worsted	Reese, Sharron			Hw	5	3		Su 84	18
Books and Reviews	Jigging...100% Hand Worsted	Reese, Sharron			S-O	8	2		Su 84	51
Books and Reviews	Jodai-gire: 7th and 8th Century Textiles in Japan from the Shosoin and Horyu-ji	Matsumoto, Kaneo			Fa	13	1		J/F 86	45
Books and Reviews	Jodai-Gire, 7th and 8th Century Textiles in Japan from the Shoso-in and Horyu-ji	Matsumoto, Kaneo			Hw	8	1		J/F 87	18

SUBJECT	TITLE	AUTHOR	IL	INST	JOUR	VOL	NO	ISS	DATE	PAGE
Books and Reviews	Johanna Brunsson: Pionjär Inom Svensk Vävkonst	Werner Gustaf, publ.	√		PWC	4	4	14		54
Books and Reviews	Joinings, Edges, and Trims	Wilson, Jean	√		Fa	11	3		M/J 84	58
Books and Reviews	Joinings, Edges, and Trims	Wilson, Jean			SS&D	15	1	57	Wi 83	103
Books and Reviews	Joinings, Edges, and Trims	Wilson, Jean			WJ	8	3	31	Wi 83	68
Books and Reviews	Joinings, Edges, and Trims	Wilson, Jean	√		PWC	3	2	8		61
Books and Reviews	Joinings, Edges and Trims: Finishing Details for Handcrafted Products	Wilson, Jean			Hw	5	1		J/F 84	22
Books and Reviews	Joy of Crafts	Blue Mountain Crafts Council, The			Iw	1	1		Fa 75	20
Books and Reviews	Joy of Hand Weaving, Second Edition, The	Tod, Osma Gallinger			H&C	15	3		Su 64	43
Books and Reviews	Joy of Handweaving, The	Gallinger, Osma			H&C	1	1		Ap 50	52
Books and Reviews	Joy of Handweaving, The	Gallinger, Osma Couch			H&C	1	3		Fa 50	62
Books and Reviews	Joy of Spinning, The	Kluger, Marilyn			SS&D	3	1	9	Wi 71	38
Books and Reviews	Joy of Spinning, The	Kluger, Marilyn			H&C	23	1		J/F 72	32
Books and Reviews	Joy of Spinning, The	Kluger, Marilyn			Iw	2	3		Sp 77	32
Books and Reviews	Junius B. Bird Conference on Andean Textiles, The	Rowe, Ann Pollard, ed.	√		WJ	12	1	45	Su 87	70
Books and Reviews	Junius B. Bird Pre-Columbian Textile Conference, May 19 and 20, 1973, The	Rowe, Ann P.; Elizabeth P. Benson; Anne-Louise Shaffer	√		Iw	5	4		Fa 80	75
Books and Reviews	Junius B. Bird Pre-Columbian Textile Conference, The	Rowe, Anne Pollard; Elizabeth P. Benson; Anne-Louise Schaffer, eds.			Fa	7	6		N/D 80	59
Books and Reviews	Jute, Fibre to Yarn	Atkinson, R. R.			H&C	16	3		Su 65	44
Books and Reviews	Kashmir Shawl, The	Pauly, Sarah Buie; Rebecca Wells Corrie			TMJ	4	2		75	80
Books and Reviews	Kaunista Kangaspuilla	Leinonen, Virpi			Hw	6	4		S/O 85	24
Books and Reviews	Kazak — Carpets of the Caucasus	Tschebull, Raoul			H&C	23	1		J/F 72	31
Books and Reviews	Keep Me Warm One Night	Burnham, Harold B.; Dorothy K. Burnham			SS&D	4	2	14	Sp 73	44
Books and Reviews	'Keep Me Warm One Night,' Early Handweaving in Eastern Canada	Burnham, Harold B.; Dorothy K. Burnham			TMJ	3	4		De 73	46
Books and Reviews	Keep Me Warm One Night: Early Handweaving in Eastern Canada	Burnham, Harold B.; Dorothy K. Burnham			H&C	24	1		J/F 73	28
Books and Reviews	Key to Weaving	Black, Mary E.			H&C	1	1		Ap 50	49
Books and Reviews	Kilim Ve Düz Dokuma Yaygilar	Acar, Belkis	√		TMJ	4	3		76	75
Books and Reviews	Kiton Acid Dye Sample Book of Wool Fibers, A	Scorgie, Jean, et al.			Hw	5	2		M/A 84	13
Books and Reviews	Knit Art	Cone, Ferne Geller	√		Fa	5	3		M/J 78	59
Books and Reviews	Knit to Fit — A Comprehensive Guide to Hand and Machine Knitting	Duncan, Ida Riley			H&C	14	3		Su 63	44
Books and Reviews	Knitted Lace Collars	Lorant, Tessa			Kn	4	1	9	Wi 87	60
Books and Reviews	Knitted Lace Doilies	Lorant, Tessa	√		Kn	4	1	9	Wi 87	60
Books and Reviews	Knitted Lace Edgings	Lorant, Tessa			Kn	1	2	2	S-S 85	79
Books and Reviews	Knitted Quilts & Flounces	Lorant, Tessa			Kn	1	2	2	S-S 85	79
Books and Reviews	Knitted Shawls & Wraps	Lorant, Tessa	√		Kn	4	1	9	Wi 87	60
Books and Reviews	Knitter's Almanac	Zimmermann, Elizabeth			Kn	1	1	1	F-W 84	14
Books and Reviews	Knitting Architect, The	Elalouf, Sion			TM			12	A/S 87	76
Books and Reviews	Knitting by Design	Erickson, Mary Anne; Eve Cohen			TM			14	D/J 87	76
Books and Reviews	Knitting & Crocheting Fun	Charles E. Tuttle Co., Inc. distr.			WJ	8	1	29	Su 83	53
Books and Reviews	Knitting from the British Isles	Starmore, Alice; Alice Matheson			Kn	2	1	3	F-W 85	79
Books and Reviews	Knitting from the Netherlands, Traditional Dutch Fishermen's Sweaters	van der Klift-Tellegen, Henriette			Kn	2	1	3	F-W 85	79

SUBJECT	TITLE	AUTHOR	IL	INST	JOUR	VOL	NO	ISS	DATE	PAGE
Books and Reviews	Knitting from the Top	Walker, Barbara			TM			9	F/M 87	76
Books and Reviews	Knitting in Plain English	Righetti, Maggie			SS&D	18	4	72	Fa 87	55
Books and Reviews	Knitting in Plain English	Righetti, Maggie			TM			11	J/J 87	73
Books and Reviews	Knitting in the Nordic Tradition	Lind, Vibeke			SS&D	18	1	69	Wi 86	38
Books and Reviews	Knitting in the Nordic Tradition	Lind, Vibeke			Kn	1	2	2	S-S 85	79
Books and Reviews	Knitting in the Nordic Tradition	Lind, Vibeke	√		Kn	3	1	5	F-W 86	70
Books and Reviews	Knitting in the Old Way	Gibson-Roberts, Priscilla A.			SS&D	17	3	67	Su 86	85
Books and Reviews	Knitting Lace	Abbey, Barbara			TM			9	F/M 87	76
Books and Reviews	Knitting Lace	Abbey, Barbara			Kn	1	2	2	S-S 85	79
Books and Reviews	Knitting Masterpieces	Herring, Ruth; Karen Manners	√		Kn	3	4	8	Fa 87	63
Books and Reviews	Knitting Masterpieces	Herring, Ruth; Karen Manners			TM			14	D/J 87	76
Books and Reviews	Knitting Now	Tubbs, Gabi	√		Kn	2	2	4	S-S 86	78
Books and Reviews	Knitting Primer, The	Specktor, Denyse			Fa	11	4		J/A 84	54
Books and Reviews	Knitting Primer, The	Specktor, Denyse			TM			6	A/S 86	84
Books and Reviews	Knitting Without Tears	Zimmermann, Elizabeth			TM			9	F/M 87	76
Books and Reviews	Knitting Without Tears	Zimmermann, Elizabeth			Kn	1	1	1	F-W 84	14
Books and Reviews	Knitting Workshop	Zimmermann, Elizabeth			Kn	1	1	1	F-W 84	14
Books and Reviews	Knots and Splices	Day, Cyrus L.			H&C	5	1		Wi 53	60
Books and Reviews	Kosode: 16th–19th Century Textiles from the Nomura Collection	Stinchecum, Amanda Mayer	√		Fa	13	3		M/J 86	59
Books and Reviews	Kosode, 16th and 19th Century Textiles from the Nomura Collection	Stinchecum, Amanda Mayer; Monica Bethe; Margot Paul			Hw	6	3		Su 85	14
Books and Reviews	Kume Himo Techniques of Japanese Plaiting	Kliot, Jules; Kaethe Kliot			WJ	3	1	9	Jy 78	35
Books and Reviews	Kumihimo, Japanese Silk Braiding Techniques	Martin, Catherine	√		WJ	11	4	44	Sp 87	73
Books and Reviews	Kumihimo: Japanese Silk Braiding Techniques	Martin, Catherine	√		Fa	14	1		J/F 87	21
Books and Reviews	Labrador Tea	Wipplinger, Michelle; Carol Reynolds; Elizabeth Black			Hw	3	2		Mr 82	22
Books and Reviews	Lace	Bath, Virginia Churchill			SS&D	11	1	41	Wi 79	32
Books and Reviews	Lace	van der Meulen-Nulle, L. W.			H&C	18	1		Wi 67	46
Books and Reviews	Lace and Lacey Weaves	Snyder, Mary E.	√		WJ	11	2	42	Fa 86	74
Books and Reviews	Lace and Lacey Weaves	Snyder, Mary E.			SS&D	4	4	16	Fa 73	63
Books and Reviews	Lace and Lacey Weaves	Snyder, Mary E.			Fa	3	1		J/F 76	4
Books and Reviews	Lace and Lacey Weaves	Snyder, Mary E.			H&C	12	2		Sp 61	59
Books and Reviews	Lace Index	Russell, Janet			Kn	1	2	2	S-S 85	79
Books and Reviews	Late Egyptian and Coptic Art	Brooklyn Museum			H&C	4	1		Wi 52	62
Books and Reviews	Latin American Brocades: Explorations in Supplementary Weft Techniques	Baizerman, Suzanne; Karen Searle			SS&D	8	2	30	Sp 77	37
Books and Reviews	Latin American Brocades: Explorations in Supplementary Weft Techniques	Baizerman, Suzanne; Karen Searle			WJ	6	4	24	Sp 82	57
Books and Reviews	Latin American Brocades: Explorations in Supplementary Weft Techniques	Baizerman, Suzanne; Karen Searle	√		Iw	3	2		Wi 78	42
Books and Reviews	Latvian Mittens	Upitis, Lizbeth	√		Kn	3	1	5	F-W 86	69
Books and Reviews	Latvian Mittens: Traditional Designs and Techniques	Upitis, Lizbeth			TM			6	A/S 86	84
Books and Reviews	Latvian Mittens: Traditional Designs and Techniques	Upitis, Lizbeth			PWC	1	1		No 81	58
Books and Reviews	Latvian Sashes, Belts and Bands	Dzevitis, Alexandra; Lilija Treimanis			WJ	7	3	27	Wi 82	49

SUBJECT	TITLE	AUTHOR	IL	INST	JOUR	VOL	NO	ISS	DATE	PAGE
Books and Reviews	Latviesu Jostas (Latvian Sashes, Belts and Bands)	Dzervitis, Aleksandra; Lilija Treimanis			SS&D	14	1	53	Wi 82	65
Books and Reviews	Latviesu Jostas/Latvian Sashes, Belts and Bands	Dzervitis, Aleksandra; Lilija Treimanis			Hw	4	3		M/J 83	12
Books and Reviews	Law (In Plain English) for Craftspeople, The	DuBoff, Leonard D.			WJ	9	3	35	Wi 85	84
Books and Reviews	Law (In Plain English) for Craftspeople, The	DuBoff, Leonard D.	√		Hw	6	2		M/A 85	71
Books and Reviews	Law (In Plain English) for Craftspeople, The	DuBoff, Leonard D.; Michael Scott, ed.			Fa	12	2		M/A 85	54
Books and Reviews	Le Flêché Authentique Du Québec	Hamelin, Véronique			WJ	8	2	30	Fa 83	63
Books and Reviews	Le Langage Du Tissu	Hugues, Patricia			WJ	8	3	31	Wi 83	65
Books and Reviews	Learn to Weave	Johnson, Nellie Sargent			H&C	1	1		Ap 50	52
Books and Reviews	Learning to Weave	Redding, Debbie	√		Fa	13	3		M/J 86	58
Books and Reviews	Learning to Weave with Debbie Redding	Redding, Debbie	√		WJ	9	4	36	Sp 85	78
Books and Reviews	Learning to Weave with Debbie Redding	Redding, Debbie	√		PWC	4	1	11		54
Books and Reviews	Legacy of the Great Wheel: Myths, History and Traditions with Practical Lessons, The	Turner, Katy			SS&D	15	1	57	Wi 83	103
Books and Reviews	Legacy of the Great Wheel, The	Turner, Katy			WJ	5	4	20	Sp 81	44
Books and Reviews	Legacy of the Great Wheel, The	Turner, Katy	√		Hw	2	3		My 81	71
Books and Reviews	Legend of the Bushwhacker Basket	Wetherbee, Martha; Nathan Taylor			SS&D	17	4	68	Fa 86	88
Books and Reviews	Legend of the Bushwhacker Basket	Wetherbee, Martha; Nathan Taylor			TM			10	A/M 87	76
Books and Reviews	Les Dentelles Aux Fuseaux Bobbin Lace (English Translation)	de Dillmont, Therese			SS&D	6	4	24	Fa 75	30
Books and Reviews	Let's Go Spinning: International Handspinning Directory and Handbook, 1971	Chapin, Doloria			H&C	22	3		Su 71	41
Books and Reviews	Letters of William Morris to His Family and Friends, The	Henderson, Philip, ed.			H&C	2	3		Su 51	61
Books and Reviews	Let's Get Technical: An Overview of Handwoven Pennsylvania Jacquard Coverlets: 1830-1860	Crosson, Janet Gray			SS&D	11	1	41	Wi 79	33
Books and Reviews	Let's Try Mushrooms for Color	Rice, Miriam C.			SS&D	6	4	24	Fa 75	29
Books and Reviews	Lichens for Vegetable Dyeing	Bolton, Eileen			H&C	24	1		J/F 73	28
Books and Reviews	Lichens for Vegetable Dyeing	Bolton, Eileen M.			H&C	12	1		Wi 61	59
Books and Reviews	Linen Heirlooms	Gallagher, Constance D. N.			WJ	8	1	29	Su 83	51
Books and Reviews	Linen Heirlooms	Gallagher, Constance D. N.			H&C	20	2		Sp 69	41
Books and Reviews	Lives and Works, Talks with Women Artists	Miller, Lynn F.; Sally S. Swenson			Fa	9	2		M/A 82	58
Books and Reviews	Living Crafts	Hughes, G. Bernard			H&C	6	1		Wi 54	63
Books and Reviews	Living with Llamas: Adventures, Photos, and a Practical Guide	Hart, Rosana	√		Fa	13	5		S/O 86	57
Books and Reviews	Logical Techniques of the Handloom Weaver Volume I, Warping and Beaming for a Treadle Loom	Wilkinson, Dorothy			H&C	16	4		Fa 65	43
Books and Reviews	Looking at Twills	Voiers, Leslie			Fa	11	4		J/A 84	54
Books and Reviews	Looking At Twills	Voiers, Leslie			SS&D	15	1	57	Wi 83	102
Books and Reviews	Looking At Twills	Voiers, Leslie			WJ	8	2	30	Fa 83	64
Books and Reviews	Looking at Twills	Voiers, Leslie			Hw	4	4		S/O 83	27
Books and Reviews	Looking at Twills	Voiers, Leslie			Hw	4	5		N/D 83	14
Books and Reviews	Looking at Twills	Voiers, Leslie			Hw	7	1		J/F 86	21
Books and Reviews	Looking at Twills	Voiers, Leslie	√		PWC	3	1	7		63
Books and Reviews	Loom and Spindle: Life Among the Early Mill Girls	Robinson, Harriet H.			Fa	9	2		M/A 82	53
Books and Reviews	Loom Book	Reed, Tim			SS&D	6	1	21	Wi 74	32

SUBJECT	TITLE	AUTHOR	IL	INST	JOUR	VOL	NO	ISS	DATE	PAGE
Books and Reviews	Loom Construction	Hjert, Jeri; Paul Von Rosensteil			SS&D	10	2	38	Sp 79	74
Books and Reviews	Loom Construction	Hjert, Jeri; Paul Von Rosenstiel			WJ	3	3	11	Ja 79	42
Books and Reviews	Loom Construction	Hjert, Jeri; Paul Von Rosenstiel			Fa	6	3		M/J 79	16
Books and Reviews	Loom Construction	Hjert, Jeri; Paul Von Rosenstiel			Iw	4	1		Wi 78	55
Books and Reviews	Loom to Build, A	Rogers, Carrie			WJ	4	2	14	Oc 79	38
Books and Reviews	Loom to Build, A	Rogers, Carrie			Iw	4	3		Su 79	66
Books and Reviews	Loom to Build, A	Rogers, Carrie M.			SS&D	11	1	41	Wi 79	32
Books and Reviews	Lore and Lure of Hooked Rugs, The	McGown, Pearl E.			H&C	18	3		Su 67	45
Books and Reviews	Lost and Found Traditions: Native American Art 1965–1985	Coe, Ralph T.	√		Hw	8	5		N/D 87	12
Books and Reviews	Lost and Found Traditions: Native American Art 1965-1985	Coe, Ralph T.			SS&D	19	1	73	Wi 87	52
Books and Reviews	Machine Knitter's Guide to Creating Fabrics, A	Lewis, Susanna E.; Julia Weissman			TM			5	J/J 86	12
Books and Reviews	Machine Knitter's Guide to Creating Fabrics: Jacquard, Lace, Intarsia, Ripple and More, A	Lewis, Susanna E.; Julia Weissman	√		Kn	3	1	5	F-W 86	71
Books and Reviews	Machine Knitter's Guide to Creating Fabrics, Jacquard, Lace, Intarsia, Ripple and More, A	Lewis, Susanna E.; Julia Weissman	√		PWC	4	2	12		53
Books and Reviews	Macrame Accessories	Meilach, Dona Z.	√		SS&D	4	3	15	Su 73	53
Books and Reviews	Macrame Book, The	Bress, Helene			SS&D	4	2	14	Sp 73	44
Books and Reviews	Macramé: Creative Design in Knotting	Meilach, Dona			H&C	22	2		Sp 71	43
Books and Reviews	Macramé: The Art of Creative Knotting	Harvey, Virginia I.			H&C	18	3		Su 67	43
Books and Reviews	Macrame, Weaving & Tapestry: Art in Fiber	Depas, Spencer			SS&D	5	1	17	Wi 73	77
Books and Reviews	Macrané: Knotting, Braiding & Twisting	Pesch, Imelda			H&C	22	2		Sp 71	45
Books and Reviews	Mad Weave Book, The	La Plantz, Shereen			TM			2	D/J 85	76
Books and Reviews	Mad Weave Book, The	LaPlantz, Shereen	√		WJ	10	2	38	Fa 85	82
Books and Reviews	Mad Weave Book, The	LaPlantz, Shereen			Hw	6	5		N/D 85	20
Books and Reviews	Made in New York State: Handwoven Coverlets 1820–1860	Partridge, Virginia			Hw	7	1		J/F 86	21
Books and Reviews	Made in New York State: Handwoven Coverlets 1820-1860	Partridge, Virginia Parslow; Rita J. Adrosko	√		Fa	13	4		J/A 86	61
Books and Reviews	Made In New York State: Handwoven Coverlets 1820-1860	Shaeffer, Margaret W. M., ed.	√		WJ	10	2	38	Fa 85	81
Books and Reviews	Made in Poland	Jarecka, Louise Llewellyn			H&C	1	3		Fa 50	64
Books and Reviews	Magdalena Abakanowicz	Jacob, Mary Jane; Magdalena Abakanowicz; Jasia Reichardt	√		Fa	10	5		S/O 83	58
Books and Reviews	Magic of Spinning, The	Channing, Marion			H&C	17	2		Sp 66	45
Books and Reviews	Magic Shuttle, The	Goodman, Deborah Lorme			WJ	8	3	31	Wi 83	65
Books and Reviews	Maker's Hand: A Close Look at Textile Structures, The	Collingwood, Peter	√		WJ	12	2	46	Fa 87	66
Books and Reviews	Maker's Hand: A Close Look at Textile Structures, The	Collingwood, Peter			TM			11	J/J 87	72
Books and Reviews	Maker's Hand: A Close Look at Textile Structures, The	Collingwood, Peter	√		PWC	5	1	15		52
Books and Reviews	Making Contemporary Rugs and Wall Hangings	Meilach, Donna			H&C	21	3		Su 70	41
Books and Reviews	Making It Legal: A Law Primer for the Craftmaker, Visual Artist, and Writer	Davidson, Marion; Martha Blue			Fa	6	6		N/D 79	51
Books and Reviews	Making It Legal: A Law Primer for the Craftmaker, Visual Artist, and Writer	Davidson, Marion; Martha Blue			Iw	5	1		Wi 79	63
Books and Reviews	Making Men's Clothes	Rhinehart, Jane			TM			7	O/N 86	72
Books and Reviews	Making Patchwork for Pleasure and Profit	Burbridge, Pauline			TM			3	F/M 86	78

SUBJECT	TITLE	AUTHOR	IL	INST	JOUR	VOL	NO	ISS	DATE	PAGE
Books and Reviews	Making Rugs for Pleasure and Profit	Koenig, Marion; Gill Speirs			WJ	6	4	24	Sp 82	60
Books and Reviews	Making Simple Clothes	Hamre, Ida; Hanne Meedam			WJ	6	4	24	Sp 82	58
Books and Reviews	Man is a Weaver	Baity, Elizabeth Chesley			H&C	2	1		Wi 50	61
Books and Reviews	Managements Workbooks for Self-Employed People	Dodd, Gerald R.			Hw	7	1		J/F 86	18
Books and Reviews	Mandala	Pasquini, Katie			Fa	11	5		S/O 84	52
Books and Reviews	Manly Art of Knitting, The	Fougner, Dave	√		Fa	5	3		M/J 78	59
Books and Reviews	Manual of Braiding, The	Speiser, Noémi			WJ	8	2	30	Fa 83	62
Books and Reviews	Manual of Braiding, The	Speiser, Noémi			Hw	4	4		S/O 83	24
Books and Reviews	Manual of Braiding, The	Speiser, Noemi	√		PWC	3	1	7		60
Books and Reviews	Manual of Engineering Drawing, A	French, Thomas; Charles Vierck			H&C	5	4		Fa 54	57
Books and Reviews	Manual of Hand-Made Bobbin Lace Work, A	Maidment, Margaret			SS&D	17	1	65	Wi 85	90
Books and Reviews	Manual of Hand-Made Bobbin Lace Work, A	Maidment, Margaret			H&C	6	2		Sp 55	62
Books and Reviews	Manual of Swedish Handweaving	Cyrus-Zetterström, Ulla	√		WJ	9	1	33	Su 84	60
Books and Reviews	Manual of Swedish Handweaving	Cyrus-Zetterström, Ulla			WJ	2	4	8	Ap 78	39
Books and Reviews	Manual of Swedish Handweaving	Cyrus-Zetterström, Ulla			SS&D	16	1	61	Wi 84	21
Books and Reviews	Manual of Swedish Handweaving	Cyrus-Zetterström, Ulla	√		PWC	3	2	8		62
Books and Reviews	Manual of Swedish Handweaving, The	Cyrus-Zetterström, Ulla			Hw	5	3		Su 84	18
Books and Reviews	Manuscript Notes on Weaving	Holmes, James			Hw	8	2		M/A 87	13
Books and Reviews	Manuscript Notes on Weaving	Holmes, James, M.S.A.	√		PWC	4	2	12		50
Books and Reviews	Maori Basketry for Beginners	Pendergrast, Mick			SS&D	9	4	36	Fa 78	82
Books and Reviews	Marion Foale's Classic Knitwear	Foale, Marion	√		Kn	3	4	8	Fa 87	62
Books and Reviews	Mary Meigs Atwater Recipe Book — Patterns for Handweavers	Mary Meigs Atwater Weavers' Guild			H&C	8	4		Fa 57	59
Books and Reviews	Mary Thomas's Book of Knitting Patterns	Thomas, Mary			Kn	1	2	2	S-S 85	79
Books and Reviews	Mary Thomas's Knitting Book	Thomas, Mary			TM			9	F/M 87	76
Books and Reviews	Master Dyers to the World—Techniques and Trade in Early Indian Dyed Cotton Textiles	Gittinger, Mattiebelle			WJ	7	4	28	Sp 83	48
Books and Reviews	Master Weaver Library, Volume 1, A Treasury for Beginners and Volume 2, All About Looms	Zielinski, S. A.			SS&D	11	3	43	Su 80	75
Books and Reviews	Master Weavers: Tapestry from the Dovecot Studios, 1912–1980	Scottish Arts Council	√		Fa	10	3		M/J 83	52
Books and Reviews	Master Weavers/Tapestry from the Dovecot Studios 1912–1980	Canongate Publishing Ltd., publ.			WJ	7	2	26	Fa 82	57
Books and Reviews	Mastercraftsmen of Ancient Peru	Sawyer, Alan R.			H&C	20	1		Wi 69	41
Books and Reviews	Masterpieces of Tapestry, from the Fourteenth to the Sixteenth Century	Souchal, Geneviève			TMJ	4	2		75	81
Books and Reviews	Mathematics in Western Culture	Kline, Morris			H&C	5	1		Wi 53	60
Books and Reviews	Maya Culture & Costume: A Catalogue of the Taylor Museum's E. B. Ricketson Collection of Guatemalan Textiles	Conte, Christine	√		WJ	10	1	37	Su 85	86
Books and Reviews	Maya of Guatemala, Their Life and Dress, The	Pettersen, Carmen L.			SS&D	8	4	32	Fa 77	72
Books and Reviews	McCall's Book of Quilts, The	McCall's Needlework and Crafts Publications, eds.			Iw	1	1		Fa 75	20
Books and Reviews	McCall's Guide — Interchangeable Yarns for Knit and Crochet Revised	Davis, Nancy, ed.			TM			1	O/N 85	76
Books and Reviews	McKay Modern English — German Dictionary	McKay, David			H&C	6	4		Fa 55	60
Books and Reviews	McKay Modern English — Swedish Dictionary	McKay, David			H&C	6	4		Fa 55	60
Books and Reviews	Meaning in Crafts	Mattie, Edward L.			H&C	10	3		Su 59	59

SUBJECT	TITLE	AUTHOR	IL	INST	JOUR	VOL	NO	ISS	DATE	PAGE
Books and Reviews	Medieval American Art — Masterpieces of the New World before Columbus	Kelemen, Pal			H&C	9	3		Su 58	60
Books and Reviews	Memory of a Landscape	Lundahl, Gunilla	√		Fa	12	4		J/A 85	48
Books and Reviews	Mennonite Quilts and Pieces	Tomlonson, Judy Schroeder			TM			3	F/M 86	78
Books and Reviews	Men's Custom Tailored Coats	Hostek, Stanley			TM			7	O/N 86	72
Books and Reviews	Men's Custom Tailored Pants	Hostek, Stanley			TM			7	O/N 86	72
Books and Reviews	Men's Custom Tailored Vests	Hostek, Stanley			TM			7	O/N 86	72
Books and Reviews	Merchants and Masterpieces: The Story of the Metropolitan Museum of Art	Tompkins, Calvin			H&C	21	3		Su 70	41
Books and Reviews	Merrimack Valley Textile Museum: A Guide to the Manuscript Collections, The	Wright, Helena, ed.			Hw	5	5		N/D 84	14
Books and Reviews	Methods of Dyeing — With Vegetable Dyes and Other Means	Pope, F. Whipple			H&C	13	1		Wi 62	44
Books and Reviews	Mexican Indian Costumes	Cordry, Donald; Dorothy Cordry			TMJ	3	4		De 73	46
Books and Reviews	Mexican Indian Costumes	Cordry, Donald; Dorothy Cordry			H&C	20	3		Su 69	41
Books and Reviews	Mexican Motifs	Tidball, Harriet			H&C	13	3		Su 62	43
Books and Reviews	Mexican Pick-Up Weave	Stirrup, Catherine A.			SS&D	3	1	9	Wi 71	38
Books and Reviews	Mexican Tapestry Weaving	Hall, Joanne			WJ	1	4	4	Ap 77	26
Books and Reviews	Mexican Tapestry Weaving	Hall, Joanne			SS&D	8	3	31	Su 77	61
Books and Reviews	Mexican Tapestry Weaving	Hall, Joanne	√		Fa	4	4		J/A 77	62
Books and Reviews	Midwest Weavers Conference Workshops, 1973	Rocky Mountain Weavers Guild			SS&D	5	3	19	Su 74	62
Books and Reviews	Millenium of Weaving in Chiapas, A	Morris, Walter F. Jr.	√		WJ	10	1	37	Su 85	87
Books and Reviews	Mittens to Knit	Becker, Mary Lamb			Kn	3	1	5	F-W 86	69
Books and Reviews	Modern Approach to Basketry with Fibers and Grasses, A	Meilach, Dona			Fa	4	1		J/F 77	43
Books and Reviews	Modern Oriental Carpets: A Buyer's Guide	Schlick, Donald			H&C	22	1		Wi 71	41
Books and Reviews	Modern Textile & Apparel Dictionary, The	Linton, George E., Ph.D. TexScD			H&C	26	2		Ap 75	24
Books and Reviews	Modern Textile Designer: Antonin Kybal	Kybal, Antonin			H&C	15	2		Sp 64	43
Books and Reviews	Modern Textile Dictionary, The	Linton, George			H&C	6	1		Wi 54	61
Books and Reviews	Modern Textile Dictionary, The	Linton, George E.			H&C	15	1		Wi 64	43
Books and Reviews	Mola Design Coloring Book: 45 Authentic Indian Designs from Panama	Shaffer, Frederick W.			Fa	11	1		J/F 84	58
Books and Reviews	Mola Design Coloring Book, The	Caraway, Caren			WJ	8	3	31	Wi 83	67
Books and Reviews	Molas	Auld, Rhoda L.	√		Fa	4	3		M/J 77	54
Books and Reviews	Molas — Folk Art of the Cuna Indians	Parker, Ann; Avon Neal	√		Fa	5	2		M/A 78	58
Books and Reviews	Molas: Folk Art of the Cuna Indians	Parker, Ann; Avon Neal			Iw	4	2		Sp 79	63
Books and Reviews	Mon Tricot 1500 Patterns	Cie des Editions de l'alma			TM			9	F/M 87	74
Books and Reviews	Monsterblad #11, Wool Weaving				H&C	10	1		Wi 59	61
Books and Reviews	Monsterblad Folder #10 Rya Rugs				H&C	9	4		Fa 58	59
Books and Reviews	Monsterblad Folder #12 Linen				H&C	9	4		Fa 58	60
Books and Reviews	Moorman Inlay Technique for Rigid Heddle Frame Looms	Searle, Karen			Hw	5	4		S/0 84	14
Books and Reviews	Moorman Inlay Technique for Rigid Heddle Frame Looms	Searle, Karen	√		PWC			6	Su 83	69
Books and Reviews	More Creative Textile Design — Color and Texture	Hartung, Rolf			H&C	16	4		Fa 65	44
Books and Reviews	More Linen Heirlooms	Gallagher, Constance			Hw	5	5		N/D 84	14
Books and Reviews	More Linen Heirlooms	Gallagher, Constance D.			SS&D	14	3	55	Su 83	61
Books and Reviews	More Linen Heirlooms	Galligher, Constance D.			WJ	7	4	28	Sp 83	48
Books and Reviews	More Than Four	Laughlin, Mary Elizabeth			SS&D	8	3	31	Su 77	61
Books and Reviews	More Than Four	Laughlin, Mary Elizabeth			Iw	2	4		Su 77	35

SUBJECT	TITLE	AUTHOR	IL	INST	JOUR	VOL	NO	ISS	DATE	PAGE
Books and Reviews	More Then Four	Laughlin, Mary Elizabeth			WJ	3	3	11	Ja 79	41
Books and Reviews	Mounting Handicraft	Kroncke, Grete			SS&D	4	2	14	Sp 73	44
Books and Reviews	Mounting Handicraft: Ideas and Instructuins for Assembling and Finishing	Kroncke, Grete			H&C	22	2		Sp 71	46
Books and Reviews	Multiple Harness Patterns from the Early 1700's	Abel, Isabel			Iw	5	1		Wi 79	65
Books and Reviews	Multiple Harness Patterns from the Early 1700's, The Snavely Patterns	Abel, Isabel I.			WJ	4	3	15	Ja 80	46
Books and Reviews	Multiple Harness Patterns from the Early 1700's — The Snavely Patterns	Abel, Isabel I.			SS&D	11	2	42	Sp 80	82
Books and Reviews	Multiple Tabby Weaves, based on Dr. William G. Bateman's Manuscript	Harvey, Virginia I., ed.			SS&D	13	2	50	Sp 82	63
Books and Reviews	Multiple Tabby Weaves. Based on Dr. William G. Bateman's Manuscript	Harvey, Virginia I., ed.			WJ	6	2	22	Fa 81	39
Books and Reviews	Multiple Tabby Weaves - Based on Dr. William G. Bateman's Manuscript	Harvey, Virginia I., ed.	√		PWC			5	Sp 83	68
Books and Reviews	Museum of Early American Tools, A	Sloane, Eric			H&C	15	3		Su 64	45
Books and Reviews	Mushrooms for Color	Rice, Miriam; Dorothy Beebee			WJ	5	2	18	Fa 80	31
Books and Reviews	Mushrooms for Color	Rice, Miriam; Dorothy Beebee			Hw	2	3		My 81	70
Books and Reviews	My Valuable Yarn Guide (second edition)				TM			1	O/N 85	76
Books and Reviews	National Directory of Shops, Galleries, Shows, Fairs: Where to Exhibit and Sell Your Work, 1982/1983.	Davis, Sally Ann			SS&D	14	2	54	Sp 83	63
Books and Reviews	National Woolcrafts Festival—Taranaki 1983 Pattern Book	National Woolcrafts Festival			WJ	8	2	30	Fa 83	62
Books and Reviews	Natural and Manmade Textile Fibers: Raw Material to Finished Fabric	Linton, George E.			H&C	18	2		Sp 67	43
Books and Reviews	Natural Basketry	Hart, Carol; Dan Hart			SS&D	8	1	29	WI 76	70
Books and Reviews	Natural Basketry	Hart, Carol; Dan Hart	√		Fa	4	1		J/F 77	43
Books and Reviews	Natural Dyes	Kierstead, Sallie Pease			SS&D	4	3	15	Su 73	53
Books and Reviews	Natural Dyes, Fast or Fugitive	Dalby, Gill			Hw	6	4		S/O 85	22
Books and Reviews	Natural Dyes for Spinners and Weavers	Wickens, Hetty			SS&D	17	2	66	Sp 86	86
Books and Reviews	Natural Dyes for Spinners and Weavers	Wickins, Hetty			WJ	8	3	31	Wi 83	67
Books and Reviews	Natural Dyes for Spinners and Weavers	Wickins, Hetty	√		PWC	3	3	9		67
Books and Reviews	Natural Dyes from the Northwest	Green, Judy			SS&D	7	2	26	Sp 76	34
Books and Reviews	Natural Dyes in the United States	Adrosko, Rita J.			SS&D	1	2	2	Mr 70	23
Books and Reviews	Natural Dyes in the United States	Adrosko, Rita J.			H&C	20	2		Sp 69	41
Books and Reviews	Natural Fiber Basketry	Smith, Sue M.			TM			10	A/M 87	76
Books and Reviews	Natural Plant Dyeing	Brooklyn Botanic Garden; Palmy Weigle, guest ed.			SS&D	5	3	19	Su 74	62
Books and Reviews	Nature and Art of Workmanship, The	Pye, David			SS&D	6	1	21	Wi 74	32
Books and Reviews	Nature and Art of Workmanship, The	Pye, David			H&C	19	4		Fa 68	42
Books and Reviews	Nature's Dyes	Gordon, Flo Ann			SS&D	4	3	15	Su 73	53
Books and Reviews	Nature's Colors	Grae, Ida			SS&D	6	2	22	Sp 75	63
Books and Reviews	Nature's Colors: Dyes from Plants	Grae, Ida			H&C	26	1		J/F 75	30
Books and Reviews	Navaho Religion, A Study of Symbolism	Reichard, Gladys A.			H&C	5	1		Wi 53	60
Books and Reviews	Navaho Weaving: Its Technic and History	Amsden, Charles Avery			SS&D	5	3	19	Su 74	62
Books and Reviews	Navajo and Hopi Weaving Techniques	Pendleton, Mary			SS&D	5	4	20	Fa 74	64
Books and Reviews	Navajo and Hopi Weaving Techniques	Pendleton, Mary			H&C	26	2		Ap 75	21
Books and Reviews	Navajo Blanket, The	Kahlenberg, Mary Hunt; Anthony Berlant			TMJ	3	4		De 73	47
Books and Reviews	Navajo Native Dyes	U. S. Department of Interior			SS&D	1	4	4	Se 70	22

SUBJECT	TITLE	AUTHOR	IL	INST	JOUR	VOL	NO	ISS	DATE	PAGE
Books and Reviews	Navajo Rugs, How to Find, Evaluate, Buy and Care for Them	Dedera, Don			SS&D	7	3	27	Su 76	34
Books and Reviews	Navajo Rugs — How to Find, Evaluate, Buy and Care for Them	Dedra, Don			WJ	3	3	11	Ja 79	41
Books and Reviews	Navajo Shepherd and Weaver	Reichard, Gladys A.			SS&D	5	3	19	Su 74	62
Books and Reviews	Navajo Techniques for Today's Weaver	Mattera, Joanne			SS&D	7	2	26	Sp 76	34
Books and Reviews	Navajo Techniques for Today's Weaver	Mattera, Joanne			Iw	1	2		Wi 76	28
Books and Reviews	Navajo Weaving: Three Centuries of Change	Kent, Kate Peck	√		WJ	11	1	41	Su 86	15
Books and Reviews	Navajo Weaving: Three Centuries of Change	Kent, Kate Peck			SS&D	18	4	72	Fa 87	55
Books and Reviews	Navajo Weaving, Three Centuries of Change	Kent, Kate Peck	√		Hw	7	2		M/A 86	88
Books and Reviews	Navajo Weaving Tradition: 1650 to the Present, The	Kaufman, Alice; Christopher Selser	√		WJ	11	1	41	Su 86	14
Books and Reviews	Needle-Made Rugs	Mathews, Sibyl			H&C	12	2		Sp 61	59
Books and Reviews	Needlework Doctor: How to Solve Every Kind of Needlework Problem, The	Davis, Mary Kay			Fa	11	6		N/D 84	56
Books and Reviews	Needlework of Mary Queen of Scotts, The	Swain, Margaret			TMJ	3	4		De 73	47
Books and Reviews	Net Making	Holdgate, Charles			H&C	24	1		J/F 73	29
Books and Reviews	New American Tapestry, The	Kaufmann, Ruth			H&C	19	3		Su 68	41
Books and Reviews	New Basketry, The	Rossbach, Ed			SS&D	8	2	30	Sp 77	37
Books and Reviews	New Basketry, The	Rossbach, Ed	√		Fa	4	2		M/A 77	41
Books and Reviews	New Design in Stitchery	Willcox, Donald J.			SS&D	2	2	6	Sp 71	34
Books and Reviews	New Design in Weaving	Willcox, Donald			H&C	22	2		Sp 71	43
Books and Reviews	New Design in Weaving	Willcox, Donald J.			SS&D	2	3	7	Su 71	26
Books and Reviews	New Designs in Crochet	MacKenzie, Clinton D.	√		Fa	5	3		M/J 78	63
Books and Reviews	New Dimensions in Needlework	Schnitzler, Jeanne; Ginny Ross			Fa	5	4		J/A 78	63
Books and Reviews	New Directions in Fair Isle Knitting	Knox, Patty			Kn	2	1	3	F-W 85	79
Books and Reviews	New Dyer, The	Vinroot, Sally; Jennie Crowder			Fa	9	4		J/A 82	53
Books and Reviews	New Furniture from Old	Yates, Raymond F.			H&C	2	4		Fa 51	63
Books and Reviews	New Handbook of Timesaving Tables for Weavers, Spinners, and Dyers, The	Roth, Bettie G.; Chris Schulz	√		WJ	10	3	39	Wi 86	72
Books and Reviews	New Handicraft Processes and Projects, 10th Edition, The	Griswold, Lester; Kathleen Griswold			H&C	24	2		M/A 73	5
Books and Reviews	New Horizons in Color	Birren, Faber			H&C	10	3		Su 59	60
Books and Reviews	New Key To Weaving	Black, Mary E.			Fa	3	1		J/F 76	4
Books and Reviews	New Key to Weaving	Black, Mary E.			H&C	9	2		Sp 58	59
Books and Reviews	New Look at Knitting...An Easier and More Creative Approach, A	Sommer, Elyse; Mike Sommer	√		Fa	5	3		M/J 78	59
Books and Reviews	New Rugs & Ryijys	Aarnio, Rauha			H&C	11	2		Sp 60	60
Books and Reviews	Nigerian Handcrafted Textiles	Eicher, Joanne Bulolz			WJ	6	4	24	Sp 82	59
Books and Reviews	Ninety-seven Needlepoint Alphabets	Borssuck, B.			Iw	1	1		Fa 75	20
Books and Reviews	Norm's Professional Yarn Finder	Danieko, Norm			TM			1	O/N 85	78
Books and Reviews	North American Dye Plants	Bliss, Anne	√		Hw	7	4		S/O 86	12
Books and Reviews	North American Indian Arts	Whiteford, Andrew; Herbert Zim			SS&D	2	2	6	Sp 71	34
Books and Reviews	Northwest Coast Indian Art: An Analysis of Form	Holm, Bill			H&C	22	3		Su 71	42
Books and Reviews	Norwegian Double Weave Pick Up...Directions and Designs	Brewer, Helen			Hw	3	5		N/D 82	12
Books and Reviews	Norwegian Double Weave Pick-Up. Directions and Designs	Brewer, Helen			WJ	7	1	25	Su 82	64
Books and Reviews	Notebook for Kenyan Dyers, A	Hindmarsh, Lorna	√		WJ	9	1	33	Su 84	59
Books and Reviews	Notes on Weaving Techniques	House, Florence E.			H&C	2	3		Su 51	62
Books and Reviews	Notes on Weaving Techniques	House, Florence E.			H&C	18	1		Wi 67	43

SUBJECT	TITLE	AUTHOR	IL	INST	JOUR	VOL	NO	ISS	DATE	PAGE
Books and Reviews	Number Knitting	Bellamy, Virginia Woods			H&C	3	4		Fa 52	61
Books and Reviews	Nya Mattor	Ingers, Gertrud			H&C	10	4		Fa 59	59
Books and Reviews	Of Coverlets—the Legacies, the Weavers	Wilson, Sadye Tune; Doris Finch Kennedy			SS&D	15	3	59	Su 84	36
Books and Reviews	Of Coverlets: The Legacies, The Weavers	Wilson, Sadye Tune; Doris Finch Kennedy			WJ	8	4	32	Sp 84	65
Books and Reviews	Of Coverlets, The Legacies, The Weavers	Wilson, Sadye Tune; Doris Finch Kennedy			WJ	8	4	32	Sp 84	65
Books and Reviews	Of Coverlets—the Legacies, the Weavers	Wilson, Sadye Tune; Doris Finch Kennedy	√		Hw	5	2		M/A 84	13
Books and Reviews	Of Coverlets—the Legacies, the Weavers	Wilson, Sadye Tune; Doris Finch Kennedy	√		PWC	3	2	8		60
Books and Reviews	Of Sheep and Men	Robertson, R. B.			H&C	8	4		Fa 57	59
Books and Reviews	Off the Loom: Creating with Fibre	Marein, Shirley			H&C	24	1		J/F 73	28
Books and Reviews	Off-Loom Weaving	Bernstein, Marion H.			SS&D	3	2	10	Sp 72	39
Books and Reviews	Off-Loom Weaving	Russell, Elfleda			Iw	1	4		Su 76	29
Books and Reviews	Off-Loom Weaving Book, The	Naumann, Rose; Raymond Hull			SS&D	4	4	16	Fa 73	63
Books and Reviews	Ojos De Dios	Klein, Chuck			H&C	24	1		J/F 73	28
Books and Reviews	Old Navajo Rugs: Their Development from 1900 to 1940	Rodee, Marion E.			Fa	8	6		N/D 81	73
Books and Reviews	Older Ways — Traditional Nova Scotian Craftsmen	Barss, Peter			WJ	6	2	22	Fa 81	40
Books and Reviews	On-Loom Card Weaving	Grey, Herbi	√		PWC			3	Oc 82	63
Books and Reviews	On-Loom Card Weaving: A Modern Extension of an Ancient Craft	Gray, Herbi			SS&D	14	2	54	Sp 83	62
Books and Reviews	On-Loom Cardweaving: A Modern Extension of an Ancient Craft	Gray, Herbi			Fa	10	3		M/J 83	54
Books and Reviews	On-Loom Cardweaving, A Modern Extension of an Ancient Craft	Gray, Herbi			WJ	7	2	26	Fa 82	60
Books and Reviews	On-Loom Cardweaving: "A Modern Extension of an Ancient Craft"	Gray, Herbi			Hw	5	4		S/O 84	14
Books and Reviews	One Hundred Embroidery Stitches	Coats and Clark			Iw	5	4		Fa 80	77
Books and Reviews	One Hundred Landskaps Vantar (Country Mittens)		√		Kn	3	1	5	F-W 86	69
Books and Reviews	One Hundred Sixty-seven International Sheep Breeds	Gnatkowski, Janice			S-O	3			79	10
Books and Reviews	One Thousand (+) Patterns	Powell, Marian			SS&D	8	3	31	Su 77	62
Books and Reviews	One Thousand (+) Patterns in 4, 6 and 8 Harness Shadow Weaves	Powell, Marian			WJ	1	3	3	Ja 77	32
Books and Reviews	Ontario Handwoven Textiles	Brett, K. B.			H&C	7	2		Sp 56	63
Books and Reviews	Opphämta Och Damast Med Skälblad Eller Dragvävstol	Johansson, Lillemor			WJ	8	2	30	Fa 83	66
Books and Reviews	Opulence, the Kimonos and Robes of Itchiku Kubota	Yamanobe, Tomoyuki			Hw	6	3		Su 85	14
Books and Reviews	Or...Alternatives to the Fig Leaf	Wittenberg, Barbara			SS&D	9	3	35	Su 78	96
Books and Reviews	Oriental Rug Repair	Stone, Peter			WJ	6	4	24	Sp 82	57
Books and Reviews	Oriental Rugs, A Comprehensive Guide	Eiland, Murray L.			TMJ	4	1		De 74	85
Books and Reviews	Oriental Rugs: A New Comprehensive Guide, Third Ed.	Eiland, Murray			Hw	3	5		N/D 82	12
Books and Reviews	Oriental Rugs Care and Repair	Amini, Majid			WJ	6	4	24	Sp 82	57
Books and Reviews	Oriental Rugs in The Metropolitan Museum of Art	Dimand, M. S.; Jean Mailey			TMJ	4	1		De 74	85
Books and Reviews	Oriental Textiles in Sweden	Geijer, Agnes			TMJ	3	2		De 71	38
Books and Reviews	Oriental Textiles in Sweden	Geijer, Agnes			H&C	3	2		Sp 52	61
Books and Reviews	Original Miniature Patterns for Hand Weaving, Part 2	Estes, Josephine E.			H&C	9	3		Su 58	63
Books and Reviews	Originals: American Women Artists	Munro, Eleanor			Iw	5	4		Fa 80	76
Books and Reviews	Overshot Weaving	Saltzman, Ellen Lewis			Fa	10	4		J/A 83	50

SUBJECT	TITLE	AUTHOR	IL	INST	JOUR	VOL	NO	ISS	DATE	PAGE
Books and Reviews	Overshot Weaving	Saltzman, Ellen Lewis			WJ	8	1	29	Su 83	51
Books and Reviews	Overshot Weaving	Saltzman, Ellen Lewis	√		Hw	5	1		J/F 84	22
Books and Reviews	Overshot Weaving	Saltzman, Ellen Lewis	√		PWC			6	Su 83	66
Books and Reviews	Pacific Basket Makers, A Living Tradition	Jones, Suzi			WJ	8	3	31	Wi 83	67
Books and Reviews	Pageant of the Rose	Gordon, Jean			H&C	4	4		Fa 53	61
Books and Reviews	Painted Warps	Eades, B. G.			H&C	15	4		Fa 64	43
Books and Reviews	Painting on Silk	Bruandet, Pierre			WJ	7	3	27	Wi 82	50
Books and Reviews	Palestinian Costume and Jewelry	Stillman, Yedida Kalfon			Iw	4	3		Su 79	65
Books and Reviews	Papyrus, Tapa, Amate & Rice Paper	Bell, Lilian A.	√		Fa	13	2		M/A 86	41
Books and Reviews	Paracas Fabrics and Nazca Needlework	Bird, Junius; Louisa Bellinger			H&C	6	3		Su 55	61
Books and Reviews	Parallel Shadow Weave	Lang, Elizabeth; Erica Dakin Voolich			PWC	5	1	15		52
Books and Reviews	Park Weaves	Harvey, Virginia I., ed.			Hw	6	3		Su 85	20
Books and Reviews	Park Weaves Based on Dr. William G. Bateman's Manuscript	Harvey, Virginia I., ed.	√		WJ	10	2	38	Fa 85	81
Books and Reviews	Park Weaves Based on Dr. William G. Batemen's Manuscript	Harvey, Virginia I., ed.	√		PWC	4	1	11		53
Books and Reviews	Park Weaves, based on Dr. William G. Batemen's unpublished manuscript	Harvey, Virginia I., ed.			SS&D	17	2	66	Sp 86	85
Books and Reviews	Pastoral Dreams	Schorsch, Anita	√		Iw	3	2		Wi 78	41
Books and Reviews	Patricia Roberts Knitting Book	Roberts, Patricia	√		Kn	2	2	4	S-S 86	79
Books and Reviews	Patricia Roberts Second Knitting Book	Roberts, Patricia	√		Kn	2	2	4	S-S 86	79
Books and Reviews	Pattern Devices for Handweavers	Keasbey, Doramay			SS&D	14	4	56	Fa 83	74
Books and Reviews	Pattern Devices for Handweavers	Keasbey, Doramay			WJ	6	4	24	Sp 82	57
Books and Reviews	Pattern Devices for Handweavers	Keasbey, Doramay			Hw	3	4		Se 82	16
Books and Reviews	Pattern Making by the Flat-Pattern Method	Hollen, Norma R.			WJ	6	4	24	Sp 82	60
Books and Reviews	Patterns for Guernseys, Jerseys and Arans, 3rd ed.	Thompson, Gladys			TM			9	F/M 87	74
Books and Reviews	Patterns for Guernseys, Jerseys & Arans	Thompson, Gladys	√		Kn	1	1	1	F-W 84	71
Books and Reviews	Patterns for Tapestry Weaving—Projects and Techniques	Harvey, Nancy	√		WJ	12	1	45	Su 87	69
Books and Reviews	Patterns for Tapestry Weaving: Projects and Techniques	Harvey, Nancy			Hw	6	1		J/F 85	16
Books and Reviews	Patterns on a Plain Weave	Steedsman, Nell			H&C	12	1		Wi 61	61
Books and Reviews	Peasant Chic	Holderness, Esther R.			SS&D	9	4	36	Fa 78	82
Books and Reviews	Pellavasta Kudottua (Flax Weaving)	Gustafsson & Saarto			H&C	10	1		Wi 59	60
Books and Reviews	Pelle's New Suit	Beskow, Elsa			Iw	2	1		Fa 76	32
Books and Reviews	Pennsylvania Dutch, American Folk Art	Kauffman, Henry			H&C	4	2		Sp 53	63
Books and Reviews	People of Eight Seasons — The Story of the Lapps	Manker, Ernst			H&C	15	3		Su 64	44
Books and Reviews	Persian Carpet Designs to Color	Reid, Mehry			WJ	8	3	31	Wi 83	67
Books and Reviews	Peru: Textiles Unlimited Shuttle Craft Guild Monographs Nos. 25 & 26, 1969	Tidball, Harriet			H&C	20	3		Su 69	43
Books and Reviews	Peruvian Textile Designs	Caraway, Caren			WJ	8	3	31	Wi 83	67
Books and Reviews	Peter Collingwood: His Weaves and Weaving	Tidball, Harriet, ed.			H&C	14	2		Sp 63	44
Books and Reviews	Peter's Prickly Pants	Wicks, Alice			SS&D	8	4	32	Fa 77	72
Books and Reviews	Peter's Prickly Pants	Wicks, Alice			Iw	2	1		Fa 76	33
Books and Reviews	Photographing Your Craft Work	Meltzer, Steve	√		WJ	11	4	44	Sp 87	74
Books and Reviews	Photographing Your Craftwork: A Hands-On Guide for Craftspeople	Meltzer, Steve			Fa	14	3		M/J 87	64
Books and Reviews	Photographing Your Craftwork; a Hands-On Guide for Craftspeople	Meltzer, Steve			Hw	7	3		M/J 86	12
Books and Reviews	Photography for Artists and Craftsmen	Schmid, Claus-Peter			SS&D	7	1	25	Wi 75	35
Books and Reviews	Pictorial Folk Art	Ford, Alice			H&C	4	3		Su 53	62

SUBJECT	TITLE	AUTHOR	IL	INST	JOUR	VOL	NO	ISS	DATE	PAGE
Books and Reviews	Pictorial Guide to American Spinning Wheels, A	Pennington, David A.; Michael B. Taylor			SS&D	7	1	25	Wi 75	35
Books and Reviews	Pictorial Guide to American Spinning Wheels, A	Pennington, David; Michael Taylor			S-O	3			79	10
Books and Reviews	Picture Knits	Rawlings, Marilyn; Jane Taylor	√		Kn	2	2	4	S-S 86	78
Books and Reviews	Pieced Clothing Variations	Porcella, Yvonne			WJ	7	2	26	Fa 82	58
Books and Reviews	Pile Weaves: Twenty-Six Techniques and How to Do Them, The	Wilson, Jean			SS&D	5	4	20	Fa 74	64
Books and Reviews	Pillow Lace	Mincoff, Elizabeth; Margaret S. Marriage			H&C	2	2		Sp 51	61
Books and Reviews	Pillow Lace in the East Midlands	Freeman, Charles			H&C	10	3		Su 59	59
Books and Reviews	Pillow Making as Art and Craft	Sommer, Elyse; Renie Adams			Iw	3	4		Su 78	45
Books and Reviews	Plain and Fancy, American Women and Their Needlework, 1700–1850	Swan, Susan Burrows			Fa	6	6		N/D 79	49
Books and Reviews	Plaited Basketry: The Woven Form	LaPlantz, Shereen	√		Fa	10	1		J/F 83	58
Books and Reviews	Plaited Basketry: The Woven Form	LaPlantz, Shereen			WJ	7	3	27	Wi 82	49
Books and Reviews	Plaited Basketry: The Woven Form	LaPlantz, Shereen	√		Hw	4	3		M/J 83	14
Books and Reviews	Plaiting Step-By-Step	Glashausser, Suellen; Carol Westfall			SS&D	9	2	34	Sp 78	49
Books and Reviews	Plant Fibers for Papermaking	Bell, Lilian A.	√		Fa	13	2		M/A 86	41
Books and Reviews	Playing with Blocks: An Exploration of Multiharness Overshot	Voolich, Erica			WJ	2	3	7	Ja 78	34
Books and Reviews	Pleasures of Pattern, The	Justema, William			H&C	20	2		Sp 69	43
Books and Reviews	Plictho of Gioanventura Rosetti, The	Edelstein, Sidney M.; Hector C. Borghetty, translators			SS&D	3	4	12	Fa 72	47
Books and Reviews	Ply-Split Camel Girths of West India	Quick, Betsy D.; Judith A. Stein			WJ	8	3	31	Wi 83	66
Books and Reviews	Polychromatic Screen Printing	Stocksdale, Joy	√		Fa	12	6		N/D 85	46
Books and Reviews	Polychrome Screen Printing	Stockdale, Joy			Hw	6	5		N/D 85	20
Books and Reviews	Popular Arts of Mexico, The	Toneyama, Kojin			SS&D	6	4	24	Fa 75	31
Books and Reviews	Popular Arts of Spanish New Mexico	Boyd, E.			TMJ	4	2		75	79
Books and Reviews	Portfolio of American Coverlets, A	Strickler, Carol			WJ	5	1	17	Su 80	47
Books and Reviews	Portfolio of American Coverlets, A Vol. V	Strickler, Carol			Hw	4	5		N/D 83	15
Books and Reviews	Portfolio of American Coverlets (Vol. 5), A	Strickler, Carol			SS&D	15	2	58	Sp 84	90
Books and Reviews	Portfolio of American Coverlets Vol. 5, A	Strickler, Carol			WJ	8	4	32	Sp 84	66
Books and Reviews	Portfolio of American Coverlets, Volume 4, A	Strickler, Carol			SS&D	12	4	48	Fa 81	62
Books and Reviews	Pour Aborder....L'ikat	Prin, Remy; Monique Prin			WJ	5	3	19	Wi 81	52
Books and Reviews	Power of Limits: Proportional Harmonies in Nature, Art and Architecture, The	Doczi, György			PWC			4	Ja 83	70
Books and Reviews	Power Sewing: New Ways to Make Fine Clothes Fast	Betzina, Sandra			Hw	7	5		N/D 86	12
Books and Reviews	Practical Applications of Dynamic Symmetry	Hambidge, Jay			H&C	19	3		Su 68	41
Books and Reviews	Practical Business and Tax Guide for the Craftsperson, A (Secong Edition)	Bair, Fred; James E. Norris			Hw	8	4		S/O 87	12
Books and Reviews	Practical Four-Shaft Weaving	Miles, Vera			H&C	14	3		Su 63	43
Books and Reviews	Practical Modern Weaving	Murray			Fa	3	1		J/F 76	6
Books and Reviews	Practical Tailoring	Liberty, J. E.			TM			7	O/N 86	72
Books and Reviews	Practical Treatise on Dying (sic) of Woollen, Cotton, and Skein Silk with the Manufacture of Broadcloth and Cassimere, A	Partridge, William			WJ	7	2	26	Fa 82	59
Books and Reviews	Prairie Wool Companion				Hw	2	4		Se 81	79
Books and Reviews	Pre-Columbian Art & Later Indian Tribal Arts	Anton, F.; F. J. Dockstoder			H&C	20	1		Wi 69	43

SUBJECT	TITLE	AUTHOR	IL	INST	JOUR	VOL	NO	ISS	DATE	PAGE
Books and Reviews	Prehistoric Textiles of the Southwest	Kent, Kate Peck			SS&D	14	4	56	Fa 83	74
Books and Reviews	Prehistoric Textiles of the Southwest	Kent, Kate Peck			Fa	10	5		S/O 83	57
Books and Reviews	Prehistoric Textiles of the Southwest	Kent, Kate Peck			WJ	8	4	32	Sp 84	66
Books and Reviews	Prehistoric Textiles of the Southwest	Kent, Kate Peck	√		Hw	4	4		S/O 83	25
Books and Reviews	Prehistoric Textiles of the Southwest	Kent, Kate Peck	√		PWC			6	Su 83	68
Books and Reviews	Pricing & Promotion	McGuire, E. Patrick; Lois Moran	√		Hw	6	2		M/A 85	71
Books and Reviews	Primary Structures of Fabrics — An Illustrated Classification, The	Emery, Irene			H&C	17	3		Su 66	43
Books and Reviews	Primer of Visual Art, A	Mundt, Ernest			H&C	4	1		Wi 52	62
Books and Reviews	Primitive Art	Boaz, Franz			H&C	4	3		Su 53	63
Books and Reviews	Primitive Art	Fraser, Douglas			H&C	14	1		Wi 63	45
Books and Reviews	Principles of Harmony & Contrast of Colors & Their Application to the Arts, The	Chevreul, M. E.			H&C	19	2		Sp 68	43
Books and Reviews	Principles of Pattern for Craftsmen and Designers, The	Proctor, Richard M.			SS&D	3	1	9	Wi 71	38
Books and Reviews	Principles of Pattern, The	Proctor, Richard			H&C	21	2		Sp 70	41
Books and Reviews	Principles of Textile Testing	Booth, J. E.			H&C	19	2		Sp 68	47
Books and Reviews	Printed Cottons of Asia — The Romance of Trade Textiles	Osumi, Tamezo			H&C	15	2		Sp 64	43
Books and Reviews	Printed Textiles: A Guide to Creative Design Fundamentals	Gentille, Terry			Fa	10	3		M/J 83	52
Books and Reviews	Printed Textiles, English & American Cottons & Linens, 1700 — 1850	Montgomery, Florence			H&C	22	1		Wi 71	41
Books and Reviews	Processing and Finishing Hand Woven Textiles	Weavers Guild of Boston, Monograph Three			WJ	6	1	21	Su 81	54
Books and Reviews	Processing and Finishing Handwoven Textiles	Handweavers Guild of Boston			SS&D	12	4	48	Fa 81	63
Books and Reviews	Producing Hand-Woven Clothing on a Small Scale	Lann, Carol K.			WJ	7	4	28	Sp 83	48
Books and Reviews	Professional Handweaving on the Fly-Shuttle Loom	Brostoff, Laya			WJ	3	3	11	Ja 79	42
Books and Reviews	Professional Handweaving on the Fly-Shuttle Loom	Brostoff, Laya			Iw	4	1		Wi 78	54
Books and Reviews	Professional Weaving on the Fly Shuttle Loom	Brostoff, Laya			SS&D	10	3	39	Su 79	36
Books and Reviews	Profitable Crafts Marketing	Jefferson, Brian T.	√		WJ	12	2	46	Fa 87	68
Books and Reviews	Profitable Crafts Marketing: A Complete Guide to Successful Selling	Jefferson, Brian	√		Hw	7	4		S/O 86	8
Books and Reviews	Promoting and Selling Your Art	Katchen, Carole			Iw	4	4		Fa 79	72
Books and Reviews	Pueblo Indian Textiles—A Living Tradition	Kent, Kate Peck			WJ	9	1	33	Su 84	60
Books and Reviews	Pueblo Indian Textiles: A Living Tradition	Kent, Kate Peck	√		Fa	11	5		S/O 84	52
Books and Reviews	Pueblo Weaving and Textile Arts	Fox, Nancy			WJ	4	2	14	Oc 79	39
Books and Reviews	Pueblo Weaving and Textile Arts	Fox, Nancy			SS&D	10	3	39	Su 79	34
Books and Reviews	Pueblo Weaving and Textile Arts	Fox, Nancy			Iw	4	1		Wi 78	53
Books and Reviews	Punkin Summer	Burress, John			H&C	9	4		Fa 58	60
Books and Reviews	Putting on the Dog	Kroll, Carol			SS&D	8	2	30	Sp 77	38
Books and Reviews	Putting on the Dog	Kroll, Carol			Iw	1	4		Su 76	29
Books and Reviews	Quilt Digest, The		√		Fa	13	4		J/A 86	63
Books and Reviews	Quilted Clothing	Laury, Jean Ray			Fa	11	1		J/F 84	58
Books and Reviews	Quilters, The	Cooper, Patricia; Norma Bradley Buferd			Iw	2	4		Su 77	35
Books and Reviews	Quilters, Women and Domestic Art, The	Cooper, Patricia; Norma Bradley Buferd			Fa	7	6		N/D 80	58
Books and Reviews	Quilting	Colby, Averil			H&C	23	4		J/A 72	26
Books and Reviews	Quiltmaker's Art, Contemporary Quilts and Their Makers, The	Mattera, Joanne, ed.	√		PWC	4	2	12		52

SUBJECT	TITLE	AUTHOR	IL	INST	JOUR	VOL	NO	ISS	DATE	PAGE
Books and Reviews	Quilts	University of Arkansas Cooperative Extension Service			Fa	14	2		M/A 87	62
Books and Reviews	Quilts to Wear	Avery, Virginia	√		Fa	10	6		N/D 83	58
Books and Reviews	Rag Rug Weaves: Patterns from Sweden	Fredlund, Jane; Birgit Wiberg	√		WJ	11	2	42	Fa 86	74
Books and Reviews	Rag Rug Weaves: Patterns from Sweden	Fredlund, Jane; Birgit Wiberg	√		Fa	13	5		S/O 86	60
Books and Reviews	Rag Rug Weaves: Patterns from Sweden	Fredlund, Jane; Birgit Wiberg			SS&D	18	2	70	Sp 87	38
Books and Reviews	Ready Reference Tables for Handweavers	Black, Mary E.; M. Joyce Chown			H&C	11	4		Fa 60	59
Books and Reviews	Rep: A Guide to Swedish Warp-Faced Rep	Carlstedt, Catherina; Ylva Kongback	√		PWC	5	2	16		53
Books and Reviews	Rep Weaves	Lundell, Laila			SS&D	19	1	73	Wi 87	51
Books and Reviews	Rep Weaves	Lundell, Laila	√		PWC	5	2	16		53
Books and Reviews	Reprints of Bette Hochberg's Textile Articles	Hochberg, Bette			WJ	7	1	25	Su 82	64
Books and Reviews	Reps, Technique De Creation De Tissage Traditionnel Et Moderne	Proulx, Bibiane April			WJ	5	1	17	Su 80	48
Books and Reviews	Reps: Technique De Creation De Tissage Traditionnel Et Moderne	Proulx, Bibiane April			SS&D	17	2	66	Sp 86	85
Books and Reviews	Repweaves	Lundell, Laila	√		WJ	12	2	46	Fa 87	65
Books and Reviews	Research Survey on the History of Wool, A	Fairservis, Walter A., Jr.			H&C	6	3		Su 55	61
Books and Reviews	Reversible Two-Color Knitting	Neighbors, Jane F.			H&C	26	5		Oc 75	14
Books and Reviews	Revolutionary Textile Design—Russia in the 1920's And 1930's	Yasinskaya, I.			Fa	12	2		M/A 85	54
Books and Reviews	Ribbon, The	Lark Book Staff; Marianne Philbin, eds.	√		Hw	6	5		N/D 85	18
Books and Reviews	Right Way to Knit: A Manual for Basic Knitting, The	Stewart, Evelyn S.			TM			9	F/M 87	76
Books and Reviews	Right Way to Macramé, The	Stewart, Evelyn Stiles			H&C	22	3		Su 71	42
Books and Reviews	Rigid Heddle Weaving	Swanson, Karen			Iw	1	2		Wi 76	28
Books and Reviews	Rigid Heddle Weaving—New and Innovative Techniques on an Easy-to-Use Loom	Swanson, Karen			SS&D	7	2	26	Sp 76	34
Books and Reviews	Robes of White Shell and Sunrise: Personal Decorative Arts of the Native American	Conn, Richard			TMJ	4	2		75	79
Books and Reviews	Robin Grey's Batiker's Guide	Grey, Robin	√		Fa	4	2		M/A 77	41
Books and Reviews	Romance of Textiles, the Story of Design in Weaing, The	Lewis, Ethel			H&C	5	2		Sp 54	61
Books and Reviews	Royal Persian and Kashmir Brocades	Anavian, Rahim; George Anavian			TMJ	4	4		77	97
Books and Reviews	Rug Book, The	Quirke, Lillian Mary			SS&D	11	4	44	Fa 80	84
Books and Reviews	Rug Hooking and Braiding	Lawless, Dorothy			H&C	4	3		Su 53	62
Books and Reviews	Rug Hooking Made Easy	Stratton, Charlotte Kimball			H&C	7	1		Wi 55	61
Books and Reviews	Rug Hooking & Rug Tapestries	Wiseman, Ann			WJ	6	1	21	Su 81	54
Books and Reviews	Rug Making — Techniques and Design	Allard, Mary			H&C	14	4		Fa 63	43
Books and Reviews	Rug Tapestries and Wool Mosaics	Wiseman, Ann			H&C	21	3		Su 70	39
Books and Reviews	Rug Techniques	Mundal, Maria			H&C	11	3		Su 60	59
Books and Reviews	Rug Weaver's Source Book, A	Ligon, Linda C., ed.	√		Fa	12	5		S/O 85	54
Books and Reviews	Rug Weaving	Lewes, Klares; Helen Hutton			H&C	13	3		Su 62	43
Books and Reviews	Rug Weaving	Lewes, Klares; Helen Hutton			H&C	13	4		Fa 62	43
Books and Reviews	Rug Weaving for Beginners	Seagroatt, Margaret			SS&D	4	1	13	Wi 72	34
Books and Reviews	Rug Weaving for Beginners: Woven Rugs, Tapestry Rugs, Knotted, Hooked and Braided Rugs	Seagroatt, Margaret			H&C	24	1		J/F 73	29

SUBJECT	TITLE	AUTHOR	IL	INST	JOUR	VOL	NO	ISS	DATE	PAGE
Books and Reviews	Rug Weaving for Everyone	Gallinger, Osma; Josephine Del Deo			H&C	9	1		Wi 57	59
Books and Reviews	Rug Weaving for Everyone	Tod, Osma; Joshphine Del Deo			H&C	17	3		Su 66	43
Books and Reviews	Rug Weaving, Technique and Design	Knight, Brian			WJ	6	3	23	Wi 81	60
Books and Reviews	Rugmaking	Droop, Joan			H&C	23	1		J/F 72	33
Books and Reviews	Rugs and Carpets of Europe and the Western World	Weeks, J. G.; D. Treganowan			H&C	21	2		Sp 70	41
Books and Reviews	Rugs and Carpets of the Orient	Larson, Knut			H&C	18	4		Fa 67	39
Books and Reviews	Rugweaver's Source Book: A Compilation of Rug Weaving Techniques, A	Ligon, Linda C., ed.	√		WJ	10	3	39	Wi 86	72
Books and Reviews	Rugweaving Techniques for Two-Harness	Mattera, Joanne			SS&D	11	2	42	Sp 80	81
Books and Reviews	Rugweaving: Techniques for Two-Harness	Mattera, Joanne			Fa	8	3		M/J 81	51
Books and Reviews	Rugweaving: Techniques for Two-Harness	Mattera, Joanne			WJ	8	4	32	Sp 84	67
Books and Reviews	Rugweaving: Techniques for Two-Harness	Mattera, Joanne			Iw	5	1		Wi 79	62
Books and Reviews	Rural Pennsylvania Clothing	Gehret, Ellen J.			SS&D	8	3	31	Su 77	61
Books and Reviews	Rush and Leafcraft	Brotherton, Germaine			Iw	3	2		Wi 78	42
Books and Reviews	Salis Weaving	Gustafson, Paula			Hw	2	4		Se 81	80
Books and Reviews	Salish Weaving	Gustafson, Paula			WJ	6	3	23	Wi 81	59
Books and Reviews	Salish Weaving—Primitive and Modern	Wells, Oliver N.			SS&D	3	2	10	Sp 72	38
Books and Reviews	Samplers, Five Centuries of a Gentle Craft	Sebba, Anne			Fa	8	4		J/A 81	34
Books and Reviews	Samplers You Can Use	Drooker, Penelope B.	√		Fa	13	2		M/A 86	41
Books and Reviews	Sasha Kagan Sweater Book, The	Kagan, Sasha	√		Kn	2	2	4	S-S 86	78
Books and Reviews	Sashes, Straps and Bands: Original Patterns in Warp-Faced Twill for the Four-Harness Loom	Johnston, Ruth; Ralph Johnston			SS&D	17	3	67	Su 86	85
Books and Reviews	Scandinavia: Contemporary Textile Art	Talley, Charles			Hw	7	5		N/D 86	14
Books and Reviews	Scandinavian Embroidery	Nielsen, Edith			Fa	5	6		N/D 78	75
Books and Reviews	Scandinavian Handweaving and Rya	CUM-Leclerc			SS&D	5	4	20	Fa 74	64
Books and Reviews	Schopferisches Weben—Creative Weaving	Kircher, Ursula			SS&D	6	3	23	Su 75	49
Books and Reviews	Scrap Fabric Crafts	Baldwin, Ed; Stevie Baldwin			WJ	7	3	27	Wi 82	48
Books and Reviews	Sculptured Needlepoint Stitchery	Projansky, Ella			Fa	5	6		N/D 78	76
Books and Reviews	Second Book of Modern Lace Knitting, The	Kinzel, Marianne			Kn	1	2	2	S-S 85	78
Books and Reviews	Second Treasury of Knitting Patterns	Walker, Barbara			Kn	1	2	2	S-S 85	79
Books and Reviews	Second Treasury of Knitting Patterns, A	Walker, Barbara			TM			9	F/M 87	74
Books and Reviews	Second Treasury of Knitting Patterns, A	Walker, Barbara G.			SS&D	2	1	5	De 70	31
Books and Reviews	Selected Canadian Spinning Wheels in Perspective: An Analytical Approach	Buxton-Keenlyside, Judith			SS&D	12	2	46	Sp 81	71
Books and Reviews	Selected Canadian Spinning Wheels in Perspective: An Analytical Approach	Buxton-Keenlyside, Judith			S-O	4			80	15
Books and Reviews	Selecting Fleece for Spinning and Yarn Gauge	Marten, Eileen			S-O	3			79	11
Books and Reviews	Self-Sufficient Weaver, The	Green, Jennifer			WJ	8	3	31	Wi 83	68
Books and Reviews	Selling Handcraft for Profit — A Directory for Skilled Craftsmen Who Have Products to Sell	Baumann, Agnes			H&C	6	4		Fa 55	59
Books and Reviews	Sett and Weaving of Tartans, The	Black, Mary E.			H&C	10	2		Sp 59	59
Books and Reviews	Setts of the Scottish Tartans, The	Stewart, Donald C.			SS&D	6	3	23	Su 75	49
Books and Reviews	Seven Hundred Years of Oriental Carpets	Erdmann, Kurt			TMJ	3	2		De 71	42
Books and Reviews	Seven Projects in Rosepath	Frey, Berta			SS&D	7	2	26	Sp 76	34
Books and Reviews	Seven Projects in Rosepath	Frey, Berta			H&C	2	1		Wi 50	59

SUBJECT	TITLE	AUTHOR	IL	INST	JOUR	VOL	NO	ISS	DATE	PAGE
Books and Reviews	Sew Sane: A Common Sense Approach to Making Your Sewing Machine Work for You	Hazen, Gale Grigg			TM			8	D/J 86	74
Books and Reviews	Sewing Machine Craft Book, The	Hall, Carolyn	√		Fa	8	4		J/A 81	62
Books and Reviews	Sewing No-No's and Know-How's—Make it Look Readymade Not Homemake	Wadlington, Mary J.			WJ	9	1	33	Su 84	61
Books and Reviews	Shade Book, The	Lindahl, Judy			WJ	7	3	27	Wi 82	50
Books and Reviews	Shadow Weave and Corkscrew Weave	Barrett, Clotilde			Iw	5	3		Su 80	71
Books and Reviews	Shaker Textile Arts	Gordon, Beverly			Fa	7	4		J/A 80	22
Books and Reviews	Shaker Textile Arts	Gordon, Beverly			SS&D	12	1	45	Wi 80	82
Books and Reviews	Shaker Textile Arts	Gordon, Beverly	√		Iw	6	1		Wi 80	73
Books and Reviews	Shaped Weaving	Krevitsky, Nik; Lois Ericson			SS&D	6	3	23	Su 75	49
Books and Reviews	Sheep Book: A Handbook for the Modern Shepherd, The	Parker, Ron			WJ	8	2	30	Fa 83	62
Books and Reviews	Sheep Book: A Handbook for the Modern Shepherd, The	Parker, Ron			S-O	8	1		Sp 84	10
Books and Reviews	Sheep Book, The	Goodyear, Carmen			Iw	2	1		Fa 76	32
Books and Reviews	Sheep Book, The	Parker, Ron			Hw	4	5		N/D 83	14
Books and Reviews	Sheep of the Lal Bagh, The	Mark, David			Iw	2	1		Fa 76	32
Books and Reviews	Shetland Pattern Book, A	Smith, Mary; Maggie Twatt	√		Kn	2	1	3	F-W 85	78
Books and Reviews	Shibori: The Inventive Art of Japanese Shaped Resist Dyeing	Wada, Yoshiko; Mary Kellogg Rice; Jane Barton	√		Fa	11	6		N/D 84	56
Books and Reviews	Shibou, the Inventive Art of Japanese Shaped Resist Dyeing	Wada, Yoshiko; Mary Kellog Rice; Jane Barton			Hw	6	3		Su 85	14
Books and Reviews	Short Dictionary of Weaving — Concisely Arranged for Quick Reference, A	Pritchard, M. E.			H&C	7	2		Sp 56	59
Books and Reviews	Shuttle-Craft Book of American Hand-Weaving	Atwater, Mary Meigs	√		PWC	4	3	13		52
Books and Reviews	Shuttle-Craft Book of American Hand-Weaving, The	Atwater, Mary Meigs			TM			11	J/J 87	72
Books and Reviews	Shuttle-Craft Book of American Hand-Weaving, The	Atwater, Mary Meigs	√		Hw	7	4		S/O 86	12
Books and Reviews	Shuttle-Craft Book of American Hand-Weaving, The	Atwater, Mary Meigs			H&C	2	2		Sp 51	64
Books and Reviews	Shuttle-Craft Book of American Hand-weaving, The	Atwater, Mary Meigs			H&C	17	4		Fa 66	43
Books and Reviews	Shuttle-Craft Book of American Handweaving, The	Atwater, Mary Meigs	√		WJ	11	3	43	Wi 87	63
Books and Reviews	Siapo: Bark Cloth Art of Samoa	Pritchard, Mary J.	√		Fa	13	5		S/O 86	56
Books and Reviews	Sidney Sheep	American Wool Council			Iw	2	1		Fa 76	32
Books and Reviews	Silk Pictures of Thomas Stevens, The	Baker, Wilma S. V.			H&C	9	2		Sp 58	61
Books and Reviews	Silk Road: Fabrics from the Han to the T'ang Dynasty, The	Museum of the Sinkiang-Uighur Antonomous Region			TMJ	4	2		75	81
Books and Reviews	Silk Roads, China Ships	Vollmer, John E.; E. J. Keall; E. Nagai-Berthrong			WJ	8	4	32	Sp 84	66
Books and Reviews	Silk Textiles of Spain — Eighth to Fifteenth Century	May, Florence			H&C	9	1		Wi 57	59
Books and Reviews	Silk Worker's Notebook, A	Kolander, Cheryl	√		WJ	10	4	40	Sp 86	82
Books and Reviews	Silk Worker's Notebook, A	Kolander, Cheryl	√		Fa	13	1		J/F 86	45
Books and Reviews	Silk Worker's Notebook, A	Kolander, Cheryl			SS&D	12	1	45	Wi 80	83
Books and Reviews	Silk Worker's Notebook, A	Kolander, Cheryl			TM			5	J/J 86	12
Books and Reviews	Silk Worker's Notebook, A	Kolander, Cheryl	√		Iw	5	1		Wi 79	60
Books and Reviews	Simple Book of Belt-Weaving, A	Hoff, Anne			SS&D	4	2	14	Sp 73	44
Books and Reviews	Simple Weaving	Alexander, Marthann			SS&D	1	2	2	Mr 70	23
Books and Reviews	Simple Weaving	Alexander, Marthann			H&C	20	4		Fa 69	42

SUBJECT	TITLE	AUTHOR	IL	INST	JOUR	VOL	NO	ISS	DATE	PAGE
Books and Reviews	Simple Weaving	Chetwynd, Hilary			H&C	20	4		Fa 69	42
Books and Reviews	Simple Weaving	Kroncke, Grete			SS&D	4	4	16	Fa 73	63
Books and Reviews	Singer Fashion Tailoring (Out of Print)	Hutton, Jessie			TM			7	O/N 86	74
Books and Reviews	Skapa Av Svampfärgat Garn	Sunström, Carla; Erik Sunström; Miriam Rice			SS&D	18	3	71	Su 87	73
Books and Reviews	Sling Braiding of the Andes; Weaver's Journal Monograph IV	Cahlander, Adele; Elayne Zorn; Ann Pollard Rowe			WJ	5	4	20	Sp 81	45
Books and Reviews	Small Webs	Lundback, Maja; Marta Rinde-Ramsback			H&C	10	4		Fa 59	60
Books and Reviews	Small Woven Tapestries	Rhodes, Mary			H&C	24	4		Au 73	5
Books and Reviews	Soft and Simple Weaving	Craft Course Publishers			WJ	3	3	11	Ja 79	43
Books and Reviews	Soft People, The Art of Dollcrafting	Pompilio, Loretta			Fa	7	2		M/A 80	43
Books and Reviews	Software for Weavers . . . A Resource	Larson, Lois	√		WJ	11	2	42	Fa 86	75
Books and Reviews	Software for Weavers: A Resource	Larson, Lois			SS&D	17	3	67	Su 86	86
Books and Reviews	Software for Weavers...A Resource	Larson, Lois			Hw	7	4		S/O 86	12
Books and Reviews	Song of the Loom: New Traditions in Navajo Weaving, The	Dockstader, Frederick J.	√		WJ	12	2	46	Fa 87	67
Books and Reviews	Sonia Delaunay	Cohen, Arthur	√		Fa	8	1		J/F 81	20
Books and Reviews	Soumak Workbook	Wilson, Jean			WJ	7	3	27	Wi 82	50
Books and Reviews	Sources of Design — Pattern & Texture	Wedd, J. A.			H&C	8	2		Sp 57	59
Books and Reviews	Southwestern Weaving	Rodee, Marian E.			SS&D	9	3	35	Su 78	94
Books and Reviews	Southwestern Weaving	Rodee, Marian E.			SS&D	9	4	36	Fa 78	81
Books and Reviews	Southwestern Weaving	Rodee, Marian E.	√		Fa	5	2		M/A 78	58
Books and Reviews	Spanish Costume Extremadura	Anderson, Ruth Matilda			H&C	3	2		Sp 52	61
Books and Reviews	Spanish Red: An Ethnogeographical Study of Cochineal and the Opuntia Cactus	Donkin, R. A.			SS&D	10	3	39	Su 79	34
Books and Reviews	Spanish Textile Tradition of New Mexico and Colorado	Museum of New Mexico Press			WJ	4	3	15	Ja 80	45
Books and Reviews	Spanish Textile Tradition of New Mexico and Colorado	Nestor, Sarah, ed.			SS&D	11	2	42	Sp 80	81
Books and Reviews	Spanish Textile Traditions of New Mexico and Colorado	Museum of International Folk Art			Fa	6	6		N/D 79	51
Books and Reviews	Speed Tailoring	Roehr, Mary			WJ	8	3	31	Wi 83	66
Books and Reviews	Speed Warping	Nyquist, Janet			SS&D	3	4	12	Fa 72	47
Books and Reviews	Spiders' Games	Morrison, Phylis			Fa	8	4		J/A 81	41
Books and Reviews	Spider's Games, A Book for Beginner Weavers	Morrison, Phylis			WJ	7	2	26	Fa 82	60
Books and Reviews	Spider's Games: A Book for Beginning Weavers	Morrison, Phylis			SS&D	11	3	43	Su 80	74
Books and Reviews	Spin, Dye and Weave Your Own Wool	Duncan, Molly			H&C	24	3		M/J 73	6
Books and Reviews	Spin, Dye & Weave Your Own Wool	Duncan, Molly			SS&D	4	3	15	Su 73	53
Books and Reviews	Spin Span Spun, Fact and Folklore for Spinners	Hochberg, Bette			WJ	4	3	15	Ja 80	45
Books and Reviews	Spin Span Spun: Fact and Folklore for Spinners	Hochberg, Bette			Fa	7	2		M/A 80	22
Books and Reviews	Spin Span Spun: Fact and Folklore for Spinners	Hochberg, Bette			SS&D	11	2	42	Sp 80	82
Books and Reviews	Spin Span Spun: Fact and Folklore for Spinners	Hochberg, Bette			S-O	3			79	10
Books and Reviews	Spin Your Own Wool	Duncan, Molly			H&C	19	4		Fa 68	41
Books and Reviews	Spin Your Own Wool	Duncan, Molly			H&C	23	3		M/J 72	27
Books and Reviews	Spinformation	Ronin, Colonel James A.			S-O	10	3		Fa 86	48
Books and Reviews	Spinners' Potluck	Illsley, Ednah			Iw	3	4		Su 78	46
Books and Reviews	Spinning and Dyeing the Natural Way	Castino, Ruth			SS&D	6	3	23	Su 75	50
Books and Reviews	Spinning and Dyeing the Natural Way	Castino, Ruth			Iw	1	2		Wi 76	28

SUBJECT	TITLE	AUTHOR	IL	INST	JOUR	VOL	NO	ISS	DATE	PAGE
Books and Reviews	Spinning and Dyeing the Natural Way	Castino, Ruth			Iw	2	3		Sp 77	32
Books and Reviews	Spinning and Spinning Wheels	Leadbeater, Eliza			S-O	3			79	10
Books and Reviews	Spinning and Weaving with Wool	Simmons, Paula	√		WJ	12	2	46	Fa 87	65
Books and Reviews	Spinning and Weaving with Wool	Simmons, Paula			WJ	2	2	6	Oc 77	35
Books and Reviews	Spinning and Weaving with Wool	Simmons, Paula			SS&D	9	2	34	Sp 78	47
Books and Reviews	Spinning and Weaving with Wool	Simmons, Paula	√		Fa	5	2		M/A 78	58
Books and Reviews	Spinning and Weaving with Wool	Simmons, Paula			Iw	3	1		Fa 77	44
Books and Reviews	Spinning for Softness and Speed	Simmons, Paula			WJ	7	2	26	Fa 82	60
Books and Reviews	Spinning for Softness and Speed	Simmons, Paula			S-O	7	2		Su 83	14
Books and Reviews	Spinning Survey	Timlin, Jean, ed.			SS&D	2	3	7	Su 71	26
Books and Reviews	Spinning Wheel Building and Restoration	Kronenberg, Bud			SS&D	12	4	48	Fa 81	63
Books and Reviews	Spinning Wheel Primer	Amos, Alden			Iw	2	3		Sp 77	33
Books and Reviews	Spinning Wheels: Spinners and Spinning	Baines, Patricia			SS&D	9	4	36	Fa 78	80
Books and Reviews	Spinning Wheels, Spinners and Spinning	Baines, Patricia			SS&D	17	3	67	Su 86	87
Books and Reviews	Spinning Wheels, Spinners and Spinning	Baines, Patricia			S-O	7	2		Su 83	15
Books and Reviews	Spinning, Wheels, Spinners and Spinning	Baines, Patricia			Iw	3	3		Sp 78	50
Books and Reviews	Spinning with a Drop Spindle	Thresh, Christine			SS&D	3	4	12	Fa 72	47
Books and Reviews	Spinning Your Own Wool Yarn	American Wool Council			S-O	4			80	15
Books and Reviews	Splendor of Persian Carpets, The	Gans-Ruedin, Erwin			Iw	5	1		Wi 79	59
Books and Reviews	Splendor of Persian Carpets, The	Gans-Ruedin, Erwin			Iw	5	3		Su 80	70
Books and Reviews	Split-Ply Twining	Harvey, Virginia I.			SS&D	7	3	27	Su 76	34
Books and Reviews	Sprang: Language and Techniques	Kliot, Jules			SS&D	5	3	19	Su 74	63
Books and Reviews	Sprang—Language and Techniques	Kliot, Jules			SS&D	6	3	23	Su 75	49
Books and Reviews	Sprang — Language & Technique	Kliot, Jules			WJ	3	1	9	Jy 78	35
Books and Reviews	Sprang Thread Twisting: A Creative Textile Technique	Skowronski, Hella; Mary Reddy			SS&D	5	3	19	Su 74	62
Books and Reviews	Spring and Summer Fashion Fabrics	Weaving Horizons			Hw	6	3		Su 85	20
Books and Reviews	Standard Handbook of Textiles, The	Hall, A. S.			H&C	17	1		Wi 66	45
Books and Reviews	Step by Step Basketry	Gilman, Rachel Seidel; Nancy Bess			SS&D	10	1	37	Wi 78	77
Books and Reviews	Step by Step Spinning and Dyeing	Svinicki, Eunice			SS&D	6	4	24	Fa 75	31
Books and Reviews	Step by Step Spinning and Dyeing	Svinicki, Eunice			Iw	2	3		Sp 77	32
Books and Reviews	Step-by-Step Knitting	Phillips, Mary Walker			SS&D	2	3	7	Su 71	26
Books and Reviews	Step-by-Step Macrame	Philips, Mary Walker			SS&D	3	1	9	Wi 71	39
Books and Reviews	Step-by-Step Macramé	Phillips, Mary Walker			SS&D	1	3	3	Ju 70	22
Books and Reviews	Step-by-Step Macramé: An Introduction to Creative Knotting	Philips, Mary Walker			H&C	21	3		Su 70	40
Books and Reviews	Step-By-Step Rugmaking	Znamierowski, Nell			SS&D	4	1	13	Wi 72	35
Books and Reviews	Step-by-Step Rugmaking	Znamierowski, Nell			H&C	23	5		S/O 72	34
Books and Reviews	Step-by-Step Tablet Weaving	Snow, Marjorie; William Snow			SS&D	5	3	19	Su 74	62
Books and Reviews	Step-by-Step Weaving	Znamierowski, Nell			H&C	18	4		Fa 67	42
Books and Reviews	Steps to a Tailored Jacket, An Illustrated Workbook	Oakley, Geraldine L.			SS&D	13	3	51	Su 82	78
Books and Reviews	Stitches in Time	Bradley, Sue	√		Kn	3	2	6	Sp 87	51
Books and Reviews	Stitches of Bobbin Lace: Structure and Classification	Kliot, Jules; Kaethe Kliot			SS&D	5	3	19	Su 74	62
Books and Reviews	Stitches of Creative Embroidery, The	Enthoven, Jacqueline			H&C	15	4		Fa 64	44
Books and Reviews	Stora Vävboken	Lundell, Laila			WJ	6	2	22	Fa 81	39
Books and Reviews	Story of Lauhala, The	Stall, Edna Williamson			WJ	8	2	30	Fa 83	63
Books and Reviews	Stricken 3	Fanderl, Liesl			Kn	1	2	2	S-S 85	79
Books and Reviews	Structure of Weaving, The	Sutton, Ann			SS&D	15	1	57	Wi 83	102
Books and Reviews	Structure of Weaving, The	Sutton, Ann			WJ	8	2	30	Fa 83	64
Books and Reviews	Structure of Weaving, The	Sutton, Ann	√		Hw	8	1		J/F 87	17
Books and Reviews	Structure of Weaving, The	Sutton, Ann	√		PWC			6	Su 83	67

SUBJECT	TITLE	AUTHOR	IL	INST	JOUR	VOL	NO	ISS	DATE	PAGE
Books and Reviews	Student Handbook of Color	Smith, Charles			H&C	18	1		Wi 67	43
Books and Reviews	Studies in Textile History: In Memory of Harold B. Burnham	Gervers, Veronika, ed.			SS&D	9	3	35	Su 78	94
Books and Reviews	Stumpwork, The Art of Raised Embroidery	Baker, Muriel			Fa	6	4		J/A 79	17
Books and Reviews	Subversive Stitch, The	Parker, Rozsika	√		Fa	13	1		J/F 86	46
Books and Reviews	Summer and Winter	Tidball, Harriet			Fa	3	1		J/F 76	4
Books and Reviews	Summer and Winter and Beyond	Barrett, Clotilde			lw	5	1		Wi 79	65
Books and Reviews	Summer and Winter and Other Two-Tie Unit Weaves	Tidball, Harriet			H&C	18	2		Sp 67	45
Books and Reviews	Summer and Winter Study at Des Moines Weavers Guild	Powell, Marian			H&C	13	2		Sp 62	44
Books and Reviews	Summer and Winter: Technique and Variations	Jefferson, Annis Lee			lw	2	4		Su 77	36
Books and Reviews	Summer & Winter and Beyond	Barrett, Clotilde			WJ	7	3	27	Wi 82	51
Books and Reviews	Supplementary Warp Patterning, Shuttle Craft Guild Monograph Seventeen, 1966	Tidball, Harriet			H&C	17	4		Fa 66	44
Books and Reviews	Supreme Persian Carpets	Amir, M. K. Zephyr			SS&D	5	2	18	Sp 74	68
Books and Reviews	Surface Design for Fabric	Proctor, Richard; Jennifer F. Lew			Hw	7	1		J/F 86	18
Books and Reviews	Surface Design for Fabric	Proctor, Richard M.; Jennifer F. Lew			TM			2	D/J 85	78
Books and Reviews	Surface Design for Fabrics	Proctor, Richard M.; Jennifer F. Lew	√		WJ	10	2	38	Fa 85	82
Books and Reviews	Surface Interest — Textiles of Today	Tidball, Harriet			H&C	12	2		Sp 61	59
Books and Reviews	Sweater Book, The	Carroll, Amy, ed.	√		Kn	2	2	4	S-S 86	78
Books and Reviews	Sweater Workshop, The	Fee, Jacqueline			TM			12	A/S 87	76
Books and Reviews	Sweater Workshop, The	Fee, Jacqueline			WJ	8	2	30	Fa 83	62
Books and Reviews	Sweater Workshop, The	Fee, Jacqueline			Hw	4	3		M/J 83	13
Books and Reviews	Swedish Handweaving	Selander, Malin			H&C	11	1		Wi 60	59
Books and Reviews	Swedish Mitten Book, Traditional Patterns from Gotlan, The	Gottfridsson, Inger; Ingrid Gottfridsson	√		Kn	3	1	5	F-W 86	69
Books and Reviews	Swedish Mitten Book: Traditional Patterns from Gotland, The	Gottfridsson, Inger; Ingrid Gottfridsson			TM			6	A/S 86	84
Books and Reviews	Swedish Patterns and Designs	Swedish Homecraft Society			H&C	2	4		Fa 51	61
Books and Reviews	Swedish Swatches—Blue Series	Selander, Malin			SS&D	3	3	11	Su 72	13
Books and Reviews	Swedish Swatches: Green Series	Selander, Malin			SS&D	10	2	38	Sp 79	74
Books and Reviews	Swedish Swatches—Red Series	Selander, Malin			SS&D	6	1	21	Wi 74	32
Books and Reviews	Swedish Swatches, Yellow Series	Selander, Malin			H&C	14	2		Sp 63	43
Books and Reviews	Swedish Swatches/Blue Series	Selander, Malin			H&C	21	1		Wi 70	41
Books and Reviews	Swedish Textile Art	Martin, Edna; Beate Sydhoff	√		Fa	10	4		J/A 83	50
Books and Reviews	Swedish Weaving	Nye, Thelma M., ed.			SS&D	4	1	13	Wi 72	34
Books and Reviews	Swedish Weaving	Nye, Thelma M., ed.			H&C	24	1		J/F 73	28
Books and Reviews	Swedish-English Weaving Glossary	Hayes, Marie			H&C	24	4		Au 73	5
Books and Reviews	Swedish-English Weaving Glossary	Hayes, Marie C.			SS&D	4	4	16	Fa 73	63
Books and Reviews	Synthetic Dyes for Natural Fibers	Knutson, Linda			Fa	10	1		J/F 83	57
Books and Reviews	Synthetic Dyes for Natural Fibers	Knutson, Linda			WJ	7	2	26	Fa 82	58
Books and Reviews	Synthetic Dyes for Natural Fibers	Knutson, Linda			Hw	4	1		J/F 83	18
Books and Reviews	Taaniko	Smith, Joyce Ronald			SS&D	7	2	26	Sp 76	34
Books and Reviews	Tabby and Twill — Wool and Worsted	Beecher, Helen Carls			H&C	4	4		Fa 53	59
Books and Reviews	Tabby is Terrific!	Boyd, Doris			lw	5	3		Su 80	71
Books and Reviews	Tailoring (Out of Print)	Bane, Allyne			TM			7	O/N 86	74
Books and Reviews	Tailoring Suits the Professional Way	Poulin, Clarence			TM			7	O/N 86	72
Books and Reviews	Tailoring: Traditional and Contemporary Techniques	Ledbetter, Marie; Linda Lansing			TM			7	O/N 86	74
Books and Reviews	Take One Spinning Wheel	Gillis, Myrtle Lovell			H&C	7	2		Sp 56	59

SUBJECT	TITLE	AUTHOR	IL	INST	JOUR	VOL	NO	ISS	DATE	PAGE
Books and Reviews	Tale of Alain, The	Zimmermann, Arnold			Kn	1	2	2	S-S 85	26
Books and Reviews	Tapa in Polynesia	Kooijman, Simon			TMJ	4	2		75	80
Books and Reviews	Tapestries	Sevensma, W. S.			H&C	17	2		Sp 66	43
Books and Reviews	Tapestries from Egypt — Woven by the Children of Harrania	Wassef, Ramses Wissa; W. Forman; B. Forman			H&C	14	4		Fa 63	43
Books and Reviews	Tapestry	Coffinet, Julien; Maurice Pianzola			H&C	23	5		S/O 72	34
Books and Reviews	Tapestry: Craft And Art	Coffinet, Julien; Maurice Pianzola			SS&D	5	4	20	Fa 74	64
Books and Reviews	Tapestry Loom Techniques	Kliot, Jules			WJ	3	1	9	Jy 78	35
Books and Reviews	Tapestry: Mirror of History	Thomson, Francis Paul			Fa	8	1		J/F 81	82
Books and Reviews	Tartans	Hesketh, Christian			H&C	13	1		Wi 62	43
Books and Reviews	Tartans: Their Art and History	Sutton, Ann; Richard Carr			SS&D	16	3	63	Su 85	9
Books and Reviews	Tartans: Their Art and History	Sutton, Ann; Richard Carr			Hw	8	3		M/J 87	17
Books and Reviews	Tassels	Hoover, Doris; Nancy Welch			WJ	7	1	25	Su 82	64
Books and Reviews	Tatsinda	Enright, Elizabeth			Iw	2	1		Fa 76	32
Books and Reviews	Tatting	Nicholls, Elgiva			H&C	17	1		Wi 66	44
Books and Reviews	Tatting — Designs from Victorian Lace Craft	Kliot, Jules; Kaethe Kliot			SS&D	11	1	41	Wi 79	32
Books and Reviews	Tatting: Designs from Victorian Lace Craft	Kliot, Jules; Kaethe Kliot			Iw	4	3		Su 79	66
Books and Reviews	Tax Reliever, The	Helleloid, Richard			SS&D	10	4	40	Fa 79	64
Books and Reviews	"Technicas Prehaspánicas del Tejido", Investigaciones XX	Mastache de Escobar, Alba Guadelupe			TMJ	3	4		De 73	47
Books and Reviews	Technique of Freeform Design, The	Searles, Nancy M.	√		WJ	9	3	35	Wi 85	84
Books and Reviews	Technique of Freeform Design, The	Searles, Nancy M.	√		Hw	5	4		S/0 84	13
Books and Reviews	Technique of Freeform Design, The	Searles, Nancy M.	√		PWC	3	3	9		67
Books and Reviews	Technique of Weaving, The	Tovey, John			SS&D	7	2	26	Sp 76	34
Books and Reviews	Technique of Weaving, The	Tovey, John			WJ	8	3	31	Wi 83	65
Books and Reviews	Technique of Weaving, The	Tovey, John			H&C	17	2		Sp 66	44
Books and Reviews	Technique of Woven Tapestry, The	Beutlich, Tadek			H&C	18	3		Su 67	44
Books and Reviews	Techniques for Designing and Weaving Warp, Weft Ikat — Double and Compound Ikat	Van Gelder, Lydia			WJ	5	3	19	Wi 81	51
Books and Reviews	Techniques of Basketry, The	Harvey, Virginia			SS&D	6	2	22	Sp 75	64
Books and Reviews	Techniques of Basketry, The	Harvey, Virginia	√		Fa	4	1		J/F 77	43
Books and Reviews	Techniques of Code Drafting	Linder, Harry P.			Hw	5	5		N/D 84	14
Books and Reviews	Techniques of Guatemalan Weaving	Bjerregaard, Lena			WJ	2	4	8	Ap 78	40
Books and Reviews	Techniques of Guatemalan Weaving	Bjerregaard, Lena			SS&D	9	4	36	Fa 78	80
Books and Reviews	Techniques of Guatemalan Weaving	Bjerregaard, Lena			Iw	3	2		Wi 78	41
Books and Reviews	Techniques of Rug Weaving, The	Collingwood, Peter			H&C	20	1		Wi 69	41
Books and Reviews	Techniques of Rya Knotting	Willcox, Donald			H&C	23	3		M/J 72	27
Books and Reviews	Techniques of Rya Knotting	Willcox, Donald A.			SS&D	3	2	10	Sp 72	38
Books and Reviews	Techniques of Sprang: Plaiting on Stretched Threads, The	Collingwood, Peter			TMJ	4	2		75	79
Books and Reviews	Techniques of Sprang, The	Collingwood, Peter			SS&D	5	2	18	Sp 74	69
Books and Reviews	Techniques of Tablet Weaving, The	Collingwood, Peter			SS&D	14	2	54	Sp 83	63
Books and Reviews	Techniques of Tablet Weaving, The	Collingwood, Peter			Fa	10	4		J/A 83	49
Books and Reviews	Techniques of Tablet Weaving, The	Collingwood, Peter			WJ	7	3	27	Wi 82	48
Books and Reviews	Techniques of Tablet Weaving, The	Collingwood, Peter	√		Hw	4	2		M/A 83	15
Books and Reviews	Techniques of Tablet Weaving, The	Collingwood, Peter	√		PWC			4	Ja 83	68
Books and Reviews	Temple, Household, Horseback: Rugs of the Tibetan Plateau	Myers, Diana K.	√		WJ	10	4	40	Sp 86	82

SUBJECT	TITLE	AUTHOR	IL	INST	JOUR	VOL	NO	ISS	DATE	PAGE
Books and Reviews	Temple, Household, Horseback: Rugs of the Tibetan Plateau	Myers, Diana K; Arthur Alden Lepper; Valrae Reynolds	√		Fa	13	2		M/A 86	41
Books and Reviews	Terraspool Method of Warping, The	Payton, Dorothy A.; Curtis Payton			H&C	2	1		Wi 50	59
Books and Reviews	Texas Quilts, Texas Women	Yabsley, Suzanne	√		Fa	12	5		S/O 85	54
Books and Reviews	Textil Bilderbok	Sampe-Hultberg, Astrid; Vera Diurson			H&C	3	3		Su 52	62
Books and Reviews	Textile Art in the Church — Vestments, Paraments, and Hangings in Contemporary Worship, Art and Architecture	Ireland, Marion P.			WJ	4	3	15	Ja 80	46
Books and Reviews	Textile Art in the Church — Vestments, Paraments, and Hangings in Contemporary Worship, Art, and Architecture	Ireland, Marion P.			H&C	22	4		Fa 71	26
Books and Reviews	Textile Art of the Andes—Catalogue of Amano Collection	Tsunoyama, Yukihiro, ed.			WJ	7	2	26	Fa 82	59
Books and Reviews	Textile Arts — A Handbook of Fabric Structure and Design, The	Birrell, Verda			H&C	10	2		Sp 59	59
Books and Reviews	Textile Book List, The	R. L. Shep, publ.			WJ	5	3	19	Wi 81	52
Books and Reviews	Textile Collections of the World	Lubell, Cecil, ed.			SS&D	8	2	30	Sp 77	37
Books and Reviews	Textile Collections of the World, Vol. 2 England	Lubell, Cecil, ed.			WJ	5	2	18	Fa 80	32
Books and Reviews	Textile Collections of the World, Vol. 3 France	Lubell, Cecil, ed.			WJ	5	2	18	Fa 80	33
Books and Reviews	Textile Collections of the World: Volume III, France	Lubell, Cecil, ed.			SS&D	9	4	36	Fa 78	82
Books and Reviews	Textile Collector's Guide	Sommer, Elyse			WJ	4	1	13	Jy 79	42
Books and Reviews	Textile Colorist, The	Birren, Faber			Fa	9	4		J/A 82	52
Books and Reviews	Textile Colorist, The	Birren, Faber			WJ	6	1	21	Su 81	53
Books and Reviews	Textile Colorist, The	Birrin, Faber			Hw	2	4		Se 81	78
Books and Reviews	Textile Conservation	Leene, J. E., ed.			SS&D	4	1	13	Wi 72	34
Books and Reviews	Textile Conservation	Leene, Jentina E., ed.			TMJ	3	4		De 73	47
Books and Reviews	Textile Conservation	Leene, Jentina E., ed.			H&C	23	6		N/D 72	41
Books and Reviews	Textile Crafts	Howard, Constance, ed.			SS&D	10	4	40	Fa 79	63
Books and Reviews	Textile Crafts	Howard, Constance, ed.			Iw	3	4		Su 78	45
Books and Reviews	Textile Design	Hunt, Antony			H&C	4	4		Fa 53	61
Books and Reviews	Textile Design and Color	Watson, William			H&C	2	1		Wi 50	62
Books and Reviews	Textile Dyeing and Printing Simplified	Proud, Nora			H&C	26	1		J/F 75	28
Books and Reviews	Textile Fibers	Parsons, L. E.; John K. Stearns			H&C	2	2		Sp 51	61
Books and Reviews	Textile Fibres, Yarns, and Fabrics	Kaswell, Ernest			H&C	4	3		Su 53	62
Books and Reviews	Textile Folk Art	Vaclavim, Antonin; Jaroslav Orel			Iw	5	1		Wi 79	61
Books and Reviews	Textile History, Vol 10, 1979; Vol 11, 1980	Pointing, K. G.; S. D. Chapman, eds.			WJ	6	3	23	Wi 81	60
Books and Reviews	Textile Industry—Information Sources	Kopycinski, Joseph V.			SS&D	6	1	21	Wi 74	32
Books and Reviews	Textile Manufacture in the Northern Roman Provinces	Wild, J. P.			H&C	21	4		Fa 70	44
Books and Reviews	Textile Museum Journal, December 1965, The	The Textile Museum			H&C	17	2		Sp 66	45
Books and Reviews	Textile Museum Journal, Vol.1, No.1	The Textile Museum			H&C	14	2		Sp 63	43
Books and Reviews	Textile Printing	Storey, Joyce			TM			8	D/J 86	72
Books and Reviews	Textile Printing & Dyeing Simplified	Proud, Nora			SS&D	6	2	22	Sp 75	64
Books and Reviews	Textile Repairing	Redden, G. O.			H&C	11	3		Su 60	59
Books and Reviews	Textile Sculpture	Waller, Irene			Fa	7	3		M/J 80	11
Books and Reviews	Textile Structure and Analysis, Shuttle Craft Guild Monograph Eighteen, 1966	Tidball, Harriet			H&C	17	4		Fa 66	44

SUBJECT	TITLE	AUTHOR	IL	INST	JOUR	VOL	NO	ISS	DATE	PAGE
Books and Reviews	Textile Techniques in Metal for Jewelers, Sculptors, and Textile Artists	Fisch, Arline M.			SS&D	7	3	27	Su 76	34
Books and Reviews	Textile Techniques in Metal for Jewelers, Sculptors and Textile Artists	Fisch, Arline M.			Fa	5	4		J/A 78	59
Books and Reviews	Textiles	Hollen, Norma; Jane Saddler			H&C	7	1		Wi 55	59
Books and Reviews	Textiles	Hollen, Norma; Jane Saddler			H&C	19	4		Fa 68	44
Books and Reviews	Textiles and Fabrics — Their Care and Preservation	Moss, A. J. Ernest			H&C	14	1		Wi 63	44
Books and Reviews	Textiles and Ornaments of India	Wheeler, Monroe, ed.			H&C	7	3		Su 56	59
Books and Reviews	Textiles Boliviens, Région de Charazani, Catalogues du Musée l'Homme	Girault, Louis			TMJ	3	3		De 72	79
Books and Reviews	Textiles, Costume and Doll Collections: in the United States and Canada	Bach, Pieter, ed.			WJ	6	4	24	Sp 82	57
Books and Reviews	Textiles for Today's Church: A Guide to Creating Fiber Art	Hahn, Roslyn			Hw	6	3		Su 85	20
Books and Reviews	Textiles from Beneath the Temple of Pachacamac, Peru	VanStan, Ina			H&C	20	3		Su 69	42
Books and Reviews	Textiles & Lacquer	Staff Members of the Tokyo National Museum			H&C	10	1		Wi 59	59
Books and Reviews	Textiles of Ancient Peru and Their Techniques	D'Harcourt, Raoul			SS&D	5	4	20	Fa 74	66
Books and Reviews	Textiles of Ancient Peru and Their Techniques	D'Harcourt, Raoul			H&C	14	1		Wi 63	43
Books and Reviews	Textiles of Baluchistan	Konieczny, M. G.			WJ	6	1	21	Su 81	54
Books and Reviews	Textiles of the Andes: Catalog of Amano Collection	Tsunoyama, Yukihiro, ed.			Hw	2	5		No 81	94
Books and Reviews	Textiles of the Andes: Catalog of the Amano Collection	Tsunoyama, Yukihiro, ed.			Fa	9	6		N/D 82	58
Books and Reviews	Textiles of the Indonesian Archipelago	Solyom, Garrett; Bronwyn Solyom			TMJ	4	2		75	81
Books and Reviews	Textiles: Properties & Behaviour	Miller, Edward			H&C	20	4		Fa 69	41
Books and Reviews	Textiles (Second Edition)	Hollen, Norma; Jane Saddler			H&C	16	4		Fa 65	44
Books and Reviews	Textures and Patterns for the Rigid Heddle Loom	Davenport, Betty	√		Hw	2	1		F-W 80	21
Books and Reviews	Textures and Patterns for the Rigid Heddle Loom	Davenport, Betty Linn			WJ	5	3	19	Wi 81	51
Books and Reviews	Thames and Hudson Manual of Dyes and Fabrics, The	Storey, Joyce			Iw	4	1		Wi 78	55
Books and Reviews	The Art and Craft of Hand Weaving, Including Fabric Design	Blumenau, Lili			H&C	14	2		Sp 63	44
Books and Reviews	Thirty Twill Variations	Morgenstern, Marvin M.			H&C	22	3		Su 71	42
Books and Reviews	Thirty-three Tonder Laces	Tonder, Meta			H&C	6	1		Wi 54	23
Books and Reviews	This Business of Art	Cochrane, Diane			Iw	4	4		Fa 79	72
Books and Reviews	Thomas Jackson Weaver	Tidball, Harriet			Fa	3	1		J/F 76	4
Books and Reviews	Thomas Jackson, Weaver, Shuttle Craft Monograph Thirteen, 1964	Tidball, Harriet			H&C	16	1		Wi 65	45
Books and Reviews	Thread Guide for Handweavers	Black, Mary E.; M. Joyce Chown			H&C	11	4		Fa 60	59
Books and Reviews	Threads in Action	Harvey, Virginia			SS&D	1	3	3	Ju 70	22
Books and Reviews	Threads in Action Monograph, Vols.1 & 2	Harvey, Virginia			H&C	21	2		Sp 70	41
Books and Reviews	Threads in Action, Vol. 2, No. 1				H&C	22	1		Wi 71	42
Books and Reviews	Three Bags Full: Spinning, Weaving and Woolcraft	Jackson, Constance; Judith Plowman			S-O	4			80	15
Books and Reviews	Thyssen-Bornemisza Collection of Oriental Rugs, The	Beattie, May H.			TMJ	3	4		De 73	46
Books and Reviews	Thyssen-Bornemisza Collection of Oriental Tugs, The	Beattie, May H.			TMJ	4	1		De 74	85
Books and Reviews	Tibetan Carpet, The	Denwood, Philip			TMJ	4	2		75	79

SUBJECT	TITLE	AUTHOR	IL	INST	JOUR	VOL	NO	ISS	DATE	PAGE
Books and Reviews	Tie-and-Dye Made Easy	Maile, Anne			H&C	23	3		M/J 72	34
Books and Reviews	Tie-Ups: The Key to Multiharness Weaving	Howard, Ruth			Hw	7	5		N/D 86	13
Books and Reviews	Ties for the Handweaver	Heartz, Robert F.			H&C	6	1		Wi 54	61
Books and Reviews	Tifaifai and Quilts of Polynesia	Hammond, Joyce D.	√		Fa	14	2		M/A 87	61
Books and Reviews	Tifaifai and Quilts of Polynesia	Hammond, Joyce D.			TM			13	O/N 87	78
Books and Reviews	To the Finish	Bogdanor, Lura Jim	√		WJ	11	1	41	Su 86	80
Books and Reviews	To the Finish	Bogdanor, Lura Jim			SS&D	17	4	68	Fa 86	88
Books and Reviews	To the Finish	Bogdanor, Lura Jim			Hw	8	3		M/J 87	16
Books and Reviews	Tour and Shop	Gilpin, Elizabeth			H&C	4	1		Wi 52	61
Books and Reviews	Tradition and Change—The New American Craftsman	Hall, Julie			SS&D	9	3	35	Su 78	95
Books and Reviews	Traditional American Crafts	Creekmore, Betsey			H&C	20	3		Su 69	41
Books and Reviews	Traditional Embroidery of Portugal	Published in Scotland			H&C	4	1		Wi 52	61
Books and Reviews	Traditional Knitting	McGregor, Sheila	√		Kn	2	1	3	F-W 85	78
Books and Reviews	Traditional Knitting	Morgan, Gwen			Kn	2	1	3	F-W 85	79
Books and Reviews	Traditional Knitting	Pearson, Michael	√		Kn	1	1	1	F-W 84	71
Books and Reviews	Traditional Knitting	Pearson, Michael	√		Kn	2	1	3	F-W 85	78
Books and Reviews	Traditional Knitting Patterns	Norbury, James			Kn	1	2	2	S-S 85	79
Books and Reviews	Traditional Knitting with Wool	Australian Wool Corporation			Kn	2	1	3	F-W 85	79
Books and Reviews	Traditional Maori Clothing—A Study of Technological Change	Mead, S. M.			SS&D	8	1	29	WI 76	71
Books and Reviews	Traditional Moroccan Loom, The	McCreary, Carol Fillips			WJ	2	1	5	Jy 77	29
Books and Reviews	Traditional Textiles of Tunisia and Related North African Weaving	Reswick, Irmtraud			SS&D	17	3	67	Su 86	88
Books and Reviews	Traditional Textiles of Tunisia and Related North African Weavings	Reswick, Irmtraud	√		Hw	7	2		M/A 86	89
Books and Reviews	Traditions in Transition: Contemporary Basket Weaving of the Southwestern Indians	Mauldin, Barbara			WJ	10	2	38	Fa 85	83
Books and Reviews	Traditions in Transition: Contemporary Basket Weaving of the Southwestern Indians	Mauldin, Barbara			Hw	7	1		J/F 86	18
Books and Reviews	Translating Tradition: Basketry Arts of the San Juan Paiutes	McGreevy, Susan Brown; Andrew Hunter Whiteford	√		WJ	11	1	41	Su 86	14
Books and Reviews	Treadled Togs	Evans, Kerry			SS&D	13	3	51	Su 82	78
Books and Reviews	Treadled Togs. A Pattern Book of Loom-Fashion Clothing	Evans, Kerry			WJ	6	2	22	Fa 81	39
Books and Reviews	Treadled Togs: A Pattern Book of Loom-Fashioned Clothing	Evans, Kerry			Hw	2	5		No 81	93
Books and Reviews	Treasure Chest of Swedish Weaving, The	Skjoldebrand, Ingerlise			WJ	7	4	28	Sp 83	48
Books and Reviews	Treasure Chest of Swedish Weaving, The	Skjoldebrand, Ingerlise	√		Hw	4	2		M/A 83	15
Books and Reviews	Treasure Chest of Swedish Weaving, The	Skjöldebrand, Ingerlise			PWC			5	Sp 83	68
Books and Reviews	Treasure Chest of Swedish Weaving, The	Skjoldebrand, Ingerlise, ed.			SS&D	14	3	55	Su 83	61
Books and Reviews	Treasures of Suzhow Embroidery	Jiangsu Handicraft Art Society			AT	8			De 87	61
Books and Reviews	Treasury of Knitting Patterns	Walker, Barbara			Kn	1	2	2	S-S 85	79
Books and Reviews	Treasury of Knitting Patterns, A	Walker, Barbara			TM			9	F/M 87	74
Books and Reviews	Treasury of Scandinavian Design, A	Zahle, Erik, ed.			H&C	15	1		Wi 64	43
Books and Reviews	Tribal Rugs: An Introduction to the Weaving of the Tribes of Iran	Housego, Jenny			Iw	4	2		Sp 79	64
Books and Reviews	Tsujigahana, the Flower of Japanese Textile Arts	Ito, Toshiko			Hw	6	3		Su 85	14
Books and Reviews	Turcoman of Iran, The	Abbot Hall Aet Gallery Catalogue			TMJ	3	3		72	80
Books and Reviews	Turkish Emboridery	Johnstone, Pauline	√		Hw	8	5		N/D 87	14

SUBJECT	TITLE	AUTHOR	IL	INST	JOUR	VOL	NO	ISS	DATE	PAGE
Books and Reviews	Turkish Textiles and Velvets	Öz, Tahsin			TMJ	3	2		De 71	38
Books and Reviews	Turkmen: Tribal Carpets and Traditions	Mackie, Louise; Jon Thompson, eds.			Hw	3	5		N/D 82	14
Books and Reviews	Tvåändsstickat		√		Kn	3	1	5	F-W 86	70
Books and Reviews	Twenty-five Original Knitting Designs	Reade, Dorothy			Kn	4	1	9	Wi 87	61
Books and Reviews	Twenty-Five Original Knitting Designs	Reade, Dorothy			Kn	1	2	2	S-S 85	79
Books and Reviews	Twills and Twill Derivatives	Landis, Lucille			SS&D	9	1	33	Wi 77	40
Books and Reviews	Two Thousand Years of Textiles	Weibel, Adele Coulin			H&C	4	1		Wi 52	59
Books and Reviews	Two-Harness Textiles: The Loom-Controlled Weaves, Shuttle Craft Guild Monograph Twenty 1967	Tidball, Harriet			H&C	18	4		Fa 67	40
Books and Reviews	Two-Harness Textiles: The Open-Work Weaves, Shuttle Craft Guild Monograph Twenty-One, 1967	Tidball, Harriet			H&C	19	1		Wi 68	44
Books and Reviews	Tzute y Jerarquia en Sololá Multipurpose Cloths and Hierarchy in Sololá	de Castellanos, Guisela Mayer; et. al.	√		WJ	11	3	43	Wi 87	65
Books and Reviews	Uncoverings 1985, Volume 6 of the research papers of American Quilt Study Group	Garoutte, Sally, ed.			TM			11	J/J 87	73
Books and Reviews	Undulating Weft Effects, Shuttle Craft Monograph Nine, 1963	Tidball, Harriet			H&C	14	3		Su 63	43
Books and Reviews	Universal Stitches for Weaving, Embroidery, and Other Fiber Arts	Hoskins, Nancy Arthur			SS&D	14	2	54	Sp 83	64
Books and Reviews	Universal Stitches for Weaving, Embroidery and Other Fiber Arts	Hoskins, Nancy Arthur			WJ	7	2	26	Fa 82	57
Books and Reviews	Universal Stitches for Weaving, Embroidery and Other Fiber Arts	Hoskins, Nancy Arthur	√		Hw	4	3		M/J 83	12
Books and Reviews	Universal Stitches for Weaving, Embroidery and Other Fiber Arts	Hoskins, Nancy Arthur	√		PWC	3	2	8		61
Books and Reviews	Universal Yarn Finder, Vol. II	Righetti, Maggie			TM			1	O/N 85	76
Books and Reviews	Unknown Craftsman, The (A Japanese Insight into Beauty)	Yanagi, Soetsu			Hw	5	5		N/D 84	12
Books and Reviews	Unlike the Lilies: Doukhobor Textile Traditions in Canada	Burnham, Dorothy K.	√		WJ	11	2	42	Fa 86	75
Books and Reviews	Unlike the Lilies: Doukhobor Textile Traditions in Canada	Burnham, Dorothy K.			TM			11	J/J 87	72
Books and Reviews	Unlike the Lilies: Doukhobor Textile Traditions In Canada	Burnham, Dorothy K.	√		Hw	8	3		M/J 87	14
Books and Reviews	Unlike the Lilies, Doukhobor Textile Traditions in Canada	Burnham, Dorothy K.	√		PWC	4	3	13		52
Books and Reviews	Use of Color and Dyeing, The	Siminoff			H&C	18	3		Su 67	45
Books and Reviews	Use of Native Craft Materials	Eberhardt, Margaret			H&C	4	2		Sp 53	63
Books and Reviews	Use of Vegetable Dyes for Beginners, The	Thurstan, Violetta			H&C	2	4		Fa 51	63
Books and Reviews	Useful Baskets	Cary, Mara	√		Iw	3	2		Wi 78	42
Books and Reviews	Using Procion Fiber Reactive Dyes for Batik, Fabric Printing and Tie-Dye	Grey			Fa	5	1		J/F 78	40
Books and Reviews	Vackra Tras Mattor och Andra Vävar (Beautiful Rag Rugs and Other Weaving)	Johnson, Astrid; Sylvia Mellqvist-Johansson; Eva-Lisa Nordin			Hw	5	2		M/A 84	13
Books and Reviews	Valuable Knitting Information (third Edition)				TM			1	O/N 85	76
Books and Reviews	Vavmonster	Selander, Malin			H&C	5	3		Su 54	58
Books and Reviews	Vegetable Dyeing	Lesch, Alma			SS&D	2	4	8	Fa 71	35
Books and Reviews	Vegetable Dyeing	Lesch, Alma			H&C	22	2		Sp 71	44
Books and Reviews	Vegetable Dyeing	Lesch, Alma			H&C	23	6		N/D 72	41
Books and Reviews	Ventilation, A Practical Guide	Clark, Nancy, et al.			Hw	7	4		S/O 86	12
Books and Reviews	Versatile Bronson	Burton, Dorothy S.			Hw	5	4		S/O 84	14
Books and Reviews	Vertical Loom — Principles and Construction, The	Kliot, Jules			WJ	3	1	9	Jy 78	35

SUBJECT	TITLE	AUTHOR	IL	INST	JOUR	VOL	NO	ISS	DATE	PAGE
Books and Reviews	Victorian Dress in Photographs	Ginsburg, Madeleine			Fa	11	4		J/A 84	54
Books and Reviews	View of Chinese Rugs from the Seventeenth to the Twentieth Century, A	Lorentz, H. A.			TMJ	3	4		De 73	47
Books and Reviews	Virginia West Swatch Book, The	West, Virginia	√		WJ	11	3	43	Wi 87	63
Books and Reviews	Virginia West Swatch Book, The	West, Virginia			SS&D	17	2	66	Sp 86	85
Books and Reviews	Virginia West Swatch Book, The	West, Virginia			Hw	7	1		J/F 86	19
Books and Reviews	Virginia West Swatch Book, The	West, Virginia	√		PWC	4	3	13		55
Books and Reviews	Visual Instructional Macrame	Paque, Joan Michaels			SS&D	3	1	9	Wi 71	39
Books and Reviews	Walk in Beauty: The Navajo and Their Blankets	Berlant, Anthony; Mary Hunt Kahlenberg			SS&D	9	2	34	Sp 78	47
Books and Reviews	Wall Clothing/Wag-Hraegel	Fox, Byrdann	√		Iw	5	2		Sp 80	77
Books and Reviews	Wall Hangings: Designing with Fabric and Thread	Rainey, Sarita R.			SS&D	3	1	9	Wi 71	39
Books and Reviews	Wall Hangings: Designing with Fabric and Thread	Rainey, Sarita R.			H&C	23	5		S/O 72	34
Books and Reviews	Wall Hangings of Today	Sherman, Vera			H&C	23	4		J/A 72	27
Books and Reviews	Warp, A Weaving Reference, The	Tate, Blair	√		WJ	10	1	37	Su 85	84
Books and Reviews	Warp: A Weaving Reference, The	Tate, Blair	√		Fa	12	3		M/J 85	54
Books and Reviews	Warp: A Weaving Reference, The	Tate, Blair			Hw	6	3		Su 85	14
Books and Reviews	Warp and Weave	LeClerc, Robert			SS&D	2	4	8	Fa 71	35
Books and Reviews	Warp and Weft, A Textile Terminology	Burnham, Dorothy K.			WJ	5	2	18	Fa 80	31
Books and Reviews	Warp and Weft, A Textile Terminology	Burnham, Dorothy K.			Fa	7	6		N/D 80	34
Books and Reviews	Warp and Weft: A Textile Terminology	Burnham, Dorothy K.			SS&D	12	2	46	Sp 81	70
Books and Reviews	Warp and Weft: A Textile Terminology	Burnham, Dorothy K.			Iw	5	4		Fa 80	76
Books and Reviews	Warp and Weft from Tibet	King, William A.			SS&D	4	4	16	Fa 73	64
Books and Reviews	Warp and Weft from Tibet	King, William A.			H&C	9	4		Fa 58	60
Books and Reviews	Warp and Weft from Tibet	King, William A.			H&C	17	4		Fa 66	45
Books and Reviews	Warp and Weft of Islam: Oriental Carpets and Weavings from Pacific Northwest Collections, The	Bacharach, Jere L.; Irene A. Bierman, ed.			SS&D	9	4	36	Fa 78	81
Books and Reviews	Warp Painting: A Manual for Weavers	Nash, Dominic			WJ	6	3	23	Wi 81	59
Books and Reviews	Warp Painting: A Manual for Weavers	Nash, Dominie			Hw	3	5		N/D 82	12
Books and Reviews	Warp with a Paddle and Beam Without Paper	Landis, Lucille	√		WJ	10	3	39	Wi 86	72
Books and Reviews	Warp-Patterned Weaves of the Andes	Rowe, Anne Pollard			SS&D	8	4	32	Fa 77	72
Books and Reviews	Warp-Weighted Loom: Studies in the History and Technology of an Ancient Implement, The	Hoffmann, Marta			Hw	5	1		J/F 84	22
Books and Reviews	Warp-Weighted Loom, Studies in the History & Technology of an Ancient Implement, The	Hoffmann, Marta			H&C	17	1		Wi 66	45
Books and Reviews	Warp-Weighted Loom, The	Hoffman, Marta			Hw	4	4		S/O 83	27
Books and Reviews	Warp/Weft/Set. A reference manual for handweavers	Beveridge, June H.			WJ	6	4	24	Sp 82	59
Books and Reviews	Warp/Weft/Sett	Beveridge, June H.			SS&D	12	2	46	Sp 81	71
Books and Reviews	Warp/Weft/Sett: A Reference Manual for Handweavers	Beveridge, June H.			Fa	8	4		J/A 81	41
Books and Reviews	Warp/Weft/Sett, A Reference Manual for Handweavers	Beveridge, June H.			Iw	6	1		Wi 80	69
Books and Reviews	Warping All By Yourself	Garrett, Cay			SS&D	5	4	20	Fa 74	64
Books and Reviews	Warping All by Yourself	Garrett, Cay			Hw	2	1		F-W 80	21
Books and Reviews	Warping All by Yourself	Garrett, Cay			Hw	4	3		M/J 83	13
Books and Reviews	Warping — All by Yourself	Garrett, Cay			H&C	26	2		Ap 75	24
Books and Reviews	Warping the Loom Alone	Folts, Teressa; David Mathieson			H&C	24	2		M/A 73	5
Books and Reviews	Washi, The World of Japanese Paper	Hughes, Sukey			Fa	6	4		J/A 79	14
Books and Reviews	Way of Working, A	Dooling, D. M., ed.			WJ	4	1	13	Jy 79	41
Books and Reviews	Way of Working, A	Dooling, D. M., ed.			Iw	4	3		Su 79	60

SUBJECT	TITLE	AUTHOR	IL	INST	JOUR	VOL	NO	ISS	DATE	PAGE
Books and Reviews	Wearable Art	da Conceicao, Maria			Fa	7	4		J/A 80	14
Books and Reviews	Wearable Crafts	Sommer, Elyse; Mike Sommer			Iw	1	4		Su 76	29
Books and Reviews	Weave a Weave	Selander, Malin	√		WJ	11	3	43	Wi 87	64
Books and Reviews	Weave a Weave	Selander, Malin	√		Fa	13	5		S/O 86	60
Books and Reviews	Weave a Weave	Selander, Malin			SS&D	19	1	73	Wi 87	52
Books and Reviews	Weave a Weave	Selander, Malin	√		Hw	7	5		N/D 86	10
Books and Reviews	Weave a Weave	Selander, Malin	√		PWC	4	3	13		55
Books and Reviews	Weave and Wear It	Andes, Ellen; Penelope Drooker; Gene Andes			WJ	4	4	16	Ap 80	26
Books and Reviews	Weave It! 28 Projects for Your Home	Meltzer, Marilyn			WJ	8	4	32	Sp 84	66
Books and Reviews	Weave It! 28 Projects for Your Home	Meltzer, Marilyn			Hw	3	2		Mr 82	20
Books and Reviews	Weave It! 28 Projects for Your Home (error-corrected WJ v6 n4 82 p61)	Meltzer, Marilyn			WJ	6	3	23	Wi 81	60
Books and Reviews	Weave with Style	Wilson, Jean			WJ	4	4	16	Ap 80	26
Books and Reviews	Weave Your Own Tweeds	Millen, Roger			H&C	7	1		Wi 55	59
Books and Reviews	Weave Your Wardrobe	Dean, Ankaret			Hw	2	5		No 81	94
Books and Reviews	Weaver's Book — Fundamentals of Handweaving, The	Tidball, Harriet			H&C	12	3		Su 61	59
Books and Reviews	Weavers Answer Book	Beck, Dorothy; Hazel Chase			SS&D	2	1	5	De 70	31
Books and Reviews	Weavers Answer Book	Beck, Dorothy; Hazel Chase			H&C	14	1		Wi 63	43
Books and Reviews	Weavers Draft Book and Clothiers Assistant, The	Hargrove, John			SS&D	10	4	40	Fa 79	64
Books and Reviews	Weavers Draft Book and Clothiers Assistant, The	Hargrove, John			WJ	7	1	25	Su 82	63
Books and Reviews	Weavers Draft Book and Clothiers Assistant, The	Hargrove, John (Compiler)			Iw	4	3		Su 79	66
Books and Reviews	Weavers' Wearables	West, Virginia			Hw	1	2		S-S 80	14
Books and Reviews	Weavers' Wisdom: 250 Aids to Happier Weaving	The Weavers Guild of Boston	√		WJ	10	3	39	Wi 86	72
Books and Reviews	Weavers' Wisdom: 250 Aids to Happier Weaving	The Weavers' Guild of Boston Corey, Rosita; Betty Shannon, eds.			SS&D	11	4	44	Fa 80	66
Books and Reviews	Weaver's Book of Fabric Design, The	Phillips, Janet			SS&D	15	3	59	Su 84	36
Books and Reviews	Weaver's Book of Fabric Design, The	Phillips, Janet	√		Hw	5	3		Su 84	16
Books and Reviews	Weaver's Book of Scottish Tartans, The	Tidball, Harriet			H&C	13	2		Sp 62	43
Books and Reviews	Weaver's Craft, The	Simpson, L. E.			H&C	1	3		Fa 50	64
Books and Reviews	Weaver's Craft, The	Simpson, L. E.; M. Weir			H&C	8	4		Fa 57	59
Books and Reviews	Weaver's Dozen, A				Hw	1	2		S-S 80	14
Books and Reviews	Weaver's Garden, A	Buchanan, Rita			SS&D	19	1	73	Wi 87	51
Books and Reviews	Weaver's Life: Ethel Mairet 1872–1952, A	Coatts, Margot			Hw	5	3		Su 84	16
Books and Reviews	Weaver's Study Course—Ideas and Techniques	Regensteiner, Else			SS&D	6	4	24	Fa 75	29
Books and Reviews	Weaver's Study Course: Ideas and Techniques	Regensteiner, Else			Fa	3	5		S/O 76	39
Books and Reviews	Weaver's Wisdon, 250 Aids to Happier Weaving	Boston Weaver's Guild Publications			WJ	5	2	18	Fa 80	31
Books and Reviews	Weaver's Word Finder	Tidball, Harriett D.			H&C	5	2		Sp 54	61
Books and Reviews	Weaves: A Design Handbook	Best, Eleanor			CW		25		Se 87	17
Books and Reviews	Weaves: A Design Handbook	Best, Eleanor	√		PWC	5	2	16		54
Books and Reviews	Weaves and Pattern Drafting	Tovey, John			H&C	21	1		Wi 70	41
Books and Reviews	Weaves of the Incas	Nass, Ulla			WJ	6	4	24	Sp 82	58
Books and Reviews	Weaves of the Incas	Nass, Ulla			Hw	3	2		Mr 82	20
Books and Reviews	Weavin' Woman, A	Stevens, Bernice A.			SS&D	3	2	10	Sp 72	38

SUBJECT	TITLE	AUTHOR	IL	INST	JOUR	VOL	NO	ISS	DATE	PAGE
Books and Reviews	Weaving	Lewis, Roger			H&C	5	3		Su 54	57
Books and Reviews	Weaving: A Creative Approach for Beginners	Creager, Clara			Fa	3	3		M/J 76	7
Books and Reviews	Weaving: A Handbook for Fiber Craftsmen	Held, Shirley			Fa	3	3		M/J 76	40
Books and Reviews	Weaving a Navajo Blanket	Reichard, Gladys A.			SS&D	6	2	22	Sp 75	64
Books and Reviews	Weaving a Tapestry	Brostoff, Laya			WJ	7	3	27	Wi 82	50
Books and Reviews	Weaving—A Timeless Craft	American Wool Council	√		Iw	3	2		Wi 78	41
Books and Reviews	Weaving and Needlecraft Color Course	Justema, William; Doris Justema			H&C	22	4		Fa 71	37
Books and Reviews	Weaving Arts of the North American Indians	Dockstader, Frederick J.			Iw	4	4		Fa 79	74
Books and Reviews	Weaving as a Hobby	Ickes, Marguerite			SS&D	1	2	2	Mr 70	23
Books and Reviews	Weaving as a Hobby	Ickis, Marguerite			H&C	20	3		Su 69	41
Books and Reviews	Weaving as an Art Form	Moorman, Theo			H&C	26	5		Oc 75	12
Books and Reviews	Weaving As an Art Form—A Personal Statement	Moorman, Theo			SS&D	6	4	24	Fa 75	30
Books and Reviews	Weaving Bands	Trotzig, Liv; Astrid Axelsson			SS&D	6	3	23	Su 75	49
Books and Reviews	Weaving Book of Peace and Patience, The	Safner, Isadora; Diane Piette			WJ	5	4	20	Sp 81	45
Books and Reviews	Weaving Book, Patterns and Ideas, The	Bress, Helene			SS&D	13	1	49	Wi 81	90
Books and Reviews	Weaving Book, The	Bress, Helene			Fa	9	2		M/A 82	58
Books and Reviews	Weaving Book, The	Bress, Helene			WJ	6	3	23	Wi 81	60
Books and Reviews	Weaving Book, The	Bress, Helene			Hw	2	5		No 81	93
Books and Reviews	Weaving: Conversion of Yarn to Fabric	Lord, P. R.; M. H. Mohamed			WJ	8	2	30	Fa 83	64
Books and Reviews	Weaving: Creative Approach for Beginners	Creager, Clara			SS&D	6	2	22	Sp 75	64
Books and Reviews	Weaving — Design and Expression	Belfer, Nancy			WJ	2	1	5	Jy 77	29
Books and Reviews	Weaving: Design and Expression	Belfer, Nancy			SS&D	7	1	25	Wi 75	34
Books and Reviews	Weaving for Beginners	Black, Mary E.			H&C	6	1		Wi 54	61
Books and Reviews	Weaving for Beginners	Rubenstone, Jessie			SS&D	8	1	29	WI 76	70
Books and Reviews	Weaving Handcraft	Alexander, Marthann			H&C	5	4		Fa 54	43
Books and Reviews	Weaving Handcraft — 15 Simple Ways to Weave	Alexander, Marthann			H&C	10	2		Sp 59	60
Books and Reviews	Weaving in Miniature	Strickler, Carol; Barbara Taggart			Iw	5	2		Sp 80	77
Books and Reviews	Weaving Inkle Bands, Shuttle Craft Guild Monograph Twenty-Seven 1969	Tidball, Harriet			H&C	21	1		Wi 70	42
Books and Reviews	Weaving is Creative	Wilson, Jean			H&C	24	2		M/A 73	5
Books and Reviews	Weaving Is Creative: The Weaver-Controlled Weaves	Wilson, Jean			SS&D	5	3	19	Su 74	62
Books and Reviews	Weaving is for Anyone	Wilson, Jean			H&C	18	3		Su 67	43
Books and Reviews	Weaving is Fun	White, A. V.			H&C	26	5		Oc 75	12
Books and Reviews	Weaving is Fun	White, A. V.			H&C	13	3		Su 62	43
Books and Reviews	Weaving is Fun	Wilson, Jean			SS&D	3	1	9	Wi 71	39
Books and Reviews	Weaving is Fun	Wilson, Jean			H&C	22	4		Fa 71	26
Books and Reviews	Weaving Lessons for Hand Looms	Snow, Edith Huntington; Laura L. Peasley			H&C	2	2		Sp 51	63
Books and Reviews	Weaving & Needlecraft Color Course	Justema, William; Doris Justema			SS&D	3	1	9	Wi 71	38
Books and Reviews	Weaving Off-Loom	Meilach, Dona; Lee E. Snow			H&C	24	4		Au 73	5
Books and Reviews	Weaving Off-Loom	Meilach, Dona Z.; Lee Erlin Snow			SS&D	4	4	16	Fa 73	63
Books and Reviews	Weaving on a Backstrap Loom: Pattern Designs from Guatemala	de Rodriguez, Judy Ziek; Nona M. Ziek			SS&D	10	3	39	Su 79	34
Books and Reviews	Weaving on a Draw-Loom	Arnold, Ruth			H&C	7	3		Su 56	59

SUBJECT	TITLE	AUTHOR	IL	INST	JOUR	VOL	NO	ISS	DATE	PAGE
Books and Reviews	Weaving on a Frame Loom: A First Project	Skoy, Mary Lonning			WJ	6	4	24	Sp 82	58
Books and Reviews	Weaving on Driftwood Looms	Craft Course Publishers			WJ	3	3	11	Ja 79	43
Books and Reviews	Weaving on Paper or Draw-Down Made Easy	Hoffman, Henry			H&C	11	1		Wi 60	59
Books and Reviews	Weaving on Simple Looms	Green, Louise; Debbie Redding			Hw	2	1		F-W 80	21
Books and Reviews	Weaving on Simple Looms	Green, Louise; Deborah Redding			lw	2	4		Su 77	36
Books and Reviews	Weaving Primer, The	Holland, Nina			lw	4	2		Sp 79	60
Books and Reviews	Weaving Rag Rugs: A Women's Craft In Western Maryland	Johnson, Geraldine Niva	√		WJ	11	2	42	Fa 86	74
Books and Reviews	Weaving Rag Rugs: A Women's Craft in Western Maryland	Johnson, Geraldine Niva	√		Hw	7	3		M/J 86	12
Books and Reviews	Weaving Roses of Rhode Island, The	Safner, Isadora M.	√		WJ	11	1	41	Su 86	74
Books and Reviews	Weaving Roses of Rhode Island, The	Safner, Isadora M.			SS&D	17	3	67	Su 86	87
Books and Reviews	Weaving Roses of Rhode Island, The	Safner, Isadora M.	√		PWC	4	2	12		50
Books and Reviews	Weaving Sourcebook: Ideas and Techniques	Regensteiner, Else			SS&D	15	2	58	Sp 84	90
Books and Reviews	Weaving Sourcebook, Ideas and Techniques	Regensteiner, Else			WJ	8	4	32	Sp 84	65
Books and Reviews	Weaving, Spinning, and Dyeing	Axford, Lavonne Brady			lw	1	2		Wi 76	28
Books and Reviews	Weaving, Spinning and Dyeing Book, The	Brown, Rachel			WJ	3	2	10	Oc 78	45
Books and Reviews	Weaving, Spinning and Dyeing Book, The	Brown, Rachel			SS&D	11	3	43	Su 80	75
Books and Reviews	Weaving, Spinning, and Dyeing Book, The	Brown, Rachel			lw	3	4		Su 78	44
Books and Reviews	Weaving, Spinning, & Dyeing: A Beginner's Manual	Hower, Virginia G.			SS&D	7	4	28	Fa 76	65
Books and Reviews	Weaving Techniques and Projects	Editors Of Sunset Magazine			SS&D	6	3	23	Su 75	49
Books and Reviews	Weaving Techniques and Projects	Gonsalve, Alyson Smith, ed.	√		Fa	3	2		M/A 76	25
Books and Reviews	Weaving Techniques and Projects	Gonsalves, Alyson Smith			SS&D	5	3	19	Su 74	62
Books and Reviews	Weaving Techniques for the Multiple-Harness Loom	Ryall, Pierre			WJ	5	1	17	Su 80	47
Books and Reviews	Weaving Techniques for the Multiple-Harness Loom	Ryall, Pierre			SS&D	11	2	42	Sp 80	83
Books and Reviews	Weaving Tricks	Gilmurray, Susan			Fa	9	4		J/A 82	53
Books and Reviews	Weaving Tricks	Gilmurray, Susan			WJ	6	1	21	Su 81	53
Books and Reviews	Weaving Tricks	Gilmurray, Susan			Hw	2	3		My 81	70
Books and Reviews	Weaving with Antique (Second Hand) Fur	Cook, Bonny			SS&D	3	2	10	Sp 72	38
Books and Reviews	Weaving with Cane and Reed: Modern Basketry	Kronke, Grete			H&C	19	3		Su 68	41
Books and Reviews	Weaving with Coconut Palm	Stevenson, George B.			WJ	8	2	30	Fa 83	65
Books and Reviews	Weaving with Foot Powered Looms	Worst, Edward F.			Fa	3	1		J/F 76	4
Books and Reviews	Weaving with Foot-Power Looms	Worst, Edward F.			SS&D	6	3	23	Su 75	49
Books and Reviews	Weaving with Linen	Patterson, Joan			H&C	9	3		Su 58	63
Books and Reviews	Weaving with Long-Eyed Heddles	VanDenburg, Niles			SS&D	8	3	31	Su 77	63
Books and Reviews	Weaving with Reeds and Fibers	Tod, Osma Gallinger; Oscar H. Benson			SS&D	7	1	25	Wi 75	34
Books and Reviews	Weaving with Style	Wilson, Jean			Hw	1	2		S-S 80	14
Books and Reviews	Weaving with Style	Wilson, Jean			lw	5	1		Wi 79	58
Books and Reviews	Weaving Without a Loom	Rainey, Sarita			H&C	17	3		Su 66	43
Books and Reviews	Weaving Without a Loom	Rainey, Sarita R.			H&C	22	3		Su 71	41
Books and Reviews	Weaving Without Tears	Thurstan, Violetta			H&C	7	4		Fa 56	60
Books and Reviews	Weaving You Can Use	Wilson, Jean			SS&D	7	2	26	Sp 76	34
Books and Reviews	Weaving You Can Wear	Wilson, Jean; Jan Burhen			SS&D	5	2	18	Sp 74	68
Books and Reviews	Weaving Your Can Use	Wilson, Jean			lw	1	2		Wi 76	28

SUBJECT	TITLE	AUTHOR	IL	INST	JOUR	VOL	NO	ISS	DATE	PAGE
Books and Reviews	Weeds — A Guide for Dyers and Herbalists	Bliss, Anne			WJ	3	2	10	Oc 78	45
Books and Reviews	Weeds: A Guide for Dyers and Herbalists	Bliss, Anne			SS&D	10	4	40	Fa 79	64
Books and Reviews	Weeds: A Guide for Dyers and Herbalists	Bliss, Anne			Iw	3	4		Su 78	45
Books and Reviews	Weft Twining, Shuttle Craft Guild Monograph Twenty-Eight, 1969	Harvey, Virginia; Harriet Tidball			H&C	21	1		Wi 70	42
Books and Reviews	West African Cloth	Kent, Kate P.			SS&D	4	1	13	Wi 72	34
Books and Reviews	Whole Craft of Spinning—From Raw Materials to the Finished Yarn, The	Kroll, Carol			WJ	8	1	29	Su 83	53
Books and Reviews	Wilcox Quilts in Hawaii, The	Schleck, Robert J.			TM			13	O/N 87	78
Books and Reviews	Wild Knitting	Jeffs, Angela, ed.			Fa	7	4		J/A 80	14
Books and Reviews	William Morris as Designer	Watkinson, Ray			H&C	19	1		Wi 68	45
Books and Reviews	William Morris: His Life, Work and Friends	Henderson, Philip			H&C	19	1		Wi 68	43
Books and Reviews	Willow, Oak and Rye	Lasansky, Jeannette			Fa	7	6		N/D 80	65
Books and Reviews	Willow, Oak and Rye	Lasansky, Jeannette			SS&D	10	4	40	Fa 79	63
Books and Reviews	Willow Spokes and Wicker Work	Stephens, Cleo M.			Iw	1	1		Fa 75	20
Books and Reviews	Wisconsin Willow...Adventures of a Basketmaker	TerBeest, Char			TM			10	A/M 87	76
Books and Reviews	Wisconsin Willow: Adventures of a Basketmaker	TerBeest, Char			Hw	7	3		M/J 86	13
Books and Reviews	Wonderful Work of the Weaver, The	Mitchell, Lillias			SS&D	4	4	16	Fa 73	63
Books and Reviews	Woodstock Craftsmen's Manual	Young, Jean			H&C	23	4		J/A 72	27
Books and Reviews	Wool and Beyond: First Australian Fibre Conference	Handweavers and Spinners Guild of Victoria			SS&D	14	2	54	Sp 83	62
Books and Reviews	Wool as an Apparel Fibre	Hopkins, Giles E.			H&C	5	1		Wi 53	59
Books and Reviews	Wool Away	Bowen, Godfrey			H&C	26	2		Ap 75	21
Books and Reviews	Wool Away-The Art and Technique of Shearing	Bowen, Godfrey			Iw	1	2		Wi 76	28
Books and Reviews	Wool Away/The Art and Technique of Shearing	Bowen, Godfrey			SS&D	7	1	25	Wi 75	35
Books and Reviews	Wool, Its Chemistry and Physics	Alexander, Peter; Robert Hudson			H&C	6	1		Wi 54	61
Books and Reviews	Wool Shrinkage and Its Prevention	Moncrieff, R. W.			H&C	6	2		Sp 55	61
Books and Reviews	Wool Trade in Tudor and Stuart England, The	Bowden, Peter			H&C	16	3		Su 65	44
Books and Reviews	Woolcraft Book, Spinning, Dyeing, Weaving, The	Jackson, Constance; Judith Plowman			WJ	6	4	24	Sp 82	59
Books and Reviews	Woolcraft Book, Spinning, Dyeing, Weaving, The	Jackson, Constance; Judith Plowman			S-O	6	4		82	10
Books and Reviews	Woolens and Tweeds, Shuttle Craft Monograph Four, 1961	Tidball, Harriet			H&C	13	1		Wi 62	43
Books and Reviews	Woolgatherings	Zimmermann, Elizabeth			Kn	1	1	1	F-W 84	14
Books and Reviews	Work of William Morris, The	Thompson, Paul			H&C	18	3		Su 67	45
Books and Reviews	Workbook for Theory of Color	Whitney, Marjorie			H&C	2	2		Sp 51	61
Books and Reviews	Working with the Wool	Bennett, Noël; Tiana Bighorse			H&C	24	2		M/A 73	5
Books and Reviews	Working with the Wool: How to Weave a Navajo Rug	Bennett, Noël; Tiana Bighorse			SS&D	5	2	18	Sp 74	68
Books and Reviews	Workshop Notes: Craft Habits Part 1(#19) Loom Types Suggested by Weaving Details	Bellinger, Louisa			H&C	11	2		Sp 60	60
Books and Reviews	Workshop Notes: Craft Habits Part 2 (#20) Spinning Fibers in Warp Yarns	Bellinger, Louisa			H&C	11	2		Sp 60	60
Books and Reviews	World of Color — An Introduction to the Theory and Use of Color in Art	Koblo, Martin			H&C	14	4		Fa 63	43
Books and Reviews	World of Indonesian Textiles, The	Warming, Wanda; Michael Gaworski	√		Fa	9	6		N/D 82	58
Books and Reviews	Worlds Within Worlds: A Journey Into the Unknown	Marten, Michael, et al.			Iw	4	2		Sp 79	64

SUBJECT	TITLE	AUTHOR	IL	INST	JOUR	VOL	NO	ISS	DATE	PAGE
Books and Reviews	Woven and Graphic Art of Anni Albers, The	Weber, Jacobs & Field	√		WJ	11	1	41	Su 86	74
Books and Reviews	Woven by Hand	Wassef, Ramses Wissa			SS&D	6	3	23	Su 75	50
Books and Reviews	Woven Fashion	Bateson, Vivienne			SS&D	16	3	63	Su 85	8
Books and Reviews	Woven Fashion	Bateson, Vivienne	√		Hw	6	2		M/A 85	72
Books and Reviews	Woven Works	Hamamura, John; Susan Hamamura			WJ	3	3	11	Ja 79	43
Books and Reviews	Woven Works	Hamamura, John; Susan Hamamura			Fa	5	6		N/D 78	73
Books and Reviews	Woven Works	Hamamura, John; Susan Hamamura			SS&D	10	3	39	Su 79	35
Books and Reviews	Woven Works	Hamamura, John; Susan Hamamura			Iw	4	3		Su 79	64
Books and Reviews	X Balam Q'ué, El Pájaro Sol: El Traje Regional De Cobán	Dieseldorff, Dr. Herbert Quirin	√		WJ	10	1	37	Su 85	85
Books and Reviews	Xenakis Technique for the Construction of four Harness Textiles, The	Xenakis, Athanasios David			WJ	3	2	10	Oc 78	46
Books and Reviews	Xenakis Technique, The	Xenakis, Athanasios David	√		Iw	3	4		Su 78	46
Books and Reviews	Yarn: A Resource Guide for Handweavers	Quinn, Celia	√		Fa	13	3		M/J 86	60
Books and Reviews	Yarn: A Resource Guide for Handweavers	Quinn, Celia			TM			1	O/N 85	78
Books and Reviews	Yarn and Cloth Calculations	Jackson, Lloyd H.			H&C	3	1		Wi 51	61
Books and Reviews	Yarn Animals You Can Make	Goerdeler, Pearl Pomeroy	√		H&C	2	3		Su 51	62
Books and Reviews	Yarn Data Handbook	Samdahl, R.			TM			1	O/N 85	76
Books and Reviews	Yarns for Textile Crafts	Lorant, Tessa			Hw	5	5		N/D 84	12
Books and Reviews	Yer Dailege: Kuna Women's Art	Salvador, Mari Lynn	√		Fa	9	1		J/F 82	58
Books and Reviews	You Can Design: An Adventure in Creating	La Pierre, Sharon			SS&D	15	3	59	Su 84	34
Books and Reviews	You Can Design, An Adventure in Creating	La Pierre, Sharon			WJ	8	3	31	Wi 83	67
Books and Reviews	You Can Weave	Black, Mary E.; Bessie R. Murray			SS&D	6	3	23	Su 75	50
Books and Reviews	Your Handspinning	Davenport, Elsie			Iw	2	3		Sp 77	31
Books and Reviews	Your Handspinning	Davenport, Elsie G.			SS&D	2	1	5	De 70	31
Books and Reviews	Your Handspinning	Davenport, Elsie G.			H&C	4	4		Fa 53	60
Books and Reviews	Your Handspinning	Davenport, Elsie G.			H&C	15	4		Fa 64	43
Books and Reviews	Your Handweaving	Davenport, Elsie G.			H&C	4	2		Sp 53	62
Books and Reviews	Your Yarn Dyeing	Davenport, Elsie G.			SS&D	4	3	15	Su 73	53
Books and Reviews	Your Yarn Dyeing — A Book for Handweavers and Spinners	Davenport, Elsie			H&C	6	4		Fa 55	61
Books and Reviews	Yvonne Porcella: A Colorful Book	Porcella, Yvonne	√		Fa	13	4		J/A 86	60
Books and Reviews, The	Art and Craft of Hand Weaving, The	Blumenau, Lili			H&C	6	3		Su 55	62
Books: Collage	Limited Editions: The Wearable Books of Lois Morrison	Rudich, Sally	√		Fa	12	3		M/J 85	91
Books: Fiber	Grrrhhhh: A Study of Social Patterns	Hickman, Deborah	√		Fa	14	4		S/O 87	23
Books: Handbound, Mixed-Media	Books Without Words	Gore, Ann	√		Fa	9	4		J/A 82	21
Books: Handmade	Conversing with Artist John Eric Broaddus	Stackel, I. M.	√		Fa	11	5		S/O 84	28
Books: Handmade, Fabric	Rubber Stamp Acts: The Little Books of Marie Combs		√		Fa	8	5		S/O 81	18
Books: Handmade, Fabric	Sas Colby	Talley, Charles	√		Fa	8	5		S/O 81	29
Books, Old: Translating Obsolete Terminology	Weaving in the Past Complete Index with Reference: Old Books — How to Read Them	Zielinski, S. A.; Robert Leclerc, ed.			MWL	21 22			'51–'73	95
Books on Tape	Weaving Texts Recorded for the Blind	Brubaker, Paul			Fa	3	5		S/O 76	35
Books: Rare Book Service	Boris Veren's Offers a Rare Book Service	Howie, Andrew	√		H&C	16	2		Sp 65	15
Books: Textile	Words in Fiber	Rowley, Kathleen	√		Fa	11	2		M/A 84	66
Bookshop	London Bookshop	Clement, Doris	√		H&C	11	1		Wi 60	11

SUBJECT	TITLE	AUTHOR	IL	INST	JOUR	VOL	NO	ISS	DATE	PAGE
Borders	Borders: Notes of a Pattern Weaver	Alvic, Philis	√	> 4	WJ	11	2	42	Fa 86	55
Borders	Coverlet: Make Someday Today, Start a Coverlet, A	van der Hoogt, Madelyn	√	√	PWC	5	1	15		24
Borders	Design for a Lunch Cloth in Three Techniques	Redfield, Gail M.	√	√	H&C	19	3		Su 68	15
Borders	Flourishing Art: USA Hmong Women Show How to Stitch Pa ndau, Their Flowery Cloth, A	Porter-Francis, Wendy	√	√	TM			9	F/M 87	33
Borders	It's a Frame-up	Valk, Gene E.	√	√	Hw	4	4		S/O 83	83
Borders	Three-Toned Blocks: Further Explorations with Long-Eyed Heddles	Broughton, Eve T.	√	> 4	WJ	9	4	36	Sp 85	72
Borders: Clothing	Designing Borders on Clothing	Knollenberg, Barbara	√	√	WJ	2	1	5	Jy 77	12
Borders: Knitted	Beginnings...	Rowley, Elaine	√	√	Kn	4	1	9	Wi 87	25
Borders: Overshot	Isolated Overshot: Linen and Cotton Teacloth	Xenakis, Athanasios David	√	> 4	PWC	3	2	8		36
Borders: Pick-Up Pattern	Off-Loom Child's Tabard		√	√	Hw	2	1		F-W 80	52, 69
Borders: Pine Tree	Pine Tree Borders, North and South	Strickler, Carol	√	> 4	Iw	5	3		Su 80	64
Borders: Twill	Linen Blend Placemats (Pam Bartl)		√	√	Hw	1	2		S-S 80	30, 56
Borders: Twill	Turkish Coat, A	Xenakis, Alexis Yiorgos	√	> 4	Hw	2	2		Mr 81	39
Borders: Weaving	Arabesque	Herring, Connie	√	√	PWC	3	1	7		47
Borders: Weaving	End and Selvage Borders	Frey, Berta	√	√	H&C	9	2		Sp 58	46
Borders: Weaving	Hand Woven Rugs: Weaves, Plain Weave, Rugs of Rag Stirps	Atwater, Mary Meigs	√	√	SCGM		29		48	3
Borders: Weaving	Mitered Corners	Sullivan, Donna	√	> 4	SS&D	15	3	59	Su 84	82
Borders: Weaving	Mitered Corners for Identical Warp and Weft Patterns	Redfield, Gail M.	√	√	H&C	14	3		Su 63	21
Borders: Weaving	Overshot Borders for Four Sides, Variations in Pattern and Plain Weave	Aldrich, Mae D.	√	> 4	H&C	15	2		Sp 64	15
Borders: Weaving, All Sides	Composition and Designing: Borders on All Sides	Zielinski, S. A.; Robert Leclerc, ed.	√	√	MWL	18			'51–'73	62
Borders: Weaving, Coverlet	Multishaft Overshot on Opposites	van der Hoogt, Madelyn	√	> 4	WJ	8	3	31	Wi 83	76
Borders: Weaving, Tabby	Composition and Designing Part 2: Pattern Weaves with Tabby Borders	Zielinski, S. A.; Robert Leclerc, ed.	√	> 4	MWL	19			'51–'73	52
Borneo	"Heads and Tales: Traditional Art of Borneo" (Exhibit)	Dyer, Carolyn Price	√		Fa	11	4		J/A 84	74
Boulevard System	Handloom Weaves: The Classification of Handloom Weaves, The Structural Group, Unit Class, Boulevard System	Tidball, Harriet	√	> 4	SCGM		33		57	26
Bound Weave	Accessories: Children's Scarves		√	√	WJ	2	4	8	Ap 78	5
Bound Weave	Bound Overshot	Xenakis, Athanasios David	√	√	PWC	3	3	9		21
Bound Weave	Bound Weave Rugs	Harrold, Yoko Tamari	√	√	WJ	2	1	5	Jy 77	20
Bound Weave	Bound Weaving	Turner, Alta R.	√	√	H&C	15	3		Su 64	10
Bound Weave	Bound Weaving	Turner, Alta R.	√	> 4	H&C	15	4		Fa 64	19
Bound Weave	Boundweave Coat (Jean Scorgie)		√	√	Hw	2	1		F-W 80	31, 75
Bound Weave	Boundweave Jacket (Jean Scorgie)		√	√	Hw	2	1		F-W 80	31, 74
Bound Weave	Boundweave: Learning from the Past	Waggoner, Phyllis	√	√	WJ	10	4	40	Sp 86	44
Bound Weave	Boundweave Rug (Debbie Redding)		√	√	Hw	3	1		Ja 82	38, 83
Bound Weave	Boundweave Rug on an Overshot Threading	Kindahl, Connie	√	√	SS&D	17	3	67	Su 86	58
Bound Weave	Canadian Weavers Design a Child's Cutter Rug		√	√	H&C	12	3		Su 61	15
Bound Weave	Carpet Bag Briefcase (Linda Ligon)		√	√	Hw	5	1		J/F 84	49, 91
Bound Weave	Children's Weft-Face Rug (Mary Skoy)		√	√	Hw	3	1		Ja 82	28, 81
Bound Weave	Double-faced, Double-woven, Three-harness Krokbragd	Holtzer, Marilyn Emerson	√	√	SS&D	14	4	56	Fa 83	46
Bound Weave	Krokbragd	Alderman, Sharon D.	√	√	Hw	2	2		Mr 81	33
Bound Weave	Krokbragd Rug (Lin Eppinger) (error-corrected Hw v2 n4 81 p22)		√	√	Hw	2	2		Mr 81	36

SUBJECT	TITLE	AUTHOR	IL	INST	JOUR	VOL	NO	ISS	DATE	PAGE
Bound Weave	Multiple Shaft Weaving — 2-Tie Four-End Block Drafts		√	> 4	WJ	6	4	24	Sp 82	48
Bound Weave	"Nina Holland: Bound Weave Rugs/Hangings" (Exhibit)	Bess, Nancy Moore	√		Fa	9	1		J/F 82	83
Bound Weave	Reversible Flamepoint Vest	Wittpenn, Ann	√	√	WJ	5	3	19	Wi 81	9
Bound Weave	Rugs for Interiors	Roach, Dianne Carol	√		SS&D	16	4	64	Fa 85	18
Bound Weave	Rugs in the Scandinavian Way		√	√	Hw	8	3		M/J 87	58
Bound Weave	Salmon Derby (Lynn Strauss)		√	> 4	Hw	7	2		M/A 86	37, I-4
Bound Weave	Shaft Switching on Boundweave (Nancy Kraushaar)		√	√	WJ	5	3	19	Wi 81	38
Bound Weave	Small Project in Bound Weave for Beginners, A	Krasnoff, Julienne H.	√	√	H&C	20	3		Su 69	13
Bound Weave	Storytelling in Boundweave	Strauss, Lynn	√	√	Hw	7	2		M/A 86	35
Bound Weave	Studies in Boundweave	Mershon, Janis	√	√	SS&D	12	2	46	Sp 81	50
Bound Weave	Swivel Explored and Contradicted		√	√	WJ	3	4	12	Ap 79	5
Bound Weave	Tapestry Effects in Boundweave Rugs	Ziebarth, Charlotte Molcar	√	√	Iw	5	1		Wi 79	23
Bound Weave	Tied Overshot Boundweave	Xenakis, Athanasios David	√	√	PWC	3	4	10		9
Bound Weave	Two Block Rug in Boundweave	Waggoner, Phyllis	√	√	WJ	12	1	45	Su 87	26
Bound Weave	Weaving and Sheepskin, Naturally	Mason, Carole	√	√	WJ	5	3	19	Wi 81	46
Bound Weave, Collingwood Variations	Boundweave	Evans, Jane	√	√	WJ	1	4	4	Ap 77	3
Bound Weave, Color Rotation	Boundweave	Evans, Jane	√	√	WJ	1	4	4	Ap 77	3
Bound Weave, Double-Faced	Bound Weave Rugs	Harrold, Yoko Tamari	√	√	WJ	2	1	5	Jy 77	20
Bound Weave, Figures	Boundweave	Evans, Jane	√	√	WJ	1	4	4	Ap 77	3
Bound Weave, Figures	Different Boundweave on Six Harnesses, A (error-corrected WJ v3 n1 insert for vol. 2)	Strickler, Carol	√	> 4	WJ	2	4	8	Ap 78	36
Bound Weave, Figures	Farmer and His Wife, Figure Boundweave, A	Pissowotski, Inge	√	√	WJ	5	4	20	Sp 81	8
Bound Weave, Figures	Figures in Boundweave	Waggoner, Phyllis	√	√	WJ	10	2	38	Fa 85	58
Bound Weave, Italian	Boundweave	Evans, Jane	√	√	WJ	1	4	4	Ap 77	3
Bound Weave, Italian	Designing Rugs for Harness-Controlled Weaving		√	> 4	WJ	4	4	16	Ap 80	27
Bound Weave, Italian	Whig Rose Study (continued)	Morgenstern, Marvin M.	√	√	WJ	7	3	27	Wi 82	23
Bound Weave, Krokbrågd	Boundweave	Evans, Jane	√	√	WJ	1	4	4	Ap 77	3
Bound Weave on Crackle	Pile Weaves, Rugs and Tapestry: Rugs in Bound Weave	Zielinski, S. A.; Robert Leclerc, ed.	√	√	MWL	14			'51–'73	56
Bound Weave on Overshot	Pile Weaves, Rugs and Tapestry: Rugs in Bound Weave	Zielinski, S. A.; Robert Leclerc, ed.	√	√	MWL	14			'51–'73	56
Bound Weave on Summer and Winter	Pile Weaves, Rugs and Tapestry: Rugs in Bound Weave	Zielinski, S. A.; Robert Leclerc, ed.	√	√	MWL	14			'51–'73	56
Bound Weave, Opposites	Boundweave	Evans, Jane	√	√	WJ	1	4	4	Ap 77	3
Bound Weave, Opposites	Christmas Boot or After Ski Boot (Jean Scorgie)		√	√	Hw	4	4		S/O 83	72, 100
Bound Weave, Rosepath	Boundweave	Evans, Jane	√	√	WJ	1	4	4	Ap 77	3
Boundweave, Flamepoint	Boundweave	Evans, Jane	√	√	WJ	1	4	4	Ap 77	3
Boutonné, Point	Weaving in Quebec: Traditional Quebecois Weaving	Barrett, Clotilde	√	√	WJ	6	4	24	Sp 82	10
Boutonné, Warp	Warp Boutonné	Lewis, Edward G.	√	√	WJ	7	2	26	Fa 82	64
Boutonné, Weft	In My Country, It's Winter	Gagné-Collard, Agathe	√	> 4	WJ	8	3	31	Wi 83	74
Box Spinner	Home Built Box Spinner	Barrow, Cynthia	√	√	WJ	2	4	8	Ap 78	43
Boxes	Gift Box Covered with Handwoven Fabrics, A	Green, Renah E.	√	√	H&C	17	4		Fa 66	12
Boxes	Jane Dunnewold	Dunnewold, Jane	√		Fa	14	3		M/J 87	23
Boxes	Silk Box	Barrett, Clotilde	√		WJ	3	2	10	Oc 78	13
Boxes	Soft Boxes: Ritual for Our Common Life	McElroy, Jane	√		Fa	10	2		M/A 83	21
Bracelets	Double-Woven Treasures from Old Peru	Cahlander, Adele	√	√	PWC			4	Ja 83	36

SUBJECT	TITLE	AUTHOR	IL	INST	JOUR	VOL	NO	ISS	DATE	PAGE
Bracelets	Unique Finish from an Amazonian Bracelet, A	Thabet, Micheline	√	√	WJ	9	3	35	Wi 85	14
Braids and Braiding	Assomption Sash, A Long Tradition in French Canada	Whitelaw, Adrienne	√	√	H&C	21	3		Su 70	12
Braids and Braiding	Braid Your Own Chenille		√	√	WJ	1	1	1	Jy 76	10
Braids and Braiding	Braiding on a Frame		√	√	WJ	2	4	8	Ap 78	22
Braids and Braiding	Chain Link Braid Made of Leather Forms a Round, Open Trimming	Sober, Marion	√	√	SS&D	4	4	16	Fa 73	50
Braids and Braiding	Finger Weaving	Cooper, Karen Coody	√	√	TM			12	A/S 87	46
Braids and Braiding	Firfletting Fringe Treatment from Norway	Searle, Karen	√	√	WJ	9	4	36	Sp 85	40
Braids and Braiding	Galloon — A French Braid with Two Wefts	Anderson, Marcile	√	√	SS&D	5	3	19	Su 74	83
Braids and Braiding	Karen Chapnick: Constructing Color	Green, Phyllis	√		Fa	13	2		M/A 86	12
Braids and Braiding	Peruvian Slings: Their Uses and Regional Variations	Noble, Carol Rasmussen	√		WJ	6	4	24	Sp 82	53
Braids and Braiding	Scandinavian Square Braid		√	√	Hw	3	2		Mr 82	75
Braids and Braiding	Skirt and Child's Dress (Halcyon Schomp) (error-corrected Hw v4 n4 83 p92)		√	√	Hw	4	3		M/J 83	46, 87
Braids and Braiding	Slentre Braiding	Bernal, Susan Scott	√	√	SS&D	9	2	34	Sp 78	63
Braids and Braiding	Triaxial Weaving of David Mooney, The	Goodman, Deborah Lerme	√	√	Fa	13	3		M/J 86	34
Braids and Braiding	Weaving on a Diamond Grid: Bedouin Style	Race, Mary E.	√	√	SS&D	12	1	45	Wi 80	20
Braids and Braiding	Working with Linen: Shirley Ruth Elgot	Perry, Pamela	√		Fa	14	2		M/A 87	32
Braids and Braiding: Bobbin	Braiding with Bobbins	Wollenberg, Jackie	√	√	SS&D	7	1	25	Wi 75	90
Braids and Braiding: Bobbin	Kumihimo	Kinoshita, Masako	√	√	SS&D	11	3	43	Su 80	19
Braids and Braiding: Bobbin	Kumihimo (error-corrected SS&D v9 n2 78 p70)	Kinoshita, Masako	√	√	SS&D	9	1	33	Wi 77	117
Braids and Braiding: Bobbin	Kumihimo: The Art of Japanese Braiding	Moss, Helen E.	√		Fa	14	1		J/F 87	20
Braids and Braiding: Bobbin	Rainbow Jacket (Sara Lamb)		√	> 4	Hw	4	1		J/F 83	45, 84
Braids and Braiding: Diagonal	Handweaving Triaxial Weaves with Braiding Techniques: Triaxial Braiding	Mooney, David R.	√	√	AT	3			My 85	99
Braids and Braiding: Double	System for Recording and Drafting Certain Types of Braids, A (error-corrected WJ v2 n1 77 insert for vol. 1)	Barrett, Clotilde; Ronnie Bohannan	√	√	WJ	1	2	2	Oc 76	20
Braids and Braiding: Drafts	System for Recording and Drafting Certain Types of Braids, A (error-corrected WJ v2 n1 77 insert for vol. 1)	Barrett, Clotilde; Ronnie Bohannan	√	√	WJ	1	2	2	Oc 76	20
Braids and Braiding: Flat Braids	Handweaving Triaxial Weaves with Braiding Techniques: Triaxial Braiding	Mooney, David R.	√	√	AT	3			My 85	99
Braids and Braiding: Flat, Square, Round	Briading Technique Documented in an Early Nineteenth-Century Japanese Treatise, "Soshun Biko", A	Kinoshita, Masako	√	√	TMJ	25			86	47
Braids and Braiding: Kumihimo	Briading Technique Documented in an Early Nineteenth-Century Japanese Treatise, "Soshun Biko", A	Kinoshita, Masako	√	√	TMJ	25			86	47
Braids and Braiding: Loop	Detective Story: Unravelling the Mystery of a 7-Loop Braid, A	Cahlander, Adele	√	√	WJ	10	1	37	Su 85	12
Braids and Braiding: Non-Flat	System for Recording and Drafting Certain Types of Braids, A (error-corrected WJ v2 n1 77 insert for vol. 1)	Barrett, Clotilde; Ronnie Bohannan	√	√	WJ	1	2	2	Oc 76	20
Braids and Braiding: Plain Weave	Unique Technique for a Braided Strap from Colombia	Cahlander, Adele	√	√	WJ	7	1	25	Su 82	56
Braids and Braiding: Slentre	Briading Technique Documented in an Early Nineteenth-Century Japanese Treatise, "Soshun Biko", A	Kinoshita, Masako	√	√	TMJ	25			86	47
Braids and Braiding: Slentre Braid	Slentre Briad	Ligon, Linda	√	√	Hw	5	1		J/F 84	109
Braids and Braiding: Sling Technique, 16-, 24-, 48-Strand Braiding	Sling Braiding in the Macusani Area of Peru	Zorn, Elayne	√	√	TMJ	19 20			80,81	41
Braids and Braiding: Split-Ply	Decorative Techniques of the Sarakatsani	Smith, Joyce	√	√	WJ	9	1	33	Su 84	14

SUBJECT	TITLE	AUTHOR	IL	INST	JOUR	VOL	NO	ISS	DATE	PAGE
Braids and Braiding: Stand and Bobbins	Briading Technique Documented in an Early Nineteenth-Century Japanese Treatise, "Soshun Biko", A	Kinoshita, Masako	√	√	TMJ	25			86	47
Braids and Braiding: Technique, Loop	Unusual Braids Produced by Loop Manipulation	Speiser, Noémi	√	√	WJ	10	1	37	Su 85	15
Braids and Braiding: Techniques	Decorative Braids Combine Well with Handwoven Material	Sober, Marion Burr	√	√	H&C	19	4		Fa 68	18
Braids and Braiding: Techniques	Kago-Uchi, The	Speiser, Noémi	√	√	AT	4			De 85	23
Braids and Braiding: Techniques, Loop-Manipulation, Eight Modes	Briading Technique Documented in an Early Nineteenth-Century Japanese Treatise, "Soshun Biko", A	Kinoshita, Masako	√	√	TMJ	25			86	47
Braids and Braiding: Triaxial Weaves	Braiding Triaxial Weaves: Enhancements and Design for Artworks	Mooney, David R.	√	√	AT	5			Ju 86	9
Braids and Braiding: Triaxial Weaves	Handweaving Triaxial Weaves with Braiding Techniques: Triaxial Braiding	Mooney, David R.	√	√	AT	3			My 85	99
Braids and Braiding: Twill	Unique Technique for a Braided Strap from Colombia	Cahlander, Adele	√	√	WJ	7	1	25	Su 82	56
Braids and Briaiding: Technique, Loop-Manipulation, Hand-Held	Briading Technique Documented in an Early Nineteenth-Century Japanese Treatise, "Soshun Biko", A	Kinoshita, Masako	√	√	TMJ	25			86	47
Braids: Woven	Latvian Folk Costume Braids	Gulbis, Elina	√	√	SS&D	4	3	15	Su 73	46
Brazil	Career on Four Continents, A	Arndt, Jessie Ash	√		H&C	21	3		Su 70	15
Brazil	Embroidered Sambas of Madeleine Colaço, The	Mathews, Kate	√		Fa	14	5		N/D 87	34
Brazilwood	Why Bother with Natural Dyeing?	Bulbach, Stanley	√	√	TM			5	J/J 86	32
British Isles	Handweavers 1800—1840	Wilson, Kax	√		Iw	5	2		Sp 80	50
Brocade	Back Strap Weaving in Zacualpan Mexico	Cooper, Jane	√	√	SS&D	5	3	19	Su 74	13
Brocade	Bath Towel Set, A	Xenakis, Athanasios David	√	> 4	PWC	1	1		No 81	24
Brocade	Brocade	Tidball, Harriet	√		SCGM		22		67	2
Brocade	Chinese Artisans At Work	Goodman, Deborah Lerme	√		Fa	13	1		J/F 86	34
Brocade	Costumes of Royal India	Levine, Betsy	√		TM			7	O/N 86	64
Brocade	Doncho for New York, A		√		H&C	15	4		Fa 64	12
Brocade	Evolution of an Artist: Morgan Clifford	Gue, Sandra	√		Fa	14	5		N/D 87	27
Brocade	Folk Textiles of Latin America	Kelemen, Pál	√		TMJ	1	4		De 65	2
Brocade	Golden Brocades, The	Wilson, Kax	√		Iw	6	1		Wi 80	66
Brocade	Graphic Weave for a Special Occasion (Carrie Rogers)		√	√	Hw	1	2		S-S 80	38
Brocade	Guatemala Weaver, The	Marks, Copeland A.	√		H&C	26	5		Oc 75	2
Brocade	Guatemalan Brocade Border, A	Simons, Phid	√	√	WJ	6	4	24	Sp 82	39
Brocade	Hopi Woven Embroidery		√	√	WJ	2	3	7	Ja 78	24
Brocade	In and On the Surface: The Tapestries of Judy Branfman	Mattera, Joanne	√		Fa	10	3		M/J 83	22
Brocade	In Pursuit of the Elusive Huipil	Marks, Copeland	√		H&C	24	4		Au 73	6
Brocade	Inside the Hangchow Brocade Factory: The Art and Craft of Mass Production	Drower, Sara	√		Fa	6	1		J/F 79	78
Brocade	Ottoman Turkish Textiles	Denny, Walter B.	√		TMJ	3	3		De 72	55
Brocade	Painting and Brocading on the Loom	Ziek, Bhakti	√	√	TM			6	A/S 86	42
Brocade	Saganishiki	Karaki, Mihoko	√		SS&D	15	3	59	Su 84	50
Brocade	Two-harness Weaves	Clark, Marion L.	√	√	H&C	14	2		Sp 63	17
Brocade	Variations on an Overshot Threading	Lermond, Charles	√	√	WJ	12	2	46	Fa 87	25
Brocade, Bouquet	Brocade: Bouquet Brocade	Tidball, Harriet	√	√	SCGM		22		67	36
Brocade, Chinese	Chinese Brocades: Development of Supplementary Weft Patterning (error-corrected WJ v11 n4 87 p78)	Drooker, Penelope	√		WJ	11	3	43	Wi 87	47
Brocade, Combinations	Brocade: Combination Brocades	Tidball, Harriet	√	√	SCGM		22		67	36
Brocade: Contemporary	Chinese Brocades: Development of Supplementary WeftPatterning (error-corrected WJ v11 n4 87 p78)	Drooker, Penelope	√		WJ	11	3	43	Wi 87	47

SUBJECT	TITLE	AUTHOR	IL	INST	JOUR	VOL	NO	ISS	DATE	PAGE
Brocade, Contemporary	Morgan Clifford: New Directions in Brocades	Gue, Sandra	√		WJ	11	4	44	Sp 87	40
Brocade, Inlay	Brocade: Inlays	Tidball, Harriet	√	√	SCGM		22		67	18
Brocade, Inlay, Casual	Brocade: Casual Inlay	Tidball, Harriet	√	√	SCGM		22		67	19
Brocade, Inlay, Decorated	Brocade: Decorated Inlays	Tidball, Harriet	√	√	SCGM		22		67	22
Brocade, Inlay, Double (Transparencies)	Brocade: Double Inlay (Transparencies)	Tidball, Harriet	√	√	SCGM		22		67	23
Brocade, Inlay, Outlined	Brocade: Underside-Turn Inlay	Tidball, Harriet	√	√	SCGM		22		67	21
Brocade, Inlay, Surface-Turn	Brocade: Surface-Turn Inlay	Tidball, Harriet	√	√	SCGM		22		67	19
Brocade, Inlay, Underside-Turn	Brocade: Underside-Turn Inlay	Tidball, Harriet	√	√	SCGM		22		67	21
Brocade, Inlay, Warp-Weft	Brocade: Warp-Weft Inlay	Tidball, Harriet	√	√	SCGM		22		67	23
Brocade, Knitting	Knit and Purl	Rowley, Elaine	√		Kn	1	1	1	F-W 84 CI	40 32
Brocade, Knitting	On Designing: Brocade Blouse	Newton, Deborah	√	√	Kn	1	1	1	F-W 84 CI	17 9
Brocade, Loom-Controlled	Blouse Fabric (Sharon Alderman)		√	√	Hw	2	3		My 81	87, 88
Brocade, Opposites	Brocade: Opposites Brocade	Tidball, Harriet	√	√	SCGM		22		67	31
Brocade, Overlay, Float	Brocade: Float Overlay Brocade	Tidball, Harriet	√	√	SCGM		22		67	24
Brocade, Overlay-Underlay	Brocade: Overlay-Underlay Brocade	Tidball, Harriet	√	√	SCGM		22		67	32
Brocade, Pick-Up	Bath Towel Set, A	Xenakis, Athanasios David	√	>4	PWC	1	1		No 81	24
Brocade, Spots	Brocade: Brocade Spots	Tidball, Harriet	√	√	SCGM		22		67	37
Brocade, Supplementary Wefts, Discontinuous	Peru, Textiles Unlimited, Part 2: Brocade	Tidball, Harriet	√	√	SCGM		26		69	29
Brocade, Supplementary-Warp	Table Turned, The (error-corrected Hw v5 n3 84 p92)	Dobrovolny, Ardis	√	>4	Hw	5	1		J/F 84	64
Brocade, Techniques	Brocade: Methods	Tidball, Harriet	√		SCGM		22		67	9
Brocade, Techniques	Painting and Brocading on the Loom	Ziek, Bhakti	√	√	TM			6	A/S 86	42
Brocade, Two-Shaft	Brocade	Tidball, Harriet			SCGM		22		67	1-50
Brocade, Warp	Miniature Cable Car from San Francisco	Ayer, Millie	√	>4	SS&D	5	4	20	Fa 74	40
Brocade, Warp	Supplementary Warp (Warp Brocade)	Wertenberger, Kathryn	√	>4	Hw	7	1		J/F 86	80
Brocade, Warp and Weft	Brocade: Warp and Weft Densities	Tidball, Harriet			SCGM		22		67	11
Brocade Weaving	Banares Brocade	DuBois, Emily	√	>4	AT	3			My 85	209
Brocade Weaving	Hanaori: An Okinawan Brocaded Textile	Miller, Dorothy	√	√	AT	1			De 83	173
Brocade, Weft	Calendar in Guatemalan Belt Weave (Evelyn Christensen)		√	√	Hw	7	2		M/A 86	69, I-14
Brocade, Weft	Time and Vision: The Work of Cynthia Schira	Janeiro, Jan	√		Fa	9	5		S/O 82	68
Brocade, Weft-Float Face	Some Weft-Float Brocaded Rugs of the Bergama-Ezine Region	Beattie, May H.	√		TMJ	3	2		De 71	20
Brocade, Wrapped	Brocade: Wrapped Brocade	Tidball, Harriet	√	√	SCGM		22		67	35
Brocade, Wrapped, Weft-Float	Guatemalan Shirt (Betty Davenport)		√	√	Hw	2	2		Mr 81	54, 72
Broché	Little Known Weaves Worth Knowing Better: Broché	Zielinski, S. A.; Robert Leclerc, ed.	√	>4	MWL	16			'51–'73	84
Bronson also see Lace, Bronson; Spot, Bronson										
Bronson	Contemporary Approach to Traditional Weaves: M's and O's	Zielinski, S. A.; Robert Leclerc, ed.	√	√	MWL	8			'51–'73	75
Bronson, Spot	Spot Weaves — Old and New: Bronson	Zielinski, S. A.; Robert Leclerc, ed.	√	>4	MWL	12			'51–'73	22
Bronson Weave	Diagonal Corduroy	Xenakis, Athanasios David	√	>4	PWC	3	4	10		51
Bronson Weave	Five Harness Pattern on a Four Harness Loom, A	Thilenius, Carol	√	√	Iw	4	3		Su 79	34
Bronson Weave	Handweaver's Instruction Manual: The Bronson Weave	Tidball, Harriet C. nee Douglas	√	√	SCGM		34		49	30
Bronson Weave	Shaker Towels: A Guild Devotes a Year of Study to Nineteenth Century Textiles (error-corrected WJ v11 n2 86 p68)	Eastlake, Sandy	√	>4	WJ	10	4	40	Sp 86	20

SUBJECT	TITLE	AUTHOR	IL	INST	JOUR	VOL	NO	ISS	DATE	PAGE
Bronson Weave	Textile Structure and Analysis, A Home Study Course in Twelve Lessons: Lessons in Weave Structure, 5. Bronson Weaves	Tidball, Harriet		√	SCGM		18		66	26
Bronson Weave	Working with the Bias	West, Virginia	√	> 4	WJ	12	1	45	Su 87	9
Bronson Weaves	Pattern and Structure in Handwoven Fabrics	Frey, Berta	√	√	H&C	6	4		Fa 55	4
Brooks Bouquet	Design for a Lunch Cloth in Three Techniques	Redfield, Gail M.	√	√	H&C	19	3		Su 68	15
Brooms	Hearth Brooms (Anne Bliss)		√	√	Hw	1	2		S-S 80	27, 57
Brushing: Cotton	Brushing Cotton	Moore, Carla S.	√		WJ	11	2	42	Fa 86	38
Brussels	Dorothy Liebes Designs Fabrics for U.S. Theatre at the Brussels World's Fair		√		H&C	9	2		Sp 58	26
Buckles	Fashion Focus: Sashes, Belts & Buckles	Snover, Susan	√	√	Hw	6	1		J/F 85	10
Bumberet Weave	Weaving Table Linens	Eychaner, Barbara Smith	√	√	TM			11	J/J 87	52
Burial Caves: West Africa	Medieval Textiles from the Tellem Caves in Central Mali, West Africa	Bedaux, Rogier M. A.; Rita Bolland	√		TMJ	19 20			80,81	65
Business Management	Financial Statements: An Aid to Financial Management	LaLena, Constance	√	√	Hw	6	2		M/A 85	33
Business Management	Sales Brochures	LaLena, Constance	√	√	Hw	6	5		N/D 85	80
Business Management	Weaving as a Professional: Production Weaving/Designing	Checker, Janet	√		WJ	6	3	23	Wi 81	29
Business Management: Financial	Borrowing from the Bank	LaLena, Constance			Hw	6	3		Su 85	33
Business Management: Financial	Break-Even Analysis	LaLena, Constance			Hw	7	4		S/O 86	60
Business Practices	Bannerworks	Strosnider, Ann	√		Fa	10	5		S/O 83	66
Business Practices	Being Professional	Dunwell, Anna	√		Fa	10	4		J/A 83	40
Business: Practices	Economics of Pricing, The	Cutcher, Hal			Fa	4	1		J/F 77	11
Business Practices	Money Matters	Beschell, Lorraine	√		Fa	5	4		J/A 78	56
Business Practices	Personal Notes on a Dyeing Art	Lapin, Claudia	√		Fa	4	4		J/A 77	60
Business Practices	Photographing Your Fiber Work	Long, Doug	√	√	Fa	4	5		S/O 77	45
Business Practices	Setting the Right Price: A Workshop with Libby Platus (error-corrected Fa v13 n1 86 p5)	Caldwell, Rebecca	√		Fa	12	5		S/O 85	51
Business Practices	Sharon La Pierre		√		Fa	4	1		J/F 77	28
Business Practices	Taking It to the Streets: Marketing Your Multiples	Clark, Noel	√		Fa	5	5		S/O 78	26
Business Practices: Planning	Planning for the Future	LaLena Constance			Hw	5	1		J/F 84	77
Business Practices: Production Efficiency	Equipment for Production Efficiency: Other Helpful Equipment	LaLena, Constance	√		Hw	5	5		N/D 84	79
Business Practices: Production Efficiency	Equipment for Production Efficiency: The Loom	LaLena, Constance			Hw	5	4		S/0 84	29
Businesses	By the Yard	Mattera, Joanne	√		TM			5	J/J 86	50
Businesses	Career Issues: Showing, Selling, and Documenting Your Work				Fa	9	5		S/O 82	52
Businesses	Hobby or Business?	Smith, William L.	√		SS&D	18	4	72	Fa 87	44
Businesses	Individual/Artistic Development: A Workshop by Francoise Grossen	Lilligren, Ingrid	√		Fa	11	3		M/J 84	45
Businesses	Managing Your Time, Part 1	LaLena, Constance	√	√	Iw	5	2		Sp 80	64
Businesses	Managing Your Time, Part 2	LaLena, Constance		√	Iw	5	3		Su 80	60
Businesses	Own Your Own				SS&D	1	4	4	Se 70	13
Businesses	Tax Tips-Education and Convention Expenses	Smith, William L.	√		SS&D	19	1	73	Wi 87	8
Businesses: Accounting	Keeping Books	LaLena, Constance	√	√	Hw	8	2		M/A 87	28
Businesses: Brushing Fabrics	Brushing Cotton	Moore, Carla S.	√		WJ	11	2	42	Fa 86	38
Businesses: Brushing Wool	Tämä on Ihana!	Scorgie, Jean	√		Hw	7	1		J/F 86	45
Businesses: Collector Wearables	Sue Nechin of First Additions	Koplos, Janet	√		Fa	10	1		J/F 83	69
Businesses: Crafts	From the High Andes to New York		√		H&C	12	1		Wi 61	53

SUBJECT	TITLE	AUTHOR	IL	INST	JOUR	VOL	NO	ISS	DATE	PAGE
Businesses: Crafts	Shop One, A Unique Craftsmen's Venture in Rochester, N. Y.		√		H&C	5	3		Su 54	45
Businesses: Fashion	Not Necessarily Seventh Ave.	Dyett, Linda	√		TM			6	A/S 86	28
Businesses: Fiber	Fiber Boom, The		√		Fa	4	4		J/A 77	20
Businesses: Papermaking	Papermaking in Chicago	Shermeta, Margo	√		Fa	11	2		M/A 84	54
Businesses: Quiltmaking	Double Lives: Can You Love Your "Work" When It's Your "Job"?	Mattera, Joanne	√		TM			10	A/M 87	62
Businesses: Small	Perfect Balance, A	LaLena, Constance	√		Hw	3	4		Se 82	77
Businesses: Specialty Yarn	Color Specialists, The		√		Kn	2	1	3	F-W 85	64
Businesses: Spinning	Door Closes for Shelburne Spinners, The	Clark, Katherine	√		SS&D	9	3	35	Su 78	34
Businesses: Spinning	Shelburne Spinners: Pushing for Perfection	Cysewski, Catherine	√		Iw	3	1		Fa 77	22
Businesses: Tapestry	Tapestry: As a Business?	Harvey, Nancy	√	√	SS&D	15	3	59	Su 84	37
Businesses: Textile	Ayottes' Designery				H&C	18	2		Sp 67	37
Businesses: Textile	Dorothy Liebes Studio				H&C	5	1		Wi 53	35
Businesses: Textile	Peggy Ives Retires — Long Established Business to C. S. Bourgeois		√		H&C	6	2		Sp 55	28
Businesses: Textile Supplies	Setting Up Shop	Ligon, Linda	√		Iw	2	4		Su 77	18
Businesses: Weaving	Business of Weaving — An Interview With Elaine P. Nixon, The	Derr, Mary	√		WJ	4	1	13	Jy 79	10
Businesses: Weaving	Can a Weaver Earn a Living? Mais Certainement!	Ryall, Pierre	√		SS&D	7	3	27	Su 76	4
Businesses: Weaving	Connie LaLena: Colonial Textiles Today	Ligon, Linda	√		Iw	3	1		Fa 77	15
Businesses: Weaving	Defining Your Business	LaLena, Constance	√		Iw	5	4		Fa 80	58
Businesses: Weaving	Do You Want to Sell Your Weaving?	Redding, Winogene B.			H&C	5	1		Wi 53	30
Businesses: Weaving	Family Hobby Becomes a Family Business	Grant, Jay S.	√		H&C	7	4		Fa 56	49
Businesses: Weaving	Help in the Studio II: Hiring a Permanent Staff	LaLena, Constance		√	Hw	4	1		J/F 83	74
Businesses: Weaving	Lee Carlin: Handweaving Entrepreneur	Ligon, Linda	√		Iw	3	1		Fa 77	26
Businesses: Weaving	Making Ends Meet At the Loom	Kosikowski, Janusz	√		SS&D	7	4	28	Fa 76	28
Businesses: Weaving	Marketing Handwoven Fabric for Apparel & Interiors	Alaniz, Leonore	√		WJ	11	4	44	Sp 87	31
Businesses: Weaving	New Weaving Shop in Santa Barbara		√		H&C	6	3		Su 55	59
Businesses: Weaving	Pricing the Production Piece	La Lena, Constance J.	√	√	SS&D	10	2	38	Sp 79	10
Businesses: Weaving	Two Weavers in Washington	Arndt, Jessie Ash			H&C	20	4		Fa 69	20
Businesses: Weaving	Weaving for a Livelihood	Hotchkiss, Ann			H&C	12	1		Wi 61	26
Businesses: Weaving	Weaving for Sale	Kossick, Ebba	√		H&C	17	3		Su 66	23
Businesses: Weaving	Weaving Together: The Ayottes of Center Sandwich, New Hampshire (Error-corrected WJ v11 n3 87 p78)	Elder, Shirley	√		WJ	11	2	42	Fa 86	30
Businesses: Weaving, Disabled	Income for the Handicapped — A Philadelphia Story	Couch, Jo-Alice	√		H&C	2	4		Fa 51	28
Businesses: Weaving, Establishing	How to Establish a Handweaving Businesss	Seeley, Anne	√		H&C	2	4		Fa 51	32
Businesses: Weaving Related	Defining Your Business	LaLena, Constance	√		Iw	5	4		Fa 80	58
Businesses: Weaving, Suppliers	Weaving Business, The	Cairns, Michael			SS&D	8	3	31	Su 77	6
Businesses: Wool	Know Your Supplier				S-O	11	3		Fa 87	41
Businesses: Wool Production	Premium Wool—A Producer's Perspective	Parker, Ron			S-O	11	3		Fa 87	39
Businesses: Yarn	American Yarn Shops: On the Endangered Species List?	Xenakis, Alexis Yiorgos	√		Kn	3	4	8	Fa 87	10
Businesses: Yarn	Bottom Line, The	Weissman, Julia	√		Kn	3	4	8	Fa 87	11
Businesses: Yarn	Dear Yarn Shop	LaBranche, Carol			Kn	3	4	8	Fa 87	10
Butternut	Why Bother with Natural Dyeing?	Bulbach, Stanley	√	√	TM			5	J/J 86	32
Buttonholes, Button Loops	Buttonholes in Boiled Wool			√	TM			12	A/S 87	8
Buttonholes, Button Loops	Correct Sewing Methods in Tailoring	Bryan, Dorothy	√	√	H&C	10	3		Su 59	25
Buttonholes, Button Loops	Garden of Fair Isles, A	Rowe, Mary	√	√	Kn	2	1	3	F-W 85	40, 8B

SUBJECT	TITLE	AUTHOR	IL	INST	JOUR	VOL	NO	ISS	DATE	PAGE
Buttonholes, Button Loops	Lesson in Cut and Sewn Handwoven Garments, A (error-corrected Hw v2 n2 81 p68)	Wertenberger, Kathryn	√	√	Hw	2	1		F-W 80	36
Buttonholes, Button Loops	Making Buttonholes		√	√	TM			1	O/N 85	6
Buttonholes, Button Loops	Two Styles of Buttonholes	Righetti, Maggie	√	√	TM			3	F/M 86	32
Buttonholes, Buttonloops	Beating the Button(hole) Blues	Moes, Dini	√	√	SS&D	15	2	58	Sp 84	64
Buttonholes: Interfacing	Making Sense of Interfacing (error-corrected TM n12 p4)	Komives, Margaret Deck	√	√	TM			10	A/M 87	58
Buttonholes: Invisible	Invisible Buttonholes			√	TM			14	D/J 87	10
Buttonholes: Knit	Cardigan Buttonholes			√	TM			9	F/M 87	4
Buttonholes: Knit	Knit Buttonholes You Won't Mind Seeing			√	TM			14	D/J 87	10
Buttons	Beads, Buttons & Findings	Green, Marilyn	√		Hw	7	5		N/D 86	84
Buttons	Buttons	Abbott, Deborah	√	√	TM			2	D/J 85	56
Buttons	Buttons: Wearable Art in Miniature	Epstein, Diana	√		Fa	12	3		M/J 85	61
Buttons	Knotted Chinese Button	Baizerman, Suzanne	√	√	WJ	9	1	33	Su 84	7
Buttons: Attaching	Buttons in Half the Time			√	TM			11	J/J 87	8
Buttons: Attaching	Easier Button Shanks			√	TM			14	D/J 87	10
Buttons: Attaching	No Dental Floss				TM			12	A/S 87	4
Buttons: Covering	Easy Covered Buttons			√	TM			10	A/M 87	12
Buttons: Sewing-On, Dental Floss	Buttons with Bite			√	TM			10	A/M 87	12
Byzantine Art	Coptic Tapestry of Byzantine Style, A	Berliner, Rudolf	√		TMJ	1	1		No 62	3
Cable Patterns	Aran Knitting	Starmore, Alice	√	√	TM			14	D/J 87	50
Cable Patterns	Diagonal Cables: A Machine Knitter's Guide to Cabling Against the Grain	Guagliumi, Susan	√	√	TM			14	D/J 87	58
Cable Stitches	Braid on the Bias (error-corrected Kn v3 n1 i5 f/w 86 p11)	Madden, Gail	√	√	Kn	2	2	4	S-S 86	35
Cable Stitches	Carnival Cable Pullover	Jensen, Candi	√	√	Kn	3	1	5	F-W 86	24
Cable Stitches	Chanel Jacket	Ratigan, Dorothy	√	√	Kn	2	2	4	S-S 86	33
Cable Stitches	Now, That's a Cabled Sweater	Yaksick, Karen	√	√	Kn	3	1	5	F-W 86	30
Cable Stitches	On Designing with Slip Stitch Bands	Newton, Deborah	√	√	Kn	3	1	5	F-W 86	21
Cable Stitches	Ropes and Braids	Lewis, Susanna E.	√	√	Kn	2	2	4	S-S 86	19
Cable Stitches	Simple Crossings for Hand Knitters	Lewis, Susanna E.	√	√	Kn	2	2	4	S-S 86	21
Cable Sweaters	Braid on the Bias (error-corrected Kn v3 n1 i5 f/w 86 p11)	Madden, Gail	√	√	Kn	2	2	4	S-S 86	35
Cadillac Upholstery	Custom Fabrics for a Classic Cadillac	Kelly, Jacquie	√	> 4	WJ	10	4	40	Sp 86	54
Caftan	Caftan (Sharon Alderman)		√	√	Hw	1	2		S-S 80	46, 65
Caftan: Northern Caucasus	Newly Excavated Caftan from the Northern Caucasus, A	Riboud, Krishna	√		TMJ	4	3		76	21
Calabrian Weave	Why Not Try Embroidery Weaves?	Jones, Jeanetta L.	√	√	H&C	17	2		Sp 66	12
Camel Girths	Split-Ply Twining: Patterns of Three Camel Girths	Harvey, Virginia I.	√	√	TIAM		1		76	31
Camera Strap	Camera Strap in Double-Weave Pick-Up	Gaston-Voûte, Suzanne	√	√	PWC			2	Ap 82	10
Camera Strap	Summer Take-along project, A	Luebbers, Karen	√	√	Hw	6	2		M/A 85	92
Canada	Assomption Sash, A Long Tradition in French Canada	Whitelaw, Adrienne	√	√	H&C	21	3		Su 70	12
Canada	Canada Council Art Bank, The	Kirby, William	√		AT	7			Ju 87	75
Canada	Canadian Classic, A	Baker, William R. M.	√		SS&D	18	3	71	Su 87	52
Canada	Canadian Handweaving (Exhibit)		√		Fa	13	3		M/J 86	55
Canada	Canadian Portfolio, A	Place, Jennifer	√		Fa	9	6		N/D 82	29
Canada	Convergence '86 Preview: Pangnirtung Weavers	Stuart, Donald	√		SS&D	16	4	64	Fa 85	70
Canada	Convergence '86 Preview: Toronto — A City in Transition	Baker, William R. M.	√		SS&D	17	1	65	Wi 85	42
Canada	Current Canadian Weaving			√	H&C	4	3		Su 53	36
Canada	Fiber Heritage of the Salish	Whonnock Spinners & Weavers	√		WJ	9	2	34	Fa 84	65
Canada	Fibre Interchange At the Banff Centre	Corpier, Leslee	√		Fa	12	4		J/A 85	40

SUBJECT	TITLE	AUTHOR	IL	INST	JOUR	VOL	NO	ISS	DATE	PAGE
Canada	Fibre-Form-Fusion: Gathering Together in Canada	Malarcher, Patricia	√		Fa	7	6		N/D 80	26
Canada	International Exposure Conference	Place, Jennifer	√		Fa	10	5		S/O 83	51
Canada	Making Weaving History	Xenakis, Alexis Yiorgos	√		PWC	4	3	13		6
Canada	New Brunswick Craft School: Hosting A Workshop by Barbara MacCallum, The	Bauer, Nancy	√		Fa	11	5		S/O 84	40
Canada	Raising the Silkworm in a Northern Climate	Szpakowski, Marceline		√	AT	2			De 84	157
Canada	South of the Border Down Canada Way	Anders, Eunice	√		SS&D	3	3	11	Su 72	6
Canada	Time Warp on the Coldstream	McIntyre, Walter	√		SS&D	15	4	60	Fa 84	50
Canada	Toronto's "unMuseum" for Textiles	Talley, Charles	√		Fa	12	4		J/A 85	43
Canada	Weaving Abroad II	Huebner, Marianne	√		H&C	21	4		Fa 70	21
Canada, British Columbia	Cowichan Country	Gibson-Roberts, Priscilla A.	√	√	Kn	3	1	5	F-W 86	61
Canada: Toronto	With Needle, Thread and Imagination			√	SS&D	1	4	4	Se 70	10
Canadian Guild of Crafts	Canadian Guild of Crafts			√	H&C	18	4		Fa 67	13
Candlewicking	Cotton Candlewicking (Jane Patrick)		√	√	Hw	3	5		N/D 82	30, 99
Cannelé	Cannelé: Create a Sumptuous Fabric That Drapes Beautifully	Broughton, Cynthia	√	√	WJ	10	3	39	Wi 86	59
Cannelé	Little Known Weaves Worth Knowing Better: Cannele	Zielinski, S. A.; Robert Leclerc, ed.	√	√	MWL	16			'51–'73	20
Cannelé	Tunic with Ribbons (Carol Powalisz)		√	√	Hw	8	1		J/F 87	52, I-8
Cannelé Ondulé	Notebook: Floats on the Surface (Betty Hagedorn)	Meyers, Ruth Nordquist, ed.	√	√	SS&D	14	3	55	Su 83	90
Canvas Weave	All Around — Year Around Shawl	Herring, Connie	√	> 4	PWC			2	Ap 82	70
Canvas Weave	Canvas Weave Elegance	Herring, Connie	√	> 4	PWC	4	1	11		23
Canvas Weave	Halfghan	Xenakis, Athanasios David	√	√	PWC	3	1	7		34
Canvas Weave	If You Have Four Harnesses	Hagarty, Harriet May		√	H&C	23	5		S/O 72	16
Canvas Weave	Red and Blue Canvas Weave Afghan	Xenakis, Athanasios David	√	√	PWC	3	1	7		22
Canvas Weave	Shuttle	Marston, Ena	√	√	SS&D	2	4	8	Fa 71	14
Canvas Weave	Simple Damask-Like Effects Using Element Diameter Differential and Element Tension Differential	Xenakis, Athanasios David	√	> 4	AT	1			De 83	317
Canvas Weave, Spot	Curtain Fabric #1 (Constance LaLena) (error-corrected Hw v7 n4 86 pl-3)		√	√	Hw	6	4		S/O 85	46, I-5
Capes	Ann Burian: Mythic Transformations	Hains, Maryellen	√		Fa	12	2		M/A 85	21
Capes	Applying the Pulled Warp Technique to Loom-Shaped Clothing	Evans, Kerry	√	√	WJ	9	3	35	Wi 85	34
Capes	Art of Fashion Design: A Handweaver's Twill Cape, The	Johnson, Judith K.	√	√	WJ	7	3	27	Wi 82	12
Capes	Autumn Sunset Cape (Leslie Voiers)		√	> 4	WJ	11	3	43	Wi 87	22
Capes	Cape by Virginia M. West		√	> 4	H&C	20	3		Su 69	21
Capes	Cape (Merna Beeny)		√	√	Hw	4	4		S/O 83	45, 95
Capes	Cape (Sharon Alderman)		√	√	Hw	2	4		Se 81	45, 84
Capes	Cape-Able Garment	Hicks, C. Norman	√	√	SS&D	6	3	23	Su 75	18
Capes	Capes Updated		√	√	H&C	26	2		Ap 75	38
Capes	Coat with Cape Sleeves (Leslie Voiers)		√	√	Hw	6	4		S/O 85	54, I-9
Capes	Contemporary Costume, Strictly Handwoven: A Cape or Coat for Winter Sports	Tidball, Harriet	√	√	SCGM		24		68	24
Capes	Contemporary Costume, Strictly Handwoven: The Nell Scott Cape	Tidball, Harriet	√	√	SCGM		24		68	12
Capes	Feather Cape, After the One Pocahontas Took to England	Frey, Berta	√	> 4	H&C	21	4		Fa 70	22
Capes	Feltmaking	Wald, Pat Boutin	√	√	S-O	1			77	46
Capes	Garments with Ethnic Flavor: Pine Tree Cape		√	> 4	WJ	2	3	7	Ja 78	16
Capes	Handwoven Cape on an Improvised Loom	Williams, Olive	√	√	H&C	22	3		Su 71	28

SUBJECT	TITLE	AUTHOR	IL	INST	JOUR	VOL	NO	ISS	DATE	PAGE
Capes	How Madame Grès Sculpts with Fabric	Cooper, Arlene	√	√	TM			10	A/M 87	50
Capes	Irish Kinsale Cloak, The	Jones, Una	√	√	WJ	8	3	31	Wi 83	35
Capes	Kinsale Cloak	Adams, Brucie	√	√	S-O	4			80	56
Capes	Llama Cape, The	Keeler, Betty			H&C	23	4		J/A 72	46
Capes	Long Sweeping Evening Cape	Roth, Bettie G.	√	> 4	WJ	6	3	23	Wi 81	26
Capes	Opera Elegance	Sylvan, Katherine	√	√	SS&D	15	4	60	Fa 84	24
Capes	Oval Cape	Sylvan, Katherine	√	√	WJ	5	3	19	Wi 81	36
Capes	Promise Kept, A	Moes, Dini	√	√	SS&D	16	3	63	Su 85	63
Capes	Ribbon Afghan and Bed Cape (Chris Switzer)		√	√	Hw	1	2		S-S 80	37, 59
Capes	Seattle Guild Garment Designs, Part 4: Edges, Closures, Capes, Dresses		√	√	SS&D	11	2	42	Sp 80	39
Capes	Shadow Weave Cape (Pat Richardson)		√	√	Hw	8	5		N/D 87	51, I-10
Capes	Snow White and a Seven-Yard Warp	Crawford, Libby	√		SS&D	2	1	5	De 70	11
Capes	Veridian Green Cape	Barrett, Clotilde	√	> 4	WJ	4	3	15	Ja 80	11
Capes	Very Special Cape, A	Alderman, Sharon D.			Hw	2	4		Se 81	46
Capes	White Circular Wrap	Richards, Iris	√	√	WJ	4	3	15	Ja 80	7
Capes	Wrapped in Style: Poncho Cape (Betty Beard)		√	√	Hw	6	1		J/F 85	41, I-14
Caps and Hats	Bag, Hat and Quesquemitl	Thorne, Sylvia; June Segermark	√	√	SS&D	3	1	9	Wi 71	18
Caps and Hats	Beginner's Hat and Scarf	Skoy, Mary Lonning	√	√	WJ	11	3	43	Wi 87	61
Caps and Hats	Bogus Bohus	Bush, Nancy	√	√	Kn	2	1	3	F-W 85	49
Caps and Hats	Bonnie Bonnet	Adams, Harriet	√	√	Kn	1	2	2	S-S 85	38
Caps and Hats	Bye, Baby Bunting	Hayes, Beth	√		S-O	10	2		Su 86	19
Caps and Hats	Caps, Hats, Mittens, Gloves, Scarves, Socks Contest Winners				S-O	10	3		Fa 86	13
Caps and Hats	Cone of Aran Hats, A	Oakley, Helen	√	√	TM			13	O/N 87	27
Caps and Hats	Cross Country Ski Set	Chadwick, Louisa	√	√	S-O	11	4		Wi 87	34
Caps and Hats	Dubbelmossa	Adams, Harriet	√	√	Kn	2	1	3	F-W 85	50, 8B
Caps and Hats	Evolution of a Project	de Grassi, Laurel	√	√	S-O	10	4		Wi 86	21
Caps and Hats	Exploring a Knitted Pattern	Bruzelius, Margaret	√	√	TM			6	A/S 86	35
Caps and Hats	Felt Vest, Hat, Mittens	Betts, Diane	√	√	S-O	9	2		Su 85	39
Caps and Hats	Felting	Askenfors, Gunilla	√	√	WJ	6	1	21	Su 81	31
Caps and Hats	Fishperson's Earflap Hat	Sherrodd, Kristie	√	√	S-O	11	3		Fa 87	53
Caps and Hats	Folk Textiles of Latin America	Kelemen, Pál	√		TMJ	1	4		De 65	2
Caps and Hats	Handbags and A Hat	Phelps, Marie	√	√	H&C	1	3		Fa 50	29
Caps and Hats	Hats, Hats, Hats	Martin, Jill			S-O	7	3		Fa 83	18
Caps and Hats	"Headlines: A Hundred Years of Hats (1840–1940)" (Exhibit)	Luddecke, Jane	√		Fa	6	6		N/D 79	78
Caps and Hats	Here Are the Last of the Hatters	Shufro, Cathy			TM			2	D/J 85	14
Caps and Hats	High-Status Caps of the Kongo and Mbundu Peoples	Gibson, Gordon D.; Cecilia R. McGurk	√		TMJ	4	4		77	71
Caps and Hats	Homage to Hats: Handmade Paper Drawing/Collages Honor a Women's Tradition	Rusoff, Beverly	√		Fa	8	1		J/F 81	80
Caps and Hats	Homemade Felt	March, Heather	√	√	TM			2	D/J 85	60
Caps and Hats	"Joan Steiner: Hats/New Sculpture" (Exhibit)	Katz, Ruth J.	√		Fa	7	5		S/O 80	72
Caps and Hats	Llama Hat	Davidsohn, Marty	√	√	PWC			4	Ja 83	65
Caps and Hats	Mohair Tam O'Shanter	Royce, Beverly; Florence Van Kleek	√	√	S-O	8	1		Sp 84	49
Caps and Hats	Mother and Daughter Bonnets	Clement, Doris	√	√	H&C	13	3		Su 62	36
Caps and Hats	Pencil Roving and the Navajo Ply	Adams, Brucie	√	√	Hw	6	1		J/F 85	75
Caps and Hats	Peruvian Hat	Ekstrom, Brenda	√	√	S-O	4			80	59
Caps and Hats	Peruvian Hat	Rowley, Elaine D.	√	√	PWC			4	Ja 83	65

SUBJECT	TITLE	AUTHOR	IL	INST	JOUR	VOL	NO	ISS	DATE	PAGE
Caps and Hats	Peruvian Straw Hat: Documenting A Declining Industry, The	Zimmer, Roni	√		Fa	12	3		M/J 85	39
Caps and Hats	Peruvian Technique for Dimensional Knotting	Bravo, Monica	√	√	WJ	12	1	45	Su 87	17
Caps and Hats	Riding the Modern Range: Stetson Hats	Goodman, Deborah Lerme	√	√	Fa	13	4		J/A 86	8
Caps and Hats	"Ruth's Madcaps" (Exhibit)	Haynes, Maryellen	√		Fa	14	4		S/O 87	9
Caps and Hats	Scandinavian Nålbinding: Needle Looped Fabric	Martinson, Kate	√	√	WJ	12	2	46	Fa 87	12
Caps and Hats	Scarf and Cap	Switzer, Chris	√	√	S-O	4			80	58
Caps and Hats	Scarf and Hat Set (Janice Jones)		√	√	Hw	4	4		S/O 83	44, 94
Caps and Hats	Scarf, Cap and Mittens Set (Marit Drenckhahn)		√	√	Hw	2	1		F-W 80	52, 78
Caps and Hats	"Shoes and Chapeaux": Visit to an Exhibition (Exhibit)			√	Fa	10	1		J/F 83	23
Caps and Hats	SPIN-OFF Book of World Records		√		S-O	7	3		Fa 83	11
Caps and Hats	Sprang and Frame Plaiting for Garments		√	√	WJ	3	3	11	Ja 79	26
Caps and Hats	Tubular Weave Vest and Hat (Sharon Lappin Lumsden)		√	√	Hw	8	1		J/F 87	48, I-6
Caps and Hats	Tulip Outfit with Loom Controlled Inlay (error-corrected WJ v6 n1 81 p28d)	Kuwabara, Nancy	√	> 4	WJ	5	3	19	Wi 81	28
Caps and Hats	Variations on a Midnight Rainbow	West, Sally	√	√	S-O	9	4		Wi 85	14
Caps and Hats	Velten—Valkning—Felting	Beukers, Henriette	√	√	Hw	4	5		N/D 83	80
Caps and Hats	Winning Woven Winter Warmers		√	> 4	Hw	7	1		J/F 86	32
Caps and Hats	Zoltán Mihalkó: Hungarian Feltmaker	Beede, Beth; Jill Garfunkel	√	√	SS&D	17	4	68	Fa 86	12
Card Weaving see Band Weaving										
Card Weaving, Double Weave	Cardwoven Double Weave, Part 2	Gray, Herbi	√	√	SS&D	15	1	57	Wi 83	92
Carding	Carded Rainbow Batts	Amos, Alden	√	√	S-O	9	1		Sp 85	19
Carding	Carders: Hand or Drum	Hochberg, Bette	√	√	S-O	3			79	40
Carding	Carding, Part 3	Hicks, C. Norman	√	√	SS&D	6	2	22	Sp 75	60
Carding	Fibre Preparation	Fraser, Victoria Keller	√		H&C	24	3		M/J 73	32
Carding	Spinner's Specialty: Heathered Yarns, A	Searle, Karen	√	√	WJ	9	2	34	Fa 84	56
Carding	What a Handweaver Can Learn from the Scottish Weaving Industry (error-corrected WJ v2 n1 77 insert for vol. 1)	Barrett, Clotilde	√	√	WJ	1	3	3	Ja 77	11
Carding, Bench	Alternates to Hand Carding	Hicks, C. Norman		√	SS&D	7	1	25	Wi 75	74
Carding: Box	Carding Box, The	Koster, Joan Bouza	√	√	SS&D	10	4	40	Fa 79	24
Carding: Color Blending	Color Blended Scarves		√	√	S-O	11	1		Sp 87	23
Carding: Color Blending	Color Games	Berent, Mary, et al.	√	√	S-O	11	1		Sp 87	21
Carding: Color Blending	Spiral Tube Socks		√	√	S-O	11	1		Sp 87	22
Carding Cotton	Spinning Cotton with the Linders	Linder, Olive; Harry Linder	√	√	WJ	11	2	42	Fa 86	14
Carding, Dog Hair	Spinning and Use of Dog's Hair, The	Pubols, Dorothy M.	√	√	WJ	4	1	13	Jy 79	36
Carding, Dog Hair	Spinning Doghair	Barrett, Clotilde	√	√	WJ	1	1	1	Jy 76	27
Carding: Hand	Proper Preparation of Fibers for Spinners	Fannin, Allen A.	√	√	H&C	20	3		Su 69	19
Carding: Machine	Bench Carding	Hicks, C. Norman	√	√	SS&D	7	2	26	Sp 76	60
Carding: Machine	Carding by Machine, Method of Fiber Preparation	Simmons, Paula	√	√	H&C	20	3		Su 69	16
Carding: Machine	Hand-Carding by Machine	Chesley, Zina Mae	√	√	SS&D	1	3	3	Ju 70	18
Carding Machines	1979 Fiberarts Equipment Directory: Carding Machines, The		√		Fa	6	2		M/A 79	57
Carding Machines	Carding Machines	Adams, Brucie	√		Iw	4	3		Su 79	54
Carding Machines	Devices to Aid in Wool Processing	Adams, Brucie	√		Hw	3	4		Se 82	69
Carding Machines	Drum Carder, The	Rossiter, Phyllis	√	√	SS&D	15	4	60	Fa 84	71
CARE	Spinning Mohair in Lesotho	Snieckus, Mary Ann	√		TM			8	D/J 86	66
Care: Hooked Rugs	Traditional Rug Hooking with a Twist	Erickson, Janet Doub	√	√	TM			12	A/S 87	30

SUBJECT	TITLE	AUTHOR	IL	INST	JOUR	VOL	NO	ISS	DATE	PAGE
Care: Knitted Cotton	Knitting with Cotton: Stitch Maneuvers Help Sweaters Stay in Shape	Dyett, Linda	√	√	TM			9	F/M 87	38
Careers: Designer/Weaver	Contemporary American Handweaving from an International Perspective	Alaniz, Leonore	√		WJ	11	3	43	Wi 87	26
Careers: Dyeing	Lifestyle: A Roundtable Discussion	Ligon, Linda	√		Iw	5	2		Sp 80	22
Careers: Handweaving, Industry	Opportunities for Handweavers in the Textile Industry				H&C	10	3		Su 59	13
Careers: Handweaving, Textile Industry	Opportunities for Handweavers in the Textile Industry		√		H&C	3	4		Fa 52	42
Careers: Spinning	Lifestyle: A Roundtable Discussion	Ligon, Linda	√		Iw	5	2		Sp 80	22
Careers: Teaching	Lifestyle: A Roundtable Discussion	Ligon, Linda	√		Iw	5	2		Sp 80	22
Careers: Textile, Part-Time	Part-Time Challenge: When Textile Art Plays a Secondary Role in One's Life, The	Bennett, Jennifer	√		Fa	10	3		M/J 83	51
Careers: Weaving	Developing Career Weavers	Johansen, Marg	√		SS&D	6	2	22	Sp 75	46
Careers: Weaving	Handweaving for a Living — How Feasible?	Carlin, Lee			SS&D	6	4	24	Fa 75	33
Careers: Weaving	In Pursuit of a Lifestyle	Grant, Susan	√		Iw	5	2		Sp 80	32
Careers: Weaving	Lifestyle: A Roundtable Discussion	Ligon, Linda	√		Iw	5	2		Sp 80	22
Careers: Weaving	Rug Weaving: One Weaver's Approach	Hand, Barbara	√	> 4	WJ	7	4	28	Sp 83	32
Caribou Hair	Caribou Hair and the Creation of a New Fabric	Goodfellow, Robin	√		AT	6			De 86	119
Caribou Hair	New Fiber for Spinners: Caribou, A	Goodfellow, Robin; Keith Slater	√		S-O	10	4		Wi 86	46
Carpet see Floor Coverings										
Carpet-Makers: Anatolian	Carpet-Makers of Western Anatolia, 1750–1914, The	Quataert, Donald			TMJ	25			86	25
Carriage Robes	Snow White and a Seven-Yard Warp	Crawford, Libby	√		SS&D	2	1	5	De 70	11
Cartoon	Bringing Tapestry into the 20th Century	Mattera, Joanne	√	√	TM			1	O/N 85	52
Cartoon	Contemporary Tapestry	Tidball, Harriet	√	√	SCGM		12		64	27
Cartoon	French Tapestry Weaving in San Francisco	Tanenbaum, Ruth	√	√	SS&D	8	3	31	Su 77	12
Cartoon	How to Weave a Transparency	Keasbey, Doramay	√	√	Hw	4	1		J/F 83	27
Cartoon	In the Gobelin Tradition: The Drouin Atelier	Gregg, Dorothy	√		SS&D	10	1	37	Wi 78	28
Cartoon	Shaped Sculptured Rugs — A Workshop with Urban Jupena		√	√	WJ	4	1	13	Jy 79	5
Cartoon	Tapestry Room from Croome Court, The		√		H&C	11	3		Su 60	30
Cartoon	Techniques of Tapestry Weaves Part 4: Developing Design for Tapestry	O'Callaghan, Kate	√	√	WJ	5	2	18	Fa 80	15
Cartoon	Weaving in San Francisco — Part 2	Prosser, Evelyn Bingham	√	√	WJ	6	3	23	Wi 81	50
Cartoon: Needlepoint	Rita Maran, Executes Designs in Yarn for Artists		√		H&C	18	1		Wi 67	14
Cartoon: Tapestry	Cartoon, The	Brostoff, Laya	√	√	Hw	3	1		Ja 82	26
Cartoon: Tapestry	Flat Tapestry Cartoon — Ready to Go, A	Swendeman, Dorothy	√	√	Hw	3	1		Ja 82	30
Casements see Window Coverings										
Cashgora	Australian Cashmere and Cashgora	Feldman-Wood, Florence	√		S-O	9	1		Sp 85	42
Cashgora	Closer Look at Cashgora, A	Presser, Fran	√	√	S-O	10	4		Wi 86	49
Cashgora	From the Woolcombers Bench: Cashgora	Dozer, Iris		√	S-O	10	2		Su 86	39
Cashgora	Spinning Australian Cashmere and Cashgora	Feldman-Wood, Florence	√	√	S-O	9	4		Wi 85	40
Cashmere	Australian Cashmere and Cashgora	Feldman-Wood, Florence	√		S-O	9	1		Sp 85	42
Cashmere	Cashmere Challenge, The	Urbanek, Karen	√	√	S-O	10	1		Sp 86	37
Cashmere	First International Cashmere Seminar	Feldman-Wood, Florence			S-O	10	1		Sp 86	39
Cashmere	Kashmir East and West	Mikosch, Elizabeth	√		TM			9	F/M 87	14
Cashmere	Spinning Australian Cashmere and Cashgora	Feldman-Wood, Florence	√	√	S-O	9	4		Wi 85	40
Cast On: Knit-Purl	Cast on in Pattern	Rowley, Elaine	√	√	Kn	3	3	7	Su 87	39
Catalogne	Table Dressing and Bedcovers			√	Fa	8	3		M/J 81	43

SUBJECT	TITLE	AUTHOR	IL	INST	JOUR	VOL	NO	ISS	DATE	PAGE
Catalogne	Weaving in Quebec: Traditional Quebecois Weaving	Barrett, Clotilde	√	√	WJ	6	4	24	Sp 82	10
Catalogues: Carpets	London Carpeted in Oriental Gardens: The 4th International Conference on Oriental Carpets	Dyer, Carolyn Price	√		Fa	11	3		M/J 84	66
Caucasia	Kazak Rugs	Tschebull, Raoul	√		TMJ	3	2		De 71	2
Caucasus	Newly Excavated Caftan from the Northern Caucasus, A	Riboud, Krishna	√		TMJ	4	3		76	21
Cedar	Melody Oakroot-Cedar Weaver	London, Bill	√	√	S-O	10	3		Fa 86	45
Cedar, Handspun	Chilkat Blanket: It Soon May Be No More, The	Eggleston, Phyllis	√	√	SS&D	7	1	25	Wi 75	44
Ceinture Fléchée	Assomption Sash, A Long Tradition in French Canada	Whitelaw, Adrienne	√	√	H&C	21	3		Su 70	12
Ceinture Flêcheé	Weaving in Quebec: Traditional Quebecois Weaving	Barrett, Clotilde	√	√	WJ	6	4	24	Sp 82	10
Celebrations	Rocky Mountain Guild Observes Colorado Centennial	Tuinsma, Frieda Z.	√		H&C	10	3		Su 59	16
Celtic Art	Ballinskelligs Tapestry Works: Ancient Art/Modern Spirit, The	Burkhauser, Jude	√		Hw	3	1		Ja 82	55
Central America	Splicing from Central America	Sober, Marion B.	√	√	H&C	22	4		Fa 71	18
Ceramics	Elizabeth MacDonald: Finding the Ties That Bind Truth and Art	Reuter, Laurel	√		Fa	14	4		S/O 87	31
Ceramics	Inspired by Fiber: Textile Sensibility in Other Media	Malarcher, Patricia	√		Fa	10	6		N/D 83	33
Ceremonial Fiber	Ruth and David Segunda		√		Fa	4	6		N/D 77	62
Ceremonial Fiber	Tapa-Making in Tonga	Raphael, Jenifer; Chad Raphael	√		Fa	13	6		N/D 86	24
Ceremonial Quilt	Heritage Quilt, The	Greenberg, Blue	√		Fa	12	2		M/A 85	90
Ceremonial Slings	Peruvian Slings: Their Uses and Regional Variations	Noble, Carol Rasmussen	√		WJ	6	4	24	Sp 82	53
Ceremonial Structures	Ceremonial Structures of Terry Jarrard Dimond, The	Hyatt, Sharyn; Teresa Mangum	√		Fa	9	4		J/A 82	66
Ceremonial Textiles	Amanda Lurie: One Weaver's Path	Lurie, Amanda	√		Fa	10	4		J/A 83	16
Ceremonial Textiles	"Ceremonial Garments" (Exhibit)	Laymon, Cynthia	√		Fa	9	6		N/D 82	82
Ceremonial Textiles	Chilkat Blanket: It Soon May Be No More, The	Eggleston, Phyllis	√	√	SS&D	7	1	25	Wi 75	44
Ceremonial Textiles	Chilkat Dancing Blanket, The	Samuel, Cheryl	√		SS&D	13	4	52	Fa 82	58
Ceremonial Textiles	Chilkat Spinning	Samuel, Alena	√	√	TM			1	O/N 85	55
Ceremonial Textiles	Embellishments on the Rain Sash	Baizerman, Suzanne	√	√	WJ	11	2	42	Fa 86	22
Ceremonial Textiles	From Baskets to Blankets (error-corrected TM i7 O/N86 p5)	Samuel, Cheryl	√	√	TM			5	J/J 86	30
Ceremonial Textiles	From English Handlooms Comes Royal Purple Velvet for Coronation Robe of Elizabeth II	Lee, Humphrey A.	√		H&C	4	2		Sp 53	17
Ceremonial Textiles	Fukusa: The Art of Giving	Lancaster, Deborah Lerme	√		Fa	13	6		N/D 86	27
Ceremonial Textiles	Garment Form As Image, The	Koplos, Janet	√		Fa	10	6		N/D 83	66
Ceremonial Textiles	Handwoven Wedding Chuppa, A	Horger, Millicent	√	√	WJ	7	4	28	Sp 83	50
Ceremonial Textiles	Hortense Amram, Designer and Weaver of Ceremonial Textiles		√	√	H&C	9	4		Fa 58	22
Ceremonial Textiles	Indian Fingerweaving, Traditional Use for Ceremonial Sashes	White, John	√	√	H&C	19	3		Su 68	4
Ceremonial Textiles	Liberty Quilts		√		TM			6	A/S 86	100
Ceremonial Textiles	Liturgical Vestment: A Contemporary Overview, The	Malarcher, Patricia	√		Fa	11	5		S/O 84	58
Ceremonial Textiles	Painted Muslin Ghost Dance Costumes of the Sioux, C–1890	Wakeland, Robin	√		Fa	8	1		J/F 81	15
Ceremonial Textiles	Paracas Needle Technique, A	Hoskins, Nancy	√	√	Iw	5	4		Fa 80	34
Ceremonial Textiles	"Patterns of Paradise: Tapa Cloth" (Exhibit)	Dyer, Carolyn	√		Fa	10	3		M/J 83	73
Ceremonial Textiles	Religious Celebration		√		SS&D	11	4	44	Fa 80	22
Ceremonial Textiles	Robes for Inspiration	Dyer, Carolyn	√		Fa	10	1		J/F 83	60

SUBJECT	TITLE	AUTHOR	IL	INST	JOUR	VOL	NO	ISS	DATE	PAGE
Ceremonial Textiles	Santa Fe Weaver Re-Creates Past	Ligon, Linda	√		Iw	1	1		Fa 75	4
Ceremonial Textiles	Symbolic or Sacred? A Personal View	Lockwood, Diana W.	√	> 4	WJ	9	3	35	Wi 85	45
Ceremonial Textiles	Tallis or Prayer Shawl, The	Derr, Mary	√	√	WJ	2	1	5	Jy 77	16
Ceremonial Textiles	Tons of Quilts at Liberty Festival	Wolff, Colette	√		TM			6	A/S 86	22
Ceremonial Textiles	Tree-Bast Fiber Textiles of Japan	Dusenbury, Mary	√	√	S-O	10	3		Fa 86	35
Ceremonial Textiles	Vestment Variations: A Weaver from the Netherlands Creates Garments for the Ecclesiastical Calendar	Jansen, Netty	√	> 4	WJ	10	3	39	Wi 86	53
Ceremonial Textiles	Weaving with the Maoris of New Zealand	Giacchina, Polly Jacobs	√	√	Fa	11	3		M/J 84	48
Ceremonial Textiles: Batak	Selected Batak Textiles: Technique and Function	Gittinger, Mattiebelle S.	√		TMJ	4	2		75	13
Ceremonial Textiles: Caps	Peruvian Technique for Dimensional Knotting	Bravo, Monica	√	√	WJ	12	1	45	Su 87	17
Ceremonial Textiles: Chilkat	Breath of Our Grandmothers, The	Samuel, Cheryl	√		WJ	8	1	29	Su 83	17
Ceremonial Textiles: India	Phulkari	Westfall, Carol D.; Dipti Desai	√		AT	6			De 86	85
Ceremonial Textiles: Japan	Obi: The Textile Art of Nishijin	Donaldson, R. Alan	√		AT	1			De 83	115
Ceremonial Textiles: Lenten Curtains	Lenten Curtains from Colonial Peru	Kelemen, Pál	√		TMJ	3	1		De 70	5
Ceremonial Textiles: Liberty Blanket	Ramah Navajo Weavers, The	D'Andrea, Pat	√		WJ	12	1	45	Su 87	44
Ceremonial Textiles: Quilts	"Quilt National '83" (Exhibit)	Roe, Nancy	√		Fa	10	5		S/O 83	82
Ceremonial Textiles: Salish	Vertical Loom (continued) Part 2, The Two-Beam Loom, The		√	√	WJ	2	1	5	Jy 77	8
Ceremonial Textiles: Ukrainian	Embroidery for the Goddess	Kelly, Mary B.	√		TM			11	J/J 87	26
Ceremonial Textiles: Wedding	Patolu and Its Techniques	De Bone, Mary Golden	√	√	TMJ	4	3		76	49
Chair Back Rest	Children's Chair Seat & Back Rest (Andrea McCormack)		√	√	Hw	3	1		Ja 82	28, 81
Chair Coverings	Sling Chair (Sharon Alderman)		√	√	Hw	6	3		Su 85	58, I-15
Chair Seat	Children's Chair Seat & Back Rest (Andrea McCormack)		√	√	Hw	3	1		Ja 82	28, 81
Chair-Seat Weaving	Chair Seats Woven of Tape and Ash Splints	Sober, Marion Burr	√	√	H&C	19	3		Su 68	13
Chair-Seat Weaving	Scintillating, Soft and Silent Seat, A	Chesley, Mariam Dolloff	√	√	Hw	5	2		M/A 84	27
Chairs: Antique	Antique Spinning Chairs	Becklake, Vera L.	√		WJ	11	2	42	Fa 86	58
Changes: Weaving	Changes in Weaving	LaLena, Constance			Hw	8	1		J/F 87	24
Channel Islands	Guernsey Tradition, The	Rowley, Elaine	√	√	Kn	1	1	1	F-W 84 CI	24 16
Channel Islands	Guernseys	Upitis, Lizbeth			Kn	1	1	1	F-W 84 CI	48 40
Charkha	Modern Charkha, The		√		H&C	9	3		Su 58	23
Charkha	More on....Charkha Techniques	Shepard, Mark	√	√	S-O	8	2		Su 84	36
Charkha	Spinning on the Charkha	Raven, Lee	√	√	S-O	7	1		Sp 83	24
Checks, Plaids, Tartans	Blue and Red Wool Plaid (Jane Patrick)		√	√	Hw	3	5		N/D 82	30, 99
Checks, Plaids, Tartans	Checkerboard Plaid		√	√	Hw	4	5		N/D 83	44
Checks, Plaids, Tartans	Child's Cape (Linda Ligon)		√	√	Hw	1	2		S-S 80	39, 63
Checks, Plaids, Tartans	Cloth for All Seasons, A		√	> 4	Hw	4	5		N/D 83	58
Checks, Plaids, Tartans	Color It Plaid	Bliss, Anne	√		Hw	4	5		N/D 83	74
Checks, Plaids, Tartans	Colorful Scarves	Waggoner, Phyllis	√	√	WJ	12	2	46	Fa 87	48
Checks, Plaids, Tartans	Composition and Designing Part 2: From Hound's Tooth to Random Patterns	Zielinski, S. A.; Robert Leclerc, ed.	√	√	MWL	19			'51–'73	71
Checks, Plaids, Tartans	Composition and Designing Part 2: Hound's Tooth in Texture and Color	Zielinski, S. A.; Robert Leclerc, ed.	√	> 4	MWL	19			'51–'73	66
Checks, Plaids, Tartans	Designer' Notebook	Myers, Ruth, ed.	√	> 4	SS&D	12	2	46	Sp 81	29
Checks, Plaids, Tartans	Desk Chair with Subtle Plaid Pattern	Lohse, Joyce	√	√	WJ	7	1	25	Su 82	24
Checks, Plaids, Tartans	Double Tartan	Xenakis, Athanasios David	√	> 4	PWC	3	1	7		42
Checks, Plaids, Tartans	Dyes of Early Tartans, The		√		Hw	4	5		N/D 83	75

SUBJECT	TITLE	AUTHOR	IL	INST	JOUR	VOL	NO	ISS	DATE	PAGE
Checks, Plaids, Tartans	Eight-Harness Check (Diane Fabeck)	Myers, Ruth, ed.	√	> 4	SS&D	12	2	46	Sp 81	29
Checks, Plaids, Tartans	Elegant Plaid Shawl, An	Kolling-Summers, Elizabeth	√	√	WJ	7	3	27	Wi 82	69
Checks, Plaids, Tartans	Evergreen	Alderman, Sharon	√	√	Hw	4	5		N/D 83	62
Checks, Plaids, Tartans	Fabrics for Interiors #4: Tartan for a Child's Room	LaLena, Constance	√		Hw	4	5		N/D 83	70
Checks, Plaids, Tartans	Fiesta Plaid	Xenakis, Athanasios David	√	√	PWC	3	1	7		39
Checks, Plaids, Tartans	Four-Harness Check (Eleanor Chase)	Myers, Ruth, ed.	√	√	SS&D	12	2	46	Sp 81	29
Checks, Plaids, Tartans	Gray Muffler (Janice Jones)		√	√	Hw	6	4		S/O 85	59, I-10
Checks, Plaids, Tartans	Gray Plaid Jacket (Mary Kay Stoehr)		√	√	Hw	6	4		S/O 85	60, I-11
Checks, Plaids, Tartans	Handspun Plaid Shirt, A (Betty Keeler)		√		Hw	4	5		N/D 83	73
Checks, Plaids, Tartans	Home Weaving: A Happy Plaid (Halcyon)		√	√	Hw	1	1		F-W 79	40
Checks, Plaids, Tartans	Houndstooth Doubleweave (Kathryn Wertenberger)		√	√	Hw	5	2		M/A 84	66, 103
Checks, Plaids, Tartans	How to Weave a Plaid Triangular Shawl	Elich-McCall, Charoltte	√	√	Hw	4	5		N/D 83	54
Checks, Plaids, Tartans	If You Have Four Harnesses	Hagarty, Harriet May		√	H&C	24	3		M/J 73	30
Checks, Plaids, Tartans	Jacket for Hiking, A	Roth, Bettie G.	√	> 4	WJ	8	3	31	Wi 83	69
Checks, Plaids, Tartans	Kilts	Branson, Branley Allan	√		Hw	4	5		N/D 83	34
Checks, Plaids,Tartans	Log Cabin Plaid		√	√	Hw	4	5		N/D 83	42
Checks, Plaids, Tartans	MacCallum Tartan Afghan (Jane Merryman)		√	√	Hw	4	5		N/D 83	Cover, 96
Checks, Plaids, Tartans	Macro Plaid, Macro Twill	Xenakis, Athanasios David	√	> 4	PWC	3	1	7		55
Checks, Plaids, Tartans	Man-Made Fibers: Baby Blankets		√	√	WJ	5	2	18	Fa 80	43
Checks, Plaids, Tartans	New HGA Textile Kits on Review		√		SS&D	12	3	47	Su 81	56
Checks, Plaids, Tartans	Notebook: Tartans	Myers, Ruth Nordquist, ed.	√	√	SS&D	13	1	49	Wi 81	24
Checks, Plaids, Tartans	Notebook: Two-or Four-Harness Check (Marion Gaum)	Myers, Ruth, ed.	√	√	SS&D	12	2	46	Sp 81	28
Checks, Plaids, Tartans	Notes on Planning Plaids			√	Hw	4	5		N/D 83	45
Checks, Plaids, Tartans	Nova Scotia Tartan, The	Black, Mary E.	√		H&C	6	2		Sp 55	26
Checks, Plaids, Tartans	Overshot Plaid		√	√	Hw	4	5		N/D 83	45
Checks, Plaids, Tartans	Plaid Blanket (Linda Ligon)		√	√	Hw	3	5		N/D 82	54, 96
Checks, Plaids, Tartans	Plaid Idea Notebook		√	√	Hw	4	5		N/D 83	41
Checks, Plaids, Tartans	Plaids (error-corrected Hw v5 n1 84 p7)	Wertenberger, Kathryn	√	√	Hw	4	5		N/D 83	50
Checks, Plaids, Tartans	Quiet Simplicity		√		Hw	4	5		N/D 83	60
Checks, Plaids, Tartans	Resist Dyeing, Curiosities and Inventions: Hound's Tooth in Texture and Colour	Zielinski, S. A.; Robert Leclerc, ed.	√	√	MWL	17			'51–'73	68
Checks, Plaids, Tartans	Roman Textiles from Vindolanda, Hexham, England	Wild, John Peter	√		TMJ	18			79	19
Checks, Plaids, Tartans	Scottish District Checks	Snyder, Mary E.	√	√	H&C	16	2		Sp 65	9
Checks, Plaids, Tartans	So You Want to Weave Tartan?	Amos, Alden		√	Hw	4	5		N/D 83	37
Checks, Plaids, Tartans	Spin a Tartan—Naturally	Adams, Brucie	√	√	Hw	4	5		N/D 83	72
Checks, Plaids, Tartans	Tartan Book: A Study Group Project, The	Haller, Jean M.	√	√	Hw	4	5		N/D 83	31
Checks, Plaids, Tartans	Tartan or Plaid?	Evans, Jane A.	√		Hw	4	5		N/D 83	33
Checks, Plaids, Tartans	Twill Plaid		√	√	Hw	4	5		N/D 83	43
Checks, Plaids, Tartans	Twill Plaid, A	Gordon, Judith	√	> 4	Hw	5	2		M/A 84	41
Checks, Plaids, Tartans	Two-Harness Textiles, The Loom-Controlled Weaves: Checks, Blended Checks	Tidball, Harriet	√	√	SCGM		20		67	19
Checks, Plaids, Tartans	Two-Harness Textiles, The Loom-Controlled Weaves: Checks, Gun Club Checks	Tidball, Harriet	√	√	SCGM		20		67	19
Checks, Plaids, Tartans	Two-Harness Textiles, The Loom-Controlled Weaves: Checks, Multi-Color Checks	Tidball, Harriet	√	√	SCGM		20		67	19

SUBJECT	TITLE	AUTHOR	IL	INST	JOUR	VOL	NO	ISS	DATE	PAGE
Checks, Plaids, Tartans	Two-Harness Textiles, The Loom-Controlled Weaves: Checks, Outline Checks	Tidball, Harriet	√	√	SCGM		20		67	18
Checks, Plaids, Tartans	Two-Harness Textiles, The Loom-Controlled Weaves: Checks, Plain and Fancy	Tidball, Harriet	√	√	SCGM		20		67	18
Checks, Plaids, Tartans	Two-Harness Textiles, The Loom-Controlled Weaves: Checks, Shadow Checks	Tidball, Harriet	√	√	SCGM		20		67	19
Checks, Plaids, Tartans	Two-Harness Textiles, The Loom-Controlled Weaves: Checks, Unequal Checks	Tidball, Harriet	√	√	SCGM		20		67	19
Checks, Plaids, Tartans	Two-Harness Textiles, The Loom-Controlled Weaves: Plaids, Asymmetrical Plaids	Tidball, Harriet	√	√	SCGM		20		67	20
Checks, Plaids, Tartans	Two-Harness Textiles, The Loom-Controlled Weaves: Plaids, Blended Plaids	Tidball, Harriet	√	√	SCGM		20		67	20
Checks, Plaids, Tartans	Two-Harness Textiles, The Loom-Controlled Weaves: Plaids, Overplaids	Tidball, Harriet		√	SCGM		20		67	21
Checks, Plaids, Tartans	Two-Harness Textiles, The Loom-Controlled Weaves: Plaids, Scotch Tartans	Tidball, Harriet			SCGM		20		67	21
Checks, Plaids, Tartans	Two-Harness Textiles, The Loom-Controlled Weaves: Plaids, Shadow Plaids	Tidball, Harriet		√	SCGM		20		67	21
Checks, Plaids, Tartans	Two-Harness Textiles, The Loom-Controlled Weaves: Plaids, Symmetrical Plaids	Tidball, Harriet	√	√	SCGM		20		67	20
Checks, Plaids, Tartans	Two-Harness Textiles, The Loom-Controlled Weaves: Plaids, Tattersall Plaids	Tidball, Harriet		√	SCGM		20		67	21
Checks, Plaids, Tartans	Two-Harness Textiles, The Loom-Controlled Weaves: Plaids, Traditional and Contemporary	Tidball, Harriet			SCGM		20		67	20
Checks, Plaids, Tartans	Two-Harness Textiles, The Loom-Controlled Weaves: Plaids, Unbalanced Plaids	Tidball, Harriet		√	SCGM		20		67	21
Checks, Plaids, Tartans	Victorian Classic: District Checks		√	√	Hw	4	5		N/D 83	66
Checks, Plaids, Tartans	Weaver of Scotland's Past	Quigley, Edward T.	√		Hw	4	5		N/D 83	35
Checks, Plaids, Tartans	Weaver's Book of Scottish Tartans: The Scottish Tartans and Their Background, The	Tidball, Harriet	√	√	SCGM		5		62	1-46
Checks, Plaids, Tartans	Weaving of the Plaid, The	Freilinger, Ida M.	√	√	SS&D	12	1	45	Wi 80	59
Checks, Plaids, Tartans	Weaving Primer, Part 1	Parks, Deborah	√	√	PWC	4	1	11		44
Checks, Plaids, Tartans	Weaving the Family Tartan	Buchanan, Rita	√	√	S-O	10	2		Su 86	36
Checks, Plaids, Tartans	Windowpane Checked Napkins (Beth Johnson)		√	√	Hw	3	3		My 82	49, 91
Checks, Plaids, Tartans	Wonderful Plaid		√		Hw	4	5		N/D 83	46
Checks, Plaids, Tartans	Woolens and Tweeds: Designing Woolen Fabrics: Scottish Woolens	Tidball, Harriet	√	√	SCGM		4		61	28
Checks, Plaids, Tartans	Woolens and Tweeds: Designing Woolen Fabrics: The District Checks	Tidball, Harriet	√	√	SCGM		4		61	29
Checks, Plaids, Tartans: District Check	Tale of a Skirt	Gaustad, Stephenie	√	√	Hw	4	5		N/D 83	68
Chenille	Cannelé: Create a Sumptuous Fabric That Drapes Beautifully	Broughton, Cynthia	√	√	WJ	10	3	39	Wi 86	59
Chenille	On Weaving Chenille Rugs	Hausner, Walter	√		H&C	3	2		Sp 52	59
Chenille	Super Rug: A Chenille "Twice-Woven" Rug	Champion, Ellen	√	√	WJ	6	4	24	Sp 82	26
Chenille, Braided	Braid Your Own Chenille		√	√	WJ	1	1	1	Jy 76	10
Chenille, Cut	Super Rug: A Chenille "Twice-Woven" Rug	Champion, Ellen	√	√	WJ	6	4	24	Sp 82	26
Chenille, Pattern Blocks	Pile Weaves, Rugs and Tapestry: Patterns in Chenille	Zielinski, S. A.; Robert Leclerc, ed.	√	√	MWL	14			'51–'73	35

SUBJECT	TITLE	AUTHOR	IL	INST	JOUR	VOL	NO	ISS	DATE	PAGE
Chenille, Woven	Doup Leno (error-corrected WJ v3 n2 78 insert p38a)		√	√	WJ	3	2	10	Oc 78	32
Chenille Woven	Shinnosuke Seino: Innovator with Wool	Schreiber, Lavonne	√		WJ	12	2	46	Fa 87	34
Chenille, Woven	Twice-Woven Rug	Rummler, Ruth	√	√	SS&D	4	2	14	Sp 73	19
Chenille, Woven	Two-Harness Textiles, The Loom-Controlled Weaves: Chenille	Tidball, Harriet	√	√	SCGM		20		67	30
Chenille, Woven	Yarn for the Weaving		√	√	PWC	3	1	7		21
Chessboard	Paired-Thread Finnweave Projects: Ben's Chessboard, The	Xenakis, Athanasios David	√	√	PWC		2		Ap 82	38
Chevron Weaves	Bateman Boulevard, Chevron, and Combination Weaves: Structures of Chevron Weaves	Bateman, Dr. William G.; Virginia I. Harvey, ed.	√	> 4	SCGM		38		87	57
Chicago	Chicago Weaving: Development and Impact	Regensteiner, Else	√		SS&D	12	1	45	Wi 80	9
Children's Weaving	Looms! For Us!	Gray, Verdelle	√		SS&D	4	1	13	Wi 72	15
Children's Weaving	Most Gratifying Work Is with Children, The	Keatley, Kathy			SS&D	2	3	7	Su 71	16
Children's Accessories	Accessories: Children's Scarves		√	√	WJ	2	4	8	Ap 78	5
Children's Accessories	Child's Nap Mat (Louise Bradley)		√	√	Hw	8	2		M/A 87	48, I-7
Children's Accessories	Weaving for the Children		√	√	Hw	8	2		M/A 87	43
Children's Clothing	Back-to-School Overblouse (Suzanne Jenkins)		√	√	Hw	2	1		F-W 80	53, 80
Children's Clothing	Bonnie Bonnet	Adams, Harriet	√	√	Kn	1	2	2	S-S 85	38
Children's Clothing	Boy's Jacket (Julie Green)		√	√	Hw	4	3		M/J 83	47, 82
Children's Clothing	Boy's Vest (Lou Cabeen)		√	√	Hw	5	4		S/0 84	42, 93
Children's Clothing	Bye, Baby Bunting	Hayes, Beth	√		S-O	10	2		Su 86	19
Children's Clothing	Children's Pinafores (Pam Bolesta)		√	√	Hw	1	1		F-W 79	38, 60
Children's Clothing	Child's Cape (Linda Ligon)		√	√	Hw	1	2		S-S 80	39, 63
Children's Clothing	Child's Easter Dress Fabric (Julie Green Edson)		√	√	Hw	3	2		Mr 82	54, 84
Children's Clothing	Child's Jumper (Julie Green Edson)		√	√	Hw	3	2		Mr 82	55, 86
Children's Clothing	Child's Play	Voiers, Leslie	√	√	SS&D	18	3	71	Su 87	22
Children's Clothing	Child's Slipover Vest		√	√	Hw	2	1		F-W 80	53, 57
Children's Clothing	Child's Tabard of Jumper (Marit Drenckhahn)		√	√	Hw	2	1		F-W 80	53, 77
Children's Clothing	Child's Windcheater	Reekie, Stephanie	√	√	S-O	6	4		82	58
Children's Clothing	Dress for Emily, A (Barbara Miller)		√	√	Hw	5	3		Su 84	50, 95
Children's Clothing	Ducky Sacque and Bonnet (Cara L. Bernhauser)		√	√	Hw	5	3		Su 84	51, 94
Children's Clothing	"Flower Child" Dress (Paula Stewart)		√	√	Hw	6	3		Su 85	48, I-9
Children's Clothing	From the Collection of Anne Poussart		√	√	WJ	7	3	27	Wi 82	62
Children's Clothing	Garden of Fair Isles, A	Rowe, Mary	√	√	Kn	2	1	3	F-W 85	40, 8B
Children's Clothing	Garments Win At 1974 Midwest Conference		√	√	SS&D	6	2	22	Sp 75	92
Children's Clothing	Girl's Tabard (Lou Cabeen)		√	√	Hw	5	4		S/0 84	42, 92
Children's Clothing	Handweaves for the Well-Dressed Baby	Currey, Ruth Dunlop	√	√	H&C	2	3		Su 51	52
Children's Clothing	Happy Dress	Sprenger, Elserine	√	√	WJ	8	3	31	Wi 83	46
Children's Clothing	Heirloom Weaving. A Christening Gown with Mary Pendergrass		√	> 4	Hw	3	4		Se 82	53
Children's Clothing	"Hugs and Kisses" Dress (Paula Stewart)		√	> 4	Hw	6	3		Su 85	48, I-10
Children's Clothing	Lacey and Thin Fabrics		√	√	WJ	2	3	7	Ja 78	4
Children's Clothing	Nora's Dress (Sharon Alderman)		√	> 4	Hw	8	2		M/A 87	43, I-3
Children's Clothing	Off-Loom Child's Tabard		√	√	Hw	2	1		F-W 80	52, 69
Children's Clothing	OshKosh B'Gosh	Rudich, Sally	√		Fa	13	5		S/0 86	16
Children's Clothing	Skirt and Child's Dress (Halcyon Schomp) (error-corrected Hw v4 n4 83 p92)		√	√	Hw	4	3		M/J 83	46, 87
Children's Clothing	Smocking	English, Trudy	√	√	SS&D	14	1	53	Wi 82	38
Children's Clothing	Sunshine Kids, The		√		Hw	4	3		M/J 83	47

SUBJECT	TITLE	AUTHOR	IL	INST	JOUR	VOL	NO	ISS	DATE	PAGE
Children's Clothing	Timeless Togs for Tiny Tots	Edson, Julie Green	√		Hw	3	2		Mr 82	54
Children's Clothing	Tucked Dress and Toddler Blouse (Kathryn Wertenberger and Nancy Kuwabara)		√	√	Hw	4	2		M/A 83	63, 100
Children's Clothing	Tulip Outfit with Loom Controlled Inlay (error-corrected WJ v6 n1 81 p28d)	Kuwabara, Nancy	√	> 4	WJ	5	3	19	Wi 81	28
Children's Clothing	Weave for the Kids?		√		Hw	5	3		Su 84	49
Children's Clothing	Weaving for the Children		√	√	Hw	8	2		M/A 87	43
Children's Clothing	What the Well-Dressed Baby Will Wear This Season	Davis, Judy Green	√	√	S-O	10	4		Wi 86	14
Children's Clothing: Booties	Samplings	Mason, Lynn DeRose	√	√	S-O	11	2		Su 87	30
Children's Clothing: Knitted	Baby Jacket	Gibson-Roberts, Priscilla A.	√	√	Kn	3	2	6	Sp 87	42
Children's Clothing: Knitted	Loving Touches: Handspinning for Babies	Hayes, Beth	√	√	S-O	11	2		Su 87	20
Children's Clothing: Knitted	Overall and Underneath	Rush, Helene	√	√	Kn	3	1	5	F-W 86	42
Children's Clothing: Knitted	Stardust Medallion Sweater	Hayes, Beth	√	√	S-O	11	2		Su 87	24
Children's Clothing: Knitted	Winter Red: A Hand and Machine Knit Combination	Lewis, Susanna	√	√	Kn	3	4	8	Fa 87	28
Children's Party Fashions	Party Dress-up		√		Hw	6	3		Su 85	48
Children's Quilts	Quilted Childhood Visions	Oberlink, Peter	√		Fa	14	1		J/F 87	6
Children's Spinning	Experiences in History	Kuwabara, Nancy	√	√	SS&D	9	1	33	Wi 77	106
Children's Spinning	Professional Spinner	Cartwright-Jones, Rhys	√		S-O	11	2		Su 87	16
Children's Stories	Storytime...The Tale of Alain	Zimmermann, Arnold			Kn	1	2	2	S-S 85	26
Children's Weaving	Egyptian Tapestries by the Children of Harrania	Davis, Peter	√		H&C	14	4		Fa 63	9
Children's Weaving	Experiences in History	Kuwabara, Nancy	√	√	SS&D	9	1	33	Wi 77	106
Children's Weaving	Planting Seeds	Greene, Susan	√		Hw	5	3		Su 84	40
Children's Weaving	Primarily Weaving	Nove, Eleanor	√		SS&D	11	4	44	Fa 80	30
Children's Weaving	Tapping the Artist Within: The Wissa Wassef Tapestries		√		H&C	26	3		M/J 75	5
Children's Weaving	Teaching Children to Weave, Need for Simple Techniques and Devices	Alexander, Marthann		√	H&C	14	1		Wi 63	19
Children's Weaving	Young Weavers in Kentucky		√		H&C	14	3		Su 63	45
Children's Weaving Projects	Children's Corner: A Picture Frame Tapestry	Champion, Ellen	√	√	WJ	4	1	13	Jy 79	19
Children's Weaving Projects	Children's Corner — A Woven Strap or Belt		√	√	WJ	3	4	12	Ap 79	38
Children's Weavings	Contemporary Egyptian Childern's Tapestries		√		Fa	4	6		N/D 77	65
Chileren's Weaving	Weaver At Five, A	Greer, Gertrude G.			H&C	2	2		Sp 51	49
Chilkat Weaving	Chilkat Dancing Blanket, The	Samuel, Cheryl	√		SS&D	13	4	52	Fa 82	58
Chimayó Weavers	Blankets of New Mexico	Kozikowski, Janusz	√		SS&D	10	1	37	Wi 78	60
Chimayó Weavers	Chimayó—A Town of Weavers	Trujillo, Lisa Rockwood	√		WJ	11	1	41	Su 86	60
China	Artisans from China Work Silken Magic	Steinhagen, Janice	√		TM			5	J/J 86	14
China	China and the Complexities of Weaving Technologies	Vollmer, John E.			AT	5			Ju 86	65
China	China: Fiber Arts in the People's Republic	Szumski, Norma J.	√		SS&D	15	1	57	Wi 83	47
China	Chinese Artisans At Work	Goodman, Deborah Lerme	√		Fa	13	1		J/F 86	34
China	Chinese Brocades: Development of Supplementary Weft Patterning (error-corrected WJ v11 n4 87 p78)	Drooker, Penelope	√		WJ	11	3	43	Wi 87	47
China	Chinese Drawloom: A Study in Weave Structure, The	Sellin, Helen	√	> 4	WJ	9	2	34	Fa 84	6
China	Chinese Influence in Colonial Peruvian Tapestries	Cammann, Schuyler	√		TMJ	1	3		De 64	21
China	Chinese Rugs	Ellis, Charles Grant	√		TMJ	2	3		De 68	35
China	"Ch'ing Dynasty Court Robes, A Splendorous Sampling" (Exhibit)	Marcoux, Alice	√		Fa	11	2		M/A 84	78
China	Conversing with Gerhardt Knodel	Park, Betty	√		Fa	12	1		J/F 85	27

SUBJECT	TITLE	AUTHOR	IL	INST	JOUR	VOL	NO	ISS	DATE	PAGE
China	Exploring Basketry in China Today	La Pierre, Sharon	√		Fa	12	4		J/A 85	54
China	Flourishing Art: China, Guizhou Women Continue to Embroider Their Legends, A	Rossi, Gail	√		TM			9	F/M 87	30
China	Guizhou Textiles	Rossi, Gail	√		SS&D	18	1	69	Wi 86	39
China	Inside the Hangchow Brocade Factory: The Art and Craft of Mass Production	Drower, Sara	√		Fa	6	1		J/F 79	78
China	Knotted Chinese Button	Baizerman, Suzanne	√	√	WJ	9	1	33	Su 84	7
China	Ko-ssu	Wilson, Kay	√		H&C	24	4		Au 73	42
China	Ming Mandarin Squares	Cammann, Schuyler	√		TMJ	4	4		77	5
China	Observations on a Chinese Drawloom	Sellin, Helen	√		WJ	8	2	30	Fa 83	6
China	On Mathematics and Treasures	Stanton, R. G.			AT	8			De 87	57
China	Sewing with Silk	Stoyer, Janet	√	√	TM			4	A/M 86	35
China	"Silk as Ceremony: The Dress of China in the Late Ch'ing Dynasty Period (1759–1911)" (Exhibit)	Mattera, Joanne	√		Fa	8	3		M/J 81	75
China	Silk Lore: The Myths of a Magical Fiber	Goodman, Deborah Lerme	√		Fa	13	1		J/F 86	42
China	Silk Makers, The		√		TM			4	A/M 86	14
China	"Silk Roads/China Ships" (Exhibit)	Sider, Sandra	√		Fa	11	4		J/A 84	74
China	Silk, the Story of a Culture	Drooker, Penelope	√		Hw	7	1		J/F 86	49
China	Tracing the Silk Road	Dyer, Carolyn	√		Fa	13	1		J/F 86	22
China	Where Did All the Silver Go? Identifying Eighteenth-Century Chinese Painted and Printed Silks	Lee-Whitman, Leanna; Maruta Skelton	√		TMJ	22			83	33
China Weave	Two Weaves from Mexico	Gubser, Elsie H.	√	√	H&C	11	3		Su 60	26
Chiné	Contemporary Satins: Chine and Ikat	Tidball, Harriet	√	√	SCGM		7		62	20
Chiné	Two-Harness Textiles, The Loom-Controlled Weaves: Decorating Plain-Weave Webs, Chiné (Warp Painting:	Tidball, Harriet	√	√	SCGM		20		67	30
Chinese Textiles	Recent Gifts of Chinese and Japanese Textiles	Hays, Mary V.	√		TMJ	4	2		75	4
Chinese Textiles	Tapestry: Technique and Tradition	Scott, Gail R.	√		H&C	22	3		Su 71	16
Chintz	Textile Arts of India	Bernier, Ronald M.	√		WJ	2	1	5	Jy 77	31
Choli Pattern	Choli Comfort		√	√	Hw	6	3		Su 85	54
Christmas see Holiday Weavings										
Chronology List: Textile History	Events in Textile History	Hochberg, Bette	√		Fa	10	2		M/A 83	52
Chronology, Textile: Peru	Peru, Textiles Unlimited: Textile Chronology	Tidball, Harriet	√		SCGM		25		68	8
Chuppa: Wedding	Handwoven Wedding Chuppa, A	Horger, Millicent	√	√	WJ	7	4	28	Sp 83	50
CIETA	On Foreign Soil But Common Ground, Textile Assembly Meets in Spain	Mailey, Jean	√		H&C	21	1		Wi 70	18
Cigar Silks	Silken Dreams of Faraway Lands	Rudich, Sally	√		Fa	12	4		J/A 85	80
Circles	Curves and Circles	Marston, Ena	√	> 4	SS&D	15	1	57	Wi 83	84
Circles	Solving the Circle	Mattera, Joanne	√	√	SS&D	7	1	25	Wi 75	67
Circles	Tapestry: Part 2—The Dreaded Circle	Harvey, Nancy	√	√	SS&D	14	4	56	Fa 83	8
Circular Weaving	Pin-Warp Collar	Porcella, Yvonne	√	√	SS&D	4	3	15	Su 73	56
Circus Costumes: Historical	Greatest Sew on Earth, The	Rogers, Georgia M.	√		TM			11	J/J 87	38
Citations	Southern California Guild Honors Atwater	Brown, Barbara	√		SS&D	9	3	35	Su 78	38
Civil War	Civil War History Preserved: The Pennsylvania Flag Project	Ashton, Mary	√		Fa	14	5		N/D 87	10
Clasped Wefts	Clasped Weft		√	√	Hw	7	4		S/O 86	58
Clasped Wefts	Resist Dyeing, Curiosities and Inventions: Clasped Wefts or Locked Weft	Zielinski, S. A.; Robert Leclerc, ed.	√	√	MWL	17			'51–'73	45
Clasped-Wefts	Blue-Bleak Embers	Colton, Mary Rawcliffe	√	√	WJ	8	4	32	Sp 84	16
Clasped-Wefts	Mug Rugs and Table Runner (Jean Scorgie)		√	√	Hw	7	4		S/O 86	58, 59 I-10
Clasped-Wefts Technique	Corded Weaves — Four Harness Cross Cords		√	> 4	WJ	4	1	13	Jy 79	25

SUBJECT	TITLE	AUTHOR	IL	INST	JOUR	VOL	NO	ISS	DATE	PAGE
Classification System: Fabrics, Multilayered	Multi-Layered Cloths: A Structured Approach	Hoskins, Janet A.	√	> 4	AT	1			De 83	137
Classification: Weaves	More About Fabrics: Key to Weaves	Zielinski, S. A.; Robert Leclerc, ed.		√	MWL	20			'51–'73	6
Cleaning: Embroidery	Washing Embroideries			√	TM			1	O/N 85	6
Cleaning: Historic Textiles	Principles of Textile Conservation Science, No. 7. Characteristics of Detergents for Cleaning Historic Textiles	Rice, James W.	√	√	TMJ	2	1		De 66	23
Cleaning Problems: Analysis	Principles of Textile Conservation Science, No. 6. The Wonders of Water in Wetcleaning	Rice, James W.	√	√	TMJ	2	1		De 66	15
Cleaning: Rugs	Washing an Antique Rug			√	TM			5	J/J 86	8
Cleaning: Tapestries	Techniques of Tapestry Weaves Part 3: Shading and Other Matters	O'Callaghan, Kate	√	√	WJ	5	1	17	Su 80	29
Cleaning Techniques	Technical Features of a Middle Horizon Tapestry Shirt from Peru, The	Bird, Junius B.; Milica Dimitrijevic Skinner	√	√	TMJ	4	1		De 74	5
Cleaning Techniques, Textiles	Ounce of Prevention: Preventing Deterioration, An	Butterfield, Mary Ann; Lotus Stack	√	√	WJ	9	4	36	Sp 85	9
Cleaning Techniques, Textiles: Detergents and Soaps	Principles of Textile Conservation Science, No. 8. Drycleaning of Fine and Fragile Textiles	Rice, James W.	√	√	TMJ	2	2		De 67	21
Cleaning Techniques, Textiles: Drycleaning Solvents	Principles of Textile Conservation Science, No. 8. Drycleaning of Fine and Fragile Textiles	Rice, James W.	√	√	TMJ	2	2		De 67	21
Cleaning Techniques, Textiles: Leather/Fiber	Principles of Textile Conservation Science, No. 10. An Investigation Into Cleaning and Conservation of Mixed Leather and Fiber Artifacts	Rice, James W.	√	√	TMJ	2	3		De 68	57
Cleaning Techniques, Textiles: Wet	Principles of Textile Conservation Science, No. 6. The Wonders of Water in Wetcleaning	Rice, James W.	√	√	TMJ	2	1		De 66	15
Closures/Fasteners	Edges, Joinings, Trims, Embellishments, Closures...and More	Wilson, Jean	√	√	Hw	2	5		No 81	42
Closures/Fasteners	Fastening Alternative, A	Mattera, Joanne	√	√	SS&D	11	3	43	Su 80	27
Closures/Fasteners	Men's Clothing		√	> 4	WJ	2	3	7	Ja 78	32
Closures/Fasteners	Moebius Vest, The	Homme, Audrey	√	√	WJ	11	4	44	Sp 87	48
Closures/Fasteners	Poncho	Hurt, Doris	√	> 4	WJ	3	3	11	Ja 79	44
Closures/Fasteners	Seattle Guild Garment Designs, Part 4: Edges, Closures, Capes and Dresses		√	√	SS&D	11	2	42	Sp 80	39
Closures/Fasteners	Thread Eyes		√	√	TM			7	O/N 86	8
Closures/Fasteners	Wasitband Closures		√	√	TM			7	O/N 86	8
Cloth Analysis see Analysis, Fabric										
Cloth, Cut-Thread	Pelete Bite: Kalabari Cut-Thread Cloth	Thieme, Otto Charles	√		Fa	10	5		S/O 83	46
Cloth Diagram	Drafts		√	√	WJ	1	1	1	Jy 76	12
Clothesline Art	Personal Flags of Everyday Life	Fraas, Gayle; Duncan Slade	√		Fa	10	1		J/F 83	99
Clothing also see Apparel, Clothing, Costume										
Clothing	Theme Issue		√		Fa	3	5		S/O 76	
Clothing, Conceptual	"Conceptual Clothing" (Exhibit)	Waller, Irene	√		Fa	14	3		M/J 87	62
Clothing, Conceptual	Through the Camera's Eye: Howard Munson's Body Coverings	Akamine, Estelle	√		Fa	14	3		M/J 87	44
Clothing Construction also see Tailoring										
Clothing Construction	Art of Fashion Design: A Handweaver's Twill Cape, The	Johnson, Judith K.	√	√	WJ	7	3	27	Wi 82	12
Clothing Construction	Beginning with Bands: Tablet Woven Garments and Accessories	Holtzer, Marilyn Emerson	√	√	WJ	9	3	35	Wi 85	28
Clothing Construction	Bits and Pieces	Knollenberg, Barbara	√	√	WJ	1	4	4	Ap 77	11
Clothing Construction	Blouse of Cards	Holtzer, Marilyn Emerson		√	SS&D	16	3	63	Su 85	20
Clothing Construction	Bog Affair, A	Homme, Audrey	√	√	PWC			3	Oc 82	44

SUBJECT	TITLE	AUTHOR	IL	INST	JOUR	VOL	NO	ISS	DATE	PAGE
Clothing Construction	Boiled Wool	Smith, Mary	√	√	TM			13	O/N 87	63
Clothing Construction	Calm and Cool...Sewing Handwoven Fabric	Krantz, Hazel	√	√	Hw	4	3		M/J 83	29
Clothing Construction	Cardigan Jacket	Evans, Kerry	√	√	WJ	5	3	19	Wi 81	10
Clothing Construction	Chenille Polo	Xenakis, Alexis Yiorgos	√	√	PWC			6	Su 83	34
Clothing Construction	Child's Play	Voiers, Leslie	√	√	SS&D	18	3	71	Su 87	22
Clothing Construction	Classic Dress, The	Hewson, Betty	√	√	Hw	5	3		Su 84	24
Clothing Construction	Clothing	Todd, Louise	√	√	H&C	24	4		Au 73	28
Clothing Construction	Coat Couture	West, Virginia	√	> 4	SS&D	14	2	54	Sp 83	48
Clothing Construction	Coat from a Blanket, A	Denecke, Gerlinda	√	√	TM			2	D/J 85	41
Clothing Construction	Cotton Jacket with Pleat	White, Jamie Leigh	√	√	WJ	7	3	27	Wi 82	68
Clothing Construction	Designed for Narrow Looms	Jennings, Lucy Anne	√	√	WJ	11	1	41	Su 86	26
Clothing Construction	Fashions by Linda Knutson and Lynn Daly		√	√	WJ	6	3	23	Wi 81	14
Clothing Construction	Felted Jacket	Bennett, Siiri	√	> 4	WJ	9	1	33	Su 84	49
Clothing Construction	Fine & Fancy: Good Sewing Techniques for Good Cloth	Bliss, Anne		√	Hw	4	1		J/F 83	38
Clothing Construction	Free and Casual Look Wool Jacket, The	McGalliard, Lorraine	√	√	WJ	6	3	23	Wi 81	8
Clothing Construction	Garments by Hanni Bureker		√	√	WJ	6	3	23	Wi 81	35
Clothing Construction	Glad Rags	Wroten, Barbara	√	√	SS&D	15	4	60	Fa 84	28
Clothing Construction	Handcrafted Clothing Construction: Some Considerations	Peterson, Jill	√		Fa	3	5		S/O 76	32
Clothing Construction	Happy Dress	Sprenger, Elserine	√	√	WJ	8	3	31	Wi 83	46
Clothing Construction	How Madame Grès Sculpts with Fabric	Cooper, Arlene	√	√	TM			10	A/M 87	50
Clothing Construction	Inlay We Trust, Part 2: Leno Inlay	Herring, Connie	√	√	PWC			6	Su 83	48
Clothing Construction	Inside an Expensive Outfit	Galpin, Mary	√	√	TM			1	O/N 85	40
Clothing Construction	Irish Kinsale Cloak, The	Jones, Una	√	√	WJ	8	3	31	Wi 83	35
Clothing Construction	Jeans: The Inside Story	Goodman, Deborah Lerme	√	√	TM			3	F/M 86	27
Clothing Construction	Lace Trilogy	Fauske, Carla	√	√	PWC			6	Su 83	52
Clothing Construction	Lesson in Cut and Sewn Handwoven Garments, A (error-corrected Hw v2 n2 81 p68)	Wertenberger, Kathryn	√	√	Hw	2	1		F-W 80	36
Clothing Construction	Linen Shift: Plain Sewing Makes the Most of Your Fabric, A	Smith, Kathleen B.	√	√	TM			9	F/M 87	46
Clothing Construction	Lining the Overshot	Moes, Dini	√	√	SS&D	13	4	52	Fa 82	64
Clothing Construction	Little Blue Dress, A	Dobsevage, David	√	√	TM			7	O/N 86	58
Clothing Construction	Little Shaping Story, A	Burgess, Leslie	√	√	Hw	4	3		M/J 83	26
Clothing Construction	Making a Great Shirt Collar	Coffin, David Page	√	√	TM			4	A/M 86	42
Clothing Construction	Making Swirly Skirts	Callaway, Grace	√	√	TM			10	A/M 87	35
Clothing Construction	Man's Shirt in Peruvian Inlay	Linder, Harry	√	> 4	WJ	4	2	14	Oc 79	8
Clothing Construction	Marvelous Mistake, A	Cramer, Pauline E.	√	√	SS&D	17	1	65	Wi 85	34
Clothing Construction	Moebius Vest, The	Homme, Audrey	√	√	WJ	11	4	44	Sp 87	48
Clothing Construction	Notes from the Tailor	Kussube, Kay; Alexis Yiorgos Xenakis		√	PWC	4	2	12		27
Clothing Construction	Panel Dress, A	Juve, Peggy	√	√	TM			12	A/S 87	29
Clothing Construction	Perfect Pair of Pants, A	Cowan, Sally	√	√	TM			7	O/N 86	26
Clothing Construction	Perfecting the Pocket	Coffin, David Page	√	√	TM			8	D/J 86	28
Clothing Construction	Raglan Rectangles	Coifman, Lucienne	√	√	SS&D	18	1	69	Wi 86	10
Clothing Construction	Rags At Work	Finch, Joan Freitag	√	√	SS&D	16	4	64	Fa 85	72
Clothing Construction	Rags to Riches: Jackets from Rags	Brones, Britta	√	√	WJ	6	3	23	Wi 81	31
Clothing Construction	Ribbon Wefts	Sewell, Suzy	√	> 4	WJ	10	3	39	Wi 86	40
Clothing Construction	Scandia Jacket		√	√	WJ	8	3	31	Wi 83	42
Clothing Construction	Sewing Handwovens	Betzina, Sandra	√	√	TM			2	D/J 85	20
Clothing Construction	Sewing Swimsuits	Callaway, Grace	√	√	TM			5	J/J 86	24
Clothing Construction	Sewing with Silk	Stoyer, Janet	√	√	TM			4	A/M 86	35
Clothing Construction	Start with a Square	Shaw, Winifred	√		SS&D	16	3	63	Su 85	50

SUBJECT	TITLE	AUTHOR	IL	INST	JOUR	VOL	NO	ISS	DATE	PAGE
Clothing Construction	Suited to Silk	Turner, Kathryn M.	√	√	SS&D	18	2	70	Sp 87	68
Clothing Construction	Summertime!	Coifman, Lucienne	√	√	SS&D	15	3	59	Su 84	74
Clothing Construction	Tailored Bog Jacket (Revisited), A	Guy, Sallie T.	√	√	SS&D	18	1	69	Wi 86	60
Clothing Construction	Tailored Vest and Skirt, A	Arnold, Ruth	√	> 4	WJ	9	3	35	Wi 85	56
Clothing Construction	Techniques of Haute Couture (error-corrected TM i7 O/N86 p5)	Rhodes, Elizabeth A.	√		TM			6	A/S 86	52
Clothing Construction	Try Shadow Weave Twill	Hewson, Betty	√	√	Hw	5	1		J/F 84	14
Clothing Construction	Tucked Dresses	Wertenberger, Kathryn; Nancy Kuwabara	√	√	Hw	4	2		M/A 83	63
Clothing Construction	Turkish Coat, A	Xenakis, Alexis Yiorgos	√	> 4	Hw	2	2		Mr 81	39
Clothing Construction	Twice Woven Bolero	Richards, Iris	√	√	WJ	4	3	15	Ja 80	24
Clothing Construction	Versatile Jacket, A	Hannah, Joyce	√	√	TM			1	O/N 85	44
Clothing Construction	Vestment Variations: A Weaver From the Netherlands Creates Garments for the Ecclesiastical Calendar	Jansen, Netty	√	> 4	WJ	10	3	39	Wi 86	53
Clothing Construction	Violet Vestment	Hahn, Roslyn	√	> 4	WJ	8	3	31	Wi 83	44
Clothing Construction	Wasteless, Waistless Dress, A	Holtzer, Marilyn F.	√	√	Hw	2	3		My 81	85
Clothing Construction	Weave and Knit Suit		√	√	WJ	8	3	31	Wi 83	18
Clothing Construction	Win's Sweaters		√	√	WJ	8	3	31	Wi 83	12
Clothing Construction	Woven Egmont Sweater	Klessen, Romy	√	√	PWC			2	Ap 82	83
Clothing Construction: Interfacings	Making Sense of Interfacing (error-corrected TM n12 p4)	Komives, Margaret Deck	√	√	TM			10	A/M 87	58
Cloud Collars, Chinese	Recent Gifts of Chinese and Japanese Textiles	Hays, Mary V.	√		TMJ	4	2		75	4
Cloud-Collar Designs	Is the Mamluk Carpet a Mandala? A Speculation	Ellis, Charles Grant	√		TMJ	4	1		De 74	30
Clown Shoes	These Toes Won't Drown in Tears of Clown	Montgomery, Larry	√		TM			11	J/J 87	14
Clowns: Pierrot	When Is Art Fashion and Fashion Art?	Martin, Richard	√		TM			11	J/J 87	12
Coats	Ahka Peacock Coat (Anita Mayer)		√	√	Hw	2	2		Mr 81	29, 79
Coats	Balenciago: The Architect of Elegant Clothing	Koda, Harold	√		TM			11	J/J 87	20
Coats	Boundweave Coat (Jean Scorgie)		√	√	Hw	2	1		F-W 80	31, 75
Coats	Brushed Wool Wrap Coat (Jean Scorgie and Kaino Leethem)		√	√	Hw	4	1		J/F 83	46, 88
Coats	Cache Valley Winter Blues: Felted Coat	Cogar, Kathryn	√	√	SS&D	17	4	68	Fa 86	16
Coats	Coat Couture	West, Virginia	√	> 4	SS&D	14	2	54	Sp 83	48
Coats	Coat for Handwoven Yardage, A	Roth, Bettie G.	√	√	WJ	7	3	27	Wi 82	6
Coats	Coat from a Blanket, A	Denecke, Gerlinda	√	√	TM			2	D/J 85	41
Coats	Coat with Cape Sleeves (Leslie Voiers)		√	√	Hw	6	4		S/O 85	54, I-9
Coats	Coat with Minimum Seams, The	Marston, Ena	√	√	SS&D	7	4	28	Fa 76	42
Coats	Contemporary Costume, Strictly Handwoven: A Fringed Coat	Tidball, Harriet	√	√	SCGM		24		68	42
Coats	Contemporary Costume, Strictly Handwoven: The Nell Scott Coat	Tidball, Harriet	√	√	SCGM		24		68	10
Coats	Couturier Fashion Design	West, Virginia	√	> 4	SS&D	13	4	52	Fa 82	34
Coats	Crochet—A Great Technique for Finishing Handwovens		√	> 4	WJ	7	3	27	Wi 82	18
Coats	Daisy Dog Fur Coat (Betty Beard)		√	√	Hw	3	2		Mr 82	62, 87
Coats	Double-Woven Treasures from Old Peru	Cahlander, Adele	√	√	PWC			4	Ja 83	36
Coats	Felted Fabric	Mayer, Anita Luvera	√	√	SS&D	15	3	59	Su 84	46
Coats	Fur Fashions	Lucas, Jerie	√	√	SS&D	15	2	58	Sp 84	26
Coats	Gala Raincoat	Moes, Dini	√	√	WJ	6	3	23	Wi 81	12
Coats	Garments with Ethnic Flavor: Desert Dusk Coat		√		WJ	2	3	7	Ja 78	16
Coats	Glit Coat (Louise B. Heite)		√	√	Hw	8	3		M/J 87	65, I-14
Coats	Gray Topcoat	Buchanan, Rita; Steve Buchanan	√	√	S-O	9	4		Wi 85	13

SUBJECT	TITLE	AUTHOR	IL	INST	JOUR	VOL	NO	ISS	DATE	PAGE
Coats	Hooded Russet Coat (Carol Thilenius)		√	√	Hw	3	4		Se 82	45, 86
Coats	I Have This Fleece...Now What?	Adams, Brucie	√	√	lw	5	4		Fa 80	62
Coats	In My Country, It's Winter	Gagné-Collard, Agathe	√	> 4	WJ	8	3	31	Wi 83	74
Coats	Irish Kinsale Cloak, The	Jones, Una	√	√	WJ	8	3	31	Wi 83	35
Coats	Japanese Shopkeeper's Coat		√	√	WJ	3	3	11	Ja 79	40
Coats	Kathy Woell Original, A	Sitko, Jane Bradley	√		SS&D	19	1	73	Wi 87	36
Coats	Lacey and Thin Fabrics		√	√	WJ	2	3	7	Ja 78	4
Coats	Making of a Coat, The	Keeler, Betty	√	√	H&C	23	1		J/F 72	20
Coats	Matelasse Double Cloth Stitched to Form the Design	Kelly, Linda	√	> 4	WJ	7	1	25	Su 82	43
Coats	Men's Clothing		√	> 4	WJ	2	3	7	Ja 78	32
Coats	Moroccan Cocoon		√	√	WJ	8	3	31	Wi 83	10
Coats	Off the Hook: Bosnian Crochet (Charlotte Winston)		√	√	Hw	2	5		No 81	45
Coats	Pine Tree Coat	Knollenberg, Barbara	√	> 4	WJ	1	2	2	Oc 76	32
Coats	Plum Special Sherpa Coat (Betty Beard)		√	√	Hw	3	1		Ja 82	36, 84
Coats	Prize-Winning Gown and Coat	Fair, Maurine	√	> 4	SS&D	2	2	6	Sp 71	16
Coats	Ravensthorpe: A Festival of Wool	Walker, Pauline; Carol Taylor	√		S-O	7	2		Su 83	16
Coats	Reversible Coat (Eileen O'Connor)		√	√	Hw	6	5		N/D 85	46, I-8
Coats	Shepherd's Dancing Coat	Fleischer, Helen	√	√	S-O	11	1		Sp 87	17
Coats	Sky Celebration	Mayer, Anita Luvera	√	√	S-O	11	2		Su 87	36
Coats	Southwest Reflections: Fiber Artists Inspired By the New Mexico Landscape	Colton, Mary Rawcliffe	√		WJ	11	1	41	Su 86	20
Coats	Sweater-Coat (Linda Urquhart)		√	√	Hw	4	4		S/O 83	41, 109
Coats	Timelessly Fashionable Turkish Coat, A	Xenakis, Alexis Yiorgos	√	√	PWC	1	1		No 81	43
Coats	Turkish Coat, A	Xenakis, Alexis Yiorgos	√	> 4	Hw	2	2		Mr 81	39
Coats	Warm and Wooly: Bright and Soft		√		Hw	1	1		F-W 79	28
Coats	Weave Three--Cocktail Skirt, Coating, Parka	Snyder, Mary	√	> 4	SS&D	6	2	22	Sp 75	34
Coats	Weaving in Quebec: Devotion to Garments	Barrett, Clotilde	√	√	WJ	6	4	24	Sp 82	18
Coats	What People Ask Before They Buy Handmade Fashions	Leslie, Victoria	√		TM			9	F/M 87	58
Coats	Wooly Rose Coat (Trudy Van Stralen)		√	√	Hw	3	3		My 82	51, 96
Coats	Wrist-to-Wrist Garment, The	Allen, Rose Mary	√	√	WJ	9	3	35	Wi 85	19
Coats, Blanket	Blanket Coat			√	TM			6	A/S 86	4
Coats, Mantles: Felt	Felt-making Craftsmen of the Anatolian and Iranian Plateaux	Gervers, Michael; Veronika Gervers	√	√	TMJ	4	1		De 74	14
Cochineal	Cochineal as a Domestic Dyestuff	Gerber, Willi; Fred Gerber		√	H&C	23	6		N/D 72	16
Cochineal	Cochineal in Colorado: or, Is Your Local Cactus Bugged? (error-corrected lw v1 n3 76 p25)	Bliss, Anne	√	√	lw	1	2		Wi 76	20
Cochineal	Diverse Dyes	Bliss, Anne	√	√	lw	3	2		Wi 78	30
Cochineal	Hooray, Hooray, The Cochineal	Arabian, Barbara		√	lw	3	3		Sp 78	25
Cochineal	Insect Dyes	Gerber, Fred	√	√	lw	3	3		Sp 78	23
Cochineal	Recipes for Cochineal Dyeing			√	lw	3	3		Sp 78	47
Cochineal	Why Bother with Natural Dyeing?	Bulbach, Stanley	√	√	TM			5	J/J 86	32
Cocoon	Moroccan Cocoon		√	√	WJ	8	3	31	Wi 83	10
Cocoon	Silk Cocoon (Karen Smith) (error-corrected Hw v8 n4 87 p I-3)		√	√	Hw	8	2		M/A 87	57, I-15
Coifs	Medieval Textiles from the Tellem Caves in Central Mali, West Africa	Bedaux, Rogier M. A.; Rita Bolland	√		TMJ	19 20			80,81	65
Collaborations	"Baker/Rapoport/Wick" in New York (Exhibit)	Park, Betty	√		Fa	4	5		S/O 77	15
Collaborations	Collaboration: A Vision of Unknown Territory	Parks, Betty	√		Fa	12	5		S/O 85	20

SUBJECT	TITLE	AUTHOR	IL	INST	JOUR	VOL	NO	ISS	DATE	PAGE
Collaborations	Collaboration in the Public Eye				Fa	12	5		S/O 85	64
Collaborations	Collaboration: Peter and Ritzi Jacobi (error-corrected Fa v13 n1 86 p6)	Corpier, Leslee	√		Fa	12	5		S/O 85	27
Collaborations	Collaborations II: Let's Do Business		√		Fa	12	5		S/O 85	66
Collaborations	Collection, The		√		WJ	3	3	11	Ja 79	30
Collaborations	Cylaine Handwoven Designs: Arlene Wohl and Lucy Matzger		√		WJ	7	3	27	Wi 82	8
Collaborations	David Johnson and Geary Jones	Rudick, Sally	√		Fa	12	5		S/O 85	18
Collaborations	Debones: Collaborative Art Works, The		√		Fa	5	2		M/A 78	55
Collaborations	Edinburg Tapestry Company		√		Fa	12	5		S/O 85	64
Collaborations	Fabric Workshop: A Philadelphia Environment Where Experimentation Reigns, The	Park, Betty	√		Fa	9	1		J/F 82	21
Collaborations	Flying Colors		√		Fa	12	5		S/O 85	65
Collaborations	"Four x Four, A Collaboration: A Special Environment " (Exhibit)	Welty, Margaret	√		Fa	7	1		J/F 80	69
Collaborations	Fran Kraynek-Prince and Neil Prince	Scarborough, Jessica	√		Fa	12	5		S/O 85	19
Collaborations	"From American Looms: Scheuer Tapestry Studio" (Exhibit) (error-corrected Fa v12 n6 85 p9)	Park, Betty	√		Fa	12	5		S/O 85	76
Collaborations	From Houston: Rochella Cooper, Anita Hickman	Vander Lee, Jana	√		Fa	3	3		M/J 76	10
Collaborations	Gathering for Enrichment: The New York Textile Study Group	Malarcher, Patricia	√		Fa	12	5		S/O 85	48
Collaborations	Grrrhhhh: A Study of Social Patterns	Hickman, Deborah	√		Fa	14	4		S/O 87	23
Collaborations	Hot Flash Fan, The		√		Fa	12	5		S/O 85	91
Collaborations	In the Shadow of Fame: Sophie Taeuber-Arp and Sonia Delaunay	Austin, Carol	√		Fa	12	5		S/O 85	50
Collaborations	Kiyomi Iwata: A Singularity of Vision	Park, Betty	√		Fa	13	1		J/F 86	10
Collaborations	Lillian Elliott and Pat Hickman: The Pleasures and Problems of Collaboration		√		Fa	12	5		S/O 85	22
Collaborations	Made by Machine: Textiles for the Eighties	Harris, Patricia; David Lyon	√		Fa	12	5		S/O 85	34
Collaborations	McDonnell Douglas		√		Fa	12	5		S/O 85	65
Collaborations	Ribbon Project: Miles of Banners for Peace, The		√		Fa	12	5		S/O 85	49
Collaborations	Rieke, Rieke — A Study in Beauty, Silence and Collaboration		√		Fa	5	6		N/D 78	35
Collaborations	Riis, Mafong Collaborate in Thread & Silver		√		SS&D	5	1	17	Wi 73	4
Collaborations	Silkworks	Goodman, Deborah Lerme	√		Fa	13	1		J/F 86	50
Collaborations	Theme Issue		√		Fa	12	5		S/O 85	
Collaborations	"Unsettled Images: Peggy Vanbianchi & Emily Standley" (Exhibit)	Rowlands-Tarbox, Jean L.	√		Fa	12	5		S/O 85	71
Collaborations	Women Faces: A Triptych		√		Fa	12	5		S/O 85	66
Collaborations	Yael Lurie — Other Places, Other Visions	Tannenbaum, Ruth	√		Fa	5	6		N/D 78	40
Collaborations: Ross/Noland/Navajo	Contemporary Navajo Weaving	Hedlund, Ann Lane	√		WJ	11	1	41	Su 86	30
Collaborations: Textile Art	Nexus: A Collaboration in Textile Art	Kuo, Susanna	√		Iw	5	3		Su 80	22
Collaborations: Weaving	Two Weavers: A Business Association Which Works	LaLena, Constance	√		Hw	2	3		My 81	66
Collagé	Alter Cloths and Shrines: The New Work of Janet Boguch	Tacker, Sylvia	√		Fa	14	5		N/D 87	6
Collagé	Fabric Collages (Exhibit)	Zerner, Amy	√		Fa	14	3		M/J 87	64
Collagé	Garment Form As Image, The	Koplos, Janet	√		Fa	10	6		N/D 83	66
Collagé	"Jacque Parsley: Collage, A New Direction" (Exhibit)	Meloy, Margaret	√		Fa	11	6		N/D 84	76
Collagé	Jerry Stefl: Fantasy, Beads, and Fiber	Matthews, Marianne R.	√		Fa	11	2		M/A 84	24
Collagé	Linda Richards-Watson: Finding the Eclectic	Rowley, Kathleen	√		Fa	10	4		J/A 83	12

SUBJECT	TITLE	AUTHOR	IL	INST	JOUR	VOL	NO	ISS	DATE	PAGE
Collagé	Liz Kregloe: A Collage of Interior Spaces	Weinstein, Ann	√		Fa	13	3		M/J 86	28
Collagé	Lynn Pierce	Pierce, Lynn	√		Fa	14	4		S/O 87	18
Collagé	On the Edge: Betye Saar — Personal Time Travels	Woelfle, Gretchen Erskine	√		Fa	9	4		J/A 82	56
Collagé	Rieke, Rieke — A Study in Beauty, Silence and Collaboration		√		Fa	5	6		N/D 78	35
Collagé	"Robin Becker and Joan Lintault: Visual Traces of the Past" (Exhibit)	Meloy, Margaret	√		Fa	11	1		J/F 84	80
Collagé	Sally Broadwell	Broadwell, Sally	√		Fa	14	4		S/O 87	19
Collagé	Vivian Poon: Exposing Facades	Rowley, Kathleen	√		Fa	13	4		J/A 86	12
Collagé	"Web Of Kentucky Thread, A" (Exhibit)	Meloy, Margaret	√		Fa	12	5		S/O 85	72
Collagé, Fabric	Art Feeds the Hungry	Harel, Uri	√		Fa	13	4		J/A 86	11
Collagé, Fabric	Dreaming, Drawing, Painting, and Stitching with Noreen Crone-Coggins	Crone-Coggins, Noreen	√		Fa	6	5		S/O 79	16
Collagé, Fabric	Fabric Speaks	Huntington, Madge	√		Fa	7	2		M/A 80	31
Collagé, Fabric	"Fiber in the Service of Art: The Work of Wilma King and Marilyn Grelle" (Exhibit)	Mathews, Rich	√		Fa	4	2		M/A 77	18
Collagé, Fabric	Floats of Fancy	Woelfle, Gretchen	√		Fa	8	2		M/A 81	52
Collagé, Fabric	"Jean Stamsta: Great Lake Series" (Exhibit)	Bard, Elizabeth A.	√		Fa	10	2		M/A 83	70
Collagé, Fabric	"Joan Schulze" (Exhibit)	Papa, Nancy	√		Fa	4	3		M/J 77	17
Collagé, Fabric	Katherine Howe "Color Card Series" Woven Paintings (Exhibit)	Dyer, Carolyn	√		Fa	7	4		J/A 80	72
Collagé, Fabric	"Lenore Tawney: A Personal World" (Exhibit)	Malarcher, Pat	√		Fa	5	6		N/D 78	63
Collagé, Fabric	Nova Scotia Weavers Arouse Interest in Wool	Major, Marjorie	√		H&C	5	1		Wi 53	28
Collagé, Fabric	Revival of Stitchery, Appliqué, and Collage	Belfer, Nancy	√		H&C	18	1		Wi 67	21
Collagé, Fabric	Sheila Hicks	Holtzer, Marilyn Emerson	√		SS&D	16	1	61	Wi 84	43
Collagé, Fabric	Stephanie Cole Kirsher	Vander Lee, Jana	√		Fa	3	6		N/D 76	11
Collagé, Fabric	"Textile Works: Lily Gilmore, Judith Moir, Sheila O'Hara" (Exhibit)	Mazur, Carole	√		Fa	8	2		M/A 81	67
Collagé, Fabric	Way of Working: Katherine Westphal and the Creative Process, A	Janeiro, Jan	√		Fa	7	6		N/D 80	35
Collagé, Fiber	Rebecca Munro: But It Turned Out All Right	Erler, Mary	√		Fa	6	6		N/D 79	28
Collagé, Fiber	Woven Collages of Arturo Sandoval, The	Park, Betty	√		Fa	6	5		S/O 79	70
Collagé, Mixed Media	"Anne Dushanko-Dobek: Silent Voices" (Exhibit)	Scheinman, Pamela	√		Fa	11	4		J/A 84	77
Collagé, Mixed Media	Joyful Hieroglyphics: For Mary Bero Anything is Possible!		√		Fa	8	5		S/O 81	40
Collagé, Mixed Media	"Unsettled Images: Peggy Vanbianchi & Emily Standley" (Exhibit)	Rowlands-Tarbox, Jean L.	√		Fa	12	5		S/O 85	71
Collagé, Mixed-Media	Illuminated Tapestries of Amy Zerner, The	Daniels, Richard	√		Fa	9	3		M/J 82	22
Collagé, Mixed-Media	Portrait of a Village	Becker, Robin; James Chressanthis	√		Fa	9	6		N/D 82	40
Collagé, Paper	Homage to Hats: Handmade Paper Drawing/Collages Honor a Women's Tradition	Rusoff, Beverly	√		Fa	8	1		J/F 81	80
Collage, Textile	From Paint to Fiber	Siewert-Miller, Elisabet	√		SS&D	3	2	10	Sp 72	18
Collapse Fabric	Are You Ready to Collapse?	Frame, Mary	√	√	S-O	11	1		Sp 87	41
Collapse Fabric	Ringlets and Waves: Undulations from Overtwist	Frame, Mary	√	√	S-O	10	4		Wi 86	28
Collapse Fabric	Save the Twist: Warping and Weaving with Overtwisted Yarns	Frame, Mary	√	√	S-O	11	2		Su 87	43
Collars, Cuffs, Yokes	Dress Yoke and Cuffs (Linda Ligon)		√	√	Hw	3	1		Ja 82	27, 87
Collars, Cuffs, Yokes	Happy Dress	Sprenger, Elserine	√	√	WJ	8	3	31	Wi 83	46
Collars, Cuffs, Yokes	Making a Great Shirt Collar	Coffin, David Page	√	√	TM			4	A/M 86	42

SUBJECT	TITLE	AUTHOR	IL	INST	JOUR	VOL	NO	ISS	DATE	PAGE
Collars, Cuffs, Yokes	Paired-Thread Finnweave Projects: The Gaza Dress, The	Xenakis, Alexis, Yiorgos	√	√	PWC			2	Ap 82	40
Collars, Cuffs, Yokes	Shirt Collars			√	TM			6	A/S 86	4
Collars, Cuffs, Yokes: Automatic-Stitched	Construction Details with Automatic Stitches	Richter, Elizabeth Lee	√	√	TM			11	J/J 87	64
Collars, Cuffs, Yokes: Knitted	Lace Collar	Drysdale, Rosemary	√	√	Kn	3	4	8	Fa 87	48
Collars, Cuffs, Yokes: Knitted	This Yoke's on You!	Glover, Medrith	√	√	Kn	3	2	6	Sp 87	35
Collars, Cuffs, Yokes: Knitted	Undies Revealed: Camisole	Upitis, Lizbeth	√	√	Kn	3	2	6	Sp 87	12
Collars, Cuffs, Yokes: Knitted	Winter Red: A Hand and Machine Knit Combination	Lewis, Susanna	√	√	Kn	3	4	8	Fa 87	28
Collars, Cuffs, Yokes: Knitted	Yoke Worksheet		√	√	Kn	3	2	6	Sp 87	30
Collections and Collecting	Art Consultants: Bridging the Gap Between Artist and Client	Goodman, Deborah Lerme	√		Fa	12	6		N/D 85	31
Collections and Collecting	Artist's Collection: Claire Zeisler, An	Lonier, Terri	√		Fa	12	6		N/D 85	29
Collections and Collecting	Atwater Collection				H&C	11	1		Wi 60	27
Collections and Collecting	Boston Museum of Fine Arts Textile Collection				SS&D	1	1	1	De 69	15
Collections and Collecting	Collections and Recollections: The Textile Museum at Sixty		√		Fa	12	6		N/D 85	76
Collections and Collecting	Convergence '74, Hurschler Collection	Hurschler, Paul; Flora Hurschler	√		SS&D	5	3	19	Su 74	43
Collections and Collecting	Corporate Collecting "Contemporary Tapestries" (Exhibit)	Dyer, Carolyn	√		Fa	4	5		S/O 77	16
Collections and Collecting	Fanfare: Fans from the Collection of the National Museum of American Art (Exhibit)	Perry, Pamela	√		Fa	12	6		N/D 85	48
Collections and Collecting	Harriet Tidball	Harvey, Virginia I.; Sylvia Tacker	√		SS&D	8	4	32	Fa 77	4
Collections and Collecting	Heirloom Linens	Furniss, Frances	√		H&C	9	2		Sp 58	11
Collections and Collecting	Ken Colwell on Collecting	Colwell, Ken	√		PWC	4	4	14		5
Collections and Collecting	Mid-Twentieth Century Textures	Mailey, Jean E.	√		H&C	8	3		Su 57	6
Collections and Collecting	Protecting Your Collection: Textile Conservation	Hutchins, Jane K.	√		Fa	12	6		N/D 85	40
Collections and Collecting	Rare Textiles and Costumes in the Collection at the University of Washington	Harvey, Virginia I.	√		H&C	15	4		Fa 64	15
Collections and Collecting	Textile Life, The	Jacobson, Gail	√		Fa	14	3		M/J 87	5
Collections and Collecting	Textile Trends: Collecting in Chicago	Lonier, Terri	√		Fa	12	6		N/D 85	26
Collections and Collecting	Textile Trends: Collecting in New York	Sider, Sandra	√		Fa	12	6		N/D 85	24
Collections and Collecting	Textile Trends: Collecting in the San Francisco Area	Scarborough, Jessica	√		Fa	12	6		N/D 85	28
Collections and Collecting	Textile Trends: Collecting in the Southwest	Elliott, Malinda	√		Fa	12	6		N/D 85	27
Collections and Collecting	Textile Trends: Collecting in Washington, D.C.	Goodman, Deborah Lerme	√		Fa	12	6		N/D 85	25
Collections and Collecting	Textile Trends: The Museum Collection	Malarcher, Patricia	√		Fa	12	6		N/D 85	23
Collections and Collecting	Textiles and Looms from Guatemala & Mexico	Grossman, Ellin F.	√		H&C	7	1		Wi 55	6
Collections and Collecting	Textiles At the Cooper Hewitt Museum	Fowler, Molly	√		SS&D	7	4	28	Fa 76	4
Collections and Collecting	Video Access to Textiles: The Helen L. Allen Textile Collection	Bard, Elizabeth A.	√		Fa	12	6		N/D 85	34
Collections and Collecting	William Morris: The Sanford and Helen Berger Collection	Austin, Carole	√		Fa	12	3		M/J 85	47
Collections and Collecting: Art Bank, Canada	Canada Council Art Bank, The	Kirby, William	√		AT	7			Ju 87	75
Collections and Collecting: Art Fabric	"Flexible Medium: Art Fabric from the Museum Collection, The" (Exhibit)	Goodman, Deborah Lerme	√		Fa	11	5		S/O 84	71
Collections and Collecting: Basketry	Basketry Collections Around the Country: A Selective List		√		Fa	11	1		J/F 84	50
Collections and Collecting: Basketry	Fine Art of Collecting Baskets, The (error-corrected TM i14 '87 p4)	Bowers, Sandra W.		√	TM			13	O/N 87	16

SUBJECT	TITLE	AUTHOR	IL	INST	JOUR	VOL	NO	ISS	DATE	PAGE
Collections and Collecting: Basketry, Ethnological	Other Ethnological Collections	Bernstein, Bruce			Fa	11	1		J/F 84	50
Collections and Collecting: Basketry, Native American	Native American Basketry	Bernstein, Bruce	√		Fa	11	1		J/F 84	50
Collections and Collecting: Basketry, Non-Native American	Non-Native American Basketry	Frye, Melinda Young	√		Fa	11	1		J/F 84	51
Collections and Collecting: Books	Healey Collection				SS&D	9	3	35	Su 78	22
Collections and Collecting: Carpets, John D. McIlhenny Collection	Carpet Collections of the Philadelphia Museum of Art	Ellis, Charles Grant	√		TMJ	17			78	29
Collections and Collecting: Carpets, Joseph Lees Williams Memorial Collection	Carpet Collections of the Philadelphia Museum of Art	Ellis, Charles Grant	√		TMJ	17			78	29
Collections and Collecting: Corporate	Woven Traditions: The Liberty Textile Collection	Roosevelt, Lynn Nanney	√		Fa	14	2		M/A 87	6
Collections and Collecting: Corporate Art	Design Concepts and Aesthetic Concerns of Corporate Art Collections	Rutherford, Karen Jenson			AT	8			De 87	193
Collections and Collecting: Costume	Textile Treasures At the Met's Costume Institute	Lonier, Terri	√		Fa	11	5		S/O 84	37
Collections and Collecting: Coverlet Drafts, 19th Century	Multiple Shaft Coverlet Drafts in the Allen-Stephenson Draft Book	Renne, Elisha	√	> 4	AT	3			My 85	125
Collections and Collecting: Crafts	Robert Pfannebecker: A Collector's Point of View	Park, Betty	√		Fa	5	4		J/A 78	42
Collections and Collecting: Early American Textiles	Early American Textiles, from Linda Belding's Collection		√		H&C	15	1		Wi 64	20
Collections and Collecting: European	European Tapestry Collections: London's Victoria & Albert Museum	Downing, Marolyn			WJ	12	1	45	Su 87	21
Collections and Collecting: European	European Textile Collections: Textile Research in Paris	Downing, Marolyn			WJ	11	2	42	Fa 86	53
Collections and Collecting: Kashmir Shawls, USA Museums	Scent of Flowers, Kishmir Shawls in the Collection of The Textile Museum, The	Mikosch, Elisabeth	√		TMJ	24			85	7
Collections and Collecting: Museums, Knitting	Collections	Upitis, Lizbeth			Kn	1	1	1	F-W 84 CI	68 7
Collections and Collecting: Oriental Carpets, Classic	Strengths of The Textile Museum's Oriental Carpet Collection, The	Ellis, Charles Grant	√		TMJ	24			85	61
Collections and Collecting: Oriental Carpets, Fragments	Strengths of The Textile Museum's Oriental Carpet Collection, The	Ellis, Charles Grant	√		TMJ	24			85	61
Collections and Collecting: Oriental Carpets, Research Value	Strengths of The Textile Museum's Oriental Carpet Collection, The	Ellis, Charles Grant	√		TMJ	24			85	61
Collections and Collecting: Oriental Carpets, Secondary Rugs	Strengths of The Textile Museum's Oriental Carpet Collection, The	Ellis, Charles Grant	√		TMJ	24			85	61
Collections and Collecting: Smithsonian	Textiles from the Smithsonian's Collection	Adrosko, Rita	√		H&C	23	2		M/A 72	20
Collections and Collecting: Spinning Wheels	Collecting Spinning Wheels	Ralph, William	√	√	H&C	24	1		J/F 73	16
Collections and Collecting: Tapestry	European Tapestry Collections: London's Victoria & Albert Museum	Downing, Marolyn			WJ	12	1	45	Su 87	21
Collections and Collecting: Textile	How a Textile Department Grew	Koplos, Janet	√		Fa	10	1		J/F 83	54
Collections and Collecting: Textile	Millions of Swatches at FIT	Kennedy, Alan			TM			11	J/J 87	18
Collections and Collecting: Textile Collections	Peru, Textiles Unlimited: Textile Collections	Tidball, Harriet	√		SCGM		25		68	14
Collections and Collecting: Textiles	Fiber Lover's Guide to the San Francisco Bay Area, A	Scarborough, Jessica	√		Fa	11	3		M/J 84	43
Collections and Collecting: Textiles	New Learns from the Old: Treasures in Museums for Today's Weavers, The	Snow, Edith Huntington	√		H&C	3	1		Wi 51	18
Collections and Collecting: Textiles	Why Not Start Your Own Museum?	Amram, Hortense	√		H&C	4	3		Su 53	28
Collections and Collecting: Tribal Rugs, Semi-Antique	Strengths of The Textile Museum's Oriental Carpet Collection, The	Ellis, Charles Grant	√		TMJ	24			85	61
Collections and Collecting: Victoria and Albert Museum	European Tapestry Collections: London's Victoria & Albert Museum	Downing, Marolyn			WJ	12	1	45	Su 87	21
Collections and Collectiong: Helen L. Allen Textile Collection	Color and Design in Andean Warp-Faced Fabrics	Femenias, Blenda	√		WJ	12	2	46	Fa 87	44

SUBJECT	TITLE	AUTHOR	IL	INST	JOUR	VOL	NO	ISS	DATE	PAGE
Collectives	Athens Tapestry Works	Many, Paul	√		Fa	5	4		J/A 78	51
Colloquy '85	Weaving Places	van der Hoogt, Madelyn	√		PWC	4	1	11		8
Colombia	Los Tejedorcitos De San Isidro		√		SS&D	6	1	21	Wi 74	80
Colonial America	Fine Fabrics: A Continuing Tradition		√		Hw	3	5		N/D 82	30
Colonial Weavers Association	HGA Education Directory, 1984	Smayda, Norma	√	>4	SS&D	15	4	60	Fa 84	6
Colonial Weavers Association	Weaver Rose — A New Perspective	Kaye, Alda Ganze	√		SS&D	8	2	30	Sp 77	8
Colonial Weaving	Dearest Daughter	Strickler, Carol	√		Hw	3	5		N/D 82	36
Colonial-Style Weavings	Blanket Snug, A		√		Hw	3	5		N/D 82	54
Colonial-Style Weavings	Blue and White		√		Hw	3	5		N/D 82	47
Colonial-Style Weavings	Linsey-Woolsey, Woolen Tweel		√		Hw	3	5		N/D 82	53
Colonial-Style Weavings	Mary Meigs Atwater		√		Hw	3	5		N/D 82	50
Colonial-Style Weavings	Old Draft, New System		√		Hw	3	5		N/D 82	55
Colonial-Style Weavings	Traditional Threadings		√		Hw	3	5		N/D 82	48
Color	Chromatic Effervescence: The Hooked Surface As a Response to My Environment	Eyerman, Linda	√		Fa	10	2		M/A 83	22
Color	Clothesline Palette: Three Hundred Yards of Color		√		Fa	9	1		J/F 82	22
Color	Color Control	Siminoff		√	SS&D	2	4	8	Fa 71	33
Color	Color Excitement	Liebler, Barbara			Hw	6	2		M/A 85	80
Color	Color Forecasting and the Weaver	Znamierowski, Nell	√		Hw	7	3		M/J 86	33
Color	Color Game	Justema, William			SS&D	3	1	9	Wi 71	11
Color	Color Specialists, The		√		Kn	2	1	3	F-W 85	64
Color	Color Symbolism in Primitive Societies (error-corrected Fa v13 n4 86 p5)	Janeiro, Jan	√		Fa	13	2		M/A 86	30
Color	Color-Order Gamp	Strickler, Carol	√	√	Iw	2	4		Su 77	24
Color	Complementary Colors	Wertenberger, Kathryn	√		Hw	6	5		N/D 85	90
Color	Costume of a Plain People, The	Schiess, Kate	√	√	TM			5	J/J 86	65
Color	Fashionable Palette of Pittsburgh Paints, The	Brenholts, Jeanne	√		Fa	14	3		M/J 87	46
Color	Fashions by Linda Knutson and Lynn Daly		√	√	WJ	6	3	23	Wi 81	14
Color	Feeling for Color. A	Vinroot, Sally	√		Hw	2	4		Se 81	47
Color	Harmony of Pinks, A		√		Hw	5	3		Su 84	58
Color	Nature: A Color Source and Inspiration for Traditional Sweaters	Gibson-Roberts, Priscilla A.	√		S-O	9	3		Fa 85	42
Color	Opinionated Knitter, The	Zimmermann, Elizabeth			Kn	2	1	3	F-W 85	8
Color	Personal Approach to Color, A	Wipplinger, Michele	√		Fa	13	2		M/A 86	31
Color	Personality of Color, The	Liebler, Barbara	√		Hw	7	4		S/O 86	80
Color	Principles of Textile Conservation Science, No. 4. The Conservation of Historical Textile Colorants	Rice, James W.	√	√	TMJ	1	2		De 63	55
Color	Sampling	Strickler, Carol	√	√	Iw	2	3		Sp 77	24
Color	Siminoff	Weigle, Palmy			SS&D	1	3	3	Ju 70	20
Color	Weave Color: A Color Sampler (Carol Strickler)		√	√	Hw	1	1		F-W 79	8
Color	Winter Colors	Beeny, Merna	√	√	Hw	4	1		J/F 83	64
Color: Analogous	Color and Dyeing	Siminoff	√	√	SS&D	2	3	7	Su 71	25
Color Analysis Algorithm	Automatic Analysis of Coloured Images	Hoskins, J. A.	√	√	AT	5			Ju 86	151
Color and Design	1 Fabric: 2 Faces	Moes, Dini	√	>4	SS&D	14	2	54	Sp 83	16
Color and Design	Alice Pickett: Rugmaker	Pickett, Alice	√		Fa	7	5		S/O 80	55
Color and Design	Andean Crossed-Warp Techniques for Decorative Trims, Part 1 — Flat Bands	Cahlander, Adele	√	√	WJ	2	4	8	Ap 78	10
Color and Design	Autumn Colors	Beeny, Merna	√		Hw	3	4		Se 82	47
Color and Design	Bound Weave Rugs	Harrold, Yoko Tamari	√	√	WJ	2	1	5	Jy 77	20
Color and Design	Bound Weaving	Turner, Alta R.	√	√	H&C	15	3		Su 64	10
Color and Design	Bound Weaving	Turner, Alta R.	√	>4	H&C	15	4		Fa 64	19

SUBJECT	TITLE	AUTHOR	IL	INST	JOUR	VOL	NO	ISS	DATE	PAGE
Color and Design	Boundweave Rug on an Overshot Threading	Kindahl, Connie	√	√	SS&D	17	3	67	Su 86	58
Color and Design	Boxed Rainbows: What to Do with a Dye Kit	Bliss, Anne	√	√	Hw	4	2		M/A 83	68
Color and Design	Bright & Bold		√	√	Hw	4	2		M/A 83	50
Color and Design	Brocade: Color	Tidball, Harriet	√		SCGM		22		67	11
Color and Design	Challenge of the Ugly Color, The	Liebler, Barbara	√		Hw	8	4		S/O 87	70
Color and Design	Co-ordinated Fabrics	Hausner, Walter		> 4	H&C	12	3		Su 61	9
Color and Design	Color and Design in Andean Warp-Faced Fabrics	Femenias, Blenda	√		WJ	12	2	46	Fa 87	44
Color and Design	Color and Structure	The Gadred Weavers	√		H&C	1	3		Fa 50	21
Color and Design	Color, Color, Color, Color—Seven Designers' Approaches		√		Hw	2	4		Se 81	27
Color and Design	Color Design for Garments	Znamierowski, Nell	√	√	Hw	7	5		N/D 86	54
Color and Design	Color & Design in Decorative Fabrics	Regensteiner, Else	√	√	H&C	9	4		Fa 58	6
Color and Design	Color Effects in Weft-faced Plain Weave (error-corrected Hw v7 n1 86 pl-3)	Davenport, Betty	√		Hw	6	5		N/D 85	12
Color and Design	Color in Summer and Winter	Alvic, Philis	√	√	WJ	7	4	28	Sp 83	64
Color and Design	Color It Plaid	Bliss, Anne		√	Hw	4	5		N/D 83	74
Color and Design	Color Play		√		Hw	5	3		Su 84	77
Color and Design	Color Rotation Trick, A		√	√	Hw	4	2		M/A 83	40
Color and Design	Color Scheming	Liebler, Barbara	√	√	Hw	5	4		S/0 84	88
Color and Design	Color Use in Patterned Weaves	Kurtz, Carol	√		SS&D	11	3	43	Su 80	22
Color and Design	Composition and Designing: Colour	Zielinski, S. A.; Robert Leclerc, ed.	√	√	MWL	18			'51–'73	31
Color and Design	Composition and Designing: Colour and Design	Zielinski, S. A.; Robert Leclerc, ed.			MWL	18			'51–'73	17
Color and Design	Composition and Designing Part 2: Random Colours	Zielinski, S. A.; Robert Leclerc, ed.			MWL	19			'51–'73	120
Color and Design	Composition and Designing Part 2: Random Patterns and Colours	Zielinski, S. A.; Robert Leclerc, ed.	√	√	MWL	19			'51–'73	115
Color and Design	Composition and Designing Part 2: Vertical Stripes in Texture and Colour	Zielinski, S. A.; Robert Leclerc, ed.	√	> 4	MWL	19			'51–'73	58
Color and Design	Considering Color		√		Hw	5	2		M/A 84	54
Color and Design	Contemporary Approach to Traditional Weaves: Colours in Crackle	Zielinski, S. A.; Robert Leclerc, ed.	√	√	MWL	8			'51–'73	21
Color and Design	Contemporary Approach to Traditional Weaves: Colours in Summer and Winter	Zielinski, S. A.; Robert Leclerc, ed.	√	> 4	MWL	7			'51–'73	119
Color and Design	Coordinates	Moes, Dini	√	√	SS&D	15	4	60	Fa 84	46
Color and Design	Counterchange, A Device for Pattern Design	Justema, William	√		H&C	19	3		Su 68	8
Color and Design	Critique: Una Flor Morada, A		√	√	Hw	4	2		M/A 83	44
Color and Design	Design and the Handweaver: Color	Atwater, Mary Meigs		√	SCGM		3		61	11
Color and Design	Design in Weaving	Berglund, Hilma	√		H&C	8	4		Fa 57	13
Color and Design	Designing Damask	Nyquist, Jan	√	> 4	SS&D	10	4	40	Fa 79	16
Color and Design	Designing for Piqué (error-corrected PWC v4 n4 i14 p33)	Sullivan, Donna	√	> 4	PWC	4	3	13		28
Color and Design	Designing with Color	Wertenberger, Kathryn		√	Hw	2	4		Se 81	32
Color and Design	Double Weave Jacket, A	Scorgie, Jean	√	√	Hw	4	4		S/O 83	48
Color and Design	Double Weaves: Polychrome Double Weave on Four Shafts	Zielinski, S. A.; Robert Leclerc, ed.	√	√	MWL	15			'51–'73	60
Color and Design	Double Weaves: Polychrome Double Weaves	Zielinski, S. A.; Robert Leclerc, ed.	√	> 4	MWL	15			'51–'73	114
Color and Design	Double Weaves: Stitching in Four Shaft Polychrome Double Weave	Zielinski, S. A.; Robert Leclerc, ed.	√	√	MWL	15			'51–'73	68
Color and Design	Double-Weave Pick-Up	Neely, Cynthia H.	√	√	TM			8	D/J 86	36
Color and Design	Drafting with Color	Kurtz, Carol	√	√	SS&D	11	1	41	Wi 79	10
Color and Design	Experimenting with Color and Two-Tie Weaving on the Rigid Heddle	Niekrasz, Jennifer	√	√	PWC	4	4	14		21

SUBJECT	TITLE	AUTHOR	IL	INST	JOUR	VOL	NO	ISS	DATE	PAGE
Color and Design	Fascination of Twills (Fourshafts): Colour Effects in Twills	Zielinski, S. A.; Robert Leclerc, ed.	√	√	MWL	9			'51–'73	80
Color and Design	Fascination of Twills (Fourshafts): More on Colours in Twills	Zielinski, S. A.; Robert Leclerc, ed.	√	> 4	MWL	9			'51–'73	85
Color and Design	Focal Point Through Color Contrast	Liebler, Barbara	√	√	Hw	4	4		S/O 83	82
Color and Design	From Simple Twills to Dobby Fantasies...A Progression	Marquess, Joyce	√	> 4	Iw	4	4		Fa 79	38
Color and Design	From White-on-White to Color	Currie, Meg	√		TM			3	F/M 86	39
Color and Design	Fukumi Shimura: Japan's Colorist Supreme	Adachi, Barbara C.	√		Fa	12	4		J/A 85	28
Color and Design	Ikat Notes: Nancy Belfer Talks About Her Recent Work	Belfer, Nancy	√		Fa	9	2		M/A 82	19
Color and Design	Ikat-Woven Images	Tacker, Sylvia	√	√	SS&D	18	1	69	Wi 86	68
Color and Design	Impressionistic Use of Color	Leibler, Barbara	√	√	Hw	4	5		N/D 83	90
Color and Design	Karen Chapnick: Constructing Color	Green, Phyllis	√		Fa	13	2		M/A 86	12
Color and Design	Little Dye Makes the Difference, A	Henrikson, Susan	√	√	Hw	4	2		M/A 83	60
Color and Design	Little Known Weaves Worth Knowing Better: Broché	Zielinski, S. A.; Robert Leclerc, ed.	√	> 4	MWL	16			'51–'73	84
Color and Design	Midwest Conference Presents Sources of Inspiration for Color		√	> 4	H&C	13	4		Fa 62	18
Color and Design	Modern Overshot (Frappé Moderne)	Collard, Agathe G.	√	√	WJ	5	4	20	Sp 81	28
Color and Design	Music for Inspiration		√	√	Hw	4	2		M/A 83	51
Color and Design	Nature Designs		√		Hw	2	4		Se 81	56
Color and Design	Nell Znamierowski: Color & Design	Liebler, Barbara	√		Hw	2	4		Se 81	40
Color and Design	Northern California Conference	Bryan, Dorothy	√	√	H&C	11	4		Fa 60	26
Color and Design	Notebook: Color Notes	Myers, Ruth Nordquist, ed.	√	√	SS&D	15	2	58	Sp 84	80
Color and Design	Notes of a Pattern Weaver	Alvic, Philis	√		SS&D	13	4	52	Fa 82	76
Color and Design	Notes of a Pattern Weaver	Alvic, Philis	√	> 4	SS&D	14	2	54	Sp 83	76
Color and Design	Notes of a Pattern Weaver	Alvic, Philis	√		SS&D	14	3	55	Su 83	66
Color and Design	One Design 2X		√		Hw	2	4		Se 81	54
Color and Design	One Warp, Many Fabrics	Liebler, Barbara	√	> 4	Iw	3	1		Fa 77	28
Color and Design	One Weaver's Viewpoint	Freeman, Claire			H&C	11	1		Wi 60	10
Color and Design	Opera Elegance	Sylvan, Katherine	√	√	SS&D	15	4	60	Fa 84	24
Color and Design	Organize to Control Your Color	Templeton, Peg	√	√	Hw	2	4		Se 81	48
Color and Design	Painting and Brocading on the Loom	Ziek, Bhakti	√	√	TM			6	A/S 86	42
Color and Design	Pile Weaves, Rugs and Tapestry: Colours in Corduroy	Zielinski, S. A.; Robert Leclerc, ed.	√	√	MWL	14			'51–'73	16
Color and Design	Planning Stripes	McDonald, Pat	√	√	Hw	2	4		Se 81	30
Color and Design	Presence of Light: The Un-Traditional Quilts of Jan Myers, The	Gutcheon, Beth	√		Fa	8	3		M/J 81	60
Color and Design	Primary Patterns	Spoering, Kathy	√	√	WJ	9	1	33	Su 84	53
Color and Design	Rainwindow: Watercolor Weaving	Schlegel, Mary	√	√	SS&D	5	2	18	Sp 74	8
Color and Design	Randall Darwall	Sayward, Jessica Lee	√		SS&D	15	2	58	Sp 84	48
Color and Design	Resist Dyeing, Curiosities and Inventions: Locked Wefts in Pattern Weaves	Zielinski, S. A.; Robert Leclerc, ed.	√	√	MWL	17			'51–'73	60
Color and Design	Reversible Flamepoint Vest	Wittpenn, Ann	√	√	WJ	5	3	19	Wi 81	9
Color and Design	Rug Based on 3-Shaft Striaght Twill		√	√	WJ	5	4	20	Sp 81	20
Color and Design	Rugs Based on Four Harness Twills (error-corrected WJ v2 n2 77 insert for vol. 2)		√	√	WJ	2	1	5	Jy 77	23
Color and Design	Rugs of Mary Veerkamp, The		√	√	Hw	4	2		M/A 83	46
Color and Design	Rya Rugs	Erickson, Johanna	√	√	SS&D	13	3	51	Su 82	36
Color and Design	Sequence of Dominance	Davis, Helen	√	√	Hw	4	2		M/A 83	42
Color and Design	Shadow Scarves (Judy Steinkoenig)		√	√	Hw	3	4		Se 82	73
Color and Design	Sheila O'Hara: Wry Humor and Virtuoso Weaving	Park, Betty	√		Fa	10	1		J/F 83	64

SUBJECT	TITLE	AUTHOR	IL	INST	JOUR	VOL	NO	ISS	DATE	PAGE
Color and Design	So You Want to Weave Tartan?	Amos, Alden		√	Hw	4	5		N/D 83	37
Color and Design	Songs in Fabric: Quiltmaker Nancy Herman Is an Unusual Musician	Rowland, Amy Zaffarano	√		Fa	9	4		J/A 82	22
Color and Design	Spot Weaves — Old and New: Polychrone Swivel	Zielinski, S. A.; Robert Leclerc, ed.	√	> 4	MWL	12			'51–'73	79
Color and Design	Spring and Summer Colors	Beeny, Merna			Hw	4	3		M/J 83	95
Color and Design	Stripe Study Group, A		√	√	Hw	4	2		M/A 83	24
Color and Design	Studies in Color and Texture through Fabric	Kramer, Helen	√		H&C	6	1		Wi 54	13
Color and Design	Summer and Winter — Part 1		√	> 4	WJ	2	4	8	Ap 78	28
Color and Design	Tabby Color	Alvic, Philis	√	√	SS&D	15	2	58	Sp 84	91
Color and Design	Taking the Guesswork Out of Color Selection	Maxson, Mary Lou	√		Hw	2	4		Se 81	44
Color and Design	Three Color Progressions and Their Use in Sweater Jackets	Sylvan, Katherine	√	√	WJ	5	4	20	Sp 81	38
Color and Design	Three-Color, Weft-Faced Block Weave	Neely, Cynthia H.	√	> 4	SS&D	15	2	58	Sp 84	74
Color and Design	Tied Overshot Boundweave	Xenakis, Athanasios David	√	√	PWC	3	4	10		9
Color and Design	Time Capsules	White, Violet	√		Hw	8	1		J/F 87	75
Color and Design	Tough Colors	Rees, Linda	√	√	Hw	2	4		Se 81	58
Color and Design	Tucked Dresses	Wertenberger, Kathryn; Nancy Kuwabara	√	√	Hw	4	2		M/A 83	63
Color and Design	Two-Harness Textiles, The Open Work Weaves: Colors	Tidball, Harriet			SCGM		21		67	3
Color and Design	Undulating Weft Effects: Designing Undulating Weft Textiles, The Colors	Tidball, Harriet		√	SCGM		9		63	4
Color and Design	Value of Value, The	Davenport, Betty	√	√	Hw	2	4		Se 81	70
Color and Design	Variations on a Theme	Liebler, Barbara	√	√	Hw	8	5		N/D 87	26
Color and Design	Variations on a Theme of Marigolds (Görel Kinersly)		√	√	Hw	5	1		J/F 84	81
Color and Design	Variations on a Twill Theme, No. 2	Marston, Ena	√	> 4	SS&D	5	3	19	Su 74	34
Color and Design	Very Special Cape, A	Alderman, Sharon D.			Hw	2	4		Se 81	46
Color and Design	Warp Color Changes in Double and Multilayer Weaves	O'Connor, Paul	√	> 4	WJ	12	2	46	Fa 87	55
Color and Design	Warp-Faced Krokbragd	Jensen, Gay; Donna Kaplan	√	> 4	WJ	12	2	46	Fa 87	62
Color and Design	Warping in Color	Moes, Dini	√	√	SS&D	14	4	56	Fa 83	24
Color and Design	Wefts of Light: Jayn Thomas' Fabric Hangings	Scarborough, Jessica	√		Fa	9	1		J/F 82	23
Color and Design	Why Do I Weave Tapestries? An Exploration of Color Theory and Tapestry Design (error-corrected Fa v7 n6 80 p8)	Griffey, Margaret	√		Fa	7	4		J/A 80	55
Color and Design	Woolens and Tweeds: Designing Woolen Fabrics: Swedish Woolens	Tidball, Harriet			SCGM		4		61	26
Color and Design	Woolens and Tweeds: Designing Woolen Fabrics: The District Checks	Tidball, Harriet	√	√	SCGM		4		61	29
Color and Design	Wrapping Your Stripes		√	√	Hw	4	2		M/A 83	48
Color and Design: Basketry	Color in the Woven Basket	Hoppe, Flo	√	√	SS&D	16	3	63	Su 85	22
Color and Design: Basketry	Kari Lønning: Exploring Color and Form in Rattan	Lønning, Kari	√	√	Fa	11	1		J/F 84	12
Color and Design: Batik	Resisting Dyes: Three Ways to Put Color in Its Place	Northup, Wendy	√	√	TM			1	O/N 85	30
Color and Design: Dyeing	New Twist on Resist	Wada, Yoshiko Iwamoto; Shelley Karpilow	√	√	TM			8	D/J 86	20
Color and Design: Dyeing	Textural Approach to Arashi Shibori, A	Beytebiere, D'Arcie	√	√	TM			8	D/J 86	24
Color and Design: Embroidery	Meaning of Folk Art in Rabari Life: A Closer Look at Mirrored Embroidery, The	Frater, Judy	√		TMJ	4	2		75	47
Color and Design: Fabrics, Interiors	Color Related Decorating Textiles Rugs, Draperies, Upholstery: Drapery and Casement Fabrics, Color and Design	Rhodes, Tonya Stalons; Harriet Tidball, ed.			SCGM		14		65	8

SUBJECT	TITLE	AUTHOR	IL	INST	JOUR	VOL	NO	ISS	DATE	PAGE
Color and Design: Fabrics, Upholstery	Color Related Decorating Textiles Rugs, Draperies, Upholstery: Upholstery Fabrics, Color and Design	Rhodes, Tonya Stalons; Harriet Tidball, ed.			SCGM		14		65	6
Color and Design: Fashions	Color Forecasting	Dyett, Linda	√		TM			3	F/M 86	22
Color and Design: Grist Patterning	Composition and Designing Part 2: Patterns in Grist	Zielinski, S. A.; Robert Leclerc, ed.	√	√	MWL	19			'51–'73	134
Color and Design: Inkle Weaving	Weaving Inkle Bands: Inkle Color Patterns and Drafts	Tidball, Harriet	√	√	SCGM		27		69	22
Color and Design: Interiors	Lever House Presents a Solution to a Unique Problem in Interior Design		√		H&C	4	3		Su 53	32
Color and Design: Knitting	Block Sweater	Morris, Sandy	√	√	Kn	2	1	3	F-W 85	56
Color and Design: Knitting	Classic, The	O'Connor, Pat	√	√	Kn	2	1	3	F-W 85	58
Color and Design: Knitting	Consider Color	Rowley, Elaine	√	√	Kn	2	1	3	F-W 85	20
Color and Design: Knitting	Fair Isle Knitting	Starmore, Alice	√	√	TM			8	D/J 86	44
Color and Design: Knitting	Kaffe Fassett		√		Kn	2	2	4	S-S 86	14
Color and Design: Knitting	Knitting with Colors	Fassett, Kaffe	√	√	TM			3	F/M 86	68
Color and Design: Knitting	Methods for Multicolored Knitting	Righetti, Maggie	√	√	TM			6	A/S 86	40
Color and Design: Knitting	Opinionated Knitter, The	Zimmermann, Elizabeth			Kn	2	1	3	F-W 85	8
Color and Design: Knitting	Sleeve Sweater	Rowley, Elaine	√	√	Kn	2	1	3	F-W 85	58
Color and Design: Knitting	Square-rigged Vests	Swansen, Meg	√	√	Kn	2	1	3	F-W 85	62
Color and Design: Knitting	Travel Sweater	Upitis, Lizbeth	√	√	Kn	2	1	3	F-W 85	58
Color and Design: Needlepoint	Color Blending in Needlepoint	Banks, Lloyd Walton	√	√	TM			10	A/M 87	24
Color and Design: Pattern Exploration	Composition and Designing Part 2: From Hound's Tooth to Random Patterns	Zielinski, S. A.; Robert Leclerc, ed.	√	√	MWL	19			'51–'73	71
Color and Design: Quilts	Log Cabins	Larzelere, Judith Ann	√	√	TM			3	F/M 86	58
Color and Design: Spinning	Beyond the Machine (The creative uses of imprecision)	d'Avila, Doris	√	√	S-O	4			80	50
Color and Design: Spinning	Color in Spinning	Adams, Brucie		√	Iw	3	2		Wi 78	34
Color and Design: Spinning	Fiber Foray: Color Exercises for the Beginner	Quinn, Celia	√	√	S-O	9	3		Fa 85	36
Color and Design: Spinning	Personal Approach to Color, A	Matlock, Ann	√		S-O	9	3		Fa 85	19
Color and Design: Spinning	Pointillist Color Effects in Spinning: A Study Program	Deems, Flo		√	S-O	4			80	53
Color and Design: Spinning	Spinning for an Ombré Project	Adams, Brucie	√	√	Hw	4	2		M/A 83	78
Color and Design: Spinning	What to do with a Rainbow	Klinect, Ann W.	√		S-O	9	3		Fa 85	26
Color and Design: Sprang	Nasca Sprang Tassels: Structure, Technique, and Order	Frame, Mary	√	√	TMJ	25			86	67
Color and Design: Tubular Bands	Andean Crossed-Warp Techniques for Decorative Trims, Part 2 — Tubular Bands (error-corrected WJ v3 n1 insert for vol. 2)	Cahlander, Adele	√	√	WJ	3	1	9	Jy 78	38
Color and Texture Effects	Block Weaves as Color and Texture Effects	Znamierowski, Nell	√	√	Hw	8	5		N/D 87	48
Color and Weave Effect	Double Weaves: Polychrome Double Weave on Four Shafts	Zielinski, S. A.; Robert Leclerc, ed.	√	√	MWL	15			'51–'73	60
Color and Weave Effects	1 Fabric: 2 Faces	Moes, Dini	√	> 4	SS&D	14	2	54	Sp 83	16
Color and Weave Effects	Automatic Analysis of Coloured Images	Hoskins, J. A.	√	√	AT	5			Ju 86	151
Color and Weave Effects	Basic Designs for Every Weaver's File	Hausner, Walter	√	√	H&C	14	4		Fa 63	22
Color and Weave Effects	Colonial Mats (Pat Epstein)		√	√	Hw	3	5		N/D 82	46, 94
Color and Weave Effects	Color and Weave Effects	O'Sullivan, Sallie	√	√	SS&D	3	4	12	Fa 72	22
Color and Weave Effects	Color and Weave Effects	Poulton, Jim	√	> 4	WJ	5	3	19	Wi 81	14
Color and Weave Effects	Color and Weave Effects with Four Harness Summer and Winter		√	√	WJ	5	2	18	Fa 80	24
Color and Weave Effects	Color Play		√		Hw	5	3		Su 84	77
Color and Weave Effects	Color-and-Weave Effects	Wertenberger, Kathryn	√	> 4	Hw	5	2		M/A 84	36
Color and Weave Effects	Composition and Designing: Colours in Simple Weaves	Zielinski, S. A.; Robert Leclerc, ed.	√	> 4	MWL	18			'51–'73	41
Color and Weave Effects	Composition and Designing Part 2: From Hound's Tooth to Random Patterns	Zielinski, S. A.; Robert Leclerc, ed.	√	√	MWL	19			'51–'73	71

SUBJECT	TITLE	AUTHOR	IL	INST	JOUR	VOL	NO	ISS	DATE	PAGE
Color and Weave Effects	Composition and Designing Part 2: Hound's Tooth in Texture and Color	Zielinski, S. A.; Robert Leclerc, ed.	√	> 4	MWL	19			'51–'73	66
Color and Weave Effects	Composition and Designing Part 2: Log Cabin	Zielinski, S. A.; Robert Leclerc, ed.	√	√	MWL	19			'51–'73	121
Color and Weave Effects	Composition and Designing Part 2: Multiblock Log Cabin and Shadow Weave	Zielinski, S. A.; Robert Leclerc, ed.	√	> 4	MWL	19			'51–'73	126
Color and Weave Effects	Composition and Designing: Pattern in Warp	Zielinski, S. A.; Robert Leclerc, ed.	√	√	MWL	18			'51–'73	79
Color and Weave Effects	Computer-Aided Design for Handweaving	Windeknecht, Margaret B.; Thomas G. Windeknecht			CW	2	1	4	Oc 80	8
Color and Weave Effects	Damask	Nyquist, Jan	√	> 4	CW	8	1	22	Se 86	3
Color and Weave Effects	Dress or Belted Jacket Fabric, Swatch #3 (Sharon Alderman)		√	√	Hw	7	4		S/O 86	24, I-4
Color and Weave Effects	Ducky Sacque and Bonnet (Cara L. Bernhauser)		√	√	Hw	5	3		Su 84	51, 94
Color and Weave Effects	Experiments in Color and Weave with Floats	Davenport, Betty	√	√	Hw	8	2		M/A 87	60
Color and Weave Effects	Fascination of Twills (Fourshafts): Colour Effects in Twills	Zielinski, S. A.; Robert Leclerc, ed.	√	√	MWL	9			'51–'73	80
Color and Weave Effects	Fascination of Twills (Fourshafts): More on Colours in Twills	Zielinski, S. A.; Robert Leclerc, ed.	√	> 4	MWL	9			'51–'73	85
Color and Weave Effects	Flamepoint Rugs for Everybody	Kirk, Betty Burian	√	√	WJ	8	4	32	Sp 84	12
Color and Weave Effects	Four Shaft Fascination	Gordon, Judith	√	√	Hw	6	1		J/F 85	12
Color and Weave Effects	Four-Shaft Double Weave with Color and Weave Effects	Scorgie, Jean; Gloria Martin	√	√	Hw	6	3		Su 85	38
Color and Weave Effects	From Cotton Patch to Cotton Patches and Then Some	Linder, Olive	√	√	WJ	5	4	20	Sp 81	48
Color and Weave Effects	Harris Tweed Jacket		√	√	Hw	2	5		No 81	49, 87
Color and Weave Effects	Houndstooth Doubleweave (Kathryn Wertenberger)		√	√	Hw	5	2		M/A 84	66, 103
Color and Weave Effects	Leamington Bags	Steedsman, Nell	√	√	SS&D	2	4	8	Fa 71	28
Color and Weave Effects	Lincoln Log Placemats (Linda Ligon)		√	√	Hw	6	1		J/F 85	61, I-15
Color and Weave Effects	Log Cabin Effects for the Rigid Heddle Loom	Davenport, Betty Lynn	√	√	Hw	8	5		N/D 87	42
Color and Weave Effects	Magnified Twill Blanket	Alderman, Sharon	√		Hw	6	5		N/D 85	53
Color and Weave Effects	Making a Color Draw-Up	TerLouw, Betty	√	√	SS&D	13	2	50	Sp 82	37
Color and Weave Effects	Notebook: Color Notes	Myers, Ruth Nordquist, ed.	√	√	SS&D	15	2	58	Sp 84	80
Color and Weave Effects	Peru, Textiles Unlimited, Part 2: Color Effect in Block Pattern	Tidball, Harriet	√	√	SCGM		26		69	4
Color and Weave Effects	Peru, Textiles Unlimited, Part 2: Plain Weave Color Effects	Tidball, Harriet	√	√	SCGM		26		69	4
Color and Weave Effects	Resist Dyeing, Curiosities and Inventions: Hound's Tooth in Texture and Colour	Zielinski, S. A.; Robert Leclerc, ed.	√	√	MWL	17			'51–'73	68
Color and Weave Effects	Shadow Weave Offers an Opportunity for Many Variations	Powell, Marian	√	√	H&C	12	3		Su 61	20
Color and Weave Effects	Silk Dyeing		√	√	WJ	3	2	10	Oc 78	21
Color and Weave Effects	Smart and Simple (Virginia West)		√	√	Hw	5	2		M/A 84	74, 94
Color and Weave Effects	Spot Weaves — Old and New: Polychrone Swivel	Zielinski, S. A.; Robert Leclerc, ed.	√	> 4	MWL	12			'51–'73	79
Color and Weave Effects	Super Scarf	Herring, Connie	√	> 4	PWC	3	1	7		28
Color and Weave Effects	Swatch #1, Wool Coat Fabric for Winter (Lillian Whipple)		√	√	Hw	7	5		N/D 86	64, I-7
Color and Weave Effects	Swatch #2, Plain Weave Check for Suiting (Virginia West)		√	√	Hw	7	5		N/D 86	62, I-6
Color and Weave Effects	Tickweave Upholstery (Sharon D. Alderman)		√	√	Hw	5	2		M/A 84	68, 105
Color and Weave Effects	Twill Color and Weave Effects...From the Computer	O'Connor, Paul	√	> 4	Iw	6	1		Wi 80	28
Color and Weave Effects	Two-Harness Textiles, The Loom-Controlled Weaves: Color-Effect Plain Weaves (Log Cabin)	Tidball, Harriet			SCGM		20		67	22

SUBJECT	TITLE	AUTHOR	IL	INST	JOUR	VOL	NO	ISS	DATE	PAGE
Color and Weave Effects	Two-Harness Textiles, The Loom-Controlled Weaves: Color-Effect Plain Weaves (Log Cabin), Surface Interest Designs	Tidball, Harriet	√	√	SCGM		20		67	24
Color and Weave Effects	Ultimate Brown Bag, The (Barbara Smith Eychaner)		√	√	Hw	7	4		S/O 86	36, I-6
Color and Weave Effects	Upholstery Fabric (Sharon Alderman)		√	√	Hw	1	1		F-W 79	42, 61
Color and Weave Effects	Weaver's Challenge	Wertenberger, Kathryn	√	√	Hw	5	1		J/F 84	27
Color and Weave Effects	Weaving and Sheepskin, Naturally	Mason, Carole	√	√	WJ	5	3	19	Wi 81	46
Color and Weave Effects	Weaving the Color Patterns of Shadow Weave		√		Hw	6	5		N/D 85	51
Color Blankets	Color Wheels and Color Blankets: Tools of the Designer	Wertenberger, Kathryn	√	√	Hw	2	4		Se 81	50
Color Blankets	Rainbow Blankets	Sullivan, Donna	√	> 4	PWC	4	4	14		27
Color Blending	Color Blended Scarves		√	√	S-O	11	1		Sp 87	23
Color Blending	Color Games	Berent, Mary, et al.	√	√	S-O	11	1		Sp 87	21
Color Blending	Spiral Tube Socks		√	√	S-O	11	1		Sp 87	22
Color Blending, On-Loom	Color Theory for Handweavers Part 2: Visual Mix	Boutin-Wald, Pat	√	√	WJ	10	3	39	Wi 86	47
Color: Braiding	Unusual Braids Produced by Loop Manipulation	Speiser, Noémi	√	√	WJ	10	1	37	Su 85	15
Color: Centroid Colors	Centroid Colors, The	Bliss, Anne	√	√	Iw	5	4		Fa 80	56
Color Chart: Hues	How to Match Colors When Dyeing Yarns or Fabrics for Textile Conservation Purposes	Rice, James W.	√	√	TMJ	2	4		De 69	27
Color Chips	Chip Making		√	√	Hw	7	5		N/D 86	92
Color: Choices	Color Me Purple	Wipplinger, Michele			Kn	2	1	3	F-W 85	70
Color: Complementary	Color and Dyeing	Siminoff	√	√	SS&D	2	3	7	Su 71	25
Color: Composition	Color and Dyeing: Color Composition for the Handweaver	Tidball, Harriet		√	SCGM		16		65	9
Color: Composition	Color Theory for Handweavers Part 1: The Basics (Photo-corrections WJ v10 n3 86 p6)	Wald, Pat Boutin	√	√	WJ	10	2	38	Fa 85	40
Color: Contrast	Focal Point Through Color Contrast	Liebler, Barbara	√	√	Hw	4	4		S/O 83	82
Color: Copy Machines	Incredible Color Copy Machine, The	Redding, Debbie	√		Hw	2	4		Se 81	74
Color: Exercises	Color	Smeltzer, Nancy	√	√	SS&D	15	2	58	Sp 84	53
Color: Exercises	Color Design for Garments	Znamierowski, Nell	√	√	Hw	7	5		N/D 86	54
Color: Exercises	Color Theory for Handweavers Part 4: More visual illusions with color	Wald, Pat Boutin	√	√	WJ	11	1	41	Su 86	37
Color: Exercises	Heathering	O'Connor, Marcie Archer	√	√	Kn	2	1	3	F-W 85	54
Color: Exercises	Planning Stripes	McDonald, Pat	√	√	Hw	2	4		Se 81	30
Color: Exercises	Value of Value, The	Davenport, Betty	√	√	Hw	2	4		Se 81	70
Color Gamp	Color Play		√		Hw	5	3		Su 84	77
Color: Graying	Color and Dyeing	Siminoff	√	√	SS&D	2	3	7	Su 71	25
Color: Harmony	Color and Dyeing: The Nature of Color and Color Harmony	Tidball, Harriet	√	√	SCGM		16		65	3
Color: Harmony	Composition and Designing: Harmonious Colouring	Zielinski, S. A.; Robert Leclerc, ed.		√	MWL	18			'51–'73	47
Color: Harmony, Munsell System	Color and Dyeing	Siminoff	√	√	SS&D	2	1	5	De 70	24
Color: Hue	Color and Dyeing	Siminoff	√	√	SS&D	2	2	6	Sp 71	30
Color: Intensity	Color and Dyeing	Siminoff	√	√	SS&D	2	2	6	Sp 71	30
Color: Mixing	Color Games	Berent, Mary, et al.	√	√	S-O	11	1		Sp 87	21
Color: Mixing	Stock Solution, The	Koehler, Glory Dail		√	SS&D	7	1	25	Wi 75	76
Color: Pattern	Color and Dyeing	Siminoff	√	√	SS&D	2	3	7	Su 71	25
Color: Pattern-Ground	Color Theory for Handweavers Part 2: Visual Mix	Boutin-Wald, Pat	√	√	WJ	10	3	39	Wi 86	47
Color: Photography	Photographing Textiles, Part 2, Color	Krasnoff, Julienne	√	√	SS&D	7	2	26	Sp 76	48

SUBJECT	TITLE	AUTHOR	IL	INST	JOUR	VOL	NO	ISS	DATE	PAGE
Color: Principles	Color Use in Patterned Weaves	Kurtz, Carol	√		SS&D	11	3	43	Su 80	22
Color: Progressions	Three Color Progressions and Their Use in Sweater Jackets	Sylvan, Katherine	√	√	WJ	5	4	20	Sp 81	38
Color: Psychology	Color Theory for Handweavers Part 3: Visual Illusions with Color	Wald, Pat Boutin	√	√	WJ	10	4	40	Sp 86	40
Color: Qualities	Color Theory for Handweavers Part 1: The Basics (Photo-corrections WJ v10 n3 86 p6)v	Wald, Pat Boutin	√	√	WJ	10	2	38	Fa 85	40
Color: Rotation	Have You Rotated Your Colors Lately?			√	Hw	7	3		M/J 86	67
Color Sequences: District Checks	Woolens and Tweeds: Designing Woolen Fabrics: The District Checks	Tidball, Harriet			SCGM		4		61	32
Color: Simultaneous Contrast	Color Theory for Handweavers Part 4: More Visual Illusions with Color	Wald, Pat Boutin	√	√	WJ	11	1	41	Su 86	37
Color Solid	Color Theory for Handweavers Part 1: The Basics (Photo-corrections WJ v10 n3 86 p6)	Wald, Pat Boutin	√	√	WJ	10	2	38	Fa 85	40
Color Solid	How to Match Colors When Dyeing Yarns or Fabrics for Textile Conservation Purposes	Rice, James W.	√	√	TMJ	2	4		De 69	27
Color: Standards	Centroid Colors, The	Bliss, Anne	√	√	Iw	5	4		Fa 80	56
Color: Symbolism	Composition and Designing: Subjective Colours	Zielinski, S. A.; Robert Leclerc, ed.		√	MWL	18			'51–'73	38
Color: Systems	Centroid Colors, The	Bliss, Anne	√	√	Iw	5	4		Fa 80	56
Color: Systems, Bergå	Color Theory for Handweavers Part 2: Visual Mix	Boutin-Wald, Pat	√	√	WJ	10	3	39	Wi 86	47
Color: Tartans	Weaver's Book of Scottish Tartans: The Tartan Colors,The	Tidball, Harriet		√	SCGM		5		62	7
Color: Theory	Color and Dyeing: Color Composition for the Handweaver	Tidball, Harriet		√	SCGM		16		65	11
Color: Theory	Color and Dyeing: The Nature of Color and Color Harmony	Tidball, Harriet	√	√	SCGM		16		65	3
Color: Theory	Color Games	Berent, Mary, et al.	√	√	S-O	11	1		Sp 87	21
Color: Theory	Color Scheming	Liebler, Barbara	√	√	Hw	5	4		S/0 84	88
Color: Theory	Color—Something Worth Dyeing For	Liebler, Barbara	√	√	Iw	3	3		Sp 78	36
Color: Theory	Color Theory Applied	Dobrovolny, Ardis	√		Hw	2	4		Se 81	33
Color: Theory	Color Theory for Handweavers Part 1: The Basics (Photo-corrections WJ v10 n3 86 p6)	Wald, Pat Boutin	√	√	WJ	10	2	38	Fa 85	40
Color: Theory	Color Theory for Handweavers Part 2: Visual Mix	Boutin-Wald, Pat	√	√	WJ	10	3	39	Wi 86	47
Color: Theory	Color Theory for Handweavers Part 3: Visual Illusions with Color	Wald, Pat Boutin	√	√	WJ	10	4	40	Sp 86	40
Color: Theory	Color Theory for Handweavers Part 4: More visual illusions with color	Wald, Pat Boutin	√	√	WJ	11	1	41	Su 86	37
Color: Theory	Color Use in Patterned Weaves	Kurtz, Carol	√		SS&D	11	3	43	Su 80	22
Color: Theory	Composition and Designing: Colour	Zielinski, S. A.; Robert Leclerc, ed.	√	√	MWL	18			'51–'73	31
Color: Theory	Designing with Color	Wertenberger, Kathryn		√	Hw	2	4		Se 81	32
Color: Theory	Mixing and Matching Colors in Dyeing	Lucey, Edmund A.	√		H&C	2	3		Su 51	26
Color: Theory	Pastel	Bliss, Anne	√	√	Hw	5	3		Su 84	86
Color: Theory	Personal Color System for Dyers, A	La Lena, Connie	√	√	Iw	3	3		Sp 78	20
Color: Theory	Practical Dyeing Method for the Fabric Conservator, A	Cooley, Theodore R.	√	√	TMJ	2	4		De 69	23
Color: Theory, Knitting	Heathering	O'Connor, Marcie Archer	√	√	Kn	2	1	3	F-W 85	54
Color: Value	Color and Dyeing	Siminoff	√	√	SS&D	2	2	6	Sp 71	30
Color: Value	Value of Value. The	Davenport, Betty	√	√	Hw	2	4		Se 81	70
Color: Visual Illusions	Color Theory for Handweavers Part 3: Visual Illusions with Color	Wald, Pat Boutin	√	√	WJ	10	4	40	Sp 86	40
Color: Visual Illusions	Color Theory for Handweavers Part 4: More visual illusions with color	Wald, Pat Boutin	√	√	WJ	11	1	41	Su 86	37

SUBJECT	TITLE	AUTHOR	IL	INST	JOUR	VOL	NO	ISS	DATE	PAGE
Color: Visual Mix	Color Theory for Handweavers Part 2: Visual Mix	Boutin-Wald, Pat	√	√	WJ	10	3	39	Wi 86	47
Color: Visual Mixing	Impressionistic Use of Color	Leibler, Barbara	√	√	Hw	4	5		N/D 83	90
Color: Warp	Warp Color Changes in Double and Multilayer Weaves	O'Connor, Paul	√	> 4	WJ	12	2	46	Fa 87	55
Color Wheel	Color and Dyeing: The Dyer's Color Wheel	Tidball, Harriet	√	√	SCGM		16		65	16
Color Wheel	Color Games	Berent, Mary, et al.	√	√	S-O	11	1		Sp 87	21
Color Wheel	Color Theory for Handweavers Part 1: The Basics (Photo-corrections WJ v10 n3 86 p6)	Wald, Pat Boutin	√	√	WJ	10	2	38	Fa 85	40
Color Wheel	Color Theory for Handweavers Part 2: Visual Mix	Boutin-Wald, Pat	√	√	WJ	10	3	39	Wi 86	47
Color Wheel	Color Wheels and Color Blankets: Tools of the Designer	Wertenberger, Kathryn	√	√	Hw	2	4		Se 81	50
Color Wheel	Creative Dyeing	Bachman, Sally	√	√	Iw	3	3		Sp 78	26
Color Wheel	How to Match Colors When Dyeing Yarns or Fabrics for Textile Conservation Purposes	Rice, James W.	√	√	TMJ	2	4		De 69	27
Color Wheel	New Look at the Standard Color Wheel, A (Kay Geary)		√		Hw	2	4		Se 81	12
Color Wheel	Personal Color System for Dyers, A	La Lena, Connie	√	√	Iw	3	3		Sp 78	20
Color Wheel: Natural Dyes	Dyeing: A Personal Palette for Tapestry	Bliss, Anne	√	√	Hw	3	1		Ja 82	66
Color-and-Weave Effects	Color-and-Weave on a Dark-Light Sequence	Windeknecht, Margaret; Thomas Windeknecht	√	√	SS&D	12	4	48	Fa 81	24
Color-and-Weave Effects	Color-and-Weave on Rosepath	Windeknecht, Margaret; Thomas Windeknecht	√	√	SS&D	13	2	50	Sp 82	8
Color-Patterned Knitting	Peruvian Mittens	Xenakis, Alexis Yiorgos	√	√	PWC			4	Ja 83	62
Colorfastness	Considerations in the Selection and Application of Natural Dyes: Mordant Selection, Part 1	Crews, Patricia	√	√	SS&D	12	2	46	Sp 81	15
Colorfastness	Considerations in the Selection and Application of Natural Dyes: Dye-plant Selection (error-corrected SS&D v12 n4 81 p8)	Crews, Patricia	√	√	SS&D	12	3	47	Su 81	52
Colorfastness	How Fast is the Color?	Bliss, Anne	√	√	Hw	5	2		M/A 84	16
Colorfastness	Notes on Color Fastness	Hausner, Walter	√	√	H&C	10	2		Sp 59	46
Colorfastness	Tests for Desired Yarn Qualities	Koehler, Glory Dail		√	SS&D	7	2	26	Sp 76	68
Colorfastness	Why Bother with Natural Dyeing?	Bulbach, Stanley	√	√	TM			5	J/J 86	32
Columbia	Hammock, The	Drooker, Penelope B.	√	√	TM			6	A/S 86	74
Combined Structure: Supplementary Warp Patterning/Plain Weave	Dal Dräll Table Runner (Nancy Klein)		√	> 4	Hw	1	2		S-S 80	25, 52
Combined Structures	More About Fabrics: Odd Weaves	Zielinski, S. A.; Robert Leclerc, ed.	√	√	MWL	20			'51–'73	41
Combined Structures: Atwater-Bronson/SpotBronson	Table Runner in Linen		√	√	PWC			5	Sp 83	25
Combined Structures: Basket Weave/Plain Weave	Autumn Sunset Cape (Leslie Voiers)		√	> 4	WJ	11	3	43	Wi 87	22
Combined Structures: Basket Weave/Plain Weave	Coat Fabric, Swatch #5 (Sharon Alderman)		√	> 4	Hw	7	4		S/O 86	24, I-5
Combined Structures: Basket Weave/Plain Weave	Keep Warm! Woolen Throw	Barrett, Clotilde	√	> 4	WJ	5	2	18	Fa 80	14
Combined Structures: Basket Weave/Plain Weave	Nora's Dress (Sharon Alderman)		√	> 4	Hw	8	2		M/A 87	43, I-3
Combined Structures: Basket Weave/Plain Weave	Shimmering Pastel Blanket (Leslie Voiers)		√	√	Hw	7	1		J/F 86	41, I-4
Combined Structures: Basket Weave/Plain Weave	Simple Scarf, Simple Luxury (error-corrected Hw v5 n1 83 p88)	Alderman, Sharon	√	√	Hw	4	4		S/O 83	64
Combined Structures: Basket Weave/Plain Weave	Simply Elegant Upholstery Fabric (Sharon Alderman)		√	> 4	Hw	6	1		J/F 85	32, I-6
Combined Structures: Basket Weave/Plain Weave	Super Scarf	Herring, Connie	√	> 4	PWC	3	1	7		28

SUBJECT	TITLE	AUTHOR	IL	INST	JOUR	VOL	NO	ISS	DATE	PAGE
Combined Structures: Basket Weave/Plain Weave/ Half-Dukagång	African Inspiration, An (Louise Bradley)		√	√	Hw	5	4		S/O 84	51, 94
Combined Structures: Basket Weave/Twill	#4: Suit or Jacket Fabric (Sharon Alderman)		√	√	Hw	8	4		S/O 87	52, I-9
Combined Structures: Basket Weave/Waffle Weave	Waffle Pillows (David Xenakis)		√	√	Hw	1	2		S-S 80	70
Combined Structures: Brocade/Basket Weave	Guatemalan Blouse (Betty Davenport)		√	√	Hw	4	2		M/A 83	55, 94
Combined Structures: Brocade/Double Weave	Morgan Clifford: New Dircetions in Brocades	Gue, Sandra	√		WJ	11	4	44	Sp 87	40
Combined Structures: Brocade/Plain Weave	Red Huiple (Betty Davenport)		√	> 4	Hw	1	2		S-S 80	45, 68
Combined Structures: Brooks Bouquet/Plain	Wedding Dress (Lise Haugh)		√	√	Hw	1	2		S-S 80	35, 64
Combined Structures: Canvas Weave/Plain Weave	Cotton Dress Fabric, Swatch #6 (Sharon Alderman)		√	√	Hw	7	4		S/O 86	24, I-5
Combined Structures: Canvas Weave/Plain Weave	Sea Crystal Dress (Vicki Tardy)		√	> 4	Hw	8	2		M/A 87	55, I-11
Combined Structures: Canvas Weave/Weft-Faced Inlay	Canvas Weave Elegance	Herring, Connie	√	> 4	PWC	4	1	11		23
Combined Structures: Crackle/Overshot	Texas Fabrics	Hardt, Blanche	√	√	H&C	8	3		Su 57	31
Combined Structures: Damask/Twill	Long Eyed Heddles	Ahrens, Jim	√	> 4	CW	6	1	16	Se 84	3
Combined Structures: Double Weave/Open Work Weave	Open Weave Casement	Cronk, Helen H.	√	> 4	H&C	13	2		Sp 62	32
Combined Structures: Double Weave/Overshot/Plain Weave	More Than Four Can Double Your Fun	Pinchin, C. Bryn	√	> 4	Hw	6	1		J/F 85	38
Combined Structures: Double Weave/Overshot/Plain Weave	Silky Dress-Up: Vest (C. Bryn Pinchin)		√	> 4	Hw	6	1		J/F 85	38, I-11
Combined Structures: Double Weave/Plain Weave	Cheery Checked Towels (Barbara Eychener)		√	> 4	Hw	3	4		Se 82	59, 82
Combined Structures: Double Weave/Plain Weave	Fur Vest (Ann Wittpenn)		√	√	Hw	4	1		J/F 83	35, 80
Combined Structures: Double Weave/Rib Overplaid	Fabrics That Go Bump (error-corrected PWC i4 83 p76)	Xenakis, Athanasios David	√	√	PWC			3	Oc 82	18
Combined Structures: Double Weave/Twill	Fur Jacket (Ann Wittpenn)		√	√	Hw	4	1		J/F 83	33, 80
Combined Structures: Double Weave/Twill	Green Plaid Blanket or Scarf (Diane Tramba)		√	> 4	Hw	2	1		F-W 80	27, 64
Combined Structures: Dukagång, Half- and Atwater-Bronson Lace	Inlay We Trust, Part 1: Half Dukagång	Herring, Connie	√	√	PWC			5	Sp 83	59
Combined Structures: Dukagäng, Inlay/Plain Weave	Dunkagäng Guest Towels (Sharon Alderman)		√	√	Hw	7	2		M/A 86	I-5
Combined Structures: Finnweave Plain Weave/Atwater-Bronson Lace	Fantastic Finnweave, Part 3	Xenakis, Athanasios David	√	√	PWC			4	Ja 83	15
Combined Structures: Finnweave Plain Weave/Leno, 1/1	Fantastic Finnweave, Part 3	Xenakis, Athanasios David	√	> 4	PWC			4	Ja 83	17
Combined Structures: Finnweave Plain Weave/Twill	Fantastic Finnweave, Part 3	Xenakis, Athanasios David	√	> 4	PWC			4	Ja 83	19
Combined Structures: Finnweave/Double Twill/Inlay	Fantastic Finnweave, Part 3	Xenakis, Athanasios David	√	> 4	PWC			4	Ja 83	22
Combined Structures: Finnweave/Log Cabin	Fantastic Finnweave, Part 3	Xenakis, Athanasios David	√	> 4	PWC			4	Ja 83	19
Combined Structures: Finnweave/Twill/Inlay	Fantastic Finnweave, Part 3	Xenakis, Athanasios David	√	> 4	PWC			4	Ja 83	22
Combined Structures: Float Weave Blocks/Plain Weave	Baby Blanket (Margaretha Essén-Hedin)		√	> 4	Hw	8	2		M/A 87	45, I-7
Combined Structures: Float Weave, Inlay/Plain Weave	Sheep Jacket (Jean Scorgie)		√	√	Hw	7	2		M/A 86	70, I-13
Combined Structures: Float Weave/Plain Weave	Baby Blanket with Light Blue Arrowpoint (Cat Brysch)		√	> 4	Hw	5	3		Su 84	50, 96

SUBJECT	TITLE	AUTHOR	IL	INST	JOUR	VOL	NO	ISS	DATE	PAGE
Combined Structures: Float Weave/Plain Weave	Baby Blanket with Pink Pattern Weave (Cat Brysch)		√	> 4	Hw	5	3		Su 84	50, 97
Combined Structures: Float Weave/Plain Weave	Cotton Lap Robe (Janice Jones)		√	> 4	Hw	7	1		J/F 86	42, I-5
Combined Structures: Float Weave/Plain Weave	Country Kitchen Checked Cloth (Margaretha Essén-Hedin) (error-corrected Hw v5 n2 84 p93) (error-corrected Hw v8 n1 87 p I-16)		√	> 4	Hw	4	5		N/D 83	58, 106
Combined Structures: Float Weave/Plain Weave	Crib Cover with Diamonds and X's (Cat Brysch)		√	> 4	Hw	5	3		Su 84	50, 96
Combined Structures: Float Weave/Plain Weave	Rio Grande Placemats (Betty Davenport)		√	√	Hw	7	4		S/O 86	57, I-11
Combined Structures: Float Weave/Plain Weave	Sandstone Pillows (Janice Jones)		√	√	Hw	5	2		M/A 84	59, 99
Combined Structures: Float Weave/Plain Weave	Springtime Curtains (Margaretha Essén-Hedin)		√	√	Hw	5	3		Su 84	72, 117
Combined Structures: Float Weave/Plain Weave	Tulip Blouse (Betty Davenport)		√	√	Hw	8	2		M/A 87	61, I-14
Combined Structures: Float Weave/Plain Weave	Winning Woven Winter Warmers		√	> 4	Hw	7	1		J/F 86	32
Combined Structures: Float Weave/Plain Weave	Wool/Mohair Coat Fabric (Sharon Alderman)		√	> 4	Hw	3	4		Se 82	41, 94
Combined Structures: Floats, Warp/Plain Weave	Pleated Curtain (Kathryn Wertenberger)		√	√	Hw	5	2		M/A 84	67, 104
Combined Structures: Gauze/"Bronson"	Leno Fabrics	Xenakis, Athanasios David	√	> 4	PWC			6	Su 83	18
Combined Structures: Gauze/Hopsack	Leno Fabrics	Xenakis, Athanasios David	√	> 4	PWC			6	Su 83	18
Combined Structures: Gauze/Plain Weave	Cardwoven Gauze	Gray, Herbi	√	√	PWC			6	Su 83	57
Combined Structures: Gauze/Plain Weave, Supplelmentary Wefts	Guatemalan Gauze Weaves: A Description and Key to Identification	Pancake, Cherri M.; Suzanne Baizerman	√	√	TMJ	19 20			80,81	1
Combined Structures: Gauze/Supplementary Warp	Leno Fabrics	Xenakis, Athanasios David	√	> 4	PWC			6	Su 83	18
Combined Structures: Gauze/Supplementary Weft	Leno Fabrics	Xenakis, Athanasios David	√	> 4	PWC			6	Su 83	18
Combined Structures: Half-Dukagång/Inlay	Lenten Pulpit Antependium (Mary Temple)		√	√	Hw	8	3		M/J 87	57, I-10
Combined Structures: Half-Dukagång/Plain Weave	Baby Pillow Case (Sigrid Piroch)		√	√	Hw	8	2		M/A 87	50, I-8
Combined Structures: Honeycomb/Plain Weave	Country Harvest Placemats (Linda Ligon)		√	√	Hw	5	4		S/0 84	48, 95
Combined Structures: Honeycomb/Plain Weave	Jelly Bean Blouse (Louise Bradley)		√	√	Hw	6	3		Su 85	50, I-11
Combined Structures: Honeycomb/Plain Weave	Rainbow Scarf (Lynne Giles)		√	> 4	Hw	8	4		S/O 87	63, I-14
Combined Structures: Honeycomb/Plain Weave	Sweet Dreams Pillow Slips (Sharon D. Alderman)		√	√	Hw	5	4		S/0 84	45, 96
Combined Structures: Hopsack/2/2 Leno	Bead Leno	Davenport, Betty	√	√	PWC			6	Su 83	62
Combined Structures: Huck/ Lace	Woven Lace and Lacey Weaves: Huck and Lace Combined	Zielinski, S. A.; Robert Leclerc, ed.	√	> 4	MWL	13			'51–'73	34
Combined Structures: Huck/ Lace, Multishaft	Woven Lace and Lacey Weaves: Huck and Lace Combined	Zielinski, S. A.; Robert Leclerc, ed.	√	> 4	MWL	13			'51–'73	39
Combined Structures: Huck Lace/Canvas Weave	Combining Lace Weaves		√	√	WJ	4	2	14	Oc 79	14
Combined Structures: Huck Lace/Huck	Huck and Huck Lace		√	> 4	WJ	1	4	4	Ap 77	33
Combined Structures: Huck Lace/Plain Weave	Accessories: Man's Scarf		√	√	WJ	4	3	15	Ja 80	40
Combined Structures: Huck Lace/Plain Weave	Batwing Sleeved Blouse (Virginia West) (error-corrected Hw v7 n2 86 p I-3)		√	> 4	Hw	7	1		J/F 86	52, I-7

SUBJECT	TITLE	AUTHOR	IL	INST	JOUR	VOL	NO	ISS	DATE	PAGE
Combined Structures: Huck Lace/Swedish Lace	Combining Lace Weaves		√	√	WJ	4	2	14	Oc 79	14
Combined Structures: Huck/ M's and O's/Overshot	Exploring the Textures: The Third Dimension	Zielinski, S. A.; Robert Leclerc, ed.	√	> 4	MWL	11			'51–'73	60
Combined Structures: Huck/Lace, Bronson	V-Neck Top with Lace Bands (Betty Davenport)		√	√	Hw	3	2		Mr 82	44, 80
Combined Structures: Huck/Plain Weave	Huck and Huck Lace		√	> 4	WJ	1	4	4	Ap 77	33
Combined Structures: Inlay/Atwater-Bronson Lace/Plain Weave	Two-Tie Inlay	Xenakis, Athanasios David	√	√	PWC	4	1	11		19
Combined Structures: Inlay/Leno Ground	Simple Inlay on a Leno Ground	Xenakis, Athanasios David; Patti Sellon	√	√	PWC	4	1	11		18
Combined Structures: Inlay/Plain Ground	Season's End Transparency (Görel Kinersly)		√	√	Hw	5	4		S/O 84	69, 105
Combined Structures: Karellian Red Pick/Plain Weave	Weaving for the Holidays (error-corrected Hw v4 n4 83 p92)		√	> 4	Hw	3	5		N/D 82	78
Combined Structures: Lace Blocks/Plain Weave	Baby Blanket (Dian Stanley)		√	√	Hw	7	3		M/J 86	74, 91
Combined Structures: Lace, Bronson /Plain Weave	Bronson Lace Afghan (Judith Drumm)		√	√	Hw	3	2		Mr 82	59, 88
Combined Structures: Lace, Bronson/Plain Weave	Country Silk Top (Betty Davenport)		√	√	Hw	5	3		Su 84	59, 102
Combined Structures: Lace, Bronson/Plain Weave	Crocus Shawl (Betty Davenport)		√	√	Hw	2	4		Se 81	56, 84
Combined Structures: Lace, Bronson/Plain Weave	Heirloom Weaving. A Christening Gown with Mary Pendergrass		√	> 4	Hw	3	4		Se 82	53
Combined Structures: Lace, Bronson/Plain Weave	Skirt/Dress Lacy Plaid Fabric #5 (Sharon D. Alderman) (error-corrected Hw v5 n5 84 p7)		√	> 4	Hw	5	3		Su 84	62, 109
Combined Structures: Lace, Bronson/Plain Weave	Table Runner		√	√	H&C	10	3		Su 59	44
Combined Structures: Lace, Bronson/Plain Weave	White Huiple (Betty Davenport)		√	√	Hw	1	2		S-S 80	45, 68
Combined Structures: Lace, Bronson/Plain Weave	White on White Shawl (Polly Scott)		√	√	Hw	7	5		N/D 86	31
Combined Structures: Lace, Bronson/Swedish Lace	Combining Lace Weaves		√	√	WJ	4	2	14	Oc 79	14
Combined Structures: Lace, Danish Medallion/Plain Weave	Warm and Wooly: Cloud-Soft Dress		√	√	Hw	1	1		F-W 79	26
Combined Structures: Lace, Loom-Controlled/Plain Weave	Lace Weave Skirt with Jacket and Top (Louise Bradley)		√	> 4	Hw	5	3		Su 84	58, 104
Combined Structures: Lace Weaves/Plain Weave	Lace Weave Gamp Tablecloth (Penelope Drooker)		√	> 4	Hw	5	3		Su 84	78, 110
Combined Structures: Lace/Plain Weave	Linen Table Mat (Janice Jones)		√	√	Hw	5	2		M/A 84	53, 98
Combined Structures: Lace/Plain Weave	My Computer Designs a Bedspread	Salsbury, Nate	√	√	Hw	3	3		My 82	80
Combined Structures: Lace/Plain Weave	Rainbow Blouse (Ruth Lantz)		√	> 4	Hw	4	1		J/F 83	45, 86
Combined Structures: Lace/Plain Weave	Why Always Four Harnesses?		√	> 4	H&C	10	2		Sp 59	6
Combined Structures: Leno/"Bronson"	Shaped Silk Sheath	Xenakis, Athanasios David; Alexis Yiorgos Xenakis	√	√	PWC			6	Su 83	39
Combined Structures: Leno, Mock/Plain Weave	Swatch Collection #11: Fabrics 6-7 (Sharon Alderman)		√	√	Hw	6	2		M/A 85	46, I-6
Combined Structures: Leno/ Plain Weave	Dress for a Summer Day		√	√	Hw	3	2		Mr 82	52
Combined Structures: Leno/Hopsack	Slightly Left of Center Jacket	Rowley, Elaine	√	√	PWC			6	Su 83	44
Combined Structures: Leno/Inlay	Inlay We Trust, Part 2: Leno Inlay	Herring, Connie	√	√	PWC			6	Su 83	48

SUBJECT	TITLE	AUTHOR	IL	INST	JOUR	VOL	NO	ISS	DATE	PAGE
Combined Structures: Leno/Overplaid	Lace Trilogy	Fauske, Carla	√	√	PWC			6	Su 83	52
Combined Structures: Leno/Overshot/Plain Weave	Leno & Borders Curtain (Constance LaLena)		√	√	Hw	5	2		M/A 84	64, 102
Combined Structures: Leno/Plain Weave	Leno Dress (Emily Law)		√	√	Hw	8	1		J/F 87	44, I-5
Combined Structures: Leno/Plain Weave	Silk/Cotton Smock (Leslie Burgess)		√	√	Hw	4	3		M/J 83	27, 86
Combined Structures: Loops, Chained/Plain Weave	Welcome Mat (Jane Patrick and Jean Anstine)		√	√	Hw	5	2		M/A 84	Cover, 96
Combined Structures: Monk's Belt/Plain Weave	"Blue Chest of Drawers" Hanging (Kerstin Åsling-Sundberg)		√	>4	Hw	8	3		M/J 87	37, I-6
Combined Structures: Monk's Belt/Plain Weave	Heritage Tablecloth (Margaretha Essén-Hedin)		√	√	Hw	8	3		M/J 87	41, I-7
Combined Structures: Monk's Belt/Plain Weave	"Maria" Rag Rug (Inga Krook)		√	√	Hw	6	3		Su 85	56, I-14
Combined Structures: Monk's Belt/Plain Weave	Rag Table Runner (Inga Krook)		√	√	Hw	8	3		M/J 87	39, I-5
Combined Structures: Monk's Belt/Plain Weave	Vest/Skirt Fabric #2 (Sharon D. Alderman)		√	√	Hw	5	4		S/O 84	57, 101
Combined Structures: Monk's Belt/Tabby	Double Weave: Plain and Patterned: The Duo-Weave, The	Tidball, Harriet	√	>4	SCGM		1		60	30
Combined Structures: M's and O's/Huckaback Lace/Basket Weave/Plain Weave	Exploring the Textures: Patterns in Texture on Four Shafts	Zielinski, S. A.; Robert Leclerc, ed.	√	√	MWL	11			'51–'73	102
Combined Structures: Openwork, Wrapping/Plain Weave	Credence Cloth (Kathleen French)		√	√	Hw	5	1		J/F 84	33, 92
Combined Structures: Overshot, Even-Tied/Uneven-Tied	Freeform Design Technique	Searles, Nancy	√	>4	PWC	3	4	10		18
Combined Structures: Overshot, Inlay/Plain Weave	Baby Blanket (Louise Bradley)		√	√	Hw	7	1		J/F 86	43, I-6
Combined Structures: Overshot, Inlay/Plain Weave	'Country' Overshot	Patrick, Jane	√	√	Hw	6	4		S/O 85	48
Combined Structures: Overshot Inlay/Plain Weave	Isolated Overshot: Inlaid Runner	Xenakis, Athanasios David	√	√	PWC	3	2	8		31
Combined Structures: Overshot Inlay/Plain Weave	Isolating a Motif		√	√	Hw	6	4		S/O 85	51
Combined Structures: Overshot, Inlay/Plain Weave	Overshot Wall Piece (Janice Jones) (error-corrected Hw v8 n1 87 p I-16)		√	√	Hw	6	4		S/O 85	50, I-7
Combined Structures: Overshot/Monk's Belt	Double Weave: Plain and Patterned: The Duo-Weave, The	Tidball, Harriet	√	>4	SCGM		1		60	30
Combined Structures: Overshot, Plain Weave	Child's Cardigan Sweater (Elizabeth Millard)		√	√	Hw	5	3		Su 84	49, 93
Combined Structures: Overshot, Rosepath/Plain Weave	Soft Surprise Guest Towels (Matilda MacGeorge)		√	√	Hw	6	4		S/O 85	86
Combined Structures: Overshot/Crackle/Summer and Winter	Patchwork	Snyder, Mary E.	√	>4	CW	2	2	5	Ja 81	2
Combined Structures: Overshot/Double Weave	Stitching Traditional Coverlet Weaves	Sellin, Helen G.	√	>4	AT	1			De 83	289
Combined Structures: Overshot/Honeycomb	Sauna Towel (Phyllis Griffith)		√	√	Hw	1	2		S-S 80	47, 54
Combined Structures: Overshot/Inlay/Plain Weave	"Flower Child" Dress (Paula Stewart)		√	√	Hw	6	3		Su 85	48, I-9
Combined Structures: Overshot/Plaid Ground	Table Mat (Janice Jones)		√	√	Hw	6	4		S/O 85	48, I-8
Combined Structures: Overshot/Plain Weave	Bound Overshot	Xenakis, Athanasios David	√	√	PWC	3	3	9		21
Combined Structures: Overshot/Plain Weave	Bouquet of Shawls, A	Templeton, Peg	√	√	Hw	5	3		Su 84	75
Combined Structures: Overshot/Plain Weave	Branding Iron Sweater (Ardis Dobrovolny)		√	√	Hw	7	4		S/O 86	68, I-14
Combined Structures: Overshot/Plain Weave	Camisole (Lou Cabeen)		√	√	Hw	4	3		M/J 83	45, 93

SUBJECT	TITLE	AUTHOR	IL	INST	JOUR	VOL	NO	ISS	DATE	PAGE
Combined Structures: Overshot/Plain Weave	Children's Pinafores (Pam Bolesta)		√	√	Hw	1	1		F-W 79	38, 60
Combined Structures: Overshot/Plain Weave	"Hugs and Kisses" Dress (Paula Stewart)		√	>4	Hw	6	3		Su 85	48, I-10
Combined Structures: Overshot/Plain Weave	Isolated Overshot: Linen and Cotton Teacloth	Xenakis, Athanasios David	√	>4	PWC	3	2	8		36
Combined Structures: Overshot/Plain Weave	Keeping Track	Ligon, Linda	√	√	Hw	8	1		J/F 87	90
Combined Structures: Overshot/Plain Weave	Napkins and Bread Cloth (Barbara Smith Eychaner)		√	√	Hw	7	4		S/O 86	54, I-11
Combined Structures: Overshot/Plain Weave	Overshot 'n Rags (Jane Patrick)		√	√	Hw	5	2		M/A 84	108
Combined Structures: Overshot/Plain Weave	Periwinkle Scarf (Linda Ligon)		√	√	Hw	8	1		J/F 87	90, I-8
Combined Structures: Overshot/Plain Weave	Pillow (Janice Jones) (error-corrected Hw v8 n1 87 p I-16)		√	√	Hw	6	4		S/O 85	49, I-8
Combined Structures: Overshot/Plain Weave	Rosepath Pinafore (Janice Jones)		√	√	Hw	7	2		M/A 86	60, I-4
Combined Structures: Overshot/Plain Weave	Scented Sachets	Xenakis, Alexis Yiorgos	√	>4	PWC	3	2	8		56
Combined Structures: Overshot/Plain Weave	Skirt and Stole (Mary Pendergrass)		√	√	Hw	1	1		F-W 79	23, 56
Combined Structures: Overshot/Plain Weave	Turned Overshot	Rowley, Elaine; Alexis Yiorgos Xenakis	√	>4	PWC	3	2	8		53
Combined Structures: Overshot/Plain Weave	Western Shirt (Louise Bradley)		√	√	Hw	3	2		Mr 82	48, 84
Combined Structures: Overshot/Twill	Christmas Vest (Yvonne Stahl)		√	>4	Hw	4	4		S/O 83	71, 101
Combined Structures: Overshot/Twill	Combining Weave Structures	London, Rhoda	√	>4	TM			3	F/M 86	56
Combined Structures: Overshot/Twill	Isolated Overshot: Razzle-dazzle Placemats	Xenakis, Athanasios David	√	>4	PWC	3	2	8		40
Combined Structures: Park/Boulevard/Twill Blocks	Bateman Legacy, The	Harvey, Virginia	√	>4	PWC	4	4	14		50
Combined Structures: Pebble Weave/Intermesh	Double-Woven Treasures from Old Peru	Cahlander, Adele	√	√	PWC			4	Ja 83	36
Combined Structures: Pile, Knotted/Plain Weave	Pile Vest (Merja Winqvist)		√	√	Hw	8	3		M/J 87	73, I-15
Combined Structures: Pile, Looped/Plain Weave	Cotton Candlewicking (Jane Patrick)		√	√	Hw	3	5		N/D 82	30, 99
Combined Structures: Pile/Plain Weave	Linen Back Scrubber (Sharon Alderman)		√	√	Hw	3	2		Mr 82	50, 92
Combined Structures: Piqué/Twill/Hopsack	Figured Piqué on a Ground of 2/2 Twill and 2/2 Hopsack	Xenakis, Athanasios David	√	>4	PWC	4	2	12		24
Combined Structures: Plain Weave/Lace, Bronson/Brook's Bouquet	Rigid Heddle Wool Curtain (Betty Davenport)		√	√	Hw	2	1		F-W 80	Cover, 72
Combined Structures: Rep, Weft/Plain Weave	Fiesta Choli (Anita Luvera Mayer)		√	√	Hw	6	3		Su 85	54, I-12
Combined Structures: Rya/Raanu	Ryijy Plus Raanu		√		SS&D	4	2	14	Sp 73	12
Combined Structures: Satin/Plain Weave	Silk Kimono (Sharon Alderman)		√	>4	Hw	1	2		S-S 80	28, 66
Combined Structures: Satin/Tabby	Contemporary Satins: Compound Satin	Tidball, Harriet	√	>4	SCGM		7		62	9
Combined Structures: Searles Lace/Plain Weave	Freeform Twill & Freeform Searles Lace	Searles, Nancy	√	>4	CW		23		Ja 87	10
Combined Structures: Simple and Compound (Plain Weave, 3/1 Twill, Discontinuous Supplementary and Complementary Wefts)	Type of Mughal Sash, A	Sonday, Milton; Nobuko Kajitani	√		TMJ	3	1		De 70	45
Combined Structures: Soumak/Plain Weave	Guatemalan Vest (Betty Davenport)		√	√	Hw	4	2		M/A 83	56, 93
Combined Structures: Spot, Bronson/Atwater-Bronson	Combining Lace Weaves		√	√	WJ	4	2	14	Oc 79	14

SUBJECT	TITLE	AUTHOR	IL	INST	JOUR	VOL	NO	ISS	DATE	PAGE
Combined Structures: Spot Bronson/Lace Bronson	Translating Four-Harness Drafts for the Single Rigid Heddle Method		√	√	PWC		5		Sp 83	22
Combined Structures: Spot, Bronson/Plain Weave	Shaker Towel III (Sharon Alderman)		√	√	Hw	3	5		N/D 82	41, 91
Combined Structures: Spot, Bronson/Plain Weave	Shaker Towel IV (Sharon Alderman)		√	√	Hw	3	5		N/D 82	39, 92
Combined Structures: Spot, Bronson/Plain Weave	Shaker Towel V (Sharon Alderman)		√	> 4	Hw	3	5		N/D 82	41, 92
Combined Structures: Sprang/Plain Weave	Sprang on the Loom	Searle, Karen	√	√	WJ	11	4	44	Sp 87	24
Combined Structures: Summer and Winter/Plain Weave	Finger Tip Towel (James Ronin)		√	> 4	Hw	1	2		S-S 80	29, 67
Combined Structures: Summer and Winter/Plain Weave	Summer Blouse in Summer and Winter, A	Sullivan, Donna	√	√	PWC	4	4	14		18
Combined Structures: Summer and Winter/Plain Weave, Weft-Faced	Rug for All Seasons, A (Falene E. Hamilton)		√	√	Hw	7	4		S/O 86	43, I-8
Combined Structures: Summer and Winter/Weave	Eight-Shaft Summer and Winter Towels		√	> 4	Hw	8	5		N/D 87	74
Combined Structures: Supplementary Warp and Weft/Plain Weave	Windowpane Scarf/Belt (Louise Bradley)		√	√	Hw	8	4		S/O 87	54, I-11
Combined Structures: Supplementary Warp, Four-block/Plain Weave	Warp-Patterned Adaptation (Carol Strickler)		√	> 4	Hw	8	3		M/J 87	I-13
Combined Structures: Supplementary Warp/Plain Weave	#3: Dress Fabric (Sharon Alderman)		√	√	Hw	8	4		S/O 87	52, I-9
Combined Structures: Supplementary Warp/Plain Weave	Supplementary Warp Top (Betty Davenport)		√	√	Hw	6	1		J/F 85	34, I-8
Combined Structures: Supplementary Warp/Plain Weave	Swatch #4 Vest (Sharon Alderman)		√	> 4	Hw	8	2		M/A 87	38, I-5
Combined Structures: Supplementary Weft, Loom-Controlled, Plain Weave	Refreshingly Simple Runner (Betty Davenport)		√	> 4	Hw	6	3		Su 85	11, I-3
Combined Structures: Tabby/Tapestry	Textiles of Coptic Egypt	Hoskins, Nancy Arthur	√	√	WJ	12	1	45	Su 87	58
Combined Structures: Tapestry/Plain Weave	Navajo Inspired Rugs (Penelope Drooker)		√	√	Hw	6	2		M/A 85	58, I-16
Combined Structures: Techniques	Four Harness Straight Draw and Combination Weaves		√	> 4	WJ	4	2	14	Oc 79	22
Combined Structures: Twill and Honeysuckle	Bedspread (Linda Ligon)		√	√	Hw	1	1		F-W 79	36, 59
Combined Structures: Twill Blocks/Plain Weave	Block Twill and Plain Weave Suit (Leslie Voiers, Phyllis Tichy)		√	> 4	Hw	8	5		N/D 87	53, I-12
Combined Structures: Twill, Broken/Plain Weave	Skirt Fabric #1 (Sharon D. Alderman)		√	> 4	Hw	5	4		S/0 84	56, 100
Combined Structures: Twill, Diaper/Twill, Point Variations	Use of the Dobby Loom for Multi-Harness Weave Manipulation, The	Renne, Elisha	√	> 4	WJ	9	3	35	Wi 85	9
Combined Structures: Twill, Dornick/Basket Weave	Swatch #4, Dornick & Basket Weave for Coat (Virginia West)		√	√	Hw	7	5		N/D 86	62, I-6
Combined Structures: Twill, Dornick/Basket Weave	Teal Skirt (Jean Scorgie)		√	√	Hw	7	5		N/D 86	42, I-8
Combined Structures: Twill, Double-Faced/Plain Weave	Turkish Coat, A	Xenakis, Alexis Yiorgos	√	> 4	Hw	2	2		Mr 81	39
Combined Structures: Twill Inlay/Plain Weave	Unbalanced Twill Braided Ribbon Inlay on Plain Weave Ground	Xenakis, Athanasios David	√	√	PWC	4	1	11		27
Combined Structures: Twill (Macro)/Hopsack Weave	Macro Plaid, Macro Twill	Xenakis, Athanasios David	√	> 4	PWC	3	1	7		55
Combined Structures: Twill/ Plain Weave	Blue Banded Shirt (Miranda Howard)		√	> 4	Hw	3	4		Se 82	66, 89
Combined Structures: Twill/ Plain Weave	Face Mitt (Jane Patrick)		√	√	Hw	3	2		Mr 82	50, 92
Combined Structures: Twill, Point/Plain Ground	Boy's Vest (Lou Cabeen)		√	√	Hw	5	4		S/0 84	42, 93

SUBJECT	TITLE	AUTHOR	IL	INST	JOUR	VOL	NO	ISS	DATE	PAGE
Combined Structures: Twill, Point/Plain Ground	Man's Vest (Lou Cabeen)		√	√	Hw	5	4		S/O 84	43, 93
Combined Structures: Twill, Reverse/Twill/Tabby	Three-Toned Blocks: Further Explorations with Long-eyed Heddles	Broughton, Eve T.	√	> 4	WJ	9	4	36	Sp 85	72
Combined Structures: Twill, Rosepath (Opposites)/Plain Weave	Handwoven Felt Mittens (Jane Kleinschmidt)		√	√	Hw	6	4		S/O 85	66, I-16
Combined Structures: Twill, Rosepath/Plain Weave	Child's Tabard of Jumper (Marit Drenckhahn)		√	√	Hw	2	1		F-W 80	53, 77
Combined Structures: Twill/Shadow Weave	Try Shadow Weave Twill	Hewson, Betty	√	√	Hw	5	1		J/F 84	14
Combined Structures: Twill, Warp-Faced/Plain Weave	Swatch #3 Skirt or Dress (Sharon Alderman)		√	> 4	Hw	8	2		M/A 87	38, I-5
Combined Structures: Twill, Weft-Faced/Twill, Warp-Faced	Freeform Twill & Freeform Searles Lace	Searles, Nancy	√	> 4	CW		23		Ja 87	10
Combined Structures: Twill/Atwater-Bronson Lace	Dog Fashions (error-corrected WJ v2 n1 77 insert for vol. 1)	Richards, Iris	√	> 4	WJ	1	3	3	Ja 77	33
Combined Structures: Twill/Basket	Double Two-Tie Twills and Basket Weave	Barrett, Clotilde	√	> 4	WJ	7	3	27	Wi 82	38
Combined Structures: Twill/Basket Weave	Man's Sport Jacket/Woman's Blazer (Sharon Alderman)		√	√	Hw	2	1		F-W 80	50, 63
Combined Structures: Twill/Leno/Plain Weave	Penny-wise Table Runner (Linda Ligon)		√	√	Hw	5	4		S/O 84	73, 109
Combined Structures: Twill/Overshot/Summer and Winter	Metamorphosis: Two-Tie Weaves and the Changeable Image	Carey, Joyce Marquess	√	> 4	AT	1			De 83	243
Combined Structures: Twill/Plain Weave	Beautiful and Bold		√	√	Hw	1	2		S-S 80	42
Combined Structures: Twill/Plain Weave	Child's Apron (Sue Ellison)		√	√	Hw	1	2		S-S 80	35, 63
Combined Structures: Twill/Plain Weave	Curtain Fabric (Constance LaLena)		√	> 4	Hw	4	5		N/D 83	70, 102
Combined Structures: Twill/Plain Weave	Lacy Linen Pillowcase (Linda Ligon)		√	√	Hw	2	5		No 81	58, 81
Combined Structures: Twill/Plain Weave	Lampas for Eight	Sullivan, Donna	√	> 4	PWC	5	2	16		34
Combined Structures: Twill/Plain Weave	On-the-Beach Cloth (Miranda Howard)		√	> 4	Hw	3	4		Se 82	67, 89
Combined Structures: Twill/Plain Weave	Placemats and Napkins for a Found Treasure (Janice Jones)		√	√	Hw	5	5		N/D 84	70, I-12
Combined Structures: Twill/Plain Weave	Placemats and Napkins for a Found Treasure (Janice Jones)		√	√	Hw	5	5		N/D 84	70, I-12
Combined Structures: Twill/Plain Weave	Poinsettia Finger Towels (Phyllis Mullin)		√	> 4	Hw	1	2		S-S 80	29, 56
Combined Structures: Twill/Plain Weave	Ribbon Blouse (Grace Hirsch)		√	√	Hw	4	1		J/F 83	44, 88
Combined Structures: Twill/Plain Weave	Rug (Pam Toller)		√	√	Hw	2	1		F-W 80	32, 77
Combined Structures: Twill/Plain Weave	Silk Necktie		√	√	Hw	2	1		F-W 80	55, 59
Combined Structures: Twill/Plain Weave	Silk Scarf (Hector Jaeger)		√	√	Hw	7	1		J/F 86	57, I-12
Combined Structures: Twill/Plain Weave	Silk Scarf (Sharon Alderman)		√	> 4	Hw	4	1		J/F 83	43, 82
Combined Structures: Twill/Plain Weave	Skirt (or Pants) Fabric (Sharon Alderman)		√	> 4	Hw	1	2		S-S 80	41, 60
Combined Structures: Twill/Plain Weave	Stars Finger Towels		√	> 4	Hw	1	2		S-S 80	55
Combined Structures: Twill/Plain Weave	Tallit (Faye Johnson)		√	√	Hw	5	1		J/F 84	35, 91
Combined Structures: Twill/Plain Weave	Twill and Plain Weave Blocks with Long-Eyed Heddles	Broughton, Eve T.	√	> 4	WJ	8	4	32	Sp 84	58
Combined Structures: Twill/Plain Weave	Twills of Charlotte Funk, The	Patrick, Jane	√		Hw	6	5		N/D 85	36
Combined Structures: Twill/Plain Weave	Two Summer Dresses on One Warp (Ritva MacLeod)		√	√	Hw	5	3		Su 84	55, 100

SUBJECT	TITLE	AUTHOR	IL	INST	JOUR	VOL	NO	ISS	DATE	PAGE
Combined Structures: Twill/Plain Weave	Type of Mughal Sash, A	Sonday, Milton; Nobuko Kajitani	√		TMJ	3	1		De 70	45
Combined Structures: Twill/Plain Weave	Weft Faced Pillows (Jane Patrick)		√	√	Hw	4	2		M/A 83	66, 98
Combined Structures: Twill/Plain Weave	Windows: Sendoni Curtains	Xenakis, Alexis Yiorgos	√	>4	PWC	4	1	11		4
Combined Structures: Twill/Plain Weave/Inlay	Blue Jacket (Jean Scorgie)				Hw	7	5		N/D 86	41, I-4
Combined Structures: Twill/Satin Piqué	Satin Piqué	Morrison, Ruth	√	>4	PWC	4	3	13		34
Combined Structures: Twill/Seersucker/Plain Weave	Greek Dower Sheet (Alexis Yiorgos Xenakis)		√	>4	Hw	1	2		S-S 80	36, 62
Combined Structures: Twill/Summer and Winter	Longest Warp in the World or, The Double Two-Tie Unit Threading System	Miller, Mary Ann	√	>4	CW	3	3	9	Ap 82	2
Combined Structures: Twill/Summer and Winter	Plaited Twill Projects: Notes of A Pattern Weaver	Alvic, Philis	√	>4	WJ	11	4	44	Sp 87	55
Combined Structures: Twill/Tapestry	Fragment, Pre-Columbian Cloth Found In Utah	Turner, Alta R.	√	√	H&C	22	1		Wi 71	20
Combined Structures: Twill/Twill	Twill on Twill (Virginia West)		√	>4	Hw	5	2		M/A 84	72, 94
Combined Structures: Waffle/Plain Weave	Child's Easter Dress Fabric (Julie Green Edson)		√	√	Hw	3	2		Mr 82	54, 84
Combined Structures: Waffle Weave/Plain Weave	Heap of Linen Towels, A (Linda Ligon)		√	√	Hw	6	2		M/A 85	54, I-12
Combined Structures: Waffle/Plain Weave	Waffle Weave Tunic (Sharon Alderman)		√	√	Hw	3	2		Mr 82	45, 82
Combined Techinques: Weave/Knit	Child's Play	Voiers, Leslie	√	√	SS&D	18	3	71	Su 87	22
Combined Techniques: Basketry/Pottery	New Direction for the Art of Basketry, A	La Pierre, Sharon	√		WJ	8	3	31	Wi 83	54
Combined Techniques: Card Weaving/Needlepoint	Needlepoint with Cardweaving	Porcella, Yvonne	√	√	SS&D	4	2	14	Sp 73	13
Combined Techniques: Crochet/Needlework	Crochet Inspired by the Trees	Moon, Ellen	√	√	TM			11	J/J 87	56
Combined Techniques: Embroidery/Block Printing	Embroidery on Block Print		√		H&C	16	4		Fa 65	20
Combined Techniques: Embroidery/Tapestry	Tapestry/Embroidery	Drooker, Penelope B.	√		Iw	5	3		Su 80	37
Combined Techniques: Felt/Knit	Velten—Valkning—Felting	Beukers, Henriette	√	√	Hw	4	5		N/D 83	80
Combined Techniques: Knit/Crochet	Fabrics That Go Bump (error-corrected PWC i4 83 p76)	Xenakis, Athanasios David	√	√	PWC			3	Oc 82	18
Combined Techniques: Knit/Crochet	Two String Sweaters	Brugger, Susan	√	√	PWC			6	Su 83	31
Combined Techniques: Loom Weaving/Card Weaving	Technique Sources Sparse—So Weaver Innovates	Carlson, Estelle	√	√	SS&D	7	1	25	Wi 75	89
Combined Techniques: Polychrome/Warp Rep	New Pick-Up Weave, A	Deru, Crescent B.	√	>4	H&C	10	4		Fa 59	26
Combined Techniques: Rya/Tapestry	Reinterpreting Rya: Irma Kukkasjärvi Energizes an Ancient Technique	Ojala, Liisa Kanning	√		WJ	9	4	36	Sp 85	26
Combined Techniques: Shaft-Switching/ Shaft-Control Weaving	Shaft-Switching Combined with Harness Control	Barrett, Clotilde	√	>4	WJ	9	1	33	Su 84	37
Combined Techniques: Shaft-Switching/Moorman Technique	Rug Weaving: One Weaver's Approach	Hand, Barbara	√	>4	WJ	7	4	28	Sp 83	32
Combined Techniques: Triaxial Braiding/Conventional Weaving	Braiding Triaxial Weaves: Enhancements and Design for Artworks	Mooney, David R.	√	√	AT	5			Ju 86	9
Combined Techniques: Weave/Appliqué/Stitchery	Weave/Appliqué/Stitchery	Belfer, Nancy	√		Iw	5	3		Su 80	41
Combined Techniques: Weave/Crochet	Combine Techniques? Why not?	Derr, Mary L.	√		WJ	7	3	27	Wi 82	19
Combined Techniques: Weave/Crochet	Complementary Crochet	Durston, Linda Moore	√	√	SS&D	15	1	57	Wi 83	68
Combined Techniques: Weave/Crochet	Creating Textures: V–, Ridge, and Post Stitches	Moon, Ellen	√	√	TM			11	J/J 87	60

149

SUBJECT	TITLE	AUTHOR	IL	INST	JOUR	VOL	NO	ISS	DATE	PAGE
Combined Techniques: Weave/Crochet	Crochet—A Great Technique for Finishing Handwovens		√	>4	WJ	7	3	27	Wi 82	18
Combined Techniques: Weave/Crochet	Slightly Left of Center Jacket	Rowley, Elaine	√	√	PWC			6	Su 83	44
Combined Techniques: Weave/Crochet	Vadmal: A Study Group from the Frozen North Warms Up to an Ancient Technique	Larson-Fleming, Susan	√	√	WJ	10	3	39	Wi 86	26
Combined Techniques: Weave/Embroidery	Weaving as Related to Embroidery	King, Bucky	√		SS&D	1	2	2	Mr 70	6
Combined Techniques: Weave/Embroidery	Weaving as Related to Embroidery	King, Bucky	√		SS&D	1	2	2	Mr 70	6
Combined Techniques: Weave/Felt	Weaving and Felt	Swendeman, Dorothy	√	√	Iw	5	3		Su 80	43
Combined Techniques: Weave/Felt	Weaving and Felt: Laminated Wefts		√		Iw	5	3		Su 80	45
Combined:Techniques: Weave/Felt/Crochet	Weaving & Felting	Berdinka, Regine	√	√	SS&D	15	2	58	Sp 84	10
Combined Techniques: Weave/Knit	Boy's Vest (Lou Cabeen)		√	√	Hw	5	4		S/O 84	42, 93
Combined Techniques: Weave/Knit	California Holiday Delight (Mary Kay Stoehr)		√	√	Hw	6	3		Su 85	41, I-6
Combined Techniques: Weave/Knit	Chenille Polo	Xenakis, Alexis Yiorgos	√	√	PWC			6	Su 83	34
Combined Techniques: Weave/Knit	Demystifying Complex Weaves: A Step-by-Step Exploration from Four to Sixteen Harnesses	Piroch, Sigrid	√	>4	WJ	10	3	39	Wi 86	8
Combined Techniques: Weave/Knit	Double Woven Quilted Vest (Yvone Stahl)		√	√	Hw	5	1		J/F 84	54, 97
Combined Techniques: Weave/Knit	Figured Piqué on a Ground of 2/2 Twill and 2/2 Hopsack	Xenakis, Athanasios David	√	>4	PWC	4	2	12		24
Combined Techniques: Weave/Knit	From Harness Sheds to Double Beds	Guagliumi, Susan Fletcher	√		Fa	10	6		N/D 83	52
Combined Techniques: Weave/Knit	Inlay We Trust, Part 2: Leno Inlay	Herring, Connie	√	√	PWC			6	Su 83	48
Combined Techniques: Weave/Knit	Inspirations from Sweaters	Brewington, Judith	√	√	WJ	7	3	27	Wi 82	14
Combined Techniques: Weave/Knit	Man's Vest (Lou Cabeen)		√	√	Hw	5	4		S/O 84	43, 93
Combined Techniques: Weave/Knit	More Moneymakers for Weavers	Klessen, Romy	√	√	PWC			2	Ap 82	9
Combined Techniques: Weave/Knit	M's and O's "Popcorn" Sweater (Mary Kay Stoehr)		√	√	Hw	5	1		J/F 84	57, 98
Combined Techniques: Weave/Knit	Quilted Vest (Susan Henrickson)		√	√	Hw	4	2		M/A 83	61, 96
Combined Techniques: Weave/Knit	Raglan Rectangles	Coifman, Lucienne	√	√	SS&D	18	1	69	Wi 86	10
Combined Techniques: Weave/Knit	Reversible Vest (Jean Scorgie)		√	√	Hw	7	4		S/O 86	66, I-13
Combined Techniques: Weave/Knit	Scandia Jacket		√	√	WJ	8	3	31	Wi 83	42
Combined Techniques: Weave/Knit	Shepherd's Dancing Coat	Fleischer, Helen	√	√	S-O	11	1		Sp 87	17
Combined Techniques: Weave/Knit	Silk	Lawrence, Mary Jo	√	√	WJ	7	3	27	Wi 82	74
Combined Techniques: Weave/Knit	Snakeskin Jacket (Mary Kay Stoehr)		√	√	Hw	5	4		S/O 84	54, 96
Combined Techniques: Weave/Knit	Sweater (Betty Beard)		√	√	Hw	1	1		F-W 79	24, 57
Combined Techniques: Weave/Knit	Turned Summer and Winter Jacket	Johnson, Melinda Raber	√	>4	WJ	8	3	31	Wi 83	58
Combined Techniques: Weave/Knit	Two String Sweaters	Brugger, Susan	√	√	PWC			6	Su 83	31
Combined Techniques: Weave/Knit	Versatile Inlay, Twill on Twill	Beard, Betty	√	√	SS&D	19	1	73	Wi 87	53

SUBJECT	TITLE	AUTHOR	IL	INST	JOUR	VOL	NO	ISS	DATE	PAGE
Combined Techniques: Weave/Knit	Vest with a Hidden Twist	Emerick, Patricia	√	√	S-O	11	4		Wi 87	36, I-46
Combined Techniques: Weave/Knit	Weave and Knit Pullover	Barrett, Clotilde	√	√	WJ	8	3	31	Wi 83	20
Combined Techniques: Weave/Knit	Weave and Knit Suit		√	√	WJ	8	3	31	Wi 83	18
Combined Techniques: Weave/Knit	Winning Woven Winter Warmers		√	> 4	Hw	7	1		J/F 86	32
Combined Techniques: Weave/Knit	Winter Colors	Beeny, Merna	√	√	Hw	4	1		J/F 83	64
Combined Techniques: Weave/Knit	Woven Egmont Sweater	Klessen, Romy	√	√	PWC			2	Ap 82	83
Combined Techniques: Weave/Knit/Crochet	Modular Clothing	Mayer, Anita	√	√	Hw	7	3		M/J 86	58
Combined Techniques: Weave/Latch-Hook	Fleecy Vest, A	Gilsdorf, Marilyn	√	√	WJ	8	4	32	Sp 84	9
Combined Techniques: Weave/Patchwork	Fascination with Form, A	Richardson, Pat	√	> 4	SS&D	12	3	47	Su 81	54
Combined Techniques: Weave/Sprang	Sprang and Weaving	Skowronski, Hella; Mary Reddy	√	√	SS&D	7	3	27	Su 76	79
Combined Techniques: Weave/Stitchery	Two Crafts, Weaving & Stitchery Combine Well	Davenport, Martha P.	√		H&C	21	3		Su 70	34
CombinedTechniques: Weave/Knit	Vadmal: A Study Group from the Frozen North Warms Up to an Ancient Technique	Larson-Fleming, Susan	√	√	WJ	10	3	39	Wi 86	26
CombinedTechniques: Weave/Knit	Wrist-to-Wrist Garment, The	Allen, Rose Mary	√	√	WJ	9	3	35	Wi 85	19
Commemorative Textiles	Bicentennial Tapestry, A	Howard, Margaret	√		SS&D	7	1	25	Wi 75	30
Commemorative Weavings	Jacquard and Woven Silk Pictures, The	Adrosko, Rita J.	√		AT	1			De 83	9
Comments: Provocative Book List	Provocative Book List: A Student Comments, A	Nestel, Susan E.			Fa	8	4		J/A 81	18
Commissions and Commissioning	Weaving Works for Worship	Paul, Jan	√		WJ	6	1	21	Su 81	40
Commissions and Commissioning	Bobbin Lace on a Grand Scale: When the Pillow Is a 12-ft. Pegboard	Lewis, Robin S.	√	√	TM			9	F/M 87	54
Commissions and Commissioning	Commercial Establishment Discovers Fiber Arts, The	Jacopetti, Alexandra	√	√	SS&D	8	2	30	Sp 77	4
Commissions and Commissioning	Commissions: Challenge and Discipline	Leffmann, Theo Claire	√		SS&D	3	3	11	Su 72	18
Commissions and Commissioning	Commissions: The Process, the Problems and the Prospects		√		Fa	6	5		S/O 79	45
Commissions and Commissioning	Contemporary Navajo Weaving	Hedlund, Ann Lane	√		WJ	11	1	41	Su 86	30
Commissions and Commissioning	Corporate Commission, The	Creager, Clara	√	√	SS&D	16	1	61	Wi 84	38
Commissions and Commissioning	Designing for an Interior: Notes of a Pattern Weaver	Alvic, Philis	√		WJ	9	4	36	Sp 85	69
Commissions and Commissioning	Fiber and Architecture: Amy Jo Lind and Maggie Nicholson		√		Fa	3	3		M/J 76	16
Commissions and Commissioning	Gerhardt Knodel	Olendorf, Donna	√		Fa	5	6		N/D 78	44
Commissions and Commissioning	Gridworks	Tacker, Sylvia	√		SS&D	16	4	64	Fa 85	30
Commissions and Commissioning	John Charles Gordon		√		Fa	4	4		J/A 77	32
Commissions and Commissioning	Notes of a Pattern Weaver	Alvic, Philis	√		WJ	10	3	39	Wi 86	65
Commissions and Commissioning	Observations	Pulleyn, Rob	√		Fa	3	3		M/J 76	38
Commissions and Commissioning	Portraits by a Weaver		√		SS&D	8	4	32	Fa 77	38
Commissions and Commissioning	Progression from Meticulous Yardage to Grand Commissions	Bernard-Boone, Ann	√		SS&D	5	1	17	Wi 73	71
Commissions and Commissioning	Sililoquy: Commission Blues	Thompson, Christine			PWC	4	1	11		9
Commissions and Commissioning	Spatial Transitions	Gilbert, James	√		SS&D	9	3	35	Su 78	12
Commissions and Commissioning	Stepping Out	Ridgeway, Terese	√		SS&D	18	1	69	Wi 86	82
Commissions and Commissioning	Talk with Jack Lenor Larsen, A		√		SS&D	12	2	46	Sp 81	11
Commissions and Commissioning	Tips for Doing Commissioned Ecclesiastical Work				Fa	4	6		N/D 77	39
Commissions and Commissioning	Weaver's Commission Workshop	Meany, Janet	√		SS&D	10	3	39	Su 79	40
Commissions and Commissioning	Weaver's Story of Two Prayer Shawls, Garments Used in Jewish Ritual, A	Schlein, Alice	√	> 4	CW	3	3	9	Ap 82	6

SUBJECT	TITLE	AUTHOR	IL	INST	JOUR	VOL	NO	ISS	DATE	PAGE
Commissions and Commissioning	Working with the Wall ... A Community Garden		√		SS&D	10	4	40	Fa 79	8
Commitment	Choosing a Focus of Study can Lead to New Growth, New Horizons, New Understanding	Chandler, Deborah			Hw	6	4		S/O 85	26
Commitment	Commitment	LaLena, Constance			Hw	2	4		Se 81	76
Comparative Analysis: Drafts, Multiple-Shaft, Coverlet	Multiple Shaft Coverlet Drafts in the Allen-Stephenson Draft Book	Renne, Elisha	√	> 4	AT	3			My 85	125
Competition also see Contest										
Competitions	Designer-Craftsmen U.S.A. 1960		√		H&C	11	3		Su 60	18
Competitions	Evening the Odds in Juried Competition	Williams, Ann			SS&D	17	3	67	Su 86	63
Competitions	Evolution of a Regional Juried Fiber Show: Fibers Unlimited, The	Rees, Linda			SS&D	17	3	67	Su 86	65
Competitions	Fibers Unlimited 1985	Tacker, Sylvia	√		SS&D	17	3	67	Su 86	68
Competitions	Fleece-to-Garment Competition in New Zealand	Ashford, Joy			SS&D	4	1	13	Wi 72	21
Competitions	HGA Greeting Card Contest Results		√		SS&D	16	2	62	Sp 85	91
Competitions	Make It With Wool		√		Hw	6	2		M/A 85	10
Competitions	Mural Contest Winner from New Zealand		√		SS&D	4	1	13	Wi 72	30
Competitions	Shear to Share	Best, Eleanor	√	√	SS&D	15	1	57	Wi 83	28
Competitions	Sheep To Shawl in Albuquerque		√		Iw	1	2		Wi 76	23
Competitions	SPIN-OFF Book of World Records		√		S-O	4			80	20
Competitions	SPIN-OFF Book of World Records		√		S-O	7	3		Fa 83	11
Competitions	SPIN-OFF Book of World Records		√		S-O	9	3		Fa 85	13
Competitions	SPIN-OFF Book of World Records				S-O	3			79	14
Competitions	SPIN-OFF Book of World Records		√		S-O	5			81	21
Competitions	SPIN-OFF Book of World Records: Caps, Scarves, Socks, Mittens, Gloves				S-O	10	3		Fa 86	13
Competitions	Spin-Weave-Wear		√	√	SS&D	16	1	61	Wi 84	70
Competitions	Wyoming Holds Golden Fleece Spinning Contest	Adams, Brucie	√		SS&D	5	4	20	Fa 74	10
Competitions: Coverlet, Awards	PWC Coverlet Hall of Fame		√		PWC	5	1	15		26
Competitions: Handspun Swatches	Handspun Swatches		√		S-O	11	3		Fa 87	17
Competitions: Lacemaking	Lacemaking Competition				TM			14	D/J 87	20
Competitions: Quilts	Liberty Quilts		√		TM			6	A/S 86	100
Competitions: Sheep-to-Shawl	From Sheep to Shawl in Four Hours	Lockwood, Sheri	√		S-O	8	2		Su 84	43
Competitions: Spinning	Fine, Finer, Finest	Raven, Lee		√	S-O	9	4		Wi 85	24
Competitions: Spinning	Fine Spinning Record Falls!				S-O	11	3		Fa 87	17
Competitions: Spinning	Sixteeneth Century Labor Day, A	Amos, Alden	√		S-O	5			81	8
Competitions: Spinning	Spinning for a Finished Product Competition	Feldman-Wood, Florence			S-O	7	4		Wi 83	30
Competitions: Spinning	Wyoming Spinners Create with Wool	Adams, Brucie	√		Iw	1	1		Fa 75	10
Competitions: Tailoring Handwovens	Make It Yourself with Handwoven Wool		√		S-O	9	1		Sp 85	12
Competitions: Weaving	Announcing the First (and last?) Mighty Fine Dish Towel Contest				Hw	3	4		Se 82	59
Competitions: Weaving	Edquist/Lloyd Team Takes Top Prize in the "Teach a Friend" Contest		√		Hw	3	3		My 82	59
Competitions: Weaving	Prize Winners: The Weaver's Journal Contest				WJ	6	1	21	Su 81	21
Competitions: Winners	King's Ranson: Contest Rusults, A		√		WJ	10	1	37	Su 85	49
Competitions: Winners	Name Draft Contest Winners		√	> 4	WJ	11	4	44	Sp 87	46
Competitions: Winners	SPIN-OFF Book of World Records				S-O	8	3		Fa 84	12
Competitions: Winners	SPIN-OFF Book of World Records: Swatch Conpetition		√		S-O	6	4		82	22
Competitions: Winners	SPIN-OFF Book of World Records: Wonnnderful Socks		√		S-O	6	4		82	21

SUBJECT	TITLE	AUTHOR	IL	INST	JOUR	VOL	NO	ISS	DATE	PAGE
Competitions: Winners	Teach a Friend to Weave — with Handspun		√		Hw	2	2		Mr 81	59
Competitions: Woolcrafts	New Zealand Fashion Parade		√		S-O	9	1		Sp 85	17
Complementary Warps	Backstrap Weaving for Penance and Profit	Coffman, Charlotte	√	√	WJ	7	1	25	Su 82	60
Complementary Warps	Complementary-Warp Weave (error-corrected WJ v7 n4 83 p4)	Coffman, Charlotte	√	√	WJ	7	3	27	Wi 82	53
Complementary Warps	Gifts from Ancient Peru	Nass, Ulla	√	√	WJ	8	1	29	Su 83	32
Complementary Warps	Weaving Processes in the Cuzco Area of Peru	Rowe, Ann Pollard	√	√	TMJ	4	2		75	30
Complementary Wefts	Decorative Weft on a Plain Weave Ground, Two Shaft Inlay and Brocade		√	√	WJ	5	4	20	Sp 81	15
Complementary Wefts	Swivel Explored and Contradicted		√	√	WJ	3	4	12	Ap 79	5
Complementary Wefts, 2-Sets	Work of a Huave Indian Weaver in Oaxaca, Mexico: Complex Weave Structures Utilizing One Warp Set and Two Complementary Weft Sets, The	Connolly, Loris	√		AT	3			My 85	7
Complementary-Warp Structure	Color and Design in Andean Warp-Faced Fabrics	Femenias, Blenda	√		WJ	12	2	46	Fa 87	44
Complementary-Warp Structures	Flat-Woven Structures Found in Nomadic and Village Weavings from the Near East and Central Asia	Wertime, John T.	√		TMJ	18			79	33
Complementary-Warp Structures, 3-Warp	Understanding Some Complex Structures from Simple Andean Looms: Steps in Analysis and Reproduction	Cahlander, Adele	√	√	AT	1			De 83	181
Complementary-Warp Structures, 4-Warp	Understanding Some Complex Structures from Simple Andean Looms: Steps in Analysis and Reproduction	Cahlander, Adele	√	√	AT	1			De 83	181
Complementary-Warp Structures, Double-Faced	Understanding Some Complex Structures from Simple Andean Looms: Steps in Analysis and Reproduction	Cahlander, Adele	√	√	AT	1			De 83	181
Complementary-Warp Structures, Intermesh	Understanding Some Complex Structures from Simple Andean Looms: Steps in Analysis and Reproduction	Cahlander, Adele	√	√	AT	1			De 83	181
Complementary-Warp Structures, Pebble	Understanding Some Complex Structures from Simple Andean Looms: Steps in Analysis and Reproduction	Cahlander, Adele	√	√	AT	1			De 83	181
Complementary-Warp Structures, Two-Faced	Understanding Some Complex Structures from Simple Andean Looms: Steps in Analysis and Reproduction	Cahlander, Adele	√	√	AT	1			De 83	181
Complementary-Weft Plain Weave	Complimentary-Weft Plain Weave — A Pick-up Technique (error-corrected WJ v5 n1 80 p28d)	Hanley, Janet	√	√	WJ	4	4	16	Ap 80	22
Complementary-Weft Plain Weave	How One Weave Leads to Another	Barrett, Clotilde	√	> 4	WJ	8	1	29	Su 83	75
Complementary-Weft Structures	Drawloom Textiles in Wool and Silk (with a Structural Analysis by Ann Pollard Rowe)	Trilling, James	√		TMJ	21			82	96
Complementary-Weft Structures	Flat-Woven Structures Found in Nomadic and Village Weavings from the Near East and Central Asia	Wertime, John T.	√		TMJ	18			79	33
Complementary-Weft Tabby	Designing Rugs for Harness-Controlled Weaving		√	> 4	WJ	4	4	16	Ap 80	27
Complementary-Weft Tabby	Swivel Explored and Contradicted		√	√	WJ	3	4	12	Ap 79	5
Complementary-Weft Tabby	Woven Miniatures		√	√	WJ	3	4	12	Ap 79	15
Complementary-Weft Tabby On Overshot	Swivel Explored and Contradicted		√	√	WJ	3	4	12	Ap 79	5
Complementary-Weft Tabby On Spot Bronson	Swivel Explored and Contradicted		√	√	WJ	3	4	12	Ap 79	5
Complementary-Weft Tabby On Summer and Winter	Swivel Explored and Contradicted		√	√	WJ	3	4	12	Ap 79	5
Complementary-Weft Tabby On Twills and Twill Derivatives	Swivel Explored and Contradicted		√	√	WJ	3	4	12	Ap 79	5
Complementary-Weft Tabby, Polychrome	Swivel Explored and Contradicted		√	√	WJ	3	4	12	Ap 79	5
Complementary-Wefts, Plain Weave, Inner Warps	Second Type of Mughal Sash, A	Sonday, Milton; Nobuko Kajitani	√		TMJ	3	2		De 71	6

153

SUBJECT	TITLE	AUTHOR	IL	INST	JOUR	VOL	NO	ISS	DATE	PAGE
Complex Weaves	Demystifying Complex Weaves: A Step-by-Step Exploration from Four to Sixteen Harnesses	Piroch, Sigrid	√	> 4	WJ	10	3	39	Wi 86	8
Complex Weaves	Double-Harness Techniques Employed in Egypt	El-Homossani, M. M.	√	> 4	AT	3			My 85	229
Complex Weaves	Drawloom Special Harness for Double Weave	Malloy, Kim, OSB	√	> 4	AT	1			De 83	77
Complex Weaves	In Pursuit of Plakhta	Golay, Myrna	√	> 4	WJ	11	3	43	Wi 87	34
Complex Weaves	Is Complex Weaving for You?	Piroch, Sigrid	√		WJ	10	2	38	Fa 85	10
Complex Weaves	Roses and Snowballs: The Development of Block Patterns in the German Linen-Weaving Tradition	Hilts, Patricia	√	> 4	AT	5			Ju 86	167
Complex Weaves	You Are Now Weaving Oakland	O'Hara, Sheila	√	> 4	AT	6			De 86	9
Complex Weaves: Beginning	Help in Bridging the Gap	Lyon, Nicki			CW	8	1	22	Se 86	24
Compositions: Fiber	"James Bassler" (Exhibit)	Malarcher, Patricia	√		Fa	8	6		N/D 81	71
Compositions, Fiber	Lynn Pierce	Pierce, Lynn	√		Fa	14	4		S/O 87	18
Compositions: Fiber	Marjorie Durko Puryear	Puryear, Marjorie Durko	√		Fa	14	4		S/O 87	19
Compositions: Mixed Media	Gertrude Parker: Metamorphosing A Humble Material	Haney, Jeanna T.	√		Fa	14	4		S/O 87	8
Compound Weaves	After Emery: Further Considerations of Fabric Classification and Terminology	Rowe, Ann Pollard	√		TMJ	23			84	53
Compound Weaves	Self-Stuffing Weft Cord Double Weave	Towner, Naomi Whiting	√	> 4	AT	3			My 85	47
Compound Weaves	Work of a Huave Indian Weaver in Oaxaca, Mexico: Complex Weave Structures Utilizing One Warp Set and Two Complementary Weft Sets, The	Connolly, Loris	√		AT	3			My 85	7
Compound Weaves: Satin-Ground Tissue Weave	Double-Harness Techniques Employed in Egypt	El-Homossani, M. M.	√	> 4	AT	3			My 85	229
Compound Weaves: Tabby, Weft-Faced	Double-Harness Techniques Employed in Egypt	El-Homossani, M. M.	√	> 4	AT	3			My 85	229
Compound Weaves: Twill, Weft-Faced	Double-Harness Techniques Employed in Egypt	El-Homossani, M. M.	√	> 4	AT	3			My 85	229
Compound Weft Weaves	Textile Structure and Analysis, A Home Study Course in Twelve Lessons: Lessons in Weave Structure, 3. Compound Weft Weaves	Tidball, Harriet		√	SCGM		18		66	25
Compu-Dobby Weaving	You Are Now Weaving Oakland	O'Hara, Sheila	√	> 4	AT	6			De 86	9
Computer Drawdowns	Faster than a Speeding Weaver	Strickler, Carol; Stewart Strickler	√		Hw	5	4		S/0 84	86
Computer Graphics	Application of Computer Generated Weaves as Texture Maps, The	Murtha, Judith Rush	√	√	AT	3			My 85	75
Computer Graphics Mode	Graphic Features on Home Computers	Strickler, Carol; Stewart Strickler		√	Hw	5	3		Su 84	89
Computer Hardware	What Computer Should I Buy?	Strickler, Stewart			Hw	8	1		J/F 87	68
Computer Language	Coming to Terms	Strickler, Carol; Stewart Strickler			Hw	4	2		M/A 83	73
Computer Networking	Computer Networking	Strickler, Carol; Stewart Strickler			Hw	8	3		M/J 87	89
Computer Programs	Computer Control of Tie-ups and Treadling Sequence	Clement, Richard	√	√	WJ	8	3	31	Wi 83	32
Computer Programs	Computer Networking	Strickler, Carol; Stewart Strickler			Hw	8	3		M/J 87	89
Computer Programs	Computer Programs				CW	4	1	10	Se 82	8
Computer Programs	Computerized Analysis of the Drawdown (addendum SS&D v13 n1 81 p4)	Hoskins, Janet A.	√	√	SS&D	13	1	49	Wi 81	76
Computer Programs	Computerized Fabric Analysis (error-corrected SS&D v14 n2 83 p4)	Hoskins, Janet A.	√	√	SS&D	14	1	53	Wi 82	26
Computer Programs	Computerized Weaving Calculations (error-corrected SS&D v12 n4 81 p8)	Jarvis, Helen		√	SS&D	12	3	47	Su 81	46
Computer Programs	Drawdown Programs for the Apple Computer	Strickler, Carol; Stewart Strickler	√		Hw	4	4		S/O 83	88
Computer Programs	Faster than a Speeding Weaver	Strickler, Carol; Stewart Strickler	√		Hw	5	4		S/0 84	86

SUBJECT	TITLE	AUTHOR	IL	INST	JOUR	VOL	NO	ISS	DATE	PAGE
Computer Programs	Jacquard Pattern Reconstructions with Computer Spreadsheets	Carr, Margaret; Helen Jarvis; Gordon Jarvis	√	√	SS&D	17	3	67	Su 86	78
Computer Programs	Linbogarn Shirt	Scorgie, Jean	√	√	WJ	7	1	25	Su 82	53
Computer Programs	Networking: Computer Enthusiasts Share Their Programs	Strickler, Stewart; Carol Strickler			Hw	6	4		S/O 85	88
Computer Programs	Posneg Program, The	Scorgie, Jean; Ann Sinclair	√	√	SS&D	13	3	51	Su 82	26
Computer Programs	Using Color Graphics: A Weaver's Experience	Strickler, Stewart; Carol Strickler	√		Hw	7	2		M/A 86	80
Computer Programs	Using the Block Patterns Program	Scorgie, Jean; Ann Sinclair	√	√	SS&D	13	4	52	Fa 82	16
Computer Programs	Using the Posneg Program	Scorgie, Jean; Ann Sinclair	√	√	SS&D	13	3	51	Su 82	28
Computer Programs	Warp/Weft Calculator for the Apple II, The	Strickler, Carol; Stewart Strickler	√	√	Hw	5	1		J/F 84	84
Computer Programs	Weave Design	Arnold, Kari Ann	√	√	SS&D	15	1	57	Wi 83	94
Computer Programs	Weave Master and Weave Master Plus, A Report (error-corrected CW v5 n3 84 p25)	Gordon, Judith	√	> 4	CW	5	1	13	Se 83	7
Computer Programs, Basic	Draft-Blender	Strickler, Carol; Stewart Strickler	√	√	Hw	8	2		M/A 87	68
Computer Programs: Basic	How to Read a Basic Program	Strickler, Stewart	√	√	Hw	4	5		N/D 83	76
Computer Programs: Basic Language	Fabric Analysis Program, A	Strickler, Carol; Stewart Strickler	√	√	Hw	7	1		J/F 86	76
Computer Programs: Cataloguing	Weavcat I on the Apple	Swantz, Sally J.	√		WJ	7	2	26	Fa 82	68
Computer Programs: Drawdown	Short and Sweet Drawdown Program for Computers, A (error-corrected WJ v7 n1 82 p36b)	Barrett, Earl	√	√	WJ	6	3	23	Wi 81	42
Computer Programs: Fabric Analysis	Computer-Aided Design Analysis	Poague, Susan	√		WJ	11	4	44	Sp 87	8
Computer: Programs, IBM-PC Basic	Computer-Assisted Weaving				CW		23		Ja 87	29
Computer Programs: Knitting	Gauge Revisor, The	Connors, Carol	√	√	Kn	3	1	5	F-W 86	54
Computer Programs: Name Draft	Name Draft (error-corrected WJ v8 n3 83 p68)		√	√	WJ	8	2	30	Fa 83	40
Computer Programs: Profile Development	Adventures of a Computer Convert (Computer Programming By A Novice)	Keasbey, Doramay	√	√	WJ	8	3	31	Wi 83	28
Computer Programs: Review	Color-and-Weave Computer Program Review	Peck, Nancy			CW	4	3	12	Ap 83	17
Computer Programs: "The Weaver"	Computer Weaving	Barrett, Clotilde	√	√	WJ	4	3	15	Ja 80	35
Computer Programs: "Video Loom"	Computer Weaving	Barrett, Clotilde	√	√	WJ	4	3	15	Ja 80	35
Computer Selection	First Steps to Buying a Home Computer	Strickler, Carol; Stewart Strickler	√	√	Hw	5	2		M/A 84	90
Computer Software	Choosing Software for Soft-Wear Work	Strickler, Carol			Hw	7	4		S/O 86	82
Computer Software	Computer Interacts: Programming The Pattern, The	Muller, Magdalena	√		SS&D	7	2	26	Sp 76	72
Computer Software	Fabric Analysis	Strickler, Carol	√		Hw	6	5		N/D 85	83
Computer Software	Interface	Ligon, Linda			Hw	4	3		M/J 83	76
Computer Software	Software Programs for the Weaver and Textile Artist	Strickler, Carol			Hw	6	3		Su 85	80
Computer Software	Software Sourcelist Update	Strickler, Carol; Stewart Strickler			Hw	5	3		Su 84	90
Computer Software	Weaver's Spreadsheet Template	Gustafson, Susan			CW	6	3	18	My 85	21
Computer Software	Weaving Software Source List				Hw	5	2		M/A 84	91
Computer Software: Embroidery	Software Choices for Weavers and Designers	Levine, Betty	√		TM			9	F/M 87	53
Computer Software: Knitting	Software Choices for Weavers and Designers	Levine, Betty	√		TM			9	F/M 87	53
Computer Software: Quilts	Software Choices for Weavers and Designers	Levine, Betty	√		TM			9	F/M 87	53
Computer Software Review	Pattern Master III (Software)	Hoskins, Janet			Hw	5	3		Su 84	18

SUBJECT	TITLE	AUTHOR	IL	INST	JOUR	VOL	NO	ISS	DATE	PAGE
Computer Software: Weaving	Computers and Weavers: Software Is Just Another Tool in the Designer's Hand	Hoskins, Janet A.	√		TM			9	F/M 87	51
Computer Softwear: Sources	Computers and Weavers: Software Is Just Another Tool in the Designer's Hand	Hoskins, Janet A.	√		TM			9	F/M 87	51
Computer Technology	Introduction to Computers for Weavers, An — Part II: What's Inside the Box?	Barrett, Earl W.	√		WJ	8	1	29	Su 83	45
Computer Technology	Introduction to Computers for Weavers—Part 3: What's Inside the Box? (cont'd); More On I/O	Barrett, Earl W.	√	√	WJ	8	2	30	Fa 83	24
Computer Weavers: Pacific Northwest	Report from Pacific Northwest	Fry, Laura			CW		25		Se 87	20
Computer-Aided Design	CAD Quilts: The Computer As a Studio Tool	Dadey, Jane	√		Fa	14	4		S/O 87	38
Computer-Controlled Loom	Computer Control of Tie-ups and Treadling Sequence	Clement, Richard	√	√	WJ	8	3	31	Wi 83	32
Computer-Digitized Video Patterns, Imaging	From Image to Woven Structure: A Video-Computer System for Textile Designers	Peterson, Lisa Lee	√	√	AT	7			Ju 87	109
Computers and Computer Applications	Adventures of a Computer Convert (Computer Programming By A Novice)	Keasbey, Doramay	√	√	WJ	8	3	31	Wi 83	28
Computers and Computer Applications	Application of Computer Generated Weaves as Texture Maps, The	Murtha, Judith Rush	√	√	AT	3			My 85	75
Computers and Computer Applications	Application of Computer-Aided Design Techniques to the Creation of Moss Crepe Weaves, The	Ping, Gu; Alan Newton	√	> 4	AT	2			De 84	185
Computers and Computer Applications	Automatic Analysis of Coloured Images	Hoskins, J. A.	√	√	AT	5			Ju 86	151
Computers and Computer Applications	CAD Quilts: The Computer As a Studio Tool	Dadey, Jane	√		Fa	14	4		S/O 87	38
Computers and Computer Applications	Color and Weave Effects	Poulton, Jim	√	> 4	WJ	5	3	19	Wi 81	14
Computers and Computer Applications	Coming to Terms	Strickler, Carol; Stewart Strickler			Hw	4	2		M/A 83	73
Computers and Computer Applications	Computer as a Design Tool, The	Strickler, Carol	√	√	Hw	8	5		N/D 87	66
Computers and Computer Applications	Computer Control of Tie-ups and Treadling Sequence	Clement, Richard	√	√	WJ	8	3	31	Wi 83	32
Computers and Computer Applications	Computer Designing at the Hemisfair				H&C	19	2		Sp 68	17
Computers and Computer Applications	Computer Generated Overshot Variations	Velderman, Pat	√		H&C	22	4		Fa 71	10
Computers and Computer Applications	Computer Imagery: True Confessions from a "Graph Paper Addict"	Carey, Joyce Marquess	√		Fa	9	2		M/A 82	17
Computers and Computer Applications	Computer Interacts: Programming the Pattern, The	Muller, Magdalena	√		SS&D	7	2	26	Sp 76	72
Computers and Computer Applications	Computer Learns to Weave, The	Huff, Karen E.	√	√	SS&D	6	4	24	Fa 75	19
Computers and Computer Applications	Computer Weaving	Barrett, Clotilde	√	√	WJ	4	3	15	Ja 80	35
Computers and Computer Applications	Computer-Aided Design Analysis	Poague, Susan	√		WJ	11	4	44	Sp 87	8
Computers and Computer Applications	Computer-Aided Design for Handweaving	Windeknecht, Margaret B.; Thomas G. Windeknecht			CW	2	1	4	Oc 80	8
Computers and Computer Applications	Computerized Analysis of the Drawdown (addendum SS&D v13 n1 81 p4)	Hoskins, Janet A.	√	√	SS&D	13	1	49	Wi 81	76
Computers and Computer Applications	Computerized Weaving Calculations (error-corrected SS&D v12 n4 81 p8)	Jarvis, Helen		√	SS&D	12	3	47	Su 81	46
Computers and Computer Applications	Computers and Weavers: Software Is Just Another Tool in the Designer's Hand	Hoskins, Janet A.	√		TM			9	F/M 87	51
Computers and Computer Applications	Computers Don't Weave (error-corrected SS&D v14 n4 83 p4)	Petrini, Marcy	√		SS&D	14	3	55	Su 83	62
Computers and Computer Applications	Computers for the Fiber Professional	LaLena, Constance		√	Hw	3	2		Mr 82	72

SUBJECT	TITLE	AUTHOR	IL	INST	JOUR	VOL	NO	ISS	DATE	PAGE
Computers and Computer Applications	Computers—Is It Still Handweaving?	Colwell, Ken	√		PWC	4	1	11		51
Computers and Computer Applications	Counterchange	Wertenberger, Kathryn	√	√	Hw	7	2		M/A 86	75
Computers and Computer Applications	Design Decisions: Software Solutions	George, Patrice	√	> 4	Hw	5	5		N/D 84	47
Computers and Computer Applications	Design of Interactive Systems for Real-Time Dobby Control	Hoskins, W. D.; J. A. Hoskins	√	√	AT	5			Ju 86	33
Computers and Computer Applications	Designing Rep Weaves with the Aid of a Computer	Bohannan, Ronnine	√	√	WJ	7	4	28	Sp 83	24
Computers and Computer Applications	Draft-Blender	Strickler, Carol; Stewart Strickler	√	√	Hw	8	2		M/A 87	68
Computers and Computer Applications	Drawdown Programs for the Apple Computer	Strickler, Carol; Stewart Strickler	√		Hw	4	4		S/O 83	88
Computers and Computer Applications	Fabric About Fabric	Cannarella, Deborah	√		TM			1	O/N 85	72
Computers and Computer Applications	Fabric Analysis	Strickler, Carol	√		Hw	6	5		N/D 85	83
Computers and Computer Applications	Five-Year Retrospective, A	Strickler, Stewart; Carol Strickler			Hw	8	4		S/O 87	60
Computers and Computer Applications	From Image to Woven Structure: A Video-Computer System for Textile Designers	Peterson, Lisa Lee	√	√	AT	7			Ju 87	109
Computers and Computer Applications	Grrrhhhh: A Study of Social Patterns	Hickman, Deborah	√		Fa	14	4		S/O 87	23
Computers and Computer Applications	High Tech—High Touch	Van Artsdalen, Martha J.	√		SS&D	18	2	70	Sp 87	54
Computers and Computer Applications	High Tech Meets High Touch: Pioneers in Art	Kaminski, Vera E.	√		Fa	13	5		S/O 86	6
Computers and Computer Applications	High-Tech Comes to Weaving: AVL Looms	Larson, Eden	√		Fa	14	4		S/O 87	36
Computers and Computer Applications	High-Tech Comes to Weaving: Macomber Looms	Henderson, Stew	√		Fa	14	4		S/O 87	35
Computers and Computer Applications	In Defense of the Computer	Strickler, Carol; Stewart Strickler	√		Hw	5	5		N/D 84	87
Computers and Computer Applications	Interface	Ligon, Linda			Hw	4	3		M/J 83	76
Computers and Computer Applications	Interface	Strickler, Carol; Stewart Strickler			Hw	3	5		N/D 82	71
Computers and Computer Applications	Interface	Strickler, Carol; Stewart Strickler			Hw	4	1		J/F 83	69
Computers and Computer Applications	Introduction to Computers for Weavers, An	Barrett, Earl W.	√	√	WJ	7	4	28	Sp 83	25
Computers and Computer Applications	Introduction to Computers for Weavers—Part 3: What's Inside the Box? (cont'd); More On I/O	Barrett, Earl W.	√	√	WJ	8	2	30	Fa 83	24
Computers and Computer Applications	Jacquard Pattern Reconstructions with Computer Spreadsheets	Carr, Margaret; Helen Jarvis; Gordon Jarvis	√	√	SS&D	17	3	67	Su 86	78
Computers and Computer Applications	Linbogarn Shirt	Scorgie, Jean	√	√	WJ	7	1	25	Su 82	53
Computers and Computer Applications	Macomber's Designers Delight Dobby, A Report	Gordon, Judith	√		CW	4	1	10	Se 82	16
Computers and Computer Applications	Margaret and Tom Windeknecht: Computer Drafts	Pilsk, Adele	√		Fa	5	5		S/O 78	18
Computers and Computer Applications	Microchips in the Sewing Room, The	Fanning, Robbie	√	√	TM			12	A/S 87	34
Computers and Computer Applications	My Computer Designs a Bedspread	Salsbury, Nate	√	√	Hw	3	3		My 82	80
Computers and Computer Applications	Name Draft (error-corrected WJ v8 n3 83 p68)		√	√	WJ	8	2	30	Fa 83	40
Computers and Computer Applications	Printers: Characteristics and Functions	Strickler, Stewart; Carol Strickler		√	Hw	7	3		M/J 86	30

SUBJECT	TITLE	AUTHOR	IL	INST	JOUR	VOL	NO	ISS	DATE	PAGE
Computers and Computer Applications	Skeleton Peg Plan for the Compu-Dobby, A	Gustafson, Susan			CW	6	3	18	My 85	24
Computers and Computer Applications	Technological Change and the Textile Industry: The Impact of the Industrial Revolution and the Computer Revolution	Thieme, Otto Charles	√		Fa	11	1		J/F 84	54
Computers and Computer Applications	Textile Designer of the Future, The	Lourie, Janice R.	√	√	H&C	17	1		Wi 66	8
Computers and Computer Applications	Textile Graphics, A New Method of Designing		√		H&C	18	1		Wi 67	19
Computers and Computer Applications	Tips on Giving Programs and Workshops on "Computers in Weaving"	Strickler, Carol	√		Hw	6	2		M/A 85	67
Computers and Computer Applications	Twill Color and Weave Effects...From the Computer	O'Connor, Paul	√	> 4	Iw	6	1		Wi 80	28
Computers and Computer Applications	Using a Computer: Four Views		√		Fa	13	5		S/O 86	7
Computers and Computer Applications	Using Color Graphics: A Weaver's Experience	Strickler, Stewart; Carol Strickler	√		Hw	7	2		M/A 86	80
Computers and Computer Applications	Using the Block Patterns Program	Scorgie, Jean; Ann Sinclair	√	√	SS&D	13	4	52	Fa 82	16
Computers and Computer Applications	Weavcat I on the Apple	Swantz, Sally J.	√		WJ	7	2	26	Fa 82	68
Computers and Computer Applications	Weave Design	Arnold, Kari Ann	√	√	SS&D	15	1	57	Wi 83	94
Computers and Computer Applications	Weaving by Computer, HemisFair Visitors Have Unique Experience		√		H&C	19	3		Su 68	11
Computers and Computer Applications	Weaving with Computers	Sowles, Susan: Theresa Ruch			SS&D	13	3	51	Su 82	30
Computers and Computer Applications	What Computer Should I Buy?	Strickler, Stewart			Hw	8	1		J/F 87	68
Computers and Computer Applications	What's in a Name? Name Drafts Drawn by Hand or Computer	Mansfield, Susan	√	√	WJ	10	3	39	Wi 86	15
Computers and Computer Applications	You Are Now Weaving Oakland	O'Hara, Sheila	√	> 4	AT	6			De 86	9
Computers and Computer Applications: Jacquard Loom	Jacquard and Woven Silk Pictures, The	Adrosko, Rita J.	√		AT	1			De 83	9
Computers: Input	Introduction to Computers for Weavers, An	Barrett, Earl W.	√	√	WJ	7	4	28	Sp 83	25
Computers: Output	Introduction to Computers for Weavers, An	Barrett, Earl W.	√	√	WJ	7	4	28	Sp 83	25
Concentration: Designing	Improving Your Concentration	Liebler, Barbara	√		Hw	6	4		S/O 85	68
Conference: Arizona	Four State Conferences	Linder, Olive	√		SS&D	10	2	38	Sp 79	30
Conference: Complex Weavers	Meeting of the Complex Weavers				CW	4	1	10	Se 82	3
Conference: Georgia	Four State Conferences	Lukasiewicz, Nancy	√		SS&D	10	2	38	Sp 79	31
Conference: Missouri	Four State Conferences	Ziemke, Dene	√		SS&D	10	2	38	Sp 79	31
Conference Speech	Fiber Horizons	LaLena, Constance			Hw	4	5		N/D 83	26
Conference: Utah	Four State Conferences	Hartford, Jane	√		SS&D	10	2	38	Sp 79	32
Conferences	American Quilt Study Group	Sears, Victoria	√		Fa	9	3		M/J 82	53
Conferences	Apprenticeship Conference				SS&D	9	4	36	Fa 78	98
Conferences	Art/Culture/Future	Scarborough, Jessica	√		Fa	13	5		S/O 86	52
Conferences	At the Tenth New England Weavers Seminar		√		SS&D	4	4	16	Fa 73	5
Conferences	California Conference at Palm Springs		√		SS&D	3	3	11	Su 72	42
Conferences	California State-wide Conference	Bryan, Dorothy	√		H&C	6	4		Fa 55	30
Conferences	California Wonderland	Newman, Mattie E.; Helen C. Stuart			SS&D	1	3	3	Ju 70	5
Conferences	Colloquy, 1985				WJ	10	2	38	Fa 85	70
Conferences	Conference of Northern California Handweavers, 1985				WJ	10	2	38	Fa 85	68
Conferences	Conference Sampler		√		SS&D	14	4	56	Fa 83	44
Conferences	Conferences: A Look Ahead				SS&D	2	2	6	Sp 71	26
Conferences	Convergence '84		√		WJ	9	1	33	Su 84	54

SUBJECT	TITLE	AUTHOR	IL	INST	JOUR	VOL	NO	ISS	DATE	PAGE
Conferences	Crossing Over—Fiber in Print	Poon, Vivian	√		Fa	10	3		M/J 83	48
Conferences	Demonstration At Northern California	Porcella, Yvonne	√		SS&D	3	4	12	Fa 72	19
Conferences	Dixie College at Las Vegas		√		SS&D	1	2	2	Mr 70	4
Conferences	Entanglements	Henzie, Susie			SS&D	3	2	10	Sp 72	45
Conferences	Feltmaking in Hungary	Beede, Beth; Jill Garfunkel	√		Fa	13	4		J/A 86	6
Conferences	Fibre-Form-Fusion: Gathering Together in Canada	Malarcher, Patricia	√		Fa	7	6		N/D 80	26
Conferences	First Conference for Ontario Weavers' Guilds	Oliphant, Carrie			H&C	6	3		Su 55	12
Conferences	First International Cashmere Seminar	Feldman-Wood, Florence			S-O	10	1		Sp 86	39
Conferences	Form and Fiber At Northern California		√		SS&D	4	3	15	Su 73	39
Conferences	Handweavers' International Festival				H&C	20	4		Fa 69	32
Conferences	Handweavers International Festival				H&C	20	2		Sp 69	33
Conferences	Handweavers International Festival	Marston, Ena			H&C	21	1		Wi 70	10
Conferences	HGA Directors to Judge At Midwest				SS&D	4	2	14	Sp 73	55
Conferences	"Hmong Art: Tradition and Change" (Exhibit)	Gordon, Beverly	√		Fa	12	6		N/D 85	36
Conferences	Intermountain Weavers: "Fiber Celebrated, 1985"	McClellan, Alice	√		SS&D	17	4	68	Fa 86	42
Conferences	International Carpet Extravaganza	Dyer, Carolyn Price	√		Fa	14	1		J/F 87	52
Conferences	International Exposure Conference	Place, Jennifer	√		Fa	10	5		S/O 83	51
Conferences	Interweave Forum: Fashion Fabrics 2	Pettigrew, Dale	√		Hw	8	4		S/O 87	76
Conferences	"K18–Stoffwechsel": A Report on the Exhibition and Symposium Held in Kassel, West Germany (Exhibit)	Vander Lee, Jana	√		Fa	10	1		J/F 83	52
Conferences	Learning Journey, A	Redding, Debbie	√		Hw	4	4		S/O 83	16
Conferences	Living Color, Northern California Conference Theme	Bryan, Dorothy	√		H&C	10	4		Fa 59	22
Conferences	Mary Snyder At News		√		SS&D	4	2	14	Sp 73	47
Conferences	Mexican Wedding	Weston, Carol	√		SS&D	2	4	8	Fa 71	30
Conferences	Michigan Conference				H&C	14	1		Wi 63	18
Conferences	Michigan Guilds Sponsor the 17th National Conference				H&C	6	1		Wi 54	31
Conferences	Michigan League Conference		√		H&C	11	4		Fa 60	31
Conferences	Michigan League of Handweavers		√	√	H&C	16	4		Fa 65	4
Conferences	Michigan Weaving, Third Conference at Hartland Shows Wide Variety		√	> 4	H&C	13	1		Wi 62	18
Conferences	Midwest Conference		√		H&C	18	1		Wi 67	36
Conferences	Midwest Conference 1967 at University of Missouri				H&C	19	1		Wi 68	42
Conferences	Midwest Conference Presents Sources of Inspiration for Color		√	> 4	H&C	13	4		Fa 62	18
Conferences	Midwest Weavers' Conference		√		WJ	9	1	33	Su 84	54
Conferences	Midwest Weavers' Conference		√		H&C	17	1		Wi 66	11
Conferences	Midwest Weavers Conference		√		H&C	14	4		Fa 63	20
Conferences	Midwest Weavers' Conference, 1985				WJ	10	2	38	Fa 85	69
Conferences	Midwest Weavers Conference Appoints John N. Payne		√		SS&D	2	3	7	Su 71	19
Conferences	National Conference in Springfield, Illinois				H&C	7	3		Su 56	43
Conferences	National Conference of Handweavers		√		H&C	3	1		Wi 51	42
Conferences	Nell Znamierowski At Texas	Maxcy, Mabel			SS&D	3	4	12	Fa 72	24
Conferences	New England Seminar				H&C	12	1		Wi 61	9
Conferences	New England Weavers Gather		√		SS&D	2	4	8	Fa 71	32
Conferences	New England Weavers' Seminar				H&C	17	4		Fa 66	39
Conferences	New England Weavers' Seminar		√		H&C	18	4		Fa 67	14
Conferences	New England Weavers' Seminar				H&C	20	1		Wi 69	21

SUBJECT	TITLE	AUTHOR	IL	INST	JOUR	VOL	NO	ISS	DATE	PAGE
Conferences	New England Weavers Seminar	Skirm, Helen W.	√		H&C	14	4		Fa 63	14
Conferences	New England Weavers' Seminar	Skirm, Helen W.			H&C	16	4		Fa 65	33
Conferences	New England Weaver's Seminar				H&C	18	1		Wi 67	33
Conferences	New York University's Annual Spring Conference on Industrial Arts	Ames, Helen B.	√		H&C	1	2		Su 50	13
Conferences	Northern California Conference				H&C	9	2		Sp 58	48
Conferences	Northern California Conference		√		H&C	17	1		Wi 66	13
Conferences	Northern California Conference	Bryan, Dorothy	√	√	H&C	8	4		Fa 57	28
Conferences	Northern California Conference	Bryan, Dorothy	√	√	H&C	11	4		Fa 60	26
Conferences	Northern California Conference	Loveland, Mary H.	√		H&C	17	3		Su 66	16
Conferences	Northern California Conference	Minton, Mary Cain	√		H&C	12	3		Su 61	30
Conferences	Northern California Conference	Minton, Mary Cain	√		H&C	13	3		Su 62	16
Conferences	Northern California Conference	Minton, Mary Cain			H&C	14	3		Su 63	20
Conferences	Northern California Conference	Minton, Mary Cain		√	H&C	15	4		Fa 64	29
Conferences	Northern California Handweavers		√		H&C	18	4		Fa 67	25
Conferences	Northern California Handweavers' Conference		√		H&C	5	4		Fa 54	21
Conferences	Northern California Handweavers Conference	Bryan, Dorothy	√		H&C	7	3		Su 56	62
Conferences	Northern California Handweavers Conference	Davis, Kathy	√		H&C	24	4		Au 73	36
Conferences	Northern California Handweavers Conference	Kennelly, Martha Mullan			H&C	22	3		Su 71	32
Conferences	Northern California Handweavers Meet		√		SS&D	7	2	26	Sp 76	50
Conferences	Northern California Handweaving Conference	Bryan, Dorothy	√		H&C	9	4		Fa 58	24
Conferences	Northern California Weavers in Their Seventeenth Session	Marston, Ena			H&C	20	4		Fa 69	18
Conferences	Northwest Conference at Seattle		√	√	H&C	8	3		Su 57	28
Conferences	Northwest Weavers Conference		√		SS&D	1	1	1	De 69	15
Conferences	On Foreign Soil But Common Ground, Textile Assembly Meets in Spain	Mailey, Jean	√		H&C	21	1		Wi 70	18
Conferences	Ontario Handspinning Seminar	Johnston, Constance	√	√	H&C	23	5		S/O 72	23
Conferences	Pacific Northwest Conference				H&C	22	3		Su 71	9
Conferences	Quilting by the Lake in Central New York	Wright, Yolanda	√		Fa	10	2		M/A 83	50
Conferences	Rainbow of Color At MLH Conference	Hancock, Charlene			SS&D	1	4	4	Se 70	21
Conferences	Second Craftsmen's Conference	Blumenau, Lili	√		H&C	9	4		Fa 58	14
Conferences	Seminar: The Flexible Medium, 1985				WJ	10	2	38	Fa 85	68
Conferences	Sense of the Individual, The	Janeiro, Jan	√		Fa	11	2		M/A 84	52
Conferences	Shaping the World Through Design	Welty, Margaret	√		Fa	9	4		J/A 82	48
Conferences	Southern California Conference		√		H&C	10	1		Wi 59	6
Conferences	Southern California Conference	Howie, Andrew J.			H&C	13	3		Su 62	21
Conferences	Southern California Conference	Marston, Ena			H&C	21	3		Su 70	30
Conferences	Southern California Guild Conference	Barrett, Katharine A.	√	√	H&C	9	1		Wi 57	15
Conferences	Spinners Explore Markets, Ideas	Bulbach, Stanley			TM			3	F/M 86	10
Conferences	Surface Design Conference 1985	Scarborough, Jessica	√		Fa	12	5		S/O 85	46
Conferences	Ted Hallman At Ottawa		√		SS&D	3	1	9	Wi 71	29
Conferences	Tradition in Transition	Torry, Barbara	√		SS&D	5	4	20	Fa 74	25
Conferences	University of Wisconsin Holds Conference for School Teachers	Crossman, Catherine	√		SS&D	5	1	17	Wi 73	60
Conferences	Weavers' Seminar, New England's Eight Biennial				H&C	20	4		Fa 69	12
Conferences	Weaving Conference for Middle Atlantic States				H&C	10	1		Wi 59	46
Conferences	West to Mid-West		√		SS&D	2	3	7	Su 71	9
Conferences	Wool on a Small Scale, 1985				WJ	10	2	38	Fa 85	70

SUBJECT	TITLE	AUTHOR	IL	INST	JOUR	VOL	NO	ISS	DATE	PAGE
Conferences	Workshop Program for Philadelphia Conference				H&C	10	2		Sp 59	16
Conferences	World Congress of Craftsmen in New York				H&C	15	2		Sp 64	12
Conferences	World Crafts Council, An American Spinner Meets Peruvian Craftsmen	Reade, Dorothy	√		H&C	20	1		Wi 69	8
Conferences: American Craft Council	Art/Culture/Future: American Craft '86	Giles, Lynne	√		Hw	7	5		N/D 86	91
Conferences: American Rabbit Breeders Association	Report on the ARBA Convention	Almond, Bonnie H.			S-O	8	2		Su 84	21
Conferences: Colloquy '85	Weaving Places	van der Hoogt, Madelyn	√		PWC	4	1	11		8
Conferences: Colloquy '86	Ken Colwell on Weaving	Colwell, Ken			PWC	4	3	13		17
Conferences: Costume	Everyday World of Fantasy, The	Smeltzer, Nancy	√		Fa	13	3		M/J 86	6
Conferences: Design	Collaborations II: Let's Do Business		√		Fa	12	5		S/O 85	66
Conferences: Fibers Cottage Industry Congress	Precious Fibers Congress	Marcus, Ruth-Claire			TM			13	O/N 87	18
Conferences: Fiberworks Symposium	Conferences: Fiberworks Symposium	Ligon, Linda	√		Iw	3	4		Su 78	26
Conferences: Former Students	Small is Beautiful	Mayer, Anita	√		Iw	6	1		Wi 80	18
Conferences: International Weavers Conference	Contemporary American Handweaving from an International Perspective	Alaniz, Leonore	√		WJ	11	3	43	Wi 87	26
Conferences: Lace	Lace and Lectures	Feldman, Betty Suter			TM			10	A/M 87	20
Conferences: Machine Knitters	Machine Knitters Meet in Seattle	Guagliumi, Susan			TM			12	A/S 87	16
Conferences: Michigan Weavers' Conference	Supplementary Warp Patterning: A Weavers' Conference	Tidball, Harriet			SCGM		17		66	31
Conferences: Northern California Handweavers	Cultures to Meet in California	Rogers, Nora	√		Hw	6	1		J/F 85	18
Conferences: Northern California Handweavers	Getting Away Close to Home	Hearst, Kate			TM			7	O/N 86	14
Conferences: Oriental Carpets	London Carpeted in Oriental Gardens: The 4th International Conference on Oriental Carpets	Dyer, Carolyn Price	√		Fa	11	3		M/J 84	66
Conferences: Quilts	Quilters Flock to Houston Festival	Wolff, Colette	√		TM			4	A/M 86	12
Conferences: SOAR	From SOAR to Rendezvous	Pettigrew, Dale			S-O	10	4		Wi 86	35
Conferences: SOAR	Second Spin-Off Autumn Retreat		√		S-O	9	1		Sp 85	44
Conferences: SOAR	SOAR 1985: Some Observations and Asides	Bulbach, Stanley			S-O	10	2		Su 86	16
Conferences: SOAR	SOAR: A High Time	Pettigrew, Dale	√		S-O	8	1		Sp 84	6
Conferences: Spinning	Planning a Regional Spinner's Gathering	Franc, Marilyn			S-O	11	4		Wi 87	16
Conferences: Spinning	Reflections: Spin-Off Rendezvous, September 13-20, 1987, YMCA of the Ozarks, Potosi, Missouri	Pettigrew, Dale	√		S-O	11	4		Wi 87	55
Conferences: Surface Design	Surface Design Conference in Kansas City	Craig-Linenberger, Gerry	√		TM			12	A/S 87	20
Conferences: Surface Design Association	Artist in Focus, The	Goldberg, Barbara B.	√		Fa	11	3		M/J 84	52
Conferences: Surface Design Association	Surface Design Association's Southeast Regional Conference	Mattera, Joanne	√		Fa	9	1		J/F 82	54
Conferences: Weaving	Looming Thoughts	Fannin, Allen; Dorothy Fannin			H&C	24	4		Au 73	17
Conferences: Weaving	New England Seminar		√		H&C	12	4		Fa 61	11
Conferences: World Craft Council	Crafts, Wine Gardens and World Friendship	Dyer, Carolyn	√		Fa	8	2		M/A 81	24
Conservation: Baskets	Common Sense Care of Baskets	Turnbaugh, Sarah P.	√	√	SS&D	9	3	35	Su 78	90
Conservation: Baskets	Giving Your Baskets a Long, Healthy Life: A Basic Guide to Basketry Conservation	Odegaard, Nancy; Dale Kronkright	√		Fa	11	1		J/F 84	43
Conservation: Degradation Factors, Biological Attack	Current Trends in Textiles Conservation and Preservation	Block, Ira			AT	8			De 87	9
Conservation: Degradation Factors, Heat	Current Trends in Textiles Conservation and Preservation	Block, Ira			AT	8			De 87	9
Conservation: Degradation Factors, Humidity	Current Trends in Textiles Conservation and Preservation	Block, Ira			AT	8			De 87	9

SUBJECT	TITLE	AUTHOR	IL	INST	JOUR	VOL	NO	ISS	DATE	PAGE
Conservation: Degradation Factors, Light	Current Trends in Textiles Conservation and Preservation	Block, Ira			AT	8			De 87	9
Conservation: Degradation Factors, Oxygen	Current Trends in Textiles Conservation and Preservation	Block, Ira			AT	8			De 87	9
Conservation: Degradation Factors, Pollutants	Current Trends in Textiles Conservation and Preservation	Block, Ira			AT	8			De 87	9
Conservation: Paper Works of Art	How to Conserve Works of Art on Paper	Shapiro, Stephen D.; Anita G. Noennig	√		Fa	11	2		M/A 84	46
Conservation: Practices	Current Trends in Textiles Conservation and Preservation	Block, Ira			AT	8			De 87	9
Conservation Science, Textiles: Acids and Acid Salts, Chemistry	Principles of Textile Conservation Science, No.13. Acids and Acid Salts for Textile Conservation	Rice, James W.	√	√	TMJ	3	1		De 70	55
Conservation Science, Textiles: Adhesives	Principles of Textile Conservation Science, No. 12. Adhesives for Textile Conservation	Rice, James W.	√	√	TMJ	2	4		De 69	34
Conservation Science, Textiles: Alkalies and Alkaline Salts, Chemistry	Principles of Textile Conservation Science, No.14. The Alkalies and Alkaline Salts	Rice, James W.	√	√	TMJ	3	1		De 70	55
Conservation Science, Textiles: Classification Fibers	Principles of Textile Conservation Science, No. 3. Classification of Fibers Found in Ancient Textiles	Rice, James W.	√	√	TMJ	1	2		De 63	21
Conservation Science, Textiles: Cleaning Solutions and Mixtures	Principles of Textile Conservation Science, No. 17. Solutions and Other Mixtures for Cleaning and Conservation of Textiles and Related Artifacts	Rice, James W.		√	TMJ	3	4		De 73	43
Conservation Science, Textiles: Colorant Classification	Principles of Textile Conservation Science, No. 4. The Conservation of Historical Textile Colorants	Rice, James W.	√	√	TMJ	1	2		De 63	55
Conservation Science, Textiles: Control Methods, Fungi and Bacteria	Principles of Textile Conservation Science, No. 2. Practical Control of Fungi and Bacteria in Fabric Specimens	Rice, James W.	√	√	TMJ	1	1		No 62	52
Conservation Science, Textiles: Detergents and Soaps	Principles of Textile Conservation Science, No. 7. Characteristics of Detergents for Cleaning Historic Textiles	Rice, James W.	√	√	TMJ	2	1		De 66	23
Conservation Science, Textiles: Drycleaning	Principles of Textile Conservation Science, No. 8. Drycleaning of Fine and Fragile Textiles	Rice, James W.	√	√	TMJ	2	2		De 67	21
Conservation Science, Textiles: Fumigants	Principles of Textile Conservation Science, No. 11. Requirements for Bulk Storage Protection Against Insect Damage	Rice, James W.	√	√	TMJ	2	4		De 69	31
Conservation Science, Textiles: Humidity	Principles of Textile Conservation Science, No. 9. How Humidity May Affect Rug, Tapestry, and Other Textile Collections	Rice, James W.	√	√	TMJ	2	3		De 68	53
Conservation Science, Textiles: Leather/Fiber	Principles of Textile Conservation Science, No. 10. An Investigation Into Cleaning and Conservation of Mixed Leather and Fiber Artifacts	Rice, James W.	√	√	TMJ	2	3		De 68	57
Conservation Science, Textiles: Oxidation Control, Chemistry	Principles of Textile Conservation Science, No.15. The Control of Oxidation in Textile Conservation	Rice, James W.	√	√	TMJ	3	1		De 70	55
Conservation Science, Textiles: Principles	Principles of Textile Conservation Science, No. 1. General Chemical and Physical Structural Features of the Natural Textile Fibers	Rice, James W.	√		TMJ	1	1		No 62	47
Conservation Science, Textiles: Reducing Agents, Strippers, Chemistry	Principles of Textile Conservation Science, No.16. The Use and Control of Reducing Agents and "Strippers"	Rice, James W.	√	√	TMJ	3	1		De 70	55
Conservation Science, Textiles: Soils and Stains, Removal Techniques (Tabulated)	Principles of Textile Conservation Science, No. 5. The Characteristics of Soils and Stains Encountered on Historic Textiles	Rice, James W.	√	√	TMJ	1	3		De 64	8
Conservation Science, Textiles: Soils and Stains, Types and Sources	Principles of Textile Conservation Science, No. 5. The Characteristics of Soils and Stains Encountered on Historic Textiles	Rice, James W.	√	√	TMJ	1	3		De 64	8

SUBJECT	TITLE	AUTHOR	IL	INST	JOUR	VOL	NO	ISS	DATE	PAGE
Conservation Science, Textiles: Useful Solution Formulae	Principles of Textile Conservation Science No. 17. Solutions and Other Mixtures for Cleaning and Conservation of Textiles and Related Artifacts	Rice, James W.		√	TMJ	3	4		De 73	43
Conservation Science, Textiles: Wet Cleaning	Principles of Textile Conservation Science, No. 6. The Wonders of Water in Wetcleaning	Rice, James W.	√	√	TMJ	2	1		De 66	15
Conservation Science: Textiles, Wet Cleaning	Tapestry Washings at the Wadsworth Atheneum	Guagliumi, Susan Fletcher	√	√	Hw	5	2		M/A 84	18
Conservation: Techniques	Common Sense and Good Housekeeping: A Basic Guide to Textile Conservation (Clarification Fa v9 n2 82 p7)	Austin, Carol	√	√	Fa	9	1		J/F 82	43
Conservation: Textile	Tapestry: A Brief Overview	Bliss, Anne	√		Iw	4	2		Sp 79	15
Conservation: Textiles	Art of Conservation: A Look Behind Closed Doors — Conserving a Tapestry Collection, The		√		Fa	9	1		J/F 82	48
Conservation: Textiles	Care Enough	Liebler, Barbara	√	√	Iw	4	2		Sp 79	42
Conservation: Textiles	Common Sense and Good Housekeeping: A Basic Guide to Textile Conservation (Clarification Fa v9 n2 82 p7)	Austin, Carol	√	√	Fa	9	1		J/F 82	43
Conservation, Textiles	Conservation Notes: A Specialized Vacuum Device for Fragil Textiles	Columbus, Joseph Vincent	√	√	TMJ	1	1		No 62	56
Conservation: Textiles	Coptic Textiles: The Art of the Ancient Weaver	Constantinides, Kathy	√		Fa	7	6		N/D 80	19
Conservation, Textiles	Coverlet Care	Strickler, Carol	√	√	Hw	6	4		S/O 85	61
Conservation: Textiles	Current Trends in Textiles Conservation and Preservation	Block, Ira			AT	8			De 87	9
Conservation, Textiles	Healing Historical Textiles	Searle, Karen	√	√	SS&D	10	4	40	Fa 79	60
Conservation, Textiles	How to Care for Your Antique Textiles	Dirks, Katherine	√	√	H&C	24	1		J/F 73	40
Conservation, Textiles	Merrimack Valley Conservation Center		√		SS&D	11	3	43	Su 80	30
Conservation: Textiles	Ounce of Prevention: Avoiding the Immediate Need for Textile Conservation, An	Butterfield, Mary Ann; Lotus Stack			WJ	9	2	34	Fa 84	39
Conservation: Textiles	Ounce of Prevention: Methods for Mounting, An	Stack, Lotus; Mary Ann Butterfield	√	√	WJ	9	3	35	Wi 85	39
Conservation: Textiles	Ounce of Prevention: Preservation and Storage, An	Butterfield, Mary Ann; Lotus Stack	√	√	WJ	10	1	37	Su 85	7
Conservation: Textiles	Ounce of Prevention: Preventing Deterioration, An	Butterfield, Mary Ann; Lotus Stack	√	√	WJ	9	4	36	Sp 85	9
Conservation, Textiles	Peru, Textiles Unlimited: Mounting and Care of Textiles	Tidball, Harriet	√		SCGM		25		68	18
Conservation: Textiles	Protecting Your Collection: Textile Conservation	Hutchins, Jane K.	√		Fa	12	6		N/D 85	40
Conservation: Textiles	Public Fiber: The Long-Range Problem of Conservation	Austin, Carole	√		Fa	14	5		N/D 87	13
Conservation: Textiles	Techniques in Textile Conservation	Brown, Geoffrey I.	√	√	S-O	10	2		Su 86	45
Conservation, Textiles	Wet-Cleaning Coverlets	McHugh, Maureen Collins	√	√	SS&D	1	3	3	Ju 70	6
Conservation: Textiles	When Moths Fly Out of Your Closet	Hochberg, Bette	√	√	Iw	4	3		Su 79	50
Conservation, Textiles: Colorant Mixing	How to Match Colors When Dyeing Yarns or Fabrics for Textile Conservation Purposes	Rice, James W.	√	√	TMJ	2	4		De 69	27
Conservation, Textiles: Dyes and Dyeing	Practical Dyeing Method for the Fabric Conservator, A	Cooley, Theodore R.	√	√	TMJ	2	4		De 69	23
Conservation Textiles: Soil and Stain Removal	What to Do About Spots and Stains			√	Hw	5	2		M/A 84	58
Conservation: Textiles, Stain Removal	Age Spots			√	TM		9		F/M 87	8
Conserving Yarn: Double Weave	Doubleweave: Some Ideas for Conserving Yarn	Cahlander, Adele`	√	√	PWC		2		Ap 82	46
Construction Plans: Box Spinner	Home Built Box Spinner	Barrow, Cynthia	√	√	WJ	2	4	8	Ap 78	43
Construction Plans: Carding Box	Carding Box, The	Koster, Joan Bouza	√	√	SS&D	10	4	40	Fa 79	24
Construction Plans: Doublejack	Doublejack	Koepp, William A.	√	√	SS&D	14	1	53	Wi 82	7
Construction Plans: Doublejack	Doublejack or Sink the Floating Selvedge	Koepp, William	√	√	WJ	9	3	35	Wi 85	67

SUBJECT	TITLE	AUTHOR	IL	INST	JOUR	VOL	NO	ISS	DATE	PAGE
Construction Plans: Lamp	Mood Lamp	Richards, Iris	√	√	WJ	3	2	10	Oc 78	44
Construction Plans: Lappet Needle	Little Known Weaves Worth Knowing Better: Lappet Weave	Zielinski, S. A.; Robert Leclerc, ed.	√	√	MWL	16			'51–'73	9
Construction Plans: Loom, Card	Modern Loom from Medieval Sources, A	Cesari, Andrea	√	√	WJ	10	2	38	Fa 85	18
Construction Plans: Loom, Floor	How to Build a Loom	Turnbull, Tom	√	√	H&C	23	3		M/J 72	3
Construction Plans: Loom, Floor	How to Build a Loom	Turnbull, Tom	√	√	H&C	23	4		J/A 72	12
Construction Plans: Loom, Frame	Braiding on a Frame		√	√	WJ	2	4	8	Ap 78	22
Construction Plans: Loom, Frame	Children's Corner: A Picture Frame Tapestry	Champion, Ellen	√	√	WJ	4	1	13	Jy 79	19
Construction Plans: Loom, Frame	Shaped Sculptured Rugs — A Workshop with Urban Jupena		√	√	WJ	4	1	13	Jy 79	5
Construction Plans: Loom, Inkle	Weaving Inkle Bands: American Inkle Loom	Tidball, Harriet	√	√	SCGM		27		69	18
Construction Plans: Loom, Inkle, Board Loom	Weaving Inkle Bands: Supplies Needed for Making a Board Loom	Tidball, Harriet		√	SCGM		27		69	2
Construction Plans: Loom, Navajo	Vertical Loom (continued) Part 3, The Navajo Loom, The		√	√	WJ	2	2	6	Oc 77	23
Construction Plans: Loom, One-Beam	Vertical Loom, The		√	√	WJ	1	3	3	Ja 77	16
Construction Plans: Loom, One-Treadle	Design for a One-Treadle Loom	Pariseau, George E., M.D.	√	√	H&C	3	3		Su 52	15
Construction Plans: Loom, Source	Building a Loom			√	TM			10	A/M 87	8
Construction Plans: Loom, Tapestry	My Life	Weldon, Lynn L.	√	√	WJ	2	2	6	Oc 77	11
Construction Plans: Loom, Two-Shaft	Part 1, Build or Buy a Loom: Building a Two-Harness Loom	Tidball, Harriet	√	√	SCGM		23		68	19
Construction Plans: Loom, Warp-Weighted	Vertical Loom (continued) — Construction of a Warp Weighted Loom, The		√	√	WJ	1	4	4	Ap 77	27
Construction Plans: Pattern Harness (Set)	Technology of Handweaving: Pattern Harness	Zielinski, S. A.; Robert Leclerc, ed.	√	√	MWL	6			'51–'73	38
Construction Plans: Pick-Up Sticks	Part 1, Build or Buy a Loom: Building a Two-Harness Loom, Pick-Up Sticks and Small Tools	Tidball, Harriet	√	√	SCGM		23		68	25
Construction Plans: Shaft-Switcher	Shaft Switching, A Simple Method Usable for Finer Setts	Herring, Connie; Athanasios David Xenakis	√	√	PWC	3	3	9		29
Construction Plans: Shed Regulator	Shed Regulator for Counterbalance Looms, The	Koepp, William	√	√	WJ	10	3	39	Wi 86	67
Construction Plans: Shed Regulator	Technology of Handweaving: Shed Regulators	Zielinski, S. A.; Robert Leclerc, ed.	√	√	MWL	6			'51–'73	29
Construction Plans: Shuttles	Part 1, Build or Buy a Loom: Building a Two-Harness Loom, Warping Board and Shuttles	Tidball, Harriet	√	√	SCGM		23		68	24
Construction Plans: Small Tools	Part 1, Build or Buy a Loom: Building a Two-Harness Loom, Pick-Up Sticks and Small Tools	Tidball, Harriet	√	√	SCGM		23		68	25
Construction Plans: Spindle	Spindle	Chesley, Zina Mae		√	SS&D	2	2	6	Sp 71	22
Construction Plans: Spinning Tools	Electric Drill Becomes A Quill Spinner and a Bobbin Winder, An	Barrett, Earl W.	√	√	WJ	1	1	1	Jy 76	19
Construction Plans: Spinning Wheel	Working Drawings for Tyrolese Type Spinning Wheel	Heintz, Kenneth G.	√	√	SS&D	4	4	16	Fa 73	61
Construction Plans: Tapestry Loom	Low Budget Tapestry Loom, A	Gilstrap, Bill; Sara Gilstrap	√	√	WJ	5	4	20	Sp 81	42
Construction Plans: Templates, Block Pick-Up	Technology of Handweaving: Templets for Finn Weave	Zielinski, S. A.; Robert Leclerc, ed.	√	√	MWL	6			'51–'73	51
Construction Plans: Twining Frame	Twined Bag, A		√	√	WJ	1	3	3	Ja 77	27
Construction Plans: Warping Board	Part 1, Build or Buy a Loom: Building a Two-Harness Loom, Warping Board and Shuttles	Tidball, Harriet	√	√	SCGM		23		68	24
Construction Plans: Yarn Storage Tree	Yarn Storage Trees	Keasbey, Doramay	√	√	SS&D	10	2	38	Sp 79	86
Construction: Saddle Bag	Weaving a Cotton Saddlebag on the Santa Elena Peninsula of Ecuador	Hagino, Jane Parker; Karen E. Stothert	√	√	TMJ	22			83	19

SUBJECT	TITLE	AUTHOR	IL	INST	JOUR	VOL	NO	ISS	DATE	PAGE
Constructions: Fabric	Building on Experience: Virginia Jacobs' Fabric Constructions	Rowland, Amy Zaffarano	√		Fa	7	4		J/A 80	39
Constructions: Fabric	Rapport with Fabric and Dye: Kiyomi Iwata, A	Malarcher, Pat	√		Fa	7	1		J/F 80	28
Constructions: Fiber	"Anne Wilson: Grid Constructions" (Exhibit)	Finkel, Marilyn	√		Fa	6	2		M/A 79	65
Constructions: Fiber	Dana Romeis: Spatial Problem-Solving	Detter, Jan	√		Fa	14	1		J/F 87	18
Constructions: Fiber	"Filaments of the Imagination" (Exhibit)	Morse, Marcia	√		Fa	8	4		J/A 81	69
Constructions: Fiber	Gerna Edens: Textile Rhythms		√		Fa	10	4		J/A 83	14
Constructions: Fiber	"Jan Wagstaff: Woven and Painted Canvas" (Exhibit)	Malarcher, Patricia	√		Fa	8	6		N/D 81	64
Constructions: Fiber	"Jarmila Machova: Fibers" (Exhibit)	Dyer, Carolyn	√		Fa	9	1		J/F 82	75
Constructions: Fiber	Joseph Alvidres	Alvidres, Joseph	√		Fa	13	2		M/A 86	15
Constructions: Fiber	Lida Gordon: An Interview	Arnow, Jan	√		Fa	6	2		M/A 79	50
Constructions: Fiber	Roberta Kremer: A Dialogue with Fiber	Bard, Elizabeth A.	√		Fa	11	4		J/A 84	24
Constructions: Fiber	"Shared Vision": A Gallery Tour with Two Artists: Jacque Parsley and Neisja Yenawine (Exhibit)	Arnow, Jan	√		Fa	8	4		J/A 81	28
Constructions: Fiber	"Sirpa Yarmolinsky: Paper and Linen Constructions" (Exhibit)	Malarcher, Patricia	√		Fa	9	1		J/F 82	84
Constructions: Fiber	Stitched, Stuffed, and Painted: The Art of Esther Luttikhuizen	Acosta, Dan	√		Fa	12	2		M/A 85	61
Constructions: Fiber	Susan Iverson: With Both Feet Firmly Planted (error-corrected Fa v3 n5 76 p2)		√		Fa	3	4		J/A 76	14
Constructions, Fiber	Why Sew Those Lines? An Interview with Giorgio Furioso and Carolyn Thomas	Paca, Al	√		Fa	7	4		J/A 80	25
Constructions: Fiber/Paper	"Cynthia Laymon: Fiber/Paper Constructions" (Exhibits)	Syverson, Gilda Morina	√		Fa	9	4		J/A 82	71
Constructions: Fiber/Wood	Extra, Extra!!		√		Fa	13	4		J/A 86	73
Constructions: Mixed Media	Alter Cloths and Shrines: The New Work of Janet Boguch	Tacker, Sylvia	√		Fa	14	5		N/D 87	6
Constructions: Mixed Media	Arturo Alonzo Sandoval	Sandoval, Arturo Alonzo	√		Fa	11	6		N/D 84	58
Constructions: Mixed Media	Creative Process: Cindy Snodgrass, The	Snodgrass, Cindy	√		Fa	11	6		N/D 84	38
Constructions: Mixed Media	Creative Process: Debra Rapport, The	Rapport, Debra	√		Fa	11	6		N/D 84	34
Constructions: Mixed Media	Creative Process: Katherine Westphal, The	Westphal, Katherine	√		Fa	11	6		N/D 84	32
Constructions: Mixed Media	Creative Process: Rosina Yue, The	Yue, Rosina	√		Fa	11	6		N/D 84	40
Constructions: Mixed Media	Creative Process: Terri Mangat, The	Mangat, Terri	√		Fa	11	6		N/D 84	36
Constructions: Mixed Media	Dorothy Caldwell: Interacting with Image and Material	Duffy, Helen	√		Fa	13	6		N/D 86	22
Constructions: Mixed Media	Ed Rossbach	Rossbach, Ed	√		Fa	11	6		N/D 84	60
Constructions: Mixed Media	Evolution of an Artist: Pam Turczyn	Turczyn, Pam	√		Fa	14	5		N/D 87	24
Constructions: Mixed Media	Fabric of Creativity: Weaving Together Left– and Right–Brain Activites, The	Miles, Candice St. Jacques	√		Fa	11	6		N/D 84	44
Constructions, Mixed Media	Fabric of Sha Sha Higby's Imagination, The	Wheater, Kathleen	√		Fa	14	3		M/J 87	35
Constructions: Mixed Media	"Glenn Brill: Recent Work" (Exhibit)	Rowley, Kathleen	√		Fa	12	1		J/F 85	72
Constructions: Mixed Media	Jody Klein: Quilted Constructions	Perry, Pamela	√		Fa	12	2		M/A 85	18
Constructions: Mixed Media	Karon Hagemeister Winzenz: Fusing Fiber, Time, and Ritual	Bard, Elizabeth A.	√		Fa	12	1		J/F 85	10
Constructions: Mixed Media	Linda Richards-Watson: Finding the Eclectic	Rowley, Kathleen	√		Fa	10	4		J/A 83	12
Constructions: Mixed Media	Memory, Metaphor, And Magic: The Art of Janet Boguch	Glowen, Ron	√		Fa	11	6		N/D 84	66
Constructions: Mixed Media	"Patricia Malarcher: Pieced Reflections" (Exhibit)	Scheinman, Pamela	√		Fa	11	2		M/A 84	77
Constructions: Mixed Media	Patricia T. Hetzler	Hetzler, Patricia T.	√		Fa	14	2		M/A 87	24
Constructions: Mixed Media	Paula Renee	Renee, Paula	√		Fa	13	6		N/D 86	3
Constructions: Mixed Media	Sas Colby	Talley, Charles	√		Fa	8	5		S/O 81	29

SUBJECT	TITLE	AUTHOR	IL	INST	JOUR	VOL	NO	ISS	DATE	PAGE
Constructions: Mixed Media	Saved Threads: Ellen Zahorec Explores Layers of Time		√		Fa	8	5		S/O 81	42
Constructions: Mixed Media	Tangential Textiles: From Quiltmaking to Points Beyond	Rowley, Kristen Carlsen	√		Fa	9	2		M/A 82	22
Constructions: Mixed Media	"Vibrant Structures" (Exhibit)	Shermeta, Margo	√		Fa	11	6		N/D 84	75
Constructions: Mixed-Media	Almost Roman Glass	Elliott, Lillian	√		Fa	10	6		N/D 83	20
Constructions: Mixed-Media	Crazy Quilt for Babies Grand, A	Greenberg, Blue	√		Fa	8	2		M/A 81	31
Constructions: Mixed-Media	Just Playing in Space: Ann McKenzie Nickolson's Textile Artwork	Koplos, Janet	√		Fa	8	2		M/A 81	34
Constructions: Mixed-Media	Katherine Virgils	Waller, Irene	√		Fa	10	5		S/O 83	12
Constructions: Mixed-Media	Lewis Knauss: New Work	Park, Betty	√		Fa	9	3		M/J 82	11
Constructions: Mixed-Media	"Lida Gordon: Recent Works" (Exhibit)	Meloy, Margaret	√		Fa	10	4		J/A 83	63
Constructions: Mixed-Media	"Local Options: The Work of Laura Strand Mills and Jo Peterson" (Exhibit)	Ferguson, Tom	√		Fa	10	3		M/J 83	69
Constructions: Mixed-Media	"Marika Contompasis: Pedestal and Wall Pieces" (Exhibits)	Dyer, Carolyn	√		Fa	9	4		J/A 82	73
Constructions: Mixed-Media	"Needle and Cloth: Ten Years Later" (Exhibit)	Hulbert, Elizabeth McKey	√		Fa	10	3		M/J 83	72
Constructions: Mixed-Media	Nets of Bernard Toale, The	Malarcher, Patricia	√		Fa	9	3		M/J 82	26
Constructions: Mixed-Media	On the Edge: Betye Saar — Personal Time Travels	Woelfle, Gretchen Erskine	√		Fa	9	4		J/A 82	56
Constructions: Mixed-Media	"Pin Rugs of Ellen Oltchick, The" (Exhibit)	Poon, Vivian	√		Fa	10	6		N/D 83	74
Constructions: Mixed-Media	Structure and Surface: The Work of Barbara MacCallum	Koplos, Janet	√		Fa	10	2		M/A 83	62
Constructions: Multimedia	Jerry Stefl: Fantasy, Beads, and Fiber	Matthews, Marianne R.	√		Fa	11	2		M/A 84	24
Constructions: Multimedia	Michael Brennand-Wood	Orlowsky, Dzvinia	√		Fa	14	1		J/F 87	26
Constructions: Neon/Fabric	Revelations: Victoria Rivers' Neon and Fabric Constructions		√		Fa	8	5		S/O 81	50
Constructions: Paper	Carol Rosen: Paper Constructions	Scheinman, Pamela	√		Fa	11	2		M/A 84	16
Constructions: Paper	Marcia Morse: A Collaboration with Paper	Rowley, Kathleen	√		Fa	11	2		M/A 84	20
Constructions: Paper	"Meri Ann Walsh: Patterned Papers" (Exhibit)	Austin, Carole	√		Fa	8	6		N/D 81	65
Constructions: Paper	Paper Art of Fritzi Huber Morrison, The	Kosta, Angela	√		Fa	11	2		M/A 84	22
Constructions: Paper	Sculptural Paper: Foundations and Directions	Scarborough, Jessica	√		Fa	11	2		M/A 84	32
Constructions: Paper	"Susan Lyman's Paper Structures" (Exhibit)	Roberts, Stephen	√		Fa	8	5		S/O 81	69
Constructions: Paper	Weaving-Drawing-Painting-Paper, A Profile of Lorelei Schott		√		WJ	6	1	21	Su 81	13
Constructions: Paper/Mixed Media	Containers of Human Experience: Fragments from the Life of Lois Polansky	Muller, Marion	√		Fa	14	5		N/D 87	32
Constructions: Paper/Thread	Mary Long Graham: Resolving Chaos and Order	Goodman, Deborah Lerme	√		Fa	13	3		M/J 86	24
Constructions: Paper/Wood	Paper and Wood Constructions (Exhibit)		√		Fa	13	5		S/O 86	54
Constructions: Screen, Mixed Media	Debra Chase: Unwearable Wearables	Lonier, Terri	√		Fa	12	3		M/J 85	12
Constructions: Textile	Dona Anderson: Edging Towards the Unknown	Tacker, Sylvia	√		Fa	12	3		M/J 85	23
Constructions: Textile	Linda Miller: Textile Constructions	Goodman, Deborah Lerme	√		Fa	12	3		M/J 85	17
Constructions: Textile	"New Wisconsin Fiber": The First Group Show of American Fiber Art In Switzerland (Exhibit)	Bard, Elizabeth A.	√		Fa	10	6		N/D 83	43
Constructions: Woven	Working with Linen: Karen Jenson Rutherford	Itter, Diane	√		Fa	14	2		M/A 87	34
Consultant: Design, Handicrafts	Weaving in Taiwan, An American Designer's Experience in Free China		√		H&C	13	1		Wi 62	10
Consultant: Textile, Strengell, Marianne	Marianne Strengell, Textile Consultant to Architects	Bemis, Marion Holden	√		H&C	8	1		Wi 56	6
Consultants: Art	Art Consultants: Bridging the Gap Between Artist and Client	Goodman, Deborah Lerme	√		Fa	12	6		N/D 85	31
Consulting Service	Rural Program Helps Artists Reach Out	Sullivan, Lia A.	√		Fa	12	5		S/O 85	42

SUBJECT	TITLE	AUTHOR	IL	INST	JOUR	VOL	NO	ISS	DATE	PAGE
Consumer's Guide: Knitting Needles	All About Knitting Needles	Dyett, Linda	√		TM			4	A/M 86	30
Consumer's Guide: Computerized Sewing Machines	Microchips in the Sewing Room, The	Fanning, Robbie	√	√	TM			12	A/S 87	34
Consumer's Guide: Sewing Machines	Needles, Loopers, and Knives	Fanning, Robbie	√	√	TM			3	F/M 86	42
Containers	Containers of Human Experience: Fragments from the Life of Lois Polansky	Muller, Marion	√		Fa	14	5		N/D 87	32
Containers	Norma Minkowitz	Minkowitz, Norma	√		Fa	13	3		M/J 86	26
Containers	Sue Pierce: Quilted Vessels	Goodman, Deborah Lerme	√		Fa	11	1		J/F 84	100
Containers: Prehistoric Bag	Prehistoric Twined Bag from Big Bone Cave, Tennessee: Manufacture, Repair, and Use, A	Kuttruff, Jenna Tedrick	√		AT	8			De 87	125
Containers: Woven	Warp-Faced Krokbragd	Jensen, Gay; Donna Kaplan	√	> 4	WJ	12	2	46	Fa 87	62
Contemporary Card Weaving	Card Weaving, A New Approach by a Chicago Weaver	Regensteiner, Else	√		H&C	16	3		Su 65	19
Contemporary Crafts	"Art of Crafts 1986" (Exhibit)		√		Fa	13	5		S/O 86	54
Contemporary Crafts	Craft Today: The American Craft Museum (Exhibit)	Sider, Sandra	√		Fa	14	2		M/A 87	54
Contemporary Crafts	"Craft Today the Poetry of the Physical" (Exhibit)		√		TM			7	O/N 86	10
Contemporary Crafts	"Currents"—Trends in Crafts (Exhibit)		√		Fa	13	5		S/O 86	53
Contemporary Crafts	Exhibition by Larsen and Riegger Indicates Broadening Field of Craft Cooperation		√		H&C	2	2		Sp 51	32
Contemporary Crafts	Weaving in the Designer Craftsmen U.S.A. 1953 Exhibition		√		H&C	5	1		Wi 53	22
Contemporary Crafts: South America	South American Crafts		√		H&C	17	2		Sp 66	16
Contemporary Craftsmen: Peru	World Crafts Council, An American Spinner Meets Peruvian Craftsmen	Reade, Dorothy	√		H&C	20	1		Wi 69	8
Contemporary Design	Designers on Design		√		Fa	10	4		J/A 83	28
Contemporary Design	Tiogruppen: When Working Together Works	Talley, Charles	√		Fa	11	6		N/D 84	41
Contemporary Design Trends	Scandinavian Design, Contemporary Trend is Toward Simplicity	Ringler, Aina	√		H&C	18	1		Wi 67	12
Contemporary Fiber	Annie Curtis Chittenden	Chittenden, Annie Curtis	√		Fa	14	5		N/D 87	11
Contemporary Fiber	"Art in Craft Media" (Exhibit)		√		Fa	13	4		J/A 86	58
Contemporary Fiber	"Barbara MacCallum: Recent Work" (Exhibit)	Schedl, Naomi Kark	√		Fa	12	4		J/A 85	68
Contemporary Fiber	Ceremonial Structures of Terry Jarrard Dimond, The	Hyatt, Sharyn; Teresa Mangum	√		Fa	9	4		J/A 82	66
Contemporary Fiber	Claire Campbell Park: Celebrating Color, Light, and Energy	Kerlin, Thomas J.	√		Fa	14	3		M/J 87	15
Contemporary Fiber	Complex Surfaces of Laura Strand Mills, The	Lancaster, Zoë Woodruff	√		Fa	14	2		M/A 87	29
Contemporary Fiber	"Contemporary Directions in Fiber" (Exhibit)	Meloy, Margaret	√		Fa	14	4		S/O 87	42
Contemporary Fiber	Fiber in Minnesota: "Traditions/Transitions II" and "Art in Architecture" (Exhibit)	Stack, Lotus	√		Fa	11	3		M/J 84	80
Contemporary Fiber	"Fiber National '84" (Exhibit)	Bard, Elizabeth A.	√		Fa	12	4		J/A 85	66
Contemporary Fiber	"Fiber National '86" (Exhibit)	Belfer, Nancy	v		Fa	14	1		J/F 87	51
Contemporary Fiber	"Fiber R/Evolution" (Exhibit)		√		TM			4	A/M 86	10
Contemporary Fiber	"Fiber R/Evolution" (Exhibit)	Levine, Betsy			TM			5	J/J 86	16
Contemporary Fiber	"Fine Focus" (Exhibit)	Rice, Nancy Newman	√		Fa	12	2		M/A 85	74
Contemporary Fiber	Grrrhhhh: A Study of Social Patterns	Hickman, Deborah	√		Fa	14	4		S/O 87	23
Contemporary Fiber	Hot Flash Fan, The		√		Fa	12	5		S/O 85	91
Contemporary Fiber	International Invitational (Exhibit)		√		Fa	14	2		M/A 87	58
Contemporary Fiber	"Karen Stoller: Fiber" (Exhibit)	Reese, Ralph Henry	√		Fa	8	1		J/F 81	96

SUBJECT	TITLE	AUTHOR	IL	INST	JOUR	VOL	NO	ISS	DATE	PAGE
Contemporary Fiber	Lee A. Malerich	Malerich, Lee A.	√		Fa	14	1		J/F 87	27
Contemporary Fiber	"Lia Cook: Shaped and Woven Constructions" (Exhibit)	Rowley, Kathleen	√		Fa	12	4		J/A 85	66
Contemporary Fiber	Lin Fife: Products of Passion (error-corrected Fa v12 n1 85 p24)	Fife, Lin	√		Fa	11	5		S/O 84	12
Contemporary Fiber	Linted Palette of Slater Barron, The	Scarborough, Jessica	√		Fa	12	4		J/A 85	42
Contemporary Fiber	"Maine Coast Artists: Fabrications" (Exhibit)	Beem, Edgar Allen	√		Fa	11	4		J/A 84	80
Contemporary Fiber	Mimi Holmes: Treasure Troves of Human Conflict	Lamberson, Peggy	√		Fa	13	6		N/D 86	20
Contemporary Fiber	On the Edge: Harmony Hammond — Collecting, Reclaiming, Connecting	Willard, Janice	√		Fa	9	4		J/A 82	58
Contemporary Fiber	On the Edge: Maureen Connor — Shaping a Response to the Past	Malarcher, Patricia	√		Fa	9	4		J/A 82	61
Contemporary Fiber	Portfolio: Why I Work in Linen, A		√		Fa	14	2		M/A 87	38
Contemporary Fiber	RISD Faculty Show (Exhibit)		√		Fa	13	4		J/A 86	59
Contemporary Fiber	"Space Sails" Soar (Exhibit)	Reid, Eve	√		Fa	13	4		J/A 86	51
Contemporary Fiber	"Tangents: Art in Fiber" (Exhibit)	Krinn, Linda	√		Fa	14	3		M/J 87	55
Contemporary Fiber	"Third Montreal Tapestry Biennial, 1984" (Exhibit)	Duffy, Helen	√		Fa	12	3		M/J 85	79
Contemporary Fiber	Time and Vision: The Work of Cynthia Schira	Janeiro, Jan	√		Fa	9	5		S/O 82	68
Contemporary Fiber	To the Walls: The 13th Lausanne Biennial (Exhibit)	Zepeda, Susan G.	√		Fa	14	4		S/O 87	41
Contemporary Fiber	"Wildlife Physics" (Exhibit)	Kitzman, Betty Lou	√		Fa	12	2		M/A 85	72
Contemporary Knitting	Mary Walker Phillips, Her New Approach to Knitting		√		H&C	16	2		Sp 65	17
Contemporary Textiles	Adela Akers, Designer-Weaver of Chicago		√		H&C	17	2		Sp 66	10
Contemporary Textiles	Art of Unweaving, The		√		Fa	10	6		N/D 83	99
Contemporary Textiles	"California Fibers: 11th Annual Show" (Exhibit)	Kosta, Angela	√		Fa	10	6		N/D 83	81
Contemporary Textiles	Canadian Portfolio, A	Place, Jennifer	√		Fa	9	6		N/D 82	29
Contemporary Textiles	Contemporary Textile Art in Scandinavia	Talley, Charles S.	√		Fa	9	6		N/D 82	43
Contemporary Textiles	Current Canadian Weaving		√		H&C	4	3		Su 53	36
Contemporary Textiles	"Current Directions: Conseie des Arts Textiles du Quebec" (Exhibit)	Newman, Rochelle	√		Fa	12	1		J/F 85	74
Contemporary Textiles	Designer-Craftsmen U.S.A. 1960		√		H&C	11	3		Su 60	18
Contemporary Textiles	Designer-Weaver in India, A	Sethna, Nelly H.	√		H&C	17	2		Sp 66	18
Contemporary Textiles	Designs from a Weaving Teacher's Studio		√		H&C	12	4		Fa 61	22
Contemporary Textiles	Dora Jung, Distinguished Finnish Weaver		√		H&C	10	2		Sp 59	14
Contemporary Textiles	"Fabric and Form: New Textile Art From Britain" (Exhibit)	Waller, Irene	√		Fa	9	6		N/D 82	80
Contemporary Textiles	"Fiber Art: An Uncommon Thread" (Exhibit)	Park, Betty	√		Fa	9	2		M/A 82	78
Contemporary Textiles	Fiber Art in Iceland	Hrafnhildur, Schram	√		Fa	9	6		N/D 82	68
Contemporary Textiles	"Fiber Images" (Exhibit)	Park, Betty	√		Fa	13	2		M/A 86	54
Contemporary Textiles	"Fifth Lodz Triennale, The" (Exhibit)	Ravarra, Patricia	√		Fa	13	3		M/J 86	50
Contemporary Textiles	"Fourth Nordic Textiltriennale" (Exhibit)	Talley, Charles	√		Fa	13	3		M/J 86	51
Contemporary Textiles	"Gail Skudera: Textile Paintings" (Exhibit)	Koplos, Janet	√		Fa	9	6		N/D 82	84
Contemporary Textiles	Great Handcraft Show at Munich				H&C	3	1		Wi 51	40
Contemporary Textiles	Innovations in Indigo	Wada, Yoshiko Iwamoto	√		Fa	13	5		S/O 86	29
Contemporary Textiles	International Textile Exhibition 1950				H&C	2	1		Wi 50	35
Contemporary Textiles	International Textile Exhibition, The	Hardin, Noma			H&C	6	1		Wi 54	28
Contemporary Textiles	International Textile Exhibition, The	Larsen, Jack Lenor	√		H&C	4	1		Wi 52	30
Contemporary Textiles	Lesley Shearer: Creation with Control	Ligon, Linda	√		Iw	2	4		Su 77	10
Contemporary Textiles	Michigan League Conference		√		H&C	11	4		Fa 60	31

SUBJECT	TITLE	AUTHOR	IL	INST	JOUR	VOL	NO	ISS	DATE	PAGE
Contemporary Textiles	Michigan Weaving, Third Conference at Hartland Shows Wide Variety		√	> 4	H&C	13	1		Wi 62	18
Contemporary Textiles	Midwest Conference		√		H&C	18	1		Wi 67	36
Contemporary Textiles	More Textiles Shown in "Good Design" 1951	Brophil, Gladys Rogers			H&C	2	2		Sp 51	38
Contemporary Textiles	New Jersey Weavers Exhibit at the Montclair Museum		√		H&C	7	3		Su 56	44
Contemporary Textiles	North California Conference	Minton, Mary Cain	√		H&C	12	3		Su 61	30
Contemporary Textiles	Northern California Conference	Bryan, Dorothy	√	√	H&C	11	4		Fa 60	26
Contemporary Textiles	Northern California Conference	Minton, Mary Cain	√		H&C	13	3		Su 62	16
Contemporary Textiles	Northern California Handweavers		√		H&C	18	4		Fa 67	25
Contemporary Textiles	Notable Collection of Textiles in Exhibition Sponsored by the Seattle Weavers' Guild		√		H&C	3	1		Wi 51	31
Contemporary Textiles	Out of the Blue: Aerial Images		√		Fa	13	5		S/O 86	44
Contemporary Textiles	"Rose Kelly: Printed, Painted and Woven Textiles" (Exhibit)	Small, Deborah	√		Fa	9	6		N/D 82	84
Contemporary Textiles	"Scandinavian Touch, The" A Traveling Exhibit (Exhibit)	Mattera, Joanna	√		Fa	10	1		J/F 83	82
Contemporary Textiles	Symposium on Contemporary Textile Art	West, Virginia	√		Fa	5	4		J/A 78	18
Contemporary Textiles	Texas Fabrics	Hardt, Blanche	√	√	H&C	8	3		Su 57	31
Contemporary Textiles	Textile Study Group, The (Exhibit)	Guagliumi, Susan	√		Fa	13	3		M/J 86	54
Contemporary Textiles	"Three Weavers: Thomasin Grim, Jane Lackey, Bhakti Ziek" (Exhibit)	Rowley, Kathleen	√		Fa	9	6		N/D 82	82
Contemporary Textiles	Weavers in the Southeast	Adams, Sally	√		H&C	20	2		Sp 69	6
Contemporary Textiles	Weaving in New Brunswick	Currey, Ruth Dunlop	√		H&C	12	1		Wi 61	29
Contemporary Textiles	Weaving in Taiwan, An American Designer's Experience in Free China		√		H&C	13	1		Wi 62	10
Contemporary Textiles	"Weaving with Lucille Landis" (Exhibit)	Hartman, Shirley G.	√		Fa	9	2		M/A 82	76
Contemporary Textiles	"Woven Works: Tradition and Innovation" (Exhibit)	White, Patrick E.	√		Fa	12	6		N/D 85	60
Contemporary Textiles: Asia	Some Contemporary Textiles in Southern Asia	Hatch, David P.	√	√	H&C	11	3		Su 60	23
Contemporary Textiles: Crete	Weaving in Crete	Znamierowski, Nell	√		H&C	15	4		Fa 64	8
Contemporary Textiles: Denmark	Modern Danish Textiles	Bryan, Dorothy	√		H&C	9	2		Sp 58	40
Contemporary Textiles: Europe	Weaving Abroad	Huebner, Marianne A.	√		H&C	21	3		Su 70	10
Contemporary Textiles: Finland	Summer with Finnish Weavers, A	Schobinger, Helen J.	√		H&C	3	2		Sp 52	12
Contemporary Textiles: Greece	Weavers in Greece	Tod, Osma Gallinger	√		H&C	19	2		Sp 68	21
Contemporary Textiles: Navajo	Navajo Weaving, Contemporary and Traditional		√		H&C	18	2		Sp 67	6
Contemporary Textiles: New Mexico	Blankets of New Mexico	Kozikowski, Janusz	√		SS&D	10	1	37	Wi 78	60
Contemporary Textiles: Rug, Handcrafted, American	American Handcrafted Rug: Past and Present, The	Stevens, Rebecca A. T.	√		TMJ	23			84	73
Contemporary Textiles: Sardinia	Design Award to Isabel Scott Fabrics for Exclusive Sardinian Import		√		H&C	13	2		Sp 62	16
Contemporary Textiles: Sardinia	Sardinian Debut, Colorful Tapestries and Rugs Interest American Weavers	Balkin, Emanuel	√		H&C	13	1		Wi 62	21
Contemporary Textiles: Sweden	Summer Study in Sweden	Schobinger, Helen J.	√		H&C	9	3		Su 58	24
Contemporary Textiles: Sweden	Swedish Textile Art Today	Widman, Dag	√		H&C	24	1		J/F 73	32
Contemporary Textiles, Sweden	Swedish Textiles Today: A Rich Tradition, A Supportive Society	Talley, Charles S.	√		Fa	8	2		M/A 81	42
Contemporary Textiles, Sweden	Well-Worn Path to Where? A View of Contemporary Swedish Textiles, The	Talley, Charles S.	√		Fa	8	2		M/A 81	44
Contemporary Weaving	Summer and Winter and Other Two-Tie Unit Weaves: Methods for Weaving Two-Tie Units, Contemporary Treatments	Tidball, Harriet	√	√	SCGM		19		66	48
Contemporary Weaving: Australia	Weaving Down Under	McKay, Isabel	√		H&C	15	3		Su 64	20
Contemporary Weaving: Denmark	Contemporary Danish Weaving		√	√	Hw	8	3		M/J 87	46
Contemporary Weaving: Finland	Contemporary Finnish Weaving		√		Hw	8	3		M/J 87	70

SUBJECT	TITLE	AUTHOR	IL	INST	JOUR	VOL	NO	ISS	DATE	PAGE
Contemporary Weaving: Iceland	Contemporary Icelandic Weaving		√		Hw	8	3		M/J 87	63
Contemporary Weaving: Norway	Contemporary Norwegian Weaving		√		Hw	8	3		M/J 87	54
Contemporary Weaving: Sweden	Contemporary Swedish Weaving		√		Hw	8	3		M/J 87	35
Contemporary Weaving: Sweden	From Hand to Hand: Swedish Weaving Today	Krondahl, Hans	√		Hw	8	3		M/J 87	34
Contest also see Competitions										
Contest Winners	"Design's n You" Contest Winners	Scorgie, Jean	√		Hw	8	4		S/O 87	31
Contest Winners	First Prize for the Holders of Hot Pots Show	Champion, Ellen	√	√	WJ	2	4	8	Ap 78	41
Contest Winners	Teachers of the Year, 1986		√		Hw	8	1		J/F 87	14
Contest Winners	Winning Woven Winter Warmers		√	> 4	Hw	7	1		J/F 86	32
Contest Winners: Vests, Handspun	Spin–Off Book of World Records		√		S-O	11	3		Fa 87	15
Contest Winners: Weaving	Handwoven "Teach a Friend to Weave" Contest, The		√		Hw	2	2		Mr 81	42
Controversies: Art/Craft	A Weaver Ponders His Craft Collection of Controversial Essays: Art or Craft	Zielinski, S. A.; Robert Leclerc, ed.			MWL	21 22			'51–'73	17
Controversies: Art/Craft	Artist Craftsman!	Bennett, Paul			H&C	24	3		M/J 73	22
Controversies: Craft/Business	A Weaver Ponders His Craft Collection of Controversial Essays: Craft or Business	Zielinski, S. A.; Robert Leclerc, ed.			MWL	21 22			'51–'73	13
Controversies: Textile Industry, Management/Labor	Technical Progress and the Evolution of Wage Arrangements in the British Cotton Weaving Industry	Jackson, K. C.; B. Pourdeyhimi	√		AT	7			Ju 87	61
Convergence see HGA										
Conversion Table: Block Weaves	Composition and Designing Part 2: Transcribing	Zielinski, S. A.; Robert Leclerc, ed.	√	> 4	MWL	19			'51–'73	50
Cooperative Workshops	Tiogruppen: When Working Together Works	Talley, Charles	√		Fa	11	6		N/D 84	41
Cooperatives/Collectives	Action in Appalachia: A Community Craft Center Bustles	Flanagan, Jane	√		SS&D	7	3	27	Su 76	96
Cooperatives/Collectives	Arachne's Children	Koster, Joan Bouza	√	√	SS&D	9	3	35	Su 78	16
Cooperatives/Collectives	Arrowcraft: Tennessee Cottage Industry	Pilsk, Adele	√		Fa	5	5		S/O 78	20
Cooperatives/Collectives	Fiber Ten	McGuire, Patricia	√		Fa	4	6		N/D 77	26
Cooperatives/Collectives	From the Great Smokies to Rockefeller Center-The Southern Highland Handicraft Guild	Hart, Robert G.	√		H&C	2	3		Su 51	5
Cooperatives/Collectives	If the Art Fits – Wear It! — Friends of the Rag	Strosnider, Ann	√		Fa	6	3		M/J 79	35
Cooperatives/Collectives	Indigenous Weft-Faced Garments of Peru	Noble, Carol Rasmussen	√		SS&D	13	3	51	Su 82	44
Cooperatives/Collectives	Interview with Linda Berry Walker...A Spinning and Dyeing Business, An	Horton, Lucy	√		Fa	4	5		S/O 77	26
Cooperatives/Collectives	Noble Tradition Preserved: An Ecuadorian Weaving Co-op, A	Llewellyn, Charles; Deborah Llewellyn	√		SS&D	11	3	43	Su 80	12
Cooperatives/Collectives	Print and Dye Works	Goldberg, Barbara; Antoinette Minichiello-Winters	√		Fa	9	3		M/J 82	25
Cooperatives/Collectives	Weaving in Donegal (error-corrected H&C v23 n3 72 p11)	McNeill, Mary	√	√	H&C	23	2		M/A 72	35
Cooperatives/Collectives	Weaving in the Austrian Tyrol		√		H&C	7	1		Wi 55	28
Cooperatives/Collectives: Afghan Crafts	Aid to Artisans	Cox-Chapman, Mally	√		TM			13	O/N 87	14
Cooperatives/Collectives: Crafts	Confluence: A Gallery	Ligon, Linda	√		Iw	2	3		Sp 77	10
Cooperatives/Collectives: Crafts	Tying Up with Others		√		H&C	26	5		Oc 75	20
Cooperatives/Collectives: Spinning	Tierra Wools Cooperative	Brown, Rachel	√	√	SS&D	18	2	70	Sp 87	62
Cooperatives/Collectives: Spinning	Vermont's Green Mountain Spinnery	Levinson, Nan	√		TM			7	O/N 86	61
Cooperatives/Collectives: Spinning Mohair	Spinning Mohair in Lesotho	Snieckus, Mary Ann	√		TM			8	D/J 86	66
Cooperatives/Collectives: Tapestry	Twelve Part Harmony: Taos Tapestry Collective		√		WJ	12	1	45	Su 87	48

SUBJECT	TITLE	AUTHOR	IL	INST	JOUR	VOL	NO	ISS	DATE	PAGE
Cooperatives/Collectives: Weaving	Albuquerque Group Proves: Co-Ops Can Work	Ligon, Linda	√		Iw	1	1		Fa 75	8
Cooperatives/Collectives: Weaving	Ramah Navajo Weavers, The	D'Andrea, Pat	√		WJ	12	1	45	Su 87	44
Cooperatives/Collectives: Weaving	Tierra Wools Cooperative	Brown, Rachel	√	√	SS&D	18	2	70	Sp 87	62
Coptic Tapestries: Monochromatic	Tapestries of Coptic Egypt, The	Hoskins, Nancy Arthur	√		AT	6			De 86	211
Coptic Tapestries: Polychromatic	Tapestries of Coptic Egypt, The	Hoskins, Nancy Arthur	√		AT	6			De 86	211
Coptic Textiles	Coptic Tapestry of Byzantine Style, A	Berliner, Rudolf	√		TMJ	1	1		No 62	3
Coptic Textiles	Coptic Textiles: The Art of the Ancient Weaver	Constantinides, Kathy	√		Fa	7	6		N/D 80	19
Coptic Textiles	"Roman Heritage: Textiles from Egypt and the Eastern Mediterranean, 300–600 A.D., The" (Exhibit)		√		Fa	9	4		J/A 82	32
Coptic Textiles	Roman Heritage, The	Angelil, Muriel	√		SS&D	13	3	51	Su 82	69
Coptic Textiles	Rugs Woven on Summer and Winter Threading		√	> 4	WJ	3	1	9	Jy 78	12
Coptic Textiles	Tapestries of Coptic Egypt, The	Hoskins, Nancy Arthur	√		AT	6			De 86	211
Coptic Textiles	Tapestry Roundel with Nilotic Scenes, A	Abdel-Malek, Laila	√		TMJ	25			86	33
Coptic Textiles	Tapestry: Technique and Tradition	Scott, Gail R.	√		H&C	22	3		Su 71	16
Coptic Textiles: Design Categories	Textiles of Coptic Egypt	Hoskins, Nancy Arthur	√	√	WJ	12	1	45	Su 87	58
Copyright Laws	Copyright	LaLena, Constance		√	Hw	4	3		M/J 83	69
Copyright Laws	Copyright Law and You, The	Malouff, Raye	√		Fa	4	6		N/D 77	53
Cord Weaves	Cord Weaves, The	Marston, Ena	√	√	SS&D	5	4	20	Fa 74	34
Cord Weaves	Corded Weaves — Four Harness Cross Cords		√	> 4	WJ	4	1	13	Jy 79	25
Cord Weaves	Horizontal Ribs & Vertical Cords	Moes, Dini	√	√	SS&D	17	4	68	Fa 86	84
Cord Weaves	Jacket in Horizontal Cord Weave, A	Duncan, Nadine	√	√	PWC			2	Ap 82	59
Cord Weaves	Plaid Idea Notebook		√	√	Hw	4	5		N/D 83	41
Cord Weaves, Bedford	More Cord Weaves	Marston, Ena	√	> 4	SS&D	6	3	23	Su 75	78
Cord Weaves, Longitudinal	Corded Weaves: Four Harness Cords for Upholstery Fabric, Drapery Material and Wallhangings		√	√	WJ	3	1	9	Jy 78	28
Cord Weaves: Self-Stuffing Weft	Self-Stuffing Weft Cord Double Weave	Towner, Naomi Whiting	√	> 4	AT	3			My 85	47
Cords and Ropes	Freestyle Embroidery: New Images with Traditional Stitches	Dahl, Caroline	√	√	TM			1	O/N 85	22
Cords and Ropes	Hot-Air Balloons	Theil, Linda	√		TM			4	A/M 86	20
Cords and Ropes	Making a Round Cord	Leavitt, Jean	√	√	TM			1	O/N 85	6
Cords and Ropes	Quick Cordmaker		√	√	TM			6	A/S 86	12
Cords and Ropes	Ropes for Every Use	Piroch, Sigrid	√	√	Hw	7	4		S/O 86	14
Cords and Ropes: Knitted	Sampler of Knit Edgings and Applied Trims, A	Newton, Deborah	√	√	TM			12	A/S 87	38
Corduroy	New Method for Pile Weave, A	Deru, Crescent	√	> 4	H&C	8	3		Su 57	16
Corduroy	Pile Weaves, Rugs and Tapestry: Colours in Corduroy	Zielinski, S. A.; Robert Leclerc, ed.	√	√	MWL	14			'51–'73	16
Corduroy	Pile Weaves, Rugs and Tapestry: Corduroy	Zielinski, S. A.; Robert Leclerc, ed.	√	√	MWL	14			'51–'73	7
Corduroy, Color-Pattern	Amazing Color-Pattern Corduroy Rug		√	> 4	PWC	3	4	10		22
Corduroy, Diagonal	Diagonal Corduroy	Xenakis, Athanasios David	√	> 4	PWC	3	4	10		51
Corduroy, Variations	Corduroy: An Account of Discovery	Alderman, Sharon D.	√	> 4	Hw	4	4		S/O 83	54
Corduroy, Wool	Corduroy: An Account of Discovery	Alderman, Sharon D.	√	> 4	Hw	4	4		S/O 83	54
Cordwainers	Old Shoes Keeping Honourable Company	Clausen, Valerie	√		TM			11	J/J 87	16
Coronet: Knitted	Coronet, A	Clayton, Clare	√	√	Kn	3	2	6	Sp 87	32
Costume also see Apparel, Clothing, Costume										
Costume	Annie Hickman: Populating an Insect World	Hempel, Toby Anne	√		Fa	14	3		M/J 87	32

SUBJECT	TITLE	AUTHOR	IL	INST	JOUR	VOL	NO	ISS	DATE	PAGE
Costume	Backstage at the Miss Universe Pageant	Loper, Bobby Ann	√		Fa	13	3		M/J 86	12
Costume	Costumes Through the Ages Stamp Collecting Kit	Smeltzer, Nancy	√		Fa	13	3		M/J 86	29
Costume	Costuming for Rock Music Videos	Pierce, Judith	√		Fa	14	3		M/J 87	51
Costume	Creative Process: Katherine Westphal, The	Westphal, Katherine	√		Fa	11	6		N/D 84	32
Costume	Debra Minsky-Jackson: Renaissance Visions in Fiber	Grunberg, Liane	√		Fa	11	4		J/A 84	68
Costume	Everyday World of Fantasy, The	Smeltzer, Nancy	√		Fa	13	3		M/J 86	6
Costume	Fabric of Sha Sha Higby's Imagination, The	Wheater, Kathleen	√		Fa	14	3		M/J 87	35
Costume	"Felt and Papermaking" (Exhibit)	Harrison, Helen A.	√		Fa	11	2		M/A 84	79
Costume	Gilbert Adrian: Creating the Hollywood Dream Style	Kinsey, Susan Buchanan	√		Fa	14	3		M/J 87	49
Costume	Liturgical Vestment: A Contemporary Overview, The	Malarcher, Patricia	√		Fa	11	5		S/O 84	58
Costume	Mummery: Philadelphia's Happy New Year	Smeltzer, Nancy	√		Fa	14	3		M/J 87	39
Costume	"Silken Threads and Silent Needles" (Exhibit)	Dunnewold, Jane	√		Fa	11	6		N/D 84	78
Costume	Theme Issue		√		Fa	11	5		S/O 84	
Costume	"Vanity Fair: A Treasure Trove from the Costume Institute" (Exhibit)	Park, Betty	√		Fa	5	3		M/J 78	15
Costume, 18th Century	Costume from the Adams Period, A	di Franco, Toni Lee	√	√	SS&D	8	1	29	WI 76	43
Costume, Children's	Handwoven Holloween, A	Palmer, Krissa Elaine	√		Hw	4	4		S/O 83	32
Costume, Circus: Home-Sewn	Greatest Sew on Earth, The	Rogers, Georgia M.	√		TM			11	J/J 87	38
Costume, Contemporary	Altered Ego: An Interview with Pat Oleszko	Lonier, Terri	√		Fa	10	1		J/F 83	26
Costume, Contemporary	Contemporary California Costume	Poon, Vivian	√		Fa	11	5		S/O 84	53
Costume, Contemporary	Conversation with Costumer Susan Nininger, A	Lonier, Terri	√		Fa	10	6		N/D 83	63
Costume, Contemporary	Conversing with Artist John Eric Broaddus	Stackel, I. M.	√		Fa	11	5		S/O 84	28
Costume, Contemporary	Costume in the Streets of New York: A Photo Essay	Gardner, George	√		Fa	11	5		S/O 84	42
Costume, Contemporary	Garment Form As Image, The	Koplos, Janet	√		Fa	10	6		N/D 83	66
Costume, Contemporary	Masks At the Heart of Disguise	Koplos, Janet	√		Fa	11	5		S/O 84	32
Costume, Contemporary	Teresa Nomura: Fabric and Fantasy	Sage, Jan	√		Fa	11	5		S/O 84	20
Costume, Dance	Bit of Rope Turns Cloth Into a Dancer's Costume, A	Grace, Leslie	√		TM			10	A/M 87	20
Costume, Dance	Costume for Dance: The Living Sculpture of Carleigh Hoff	Parshall, Priscilla	√		Fa	8	1		J/F 81	28
Costume, Dance	Leanne Mahoney: Costuming for Ballet	Tejeda, Christina	√		Fa	11	5		S/O 84	64
Costume, Dance	Patricia Bulitt: Gutsongs and Other Dances	Scarborough, Jessica	√		Fa	11	5		S/O 84	50
Costume, Dance	Whence the Tutu?	Austin, Carole	√		Fa	11	5		S/O 84	46
Costume, Design	One-of-a-Kind Garment in Beiderwand, A	Alvic, Philis	√		WJ	9	1	33	Su 84	51
Costume, France	"Splendor of French Style, The" Textiles from Joan of Arc to Napoleon III (Exhibit)	Guagliumi, Susan	√		Fa	13	4		J/A 86	13
Costume, Metal/Fiber	Mary Sue Kern: Embodied Dualities	Logiudice, JoEL	√		Fa	13	5		S/O 86	26
Costume, Miniature	Costumes on a Small Scale	Caldwell, Rebecca	√		Fa	11	5		S/O 84	87
Costume, Opera	Jill Lindgren: Costuming for Opera	Elliott, Malinda	√		Fa	11	5		S/O 84	62
Costume, Resources	Advisers Guide to Costume Resources, An (error-corrected Fa v12 n1 85 p24)	Caldwell, Rebecca			Fa	11	5		S/O 84	48
Costume, Resources	Advisers Guide to Costume Resources, An (error-corrected Fa v12 n1 85 p24)	Caldwell, Rebecca			Fa	11	5		S/O 84	48
Costume, Style Evolution	Clothing Change Through Contact: Traditional Guatemalan Dress	Fisher, Abby Sue	√		WJ	10	3	39	Wi 86	60
Costume, Theater	Contemporary California Costume	Poon, Vivian	√		Fa	11	5		S/O 84	53

SUBJECT	TITLE	AUTHOR	IL	INST	JOUR	VOL	NO	ISS	DATE	PAGE
Costume, Theater	Jeannie Davidson: Costuming for Shakespearean Theater	Rowley, Kathleen	√		Fa	11	5		S/O 84	66
Costume Traditions: China	"Silk as Ceremony: The Dress of China in the Late Ch'ing Dynasty Period (1759–1911)" (Exhibit)	Mattera, Joanne	√		Fa	8	3		M/J 81	75
Costume Traditions: China, Ming Dynasty	Chinese Textile in Seventeenth Century Spain, A	Cammann, Schuyler	√		TMJ	1	4		De 65	57
Costume Traditions: Colonial America	Making Clothes in Colonial Style	Morris, Gitta	√		TM			6	A/S 86	20
Costume Traditions: Ecuador	Costume and Weaving in Saraguro, Ecuador	Meisch, Lynn Ann	√		TMJ	19 20			80,81	55
Costume Traditions: Europe, Prehistoric	Historical Components of Regional Costume in South-Eastern Europe, The	Gervers, Veronika	√		TMJ	4	2		75	61
Costume Traditions: Europe, Western	Historical Components of Regional Costume in South-Eastern Europe, The	Gervers, Veronika	√		TMJ	4	2		75	61
Costume Traditions: Greece	Decorative Techniques of the Sarakatsani	Smith, Joyce	√	√	WJ	9	1	33	Su 84	14
Costume Traditions: Greece	Greek Chemises: Cut and Construction	Welters, Linda	√	√	WJ	10	1	37	Su 85	40
Costume Traditions: Guatemala	Clothing Change Through Contact: Traditional Guatemalan Dress	Fisher, Abby Sue	√		WJ	10	3	39	Wi 86	60
Costume Traditions: Ikat-Dyed, Japan	Kasuri: A Japanese Textile	Dusenbury, Mary	√		TMJ	17			78	41
Costume Traditions: India	"Costumes of Royal India, The" (Exhibit)	McCann, Kathleen	√		Fa	13	1		J/F 86	58
Costume Traditions: India	Meaning of Folk Art in Rabari Life: A Closer Look at Mirrored Embroidery, The	Frater, Judy	√		TMJ	4	2		75	47
Costume Traditions: Japan	Obi: The Textile Art of Nishijin	Donaldson, R. Alan	√		AT	1			De 83	115
Costume Traditions: Latvia	Latvian Folk Costume Braids	Gulbis, Elina	√	√	SS&D	4	3	15	Su 73	46
Costume Traditions: Mollie Costume, 18th Century	Eighteenth Century Mollie Costume	Spray, Kathy	√		WJ	6	3	23	Wi 81	38
Costume Traditions: Native Americans	Costumes Highlight Texas Conference		√		SS&D	3	4	12	Fa 72	24
Costume Traditions: Norway	Card Woven Belt of East Telemark—An Adaptation of a Traditional Norwegian Technique	Nelson, Lila	√	√	WJ	9	1	33	Su 84	30
Costume Traditions: Ottoman Turkey	Historical Components of Regional Costume in South-Eastern Europe, The	Gervers, Veronika	√		TMJ	4	2		75	61
Costume Traditions: Palestine	Seen Around the Country: Palestinian Costume Exhibit in New Mexico	Ulrich, Kenn	√		SS&D	9	4	36	Fa 78	84
Costume Traditions: Peru	Indigenous Weft-Faced Garments of Peru	Noble, Carol Rasmussen	√		SS&D	13	3	51	Su 82	44
Costume Traditions: Peru	Technical Features of a Middle Horizon Tapestry Shirt from Peru, The	Bird, Junius B.; Milica Dimitrijevic Skinner	√		TMJ	4	1		De 74	5
Costume Traditions: Peru	Technical Features of Inca Tapestry Tunics	Rowe, Ann Pollard	√		TMJ	17			78	5
Costume Traditions: Rome and Byzantium	Historical Components of Regional Costume in South-Eastern Europe, The	Gervers, Veronika	√		TMJ	4	2		75	61
Costume Traditions: Russia	Russian Costumes At The Metropolitan Museum		√		SS&D	8	3	31	Su 77	88
Costume Traditions: Southeast Asia	Dress and Design in Highland Southeast Asia: The Hmong (Miao) and the Yao	Adams, Monni	√		TMJ	4	1		De 74	51
Costume Traditions: The Steppes	Historical Components of Regional Costume in South-Eastern Europe, The	Gervers, Veronika	√		TMJ	4	2		75	61
Cottage Industries	Bhotiya Woolens from India	Willis, Elizabeth Bayley	√		H&C	5	2		Sp 54	4
Cottage Industries	Convergence '86 Preview: Pangnirtung Weavers	Stuart, Donald	√		SS&D	16	4	64	Fa 85	70
Cottage Industries	Exploring a Knitted Pattern	Bruzelius, Margaret	√	√	TM			6	A/S 86	35
Cottage Industries	Knitting for a Living (error-corrected TM i6 A/S86 p6)	Guagliumi, Susan	√		TM			4	A/M 86	38
Cottage Industries	Nantucket Looms and Sam Kasten	Erickson, Johanna	√		SS&D	17	3	67	Su 86	70
Cottage Industries	New Philippine Textiles	Gele, Emilé	√		H&C	5	3		Su 54	14
Cottage Industries	Robozos of Tenancingo	Hewitt, T. H.	√	√	H&C	8	3		Su 57	19
Cottage Industries	Silks from Siam	Woodward, Carol H.	√		H&C	2	3		Su 51	23
Cottage Industries	Story of the Johnson Rugs, The	Gallinger, Osma Couch	√		H&C	7	2		Sp 56	28

SUBJECT	TITLE	AUTHOR	IL	INST	JOUR	VOL	NO	ISS	DATE	PAGE
Cottage Industries	Time Warp on the Coldstream	McIntyre, Walter	√		SS&D	15	4	60	Fa 84	50
Cottage Industries	Traditional Felt Rugmaking in Turkey	Ispay, Francis	√	√	Fa	13	4		J/A 86	18
Cottage Industries	Weavers of Bali	Hannon, Farrell	√		SS&D	18	4	72	Fa 87	46
Cottage Industries	Wool on a Small Scale: A Large Success	de la Cruz, Catherine Jacinta			S-O	9	4		Wi 85	21
Cottage Industries	Yuki Tsumugi	Urbanek, Karen	√	√	S-O	10	1		Sp 86	42
Cottage Industries: Bandhani (Tie Dye)	Bandhani (Tie Dye)	Westfall, Carol D.; Dipti Desai	√		AT	8			De 87	19
Cottage Industries: Batik, Java	Batik Making and the Royal Javanese Cemetery at Imogiri	Joseph, Rebecca M.	√		TMJ	24			85	83
Cottage Industries: Carpets, Anatolian	Carpet-Makers of Western Anatolia, 1750–1914, The	Quataert, Donald			TMJ	25			86	25
Cottage Industries: Embroidery	Gujarati Embroidery	Westfall, Carol D.; Dipti Desai	√		AT	8			De 87	29
Cottage Industries: Fiber Production	Precious Fibers Congress	Marcus, Ruth-Claire			TM			13	O/N 87	18
Cottage Industries: Goat-to-Garment	Ontario Mohair Company, The	Schaffernicht, Elisabeth	√		S-O	7	3		Fa 83	26
Cottage Industries: Knitting	Arctic Handknitted, One Hundred Per Cent Qiviut	Griffiths, Helen M.	√		H&C	22	2		Sp 71	6
Cottage Industries: Navajo Weaving	Contemporary Navajo Weaving	Hedlund, Ann Lane	√		WJ	11	1	41	Su 86	30
Cottage Industries: Spinning	Allen Farm Sheep and Wool Company	Erickson, Johanna	√		SS&D	17	3	67	Su 86	25
Cottage Industries: Spinning	Spinning Mohair in Lesotho	Snieckus, Mary Ann	√		TM			8	D/J 86	66
Cottage Industries: Textiles	Warping it Up with Andrea	Duffy, Joe	√		SS&D	17	1	65	Wi 85	49
Cottage Industries: Weaving	Arrowcraft: Tennessee Cottage Industry	Pilsk, Adele	√		Fa	5	5		S/O 78	20
Cottage Industries: Weaving	Berea College Fireside Industries Now Employ Sixty Weavers	Stahl, Sam	√		H&C	19	2		Sp 68	5
Cottage Industries: Weaving	Chimayó—A Town of Weavers	Trujillo, Lisa Rockwood	√		WJ	11	1	41	Su 86	60
Cottage Industries: Weaving	Elliot Weavers of Dublin	Burow, Nellie B.			SS&D	1	1	1	De 69	16
Cottage Industries: Weaving	Journey Through Greece, Two Americans in Search of Native Weaving	Znamierowski, Nell	√		H&C	14	2		Sp 63	8
Cottage Industries: Weaving	Keeping Tradition Alive	Wilcox, Don	√		Fa	14	1		J/F 87	44
Cottage Industries: Weaving	Los Tejedorcitos De San Isidro		√		SS&D	6	1	21	Wi 74	80
Cottage Industries: Weaving	Ossie Phillips: A Tradition of Mountain Weaving	Sheward, Cynthia M.	√		Fa	14	2		M/A 87	25
Cottage Industries: Weaving	Sixty Years of Weaving At Arrowmont	Johnson, Debbie	√		Fa	12	5		S/O 85	39
Cottage Industries: Weaving	Textile Arts of Multan, Pakistan	Shahzaman, Mahboob	√	> 4	SS&D	4	3	15	Su 73	8
Cottage Industries: Weaving	Tweed Weavers of Glenmore, The	Burkhauser, Jude	√		Hw	3	3		My 82	56
Cottage Industries: Weaving	Valhalla Weavers of North Carolina, The		√		H&C	4	2		Sp 53	48
Cottage Industries: Weaving	Vestments from the KilBride Workshop		√		H&C	15	3		Su 64	12
Cottage Industries: Weaving, Ireland	Irish Weaving	Clement, Doris; Ted Clement	√		H&C	21	2		Sp 70	4
Cottage Industries: Wool	Wool as a Cottage Industry	Simmons, Paula	√		S-O	9	2		Su 85	42
Cotton	Before Heddles Were Invented	Bird, Junius B.	√		H&C	3	3		Su 52	5
Cotton	China and the Complexities of Weaving Technologies	Vollmer, John E.			AT	5			Ju 86	65
Cotton	Cotton		√		WJ	11	2	42	Fa 86	9
Cotton	Cotton		√		WJ	4	2	14	Oc 79	4
Cotton	Cotton, Cool and Comfy	Gibson-Roberts, Priscilla A.	√	√	Kn	3	2	6	Sp 87	48
Cotton	Cotton Glossary	Schmoller, Irene Laughing Cloud			WJ	11	2	42	Fa 86	13
Cotton	Cotton in the Natural Dyepot	Baker, Ella	√	√	S-O	9	3		Fa 85	29
Cotton	Cotton: Legacy of Gods & Kings	Schmoller, Irene Laughing Cloud	√		WJ	11	2	42	Fa 86	11
Cotton	Cotton Plays a Vital Role	Hausner, Walter	√		H&C	3	3		Su 52	8
Cotton	Cotton: What Should You Ask For?	Linder, Olive			S-O	8	3		Fa 84	36

SUBJECT	TITLE	AUTHOR	IL	INST	JOUR	VOL	NO	ISS	DATE	PAGE
Cotton	Discover Cotton Spinning	Ajeman, Norma; Irene Laughing Cloud Schmoller	√	√	WJ	8	3	31	Wi 83	49
Cotton	Fiber Foray: Ginned Cotton	Quinn, Celia	√	√	S-O	9	2		Su 85	26
Cotton	Inspiration for New Designs in Cotton	Hausner, Walter	√		H&C	3	4		Fa 52	23
Cotton	King Cotton Is Back	Linder, Olive; Harry Linder	√		SS&D	5	2	18	Sp 74	65
Cotton	Making Sense of Interfacing (error-corrected TM n12 p4)	Komives, Margaret Deck	√	√	TM			10	A/M 87	58
Cotton	Mercerizing: Not for Everyone	Amos, Alden	√		S-O	9	2		Su 85	30
Cotton	My Affair with King Cotton	Franklin, Sue	√	√	TM			9	F/M 87	39
Cotton	Quinn's Spinning Notes	Quinn, Cecelia			S-O	5			81	55
Cotton	Spinning Cotton with the Linders	Linder, Olive; Harry Linder	√	√	WJ	11	2	42	Fa 86	14
Cotton	Theme Issue		√		WJ	11	2	42	Fa 86	
Cotton	Understanding Cotton Fiber & Yarns	Ayotte, Robert; Roberta Ayotte	√		WJ	11	2	42	Fa 86	27
Cotton	Vegetable Lamb of Tartary, The	Ligon, Linda	√		lw	1	4		Su 76	9
Cotton	Yarns and Fibers: Cotton	Zielinski, S. A.; Robert Leclerc, ed.			MWL	4			'51–'73	26
Cotton: Breeding	In Search of Colored Cotton	Fox, Sally	√	√	S-O	11	4		Wi 87	48
Cotton: Breeding	Naturally Colored Cottons	Fox, Sally	√		S-O	11	1		Sp 87	29
Cotton: Brown	Acadian Brown Cotton	Exner, Beatrice B.	√		H&C	11	4		Fa 60	22
Cotton, Brown	Acadian Cotton Spinning	Schiller, Elaine Z.	√	√	SS&D	5	3	19	Su 74	75
Cotton: Brown	Cotton of a Different Color	Campbell, John; Susan Campbell		√	WJ	4	2	14	Oc 79	20
Cotton, Brown	Discover Cotton Spinning	Ajeman, Norma; Irene Laughing Cloud Schmoller	√	√	WJ	8	3	31	Wi 83	49
Cotton: Brown Acadian	L'Amour de Maman: The Acadian Textile Heritage	Rossetter, Tabitha Wilson	√		Fa	8	3		M/J 81	29
Cotton: Characteristics	Finishing Handspun Cotton	Linder, Harry	√	√	S-O	2			78	30
Cotton: Colonial America	Fleecing of the American Colonies, The	Liebler, Barbara	√		lw	2	1		Fa 76	21
Cotton: Colored	In Search of Colored Cotton	Fox, Sally	√	√	S-O	11	4		Wi 87	48
Cotton: Colored	Naturally Colored Cottons	Fox, Sally	√		S-O	11	1		Sp 87	29
Cotton: Downproof, Source	Downproof Cotton			√	TM			10	A/M 87	8
Cotton: Ginning	In Search of Colored Cotton	Fox, Sally	√	√	S-O	11	4		Wi 87	48
Cotton: Growing Restrictions	Naturally Colored Cottons	Fox, Sally	√		S-O	11	1		Sp 87	29
Cotton: Origin Countries	Naturally Colored Cottons	Fox, Sally	√		S-O	11	1		Sp 87	29
Cotton: Qualities	Knitting with Cotton: Stitch Maneuvers Help Sweaters Stay in Shape	Dyett, Linda	√	√	TM			9	F/M 87	38
Cotton: Spun/Unspun	Cotton: An Invitation	Hagan, Kathleen	√		WJ	4	2	14	Oc 79	12
Cotton: Wild Species	Naturally Colored Cottons	Fox, Sally	√		S-O	11	1		Sp 87	29
Counterchange	Counterchange	Wertenberger, Kathryn	√	√	Hw	7	2		M/A 86	75
Counterchange	Counterchange, A Device for Pattern Design	Justema, William	√		H&C	19	3		Su 68	8
Counterchange	Counterchange & New Color	Sonday, Milton	√		H&C	20	3		Su 69	23
Counters, Yardage	How to Warp with a Paddle—Beam Without Paper, Part 1	Landis, Lucille	√	√	SS&D	16	1	61	Wi 84	72
Counters, Yardage	Warp Yardage Counters		√		SS&D	16	1	61	Wi 84	72
Courses see Education										
Coverlet see Bed Coverings										
Coverlet Traditions: Illinois	History Lives on at Bishop Hill	Rohrer, Marge	√		lw	4	3		Su 79	43
Coverlet Traditions: Kentucky	Coverlet Tradition in Kentucky, The	Guy, Sallie T.	√		lw	4	3		Su 79	35
Coverlet Traditions: Lancaster County, Pa.	Weaving Drafts and Diaper Twills in Lancaster County	Crosson, Janet Gray	√	> 4	lw	4	3		Su 79	40
Coverlet Traditions: North Carolina	Jane Cox: Her Draft for Counterpins	Pinchin, C. B.	√	√	lw	4	3		Su 79	31

SUBJECT	TITLE	AUTHOR	IL	INST	JOUR	VOL	NO	ISS	DATE	PAGE
Coverlet Traditions: Tennessee	Coverlets	Wilson, Sadye Tune; Doris Finch Kennedy	√		SS&D	14	4	56	Fa 83	34
Coverlet Weavers	Coverlet Tradition in Kentucky, The	Guy, Sallie T.	√		lw	4	3		Su 79	35
Coverlet Weavers: Indiana, 19th Century	Art of Indiana Coverlets, The	Gilfoy, Peggy S.	√		AT	2			De 84	69
Coverlet Weavers: Maryland, 19th Century	Artifacts Don't "Lie"	Anderson, Clarita	√		AT	7			Ju 87	9
Coverlet Weavers: Ohio, 19th Century	Ohio's Woven Coverlets: Textile Industry in a Rural Economy	Cunningham, Patricia A.	√		AT	2			De 84	165
Coverlet Weavers: Welty, John B.	Artifacts Don't "Lie"	Anderson, Clarita	√		AT	7			Ju 87	9
Coverlet Weaving: 19th Century	Doubleweave: A Popular Technique of the 19th Century Coverlet Weaver	Colwell, Ken	√	> 4	PWC			2	Ap 82	53
Coverlet Weaving: Loom Types Used	Doubleweave: A Popular Technique of the 19th Century Coverlet Weaver	Colwell, Ken	√	> 4	PWC			2	Ap 82	53
Cow Hair	Immigrant Memories	Butcher-Younghans, Sherry	√		WJ	9	4	36	Sp 85	44
Cowls	How Madame Grès Sculpts with Fabric	Cooper, Arlene	√	√	TM			10	A/M 87	50
Crabbing	Tracking, the Mystery of the Crinkling Cloth	Alderman, Sharon	√	√	Hw	6	4		S/O 85	31
Crackle, Quasi-	Unharnessing the Summer and Winter Weave	Xenakis, Athanasios David	√		lw	4	4		Fa 79	42
Crackle Weave	Church Paraments in Crackle Weave	Murphy, Mathilda C.	√	> 4	SS&D	5	3	19	Su 74	54
Crackle Weave	Contemporary Approach to Traditional Weaves: Crackle and Twill	Zielinski, S. A.; Robert Leclerc, ed.	√	√	MWL	8			'51–'73	17
Crackle Weave	Contemporary Approach to Traditional Weaves: Crackle, Old and New	Zielinski, S. A.; Robert Leclerc, ed.	√	√	MWL	8			'51–'73	9
Crackle Weave	Crackle		√	√	WJ	3	3	11	Ja 79	32
Crackle Weave	Crackle Christmas Runner (Jean Scorgie)		√	√	Hw	8	4		S/O 87	58, I-13
Crackle Weave	Crackle Stole and Pillow (Nell Znamierowski)		√	√	Hw	8	5		N/D 87	49, I-9
Crackle Weave	Crackle Weave		√	√	Hw	8	5		N/D 87	48
Crackle Weave	Crackle Weave and Its Possible Variations	Snyder, Mary E.	√	> 4	H&C	13	1		Wi 62	13
Crackle Weave	Crackle Weave Luncheon Cloth (Gladys Strong)		√	√	Hw	3	5		N/D 82	51, 95
Crackle Weave	Crackle Weave, Part 1	Lyon, Nancy	√	√	SS&D	19	1	73	Wi 87	21
Crackle Weave	Designing Rugs for Harness-Controlled Weaving		√	> 4	WJ	4	4	16	Ap 80	27
Crackle Weave	Fashion Show of Handwoven Garments		√	> 4	WJ	3	3	11	Ja 79	5
Crackle Weave	Five Crackle Weave Projects	Macomber, Dorothea	√	√	H&C	9	3		Su 58	42
Crackle Weave	From Portraits to Textile Designs		√	> 4	H&C	11	1		Wi 60	20
Crackle Weave	Hand Woven Rugs: Weaves, Crackle	Atwater, Mary Meigs	√	√	SCGM		29		48	19
Crackle Weave	Handweaver's Instruction Manual: The Crackle Weave	Tidball, Harriet C. nee Douglas	√	√	SCGM		34		49	28
Crackle Weave	Handwoven Wedding Chuppa, A	Horger, Millicent	√	√	WJ	7	4	28	Sp 83	50
Crackle Weave	Holiday Tabard (Kathryn Wertenberger)		√	√	Hw	2	1		F-W 80	54, 59
Crackle Weave	Multiple Harness Crackle		√	> 4	WJ	4	1	13	Jy 79	15
Crackle Weave	Northwest Conference at Seattle		√	√	H&C	8	3		Su 57	28
Crackle Weave	Pattern and Structure in Handwoven Fabrics	Frey, Berta	√	√	H&C	6	4		Fa 55	4
Crackle Weave	Stitching Traditional Coverlet Weaves	Sellin, Helen G.	√	> 4	AT	1			De 83	289
Crackle Weave	Swivel Variations for Four Harness Looms	James, Ona	√	√	H&C	14	4		Fa 63	11
Crackle Weave	Violet Vestment	Hahn, Roslyn	√	> 4	WJ	8	3	31	Wi 83	44
Crackle Weave	Weaving Towels As a Means of Learning the Basic Four-Shaft Weaves	Barrett, Clotilde	√	√	WJ	8	2	30	Fa 83	11
Crackle Weave, 4- Shaft, 12-Block	Contemporary Approach to Traditional Weaves: 12-Block Crackle on Four Shafts	Zielinski, S. A.; Robert Leclerc, ed.	√	√	MWL	8			'51–'73	55
Crackle Weave, 4-Shaft, 12-Block	Contemporary Approach to Traditional Weaves: 12-Block Crackle and Overshot	Zielinski, S. A.; Robert Leclerc, ed.	√	> 4	MWL	7			'51–'73	74

SUBJECT	TITLE	AUTHOR	IL	INST	JOUR	VOL	NO	ISS	DATE	PAGE
Crackle Weave, 4-Shaft, 8-Block	Contemporary Approach to Traditional Weaves: 8-Block Crackle on Four Shafts	Zielinski, S. A.; Robert Leclerc, ed.	√	√	MWL	8			'51–'73	47
Crackle Weave, 6-Shaft, Warp Crackle,	Contemporary Approach to Traditional Weaves: Production Drafts — Projects for Six-Shaft Warp Crackle	Zielinski, S. A.; Robert Leclerc, ed.	√	> 4	MWL	8			'51–'73	44
Crackle Weave, Block Design	Contemporary Approach to Traditional Weaves: Free Patterns in Crackle	Zielinski, S. A.; Robert Leclerc, ed.	√	√	MWL	8			'51–'73	26
Crackle Weave, Color Placement	Contemporary Approach to Traditional Weaves: Colours in Crackle	Zielinski, S. A.; Robert Leclerc, ed.	√	√	MWL	8			'51–'73	21
Crackle Weave System	Handloom Weaves: The Classification of Handloom Weaves, The Structural Group, Twill Derivative Class, Crackle Weave System	Tidball, Harriet	√	√	SCGM		33		57	19
Crackle Weave, Transcribed From Block Weaves	Contemporary Approach to Traditional Weaves: Practical Project for Warp Crackle	Zielinski, S. A.; Robert Leclerc, ed.	√	√	MWL	8			'51–'73	37
Crackle Weave, Two-Harness (Sets) Weaving	Little Known Weaves Worth Knowing Better: Two-Harness Method	Zielinski, S. A.; Robert Leclerc, ed.	√	> 4	MWL	16			'51–'73	35
Crackle Weave with Floats of Four	Contemporary Approach to Traditional Weaves: Crackle with Floats of Four	Zielinski, S. A.; Robert Leclerc, ed.	√	√	MWL	8			'51–'73	65
Crackle Weave, Without Incidentals	Contemporary Approach to Traditional Weaves: Crackle Without Incidentals	Zielinski, S. A.; Robert Leclerc, ed.	√	√	MWL	8			'51–'73	30
Craft Center	Action in Appalachia: A Community Craft Center Bustles	Flanagan, Jane	√		SS&D	7	3	27	Su 76	96
Craft Center	Clinch Valley: Each One Teach Others	Mayer, Alice W.	√		SS&D	2	2	6	Sp 71	31
Craft Center	Country Roads, A Craft Market and a Weaving Center		√		H&C	18	3		Su 67	30
Craft Center	Memorial Craft Center for Florida Weaver		√		H&C	6	1		Wi 54	25
Craft Center	New Jersey Craft Center				H&C	8	1		Wi 56	15
Craft Center	Old Mill Houses Brookfield Craft Center				H&C	12	3		Su 61	48
Craft Center	Tryon Crafts				H&C	13	3		Su 62	27
Craft Center	Tying Up with Others		√		H&C	26	5		Oc 75	20
Craft Center	Weavers Guild of Minnesota, Textile Workshop	Nunneley, Faithe			H&C	22	1		Wi 71	13
Craft Center	Worcester Craft Center				H&C	11	4		Fa 60	11
Craft Center: Bali	Weavers of Bali	Hannon, Farrell	√		SS&D	18	4	72	Fa 87	46
Craft Center: Disabled	Comminicating Through Craft	de Mar, Lola	√		Fa	14	1		J/F 87	38
Craft Center: Weaving	Quicksand Craft Center: A New Way of Life for Kentucky Mountain Women	Guy, Sallie T.	√		Hw	2	4		Se 81	16
Craft Essay	Craft As Contemplative Encounter	Centner, David J., O.C.D.			Iw	4	3		Su 79	60
Craft Fairs	Craft Fairs: To Show or Not to Show	Goodman, Deborah Lerme	√		Fa	12	2		M/A 85	50
Craft Fairs	Fair at the Top	Donahue, Patric	√		H&C	21	4		Fa 70	18
Craft Fairs	Negotiating the Craft Fair Circuit: Important First Steps	Scott, Michael			Fa	12	2		M/A 85	50
Craft Market	Rhinebeck '80		√		SS&D	11	4	44	Fa 80	40
Craft Program	New Craft Program at St. Benedict's Monastery	Russell, Harold W.			SS&D	2	3	7	Su 71	24
Craft Programs	New York State Sponsors Weaving in New Craft Project at Woodstock		√		H&C	3	2		Sp 52	41
Craft Traditions: Nova Scotia	Basketry Traditions of Nova Scotia, The	Gordon, Joleen	√		SS&D	17	2	66	Sp 86	52
Crafts	Bridging the Gap Between Craft Artists and Interior Designers	Kraus, William	√		SS&D	16	4	64	Fa 85	37
Crafts	Chase Home	McCarthy, Bridget Beatty	√		SS&D	16	4	64	Fa 85	44
Crafts	Chase Home: Utah Arts Council	Burke, Dan E.	√		SS&D	16	4	64	Fa 85	40
Crafts	Common Denominator of the Handicrafts, The	Ford, Toni	√		H&C	3	1		Wi 51	23
Crafts	National Crafts Planning Project: A Report to the HGA Membership	Dieterich, Mary			SS&D	12	4	48	Fa 81	75
Crafts	Shop One, A Unique Craftsmen's Venture In Rochester, N. Y.		√		H&C	5	3		Su 54	45

SUBJECT	TITLE	AUTHOR	IL	INST	JOUR	VOL	NO	ISS	DATE	PAGE
Craftsman and Social Conscience	Craftsman and Social Conscience: E. F. Schumacher, The	Hepburn, Ian			Hw	6	1		J/F 85	20
Craftsman and Social Conscience	Craftsman and Social Conscience, Part 2: Mahatma Gandhi, The	Hepburn, Ian			Hw	5	5		N/D 84	22
Craftsman and Social Conscience	Craftsman and Social Conscience: William Morris, The	Hepburn, Ian			Hw	5	4		S/O 84	26
Crash	Body as Canvas, The	Koda, Harold	√		TM			8	D/J 86	56
Creative Process	African Artist in a Dying Trade, An	Kessler, Cristina	√	√	Fa	11	6		N/D 84	51
Creative Process	Arturo Alonzo Sandoval	Sandoval, Arturo Alonzo	√		Fa	11	6		N/D 84	58
Creative Process	Blocked, A First-Person Account	Howe, Cathe			Fa	11	6		N/D 84	55
Creative Process	Creative Cycle: Recharging, The	Rowley, Kathleen			Fa	11	6		N/D 84	54
Creative Process	Creative Process: Cindy Snodgrass, The	Snodgrass, Cindy	√		Fa	11	6		N/D 84	38
Creative Process	Creative Process: Debra Rapport, The	Rapport, Debra	√		Fa	11	6		N/D 84	34
Creative Process	Creative Process: Fiber Artists At Work, The		√		Fa	11	6		N/D 84	31
Creative Process	Creative Process: Katherine Westphal, The	Westphal, Katherine	√		Fa	11	6		N/D 84	32
Creative Process	Creative Process: Rosina Yue, The	Yue, Rosina	√		Fa	11	6		N/D 84	40
Creative Process	Creative Process: Terri Mangat, The	Mangat, Terri	√		Fa	11	6		N/D 84	36
Creative Process	Design by Decision: A Practical Approach to the Creative Process	Hall, Carolyn Vosburg	√		Fa	8	2		M/A 81	13
Creative Process	Ed Rossbach	Rossbach, Ed	√		Fa	11	6		N/D 84	60
Creative Process	Individual/Artistic Development: A Workshop by Francoise Grossen	Lilligren, Ingrid	√		Fa	11	3		M/J 84	45
Creative Process	Junque Quilts	Murray, Clare	√		Fa	14	4		S/O 87	6
Creative Process	Layne Goldsmith: Felted Worlds	Baldwin, P. H.	√		Fa	11	6		N/D 84	24
Creative Process	Memory, Metaphor, and Magic: The Art of Janet Boguch	Glowen, Ron	√		Fa	11	6		N/D 84	66
Creative Process	Probing the Creative Process: A Book List to Begin With	Austin, Carole	√		Fa	11	6		N/D 84	53
Creative Process	Sharon Marcus: Designing for Tapestry, One Approach to the Creative Process	Marcus, Sharon	√		Fa	11	6		N/D 84	26
Creative Process	Sources: A.K.A. The Muse	Janeiro, Jan	√		Fa	11	6		N/D 84	52
Creative Process	Tiogruppen: When Working Together Works	Talley, Charles	√		Fa	11	6		N/D 84	41
Creative Process	When Prison Is Home: Challenging the Creative Spirit	Scarborough, Jessica	√		Fa	11	6		N/D 84	69
Creative Process: Left- and Right-Brain	Fabric of Creativity: Weaving Together Left– and Right–Brain Activites, The	Miles, Candice St. Jacques	√		Fa	11	6		N/D 84	44
Creativity	Cardiac Algorithms or the Heart's Way of Inferring Meaning from Pattern	Courtney, Elizabeth	√		AT	5			Ju 86	51
Creativity	Creative Overshot: Begin with a Line	Windeknecht, Margaret B.	√	√	SCGM		31		78	22
Creativity	Creative Two Harness Weaving	Liebler, Barbara	√	√	Iw	4	4		Fa 79	64
Creativity	Creativity	Humphery, Laney			Hw	6	3		Su 85	22
Creativity	Education of the Creative Craftsman	Brennan, Harold J.			H&C	11	3		Su 60	13
Creativity	Evolution of a Project	de Grassi, Laurel	√	√	S-O	10	4		Wi 86	21
Creativity	Evolution of a Weaving, The	Kearney, Kathleen	√	√	SS&D	12	1	45	Wi 80	64
Creativity	Handspun: Inspiration from Commercial Sources	Mintzer, Arlene	√		S-O	10	2		Su 86	33
Creativity	In the Beginning	Van Gelder, Lydia	√		S-O	10	2		Su 86	43
Creativity	Journey in Thread, A	Rees, Linda	√		Hw	5	5		N/D 84	99
Creativity	Lesley Shearer: Creation with Control	Ligon, Linda	√		Iw	2	4		Su 77	10
Creativity	Mathematical Design Concepts Relative to Aesthetic Concerns	Michaels-Paque, J.	√		AT	8			De 87	155
Creativity	On Designing and Creativity	Smith, Barbara			Hw	5	5		N/D 84	96
Creativity	Organization Lets Creativity Flow	Shurtleff, Chris Ann	√		Hw	7	5		N/D 86	74
Creativity	Ringlets and Waves: Undulations from Overtwist	Frame, Mary	√	√	S-O	10	4		Wi 86	28

SUBJECT	TITLE	AUTHOR	IL	INST	JOUR	VOL	NO	ISS	DATE	PAGE
Creativity	Teaching Children How to Knit	Baker, Ella			S-O	10	2		Su 86	42
Creativity	Variations on One Warp	Alvic, Philis	√		SS&D	12	4	48	Fa 81	70
Creativity	Way of Working: Katherine Westphal and the Creative Process, A	Janeiro, Jan	√		Fa	7	6		N/D 80	35
Creativity	Weaver of Images	Brownlee-Ramsdale, Sandra	√		AT	6			De 86	147
Creativity	Weaving, 'riting, and 'rithmetic	Tate, Blair	√		AT	6			De 86	57
Crepe, Modified	Icicle Dress (Mary McGuinness)		√	√	Hw	8	1		J/F 87	45, I-4
Crepe Weave	Add a New Twist to Your Spinning	Hochberg, Bette	√	√	S-O	5			81	42
Crepe Weave	Application of Computer-Aided Design Techniques to the Creation of Moss Crepe Weaves, The	Ping, Gu; Alan Newton	√	> 4	AT	2			De 84	185
Crepe Weave	Experimenting with Silk Crepe	Quinn, Celia	√	√	S-O	10	4		Wi 86	36
Crepe Weave	Exploring the Textures: Crepe	Zielinski, S. A.; Robert Leclerc, ed.	√	> 4	MWL	11			'51–'73	68
Crepe Weave	If You Have Four Harnesses	Hagarty, Harriet May		√	H&C	23	5		S/O 72	16
Crepe Weave	Jacket (Nell Znamierowski)		√	> 4	Hw	7	3		M/J 86	34, I-6
Crepe Weave	Multiple Harness Weaving Course Part 5. Twill Derivatives (continued)		√	> 4	WJ	5	3	19	Wi 81	12
Crepe Weave	Scarf (Nell Znamierowski)		√	> 4	Hw	7	3		M/J 86	34, I-6
Crepe Weave	Shirt with Marbled Inset (Anne Bliss)		√	√	Hw	4	3		M/J 83	49, 82
Crepe Weave	Tailored Vest and Skirt, A	Arnold, Ruth	√	> 4	WJ	9	3	35	Wi 85	56
Crepe-Effect, Tabby	More About Fabrics: Tabby	Zielinski, S. A.; Robert Leclerc, ed.	√	√	MWL	20			'51–'73	19
Crete	Weaving in Crete	Znamierowski, Nell	√		H&C	15	4		Fa 64	8
Crib Blanket	Patchwork Designs in Summer and Winter	Davenport, Betty	√	√	PWC	1	1		No 81	27
Crinoline	Making Swirly Skirts	Callaway, Grace	√	√	TM			10	A/M 87	35
Critique	Further Thoughts on "The Artist & The Quilt"	Dunnewold, Jane			Fa	11	2		M/A 84	56
Critique: Classroom	Rugweaving: Teaching on Two Harnesses	Mattera, Joanne	√	√	Iw	5	1		Wi 79	27
Critique: Workshop	Individual/Artistic Development: A Workshop by Francoise Grossen	Lilligren, Ingrid	√		Fa	11	3		M/J 84	45
Crochet	Albert Lohnes		√		Fa	5	3		M/J 78	53
Crochet	Alice's Apron	Meltzer, Bonnie	√		SS&D	5	2	18	Sp 74	29
Crochet	Andrea Uravitch		√		Fa	3	6		N/D 76	14
Crochet	Andrea V. Uravitch, "Wild and Domestic" (Exhibit)	Stevens, Rebecca A. T.	√		Fa	10	2		M/A 83	71
Crochet	Annie Dempsey: Sculptural Crochet (Exhibit)	Lindley, Susan	√		Fa	9	2		M/A 82	76
Crochet	Bogs	Fauske, Clara	√	√	PWC			3	Oc 82	39
Crochet	Carla's Zebra Top	Fauske, Carla	√	√	PWC			2	Ap 82	88
Crochet	Carol Hoffman: Research in Molecular Crochet		√		Fa	3	4		J/A 76	18
Crochet	Combine Techniques? Why not?	Derr, Mary L.	√		WJ	7	3	27	Wi 82	19
Crochet	Complementary Crochet	Durston, Linda Moore	√	√	SS&D	15	1	57	Wi 83	68
Crochet	Cows in Fiber	Timmons, Chris	√		Fa	11	4		J/A 84	55
Crochet	Creative Clothing: Surface Embellishment	Mayer, Anita Luvera	√	√	WJ	11	3	43	Wi 87	30
Crochet	Crochet—A Great Technique for Finishing Handwovens		√	> 4	WJ	7	3	27	Wi 82	18
Crochet	Crochet a Waistband			√	TM			4	A/M 86	8
Crochet	Crochet as a Madness	Horton, Lucy	√		Fa	5	3		M/J 78	22
Crochet	Crochet Pattern for Pinwheel Spread	Cannarella, Deborah	√	√	TM			7	O/N 86	18
Crochet	Crochet Trim		√	√	Hw	7	3		M/J 86	53
Crochet	Crocheted Cream Puffs? What You See Is Not What You Get	Fedders, Pat	√		Fa	8	5		S/O 81	16
Crochet	Crocheter Gets Wired, A	Carlton, Bronwyn	√		Fa	7	1		J/F 80	31
Crochet	Cynthia Gale-Nosek: Searching for the Limits of Crochet	Gale-Nosek, Cynthia	√		Fa	11	4		J/A 84	49

SUBJECT	TITLE	AUTHOR	IL	INST	JOUR	VOL	NO	ISS	DATE	PAGE
Crochet	Dazzling with Sequins	Kelsey, Barbara Shomer	√	√	TM			1	O/N 85	60
Crochet	"Dione Christensen Fiberworks" (Exhibit)	Meyer, Florence	√		Fa	6	2		M/A 79	63
Crochet	Elizabeth Tuttle: Pointillist Crochet	Demske, Barbara	√		Fa	7	4		J/A 80	48
Crochet	Fiber and Architecture: Marge Walters		√		Fa	3	3		M/J 76	33
Crochet	Fiber Mandalas: Doilies As Spiritual Art	Maines, Rachel	√		Fa	9	3		M/J 82	17
Crochet	Hammock, The	Drooker, Penelope B.	√	√	TM			6	A/S 86	74
Crochet	Howard Zabler		√		Fa	5	3		M/J 78	54
Crochet	Jane Rake's Crochet	Dunn, Katherine	√		Fa	6	3		M/J 79	62
Crochet	Jappie King Black: The Siren and Other Tempting Crocheted Beings (error-corrected Fa v8 n2 81 p7)	West, Virginia	√		Fa	7	6		N/D 80	14
Crochet	Lace Trilogy	Fauske, Carla	√	√	PWC			6	Su 83	52
Crochet	Lampshade Transfigured, A	Fauske, Carla	√	√	PWC	1	1		No 81	55
Crochet	Mind Boggling Bogs	Klessen, Romy	√	√	PWC			3	Oc 82	40
Crochet	New Look At Crochet, A	Lep, Annette	√		TM			9	F/M 87	86
Crochet	"Norma Minkowitz" (Exhibit)	Grover, Donald	√		Fa	6	5		S/O 79	77
Crochet	On the Other Foot: The Shoe Sculptures of Norma Minkowitz		√		Fa	10	1		J/F 83	13
Crochet	Portfolio: Why I Work in Linen, A		√		Fa	14	2		M/A 87	40
Crochet	Renie Breskin Adams: Artist...Teacher...Self-Seeker	Sommer, Elyse	√		Fa	5	3		M/J 78	36
Crochet	Resemblance to Afghans; Crochet Rubbings?, A	Elliott, Sally	√		Fa	8	3		M/J 81	48
Crochet	Romy's One-Shouldered Bodice	Klessen, Romy	√	√	PWC			2	Ap 82	87
Crochet	Ruth and David Segunda		√		Fa	4	6		N/D 77	62
Crochet	Shaped Silk Sheath	Xenakis, Athanasios David; Alexis Xenakis Yiorgos	√	√	PWC			6	Su 83	39
Crochet	Sharon Hedges	Malarcher, Pat	√		Fa	5	3		M/J 78	56
Crochet	Spinning Fibers for Crochet	Linder, Harry P.	√	√	S-O	10	1		Sp 86	30
Crochet	Ten Years and Ten Pounds of Crochet	Cannarella, Deborah	√		TM			1	O/N 85	80
Crochet	Textile Life, The	Jacobson, Gail	√		Fa	14	3		M/J 87	5
Crochet	Three Personal Statements: Norma Minkowitz, Gillian Bull, Mardel Esping		√		Fa	3	5		S/O 76	19
Crochet	Touch of the Poet: Wearables by Denise Welsh-May, A	Park, Betty	√		Fa	6	6		N/D 79	52
Crochet	Two String Sweaters	Brugger, Susan	√	√	PWC			6	Su 83	31
Crochet	Windows: Sendoni Curtains	Xenakis, Alexis Yiorgos	√	> 4	PWC	4	1	11		4
Crochet: Abbreviations	Creating Textures: V–, Ridge, and Post Stitches	Moon, Ellen	√	√	TM			11	J/J 87	60
Crochet: Cables	Crocheting Wearable Fabric	McGoveran, Mary	√	√	TM			9	F/M 87	62
Crochet: Characteristics	Crochet Inspired by the Trees	Moon, Ellen	√	√	TM			11	J/J 87	56
Crochet: Double	Crocheting Wearable Fabric	McGoveran, Mary	√	√	TM			9	F/M 87	62
Crochet: Hooks and Yarn Sizes	Crocheting Wearable Fabric	McGoveran, Mary	√	√	TM			9	F/M 87	62
Crochet: Knit Patterns	Crocheting Wearable Fabric	McGoveran, Mary	√	√	TM			9	F/M 87	62
Crochet: Relief Flanges	Creating Textures: V–, Ridge, and Post Stitches	Moon, Ellen	√	√	TM			11	J/J 87	60
Crochet: Ribbing	Crocheting Wearable Fabric	McGoveran, Mary	√	√	TM			9	F/M 87	62
Crochet: Single	Three Color Basket in Single Crochet	Klessen, Romy	√	√	PWC			4	Ja 83	60
Crochet: Stitch, Proportions	Romy's Soapbox	Klessen, Romy	√	√	PWC			2	Ap 82	88
Crochet: Stitches	Creating Textures: V–, Ridge, and Post Stitches	Moon, Ellen	√	√	TM			11	J/J 87	60
Crochet: Stitches	Crochet Inspired by the Trees	Moon, Ellen	√	√	TM			11	J/J 87	56
Crochet: Stitches	Crocheting Wearable Fabric	McGoveran, Mary	√	√	TM			9	F/M 87	62
Crochet: Texture	Creating Textures: V–, Ridge, and Post Stitches	Moon, Ellen	√	√	TM			11	J/J 87	60

SUBJECT	TITLE	AUTHOR	IL	INST	JOUR	VOL	NO	ISS	DATE	PAGE
Crochet: Triangles	Creating Textures: V–, Ridge, and Post Stitches	Moon, Ellen	√	√	TM			11	J/J 87	60
Crochet vs. Crochet	Crocheting Wearable Fabric	McGoveran, Mary	√	√	TM			9	F/M 87	62
Crochet vs. Knitting	Crocheting Wearable Fabric	McGoveran, Mary	√	√	TM			9	F/M 87	62
Crochet vs. Knitting	Knitting Vs. Crochet				TM			11	J/J 87	4
Crocheting Handspun	Creative Knitwear		√		S-O	3			79	62
Crocheting Handspun	Crocheted Baby Bib, A	Linder, Harry P.	√	√	S-O	10	1		Sp 86	32
Crocheting Handspun	Have Spindle Will Travel	Ruane, Joan	√	√	S-O	7	4		Wi 83	38
Crocheting Handspun	Jean Newsted's Angora Scarf		√		S-O	9	3		Fa 85	13
Crocheting Handspun	Two Blankets: A Blanket for Baby Gregory	Smith, Kenneth Loyal	√		S-O	10	1		Sp 86	22
Cross Weave	Woven Lace and Lacey Weaves: Cross Weave	Zielinski, S. A.; Robert Leclerc, ed.	√	√	MWL	13			'51–'73	64
Crossed-Warp, Andean	Andean Crossed-Warp Techniques for Decorative Trims, Part 1 — Flat Bands	Cahlander, Adele	√	√	WJ	2	4	8	Ap 78	10
Crossed-Warp, Andean	Andean Crossed-Warp Techniques for Decorative Trims, Part 2 — Tubular Bands (error-corrected WJ v3 n1 insert for vol. 2)	Cahlander, Adele	√	√	WJ	3	1	9	Jy 78	38
Cuffs see Collars, Cuffs, Yokes										
Culottes	Skirts Become Culottes		√	√	TM			10	A/M 87	6
Cultivation: Cotton	Cotton		√		WJ	4	2	14	Oc 79	4
Cultivation: Cotton	My Affair with King Cotton	Franklin, Sue	√	√	T			9	F/M 87	39
Cultivation: Cotton, Brown	Cotton of a Different Color	Campbell, John; Susan Campbell		√	WJ	4	2	14	Oc 79	20
Cultivation: Dye Plants	Dye Garden	Walbridge, T.		√	SS&D	8	2	30	Sp 77	63
Cultivation: Dye Plants	Dyer's Garden Is Feature of Landscape Plan	Kramer, Jack	√	√	SS&D	4	4	16	Fa 73	35
Cultivation: Dye Plants	Grow Your Own Colors: Plant a Dye Garden (error-corrected S-O v11 n2 '87 p7)	Buchanan, Rita	√	√	S-O	11	1		Sp 87	35
Cultivation: Dye Plants	Planting a Dye Garden	Magoffin, Connie	√	√	WJ	10	2	38	Fa 85	36
Cultivation: Flax	Continuous Thread: From Flax Seed to Linen Cloth, The	Calhoun, Wheeler; Lee Kirschner	√		S-O	7	1		Sp 83	28
Cultivation: Flax	Flax	Miller, Suzanne	√	√	WJ	7	2	26	Fa 82	12
Cultivation: Flax	Raising Flax in Your Garden	McRae, Annette	√		S-O	3			79	4
Cultivation: Flax	Virginia's Handy Tips for Flax Growing	Handy, Virginia		√	S-O	10	3		Fa 86	44
Cultivation: Indigo	Personal Exploration of Indigo, A	Miller, Dorothy	√	√	Fa	13	5		S/O 86	32
Cultivation: Ramie	Ramie	Cobb, Lorie	√		S-O	10	3		Fa 86	40
Cultivation: Teasels	Teasels	Leadbeater, Eliza	√	√	Hw	2	5		No 81	54
Cultivation: Willow	Basket Willow: Cultivating and Gathering the Withy	Hart, Carol	√	√	TM			3	F/M 86	63
Cultlivation: Madder	Madder Saga, The	Jones, Marilyn	√		SS&D	13	2	50	Sp 82	28
Cuna Cachi Weaving: Technique	Cuna Cachi: A Study of Hammock Weaving Among the Cuna Indians of The San Blas Islands	Lambert, Anne M.	√	√	AT	5			Ju 86	105
Curtains see Window Coverings										
Curves: Sewing	Shapely Curves	Anthony, Janice	√	√	TM			11	J/J 87	30
Cushions and Pillows	Afghan and Pillow Set	D'Ambrosio, Gina	√	√	S-O	11	2		Su 87	14
Cushions and Pillows	Bedspread and Pillow (Beatrice E. Reeve)		√	√	H&C	12	3		Su 61	55
Cushions and Pillows	Beyond the Fringe	Wertenberger, Kathryn	√	> 4	Hw	2	5		No 81	27
Cushions and Pillows	Casual Cushions	McFeely, Nancy W.	√	√	SS&D	3	1	9	Wi 71	9
Cushions and Pillows	Celtic Knot Box Cushion	Xenakis, Athanasios David	√	√	PWC	3	4	10		60
Cushions and Pillows	Crackle Stole and Pillow (Nell Znamierowski)		√	√	Hw	8	5		N/D 87	49, I-9
Cushions and Pillows	Cushion Creations	Speth, Lottie	√	√	SS&D	15	1	57	Wi 83	38
Cushions and Pillows	Cushion (Margaretha Essén-Hedin)		√	√	Hw	5	3		Su 84	72, 118

SUBJECT	TITLE	AUTHOR	IL	INST	JOUR	VOL	NO	ISS	DATE	PAGE
Cushions and Pillows	Desert Triptych: Three Tapestry Pillows (Carol Kampert)		√	√	Hw	3	1		Ja 82	Cover, 89
Cushions and Pillows	Designing for Piqué (error-corrected PWC v4 n4 i14 '87 p33)	Sullivan, Donna	√	> 4	PWC	4	3	13		28
Cushions and Pillows	Different BUT Related	Smith, Dorothy N.	√	√	WJ	7	1	25	Su 82	32
Cushions and Pillows	Discarded Fur Pieces for Rugs and Pillows	Cook, Bonny	√	√	SS&D	4	3	15	Su 73	20
Cushions and Pillows	Diversified Plain Weave Pillow (Kathryn Wertenberger)		√	> 4	Hw	8	5		N/D 87	62, I-15
Cushions and Pillows	Double Corduroy Pillows (Pam Bolesta)		√	√	Hw	2	1		F-W 80	32, 60
Cushions and Pillows	Easy Weaving for Easy Living		√	√	Hw	1	2		S-S 80	48
Cushions and Pillows	Erica: The new Rigid Heddle Loom	Cooper, Frayda	√		H&C	26	5		Oc 75	25
Cushions and Pillows	Fireside Throw and Pillow (Betty Davenport)		√	√	Hw	8	1		J/F 87	72, I-13
Cushions and Pillows	Five Pillows on One Warp (Sharon D. Alderman)		√	> 4	Hw	3	3		My 82	38, 93
Cushions and Pillows	Floor's the Limit, The	Xenakis, Athanasios David	√	> 4	PWC	3	3	9		12
Cushions and Pillows	Four Is Not Always Enough	Sullivan, Donna	√	> 4	PWC	4	3	13		18
Cushions and Pillows	Furry Pillow	Cox, Dorothy	√	√	WJ	7	2	26	Fa 82	56
Cushions and Pillows	Gunclub Checks (Judy Steinkoenig)		√	√	Hw	4	5		N/D 83	66, 106
Cushions and Pillows	Homemade Felt	March, Heather	√	√	TM			2	D/J 85	60
Cushions and Pillows	It Still Can Be Beautiful: Although Utilitarian	Rutkovsky, Fran Cutrell	√	√	SS&D	7	3	27	Su 76	57
Cushions and Pillows	Lynn's Pillows	Tedder, Lynn	√	√	PWC	4	3	13		25
Cushions and Pillows	Michigan Weaving, Third Conference at Hartland Shows Wide Variety		√	> 4	H&C	13	1		Wi 62	18
Cushions and Pillows	Name Draft (error-corrected WJ v8 n3 83 p68)		√	√	WJ	8	2	30	Fa 83	40
Cushions and Pillows	Overshot Derived from 2/2 Twill: Apricot Accents	Lyon, Linda	√	√	PWC	3	2	8		21
Cushions and Pillows	Overshot Pillow (Sue Ellison)		√	√	Hw	1	1		F-W 79	36, 60
Cushions and Pillows	Pastel Throw and Pillow (Halcyon Schomp)		√	√	Hw	8	1		J/F 87	74, I-15
Cushions and Pillows	Peculiar Piqué Pillow	Lyon, Linda	√	> 4	PWC	4	2	12		30
Cushions and Pillows	Pick-Up Piqué (error-corrected SS&D v19 n1 87 p33)	Fletcher, Joyce	√	√	SS&D	18	4	72	Fa 87	60
Cushions and Pillows	Pillow and Table Runner in Summer and Winter Weave	Xenakis, Athanasios David	√	√	PWC	1	1		No 81	21
Cushions and Pillows	Pillow (Janice Jones) (error-corrected Hw v8 n1 87 p I-16)		√	√	Hw	6	4		S/O 85	49, I-8
Cushions and Pillows	Pillow Pair (Janice Jones)		√	√	Hw	7	4		S/O 86	52, I-12
Cushions and Pillows	Plaid Blanket and Pillow (Margaretha Essén-Hedin)		√	> 4	Hw	8	1		J/F 87	71, I-14
Cushions and Pillows	Project Notebook, A	Ligon, Linda	√	√	Iw	3	1		Fa 77	31
Cushions and Pillows	Projects At Chautauqua Summer School	Snyder, Mary E.	√	√	H&C	23	3		M/J 72	14
Cushions and Pillows	Sandstone Pillows (Janice Jones)		√	√	Hw	5	2		M/A 84	59, 99
Cushions and Pillows	Simple Pillow, A	Kopette, Linda	√	√	SS&D	4	1	13	Wi 72	36
Cushions and Pillows	Striped Pillows (Carol Klippenstein)		√	√	Hw	1	1		F-W 79	36, 60
Cushions and Pillows	Tapestry Face Pillows (Sharon La Pierre)		√	√	SS&D	4	2	14	Sp 73	9
Cushions and Pillows	Three Double Weave Pillows (Laurel Howard) (error-corrected Hw v2 n2 81 p68)		√	> 4	Hw	2	1		F-W 80	32, 76
Cushions and Pillows	Three in One	Moes, Dini	√	√	SS&D	18	2	70	Sp 87	74
Cushions and Pillows	Thrum Pillows (Betty Davenport)		√	√	Hw	5	5		N/D 84	66, I-10
Cushions and Pillows	Traditional Berber Weaving in Central Morocco	Forelli, Sally; Jeanette Harries	√		TMJ	4	4		77	41
Cushions and Pillows	Twill Block and Stripe Pillows (Pam Pawl)		√	> 4	Hw	6	5		N/D 85	52, I-11

SUBJECT	TITLE	AUTHOR	IL	INST	JOUR	VOL	NO	ISS	DATE	PAGE
Cushions and Pillows	Two Floor Pillows for the Rigid Heddle Loom	Christensen, Joanne	√	√	Hw	2	2		Mr 81	56
Cushions and Pillows	Variations on a Landes Theme	Coutts, Lucele	√	√	WJ	8	4	32	Sp 84	24
Cushions and Pillows	Variations on a Theme of Marigolds (Görel Kinersly)		√	√	Hw	5	1		J/F 84	81
Cushions and Pillows	Waffle Pillows (David Xenakis)		√	√	Hw	1	2		S-S 80	70
Cushions and Pillows	Weaving in Donegal (error-corrected H&C v23 n3 72 p11)	McNeill, Mary	√	√	H&C	23	2		M/A 72	35
Cushions and Pillows	Weft Faced Pillows (Jane Patrick)		√	√	Hw	4	2		M/A 83	66, 98
Cutch	Why Bother with Natural Dyeing?	Bulbach, Stanley	√	√	TM			5	J/J 86	32
Cyprus	Weavers of Cyprus	Macdonald, Elizabeth	√		H&C	5	4		Fa 54	24
Damask	Contemporary Approach to Traditional Weaves: Modern Damask and Other Turned Twills	Zielinski, S. A.; Robert Leclerc, ed.	√	> 4	MWL	8			'51–'73	83
Damask	Contemporary Satins: A Damask Table Cloth Pattern	Tidball, Harriet	√	√	SCGM		7		62	15
Damask	Contemporary Satins: Damask	Tidball, Harriet	√	> 4	SCGM		7		62	12
Damask	Contemporary Use of Traditional Damask, A	Lalena, Constance	√		WJ	8	1	29	Su 83	69
Damask	Damask	Nyquist, Jan	√	> 4	CW	8	1	22	Se 86	3
Damask	Damask on a Drawloom	Keasbey, Doramay	√	> 4	SS&D	8	1	29	WI 76	63
Damask	Damask with a Sword	Keasbey, Doramay	√	> 4	CW	7	2	20	Ja 86	16
Damask	Designing Damask	Nyquist, Jan	√	> 4	SS&D	10	4	40	Fa 79	16
Damask	Dora Jung: The Artist and the Person	Talley, Charles	√		Fa	12	1		J/F 85	39
Damask	Fabrics for Interiors #9: Contemporary Damask Fabrics for a Bedroom	LaLena, Constance	√		Hw	7	2		M/A 86	64
Damask	Fantastic Finnweave, Part 3	Xenakis, Athanasios David	√	> 4	PWC			4	Ja 83	29
Damask	Five Harness Damask	Steele, Zella	√	> 4	H&C	18	1		Wi 67	20
Damask	Four-Harness Damask	Foster, Frances A.	√	√	H&C	9	1		Wi 57	23
Damask	Long Eyed Heddles	Ahrens, Jim	√	> 4	CW	6	1	16	Se 84	3
Damask	Multiple Shaft Weaving, Twill and Satin Blocks, Damask		√	> 4	WJ	5	4	20	Sp 81	10
Damask	Notes on the Damask Weave	Ahrens, Jim		> 4	CW	2	1	4	Oc 80	6
Damask	Origins: Damask	Wilson, Kax			Hw	2	3		My 81	68
Damask	Penland's Damask Loom		√		H&C	6	3		Su 55	24
Damask	Pick-Up Damask	Drooker, Penelope B.	√	> 4	SS&D	11	1	41	Wi 79	38
Damask	Small Damask Designs	Pennington, Fred A.	√		H&C	6	3		Su 55	54
Damask	Vestment Variations: A Weaver From the Netherlands Creates Garments for the Ecclesiastical Calendar	Jansen, Netty	√	> 4	WJ	10	3	39	Wi 86	53
Damask	Weaving Damask	Arnold, Ruth	√	> 4	H&C	6	3		Su 55	4
Damask	Weaving Damask on a Damask Loom	Steele, Zella	√		H&C	21	4		Fa 70	4
Damask, Block	Roses and Snowballs: The Development of Block Patterns in the German Linen-Weaving Tradition	Hilts, Patricia	√	> 4	AT	5			Ju 86	167
Damask, Demi-	Swatch #2, Winter Coat Fabric (Malin Salander)		√	√	Hw	7	5		N/D 86	60, I-5
Damask, Double	Contemporary Satins: Double Damask	Tidball, Harriet	√	> 4	SCGM		7		62	13
Damask, Double	Damask	Nyquist, Jan	√	> 4	CW	8	1	22	Se 86	3
Damask, False	Damask	Nyquist, Jan	√	> 4	CW	8	1	22	Se 86	3
Damask, False	Designing Damask	Nyquist, Jan	√	> 4	SS&D	10	4	40	Fa 79	16
Damask, False	Eight Harness Linen from Elizabeth Kackenmeister		√	> 4	H&C	15	1		Wi 64	34
Damask, False (Twill)	Bedspread (Marilyn Dillard)		√	√	Hw	4	4		S/O 83	60, 105
Damask, Half-	Little Known Weaves Worth Knowing Better: Demi-Damassé	Zielinski, S. A.; Robert Leclerc, ed.	√	√	MWL	16			'51–'73	109
Damask, Half- , on Crackle	Little Known Weaves Worth Knowing Better: Demi-Damassé	Zielinski, S. A.; Robert Leclerc, ed.	√	√	MWL	16			'51–'73	109

SUBJECT	TITLE	AUTHOR	IL	INST	JOUR	VOL	NO	ISS	DATE	PAGE
Damask, Half-, on Summer and Winter	Little Known Weaves Worth Knowing Better: Demi-Damassé	Zielinski, S. A.; Robert Leclerc, ed.	√	√	MWL	16			'51–'73	109
Damask, Inlay	Contemporary Satins: Pick-Up and Inlay Damask	Tidball, Harriet	√	√	SCGM		7		62	16
Damask Knitting	Knitter's Puzzle: Damask Knitting with Your Handspun, A	Howard, Miranda	√	√	S-O	9	1		Sp 85	36
Damask, Pick-Up	Contemporary Satins: Pick-Up and Inlay Damask	Tidball, Harriet	√	√	SCGM		7		62	16
Damask, Pick-Up	Damask	Mudge, Christine	√	> 4	Iw	6	1		Wi 80	46
Damask System	Handloom Weaves: The Classification of Handloom Weaves, The Structural Group, Unit Class, Damask	Tidball, Harriet	√	> 4	SCGM		33		57	28
Damask, Turned	Drafting: A Personal Approach, Part 3	Alvic, Philis	√	> 4	SS&D	13	3	51	Su 82	40
Damask, Twill	Four Harness Damask — A Pick-up Weave	Merritt, Elveana	√	√	WJ	5	1	17	Su 80	20
Damask, Two-Block	Tablecloth and Six Napkins in Two-Block Damask (Janet Carper)		√	> 4	Hw	4	3		M/J 83	54, 94
Damask, Two-Harness (Sets)	Little Known Weaves Worth Knowing Better: Two-Harness Method	Zielinski, S. A.; Robert Leclerc, ed.	√	> 4	MWL	16			'51–'73	31
Damask Weaver	Dora Jung, Distinguished Finnish Weaver		√		H&C	10	2		Sp 59	14
Dance and Fiber	Costume for Dance: The Living Sculpture of Carleigh Hoff	Parshall, Priscilla	√		Fa	8	1		J/F 81	28
Dance and Fiber	"Diaghilev—Costumes and Designs of the Ballets Russes" (Exhibit)	Grover, Donald	√		Fa	6	3		M/J 79	79
Dance and Fiber	Fabric of Movement, The	Lyon, David	√		Fa	13	3		M/J 86	76
Dance and Fiber	Interweavings, A Dance	Arouh, Leslie	√		Fa	7	1		J/F 80	16
Dance and Fiber	Patricia Bulitt: Gutsongs and Other Dances	Scarborough, Jessica	√		Fa	11	5		S/O 84	50
Darning Knits	On Darning Knits			√	TM			7	O/N 86	4
Darning Techniques	Darn That Hole	Markrich, Lilo	√	√	TM			5	J/J 86	38
Darts	How to Mark Darts		√	√	TM			2	D/J 85	8
Darts	Stanley Hostek on Darts	Hostek, Stanley	√	√	TM			14	D/J 87	67
Darts: Variations	Playing with Darts	Abbott, Deborah	√	√	TM			14	D/J 87	64
Dating Historical Textiles: Dated Painting	Turkish Carpet with Spots and Stripes, A	Mackie, Louise W.	√		TMJ	4	3		76	4
Daze	Body as Canvas, The	Koda, Harold	√		TM			8	D/J 86	56
Decorative Arts also see Interiors										
Decorative Arts	Cooper-Hewitt Museum, The	Park, Betty	√		Fa	9	5		S/O 82	13
Decorative Arts	Textile Designs from Wallpaper	Justema, William	√		H&C	16	1		Wi 65	5
Definitions: Leno, Doup	Doup Leno: Definitions	Skowronski, Hella; Sylvia Tacker	√		SCGM		32		80	6
Definitions: Weaving	Creative Monk's Belt: Definitions	Windeknecht, Margaret B.			SCGM		30		76	4
Definitions: Weaving	Creative Overshot: Definitions	Windeknecht, Margaret B.	√		SCGM		31		78	5
Degradation: Textiles	Ultraviolet Absorbers: A Treatment to Reduce Fading and Degradation of Textiles	Crews, Particia Cox; Barbara M. Reagan			AT	8			De 87	43
Deknotting	Treasury for Beginners: Deknotting	Zielinski, S. A.; Robert Leclerc, ed.		√	MWL	1			'51–'73	41
Demonstrations and Demonstrating	Are Those Colors Really from Plants?	Brough, Hazel	√	√	SS&D	8	4	32	Fa 77	67
Demonstrations and Demonstrating	Art of Conservation: A Look Behind Closed Doors — Conserving a Tapestry Collection, The			√	Fa	9	1		J/F 82	48
Demonstrations and Demonstrating	Early American Craftsman's Holiday, An	Wellman, Kathryn	√		H&C	2	2		Sp 51	30
Demonstrations and Demonstrating	Flax — From Seed to Yarn	Parslow, Virginia	√		H&C	3	2		Sp 52	30
Demonstrations and Demonstrating	Fleece to Fibers At Museum of Man	Cox, Penni	√		SS&D	5	4	20	Fa 74	50
Demonstrations and Demonstrating	From Sheep to Shawl	Thorne, Sylvia	√		H&C	17	1		Wi 66	36

SUBJECT	TITLE	AUTHOR	IL	INST	JOUR	VOL	NO	ISS	DATE	PAGE
Demonstrations and Demonstrating	Grandadddy of Sheep-To-Shawls: The Newberry Coat 1811, The				S-O	6	4		82	20
Demonstrations and Demonstrating	Jacquard Demonstration		√		SS&D	2	3	7	Su 71	12
Demonstrations and Demonstrating	New Zealand Woolcrafts Festival	Guy, Sallie T.	√		SS&D	14	4	56	Fa 83	28
Demonstrations and Demonstrating	Paid Spinning Demonstrations	Hicks, C. Norman			SS&D	7	3	27	Su 76	46
Demonstrations and Demonstrating	Seminars on Early American Crafts	MacFarlane, Janet R.	√		H&C	2	2		Sp 51	29
Demonstrations and Demonstrating	Shear to Share	Best, Eleanor	√	√	SS&D	15	1	57	Wi 83	28
Demonstrations and Demonstrating	Sheep to Shawl: A Wonderful Show	Steinberg, Natali	√		S-O	6	4		82	41
Demonstrations and Demonstrating	Weavers Demonstrate for Mrs. Johnson		√		H&C	19	4		Fa 68	11
Demonstrations and Demonstrating: Colonial Weaving	Weaving with the Past	Schliske, Doreen	√		Hw	3	5		N/D 82	15
Demonstrations and Demonstrating: Jacquard Weaving	Restoring an Old Loom	Adrosko, Rita J.	√	√	H&C	15	3		Su 64	16
Demonstrations and Demonstrating: Sheep-to-Shawl	Ewe Can't Win This Wrestling Match	Byers, Patricia			TM			10	A/M 87	18
Demonstrations and Demonstrating: Spinning	But Why Does it Spin?	Bradley, Louise	√		S-O	5			81	10
Demonstrations and Demonstrating: Spinning	Demonstrating at the Smithsonian	Bielenberg, Kristina	√		H&C	24	1		J/F 73	19
Demonstrations and Demonstrating: Spinning	Demonstration Do's and Don'ts	Dokka, Margaret		√	SS&D	7	3	27	Su 76	64
Demonstrations and Demonstrating: Spinning	Handspinning in New Hampshire	Brackett, Thelma	√		H&C	17	1		Wi 66	18
Demonstrations and Demonstrating: Spinning	Linen Demonstrations				H&C	16	1		Wi 65	13
Demonstrations and Demonstrating: Spinning	Lions and Tigers and.....Sheep?	Johnson, Ginger R.	√		S-O	8	2		Su 84	24
Demonstrations and Demonstrating: Spinning	Planning a Spinning Demonstration	Reynolds, Donna			S-O	9	2		Su 85	17
Demonstrations and Demonstrating: Spinning	Song of the Bobbin	Nelson, Lois	√		SS&D	4	3	15	Su 73	42
Demonstrations and Demonstrating: Spinning	Spindle	Chesley, Zina Mae			SS&D	2	1	5	De 70	16
Demonstrations and Demonstrating: Spinning	Spinning at the Smithsonian	Epskamp, Sally	√		S-O	5			81	35
Demonstrations and Demonstrating: Spinning	Spinning Demonstrations	Sumpter, Frances R.			SS&D	3	4	12	Fa 72	31
Demonstrations and Demonstrating: Spinning	Strawbery Banke, A Restored New England Village	Currey, Ruth Dunlop	√		H&C	22	2		Sp 71	14
Demonstrations and Demonstrating: Spinning	String into Fuzz	Weddle, Diane	√		S-O	5			81	12
Demonstrations and Demonstrating: Spinning	Teaching the Blind to Spin: A Group Session	Gonzales, Carolyn	√		SS&D	10	3	39	Su 79	90
Demonstrations and Demonstrating: Spinning, Dyeing, Weaving	Demonstrators Revive Old Textile Arts		√		H&C	12	2		Sp 61	25
Demonstrations and Demonstrating: Spinning Flax	Linen Demonstration, Mary Alice Amos		√		H&C	16	2		Sp 65	30
Demonstrations and Demonstrating: Weaving	Demonstrating at the Smithsonian	Bielenberg, Kristina	√		H&C	24	1		J/F 73	19
Demonstrations and Demonstrating: Weaving	Demonstrating How Cloth Is Made	Guy, Sallie T.		√	SS&D	6	2	22	Sp 75	24
Demonstrations and Demonstrating: Weaving	Strawbery Banke, A Restored New England Village	Currey, Ruth Dunlop	√		H&C	22	2		Sp 71	14
Demonstrations and Demonstrating: Weaving	Weaver Who Wastes Not, A	Porcella, Yvonne	√	√	SS&D	6	4	24	Fa 75	8

SUBJECT	TITLE	AUTHOR	IL	INST	JOUR	VOL	NO	ISS	DATE	PAGE
Demonstrations and Demonstrating: Weaving	Weaving Demonstrations	Anderson, J.	√	√	H&C	15	4		Fa 64	14
Demonstrations and Demonstrating: Weaving, Spinning, 18th Century	Williamsburg Weaving	Brown, Bonnie	√		H&C	12	2		Sp 61	30
Denim	Denim Production: The Making of an American Staple	Rudich, Sally	√		Fa	13	5		S/O 86	11
Denim	Jeans: The Inside Story	Goodman, Deborah Lerme	√	√	TM			3	F/M 86	27
Denim	Lee Company	Rudich, Sally	√		Fa	13	5		S/O 86	13
Denim	Levi Strauss & Co.	Scarborough, Jessica	√		Fa	13	5		S/O 86	17
Denim	OshKosh B'Gosh	Rudich, Sally	√		Fa	13	5		S/O 86	16
Denim	Wrangler	Rudich, Sally	√		Fa	13	5		S/O 86	12
Denmark	At Home in a Changing World	Talley, Charles	√		Hw	8	3		M/J 87	44
Denmark	Contemporary Danish Weaving		√	√	Hw	8	3		M/J 87	46
Denmark	Danish Design: Form Follows Function		√	√	Hw	8	3		M/J 87	50
Denmark	Danish Twined Rag Rugs: Lillie Sherwood's Legacy	Irwin, Bobbie	√	√	WJ	10	4	40	Sp 86	32
Denmark	Denmark's Vaeveboden	Hill, Patricia C.	√	>4	H&C	5	2		Sp 54	16
Denmark	Linen Undergarments: A Proud Danish Heritage	Todd-Cope, Louise	√		Fa	14	2		M/A 87	51
Denmark	Modern Danish Textiles	Bryan, Dorothy	√		H&C	9	2		Sp 58	40
Denmark	Structure and Form in the Weaving of John Becker	Swannie, Suzanne	√		AT	6			De 86	173
Denmark	Textiles from an Ancient Danish Tomb	Zethraus, Kamma	√		H&C	6	2		Sp 55	46
Denmark	U.S. Students Visit Danish Yarn Company				H&C	19	4		Fa 68	34
Denting, Spaced	Inlay Techniques	Barrett, Clotilde	√	√	WJ	1	1	1	Jy 76	3
Denting, Spaced	Space-Dented Warp	Fry, Laura	√	√	WJ	4	3	15	Ja 80	26
Denting, Variations	Swatch #4, Linen Suit Fabric for Spring (Lillian Whipple)		√	√	Hw	7	5		N/D 86	64, I-7
Denting, Variations	Verticals	O'Shaughnessy, Marjorie	√	>4	SS&D	15	1	57	Wi 83	8
Design Analysis/Classification Textiles: African Caps	High-Status Caps of the Kongo and Mbundu Peoples	Gibson, Gordon D.; Cecilia R. McGurk	√		TMJ	4	4		77	71
Design Analysis/Classification Textiles: Anatolian Rugs	Anatolian Rugs: An Essay on Method	Denny, Walter B.	√		TMJ	3	4		De 73	7
Design Analysis/Classification Textiles: Asian	Flat-Woven Structures Found in Nomadic and Village Weavings from the Near East and Central Asia	Wertime, John T.	√		TMJ	18			79	33
Design Analysis/Classification Textiles: Banners	Group of Silk Islamic Banners, A	Denny, Walter B.	√		TMJ	4	1		De 74	67
Design Analysis/Classification Textiles: Batak Textiles	Selected Batak Textiles: Technique and Function	Gittinger, Mattiebelle S.	√		TMJ	4	2		75	13
Design Analysis/Classification Textiles: Batik	Conversations with a Batik Master	Gittinger, Mattiebelle S.	√		TMJ	18			79	25
Design Analysis/Classification Textiles: Batik	Symbolic Scenes in Javanese Batik	Adams, Monni	√		TMJ	3	1		De 70	25
Design Analysis/Classification Textiles: Batik	Van Zuylen Batik, Pekalongan, Central Java (1890-1946)	de Raadt-Apell, M. J.	√		TMJ	19 20			80,81	75
Design Analysis/Classification Textiles: Batik, Ikat	Additions to the Indonesian Collection	Gittinger, Mattiebelle S.	√		TMJ	4	3		76	43
Design Analysis/Classification Textiles: Berber Textiles	Traditional Berber Weaving in Central Morocco	Forelli, Sally; Jeanette Harries	√		TMJ	4	4		77	41
Design Analysis/Classification Textiles: Caftan	Newly Excavated Caftan from the Northern Caucasus, A	Riboud, Krishna	√		TMJ	4	3		76	21
Design Analysis/Classification Textiles: Carpet Depicted in Chinese Painting	Oriental Rug of A. D. 1280, An	Laing, Ellen Johnston	√		TMJ	4	1		De 74	82
Design Analysis/Classification Textiles: Carpets	Gifts from Kashan to Cairo	Ellis, Charles Grant	√		TMJ	1	1		No 62	33
Design Analysis/Classification Textiles: Carpets, Herat	Some Compartment Designs for Carpets, and Herat	Ellis, Charles Grant	√		TMJ	1	4		De 65	42

SUBJECT	TITLE	AUTHOR	IL	INST	JOUR	VOL	NO	ISS	DATE	PAGE
Design Analysis/Classification Textiles: Carpets, Mamluk	Is the Mamluk Carpet a Mandala? A Speculation	Ellis, Charles Grant	√		TMJ	4	1		De 74	30
Design Analysis/Classification Textiles: Carpets, Mamluk	Mysteries of the Misplaced Mamluks	Ellis, Charles Grant	√		TMJ	2	2		De 67	2
Design Analysis/Classification Textiles: Carpets, Persian	Some Compartment Designs for Carpets, and Herat	Ellis, Charles Grant	√		TMJ	1	4		De 65	42
Design Analysis/Classification Textiles: Carpets, Persian, Five-Medallion	Symbolic Meanings in Oriental Rug Patterns: Part 3	Cammann, Schuyler V.R.	√		TMJ	3	3		De 72	42
Design Analysis/Classification Textiles: Carpets, Spanish	Two Remarkable Fifteenth Century Carpets from Spain	Mackie, Louise W.	√		TMJ	4	4		77	15
Design Analysis/Classification Textiles: Chinese Silks, 18th Century	Where Did All the Silver Go? Identifying Eighteenth-Century Chinese Painted and Printed Silks	Lee-Whitman, Leanna; Maruta Skelton	√		TMJ	22			83	33
Design Analysis/Classification Textiles: Cloth Fragment	Classical Greek Textiles from Nymphaeum	Wild, John Peter	√		TMJ	4	4		77	33
Design Analysis/Classification Textiles: Drawloom	Drawloom Textiles in Wool and Silk (with a Structural Analysis by Ann Pollard Rowe)	Trilling, James	√		TMJ	21			82	96
Design Analysis/Classification Textiles: Egyptian Carpets, Mameluks	Symbolic Meanings in Oriental Rug Patterns: Part 3	Cammann, Schuyler V.R.	√		TMJ	3	3		De 72	42
Design Analysis/Classification Textiles: Embroideries, Turkish	Some Unusual Turkish Embroideries of the Early Eighteenth Century	Johnstone, Pauline	√		TMJ	24			85	75
Design Analysis/Classification Textiles: Embroidery, Rabari	Meaning of Folk Art in Rabari Life: A Closer Look at Mirrored Embroidery, The	Frater, Judy	√		TMJ	4	2		75	47
Design Analysis/Classification Textiles: European Shawls	Woven Structures of European Shawls in The Textile Museum Collection, The	Rowe, Ann Pollard			TMJ	24			85	55
Design Analysis/Classification Textiles: Hmong and Yao	Dress and Design in Highland Southeast Asia: The Hmong (Miao) and the Yao	Adams, Monni	√		TMJ	4	1		De 74	51
Design Analysis/Classification Textiles: Ikat	Designs in Sumba Textiles, Local Meanings and Foreign Influences	Adams, Monni	√		TMJ	3	2		De 71	28
Design Analysis/Classification Textiles: Interlace Patterns	Appendix I: The Development of Interlace and Related Patterns	Trilling, James	√		TMJ	21			82	104
Design Analysis/Classification Textiles: Islamic Rugs	Iconography of Everyday Life in Nineteenth-Century Middle Eastern Rugs, The	Paquin, Gerard A.	√		TMJ	22			83	5
Design Analysis/Classification Textiles: Islamic Rugs	Symbolic Meanings in Oriental Rug Patterns: Part 1	Cammann, Schuyler V.R.	√		TMJ	3	3		De 72	5
Design Analysis/Classification Textiles: Kashmir Shawls	Catalogue of Kashmir Shawls in The Textile Museum	Mikosch, Elisabeth	√		TMJ	24			85	23
Design Analysis/Classification Textiles: Kashmir Shawls	Scent of Flowers, Kishmir Shawls in the Collection of The Textile Museum, The	Mikosch, Elisabeth	√		TMJ	24			85	7
Design Analysis/Classification Textiles: Kasuri/Ikat Weaving, Japan	Kasuri: A Japanese Textile	Dusenbury, Mary	√		TMJ	17			78	41
Design Analysis/Classification Textiles: Kesa	Distant Mountains: The Influence of Funzo-e on the Tradition of Buddhist Clerical Robes in Japan	Lyman, Marie	√		TMJ	23			84	25
Design Analysis/Classification Textiles: Kesa	Kesa: Its Sacred and Secular Aspects	Kennedy, Alan	√		TMJ	22			83	67
Design Analysis/Classification Textiles: Lenten Curtains	Lenten Curtains from Colonial Peru	Kelemen, Pál	√		TMJ	3	1		De 70	5
Design Analysis/Classification Textiles: Mandarin Squares	Ming Mandarin Squares	Cammann, Schuyler	√		TMJ	4	4		77	5
Design Analysis/Classification Textiles: Methodology Reliability	Coptic Tapestry of Byzantine Style, A	Berliner, Rudolf	√		TMJ	1	1		No 62	3
Design Analysis/Classification Textiles: Mughal Sash	Second Type of Mughal Sash, A	Sonday, Milton; Nobuko Kajitani	√		TMJ	3	2		De 71	6
Design Analysis/Classification Textiles: Mughal Sash	Type of Mughal Sash, A	Sonday, Milton; Nobuko Kajitani	√		TMJ	3	1		De 70	45
Design Analysis/Classification Textiles: Mughal Textiles	Preliminary Report on a Group of Important Mughal Textiles, A	Smart, Ellen S.	√		TMJ	25			86	5
Design Analysis/Classification Textiles: Nasca Sprang Tassels	Nasca Sprang Tassels: Structure, Technique, and Order	Frame, Mary	√	√	TMJ	25			86	67

SUBJECT	TITLE	AUTHOR	IL	INST	JOUR	VOL	NO	ISS	DATE	PAGE
Design Analysis/Classification Textiles: Ottoman Turkish Textiles	Ottoman Turkish Textiles	Denny, Walter B.	√		TMJ	3	3		De 72	55
Design Analysis/Classification Textiles: Paracas Mantle	Identifying Hands at Work on a Paracas Mantle	Paul, Anne; Susan A. Niles	√		TMJ	23			84	5
Design Analysis/Classification Textiles: Paracas Mantles	Re-Establishing Provenience of Two Paracas Mantles	Paul, Anne			TMJ	19 20			80,81	35
Design Analysis/Classification Textiles: Persian Carpets	Symbolic Meanings in Oriental Rug Patterns: Part 2	Cammann, Schuyler V.R.	√		TMJ	3	3		De 72	22
Design Analysis/Classification Textiles: Persian Carpets, Five-Medallion	Symbolic Meanings in Oriental Rug Patterns: Part 3	Cammann, Schuyler V.R.	√		TMJ	3	3		De 72	42
Design Analysis/Classification Textiles: Peruvian Textiles	Interlocking Warp and Weft in the Nasca 2 Style	Rowe, Ann Pollard	√		TMJ	3	3		De 72	67
Design Analysis/Classification Textiles: Pile, Weft-Loop, Patterned	Textiles with Patterns in Weft-Loop Pile	Trilling, James	√		TMJ	21			82	93
Design Analysis/Classification Textiles: Resist-Dyed	Resist-Dyed Textiles	Trilling, James	√		TMJ	21			82	102
Design Analysis/Classification Textiles: Rugs, Brocade	Some Weft-Float Brocaded Rugs of the Bergama-Ezine Region	Beattie, May H.	√		TMJ	3	2		De 71	20
Design Analysis/Classification Textiles: Rugs, Chinese	Chinese Rugs	Ellis, Charles Grant	√		TMJ	2	3		De 68	35
Design Analysis/Classification Textiles: Rugs, Kazak	Kazak Rugs	Tschebull, Raoul	√		TMJ	3	2		De 71	2
Design Analysis/Classification Textiles: Rugs, Kilim, Kurdish	Kurdish Kilim Weaving in the Van-Hakkari District of Eastern Turkey	Landreau, Anthony N.	√	√	TMJ	3	4		De 73	27
Design Analysis/Classification Textiles: Rugs, Kirman	Kirman's Heritage in Washington: Vase Rugs in The Textile Museum	Ellis, Charles Grant	√		TMJ	2	3		De 68	17
Design Analysis/Classification Textiles: Rugs, Ottoman Prayer	Ottoman Prayer Rugs, The	Ellis, Charles Grant	√		TMJ	2	4		De 69	5
Design Analysis/Classification Textiles: Rugs, Soumak	Soumak-Woven Rug in a 15th Century International Sytle, A	Ellis, Charles Grant	√		TMJ	1	2		De 63	3
Design Analysis/Classification Textiles: Rugs, Turkish	Turkish Carpet with Spots and Stripes, A	Mackie, Louise W.	√		TMJ	4	3		76	4
Design Analysis/Classification Textiles: State of Research	Remarks on Some Tapestries from Egypt	Berliner, Rudolf	√		TMJ	1	4		De 65	20
Design Analysis/Classification Textiles: Tapestries, Coptic	Remarks on Some Tapestries from Egypt	Berliner, Rudolf	√		TMJ	1	4		De 65	20
Design Analysis/Classification Textiles: Tapestries, Late Roman	Tapestries	Trilling, James	√		TMJ	21			82	29
Design Analysis/Classification Textiles: Tapestries, Middle Horizon, Early	Peruvian Textile Fragment from the Beginning of the Middle Horizon	Conklin, William J	√		TMJ	3	1		De 70	15
Design Analysis/Classification Textiles: Tapestries, Peru	Chinese Influence in Colonial Peruvian Tapestries	Cammann, Schuyler	√		TMJ	1	3		De 64	21
Design Analysis/Classification Textiles: Tapestry Roundel	Tapestry Roundel with Nilotic Scenes, A	Abdel-Malek, Laila	√		TMJ	25			86	33
Design Analysis/Classification Textiles: Tapestry Roundels, Coptic	Horsemen in Tapestry Roundels Found in Egypt	Berliner, Rudolf	√		TMJ	1	2		De 63	39
Design Analysis/Classification Textiles: Tapestry Shirt	Technical Features of a Middle Horizon Tapestry Shirt from Peru, The	Bird, Junius B.; Milica Dimitrijevic Skinner	√		TMJ	4	1		De 74	5
Design Analysis/Classification Textiles: Tapestry Tunics, Inca	Technical Features of Inca Tapestry Tunics	Rowe, Ann Pollard	√		TMJ	17			78	5
Design Analysis/Classification Textiles: Theory	Coptic Tapestry of Byzantine Style, A	Berliner, Rudolf	√		TMJ	1	1		No 62	3
Design Analysis/Classification Textiles: Tiahuanaco Tapestry Design	Tiahuanaco Tapestry Design	Sawyer, Alan R.	√		TMJ	1	2		De 63	27
Design Analysis/Classification Textiles: Tunics, Musician, Peru	Textile Evidence for Huari Music	Rowe, Ann Pollard	√		TMJ	18			79	5
Design Analysis/Classification Textiles: West African	Medieval Textiles from the Tellem Caves in Central Mali, West Africa	Bedaux, Rogier M. A.; Rita Bolland	√		TMJ	19 20			80,81	65
Design Analysis/Classifiction Textiles: Tapestries	More About the Developing Islamic Style in Tapestries	Berliner, Rudolf	√		TMJ	2	1		De 66	3

SUBJECT	TITLE	AUTHOR	IL	INST	JOUR	VOL	NO	ISS	DATE	PAGE
Design: Definition	Composition and Designing: Design	Zielinski, S. A.; Robert Leclerc, ed.			MWL	18			'51–'73	14
Design Elements: Composition	Designs in Sumba Textiles, Local Meanings and Foreign Influences	Adams, Monni	√		TMJ	3	2		De 71	28
Design Elements: Purpose	Design and the Handweaver: Elements of Design: Purpose	Atwater, Mary Meigs			SCGM		3		61	3
Design Evolution: Eagle Motif	Use of Eagles as a Decorative and Symbolic Motif in 19th Century American Coverlets, The	Anderson, Clarita; Jo B. Paoletti	√		AT	3			My 85	173
Design Evolution: Kashmir Shawls	Scent of Flowers, Kishmir Shawls in the Collection of The Textile Museum, The	Mikosch, Elisabeth	√		TMJ	24			85	7
Design Evolution: Tapestries	More About the Developing Islamic Style in Tapestries	Berliner, Rudolf	√		TMJ	2	1		De 66	3
Design Evolution: Tapestry Roundels, Coptic	Horsemen in Tapestry Roundels Found in Egypt	Berliner, Rudolf	√		TMJ	1	2		De 63	39
Design Evolution: Tiahuanaco Tapestry	Tiahuanaco Tapestry Design	Sawyer, Alan R.	√		TMJ	1	2		De 63	27
Design Motifs: Blazons, Mamluk	Mysteries of the Misplaced Mamluks	Ellis, Charles Grant	√		TMJ	2	2		De 67	2
Design: Warping Sticks	Warping and Weaving Mitla Cloth on the Backstrap Loom	Knottenbelt, Maaike	√	√	TMJ	22			83	53
Designer also see People										
Designer Collections	Alexander Julian: Cut of a Different Cloth	De Leon, Sherry	√		Fa	12	3		M/J 85	64
Designer Collections	Annikki Karvinen: Finnish Designer of Wovens	Talley, Charles	√		Fa	13	4		J/A 86	16
Designer Collections	Designer Collection: Lillian Whipple		√	√	Hw	7	5		N/D 86	64
Designer Collections	Designer Collection: Malin Selander		√	√	Hw	7	5		N/D 86	60
Designer Collections	Designer Collection: Virginia West		√	√	Hw	7	5		N/D 86	62
Designer Collections: Fabrics, Interiors	Terra Nova: Jack Lenor Larsen	Larson-Fleming, Susan	√		WJ	11	1	41	Su 86	49
Designer Collections: Knitwear	Knitted Palette of Brenda French, The	Pierce, Judith	√		Fa	13	2		M/A 86	43
Designer Collections: Veness, Tim	Notes on Designing for Drape	Veness, Tim	√		Hw	7	5		N/D 86	76
Designer: Interiors	Fiber and Architecture: Dennis Jenkins		√		Fa	3	3		M/J 76	35
Designer: Interiors	Fiber and Architecture: Richard Worthen		√		Fa	3	3		M/J 76	32
Designer: Theater	Fiber as Set Design: The Work of Clayton Karkosh and Associates		√		Fa	3	4		J/A 76	34
Designer/Craftsmen: Textile Industry	Craftsmen in Industry				H&C	16	1		Wi 65	8
Designer/Weaver	Adapting Handwoven Fabrics to Interior Design	Storey, Walter Rendell	√		H&C	4	3		Su 53	8
Designer/Weaver	Adela Akers, Designer-Weaver of Chicago		√		H&C	17	2		Sp 66	10
Designer/Weaver	Albertje Koopman		√		Hw	4	1		J/F 83	56
Designer/Weaver	Alice Hindson, Expert on the Draw-loom	Arnold, Ruth	√		H&C	10	4		Fa 59	12
Designer/Weaver	Ana Rossell: Weaving with Flair for C. A. R. E.	Ligon, Linda	√		Iw	3	1		Fa 77	18
Designer/Weaver	Anita Mayer	Wilson, Jean	√		Hw	2	2		Mr 81	28
Designer/Weaver	Anni Albers — Innovator in Textile Design		√		H&C	10	4		Fa 59	6
Designer/Weaver	Artist/Designer: Two Approaches to Fabric	Kinsella, Pat	√		AT	3			My 85	57
Designer/Weaver	Bringing Freedom to Fibers: Loni Parker	Brough, Hazel	√		SS&D	7	3	27	Su 76	44
Designer/Weaver	By the Yard	Mattera, Joanne	√		TM			5	J/J 86	50
Designer/Weaver	Canadian Classic, A	Baker, William R. M.	√		SS&D	18	3	71	Su 87	52
Designer/Weaver	Crane Day Designs	Colton, Mary Rawcliffe	√		SS&D	18	2	70	Sp 87	48
Designer/Weaver	Dale Goffigan: Textile Designer		√		Fa	12	3		M/J 85	66
Designer/Weaver	Dalsgaard Tapestries, The	Clement, Doris W.	√		H&C	17	1		Wi 66	6
Designer/Weaver	Decorative Miniatures in Silk by Jadwiga Rakowska		√		H&C	10	2		Sp 59	22
Designer/Weaver	Designer-Weaver in India, A	Sethna, Nelly H.	√		H&C	17	2		Sp 66	18
Designer/Weaver	Diane Wiersba	Gilfoy, Peggy S.	√		H&C	15	3		Su 64	19

SUBJECT	TITLE	AUTHOR	IL	INST	JOUR	VOL	NO	ISS	DATE	PAGE
Designer/Weaver	Don Bujnowski		√		H&C	13	4		Fa 62	31
Designer/Weaver	Dora Jung, Distinguished Finnish Weaver		√		H&C	10	2		Sp 59	14
Designer/Weaver	Dorothy Dodge: Boldness in Fiber		√		SS&D	6	3	23	Su 75	4
Designer/Weaver	Dorothy Liebes		√		H&C	11	2		Sp 60	18
Designer/Weaver	Edith Huntington Snow, Weaver, Artist, Craftsman (Reprint)	Jarecka, Louise Llewellyn	√		H&C	26	2		Ap 75	10
Designer/Weaver	Eia Lampe Advocates Classical Weaving Techniques For Today		√		H&C	17	2		Sp 66	6
Designer/Weaver	Eleen Auvil, Versatile Designer Weaver		√		H&C	20	1		Wi 69	11
Designer/Weaver	Ella Bolster		√	> 4	H&C	12	2		Sp 61	26
Designer/Weaver	Ellen Krucker	Busby, Robert J.			H&C	20	1		Wi 69	44
Designer/Weaver	Ellen Siegel, Designer for the Handloom and Power Loom		√		H&C	15	1		Wi 64	6
Designer/Weaver	Emily Belding, Textile Designer		√		H&C	7	1		Wi 55	26
Designer/Weaver	Fabrics from the Looms of Karl Laurell		√		H&C	2	4		Fa 51	9
Designer/Weaver	Fiber World of Leah Orr, The	Orr, Leah	√		SS&D	9	3	35	Su 78	8
Designer/Weaver	Frances van Hall	Bryan, Dorothy	√		H&C	11	2		Sp 60	43
Designer/Weaver	Francisca Mayer, Designer-Weaver in the Peruvian Highland	Boyer, Ruth McDonald	√		H&C	19	2		Sp 68	18
Designer/Weaver	From Canvas to Fabric...Jeffrey Aronoff 1980 Coty Award Winner		√		SS&D	11	4	44	Fa 80	50
Designer/Weaver	Greta, Lein, Young Norweigan Designer-Weaver	Nygards-Kers, Ingrid	√		H&C	14	1		Wi 63	15
Designer/Weaver	Hal Painter, Weaver of Tapestries and Rugs		√		H&C	16	3		Su 65	10
Designer/Weaver	Hans Krondahl		√		SS&D	5	3	19	Su 74	4
Designer/Weaver	Hella Skowronski		√		H&C	11	4		Fa 60	18
Designer/Weaver	Ida Dean Grae				H&C	14	3		Su 63	4
Designer/Weaver	Ida Grae—A Totally Textural Experience	Kaplan, Suzan	√		SS&D	5	4	20	Fa 74	4
Designer/Weaver	Interview with Albertje Koopman, An	LaLena, Constance	√		Hw	7	3		M/J 86	89
Designer/Weaver	Interview with Jack Lenor Larsen, An		√		WJ	7	1	25	Su 82	10
Designer/Weaver	Interview with Susan Klebanoff, An		√		SS&D	13	3	51	Su 82	34
Designer/Weaver	Isabel Scott, Handweaver and Designer	Storey, Walter Rendell	√		H&C	4	2		Sp 53	14
Designer/Weaver	Jack Lenor Larsen		√		SS&D	15	4	60	Fa 84	22
Designer/Weaver	Jack Lenor Larsen		√		H&C	11	2		Sp 60	22
Designer/Weaver	Jack Lenor Larsen	Znamierowski, Nell	√		H&C	22	3		Su 71	6
Designer/Weaver	"Jack Lenor Larsen: 30 Years of Creative Textiles" (Exhibit)	Zoppetti, Patti	√		Fa	9	5		S/O 82	82
Designer/Weaver	Jack Lenor Larsen: Convergence '76 Keynoter		√		SS&D	7	1	25	Wi 75	4
Designer/Weaver	Jackie von Ladau, Versatile Weaver	Clement, Doris	√	√	H&C	10	3		Su 59	20
Designer/Weaver	James and Marie Howell, Designers		√		H&C	10	2		Sp 59	11
Designer/Weaver	John Charles Gordon, An Explorer in Materials		√		H&C	20	1		Wi 69	19
Designer/Weaver	Julia Keiner, Brings Fabrics from Israel		√		H&C	15	2		Sp 64	22
Designer/Weaver	Karen Stoller		√		SS&D	11	4	44	Fa 80	79
Designer/Weaver	Kenneth J. Uyemura: A Feeling of Relatedness		√		SS&D	4	3	15	Su 73	45
Designer/Weaver	Kerstin Ekengren	af Kleen, Nils E.	√		H&C	15	2		Sp 64	18
Designer/Weaver	Kjeld Juul-Hansen		√		H&C	9	2		Sp 58	29
Designer/Weaver	Klara Cherepov, A Career in Two Countries	Landis, Bruce	√		H&C	18	3		Su 67	19
Designer/Weaver	Laurie Herrick, Contemporary Weaver and Teacher	Furniss, Frances	√		H&C	18	4		Fa 67	10
Designer/Weaver	Lea Van Puymbroeck Miller, Innovator in Handweaving	Boyer, Ruth M.	√		H&C	20	2		Sp 69	15
Designer/Weaver	Lee Carlin: Handweaving Entrepreneur	Ligon, Linda	√		Iw	3	1		Fa 77	26

SUBJECT	TITLE	AUTHOR	IL	INST	JOUR	VOL	NO	ISS	DATE	PAGE
Designer/Weaver	Legacy of Color and Texture: Dorothy Liebes, 1899-1972, A	Weltge, Sigrid	√		Iw	4	3		Su 79	25
Designer/Weaver	Lenore Tawney		√		H&C	13	2		Sp 62	6
Designer/Weaver	Lewis Mayhew, Versatile Northwest Weaver		√		H&C	14	3		Su 63	9
Designer/Weaver	Lia Cook, An Interview	Papa, Nancy	√		Iw	4	4		Fa 79	24
Designer/Weaver	Libby Platus: Heroic Fiber Sculpture		√		SS&D	6	4	24	Fa 75	4
Designer/Weaver	Malin Selander	Cromstedt, Cathrine	√		H&C	17	1		Wi 66	22
Designer/Weaver	Manfred Goldschmidt		√		H&C	11	3		Su 60	20
Designer/Weaver	Marg Johansen, An American Represented in International Tapestry Show		√		H&C	17	1		Wi 66	20
Designer/Weaver	Margareta Nettles — Weaver, Designer	Slater, Deborah	√		H&C	23	1		J/F 72	22
Designer/Weaver	Margareta Ohberg, From Sweden to a Long Career in America		√		H&C	12	3		Su 61	17
Designer/Weaver	Marianne Strengell		√		H&C	13	4		Fa 62	14
Designer/Weaver	Marion Stewart		√		H&C	13	4		Fa 62	17
Designer/Weaver	Marli Ehrman		√		H&C	11	2		Sp 60	25
Designer/Weaver	Martha Pollock	Bryan, Dorothy	√		H&C	7	4		Fa 56	7
Designer/Weaver	Mary Crovatt Hambidge	Schaller, Karin	√		Fa	11	5		S/O 84	24
Designer/Weaver	Matias Lozano, Designer Weaver		√		H&C	10	1		Wi 59	28
Designer/Weaver	Nell Znamierowski: Color & Design	Liebler, Barbara	√		Hw	2	4		Se 81	40
Designer/Weaver	Nell Znamierowski, Weaver-Designer	Znamierowski, Nell	√		SS&D	3	4	12	Fa 72	16
Designer/Weaver	Pat White: The "Small Things" Are Her Signature	Park, Betty	√	√	SS&D	13	3	51	Su 82	58
Designer/Weaver	Pauline Dutterer, Designer and Weaver		√		H&C	3	2		Sp 52	28
Designer/Weaver	Peter Collingwood, English Rug Weaver		√		H&C	11	4		Fa 60	12
Designer/Weaver	Peter Collingwood, His Weaves and Weaving: Peter Collingwood-Designer and Weaver	Tidball, Harriet	√		SCGM		8		63	44
Designer/Weaver	Philis Schroeder: No Room for Error		√		SS&D	6	3	23	Su 75	5
Designer/Weaver	Polly Yori (error-corrected H&C v21 n3 70 p45)	Marston, Ena	√	> 4	H&C	21	1		Wi 70	19
Designer/Weaver	Profile: Robert L. Kidd	Fleming, Ray Frost	√		H&C	23	5		S/O 72	9
Designer/Weaver	Robert D. Sailors		√		H&C	16	4		Fa 65	6
Designer/Weaver	Robert Harnden — Diplomat & Weaver	Schobinger, Helen J.	√		H&C	11	1		Wi 60	16
Designer/Weaver	Roy Ginstrom, Versatile Handweaver and Designer of Fabrics for Power Looms		√		H&C	13	3		Su 62	6
Designer/Weaver	Sara Matsson Anliot	Bryan, Dorothy	√		H&C	11	3		Su 60	10
Designer/Weaver	SS&D Interview: Cynthia Schira (error-corrected SS&D v10 n2 79 p56)	Park, Betty	√		SS&D	10	1	37	Wi 78	4
Designer/Weaver	SS&D Interview: Else Regensteiner	Towner, Naomi Whiting	√		SS&D	10	2	38	Sp 79	4
Designer/Weaver	Summer and Winter Garments (Melinda Raber Johnson)		√	√	WJ	11	3	43	Wi 87	44
Designer/Weaver	Susan B. Goldberg		√		H&C	16	4		Fa 65	12
Designer/Weaver	Taproot: Jack Lenor Larsen	Goldin, Susan	√		Iw	4	3		Su 79	17
Designer/Weaver	Terra Nova: Jack Lenor Larsen	Larson-Fleming, Susan	√		WJ	11	1	41	Su 86	49
Designer/Weaver	Textiles Designed for Contemporary Furniture		√		H&C	12	2		Sp 61	17
Designer/Weaver	Theo Moorman, English Tapestry Weaver in San Francisco	Marston, Ena	√	√	H&C	20	1		Wi 69	12
Designer/Weaver	Tina McMorran	Chalmers, Marjorie	√		SS&D	3	3	11	Su 72	23
Designer/Weaver	Trude Guermonprez	Bryan, Dorothy	√		H&C	11	2		Sp 60	30
Designer/Weaver	Tzaims Luksus		√		H&C	14	1		Wi 63	12
Designer/Weaver	Versatile Swedish Weaver, Ann-Mari Hoke, A		√		H&C	8	2		Sp 57	20
Designer/Weaver	Weaver Profile: Mahota Handwovens	Irwin, Bobbie	√		Hw	8	5		N/D 87	35

SUBJECT	TITLE	AUTHOR	IL	INST	JOUR	VOL	NO	ISS	DATE	PAGE
Designer/Weaver	"Woven and Graphic Art of Anni Albers, The" (Exhibit)	Malarcher, Patricia	√		Fa	13	1		J/F 86	62
Designers	Designers on Design		√		Fa	10	4		J/A 83	28
Designers: Fabrics	Tiogruppen: When Working Together Works	Talley, Charles	√		Fa	11	6		N/D 84	41
Designers: Fashion	Revivified Past, A	Upitis, Lizbeth	√		Kn	3	1	5	F-W 86	12
Designers: Knitting	American Designers		√		Kn	3	1	5	F-W 86	16
Designers: Knitwear	Knitting for a Living (error-corrected TM i6 A/S86 p6)	Guagliumi, Susan	√		TM			4	A/M 86	38
Designers: Knitwear	Succeeding with the Knitting Machine	Mattera, Joanne	√		TM			2	D/J 85	50
Designers: Textile	In the Shadow of Fame: Sophie Taeuber-Arp and Sonia Delaunay	Austin, Carol	√		Fa	12	5		S/O 85	50
Designers: Textiles	Knoll Textiles		√		H&C	9	3		Su 58	12
Designer's Notebook	Early Fabrics	Myers, Ruth, ed.	√	√	SS&D	12	3	47	Su 81	67
Designs and Designing	Creativity	Humphery, Laney			Hw	6	3		Su 85	22
Designs and Designing	Design for Interiors	Stewart-Pollack, Julie	√		Hw	5	2		M/A 84	52
Designs and Designing	Functional or Decorative Design	Liebler, Barbara			Hw	8	1		J/F 87	12
Designs and Designing	How I Design	Miller, Mary Jane	√	√	TM			8	D/J 86	10
Designs and Designing	Italy at Work — Her Renaissance in Design Today		√		H&C	2	1		Wi 50	41
Designs and Designing	Journey in Thread, A	Rees, Linda	√		Hw	5	5		N/D 84	99
Designs and Designing	Katie Pasquini: Mandala Quilts	Pasquini, Katie	√		Fa	10	4		J/A 83	20
Designs and Designing	Lines and Shapes in Interior Spaces		√		Hw	5	2		M/A 84	52
Designs and Designing	On Designing and Creativity	Smith, Barbara			Hw	5	5		N/D 84	96
Designs and Designing	On Making Good Cloth	Darwall, Randall	√		Hw	7	5		N/D 86	22
Designs and Designing	What a Handweaver Can Learn from the Scottish Weaving Industry (error-corrected WJ v2 n1 77 insert for vol. 1)	Barrett, Clotilde	√	√	WJ	1	3	3	Ja 77	11
Designs and Designing	Working with Material	Albers, Anni			Iw	3	2		Wi 78	12
Designs and Designing: Adapting Weaves	Adapting a Weave to Your Purpose	Liebler, Barbara	√	√	Iw	4	3		Su 79	52
Designs and Designing: Andean Trims	Andean Crossed-Warp Techniques for Decorative Trims, Part 1 — Flat Bands	Cahlander, Adele	√	√	WJ	2	4	8	Ap 78	10
Designs and Designing: Apparel	Barbara Knollenberg, Fashion Designer, A Personal Story		√		WJ	6	3	23	Wi 81	10
Designs and Designing: Apparel	Loom-Shaped Garment, A	Haynes, Albertje Koopman	√	√	SS&D	9	1	33	Wi 77	83
Designs and Designing: Apparel Fabrics	Designing Handwoven Clothing	Thomason, Roger	√		SS&D	10	1	37	Wi 78	88
Designs and Designing: Apparel Fabrics	Weaving for Ethnic Clothing	Marston, Ena	√	√	SS&D	10	1	37	Wi 78	42
Designs and Designing: Architectural Textiles	Weaver's Commission Workshop	Meany, Janet	√		SS&D	10	3	39	Su 79	40
Designs and Designing: Basics	Return to Basic Disciplines	Stark, Ruthellen	√		SS&D	2	1	5	De 70	10
Designs and Designing: Baskets	Wickerwork Basket Weaving in Four-Strand Designs (error-corrected SS&D v14 n1 82 p6)	Jensen, Elizabeth Jane	√	√	SS&D	13	4	52	Fa 82	20
Designs and Designing: Beadwork	Contemporary Appliqued Beadwork: Design Ideas	Woodsmall, Annabel Whitney	√	√	TIAM			2		79	9
Designs and Designing: Beadwork Application Process	Contemporary Appliqued Beadwork: The Application Process	Woodsmall, Annabel Whitney	√	√	TIAM			2		79	12
Designs and Designing: Bedspreads	Designing Bedspreads for Use in Modern Interiors	Frey, Berta	√		H&C	13	3		Su 62	9
Designs and Designing: Beiderwand	Beiderwand	Gordon, Judith	√	>4	CW	1	2	2	Fe 80	1
Designs and Designing: Belts	Bevy of Belts, A	Karjala, Beth	√	√	Hw	8	1		J/F 87	46
Designs and Designing: Bergman Weaves	Bergman	Alvic, Philis	√	>4	CW	2	1	4	Oc 80	10
Designs and Designing: Bias	Working with the Bias	West, Virginia	√	>4	WJ	12	1	45	Su 87	9
Designs and Designing: Blankets	Four Blankets		√		Hw	7	1		J/F 86	40

SUBJECT	TITLE	AUTHOR	IL	INST	JOUR	VOL	NO	ISS	DATE	PAGE
Designs and Designing: Block Patterns	Summer and Winter: A Rug for All Seasons (Falene E. Hamilton)		√	√	Hw	7	4		S/O 86	42
Designs and Designing: Block Patterns	Summer and Winter and Other Two-Tie Unit Weaves: Drafts and Patterns	Tidball, Harriet	√	> 4	SCGM		19		66	17
Designs and Designing: Block Patterns, Damask	Contemporary Satins: Three-Block Patterns	Tidball, Harriet	√	> 4	SCGM		7		62	14
Designs and Designing: Block Patterns, Figures	Summer and Winter and Other Two-Tie Unit Weaves: Drafts and Patterns	Tidball, Harriet	√	> 4	SCGM		19		66	31
Designs and Designing: Block Patterns, Pine Trees	Summer and Winter and Other Two-Tie Unit Weaves: Drafts and Patterns	Tidball, Harriet	√	> 4	SCGM		19		66	28
Designs and Designing: Block Patterns, Texture	Exploring the Textures: Designing the Texture	Zielinski, S. A.; Robert Leclerc, ed.	√	> 4	MWL	11			'51–'73	74
Designs and Designing: Block Patterns, Velvet	Pile Weaves, Rugs and Tapestry: Patterns in Velvet Rugs	Zielinski, S. A.; Robert Leclerc, ed.	√	√	MWL	14			'51–'73	70
Designs and Designing: Block Weaves, Uneven-Tied	Uneven-Tied Overshot	Searles, Nancy	√	> 4	PWC	3	4	10		14
Designs and Designing: Blocks	Alphabet Soup	Chandler, Deborah	√	> 4	Hw	8	5		N/D 87	90
Designs and Designing: Blocks	Atwater-Bronson Lace — Turned		√	√	WJ	2	4	8	Ap 78	20
Designs and Designing: Blocks	Block: An Exploration of Weaves, The	Strickler, Carol	√		Hw	8	5		N/D 87	41
Designs and Designing: Blocks	Block Drafting, Profile Drafts, and a Few Other Related Things	Redding, Debbie	√	> 4	Hw	4	3		M/J 83	19
Designs and Designing: Blocks	Block Weaves Part 1, Profile Drafts and Block Designs (error-corrected WJ v2 n4 78 insert for vol. 2)		√	> 4	WJ	2	3	7	Ja 78	6
Designs and Designing: Blocks	Block Weaves Part 2, Atwater Bronson Lace		√	> 4	WJ	2	3	7	Ja 78	10
Designs and Designing: Blocks	Blocks and Warp-Faced Weaving			√	Hw	8	5		N/D 87	61
Designs and Designing: Blocks	Blocks in Production	LaLena, Constance	√	√	Hw	8	5		N/D 87	22
Designs and Designing: Blocks	Coverlet Weaves Using Two Ties	Barrett, Clotilde	√	> 4	WJ	3	4	12	Ap 79	26
Designs and Designing: Blocks	Designing Block Weaves	Kurtz, Carol	√	> 4	SS&D	11	2	42	Sp 80	5
Designs and Designing: Blocks	Designing Damask	Nyquist, Jan	√	> 4	SS&D	10	4	40	Fa 79	16
Designs and Designing: Blocks	Designing with Loom-Woven Open Weaves	Marston, Ena	√	√	SS&D	13	1	49	Wi 81	22
Designs and Designing: Blocks	Designs in Summer-and-Winter	Barrett, Ruth L.	√	> 4	H&C	12	4		Fa 61	34
Designs and Designing: Blocks	Diversified Plain Weave	Wertenberger, Kathryn	√	> 4	Hw	8	5		N/D 87	62
Designs and Designing: Blocks	Drafting: A Personal Approach, Part 2	Alvic, Philis	√	> 4	SS&D	13	2	50	Sp 82	46
Designs and Designing: Blocks	Eighteenth Century German Court Weaver: Johann Michael Frickinger, An	Hilts, Patricia	√		SS&D	11	4	44	Fa 80	16
Designs and Designing: Blocks	Handwoven Trees	Wertenberger, Kathryn	√	> 4	Hw	5	5		N/D 84	90
Designs and Designing: Blocks	How to Weave Your Own Designs	Arnold, Ruth	√	> 4	H&C	11	3		Su 60	6
Designs and Designing: Blocks	Lines, Squares, Rectangles	Marston, Ena	√	√	SS&D	14	3	55	Su 83	72
Designs and Designing: Blocks	Loom Controlled Designs		√	> 4	WJ	3	3	11	Ja 79	18
Designs and Designing: Blocks	Mattor (error-corrected WJ v2 n1 77 insert for vol. 1)	Dunham, Miriam	√	√	WJ	1	4	4	Ap 77	21
Designs and Designing: Blocks	Megablocks	Patrick, Jane	√	√	Hw	4	1		J/F 83	60
Designs and Designing: Blocks	Monk's Belt and Ways to Think of Blocks		√	> 4	Hw	8	5		N/D 87	57
Designs and Designing: Blocks	Multiple Harness Crackle		√	> 4	WJ	4	1	13	Jy 79	15
Designs and Designing: Blocks	New Design for Place Mats	Frey, Berta	√	> 4	H&C	6	4		Fa 55	28
Designs and Designing: Blocks	Notes of a Pattern Weaver	Alvic, Philis	√		SS&D	13	4	52	Fa 82	76
Designs and Designing: Blocks	Notes of a Pattern Weaver	Alvic, Philis	√	> 4	SS&D	14	2	54	Sp 83	76
Designs and Designing: Blocks	Notes of a Pattern Weaver	Alvic, Philis	√	> 4	SS&D	14	4	56	Fa 83	82
Designs and Designing: Blocks	Patchwork Designs in Summer and Winter	Davenport, Betty	√	√	PWC	1	1		No 81	27
Designs and Designing: Blocks	Personal Approach to Drafting, A	Alvic, Philis	√	> 4	SS&D	13	1	49	Wi 81	32
Designs and Designing: Blocks	Point Block Progression: Notes of a Pattern Weaver	Alvic, Philis	√	> 4	WJ	10	4	40	Sp 86	67
Designs and Designing: Blocks	Practical Weave for Rugs (Reprint), A	Atwater, Mary Meigs	√	> 4	H&C	26	1		J/F 75	7
Designs and Designing: Blocks	Profile Drafting: Getting the Big Picture	Alderman, Sharon	√	> 4	Hw	8	5		N/D 87	44
Designs and Designing: Blocks	Rug Based on 3-Shaft Striaght Twill		√	√	WJ	5	4	20	Sp 81	20

SUBJECT	TITLE	AUTHOR	IL	INST	JOUR	VOL	NO	ISS	DATE	PAGE
Designs and Designing: Blocks	Rugs Woven on Summer and Winter Threading		√	> 4	WJ	3	1	9	Jy 78	12
Designs and Designing: Blocks	Shaft-Switch Rugs with Pinstripe Pattern Areas		√	√	WJ	5	2	18	Fa 80	28
Designs and Designing: Blocks	Shaft-Switching on 3-End Drafts: Striped Patterns, Part 1		√	√	WJ	6	1	21	Su 81	7
Designs and Designing: Blocks	Single-Tied Unit Weave		√	> 4	Hw	8	5		N/D 87	54
Designs and Designing: Blocks	Southwest Collection, The		√	√	Hw	7	4		S/O 86	52
Designs and Designing: Blocks	Summer and Winter for Four Shafts	Allen, Debbie	√	√	Hw	8	5		N/D 87	86
Designs and Designing: Blocks	Summer and Winter — Part 1		√	> 4	WJ	2	4	8	Ap 78	28
Designs and Designing: Blocks	System in Symbols, A	The Gadred Weavers	√	> 4	H&C	2	1		Wi 50	16
Designs and Designing: Blocks	Taking Charge of Your Design	West, Virginia	√	> 4	Hw	8	5		N/D 87	46
Designs and Designing: Blocks	Three-Toned Blocks, Part 1: Simple Pattern	Broughton, Eve T.	√	> 4	CW	6	1	16	Se 84	12
Designs and Designing: Blocks	Two-Tie Unit for Rugs, Part 1: The Double-Faced Stuffer Weave and Summer-and-Winter, The	Windeknecht, Margaret	√	> 4	SS&D	16	1	61	Wi 84	82
Designs and Designing: Blocks	Variations on a Landes Theme	Coutts, Lucele	√	√	WJ	8	4	32	Sp 84	24
Designs and Designing: Blocks	Warp-pattern Weaving	Frey, Berta	√	√	H&C	10	3		Su 59	9
Designs and Designing: Blocks	Weaving Block Twills		√	> 4	Hw	8	5		N/D 87	52
Designs and Designing: Blocks	Weft-Faced Weaving of Block Weaves		√	√	Hw	8	5		N/D 87	59
Designs and Designing: Blocks, Alternating	Three-Toned Blocks, Part 3: Alternating Designs	Broughton, Eve T.	√	> 4	CW	6	3	18	My 85	10
Designs and Designing: Blocks, Combined	Roses and Snowballs: The Development of Block Patterns in the German Linen-Weaving Tradition	Hilts, Patricia	√	> 4	AT	5			Ju 86	167
Designs and Designing: Blocks, Computer-Aided	Posneg Program, The	Scorgie, Jean; Ann Sinclair	√	√	SS&D	13	3	51	Su 82	26
Designs and Designing: Blocks, Crackle Weave	Contemporary Approach to Traditional Weaves: Free Patterns in Crackle	Zielinski, S. A.; Robert Leclerc, ed.	√	√	MWL	8			'51–'73	26
Designs and Designing: Blocks, Single	Roses And Snowballs: The Development of Block Patterns in the German Linen-Weaving Tradition	Hilts, Patricia	√	> 4	AT	5			Ju 86	167
Designs and Designing: Blocks, Turned	Drafting: A Personal Approach, Part 3	Alvic, Philis	√	> 4	SS&D	13	3	51	Su 82	40
Designs and Designing: Borders	It's a Frame-up	Valk, Gene E.	√	√	Hw	4	4		S/O 83	83
Designs and Designing: Borders, Clothing	Designing Borders on Clothing	Knollenberg, Barbara	√	√	WJ	2	1	5	Jy 77	12
Designs and Designing: Bound Weave	Studies in Boundweave	Mershon, Janis	√	√	SS&D	12	2	46	Sp 81	50
Designs and Designing: Card Weaving	Card Weaving	Frey, Berta	√	√	H&C	18	3		Su 67	8
Designs and Designing: Card Weaving	Cardweaving Patterns on a 4-Shaft Loom	Ohman, Polly	√	√	WJ	6	4	24	Sp 82	36
Designs and Designing: Card Weaving	Diagonal Triple-turn Cardweaving	Holtzer, Marilyn	√	√	SS&D	11	2	42	Sp 80	100
Designs and Designing: Chenille	Pile Weaves, Rugs and Tapestry: Free Patterns in Chenille	Zielinski, S. A.; Robert Leclerc, ed.	√	√	MWL	14			'51–'73	43
Designs and Designing: Chimayó Style	Chimayó—A Town of Weavers	Trujillo, Lisa Rockwood	√		WJ	11	1	41	Su 86	60
Designs and Designing: Circular	Weaving on a Round Loom	Priest, Alice B.	√	√	H&C	19	2		Sp 68	35
Designs and Designing: Clothing	Beautiful Fabric Is Not Enough	Lommen, Sandy	√	√	SS&D	15	2	58	Sp 84	40
Designs and Designing: Clothing	Dazzling Designs	Eagle, Elsie	√	√	SS&D	15	1	57	Wi 83	19
Designs and Designing: Clothing	Designing Your Handwoven Garments	Scorgie, Jean	√	√	Hw	7	5		N/D 86	40
Designs and Designing: Clothing	Dress and Design in Highland Southeast Asia: The Hmong (Miao) and the Yao	Adams, Monni	√		TMJ	4	1		De 74	51
Designs and Designing: Clothing	Little Blue Dress, A	Dobsevage, David	√	√	TM			7	O/N 86	58
Designs and Designing: Clothing	Loom Designed Garments	Thomason, Roger	√		SS&D	1	3	3	Ju 70	10
Designs and Designing: Clothing	Pat White: The "Small Things" Are Her Signature	Park, Betty	√	√	SS&D	13	3	51	Su 82	58
Designs and Designing: Clothing	Sculptor's Approach to Clothing Design, A	Liebler, Barbara	√	√	Hw	5	1		J/F 84	76

SUBJECT	TITLE	AUTHOR	IL	INST	JOUR	VOL	NO	ISS	DATE	PAGE
Designs and Designing: Clothing	Seattle Guild Garment Designs, Part 1	Noble, Judy	√	√	SS&D	10	3	39	Su 79	26
Designs and Designing: Clothing	Seattle Guild Garment Designs, Part 2: Completing the Top		√	√	SS&D	10	4	40	Fa 79	71
Designs and Designing: Clothing	Seattle Guild Garment Designs, Part 3, Skirts and Pants		√	√	SS&D	11	1	41	Wi 79	20
Designs and Designing: Clothing	Seattle Guild Garment Designs, Part 4: Edges, Closures, Capes and Dresses		√	√	SS&D	11	2	42	Sp 80	39
Designs and Designing: Color and Weave Motif Development	Automatic Analysis of Coloured Images	Hoskins, J. A.	√	√	AT	5			Ju 86	151
Designs and Designing: Color and Weave Patterns	Automatic Analysis of Coloured Images	Hoskins, J. A.	√	√	AT	5			Ju 86	151
Designs and Designing: Color Variations	Undulating Weft Effects: Variations from Designing, Variations Based on Color	Tidball, Harriet	√	√	SCGM		9		63	20
Designs and Designing: Composition	Concerns and Influences in My Work	Kidd, Jane	√		AT	6			De 86	135
Designs and Designing: Computer-Aided	Automatic Analysis of Coloured Images	Hoskins, J. A.	√	√	AT	5			Ju 86	151
Designs and Designing: Computer-Aided	CAD Quilts: The Computer As a Studio Tool	Dadey, Jane	√		Fa	14	4		S/O 87	38
Designs and Designing: Computer-Aided	Charting Intarsia Designs	Guagliumi, Susan	√	√	TM			10	A/M 87	69
Designs and Designing: Computer-Aided	Computer as a Design Tool, The	Strickler, Carol	√	√	Hw	8	5		N/D 87	66
Designs and Designing: Computer-Aided	Computer-Aided Design Analysis	Poague, Susan	√		WJ	11	4	44	Sp 87	8
Designs and Designing: Computer-Aided	Computer-Aided Design for Handweaving	Windeknecht, Margaret B.; Thomas G. Windeknecht			CW	2	1	4	Oc 80	8
Designs and Designing: Computer-Aided	Computers and Weavers: Software Is Just Another Tool in the Designer's Hand	Hoskins, Janet A.	√		TM			9	F/M 87	51
Designs and Designing: Computer-Aided	Design Decisions: Software Solutions	George, Patrice	√	> 4	Hw	5	5		N/D 84	47
Designs and Designing: Computer-Aided	Designing Rep Weaves with the Aid of a Computer	Bohannan, Ronnine	√	√	WJ	7	4	28	Sp 83	24
Designs and Designing: Computer-Aided	Handwoven Velvet of Barbara Pickett, The	Cohn, Lisa	√	√	Hw	8	1		J/F 87	20
Designs and Designing: Computer-Aided	Linbogarn Shirt	Scorgie, Jean	√	√	WJ	7	1	25	Su 82	53
Designs and Designing: Computer-Aided	My Computer Designs a Bedspread	Salsbury, Nate	√	√	Hw	3	3		My 82	80
Designs and Designing: Computer-Aided	Textile Graphics, A New Method of Designing		√		H&C	18	1		Wi 67	19
Designs and Designing: Computer-Aided	Twill Color and Weave Effects...From the Computer	O'Connor, Paul	√	> 4	lw	6	1		Wi 80	28
Designs and Designing: Concentration	Improving Your Concentration	Liebler, Barbara	√		Hw	6	4		S/O 85	68
Designs and Designing: Conceptual	Approach to Teaching Design, An	Pickett, Barbara Setsu	√	√	lw	3	2		Wi 78	16
Designs and Designing: Conceptual	Conceptual Design in Weaving	Towner, Naomi Whiting	√		lw	3	2		Wi 78	14
Designs and Designing: Conceptual	Design Concept, The	Liebler, Barbara	√		lw	3	2		Wi 78	28
Designs and Designing: Conceptual	Dolly Curtis: Contrasts	Ligon, Linda	√		lw	3	4		Su 78	24
Designs and Designing: Conceptual	Mathematical Design Concepts Relative to Aesthetic Concerns	Michaels-Paque, J.	√		AT	8			De 87	155
Designs and Designing: Conceptual	Warren Seelig: A Conversation	Ligon, Linda	√		lw	3	2		Wi 78	20
Designs and Designing: Continuity	Continuity of Patterning	Liebler, Barbara	√		Hw	6	1		J/F 85	92
Designs and Designing: Continuity	Sculptor's Approach to Clothing Design, A	Liebler, Barbara	√	√	Hw	5	1		J/F 84	76
Designs and Designing: Control System, Dobby Loom, Microcomputer-controlled.	Design of Interactive Systems for Real-Time Dobby Control	Hoskins, W. D.; J. A. Hoskins	√	√	AT	5			Ju 86	33

SUBJECT	TITLE	AUTHOR	IL	INST	JOUR	VOL	NO	ISS	DATE	PAGE
Designs and Designing: Cord Weaves	Secret of a Corrugated Surface: Bedford Cord, The (error-corrected Hw v6 n3 85 p 1-2)	Alderman, Sharon	√	> 4	Hw	6	1		J/F 85	27
Designs and Designing: Corduroy, Color-Pattern	Amazing Color-Pattern Corduroy Rug		√	> 4	PWC	3	4	10		22
Designs and Designing: Couturier Fabrics	Couturier Fashion Design	West, Virginia	√	> 4	SS&D	13	4	52	Fa 82	34
Designs and Designing: Couturier Fabrics	Couturier Fashions: Part 1, Couturier Fabric Design	West, Virginia	√	√	SS&D	13	3	51	Su 82	8
Designs and Designing: Curves	Shapely Curves	Anthony, Janice	√	√	TM			11	J/J 87	30
Designs and Designing: Decorative Arts	Design Reform, 1875–1920 (Exhibit)		√		Fa	14	2		M/A 87	59
Designs and Designing: Denmark	Danish Design: Form Follows Function		√	√	Hw	8	3		M/J 87	50
Designs and Designing: Design Elements	Exercises in Design	McNair, Peg	√	√	SS&D	11	2	42	Sp 80	55
Designs and Designing: Design Elements	Making the Most of Your Weave	Barnes, Muriel	√	> 4	H&C	19	4		Fa 68	15
Designs and Designing: Design Evolution	Evolution of a Weaving, The	Kearney, Kathleen	√	√	SS&D	12	1	45	Wi 80	64
Designs and Designing: Design Evolution	Three Faces of the Eight-Pointed Star Motif (error-corrected SS&D v14 n4 83 p4)	Coffman, Charlotte	√	√	SS&D	14	3	55	Su 83	56
Designs and Designing: Design Manipulation	Different BUT Related	Smith, Dorothy N.	√	√	WJ	7	1	25	Su 82	32
Designs and Designing: Distorted Warps/Wefts	Manipulated Warps or Having Fun with Controlled Distortion	Foster, Robert	√		H&C	16	2		Sp 65	12
Designs and Designing: Distortion	Tiahuanaco Tapestry Design	Sawyer, Alan R.	√		TMJ	1	2		De 63	27
Designs and Designing: Double Corduroy	Peter Collingwood, His Weaves and Weaving: Double Corduroy Pile Rugs	Collingwood, Peter; Harriet Tidball, ed.	√	√	SCGM		8		63	3
Designs and Designing: Double-Weave Drafts	Double Weaves: Analysis and Synthesis	Zielinski, S. A.; Robert Leclerc, ed.	√	> 4	MWL	15			'51–'73	135
Designs and Designing: Draft-Aided	Corduroy: An Account of Discovery	Alderman, Sharon D.	√	> 4	Hw	4	4		S/O 83	54
Designs and Designing: Dynamic Symmetry	Color & Design in Decorative Fabrics	Regensteiner, Else	√	√	H&C	9	4		Fa 58	6
Designs and Designing: Dynamic Symmetry	Excerpt from Geometric Design in Weaving, An	Regensteiner, Else	√	√	WJ	11	4	44	Sp 87	13
Designs and Designing: Dynamic/Static	Dynamic Design	Liebler, Barbara		√	Hw	6	5		N/D 85	89
Designs and Designing: Early American	Coverlets and Bedspreads: Variety in Early American Design	Saulpaugh, Dassah	√		H&C	17	4		Fa 66	8
Designs and Designing: Ecclesiastical/Liturgical Weavings	Vestment Variations: A Weaver From the Netherlands Creates Garments for the Ecclesiastical Calendar	Jansen, Netty	√	> 4	WJ	10	3	39	Wi 86	53
Designs and Designing: Egyptian Tapestries, Theatrical Influence	Tapestries from Egypt Influenced by Theatrical Performances	Berliner, Rudolf	√		TMJ	1	3		De 64	35
Designs and Designing: Element, Variations	Variations on a Theme	Liebler, Barbara	√	√	Hw	8	5		N/D 87	26
Designs and Designing: Elements	Design and the Handweaver: Elements of Design: Purpose	Atwater, Mary Meigs			SCGM		3		61	3
Designs and Designing: Elements	Techniques of Tapestry Weaves Part 4: Developing Design for Tapestry	O'Callaghan, Kate	√	√	WJ	5	2	18	Fa 80	15
Designs and Designing: Elements	What if...Vest	Davenport, Betty	√		Hw	5	4		S/O 84	75
Designs and Designing: Embroidery	Freestyle Embroidery: New Images with Traditional Stitches	Dahl, Caroline	√	√	TM			1	O/N 85	22
Designs and Designing: Embroidery	Point of View (Renie Breskin Adams)		√		TM			7	O/N 86	92
Designs and Designing: Exercises	Design Exercises for Inspiration and Fun	McNair, Peg	√	√	Fa	14	1		J/F 87	47
Designs and Designing: Fabrics	But What Do I Do with It?	Alderman, Sharon D.	√	√	Hw	7	5		N/D 86	50
Designs and Designing: Fabrics	Color Design for Garments	Znamierowski, Nell	√	√	Hw	7	5		N/D 86	54
Designs and Designing: Fabrics	Composition and Designing: Designing New Fabrics	Zielinski, S. A.; Robert Leclerc, ed.	√	√	MWL	18			'51–'73	53
Designs and Designing: Fabrics	Coordinates	Moes, Dini	√	√	SS&D	15	4	60	Fa 84	46

SUBJECT	TITLE	AUTHOR	IL	INST	JOUR	VOL	NO	ISS	DATE	PAGE
Designs and Designing: Fabrics	Handwoven Fabric: Beginnings, Decision Making	Alderman, Sharon			Hw	3	2		Mr 82	31
Designs and Designing: Fabrics	Handwoven Fabrics in New Ships		√		H&C	9	4		Fa 58	19
Designs and Designing: Fabrics	Notes on Designing for Drape	Veness, Tim	√		Hw	7	5		N/D 86	76
Designs and Designing: Fabrics	On Designing Fabric for Suits	Byers, Pat			TM			6	A/S 86	24
Designs and Designing: Fabrics	On Designing Fashion Fabrics	Sutton, Ann	√	√	Hw	7	5		N/D 86	66
Designs and Designing: Fabrics, Window Coverings	Color Related Decorating Textiles Rugs, Draperies, Upholstery: The Textile Designs	Rhodes, Tonya Stalons; Harriet Tidball, ed.			SCGM		14		65	10
Designs and Designing: Fabrics, Woolen	Woolens and Tweeds: Designing Woolen Fabrics	Tidball, Harriet		√	SCGM		4		61	26
Designs and Designing: Fabrics, Woolen	Woolens and Tweeds: Designing Woolen Fabrics: New Designs for Woolens	Tidball, Harriet	√	√	SCGM		4		61	38
Designs and Designing: Fibonacci Series	Bright & Bold		√	√	Hw	4	2		M/A 83	50
Designs and Designing: Fibonacci Series	Fibonacci Series, The		√	√	Hw	4	2		M/A 83	45
Designs and Designing: Figured Silks	Designs in Ancient Figured Silks	Blumenau, Lili	√		H&C	2	1		Wi 50	5
Designs and Designing: Figures, Bound Weave	Figures in Boundweave	Waggoner, Phyllis	√	√	WJ	10	2	38	Fa 85	58
Designs and Designing: Finishes	Sampler of Knit Edgings and Applied Trims, A	Newton, Deborah	√	√	TM			12	A/S 87	38
Designs and Designing: Five-Dimensional	Mathematical Design Concepts Relative to Aesthetic Concerns	Michaels-Paque, J.	√		AT	8			De 87	155
Designs and Designing: Foreign Influences	Designs in Sumba Textiles, Local Meanings and Foreign Influences	Adams, Monni	√		TMJ	3	2		De 71	28
Designs and Designing: Freeform Techniques	Freeform Design Technique	Searles, Nancy	√	> 4	PWC	3	4	10		18
Designs and Designing: Garment Shapes	Shapes of Garments, The (Reprint)	Burnham, Dorothy K.			TM			9	F/M 87	50
Designs and Designing: Geometric	Color and Design in Andean Warp-Faced Fabrics	Femenias, Blenda	√		WJ	12	2	46	Fa 87	44
Designs and Designing: Geometric	Double Weave Pick-Up with Straight Diagonal Lines	Wolter, Edith L.	√	√	WJ	7	4	28	Sp 83	61
Designs and Designing: Geometric	Excerpt from Geometric Design in Weaving, An	Regensteiner, Else	√	√	WJ	11	4	44	Sp 87	13
Designs and Designing: Geometric	Mathematical Design Concepts Relative to Aesthetic Concerns	Michaels-Paque, J.	√		AT	8			De 87	155
Designs and Designing: Geometric	Woven Circles and Cones	Henzie, Susie	√	√	SS&D	10	4	40	Fa 79	58
Designs and Designing: Geometric Designs	Design and the Handweaver: Pattern	Atwater, Mary Meigs	√	√	SCGM		3		61	17
Designs and Designing: Geometric Designs	Original Fabrics of Kaftan, The	El-Homossani, M. M.	√	> 4	AT	1			De 83	263
Designs and Designing: Geometric, Proportion	Geometric Proportions As a Design Tool	Templeton, Peg	√	√	WJ	4	4	16	Ap 80	8
Designs and Designing: German Linen Weaves	Seventeenth and Eighteenth Century Twills: The German Linen Tradition	Hilts, Patricia	√	> 4	AT	3			My 85	139
Designs and Designing: Gloves, Knit	Handknitting Gloves	Newton, Deborah	√	√	TM			14	D/J 87	24
Designs and Designing: Graphed Images	Portraits in Double Weave	Strickler, Carol	√	√	WJ	1	3	3	Ja 77	30
Designs and Designing: Graphic Aids	Charting Intarsia Designs	Guagliumi, Susan	√	√	TM			10	A/M 87	69
Designs and Designing: Grid	Excerpt from Geometric Design in Weaving, An	Regensteiner, Else	√	√	WJ	11	4	44	Sp 87	13
Designs and Designing: Hand Loom	Problems in Designing for Hand and Power Looms	Hausner, Walter	√		H&C	3	1		Wi 51	33
Designs and Designing: Hmong Textiles	Flourishing Art: USA Hmong Women Show How to Stitch Pa ndau, Their Flowery Cloth, A	Porter-Francis, Wendy	√	√	TM			9	F/M 87	33
Designs and Designing: Hooking	Designs in Rughooking		√		H&C	23	3		M/J 72	51

SUBJECT	TITLE	AUTHOR	IL	INST	JOUR	VOL	NO	ISS	DATE	PAGE
Designs and Designing: Hooking	Hooked on Texture: Unconventional Punch-Needle Rugs	Crouse, Gloria E.	√	√	TM			14	D/J 87	68
Designs and Designing: Hooking	Hooked on Texture: Unconventional Punch-Needle Rugs	Crouse, Gloria E.	√	√	TM			14	D/J 87	68
Designs and Designing: Huck, Multi-Harness	Multi-Harness Huck: Learn About the Structure of This Family of Weaves and Design Your Own Variations	Barrett, Clotilde	√	> 4	WJ	10	4	40	Sp 86	11
Designs and Designing: Ikat	Revival of Ikat	Rushfelt, Joy M.	√	√	H&C	19	2		Sp 68	14
Designs and Designing: Ikat	Tying Warp Ikat on the Loom	Hannon, Farrell	√	√	WJ	8	1	29	Su 83	41
Designs and Designing: Ikat	Warp Ikat Part 2: Quick Design Effects	Reiss, Zenaide	√	√	SS&D	13	1	49	Wi 81	16
Designs and Designing: Industry	Designing for Industry	Speth, Lottie	√		SS&D	2	4	8	Fa 71	21
Designs and Designing: Industry, Textile	Ellen Siegel, Designer for the Handloom and Power Loom		√		H&C	15	1		Wi 64	6
Designs and Designing: Industry, Textile	Roy Ginstrom, Versatile Handweaver and Designer of Fabrics for Power Looms		√		H&C	13	3		Su 62	6
Designs and Designing: Industry, Textile	Textiles Designed for Contemporary Furniture		√		H&C	12	2		Sp 61	17
Designs and Designing: Industry, Textile	Weaving Weights and Qualities	Blumenau, Lili			H&C	8	2		Sp 57	9
Designs and Designing: Industry, Textiles	William Morris, A Twentieth Century View of His Woven Textiles	Morris, Barbara J.	√		H&C	12	2		Sp 61	6
Designs and Designing: Industry, Textiles	William Morris, His Designs for Carpets & Tapestries	Morris, Barbara J.	√		H&C	12	4		Fa 61	18
Designs and Designing: Inkle Bands	Designing Inkle Bands	Davenport, Betty	√	√	PWC			4	Ja 83	56
Designs and Designing: Interiors	Designing for an Interior: Notes of a Pattern Weaver	Alvic, Philis	√		WJ	9	4	36	Sp 85	69
Designs and Designing: Intuitive, On-Loom	Weaver of Images	Brownlee-Ramsdale, Sandra	√		AT	6			De 86	147
Designs and Designing: Jacquard Weaving	Jacquard Weaving	Goldschmidt, Manfred			H&C	23	4		J/A 72	35
Designs and Designing: Knitted Gloves	Handknitting Gloves	Newton, Deborah	√	√	TM			14	D/J 87	24
Designs and Designing: Knitting	American Designers		√		Kn	3	1	5	F-W 86	16
Designs and Designing: Knitting	Be Your Own Designer	Lewis, Susanna	√	√	Kn	3	1	5	F-W 86	48
Designs and Designing: Knitting	Braid on the Bias (error-corrected Kn v3 n1 i5 f/w 86 p11)	Madden, Gail	√	√	Kn	2	2	4	S-S 86	35
Designs and Designing: Knitting	Contrasting Textures	Rowley, Elaine			Kn	2	2	4	S-S 86	67
Designs and Designing: Knitting	Conversion Factor, The	Barnes, Galer	√	√	Kn	3	1	5	F-W 86	54
Designs and Designing: Knitting	Creative Knitwear		√		S-O	3			79	62
Designs and Designing: Knitting	Designing with Ribs	Newton, Deborah	√	√	Kn	2	2	4	S-S 86	62
Designs and Designing: Knitting	Double-Breasted Jacket in Mosiac	Newton, Deborah	√	√	Kn	2	1	3	F-W 85	45, 8B
Designs and Designing: Knitting	Fair Isle in Natural Colors, The	Gibson-Roberts, Priscilla A.	√	√	Kn	2	1	3	F-W 85	34
Designs and Designing: Knitting	Fair Isle Knitting	Starmore, Alice	√	√	TM			8	D/J 86	44
Designs and Designing: Knitting	Fine Yarns: Special and Accessible	Newton, Deborah	√	√	Kn	3	4	8	Fa 87	16
Designs and Designing: Knitting	Garter Stitch Ribwarmer	Zimmermann, Elizabeth	√	√	Kn	3	1	5	F-W 86	46
Designs and Designing: Knitting	Hollow Oak Vest	Rush, Helene	√	√	Kn	2	2	4	S-S 86	30
Designs and Designing: Knitting	Jackie's Sweaters: Blouson, Dolman, Striped Silk	Kroeger, Jackie	√	√	Kn	1	1	1	F-W 84 CI	41 33
Designs and Designing: Knitting	Kaffe Fassett		√		Kn	2	2	4	S-S 86	14
Designs and Designing: Knitting	Knitters, Make a Trip to the Fabric Store	Guagliumi, Susan	√	√	TM			7	O/N 86	35
Designs and Designing: Knitting	Knitting a Seamless Sweater	Zimmermann, Elizabeth	√	√	TM			7	O/N 86	47
Designs and Designing: Knitting	Knitting from a Paper Pattern	Keeler, Betty	√	√	S-O	8	4		Wi 84	23
Designs and Designing: Knitting	Michelin Man Sweater	Zimmermann, Elizabeth	√	√	Kn	2	2	4	S-S 86	72
Designs and Designing: Knitting	My Knit Suit	Klinect, Ann W.	√		S-O	10	1		Sp 86	40
Designs and Designing: Knitting	Number Knitting — A New Way with an Old Art	Jarecka, Louise Llewellyn	√	√	H&C	2	1		Wi 50	22

SUBJECT	TITLE	AUTHOR	IL	INST	JOUR	VOL	NO	ISS	DATE	PAGE
Designs and Designing: Knitting	On Designing: Brocade Blouse	Newton, Deborah	√	√	Kn	1	1	1	F-W 84 CI	17 9
Designs and Designing: Knitting	On Designing in 2 Dimensions: Shawls and Scarves	Newton, Deborah	√	√	Kn	4	1	9	Wi 87	30
Designs and Designing: Knitting	On Designing with Lace	Newton, Deborah	√	√	Kn	1	2	2	S-S 85	21
Designs and Designing: Knitting	On Designing with Slip Stitch Bands	Newton, Deborah	√	√	Kn	3	1	5	F-W 86	21
Designs and Designing: Knitting	Perfect Pleats	Rowley, Elaine		√	Kn	3	2	6	Sp 87	24
Designs and Designing: Knitting	Pleats in Hand-Knit Fabrics	Newton, Deborah	√	√	Kn	3	2	6	Sp 87	23
Designs and Designing: Knitting	Tale of Two Knitters, A	Preen, Maureen	√		S-O	8	4		Wi 84	19
Designs and Designing: Knitting	Thoughts on Sweater Design	Dewees, Libby	√		S-O	9	3		Fa 85	47
Designs and Designing: Knitting	Welts and Bobbles: Crop Top	Dana, Zelda	√	√	Kn	2	2	4	S-S 86	38
Designs and Designing: Knots and Knotting	Panel — A Statement of Unity, The	Zachofsky, Toni	√		H&C	22	4		Fa 71	20
Designs and Designing: Krokbrågd	Summer and Winter Revisited, Part 2: I. On Designing with Krokbragd, Krokbragd Mug Rugs	Lyon, Linda	√	√	PWC			2	Ap 82	63
Designs and Designing: Lace	Tarascan Lace (error-corrected WJ v9 n1 84 p70)	Thabet, Micheline	√	√	WJ	8	4	32	Sp 84	48
Designs and Designing: Lampshades	Designing Lamp Shades		√	√	H&C	8	4		Fa 57	24
Designs and Designing: Lampas	Contrails Coverlet	Kelly, Jacquie	√	>4	PWC	5	1	15		48
Designs and Designing: Lampshades	Composition and Designing: Lamp Shades	Zielinski, S. A.; Robert Leclerc, ed.	√	√	MWL	18			'51–'73	85
Designs and Designing: Leno, Doup	Exploring Doup Leno	Laughlin, Mary Elizabeth	√	>4	CW	4	3	12	Ap 83	3
Designs and Designing: Light	Using Light as a Design Element	Liebler, Barbara	√		Hw	5	3		Su 84	88
Designs and Designing: Machine Knitting	Appropriate Designs for Short-Row and Slip Intarsia	Guagliumi, Susan	√	√	TM			10	A/M 87	70
Designs and Designing: Machine Knitting	Knitting Machine: A Creative Tool, The	Mendelson, Linda	√	√	Fa	5	3		M/J 78	32
Designs and Designing: Machine Knitting	Thread Weaving	Sample, Joan	√	√	TM			8	D/J 86	64
Designs and Designing: Material Variations	Undulating Weft Effects: Variations from Designing, Variations Based on Materials	Tidball, Harriet	√		SCGM		9		63	22
Designs and Designing: Mathematical Concepts	Mathematical Design Concepts Relative to Aesthetic Concerns	Michaels-Paque, J.	√		AT	8			De 87	155
Designs and Designing: Medallion Quilts	Medallion Quilting	Miller, Kristin	√	√	TM			14	D/J 87	60
Designs and Designing: Mexican Motifs, Primitive	Mexican Motifs: Mexico, Land of Contrasts	Tidball, Harriet	√		SCGM		6		62	1
Designs and Designing: Mini-Drawdowns	New Multi-Harness Drawdown Technique, A	Salsbury, Nate	√	>4	Iw	6	1		Wi 80	57
Designs and Designing: Miscellaneous Yarns	Using Unplanned Yarn in a Planned Project	Chandler, Deborah	√		Hw	8	2		M/A 87	24
Designs and Designing: Module	Excerpt from Geometric Design in Weaving, An	Regensteiner, Else	√	√	WJ	11	4	44	Sp 87	13
Designs and Designing: Modules	Modular Clothing	Mayer, Anita	√	√	Hw	7	3		M/J 86	58
Designs and Designing: Modules	Modular Design Applied: A Man's Robe		√	√	Hw	4	2		M/A 83	52
Designs and Designing: Modules	Module, a Basis for Textile Design, The	Justema, William	√	√	H&C	18	1		Wi 67	9
Designs and Designing: Modules	Stripe as a Design Module, The	Liebler, Barbara	√	√	Hw	4	2		M/A 83	52
Designs and Designing: Modules Technique	Roses and Snowballs: The Development of Block Patterns in the German Linen-Weaving Tradition	Hilts, Patricia	√	>4	AT	5			Ju 86	167
Designs and Designing: Motif	Additions to the Indonesian Collection	Gittinger, Mattiebelle S.	√		TMJ	4	3		76	43
Designs and Designing: Motif Evolution	Autumn Leaves, A Design in Summer-and-Winter	Arnold, Ruth	√	√	H&C	14	3		Su 63	14
Designs and Designing: Napkins	Accent on Napkins	Guy, Sallie T.	√	√	Hw	8	1		J/F 87	60
Designs and Designing: Narrow Fabrics	Designed for Narrow Looms	Jennings, Lucy Anne	√	√	WJ	11	1	41	Su 86	26
Designs and Designing: Narrow Fabrics	Making Narrow Looms Do Big Jobs	Kling, Mary Nell	√		H&C	2	1		Wi 50	13

SUBJECT	TITLE	AUTHOR	IL	INST	JOUR	VOL	NO	ISS	DATE	PAGE
Designs and Designing: Native Americans	Indian Weavers and Contemporary Design		√		H&C	3	2		Sp 52	4
Designs and Designing: Obi	Obi: The Textile Art of Nishijin	Donaldson, R. Alan	√		AT	1			De 83	115
Designs and Designing: Openwork, Weft-Wrap	Weft-Wrap Openwork Technique	Atwood, Betty	√	√	AT	3			My 85	65
Designs and Designing: Opphämta	Designing for the Opphämta Loom	Johns, Greg	√	> 4	PWC	3	4	10		68
Designs and Designing: Overshot	Bound Overshot	Xenakis, Athanasios David	√	√	PWC	3	3	9		21
Designs and Designing: Overshot Block Patterns	Even-Tied Overshot	Xenakis, Athanasios David	√	> 4	PWC	3	3	9		40
Designs and Designing: Overshot Blocks	Multishaft Overshot on Opposites	van der Hoogt, Madelyn	√	> 4	WJ	8	3	31	Wi 83	76
Designs and Designing: Overshot Patterns	Floor's the Limit, The	Xenakis, Athanasios David	√	> 4	PWC	3	3	9		12
Designs and Designing: Overshot, Shaft-Switching Technique	Even-Tied Overshot on Four Shafts with Shaft Switching	Herring, Connie; Athanasios David Xenakis	√	√	PWC	3	3	9		44
Designs and Designing: Overshot, Tied	In Timeless Form	Herring, Connie	√	√	PWC	3	3	9		35
Designs and Designing: Paper Weaving	Paper Weaving	Scanlin, Tommye McClure	√	√	Hw	7	4		S/O 86	28
Designs and Designing: Pattern Blocks	Pattern Blocks, Basic Tool for Design	Frey, Berta	√	> 4	H&C	19	2		Sp 68	8
Designs and Designing: Pattern, Brocade, Pick-Up	Part 2, Patterns for Pick-Up and Brocade	Tidball, Harriet	√		SCGM		23		68	26
Designs and Designing: Pattern Principles	Learning to See Pattern	Morrison, Skye	√	√	TM			2	D/J 85	44
Designs and Designing: Pattern, Small	Composition and Designing: Small Patterns	Zielinski, S. A.; Robert Leclerc, ed.	√	√	MWL	18			'51–'73	67
Designs and Designing: Pattern-Ground Weaves	Multiple Shaft Weaving: M's and O's with Two Foundation Shafts	Evans, Jane	√	> 4	WJ	6	1	21	Su 81	27
Designs and Designing: Peruvian Tapestries, Chinese Influence	Chinese Influence in Colonial Peruvian Tapestries	Cammann, Schuyler	√		TMJ	1	3		De 64	21
Designs and Designing: Peruvian Textiles, Ancient	Peru, Textiles Unlimited: Peruvian Textile Designing	Tidball, Harriet	√		SCGM		25		68	24
Designs and Designing: Philosophy	Toward Abstraction and Simplicity	Moorman, Theo	√		SS&D	3	1	9	Wi 71	30
Designs and Designing: Pile Weaves, Chenille	Pile Weaves, Rugs and Tapestry: The Ultimate in Chenille	Zielinski, S. A.; Robert Leclerc, ed.	√	√	MWL	14			'51–'73	49
Designs and Designing: Piqué	Designing for Piqué (error-corrected PWC v4 n4 i14 p33)	Sullivan, Donna	√	> 4	PWC	4	3	13		28
Designs and Designing: Piqué	Planning Figured Piqué Designs on Pre-Marked Graph Paper	Xenakis, Athanasios David	√	> 4	PWC	4	2	12		16
Designs and Designing: Piqué, Charting	Pick Up Pick-Up Piqué (error-corrected PWC v4 n4 i14 p33)		√	√	PWC	4	3	13		23
Designs and Designing: Piqué, Figured	Pick-Up Piqué (error-corrected SS&D v19 n1 87 p33)	Fletcher, Joyce	√	√	SS&D	18	4	72	Fa 87	60
Designs and Designing: Piqué, Stitcher Warp Patterns	Stitcher Designer Hints for Loom-Controlled Figured Piqué	van der Hoogt, Madelyn	√	> 4	PWC	4	3	13		48
Designs and Designing: Plaids	Notes on Planning Plaids			√	Hw	4	5		N/D 83	45
Designs and Designing: Plaiting	Plaiting: Non-Loom Weaving	Laky, Gyöngy	√	√	SS&D	12	2	46	Sp 81	33
Designs and Designing: Ponchos	Composition and Designing: Ponchos	Zielinski, S. A.; Robert Leclerc, ed.	√	√	MWL	18			'51–'73	81
Designs and Designing: Positive/Negative Space	Counterchange	Wertenberger, Kathryn	√	√	Hw	7	2		M/A 86	75
Designs and Designing: Power Loom	Problems in Designing for Hand and Power Looms	Hausner, Walter	√		H&C	3	1		Wi 51	33
Designs and Designing: Principles	Effective Designing	La Pierre, Sharon	√		SS&D	11	3	43	Su 80	36
Designs and Designing: Principles	Mathematical Design Concepts Relative to Aesthetic Concerns	Michaels-Paque, J.	√		AT	8			De 87	155
Designs and Designing: Problems	Problems in Designing for Hand and Power Looms	Hausner, Walter	√		H&C	3	1		Wi 51	33
Designs and Designing: Process	Interview with Jhane Barnes: Designer, Weaver, Spinner, An	Lonier, Terri	√		Fa	10	4		J/A 83	55

SUBJECT	TITLE	AUTHOR	IL	INST	JOUR	VOL	NO	ISS	DATE	PAGE
Designs and Designing: Process	Windworks: A Way of Working	Frasier, Debra	√		Fa	10	4		J/A 83	58
Designs and Designing: Process Exercises	Exercises in Design	McNair, Peg	√	√	SS&D	11	2	42	Sp 80	55
Designs and Designing: Profile Block	Tablecloth in Bergman Weave	Morrison, Ruth	√	>4	PWC	4	4	14		38
Designs and Designing: Profile Blocks	The Longest Warp in the World or, The Double Two-Tie Unit Threading System	Miller, Mary Ann	√	>4	CW	3	3	9	Ap 82	2
Designs and Designing: Profile Drafts	More Harnesses Make the Difference	Wertenberger, Kathryn	√	>4	Hw	2	3		My 81	40
Designs and Designing: Profile Drafts	Undulating Twills	Carey, Joyce Marquess	√	>4	Iw	6	1		Wi 80	31
Designs and Designing: Profile Drafts	Why Always Four Harnesses?		√	>4	H&C	10	2		Sp 59	6
Designs and Designing: Profile Patterns	Contemporary Approach to Traditional Weaves: Modern Patterns for Traditional Weaves	Zielinski, S. A.; Robert Leclerc, ed.	√	>4	MWL	8			'51–'73	89
Designs and Designing: Progression	Change of Heart and Other Progressive Ideas, A	Carey, Joyce Marquess	√	>4	PWC	3	3	9		18
Designs and Designing: Proportion	Color & Design in Decorative Fabrics	Regensteiner, Else	√	√	H&C	9	4		Fa 58	6
Designs and Designing: Proportion	Fibonacci Series, The		√	√	Hw	4	2		M/A 83	45
Designs and Designing: Proportions	Composition and Designing: Proportions	Zielinski, S. A.; Robert Leclerc, ed.	√	√	MWL	18			'51–'73	48
Designs and Designing: Quilts	Double Lives: Can You Love Your "Work" When It's Your "Job"?	Mattera, Joanne	√		TM			10	A/M 87	62
Designs and Designing: Quilts	Hawaiian Quilt, The	White-Hansen, Sue Ellen	√	√	TM			13	O/N 87	22
Designs and Designing: Quilts	Log Cabins	Larzelere, Judith Ann	√	√	TM			3	F/M 86	58
Designs and Designing: Rag Rugs	Rag Rugs		√	√	WJ	4	1	13	Jy 79	22
Designs and Designing: Rags	From Rags to Riches	Krook, Inga	√	√	Hw	4	3		M/J 83	32
Designs and Designing: Redesign	Big Work from Small Looms	Liebler, Barbara	√		Hw	2	2		Mr 81	61
Designs and Designing: Repetition	Repetition	Liebler, Barbara	√	√	Hw	6	3		Su 85	92
Designs and Designing: Repetition	Repetition Repetition Repetition		√	√	Hw	4	2		M/A 83	49
Designs and Designing: Repetition, Variations	Variations on a Theme	Liebler, Barbara	√	√	Hw	8	5		N/D 87	26
Designs and Designing: Rigid-Heddle Weaving	Small Projects of Interest to Beginning Weavers	Freeman, Claire	√	√	H&C	20	4		Fa 69	9
Designs and Designing: Rugs	Designing Rugs for Harness-Controlled Weaving		√	>4	WJ	4	4	16	Ap 80	27
Designs and Designing: Rugs	Ed Oppenheimer: Rugs	Ligon, Linda	√		Iw	5	1		Wi 79	31
Designs and Designing: Rugs	Notes from a Rugweaver's Journal	Schomp, Halcyon; Hector Jaeger	√	√	Hw	3	4		Se 82	35
Designs and Designing: Rugs	Observations on the Six-End Block Draft for Rug Weaving	Schlein, Alice	√	√	WJ	6	4	24	Sp 82	30
Designs and Designing: Rugs	Painted Rug Designs: Trader Hubbell's Influence on Navajo Weaving	Blue, Martha	√		Fa	14	5		N/D 87	5
Designs and Designing: Rugs	Perspective on Rug Design, A	Stanley, Martha			WJ	7	2	26	Fa 82	66
Designs and Designing: Rugs	Peter Collingwood, His Weaves and Weaving: On Rug Designing	Collingwood, Peter; Harriet Tidball, ed.	√	√	SCGM		8		63	1
Designs and Designing: Rugs	Rag Rugs, Not Always Made from Rags	Erickson, Johanna	√	√	TM			3	F/M 86	40
Designs and Designing: Rugs	Rug Techniques-An Overview	Stanley, Martha	√		WJ	6	4	24	Sp 82	34
Designs and Designing: Rugs	Rug Weaving...Design Considerations	Stanley, Martha Alice	√		Iw	5	1		Wi 79	20
Designs and Designing: Rugs, Profile Blocks	Hand Woven Rugs: Weaves, Two-Warp Weave, Eignt-Harness Patterns	Atwater, Mary Meigs	√	>4	SCGM		29		48	25
Designs and Designing: Rugs, Profile Blocks	Hand Woven Rugs: Weaves, Two-Warp Weave, Four-Harness Patterns	Atwater, Mary Meigs	√	√	SCGM		29		48	24
Designs and Designing: Rugs, Rag	"Maria" Rag Rug	Krook, Inga	√	√	Hw	6	3		Su 85	56
Designs and Designing: Rugs, Shaft-Switching	Shaft-Switching on 3-End Drafts		√	√	WJ	5	4	20	Sp 81	24
Designs and Designing: Sari	Patolu and Its Techniques	De Bone, Mary Golden	√	√	TMJ	4	3		76	49
Designs and Designing: Satin	Contemporary Satins: Designing in Satins	Tidball, Harriet	√	√	SCGM		7		62	18

SUBJECT	TITLE	AUTHOR	IL	INST	JOUR	VOL	NO	ISS	DATE	PAGE
Designs and Designing: Satin Counts	Contemporary Satins: Satin Counts	Tidball, Harriet	√	> 4	SCGM		7		62	3
Designs and Designing: Satin Weaves	Satin — The Designer Weave	Nyquist, Jan	√	> 4	CW	7	3	21	My 86	15
Designs and Designing: Scale	Relative Scale	Liebler, Barbara	√	√	Hw	5	2		M/A 84	78
Designs and Designing: Scandinavian	Scandinavian Design, Contemporary Trend is Toward Simplicity	Ringler, Aina	√		H&C	18	1		Wi 67	12
Designs and Designing: Selvages	Design It		√		Hw	6	1		J/F 85	61
Designs and Designing: Selvages	Flaunt It		√	√	Hw	6	1		J/F 85	65
Designs and Designing: Sequence of Dominance	Critique: Una Flor Morada, A		√	√	Hw	4	2		M/A 83	44
Designs and Designing: Sequence of Dominance	Sequence of Dominance	Davis, Helen	√	√	Hw	4	2		M/A 83	42
Designs and Designing: Shadow Weave	Shadow Weave		√	√	Hw	6	5		N/D 85	51
Designs and Designing: Shadow Weave "Twill" Blocks	Magnified Twill Blanket	Alderman, Sharon	√		Hw	6	5		N/D 85	53
Designs and Designing: Shaft-Switching	Shaft Switch Technique (error-corrected WJ v6 n1 81 p28d)		√	√	WJ	5	1	17	Su 80	5
Designs and Designing: Shaft-Switching	Shaft Switching on a Jack Loom	Wilson, Sadye Tune	√	√	SS&D	10	1	37	Wi 78	70
Designs and Designing: Sleying	Designing in the Reed	Hausner, Walter	√	√	H&C	8	2		Sp 57	10
Designs and Designing: Source, Feathers	Ongoing Feather: Jan Janeirós Search for a Personal Metaphor, The	Talley, Charles	√		Fa	6	4		J/A 79	46
Designs and Designing: Sources	African Motifs, Interpreted by Jack Lenore Larsen in His Newest Fabrics		√		H&C	14	2		Sp 63	6
Designs and Designing: Sources	Ancient Textiles, a Fascinating Study		√		H&C	9	2		Sp 58	23
Designs and Designing: Sources	Autumn Leaves, A Design in Summer-and-Winter	Arnold, Ruth	√	√	H&C	14	3		Su 63	14
Designs and Designing: Sources	Building on a Tradition	Alvic, Philis	√		Iw	4	3		Su 79	45
Designs and Designing: Sources	Cooper Union Museum, A Rich Source of Ideas for Designers and Weavers, The		√		H&C	13	3		Su 62	18
Designs and Designing: Sources	Courting the Muse	Liebler, Barbara	√		Hw	5	5		N/D 84	37
Designs and Designing: Sources	Design Concept, The	Liebler, Barbara	√		Iw	3	2		Wi 78	28
Designs and Designing: Sources	Documents & Design	Justema, William	√		H&C	21	4		Fa 70	40
Designs and Designing: Sources	Fabric Design, An Approach by a Young Weaver	Carson, Candace	√	√	H&C	20	1		Wi 69	16
Designs and Designing: Sources	Fabric Ornamentation	Kaufman, Glen	√		H&C	17	1		Wi 66	14
Designs and Designing: Sources	Ideas Are Where You Find Them	Breeze, Helen	√	> 4	H&C	3	2		Sp 52	22
Designs and Designing: Sources	Miniature Musical Drafts	Newman, Margaret	√	√	SS&D	4	4	16	Fa 73	70
Designs and Designing: Sources	New Learns from the Old: Treasurers in Museums for Today's Weavers, The	Snow, Edith Huntington	√		H&C	3	1		Wi 51	18
Designs and Designing: Sources	Old & New Uses for Double Weave	Macomber, Dorothea	√	√	H&C	8	4		Fa 57	16
Designs and Designing: Sources	Persian Handcrafted Items	Brockway, Edith	√		H&C	26	5		Oc 75	16
Designs and Designing: Sources	Rare Peruvian Textiles		√		H&C	9	2		Sp 58	18
Designs and Designing: Sources	Secret Treasures of Tibet	Wiltsie-Vaniea, Anne	√		SS&D	18	3	71	Su 87	60
Designs and Designing: Sources	Stennett Heaton: He Finds Beauty in the Mini World		√		SS&D	7	1	25	Wi 75	8
Designs and Designing: Sources	Textile Motifs from Folk Art		√		H&C	8	3		Su 57	10
Designs and Designing: Sources	Weaving, 'riting, and 'rithmetic	Tate, Blair	√		AT	6			De 86	57
Designs and Designing: Sources, Aerial Images	Out of the Blue: Aerial Images		√		Fa	13	5		S/O 86	44
Designs and Designing: Sources, Algebra	Variations on an Algebraic Equation	Redfield, Gail	√	> 4	H&C	10	3		Su 59	46
Designs and Designing: Sources, Algebraic	Two Weavers in a Trailer		√	> 4	H&C	4	2		Sp 53	20
Designs and Designing: Sources, Ancient Civilizations	Weavers in Greece	Tod, Osma Gallinger	√		H&C	19	2		Sp 68	21
Designs and Designing: Sources, Art	Master's Palette, A		√	√	Hw	4	2		M/A 83	49

SUBJECT	TITLE	AUTHOR	IL	INST	JOUR	VOL	NO	ISS	DATE	PAGE
Designs and Designing: Sources, Art	Shawl After Edgar Degas	Straight, Dixie	√		Hw	5	5		N/D 84	64
Designs and Designing: Sources, Art	Tapestries to Wear	Mayer, Anita Luvera	√	√	Hw	5	5		N/D 84	54
Designs and Designing: Sources, Colors	Outrageous Colors	Wertenberger, Kathryn	√		Hw	5	5		N/D 84	68
Designs and Designing: Sources, Commercial Fabric	Four Shaft Fascination	Gordon, Judith	√	√	Hw	6	1		J/F 85	12
Designs and Designing: Sources, Commercial Fabric	Spots or Stripes?	Gordon, Judith	√	> 4	Hw	5	4		S/O 84	36
Designs and Designing: Sources, Commercial Fabric	Suitable Subtleties	Gordon, Judith	√	> 4	Hw	5	3		Su 84	22
Designs and Designing: Sources, Commercial Fabric	Tisket, a Tasket, A	Gordon, Judith	√	> 4	Hw	5	5		N/D 84	34
Designs and Designing: Sources, Commercial Fabric	Twill Plaid, A	Gordon, Judith	√	> 4	Hw	5	2		M/A 84	41
Designs and Designing: Sources: Coverlet Patterns	Inspiration	Alvic, Philis	√		WJ	8	1	29	Su 83	65
Designs and Designing: Sources, Ethnic Textiles	Double Woven Bag Inspired by a South American Bag, A	Barrett, Clotilde	√	√	WJ	1	2	2	Oc 76	29
Designs and Designing: Sources: Ethnic Textiles	Guatemalan Stripes	Davenport, Betty	√	√	Hw	4	2		M/A 83	54
Designs and Designing: Sources, Ethnic Textiles	Woven Inspiration from West African Textiles	Renne, Elisha	√	√	WJ	10	4	40	Sp 86	60
Designs and Designing: Sources, Fish	Fish Provide the Ideas for a Series of Colorful Bookmarks	Allan, G. Ernestine	√	√	H&C	16	4		Fa 65	17
Designs and Designing: Sources, Historic Weaving Drafts	Notes of a Pattern Weaver	Alvic, Philis	√	> 4	SS&D	14	4	56	Fa 83	82
Designs and Designing: Sources, Literary	Inspiring Words	Strickler, Carol	√		Hw	5	5		N/D 84	44
Designs and Designing: Sources (Microphotographs)	Scientific Research Suggests Ideas for Fabric Designs		√		H&C	15	3		Su 64	5
Designs and Designing: Sources, Museum Collections	Textile Designs from Wallpaper	Justema, William	√		H&C	16	1		Wi 65	5
Designs and Designing: Sources, Music	Music for Inspiration		√	√	Hw	4	2		M/A 83	51
Designs and Designing: Sources: Native American Art	Terra Nova: Jack Lenor Larsen	Larson-Fleming, Susan	√		WJ	11	1	41	Su 86	49
Designs and Designing: Sources, Native American Dress	Weaver Profile: Mahota Handwovens	Irwin, Bobbie	√		Hw	8	5		N/D 87	35
Designs and Designing: Sources, Nature	Changing Seasons, The	Schomp, Halcyon; Hector Jaeger	√		Hw	5	5		N/D 84	61
Designs and Designing: Sources, Nature	Fall Foliage	Voiers, Leslie	√		Hw	5	5		N/D 84	69
Designs and Designing: Sources, Nature	Harts and Flowers: Sweden's Märta Måås-Fjetterstrom's Designs Inspired a Textile Renaissance	Selkurt, Claire	√		WJ	9	4	36	Sp 85	30
Designs and Designing: Sources, Nature	Maine Coast Memories	Jaeger, Hector; Halcyon Schomp	√		Hw	5	5		N/D 84	72
Designs and Designing: Sources: Nature	Southwest Reflections: Fiber Artists Inspired by the New Mexico Landscape	Colton, Mary Rawcliffe	√		WJ	11	1	41	Su 86	20
Designs and Designing: Sources, Nature	Weaving Memories	Alderman, Sharon D.	√		Hw	5	5		N/D 84	57
Designs and Designing: Sources, Old China	Found Treasures	Jones, Janice	√		Hw	5	5		N/D 84	70
Designs and Designing: Sources, Old Textiles	Crazy Quilt Wrap	Stoehr, Mary Kay	√		Hw	5	5		N/D 84	71
Designs and Designing: Sources, Old Textiles	Paisley-Inspired	Dobrovolny, Ardis	√		Hw	5	5		N/D 84	67
Designs and Designing: Sources, Old Textiles	Reinterpreting Old Weaves for Today and Tomorrow	Essén-Hedin, Margaretha	√		Hw	8	3		M/J 87	40
Designs and Designing: Sources, Old Textiles	Swatch Collection #15	Alderman, Sharon	√	√	Hw	8	2		M/A 87	38

SUBJECT	TITLE	AUTHOR	IL	INST	JOUR	VOL	NO	ISS	DATE	PAGE
Designs and Designing: Sources, Old Textiles	There's More to an Old Friar's Blanket than Monk's Belt	Centner, David J., OCD	√		Hw	5	5		N/D 84	41
Designs and Designing: Sources, Old Textiles	Thrums	Davenport, Betty	√		Hw	5	5		N/D 84	66
Designs and Designing: Sources, Quilts	Textile-Inspired Architecture	Smeltzer, Nancy	√		Fa	14	4		S/O 87	5
Designs and Designing: Sources, Ritual	JoAnn Giordano: A Modern Mythology	Malarcher, Patricia	√		Fa	13	6		N/D 86	13
Designs and Designing: Sources, Textile	Elizabeth MacDonald: Finding the Ties That Bind Truth and Art	Reuter, Laurel	√		Fa	14	4		S/O 87	31
Designs and Designing: Sources, Textile Mill Samples	Lace & Flowers: Vintage Inspiration	George, Patrice	√	> 4	Hw	8	5		N/D 87	68
Designs and Designing: Sources, Victorian Clothing	Weddding Dress, My	Caliendo, Karen	√		Hw	5	5		N/D 84	76
Designs and Designing: Sources, Vintage Swatch Albums	Inspiration from Woven Samples of the Past or...a Bunch of Us Last Sunday	Bradley, Louise	√		Hw	5	5		N/D 84	50
Designs and Designing: Sources, Wallpapers	Textiles Related to Wallpapers	Backlin-Landman, Hedy	√		H&C	16	3		Su 65	16
Designs and Designing: Space	Representational Space	Liebler, Barbara		√	Hw	7	3		M/J 86	62
Designs and Designing: Space	Spaced Out	Liebler, Barbara	√		Hw	7	2		M/A 86	86
Designs and Designing: Space-Dyed Yarn	Special Warp Effects with Space-Dyed Yarn	Bohannan, Ronnine	√	√	Hw	7	3		M/J 86	50
Designs and Designing: Spaced Warps	Undulating Weft Effects: Variations from Designing, Spaced Warp	Tidball, Harriet	√	√	SCGM		9		63	20
Designs and Designing: Spanish Textiles, Chinese Influence	Chinese Textile in Seventeenth Century Spain, A	Cammann, Schuyler	√		TMJ	1	4		De 65	57
Designs and Designing: Stitcher Warps	Designing for Piqué (error-corrected PWC v4 n4 i14 p33)	Sullivan, Donna	√	> 4	PWC	4	3	13		28
Designs and Designing: Stripes	Color Rotation Trick, A		√	√	Hw	4	2		M/A 83	40
Designs and Designing: Stripes	Composition and Designing: Stripes	Zielinski, S. A.; Robert Leclerc, ed.	√	√	MWL	18			'51–'73	72
Designs and Designing: Stripes	Planning and Weaving New Stripes	Blumenau, Lili	√	√	H&C	4	4		Fa 53	9
Designs and Designing: Stripes	Stripe Study Group, A		√	√	Hw	4	2		M/A 83	24
Designs and Designing: Stripes	Stripes		√	√	Hw	4	2		M/A 83	40
Designs and Designing: Stripes	Swatch Collection #7	Alderman, Sharon	√		Hw	4	2		M/A 83	58
Designs and Designing: Structure and Composition	Weaving, 'riting, and 'rithmetic	Tate, Blair	√		AT	6			De 86	57
Designs and Designing: Structure/Form	Structure and Form in the Weaving of John Becker	Swannie, Suzanne	√		AT	6			De 86	173
Designs and Designing: Stylization	Tiahuanaco Tapestry Design	Sawyer, Alan R.	√		TMJ	1	2		De 63	27
Designs and Designing: Suit, Knitted	Knitting Odyssey, A	Dyett, Linda	√	√	TM			13	O/N 87	48
Designs and Designing: Supplementary Weft	Decorative Weft on a Plain Weave Ground, Two Shaft Inlay and Brocade		√	√	WJ	5	4	20	Sp 81	15
Designs and Designing: Surface Design	Surface Attraction	Mattera, Joanne	√		TM			7	O/N 86	20
Designs and Designing: Surface Interest	Surface Interest — Textiles of Today: Surface Interest Designs with Drafts, Group 1, Accented Designs	Tidball, Harriet			SCGM		2		61	7
Designs and Designing: Sweaters	Converting Images Into Sweaters	MacHenry, Rachel	√	√	TM			10	A/M 87	72
Designs and Designing: Sweaters	Crochet Inspired by the Trees	Moon, Ellen	√	√	TM			11	J/J 87	56
Designs and Designing: Sweaters	Custom-Shaped Sweaters			√	TM			10	A/M 87	6
Designs and Designing: Swedish	Swedish Design	Krondahl, Hans	√		Hw	4	2		M/A 83	29
Designs and Designing: Tabby, Techniques	Tabby Weave, Ways to Make It More Interesting	Hausner, Walter	√		H&C	12	4		Fa 61	6
Designs and Designing: Tablet Weaving	Double-Faced 3/1 Broken Twill Woven on Tablets	Collingwood, Peter	√	√	AT	1			De 83	91
Designs and Designing: Tapestry	Contemporary Tapestries, A Midwest Designer's Approach	McDaniel, Claribel	√		H&C	13	1		Wi 62	9
Designs and Designing: Tapestry	Harmony by Contrast	Newman, Rochelle	√		SS&D	14	3	55	Su 83	92

SUBJECT	TITLE	AUTHOR	IL	INST	JOUR	VOL	NO	ISS	DATE	PAGE
Designs and Designing: Tapestry	Linda Fox La France: Designer — Tapestry Weaver	Hunt, Elizabeth Ann	√		Iw	4	2		Sp 79	36
Designs and Designing: Tapestry	Notes for a Potential Tapestry Weaver	Schira, Cynthia	√	√	H&C	19	4		Fa 68	12
Designs and Designing: Tapestry	Preparation and the Tapestry, The	Bick, Georgie	√		SS&D	2	2	6	Sp 71	6
Designs and Designing: Tapestry	Tapestry Gunner	Henry, Patti	√	√	TM			7	O/N 86	40
Designs and Designing: Tapestry	Tapestry: Part 2—The Dreaded Circle	Harvey, Nancy	√	√	SS&D	14	4	56	Fa 83	8
Designs and Designing: Tapestry	Tapestry Weaving and Design	Crump, Nancy	√	√	Iw	4	2		Sp 79	24
Designs and Designing: Tapestry	Techniques of Tapestry Weaves Part 4: Developing Design for Tapestry	O'Callaghan, Kate	√	√	WJ	5	2	18	Fa 80	15
Designs and Designing: Tapestry	Uno Mas — The Secret of Mexican Tapestry	Hall, Joanne	√	√	SS&D	5	3	19	Su 74	88
Designs and Designing: Tapestry, Composition	Contemporary Tapestry	Tidball, Harriet	√	√	SCGM		12		64	33
Designs and Designing: Tartans	So You Want to Weave Tartan?	Amos, Alden		√	Hw	4	5		N/D 83	37
Designs and Designing: Technique	Design by Decision: A Practical Approach to the Creative Process	Hall, Carolyn Vosburg	√		Fa	8	2		M/A 81	13
Designs and Designing: Technique	Elizabeth Tuttle: Pointillist Crochet	Demske, Barbara	√		Fa	7	4		J/A 80	48
Designs and Designing: Technique	Haptic Visions	Brubaker, Paul			WJ	11	4	44	Sp 87	59
Designs and Designing: Technique	Merry Holoien: A Harmony of Color and Sound	Ormseth, Laurie	√		Fa	13	2		M/A 86	6
Designs and Designing: Techniques	Argyle: The Transformation of a Classical Pattern Through the Design Process	Faust, Regine	√		Fa	9	4		J/A 82	24
Designs and Designing: Techniques	Basic Weaves, Tool to Develop Fabric Structures (error-corrected H&C v20 n4 69 p43)	Hausner, Walter	√	√	H&C	20	3		Su 69	4
Designs and Designing: Techniques	Counterchange, A Device for Pattern Design	Justema, William	√		H&C	19	3		Su 68	8
Designs and Designing: Techniques	Cut, Paste, and Copy	Wolff, Colette	√	√	TM			8	D/J 86	52
Designs and Designing: Techniques	Design in Handwoven Screens, Part 1	Rossbach, Ed	√	√	H&C	6	1		Wi 54	16
Designs and Designing: Techniques	Design in Handwoven Screens, Part 2	Rossbach, Ed	√		H&C	6	3		Su 55	16
Designs and Designing: Techniques	Designing for Finnweave	Xenakis, Athanasios David	√	√	PWC			2	Ap 82	50
Designs and Designing: Techniques	Designing with Modules	Sullivan, Donna	√	√	SS&D	16	4	64	Fa 85	54
Designs and Designing: Techniques	Experiments in Design by an Ohio Weaver		√		H&C	17	3		Su 66	22
Designs and Designing: Techniques	Fascination with Form, A	Richardson, Pat	√	> 4	SS&D	12	3	47	Su 81	54
Designs and Designing: Techniques	Module, a Basis for Textile Design, The	Justema, William	√	√	H&C	18	1		Wi 67	9
Designs and Designing: Techniques	Notes on Design from Grace Marvin			√	H&C	16	3		Su 65	36
Designs and Designing: Techniques	Raffia Tapestries	Del Deo, Josephine	√	√	H&C	9	1		Wi 57	20
Designs and Designing: Techniques	Reed as a Design Element, The	Hausner, Walter			H&C	21	4		Fa 70	20
Designs and Designing: Techniques	Roses and Snowballs: The Development of Block Patterns in the German Linen-Weaving Tradition	Hilts, Patricia	√	> 4	AT	5			Ju 86	167
Designs and Designing: Techniques	Solving the Circle	Mattera, Joanne	√	√	SS&D	7	1	25	Wi 75	67
Designs and Designing: Techniques	Tapestries in Rope	Smith, John	√	√	H&C	17	1		Wi 66	10
Designs and Designing: Techniques	Textile Designer of the Future, The	Lourie, Janice R.	√	√	H&C	17	1		Wi 66	8
Designs and Designing: Techniques	Textile Designs from Wallpaper	Justema, William	√		H&C	16	1		Wi 65	5
Designs and Designing: Techniques	Turned Drafts, A Useful Technique for Variety		√	√	H&C	19	3		Su 68	30

SUBJECT	TITLE	AUTHOR	IL	INST	JOUR	VOL	NO	ISS	DATE	PAGE
Designs and Designing: Techniques, Double Weaves	Designing Four-Shaft Double Weaves	Muller, Donna	√	√	WJ	7	4	28	Sp 83	56
Designs and Designing: Techniques, Finnweave	Fantastic Finnweave, Part 1	Xenakis, Athanasios David	√	√	PWC			2	Ap 82	18
Designs and Designing: Techniques, Interdiciplinary	Mathematical Design Concepts Relative to Aesthetic Concerns	Michaels-Paque, J.	√		AT	8			De 87	155
Designs and Designing: Techniques, Kantha	Kantha	Westfall, Carol D.; Dipti Desai	√	√	AT	7			Ju 87	161
Designs and Designing: Techniques, MasterWeaver Loom	MasterWeaver Loom: A New Concept in Hand-Weaving, The	El-Homossani, Dr. M. M.	√	√	WJ	8	4	32	Sp 84	54
Designs and Designing: Techniques, Miniatures	Miniatures, Fine Threads, Complex Weaves	Piroch, Sigrid		√	CW	7	2	20	Ja 86	3
Designs and Designing: Techniques, Twill, Free-Form	Freeform Twill & Freeform Searles Lace	Searles, Nancy	√	> 4	CW		23		Ja 87	10
Designs and Designing: Techniques, Warp Rep	Four-Block Warp Rep (error-corrected WJ v8 n1 83 p50)	Robitaille, Annette	√	> 4	WJ	7	4	28	Sp 83	16
Designs and Designing: Terminology	Composition and Designing: Terminology of Designing	Zielinski, S. A.; Robert Leclerc, ed.	√		MWL	18			'51–'73	7
Designs and Designing: Tessellation	Excerpt from Geometric Design in Weaving, An	Regensteiner, Else	√	√	WJ	11	4	44	Sp 87	13
Designs and Designing: Textile	Anni Albers — Innovator in Textile Design		√		H&C	10	4		Fa 59	6
Designs and Designing: Textile	Cut, Paste, and Copy	Wolff, Colette	√	√	TM			8	D/J 86	52
Designs and Designing: Textile	From Portraits to Textile Designs		√	> 4	H&C	11	1		Wi 60	20
Designs and Designing: Textile	Independent Design Study At Philadelphia Textile College				H&C	22	4		Fa 71	22
Designs and Designing: Textile Industry	Colour, Texture, Ornament, Line: A Question for Managers—Do You Know How Your Designers Think?	Willock, Jack			AT	4			De 85	97
Designs and Designing: Textile Industry	Handweaving in the Textile Industry	Hausner, Walter A.			H&C	9	1		Wi 57	28
Designs and Designing: Textile Industry	Industrial Fabric & the Woven Form	Zausner, Judith	√		H&C	23	6		N/D 72	43
Designs and Designing: Textile Industry	Opportunities for Handweavers in the Textile Industry		√		H&C	3	4		Fa 52	42
Designs and Designing: Textile, Peruvian Influence	Peru, Textiles Unlimited: Peruvian Models for Modern Weavers	Tidball, Harriet	√		SCGM		25		68	26
Designs and Designing: Textile Printing	"Patterns" with a Look at Japanese Printing with Stencils (Exhibit)	Dyer, Carolyn	√		Fa	4	5		S/O 77	10
Designs and Designing: Texture	Of Treasures & Textures	Liebler, Barbara			Hw	8	2		M/A 87	22
Designs and Designing: Texture	Texture as Stripe		√	√	Hw	4	2		M/A 83	66
Designs and Designing: Theme, Variations	Variations on a Theme	Liebler, Barbara	√	√	Hw	8	5		N/D 87	26
Designs and Designing: Thought Process	Laura Militzer Bryant: Thought Process	Bryant, Laura Militzer	√		Fa	10	4		J/A 83	52
Designs and Designing: Three Dimensional Textiles, Computer-Aided	Application of Computer Generated Weaves as Texture Maps, The	Murtha, Judith Rush	√	√	AT	3			My 85	75
Designs and Designing: Three-Dimensional	Leora K. Stewart: Form in Three-Dimensional Space		√		SS&D	1	4	4	Se 70	5
Designs and Designing: Tie-Ups	Designing from the Tie-Up, A Multiharness Tool (error-corrected Iw v5 n1 79 p10)	Alderman, Sharon D.	√	> 4	Iw	4	4		Fa 79	30
Designs and Designing: Tie-Ups	Multi-Harness Overshot "Trials"	Deygout, Françoise	√	> 4	CW		24		My 87	3
Designs and Designing: Tradition/Innovation	Structure and Form in the Weaving of John Becker	Swannie, Suzanne	√		AT	6			De 86	173
Designs and Designing: Translating Patterns	Ideas Are Where You Find Them	Breeze, Helen	√	> 4	H&C	3	2		Sp 52	22
Designs and Designing: Triaxial Weaves	Braiding Triaxial Weaves: Enhancements and Design for Artworks	Mooney, David R.	√	√	AT	5			Ju 86	9
Designs and Designing: Tubular Weaving	Andean Crossed-Warp Techniques for Decorative Trims, Part 2 — Tubular Bands (error-corrected WJ v3 n1 insert for vol. 2)	Cahlander, Adele	√	√	WJ	3	1	9	Jy 78	38
Designs and Designing: Twill	Designing Fancy Twills in Double Two-Tie Unit Weave	Kelly, Jacquie	√	> 4	Iw	6	1		Wi 80	49

SUBJECT	TITLE	AUTHOR	IL	INST	JOUR	VOL	NO	ISS	DATE	PAGE
Designs and Designing: Twill	Twills of Charlotte Funk, The	Patrick, Jane	√		Hw	6	5		N/D 85	36
Designs and Designing: Twill	Yarn Twist and Twills			√	Hw	6	5		N/D 85	44
Designs and Designing: Twill Blocks/Stripes	Twill in Blocks and Stripes		√		Hw	6	5		N/D 85	52
Designs and Designing: Twill, Diagonals, Reversals	Very Basics of Weaving Drafting: Two and Three Shafts, The	Carey, Joyce Marquess	√	√	WJ	6	2	22	Fa 81	50
Designs and Designing: Twill, Multishaft	Fascination of Twills (Multishafts): How to Design Diamond Twills on Six and Eight Shafts	Zielinski, S. A.; Robert Leclerc, ed.	√	> 4	MWL	10			'51–'73	72
Designs and Designing: Twill, Undulating	Twill with a Twist	Keasbey, Doramay	√	> 4	Hw	6	5		N/D 85	31
Designs and Designing: Twill, Unit Structure, 2-Tie, Double	Twills in Double Two-Tie Unit Weave	van der Hoogt, Madelyn	√	> 4	Hw	6	5		N/D 85	64
Designs and Designing: Twining, Split-Ply	Split-Ply Twining: Designing with Split-Ply Twining	Harvey, Virginia I.		√	TIAM		1		76	25
Designs and Designing: Twining, Split-Ply, Three-Dimensional Designs	Split-Ply Twining: Three-Dimensional Designs	Harvey, Virginia I.	√	√	TIAM		1		76	37
Designs and Designing: Undulating Weft Textiles	Undulating Weft Effects: Designing Undulating Weft Textiles	Tidball, Harriet		√	SCGM		9		63	4
Designs and Designing: Unit Structure, 2-Tie, Double	Stitcher Designer Hints for Loom-Controlled Figured Piqué	van der Hoogt, Madelyn	√	> 4	PWC	4	3	13		48
Designs and Designing: Upholstery	Designing Satisfactory Upholstery Fabrics		√		H&C	4	1		Wi 52	20
Designs and Designing: Upholstery Fabric	Weaving Upholstery, The Qualities of a Sound Fabric	Regensteiner, Else	√		H&C	14	1		Wi 63	10
Designs and Designing: Video Digitizer System	From Image to Woven Structure: A Video-Computer System for Textile Designers	Peterson, Lisa Lee	√	√	AT	7			Ju 87	109
Designs and Designing: Waffle Weave	Beauty and Warmth: A Throw in Waffle Weave		√		Hw	6	5		N/D 85	55
Designs and Designing: Warp Stripes	Evergreen	Alderman, Sharon	√	√	Hw	4	5		N/D 83	62
Designs and Designing: Weaving	Artist and Industry — A Cooperative Effort		√		Hw	8	3		M/J 87	71
Designs and Designing: Weaving	Color-and-Weave on a Dark-Light Sequence	Windeknecht, Margaret; Thomas Windeknecht	√	√	SS&D	12	4	48	Fa 81	24
Designs and Designing: Weaving	Color-and-Weave on Rosepath	Windeknecht, Margaret; Thomas Windeknecht	√	√	SS&D	13	2	50	Sp 82	8
Designs and Designing: Weaving	Complementary-Warp Weave (error-corrected WJ v7 n4 83 p4)	Coffman, Charlotte	√	√	WJ	7	3	27	Wi 82	53
Designs and Designing: Weaving	Creating Textiles for Today's Interiors	Vogel, Edna	√		H&C	3	1		Wi 51	5
Designs and Designing: Weaving	Curves and Circles	Marston, Ena	√	> 4	SS&D	15	1	57	Wi 83	84
Designs and Designing: Weaving	Design and the Handweaver	Atwater, Mary Meigs	√	√	SCGM		3		61	1-26
Designs and Designing: Weaving	Design for Torah Cover Based on 'Torah is Truth' and 'Tree of Life'	Lebovitz, Constance	√	√	SS&D	4	4	16	Fa 73	18
Designs and Designing: Weaving	Design Variations in Simple Textures	Hausner, Walter	√	√	H&C	8	1		Wi 56	12
Designs and Designing: Weaving	Designing for the Custom Trade	Frank, Elizabeth	√		H&C	3	1		Wi 51	44
Designs and Designing: Weaving	Designing Rep Weave	Ridgeway, Terese	√	> 4	SS&D	16	3	63	Su 85	28
Designs and Designing: Weaving	Exploring Wedge Weave	Mattera, Joanne	√	√	Iw	3	2		Wi 78	24
Designs and Designing: Weaving	Fabric About Fabric	Cannarella, Deborah	√		TM			1	O/N 85	72
Designs and Designing: Weaving	Grouped Warp Threads	Davison, Marguerite Porter	√	√	H&C	26	3		M/J 75	24
Designs and Designing: Weaving	Journey in Progress, A	Chittenden, Annie Curtis	√	√	SS&D	17	4	68	Fa 86	50
Designs and Designing: Weaving	Marianne Strengell, Textile Consultant to Architects	Bemis, Marion Holden	√		H&C	8	1		Wi 56	6
Designs and Designing: Weaving	Marianne Strengell's Approach to Design	Bryan, Dorothy	√		H&C	11	4		Fa 60	29
Designs and Designing: Weaving	Notes of a Pattern Weaver	Alvic, Philis	√		SS&D	14	3	55	Su 83	66
Designs and Designing: Weaving	One Warp, Many Fabrics	Liebler, Barbara	√	> 4	Iw	3	1		Fa 77	28
Designs and Designing: Weaving	One Weaver's Approach to Designing Yardage	Alderman, Sharon	√	√	Iw	3	2		Wi 78	22
Designs and Designing: Weaving	One Weaver's Viewpoint	Freeman, Claire			H&C	11	1		Wi 60	10

SUBJECT	TITLE	AUTHOR	IL	INST	JOUR	VOL	NO	ISS	DATE	PAGE
Designs and Designing: Weaving	Planning Clothing Fabrics, Suggestions for Exploring Basic Weaves	Snyder, Mary E.	√	>4	H&C	15	1		Wi 64	9
Designs and Designing: Weaving	Planning for Threading and Treadling	Wertenberger, Kathryn	√	√	Hw	2	2		Mr 81	47
Designs and Designing: Weaving	Rainwindow: Watercolor Weaving	Schlegel, Mary	√	√	SS&D	5	2	18	Sp 74	8
Designs and Designing: Weaving	Rugs for Interiors	Roach, Dianne Carol	√		SS&D	16	4	64	Fa 85	18
Designs and Designing: Weaving	Sampler to Aid in Designing Fabrics, A		√	√	H&C	5	4		Fa 54	22
Designs and Designing: Weaving	Sixteen-Harness Design for Draperies, A	Fishback, John S.	√	>4	H&C	11	1		Wi 60	24
Designs and Designing: Weaving	Stars & Roses Or Designing and Drafting Overshot	Marston, Ena	√	√	SS&D	4	3	15	Su 73	27
Designs and Designing: Weaving	Syllabus for Success	Michaels-Paque, Joan	√	√	SS&D	15	3	59	Su 84	11
Designs and Designing: Weaving	Toward Professionalism in Weaving	Bradley, David H.			H&C	8	4		Fa 57	19
Designs and Designing: Weaving	Two-harness Weaves	Freeman, Claire	√	√	H&C	11	4		Fa 60	40
Designs and Designing: Weaving	Use of Novelty Yarns in Weaving, The	Blumenau, Lili	√		H&C	3	2		Sp 52	16
Designs and Designing: Weaving	Variations on One Warp	Alvic, Philis	√		SS&D	12	4	48	Fa 81	70
Designs and Designing: Weaving	Verticals	O'Shaughnessy, Marjorie	√	>4	SS&D	15	1	57	Wi 83	8
Designs and Designing: Weaving	Warp-Faced Weaving, Part 1	Jensen, Gay	√	√	Hw	3	3		My 82	42
Designs and Designing: Weaving	Weaver-Designer Plans a Fabric, The	Blumenau, Lili	√		H&C	3	1		Wi 51	8
Designs and Designing: Weaving	Weaving Ripples and Curves	Irvine, Marie M.	√	√	SS&D	12	1	45	Wi 80	52
Designs and Designing: Weaving, 6-Block Patterns	Summer and Winter and Other Two-Tie Unit Weaves: Variations on a Six-Block Diamond Threading	Tidball, Harriet	√		SCGM		19		66	58
Designs and Designing: Weaving, Block Patterns	Composition and Designing Part 2: Numerical Patterns	Zielinski, S. A.; Robert Leclerc, ed.	√	√	MWL	19			'51–'73	40
Designs and Designing: Weaving, Block Patterns	Composition and Designing Part 2: Pattern Variations: How to Find the Number	Zielinski, S. A.; Robert Leclerc, ed.		√	MWL	19			'51–'73	25
Designs and Designing: Weaving, Block Patterns	Creative Overshot: Create a Layout	Windeknecht, Margaret B.	√	√	SCGM		31		78	18
Designs and Designing: Weaving, Block Patterns	Workshop at Home, Weaving Summer and Winter	Arnold, Ruth	√	√	H&C	9	3		Su 58	6
Designs and Designing: Weaving, Block Patterns, Profiles	Composition and Designing Part 2: Variations of Four Block Patterns	Zielinski, S. A.; Robert Leclerc, ed.	√	√	MWL	19			'51–'73	20
Designs and Designing: Weaving, Blocks Combined	Creative Monk's Belt: Putting the Blocks Together	Windeknecht, Margaret B.	√	>4	SCGM		30		76	25
Designs and Designing: Weaving, Border Variations	Undulating Weft Effects: Variations from Designing, Borders	Tidball, Harriet	√	√	SCGM		9		63	25
Designs and Designing: Weaving, Borders	End and Selvage Borders	Frey, Berta	√	√	H&C	9	2		Sp 58	46
Designs and Designing: Weaving, Brocade	Brocade: Sampling and Designing	Tidball, Harriet	√	√	SCGM		22		67	13
Designs and Designing: Weaving, Brocade	Brocade: Studying Design	Tidball, Harriet	√		SCGM		22		67	17
Designs and Designing: Weaving Chenille	Pile Weaves, Rugs and Tapestry: Chenille or Twice-Woven Fabric	Zielinski, S. A.; Robert Leclerc, ed.	√	√	MWL	14			'51–'73	26
Designs and Designing: Weaving, Color	Design and the Handweaver: Color	Atwater, Mary Meigs		√	SCGM		3		61	11
Designs and Designing: Weaving: Computer-Aided	Application of Computer Generated Weaves as Texture Maps, The	Murtha, Judith Rush	√	√	AT	3			My 85	75
Designs and Designing: Weaving, Computer-Aided Techniques	Application of Computer-Aided Design Techniques to the Creation of Moss Crepe Weaves, The	Ping, Gu; Alan Newton	√	>4	AT	2			De 84	185
Designs and Designing: Weaving, Conceptual	Characteristics of Handweaves	Howell, Marie	√		H&C	12	1		Wi 61	18
Designs and Designing: Weaving Drafts	Designing Drafts	Kurtz, Carol	√	√	SS&D	10	4	40	Fa 79	28
Designs and Designing: Weaving, Drafts	Drafting with Color	Kurtz, Carol	√	√	SS&D	11	1	41	Wi 79	10
Designs and Designing: Weaving, Handloom	Design for Hand & Power Loom	Hausner, Walter			H&C	21	1		Wi 70	11
Designs and Designing: Weaving Industry	Artist/Designer: Two Approaches to Fabric	Kinsella, Pat	√		AT	3			My 85	57

SUBJECT	TITLE	AUTHOR	IL	INST	JOUR	VOL	NO	ISS	DATE	PAGE
Designs and Designing: Weaving Industry	Working As a Handweaver; Some Reflections and Techniques	Bradley, Ann			SS&D	5	2	18	Sp 74	61
Designs and Designing: Weaving, Leno, Simple Patterns	Two-Harness Textiles, The Open Work Weaves: Gauze and Leno, The Crossed-Warp Weaves, Simple Leno Patterns	Tidball, Harriet	√	√	SCGM		21		67	30
Designs and Designing: Weaving, Modern	Composition and Designing: Traditional and Modern Designing	Zielinski, S. A.; Robert Leclerc, ed.	√	√	MWL	18			'51–'73	24
Designs and Designing: Weaving, Outline Method Variations	Undulating Weft Effects: Variations from Designing, Variations Based on Outline Method	Tidball, Harriet	√	√	SCGM		9		63	23
Designs and Designing: Weaving, Pattern	Design and the Handweaver: Pattern	Atwater, Mary Meigs	√	√	SCGM		3		61	17
Designs and Designing: Weaving, Pattern in Twist	Composition and Designing: Patterns in Twist	Zielinski, S. A.; Robert Leclerc, ed.	√	√	MWL	18			'51–'73	75
Designs and Designing: Weaving, Pick-Up	Loom-Controlled Adaptation of a Mexican Pick-Up Pattern Technique	Keasbey, Doramay	√	> 4	CW	6	2	17	Ja 85	19
Designs and Designing: Weaving, Power Loom	Design for Hand & Power Loom	Hausner, Walter			H&C	21	1		Wi 70	11
Designs and Designing: Weaving, Proportion	Design and the Handweaver: Proportion	Atwater, Mary Meigs	√	√	SCGM		3		61	5
Designs and Designing: Weaving, Sculpture	Ken Weaver on Rep Weaving	Weaver, Ken	√		WJ	7	4	28	Sp 83	20
Designs and Designing: Weaving, Sources	Adaptations of Primitive Warp-Pattern Weaves	Landreau, Tony	√	√	H&C	8	1		Wi 56	25
Designs and Designing: Weaving, Sources	Contemporary Textile Designs from Ancient Sources		√	> 4	H&C	7	4		Fa 56	29
Designs and Designing: Weaving, Sources	Designs in Old Linen Tablecloths	Gubser, Elsie H.	√	> 4	H&C	9	3		Su 58	21
Designs and Designing: Weaving, Sources	Miniatures Adapted from Colonial Patterns	Gibbs, Emily	√	√	H&C	8	2		Sp 57	26
Designs and Designing: Weaving, Sources	New York Handweavers at Cooper Union Museum		√		H&C	7	4		Fa 56	20
Designs and Designing: Weaving, Stripes	Two-Harness Textiles, The Loom-Controlled Weaves: Stripes and Bands, Stripe Diagrams	Tidball, Harriet	√	√	SCGM		20		67	16
Designs and Designing: Weaving, Tartans, Contemporary	Weaver's Book of Scottish Tartans: Contemporary Adaptations in Tartans, The	Tidball, Harriet			SCGM		5		62	7
Designs and Designing: Weaving, Techniques	Design in Weaving	Berglund, Hilma	√		H&C	8	4		Fa 57	13
Designs and Designing: Weaving, Techniques	First Step in Designing Textures, A	Hausner, Walter	√	√	H&C	9	2		Sp 58	14
Designs and Designing: Weaving, Texture	Design and the Handweaver: Texture	Atwater, Mary Meigs		√	SCGM		3		61	9
Designs and Designing: Weaving, Three-Dimensional	Woven Circles and Cones	Henzie, Susie	√	√	SS&D	10	4	40	Fa 79	58
Designs and Designing: Weaving, Traditional	Composition and Designing: Traditional and Modern Designing	Zielinski, S. A.; Robert Leclerc, ed.	√	√	MWL	18			'51–'73	24
Designs and Designing: With Buttons	Buttons	Abbott, Deborah	√	√	TM			2	D/J 85	56
Designs and Desingnig: Sources	'lectric Ikat Wins WHFL Award		√	√	SS&D	5	3	19	Su 74	92
Designs and Desingnig: Weaving, 2-Shaft	Two-Harness Designs	Bryan, Dorothy	√		H&C	9	3		Su 58	28
Designs: Charted	Alexis' Favorite	Rowley, Elaine	√	√	Kn	1	1	1	F-W 84 CI	46,56B 48
Designs: Charted	Alpaca Vest	Newton, Deborah	√	√	Kn	3	4	8	Fa 87	21
Designs: Charted	Alphabet Soup	Chandler, Deborah	√	> 4	Hw	8	5		N/D 87	90
Designs: Charted	Amazing Color-Pattern Corduroy Rug		√	> 4	PWC	3	4	10		22
Designs: Charted	And a Necklace, Too	Upitis, Lizbeth	√	√	Kn	2	2	4	S-S 86	48
Designs: Charted	Andean Crossed-Warp Techniques for Decorative Trims, Part 1 — Flat Bands	Cahlander, Adele	√	√	WJ	2	4	8	Ap 78	10

209

SUBJECT	TITLE	AUTHOR	IL	INST	JOUR	VOL	NO	ISS	DATE	PAGE
Designs: Charted	Andean Crossed-Warp Techniques for Decorative Trims, Part 2 — Tubular Bands (error-corrected WJ v3 n1 insert for vol. 2)	Cahlander, Adele	√	√	WJ	3	1	9	Jy 78	38
Designs: Charted	Autumn Leaves, A Design in Summer-and-Winter	Arnold, Ruth	√	√	H&C	14	3		Su 63	14
Designs: Charted	Babushkas	Upitis, Lizbeth	√	√	Kn	4	1	9	Wi 87	48
Designs: Charted	Beaded Sweater	Diven, Gail; Rosemary Drysdale	√	√	Kn	2	2	4	S-S 86	50
Designs: Charted	Beyond the Fringe	Wertenberger, Kathryn	√	> 4	Hw	2	5		No 81	27
Designs: Charted	Block Weaves Part 1, Profile Drafts and Block Designs (error-corrected WJ v2 n4 78 insert for vol. 2)		√	> 4	WJ	2	3	7	Ja 78	6
Designs: Charted	Block Weaves Part 2, Atwater Bronson Lace		√	> 4	WJ	2	3	7	Ja 78	10
Designs: Charted	Blooming Leaf	Xenakis, Athanasios David	√	√	PWC	3	3	9		51
Designs: Charted	Bogus Bohus	Bush, Nancy	√	√	Kn	2	1	3	F-W 85	49
Designs: Charted	Bonnie Bonnet	Adams, Harriet	√	√	Kn	1	2	2	S-S 85	38
Designs: Charted	Borders: Notes of a Pattern Weaver	Alvic, Philis	√	> 4	WJ	11	2	42	Fa 86	55
Designs: Charted	Boundweave	Evans, Jane	√	√	WJ	1	4	4	Ap 77	3
Designs: Charted	Braid on the Bias (error-corrected Kn v3 n1 i5 f/w 86 p11)	Madden, Gail	√	√	Kn	2	2	4	S-S 86	35
Designs: Charted	Camera Strap in Double-Weave Pick-Up	Gaston-Voûte, Suzanne	√	√	PWC			2	Ap 82	10
Designs: Charted	Carnival Cable Pullover	Jensen, Candi	√	√	Kn	3	1	5	F-W 86	24
Designs: Charted	Cartoon, The	Brostoff, Laya	√	√	Hw	3	1		Ja 82	26
Designs: Charted	Celtic Knot Box Cushion	Xenakis, Athanasios David	√	√	PWC	3	4	10		60
Designs: Charted	Chanel Jacket	Ratigan, Dorothy	√	√	Kn	2	2	4	S-S 86	33
Designs: Charted	Christmas Gretings from the Weaver's Journal Staff		√	> 4	WJ	3	2	10	Oc 78	41
Designs: Charted	Complementary-Warp Weave (error-corrected WJ v7 n4 83 p4)	Coffman, Charlotte	√	√	WJ	7	3	27	Wi 82	53
Designs: Charted	Coronet, A	Clayton, Clare	√	√	Kn	3	2	6	Sp 87	32
Designs: Charted	Cotton Hanging — On a Chinese Folk Motif	Xenakis, Athanasios David	√	√	PWC	1	1		No 81	39
Designs: Charted	Coverlet Weaves on a Rigid-Heddle (David Xenakis)		√	√	Hw	2	1		F-W 80	38
Designs: Charted	Coverlet Weaves Using Two Ties	Barrett, Clotilde	√	> 4	WJ	3	4	12	Ap 79	26
Designs: Charted	Designing for Finnweave	Xenakis, Athanasios David	√	√	PWC			2	Ap 82	50
Designs: Charted	Designing for the Opphämta Loom	Johns, Greg	√	> 4	PWC	3	4	10		68
Designs: Charted	Designing Rugs for Harness-Controlled Weaving		√	> 4	WJ	4	4	16	Ap 80	27
Designs: Charted	Different Boundweave on Six Harnesses, A (error-corrected WJ v3 n1 vol. 2 insert)	Strickler, Carol	√	> 4	WJ	2	4	8	Ap 78	36
Designs: Charted	Different Floats for Different Folks		√	√	PWC			5	Sp 83	31
Designs: Charted	Double Piqué, Double Weave (error-corrected PWC v4 n4 i14 p33)	van der Hoogt, Madelyn	√	> 4	PWC	4	3	13		40
Designs: Charted	Double Weave, Finnweave and Mexican Variations	Frey, Berta	√	√	H&C	12	2		Sp 61	12
Designs: Charted	Double Weave Pick-Up with Straight Diagonal Lines	Wolter, Edith L.	√	√	WJ	7	4	28	Sp 83	61
Designs: Charted	Double-Woven Treasures from Old Peru	Cahlander, Adele	√	√	PWC			4	Ja 83	36
Designs: Charted	Dubbelmossa	Adams, Harriet	√	√	Kn	2	1	3	F-W 85	50, 8B
Designs: Charted	Even-Tied Overshot on a Rigid Heddle Loom	Xenakis, Athanasios David	√	√	PWC	3	3	9		46
Designs: Charted	Even-Tied Overshot on Four Shafts with Shaft Switching	Herring, Connie; Athanasios David Xenakis	√	√	PWC	3	3	9		44
Designs: Charted	Experimenting with Color and Two-Tie Weaving on the Rigid Heddle	Niekrasz, Jennifer	√	√	PWC	4	4	14		21
Designs: Charted	Exploring a Knitted Pattern	Bruzelius, Margaret	√	√	TM			6	A/S 86	35

SUBJECT	TITLE	AUTHOR	IL	INST	JOUR	VOL	NO	ISS	DATE	PAGE
Designs: Charted	Fair Isle in Natural Colors, The	Gibson-Roberts, Priscilla A.	√	√	Kn	2	1	3	F-W 85	34
Designs: Charted	Fair Isle Knitting	Starmore, Alice	√	√	TM			8	D/J 86	44
Designs: Charted	Fantastic Finnweave, Part 1	Xenakis, Athanasios David	√	√	PWC			2	Ap 82	18
Designs: Charted	Fantastic Finnweave, Part 2: Single-Thread Projects	Xenakis, Athanasios David	√	√	PWC			3	Oc 82	14
Designs: Charted	Fantastic Finnweave, Part 3	Xenakis, Athanasios David	√	> 4	PWC			4	Ja 83	10
Designs: Charted	Farmer and His Wife, Figure Boundweave, A	Pissowotski, Inge	√	√	WJ	5	4	20	Sp 81	8
Designs: Charted	Faroese Shawls	Swansen, Meg	√	√	Kn	4	1	9	Wi 87	26
Designs: Charted	Figured Piqué Patterning with the Double Two-Tie System (error-corrected PWC v4 n3 i13 p4)	Xenakis, Athanasios David; Patti Sellon	√	> 4	PWC	4	2	12		20
Designs: Charted	Finnish Lace: a Leno Variation	Egen, Su	√	√	Hw	7	2		M/A 86	49
Designs: Charted	Finnweave	Barrett, Clotilde	√	> 4	WJ	11	4	44	Sp 87	25
Designs: Charted	Fishperson's Earflap Hat	Sherrodd, Kristie	√	√	S-O	11	3		Fa 87	53
Designs: Charted	Flat Tapestry Cartoon — Ready to Go, A	Swendeman, Dorothy	√	√	Hw	3	1		Ja 82	30
Designs: Charted	Four Harness Damask — A Pick-up Weave	Merritt, Elveana	√	√	WJ	5	1	17	Su 80	20
Designs: Charted	Four-Block Double Weave on Four Shafts	Barrett, Clotilde	√	√	WJ	8	1	29	Su 83	72
Designs: Charted	Four-Block Warp Rep (error-corrected WJ v8 n1 83 p50)	Robitaille, Annette	√	> 4	WJ	7	4	28	Sp 83	16
Designs: Charted	Four-Shaft, Two-Block Warp-Faced Rep Floor Covering	Kolling-Summers, Elizabeth	√	√	WJ	7	4	28	Sp 83	15
Designs: Charted	Four-Shaft Unbalanced Twill Braided Ribbon Inlay on Plain Weave Ground	Xenakis, Athanasios David	√	√	PWC	4	1	11		27
Designs: Charted	Fringes from Warp Ends	Brooks, Marguerite G.	√	√	H&C	6	1		Wi 54	46
Designs: Charted	Fun with Bronson Lace Variations	Davenport, Betty	√	√	PWC			5	Sp 83	46
Designs: Charted	Gaffer's Gansey	Zimmermann, Elizabeth	√	√	Kn	1	1	1	F-W 84 CI	36,56B 28
Designs: Charted	Gansey in Handspun, The	Gibson-Roberts, Priscilla A.	√	√	Kn	1	1	1	F-W 84 CI	32,56B 24
Designs: Charted	Gansey with Yoke	Farley, Sidna	√	√	Kn	3	2	6	Sp 87	27
Designs: Charted	Garden of Fair Isles, A	Rowe, Mary	√	√	Kn	2	1	3	F-W 85	40, 8B
Designs: Charted	Grandma's Checkerboard Lace	Yaksick, Karen	√	√	Kn	4	1	9	Wi 87	52
Designs: Charted	Graphic Weave for a Special Occasion (Carrie Rogers)		√	√	Hw	1	2		S-S 80	38
Designs: Charted	Guatemala Visited	Atwater, Mary Meigs	√	√	SCGM		15		65	19
Designs: Charted	Guatemala Visited	Atwater, Mary Meigs	√	√	SCGM		15		65	41
Designs: Charted	Guatemalan Brocade Border, A	Simons, Phid	√	√	WJ	6	4	24	Sp 82	39
Designs: Charted	Guernseys	Upitis, Lizbeth			Kn	1	1	1	F-W 84 CI	48 40
Designs: Charted	Hand Woven Rugs: Weaves, Two-Warp Weave, Pick-Up Method	Atwater, Mary Meigs	√	√	SCGM		29		48	26
Designs: Charted	Happy Dress	Sprenger, Elserine	√	√	WJ	8	3	31	Wi 83	46
Designs: Charted	Highlands Shawl	Bush, Nancy	√	√	Kn	4	1	9	Wi 87	40
Designs: Charted	Holiday Runners	Skoy, Mary	√	> 4	WJ	12	2	46	Fa 87	22
Designs: Charted	Home Weaving: Linen'n Lace	Xenakis, Athanasios David	√	√	Hw	1	1		F-W 79	44
Designs: Charted	How to Weave a Transparency	Keasbey, Doramay	√	√	Hw	4	1		J/F 83	27
Designs: Charted	How to Weave Your own Designs	Arnold, Ruth	√	> 4	H&C	11	3		Su 60	6
Designs: Charted	Imperial Tulip and Prairie Flower		√	√	PWC			5	Sp 83	15
Designs: Charted	In Pursuit of Plakhta	Golay, Myrna	√	> 4	WJ	11	3	43	Wi 87	34
Designs: Charted	Inkle Belt (Miranda Howard)		√	√	Hw	2	5		No 81	36, 90
Designs: Charted	Inlay We Trust, Part 1: Half Dukagång	Herring, Connie	√	√	PWC			5	Sp 83	59
Designs: Charted	Inlay We Trust Part 3: Pillow Based on Greek Inlay Technique	Herring, Connie	√	√	PWC	3	4	10		44

SUBJECT	TITLE	AUTHOR	IL	INST	JOUR	VOL	NO	ISS	DATE	PAGE
Designs: Charted	Inscribing a Coverlet	Beevers, Sue	√	√	PWC	5	2	16		16
Designs: Charted	Inspiration in Boundweave	Strauss, Lynn	√	> 4	Hw	7	2		M/A 86	38
Designs: Charted	Instructions: Pick-Up Figured Piqué (error-corrected PWC v4 n3 i13 p4)	Xenakis, Athanasios David	√	√	PWC	4	2	12		39
Designs: Charted	Intarsia Shawl	Lewis, Susanna	√	√	Kn	4	1	9	Wi 87	46
Designs: Charted	Isolated Overshot: Inlaid Runner	Xenakis, Athanasios David	√	√	PWC	3	2	8		31
Designs: Charted	Karellian Red Pick	Howard, Miranda	√	√	Hw	2	5		No 81	36
Designs: Charted	Karellian Red Pick Dress (Miranda Howard)		√	√	Hw	2	5		No 81	36, 90
Designs: Charted	Knit and Purl	Rowley, Elaine	√		Kn	1	1	1	F-W 84 CI	40 32
Designs: Charted	Knitted Yarn Over: This Simple Stitch Creates a Hole in the Fabric, The	MacNulty, Shirley W.	√	√	TM			10	A/M 87	38
Designs: Charted	Lace and Knots	Newton, Deborah	√	√	Kn	3	4	8	Fa 87	20
Designs: Charted	Lace Curtains	Higginbotham, Charles	√	√	Kn	1	2	2	S-S 85	40
Designs: Charted	Lace from Hand to Machine	Lewis, Susanna E.	√	√	Kn	1	2	2	S-S 85	71
Designs: Charted	Lace Garland	Ocker, Emily	√	√	Kn	4	1	9	Wi 87	38
Designs: Charted	Lace Shawl	Newton, Deborah	√	√	Kn	4	1	9	Wi 87	54
Designs: Charted	Lace-Weave Tunic	Rowley, Elaine	√	√	PWC			5	Sp 83	18
Designs: Charted	Lampshade Transfigured, A	Fauske, Carla	√	√	PWC	1	1		No 81	55
Designs: Charted	Latvian Wedding Mittens	Upitis, Lizbeth	√	√	PWC			2	Ap 82	92
Designs: Charted	Little Knitting on the Side, A	Glover, Medrith	√	√	Kn	2	1	3	F-W 85	38
Designs: Charted	Llama Hat	Davidsohn, Marty	√	√	PWC			4	Ja 83	65
Designs: Charted	Long Sweeping Evening Cape	Roth, Bettie G.	√	> 4	WJ	6	3	23	Wi 81	26
Designs: Charted	Loom Controlled Designs		√	> 4	WJ	3	3	11	Ja 79	18
Designs: Charted	Martha Washington's Inaugural Gown	Reams, Dorothy E.	√		SS&D	7	3	27	Su 76	15
Designs: Charted	MasterWeaver Loom: A New Concept in Hand-Weaving, The	El-Homossani, Dr. M. M.	√	√	WJ	8	4	32	Sp 84	54
Designs: Charted	Mitten Miniatures	Upitis, Lizbeth	√	√	Kn	4	1	9	Wi 87	50
Designs: Charted	Multiple Shaft Weaving — 2-Tie Four-End Block Drafts		√	> 4	WJ	6	4	24	Sp 82	48
Designs: Charted	Navajo Saddle Blanket Patterns	Barrett, Clotilde	√	√	WJ	11	1	41	Su 86	56
Designs: Charted	Notes on Plaiting in the Upper Amazon Basin, Peru	Blinks, Anne	√	√	Iw	5	4		Fa 80	51
Designs: Charted	Now, That's a Cabled Sweater	Yaksick, Karen	√	√	Kn	3	1	5	F-W 86	30
Designs: Charted	Number Knitting — A New Way with an Old Art	Jarecka, Louise Llewellyn	√	√	H&C	2	1		Wi 50	22
Designs: Charted	Observations on the Six-End Block Draft for Rug Weaving	Schlein, Alice	√	√	WJ	6	4	24	Sp 82	30
Designs: Charted	On Designing: Brocade Blouse	Newton, Deborah	√	√	Kn	1	1	1	F-W 84 CI	17 9
Designs: Charted	On Designing with Slip Stitch Bands	Newton, Deborah	√	√	Kn	3	1	5	F-W 86	21
Designs: Charted	Orchid Shawl	Xenakis, Athanasios David	√	√	PWC			5	Sp 83	38
Designs: Charted	Paired-Thread Finnweave Projects: Ben's Chessboard, The	Xenakis, Athanasios David	√	√	PWC			2	Ap 82	38
Designs: Charted	Paired-Thread Finnweave Projects: Five Placemats Based on a Chinese Lattice Design, The	Xenakis, Athanasios David	√	√	PWC			2	Ap 82	34
Designs: Charted	Paired-Thread Finnweave Projects: Lynn's Zebra, The	Xenakis, Athanasios David	√	√	PWC			2	Ap 82	36
Designs: Charted	Paired-Thread Finnweave Projects: Medusa, the Gorgeous Gorgon, The	Xenakis, Athanasios David	√	√	PWC			2	Ap 82	43
Designs: Charted	Paired-Thread Finnweave Projects: The Gaza Dress, The	Xenakis, Alexis, Yiorgos	√	√	PWC			2	Ap 82	40
Designs: Charted	Part 2, Patterns for Pick-Up and Brocade	Tidball, Harriet	√		SCGM		23		68	26

SUBJECT	TITLE	AUTHOR	IL	INST	JOUR	VOL	NO	ISS	DATE	PAGE
Designs: Charted	Particular Guernsey, A	Rowley, Elaine	√	√	Kn	1	1	1	F-W 84 CI	25,56A 17
Designs: Charted	Patchwork Designs in Summer and Winter	Davenport, Betty	√	√	PWC	1	1		No 81	27
Designs: Charted	Patolu and Its Techniques	De Bone, Mary Golden	√	√	TMJ	4	3		76	49
Designs: Charted	Peruvian Hat	Rowley, Elaine D.	√	√	PWC		4		Ja 83	65
Designs: Charted	Peruvian Mittens	Xenakis, Alexis Yiorgos	√	√	PWC		4		Ja 83	62
Designs: Charted	Pick-Up Patterned Double Weave	Keasbey, Doramay	√	√	Hw	5	2		M/A 84	80
Designs: Charted	Pick-Up Piqué (error-corrected SS&D v19 n1 87 p33)	Fletcher, Joyce	√	√	SS&D	18	4	72	Fa 87	60
Designs: Charted	Pillow and Table Runner in Summer and Winter Weave	Xenakis, Athanasios David	√	√	PWC	1	1		No 81	21
Designs: Charted	Planning Figured Piqué Designs on Pre-Marked Graph Paper	Xenakis, Athanasios David	√	>4	PWC	4	2	12		16
Designs: Charted	Point Block Progression: Notes of a Pattern Weaver	Alvic, Philis	√	>4	WJ	10	4	40	Sp 86	67
Designs: Charted	Quatrefoil	Xenakis, Athanasios David	√	√	PWC	3	3	9		53
Designs: Charted	Rep Weaves	Proulx, Bibiane April	√	>4	WJ	7	4	28	Sp 83	10
Designs: Charted	Revival of Double Weave in Scandinavia	Schrum, Louaine M.	√	√	H&C	8	1		Wi 56	22
Designs: Charted	Ropes and Braids	Lewis, Susanna E.	√	√	Kn	2	2	4	S-S 86	19
Designs: Charted	Rugs Woven on Summer and Winter Threading		√	>4	WJ	3	1	9	Jy 78	12
Designs: Charted	Shaft-Switch Rugs with Pinstripe Pattern Areas		√	√	WJ	5	2	18	Fa 80	28
Designs: Charted	Shaft-Switching on 3-End Drafts		√	√	WJ	5	4	20	Sp 81	24
Designs: Charted	Shaft-Switching on 3-End Drafts: Striped Patterns, Part 1		√	√	WJ	6	1	21	Su 81	7
Designs: Charted	Shaft-Switching on 3-end Drafts: Striped Patterns, Part 2		√	√	WJ	6	2	22	Fa 81	16
Designs: Charted	Shaft-Switching to Create Tapestry Effects	Green, Andrea	√	√	WJ	8	4	32	Sp 84	36
Designs: Charted	Sheep of a Sweater, A	Lambersten, Martha	√	√	Kn	3	4	8	Fa 87	51
Designs: Charted	Shetland Lace Wedding Handkerchief, A (error-corrected TM n12 87 p4)	Korach, Alice	√	√	TM			11	J/J 87	42
Designs: Charted	Shirt for All Seasons, A	Rush, Helene	√	√	Kn	3	2	6	Sp 87	25
Designs: Charted	Sidna's Shetland Shawl	Farley, Sidna	√	√	Kn	4	1	9	Wi 87	22
Designs: Charted	Six Ways to Wear Your Lace	Beugler, Eugen	√	√	Kn	4	1	9	Wi 87	44
Designs: Charted	Something Out of Nothing	Spencer, Edith L.	√	√	H&C	8	3		Su 57	14
Designs: Charted	St. Ives Cardigan	Bush, Nancy	√	√	Kn	3	2	6	Sp 87	28
Designs: Charted	Star and Diamond	Xenakis, Athanasios David	√	√	PWC	3	3	9		49
Designs: Charted	Stonington Shawl	Zimmermann, Elizabeth	√	√	Kn	1	2	2	S-S 85	60, 72B
Designs: Charted	Storytelling in Boundweave	Strauss, Lynn	√	√	Hw	7	2		M/A 86	35
Designs: Charted	Summer and Winter and Other Two-Tie Unit Weaves: Variations on a Six-Block Diamond Threading	Tidball, Harriet	√		SCGM		19		66	58
Designs: Charted	Summer and Winter — Part 1		√	>4	WJ	2	4	8	Ap 78	28
Designs: Charted	Summer and Winter Revisited Part 4: Turned Pebble Weave	Xenakis, Athanasios David	√	√	PWC		4		Ja 83	52
Designs: Charted	Summer and Winter Unharnessed	Xenakis, Athanasios David	√	√	PWC	1	1		No 81	10
Designs: Charted	Supplementary Warp Patterning: Native American Warp Pick-Up	Tidball, Harriet	√	√	SCGM		17		66	15
Designs: Charted	T-Sweater	Rowley, Elaine	√	√	Kn	1	2	2	S-S 85	34, 72A
Designs: Charted	Tablecloth in Summer and Winter	Xenakis, Athanasios David	√	√	PWC	1	1		No 81	16
Designs: Charted	Tarascan Lace		√	√	WJ	2	3	7	Ja 78	21
Designs: Charted	Tarascan Lace	Jenkins, Evelyn	√	√	H&C	11	1		Wi 60	12

SUBJECT	TITLE	AUTHOR	IL	INST	JOUR	VOL	NO	ISS	DATE	PAGE
Designs: Charted	Tarascan Lace (error-corrected WJ v9 n1 84 p70)	Thabet, Micheline	√	√	WJ	8	4	32	Sp 84	48
Designs: Charted	Ten-Harness Design for a Towel	Gubser, Elsie H.	√	> 4	H&C	9	4		Fa 58	28
Designs: Charted	Thirty-Button Classic	Gibson-Roberts, Priscilla A.	√	√	S-O	11	1		Sp 87	32
Designs: Charted	Tied Overshot Boundweave	Xenakis, Athanasios David	√	√	PWC	3	4	10		9
Designs: Charted	Tiffany's Gansey	Adams, Harriet	√	√	Kn	1	1	1	F-W 84 CI	29,56A 21
Designs: Charted	Traditional Fair Isle Sweater	Upitis, Lizbeth	√	√	Kn	2	1	3	F-W 85	26, 8B
Designs: Charted	Traditional Stockings: A Girl's Stocking (Lizbeth Upitis)		√	√	Kn	1	2	2	S-S 85	68
Designs: Charted	Tulip Outfit with Loom Controlled Inlay (error-corrected WJ v6 n1 81 p28d)	Kuwabara, Nancy	√	> 4	WJ	5	3	19	Wi 81	28
Designs: Charted	Turned Summer and Winter Jacket	Johnson, Melinda Raber	√	> 4	WJ	8	3	31	Wi 83	58
Designs: Charted	Twill and Plain Weave Blocks with Long-Eyed Heddles	Broughton, Eve T.	√	> 4	WJ	8	4	32	Sp 84	58
Designs: Charted	Two Alpaca and Wool Scarves	Xenakis, Athanasios David	√	> 4	PWC	3	4	10		40
Designs: Charted	Two Floor Pillows for the Rigid Heddle Loom	Christensen, Joanne	√	√	Hw	2	2		Mr 81	56
Designs: Charted	Two Weaves from Mexico	Gubser, Elsie H.	√	√	H&C	11	3		Su 60	26
Designs: Charted	Two-Harness Textiles, The Loom-Controlled Weaves: Stripes and Bands, Stripe Diagrams	Tidball, Harriet	√	√	SCGM		20		67	16
Designs: Charted	Two-Tie Inlay	Xenakis, Athanasios David	√	√	PWC	4	1	11		19
Designs: Charted	Undies Revealed: Camisole	Upitis, Lizbeth	√	√	Kn	3	2	6	Sp 87	12
Designs: Charted	Undies Revealed: Petticoat	Rowley, Elaine	√	√	Kn	3	2	6	Sp 87	13
Designs: Charted	Unharnessing the Summer and Winter Weave	Xenakis, Athanasios David	√		Iw	4	4		Fa 79	42
Designs: Charted	Variations On A Landes Theme	Coutts, Lucele	√	√	WJ	8	4	32	Sp 84	24
Designs: Charted	Vestment Variations: A Weaver from the Netherlands Creates Garments for the Ecclesiastical Calendar	Jansen, Netty	√	> 4	WJ	10	3	39	Wi 86	53
Designs: Charted	Victorian Garden (error-corrected PWC i8 p66)	Xenakis, Athanasios David	√	√	PWC	3	1	7		31
Designs: Charted	Violet Vestment	Hahn, Roslyn	√	> 4	WJ	8	3	31	Wi 83	44
Designs: Charted	Weaving and Sheepskin, Naturally	Mason, Carole	√	√	WJ	5	3	19	Wi 81	46
Designs: Charted	Weaving Damask	Arnold, Ruth	√	> 4	H&C	6	3		Su 55	4
Designs: Charted	Weaving in Quebec: Traditional Quebecois Weaving	Barrett, Clotilde	√	√	WJ	6	4	24	Sp 82	10
Designs: Charted	Weaving Rya and Flossa Rugs	af Kleen, Elizabeth	√	√	H&C	13	3		Su 62	29
Designs: Charted	Weaving the Girdle of Rameses	Hilts, Patricia	√	> 4	WJ	9	1	33	Su 84	22
Designs: Charted	Weaving With Ramie		√	> 4	WJ	8	2	30	Fa 83	80
Designs: Charted	White on White	Lyon, Linda	√	√	PWC	3	3	9		60
Designs: Charted	Windows: Sendoni Curtains	Xenakis, Alexis Yiorgos	√	> 4	PWC	4	1	11		4
Designs: Charted	Winter Birches: The Blouse	Upitis, Lizbeth	√	√	Kn	1	2	2	S-S 85	46, 72B
Designs: Charted	Winter Birches: The Jacket	Upitis, Lizbeth	√	√	Kn	1	2	2	S-S 85	44
Designs: Charted	Winter Red: A Hand and Machine Knit Combination	Lewis, Susanna	√	√	Kn	3	4	8	Fa 87	28
Designs: Charted	Wool Skirt and Shawl	Crosby, Roberta	√	√	PWC			5	Sp 83	55
Designs: Charted	Wymple in Tyme, A	Gibson-Roberts, Priscilla A.	√	√	Kn	3	4	8	Fa 87	56
Designs: Charted, Inkle	Four Projects from Mrs. Elsie H. Gubser	Gubser, Elsie H.	√	√	H&C	6	3		Su 55	49
Designs, Charted, Inkle	What and Why of "Inkle"	Atwater, Mary Meigs	√	√	H&C	3	2		Sp 52	18
Designs: Charted, On Lines	Fantastic Finnweave, Part 2	Xenakis, Athanasios David	√	√	PWC			3	Oc 82	10

SUBJECT	TITLE	AUTHOR	IL	INST	JOUR	VOL	NO	ISS	DATE	PAGE
Designs: Charted, On Spaces	Fantastic Finnweave, Part 2	Xenakis, Athanasios David	√	√	PWC			3	Oc 82	10
Designs: Charting	Charting Intarsia Designs	Guagliumi, Susan	√	√	TM			10	A/M 87	69
Detergents: Molecular Structure and Characteristics	Principles of Textile Conservation Science, No. 7. Characteristics of Detergents for Cleaning Historic Textiles	Rice, James W.	√	√	TMJ	2	1		De 66	23
Diaper	Sarah Fowler's Book of Drafts, Part 3	North, Lois	√	>4	SS&D	6	3	23	Su 75	74
Diaper, Two-Harness (Sets)	Little Known Weaves Worth Knowing Better: Two-Harness Method	Zielinski, S. A.; Robert Leclerc, ed.	√	>4	MWL	16			'51–'73	31
Dimai	Dimai	Petraitis, Ada	√	>4	CW	5	3	15	My 84	5
Dimai	Dimai or Tied Lithuanian (Computer Drafts-Eleanor Best)	Petraitis, Ada	√	>4	CW	4	2	11	Ja 83	16
Dimai	Lithuanian Pervarai: Producing a Twenty Shaft Pattern on a Twelve Shaft Loom	Meek, M. Kati	√	>4	AT	1			De 83	159
Dimai, Ground	Introduction to Tied Unit Weaves, An	Kelly, Jacquie	√	>4	PWC	4	4	14		40
Dimai, Tied-Lithuanian	Introduction to Tied Unit Weaves, An	Kelly, Jacquie	√	>4	PWC	4	4	14		40
Dimity	Fascination of Twills (Fourshafts): Dimity	Zielinski, S. A.; Robert Leclerc, ed.	√	√	MWL	9			'51–'73	24
Dimity	Notebook: Some Light Behind the Weave (Barbara Keller)	Myers, Ruth Nordquist, ed.	√	>4	SS&D	13	3	51	Su 82	16
Dimity	Shaker Towels: A Guild Devotes a Year of Study to Nineteenth Century Textiles (error-corrected WJ v11 n2 86 p68)	Eastlake, Sandy	√	>4	WJ	10	4	40	Sp 86	20
Dimity Cord	Fascination of Twills (Fourshafts): Dimity	Zielinski, S. A.; Robert Leclerc, ed.	√	√	MWL	9			'51–'73	24
Dimity, Patterned	Fascination of Twills (Fourshafts): Dimity	Zielinski, S. A.; Robert Leclerc, ed.		√	MWL	9			'51–'73	24
Dimity, Patterned	Fascination of Twills (Fourshafts): Dimity	Zielinski, S. A.; Robert Leclerc, ed.	√	√	MWL	9			'51–'73	24
Dimity, Two-Harness (Sets)	Little Known Weaves Worth Knowing Better: Two-Harness Method	Zielinski, S. A.; Robert Leclerc, ed.	√	>4	MWL	16			'51–'73	31
Dimity, Variations	Dimity Delight	Sullivan, Donna	√	>4	PWC	5	1	15		17
Dimity Weave	Little Known Weaves Worth Knowing Better: Dimity	Zielinski, S. A.; Robert Leclerc, ed.	√	√	MWL	16			'51–'73	56
Dinner Party, The	History in Stitches, A	Mattera, Joanne	√		Fa	7	3		M/J 80	37
Dinner Party, The	Judy Chicago's Dinner Party: A Review	Mattera, Joanne	√		Fa	7	3		M/J 80	16
Dinner Party, The	Right Out of History	Mattera, Joanne	√		Fa	9	3		M/J 82	55
Disabled also see Therapy/Rehabilitation										
Disabled	Arbutus Crafts				SS&D	2	1	5	De 70	17
Disabled	Comminicating Through Craft	de Mar, Lola	√		Fa	14	1		J/F 87	38
Disabled	Income for the Handicapped — A Philadelphia Story	Couch, Jo-Alice	√		H&C	2	4		Fa 51	28
Disabled	Weaving for the Mentally Handicapped	Kille, Eleanor C., O.T.R.	√		H&C	4	4		Fa 53	26
Disabled: Blind	Blind Woman Is in My Weaving Class ... What Do I Do Now?, A	Zinsmeister, Anna	√		Fa	14	1		J/F 87	42
Disabled: Blind	Haptic Visions	Brubaker, Paul			WJ	11	4	44	Sp 87	59
Disabled: Blind	Kenneth Spaulding's Triumph: The Will to Weave	Spaulding, K. B., Jr.	√	√	SS&D	7	1	25	Wi 75	18
Disabled: Blind	Story of Henry Reynolds, The		√		H&C	4	2		Sp 53	23
Disabled: Blind	Story of the Johnson Rugs, The	Gallinger, Osma Couch	√		H&C	7	2		Sp 56	28
Disabled: Blind	Teaching the Blind to Spin: A Group Session	Gonzales, Carolyn	√		SS&D	10	3	39	Su 79	90
Disabled: Blind	Teaching the Blind to Spin: An Impromptu Lesson	Chapin, Doloria		√	SS&D	10	3	39	Su 79	91
Disabled: Blind	Weaving Program at the Guild for the Jewish Blind		√		H&C	10	2		Sp 59	29
Disabled: Blind	Weaving Texts Recorded for the Blind				Fa	3	5		S/O 76	35
Disabled: Blind/Deaf	Klara Johnson: A Weaver's Vision Realized	Magoffin, Connie	√	√	WJ	11	4	44	Sp 87	62

SUBJECT	TITLE	AUTHOR	IL	INST	JOUR	VOL	NO	ISS	DATE	PAGE
Disabled: Special Education	Fiber is "Special"	Jackson, Mary Lynn; Cheryl McWilliams	√		SS&D	15	2	58	Sp 84	13
Disabled: Veterans	Welsh Wool Yarn Factory Hires Disabled Veterans	Hetherington, E.	√		SS&D	5	1	17	Wi 73	28
Disasters: Spinning	Oops!		√		S-O	11	3		Fa 87	37
Discipline	Choosing a Focus of Study Can Lead to New Growth, New Horizons, New Understanding	Chandler, Deborah			Hw	6	4		S/O 85	26
Discontinuous Warp	Scaffold Weaving: A Contemporary Garment Inspired by an Ancient Technique	Searle, Karen	√	√	WJ	10	2	38	Fa 85	65
Discontinuous Weft	Scaffold Weaving: A Contemporary Garment Inspired by an Ancient Technique	Searle, Karen	√	√	WJ	10	2	38	Fa 85	65
Display Stands	Notes of a Pattern Weaver	Alvic, Philis	√		SS&D	13	4	52	Fa 82	76
Disposal: Dyestuffs	Disposing of Dyestuffs			√	TM			2	D/J 85	8
Distaffs	Distaff, The	Henzie, Suzie	√	√	WJ	7	2	26	Fa 82	10
Distaffs	Distaffs: Scanning through History	Henzie, Susie	√		SS&D	9	4	36	Fa 78	56
Distaffs	Dressing the Distaff	Henzie, Susie	√	√	SS&D	10	1	37	Wi 78	12
Distaffs	Spindle and Distaff	Florentine, Gemma	√	√	TM			2	D/J 85	33
Distaffs	Suitcase Distaff, A	Linder, Harry; Olive Linder	√	√	S-O	10	2		Fa 86	33
Distaffs: Dressing	Distaff, The	Henzie, Suzie	√	√	WJ	7	2	26	Fa 82	10
Distaffs: Types	Looking at Distaffs	Hochberg, Bette	√		Iw	3	3		Sp 78	43
Distorted Weft	Unusual Drapery with Distorted Wefts (Jeanetta L. Jones)		√	√	H&C	15	2		Sp 64	36
Distorted Weft: Basket/Tabby	Little Known Weaves Worth Knowing Better: Distorted Weft	Zielinski, S. A.; Robert Leclerc, ed.	√	>4	MWL	16			'51–'73	79
Distorted Weft: Bronson	Little Known Weaves Worth Knowing Better: Distorted Weft	Zielinski, S. A.; Robert Leclerc, ed.	√	>4	MWL	16			'51–'73	79
Distorted Weft: Cannelé	Little Known Weaves Worth Knowing Better: Distorted Weft	Zielinski, S. A.; Robert Leclerc, ed.	√	>4	MWL	16			'51–'73	79
Distorted Weft: Honeycomb	Little Known Weaves Worth Knowing Better: Distorted Weft	Zielinski, S. A.; Robert Leclerc, ed.	√	>4	MWL	16			'51–'73	79
Distorted Weft: Patterning	Little Known Weaves Worth Knowing Better: Distorted Weft	Zielinski, S. A.; Robert Leclerc, ed.	√	>4	MWL	16			'51–'73	79
Diversified Plain Weave	Diversified Plain Weave	Wertenberger, Kathryn	√	>4	Hw	8	5		N/D 87	62
Diversified Plain Weave	Klara Cherepov's Diversified Plain Weave	Weigle, Palmy	√	>4	SS&D	6	1	21	Wi 74	55
Diversified Plain Weave, Two-Block	Diversified Plain Weave Pillow (Kathryn Wertenberger)		√	>4	Hw	8	5		N/D 87	62, I-15
Dobby Chain Links	Twist Ties			√	CW	1	1	1	De 79	2
Dobby Lag Chain	Dobby Loom Explained, The	Colwell, Ken	√	√	SS&D	11	4	44	Fa 80	7
Dobby Lag Systems	Dobby Loom Explained, The	Colwell, Ken	√	√	SS&D	11	4	44	Fa 80	7
Dobby Peg Plans	Skeleton Peg Plan for the Compu-Dobby, A	Gustafson, Susan			CW	6	3	18	My 85	24
Dobby Weaving	Dobby Loom: A Workbench Report, The	Bendich, Hilary	√		SS&D	11	4	44	Fa 80	79
Dobby Weaving	Dobby Loom Explained, The	Colwell, Ken	√	√	SS&D	11	4	44	Fa 80	7
Dobby Weaving	From Simple Twills to Dobby Fantasies...A Progression	Marquess, Joyce	√	>4	Iw	4	4		Fa 79	38
Dobby Weaving	Lia Cook, An Interview	Papa, Nancy	√		Iw	4	4		Fa 79	24
Dobby Weaving	Lia Cook: Exploring the Territory Where Painting and Textiles Meet	Alexander, Judy	√		Fa	9	5		S/O 82	28
Dobby Weaving	Modification of the AVL Dobby Loom for Execution of Multi-Shaft Two-Tie Block Weaves	Gustafson, Susan L.	√	√	AT	1			De 83	235
Dobby Weaving	Single Thread Harness Pattern Weaving	Fry, Laura	√	>4	CW	5	1	13	Se 83	14
Dobby Weaving	Textile Arts of Multan, Pakistan	Shahzaman, Mahboob	√	>4	SS&D	4	3	15	Su 73	8
Dobby Weaving	Time Warp on the Coldstream	McIntyre, Walter	√		SS&D	15	4	60	Fa 84	50
Dobby Weaving	Weaver's Story of Two Prayer Shawls, Garments Used in Jewish Ritual, A	Schlein, Alice	√	>4	CW	3	3	9	Ap 82	6

SUBJECT	TITLE	AUTHOR	IL	INST	JOUR	VOL	NO	ISS	DATE	PAGE
Dobby Weaving	Weaving on a Dobby Loom	Ligon, Linda	√		Iw	1	4		Su 76	10
Documentation Findings: Silks, 18th Century, Painterly and Coloration Characteristics	Where Did All the Silver Go? Identifying Eighteenth-Century Chinese Painted and Printed Silks	Lee-Whitman, Leanna; Maruta Skelton	√		TMJ	22			83	33
Documentation Findings: Silks, 18th Century, Painting and Printing Techniques	Where Did All the Silver Go? Identifying Eighteenth-Century Chinese Painted and Printed Silks	Lee-Whitman, Leanna; Maruta Skelton	√		TMJ	22			83	33
Documentation Findings: Silks, 18th Century, Physical Characteristics	Where Did All the Silver Go? Identifying Eighteenth-Century Chinese Painted and Printed Silks	Lee-Whitman, Leanna; Maruta Skelton	√		TMJ	22			83	33
Documentation Findings: Silks, 18th Century, Pigment Analysis Data	Where Did All the Silver Go? Identifying Eighteenth-Century Chinese Painted and Printed Silks	Lee-Whitman, Leanna; Maruta Skelton	√		TMJ	22			83	33
Documentation Techniques: Coverlets	Analysis and Documentation of Coverlets (error-corrected AT v3 85 p269)	Ulasewicz, Connie; Clarita Anderson; Steven M. Spivak	√	> 4	AT	2			De 84	113
Documentations: Coverlets	Coverlet Homeconing '86	Thoeming, Bette; Kay Hulquist	√	√	Hw	8	5		N/D 87	70
Documentations: Coverlets	Coverlet Information Sheet	Strickler, Carol	√	√	Iw	6	1		Wi 80	55
Documentations: Coverlets	Coverlet Information Sheets, Nos. 1-4	Strickler, Carol	√	> 4	Iw	3	1		Fa 77	38
Documentations: Coverlets	Coverlet Information Sheets, Nos. 2.1—2.2	Strickler, Carol	√	√	Iw	3	4		Su 78	41
Documentations: Coverlets	Coverlet Information Sheets, Nos. 2.3—2.4	Strickler, Carol	√	√	Iw	4	1		Wi 78	51
Documentations: Coverlets	Coverlet Information Sheets, Nos. 2.5—2.6	Strickler, Carol	√	√	Iw	4	2		Sp 79	57
Documentations: Coverlets	Coverlet Information Sheets, Nos. 3.1	Strickler, Carol	√	√	Iw	4	4		Fa 79	52
Documentations: Coverlets	Coverlet Information Sheets, Nos. 5—6	Strickler, Carol	√	> 4	Iw	3	2		Wi 78	36
Documentations: Coverlets	Coverlets	Wilson, Sadye Tune; Doris Finch Kennedy	√		SS&D	14	4	56	Fa 83	34
Documentations: Coverlets	Three-R's of Coverlets: Revival, Restoration, Research	Sellin, Helen; Peggy Hoyt			PWC	5	2	16		33
Documentations: Procedures	Coverlet Homeconing '86	Thoeming, Bette; Kay Hulquist	√	√	Hw	8	5		N/D 87	70
Documentations: Straw Hat, Industry	Peruvian Straw Hat: Documenting a Declining Industry, The	Zimmer, Roni	√		Fa	12	3		M/J 85	39
Documentations: Textile Collection	Documenting Your Textile Collection	Metzler-Smith, Sandra J.			Fa	9	5		S/O 82	55
Dog Breeds	Fur Fashions	Lucas, Jerie	√	√	SS&D	15	2	58	Sp 84	26
Dog Breeds	Spinning and Use of Dog's Hair, The	Pubols, Dorothy M.	√	√	WJ	4	1	13	Jy 79	36
Dog Fashions	Dog Fashions (error-corrected WJ v2 n1 77 insert for vol. 1)	Richards, Iris	√	> 4	WJ	1	3	3	Ja 77	33
Dog Hair	Dealing with Dog Hair	Murrow, Romedy	√		S-O	8	1		Sp 84	36
Dog Hair	Fur Fashions	Lucas, Jerie	√	√	SS&D	15	2	58	Sp 84	26
Dog Hair	Hair of the Dog, The	Adams, Brucie	√	√	Hw	3	2		Mr 82	62
Dog Hair	Handspuns for Tapestries	Szumski, Norma; Phyllis Clemmer; Clotilde Barrett	√		WJ	6	2	22	Fa 81	41
Dog Hair	Spinning Doghair	Barrett, Clotilde	√	√	WJ	1	1	1	Jy 76	27
Dogwood	Basket Willow: Cultivating and Gathering the Withy	Hart, Carol	√	√	TM			3	F/M 86	63
Doll Clothing	Antique Madras Plaid (Constance LaLena)		√	√	Hw	3	3		My 82	53, 91
Doll Clothing	Miniature Garments	Wood, Irene K.	√		SS&D	11	2	42	Sp 80	60
Doll House Furnishings: Handwoven	Home Weaving: It's the Little Things that Count		√	√	Hw	1	1		F-W 79	38
Doll Making	Half Magic, Half Fiber	Parry, Nancy	√		TM			12	A/S 87	16
Dollhouses	Dollhouse, The		√	√	SS&D	14	2	54	Sp 83	44
Dolls	Brief Creative Tale, A	Kosta, Angela	√		Fa	11	6		N/D 84	95
Dolls	Cut from the Same Cloth	Andrews, Kathy Boals	√		Fa	13	3		M/J 86	21
Dolls	Fantasy Figures: Shelly Fowler's Fabric Dolls	Place, Jennifer	√		Fa	10	1		J/F 83	16

SUBJECT	TITLE	AUTHOR	IL	INST	JOUR	VOL	NO	ISS	DATE	PAGE
Dolls	Floppy Dolls (error-corrected SS&D v9 n2 78 p70)	Fitch, Betsy	√	√	SS&D	9	1	33	Wi 77	22
Dolls	Half Magic, Half Fiber	Parry, Nancy	√		TM			12	A/S 87	16
Dolls	Lenore Davis: Figuring in Cloth	Frasier, Debra	√		Fa	10	5		S/O 83	10
Dolls	Mimi Holmes: Treasure Troves of Human Conflict	Lamberson, Peggy	√		Fa	13	6		N/D 86	20
Dolls	Mysterious Figurines of Keiko Yamaguchi, The	Hempel, Toby Anne	√		Fa	14	4		S/O 87	16
Dolls	Nancy Greaver		√		Fa	4	4		J/A 77	51
Dolls	Nek Chand's Fantasy Garden	Ziek, Bhakti	√		TM			3	F/M 86	88
Dolls	Stepping Out (Lenore Davis)		√		TM			8	D/J 86	84
Dolls	Sven Scandinavian				Kn	1	1	1	F-W 84 CI	58 48
Dolls	Woven Rag Doll, A	Foeley, Cora V.	√	√	H&C	17	3		Su 66	17
Dolls: Fashion	Costumes on a Small Scale	Caldwell, Rebecca	√		Fa	11	5		S/O 84	87
Dolls: Knitted	Dolls: Knitted and Woven	Laury, Jean Ray	√	√	H&C	26	5		Oc 75	36
Dolls, Paper	What a Doll! Provocative Paper Dolls, A Captivating Idea	Gould, Mary	√	√	Fa	8	1		J/F 81	78
Dolls: Woven	Dolls: Knitted and Woven	Laury, Jean Ray	√	√	H&C	26	5		Oc 75	36
Dornick, Two-Harness (Sets)	Little Known Weaves Worth Knowing Better: Two-Harness Method	Zielinski, S. A.; Robert Leclerc, ed.	√	> 4	MWL	16			'51–'73	31
Dotted Swiss	Special Summer Vest, A	Jennings, Lucy Anne	√	> 4	WJ	9	3	35	Wi 85	42
Double Binding Technique	Double Binding Technique			√	Hw	4	3		M/J 83	36
Double Binding Technique	From Rags to Riches	Krook, Inga	√	√	Hw	4	3		M/J 83	32
Double Cloth, Double-Width	California Poppy Tablecloth and Napkins (Jean Scorgie)		√	√	Hw	6	3		Su 85	61, I-16
Double Corduroy	Cotton String Rug (Jean Bendon)		√	√	Hw	3	2		Mr 82	51, 90
Double Corduroy	Double Corduroy Rug (error-corrected WJ v11 n3 87 p78)	Waggoner, Phyllis	√	√	WJ	11	2	42	Fa 86	42
Double Knitting	Double Knitting	Rowley, Elaine		√	Kn	3	4	8	Fa 87	60
Double Knitting	V-Neck Jacket	Upitis, Lizbeth	√	√	Kn	3	4	8	Fa 87	37
Double Knitting	Windowpane Jacket: In Double Knit and Garter Stitch	Ellman, Norma	√	√	Kn	3	4	8	Fa 87	40
Double Summer and Winter and Twill	Summer and Winter and Other Two-Tie Unit Weaves: Methods for Weaving Two-Tie Units, Double-Summer and Winter-Twill	Tidball, Harriet	√	> 4	SCGM		19		66	56
Double Two-Tie Unit Weave see Unit Structure										
Double Warp Beams	Tale of Tucks, A (error-corrected SS&D v7 n1 75 p63)	Guagliumi, Susan	√	> 4	SS&D	7	1	25	Wi 75	56
Double Weave also see Finnweave; Mexican Weave										
Double Weave	Artifacts Don't "Lie"	Anderson, Clarita	√		AT	7			Ju 87	9
Double Weave	Backed Weaves: Part 1	Marston, Ena	√	> 4	SS&D	8	3	31	Su 77	64
Double Weave	Backed Weaves, Part 2	Marston, Ena	√	> 4	SS&D	8	4	32	Fa 77	50
Double Weave	Bolivian Highland Weaving, Part 1	Cason, Marjorie; Adele Cahlander	√		SS&D	6	2	22	Sp 75	4
Double Weave	Coat for Handwoven Yardage, A	Roth, Bettie G.	√	> 4	WJ	7	3	27	Wi 82	6
Double Weave	Colonial Coverlets, Part 4: Doubleweave	Liebler, Barbara	√	√	Iw	2	1		Fa 76	29
Double Weave	Decorative Miniatures in Silk by Jadwiga Rakowska		√		H&C	10	2		Sp 59	22
Double Weave	Designing Rugs for Harness-Controlled Weaving		√	> 4	WJ	4	4	16	Ap 80	27
Double Weave	Double Weave	Wertenberger, Kathryn	√	> 4	Hw	5	4		S/O 84	81
Double Weave	Double Weave, First Steps in Development	Hausner, Walter	√	> 4	H&C	15	2		Sp 64	10
Double Weave	Double Weave for Fiber Art	Rucker, Karon	√	√	SS&D	9	2	34	Sp 78	19
Double Weave	Double Weave on a Rigid Heddle Loom	Gaston-Voûte, Suzanne	√	√	SS&D	8	3	31	Su 77	70

SUBJECT	TITLE	AUTHOR	IL	INST	JOUR	VOL	NO	ISS	DATE	PAGE
Double Weave	Double Weave: Plain and Patterned, The	Tidball, Harriet	√		SCGM		1		60	1-34
Double Weave	Double Weave Project for the Beginner	Krasnoff, Julienne	√	√	H&C	21	4		Fa 70	11
Double Weave	Double Weaves	Zielinski, S. A.; Robert Leclerc, ed.	√	√	MWL	15			'51–'73	9
Double Weave	Double Woven House Boots	MacDonald, Margaret	√	> 4	WJ	6	4	24	Sp 82	44
Double Weave	Double-faced, Double-woven, Three-harness Krokbragd	Holtzer, Marilyn Emerson	√	√	SS&D	14	4	56	Fa 83	46
Double Weave	Double-Woven Treasures from Old Peru	Cahlander, Adele	√	√	PWC			4	Ja 83	36
Double Weave	Doublecloth Coverlets	Shermeta, Margo	√		Fa	13	5		S/O 86	6
Double Weave	Doubleweave: A Popular Technique of the 19th Century Coverlet Weaver	Colwell, Ken	√	> 4	PWC			2	Ap 82	53
Double Weave	Doubleweave Jacket: 4-Shaft Version (Jean Scorgie)		√	√	Hw	4	4		S/O 83	48, 99
Double Weave	Doubleweave Jacket: 8-Shaft Version (Jean Scorgie)		√	> 4	Hw	4	4		S/O 83	48, 99
Double Weave	Doubleweave: Some Ideas for Conserving Yarn	Cahlander, Adele	√	√	PWC			2	Ap 82	46
Double Weave	Drawloom Special Harness for Double Weave	Malloy, Kim, OSB	√	> 4	AT	1			De 83	77
Double Weave	Embroidery on the Loom	Drooker, Penelope B.	√	√	SS&D	9	3	35	Su 78	60
Double Weave	Evolution of an Idea: Olive and Harry Develop Some New Angles on Weaving a Stole, The	Linder, Olive; Harry Linder	√	> 4	Hw	5	1		J/F 84	66
Double Weave	Figure-in-the-Round, A Caricature	Lebovitz, Connie	√	√	SS&D	6	1	21	Wi 74	5
Double Weave	Finnish Techniques	Tanner, Kersten	√		SS&D	6	3	23	Su 75	45
Double Weave	Finnweave	Barrett, Clotilde	√	> 4	WJ	11	4	44	Sp 87	25
Double Weave	Finnweave Can Be Fun	Ringler, Aina	√	√	H&C	9	4		Fa 58	12
Double Weave	First Prize for the Holders of Hot Pots Show	Champion, Ellen	√	√	WJ	2	4	8	Ap 78	41
Double Weave	Five Block Double Weave Using the Glimåkra Long Eyed Heddle Accessory	Tramba, Diane	√	> 4	WJ	7	3	27	Wi 82	45
Double Weave	Four-Shaft Double Weave With Color and Weave Effects	Scorgie, Jean; Gloria Martin	√	√	Hw	6	3		Su 85	38
Double Weave	From California, Double Woven Fabrics for Varied Uses	Bryan, Dorothy	√	√	H&C	12	3		Su 61	6
Double Weave	Gang: Technical And Conceptual Applications to Loom Controlled Weave Structures	Towner, Naomi Whiting	√	> 4	AT	5			Ju 86	91
Double Weave	How One Weave Leads to Another	Barrett, Clotilde	√	> 4	WJ	8	1	29	Su 83	75
Double Weave	Layered Fabrics: Four-Harness, Two-Color Double Cloth, Part 1	Marston, Ena	√	√	SS&D	6	1	21	Wi 74	28
Double Weave	Layered Fabrics on Eight Harnesses	Marston, Ena	√	> 4	SS&D	6	4	24	Fa 75	50
Double Weave	Longest Warp in the World or, The Double Two-Tie Unit Threading System	Miller, Mary Ann	√	> 4	CW	3	3	9	Ap 82	2
Double Weave	Making Narrow Looms Do Big Jobs	Kling, Mary Nell	√		H&C	2	1		Wi 50	13
Double Weave	Maurine Fair	Ligon, Linda	√	> 4	Iw	2	2		Wi 77	20
Double Weave	Michigan Weaving, Third Conference at Hartland Shows Wide Variety		√	> 4	H&C	13	1		Wi 62	18
Double Weave	Mind Boggling Bogs	Herring, Connie	√	√	PWC			3	Oc 82	36
Double Weave	Obsession with Trees, An	MacNutt, Dawn	√	√	SS&D	9	4	36	Fa 78	88
Double Weave	Old & New Uses for Double Weave	Macomber, Dorothea	√	√	H&C	8	4		Fa 57	16
Double Weave	Paired-Thread Finnweave Projects: A Chessboard for the Nonfinn with Eight Harnesses, The	Xenakis, Athanasios David	√	> 4	PWC			2	Ap 82	38
Double Weave	"Patch" by Ted Hallman, At the Smithsonian		√		SS&D	4	4	16	Fa 73	23
Double Weave	Patterned Double Weave		√	√	Hw	7	2		M/A 86	56
Double Weave	Polychrome Double Weave (error-corrected SS&D v7 n1 75 p64)	Marston, Ena	√	> 4	SS&D	7	1	25	Wi 75	52
Double Weave	Portraits in Double Weave	Strickler, Carol	√	√	WJ	1	3	3	Ja 77	30

SUBJECT	TITLE	AUTHOR	IL	INST	JOUR	VOL	NO	ISS	DATE	PAGE
Double Weave	Rag Vest (Susan Snover)		√	√	Hw	4	1		J/F 83	44, 86
Double Weave	Rainwindow: Watercolor Weaving	Schlegel, Mary	√	√	SS&D	5	2	18	Sp 74	8
Double Weave	Red, Brown and Ecru Mat (Gloria Martin)		√	√	Hw	6	3		Su 85	38, I-15
Double Weave	Rena Thompson: Echoes of Intuitive Truths	Park, Betty	√		Fa	13	2		M/A 86	46
Double Weave	Revival of Double Weave in Scandinavia	Schrum, Louaine M.	√	√	H&C	8	1		Wi 56	22
Double Weave	Roses and Snowballs: The Development of Block Patterns in the German Linen-Weaving Tradition	Hilts, Patricia	√	>4	AT	5			Ju 86	167
Double Weave	Self-Stuffing Weft Cord Double Weave	Towner, Naomi Whiting	√	>4	AT	3			My 85	47
Double Weave	Some Additional Notes on the Damask—Threading the Pattern Harnesses	Ahrens, Jim	√	>4	CW	6	2	17	Ja 85	3
Double Weave	Stars, Diamonds, Tables, and Sunrise: Motifs and Structures of Woven Coverlets	Cabeen, Lou	√	√	TM			14	D/J 87	32
Double Weave	Tablecloth in Double Weave, A	Robinson, Irma	√	>4	H&C	8	4		Fa 57	44
Double Weave	Tea Cloth (Sharon Alderman)		√	√	Hw	2	1		F-W 80	43, 76
Double Weave	Technique & History of the Polish Double-weave, The	Wimmer, Gayle	√		H&C	24	3		M/J 73	8
Double Weave	Textile Structure and Analysis, A Home Study Course in Twelve Lessons: Lessons in Weave Structure, 9. Double Weave	Tidball, Harriet		>4	SCGM		18		66	28
Double Weave	Turned Drafts in Double Two-Tie Unit Weave	van der Hoogt, Madelyn	√	>4	WJ	9	2	34	Fa 84	13
Double Weave	Twenty-Harness Madness	Moore, Gen	√	>4	SS&D	12	4	48	Fa 81	46
Double Weave	Warp Color Changes in Double and Multilayer Weaves	O'Connor, Paul	√	>4	WJ	12	2	46	Fa 87	55
Double Weave	Weaving a City Skyline	Wennerstrom, Ann K.	√	√	WJ	7	1	25	Su 82	30
Double Weave	Woven Structures of European Shawls in The Textile Museum Collection, The	Rowe, Ann Pollard			TMJ	24			85	55
Double Weave, Angled	Double-Faced Krokbragd	Holtzer, Marilyn Emerson	√	>4	WJ	9	4	36	Sp 85	59
Double Weave, Backed Weaves, Surface Interest	Surface Interest — Textiles of Today: Surface Interest Designs with Drafts, Group 5, Backed-Fabric Designs	Tidball, Harriet	√	>4	SCGM		2		61	18
Double Weave, Basket Weave	Double Weave: Plain and Patterned: A Double-fold Blanket Weave by Mary Atwater, The	Tidball, Harriet	√	√	SCGM		1		60	26
Double Weave, Blocks	But What's the Tie-Up?	van der Hoogt, Madelyn	√	>4	PWC	5	1	15		36
Double Weave, Blocks	Double Weave Runner (Miranda Howard)		√	>4	Hw	6	3		Su 85	36, I-16
Double Weave, Blocks	Double Weave Table Runner (Robert P. Owen)		√	>4	Hw	8	5		N/D 87	41, 76
Double Weave, Blocks	Reversible Vest (Jean Scorgie)		√	√	Hw	7	4		S/O 86	66, I-13
Double Weave, Blocks, Integrated, "Pockets"	Double Weaves: Pattern in Double Weaves	Zielinski, S. A.; Robert Leclerc, ed.	√	>4	MWL	15			'51–'73	104
Double Weave Class	Handloom Weaves: The Classification of Handloom Weaves, The Structural Group, The Double Weave Class	Tidball, Harriet		√	SCGM		33		57	33
Double Weave, Complementary Warp	Double-Woven Treasures from Old Peru	Cahlander, Adele	√	√	PWC			4	Ja 83	36
Double Weave, Divided Side	Sweater (Betty Beard)		√	√	Hw	1	1		F-W 79	24, 57
Double Weave, Divided Top	Double Woven Vest (Betty Beard)		√	√	Hw	1	1		F-W 79	24, 57
Double Weave, Double Harness	Double & Triple Harness Double-Cloth	Fabeck, Diane	√	>4	CW	7	3	21	My 86	7
Double Weave, Double Twill, Stitched	Double Tartan	Xenakis, Athanasios David	√	>4	PWC	3	1	7		42
Double Weave, Double Width	twill ^ 2 = Double Width Afghans	Guy, Sallie T.	√	>4	SS&D	15	1	57	Wi 83	34
Double Weave, Double Width	Winter Wrap-Ups Revisited	Deschaines, Sybil	√	>4	SS&D	16	1	61	Wi 84	26
Double Weave, Double-Width	Baby Blanket		√	√	H&C	10	4		Fa 59	20
Double Weave, Double-Width	Contemporary Costume, Strictly Handwoven: Double Width and Tubular Weaving	Tidball, Harriet	√	√	SCGM		24		68	4

SUBJECT	TITLE	AUTHOR	IL	INST	JOUR	VOL	NO	ISS	DATE	PAGE
Double Weave, Double-Width	Dolman Top (Elaine Rowley)		√	√	Hw	1	2		S-S 80	45, 67
Double Weave, Double-Width	Double Weave: Plain and Patterned: A Double-fold Blanket Weave by Mary Atwater, The	Tidball, Harriet	√	√	SCGM		1		60	26
Double Weave, Double-Width	Double Weaves: Double Weaves Circular and Double-Width Cloth	Zielinski, S. A.; Robert Leclerc, ed.	√	>4	MWL	15			'51–'73	90
Double Weave, Double-Width	Double Weaves: Double Width	Zielinski, S. A.; Robert Leclerc, ed.	√	>4	MWL	15			'51–'73	125
Double Weave, Double-Width	Double Weaves: Practice in Double Width Fabrics	Zielinski, S. A.; Robert Leclerc, ed.			MWL	15			'51–'73	132
Double Weave, Double-Width	Double Width Weaving: Dealing with the Fold	Guy, Sallie T.			CW	5	3	15	My 84	17
Double Weave, Double-Width	Four Harness Double Width Weaving	Frey, Berta	√	√	H&C	12	1		Wi 61	6
Double Weave, Double-Width	Handloom Weaves: The Classification of Handloom Weaves, The Structural Group, The Double Weave Class, Double-Width Pattern System	Tidball, Harriet	√	>4	SCGM		33		57	34
Double Weave, Double-Width	Layered Fabrics: Four-Harness, Two-Color Double Cloth, Part 2	Marston, Ena	√	√	SS&D	6	2	22	Sp 75	56
Double Weave, Double-Width	Spring Ensemble (Ronnine Bohannan)		√	√	Hw	6	2		M/A 85	56, I-13
Double Weave, Fabric	Double Weave: Plain and Patterned: Clothing Textiles in Double Weave, The	Tidball, Harriet	√	>4	SCGM		1		60	31
Double Weave, Finnish	Double Weave, Finnweave and Mexican Variations	Frey, Berta	√	√	H&C	12	2		Sp 61	12
Double Weave, Four-Color	Double Weave in Four Colors Part 1	Broughton, Eve	√	>4	CW		23		Ja 87	3
Double Weave, Four-Color	Double Weave in Four Colors Part 2	Broughton, Eve	√	>4	CW		24		My 87	17
Double Weave, Four-Shaft	Handloom Weaves: The Classification of Handloom Weaves, The Structural Group, The Double Weave Class, Four-Harness Double Weave System	Tidball, Harriet	√	√	SCGM		33		57	33
Double Weave, Hems	Double Weaves: Hems in Four Shaft Double Weaving	Zielinski, S. A.; Robert Leclerc, ed.	√	√	MWL	15			'51–'73	76
Double Weave, Jacquard	Art of Indiana Coverlets, The	Gilfoy, Peggy S.	√		AT	2			De 84	69
Double Weave, Layers	Parka (Betty Beard)		√	√	Hw	1	1		F-W 79	18, 53
Double Weave, Leno	Double Weaves: Leno in Double Weave on Four Shafts	Zielinski, S. A.; Robert Leclerc, ed.	√	√	MWL	15			'51–'73	72
Double Weave, Log Cabin	Double Weave: Plain and Patterned: Log Cabin, The	Tidball, Harriet	√	√	SCGM		1		60	25
Double Weave, Mexican	Double Weave, Finnweave and Mexican Variations	Frey, Berta	√	√	H&C	12	2		Sp 61	12
Double Weave, Miniature	Miniature World, A	Piroch, Sigrid	√	>4	PWC	5	2	16		26
Double Weave, Multiblock Patterns	Double Weaves: Double Weaves Multi-Block Patterns	Zielinski, S. A.; Robert Leclerc, ed.	√	>4	MWL	15			'51–'73	107
Double Weave, Multilayered	Double Weaves: Double Width	Zielinski, S. A.; Robert Leclerc, ed.	√	>4	MWL	15			'51–'73	125
Double Weave, Overshot	Double Weave: Plain and Patterned: Overshot, The	Tidball, Harriet	√	>4	SCGM		1		60	26
Double Weave, Patterned	Double Weave on Eight Harnesses for Patterned Fabrics	Frey, Berta	√	>4	H&C	12	3		Su 61	23
Double Weave, Patterned	Handloom Weaves: The Classification of Handloom Weaves, The Structural Group, The Double Weave Class, Patterned Double Weave System	Tidball, Harriet	√	>4	SCGM		33		57	34
Double Weave, Patterned	Use of Long-Eyed Heddles for Patterned Double Weave, The	Howard, Ruth	√	>4	WJ	6	2	22	Fa 81	35
Double Weave, Pebble	Double-Woven Treasures from Old Peru	Cahlander, Adele	√	√	PWC			4	Ja 83	36
Double Weave, Pick-Up	Camera Strap in Double-Weave Pick-Up	Gaston-Voûte, Suzanne	√	√	PWC			2	Ap 82	10
Double Weave, Pick-Up	Double Weave Pick-Up with Straight Diagonal Lines	Wolter, Edith L.	√	√	WJ	7	4	28	Sp 83	61
Double Weave, Pick-Up	Double Weave: Plain and Patterned: Decorative Patterns in Double Weave by Pick-Up Methods, The	Tidball, Harriet	√	√	SCGM		1		60	11

SUBJECT	TITLE	AUTHOR	IL	INST	JOUR	VOL	NO	ISS	DATE	PAGE
Double Weave, Pick-Up	Double Weave Runner (Jean Scorgie, Kathe Fletcher)		√	√	Hw	7	2		M/A 86	57, I-10
Double Weave, Pick-Up	Double-Weave Pick-Up	Neely, Cynthia H.	√	√	TM			8	D/J 86	36
Double Weave, Pick-Up	Fantastic Finnweave, Part 3	Xenakis, Athanasios David	√	> 4	PWC			4	Ja 83	28
Double Weave, Pick-Up	Garments with Ethnic Flavor: Mexican Motif Skirt		√	√	WJ	2	3	7	Ja 78	13
Double Weave, Pick-Up	Inspired Double Weave		√		Hw	7	2		M/A 86	58
Double Weave, Pick-Up	Name Draft Contest Winners		√	> 4	WJ	11	4	44	Sp 87	46
Double Weave, Pick-Up	Peru, Textiles Unlimited, Part 2: Double Weave	Tidball, Harriet	√	√	SCGM		26		69	33
Double Weave, Pick-Up	Pick-Up Patterned Double Weave	Keasbey, Doramay	√	√	Hw	5	2		M/A 84	80
Double Weave, Pick-Up	Step on It: Nancy Searle's Technique for Patterned Double Weave	Searle, Nancy	√	√	Hw	4	3		M/J 83	67
Double Weave, Pick-Up	Summer and Winter Revisited, Part 1: Two-Heddle Double Cloth	Xenakis, Athanasios David	√	√	PWC			2	Ap 82	61
Double Weave, Pick-Up	Understanding Some Complex Structures from Simple Andean Looms: Steps in Analysis and Reproduction	Cahlander, Adele	√	√	AT	1			De 83	181
Double Weave, Pick-Up	Woven Banner: For the Class Of '76, A	Thomen, Lydia	√	√	SS&D	7	2	26	Sp 76	7
Double Weave, Pick-Up, Finnweave Method	Double Weave: Plain and Patterned: The Finnweave Method, The	Tidball, Harriet	√	√	SCGM		1		60	16
Double Weave, Pick-Up, Mexican Method	Double Weave: Plain and Patterned: The Paired Thread or Mexican Method, The	Tidball, Harriet	√	√	SCGM		1		60	14
Double Weave, Pick-Up, Norwegian Method	Double Weave: Plain and Patterned: The Norwegian Method, The	Tidball, Harriet	√	√	SCGM		1		60	16
Double Weave, Pick-Up, Peruvian Method	Double Weave: Plain and Patterned: The Continuous Weft or Peruvian Method, The	Tidball, Harriet	√	√	SCGM		1		60	18
Double Weave Pick-Up, Pocket Figures	Double Weave: Plain and Patterned: Pick-Up Pocket Figures, Twill Background, The	Tidball, Harriet	√	> 4	SCGM		1		60	33
Double Weave, Pick-Up, Polychrome	Peru, Textiles Unlimited, Part 2: Double Weave	Tidball, Harriet	√	√	SCGM		26		69	35
Double Weave: Pick-Up, Shed-Shuttle	Double Weaves: Finn Weave	Zielinski, S. A.; Robert Leclerc, ed.	√	√	MWL	15			'51–'73	38
Double Weave, Pick-Up, Shed-Shuttle	Double Weaves: Practice of Finn Weave	Zielinski, S. A.; Robert Leclerc, ed.	√	√	MWL	15			'51–'73	44
Double Weave, Pick-Up, Single	Double Weave: Plain and Patterned: The Single Pick-Up Method, The	Tidball, Harriet	√	√	SCGM		1		60	12
Double Weave: Pick-Up, Split-Shed	Double Weaves: Finn Weave	Zielinski, S. A.; Robert Leclerc, ed.	√	√	MWL	15			'51–'73	38
Double Weave, Piqué	Double Piqué, Double Weave (error-corrected PWC v4 n4 i14 p33)	van der Hoogt, Madelyn	√	> 4	PWC	4	3	13		40
Double Weave, Plain	Understanding Some Complex Structures from Simple Andean Looms: Steps in Analysis and Reproduction	Cahlander, Adele	√	√	AT	1			De 83	181
Double Weave, Pocket	Double Weave: Plain and Patterned: The Pocket Weave, The	Tidball, Harriet	√	> 4	SCGM		1		60	27
Double Weave, Polychrome	Double Weave: Plain and Patterned: Double Weave Polychrome, The	Tidball, Harriet	√	> 4	SCGM		1		60	33
Double Weave, Polychrome	Double Weaves: Polychrome Double Weave on Four Shafts	Zielinski, S. A.; Robert Leclerc, ed.	√	√	MWL	15			'51–'73	60
Double Weave, Polychrome	Double Weaves: Polychrome Double Weaves	Zielinski, S. A.; Robert Leclerc, ed.	√	> 4	MWL	15			'51–'73	114
Double Weave, Quilted	Handloom Weaves: The Classification of Handloom Weaves, The Structural Group, The Double Weave Class, Quilted Double Weave System	Tidball, Harriet	√	> 4	SCGM		33		57	34
Double Weave, Single Harness (Set)	Double & Triple Harness Double-Cloth	Fabeck, Diane	√	> 4	CW	7	3	21	My 86	7
Double Weave, Stitched	Designing Four-Shaft Double Weaves	Muller, Donna	√	√	WJ	7	4	28	Sp 83	56
Double Weave, Stitched	Double Weave Blocks on Eight	Howard, Miranda	√	> 4	Hw	6	3		Su 85	36
Double Weave, Stitched	Four-Block Double Weave on Four Shafts	Barrett, Clotilde	√	√	WJ	8	1	29	Su 83	72

222

SUBJECT	TITLE	AUTHOR	IL	INST	JOUR	VOL	NO	ISS	DATE	PAGE
Double Weave, Stitched	From Sample to Finished Product	Keasbey, Doramay	√	>4	SS&D	15	3	59	Su 84	62
Double Weave, Stitched	Loom Controlled Quilted Fabrics	Bardwell, Kathryn	√	√	WJ	7	1	25	Su 82	39
Double Weave, Stitched	Matelasse Double Cloth Stitched to Form the Design	Kelly, Linda	√	>4	WJ	7	1	25	Su 82	43
Double Weave, Stitched	Pile Weaves, Rugs and Tapestry: Handwoven Furcoat	Zielinski, S. A.; Robert Leclerc, ed.	√	>4	MWL	14			'51–'73	21
Double Weave, Stitched	Quilted Bedspread		√	>4	H&C	16	3		Su 65	16, 46
Double Weave, Stitched	Quilted Double Woven Baby Blanket, A		√	>4	H&C	10	1		Wi 59	13
Double Weave, Stitched	Quilted Fabrics, A Method of Draft Writing for Individual Designs	Frey, Berta	√	>4	H&C	14	4		Fa 63	17
Double Weave, Stitched	Quilted Placemat and Napkin (Henrietta Dyk)		√	>4	Hw	5	1		J/F 84	61, 104
Double Weave, Stitched	Reversible Jacket in Double Weave, A	Evans, Jane	√	>4	WJ	3	1	9	Jy 78	23
Double Weave, Stitched	Reversible Matelasse Jacket	Champion, Ellen	√	>4	WJ	7	1	25	Su 82	41
Double Weave, Stitched	Simple Matelasse by the Pick-Up Method		√	√	WJ	7	1	25	Su 82	40
Double Weave, Stitched	Stitched Double Cloth—Matelassé		√		WJ	7	1	25	Su 82	37
Double Weave, Stitched	Stitched Double Cloth Vest		√	√	WJ	7	1	25	Su 82	38
Double Weave, Stitched	Stitching Traditional Coverlet Weaves	Sellin, Helen G.	√	>4	AT	1			De 83	289
Double Weave, Stitched Layers	Double Weaves: Double Weave Stitching	Zielinski, S. A.; Robert Leclerc, ed.	√	√	MWL	15			'51–'73	51
Double Weave, Stitched Layers	Double Weaves: Double Weaves Circular and Double-Width Cloth	Zielinski, S. A.; Robert Leclerc, ed.	√	>4	MWL	15			'51–'73	90
Double Weave, Stitched Layers	Double Weaves: Stitched Layers	Zielinski, S. A.; Robert Leclerc, ed.	√	>4	MWL	15			'51–'73	99
Double Weave, Stitched Layers	Stitched Doublecloths	Hoskins, Janet A.	√	>4	CW	3	1	7	Se 81	1
Double Weave, Stitched Layers, Invisible Stitching	Double Weaves: Problems in Double Weaves Stitching	Zielinski, S. A.; Robert Leclerc, ed.	√	>4	MWL	15			'51–'73	144
Double Weave, Stitched Layers, Quilting	Double Weaves: Quilting or Quilt Weave	Zielinski, S. A.; Robert Leclerc, ed.	√	>4	MWL	15			'51–'73	148
Double Weave, Stitched Layers, Quilting, Wadding	Double Weaves: Quilting or Quilt Weave	Zielinski, S. A.; Robert Leclerc, ed.	√	>4	MWL	15			'51–'73	148
Double Weave, Stitched Layers, Vertical Stitching	Double Weaves: Vertical Stitching on Four Shafts	Zielinski, S. A.; Robert Leclerc, ed.	√	√	MWL	15			'51–'73	55
Double Weave, Stitched, Loom-Controlled	Double Weave: Plain and Patterned: An Unusual Double Weave Blanket, The	Tidball, Harriet	√	>4	SCGM		1		60	32
Double Weave, Stitched, Loom-Controlled	Double Weave: Plain and Patterned: Quilted Double Fabrics, The	Tidball, Harriet	√	>4	SCGM		1		60	28
Double Weave, Stitched, Padded	Loom Quilted Double Weave Bedspread (Wendy McKay)		√	>4	Hw	8	4		S/O 87	88, I-15
Double Weave, Stitched, Padded	Masculine Element, The (Pam Bolesta)		√	√	Hw	2	1		F-W 80	34
Double Weave, Stitched, Padded	More Than Four can Double Your Fun	Pinchin, C. Bryn	√	>4	Hw	6	1		J/F 85	38
Double Weave, Stitched, Padded	Silky Dress-Up: Vest (C. Bryn Pinchin)		√	>4	Hw	6	1		J/F 85	38, I-11
Double Weave, Stitched, Padded	Ski Vest (Pam Bolesta)		√	√	Hw	2	1		F-W 80	34, 61
Double Weave, Stitched, Padded	Two for Tea (Sharon Alderman)		√	√	Hw	2	1		F-W 80	42
Double Weave, Stitched, Polychrome	Double Weaves: Stitching in Four Shaft Polychrome Double Weave	Zielinski, S. A.; Robert Leclerc, ed.	√	√	MWL	15			'51–'73	68
Double Weave, Stitched, Stuffed	Double Woven Quilted Vest (Yvone Stahl)		√	√	Hw	5	1		J/F 84	54, 97
Double Weave, Stitched, Stuffed	Keep Warm! Foot Cozy	Barrett, Clotilde	√	√	WJ	5	2	18	Fa 80	12
Double Weave, Stitched, Surface Interest	Surface Interest — Textiles of Today: Surface Interest Designs with Drafts, Group 4, Double-Faced Designs	Tidball, Harriet	√	>4	SCGM		2		61	16
Double Weave, Stitched/Stuffed, Surface Interest	Surface Interest — Textiles of Today: Surface Interest Designs with Drafts, Group 5, Backed-Fabric Designs	Tidball, Harriet	√	>4	SCGM		2		61	18
Double Weave, Stuffed	Modular Weaves to Be Stuffed on the Loom	Russell, Joan	√	√	SS&D	5	4	20	Fa 74	97
Double Weave, Stuffed	Twentieth Century Rug	Hofstrom, Juanita	√	√	H&C	22	1		Wi 71	16
Double Weave, Tabby	Double Weave: Plain and Patterned: Tabby, The	Tidball, Harriet	√	√	SCGM		1		60	24
Double Weave, Techniques	On the Double!	Ligon, Linda	√	√	Hw	4	3		M/J 83	64

SUBJECT	TITLE	AUTHOR	IL	INST	JOUR	VOL	NO	ISS	DATE	PAGE
Double Weave, Tubular	Accessories: Double Woven Bag		√	√	WJ	2	4	8	Ap 78	7
Double Weave, Tubular	Child's Nap Mat (Louise Bradley)		√	√	Hw	8	2		M/A 87	48, I-7
Double Weave, Tubular	Contemporary Costume, Strictly Handwoven: Double Width and Tubular Weaving	Tidball, Harriet	√	√	SCGM		24		68	4
Double Weave, Tubular	Double Weaves: Double Weaves Circular and Double-Width Cloth	Zielinski, S. A.; Robert Leclerc, ed.	√	>4	MWL	15			'51–'73	90
Double Weave, Tubular	Double Weaves: Double Weaving Circular Cloth	Zielinski, S. A.; Robert Leclerc, ed.	√	√	MWL	15			'51–'73	48
Double Weave, Tubular	Double Woven Bag Inspired by a South American Bag, A	Barrett, Clotilde	√	√	WJ	1	2	2	Oc 76	29
Double Weave, Tubular	Double Woven Mailbag with Name Tags	Verlinden, Lieve	√	√	WJ	7	1	25	Su 82	34
Double Weave, Tubular	Double Woven Tea Cosy		√	>4	WJ	2	1	5	Jy 77	15
Double Weave, Tubular	Doubleweave Bag (Pam Bolesta)		√	√	Hw	1	1		F-W 79	20, 53
Double Weave, Tubular	Floppy Dolls (error-corrected SS&D v9 n2 78 p70)	Fitch, Betsy	√	√	SS&D	9	1	33	Wi 77	22
Double Weave, Tubular	Houndstooth Doubleweave (Kathryn Wertenberger)		√	√	Hw	5	2		M/A 84	66, 103
Double Weave, Tubular	Jacket Inspired by West African Narrow Strip Weaving	Bradley, Louise	√	√	WJ	5	3	19	Wi 81	31
Double Weave, Tubular	Jumpsuits, Anyone?	Fieldman, M. Lucille	√	>4	SS&D	7	3	27	Su 76	60
Double Weave, Tubular	Mind Boggling Bogs	Herring, Connie	√	√	PWC			3	Oc 82	36
Double Weave, Tubular	Multi-Layered Tubular Hangings	Maxcy, Mabel E.	√	√	SS&D	4	4	16	Fa 73	12
Double Weave, Tubular	Six Little Sachets (Dixie Straight)		√	√	Hw	6	4		S/O 85	64, I-14
Double Weave, Tubular	Sweater (Betty Beard)		√	√	Hw	1	1		F-W 79	24, 57
Double Weave, Tubular	Tale of Tucks, A (error-corrected SS&D v7 n1 75 p63)	Guagliumi, Susan	√	>4	SS&D	7	1	25	Wi 75	56
Double Weave, Tubular	Textured Cottons: Seamless, No-Sweat Shirt	Rasmussen, Peg	√	√	WJ	6	3	23	Wi 81	25
Double Weave, Tubular	"The Robe," is Woven on a California Handloom	Marshall, Bertha	√		H&C	4	3		Su 53	14
Double Weave, Tubular	Tubular Double Weave	Lumsden, Sharon Lappin	√	√	Hw	8	1		J/F 87	49
Double Weave, Tubular	Tubular Double Weave: The Basics		√	√	Hw	8	1		J/F 87	51
Double Weave, Tubular	Tubular Weave Vest and Hat (Sharon Lappin Lumsden)		√	√	Hw	8	1		J/F 87	48, I-6
Double Weave, Tubular	Two Tubes in Double Weave (error-corrected SS&D v5 n4 74 p69)	Neale, Mary Beth	√	>4	SS&D	5	3	19	Su 74	8
Double Weave, Tubular	Vertical Pockets	Krasnoff, Julienne Hallen	√	√	H&C	21	1		Wi 70	21
Double Weave, Tubular	Weaver's Work Apron: A Project in Double Weave		√	√	WJ	7	2	26	Fa 82	27
Double Weave, Tubular	White Circular Wrap	Richards, Iris	√	√	WJ	4	3	15	Ja 80	7
Double Weave, Tubular, Stuffed	Fashions by Linda Knutson and Lynn Daly		√	√	WJ	6	3	23	Wi 81	14
Double Weave, Tubular, Twill	Three Double Weave Pillows (Laurel Howard) (error-corrected Hw v2 n2 81 p68)		√	>4	Hw	2	1		F-W 80	32, 76
Double Weave, Tucks	Tuck Tactics	Speth, Lottie	√	√	SS&D	15	3	59	Su 84	80
Double Weave, Tucks	Tuck Weaving	Frey, Berta	√	√	H&C	9	4		Fa 58	11
Double Weave, Twill	Double Weave: Plain and Patterned: Twill, The	Tidball, Harriet	√	>4	SCGM		1		60	25
Double Weave, Twill, Double-Faced	Handloom Weaves: The Classification of Handloom Weaves, The Structural Group, The Double Weave Class, Twill Double-Face Weave System	Tidball, Harriet	√	>4	SCGM		33		57	34
Double Weave, Two-Block	#2: Vest Fabric (Sharon Alderman)		√	>4	Hw	8	4		S/O 87	52, I-8
Double Weave, Two-Block, Fringes	Double Weave: Plain and Patterned: Block Fringes, The	Tidball, Harriet	√	>4	SCGM		1		60	32
Double Weave, Two-Block, Texture Variations	Double Weave: Plain and Patterned: Texture Variations in Two Block Double Weave, The	Tidball, Harriet	√	>4	SCGM		1		60	22
Double Weave, Two-Faced Patterns	Double-Woven Treasures from Old Peru	Cahlander, Adele	√	√	PWC			4	Ja 83	36

SUBJECT	TITLE	AUTHOR	IL	INST	JOUR	VOL	NO	ISS	DATE	PAGE
Double Weave, Two-Warp	Double Weave: Plain and Patterned: Pleats and Tucks, The	Tidball, Harriet	√	> 4	SCGM		1		60	32
Double Weave, Two-Warp	Double Weaves: Two Warp Double Weaves	Zielinski, S. A.; Robert Leclerc, ed.	√	> 4	MWL	15			'51–'73	122
Double Weave, Two-Warp	Double Weaves: Two-Warp Weaves	Zielinski, S. A.; Robert Leclerc, ed.	√	√	MWL	15			'51–'73	22
Double Weave, Two-Warp, Pick-Up	Double Weave: Plain and Patterned: The Pick-Up Duo-Weave, The	Tidball, Harriet	√	√	SCGM		1		60	31
Double Weave, Warp-Faced	Double-Woven Treasures from Old Peru	Cahlander, Adele	√	√	PWC			4	Ja 83	36
Double Weave, Warp-Faced	Understanding Some Complex Structures from Simple Andean Looms: Steps in Analysis and Reproduction	Cahlander, Adele	√	√	AT	1			De 83	181
Double Weave, Warp-Faced	Warp-Faced Double Cloth: Adaptation of an Andean Technique for the Treadle Loom	Cahlander, Adele	√	√	WJ	10	4	40	Sp 86	72
Double Weave, Warp-Faced	Weaving on a Diamond Grid: Bedouin Style	Race, Mary E.	√	√	SS&D	12	1	45	Wi 80	20
Double Weave, Warp-Faced	Weaving the Girdle of Rameses on Nine Harnesses	Parkinson, Alberta	√	> 4	CW	3	2	8	Ja 82	1
Double-Beam Weaving	Corded Rep Weave and Velvet Rugs	Proulx, Bibiane April	√	√	SS&D	17	3	67	Su 86	80
Double-Faced Stuffer Weave	Summer and Winter and Other Two-Tie Unit Weaves: Methods for Weaving Two-Tie Units, Double-Faced Stuffer Weave	Tidball, Harriet	√	> 4	SCGM		19		66	52
Double-Faced Stuffer Weave	Two-Tie Unit for Rugs: Part 1, The Double-Faced Stuffer Weave and Summer-and-Winter, The	Windeknecht, Margaret	√	> 4	SS&D	16	1	61	Wi 84	82
Double-Faced Stuffer Weave	Two-Tie Unit for Rugs: Part 2 Warping and Weaving Methods, The	Windeknecht, Margaret	√	> 4	SS&D	16	2	62	Sp 85	34
Double-Faced Stuffer Weave	Two-Tie Unit for Rugs: Part 2 Warping and Weaving Methods, The	Windeknecht, Margaret	√	> 4	SS&D	16	2	62	Sp 85	34
Double-Faced Weave	Rugs Woven on Summer and Winter Threading		√	> 4	WJ	3	1	9	Jy 78	12
Double-Faced Weaves	Backstrap Weaving for Penance and Profit	Coffman, Charlotte	√	√	WJ	7	1	25	Su 82	60
Double-Faced Weaves	Bath Towel Set, A	Xenakis, Athanasios David	√	> 4	PWC	1	1		No 81	24
Double-Faced Weaves	Contemporary Satins: Double Satin	Tidball, Harriet	√	> 4	SCGM		7		62	10
Double-Faced Weaves	Double Weaves: Double Weaves Circular and Double-Width Cloth	Zielinski, S. A.; Robert Leclerc, ed.	√	> 4	MWL	15			'51–'73	95
Double-Faced Weaves	Double-Faced 3/1 Broken Twill Woven on Tablets	Collingwood, Peter	√	√	AT	1			De 83	91
Double-Faced Weaves	Double-Faced Cloth: One Cloth, Two Appearances	Alderman, Sharon	√	> 4	Hw	3	4		Se 82	61
Double-Faced Weaves	Felted Jacket	Bennett, Siiri	√	> 4	WJ	9	1	33	Su 84	49
Double-Faced Weaves	From Rags to Riches	Krook, Inga	√	√	Hw	4	3		M/J 83	32
Double-Faced Weaves	Multiple Rigid Heddle Adventure, Part 1, The	Xenakis, Athanasios David	√	√	PWC	3	4	10		34
Double-Faced Weaves	Warp Stuffer Weave with Shaft Switching Applications	Evans, Jane A.	√	> 4	Hw	4	3		M/J 83	72
Double-Faced Weaves	Weaving Primer	Parks, Deborah	√	√	PWC	3	3	9		4
Double-Faced Weaves	Work of a Huave Indian Weaver in Oaxaca, Mexico: Complex Weave Structures Utilizing One Warp Set and Two Complementary Weft Sets, The	Connolly, Loris	√		AT	3			My 85	7
Double-Faced Weaves: Pick-Up	Fantastic Finnweave, Part 3	Xenakis, Athanasios David	√	> 4	PWC			4	Ja 83	22
Double-Faced Weaves, Surface Interest	Surface Interest — Textiles of Today: Surface Interest Designs with Drafts, Group 4, Double-Faced Designs	Tidball, Harriet	√	> 4	SCGM		2		61	16
Double-Harness Weaving	Damask on a Drawloom	Keasbey, Doramay	√	> 4	SS&D	8	1	29	WI 76	63
Double-Harness Weaving see Two-Harness (Sets) Weaving										
Double-Warp Overlay	Rug Weaving: One Weaver's Approach	Hand, Barbara	√	> 4	WJ	7	4	28	Sp 83	32

SUBJECT	TITLE	AUTHOR	IL	INST	JOUR	VOL	NO	ISS	DATE	PAGE
Doublejack	Doublejack	Koepp, William A.	√	√	SS&D	14	1	53	Wi 82	7
Doubling	Spinning in Bolivia	Meisch, Lynn A.	√	√	S-O	10	1		Sp 86	25
Doups	Exploring Doup Leno	Laughlin, Mary Elizabeth	√	> 4	CW	4	3	12	Ap 83	3
Doups	Hanaori: An Okinawan Brocaded Textile	Miller, Dorothy	√	√	AT	1			De 83	173
Doups: Constructing	Doup Leno: Doups	Skowronski, Hella; Sylvia Tacker	√	√	SCGM		32		80	11
Doups: Installing	Doupe Leno for the Rigid Heddle Loom	Xenakis, Athanasios David	√	√	PWC		6		Su 83	14
Doups: Tying	Doupe Leno for the Harness Loom	Xenakis, Alexis Yiorgos; Elaine Rowley	√	√	PWC		6		Su 83	10
Down and Feathers	Feather Cape, After the One Pocahontas Took to England	Frey, Berta	√	> 4	H&C	21	4		Fa 70	22
Down and Feathers	Hawaiian Feather Techniques	Kwiatkowski, Ron	√	√	Iw	1	4		Su 76	16
Down and Feathers	Inca Feathers	Kwiatkowski, Ron	√	√	Iw	1	2		Wi 76	16
Down and Feathers	Plumage in the Dyepot	Brown, Melissa J.	√	√	SS&D	9	1	33	Wi 77	103
Down and Feathers	Spinning with Down and Knitting with Feathers	von Ammon, Helen	√		S-O	10	4		Wi 86	15
Down and Feathers	Trimming the Southwestern Look	Chaudet, Annette	√	√	WJ	11	1	41	Su 86	35
Down and Feathers	Warmth for a Cool Climate: Handspun Wool & Milkweed Down	Danielson, Esther	√	√	SS&D	17	4	68	Fa 86	24
Drafts and Drafting	Drafts with Many Uses		√	> 4	H&C	16	3		Su 65	34
Drafts and Drafting	Handweaver's Instruction Manual: The Drafts	Tidball, Harriet C. nee Douglas	√		SCGM		34		49	34
Drafts and Drafting	If You Have 4 Harnesses	Hagarty, Harriet May		√	H&C	24	2		M/A 73	44
Drafts and Drafting	Pattern and Structure in Handwoven Fabrics	Frey, Berta	√	√	H&C	6	4		Fa 55	4
Drafts and Drafting: 1-2-1 Tie, 10-End Block, Boulevard Weave	Bateman Boulevard, Chevron, and Combination Weaves: Boulevard Structures, Division 2	Bateman, Dr. William G.; Virginia I. Harvey, ed.	√	> 4	SCGM		38		87	48
Drafts and Drafting: 1-2-1 Tie, 12-End Block, Boulevard Weave	Bateman Boulevard, Chevron, and Combination Weaves: Boulevard Structures, Division 3	Bateman, Dr. William G.; Virginia I. Harvey, ed.	√	> 4	SCGM		38		87	54
Drafts and Drafting: 1-2-1 Tie, 6-End Block, Boulevard Weave	Bateman Boulevard, Chevron, and Combination Weaves: Boulevard Structures, Division 1	Bateman, Dr. William G.; Virginia I. Harvey, ed.	√	> 4	SCGM		38		87	17
Drafts and Drafting: 1-2-1 Tie, 8-End Block, Boulevard Weave	Bateman Boulevard, Chevron, and Combination Weaves: Boulevard Structures, Division 2	Bateman, Dr. William G.; Virginia I. Harvey, ed.	√	> 4	SCGM		38		87	37
Drafts and Drafting: 1-2-3-2-1 Tie, 10-End Block, Bateman Chevron Weaves	Bateman Boulevard, Chevron, and Combination Weaves: Chevron Structures, Division 1	Bateman, Dr. William G.; Virginia I. Harvey, ed.	√	> 4	SCGM		38		87	59
Drafts and Drafting: 1-2-3-2-1 Tie, 12-End Block, Bateman Chevron Weaves	Bateman Boulevard, Chevron, and Combination Weaves: Chevron Structures, Division 2	Bateman, Dr. William G.; Virginia I. Harvey, ed.	√	> 4	SCGM		38		87	62
Drafts and Drafting: 1-2-3-2-1 Tie, 14-End Block, Bateman Chevron Weaves	Bateman Boulevard, Chevron, and Combination Weaves: Chevron Structures, Division 3	Bateman, Dr. William G.; Virginia I. Harvey, ed.	√	> 4	SCGM		38		87	69
Drafts and Drafting: 1-2-3-2-1 Tie, 16-End Block, Bateman Chevron Weaves	Bateman Boulevard, Chevron, and Combination Weaves: Chevron Structures, Division 4	Bateman, Dr. William G.; Virginia I. Harvey, ed.	√	> 4	SCGM		38		87	72
Drafts and Drafting: 1-2-3-2-1 Tie, 20-End Block, Bateman Chevron Weaves	Bateman Boulevard, Chevron, and Combination Weaves: Chevron Structures, Division 5	Bateman, Dr. William G.; Virginia I. Harvey, ed.	√	> 4	SCGM		38		87	80
Drafts and Drafting: 2-Shaft	Little Known Weaves Worth Knowing Better: Drafts for Two Shafts	Zielinski, S. A.; Robert Leclerc, ed.	√	√	MWL	16			'51–'73	38
Drafts and Drafting: 2-Tie Unit Structure	Summer and Winter and Other Two-Tie Unit Weaves: The Two-Tie Unit System	Tidball, Harriet	√	> 4	SCGM		19		66	4
Drafts and Drafting: 3-Shaft	Double-faced, Double-woven, Three-harness Krokbragd	Holtzer, Marilyn Emerson	√	√	SS&D	14	4	56	Fa 83	46
Drafts and Drafting: 3-Shaft	Little Known Weaves Worth Knowing Better: Three-Shaft Weaves	Zielinski, S. A.; Robert Leclerc, ed.	√	√	MWL	16			'51–'73	47
Drafts and Drafting: 3-Shaft	Mexican Motifs: A Mexican Quesquimitl	Tidball, Harriet	√	√	SCGM		6		62	13

SUBJECT	TITLE	AUTHOR	IL	INST	JOUR	VOL	NO	ISS	DATE	PAGE
Drafts and Drafting: 7-Shaft Blocks, Tag Weave (Tag Treadling)	Bateman Park Weaves: Division I — Seven-Harness Blocks, Tag Weave or Tag Treadling	Bateman, Dr. William G.; Virginia I. Harvey, ed.	√	>4	SCGM		37		84	27
Drafts and Drafting: Adapting Techniques	Notebook: Adapting Large Overshot Patterns	Meyers, Ruth Nordquist, ed.	√	>4	SS&D	14	4	56	Fa 83	16
Drafts and Drafting: Adjusting Drafts	Adjusting the Draft	Frey, Berta	√	>4	H&C	10	1		Wi 59	14
Drafts and Drafting: Algebraic	Variations on an Algebraic Equation	Redfield, Gail	√	>4	H&C	10	3		Su 59	46
Drafts and Drafting: Backed Weaves	Backed Weaves, Part 2	Marston, Ena	√	>4	SS&D	8	4	32	Fa 77	50
Drafts and Drafting: Barley Corn	Thomas Jackson, Weaver: 17th and 18th Century Records	Tidball, Harriet	√	>4	SCGM		13		64	21
Drafts and Drafting: Basic Weaves	Basic Weaves, Tool to Develop Fabric Structures (error-corrected H&C v20 n4 69 p43)	Hausner, Walter	√	√	H&C	20	3		Su 69	4
Drafts and Drafting: Bateman Blend Weaves	Bateman Blend Weaves Extended Beyond Eight Harnesses, Part 1	Harvey, Virginia I.	√	>4	CW	4	3	12	Ap 83	9
Drafts and Drafting: Bateman Blend Weaves	Bateman Blend Weaves Extended Beyond Eight Harnesses, Part 2	Harvey, Virginia I.	√	>4	CW	5	1	13	Se 83	3
Drafts and Drafting: Bateman Blend Weaves, 3-Tie Blocks	Bateman Blend Weaves: Three-Tie and Four-Tie Blocks	Bateman, Dr. William G.; Virginia I. Harvey, ed.	√	>4	SCGM		36		82	120
Drafts and Drafting: Bateman Blend Weaves, 4-Tie Blocks	Bateman Blend Weaves: Three-Tie and Four-Tie Blocks	Bateman, Dr. William G.; Virginia I. Harvey, ed.	√	>4	SCGM		36		82	120
Drafts and Drafting: Bateman Blend Weaves, Basic Blocks	Bateman Blend Weaves: The Structures of the Bateman Blend System	Bateman, Dr. William G.; Virginia I. Harvey, ed.	√	>4	SCGM		36		82	14
Drafts and Drafting: Bateman Blend Weaves, Division A, Unit Structure, 6-Tie, 6-Thread Blocks	Bateman Blend Weaves: Division A — Six-Thread Blocks	Bateman, Dr. William G.; Virginia I. Harvey, ed.	√	>4	SCGM		36		82	21
Drafts and Drafting: Bateman Blend Weaves, Division B, Unit Structure, 2-Tie, 8-Thread Blocks	Bateman Blend Weaves: Division B — Eight-Thread Blocks	Bateman, Dr. William G.; Virginia I. Harvey, ed.	√	>4	SCGM		36		82	51
Drafts and Drafting: Bateman Blend Weaves, Division C, Unit Structure, 2-Tie, 10-Thread Blocks	Bateman Blend Weaves: Division C — Ten-Thread Blocks	Bateman, Dr. William G.; Virginia I. Harvey, ed.	√	>4	SCGM		36		82	72
Drafts and Drafting: Bateman Blend Weaves, Division D, Unit Structure, 2-Tie, 12-Thread Blocks	Bateman Blend Weaves: Division D — Twelve-Thread Blocks	Bateman, Dr. William G.; Virginia I. Harvey, ed.	√	>4	SCGM		36		82	109
Drafts and Drafting: Bateman Blend Weaves, Notation System	Bateman Blend Weaves: Explanation of Forms	Bateman, Dr. William G.; Virginia I. Harvey, ed.	√	>4	SCGM		36		82	9
Drafts and Drafting: Bateman Blend Weaves, Variations A, B, C Blocks	Bateman Blend Weaves: Variations of A, B, and C Blocks	Bateman, Dr. William G.; Virginia I. Harvey, ed.	√	>4	SCGM		36		82	112
Drafts and Drafting: Bateman Chevron Weave Structures	Bateman Boulevard, Chevron, and Combination Weaves: Structures of Chevron Weaves	Bateman, Dr. William G.; Virginia I. Harvey, ed.	√	>4	SCGM		38		87	57
Drafts and Drafting: Bateman Combination Weaves (Park, Boulevard, Chevron)	Bateman Boulevard, Chevron, and Combination Weaves: Structures of Combination Weaves	Bateman, Dr. William G.; Virginia I. Harvey, ed.	√	>4	SCGM		38		87	82
Drafts and Drafting: Bateman Multiple Tabby Weaves	Extending Dr. William G. Bateman's Multiple Tabby Weaves Beyond Eight Harnesses (error-corrected CW v4 n3 83 p12)	Harvey, Virginia I.	√	>4	CW	4	2	11	Ja 83	4
Drafts and Drafting: Bateman Multiple Tabby Weaves, 6-Shaft	Multiple Tabby Weaves: Six-Harness Multiple Tabby Weaves	Bateman, Dr. William G.; Virginia I. Harvey, ed.	√	>4	SCGM		35		81	59
Drafts and Drafting: Bateman Multiple Tabby Weaves, Basic Blocks	Multiple Tabby Weaves: The Basic Blocks	Bateman, Dr. William G.; Virginia I. Harvey, ed.	√	√	SCGM		35		81	20
Drafts and Drafting: Bateman Multiple Tabby Weaves, Eight-Shaft	Multiple Tabby Weaves: Eight-Harness Multiple Tabby Weaves	Bateman, Dr. William G.; Virginia I. Harvey, ed.	√	>4	SCGM		35		81	70
Drafts and Drafting: Bateman Multiple Tabby Weaves, Expanding Blocks	Multiple Tabby Weaves: Expanding the Blocks	Bateman, Dr. William G.; Virginia I. Harvey, ed.	√	√	SCGM		35		81	46
Drafts and Drafting: Bateman Multiple Tabby Weaves, Notation System	Multiple Tabby Weaves: Explanation of Forms	Bateman, Dr. William G.; Virginia I. Harvey, ed.	√	√	SCGM		35		81	15

SUBJECT	TITLE	AUTHOR	IL	INST	JOUR	VOL	NO	ISS	DATE	PAGE
Drafts and Drafting: Bateman Multiple Tabby Weaves, Rearranging Block Threading	Multiple Tabby Weaves: Rearranging the Threading Within the Blocks	Bateman, Dr. William G.; Virginia I. Harvey, ed.	√	√	SCGM		35		81	26
Drafts and Drafting: Bateman Park Weaves, Basic Blocks, Rules	Bateman Park Weaves: Park Weave Rules	Bateman, Dr. William G.; Virginia I. Harvey, ed.	√	> 4	SCGM		37		84	18
Drafts and Drafting: Bateman Park Weaves, Division I, Unit Structure,1-Tie, 7-Shaft Blocks	Bateman Park Weaves: Division I — Seven-Harness Blocks	Bateman, Dr. William G.; Virginia I. Harvey, ed.	√	> 4	SCGM		37		84	19
Drafts and Drafting Bateman Park Weaves, Division II, , Unit Structure, 1-Tie, Blocks, Variable Thread Blocks, 8-Shaft	Bateman Park Weaves: Division II — Blocks of Varying Sizes Combined in a Draft	Bateman, Dr. William G.; Virginia I. Harvey, ed.	√	> 4	SCGM		37		84	88
Drafts and Drafting: Bateman Park Weaves, Division II, Unit Structure, 1-Tie, 4-Thread Blocks, 8-Shaft	Bateman Park Weaves: Division II — Eight-Harness Blocks	Bateman, Dr. William G.; Virginia I. Harvey, ed.	√	> 4	SCGM		37		84	48
Drafts and Drafting: Bateman Park Weaves, Division II, Unit Structure, 1-Tie, 8-Thread Blocks, 8-Shaft	Bateman Park Weaves: Division II — Eight-Harness Blocks, Eight-Thread Blocks	Bateman, Dr. William G.; Virginia I. Harvey, ed.	√	> 4	SCGM		37		84	74
Drafts and Drafting: Bateman Park Weaves, Division II, Unit Structure, 1-Tie, 6-Thread Blocks, 8-Shaft	Bateman Park Weaves: Division II — Eight-Harness Blocks, Six-Thread Blocks	Bateman, Dr. William G.; Virginia I. Harvey, ed.	√	> 4	SCGM		37		84	60
Drafts and Drafting: Bateman Park Weaves, Division II, Unit Structure, 1-Tie, 10-Thread Blocks, 8-Shaft	Bateman Park Weaves: Division II — Eight-Harness Blocks, Ten-Thread Blocks	Bateman, Dr. William G.; Virginia I. Harvey, ed.	√	> 4	SCGM		37		84	79
Drafts and Drafting: Bateman Park Weaves, Division II, Unit Structure, 1-Tie, 12-Thread Blocks, 8-Shaft	Bateman Park Weaves: Division II — Eight-Harness Blocks, Twelve-Thread Blocks	Bateman, Dr. William G.; Virginia I. Harvey, ed.	√	> 4	SCGM		37		84	83
Drafts and Drafting: Bateman Park Weaves, Notation System	Bateman Park Weaves: Explanation of Forms	Bateman, Dr. William G.; Virginia I. Harvey, ed.	√	> 4	SCGM		37		84	11
Drafts and Drafting: Bateman Park Weaves, Special Directions	Bateman Park Weaves: Special Directions	Bateman, Dr. William G.; Virginia I. Harvey, ed.		√	SCGM		37		84	14
Drafts and Drafting: Bedford Cord	Secret of a Corrugated Surface: Bedford Cord, The (error-corrected Hw v6 n3 85 p l-2)	Alderman, Sharon	√	> 4	Hw	6	1		J/F 85	27
Drafts and Drafting: Beginning	Treasury for Beginners: A Weaving Draft	Zielinski, S. A.; Robert Leclerc, ed.	√	√	MWL	1			'51–'73	45
Drafts and Drafting: Beginning	Treasury for Beginners: Drafting for Beginners	Zielinski, S. A.; Robert Leclerc, ed.	√	√	MWL	1			'51–'73	47
Drafts and Drafting: Beginning	Treasury for Beginners: Practical Suggestions on Drafting	Zielinski, S. A.; Robert Leclerc, ed.	√	√	MWL	1			'51–'73	52
Drafts and Drafting: Beiderwand, 2:1	Beiderwand	Gordon, Judith	√	> 4	CW	1	2	2	Fe 80	1
Drafts and Drafting: Bird's Eye	Thomas Jackson, Weaver: 17th and 18th Century Records	Tidball, Harriet	√	> 4	SCGM		13		64	21
Drafts and Drafting: Blended	"Sand Dunes and Dune Grass": Two Garments from a Blended Draft (Ardis Dobrovolny)		√	√	Hw	6	2		M/A 85	57, l-14
Drafts and Drafting: Blended Drafts	Blended Drafts	Strickler, Carol	√	> 4	Hw	6	2		M/A 85	37
Drafts and Drafting: Blocks	Bergman: Notes of a Pattern Weaver	Alvic, Philis	√	> 4	WJ	10	1	37	Su 85	64
Drafts and Drafting: Blocks	Blocks and Profiles	Carey, Joyce Marquess	√	√	WJ	7	2	26	Fa 82	33
Drafts and Drafting: Blocks	But What's the Tie-Up?	van der Hoogt, Madelyn	√	> 4	PWC	5	1	15		36
Drafts and Drafting: Blocks	Coverlet from Start to Finish, A	van der Hoogt, Madelyn	√	√	PWC	5	1	15		20
Drafts and Drafting: Blocks	Crackle Weave and Its Possible Variations	Snyder, Mary E.	√	> 4	H&C	13	1		Wi 62	13
Drafts and Drafting: Blocks	Creative Monk's Belt	Windeknecht, Margaret B.	√	> 4	SS&D	9	1	33	Wi 77	28
Drafts and Drafting: Blocks	Creative Monk's Belt: Using the Block Prinicple	Windeknecht, Margaret B.	√	√	SCGM		30		76	9
Drafts and Drafting: Blocks	Designing Block Weaves	Kurtz, Carol	√	> 4	SS&D	11	2	42	Sp 80	5
Drafts and Drafting: Blocks	Double & Triple Harness Double-Cloth	Fabeck, Diane	√	> 4	CW	7	3	21	My 86	7

228

SUBJECT	TITLE	AUTHOR	IL	INST	JOUR	VOL	NO	ISS	DATE	PAGE
Drafts and Drafting: Blocks	Double Two-Tie System Applied to Overshot	Xenakis, Athanasios David	√	>4	PWC	3	3	9		7
Drafts and Drafting: Blocks	Double Weave in Four Colors Part 1	Broughton, Eve	√	>4	CW		23		Ja 87	3
Drafts and Drafting: Blocks	Double Weave on Eight Harnesses for Patterned Fabrics	Frey, Berta	√	>4	H&C	12	3		Su 61	23
Drafts and Drafting: Blocks	Even-Tied Overshot	Xenakis, Athanasios David	√	>4	PWC	3	3	9		40
Drafts and Drafting: Blocks	Even-Tied Overshot on Four Shafts with Shaft Switching	Herring, Connie; Athanasios David Xenakis	√	√	PWC	3	3	9		44
Drafts and Drafting: Blocks	Figured Piqué Patterning with the Double Two-Tie System (error-corrected PWC v4 n3 i13 p4)	Xenakis, Athanasios David; Patti Sellon	√	>4	PWC	4	2	12		20
Drafts and Drafting: Blocks	Five Crackle Weave Projects	Macomber, Dorothea	√	√	H&C	9	3		Su 58	42
Drafts and Drafting: Blocks	Four-Shaft Primer: Tie Talk	Sullivan, Donna	√	>4	PWC	4	4	14		14
Drafts and Drafting: Blocks	Four-Shaft, Two-Block Warp-Faced Rep Floor Covering	Kolling-Summers, Elizabeth	√	√	WJ	7	4	28	Sp 83	15
Drafts and Drafting: Blocks	Lines, Squares, Rectangles	Marston, Ena	√	√	SS&D	14	3	55	Su 83	72
Drafts and Drafting: Blocks	Mexican Caprice	Snyder, Mary E.	√	>4	CW	2	2	5	Ja 81	7
Drafts and Drafting: Blocks	More Harnesses Make the Difference	Wertenberger, Kathryn	√	>4	Hw	2	3		My 81	40
Drafts and Drafting: Blocks	Multi-Harness Huck: Learn About the Structure of This Family of Weaves and Design Your Own Variations	Barrett, Clotilde	√	>4	WJ	10	4	40	Sp 86	11
Drafts and Drafting: Blocks	Multiple Harness Weaving Course Part 4: Twill Derivatives (cont'd)	Searles, Nancy M.	√	>4	WJ	5	2	18	Fa 80	19
Drafts and Drafting: Blocks	Multiple Shaft Weaving — Threading for 2-or-more-tie Block Weaves		√	>4	WJ	6	2	22	Fa 81	42
Drafts and Drafting: Blocks	Multiple Shaft Weaving — Tie-Ups for 2-or-More-Tie Block Weaves		√	>4	WJ	6	3	23	Wi 81	41
Drafts and Drafting: Blocks	Multiple Shaft Weaving, Twill and Satin Blocks, Damask		√	>4	WJ	5	4	20	Sp 81	10
Drafts and Drafting: Blocks	Notes from a Rugweaver's Journal	Schomp, Halcyon; Hector Jaeger	√	√	Hw	3	4		Se 82	35
Drafts and Drafting: Blocks	Observations on the Six-End Block Draft for Rug Weaving	Schlein, Alice	√	√	WJ	6	4	24	Sp 82	30
Drafts and Drafting: Blocks	One Warp, Many Fabrics	Liebler, Barbara	√	>4	Iw	3	1		Fa 77	28
Drafts and Drafting: Blocks	Overshot Derived from 2/2 Twill	Xenakis, Athanasios David	√	√	PWC	3	2	8		7
Drafts and Drafting: Blocks	Pattern Blocks, Basic Tool for Design	Frey, Berta	√	>4	H&C	19	2		Sp 68	8
Drafts and Drafting: Blocks	Personal Approach to Drafting, A	Alvic, Philis	√	>4	SS&D	13	1	49	Wi 81	32
Drafts and Drafting: Blocks	Point Block Progression: Notes of a Pattern Weaver	Alvic, Philis	√	>4	WJ	10	4	40	Sp 86	67
Drafts and Drafting: Blocks	Practical Weave for Rugs (Reprint), A	Atwater, Mary Meigs	√	>4	H&C	26	1		J/F 75	7
Drafts and Drafting: Blocks	Rep Weaves	Proulx, Bibiane April	√	>4	WJ	7	4	28	Sp 83	10
Drafts and Drafting: Blocks	Shaft Switch Technique (error-corrected WJ v6 n1 81 p28d)		√	√	WJ	5	1	17	Su 80	5
Drafts and Drafting: Blocks	Shaft Switch Techniques (error-corrected WJ v5 n1 80 p5)	Busse, Jane	√	√	WJ	4	4	16	Ap 80	11
Drafts and Drafting: Blocks	Shaft-Switching Combined with Harness Control	Barrett, Clotilde	√	>4	WJ	9	1	33	Su 84	37
Drafts and Drafting: Blocks	Six-Harness M's and O's	Jackson, Marguerite	√	>4	H&C	9	3		Su 58	15
Drafts and Drafting: Blocks	Some Interpretations of Compass and Double Square		√	>4	H&C	4	4		Fa 53	18
Drafts and Drafting: Blocks	System in Symbols, A	The Gadred Weavers	√	>4	H&C	2	1		Wi 50	16
Drafts and Drafting: Blocks	Three-Toned Blocks, Part 1: Simple Pattern	Broughton, Eve T.	√	>4	CW	6	1	16	Se 84	12
Drafts and Drafting: Blocks	Three-Toned Blocks, Part 2: Reverses	Broughton, Eve T.	√	>4	CW	6	2	17	Ja 85	10
Drafts and Drafting: Blocks	Variations in the Honeysuckle Design	Frey, Berta	√	>4	H&C	1	3		Fa 50	26
Drafts and Drafting: Blocks	Warp Faced Patterning	Riccardi, Mary Elinor Steinbaugh	√	√	SS&D	10	2	38	Sp 79	40
Drafts and Drafting: Blocks	Weaver's Challenge	Wertenberger, Kathryn	√	√	Hw	5	1		J/F 84	27

SUBJECT	TITLE	AUTHOR	IL	INST	JOUR	VOL	NO	ISS	DATE	PAGE
Drafts and Drafting: Blocks, 3-End	Weaving a Wall Hanging	Collingwood, Peter	√	√	H&C	11	4		Fa 60	15
Drafts and Drafting: Blocks, Alternating	Three-Toned Blocks, Part 3: Alternating Designs	Broughton, Eve T.	√	> 4	CW	6	3	18	My 85	10
Drafts and Drafting: Blocks Draft	Block Drafting, Profile Drafts, and a Few Other Related Things	Redding, Debbie	√	> 4	Hw	4	3		M/J 83	19
Drafts and Drafting: Blocks Draft	Deciphering Drafts	Keasbey, Doramay	√	> 4	PWC	4	4	14		30
Drafts and Drafting: Blocks Draft	Introduction to Tied Unit Weaves, An	Kelly, Jacquie	√	> 4	PWC	4	4	14		40
Drafts and Drafting: Blocks, Extended	Extending Dr. Bateman's Park Weaves	Harvey, Virginia I.	√	> 4	CW	6	3	18	My 85	3
Drafts and Drafting: Blocks (Four Blocks/Four Shafts)	Summer-and-Winter, Experiments with Four Blocks on Four Harnesses	Aldrich, Mae D.	√	√	H&C	17	4		Fa 66	21
Drafts and Drafting: Blocks, Half-Tone	Eight-Shaft Overshot on Opposites	van der Hoogt, Madelyn; Margaret Heller	√	> 4	PWC	4	4	14		34
Drafts and Drafting: Blocks, Long-Eyed Heddles	Ups and Downs of the Long-Eyed Heddle	Swales, Lois	√	> 4	CW	5	2	14	Ja 84	8
Drafts and Drafting: Blocks, Overshot	Eight-Shaft Overshot on Opposites	van der Hoogt, Madelyn; Margaret Heller	√	> 4	PWC	4	4	14		34
Drafts and Drafting: Blocks, Pattern-Ground	Multiple Shaft Weaving: M's and O's with Two Foundation Shafts	Evans, Jane	√	> 4	WJ	6	1	21	Su 81	27
Drafts and Drafting: Blocks Techniques	Huckaback Lace, A Study of Fabric Structure	Needham, Bertha B.	√	> 4	H&C	12	3		Su 61	26
Drafts and Drafting: Blocks, Three-Toned	Three-Toned Blocks: Further Explorations with Long-eyed Heddles	Broughton, Eve T.	√	> 4	WJ	9	4	36	Sp 85	72
Drafts and Drafting: Blocks, Tied	Drafting: A Personal Approach, Part 2	Alvic, Philis	√	> 4	SS&D	13	2	50	Sp 82	46
Drafts and Drafting: Blocks Tied	Kuvikas	Schoenfeld, Klara	√	> 4	H&C	12	2		Sp 61	20
Drafts and Drafting: Blocks, Tied	Tied Lithuanian: Notes of a Pattern Weaver	Alvic, Philis	√	> 4	WJ	9	3	35	Wi 85	50
Drafts and Drafting: Blocks, Two-Harness(Sets) System	Weaving Damask	Arnold, Ruth	√	> 4	H&C	6	3		Su 55	4
Drafts and Drafting: Borders	Composition and Designing Part 2: Pattern Weaves with Tabby Borders	Zielinski, S. A.; Robert Leclerc, ed.	√	> 4	MWL	19			'51–'73	52
Drafts and Drafting: Borders	Mitered Corners for Identical Warp and Weft Patterns	Redfield, Gail M.	√	√	H&C	14	3		Su 63	21
Drafts and Drafting: Borders	Overshot Borders for Four Sides, Variations in Pattern and Plain Weave	Aldrich, Mae D.	√	> 4	H&C	15	2		Sp 64	15
Drafts and Drafting: Borders, Tabby	Composition and Designing Part 2: Pattern Weaves with Tabby Borders	Zielinski, S. A.; Robert Leclerc, ed.	√	> 4	MWL	19			'51–'73	52
Drafts and Drafting: Boulevard, and Chevron Weaves: Special Information	Bateman Boulevard, Chevron, and Combination Weaves: Rules and Special Information	Bateman, Dr. William G.; Virginia I. Harvey, ed.	√	> 4	SCGM		38		87	15
Drafts and Drafting: Boulevard, Chevron, and Combination Weaves: Notation System	Bateman Boulevard, Chevron, and Combination Weaves: Explanation of Forms	Bateman, Dr. William G.; Virginia I. Harvey, ed.	√	> 4	SCGM		38		87	11
Drafts and Drafting: Boulevard, Chevron, and Combination Weaves: Relationship	Bateman Boulevard, Chevron, and Combination Weaves: Relationship	Bateman, Dr. William G.; Virginia I. Harvey, ed.	√	> 4	SCGM		38		87	14
Drafts and Drafting: Boulevard Weaves: Structures	Bateman Boulevard, Chevron, and Combination Weaves: Boulevard Structures	Bateman, Dr. William G.; Virginia I. Harvey, ed.	√	> 4	SCGM		38		87	16
Drafts and Drafting: Braids, Flat	System for Recording and Drafting Certain Types of Braids, A (error-corrected WJ v2 n1 77 insert for vol. 1)	Barrett, Clotilde; Ronnie Bohannan	√	√	WJ	1	2	2	Oc 76	20
Drafts and Drafting: Callomanko	Thomas Jackson, Weaver: 17th and 18th Century Records	Tidball, Harriet	√	> 4	SCGM		13		64	18
Drafts and Drafting: Card Weaving	Double-and Double-Faced Cloth on Six-Hole Cards	Holtzer, Marilyn F.	√	√	Iw	5	2		Sp 80	66
Drafts and Drafting: Coded	Hanging Based on HGA Name Draft to Decorate New Offices	Fuchs, Rudolph	√	√	SS&D	5	4	20	Fa 74	14
Drafts and Drafting: Coded	New HGA Name Draft: Miniature Coverlet in Overshot, A	Marston, Ena	√	√	SS&D	12	3	47	Su 81	12
Drafts and Drafting: Color and Weave Effects	Drafts		√	√	WJ	1	1	1	Jy 76	12

SUBJECT	TITLE	AUTHOR	IL	INST	JOUR	VOL	NO	ISS	DATE	PAGE
Drafts and Drafting: Color Technique	Drafting with Color	Kurtz, Carol	√	√	SS&D	11	1	41	Wi 79	10
Drafts and Drafting: Combination Weaves	Patchwork	Snyder, Mary E.	√	>4	CW	2	2	5	Ja 81	2
Drafts and Drafting: Combined Structures	Double Weave	Wertenberger, Kathryn	√	>4	Hw	5	4		S/O 84	81
Drafts and Drafting: Combined Structures, Adjoining	Four Harness Straight Draw and Combination Weaves		√	>4	WJ	4	2	14	Oc 79	22
Drafts and Drafting: Combining Structures	Combining Weave Structures	London, Rhoda	√	>4	TM			3	F/M 86	56
Drafts and Drafting: Complete Draft	Creative Drafting and Analysis: Drafting Lesson 1	Zielinski, S. A.; Robert Leclerc, ed.	√	√	MWL	3			'51–'73	7
Drafts and Drafting: Complex Weaves	Demystifying Complex Weaves: A Step-by-Step Exploration from Four to Sixteen Harnesses	Piroch, Sigrid	√	>4	WJ	10	3	39	Wi 86	8
Drafts and Drafting: Compound Weaves, Piqué	Planning Figured Piqué Designs on Pre-Marked Graph Paper	Xenakis, Athanasios David	√	>4	PWC	4	2	12		16
Drafts and Drafting: Conversion Technique	Shadowweave, Part 3 — Marian Powell's Shadow Weave Conversion	Barrett, Clotilde	√	>4	WJ	1	3	3	Ja 77	25
Drafts and Drafting: Converting Color Draft to Threading Draft	Warp-Faced 2/2 Twill: Part 2	Jensen, Gay	√	√	Hw	3	4		Se 82	50
Drafts and Drafting: Corduroy	Corduroy: An Account of Discovery	Alderman, Sharon D.	√	>4	Hw	4	4		S/O 83	54
Drafts and Drafting: Countermarch	Skillbragd Runner (Myrna Golay)		√	>4	Hw	8	3		M/J 87	61, I-12
Drafts and Drafting: Countermarch	Warp-Patterned Adaptation (Carol Strickler)		√	>4	Hw	8	3		M/J 87	I-13
Drafts and Drafting: Crackle Weave, 4-Shaft Crackle in Warp	Contemporary Approach to Traditional Weaves: Production Drafts; Four-Shaft Crackle in Warp	Zielinski, S. A.; Robert Leclerc, ed.	√	>4	MWL	8			'51–'73	60
Drafts and Drafting: Creative Drafting, Traps	Creative Drafting and Analysis: Traps in Creative Drafting	Zielinski, S. A.; Robert Leclerc, ed.	√	>4	MWL	3			'51–'73	67
Drafts and Drafting: Creative, Traps	Composition and Designing Part 2: Traps in Creative Drafting	Zielinski, S. A.; Robert Leclerc, ed.	√	√	MWL	19			'51–'73	138
Drafts and Drafting: Curly Weave	Undulating Weft Effects: The Drafts, Curly Weave	Tidball, Harriet	√	√	SCGM		9		63	10
Drafts and Drafting: Damask	Contemporary Satins: Damask	Tidball, Harriet	√	>4	SCGM		7		62	12
Drafts and Drafting: Damask	Damask	Nyquist, Jan	√	>4	CW	8	1	22	Se 86	3
Drafts and Drafting: Damask	Notes on the Damask Weave	Ahrens, Jim		>4	CW	2	1	4	Oc 80	6
Drafts and Drafting: Damask Diaper	Thomas Jackson, Weaver: 17th and 18th Century Records	Tidball, Harriet	√	>4	SCGM		13		64	30
Drafts and Drafting: Derivatives	Shadowweave, Part 1 (error-corrected WJ v2 n1 77 errata sheet vol. 1)	Barrett, Clotilde	√	>4	WJ	1	1	1	Jy 76	13
Drafts and Drafting: Design	Designing Drafts	Kurtz, Carol	√	√	SS&D	10	4	40	Fa 79	28
Drafts and Drafting: Design	Ways to Weave Overshot: Part 3	Marston, Ena	√	√	SS&D	12	2	46	Sp 81	6
Drafts and Drafting: Designing Twills	Changing the Angle of the Twill Diagonal Line	Laughlin, Elizabeth	√	>4	SS&D	7	4	28	Fa 76	11
Drafts and Drafting: Diaper	Thomas Jackson, Weaver: 17th and 18th Century Records	Tidball, Harriet	√	>4	SCGM		13		64	26
Drafts and Drafting: Double Weave	Double Weave: Plain and Patterned: Double Weave Structure, Drafts and Graphic Forms, The	Tidball, Harriet	√	√	SCGM		1		60	8
Drafts and Drafting: Double Weave, Double-Width	Double Weave: Plain and Patterned: Double Width and Tubular Cloth, The	Tidball, Harriet	√	>4	SCGM		1		60	24
Drafts and Drafting: Double Weave, Four-Shaft	Double Weave: Plain and Patterned: Four-Harness Drafts and Tie-ups, The	Tidball, Harriet	√	√	SCGM		1		60	10
Drafts and Drafting: Double Weave, Multiblock Patterns	Double Weaves: Double Weaves Multi-Block Patterns	Zielinski, S. A.; Robert Leclerc, ed.	√	>4	MWL	15			'51–'73	107
Drafts and Drafting: Double Weave, Self-Stitched	Stitched Doublecloths	Hoskins, Janet A.	√	>4	CW	3	1	7	Se 81	1
Drafts and Drafting: Double Weave, Stitched, Pick-Up	Double Weave: Plain and Patterned: Quilting by the Pick-Up Method, The	Tidball, Harriet	√	>4	SCGM		1		60	29
Drafts and Drafting: Double Weave Surface Connections	Designing Four-Shaft Double Weaves	Muller, Donna	√	√	WJ	7	4	28	Sp 83	56

SUBJECT	TITLE	AUTHOR	IL	INST	JOUR	VOL	NO	ISS	DATE	PAGE
Drafts and Drafting: Double Weave, Three- and Four-Block	Double Weave: Plain and Patterned: Three and Four Block Double Weave, The	Tidball, Harriet	√	> 4	SCGM		1		60	23
Drafts and Drafting: Double Weave, Tubular	Double Weave: Plain and Patterned: Double Width and Tubular Cloth, The	Tidball, Harriet	√	> 4	SCGM		1		60	24
Drafts and Drafting: Double Weave, Two-Block	Double Weave: Plain and Patterned: Two Block Double Weave, The	Tidball, Harriet	√	> 4	SCGM		1		60	19
Drafts and Drafting: Double Weave, Two-Block	Double Weave: Plain and Patterned: Two Block Drafts and Tie-Ups, The	Tidball, Harriet	√	> 4	SCGM		1		60	21
Drafts and Drafting: Double Weave, Two-Warp, Combined Weaves	Double Weave: Plain and Patterned: The Duo-Weave, The	Tidball, Harriet	√	> 4	SCGM		1		60	30
Drafts and Drafting: Double Weaves	Creative Drafting and Analysis: Drafts for Double Weaves	Zielinski, S. A.; Robert Leclerc, ed.	√	> 4	MWL	3			'51–'73	54
Drafts and Drafting: Double Weaves	Double Weaves: Analysis and Synthesis	Zielinski, S. A.; Robert Leclerc, ed.	√	> 4	MWL	15			'51–'73	135
Drafts and Drafting: Double Weaves	Double Weaves: Drafts for Double Weaves	Zielinski, S. A.; Robert Leclerc, ed.	√	> 4	MWL	15			'51–'73	83
Drafts and Drafting: Draft Analysis	Multiple Harness Weaving Course — Introduction (error-corrected WJ v5 n1 80 insert p28d)		√	> 4	WJ	4	2	14	Oc 79	32
Drafts and Drafting: Draft Forms	Thomas Jackson, Weaver: 17th and 18th Century Records	Tidball, Harriet	√		SCGM		13		64	11
Drafts and Drafting: Draw-Down	Creative Drafting and Analysis: Drafting Lesson 2	Zielinski, S. A.; Robert Leclerc, ed.	√	√	MWL	3			'51–'73	10
Drafts and Drafting: Draw-Down	Handweaver's Instruction Manual: Developing Drafts on Paper	Tidball, Harriet C. nee Douglas	√	√	SCGM		34		49	32
Drafts and Drafting: Draw-Down	New Multi-Harness Drawdown Technique, A	Salsbury, Nate	√	> 4	lw	6	1		Wi 80	57
Drafts and Drafting: Draw-Down	Pattern Sticks, Invention of Astrid Swenson of Queens College		√	√	H&C	19	4		Fa 68	21
Drafts and Drafting: Draw-Up	Making a Color Draw-Up	TerLouw, Betty	√	√	SS&D	13	2	50	Sp 82	37
Drafts and Drafting: Drawdowns	Drafting	Nyquist, Janet	√	√	SS&D	1	2	2	Mr 70	16
Drafts and Drafting: Drawdowns, Computer-Assisted	Computerized Analysis of the Drawdown (addendum SS&D v13 n1 81 p4)	Hoskins, Janet A.	√	√	SS&D	13	1	49	Wi 81	76
Drafts and Drafting: Drawloom	All About Looms: Draw-Looms	Zielinski, S. A.; Robert Leclerc, ed.	√	> 4	MWL	2			'51–'73	63
Drafts and Drafting: Drawloom, Split-Harness	Split-Harness Drawloom, The	Malloy, Kim, OSB	√	> 4	CW	2	1	4	Oc 80	3
Drafts and Drafting: Drop-Turnover Repeat	Composition and Designing Part 2: Drop-Turnover Repeat	Zielinski, S. A.; Robert Leclerc, ed.	√	√	MWL	19			'51–'73	87
Drafts and Drafting: Exercises	Drafting 101: Literacy in Weaving (error-corrected Hw v4 n1 83 p24)	Redding, Debbie	√	√	Hw	3	5		N/D 82	73
Drafts and Drafting: Exercises	Drafting 101: Literacy in Weaving, Part 2	Redding, Debbie	√	√	Hw	4	1		J/F 83	24
Drafts and Drafting: Expanding Drafts	twill ^ 2 = Double Width Afghans	Guy, Sallie T.	√	> 4	SS&D	15	1	57	Wi 83	34
Drafts and Drafting: Expansion	Expanded Point Twill	McCeary, Gay	√	> 4	lw	4	3		Su 79	37
Drafts and Drafting: Extended Motifs	Shadowweave, Part 1 (error-corrected WJ v2 n1 77 errata sheet vol. 1)	Barrett, Clotilde	√	> 4	WJ	1	1	1	Jy 76	13
Drafts and Drafting: Figures	Christmas Vest (Yvonne Stahl)		√	> 4	Hw	4	4		S/O 83	71, 101
Drafts and Drafting: Floating Warp	Five Harness Pattern on a Four Harness Loom, A	Thilenius, Carol	√	√	lw	4	3		Su 79	34
Drafts and Drafting: Foreign Literature	Creative Drafting and Analysis: Drafts in Foreign Literature	Zielinski, S. A.; Robert Leclerc, ed.	√	> 4	MWL	3			'51–'73	71
Drafts and Drafting: Gauze Weaves	Gauze Weave: Pick-up Versus Bead Gauze	Sullivan, Donna	√	√	SS&D	17	3	67	Su 86	14
Drafts and Drafting: Geometric Designs	Qotny & Alaga: Traditional Striped Fabrics for the Middle Eastern Kaftan	El-Homossani, M. M.	√	> 4	WJ	10	1	37	Su 85	33
Drafts and Drafting: Graphic System	Handweaver's Instruction Manual: The Draft, Modern Graphic Draft	Tidball, Harriet C. nee Douglas	√	√	SCGM		34		49	10
Drafts and Drafting: Honeycomb	Undulating Weft Effects: The Drafts, Honeycomb	Tidball, Harriet	√	√	SCGM		9		63	7
Drafts and Drafting: Honeycomb, Multishaft	Undulating Weft Effects: The Drafts, Multiple-Shaft Honeycomb	Tidball, Harriet	√	> 4	SCGM		9		63	12

SUBJECT	TITLE	AUTHOR	IL	INST	JOUR	VOL	NO	ISS	DATE	PAGE
Drafts and Drafting: Huck	Thomas Jackson, Weaver: 17th and 18th Century Records	Tidball, Harriet	√	√	SCGM		13		64	16
Drafts and Drafting: Inkle	Inkle Weaving, Fun and Challenge	Anderson, Marcile	√	√	SS&D	5	4	20	Fa 74	29
Drafts and Drafting: Inkle	What and Why of "Inkle"	Atwater, Mary Meigs	√	√	H&C	3	2		Sp 52	18
Drafts and Drafting: Inkle Weave	Little Known Weaves Worth Knowing Better: Inkle Drafts	Zielinski, S. A.; Robert Leclerc, ed.	√	√	MWL	16			'51–'73	114
Drafts and Drafting: Inkle Weaving, Color	Weaving Inkle Bands: Inkle Color Patterns and Drafts	Tidball, Harriet	√	√	SCGM		27		69	22
Drafts and Drafting: Integrated Drafts	Anyone Can Blend	Kessenich, Loraine	√	√	H&C	7	1		Wi 55	22
Drafts and Drafting: Integrated Drafts, Computer-Aided	Draft-Blender	Strickler, Carol; Stewart Strickler	√	√	Hw	8	2		M/A 87	68
Drafts and Drafting: Integrated Weaves, Balanced	Balanced Integrated Weaves	Marston, Ena	√	>4	SS&D	8	1	29	WI 76	10
Drafts and Drafting: Integrated Weaves, Unbalanced	More Integrated Weaves	Marston, Ena	√	>4	SS&D	8	2	30	Sp 77	20
Drafts and Drafting: John Murphy's Drafts	More About Fabrics: Murphy's Drafts	Zielinski, S. A.; Robert Leclerc, ed.	√	>4	MWL	20			'51–'73	93
Drafts and Drafting: Lace, Searles, Free-Form	Freeform Twill & Freeform Searles Lace	Searles, Nancy	√	>4	CW		23		Ja 87	10
Drafts and Drafting: Lace, Searles, Traditional	Freeform Twill & Freeform Searles Lace	Searles, Nancy	√	>4	CW		23		Ja 87	10
Drafts and Drafting: Lampas	Contrails Coverlet	Kelly, Jacquie	√	>4	PWC	5	1	15		48
Drafts and Drafting: Lampas	Lampas	Kelly, Jacquie	√	>4	PWC	5	1	15		46
Drafts and Drafting: Leno, Doup	Doup Leno: Drafts for Four Harness Looms	Skowronski, Hella; Sylvia Tacker	√	√	SCGM		32		80	24
Drafts and Drafting: Leno, Doup	Experimenting with Leno Weaves	Chetwynd, Hilary	√	√	SS&D	5	3	19	Su 74	29
Drafts and Drafting: Leno, Doup	What is Leno?	Frey, Berta	√	>4	H&C	6	2		Sp 55	4
Drafts and Drafting: Leno, Doup, Multishaft	Doup Leno: Drafts for Multiple Harness Looms	Skowronski, Hella; Sylvia Tacker	√	>4	SCGM		32		80	36
Drafts and Drafting: Linear Zigzag	Undulating Weft Effects: The Drafts, Interrupted Linear Zigzag	Tidball, Harriet	√	>4	SCGM		9		63	17
Drafts and Drafting: Linsey Woolsey	Thomas Jackson, Weaver: 17th and 18th Century Records	Tidball, Harriet	√	√	SCGM		13		64	17
Drafts and Drafting: Long-Eyed Heddle	Oscar Knopf's Ingenious Invention	Miller, Ethel E.	√	>4	H&C	10	2		Sp 59	24
Drafts and Drafting: Long-Eyed Heddles	Long-Eyed Heddles and Rising Shed Looms	Fabeck, Diane	√	>4	Iw	4	4		Fa 79	28
Drafts and Drafting: Long-Eyed Heddles	Use Of Long-Eyed Heddles, The	Koob, Katherine; Barbara Keller; Ruth Howard	√	>4	CW	1	3	3	Ap 80	1
Drafts and Drafting: Manifold Drafts	Shadow Weave — Part 4. The Relationship Between Shadow Weave and Corkscrew Weave		√	>4	WJ	1	4	4	Ap 77	30
Drafts and Drafting: Miniaturizing	Traditional Teddy: Overshot in Miniature	Sullivan, Donna	√	√	PWC	5	2	16		14
Drafts and Drafting: Miniaturizing	Woven and Other Textile Miniatures (error-corrected WJ v2 n1 77 insert for vol. 1)		√	√	WJ	1	4	4	Ap 77	16
Drafts and Drafting: Mitered Corners	Mitered Corners	Sullivan, Donna	√	>4	SS&D	15	3	59	Su 84	82
Drafts and Drafting: Multiharness Weaves	Creative Drafting and Analysis: Drafts for 8 Frames	Zielinski, S. A.; Robert Leclerc, ed.	√	>4	MWL	3			'51–'73	61
Drafts and Drafting: Multiple-Harness (Sets) Weaving	Double & Triple Harness Double-Cloth	Fabeck, Diane	√	>4	CW	7	3	21	My 86	7
Drafts and Drafting: Multiple-Harness	In Search of Jacob Angstadt: A Master Weaver Lives Again		√		SS&D	7	2	26	Sp 76	27
Drafts and Drafting: Multiple-Shaft Weaves	Multiple Shaft Coverlet Drafts in the Allen-Stephenson Draft Book	Renne, Elisha	√	>4	AT	3			My 85	125
Drafts and Drafting: M's and O's	Thomas Jackson, Weaver: 17th and 18th Century Records	Tidball, Harriet	√	√	SCGM		13		64	16
Drafts and Drafting: M's and O's	Undulating Weft Effects: The Drafts, Various Interlacement Foundations	Tidball, Harriet	√	√	SCGM		9		63	13

SUBJECT	TITLE	AUTHOR	IL	INST	JOUR	VOL	NO	ISS	DATE	PAGE
Drafts and Drafting: Name Drafts	Merry Christmas—A Name Draft	Bliven, Jeanette; Norma Smayda	√	√	Hw	4	4		S/O 83	74
Drafts and Drafting: Name Drafts	Name Drafting	Mitchell, Peter	√	√	Hw	3	2		Mr 82	34
Drafts and Drafting: Notation Systems	Handweaver's Instruction Manual: The Draft, Systems of Notation	Tidball, Harriet C. nee Douglas	√	√	SCGM		34		49	10
Drafts and Drafting: Notation Variations	Coverlet from Start to Finish, A	van der Hoogt, Madelyn	√	√	PWC	5	1	15		20
Drafts and Drafting: Notation Variations	Deciphering Drafts	Keasbey, Doramay	√	>4	PWC	4	4	14		30
Drafts and Drafting: Ondulé	Undulating Weft Effects: The Drafts, Ondulé	Tidball, Harriet	√		SCGM		9		63	18
Drafts and Drafting: Opposites	Creative Monk's Belt: Opposites in Drafting and Weaving	Windeknecht, Margaret B.	√	√	SCGM		30		76	12
Drafts and Drafting: Opposites, Variations	Creative Monk's Belt: Variations on Opposites	Windeknecht, Margaret B.	√	√	SCGM		30		76	14
Drafts and Drafting: Overshot	Stars, Diamonds, Tables, and Sunrise: Motifs and Structures of Woven Coverlets	Cabeen, Lou	√	√	TM			14	D/J 87	32
Drafts and Drafting: Overshot	Stars & Roses Or Designing and Drafting Overshot	Marston, Ena	√	√	SS&D	4	3	15	Su 73	27
Drafts and Drafting: Overshot, Borders	Handweaver's Instruction Manual: The Overshot Weave, Drafting Borders	Tidball, Harriet C. nee Douglas	√	√	SCGM		34		49	27
Drafts and Drafting: Overshot, Converted Line	Creative Overshot: Begin with A Line	Windeknecht, Margaret B.	√	√	SCGM		31		78	22
Drafts and Drafting: Overshot, Expanded Twill	Creative Overshot: Expand a Twill	Windeknecht, Margaret B.	√	√	SCGM		31		78	15
Drafts and Drafting: Overshot, Twill Derivative	Creative Overshot: Overshot as a Twill Derivative	Windeknecht, Margaret B.	√	√	SCGM		31		78	12
Drafts and Drafting: Overshot, Variations	Creative Overshot: Eight-Harness Overshot	Windeknecht, Margaret B.	√	>4	SCGM		31		78	54
Drafts and Drafting: Pattern Analysis, Technique	Pattern Analysis	Gallagher, Constance D.	√	√	H&C	19	4		Fa 68	6
Drafts and Drafting: Pattern, Balance	Handweaver's Instruction Manual: Pattern Arrangement, Balancing the Pattern	Tidball, Harriet C. nee Douglas		√	SCGM		34		49	12
Drafts and Drafting: Pattern Enlargement	Design in Weaving: Tailoring an Overshot	Alderman, Sharon D.	√	√	Hw	3	1		Ja 82	68
Drafts and Drafting: Pattern Harness (Set)	Technology of Handweaving: Pattern Harness	Zielinski, S. A.; Robert Leclerc, ed.	√	√	MWL	6			'51–'73	45
Drafts and Drafting: Pattern Reduction	Design in Weaving: Tailoring an Overshot	Alderman, Sharon D.	√	√	Hw	3	1		Ja 82	68
Drafts and Drafting: Pattern-Ground Weaves	Double Two-Tie Twills and Basket Weave	Barrett, Clotilde	√	>4	WJ	7	3	27	Wi 82	38
Drafts and Drafting: Pattern-Ground Weaves	Figured Piqué on a Ground of 2/2 Twill and 2/2 Hopsack	Xenakis, Athanasios David	√	>4	PWC	4	2	12		24
Drafts and Drafting: Pattern-Ground Weaves	Five Block Double Weave Using the Glimåkra Long Eyed Heddle Accessory	Tramba, Diane	√	>4	WJ	7	3	27	Wi 82	45
Drafts and Drafting: Pattern-Ground Weaves	Four + Four: An Introduction to Those Extra Harnesses	Howard, Miranda	√	>4	Hw	3	4		Se 82	66
Drafts and Drafting: Pattern-Ground Weaves	Instructions: Pick-Up Figured Piqué (error-corrected PWC v4 n3 i13 p4)	Xenakis, Athanasios David	√	√	PWC	4	2	12		39
Drafts and Drafting: Pattern-Ground Weaves	Multiple Shaft Weaving, Twill and Satin Blocks, Damask		√	>4	WJ	5	4	20	Sp 81	10
Drafts and Drafting: Pattern-Ground Weaves	Planning Figured Piqué Designs on Pre-Marked Graph Paper	Xenakis, Athanasios David	√	>4	PWC	4	2	12		16
Drafts and Drafting: Pattern-Ground Weaves, Huck	Multi-Harness Huck: Learn About the Structure of This Family of Weaves and Design Your Own Variations	Barrett, Clotilde	√	>4	WJ	10	4	40	Sp 86	11
Drafts and Drafting: Point Twill/Complex Twill	Multiple Shaft Coverlet Drafts in the Allen-Stephenson Draft Book	Renne, Elisha	√	>4	AT	3			My 85	125
Drafts and Drafting: Profile Development	Overshot Sampler Bedspread for a Narrow Loom, An	Keasbey, Doramay	√	√	PWC	5	1	15		42
Drafts and Drafting: Profile Drafts	Blanket Weave, The	Robitaille, Annette	√	>4	WJ	8	4	32	Sp 84	62
Drafts and Drafting: Profile Drafts	Block Drafting, Profile Drafts, and a Few Other Related Things	Redding, Debbie	√	>4	Hw	4	3		M/J 83	19

SUBJECT	TITLE	AUTHOR	IL	INST	JOUR	VOL	NO	ISS	DATE	PAGE
Drafts and Drafting: Profile Drafts	Block Weaves Part 1, Profile Drafts and Block Designs (error-corrected WJ v2 n4 78 insert for vol. 2)		√	> 4	WJ	2	3	7	Ja 78	6
Drafts and Drafting: Profile Drafts	Block Weaves Part 2, Atwater Bronson Lace		√	> 4	WJ	2	3	7	Ja 78	10
Drafts and Drafting: Profile Drafts	Blocks and Profiles	Carey, Joyce Marquess	√	√	WJ	7	2	26	Fa 82	33
Drafts and Drafting: Profile Drafts	But What's the Tie-Up?	van der Hoogt, Madelyn	√	> 4	PWC	5	1	15		36
Drafts and Drafting: Profile Drafts	Contrails Coverlet	Kelly, Jacquie	√	> 4	PWC	5	1	15		48
Drafts and Drafting: Profile Drafts	Curves and Circles	Marston, Ena	√	> 4	SS&D	15	1	57	Wi 83	84
Drafts and Drafting: Profile Drafts	Deciphering Drafts	Keasbey, Doramay	√	> 4	PWC	4	4	14		30
Drafts and Drafting: Profile Drafts	Designing Block Weaves	Kurtz, Carol	√	> 4	SS&D	11	2	42	Sp 80	5
Drafts and Drafting: Profile Drafts	Expanded Point Twill	McCeary, Gay	√	> 4	lw	4	3		Su 79	37
Drafts and Drafting: Profile Drafts	Four-Block Warp Rep (error-corrected WJ v8 n1 83 p50)	Robitaille, Annette	√	> 4	WJ	7	4	28	Sp 83	16
Drafts and Drafting: Profile Drafts	Handweaver's Instruction Manual: The Draft, The Profile Draft	Tidball, Harriet C. nee Douglas	√	√	SCGM		34		49	10
Drafts and Drafting: Profile Drafts	Huck and Huck Lace		√	> 4	WJ	1	4	4	Ap 77	33
Drafts and Drafting: Profile Drafts	Megablocks	Patrick, Jane	√	√	Hw	4	1		J/F 83	60
Drafts and Drafting: Profile Drafts	More Harnesses Make the Difference	Wertenberger, Kathryn	√	> 4	Hw	2	3		My 81	40
Drafts and Drafting: Profile Drafts	Multiple Shaft Weaving — 2-Tie Four-End Block Drafts		√	> 4	WJ	6	4	24	Sp 82	48
Drafts and Drafting: Profile Drafts	Multishaft Overshot on Opposites	van der Hoogt, Madelyn	√	> 4	WJ	8	3	31	Wi 83	76
Drafts and Drafting: Profile Drafts	Norse Kjøkken	Rowley, Elaine	√	√	PWC	3	1	7		16
Drafts and Drafting: Profile Drafts	Overshot Derived from 2/2 Twill	Xenakis, Athanasios David	√	√	PWC	3	2	8		7
Drafts and Drafting: Profile Drafts	Personal Approach to Drafting, A	Alvic, Philis	√	> 4	SS&D	13	1	49	Wi 81	32
Drafts and Drafting: Profile Drafts	Pine Tree Borders, North and South	Strickler, Carol	√	> 4	lw	5	3		Su 80	64
Drafts and Drafting: Profile Drafts	Practical Weave for Rugs, A	Atwater, Mary Meigs	√	> 4	H&C	5	2		Sp 54	24
Drafts and Drafting: Profile Drafts	Rep Weaves	Proulx, Bibiane April	√	> 4	WJ	7	4	28	Sp 83	10
Drafts and Drafting: Profile Drafts	Rugs Woven on Summer and Winter Threading		√	> 4	WJ	3	1	9	Jy 78	12
Drafts and Drafting: Profile Drafts	Sarah Fowler's Book of Drafts, Part 3	North, Lois	√	> 4	SS&D	6	3	23	Su 75	74
Drafts and Drafting: Profile Drafts	Six-Harness M's and O's	Jackson, Marguerite	√	> 4	H&C	9	3		Su 58	15
Drafts and Drafting: Profile Drafts	Some Interpretations of Compass and Double Square		√	> 4	H&C	4	4		Fa 53	18
Drafts and Drafting: Profile Drafts	Summer and Winter — A Stock of Options	Minard, Juanita	√	√	SS&D	10	3	39	Su 79	42
Drafts and Drafting: Profile Drafts	Summer and Winter and Other Two-Tie Unit Weaves: Drafts and Patterns	Tidball, Harriet	√	> 4	SCGM		19		66	17
Drafts and Drafting: Profile Drafts	Summer and Winter and Other Two-Tie Unit Weaves: Summer and Winter Tie-Ups	Tidball, Harriet	√	> 4	SCGM		19		66	7
Drafts and Drafting: Profile Drafts	Summer and Winter — Part 1		√	> 4	WJ	2	4	8	Ap 78	28
Drafts and Drafting: Profile Drafts	System in Symbols, A	The Gadred Weavers	√	> 4	H&C	2	1		Wi 50	16
Drafts and Drafting: Profile Drafts	Treasury for Beginners: Theory of the Profiles	Zielinski, S. A.; Robert Leclerc, ed.	√	√	MWL	1			'51–'73	63
Drafts and Drafting: Profile Drafts	Turned Drafts in Double Two-Tie Unit Weave	van der Hoogt, Madelyn	√	> 4	WJ	9	2	34	Fa 84	13
Drafts and Drafting: Profile Drafts	Two-Tie Unit for Rugs: Part 1, The Double-Faced Stuffer Weave and Summer-and-Winter, The	Windeknecht, Margaret	√	> 4	SS&D	16	1	61	Wi 84	82
Drafts and Drafting: Profile Drafts	Use of Long-Eyed Heddles for Patterned Double Weave, The	Howard, Ruth	√	> 4	WJ	6	2	22	Fa 81	35
Drafts and Drafting: Profile Drafts	Using a Profile Draft		√	√	Hw	1	2		S-S 80	66
Drafts and Drafting: Profile Drafts	Warp Faced Patterning	Riccardi, Mary Elinor Steinbaugh	√	√	SS&D	10	2	38	Sp 79	40
Drafts and Drafting: Profile Drafts	Warp-pattern Weaving	Frey, Berta	√	√	H&C	10	3		Su 59	9
Drafts and Drafting: Profile Drafts	Weaving Drafts and Diaper Twills in Lancaster County	Crosson, Janet Gray	√	> 4	lw	4	3		Su 79	40
Drafts and Drafting: Profile Drafts	Workshop at Home, Weaving Summer and Winter	Arnold, Ruth	√	√	H&C	9	3		Su 58	6

SUBJECT	TITLE	AUTHOR	IL	INST	JOUR	VOL	NO	ISS	DATE	PAGE
Drafts and Drafting: Profile Drafts, Satin Piqué	Satin Piqué	Morrison, Ruth	√	> 4	PWC	4	3	13		34
Drafts and Drafting: Profile Drafts, Substituting	Summer and Winter and Other Two-Tie Unit Weaves: Profile Substituting	Tidball, Harriet	√	> 4	SCGM		19		66	6
Drafts and Drafting: Profile Drafts, Variable Threading	Composition and Designing Part 2: Transcribing	Zielinski, S. A.; Robert Leclerc, ed.	√	> 4	MWL	19			'51–'73	44
Drafts and Drafting: Profile Draw Down	Dimai	Petraitis, Ada	√	> 4	CW	5	3	15	My 84	5
Drafts and Drafting: Profile, Lampas	Lampas for Eight	Sullivan, Donna	√	> 4	PWC	5	2	16		34
Drafts and Drafting: Profile, Miniatures	Miniature World, A	Piroch, Sigrid	√	> 4	PWC	5	2	16		26
Drafts and Drafting: Profile Notation	Roses and Snowballs: The Development of Block Patterns in the German Linen-Weaving Tradition	Hilts, Patricia	√	> 4	AT	5			Ju 86	167
Drafts and Drafting: Profile Patterns	Creative Drafting and Analysis: Drafting Lesson 8	Zielinski, S. A.; Robert Leclerc, ed.	√	> 4	MWL	3			'51–'73	30
Drafts and Drafting: Profile Patterns, 2-Block Variations	Creative Drafting and Analysis: Drafting Lesson 11	Zielinski, S. A.; Robert Leclerc, ed.	√	> 4	MWL	3			'51–'73	39
Drafts and Drafting: Profile Patterns, 3-Block or More, Variations	Creative Drafting and Analysis: Drafting Lesson 13	Zielinski, S. A.; Robert Leclerc, ed.	√	> 4	MWL	3			'51–'73	46
Drafts and Drafting: Profile Patterns, 3-Block Variations	Creative Drafting and Analysis: Drafting Lesson 12 (variations of 3-block patterns)	Zielinski, S. A.; Robert Leclerc, ed.	√	> 4	MWL	3			'51–'73	43
Drafts and Drafting: Profile, Stitcher Drafts	Stitcher Designer Hints For Loom-Controlled Figured Piqué	van der Hoogt, Madelyn	√	> 4	PWC	4	3	13		48
Drafts and Drafting: Profile, Technique	Profile Drafting: Getting the Big Picture	Alderman, Sharon	√	> 4	Hw	8	5		N/D 87	44
Drafts and Drafting: Profiles, Stripes	Thomas Jackson, Weaver: 17th and 18th Century Records	Tidball, Harriet	√	> 4	SCGM		13		64	35
Drafts and Drafting: Random Drafts, Satin	Composition and Designing Part 2: Random Satins	Zielinski, S. A.; Robert Leclerc, ed.	√	> 4	MWL	19			'51–'73	83
Drafts and Drafting: Random Drafts Woven As-Drawn-In	Composition and Designing Part 2: Four Shaft Random Drafts Woven-As-Drawn-In	Zielinski, S. A.; Robert Leclerc, ed.	√	√	MWL	19			'51–'73	98
Drafts and Drafting: Random Number Drafts	Composition and Designing Part 2: Random Drafts	Zielinski, S. A.; Robert Leclerc, ed.	√	√	MWL	19			'51–'73	79
Drafts and Drafting: Reduction	Expanded Point Twill	McCeary, Gay	√	> 4	lw	4	3		Su 79	37
Drafts and Drafting: Reduction	Historical American Weaving in Miniature	Strickler, Carol; Barbara Taggart	√	√	lw	4	3		Su 79	48
Drafts and Drafting: Rigid-Heddle	Double Two-Tie Unit Weave: An Expansion of Options for Rigid Heddle Weaving, The	Xenakis, Athanasios David	√	√	lw	5	1		Wi 79	39
Drafts and Drafting: Satin	Contemporary Satins: Drafting Satin	Tidball, Harriet	√	> 4	SCGM		7		62	7
Drafts and Drafting: Satin	Contemporary Satins: Satin Counts	Tidball, Harriet	√	> 4	SCGM		7		62	3
Drafts and Drafting: Satin	Satin — The Designer Weave	Nyquist, Jan	√	> 4	CW	7	3	21	My 86	15
Drafts and Drafting: Satin	Satin — The Designer Weave (error-corrected SS&D v10 n4 79 p66)	Nyquist, Janet	√	> 4	SS&D	10	3	39	Su 79	77
Drafts and Drafting: Satin	Thomas Jackson, Weaver: 17th and 18th Century Records	Tidball, Harriet	√	> 4	SCGM		13		64	18
Drafts and Drafting: Satin, Double Stitched	Contemporary Satins: Double Stitched Satin	Tidball, Harriet	√	> 4	SCGM		7		62	8
Drafts and Drafting: Satinet	Thomas Jackson, Weaver: 17th and 18th Century Records	Tidball, Harriet	√	> 4	SCGM		13		64	20
Drafts and Drafting: Satins, Long-Eyed Heddles	Satin and Long-Eyed Heddles	Hoskins, Janet A.; W. D. Hoskins	√	> 4	WJ	6	1	21	Su 81	25
Drafts and Drafting: Scandinavian Style	Creative Weave Drafting, Scandinavian Style	Snow, Jean Brooker	√	> 4	SS&D	17	4	68	Fa 86	61
Drafts and Drafting: Scrambled Drafts	Contemporary Approach to Traditional Weaves: New Patterns in Traditional Weaves	Zielinski, S. A.; Robert Leclerc, ed.	√	> 4	MWL	8			'51–'73	86
Drafts and Drafting: Scrambled Drafts	Creative Drafting and Analysis: Scrambled Drafts	Zielinski, S. A.; Robert Leclerc, ed.	√	> 4	MWL	3			'51–'73	77
Drafts and Drafting: Selvages, 2-Tie Unit System	Summer and Winter and Other Two-Tie Unit Weaves: Selvages	Tidball, Harriet	√	> 4	SCGM		19		66	10

SUBJECT	TITLE	AUTHOR	IL	INST	JOUR	VOL	NO	ISS	DATE	PAGE
Drafts and Drafting: Seventeen Pattern Types	Seventeen Pattern Types, A Study of Repeat Patterns in Two Dimensions	Elliott, Verda	√	>4	CW		25		Se 87	23
Drafts and Drafting: Shadow Weave	Shadowweave, Part 1 (error-corrected WJ v2 n1 77 insert for vol. 1)	Barrett, Clotilde	√	>4	WJ	1	1	1	Jy 76	13
Drafts and Drafting: Shed Drafts, Abbreviated	More About Larch Trees	The Gadred Weavers	√	>4	H&C	2	3		Su 51	28
Drafts and Drafting: Shed Drafts, Master	More About Larch Trees	The Gadred Weavers	√	>4	H&C	2	3		Su 51	28
Drafts and Drafting: Short Draft	Treasury for Beginners: Analysis of Patterns	Zielinski, S. A.; Robert Leclerc, ed.	√	√	MWL	1			'51–'73	60
Drafts and Drafting: Spider Weave	Undulating Weft Effects: The Drafts, Linear Zigzag or Spider Weave	Tidball, Harriet	√	√	SCGM		9		63	16
Drafts and Drafting: Spot Weave	Thomas Jackson, Weaver: 17th and 18th Century Records	Tidball, Harriet	√	>4	SCGM		13		64	22
Drafts and Drafting: Spot Weave	Undulating Weft Effects: The Drafts, Various Interlacement Foundations	Tidball, Harriet	√	√	SCGM		9		63	13
Drafts and Drafting: Star and Diamond Patterns	Multiple Shaft Coverlet Drafts in the Allen-Stephenson Draft Book	Renne, Elisha	√	>4	AT	3			My 85	125
Drafts and Drafting: Stripes, Vertical	Composition and Designing Part 2: Vertical Stripes in Texture and Colour	Zielinski, S. A.; Robert Leclerc, ed.	√	>4	MWL	19			'51–'73	58
Drafts and Drafting: Style, 19th Century	Multiple Shaft Coverlet Drafts in the Allen-Stephenson Draft Book	Renne, Elisha	√	>4	AT	3			My 85	125
Drafts and Drafting: Summer and Winter	Summer and Winter and Other Two-Tie Unit Weaves: The Two-Tie Unit System	Tidball, Harriet	√	>4	SCGM		19		66	4
Drafts and Drafting: Summer and Winter	Undulating Weft Effects: The Drafts, Various Interlacement Foundations	Tidball, Harriet	√	√	SCGM		9		63	14
Drafts and Drafting: Superimposed Drafts	All About Looms: Draw-Looms	Zielinski, S. A.; Robert Leclerc, ed.	√	>4	MWL	2			'51–'73	50
Drafts and Drafting: Supplementary Warps	Supplementary Warp Patterning: Drafts	Tidball, Harriet	√	>4	SCGM		17		66	3
Drafts and Drafting: Symbols	System in Symbols, A	The Gadred Weavers	√	>4	H&C	2	1		Wi 50	16
Drafts and Drafting: Systems	Handloom Weaves: Draft Conventions	Tidball, Harriet	√	√	SCGM		33		57	4
Drafts and Drafting: Systems, Multiple-Shaft Weaving	Multiple Harness Weaving Course — Introduction (error-corrected WJ v5 n1 80 insert p28d)		√	>4	WJ	4	2	14	Oc 79	32
Drafts and Drafting: Tablet Weaving	New Way to Draft Double-Twist/Double-Turn Tablet Weaving, A	Doleman, Paul	√	√	SS&D	11	4	44	Fa 80	42
Drafts and Drafting: Tape Loom	Setting Up a Tape Loom	Crawford, Grace Post	√	√	H&C	12	1		Wi 61	19
Drafts and Drafting: Technique	Brighton Honeycomb	Muller, Donna	√	>4	CW	5	3	15	My 84	12
Drafts and Drafting: Technique	More Logical Method of Drafting, A	Hoyt, Peggy	√	>4	CW	5	3	15	My 84	22
Drafts and Drafting: Technique	The Longest Warp in the World or, The Double Two-Tie Unit Threading System	Miller, Mary Ann	√	>4	CW	3	3	9	Ap 82	2
Drafts and Drafting: Techniques	Basic Drafting	Kurtz, Carol	√	√	SS&D	10	3	39	Su 79	18
Drafts and Drafting: Techniques	Blended Drafts	Strickler, Carol	√	>4	Hw	6	2		M/A 85	37
Drafts and Drafting: Techniques	Block Drafting, Profile Drafts, and a Few Other Related Things	Redding, Debbie	√	>4	Hw	4	3		M/J 83	19
Drafts and Drafting: Techniques	Blocks and Profiles	Carey, Joyce Marquess	√	√	WJ	7	2	26	Fa 82	33
Drafts and Drafting: Techniques	Cloth Analysis — The Draft from the Fabric	Frey, Berta	√	√	H&C	2	4		Fa 51	11
Drafts and Drafting: Techniques	Demystifying Complex Weaves: A Step-by-Step Exploration from Four to Sixteen Harnesses	Piroch, Sigrid	√	>4	WJ	10	3	39	Wi 86	8
Drafts and Drafting: Techniques	Designing Drafts	Kurtz, Carol	√	√	SS&D	10	4	40	Fa 79	28
Drafts and Drafting: Techniques	Discerning the Pattern	Keasbey, Doramay	√	√	SS&D	7	2	26	Sp 76	84
Drafts and Drafting: Techniques	Don't Avoid the Draft, Learn to Read It!	Redding, Debbie	√	√	Hw	2	1		F-W 80	12
Drafts and Drafting: Techniques	Double-Faced Cloth: One Cloth, Two Appearances	Alderman, Sharon	√	>4	Hw	3	4		Se 82	61
Drafts and Drafting: Techniques	Doupe Leno for the Harness Loom	Xenakis, Alexis Yiorgos; Elaine Rowley	√	√	PWC			6	Su 83	10
Drafts and Drafting: Techniques	Drafting in Color	Nyquist, Janet	√	√	SS&D	1	1	1	De 69	5

SUBJECT	TITLE	AUTHOR	IL	INST	JOUR	VOL	NO	ISS	DATE	PAGE
Drafts and Drafting: Techniques	Drafting Plans for 4-Harness Rosepath Motifs	Strickler, Carol	√	√	SS&D	5	1	17	Wi 73	58
Drafts and Drafting: Techniques	Drafts		√	√	WJ	1	1	1	Jy 76	12
Drafts and Drafting: Techniques	Four Harness Damask — A Pick-up Weave	Merritt, Elveana	√	√	WJ	5	1	17	Su 80	20
Drafts and Drafting: Techniques	Four Harness Double Width Weaving	Frey, Berta	√	√	H&C	12	1		Wi 61	6
Drafts and Drafting: Techniques	Four-Block Warp Rep (error-corrected WJ v8 n1 83 p50)	Robitaille, Annette	√	> 4	WJ	7	4	28	Sp 83	16
Drafts and Drafting: Techniques	How to Weave Your own Designs	Arnold, Ruth	√	> 4	H&C	11	3		Su 60	6
Drafts and Drafting: Techniques	Let's Pull Together	Barrett, Clotilde	√	√	WJ	8	1	29	Su 83	85
Drafts and Drafting: Techniques	Loom Controlled Designs		√	> 4	WJ	3	3	11	Ja 79	18
Drafts and Drafting: Techniques	Method of Drafting	Nyquist, Janet	√	√	SS&D	1	1	1	De 69	4
Drafts and Drafting: Techniques	Miniature Musical Drafts	Newman, Margaret	√	√	SS&D	4	4	16	Fa 73	70
Drafts and Drafting: Techniques	Multiple Harness Weaving Course — Introduction (error-corrected WJ v5 n1 80 insert p28d)		√	> 4	WJ	4	2	14	Oc 79	32
Drafts and Drafting: Techniques	Multiple Harness Weaving Course — Part 2: Twills and Satins, With Contribution by Nancy Searles		√	> 4	WJ	4	4	16	Ap 80	16
Drafts and Drafting: Techniques	My Computer Designs a Bedspread	Salsbury, Nate	√	√	Hw	3	3		My 82	80
Drafts and Drafting: Techniques	Name Draft (error-corrected WJ v8 n3 83 p68)		√	√	WJ	8	2	30	Fa 83	40
Drafts and Drafting: Techniques	New Ways with Old Drafts (error-corrected H&C v2 n4 51 p64)	Frey, Berta	√	√	H&C	2	3		Su 51	8
Drafts and Drafting: Techniques	Quilted Fabrics, A Method of Draft Writing for Individual Designs	Frey, Berta	√	> 4	H&C	14	4		Fa 63	17
Drafts and Drafting: Techniques	Toward a Standard Drafting System	Gottdiener, Jennifer	√	> 4	H&C	24	2		M/A 73	12
Drafts and Drafting: Techniques	Treadle as Drawn In	Frey, Berta	√	> 4	H&C	5	3		Su 54	24
Drafts and Drafting: Techniques	Weave Analysis	Carey, Joyce Marquess	√	> 4	WJ	7	1	25	Su 82	45
Drafts and Drafting: Techniques	Weaving Draft: Road Map to Success, The	Liebler, Barbara	√		Iw	1	2		Wi 76	26
Drafts and Drafting: Techniques	Weaving Music	Henneberger, Karel	√	> 4	SS&D	16	4	64	Fa 85	6
Drafts and Drafting: Techniques	Weaving on Paper		√	> 4	SS&D	3	3	11	Su 72	34
Drafts and Drafting: Techniques	What is a Draft?	Frey, Berta	√	√	H&C	9	1		Wi 57	11
Drafts and Drafting: Techniques, Bands	Weaving the Girdle of Rameses	Hilts, Patricia	√	> 4	WJ	9	1	33	Su 84	22
Drafts and Drafting: Techniques, Basic	Drafting 101: Literacy in Weaving (error-corrected Hw v4 n1 83 p24)	Redding, Debbie	√	√	Hw	3	5		N/D 82	73
Drafts and Drafting: Techniques, Basic	Drafting 101: Literacy in Weaving, Part 2	Redding, Debbie	√	√	Hw	4	1		J/F 83	24
Drafts and Drafting: Techniques, Basics	Very Basics of Weaving Drafting: Two and Three Shafts, The	Carey, Joyce Marquess	√	√	WJ	6	2	22	Fa 81	50
Drafts and Drafting: Techniques, Loom-Stitching	Matelasse Double Cloth Stitched to Form the Design	Kelly, Linda	√	> 4	WJ	7	1	25	Su 82	43
Drafts and Drafting: Techniques, Name Drafts	What's in a Name? Name Drafts Drawn by Hand or Computer	Mansfield, Susan	√	√	WJ	10	3	39	Wi 86	15
Drafts and Drafting: Techniques, Twill	Multiple Harness Weaving Course — Part I (error-corrected WJ v4 n4 80 p16)		√	> 4	WJ	4	3	15	Ja 80	14
Drafts and Drafting: Threading	Multiple Shaft Weaving — Threading for 2-or-More-Tie Block Weaves		√	> 4	WJ	6	2	22	Fa 81	42
Drafts and Drafting: Threading	Overshot Derived from 2/2 Twill	Xenakis, Athanasios David	√	√	PWC	3	2	8		7
Drafts and Drafting: Threading Draft Conversions	Shadow Weave	Evans, Jane	√	√	SS&D	15	4	60	Fa 84	57
Drafts and Drafting: Threading Full Drafts	Creative Drafting and Analysis: Drafting Lesson 5	Zielinski, S. A.; Robert Leclerc, ed.	√	√	MWL	3			'51–'73	20
Drafts and Drafting: Threading Notation Systems	Creative Drafting and Analysis: Drafting Lesson 7	Zielinski, S. A.; Robert Leclerc, ed.	√	> 4	MWL	3			'51–'73	27
Drafts and Drafting: Threading Patterns	Sarah Fowler's Book of Drafts, Part 1	North, Lois	√	> 4	SS&D	6	1	21	Wi 74	8

SUBJECT	TITLE	AUTHOR	IL	INST	JOUR	VOL	NO	ISS	DATE	PAGE
Drafts and Drafting: Threading Profile Drafts	Creative Drafting and Analysis: Drafting Lesson 8	Zielinski, S. A.; Robert Leclerc, ed.	√	>4	MWL	3			'51–'73	30
Drafts and Drafting: Threading Profile Drafts	Creative Drafting and Analysis: Drafting Lesson 9	Zielinski, S. A.; Robert Leclerc, ed.	√	>4	MWL	3			'51–'73	33
Drafts and Drafting: Threading Profile Drafts, Non-Unit Structures	Creative Drafting and Analysis: Drafting Lesson 10	Zielinski, S. A.; Robert Leclerc, ed.	√	√	MWL	3			'51–'73	36
Drafts and Drafting: Threading Schedule	Handweaver's Instruction Manual: Pattern Arrangement, Threading Schedules	Tidball, Harriet C. nee Douglas		√	SCGM		34		49	12
Drafts and Drafting: Threading Short Drafts	Creative Drafting and Analysis: Drafting Lesson 6	Zielinski, S. A.; Robert Leclerc, ed.	√	√	MWL	3			'51–'73	24
Drafts and Drafting: Threading Short Drafts, Notation Systems	Creative Drafting and Analysis: Short Drafts	Zielinski, S. A.; Robert Leclerc, ed.	√	>4	MWL	3			'51–'73	49
Drafts and Drafting: Threading Translations	Spanish Colonial Loom: A Contemporary Loom-Maker Uses Traditional Tools to Construct a Replica for the Albuquerque Museum	Edwards, Jack	√	√	WJ	11	1	41	Su 86	16
Drafts and Drafting: Threading Unit Drafts	Creative Drafting and Analysis: Drafting Lesson 8	Zielinski, S. A.; Robert Leclerc, ed.	√	>4	MWL	3			'51–'73	30
Drafts and Drafting: Threading Unit Drafts	Creative Drafting and Analysis: Drafting Lesson 9	Zielinski, S. A.; Robert Leclerc, ed.	√	>4	MWL	3			'51–'73	33
Drafts and Drafting: Three-Shaft Weaves	Very Basics of Weaving Drafting: Two and Three Shafts, The	Carey, Joyce Marquess	√	√	WJ	6	2	22	Fa 81	50
Drafts and Drafting: Tie Group, Block Separation Ties	Bateman Blend Weaves: The Structures of the Bateman Blend System	Bateman, Dr. William G.; Virginia I. Harvey, ed.	√	>4	SCGM		36		82	14
Drafts and Drafting: Tie Ups, Hand Loom Conversion	Handweaver's Instruction Manual: The Tie-Up, Hand Loom Conversion	Tidball, Harriet C. nee Douglas			SCGM		34		49	11
Drafts and Drafting: Tie Ups, Rising Shed	Handweaver's Instruction Manual: The Tie-Up, Rising Shed	Tidball, Harriet C. nee Douglas	√	√	SCGM		34		49	11
Drafts and Drafting: Tie Ups, Sinking Shed	Handweaver's Instruction Manual: The Tie-Up, Sinking Shed	Tidball, Harriet C. nee Douglas	√	√	SCGM		34		49	11
Drafts and Drafting: Tie Ups, Standard Tie-Up	Handweaver's Instruction Manual: The Tie-Up, Standard Tie-Up	Tidball, Harriet C. nee Douglas		√	SCGM		34		49	11
Drafts and Drafting: Tie-Down Warps	Analysis of Star and Diamond Weave Structures, An (error-corrected SS&D v10 n1 78 p101)	Anderson, Clarita; Judith Gordon; Naomi Whiting Towner	√	>4	SS&D	9	4	36	Fa 78	71
Drafts and Drafting: Tie-Down Warps	Overshot: The Weave and the Designs	Marston, Ena	√	>4	SS&D	11	2	42	Sp 80	74
Drafts and Drafting: Tie-Down Warps	Summer and Winter — A Stock of Options	Minard, Juanita	√	√	SS&D	10	3	39	Su 79	42
Drafts and Drafting: Tie-Ups	Designing from the Tie-Up, A Multiharness Tool (error-corrected lw v5 n1 79 p10)	Alderman, Sharon D.	√	>4	lw	4	4		Fa 79	30
Drafts and Drafting: Tie-Ups	How to Determine Tie-Up for Multi-Harness Huck Lace Patterns	Quinn, Eva		>4	SS&D	1	3	3	Ju 70	16
Drafts and Drafting: Tie-Ups	Overshot Derived from 2/2 Twill	Xenakis, Athanasios David	√	√	PWC	3	2	8		7
Drafts and Drafting: Tie-Ups	Sixteen-Harness Design for Draperies, A	Fishback, John S.	√	>4	H&C	11	1		Wi 60	24
Drafts and Drafting: Tie-Ups	Treasury for Beginners: The Logic of Tie-Ups	Zielinski, S. A.; Robert Leclerc, ed.	√	>4	MWL	1			'51–'73	82
Drafts and Drafting: Tie-ups, Complex	Demystifying Complex Weaves: A Step-by-Step Exploration from Four to Sixteen Harnesses	Piroch, Sigrid	√	>4	WJ	10	3	39	Wi 86	8
Drafts and Drafting: Tie-Ups, Damask	Are You Pegging, Tyeing-Up or Punching the Computer?	Best, Eleanor	√	>4	CW	3	2	8	Ja 82	8
Drafts and Drafting: Tie-Ups, Double Weave	Are You Pegging, Tyeing-Up or Punching the Computer?	Best, Eleanor	√	>4	CW	3	2	8	Ja 82	8
Drafts and Drafting: Tie-Ups, M's and O's, 2-Tie	Are You Pegging, Tyeing-Up or Punching the Computer?	Best, Eleanor	√	>4	CW	3	2	8	Ja 82	8
Drafts and Drafting: Tie-Ups Summer and Winter	Summer and Winter and Other Two-Tie Unit Weaves: Summer and Winter Tie-Ups	Tidball, Harriet	√	>4	SCGM		19		66	7
Drafts and Drafting: Translating	Translating Four-Harness Drafts for the Single Rigid Heddle Method		√	√	PWC			5	Sp 83	22
Drafts and Drafting: Translating	Translating Four-Harness Drafts for the Single Rigid Heddle Method		√	√	PWC			5	Sp 83	22

SUBJECT	TITLE	AUTHOR	IL	INST	JOUR	VOL	NO	ISS	DATE	PAGE
Drafts and Drafting: Translating, Card Weaving to Loom	Card Weaving, Patterns Translated to a Handloom	Priest, Alice R.	√	√	H&C	12	2		Sp 61	15
Drafts and Drafting: Transposed Threading & Treadling	Skirt with Warp Stripe Pattern	Frey, Berta	√	√	H&C	14	2		Sp 63	38
Drafts and Drafting: Treadling	Creative Drafting and Analysis: Drafting Lesson 3	Zielinski, S. A.; Robert Leclerc, ed.	√	√	MWL	3			'51–'73	14
Drafts and Drafting: Treadling	Overshot Derived from 2/2 Twill	Xenakis, Athanasios David	√	√	PWC	3	2	8		7
Drafts and Drafting: Treadling	Sixteen-Harness Design for Draperies, A	Fishback, John S.	√	>4	H&C	11	1		Wi 60	24
Drafts and Drafting: Treadling As-Drawn-In	Creative Drafting and Analysis: Drafting Lesson 3	Zielinski, S. A.; Robert Leclerc, ed.	√	√	MWL	3			'51–'73	14
Drafts and Drafting: Treadling, Basic	Creative Drafting and Analysis: Drafting Lesson 4	Zielinski, S. A.; Robert Leclerc, ed.	√	√	MWL	3			'51–'73	17
Drafts and Drafting: Treadling Rose Fashion	Creative Drafting and Analysis: Drafting Lesson 4	Zielinski, S. A.; Robert Leclerc, ed.	√	√	MWL	3			'51–'73	17
Drafts and Drafting: Treadling Variations	Metamorphosis: Two-Tie Weaves and the Changeable Image	Carey, Joyce Marquess	√	>4	AT	1			De 83	243
Drafts and Drafting: True-Shed Loom	Fabrics from a New Type Multi-Harness Loom	Cory, Sue Armstrong	√	>4	H&C	10	1		Wi 59	24
Drafts and Drafting: Turned Drafts	Atwater-Bronson Lace — Turned		√	√	WJ	2	4	8	Ap 78	20
Drafts and Drafting: Turned Drafts	Composition and Designing: Pattern in Warp	Zielinski, S. A.; Robert Leclerc, ed.	√	√	MWL	18			'51–'73	79
Drafts and Drafting: Turned Drafts	Dimity Delight	Sullivan, Donna	√	>4	PWC	5	1	15		17
Drafts and Drafting: Turned Drafts	Drafting: A Personal Approach, Part 3	Alvic, Philis	√	>4	SS&D	13	3	51	Su 82	40
Drafts and Drafting: Turned Drafts	How One Weave Leads to Another	Barrett, Clotilde	√	>4	WJ	8	1	29	Su 83	75
Drafts and Drafting: Turned Drafts	Lithuanian Pervarai: Producing a Twenty Shaft Pattern on a Twelve Shaft Loom	Meek, M. Kati	√	>4	AT	1			De 83	159
Drafts and Drafting: Turned Drafts	Merry Christmas!	Barrett, Clotilde	√	>4	WJ	8	2	30	Fa 83	36
Drafts and Drafting: Turned Drafts	Mitered Corners	Sullivan, Donna	√	>4	SS&D	15	3	59	Su 84	82
Drafts and Drafting: Turned Drafts	Shadow Weave — Part 4. The Relationship Between Shadow Weave and Corkscrew Weave		√	>4	WJ	1	4	4	Ap 77	30
Drafts and Drafting: Turned Drafts	Some Experiments with Turned Drafts	Carter, Helen H.	√	>4	CW	5	2	14	Ja 84	3
Drafts and Drafting: Turned Drafts	Supplementary Warp Patterns		√	>4	WJ	2	3	7	Ja 78	26
Drafts and Drafting: Turned Drafts	Table Turned, The (error-corrected Hw v5 n3 84 p92)	Dobrovolny, Ardis	√	>4	Hw	5	1		J/F 84	64
Drafts and Drafting: Turned Drafts	Take Advantage of Turned Drafts	Moes, Dini	√	>4	SS&D	13	2	50	Sp 82	58
Drafts and Drafting: Turned Drafts	Turned Drafts	Wertenberger, Kathryn	√	>4	Hw	6	3		Su 85	90
Drafts and Drafting: Turned Drafts	Turned Drafts, A Useful Technique for Variety		√	√	H&C	19	3		Su 68	30
Drafts and Drafting: Turned Drafts	Turned Drafts in Double Two-Tie Unit Weave	van der Hoogt, Madelyn	√	>4	WJ	9	2	34	Fa 84	13
Drafts and Drafting: Turned Drafts	Turned Overshot	Rowley, Elaine; Alexis Yiorgos Xenakis	√	>4	PWC	3	2	8		53
Drafts and Drafting: Turned Drafts	Turned Summer and Winter Jacket	Johnson, Melinda Raber	√	>4	WJ	8	3	31	Wi 83	58
Drafts and Drafting: Turned Drafts	Warp-Faced Krokbragd	Jensen, Gay; Donna Kaplan	√	>4	WJ	12	2	46	Fa 87	62
Drafts and Drafting:Turned Drafts	Woven Lace and Lacey Weaves: Turned Lace for Eight Shafts	Zielinski, S. A.; Robert Leclerc, ed.	√	>4	MWL	13			'51–'73	45
Drafts and Drafting: Turned Drafts	Woven Lace and Lacey Weaves: Turned Lace for Four Frames	Zielinski, S. A.; Robert Leclerc, ed.	√	√	MWL	13			'51–'73	12
Drafts and Drafting: Turned Drafts, Crackle	Contemporary Approach to Traditional Weaves: Production Drafts-Four-Shaft Crackle in Warp	Zielinski, S. A.; Robert Leclerc, ed.	√	>4	MWL	8			'51–'73	60
Drafts and Drafting: Twill	If You Have Four Harnesses	Hagerty, Harriet May	√	√	H&C	26	1		J/F 75	24
Drafts and Drafting: Twill	Versatile Twill	Liebler, Barbara	√	√	lw	6	1		Wi 80	26
Drafts and Drafting: Twill, Block-Pattern Style	Seventeenth and Eighteenth Century Twills: The German Linen Tradition	Hilts, Patricia	√	>4	AT	3			My 85	139
Drafts and Drafting: Twill, Blocks	Huguenot Coverlets	Strickler, Carol	√	>4	WJ	1	2	2	Oc 76	8
Drafts and Drafting: Twill Blocks	New Multi-Harness Drawdown Technique, A	Salsbury, Nate	√	>4	lw	6	1		Wi 80	57

SUBJECT	TITLE	AUTHOR	IL	INST	JOUR	VOL	NO	ISS	DATE	PAGE
Drafts and Drafting: Twill, Broken	Seventeenth and Eighteenth Century Twills: The German Linen Tradition	Hilts, Patricia	√	>4	AT	3			My 85	139
Drafts and Drafting: Twill Derivatives	Multiple Harness Weaving Course Part 5. Twill Derivatives (continued)		√	>4	WJ	5	3	19	Wi 81	12
Drafts and Drafting: Twill, Diaper	Weaving Drafts and Diaper Twills in Lancaster County	Crosson, Janet Gray	√	>4	Iw	4	3		Su 79	40
Drafts and Drafting: Twill, Expanded	Undulating Twills	Carey, Joyce Marquess	√	>4	Iw	6	1		Wi 80	31
Drafts and Drafting: Twill, Free-Form	Freeform Twill & Freeform Searles Lace	Searles, Nancy	√	>4	CW		23		Ja 87	10
Drafts and Drafting: Twill, Herringbone	Fascination of Twills (Fourshafts): Twills-3	Zielinski, S. A.; Robert Leclerc, ed.	√	>4	MWL	9			'51–'73	17
Drafts and Drafting: Twill, Point	Seventeenth and Eighteenth Century Twills: The German Linen Tradition	Hilts, Patricia	√	>4	AT	3			My 85	139
Drafts and Drafting: Twill, Point, Double	Fascination of Twills (Fourshafts): Twills-3	Zielinski, S. A.; Robert Leclerc, ed.	√	>4	MWL	9			'51–'73	17
Drafts and Drafting: Twill, Point, Extended	Huguenot Coverlets	Strickler, Carol	√	>4	WJ	1	2	2	Oc 76	8
Drafts and Drafting: Twill Threading/Satin Tie-Up	Damask	Mudge, Christine	√	>4	Iw	6	1		Wi 80	46
Drafts and Drafting: Twill, Unit Structure, 2-Tie, Double	Twills in Double Two-Tie Unit Weave	van der Hoogt, Madelyn	√	>4	Hw	6	5		N/D 85	64
Drafts and Drafting: Two-Harness (Sets) Method	Little Known Weaves Worth Knowing Better: Two-Harness Method	Zielinski, S. A.; Robert Leclerc, ed.	√	>4	MWL	16			'51–'73	23
Drafts and Drafting: Two-Harness (Sets) System	Patterns Woven in Lace	Keasbey, Doramay	√	>4	CW	3	2	8	Ja 82	11
Drafts and Drafting: Two-Harness (Sets) Weaving	Double & Triple Harness Double-Cloth	Fabeck, Diane	√	>4	CW	7	3	21	My 86	7
Drafts and Drafting: Two-Harness (Sets) Weaving	Five Block Double Weave Using the Glimåkra Long Eyed Heddle Accessory	Tramba, Diane	√	>4	WJ	7	3	27	Wi 82	45
Drafts and Drafting: Two-Shaft Weaves	Very Basics of Weaving Drafting: Two and Three Shafts, The	Carey, Joyce Marquess	√	√	WJ	6	2	22	Fa 81	50
Drafts and Drafting: Two-Warp Technique	Hand Woven Rugs: Weaves, Two-Warp Weave, Eignt-Harness Patterns	Atwater, Mary Meigs	√	>4	SCGM		29		48	25
Drafts and Drafting: Two-Warp Technique	Hand Woven Rugs: Weaves, Two-Warp Weave, Four-Harness Patterns	Atwater, Mary Meigs	√	√	SCGM		29		48	24
Drafts and Drafting: Typewriter	Treasury for Beginners: Modernized Drafting	Zielinski, S. A.; Robert Leclerc, ed.	√	√	MWL	1			'51–'73	113
Drafts and Drafting: Undulating Warp Conversion	Undulating Weft Effects: The Drafts, Undulating Warp Conversion	Tidball, Harriet	√	>4	SCGM		9		63	19
Drafts and Drafting: Unit Blocks	How to Weave Your own Designs	Arnold, Ruth	√	>4	H&C	11	3		Su 60	6
Drafts and Drafting: Unit Structure	But What's the Tie-Up?	van der Hoogt, Madelyn	√	>4	PWC	5	1	15		36
Drafts and Drafting: Unit Structure	Deciphering Drafts	Keasbey, Doramay	√	>4	PWC	4	4	14		30
Drafts and Drafting: Unit Structure	Double Two-Tie System Applied to Overshot	Xenakis, Athanasios David	√	>4	PWC	3	3	9		7
Drafts and Drafting: Unit Structure	Even-Tied Overshot	Xenakis, Athanasios David	√	>4	PWC	3	3	9		40
Drafts and Drafting: Unit Structure	Introduction to Tied Unit Weaves, An	Kelly, Jacquie	√	>4	PWC	4	4	14		40
Drafts and Drafting: Unit Structure	Twill Derivative and Unit Classes	Wilson, Patricia	√	√	SS&D	3	3	11	Su 72	38
Drafts and Drafting: Unit Structure, 2-Tie	Bateman Blend Weaves: The Structures of the Bateman Blend System	Bateman, Dr. William G.; Virginia I. Harvey, ed.	√	>4	SCGM		36		82	14
Drafts and Drafting: Unit Structure, 2-Tie	S&W Wrapper	Sullivan, Donna	√	√	SS&D	15	1	57	Wi 83	24
Drafts and Drafting: Unit Structure, 2-Tie	Sixteen-Harness Beiderwand Coverlet	Hoskinson, Marian K.	√	>4	SS&D	14	4	56	Fa 83	19
Drafts and Drafting: Unit Structure, 2-Tie	Two-Tie Unit for Rugs: Part 1, The Double-Faced Stuffer Weave and Summer-and-Winter, The	Windeknecht, Margaret	√	>4	SS&D	16	1	61	Wi 84	82
Drafts and Drafting: Unit, Structure, 2-Tie	Two-Tie Unit for Rugs: Part 2 Warping and Weaving Methods, The	Windeknecht, Margaret	√	>4	SS&D	16	2	62	Sp 85	34
Drafts and Drafting: Unit Structure, 2-Tie, Double	Figured Piqué Patterning with the Double Two-Tie System (error-corrected PWC v4 n3 i13 p4)	Xenakis, Athanasios David; Patti Sellon	√	>4	PWC	4	2	12		20

SUBJECT	TITLE	AUTHOR	IL	INST	JOUR	VOL	NO	ISS	DATE	PAGE
Drafts and Drafting: Unit Structure, 2-Tie, Double	Planning Figured Piqué Designs on Pre-Marked Graph Paper	Xenakis, Athanasios David	√	> 4	PWC	4	2	12		16
Drafts and Drafting: Unit Structure, 3-Tie	Bateman Blend Weaves: The Structures of the Bateman Blend System	Bateman, Dr. William G.; Virginia I. Harvey, ed.	√	> 4	SCGM		36		82	14
Drafts and Drafting: Unit Structure, 4-Tie	Bateman Blend Weaves: The Structures of the Bateman Blend System	Bateman, Dr. William G.; Virginia I. Harvey, ed.	√	> 4	SCGM		36		82	14
Drafts and Drafting: Unit Structure, Uneven-Tied	Uneven-Tied Overshot	Searles, Nancy	√	> 4	PWC	3	4	10		14
Drafts and Drafting: Variations	Variations on a Draft	Marston, Ena	√	√	SS&D	3	1	9	Wi 71	13
Drafts and Drafting: Waffle Variations	Waffle Weave	Wertenberger, Kathryn	√	> 4	Hw	8	4		S/O 87	83
Drafts and Drafting: Weave Drafts	Composition and Designing: Designing New Fabrics	Zielinski, S. A.; Robert Leclerc, ed.	√	√	MWL	18			'51–'73	53
Drape/Hand	Notes on Designing for Drape	Veness, Tim	√		Hw	7	5		N/D 86	76
Draperies see Window Coverings										
Draping	Draping a Blouse	Sperry, Ellen	√	√	TM			3	F/M 86	46
Draw-Frame Device	Draw Frame Device	Jansons, Ilga	√	√	SS&D	10	4	40	Fa 79	90
Drawdowns	Tie Ups, Pegplans & Drawdowns		√	> 4	CW	8	1	22	Se 86	27
Drawdowns, Peg Plans, Tie-Ups	Tie Ups, Pegplans & Drawdowns		√	> 4	CW	8	1	22	Se 86	27
Drawdowns: Techniques	New Multi-Harness Drawdown Technique, A	Salsbury, Nate	√	> 4	Iw	6	1		Wi 80	57
Drawing/Painting	Beth Ames Swartz: A Painter's Way with Paper	Krapes, Shelley	√		Fa	9	4		J/A 82	19
Drawing/Painting	"Frank Gardner: Aleatory Works" (Exhibit)	Guagliumi, Susan	√		Fa	9	2		M/A 82	75
Drawing/Painting	Homage to Hats: Handmade Paper Drawing/Collages Honor a Women's Tradition	Rusoff, Beverly	√		Fa	8	1		J/F 81	80
Drawing/Painting	"Jan Wagstaff: Woven and Painted Canvas" (Exhibit)	Malarcher, Patricia	√		Fa	8	6		N/D 81	64
Drawing/Painting	"Jody Klein's Paper Quilts" (Exhibit)	Storey, Isabelle B.	√		Fa	8	6		N/D 81	70
Drawing/Painting	On the Edge: Betye Saar — Personal Time Travels	Woelfle, Gretchen Erskine	√		Fa	9	4		J/A 82	56
Drawing/Painting	On the Edge: Harmony Hammond — Collecting, Reclaiming, Connecting	Willard, Janice	√		Fa	9	4		J/A 82	58
Drawing/Painting	Resemblance to Afghans; Crochet Rubbings?, A	Elliott, Sally	√		Fa	8	3		M/J 81	48
Drawing/Painting	Saved Threads: Ellen Zahorec Explores Layers of Time		√		Fa	8	5		S/O 81	42
Drawing/Painting	Therese May: Moving Freely from Fabric to Paint and Back Again	Huffaker, Katherine	√		Fa	9	1		J/F 82	26
Drawing/Painting	Timeless Stitches: Myrna Shiras' Stitched Drawings	Schwartz, Joyce B.	√		Fa	8	3		M/J 81	65
Drawloom	Drawloom Textiles in Wool and Silk (with a Structural Analysis by Ann Pollard Rowe)	Trilling, James	√		TMJ	21			82	96
Drawloom: Construction and Adapting	Converting a 10-Shaft Drawloom to 25 Shafts	Hoyt, Peggy		√	CW	7	1	19	Se 85	3
Drawloom, Two-Harness (Sets) System	Penland's Damask Loom			√	H&C	6	3		Su 55	24
Drawloom, Two-Harness (Sets) System	Weaving Damask	Arnold, Ruth	√	> 4	H&C	6	3		Su 55	4
Drawloom Weaving	Additions to the Indonesian Collection	Gittinger, Mattiebelle S.	√		TMJ	4	3		76	43
Drawloom Weaving	Artisans from China Work Silken Magic	Steinhagen, Janice	√		TM			5	J/J 86	14
Drawloom Weaving	Banares Brocade	DuBois, Emily	√	> 4	AT	3			My 85	209
Drawloom Weaving	Chinese Brocades: Development of Supplementary Weft Patterning (error-corrected WJ v11 n4 87 p78)	Drooker, Penelope	√		WJ	11	3	43	Wi 87	47
Drawloom Weaving	Chinese Drawloom: A Study in Weave Structure, The	Sellin, Helen	√	> 4	WJ	9	2	34	Fa 84	6
Drawloom Weaving	Drawloom Basics	van der Hoogt, Madelyn	√	> 4	Hw	7	2		M/A 86	61
Drawloom Weaving	Drawloom Textiles in Wool and Silk (with a Structural Analysis by Ann Pollard Rowe)	Trilling, James	√		TMJ	21			82	96

SUBJECT	TITLE	AUTHOR	IL	INST	JOUR	VOL	NO	ISS	DATE	PAGE
Drawloom Weaving	How to Weave Your own Designs	Arnold, Ruth	√	> 4	H&C	11	3		Su 60	6
Drawloom Weaving	Kashmir or Paisley; Romance of the Shawl	Wilson, Kax	√		Iw	4	4		Fa 79	34
Drawloom Weaving	Newly Excavated Caftan from the Northern Caucasus, A	Riboud, Krishna	√		TMJ	4	3		76	21
Drawloom Weaving	Newly Excavated Caftan from the Northern Caucasus, A	Riboud, Krishna	√		TMJ	4	3		76	21
Drawloom Weaving	Original Fabrics of Kaftan, The	El-Homossani, M. M.	√	> 4	AT	1			De 83	263
Drawloom Weaving	Portfolio: Harriet Jenny		√		Hw	7	1		J/F 86	36
Drawloom Weaving (10-Pattern Shafts)	Display Towel (Astrid Sonesson)		√	> 4	Hw	8	3		M/J 87	43, I-4
Drawloom Weaving: Single-Thread Harness Pattern Weaving	Single Thread Harness Pattern Weaving	Fry, Laura	√	> 4	CW	5	1	13	Se 83	14
Drawloom Weaving, Split-Harness	Split-Harness Drawloom, The	Malloy, Kim, OSB	√	> 4	CW	2	1	4	Oc 80	3
Drawlooms, Comparative Analysis	Support System for Drawloom Weavers, A	van der Hoogt, Madelyn			CW	7	2	20	Ja 86	10
Drawn Threadwork	Drawn Threadwork	Duroy, Marie-Pierre	√	√	TM			8	D/J 86	41
Dreams, Mysteries, Visions	Theme Issue		√		Fa	7	3		M/J 80	
Dress Forms	Drafter, The Draper, The Flat Patternmaker, The	Nebesar, Rebecca Lanxner	√	√	TM			11	J/J 87	33
Dress Forms	Draping a Blouse	Sperry, Ellen	√	√	TM			3	F/M 86	46
Dress Forms: Source	Dress Forms			√	TM			11	J/J 87	11
Dresses and Gowns	Applying the Pulled Warp Technique to Loom-Shaped Clothing	Evans, Kerry	√	√	WJ	9	3	35	Wi 85	34
Dresses and Gowns	Balenciago: The Architect of Elegant Clothing	Koda, Harold	√		TM			11	J/J 87	20
Dresses and Gowns	Beautiful Fabric Is Not Enough	Lommen, Sandy	√	√	SS&D	15	2	58	Sp 84	40
Dresses and Gowns	Classic Dress, The	Hewson, Betty	√	√	Hw	5	3		Su 84	24
Dresses and Gowns	Contemporary Costume, Strictly Handwoven: A Dinner Dress	Tidball, Harriet	√	√	SCGM		24		68	22
Dresses and Gowns	Contemporary Costume, Strictly Handwoven: A Dress in Two Pieces	Tidball, Harriet	√	√	SCGM		24		68	18
Dresses and Gowns	Contemporary Costume, Strictly Handwoven: A Party Dress	Tidball, Harriet	√	√	SCGM		24		68	23
Dresses and Gowns	Contemporary Costume, Strictly Handwoven: A Sweater Dress	Tidball, Harriet	√	√	SCGM		24		68	39
Dresses and Gowns	Contemporary Costume, Strictly Handwoven: An Outdoor Dress	Tidball, Harriet	√	√	SCGM		24		68	36
Dresses and Gowns	Contemporary Costume, Strictly Handwoven: The Coat Dress	Tidball, Harriet	√	√	SCGM		24		68	17
Dresses and Gowns	Contemporary Costume, Strictly Handwoven: The Peter Pan Dress	Tidball, Harriet	√	√	SCGM		24		68	20
Dresses and Gowns	Contemporary Costume, Strictly Handwoven: The Tonya Rhodes Dress	Tidball, Harriet	√	√	SCGM		24		68	32
Dresses and Gowns	Contemporary Gown, Traditional Flavor	Linder, Olive	√	> 4	SS&D	6	3	23	Su 75	51
Dresses and Gowns	Design a Dress—On the Loom	Holland, Nina	√	√	SS&D	6	2	22	Sp 75	37
Dresses and Gowns	Designed for Narrow Looms	Jennings, Lucy Anne	√	√	WJ	11	1	41	Su 86	26
Dresses and Gowns	Dress for a Summer Day (Helen Moseley Gant)		√	√	Hw	3	2		Mr 82	52
Dresses and Gowns	Dress (size 14) Shaped on Loom (size 24")	Roth, Bettie	√	√	SS&D	3	1	9	Wi 71	17
Dresses and Gowns	Fashion Show of Handwoven Garments		√	> 4	WJ	3	3	11	Ja 79	5
Dresses and Gowns	From the Collection of Anne Poussart		√	√	WJ	7	3	27	Wi 82	62
Dresses and Gowns	Garments Win At 1974 Midwest Conference		√	√	SS&D	6	2	22	Sp 75	92
Dresses and Gowns	Garments with Ethnic Flavor: Blue and White Twill Dress		√	√	WJ	2	3	7	Ja 78	18
Dresses and Gowns	Garments with Ethnic Flavor: Dress Inspired by the American Southwest		√	√	WJ	2	3	7	Ja 78	17
Dresses and Gowns	Garments with Ethnic Flavor: Ethnic Dress with Supplementary Warp		√	√	WJ	2	3	7	Ja 78	14

SUBJECT	TITLE	AUTHOR	IL	INST	JOUR	VOL	NO	ISS	DATE	PAGE
Dresses and Gowns	Garments with Ethnic Flavor: Mexican Embroidery Combined with Handwoven Yardage		√	> 4	WJ	2	3	7	Ja 78	17
Dresses and Gowns	Greek Chemises: Cut and Construction	Welters, Linda	√	√	WJ	10	1	37	Su 85	40
Dresses and Gowns	Handwoven Silk Garments: Blue Silk Dress	Alvic, Philis	√	> 4	WJ	3	2	10	Oc 78	27
Dresses and Gowns	Handwoven Silk Garments: Ikat Dress	Schreiber, LaVonne	√	√	WJ	3	2	10	Oc 78	30
Dresses and Gowns	How Madame Grès Sculpts with Fabric	Cooper, Arlene	√	√	TM			10	A/M 87	50
Dresses and Gowns	Icicle Dress (Mary McGuinness)		√	√	Hw	8	1		J/F 87	45, I-4
Dresses and Gowns	Jewel Dress (Betty Beard)		√	√	Hw	6	3		Su 85	46, I-8
Dresses and Gowns	Karellian Red Pick Dress (Miranda Howard)		√	√	Hw	2	5		No 81	36, 90
Dresses and Gowns	Lacey and Thin Fabrics		√	√	WJ	2	3	7	Ja 78	4
Dresses and Gowns	Leno Dress (Emily Law)		√	√	Hw	8	1		J/F 87	44, I-5
Dresses and Gowns	Little Blue Dress, A	Dobsevage, David	√	√	TM			7	O/N 86	58
Dresses and Gowns	Marvelous Mistake, A	Cramer, Pauline E.	√	√	SS&D	17	1	65	Wi 85	34
Dresses and Gowns	Michigan Weaving, Third Conference at Hartland Shows Wide Variety		√	√	H&C	13	1		Wi 62	18
Dresses and Gowns	Olive Dress (Jean Scorgie)		√	> 4	Hw	7	5		N/D 86	44, I-3
Dresses and Gowns	Orange Gown Has Brass Trim	Dickinson, Hattie K.	√	√	SS&D	3	4	12	Fa 72	33
Dresses and Gowns	Paired-Thread Finnweave Projects: The Gaza Dress, The	Xenakis, Alexis, Yiorgos	√	√	PWC			2	Ap 82	40
Dresses and Gowns	Panel Dress, A	Juve, Peggy	√	√˙	TM			12	A/S 87	29
Dresses and Gowns	Prize-Winning Gown and Coat	Fair, Maurine	√	> 4	SS&D	2	2	6	Sp 71	16
Dresses and Gowns	Promise Kept, A	Moes, Dini	√	√	SS&D	16	3	63	Su 85	63
Dresses and Gowns	Sea Crystal Dress (Vicki Tardy)		√	> 4	Hw	8	2		M/A 87	55, I-11
Dresses and Gowns	Seattle Guild Garment Designs, Part 4: Edges, Closures, Capes and Dresses		√	√	SS&D	11	2	42	Sp 80	39
Dresses and Gowns	Seersucker Dress (Sharon Alderman)		√	√	Hw	4	3		M/J 83	42, 79
Dresses and Gowns	Shaped Silk Sheath	Xenakis, Athanasios David; Alexis Yiorgos Xenakis	√	√	PWC			6	Su 83	39
Dresses and Gowns	Space-Dented Warp	Fry, Laura	√	√	WJ	4	3	15	Ja 80	26
Dresses and Gowns	Sprang and Frame Plaiting for Garments		√	√	WJ	3	3	11	Ja 79	26
Dresses and Gowns	Summertime!	Coifman, Lucienne	√	√	SS&D	15	3	59	Su 84	74
Dresses and Gowns	Supplementary Warp Patterning: Dresses Styled From Warp Pattern Fabrics	Tidball, Harriet	√	> 4	SCGM		17		66	31
Dresses and Gowns	Taste of Honey(comb), A	Rasmussen, Peg	√	√	SS&D	16	2	62	Sp 85	6
Dresses and Gowns	Textured Cottons: Dress and Sauna Robe	Henrikson, Sue	√	> 4	WJ	6	3	23	Wi 81	20
Dresses and Gowns	Tucked Dress and Toddler Blouse (Kathryn Wertenberger and Nancy Kuwabara)		√	√	Hw	4	2		M/A 83	63, 100
Dresses and Gowns	Twilight Dress (Mary Kay Stoehr)		√	√	Hw	7	3		M/J 86	51, I-12
Dresses and Gowns	Two Summer Dresses on One Warp (Ritva MacLeod)		√	√	Hw	5	3		Su 84	55, 100
Dresses and Gowns	Warm and Wooly: Cloud-soft Dress		√	√	Hw	1	1		F-W 79	26
Dresses and Gowns	Wasteless, Waistless Dress. A	Holtzer, Marilyn F.	√	√	Hw	2	3		My 81	85
Dresses and Gowns	Wear Your Best Apron	MacNutt, Dawn	√	√	SS&D	8	4	32	Fa 77	65
Dresses and Gowns	Wearing Handwovens with Style	Mayer, Anita	√	√	WJ	10	3	39	Wi 86	22
Dresses and Gowns	Weaver Who Wastes Not, A	Porcella, Yvonne	√	√	SS&D	6	4	24	Fa 75	8
Dresses and Gowns	Weaving the Night Fantastic	Lyon, Linda	√	> 4	PWC			5	Sp 83	51
Dresses and Gowns	Weddding Dress, My	Caliendo, Karen	√		Hw	5	5		N/D 84	76
Dresses and Gowns	Wedding Dress (Lise Haugh)		√	√	Hw	1	2		S-S 80	35, 64
Dresses and Gowns	Yosemite Dress Inspired by Snow and Sugar Pines	Durr, Judy	√		SS&D	5	3	19	Su 74	20
Dresses and Gowns: Inaugural	Martha Washington's Inaugural Gown	Reams, Dorothy E.	√		SS&D	7	3	27	Su 76	15
Dresses and Gowns: Weddding	Three Adventures of a Wedding Dress	Chapin, Doloria	√	√	SS&D	4	3	15	Su 73	51

SUBJECT	TITLE	AUTHOR	IL	INST	JOUR	VOL	NO	ISS	DATE	PAGE
Dresses and Gowns: Wedding	Balenciago: The Architect of Elegant Clothing	Koda, Harold	√		TM			11	J/J 87	20
Dresses and Gowns: Wedding	Handspun Wedding Gown, A	Anderson, Arlene	√	√	S-O	8	4		Wi 84	13
Dresses and Gowns: Wedding	Handwoven Silk Garments: A Wedding Dress	Best, Eleanor	√	√	WJ	3	2	10	Oc 78	28
Dresses and Gowns: Wedding	Heirloom Wedding Dress	Ellman, Norma	√	√	Kn	3	2	6	Sp 87	31
Dresses, Draped-Pattern Method	Drafter, The Draper, The Flat Patternmaker, The	Nebesar, Rebecca Lanxner	√	√	TM			11	J/J 87	33
Dressing Loom	Handweaver's Instruction Manual: Dressing the Loom, Chain Warping	Tidball, Harriet C. nee Douglas	√	√	SCGM		34		49	13
Dressing Loom	Vertical Loom, The		√	√	WJ	1	3	3	Ja 77	16
Dressing Loom	Weaving a Cotton Saddlebag on the Santa Elena Peninsula of Ecuador	Hagino, Jane Parker; Karen E. Stothert	√	√	TMJ	22			83	19
Dressing Loom	What a Handweaver Can Learn from the Scottish Weaving Industry (error-corrected WJ v2 n1 77 insert for vol. 1)	Barrett, Clotilde	√	√	WJ	1	3	3	Ja 77	11
Dressing Loom: Navajo	Vertical Loom (continued) Part 3, The Navajo Loom, The		√	√	WJ	2	2	6	Oc 77	23
Dressing Loom: Warp-Weighted	Vertical Loom (continued) — Construction of a Warp Weighted Loom, The		√	√	WJ	1	4	4	Ap 77	27
Dressing Up	Theme Issue		√		Fa	14	3		M/J 87	
Drop-Turnover Repeat	Composition and Designing Part 2: Drop-Turnover Repeat	Zielinski, S. A.; Robert Leclerc, ed.	√	√	MWL	19			'51–'73	87
Dropped Weaves: Plain Weave	Little Known Weaves Worth Knowing Better: Dropped Weaves	Zielinski, S. A.; Robert Leclerc, ed.	√	> 4	MWL	16			'51–'73	11
Dropped Weaves: Twill	Little Known Weaves Worth Knowing Better: Dropped Weaves	Zielinski, S. A.; Robert Leclerc, ed.	√	> 4	MWL	16			'51–'73	15
Drycleaning Agents (List): Solvents and Detergents	Principles of Textile Conservation Science, No. 8. Drycleaning of Fine and Fragile Textiles	Rice, James W.	√	√	TMJ	2	2		De 67	21
Drycleaning Systems: Textile	Principles of Textile Conservation Science, No. 8. Drycleaning of Fine and Fragile Textiles	Rice, James W.	√	√	TMJ	2	2		De 67	21
Drycleaning: Textiles	Principles of Textile Conservation Science, No. 8. Drycleaning of Fine and Fragile Textiles	Rice, James W.	√	√	TMJ	2	2		De 67	21
Drying Frames	Woolly Boards		√		Kn	2	1	3	F-W 85	16
Drying Tenter	What a Handweaver Can Learn from the Scottish Weaving Industry (error-corrected WJ v2 n1 77 errata sheet for vol. 1)	Barrett, Clotilde	√	√	WJ	1	3	3	Ja 77	11
Dubbelmossa	Dubbelmossa	Adams, Harriet	√	√	Kn	2	1	3	F-W 85	50, 8B
Dukagång	Decorative Weft on a Plain Weave Ground, Two Shaft Inlay and Brocade		√	√	WJ	5	4	20	Sp 81	15
Dukagång	Dunkagäng Ideas		√		Hw	7	2		M/A 86	44
Dukagång	Dunkagäng, the Stuff of Hearts and Flowers	Alderman, Sharon	√	√	Hw	7	2		M/A 86	41
Dukagång	Enlarged Patterns: A Fresh Look at Old Techniques	McClelland, Patricia Polett	√	> 4	WJ	7	4	28	Sp 83	68
Dukagång	Happy Dress	Sprenger, Elserine	√	√	WJ	8	3	31	Wi 83	46
Dukagång	Loom Shaped Top with Dukagång Inlay	Searle, Karen	√	√	WJ	11	3	43	Wi 87	8
Dukagång	Technique is Dukagang	Teilmann, Nina	√	√	SS&D	3	3	11	Su 72	22
Dukagång	Traditional Dukagång for Contemporary Textiles		√	√	Hw	8	3		M/J 87	57
Dukagång	Traditional Ways with Dunkagäng	Post, Margaret	√	√	Hw	7	2		M/A 86	42
Dukagång	Why Not Try Embroidery Weaves?	Jones, Jeanetta L.	√	√	H&C	17	2		Sp 66	12
Dukagång, Half-	Inlay Techniques	Barrett, Clotilde	√	√	WJ	1	1	1	Jy 76	3
Dukagång, Half–	Inlay We Trust, Part 1: Half Dukagång	Herring, Connie	√	√	PWC			5	Sp 83	59
Dukagång, Half-	Springtime Curtains (Margaretha Essén-Hedin)		√	√	Hw	5	3		Su 84	72, 117

SUBJECT	TITLE	AUTHOR	IL	INST	JOUR	VOL	NO	ISS	DATE	PAGE
Dukagång, Half-	Turned Drafts in Double Two-Tie Unit Weave	van der Hoogt, Madelyn	√	> 4	WJ	9	2	34	Fa 84	13
Dye Analyses: Technique	Turkish Carpet with Spots and Stripes, A	Mackie, Louise W.	√		TMJ	4	3		76	4
Dye Painting	Lenore Davis: Dye Painted Soft Sculpture		√	√	Fa	5	1		J/F 78	68
Dye Plant Garden	Planting a Dye Garden	Magoffin, Connie	√	√	WJ	10	2	38	Fa 85	36
Dye Plants	Ann Bliss: Writing a Book About Her Friends		√		Fa	3	5		S/O 76	15
Dye Plants	Bindweeds	Bliss, Anne	√	√	Hw	6	5		N/D 85	86
Dye Plants	Considerations in the Selection and Application of Natural Dyes: Dye-plant Selection (error-corrected SS&D v12 n4 81 p8)	Crews, Patricia	√	√	SS&D	12	3	47	Su 81	52
Dye Plants	Dandelion Dye and Other Delights	Bliss, Anne	√	√	lw	2	3		Sp 77	22
Dye Plants	Dye Garden	Walbridge, T.		√	SS&D	8	2	30	Sp 77	63
Dye Plants	Dyer's Garden Is Feature of Landscape Plan	Kramer, Jack	√	√	SS&D	4	4	16	Fa 73	35
Dye Plants	Dyes of Early Tartans, The		√		Hw	4	5		N/D 83	75
Dye Plants	Grow Your Own Colors: Plant A Dye Garden (error-corrected S-O v11 n2 '87 p7)	Buchanan, Rita	√	√	S-O	11	1		Sp 87	35
Dye Plants	Lovely Dyes from Rank Weeds	Bliss, Anne	√		lw	3	4		Su 78	38
Dye Plants	Prairie Plants: Natives and Immigrants	Bliss, Anne	√	√	Hw	3	4		Se 82	74
Dye Plants	Spring Greens (make more than green!)	Bliss, Anne	√	√	Hw	3	2		Mr 82	69
Dye Plants	Textile Fiber and Dye Garden		√		H&C	10	2		Sp 59	23
Dye Plants	This Year, Plan and Plant a Dye Patch	Bliss, Anne	√	√	lw	2	2		Wi 77	28
Dye Plants	This Year, Plan and Plant a Dye Patch	Bliss, Anne	√	√	lw	2	2		Wi 77	28
Dye Plants	Thistles	Bliss, Anne	√	√	Hw	7	1		J/F 86	84
Dye Plants	Woad: A Medieval Dye	Austin, Carol	√		Fa	13	3		M/J 86	29
Dye Plants: Poisonous	Poisonous Dye Plants	Ellis, Jennie Faye		√	SS&D	4	2	14	Sp 73	46
Dyeing Basketry Materials	Confetti Basketry	Brown, Sally	√	√	SS&D	18	3	71	Su 87	9
Dyeing Cloth	Summer Shades	Koster, Joan Bouza	√	√	SS&D	18	3	71	Su 87	40
Dyeing Cotton	Dyed Cotton Rug in Overshot	Wright, Gilbert	√	√	WJ	7	4	28	Sp 83	81
Dyeing Cotton	Dyeing with Fiber Reactive Dyes on Cotton	Read, Kay	√	√	WJ	4	2	14	Oc 79	42
Dyeing Cotton	Mineral Dyes 2, The	Liles, James N.	√	√	SS&D	13	4	52	Fa 82	60
Dyeing Cotton	Mineral Dyes, The	Liles, James N.	√	√	SS&D	13	3	51	Su 82	54
Dyeing Cotton	Putting the King in the Pot	Bliss, Anne	√	√	lw	1	4		Su 76	20
Dyeing Cotton Lint	Dyeing and Spinning Cotton Lint	Linder, Harry; Olive Linder	√	√	SS&D	10	2	38	Sp 79	62
Dyeing Easter Eggs	Easter Fun!		√	√	Hw	1	2		S-S 80	39
Dyeing Fabric	Dyeing by the Yard	Bliss, Anne	√		lw	5	2		Sp 80	60
Dyeing Fabric	Rapport with Fabric and Dye: Kiyomi Iwata, A	Malarcher, Pat	√		Fa	7	1		J/F 80	28
Dyeing Fabric, Piece-Dyed	Dyeing by the Yard	Bliss, Anne	√		lw	5	2		Sp 80	60
Dyeing Fabric, Space-Dyed	Dyeing by the Yard	Bliss, Anne	√		lw	5	2		Sp 80	60
Dyeing Fabric, Yarn-Dyed	Dyeing by the Yard	Bliss, Anne	√		lw	5	2		Sp 80	60
Dyeing Flax	Maori and Pakeha of New Zealand Use Wool and Phormium Tenax	Duncan, Molly	√	√	SS&D	5	1	17	Wi 73	65
Dyeing Fleece	Rainbow Fleece: A Happy Hazard Approach to Chemical Dyeing	Lorance, Marilyn	√	√	Hw	2	4		Se 81	68
Dyeing Fleece, Handspun	Dyeing by the Yard	Bliss, Anne	√		lw	5	2		Sp 80	60
Dyeing Linen	Chemical Dyeing of Linen	Gwynne, Elaine	√	√	WJ	7	2	26	Fa 82	23
Dyeing Linen	History of Linen, A	Mattera, Joanne	√	√	SS&D	8	3	31	Su 77	16
Dyeing Linen	Mineral Dyes 2, The	Liles, James N.	√	√	SS&D	13	4	52	Fa 82	60
Dyeing Linen	Mineral Dyes, The	Liles, James N.	√	√	SS&D	13	3	51	Su 82	54
Dyeing Paper Pulp	Personal Exploration of Indigo, A	Miller, Dorothy	√	√	Fa	13	5		S/O 86	32
Dyeing Reed	Twill Woven Market Basket	Daugherty, Robin Taylor	√	√	Hw	6	1		J/F 85	80

SUBJECT	TITLE	AUTHOR	IL	INST	JOUR	VOL	NO	ISS	DATE	PAGE
Dyeing Silk	Art of Silk Dyeing, The (Photo-corrections WJ v10 n3 86 p6)	Wipplinger, Michelle	√	√	WJ	10	2	38	Fa 85	46
Dyeing Silk	Dye! Silk!		√	√	Hw	4	1		J/F 83	48
Dyeing Silk	Fixing to Dye: Confessions of a Silk Addict	Lapin, Claudia	√	√	Fa	5	1		J/F 78	30
Dyeing Silk	Handwoven Silk Garments: Ikat Dress	Schreiber, LaVonne	√	√	WJ	3	2	10	Oc 78	30
Dyeing Silk	Handwoven Silk Garments: Ikat Kimono	Barnett-Westfall, Lynn	√	√	WJ	3	2	10	Oc 78	30
Dyeing Silk	Handwoven Silk Garments: Ikat Shirt	Utzinger, Karen	√	√	WJ	3	2	10	Oc 78	29
Dyeing Silk	How to Dye and Starch Silk	Bromberg, Kay	√	√	WJ	5	1	17	Su 80	43
Dyeing Silk	Introduction to Silk Dyeing, An	Walsh, Joan Lea		√	WJ	3	2	10	Oc 78	14
Dyeing Silk	Natural Dyeing of Silk Fiber	Kolander, Cheryl	√	√	SS&D	9	2	34	Sp 78	58
Dyeing Silk	Production Dyeing with Natural Dyes	Van Stralen, Trudy	√	√	S-O	11	4		Wi 87	57
Dyeing Silk	Silk	Chadwick, A.	√	√	WJ	3	2	10	Oc 78	6
Dyeing Silk	Silk and Fiber Reactive Dyes		√	√	WJ	3	2	10	Oc 78	24
Dyeing Silk	Silk Dyeing		√	√	WJ	3	2	10	Oc 78	21
Dyeing Silk	Silk: Spinner's Luxury		√	√	Hw	5	4		S/O 84	85
Dyeing Silk	Tips for Dyeing Silk	Bliss, Anne		√	Hw	7	1		J/F 86	61
Dyeing Wool	Mineral Dyes, The	Liles, James N.	√	√	SS&D	13	3	51	Su 82	54
Dyeing Wool	Production Dyeing with Natural Dyes	Van Stralen, Trudy	√	√	S-O	11	4		Wi 87	57
Dyeing Wool	Recent Success of Carole Lubove-Klein: An Inspiring Yarn, The	McGuire, Patricia	√		Fa	9	5		S/O 82	20
Dyeing Wool/Non-Wool Blends	Dyeing of Wool Blends	Mayer, Francis	√	√	WJ	2	4	8	Ap 78	26
Dyes and Dyeing	American Sojourn of African Textiles, An	Lonier, Terri	√		Fa	11	1		J/F 84	66
Dyes and Dyeing	Ann Bliss: Writing a Book About Her Friends		√		Fa	3	5		S/O 76	15
Dyes and Dyeing	Building Your Own Steam Cabinet	Yannie, Barbara	√	√	Fa	5	1		J/F 78	32
Dyes and Dyeing	Casting Shadows: The Work of Pam Scheinman	Scheinman, Pam	√		Fa	5	1		J/F 78	60
Dyes and Dyeing	Color and Dyeing	Tidball, Harriet			SCGM		16		65	1-54
Dyes and Dyeing	Cracked, Pots, Snaggled Skeins and Other Dyeing Dilemmas	Bliss, Anne	√	√	Hw	2	5		No 81	68
Dyes and Dyeing	Excellence of Spinning, Vitality of Dyes Impress Visitor to 'Down Under'	Barker, Mary	√		SS&D	4	4	16	Fa 73	46
Dyes and Dyeing	Gioanventura Rosetti and His Dye Book—1548 A. D.	Bliss, Anne	√		Iw	3	1		Fa 77	36
Dyes and Dyeing	Hand-Painted Silk	Jaffie, H. R.	√		Fa	10	5		S/O 83	17
Dyes and Dyeing	How Fast is the Color?	Bliss, Anne	√	√	Hw	5	2		M/A 84	16
Dyes and Dyeing	Mary Frances Davidson: A Tribute	Pilsk, Adele	√		Fa	5	1		J/F 78	58
Dyes and Dyeing	"Master Dyers to the World" (Exhibit)	Sider, Sandra	√		Fa	11	1		J/F 84	83
Dyes and Dyeing	"Michael Olszewski: Pleated and Stitched Silk" (Exhibit)	Poon, Vivian	√		Fa	11	3		M/J 84	78
Dyes and Dyeing	Mixing and Matching Colors in Dyeing	Lucey, Edmund A.	√		H&C	2	3		Su 51	26
Dyes and Dyeing	Paper Clothing, East	Sahlstrand, Margaret	√	√	Fa	11	2		M/A 84	36
Dyes and Dyeing	Personal Exploration of Indigo, A	Miller, Dorothy	√	√	Fa	13	5		S/O 86	32
Dyes and Dyeing	Ruth Anderson, Custom Dyer	Kline, Michael	√		Fa	9	5		S/O 82	27
Dyes and Dyeing	Sampler of Surface Design, A	Westphal, Katherine	√		Fa	10	5		S/O 83	39
Dyes and Dyeing	Siminoff	Weigle, Palmy			SS&D	1	3	3	Ju 70	20
Dyes and Dyeing	Theme Issue		√		Fa	5	1		J/F 78	
Dyes and Dyeing	Virginia Davis	Malarcher, Patricia	√		Fa	10	5		S/O 83	14
Dyes and Dyeing	"Weaver's Life, Ethel Mairet, 1872–1952, A" (Exhibit)	Waller, Irene	√		Fa	11	4		J/A 84	78
Dyes and Dyeing: 17th Century	Some Remarks on the Work of Markham	Stanton, R. G.; J. L. Allston	√	√	AT	2			De 84	95
Dyes and Dyeing: Airbrush	Cindy Owings: Applying Dyes with an Airbrush		√	√	Fa	5	1		J/F 78	66
Dyes and Dyeing: Ancient Dyes	Peru, Textiles Unlimited: Textile Characteristics, Dyes	Tidball, Harriet	√		SCGM		25		68	20

SUBJECT	TITLE	AUTHOR	IL	INST	JOUR	VOL	NO	ISS	DATE	PAGE
Dyes and Dyeing: Cellulose Fibers	Dyeing with Fiber Reactive Dyes on Cotton	Read, Kay	√	√	WJ	4	2	14	Oc 79	42
Dyes and Dyeing: Chemical	Acid Dyeing	Kormos, Antonia	√	√	SS&D	15	2	58	Sp 84	34
Dyes and Dyeing: Chemical	Acid Dyes, Part 1, The	Koehler, Glory Dail		√	SS&D	6	3	23	Su 75	53
Dyes and Dyeing: Chemical	Acid Dyes, Part 2, The	Koehler, Glory Dail		√	SS&D	6	4	24	Fa 75	78
Dyes and Dyeing: Chemical	Bouquet of Shawls, A	Templeton, Peg	√	√	Hw	5	3		Su 84	75
Dyes and Dyeing: Chemical	Chemical Dyeing of Linen	Gwynne, Elaine	√	√	WJ	7	2	26	Fa 82	23
Dyes and Dyeing: Chemical	Chemical Dyeing, Part 2	Koehler, Glory Dail		√	SS&D	6	2	22	Sp 75	59
Dyes and Dyeing: Chemical	Chemical Dyeing: Preparation, Part 1	Koehler, Glory Dail		√	SS&D	6	1	21	Wi 74	70
Dyes and Dyeing: Chemical	Color and Dyeing: Chemicals Used in Dyeing	Tidball, Harriet		√	SCGM		16		65	15
Dyes and Dyeing: Chemical	Color and Dyeing: Dyeing Animal Fibers and Nylon with Benzyl Dyes	Tidball, Harriet		√	SCGM		16		65	31
Dyes and Dyeing: Chemical	Color and Dyeing: Dyeing Vegetable Fibers and Rayon with Chlorantine Dyes	Tidball, Harriet		√	SCGM		16		65	32
Dyes and Dyeing: Chemical	Color and Dyeing: The Dyes	Tidball, Harriet		√	SCGM		16		65	13
Dyes and Dyeing: Chemical	Color Control	Siminoff		√	SS&D	2	4	8	Fa 71	33
Dyes and Dyeing: Chemical	Commercial Dyes for Handweaving	Lucey, Edmund A.			H&C	1	3		Fa 50	54
Dyes and Dyeing: Chemical	Conflict Resolved: The Hows and Whys of Hand-Dyed Relief Painting, A	Kroetsch, Glenn	√		Fa	8	4		J/A 81	13
Dyes and Dyeing: Chemical	Dip Dyeing	Hausner, Walter	√	√	H&C	22	2		Sp 71	12
Dyes and Dyeing: Chemical	Direct Dyes	Koehler, Glory Dail	√	√	SS&D	7	3	27	Su 76	88
Dyes and Dyeing: Chemical	Dye! Silk!		√	√	Hw	4	1		J/F 83	48
Dyes and Dyeing: Chemical	Dye-Recipe Query			√	TM			5	J/J 86	4
Dyes and Dyeing: Chemical	Dyed Cotton Rug in Overshot	Wright, Gilbert	√	√	WJ	7	4	28	Sp 83	81
Dyes and Dyeing: Chemical	Dyeing and Spinning Cotton Lint	Linder, Harry; Olive Linder	√	√	SS&D	10	2	38	Sp 79	62
Dyes and Dyeing: Chemical	Dyeing with Fiber Reactive Dyes on Cotton	Read, Kay	√	√	WJ	4	2	14	Oc 79	42
Dyes and Dyeing: Chemical	Dyeing with the Direct or Substantive Colors	Lucey, Edmund A.		√	H&C	2	1		Wi 50	52
Dyes and Dyeing: Chemical	Dyes for Painting Warps	Bliss, Anne	√	√	Hw	5	4		S/O 84	65
Dyes and Dyeing: Chemical	Fiber Reactive Dyes	Ridgeway, Teresa	√	√	SS&D	13	1	49	Wi 81	34
Dyes and Dyeing: Chemical	Fullus: Ikat Blankets of Tarabuco, Bolivia	Meisch, Lynn A.	√	√	WJ	10	1	37	Su 85	54
Dyes and Dyeing: Chemical	Getting Started with Chemical Dyes	Knutson, Linda	√	√	S-O	8	3		Fa 84	39
Dyes and Dyeing: Chemical	Introduction for the Use of Procion Dyes	Wight, James	√		Fa	3	1		J/F 76	11
Dyes and Dyeing: Chemical	Little Dye Makes the Difference, A	Henrikson, Susan	√	√	Hw	4	2		M/A 83	60
Dyes and Dyeing: Chemical	Multi-Color, One Pot Dyeing	Henrikson, Susan	√	√	WJ	8	4	32	Sp 84	39
Dyes and Dyeing: Chemical	Notes on Color Fastness	Hausner, Walter	√	√	H&C	10	2		Sp 59	46
Dyes and Dyeing: Chemical	Painting and Brocading on the Loom	Ziek, Bhakti	√	√	TM			6	A/S 86	42
Dyes and Dyeing: Chemical	Procion M: The Thick and the Thin	Deschamps, Kalli	√	√	Iw	3	4		Su 78	40
Dyes and Dyeing: Chemical	Rainbow Dyeing	Rowe, Erica	√	√	WJ	8	2	30	Fa 83	31
Dyes and Dyeing: Chemical	Shigeki and Shihoko Fukumoto: Balancing Art and Function	Lancaster, Zöe Woodruff	√		Fa	13	6		N/D 86	5
Dyes and Dyeing: Chemical	Sky Celebration	Mayer, Anita Luvera	√	√	S-O	11	2		Su 87	36
Dyes and Dyeing: Chemical	Space Dyeing with Fiber-Reactive Dyes	Knutson, Linda	√	√	WJ	8	1	29	Su 83	89
Dyes and Dyeing: Chemical	Spinning Mohair in Lesotho	Snieckus, Mary Ann	√		TM			8	D/J 86	66
Dyes and Dyeing: Chemical	Spray Dyeing to Obtain Space-Dyed Yarns	Shapiro, Brenda	√	√	SS&D	15	4	60	Fa 84	54
Dyes and Dyeing: Chemical	Sprinkle, Dump and Dapple	Rabinowe, Victoria	√	√	SS&D	4	3	15	Su 73	55
Dyes and Dyeing: Chemical	Summer Shades	Koster, Joan Bouza	√	√	SS&D	18	3	71	Su 87	40
Dyes and Dyeing: Chemical	Sweater of Many Colors, A	McIntee, Polly	√	√	S-O	11	2		Su 87	15
Dyes and Dyeing: Chemical	Using Procion Dyes	Stetson, G. Robert	√	√	Iw	3	3		Sp 78	31
Dyes and Dyeing: Chemical	Vat Dyes	Koehler, Glory Dail		√	SS&D	8	1	29	Wi 76	37
Dyes and Dyeing: Chemical	Why Bother with Natural Dyeing?	Bulbach, Stanley	√	√	TM			5	J/J 86	32
Dyes and Dyeing: Chemical	Wool Dyed the Procion Way	Windeknecht, Margaret B.	√	√	SS&D	6	4	24	Fa 75	89

SUBJECT	TITLE	AUTHOR	IL	INST	JOUR	VOL	NO	ISS	DATE	PAGE
Dyes and Dyeing: Chemical, Cold-Water	Resist Dyeing, Curiosities and Inventions: Resist Dyeing	Zielinski, S. A.; Robert Leclerc, ed.			MWL	17			'51–'73	7
Dyes and Dyeing: Chemical, Dye Mixing	Creative Dyeing	Bachman, Sally	√	√	Iw	3	3		Sp 78	26
Dyes and Dyeing: Chemical, Dye Mixing	Personal Color System for Dyers, A	La Lena, Connie	√	√	Iw	3	3		Sp 78	20
Dyes and Dyeing: Chemistry	Some Preliminary Chemistry for Dyers	Viditz-Ward, Anton	√	√	Iw	3	3		Sp 78	29
Dyes and Dyeing: Colorant Molecular Structure	Principles of Textile Conservation Science, No. 4. The Conservation of Historical Textile Colorants	Rice, James W.	√	√	TMJ	1	2		De 63	55
Dyes and Dyeing: Colorant Testing Methods	Principles of Textile Conservation Science, No. 4. The Conservation of Historical Textile Colorants	Rice, James W.	√	√	TMJ	1	2		De 63	55
Dyes and Dyeing: Colors	Centroid Colors, The	Bliss, Anne	√	√	Iw	5	4		Fa 80	56
Dyes and Dyeing: Commercial	Color Forecasting	Dyett, Linda	√		TM			3	F/M 86	22
Dyes and Dyeing: Cross Dyeing	Color and Dyeing: Dyeing Variations	Tidball, Harriet		√	SCGM		16		65	37
Dyes and Dyeing: Custom	Dyeing to Order	Henrikson, Sue	√		Hw	3	3		My 82	45
Dyes and Dyeing: Dip-Dyeing	Passion for Elegance: Master Dyer Marian Clayden Creates Clothing by Listening to the Fabric, A	Levine, Betsy	√	√	TM			14	D/J 87	36
Dyes and Dyeing: Dip-Dyeing	Resist Dyeing, Curiosities and Inventions: Kasuri on Inkle Loom	Zielinski, S. A.; Robert Leclerc, ed.	√	√	MWL	17			'51–'73	39
Dyes and Dyeing: Dipping	Ikats of Joan Hausrath: A Painterly Approach to Weaving, The	Dunn, Roger T.	√		Fa	8	6		N/D 81	48
Dyes and Dyeing: Dye Kit	Boxed Rainbows: What to Do with a Dye Kit	Bliss, Anne	√	√	Hw	4	2		M/A 83	68
Dyes and Dyeing: Dye Kit	Color Specialists, The		√		Kn	2	1	3	F-W 85	64
Dyes and Dyeing: Dye Laboratory, Portable	Vacation Dye Samples	Martin, Jill	√	√	Hw	4	3		M/J 83	58
Dyes and Dyeing: Dye Painting	K. Lee Manuel: Wearable Dreams		√		Fa	3	5		S/O 76	12
Dyes and Dyeing: Dye/Stain	Juicy Fruits and Nut Hulls: (is it a dye or a stain?)	Bliss, Anne	√		Hw	4	4		S/O 83	80
Dyes and Dyeing: Dyes/Uses (Chart)	Fiberarts Special: Dyes and Dyeing Chart, A (error-corrected Fa v5 n2 78 p58)			√	Fa	5	1		J/F 78	34
Dyes and Dyeing: Edge-Dyeing	Passion for Elegance: Master Dyer Marian Clayden Creates Clothing by Listening to the Fabric, A	Levine, Betsy	√	√	TM			14	D/J 87	36
Dyes and Dyeing: Fabric	Personal Notes on a Dyeing Art	Lapin, Claudia	√		Fa	4	4		J/A 77	60
Dyes and Dyeing: Fiber Reactive Dyes	Silk and Fiber Reactive Dyes		√	√	WJ	3	2	10	Oc 78	24
Dyes and Dyeing: Fiber-Mix	Fiber-Mix Dyeing of Textiles	Arnold, Kari	√	√	SS&D	16	2	62	Sp 85	46
Dyes and Dyeing: Fibers, Animal	Color and Dyeing: Dyeing Animal Fibers and Nylon with Benzyl Dyes	Tidball, Harriet		√	SCGM		16		65	31
Dyes and Dyeing: Fibers, Man-Made	Color and Dyeing: Dyeing Animal Fibers and Nylon with Benzyl Dyes	Tidball, Harriet		√	SCGM		16		65	31
Dyes and Dyeing: Fibers, Man-Made	Color and Dyeing: Dyeing Vegetable Fibers and Rayon with Chlorantine Dyes	Tidball, Harriet		√	SCGM		16		65	32
Dyes and Dyeing: Fibers, Vegetable	Color and Dyeing: Dyeing Vegetable Fibers and Rayon with Chlorantine Dyes	Tidball, Harriet		√	SCGM		16		65	32
Dyes and Dyeing: Hazards	Memo to All Concerned Craftsmen (error-corrected SS&D v10 n4 79 p66)	Towner, Naomi Whiting			SS&D	10	3	39	Su 79	10
Dyes and Dyeing: History	Why Bother with Natural Dyeing?	Bulbach, Stanley	√	√	TM			5	J/J 86	32
Dyes and Dyeing: Insects	Cochineal in Colorado: or, Is Your Local Cactus Bugged? (error-corrected Iw v1 n3 76 p25)	Bliss, Anne	√	√	Iw	1	2		Wi 76	20
Dyes and Dyeing: Japanese Technique	Surface Design Association's Southeast Regional Conference	Mattera, Joanne	√		Fa	9	1		J/F 82	54
Dyes and Dyeing: Leaf Printing	Leaf Printing	Ligon, Linda	√	√	Hw	4	3		M/J 83	60
Dyes and Dyeing: Marbling	Marbling Cloth	Bliss, Anne	√	√	Hw	4	3		M/J 83	56
Dyes and Dyeing: Mineral	Mineral Dyes 2, The	Liles, James N.	√	√	SS&D	13	4	52	Fa 82	60
Dyes and Dyeing: Mineral	Mineral Dyes, The	Liles, James N.	√	√	SS&D	13	3	51	Su 82	54

SUBJECT	TITLE	AUTHOR	IL	INST	JOUR	VOL	NO	ISS	DATE	PAGE
Dyes and Dyeing: Mordants	Bancroft's Mordant: A Useful One-Pot Natural Dye Technique	Liles, James N.; Dale Liles	√	√	SS&D	15	3	59	Su 84	76
Dyes and Dyeing: Mordants	Color and Dyeing: "Home Dyeing with Natural Dyes"	Tidball, Harriet		√	SCGM		16		65	39
Dyes and Dyeing: Mordants	Considerations in the Selection and Application of Natural Dyes: Mordant Selection, Part 1	Crews, Patricia	√	√	SS&D	12	2	46	Sp 81	15
Dyes and Dyeing: Mordants	Dyes from the Herb Garden	King, Helen	√	√	TM			6	A/S 86	58
Dyes and Dyeing: Mordants	Introduction to Silk Dyeing, An	Walsh, Joan Lea		√	WJ	3	2	10	Oc 78	14
Dyes and Dyeing: Mordants	Problem Solving	Bliss, Anne; with Margaret Emerson		√	Iw	3	3		Sp 78	34
Dyes and Dyeing: Mordants	Production Dyeing with Natural Dyes	Van Stralen, Trudy	√	√	S-O	11	4		Wi 87	57
Dyes and Dyeing: Mordants	Why Bother with Natural Dyeing?	Bulbach, Stanley	√	√	TM			5	J/J 86	32
Dyes and Dyeing: Mordants and Additives	Color Variations: Uses for Mordants and Additives	Bliss, Anne		√	Hw	5	1		J/F 84	80
Dyes and Dyeing: Mordants, Hardware	Mother-Wit and the Dyepot	Handy-Marchello, Barbara		√	WJ	9	2	34	Fa 84	25
Dyes and Dyeing: Mordants, Mud	Kumejima Dorozome: The Vegetable Dye and Mud Mordanting Process of Silk Tsugumi	Miller, Dorothy	√	√	AT	5			Ju 86	131
Dyes and Dyeing: Mordants, Multiple	Polychroma: Natural Dye Methods	Piroch, Sigrid	√	√	SS&D	17	2	66	Sp 86	26
Dyes and Dyeing: Mottled Dyeing	Color and Dyeing: Dyeing Variations	Tidball, Harriet		√	SCGM		16		65	37
Dyes and Dyeing: Native Americans	From Body Paint to Buffalo Hides	Bliss, Anne	√	√	Iw	4	1		Wi 78	42
Dyes and Dyeing: Natural Dye Printing	Printing with Natural Dyes: An Historical Perspective			√	Hw	3	5		N/D 82	66
Dyes and Dyeing: Natural Dye Printing	What's the Madder with Calico?			√	Hw	3	5		N/D 82	67
Dyes and Dyeing: Natural Materials	Adventures in Dyeing Wood and Bark (error-corrected SS&D v9 n4 78 p34)	Hearne, Gladys	√	√	SS&D	9	3	35	Su 78	20
Dyes and Dyeing: Natural Materials	Alkanet	Gerber, Frederick		√	Iw	5	3		Su 80	66
Dyes and Dyeing: Natural Materials	Andes Tradition, An	McConnell, Kathleen	√	√	SS&D	18	2	70	Sp 87	29
Dyes and Dyeing: Natural Materials	Annatto: Color for Complexions, Cheese and Cloth	Bliss, Anne	√	√	Hw	5	5		N/D 84	82
Dyes and Dyeing: Natural Materials	Arctic Adventures with Qiviut	Hudson, Marjorie; Kathy Sparks	√	√	S-O	11	3		Fa 87	47
Dyes and Dyeing: Natural Materials	Are Those Colors Really from Plants?	Brough, Hazel	√	√	SS&D	8	4	32	Fa 77	67
Dyes and Dyeing: Natural Materials	Bindweeds	Bliss, Anne	√	√	Hw	6	5		N/D 85	86
Dyes and Dyeing: Natural Materials	Blood-Root in Your Own Back Yard	Loftis, Doris			SS&D	1	3	3	Ju 70	22
Dyes and Dyeing: Natural Materials	Chaos in the Kitchen, Part 2	Gerber, Willi; Fred Gerber	√	√	SS&D	5	4	20	Fa 74	92
Dyes and Dyeing: Natural Materials	Christmas Tree Dye — A Natural!	Rossiter, Phyllis	√	√	S-O	9	4		Wi 85	22
Dyes and Dyeing: Natural Materials	Color and Dyeing: "Home Dyeing with Natural Dyes"	Tidball, Harriet		√	SCGM		16		65	39
Dyes and Dyeing: Natural Materials	Color Magic from Lichen Dyebaths	Casselman, Karen Leigh	√	√	SS&D	17	2	66	Sp 86	74
Dyes and Dyeing: Natural Materials	Common Plants Yield Dyes for Homespun Yarn			√	H&C	2	4		Fa 51	16
Dyes and Dyeing: Natural Materials	Considerations in the Selection and Application of Natural Dyes: Mordant Selection, Part 1	Crews, Patricia	√	√	SS&D	12	2	46	Sp 81	15
Dyes and Dyeing: Natural Materials	Considerations in the Selection and Application of Natural Dyes: Dye-plant Selection (error-corrected SS&D v12 n4 81 p8)	Crews, Patricia	√	√	SS&D	12	3	47	Su 81	52
Dyes and Dyeing: Natural Materials	Control Dyeing with Indigo	Taggart, Barbara		√	SS&D	5	3	19	Su 74	53

SUBJECT	TITLE	AUTHOR	IL	INST	JOUR	VOL	NO	ISS	DATE	PAGE
Dyes and Dyeing: Natural Materials	Costume and Weaving in Saraguro, Ecuador	Meisch, Lynn Ann	√		TMJ	19 20			80,81	55
Dyes and Dyeing: Natural Materials	Cotton in the Natural Dyepot	Baker, Ella	√	√	S-O	9	3		Fa 85	29
Dyes and Dyeing: Natural Materials	Currants: Not Just for Eating	Bliss, Anne	√	√	Hw	7	4		S/O 86	74
Dyes and Dyeing: Natural Materials	Daisy, Daisy, Give Me Your Color, Do	Bliss, Anne	√	√	Hw	6	4		S/O 85	80
Dyes and Dyeing: Natural Materials	Dandelion Dye and Other Delights	Bliss, Anne	√	√	Iw	2	3		Sp 77	22
Dyes and Dyeing: Natural Materials	Diverse Dyes	Bliss, Anne	√	√	Iw	3	2		Wi 78	30
Dyes and Dyeing: Natural Materials	Don't Cry...Dye	Bliss, Anne	√	√	Hw	2	2		Mr 81	50
Dyes and Dyeing: Natural Materials	Dye Session in the Park	McCartney, Doris			SS&D	1	2	2	Mr 70	22
Dyes and Dyeing: Natural Materials	Dyeing and Spinning Cotton Lint	Linder, Harry; Olive Linder	√	√	SS&D	10	2	38	Sp 79	62
Dyes and Dyeing: Natural Materials	Dyeing by the Yard	Bliss, Anne	√		Iw	5	2		Sp 80	60
Dyes and Dyeing: Natural Materials	Dyeing Gold and Yellow	Blackburn, Edna	√	√	TM			1	O/N 85	28
Dyes and Dyeing: Natural Materials	Dyeing in the Black Hills	Daly, Lynn	√		Iw	1	4		Su 76	18
Dyes and Dyeing: Natural Materials	Dyeing in the Rockies	Bliss, Anne	√	√	SS&D	8	1	29	WI 76	14
Dyes and Dyeing: Natural Materials	Dyeing Natural Materials	Taggart, Barbara			SS&D	4	4	16	Fa 73	57
Dyes and Dyeing: Natural Materials	Dyeing with Bark	Lohmolder, Jo		√	SS&D	5	2	18	Sp 74	76
Dyes and Dyeing: Natural Materials	Dyeing with Lichens	Gerber, Willi; Fred Gerber	√	√	H&C	20	2		Sp 69	13
Dyes and Dyeing: Natural Materials	Dyeing with Tree Blossoms	Held, Shirley	√	√	SS&D	8	4	32	Fa 77	41
Dyes and Dyeing: Natural Materials	Dyepot	Taggart, Barbara			SS&D	2	4	8	Fa 71	29
Dyes and Dyeing: Natural Materials	Dyes from Mushrooms: A Spectrum of Extraordinary Color	Rice, Miriam	√	√	TM			10	A/M 87	44
Dyes and Dyeing: Natural Materials	Dyes from Oak Galls	Bliss, Anne	√	√	Iw	6	1		Wi 80	64
Dyes and Dyeing: Natural Materials	Dyes from the Herb Garden	King, Helen	√	√	TM			6	A/S 86	58
Dyes and Dyeing: Natural Materials	Dyes of Mexico	Wipplinger, Michele	√	√	S-O	9	3		Fa 85	32
Dyes and Dyeing: Natural Materials	Exotic Woods for the Dyepot	Held, Shirley E.	√	√	SS&D	9	4	36	Fa 78	48
Dyes and Dyeing: Natural Materials	From a Dyer's Diary	Griffin, Gertrude	√		SS&D	4	1	13	Wi 72	11
Dyes and Dyeing: Natural Materials	Fukumi Shimura: Japan's Colorist Supreme	Adachi, Barbara C.	√		Fa	12	4		J/A 85	28
Dyes and Dyeing: Natural Materials	Grow Your Own Colors: Plant a Dye Garden (error-corrected S-O v11 n2 '87 p7)	Buchanan, Rita	√	√	S-O	11	1		Sp 87	35
Dyes and Dyeing: Natural Materials	Home Dyeing with Native Plants Provides Wide Range of Colors	Langton, Janet F.		√	H&C	19	3		Su 68	16
Dyes and Dyeing: Natural Materials	Ida Grae—A Totally Textural Experience	Kaplan, Suzan	√		SS&D	5	4	20	Fa 74	4
Dyes and Dyeing: Natural Materials	Insect Dyes	Gerber, Fred	√	√	Iw	3	3		Sp 78	23
Dyes and Dyeing: Natural Materials	Interview with Linda Berry Walker...A Spinning and Dyeing Business, An	Horton, Lucy	√		Fa	4	5		S/O 77	26
Dyes and Dyeing: Natural Materials	Introduction to Silk Dyeing, An	Walsh, Joan Lea		√	WJ	3	2	10	Oc 78	14

SUBJECT	TITLE	AUTHOR	IL	INST	JOUR	VOL	NO	ISS	DATE	PAGE
Dyes and Dyeing: Natural Materials	Investigative Method—A Tool for Study, Part 1	Gerber, Fred	√	√	SS&D	6	1	21	Wi 74	62
Dyes and Dyeing: Natural Materials	Juicy Fruits and Nut Hulls: (is it a dye or a stain?)	Bliss, Anne	√		Hw	4	4		S/O 83	80
Dyes and Dyeing: Natural Materials	Kumejima Dorozome: The Vegetable Dye and Mud Mordanting Process of Silk Tsugumi	Miller, Dorothy	√	√	AT	5			Ju 86	131
Dyes and Dyeing: Natural Materials	Last Species: Osage Orange, Bois d'Arc, Horse Apple, Hedge Apple, The	Bliss, Anne	√	√	Iw	1	3		Sp 76	24
Dyes and Dyeing: Natural Materials	Lichens	Wipplinger, Michele	√	√	S-O	10	2		Su 86	34
Dyes and Dyeing: Natural Materials	Lichens As Dyestuffs	Shaw, Lynn C.	√	√	SS&D	5	2	18	Sp 74	28
Dyes and Dyeing: Natural Materials	Lingonberries in the Pot	Colson, Lois	√		SS&D	3	1	9	Wi 71	33
Dyes and Dyeing: Natural Materials	Lovely Dyes from Rank Weeds	Bliss, Anne	√		Iw	3	4		Su 78	38
Dyes and Dyeing: Natural Materials	Martin's Creek Settlement: A Pictorial Weaving	Thompson, Kathleen; Alice Tipton	√		S-O	9	3		Fa 85	39
Dyes and Dyeing: Natural Materials	Milkweed and Balduinea in the Dyepot	Gerber, Fred; Willi Gerber	√	√	H&C	22	3		Su 71	23
Dyes and Dyeing: Natural Materials	Mushroom Dyes	Meltzer-Smith, Sandra Jo	√		SS&D	11	3	43	Su 80	53
Dyes and Dyeing: Natural Materials	Natural Dyeing in Wisconsin	Rigby, M. Edith	√	√	SS&D	12	2	46	Sp 81	8
Dyes and Dyeing: Natural Materials	Natural Dyeing of Silk Fiber	Kolander, Cheryl	√	√	SS&D	9	2	34	Sp 78	58
Dyes and Dyeing: Natural Materials	Nature's Colors, Naturally	Lorance, Marilyn	√		SS&D	10	1	37	Wi 78	49
Dyes and Dyeing: Natural Materials	Navajo Way, The	Jolley, Ginger	√	√	S-O	11	4		Wi 87	38
Dyes and Dyeing: Natural Materials	Notes on Vegetable Dyeing	Gerber, Fred; Willi Gerber		√	H&C	23	3		M/J 72	28
Dyes and Dyeing: Natural Materials	Novelty Yarns: Creation in Color and Texture	Dick, Barbara Ann	√	√	SS&D	12	3	47	Su 81	32
Dyes and Dyeing: Natural Materials	Old Man's Beard, the Reindeer's Moss and the Stag's Horn, The	Bliss, Anne	√	√	Hw	7	2		M/A 86	72
Dyes and Dyeing: Natural Materials	On Dyeing with Madder	Bliss, Anne	√	√	Iw	5	1		Wi 79	48
Dyes and Dyeing: Natural Materials	Pine Needle Basketry	Washington, Misti	√	√	SS&D	16	4	64	Fa 85	46
Dyes and Dyeing: Natural Materials	Plant Pigments and Natural Dyeing	Williams, Sharon Flynn	√	√	SS&D	14	2	54	Sp 83	32
Dyes and Dyeing: Natural Materials	Polychroma: Natural Dye Methods	Piroch, Sigrid	√	√	SS&D	17	2	66	Sp 86	26
Dyes and Dyeing: Natural Materials	Prairie Plants: Natives and Immigrants	Bliss, Anne	√	√	Hw	3	4		Se 82	74
Dyes and Dyeing: Natural Materials	Production Dyeing with Natural Dyes	Van Stralen, Trudy	√	√	S-O	11	4		Wi 87	57
Dyes and Dyeing: Natural Materials	Purple in Antiquity	Davidson, Mary Frances			SS&D	2	1	5	De 70	26
Dyes and Dyeing: Natural Materials	Q & A on Vegetable Dyes	Oswald, Francis		√	SS&D	1	1	1	De 69	11
Dyes and Dyeing: Natural Materials	Quercitron, The Forgotten Dyestuff, Producer of Clear, Bright Colors	Gerber, Willi; Fred Gerber	√		SS&D	5	1	17	Wi 73	25
Dyes and Dyeing: Natural Materials	Recipes for Cochineal Dyeing			√	Iw	3	3		Sp 78	47
Dyes and Dyeing: Natural Materials	Reds and More Reds	Taggart, Barbara		√	SS&D	5	1	17	Wi 73	57
Dyes and Dyeing: Natural Materials	Ruth Clark, Tapestry Weaver	Olson, Mabel C.	√	√	H&C	9	1		Wi 57	29
Dyes and Dyeing: Natural Materials	SOAR Dyeworks	Bliss, Anne	√	√	S-O	10	2		Su 86	44

SUBJECT	TITLE	AUTHOR	IL	INST	JOUR	VOL	NO	ISS	DATE	PAGE
Dyes and Dyeing: Natural Materials	Spring Greens (make more than green!)	Bliss, Anne	√	√	Hw	3	2		Mr 82	69
Dyes and Dyeing: Natural Materials	Stalking the Wild Mushroom	Pepin, Yvonne	√	√	SS&D	16	4	64	Fa 85	22
Dyes and Dyeing: Natural Materials	Straining Dyestuffs			√	TM			11	J/J 87	8
Dyes and Dyeing: Natural Materials	Study of Andean Spinning in the Cuzco Region, A	Goodell, Miss Grace	√	√	TMJ	2	3		De 68	2
Dyes and Dyeing: Natural Materials	Successful Experiment. Michigan Group Explores Natural Dyes	Boydston, Kay	√	√	H&C	14	1		Wi 63	11
Dyes and Dyeing: Natural Materials	Summer Harvest, Winter Jacket	O'Connor, Marina	√	√	S-O	11	2		Su 87	13
Dyes and Dyeing: Natural Materials	Supermarket Dyeing	Taggart, Barbara		√	SS&D	3	2	10	Sp 72	34
Dyes and Dyeing: Natural Materials	Sweater of Many Colors, A	McIntee, Polly	√	√	S-O	11	2		Su 87	15
Dyes and Dyeing: Natural Materials	Sweetgrass, Cedar & Sage: Portrait of a Southwestern Weaver	Schevill, Margot	√		WJ	10	1	37	Su 85	24
Dyes and Dyeing: Natural Materials	"The Robe," is Woven on a California Handloom	Marshall, Bertha	√		H&C	4	3		Su 53	14
Dyes and Dyeing: Natural Materials	This Year, Plan and Plant a Dye Patch	Bliss, Anne	√	√	Iw	2	2		Wi 77	28
Dyes and Dyeing: Natural Materials	Thistles	Bliss, Anne	√	√	Hw	7	1		J/F 86	84
Dyes and Dyeing: Natural Materials	Tie-Dye...Naturally	Bliss, Anne	√	√	Iw	4	3		Su 79	58
Dyes and Dyeing: Natural Materials	Tina McMorran	Stevens, Bernice A.	√		H&C	15	3		Su 64	14
Dyes and Dyeing: Natural Materials	Tyrian Purple	Robinson, John P., Jr.	√		H&C	24	1		J/F 73	30
Dyes and Dyeing: Natural Materials	Uncommon Dyewood: Manzanita—From the Chaparral, An	Hall, Joanne Arvidson	√	√	SS&D	7	3	27	Su 76	55
Dyes and Dyeing: Natural Materials	Unnatural Acts with Natural Dyes or How I Learned To Love the Weed	Grant, Susan	√		Fa	5	1		J/F 78	48
Dyes and Dyeing: Natural Materials	Unusual Colors from Experiments with Vegetable Dyes	Cranch, George E.		√	H&C	13	3		Su 62	13
Dyes and Dyeing: Natural Materials	Using Natural Dyes	Bliss, Anne		√	S-O	8	3		Fa 84	42
Dyes and Dyeing: Natural Materials	Viditz-Ward Dyes in Evergreen; Students Still Blue	Ritchey, Janet	√		Iw	2	4		Su 77	13
Dyes and Dyeing: Natural Materials	Weaving the Family Tartan	Buchanan, Rita	√	√	S-O	10	2		Su 86	36
Dyes and Dyeing: Natural Materials	Why Bother with Natural Dyeing?	Bulbach, Stanley	√	√	TM			5	J/J 86	32
Dyes and Dyeing: Natural Materials	Winter Dyeing with Umbilicate Lichens (error-corrected SS&D v9 n4 78 p34)	Casselman, Karen L.	√	√	SS&D	9	2	34	Sp 78	8
Dyes and Dyeing: Natural Materials	Wool — Plants — Color	Mercer, Paul	√	√	H&C	22	1		Wi 71	12
Dyes and Dyeing: Natural Materials, Balduinea	Milkweed and Balduinea in the Dyepot (Reprint)	Gerber, Fred; Willi Gerber	√	√	H&C	26	1		J/F 75	19
Dyes and Dyeing: Natural Materials, Brazilwood	Get Some Razzle Dazzle—Try "Brazzle"	Bliss, Anne		√	Iw	2	4		Su 77	28
Dyes and Dyeing: Natural Materials, Cochineal	Cochineal as a Domestic Dyestuff	Gerber, Willi; Fred Gerber		√	H&C	23	6		N/D 72	16
Dyes and Dyeing: Natural Materials, Indigo	Chaos in the Kitchen: Part 1	Gerber, Willi; Fred Gerber	√	√	SS&D	5	3	19	Su 74	70
Dyes and Dyeing: Natural Materials, Indigo	Indigo, Discovery of Plants and Experiments in Dyeing	Gerber, Willi; Fred Gerber	√	√	H&C	26	3		M/J 75	11
Dyes and Dyeing: Natural Materials, Lichen	On Lichen Dyeing	Oakland, Amy		√	H&C	24	2		M/A 73	20
Dyes and Dyeing: Natural Materials, Milkweed	Milkweed and Balduinea in the Dyepot (Reprint)	Gerber, Fred; Willi Gerber	√	√	H&C	26	1		J/F 75	19
Dyes and Dyeing: Natural Materials, Orchils	Chaos in the Kitchen: Part 1	Gerber, Willi; Fred Gerber	√	√	SS&D	5	3	19	Su 74	70

SUBJECT	TITLE	AUTHOR	IL	INST	JOUR	VOL	NO	ISS	DATE	PAGE
Dyes and Dyeing: Natural Materials, Quercitron	Quercitron, The Forgotten Dyestuffs, Producer of Clear Bright Colors: Part 2	Gerber, Willi; Fred Gerber	√	√	SS&D	5	2	18	Sp 74	87
Dyes and Dyeing: Natural Materials, Ramie	Miyako Jofu	Miller, Dorothy	√	√	AT	7			Ju 87	85
Dyes and Dyeing: Natural Materials, Spice	Spice Dyeing	Reesor, Tracy		√	WJ	6	4	24	Sp 82	47
Dyes and Dyeing: Natural Materials: Trees	Dyeing with Willows, Cottonwoods, Aspens and Poplars	Bliss, Anne	√	√	Iw	5	3		Su 80	54
Dyes and Dyeing: Natural Materials, Weld	Ancient Yellow Goes Modern, An	Bliss, Anne	√	√	Iw	4	2		Sp 79	44
Dyes and Dyeing: Natural Materials, Woad	Getting Woaded for Winter	Bliss, Anne	√	√	Iw	2	1		Fa 76	22
Dyes and Dyeing: Natural vs Synthetic	Natural Dye Myth, The	Tillett, Leslie	√		Iw	4	2		Sp 79	55
Dyes and Dyeing: Navajo	Dyepot	Taggart, Barbara			SS&D	3	4	12	Fa 72	35
Dyes and Dyeing: Navajo	Navajo: Textiles, Blankets, Rugs, Tapestries	Morrow, Mable	√	√	SS&D	2	1	5	De 70	5
Dyes and Dyeing: Overdying, Chemical	Minor Miracles — New Life for Old Yarn	Bliss, Anne	√	√	Hw	8	4		S/O 87	68
Dyes and Dyeing: Overdying, Natural Dyes	Minor Miracles — New Life for Old Yarn	Bliss, Anne	√	√	Hw	8	4		S/O 87	68
Dyes and Dyeing: Painting	Sensuous Silk: Cedrus Monte's Painted Silk Garments	Gilliland, David	√		Fa	8	1		J/F 81	17
Dyes and Dyeing: Paper	Paper Art of Fritzi Huber Morrison, The	Kosta, Angela	√		Fa	11	2		M/A 84	22
Dyes and Dyeing: Paper	Paper Clothing: West	Koplos, Janet	√		Fa	11	2		M/A 84	39
Dyes and Dyeing: Pastels	Pastel	Bliss, Anne	√	√	Hw	5	3		Su 84	86
Dyes and Dyeing: Piece Dyeing	Color and Dyeing: Dyeing Variations	Tidball, Harriet		√	SCGM		16		65	37
Dyes and Dyeing: Piece Dyeing	Silk Dyeing		√	√	WJ	3	2	10	Oc 78	21
Dyes and Dyeing: Pigments, Plant	Plant Pigments and Natural Dyeing	Williams, Sharon Flynn	√	√	SS&D	14	2	54	Sp 83	32
Dyes and Dyeing: Plaid	Color It Plaid	Bliss, Anne		√	Hw	4	5		N/D 83	74
Dyes and Dyeing: Preparation Dye Concentrate	Color and Dyeing: Dyeing Processes, Preparing a Dye Concentrate	Tidball, Harriet		√	SCGM		16		65	24
Dyes and Dyeing: Preparation Dye Solution	Color and Dyeing: Dyeing Processes, Preparing the Dye Solution	Tidball, Harriet	√	√	SCGM		16		65	23
Dyes and Dyeing: Preparation Dyebath	Color and Dyeing: Dyeing Processes, Preparing the Dyebath	Tidball, Harriet	√	√	SCGM		16		65	24
Dyes and Dyeing: Preparation Yarn	Color and Dyeing: Dyeing Processes, Preparing the Yarn for Dyeing	Tidball, Harriet	√	√	SCGM		16		65	21
Dyes and Dyeing: Problems/Solutions	Cracked, Pots, Snaggled Skeins and Other Dyeing Dilemmas	Bliss, Anne	√	√	Hw	2	5		No 81	68
Dyes and Dyeing: Properties of Dye Classes	Principles of Textile Conservation Science, No. 4. The Conservation of Historical Textile Colorants	Rice, James W.	√	√	TMJ	1	2		De 63	55
Dyes and Dyeing: Quality	Importance of Quality in the Art of Dyeing, The	McManus, Fran			S-O	7	2		Su 83	10
Dyes and Dyeing: Records	Color and Dyeing: Dyeing Processes, Records and Marking the Notes	Tidball, Harriet	√	√	SCGM		16		65	30
Dyes and Dyeing: Resist	Ana Lisa Hedstrom: The Intuitive Language of Shibori	Scarborough, Jessica	√		Fa	13	1		J/F 86	26
Dyes and Dyeing: Resist	Anne McKenzie Nickolson	Nickolson, Anne McKenzie	√		Fa	12	6		N/D 85	20
Dyes and Dyeing: Resist	Art of Stitched Shibori, The (error-corrected Fa v12 n3 85 p8)	Wada, Yoshiko; Mary Kellogg Rice, Jane Barton	√		Fa	12	2		M/A 85	55
Dyes and Dyeing: Resist	Art Wear of Peggy Juve, The	Tacker, Sylvia	√		Fa	14	1		J/F 87	25
Dyes and Dyeing: Resist	"Contemporary Shibori" (Exhibit)	Howe, Cathe	√		Fa	11	3		M/J 84	82
Dyes and Dyeing: Resist	"Dyer's Art: Ikat, Batik, Plangi, The" (Exhibit)	Dyer, Carolyn	√		Fa	5	4		J/A 78	11
Dyes and Dyeing: Resist	D'Arcie Beytebiere: Windswept Designs in Pleated Silk	Tacker, Sylvia	√		Fa	13	1		J/F 86	28
Dyes and Dyeing: Resist	Innovations in Indigo	Wada, Yoshiko Iwamoto	√		Fa	13	5		S/O 86	29
Dyes and Dyeing: Resist	Kasuri and I	Robinson, Irma	√		SS&D	1	2	2	Mr 70	19

SUBJECT	TITLE	AUTHOR	IL	INST	JOUR	VOL	NO	ISS	DATE	PAGE
Dyes and Dyeing: Resist	Limited-Edition Vests	Stocksdale, Joy	√	√	TM			4	A/M 86	60
Dyes and Dyeing: Resist	Microwave Dyeing	Mortensen, Diane	√	√	SS&D	10	4	40	Fa 79	12
Dyes and Dyeing: Resist	New Twist on Resist	Wada, Yoshiko Iwamoto; Shelley Karpilow	√	√	TM			8	D/J 86	20
Dyes and Dyeing: Resist	Passion for Elegance: Master Dyer Marian Clayden Creates Clothing by Listening to the Fabric, A	Levine, Betsy	√	√	TM			14	D/J 87	36
Dyes and Dyeing: Resist	Peru, Textiles Unlimited: Tie-Dye, Ikat, Painting	Tidball, Harriet	√		SCGM		25		68	32
Dyes and Dyeing: Resist	Resist-Dyed Textiles	Trilling, James	√		TMJ	21			82	102
Dyes and Dyeing: Resist	Resisting Dyes: Three Ways to Put Color in Its Place	Northup, Wendy	√	√	TM			1	O/N 85	30
Dyes and Dyeing: Resist	Space Dyeing with Fiber-Reactive Dyes	Knutson, Linda	√	√	WJ	8	1	29	Su 83	89
Dyes and Dyeing: Resist	Textural Approach to Arashi Shibori, A	Beytebiere, D'Arcie	√	√	TM			8	D/J 86	24
Dyes and Dyeing: Resist	Wall Hangings of Judith Content, The	Scarborough, Jessica	√		Fa	13	2		M/A 86	10
Dyes and Dyeing: Resist	Wealth of Fiber: Nigeria's Adire Cloth , A	Ulrich, George	√		Fa	13	5		S/O 86	39
Dyes and Dyeing: Resist, Batik	Batik Making and the Royal Javanese Cemetery at Imogiri	Joseph, Rebecca M.	√		TMJ	24			85	83
Dyes and Dyeing: Resist, Batik	Dyeing with Fiber Reactive Dyes on Cotton	Read, Kay	√	√	WJ	4	2	14	Oc 79	42
Dyes and Dyeing: Resist, Batik	Resist Dyeing, Curiosities and Inventions: Batik 1	Zielinski, S. A.; Robert Leclerc, ed.	√	√	MWL	17			'51–'73	21
Dyes and Dyeing: Resist, Batik	Resist Dyeing, Curiosities and Inventions: Crackle in Batik	Zielinski, S. A.; Robert Leclerc, ed.		√	MWL	17			'51–'73	36
Dyes and Dyeing: Resist, Batik	Symbolic Scenes in Javanese Batik	Adams, Monni	√		TMJ	3	1		De 70	25
Dyes and Dyeing: Resist, Batik, Technique	Van Zuylen Batik, Pekalongan, Central Java (1890-1946)	de Raadt-Apell, M. J.	√	√	TMJ	19,20			80,81	75
Dyes and Dyeing: Resist, Clamp Technique	Clamp and Discharge Demonstration (error-corrected Fa v5 n3 78 p3)	Meilach, Dona Z.	√	√	Fa	5	1		J/F 78	45
Dyes and Dyeing: Resist, Combined Techniques	Resist Dyeing, Curiosities and Inventions: Clasped Wefts or Locked Weft	Zielinski, S. A.; Robert Leclerc, ed.	√		MWL	17			'51–'73	40
Dyes and Dyeing: Resist Dyeing	Color and Dyeing: Dyeing Variations	Tidball, Harriet		√	SCGM		16		65	37
Dyes and Dyeing: Resist, Ikat	Basic Ikat	Carlson, Estelle	√	√	Iw	5	3		Su 80	27
Dyes and Dyeing: Resist, Ikat	Brushstrokes of Color	Bohannan, Ronnine	√	√	Hw	5	3		Su 84	56
Dyes and Dyeing: Resist, Ikat	Contemporary Satins: Chine and Ikat	Tidball, Harriet	√		SCGM		7		62	20
Dyes and Dyeing: Resist, Ikat	Ikat Striped Ruana and Skirt	Colton, Mary Rawcliffe	√	√	Hw	5	4		S/O 84	60
Dyes and Dyeing: Resist, Ikat	Ikat with Ease	Bliss, Anne	√	√	Hw	2	4		Se 81	60
Dyes and Dyeing: Resist, Ikat	Ikat-Woven Images	Tacker, Sylvia	√	√	SS&D	18	1	69	Wi 86	68
Dyes and Dyeing: Resist, Ikat	Kimono	Colton, Mary Rawcliffe	√	√	SS&D	15	1	57	Wi 83	30
Dyes and Dyeing: Resist, Ikat	New Technique for Pulled-Warp Ikat, A	Wu, Han-Lien	√	√	Iw	5	3		Su 80	29
Dyes and Dyeing: Resist, Ikat	Notes on Ikat Weaving	Schira, Cynthia	√	√	H&C	24	2		M/A 73	6
Dyes and Dyeing: Resist, Ikat	Sumbanese Ikat	Hannon, Farrell	√	√	WJ	8	1	29	Su 83	38
Dyes and Dyeing: Resist, Ikat	Tying Warp Ikat on the Loom	Hannon, Farrell	√	√	WJ	8	1	29	Su 83	41
Dyes and Dyeing: Resist, Ikat, Double	Patolu and Its Techniques	De Bone, Mary Golden	√	√	TMJ	4	3		76	49
Dyes and Dyeing: Resist, Indigo	Shigeki and Shihoko Fukumoto: Balancing Art and Function	Lancaster, Zöe Woodruff	√		Fa	13	6		N/D 86	5
Dyes and Dyeing: Resist, Jaspé	Jaspé Weaving	Young, Helen Daniels	√	√	H&C	5	3		Su 54	30
Dyes and Dyeing: Resist, Kasuri	Kasuri: A Japanese Textile	Dusenbury, Mary	√		TMJ	17			78	41
Dyes and Dyeing: Resist, Kasuri	Kasuri: The Japanese Ikat	Schrieber, La Vonne	√	√	SS&D	14	1	53	Wi 82	22
Dyes and Dyeing: Resist, Kasuri	Kumejima Dorozome: The Vegetable Dye and Mud Mordanting Process of Silk Tsugumi	Miller, Dorothy	√	√	AT	5			Ju 86	131
Dyes and Dyeing: Resist, Kasuri	Resist Dyeing, Curiosities and Inventions: Kasuri on Inkle Loom	Zielinski, S. A.; Robert Leclerc, ed.	√	√	MWL	17			'51–'73	38
Dyes and Dyeing: Resist, On-Loom	Resist Dyeing, Curiosities and Inventions: Kasuri on Inkle Loom	Zielinski, S. A.; Robert Leclerc, ed.	√	√	MWL	17			'51–'73	38

SUBJECT	TITLE	AUTHOR	IL	INST	JOUR	VOL	NO	ISS	DATE	PAGE
Dyes and Dyeing: Resist, Shibori	Resist Dyeing, Curiosities and Inventions: Shibori	Zielinski, S. A.; Robert Leclerc, ed.	√	√	MWL	17			'51–'73	10
Dyes and Dyeing: Resist, Silk Screen	Resist Dyeing, Curiosities and Inventions: Batik 2	Zielinski, S. A.; Robert Leclerc, ed.	√	√	MWL	17			'51–'73	30
Dyes and Dyeing: Resist, Technique	Resist Dyeing, Curiosities and Inventions: Resist Dyeing	Zielinski, S. A.; Robert Leclerc, ed.	√		MWL	17			'51–'73	7
Dyes and Dyeing: Resist, Technique	Revival of Ikat	Rushfelt, Joy M.	√	√	H&C	19	2		Sp 68	14
Dyes and Dyeing: Resist, Technique	Tie Dyeing in India (error-corrected H&C v14 n2 63 p46)	Arness, Judith Russell	√	√	H&C	14	1		Wi 63	6
Dyes and Dyeing: Resist, Techniques	Bandhana (Tie Dye)	Westfall, Carol D.; Dipti Desai	√		AT	8			De 87	19
Dyes and Dyeing: Resist, Tie-Dye	African Artist in a Dying Trade, An	Kessler, Cristina	√	√	Fa	11	6		N/D 84	51
Dyes and Dyeing: Resist, Tie-Dye	Bandhana (Tie Dye)	Westfall, Carol D.; Dipti Desai	√		AT	8			De 87	19
Dyes and Dyeing: Resist, Tie-Dye	Chaos in the Kitchen: Part 1	Gerber, Willi; Fred Gerber	√	√	SS&D	5	3	19	Su 74	70
Dyes and Dyeing: Resist, Tie-Dye	Chaos in the Kitchen, Part 2	Gerber, Willi; Fred Gerber	√	√	SS&D	5	4	20	Fa 74	92
Dyes and Dyeing: Resist, Tie-Dye	Jaspe Process, The	Lopez, Beatriz	√	√	SS&D	8	3	31	Su 77	54
Dyes and Dyeing: Resist, Tie-Dye	Marian Clayden: Fabric Dyer	Meilach, Dona Z.	√		Fa	5	1		J/F 78	43
Dyes and Dyeing: Resist, Tie-Dye	Rabari Lodi: Creating A Fabric Through Social Alliance, The	Frater, Judy	√	√	WJ	10	1	37	Su 85	28
Dyes and Dyeing: Resist, Tie-Dye	Tie-Dyed Warp	Weintraub, Fran	√	√	SS&D	4	1	13	Wi 72	38
Dyes and Dyeing: Resist, Tie-Dye	Tiedyeing an Art on the Island of Sumba	Adams, Moni	√	√	H&C	22	1		Wi 71	9
Dyes and Dyeing: Resist, Tie-Dyeing	Peter Collingwood, His Weaves and Weaving: A Rug in Tie-Dye	Collingwood, Peter; Harriet Tidball, ed.	√	√	SCGM		8		63	8
Dyes and Dyeing: Resist, Tie-Dyeing	Tie-Dye...Naturally	Bliss, Anne	√	√	Iw	4	3		Su 79	58
Dyes and Dyeing: Resist, Tsutsugaki	Japanese Country Textiles (Exhibit)	Rowley, Kathleen	√		Fa	13	5		S/O 86	49
Dyes and Dyeing: Resist/Caustic Soda	Exploration of Caustic Soda, An	Bissell, June M.	√		Fa	7	6		N/D 80	43
Dyes and Dyeing: Rope	Manipulated Rope	Meilach, Dona Z.	√		Fa	5	1		J/F 78	46
Dyes and Dyeing: Skill	How Much Dye Can a Dyebath Dye if a Dyebath Can Dye Dye?	Bliss, Anne	√	√	Hw	6	2		M/A 85	85
Dyes and Dyeing: Solar	Nature's Colors, Naturally	Lorance, Marilyn	√		SS&D	10	1	37	Wi 78	49
Dyes and Dyeing: Solar	Stained Glass Vest	Shull, Paula	√	√	S-O	11	4		Wi 87	29
Dyes and Dyeing: Space Dyeing	Microwave Dyeing	Mortensen, Diane	√	√	SS&D	10	4	40	Fa 79	12
Dyes and Dyeing: Space Dyeing	Random Warp Dyeing: A Spontaneous Steam Dye Process	D'Ambrosio, Gina	√	√	WJ	10	3	39	Wi 86	42
Dyes and Dyeing: Space Dyeing	Space Dyeing with Fiber-Reactive Dyes	Knutson, Linda	√	√	WJ	8	1	29	Su 83	89
Dyes and Dyeing: Space-Dyeing	Unlocking the Secret of Space-Dyed Yarn for a Weft-Wise Design	Stoehr, Mary Kay	√	√	Hw	7	3		M/J 86	52
Dyes and Dyeing: Space-Dyeing, Techniques	Do It Yourself Guide to Space-Dyed Yarn	Bliss, Anne	√	√	Hw	7	3		M/J 86	55
Dyes and Dyeing: Spot Dyeing	Color and Dyeing: Dyeing Variations	Tidball, Harriet		√	SCGM		16		65	37
Dyes and Dyeing: Spray	Cynthia Pannucci: Relocating, Creating, Connecting	Mattera, Joanne	√		Fa	9	3		M/J 82	23
Dyes and Dyeing: Stock Dyeing	Color and Dyeing: Dyeing Variations	Tidball, Harriet		√	SCGM		16		65	37
Dyes and Dyeing: Synthetic	Designer Yarn — A Use for Acid Dyes	Omer, Martha			S-O	6	4		82	56
Dyes and Dyeing: Synthetic	Dyeing with the Synthetics	Bliss, Anne	√	√	Hw	6	1		J/F 85	69
Dyes and Dyeing: Synthetic	Point of Departure	Ligon, Linda	√	√	S-O	10	2		Su 86	53
Dyes and Dyeing: Synthetic	Thoughts on Sweater Design	Dewees, Libby	√		S-O	9	3		Fa 85	47
Dyes and Dyeing: Synthetic	"Union" Dyes and Another Look at a "Rainbow" Pot	Henrikson, Susan			S-O	6	4		82	16
Dyes and Dyeing: Synthetic Dyes	Introduction to Silk Dyeing, An	Walsh, Joan Lea		√	WJ	3	2	10	Oc 78	14
Dyes and Dyeing: Tapa Cloth	"Patterns of Paradise: Tapa Cloth" (Exhibit)	Dyer, Carolyn	√		Fa	10	3		M/J 83	73
Dyes and Dyeing: Techniques	Acid Dyeing	Kormos, Antonia	√	√	SS&D	15	2	58	Sp 84	34

SUBJECT	TITLE	AUTHOR	IL	INST	JOUR	VOL	NO	ISS	DATE	PAGE
Dyes and Dyeing: Techniques	Acid Dyes, Part 2, The	Koehler, Glory Dail		√	SS&D	6	4	24	Fa 75	78
Dyes and Dyeing: Techniques	Alkanet	Gerber, Frederick		√	Iw	5	3		Su 80	66
Dyes and Dyeing: Techniques	Ancient Yellow Goes Modern, An	Bliss, Anne	√	√	Iw	4	2		Sp 79	44
Dyes and Dyeing: Techniques	Art of Silk Dyeing, The (Photo-corrections WJ v10 n3 86 p6)	Wipplinger, Michelle	√	√	WJ	10	2	38	Fa 85	46
Dyes and Dyeing: Techniques	Chaos in the Kitchen: Part 1	Gerber, Willi; Fred Gerber	√	√	SS&D	5	3	19	Su 74	70
Dyes and Dyeing: Techniques	Christmas Tree Dye — A Natural!	Rossiter, Phyllis	√	√	S-O	9	4		Wi 85	22
Dyes and Dyeing: Techniques	Color and Dyeing: Dyeing Processes, Dyeing the Yarn	Tidball, Harriet	√	√	SCGM		16		65	26
Dyes and Dyeing: Techniques	Color and Dyeing: "Home Dyeing with Natural Dyes"	Tidball, Harriet		√	SCGM		16		65	39
Dyes and Dyeing: Techniques	Color and Dyeing: Methods	Tidball, Harriet	√	√	SCGM		16		65	34
Dyes and Dyeing: Techniques	Color Magic from Lichen Dyebaths	Casselman, Karen Leigh	√	√	SS&D	17	2	66	Sp 86	74
Dyes and Dyeing: Techniques	Confessions of a Mad Spinner	de la Garza, Phyllis			S-O	5			81	15
Dyes and Dyeing: Techniques	Creative Dyeing	Bachman, Sally	√	√	Iw	3	3		Sp 78	26
Dyes and Dyeing: Techniques	Crochet Inspired by the Trees	Moon, Ellen	√	√	TM			11	J/J 87	56
Dyes and Dyeing: Techniques	Dip Dyeing	Hausner, Walter	√	√	H&C	22	2		Sp 71	12
Dyes and Dyeing: Techniques	Direct Dyes	Koehler, Glory Dail	√	√	SS&D	7	3	27	Su 76	88
Dyes and Dyeing: Techniques	Diverse Dyes	Bliss, Anne	√	√	Iw	3	2		Wi 78	30
Dyes and Dyeing: Techniques	Dye and Spin Workshops on Nantucket	Beinecke, Mary Ann	√	√	SS&D	4	1	13	Wi 72	12
Dyes and Dyeing: Techniques	Dyeing: A Personal Palette for Tapestry	Bliss, Anne	√	√	Hw	3	1		Ja 82	66
Dyes and Dyeing: Techniques	Dyeing Gold and Yellow	Blackburn, Edna	√	√	TM			1	O/N 85	28
Dyes and Dyeing: Techniques	Dyeing in the Rockies	Bliss, Anne	√	√	SS&D	8	1	29	WI 76	14
Dyes and Dyeing: Techniques	Dyeing Mohair and the Random Effect	Russell, Barbara	√	√	S-O	6	4		82	54
Dyes and Dyeing: Techniques	Dyeing of Wool Blends	Mayer, Francis	√	√	WJ	2	4	8	Ap 78	26
Dyes and Dyeing: Techniques	Dyeing with Fiber Reactive Dyes on Cotton	Read, Kay	√	√	WJ	4	2	14	Oc 79	42
Dyes and Dyeing: Techniques	Dyeing with Lichens	Gerber, Willi; Fred Gerber	√	√	H&C	20	2		Sp 69	13
Dyes and Dyeing: Techniques	Dyeing with the Direct or Substantive Colors	Lucey, Edmund A.		√	H&C	2	1		Wi 50	52
Dyes and Dyeing: Techniques	Dyeing with Tree Blossoms	Held, Shirley	√	√	SS&D	8	4	32	Fa 77	41
Dyes and Dyeing: Techniques	Dyes for Handspuns: Fiber to Yarn	Bliss, Anne		√	S-O	6	4		82	52
Dyes and Dyeing: Techniques	Dyes From Mushrooms: A Spectrum of Extraordinary Color	Rice, Miriam	√	√	TM			10	A/M 87	44
Dyes and Dyeing: Techniques	"Easy As Pie" Dye Method, An	Stevens, Connie	√	√	S-O	9	1		Sp 85	22
Dyes and Dyeing: Techniques	Fiber-Mix Dyeing of Textiles	Arnold, Kari	√	√	SS&D	16	2	62	Sp 85	46
Dyes and Dyeing: Techniques	From a Dyer's Diary	Griffin, Gertrude		√	SS&D	1	3	3	Ju 70	21
Dyes and Dyeing: Techniques	Hints for Dyeing	Bliss, Anne			S-O	9	3		Fa 85	53
Dyes and Dyeing: Techniques	Home Dyeing with Native Plants Provides Wide Range of Colors	Langton, Janet F.		√	H&C	19	3		Su 68	16
Dyes and Dyeing: Techniques	How to Dye and Starch Silk	Bromberg, Kay	√	√	WJ	5	1	17	Su 80	43
Dyes and Dyeing: Techniques	How to Match Colors When Dyeing Yarns or Fabrics for Textile Conservation Purposes	Rice, James W.	√	√	TMJ	2	4		De 69	27
Dyes and Dyeing: Techniques	Ikat with Ease	Bliss, Anne	√	√	Hw	2	4		Se 81	60
Dyes and Dyeing: Techniques	Indigo	Weigle, Palmy	√	√	SS&D	8	3	31	Su 77	67
Dyes and Dyeing: Techniques	Indigo, Discovery of Plants and Experiments in Dyeing	Gerber, Willi; Fred Gerber	√	√	H&C	19	4		Fa 68	4
Dyes and Dyeing: Techniques	Indigo Dyeing			√	TM			3	F/M 86	8
Dyes and Dyeing: Techniques	Indigo Dyeing and the Problems of Crocking	Pendergrass, Mary	√	√	WJ	4	3	15	Ja 80	30
Dyes and Dyeing: Techniques	Indigo—The all Time Favorite Blue	Bliss, Anne	√	√	Hw	2	3		My 81	60
Dyes and Dyeing: Techniques	Investigative Method—A Tool for Study, Part 1	Gerber, Fred	√	√	SS&D	6	1	21	Wi 74	62
Dyes and Dyeing: Techniques	Investigative Method—A Tool for Study, Part 2	Gerber, Fred		√	SS&D	6	2	22	Sp 75	53

SUBJECT	TITLE	AUTHOR	IL	INST	JOUR	VOL	NO	ISS	DATE	PAGE
Dyes and Dyeing: Techniques	Investigative Method — A Tool for Study, Part 3	Gerber, Fred; Juanita Gerber		√	SS&D	6	4	24	Fa 75	69
Dyes and Dyeing: Techniques	Kumejima Dorozome: The Vegetable Dye and Mud Mordanting Process of Silk Tsugumi	Miller, Dorothy	√	√	AT	5			Ju 86	131
Dyes and Dyeing: Techniques	Learning the Flax of Life	Murrow, Romedy	√	√	S-O	9	3		Fa 85	49
Dyes and Dyeing: Techniques	Microwave Dyeing	Mortensen, Diane	√	√	SS&D	10	4	40	Fa 79	12
Dyes and Dyeing: Techniques	Milkweed and Balduinea in the Dyepot	Gerber, Fred; Willi Gerber	√	√	H&C	22	3		Su 71	23
Dyes and Dyeing: Techniques	Milkweed and Balduinea in the Dyepot (Reprint)	Gerber, Fred; Willi Gerber	√	√	H&C	26	1		J/F 75	19
Dyes and Dyeing: Techniques	Mineral Dyes 2, The	Liles, James N.	√	√	SS&D	13	4	52	Fa 82	60
Dyes and Dyeing: Techniques	Mineral Dyes, The	Liles, James N.	√	√	SS&D	13	3	51	Su 82	54
Dyes and Dyeing: Techniques	Multi-Color, One Pot Dyeing	Henrikson, Susan	√	√	WJ	8	4	32	Sp 84	39
Dyes and Dyeing: Techniques	Nature's Colors, Naturally	Lorance, Marilyn	√		SS&D	10	1	37	Wi 78	49
Dyes and Dyeing: Techniques	New Twist on Resist	Wada, Yoshiko Iwamoto; Shelley Karpilow	√	√	TM			8	D/J 86	20
Dyes and Dyeing: Techniques	Notes on Color Fastness	Hausner, Walter	√	√	H&C	10	2		Sp 59	46
Dyes and Dyeing: Techniques	On Dyeing with Madder	Bliss, Anne	√	√	Iw	5	1		Wi 79	48
Dyes and Dyeing: Techniques	Onion Gold	Kolander, Cheryl	√	√	S-O	9	3		Fa 85	40
Dyes and Dyeing: Techniques	Personal Color System for Dyers, A	La Lena, Connie	√	√	Iw	3	3		Sp 78	20
Dyes and Dyeing: Techniques	Plumage in the Dyepot	Brown, Melissa J.	√	√	SS&D	9	1	33	Wi 77	103
Dyes and Dyeing: Techniques	Polychroma: Natural Dye Methods	Piroch, Sigrid	√	√	SS&D	17	2	66	Sp 86	26
Dyes and Dyeing: Techniques	Practical Dyeing Method for the Fabric Conservator, A	Cooley, Theodore R.	√	√	TMJ	2	4		De 69	23
Dyes and Dyeing: Techniques	Preparing, Spinning and Dyeing Mohair	Russell, Barbara		√	S-O	7	3		Fa 83	52
Dyes and Dyeing: Techniques	Problem Solving	Bliss, Anne; with Margaret Emerson		√	Iw	3	3		Sp 78	34
Dyes and Dyeing: Techniques	Procion M: The Thick and the Thin	Deschamps, Kalli	√	√	Iw	3	4		Su 78	40
Dyes and Dyeing: Techniques	Production Dyeing with Natural Dyes	Van Stralen, Trudy	√	√	S-O	11	4		Wi 87	57
Dyes and Dyeing: Techniques	Putting the King in the Pot	Bliss, Anne	√	√	Iw	1	4		Su 76	20
Dyes and Dyeing: Techniques	Rainbow Fleece: A Happy Hazard Approach to Chemical Dyeing	Lorance, Marilyn	√	√	Hw	2	4		Se 81	68
Dyes and Dyeing: Techniques	Random Warp Dyeing: A Spontaneous Steam Dye Process	D'Ambrosio, Gina	√	√	WJ	10	3	39	Wi 86	42
Dyes and Dyeing: Techniques	Second Look at Soft Drink Mix Dyes, A	Bloedel, Linda		√	WJ	9	2	34	Fa 84	24
Dyes and Dyeing: Techniques	Silk and Fiber Reactive Dyes		√	√	WJ	3	2	10	Oc 78	24
Dyes and Dyeing: Techniques	Silk Dyeing		√	√	WJ	3	2	10	Oc 78	21
Dyes and Dyeing: Techniques	Some New Rules for Dyeing	Mies, Mary; Betty Bernstein	√	√	SS&D	11	3	43	Su 80	9
Dyes and Dyeing: Techniques	Spice Dyeing	Reesor, Tracy		√	WJ	6	4	24	Sp 82	47
Dyes and Dyeing: Techniques	Spray Dyeing to Obtain Space-Dyed Yarns	Shapiro, Brenda	√	√	SS&D	15	4	60	Fa 84	54
Dyes and Dyeing: Techniques	Sprinkle, Dump and Dapple	Rabinowe, Victoria	√	√	SS&D	4	3	15	Su 73	55
Dyes and Dyeing: Techniques	Stock Solution, The	Koehler, Glory Dail		√	SS&D	7	1	25	Wi 75	76
Dyes and Dyeing: Techniques	Stretching Fabric in Small Spaces	Levy, Julie	√	√	TM			3	F/M 86	34
Dyes and Dyeing: Techniques	Summer Shades	Koster, Joan Bouza	√	√	SS&D	18	3	71	Su 87	40
Dyes and Dyeing: Techniques	Surface Design Techniques — The Basics	Bliss, Anne	√	√	Hw	8	1		J/F 87	78
Dyes and Dyeing: Techniques	Textural Approach to Arashi Shibori, A	Beytebiere, D'Arcie	√	√	TM			8	D/J 86	24
Dyes and Dyeing: Techniques	Tiedyeing an Art on the Island of Sumba	Adams, Moni	√	√	H&C	22	1		Wi 71	9
Dyes and Dyeing: Techniques	Traditional Berber Weaving in Central Morocco	Forelli, Sally; Jeanette Harries	√		TMJ	4	4		77	41
Dyes and Dyeing: Techniques	Uncommon Dyewood: Manzanita—From the Chaparral, An	Hall, Joanne Arvidson	√	√	SS&D	7	3	27	Su 76	55
Dyes and Dyeing: Techniques	Using Procion Dyes	Stetson, G. Robert	√	√	Iw	3	3		Sp 78	31
Dyes and Dyeing: Techniques	Vat Dyes	Koehler, Glory Dail		√	SS&D	8	1	29	WI 76	37
Dyes and Dyeing: Techniques	Weaver Dyes, A	Glantz, Mary Ann	√		SS&D	2	3	7	Su 71	23

SUBJECT	TITLE	AUTHOR	IL	INST	JOUR	VOL	NO	ISS	DATE	PAGE
Dyes and Dyeing: Techniques	Why Bother with Natural Dyeing?	Bulbach, Stanley	√	√	TM			5	J/J 86	32
Dyes and Dyeing: Techniques	Winter Dyeing with Umbilicate Lichens (error-corrected SS&D v9 n4 78 p34)	Casselman, Karen L.	√	√	SS&D	9	2	34	Sp 78	8
Dyes and Dyeing: Techniques	Wonderful Worsted	Dozer, Iris L.	√	√	SS&D	15	3	59	Su 84	26
Dyes and Dyeing: Techniques	Wool Dyed the Procion Way	Windeknecht, Margaret B.	√	√	SS&D	6	4	24	Fa 75	89
Dyes and Dyeing: Techniques	Wool Dyeing and Mothproofing for the Handweaver	Mayer, Francis		√	WJ	2	3	7	Ja 78	41
Dyes and Dyeing: Techniques, Bundle	Dye a Bundle	Bliss, Anne	√	√	Hw	5	3		Su 84	87
Dyes and Dyeing: Techniques, Chemicals	Color and Dyeing: Chemical Dyeing	Tidball, Harriet		√	SCGM		16		65	13
Dyes and Dyeing: Techniques, Kool-Aid	Safe Dye for Children, A	Gilsdorf, Marilyn	√	√	WJ	8	4	32	Sp 84	47
Dyes and Dyeing: Techniques, Microwave	Two Easy Dye Methods	Hessler, Jean	√	√	Hw	8	2		M/A 87	86
Dyes and Dyeing: Techniques, One-Pot	Bancroft's Mordant: A Useful One-Pot Natural Dye Technique	Liles, James N.; Dale Liles	√	√	SS&D	15	3	59	Su 84	76
Dyes and Dyeing: Techniques, Oven	Two Easy Dye Methods	Hessler, Jean	√	√	Hw	8	2		M/A 87	86
Dyes and Dyeing: Techniques, Overdye	Overdyeing Your Yarns: A Way to Increase Your Palette	Warner, Lucy Ann	√	√	Fa	5	1		J/F 78	37
Dyes and Dyeing: Techniques, Percentage Ratio	Chemical Dyeing of Linen	Gwynne, Elaine	√	√	WJ	7	2	26	Fa 82	23
Dyes and Dyeing: Techniques, Rainbow	Rainbow Dyeing	Rowe, Erica	√	√	WJ	8	2	30	Fa 83	31
Dyes and Dyeing: Techniques, Solar	Solar Dyeing: A New Look At Fermentation	Bliss, Anne	√	√	Iw	1	1		Fa 75	12
Dyes and Dyeing: Techniques, Sprinkle	Hand-Dyed Angora Bunny Scarf	Hart, Jacque	√	√	S-O	11	4		Wi 87	26
Dyes and Dyeing: Techniques, Timing	Time Element, The	Thilenius, Carol	√	√	Iw	4	4		Fa 79	56
Dyes and Dyeing: Techniques, Top Dyeing	Chemical Dyeing of Linen	Gwynne, Elaine	√	√	WJ	7	2	26	Fa 82	23
Dyes and Dyeing: Tips	Tips on Home Dyeing	Hurry, Gaynel		√	H&C	22	4		Fa 71	19
Dyes and Dyeing: Top Dyeing	Color and Dyeing: Dyeing Variations	Tidball, Harriet		√	SCGM		16		65	37
Dyes and Dyeing: Tritik Discharge	Carol Westfall: Adapting Dye Transfer Methods	Park, Betty	√		Fa	5	1		J/F 78	64
Dyes and Dyeing: Turkey Red	On Dyeing with Madder	Bliss, Anne	√	√	Iw	5	1		Wi 79	48
Dyes and Dyeing: Union Dyeing	Color and Dyeing: Dyeing Variations	Tidball, Harriet		√	SCGM		16		65	37
Dyes and Dyeing: Varicolored Dyeing	Color and Dyeing: Dyeing Variations	Tidball, Harriet		√	SCGM		16		65	37
Dyes and Dyeing: Warp Dyeing	Color and Dyeing: Dyeing Variations	Tidball, Harriet		√	SCGM		16		65	37
Dyes and Dyeing: Wool	Q & A on Wool Dyeing	Oswald, Francis		√	SS&D	1	1	1	De 69	11
Dyes and Dyeing: Wool	Woolens and Tweeds: From Fleece to Woolen Yarn: Dyeing	Tidball, Harriet			SCGM		4		61	8
Dyes and Dyeing: Workshops	"Dye-In" in Detail: For Novices in Nova Scotia, A	Lock, Carolyn		√	SS&D	7	2	26	Sp 76	36
Dyes and Dyeing: Workshops	Dyepot in Australia	Taggart, Barbara	√	√	SS&D	5	4	20	Fa 74	56
Dyes and Dyeing: Workshops	New Hampshire Gives Dyeshop	Mitiguy, Harriet			SS&D	3	3	11	Su 72	21
Dyes and Dyeing: Workshops	We Dyed in the Woods	Castino, Ruth	√	√	SS&D	4	3	15	Su 73	22
Dyes and Dyeing: Yardage	Clothesline Palette: Three Hundred Yards of Color		√		Fa	9	1		J/F 82	22
Dyes: For Cellulose Acetate, Nylon, Polyester	Dyeing with the Synthetics	Bliss, Anne	√	√	Hw	6	1		J/F 85	69
Dyes: For Cotton, Linen, Cellulose	Dyeing with the Synthetics	Bliss, Anne	√	√	Hw	6	1		J/F 85	69
Dyes: For Protein Fiber	Dyeing with the Synthetics	Bliss, Anne	√	√	Hw	6	1		J/F 85	69
Dyes: For Viscose Rayon	Dyeing with the Synthetics	Bliss, Anne	√	√	Hw	6	1		J/F 85	69
Dyes: Types	Dyeing with the Synthetics	Bliss, Anne	√	√	Hw	6	1		J/F 85	69
Early American Crafts	Early American Craftsman's Holiday, An	Wellman, Kathryn	√		H&C	2	2		Sp 51	30
Early American Crafts	Seminars on Early American Crafts	MacFarlane, Janet R.	√		H&C	2	2		Sp 51	29

SUBJECT	TITLE	AUTHOR	IL	INST	JOUR	VOL	NO	ISS	DATE	PAGE
Early American Fabrics	Williamsburg Weaving	Brown, Bonnie	√		H&C	12	2		Sp 61	30
Early American Linens	Early American Linens	Gallagher, Constance	√	>4	H&C	15	3		Su 64	7
Early American Textile Designs	Coverlets and Bedspreads: Variety in Early American Design	Saulpaugh, Dassah	√		H&C	17	4		Fa 66	8
Early American Textile Designs	Pennington Linens, Iowa Weaver Collects Old Designs		√		H&C	16	3		Su 65	14
Early American: Textiles	Early American Handwoven Linens	Gallagher, Constance D.			SS&D	1	1	1	De 69	12
Early American Textiles	Early American Textiles, from Linda Belding's Collection		√		H&C	15	1		Wi 64	20
Early American Textiles	Peter Stauffer — Early 19th Century Weaver	Rogers, Grace L.	√	>4	H&C	7	1		Wi 55	12
Early American: Textiles	Weaver Rose — A New Perspective	Kaye, Alda Ganze	√		SS&D	8	2	30	Sp 77	8
Early American: Weaving	Martha Washington's Inaugural Gown	Reams, Dorothy E.	√		SS&D	7	3	27	Su 76	15
Easter see Holiday Weavings										
Easy Projects	Keep It Simple		√	√	Hw	8	3		M/J 87	91
Easy Projects	Ruana for Beginners, A	Rose, Violet	√	√	Hw	8	4		S/O 87	48
Ecclesiastical/Liturgical Embroidery	Sten Kauppi		√		H&C	5	1		Wi 53	48
Ecclesiastical/Liturgical Fiber	Dina Barzel		√		Fa	4	6		N/D 77	38
Ecclesiastical/Liturgical Fiber	Ecclesiastical Fiber	Eggers, Conni	√		Fa	4	6		N/D 77	36
Ecclesiastical/Liturgical Fiber	Emma & Felix Senger		√		Fa	4	6		N/D 77	44
Ecclesiastical/Liturgical Fiber	Kai Walters	Pilsk, Adele	√		Fa	4	6		N/D 77	42
Ecclesiastical/Liturgical Fiber	Marjorie Coffey	Coffey, Marjorie	√		Fa	4	6		N/D 77	40
Ecclesiastical/Liturgical Fiber	Mary Becker		√		Fa	4	6		N/D 77	39
Ecclesiastical/Liturgical Weavings	Advent Chasuble, An	Droege, Carol	√		SS&D	17	1	65	Wi 85	41
Ecclesiastical/Liturgical Weavings	Ark Curtain	Howell, Marie	√		H&C	15	2		Sp 64	37
Ecclesiastical/Liturgical Weavings	Award to Church in Rochester				H&C	18	3		Su 67	40
Ecclesiastical/Liturgical Weavings	Chasubles from Marjorie January's Looms		√		H&C	19	1		Wi 68	18
Ecclesiastical/Liturgical Weavings	Church Paraments in Crackle Weave	Murphy, Mathilda C.	√	>4	SS&D	5	3	19	Su 74	54
Ecclesiastical/Liturgical Weavings	Communion Vestments, Designed and Woven by a Clergyman		√		H&C	16	1		Wi 65	10
Ecclesiastical/Liturgical Weavings	Contemporary Religious Art in California	Bryan, Dorothy	√		H&C	4	1		Wi 52	7
Ecclesiastical/Liturgical Weavings	Contemporary Vestments	Markey, Barbara R.	√		H&C	9	3		Su 58	11
Ecclesiastical/Liturgical Weavings	Design for Torah Cover Based on 'Torah is Truth' and 'Tree of Life'	Lebovitz, Constance	√	√	SS&D	4	4	16	Fa 73	18
Ecclesiastical/Liturgical Weavings	Dossal Woven by the Rev. L. Harold Hinrichs For His Church, A		√		H&C	20	3		Su 69	11
Ecclesiastical/Liturgical Weavings	Draperies for a Synagogue		√		H&C	9	4		Fa 58	45
Ecclesiastical/Liturgical Weavings	Early Christian Church Curtains	Austin, Carole	√		Fa	14	2		M/A 87	28
Ecclesiastical/Liturgical Weavings	Ecclesiastical Tapestries		√		H&C	8	3		Su 57	50
Ecclesiastical/Liturgical Weavings	Ecclesiastical Weaving		√	√	H&C	13	1		Wi 62	34
Ecclesiastical/Liturgical Weavings	Ecclesiastical Weaving	King, Bucky	√		WJ	6	1	21	Su 81	35
Ecclesiastical/Liturgical Weavings	Ecclesiastical Weaving, Part 1	Ziemke, Dene	√		SS&D	9	3	35	Su 78	31
Ecclesiastical/Liturgical Weavings	Ecclesiastical Weaving, Part 2	Ziemke, Dene	√	√	SS&D	9	4	36	Fa 78	42
Ecclesiastical/Liturgical Weavings	Ecclesiastical Weaving, Part 3	Ziemke, Dene	√		SS&D	10	1	37	Wi 78	46
Ecclesiastical/Liturgical Weavings	Ecclesiastical Weaving, Part 4	Ziemke, Dene	√		SS&D	10	2	38	Sp 79	65
Ecclesiastical/Liturgical Weavings	Ecclesiastical Weavings of Diana Lockwood, The		√	>4	WJ	4	3	15	Ja 80	18
Ecclesiastical/Liturgical Weavings	Eucharistic Vestments, The	Malloy, Kim, OSB	√	√	WJ	6	1	21	Su 81	37
Ecclesiastical/Liturgical Weavings	Fabrics from a New Type Multi-Harness Loom	Cory, Sue Armstrong	√	>4	H&C	10	1		Wi 59	24
Ecclesiastical/Liturgical Weavings	Fiber and Architecture: Wilcke Smith		√		Fa	3	3		M/J 76	18
Ecclesiastical/Liturgical Weavings	Greta, Lein, Young Norweigan Designer-Weaver	Nygards-Kers, Ingrid	√		H&C	14	1		Wi 63	15
Ecclesiastical/Liturgical Weavings	Handwoven Applique on Handwoven Fabrics Used by Hortense Amram in Ecclesiastical Design		√	√	H&C	13	2		Sp 62	20

SUBJECT	TITLE	AUTHOR	IL	INST	JOUR	VOL	NO	ISS	DATE	PAGE
Ecclesiastical/Liturgical Weavings	Hortense Amram, Designer and Weaver of Ceremonial Textiles		√	√	H&C	9	4		Fa 58	22
Ecclesiastical/Liturgical Weavings	Jewish Ceremonial Textiles		√		H&C	7	4		Fa 56	18
Ecclesiastical/Liturgical Weavings	Laurie Herrick		√		Fa	4	6		N/D 77	43
Ecclesiastical/Liturgical Weavings	Lenten Curtains from Colonial Peru	Kelemen, Pál	√		TMJ	3	1		De 70	5
Ecclesiastical/Liturgical Weavings	Lenten Pulpit Antependium (Mary Temple)		√	√	Hw	8	3		M/J 87	57, I-10
Ecclesiastical/Liturgical Weavings	Liturgical Textiles	Quigley, Viola Joyce	√	> 4	H&C	11	3		Su 60	53
Ecclesiastical/Liturgical Weavings	"Marie Lyman: Liturgical Vestments" (Exhibit)	Griffin, Rachel	√		Fa	7	3		M/J 80	77
Ecclesiastical/Liturgical Weavings	Marion Stewart		√		H&C	13	4		Fa 62	17
Ecclesiastical/Liturgical Weavings	Marjorie Pohlman		√		Fa	4	6		N/D 77	45
Ecclesiastical/Liturgical Weavings	Modern Church Textiles	Howell, Marie	√		H&C	13	3		Su 62	20
Ecclesiastical/Liturgical Weavings	Open-Weave Altar Hanging	McIntosh, Joan W.	√		SS&D	4	2	14	Sp 73	15
Ecclesiastical/Liturgical Weavings	Prayer Shawls	Bercey, Lee	√	√	H&C	20	1		Wi 69	20
Ecclesiastical/Liturgical Weavings	Pure Silk Ecclesiastical Vestments		√	√	SS&D	4	1	13	Wi 72	16
Ecclesiastical/Liturgical Weavings	Reflections on the Chasuble	Centner, The Rev. David J., O.C.D.	√		Hw	5	1		J/F 84	36
Ecclesiastical/Liturgical Weavings	Religious Celebration		√		SS&D	11	4	44	Fa 80	22
Ecclesiastical/Liturgical Weavings	Seasonal Stoles	Rizner, Constance Bufkin	√	√	SS&D	18	2	70	Sp 87	22
Ecclesiastical/Liturgical Weavings	Show Stopper: Easter Chasuble		√		SS&D	6	2	22	Sp 75	47
Ecclesiastical/Liturgical Weavings	Some Practical Suggestions for Making Ecclesiastical Vesture	Jacopin, Armand J.	√		H&C	9	3		Su 58	18
Ecclesiastical/Liturgical Weavings	Special Piece—A Special Place, A	Harvey, Nancy	√		WJ	8	1	29	Su 83	67
Ecclesiastical/Liturgical Weavings	St. Mary's Weavers		√		H&C	10	1		Wi 59	30
Ecclesiastical/Liturgical Weavings	Stepping Out	Ridgeway, Terese	√		SS&D	18	1	69	Wi 86	82
Ecclesiastical/Liturgical Weavings	Structure and Form in the Weaving of John Becker	Swannie, Suzanne	√		AT	6			De 86	173
Ecclesiastical/Liturgical Weavings	Suggestions for Weavers of Liturgical Textiles	Ormond, Helen C.	√	√	H&C	10	3		Su 59	29
Ecclesiastical/Liturgical Weavings	Symbolic or Sacred? A Personal View	Lockwood, Diana W.	√	> 4	WJ	9	3	35	Wi 85	45
Ecclesiastical/Liturgical Weavings	Talbot Weavers' Golden Anniversary (error-corrected H&C v5 n4 54 p43)		√		H&C	5	3		Su 54	4
Ecclesiastical/Liturgical Weavings	Tale of a Talis, A	Sylvan, Katherine	√	√	WJ	6	1	21	Su 81	42
Ecclesiastical/Liturgical Weavings	Tallis or Prayer Shawl, The	Derr, Mary	√	√	WJ	2	1	5	Jy 77	16
Ecclesiastical/Liturgical Weavings	Tapestries at Temple Emanu-El	Golub, Ina	√		SS&D	14	1	53	Wi 82	41
Ecclesiastical/Liturgical Weavings	Tapestry for a Midwest Chapel	Helfman, Muriel Nezhnie	√		H&C	21	2		Sp 70	8
Ecclesiastical/Liturgical Weavings	Temple Tapestry	Rapp, Sylvia	√		SS&D	15	2	58	Sp 84	24
Ecclesiastical/Liturgical Weavings	"The Robe," is Woven on a California Handloom	Marshall, Bertha	√		H&C	4	3		Su 53	14
Ecclesiastical/Liturgical Weavings	Theo Moorman: A Conversation with a Very Special Person		√		Fa	3	4		J/A 76	22
Ecclesiastical/Liturgical Weavings	Thousand Years of Western Vestments: Raiment for the Lord's Service, A		√		SS&D	7	2	26	Sp 76	8
Ecclesiastical/Liturgical Weavings	Tree of Life	Renee, Paula	√		SS&D	17	2	66	Sp 86	80
Ecclesiastical/Liturgical Weavings	Vestment Variations: A Weaver From the Netherlands Creates Garments for the Ecclesiastical Calendar	Jansen, Netty	√	> 4	WJ	10	3	39	Wi 86	53
Ecclesiastical/Liturgical Weavings	Vestments by Indian Craftsmen: A Cooperative Enterprise of the Lummis, Navajos, and Sioux		√		H&C	18	1		Wi 67	6
Ecclesiastical/Liturgical Weavings	Vestments from the KilBride Workshop		√		H&C	15	3		Su 64	12
Ecclesiastical/Liturgical Weavings	Violet Vestment	Hahn, Roslyn	√	> 4	WJ	8	3	31	Wi 83	44
Ecclesiastical/Liturgical Weavings	We Like Weaving	Anita, Sister M.	√	> 4	H&C	22	1		Wi 71	17
Ecclesiastical/Liturgical Weavings	Weaver's Story of Two Prayer Shawls, Garments Used in Jewish Ritual, A	Schlein, Alice	√	> 4	CW	3	3	9	Ap 82	6
Ecclesiastical/Liturgical Weavings	Weaving a Tribute for Their Church		√		H&C	2	4		Fa 51	23
Ecclesiastical/Liturgical Weavings	Weaving Ecclesiastical Stoles and Chasubles	Reed, Kathy	√	√	WJ	6	1	21	Su 81	46

SUBJECT	TITLE	AUTHOR	IL	INST	JOUR	VOL	NO	ISS	DATE	PAGE
Ecclesiastical/Liturgical Weavings	Weaving for the Church—A Challenge	Hahn, Roslyn J.	√		Hw	5	1		J/F 84	32
Ecclesiastical/Liturgical Weavings	Weaving Works for Worship	Paul, Jan	√		WJ	6	1	21	Su 81	40
Ecclesiastical/Liturgical Weavings: Contemporary	Liturgical Vestment: A Contemporary Overview, The	Malarcher, Patricia	√		Fa	11	5		S/O 84	58
Ecuador	Backstrap Weaving for Penance and Profit	Coffman, Charlotte	√	√	WJ	7	1	25	Su 82	60
Ecuador	Costume and Weaving in Saraguro, Ecuador	Meisch, Lynn Ann	√		TMJ	19 20			80,81	55
Ecuador	Hamaca from Ecuador	Bowman, Susan	√	√	SS&D	10	3	39	Su 79	52
Ecuador	Indian Textiles from Ecuador		√		H&C	10	1		Wi 59	19
Ecuador	Noble Tradition Preserved: An Ecuadorian Weaving Co-op, A	Llewellyn, Charles; Deborah Llewellyn	√		SS&D	11	3	43	Su 80	12
Ecuador	Primitive Indian Designs Inspire Ecuador's Gift to United Nations		√		H&C	4	1		Wi 52	13
Ecuador	Spinning in Ecuador	Meisch, Lynn Ann	√	√	S-O	4			80	24
Ecuador	Weaving a Cotton Saddlebag on the Santa Elena Peninsula of Ecuador	Hagino, Jane Parker; Karen E. Stothert	√	√	TMJ	22			83	19
Ecuadorian Weaving	Costume and Weaving in Saraguro, Ecuador	Meisch, Lynn Ann	√		TMJ	19 20			80,81	55
Edinburgh Tapestry Company	Imagery Is Personal in Tapestry Today	Clausen, Valerie	√		TM			9	F/M 87	66
Editors: American Knitting	American Knitting Editors				Kn	2	2	4	S-S 86	68
Education: Adult Classes, Weaving	Weaving Classes in Milwaukee		√		H&C	11	3		Su 60	44
Education: Art Center, Mendocino Textile Apprenticeship Program	Livin' and Workin' on the Land: Fiber Art Outside the Mainstream	Talley, Charles S.	√		Fa	8	6		N/D 81	38
Education: Atelier, Tapestry	In the Gobelin Tradition: The Drouin Atelier	Gregg, Dorothy	√		SS&D	10	1	37	Wi 78	28
Education: Books on Tape	Weaving Texts Recorded for the Blind	Brubaker, Paul			Fa	3	5		S/O 76	35
Education: Classes, Papermaking	Learning Papermaking in Nantucket	Bach, Ann	√		Fa	11	2		M/A 84	47
Education: Classes, Weaving	Shinnosuke Seino: Innovator with Wool	Schreiber, Lavonne	√		WJ	12	2	46	Fa 87	34
Education: Classes/Workshops, Papermaking	Papermaking Classes and Workshops: A Selective List	Howe, Cathe	√		Fa	11	2		M/A 84	47
Education: Community Classes, Weaving	Arts & Crafts Program at Riverside Church		√		H&C	11	2		Sp 60	27
Education: Community Classes, Weaving	Marli Ehrman		√		H&C	11	2		Sp 60	25
Education: Community Classes, Weaving	Richmond Art Center, A Unique Adventure, The	Bryan, Dorothy	√		H&C	3	3		Su 52	34
Education: Community Classes, Weaving	Weaving Project for Young and Old		√		H&C	14	4		Fa 63	32
Education: Community Craft Programs	Westchester County Crafts Program	Kiser, Charlotte E.	√		H&C	3	1		Wi 51	38
Education: Community Programs, Crafts	St. John's Cathedral Project	Murray, Megan	√		Fa	10	4		J/A 83	45
Education: Community Project, Weaving	Future Weavers	Holroyd, Ruth N.	√		SS&D	2	3	7	Su 71	13
Education: Correspondence Course, Weaving	Polly Yori (error-corrected H&C v21 n3 70 p45)	Marston, Ena	√	> 4	H&C	21	1		Wi 70	19
Education: Crafts	Crafts in Education, Part 2, The	Brennan, Harold J.			H&C	6	2		Sp 55	15
Education: Elementary, Projects, Wearable Art	Wearable Art at P. S. 152	Wallach, Nancy	√		Fa	7	6		N/D 80	25
Education: Elementary, Public Park Service Program	Day in the Life of a Millgirl	Salinger, Maude	√		SS&D	17	4	68	Fa 86	78
Education: Graduate School, Fiber Arts	Graduate School...Is It Right For You?	Huey, Carol			Iw	5	4		Fa 80	71
Education: Graduate Students	Teacher/Student Interface: Two Views of Education	Obeymeyer, Lindsay; Maria Katsaros	√		Fa	14	1		J/F 87	34
Education: Historic Sites, Crafts Program	With Needle, Thread and Imagination		√		SS&D	1	4	4	Se 70	10
Education: Home Study Course, Weaving	Textile Structure and Analysis, A Home Study Course in Twelve Lessons	Tidball, Harriet	√	√	SCGM		18		66	1-31

SUBJECT	TITLE	AUTHOR	IL	INST	JOUR	VOL	NO	ISS	DATE	PAGE
Education: Home Study Programs	Exploration of Materials, The	Waller, Irene	√	√	SS&D	8	4	32	Fa 77	55
Education: Instructions, Taped	Kenneth Spaulding's Triumph: The Will to Weave	Spaulding, K. B., Jr.	√	√	SS&D	7	1	25	Wi 75	18
Education: Lessons (15), Tapestry, Composition	Contemporary Tapestry	Tidball, Harriet	√	√	SCGM		12		64	35
Education: Lessons, Tapestry Weaving	Contemporary Tapestry	Tidball, Harriet	√	√	SCGM		12		64	34
Education: Mini-Courses, Weaving	Mini-Course—Maxi-Success	Ziemke, Dene	√		SS&D	6	2	22	Sp 75	88
Education: Museum Classes, Crafts	Spinners & Weavers in New Zealand Use Native Materials	Duncan, Molly	√		H&C	21	1		Wi 70	14
Education: Museum Classes, Design	Documents & Design	Justema, William	√		H&C	21	4		Fa 70	40
Education: Museum Classes, Fabric Analysis	On Foreign Soil But Common Ground, Textile Assembly Meets in Spain	Mailey, Jean	√		H&C	21	1		Wi 70	18
Education: Museum Classes, Weaving	Designs from a Weaving Teacher's Studio		√		H&C	12	4		Fa 61	22
Education: Museum Classes, Weaving	Fiftieth Anniversary for Newark Museum		√		H&C	10	2		Sp 59	9
Education: Museum Classes, Weaving	Montclair Museum Classes	Turner, Alta R.	√		H&C	11	4		Fa 60	25
Education: Museum Classes, Weaving	Weavers at Montclair Museum		√	√	H&C	20	1		Wi 69	30
Education: Museum Classes, Weaving	Weaving Classes in an Art Gallery	Holroyd, Ruth N.	√	√	H&C	22	4		Fa 71	12
Education: Museum Classes, Weaving	Weaving Courses at the Newark Museum	Reeve, Beatrice	√		H&C	4	4		Fa 53	33
Education: Museum Courses, Crafts	Thousand Islands Museum Craft School	Barnes, Muriel			SS&D	1	3	3	Ju 70	4
Education: Museum Courses, Weaving	Contemporary Hangings at Brookfield	Gotthoffer, Esther	√		SS&D	1	1	1	De 69	2
Education: Museum Programs, Textile	Weaving at Fort Hunter Museum	Meigs, Margaret Wister	√		H&C	4	2		Sp 53	26
Education: Museum Programs, Weaving	New Jersey Weavers Exhibit at the Montclair Museum		√		H&C	7	3		Su 56	44
Education: Out-Reach Program, Weaving	Weaving Vehicle, The	Mavigliano, George J.	√		SS&D	8	3	31	Su 77	79
Education: Primary, Teaching, Weaving	Planting Seeds	Greene, Susan	√		Hw	5	3		Su 84	40
Education: Primary, Weaving	Each One Picked a Color—4th and 5th Graders Weave a Blanket	Hanna, Linda	√		WJ	9	1	33	Su 84	34
Education: Primary, Weaving	Fifth Grade Weavers in California	Marshall, Bertha	√		H&C	5	1		Wi 53	31
Education: Primary, Weaving	Miniature Weavers on Full-Size Looms		√		SS&D	2	1	5	De 70	23
Education: Programs, Textile Design	If Fashion Starts in the Fabric, Where Are Our Fabric Designers?	Humphries, Mary; Carol Outram			CW	3	1	7	Se 81	4
Education: Programs, Textiles	Textile Apprenticeship in Northern California	Montgomery, Larry			TM			9	F/M 87	20
Education: School, Spinning	Door Closes for Shelburne Spinners, The	Clark, Katherine	√		SS&D	9	3	35	Su 78	34
Education: Schools, Craft	Guide to Weaving Schools and Craft Schools, A	Pettigrew, Dale			Hw	5	3		Su 84	33
Education: Schools, Crafts	Common Denominator of the Handicrafts, The	Ford, Toni	√		H&C	3	1		Wi 51	23
Education: Schools, Crafts	Education of the Creative Craftsman	Brennan, Harold J.			H&C	11	3		Su 60	13
Education: Schools, Crafts	Haystack Mountain School of Crafts, The	Merrit, Francis S.	√		H&C	3	1		Wi 51	29
Education: Schools, Crafts	New Brunswick Craft School: Hosting A Workshop by Barbara MacCallum, The	Bauer, Nancy	√		Fa	11	5		S/O 84	40
Education: Schools, Crafts	Penland School of Crafts, The	Brown, William J.			H&C	16	3		Su 65	21
Education: Schools, Crafts	Penland School of Handicrafts		√		H&C	23	2		M/A 72	8
Education: Schools, Crafts	Sixty Years of Weaving At Arrowmont	Johnson, Debbie	√		Fa	12	5		S/O 85	39
Education: Schools, Design	Jacquard Project: Selections from the Current Exhibition, The		√		Fa	9	2		M/A 82	36
Education: Schools, Dyeing	Three Weeks At Nantucket				SS&D	2	1	5	De 70	19

SUBJECT	TITLE	AUTHOR	IL	INST	JOUR	VOL	NO	ISS	DATE	PAGE
Education: Schools, Fabric Arts	San Francisco School of Fabric Arts, The	Papa, Nancy	√		Fa	6	1		J/F 79	13
Education: Schools, Fashion Design	Education in Fashion and Fabric: Program at the Fashion Institute of Technology	Stout, Pola	√		H&C	16	3		Su 65	6
Education: Schools, Handicrafts	Penland's First 25 Years		√		H&C	5	2		Sp 54	8
Education: Schools, Kimono Technology	Visiting the Kimono School	Hannah, Joyce	√		TM			4	A/M 86	16
Education: Schools, Lace	Lace Is My Career. Wire Is My Specialty		√		Fa	14	4		S/O 87	61
Education: Schools, Native American	Mable Morrow–Appreciation for Indian Arts, Part 1	Maxcy, Mabel E.	√		SS&D	5	1	17	Wi 73	29
Education: Schools, Spinning	Shelburne Spinners: Pushing for Perfection	Cysewski, Catherine	√		Iw	3	1		Fa 77	22
Education: Schools, Tapestry	Weaving in San Francisco — Part 1	Prosser, Evelyn Bingham	√		WJ	6	2	22	Fa 81	44
Education: Schools, Textile	Fiberworks' Tenth Anniversary	Smith, J. Weldon	√		Fa	10	5		S/O 83	49
Education: Schools, Textile	Handarbetets vanner: Artists and Craftsmakers Collaborate in Sweden	Talley, Charles	√		Fa	10	3		M/J 83	56
Education: Schools, Textile	In Memorium: Fiberworks Center for the Textile Arts 1973–1987	Talley, Charles	√		Fa	14	5		N/D 87	44
Education: Schools, Textile	Pacific Basin School Closes	London, Rhoda			TM			7	O/N 86	10
Education: Schools, Textile	Summer Study in Sweden	Schobinger, Helen J.	√		H&C	9	3		Su 58	24
Education: Schools, Textile	Textile Students Take Looms Outdoors At RIT	Lenderman, Max	√		SS&D	5	4	20	Fa 74	8
Education: Schools, Textile Design Program	School for American Craftsmen	Johnston, Dr. Robert N.	√		H&C	23	2		M/A 72	17
Education: Schools, Textile Programs	Fibre Interchange At the Banff Centre	Corpier, Leslee	√		Fa	12	4		J/A 85	40
Education: Schools, Weaving	Career on Four Continents, A	Arndt, Jessie Ash	√		H&C	21	3		Su 70	15
Education: Schools, Weaving	Chicago Weaving: Development and Impact	Regensteiner, Else	√		SS&D	12	1	45	Wi 80	9
Education: Schools, Weaving	Edith Huntington Snow, Weaver, Artist, Craftsman (Reprint)	Jarecka, Louise Llewellyn	√		H&C	26	2		Ap 75	10
Education: Schools, Weaving	Guide to Weaving Schools and Craft Schools, A	Pettigrew, Dale			Hw	5	3		Su 84	33
Education: Schools, Weaving	Learning Journey, A	Redding, Debbie	√		Hw	4	4		S/O 83	16
Education: Schools, Weaving	Learning to Weave in Japan	Schrieber, LaVonne	√		WJ	8	1	29	Su 83	79
Education: Schools, Weaving	Learning to Weave in Sweden	Chase, Mary A.	√		H&C	24	3		M/J 73	7
Education: Schools, Weaving	Mannings — A Weavers Paradise, The	Geehr, Peg	√		H&C	26	1		J/F 75	15
Education: Schools, Weaving	Margaret Carter, A Weaver in Three States	Currey, Ruth Dunlop	√		H&C	21	4		Fa 70	12
Education: Schools, Weaving	New Carpet-Making School for Vragiana	Wile, Leslie	√		SS&D	4	2	14	Sp 73	17
Education: Schools, Weaving	Scholarship Report: Fuchs At Varpapuu	Fuchs, Douglas Eric	√		SS&D	7	1	25	Wi 75	92
Education: Schools, Weaving	Study Opportunities: Mexican Tapestry Weaving in San Miguel	de la Garza, Phyllis	√		Hw	3	1		Ja 82	62
Education: Schools, Weaving	Waulking Tweeds at the Marshfield School of Weaving	Gallagher, Kate	√		Hw	6	4		S/O 85	10
Education: Schools, Weaving	Weavers in the Southeast	Adams, Sally	√		H&C	20	2		Sp 69	6
Education: Schools, Weaving	Weaving Places	Xenakis, Alexis Yiorgos	√		PWC	4	2	12		28
Education: Schools, Weaving	Webschule Sindelfingen	McKeown, Alice	√	√	SS&D	6	3	23	Su 75	8
Education: Schools, Weaving and Craft	Guide to Weaving Schools and Craft Schools, A	Pettigrew, Dale			Hw	5	3		Su 84	33
Education: Schools, Weaving Courses	At the Cranbrook Academy of Art	Larsen, Jack Lenor	√		H&C	3	2		Sp 52	24
Education: Schools, Weaving Courses	Craft Classes in London, Ontario	Schoenfeld, Klara	√		H&C	3	1		Wi 51	47
Education: Schools, Weaving Curriculum	Weaving Now a Major Course		√		H&C	11	3		Su 60	17
Education: Schools, Weaving (Italy)	Salute to Italy: Paola Besana		√		SS&D	16	2	62	Sp 85	25
Education: Schools, Weaving Program	Cincinnati Weaving School				H&C	18	4		Fa 67	34

SUBJECT	TITLE	AUTHOR	IL	INST	JOUR	VOL	NO	ISS	DATE	PAGE
Education: Schools, Weaving Program	Greek Craft Summer: The American Farm School	Regensteiner, Else	√		SS&D	7	3	27	Su 76	100
Education: Schools, Weaving Program	Projects At Chautauqua Summer School	Snyder, Mary E.	√	√	H&C	23	3		M/J 72	14
Education: Schools, Weaving Program	School for American Craftsmen	Johnston, Dr. Robert N.	√		H&C	23	2		M/A 72	17
Education: Schools, Weaving Programs	Expanded Program for the Craft Students League		√		H&C	8	3		Su 57	12
Education: Schools, Weaving Programs	Handweaving for Industry: The Program at the Rhode Island School of Design	Heath, Howard	√		H&C	2	4		Fa 51	14
Education: Schools, Weaving Programs	Mills College Weavers	Byran, Dorothy	√		H&C	8	3		Su 57	22
Education: Schools, Weaving Programs	School Listings				H&C	24	1		J/F 73	38
Education: Schools, Weaving Programs	School of the Art Institute	Regensteiner, Else	√		SS&D	3	1	9	Wi 71	27
Education: Schools, Weaving Programs	School of the Art Institute of Chicago Offers Weaving Classes	Regensteiner, Else	√		H&C	5	2		Sp 54	28
Education: Schools, Weaving Programs	Summer Course at the Banff School of Fine Arts		√		H&C	6	2		Sp 55	21
Education: Schools, Weaving, Sweden	Sätergläntan School in Sweden, Landmark in the History of Handweaving, The	Longbers, Ingeborg	√		H&C	1	3		Fa 50	4
Education: Schools, Weaving, Sweden	Swedish Workshop		√	√	H&C	12	4		Fa 61	12
Education: Secondary, Navajo Dyeing	Navajo Way, The	Esping, Mardel	√	√	Iw	2	2		Wi 77	30
Education: Secondary, Navajo Spinning	Navajo Way, The	Esping, Mardel	√	√	Iw	2	2		Wi 77	30
Education: Secondary, Navajo Weaving	Navajo Way, The	Esping, Mardel	√	√	Iw	2	2		Wi 77	30
Education: Secondary, Spinning	Kansans Learn There's More Than One Way to Skin a Sheep	Reed, Brice	√		Iw	1	1		Fa 75	18
Education: Secondary, Textile Courses	Textiles 101/102, You're Looking Good	Carbee, Gail	√		Fa	3	3		M/J 76	42
Education: Secondary, Weaving	Continuation School Program, A	Bryan, Dorothy	√	√	H&C	6	4		Fa 55	23
Education: Secondary, Weaving	Weaving as Art at Hellgate High	Deschamps, Kalli	√		Iw	1	2		Wi 76	25
Education: Secondary, Weaving	Weaving in High School	Lebovitz, Constance	√		SS&D	7	4	28	Fa 76	19
Education: Secondary, Weaving Program	Young Weavers in the Ozarks	Lyon, Marge	√	√	H&C	8	2		Sp 57	15
Education: Secondary, Weaving Programs	Experiences in Organizing School Weaving Departments	Frey, Berta			H&C	5	4		Fa 54	26
Education: Seminars, Textile Crafts	Seminars on Early American Crafts	MacFarlane, Janet R.	√		H&C	2	2		Sp 51	29
Education: Seminars, Weaving	Weavers' Seminar in Massachusetts	Clark, Eleanor W.	√		H&C	6	4		Fa 55	9
Education: Settlement School	Pi Beta Phi Settlement School				H&C	14	2		Sp 63	12
Education: Settlement Schools	Quicksand Craft Center: A New Way of Life for Kentucky Mountain Women	Guy, Sallie T.	√		Hw	2	4		Se 81	16
Education: Studio–Production Program, Fiber	Banff Experience: A Personal View of Fibre Interchange 1980, The	Irwin, Kim	√		Fa	8	4		J/A 81	35
Education: Studio-Teaching, Weaving	Learning to Weave in Japan	Schrieber, LaVonne	√		WJ	8	1	29	Su 83	79
Education: Study Course, Gauze Weaves	Gauze At Moore College of Art	Todd, Louise	√		SS&D	3	3	11	Su 72	20
Education: Study Course, Twill Derivative Weaves	Multiple Harness Weaving Course Part 4: Twill Derivatives (cont'd)	Searles, Nancy M.	√	> 4	WJ	5	2	18	Fa 80	19
Education: Study Courses, Correspondence	Weaving Together: The Ayottes of Center Sandwich, New Hampshire (Error-corrected WJ v11 n3 87 p78)	Elder, Shirley	√		WJ	11	2	42	Fa 86	30
Education: Study Courses, Multiple-Harness Weaving	Multiple Harness Weaving Course — Part 3: Twill Derivatives		√	> 4	WJ	5	1	17	Su 80	40
Education: Study Courses, Multiple-Harness Weaving	Multiple Harness Weaving Course Part 5. Twill Derivatives (continued)		√	> 4	WJ	5	3	19	Wi 81	12

SUBJECT	TITLE	AUTHOR	IL	INST	JOUR	VOL	NO	ISS	DATE	PAGE
Education: Study Courses, Tapestry	Contemporary Tapestry: On Looms, Warping, Setting Up Tapestry Study Course — Part 1	O'Callaghan, Kate	√	√	WJ	4	3	15	Ja 80	41
Education: Study Courses, Tapestry	Techniques of Tapestry Weaves Part 2: Making a Sampler	O'Callaghan, Kate	√	√	WJ	4	4	16	Ap 80	45
Education: Study Courses, Tapestry	Techniques of Tapestry Weaves Part 4: Developing Design for Tapestry	O'Callaghan, Kate	√	√	WJ	5	2	18	Fa 80	15
Education: Study Courses, Tapestry Weaving	Techniques of Tapestry Weaves Part 3: Shading and Other Matters	O'Callaghan, Kate	√	√	WJ	5	1	17	Su 80	29
Education: Study Courses, Weaving	Multiple Harness Weaving Course — Introduction (error-corrected WJ v5 n1 80 insert p28d)		√	> 4	WJ	4	2	14	Oc 79	32
Education: Study Courses, Weaving	Multiple Harness Weaving Course — Part 2: Twills and Satins, With Contribution by Nancy Searles		√	> 4	WJ	4	4	16	Ap 80	16
Education: Study Courses, Weaving	Multiple Harness Weaving Course — Part I (error-corrected WJ v4 n4 80 p16)		√	> 4	WJ	4	3	15	Ja 80	14
Education: Study Group, Weaving	Study Group Project, A	Searles, Nancy M.	√		Hw	2	5		No 81	16
Education: Study Groups	Color Games	Berent, Mary, et al.	√	√	S-O	11	1		Sp 87	21
Education: Study Groups, Garment Design	Seattle Guild Garment Designs, Part 1	Noble, Judy	√	√	SS&D	10	3	39	Su 79	26
Education: Study Groups, Garment Design	Seattle Guild Garment Designs, Part 2: Completing the Top		√	√	SS&D	10	4	40	Fa 79	71
Education: Study Groups, Garment Design	Seattle Guild Garment Designs, Part 3, Skirts and Pants		√	√	SS&D	11	1	41	Wi 79	20
Education: Study Groups, Spinning	Woolworth: Experiments in Spinning	Lorance, Marilyn			S-O	3			79	38
Education: Study Groups, Textile	Gathering for Enrichment: The New York Textile Study Group	Malarcher, Patricia	√		Fa	12	5		S/O 85	48
Education: Study Groups, Weaving	Experiment in Group Study	Bryan, Dorothy	√	> 4	H&C	10	3		Su 59	6
Education: Study Groups, Weaving	Projects Spark Interest	Rothacker, Chet			Hw	1	2		S-S 80	15
Education: Study Groups, Weaving	Stripe Study Group, A		√	√	Hw	4	2		M/A 83	24
Education: Study Groups, Weaving	Supplementary Warp Patterning: A Productive Study Group	Tidball, Harriet	√		SCGM		17		66	31
Education, Study Groups: Weaving	Tartan Book: A Study Group Project, The	Haller, Jean M.	√	√	Hw	4	5		N/D 83	31
Education: Study Groups, Weaving	Twenty-Five Weavers, California Study Group Has Varied Programs, The	Howie, Andrew J.	√	√	H&C	13	2		Sp 62	21
Education: Study Groups, Weaving	Variations on a Theme: A Seattle Weavers' Guild Study Group Project	Sullivan, Jean H.	√	√	Hw	8	2		M/A 87	64
Education: Study Groups, Weaving Program	No Weavers Nearby? Form a Beginning Class—And a Guild	Zorick, Jean	√		SS&D	5	4	20	Fa 74	87
Education: Study Groups, Weaving Program	Program for a Study Group	Regensteiner, Else		√	SS&D	3	2	10	Sp 72	10
Education: Study Groups, Weaving Program	Program for a Study Group	Regensteiner, Else		√	SS&D	3	3	11	Su 72	43
Education: Study Groups, Weaving Program	Program for a Study Group	Regensteiner, Else		√	SS&D	3	4	12	Fa 72	42
Education: Study Groups, Weaving Program	Program for a Study Group, Part 4	Regensteiner, Else		√	SS&D	4	1	13	Wi 72	25
Education: Study Groups, Weaving Program	Program for a Study Group, Part 5	Regensteiner, Else		√	SS&D	4	2	14	Sp 73	43
Education: Study Groups, Weaving Program	Program for a Study Group, Part 6	Regensteiner, Else			SS&D	4	3	15	Su 73	40
Education: Study Groups, Weaving Program	Program for a Study Group, Part 7	Regensteiner, Else		√	SS&D	4	4	16	Fa 73	43
Education: Study Groups, Weaving Program	Program for a Study Group, Part 8	Regensteiner, Else			SS&D	5	1	17	Wi 73	51
Education: Study Groups, Weaving Program	Seattle Guild Garment Designs, Part 4: Edges, Closures, Capes and Dresses		√	√	SS&D	11	2	42	Sp 80	39

SUBJECT	TITLE	AUTHOR	IL	INST	JOUR	VOL	NO	ISS	DATE	PAGE
Education: Study Groups, Weaving Program	Study Groups — A Personal View	Nunneley, Faithe			SS&D	2	2	6	Sp 71	14
Education: Study Groups, Weaving Program	Weavers Study Group				Fa	3	6		N/D 76	43
Education: Study Program, Dyeing	Pointillist Color Effects in Spinning: A Study Program	Deems, Flo		√	S-O	4			80	53
Education: Study Program, Spinning	Craft to College Credit	Bowman, Cora			S-O	9	2		Su 85	48
Education: Study Programs, Computer Weaving	Weaving with Computers	Sowles, Susan: Theresa Ruch			SS&D	13	3	51	Su 82	30
Education: Study Programs, Looms	Ethnic Looms	Jorstad, Caroline	√		SS&D	13	4	52	Fa 82	40
Education: Summer Camp, Weaving	Camp Culhane, It's All in the Family	Culhane, Isabel	√		SS&D	6	3	23	Su 75	23
Education: Summer Classes, Children's Weaving	Young Weavers in Kentucky		√		H&C	14	3		Su 63	45
Education: Swatch-Swap	Learning from the Learning Exchange	Petrini, Marcy	√	> 4	SS&D	18	1	69	Wi 86	62
Education: Teaching	Creative Solutions	Chandler, Deborah		√	Hw	6	3		Su 85	28
Education: Teaching	Getting the Most Out of a Class	Chandler, Deborah			Hw	7	5		N/D 86	16
Education: Teaching	On Learning	Chandler, Deborah			Hw	7	4		S/O 86	20
Education: Teaching	Paper Weaving	Scanlin, Tommye McClure	√	√	Hw	7	4		S/O 86	28
Education: Teaching	**Teacher**/Student Interface: Two Views of Education	Kosta, Angela	√		Fa	14	1		J/F 87	31
Education: Teaching, Basketry	Basketmaker's Year "Down Under", A	Malarcher, Patricia	√		Fa	8	4		J/A 81	47
Education: Teaching, Competency	Cutcher's Corner	Cutcher, Hal; Elaine Cutcher			Fa	3	4		J/A 76	40
Education: Teaching, Crafts	Craft Arts in Education, The	Brennan, Harold J.			H&C	6	1		Wi 54	12
Education: Teaching, Design	Approach to Teaching Design, An	Pickett, Barbara Setsu	√	√	Iw	3	2		Wi 78	16
Education: Teaching, Design	Conceptual Design in Weaving	Towner, Naomi Whiting	√		Iw	3	2		Wi 78	14
Education: Teaching, Design	Warren Seelig: A Conversation	Ligon, Linda	√		Iw	3	2		Wi 78	20
Education: Teaching, Disabled	Blind Woman Is in My Weaving Class ... What Do I Do Now?, A	Zinsmeister, Anna	√		Fa	14	1		J/F 87	42
Education, Teaching: Elementary	Julie Green: The World of Fiber	Lyon, David	√		Fa	14	1		J/F 87	40
Education: Teaching, Fiber Arts	Gerhardt Knodel	Olendorf, Donna	√		Fa	5	6		N/D 78	44
Education: Teaching, Knitting	Teaching Children How to Knit	Baker, Ella			S-O	10	2		Su 86	42
Education, Teaching, Learning Disabled	Comminicating Through Craft	de Mar, Lola	√		Fa	14	1		J/F 87	38
Education: Teaching, Lesson Plans	How to Teach Hands-On Skills: The Basics of Lesson Planning	Waagen, Alice K.		√	SS&D	17	2	66	Sp 86	65
Education: Teaching, Lesson Plans	Weaving Classes in an Art Gallery	Holroyd, Ruth N.	√	√	H&C	22	4		Fa 71	12
Education: Teaching, Prison	Teaching At a Men's Prison	Plevin, Ann	√		Fa	14	1		J/F 87	36
Education: Teaching, Quilting	Quilting by the Lake in Central New York	Wright, Yolanda	√		Fa	10	2		M/A 83	50
Education: Teaching, Senior Citizens	Teaching Fiber to the Elderly: A Personal Experience	Bryan, Linda Nelson	√		Fa	4	6		N/D 77	60
Education: Teaching, Sewing	Techniques of Haute Couture (error-corrected TM i7 O/N86 p5)	Rhodes, Elizabeth A.	√	√	TM			6	A/S 86	52
Education: Teaching, Spinning	Beginning Spinning with Minimal Equipment	Ellison, Nancy	√	√	S-O	4			80	37
Education: Teaching, Spinning	Easing the Beginner's Fears	Irwin, Bobbie		√	S-O	10	4		Wi 86	24
Education: Teaching, Spinning	Guilds for Spinners	Rowe, Erica	√		S-O	3			79	35
Education: Teaching, Spinning	Handspinning Project, The	Keefe, Carolyn	√		S-O	3			79	32
Education: Teaching, Spinning	Kansans Learn There's More Than One Way to Skin a Sheep	Reed, Brice	√		Iw	1	1		Fa 75	18
Education: Teaching, Spinning	Six of One, Half a Dozen of the Other (a roundtable discussion with six spinners)		√		S-O	5			81	51
Education: Teaching, Spinning	Spinning and Weaving in a Country School	Adams, Brucie	√		Iw	1	3		Sp 76	29
Education: Teaching, Spinning	Spinning in the Classroom	Posner, Sally	√		S-O	2			78	37

SUBJECT	TITLE	AUTHOR	IL	INST	JOUR	VOL	NO	ISS	DATE	PAGE
Education: Teaching, Spinning	Spinning Teachers Extraordinaire	Chandler, Deborah			S-O	10	4		Wi 86	10
Education: Teaching, Spinning	Teacher's Tricks	Grayson, Persis	√	√	S-O	10	1		Sp 86	10
Education: Teaching, Spinning	Your Spinning Teacher	Ericson, Virginia D.	√		S-O	1			77	36
Education: Teaching, Stitchery	Jacqueline Enthoven: Portrait of a Stitchery Teacher	Szajman, Rena	√		Fa	4	3		M/J 77	45
Education: Teaching, Weaving	A Weaver Ponders His Craft, Collection of Controversial Essays: Teaching	Zielinski, S. A.; Robert Leclerc, ed.		√	MWL	21 22			'51–'73	21
Education: Teaching, Weaving	Anni Albers — Innovator in Textile Design		√		H&C	10	4		Fa 59	6
Education: Teaching, Weaving	Edna Minor of the Craft Students League		√		H&C	4	3		Su 53	4
Education: Teaching, Weaving	Fabric Encounter	Kaplan, Susan	√		H&C	24	4		Au 73	19
Education: Teaching, Weaving	Fabrics from Israel	Keiner, Julia	√		H&C	5	4		Fa 54	30
Education: Teaching, Weaving	How to Succeed at Teaching (By Really Trying)	Redding, Debbie			Iw	4	4		Fa 79	48
Education: Teaching, Weaving	Ida Dean Grae — Imaginative Teacher	Brayn, Dorothy	√		H&C	6	2		Sp 55	16
Education: Teaching, Weaving	Kay Geary	Bryan, Dorothy	√		H&C	3	2		Sp 52	26
Education: Teaching, Weaving	Lea Van Puymbroeck Miller, Innovator in Handweaving	Boyer, Ruth M.	√		H&C	20	2		Sp 69	15
Education: Teaching, Weaving	Lysbeth Wallace Discusses Teaching Methods		√		H&C	15	1		Wi 64	18
Education: Teaching, Weaving	"Mama" Gravander	Bryan, Dorothy	√		H&C	5	4		Fa 54	4
Education: Teaching, Weaving	Mary E. Heickman, Texas Weaver and Teacher	Morse, Martha	√		H&C	17	3		Su 66	18
Education: Teaching, Weaving	Most Gratifying Work Is with Children, The	Keatley, Kathy			SS&D	2	3	7	Su 71	16
Education: Teaching, Weaving	Myra L. Davis, Master Weaver	Clement, Doris	√		H&C	12	1		Wi 61	24
Education: Teaching, Weaving	"Not a Child's Toy"	Cahlander, Adele W.	√	√	SS&D	3	3	11	Su 72	32
Education: Teaching, Weaving	On Teaching Weaving	Ux, Katherine	√		H&C	11	3		Su 60	48
Education: Teaching, Weaving	On Teaching Weaving	Zielinski, S. A.	√		H&C	19	1		Wi 68	38
Education: Teaching, Weaving	Peter Collingwood, English Rug Weaver		√		H&C	11	4		Fa 60	12
Education: Teaching, Weaving	Robert Harnden — Diplomat & Weaver	Schobinger, Helen J.	√		H&C	11	1		Wi 60	16
Education: Teaching, Weaving	Rugweaving: Teaching on Two Harnesses	Mattera, Joanne	√	√	Iw	5	1		Wi 79	27
Education: Teaching, Weaving	Sara Matsson Anliot	Bryan, Dorothy	√		H&C	11	3		Su 60	10
Education: Teaching, Weaving	School Psychologist Finds Weaving Valuable	Griswold, Irene T.			SS&D	5	1	17	Wi 73	73
Education: Teaching, Weaving	Sherrie Smith	Ligon, Linda	√		Iw	2	1		Fa 76	10
Education: Teaching, Weaving	Spinning and Weaving in a Country School	Adams, Brucie	√		Iw	1	3		Sp 76	29
Education: Teaching, Weaving	Suggestions for the Beginning Weaver	Gulick, Evelyn M.	√	√	H&C	19	1		Wi 68	12
Education: Teaching, Weaving	Teaching Children to Weave, Need for Simple Techniques and Devices	Alexander, Marthann		√	H&C	14	1		Wi 63	19
Education: Teaching, Weaving	Teaching on a Shoe-String Budget	Posner, Sally	√		SS&D	5	1	17	Wi 73	9
Education: Teaching, Weaving	Teaching the Blind to Weave	Bradford, Eileen			H&C	6	1		Wi 54	26
Education: Teaching, Weaving	Weavers in Cleveland	Rial, Katherine	√		H&C	6	3		Su 55	26
Education: Teaching, Weaving	Weaving as Art at Hellgate High	Deschamps, Kalli	√		Iw	1	2		Wi 76	25
Education: Teaching, Weaving	Weaving for the Blind	Lees, Maureen V.	√	√	H&C	8	2		Sp 57	22
Education: Teaching, Weaving	Weaving in New Brunswick	Currey, Ruth Dunlop	√		H&C	12	1		Wi 61	29
Education: Teaching, Weaving	Weaving Workshop with Barbara Wittenberg: Sharing is Pervasive, A	Aikin, Patti	√		Fa	8	4		J/A 81	21
Education: Teaching, Weaving, Tape Recorder	Weaving Lessons by a Tape Recorder				H&C	10	4		Fa 59	21
Education: Tertiary, Design	Design Courses Precede Weaving at the University of Kansas	Fitzgerald, Jeanne			H&C	4	2		Sp 53	34
Education: Tertiary, Fiber	Open Jurying in Pittsburg: Putting Your Work on the Line (Exhibit)	Myrinx, Elaine	√		Fa	6	2		M/A 79	23
Education: Tertiary, Independent Study	Independent Design Study At Philadelphia Textile College				H&C	22	4		Fa 71	22
Education: Tertiary, Mini-Session, Weaving	Mini-Session Increases Weaving Program 4-Fold	Jackie, Erma; Kenneth G. Heintz	√		SS&D	4	4	16	Fa 73	53

SUBJECT	TITLE	AUTHOR	IL	INST	JOUR	VOL	NO	ISS	DATE	PAGE
Education: Tertiary, Textiles	This College Training Unites Craft and Industry		√		H&C	2	2		Sp 51	12
Education: Tertiary, Weaving	Collegiate Weavers: Buffalo, New York	Belfer, Nancy	√		SS&D	9	3	35	Su 78	85
Education: Tertiary, Weaving	Design Courses Precede Weaving at the University of Kansas	Fitzgerald, Jeanne			H&C	4	2		Sp 53	34
Education: Tertiary, Weaving	Handweaving at North Texas State College	Fuchs, Rudolph	√		H&C	2	2		Sp 51	14
Education: Tertiary, Weaving	Handweaving in Memphis	Hansen, Helen; Meade Nichol	√		H&C	8	1		Wi 56	19
Education: Tertiary, Weaving	Missouri Weaving Classes		√		H&C	19	3		Su 68	44
Education: Tertiary, Weaving	New Weaving Room for Teachers College				H&C	10	1		Wi 59	56
Education: Tertiary, Weaving	Rugweaving: Teaching on Two Harnesses	Mattera, Joanne	√	√	Iw	5	1		Wi 79	27
Education: Tertiary, Weaving	School for American Craftsmen Observes Its Tenth Anniversary, The	Laurell, Karl	√		H&C	4	4		Fa 53	12
Education: Tertiary, Weaving	Student Insights		√		SS&D	8	1	29	WI 76	54
Education: Tertiary, Weaving	Students Display Diversity: More from the College Campus		√		SS&D	7	3	27	Su 76	48
Education: Tertiary, Weaving	Today's Conscious Aesthetic Philosophy 'Asks Us to Rationalize the Non-Rational'	McCarthy, Judy; Sue Ferguson	√		SS&D	4	4	16	Fa 73	54
Education: Tertiary, Weaving	Training in Handweaving Offered on the Pacific Coast	Bryan, Dorothy	√		H&C	2	2		Sp 51	16
Education: Tertiary, Weaving	Weaving Activity Booms on Campus		√		SS&D	6	3	23	Su 75	35
Education: Tertiary, Weaving	Weaving Again Offered at Texas Women's University	Maxcy, Mabel E.	√		H&C	20	4		Fa 69	21
Education: Tertiary, Weaving	Weaving at State University of Iowa	Rouse, Mary	√		H&C	4	3		Su 53	24
Education: Tertiary, Weaving	Weaving Classes Show Growth at San Jose State College	Hatch, David P.	√	> 4	H&C	13	2		Sp 62	23
Education: Tertiary, Weaving	Youth Will Be Served: Young Weavers Demonstrate Eloquence on the Loom		√		SS&D	7	2	26	Sp 76	44
Education: Tertiary, Weaving Courses	Kansas University, An Interview with Evelyn DeGraw (error-corrected H&C v22 n2 71 p4)	Lee, Jane	√		H&C	22	1		Wi 71	6
Education: Tertiary, Weaving Courses	Weaving in a College Art Department	Pease, Marion D.	√		H&C	3	4		Fa 52	20
Education: Tertiary, Weaving Program	Young Weavers in the Ozarks	Lyon, Marge	√	√	H&C	8	2		Sp 57	15
Education: Weaving, Program for Children	Weaving Program for Children, A	Knight, Martha R.	√		H&C	2	3		Su 51	58
Education: Workshops, Basketry	Brookfield Basketry Institute, The	Smith, Sue M.	√		Fa	12	2		M/A 85	46
Education: Workshops, Basketry, Coiling	Basketry Workshop & Show at the Fairtree Gallery, A	Hansen, Debby; Betty Morris	√	√	H&C	24	3		M/J 73	43
Education: Workshops, Computer	Tips on Giving Programs and Workshops on "Computers in Weaving"	Strickler, Carol	√		Hw	6	2		M/A 85	67
Education: Workshops, Coverlet Weaving	History Lives on at Bishop Hill	Rohrer, Marge	√		Iw	4	3		Su 79	43
Education: Workshops, Dyeing	Contemporary Texas Natural Dye Workshop	Young, Athalie Child	√		SS&D	1	4	4	Se 70	18
Education: Workshops, Dyeing	Dye and Spin Workshops on Nantucket	Beinecke, Mary Ann	√	√	SS&D	4	1	13	Wi 72	12
Education: Workshops, Dyeing	Weaving in the Woods	Painter, Hal	√		SS&D	5	2	18	Sp 74	73
Education: Workshops, Dyeing	Workshop Tour to Sweden	Young, Dorothy M.	√		SS&D	4	2	14	Sp 73	41
Education: Workshops, Embroidery	Las Artistas Del Valle: Images of Everyday Life in Colorado's San Luis Valley	Reith, Stephanie J.	√		Fa	10	3		M/J 83	24
Education: Workshops: Embroidery	Workshop with Needle Artist Constance Howard, A	Hearst, Kate	√		TM			14	D/J 87	18
Education: Workshops, Macramé	Macramé Workshop	Koehler, Nancy J.	√		H&C	21	4		Fa 70	28
Education: Workshops, Spinning	Learn to Spin on Our Sheep Farm	Jones, Mrs. Gary	√		SS&D	2	3	7	Su 71	18
Education: Workshops, Spinning	Workshop Tour to Sweden	Young, Dorothy M.	√		SS&D	4	2	14	Sp 73	41
Education: Workshops, Spinning	Your Spinning Teacher	Ericson, Virginia D.	√		S-O	1			77	36
Education: Workshops, Tapestry, Gobelins	Two Weeks in the South of France: At a Gobelins Tapestry Workshop	Lucas, Mary	√		Fa	8	4		J/A 81	38

SUBJECT	TITLE	AUTHOR	IL	INST	JOUR	VOL	NO	ISS	DATE	PAGE
Education: Workshops, Textile	Mary Woodard Davis Promotes Craft in Santa Fe	Ligon, Linda	√		lw	1	1		Fa 75	6
Education: Workshops, Textile, By Native Americans	Mary Woodard Davis Promotes Craft in Santa Fe	Ligon, Linda	√		lw	1	1		Fa 75	6
Education: Workshops, Weaving	Art of Ixchel: Learning to Weave in Guatemala and Rhode Island, The	Schevill, Margot	√	√	WJ	8	1	29	Su 83	57
Education: Workshops, Weaving	California Workshop	Hayfield, Jesse	√	> 4	H&C	10	4		Fa 59	40
Education: Workshops, Weaving	Circuit Riding Weavers		√		H&C	10	1		Wi 59	11
Education: Workshops, Weaving	Collingwood Rug Workshop	Bogdanor, Lura Jim			SS&D	1	4	4	Se 70	11
Education: Workshops, Weaving	Experiences with a Weaving Workshop	Redfield, Gail M.			H&C	6	1		Wi 54	58
Education: Workshops, Weaving	Experimental Workshop Tests New Approaches To Weaving	Currey, Ruth	√		H&C	21	4		Fa 70	19
Education: Workshops, Weaving	Fashioning a Workshop	Koopman, Albertje	√	√	SS&D	16	1	61	Wi 84	29
Education: Workshops, Weaving	Fundraising Brings Kasuri Kimono Weaver to Nashville Workshop	Wilson, Sadye Tune	√		SS&D	9	2	34	Sp 78	4
Education: Workshops, Weaving	Guatemala Weaving Workshop	Kingsmill, Sally	√		H&C	26	3		M/J 75	28
Education: Workshops, Weaving	Louise Todd: How Else Can This Be Woven?	TerLouw, Eliszabeth	√		SS&D	2	2	6	Sp 71	20
Education: Workshops, Weaving	Noble Tradition Preserved: An Ecuadorian Weaving Co-op, A	Llewellyn, Charles; Deborah Llewellyn	√		SS&D	11	3	43	Su 80	12
Education: Workshops, Weaving	Ontario Workshop	Kellett, Althea			SS&D	3	1	9	Wi 71	12
Education: Workshops, Weaving	Organizing a Weaving Workshop	Pendleton, Mary		√	H&C	5	2		Sp 54	44
Education: Workshops, Weaving	Swedish Workshop		√	√	H&C	12	4		Fa 61	12
Education: Workshops, Weaving	Theo Moorman, English Tapestry Weaver in San Francisco	Marston, Ena	√	√	H&C	20	1		Wi 69	12
Education: Workshops, Weaving	Weaving in New Brunswick	Currey, Ruth Dunlop	√		H&C	12	1		Wi 61	29
Education: Workshops, Weaving	Weaving in Quebec	Barrett, Clotilde	√	√	WJ	6	4	24	Sp 82	8
Education: Workshops, Weaving	Weaving in the Woods	Painter, Hal	√		SS&D	5	2	18	Sp 74	73
Education: Workshops, Weaving	Weaving Workshop with Barbara Wittenberg: Sharing is Pervasive, A	Aikin, Patti	√		Fa	8	4		J/A 81	21
Education: Workshops, Weaving	Workshop Tour to Sweden	Young, Dorothy M.	√		SS&D	4	2	14	Sp 73	41
Education: Workshops, Weaving	Workshops at Banff		√		SS&D	2	3	7	Su 71	10
Education: Workshops, Weaving (Children)	Experiences in History	Kuwabara, Nancy	√	√	SS&D	9	1	33	Wi 77	106
Edward C. Blum Design Laboratory (NYC)	Millions of Swatches at FIT	Kennedy, Alan			TM			11	J/J 87	18
Efficiency, Production	Equipment for Production Efficiency: The Loom	LaLena, Constance			Hw	5	4		S/O 84	29
Egypt	Contemporary Egyptian Children's Tapestries		√		Fa	4	6		N/D 77	65
Egypt	Coptic Tapestry of Byzantine Style, A	Berliner, Rudolf	√		TMJ	1	1		No 62	3
Egypt	Double-Harness Techniques Employed in Egypt	El-Homossani, M. M.	√	> 4	AT	3			My 85	229
Egypt	Egyptian Tapestries by the Children of Harrania	Davis, Peter	√		H&C	14	4		Fa 63	9
Egypt	Horsemen in Tapestry Roundels Found in Egypt	Berliner, Rudolf	√		TMJ	1	2		De 63	39
Egypt	Is the Mamluk Carpet a Mandala? A Speculation	Ellis, Charles Grant	√		TMJ	4	1		De 74	30
Egypt	Mysteries of the Misplaced Mamluks	Ellis, Charles Grant	√		TMJ	2	2		De 67	2
Egypt	Native Craftsmen Produce for Nile Hilton Hotel		√		H&C	11	3		Su 60	54
Egypt	Problem of Twist, A	Gordon, Judith	√	√	SS&D	12	4	48	Fa 81	28
Egypt	Roman Heritage, The	Angelil, Muriel	√		SS&D	13	3	51	Su 82	69
Egypt	Tapestries from Egypt Influenced by Theatrical Performances	Berliner, Rudolf	√		TMJ	1	3		De 64	35
Egypt	Tapestries of Coptic Egypt, The	Hoskins, Nancy Arthur	√		AT	6			De 86	211
Egypt	Tapestry Roundel with Nilotic Scenes, A	Abdel-Malek, Laila	√		TMJ	25			86	33

SUBJECT	TITLE	AUTHOR	IL	INST	JOUR	VOL	NO	ISS	DATE	PAGE
Egypt	Tapping the Artist Within: The Wissa Wassef Tapestries		√		H&C	26	3		M/J 75	5
Egypt	Textile Remains from a Late Temple in Egyptian Nubia	Adams, Nettie K.	√		AT	8			De 87	85
Egypt	Textiles of Coptic Egypt	Hoskins, Nancy Arthur	√	√	WJ	12	1	45	Su 87	58
Egypt	Weaving the Girdle of Rameses	Hilts, Patricia	√	>4	WJ	9	1	33	Su 84	22
Egypt: Ethnic, Religious, Cultural Conditions	Remarks on Some Tapestries from Egypt	Berliner, Rudolf	√		TMJ	1	4		De 65	20
Elastic	Easy Elastic		√	√	TM			2	D/J 85	6
Elastic, Knitting	Putting Knitted Pieces Together	Guagliumi, Susan	√	√	TM			11	J/J 87	45
Elastic Thread	Coping with Elastic Thread			√	TM			12	A/S 87	10
Elastic, Waistbands	No-Snag Elastic			√	TM			9	F/M 87	10
Element Diameter Differential	Simple Damask-Like Effects Using Element Diameter Differential and Element Tension Differential	Xenakis, Athanasios David	√	>4	AT	1			De 83	317
Element Tension Differential	Simple Damask-Like Effects Using Element Diameter Differential and Element Tension Differential	Xenakis, Athanasios David	√	>4	AT	1			De 83	317
Embellishments	Claire Zeisler's Fragments and Dashes	Levine, Betsy	√		TM			1	O/N 85	84
Embellishments	Creative Clothing: Surface Embellishment	Mayer, Anita Luvera	√	√	WJ	11	3	43	Wi 87	30
Embellishments	Edges, Joinings, Trims, Embellishments, Closures...and More	Wilson, Jean	√	√	Hw	2	5		No 81	42
Embellishments	Finishes and Embellishments	King, Bucky; Susan W. Gilmurray	√	√	SS&D	3	4	12	Fa 72	28
Embellishments: Cord Embroidery	Celtic Knot Box Cushion	Xenakis, Athanasios David	√	√	PWC	3	4	10		60
Embellishments: Embroidery	Guatemalan Gauze Weaves: A Description and Key to Identification	Pancake, Cherri M.; Suzanne Baizerman	√	√	TMJ	19 20			80,81	1
Embellishments: Sash Ring	Embellishments on the Rain Sash	Baizerman, Suzanne	√	√	WJ	11	2	42	Fa 86	22
Embellishments: Techniques	Peru, Textiles Unlimited: Textile Characteristics, Ornamental Techniques	Tidball, Harriet	√		SCGM		25		68	20
Embossing: Paper	Paper Clothing, East	Sahlstrand, Margaret	√	√	Fa	11	2		M/A 84	36
Embroidering Yarn, Handspun	Nature: A Color Source and Inspiration for Traditional Sweaters	Gibson-Roberts, Priscilla A.	√		S-O	9	3		Fa 85	42
Embroidery	All That Glitters: Shisha by Machine	Fanning, Robbie	√	√	TM			1	O/N 85	63
Embroidery	Anne McKenzie Nickolson	Nickolson, Anne McKenzie	√		Fa	12	6		N/D 85	20
Embroidery	Balenciago: The Architect of Elegant Clothing	Koda, Harold	√		TM			11	J/J 87	20
Embroidery	"Birth Project, The" First Showing of Judy Chicago's New Work (Exhibit)	von Kreisler-Bomben, Kristin	√		Fa	10	1		J/F 83	81
Embroidery	Caroline Dahl	Dahl, Caroline	√		Fa	13	3		M/J 86	27
Embroidery	Chinese Brushwork Converted Into Classical Embroidery	Stickler, John C.	√		H&C	22	2		Sp 71	11
Embroidery	Christmas Cards		√	>4	WJ	7	2	26	Fa 82	54
Embroidery	Christmas Embroidery in Pakistan	Garland, Mary	√		TM			14	D/J 87	90
Embroidery	Comminicating Through Craft	de Mar, Lola	√		Fa	14	1		J/F 87	38
Embroidery	Contemporary Embroidery		√		H&C	17	3		Su 66	4
Embroidery	Costumes of Royal India	Levine, Betsy	√		TM			7	O/N 86	64
Embroidery	Design by Decision: A Practical Approach to the Creative Process	Hall, Carolyn Vosburg	√		Fa	8	2		M/A 81	13
Embroidery	Embroidered Jacket (Carol Powalisz)		√	√	Hw	8	4		S/O 87	46, I-7
Embroidery	Embroidered Life, An (error-corrected Fa v7 n4 80 p6)	Alonso, Harriet	√		Fa	7	3		M/J 80	66
Embroidery	Embroidered Neckpieces of Theodora Elston, The	Sacks, Star M.	√		Fa	6	3		M/J 79	51
Embroidery	Embroidered Sambas of Madeleine Colaço, The	Mathews, Kate	√		Fa	14	5		N/D 87	34
Embroidery	"Embroiderer's Guild of America, 11th Biennial Exhibition" (Exhibit)	Itter, Diane	√		Fa	12	2		M/A 85	76
Embroidery	Embroidery on the Loom	Drooker, Penelope B.	√	√	SS&D	9	3	35	Su 78	60

SUBJECT	TITLE	AUTHOR	IL	INST	JOUR	VOL	NO	ISS	DATE	PAGE
Embroidery	"Embroidery Through the Ages" (Exhibit)	Grover, Donald	√		Fa	5	6		N/D 78	62
Embroidery	"Flexible Medium: Art Fabric from the Museum Collection, The" (Exhibit)	Goodman, Deborah Lerme	√		Fa	11	5		S/O 84	71
Embroidery	Flourishing Art: USA Hmong Women Show How to Stitch Pa ndau, Their Flowery Cloth, A	Porter-Francis, Wendy	√	√	TM			9	F/M 87	33
Embroidery	Folk Textiles of Latin America	Kelemen, Pál	√		TMJ	1	4		De 65	2
Embroidery	Handwoven Silk Garments: A Wedding Dress	Best, Eleanor	√	√	WJ	3	2	10	Oc 78	28
Embroidery	Hiroko Ogawa: Keeping Alive the Art of Sashiko	Scarborough, Jessica	√		Fa	12	2		M/A 85	12
Embroidery	Interlocking Warp and Weft in the Nasca 2 Style	Rowe, Ann Pollard	√		TMJ	3	3		De 72	67
Embroidery	Just Playing in Space: Ann McKenzie Nickolson's Textile Artwork	Koplos, Janet	√		Fa	8	2		M/A 81	34
Embroidery	Kantha	Westfall, Carol D.; Dipti Desai	√	√	AT	7			Ju 87	161
Embroidery	Kantha Cloths of Bengal: The Sari Transformed	Gupta, Asha	√		Fa	9	6		N/D 82	19
Embroidery	Kashmir East and West	Mikosch, Elizabeth	√		TM			9	F/M 87	14
Embroidery	Keeping Culture Alive with Needle and Thread	White, Virginia L.	√		Fa	9	3		M/J 82	40
Embroidery	Lee A. Malerich	Malerich, Lee A.	√		Fa	14	1		J/F 87	27
Embroidery	Liberated Embroidery		√		Fa	9	3		M/J 82	35
Embroidery	"Linda Maxwell and Caroline Dahl: Terror Sampler and Other Dogs" (Exhibit)	Poon, Vivian	√		Fa	11	6		N/D 84	79
Embroidery	"Nancy Hemenway: Aqua Lapis" (Exhibit)	Skudera, Gail	√		Fa	11	5		S/O 84	72
Embroidery	National Standards Council of American Embroiderers	Waxler, Dorothy V.	√		Fa	9	3		M/J 82	56
Embroidery	Persian Legend in Silk		√		TM			14	D/J 87	92
Embroidery	Personal Touch, A		√	√	Hw	3	5		N/D 82	43
Embroidery	Perspective on Embroidery: In Answer to Emery, A	From, Dot	√		AT	6			De 86	195
Embroidery	Point of View (Renie Breskin Adams)		√		TM			7	O/N 86	92
Embroidery	Re-Establishing Provenience of Two Paracas Mantles	Paul, Anne			TMJ	19 20			80,81	35
Embroidery	Recent Gifts of Chinese and Japanese Textiles	Hays, Mary V.	√		TMJ	4	2		75	4
Embroidery	"Ritual Narratives" (Exhibit)		√		Fa	13	3		M/J 86	57
Embroidery	Rue Furch		√		Fa	4	3		M/J 77	42
Embroidery	Sampler of Surface Design, A	Westphal, Katherine	√		Fa	10	5		S/O 83	39
Embroidery	"Silken Threads and Silent Needles" (Exhibit)	Dunnewold, Jane	√		Fa	11	6		N/D 84	78
Embroidery	"Splendor of French Style, The" Textiles from Joan of Arc to Napoleon III (Exhibit)	Guagliumi, Susan	√		Fa	13	4		J/A 86	13
Embroidery	Tapestry and Embroidery	Drooker, Penelope B.	√		Iw	5	3		Su 80	37
Embroidery	Textile Arts of India	Bernier, Ronald M.	√		WJ	2	1	5	Jy 77	31
Embroidery	"Thomas Lundberg" (Exhibit)	Itter, Diane	√		Fa	10	4		J/A 83	67
Embroidery	Threads of Gold	Austin, Carole	√		Fa	13	4		J/A 86	10
Embroidery	Verina Warren	Scarborough, Jessica	√		Fa	13	4		J/A 86	26
Embroidery: Background Fabrics	Jacqueline Enthoven, Suggests Handwoven Fabrics for Embroidery		√		H&C	17	4		Fa 66	19
Embroidery: Brocade-Style	On Mathematics and Treasures	Stanton, R. G.			AT	8			De 87	57
Embroidery: Canvas	Paulus Berensohn: A Potter Discovers Canvas Embroidery	Grover, Donald	√		Fa	6	5		S/O 79	28
Embroidery: Colcha	Colcha Embroidery			√	TM			6	A/S 86	8
Embroidery: Cord	Celtic Knot Box Cushion	Xenakis, Athanasios David	√	√	PWC	3	4	10		60
Embroidery: Double-Sided	Chinese Artisans At Work	Goodman, Deborah Lerme	√		Fa	13	1		J/F 86	34

SUBJECT	TITLE	AUTHOR	IL	INST	JOUR	VOL	NO	ISS	DATE	PAGE
Embroidery: Double-Sided	On Mathematics and Treasures	Stanton, R. G.			AT	8			De 87	57
Embroidery: Double-Sided, Double Image	Two-Sided Embroidery				TM			8	D/J 86	4
Embroidery: Double-Sided, Double-Image	Artisans from China Work Silken Magic	Steinhagen, Janice	√		TM			5	J/J 86	14
Embroidery: Double-Sided, Double-Image	Double Embroidery				TM			11	J/J 87	4
Embroidery: Double-Sided Embroidery	On Mathematics and Treasures	Stanton, R. G.			AT	8			De 87	57
Embroidery: Emery's Concept	Perspective on Embroidery: In Answer to Emery, A	From, Dot	√		AT	6			De 86	195
Embroidery: Fine (Micro-)	On Mathematics and Treasures	Stanton, R. G.			AT	8			De 87	57
Embroidery: From's Concept	Perspective on Embroidery: In Answer to Emery, A	From, Dot	√		AT	6			De 86	195
Embroidery: Gujarati	Gujarati Embroidery	Westfall, Carol D.; Dipti Desai	√		AT	8			De 87	29
Embroidery: Hair	On Mathematics and Treasures	Stanton, R. G.			AT	8			De 87	57
Embroidery: Hispanic, Colcha	Las Artistas Del Valle: Images of Everyday Life in Colorado's San Luis Valley	Reith, Stephanie J.	√		Fa	10	3		M/J 83	24
Embroidery: Hmong	Flourishing Art: China, Guizhou Women Continue to Embroider Their Legends, A	Rossi, Gail	√		TM			9	F/M 87	30
Embroidery: Hmong and Yao	Dress and Design in Highland Southeast Asia: The Hmong (Miao) and the Yao	Adams, Monni	√		TMJ	4	1		De 74	51
Embroidery: Japanese	Japan's Masterful Embroideries	Markrich, Lilo	√		TM			12	A/S 87	68
Embroidery: Japanese, Traditional	Spirit Exits Through the Embroiderer's Hands, The	Colwell, Katherine	√	√	TM			12	A/S 87	18
Embroidery: Knot	On Mathematics and Treasures	Stanton, R. G.			AT	8			De 87	57
Embroidery: Machine	Barbara Smith: Views from Within	Lucas, Jane	√		Fa	10	5		S/O 83	18
Embroidery: Mexican	Garments with Ethnic Flavor: Mexican Embroidery Combined with Handwoven Yardage		√	> 4	WJ	2	3	7	Ja 78	17
Embroidery: Mirrored	Meaning of Folk Art in Rabari Life: A Closer Look at Mirrored Embroidery, The	Frater, Judy	√		TMJ	4	2		75	47
Embroidery: Pueblo, Contemporary	Sweetgrass, Cedar & Sage: Portrait of a Southwestern Weaver	Schevill, Margot	√		WJ	10	1	37	Su 85	24
Embroidery: Rabari Style	Rabari Lodi: Creating a Fabric Through Social Alliance, The	Frater, Judy	√	√	WJ	10	1	37	Su 85	28
Embroidery: Random Stitch	On Mathematics and Treasures	Stanton, R. G.			AT	8			De 87	57
Embroidery, Schiffli	Schiffli Embroidery		√		Fa	9	3		M/J 82	49
Embroidery: Skills	Identifying Hands at Work on a Paracas Mantle	Paul, Anne; Susan A. Niles	√		TMJ	23			84	5
Embroidery: Stitches	Guilding The Lily: Embroidery Stitches in Victorian Crazy Quilts	Horton, Margaret	√	√	TM			10	A/M 87	48
Embroidery: Stitches	Tapestry and Embroidery	Drooker, Penelope B.	√	√	Iw	5	3		Su 80	40
Embroidery: Suzhou	On Mathematics and Treasures	Stanton, R. G.			AT	8			De 87	57
Embroidery: Tambour	Some Unusual Turkish Embroideries of the Early Eighteenth Century	Johnstone, Pauline	√		TMJ	24			85	75
Embroidery: Tambour	Tambour Embroidery		√	√	TM			12	A/S 87	6
Embroidery: Techniques	Freestyle Embroidery: New Images with Traditional Stitches	Dahl, Caroline	√	√	TM			1	O/N 85	22
Embroidery Traditions: China	On Mathematics and Treasures	Stanton, R. G.			AT	8			De 87	57
Embroidery: Turkish	Some Unusual Turkish Embroideries of the Early Eighteenth Century	Johnstone, Pauline	√		TMJ	24			85	75
Embroidery: Ukrainian Designs	Embroidery for the Goddess	Kelly, Mary B.	√		TM			11	J/J 87	26
Embroidery: Weave	Little Known Weaves Worth Knowing Better: Two-Harness Method	Zielinski, S. A.; Robert Leclerc, ed.	√	> 4	MWL	16			'51–'73	37
Embroidery: Woven	Decorative Weft on a Plain Weave Ground, Two Shaft Inlay and Brocade		√	√	WJ	5	4	20	Sp 81	15
Embroidery: Woven	Garments with Ethnic Flavor: Dress Inspired by the American Southwest		√	√	WJ	2	3	7	Ja 78	17

SUBJECT	TITLE	AUTHOR	IL	INST	JOUR	VOL	NO	ISS	DATE	PAGE
Embroidery: Woven	Guatemalan Brocade Border, A	Simons, Phid	√	√	WJ	6	4	24	Sp 82	39
Embroidery: Woven	Hopi Woven Embroidery		√	√	WJ	2	3	7	Ja 78	24
Embroidery: Woven	Smålands Weave on Eight Shafts	Shannon, Eileen	√	> 4	WJ	9	1	33	Su 84	47
Embroidery: Woven	Why Not Try Embroidery Weaves?	Jones, Jeanetta L.	√	√	H&C	17	2		Sp 66	12
Employees	Help in the Studio I: Evaluating Your Needs	LaLena, Constance	√		Hw	3	5		N/D 82	81
Employees	Help in the Studio II: Hiring a Permanent Staff	LaLena, Constance		√	Hw	4	1		J/F 83	74
Endangered Species	Saving the Navajo Sheep	Timmons, Chris	√		Fa	11	3		M/J 84	54
Endangered: Tropical Rain Forest	Protesting a Worldwide Danger		√		Fa	14	1		J/F 87	77
England	Bernard Barton Spinning Wheel — 1766, The		√		S-O	7	4		Wi 83	16
England	Coventry Tapestry, The Largest Woven in Modern Times, The		√		H&C	14	1		Wi 63	18
England	Fabric of the Lake District: Herdwick Sheep	Humphries, Andrew B.	√		S-O	8	4		Wi 84	45
England	Ravensthorpe: A Festival of Wool	Walker, Pauline; Carol Taylor	√		S-O	7	2		Su 83	16
England	Roman Textiles from Vindolanda, Hexham, England	Wild, John Peter	√		TMJ	18			79	19
England	Silk Production of Lullingstone and Whitchurch, The	Rubbert, Toni	√		Hw	3	4		Se 82	27
England	Story of Reticella, The	Cave, OEnone	√		H&C	11	3		Su 60	14
England	Technical Progress and the Evolution of Wage Arrangements in the British Cotton Weaving Industry	Jackson, K. C.; B. Pourdeyhimi	√		AT	7			Ju 87	61
England	Three English Tapestry Weavers	Liebler, Barbara	√		Hw	3	1		Ja 82	60
England	Vestments from the KilBride Workshop		√		H&C	15	3		Su 64	12
England	Weaving Abroad II	Huebner, Marianne	√		H&C	21	4		Fa 70	21
England	William Morris, A Twentieth Century View of His Woven Textiles	Morris, Barbara J.	√		H&C	12	2		Sp 61	6
England	William Morris, His Designs for Carpets & Tapestries	Morris, Barbara J.	√		H&C	12	4		Fa 61	18
England: York County	Thomas Jackson, Weaver: 17th and 18th Century Records	Tidball, Harriet	√		SCGM		13		64	8
Environmental/Public Fiber	Gates: Project for Central Park, The		√		Fa	9	4		J/A 82	92
Environmental Art	Design Concepts and Aesthetic Concerns of Corporate Art Collections	Rutherford, Karen Jenson			AT	8			De 87	193
Environmental Art: Fiber/Music	Cardiac Algorithms or the Heart's Way of Inferring Meaning from Pattern	Courtney, Elizabeth	√		AT	5			Ju 86	51
Environmental Fiber	Arvada Project, The	Heath, Jennifer	√		Fa	5	4		J/A 78	45
Environmental Fiber	Building on Experience: Virginia Jacobs' Fabric Constructions	Rowland, Amy Zaffarano	√		Fa	7	4		J/A 80	39
Environmental Fiber	Cindy Snodgrass: Wind Sculptures	Wilson, Karen	√		Fa	6	5		S/O 79	56
Environmental Fiber	Fiber and Architecture: Dennis Jenkins		√		Fa	3	3		M/J 76	35
Environmental Fiber	"Four x Four, A Collaboration: A Special Environment " (Exhibit)	Welty, Margaret	√		Fa	7	1		J/F 80	69
Environmental Fiber	Grau-Garriga: An Interview	Nelson, Susan Venable; Valerie Bechtol	√		Fa	5	4		J/A 78	32
Environmental Fiber	Ice Tapestries: The Environmental Art of Phyllis Dukes	Scarborough, Jessica	√		Fa	6	5		S/O 79	26
Environmental Fiber	Kliots of Berkeley, The	Talley, Charles S.	√		Fa	7	4		J/A 80	44
Environmental Sculpture	Jim Grashow: Inspired by Architecture		√		Fa	12	1		J/F 85	62
Environmental/Public Fiber	Clothesline Palette: Three Hundred Yards of Color		√		Fa	9	1		J/F 82	22
Environmental/Public Fiber	Conversation with Barbara Shawcroft: A Sculptor in Fiber, A	Mattera, Joanna	√		Fa	8	4		J/A 81	58
Environmental/Public Fiber	Dionysian Spirits: Dennis Valinski's Sculptures of Life	Snodgrass, Cindy	√		Fa	8	5		S/O 81	48
Environmental/Public Fiber	Fraas—Slade: Painted Views	Reith, Stephanie	√		Fa	8	5		S/O 81	32

SUBJECT	TITLE	AUTHOR	IL	INST	JOUR	VOL	NO	ISS	DATE	PAGE
Environmental/Public Fiber	George Brett: Webs of a Mad Spider	McMillan, Sam	√		Fa	8	6		N/D 81	32
Environmental/Public Fiber	Here Today, Gone Tomorrow: The Transitory Sculpture of Virginia Gunter	Mattera, Joanne	√		Fa	8	2		M/A 81	18
Environmental/Public Fiber	Karon Hagemeister Winzenz: Fusing Fiber, Time, and Ritual	Bard, Elizabeth A.	√		Fa	12	1		J/F 85	10
Environmental/Public Fiber	Papermaking in the U.S.A.	Toale, Bernard	√		Fa	9	4		J/A 82	34
Environmental/Public Fiber	"Voyage Continued" An Illuminating Experience (Exhibit)	Malarcher, Patricia	√		Fa	8	2		M/A 81	16
Environmental/Public Fiber	Windworks: A Way of Working	Frasier, Debra	√		Fa	10	4		J/A 83	58
Environmental/Public Fiber	Yurt in Artpark, The	Brennan, Joan	√		Fa	9	3		M/J 82	19
Environmental/Public Sculpture	Enduring Art of Jagoda Buic, The	Mathews, Rich	√		Fa	11	4		J/A 84	64
Environmental/Public Sculpture	Joyce Chown's "Fabricated Structure: Weir"	Weir, Jean; Joyce Chown	√		Fa	11	4		J/A 84	39
Environmental/Public Sculpture	"Terminal": Drawing in Three Dimensions	Lyman, Susan	√		Fa	11	4		J/A 84	60
Environmental/Public Sculpture	Visual Language of Bella Feldman, The	Scarborough, Jessica	√		Fa	11	4		J/A 84	30
Environments: Fiber	"Karen Armstrong's Jungle Happening" (Exhibit)	Kerr, Connie	√		Fa	6	2		M/A 79	19
Equipment and Accessories also see Specific Items										
Equipment and Accessories	Directory of Plans for Weaving and Spinning Equipment	Hammock, Noël			SS&D	6	2	22	Sp 75	27
Equipment and Accessories	Fiberarts Equipment Directory 1979: Looms, The		√		Fa	6	1		J/F 79	28
Equipment and Accessories	Fiberarts Equipment Directory 1979, The (Addenda Fa v6 n2 79 p56)		√		Fa	6	1		J/F 79	27
Equipment and Accessories	Weaving in the Urban Tradition	Bulback, Stanley	√		SS&D	12	3	47	Su 81	7
Equipment and Accessories: Batik	Resisting Dyes: Three Ways to Put Color in Its Place	Northup, Wendy	√	√	TM			1	O/N 85	30
Equipment and Accessories: Bobbin Winders	Handweaver's Instruction Manual: Additional Equipment, Bobbin Winder	Tidball, Harriet C. nee Douglas			SCGM		34		49	5
Equipment and Accessories: Bobbin Winders	Technology of Handweaving: Bobbin Winders	Zielinski, S. A.; Robert Leclerc, ed.			MWL	6			'51–'73	68
Equipment and Accessories: Bobbins	Handweaver's Instruction Manual: Additional Equipment, Bobbins	Tidball, Harriet C. nee Douglas			SCGM		34		49	5
Equipment and Accessories: Bobbins	Technology of Handweaving: Shuttles, Bobbins, Quills	Zielinski, S. A.; Robert Leclerc, ed.	√	√	MWL	6			'51–'73	10
Equipment and Accessories: Braiding Stool	Kumihimo	Kinoshita, Masako	√	√	SS&D	11	3	43	Su 80	19
Equipment and Accessories: Complex Weaving	New Items for Complex Weavers	Colwell, Ken	√		CW	2	3	6	Ap 81	5
Equipment and Accessories: Conservation, Vacuum Device	Conservation Notes: A Specialized Vacuum Device for Fragil Textiles	Columbus, Joseph Vincent	√	√	TMJ	1	1		No 62	56
Equipment and Accessories: Doubling Stand	Technology of Handweaving: Doubling Stand	Zielinski, S. A.; Robert Leclerc, ed.	√	√	MWL	6			'51–'73	26
Equipment and Accessories: Drafting Tools	Pattern Sticks, Invention of Astrid Swenson of Queens College		√	√	H&C	19	4		Fa 68	21
Equipment and Accessories: Drawing-In Hook	Handweaver's Instruction Manual: Additional Equipment, Drawing-in Hook	Tidball, Harriet C. nee Douglas			SCGM		34		49	6
Equipment and Accessories: Drawloom Attachment	Oscar Knopf's Ingenious Invention	Miller, Ethel E.	√	> 4	H&C	10	2		Sp 59	24
Equipment and Accessories: Drum Carders	Exotic Fiber Blends	Royce, Beverly	√	√	S-O	9	4		Wi 85	43
Equipment and Accessories: Dyeing	Building Your Own Steam Cabinet	Yannie, Barbara	√	√	Fa	5	1		J/F 78	32
Equipment and Accessories: Dyeing	Color and Dyeing: Equipment for Dyeing	Tidball, Harriet	√	√	SCGM		16		65	17
Equipment and Accessories: Dyeing	Color and Dyeing: Equipment for Dyeing, Equipment for Precision Dyeing	Tidball, Harriet		√	SCGM		16		65	20
Equipment and Accessories: Dyeing	Color and Dyeing: Equipment for Dyeing, Equipment for Teaspoon Dyeing	Tidball, Harriet	√	√	SCGM		16		65	19
Equipment and Accessories: Dyeing	Color and Dyeing: Equipment for Dyeing, Yarn Measuring and Weighing	Tidball, Harriet	√	√	SCGM		16		65	17

SUBJECT	TITLE	AUTHOR	IL	INST	JOUR	VOL	NO	ISS	DATE	PAGE
Equipment and Accessories: Dyeing, Winding Frame	Balinese Ikat	Hannon, Farrell	√	√	WJ	5	1	17	Su 80	49
Equipment and Accessories: Flying Shuttles	Technology of Handweaving: Flying Shuttle	Zielinski, S. A.; Robert Leclerc, ed.	√	√	MWL	6			'51–'73	56
Equipment and Accessories: Heddle-Switching Device	Changing Patterns in Midstream, Rethreading Made Unnecessary by New Device	Ziegler, Luise	√	√	H&C	13	2		Sp 62	12
Equipment and Accessories: Heddles	Handweaver's Instruction Manual: Additional Equipment, Heddles	Tidball, Harriet C. nee Douglas			SCGM		34		49	6
Equipment and Accessories: Hooking	Tapestry Gunner	Henry, Patti	√	√	TM			7	O/N 86	40
Equipment and Accessories: Importing	Consider Importing	Ziemke, Dene			SS&D	4	1	13	Wi 72	41
Equipment and Accessories: Knitting, Wooly Boards	Woolly Boards		√		Kn	2	1	3	F-W 85	16
Equipment and Accessories: Lease Rods	Technology of Handweaving: The Lease and the Lease Rods	Zielinski, S. A.; Robert Leclerc, ed.	√	√	MWL	6			'51–'73	17
Equipment and Accessories: Leash Sticks	Handweaver's Instruction Manual: Additional Equipment, Leash Sticks	Tidball, Harriet C. nee Douglas			SCGM		34		49	6
Equipment and Accessories: Loom	Doublejack	Koepp, William A.	√	√	SS&D	14	1	53	Wi 82	7
Equipment and Accessories: Loom Bench	Handweaver's Instruction Manual: Additional Equipment, Loom Bench	Tidball, Harriet C. nee Douglas			SCGM		34		49	6
Equipment and Accessories: Loom Benches	1979 Fiberarts Equipment Directory: Loom Benches, The		√		Fa	6	1		J/F 79	59
Equipment and Accessories: Loom Cord	Handweaver's Instruction Manual: Additional Equipment, Loom Cord	Tidball, Harriet C. nee Douglas			SCGM		34		49	6
Equipment and Accessories: Papermaking	Papermaking: Where It's Coming From	Hughey, Michael W.	√	√	SS&D	10	4	40	Fa 79	45
Equipment and Accessories: Pattern Harness (Set)	Technology of Handweaving: Pattern Harness	Zielinski, S. A.; Robert Leclerc, ed.	√	√	MWL	6			'51–'73	38
Equipment and Accessories: Pick-Up Sticks	Five, Six, Pick-up Sticks		√	√	Hw	7	2		M/A 86	53
Equipment and Accessories: Pick-Up Sticks	Handweaver's Instruction Manual: Additional Equipment, Pick-Up Sticks	Tidball, Harriet C. nee Douglas			SCGM		34		49	6
Equipment and Accessories: Plying	Two Heads Are Better Than One, or A Story with a Good Twist	Kirschner, Lee	√	√	S-O	8	4		Wi 84	42
Equipment and Accessories: Plying Machine	Contemporary Uses for an Ancient Fiber: Spanish Moss	Elliott, Douglas B.	√	√	SS&D	9	2	34	Sp 78	51
Equipment and Accessories: Quills	Technology of Handweaving: Quills	Zielinski, S. A.; Robert Leclerc, ed.		√	MWL	6			'51–'73	16
Equipment and Accessories: Quills	Technology of Handweaving: Shuttles, Bobbins, Quills	Zielinski, S. A.; Robert Leclerc, ed.	√	√	MWL	6			'51–'73	10
Equipment and Accessories: Raddles	Technology of Handweaving: Raddles	Zielinski, S. A.; Robert Leclerc, ed.	√	√	MWL	6			'51–'73	21
Equipment and Accessories: Reeds	Choosing the Right Reed		√	√	Hw	7	4		S/O 86	85
Equipment and Accessories: Reeds	Designing in the Reed	Hausner, Walter	√	√	H&C	8	2		Sp 57	10
Equipment and Accessories: Reeds	Handweaver's Instruction Manual: Additional Equipment, Reeds	Tidball, Harriet C. nee Douglas			SCGM		34		49	6
Equipment and Accessories: Reeds	Reeds Too Fine? There is a Way	Moes, Dini	√	√	SS&D	14	4	56	Fa 83	27
Equipment and Accessories: Reeds	Sett and the Hand of the Fabric	Roth, Bettie G.	√	√	SS&D	12	3	47	Su 81	16
Equipment and Accessories: Reeds	Working Weaver—Reeds: Increasing Their Efficiency	Checkowy, Edna	√	√	SS&D	16	4	64	Fa 85	12
Equipment and Accessories: Reeds, Sectional	Ruana	Sylvan, Katherine	√	√	WJ	5	3	19	Wi 81	34
Equipment and Accessories: Reeds, Types	Reed as a Design Element, The	Hausner, Walter			H&C	21	4		Fa 70	20
Equipment and Accessories: Resist Dyeing	Limited-Edition Vests	Stocksdale, Joy	√	√	TM			4	A/M 86	60

SUBJECT	TITLE	AUTHOR	IL	INST	JOUR	VOL	NO	ISS	DATE	PAGE
Equipment and Accessories: Russ-Knotting	Russ-Knotting from Sweden	Swenson, Astrid	√	√	SS&D	4	3	15	Su 73	24
Equipment and Accessories: Shed Regulators	Technology of Handweaving: Shed Regulators	Zielinski, S. A.; Robert Leclerc, ed.	√	√	MWL	6			'51–'73	29
Equipment and Accessories: Shuttle Races	Technology of Handweaving: Shuttles and Shuttle-Races	Zielinski, S. A.; Robert Leclerc, ed.	√	√	MWL	6			'51–'73	7
Equipment and Accessories: Shuttles	Handweaver's Instruction Manual: Additional Equipment, Shuttles	Tidball, Harriet C. nee Douglas	√		SCGM		34		49	5
Equipment and Accessories: Shuttles	Technology of Handweaving: Shuttles and Shuttle-Races	Zielinski, S. A.; Robert Leclerc, ed.	√	√	MWL	6			'51–'73	7
Equipment and Accessories: Shuttles	Technology of Handweaving: Shuttles, Bobbins, Quills	Zielinski, S. A.; Robert Leclerc, ed.	√	√	MWL	6			'51–'73	10
Equipment and Accessories: Skein Holder	Handweaver's Instruction Manual: Additional Equipment, Skein Holder	Tidball, Harriet C. nee Douglas			SCGM		34		49	5
Equipment and Accessories: Spindles	Christmas Tree Tip Makes a Drop Spindle	Wollenberg, Jackie	√	√	SS&D	6	1	21	Wi 74	60
Equipment and Accessories: Spindles, Drop	Drop Spindles	Vernon, Jeane	√		SS&D	4	4	16	Fa 73	45
Equipment and Accessories: Spinning	But Why Does it Spin?	Bradley, Louise	√		S-O	5			81	10
Equipment and Accessories: Spinning	Carders: Hand or Drum	Hochberg, Bette	√	√	S-O	3			79	40
Equipment and Accessories: Spinning	Carding Box, The	Koster, Joan Bouza	√	√	SS&D	10	4	40	Fa 79	24
Equipment and Accessories: Spinning	Carding Machines	Adams, Brucie	√		Iw	4	3		Su 79	54
Equipment and Accessories: Spinning	Colonial Equipment	Pennington, David; Michael Taylor	√		S-O	2			78	40
Equipment and Accessories: Spinning	Directory of Plans for Weaving and Spinning Equipment	Hammock, Noël			SS&D	6	2	22	Sp 75	27
Equipment and Accessories: Spinning	Hooked Stick	Quinn, Celia	√	√	S-O	9	2		Su 85	34
Equipment and Accessories: Spinning	Journey Through Greece, Two Americans in Search of Native Weaving	Znamierowski, Nell	√		H&C	14	2		Sp 63	8
Equipment and Accessories: Spinning	One-Spindle Twister	Russell, Harold W.; Walter W. Ingenthron, Jr.	√		SS&D	3	1	9	Wi 71	10
Equipment and Accessories: Spinning	Suitcase Distaff, A	Linder, Harry; Olive Linder	√	√	S-O	10	2		Fa 86	33
Equipment and Accessories: Spinning	There's An Old Spinning Wheel in the Parlor	Rossiter, Phyllis	√		S-O	9	1		Sp 85	31
Equipment and Accessories: Spinning	Weaving and Tailoring Handpun Yardage	Simmons, Paula	√	√	S-O	2			78	48
Equipment and Accessories: Spinning, Bobbin Winders	Electric Drill Becomes a Quill Spinner and a Bobbin Winder, An	Barrett, Earl W.	√	√	WJ	1	1	1	Jy 76	19
Equipment and Accessories: Spinning, High-Whorl Lap Spindle	High-Whorl Lap Spindle, The	Heite, Louise	√	√	S-O	10	1		Sp 86	36
Equipment and Accessories: Spinning, Spinning Quill	Electric Drill Becomes a Quill Spinner and a Bobbin Winder, An	Barrett, Earl W.	√	√	WJ	1	1	1	Jy 76	19
Equipment and Accessories: Spinning Whorls	Spanish Colonial Spindle Whorls: The History and the Art	Spradley, J. L.	√	√	S-O	7	1		Sp 83	35
Equipment and Accessories: Spool Rack	Handweaver's Instruction Manual: Additional Equipment, Spool Rack	Tidball, Harriet C. nee Douglas	√		SCGM		34		49	5
Equipment and Accessories: Swifts	Yarns and Fibers: Skeins and Swifts	Zielinski, S. A.; Robert Leclerc, ed.	√	√	MWL	4			'51–'73	9
Equipment and Accessories: Tailoring	Sewing Handwovens	Betzina, Sandra	√	√	TM			2	D/J 85	20
Equipment and Accessories, Tailoring	Tailoring Handwoven Fabrics	Bryan, Dorothy	√		H&C	10	2		Sp 59	17
Equipment and Accessories: Tapestry	Notes for a Potential Tapestry Weaver	Schira, Cynthia	√	√	H&C	19	4		Fa 68	12
Equipment and Accessories: Tatting	Tatting	Suter, Betty	√	√	TM			6	A/S 86	64
Equipment and Accessories: Temples and Stretchers	Technology of Handweaving: Templets for Finn Weave	Zielinski, S. A.; Robert Leclerc, ed.	√	√	MWL	6			'51–'73	51

SUBJECT	TITLE	AUTHOR	IL	INST	JOUR	VOL	NO	ISS	DATE	PAGE
Equipment and Accessories: Temples and Stretchers	Technology of Handweaving: Templets or Stretchers	Zielinski, S. A.; Robert Leclerc, ed.	√	√	MWL	6			'51–'73	48
Equipment and Accessories: Tensioner	Handweaver's Instruction Manual: Additional Equipment, Tensioner	Tidball, Harriet C. nee Douglas			SCGM		34		49	6
Equipment and Accessories: Textile	Textiles from the Smithsonian's Collection	Adrosko, Rita	√		H&C	23	2		M/A 72	20
Equipment and Accessories: Textile, Miscellaneous	1979 Fiberarts Equipment Directory: Miscellaneous, The		√		Fa	6	2		M/A 79	58
Equipment and Accessories: Textiles	Textile Equipment & Inventions Fair	Utzinger, Karen	√		SS&D	3	2	10	Sp 72	44
Equipment and Accessories: Warping	Angel Sticks, An Aid to Warping	Walrath, E. K.	√	√	H&C	20	3		Su 69	15
Equipment and Accessories: Warping	Everything a Weaver Should Know About Warps and Warping: Warping & Warping Equipment	Zielinski, S. A.; Robert Leclerc, ed.	√	√	MWL	5			'51–'73	7
Equipment and Accessories: Warping Board	Handweaver's Instruction Manual: Additional Equipment, Warping Board	Tidball, Harriet C. nee Douglas	√		SCGM		34		49	5
Equipment and Accessories: Warping, Horizontal Warping Mill	Everything a Weaver Should Know About Warps and Warping: Horizontal Warping Mill	Zielinski, S. A.; Robert Leclerc, ed.	√	√	MWL	5			'51–'73	14
Equipment and Accessories: Warping, Horizontal Warping Mill, The Heck Block	Everything a Weaver Should Know About Warps and Warping: Horizontal Warping Mill — The Heck Block	Zielinski, S. A.; Robert Leclerc, ed.	√	√	MWL	5			'51–'73	22
Equipment and Accessories: Warping, Mill	Everything a Weaver Should Know About Warps and Warping: The Warping Mill	Zielinski, S. A.; Robert Leclerc, ed.		√	MWL	5			'51–'73	27
Equipment and Accessories: Warping Paddles	How to Warp with a Paddle—Beam Without Paper, Part 1	Landis, Lucille	√	√	SS&D	16	1	61	Wi 84	72
Equipment and Accessories: Warping Paddles	Technology of Handweaving: Paddles	Zielinski, S. A.; Robert Leclerc, ed.	√	√	MWL	6			'51–'73	80
Equipment and Accessories: Warping, Sett Indicator	Everything a Weaver Should Know About Warps and Warping: Sett Indicator	Zielinski, S. A.; Robert Leclerc, ed.	√	√	MWL	5			'51–'73	59
Equipment and Accessories: Warping, Tension Box	Everything a Weaver Should Know About Warps and Warping: Sectional Warp Beam	Zielinski, S. A.; Robert Leclerc, ed.	√	√	MWL	5			'51–'73	34
Equipment and Accessories: Weaving	Braille Pattern Board Developed for Wasinger	Tope, Carolyn	√		SS&D	4	3	15	Su 73	18
Equipment and Accessories: Weaving	Creative Equipment		√		Iw	3	4		Su 78	35
Equipment and Accessories: Weaving	Directory of Plans for Weaving and Spinning Equipment	Hammock, Noël			SS&D	6	2	22	Sp 75	27
Equipment and Accessories: Weaving	Equipment for Production Efficiency: Other Helpful Equipment	LaLena, Constance	√		Hw	5	5		N/D 84	79
Equipment and Accessories: Weaving	Hand Teasels and Shears		√		SS&D	2	2	6	Sp 71	18
Equipment and Accessories: Weaving	Making & Using the Loop Heddle Jig (error-corrected SS&D v13 n2 81 p4)	Towne, Carroll A.	√	√	SS&D	13	1	49	Wi 81	10
Equipment and Accessories: Weaving	Techniques for Better Weaving (error-corrected TM i9 D/J 86 p4)	Osterkamp, Peggy	√	√	TM			7	O/N 86	42
Equipment and Accessories: Weaving	Textile Arts of Multan, Pakistan	Shahzaman, Mahboob	√	> 4	SS&D	4	3	15	Su 73	8
Equipment and Accessories: Weaving	Tools of the Trade	Chandler, Deborah	√		Hw	6	1		J/F 85	23
Equipment and Accessories: Weaving	Yarn Storage Trees	Keasbey, Doramay	√	√	SS&D	10	2	38	Sp 79	86
Equipment and Accessories: Weaving, Bubbler	Rug Weaving: How to Avoid Drawing-in of the Warp	Stanley, Martha	√	√	WJ	6	2	22	Fa 81	10
Equipment and Accessories: Weaving, Heddle Bar	Weaving in Quebec: New Ideas and Techniques	Barrett, Clotilde	√	√	WJ	6	4	24	Sp 82	16
Equipment and Accessories: Weaving, Heddle Jig	Tie Your Own String Heddles	Perrault, Joe	√	√	WJ	11	1	41	Su 86	65
Equipment and Accessories: Weaving, Heddle Rack	Tie Your Own String Heddles	Perrault, Joe	√	√	WJ	11	1	41	Su 86	65
Equipment and Accessories: Weaving, Shuttles	Knowledge of Shuttles is Important	Carter, Bill	√		H&C	2	3		Su 51	31

SUBJECT	TITLE	AUTHOR	IL	INST	JOUR	VOL	NO	ISS	DATE	PAGE
Equipment and Accesssories: Sewing	Proper Sewing Equipment	Betzina, Sandra	√		Hw	7	5		N/D 86	72
Equipment, Constructihg and Adapting	Evolution of the Multi-Loom, The	Brokaw, Edith H., O.T.R.	√		H&C	3	4		Fa 52	9
Equipment, Constructing and Adapting	From the Weaver's Bench: Full Width Projects	Elam, E. T.		√	H&C	23	5		S/O 72	30
Equipment: Constructing and Adapting	Reeds Too Fine? There is a Way	Moes, Dini	√	√	SS&D	14	4	56	Fa 83	27
Equipment, Constructing and Adapting: Reed Support	Can You Use Comfort, Sley & Thread in the Same Sentence?	Gustafson, Susan L.	√	√	CW	8	1	22	Se 86	11
Equipment, Constructing and Adapting: Shaft Support	Can You Use Comfort, Sley & Thread in the Same Sentence?	Gustafson, Susan L.	√	√	CW	8	1	22	Se 86	11
Equipment, Constructing and Adapting: Spinning	From Bobbin Flyer to Electric Spinner	Holborn, Joan	√	√	S-O	3			79	44
Equipment: Constructing and Adapting, Spinning	Home Built Box Spinner	Barrow, Cynthia	√	√	WJ	2	4	8	Ap 78	43
Equipment: Constructing and Adapting: Spinning	"Workbench" Wheel and Reel		√	√	SS&D	4	1	13	Wi 72	24
Equipment, Constructing and Adapting: Spinning Spindles	Teacher's Tricks	Grayson, Persis	√	√	S-O	10	1		Sp 86	10
Equipment, Constructing and Adapting: Weaving	Tools You Can Make		√	√	H&C	3	3		Su 52	28
Equipment, Repair and Maintenance: Spinning	Great Wheel, The	Turner, Katy	√	√	S-O	3			79	46
Equipment, Repair and Maintenance: Weaving	Technology of Handweaving: Taking Care of the Equipment	Zielinski, S. A.; Robert Leclerc, ed.		√	MWL	6			'51–'73	74
Errors/Solutions: Warping	Rx: Winding and Threading Errors	Guy, Sallie T.	√	√	Hw	2	5		No 81	66
Errors/Solutions: Weaving	Avoiding and Repairing Weaving Errors	Alderman, Sharon D.	√	√	Hw	2	5		No 81	60
Ethics	On the Use of Borrowed Patterns and Designs	Ligon, Linda			Hw	4	4		S/O 83	30
Ethnic Designs	Pueblo Deco	Sitko, Jane Bradley	√		SS&D	18	4	72	Fa 87	40
Ethnic Textiles	Adaptations of Primitive Warp-Pattern Weaves	Landreau, Tony	√	√	H&C	8	1		Wi 56	25
Ethnic Textiles	Art and Romance of Peasant Clothes, The		√		SS&D	9	2	34	Sp 78	76
Ethnic Textiles	Bit of Rope Turns Cloth Into a Dancer's Costume, A	Grace, Leslie	√		TM			10	A/M 87	20
Ethnic Textiles	Card Woven Belt of East Telemark—An Adaptation of a Traditional Norwegian Technique	Nelson, Lila	√	√	WJ	9	1	33	Su 84	30
Ethnic Textiles	Clothing Change Through Contact: Traditional Guatemalan Dress	Fisher, Abby Sue	√		WJ	10	3	39	Wi 86	60
Ethnic Textiles	Clothing from Rectangles	Liebler, Barbara	√	√	Iw	5	4		Fa 80	52
Ethnic Textiles	Contemporary Egyptian Childern's Tapestries		√		Fa	4	6		N/D 77	65
Ethnic Textiles	Culture That Supports Culture, A		√		Fa	10	4		J/A 83	84
Ethnic Textiles	Decorative Techniques of the Sarakatsani	Smith, Joyce	√	√	WJ	9	1	33	Su 84	14
Ethnic Textiles	Detective Story: Unravelling the Mystery of a 7-Loop Braid, A	Cahlander, Adele	√	√	WJ	10	1	37	Su 85	12
Ethnic Textiles	Ethnic Costume		√		SS&D	12	1	45	Wi 80	16
Ethnic Textiles	Ethnic Inspired Jacket	Hurt, Doris	√	√	WJ	4	4	16	Ap 80	43
Ethnic Textiles	Fashion Trends	Nelipovitch, Kate; Susan Hick	√		WJ	6	3	23	Wi 81	6
Ethnic Textiles	Fiber Heritage of the Salish	Whonnock Spinners & Weavers	√		WJ	9	2	34	Fa 84	65
Ethnic Textiles	Folkwear: In the Company of Some Friends		√		Fa	3	5		S/O 76	36
Ethnic Textiles	Fullus: Ikat Blankets of Tarabuco, Bolivia	Meisch, Lynn A.	√	√	WJ	10	1	37	Su 85	54
Ethnic Textiles	Greek Chemises: Cut and Construction	Welters, Linda	√	√	WJ	10	1	37	Su 85	40
Ethnic Textiles	Guatemala: Weaving, People	Frost, Gordon	√		Iw	5	4		Fa 80	30
Ethnic Textiles	Guatemalan Brocade Border, A	Simons, Phid	√	√	WJ	6	4	24	Sp 82	39

SUBJECT	TITLE	AUTHOR	IL	INST	JOUR	VOL	NO	ISS	DATE	PAGE
Ethnic Textiles	Guatemalan Stripes	Davenport, Betty	√	√	Hw	4	2		M/A 83	54
Ethnic Textiles	In the Dark of the Swamp...Seminole Patchwork		√	√	Fa	4	3		M/J 77	38
Ethnic Textiles	Jerga: A Twill in Harmony with its Heritage	Wilson, Kax	√		Hw	6	5		N/D 85	60
Ethnic Textiles	Kaleidoscopic Tour of Turkey, A	Dyer, Carol; Carel Bertram	√		Fa	7	5		S/O 80	48
Ethnic Textiles	Kantha Cloths of Bengal: The Sari Transformed	Gupta, Asha	√		Fa	9	6		N/D 82	19
Ethnic Textiles	Kumejima Kasuri: A Visit to a Remote Japanese Silk Center	Mitchell, Alison	√	√	WJ	10	1	37	Su 85	59
Ethnic Textiles	Las Artistas Del Valle: Images of Everyday Life in Colorado's San Luis Valley	Reith, Stephanie J.	√		Fa	10	3		M/J 83	24
Ethnic Textiles	Mayan Folk Textiles: Symbol of a Society	Dieterich, Mary	√		Hw	6	3		Su 85	64
Ethnic Textiles	Mexican Travelogue, A	Hewitt, T. H.	√		H&C	3	3		Su 52	22
Ethnic Textiles	"Our Shining Heritage: Textile Arts of the Slavs and Their Neighbors" (Exhibit)	Mackin, Jeanne	√		Fa	8	4		J/A 81	75
Ethnic Textiles	Overshot Overlay for Ethnic Clothing	Marston, Ena	√		SS&D	9	3	35	Su 78	88
Ethnic Textiles	Paisley Shawls: A Democratic Fashion	Goodman, Deborah Lerme	√		Fa	12	3		M/J 85	52
Ethnic Textiles	Paper Clothing, East	Sahlstrand, Margaret	√	√	Fa	11	2		M/A 84	36
Ethnic Textiles	Pelete Bite: Kalabari Cut-Thread Cloth	Thieme, Otto Charles	√		Fa	10	5		S/O 83	46
Ethnic Textiles	Qotny & Alaga: Traditional Striped Fabrics for the Middle Eastern Kaftan	El-Homossani, M. M.	√	> 4	WJ	10	1	37	Su 85	33
Ethnic Textiles	Rabari Lodi: Creating a Fabric Through Social Alliance, The	Frater, Judy	√	√	WJ	10	1	37	Su 85	28
Ethnic Textiles	Revivified Past, A	Upitis, Lizbeth	√		Kn	3	1	5	F-W 86	12
Ethnic Textiles	"Silken Threads and Silent Needles" (Exhibit)	Dunnewold, Jane	√		Fa	11	6		N/D 84	78
Ethnic Textiles	Sweetgrass, Cedar & Sage: Portrait of a Southwestern Weaver	Schevill, Margot	√		WJ	10	1	37	Su 85	24
Ethnic Textiles	Three Personal Statements: Norma Minkowitz, Gillian Bull, Mardel Esping		√		Fa	3	5		S/O 76	19
Ethnic Textiles	Toronto's "unMuseum" for Textiles	Talley, Charles	√		Fa	12	4		J/A 85	43
Ethnic Textiles	Villanueva Tapestries		√		Fa	4	3		M/J 77	45
Ethnic Textiles	Wadmal — A Felted Fabric	Snover, Susan; Jean Sullivan	√	√	SS&D	11	2	42	Sp 80	89
Ethnic Textiles	Warp-Faced Double Cloth: Adaptation of an Andean Technique for the Treadle Loom	Cahlander, Adele	√	√	WJ	10	4	40	Sp 86	72
Ethnic Textiles	Weaving For Ethnic Clothing	Marston, Ena	√	√	SS&D	10	1	37	Wi 78	42
Ethnic Textiles	Weaving Out of One's Own Tradition	Centner, David			Iw	5	4		Fa 80	32
Ethnic Textiles	Weaving Tradition in the Andes, A	Adelson, Laurie; Bruce Takami	√		Fa	6	4		J/A 79	22
Ethnic Textiles	Yurts (Not Your Average Dwelling)	Landess, Susan	√		Fa	5	6		N/D 78	26
Ethnic Textiles	Yvonne Porcella		√		Fa	4	5		S/O 77	52
Ethnic Textiles	Yvonne Porcella: A Modern Master of the Ethnic Clothing Tradition	Avery, Virginia	√		Fa	8	1		J/F 81	63
Ethnic Textiles, Reinterpreting	Modern Interpretations of Ethnic Garments	Dickey, Enola	√	√	SS&D	9	2	34	Sp 78	28
Ethnic-Inspired Textiles: Cape	Garments with Ethnic Flavor: Pine Tree Cape		√	> 4	WJ	2	3	7	Ja 78	16
Ethnic-Inspired Textiles: Coat	Garments with Ethnic Flavor: Desert Dusk Coat		√		WJ	2	3	7	Ja 78	16
Ethnic-Inspired Textiles: Coat	Turkish Coat, A	Xenakis, Alexis Yiorgos	√	> 4	Hw	2	2		Mr 81	39
Ethnic-Inspired Textiles: Dress	Garments with Ethnic Flavor: Blue and White Twill Dress		√	√	WJ	2	3	7	Ja 78	18
Ethnic-Inspired Textiles: Dress	Garments with Ethnic Flavor: Dress Inspired by the American Southwest		√	√	WJ	2	3	7	Ja 78	17
Ethnic-Inspired Textiles: Dress	Garments with Ethnic Flavor: Ethnic Dress with Supplementary Warp		√	√	WJ	2	3	7	Ja 78	14

SUBJECT	TITLE	AUTHOR	IL	INST	JOUR	VOL	NO	ISS	DATE	PAGE
Ethnic-Inspired Textiles: Garments	Garments with Ethnic Flavor				WJ	2	3	7	Ja 78	13
Ethnic-Inspired Textiles: Skirt	Garments with Ethnic Flavor: Mexican Motif Skirt		√	√	WJ	2	3	7	Ja 78	13
Etymology: Weaving	Weaving a Web	Wolfe, Susan			PWC	4	3	13		5
Europe	European Craft Tour, A	Polaski, Lois	√		H&C	23	1		J/F 72	16
Europe	Handweaver & Craftsman Tour of Europe, 1972	Polaski, Lois	√		H&C	23	2		M/A 72	13
Europe	Kashmiri to Paisley: Evolution of the Paisley shawl	Larson-Fleming, Susan	√		WJ	11	3	43	Wi 87	37
Europe	Weaver's Journey, A	Gonzalez, Loraine			H&C	15	2		Sp 64	33
Europe	Weaving Abroad	Huebner, Marianne A.	√		H&C	21	3		Su 70	10
Europe	Weaving Abroad II	Huebner, Marianne	√		H&C	21	4		Fa 70	21
European Shawls: Double-Woven	Woven Structures of European Shawls in The Textile Museum Collection, The	Rowe, Ann Pollard			TMJ	24			85	55
European Shawls: Reversible	Woven Structures of European Shawls in The Textile Museum Collection, The	Rowe, Ann Pollard			TMJ	24			85	55
European Shawls: Twill-Woven	Woven Structures of European Shawls in The Textile Museum Collection, The	Rowe, Ann Pollard			TMJ	24			85	55
Evaluation: Weaving Skills	Evaluating Your Work for the Market	Hoffmann, Jenet	√		SS&D	10	4	40	Fa 79	80
Events	African American Thread Fare	White, Marcia	√		Fa	9	6		N/D 82	56
Events: Fabric Encounter	Fabric Encounter	Kaplan, Susan	√		H&C	24	4		Au 73	19
Events: National Spinning and Weaving Week	National Spinning & Weaving Week, 1982: "A Blanket of Joy"		√		Hw	3	3		My 82	28
Events: National Spinning and Weaving Week	Spinning and Weaving Week Celebrated Nationwide		√		Hw	2	5		No 81	8
Exclusivity	A Weaver Ponders His Craft, Collection of Controversial Essays: Exclusivity	Zielinski, S. A.; Robert Leclerc, ed.			MWL	21 22			'51–'73	47
Exercise	Yoga For Weavers	McCloud, Nena	√		Fa	5	2		M/A 78	40
Exercises	Weaving is a Pain in the...	Chandler, Deborah	√	√	Hw	6	2		M/A 85	26
Exhibition Designers	Behind the Scenes: A Museum Installation	Goodman, Deborah Lerme	√		Fa	13	3		M/J 86	42
Exhibits and Ehxibiting	At the Studio of Lenore Tawney		√		H&C	16	2		Sp 65	35
Exhibits and Eshibiting	Aritst's Suggestions for More Effective Display of Handweaving, An	Hamilton, Stephen		√	H&C	13	2		Sp 62	10
Exhibits and Exhibiting	8th International Biennial of Tapestry: Three Perspectives, The	Marston, Ena; Shirley E. Held; Esther Dendel	√		SS&D	9	1	33	Wi 77	4
Exhibits and Exhibiting	American Sojourn of African Textiles, An	Lonier, Terri	√		Fa	11	1		J/F 84	66
Exhibits and Exhibiting	Anni Albers — Innovator in Textile Design		√		H&C	10	4		Fa 59	6
Exhibits and Exhibiting	Art and Romance of Peasant Clothes, The		√		SS&D	9	2	34	Sp 78	76
Exhibits and Exhibiting	Art of Working with Linen, The		√		Fa	14	2		M/A 87	9
Exhibits and Exhibiting	"Art Quilt, The" (Exhibit)	McMorris, Penny; Kile, Michael	√		TM			7	O/N 86	30
Exhibits and Exhibiting	Artwear/ACE Expo		√		WJ	12	1	45	Su 87	35
Exhibits and Exhibiting	At the Pittsburgh Exhibit		√		SS&D	3	4	12	Fa 72	44
Exhibits and Exhibiting	Aubussons on Tour		√		H&C	13	4		Fa 62	20
Exhibits and Exhibiting	Bauhaus Weaving	Dodge, Dorothy	√		H&C	22	4		Fa 71	17
Exhibits and Exhibiting	Bellevue Fair	Kobler, Virginia	√		H&C	18	1		Wi 67	26
Exhibits and Exhibiting	Best Foot Forward: The Weavers Guild of Pittsburgh	McGuire, Patricia	√		SS&D	7	1	25	Wi 75	41
Exhibits and Exhibiting	Biennale, The	Taylor, Dianne; Elmer Taylor	√		SS&D	12	4	48	Fa 81	54
Exhibits and Exhibiting	Biennale, The	Waller, Irene	√		SS&D	14	4	56	Fa 83	20
Exhibits and Exhibiting	Biennale/Another View, The	Coifman, Lucienne	√		SS&D	15	1	57	Wi 83	76
Exhibits and Exhibiting	But Is It Tapestry?	Meltzer, Marilyn	√		SS&D	5	3	19	Su 74	39
Exhibits and Exhibiting	California Designed	Bryan, Dorothy	√		H&C	7	1		Wi 55	30
Exhibits and Exhibiting	California Exposition Art Show		√		SS&D	3	2	10	Sp 72	14

SUBJECT	TITLE	AUTHOR	IL	INST	JOUR	VOL	NO	ISS	DATE	PAGE
Exhibits and Exhibiting	Canada's Handwoven Heritage		√		Hw	7	4		S/O 86	89
Exhibits and Exhibiting	Cincinnati Celebrates '76	Berger, Florence S.	√		SS&D	8	2	30	Sp 77	60
Exhibits and Exhibiting	COE Retrospective	Drooker, Penelope			SS&D	15	4	60	Fa 84	19
Exhibits and Exhibiting	Conferences: Convergence '78	Ligon, Linda; with Barbara Gentry	√		Iw	3	4		Su 78	28
Exhibits and Exhibiting	Connecticut Weavers Use New Display Methods				H&C	12	2		Sp 61	52
Exhibits and Exhibiting	Contemporary Embroidery		√		H&C	17	3		Su 66	4
Exhibits and Exhibiting	Contemporary Handweavers at the De Young Museum	Crockett, Candace	√		SS&D	2	2	6	Sp 71	4
Exhibits and Exhibiting	Contemporary Handweaving for the Home, Memphis Guild Exhibition	Miller, Carolyn A.			H&C	10	2		Sp 59	20
Exhibits and Exhibiting	Contemporary Hangings at Brookfield	Gotthoffer, Esther	√		SS&D	1	1	1	De 69	2
Exhibits and Exhibiting	Contemporary Indiana Weavers		√		H&C	18	4		Fa 67	9
Exhibits and Exhibiting	"Contemporary Weaving" (Exhibit)		√		Fa	3	1		J/F 76	5
Exhibits and Exhibiting	Convergence '84, Dallas				SS&D	15	2	58	Sp 84	46
Exhibits and Exhibiting	Convergence '84, Dallas	Dailey, Linda	√		SS&D	15	4	60	Fa 84	38
Exhibits and Exhibiting	Coudre A Main: Costumes by Hand	Tacker, Sylvia	√		Fa	12	2		M/A 85	49
Exhibits and Exhibiting	Country of Origin, USA: A Decade of Contemporary Rugs	Stevens, Rebeccah A. T.	√		Fa	11	3		M/J 84	60
Exhibits and Exhibiting	Courtyard, Bazaar, Temple: Traditions in Indian Textile Expression		√		SS&D	13	4	52	Fa 82	44
Exhibits and Exhibiting	Creative Crafts Council Exhibit		√		SS&D	2	2	6	Sp 71	24
Exhibits and Exhibiting	Creative Weavers Show Diversity in Juried Exhibit		√		SS&D	4	4	16	Fa 73	48
Exhibits and Exhibiting	Cut from the Same Cloth	Andrews, Kathy Boals	√		Fa	13	3		M/J 86	21
Exhibits and Exhibiting	De Cordova Exhibit	Corey, Rosita	√		SS&D	3	4	12	Fa 72	46
Exhibits and Exhibiting	Designer-Craftsmen U.S.A. 1960		√		H&C	11	3		Su 60	18
Exhibits and Exhibiting	Discovering Canada's Handwoven Heritage		√		SS&D	17	3	67	Su 86	40
Exhibits and Exhibiting	Dr. Elisabeth Moses of the M. H. de Young Museum	Bryan, Dorothy	√		H&C	7	2		Sp 56	16
Exhibits and Exhibiting	East-West		√		SS&D	11	4	44	Fa 80	28
Exhibits and Exhibiting	Evolution of a Regional Juried Fiber Show: Fibers Unlimited, The	Rees, Linda			SS&D	17	3	67	Su 86	65
Exhibits and Exhibiting	Exercises in Color		√	√	H&C	16	2		Sp 65	36
Exhibits and Exhibiting	Exhibition by Larsen and Riegger Indicates Broadening Field of Craft Cooperation		√		H&C	2	2		Sp 51	32
Exhibits and Exhibiting	Exhibition Spaces	Kerr, Connie	√		SS&D	14	3	55	Su 83	8
Exhibits and Exhibiting	FABRICation '72		√		SS&D	3	4	12	Fa 72	13
Exhibits and Exhibiting	Fabrications '75, San Diego	Neuner, Norma	√		SS&D	6	3	23	Su 75	29
Exhibits and Exhibiting	Fabrics International		√		H&C	13	1		Wi 62	6
Exhibits and Exhibiting	Fiber and Politics		√		Fa	13	3		M/J 86	20
Exhibits and Exhibiting	Fiber Structures: A Preview		√		SS&D	7	2	26	Sp 76	92
Exhibits and Exhibiting	Fiber Talks—Eloquently	Wiley, Lois	√		SS&D	9	4	36	Fa 78	92
Exhibits and Exhibiting	"Fibers" At Tactile Gallery		√	√	SS&D	6	2	22	Sp 75	14
Exhibits and Exhibiting	Fibers Unlimited 1980: Whatcom Textile Guild	McNair, Peg	√		Hw	2	3		My 81	20
Exhibits and Exhibiting	Fibers Unlimited 1985	Tacker, Sylvia	√		SS&D	17	3	67	Su 86	68
Exhibits and Exhibiting	Fiberscene		√		SS&D	11	4	44	Fa 80	65
Exhibits and Exhibiting	Fiberscene		√		SS&D	12	1	45	Wi 80	24
Exhibits and Exhibiting	Fiberscene		√		SS&D	12	2	46	Sp 81	55
Exhibits and Exhibiting	Fiberscene		√		SS&D	12	3	47	Su 81	31
Exhibits and Exhibiting	Fiberscene		√		SS&D	12	4	48	Fa 81	44
Exhibits and Exhibiting	Fiberscene		√		SS&D	13	2	50	Sp 82	44
Exhibits and Exhibiting	Fiberscene		√		SS&D	14	1	53	Wi 82	70

SUBJECT	TITLE	AUTHOR	IL	INST	JOUR	VOL	NO	ISS	DATE	PAGE
Exhibits and Exhibiting	Fiberscene		√		SS&D	14	2	54	Sp 83	74
Exhibits and Exhibiting	Fiberscene		√		SS&D	15	2	58	Sp 84	56
Exhibits and Exhibiting	Fiberscene (error-corrected SS&D v14 n4 83 p4)				SS&D	14	3	55	Su 83	48
Exhibits and Exhibiting	Fiberworks: At The Cleveland Museum of Art		√		SS&D	8	4	32	Fa 77	34
Exhibits and Exhibiting	Fifth International Tapestry Exhibit	Wick, Susan	√		H&C	22	4		Fa 71	16
Exhibits and Exhibiting	First World Crafts Exhibition		√		SS&D	5	3	19	Su 74	40
Exhibits and Exhibiting	For the Floor: An International Exhibit of Contemporary Artists' Rugs	Wolff, Colette	√		Hw	6	2		M/A 85	20
Exhibits and Exhibiting	For the Floor: The World at Our Feet	Busch, Akiko	√		SS&D	16	3	63	Su 85	54
Exhibits and Exhibiting	From the Far West: Carpets and Textiles of Morocco	West, Virginia	√		Hw	2	3		My 81	14
Exhibits and Exhibiting	Further Thoughts on "The Artist & The Quilt"	Dunnewold, Jane			Fa	11	2		M/A 84	56
Exhibits and Exhibiting	Governors' Conference Features Fiber	Hazlett, Paula Renee	√		SS&D	13	1	49	Wi 81	14
Exhibits and Exhibiting	Great Handcraft Show at Munich				H&C	3	1		Wi 51	40
Exhibits and Exhibiting	Great Variety Shown in Earth, Fire, and Fibre Exhibition in Alaska		√		SS&D	5	3	19	Su 74	84
Exhibits and Exhibiting	Handweaving in Effective Settings	Bryan, Dorothy	√		H&C	12	1		Wi 61	10
Exhibits and Exhibiting	Handwoven Rugs from the Northwest	Disney, Jean	√		H&C	6	4		Fa 55	42
Exhibits and Exhibiting	Hangups		√		Fa	3	6		N/D 76	6
Exhibits and Exhibiting	Heirloom Linens	Furniss, Frances	√		H&C	9	2		Sp 58	11
Exhibits and Exhibiting	High Tech—High Touch	Van Artsdalen, Martha J.	√		SS&D	18	2	70	Sp 87	54
Exhibits and Exhibiting	Houston "Stalagtite"		√		SS&D	3	4	12	Fa 72	7
Exhibits and Exhibiting	Impressions of an Exposition	Levy, Julie			TM			8	D/J 86	12
Exhibits and Exhibiting	Indian Textiles from Ecuador		√		H&C	10	1		Wi 59	19
Exhibits and Exhibiting	Influence from the East: Textiles and Textile Patterns in Western Art	Park, Betty	√		Fa	12	2		M/A 85	22
Exhibits and Exhibiting	Intermountain Weavers: "Fiber Celebrated, 1985"	McClellan, Alice	√		SS&D	17	4	68	Fa 86	42
Exhibits and Exhibiting	International Textile Exhibition 1950				H&C	2	1		Wi 50	35
Exhibits and Exhibiting	International Textile Exhibition, The	Hardin, Noma			H&C	6	1		Wi 54	28
Exhibits and Exhibiting	International Textile Exhibition, The	Larsen, Jack Lenor	√		H&C	4	1		Wi 52	30
Exhibits and Exhibiting	Jack Lenor Larsen	Znamierowski, Nell	√		H&C	22	3		Su 71	6
Exhibits and Exhibiting	Judy Chicago: The Second Decade	Keener, Terrah	√		SS&D	15	4	60	Fa 84	30
Exhibits and Exhibiting	Juried Exhibit from Pattern to Free- Form	Rupp, Michael	√		SS&D	6	1	21	Wi 74	42
Exhibits and Exhibiting	Lace and Cashmere		√		TM			8	D/J 86	12
Exhibits and Exhibiting	Lace Constructions from Czechoslovakia				H&C	15	4		Fa 64	34
Exhibits and Exhibiting	Larger Weaving Section for Women's International		√		H&C	8	2		Sp 57	14
Exhibits and Exhibiting	Lausanne Biennale: The Scene of an Adventure, The	Ritschard, Mlle. Claude	√		Iw	4	2		Sp 79	19
Exhibits and Exhibiting	Lenore Tawney		√		H&C	13	2		Sp 62	6
Exhibits and Exhibiting	Logistics Solved in Seattle	Noble, Judy	√		SS&D	6	3	23	Su 75	92
Exhibits and Exhibiting	Maggie Riegler Exhibit Tours USA		√		SS&D	4	1	13	Wi 72	32
Exhibits and Exhibiting	Making of an Exhibition: An Insider's Report, The	Wolff, Colette	√		Fa	12	3		M/J 85	46
Exhibits and Exhibiting	Material Matters: Textile Gifts to the Cleveland Museum of Art	McClelland, Elizabeth	√		Fa	12	3		M/J 85	50
Exhibits and Exhibiting	Michigan Weaving, Third Conference at Hartland Shows Wide Variety		√		H&C	13	1		Wi 62	18
Exhibits and Exhibiting	Mississippi River Craft Show		√		H&C	14	3		Su 63	35
Exhibits and Exhibiting	Monk's Belt	Moes, Dini	√	√	SS&D	18	4	72	Fa 87	52
Exhibits and Exhibiting	More Textiles Shown in "Good Design" 1951	Brophil, Gladys Rogers			H&C	2	2		Sp 51	38
Exhibits and Exhibiting	National Mini Tapestry Exhibit	Cameron, Carolyn W.	√		SS&D	9	3	35	Su 78	48

SUBJECT	TITLE	AUTHOR	IL	INST	JOUR	VOL	NO	ISS	DATE	PAGE
Exhibits and Exhibiting	New Elegance: Contemporary Art Wear, The	Van Artsdalen, Martha	√		SS&D	16	1	61	Wi 84	50
Exhibits and Exhibiting	New England Crafts at Worcester	Currey, Ruth Dunlop	√		H&C	7	1		Wi 55	18
Exhibits and Exhibiting	New England Weavers at Old Slater Mill		√		H&C	9	1		Wi 57	22
Exhibits and Exhibiting	New Italian Renaissance Follows Liberation, A				H&C	3	1		Wi 51	10
Exhibits and Exhibiting	New Jersey Weavers Exhibit at the Montclair Museum		√		H&C	7	3		Su 56	44
Exhibits and Exhibiting	New York Handweavers at Cooper Union Museum		√		H&C	7	4		Fa 56	20
Exhibits and Exhibiting	Next to the Skin		√		SS&D	15	4	60	Fa 84	42
Exhibits and Exhibiting	Ninth International Biennial of Tapestry: A Prime Reflector, The	West, Virginia	√		SS&D	11	1	41	Wi 79	96
Exhibits and Exhibiting	Norwegian Tapestries		√		H&C	10	4		Fa 59	46
Exhibits and Exhibiting	Notable Collection of Textiles in Exhibition Sponsored by the Seattle Weavers' Guild		√		H&C	3	1		Wi 51	31
Exhibits and Exhibiting	Nova Scotia Designer Craftsmen: Profile '81	Budgey, Elfriede	√		SS&D	13	1	49	Wi 81	30
Exhibits and Exhibiting	On Exhibiting: A Few Caveats	Rees, Linda		√	SS&D	7	1	25	Wi 75	60
Exhibits and Exhibiting	People on Exhibit At Henry Gallery	Noble, Judy	√		SS&D	6	1	21	Wi 74	84
Exhibits and Exhibiting	Philadelphia Guild Point System	Schlegel, Mary		√	SS&D	4	4	16	Fa 73	4
Exhibits and Exhibiting	Picasso, The Weaver		√		SS&D	11	4	44	Fa 80	15
Exhibits and Exhibiting	Pittsburgh Weavers Guild Exhibition				SS&D	3	1	9	Wi 71	16
Exhibits and Exhibiting	Planning an Exhibition	Wellman, Kathryn, O.T.R.	√		H&C	3	4		Fa 52	26
Exhibits and Exhibiting	Polish Art Weaving 1960-1976		√		SS&D	9	1	33	Wi 77	120
Exhibits and Exhibiting	Portland Weavers Scholarship Show	Turner, Kathryn	√		SS&D	6	1	21	Wi 74	79
Exhibits and Exhibiting	Presence of Light, The	Park, Betty	√		SS&D	15	4	60	Fa 84	36
Exhibits and Exhibiting	Preview...Convergence '82, A		√		SS&D	13	3	51	Su 82	65
Exhibits and Exhibiting	Quilt National '85	Levine, Betsy	√		TM			2	D/J 85	10
Exhibits and Exhibiting	Rocky Mountain Guild Observes Colorado Centennial	Tuinsma, Frieda Z.	√		H&C	10	3		Su 59	16
Exhibits and Exhibiting	Rocky Mountain Weavers Display Fabrics for the Home	Matty, Norma P.	√		H&C	12	4		Fa 61	9
Exhibits and Exhibiting	Roman Heritage, The	Angelil, Muriel	√		SS&D	13	3	51	Su 82	69
Exhibits and Exhibiting	Rugs: An Exhibition of Contemporary Handwoven Floorcoverings	Smayda, Norma			SS&D	17	4	68	Fa 86	83
Exhibits and Exhibiting	Russian Costumes At The Metropolitan Museum		√		SS&D	8	3	31	Su 77	88
Exhibits and Exhibiting	Second Annual Handcrafted Wool Showcase	Kirk, Ray	√		S-O	3			79	6
Exhibits and Exhibiting	Seen Around the Country		√		SS&D	10	4	40	Fa 79	92
Exhibits and Exhibiting	Seen Around the Country				SS&D	11	1	41	Wi 79	94
Exhibits and Exhibiting	Seen Around the Country		√		SS&D	11	3	43	Su 80	38
Exhibits and Exhibiting	Seen Around the Country: A Letter from England (error-corrected SS&D v10 n3 79 p75)	Waller, Irene	√		SS&D	10	2	38	Sp 79	103
Exhibits and Exhibiting	Seen Around the Country: Colorado Fibers	Boland, Loay C.	√		SS&D	10	1	37	Wi 78	84
Exhibits and Exhibiting	Seen Around the Country: Contemporary Fiber Statements		√		SS&D	10	3	39	Su 79	4
Exhibits and Exhibiting	Seen Around the Country: Fiber at the Torpedo Factory	Kasper, Susan; Roslyn Logsdon	√		SS&D	9	4	36	Fa 78	86
Exhibits and Exhibiting	Seen Around the Country: Fibers Unlimited 1978	Noble, Judy	√		SS&D	10	2	38	Sp 79	101
Exhibits and Exhibiting	Seen Around the Country: Insights Into Lenore Tawney		√		SS&D	10	2	38	Sp 79	98
Exhibits and Exhibiting	Seen Around the Country: Palestinian Costume Exhibit in New Mexico	Ulrich, Kenn	√		SS&D	9	4	36	Fa 78	84
Exhibits and Exhibiting	Seen Around the Country: Threads Unlimited IV	Barrett, Clotilde	√		SS&D	10	1	37	Wi 78	84

SUBJECT	TITLE	AUTHOR	IL	INST	JOUR	VOL	NO	ISS	DATE	PAGE
Exhibits and Exhibiting	sere-chrysalis-seer		√		PWC	4	2	12		34
Exhibits and Exhibiting	Seven Valley Weavers				H&C	20	4		Fa 69	36
Exhibits and Exhibiting	Seventh Lausanne Biennial, The		√		SS&D	7	2	26	Sp 76	41
Exhibits and Exhibiting	Show Stopper: Con-Tex-Ture		√		SS&D	6	2	22	Sp 75	80
Exhibits and Exhibiting	Show Stopper: Easter Chasuble		√		SS&D	6	2	22	Sp 75	47
Exhibits and Exhibiting	Show Strategies (error-corrected SS&D v19 n1 87 p33)	Itter, Diane	√		SS&D	18	4	72	Fa 87	26
Exhibits and Exhibiting	Show Strategies, Part 2	Itter, Diane	√		SS&D	19	1	73	Wi 87	28
Exhibits and Exhibiting	Show-Stoppers		√		SS&D	5	4	20	Fa 74	45
Exhibits and Exhibiting	Show-Stoppers		√		SS&D	6	1	21	Wi 74	12
Exhibits and Exhibiting	Showtime '83		√		SS&D	14	4	56	Fa 83	52
Exhibits and Exhibiting	Siminoff Textiles	Trayer, Blanche C.	√		H&C	9	1		Wi 57	18
Exhibits and Exhibiting	Small Expressions/Large Celebrations		√		SS&D	15	4	60	Fa 84	41
Exhibits and Exhibiting	Southern California Show		√		H&C	14	3		Su 63	30
Exhibits and Exhibiting	Southwestern Spanish Textiles (error-corrected SS&D v9 n4 78 p34)	Spillman, Trish; Marion Rinehart	√		SS&D	9	3	35	Su 78	56
Exhibits and Exhibiting	St. Louis Guild 50th Anniversary	Ziemke, Dene	√		SS&D	6	3	23	Su 75	93
Exhibits and Exhibiting	St. Mary's Weavers		√		H&C	10	1		Wi 59	30
Exhibits and Exhibiting	Stitchery '66	King, Bucky	√		H&C	18	1		Wi 67	25
Exhibits and Exhibiting	Structure and Surface: The Work of Barbara MacCallum	Koplos, Janet	√		Fa	10	2		M/A 83	62
Exhibits and Exhibiting	Swedish Touch, The		√		SS&D	4	1	13	Wi 72	22
Exhibits and Exhibiting	Texas Fabrics	Hardt, Blanche	√	√	H&C	8	3		Su 57	31
Exhibits and Exhibiting	Textiles from India		√		H&C	6	3		Su 55	9
Exhibits and Exhibiting	Textiles on Display: The Installation of Fiber Exhibitions	Rees, Linda	√	√	SS&D	17	4	68	Fa 86	38
Exhibits and Exhibiting	Textiles USA		√		H&C	7	4		Fa 56	24
Exhibits and Exhibiting	Three British Weavers	Held, Shirley E.			H&C	23	6		N/D 72	33
Exhibits and Exhibiting	Thurid Clark		√		Fa	3	6		N/D 76	8
Exhibits and Exhibiting	Tradition and Change: Fiber '79	Martin, Elaine	√		Iw	5	2		Sp 80	72
Exhibits and Exhibiting	Traditional Lithuanian Weaving in Chicago	Meek, M. Kati	√		SS&D	17	3	67	Su 86	50
Exhibits and Exhibiting	Twelfth International Tapestry Biennale, The	Coifman, Lucienne	√		SS&D	17	2	66	Sp 86	45
Exhibits and Exhibiting	Twelfth International Tapestry Biennale, The	Waller, Irene	√		SS&D	17	2	66	Sp 86	42
Exhibits and Exhibiting	Two Exhibitions in Sweden	Stockenstrom, Ann-Marie v.	√		H&C	18	1		Wi 67	22
Exhibits and Exhibiting	Valberg Rugs on View		√		H&C	9	1		Wi 57	25
Exhibits and Exhibiting	Wearables in the Market Place: Reporting on a Survey	Dunnewold, Jane	√		Fa	12	3		M/J 85	48
Exhibits and Exhibiting	Weaving and Light: Creative Ideas and Techniques for Your Next Show	Hafermann, Candy Kreitlow	√	√	Iw	5	3		Su 80	34
Exhibits and Exhibiting	Weaving in the Designer Craftsmen U.S.A. 1953 Exhibition		√		H&C	5	1		Wi 53	22
Exhibits and Exhibiting	Weaving of Saudi Arabia		√		SS&D	14	2	54	Sp 83	20
Exhibits and Exhibiting	Web of India, The	Malarcher, Patricia	√		SS&D	13	2	50	Sp 82	38
Exhibits and Exhibiting	Weigle—Hubbell Exhibit	McKinley, Sally	√		SS&D	3	1	9	Wi 71	36
Exhibits and Exhibiting	Western Handweaving 1957	Bryan, Dorothy	√		H&C	8	4		Fa 57	6
Exhibits and Exhibiting	Whitewater Birds At Wisconsin Show		√	√	SS&D	2	2	6	Sp 71	10
Exhibits and Exhibiting	"Wildfire" Wins Best-in-Show		√		SS&D	4	1	13	Wi 72	39
Exhibits and Exhibiting	William Morris: The Sanford and Helen Berger Collection	Austin, Carole	√		Fa	12	3		M/J 85	47
Exhibits and Exhibiting	World Trade Fair		√		H&C	8	3		Su 57	44
Exhibits and Exhibiting	Young Americans 1958		√		H&C	9	4		Fa 58	46
Exhibits and Exhibiting: Alaska	"Fiber Feelings" (Exhibit)	King, Dianne Hennessy	√		Fa	5	5		S/O 78	70
Exhibits and Exhibiting: Arizona	"Tina Johnson-Depuy Soft Jewelry" (Exhibit)	Cardinale, Robert L.	√		Fa	6	3		M/J 79	81

SUBJECT	TITLE	AUTHOR	IL	INST	JOUR	VOL	NO	ISS	DATE	PAGE
Exhibits and Exhibiting: Arkansas	Italian Textiles (Exhibit)		√		Fa	14	1		J/F 87	69
Exhibits and Exhibiting: California	"American Quilts: A Handmade Legacy" (Exhibit)	Janeiro, Jan	√		Fa	8	4		J/A 81	72
Exhibits and Exhibiting: California	"Anne Wilson: Recent Work" (Exhibit)	Arajs, Ilze	√		Fa	11	4		J/A 84	75
Exhibits and Exhibiting: California	"Art and Romance of Peasant Clothing, The" (Exhibit)	Dyer, Carolyn	√		Fa	5	3		M/J 78	16
Exhibits and Exhibiting: California	"Art Fabric '77: The Contemporary American Tapestry" (Exhibit)	Papa, Nancy	√		Fa	4	4		J/A 77	12
Exhibits and Exhibiting: California	"Art Fabric: Mainstream, The" (Exhibit)	Janeiro, Jan	√		Fa	8	5		S/O 81	70
Exhibits and Exhibiting: California	"Art of African Masquerade, The" (Exhibit)	Dyer, Carolyn Price	√		Fa	13	3		M/J 86	56
Exhibits and Exhibiting: California	"Art of the Cuna, The" (Exhibit)	Williams, Dai	√		Fa	10	4		J/A 83	64
Exhibits and Exhibiting: California	"Arts of Ghana" (Exhibit)	Dyer, Carolyn	√		Fa	5	1		J/F 78	19
Exhibits and Exhibiting: California	"Arts of Indian Asia: The Joy of Artistic Expression, The" (Exhibit)	Dyer, Carolyn	√		Fa	5	5		S/O 78	64
Exhibits and Exhibiting: California	"At the Edge of Asia: Five Centuries of Turkish Textiles" (Exhibit)	Dyer, Carolyn Price	√		Fa	10	4		J/A 83	65
Exhibits and Exhibiting: California	"Barbara Shawcroft: Nets, Rope, and Cloth" (Exhibit)	Finucane, Brigid	√		Fa	12	4		J/A 85	68
Exhibits and Exhibiting: California	"Basket and Paper Invitational Show" (Exhibit)	Howe, Cathe	√		Fa	12	3		M/J 85	71
Exhibits and Exhibiting: California	"Baskets in La Jolla" (Exhibit)	Blaylock, Mary P.	√		Fa	11	1		J/F 84	79
Exhibits and Exhibiting: California	"Bella Tabak Feldman: Recent Sculpture" (Exhibit)	Scarborough, Jessica	√		Fa	10	2		M/A 83	70
Exhibits and Exhibiting: California	"Birth Project, The" First Showing of Judy Chicago's New Work (Exhibit)	von Kreisler-Bomben, Kristin	√		Fa	10	1		J/F 83	81
Exhibits and Exhibiting: California	"California Fibers: 11th Annual Show" (Exhibit)	Kosta, Angela	√		Fa	10	6		N/D 83	81
Exhibits and Exhibiting: California	"California Women in Crafts" (Exhibit)	Dyer, Carolyn	√		Fa	4	2		M/A 77	10
Exhibits and Exhibiting: California	"Camel Belts from the Great Indian Desert" (Exhibit)	Janeiro, Jan	√		Fa	10	6		N/D 83	75
Exhibits and Exhibiting: California	"Carolyn Prince Batchelor: Vessels" (Exhibit)	Lilligren, Ingrid	√		Fa	12	3		M/J 85	77
Exhibits and Exhibiting: California	"Contemporary Japanese Tapestry, The" (Exhibit)	Glass, Laurie H.	√		Fa	4	6		N/D 77	22
Exhibits and Exhibiting: California	"Contemporary Shibori" (Exhibit)	Howe, Cathe	√		Fa	11	3		M/J 84	82
Exhibits and Exhibiting: California	Corporate Collecting "Contemporary Tapestries" (Exhibit)	Dyer, Carolyn	√		Fa	4	5		S/O 77	16
Exhibits and Exhibiting: California	"Daniel Graffin: Traces" (Exhibit)	Janeiro, Jan	√		Fa	7	2		M/A 80	73
Exhibits and Exhibiting: California	"Deborah Corsini: Tapestries" (Exhibit)	Talley, Charles S.	√		Fa	7	5		S/O 80	68
Exhibits and Exhibiting: California	"Deborah Warner's Visual Journal" (Exhibit)	Poon, Vivian	√		Fa	10	6		N/D 83	76
Exhibits and Exhibiting: California	"Detailed Directions in Fiber" (Exhibit)	Van Gelder, Lydia	√		Fa	9	3		M/J 82	77
Exhibits and Exhibiting: California	"Dominic DiMare: New Work" (Exhibit)	Janeiro, Jan	√		Fa	8	2		M/A 81	63
Exhibits and Exhibiting: California	"Dorte Christjansen" (Exhibit)	Dyer, Carolyn	√		Fa	6	2		M/A 79	62
Exhibits and Exhibiting: California	"Dowries from Kutch: A Women's Folk Art Tradition in India" (Exhibit)	Dyer, Carolyn	√		Fa	7	1		J/F 80	70
Exhibits and Exhibiting: California	"Dyer's Art: Ikat, Batik, Plangi, The" (Exhibit)	Dyer, Carolyn	√		Fa	5	4		J/A 78	11
Exhibits and Exhibiting: California	"Elegant Art: Fantasy and Fashion in the Eighteenth Century, An" (Exhibit)	Dyer, Carolyn Price	√		Fa	10	4		J/A 83	66
Exhibits and Exhibiting: California	"Ellie Fidler — Tapestries" (Exhibit)	Tanenbaum, Ruth	√		Fa	5	4		J/A 78	14
Exhibits and Exhibiting: California	Ethnic Textile Art at U.C.L.A. — "Afro-American Arts of the Suriname Rain Forest" (Exhibit)	Dyer, Carolyn	√		Fa	8	2		M/A 81	59
Exhibits and Exhibiting: California	Ethnic Textile Art at U.C.L.A. — "Yer Dailege: Kuna Women's Art" (Exhibit)	Dyer, Carolyn	√		Fa	8	2		M/A 81	59
Exhibits and Exhibiting: California	"Fabled Fabrics: Bolivian Fabrics from the Hill Collection" (Exhibit)	Dyer, Carolyn	√		Fa	9	6		N/D 82	84
Exhibits and Exhibiting: California	"Fabrications" (Exhibit)	Talley, Charles	√		Fa	6	4		J/A 79	76
Exhibits and Exhibiting: California	"Fantasy Clothes/Fantastic Costumes" (Exhibit)	Dyer, Carolyn	√		Fa	4	2		M/A 77	11

SUBJECT	TITLE	AUTHOR	IL	INST	JOUR	VOL	NO	ISS	DATE	PAGE
Exhibits and Exhibiting: California	Fiber Artists Find New Showcase in San Diego (Exhibit)	Meilach, Dona	√		Fa	3	4		J/A 76	8
Exhibits and Exhibiting: California	"Fiber Departures" (Exhibit)	Dyer, Carolyn	√		Fa	4	3		M/J 77	9
Exhibits and Exhibiting: California	"Fiber Structure National" (Exhibit)	Dyer, Carolyn	√		Fa	8	5		S/O 81	75
Exhibits and Exhibiting: California	"Fiberworks 1976" (Exhibit)	Papa, Nancy	√		Fa	4	1		J/F 77	9
Exhibits and Exhibiting: California	"Five Artists: Quilts" (Exhibit)	Scarborough, Jessica	√		Fa	13	5		S/O 86	47
Exhibits and Exhibiting: California	Flour Sacks on Display (Exhibit)		√		Fa	14	1		J/F 87	70
Exhibits and Exhibiting: California	"Four x Four, A Collaboration: A Special Environment " (Exhibit)	Welty, Margaret	√		Fa	7	1		J/F 80	69
Exhibits and Exhibiting: California	"Fukusa: The Shojiro Nomura Collection" (Exhibit)	Janeiro, Jan	√		Fa	11	3		M/J 84	79
Exhibits and Exhibiting: California	"Glenn Brill: Recent Work" (Exhibit)	Rowley, Kathleen	√		Fa	12	1		J/F 85	72
Exhibits and Exhibiting: California	"Grass" (Exhibit)	Dyer, Carolyn	√		Fa	4	1		J/F 77	5
Exhibits and Exhibiting: California	Gyongy Laky's Transformations (Exhibit)		√		Fa	13	4		J/A 86	54
Exhibits and Exhibiting: California	"Heads and Tales: Traditional Art of Borneo" (Exhibit)	Dyer, Carolyn Price	√		Fa	11	4		J/A 84	74
Exhibits and Exhibiting: California	"Ikats of Orissa" (Exhibit)	De Bone, Mary	√		Fa	11	1		J/F 84	82
Exhibits and Exhibiting: California	"Indonesia: The Fabled Islands of Spice" (Exhibit)	Dyer, Carolyn	√		Fa	6	2		M/A 79	71
Exhibits and Exhibiting: California	"Innerskins/Outerskins: Gut and Fishskin" (Exhibit)		√		TM			14	D/J 87	20
Exhibits and Exhibiting: California	"Introductions '80" Emily DuBois and Sylvia Seventy (Exhibit)	Janeiro, Jan	√		Fa	7	6		N/D 80	70
Exhibits and Exhibiting: California	Jaki Ernst "Fibre Graphics and Soft Sculpture" (Exhibit)	Gilsenan, Nancy	√		Fa	7	6		N/D 80	69
Exhibits and Exhibiting: California	"Jan Janeiro: Recent Textiles" (Exhibit)	Talley, Charles S.	√		Fa	8	2		M/A 81	65
Exhibits and Exhibiting: California	"Janet Boguch: Delivered Runes" (Exhibit)	Janeiro, Jan	√		Fa	6	5		S/O 79	83
Exhibits and Exhibiting: California	"Jarmila Machova: Fibers" (Exhibit)	Dyer, Carolyn	√		Fa	9	1		J/F 82	75
Exhibits and Exhibiting: California	"Jean Ray Laury — Exhibit of Stitchery" (Exhibit)	Gutcheon, Beth	√		Fa	6	2		M/A 79	66
Exhibits and Exhibiting: California	"Jean Ray Laury: Quilted Work" (Exhibit)	Sprague, Mary	√		Fa	9	1		J/F 82	84
Exhibits and Exhibiting: California	"Jennifer Gottdiener: Installation — Thread as Volume" (Exhibit)	Welty, Margaret	√		Fa	7	5		S/O 80	70
Exhibits and Exhibiting: California	"Julia Mitchell: Landscape Tapestries" (Exhibit)	Poon, Vivian	√		Fa	10	6		N/D 83	80
Exhibits and Exhibiting: California	Katherine Howe "Color Card Series" Woven Paintings (Exhibit)	Dyer, Carolyn	√		Fa	7	4		J/A 80	72
Exhibits and Exhibiting: California	"Knowing the Ropes" (Exhibit)	Janeiro, Jan	√		Fa	6	4		J/A 79	72
Exhibits and Exhibiting: California	"Ladders and Windows" (Exhibit)	Kester, Bernard	√		Fa	13	4		J/A 86	52
Exhibits and Exhibiting: California	"Left on the Loom" (Exhibit)	Dyer, Carolyn	√		Fa	5	2		M/A 78	16
Exhibits and Exhibiting: California	"Leroy Wilce: Adobe Walls" (Exhibit)	Dyer, Carolyn	√		Fa	4	4		J/A 77	17
Exhibits and Exhibiting: California	"Lia Cook" (Exhibit)	Park, Betty	√		Fa	5	5		S/O 78	72
Exhibits and Exhibiting: California	"Lia Cook: Shaped and Woven Constructions" (Exhibit)	Rowley, Kathleen	√		Fa	12	4		J/A 85	66
Exhibits and Exhibiting: California	"Linda Maxwell and Caroline Dahl: Terror Sampler and Other Dogs" (Exhibit)	Poon, Vivian	√		Fa	11	6		N/D 84	79
Exhibits and Exhibiting: California	"Loom, the Needle, and the Dye Pot, The" (Exhibit)	Dyer, Carolyn	√		Fa	5	1		J/F 78	20
Exhibits and Exhibiting: California	"Marika Contompasis: Pedestal and Wall Pieces" (Exhibits)	Dyer, Carolyn	√		Fa	9	4		J/A 82	73
Exhibits and Exhibiting: California	"Meri Ann Walsh: Patterned Papers" (Exhibit)	Austin, Carole	√		Fa	8	6		N/D 81	65
Exhibits and Exhibiting: California	"Michael Olszewski: Pleated and Stitched Silk" (Exhibit)	Poon, Vivian	√		Fa	11	3		M/J 84	78
Exhibits and Exhibiting: California	"Mingei — The Folk Arts of Japan" (Exhibit)	Meilach, Dona Z.	√		Fa	4	2		M/A 77	10
Exhibits and Exhibiting: California	"Modern Aubusson Tapestry, The" (Exhibit)	Tanenbaum, Ruth	√		Fa	5	3		M/J 78	14

SUBJECT	TITLE	AUTHOR	IL	INST	JOUR	VOL	NO	ISS	DATE	PAGE
Exhibits and Exhibiting: California	"Nance O'Banion: Handmade Paper and Bamboo Painting" (Exhibit)	Janeiro, Jan	√		Fa	7	4		J/A 80	15
Exhibits and Exhibiting: California	"Nance O'Banion: Painted Paper Skin Series" (Exhibits)	Rowley, Kathleen	√		Fa	9	4		J/A 82	70
Exhibits and Exhibiting: California	"Nance O'Banion: Rocks, Curtains, Windows, and Walls" (Exhibit)	Talley, Charles	√		Fa	12	5		S/O 85	69
Exhibits and Exhibiting: California	"Nancy Youdelman: Shattered Glass" (Exhibit)	Woelfle, Gretchen	√		Fa	7	3		M/J 80	74
Exhibits and Exhibiting: California	"Neda Al Hilali" (Exhibit)	Janeiro, Jan	√		Fa	9	3		M/J 82	75
Exhibits and Exhibiting: California	"Paper Clothing and More in San Francisco" (Exhibit)	Scarborough, Jessica	√		Fa	11	2		M/A 84	75
Exhibits and Exhibiting: California	"Paper Sources" (Exhibit)	Papa, Nancy	√		Fa	5	4		J/A 78	16
Exhibits and Exhibiting: California	"Patterns" with a Look at Japanese Printing with Stencils (Exhibit)	Dyer, Carolyn	√		Fa	4	5		S/O 77	10
Exhibits and Exhibiting: California	"People and Art of the Philippines, The" (Exhibit)	Dyer, Carolyn	√		Fa	9	3		M/J 82	84
Exhibits and Exhibiting: California	"Pin Rugs of Ellen Oltchick, The" (Exhibit)	Poon, Vivian	√		Fa	10	6		N/D 83	74
Exhibits and Exhibiting: California	"Poetry for the Body, Clothing for the Spirit" (Exhibit)	Hickman, Pat	√		Fa	10	5		S/O 83	75
Exhibits and Exhibiting: California	"Power Garments" (Exhibit)	Papa, Nancy	√		Fa	5	1		J/F 78	13
Exhibits and Exhibiting: California	"Quilts: A Tradition of Variations" (Exhibit)	Rowley, Kathleen	√		Fa	10	2		M/A 83	68
Exhibits and Exhibiting: California	"Renaissance Costume and Textiles: 1450–1620" (Exhibit)	Dyer, Carolyn	√		Fa	6	6		N/D 79	70
Exhibits and Exhibiting: California	"Ritual Narratives" (Exhibit)		√		Fa	13	3		M/J 86	57
Exhibits and Exhibiting: California	"Romanian Folk Textiles" (Exhibit)	Dyer, Carolyn	√		Fa	5	3		M/J 78	11
Exhibits and Exhibiting: California	"Rose Kelly: Printed, Painted and Woven Textiles" (Exhibit)	Small, Deborah	√		Fa	9	6		N/D 82	84
Exhibits and Exhibiting: California	"Salute to California: Fifty Years of Fashion, 1930–1980" (Exhibit)	Dyer, Carolyn	√		Fa	8	1		J/F 81	95
Exhibits and Exhibiting: California	"Seven Sonoma County Fibre Artists" (Exhibit)	Robinson, Sharon	√		Fa	3	4		J/A 76	6
Exhibits and Exhibiting: California	"Southern California Designer Crafts" (Exhibit)	Dyer, Carolyn	√		Fa	5	2		M/A 78	14
Exhibits and Exhibiting: California	"Tapestries of Trude Guermonprez: A Retrospective, The" (Exhibit)	Rowley, Kathleen	√		Fa	10	3		M/J 83	68
Exhibits and Exhibiting: California	"Tenth Annual Textile Exhibition" (Exhibit)	Papa, Nancy	√		Fa	5	4		J/A 78	13
Exhibits and Exhibiting: California	"Textile Traditions of Indonesia" (Exhibit)	Dyer, Carolyn	√		Fa	5	1		J/F 78	15
Exhibits and Exhibiting: California	"Textiles by Pat Kinsella and Sheila O'Hara" (Exhibit)	Janeiro, Jan	√		Fa	6	3		M/J 79	72
Exhibits and Exhibiting: California	"Third Annual Fiber Show" (Exhibit)	Papa, Nancy	√		Fa	5	6		N/D 78	65
Exhibits and Exhibiting: California	"Thomasin Grim: New Work" (Exhibit)	Scarborough, Jessica	√		Fa	11	5		S/O 84	73
Exhibits and Exhibiting: California	"Three Living Treasures from California" (Exhibit)	Brandford, Joanne Segal; Sandra Dickey Harner	√		Fa	12	5		S/O 85	70
Exhibits and Exhibiting: California	"Three Weavers: Thomasin Grim, Jane Lackey, Bhakti Ziek" (Exhibit)	Rowley, Kathleen	√		Fa	9	6		N/D 82	82
Exhibits and Exhibiting: California	"Toys and Games" (Exhibit)	Meilach, Dona Z.	√		Fa	4	1		J/F 77	7
Exhibits and Exhibiting: California	"Traditional Japanese Designs: The Tom and Frances Blakemore Collection of Textiles Stencils and Costumes" (Exhibit)	Dyer, Carolyn	√		Fa	7	3		M/J 80	81
Exhibits and Exhibiting: California	"Transformation: UCLA Alumnae In Fiber" (Exhibit)	Dyer, Carolyn	√		Fa	6	4		J/A 79	67
Exhibits and Exhibiting: California	"Wearable Folk Art" (Exhibit)	Dyer, Carolyn	√		Fa	6	3		M/J 79	82
Exhibits and Exhibiting: California	"Weaver's Art: Selected Rug Traditions of the Middle East and China, A" (Exhibit)	Talley, Charles	√		Fa	6	5		S/O 79	76
Exhibits and Exhibiting: California	"Works In, On, and of Paper" (Exhibit)	Les, Kathleen	√		Fa	6	5		S/O 79	79
Exhibits and Exhibiting: Canada	Abstracted Wearables (Exhibit)				Fa	14	2		M/A 87	61
Exhibits and Exhibiting: Canada	"Anke Van Ginhoven: Tapestries 1977" (Exhibit)	Cantieni, Graham	√		Fa	5	1		J/F 78	21
Exhibits and Exhibiting: Canada	Canadian Handweaving (Exhibit)		√		Fa	13	3		M/J 86	55
Exhibits and Exhibiting: Canada	"Fiberous": Fiber as a Source of Inspiration (Exhibit)	Willard, Janice	√		Fa	10	1		J/F 83	80

SUBJECT	TITLE	AUTHOR	IL	INST	JOUR	VOL	NO	ISS	DATE	PAGE
Exhibits and Exhibiting: Canada	"Focus on Handwoven Fabric: Ontario Handweavers and Spinners" (Exhibits)	Place, Jennifer	√		Fa	9	4		J/A 82	74
Exhibits and Exhibiting: Canada	"In the Presence of the Dragon Throne" (Exhibit)	Szajman, Rena	√		Fa	4	3		M/J 77	13
Exhibits and Exhibiting: Canada	"Patricia McClelland: Woven Work" (Exhibit)	MacNutt, Dawn	√		Fa	7	5		S/O 80	74
Exhibits and Exhibiting: Canada	"Third Montreal Tapestry Biennial, 1984" (Exhibit)	Duffy, Helen	√		Fa	12	3		M/J 85	79
Exhibits and Exhibiting: Canada	"Trees and Other Things" (Exhibit)	Hillis, Anne	√		Fa	5	4		J/A 78	17
Exhibits and Exhibiting: Collaborative	Interweavings	Stewart, Laura	√		Fa	11	3		M/J 84	47
Exhibits and Exhibiting: Colorado	"Art of Crafts 1986" (Exhibit)		√		Fa	13	5		S/O 86	54
Exhibits and Exhibiting: Colorado	Overview, An	Paterson, Kathy	√		Fa	3	5		S/O 76	6
Exhibits and Exhibiting: Colorado	Pikes Peak Weavers Guild First Fibre Arts Festival (Exhibit)	Fife, Lin	√		Fa	3	5		S/O 76	6
Exhibits and Exhibiting: Colorado	"Private Spaces, Private Lives" A Juried Fiber Show (Exhibit)	Hunt, Elizabeth Ann	√		Fa	7	6		N/D 80	75
Exhibits and Exhibiting: Colorado	"Revolution in Fiber Art" (Exhibit)		√		Fa	3	3		M/J 76	7
Exhibits and Exhibiting: Colorado	"Shoes and Chapeaux": Visit to an Exhibition (Exhibit)		√		Fa	10	1		J/F 83	23
Exhibits and Exhibiting: Colorado	"Wearable Art" (Exhibit)	Hunt, E. Ann	√		Fa	6	3		M/J 79	78
Exhibits and Exhibiting: Connecticut	"Art Couture '82" (Exhibit)	Guagliumi, Sasan	√		Fa	10	1		J/F 83	84
Exhibits and Exhibiting: Connecticut	"Art Couture VII" (Exhibit)	Guagliumi, Susan Fletcher	√		Fa	12	3		M/J 85	78
Exhibits and Exhibiting: Connecticut	"Dolly Curtis Textile Graphics" (Exhibit)	Reed, Irene C.	√		Fa	6	2		M/A 79	70
Exhibits and Exhibiting: Connecticut	"Frank Gardner: Aleatory Works" (Exhibit)	Guagliumi, Susan	√		Fa	9	2		M/A 82	75
Exhibits and Exhibiting: Connecticut	"Kari Lønning — Mary Billingsley" (Exhibit)	Beede, Beth	√		Fa	6	6		N/D 79	69
Exhibits and Exhibiting: Connecticut	"Lenore Tawney: A Personal World" (Exhibit)	Malarcher, Pat	√		Fa	5	6		N/D 78	63
Exhibits and Exhibiting: Connecticut	"Soft As Silk" (Exhibit)	Guagliumi, Susan	√		Fa	10	1		J/F 83	78
Exhibits and Exhibiting: Connecticut	"Splendor of French Style, The" Textiles from Joan of Arc to Napoleon III (Exhibit)	Guagliumi, Susan	√		Fa	13	4		J/A 86	13
Exhibits and Exhibiting: Connecticut	Textile Study Group, The (Exhibit)	Guagliumi, Susan	√		Fa	13	3		M/J 86	54
Exhibits and Exhibiting: Connecticut	"Weaving with Lucille Landis" (Exhibit)	Hartman, Shirley G.	√		Fa	9	2		M/A 82	76
Exhibits and Exhibiting: Crafts	Washington Perspective		√		SS&D	15	3	59	Su 84	53
Exhibits and Exhibiting: Denmark	" 'Genuine' Orientals from Denmark" (Exhibit)	Studsgarth, Randi	√		Fa	8	2		M/A 81	64
Exhibits and Exhibiting: Denmark	Show Your Work in Denmark	Vilsbøll, Anne	√		TM			14	D/J 87	16
Exhibits and Exhibiting: District of Columbia	"22 Polish Textile Artists" (Exhibit)	Park, Betty	√		Fa	4	5		S/O 77	8
Exhibits and Exhibiting: District of Columbia	Andrea V. Uravitch, "Wild and Domestic" (Exhibit)	Stevens, Rebecca A. T.	√		Fa	10	2		M/A 83	71
Exhibits and Exhibiting: District of Columbia	"Belgian Lace" (Exhibit)		√		Fa	7	4		J/A 80	66
Exhibits and Exhibiting: District of Columbia	"Century of Change in Guatemalan Textiles, A" (Exhibit)	Brown, Arleen Emery	√		Fa	9	3		M/J 82	79
Exhibits and Exhibiting: District of Columbia	"Fabled Cloth: Batik from Java's North Coast" (Exhibit)	Goodman, Deborah Lerme	√		Fa	12	4		J/A 85	58
Exhibits and Exhibiting: District of Columbia	Fanfare: Fans from the Collection of the National Museum of American Art (Exhibit)	Perry, Pamela	√		Fa	12	6		N/D 85	48
Exhibits and Exhibiting: District of Columbia	"Fiber 82: Miniatures" (Exhibit)	Brown, Arleen Emery	√		Fa	9	4		J/A 82	72
Exhibits and Exhibiting: District of Columbia	"Five Women from Texas" (Exhibit)	Leach, Vivian	√		Fa	6	1		J/F 79	86

SUBJECT	TITLE	AUTHOR	IL	INST	JOUR	VOL	NO	ISS	DATE	PAGE
Exhibits and Exhibiting: District of Columbia	"Flexible Medium: Art Fabric From The Museum Collection, The" (Exhibit)	Goodman, Deborah Lerme	√		Fa	11	5		S/O 84	71
Exhibits and Exhibiting: District of Columbia	"Flowers of the Yayla: Yoruk Weaving of the Toros Mountains" (Exhibit)	Bloom, Mary Jane	√		Fa	11	3		M/J 84	76
Exhibits and Exhibiting: District of Columbia	"Forms in Fiber" (Exhibit)	Brown, Arleen Emery	√		Fa	7	5		S/O 80	73
Exhibits and Exhibiting: District of Columbia	"Glorious Knits of Kaffe Fassett, The" (Exhibit)	McCann, Kathleen	√		Fa	13	2		M/A 86	53
Exhibits and Exhibiting: District of Columbia	Historic Persian Handiwork at the Textile Museum (Exhibit)	Dyer, Carolyn Price	√		Fa	14	5		N/D 87	42
Exhibits and Exhibiting: District of Columbia	"History of Knitting" (Exhibit)	Park, Betty	√		Fa	5	3		M/J 78	10
Exhibits and Exhibiting: District of Columbia	"Joyce Kozloff" An Interior Decorated (Exhibit)	Greenberg, Blue	√		Fa	8	1		J/F 81	89
Exhibits and Exhibiting: District of Columbia	"Old Traditions/New Directions" (Exhibit)	West, Virginia	√		Fa	8	6		N/D 81	66
Exhibits and Exhibiting: District of Columbia	"Painted Weavings" Lia Cook and Neda Al-Hilali (Exhibit)	Park, Betty	√		Fa	8	1		J/F 81	88
Exhibits and Exhibiting: District of Columbia	"Printed, Painted, and Dyed: The New Fabric Surface" (Exhibit)	Hecker, Carolyn	√		Fa	5	6		N/D 78	71
Exhibits and Exhibiting: District of Columbia	"Roman Heritage: Textiles from Egypt and the Eastern Mediterranean, 300–600 A.D., The" (Exhibit)		√		Fa	9	4		J/A 82	32
Exhibits and Exhibiting: District of Columbia	"Song of the Loom: New Traditions in Navajo Weaving, The" (Exhibit)		√		TM			11	J/J 87	18
Exhibits and Exhibiting: District of Columbia	"Threads" (Exhibit)	Kurtz, Carol	√		Fa	10	4		J/A 83	62
Exhibits and Exhibiting: District of Columbia	"Turkmen: Tribal Carpets and Traditions" (Exhibit)	Dyer, Carol	√		Fa	8	3		M/J 81	70
Exhibits and Exhibiting: District of Columbia	Washington Fiber	Mathews, Rich	√		Fa	3	5		S/O 76	9
Exhibits and Exhibiting: District of Columbia	"Woven and Graphic Art of Anni Albers, The" (Exhibit)	Malarcher, Patricia	√		Fa	13	1		J/F 86	62
Exhibits and Exhibiting: Embroidery	Point of View (Renie Breskin Adams)		√		TM			7	O/N 86	92
Exhibits and Exhibiting: England	"Conceptual Clothing" (Exhibit)	Waller, Irene	√		Fa	14	3		M/J 87	62
Exhibits and Exhibiting: England	"Fabric and Form: New Textile Art from Britain" (Exhibit)	Waller, Irene	√		Fa	9	6		N/D 82	80
Exhibits and Exhibiting: England	"Gaudy Ladies" (Exhibit)		√		Fa	8	4		J/A 81	44
Exhibits and Exhibiting: England	"Issey Miyake: Fashion Without Taboos" (Exhibit)	Mathews, Cleve	√		Fa	12	3		M/J 85	70
Exhibits and Exhibiting: England	"Miniature Textiles: 4th International Exhibition" (Exhibit)	Talley, Charles S.	√		Fa	8	3		M/J 81	72
Exhibits and Exhibiting: England	Paper Abroad (Exhibit)	Waller, Irene	√		Fa	11	2		M/A 84	82
Exhibits and Exhibiting: England	"Weaver's Life, Ethel Mairet, 1872–1952, A" (Exhibit)	Waller, Irene	√		Fa	11	4		J/A 84	78
Exhibits and Exhibiting: Fashion Design	Body as Canvas, The	Koda, Harold	√		TM			8	D/J 86	56
Exhibits and Exhibiting: Finland	"Swiss Tapestries" (Exhibit)	Talley, Charles S.	√		Fa	7	6		N/D 80	74
Exhibits and Exhibiting: Florida	"Frontiers of Contemporary Weaving" (Exhibit)	Clark, Barbara	√		Fa	4	1		J/F 77	6
Exhibits and Exhibiting: Florida	"Needle Expressions '80" (Exhibit)		√		Fa	8	1		J/F 81	93
Exhibits and Exhibiting: France	Paris Museum Surveys Fashion	Colton, Sarah	√		Fa	14	3		M/J 87	6
Exhibits and Exhibiting: Georgia	"Fibrations" (Exhibit)	Silver, Elizabeth	√		Fa	6	5		S/O 79	85
Exhibits and Exhibiting: Georgia	"Local Options: The Work of Laura Strand Mills and Jo Peterson" (Exhibit)	Ferguson, Tom	√		Fa	10	3		M/J 83	69
Exhibits and Exhibiting: Georgia	"Quilts of Patsy Allen, The" (Exhibit)	Laymon, Cynthia	√		Fa	10	6		N/D 83	76
Exhibits and Exhibiting: Germany	"Jagoda Buic" (Exhibit)	Mathews, Rich	√		Fa	4	5		S/O 77	13
Exhibits and Exhibiting: Germany	"K18–Stoffwechsel": A Report on the Exhibition and Symposium Held in Kassel, West Germany (Exhibit)	Vander Lee, Jana	√		Fa	10	1		J/F 83	52
Exhibits and Exhibiting: Guilds	Guild Show or Sale, A	LaLena, Constance			Hw	6	4		S/O 85	72

SUBJECT	TITLE	AUTHOR	IL	INST	JOUR	VOL	NO	ISS	DATE	PAGE
Exhibits and Exhibiting: Hawaii	"Filaments of the Imagination" (Exhibit)	Morse, Marcia	√		Fa	8	4		J/A 81	69
Exhibits and Exhibiting: Hawaii	Japanese Country Textiles (Exhibit)	Rowley, Kathleen	√		Fa	13	5		S/O 86	49
Exhibits and Exhibiting: Hooking	Hooking Wild Horses (Zorach, Marguerite)		√		TM			10	A/M 87	88
Exhibits and Exhibiting: Illinois	"Becky Clark Fiber" (Exhibit)	Farber, Deborah	√		Fa	6	1		J/F 79	89
Exhibits and Exhibiting: Illinois	"Claire Zeisler" (Exhibit)	Richerson, Suzanne	√		Fa	6	4		J/A 79	69
Exhibits and Exhibiting: Illinois	"Critters and Cohorts" (Exhibit)	Clark, Becky	√		Fa	4	6		N/D 77	13
Exhibits and Exhibiting: Illinois	"Fiber Art: Tapestries and Wall Hangings" (Exhibit)	Koplos, Janet	√		Fa	6	6		N/D 79	75
Exhibits and Exhibiting: Illinois	"Fiber Directions" (Exhibit)		√		Fa	14	1		J/F 87	70
Exhibits and Exhibiting: Illinois	"Fiber in Focus" (Exhibit)	Skudera, Gail	√		Fa	10	6		N/D 83	82
Exhibits and Exhibiting: Illinois	"Gail Skudera: Textile Paintings" (Exhibit)	Koplos, Janet	√		Fa	9	6		N/D 82	84
Exhibits and Exhibiting: Illinois	"Hmong Art: Tradition and Change" (Exhibit)	Gordon, Beverly	√		Fa	12	6		N/D 85	36
Exhibits and Exhibiting: Illinois	Interview with Mary Jane Jacob, An	Park, Betty	√		Fa	9	6		N/D 82	13
Exhibits and Exhibiting: Illinois	"Janet Markarian" (Exhibit)	Skudera, Gail	√		Fa	13	4		J/A 86	53
Exhibits and Exhibiting: Illinois	"Karen Jenson Rutherford: Wall Hangings" (Exhibit)	Towner, Naomi Whiting	√		Fa	7	6		N/D 80	72
Exhibits and Exhibiting: Illinois	"Karen Stahlecker" (Exhibit)	Shermeta, Margo	√		Fa	10	5		S/O 83	80
Exhibits and Exhibiting: Illinois	"Kathryn Lipke/Fiber-Paper-Pulp: Works in Handmade Paper" (Exhibit)	Piazza, Virginia	√		Fa	4	4		J/A 77	13
Exhibits and Exhibiting: Illinois	"Lynn Hall: Figure and Furniture" (Exhibit)	Shermeta, Margo	√		Fa	12	1		J/F 85	73
Exhibits and Exhibiting: Illinois	"Magdalena Abakanowicz" (Exhibit)	Koplos, Janet	√		Fa	10	2		M/A 83	66
Exhibits and Exhibiting: Illinois	"Nancy Hemenway: Aqua Lapis" (Exhibit)	Skudera, Gail	√		Fa	11	5		S/O 84	72
Exhibits and Exhibiting: Illinois	"New American Paperworks" (Exhibit) (error-corrected Fa v13 n3 86 p5)	Shermeta, Margo	√		Fa	13	1		J/F 86	64
Exhibits and Exhibiting: Illinois	"New Dimensions in Handmade Paper" (Exhibit)	Koplos, Janet	√		Fa	8	5		S/O 81	72
Exhibits and Exhibiting: Illinois	"Patterns of Paradise: Tapa Cloth" (Exhibit)	Dyer, Carolyn	√		Fa	10	3		M/J 83	73
Exhibits and Exhibiting: Illinois	"Patti Mitchem: Rep Weave Hangings" (Exhibit)	Barnett-Westfall, Lynn	√		Fa	8	3		M/J 81	67
Exhibits and Exhibiting: Illinois	"Sources of Inspiration" (Exhibit)		√		Fa	14	1		J/F 87	50
Exhibits and Exhibiting: Illinois	"Survey of Illinois Fiber" (Exhibit)	Jensen, Janet	√		Fa	5	5		S/O 78	69
Exhibits and Exhibiting: Illinois	"Vibrant Structures" (Exhibit)	Shermeta, Margo	√		Fa	11	6		N/D 84	75
Exhibits and Exhibiting: Illinois	"Woven, Tied, and Knotted" (Exhibit)	Koplos, Janet	√		Fa	9	2		M/A 82	82
Exhibits and Exhibiting: Indiana	"Embroiderer's Guild of America, 11th Biennial Exhibition" (Exhibit)	Itter, Diane	√		Fa	12	2		M/A 85	76
Exhibits and Exhibiting: Indiana	"Fiber Structures and Fabric Surfaces" (Exhibit)	Itter, Diane	√		Fa	7	1		J/F 80	67
Exhibits and Exhibiting: Indiana	"Images of the Moslem World" (Exhibit)		√		Fa	14	5		N/D 87	42
Exhibits and Exhibiting: Indiana	"Patricia Campbell: The Modular Form" (Exhibit)	Itter, Diane	√		Fa	11	3		M/J 84	75
Exhibits and Exhibiting: Indiana	"Thomas Lundberg" (Exhibit)	Itter, Diane	√		Fa	10	4		J/A 83	67
Exhibits and Exhibiting: Iowa	"Barbara MacCallum: Recent Work" (Exhibit)	Schedl, Naomi Kark	√		Fa	12	4		J/A 85	68
Exhibits and Exhibiting: Iowa	"Beds, Sweet Dreams, and Other Things" (Exhibit)	Bissell, June	√		Fa	6	4		J/A 79	70
Exhibits and Exhibiting: Iowa	"Fiber Invitational" (Exhibit)	Richerson, Suzanne	√		Fa	8	4		J/A 81	76
Exhibits and Exhibiting: Iowa	"In the Garden of Strange Gods" (Exhibit)	McDonald, Julie Jensen	√		Fa	14	4		S/O 87	41
Exhibits and Exhibiting: Iowa	"Naomi Kark Schedl: Coverings, Enclosures, and Pathways" (Exhibit)	Richerson, Suzanne	√		Fa	11	4		J/A 84	73
Exhibits and Exhibiting: Iowa	"Priscilla Sage: Small Paintings and Fiber Sculpture" (Exhibit)	Richerson, Suzanne	√		Fa	8	3		M/J 81	69
Exhibits and Exhibiting: Iowa	"Woven Works: Tradition and Innovation" (Exhibit)	White, Patrick E.	√		Fa	12	6		N/D 85	60
Exhibits and Exhibiting: Israel	"Hedi Taryan: The Infinity of Small Things" (Exhibit)	Chamish, Barry	√		Fa	10	5		S/O 83	79
Exhibits and Exhibiting: Japan	"Fiber Works — Americas & Japan" (Exhibit)	Kato, Kuniko Lucy	√		Fa	5	1		J/F 78	10

SUBJECT	TITLE	AUTHOR	IL	INST	JOUR	VOL	NO	ISS	DATE	PAGE
Exhibits and Exhibiting: Japan	"Kimono As Art: Modern Textile Works by Kako Moriguchi, Rikizo Munehiro, and Fukumi Shimura" (Exhibit)	Koplos, Janet	√		Fa	13	1		J/F 86	60
Exhibits and Exhibiting: Kansas	"Chris Wolf Edmonds" (Exhibit)	Brackman, Barbara	√		Fa	11	5		S/O 84	72
Exhibits and Exhibiting: Kansas	"Pamela Gustavson Johnson: Constructivist Quilts" (Exhibit)	Brackman, Barbara	√		Fa	10	2		M/A 83	68
Exhibits and Exhibiting: Kentucky	"Ann Stewart Anderson: New Work" (Exhibit)	Arnow, Jan	√		Fa	7	1		J/F 80	64
Exhibits and Exhibiting: Kentucky	"Contemporary Directions in Fiber" (Exhibit)	Meloy, Margaret	√		Fa	14	4		S/O 87	42
Exhibits and Exhibiting: Kentucky	"Distilling the Essence of Basketry" (Exhibit)	Anderson, Ann Stewart	√		Fa	13	2		M/A 86	52
Exhibits and Exhibiting: Kentucky	"Forms and Surfaces" (Exhibit)		√		Fa	8	4		J/A 81	68
Exhibits and Exhibiting: Kentucky	"Jacque Parsley: Avallon Series" (Exhibit)	Anderson, Ann Stewart	√		Fa	9	5		S/O 82	82
Exhibits and Exhibiting: Kentucky	"Jacque Parsley: Collage, A New Direction" (Exhibit)	Meloy, Margaret	√		Fa	11	6		N/D 84	76
Exhibits and Exhibiting: Kentucky	"Kentucky Quilt Project: 1800–1900, The" (Exhibit)		√		Fa	10	2		M/A 83	51
Exhibits and Exhibiting: Kentucky	"Lida Gordon: Recent Works" (Exhibit)	Meloy, Margaret	√		Fa	10	4		J/A 83	63
Exhibits and Exhibiting: Kentucky	"Paper and Felt Redefined" (Exhibit)	Ogden, Anne	√		Fa	5	2		M/A 78	17
Exhibits and Exhibiting: Kentucky	"Robin Becker and Joan Lintault: Visual Traces of the Past" (Exhibit)	Meloy, Margaret	√		Fa	11	1		J/F 84	80
Exhibits and Exhibiting: Kentucky	"Shared Vision": A Gallery Tour with Two Artists: Jacque Parsley and Neisja Yenawine (Exhibit)	Arnow, Jan	√		Fa	8	4		J/A 81	28
Exhibits and Exhibiting: Kentucky	"Surface Design: Approaches '78" (Exhibit)	Arnow, Jan	√		Fa	6	2		M/A 79	67
Exhibits and Exhibiting: Kentucky	"Web of Kentucky Thread, A" (Exhibit)	Meloy, Margaret	√		Fa	12	5		S/O 85	72
Exhibits and Exhibiting: Kentucky	"Works in Fiber" (Exhibit)	Arnow, Jan	√		Fa	8	2		M/A 81	61
Exhibits and Exhibiting: London	"Third International Exhibition of Miniature Textiles 1978" (Exhibit)	Spencer, Patricia	√		Fa	6	1		J/F 79	90
Exhibits and Exhibiting: Maine	"Maine Coast Artists: Fabrications" (Exhibit)	Beem, Edgar Allen	√		Fa	11	4		J/A 84	80
Exhibits and Exhibiting: Maine	"Statements in Fibre" (Exhibit)	Wagner, Liz	√		Fa	6	1		J/F 79	88
Exhibits and Exhibiting: Maryland	"Focus on Fiber" (Exhibit)	Hecker, Carolyn	√		Fa	6	3		M/J 79	83
Exhibits and Exhibiting: Maryland	"Tangents: Art In Fiber" (Exhibit)	Krinn, Linda	√		Fa	14	3		M/J 87	55
Exhibits and Exhibiting: Massachuesetts	"Micala Sidore: Sign Language" (Exhibit)	Temple, Nancy	√		Fa	12	3		M/J 85	72
Exhibits and Exhibiting: Massachusetts	"Anne Flaten Pixley" (Exhibit)	Mattera, Joanne	√		Fa	6	6		N/D 79	68
Exhibits and Exhibiting: Massachusetts	"Barbara Heilmann-Levine: Tapestries and Paintings" (Exhibit)	Pasquine, Ruth	√		Fa	10	2		M/A 83	69
Exhibits and Exhibiting: Massachusetts	"Basketry: Tradition in New Form" (Exhibit)	Scarborough, Jessica	√		Fa	9	3		M/J 82	83
Exhibits and Exhibiting: Massachusetts	"Beyond the Fringe" (Exhibit)	Einstein, Sylvia	√		Fa	7	2		M/A 80	70
Exhibits and Exhibiting: Massachusetts	"Boston Seven: A Fiber Show, The" (Exhibit)	Goldman, Judy Ann	√		Fa	6	3		M/J 79	73
Exhibits and Exhibiting: Massachusetts	"Carol Mecagni: Illuminated Tapestries" (Exhibit)	Newman, Rochelle	√		Fa	9	2		M/A 82	79
Exhibits and Exhibiting: Massachusetts	"Current Directions: Conseie des Arts Textiles du Quebec" (Exhibit)	Newman, Rochelle	√		Fa	12	1		J/F 85	74
Exhibits and Exhibiting: Massachusetts	Design Reform, 1875–1920 (Exhibit)		√		Fa	14	2		M/A 87	59
Exhibits and Exhibiting: Massachusetts	"Fabric Constructions: The Art Quilt" (Exhibit)	Klein, Jody	√		Fa	11	2		M/A 84	81
Exhibits and Exhibiting: Massachusetts	"Fiber/Fabric '81" (Exhibit)	Scarborough, Jessica	√		Fa	8	4		J/A 81	74
Exhibits and Exhibiting: Massachusetts	"Fibers: From Function to Formalization" (Exhibit)	Scarborough, Jessica	√		Fa	9	1		J/F 82	76

SUBJECT	TITLE	AUTHOR	IL	INST	JOUR	VOL	NO	ISS	DATE	PAGE
Exhibits and Exhibiting: Massachusetts	"Jody Klein's Paper Quilts" (Exhibit)	Storey, Isabelle B.	√		Fa	8	6		N/D 81	70
Exhibits and Exhibiting: Massachusetts	"Michael James: A Ten-Year Retrospective" (Exhibit)	Klein, Jody	√		Fa	11	2		M/A 84	80
Exhibits and Exhibiting: Massachusetts	"New England Images" (Exhibit)	Harris, Patricia; David Lyon	√		Fa	10	6		N/D 83	78
Exhibits and Exhibiting: Massachusetts	"Radka Donnell-Vogt: Patchwork Quilts" (Exhibit)	Chase, Pattie	√		Fa	7	5		S/O 80	76
Exhibits and Exhibiting: Massachusetts	"Show of Complements, A" (Exhibit)	Schevill, Margot Blum	√		Fa	13	4		J/A 86	50
Exhibits and Exhibiting: Massachusetts	"Show of Fans, A" (Exhibit)	Goodman, Deborah Lerme	√		Fa	12	6		N/D 85	56
Exhibits and Exhibiting: Massachusetts	"Silk as Ceremony: The Dress of China in the Late Ch'ing Dynasty Period (1759–1911)" (Exhibit)	Mattera, Joanne	√		Fa	8	3		M/J 81	75
Exhibits and Exhibiting: Massachusetts	"Ten Boston Fiber Artists" (Exhibit)	Serenyi, Peter	√		Fa	5	5		S/O 78	67
Exhibits and Exhibiting: Massachusetts	"Theo Moorman: Experiments in Weaving" (Exhibit)	Dunwell, Anna	√		Fa	9	5		S/O 82	80
Exhibits and Exhibiting: Massachusetts	"Throbbing Needles II" (Exhibit)	Mattera, Joanne	√		Fa	7	2		M/A 80	71
Exhibits and Exhibiting: Mexico	"Structures in Fiber" (Exhibit)	Padin, Carmen	√		Fa	5	6		N/D 78	70
Exhibits and Exhibiting: Michigan	"Anne Wilson: Grid Constructions" (Exhibit)	Finkel, Marilyn	√		Fa	6	2		M/A 79	65
Exhibits and Exhibiting: Michigan	"Artist Collects: Historic Fabrics from the Collection of Gerhardt Krodel, An" (Exhibit) (error-corrected Fa v7 n4 80 p6)	Constantinides, Kathy	√		Fa	7	3		M/J 80	78
Exhibits and Exhibiting: Michigan	"Connections" (Exhibit)	Constantinides, Kathy	√		Fa	6	4		J/A 79	74
Exhibits and Exhibiting: Michigan	"Entanglements" (Exhibit)	Markle, Marsha	√		Fa	4	2		M/A 77	16
Exhibits and Exhibiting: Michigan	"Felt: A Rich Tradition and Current Involvements" (Exhibit)	Constantinides, Kathy	√		Fa	6	3		M/J 79	74
Exhibits and Exhibiting: Michigan	"Gerhardt Knodel—Makes Places to Be" (Exhibit)	Livingstone, Joan	√		Fa	10	3		M/J 83	71
Exhibits and Exhibiting: Michigan	"Ruth's Madcaps" (Exhibit)	Haynes, Maryellen	√		Fa	14	4		S/O 87	9
Exhibits and Exhibiting: Michigan	Seventeen Pattern Types, A Study of Repeat Patterns in Two Dimensions	Elliott, Verda	√	> 4	CW		25		Se 87	23
Exhibits and Exhibiting: Michigan	"Space Sails: American Banners" (Exhibit)	Deyo, Diane	√		Fa	9	5		S/O 82	82
Exhibits and Exhibiting: Michigan	"Space Sails" Soar (Exhibit)	Reid, Eve	√		Fa	13	4		J/A 86	51
Exhibits and Exhibiting: Michigan	"Wildlife Physics" (Exhibit)	Kitzman, Betty Lou	√		Fa	12	2		M/A 85	72
Exhibits and Exhibiting: Michigan	"Women of Fiber: Six Michigan Artists" (Exhibit)	Reid, Eve	√		Fa	8	5		S/O 81	74
Exhibits and Exhibiting: Minnesota	Artwear '87 (Exhibit)		√		Fa	14	2		M/A 87	58
Exhibits and Exhibiting: Minnesota	Fiber in Minnesota: "Traditions/Transitions II" and "Art in Architecture" (Exhibit)	Stack, Lotus	√		Fa	11	3		M/J 84	80
Exhibits and Exhibiting: Minnesota	"German Wearable Textiles" (Exhibit)	Van Til, Reinder	√		Fa	12	6		N/D 85	59
Exhibits and Exhibiting: Minnesota	"Ideas and Capabilities: Barbara Sykes' Fiber Constructions" (Exhibit)	Blakely, Deborah	√		Fa	8	1		J/F 81	94
Exhibits and Exhibiting: Missouri	"Fiber Forms: Linda Eyerman, Jane Sauer" (Exhibit)	Degener, Patricia	√		Fa	8	3		M/J 81	73
Exhibits and Exhibiting: Missouri	"Fine Focus" (Exhibit)	Rice, Nancy Newman	√		Fa	12	2		M/A 85	74
Exhibits and Exhibiting: Missouri	"Mini Tapestry Exhibit" (Exhibit)	Bockelman, JoAnne	√		Fa	5	4		J/A 78	12
Exhibits and Exhibiting: Missouri	"Other Baskets" An Invitational Show in St. Louis (Exhibit)	Degener, Patricia	√		Fa	10	1		J/F 83	76
Exhibits and Exhibiting: Nebraska	"Material/Culture" (Exhibit)	Ross, Douglas	√		Fa	14	2		M/A 87	55
Exhibits and Exhibiting: New Jersey	"Anne Dushanko-Dobek: Silent Voices" (Exhibit)	Scheinman, Pamela	√		Fa	11	4		J/A 84	77
Exhibits and Exhibiting: New Jersey	"Anni Albers: Current Work" (Exhibit)	Guyer, Niki	√		Fa	6	6		N/D 79	72

SUBJECT	TITLE	AUTHOR	IL	INST	JOUR	VOL	NO	ISS	DATE	PAGE
Exhibits and Exhibiting: New Jersey	"Contemporary Fiber Art" (Exhibit)	Guyer, Niki	√		Fa	5	6		N/D 78	66
Exhibits and Exhibiting: New Jersey	"From American Looms: Scheuer Tapestry Studio" (Exhibit) (error-corrected Fa v12 n6 85 p9)	Park, Betty	√		Fa	12	5		S/O 85	76
Exhibits and Exhibiting: New Jersey	"In Praise of Heroes" (Exhibit)	Malarcher, Patricia	√		Fa	10	1		J/F 83	78
Exhibits and Exhibiting: New Jersey	"Joy Saville: Contemporary Quilting" (Exhibits)	Park, Betty	√		Fa	9	4		J/A 82	72
Exhibits and Exhibiting: New Jersey	"New Elegance: Contemporary Wearable Art, The" (Exhibit)	Malarcher, Patricia	√		Fa	12	4		J/A 85	44
Exhibits and Exhibiting: New Jersey	"Patricia Malarcher: Pieced Reflections" (Exhibit)	Scheinman, Pamela	√		Fa	11	2		M/A 84	77
Exhibits and Exhibiting: New Jersey	"Patterns" (Exhibit)	Malarcher, Patricia	√		Fa	10	2		M/A 83	76
Exhibits and Exhibiting: New Jersey	"Ruth Geneslaw/Pat Malarcher" (Exhibit)	Guyar, Niki	√		Fa	6	4		J/A 79	66
Exhibits and Exhibiting: New Mexico	"Art in Craft Media" (Exhibit)		√		Fa	13	4		J/A 86	58
Exhibits and Exhibiting: New Mexico	"Kimono East/Kimono West" (Exhibit)	Lusk, Jennie	√		Fa	7	5		S/O 80	71
Exhibits and Exhibiting: New Mexico	"Peg McNair/Tapestries" (Exhibit)	Petersen, Jill	√		Fa	4	3		M/J 77	12
Exhibits and Exhibiting: New Mexico	"Quilts as Textile Art: Collection of Mary Woodard Davis" (Exhibit)		√		Fa	3	2		M/A 76	8
Exhibits and Exhibiting: New Mexico	"Textile Works: Lily Gilmore, Judith Moir, Sheila O'Hara" (Exhibit)	Mazur, Carole	√		Fa	8	2		M/A 81	67
Exhibits and Exhibiting: New Mexico	"Textiles New Mexico 1976" (Exhibit)	Warner, Lucy Ann	√		Fa	3	2		M/A 76	12
Exhibits and Exhibiting: New Mexico	"Textiles New Mexico 1978" (Exhibit)	Tatum, Phyllis	√		Fa	5	4		J/A 78	10
Exhibits and Exhibiting: New Mexico	"Weavers of the Jade Needle" An Exhibition of Highland Guatemalan Textiles (Exhibit)	Stout, Carol	√		Fa	3	2		M/A 76	30
Exhibits and Exhibiting: New York	"100% Wool" (Exhibit)	Goldin, Susan	√		Fa	4	6		N/D 77	18
Exhibits and Exhibiting: New York	"Akiko Kotani" (Exhibit)	Malarcher, Patricia	√		Fa	8	4		J/A 81	73
Exhibits and Exhibiting: New York	"American Hooked Rugs: 1850–1957" (Exhibit)	Scarborough, Jessica	√		Fa	8	6		N/D 81	68
Exhibits and Exhibiting: New York	"Ann Trusty: Grid and Pattern" (Exhibit)	Stiles, David	√		Fa	9	1		J/F 82	79
Exhibits and Exhibiting: New York	"Art of Basketry, The" (Exhibit)	Park, Betty	√		Fa	4	2		M/A 77	9
Exhibits and Exhibiting: New York	"Art to Wear" (Exhibit)	Murray, Megan	√		Fa	11	1		J/F 84	76
Exhibits and Exhibiting: New York	"Artists in Aprons" (Exhibit)	Alonzo, Harriet	√		Fa	6	3		M/J 79	76
Exhibits and Exhibiting: New York	"Aurelia Muñoz" (Exhibit)	Park, Betty	√		Fa	4	6		N/D 77	21
Exhibits and Exhibiting: New York	"Baker/Rapoport/Wick" in New York (Exhibit)	Park, Betty	√		Fa	4	5		S/O 77	15
Exhibits and Exhibiting: New York	"Baltimore Album Quilts" (Exhibit)	Park, Betty	√		Fa	8	6		N/D 81	69
Exhibits and Exhibiting: New York	"Basket-Maker's Art, The" (Exhibit)	Grover, Donald	√		Fa	6	6		N/D 79	73
Exhibits and Exhibiting: New York	"Baskets of Akwesasne" (Exhibit)	Doyle, Claire	√		Fa	11	1		J/F 84	77
Exhibits and Exhibiting: New York	"Bernard Toale: Works in Fiber" (Exhibit)	Malarcher, Patricia	√		Fa	7	2		M/A 80	65
Exhibits and Exhibiting: New York	"Ceremonial Works" (Exhibit)		√		Fa	13	2		M/A 86	56
Exhibits and Exhibiting: New York	"Claire Zeisler" (Exhibit)	Mathews, Rich	√		Fa	4	1		J/F 77	12
Exhibits and Exhibiting: New York	"Constance Dodge: Mind Feelings" (Exhibit)	Flanagan, Jeanne	√		Fa	9	3		M/J 82	82
Exhibits and Exhibiting: New York	"Costumes of Royal India, The" (Exhibit)	McCann, Kathleen	√		Fa	13	1		J/F 86	58
Exhibits and Exhibiting: New York	Craft Today: The American Craft Museum (Exhibit)	Sider, Sandra	√		Fa	14	2		M/A 87	54
Exhibits and Exhibiting: New York	"Craft Today the Poetry of the Physical" (Exhibit)		√		TM			7	O/N 86	10
Exhibits and Exhibiting: New York	"Cynthia Schira" (Exhibit)	Park, Betty	√		Fa	5	3		M/J 78	13
Exhibits and Exhibiting: New York	"Diaghilev—Costumes and Designs of the Ballets Russes" (Exhibit)	Grover, Donald	√		Fa	6	3		M/J 79	79

SUBJECT	TITLE	AUTHOR	IL	INST	JOUR	VOL	NO	ISS	DATE	PAGE
Exhibits and Exhibiting: New York	"Dione Christensen Fiberworks" (Exhibit)	Meyer, Florence	√		Fa	6	2		M/A 79	63
Exhibits and Exhibiting: New York	"Dominic Di Mare" (Exhibit)	Park, Betty	√		Fa	4	3		M/J 77	8
Exhibits and Exhibiting: New York	"Embroidery Through the Ages" (Exhibit)	Grover, Donald	√		Fa	5	6		N/D 78	62
Exhibits and Exhibiting: New York	"Eyedazzlers!" (Exhibit)	Lonier, Terri	√		Fa	11	3		M/J 84	77
Exhibits and Exhibiting: New York	"Fashion and Surrealism" (Exhibit)		√		TM			14	D/J 87	16
Exhibits and Exhibiting: New York	"Fashions of the Hapsburg Era: Austria-Hungary" (Exhibit)	Malarcher, Patricia	√		Fa	7	3		M/J 80	75
Exhibits and Exhibiting: New York	"Felt and Papermaking" (Exhibit)	Harrison, Helen A.	√		Fa	11	2		M/A 84	79
Exhibits and Exhibiting: New York	"Felting" (Exhibit)	Park, Betty	√		Fa	7	6		N/D 80	71
Exhibits and Exhibiting: New York	"Ferne Jacobs: New Works" (Exhibit)	Park, Betty	√		Fa	6	1		J/F 79	84
Exhibits and Exhibiting: New York	"Fiber Art: An Uncommon Thread" (Exhibit)	Park, Betty	√		Fa	9	2		M/A 82	78
Exhibits and Exhibiting: New York	"Fiber Drawings: Works in Thread on Paper" (Exhibit)	Krapes, Shelley	√		Fa	5	5		S/O 78	65
Exhibits and Exhibiting: New York	"Fiber from the Marietta College Crafts National" (Exhibit)	Murray, Megan	√		Fa	11	2		M/A 84	76
Exhibits and Exhibiting: New York	"Fiber National '84" (Exhibit)	Bard, Elizabeth A.	√		Fa	12	4		J/A 85	66
Exhibits and Exhibiting: New York	"Fiber National '86" (Exhibit)	Belfer, Nancy	√		Fa	14	1		J/F 87	51
Exhibits and Exhibiting: New York	"For the Floor" (Exhibit)	Sider, Sandra	√		Fa	12	6		N/D 85	61
Exhibits and Exhibiting: New York	"Frank Lincoln Viner—Fantaisie: Constructions and Objects" (Exhibit)	Malarcher, Pat	√		Fa	7	1		J/F 80	73
Exhibits and Exhibiting: New York	"Glory of Russian Costumes, The" (Exhibit)	Vander Lee, Jana	√		Fa	4	3		M/J 77	15
Exhibits and Exhibiting: New York	"Great American Foot, The" (Exhibit)	Grover, Donald	√		Fa	5	4		J/A 78	15
Exhibits and Exhibiting: New York	"Hair" (Exhibit)	Alonzo, Harriet	√		Fa	7	6		N/D 80	73
Exhibits and Exhibiting: New York	"Hawaiian Quilts: Treasures of an Island Folk Art" (Exhibit)	Alonso, Harriet	√		Fa	6	6		N/D 79	77
Exhibits and Exhibiting: New York	"Historic Spanish Lace" (Exhibit)		√		Fa	14	1		J/F 87	54
Exhibits and Exhibiting: New York	"Infrastructure" (Exhibit)	Malarcher, Patricia	√		Fa	11	4		J/A 84	76
Exhibits and Exhibiting: New York	"Interlacing: The Elemental Fabric" (Exhibit)		√		Fa	14	3		M/J 87	62
Exhibits and Exhibiting: New York	"Interlacings" At American Craft Museum (Exhibit)		√		TM			11	J/J 87	15
Exhibits and Exhibiting: New York	"James Bassler" (Exhibit)	Malarcher, Patricia	√		Fa	8	6		N/D 81	71
Exhibits and Exhibiting: New York	"Jan Wagstaff: Woven and Painted Canvas" (Exhibit)	Malarcher, Patricia	√		Fa	8	6		N/D 81	64
Exhibits and Exhibiting: New York	"Jayn Thomas" (Exhibit)	Malarcher, Patricia	√		Fa	10	5		S/O 83	81
Exhibits and Exhibiting: New York	"Joan Livingstone: Lamia Lemures" (Exhibit)	Malarcher, Patricia	√		Fa	7	4		J/A 80	67
Exhibits and Exhibiting: New York	"Joan Livingstone/Recent Work: Felt/Wood" (Exhibit)	Park, Betty	√		Fa	4	4		J/A 77	14
Exhibits and Exhibiting: New York	"Joan Steiner: Hats/New Sculpture" (Exhibit)	Katz, Ruth J.	√		Fa	7	5		S/O 80	72
Exhibits and Exhibiting: New York	"Joanne Brandford: Recent Nets" (Exhibit)	Park, Betty	√		Fa	11	6		N/D 84	77
Exhibits and Exhibiting: New York	"Joanne Segal Brandford — Nets" (Exhibit)	Park, Betty	√		Fa	5	3		M/J 78	17
Exhibits and Exhibiting: New York	"John McQueen" (Exhibit)		√		Fa	4	4		J/A 77	14
Exhibits and Exhibiting: New York	"Josef Grau-Garriga" (Exhibit)	Grover, Donald	√		Fa	5	2		M/A 78	13
Exhibits and Exhibiting: New York	"Kiyomi Iwata: Works in Fiber" (Exhibit)	Malarcher, Patricia	√		Fa	9	2		M/A 82	77
Exhibits and Exhibiting: New York	"Lace" (Exhibit)	Lo Presti, Louise	√		Fa	9	6		N/D 82	79
Exhibits and Exhibiting: New York	"Landscapes" (Exhibit)	Clardy, Andrea	√		Fa	5	2		M/A 78	10
Exhibits and Exhibiting: New York	"Leora Stewart: New Works—Deborah Warner: Four Corners Journal" (Exhibit)	Malarcher, Patricia	√		Fa	6	6		N/D 79	71
Exhibits and Exhibiting: New York	"Macungie Notes — Lewis Knauss" (Exhibit)	Park, Betty	√		Fa	5	2		M/A 78	15
Exhibits and Exhibiting: New York	"Mariyo Yagi" (Exhibit)	Park, Betty	√		Fa	5	1		J/F 78	19
Exhibits and Exhibiting: New York	"Master Dyers to the World" (Exhibit)	Sider, Sandra	√		Fa	11	1		J/F 84	83

SUBJECT	TITLE	AUTHOR	IL	INST	JOUR	VOL	NO	ISS	DATE	PAGE
Exhibits and Exhibiting: New York	"Maximum Coverage: Wearables by Contemporary American Artists" (Exhibit)	Risseeuw, Mary	√		Fa	8	1		J/F 81	93
Exhibits and Exhibiting: New York	"Michelle Lester: New Tapestries" (Exhibit)	Park, Betty	√		Fa	6	1		J/F 79	85
Exhibits and Exhibiting: New York	"Nancy Moore Bess: Baskets" (Exhibit)	Waller, Elsa	√		Fa	7	5		S/O 80	74
Exhibits and Exhibiting: New York	"Needle and Cloth: Ten Years Later" (Exhibit)	Hulbert, Elizabeth McKey	√		Fa	10	3		M/J 83	72
Exhibits and Exhibiting: New York	"New Works in Batik by Laura Adasko" (Exhibit)	Gutcheon, Beth	√		Fa	5	3		M/J 78	12
Exhibits and Exhibiting: New York	"Nina Holland: Bound Weave Rugs/Hangings" (Exhibit)	Bess, Nancy Moore	√		Fa	9	1		J/F 82	83
Exhibits and Exhibiting: New York	"Norma Minkowitz" (Exhibit)	Grover, Donald	√		Fa	6	5		S/O 79	77
Exhibits and Exhibiting: New York	"Olga de Amaral" (Exhibit)	Grover, Donald	√		Fa	5	1		J/F 78	18
Exhibits and Exhibiting: New York	"Our Shining Heritage: Textile Arts of the Slavs and Their Neighbors" (Exhibit)	Mackin, Jeanne	√		Fa	8	4		J/A 81	75
Exhibits and Exhibiting: New York	Paper and Wood Constructions (Exhibit)		√		Fa	13	5		S/O 86	54
Exhibits and Exhibiting: New York	Paper: Three Shows At the American Craft Museums (Exhibit)	Lonier, Terri	√		Fa	9	5		S/O 82	84
Exhibits and Exhibiting: New York	"Partners in Art: Brushwork by Lee, Dong Chun and Embroidery by Yu, Chug Hee" (Exhibit)	Backer, Ellen	√		Fa	4	3		M/J 77	16
Exhibits and Exhibiting: New York	"Presence of Light, The" (Exhibit)	Talley, Charles	√		Fa	12	2		M/A 85	72
Exhibits and Exhibiting: New York	"Quilt National '83" (Exhibit)	Roe, Nancy	√		Fa	10	5		S/O 83	82
Exhibits and Exhibiting: New York	"Ruth Kao: Silk Sense" (Exhibit)	Sider, Sandra	√		Fa	12	1		J/F 85	72
Exhibits and Exhibiting: New York	"Scandinavian Touch, The" A Traveling Exhibit (Exhibit)	Mattera, Joanna	√		Fa	10	1		J/F 83	82
Exhibits and Exhibiting: New York	"Sculpture of Claire Zeisler" (Exhibit)	Malarcher, Patricia	√		Fa	12	6		N/D 85	57
Exhibits and Exhibiting: New York	"Sherri Smith: New Works" (Exhibit)	Malarcher, Pat	√		Fa	5	5		S/O 78	75
Exhibits and Exhibiting: New York	Shihoko Fukumoto (Exhibit)		√		Fa	14	2		M/A 87	61
Exhibits and Exhibiting: New York	"Show Biz" (Exhibit)	Scheinman, Pamela	√		Fa	7	4		J/A 80	69
Exhibits and Exhibiting: New York	"Silk Roads/China Ships" (Exhibit)	Sider, Sandra	√		Fa	11	4		J/A 84	74
Exhibits and Exhibiting: New York	"Sirpa Yarmolinsky: Paper and Linen Constructions" (Exhibit)	Malarcher, Patricia	√		Fa	9	1		J/F 82	84
Exhibits and Exhibiting: New York	"Skin Forms: Innovations in Leather" (Exhibit)	Mackin, Jeanne	√		Fa	7	2		M/A 80	67
Exhibits and Exhibiting: New York	"Suellen Glashausser — Fences" (Exhibit)	Malarcher, Pat	√		Fa	6	3		M/J 79	77
Exhibits and Exhibiting: New York	"Susan Goldin: Windows" (Exhibit)	Malarcher, Patricia	√		Fa	9	3		M/J 82	76
Exhibits and Exhibiting: New York	"Susan Lyman's Paper Structures" (Exhibit)	Roberts, Stephen	√		Fa	8	5		S/O 81	69
Exhibits and Exhibiting: New York	"Tapestries by Janet Taylor" (Exhibit)	Malarcher, Patricia	√		Fa	9	5		S/O 82	81
Exhibits and Exhibiting: New York	"Vanity Fair: A Treasure Trove from the Costume Institute" (Exhibit)	Park, Betty	√		Fa	5	3		M/J 78	15
Exhibits and Exhibiting: New York	"Wall Hangings: The New Classicism" (Exhibit)	Grover, Donald	√		Fa	4	4		J/A 77	10
Exhibits and Exhibiting: New York	"Wearables" (Exhibit)	Grover, Donald	√		Fa	6	6		N/D 79	76
Exhibits and Exhibiting: New York	"Weaving Without Fiber" (Exhibit)	Hempel, Toby Anne	√		Fa	13	5		S/O 86	48
Exhibits and Exhibiting: New York	Whitney Museum of American Art, The (Exhibit)	Park, Betty	√		Fa	9	2		M/A 82	11
Exhibits and Exhibiting: New York	"With or Without a Loom" (Exhibit)	Rowley, Kristin Carlsen	√		Fa	8	5		S/O 81	67
Exhibits and Exhibiting: New York	"Women Artists: Clay, Fiber, Metal" (Exhibit)	Malarcher, Patricia	√		Fa	5	2		M/A 78	11
Exhibits and Exhibiting: New York	"Young Americans: Fiber, Wood, Plastic, Leather" (Exhibit)	Malarcher, Patricia	√		Fa	4	6		N/D 77	14
Exhibits and Exhibiting: New York	"Yves Saint Laurent: 25 Years Of Design" (Exhibit)	Lonier, Terri	√		Fa	12	1		J/F 85	76
Exhibits and Exhibiting: North Carolina	"Ceremonial Garments" (Exhibit)	Laymon, Cynthia	√		Fa	9	6		N/D 82	82
Exhibits and Exhibiting: North Carolina	"Cynthia Laymon: Fiber/Paper Constructions" (Exhibits)	Syverson, Gilda Morina	√		Fa	9	4		J/A 82	71

SUBJECT	TITLE	AUTHOR	IL	INST	JOUR	VOL	NO	ISS	DATE	PAGE
Exhibits and Exhibiting: North Carolina	"Evolution of Fashion, 1909–1919, The" (Exhibit)		√		Fa	8	1		J/F 81	92
Exhibits and Exhibiting: North Carolina	"Festival of Weaving" (Exhibit)	Greenberg, Blue	√		Fa	7	4		J/A 80	71
Exhibits and Exhibiting: North Carolina	"Fibers" (Exhibit)	Meyer, Zach	√		Fa	4	4		J/A 77	11
Exhibits and Exhibiting: North Carolina	"Fibers Southeast 1979" (Exhibit)	Johnson, Elma	√		Fa	6	2		M/A 79	68
Exhibits and Exhibiting: North Carolina	"Headlines: A Hundred Years of Hats (1840–1940)" (Exhibit)	Luddecke, Jane	√		Fa	6	6		N/D 79	78
Exhibits and Exhibiting: North Carolina	International Invitational (Exhibit)		√		Fa	14	2		M/A 87	58
Exhibits and Exhibiting: North Carolina	"Martha Matthews: Tapestry" (Exhibit)	Laymon, Cynthia	√		Fa	9	1		J/F 82	85
Exhibits and Exhibiting: North Carolina	Mountain Heritage, A (Exhibit)		√		Fa	13	4		J/A 86	58
Exhibits and Exhibiting: North/South Carolina	"North/South Carolina Fibers Competition" (Exhibit)	Laymon, Cynthia	√		Fa	10	4		J/A 83	68
Exhibits and Exhibiting: Norway	"Fourth Nordic Textiltriennale" (Exhibit)	Talley, Charles	√		Fa	13	3		M/J 86	51
Exhibits and Exhibiting: Ohio	"Basketry Today: And Quilts from the Collection of Phyllis Haders" (Exhibits)	von Weise, Wenda	√		Fa	9	4		J/A 82	75
Exhibits and Exhibiting: Ohio	"Cloth Forms" (Exhibits)	Skudera, Gail	√		Fa	9	4		J/A 82	76
Exhibits and Exhibiting: Ohio	"Contemporary Quilts" (Exhibit)		√		Fa	8	3		M/J 81	74
Exhibits and Exhibiting: Ohio	"Emerging Quiltmakers" (Exhibit)	McMorris, Penny	√		Fa	12	1		J/F 85	75
Exhibits and Exhibiting: Ohio	"Fiber Forms '78" (Exhibit)	Patton, Ellen	√		Fa	5	5		S/O 78	66
Exhibits and Exhibiting: Ohio	"Fiber Techniques: The Weaver's Guild of Greater Cincinnati" (Exhibit)	Fedders, Pat	√		Fa	8	1		J/F 81	91
Exhibits and Exhibiting: Ohio	"Fiberworks" (Exhibit)	Park, Betty	√		Fa	4	6		N/D 77	10
Exhibits and Exhibiting: Ohio	"Interweave '78" (Exhibit)	Yarnell, Grace	√		Fa	5	6		N/D 78	69
Exhibits and Exhibiting: Ohio	"Interweave 79" (Exhibit)	Constantinides, Kathy	√		Fa	7	1		J/F 80	66
Exhibits and Exhibiting: Ohio	"Lilian Tyrrell: Tapestries" (Exhibit)	McClelland, Elizabeth	√		Fa	11	6		N/D 84	76
Exhibits and Exhibiting: Ohio	"Microfibers" (Exhibit)	McClelland, Elizabeth	√		Fa	8	2		M/A 81	66
Exhibits and Exhibiting: Ohio	"Quilt National '79" (Exhibit)	Gutcheon, Beth	√		Fa	6	5		S/O 79	80
Exhibits and Exhibiting: Ohio	"Quilt National '85": A Proving Ground (Exhibit)	Roe, Nancy	√		Fa	12	6		N/D 85	58
Exhibits and Exhibiting: Ohio	"Quilt National '87" (Exhibit)		√		Fa	14	3		M/J 87	62
Exhibits and Exhibiting: Ohio	"Quilts by Jane Reeves" (Exhibit)b		√		Fa	14	1		J/F 87	71
Exhibits and Exhibiting: Ohio	"Quilts—Innovation and Tradition" (Exhibit)	Barnard, Eileen Wolford	√		Fa	10	3		M/J 83	72
Exhibits and Exhibiting: Oregon	Annie Dempsey: Sculptural Crochet (Exhibit)	Lindley, Susan	√		Fa	9	2		M/A 82	76
Exhibits and Exhibiting: Oregon	"Crafts Northwest, Circa 1980" (Exhibit)	Evans, Rojean; Louise Klemperer	√		Fa	7	5		S/O 80	75
Exhibits and Exhibiting: Oregon	"Marie Lyman: Liturgical Vestments" (Exhibit)	Griffin, Rachel	√		Fa	7	3		M/J 80	77
Exhibits and Exhibiting: Oregon	"Sherri Smith: Recent Work" (Exhibit)	Kirkland, Lawrence P.	√		Fa	7	4		J/A 80	63
Exhibits and Exhibiting: Organizing	Organizing a Major Textile Show	Papa, Nancy		√	SS&D	8	1	29	WI 76	28
Exhibits and Exhibiting: Pennsylvainia	"Voyage Continued" An Illuminating Experience (Exhibit)	Malarcher, Patricia	√		Fa	8	2		M/A 81	16
Exhibits and Exhibiting: Pennsylvania	"Amy Lipshie: Tapestries" (Exhibit)	Park, Betty	√		Fa	12	3		M/J 85	76
Exhibits and Exhibiting: Pennsylvania	"Art Couture/Haute Couture" (Exhibit)	McGuire, Patricia	√		Fa	9	1		J/F 82	86
Exhibits and Exhibiting: Pennsylvania	"Birth Symbol in Traditional Women's Art, The" (Exhibit)	Vanco, John	√		Fa	13	3		M/J 86	52
Exhibits and Exhibiting: Pennsylvania	"Diane Itter: Recent Work" (Exhibit)	Park, Betty	√		Fa	8	5		S/O 81	68
Exhibits and Exhibiting: Pennsylvania	"Fiber Images" (Exhibit)	Park, Betty	√		Fa	13	2		M/A 86	54

SUBJECT	TITLE	AUTHOR	IL	INST	JOUR	VOL	NO	ISS	DATE	PAGE
Exhibits and Exhibiting: Pennsylvania	"Fiber Invitational" (Exhibit)	Bywater, William	√		Fa	7	2		M/A 80	66
Exhibits and Exhibiting: Pennsylvania	"Fiber Structures" Convergence '76 (Exhibit)	Mathews-Pulleyn, Kathryn	√		Fa	3	4		J/A 76	12
Exhibits and Exhibiting: Pennsylvania	"Harmonist Needlework and Textiles" (Exhibit)	Thomas, Kay	√		Fa	7	6		N/D 80	68
Exhibits and Exhibiting: Pennsylvania	"Karen Armstrong's Jungle Happening" (Exhibit)	Kerr, Connie	√		Fa	6	2		M/A 79	19
Exhibits and Exhibiting: Pennsylvania	"Karen Stoller: Fiber" (Exhibit)	Reese, Ralph Henry	√		Fa	8	1		J/F 81	96
Exhibits and Exhibiting: Pennsylvania	Open Jurying in Pittsburg: Putting Your Work on the Line (Exhibit)	Myrinx, Elaine	√		Fa	6	2		M/A 79	23
Exhibits and Exhibiting: Pennsylvania	"Redefining the American Quilt" (Exhibit)		√		Fa	14	4		S/O 87	43
Exhibits and Exhibiting: Pennsylvania	"Stitcherhood Is Powerful" (Exhibit)	McGuire, Patricia	√		Fa	5	6		N/D 78	68
Exhibits and Exhibiting: Pennsylvania	"Stitchery '77" (Exhibit)	Pierucci, Louise	√		Fa	4	3		M/J 77	11
Exhibits and Exhibiting: Pennsylvania	"Stitchery '79" (Exhibit)	Kerr, Connie	√		Fa	6	5		S/O 79	78
Exhibits and Exhibiting: Philippines	"Fiber As Art" An Exhibition in the Philippines (Exhibit)		√		Fa	7	6		N/D 80	76
Exhibits and Exhibiting: Planning	Fun Approach to a Guild Show or Sale, The	Routh, Carol			Hw	8	2		M/A 87	32
Exhibits and Exhibiting: Planning	Preparing for a Show	Summa, Susan	√		Fa	10	4		J/A 83	44
Exhibits and Exhibiting: Planning	What to do with a Great Idea?	Mann, Joyce P.			Hw	4	3		M/J 83	16
Exhibits and Exhibiting: Poland	"Fifth Lodz Triennale, The" (Exhibit)	Ravarra, Patricia	√		Fa	13	3		M/J 86	50
Exhibits and Exhibiting: Quilts	Fashionable Quilts	Wolff, Colette	√		TM			10	A/M 87	16
Exhibits and Exhibiting: Quilts	Quilt Lovers, Take Notice				TM			10	A/M 87	22
Exhibits and Exhibiting: Quilts	Quilt National on Tour		√		TM			13	O/N 87	14
Exhibits and Exhibiting: Rhode Island	"Ch'ing Dynasty Court Robes, A Splendorous Sampling" (Exhibit)	Marcoux, Alice	√		Fa	11	2		M/A 84	78
Exhibits and Exhibiting: Rhode Island	Jacquard Project: Selections from the Current Exhibition, The		√		Fa	9	2		M/A 82	36
Exhibits and Exhibiting: Rhode Island	"Needlework" (Exhibit)	Krueger, Glee	√		Fa	9	3		M/J 82	78
Exhibits and Exhibiting: Rhode Island	"Paper" (Exhibit)	Toale, Bernard	√		Fa	7	5		S/O 80	69
Exhibits and Exhibiting: Rhode Island	RISD Faculty Show (Exhibit)		√		Fa	13	4		J/A 86	59
Exhibits and Exhibiting: SITES	"Patterns and Sources of Navajo Weaving" (Exhibit)	Mattera, Joanne	√		Fa	7	4		J/A 80	68
Exhibits and Exhibiting: Solo Show	That First Solo Show	Beschell, Lorraine	√	√	Iw	5	1		Wi 79	53
Exhibits and Exhibiting: South Carolina	"National Crafts '81: Works by the 1981 National Endowment for the Arts Craft Fellows" (Exhibit)	Mattera, Joanne	√		Fa	9	1		J/F 82	82
Exhibits and Exhibiting: South Carolina	"Needle Expressions '84" (Exhibit)	Koplos, Janet	√		Fa	12	2		M/A 85	74
Exhibits and Exhibiting: Switzerland	"Cynthia Schira" (Exhibit)	Zopetti, Patti	√		Fa	6	4		J/A 79	73
Exhibits and Exhibiting, Switzerland	Eleventh International Biennial of Tapestry, The	Taylor, Elmer; Dianne Taylor	√		Fa	10	5		S/O 83	33
Exhibits and Exhibiting: Switzerland	"Jack Lenor Larsen: 30 Years of Creative Textiles" (Exhibit)	Zoppetti, Patti	√		Fa	9	5		S/O 82	82
Exhibits and Exhibiting: Switzerland	Lausanne Notebook: Our Special Report on the 8th Lausanne Biennial of Tapestry, A	Mathews, Rich	√		Fa	4	5		S/O 77	30
Exhibits and Exhibiting: Switzerland	"New Wisconsin Fiber": The First Group Show of American Fiber Art in Switzerland (Exhibit)	Bard, Elizabeth A.	√		Fa	10	6		N/D 83	43
Exhibits and Exhibiting: Switzerland	"Ninth International Biennial of Tapestry" (Exhibit)	Pulleyn, Rob	√		Fa	6	4		J/A 79	62

SUBJECT	TITLE	AUTHOR	IL	INST	JOUR	VOL	NO	ISS	DATE	PAGE
Exhibits and Exhibiting: Switzerland	Paper Abroad (Exhibit)	Waller, Irene	√		Fa	11	2		M/A 84	82
Exhibits and Exhibiting: Switzerland	"Tenth International Biennial of Tapestry: Four Views" (Exhibit)	Shawcroft, Barbara	√		Fa	8	6		N/D 81	52
Exhibits and Exhibiting: Switzerland	To the Walls: The 13th Lausanne Biennial (Exhibit)	Zepeda, Susan G.	√		Fa	14	4		S/O 87	41
Exhibits and Exhibiting: Switzerland	Twelfth International Biennial of Tapestry	Taylor, Dianne; Elmer Taylor	√		Fa	12	6		N/D 85	50
Exhibits and Exhibiting: Tennessee	"Contemporary African American Crafts" (Exhibit)	Pilsk, Adele	√		Fa	6	6		N/D 79	74
Exhibits and Exhibiting: Tennessee	"Currents"—Trends in Crafts (Exhibit)		√		Fa	13	5		S/O 86	53
Exhibits and Exhibiting: Tennessee	"Fabric/Nexus: New Connections" (Exhibit)	Moldovan, George	√		Fa	10	3		M/J 83	70
Exhibits and Exhibiting: Tennessee	"Patchwork Garden, A" (Exhibit)	Hetzler, Patricia	√		Fa	8	5		S/O 81	73
Exhibits and Exhibiting: Tennessee	Quilts at Arrowmont (Exhibit)		√		Fa	13	3		M/J 86	53
Exhibits and Exhibiting: Texas	"Artists' Quilts" (Exhibit)	Woelfle, Gretchen	√		Fa	8	4		J/A 81	70
Exhibits and Exhibiting: Texas	"Charms" (Exhibit)	Vander Lee, Jana	√		Fa	3	3		M/J 76	6
Exhibits and Exhibiting: Texas	"Common Threads Shared" (Exhibit)	Dishough, Susanne	√		Fa	4	6		N/D 77	16
Exhibits and Exhibiting: Texas	"Decade of Fibers, A" (Exhibit)	Franklin, Sue	√		Fa	5	1		J/F 78	17
Exhibits and Exhibiting: Texas	"Eleanor Merrill" (Exhibit)	Vander Lee, Jana	√		Fa	4	1		J/F 77	8
Exhibits and Exhibiting: Texas	"Fiber" (Exhibit)	Vander Lee, Jana	√		Fa	3	2		M/A 76	9
Exhibits and Exhibiting: Texas	"Fibers '76" (Exhibit)		√		Fa	3	2		M/A 76	7
Exhibits and Exhibiting: Texas	"Flemish Tapestries of Willem De Kempeneer" (Exhibit)	Vander Lee, Jana	√		Fa	3	5		S/O 76	7
Exhibits and Exhibiting: Texas	"Houston Designer-Craftsmen 1976" (Exhibit)	Vander Lee, Jana	√		Fa	3	4		J/A 76	9
Exhibits and Exhibiting: Texas	"Jackie Winsor" (Exhibit)	Malarcher, Pat	√		Fa	6	4		J/A 79	68
Exhibits and Exhibiting: Texas	"Silken Threads and Silent Needles" (Exhibit)	Dunnewold, Jane	√		Fa	11	6		N/D 84	78
Exhibits and Exhibiting: Texas	"Surface Design South Central" (Exhibit)	Erhler, Mary	√		Fa	6	4		J/A 79	75
Exhibits and Exhibiting: Texas	"Weavers I: The Contemporary Handweavers of Houston" (Exhibit)	Vander Lee, Jana	√		Fa	3	2		M/A 76	8
Exhibits and Exhibiting: Utah	"Theme Show in Utah, A" (Exhibit)	Alderman, Sharon D.	√		Fa	8	3		M/J 81	68
Exhibits and Exhibiting: Vermont	Portraits of Aging (Exhibit)		√		Fa	13	4		J/A 86	54
Exhibits and Exhibiting: Vermont	"Recent Work by Elsa Waller" (Exhibit)	Harrington, Elaine	√		Fa	8	4		J/A 81	71
Exhibits and Exhibiting: Virginia	"Free Flow" (Exhibit)	Hecker, Carolyn	√		Fa	5	5		S/O 78	73
Exhibits and Exhibiting: Virginia	"Karen Swanson" (Exhibit)	Sunshine, Joanna	√		Fa	4	2		M/A 77	13
Exhibits and Exhibiting: Virginia	"Mary Walker Phillips — Wall Hangings" (Exhibit)	Mathews, Richard; Joan Burton	√		Fa	3	4		J/A 76	8
Exhibits and Exhibiting: Virginia	"Michelle Morris: Tapestries and Related Work" (Exhibit)	Fitt, Cate	√		Fa	7	4		J/A 80	65
Exhibits and Exhibiting: Virginia	"Patti Glazer, Woven Tapestry" (error-corrected Fa v3 n5 76 p2) (Exhibit)	Mathews, Richard	√		Fa	3	4		J/A 76	6
Exhibits and Exhibiting: Washington	"Common Cord, The" Central Asian Textiles (Exhibit)	Prinzing, Debra	√		Fa	14	3		M/J 87	56
Exhibits and Exhibiting: Washington	"Fibers Unlimited 1979" (Exhibit)	Davidian, Robert	√		Fa	7	2		M/A 80	69
Exhibits and Exhibiting: Washington	"Fibers Unlimited" (Exhibit)	Sherwood, Thomas	√		Fa	5	1		J/F 78	14
Exhibits and Exhibiting: Washington	International Tapestry (Exhibit)		√		Fa	13	4		J/A 86	59
Exhibits and Exhibiting: Washington	"Pat Rutledge: Batiks" (Exhibit)	Ellis, Betty	√		Fa	9	1		J/F 82	77
Exhibits and Exhibiting: Washington	"Unsettled Images: Peggy Vanbianchi & Emily Standley" (Exhibit)	Rowlands-Tarbox, Jean L.	√		Fa	12	5		S/O 85	71
Exhibits and Exhibiting: West Germany	"Ritzi and Peter Jacobi" (Exhibit)	Mathews, Rich	√		Fa	4	5		S/O 77	12
Exhibits and Exhibiting: Wisconsin	"Assemblage: Wisconsin Paper" (Exhibit)	Bard, Elizabeth	√		Fa	11	1		J/F 84	78

SUBJECT	TITLE	AUTHOR	IL	INST	JOUR	VOL	NO	ISS	DATE	PAGE
Exhibits and Exhibiting: Wisconsin	"Basketworks": Visit to an Exhibition (Exhibit)		√		Fa	9	1		J/F 82	17
Exhibits and Exhibiting: Wisconsin	"Contemporary Quilting: A Renaissance" (Exhibit)	Lauter, Estella	√		Fa	9	1		J/F 82	78
Exhibits and Exhibiting: Wisconsin	"Coverlets: An American Tradition" (Exhibit)	Lowell-LaRoque, Jane	√		Fa	7	1		J/F 80	71
Exhibits and Exhibiting: Wisconsin	"Fiber R/Evolution" (Exhibit)		√		TM			4	A/M 86	10
Exhibits and Exhibiting: Wisconsin	"Fiber R/Evolution" (Exhibit)	Levine, Betsy			TM			5	J/J 86	16
Exhibits and Exhibiting: Wisconsin	"Fiber R/Evolution" (Exhibit)	Rudich, Sally	√		Fa	13	4		J/A 86	45
Exhibits and Exhibiting: Wisconsin	"Jean Stamsta: Great Lake Series" (Exhibit)	Bard, Elizabeth A.	√		Fa	10	2		M/A 83	70
Exhibits and Exhibiting: Wisconsin	"Made in Wisconsin: An Exhibition of Recent Works In-Of-And-On Handmade Paper" (Exhibit)	Hagemeister-Winzenz, Karon	√		Fa	5	4		J/A 78	19
Exhibits and Exhibiting: Wisconsin	Review/Discussion of Artspace's Innovative Yet Flawed "Fiber Freely Interpreted", A (Exhibit)		√		Fa	4	2		M/A 77	38
Exhibits and Exhibiting: Wisconsin	"Seventh Annual Twin Ports Fibers Invitational" (Exhibit)	LaRoque, Jane V. Lowell	√		Fa	7	3		M/J 80	80
Exhibits and Exhibiting: Wisconsin	"Wisconsin Fiber Miniatures" (Exhibit)	Lowell-LaRoque, Jane V.	√		Fa	6	5		S/O 79	84
Exhibits and Exhibitinh: New York	"Works in Miniature" (Exhibit)	Malarcher, Patricia	√		Fa	7	3		M/J 80	82
Extra-Weft Wrapping	Flat-Woven Structures Found in Nomadic and Village Weavings from the Near East and Central Asia	Wertime, John T.	√		TMJ	18			79	33
Eyeglass Case	How to Weave Your own Designs	Arnold, Ruth	√	> 4	H&C	11	3		Su 60	6
Eyelash Cloth	Double Weave: Plain and Patterned: Block Fringes, The	Tidball, Harriet	√	> 4	SCGM		1		60	32
Eyelash Cloth	Notebook: Floats on the Surface (Esther Flory)	Meyers, Ruth Nordquist, ed.	√	√	SS&D	14	3	55	Su 83	90
Fabric	But What Do I Do With It?	Alderman, Sharon D.	√	√	Hw	7	5		N/D 86	50
Fabric	Theme Issue		√		Fa	9	1		J/F 82	
Fabric, Accent	Fabric #3: Accent Fabric (Constance LaLena)		√	√	Hw	6	3		Su 85	62, I-5
Fabric, Accent	Fabric #4: Accent Fabric (Constance LaLena)		√	√	Hw	6	3		Su 85	62, I-5
Fabric, Alaga, Stripe	Qotny & Alaga: Traditional Striped Fabrics for the Middle Eastern Kaftan	El-Homossani, M. M.	√	> 4	WJ	10	1	37	Su 85	33
Fabric, Apparel	1 Fabric: 2 Faces	Moes, Dini	√	> 4	SS&D	14	2	54	Sp 83	16
Fabric, Apparel	Air Robe	Dedekam, Phyllis	√	√	SS&D	18	3	71	Su 87	47
Fabric, Apparel	Basic Sewing Techniques in Handling Handwoven Fabrics for Garments.	Knollenberg, Barbara	√	√	WJ	1	1	1	Jy 76	25
Fabric, Apparel	Blue and Red Wool Plaid (Jane Patrick)		√	√	Hw	3	5		N/D 82	30, 99
Fabric, Apparel	Broadcloth and Doeskin	Ponting, K. G.			WJ	7	2	26	Fa 82	38
Fabric, Apparel	Canadian Classic, A	Baker, William R. M.	√		SS&D	18	3	71	Su 87	52
Fabric, Apparel	Canadian Clothing Fabrics		√	√	H&C	14	2		Sp 63	15
Fabric, Apparel	Cape by Virginia M. West		√	> 4	H&C	20	3		Su 69	21
Fabric, Apparel	Child's Dress Pattern	Deygout, Françoise	√	> 4	CW		24		My 87	13
Fabric, Apparel	Coat Couture	West, Virginia	√	> 4	SS&D	14	2	54	Sp 83	48
Fabric, Apparel	Contemporary Satins: An Alphabet of Satin Designs	Tidball, Harriet	√	> 4	SCGM		7		62	22
Fabric, Apparel	Dazzling Designs	Eagle, Elsie	√	√	SS&D	15	1	57	Wi 83	19
Fabric, Apparel	Design Decisions: Software Solutions	George, Patrice	√	> 4	Hw	5	5		N/D 84	47
Fabric, Apparel	Design in Wool on Eight Harnesses, A		√	>4	H&C	14	2		Sp 63	36
Fabric, Apparel	Designing for Industry	Speth, Lottie	√		SS&D	2	4	8	Fa 71	21
Fabric, Apparel	Designing Handwoven Clothing	Thomason, Roger	√		SS&D	10	1	37	Wi 78	88
Fabric, Apparel	Diversity of Fabrics Comes from the Looms of Joseph D. Acton and Bret Carberry of Philadelphia, A		√		H&C	4	2		Sp 53	4
Fabric, Apparel	Double-Faced Fabric (Sharon Alderman)		√	> 4	Hw	3	4		Se 82	41, 95

SUBJECT	TITLE	AUTHOR	IL	INST	JOUR	VOL	NO	ISS	DATE	PAGE
Fabric, Apparel	Dress for a Summer Day		√	√	Hw	3	2		Mr 82	52
Fabric, Apparel	Experimenting with Leno Weaves	Chetwynd, Hilary	√	√	SS&D	5	3	19	Su 74	29
Fabric, Apparel	Fabric Design, An Approach by a Young Weaver	Carson, Candace	√	√	H&C	20	1		Wi 69	16
Fabric, Apparel	Fabric for Clothing	Marston, Ena	√		SS&D	13	3	51	Su 82	52
Fabric, Apparel	Fabrics for Spring Ensembles	Wertenberger, Kathryn	√	√	Hw	6	2		M/A 85	82
Fabric, Apparel	Fabrics from a Prairie Loom		√		H&C	4	2		Sp 53	30
Fabric, Apparel	Frances van Hall	Bryan, Dorothy	√		H&C	11	2		Sp 60	43
Fabric, Apparel	From Elsie H. Gubser's Studio		√	> 4	H&C	7	3		Su 56	24
Fabric, Apparel	From English Handlooms Comes Royal Purple Velvet for Coronation Robe of Elizabeth II	Lee, Humphrey A.	√		H&C	4	2		Sp 53	17
Fabric, Apparel	Gordons, Weavers at the Greenbrier Art Colony, The		√	> 4	H&C	16	3		Su 65	18
Fabric, Apparel	Grace Marvin, Her Ideas on Making Clothing from Handwoven Fabrics		√	√	H&C	13	3		Su 62	14
Fabric, Apparel	Hand Woven Garments	Piper, Aris	√	> 4	WJ	5	3	19	Wi 81	24
Fabric, Apparel	Handweaves for Men's Wear		√		H&C	9	2		Sp 58	42
Fabric, Apparel	Handwoven Designs for the Custom Trade	Frank, Elizabeth	√		H&C	3	1		Wi 51	44
Fabric, Apparel	Handwoven Fabric: Beginnings, Decision Making	Alderman, Sharon			Hw	3	2		Mr 82	31
Fabric, Apparel	Handwoven Swatch Collection #1	Alderman, Sharon	√		Hw	1	2		S-S 80	41
Fabric, Apparel	Handwoven Swatch Collection #2	Alderman, Sharon	√		Hw	2	1		F-W 80	50
Fabric, Apparel	Handwoven Swatch Collection #3 (Sharon Alderman)		√		Hw	2	3		My 81	87
Fabric, Apparel	If You Have Four Harnesses	Hagarty, Harriet May	√	> 4	H&C	24	1		J/F 73	11
Fabric, Apparel	Janet Nyquist, Custom Weaver of Apparel Fabrics		√	√	H&C	16	1		Wi 65	16
Fabric, Apparel	Lewis Mayhew, Versatile Northwest Weaver		√		H&C	14	3		Su 63	9
Fabric, Apparel	Linen	Shaffer, Christine H.	√		H&C	12	2		Sp 61	29
Fabric, Apparel	Marketing Handwoven Fabric for Apparel & Interiors	Alaniz, Leonore	√		WJ	11	4	44	Sp 87	31
Fabric, Apparel	Matter of Style: Swatch Collection #5, A	Alderman, Sharon	√		Hw	3	2		Mr 82	8
Fabric, Apparel	Midwest Conference Presents Sources of Inspiration for Color		√	> 4	H&C	13	4		Fa 62	18
Fabric, Apparel	Modern Interpretations of Ethnic Garments	Dickey, Enola	√	√	SS&D	9	2	34	Sp 78	28
Fabric, Apparel	New England Weavers' Seminar		√		H&C	18	4		Fa 67	14
Fabric, Apparel	Notebook: Blouse Fabric (Avis Black) (error-corrected SS&D v17 n3 86 p5)	Myers, Ruth, ed.	√	√	SS&D	12	3	47	Su 81	67
Fabric, Apparel	Peggy Ives Retires — Long Established Business to C. S. Bourgeois		√		H&C	6	2		Sp 55	28
Fabric, Apparel	Persian Handcrafted Items	Brockway, Edith	√		H&C	26	5		Oc 75	16
Fabric: Apparel	Pine Tree Coat	Knollenberg, Barbara	√	> 4	WJ	1	2	2	Oc 76	32
Fabric, Apparel	Planning Clothing Fabrics, Suggestions for Exploring Basic Weaves	Snyder, Mary E.	√	> 4	H&C	15	1		Wi 64	9
Fabric, Apparel	Prize-Winning Gown and Coat	Fair, Maurine	√	> 4	SS&D	2	2	6	Sp 71	16
Fabric, Apparel	Projects with Cotton		√	√	WJ	4	2	14	Oc 79	28
Fabric, Apparel	Reflections on 7560 Weft Picks	Ligon, Linda	√	> 4	Hw	8	3		M/J 87	98
Fabric, Apparel	Shadowweave, Part 1 (error-corrected WJ v2 n1 77 insert for vol. 1)	Barrett, Clotilde	√	> 4	WJ	1	1	1	Jy 76	13
Fabric, Apparel	Southern California Show		√	> 4	H&C	14	3		Su 63	30
Fabric, Apparel	Sprang and Frame Plaiting for Garments		√	√	WJ	3	3	11	Ja 79	26
Fabric, Apparel	Summer and Winter Suiting	Upson, Frieda	√	> 4	SS&D	12	1	45	Wi 80	62
Fabric, Apparel	Supplementary Weft Float Patterning	Marston, Ena	√	√	SS&D	9	4	36	Fa 78	63
Fabric, Apparel	Surface Interest Has Become A Favorite for Apparel Fabrics	Slason, Helen	√	> 4	H&C	18	3		Su 67	22

SUBJECT	TITLE	AUTHOR	IL	INST	JOUR	VOL	NO	ISS	DATE	PAGE
Fabric, Apparel	Swatch #1, Basket Weave (Diana Sanderson)		√	√	Hw	7	5		N/D 86	46, I-4
Fabric, Apparel	Swatch #1: Reversing Twill Warp and Weft (Sharon Alderman)		√	√	Hw	6	5		N/D 85	48, I-9
Fabric, Apparel	Swatch #2, Basket Weave (Diana Sanderson)		√	√	Hw	7	5		N/D 86	46, I-4
Fabric, Apparel	Swatch #3: Granite Weave Tweed (Sharon Alderman)		√	√	Hw	6	5		N/D 85	48, I-10
Fabric, Apparel	Swatch #3, Twill (Diana Sanderson)		√	√	Hw	7	5		N/D 86	46, I-4
Fabric, Apparel	Swatch #4: Dark Blue Dornick Twill with Silk Stripes (Sharon Alderman)		√	√	Hw	6	5		N/D 85	48, I-10
Fabric, Apparel	Swatch #4, Twill (Diana Sanderson)		√	√	Hw	7	5		N/D 86	46, I-5
Fabric, Apparel	Swatch #5: Bluish-red Warp-striped Worsted (Sharon Alderman)		√	> 4	Hw	6	5		N/D 85	48, I-10
Fabric, Apparel	Swatch #5, Twill (Diana Sanderson)		√	√	Hw	7	5		N/D 86	46, I-5
Fabric, Apparel	Swatch #6: Blue-Red Tweed (Sharon Alderman)		√	√	Hw	6	5		N/D 85	48, I-11
Fabric, Apparel	Swatch Collection #11	Alderman, Sharon	√		Hw	6	2		M/A 85	46
Fabric, Apparel	Swatch Collection #11: Fabrics 1-5 (Sharon Alderman)		√	> 4	Hw	6	2		M/A 85	46, I-5
Fabric, Apparel	Swatch Collection #11: Fabrics 6-7 (Sharon Alderman)		√	√	Hw	6	2		M/A 85	46, I-6
Fabric, Apparel	Swatch Collection #11: Fabrics 8-10 (Sharon Alderman)		√	√	Hw	6	2		M/A 85	46, I-7
Fabric, Apparel	Swatch Collection #13	Alderman, Sharon	√		Hw	7	3		M/J 86	28
Fabric, Apparel	Swatch Collection #6	Alderman, Sharon	√		Hw	3	4		Se 82	41
Fabric, Apparel	Swatch Collection #8	Alderman, Sharon	√		Hw	4	4		S/O 83	52
Fabric, Apparel	Textile Arts of Multan, Pakistan: Part 2	Shahzaman, Mahboob	√	> 4	SS&D	4	4	16	Fa 73	65
Fabric, Apparel	Tuck Weaving	Frey, Berta	√	√	H&C	9	4		Fa 58	11
Fabric, Apparel	We Like Weaving	Anita, Sister M.	√	> 4	H&C	22	1		Wi 71	17
Fabric, Apparel	Weave Three--Cocktail Skirt, Coating, Parka	Snyder, Mary	√	> 4	SS&D	6	2	22	Sp 75	34
Fabric, Apparel	Weavers of Rabun, The		√		H&C	7	2		Sp 56	6
Fabric, Apparel	Weaver's Notebook		√	> 4	SS&D	10	1	37	Wi 78	32
Fabric, Apparel	Weaving Fabrics for Men's Wear	Jones, Alice Varney	√		H&C	1	1		Ap 50	40
Fabric, Apparel	Weaving Skirts	Wood, Gerry	√	> 4	H&C	9	4		Fa 58	18
Fabric, Apparel	What a Handweaver Can Learn from the Scottish Weaving Industry (error-corrected WJ v2 n1 77 insert for vol. 1)	Barrett, Clotilde	√	√	WJ	1	3	3	Ja 77	11
Fabric, Apparel	When You Plan to Sell	af Kleen, Elisabeth; Nils af Kleen	√	√	H&C	14	3		Su 63	32
Fabric, Apparel	Why Multi-Harness Weaves for Clothing Fabrics	Hoskinson, Marian K.			CW	3	2	8	Ja 82	13
Fabric, Apparel	Woolens from a 20-inch Loom	Skirm, Helen W.	√	√	H&C	9	1		Wi 57	26
Fabric, Apparel: Blouse	Blouse Fabric (Sharon Alderman)		√	√	Hw	2	3		My 81	87, 88
Fabric, Apparel: Blouse	Blouse (Sharon Alderman)		√	√	Hw	1	2		S-S 80	41, 60
Fabric, Apparel: Blouse	Blouse (Sharon Alderman)		√	√	Hw	2	4		Se 81	36, 88
Fabric, Apparel: Blouse	Swatch #3, Striped Fabric for Blouse (Virginia West)		√	√	Hw	7	5		N/D 86	62, I-6
Fabric, Apparel: Blouse	Swatch #4: Blouse Fabric (Sharon Alderman)		√	√	Hw	7	3		M/J 86	28, I-5
Fabric, Apparel: Blouse	Swatch #5 Blouse (Sharon Alderman) (error-corrected Hw v8 n4 87 p I-3)		√	√	Hw	8	2		M/A 87	38, I-5
Fabric, Apparel: Blouse	Swatch #5, Silk Blouse Fabric (Lillian Whipple)		√	> 4	Hw	7	5		N/D 86	64, I-7
Fabric, Apparel: Blouse, Dress	Blouse/Dress (Sharon Alderman)		√	√	Hw	2	1		F-W 80	50, 63
Fabric, Apparel: Blouse, Dress	Swatch #1, Blouse Fabric (Malin Salander)		√	√	Hw	7	5		N/D 86	60, I-5

SUBJECT	TITLE	AUTHOR	IL	INST	JOUR	VOL	NO	ISS	DATE	PAGE
Fabric, Apparel: Blouse, Dress	Swatch #1, Huck Lace for Blouse or Dress (Virginia West)		√	√	Hw	7	5		N/D 86	62, I-6
Fabric, Apparel: Blouse/Shirt	Blouse/Shirt (Sharon Alderman)		√	√	Hw	4	2		M/A 83	58, 92
Fabric, Apparel: Caftan	Seersucker for Caftan (Sharon Alderman)		√	√	Hw	1	2		S-S 80	41, 60
Fabric, Apparel: Cape	Technical Information for Cape Fabric (Sharon Alderman)		√	√	Hw	5	5		N/D 84	60, I-14
Fabric, Apparel: Children's Clothing	Cotton Shirt and Children's Dresses Fabric (Lillemor Johansson and Astrid Linderoth)		√	√	Hw	4	2		M/A 83	32, 82
Fabric, Apparel: Coat	Coat Fabric, Swatch #5 (Sharon Alderman)		√	>4	Hw	7	4		S/O 86	24, I-5
Fabric, Apparel: Coat	Daisy Dog Fur Coat (Betty Beard)		√	√	Hw	3	2		Mr 82	62, 87
Fabric, Apparel: Coat	Irish Weaving	Clement, Doris; Ted Clement	√	>4	H&C	21	2		Sp 70	4
Fabric, Apparel: Coat	More About Fabrics: Practical Projects for Basket and Twill	Zielinski, S. A.; Robert Leclerc, ed.	√	√	MWL	20			'51–'73	35
Fabric, Apparel: Coat	Pile Weaves, Rugs and Tapestry: Handwoven Furcoat	Zielinski, S. A.; Robert Leclerc, ed.	√	>4	MWL	14			'51–'73	21
Fabric, Apparel: Coat	Swatch #1, Wool Coat Fabric for Winter (Lillian Whipple)		√	√	Hw	7	5		N/D 86	64, I-7
Fabric, Apparel: Coat	Swatch #2, Winter Coat Fabric (Malin Salander)		√	√	Hw	7	5		N/D 86	60, I-5
Fabric, Apparel: Coat	Swatch #4, Dornick & Basket Weave for Coat (Virginia West)		√	√	Hw	7	5		N/D 86	62, I-6
Fabric, Apparel: Coat	Wool/Mohair Coat Fabric (Sharon Alderman)		√	>4	Hw	3	4		Se 82	41, 94
Fabric, Apparel: Coat	Wooly Rose Coat (Trudy Van Stralen)		√	√	Hw	3	3		My 82	51, 96
Fabric, Apparel: Coat, Jacket	Coat/Jacket Fabric #4 (Sharon D. Alderman)		√	√	Hw	5	4		S/O 84	56, 102
Fabric, Apparel: Doll Dress	Antique Madras Plaid (Constance LaLena)		√	√	Hw	3	3		My 82	53, 91
Fabric, Apparel: Dress	Child's Easter Dress Fabric (Julie Green Edson)		√	√	Hw	3	2		Mr 82	54, 84
Fabric, Apparel: Dress	Cotton Dress Fabric, Swatch #6 (Sharon Alderman)		√	√	Hw	7	4		S/O 86	24, I-5
Fabric, Apparel: Dress	Dress Fabric, #3 (Sharon Alderman)		√	√	Hw	8	4		S/O 87	52, I-9
Fabric, Apparel: Dress	Dress Fabric (Sharon Alderman)		√	>4	Hw	1	2		S-S 80	41, 61
Fabric, Apparel: Dress	Dress (Sharon Alderman)		√	√	Hw	2	1		F-W 80	50, 62
Fabric, Apparel: Dress	Ribweave Dress Fabric (Julia Green)		√	√	Hw	3	1		Ja 82	37, 87
Fabric, Apparel: Dress	Swatch #2: Plain Twill Blue Tweed for Skirt (Sharon Alderman)		√	√	Hw	6	5		N/D85	48, I-9
Fabric, Apparel: Dress	Swatch #2 Shirtwaist Dress (Sharon Alderman)		√	√	Hw	8	2		M/A 87	38, I-4
Fabric, Apparel: Dress	Swatch #3, Cotton Dress Fabric for Summer (Lillian Whipple)		√	√	Hw	7	5		N/D 86	64, I-7
Fabric, Apparel: Dress	White Dress (Sharon Alderman)		√	>4	Hw	2	3		My 81	88
Fabric, Apparel: Dress	Worsted Dress (Sharon Alderman)		√	√	Hw	3	4		Se 82	41, 95
Fabric, Apparel: Dress, Blouse	Dress/Blouse Fabric (Sharon Alderman)		√	√	Hw	3	2		Mr 82	9, 79
Fabric, Apparel: Dress, Jacket	Dress or Belted Jacket Fabric, Swatch #3 (Sharon Alderman)		√	√	Hw	7	4		S/O 86	24, I-4
Fabric, Apparel: Dresses	Supplementary Warp Patterning: Dresses Styled From Warp Pattern Fabrics	Tidball, Harriet	√	>4	SCGM		17		66	33-43
Fabric, Apparel: Dresses and Gowns	Dress (Sharon Alderman)		√	√	Hw	2	4		Se 81	36, 87
Fabric, Apparel: Handwoven	Planned Weaving for Your Wardrobe	Page, Marta	√		H&C	2	4		Fa 51	30
Fabric, Apparel: Jacket	Bits and Pieces	Knollenberg, Barbara	√	√	WJ	1	4	4	Ap 77	11
Fabric, Apparel: Jacket	Cotton/Linen Jacket (Sharon Alderman)		√	√	Hw	4	2		M/A 83	58, 92
Fabric, Apparel: Jacket	Jacket Fabric #3 (Sharon D. Alderman)		√	√	Hw	5	4		S/O 84	56, 102
Fabric, Apparel: Jacket	Jacket Fabric #6 (Sharon D. Alderman)		√	>4	Hw	5	3		Su 84	62, 109
Fabric, Apparel: Jacket	Jacket Fabric (Sharon Alderman)		√	√	Hw	2	3		My 81	87, 83

SUBJECT	TITLE	AUTHOR	IL	INST	JOUR	VOL	NO	ISS	DATE	PAGE
Fabric, Apparel: Jacket	Jacket or Coat (Sharon Alderman)		√	√	Hw	2	4		Se 81	36, 86
Fabric, Apparel: Jacket	Jacket (Sharon Alderman)		√	√	Hw	1	2		S-S 80	41, 61
Fabric, Apparel: Jacket	Jacket (Sharon Alderman)		√	>4	Hw	2	1		F-W 80	50, 62
Fabric, Apparel: Jacket	Man's Sport Jacket/Woman's Blazer (Sharon Alderman)		√	√	Hw	2	1		F-W 80	50, 63
Fabric, Apparel: Jacket	One Pattern, One Warp (Louise Bradley)		√	√	Hw	3	3		My 82	34, 97
Fabric, Apparel: Jacket	Plum Wooly Jacket (Linda Ligon)		√	√	Hw	5	1		J/F 84	46, 108
Fabric, Apparel: Jacket	Striped Cotton Jacket (Sharon Alderman)		√	√	Hw	4	2		M/A 83	58, 90
Fabric, Apparel: Jacket	Suit or Jacket Fabric, #4 (Sharon Alderman)		√	√	Hw	8	4		S/O 87	52, I-9
Fabric, Apparel: Jacket	Swatch #3, Jacket Fabric (Malin Salander)		√	√	Hw	7	5		N/D 86	60, I-5
Fabric, Apparel: Jacket	Swatch #3: Linen Jacket Fabric (Sharon Alderman)		√	√	Hw	7	3		M/J 86	28, I-4
Fabric, Apparel: Jacket	Three Hand-Dyed Jackets (Sue Henrikson)		√	√	Hw	3	3		My 82	45, 96
Fabric, Apparel: Jacket	Tweed Jacket Fabric, Swatch #1 (Sharon Alderman)		√	√	Hw	7	4		S/O 86	24, I-4
Fabric, Apparel: Jacket	Woolen Jacket (Sharon Alderman)		√	√	Hw	3	4		Se 82	41, 95
Fabric, Apparel: Jacket, Coat	Jacket/Coat, Fabric #1 (Sharon Alderman)		√	√	Hw	8	4		S/O 87	52, I-8
Fabric, Apparel: Jacket, Coat	Swatch #5, Medallions for Jacket or Coat (Virginia West)		√	>4	Hw	7	5		N/D 86	62, I-6
Fabric, Apparel: Jacket, Vest	Jacket or Vest Fabric (Sharon Alderman)		√	√	Hw	3	2		Mr 82	9, 78
Fabric, Apparel: Jacket, Vest	Jacket/Vest Fabric, Swatch #2 (Sharon Alderman)		√	√	Hw	7	4		S/O 86	24, I-4
Fabric, Apparel: Jackets	More About Fabrics: Practical Projects for Basket and Twill	Zielinski, S. A.; Robert Leclerc, ed.	√	√	MWL	20			'51–'73	35
Fabric, Apparel: Jumper	Child's Jumper (Julie Green Edson)		√	√	Hw	3	2		Mr 82	55, 86
Fabric, Apparel: Miniature	Joy to the World		√	√	WJ	6	2	22	Fa 81	59
Fabric, Apparel: Movie Costumes	Circuit Riding Weavers		√		H&C	10	1		Wi 59	11
Fabric, Apparel: Robe	Bathrobe (Linda Ligon)		√	√	Hw	3	2		Mr 82	50, 91
Fabric, Apparel: Shirt	Cotton Shirt and Children's Dresses Fabric (Lillemor Johansson and Astrid Linderoth)		√	√	Hw	4	2		M/A 83	32, 82
Fabric, Apparel: Shirt	Man's Shirt (Sue Hendrikson)		√	√	Hw	3	2		Mr 82	49, 83
Fabric, Apparel: Shirt	Western Shirt (Louise Bradley)		√	√	Hw	3	2		Mr 82	48, 84
Fabric, Apparel: Shirt, Dress	Plaid Shirt/Dress Fabric (Sharon Alderman)		√	√	Hw	4	4		S/O 83	52, 96
Fabric, Apparel: Shrug	Shrug/Shannon Sweater/Shawl Fabric (Sharon Alderman)		√	√	Hw	2	3		My 81	87, 89
Fabric, Apparel: Skirt	Dirndl Skirt/Divided Skirt Fabric (Sharon Alderman)		√	√	Hw	3	2		Mr 82	9, 80
Fabric, Apparel: Skirt	Shetland Skirt (Sharon Alderman)		√	√	Hw	2	4		Se 81	36, 85
Fabric, Apparel: Skirt	Skirt Fabric #1 (Sharon D. Alderman)		√	>4	Hw	5	4		S/0 84	56, 100
Fabric, Apparel: Skirt	Skirt Fabric #5 (Sharon D. Alderman)		√	√	Hw	5	4		S/0 84	56, 102
Fabric, Apparel: Skirt	Skirt Fabric (Sharon Alderman)		√	√	Hw	2	3		My 81	87, 89
Fabric, Apparel: Skirt	Skirt Fabric (Sharon Alderman)		√	√	Hw	4	4		S/O 83	52, 95
Fabric, Apparel: Skirt	Skirt (Sharon Alderman)		√	√	Hw	2	1		F-W 80	50, 62
Fabric, Apparel: Skirt	Skirt (Sharon Alderman)		√	√	Hw	4	2		M/A 83	58, 91
Fabric, Apparel: Skirt	Swatch #1: Skirt Fabric (Sharon Alderman)		√	√	Hw	7	3		M/J 86	28, I-4
Fabric, Apparel: Skirt	Swatch #2: Plain Twill Blue Tweed for Skirt (Sharon Alderman)		√	√	Hw	6	5		N/D 85	48, I-10
Fabric, Apparel: Skirt	Swatch #4, Skirt Fabric (Malin Salander)		√	√	Hw	7	5		N/D 86	60, I-6
Fabric, Apparel: Skirt	Swatch Collection Skirt (Sharon Alderman)		√	√	Hw	4	1		J/F 83	68, 94
Fabric, Apparel: Skirt	Teal Skirt (Jean Scorgie)		√	√	Hw	7	5		N/D 86	42, I-8
Fabric, Apparel: Skirt	Tweed Skirt (Sharon Alderman)		√	√	Hw	2	4		Se 81	36, 86

SUBJECT	TITLE	AUTHOR	IL	INST	JOUR	VOL	NO	ISS	DATE	PAGE
Fabric, Apparel: Skirt	Worsted Skirt (Sharon Alderman)		√	√	Hw	3	4		Se 82	41, 94
Fabric, Apparel: Skirt, Dress	Cotton Skirt or Dress (Sharon Alderman)		√	√	Hw	3	4		Se 82	41, 94
Fabric, Apparel: Skirt, Dress	Skirt/Dress Fabric #1 (Sharon D. Alderman)		√	√	Hw	5	3		Su 84	62, 108
Fabric, Apparel: Skirt, Dress	Skirt/Dress Fabric #2 & #3 (Sharon D. Alderman)		√	√	Hw	5	3		Su 84	62, 108
Fabric, Apparel: Skirt, Dress	Skirt/Dress Fabric (Sharon Alderman)		√	√	Hw	2	3		My 81	87, 89
Fabric, Apparel: Skirt, Dress	Skirt/Dress Lacy Plaid Fabric #5 (Sharon D. Alderman) (error-corrected Hw v5 n5 84 p7)		√	> 4	Hw	5	3		Su 84	62, 109
Fabric, Apparel: Skirt, Dress	Skirt/Dress (Sharon Alderman)		√	√	Hw	4	2		M/A 83	58, 90
Fabric, Apparel: Skirt, Dress	Swatch #1 Skirt or Dress (Sharon Alderman)		√	√	Hw	8	2		M/A 87	38, I-4
Fabric, Apparel: Skirt, Dress	Swatch #3 Skirt or Dress (Sharon Alderman)		√	> 4	Hw	8	2		M/A 87	38, I-5
Fabric, Apparel: Skirt, Jacket	Striped Skirt/Jacket (Sharon Alderman)		√	√	Hw	4	4		S/O 83	52, 96
Fabric, Apparel: Skirt, Pants	Skirt (or Pants) fabric (Sharon Alderman)		√	> 4	Hw	1	2		S-S 80	41, 60
Fabric, Apparel: Skirt, Slacks	Skirt/Slacks Fabric #4 (Sharon D. Alderman)		√	√	Hw	5	3		Su 84	62, 109
Fabric, Apparel: Skirt, Slacks	Skirt/Slacks Fabric (Sharon Alderman)		√	√	Hw	4	4		S/O 83	52, 96
Fabric, Apparel: Skirts	More About Fabrics: Practical Projects for Basket and Twill	Zielinski, S. A.; Robert Leclerc, ed.	√	√	MWL	20			'51–'73	35
Fabric, Apparel: Slacks, Suit	Slacks/Suit Fabric (Sharon Alderman)		√	√	Hw	3	2		Mr 82	9, 80
Fabric, Apparel: Suit	Skirt or Suit , Fabric #5 (Sharon Alderman		√	√	Hw	8	4		S/O 87	52, I-9
Fabric, Apparel: Suit	Swatch #2, Lightweight Wool Suit Fabric for Fall (Lillian Whipple)		√	> 4	Hw	7	5		N/D 86	64, I-7
Fabric, Apparel: Suit	Swatch #4, Linen Suit Fabric for Spring (Lillian Whipple)		√	√	Hw	7	5		N/D 86	64, I-7
Fabric, Apparel: Suiting	More About Fabrics: Practical Projects for Basket and Twill	Zielinski, S. A.; Robert Leclerc, ed.	√	√	MWL	20			'51–'73	37
Fabric, Apparel: Suiting	More About Fabrics: Practical Projects for Basket and Twill	Zielinski, S. A.; Robert Leclerc, ed.	√	√	MWL	20			'51–'73	35
Fabric, Apparel: Suiting	Swatch #2, Plain Weave Check for Suiting (Virginia West)		√	√	Hw	7	5		N/D 86	62, I-6
Fabric, Apparel: Tee-Top	Swatch #2: Tee-Top Fabric (Sharon Alderman)		√	> 4	Hw	7	3		M/J 86	28, I-4
Fabric, Apparel: Top	V-Neck Top with Lace Bands (Betty Davenport)		√	√	Hw	3	2		Mr 82	44, 80
Fabric, Apparel: Tunic	Waffle Weave Tunic (Sharon Alderman)		√	√	Hw	3	2		Mr 82	45, 82
Fabric, Apparel: Tunic, Vest	Tunic/Loose Vest Fabric (Sharon Alderman)		√	> 4	Hw	3	2		Mr 82	9, 78
Fabric, Apparel: Vest	Swatch #4 Vest (Sharon Alderman)		√	> 4	Hw	8	2		M/A 87	38, I-5
Fabric, Apparel: Vest	Swatch Collection Vest (Sharon Alderman)		√	> 4	Hw	4	1		J/F 83	68, 94
Fabric, Apparel: Vest	Vest, Fabric #2 (Sharon Alderman)		√	> 4	Hw	8	4		S/O 87	52, I-8
Fabric, Apparel: Vest, Jacket	Corduroy Vest/Jacket Fabric (Sharon Alderman)		√	> 4	Hw	4	4		S/O 83	52, 98
Fabric, Apparel: Vest, Skirt	Vest/Skirt Fabric #2 (Sharon D. Alderman)		√	> 4	Hw	5	4		S/0 84	57, 101
Fabric, Apparel: Vest, Sweater	Soft Vest or Sweater Fabric, Swatch #4 (Sharon Alderman)		√	√	Hw	7	4		S/O 86	24, I-4
Fabric, Apparel: Wedding Dress	Wedding Dress Fabric (Sharon Condie)		√	√	Hw	4	3		M/J 83	55, 82
Fabric, Backed	Backed Cloth on Four Harnesses		√	√	WJ	4	1	13	Jy 79	30
Fabric, Backed	Josephina's Suit	Koopman, Albertje	√	> 4	WJ	4	4	16	Ap 80	50
Fabric, Backed	Tisket, a Tasket, A	Gordon, Judith	√	> 4	Hw	5	5		N/D 84	34
Fabric, Bed Covering	Upholstery and Bed Covering Fabric, Fabric #3 (Constance LaLena)		√	> 4	Hw	7	2		M/A 86	64, I-12
Fabric, Bedding	Blue and White Bed Ticking (Jane Patrick)		√	√	Hw	3	5		N/D 82	30, 99
Fabric, Bookbinding	Book That's Bound to Please, A	Ligon, Linda	√	√	Hw	4	4		S/O 83	67
Fabric, Broadcloth	Broadcloth and Doeskin	Ponting, K. G.			WJ	7	2	26	Fa 82	38

SUBJECT	TITLE	AUTHOR	IL	INST	JOUR	VOL	NO	ISS	DATE	PAGE
Fabric Bumps: Crochet	Fabrics That Go Bump (error-corrected PWC i4 83 p76)	Xenakis, Athanasios David	√	√	PWC			3	Oc 82	18
Fabric Bumps: Knit	Fabrics That Go Bump (error-corrected PWC i4 83 p76)	Xenakis, Athanasios David	√	√	PWC			3	Oc 82	18
Fabric Bumps: Woven	Fabrics That Go Bump (error-corrected PWC i4 83 p76)	Xenakis, Athanasios David	√	√	PWC			3	Oc 82	18
Fabric, Caribou Hair/Wool	Caribou Hair and the Creation of a New Fabric	Goodfellow, Robin	√		AT	6			De 86	119
Fabric, Chintz	Preliminary Report on a Group of Important Mughal Textiles, A	Smart, Ellen S.	√		TMJ	25			86	5
Fabric, Collapse	Vest with a Hidden Twist	Emerick, Patricia	√	√	S-O	11	4		Wi 87	36, I-46
Fabric Collections	African Motifs, Interpreted by Jack Lenore Larsen in His Newest Fabrics		√		H&C	14	2		Sp 63	6
Fabric, Collections	Fabrics for Interiors #11: The Southwest Collection	LaLena, Constance J.	√	√	Hw	8	4		S/O 87	36
Fabric Collections: Interiors	Cozy Retreat, A	LaLena, Constance	√		Hw	5	2		M/A 84	65
Fabric Collections: Interiors	Fabrics for Interiors #1	LaLena, Constance	√		Hw	3	4		Se 82	33
Fabric Collections: Interiors	Fabrics for Interiors #4: Tartan for a Child's Room	LaLena, Constance	√		Hw	4	5		N/D 83	70
Fabric Collections: Interiors	Fabrics for Interiors #6	LaLena, Constance	√		Hw	5	5		N/D 84	32
Fabric Collections: Interiors	Fabrics for Interiors #7	LaLena, Constance	√		Hw	6	3		Su 85	62
Fabric Collections: Interiors	Fabrics for Interiors, #9	LaLena, Constance	√	> 4	Hw	7	2		M/A 86	64, I-12
Fabric Collections: Interiors	Home Comfort	Wertenberger, Kathryn	√		Hw	5	2		M/A 84	66
Fabric Collections: Interiors	Work with Style	Alderman, Sharon D.	√		Hw	5	2		M/A 84	68
Fabric Collections: Upholstery	Designer Fabrics for Upholstery	West, Virginia	√		Hw	5	2		M/A 84	72
Fabric, Colonial	Colonial Fabrics: A Glossary	Patrick, Jane	√		Hw	3	5		N/D 82	25
Fabric, Colonial America	Fine Fabrics: A Continuing Tradition		√		Hw	3	5		N/D 82	30
Fabric, Color	Desperate Need for Chartreuse, The	Phillips, Constance			TM			1	O/N 85	14
Fabric, Commemorative	"In Praise of Heroes" (Exhibit)	Malarcher, Patricia	√		Fa	10	1		J/F 83	78
Fabric, Contemporary	Edna Minor of the Craft Students League		√		H&C	4	3		Su 53	4
Fabric, Coordinated	Fall Wrap Up — Weaves and Fabrics for Classic Garments		√	√	Hw	8	4		S/O 87	40
Fabric, Cotton	Cotton: Legacy of Gods & Kings	Schmoller, Irene Laughing Cloud	√		WJ	11	2	42	Fa 86	11
Fabric, Crochet	Crocheting Wearable Fabric	McGoveran, Mary	√	√	TM			9	F/M 87	62
Fabric, Custom-Woven	Deborah Ann Abbott: Power Loom Weaving on a New Hampshire Farm	Mattera, Joanne	√		Fa	9	1		J/F 82	35
Fabric Design	Theme Issue		√		WJ	11	4	44	Sp 87	
Fabric, Doeskin	Broadcloth and Doeskin	Ponting, K. G.			WJ	7	2	26	Fa 82	38
Fabric, Drapery	At the Window		√		Hw	5	2		M/A 84	46
Fabric, Drapery	Curtain Fabric #1 (Constance LaLena) (error-corrected Hw v7 n4 86 pl-3)		√	√	Hw	6	4		S/O 85	46, I-5
Fabric, Drapery	Curtain, Fabric #5 (Constance LaLena)		√	√	Hw	8	4		S/O 87	36, I-4
Fabric, Drapery	Drapery Fabric (Constance LaLena)		√	√	Hw	3	4		Se 82	33, 84
Fabric, Drapery	Drapery for a Club	Uhlmann, Ilse Etta	√		H&C	12	1		Wi 61	48
Fabric, Drapery	Drapery/Curtain Fabric (Constance LaLena)		√	√	Hw	4	1		J/F 83	66, 91
Fabric, Drapery	Fabric #1 Curtains (Constance LaLena)		√	√	Hw	8	2		M/A 87	52, I-9
Fabric, Drapery	Fabric #5: Casement or Curtain Fabric (Constance LaLena)		√	√	Hw	6	3		Su 85	62, I-5
Fabric, Drapery	Midwest Weavers Conference		√	√	H&C	14	4		Fa 63	20
Fabric, Drapery	Monk's Belt Drapery (Constance LaLena)		√	√	Hw	5	2		M/A 84	64, 102
Fabric, Drapery	Projects with Cotton		√	√	WJ	4	2	14	Oc 79	28
Fabric, Drapery	Sixteen-Harness Design for Draperies, A	Fishback, John S.	√	> 4	H&C	11	1		Wi 60	24
Fabric, Drapery	Supplementary Warp Patterning: Contemporary Draperies in Supplementary Warp	Tidball, Harriet	√		SCGM		17		66	28

SUBJECT	TITLE	AUTHOR	IL	INST	JOUR	VOL	NO	ISS	DATE	PAGE
Fabric, Drapery	Unusual Drapery with Distorted Wefts (Jeanetta L. Jones)		√	√	H&C	15	2		Sp 64	36
Fabric, Drapery and Casement	Color Related Decorating Textiles Rugs, Draperies, Upholstery: Drapery and Casement Fabrics	Rhodes, Tonya Stalons; Harriet Tidball, ed.			SCGM		14		65	8
Fabric, Embossed	Embossed Silk (Jane Patrick)		√	√	Hw	3	5		N/D 82	30, 98
Fabric, Evaluating	Techniques of Haute Couture (error-corrected TM i7 O/N86 p5)	Rhodes, Elizabeth A.	√	√	TM			6	A/S 86	52
Fabric, Felted	Wadmal — A Felted Fabric	Snover, Susan; Jean Sullivan	√	√	SS&D	11	2	42	Sp 80	89
Fabric Flowers: Technique	Making Fabric Flowers	Ritch, Diane; Yoshiko Iwamoto Wada	√	√	TM			13	O/N 87	68
Fabric, Furnishings, Temple	Textile Remains from a Late Temple in Egyptian Nubia	Adams, Nettie K.	√		AT	8			De 87	85
Fabric, Handwoven	Coat for Handwoven Yardage, A	Roth, Bettie G.	√	√	WJ	7	3	27	Wi 82	6
Fabric, Handwoven	Couturier Fashions: Part 1, Couturier Fabric Design	West, Virginia	√	√	SS&D	13	3	51	Su 82	8
Fabric, Handwoven	Emphasis on Handwoven Fabrics in the Architect's Design		√		H&C	6	1		Wi 54	20
Fabric, Handwoven	Fabric for Clothing	Marston, Ena	√		SS&D	13	3	51	Su 82	52
Fabric, Handwoven	"Focus on Handwoven Fabric: Ontario Handweavers and Spinners" (Exhibits)	Place, Jennifer	√		Fa	9	4		J/A 82	74
Fabric, Handwoven	Garments by Hanni Bureker		√	√	WJ	6	3	23	Wi 81	35
Fabric, Handwoven	Garments from the Loom: Handweaver Randall Darwall Focuses on the Cloth	Mattera, Joanne	√		Fa	10	1		J/F 83	20
Fabric, Handwoven	Hand Woven Garments	Piper, Aris	√	> 4	WJ	5	3	19	Wi 81	24
Fabric, Handwoven	Handwoven Designs for the Custom Trade	Frank, Elizabeth	√		H&C	3	1		Wi 51	44
Fabric, Handwoven	Ken Colwell on Weaving	Colwell, Ken			PWC	4	3	13		17
Fabric, Handwoven	Margaret Carter, A Weaver In Three States	Currey, Ruth Dunlop	√		H&C	21	4		Fa 70	12
Fabric, Handwoven	Marketing Handwoven Fabric for Apparel & Interiors	Alaniz, Leonore	√		WJ	11	4	44	Sp 87	31
Fabric, Handwoven	Mexican Motifs: A Fine Cotton Warp-Pattern Fabric	Tidball, Harriet	√	√	SCGM		6		62	18
Fabric, Handwoven	Nantucket Looms and Sam Kasten	Erickson, Johanna	√		SS&D	17	3	67	Su 86	70
Fabric, Handwoven	Nova Scotia Weavers Arouse Interest in Wool	Major, Marjorie	√		H&C	5	1		Wi 53	28
Fabric, Handwoven	Ohio Weaving Venture, An	Pendleton, Mary	√		H&C	4	4		Fa 53	23
Fabric, Handwoven	Sett and the Hand of the Fabric	Roth, Bettie G.	√	√	SS&D	12	3	47	Su 81	16
Fabric, Handwoven	Sewing Handwovens	Betzina, Sandra	√	√	TM			2	D/J 85	20
Fabric, Handwoven	Story of a Piece of Weaving		√	√	SS&D	6	1	21	Wi 74	85
Fabric, Handwoven	Texture with Handspun	Page, Judy	√	√	WJ	6	2	22	Fa 81	20
Fabric, Handwoven	Tracking, the Mystery of the Crinkling Cloth	Alderman, Sharon	√	√	Hw	6	4		S/O 85	31
Fabric, Heat Resistant	Hot-Air Balloons	Theil, Linda	√		TM			4	A/M 86	20
Fabric, Ikat	Guatemala Visited	Atwater, Mary Meigs	√		SCGM		15		65	44
Fabric, Interiors	Accent Fabric (Constance LaLena)		√	√	Hw	3	4		Se 82	33, 84
Fabric, Interiors	Accent Fabric (Constance LaLena)		√	√	Hw	4	1		J/F 83	66, 91
Fabric, Interiors	Accent Fabric, Fabric #4 (Constance LaLena)		√	√	Hw	5	5		N/D 84	32, I-5
Fabric, Interiors	Accent Tweed Check, Fabric #5 (Constance LaLena)		√	√	Hw	5	5		N/D 84	32, I-5
Fabric, Interiors	Adapting Handwoven Fabrics to Interior Design	Storey, Walter Rendell	√		H&C	4	3		Su 53	8
Fabric, Interiors	African Motifs, Interpreted by Jack Lenore Larsen in His Newest Fabrics		√		H&C	14	2		Sp 63	6
Fabric, Interiors	Basic Fabric, Fabric #4 (Constance LaLena)		√		Hw	7	2		M/A 86	64, I-12
Fabric, Interiors	Bridging the Gap Between Craft Artists and Interior Designers	Kraus, William	√		SS&D	16	4	64	Fa 85	37

SUBJECT	TITLE	AUTHOR	IL	INST	JOUR	VOL	NO	ISS	DATE	PAGE
Fabric, Interiors	California Designed	Bryan, Dorothy	√		H&C	7	1		Wi 55	30
Fabric, Interiors	Casement Cloth (Constance LaLena)		√	√	Hw	3	4		Se 82	33, 84
Fabric, Interiors	Casual and Comfortable		√		Hw	5	2		M/A 84	45
Fabric, Interiors	Chase Home	McCarthy, Bridget Beatty	√		SS&D	16	4	64	Fa 85	44
Fabric, Interiors	Chase Home: Utah Arts Council	Burke, Dan E.	√		SS&D	16	4	64	Fa 85	40
Fabric, Interiors	Checked Patio Furniture Cover (Constance LaLena)		√	√	Hw	4	3		M/J 83	50, 84
Fabric, Interiors	Co-ordinated Fabrics	Hausner, Walter		> 4	H&C	12	3		Su 61	9
Fabric, Interiors	Color & Design in Decorative Fabrics	Regensteiner, Else	√	√	H&C	9	4		Fa 58	6
Fabric, Interiors	Colorful Blinds and Fabrics from Texas		√		H&C	6	4		Fa 55	14
Fabric, Interiors	Contemporary Textile Designs from Ancient Sources		√	> 4	H&C	7	4		Fa 56	29
Fabric, Interiors	Corded Weaves: Four Harness Cords for Upholstery Fabric, Drapery Material and Wallhangings		√	√	WJ	3	1	9	Jy 78	28
Fabric, Interiors	Country Lace Cloth (Bryn Pinchin)		√	> 4	Hw	6	4		S/O 85	44, I-6
Fabric, Interiors	Country Roads, A Craft Market and a Weaving Center		√		H&C	18	3		Su 67	30
Fabric, Interiors	Coverlet or Bedspread (Constance LaLena)		√	√	Hw	4	5		N/D 83	70, 102
Fabric, Interiors	Creating Textiles for Today's Interiors	Vogel, Edna	√		H&C	3	1		Wi 51	5
Fabric, Interiors	Curtain Fabric (Constance LaLena)		√	> 4	Hw	4	5		N/D 83	70, 102
Fabric, Interiors	Cushion Fabric #2 (Constance LaLena)		√	√	Hw	6	4		S/O 85	46, I-5
Fabric, Interiors	Dale Goffigan: Textile Designer		√		Fa	12	3		M/J 85	66
Fabric, Interiors	Decorator's Use of Handwoven Fabrics, A	Storey, Walter Rendell	√		H&C	4	4		Fa 53	4
Fabric, Interiors	Design by the Yard: Today's Fabric Innovators	Scarborough, Jessica	√		Fa	12	5		S/O 85	30
Fabric, Interiors	Designer Notes on Fabrics for Interiors	LaLena, Constance	√		Hw	3	4		Se 82	34
Fabric, Interiors	Designing Lamp Shades		√	√	H&C	8	4		Fa 57	24
Fabric, Interiors	Dish Towelling #4 (Constance LaLena)		√	√	Hw	6	4		S/O 85	46, I-6
Fabric, Interiors	Diversified Plain Weave	Wertenberger, Kathryn	√	> 4	Hw	8	5		N/D 87	62
Fabric, Interiors	Diversity of Fabrics Comes from the Looms of Joseph D. Acton and Bret Carberry of Philadelphia, A		√		H&C	4	2		Sp 53	4
Fabric, Interiors	Dorothy Liebes		√		H&C	11	2		Sp 60	18
Fabric, Interiors	Doubleface Twill (Constance LaLena)		√	> 4	Hw	5	2		M/A 84	64, 102
Fabric, Interiors	Doup Leno	Skowronski, Hella; Sylvia Tacker	√	√	TM			4	A/M 86	56
Fabric, Interiors	Draperies for a Synagogue		√		H&C	9	4		Fa 58	45
Fabric, Interiors	Drapery by Dorothy Piercy		√	√	H&C	15	1		Wi 64	35
Fabric, Interiors	Drapery Fabric, Fabric #1 (Constance LaLena)		√	√	Hw	5	5		N/D 84	33, I-5
Fabric, Interiors	Eight-Harness Drapery from the Loom of Doris Cochran		√	> 4	H&C	13	2		Sp 62	11
Fabric, Interiors	Ellen Siegel, Designer for the Handloom and Power Loom		√		H&C	15	1		Wi 64	6
Fabric, Interiors	Emphasis on Handwoven Fabrics in the Architect's Design		√		H&C	6	1		Wi 54	20
Fabric, Interiors	Exercises in Color		√	√	H&C	16	2		Sp 65	36
Fabric, Interiors	Fabric 2 Accessories or Upholstery (Constance LaLena)		√	√	Hw	8	2		M/A 87	52, I-9
Fabric, Interiors	Fabric 3 Accessories or Upholstery (Constance LaLena)		√	√	Hw	8	2		M/A 87	52, I-10
Fabric, Interiors	Fabric 4 Coverlet/Bedspread Fabric (Constance LaLena)		√	√	Hw	8	2		M/A 87	52, I-10
Fabric, Interiors	Fabrics for a Country Kitchen	LaLena, Constance	√		Hw	6	4		S/O 85	46
Fabric, Interiors	Fabrics for a Glasshouse	Uhlmann, Ilse Etta	√		H&C	9	2		Sp 58	49
Fabric, Interiors	Fabrics for Interiors	VanSlyke, Gail Rutter		√	WJ	3	1	9	Jy 78	5

SUBJECT	TITLE	AUTHOR	IL	INST	JOUR	VOL	NO	ISS	DATE	PAGE
Fabric, Interiors	Fabrics for Interiors 10	LaLena, Constance	√	√	Hw	8	2		M/A 87	52
Fabric, Interiors	Fabrics for Interiors 2	LaLena, Constance	√		Hw	4	1		J/F 83	66
Fabric, Interiors	Fabrics for Interiors 3	LaLena, Constance	√		Hw	4	3		M/J 83	50
Fabric, Interiors	Fabrics for Interiors 4: Tartan for a Child's Room	LaLena, Constance	√		Hw	4	5		N/D 83	70
Fabric, Interiors	Fabrics for Interiors 8	LaLena, Constance	√		Hw	6	4		S/O 85	46
Fabric, Interiors	Fabrics for Interiors 9: Contemporary Damask Fabrics for a Bedroom	LaLena, Constance	√		Hw	7	2		M/A 86	64
Fabric, Interiors	Fabrics from a Prairie Loom		√		H&C	4	2		Sp 53	30
Fabric, Interiors	Fabrics from Karen Bulow's Looms	Storey, Walter Rendell	√		H&C	5	1		Wi 53	14
Fabric, Interiors	Fabrics to the Fore in Homefurnishings		√		H&C	3	3		Su 52	30
Fabric, Interiors	Fiberglas Designs		√		H&C	19	3		Su 68	32
Fabric, Interiors	Fiberglas Fabrics		√		H&C	15	4		Fa 64	5
Fabric, Interiors	Fiberworks and Interior Decorating	Rau, Joanne	√		SS&D	13	1	49	Wi 81	45
Fabric, Interiors	Frances van Hall	Bryan, Dorothy	√		H&C	11	2		Sp 60	43
Fabric, Interiors	From California, Double Woven Fabrics for Varied Uses	Bryan, Dorothy	√	√	H&C	12	3		Su 61	6
Fabric, Interiors	Goose-eye Twill (Constance LaLena)		√	√	Hw	5	2		M/A 84	63, 100
Fabric, Interiors	Hand Towelling #5 (Constance LaLena)		√	√	Hw	6	4		S/O 85	46, I-6
Fabric, Interiors	Handweaver Plans an Interior, A	Bryan, Dorothy	√		H&C	6	1		Wi 54	8
Fabric, Interiors	Handweaver's Place in the U. S. Textile Market, The	Kaufmann, Edgar, Jr.	√		H&C	5	4		Fa 54	11
Fabric, Interiors	Handweaving in Effective Settings	Bryan, Dorothy	√		H&C	12	1		Wi 61	10
Fabric, Interiors	Handweaving in Period and Contemporary Interiors	Bryan, Dorothy	√		H&C	4	4		Fa 53	16
Fabric, Interiors	Handwoven Fabrics: Accents of Distinction in Interior Design	Storey, Walter Rendell	√		H&C	4	1		Wi 52	4
Fabric, Interiors	Handwoven Fabrics in New Ships		√		H&C	9	4		Fa 58	19
Fabric, Interiors	Handwoven Fabrics on the High Seas	Ames, Helen B.	√		H&C	2	2		Sp 51	9
Fabric, Interiors	Hella Skowronski		√		H&C	11	4		Fa 60	18
Fabric, Interiors	Historic Textiles for Contemporary Spaces	Lonier, Terri	√		Fa	12	1		J/F 85	64
Fabric, Interiors	Houndstooth Doubleweave (Kathryn Wertenberger)		√	√	Hw	5	2		M/A 84	66, 103
Fabric, Interiors	Interview with Jack Lenor Larsen		√		WJ	7	1	25	Su 82	10
Fabric, Interiors	Isabel Scott Fabrics		√		H&C	9	1		Wi 57	8
Fabric, Interiors	Isabel Scott, Handweaver and Designer	Storey, Walter Rendell	√		H&C	4	2		Sp 53	14
Fabric, Interiors	Jack Lenor Larsen		√		SS&D	15	4	60	Fa 84	22
Fabric, Interiors	Jack Lenor Larsen		√		H&C	11	2		Sp 60	22
Fabric, Interiors	James and Marie Howell, Designers		√		H&C	10	2		Sp 59	11
Fabric, Interiors	Julia Keiner, Brings Fabrics from Israel		√		H&C	15	2		Sp 64	22
Fabric, Interiors	Kjeld Juul-Hansen		√		H&C	9	2		Sp 58	29
Fabric, Interiors	Klara Cherepov, A Career in Two Countries	Landis, Bruce	√		H&C	18	3		Su 67	19
Fabric, Interiors	Knoll Textiles		√		H&C	9	3		Su 58	12
Fabric, Interiors	Laurie Herrick, Contemporary Weaver and Teacher	Furniss, Frances	√		H&C	18	4		Fa 67	10
Fabric, Interiors	Leno & Borders Curtain (Constance LaLena)		√	√	Hw	5	2		M/A 84	64, 102
Fabric, Interiors	Linen	Shaffer, Christine H.	√		H&C	12	2		Sp 61	29
Fabric, Interiors	Linen and Silk Drapery		√	√	H&C	18	3		Su 67	10
Fabric, Interiors	Made by Machine: Textiles for the Eighties	Harris, Patricia; David Lyon	√		Fa	12	5		S/O 85	34
Fabric, Interiors	Manfred Goldschmidt		√		H&C	11	3		Su 60	20
Fabric, Interiors	Maria Kipp — Her Career as a Weaver	Bryan, Dorothy	√		H&C	3	1		Wi 51	15
Fabric, Interiors	Marianne Granville, Designer with Old World Background	Harvey, Jane	√		H&C	16	4		Fa 65	16

SUBJECT	TITLE	AUTHOR	IL	INST	JOUR	VOL	NO	ISS	DATE	PAGE
Fabric, Interiors	Marianne Strengell, Textile Consultant to Architects	Bemis, Marion Holden	√		H&C	8	1		Wi 56	6
Fabric, Interiors	Marketing Handwoven Fabric for Apparel & Interiors	Alaniz, Leonore	√		WJ	11	4	44	Sp 87	31
Fabric, Interiors	Marli Ehrman		√		H&C	11	2		Sp 60	25
Fabric, Interiors	Martha Pollock	Bryan, Dorothy	√		H&C	7	4		Fa 56	7
Fabric, Interiors	Mat Fabric #3		√	√	Hw	6	4		S/O 85	46, I-5
Fabric, Interiors	Michigan League of Handweavers		√	√	H&C	16	4		Fa 65	4
Fabric, Interiors	Nantucket Looms, Fabrics by Island Weavers in Restored Inn	Chesrown, Melva A.	√		H&C	14	4		Fa 63	6
Fabric, Interiors	Nantucket Looms, Versatile Uses For Island Fabrics		√		H&C	20	2		Sp 69	18
Fabric, Interiors	Native Craftsmen Produce for Nile Hilton Hotel		√		H&C	11	3		Su 60	54
Fabric, Interiors	New Craft Program Will be Given on Nantucket Island		√		H&C	16	1		Wi 65	14
Fabric, Interiors	Northern California Conference	Bryan, Dorothy	√	√	H&C	8	4		Fa 57	28
Fabric, Interiors	Old World Weavers at Work in the New	Kamola, Stephanie	√	√	H&C	7	2		Sp 56	24
Fabric, Interiors	Optic Twill (Constance LaLena)		√	√	Hw	5	2		M/A 84	64, 100
Fabric, Interiors	Patterns from the Weaver's Guild		√	√	H&C	26	5		Oc 75	29
Fabric, Interiors	Persian Handcrafted Items	Brockway, Edith	√		H&C	26	5		Oc 75	16
Fabric, Interiors	Personalized Interiors		√		Hw	5	2		M/A 84	44
Fabric, Interiors	Practical Projects	Plath, Iona	√	√	H&C	15	4		Fa 64	17
Fabric, Interiors	Projects with Cotton		√	√	WJ	4	2	14	Oc 79	28
Fabric, Interiors	Pueblo Deco	Sitko, Jane Bradley	√		SS&D	18	4	72	Fa 87	40
Fabric, Interiors	Rancocas Fabrics		√		H&C	8	2		Sp 57	41
Fabric, Interiors	Robert D. Sailors		√		H&C	16	4		Fa 65	6
Fabric, Interiors	Rocky Mountain Weavers Display Fabrics for the Home	Matty, Norma P.	√		H&C	12	4		Fa 61	9
Fabric, Interiors	Roller Shade for Window, Fabric #1 (Constance LaLena)		√	> 4	Hw	7	2		M/A 86	64, I-12
Fabric, Interiors	Roy Ginstrom, Versatile Handweaver and Designer of Fabrics for Power Looms		√		H&C	13	3		Su 62	6
Fabric, Interiors	Rug, Fabric #1 (Constance LaLena)		√	√	Hw	8	4		S/O 87	36, I-3
Fabric, Interiors	Seat and Back for Director's Chairs (Constance LaLena)		√	√	Hw	4	3		M/J 83	50, 85
Fabric, Interiors	Siminoff Textiles	Trayer, Blanche C.	√		H&C	9	1		Wi 57	18
Fabric, Interiors	Simple Rustic Fabrics for a Den	LaLena, Constance	√		Hw	5	5		N/D 84	33
Fabric, Interiors	Slipcover Fabric #1 (Constance LaLena)		√	> 4	Hw	4	3		M/J 83	50, 85
Fabric, Interiors	Slipcover Fabric #2 (Constance LaLena)		√	> 4	Hw	4	3		M/J 83	50, 85
Fabric, Interiors	Space-Dented Warp	Fry, Laura	√	√	WJ	4	3	15	Ja 80	26
Fabric, Interiors	Studies in Color and Texture through Fabric	Kramer, Helen	√		H&C	6	1		Wi 54	13
Fabric, Interiors	Summer and Winter Accent (Kathryn Wertenberger)		√	> 4	Hw	5	2		M/A 84	66, 104
Fabric, Interiors	Summer Whites	LaLena, Constance	√		Hw	4	3		M/J 83	51
Fabric, Interiors	Susan B. Goldberg		√		H&C	16	4		Fa 65	12
Fabric, Interiors	Textiles in the United Nations Buildings	Blumenau, Lili	√		H&C	4	1		Wi 52	10
Fabric, Interiors	Textiles Related to Wallpapers	Backlin-Landman, Hedy	√		H&C	16	3		Su 65	16
Fabric, Interiors	To Dress Your Room: Dress Your Loom	Shrauger, Carolyn	√		SS&D	7	3	27	Su 76	61
Fabric, Interiors	Trends for Fashionable Interiors	Hick, Susan	√		WJ	7	1	25	Su 82	18
Fabric, Interiors	Trude Guermonprez	Bryan, Dorothy	√		H&C	11	2		Sp 60	30
Fabric, Interiors	Tweed Stripe Upholstery, Fabric #3 (Constance LaLena)		√	√	Hw	5	5		N/D 84	32, I-5
Fabric, Interiors	Tweed Upholstery, Fabric #2 (Constance LaLena)		√	√	Hw	5	5		N/D 84	32, I-5
Fabric, Interiors	Twill Accent Fabrics (Sharon D. Alderman)		√	> 4	Hw	5	2		M/A 84	69, 107

SUBJECT	TITLE	AUTHOR	IL	INST	JOUR	VOL	NO	ISS	DATE	PAGE
Fabric, Interiors	Tzaims Luksus		√		H&C	14	1		Wi 63	12
Fabric, Interiors	Weaving for Interior Spaces: A Reader Notebook		√		Hw	5	2		M/A 84	42
Fabric, Interiors	Weaving with Native Materials	Fuchs, Rudolph	√		H&C	2	4		Fa 51	21
Fabric, Interiors	West Coast Weaving in Modern Interiors	Bryan, Dorothy	√		H&C	3	4		Fa 52	7
Fabric, Interiors	Wool for Sheer Draperies and Upholstery	Frey, Berta	√		H&C	2	4		Fa 51	44
Fabric, Interiors	Woven Wood, Speciality of Robert Webb		√		H&C	16	2		Sp 65	19
Fabric, Interiors	Yardage (Constance LaLena)		√	√	Hw	4	5		N/D 83	70, 102
Fabric, Interiors: Handwoven	Handwoven Fabrics in the S. S. United States		√		H&C	4	1		Wi 52	15
Fabric, Interiors: Selection	Selection of Fabrics for Interiors		√		H&C	10	4		Fa 59	30
Fabric, International	Fabrics International		√		H&C	13	1		Wi 62	6
Fabric, Lampas	Chinese Drawloom: A Study in Weave Structure, The	Sellin, Helen	√	>4	WJ	9	2	34	Fa 84	6
Fabric, Mail-Order Clubs	Another Fabric Club				TM			8	D/J 86	4
Fabric, Marbleized	Sandra Holzman: Marbleized Fabrics	Piucci, Joanna	√		Fa	10	5		S/O 83	21
Fabric: Matelassé	Magic of Matelassé, The	West, Virginia	√	>4	PWC	4	3	13		44
Fabric, Matelassé	Matelasse Double Cloth Stitched to Form the Design	Kelly, Linda	√	>4	WJ	7	1	25	Su 82	43
Fabric, Matelassé	Simple Matelasse by the Pick-Up Method		√	√	WJ	7	1	25	Su 82	40
Fabric, Matelassé	Stitched Double Cloth—Matelassé		√		WJ	7	1	25	Su 82	37
Fabric, Matellassé	Reversible Matelasse Jacket	Champion, Ellen	√	>4	WJ	7	1	25	Su 82	41
Fabric, Metallic	Lamé	Boyce, Ann	√		TM			8	D/J 86	32
Fabric, Multi-Purpose	Swatch #5: Multi-purpose #1 (Sharon Alderman)		√	√	Hw	7	3		M/J 86	28, I-5
Fabric, Multi-Purpose	Swatch #6: Multi-purpose #2 (Sharon Alderman)		√	√	Hw	7	3		M/J 86	28, I-5
Fabric, Multilayered	Multi-Layered Cloths: A Structured Approach	Hoskins, Janet A.	√	>4	AT	1			De 83	137
Fabric, Narrow	Garments from Narrow Fabrics	Davenport, Betty	√	√	Hw	6	2		M/A 85	18
Fabric, Narrow	Put It Together: Large Cloths from Small Looms	Davenport, Betty	√	√	Hw	8	1		J/F 87	73
Fabric, Ornamentation	Fabric Ornamentation	Kaufman, Glen	√		H&C	17	1		Wi 66	14
Fabric, Painted	Ana Lisa Hedstrom: The Intuitive Language Of Shibori	Scarborough, Jessica	√		Fa	13	1		J/F 86	26
Fabric, Painted	Art to Wear — Three Innovators: Cate Fitt, Emma Vesey, Dina Schwartz Knapp		√		Fa	8	1		J/F 81	67
Fabric, Painted	Art Wear of Peggy Juve, The	Tacker, Sylvia	√		Fa	14	1		J/F 87	25
Fabric, Painted	Artist's Need for Needlework, An	Benanti, Gigi	√		TM			9	F/M 87	20
Fabric, Painted	Barbara Smith: Views from Within	Lucas, Jane	√		Fa	10	5		S/O 83	18
Fabric, Painted	Conflict Resolved: The Hows and Whys of Hand-Dyed Relief Painting, A	Kroetsch, Glenn	√		Fa	8	4		J/A 81	13
Fabric, Painted	Connie McEntire Lehman's Side Glances from Drawings Into Dye-Painted Hangings	Clurman, Irene	√		Fa	8	5		S/O 81	26
Fabric, Painted	Conversation with Claire Zeisler, A	Koplos, Janet	√		Fa	10	4		J/A 83	25
Fabric, Painted	Fabric Painting in India: The Kalamkaris of J. Gurappa Chetty	Lintault, M. Joan	√		Fa	9	1		J/F 82	64
Fabric, Painted	Fabric Painting in New York	Katz, Ruth J.	√		Fa	9	1		J/F 82	61
Fabric, Painted	Fashionable Palette of Pittsburgh Paints, The	Brenholts, Jeanne	√		Fa	14	3		M/J 87	46
Fabric, Painted	Floats of Fancy	Woelfle, Gretchen	√		Fa	8	2		M/A 81	52
Fabric, Painted	Fondness for Rabbits: Nancy Erickson's Quilts Deliver a Serious Message in a Soft Medium, A		√		Fa	8	6		N/D 81	17
Fabric, Painted	Fraas—Slade: Painted Views	Reith, Stephanie	√		Fa	8	5		S/O 81	32
Fabric, Painted	Funeral	Knauer, Katherine	√		Fa	13	6		N/D 86	30
Fabric, Painted	"Gail Skudera: Textile Paintings" (Exhibit)	Koplos, Janet	√		Fa	9	6		N/D 82	84
Fabric, Painted	Hand-Painted Silk	Jaffie, H. R.	√		Fa	10	5		S/O 83	17

SUBJECT	TITLE	AUTHOR	IL	INST	JOUR	VOL	NO	ISS	DATE	PAGE
Fabric, Painted	Images in Sharpe Focus: Susan Sharpe's Quilts Are Drawn, Painted and Stitched	Jernigan, Bonnie	√		Fa	10	2		M/A 83	19
Fabric, Painted	Improvs on Silk: The Fabric Painting of Susan Daniel	Fitt, Cate	√		Fa	8	5		S/O 81	45
Fabric, Painted	"Jacque Parsley: Avallon Series" (Exhibit)	Anderson, Ann Stewart	√		Fa	9	5		S/O 82	82
Fabric, Painted	Janice Anthony's Contemporary Quilts	Henderson, Stew	√		Fa	13	4		J/A 86	22
Fabric, Painted	Jerri Finch-Hurley: Quilted Paintings	Wonder, Danny	√		Fa	11	2		M/A 84	27
Fabric, Painted	Julia Hill: Art and Textile Lab	Lancaster, Zöe Woodruff	√		Fa	12	3		M/J 85	11
Fabric, Painted	Just Playing in Space: Ann McKenzie Nickolson's Textile Artwork	Koplos, Janet	√		Fa	8	2		M/A 81	34
Fabric, Painted	Kate Woolstenhulme: A Sense of Place	Walters, Roberta	√		Fa	10	2		M/A 83	56
Fabric, Painted	Lenore Davis: Figuring in Cloth	Frasier, Debra	√		Fa	10	5		S/O 83	10
Fabric, Painted	Lia Cook: Exploring the Territory Where Painting and Textiles Meet	Alexander, Judy	√		Fa	9	5		S/O 82	28
Fabric, Painted	Linda Levin: Quilted Impressions	Goodman, Deborah Lerme	√		Fa	14	2		M/A 87	13
Fabric, Painted	"Maine Coast Artists: Fabrications" (Exhibit)	Beem, Edgar Allen	√		Fa	11	4		J/A 84	80
Fabric, Painted	Making Fabric Flowers	Ritch, Diane; Yoshiko Iwamoto Wada	√	√	TM			13	O/N 87	68
Fabric, Painted	Martin Peavy: An Improvisational Approach to Rugs	Peavy, Martin	√		Fa	11	3		M/J 84	22
Fabric, Painted	Merry Holoien: A Harmony of Color and Sound	Ormseth, Laurie	√		Fa	13	2		M/A 86	6
Fabric, Painted	"Michael Olszewski: Pleated and Stitched Silk" (Exhibit)	Poon, Vivian	√		Fa	11	3		M/J 84	78
Fabric, Painted	Painted Cloth Gardens on Wheels	Wilcox, Don	√		TM			9	F/M 87	18
Fabric, Painted	Painted Muslin Ghost Dance Costumes of the Sioux, C–1890	Wakeland, Robin	√		Fa	8	1		J/F 81	15
Fabric, Painted	Painted Surface, The (error-corrected Fa v9 n4 82 p9)		√		Fa	9	3		M/J 82	64
Fabric, Painted	Painted-Silk Clothing	Juve, Peggy	√	√	TM			12	A/S 87	24
Fabric, Painted	Pittsburg Artists Create Kimono Canvases		√		Fa	13	3		M/J 86	7
Fabric, Painted	"Rose Kelly: Printed, Painted and Woven Textiles" (Exhibit)	Small, Deborah	√		Fa	9	6		N/D 82	84
Fabric, Painted	Sampler of Surface Design, A	Westphal, Katherine	√		Fa	10	5		S/O 83	39
Fabric, Painted	Sensuous Silk: Cedrus Monte's Painted Silk Garments	Gilliland, David	√		Fa	8	1		J/F 81	17
Fabric, Painted	Soft Boxes: Ritual for Our Common Life	McElroy, Jane	√		Fa	10	2		M/A 83	21
Fabric, Painted	Stitched, Stuffed, and Painted: The Art of Esther Luttikhuizen	Acosta, Dan	√		Fa	12	2		M/A 85	61
Fabric, Painted	Surface Designers Meet in Nantucket	Northup, Wendy			TM			9	F/M 87	16
Fabric, Painted	Therese May: Risking to Grow	Scarborough, Jessica	√		Fa	12	4		J/A 85	15
Fabric, Painted	Wear an Original Painting: Melody Weiler's Airbrushed Shirtscapes	Speight, Jerry	√	√	Fa	8	1		J/F 81	13
Fabric, Painted: Airbrush	Jerri Finch-Hurley	Finch-Hurley, Jerri	√		Fa	13	1		J/F 86	18
Fabric, Painted: Chintz, Cotton	Preliminary Report on a Group of Important Mughal Textiles, A	Smart, Ellen S.	√		TMJ	25			86	5
Fabric, Painted: Cotton	Lenten Curtains from Colonial Peru	Kelemen, Pál	√		TMJ	3	1		De 70	5
Fabric, Painted, Resist	"Art to Wear" (Exhibit)	Murray, Megan	√		Fa	11	1		J/F 84	76
Fabric, Painting	K. Lee Manuel: Wearable Dreams		√		Fa	3	5		S/O 76	12
Fabric, Paper	Paper Clothing, East	Sahlstrand, Margaret	√	√	Fa	11	2		M/A 84	36
Fabric, Paper	Shifu: A Handwoven Paper Textile of Japan	Miller, Dorothy	√	√	AT	4			De 85	43
Fabric, Period	By the Yard	Mattera, Joanne	√		TM			5	J/J 86	50
Fabric, Period: 18th Century	Eighteenth Century Mollie Costume	Spray, Kathy	√		WJ	6	3	23	Wi 81	38
Fabric, Pictorial	"In Praise of Heroes" (Exhibit)	Malarcher, Patricia	√		Fa	10	1		J/F 83	78
Fabric, Printed	Adinkra: Weft African Textile of Pride	Rex, Chris	√		Fa	9	6		N/D 82	36
Fabric, Printed	Behind the Scenes: A Fabric Printer	Lancaster, Zoe Woodruff	√		Fa	13	3		M/J 86	44

SUBJECT	TITLE	AUTHOR	IL	INST	JOUR	VOL	NO	ISS	DATE	PAGE
Fabric, Printed	Maridadi West: A Fort Collins, Colorado Fabric Design Studio with Its Roots in East Africa	Mattera, Joanne	√		Fa	9	2		M/A 82	24
Fabric, Printed	Marvelous Mezzaro, The	Wasiqullah, Alexandra	√		Fa	10	5		S/O 83	29
Fabric, Printed	Printed Fabric: Another View		√		Fa	9	1		J/F 82	100
Fabric, Printed	Rubber Stamping on Fabric	Goodman, Deborah Lerme	√		Fa	13	2		M/A 86	38
Fabric, Printed	Southwestern Rhythms of Harwood Steiger Fabrics, The	Beeaff, Dianne Ebertt	√		Fa	13	2		M/A 86	29
Fabric, Printed	"Splendor of French Style, The" Textiles from Joan of Arc to Napoleon III (Exhibit)	Guagliumi, Susan	√		Fa	13	4		J/A 86	13
Fabric, Printed	Textile Arts of India	Bernier, Ronald M.	√		WJ	2	1	5	Jy 77	31
Fabric, Printing	Limited-Edition Vests	Stocksdale, Joy	√	√	TM			4	A/M 86	60
Fabric, Printing	Surface Attraction	Mattera, Joanne	√		TM			7	O/N 86	20
Fabric Printing: Natural Dyes	Printing with Natural Dyes: An Historical Perspective		√		Hw	3	5		N/D 82	66
Fabric, Qotny, Stripe	Qotny & Alaga: Traditional Striped Fabrics for the Middle Eastern Kaftan	El-Homossani, M. M.	√	> 4	WJ	10	1	37	Su 85	33
Fabric, Quality	On Making Good Cloth	Darwall, Randall	√		Hw	7	5		N/D 86	22
Fabric, Quilted	Art to Wear — Three Innovators: Cate Fitt, Emma Vesey, Dina Schwartz Knapp		√		Fa	8	1		J/F 81	67
Fabric, Quilted	Heritage Project: Quilted Vest, A	King, Lorna J.	√	√	WJ	4	3	15	Ja 80	28
Fabric, Ramie	Miyako Jofu	Miller, Dorothy	√	√	AT	7			Ju 87	85
Fabric, Silk	China and the Complexities of Weaving Technologies	Vollmer, John E.			AT	5			Ju 86	65
Fabric, Smoked	Flourishing Art: China, Guizhou Women Continue to Embroider Their Legends, A	Rossi, Gail	√		TM			9	F/M 87	30
Fabric Stabilizer	So There Is a Use for Fancy Machine Stitches	Richter, Elizabeth Lee	√	√	TM			11	J/J 87	62
Fabric Strips: Preparation	Two Block Rug in Boundweave	Waggoner, Phyllis	√	√	WJ	12	1	45	Su 87	26
Fabric Structure: Classification and Terminology	After Emery: Further Considerations of Fabric Classification and Terminology	Rowe, Ann Pollard	√		TMJ	23			84	53
Fabric Structures	"Cloth Forms" (Exhibits)	Skudera, Gail	√		Fa	9	4		J/A 82	76
Fabric Swatches	Millions of Swatches at FIT	Kennedy, Alan			TM			11	J/J 87	18
Fabric, Synthetic	Hot-Air Balloons	Theil, Linda	√		TM			4	A/M 86	20
Fabric, Synthetic	Imitating the Silkworm	Stetson, G. Robert; Cathy Shufro; Dennis Danaher	√		TM			5	J/J 86	42
Fabric, Synthetic	Polyester in Japan	Wasserman, Andrea Stix	√		TM			5	J/J 86	20
Fabric, Towelling	Fabric #5 Towels (Constance LaLena)		√	√	Hw	8	2		M/A 87	52, I-10
Fabric, Two-Faced	Notebook: One Fabric — Two Faces	Myers, Ruth Nordquist	√	> 4	SS&D	13	2	50	Sp 82	16
Fabric, Two-Warp	Double Weaves: Two-Warp Fabrics	Zielinski, S. A.; Robert Leclerc, ed.	√	√	MWL	15			'51–'73	16
Fabric, Two-Warp	Double Weaves: Two-Warp Weaves	Zielinski, S. A.; Robert Leclerc, ed.	√	√	MWL	15			'51–'73	17
Fabric Types: 1-Plane, Primary	Multi-Layered Cloths: A Structured Approach	Hoskins, Janet A.	√	> 4	AT	1			De 83	137
Fabric Types: 2-Planes, Secondary	Multi-Layered Cloths: A Structured Approach	Hoskins, Janet A.	√	> 4	AT	1			De 83	137
Fabric Types: 3-Planes, Ternary	Multi-Layered Cloths: A Structured Approach	Hoskins, Janet A.	√	> 4	AT	1			De 83	137
Fabric Types: 4-Planes, Quatenary	Multi-Layered Cloths: A Structured Approach	Hoskins, Janet A.	√	> 4	AT	1			De 83	137
Fabric, Upholstery	Upholstery Fabric 1 (Constance LaLena)		√	√	Hw	3	4		Se 82	33, 84
Fabric, Upholstery	Basket Squares (Virginia West)		√	√	Hw	5	2		M/A 84	74, 94
Fabric, Upholstery	Bedford Cord Upholstery (Kathryn Wertenberger)		√	√	Hw	5	2		M/A 84	66, 104
Fabric, Upholstery	Color Related Decorating Textiles Rugs, Draperies, Upholstery: Upholstery Fabrics	Rhodes, Tonya Stalons; Harriet Tidball, ed.			SCGM		14		65	6

SUBJECT	TITLE	AUTHOR	IL	INST	JOUR	VOL	NO	ISS	DATE	PAGE
Fabric, Upholstery	Contemporary Satins: An Alphabet of Satin Designs	Tidball, Harriet	√	> 4	SCGM		7		62	22
Fabric, Upholstery	Corded Weaves: Four Harness Cords for Upholstery Fabric, Drapery Material and Wallhangings		√	√	WJ	3	1	9	Jy 78	28
Fabric, Upholstery	Custom Fabrics for a Classic Cadillac	Kelly, Jacquie	√	> 4	WJ	10	4	40	Sp 86	54
Fabric, Upholstery	Designing Satisfactory Upholstery Fabrics		√		H&C	4	1		Wi 52	20
Fabric, Upholstery	Desk Chair with Subtle Plaid Pattern	Lohse, Joyce	√	√	WJ	7	1	25	Su 82	24
Fabric, Upholstery	Eight Shaft Warp Rep Honeycomb (Virginia West)		√	> 4	Hw	5	2		M/A 84	72, 95
Fabric, Upholstery	Fabric #1: Upholstery Fabric (Constance LaLena)		√	√	Hw	6	3		Su 85	62, I-4
Fabric, Upholstery	Fabric #2: Upholstery Fabric (Constance LaLena)		√	√	Hw	6	3		Su 85	62, I-4
Fabric, Upholstery	Fabrics for Interiors	VanSlyke, Gail Rutter		√	WJ	3	1	9	Jy 78	5
Fabric, Upholstery	Grouped Warp Threads	Davison, Marguerite Porter	√	√	H&C	26	3		M/J 75	24
Fabric, Upholstery	Honeycomb Upholstery (Constance LaLena)		√	> 4	Hw	4	1		J/F 83	66, 91
Fabric, Upholstery	Mattweave Upholstery (Sharon D. Alderman)		√	√	Hw	5	2		M/A 84	68, 105
Fabric, Upholstery	Michigan Weaving, Third Conference at Hartland Shows Wide Variety		√	> 4	H&C	13	1		Wi 62	18
Fabric, Upholstery	New Method for Pile Weave, A	Deru, Crescent	√	√	H&C	8	3		Su 57	16
Fabric, Upholstery	Nubby Upholstery (Kathryn Wertenberger)		√	> 4	Hw	5	2		M/A 84	66, 103
Fabric, Upholstery	On Handwoven Upholstery	Ligon, Linda	√	> 4	Hw	3	2		Mr 82	58
Fabric, Upholstery	Overshot Upholstery (Sharon Alderman) (error-corrected Hw v3 n3 82 p87)		√	√	Hw	3	1		Ja 82	69, 82
Fabric, Upholstery	Plain Weave Upholstery (Kathryn Wertenberger)		√	√	Hw	5	2		M/A 84	66, 104
Fabric, Upholstery	Plaited Twills		√	> 4	WJ	7	4	28	Sp 83	76
Fabric, Upholstery	Pleated Curtain (Kathryn Wertenberger)		√	√	Hw	5	2		M/A 84	67, 104
Fabric, Upholstery	Pueblo Deco	Sitko, Jane Bradley	√		SS&D	18	4	72	Fa 87	40
Fabric, Upholstery	Right Side or Wrong — Hard to Tell		√		H&C	2	4		Fa 51	24
Fabric, Upholstery	Seat for All Seasons, A	Rasmussen, Peg	√	√	WJ	6	2	22	Fa 81	21
Fabric, Upholstery	Simply Elegant Upholstery Fabric (Sharon Alderman)		√	> 4	Hw	6	1		J/F 85	32, I-6
Fabric, Upholstery	Smart and Simple (Virginia West)		√	√	Hw	5	2		M/A 84	74, 94
Fabric, Upholstery	Spot Bronson (Virginia West)		√	√	Hw	5	2		M/A 84	74, 94
Fabric, Upholstery	Striped Upholstery, Fabric #3 (Constance LaLena)		√	√	Hw	8	4		S/O 87	36, I-4
Fabric, Upholstery	Syncopated Log Cabin (Virginia West)		√	√	Hw	5	2		M/A 84	72, 94
Fabric, Upholstery	Textiles Designed for Contemporary Furniture		√		H&C	12	2		Sp 61	17
Fabric, Upholstery	Tickweave Upholstery (Sharon D. Alderman)		√	√	Hw	5	2		M/A 84	68, 105
Fabric, Upholstery	Twill on Twill (Virginia West)		√	> 4	Hw	5	2		M/A 84	72, 94
Fabric, Upholstery	Twill Upholstery Fabric (Constance LaLena)		√	√	Hw	4	1		J/F 83	66, 91
Fabric, Upholstery	Undulating Twill Upholstery (Sharon Alderman)		√	√	Hw	3	1		Ja 82	69, 82
Fabric, Upholstery	Unusual Upholstery from Discarded Stockings	Ross, Marjorie Ruth	√	√	H&C	8	2		Sp 57	47
Fabric, Upholstery	Upholstery	Wendler, Maxine	√	√	WJ	7	1	25	Su 82	22
Fabric, Upholstery	Upholstery and Accent Fabric #4 (Constance LaLena)		√	√	Hw	8	4		S/O 87	36, I-4
Fabric, Upholstery	Upholstery and Bed Covering Fabric, Fabric #3 (Constance LaLena)		√	> 4	Hw	7	2		M/A 86	64, I-12
Fabric, Upholstery	Upholstery Fabric 2 (Constance LaLena)		√	> 4	Hw	3	4		Se 82	33, 84

SUBJECT	TITLE	AUTHOR	IL	INST	JOUR	VOL	NO	ISS	DATE	PAGE
Fabric, Upholstery	Upholstery Fabric (Constance LaLena)		√	√	Hw	4	5		N/D 83	70, 102
Fabric, Upholstery	Upholstery Fabric, Fabric #2 (Constance LaLena)		√	>4	Hw	7	2		M/A 86	64, I-12
Fabric, Upholstery	Upholstery Fabric (Sharon Alderman)		√	√	Hw	1	1		F-W 79	42, 61
Fabric, Upholstery	Upholstery or Cushion, Fabric #2 (Constance LaLena)		√	√	Hw	8	4		S/O 87	36, I-3
Fabric, Upholstery	Weaver's Notebook		√	√	SS&D	9	4	36	Fa 78	100
Fabric, Upholstery	Weaver's Notebook		√	√	SS&D	9	4	36	Fa 78	101
Fabric, Upholstery	Weaver's Notebook		√	√	SS&D	10	1	37	Wi 78	33
Fabric, Upholstery	Weaving Upholstery, The Qualities of a Sound Fabric	Regensteiner, Else	√		H&C	14	1		Wi 63	10
Fabric, Upholstery, Automobile	Handloom in the Automobile Industry, The	Clement, Doris	√		H&C	10	3		Su 59	61
Fabric, Vadmal	Vadmal: A Study Group from the Frozen North Warms Up to an Ancient Technique	Larson-Fleming, Susan	√	√	WJ	10	3	39	Wi 86	26
Fabric, Very Wide	Peru, Textiles Unlimited: Textile Characteristics, Very Wide Fabrics	Tidball, Harriet	√		SCGM		25	68		20
Fabric, Window Coverings	Color Related Decorating Textiles Rugs, Draperies, Upholstery: Drapery and Casement Fabrics, Weaving Six Yards of Drapery	Rhodes, Tonya Stalons; Harriet Tidball, ed.		√	SCGM		14	65		9
Fabric, Window Coverings	Color Related Decorating Textiles Rugs, Draperies, Upholstery: The Textile Designs	Rhodes, Tonya Stalons; Harriet Tidball, ed.			SCGM		14	65		10
Fabric, Xerography	Color Xerography and the Fiber Artist	Theil, Linda	√		Fa	8	5		S/O 81	59
Fabric-Strip Hooking	Chromatic Effervescence: The Hooked Surface As a Response to My Environment	Eyerman, Linda	√		Fa	10	2		M/A 83	22
Fabric-Strip Weaving	Annikki Karvinen: Finnish Designer of Wovens	Talley, Charles	√		Fa	13	4		J/A 86	16
Fabric-Strip Weaving	Beyond Rags: Fabric Strip Design	Larson-Fleming, Susan	√	√	WJ	9	4	36	Sp 85	47
Fabric-Strip Weaving	California Rags	Saulson, Sarah F.	√	√	SS&D	18	1	69	Wi 86	44
Fabric-Strip Weaving	Glad Rags	Wroten, Barbara	√	√	SS&D	15	4	60	Fa 84	28
Fabric-Strip Weaving	Margrit Schmidtke: An Evolving Artist	Schmidtke, Sheila	√		Fa	13	5		S/O 86	42
Fabric-Strip Weaving	No More Hot Hands—A Handwoven Skillet Holder!		√	√	Hw	8	3		M/J 87	23
Fabric-Strip Weaving	Poppana!		√	√	Hw	8	3		M/J 87	74
Fabric-Strip Weaving	Rag Rugs, Not Always Made from Rags	Erickson, Johanna	√	√	TM			3	F/M 86	40
Fabric-Strip Weaving	Rags to Riches: Jackets from Rags	Brones, Britta	√	√	WJ	6	3	23	Wi 81	31
Fabric-Strip Weaving	Ribbon Wefts	Sewell, Suzy	√	>4	WJ	10	3	39	Wi 86	40
Fabric-Strip Weaving	Summer and Winter Poppana Table Mat (Janice Jones)		√	√	Hw	8	5		N/D 87	87, I-16
Fabric-Strip Weaving	Two Block Rug in Boundweave	Waggoner, Phyllis	√	√	WJ	12	1	45	Su 87	26
Fabric/Acoustics	Judit Kele: The Sound of the Way It Feels	Colton, Sarah	√		Fa	14	3		M/J 87	42
Facings	Let's Face It!	Bradley, Louise	√	√	Hw	8	1		J/F 87	34
Fading: Textiles	Ultraviolet Absorbers: A Treatment To Reduce Fading and Degradation of Textiles	Crews, Patricia Cox; Barbara M. Reagan			AT	8			De 87	43
Failure	My Success Is Absolutely Assured	Chandler, Deborah	√		Hw	7	1		J/F 86	23
Fair Isle Knitting	Fair Isle in Natural Colors, The	Gibson-Roberts, Priscilla A.	√	√	Kn	2	1	3	F-W 85	34
Fair Isle Knitting	Fair Isle Knitting	Starmore, Alice	√	√	TM			8	D/J 86	44
Fair Isle Knitting	Garden of Fair Isles, A	Rowe, Mary	√	√	Kn	2	1	3	F-W 85	40, 8B
Fair Isle Knitting	Little Knitting on the Side, A	Glover, Medrith	√	√	Kn	2	1	3	F-W 85	38
Fair Isle Knitting	Methods for Multicolored Knitting	Righetti, Maggie	√	√	TM			6	A/S 86	40
Fair Isle Knitting	Notes of a Textile Sleuth	Upitis, Lizbeth	√	√	Kn	2	1	3	F-W 85	22
Fair Isle Knitting	Opinionated Knitter, The	Zimmermann, Elizabeth			Kn	2	1	3	F-W 85	8
Fair Isle Knitting	Traditional Fair Isle Sweater	Upitis, Lizbeth	√	√	Kn	2	1	3	F-W 85	26, 8B
Fair Isle Knitting: Machine	Appropriate Designs for Short-Row and Slip Intarsia	Guagliumi, Susan	√	√	TM			10	A/M 87	70

SUBJECT	TITLE	AUTHOR	IL	INST	JOUR	VOL	NO	ISS	DATE	PAGE
Fairs	Future Weavers	Holroyd, Ruth N.	√		SS&D	2	3	7	Su 71	13
Fairs	Handweaving from Many Countries at the International Trade Fair	Brophil, Gladys Rogers	√		H&C	1	3		Fa 50	31
Fairs	Textile Equipment & Inventions Fair	Utzinger, Karen	√		SS&D	3	2	10	Sp 72	44
Fairs	Two Hundred Years of Textile Crafts	Strickler, Carol	√		Iw	1	3		Sp 76	26
Fairs	World's Fair, New York				H&C	15	3		Su 64	23
Fairs	York State Craftsmen				H&C	20	2		Sp 69	38
Fairs: Crafts	Abbey of Regina Laudis, O.S.B. from Notes of the Abbey Community		√		SS&D	16	3	63	Su 85	42
Fairs: Crafts	Come to the Fair				SS&D	1	3	3	Ju 70	11
Fame and Fortune	Theme Issue		√		Fa	9	5		S/O 82	
Fannin Weaving Mill	Determination and Innovation: A Successful Weaving Mill	Fago, D'Ann Calhoun	√		TM			14	D/J 87	14
Fans	Fanfare: Fans from the Collection of the National Museum of American Art (Exhibit)	Perry, Pamela	√		Fa	12	6		N/D 85	48
Fans	Paper Art of Fritzi Huber Morrison, The	Kosta, Angela	√		Fa	11	2		M/A 84	22
Fans	Pieces of History	Meyers, Judith Philipp	√		Fa	14	5		N/D 87	54
Fans	"Show of Fans, A" (Exhibit)	Goodman, Deborah Lerme	√		Fa	12	6		N/D 85	56
Fans, Contemporary	Fans and Fan Imagery	Howe, Katherine; Joanne Mattera	√		Fa	9	4		J/A 82	26
Faroe Islands	Faroese Shawls	Swansen, Meg	√	√	Kn	4	1	9	Wi 87	26
Fashion	Albertje Koopman		√		Hw	4	1		J/F 83	56
Fashion	"Art Couture VII" (Exhibit)	Guagliumi, Susan Fletcher	√		Fa	12	3		M/J 85	78
Fashion	Art to Wear — Three Innovators: Cate Fitt, Emma Vesey, Dina Schwartz Knapp		√		Fa	8	1		J/F 81	67
Fashion	Choli Comfort		√	√	Hw	6	3		Su 85	54
Fashion	Contemporary American Handweaving from an International Perspective	Alaniz, Leonore	√		WJ	11	3	43	Wi 87	26
Fashion	Cool and Casual Cotton		√		Hw	6	3		Su 85	42
Fashion	"Design's on You" Contest Winners	Scorgie, Jean	√		Hw	8	4		S/O 87	31
Fashion	"Evolution of Fashion, 1909–1919, The" (Exhibit)		√		Fa	8	1		J/F 81	92
Fashion	Fashionable Palette of Pittsburgh Paints, The	Brenholts, Jeanne	√		Fa	14	3		M/J 87	46
Fashion	Fashionable Threads		√		SS&D	8	4	32	Fa 77	70
Fashion	Fiesta! Wear!		√		Hw	6	3		Su 85	41
Fashion	Garments from the Loom: Handweaver Randall Darwall Focuses on the Cloth	Mattera, Joanne	√		Fa	10	1		J/F 83	20
Fashion	Handwoven Clothing Today: The Couturier Touch	West, Virginia	√		Fa	8	1		J/F 81	39
Fashion	Knitted Palette of Brenda French, The	Pierce, Judith	√		Fa	13	2		M/A 86	43
Fashion	Marketing Handwoven Fabric for Apparel & Interiors	Alaniz, Leonore	√		WJ	11	4	44	Sp 87	31
Fashion	Ole! Summer Fun		√		Hw	6	3		Su 85	52
Fashion	Our Time Has Come	Lott, Gwynne			WJ	2	3	7	Ja 78	3
Fashion	Paris Museum Surveys Fashion	Colton, Sarah	√		Fa	14	3		M/J 87	6
Fashion	Party Ensemble with Style		√	√	Hw	6	3		Su 85	44
Fashion	Relax...in Comfort and Style		√		Hw	6	3		Su 85	50
Fashion	Return of the Rag, The	Basa, Lynn	√		Fa	14	3		M/J 87	29
Fashion	Santa Fe Weaving Center, The	Elliott, Malinda	√		Fa	9	5		S/O 82	32
Fashion	Sensuous Silk: Cedrus Monte's Painted Silk Garments	Gilliland, David	√		Fa	8	1		J/F 81	17
Fashion	Simply Elegant		√	√	Hw	6	3		Su 85	46
Fashion	"Splendor of French Style, The" Textiles from Joan of Arc to Napoleon III (Exhibit)	Guagliumi, Susan	√		Fa	13	4		J/A 86	13
Fashion	"Splendor of French Style, The" Textiles from Joan of Arc to Napoleon III (Exhibit)	Guagliumi, Susan	√		Fa	13	4		J/A 86	13

SUBJECT	TITLE	AUTHOR	IL	INST	JOUR	VOL	NO	ISS	DATE	PAGE
Fashion	Spring!		√	√	Hw	8	2		M/A 87	55
Fashion	Surface Design and the Garment Form	Reith, Stephanie J.	√		Fa	8	1		J/F 81	34
Fashion	Timelessness and Style ... Select a Pattern for Handwoven Fabric (error-corrected WJ v6 n1 81 p28d)	Davis, Helen B.	√		WJ	5	3	19	Wi 81	6
Fashion	Wear an Original Painting: Melody Weiler's Airbrushed Shirtscapes	Speight, Jerry	√	√	Fa	8	1		J/F 81	13
Fashion	"Yves Saint Laurent: 25 Years of Design" (Exhibit)	Lonier, Terri	√		Fa	12	1		J/F 85	76
Fashion	Yvonne Porcella: A Modern Master of the Ethnic Clothing Tradition	Avery, Virginia	√		Fa	8	1		J/F 81	63
Fashion Arts	"Fashion and Surrealism" (Exhibit)		√		TM			14	D/J 87	16
Fashion Collections	Ana Rossell: Weaving with Flair for C. A. R. E.	Ligon, Linda	√		Iw	3	1		Fa 77	18
Fashion Collections	Crane Day Designs	Colton, Mary Rawcliffe	√		SS&D	18	2	70	Sp 87	48
Fashion Collections	Deborah Ann Abbott: Power Loom Weaving on a New Hampshire Farm	Mattera, Joanne	√		Fa	9	1		J/F 82	35
Fashion Collections	From the Collection of Anne Poussart		√	√	WJ	7	3	27	Wi 82	62
Fashion Collections	Keeping Tradition Alive	Wilcox, Don	√		Fa	14	1		J/F 87	44
Fashion Collections	Lee Carlin: Handweaving Entrepreneur	Ligon, Linda	√		Iw	3	1		Fa 77	26
Fashion Collections	Pleats, Pleats, Pleats: For Sculptural Garments and Sculpture Itself		√		Fa	9	1		J/F 82	40
Fashion Collections	Surface Attraction	Mattera, Joanne	√		TM			7	O/N 86	20
Fashion Collections	Weaver Profile: Mahota Handwovens	Irwin, Bobbie	√		Hw	8	5		N/D 87	35
Fashion Collections: Ammann, Anneliese	For Anneliese Ammann, Simplicity is Key to Woven Garments	Kaspar, Patricia	√		WJ	7	3	27	Wi 82	70
Fashion Collections: Michael Kors	Diary of a Collection	Mattera, Joanne	√		TM			13	O/N 87	36
Fashion Design	Education in Fashion and Fabric: Program at the Fashion Institute of Technology	Stout, Pola	√		H&C	16	3		Su 65	6
Fashion Design	Passion for Elegance: Master Dyer Marian Clayden Creates Clothing by Listening to the Fabric, A	Levine, Betsy	√	√	TM			14	D/J 87	36
Fashion Design	Summer and Winter Garments (Melinda Raber Johnson)		√	√	WJ	11	3	43	Wi 87	44
Fashion Design	Wearing Handwovens with Style	Mayer, Anita	√	√	WJ	10	3	39	Wi 86	22
Fashion Designers	Alexander Julian		√		Hw	7	5		N/D 86	39
Fashion Designers	Barbara Knollenberg, Fashion Designer, A Personal Story		√		WJ	6	3	23	Wi 81	10
Fashion Designers	Body as Canvas, The	Koda, Harold	√		TM			8	D/J 86	56
Fashion Designers	Color Forecasting	Dyett, Linda	√		TM			3	F/M 86	22
Fashion Designers	Costuming for Rock Music Videos	Pierce, Judith	√		Fa	14	3		M/J 87	51
Fashion Designers	Diary of a Collection	Mattera, Joanne	√		TM			13	O/N 87	36
Fashion Designers	Five Fibre Pieces	Dean, Ankaret	√	√	SS&D	18	2	70	Sp 87	8
Fashion Designers	Gilbert Adrian: Creating the Hollywood Dream Style	Kinsey, Susan Buchanan	√		Fa	14	3		M/J 87	49
Fashion Designers	How Madame Grès Sculpts with Fabric	Cooper, Arlene	√	√	TM			10	A/M 87	50
Fashion Designers	Inside an Expensive Outfit	Galpin, Mary	√	√	TM			1	O/N 85	40
Fashion Designers	Interview with Jhane Barnes: Designer, Weaver, Spinner, An	Lonier, Terri	√		Fa	10	4		J/A 83	55
Fashion Designers	Jhane Barnes		√		Hw	7	5		N/D 86	38
Fashion Designers	Jhane Barnes: A Convergence '88 Chicago Preview		√		SS&D	18	4	72	Fa 87	12
Fashion Designers	Leni Hoch: "...To Hell with These Loom-Shaped Garments"	Grant, Susan	√		Fa	5	5		S/O 78	46
Fashion Designers	Maria Rodriguez		√		Hw	7	5		N/D 86	37
Fashion Designers	Not Necessarily Seventh Ave.	Dyett, Linda	√		TM			6	A/S 86	28
Fashion Designers	"Yves Saint Laurent: 25 Years of Design" (Exhibit)	Lonier, Terri	√		Fa	12	1		J/F 85	76

SUBJECT	TITLE	AUTHOR	IL	INST	JOUR	VOL	NO	ISS	DATE	PAGE
Fashion Designers: Kleibacker, Charles	Techniques of Haute Couture (error-corrected TM i7 O/N86 p5)	Rhodes, Elizabeth A.	√	√	TM			6	A/S 86	52
Fashion: Eighteenth Century	"Elegant Art: Fantasy and Fashion in the Eighteenth Century, An" (Exhibit)	Dyer, Carolyn Price	√		Fa	10	4		J/A 83	66
Fashion Fabric: Handspun	Couturier Fashions: Part 1, Couturier Fabric Design	West, Virginia	√	√	SS&D	13	3	51	Su 82	8
Fashion Fabric: Handspun	Designing the Line	Drooker, Penelope	√		SS&D	11	2	42	Sp 80	12
Fashion Fabric: Handspun	Pat White: The "Small Things" Are Her Signature	Park, Betty	√	√	SS&D	13	3	51	Su 82	58
Fashion Fabrics	Air Robe	Dedekam, Phyllis	√	√	SS&D	18	3	71	Su 87	47
Fashion Fabrics	Alexander Julian: Cut of a Different Cloth	De Leon, Sherry	√		Fa	12	3		M/J 85	64
Fashion Fabrics	Art of Fashion Design: A Handweaver's Twill Cape, The	Johnson, Judith K.	√	√	WJ	7	3	27	Wi 82	12
Fashion Fabrics	Barbara Knollenberg, Fashion Designer, A Personal Story		√		WJ	6	3	23	Wi 81	10
Fashion Fabrics	Canadian Classic, A	Baker, William R. M.	√		SS&D	18	3	71	Su 87	52
Fashion Fabrics	Couturier Fashion Design	West, Virginia	√	> 4	SS&D	13	4	52	Fa 82	34
Fashion Fabrics	Cylaine Handwoven Designs: Arlene Wohl and Lucy Matzger		√		WJ	7	3	27	Wi 82	8
Fashion Fabrics	Designer Collection: Lillian Whipple		√	√	Hw	7	5		N/D 86	64
Fashion Fabrics	Designer Collection: Malin Selander		√	√	Hw	7	5		N/D 86	60
Fashion Fabrics	Designer Collection: Virginia West		√	√	Hw	7	5		N/D 86	62
Fashion Fabrics	Education in Fashion and Fabric: Program at the Fashion Institute of Technology	Stout, Pola	√		H&C	16	3		Su 65	6
Fashion Fabrics	Ellen Hauptli's Pleats	Levine, Betsy	√		TM			5	J/J 86	48
Fashion Fabrics	Fabric Design, An Approach by a Young Weaver	Carson, Candace	√	√	H&C	20	1		Wi 69	16
Fashion Fabrics	Fabrics for Spring Ensembles	Wertenberger, Kathryn	√	√	Hw	6	2		M/A 85	82
Fashion Fabrics	Fashion Trends	Hick, Susan	√		WJ	9	2	34	Fa 84	10
Fashion Fabrics	Fashions by Linda Knutson and Lynn Daly		√	√	WJ	6	3	23	Wi 81	14
Fashion Fabrics	Five Fibre Pieces	Dean, Ankaret	√	√	SS&D	18	2	70	Sp 87	8
Fashion Fabrics	From Portraits to Textile Designs		√	> 4	H&C	11	1		Wi 60	20
Fashion Fabrics	High Fashion in Handweaving	Bryan, Dorothy	√		H&C	2	1		Wi 50	20
Fashion Fabrics	If Fashion Starts in the Fabric, Where Are Our Fabric Designers?	Humphries, Mary; Carol Outram			CW	3	1	7	Se 81	4
Fashion Fabrics	Kathy Woell Original, A	Sitko, Jane Bradley	√		SS&D	19	1	73	Wi 87	36
Fashion Fabrics	Malin Selander	Cromstedt, Cathrine	√		H&C	17	1		Wi 66	22
Fashion Fabrics	Not Necessarily Seventh Ave.	Dyett, Linda	√		TM			6	A/S 86	28
Fashion Fabrics	On Designing Fashion Fabrics	Sutton, Ann	√	√	Hw	7	5		N/D 86	66
Fashion Fabrics	One-of-a-Kind Garment in Beiderwand, A	Alvic, Philis	√		WJ	9	1	33	Su 84	51
Fashion Fabrics	Plymouth Colony Farms Fashions		√		H&C	4	1		Wi 52	41
Fashion Fabrics	Spinners and Weavers of Modern Greece		√		H&C	1	2		Su 50	30
Fashion Fabrics	Suited to Silk	Turner, Kathryn M.	√	√	SS&D	18	2	70	Sp 87	68
Fashion Fabrics	Swatch Collection #12: Classic Fabrics for City Fashions	Alderman, Sharon D.	√	√	Hw	6	5		N/D 85	48
Fashion Fabrics	Swatch Collection #13	Alderman, Sharon	√		Hw	7	3		M/J 86	28
Fashion Fabrics	Tzaims Luksus		√		H&C	14	1		Wi 63	12
Fashion Fabrics	Weavers of Rabun, The		√		H&C	7	2		Sp 56	6
Fashion Garments: Handmade	What People Ask Before They Buy Handmade Fashions	Leslie, Victoria	√		TM			9	F/M 87	58
Fashion Houses: Balenciago	Balenciago: The Architect of Elegant Clothing	Koda, Harold	√		TM			11	J/J 87	20
Fashion Houses: Chanel	Knitting Odyssey, A	Dyett, Linda	√	√	TM			13	O/N 87	48
Fashion Houses: Chanel	When Is Art Fashion and Fashion Art?	Martin, Richard	√		TM			11	J/J 87	12
Fashion Institute of Technology	Balenciago: The Architect of Elegant Clothing	Koda, Harold	√		TM			11	J/J 87	20
Fashion Institute of Technology (NYC)	Millions of Swatches at FIT	Kennedy, Alan			TM			11	J/J 87	18

SUBJECT	TITLE	AUTHOR	IL	INST	JOUR	VOL	NO	ISS	DATE	PAGE
Fashion: Knitwear	Body in Question, The	Rowley, Elaine			Kn	3	2	6	Sp 87	54
Fashion: Late 19th—Early 20th Century	"Fashions of the Hapsburg Era: Austria-Hungary" (Exhibit)	Malarcher, Patricia	√		Fa	7	3		M/J 80	75
Fashion, Nine-to-Five	Nine-to-Five		√		Hw	5	1		J/F 84	43
Fashion, Parody	Girls Who Wear Cactus	Akamine, Estelle	√		TM			4	A/M 86	66
Fashion Shows	"Art Couture/Haute Couture" (Exhibit)	McGuire, Patricia	√		Fa	9	1		J/F 82	86
Fashion Shows	Collegiate Fashion Show Highlights Textile Program	Belfer, Nancy	√		Fa	14	1		J/F 87	6
Fashion Shows	Convergence '86 Fashions	Dean, Ankaret	√		SS&D	18	1	69	Wi 86	16
Fashion Shows	Fashion Ballet	Hartford, Jane	√		SS&D	6	1	21	Wi 74	85
Fashion Shows	Governors' Conference Features Fiber	Hazlett, Paula Renee	√		SS&D	13	1	49	Wi 81	14
Fashion Shows: Convergence	Five Fibre Pieces	Dean, Ankaret	√	√	SS&D	18	2	70	Sp 87	8
Fashion: Silhouettes	Underneath It All: A Brief History of Underwear and Fashion's Changing Silhouette	Singletary, Suzanne	√		Fa	11	5		S/O 84	44
Fashion Trends	Body as Canvas, The	Koda, Harold	√		TM			8	D/J 86	56
Fashion Trends	Clothing	Todd, Louise	√	√	H&C	24	4		Au 73	28
Fashion Trends	Color Forecasting	Dyett, Linda	√		TM			3	F/M 86	22
Fashion Trends	Designing the Line	Drooker, Penelope	√		SS&D	11	2	42	Sp 80	12
Fashion Trends	Fashion Tour		√		SS&D	12	1	45	Wi 80	48
Fashion Trends	Fashion Trends		√		WJ	9	3	35	Wi 85	24
Fashion Trends	Fashion Trends	Hick, Susan	√		WJ	9	1	33	Su 84	12
Fashion Trends	Fashion Trends	Hick, Susan	√		WJ	9	2	34	Fa 84	10
Fashion Trends	Fashion Trends	Hick, Susan	√		WJ	7	2	26	Fa 82	16
Fashion Trends	Fashion Trends	Hick, Susan	√		WJ	7	3	27	Wi 82	16
Fashion Trends	Fashion Trends	Hick, Susan	√		WJ	7	4	28	Sp 83	40
Fashion Trends	Fashion Trends	Hick, Susan	√		WJ	8	2	30	Fa 83	28
Fashion Trends	Fashion Trends	Hick, Susan	√		WJ	8	3	31	Wi 83	26
Fashion Trends	Fashion Trends	Hick, Susan	√		WJ	8	4	32	Sp 84	56
Fashion Trends	Fashion Trends	Nelipovitch, Kate; Susan Hick	√		WJ	6	3	23	Wi 81	6
Fashion Trends	Fashion Trends: Fall	Hick, Susan	√		WJ	10	1	37	Su 85	20
Fashion Trends	Fashion Trends: Fall	Hick, Susan	√		WJ	11	1	41	Su 86	54
Fashion Trends	Fashion Trends: Spring	Hick, Susan	√		WJ	10	3	39	Wi 86	38
Fashion Trends	Fashion Trends: Summer	Hick, Susan	√		WJ	9	4	36	Sp 85	20
Fashion Trends	Fashion Trends: Summer	Hick, Susan	√		WJ	10	4	40	Sp 86	52
Fashion Trends	Fashion Trends: Winter	Hick, Susan	√		WJ	10	2	38	Fa 85	24
Fashion Trends	High Fashion in Handweaving	Bryan, Dorothy	√		H&C	2	1		Wi 50	20
Fashion Trends	Not Necessarily Seventh Ave.	Dyett, Linda	√		TM			6	A/S 86	28
Fashion Trends	"Yves Saint Laurent: 25 Years of Design" (Exhibit)	Lonier, Terri	√		Fa	12	1		J/F 85	76
Fashion Trends: Apparel	Black		√		Hw	4	1		J/F 83	44
Fashion Trends: Apparel	Fall '85 Fashion Scene	Patrick, Jane	√		Hw	6	3		Su 85	18
Fashion Trends: Apparel	Matter of Style, A		√	√	Hw	3	3		My 82	4
Fashion Trends: Apparel	Matter of Style, A		√		Hw	4	1		J/F 83	43
Fashion Trends: Apparel	Matter of Style, A	Ligon, Linda	√		Hw	2	5		No 81	4
Fashion Trends: Apparel	Matter of Style, A	Ligon, Linda	√		Hw	4	1		J/F 83	14
Fashion Trends: Apparel	Matter of Style, A	Ligon, Linda	√		Hw	4	4		S/O 83	14
Fashion Trends: Apparel	Matter of Style, A	Ligon, Linda	√		Hw	4	5		N/D 83	12
Fashion Trends: Apparel	Matter of Style. A	Patrick, Jane			Hw	5	4		S/O 84	28
Fashion Trends: Color	Color Forecasting and the Weaver	Znamierowski, Nell	√		Hw	7	3		M/J 86	33
Fashion Trends: Color	Matter of Style. A				Hw	3	4		Se 82	5
Fashion Trends: Color	Matter of Style, A	Ligon, Linda	√		Hw	2	4		Se 81	4
Fashion Trends: Color	Matter of Style, A	Ligon, Linda	√		Hw	4	2		M/A 83	6
Fashion Trends: Formalwear	Tuxedo 100 Years Later, The	Shufro, Cathy	√		TM			7	O/N 86	54

SUBJECT	TITLE	AUTHOR	IL	INST	JOUR	VOL	NO	ISS	DATE	PAGE
Fashion Trends: Interiors	Matter of Style, A		√		Hw	3	1		Ja 82	14
Fashion Trends: Knitting	American Knitting Editors				Kn	2	2	4	S-S 86	68
Fashion Trends: Knitting, Ethnic Textiles	Revivified Past, A	Upitis, Lizbeth	√		Kn	3	1	5	F-W 86	12
Fashion Trends: Knitting, Ponchos	Rag Trade: Picture Postcard, The (Susanna Lewis)	Weissman, Julia	√		Kn	3	1	5	F-W 86	68
Fashion Trends: Knitting, Sweaters	Rag Trade, The	Weissman, Julia	√		Kn	1	1	1	F-W 84	70 CI 53
Fashion Trends: Knitting, Sweaters	Rag Trade, The	Weissman, Julia	√		Kn	1	2	2	S-S 85	53
Fashion Trends: Knitting, Sweaters	Rag Trade, The	Weissman, Julia	√		Kn	2	2	4	S-S 86	59
Fashion Trends: Knitting, Sweaters	Rag Trade, The	Weissman, Julia	√		Kn	2	1	3	F-W 85	76
Fashion Trends: Rugs	Return of the Magic Carpets	Sortor, David	√		H&C	5	3		Su 54	16
Fashion: Undergarments	Tempting and Tempestuous	Upitis, Lizbeth	√		Kn	3	2	6	Sp 87	8
Fashion, Vintage	Way We Wore: San Francisco's Museum of Vintage Fashion, The	Scarborough, Jessica	√		Fa	14	5		N/D 87	5
Feathers see Down and Feathers										
Featherwork	Fabulous Plumage of Mae Augarten, The	Forscey, Suzon	√		Fa	6	3		M/J 79	65
Featherwork	Santa Fe Weaver Re-Creates Past	Ligon, Linda	√		Iw	1	1		Fa 75	4
Featherwork: Techniques	Hawaiian Feather Techniques	Kwiatkowski, Ron	√	√	Iw	1	4		Su 76	16
Featherwork: Techniques	Inca Feathers	Kwiatkowski, Ron	√	√	Iw	1	2		Wi 76	16
Featherwork: Techniques, Ancient Peruvian	Peru, Textiles Unlimited: Feather Work	Tidball, Harriet	√		SCGM		25		68	31
Felt and Feltmaking	Chad Alice Hagen's Felt Work	Bard, Elizabeth A.	√		Fa	13	4		J/A 86	30
Felt and Feltmaking	Choosing the Fiber for Feltmaking	Spark, Pat	√	√	SS&D	17	4	68	Fa 86	20
Felt and Feltmaking	Contemporary Felting	Mattera, Joanne	√	√	SS&D	7	2	26	Sp 76	89
Felt and Feltmaking	Do It Yourself	Oren, Linda Lowe	√	√	SS&D	11	1	41	Wi 79	59
Felt and Feltmaking	Felt		√		SS&D	11	1	41	Wi 79	47
Felt and Feltmaking	"Felt: A Rich Tradition and Current Involvements" (Exhibit)	Constantinides, Kathy	√		Fa	6	3		M/J 79	74
Felt and Feltmaking	Felt and Paper: A Portfolio		√		Fa	13	4		J/A 86	35
Felt and Feltmaking	"Felt and Papermaking" (Exhibit)	Harrison, Helen A.	√		Fa	11	2		M/A 84	79
Felt and Feltmaking	Felted Paper: A New Technique	Newby, Alice Bartholomew	√	√	Fa	9	4		J/A 82	42
Felt and Feltmaking	Felted Wool Landscapes	Showalter, Pat	√	√	S-O	9	3		Fa 85	22
Felt and Feltmaking	Felting	Askenfors, Gunilla	√	√	WJ	6	1	21	Su 81	31
Felt and Feltmaking	"Felting" (Exhibit)	Park, Betty	√		Fa	7	6		N/D 80	71
Felt and Feltmaking	Feltmaking	Salzman, Myra	√		SS&D	14	2	54	Sp 83	42
Felt and Feltmaking	Feltmaking	Wald, Pat Boutin	√	√	S-O	1			77	46
Felt and Feltmaking	Feltmaking Experience, A	Betts, Diane	√	√	S-O	9	2		Su 85	39
Felt and Feltmaking	Feltmaking in Hungary	Beede, Beth; Jill Garfunkel	√		Fa	13	4		J/A 86	6
Felt and Feltmaking	Feltmaking in India: A Remnant of the Past	MacDougal, Marleah Drexler	√		Fa	6	6		N/D 79	10
Felt and Feltmaking	Feltmaking: Instant Delight	Green, Louise	√	√	Iw	3	4		Su 78	18
Felt and Feltmaking	Feltmaking Now: The Exciting Revival of an Ancient Technique	Gordon, Beverly	√		Fa	6	6		N/D 79	43
Felt and Feltmaking	Freeform Felt	Shirley, Roz	√	√	SS&D	18	3	71	Su 87	81
Felt and Feltmaking	Gayle Luchessa	Papa, Nancy	√		Fa	4	5		S/O 77	56
Felt and Feltmaking	Goody Twoshoes: Gaza Bowen, An Extraordinary Shoemaker		√		Fa	8	5		S/O 81	13
Felt and Feltmaking	Groupwork with Dutch Feltmaker Inge Evers	Clark, Sherry	√	√	SS&D	17	4	68	Fa 86	28
Felt and Feltmaking	Hand-Felted Mittens (Sara Lamb)		√	√	Hw	4	5		N/D 83	84
Felt and Feltmaking	Handwoven Felt Mittens (Jane Kleinschmidt)		√	√	Hw	6	4		S/O 85	66, I-16
Felt and Feltmaking	Homemade Felt	March, Heather	√	√	TM			2	D/J 85	60

SUBJECT	TITLE	AUTHOR	IL	INST	JOUR	VOL	NO	ISS	DATE	PAGE
Felt and Feltmaking	How a "Secret" Spread	Heimstadt, Leslie	√		SS&D	11	1	41	Wi 79	50
Felt and Feltmaking	"Joan Livingstone: Lamia Lemures" (Exhibit)	Malarcher, Patricia	√		Fa	7	4		J/A 80	67
Felt and Feltmaking	"Joan Livingstone/Recent Work: Felt/Wood" (Exhibit)	Park, Betty	√		Fa	4	4		J/A 77	14
Felt and Feltmaking	Layne Goldsmith: Felted Worlds	Baldwin, P. H.	√		Fa	11	6		N/D 84	24
Felt and Feltmaking	Lida Gordon: An Interview	Arnow, Jan	√		Fa	6	2		M/A 79	50
Felt and Feltmaking	Making Felt with Mohair	Daugherty, Robin Taylor	√	√	S-O	7	3		Fa 83	48
Felt and Feltmaking	Merry Holoien: A Harmony of Color and Sound	Ormseth, Laurie	√		Fa	13	2		M/A 86	6
Felt and Feltmaking	More Than Just a Fling	Kaufman, Deborah	√		Fa	7	3		M/J 80	54
Felt and Feltmaking	Pioneer Spirit of Carole Beadle: At the Frontier of Feltmaking, The	Howe, Cathe	√		Fa	6	6		N/D 79	36
Felt and Feltmaking	Portfolio of Contemporary Fiber Sculpture, A		√		Fa	11	4		J/A 84	34
Felt and Feltmaking	Reversible Felted Wool Vest (Pam Bolesta)		√	√	Hw	1	1		F-W 79	20, 54
Felt and Feltmaking	Shelters and Symbols	Gordon, Beverly	√	√	SS&D	11	1	41	Wi 79	53
Felt and Feltmaking	Shinnosuke Seino: Innovator With Wool	Schreiber, Lavonne	√		WJ	12	2	46	Fa 87	34
Felt and Feltmaking	Touch of the Poet: Wearables by Denise Welsh-May, A	Park, Betty	√		Fa	6	6		N/D 79	52
Felt and Feltmaking	Traditional Felt Rugmaking in Turkey	Ispay, Francis	√	√	Fa	13	4		J/A 86	18
Felt and Feltmaking	Variations on a Midnight Rainbow	West, Sally	√	√	S-O	9	4		Wi 85	14
Felt and Feltmaking	Velten—Valkning—Felting	Beukers, Henriette	√	√	Hw	4	5		N/D 83	80
Felt and Feltmaking	Weaving and Felt	Swendeman, Dorothy	√	√	Iw	5	3		Su 80	43
Felt and Feltmaking	Weaving and Felt: Laminated Wefts		√		Iw	5	3		Su 80	45
Felt and Feltmaking	Weaving & Felting	Berdinka, Regine	√	√	SS&D	15	2	58	Sp 84	10
Felt and Feltmaking	Yurt in Artpark, The	Brennan, Joan	√		Fa	9	3		M/J 82	19
Felt and Feltmaking	Yurts (Not Your Average Dwelling)	Landess, Susan	√		Fa	5	6		N/D 78	26
Felt and Feltmaking	Zoltán Mihalkó: Hungarian Feltmaker	Beede, Beth; Jill Garfunkel	√	√	SS&D	17	4	68	Fa 86	12
Felt and Feltmaking: Caribou Hair and Wool	Caribou Hair and the Creation of a New Fabric	Goodfellow, Robin	√		AT	6			De 86	119
Felt and Feltmaking: Industrial	Manufacture of Industrial Felt, The	Goodman, Deborah Lerme	√	√	Fa	13	4		J/A 86	20
Felt and Feltmaking: Technique	Felt-making Craftsmen of the Anatolian and Iranian Plateaux	Gervers, Michael; Veronika Gervers	√	√	TMJ	4	1		De 74	14
Felt and Paper	Theme Issue		√		Fa	13	4		J/A 86	
Felting	Cache Valley Winter Blues: Felted Coat	Cogar, Kathryn	√	√	SS&D	17	4	68	Fa 86	16
Felting	Felted Fabric	Mayer, Anita Luvera	√	√	SS&D	15	3	59	Su 84	46
Felting	Felted Jacket	Bennett, Siiri	√	> 4	WJ	9	1	33	Su 84	49
Felting	Riding the Modern Range: Stetson Hats	Goodman, Deborah Lerme	√	√	Fa	13	4		J/A 86	8
Felting	Superwash Wool	Donnelly, Robert	√		S-O	10	2		Su 86	49
Felting	Wadmal — A Felted Fabric	Snover, Susan; Jean Sullivan	√	√	SS&D	11	2	42	Sp 80	89
Felting	Warmth for a Cool Climate: Handspun Wool & Milkweed Down	Danielson, Esther	√	√	SS&D	17	4	68	Fa 86	24
Felting	Weaving Primer	Parks, Deborah	√	√	PWC	3	4	10		4
Felting	Why Wool Felts	Mattera, Joanne	√		Fa	6	6		N/D 79	48
Felting	Woven Felted Boots		√	√	WJ	7	1	25	Su 82	28
Felting: Handknit Fabric	Felting Knit Mohair	Mitchell, Suzanne	√	√	TM			13	O/N 87	66
Felting: Handwoven Fabric	Boiled Wool	Smith, Mary	√	√	TM			13	O/N 87	63
Fences	Divided Spaces: The Fences of Japan	Bess, Nancy Moore	√		Fa	14	4		S/O 87	28
Festivals	Korean Journal	Blickenstaff, Maxine L.	√		SS&D	7	2	26	Sp 76	52
Festivals	New Zealand Woolcrafts Festival	Guy, Sallie T.	√		SS&D	14	4	56	Fa 83	28
Festivals	Ravensthorpe: A Festival of Wool	Walker, Pauline; Carol Taylor	√		S-O	7	2		Su 83	16
Festivals	Tons of Quilts at Liberty Festival	Wolff, Colette	√		TM			6	A/S 86	22

SUBJECT	TITLE	AUTHOR	IL	INST	JOUR	VOL	NO	ISS	DATE	PAGE
Festivals: Woolcraft Society	Knitter's Journey: New Zealand, A	Zimmermann, Elizabeth	√		Kn	4	1	9	Wi 87	18
Fiber and Architecture	Theme Issue		√		Fa	3	3		M/J 76	
Fiber Art: Conversations	Fiber Conversations, Scandinavian/American-Style	Goodman, Deborah Lerme	√		Fa	10	6		N/D 83	53
Fiber Artist	Dementia	Rogers, Fran			S-O	9	4		Wi 85	51
Fiber Artists	Making a Living: Eight Fiber Artists Tell How They Do It	Rowley, Kathleen	√		Fa	9	5		S/O 82	38
Fiber Arts	"North/South Carolina Fibers Competition" (Exhibit)	Laymon, Cynthia	√		Fa	10	4		J/A 83	68
Fiber Community	Fiber on Martha's Vineyard	Erickson, Johanna	√		Fa	11	4		J/A 84	46
Fiber, Contemporary	"Infrastructure" (Exhibit)	Malarcher, Patricia	√		Fa	11	4		J/A 84	76
Fiber Designer	Marjorie Ford-Pohlmann: Fiber Design Professional	LaLena, Constance	√		Hw	5	3		Su 84	82
Fiber & Education	Theme Issue		√		Fa	14	1		J/F 87	
Fiber, Painted	"Jan Wagstaff: Woven and Painted Canvas" (Exhibit)	Malarcher, Patricia	√		Fa	8	6		N/D 81	64
Fiber, Painted	"Meri Ann Walsh: Patterned Papers" (Exhibit)	Austin, Carole	√		Fa	8	6		N/D 81	65
Fiber Trends	Questions of Style: Contemporary Trends in the Fiber Arts	Howe-Echt, Katherine	√		Fa	7	2		M/A 80	38
Fiber, U.S.A.	"Fiber R/Evolution" (Exhibit)	Rudich, Sally	√		Fa	13	4		J/A 86	45
Fiber-to-Fabric	Fiber Foray: Working with Kid Mohair	Quinn, Celia	√	√	S-O	10	1		Sp 86	44
Fiber-to-Fabric	Fleece to Fabric		√		SS&D	3	2	10	Sp 72	33
Fiber-to-Fabric	Fleece to Fibers At Museum of Man	Cox, Penni	√		SS&D	5	4	20	Fa 74	50
Fiber-to-Fabric	Focus On Flax: From Flax to Fabric with Virginia Handy	Christian, Donna Allgaier	√		S-O	10	3		Fa 86	22
Fiber-to-Fabric	From Sheep to Skirt in Five Days	Copestick, Myrtis Gorst	√	√	H&C	3	3		Su 52	25
Fiber-to-Fabric	Llama Cape, The	Keeler, Betty			H&C	23	4		J/A 72	46
Fiber-to-Fabric	Making of a Coat, The	Keeler, Betty	√	√	H&C	23	1		J/F 72	20
Fiber-to-Fabric	Spin-Weave-Wear		√	√	SS&D	16	1	61	Wi 84	70
Fiber-to-Fabric	Warped-Faced Ruana	D'Ambrosio, Gina	√	√	S-O	10	2		Su 86	17
Fiber-to-Fabric	Weaving the Family Tartan	Buchanan, Rita	√	√	S-O	10	2		Su 86	36
Fiber-to-Fabric	Wonderful Worsted	Dozer, Iris L.	√	√	SS&D	15	3	59	Su 84	26
Fiber-to-Fabric	Wool — That Wonderful Natural Fiber	Derr, Mary L.	√	√	WJ	2	2	6	Oc 77	2
Fiber-to-Fabric: Costs	From Lamb to Rack: Wool	Hodges, Eva			Hw	4	2		M/A 83	101
Fiber-to-Fabric: Kasuri Process	Kumejima Dorozome: The Vegetable Dye and Mud Mordanting Process of Silk Tsugumi	Miller, Dorothy	√	√	AT	5			Ju 86	131
Fiber-to-Garment	Ravensthorpe: A Festival of Wool	Walker, Pauline; Carol Taylor	√		S-O	7	2		Su 83	16
Fiber-to-Yarn	Woolens and Tweeds: From Fleece to Woolen Yarn	Tidball, Harriet	√	√	SCGM		4		61	7
Fiberglass	Fiberglas Designs		√		H&C	19	3		Su 68	32
Fiberglass Screening	Girls Who Wear Cactus	Akamine, Estelle	√		TM			4	A/M 86	66
Fibergraphics	Debones: Collaborative Art Works, The		√		Fa	5	2		M/A 78	55
Fibers also see Specific Fibers										
Fibers	Hot and Cold Running Fiber	Phillips, Constance			TM			3	F/M 86	12
Fibers	Selecting Fibers — Spinner's Choice				S-O	8	3		Fa 84	21
Fibers, Animal	China and the Complexities of Weaving Technologies	Vollmer, John E.			AT	5			Ju 86	65
Fibers, Animal	Closer Look at Cashgora, A	Presser, Fran	√	√	S-O	10	4		Wi 86	49
Fibers, Animal	Fibers for Spinning		√		WJ	9	2	34	Fa 84	42
Fibers, Animal	New Fiber for Spinners: Caribou, A	Goodfellow, Robin; Keith Slater	√		S-O	10	4		Wi 86	46
Fibers, Animal	Qiviut — The Ultimate Luxury Fiber	Gibson-Roberts, Priscilla A.	√	√	Kn	3	4	8	Fa 87	58
Fibers, Animal	Spinning and Use of Dog's Hair, The	Pubols, Dorothy M.	√	√	WJ	4	1	13	Jy 79	36
Fibers, Animal	Spinning Doghair	Barrett, Clotilde	√	√	WJ	1	1	1	Jy 76	27

322

SUBJECT	TITLE	AUTHOR	IL	INST	JOUR	VOL	NO	ISS	DATE	PAGE
Fibers, Animal	Zoo Story	Sermon, Margaret	√		SS&D	2	4	8	Fa 71	10
Fibers, Animal: Caribou	Caribou Hair and the Creation of a New Fabric	Goodfellow, Robin	√		AT	6			De 86	119
Fibers, Animal: Karakul	Know Your Fibers: Karakul	Ligon, Linda	√		Iw	2	3		Sp 77	12
Fibers, Animal: Llama	Llamas	Switzer, Chris	√	√	S-O	5			81	31
Fibers, Animal: Vicuna	Paco-Vicuna: An Endangered Species		√		S-O	5			81	34
Fibers, Bast	China and the Complexities of Weaving Technologies	Vollmer, John E.			AT	5			Ju 86	65
Fibers, Bast: ASA	Distant Mountains: The Influence of Funzo-e on the Tradition of Buddhist Clerical Robes in Japan	Lyman, Marie	√		TMJ	23			84	25
Fibers, Blending	What a Handweaver Can Learn from the Scottish Weaving Industry (error-corrected WJ v2 n1 77 insert for vol. 1)	Barrett, Clotilde	√	√	WJ	1	3	3	Ja 77	11
Fibers, Characteristics	Designing the Warp: Parallel Considerations	Criscola, Jeanne	√	√	TM			1	O/N 85	66
Fibers, Characteristics	Fiber Facts for Finishing Fabrics	Hochberg, Bette	√	√	Hw	2	5		No 81	62
Fibers, Characteristics	Fibers for Spinning		√		WJ	9	2	34	Fa 84	42
Fibers, Characteristics	For Beginning Weavers — What Yarns Can I Use?	Frey, Berta	√	√	H&C	17	2		Sp 66	17
Fibers, Characteristics	Handspinner's Choice, The	Gibson-Roberts, Priscilla A.	√	√	Kn	1	2	2	S-S 85	56
Fibers, Characteristics	Hints on Weaving and Finishing Rugs		√	√	WJ	2	2	6	Oc 77	16
Fibers, Characteristics	In Brief: Fiber Notes	Veness, Tim	√	√	Hw	7	5		N/D 86	53
Fibers, Characteristics	Understanding Yarns	Redding, Debbie	√		Hw	5	1		J/F 84	18
Fibers, Characteristics	Which Fiber?	Liebler, Barbara	√		Iw	4	1		Wi 78	48
Fibers, Characteristics	Yarn Shop Dilemma, The	Liebler, Barbara	√	√	Iw	1	1		Fa 75	16
Fibers, Characteristics	Yarns and Fibers: Silk and Rayon	Zielinski, S. A.; Robert Leclerc, ed.			MWL	4			'51–'73	57
Fibers, Characteristics: Angora	Angora: Frivolous Fluff or Fantistic Fiber?	Rowe, Erica	√	√	S-O	8	2		Su 84	13
Fibers, Characteristics: Animal	Angora Goats and Mohair	Chastant, Kathryn Ross	√	√	S-O	7	3		Fa 83	29
Fibers, Characteristics: Bast Fibers	Survey of Leaf and Stem Fibers, A	Buchanan, Rita	√		S-O	10	3		Fa 86	24
Fibers, Characteristics: Caribou Hair	Caribou Hair and the Creation of a New Fabric	Goodfellow, Robin	√		AT	6			De 86	119
Fibers, Characteristics: Cotton	Cotton		√		WJ	4	2	14	Oc 79	4
Fibers, Characteristics: Cotton	Cotton Plays a Vital Role	Hausner, Walter	√		H&C	3	3		Su 52	8
Fibers, Characteristics: Cotton	Cotton: What Should You Ask For?	Linder, Olive			S-O	8	3		Fa 84	36
Fibers, Characteristics: Cotton	Discover Cotton Spinning	Ajeman, Norma; Irene Laughing Cloud Schmoller	√	√	WJ	8	3	31	Wi 83	49
Fibers, Characteristics: Cotton	Peru, Textiles Unlimited: Textile Characteristics, Fibers	Tidball, Harriet	√		SCGM		25		68	20
Fibers, Characteristics: Cotton	Spinning Cotton with the Linders	Linder, Olive; Harry Linder	√	√	WJ	11	2	42	Fa 86	14
Fibers, Characteristics: Cotton	Understanding Cotton Fiber & Yarns	Ayotte, Robert; Roberta Ayotte	√		WJ	11	2	42	Fa 86	27
Fibers, Characteristics: Karakul	Karakul	Walker, Linda Berry	√		Hw	3	2		Mr 82	60
Fibers, Characteristics: Llama Wool	Llama Wool	Smith, Carolyn	√	√	S-O	11	2		Su 87	32
Fibers, Characteristics: Man-Made	Characteristics of Man-made Yarns	Hausner, Walter	√		H&C	6	3		Su 55	19
Fibers, Characteristics: Natural Fibers	Principles of Textile Conservation Science, No. 1. General Chemical and Physical Structural Features of the Natural Textile Fibers	Rice, James W.	√		TMJ	1	1		No 62	47
Fibers, Characteristics: Plant	Learning the Ropes: Abaca	Coffman, Charlotte	√	√	S-O	7	4		Wi 83	40
Fibers, Characteristics: Plant	Ruffles and Ridges: A Scanning Electron Microscopy Study of Vegetable Fibers	Rowe, Erica	√		S-O	4			80	30
Fibers, Characteristics: Plant	Using the Fibers of Native Plants	Buchanan, Rita	√	√	S-O	9	4		Wi 85	29

SUBJECT	TITLE	AUTHOR	IL	INST	JOUR	VOL	NO	ISS	DATE	PAGE
Fibers, Characteristics: Silk	Shiny and Un	Gibson-Roberts, Priscilla A.	√		Kn	2	2	4	S-S 86	58
Fibers, Characteristics: Synthetic	Yarns and Fibers: Synthetic Yarns	Zielinski, S. A.; Robert Leclerc, ed.			MWL	4			'51–'73	54
Fibers, Characteristics: Wool	Peru, Textiles Unlimited: Textile Characteristics, Fibers	Tidball, Harriet	√		SCGM		25		68	20
Fibers, Characteristics, Wool	Raw Wool Values, How They Determine The End Use	Innes, J. Alisdair		√	H&C	15	1		Wi 64	15
Fibers, Classification: Synthetic	Fibers — From Where to Where?	Richards, H. Rex	√		S-O	2			78	33
Fibers, Exotic: Qiviut	Musk Ox, and Miscellaneous	Adams, Brucie	√	√	Iw	4	2		Sp 79	46
Fibers, Fiberglass	Fiberglas Fabrics		√		H&C	15	4		Fa 64	5
Fibers, Furlike	"Anne Wilson: Recent Work" (Exhibit)	Arajs, Ilze	√		Fa	11	4		J/A 84	75
Fibers, Identifying	Designing the Warp: Parallel Considerations	Criscola, Jeanne	√	√	TM			1	O/N 85	66
Fibers, Identifying	Guide to Spinning Other Fibers, A	Hochberg, Bette	√		S-O	1			77	15
Fibers, Identifying: Electron Micrography	Fibers	Abrahams, Howard	√		Iw	1	3		Sp 76	8
Fibers, Identifying: Plant	Ruffles and Ridges: A Scanning Electron Microscopy Study of Vegetable Fibers	Rowe, Erica	√		S-O	4			80	30
Fibers, Man-Made	Characteristics of Man-made Yarns	Hausner, Walter	√		H&C	6	3		Su 55	19
Fibers, Man-Made	Current Developments in Man-made Yarns and Fibers	Hausner, Walter			H&C	9	3		Su 58	41
Fibers, Man-Made	Developments in Man-made Fibers	Hausner, Walter			H&C	11	1		Wi 60	31
Fibers, Man-Made	Developments in Man-Made Fibers	Hausner, Walter			H&C	12	1		Wi 61	13
Fibers, Man-Made	Fiberglas Fabrics		√		H&C	15	4		Fa 64	5
Fibers, Man-Made	Man-Made Fibers	Hausner, Walter	√		WJ	9	3	35	Wi 85	61
Fibers, Man-Made	New Developments in Man-Made Fibers	Hausner, Walter			H&C	7	3		Su 56	12
Fibers, Man-Made	Synthetic Fibers, A Personal Assessment	Mattera, Joanne	√	√	Iw	4	2		Sp 79	48
Fibers, Man-Made: Orlon	New Man-Made Fiber Developed for Handweavers, A	Laurell, Karl	√	√	H&C	5	1		Wi 53	27
Fibers, Man-Made: Polycrest	Handweaves in a New Fiber		√		H&C	17	3		Su 66	32
Fibers, Man-Made: Rayon	Fringe Using a Gold Knubby Rayon	Everett, Marion	√	√	WJ	5	2	18	Fa 80	42
Fibers, Man-Made: Rayon	Man-Made Fibers: Baby Blankets		√	√	WJ	5	2	18	Fa 80	43
Fibers, Man-Made: Rayon	Man-Made Fibers: Rayon: Man-Made Cellulosic Fiber				WJ	5	2	18	Fa 80	38
Fibers, Man-Made: Rayon	Man-Made Fibers: Table Runner		√	> 4	WJ	5	2	18	Fa 80	45
Fibers, Man-Made, Rayon	Yarns and Fibers: Silk and Rayon	Zielinski, S. A.; Robert Leclerc, ed.			MWL	4			'51–'73	57
Fibers, Man-Made: Types	Man-Made Fibers				WJ	5	2	18	Fa 80	36
Fibers, Man-Made: Types	Man-Made Fibers: Man-Made Fibers for the Handweaver (error-corrected WJ v5 n3 81 p52)		√		WJ	5	2	18	Fa 80	39
Fibers, Painted	Metamorphosis in Maine: The Art of Barbara Lambert	Levy, Beverly Sauer	√		Fa	11	3		M/J 84	20
Fibers, Papermaking	How Does Your Garden Grow? Plant Fibers and Handmade Paper	Plummer, Beverly	√		Fa	6	4		J/A 79	34
Fibers, Plant	Corn Silk Challenge, The	Gherity, Delle		√	SS&D	7	3	27	Su 76	9
Fibers, Plant	Cotton Plays a Vital Role	Hausner, Walter	√		H&C	3	3		Su 52	8
Fibers, Plant	Discover Cotton Spinning	Ajeman, Norma; Irene Laughing Cloud Schmoller	√	√	WJ	8	3	31	Wi 83	49
Fibers, Plant	Fibers for Spinning		√		WJ	9	2	34	Fa 84	42
Fibers, Plant	From Ramie Top to Ramie Top	Knishern, Edna Maki	√	√	SS&D	9	2	34	Sp 78	78
Fibers, Plant	Hal Painter Explores the Possibilities of Raffia		√		H&C	3	4		Fa 52	28
Fibers, Plant	History of Bast Fibers, A	Mattera, Joanne	√		SS&D	8	4	32	Fa 77	27
Fibers: Plant	Natural Fiber Basketry	Smith, Sue M.	√		SS&D	15	3	59	Su 84	23
Fibers, Plant	Piña	Wallace, Lysbeth	√		WJ	8	2	30	Fa 83	77
Fibers, Plant	Plant Fibers		√	√	WJ	8	2	30	Fa 83	67

SUBJECT	TITLE	AUTHOR	IL	INST	JOUR	VOL	NO	ISS	DATE	PAGE
Fibers, Plant	Survey of Leaf and Stem Fibers, A	Buchanan, Rita	√		S-O	10	3		Fa 86	24
Fibers, Plant	Using the Fibers of Native Plants	Buchanan, Rita	√	√	S-O	9	4		Wi 85	29
Fibers, Plant	Weaving with Ramie		√	> 4	WJ	8	2	30	Fa 83	80
Fibers, Plant: Bast	Yarns and Fibers: Coarse Fibers of the Linen Family	Zielinski, S. A.; Robert Leclerc, ed.			MWL	4			'51–'73	74
Fibers, Plant: Cotton	Cotton		√		WJ	4	2	14	Oc 79	4
Fibers, Plant: Cotton	Cotton of a Different Color	Campbell, John; Susan Campbell		√	WJ	4	2	14	Oc 79	20
Fibers, Plant: Cotton	Understanding Cotton Fiber & Yarns	Ayotte, Robert; Roberta Ayotte	√		WJ	11	2	42	Fa 86	27
Fibers, Preparation: Animal	Some Hints on Spinning Musk Ox Wool	Cornwall, E. Marguerite	√	√	S-O	7	1		Sp 83	20
Fibers, Preparation: Cedar Bark	Cedar Bark, A Versatile Natural Weaving Material	Wilson, Patricia	√	√	H&C	20	3		Su 69	7
Fibers, Preparation: Wool	Sweater's Tale, A	Owens, Julie	√	√	Hw	6	4		S/O 85	82
Fibers, Processed	Prepared Fibers: A Sourcelist	Adams, Brucie			Hw	2	5		No 81	71
Fibers, Processing	Banares Brocade	DuBois, Emily	√	> 4	AT	3			My 85	209
Fibers, Processing	Chemical Dyeing, Part 2	Koehler, Glory Dail		√	SS&D	6	2	22	Sp 75	59
Fibers, Processing	Chemical Dyeing: Preparation, Part 1	Koehler, Glory Dail		√	SS&D	6	1	21	Wi 74	70
Fibers, Processing	Spindle	Chesley, Zina Mae			SS&D	1	2	2	Mr 70	20
Fibers, Processing: Animal	Angora Goats and Mohair	Chastant, Kathryn Ross	√	√	S-O	7	3		Fa 83	29
Fibers, Processing: Animal	Beverley Royce's "Recipe" for Merino	Royce, Beverly	√	√	S-O	5			81	49
Fibers, Processing: Animal	Breeds of Sheep for Spinners: Corriedale	Nickerson, Signe	√	√	S-O	10	4		Wi 86	18
Fibers, Processing: Animal	Carders: Hand or Drum	Hochberg, Bette	√	√	S-O	3			79	40
Fibers, Processing: Animal	Carding by Machine, Method of Fiber Preparation	Simmons, Paula	√	√	H&C	20	3		Su 69	16
Fibers, Processing: Animal	Dealing with Dog Hair	Murrow, Romedy	√		S-O	8	1		Sp 84	36
Fibers, Processing: Animal	Felt-making Craftsmen of the Anatolian and Iranian Plateaux	Gervers, Michael; Veronika Gervers	√	√	TMJ	4	1		De 74	14
Fibers, Processing: Animal	From the Woolcombers Bench: Cashgora	Dozer, Iris		√	S-O	10	2		Su 86	39
Fibers, Processing: Animal	Guide to Spinning Other Fibers, A	Hochberg, Bette	√		S-O	1			77	15
Fibers, Processing: Animal	Kurdish Kilim Weaving in the Van-Hakkari District of Eastern Turkey	Landreau, Anthony N.	√	√	TMJ	3	4		De 73	27
Fibers Processing: Animal	Llama Cape, The	Keeler, Betty			H&C	23	4		J/A 72	46
Fibers, Processing: Animal	On Preparing Fleece		√		S-O	1			77	32
Fibers, Processing: Animal	Pet Yarn	Kroll, Carol	√		S-O	1			77	18
Fibers, Processing: Animal	Preparing, Spinning and Dyeing Mohair	Russell, Barbara		√	S-O	7	3		Fa 83	52
Fibers, Processing: Animal	Proper Preparation of Fibers for Spinners	Fannin, Allen A.	√	√	H&C	20	3		Su 69	19
Fibers, Processing: Animal	Qiviut — The Ultimate Luxury Fiber	Gibson-Roberts, Priscilla A.	√	√	Kn	3	4	8	Fa 87	58
Fibers, Processing: Animal	Scouring a Fleece	Wallace, Meg		√	WJ	1	2	2	Oc 76	18
Fibers, Processing: Animal	Spinning Australian Cashmere and Cashgora	Feldman-Wood, Florence	√	√	S-O	9	4		Wi 85	40
Fibers, Processing: Animal	Spinning Lesson, A	Muller, Ann	√	√	H&C	2	3		Su 51	17
Fibers, Processing: Animal	Spinning Traditional Knitting Yarns for Ethnic Sweaters	Gibson-Roberts, Priscilla A.	√	√	S-O	8	4		Wi 84	26
Fibers, Processing: Animal	Using a Drop Spindle	Hicks, C. Norman		√	SS&D	5	4	20	Fa 74	79
Fibers, Processing: Animal	Weaving with Handspun Alpaca	Anderson, J.	√		H&C	17	2		Sp 66	20
Fibers, Processing: Animal	When You Begin to Spin	Simmons, Paula	√	√	H&C	17	3		Su 66	8
Fibers, Processing: Animal	Wonderful Worsted	Dozer, Iris	√	√	S-O	7	2		Su 83	32
Fibers, Processing: Animal	Wonderful Worsted II: Alternate Methods of Woolcombing	Dozier, Iris	√	√	S-O	7	4		Wi 83	21
Fibers, Processing: Animal	Wool Dyeing and Mothproofing for the Handweaver	Mayer, Francis		√	WJ	2	3	7	Ja 78	41
Fibers, Processing: Animal	Spinning and Use of Dog's Hair, The	Pubols, Dorothy M.	√	√	WJ	4	1	13	Jy 79	36
Fibers, Processing: Banana	Banana, Ramie, and Hemp in Okinawa (error-corrected Fa v14 n3 87 p4)	Miller, Dorothy	√		Fa	14	2		M/A 87	46

SUBJECT	TITLE	AUTHOR	IL	INST	JOUR	VOL	NO	ISS	DATE	PAGE
Fibers, Processing: Bast	Some Remarks on the Work of Markham	Stanton, R. G.; J. L. Allston	√	√	AT	2			De 84	95
Fibers, Processing: Bast	Twined Bags and Pouches of the Eastern Woodlands	White, John Kennardh	√	√	H&C	20	3		Su 69	8
Fibers, Processing: Commercial	Wool: Mill-Prepared for Handspinners	Wheeler, Barbara R.	√		S-O	8	3		Fa 84	23
Fibers, Processing: Cotton	Discover Cotton Spinning	Ajeman, Norma; Irene Laughing Cloud Schmoller	√	√	WJ	8	3	31	Wi 83	49
Fibers, Processing: Cotton	Spinning Cotton with the Linders	Linder, Olive; Harry Linder	√	√	WJ	11	2	42	Fa 86	14
Fibers, Processing: Cotton	Yarns and Fibers: Cotton	Zielinski, S. A.; Robert Leclerc, ed.			MWL	4			'51–'73	26
Fibers, Processing: Dog Hair	Spinning Doghair	Barrett, Clotilde	√	√	WJ	1	1	1	Jy 76	27
Fibers, Processing: Dogwood	Basket Willow: Cultivating and Gathering the Withy	Hart, Carol	√	√	TM			3	F/M 86	63
Fibers, Processing: Flax	Flax	Miller, Suzanne	√	√	WJ	7	2	26	Fa 82	12
Fibers, Processing: Flax	Flax — from Seed to Yarn	Parslow, Virginia	√		H&C	3	2		Sp 52	30
Fibers, Processing: Flax	Flax Processing	Chase, Mary A.	√	√	WJ	7	2	26	Fa 82	5
Fibers, Processing: Flax	History of Linen, A	Mattera, Joanne	√	√	SS&D	8	3	31	Su 77	16
Fibers, Processing: Hemp	Banana, Ramie, and Hemp in Okinawa (error-corrected Fa v14 n3 87 p4)	Miller, Dorothy	√		Fa	14	2		M/A 87	46
Fibers, Processing: Kudzu	Kudzu: The Noxious Weed Transformed	Buchanan, Rita	√		Fa	14	2		M/A 87	48
Fibers, Processing: Linen	Yarns and Fibers: Linen	Zielinski, S. A.; Robert Leclerc, ed.		√	MWL	4			'51–'73	15
Fibers, Processing: Llama Wool	Llama Wool	Smith, Carolyn	√	√	S-O	11	2		Su 87	32
Fibers, Processing: Piña	Piña	Wallace, Lysbeth	√		WJ	8	2	30	Fa 83	77
Fibers, Processing: Plant	At Homewith Flax	Reese, Sharron			S-O	10	3		Fa 86	19
Fibers, Processing: Plant	Continuous Thread, Part 2: From Flax Seed to Linen Cloth, The	Calhoun, Wheeler; Lee Kirschner	√	√	S-O	7	2		Su 83	44
Fibers, Processing: Plant	Continuous Thread, Part 3: From Flax Seed to Linen Cloth, The	Calhoun, Wheeler; Lee Kirschner	√	√	S-O	7	4		Wi 83	35
Fibers, Processing: Plant	Flax (error-corrected S-O V3 79 p11)	Leadbeater, Eliza	√	√	S-O	2			78	18
Fibers, Processing: Plant	Flax: Yarn Design Determines Choice	Leadbeater, Eliza	√	√	S-O	8	3		Fa 84	34
Fibers, Processing: Plant	Florida Weaver's Use of Native Materials, A	Ames, Helen B.	√	√	H&C	4	2		Sp 53	50
Fibers, Processing: Plant	Kudzu	Foster, Ann	√		S-O	3			79	23
Fibers, Processing: Plant	Learning the Ropes: Abaca	Coffman, Charlotte	√	√	S-O	7	4		Wi 83	40
Fibers, Processing: Plant	L'Amour de Maman: The Acadian Textile Heritage	Rossetter, Tabitha Wilson	√		Fa	8	3		M/J 81	29
Fibers, Processing: Plant	Preparing Plant Fibers for Handweaving	Ford, Toni	√	√	H&C	2	1		Wi 50	10
Fibers, Processing: Plant	Ramie	Quinn, Celia	√	√	S-O	8	4		Wi 84	50
Fibers, Processing: Plant	Virginia's Handy Tips for Flax Growing	Handy, Virginia		√	S-O	10	3		Fa 86	44
Fibers, Processing, Plant	Weaving with the Maoris of New Zealand	Giacchina, Polly Jacobs	√	√	Fa	11	3		M/J 84	48
Fibers, Processing: Plant	Yarns and Fibers: Unusual Yarns - 1	Zielinski, S. A.; Robert Leclerc, ed.		√	MWL	4			'51–'73	79
Fibers, Processing: Plant, Paper Mulberry	Shifu: A Handwoven Paper Textile of Japan	Miller, Dorothy	√	√	AT	4			De 85	43
Fibers, Processing: Plant, Ramie	Miyako Jofu	Miller, Dorothy	√	√	AT	7			Ju 87	85
Fibers, Processing: Qiviut	Arctic Adventures with Qiviut	Hudson, Marjorie; Kathy Sparks	√	√	S-O	11	3		Fa 87	47
Fibers, Processing: Ramie	Banana, Ramie, and Hemp in Okinawa (error-corrected Fa v14 n3 87 p4)	Miller, Dorothy	√		Fa	14	2		M/A 87	46
Fibers, Processing: Silk	Fiber Foray: Spinning Silk Cocoons	Quinn, Celia	√	√	S-O	8	2		Su 84	27
Fibers, Processing: Silk	History of Silk, A	Mattera, Joanne	√	√	SS&D	8	2	30	Sp 77	24
Fibers, Processing: Silk	How to Scour Silk	Bromberg, Kay	√	√	WJ	4	4	16	Ap 80	40
Fibers, Processing: Silk	Keeping Silkworms: The Art of Sericulture	Fenner, Monnie	√	√	S-O	8	2		Su 84	29
Fibers, Processing: Silk	Kumejima Dorozome: The Vegetable Dye and Mud Mordanting Process of Silk Tsugumi	Miller, Dorothy	√	√	AT	5			Ju 86	131

SUBJECT	TITLE	AUTHOR	IL	INST	JOUR	VOL	NO	ISS	DATE	PAGE
Fibers, Processing: Silk	Preparing Silk in Kumejima	Mitchell, Alison	√	√	WJ	10	2	38	Fa 85	53
Fibers, Processing: Silk	Silk	Chadwick, A.	√	√	WJ	3	2	10	Oc 78	6
Fibers, Processing: Silk	Silk: A Fiber of Many Faces	Quinn, Celia	√	√	S-O	8	3		Fa 84	30
Fibers, Processing: Silk	Silk Dyeing		√	√	WJ	3	2	10	Oc 78	21
Fibers, Processing: Silk	Silk: Working with Reeled, Spun, and Mawata		√	√	S-O	5			81	46
Fibers, Processing: Silk	Spinning Silk	Sullivan, Donna	√	√	SS&D	16	2	62	Sp 85	39
Fibers, Processing: Silk	Wild Silk	Kolander, Cheryl	√	√	Iw	2	3		Sp 77	8
Fibers, Processing: Sisal	Sisal Production in Highland Guatemala	Ventura, Carol	√	√	Fa	14	2		M/A 87	44
Fibers, Processing: Willow	Basket Willow: Cultivating and Gathering the Withy	Hart, Carol	√	√	TM			3	F/M 86	63
Fibers, Processing, Wool	Commercial Materials in Modern Navajo Rugs	Hedlund, Ann Lane	√		TMJ	25			86	83
Fibers, Processing: Wool	Devices to Aid in Wool Processing	Adams, Brucie	√		Hw	3	4		Se 82	69
Fibers, Processing: Wool	Drum Carder, The	Rossiter, Phyllis	√	√	SS&D	15	4	60	Fa 84	71
Fibers, Processing: Wool	Fibre Preparation	Fraser, Victoria Keller	√		H&C	24	3		M/J 73	32
Fibers, Processing: Wool	Handspun Yarns from Black Sheep Wool	Simmons, Paula	√	√	H&C	14	3		Su 63	6
Fibers, Processing: Wool	I Have This Fleece...Now What?	Adams, Brucie	√	√	Iw	5	4		Fa 80	62
Fibers, Processing: Wool	If You Want to Work with the Best Wool Yarns, Spin Them Yourself	Bulback, Stanley	√	√	TM			13	O/N 87	56
Fibers, Processing: Wool	Navajo Way, The	Jolley, Ginger	√	√	S-O	11	4		Wi 87	38
Fibers, Processing: Wool	New Approach to a Traditional Design	Ziegler, Luise	√	√	H&C	14	3		Su 63	11
Fibers, Processing: Wool	Preparing a Columbia Fleece for Handweaving	Wilson, Helen		√	WJ	2	2	6	Oc 77	22
Fibers, Processing: Wool	Some Remarks on the Work of Markham	Stanton, R. G.; J. L. Allston	√	√	AT	2			De 84	95
Fibers, Processing: Wool	Spinning a Gossamer Web	Gibson-Roberts, Priscilla A.	√	√	Kn	4	1	9	Wi 87	62
Fibers, Processing: Wool	Wool — That Wonderful Natural Fiber	Derr, Mary L.	√	√	WJ	2	2	6	Oc 77	2
Fibers, Processing: Wool	Woolcombing	Adams, Brucie	√	√	Iw	3	3		Sp 78	41
Fibers, Processing: Wool	Woolens and Tweeds:From Fleece to Woolen Yarn: Sorting and Scouring	Tidball, Harriet	√		SCGM		4		61	7
Fibers, Processing: Wool, Carding	Woolens and Tweeds: From Fleece to Woolen Yarn: Carding	Tidball, Harriet	√	√	SCGM		4		61	8
Fibers, Processing: Wool, Oiling	Woolens and Tweeds: From Fleece to Woolen Yarn: Oiling	Tidball, Harriet	√	√	SCGM		4		61	8
Fibers, Properties	Common Sense Care of Baskets	Turnbaugh, Sarah P.	√	√	SS&D	9	3	35	Su 78	90
Fibers, Properties	Designing the Warp: Parallel Considerations	Criscola, Jeanne	√	√	TM			1	O/N 85	66
Fibers, Properties	Fiber Properties: Tenacity	Raven, Lee	√		S-O	7	1		Sp 83	38
Fibers, Properties	Fibers	Abrahams, Howard	√		Iw	1	3		Sp 76	8
Fibers, Properties	Fibre Properties That Affect Weaving	Hochberg, Bette	√	√	SS&D	13	2	50	Sp 82	72
Fibers, Properties: Caribou Hair	Caribou Hair and the Creation of a New Fabric	Goodfellow, Robin	√		AT	6			De 86	119
Fibers, Properties: Caribou Hair	New Fiber for Spinners: Caribou, A	Goodfellow, Robin; Keith Slater	√		S-O	10	4		Wi 86	46
Fibers, Properties: Cotton	Yarns and Fibers: Cotton	Zielinski, S. A.; Robert Leclerc, ed.			MWL	4			'51–'73	26
Fibers, Properties: Linen	Yarns and Fibers: Linen	Zielinski, S. A.; Robert Leclerc, ed.			MWL	4			'51–'73	15
Fibers, Properties: Man-Made	Characteristics of Man-made Yarns	Hausner, Walter	√		H&C	6	3		Su 55	19
Fibers, Properties: Plant	Flax (error-corrected S-O V3 79 p11)	Leadbeater, Eliza	√	√	S-O	2			78	18
Fibers, Properties: Silk	Introduction to Silk Dyeing, An	Walsh, Joan Lea		√	WJ	3	2	10	Oc 78	14
Fibers, Properties: Silk	Silk	Chadwick, A.	√	√	WJ	3	2	10	Oc 78	6
Fibers, Properties: Wool	Wool — Most Versatile of Fibers, Part 1	Kiessling, Robert H.	√		H&C	2	3		Su 51	13
Fibers, Reactive Properties	Fiber Facts for Finishing Fabrics	Hochberg, Bette	√	√	Hw	2	5		No 81	62

SUBJECT	TITLE	AUTHOR	IL	INST	JOUR	VOL	NO	ISS	DATE	PAGE
Fibers, Recognition Characteristics: Natural Fibers	Principles of Textile Conservation Science, No. 3. Classification of Fibers Found in Ancient Textiles	Rice, James W.	√	√	TMJ	1	2		De 63	21
Fibers, Reflective	Using Light as a Design Element	Liebler, Barbara	√		Hw	5	3		Su 84	88
Fibers, Selecting	Which Fiber?	Liebler, Barbara	√		Iw	4	1		Wi 78	48
Fibers, Spinning	Fibers for Spinning		√		WJ	9	2	34	Fa 84	42
Fibers, Structure	Fibers	Abrahams, Howard	√		Iw	1	3		Sp 76	8
Fibers, Structure: Chemical and Physical	Principles of Textile Conservation Science, No. 1. General Chemical and Physical Structural Features of the Natural Textile Fibers	Rice, James W.	√		TMJ	1	1		No 62	47
Fibers, Structure: Chemical and Physical	Principles of Textile Conservation Science, No. 3. Classification of Fibers Found in Ancient Textiles	Rice, James W.	√	√	TMJ	1	2		De 63	21
Fibers, Structure: Cotton	Vegetable Lamb of Tartary, The	Ligon, Linda	√		Iw	1	4		Su 76	9
Fibers, Structure: Flax	Flax Processing	Chase, Mary A.	√	√	WJ	7	2	26	Fa 82	5
Fibers, Structure: Theories	Principles of Textile Conservation Science, No. 1. General Chemical and Physical Structural Features of the Natural Textile Fibers	Rice, James W.	√		TMJ	1	1		No 62	47
Fibers, Structure: Wool	Wool Fibre Structure	Australian Wool Board	√		SS&D	4	3	15	Su 73	60
Fibers, Synthetic	Characteristics of Man-made Yarns	Hausner, Walter	√		H&C	6	3		Su 55	19
Fibers, Synthetic	Synthetic Fibers, A Personal Assessment	Mattera, Joanne	√	√	Iw	4	2		Sp 79	48
Fibers, Types	In Brief: Fiber Notes	Veness, Tim	√	√	Hw	7	5		N/D 86	53
Fibers, Unspun	Enhance with Unspuns	Fowler, Mary Jean	√		SS&D	7	3	27	Su 76	33
Field Study: Spinning, Peru	Study of Andean Spinning in the Cuzco Region, A	Goodell, Miss Grace	√	√	TMJ	2	3		De 68	2
Field Study: Yarn Production Rate, Peru	Handspun Yarn Production Rates in the Cuzco Region of Peru	Bird, Junius B.	√		TMJ	2	3		De 68	9
Figure, Human	Lenore Davis: Figuring in Cloth	Frasier, Debra	√		Fa	10	5		S/O 83	10
Figures	Mysterious Figurines of Keiko Yamaguchi, The	Hempel, Toby Anne	√		Fa	14	4		S/O 87	16
Figures, Bound Weave	Different Boundweave on Six Harnesses, A (error-corrected WJ v3 n1 insert for vol. 2)	Strickler, Carol	√	> 4	WJ	2	4	8	Ap 78	36
Figures, Tapestry	Hope and Phillip Holtzman	Holtzman, Hope; Phillip Holtzman	√		Fa	14	2		M/A 87	23
Files and Filing	Practical Vertical File for Handweavers, A	Thorpe, Heather G.	√		H&C	6	2		Sp 55	54
Files and Filing: Organization	Treasury for Beginners: Organizing Materials	Zielinski, S. A.; Robert Leclerc, ed.	√	√	MWL	1			'51–'73	120
Film	Quilts in Women's Lives	Mattera, Joanne	√		Fa	9	3		M/J 82	54
Film	Right Out of History	Mattera, Joanne	√		Fa	9	3		M/J 82	55
Film Reviews	Oaksie. A 16mm Color Film	Appalshop Films			SS&D	11	4	44	Fa 80	67
Findings	Beads, Buttons & Findings	Green, Marilyn	√		Hw	7	5		N/D 86	84
Finger Weaving	Assomption Sash, A Long Tradition in French Canada	Whitelaw, Adrienne	√	√	H&C	21	3		Su 70	12
Finger Weaving	Finger Weaving Being Revived by Cherokees (error-corrected SS&D v5 n4 74 p69)	Coulter, Doris	√	√	SS&D	5	3	19	Su 74	55
Finger Weaving	Fingerweaving: Two Perspectives, The Historic View	Turner, Alta R.	√	√	SS&D	6	4	24	Fa 75	44
Finger Weaving	Fingerweaving: Two Perspectives, The Practical Lesson	Lee, Pamela	√	√	SS&D	6	4	24	Fa 75	44
Finger Weaving	Fingerwoven Ruana (Linda Ligon)		√	√	Hw	1	1		F-W 79	18, 52
Finger Weaving	Hungarian Weaving	Allen, Jane Ingram	√	√	SS&D	10	3	39	Su 79	93
Finger Weaving	Indian Fingerweaving, Traditional Use for Ceremonial Sashes	White, John	√	√	H&C	19	3		Su 68	4
Finger Weaving	Maori and Pakeha of New Zealand Use Wool and Phormium Tenax	Duncan, Molly	√	√	SS&D	5	1	17	Wi 73	65
Finger Weaving	Obi: The Textile Art of Nishijin	Donaldson, R. Alan	√		AT	1			De 83	115
Finger Weaving, Cherokee	Revival of Cherokee Arts and Crafts, The	Parris, John	√		H&C	4	2		Sp 53	9

SUBJECT	TITLE	AUTHOR	IL	INST	JOUR	VOL	NO	ISS	DATE	PAGE
Finger Weaving: Techniques	Finger Weaving	Cooper, Karen Coody	√	√	TM			12	A/S 87	46
Finger-Controlled Weaving	Finger Control: Or Getting the Most Out of Your Loom	Patrick, Jane	√	√	Hw	4	2		M/A 83	70
Fingernail Weaving	Fingernail Weaving: The Crystallized Art of Patience	Kinoshita, Takeshi	√	√	SS&D	13	1	49	Wi 81	26
Finishes	Andean Crossed-Warp Techniques for Decorative Trims, Part 1 — Flat Bands	Cahlander, Adele	√	√	WJ	2	4	8	Ap 78	10
Finishes	Basic Sewing Techniques in Handling Handwoven Fabrics for Garments	Knollenberg, Barbara	√	√	WJ	1	1	1	Jy 76	25
Finishes	Beyond the Fringe	Wertenberger, Kathryn	√	> 4	Hw	2	5		No 81	27
Finishes	Bobbin Lace, Part 7: A Simple Edging & Corner Pattern	Southard, Doris	√	√	SS&D	7	1	25	Wi 75	79
Finishes	Choosing End Finishes for Towels and Table Linens		√		Hw	1	2		S-S 80	55
Finishes	Cocoon Wrap Jacket, The		√	√	WJ	5	3	19	Wi 81	18
Finishes	Complementary Crochet	Durston, Linda Moore	√	√	SS&D	15	1	57	Wi 83	68
Finishes	Coverlet Weaving	Williams, Ann	√	√	SS&D	14	4	56	Fa 83	32
Finishes	Creative Monk's Belt: The Finished Product	Windeknecht, Margaret B.	√	√	SCGM		30		76	37
Finishes	Decorative Braids Combine Well with Handwoven Material	Sober, Marion Burr	√	√	H&C	19	4		Fa 68	18
Finishes	Double Two-Tie Twills and Basket Weave	Barrett, Clotilde	√	> 4	WJ	7	3	27	Wi 82	38
Finishes	Edges, Joinings, Trims, Embellishments, Closures...and more	Wilson, Jean	√	√	Hw	2	5		No 81	42
Finishes	Finishes and Embellishments	King, Bucky; Susan W. Gilmurray	√	√	SS&D	3	4	12	Fa 72	28
Finishes	Finishing Handwoven Fabrics	Nelson, Cornelia W.; William O. Nelson			H&C	4	4		Fa 53	32
Finishes	Guatamalan Finishes	Gotthoffer, Esther	√		H&C	22	1		Wi 71	18
Finishes	Guatemalan Brocade Border, A	Simons, Phid	√	√	WJ	6	4	24	Sp 82	39
Finishes	Inspirations from Sweaters	Brewington, Judith	√	√	WJ	7	3	27	Wi 82	14
Finishes	Joinings, Edges and Trims	Wilson, Jean	√	√	SS&D	14	3	55	Su 83	50
Finishes	Knotting Stitches for Weavers	Hoskins, Nancy Arthur	√	√	SS&D	15	3	59	Su 84	6
Finishes	Macramé	Harvey, Virginia Isham	√	√	H&C	19	4		Fa 68	8
Finishes	Macramé, Ideal for Finishing Edges	Harvey, Virginia Isham	√	√	H&C	18	2		Sp 67	15
Finishes	Macramé, Knotting Can Add Pattern	Harvey, Virginia Isham	√	√	H&C	18	3		Su 67	13
Finishes	Methods of Finishing Handwoven Fabrics: Edges and Fringes	Lytle, Edwina	√	√	H&C	8	4		Fa 57	26
Finishes	Methods of Finishing Handwoven Fabrics: The Noel Stitch	Van Cleve, Kate	√	√	H&C	8	4		Fa 57	27
Finishes	Nez Percé Indian Art and Craft Revival	Connette, Ann	√	√	H&C	21	4		Fa 70	5
Finishes	Oriental Hem Stitch	Post, Margaret	√	√	SS&D	8	2	30	Sp 77	59
Finishes	Rugs Woven on Summer and Winter Threading		√	> 4	WJ	3	1	9	Jy 78	12
Finishes	Seattle Guild Garment Designs, Part 4: Edges, Closures, Capes and Dresses		√	√	SS&D	11	2	42	Sp 80	39
Finishes	Secret Treasures of Tibet	Wiltsie-Vaniea, Anne	√		SS&D	18	3	71	Su 87	60
Finishes	Shaker Technique: Part 2, Rag Rugs, The	Gordon, Beverly	√	√	SS&D	8	1	29	WI 76	83
Finishes	Special Andean Tubular Trim—Woven Without Heddles, A	Cahlander, Adele; Ed Franquemont; Barbara Bergman	√	√	WJ	6	3	23	Wi 81	54
Finishes	Stitches	Wilson, Jean	√	√	SS&D	15	4	60	Fa 84	67
Finishes	Story of My Dining Room Rug, The	Rogers, Carrie M.	√	√	WJ	6	4	24	Sp 82	24
Finishes	Tacky–to–Tasteful—Finishing Touches for Household Linens	Bradley, Louise	√	√	Hw	8	3		M/J 87	27
Finishes	Tagari: A Greek Saddlebag of Handspun Wools, The	Koster, Joan Boura	√	√	WJ	6	2	22	Fa 81	24
Finishes	Taste of Honey(comb), A	Rasmussen, Peg	√	√	SS&D	16	2	62	Sp 85	6
Finishes	Varied Hemstitching, Used for Finishing	West, Virginia M.	√	√	H&C	18	2		Sp 67	19

SUBJECT	TITLE	AUTHOR	IL	INST	JOUR	VOL	NO	ISS	DATE	PAGE
Finishes	Versatile Inlay, Twill on Twill	Beard, Betty	√	√	SS&D	19	1	73	Wi 87	53
Finishes	Weaving on a Diamond Grid: Bedouin Style	Race, Mary E.	√	√	SS&D	12	1	45	Wi 80	20
Finishes	Wire Your Wall Hangings	Adams, Carol; Patricia L. Magee	√	√	SS&D	15	1	57	Wi 83	100
Finishes: Attaching	Croched Edgings on Wovens			√	TM			11	J/J 87	6
Finishes: Automatic-Stitched	Construction Details with Automatic Stitches	Richter, Elizabeth Lee	√	√	TM			11	J/J 87	64
Finishes: Basketry	Confetti Basketry	Brown, Sally	√	√	SS&D	18	3	71	Su 87	9
Finishes: Bias Binding	Biased Toward Bias	Bradley, Louise	√	√	Hw	6	3		Su 85	24
Finishes: Binding, Knitted	Coat for Handwoven Yardage, A	Roth, Bettie G.	√	√	WJ	7	3	27	Wi 82	6
Finishes: Binding, Leather	Binding Handwoven Garments with Leather	Knollenberg, Barbara	√	√	WJ	1	3	3	Ja 77	22
Finishes: Binding, Ultrasuede	Stitched Double Cloth Vest		√	√	WJ	7	1	25	Su 82	38
Finishes: Braid, Flat	Weaver's Work Apron: A Project in Double Weave		√	√	WJ	7	2	26	Fa 82	27
Finishes: Braided	Kurdish Kilim Weaving in the Van-Hakkari District of Eastern Turkey	Landreau, Anthony N.	√	√	TMJ	3	4		De 73	27
Finishes: Braided	Weaving a Cotton Saddlebag on the Santa Elena Peninsula of Ecuador	Hagino, Jane Parker; Karen E. Stothert	√	√	TMJ	22			83	19
Finishes: Braids	Skirt and Child's Dress (Halcyon Schomp) (error-corrected Hw v4 n4 83 p92)		√	√	Hw	4	3		M/J 83	46, 87
Finishes: Chained Loops	Hints on Weaving and Finishing Rugs		√	√	WJ	2	2	6	Oc 77	16
Finishes: Coverlets	Coverlet: Weaving and Finishing Hints, A	van der Hoogt, Madelyn	√	√	PWC	5	1	15		34
Finishes: Crochet	Crochet—A Great Technique for Finishing Handwovens		√	> 4	WJ	7	3	27	Wi 82	18
Finishes: Crochet	Crochet Trim		√	√	Hw	7	3		M/J 86	53
Finishes: Crochet	Greek Dower Sheet, A	Xenakis, Alexis Yiorgos	√		Hw	1	2		S-S 80	36
Finishes: Crochet	Moebius Vest, The	Homme, Audrey	√	√	WJ	11	4	44	Sp 87	48
Finishes: Crochet	Off the Hook: Bosnian Crochet (Charlotte Winston)		√	√	Hw	2	5		No 81	45
Finishes: Crochet	Other Finishes for Finnweave	Xenakis, Athanasios David		√	PWC			2	Ap 82	49
Finishes: Crochet	Putting Knitted Pieces Together	Guagliumi, Susan	√	√	TM			11	J/J 87	45
Finishes: Crochet	Some Edgings	Ligon, Linda	√	√	Hw	4	1		J/F 83	42
Finishes: Crochet	Wrist-to-Wrist Garment, The	Allen, Rose Mary	√	√	WJ	9	3	35	Wi 85	19
Finishes: Crochet Trim	Loom Shaped Top with Dukagång Inlay	Searle, Karen	√	√	WJ	11	3	43	Wi 87	8
Finishes: Damascus Edge	Hints on Weaving and Finishing Rugs		√	√	WJ	2	2	6	Oc 77	16
Finishes: Damascus Edge	Navajo Saddle Blanket Patterns	Barrett, Clotilde	√	√	WJ	11	1	41	Su 86	56
Finishes: Damascus Edge	Navajo Saddle Blanket Patterns	Barrett, Clotilde	√	√	WJ	1	1	1	Jy 76	22
Finishes: Edging	California Poppy Tablecloth and Napkins	Scorgie, Jean	√	√	Hw	6	3		Su 85	60
Finishes: Flat-Fabric	Sampler of Knit Edgings and Applied Trims, A	Newton, Deborah	√	√	TM			12	A/S 87	38
Finishes: Fringe	Afghans: Things to Consider and Finishes	Xenakis, Athanasios David	√	√	PWC	3	1	7		10
Finishes: Fringe	Bobbin Lace: Part 5, A Fringe	Southard, Doris	√	√	SS&D	6	3	23	Su 75	60
Finishes: Fringe	Embellishments on the Rain Sash	Baizerman, Suzanne	√	√	WJ	11	2	42	Fa 86	22
Finishes: Fringe	Fancy Coverlet Fringes	McGeary, Gay	√	√	Hw	2	5		No 81	38
Finishes: Fringe	Firfletting Fringe Treatment from Norway	Searle, Karen	√	√	WJ	9	4	36	Sp 85	40
Finishes: Fringe	Fringe Elements	Bradley, Louise	√	√	Hw	5	4		S/O 84	22
Finishes: Fringe	Fringes from Warp Ends	Brooks, Marguerite G.	√	√	H&C	6	1		Wi 54	46
Finishes: Fringe	Garments Made from Simple Patterns: A Vest		√	√	WJ	2	3	7	Ja 78	37
Finishes: Fringe	Gift to My Country: Lincoln Bedroom Coverlet, A	Jarvis, Helen N.	√	√	SS&D	9	4	36	Fa 78	17
Finishes: Fringe	Handwoven Wedding Chuppa, A	Horger, Millicent	√	√	WJ	7	4	28	Sp 83	50
Finishes: Fringe	Happy Ending, A	Liebler, Barbara	√	√	Iw	1	4		Su 76	22
Finishes: Fringe	Happy Ending, II, A	Liebler, Barbara	√	√	Iw	2	1		Fa 76	24

SUBJECT	TITLE	AUTHOR	IL	INST	JOUR	VOL	NO	ISS	DATE	PAGE
Finishes: Fringe	Hemstitched Fringe on the Loom	Neher, Evelyn C.	√	√	H&C	2	2		Sp 51	8
Finishes: Fringe	Latvian Wedding Mittens	Upitis, Lizbeth	√	√	PWC			2	Ap 82	92
Finishes: Fringe	New Twist in Making Fringe, A	Kniskern, Verne B.	√	√	Hw	6	1		J/F 85	7
Finishes: Fringe	Orchid Shawl	Xenakis, Athanasios David	√	√	PWC			5	Sp 83	38
Finishes: Fringe	Other Finishes for Finnweave	Xenakis, Athanasios David		√	PWC			2	Ap 82	49
Finishes: Fringe	Peru, Textiles Unlimited, Part 2: Fringes and Tabs	Tidball, Harriet	√	√	SCGM		26		69	41
Finishes: Fringe	Woven Swing		√	√	WJ	3	1	9	Jy 78	46
Finishes: Fringe, Card Woven	Card Woven Fringe: The ABCD's for the Beginner	Searle, Karen	√	√	WJ	10	2	38	Fa 85	21
Finishes: Fringe, Card-Woven	Dhabla Weaving in India	De Bone, Mary	√	√	SS&D	8	3	31	Su 77	9
Finishes: Fringe, Crochet	Poncho	Hurt, Doris	√	> 4	WJ	3	3	11	Ja 79	44
Finishes: Fringe, Decorative Ring	Braiding on a Frame		√	√	WJ	2	4	8	Ap 78	22
Finishes: Fringe, Gathering Knot	Refreshingly Simple Runner (Betty Davenport)		√	> 4	Hw	6	3		Su 85	11, I-3
Finishes: Fringe, Hooked and Knotted	Hooked on Texture: Unconventional Punch-Needle Rugs	Crouse, Gloria E.	√	√	TM			14	D/J 87	68
Finishes: Fringe, On-Loom	Cocoon Wrap Jacket, The		√	√	WJ	5	3	19	Wi 81	18
Finishes: Fringe, Plied	Other Finishes for Finnweave	Xenakis, Athanasios David		√	PWC			2	Ap 82	49
Finishes: Fringe, Plied	Weaving Primer	Parks, Deborah	√	√	PWC	4	2	12		36
Finishes: Fringe, Ritual	Tale of a Talis, A	Sylvan, Katherine	√	√	WJ	6	1	21	Su 81	42
Finishes: Fringe Ties, Mexican	Hand Woven Rugs: Various Fringe Ties	Atwater, Mary Meigs	√	√	SCGM		29		48	27
Finishes: Fringe Ties, Neolithic	Hand Woven Rugs: Various Fringe Ties	Atwater, Mary Meigs	√	√	SCGM		29		48	27
Finishes: Fringe Ties, Philippine	Hand Woven Rugs: Various Fringe Ties	Atwater, Mary Meigs	√	√	SCGM		29		48	27
Finishes: Fringe Ties, Sword-Point	Hand Woven Rugs: Various Fringe Ties	Atwater, Mary Meigs	√	√	SCGM		29		48	27
Finishes: Fringe, Woven	Fancy Coverlet Fringes	McGeary, Gay	√	√	Hw	2	5		No 81	38
Finishes: Fringe, Woven	Fringe Using a Gold Knubby Rayon	Everett, Marion	√	√	WJ	5	2	18	Fa 80	42
Finishes: Fringe, Woven	Lacey and Thin Fabrics		√	√	WJ	2	3	7	Ja 78	4
Finishes: Fringe, Woven	Overshot Sampler Bedspread for a Narrow Loom, An	Keasbey, Doramay	√	√	PWC	5	1	15		42
Finishes: Fringe, Woven	Western Shirt (Louise Bradley)		√	√	Hw	3	2		Mr 82	48, 84
Finishes: Fringe, Woven Picot	Woven Fringes		√	> 4	WJ	3	3	11	Ja 79	14
Finishes: Frogs, Handmade	Poncho	Hurt, Doris	√	> 4	WJ	3	3	11	Ja 79	44
Finishes: Greek Costume	Decorative Techniques of the Sarakatsani	Smith, Joyce	√	√	WJ	9	1	33	Su 84	14
Finishes: Half-Damascus	Shaft-Switching to Create Tapestry Effects	Green, Andrea	√	√	WJ	8	4	32	Sp 84	36
Finishes: Half-Damascus Edge	Hints on Weaving and Finishing Rugs		√	√	WJ	2	2	6	Oc 77	16
Finishes: Half-Hitch, Double	Placemats	DeRoy, Paul	√	> 4	WJ	1	3	3	Ja 77	4
Finishes: Hems	Other Finishes for Finnweave	Xenakis, Athanasios David		√	PWC			2	Ap 82	49
Finishes: Hemstitching	Hemstitched Finish	Kackenmeister, Elizabeth	√	√	H&C	16	2		Sp 65	37
Finishes: Hemstitching	Hemstitching for Linens	Baizerman, Suzanne	√	√	WJ	10	4	40	Sp 86	25
Finishes: Hemstitching	Lacy Linen Pillowcase (Linda Ligon)		√	√	Hw	2	5		No 81	58, 81
Finishes: Hemstitchnig	Keep Warm! Large Rectangular Shawl	Sylvan, Katherine	√	> 4	WJ	5	2	18	Fa 80	10
Finishes: Hemstitchnig	Placemats	DeRoy, Paul	√	> 4	WJ	1	3	3	Ja 77	4
Finishes: Indian Edge	Hints on Weaving and Finishing Rugs		√	√	WJ	2	2	6	Oc 77	16
Finishes: Inkle Bands	Inkle Bands as Finishing Details on Garments	Brones, Britta	√	√	WJ	7	3	27	Wi 82	35
Finishes: Inkle Bands	Weaving Inkle Bands: Finishing Bands	Tidball, Harriet	√	√	SCGM		27		69	40
Finishes: Inkle Bands, Fringes	Weaving Inkle Bands: Variations, Embellishments, Finishes, Fringes	Tidball, Harriet		√	SCGM		27		69	27
Finishes: Inkle Bands, Inkle-Fringe Warp	Weaving Inkle Bands: Variations, Embellishments, Finishes, Inkle-Fringe Warp	Tidball, Harriet	√	√	SCGM		27		69	28

SUBJECT	TITLE	AUTHOR	IL	INST	JOUR	VOL	NO	ISS	DATE	PAGE
Finishes: Inkle Bands, Picots	Weaving Inkle Bands: Variations, Embellishments, Finishes, Picots	Tidball, Harriet		√	SCGM		27		69	27
Finishes: Inkle Bands, Variations	Weaving Inkle Bands: Variations, Embellishments, Finishes, Ghiordes Knot Fringes and Tassels	Tidball, Harriet	√	√	SCGM		27		69	27
Finishes: Knit	In My Country, It's Winter	Gagné-Collard, Agathe	√	> 4	WJ	8	3	31	Wi 83	74
Finishes: Knitted	Sampler of Knit Edgings and Applied Trims, A	Newton, Deborah	√	√	TM			12	A/S 87	38
Finishes: Kumi-Himo Braid	Jacket for Hiking, A	Roth, Bettie G.	√	> 4	WJ	8	3	31	Wi 83	69
Finishes: Leather	Garments Made from Simple Patterns: Two Tabards		√	> 4	WJ	2	3	7	Ja 78	35
Finishes: Leather	Men's Clothing		√	> 4	WJ	2	3	7	Ja 78	32
Finishes: Machine Knitting	Knitters, Make a Trip to the Fabric Store	Guagliumi, Susan	√	√	TM			7	O/N 86	35
Finishes: Machine Stitched	Attaching Trims by Machine		√	√	TM			11	J/J 87	6
Finishes: Maori Braid	Four-End Block Draft or Summer and Winter	McClanathan, Barbara	√	√	WJ	8	4	32	Sp 84	22
Finishes: Maori Edge	Hints on Weaving and Finishing Rugs		√	√	WJ	2	2	6	Oc 77	16
Finishes: Native American Style	Trimming the Southwestern Look	Chaudet, Annette	√	√	WJ	11	1	41	Su 86	35
Finishes: Peruvian Needle Stitch	California Holiday Delight (Mary Kay Stoehr)		√	√	Hw	6	3		Su 85	41, I-6
Finishes: Phillipine Edge	Hints on Weaving and Finishing Rugs		√	√	WJ	2	2	6	Oc 77	16
Finishes: Phillipine Edge	Quick Thick Rug, A		√	√	WJ	7	4	28	Sp 83	43
Finishes: Piping	On the Edge		√	√	Hw	4	4		S/O 83	34
Finishes: Piping, Woven	Autumn Sunset Cape (Leslie Voiers)		√	> 4	WJ	11	3	43	Wi 87	22
Finishes: Pom-Pom	Beginner's Hat and Scarf	Skoy, Mary Lonning	√	√	WJ	11	3	43	Wi 87	61
Finishes: Ribbing, Knit	Machine Knit Ribbing for Woven Goods	Owens, Julie	√	√	Hw	6	2		M/A 85	30
Finishes: Rolled Edge, Woven	Peru, Textiles Unlimited, Part 2: The No-Salvage or Rolled Edge	Tidball, Harriet	√	√	SCGM		26		69	36
Finishes: Rolled Ends, Woven	Peru, Textiles Unlimited, Part 2: Rolled Ends	Tidball, Harriet	√	√	SCGM		26		69	37
Finishes: Rugs	Boundweave Rug on an Overshot Threading	Kindahl, Connie	√	√	SS&D	17	3	67	Su 86	58
Finishes: Rugs, Card Weaving	Peter Collingwood, His Weaves and Weaving: Rug Finishes	Collingwood, Peter; Harriet Tidball, ed.	√	√	SCGM		8		63	15
Finishes: Rugs, Cording	Peter Collingwood, His Weaves and Weaving: Rug Finishes	Collingwood, Peter; Harriet Tidball, ed.	√	√	SCGM		8		63	15
Finishes: Rugs, Damascus Edge	Peter Collingwood, His Weaves and Weaving: Rug Finishes	Collingwood, Peter; Harriet Tidball, ed.	√	√	SCGM		8		63	15
Finishes: Rugs, Double Hitches	Peter Collingwood, His Weaves and Weaving: Rug Finishes	Collingwood, Peter; Harriet Tidball, ed.	√	√	SCGM		8		63	15
Finishes: Rugs, Indian Edge	Peter Collingwood, His Weaves and Weaving: Rug Finishes	Collingwood, Peter; Harriet Tidball, ed.	√	√	SCGM		8		63	15
Finishes: Rugs, Knots	Peter Collingwood, His Weaves and Weaving: Rug Finishes	Collingwood, Peter; Harriet Tidball, ed.	√	√	SCGM		8		63	15
Finishes: Rugs, Maori Edge	Peter Collingwood, His Weaves and Weaving: Rug Finishes	Collingwood, Peter; Harriet Tidball, ed.	√	√	SCGM		8		63	15
Finishes: Rugs, Philippine Edge	Peter Collingwood, His Weaves and Weaving: Rug Finishes	Collingwood, Peter; Harriet Tidball, ed.	√	√	SCGM		8		63	15
Finishes: Rugs, Plain Weave/Twining/Soumak	Peter Collingwood, His Weaves and Weaving: The Slowest Rug Finish in the World	Collingwood, Peter; Harriet Tidball, ed.	√	√	SCGM		8		63	23
Finishes: Rugs, Plaiting	Peter Collingwood, His Weaves and Weaving: Rug Finishes	Collingwood, Peter; Harriet Tidball, ed.	√	√	SCGM		8		63	15
Finishes: Rugs, Plying	Peter Collingwood, His Weaves and Weaving: Rug Finishes	Collingwood, Peter; Harriet Tidball, ed.	√	√	SCGM		8		63	15
Finishes: Rugs, Protectors, Warp	Peter Collingwood, His Weaves and Weaving: Rug Finishes	Collingwood, Peter; Harriet Tidball, ed.	√	√	SCGM		8		63	15
Finishes: Rugs: Protectors, Warp and Weft	Peter Collingwood, His Weaves and Weaving: Rug Finishes	Collingwood, Peter; Harriet Tidball, ed.	√	√	SCGM		8		63	15
Finishes: Rugs, Protectors, Weft	Peter Collingwood, His Weaves and Weaving: Rug Finishes	Collingwood, Peter; Harriet Tidball, ed.	√	√	SCGM		8		63	15

SUBJECT	TITLE	AUTHOR	IL	INST	JOUR	VOL	NO	ISS	DATE	PAGE
Finishes: Rugs, Rug-Knot	Hand Woven Rugs: Various Fringe Ties	Atwater, Mary Meigs	√	√	SCGM		29		48	27
Finishes: Rugs, Woven Edge	Peter Collingwood, His Weaves and Weaving: Rug Finishes	Collingwood, Peter; Harriet Tidball, ed.	√	√	SCGM		8		63	15
Finishes: Stitchery	Stitched Finishes in the Guatemalan Tradition	Pancake, Cherri; Karen Searle; Sue Baizerman	√	√	Hw	2	5		No 81	29
Finishes: Tabs, Woven	Peru, Textiles Unlimited, Part 2: Fringes and Tabs	Tidball, Harriet	√	√	SCGM		26		69	41
Finishes: Tape, Knitted	Horizontal Ribs & Vertical Cords	Moes, Dini	√	√	SS&D	17	4	68	Fa 86	84
Finishes: Tape, Twill	Vadmal Jacket (Janice Jones)		√	√	Hw	8	4		S/O 87	45, I-7
Finishes: Tape, Woven	Woven Tape for Coat (Carol Thilenius)		√	√	Hw	3	4		Se 82	45, 86
Finishes: Tapestry	Contemporary Tapestry	Tidball, Harriet			SCGM		12		64	24
Finishes: Tassels	Weaving a Cotton Saddlebag on the Santa Elena Peninsula of Ecuador	Hagino, Jane Parker; Karen E. Stothert	√	√	TMJ	22			83	19
Finishes: Tassels and Tassel Making	Peru, Textiles Unlimited, Part 2: Tassels	Tidball, Harriet	√	√	SCGM		26		69	43
Finishes: Techniques, Rugs	Rug Finishes: An Overview	Stanley, Martha	√		Hw	2	5		No 81	32
Finishes: Techniques, Rugs	Sampling of Rug Finishes, A		√	√	Hw	2	5		No 81	34
Finishes: Tubular Edge-Binding	Tubular Edge-Binding from Bolivia, A	Cahlander, Adele; Marjorie Cason	√	√	WJ	1	4	4	Ap 77	13
Finishes: Tubular Tapes, Woven	Peru, Textiles Unlimited, Part 2: Tubular Tapes	Tidball, Harriet	√	√	SCGM		26		69	37
Finishes: Twined Edge	Hints on Weaving and Finishing Rugs		√	√	WJ	2	2	6	Oc 77	16
Finishes: Twined, Weft	Selected Batak Textiles: Technique and Function	Gittinger, Mattiebelle S.	√		TMJ	4	2		75	13
Finishes: Twining, Split-Ply	Split-Ply Twining: Finishing	Harvey, Virginia I.	√	√	TIAM		1		76	44
Finishes: Twining, Weft	Weft Twining: The Structures of Weft Twining, Finishing a Twined, Braided or Chained Textile	Harvey, Virginia I.; Harriet Tidball	√	√	SCGM		28		69	28
Finishes: Woven Edge	Hints on Weaving and Finishing Rugs		√	√	WJ	2	2	6	Oc 77	16
Finishes/Shared Traditions	Creative Clothing: Surface Embellishment	Mayer, Anita Luvera	√	√	WJ	11	3	43	Wi 87	30
Finishes/Shared Traditions	Finishes for Vadmal	Baizerman, Suzanne	√	√	WJ	10	3	39	Wi 86	30
Finishes/Shared Traditions	Trimming the Southwestern Look	Chaudet, Annette	√	√	WJ	11	1	41	Su 86	35
Finishes/Shared Traditions: Braiding	Detective Story: Unravelling the Mystery of a 7-Loop Braid, A	Cahlander, Adele	√	√	WJ	10	1	37	Su 85	12
Finishes/Shared Traditions: Fringe	Card Woven Fringe: The ABCD's for the Beginner	Searle, Karen	√	√	WJ	10	2	38	Fa 85	21
Finishes/Shared Traditions: Fringe	Unique Finish from an Amazonian Bracelet, A	Thabet, Micheline	√	√	WJ	9	3	35	Wi 85	14
Finishes/Shared Traditions: Knotting	Divide . . . and Conquer	Baizerman, Suzanne	√		WJ	9	2	34	Fa 84	61
Finishes/Shared Traditions: Knotting	Knotted Chinese Button	Baizerman, Suzanne	√	√	WJ	9	1	33	Su 84	7
Finishing	Beginnings...	Rowley, Elaine	√	√	Kn	4	1	9	Wi 87	25
Finishing	Beyond the Fringe	Wertenberger, Kathryn	√	> 4	Hw	2	5		No 81	27
Finishing	Boundweave Rug on an Overshot Threading	Kindahl, Connie	√	√	SS&D	17	3	67	Su 86	58
Finishing	Bringing Tapestry into the 20th Century	Mattera, Joanne	√		TM			1	O/N 85	48
Finishing	Broadcloth and Doeskin	Ponting, K. G.			WJ	7	2	26	Fa 82	38
Finishing	Continuous Thread, Part 3: From Flax Seed to Linen Cloth, The	Calhoun, Wheeler; Lee Kirschner	√	√	S-O	7	4		Wi 83	35
Finishing	Designing Handwoven Clothing	Thomason, Roger	√		SS&D	10	1	37	Wi 78	88
Finishing	Finishing Handwoven Fabrics	Alderman, Sharon D.	√	√	SS&D	9	1	33	Wi 77	13
Finishing	Finishing Handwoven Fabrics	Lucey, Edmund A.	√		H&C	1	2		Su 50	24
Finishing	Finishing Mohair Yarns and Goods				S-O	7	3		Fa 83	62
Finishing	Finishing Wool and Linen	Mudge, Christine S.		√	SS&D	9	3	35	Su 78	41
Finishing	Gala Raincoat	Moes, Dini	√	√	WJ	6	3	23	Wi 81	12
Finishing	Getting it Straight	Bradley, Louise	√	√	Hw	6	5		N/D 85	23
Finishing	Hemming Ways	Wroten, Barbara	√	√	SS&D	18	3	71	Su 87	74

SUBJECT	TITLE	AUTHOR	IL	INST	JOUR	VOL	NO	ISS	DATE	PAGE
Finishing	Ins and Outs of Hand Quilting, The	Giganti, Maria; Carol Clyne	√	√	TM			2	D/J 85	64
Finishing	Insulating Window Covering	Svenson, Mary Jane	√	√	WJ	6	1	21	Su 81	18
Finishing	It's Good to be All Wet, Sometimes	Redding, Debbie	√	√	Hw	2	3		My 81	22
Finishing	Knitting with Colors	Fassett, Kaffe	√	√	TM			3	F/M 86	68
Finishing	Let's Face It!	Bradley, Louise	√	√	Hw	8	1		J/F 87	34
Finishing	Original Fabrics of Kaftan, The	El-Homossani, M. M.	√	>4	AT	1			De 83	263
Finishing	Pine Tree Coat	Knollenberg, Barbara	√	>4	WJ	1	2	2	Oc 76	32
Finishing	Professional Finishing: Hints for Beginners, Reminders for Old Hands	Beschell, Lorraine	√		Fa	5	6		N/D 78	54
Finishing	Raglan Rectangles	Coifman, Lucienne	√	√	SS&D	18	1	69	Wi 86	10
Finishing	Rags to Riches: Jackets from Rags	Brones, Britta	√	√	WJ	6	3	23	Wi 81	31
Finishing	Ribbed Piqué	Sullivan, Donna	√	√	SS&D	18	3	71	Su 87	30
Finishing	Seaming and Finishing	Thompson, Chris	√	√	PWC			3	Oc 82	46
Finishing	Sewing Handwovens	Betzina, Sandra	√	√	TM			2	D/J 85	20
Finishing	Six of One, Half a Dozen of the Other (a roundtable discussion with six spinners)		√		S-O	5			81	51
Finishing	Suggestions for Finishing Handwoven Fabrics	Hausner, Walter	√	√	H&C	10	4		Fa 59	9
Finishing	Tacky–To–Tasteful—Finishing Touches for Household Linens	Bradley, Louise	√	√	Hw	8	3		M/J 87	27
Finishing	Teasels	Leadbeater, Eliza	√	√	Hw	2	5		No 81	54
Finishing	Three Spun Threads	Royce, Beverly	√	√	S-O	9	1		Sp 85	39
Finishing	Traditional Methods of Finishing Cloth by Hand	Gordon, Beverly	√	√	Iw	5	4		Fa 80	66
Finishing	Weaving Tweeds	Hotchkiss, Clifford; Ann Hotchkiss		√	H&C	13	2		Sp 62	14
Finishing	Weaving with Handspun Yarns: Suggestions for Beginning Spinners	Simmons, Paula	√	√	H&C	17	4		Fa 66	4
Finishing	Working with Wool	Healey, Edna O.	√	√	SS&D	2	4	8	Fa 71	15
Finishing: Brushing	Brushing			√	Hw	4	1		J/F 83	46
Finishing: Brushing	Finishing Fabric	Fry, Laura	√		CW	7	1	19	Se 85	18
Finishing: Brushing	Tämä on Ihana!	Scorgie, Jean	√		Hw	7	1		J/F 86	45
Finishing: Burling	Woolens and Tweeds: The Finishing of Woolen Fabrics, Burling	Tidball, Harriet		√	SCGM		4		61	23
Finishing: Collapse Fabric	Save the Twist: Warping and Weaving with Overtwisted Yarns	Frame, Mary	√	√	S-O	11	2		Su 87	43
Finishing: Construction Pressing	Pressing Need, Or the Ironing of It, A	Bradley, Louise	√	√	Hw	7	4		S/O 86	71
Finishing: Corners	Classy Corners	Bradley, Louise	√	√	Hw	6	1		J/F 85	86
Finishing: Cotton	Brushing Cotton	Moore, Carla S.	√		WJ	11	2	42	Fa 86	38
Finishing: Cotton, Handspun	Finishing Handspun Cotton	Linder, Harry	√	√	S-O	2			78	30
Finishing: Coverlets	Coverlet: Weaving and Finishing Hints, A	van der Hoogt, Madelyn	√	√	PWC	5	1	15		34
Finishing: Crochet	Crochet Inspired by the Trees	Moon, Ellen	√	√	TM			11	J/J 87	56
Finishing: Design Variables	Characteristics of Handweaves	Howell, Marie	√		H&C	12	1		Wi 61	18
Finishing: Embossed	Embossed Silk (Jane Patrick)		√	√	Hw	3	5		N/D 82	30, 98
Finishing: Fabric	Fiber Facts for Finishing Fabrics	Hochberg, Bette	√	√	Hw	2	5		No 81	62
Finishing: Fabric	Finishing Fabric	Fry, Laura	√		CW	7	1	19	Se 85	18
Finishing: Garments	Finishing Handwoven Garments: A Beginner's Guide	Raikos, Pam	√	√	SS&D	12	4	48	Fa 81	40
Finishing: Handspun Yarn	Finishing a Woolen Knitting Yarn	Gibson-Roberts, Priscilla A.			S-O	9	2		Su 85	38
Finishing: Handwoven Fabric	Finishing Handwoven Materials	Thilenius, Carol	√	√	Iw	2	3		Sp 77	16
Finishing: Handwoven Fabric	More About Fabrics: Finishing of Handwoven Fabrics	Zielinski, S. A.; Robert Leclerc, ed.		√	MWL	20			'51–'73	77
Finishing: Handwoven Fabrics	What a Handweaver Can Learn from the Scottish Weaving Industry (error-corrected WJ v2 n1 77 insert for vol. 1)	Barrett, Clotilde	√	√	WJ	1	3	3	Ja 77	11

SUBJECT	TITLE	AUTHOR	IL	INST	JOUR	VOL	NO	ISS	DATE	PAGE
Finishing: Home Sewing	Woolens and Tweeds: The Finishing of Woolen Fabrics, For Those Who Sew at Home	Tidball, Harriet	√	√	SCGM		4		61	25
Finishing: Knitting, Techniques	Putting Knitted Pieces Together	Guagliumi, Susan	√	√	TM			11	J/J 87	45
Finishing: Linen	Methods of Finishing Handwoven Fabrics: Finishing Linen	Arnold, Ruth	√	√	H&C	8	4		Fa 57	27
Finishing: Metal	Silver and Gold	Bramhall, Pat; Butch Bramhall	√	√	SS&D	19	1	73	Wi 87	40
Finishing: Needle Lace	Needle Lace	Kaiser, Eunice	√	√	TM			13	O/N 87	40
Finishing: Needle Weaving	Ruana	Sylvan, Katherine	√	√	WJ	5	3	19	Wi 81	34
Finishing: Orlon	New Man-Made Fiber Developed for Handweavers, A	Laurell, Karl	√	√	H&C	5	1		Wi 53	27
Finishing: Pounding	Miyako Jofu	Miller, Dorothy	√	√	AT	7			Ju 87	85
Finishing: Silicone	New Finishing Process				H&C	8	1		Wi 56	44
Finishing: Special Finishes	Woolens and Tweeds: The Finishing of Woolen Fabrics: Special Finishes	Tidball, Harriet		√	SCGM		4		61	23
Finishing: Steaming	Woolens and Tweeds: The Finishing of Woolen Fabrics: Steaming	Tidball, Harriet		√	SCGM		4		61	22
Finishing: Sweaters	Putting Knitted Pieces Together	Guagliumi, Susan	√	√	TM			11	J/J 87	45
Finishing: Tailor	Woolens and Tweeds: The Finishing of Woolen Fabrics: The Weaver and the Tailor	Tidball, Harriet	√	√	SCGM		4		61	24
Finishing: Tapestries	Techniques of Tapestry Weaves Part 3: Shading and Other Matters	O'Callaghan, Kate	√	√	WJ	5	1	17	Su 80	29
Finishing: Techniques	Traditional Methods of Finishing Cloth by Hand	Gordon, Beverly	√	√	Iw	5	4		Fa 80	66
Finishing: Tweed	Use a Hothead				SS&D	5	2	18	Sp 74	52
Finishing: Wool	Finishing Notes		√		Hw	2	5		No 81	53
Finishing: Wool	Finishing Wool: Three Approaches		√		Hw	2	5		No 81	51
Finishing: Wool	More About Fabrics: Finishing of Wool	Zielinski, S. A.; Robert Leclerc, ed.		√	MWL	20			'51–'73	81
Finishing: Wool	Shinnosuke Seino: Innovator with Wool	Schreiber, Lavonne	√		WJ	12	2	46	Fa 87	34
Finishing: Wool	Wool Finishing	Mayer, Francis		√	WJ	3	1	9	Jy 78	31
Finishing: Woolens	Methods of Finishing Handwoven Fabrics: Finishing Woolens	Cate, Katharine F.	√	√	H&C	8	4		Fa 57	26
Finishing: Woolens, Historic Methods	Woolens and Tweeds: The Finishing of Woolen Fabrics: Historic Methods	Tidball, Harriet			SCGM		4		61	20
Finishing: Woolens Home Methods	Woolens and Tweeds: The Finishing of Woolen Fabrics: Home Methods	Tidball, Harriet		√	SCGM		4		61	21
Finland	Artist and Industry — A Cooperative Effort		√		Hw	8	3		M/J 87	71
Finland	Contemporary Finnish Weaving		√		Hw	8	3		M/J 87	70
Finland	Dora Jung, Distinguished Finnish Weaver		√		H&C	10	2		Sp 59	14
Finland	Finland's Rya Rugs	The Finnish Consulate General of New York	√		SS&D	13	4	52	Fa 82	54
Finland	Finnish Ryijy (Rya)		√	√	Hw	8	3		M/J 87	72
Finland	Finnish Textile Art: From Byzantine to Bauhaus	Rantanen, Kristi	√		Hw	8	3		M/J 87	68
Finland	Finnish Transparent Weaving	Utzinger, Karin	√	√	WJ	5	1	17	Su 80	34
Finland	Karelian Red-Picking	Ruchti, Willie Jager	√	> 4	WJ	5	2	18	Fa 80	34
Finland	Linen in Finland	Haglich, Sr. Bianca; Raija Ranne	√	√	SS&D	8	3	31	Su 77	84
Finland	Poppana!		√	√	Hw	8	3		M/J 87	74
Finland	Reinterpreting Rya: Irma Kukkasjärvi Energizes an Ancient Technique	Ojala, Liisa Kanning	√		WJ	9	4	36	Sp 85	26
Finland	Ryijy Plus Raanu		√		SS&D	4	2	14	Sp 73	12
Finland	Scholarship Report: Fuchs At Varpapuu	Fuchs, Douglas Eric	√		SS&D	7	1	25	Wi 75	92
Finland	Stacks and Racks of Handwovens in Finland		√		SS&D	5	2	18	Sp 74	91
Finland	Summer with Finnish Weavers, A	Schobinger, Helen J.	√		H&C	3	2		Sp 52	12

SUBJECT	TITLE	AUTHOR	IL	INST	JOUR	VOL	NO	ISS	DATE	PAGE
Finland	Verkkonauhaa	Tacker, Sylvia	√	√	SS&D	11	4	44	Fa 80	12
Finnknit	Finns Can Knit Too or How to Knit a Finn	Rowley, Elaine D.	√	√	PWC			2	Ap 82	76
Finnweave also see Double Weave										
Finnweave	Fantastic Finnweave, Part 3	Xenakis, Athanasios David	√	>4	PWC			4	Ja 83	10
Finnweave	Finnish Techniques	Tanner, Kersten	√		SS&D	6	3	23	Su 75	45
Finnweave	Handbag in Finnweave		√	√	H&C	16	1		Wi 65	33
Finnweave	Vertical Pockets	Krasnoff, Julienne Hallen	√	√	H&C	21	1		Wi 70	21
Finnweave, Contemporary	Finnweave in Norway: Yesterday and Today	Nelson, Lila	√		PWC			2	Ap 82	14
Finnweave, Loom-Controlled	Finnweave	Barrett, Clotilde	√	>4	WJ	11	4	44	Sp 87	25
Finnweave, Paired-Thread	Fantastic Finnweave, Part 1	Xenakis, Athanasios David	√	√	PWC			2	Ap 82	18
Finnweave, Paired-Thread	Paired-Thread Finnweave Projects: Five Placemats Based on a Chinese Lattice Design, The	Xenakis, Athanasios David	√	√	PWC			2	Ap 82	34
Finnweave, Paired-Thread, Discontinuous Wefts	Paired-Thread Finnweave Projects: The Gaza Dress, The	Xenakis, Alexis, Yiorgos	√	√	PWC			2	Ap 82	40
Finnweave, Pick-Up	Double Weaves: Finn Weave	Zielinski, S. A.; Robert Leclerc, ed.	√	√	MWL	15			'51–'73	38
Finnweave, Pick-Up	Finnweave	Barrett, Clotilde	√	>4	WJ	11	4	44	Sp 87	25
Finnweave, Pick-Up	Finnweave Can Be Fun	Ringler, Aina	√	√	H&C	9	4		Fa 58	12
Finnweave, Pick-Up	Portraits in Double Weave	Strickler, Carol	√	√	WJ	1	3	3	Ja 77	30
Finnweave, Pick-Up, Shed-Shuttle	Double Weaves: Practice of Finn Weave	Zielinski, S. A.; Robert Leclerc, ed.	√	√	MWL	15			'51–'73	44
Finnweave, Single Thread	Fantastic Finnweave, Part 2	Xenakis, Athanasios David	√	√	PWC			3	Oc 82	10
Finnweave, Single Thread	Fantastic Finnweave, Part 2: Single-Thread Projects	Xenakis, Athanasios David	√	√	PWC			3	Oc 82	14
Finnweave Templates	Technology of Handweaving: Templets for Finn Weave	Zielinski, S. A.; Robert Leclerc, ed.	√	√	MWL	6			'51–'73	51
Firfletting	Firfletting Fringe Treatment from Norway	Searle, Karen	√	√	WJ	9	4	36	Sp 85	40
Fishskin	"Innerskins/Outerskins: Gut and Fishskin" (Exhibit)		√		TM			14	D/J 87	20
Fitting	Body in Question, The	Rowley, Elaine			Kn	3	2	6	Sp 87	54
Fitting	Little Shaping Story, A	Burgess, Leslie	√	√	Hw	4	3		M/J 83	26
Fitting	More to Fitting			√	TM			13	O/N 87	4
Fitting	Perfect Fit	Allen, Alice	√	√	TM			12	A/S 87	71
Fitting	Plastic Pattern Promises Perfect Fit, A	Fanning, Robbie			TM			12	A/S 87	20
Fitting	Tailoring Handwoven Fabrics	Bryan, Dorothy	√		H&C	10	2		Sp 59	17
Fitting: Knitting	Opinionated Knitter, The	Zimmermann, Elizabeth			Kn	1	2	2	S-S 85	12
Fitting, Pants	Fitting Pants			√	TM			9	F/M 87	4
Fitting, Pants	More About Fitting Pants			√	TM			11	J/J 87	4
Fitting, Pants	More About Pants			√	TM			10	A/M 87	4
Fixed-Warp Weaving	Indian Fingerweaving, Traditional Use for Ceremonial Sashes	White, John	√	√	H&C	19	3		Su 68	4
Flags see Banners/Flags										
Flame Retardants	Things to Know and Tell About Flame Retardants	Pater, Stephen			WJ	8	2	30	Fa 83	50
Flamepoint	Flamepoint Rugs for Everybody	Kirk, Betty Burian	√	√	WJ	8	4	32	Sp 84	12
Flamepoint	Reversible Flamepoint Vest	Wittpenn, Ann	√	√	WJ	5	3	19	Wi 81	9
Flamepoint on Overshot	Notebook: Warmables (Alice Millette)	Meyers, Ruth Nordquist, ed.	√	√	SS&D	15	1	57	Wi 83	80
Flameproofing	Flameproofing Fibers	Platus, Libby	√	√	SS&D	8	2	30	Sp 77	29
Flameproofing	Techniques of Tapestry Weaves Part 3: Shading and Other Matters	O'Callaghan, Kate	√	√	WJ	5	1	17	Su 80	29
Flameproofing: Cotton	Flameproofing Fabrics			√	TM			2	D/J 85	8
Flameproofing: Cotton	Follow-Up on Flameproofing			√	TM			3	F/M 86	6

SUBJECT	TITLE	AUTHOR	IL	INST	JOUR	VOL	NO	ISS	DATE	PAGE
Flameproofing Recipe	Fireproofing	Schlegel, Lee-lee			Fa	5	1		J/F 78	8
Flax	At Home with Flax	Reese, Sharron			S-O	10	3		Fa 86	19
Flax	Continuous Thread: From Flax Seed to Linen Cloth, The	Calhoun, Wheeler; Lee Kirschner	√		S-O	7	1		Sp 83	28
Flax	Continuous Thread, Part 2: From Flax Seed to Linen Cloth, The	Calhoun, Wheeler; Lee Kirschner	√	√	S-O	7	2		Su 83	44
Flax	Continuous Thread, Part 3: From Flax Seed to Linen Cloth, The	Calhoun, Wheeler; Lee Kirschner	√	√	S-O	7	4		Wi 83	35
Flax	Distaff, The	Henzie, Suzie	√	√	WJ	7	2	26	Fa 82	10
Flax	Dressing the Distaff	Henzie, Susie	√	√	SS&D	10	1	37	Wi 78	12
Flax	Fiber Foray: Getting Started with Line Flax	Quinn, Celia	√	√	S-O	9	4		Wi 85	46
Flax	Flax	Miller, Suzanne	√	√	WJ	7	2	26	Fa 82	12
Flax	Flax (error-corrected S-O V3 79 p11)	Leadbeater, Eliza	√	√	S-O	2			78	18
Flax	Flax — From Seed to Yarn	Parslow, Virginia	√		H&C	3	2		Sp 52	30
Flax	Flax Processing	Chase, Mary A.	√	√	WJ	7	2	26	Fa 82	5
Flax	Flax: Yarn Design Determines Choice	Leadbeater, Eliza	√	√	S-O	8	3		Fa 84	34
Flax	Focus on Flax: From Flax to Fabric with Virginia Handy	Christian, Donna Allgaier	√		S-O	10	3		Fa 86	22
Flax	History of Linen, A	Mattera, Joanne	√	√	SS&D	8	3	31	Su 77	16
Flax	Impatient Spinner's Way to Spin Flax, The	Gordon, Carol	√	√	S-O	10	4		Wi 86	42
Flax	Learning the Flax of Life	Murrow, Romedy	√	√	S-O	9	3		Fa 85	49
Flax	Line Flax Spinning	Heyl, Maxine; Linda Wilson	√	√	WJ	7	2	26	Fa 82	20
Flax	Linen Lore	Goodman, Deborah Lerme	√		Fa	14	2		M/A 87	16
Flax	Plant Fibers		√	√	WJ	8	2	30	Fa 83	67
Flax	Spinning Flax	Fannin, Allen A.	√	√	H&C	18	2		Sp 67	21
Flax	Tapestry Weaving with Unspun Flax	Westerink, Claire	√	√	WJ	11	2	42	Fa 86	49
Flax	Virginia's Handy Tips for Flax Growing	Handy, Virginia		√	S-O	10	3		Fa 86	44
Flax: Felted	Felted Paper: A New Technique	Newby, Alice Bartholomew	√	√	Fa	9	4		J/A 82	42
Flax: New Zealand	Maori and Pakeha of New Zealand Use Wool and Phormium Tenax	Duncan, Molly	√	√	SS&D	5	1	17	Wi 73	65
Flax, New Zealand	Plant Fibers		√	√	WJ	8	2	30	Fa 83	67
Flax, New Zealand	Survey of Leaf and Stem Fibers, A	Buchanan, Rita	√		S-O	10	3		Fa 86	24
Flax: New Zealand	Weaving with the Maoris of New Zealand	Giacchina, Polly Jacobs	√	√	Fa	11	3		M/J 84	48
Flax Tow	Slave Shirt Woven for Booker T. Washington Museum		√		H&C	19	3		Su 68	21
Flea Markets	Shopping Foreign Flea Markets	Austin, Carol	√		Fa	12	6		N/D 85	45
Fleece Characteristics	Spinning Down Under: What Are You Going to Do with the Yarn?	De Boer, Janet	√		S-O	1			77	23
Fleece Characteristics: Border Leicester	Border Leicester	Walker, Linda Berry	√	√	Hw	2	3		My 81	64
Fleece Characteristics: Cheviot, Border	Border Cheviot	Walker, Linda Berry	√	√	Hw	4	1		J/F 83	63
Fleece Characteristics: Cheviot, North Country	North Country Cheviot	Walker, Linda Berry	√	√	Hw	4	1		J/F 83	63
Fleece, Characteristics: Clun Forest	Clun Forest	Walker, Linda Berry	√		Iw	6	1		Wi 80	62
Fleece, Characteristics: Corriedale	Corriedale	Walker, Linda Berry	√		Hw	3	1		Ja 82	73
Fleece Characteristics: Cotswold	Cotswold	Walker, Linda Berry	√	√	Hw	3	4		Se 82	71
Fleece, Characteristics: Jacob	Jacob	Walker, Linda Berry	√	√	Iw	5	4		Fa 80	64
Fleece, Characteristics: Lincoln	Lincoln	Walker, Linda Berry	√	√	Iw	5	1		Wi 79	52
Fleece, Characteristics: Merino	Merino	Walker, Linda Berry	√	√	Iw	5	3		Su 80	59
Fleece, Characteristics: Perendale	Perendale	Walker, Linda Berry	√	√	Hw	2	4		Se 81	69
Fleece, Characteristics: Rambouillet	Rambouillet	Walker, Linda Berry	√	√	Iw	4	3		Su 79	55
Fleece, Characteristics: Romney	Romney	Walker, Linda Berry	√		Iw	5	2		Sp 80	63

SUBJECT	TITLE	AUTHOR	IL	INST	JOUR	VOL	NO	ISS	DATE	PAGE
Fleece, Characteristics: Scottish Blackface	Scottish Blackface	Walker, Linda Berry	√	√	Iw	4	4		Fa 79	60
Fleece: Columbia	Preparing a Columbia Fleece for Handweaving	Wilson, Helen		√	WJ	2	2	6	Oc 77	22
Fleece: Evaluating	If You Want to Work with the Best Wool Yarns, Spin Them Yourself	Bulback, Stanley	√	√	TM			13	O/N 87	56
Fleece Preparation	Kiwicraft	Horne, Beverley	√	√	S-O	3			79	52
Fleece Preparation	Spinning in the Grease	Ekstrom, Brenda	√	√	S-O	3			79	50
Fleece: Skirting	There's More Than One Way to Shear a Sheep	Parker, Ron; Teresa Parker	√	√	TM			13	O/N 87	61
Fleece-to-Apparel	From Lamb to Rack: Wool	Hodges, Eva			Hw	4	2		M/A 83	101
Fleece-to-Garment	Fleece-to-Garment Competition in New Zealand	Ashford, Joy			SS&D	4	1	13	Wi 72	21
Fleeces	From Spinner to Weaver	Kluge, Gini	√		S-O	8	1		Sp 84	43
Fleeces	Handspinner's Guide to Fleece Selection and Evaluation, A	Hiersch, Vicki			S-O	7	4		Wi 83	50
Fleeces	Pennyroyal Pick-up	Reedy, Dorrie		√	SS&D	15	1	57	Wi 83	79
Fleeces	Selecting Wool for Handspinning (error-corrected SS&D v13 n1 81 p4)	Fleet, Malcolm		√	SS&D	12	4	48	Fa 81	66
Fleeces	Wool: Choosing a Domestic Fleece	Walker, Linda Berry	√		S-O	8	3		Fa 84	21
Fleeces	Wool Forum: Producers and Consumers vs Bureaucracy	Parker, Ron; Teresa Parker			S-O	10	4		Si 86	7
Fleeces	Wool on the Hoof	Lis, Mary Jane	√	√	SS&D	12	4	48	Fa 81	64
Fleeces: British	Wool: Selecting British Fleeces	Leadbeater, Eliza			S-O	8	3		Fa 84	25
Flicking	Angora Goats and Mohair	Chastant, Kathryn Ross	√	√	S-O	7	3		Fa 83	29
Flicking	Spinning a Gossamer Web	Gibson-Roberts, Priscilla A.	√	√	Kn	4	1	9	Wi 87	62
Float Weave	Fabric #5 Towels (Constance LaLena)		√	√	Hw	8	2		M/A 87	52, I-10
Float Weave	Supplementary Weft Float Patterning	Marston, Ena	√	√	SS&D	9	4	36	Fa 78	63
Float Weave, Deflected Wefts	Notebook: Floats on the Surface (Diane Ruch)	Meyers, Ruth Nordquist, ed.	√	√	SS&D	14	3	55	Su 83	90
Float Weave: Overshot Effect	Hand Towels in Overshot Effect	Davenport, Betty	√	√	PWC	3	2	8		48
Float Weave: Plain-Weave-Derived	Flat-Woven Structures Found in Nomadic and Village Weavings from the Near East and Central Asia	Wertime, John T.	√		TMJ	18			79	33
Float Weave: Warp and Weft	Border Squares Curtain (Sharon D. Alderman)		√	>4	Hw	5	2		M/A 84	69, 106
Float Weave: Warp-Faced	Warping and Weaving Mitla Cloth on the Backstrap Loom	Knottenbelt, Maaike	√	√	TMJ	22			83	53
Float Weave: Weft	Leno Sampler Wallhanging (Betty Davenport)		√	√	Hw	7	2		M/A 86	47, I-8
Float Weave: Weft-Faced	Three-Color, Weft-Faced Block Weave	Neely, Cynthia H.	√	>4	SS&D	15	2	58	Sp 84	74
Floating Warps	Double-faced, Double-woven, Three-harness Krokbragd	Holtzer, Marilyn Emerson	√	√	SS&D	14	4	56	Fa 83	46
Flocati	Handwoven Flocati of Epirus, The	Gans, Naomi Beth; Catherine Haywood	√	√	SS&D	12	3	47	Su 81	35
Flokates	Chule: Freedom to Weave		√		Iw	4	4		Fa 79	47
Flokates	Chule's Wool Creations	Carter, Dianne	√		SS&D	17	4	68	Fa 86	30
Flood Damage	Minimizing Water Damage	Ziemke, Dene		√	SS&D	9	2	34	Sp 78	56
Floor Covering: Carpets, A.D. 1280, Depicted in Painting	Oriental Rug of A. D. 1280, An	Laing, Ellen Johnston	√		TMJ	4	1		De 74	82
Floor Coverings: Bathmats, Rag	Sock Top Bathmat (Paula Pfaff)		√	√	WJ	10	4	40	Sp 86	49
Floor Coverings: Carpets	Carpet Collections of the Philadelphia Museum of Art	Ellis, Charles Grant	√		TMJ	17			78	29
Floor Coverings: Carpets	International Carpet Extravaganza	Dyer, Carolyn Price	√		Fa	14	1		J/F 87	52
Floor Coverings: Carpets	London Carpeted in Oriental Gardens: The 4th International Conference on Oriental Carpets	Dyer, Carolyn Price	√		Fa	11	3		M/J 84	66
Floor Coverings: Carpets	New Carpet-Making School for Vragiana	Wile, Leslie	√		SS&D	4	2	14	Sp 73	17
Floor Coverings: Carpets	Secret Treasures of Tibet	Wiltsie-Vaniea, Anne	√		SS&D	18	3	71	Su 87	60

SUBJECT	TITLE	AUTHOR	IL	INST	JOUR	VOL	NO	ISS	DATE	PAGE
Floor Coverings: Carpets	Stanley Bulbach	McManus, Fran	√		S-O	8	2		Su 84	55
Floor Coverings: Carpets	Tribute to a Famous Weaver	Wilkinson, Dorothy	√		H&C	17	4		Fa 66	32
Floor Coverings: Carpets	"Turkmen: Tribal Carpets and Traditions" (Exhibit)	Dyer, Carol	√		Fa	8	3		M/J 81	70
Floor Coverings: Carpets	Why Bother with Natural Dyeing?	Bulbach, Stanley	√	√	TM			5	J/J 86	32
Floor Coverings: Carpets	William Morris, His Designs for Carpets & Tapestries	Morris, Barbara J.	√		H&C	12	4		Fa 61	18
Floor Coverings: Carpets, Afghan	Afghan Carpet Weavers		√		H&C	24	3		M/J 73	27
Floor Coverings: Carpets, Anatolian	Carpet-Makers of Western Anatolia, 1750–1914, The	Quataert, Donald			TMJ	25			86	25
Floor Coverings: Carpets, Axminster	Nineteenth Century American Carpets		√		WJ	4	4	16	Ap 80	53
Floor Coverings: Carpets, Brussels	Nineteenth Century American Carpets		√		WJ	4	4	16	Ap 80	53
Floor Coverings: Carpets, Chenille	Nineteenth Century American Carpets		√		WJ	4	4	16	Ap 80	53
Floor Coverings: Carpets, Compartment, Herat	Some Compartment Designs for Carpets, and Herat	Ellis, Charles Grant	√		TMJ	1	4		De 65	42
Floor Coverings: Carpets, Compartment, Persian	Some Compartment Designs for Carpets, and Herat	Ellis, Charles Grant	√		TMJ	1	4		De 65	42
Floor Coverings: Carpets, Egyptian, Mameluks	Symbolic Meanings in Oriental Rug Patterns: Part 3	Cammann, Schuyler V.R.	√		TMJ	3	3		De 72	42
Floor Coverings: Carpets, Ingrain	Nineteenth Century American Carpets		√		WJ	4	4	16	Ap 80	53
Floor Coverings: Carpets, Kashan	Gifts from Kashan to Cairo	Ellis, Charles Grant	√		TMJ	1	1		No 62	33
Floor Coverings: Carpets, Looped-Pile	Nineteenth Century American Carpets		√		WJ	4	4	16	Ap 80	53
Floor Coverings: Carpets, Mamluk	Is the Mamluk Carpet a Mandala? A Speculation	Ellis, Charles Grant	√		TMJ	4	1		De 74	30
Floor Coverings: Carpets, Mamluk	Mysteries of the Misplaced Mamluks	Ellis, Charles Grant	√		TMJ	2	2		De 67	2
Floor Coverings: Carpets, Miniature	Carpets in Miniature		√		Fa	11	3		M/J 84	99
Floor Coverings: Carpets, Oriental	Strengths of The Textile Museum's Oriental Carpet Collection, The	Ellis, Charles Grant	√		TMJ	24			85	61
Floor Coverings: Carpets, Ottoman	Gifts from Kashan to Cairo	Ellis, Charles Grant	√		TMJ	1	1		No 62	33
Floor Coverings: Carpets, Persian	Ardabil Puzzle, The	Weaver, Martin E.	√		TMJ	23			84	43
Floor Coverings: Carpets, Persian	Little Gems of Ardebil, The	Ellis, Charles Grant	√		TMJ	1	3		De 64	18
Floor Coverings: Carpets, Persian	Symbolic Meanings in Oriental Rug Patterns: Part 2	Cammann, Schuyler V.R.	√		TMJ	3	3		De 72	22
Floor Coverings: Carpets, Persian, Five-Medallion	Symbolic Meanings in Oriental Rug Patterns: Part 3	Cammann, Schuyler V.R.	√		TMJ	3	3		De 72	42
Floor Coverings: Carpets, Pile, Knotted	Afghan Carpets	Spooner, Brian	√		SS&D	5	2	18	Sp 74	41
Floor Coverings: Carpets, Spanish, Armorial	Two Remarkable Fifteenth Century Carpets from Spain	Mackie, Louise W.	√		TMJ	4	4		77	15
Floor Coverings: Carpets, Summer (Floorcloth)	Preliminary Report on a Group of Important Mughal Textiles, A	Smart, Ellen S.	√		TMJ	25			86	5
Floor Coverings: Carpets, Velvet	Nineteenth Century American Carpets		√		WJ	4	4	16	Ap 80	53
Floor Coverings: Carpets, Wilton	Nineteenth Century American Carpets		√		WJ	4	4	16	Ap 80	53
Floor Coverings: Floorcloths	Controlled Chaos: The Floorcloths of Carmon Slater	Fife, Lin	√		Fa	12	5		S/O 85	16
Floor Coverings: Floorcloths	Floorcloths: A New Look at an Old Technique	Holland, Nina	√		Fa	7	5		S/O 80	34
Floor Coverings: Floorcloths	Joan McCandlish	McCandlish, Joan	√		Fa	14	4		S/O 87	18
Floor Coverings: Floorcloths, Cotton, Painted	Preliminary Report on a Group of Important Mughal Textiles, A	Smart, Ellen S.	√		TMJ	25			86	5
Floor Coverings: Mats	"With or Without a Loom" (Exhibit)	Rowley, Kristin Carlsen	√		Fa	8	5		S/O 81	67
Floor Coverings: Rugs	"Adding" Treadles for a Complex Weave	Windeknecht, Margaret	√	> 4	CW	3	3	9	Ap 82	4
Floor Coverings: Rugs	Alice Pickett: Rugmaker	Pickett, Alice	√		Fa	7	5		S/O 80	55
Floor Coverings: Rugs	All White Overshot Rug (error-corrected WJ v7 n1 82 p36b)	Kendahl, Connie	√	√	WJ	6	4	24	Sp 82	23

SUBJECT	TITLE	AUTHOR	IL	INST	JOUR	VOL	NO	ISS	DATE	PAGE
Floor Coverings: Rugs	Anne Brooke's Impeccable Woven Rugs	West, Virginia	√		Fa	6	6		N/D 79	24
Floor Coverings: Rugs	Baa, Baa, Black Sheep, Have You Any Wool?	Bulbach, Stanley	√		S-O	9	2		Su 85	44
Floor Coverings: Rugs	Bedside Runner		√	√	S-O	7	3		Fa 83	57
Floor Coverings: Rugs	Behind the Scenes: A "Missing" Tradition	Goodman, Deborah Lerme	√		Fa	13	3		M/J 86	46
Floor Coverings: Rugs	Black & White Rug (Jette Kai)		√	√	Hw	8	3		M/J 87	50, I-8
Floor Coverings: Rugs	Block Weave Rug (Jean Scorgie, Janice Jones)		√	√	Hw	8	5		N/D 87	58, I-14
Floor Coverings: Rugs	Blue-Bleak Embers	Colton, Mary Rawcliffe	√	√	WJ	8	4	32	Sp 84	16
Floor Coverings: Rugs	Bound Rosepath Rug (Phyllis Waggoner)		√	√	Hw	8	3		M/J 87	59, I-11
Floor Coverings: Rugs	Boundweave		√		Hw	3	1		Ja 82	38
Floor Coverings: Rugs	Boundweave	Evans, Jane	√	√	WJ	1	4	4	Ap 77	3
Floor Coverings: Rugs	Boundweave: Learning from the Past	Waggoner, Phyllis	√	√	WJ	10	4	40	Sp 86	44
Floor Coverings: Rugs	Boundweave Rug on an Overshot Threading	Kindahl, Connie	√	√	SS&D	17	3	67	Su 86	58
Floor Coverings: Rugs	Broken Twill Rug (Halcyon)		√	√	Hw	1	1		F-W 79	31, 58
Floor Coverings: Rugs	Carpets for a Historic Philadelphia House	Scott, Chester M.	√	√	H&C	16	3		Su 65	13
Floor Coverings: Rugs	Chenille Rugs from California	Bryan, Dorothy			H&C	2	3		Su 51	22
Floor Coverings: Rugs	Children's Weft-Face Rug (Mary Skoy)		√	√	Hw	3	1		Ja 82	28, 81
Floor Coverings: Rugs	Chinese Rugs	Ellis, Charles Grant	√		TMJ	2	3		De 68	35
Floor Coverings: Rugs	Choosing a Loom, One Weaver's Experience with a Countermarch	Hoyt, Peggy	√	> 4	CW	4	1	10	Se 82	14
Floor Coverings: Rugs	Complimentary-Weft Plain Weave — A Pick-up Technique (error-corrected WJ v5 n1 80 p28d)	Hanley, Janet	√	√	WJ	4	4	16	Ap 80	22
Floor Coverings: Rugs	Contemporary Alpujarra Rugs	Lorton, Henni	√		H&C	4	4		Fa 53	28
Floor Coverings: Rugs	Conversation with Ed Oppenheimer, A	Pulleyn, Rob	√		Fa	4	4		J/A 77	24
Floor Coverings: Rugs	Corkscrew Weave	Barrett, Clotilde	√	> 4	WJ	5	1	17	Su 80	16
Floor Coverings: Rugs	Cows in Fiber	Timmons, Chris	√		Fa	11	4		J/A 84	55
Floor Coverings: Rugs	Crackle		√	√	WJ	3	3	11	Ja 79	32
Floor Coverings: Rugs	Critique: Una Flor Morada, A		√	√	Hw	4	2		M/A 83	44
Floor Coverings: Rugs	Desert Sunset Rugs (Hector and Halcyon)		√	√	Hw	1	2		S-S 80	32, 58
Floor Coverings: Rugs	Designing Rugs for Harness-Controlled Weaving		√	> 4	WJ	4	4	16	Ap 80	27
Floor Coverings: Rugs	Double-faced, Double-woven, Three-harness Krokbragd	Holtzer, Marilyn Emerson	√	√	SS&D	14	4	56	Fa 83	46
Floor Coverings: Rugs	Double-Faced Krokbragd	Holtzer, Marilyn Emerson	√	> 4	WJ	9	4	36	Sp 85	59
Floor Coverings: Rugs	Doup Leno (error-corrected WJ v3 n2 78 insert p38a)		√	√	WJ	3	2	10	Oc 78	32
Floor Coverings: Rugs	Easy Striped Knits	Walker, Barbara G.	√	√	TM			4	A/M 86	54
Floor Coverings: Rugs	Ed Oppenheimer: Rugs	Ligon, Linda	√		Iw	5	1		Wi 79	31
Floor Coverings: Rugs	Extra-Warp Woven-Pile	Sullivan, Donna	√	√	SS&D	17	1	65	Wi 85	19
Floor Coverings: Rugs	Fabrics for Interiors	VanSlyke, Gail Rutter		√	WJ	3	1	9	Jy 78	5
Floor Coverings: Rugs	Fantastic Finnweave, Part 3	Xenakis, Athanasios David	√	√	PWC			4	Ja 83	11
Floor Coverings: Rugs	Flamepoint Rugs for Everybody	Kirk, Betty Burian	√	√	WJ	8	4	32	Sp 84	12
Floor Coverings: Rugs	"For the Floor" (Exhibit)	Sider, Sandra	√		Fa	12	6		N/D 85	61
Floor Coverings: Rugs	For the Floor: The World at Our Feet	Busch, Akiko	√		SS&D	16	3	63	Su 85	54
Floor Coverings: Rugs	Four-End Block Draft or Summer and Winter	McClanathan, Barbara	√	√	WJ	8	4	32	Sp 84	22
Floor Coverings: Rugs	From Straw Mats to Hooked Rugs: Floor Coverings of the 19th Century	Thieme, Otto Charles	√		Fa	11	3		M/J 84	55
Floor Coverings: Rugs	" 'Genuine' Orientals from Denmark" (Exhibit)	Studsgarth, Randi	√		Fa	8	2		M/A 81	64
Floor Coverings: Rugs	Ghost Rugs	Kozikowski, Janusz; Nancy Kozikowski	√		Iw	4	1		Wi 78	24
Floor Coverings: Rugs	Ginger Jolley: Inspired by Navajo Weaving	Jolley, Ginger	√		Fa	11	3		M/J 84	36

SUBJECT	TITLE	AUTHOR	IL	INST	JOUR	VOL	NO	ISS	DATE	PAGE
Floor Coverings: Rugs	Hal Painter, Weaver of Tapestries and Rugs		√		H&C	16	3		Su 65	10
Floor Coverings: Rugs	Hand Woven Rugs: Equipment	Atwater, Mary Meigs			SCGM		29		48	1-28
Floor Coverings: Rugs	Hand Woven Rugs: Weaves, Crackle	Atwater, Mary Meigs	√	√	SCGM		29		48	19
Floor Coverings: Rugs	Hand Woven Rugs: Weaves, Four-Harness Overshot, Indian Saddle-Blanket Weave	Atwater, Mary Meigs	√	√	SCGM		29		48	18
Floor Coverings: Rugs	Hand Woven Rugs: Weaves, Four-Harness Overshot, No-Tabby Technique	Atwater, Mary Meigs	√	√	SCGM		29		48	15
Floor Coverings: Rugs	Hand Woven Rugs: Weaves, Plain Weave	Atwater, Mary Meigs			SCGM		29		48	3
Floor Coverings: Rugs	Hand Woven Rugs: Weaves, Plain Weave, Swedish "Matta" Technique	Atwater, Mary Meigs	√	√	SCGM		29		48	7
Floor Coverings: Rugs	Hand Woven Rugs: Weaves, Summer and Winter	Atwater, Mary Meigs	√	√	SCGM		29		48	21
Floor Coverings: Rugs	Hand Woven Rugs: Weaves, Two-Warp Weave	Atwater, Mary Meigs			SCGM		29		48	21
Floor Coverings: Rugs	Hand Woven Rugs: Weaves, Two-Warp Weave, Pick-Up Method	Atwater, Mary Meigs	√	√	SCGM		29		48	26
Floor Coverings: Rugs	Handweaving in Spain	Arnold, Ruth	√		H&C	8	4		Fa 57	10
Floor Coverings: Rugs	Handwoven Rugs from the Northwest	Disney, Jean	√		H&C	6	4		Fa 55	42
Floor Coverings: Rugs	Harts and Flowers: Sweden's Märta Määs-Fjetterstrom's Designs Inspired a Textile Renaissance	Selkurt, Claire	√		WJ	9	4	36	Sp 85	30
Floor Coverings: Rugs	Hints on Weaving and Finishing Rugs		√	√	WJ	2	2	6	Oc 77	16
Floor Coverings: Rugs	In Production? Rug Weaving	Fawkes, Judith Poxson	√		Iw	5	1		Wi 79	36
Floor Coverings: Rugs	Indian Textiles from Ecuador		√		H&C	10	1		Wi 59	19
Floor Coverings: Rugs	Indian Weavers and Contemporary Design		√		H&C	3	2		Sp 52	4
Floor Coverings: Rugs	Inkle Rug (Robin Wilton)		√	√	Hw	1	1		F-W 79	31, 58
Floor Coverings: Rugs	Jane Rademacher: A Working Weaver in Rural Wisconsin	Lowell-LaRoque, Jane V.	√		Fa	6	2		M/A 79	21
Floor Coverings: Rugs	Janet Swanson	Swanson, Janet	√		Fa	7	5		S/O 80	43
Floor Coverings: Rugs	Janusz Kozikowski	Kozikowski, Janusz	√		Fa	7	5		S/O 80	43
Floor Coverings: Rugs	Joan Gilfallan	Gilfallan, Joan	√		Fa	7	5		S/O 80	43
Floor Coverings: Rugs	Julia Keiner, Brings Fabrics from Israel		√		H&C	15	2		Sp 64	22
Floor Coverings: Rugs	Kristin Carlsen Rowley: Rugmaker	Rowley, Kristin Carlsen	√		Fa	7	5		S/O 80	52
Floor Coverings: Rugs	Krokbragd	Alderman, Sharon D.	√	√	Hw	2	2		Mr 81	33
Floor Coverings: Rugs	Krokbragd Rug (Lin Eppinger) (error-corrected Hw v2 n4 81 p22)		√	√	Hw	2	2		Mr 81	36
Floor Coverings: Rugs	'lectric Ikat Wins WHFL Award		√	√	SS&D	5	3	19	Su 74	92
Floor Coverings: Rugs	Leslie Ann Demane		√		Fa	4	5		S/O 77	55
Floor Coverings: Rugs	Loom Controlled Designs		√	> 4	WJ	3	3	11	Ja 79	18
Floor Coverings: Rugs	Maine Coast Rug (Halcyon Schomp and Hector Jaeger)		√	√	Hw	5	5		N/D 84	72, I-14
Floor Coverings: Rugs	Mattor (error-corrected WJ v2 n1 77 insert for vol. 1)	Dunham, Miriam	√	√	WJ	1	4	4	Ap 77	21
Floor Coverings: Rugs	Meet, Cross, and Separate	Holtzer, Marilyn Emerson	√	√	SS&D	16	3	63	Su 85	17
Floor Coverings: Rugs	Meet-and-Separate Technique	Martin, Mary	√	√	WJ	8	4	32	Sp 84	14
Floor Coverings: Rugs	Morning Glory	Bulbach, Stanley	√	√	S-O	9	1		Sp 85	15
Floor Coverings: Rugs	Multiple Harness Crackle		√	> 4	WJ	4	1	13	Jy 79	15
Floor Coverings: Rugs	Multiple Shaft Weaving — 2-Tie Four-End Block Drafts		√	> 4	WJ	6	4	24	Sp 82	48
Floor Coverings: Rugs	Navajo Inspired Rugs (Penelope Drooker)		√	√	Hw	6	2		M/A 85	58, I-16
Floor Coverings: Rugs	Navajo Saddle Blanket Patterns	Barrett, Clotilde	√	√	WJ	1	1	1	Jy 76	22
Floor Coverings: Rugs	"Nina Holland: Bound Weave Rugs/Hangings" (Exhibit)	Bess, Nancy Moore	√		Fa	9	1		J/F 82	83
Floor Coverings: Rugs	Notes from a Rugweaver's Journal	Schomp, Halcyon; Hector Jaeger	√	√	Hw	3	4		Se 82	35

SUBJECT	TITLE	AUTHOR	IL	INST	JOUR	VOL	NO	ISS	DATE	PAGE
Floor Coverings: Rugs	Observations on the Six-End Block Draft for Rug Weaving	Schlein, Alice	√	√	WJ	6	4	24	Sp 82	30
Floor Coverings: Rugs	On Rugs and Rug Weaving		√	⟨	Hw	5	2		M/A 84	75
Floor Coverings: Rugs	On Weaving Chenille Rugs	Hausner, Walter	√		H&C	3	2		Sp 52	59
Floor Coverings: Rugs	Overshot Derived from 2/2 Twill: Ornamental Throw Rug in Overshot	Davidsohn, Marty	√	√	PWC	3	2	8		22
Floor Coverings: Rugs	Painted Rug Designs: Trader Hubbell's Influence on Navajo Weaving	Blue, Martha	√		Fa	14	5		N/D 87	5
Floor Coverings: Rugs	Perspective on Rug Design, A	Stanley, Martha			WJ	7	2	26	Fa 82	66
Floor Coverings: Rugs	Peter Collingwood, English Rug Weaver		√		H&C	11	4		Fa 60	12
Floor Coverings: Rugs	Peter Collingwood, His Weaves and Weaving: A Flat Weave For Rugs, Pick-Up or Harness Controlled	Collingwood, Peter; Harriet Tidball, ed.	√	√	SCGM		8		63	11
Floor Coverings: Rugs	Peter Collingwood, His Weaves and Weaving: A Flat Weave For Rugs, Pick-Up or Harness Controlled	Collingwood, Peter; Harriet Tidball, ed.	√	√	SCGM		8		63	11
Floor Coverings: Rugs	Peter Collingwood, His Weaves and Weaving: A Patterned Flat Weave For Rugs	Collingwood, Peter; Harriet Tidball, ed.	√	√	SCGM		8		63	14
Floor Coverings: Rugs	Pile Weaves, Rugs and Tapestry: Rugs in Bound Weave	Zielinski, S. A.; Robert Leclerc, ed.	√	√	MWL	14			'51–'73	56
Floor Coverings: Rugs	Practical Weave for Rugs (Reprint), A	Atwater, Mary Meigs	√	> 4	H&C	26	1		J/F 75	7
Floor Coverings: Rugs	Primitive Indian Designs Inspire Ecuador's Gift to United Nations		√		H&C	4	1		Wi 52	13
Floor Coverings: Rugs	Projects for a Six-Dent Rigid Heddle Backstrap Loom	Swanson, Karen	√	√	H&C	21	4		Fa 70	9
Floor Coverings: Rugs	Quick Thick Rug, A		√	√	WJ	7	4	28	Sp 83	43
Floor Coverings: Rugs	Rag Rugs	Michaelis, Aimida	√		SS&D	2	4	8	Fa 71	25
Floor Coverings: Rugs	Rag Rugs, Not Always Made from Rags	Erickson, Johanna	√	√	TM			3	F/M 86	40
Floor Coverings: Rugs	Recycling—Ragtime	Ligon, Linda	√	√	Iw	3	4		Su 78	22
Floor Coverings: Rugs	Result of Weaving Rugs, The	Brooke, Anne	√		WJ	7	4	28	Sp 83	39
Floor Coverings: Rugs	Rib Weave Rug (Mary Veercamp) (error-corrected Hw v4 n4 83 p92)		√	√	Hw	4	2		M/A 83	47, 84
Floor Coverings: Rugs	Ripsmatta Rug (Diane Tramba, Marianne Goddard, Joanne Tallarovie)		√	> 4	Hw	2	3		My 81	45, 83
Floor Coverings: Rugs	Rosemary R. Olmsted: Following Krokbragd's Crooked Path	Olmsted, Rosemary R.	√		Fa	11	3		M/J 84	28
Floor Coverings: Rugs	Round Rug Woven on a Hula Hoop, A	Pemberton, Mildred	√	√	H&C	20	3		Su 69	12
Floor Coverings: Rugs	Rug Based on 3-Shaft Striaght Twill		√	√	WJ	5	4	20	Sp 81	20
Floor Coverings: Rugs	Rug (Marilyn Dillard)		√	√	Hw	4	4		S/O 83	60, 105
Floor Coverings: Rugs	Rug (Pam Toller)		√	√	Hw	2	1		F-W 80	32, 77
Floor Coverings: Rugs	Rug Weaving...Design Considerations	Stanley, Martha Alice	√		Iw	5	1		Wi 79	20
Floor Coverings: Rugs	Rug Weaving: How to Avoid Drawing-in of the Warp	Stanley, Martha	√	√	WJ	6	2	22	Fa 81	10
Floor Coverings: Rugs	Rug Weaving: One Weaver's Approach	Hand, Barbara	√	> 4	WJ	7	4	28	Sp 83	32
Floor Coverings: Rugs	Rug Weaving: Rug Yarns	Stanley, Martha	√		WJ	6	3	23	Wi 81	44
Floor Coverings: Rugs	Rug Weaving with Natural Dyed Yarns	Fisher, Pat	√	√	SS&D	2	2	6	Sp 71	28
Floor Coverings: Rugs	Rugs: An Exhibition of Contemporary Handwoven Floorcoverings	Smayda, Norma			SS&D	17	4	68	Fa 86	83
Floor Coverings: Rugs	Rugs and Carpets — Their Importance in Interior Design		√		H&C	3	4		Fa 52	30
Floor Coverings: Rugs	Rugs and Carpets, Their Importance in Interior Design		√		H&C	4	1		Wi 52	22
Floor Coverings: Rugs	Rugs Based on Four Harness Twills (error-corrected WJ v2 n2 77 insert for vol. 2)		√	√	WJ	2	1	5	Jy 77	23
Floor Coverings: Rugs	Rugs for Interiors	Roach, Dianne Carol	√		SS&D	16	4	64	Fa 85	18
Floor Coverings: Rugs	Rugs for the Dream Auction	Moes, Dini	√	√	SS&D	17	2	66	Sp 86	58
Floor Coverings: Rugs	Rugs of Mary Veerkamp, The		√	√	Hw	4	2		M/A 83	46
Floor Coverings: Rugs	Rugs on a Three-End Block Draft	Kindahl, Connie	√	√	WJ	8	4	32	Sp 84	19

SUBJECT	TITLE	AUTHOR	IL	INST	JOUR	VOL	NO	ISS	DATE	PAGE
Floor Coverings: Rugs	Rugs Woven on Summer and Winter Threading		√	> 4	WJ	3	1	9	Jy 78	12
Floor Coverings: Rugs	Rugweaving: Teaching on Two Harnesses	Mattera, Joanne	√	√	Iw	5	1		Wi 79	27
Floor Coverings: Rugs	Shadow Weave Rug on Four Harnesses		√	√	WJ	4	4	16	Ap 80	24
Floor Coverings: Rugs	Shaft Switch Techniques (error-corrected WJ v5 n1 80 p5)	Busse, Jane	√	√	WJ	4	4	16	Ap 80	11
Floor Coverings: Rugs	Shaft Switching on Boundweave (Nancy Kraushaar)		√	√	WJ	5	3	19	Wi 81	38
Floor Coverings: Rugs	Shaft-Switch Rugs with Pinstripe Pattern Areas		√	√	WJ	5	2	18	Fa 80	28
Floor Coverings: Rugs	Shaft-Switching Device of Richard Shultz		√	√	WJ	8	4	32	Sp 84	35
Floor Coverings: Rugs	Shaft-Switching Device of William Koepp		√	√	WJ	8	4	32	Sp 84	32
Floor Coverings: Rugs	Shaft-Switching on 3-End Drafts: Striped Patterns, Part 1		√	√	WJ	6	1	21	Su 81	7
Floor Coverings: Rugs	Shaft-Switching to Create Tapestry Effects	Green, Andrea	√	√	WJ	8	4	32	Sp 84	36
Floor Coverings: Rugs	Some Weft-Float Brocaded Rugs of the Bergama-Ezine Region	Beattie, May H.	√		TMJ	3	2		De 71	20
Floor Coverings: Rugs	"Song of the Loom: New Traditions In Navajo Weaving, The" (Exhibit)		√		TM			11	J/J 87	18
Floor Coverings: Rugs	Sonja Flavin: Weaving for the Classics	Sobieszek, Robert A.	√		Fa	11	3		M/J 84	70
Floor Coverings: Rugs	Southwest Reflections: Fiber Artists Inspired by the New Mexico Landscape	Colton, Mary Rawcliffe	√		WJ	11	1	41	Su 86	20
Floor Coverings: Rugs	Spinning Doghair	Barrett, Clotilde	√	√	WJ	1	1	1	Jy 76	27
Floor Coverings: Rugs	Spot Weave Rug	Hanley, Janet	√	√	WJ	3	4	12	Ap 79	40
Floor Coverings: Rugs	Story of the Johnson Rugs, The	Gallinger, Osma Couch	√		H&C	7	2		Sp 56	28
Floor Coverings: Rugs	Summer and Winter Rug (Jean Anstine) (error-corrected Hw v4 n2 83 p80)		√	√	Hw	3	5		N/D 82	48, 87
Floor Coverings: Rugs	Super Rug: A Chenille "Twice-Woven" Rug	Champion, Ellen	√	√	WJ	6	4	24	Sp 82	26
Floor Coverings: Rugs	Sweetgrass, Cedar & Sage: Portrait of a Southwestern Weaver	Schevill, Margot	√		WJ	10	1	37	Su 85	24
Floor Coverings: Rugs	Tapestry Effects in Boundweave Rugs	Ziebarth, Charlotte Molcar	√	√	Iw	5	1		Wi 79	23
Floor Coverings: Rugs	Textile Arts of Multan, Pakistan: Part 2	Shahzaman, Mahboob	√	> 4	SS&D	4	4	16	Fa 73	65
Floor Coverings: Rugs	Textured Rugs from the Pacific Coast		√		H&C	3	3		Su 52	37
Floor Coverings: Rugs	Theme Issue		√		Fa	7	5		S/O 80	
Floor Coverings: Rugs	Theme Issue		√		Fa	11	3		M/J 84	
Floor Coverings: Rugs	Three-Color, Weft-Faced Block Weave	Neely, Cynthia H.	√	> 4	SS&D	15	2	58	Sp 84	74
Floor Coverings: Rugs	Twentieth Century Rug	Hofstrom, Juanita	√	√	H&C	22	1		Wi 71	16
Floor Coverings: Rugs	Twill and Plain Weave Blocks with Long-Eyed Heddles	Broughton, Eve T.	√	> 4	WJ	8	4	32	Sp 84	58
Floor Coverings: Rugs	Twill Rugs (Marilyn Dillard)		√	√	Hw	6	5		N/D 85	Cover, I-5
Floor Coverings: Rugs	Two-Harness Rugs	Van Cleve, Kate	√		H&C	4	2		Sp 53	53
Floor Coverings: Rugs	Two-Tie Unit for Rugs: Part 1, The Double-Faced Stuffer Weave and Summer-and-Winter, The	Windeknecht, Margaret	√	> 4	SS&D	16	1	61	Wi 84	82
Floor Coverings: Rugs	Two-Tie Unit for Rugs: Part 2 Warping and Weaving Methods, The	Windeknecht, Margaret	√	> 4	SS&D	16	2	62	Sp 85	34
Floor Coverings: Rugs	V'Soske Rugs Through the Years	V'Soske, Vesta S.	√		H&C	5	4		Fa 54	8
Floor Coverings: Rugs	Warp-Faced Krokbragd	Jensen, Gay; Donna Kaplan	√	> 4	WJ	12	2	46	Fa 87	62
Floor Coverings: Rugs	Warp-Faced Rugs	Giles, Lynne	√		Hw	7	4		S/O 86	40
Floor Coverings: Rugs	"Weaver's Art: Selected Rug Traditions of the Middle East and China, A" (Exhibit)	Talley, Charles	√		Fa	6	5		S/O 79	76
Floor Coverings: Rugs	Weaving a Tribute for Their Church		√		H&C	2	4		Fa 51	23
Floor Coverings: Rugs	Wedge Weave: A New Approach	Noble, Carol Rasmussen	√	√	WJ	5	2	18	Fa 80	49
Floor Coverings: Rugs	Weft Ikat for Rugs	Van Gelder, Lydia	√	√	WJ	5	4	20	Sp 81	31
Floor Coverings: Rugs	Working with the Wall ... A Community Garden		√		SS&D	10	4	40	Fa 79	8
Floor Coverings: Rugs, Aaklae	Rugs by an Architect		√	√	H&C	13	4		Fa 62	6

SUBJECT	TITLE	AUTHOR	IL	INST	JOUR	VOL	NO	ISS	DATE	PAGE
Floor Coverings: Rugs, Anatolian	Anatolian Rugs: An Essay on Method	Denny, Walter B.	√		TMJ	3	4		De 73	7
Floor Coverings: Rugs, Anatolian	"Flowers of the Yayla: Yoruk Weaving of the Toros Mountains" (Exhibit)	Bloom, Mary Jane	√		Fa	11	3		M/J 84	76
Floor Coverings: Rugs, Anatolian	Textile Museum's White-Ground Rug, The		√		SS&D	8	4	32	Fa 77	45
Floor Coverings: Rugs, Backing	Weaving Rya and Flossa Rugs	af Kleen, Elizabeth	√	√	H&C	13	3		Su 62	29
Floor Coverings: Rugs, Color Mixing	Effective Weave for Rugs, An		√	√	H&C	11	1		Wi 60	26
Floor Coverings: Rugs, Contemporary	Country of Origin, USA: A Decade of Contemporary Rugs	Stevens, Rebeccah A. T.	√		Fa	11	3		M/J 84	60
Floor Coverings: Rugs, Contemporary	For the Floor: An International Exhibit of Contemporary Artists' Rugs	Wolff, Colette	√		Hw	6	2		M/A 85	20
Floor Coverings: Rugs, Cotton	Dyed Cotton Rug in Overshot	Wright, Gilbert	√	√	WJ	7	4	28	Sp 83	81
Floor Coverings: Rugs, Fabric-Strip	Two Block Rug in Boundweave	Waggoner, Phyllis	√	√	WJ	12	1	45	Su 87	26
Floor Coverings: Rugs, Felt	Felt-making Craftsmen of the Anatolian and Iranian Plateaux	Gervers, Michael; Veronika Gervers	√	√	TMJ	4	1		De 74	14
Floor Coverings: Rugs, Felt	Traditional Felt Rugmaking in Turkey	Ispay, Francis	√	√	Fa	13	4		J/A 86	18
Floor Coverings: Rugs, Felted	Rugs: Jun Tomita, Weaver		√		Fa	9	2		M/A 82	61
Floor Coverings: Rugs, Fleece	Fleece Rug	Hochberg, Bette	√	√	Hw	2	2		Mr 81	52
Floor Coverings: Rugs, Fleece	Fleece Rug (Elizabeth Ligon)		√	√	Hw	2	2		Mr 81	52, 80
Floor Coverings: Rugs, Flossa	Four Projects from Mrs. Elsie H. Gubser	Gubser, Elsie H.	√	√	H&C	6	3		Su 55	49
Floor Coverings: Rugs, Flossa	Hand Woven Rugs: Weaves, Plain Weave, Tapestry Techniques	Atwater, Mary Meigs	√	√	SCGM		29		48	11
Floor Coverings: Rugs, Flossa	Kerstin Ekengren	af Kleen, Nils E.	√		H&C	15	2		Sp 64	18
Floor Coverings: Rugs, Flossa	Weaving Rya and Flossa Rugs	af Kleen, Elizabeth	√	√	H&C	13	3		Su 62	29
Floor Coverings: Rugs, Fur	Discarded Fur Pieces for Rugs and Pillows	Cook, Bonny	√	√	SS&D	4	3	15	Su 73	20
Floor Coverings: Rugs, Fur, Imitation	Mystery of Pile Rugs, The	Austin, Carole	√		Fa	13	6		N/D 86	1
Floor Coverings: Rugs, Handcrafted, American	American Handcrafted Rug: Past and Present, The	Stevens, Rebecca A. T.	√		TMJ	23			84	73
Floor Coverings: Rugs, Hooked	"American Hooked Rugs: 1850–1957" (Exhibit)	Scarborough, Jessica	√		Fa	8	6		N/D 81	68
Floor Coverings: Rugs, Hooked	Chromatic Effervescence: The Hooked Surface As a Response to My Environment	Eyerman, Linda	√		Fa	10	2		M/A 83	22
Floor Coverings: Rugs, Hooked	Designs in Rughooking		√		H&C	23	3		M/J 72	51
Floor Coverings: Rugs, Hooked	Dolphin Rug	Bahr, Ann	√	√	H&C	21	2		Sp 70	36
Floor Coverings: Rugs, Hooked	Exuberant Art of Elizabeth Browning Jackson, The	Place, Jennifer	√		Fa	10	6		N/D 83	12
Floor Coverings: Rugs, Hooked	Hooked on Texture: Unconventional Punch-Needle Rugs	Crouse, Gloria E.	√	√	TM			14	D/J 87	68
Floor Coverings: Rugs, Hooked	Hooking Wild Horses (Zorach, Marguerite)		√		TM			10	A/M 87	88
Floor Coverings: Rugs, Hooked	Rug Craftsmen	Olmsted, Anna W.	√		H&C	18	2		Sp 67	27
Floor Coverings: Rugs, Hooked	Rug for a Beginner	Holmes, Cora	√		S-O	10	1		Sp 86	24
Floor Coverings: Rugs, Hooked	Rug Hooking for Relaxation	Sizer, Theodore	√	√	H&C	17	2		Sp 66	8
Floor Coverings: Rugs, Hooked	Rug Hooking: The Flourishing of a Time-Honored Technique	Moshimer, Joan	√	√	Fa	7	5		S/O 80	37
Floor Coverings: Rugs, Hooked	Rugs Are Art				TM			13	O/N 87	4
Floor Coverings: Rugs, Hooked	Three Moods of Hooking Rugs, The	Oakley, Helen			TM			2	D/J 85	10
Floor Coverings: Rugs, Hooked	Traditional Rug Hooking with a Twist	Erickson, Janet Doub	√	√	TM			12	A/S 87	30
Floor Coverings: Rugs, Hooked	Truth About American Hooking, The	Fallier, Jeanne H.	√	√	TM			14	D/J 87	20
Floor Coverings: Rugs, Iran	Kings, Heroes, Lovers: Pictorial Rugs From the Tribes and Villages of Iran	Goodman, Deborah Lerme	√		Fa	11	3		M/J 84	38
Floor Coverings: Rugs, Islamic, 19th Century	Iconography of Everyday Life in Nineteenth-Century Middle Eastern Rugs, The	Paquin, Gerard A.	√		TMJ	22			83	5
Floor Coverings: Rugs, Kazak	Kazak Rugs	Tschebull, Raoul	√		TMJ	3	2		De 71	2

SUBJECT	TITLE	AUTHOR	IL	INST	JOUR	VOL	NO	ISS	DATE	PAGE
Floor Coverings: Rugs, Kilim, Kurdish	Kurdish Kilim Weaving in the Van-Hakkari District of Eastern Turkey	Landreau, Anthony N.	√	√	TMJ	3	4		De 73	27
Floor Coverings: Rugs; Kirman, Vase Rugs	Kirman's Heritage in Washington: Vase Rugs in The Textile Museum	Ellis, Charles Grant	√		TMJ	2	3		De 68	17
Floor Coverings: Rugs, Knitted	Knitted Rugs	Austin, Carole	√		Fa	11	3		M/J 84	57
Floor Coverings: Rugs, Knotted	Bhotiya Woolens from India	Willis, Elizabeth Bayley	√		H&C	5	2		Sp 54	4
Floor Coverings: Rugs, Knotted	Weavers in Iran, Thousands at Work on Primitive Looms	Leclerc, Robert	√		H&C	21	2		Sp 70	9
Floor Coverings: Rugs, Latch-Hook	Vera Tonrey's Latch Hook Rug		√		S-O	9	3		Fa 85	14
Floor Coverings: Rugs, Linen	Linen Rug		√	√	Hw	2	3		My 81	50, 82
Floor Coverings: Rugs, Miniature	Woven Miniatures		√	√	WJ	3	4	12	Ap 79	15
Floor Coverings: Rugs, Morocco	Traditional Berber Weaving in Central Morocco	Forelli, Sally; Jeanette Harries	√		TMJ	4	4		77	41
Floor Coverings: Rugs, Navajo	Auctioning Rugs Among the Navajos	Marcus, Ruth-Claire	√		TM			6	A/S 86	16
Floor Coverings: Rugs, Navajo	Commercial Materials in Modern Navajo Rugs	Hedlund, Ann Lane	√		TMJ	25			86	83
Floor Coverings: Rugs, Navajo	D. Y. Begay: A Navajo Weaver in New York City	Harvey, Nancy	√		SS&D	17	4	68	Fa 86	32
Floor Coverings: Rugs, Navajo	Exploring a Tradition: Navajo Rugs, Classic and Contemporary	Elliott, Malinda	√		Fa	11	3		M/J 84	32
Floor Coverings: Rugs, Navajo	"Eyedazzlers!" (Exhibit)	Lonier, Terri	√		Fa	11	3		M/J 84	77
Floor Coverings: Rugs, Navajo	Navajo: Textiles, Blankets, Rugs, Tapestries	Morrow, Mable	√	√	SS&D	1	4	4	Se 70	3
Floor Coverings: Rugs, Navajo	Navajo: Textiles, Blankets, Rugs, Tapestries	Morrow, Mable	√	√	SS&D	2	1	5	De 70	5
Floor Coverings: Rugs, Navajo	Navajo Weaving, Contemporary and Traditional		√		H&C	18	2		Sp 67	6
Floor Coverings: Rugs, Navajo	Pearl Sunrise: Weaving the "Old Way"	Sunrise, Pearl	√		Fa	11	3		M/J 84	34
Floor Coverings: Rugs, Navajo	Rugs Woven on Summer and Winter Threading		√	> 4	WJ	3	1	9	Jy 78	12
Floor Coverings: Rugs, Navajo Saddle Blanket	Navajo Saddle Blanket Patterns	Barrett, Clotilde	√	√	WJ	11	1	41	Su 86	56
Floor Coverings: Rugs, Oriental	Ordinary Weaver and Her Extraordinary Rugs, An	Xenakis, Alexis Yiorgos	√		PWC	4	2	12		4
Floor Coverings: Rugs, Oriental	Return of the Magic Carpets	Sortor, David	√		H&C	5	3		Su 54	16
Floor Coverings: Rugs, Oriental	Symbolic Meanings in Oriental Rug Patterns: Part 1	Cammann, Schuyler V.R.	√		TMJ	3	3		De 72	5
Floor Coverings: Rugs, Oriental	Washington Hajji Baba, The	Jones, H. McCoy	√		TMJ	2	2		De 67	35
Floor Coverings: Rugs, Ottoman, Prayer Rugs	Ottoman Prayer Rugs, The	Ellis, Charles Grant	√		TMJ	2	4		De 69	5
Floor Coverings: Rugs, Painted	Martin Peavy: An Improvisational Approach to Rugs	Peavy, Martin	√		Fa	11	3		M/J 84	22
Floor Coverings: Rugs, Paper	Rugs: Lin Fife, Papermaker		√		Fa	9	2		M/A 82	61
Floor Coverings: Rugs, Pile	Color Related Decorating Textiles Rugs, Draperies, Upholstery: Double Corduroy Pile Rugs, Other Floated Pile Rugs	Rhodes, Tonya Stalons; Harriet Tidball, ed.			SCGM		14		65	1
Floor Coverings: Rugs, Pile	Cotton String Rug (Jean Bendon)		√	√	Hw	3	2		Mr 82	51, 90
Floor Coverings: Rugs, Pile	Double Corduroy (Marilyn Dillard)		√	√	Hw	7	4		S/O 86	44
Floor Coverings: Rugs, Pile	Double Corduroy Rug (Marilyn Dillard)		√	√	Hw	7	4		S/O 86	45, I-9
Floor Coverings: Rugs, Pile	Double Corduroy with Varied Pile	Collingwood, Peter	√	√	Hw	7	4		S/O 86	47
Floor Coverings: Rugs, Pile	Hand Woven Rugs: Weaves, Plain Weave, Rugs with Knotted Pile	Atwater, Mary Meigs	√	√	SCGM		29		48	10
Floor Coverings: Rugs, Pile	Martha Opdahl	Opdahl, Martha	√		Fa	13	4		J/A 86	27
Floor Coverings: Rugs, Pile	Mystery of Pile Rugs, The	Austin, Carole	√		Fa	13	6		N/D 86	1
Floor Coverings: Rugs, Pile	Native Craftsmen Produce for Nile Hilton Hotel		√		H&C	11	3		Su 60	54
Floor Coverings: Rugs, Pile	New Method for Pile Weave, A	Deru, Crescent	√	√	H&C	8	3		Su 57	16
Floor Coverings: Rugs, Pile	Pile Weaves, Rugs and Tapestry: Chenille	Zielinski, S. A.; Robert Leclerc, ed.	√	√	MWL	14			'51–'73	26

SUBJECT	TITLE	AUTHOR	IL	INST	JOUR	VOL	NO	ISS	DATE	PAGE
Floor Coverings: Rugs, Pile	Pile Weaves, Rugs and Tapestry: Free Patterns in Chenille	Zielinski, S. A.; Robert Leclerc, ed.	√	√	MWL	14			'51–'73	43
Floor Coverings: Rugs, Pile	Pile Weaves, Rugs and Tapestry: The Ultimate in Chenille	Zielinski, S. A.; Robert Leclerc, ed.	√	√	MWL	14			'51–'73	49
Floor Coverings: Rugs, Pile	Rug from Thrums, A	Kaleda, Ruth	√	√	H&C	13	3		Su 62	41
Floor Coverings: Rugs, Pile	Weaving in Quebec: New Traditions	Barrett, Clotilde	√	√	WJ	6	4	24	Sp 82	14
Floor Coverings: Rugs, Pile, Corduroy	Amazing Color-Pattern Corduroy Rug		√	> 4	PWC	3	4	10		22
Floor Coverings: Rugs, Pile, Double Corduroy	Color Related Decorating Textiles Rugs, Draperies, Upholstery: Double Corduroy Pile Rugs	Rhodes, Tonya Stalons; Harriet Tidball, ed.			SCGM		14		65	1
Floor Coverings: Rugs, Pile, Double Corduroy	Peter Collingwood, His Weaves and Weaving: Double Corduroy Pile Rugs	Collingwood, Peter; Harriet Tidball, ed.	√	√	SCGM		8		63	3
Floor Coverings: Rugs, Pile, Knotted	Knotted and Tufted Rugs	Bryan, Dorothy	√	√	H&C	9	1		Wi 57	4
Floor Coverings: Rugs, Pile, Knotted	Knotted Rugs		√		H&C	16	1		Wi 65	37
Floor Coverings: Rugs, Pile, Looped	Weaving with Lofty Yarns	Frey, Berta	√	√	H&C	18	2		Sp 67	35
Floor Coverings: Rugs, Pile, Patterned	Pile Weaves, Rugs and Tapestry: Patterns in Velvet Rugs	Zielinski, S. A.; Robert Leclerc, ed.	√	√	MWL	14			'51–'73	70
Floor Coverings: Rugs, Pile, Tied, Unspun Wool	Hand Woven Rugs: Weaves, Plain Weave, Pile, Tied	Atwater, Mary Meigs	√	√	SCGM		29		48	14
Floor Coverings: Rugs, Pile, Tufted	Knotted and Tufted Rugs	Bryan, Dorothy	√	√	H&C	9	1		Wi 57	4
Floor Coverings: Rugs, Pile, Velvet	Corded Rep Weave and Velvet Rugs	Proulx, Bibiane April	√	√	SS&D	17	3	67	Su 86	80
Floor Coverings: Rugs, Pile, Velvet	Pile Weaves, Rugs and Tapestry: Velvet Rugs	Zielinski, S. A.; Robert Leclerc, ed.	√	√	MWL	14			'51–'73	65
Floor Coverings: Rugs, Pile, Warpless	Pile Weaves, Rugs and Tapestry: Pile Rugs Without Warp	Zielinski, S. A.; Robert Leclerc, ed.	√	√	MWL	14			'51–'73	86
Floor Coverings: Rugs, Pin	"Pin Rugs of Ellen Oltchick, The" (Exhibit)	Poon, Vivian	√		Fa	10	6		N/D 83	74
Floor Coverings: Rugs, Rag	Barefoot Comfort Rag Rug (Linda Ligon)		√	√	Hw	5	4		S/O 84	70, 105
Floor Coverings: Rugs, Rag	Double Corduroy Rug (error-corrected WJ v11 n3 87 p78)	Waggoner, Phyllis	√	√	WJ	11	2	42	Fa 86	42
Floor Coverings: Rugs, Rag	From Cotton Patch to Cotton Patches and Then Some	Linder, Olive	√	√	WJ	5	4	20	Sp 81	48
Floor Coverings: Rugs, Rag	From Rags to Riches	Krook, Inga	√	√	Hw	4	3		M/J 83	32
Floor Coverings: Rugs, Rag	From Rags to Riches: Artful Recycling	Loud, Dana	√		Fa	13	5		S/O 86	23
Floor Coverings: Rugs, Rag	Hand Woven Rugs: Weaves, Plain Weave, Rugs of Rag Stirps	Atwater, Mary Meigs	√	√	SCGM		29		48	3
Floor Coverings: Rugs, Rag	Log Cabin Rag Rugs	Meany, Janet K.	√	√	WJ	9	4	36	Sp 85	50
Floor Coverings: Rugs, Rag	"Maria" Rag Rug (Inga Krook)		√	√	Hw	6	3		Su 85	56, I-14
Floor Coverings: Rugs, Rag	Mystery Sun Rug	Oles, Jery	√	> 4	WJ	8	4	32	Sp 84	10
Floor Coverings: Rugs, Rag	Pile Weaves, Rugs and Tapestry: Catalogne or Plain Rag Rugs	Zielinski, S. A.; Robert Leclerc, ed.		√	MWL	14			'51–'73	74
Floor Coverings: Rugs, Rag	Pushing the Limits with Rags	Linder, Olive	√	√	Hw	2	3		My 81	51
Floor Coverings: Rugs, Rag	Rag Rug Traditions	Meany, Janet K.	√		WJ	9	4	36	Sp 85	56
Floor Coverings: Rugs, Rag	Rag Rugs		√	√	WJ	4	1	13	Jy 79	22
Floor Coverings: Rugs, Rag	Rag Rugs: Helen Gushee Helps Keep a Tradition Alive	Woelfle, Gretchen	√		Fa	7	5		S/O 80	31
Floor Coverings: Rugs, Rag	Rag Rugs on Overshot Threading	Snover, Susan	√	√	WJ	5	4	20	Sp 81	22
Floor Coverings: Rugs, Rag	Rag Rugs with Overlapping Weft Ends	White, Ruth	√	√	WJ	6	4	24	Sp 82	28
Floor Coverings: Rugs, Rag	Rags (Susan Snover)		√	√	Hw	2	3		My 81	43
Floor Coverings: Rugs, Rag	Rags to Rugs (error-corrected H&C v14 n1 63 p46)	Shaver, Bee	√	√	H&C	13	4		Fa 62	40
Floor Coverings: Rugs, Rag	Rags Unlimited	Evans, Jane A.	√	> 4	Hw	2	3		My 81	44
Floor Coverings: Rugs, Rag	Ragtime	Erickson, Johanna	√	√	SS&D	14	3	55	Su 83	41
Floor Coverings: Rugs, Rag	Rugs in the American Tradition, Ruth Place Finds a Continuing Demand		√		H&C	19	2		Sp 68	20

SUBJECT	TITLE	AUTHOR	IL	INST	JOUR	VOL	NO	ISS	DATE	PAGE
Floor Coverings: Rugs, Rag	Shaker Technique: Part 2, Rag Rugs, The	Gordon, Beverly	√	√	SS&D	8	1	29	WI 76	83
Floor Coverings: Rugs, Rag	Soumak Rug (Jean Scorgie)		√	√	Hw	6	4		S/O 85	41, I-4
Floor Coverings: Rugs, Rag	Stenciled Rag Rug (Betty Oldenberg)		√	√	Hw	5	3		Su 84	74
Floor Coverings: Rugs, Rag	Story of My Dining Room Rug, The	Rogers, Carrie M.	√	√	WJ	6	4	24	Sp 82	24
Floor Coverings: Rugs, Rag	Toothbrush Handle Rugs: Nålbinding with Rags	Nelson, Lila	√	√	WJ	12	2	46	Fa 87	16
Floor Coverings: Rugs, Rag	Twill Wool Rag Rug (Mary Kay Stoehr)		√	> 4	Hw	5	2		M/A 84	57, 95
Floor Coverings: Rugs, Rag	Weaving in Quebec: Traditional Quebecois Weaving	Barrett, Clotilde	√	√	WJ	6	4	24	Sp 82	10
Floor Coverings: Rugs, Rag, Miniatures	Home Weaving: It's the Little Things that Count		√	√	Hw	1	1		F-W 79	38
Floor Coverings: Rugs, Rag, Warp-Faced	If You Have Four Harnesses		√	√	H&C	24	4		Au 73	39
Floor Coverings: Rugs, Rep	Designing Rep Weave	Ridgeway, Terese	√	√	SS&D	16	3	63	Su 85	28
Floor Coverings: Rugs, Rep	Designing Rep Weaves with the Aid of a Computer	Bohannan, Ronnine	√	√	WJ	7	4	28	Sp 83	24
Floor Coverings: Rugs, Rep	Four-Block Warp Rep (error-corrected WJ v8 n1 83 p50)	Robitaille, Annette	√	> 4	WJ	7	4	28	Sp 83	16
Floor Coverings: Rugs, Rep	Four-Shaft, Two-Block Warp-Faced Rep Floor Covering	Kolling-Summers, Elizabeth	√	√	WJ	7	4	28	Sp 83	15
Floor Coverings: Rugs, Rep	Weaving in Quebec: New Traditions	Barrett, Clotilde	√	√	WJ	6	4	24	Sp 82	14
Floor Coverings: Rugs, Rippsmatta	Mattor (error-corrected WJ v2 n1 77 insert for vol. 1)	Dunham, Miriam	√	√	WJ	1	4	4	Ap 77	21
Floor Coverings: Rugs, Rippsmatta	Shadowweave, Part 2 — Unbalanced Shadowweave (error-corrected WJ v2 n1 77 insert for vol. 1)	Barrett, Clotilde	√	> 4	WJ	1	2	2	Oc 76	14
Floor Coverings: Rugs, Room-Sized	Start with a Room-Sized Rug and Work Up	Johnston, Coleen	√		Hw	8	4		S/O 87	85
Floor Coverings: Rugs, Rya	Finland's Rya Rugs	The Finnish Consulate General of New York	√		SS&D	13	4	52	Fa 82	54
Floor Coverings: Rugs, Rya	Finnish Techniques	Tanner, Kersten	√		SS&D	6	3	23	Su 75	45
Floor Coverings: Rugs, Rya	Reinterpreting Rya: Irma Kukkasjärvi Energizes an Ancient Technique	Ojala, Liisa Kanning	√		WJ	9	4	36	Sp 85	26
Floor Coverings: Rugs, Rya	Rya Rugs		√		H&C	10	4		Fa 59	10
Floor Coverings: Rugs, Rya	Rya Rugs	Erickson, Johanna	√	√	SS&D	13	3	51	Su 82	36
Floor Coverings: Rugs, Rya	Valberg Rugs on View		√		H&C	9	1		Wi 57	25
Floor Coverings: Rugs, Rya	Weaving Rya and Flossa Rugs	af Kleen, Elizabeth	√	√	H&C	13	3		Su 62	29
Floor Coverings: Rugs, Rya, Sculptured	Shaped Sculptured Rugs — A Workshop with Urban Jupena		√	√	WJ	4	1	13	Jy 79	5
Floor Coverings: Rugs, Scandinavian	Rugs in the Scandinavian Way		√	√	Hw	8	3		M/J 87	58
Floor Coverings: Rugs, Shaft-Switching	Shaft-Switching Combined with Harness Control	Barrett, Clotilde	√	> 4	WJ	9	1	33	Su 84	37
Floor Coverings: Rugs, Shaft-Switching	Shaft-Switching on Rising Shed Looms Using Weighted Floating Heddles	Harse, Crys	√	√	WJ	9	4	36	Sp 85	63
Floor Coverings: Rugs, Shaker	Shaker Textiles	Hillenburg, Nancy	√	√	WJ	8	1	29	Su 83	22
Floor Coverings: Rugs, Silk-Screen	Rugs: Jo Ann Giordano, Silk Screener		√		Fa	9	2		M/A 82	60
Floor Coverings: Rugs, Soumak	Hand Woven Rugs: Weaves, Plain Weave, Soumak Technique	Atwater, Mary Meigs	√	√	SCGM		29		48	11
Floor Coverings: Rugs, Soumak	Soumak-Woven Rug in a 15th Century International Sytle, A	Ellis, Charles Grant	√		TMJ	1	2		De 63	3
Floor Coverings: Rugs, Stenciled	Stenciled Rag Rug (Betty Oldenberg)		√	√	Hw	5	3		Su 84	74
Floor Coverings: Rugs, Tapestry	Hand Woven Rugs: Weaves, Plain Weave, Tapestry Techniques	Atwater, Mary Meigs	√	√	SCGM		29		48	11
Floor Coverings: Rugs, Tapestry	Home Weaving: A Trio of Rugs		√	√	Hw	1	1		F-W 79	30
Floor Coverings: Rugs, Tapestry	Sam Kasten's Blue-Beige Tapestry Rug		√		SS&D	17	3	67	Su 86	72
Floor Coverings: Rugs, Tapestry Weave	Pile Weaves, Rugs and Tapestry: True Tapestry and Rugs	Zielinski, S. A.; Robert Leclerc, ed.		√	MWL	14			'51–'73	76

SUBJECT	TITLE	AUTHOR	IL	INST	JOUR	VOL	NO	ISS	DATE	PAGE
Floor Coverings: Rugs, Tapestry Weave, Rolag	Pile Weaves, Rugs and Tapestry: Rolag Tapestry	Zielinski, S. A.; Robert Leclerc, ed.		√	MWL	14			'51–'73	83
Floor Coverings: Rugs, Techniques	Rug Techniques-An Overview	Stanley, Martha	√		WJ	6	4	24	Sp 82	34
Floor Coverings: Rugs, Tie-Dyeing	Peter Collingwood, His Weaves and Weaving: A Rug in Tie-Dye	Collingwood, Peter; Harriet Tidball, ed.	√	√	SCGM		8		63	8
Floor Coverings: Rugs, Tufted	Hand Woven Rugs: Weaves, Plain Weave, Picked-Up Tufting	Atwater, Mary Meigs	√	√	SCGM		29		48	7
Floor Coverings: Rugs, Tufted	Tufted Rugs of Martha Opdahl, The	Piucci, Joanna A.	√		Fa	11	3		M/J 84	15
Floor Coverings: Rugs, Turkey	Kaleidoscopic Tour of Turkey, A	Dyer, Carol; Carel Bertram	√		Fa	7	5		S/O 80	48
Floor Coverings: Rugs, Turkish	Turkish Carpet with Spots and Stripes, A	Mackie, Louise W.	√		TMJ	4	3		76	4
Floor Coverings: Rugs, Twice-Woven	Hand Woven Rugs: Weaves, Plain Weave, Twice-Woven Rugs	Atwater, Mary Meigs	√	√	SCGM		29		48	5
Floor Coverings: Rugs, Twice-Woven	Twice-Woven Rug	Rummler, Ruth	√	√	SS&D	4	2	14	Sp 73	19
Floor Coverings: Rugs, Twined	Danish Twined Rag Rugs: Lillie Sherwood's Legacy	Irwin, Bobbie	√	√	WJ	10	4	40	Sp 86	32
Floor Coverings: Rugs, Unspun Fleece	Mary Bridget Plaisted, Colorado Weaver		√	√	H&C	22	1		Wi 71	15
Floor Coverings: Runners	Skillbragd Runner (Myrna Golay)		√	> 4	Hw	8	3		M/J 87	61, I-12
Floor Coverings: Sculpture	Fragil Landscape	Akamine, Estelle	√		TM			5	J/J 86	88
Florida	Indigo, Discovery of Plants and Experiments in Dyeing	Gerber, Willi; Fred Gerber	√	√	H&C	26	3		M/J 75	11
Florida	Weaving With Florida's Native Materials	Henderson, Helen	√	√	H&C	9	2		Sp 58	7
Flossa	How Much Yarn for the Job? Rya and Flossa	Towner, Naomi W.	√	√	SS&D	8	4	32	Fa 77	14
Flossa Technique	Hand Woven Rugs: Weaves, Plain Weave, Tapestry Techniques	Atwater, Mary Meigs	√	√	SCGM		29		48	11
Flour Sacks	Flour Sacks on Display (Exhibit)		√		Fa	14	1		J/F 87	70
Flowers: Fabric	Making Fabric Flowers	Ritch, Diane; Yoshiko Iwamoto Wada	√	√	TM			13	O/N 87	68
Flowers: Woven	Handwoven or Leather Flowers	Richards, Iris	√	√	WJ	4	1	13	Jy 79	34
Fly-Shuttle Weaving	Fly-Shuttle Looms Enhance Weaving Pleasure	Brostoff, Laya	√		SS&D	6	2	22	Sp 75	74
Folk Art	Embroidery for the Goddess	Kelly, Mary B.	√		TM			11	J/J 87	26
Folk Art	M.O.I.F.A.	Livingston, Lois; Marion Rinehart	√		SS&D	14	3	55	Su 83	46
Folk Art	Meaning of Folk Art in Rabari Life: A Closer Look at Mirrored Embroidery, The	Frater, Judy	√		TMJ	4	2		75	47
Folk Art	"Mingei — The Folk Arts of Japan" (Exhibit)	Meilach, Dona Z.	√		Fa	4	2		M/A 77	10
Folk Art	Textile Motifs from Folk Art		√		H&C	8	3		Su 57	10
Folk Art: India	Meaning of Folk Art in Rabari Life: A Closer Look at Mirrored Embroidery, The	Frater, Judy	√		TMJ	4	2		75	47
Folk Art: Poland	Technique & History of the Polish Double-weave, The	Wimmer, Gayle	√		H&C	24	3		M/J 73	8
Folk Art: Textiles, Latin America	Folk Textiles of Latin America	Kelemen, Pál	√		TMJ	1	4		De 65	2
Folk Art: Textiles, Peru	General Patterson's Tapestry	Sellschopp, Dr. E. A.	√		TMJ	2	4		De 69	2
Folk Craft	Temari: Threads to the Past	Beall, Karen F.	√		Fa	14	2		M/A 87	7
Folk Weaving	Woven Woolen Whimseys		√	√	WJ	2	2	6	Oc 77	14
Folklore	Folklore of Puppeteer Joan Mickelson, The	Van Til, Reinder	√		Fa	13	1		J/F 86	14
Folklore	Linen Lore	Goodman, Deborah Lerme	√		Fa	14	2		M/A 87	16
Folklore	Myth, Music, and Magic: The Needlework of Pilar Coover	Schevill, Margot Blum	√	√	TM			14	D/J 87	30
Folklore	Spiders: Masters of Natural Textiles	Palmer, Jacqueline M.	√		Fa	14	4		S/O 87	33
Folktales	In the Web of Superstition: Myths and Folktales About Nets	Nappen, Barbara	√		Fa	9	3		M/J 82	30
Folktales	Linen Lore	Goodman, Deborah Lerme	√		Fa	14	2		M/A 87	16

SUBJECT	TITLE	AUTHOR	IL	INST	JOUR	VOL	NO	ISS	DATE	PAGE
Folktales	Na´ashje´ii Asdzaa—Spider Woman		√		S-O	1			77	11
Folktales	Three Spinsters, The				S-O	1			77	55
Folktales: Iran	Rostam and Akvan the Demon		√		Fa	11	3		M/J 84	41
Folkwear	"Art and Romance of Peasant Clothing, The" (Exhibit)	Dyer, Carolyn	√		Fa	5	3		M/J 78	16
Folkwear	Fashion Trends	Nelipovitch, Kate; Susan Hick	√		WJ	6	3	23	Wi 81	6
Folkwear Patterns	Folkwear: In the Company of Some Friends		√		Fa	3	5		S/O 76	36
Footstools	Kitt Miller: Art Among Friends	Wolfe, Gregory	√		Fa	14	3		M/J 87	10
Footwear	Accessories: Bags and Slippers		√	√	WJ	5	3	19	Wi 81	42
Footwear	Accessories: Hot Foot		√	√	WJ	2	4	8	Ap 78	9
Footwear	Accessories: Woven Clogs		√	√	WJ	4	3	15	Ja 80	39
Footwear	Christmas Boot or After Ski Boot (Jean Scorgie)		√	√	Hw	4	4		S/O 83	72, 100
Footwear	Didier Legrand: Magic Afoot	Monico, Michele	√		Fa	12	4		J/A 85	12
Footwear	Double Woven House Boots	MacDonald, Margaret	√	> 4	WJ	6	4	24	Sp 82	44
Footwear	Few Words About Feet, Shoes and Other Things We Walk On, A	Katz, Ruth J.	√		Fa	6	3		M/J 79	53
Footwear	Goody Twoshoes: Gaza Bowen, An Extraordinary Shoemaker		√		Fa	8	5		S/O 81	13
Footwear	"Great American Foot, The" (Exhibit)	Grover, Donald	√		Fa	5	4		J/A 78	15
Footwear	Judith Sarchielli: Mukluk Maker	Sarchielli, Judith	√		Fa	5	6		N/D 78	23
Footwear	Keep Warm! Foot Cozy	Barrett, Clotilde	√	√	WJ	5	2	18	Fa 80	12
Footwear	Mukluks (Bridget McNamara)		√	√	Hw	1	1		F-W 79	20, 54
Footwear	Old Shoes Keeping Honourable Company	Clausen, Valerie	√		TM			11	J/J 87	16
Footwear	On the Other Foot: The Shoe Sculptures of Norma Minkowitz		√		Fa	10	1		J/F 83	13
Footwear	Shoemaker's Art, The	Bowen, Gaza	√	√	TM			5	J/J 86	56
Footwear	"Shoes and Chapeaux": Visit to an Exhibition (Exhibit)		√		Fa	10	1		J/F 83	23
Footwear	These Toes Won't Drown in Tears of Clown	Montgomery, Larry	√		TM			11	J/J 87	14
Footwear	Woven Felted Boots		√	√	WJ	7	1	25	Su 82	28
Foreign Literature: Drafts	Creative Drafting and Analysis: Drafts in Foreign Literature	Zielinski, S. A.; Robert Leclerc, ed.	√	> 4	MWL	3			'51–'73	71
Formalwear: Men's	Tuxedo 100 Years Later, The	Shufro, Cathy	√		TM			7	O/N 86	54
Foundations: Aesthetic Understanding	Alexander Julian's Foundation for Aesthetic Understanding	Lancaster, Zöe Woodruff	√		Fa	14	1		J/F 87	24
Four-Selvage Textiles	Understanding Some Complex Structures from Simple Andean Looms: Steps in Analysis and Reproduction	Cahlander, Adele	√	√	AT	1			De 83	181
Four-Shaft Weaving	Patterns from the Weaver's Guild		√	√	H&C	26	5		Oc 75	29
Fragments, Textile	Rummaging for Treasures	Strickler, Carol	√		SS&D	3	4	12	Fa 72	20
Frame Loom Weaving	Plain Weave — Plane Weave	Carey, Joyce Marquess	√	√	PWC	3	4	10		56
Frame-Loom Weaving	How to Weave a Plaid Triangular Shawl	Elich-McCall, Charoltte	√	√	Hw	4	5		N/D 83	54
France	French Weaving 1972	Watt, Ruth	√		H&C	23	6		N/D 72	48
France	Gobelins Royal Tapestry Works: Tradition and Change in France	Rex, Chris	√		Fa	10	3		M/J 83	58
Friends of the Rag	If the Art Fits – Wear It! — Friends of the Rag	Strosnider, Ann	√		Fa	6	3		M/J 79	35
Friends of the Rag	Return of the Rag, The	Basa, Lynn	√		Fa	14	3		M/J 87	29
Fringe see Finishes										
Fringe, Woven	Notebook: "Someday" File, The (Wisconsin Fedeeration of Handweavers)	Myers, Ruth Nordquist,ed.	√		SS&D	15	3	59	Su 84	66
Fruit, Woven	Loom Woven Baskets	Bowman, Gloria	√	√	WJ	10	4	40	Sp 86	37
Fukusa	Fukusa: The Art of Giving	Lancaster, Deborah Lerme	√		Fa	13	6		N/D 86	27

SUBJECT	TITLE	AUTHOR	IL	INST	JOUR	VOL	NO	ISS	DATE	PAGE
Fukusa	"Fukusa: The Shojiro Nomura Collection" (Exhibit)	Janeiro, Jan	√		Fa	11	3		M/J 84	79
Fukusa: Embroidered	Japan's Masterful Embroideries	Markrich, Lilo	√		TM			12	A/S 87	68
Fulling	Finishing Notes		√		Hw	2	5		No 81	53
Fulling	Irish Kinsale Cloak, The	Jones, Una	√	√	WJ	8	3	31	Wi 83	35
Fulling	More About Fabrics: Finishing of Wool	Zielinski, S. A.; Robert Leclerc, ed.		√	MWL	20			'51–'73	81
Fulling	Three Color Progressions and Their Use in Sweater Jackets	Sylvan, Katherine	√	√	WJ	5	4	20	Sp 81	38
Fulling	Traditional Methods of Finishing Cloth by Hand	Gordon, Beverly	√	√	Iw	5	4		Fa 80	66
Fulling	Vadmal: A Study Group from the Frozen North Warms up to an Ancient Technique	Larson-Fleming, Susan	√	√	WJ	10	3	39	Wi 86	26
Fulling	Vadmal Jacket (Janice Jones)		√	√	Hw	8	4		S/O 87	45, I-7
Fulling	Velten—Valkning—Felting	Beukers, Henriette	√	√	Hw	4	5		N/D 83	80
Fulling	Wool Finishing	Mayer, Francis		√	WJ	3	1	9	Jy 78	31
Fulling	Wooly Woolens	Thilenius, Carol; Marion Simpson	√	√	Hw	3	4		Se 82	44
Fulling	Wrap Up Your Warp	Voiers, Leslie	√	> 4	SS&D	18	1	69	Wi 86	49
Fulling: Knitting	Fulled Blazer	Newton, Deborah	√	√	Kn	3	1	5	F-W 86	38
Fulling: Knitting	Fulled Knitting	Upitis, Lizbeth	√	√	Kn	3	1	5	F-W 86	34
Fulling: Knitting	Fulling Notes	Newton, Deborah	√	√	Kn	3	1	5	F-W 86	37
Fulling: Knitting	Just an Idea	Beetem, Debra		√	Kn	3	1	5	F-W 86	37
Fulling: Knitting	Little Knowledge, A	Rowley, Elaine		√	Kn	3	1	5	F-W 86	41
Fund Raising: Camel Fund	Gravander Spinners, Raising Funds to Buy a Camel, The	McKinley, Esther D.	√		H&C	18	2		Sp 67	12
Fundraising	Fundraising Brings Kasuri Kimono Weaver to Nashville Workshop	Wilson, Sadye Tune	√		SS&D	9	2	34	Sp 78	4
Fundraising	Rugs for the Dream Auction	Moes, Dini	√	√	SS&D	17	2	66	Sp 86	58
Fur	Discarded Fur Pieces for Rugs and Pillows	Cook, Bonny	√	√	SS&D	4	3	15	Su 73	20
Fur	Furry Pillow	Cox, Dorothy	√	√	WJ	7	2	26	Fa 82	56
Fur	Karakul	Walker, Linda Berry	√		Hw	3	2		Mr 82	60
Fur	Riding the Modern Range: Stetson Hats	Goodman, Deborah Lerme	√	√	Fa	13	4		J/A 86	8
Fur	Touch of Fur, A	Dickey, Enola	√	√	SS&D	8	4	32	Fa 77	85
Fur	Weaving and Sheepskin, Naturally	Mason, Carole	√	√	WJ	5	3	19	Wi 81	46
Fur	Weaving in the Fur Weft	Patrick, Jane; Ann Wittpenn	√	√	Hw	4	1		J/F 83	33
Fur	Weaving with Fur for A Bag	Keeler, Betty	√	√	H&C	26	1		J/F 75	22
Fur: Pile, Loop, Cut	Double Two-Tie Twills and Basket Weave	Barrett, Clotilde	√	> 4	WJ	7	3	27	Wi 82	38
Fur, Rabbit	Recipe for Tanning Rabbit Fur	Clemmer, Phyllis	√	√	WJ	8	3	31	Wi 83	16
Furniture	Exuberant Art of Elizabeth Browning Jackson, The	Place, Jennifer	√		Fa	10	6		N/D 83	12
Furniture	Pueblo Deco	Sitko, Jane Bradley	√		SS&D	18	4	72	Fa 87	40
Furniture: Hassock	Furniture in Coiled Basketry Technique		√	√	WJ	3	1	9	Jy 78	22
Furniture: Sculpture	Fiber and Architecture: Dennis Jenkins		√		Fa	3	3		M/J 76	35
Furniture: Spinning Chairs	Antique Spinning Chairs	Becklake, Vera L.	√		WJ	11	2	42	Fa 86	58
Furniture: Swing, Woven	Woven Swing		√	√	WJ	3	1	9	Jy 78	46
Furniture/Fabric	Liza Lamb	Rowley, Kristin	√		Fa	13	5		S/O 86	18
Furoshiki Bag	Bags	Meiling, Nancy	√	√	WJ	6	3	23	Wi 81	40
Fusing: Fabric	When a Fusing Fails	Coffin, David Page	√	√	TM			10	A/M 87	61
Fustic	Why Bother with Natural Dyeing?	Bulbach, Stanley	√	√	TM			5	J/J 86	32
Futura 2000	Body as Canvas, The	Koda, Harold	√		TM			8	D/J 86	56
Gadgets, Handweaving	Technology of Handweaving: Gadgets	Zielinski, S. A.; Robert Leclerc, ed.			MWL	6			'51–'73	76

Galleries see Museums and Galleries

SUBJECT	TITLE	AUTHOR	IL	INST	JOUR	VOL	NO	ISS	DATE	PAGE
Games see Puzzles and Games										
Gang Weaving Concept: Drafts and Drafting	Gang: Technical and Conceptual Applications to Loom Controlled Weave Structures	Towner, Naomi Whiting	√	> 4	AT	5			Ju 86	91
Gang Weaving Concept: Looms	Gang: Technical and Conceptual Applications to Loom Controlled Weave Structures	Towner, Naomi Whiting	√	> 4	AT	5			Ju 86	91
Gang Weaving Concept: Weave Structures	Gang: Technical and Conceptual Applications to Loom Controlled Weave Structures	Towner, Naomi Whiting	√	> 4	AT	5			Ju 86	91
Gathering: Machine	Making Swirly Skirts	Callaway, Grace	√	√	TM			10	A/M 87	35
Gathers	Easy Way to Gather Fabric, An			√	TM			5	J/J 86	10
Gating	Treasury for Beginners: Gating	Zielinski, S. A.; Robert Leclerc, ed.	√	√	MWL	1			'51–'73	27
Gauge: Knitting	Putting Knitted Pieces Together	Guagliumi, Susan	√	√	TM			11	J/J 87	45
Gauze or Leno Class	Handloom Weaves: The Classification of Handloom Weaves, The Structural Group, The Gauze or Leno Class	Tidball, Harriet	√	√	SCGM		33		57	38
Gauze Weaves also see Leno; Openwork Weaves										
Gauze Weaves	Doupe Leno for the Harness Loom	Xenakis, Alexis Yiorgos; Elaine Rowley	√	√	PWC			6	Su 83	10
Gauze Weaves	Doupe Leno for the Rigid Heddle Loom	Xenakis, Athanasios David	√	√	PWC			6	Su 83	14
Gauze Weaves	Folk Textiles of Latin America	Kelemen, Pál	√		TMJ	1	4		De 65	2
Gauze Weaves	Guatemalan Gauze Weaves: A Description and Key to Identification	Pancake, Cherri M.; Suzanne Baizerman	√	√	TMJ	19 20			80,81	1
Gauze Weaves	Leno Fabrics	Xenakis, Athanasios David	√	√	PWC			6	Su 83	18
Gauze Weaves	Mexican Motifs: A Cotton Shawl in Leno or Gauze Weave	Tidball, Harriet	√	√	SCGM		6		62	16
Gauze Weaves	Peru, Textiles Unlimited, Part 2: Gauze	Tidball, Harriet	√	√	SCGM		26		69	46
Gauze Weaves	Quadruple Cloth, A Gauze Application	Edman, Larry E.	√	> 4	PWC			2	Ap 82	72
Gauze Weaves	Simple Damask-Like Effects Using Element Diameter Differential and Element Tension Differential	Xenakis, Athanasios David	√	> 4	AT	1			De 83	317
Gauze Weaves	Tarascan Lace		√	√	WJ	2	3	7	Ja 78	21
Gauze Weaves	Three Ancient Peruvian Gauze Looms	Rowe, Ann Pollard; Junius B. Bird	√		TMJ	19 20			80,81	27
Gauze Weaves	Weaving Primer	Ingebretsen, Catherine	√	√	PWC			6	Su 83	4
Gauze Weaves	Wool Skirt and Shawl	Crosby, Roberta	√	√	PWC			5	Sp 83	55
Gauze Weaves	Woven Lace and Lacey Weaves: Cross Weave	Zielinski, S. A.; Robert Leclerc, ed.	√	√	MWL	13			'51–'73	64
Gauze Weaves, Bead	Gauze Weave: Pick-up Versus Bead Gauze	Sullivan, Donna	√	√	SS&D	17	3	67	Su 86	14
Gauze Weaves: Card Woven	Cardwoven Gauze	Gray, Herbi	√	√	PWC			6	Su 83	57
Gauze Weaves, Crossed-Warps	Doup Leno	Skowronski, Hella; Sylvia Tacker	√	√	TM			4	A/M 86	56
Gauze Weaves: Identification	Guatemalan Gauze Weaves: A Description and Key to Identification	Pancake, Cherri M.; Suzanne Baizerman	√	√	TMJ	19 20			80,81	1
Gauze Weaves, Leno	Gifts from Ancient Peru	Nass, Ulla	√	√	WJ	8	1	29	Su 83	32
Gauze Weaves, Leno	Tarascan Lace (error-corrected WJ v9 n1 84 p70)	Thabet, Micheline	√	√	WJ	8	4	32	Sp 84	48
Gauze Weaves, Peruvian	Pick-Up Leno, A Two-harness Loom Technique	Wallace, Meg	√	√	WJ	1	2	2	Oc 76	3
Gauze Weaves, Pick-up	Gauze Weave: Pick-up Versus Bead Gauze	Sullivan, Donna	√	√	SS&D	17	3	67	Su 86	14
Genealogy of Weaves	Weaving in the Past Complete Index with Reference: Genealogy of Weaves	Zielinski, S. A.; Robert Leclerc, ed.	√		MWL	21 22			'51–'73	71
Germany	Eighteenth Century German Court Weaver: Johann Michael Frickinger, An	Hilts, Patricia	√		SS&D	11	4	44	Fa 80	16

SUBJECT	TITLE	AUTHOR	IL	INST	JOUR	VOL	NO	ISS	DATE	PAGE
Germany	Post-War Influences in West German Weaving	Reiser, Bertl	√		H&C	4	3		Su 53	11
Germany	Roses and Snowballs: The Development of Block Patterns in the German Linen-Weaving Tradition	Hilts, Patricia	√	>4	AT	5			Ju 86	167
Germany	Seventeenth and Eighteenth Century Twills: The German Linen Tradition	Hilts, Patricia	√	>4	AT	3			My 85	139
Germany	Webschule Sindelfingen	McKeown, Alice	√	√	SS&D	6	3	23	Su 75	8
Germany, Western	Western German Weavers	Abbott, Edith E.	√		H&C	8	4		Fa 57	22
Gift Wrap	Machine-Stitched Gift Wrap			√	TM			10	A/M 87	12
Gigging	What a Handweaver Can Learn from the Scottish Weaving Industry (error-corrected WJ v2 n1 77 insert for vol. 1)	Barrett, Clotilde	√	√	WJ	1	3	3	Ja 77	11
Ginning	In Search of Colored Cotton	Fox, Sally	√	√	S-O	11	4		Wi 87	48
Girdle of Rameses	Weaving the Girdle of Rameses	Hilts, Patricia	√	>4	WJ	9	1	33	Su 84	22
Girdles, Fiesta	Guatemala Visited	Atwater, Mary Meigs	√	√	SCGM		15		65	17
Glass	Cid Suntrader: Weaving with Glass	Suntrader, Cid	√		Fa	14	4		S/O 87	5
Glass	Inspired by Fiber: Textile Sensibility in Other Media	Malarcher, Patricia	√		Fa	10	6		N/D 83	33
Glass, Fake	Almost Roman Glass	Elliott, Lillian	√		Fa	10	6		N/D 83	20
Glass, Stained	Continuing Tradition, A		√		Fa	9	2		M/A 82	100
Glimäkra Looms	Glimakra Looms' N Yarns	Xenakis, Alexis Yiorgos	√		PWC	4	1	11		48
Glit	Glit — An Icelandic Inlay Technique	Heite, Louise B.	√	√	Hw	8	3		M/J 87	64
Glossary: Basketry	Giving Your Baskets a Long, Healthy Life: A Basic Guide to Basketry Conservation	Odegaard, Nancy; Dale Kronkright	√		Fa	11	1		J/F 84	43
Glossary: Basketry	Making an Open-Weave Willow Basket	Hart, Carol	√	√	TM			4	A/M 86	24
Glossary: Bateman Blend Weaves, Weaving Terms	Bateman Blend Weaves: Definitions	Bateman, Dr. William G.; Virginia I. Harvey, ed.	√		SCGM		36		82	6
Glossary: Bateman Boulevard, Chevron, and Combination Weaves	Bateman Boulevard, Chevron, and Combination Weaves: Definitions	Bateman, Dr. William G.; Virginia I. Harvey, ed.	√	>4	SCGM		38		87	6
Glossary: Bateman Multiple Tabby Weaves, Weaving Terms	Multiple Tabby Weaves: Definitions	Bateman, Dr. William G.; Virginia I. Harvey, ed.	√		SCGM		35		81	9
Glossary: Bateman Park Weaves, Weaving Terms	Bateman Park Weaves: Definitions	Bateman, Dr. William G.; Virginia I. Harvey, ed.	√		SCGM		37		84	6
Glossary: Brocade, Banares	Banares Brocade	DuBois, Emily	√	>4	AT	3			My 85	209
Glossary: CAD Features	"In the Garden of Strange Gods" (Exhibit)	McDonald, Julie Jensen	√		Fa	14	4		S/O 87	41
Glossary: Carding	Drum Carder, The	Rossiter, Phyllis	√	√	SS&D	15	4	60	Fa 84	71
Glossary: Checks	Victorian Classic: District Checks		√	√	Hw	4	5		N/D 83	66
Glossary: Clothing Construction	Seattle Guild Garment Designs, Part 1	Noble, Judy	√	√	SS&D	10	3	39	Su 79	26
Glossary: Colonial Fabrics	Colonial Fabrics: A Glossary	Patrick, Jane	√		Hw	3	5		N/D 82	25
Glossary: Color	Color Theory for Handweavers Part 4: More visual illusions with color	Wald, Pat Boutin	√	√	WJ	11	1	41	Su 86	37
Glossary: Color	Complementary Colors	Wertenberger, Kathryn	√		Hw	6	5		N/D 85	90
Glossary: Color	Designing with Color	Wertenberger, Kathryn		√	Hw	2	4		Se 81	32
Glossary: Color	Why Do I Weave Tapestries? An Exploration of Color Theory and Tapestry Design (error-corrected Fa v7 n6 80 p8)	Griffey, Margaret	√		Fa	7	4		J/A 80	55
Glossary: Cotton	Cotton Glossary	Schmoller, Irene Laughing Cloud			WJ	11	2	42	Fa 86	13
Glossary: Cotton Fabrics	Cotton: Legacy of Gods & Kings	Schmoller, Irene Laughing Cloud	√		WJ	11	2	42	Fa 86	11
Glossary: Design	Composition and Designing: Terminology of Designing	Zielinski, S. A.; Robert Leclerc, ed.	√		MWL	18			'51–'73	7
Glossary: Dyeing	Glossary of Dyeing Terms				Fa	5	1		J/F 78	36
Glossary: Embroidery	Freestyle Embroidery: New Images with Traditional Stitches	Dahl, Caroline	√	√	TM			1	O/N 85	22
Glossary: English-Spanish Weaving Terms	Weaving a Cotton Saddlebag on the Santa Elena Peninsula of Ecuador	Hagino, Jane Parker; Karen E. Stothert	√	√	TMJ	22			83	19

SUBJECT	TITLE	AUTHOR	IL	INST	JOUR	VOL	NO	ISS	DATE	PAGE
Glossary: Fabric Names, Origins	What's in a Name?				Fa	10	2		M/A 83	46
Glossary: Kashmir Shawls	Scent of Flowers, Kishmir Shawls in the Collection of The Textile Museum, The	Mikosch, Elisabeth	√		TMJ	24			85	7
Glossary: Kasuri Techniques	Kasuri: A Japanese Textile	Dusenbury, Mary	√		TMJ	17			78	41
Glossary: Leno, Doup	Exploring Doup Leno	Laughlin, Mary Elizabeth	√	> 4	CW	4	3	12	Ap 83	3
Glossary: Lichen Dyeing	Color Magic from Lichen Dyebaths	Casselman, Karen Leigh	√	√	SS&D	17	2	66	Sp 86	74
Glossary: Machine Knitting	Winter Red: A Hand and Machine Knit Combination	Lewis, Susanna	√	√	Kn	3	4	8	Fa 87	28
Glossary: Man-Made Fibers, Technology	Man-Made Fibers	Hausner, Walter	√		WJ	9	3	35	Wi 85	61
Glossary: Novelty Yarns	Evening Bags that Shine with Flash & Glitter	Piroch, Sigrid	√	√	Hw	6	1		J/F 85	36
Glossary: Novelty Yarns	Supplementary Warp for Novelty Yarns	Davenport, Betty	√	√	Hw	6	1		J/F 85	34
Glossary: Piqué	Ribbed Piqué	Sullivan, Donna	√	√	SS&D	18	3	71	Su 87	30
Glossary: Quichua Weaving	Noble Tradition Preserved: An Ecuadorian Weaving Co-op, A	Llewellyn, Charles; Deborah Llewellyn	√		SS&D	11	3	43	Su 80	12
Glossary: Selvages	Edges of Knitting, The	Gaffey, Theresa	√	√	TM			5	J/J 86	54
Glossary: Silk	Introduction to Silk Dyeing, An	Walsh, Joan Lea		√	WJ	3	2	10	Oc 78	14
Glossary: Sling Braiding	Sling Braiding in the Macusani Area of Peru	Zorn, Elayne	√	√	TMJ	19 20			80,81	41
Glossary: Spinning	Glossary				S-O	1			77	6
Glossary: Spinning	Irregularity in Handspun Part 2	Simmons, Paula	√	√	H&C	21	1		Wi 70	20
Glossary: Spinning	Spinning in Bolivia	Meisch, Lynn A.	√	√	S-O	10	1		Sp 86	25
Glossary: Spinning	Wonderful Worsted	Dozer, Iris	√	√	S-O	7	2		Su 83	35
Glossary: Split-Ply Twining Terms	Split-Ply Twining: Definition of Terms	Harvey, Virginia I.	√	√	TIAM		1		76	5
Glossary: Stitches and Attachments	Buyer's Guide to Sewing Machines, A	Piucci, Joanna	√		Fa	10	2		M/A 83	39
Glossary: Stripes	Glossary of Stripes, A				Hw	4	2		M/A 83	48
Glossary: Swedish Weaving Terms	Glossary Swedish Weaving Terms				Hw	4	2		M/A 83	102
Glossary: Tartan Terms	Weaver's Book of Scottish Tartans: Tartan Terms, The	Tidball, Harriet			SCGM		5		62	12
Glossary: Texture Stitches	Texture Stitches for Needlepoint	Hamer, Rosalie	√	√	TM			5	J/J 86	62
Glossary: Tied Weaves	Tied Weave Glossary	Kelly, Jacquie			PWC	4	4	14		44
Glossary: Turkish Rug Terms	Anatolian Rugs: An Essay on Method	Denny, Walter B.	√		TMJ	3	4		De 73	7
Glossary: Twill	Twill Basics		√	√	Hw	6	5		N/D 85	57
Glossary: Twining, Weft	Weft Twining: Definitions	Harvey, Virginia I.; Harriet Tidball			SCGM		28		69	1
Glossary: Wool	Fleece in the Hands of a New Zealand Spinner	Horne, Beverley	√		S-O	2			78	24
Glossary: Wool	Selecting Wool for Handspinning (error-corrected SS&D v13 n1 81 p4)	Fleet, Malcolm		√	SS&D	12	4	48	Fa 81	66
Gloves see Mittens and Gloves										
Goat Raising	Raising Angora Goats in Texas	Franklin, Sue			TM			8	D/J 86	12
God's Eyes	For Good Health and Long Life	Fair, Maurine	√		SS&D	3	1	9	Wi 71	34
God's Eyes	From Peru, Gods Eyes on a Stick	Atwood, Betty	√	√	SS&D	5	1	17	Wi 73	8
God's Eyes	Notes of a Pattern Weaver	Alvic, Philis	√	√	SS&D	15	1	57	Wi 83	74
God's Eyes	Ojo de Dios	Champion, Ellen	√	√	WJ	4	2	14	Oc 79	40
God's Eyes	Toys and Other Fun Stuff	Ligon, Linda	√		Iw	2	1		Fa 76	13
Gondola	Ballooning Art Form: The Making of a Hot Air Balloon Basket, A		√		SS&D	11	4	44	Fa 80	8
Gores	Linen Shift: Plain Sewing Makes the Most of Your Fabric, A	Smith, Kathleen B.	√	√	TM			9	F/M 87	46
Gowns see Dresses and Gowns										
Grain, Fabric	Keeping Track of the Grain			√	TM			9	F/M 87	12
Grain, Fabric: Establishing	Fabric Grain		√	√	TM			13	O/N 87	6
Grants	Brief Bibliography of Grant References, A	Polster, Joanne			Fa	11	4		J/A 84	50

SUBJECT	TITLE	AUTHOR	IL	INST	JOUR	VOL	NO	ISS	DATE	PAGE
Grants	Fundraising Brings Kasuri Kimono Weaver to Nashville Workshop	Wilson, Sadye Tune	√		SS&D	9	2	34	Sp 78	4
Grants	Grant Fellowships for the Fiber Artist	Itter, Diane			Fa	11	4		J/A 84	50
Grants	State Grant — A Two-Way Street, The	Curtis, Dolly	√		SS&D	8	4	32	Fa 77	8
Graph Paper	Pre-Marked Graph Paper for Your Designing Enjoyment		√		PWC	4	2	12		54
Graphs see Drafts and Drafting										
Grass	"Grass" (Exhibit)	Dyer, Carolyn	√		Fa	4	1		J/F 77	5
Great Britain	British Revival in Handweaving, The	Hall, Wendy	√		H&C	4	3		Su 53	21
Great Britain	British Versatility	Leek, Yvonne B.			SS&D	6	3	23	Su 75	41
Great Britain	Knitting Craft in Great Britain, The	Kinder, Kathleen	√		Fa	11	4		J/A 84	42
Great Britain	Native British Sheep: The Rare Breeds	Leadbeater, Eliza	√		S-O	3			79	19
Great Britain	Wools of Britain, The	Seagroatt, Margaret	√		H&C	24	2		M/A 73	33
Great Britian	Through the "Almanack" Office Window	Parr, Rowena			S-O	11	3		Fa 87	36
Greece	Arachne's Children	Koster, Joan Bouza	√	√	SS&D	9	3	35	Su 78	16
Greece	Classical Greek Textiles from Nymphaeum	Wild, John Peter	√		TMJ	4	4		77	33
Greece	Classical Greek Textiles from Nymphaeum	Wild, John Peter	√		TMJ	4	4		77	33
Greece	Decorative Techniques of the Sarakatsani	Smith, Joyce	√	√	WJ	9	1	33	Su 84	14
Greece	Greek Craft Summer: The American Farm School	Regensteiner, Else	√		SS&D	7	3	27	Su 76	100
Greece	Greek Dower Sheet, A	Xenakis, Alexis Yiorgos	√		Hw	1	2		S-S 80	36
Greece	Handwoven Flocati of Epirus, The	Gans, Naomi Beth; Catherine Haywood	√	√	SS&D	12	3	47	Su 81	35
Greece	Inlay We Trust Part 3: Pillow Based on Greek Inlay Technique	Herring, Connie	√	√	PWC	3	4	10		44
Greece	Journey Through Greece, Two Americans in Search of Native Weaving	Znamierowski, Nell	√		H&C	14	2		Sp 63	8
Greece	Mistra	Xenakis, Alexis Yiorgos	√		Kn	2	2	4	S-S 86	56
Greece	New Carpet-Making School for Vragiana	Wile, Leslie	√		SS&D	4	2	14	Sp 73	17
Greece	Portrait of a Village	Becker, Robin; James Chressanthis	√		Fa	9	6		N/D 82	40
Greece	Search for Handweaving in Greece, A (error-corrected H&C v21 n3 70 p42)	Turner, Alta R.	√		H&C	21	2		Sp 70	16
Greece	Spinners and Weavers of Modern Greece		√		H&C	1	2		Su 50	30
Greece	Tagari: A Greek Saddlebag of Handspun Wools, The	Koster, Joan Boura	√	√	WJ	6	2	22	Fa 81	24
Greece	Textile Life, The	Jacobson, Gail	√		Fa	14	3		M/J 87	5
Greece	Weavers in Greece	Tod, Osma Gallinger	√		H&C	19	2		Sp 68	21
Greece	Windows: Kouverta	Xenaxis, Alexis Yiorgos	√	√	PWC	5	1	15		14
Greece	Windows: Sendoni Curtains	Xenakis, Alexis Yiorgos	√	> 4	PWC	4	1	11		4
Greeting Cards: Woven, Convalescent Cards	Merry Christmas, Handweavers: Greeting Cards for Other Occassions	Tidball, Harriet	√	√	SCGM		10		63	17
Greeting Cards: Woven, Note Cards	Merry Christmas, Handweavers: Greeting Cards for Other Occassions	Tidball, Harriet	√	√	SCGM		10		63	17
Group Projects	Groupwork with Dutch Feltmaker Inge Evers	Clark, Sherry	√	√	SS&D	17	4	68	Fa 86	28
Group Projects	Variations on a Theme: A Seattle Weavers' Guild Study Group Project	Sullivan, Jean H.	√	√	Hw	8	2		M/A 87	64
Group Projects	Wadmal — A Felted Fabric	Snover, Susan; Jean Sullivan	√	√	SS&D	11	2	42	Sp 80	89
Group Projects: Coverlet Documentations	Three-R's of Coverlets: Revival, Restoration, Research	Sellin, Helen; Peggy Hoyt			PWC	5	2	16		33
Group Projects: Coverlets	Weavers' Friendship Coverlet	Best, Eleanor	√	√	Hw	3	5		N/D 82	68
Group Projects: Place Mats, Insulated	Rainbow on the Table, A (Sharon Hakala, Carol Isleib, Carol Shabaz, Ruth Stump)	Isleib, Carol	√	√	Hw	5	3		Su 84	46

SUBJECT	TITLE	AUTHOR	IL	INST	JOUR	VOL	NO	ISS	DATE	PAGE
Group Projects: Quilting	Group of Quilters Fit Ideas to Theme of Gift	Barnett, Linda Lowman	√		TM		7		O/N 86	33
Group Projects: Quilting	Quilting for World Peace	Shufro, Cathy	√		TM		10		A/M 87	14
Group Projects: Tapestry	Diamond Odyssey		√		SS&D	14	4	56	Fa 83	40
Group Projects: Weaving	Each One Picked a Color—4th and 5th Graders Weave a Blanket	Hanna, Linda	√		WJ	9	1	33	Su 84	34
Group Projects: Weaving	World's Wildest Weaving, The	Herring, Connie	√		PWC	1	1		No 81	41
Group Projects: Weaving, Supplementary Warp Patterning (Dress Fabrics)	Supplementary Warp Patterning: Dresses Styled From Warp Pattern Fabrics	Tidball, Harriet	√	> 4	SCGM		17		66	33-43
Grouped-Thread Class	Handloom Weaves: The Classification of Handloom Weaves, The Structural Group, The Grouped-Thread Class	Tidball, Harriet		√	SCGM		33		57	30
Grouped-Thread Weaves	Textile Structure and Analysis, A Home Study Course in Twelve Lessons: Lessons in Weave Structure, 8. Grouped-Thread Weaves	Tidball, Harriet		> 4	SCGM		18		66	28
Guage: Knitting	Conversion Factor, The	Barnes, Galer	√	√	Kn	3	1	5	F-W 86	54
Guage: Knitting	Gauge Revisor, The	Connors, Carol	√	√	Kn	3	1	5	F-W 86	54
Guatemala	Adventures with Guatemalan Weaving	Young, Helen Daniels	√		H&C	4	1		Wi 52	26
Guatemala	Art of Ixchel: Learning to Weave in Guatemala and Rhode Island, The	Schevill, Margot	√	√	WJ	8	1	29	Su 83	57
Guatemala	Backstrap Weaving in MesoAmerica	Baizerman, Suzanne; Karen Searle	√	√	Iw	5	4		Fa 80	38
Guatemala	"Century of Change in Guatemalan Textiles, A" (Exhibit)	Brown, Arleen Emery	√		Fa	9	3		M/J 82	79
Guatemala	Clothing Change Through Contact: Traditional Guatemalan Dress	Fisher, Abby Sue	√		WJ	10	3	39	Wi 86	60
Guatemala	Clothing from Rectangles	Liebler, Barbara	√	√	Iw	5	4		Fa 80	52
Guatemala	Cristi — Sketch of a Guatemalan Weaver	Nash, Jeanne; Jeanne Schmelzer	√		Iw	5	4		Fa 80	28
Guatemala	Divide . . . and Conquer	Baizerman, Suzanne	√		WJ	9	2	34	Fa 84	61
Guatemala	Guatamalan Finishes	Gotthoffer, Esther	√		H&C	22	1		Wi 71	18
Guatemala	Guatemala Visited	Atwater, Mary Meigs	√		SCGM		15		65	1-46
Guatemala	Guatemala Weaver, The	Marks, Copeland A.	√		H&C	26	5		Oc 75	2
Guatemala	Guatemala: Weaving, People	Frost, Gordon	√		Iw	5	4		Fa 80	30
Guatemala	Guatemala Weaving Workshop	Kingsmill, Sally	√		H&C	26	3		M/J 75	28
Guatemala	Guatemalan Gauze Weaves: A Description and Key to Identification	Pancake, Cherri M.; Suzanne Baizerman	√	√	TMJ	19 20			80,81	1
Guatemala	Guatemalan Looms	Young, Helen Daniels	√		H&C	4	3		Su 53	16
Guatemala	Guatemalan Stripes	Davenport, Betty	√	√	Hw	4	2		M/A 83	54
Guatemala	In Pursuit of the Elusive Huipil	Marks, Copeland	√		H&C	24	4		Au 73	6
Guatemala	Jacquard Weaving in Huehuetenango	Anderson, Marilyn	√		Fa	9	2		M/A 82	31
Guatemala	Jaspe Process, The	Lopez, Beatriz	√	√	SS&D	8	3	31	Su 77	54
Guatemala	Mayan Folk Textiles: Symbol of a Society	Dieterich, Mary	√		Hw	6	3		Su 85	64
Guatemala	Nahuala Spinning	Linder, Harry; Olive Linder	√		S-O	2			78	23
Guatemala	Painting and Brocading on the Loom	Ziek, Bhakti	√	√	TM		6		A/S 86	42
Guatemala	Sisal Production in Highland Guatemala	Ventura, Carol	√		Fa	14	2		M/A 87	44
Guatemala	Stitched Finishes in the Guatemalan Tradition	Pancake, Cherri; Karen Searle; Sue Baizerman	√	√	Hw	2	5		No 81	29
Guatemala	Textiles and Looms from Guatemala & Mexico	Grossman, Ellin F.	√		H&C	7	1		Wi 55	6
Guatemala	"Weavers of the Jade Needle" An Exhibition of Highland Guatemalan Textiles (Exhibit)	Stout, Carol	√		Fa	3	2		M/A 76	30
Guatemala	Weavings of the Guatemalan Highland Maya	Marks, Copeland H.	√	√	SS&D	7	4	28	Fa 76	88
Guatemalan Belt Weave	Calendar in Guatemalan Belt Weave (Evelyn Christensen)		√	√	Hw	7	2		M/A 86	69, I-14

SUBJECT	TITLE	AUTHOR	IL	INST	JOUR	VOL	NO	ISS	DATE	PAGE
Guatemalan Brocade	Guatemalan Brocade Border, A	Simons, Phid	√	√	WJ	6	4	24	Sp 82	39
Guatemalan Skip Weave	Why Not Try Embroidery Weaves?	Jones, Jeanetta L.	√	√	H&C	17	2		Sp 66	12
Guernsey, Gansey, Aran	Aran Knitting	Starmore, Alice	√	√	TM			14	D/J 87	50
Guernsey, Gansey, Aran	Cone of Aran Hats, A	Oakley, Helen	√	√	TM			13	O/N 87	27
Guernsey, Gansey, Aran	Fair Isle Knitting	Starmore, Alice	√	√	TM			8	D/J 86	44
Guernsey, Gansey, Aran	Gaffer's Gansey	Zimmermann, Elizabeth	√	√	Kn CI	1	1	1	F-W 84	36,56B 28
Guernsey, Gansey, Aran	Gansey in Handspun, The	Gibson-Roberts, Priscilla A.	√	√	Kn CI	1	1	1	F-W 84	32,56B 24
Guernsey, Gansey, Aran	Gansey with Yoke	Farley, Sidna	√	√	Kn	3	2	6	Sp 87	27
Guernsey, Gansey, Aran	Gooden Gansey Sweaters	Gallagher, Marten	√		Fa	12	6		N/D 85	12
Guernsey, Gansey, Aran	Guernseys	Upitis, Lizbeth			Kn CI	1	1	1	F-W 84	48 40
Guernsey, Gansey, Aran	Josh's Gansey	Camper, Dorothy	√	√	Kn CI	1	1	1	F-W 84	28 20
Guernsey, Gansey, Aran	Particular Guernsey, A	Rowley, Elaine	√	√	Kn CI	1	1	1	F-W 84	25,56A 17
Guernsey, Gansey, Aran	Tiffany's Gansey	Adams, Harriet	√	√	Kn CI	1	1	1	F-W 84	29,56A 21
Guide: Textiles	Fiber Lover's Guide to the San Francisco Bay Area, A	Scarborough, Jessica	√		Fa	11	3		M/J 84	43
Guilds: Crafts	Handicraft Club of Rhode Island, The	Batchelder, Helen Tilton	√		H&C	7	1		Wi 55	15
Guilds: Crafts	League of New Hampshire Arts and Crafts, The				H&C	8	3		Su 57	21
Guilds: Crafts	League of New Hampshire Craftsmen	Drooker, Penelope B.	√		SS&D	9	1	33	Wi 77	42
Guilds: Crafts	Persis Grayson, Weaver & Spinner	Amos, Mary Alice	√		H&C	19	1		Wi 68	10
Guilds: Crafts	Society of Arts and Crafts, Boston, The				H&C	15	1		Wi 64	13
Guilds: Periodical Pool	Periodical Pool	Thorpe, Heather G.			H&C	6	3		Su 55	31
Guilds: Programs	Guild Programs Within the Budget	Spiegel, Nancy			H&C	8	2		Sp 57	46
Guilds: Programs	Program Suggestions for Weavers' Guilds	Frey, Berta	√		H&C	7	1		Wi 55	29
Guilds: Weavers'/ Spinners'	Weavers Guild of Greater Cincinnati	Lewis, Elsie M.	√	√	H&C	3	3		Su 52	44
Guilds: Weavers'/Spinners	Boston Celebrates Its Fiftieth	Stanwood, Creighton	√		SS&D	3	3	11	Su 72	10
Guilds: Weavers'/Spinners'	Cleveland West At Home & Flower Show		√		SS&D	3	4	12	Fa 72	43
Guilds: Weavers'/Spinners'	Contemporary Handweavers at the De Young Museum	Crockett, Candace	√		SS&D	2	2	6	Sp 71	4
Guilds: Weavers'/Spinners'	Creative Value of Group Effort		√		SS&D	1	3	3	Ju 70	8
Guilds: Weavers'/Spinners'	Lexington Fair in November	Parsons, Bernice	√		SS&D	3	4	12	Fa 72	6
Guilds: Weavers'/Spinners'	Potomac Craftsmen Select a New Home	Keasbey, Doramay	√		SS&D	4	1	13	Wi 72	40
Guilds: Weavers'/Spinners'	South of the Border Down Canada Way	Anders, Eunice	√		SS&D	3	3	11	Su 72	6
Guilds: Weavers'/Spinners'	Talk 'N' Tabby				SS&D	1	4	4	Se 70	19
Guilds: Weavers'/Spinners'	Twenty Weavers of D. C.				SS&D	3	1	9	Wi 71	24
Guilds: Weavers'/Spinners'	Values of Local Guilds	Ross, Ruth Custer			SS&D	4	2	14	Sp 73	7
Guilds: Weavers/Spinners	What Makes a Good Guild?	Ashwell, Eleanor V.			SS&D	2	1	5	De 70	7
Guilds: Weavers'/Spinners'	Acadians Honor Tapestry Master	Whitney, Gladys	√		SS&D	6	4	24	Fa 75	7
Guilds: Weavers'/Spinners'	Arizona Guild Weaves for the Govenor	Comings, Marian	√		H&C	7	2		Sp 56	44
Guilds: Weavers'/Spinners'	Arts and Crafts Society of Portland, Oregon, The				H&C	1	3		Fa 50	44
Guilds: Weavers'/Spinners'	Associated Hand Weavers				H&C	7	3		Su 56	41
Guilds: Weavers'/Spinners'	Associated Handweavers at Philadelphia	Schobinger, Helen J.	√		H&C	3	1		Wi 51	37
Guilds: Weavers'/Spinners'	Baltimore Guild Anniversary				H&C	20	4		Fa 69	31
Guilds: Weavers'/Spinners'	Bicentennial Tapestry, A	Howard, Margaret	√		SS&D	7	1	25	Wi 75	30
Guilds: Weavers'/Spinners'	Boston Guild Sales	Gallagher, Constance; Evelyn Bustead	√		H&C	11	4		Fa 60	49
Guilds: Weavers'/Spinners'	Chicago Weavers				H&C	11	1		Wi 60	49
Guilds: Weavers'/Spinners'	Chicago Weaving: Development and Impact	Regensteiner, Else	√		SS&D	12	1	45	Wi 80	9
Guilds: Weavers'/Spinners'	Connecticut Weavers		√		H&C	7	2		Sp 56	31

SUBJECT	TITLE	AUTHOR	IL	INST	JOUR	VOL	NO	ISS	DATE	PAGE
Guilds: Weavers'/Spinners'	Contemporary Handweavers of Texas		√		H&C	2	1		Wi 50	55
Guilds: Weavers'/Spinners'	Cooperative Weaving Project, A	Amram, Hortense	√		H&C	5	4		Fa 54	31
Guilds: Weavers'/Spinners'	Craft Classes in London, Ontario	Schoenfeld, Klara	√		H&C	3	1		Wi 51	47
Guilds: Weavers'/Spinners'	Des Moines Weavers Learn to Spin	Seeburger, Marze Marvin	√		H&C	6	1		Wi 54	56
Guilds: Weavers'/Spinners'	Designer-Weavers of Washington, D. C.				H&C	9	2		Sp 58	27
Guilds: Weavers'/Spinners'	Diamond Odyssey		√		SS&D	14	4	56	Fa 83	40
Guilds: Weavers'/Spinners'	Ethnic Looms	Jorstad, Caroline	√		SS&D	13	4	52	Fa 82	40
Guilds: Weavers'/Spinners'	Eugene Spinners, The	Reade, Dorothy	√		H&C	18	3		Su 67	20
Guilds: Weavers'/Spinners'	Fiber Exhibition	Rhodes, Maribelle N.			H&C	23	1		J/F 72	35
Guilds: Weavers'/Spinners'	From Sheep to Shawl	Thorne, Sylvia	√		H&C	17	1		Wi 66	36
Guilds: Weavers'/Spinners'	Gravander Spinners, Raising Funds to Buy a Camel, The	McKinley, Esther D.	√		H&C	18	2		Sp 67	12
Guilds: Weavers'/Spinners'	Greater Lansing Weavers' Guild		√		H&C	8	2		Sp 57	28
Guilds: Weavers'/Spinners'	Growth in Minneapolis				SS&D	5	1	17	Wi 73	61
Guilds: Weavers'/Spinners'	Guild in Focus: Fiber Artisans, A	Kline, Martha	√		Fa	11	5		S/O 84	47
Guilds: Weavers'/Spinners'	Guild Video-tapes the Wool Process				SS&D	8	4	32	Fa 77	90
Guilds: Weavers'/Spinners'	Guilds for Spinners	Rowe, Erica	√		S-O	3			79	35
Guilds: Weavers'/Spinners'	Handweavers' Guild of Westchester				H&C	18	1		Wi 67	33
Guilds: Weavers'/Spinners'	Happy Anniversary, Too	Aikin, Patti			SS&D	16	1	61	Wi 84	45
Guilds: Weavers'/Spinners'	Hui Mea Hana of Honolulu	Judd, Eva Marie	√	√	H&C	8	4		Fa 57	51
Guilds: Weavers'/Spinners'	Installation Ceremony of Guild Officers, Verde Valley	Gaudy, Betty			Hw	7	5		N/D 86	15
Guilds: Weavers'/Spinners'	Intermountain Weavers: "Fiber Celebrated, 1985"	McClellan, Alice	√		SS&D	17	4	68	Fa 86	42
Guilds: Weavers'/Spinners'	Lincoln, Nebraska Weavers' Guild		√		H&C	4	2		Sp 53	44
Guilds: Weavers'/Spinners'	Love-Spinning Farewell in Hawaii	McCarty, Carole	√		SS&D	6	1	21	Wi 74	41
Guilds: Weavers'/Spinners'	Marli-Weavers of Chicago, The	Uhlman, Ilse Etta	√		H&C	4	1		Wi 52	9
Guilds: Weavers'/Spinners'	Memphis Guild of Handloom Weavers, The	Quigley, Viola J.	√		H&C	2	3		Su 51	50
Guilds: Weavers'/Spinners'	Memphis Guild Sponsors Textile Room		√		H&C	7	2		Sp 56	27
Guilds: Weavers'/Spinners'	Michigan Guild Project: A Four-Panel Folding Screen	James, Esther	√	√	SS&D	9	1	33	Wi 77	114
Guilds: Weavers'/Spinners'	Michigan Guilds Sponsor the 17th National Conference				H&C	6	1		Wi 54	31
Guilds: Weavers'/Spinners'	Michigan League of Handweavers	Neeland, Muriel M.			H&C	17	4		Fa 66	18
Guilds: Weavers'/Spinners'	MidAtlantic Fiber Association	Van Artsdalen, Martha	√		SS&D	17	2	66	Sp 86	10
Guilds: Weavers'/Spinners'	Milwaukee Weavers' Guild		√		H&C	2	4		Fa 51	39
Guilds: Weavers'/Spinners'	Minneapolis Beehive Buzzes	Searle, Karen	√		SS&D	6	3	23	Su 75	48
Guilds: Weavers'/Spinners'	Minnesota Weavers Guild, The	Nodland, Marie	√		H&C	22	3		Su 71	12
Guilds: Weavers'/Spinners'	Museum Treasures Inspire Philadelphia Weavers		√		H&C	5	3		Su 54	19
Guilds: Weavers'/Spinners'	Natural Dyeing in Wisconsin	Rigby, M. Edith	√	√	SS&D	12	2	46	Sp 81	8
Guilds: Weavers'/Spinners'	New Hampshire Guild				H&C	7	1		Wi 55	48
Guilds: Weavers'/Spinners'	New Hampshire Weavers, The	Morrison, Harriet B.			H&C	1	2		Su 50	54
Guilds: Weavers'/Spinners'	New Omaha Weaver's Guild Stresses Quality Production, The		√		H&C	1	2		Su 50	53
Guilds: Weavers'/Spinners'	New York Guild				H&C	7	1		Wi 55	21
Guilds: Weavers'/Spinners'	New York Guild of Handweavers		√	√	H&C	9	3		Su 58	20
Guilds: Weavers'/Spinners'	New Zealand Spinners	Robinson, Margaret	√		H&C	10	3		Su 59	23
Guilds: Weavers'/Spinners'	North Shore Weavers Guild	Hamilton, Eva B.			H&C	20	4		Fa 69	33
Guilds: Weavers'/Spinners'	Northeastern Pennsylvania Guild				H&C	7	2		Sp 56	30
Guilds: Weavers'/Spinners'	Northwest Arkansas Guild	Elliott, Blanche E.			H&C	7	1		Wi 55	50
Guilds: Weavers'/Spinners'	One Guild's Story: From Founding an Organization to Building Its Image	Piroch, Sigrid	√		WJ	12	2	46	Fa 87	30
Guilds: Weavers'/Spinners'	Onondaga Weavers				H&C	17	1		Wi 66	21
Guilds: Weavers'/Spinners'	Philadelphia Weavers' Guild				H&C	7	1		Wi 55	43

SUBJECT	TITLE	AUTHOR	IL	INST	JOUR	VOL	NO	ISS	DATE	PAGE
Guilds: Weavers'/Spinners'	Pinellas Weavers	Aldrich, Mae D.			H&C	20	2		Sp 69	12
Guilds: Weavers'/Spinners'	Portage Trail Weavers		√		H&C	13	4		Fa 62	30
Guilds: Weavers'/Spinners'	Portland Guild's Yarn Shop		√		H&C	6	3		Su 55	55
Guilds: Weavers'/Spinners'	Potomac Craftsmen	Arness, Judidth R.			H&C	15	4		Fa 64	18
Guilds: Weavers'/Spinners'	Princeton Weavers Guild	Hoisington, Gladys			H&C	16	2		Sp 65	41
Guilds: Weavers'/Spinners'	Projects Spark Interest	Rothacker, Chet			Hw	1	2		S-S 80	15
Guilds: Weavers'/Spinners'	Raising Silkworms, The Glenna Harris Guild's Project	Pentler, Fumiko	√	√	H&C	20	1		Wi 69	14
Guilds: Weavers'/Spinners'	Rochester Weavers, New York Guild Sponsors Variety of Projects (error-corrected H&C v14 n1 63 p46)	Clement, Doris	√	√	H&C	13	4		Fa 62	12
Guilds: Weavers'/Spinners'	Rocky Mountain Guild Observes Colorado Centennial	Tuinsma, Frieda Z.	√		H&C	10	3		Su 59	16
Guilds: Weavers'/Spinners'	Salish Weaving	Boxberger, Daniel L.	√		SS&D	13	4	52	Fa 82	30
Guilds: Weavers'/Spinners'	Seattle Guild Garment Designs, Part 1	Noble, Judy	√	√	SS&D	10	3	39	Su 79	26
Guilds: Weavers'/Spinners'	Seattle Guild Garment Designs, Part 2: Completing the Top		√	√	SS&D	10	4	40	Fa 79	71
Guilds: Weavers'/Spinners'	Seattle Guild Garment Designs, Part 3, Skirts and Pants		√	√	SS&D	11	1	41	Wi 79	20
Guilds: Weavers'/Spinners'	Seattle Guild Garment Designs, Part 4: Edges, Closures, Capes and Dresses		√	√	SS&D	11	2	42	Sp 80	39
Guilds: Weavers'/Spinners'	Seattle Weavers' Guild, The	Robinson, Irma F.	√		H&C	1	1		Ap 50	34
Guilds: Weavers'/Spinners'	Seven Valley Weavers				H&C	20	4		Fa 69	36
Guilds: Weavers'/Spinners'	South Florida Handweavers		√		H&C	6	4		Fa 55	44
Guilds: Weavers'/Spinners'	Southern California Guild Honors Atwater	Brown, Barbara	√		SS&D	9	3	35	Su 78	38
Guilds: Weavers'/Spinners'	Southern California Hand Weavers Guild, The	Brownell, Effielee E.	√		H&C	6	2		Sp 55	30
Guilds: Weavers'/Spinners'	Spirit of St. Louis, The	Norton, Mary K.			SS&D	7	4	28	Fa 76	35
Guilds: Weavers'/Spinners'	St Louis Guild	Simpson, Jeanne W.	√	√	H&C	9	1		Wi 57	44
Guilds: Weavers'/Spinners'	St. Louis Weavers' Guild	Norton, Mary K.			H&C	17	4		Fa 66	23
Guilds: Weavers'/Spinners'	Tacoma Weavers Guild	Jeklin, Mrs. Lewis	√		H&C	9	1		Wi 57	14
Guilds: Weavers'/Spinners'	Textile Arts Club of Cleveland, Ohio	Collacott, Margaret C.			H&C	6	3		Su 55	25
Guilds: Weavers'/Spinners'	Tulsa Handweavers				H&C	14	4		Fa 63	21
Guilds: Weavers'/Spinners'	Utah Guild Sheep to Shawl	Hartford, Jane	√		SS&D	8	2	30	Sp 77	23
Guilds: Weavers'/Spinners'	Wadmal — A Felted Fabric	Snover, Susan; Jean Sullivan	√	√	SS&D	11	2	42	Sp 80	89
Guilds: Weavers'/Spinners'	Weaver Who Wastes Not, A	Porcella, Yvonne	√	√	SS&D	6	4	24	Fa 75	8
Guilds: Weavers'/Spinners'	Weavers Guild of Boston				H&C	18	1		Wi 67	19
Guilds: Weavers'/Spinners'	Weavers' Guild of Boston, The	Van Cleve, Kate	√		H&C	3	1		Wi 51	55
Guilds: Weavers'/Spinners'	Weavers Guild of Kalamazoo Profile				SS&D	12	2	46	Sp 81	86
Guilds: Weavers'/Spinners'	Weavers Guild of Minnesota, Textile Workshop	Nunneley, Faithe			H&C	22	1		Wi 71	13
Guilds: Weavers'/Spinners'	Weavers' Guild of St. Louis	Varney, Ethel B.			H&C	6	2		Sp 55	50
Guilds: Weavers'/Spinners'	Weavers' Guilds Expand Activities				H&C	4	4		Fa 53	11
Guilds: Weavers'/Spinners'	Weavers in Wisconsin				H&C	11	1		Wi 60	21
Guilds: Weavers'/Spinners'	Weavers of Spokane	Cain, Lois	√		H&C	6	4		Fa 55	26
Guilds: Weavers'/Spinners'	Weavers Were Founders of Potomac Craftsmen	Cochran, Doris M.			H&C	6	2		Sp 55	48
Guilds: Weavers'/Spinners'	Weaver's Guild of Rochester, New York, The		√		H&C	2	1		Wi 50	57
Guilds: Weavers'/Spinners'	Weaving Down Under	McKay, Isabel	√		H&C	15	3		Su 64	20
Guilds: Weavers'/Spinners'	Weaving with Computers	Sowles, Susan: Theresa Ruch			SS&D	13	3	51	Su 82	30
Guilds: Weavers'/Spinners'	Wheels Turn for French Revolution		√		Iw	1	1		Fa 75	14
Guilds: Weavers'/Spinners'	Wisconsin Federation of Hand Weavers Sponsors State Show				H&C	3	4		Fa 52	56

SUBJECT	TITLE	AUTHOR	IL	INST	JOUR	VOL	NO	ISS	DATE	PAGE
Guilds: Weavers'/Spinners', Arizona Desert Weavers and Spinners	Guild Life Crisis	Dozer, Iris			S-O	10	1		Sp 86	18
Guilds: Weavers'/Spinners', Aurora Colony Handspinners Guild	Aurora Colony Antique Spinning Wheel Showcase	Cobb, Lorie	√		S-O	10	3		Fa 86	43
Guilds: Weavers'/Spinners', Projects	Fun Approach to a Guild Show or Sale, The	Routh, Carol			Hw	8	2		M/A 87	32
Guilds: Weavers'/Spinners', Projects	Variations on a Theme: A Seattle Weavers' Guild Study Group Project	Sullivan, Jean H.	√	√	Hw	8	2		M/A 87	64
Guilds: Weavers'/Spinners', Sitka, Alaska	Spinning in a Special Climate	Allen, Marian			S-O	11	3		Fa 87	50
Guilds: Weaving Projects	Rochester Weavers, New York Guild Sponsors Variety of Projects (error-corrected H&C v14 n1 63 p46)	Clement, Doris	√	√	H&C	13	4		Fa 62	12
Guinness-Size Weaving	World's Wildest Weaving, The	Herring, Connie	√		PWC	1	1		No 81	41
Gulla Baskets	Afro-American Sweetgrass Basketry	Johnson, Beth	√		Fa	9	5		S/O 82	23
Gussets	Linen Shift: Plain Sewing Makes the Most of Your Fabric, A	Smith, Kathleen B.	√	√	TM			9	F/M 87	46
Gussets	Poetry of Sleeves: Shaping and Sewing Cloth to Fit the Arm, The	Nebesar, Rebecca Lanxner	√	√	TM			9	F/M 87	24
Gut	"Innerskins/Outerskins: Gut and Fishskin" (Exhibit)		√		TM			14	D/J 87	20
Gutwork	Gertrude Parker: Metamorphosing a Humble Material	Haney, Jeanna T.	√		Fa	14	4		S/O 87	8
Gutwork	Gutwork	Hickman, Pat	√		Fa	7	6		N/D 80	46
Gutwork	Patricia Bulitt: Gutsongs and Other Dances	Scarborough, Jessica	√		Fa	11	5		S/O 84	50
Hair Coiling	Wearable Coils: Nigerian Hair Sculpture	Rosen, Norma	√		Fa	12	4		J/A 85	33
Hair Sculpture	Hair As a Sculptor's Medium	Akamine, Estelle	√		Fa	14	3		M/J 87	24
Hair Sculpture	Wearable Coils: Nigerian Hair Sculpture	Rosen, Norma	√		Fa	12	4		J/A 85	33
Hair Styling	Hair Dressing as a Fiber Art	Yehling, Carol	√		Fa	7	1		J/F 80	20
Hair Styling	"Hair" (Exhibit)	Alonzo, Harriet	√		Fa	7	6		N/D 80	73
Hair Styling: Nigeria	Wearable Coils: Nigerian Hair Sculpture	Rosen, Norma	√		Fa	12	4		J/A 85	33
Haircloth	Tailor's Logic	Hostek, Stanley	√	√	TM			14	D/J 87	42
Haiti	Haitian Voodoo Banners: Dazzling Invitations to the Spirits	Lorenzo, Lauri	√		Fa	13	6		N/D 86	11
Half-Basket	Roman Textiles from Vindolanda, Hexham, England	Wild, John Peter	√		TMJ	18			79	19
Halkrus	Traditional Texture Weaves: Halkrus or Honeycomb	Zielinski, S. A.; Robert Leclerc, ed.	√	√	MWL	11			'51–'73	14
Hammocks	"Cocoon" Hammock	Drooker, Penelope B.	√	> 4	WJ	5	4	20	Sp 81	46
Hammocks	Cuna Cachi: A Study of Hammock Weaving Among the Cuna Indians of the San Blas Islands	Lambert, Anne M.	√	√	AT	5			Ju 86	105
Hammocks	Easy Weaving for Easy Living		√	√	Hw	1	2		S-S 80	48
Hammocks	Hamaca from Ecuador	Bowman, Susan	√	√	SS&D	10	3	39	Su 79	52
Hammocks	Hammock, The	Drooker, Penelope B.	√	√	TM			6	A/S 86	74
Hammocks	Hammocks	Earth Guild	√	√	SS&D	14	3	55	Su 83	24
Hammocks	Hammocks — A Swing Story	Bowman, Susan; Susan Guagliumi; Olive Linder			SS&D	10	3	39	Su 79	52
Hammocks	Knotted Netting Methods	Guagliumi, Susan	√	√	SS&D	10	3	39	Su 79	86
Hammocks	Sisal for Hammocks	Hannah, Joyce	√		TM			6	A/S 86	18
Hammocks	Sprang Time	Linder, Olive			SS&D	10	3	39	Su 79	88
Hammocks: Netted	Netted Hammock		√	√	WJ	4	1	13	Jy 79	43
Hammocks: Woven	Combining Lace Weaves		√	√	WJ	4	2	14	Oc 79	14
Hams	Irons, Boards, and Presses: A Survey of the Tools That Beautify Sewing	Coffin, David Page	√		TM			10	A/M 87	40
Hanaori: Flower Weaving	Hanaori: An Okinawan Brocaded Textile	Miller, Dorothy	√	√	AT	1			De 83	173

SUBJECT	TITLE	AUTHOR	IL	INST	JOUR	VOL	NO	ISS	DATE	PAGE
Handicapped see Disabled; and Therapy/Rehabilitation										
Handkerchiefs	Shetland Lace	Korach, Alice	√	√	TM			11	J/J 87	40
Handkerchiefs: Political	Handkerchiefs and Politics	Austin, Carole	√		Fa	12	3		M/J 85	51
Handkerchiefs, Silk	More About Fabrics: Practical Projects in Tabby	Zielinski, S. A.; Robert Leclerc, ed.	√	√	MWL	20			'51–'73	29
Handkerchiefs: Wedding	Shetland Lace Wedding Handkerchief, A (error-corrected TM n12 87 p4)	Korach, Alice	√	√	TM			11	J/J 87	42
Handloom Weaving	Handloom Weaves	Tidball, Harriet			SCGM		33		57	1
Handloom Weaving: Loom-Controlled	Handloom Weaves, The	Tidball, Harriet			SCGM		33		57	I-38
Handspinning	Handspinning: The Unexamined Life	Fannin, Allen	√		S-O	10	2		Su 86	35
Handspun	Thread Weaving	Sample, Joan	√	√	TM			8	D/J 86	64
Handweavers Guild of America see HGA										
Handweaving	Handweavers 1800—1840	Wilson, Kax	√		Iw	5	2		Sp 80	50
Handweaving	Handweaver's Instruction Manual: The Introduction	Tidball, Harriet C. nee Douglas	√	√	SCGM		34		49	1-41
Handweaving	Handweaving for Pleasure and Profit	Pasco, Henry H.			H&C	20	4		Fa 69	7
Handweaving	Universality of Handweaving, The				SS&D	4	1	13	Wi 72	11
Handweaving 1950	American Handweaving, A Mid-Century Viewpoint	Frey, Berta	√		H&C	1	1		Ap 50	5
Handweaving 1950	Handweaving in the South Today	Ford, Toni	√		H&C	1	1		Ap 50	14
Handweaving 1950 — 1969	Twenty Years of Handweaving	Linton, Dr. George E.			H&C	20	2		Sp 69	11
Handweaving 1965	Handweaving 1965	Frey, Berta			H&C	16	2		Sp 65	6
Handweaving 1969	Handweaving 1969	Regensteiner, Else	√		H&C	20	2		Sp 69	4
Handweaving 1970	Tradition, Innovation — Identity	Regensteiner, Else	√		SS&D	1	2	2	Mr 70	3
Handweaving: Canada	Canadian Handweaving (Exhibit)		√		Fa	13	3		M/J 86	55
Handweaving: Characteristics	Characteristics of Handweaves	Howell, Marie	√		H&C	12	1		Wi 61	18
Handweaving: Commercial, Mexico	Mexican Motifs: Mexican Commercial Handweaving	Tidball, Harriet	√		SCGM		6		62	21
Handweaving: Contemporary	Contemporary American Handweaving from an International Perspective	Alaniz, Leonore	√		WJ	11	3	43	Wi 87	26
Handweaving: Everyday Living	Handweaving in Everyday Living	Green, Harry B.			H&C	10	4		Fa 59	24
Handweaving: Greece	Search for Handweaving in Greece, A (error-corrected H&C v21 n3 70 p42)	Turner, Alta R.	√		H&C	21	2		Sp 70	16
Handweaving: International	Contemporary American Handweaving from an International Perspective	Alaniz, Leonore	√		WJ	11	3	43	Wi 87	26
Handweaving: Knots	Peter Collingwood, His Weaves and Weaving: Knots Used in Handweaving	Collingwood, Peter; Harriet Tidball, ed.	√	√	SCGM		8		63	28
Handweaving: Review	Review of Handweaving, A	Laurell, Karl	√		H&C	15	1		Wi 64	14
Handweaving: Revival	British Revival in Handweaving, The	Hall, Wendy	√		H&C	4	3		Su 53	21
Handweaving: Revival	Quarter Century of Handweavers' Progress, A	Atwater, Mary Meigs	√		H&C	2	2		Sp 51	5
Handweaving: Southeast	Weavers in the Southeast	Adams, Sally	√		H&C	20	2		Sp 69	6
Handweaving Trends 1950 — 1969	Note from Berta Frey, A				H&C	20	2		Sp 69	30
Handweaving1960	American Handweaving 1960		√		H&C	11	2		Sp 60	5
Hanging Textiles	Contemporary Tapestry	Tidball, Harriet	√	√	SCGM		12		64	25
Hanging Textiles	Rods for Wall Hanging			√	TM			3	F/M 86	8
Hanging Textiles	Transparent Weaving with Handspun Cotton Weft	Green, Andrea	√	√	WJ	8	2	30	Fa 83	44
Hanging Textiles	Weaving a City Skyline	Wennerstrom, Ann K.	√	√	WJ	7	1	25	Su 82	30
Hanging Textiles	Working Out Your Hangups	Liebler, Barbara	√	√	Iw	2	2		Wi 77	24
Hanging Textiles: Techniques	Simple Ways to Hang a Weaving	Graves, John; Susan Graves	√	√	WJ	10	4	40	Sp 86	69
Hangings	Beyond Quilting	Dyett, Linda	√	√	TM			5	J/J 86	70
Hangings	Christmas Transparencies (Görel Kinersly)		√	√	Hw	6	4		S/O 85	66, I-16

SUBJECT	TITLE	AUTHOR	IL	INST	JOUR	VOL	NO	ISS	DATE	PAGE
Hangings	Felted Wool Landscapes	Showalter, Pat	√	√	S-O	9	3		Fa 85	22
Hangings	Folk Textiles of Latin America	Kelemen, Pál	√		TMJ	1	4		De 65	2
Hangings	Martin's Creek Settlement: A Pictorial Weaving	Thompson, Kathleen; Alice Tipton	√		S-O	9	3		Fa 85	39
Hangings	Multi-Layered Tubular Hangings	Maxcy, Mabel E.	√	√	SS&D	4	4	16	Fa 73	12
Hangings	Reversible Cardwoven Hanging	Bradshaw, Susan	√		S-O	10	4		Wi 86	16
Hangings: Macrolace	Bobbin Lace on a Grand Scale: When the Pillow Is a 12-ft. Pegboard	Lewis, Robin S.	√	√	TM			9	F/M 87	54
Harness Lace	Complex "Harness Lace"	Nass, Ulla	√	√	SS&D	9	3	35	Su 78	4
Harness Lace	Gifts from Ancient Peru	Nass, Ulla	√	√	WJ	8	1	29	Su 83	32
Harness Lace	"Harness Lace:" A New Leno Set-Up	Nass, Ulla	√	√	SS&D	8	2	30	Sp 77	56
Harris Tweeds	Happy Weaver of the Isle of Harris, The	Ham, Phebe D.	√		SS&D	1	2	2	Mr 70	12
Harris Tweeds	Romance of Harris Tweeds, The	Fairbairn, J. E.	√		H&C	2	3		Su 51	21
Hat Band	Hat Band (Barbara Elkins)		√	√	Hw	2	1		F-W 80	35, 69
Hatching	Hatching	Marston, Ena	√	√	SS&D	10	3	39	Su 79	56
Hats and Caps	Stylish No-Sew Hat	Anderson, Barbara	√	√	WJ	6	3	23	Wi 81	39
Haute Couture	Techniques of Haute Couture (error-corrected TM i7 O/N86 p5)	Rhodes, Elizabeth A.	√	√	TM			6	A/S 86	52
Hawaii	Dogbones from Trees?	Jackson, Mariechen	√		SS&D	2	1	5	De 70	18
Hawaii	Hawaiian Feather Techniques	Kwiatkowski, Ron	√	√	Iw	1	4		Su 76	16
Hawaii	Hawaiian Quilt, The	White-Hansen, Sue Ellen	√	√	TM			13	O/N 87	22
Hawaii	Hawaiian Quilting: Tradition Through Change	Akana, Elizabeth A.	√		Fa	9	3		M/J 82	62
Hawaii	Hui Mea Hana of Honolulu	Judd, Eva Marie	√	√	H&C	8	4		Fa 57	51
Hawaii	Legend of Maui and the Sun, The		√		SS&D	1	3	3	Ju 70	3
Hawaii	Love-Spinning Farewell in Hawaii	McCarty, Carole	√		SS&D	6	1	21	Wi 74	41
Hawaii	Protest in Hawaii		√		SS&D	2	3	7	Su 71	10
Hawaii	Wailani Johansen, Quiltmaker: Sharing the Tradition of the Hawaiian Quilt	Rex, Chris	√		Fa	9	3		M/J 82	60
Hawaii	Weaving in Hawaii	Robinson, Hester A.	√		H&C	3	4		Fa 52	12
Hazards	Memo to All Concerned Craftsmen (error-corrected SS&D v10 n4 79 p66)	Towner, Naomi Whiting			SS&D	10	3	39	Su 79	10
Hazards	Protecting Yourself: Fiber Art Hazards and Precautions	Rossol, Monona	√		Fa	12	6		N/D 85	42
Hazards	Rules for Using Paints, Inks, and Dyes	Rossol, Monona	√		Fa	12	6		N/D 85	42
Hazards: Chemical Dyes	Rainbow Dyeing	Rowe, Erica	√	√	WJ	8	2	30	Fa 83	31
Hazards: Drycleaning Solvents	Principles of Textile Conservation Science, No. 8. Drycleaning of Fine and Fragile Textiles	Rice, James W.	√	√	TMJ	2	2		De 67	21
Hazards: Dye	Carcinogens in Dyes			√	TM			6	A/S 86	4
Hazards: Dye	Chemical Safety In Dyeing			√	TM			7	O/N 86	4
Hazards: Dyeing	Chemical Dyeing of Linen	Gwynne, Elaine	√	√	WJ	7	2	26	Fa 82	23
Hazards: Dyeing	Dyeing Dangers	Reagan, Trudy		√	Fa	5	1		J/F 78	36
Hazards: Dyeing	Dyeing with Fiber Reactive Dyes on Cotton	Read, Kay	√	√	WJ	4	2	14	Oc 79	42
Hazards: Dyeing	Exploration of Caustic Soda, An	Bissell, June M.	√		Fa	7	6		N/D 80	43
Hazards: Dyeing	Hazards of Dyes by Class	Rossol, Monona	√		Fa	12	6		N/D 85	43
Hazards: Dyeing	Hazards of Mordants and Dye-Assisting Chemicals	Rossol, Monona	√		Fa	12	6		N/D 85	43
Hazards: Dyes	Safety Tip for Fiber-Reactive Dyes, A			√	TM			5	J/J 86	10
Hazards: Eye	Chemical Eye Injuries and Contact Lenses: A Dangerous Combination	Holtzer, Marilyn	√		SS&D	12	1	45	Wi 80	7
Hazards: Spinning	Words to the Wise	Parsons, Jane			S-O	11	1		Sp 87	28
Hazards: Wax	Toxicity of Wax			√	TM			5	J/J 86	8
Headbands	Guatemala Visited	Atwater, Mary Meigs	√	√	SCGM		15		65	23
Health and Safety	Anthrax!		√		Fa	3	2		M/A 76	10
Health and Safety	Anthrax Reported				SS&D	9	4	36	Fa 78	32

SUBJECT	TITLE	AUTHOR	IL	INST	JOUR	VOL	NO	ISS	DATE	PAGE
Health and Safety	Bancroft's Mordant: A Useful One-Pot Natural Dye Technique	Liles, James N.; Dale Liles	√	√	SS&D	15	3	59	Su 84	76
Health and Safety	Chemical Eye Injuries and Contact Lenses: A Dangerous Combination	Holtzer, Marilyn	√		SS&D	12	1	45	Wi 80	7
Health and Safety	Dyepot	Koehler, Glory Dail			SS&D	7	4	28	Fa 76	58
Health and Safety	Hazards Faced by Weavers	Goodyear, Nancy L.		√	SS&D	13	3	51	Su 82	15
Health and Safety	Health and Safety Hazards in the Fiber Studio	LaLena, Constance	√	√	Hw	4	5		N/D 83	79
Health and Safety	Memo to All Concerned Craftsmen (error-corrected SS&D v10 n4 79 p66)	Towner, Naomi Whiting			SS&D	10	3	39	Su 79	10
Health and Safety	Microwave Dyeing	Mortensen, Diane	√	√	SS&D	10	4	40	Fa 79	12
Health and Safety	Poisonous Dye Plants	Ellis, Jennie Faye		√	SS&D	4	2	14	Sp 73	46
Health and Safety	Tests for Desired Yarn Qualities	Koehler, Glory Dail		√	SS&D	7	2	26	Sp 76	68
Health and Safety	Weaving is a Pain in the...	Chandler, Deborah	√	√	Hw	6	2		M/A 85	26
Health and Safety	Weaving with a Strong Back	Brostoff, Laya	√		Hw	3	3		My 82	41
Health and Safety: Anthrax	Anthrax Sterilization Methods and Their Effects on Fibers	Towner, Naomi Whiting; Helen Cushman		√	SS&D	7	3	27	Su 76	94
Health and Safety: Anthrax	Contaminated Yarn				SS&D	7	2	26	Sp 76	39
Health and Safety: Carpal Tunnel Syndrome	Words to the Wise	Parsons, Jane			S-O	11	1		Sp 87	28
Health and Safety: Pain	Happy Endings	Ligon, Linda	√	√	Hw	8	5		N/D 87	99
Hebrides, Outer	Tweed of Harris, The	Johnson, Beth	√		Hw	2	5		No 81	47
Heddle Construction: String, Continuous	Warping and Weaving Mitla Cloth on the Backstrap Loom	Knottenbelt, Maaike	√	√	TMJ	22			83	53
Heddle Rod, Multiple	Warping and Weaving Mitla Cloth on the Backstrap Loom	Knottenbelt, Maaike	√	√	TMJ	22			83	53
Heddle Rod, Single	Weaving a Cotton Saddlebag on the Santa Elena Peninsula of Ecuador	Hagino, Jane Parker; Karen E. Stothert	√	√	TMJ	22			83	19
Heddles	Heddles, The Many Advantages of Using a Variety	Walrath, E. K.	√		H&C	17	4		Fa 66	20
Heddles: Continuous Element	Patolu and Its Techniques	De Bone, Mary Golden	√	√	TMJ	4	3		76	49
Heddles, Doup	Doup Leno (error-corrected WJ v3 n2 78 insert p38a)		√	√	WJ	3	2	10	Oc 78	32
Heddles: Doup, Steel	Leno with Steel Doup Heddles	Barrett, Clotilde	√	√	WJ	6	3	23	Wi 81	48
Heddles: Gauze Weaving	Two-Harness Textiles, The Open Work Weaves: Gauze and Leno, The Crossed-Warp Weaves, The Gauze Heddle	Tidball, Harriet	√	√	SCGM		21		67	22
Heddles: Interlinked, Two-Way	Understanding Some Complex Structures from Simple Andean Looms: Steps in Analysis and Reproduction	Cahlander, Adele	√	√	AT	1			De 83	181
Heddles: Loop	Andean Crossed-Warp Techniques for Decorative Trims, Part 2 — Tubular Bands (error-corrected WJ v3 n1 insert for vol. 2)	Cahlander, Adele	√	√	WJ	3	1	9	Jy 78	38
Heddles: Pattern, Extra-Long	Pattern Weaving, Laotian Style	Keasbey, Doramay	√	√	Hw	2	3		My 81	54
Heddles: Pattern Heddle Stick	Brocade: The Pattern Heddle	Tidball, Harriet	√	√	SCGM		22		67	7
Heddles: Rectangular Eye	Knotless Cords and Heddles on a Counter-march Loom (error-corrected SS&D v12 n3 81 p6)	Kinersly, Görel A. B.	√	√	SS&D	12	2	46	Sp 81	18
Heddles, Repair	Satisfactory Repair Heddles	Heintz, Dr. Kenneth G.	√	√	SS&D	4	3	15	Su 73	43
Heddles: Shaft-Switching Adaptations	Shaft Switch Technique (error-corrected WJ v6 n1 81 p28d)		√	√	WJ	5	1	17	Su 80	5
Heddles, String	Dear Heddle		√	√	WJ	1	2	2	Oc 76	35
Heddles: String	Tie Your Own String Heddles	Perrault, Joe	√	√	WJ	11	1	41	Su 86	65
Heddles: String	Vertical Loom (continued) — Construction of a Warp Weighted Loom, The		√	√	WJ	1	4	4	Ap 77	27
Heddles: String, Continuous	Cuna Cachi: A Study of Hammock Weaving Among the Cuna Indians of the San Blas Islands	Lambert, Anne M.	√	√	AT	5			Ju 86	105
Heddles: String, Tying	Complementary-Warp Weave (error-corrected WJ v7 n4 83 p4)	Coffman, Charlotte	√	√	WJ	7	3	27	Wi 82	53

SUBJECT	TITLE	AUTHOR	IL	INST	JOUR	VOL	NO	ISS	DATE	PAGE
Heddles: Tying, Inkle Loom	Weaving Inkle Bands: Preparing the Board Loom and Weaving, Heddle Making	Tidball, Harriet	√	√	SCGM		27		69	6
Heddles: Tying Techniques	Tie Your Own String Heddles	Perrault, Joe	√	√	WJ	11	1	41	Su 86	65
Heddles: Weighted	Shaft-Switching on Rising Shed Looms Using Weighted Floating Heddles	Harse, Crys	√	√	WJ	9	4	36	Sp 85	63
Heirloom Weaving	For a Summer Bride		√		Hw	4	3		M/J 83	55
Heirloom Weaving	Heirloom Weaving. A Christening Gown with Mary Pendergrass		√	> 4	Hw	3	4		Se 82	53
Heirlooms	Emotional Value				TM			14	D/J 87	4
Heirlooms	Granny's Coverlet (or how do you tell if your coverlet's real?)	Strickler, Carol		√	S-O	6	4		82	26
Heirlooms	Great-Grandmother's Linens	Mattera, Joanne	√		TM			3	F/M 86	86
Heirlooms	Greek Dower Sheet, A	Xenakis, Alexis Yiorgos	√		Hw	1	2		S-S 80	36
Heirlooms	Handing Down More Than Just a Quilt	Hamilton, Carolyn	√		TM			12	A/S 87	86
Heirlooms	Heirloom Christmas, An		√	√	Hw	8	4		S/O 87	56
Heirlooms	Heirloom Wedding Dress	Ellman, Norma	√	√	Kn	3	2	6	Sp 87	31
Heirlooms	Heirlooms Don't Just Happen	Staines, Barbara			S-O	6	4		82	35
Heirlooms	Hey, Sailor, Let Me Shorten Your Sleeve	Violante, Elizabeth	√		TM			6	A/S 86	98
Heirlooms	Linen Bed Sheets		√		TM			4	A/M 86	86
Heirlooms	Ten Years and Ten Pounds of Crochet	Cannarella, Deborah	√		TM			1	O/N 85	80
Heirlooms: Linens	Heirloom Linens	Furniss, Frances	√		H&C	9	2		Sp 58	11
Heirlooms: Weaving Arts	Heirlooms At Montana		√		SS&D	1	4	4	Se 70	8
Help: Craft Production, Needy Countries	A Weaver Ponders His Craft, Collection of Controversial Essays: How to Help	Zielinski, S. A.; Robert Leclerc, ed.		√	MWL	21 22			'51–'73	31
Helpful Hints: Dyeing	Hints for Dyeing	Bliss, Anne			S-O	9	3		Fa 85	53
Helpful Hints: Fleece Selection	Fleece in the Hands of a New Zealand Spinner	Horne, Beverley	√		S-O	2			78	24
Helpful Hints: Linen, Weft	Dear Heddle		√	√	WJ	1	1	1	Jy 76	8
Helpful Hints: Narrow-Loom Weaving	Making Narrow Looms Do Big Jobs	Kling, Mary Nell	√		H&C	2	1		Wi 50	13
Helpful Hints: Spinning	Designing Yarn	Noble, Judith G.	√		S-O	2			78	53
Helpful Hints: Spinning	Easing the Beginner's Fears	Irwin, Bobbie		√	S-O	10	4		Wi 86	24
Helpful Hints: Spinning	Fine, Finer, Finest	Raven, Lee		√	S-O	9	4		Wi 85	24
Helpful Hints: Spinning	Fleece in the Hands of a New Zealand Spinner	Horne, Beverley			S-O	2			78	24
Helpful Hints: Spinning	Problems With Your Flyer and Bobbin Wheel Spinning	Raven, Lee	√	√	S-O	11	4		Wi 87	23
Helpful Hints: Spinning	Production Handspinning	Carlin, Lee J.	√		S-O	1			77	50
Helpful Hints: Spinning	Tips on Spinning a Wool Embroidery Yarn	Gibson-Roberts, Priscilla A.	√	√	S-O	9	3		Fa 85	46
Helpful Hints: Splicing Weft	Method of Splicing a Weft, A		√	√	H&C	2	2		Sp 51	59
Helpful Hints: Spoolrack, Tangle	Dear Heddle		√	√	WJ	1	1	1	Jy 76	8
Helpful Hints: Stabilize Loom	Tricks of the Trade	Gubser, Elsie H.	√		H&C	6	4		Fa 55	29
Helpful Hints: Warps and Warping	Tricks of the Trade	Gubser, Elsie H.	√		H&C	6	4		Fa 55	29
Helpful Hints: Warps and Warping	Wrap Up Your Warp	Voiers, Leslie	√	> 4	SS&D	18	1	69	Wi 86	49
Helpful Hints: Weaving	Have You Tried This?	Thorpe, Heather G.			H&C	8	1		Wi 56	29
Helpful Hints: Weaving	Something Out of Nothing	Spencer, Edith L.	√	√	H&C	8	3		Su 57	14
Helpful Hints: Weaving	Try Something Different	Krasnoff, Julienne	√	√	H&C	21	2		Sp 70	19
Helpful Suggestions: Weaving	Peter Collingwood, His Weaves and Weaving: Some Practical Hints, Notes on Collingwood Lectures	Fitzgerald, Nathallie	√	√	SCGM		8		63	40
Hemp	Banana, Ramie, and Hemp in Okinawa (error-corrected Fa v14 n3 87 p4)	Miller, Dorothy	√		Fa	14	2		M/A 87	46
Hemp	Plant Fibers		√	√	WJ	8	2	30	Fa 83	67
Hemp	Survey of Leaf and Stem Fibers, A	Buchanan, Rita	√		S-O	10	3		Fa 86	24
Hems	Hems			√	TM			5	J/J 86	10

SUBJECT	TITLE	AUTHOR	IL	INST	JOUR	VOL	NO	ISS	DATE	PAGE
Hems, Double Weave	Double Weaves: Hems in Four Shaft Double Weaving	Zielinski, S. A.; Robert Leclerc, ed.	√	√	MWL	15			'51–'73	76
Hems, Hand-Rolled	Hand-Rolled Hems		√	√	TM			10	A/M 87	10
Hems, Knitted	Sampler of Knit Edgings and Applied Trims, A	Newton, Deborah	√	√	TM			12	A/S 87	38
Hemstitching	Afghans: Things to Consider and Finishes	Xenakis, Athanasios David	√	√	PWC	3	1	7		10
Hemstitching	Hemstitch in Time, A	Ligon, Linda	√	√	Hw	8	2		M/A 87	98
Hemstitching	Hemstitching	West, Virginia	√	√	Hw	2	5		No 81	56
Hemstitching	Oriental Hem Stitch	Post, Margaret	√	√	SS&D	8	2	30	Sp 77	59
Hemstitching	So There Is a Use for Fancy Machine Stitches	Richter, Elizabeth Lee	√	√	TM			11	J/J 87	62
Hemstitching	Virginia West's Hemstitching Method		√	√	Hw	2	5		No 81	59
Hemstitching	Weaving in Quebec: Traditional Quebecois Weaving	Barrett, Clotilde	√	√	WJ	6	4	24	Sp 82	10
Hemstitching: Automatic-Stitched	Construction Details with Automatic Stitches	Richter, Elizabeth Lee	√	√	TM			11	J/J 87	64
Hemstitching: Techniques	Hemstitching for Linens	Baizerman, Suzanne	√	√	WJ	10	4	40	Sp 86	25
Hemstitching: Types	Varied Hemstitching, Used for Finishing	West, Virginia M.	√	√	H&C	18	2		Sp 67	19
Henequen	Plant Fibers: Soft Fibers		√	√	WJ	8	2	30	Fa 83	67
Henequen	Survey of Leaf and Stem Fibers, A	Buchanan, Rita	√		S-O	10	3		Fa 86	24
Heraldry	Banners		√	√	SS&D	11	4	44	Fa 80	47
Herbs	Dyes from the Herb Garden	King, Helen	√	√	TM			6	A/S 86	58
Herbs	Herbal Moth Repellents: Safeguard or Sentiment?	Buchanan, Rita			S-O	10	2		Su 86	25
Herbs	Herbs for a Healthy Angora	McConnell, Kathleen	√		S-O	8	1		Sp 84	38
Herringbone Stitch	School for Knitters		√	√	Kn	3	2	6	Sp 87	3
Hessian Weave	Contemporary Fabrics from an Australia Handweaving Mill	Daniel, Robert	√		H&C	16	1		Wi 65	18
HGA	Biennial Report — HGA and the Future		√		SS&D	3	4	12	Fa 72	10
HGA	Biennial Report — HGA As It Is Today		√		SS&D	3	4	12	Fa 72	8
HGA	Biennial Report: Responsibility of Growth		√		SS&D	5	4	20	Fa 74	18
HGA	By-Laws of Handweavers Guild of America, Inc.				SS&D	3	2	10	Sp 72	41
HGA	Certificate of Incorporation of Handweavers Guild of America, Inc.				SS&D	3	2	10	Sp 72	40
HGA	Focus on the HGA Board of Directors		√		SS&D	10	1	37	Wi 78	52
HGA	Focus on the HGA Board of Directors		√		SS&D	10	3	39	Su 79	45
HGA	From the President				SS&D	2	3	7	Su 71	4
HGA	HGA Board Candidates: Vote for Three		√		SS&D	10	2	38	Sp 79	48
HGA	HGA Executive Board		√		SS&D	2	3	7	Su 71	5
HGA	In the Beginning				SS&D	1	1	1	De 69	1
HGA	Report — Board of Directors		√		SS&D	3	4	12	Fa 72	12
HGA	Respectfully Submitted	Holcombe, Elizabeth	√		SS&D	2	3	7	Su 71	4
HGA	Revised HGA By-Laws				SS&D	7	4	28	Fa 76	92
HGA	Tradition, Innovation — Identity	Regensteiner, Else	√		SS&D	1	2	2	Mr 70	3
HGA: Awards	Goldenrod Poncho Wins HGA Award	Hunter, Frances	√	√	SS&D	5	4	20	Fa 74	95
HGA: Awards	HGA Judges Choice Awards 1986				SS&D	18	3	71	Su 87	90
HGA: Awards	HGA Scholarship	Braun, Susan G.	√		SS&D	18	1	69	Wi 86	9
HGA: Awards	HGA Showcase (error-corrected SS&D v10 n3 79 p75)		√		SS&D	10	2	38	Sp 79	58
HGA: Awards	Judges Choice Awards—Summer 1973		√		SS&D	5	1	17	Wi 73	85
HGA: Awards	Show Stopper—Deborah Hughes		√		SS&D	6	3	23	Su 75	40
HGA: Awards	Showtime '81: The HGA Winner's Circle		√		SS&D	12	3	47	Su 81	21
HGA: Certificate of Excellence	Certificates of Excellence: What Goes On	Nunneley, Faithe	√		SS&D	10	1	37	Wi 78	36
HGA: Certificate of Excellence in Handspinning	Certificate of Excellence in Handspinning				SS&D	12	2	46	Sp 81	13

SUBJECT	TITLE	AUTHOR	IL	INST	JOUR	VOL	NO	ISS	DATE	PAGE
HGA: Certificate of Excellence in Handspinning	Certificate of Excellence in Handspinning	Champion, Ellen			S-O	11	3		Fa 87	28
HGA: Certificate of Excellence in Handspinning	Certificate of Excellence in Handspinning, The	Shaffer-Meyer, Rima; Arlene M. Stein			SS&D	13	2	50	Sp 82	35
HGA: Certificate of Excellence in Handspinning	Certificate of Excellence, The	Redman, Jane	√		SS&D	8	1	29	WI 76	46
HGA: Certificate of Excellence in Handspinning	COE in Handspinning, The	Shaffer-Meyer, Rima			SS&D	15	2	58	Sp 84	25
HGA: Certificate Of Excellence in Handspinning	Handbook of Requirements for HGA Certificate of Excellence				SS&D	6	3	23	Su 75	48A
HGA: Certificate of Excellence in Handspinning	Handspun into Lace	Fournier, Jane	√	√	SS&D	17	4	68	Fa 86	70
HGA Certificate of Excellence in Handspinning	HGA Spinning Program	Lorance, Marilyn			SS&D	11	2	42	Sp 80	67
HGA: Certificate of Excellence in Handspinning	Kathy Mincer: In Pursuit of Excellence	Linder, Olive	√		SS&D	13	2	50	Sp 82	31
HGA: Certificate of Excellence in Handspinning	Report on the HGA Handspinning Certificate of Excellence, A	Lorance, Marilyn			S-O	4			80	6
HGA: Certificate of Excellence in Handspinning	Thoughts on The Certificate of Excellence in Handspinning	Dozer, Iris	√		SS&D	17	4	68	Fa 86	67
HGA Certificate of Excellence in Handweaving	Applicant #029: Antonia Kormos	Wertheimer, Sheila	√		SS&D	10	2	38	Sp 79	68
HGA: Certificate of Excellence in Handweaving	Applicant 3-86	Sullivan, Donna	√		SS&D	18	4	72	Fa 87	32
HGA: Certificate of Excellence in Handweaving	Certificate Holders: Now What? Part 2, The	Alderman, Sharon D.	√		SS&D	12	4	48	Fa 81	52
HGA: Certificate of Excellence in Handweaving	Certificate Holders: Now What?, The	Alderman, Sharon D.	√		SS&D	12	2	46	Sp 81	41
HGA: Certificate of Excellence in Handweaving	Certificate Holders: What Now? Part 3, The	Alderman, Sharon D.	√		SS&D	13	2	50	Sp 82	60
HGA: Certificate of Excellence in Handweaving	Certificate of Excellence in Handweaving: COE Holders, The	Drooker, Penelope B.	√		SS&D	14	1	53	Wi 82	49
HGA: Certificate of Excellence in Handweaving	Certificate of Excellence to be Offered	Regensteiner, Else			SS&D	5	4	20	Fa 74	52
HGA: Certificate of Excellence in Handweaving	Certificate Success	Drooker, Penelope	√		SS&D	16	1	61	Wi 84	66
HGA: Certificate of Excellence in Handweaving	Certificate: Where Artist and Artisan Meet	Redman, Jane	√	> 4	SS&D	8	2	30	Sp 77	48
HGA: Certificate of Excellence in Handweaving	COE Diary, A	Drooker, Penelope			SS&D	16	2	62	Sp 85	30
HGA: Certificate of Excellence in Handweaving	COE Retrospective	Drooker, Penelope			SS&D	15	4	60	Fa 84	19
HGA: Certificate of Excellence in Handweaving	Crate Expectations	Drooker, Penelope	√		SS&D	16	1	61	Wi 84	69
HGA: Certificate of Excellence in Handweaving	HGA Certificate of Excellence: A Report	Ligon, Linda	√		Iw	2	2		Wi 77	8
HGA: Competition Winners	Small Expressions 1987 Winners Showcase		√		SS&D	19	1	73	Wi 87	81
HGA: Consulting Service	HGA Presents — A New Consulting Service				SS&D	2	2	6	Sp 71	22
HGA: Convergences	Appraisal of Convergence '72, An	Henzie, Susie			SS&D	3	4	12	Fa 72	41
HGA: Convergences	By the Bay—Convergence '74				SS&D	5	2	18	Sp 74	10
HGA: Convergences	Challenge, Exploration				SS&D	3	2	10	Sp 72	23
HGA: Convergences	Conferences: Convergence '78	Ligon, Linda; with Barbara Gentry	√		Iw	3	4		Su 78	28
HGA: Convergences	Conferences: Where Do We Go From Here?	Tillett, Leslie			Iw	3	4		Su 78	32
HGA: Convergences	Convergence '72 — General Information				SS&D	3	2	10	Sp 72	25
HGA: Convergences	Convergence '72 — Program and People				SS&D	3	2	10	Sp 72	24
HGA: Convergences	Convergence '72 — The Convention				SS&D	3	1	9	Wi 71	23
HGA: Convergences	Convergence '72 — The Program				SS&D	3	1	9	Wi 71	24
HGA: Convergences	Convergence '72 — The Workshops				SS&D	3	1	9	Wi 71	22

SUBJECT	TITLE	AUTHOR	IL	INST	JOUR	VOL	NO	ISS	DATE	PAGE
HGA: Convergences	Convergence '74, Events Calendar				SS&D	5	3	19	Su 74	45
HGA: Convergences	Convergence '74 — General Information				SS&D	5	1	17	Wi 73	46
HGA: Convergences	Convergence '74 — HGA's Great Gathering		√		SS&D	4	4	16	Fa 73	8
HGA: Convergences	Convergence '74, Hurschler Collection	Hurschler, Paul; Flora Hurschler	√		SS&D	5	3	19	Su 74	43
HGA: Convergences	Convergence '74 — Seminars And Workshops				SS&D	5	1	17	Wi 73	11
HGA: Convergences	Convergence '74, Speakers		√		SS&D	5	3	19	Su 74	44
HGA: Convergences	Convergence '76		√		SS&D	6	3	23	Su 75	27
HGA: Convergences	Convergence '76: Fiber Craftsmen in Action		√		SS&D	7	4	28	Fa 76	106
HGA: Convergences	Convergence '76—Visit to an Old Weaving Village Plus a Riverboat Cruise		√		SS&D	6	1	21	Wi 74	47
HGA: Convergences	Convergence '78 Information				SS&D	9	1	33	Wi 77	55
HGA: Convergences	Convergence '78 Update: Visions and Revisions	Stoller, Irene			SS&D	9	2	34	Sp 78	102
HGA: Convergences	Convergence '80 Registration Information				SS&D	11	1	41	Wi 79	69
HGA: Convergences	Convergence '82		√		SS&D	13	4	52	Fa 82	41
HGA: Convergences	Convergence '82	Price, Susan			Fa	9	6		N/D 82	54
HGA: Convergences	Convergence '82: Registration Information				SS&D	13	1	49	Wi 81	51
HGA: Convergences	Convergence '84	Redding, Debbie			Hw	5	4		S/O 84	17
HGA: Convergences	Convergence '84	Rowley, Kathleen	√		Fa	12	2		M/A 85	42
HGA: Convergences	Convergence '84 Conference Information				SS&D	15	1	57	Wi 83	51
HGA: Convergences	Convergence '84 Conference Information				SS&D	15	1	57	Wi 83	51
HGA: Convergences	Convergence '84: Dallas	Dailey, Linda	√		SS&D	15	4	60	Fa 84	38
HGA: Convergences	Convergence '86				Hw	8	1		J/F 87	28
HGA: Convergences	Convergence '86	Marcus, Ruth-Claire			TM			8	D/J 86	10
HGA: Convergences	Convergence '86 Co-Hosts: The Ontario Crafts Council and The Ontario Handweavers and Spinners	Wyndham, Lois	√		SS&D	17	3	67	Su 86	38
HGA: Convergences	Convergence '86 Fashions	Dean, Ankaret	√		SS&D	18	1	69	Wi 86	16
HGA Convergences	Convergence '86 Preview: Keynote Speaker Dorothy Burnham	Dean, Ankaret	√		SS&D	16	3	63	Su 85	32
HGA: Convergences	Convergence '86 Preview: Pangnirtung Weavers	Stuart, Donald	√		SS&D	16	4	64	Fa 85	70
HGA: Convergences	Convergence '86 Preview: Toronto — A City in Transition	Baker, William R. M.	√		SS&D	17	1	65	Wi 85	42
HGA: Convergences	Convergence '86 Seventh Biennial Conference Information (error-corrected SS&D v17 n2 86 p41)		√		SS&D	17	1	65	Wi 85	57
HGA: Convergences	Convergence '88	Gordon, Judith			CW		25		Se 87	10
HGA: Convergences	Convergence in the Rockies				SS&D	8	4	32	Fa 77	75
HGA: Convergences	Convergence Preview — Six Peaks, A		√		SS&D	11	2	42	Sp 80	47
HGA: Convergences	Coverlet for Convergence 1988, A		√	√	SS&D	19	1	73	Wi 87	46
HGA: Convergences	Discovering Canada's Handwoven Heritage		√		SS&D	17	3	67	Su 86	40
HGA: Convergences	"Fiber Structures" Convergence '76 (Exhibit)	Mathews-Pulleyn, Kathryn	√		Fa	3	4		J/A 76	12
HGA: Convergences	Guild Shows At Convergence '74		√		SS&D	4	2	14	Sp 73	13
HGA: Convergences	HGA Convergence '88, Registration Material		√		SS&D	19	1	73	Wi 87	82
HGA: Convergences	Introducing: Alice Partanen				SS&D	4	3	15	Su 73	17
HGA: Convergences	It Happened in Pittsburgh		√		SS&D	7	4	28	Fa 76	84
HGA: Convergences	Ken Colwell on Weaving	Colwell, Ken			PWC	4	3	13		17
HGA: Convergences	Keynote in Chicago: Knodel	Livingstone, Joan	√		SS&D	18	3	71	Su 87	37
HGA: Convergences	Marilyn Pappas: Cranbrook Workshop				SS&D	3	2	10	Sp 72	46

SUBJECT	TITLE	AUTHOR	IL	INST	JOUR	VOL	NO	ISS	DATE	PAGE
HGA: Convergences	Michigan in '72 — Cranbrook Workshops				SS&D	2	4	8	Fa 71	11
HGA: Convergences	More Than Just Motor City	Loftis, Doris			SS&D	3	1	9	Wi 71	37
HGA: Convergences	Photographer at Convergence, The	Brown, Carolyn		√	SS&D	17	2	66	Sp 86	61
HGA: Convergences	Preview...Convergence '82, A		√		SS&D	13	3	51	Su 82	65
HGA: Convergences	San Francisco Invites HGA In '74	Porcella, Yvonne	√		SS&D	4	1	13	Wi 72	19
HGA: Convergences	Special Interest Groups — Leaders & Topics				SS&D	3	3	11	Su 72	16
HGA: Convergences	Turkoman Yurt, The		√	√	SS&D	10	1	37	Wi 78	24
HGA: Convergences	Weavers Bag — From Many Lands to Convergence '74, The	West, Virginia	√	√	SS&D	5	1	17	Wi 73	38
HGA: Convergences	Weavers Bag — From Montana to Convergence '74, The	Burlew, Margaret	√	√	SS&D	5	1	17	Wi 73	39
HGA: Convergences	Where Do We Go From Here?	Tillett, Leslie			SS&D	10	1	37	Wi 78	18
HGA: Convergences 76: Speaker	Jack Lenor Larsen: Convergence '76 Keynoter		√		SS&D	7	1	25	Wi 75	4
HGA: Convergences 76: Speaker	Shuttle Power	Hanks, Nancy	√		SS&D	7	4	28	Fa 76	45
HGA: History	First Fifteen Years, The	Henzie, Susie			SS&D	16	1	61	Wi 84	44
HGA: History	Happy Anniversary, Too	Aikin, Patti			SS&D	16	1	61	Wi 84	45
HGA: History	HGA Keepsakes		√		SS&D	16	1	61	Wi 84	46
HGA: History	HGA Presidents Past and Present		√		SS&D	16	1	61	Wi 84	8
HGA: International Committee	Universality of Handweaving, The				SS&D	4	1	13	Wi 72	11
HGA: Learning Exchange	Learning from the Learning Exchange	Petrini, Marcy	√	> 4	SS&D	18	1	69	Wi 86	62
HGA: Rep	Profile of a State Rep	Cramer, Pauline Ellis	√		SS&D	15	4	60	Fa 84	89
HGA Rep	Profile of an HGA Rep		√		SS&D	16	1	61	Wi 84	9
HGA Rep	Profile of an HGA Rep		√		SS&D	16	2	62	Sp 85	58
HGA Rep: Colton, Mary Rawcliffe	Profile of an HGA Rep		√		SS&D	17	4	68	Fa 86	89
HGA Rep: Crary, Sharon	Profile of an HGA Rep		√		SS&D	17	2	66	Sp 86	84
HGA Rep: Dessureau, Barbara	Profile of an HGA Rep		√		SS&D	16	3	63	Su 85	87
HGA Rep: Evans, Jane	Profile of an HGA Rep		√		SS&D	17	3	67	Su 86	84
HGA Rep: Glover, Elvira	Profile of an HGA Rep	Keen, Annette	√		SS&D	19	1	73	Wi 87	49
HGA Rep: Keen, Annette	Profile of an HGA Rep		√		SS&D	18	4	72	Fa 87	73
HGA Rep: Lala, Susan	Profile of an HGA Rep		√		SS&D	16	4	64	Fa 85	87
HGA Rep: Meany, Janet	Profile of an HGA Rep		√		SS&D	17	1	65	Wi 85	89
HGA Rep: Petrini, Marcy F.	Profile of an HGA Rep		√		SS&D	18	1	69	Wi 86	37
HGA Rep: Smayda, Norma	Profile of an HGA Rep	Smayda, Susan	√		SS&D	15	2	58	Sp 84	39
HGA Rep: Turner, Kathryn	Profile of an HGA Rep		√		SS&D	18	2	70	Sp 87	39
HGA: Scholarship Fund	Berta Frey Book Will Benefit Scholarship Fund				SS&D	3	4	12	Fa 72	32
HGA: Scholarship Fund	In Honor of Berta Frey	Johnson, Garnette			SS&D	3	2	10	Sp 72	4
HGA: Scholarships	1977 HGA Scholarships (error-corrected SS&D v9 n2 78 p70)		√		SS&D	9	1	33	Wi 77	46
HGA Scholarships	HGA Scholarship	Braun, Susan G.	√		SS&D	18	1	69	Wi 86	9
HGA: Scholarships	HGA Scholarship Winners Challenge The Future		√		SS&D	6	4	24	Fa 75	43
HGA: Scholarships	HGA Scholarships '79		√		SS&D	10	4	40	Fa 79	96
HGA: Scholarships	More 1978 Scholarships		√		SS&D	10	1	37	Wi 78	107
HGA: Scholarships	Scholarship Committee Outlines Program				SS&D	4	3	15	Su 73	7
HGA Scholarships	Scholarship in Action		√		SS&D	7	4	28	Fa 76	108
HGA: Scholarships	Scholarship Report: Fuchs At Varpapuu	Fuchs, Douglas Eric	√		SS&D	7	1	25	Wi 75	92
HGA: Scholarships	Scholarship Winner Has Impressive Credentials				SS&D	6	3	23	Su 75	72
HGA: Scholarships	Scholarship Winners Announced				SS&D	5	4	20	Fa 74	47
HGA: Scholarships	Scholarships '78		√		SS&D	9	4	36	Fa 78	44
HGA: Scholarships	Summer Scholarship to Finland, 1975				SS&D	6	1	21	Wi 74	25
HGA Scholarships: Hein, Jennifer	HGA Scholarship Award		√		SS&D	18	4	72	Fa 87	50

SUBJECT	TITLE	AUTHOR	IL	INST	JOUR	VOL	NO	ISS	DATE	PAGE
HGA Scholarships: Miller, Linda	HGA Scholarship Award	Braun, Suzan G.	√		SS&D	16	3	63	Su 85	62
HGA: Surveys	HGA Membership Survey Findings				SS&D	9	4	36	Fa 78	78
Hieroglyphics: Mexican Codices	Heritage in Tapestry, A	Arvonio, John	√		H&C	23	4		J/A 72	9
Hippari	Versatile Jacket, A	Hannah, Joyce	√	√	TM			1	O/N 85	44
Hispanic-Americans	Blankets of New Mexico	Kozikowski, Janusz	√		SS&D	10	1	37	Wi 78	60
Historian: Textile	Making Weaving History	Xenakis, Alexis Yiorgos	√		PWC	4	3	13		6
Historic Sites	Convergence '76—Visit to an Old Weaving Village Plus a Riverboat Cruise		√		SS&D	6	1	21	Wi 74	47
Historic Sites	Old Sturbridge Village		√		H&C	1	1		AP 50	16
Historic Sites	Weaving at Fort Hunter Museum	Meigs, Margaret Wister	√		H&C	4	2		Sp 53	26
Historic Sites: Bates-Scofield Homestead	Kitchen Curtains for a Restored 18th Century Homestead		√	√	H&C	19	3		Su 68	28
Historic Sites: Cedar Grove	Carpets for a Historic Philadelphia House	Scott, Chester M.	√	√	H&C	16	3		Su 65	13
Historic Sites: Hubbel Trading Post	Painted Rug Designs: Trader Hubbell's Influence on Navajo Weaving	Blue, Martha	√		Fa	14	5		N/D 87	5
Historic Sites: Jared Coffin House	Nantucket Looms, Fabrics by Island Weavers in Restored Inn	Chesrown, Melva A.	√		H&C	14	4		Fa 63	6
Historic Sites: Locust Grove	Weaving at Locust Grove	Lutz, Mrs. William C.	√		H&C	19	1		Wi 68	31
Historic Sites: Mt. Vernon	Martha Washington's Inaugural Gown	Reams, Dorothy E.	√		SS&D	7	3	27	Su 76	15
Historic Sites: Old Economy Village	Linens At Old Economy, The	Gallagher, Constance Dann	√	> 4	SS&D	7	3	27	Su 76	84
Historic Sites: Old Slater Mill	New England Weavers at Old Slater Mill		√		H&C	9	1		Wi 57	22
Historic Sites: Slater Mill Historic Site	Slater Mill Historic Site, The	Rubbert, Toni Condon	√		S-O	8	2		Su 84	42
Historic Sites: Strawberry Banke	Strawbery Banke, A Restored New England Village	Currey, Ruth Dunlop	√		H&C	22	2		Sp 71	14
Historic Sites: Williamsburg	Norman Kennedy — Weaver at Williamsburg	Slater, Deborah	√		H&C	23	1		J/F 72	23
Historic Sites: Williamsburg	Williamsburg Weaving	Brown, Bonnie	√		H&C	12	2		Sp 61	30
Historical Baskets	Giving Your Baskets a Long, Healthy Life: A Basic Guide to Basketry Conservation	Odegaard, Nancy; Dale Kronkright	√		Fa	11	1		J/F 84	43
Historical Books: (England)	Few Observations on "Remains", A	Stanton, R. G.	√		AT	4			De 85	9
Historical Books: Weaving, 18th Century	Eighteenth Century German Court Weaver: Johann Michael Frickinger, An	Hilts, Patricia	√		SS&D	11	4	44	Fa 80	16
Historical Costume	Culture & Costume in Edo Japan	Staples, Loretta	√		SS&D	12	1	45	Wi 80	26
Historical Costume	Ethnic Costume		√		SS&D	12	1	45	Wi 80	16
Historical Costume	"Vanity Fair: A Treasure Trove from the Costume Institute" (Exhibit)	Park, Betty	√		Fa	5	3		M/J 78	15
Historical Costume: Buddhist Monk Robes	Distant Mountains: The Influence of Funzo-e on the Tradition of Buddhist Clerical Robes in Japan	Lyman, Marie	√		TMJ	23			84	25
Historical Costume: Buddhist Monk Robes	Kesa: Its Sacred and Secular Aspects	Kennedy, Alan	√		TMJ	22			83	67
Historical Costumes	Rare Textiles and Costumes in the Collection at the University of Washington	Harvey, Virginia I.	√		H&C	15	4		Fa 64	15
Historical Costumes	Russian Costumes At The Metropolitan Museum		√		SS&D	8	3	31	Su 77	88
Historical Coverlets: Colonial Coverlet Guild of America	Stars, Diamonds, Tables, and Sunrise: Motifs and Structures of Woven Coverlets	Cabeen, Lou	√	√	TM			14	D/J 87	32
Historical Dye Books: 16th Century	Gioanventura Rosetti and His Dye Book—1548 A. D.	Bliss, Anne	√		Iw	3	1		Fa 77	36
Historical Equipment: Textile	Merrimack Valley Museum		√		H&C	17	3		Su 66	29
Historical Journals: Fiennes, Celia	English Textiles Referred to by Celia Fiennes	Stewart, Imogen	√		AT	4			De 85	67
Historical Lace	"Historic Spanish Lace" (Exhibit)		√		Fa	14	1		J/F 87	54
Historical Lace	Story of Reticella, The	Cave, OEnone	√		H&C	11	3		Su 60	14
Historical Looms: 19th Century	Saga of a Fancy Woolen Loom, The	Gross, Laurence F.	√		SS&D	9	3	35	Su 78	25
Historical Manuscripts: "Soshun Biko"	Briading Technique Documented in an Early Nineteenth-Century Japanese Treatise, "Soshun Biko", A	Kinoshita, Masako	√	√	TMJ	25			86	47

SUBJECT	TITLE	AUTHOR	IL	INST	JOUR	VOL	NO	ISS	DATE	PAGE
Historical Painting: Carpet Depicted in Chinese Painting	Oriental Rug of A. D. 1280, An	Laing, Ellen Johnston	√		TMJ	4	1		De 74	82
Historical Snippets: Textiles, Royal Endorsement	Historical Question				AT	7			Ju 87	187
Historical Spinning Equipment	Colonial Equipment	Pennington, David; Michael Taylor	√		S-O	2			78	40
Historical Spinning Wheel	Patent Pendulum Spinning Wheel, The		√		H&C	20	3		Su 69	33
Historical Tartan Setts	Weaver's Book of Scottish Tartans: The Tartan Setts, Listing of 260 Tartan Setts, The	Tidball, Harriet	√	√	SCGM		5		62	23
Historical Textile Equipment	Winterthur Museum (error-corrected SS&D v13 n3 82 p4)	Sitko, Jane Bradley	√		SS&D	13	2	50	Sp 82	24
Historical Textile Mills	Saga of a Fancy Woolen Loom, The	Gross, Laurence F.	√		SS&D	9	3	35	Su 78	25
Historical Textiles	"Artist Collects: Historic Fabrics from the Collection of Gerhardt Krodel, An" (Exhibit) (error-corrected Fa v7 n4 80 p6)	Constantinides, Kathy	√		Fa	7	3		M/J 80	78
Historical Textiles	Barberini Tapestries		√		H&C	17	1		Wi 66	33
Historical Textiles	Color and Design in Andean Warp-Faced Fabrics	Femenias, Blenda	√		WJ	12	2	46	Fa 87	44
Historical Textiles	Early American Textiles, from Linda Belding's Collection		√		H&C	15	1		Wi 64	20
Historical Textiles	"Evolution of Fashion, 1909–1919, The" (Exhibit)		√		Fa	8	1		J/F 81	92
Historical Textiles	Inspiration from the Past: Textile Treasures in the World of New York City Auctions	Sider, Sandra	√		Fa	11	6		N/D 84	62
Historical Textiles	Kashmiri to Paisley: Evolution of the Paisley shawl	Larson-Fleming, Susan	√		WJ	11	3	43	Wi 87	37
Historical Textiles	Linens At Old Economy, The	Gallagher, Constance Dann	√	> 4	SS&D	7	3	27	Su 76	84
Historical Textiles	Linsey-Woolseys at the Sheburne Museum, The (error-corrected SS&D v16 n3 85 p90)	Noordaa, Titia Vander	√		SS&D	16	2	62	Sp 85	59
Historical Textiles	Material Matters: Textile Gifts to the Cleveland Museum of Art	McClelland, Elizabeth	√		Fa	12	3		M/J 85	50
Historical Textiles	Museum Textiles: How to Get at Them and Use Them	Gordon, Beverly	√		WJ	8	1	29	Su 83	14
Historical Textiles	Nineteenth Century Tapestry in Billedvev, A	Nelson, Lila	√		WJ	10	2	38	Fa 85	26
Historical Textiles	Painted Muslin Ghost Dance Costumes of the Sioux, C–1890	Wakeland, Robin	√		Fa	8	1		J/F 81	15
Historical Textiles	Point Twill 125 Years Old	Stuart, Helen C.	√	√	SS&D	3	4	12	Fa 72	41
Historical Textiles	Rare Textiles and Costumes in the Collection at the University of Washington	Harvey, Virginia I.	√		H&C	15	4		Fa 64	15
Historical Textiles	Southwest Indian Twill Tapestry	Atwood, Betty	√		WJ	8	1	29	Su 83	35
Historical Textiles	Textiles At The Cooper Hewitt Museum	Fowler, Molly	√		SS&D	7	4	28	Fa 76	4
Historical Textiles	Weaving the Girdle of Rameses	Hilts, Patricia	√	> 4	WJ	9	1	33	Su 84	22
Historical Textiles	Winterthur Museum (error-corrected SS&D v13 n3 82 p4)	Sitko, Jane Bradley	√		SS&D	13	2	50	Sp 82	24
Historical Textiles: 18th Century	Anatomy of a Quilted Counterpane (page revised WJ v9 n1 84 p70)	Adrosko, Rita J.	√		WJ	8	4	32	Sp 84	42
Historical Textiles: 19th Century	Jacquard Loomed: Turn-of-the-Century Fabrics	Marcoux, Alice	√		Fa	9	2		M/A 82	35
Historical Textiles: 19th Century	Uncovering the Life and Weaving of John E. Schneider	Thieme, Otto Charles	√		SS&D	9	2	34	Sp 78	80
Historical Textiles: Baltimore Friendship Quilt	Mastering the Art of Hand Appliqué	Wolff, Colette	√	√	TM			4	A/M 86	49
Historical Textiles: Banners, Islamic	Group of Silk Islamic Banners, A	Denny, Walter B.	√		TMJ	4	1		De 74	67
Historical Textiles: Batik	Van Zuylen Batik, Pekalongan, Central Java (1890-1946)	de Raadt-Apell, M. J.	√		TMJ	19 20			80,81	75
Historical Textiles: Batik, Java	Symbolic Scenes in Javanese Batik	Adams, Monni	√		TMJ	3	1		De 70	25

SUBJECT	TITLE	AUTHOR	IL	INST	JOUR	VOL	NO	ISS	DATE	PAGE
Historical Textiles: Caftan	Newly Excavated Caftan from the Northern Caucasus, A	Riboud, Krishna	√		TMJ	4	3		76	21
Historical Textiles: Carpets	Carpet Collections of the Philadelphia Museum of Art	Ellis, Charles Grant	√		TMJ	17			78	29
Historical Textiles: Carpets	Gifts from Kashan to Cairo	Ellis, Charles Grant	√		TMJ	1	1		No 62	33
Historical Textiles: Carpets	Some Compartment Designs for Carpets, and Herat	Ellis, Charles Grant	√		TMJ	1	4		De 65	42
Historical Textiles: Carpets, Anatolian	Carpet-Makers of Western Anatolia, 1750–1914, The	Quataert, Donald			TMJ	25			86	25
Historical Textiles: Carpets, Iran	Ardabvil Puzzle, The	Weaver, Martin E.	√		TMJ	23			84	43
Historical Textiles: Carpets, Mamluk	Mysteries of the Misplaced Mamluks	Ellis, Charles Grant	√		TMJ	2	2		De 67	2
Historical Textiles: Carpets, Persian	Little Gems of Ardebil, The	Ellis, Charles Grant	√		TMJ	1	3		De 64	18
Historical Textiles: Carpets, Persian, Five-Medallion	Symbolic Meanings in Oriental Rug Patterns: Part 3	Cammann, Schuyler V.R.	√		TMJ	3	3		De 72	42
Historical Textiles: Carpets, Spanish, Fifteenth Century	Two Remarkable Fifteenth Century Carpets from Spain	Mackie, Louise W.	√		TMJ	4	4		77	15
Historical Textiles: China	"In the Presence of the Dragon Throne" (Exhibit)	Szajman, Rena	√		Fa	4	3		M/J 77	13
Historical Textiles: China	Ko-ssu	Wilson, Kay	√		H&C	24	4		Au 73	42
Historical Textiles: Chinese	Recent Gifts of Chinese and Japanese Textiles	Hays, Mary V.	√		TMJ	4	2		75	4
Historical Textiles: Chinese Silks, 18th Century	Where Did All the Silver Go? Identifying Eighteenth-Century Chinese Painted and Printed Silks	Lee-Whitman, Leanna; Maruta Skelton	√		TMJ	22			83	33
Historical Textiles: Coptic	Remarks on Some Tapestries from Egypt	Berliner, Rudolf	√		TMJ	1	4		De 65	20
Historical Textiles: Costume	English Textiles Referred to by Celia Fiennes	Stewart, Imogen	√		AT	4			De 85	67
Historical Textiles: Costume	Textile Treasures At the Met's Costume Institute	Lonier, Terri	√		Fa	11	5		S/O 84	37
Historical Textiles: Costumes	Martha Washington's Inaugural Gown	Reams, Dorothy E.	√		SS&D	7	3	27	Su 76	15
Historical Textiles: Coverlet	Early American Coverlet of the Summer and Winter Type		√	> 4	WJ	3	4	12	Ap 79	35
Historical Textiles: Coverlets	Handwoven American Coverlets of the Overshot Type	Carey, Joyce Marquess	√	> 4	PWC	3	3	9		24
Historical Textiles: Coverlets	Historic Coverlets		√		H&C	7	3		Su 56	18
Historical Textiles: Damask	Contemporary Use of Traditional Damask, A	Lalena, Constance	√		WJ	8	1	29	Su 83	69
Historical Textiles: Early 19th Century	Designs from Serff Patterns	Abel, Isabel I.	√	> 4	H&C	11	4		Fa 60	6
Historical Textiles: Early 19th Century	Peter Stauffer — Early 19th Century Weaver	Rogers, Grace L.	√	> 4	H&C	7	1		Wi 55	12
Historical Textiles: Egypt	Coptic Textiles: The Art of the Ancient Weaver	Constantinides, Kathy	√		Fa	7	6		N/D 80	19
Historical Textiles: Egypt	Linen: The Enduring Thread of History	Hoskins, Nancy Arthur	√		Fa	14	2		M/A 87	42
Historical Textiles: Egyptian Carpets, Mameluks	Symbolic Meanings in Oriental Rug Patterns: Part 3	Cammann, Schuyler V.R.	√		TMJ	3	3		De 72	42
Historical Textiles: Embroideries	Persian Legend In Silk		√		TM			14	D/J 87	92
Historical Textiles: England, 17th and 18th Centuries	English Textiles Referred to by Celia Fiennes	Stewart, Imogen	√		AT	4			De 85	67
Historical Textiles: Fashion Fabrics	English Textiles Referred to by Celia Fiennes	Stewart, Imogen	√		AT	4			De 85	67
Historical Textiles: Harmonist	"Harmonist Needlework and Textiles" (Exhibit)	Thomas, Kay	√		Fa	7	6		N/D 80	68
Historical Textiles: Identification	Granny's Coverlet (or how do you tell if your coverlet's real?)	Strickler, Carol		√	S-O	6	4		82	26
Historical Textiles: Ikat, Double (Warp/Weft)	Kasuri: A Japanese Textile	Dusenbury, Mary	√		TMJ	17			78	41
Historical Textiles: Indonesia	Additions to the Indonesian Collection	Gittinger, Mattiebelle S.	√		TMJ	4	3		76	43
Historical Textiles: Interior Furnishings	English Textiles Referred to by Celia Fiennes	Stewart, Imogen	√		AT	4			De 85	67

SUBJECT	TITLE	AUTHOR	IL	INST	JOUR	VOL	NO	ISS	DATE	PAGE
Historical Textiles: Interiors	Historic Textiles for Contemporary Spaces	Lonier, Terri	√		Fa	12	1		J/F 85	64
Historical Textiles: Japanese	Recent Gifts of Chinese and Japanese Textiles	Hays, Mary V.	√		TMJ	4	2		75	4
Historical Textiles: Labels, Woven	Marks of Distinction: Woven Labels 1900–1940	Kluge, Chris	√		Fa	8	1		J/F 81	24
Historical Textiles: Latin America	Folk Textiles of Latin America	Kelemen, Pál	√		TMJ	1	4		De 65	2
Historical Textiles: Lenten Curtains, Peru	Lenten Curtains from Colonial Peru	Kelemen, Pál	√		TMJ	3	1		De 70	5
Historical Textiles: Mandarin Squares	Chinese Textile in Seventeenth Century Spain, A	Cammann, Schuyler	√		TMJ	1	4		De 65	57
Historical Textiles: Mandarin Squares	Ming Mandarin Squares	Cammann, Schuyler	√		TMJ	4	4		77	5
Historical Textiles: Mughal, Seventeenth Century	Preliminary Report on a Group of Important Mughal Textiles, A	Smart, Ellen S.	√		TMJ	25			86	5
Historical Textiles: Needlework	"Needlework" (Exhibit)	Krueger, Glee	√		Fa	9	3		M/J 82	78
Historical Textiles: Ottoman Turkish Textiles	Ottoman Turkish Textiles	Denny, Walter B.	√		TMJ	3	3		De 72	55
Historical Textiles: Persian	Historic Persian Handiwork at the Textile Museum (Exhibit)	Dyer, Carolyn Price	√		Fa	14	5		N/D 87	42
Historical Textiles: Peru	Double-Woven Treasures from Old Peru	Cahlander, Adele	√	√	PWC			4	Ja 83	36
Historical Textiles: Peru	Gifts from Ancient Peru	Nass, Ulla	√	√	WJ	8	1	29	Su 83	32
Historical Textiles: Peruvian Mantle	Swatch Collection #15	Alderman, Sharon	√	√	Hw	8	2		M/A 87	38
Historical Textiles: Quilts	When You See This Remember Me		√		Fa	9	5		S/O 82	100
Historical Textiles: Rugs, 15th Century	Soumak-Woven Rug in a 15th Century International Sytle, A	Ellis, Charles Grant	√		TMJ	1	2		De 63	3
Historical Textiles: Rugs, Anatolian	Anatolian Rugs: An Essay on Method	Denny, Walter B.	√		TMJ	3	4		De 73	7
Historical Textiles: Rugs, China	Chinese Rugs	Ellis, Charles Grant	√		TMJ	2	3		De 68	35
Historical Textiles: Rugs, Flat-Weaves	Some Weft-Float Brocaded Rugs of the Bergama-Ezine Region	Beattie, May H.	√		TMJ	3	2		De 71	20
Historical Textiles: Rugs, Iran	Kings, Heroes, Lovers: Pictorial Rugs From the Tribes and Villages of Iran	Goodman, Deborah Lerme	√		Fa	11	3		M/J 84	38
Historical Textiles: Rugs, Islamic	Symbolic Meanings in Oriental Rug Patterns: Part 1	Cammann, Schuyler V.R.	√		TMJ	3	3		De 72	5
Historical Textiles: Rugs, Kazak	Kazak Rugs	Tschebull, Raoul	√		TMJ	3	2		De 71	2
Historical Textiles: Rugs, Kilim, Kurdish	Kurdish Kilim Weaving in the Van-Hakkari District of Eastern Turkey	Landreau, Anthony N.	√	√	TMJ	3	4		De 73	27
Historical Textiles: Rugs, Kirman Vase Rugs	Kirman's Heritage in Washington: Vase Rugs in The Textile Museum	Ellis, Charles Grant	√		TMJ	2	3		De 68	17
Historical Textiles: Rugs, Ottoman Prayer	Ottoman Prayer Rugs, The	Ellis, Charles Grant	√		TMJ	2	4		De 69	5
Historical Textiles: Rugs, Persian	Symbolic Meanings in Oriental Rug Patterns: Part 2	Cammann, Schuyler V.R.	√		TMJ	3	3		De 72	22
Historical Textiles: Rugs, Sweden	From Mexico to Rumania to Sweden	Landreau, Anthony N.	√		TMJ	2	4		De 69	37
Historical Textiles: Rugs, Turkish	Turkish Carpet with Spots and Stripes, A	Mackie, Louise W.	√		TMJ	4	3		76	4
Historical Textiles: Russia	"Glory of Russian Costumes, The" (Exhibit)	Vander Lee, Jana	√		Fa	4	3		M/J 77	15
Historical Textiles: Samplers	Stitch in Time, A	Harris, Patricia; David Lyon	√		Fa	12	2		M/A 85	27
Historical Textiles: Sashes, Mughal	Second Type of Mughal Sash, A	Sonday, Milton; Nobuko Kajitani	√		TMJ	3	2		De 71	6
Historical Textiles: Sashes, Mughal	Type of Mughal Sash, A	Sonday, Milton; Nobuko Kajitani	√		TMJ	3	1		De 70	45
Historical Textiles: Shaker	Personal Touch, A		√	√	Hw	3	5		N/D 82	43
Historical Textiles: Silks, Figured	On Eighteenth Century Flowered Silk Weaving as an Inspiration for Todays Complex Weavers	Fairbanks, Dale			CW	7	1	19	Se 85	8
Historical Textiles: Sprang	Listening to Threads	Reynders-Baas, Coby	√		WJ	11	4	44	Sp 87	21
Historical Textiles: Tapestries	Coptic Tapestry of Byzantine Style, A	Berliner, Rudolf	√		TMJ	1	1		No 62	3

SUBJECT	TITLE	AUTHOR	IL	INST	JOUR	VOL	NO	ISS	DATE	PAGE
Historical Textiles: Tapestries	Modern Handweaver Restores Famous Tapestries, A		√	√	H&C	3	2		Sp 52	9
Historical Textiles: Tapestries	More About the Developing Islamic Style in Tapestries	Berliner, Rudolf	√		TMJ	2	1		De 66	3
Historical Textiles: Tapestries, Coptic	Rudolf Berliner Memorial		√		TMJ	2	4		De 69	41
Historical Textiles: Tapestries, Egypt	Tapestries from Egypt Influenced by Theatrical Performances	Berliner, Rudolf	√		TMJ	1	3		De 64	35
Historical Textiles: Tapestries, Middle Horizon, Early	Peruvian Textile Fragment from the Beginning of the Middle Horizon	Conklin, William J	√		TMJ	3	1		De 70	15
Historical Textiles: Tapestries, Peru	Chinese Influence in Colonial Peruvian Tapestries	Cammann, Schuyler	√		TMJ	1	3		De 64	21
Historical Textiles: Tapestries, Peru	General Patterson's Tapestry	Sellschopp, Dr. E. A.	√		TMJ	2	4		De 69	2
Historical Textiles: Tapestry Roundels, Coptic	Horsemen in Tapestry Roundels Found in Egypt	Berliner, Rudolf	√		TMJ	1	2		De 63	39
Historical Textiles: Tassels Nasca Period	Nasca Sprang Tassels: Structure, Technique, and Order	Frame, Mary	√	√	TMJ	25			86	67
Historical Textiles: The Netherlands	Listening to Threads	Reynders-Baas, Coby	√		WJ	11	4	44	Sp 87	21
Historical Textiles: Turkey, Early 18th Century	Some Unusual Turkish Embroideries of the Early Eighteenth Century	Johnstone, Pauline	√		TMJ	24			85	75
Historical Textiles: World	"Loom, the Needle, and the Dye Pot, The" (Exhibit)	Dyer, Carolyn	√		Fa	5	1		J/F 78	20
Historical Tools	Antique Fiber Tools		√		WJ	9	2	34	Fa 84	29
Historical Weaving Books	In Search of Jacob Angstadt: A Master Weaver Lives Again		√		SS&D	7	2	26	Sp 76	27
Historical Weaving Documents	Summer-and-Winter as Developed in the Nineties	Frey, Berta	√	√	H&C	21	2		Sp 70	11
Historical Weaving Drafts	Designs for Today from Great-Grandmother's Drafts	Riswold, Margaret	√	√	H&C	3	3		Su 52	20
Historical Weaving Drafts	Designs from 18 Century Drafts		√		H&C	13	4		Fa 62	9
Historical Weaving Drafts	Eighteenth Century Weaving Puzzle, An	North, Lois	√	√	H&C	10	3		Su 59	14
Historical Weaving Drafts	Jane Cox: Her Draft for Counterpins	Pinchin, C. B.	√	√	Iw	4	3		Su 79	31
Historical Weaving Drafts	More About Fabrics: Murphy's Drafts	Zielinski, S. A.; Robert Leclerc, ed.	√	> 4	MWL	20			'51–'73	93
Historical Weaving Drafts	Multiple Shaft Coverlet Drafts in the Allen-Stephenson Draft Book	Renne, Elisha	√	> 4	AT	3			My 85	125
Historical Weaving Drafts	New Zealand Interpretation of Compass and Double Square, A		√	√	H&C	8	4		Fa 57	20
Historical Weaving Drafts	Sarah Fowler's Book of Drafts, Part 1	North, Lois	√	> 4	SS&D	6	1	21	Wi 74	8
Historical Weaving Drafts	Sarah Fowler's Book of Drafts, Part 2		√	> 4	SS&D	6	2	22	Sp 75	78
Historical Weaving Drafts	Sarah Fowler's Book of Drafts, Part 3	North, Lois	√	>4	SS&D	6	3	23	Su 75	74
Historical Weaving Drafts	Sarah Fowler's Book of Drafts, Part 4	North, Lois	√	> 4	SS&D	6	4	24	Fa 75	84
Historical Weaving Drafts	Thomas Jackson, Weaver: 17th and 18th Century Records	Tidball, Harriet	√		SCGM		13		64	1
Historical Weaving Drafts	Use of the Dobby Loom for Multi-Harness Weave Manipulation, The	Renne, Elisha	√	> 4	WJ	9	3	35	Wi 85	9
Historical Weaving Drafts	Weaving Drafts and Diaper Twills in Lancaster County	Crosson, Janet Gray	√	> 4	Iw	4	3		Su 79	40
Historical Weaving Drafts, 19th Century	Designs from Serff Patterns	Abel, Isabel I.	√	> 4	H&C	11	4		Fa 60	6
Historical Weaving Patterns: Swedish	Family Patterns	Mickelson, Sylvia			SS&D	2	4	8	Fa 71	17
History	Angora Goats and Mohair	Chastant, Kathryn Ross	√	√	S-O	7	3		Fa 83	29
History: A. H. Rice Company	A. H. Rice Company: Maker of Silk Thread	Goodman, Deborah Lerme	√		Fa	13	1		J/F 86	54
History: Acadians	L'Amour de Maman: The Acadian Textile Heritage	Rossetter, Tabitha Wilson	√		Fa	8	3		M/J 81	29
History: African Textiles	American Sojourn of African Textiles, An	Lonier, Terri	√		Fa	11	1		J/F 84	66
History: Alpujarra Rugs	Contemporary Alpujarra Rugs	Lorton, Henni	√		H&C	4	4		Fa 53	28
History: Ancient Peru	Peru, Textiles Unlimited: Ancient Peru	Tidball, Harriet	√		SCGM		25		68	1

SUBJECT	TITLE	AUTHOR	IL	INST	JOUR	VOL	NO	ISS	DATE	PAGE
History: Apparel, 11th-17th Centuries	Few Observations on "Remains", A	Stanton, R. G.	√		AT	4			De 85	9
History: Argyle	Argyle: The Transformation of a Classical Pattern Through the Design Process	Faust, Regine	√		Fa	9	4		J/A 82	24
History: Armor	Basketry Armor	Austin, Carole	√		Fa	14	1		J/F 87	28
History: Arrowmont School of Arts and Crafts	Sixty Years of Weaving At Arrowmont	Johnson, Debbie	√		Fa	12	5		S/O 85	39
History: Automatic Loom Development, 1857—1900	Development of Weaving Using Automatic Looms, The	Pourdeyhimi, B.; K. C. Jackson; K. Hepworth			AT	4			De 85	107
History: Automatic Loom Development, 1900—1920	Development of Weaving Using Automatic Looms, The	Pourdeyhimi, B.; K. C. Jackson; K. Hepworth			AT	4			De 85	107
History: Automatic Loom Development, British Made	Development of Weaving Using Automatic Looms, The	Pourdeyhimi, B.; K. C. Jackson; K. Hepworth			AT	4			De 85	107
History: Automatic Loom Development, Post World War II	Development of Weaving Using Automatic Looms, The	Pourdeyhimi, B.; K. C. Jackson; K. Hepworth			AT	4			De 85	107
History: Automatic Loom Development, Prior to1857	Development of Weaving Using Automatic Looms, The	Pourdeyhimi, B.; K. C. Jackson; K. Hepworth			AT	4			De 85	107
History: Automatic Loom Development, USA Made	Development of Weaving Using Automatic Looms, The	Pourdeyhimi, B.; K. C. Jackson; K. Hepworth			AT	4			De 85	107
History: Automatic Looms (England)	Note on the Diffusion of the Automatic Loom Within the British Cotton Industry, A	Pourdeyhimi, B.; K. C. Jackson	√		AT	6			De 86	101
History: Bandanna	Highlights in Bandanna History		√		Fa	12	3		M/J 85	45
History: Banners, Labor	Labor Banners of Australia	Mancini, Anne	√		Fa	14	5		N/D 87	36
History: Barocade Weaving, India	Banares Brocade	DuBois, Emily	√	> 4	AT	3			My 85	209
History: Basketry	Basketry...A New Approach to an Old Art Form	Meilach, Dona	√	√	Fa	4	1		J/F 77	16
History: Basketry, Southeast USA	Appalachian Basketry	Overcast, Roy	√		Fa	4	1		J/F 77	20
History: Baskets	"Baskets of Akwesasne" (Exhibit)	Doyle, Claire	√		Fa	11	1		J/F 84	77
History: Baskets	Thinking About Historical Baskets	Rossbach, Ed	√		Fa	11	1		J/F 84	32
History: Basque Sheepmen	Amazing Basques and Their Sheep, The	Dayton, Rita	√		S-O	3			79	19
History: Bast Fibers	History of Bast Fibers, A	Mattera, Joanne	√		SS&D	8	4	32	Fa 77	27
History: Batik, Java	Batik Making and the Royal Javanese Cemetery at Imogiri	Joseph, Rebecca M.	√		TMJ	24			85	83
History: Bauhaus	Bauhaus Weaving	Dodge, Dorothy	√		H&C	22	4		Fa 71	17
History: Beads and Beading	Contemporary Appliqued Beadwork: Introduction	Woodsmall, Annabel Whitney	√		TIAM		2		79	5
History: Berea College Fireside Industries	Berea College Fireside Industries Now Employ Sixty Weavers	Stahl, Sam	√		H&C	19	2		Sp 68	5
History: Biennale, Lausanne	Brief History of the International Biennial of Tapestry or "Watch Out for Women Who Knit", A	Taylor, Dianne	√		Fa	10	5		S/O 83	43
History: Biennale, Lausanne	Lausanne Notebook: Our Special Report on the 8th Lausanne Biennial of Tapestry, A	Mathews, Rich	√		Fa	4	5		S/O 77	30
History: Block Pattern Weaving	Roses and Snowballs: The Development of Block Patterns in the German Linen-Weaving Tradition	Hilts, Patricia	√	> 4	AT	5			Ju 86	167
History: Bobbin Lace	Bawdry History of a Precious Commodity, The	McIlvain, Myra Hargrave	√		Fa	13	3		M/J 86	14
History: Bohus Knitting	Bogus Bohus	Bush, Nancy	√	√	Kn	2	1	3	F-W 85	49
History: Braiding	Briading Technique Documented in an Early Nineteenth-Century Japanese Treatise, "Soshun Biko", A	Kinoshita, Masako	√	√	TMJ	25			86	47
History: Brazilwood	Get Some Razzle Dazzle—Try "Brazzle"	Bliss, Anne		√	Iw	2	4		Su 77	28
History: Brocades	Chinese Brocades: Development of Supplementary Weft Patterning (error-corrected WJ v11 n4 87 p78)	Drooker, Penelope	√		WJ	11	3	43	Wi 87	47

SUBJECT	TITLE	AUTHOR	IL	INST	JOUR	VOL	NO	ISS	DATE	PAGE
History: Brocades	Golden Brocades, The	Wilson, Kax	√		Iw	6	1		Wi 80	66
History: Buttons	Buttons	Abbott, Deborah	√	√	TM			2	D/J 85	56
History: Buttons	Buttons: Wearable Art in Miniature	Epstein, Diana	√		Fa	12	3		M/J 85	61
History: Caps, High Status, West Central Africa	High-Status Caps of the Kongo and Mbundu Peoples	Gibson, Gordon D.; Cecilia R. McGurk	√		TMJ	4	4		77	71
History: Card Weaving	Considering Cardweaving	Crockett, Candace	√		H&C	22	3		Su 71	13
History: Chasuble	Reflections on the Chasuble	Centner, The Rev. David J., O.C.D.	√		Hw	5	1		J/F 84	36
History: Cherokee Basketry	Doubleweave Basketry of the Cherokees	Ligon, Linda	√		Iw	4	1		Wi 78	28
History: Chilkat Blanket	Weft Twining: History, The Chilkat Blanket	Harvey, Virginia I.; Harriet Tidball	√		SCGM		28		69	5
History: Chimayó Weaving	Chimayó—A Town of Weavers	Trujillo, Lisa Rockwood	√		WJ	11	1	41	Su 86	60
History: Chinese and Western-Origin Silks, 18th Century	Where Did All the Silver Go? Identifying Eighteenth-Century Chinese Painted and Printed Silks	Lee-Whitman, Leanna; Maruta Skelton	√		TMJ	22			83	33
History: Chinese Textiles	China and the Complexities of Weaving Technologies	Vollmer, John E.			AT	5			Ju 86	65
History: Church Curtains	Early Christian Church Curtains	Austin, Carole	√		Fa	14	2		M/A 87	28
History: Churro Sheep	Return of the Churro, The	Alderman, Sharon D.	√		S-O	8	1		Sp 84	46
History: Cloaks	Irish Kinsale Cloak, The	Jones, Una	√	√	WJ	8	3	31	Wi 83	35
History: Cochineal	Cochineal as a Domestic Dyestuff	Gerber, Willi; Fred Gerber		√	H&C	23	6		N/D 72	16
History: Cochineal	Insect Dyes	Gerber, Fred	√	√	Iw	3	3		Sp 78	23
History: Complex Weavers	Complex Weavers: A History of the Group, The	Best, Eleanor	√		SS&D	12	2	46	Sp 81	19
History: Containers	Janet Markarian: From Baskets to Bags, Containers Transformed	Koplos, Janet	√		Fa	11	1		J/F 84	16
History: Coptic Weaving	Textiles of Coptic Egypt	Hoskins, Nancy Arthur	√	√	WJ	12	1	45	Su 87	58
History: Corduroy	Corde du Roi	Wilson, Kax	√		Iw	5	3		Su 80	49
History: Costume	Contemporary California Costume	Poon, Vivian	√		Fa	11	5		S/O 84	53
History: Costume	"Silken Threads and Silent Needles" (Exhibit)	Dunnewold, Jane	√		Fa	11	6		N/D 84	78
History: Costume	Where's the Sport in Sportswear?	McComb, Richard	√		TM			2	D/J 85	36
History: Costume, China	"Silk as Ceremony: The Dress of China in the Late Ch'ing Dynasty Period (1759–1911)" (Exhibit)	Mattera, Joanne	√		Fa	8	3		M/J 81	75
History: Costume, Miniature	Costumes on a Small Scale	Caldwell, Rebecca	√		Fa	11	5		S/O 84	87
History: Costume, Renaissance	"Renaissance Costume and Textiles: 1450–1620" (Exhibit)	Dyer, Carolyn	√		Fa	6	6		N/D 79	70
History: Cotton	Cotton		√		WJ	4	2	14	Oc 79	4
History: Cotton	Cotton, Cool and Comfy	Gibson-Roberts, Priscilla A.	√	√	Kn	3	2	6	Sp 87	48
History: Cotton	Cotton Plays a Vital Role	Hausner, Walter	√		H&C	3	3		Su 52	8
History: Cotton	Naturally Colored Cottons	Fox, Sally	√		S-O	11	1		Sp 87	29
History: Cotton	Vegetable Lamb of Tartary, The	Ligon, Linda	√		Iw	1	4		Su 76	9
History: Cotton	Yarns and Fibers: Cotton	Zielinski, S. A.; Robert Leclerc, ed.			MWL	4			'51–'73	26
History: Coverlet Patterns	Art of Indiana Coverlets, The	Gilfoy, Peggy S.	√		AT	2			De 84	69
History: Coverlet Research	Analysis and Documentation of Coverlets (error-corrected AT v3 85 p269)	Ulasewicz, Connie; Clarita Anderson; Steven M. Spivak	√	> 4	AT	2			De 84	113
History: Coverlet Weavers, 19th Century	Artifacts Don't "Lie"	Anderson, Clarita	√		AT	7			Ju 87	9
History: Coverlet Weaving, Indiana	Art of Indiana Coverlets, The	Gilfoy, Peggy S.	√		AT	2			De 84	69
History: Coverlet Weaving, Ohio	Ohio's Woven Coverlets: Textile Industry in a Rural Economy	Cunningham, Patricia A.	√		AT	2			De 84	165
History: Coverlets	Historic Coverlets		√		H&C	7	3		Su 56	18
History: Crafts, Cherokee	Cherokee Weavers Used Looms Over Two Hundred Years Ago	Coulter, Doris M.	√		H&C	18	3		Su 67	17

SUBJECT	TITLE	AUTHOR	IL	INST	JOUR	VOL	NO	ISS	DATE	PAGE
History: Currants	Currants: Not Just for Eating	Bliss, Anne	√	√	Hw	7	4		S/O 86	74
History: Damask	Origins: Damask	Wilson, Kax			Hw	2	3		My 81	68
History: Damask	Weaving Damask	Arnold, Ruth	√	> 4	H&C	6	3		Su 55	4
History: Design, Sweden	Swedish Design	Krondahl, Hans	√		Hw	4	2		M/A 83	30
History: Distaffs	Distaffs: Scanning through History	Henzie, Susie	√		SS&D	9	4	36	Fa 78	56
History: District Checks	Woolens and Tweeds: Designing Woolen Fabrics: The District Checks	Tidball, Harriet			SCGM		4		61	30
History: Dobby Weaving	Dobby Loom Explained, The	Colwell, Ken	√	√	SS&D	11	4	44	Fa 80	7
History: Double Weave	Double Weave: Plain and Patterned: History of the Double Weave, The	Tidball, Harriet	√		SCGM		1		60	1
History: Double Weave	Revival of Double Weave in Scandinavia	Schrum, Louaine M.	√	√	H&C	8	1		Wi 56	22
History: Double Weave	Technique & History of the Polish Double-weave, The	Wimmer, Gayle	√		H&C	24	3		M/J 73	8
History: Dovecot Studios	Dovecot Studios	Soroka, Joanne	√		SS&D	12	4	48	Fa 81	36
History: Dovecote Studios, Edinburgh Tapestry Company	Tapestry Weavers of Edinburgh, The	Lister, John A.	√		H&C	12	1		Wi 61	22
History: Drawloom	Damask on a Drawloom	Keasbey, Doramay	√	> 4	SS&D	8	1	29	WI 76	63
History: Dyeing	Bancroft's Mordant: A Useful One-Pot Natural Dye Technique	Liles, James N.; Dale Liles	√	√	SS&D	15	3	59	Su 84	76
History: Dyeing	Gioanventura Rosetti and His Dye Book—1548 A. D.	Bliss, Anne	√		Iw	3	1		Fa 77	36
History: Dyeing	"Master Dyers to the World" (Exhibit)	Sider, Sandra	√		Fa	11	1		J/F 84	83
History: Dyes and Dyeing	Color and Dyeing: The Home Dyer	Tidball, Harriet			SCGM		16		65	1
History: Dyes and Dyeing	Thomas Jackson, Weaver: 17th and 18th Century Records	Tidball, Harriet			SCGM		13		64	15
History: Dyes, Annatto Seed	Annatto: Color for Complexions, Cheese and Cloth	Bliss, Anne	√	√	Hw	5	5		N/D 84	82
History: Dyes, Native American	From Body Paint to Buffalo Hides	Bliss, Anne	√	√	Iw	4	1		Wi 78	42
History: Eagle Motifs	Use of Eagles as a Decorative and Symbolic Motif in 19th Century American Coverlets, The	Anderson, Clarita; Jo B. Paoletti	√		AT	3			My 85	173
History: Ecclesiastical/Liturgical Fiber	Ecclesiastical Fiber	Eggers, Conni	√		Fa	4	6		N/D 77	36
History: Egyptian Carpets, Mameluks	Symbolic Meanings in Oriental Rug Patterns: Part 3	Cammann, Schuyler V.R.	√		TMJ	3	3		De 72	42
History: Embroidery, Rabari	Meaning of Folk Art in Rabari Life: A Closer Look at Mirrored Embroidery, The	Frater, Judy	√		TMJ	4	2		75	47
History: Environmental Art	Design Concepts and Aesthetic Concerns of Corporate Art Collections	Rutherford, Karen Jenson			AT	8			De 87	193
History: Eskimo	Patricia Bulitt: Gutsongs and Other Dances	Scarborough, Jessica	√		Fa	11	5		S/O 84	50
History: Fabric Ornamentation	Fabric Ornamentation	Kaufman, Glen	√		H&C	17	1		Wi 66	14
History: Fabric Printing	Printing with Natural Dyes: An Historical Perspective		√		Hw	3	5		N/D 82	66
History: Fabric Printing	What's the Madder with Calico?		√		Hw	3	5		N/D 82	67
History: Fair Isle Knitting	Notes of a Textile Sleuth	Upitis, Lizbeth	√	√	Kn	2	1	3	F-W 85	22
History: Fans	Fanfare: Fans from the Collection of the National Museum of American Art (Exhibit)	Perry, Pamela	√		Fa	12	6		N/D 85	48
History: Fashion	Return of the Reticule	Upitis, Lizbeth	√		Kn	2	2	4	S-S 86	44
History: Fashion	Revivified Past, A	Upitis, Lizbeth	√		Kn	3	1	5	F-W 86	12
History: Fashion, Hapsburg Era	"Fashions of the Hapsburg Era: Austria-Hungary" (Exhibit)	Malarcher, Patricia	√		Fa	7	3		M/J 80	75
History: Featherwork, Inca	Inca Feathers	Kwiatkowski, Ron	√	√	Iw	1	2		Wi 76	16
History: Felt and Feltmaking	Shelters and Symbols	Gordon, Beverly	√	√	SS&D	11	1	41	Wi 79	53
History: Feltmaking	Feltmaking Now: The Exciting Revival of an Ancient Technique	Gordon, Beverly	√		Fa	6	6		N/D 79	43
History: Feltmaking, Turkey	Felt-making Craftsmen of the Anatolian and Iranian Plateaux	Gervers, Michael; Veronika Gervers	√	√	TMJ	4	1		De 74	14
History: Fiber, U.S.A. (1950–1970)	"Fiber R/Evolution" (Exhibit)	Rudich, Sally	√		Fa	13	4		J/A 86	45

SUBJECT	TITLE	AUTHOR	IL	INST	JOUR	VOL	NO	ISS	DATE	PAGE
History: Finger Weaving	Fingerweaving: Two Perspectives, The Historic View	Turner, Alta R.	√	√	SS&D	6	4	24	Fa 75	44
History: Finishing	Traditional Methods of Finishing Cloth by Hand	Gordon, Beverly	√	√	Iw	5	4		Fa 80	66
History: Finnweave	Finnweave in Norway: Yesterday and Today	Nelson, Lila	√		PWC			2	Ap 82	14
History: Fishermen's Sweaters	Knitting from the Netherlands: Traditional Dutch Fishermen's Sweaters	Van der Klift-Tellegen, Henriette	√		Fa	12	4		J/A 85	45
History: Floorcloths	Floorcloths: A New Look at an Old Technique	Holland, Nina	√		Fa	7	5		S/O 80	34
History: Fulling	Traditional Methods of Finishing Cloth by Hand	Gordon, Beverly	√	√	Iw	5	4		Fa 80	66
History: Gauze Weaves	Guatemalan Gauze Weaves: A Description and Key to Identification	Pancake, Cherri M.; Suzanne Baizerman	√	√	TMJ	19 20			80,81	1
History: Gilmore Looms	E.E. Gilmore, Loom Builder and Weaver	Watson, Aleta	√		H&C	23	5		S/O 72	24
History: Gobelins Tapestries	Gobelin Tapestries	Frech, Mary L.	√		H&C	26	1		J/F 75	12
History: Hairstyle	"Hair" (Exhibit)	Alonzo, Harriet	√		Fa	7	6		N/D 80	73
History: Hambidge Center	Mary Crovatt Hambidge	Schaller, Karin	√		Fa	11	5		S/O 84	24
History: Hand Knitting	Bishop of Leicester, The	Rutt, Richard	√		Kn	4	1	9	Wi 87	10
History: Handicraft Club of Rhode Island	Handicraft Club of Rhode Island, The	Batchelder, Helen Tilton	√		H&C	7	1		Wi 55	15
History: Handspinning	Reading History in the Classifieds	Robson, Deborah			S-O	11	3		Fa 87	20
History: Handweaving	Eleven Years Ago in Handweaving				Hw	7	1		J/F 86	22
History: Handweaving	Fifteen Years Ago in Handweaving				Hw	6	4		S/O 85	14
History: Handweaving	Fifty Years Ago in Handweaving				Hw	6	1		J/F 85	14
History: Handweaving	Fifty Years Ago in Handweaving: E. E. Gilmore, A Lifetime of Weaving		√		Hw	7	2		M/A 86	22
History: Handweaving	Forty Years Ago in Handweaving		√		Hw	5	4		S/0 84	32
History: Handweaving	On Time, Tools, and Techniques	The Gadred Weavers	√		H&C	2	4		Fa 51	18
History: Handweaving	One Hundred Sixty Years of Craftsmanship	Ligon, Linda	√		Iw	1	3		Sp 76	17
History: Handweaving	One Hundred Years Ago in Handweaving				Hw	7	3		M/J 86	27
History: Handweaving	One Hundred Years Ago in Handweaving: Handweaving as a Domestic Art	Waagen, Alice K.			Hw	6	3		Su 85	8
History: Handweaving	Quarter Century of Handweavers' Progress, A	Atwater, Mary Meigs	√		H&C	2	2		Sp 51	5
History: Handweaving	Thirty Years Ago in Handweaving				Hw	5	2		M/A 84	31
History: Handweaving	Thirty Years Ago in Handweaving				Hw	5	3		Su 84	9
History: Handweaving	Thirty Years Ago in Handweaving		√		Hw	5	5		N/D 84	18
History: Handweaving	Twenty-Five Years Ago in Handweaving				Hw	5	1		J/F 84	24
History: Handweaving	Twenty-Five Years Ago in Handweaving				Hw	6	2		M/A 85	15
History: Handweaving, British Isles	Handweavers 1800—1840	Wilson, Kax	√		Iw	5	2		Sp 80	50
History: Harris Tweed	Tweed of Harris, The	Johnson, Beth	√		Hw	2	5		No 81	47
History: Hats (1840–1940)	"Headlines: A Hundred Years of Hats (1840–1940)" (Exhibit)	Luddecke, Jane	√		Fa	6	6		N/D 79	78
History: Herdwick Sheep	Fabric of the Lake District: Herdwick Sheep	Humphries, Andrew B.	√		S-O	8	4		Wi 84	45
History: Hmong	Flourishing Art: China, Guizhou Women Continue to Embroider Their Legends, A	Rossi, Gail	√		TM			9	F/M 87	30
History: Home Dyeing	Color and Dyeing: "Home Dyeing with Natural Dyes"	Tidball, Harriet		√	SCGM		16		65	39
History: Indigo	Indigo, Discovery of Plants and Experiments in Dyeing	Gerber, Willi; Fred Gerber	√	√	H&C	26	3		M/J 75	11
History: Indigo, U.S.A.	Indigo, Discovery of Plants and Experiments in Dyeing	Gerber, Willi; Fred Gerber	√	√	H&C	19	4		Fa 68	4
History: Indonesian Textiles	Indonesian Textiles at The Textile Museum	Adams, Monni	√		TMJ	3	1		De 70	41
History: Islamic Rugs	Symbolic Meanings in Oriental Rug Patterns: Part 1	Cammann, Schuyler V.R.	√		TMJ	3	3		De 72	5

SUBJECT	TITLE	AUTHOR	IL	INST	JOUR	VOL	NO	ISS	DATE	PAGE
History: Jacquard Loom	Jackie von Ladau, Versatile Weaver	Clement, Doris	√	√	H&C	10	3		Su 59	20
History: Jacquard Loom	Jacquard and Woven Silk Pictures, The	Adrosko, Rita J.	√		AT	1			De 83	9
History: Jacquard Weaving	Jacquard and Woven Silk Pictures, The	Adrosko, Rita J.	√		AT	1			De 83	9
History: Jacquard Weaving	Jacquard, Jacquard	Laing, K. M.	√		TM			3	F/M 86	10
History: Japanese Weaving	Japanese Weaves Provide Ideas for Experiment	Freeman, Claire	√	√	H&C	21	1		Wi 70	4
History: Japanese Weaving	Learning to Weave in Japan	Schrieber, LaVonne	√		WJ	8	1	29	Su 83	79
History: Jerga	Jerga: A Twill in Harmony with its Heritage	Wilson, Kax	√		Hw	6	5		N/D 85	60
History: Kaftan	Original Fabrics of Kaftan, The	El-Homossani, M. M.	√	> 4	AT	1			De 83	263
History: Kago-Uchi	Kago-Uchi, The	Speiser, Noémi	√	√	AT	4			De 85	23
History: Kantha	Kantha	Westfall, Carol D.; Dipti Desai	√	√	AT	7			Ju 87	161
History: Kashmir Shawl	Kashmir East and West	Mikosch, Elizabeth	√		TM			9	F/M 87	14
History: Kashmir Shawl	Kashmir or Paisley; Romance of the Shawl	Wilson, Kax	√		Iw	4	4		Fa 79	34
History: Kashmir Shawl	Kashmiri to Paisley: Evolution of the Paisley shawl	Larson-Fleming, Susan	√		WJ	11	3	43	Wi 87	37
History: Kashmir Shawl	Scent of Flowers, Kishmir Shawls in the Collection of The Textile Museum, The	Mikosch, Elisabeth	√		TMJ	24			85	7
History: Kashmir Shawls	Paisley Shawls: A Democratic Fashion	Goodman, Deborah Lerme	√		Fa	12	3		M/J 85	52
History: Kasuri/Ikat Weaving, Japan	Kasuri: A Japanese Textile	Dusenbury, Mary	√		TMJ	17			78	41
History: Kesa	Kesa: Its Sacred and Secular Aspects	Kennedy, Alan	√		TMJ	22			83	67
History: Kilts	Kilts	Branson, Branley Allan	√		Hw	4	5		N/D 83	34
History: Kimono	Kimono East/West	Wada, Yoshiko	√		Fa	9	1		J/F 82	19
History: Knitting	Arans: A Saga in Wool (error-corrected S-O V4 80 p4)	Schlegel, Lee-lee	√	√	S-O	3			79	56
History: Knitting	Guernseys	Upitis, Lizbeth			Kn	1	1	1	F-W 84 CI	48 40
History: Knitting, Fair Isle	Fair Isle Knitting	Starmore, Alice	√	√	TM			8	D/J 86	44
History: Knitting Machines	History of the Knitting Machine		√		Fa	9	2		M/A 82	44
History: Knots	Leonardo's Knot	Austin, Carole	√		Fa	12	2		M/A 85	43
History: Knotting, Chinese	Nelson Chang: Champion of Chinese Knotting	Westbrook, John R.,	√		Fa	14	3		M/J 87	6
History: Ko-Ssu	Ko-ssu	Wilson, Kay	√		H&C	24	4		Au 73	42
History: Kumihimo	Kumihimo: The Art of Japanese Braiding	Moss, Helen E.	√		Fa	14	1		J/F 87	20
History: Lace	Contemporary Lace of Susan Wood, The	Darling, Drew	√		Fa	11	6		N/D 84	22
History: Lace, Battenberg	Battenberg Lace: Making Lace with Woven Tape and a Needle	Kliot, Jules; Kaethe Kliot	√	√	TM			10	A/M 87	30
History: Lace Making, Sweden	Picture Lace	Larson-Fleming, Susan	√		WJ	9	4	36	Sp 85	42
History: Leclerc Looms	LeClerc Loom Corporation, A Story of Three Generations, The	Holland, Nina	√		H&C	24	3		M/J 73	20
History: Leno Weave	What is Leno?	Frey, Berta	√	> 4	H&C	6	2		Sp 55	4
History: Ligetuhr Arbeit	Ligetuhr Arbeit: A Seventeenth-Century Compound Mounting and a Family of Associated Weaves	Hilts, Patricia	√	> 4	AT	7			Ju 87	31
History: Linen	History of Linen, A	Mattera, Joanne	√	√	SS&D	8	3	31	Su 77	16
History: Linen	Linen: A Brief History				WJ	7	2	26	Fa 82	46
History: Linen	Linen: The Enduring Thread of History	Hoskins, Nancy Arthur	√		Fa	14	2		M/A 87	42
History: Lithuanian Weaving	Lithuanian Pervarai: Producing a Twenty Shaft Pattern on a Twelve Shaft Loom	Meek, M. Kati	√	> 4	AT	1			De 83	159
History: Living	Weaving with the Past	Schliske, Doreen	√		Hw	3	5		N/D 82	15
History: Looms	Witch Engine! The Machinations of the Dobby	Cutcher, Hal	√		Iw	2	4		Su 77	22
History: Looms, Card	Modern Loom from Medieval Sources, A	Cesari, Andrea	√	√	WJ	10	2	38	Fa 85	18
History: Looms, East Asia	China and the Complexities of Weaving Technologies	Vollmer, John E.			AT	5			Ju 86	65
History: Looms, Tape	Tape Looms	Van Artsdalen, Martha	√		SS&D	15	4	60	Fa 84	15

SUBJECT	TITLE	AUTHOR	IL	INST	JOUR	VOL	NO	ISS	DATE	PAGE
History: Machine Knitting	Knitting Craft in Great Britain, The	Kinder, Kathleen	√		Fa	11	4		J/A 84	42
History: Madder	Madder Saga, The	Jones, Marilyn	√		SS&D	13	2	50	Sp 82	28
History: Madder	On Dyeing with Madder	Bliss, Anne	√	√	Iw	5	1		Wi 79	48
History: Mandala	Fiber Mandalas: Doilies As Spiritual Art	Maines, Rachel	√		Fa	9	3		M/J 82	17
History: Masks	Masks At the Heart of Disguise	Koplos, Janet	√		Fa	11	5		S/O 84	32
History: Mattor	Mattor (error-corrected WJ v2 n1 77 insert for vol. 1)	Dunham, Miriam	√	√	WJ	1	4	4	Ap 77	21
History: Men Knitters	Manly Art of Knitting...What's Become Of It, The	Weissman, Julia			Kn	3	2	6	Sp 87	15
History: Mercerizing	Mercerizing: Not for Everyone	Amos, Alden	√		S-O	9	2		Su 85	30
History: Metallic Yarn	Back to the Gold Standard	Siminoff	√		H&C	1	3		Fa 50	24
History: Mezzaro	Marvelous Mezzaro, The	Wasiqullah, Alexandra	√		Fa	10	5		S/O 83	29
History: Mineral Dyes	Mineral Dyes, The	Liles, James N.	√	√	SS&D	13	3	51	Su 82	54
History: Mohair Industry	Mohair: A Multimillion Dollar Industry for Australia	Gray, Isabel			S-O	8	4		Wi 84	47
History: Mummery	Mummery: Philadelphia's Happy New Year	Smeltzer, Nancy	√		Fa	14	3		M/J 87	39
History: Musk Ox	Musk Ox, The	Howard, Helen Griffiths	√		S-O	7	1		Sp 83	16
History: Musk Ox/Qiviut	Qiviut from the Musk Ox		√		H&C	18	3		Su 67	5
History: Native American Weaving	Indian Weavers and Contemporary Design		√		H&C	3	2		Sp 52	4
History: Native Americans, Cherokee	Revival of Cherokee Arts and Crafts, The	Parris, John	√		H&C	4	2		Sp 53	9
History: Navajo Weaving	Commercial Materials in Modern Navajo Rugs	Hedlund, Ann Lane	√		TMJ	25			86	83
History: Navajo Weaving	Contemporary Navajo Weaving	Hedlund, Ann Lane	√		WJ	11	1	41	Su 86	30
History: Navajo Weaving	Exploring a Tradition: Navajo Rugs, Classic and Contemporary	Elliott, Malinda	√		Fa	11	3		M/J 84	32
History: Navajo Weaving	"Eyedazzlers!" (Exhibit)	Lonier, Terri	√		Fa	11	3		M/J 84	77
History: Navajo Weaving	Navajo Weaving, Contemporary and Traditional		√		H&C	18	2		Sp 67	6
History: Needlework	Yesterday's Necessity — Today's Choice	Goodrick, Gail L.			S-O	7	2		Su 83	30
History: Needlework, American	C.H.A.N. for Short: The Story of Rachel Maines	Alonso, Harriet	√		Fa	8	3		M/J 81	13
History: Nishijin Weaving	Obi: The Textile Art of Nishijin	Donaldson, R. Alan	√		AT	1			De 83	115
History: Northwest Coast Indians	Totems in Tapestry	Swingle, Daphne	√		H&C	22	2		Sp 71	5
History: Norway	Weaving in Rural Norway: A Living Tradition	Nelson, Lila	√		Hw	8	3		M/J 87	52
History: Nubian Textiles, Late Classical	Textile Remains from a Late Temple in Egyptian Nubia	Adams, Nettie K.	√		AT	8			De 87	85
History: Osage Orange	The Last Species: Osage Orange, Bois d'Arc, Horse Apple, Hedge Apple	Bliss, Anne	√	√	Iw	1	3		Sp 76	24
History: Overshot	'Country' Overshot	Patrick, Jane	√	√	Hw	6	4		S/O 85	48
History: Painted Fabrics	Painted Silk	Bliss, Anne	√	√	Hw	4	1		J/F 83	50
History: Paisley	Paisley	Badone, Donalda	√		Hw	8	1		J/F 87	39
History: Paisley Shawl	Kashmir or Paisley; Romance of the Shawl	Wilson, Kax	√		Iw	4	4		Fa 79	34
History: Paisley Shawl	Kashmiri to Paisley: Evolution of the Paisley shawl	Larson-Fleming, Susan	√		WJ	11	3	43	Wi 87	37
History: Paper Cloth	Paper Clothing, East	Sahlstrand, Margaret	√	√	Fa	11	2		M/A 84	36
History: Paper Clothing	Paper Clothing: West	Koplos, Janet	√		Fa	11	2		M/A 84	39
History: Papercuts	Claudia Hopf: Drawing with Scissors	Timmons, Christine	√		Fa	11	2		M/A 84	99
History: Papermaking	Dard Hunter Paper Museum, The	Bard, Elizabeth A.	√		Fa	11	2		M/A 84	43
History: Papermaking	Papermaking: Where It's Coming From	Hughey, Michael W.	√	√	SS&D	10	4	40	Fa 79	45
History: Pattern Weaves	Structure and Form in the Weaving of John Becker	Swannie, Suzanne	√		AT	6			De 86	173
History: Penland School of Handicrafts	Penland School of Handicrafts		√		H&C	23	2		M/A 72	8

SUBJECT	TITLE	AUTHOR	IL	INST	JOUR	VOL	NO	ISS	DATE	PAGE
History: Persian Carpets	Symbolic Meanings in Oriental Rug Patterns: Part 2	Cammann, Schuyler V.R.	√		TMJ	3	3		De 72	22
History: Persian Carpets, Five-Medallion	Symbolic Meanings in Oriental Rug Patterns: Part 3	Cammann, Schuyler V.R.	√		TMJ	3	3		De 72	42
History: Peruvian Textiles	Chavin Textiles and the Origins of Peruvian Weaving	Conklin, William J	√		TMJ	3	2		De 71	13
History: Photographic Processes on Fabric	Blues in the Light: Cyanotype on Fabric	Sider, Sandra	√		Fa	13	5		S/O 86	34
History: Pi Beta Phi Settlement School	Pi Beta Phi Settlement School				H&C	14	2		Sp 63	12
History: Pile Weave	Color Related Decorating Textiles Rugs, Draperies, Upholstery: Double Corduroy Pile Rugs, History	Rhodes, Tonya Stalons; Harriet Tidball, ed.			SCGM		14		65	1
History: Plant Fibers	Plant Fibers		√	√	WJ	8	2	30	Fa 83	67
History: Pomo Basketry	Family Album of Pomo Baskets, A	Metzler, Sandra	√		Fa	11	1		J/F 84	63
History: Pueblo Weaving	Pueblo Weaving: A Renaissance	Sakiestewa, Ramona	√		Iw	4	1		Wi 78	34
History: Pueblo Weaving	Pueblo Weaving, An Ancient Art: Hopi Keep to Their Traditional Designs		√		H&C	19	1		Wi 68	5
History: Qiviut	Qiviut Update	Griffiths, Helen M.	√		SS&D	7	4	28	Fa 76	60
History: Quercitron	Quercitron, The Forgotten Dyestuff, Producer of Clear, Bright Colors	Gerber, Willi; Fred Gerber	√		SS&D	5	1	17	Wi 73	25
History: Quilts, Hawaii	Hawaiian Quilt, The	White-Hansen, Sue Ellen	√	√	TM			13	O/N 87	22
History: Quilts, Hawaii	"Hawaiian Quilts: Treasures of an Island Folk Art" (Exhibit)	Alonso, Harriet	√		Fa	6	6		N/D 79	77
History: Quilts, Slave	Slave Quilts: Threads of History	Grabiner, Dana M.	√		Fa	13	5		S/O 86	22
History: Rabari Lodi	Rabari Lodi: Creating a Fabric Through Social Alliance, The	Frater, Judy	√	√	WJ	10	1	37	Su 85	28
History: Rag Weaving	Rag Rug Traditions	Meany, Janet K.	√		WJ	9	4	36	Sp 85	56
History: Rag Weaving, Sweden	Rag Weaving: A History of Necessity		√		Hw	8	3		M/J 87	38
History: Reticella	Story of Reticella, The	Cave, OEnone	√		H&C	11	3		Su 60	14
History: Ribbon Fashions	Rapt with Ribbons	Nager, Sandra	√		TM			12	A/S 87	14
History: Robes	"Ch'ing Dynasty Court Robes, A Splendorous Sampling" (Exhibit)	Marcoux, Alice	√		Fa	11	2		M/A 84	78
History: Robes	Robes for Inspiration	Dyer, Carolyn	√		Fa	10	1		J/F 83	60
History: Rose Symbol	Floral Symbolism: The Western Rose	Austin, Carole	√		Fa	13	2		M/A 86	42
History: Royal Gobelins Factory	In the Gobelin Tradition: The Drouin Atelier	Gregg, Dorothy	√		SS&D	10	1	37	Wi 78	28
History: Rug Weaving	Rugs and Carpets — Their Importance in Interior Design		√		H&C	3	4		Fa 52	30
History: Rugs	Country of Origin, USA: A Decade of Contemporary Rugs	Stevens, Rebeccah A. T.	√		Fa	11	3		M/J 84	60
History: Rugs	London Carpeted in Oriental Gardens: The 4th International Conference on Oriental Carpets	Dyer, Carolyn Price	√		Fa	11	3		M/J 84	66
History: Rugs	Sonja Flavin: Weaving for the Classics	Sobieszek, Robert A.	√		Fa	11	3		M/J 84	70
History: Rugs, 19th Century	From Straw Mats to Hooked Rugs: Floor Coverings of the 19th Century	Thieme, Otto Charles	√		Fa	11	3		M/J 84	55
History: Rugs, Handcrafted, American	American Handcrafted Rug: Past and Present, The	Stevens, Rebecca A. T.	√		TMJ	23			84	73
History: Rugs, Hooked	Rug Hooking: The Flourishing of a Time-Honored Technique	Moshimer, Joan	√	√	Fa	7	5		S/O 80	37
History: Rugs, Iran	Kings, Heroes, Lovers: Pictorial Rugs From the Tribes and Villages of Iran	Goodman, Deborah Lerme	√		Fa	11	3		M/J 84	38
History: Rugs, Knitted	Knitted Rugs	Austin, Carole	√		Fa	11	3		M/J 84	57
History: Rya	Finland's Rya Rugs	The Finnish Consulate General of New York	√		SS&D	13	4	52	Fa 82	54
History: Rya	Finnish Ryijy (Rya)		√	√	Hw	8	3		M/J 87	72
History: Salish Robes	From Baskets to Blankets (error-corrected TM i7 O/N86 p5)	Samuel, Cheryl	√	√	TM			5	J/J 86	30
History: Samplers, Stitchery	Stitch in Time, A	Harris, Patricia; David Lyon	√		Fa	12	2		M/A 85	27

SUBJECT	TITLE	AUTHOR	IL	INST	JOUR	VOL	NO	ISS	DATE	PAGE
History: San Francisco Tapestry Workshop	Weaving in San Francisco — Part 1	Prosser, Evelyn Bingham	√		WJ	6	2	22	Fa 81	44
History: Sari	Patolu and Its Techniques	De Bone, Mary Golden	√	√	TMJ	4	3		76	49
History: Scotland	Weaver's Book of Scottish Tartans: The Scottish Tartans and Their Background: Scottish History, The	Tidball, Harriet	√		SCGM		5		62	4
History: Scottish Tartans	Weaver's Book of Scottish Tartans: The Scottish Tartans and Their Background, The	Tidball, Harriet	√		SCGM		5		62	1
History: Scottish Tartans, Highland Dress	Weaver's Book of Scottish Tartans: The Scottish Tartans and Their Background: Highland Dress, The	Tidball, Harriet	√		SCGM		5		62	2
History: Scottish Tartans, Sett-Stick	Weaver's Book of Scottish Tartans: The Scottish Tartans and Their Background: The Sett-Stick, The	Tidball, Harriet	√	√	SCGM		5		62	3
History: Seersucker	Origins	Wilson, Kax	√		Iw	4	4		Fa 79	51
History: Sericulture, Mormon	Saints and the Silkworms, The	Alderman, Sharon	√	√	Iw	3	4		Su 78	15
History: Shaker Baskets	Shaker Baskets Today	Wetherbee, Martha	√		SS&D	19	1	73	Wi 87	60
History: Shaker Rugs	Shaker Technique: Part 2, Rag Rugs, The	Gordon, Beverly	√	√	SS&D	8	1	29	WI 76	83
History: Shakers	Hands to Work and Hearts to God	Erf, Mary Elva	√	√	WJ	8	1	29	Su 83	25
History: Shakers	Shaker Textiles	Hillenburg, Nancy	√	√	WJ	8	1	29	Su 83	22
History: Shawls	Ah, Shawls!	Upitis, Lizbeth	√		Kn	4	1	9	Wi 87	14
History: Sheep Breeds, Britain	Wools of Britain, The	Seagroatt, Margaret	√		H&C	24	2		M/A 73	33
History: Sheep Breeds, Cotswold	Cotswold	Murray, Gwen B.	√		S-O	11	1		Sp 87	47
History: Sheep, Churro	Churro Sheep in the Navajo Tradition	McNeal, Dr. Lyle G.	√		WJ	10	2	38	Fa 85	31
History: Sheep, Columbia	Columbia, The	Adams, Brucie	√		Iw	3	4		Su 78	36
History: Sheep, Merino	Experiments with Merino	Adams, Brucie	√	√	Iw	5	1		Wi 79	50
History: Sheep Raising	Wool — That Wonderful Natural Fiber	Derr, Mary L.	√	√	WJ	2	2	6	Oc 77	2
History: Sheep-to-Shawl Competitions	Grandaddy of Sheep-to-Shawls: The Newberry Coat 1811, The				S-O	6	4		82	20
History: Sheepherding, Ireland	Shepherds of Glenmore, The	Burkhauser, Jude	√		S-O	6	4		82	36
History: Silk	"Common Cord, The" Central Asian Textiles (Exhibit)	Prinzing, Debra	√		Fa	14	3		M/J 87	56
History: Silk	History of Silk, A	Mattera, Joanne	√	√	SS&D	8	2	30	Sp 77	24
History: Silk	Mistra	Xenakis, Alexis Yiorgos	√		Kn	2	2	4	S-S 86	56
History: Silk	Sensuous Silk	West, Virginia	√		Hw	7	1		J/F 86	52
History: Silk	Silk		√		S-O	1			77	34
History: Silk	Silk Lore: The Myths of a Magical Fiber	Goodman, Deborah Lerme	√		Fa	13	1		J/F 86	42
History: Silk	Silk, the Story of a Culture	Drooker, Penelope	√		Hw	7	1		J/F 86	49
History: Silk Industry	Silk City: Paterson, New Jersey	Malarcher, Patricia	√		Fa	13	1		J/F 86	31
History: Silk Pictures, Woven	Jacquard and Woven Silk Pictures, The	Adrosko, Rita J.	√		AT	1			De 83	9
History: Silk Road	Tracing the Silk Road	Dyer, Carolyn	√		Fa	13	1		J/F 86	22
History: Silk Weaving, England	From English Handlooms Comes Royal Purple Velvet for Coronation Robe of Elizabeth II	Lee, Humphrey A.	√		H&C	4	2		Sp 53	17
History: Silk Weaving Industry	On Eighteenth Century Flowered Silk Weaving as an Inspiration for Todays Complex Weavers	Fairbanks, Dale			CW	7	1	19	Se 85	8
History: Smock	Handwoven Smocks	Short, Melba Ellis	√	√	Hw	5	3		Su 84	66
History: Southern Highland Handicraft Guild	Persis Grayson, Weaver & Spinner	Amos, Mary Alice	√		H&C	19	1		Wi 68	10
History: Spanish Moss	Contemporary Uses for an Ancient Fiber: Spanish Moss	Elliott, Douglas B.	√	√	SS&D	9	2	34	Sp 78	51
History: Spider Silk	Spiders: Masters of Natural Textiles	Palmer, Jacqueline M.	√		Fa	14	4		S/O 87	33
History: "Spindle City"	"Spindle City," Lowell, Massachusetts	Scarborough, Jessica	√		Fa	9	2		M/A 82	53
History: Spindles	High Whorl Spindle, The	Hochberg, Bette	√	√	SS&D	11	1	41	Wi 79	12

SUBJECT	TITLE	AUTHOR	IL	INST	JOUR	VOL	NO	ISS	DATE	PAGE
History: Spinning	Colonial Equipment	Pennington, David; Michael Taylor	√		S-O	2			78	40
History: Spinning	Kiwicraft	Horne, Beverley	√	√	S-O	3			79	52
History: Spinning	Leonardo Da Vinci's Ideas on the Mechanization of Spinning	Born, W.			S-O	2			78	47
History: Spinning	Llamas	Switzer, Chris	√	√	S-O	5			81	31
History: Spinning	Looming Thoughts	Fannin, Allen	√		S-O	1			77	12
History: Spinning	Na´ashje´ii Asdzaa—Spider Woman		√		S-O	1			77	11
History: Spinning	Nahuala Spinning	Linder, Harry; Olive Linder	√		S-O	2			78	23
History: Spinning	Spanish Colonial Spindle Whorls: The History and the Art	Spradley, J. L.	√	√	S-O	7	1		Sp 83	35
History: Spinning	Spinning in Ecuador	Meisch, Lynn Ann	√	√	S-O	4			80	24
History: Spinning	Spinning in the Southwest — Prehistoric, Historic, and Contemporary	Lawrence, Ramona Sakiestewa	√		S-O	1			77	8
History: Spinning	Spinning with Gandhi	Grant, Susan	√		S-O	2			78	15
History: Spinning	There's An Old Spinning Wheel in the Parlor	Rossiter, Phyllis	√		S-O	9	1		Sp 85	31
History: Spinning	Women as Spinners: New England Spinsters	Gordon, Beverly	√		S-O	3			79	16
History: Spinning, America, 18th Century	Handweaving and the Powerloom in 18th Century America	Cooper, Grace Rogers	√		H&C	22	4		Fa 71	5
History: Spinning Wheels	Bernard Barton Spinning Wheel — 1766, The		√		S-O	7	4		Wi 83	16
History: Spinning Wheels	Misunderstood Spinning Wheel, The	Kronenberg, Bud	√	√	SS&D	12	3	47	Su 81	11
History: Spinning Wheels	Short History of the Spinning Wheel, A	Swenson, Astrid	√		SS&D	7	3	27	Su 76	40
History: Sprang	Listening to Threads	Reynders-Baas, Coby	√		WJ	11	4	44	Sp 87	21
History: Sprang	Nasca Sprang Tassels: Structure, Technique, and Order	Frame, Mary	√	√	TMJ	25			86	67
History: Sprang	World of Ancient and Modern Sprang, The	Collingwood, Peter	√	√	SS&D	5	1	17	Wi 73	90
History: Star Spangled Banner	Star Spangled Banner, The	West, Virginia M.	√		H&C	15	2		Sp 64	13
History: Stitchery	History of Texture Stitches, A	Markrich, Lilo	√		TM			5	J/J 86	63
History: Stockings, Knitted Lace	Lace and Legs	Upitis, Lizbeth	√		Kn	1	2	2	S-S 85	64
History: Suits, Chanel-Lagerfeld Style	Knitting Odyssey, A	Dyett, Linda	√	√	TM			13	O/N 87	48
History: Summer and Winter Weave	Summer and Winter and Other Two-Tie Unit Weaves: History of the Summer and Winter Weave	Tidball, Harriet			SCGM		19		66	2
History: T-Shirts	Tons of T's	Upitis, Lizbeth	√		Kn	3	3	7	Su 87	8
History: Tabby Weave	Tabby Weave, Ways to Make It More Interesting	Hausner, Walter	√		H&C	12	4		Fa 61	6
History: Table Linens	History of Table Linens, A				Hw	8	3		M/J 87	40
History: Taffeta	Origins	Wilson, Kax			Iw	5	1		Wi 79	47
History: Tape-Loom Weaving	Tape Loom — Then and Now, The	Chesley, Mariam Dolloff	√		Hw	3	5		N/D 82	56
History: Tapestry	Aubusson Tapestry	Larochette, Jean-Pierre	√		SS&D	13	4	52	Fa 82	5
History: Tapestry	Tapestry: A Brief Overview	Bliss, Anne	√		Iw	4	2		Sp 79	15
History: Tapestry	Tapestry: Technique and Tradition	Scott, Gail R.	√		H&C	22	3		Su 71	16
History: Tapestry, Ireland	Ballinskelligs Tapestry Works: Ancient Art/Modern Spirit, The	Burkhauser, Jude	√		Hw	3	1		Ja 82	55
History: Tapestry, Mexico	Study Opportunities: Mexican Tapestry Weaving in San Miguel	de la Garza, Phyllis	√		Hw	3	1		Ja 82	62
History: Tapestry Room from Croome Court	Tapestry Room from Croome Court, The		√		H&C	11	3		Su 60	30
History: Tapestry Weaving	Tapestry and Today's Weavers		√	√	H&C	5	1		Wi 53	4
History: Tartan Dyes	Dyes of Early Tartans, The		√		Hw	4	5		N/D 83	75
History: Tatting	Tatting	Tooker, Dorothy	√		SS&D	17	4	68	Fa 86	74
History: Teasels	Teasels	Leadbeater, Eliza	√	√	Hw	2	5		No 81	54
History: Tents	Tents in History	Austin, Carole	√		Fa	12	4		J/A 85	47

SUBJECT	TITLE	AUTHOR	IL	INST	JOUR	VOL	NO	ISS	DATE	PAGE
History: Tenugui	Tenugui: Decorative Japanese Hand Towels		√		Fa	9	6		N/D 82	25
History: Textilately	From Fibre to Haute Coutoure on World Postage Stamps	Cysarz, J. M.	√		AT	4			De 85	89
History: Textile Art, Late Roman, Early Byzantine	Roman Heritage: Introduction, The	Trilling, James	√		TMJ	21			82	11
History: Textile Arts, 17th Century	Some Remarks on the Work of Markham	Stanton, R. G.; J. L. Allston	√	√	AT	2			De 84	95
History: Textile Education	Learning to Weave in Japan	Schrieber, LaVonne	√		WJ	8	1	29	Su 83	79
History: Textile Industry	Museum of American Textile History	Saulson, Sarah Fusfeld	√		SS&D	17	4	68	Fa 86	80
History: Textile Industry	Technological Change and the Textile Industry: The Impact of the Industrial Revolution and the Computer Revolution	Thieme, Otto Charles	√		Fa	11	1		J/F 84	54
History: Textile Machinery Patents, American	Nineteenth Century License Agreements for Fancy Weaving Machines	Anderson, Clarita; Steven M. Spivak	√		AT	8			De 87	67
History: Textile Machinery Patents, British	Nineteenth Century License Agreements for Fancy Weaving Machines	Anderson, Clarita; Steven M. Spivak	√		AT	8			De 87	67
History: Textile Mill Girls	Mill Girls of 'Spindle City,' The	Rubbert, Toni Condon	√		S-O	10	1		Sp 86	16
History: Textile Mills	Day in the Life of a Millgirl	Salinger, Maude	√		SS&D	17	4	68	Fa 86	78
History: Textile Mills	"Spindle City," Lowell, Massachusetts	Scarborough, Jessica	√		Fa	9	2		M/A 82	53
History: Textile Mills	Tour Through Merrimack Valley Textile Museum, A	Britton, Nancy	√		Fa	9	2		M/A 82	52
History: Textile Trade Unions (Britian)	Technical Progress and the Evolution of Wage Arrangements in the British Cotton Weaving Industry	Jackson, K. C.; B. Pourdeyhimi	√		AT	7			Ju 87	61
History: Textiles	Events in Textile History	Hochberg, Bette	√		Fa	10	2		M/A 83	52
History: Textiles	Inspiration from the Past: Textile Treasures in the World of New York City Auctions	Sider, Sandra	√		Fa	11	6		N/D 84	62
History: Textiles, Borneo	"Heads and Tales: Traditional Art of Borneo" (Exhibit)	Dyer, Carolyn Price	√		Fa	11	4		J/A 84	74
History: Textiles, China	"Silk Roads/China Ships" (Exhibit)	Sider, Sandra	√		Fa	11	4		J/A 84	74
History: Textiles, Ecuador	Weaving a Cotton Saddlebag on the Santa Elena Peninsula of Ecuador	Hagino, Jane Parker; Karen E. Stothert	√	√	TMJ	22			83	19
History: Textiles, Egypt	Tapestries of Coptic Egypt, The	Hoskins, Nancy Arthur	√		AT	6			De 86	211
History: Textiles, Home Production	Early Home Textile Production in Chautauqua County, New York	Fahnestock, Ann			S-O	6	4		82	32
History: Textiles, Little Tennessee River Valley	Prehistoric Textiles Revealed by Potsherds	Kuttruff, Jenna Tedrick	√		SS&D	11	3	43	Su 80	40
History: Textiles, Mid-Twentieth Century	Mid-Twentieth Century Textures	Mailey, Jean E.	√		H&C	8	3		Su 57	6
History: Textiles, Peru	Rare Peruvian Textiles		√		H&C	9	2		Sp 58	18
History: Textiles, Peru	Vignettes from Peru	Wilson, Kax	√		Iw	5	4		Fa 80	46
History: The Penland School of Crafts	Penland School of Crafts, The	Brown, William J.			H&C	16	3		Su 65	21
History: The Society of Arts and Crafts of Boston, Massachusetts	Society of Arts and Crafts of Boston, Massachusetts, The	Van Cleve, Kate	√		H&C	1	2		Su 50	5
History: The Weaving Room	Ossie Phillips: A Tradition of Mountain Weaving	Sheward, Cynthia M.	√		Fa	14	2		M/A 87	25
History: Thistle	Thistles	Bliss, Anne	√	√	Hw	7	1		J/F 86	84
History: Thread, Gold	Threads of Gold	Austin, Carole	√		Fa	13	4		J/A 86	10
History: Toothbrush Rugs	Toothbrush Handle Rugs: Nålbinding With Rags	Nelson, Lila	√	√	WJ	12	2	46	Fa 87	16
History: Trade Materials, Navajo Weaving	Commercial Materials in Modern Navajo Rugs	Hedlund, Ann Lane	√		TMJ	25			86	83
History: Tree-Bast Fiber Textiles, Japan	Tree-Bast Fiber Textiles of Japan	Dusenbury, Mary	√	√	S-O	10	3		Fa 86	35
History: Triaxial Weaving	Triaxial Weaves and Weaving: An Exploration for Hand Weavers	Mooney, David R.	√	√	AT	2			De 84	9
History: Tutu	Whence the Tutu?	Austin, Carole	√		Fa	11	5		S/O 84	46
History: Tweed	Tweed	Wilson, Kax	√		Iw	5	2		Sp 80	59

SUBJECT	TITLE	AUTHOR	IL	INST	JOUR	VOL	NO	ISS	DATE	PAGE
History: Twills, 17th and 18th Century, Germany	Seventeenth and Eighteenth Century Twills: The German Linen Tradition	Hilts, Patricia	√	> 4	AT	3			My 85	139
History: Twining, Weft	Weft Twining: History	Harvey, Virginia I.; Harriet Tidball			SCGM		28		69	2
History: Two-Shaft Looms	Don't Overlook Two Harness Looms	Brown, Harriette J.	√		H&C	5	3		Su 54	10
History: Tyrian Purple	Purple in Antiquity	Davidson, Mary Frances			SS&D	2	1	5	De 70	26
History: Tyrian Purple Dye	Tyrian Purple	Robinson, John P., Jr.	√		H&C	24	1		J/F 73	30
History: Undergarments	Tempting and Tempestuous	Upitis, Lizbeth	√		Kn	3	2	6	Sp 87	8
History: Underwear	Underneath It All: A Brief History of Underwear and Fashion's Changing Silhouette	Singletary, Suzanne	√		Fa	11	5		S/O 84	44
History: Undulating Weft Textiles	Undulating Weft Effects (Honeycomb)	Tidball, Harriet	√		SCGM		9		63	1
History: Vadmal	Vadmal: A Study Group from the Frozen North Warms Up to an Ancient Technique	Larson-Fleming, Susan	√	√	WJ	10	3	39	Wi 86	26
History: Vestments	Thousand Years of Western Vestments: Raiment for the Lord's Service, A		√		SS&D	7	2	26	Sp 76	8
History: Waistcoats	Colorful Waistcoats Woven by Elsie H. Gubser		√	√	H&C	18	1		Wi 67	18
History: Warp Twining	Hungarian Weaving	Allen, Jane Ingram	√	√	SS&D	10	3	39	Su 79	93
History: Warp Wrapping	Chavin Textiles and the Origins of Peruvian Weaving	Conklin, William J	√		TMJ	3	2		De 71	13
History: Weaving	Saint Severus: Parton Saint of Weavers	Moes, Dini	√		SS&D	16	2	62	Sp 85	58
History: Weaving	Weaving in the Past, Complete Index with Reference: The History of Handweaving	Zielinski, S. A.; Robert Leclerc, ed.			MWL	21 22			'51–'73	77
History Weaving: 17th and 18th Century	Thomas Jackson, Weaver: 17th and 18th Century Records	Tidball, Harriet	√		SCGM		13		64	1
History: Weaving, America, 18th Century	Handweaving and the Powerloom in 18th Century America	Cooper, Grace Rogers	√		H&C	22	4		Fa 71	5
History: Weaving, Canada	Making Weaving History	Xenakis, Alexis Yiorgos	√		PWC	4	3	13		6
History: Weaving Equipment, China	China and the Complexities of Weaving Technologies	Vollmer, John E.			AT	5			Ju 86	65
History: Weaving, Figured Silk	Weaves in Figured Silks	Blumenau, Lili	√	√	H&C	2	2		Sp 51	25
History: Weaving, Figured Silks	Designs in Ancient Figured Silks	Blumenau, Lili	√		H&C	2	1		Wi 50	5
History: Weaving, Greece	Search for Handweaving in Greece, A (error-corrected H&C v21 n3 70 p42)	Turner, Alta R.	√		H&C	21	2		Sp 70	16
History: Weaving, India	Handweaving in India Today	King, Edith B.; Earl L. King	√		H&C	7	4		Fa 56	10
History: Weaving, Satin	Contemporary Satins: History	Tidball, Harriet	√		SCGM		7		62	1
History: Weaving Technology	Structure and Form in the Weaving of John Becker	Swannie, Suzanne	√		AT	6			De 86	173
History: Weaving Technology, China	China and the Complexities of Weaving Technologies	Vollmer, John E.			AT	5			Ju 86	65
History: Weaving Time-Line	Thread That Runs So True — A Weaving Time Line	Strickler, Carol	√		Hw	3	5		N/D 82	45
History: Weaving, Wales	Wool Gathering in Wales	Clement, Doris; Ted Clement	√		H&C	23	1		J/F 72	26
History: Weft-Faced Compound Weaves	Double-Harness Techniques Employed in Egypt	El-Homossani, M. M.	√	> 4	AT	3			My 85	229
History: Weir	Joyce Chown's "Fabricated Structure: Weir"	Weir, Jean; Joyce Chown	√		Fa	11	4		J/A 84	39
History: Woodland Indian Bay Weaving	Reviving the Lost Art of Woodland Indian Bag Weaving	King, Rod	√		Fa	13	2		M/A 86	27
History: Wool, Wales	Weaving in Wales	Kemp, Gwendoline	√		H&C	6	2		Sp 55	24
History: Woolens, America	Woolens and Tweeds: History of Woolens in America	Tidball, Harriet			SCGM		4		61	3
History: Words/Fiber	Words in Fiber	Rowley, Kathleen	√		Fa	11	2		M/A 84	66
History: Xerox	Color Xerography and the Fiber Artist	Theil, Linda	√		Fa	8	5		S/O 81	59
Hmong	Flourishing Art: China, Guizhou Women Continue to Embroider Their Legends, A	Rossi, Gail	√		TM			9	F/M 87	30

SUBJECT	TITLE	AUTHOR	IL	INST	JOUR	VOL	NO	ISS	DATE	PAGE
Hmong	Flourishing Art: USA Hmong Women Show How to Stitch Pa ndau, Their Flowery Cloth, A	Porter-Francis, Wendy	√	√	TM			9	F/M 87	33
Hmong	"Hmong Art: Tradition and Change" (Exhibit)	Gordon, Beverly	√		Fa	12	6		N/D 85	36
Hmong	Keeping Culture Alive with Needle and Thread	White, Virginia L.	√		Fa	9	3		M/J 82	40
Hmong	Keeping Tradition Alive	Wilcox, Don	√		Fa	14	1		J/F 87	44
Hmong	Night Stories	White, Virginia	√		TM			11	J/J 87	82
Hmong Textile Outlet	Hmong Catalogue				TM			11	J/J 87	4
Holiday Costume	Mummery: Philadelphia's Happy New Year	Smeltzer, Nancy	√		Fa	14	3		M/J 87	39
Holiday Crocheting: Christmas	Crocheted and Knitted "Precious Littles"	Rowley, Elaine D.	√	√	PWC			3	Oc 82	58
Holiday Embroidery: Christmas	Christmas Embroidery in Pakistan	Garland, Mary	√		TM			14	D/J 87	90
Holiday Knitting: Christmas	Crocheted and Knitted "Precious Littles"	Rowley, Elaine D.	√	√	PWC			3	Oc 82	58
Holiday Plaiting: Christmas	Man-Made Fibers: Season's Greetings		√	√	WJ	5	2	18	Fa 80	46
Holiday Weaving: Christmas	Basketry Drop Spindle	Coutts, Lucele	√		SS&D	11	4	44	Fa 80	49
Holiday Weaving: Christmas	Christmas Card	Nyquist, Janet	√	>4	CW	1	2	2	Fe 80	11
Holiday Weaving: Christmas	Christmas Card by Marjorie Beattie Ellis, A		√	√	H&C	20	3		Su 69	29
Holiday Weaving: Christmas	Christmas Card Contest Winners		√	√	SS&D	2	2	6	Sp 71	32
Holiday Weaving: Christmas	Christmas Cards		√	>4	WJ	7	2	26	Fa 82	54
Holiday Weaving: Christmas	Christmas Cards	Clement, Doris	√		H&C	15	2		Sp 64	20
Holiday Weaving: Christmas	Christmas Decorations		√	>4	H&C	6	4		Fa 55	12
Holiday Weaving: Christmas	Christmas Greeting, A	Strand, Victoria	√	>4	H&C	12	4		Fa 61	17
Holiday Weaving: Christmas	Christmas Gretings from the Weaver's Journal Staff		√	>4	WJ	3	2	10	Oc 78	41
Holiday Weaving: Christmas	Christmas Is Coming: An Advent Calendar	Erf, Mary Elva	√	>4	SS&D	7	4	28	Fa 76	20
Holiday Weaving: Christmas	Christmas Is Coming: Woven Ornaments	Wertenberger, Kathryn	√	√	SS&D	7	4	28	Fa 76	21
Holiday Weaving: Christmas	Christmas Joy		√		Hw	6	4		S/O 85	63
Holiday Weaving: Christmas	Christmas Miniatures, Part 1: Summer and Winter Coverlets	Lyon, Linda	√	√	PWC			3	Oc 82	50
Holiday Weaving: Christmas	Christmas Miniatures, Part 2: Krokbragd Bellpulls (error-corrected PWC i4 83 p76)	Xenakis, Athanasios David	√	>4	PWC			3	Oc 82	52
Holiday Weaving: Christmas	Christmas Project, A	Richards, Iris	√	√	WJ	1	2	2	Oc 76	12
Holiday Weaving: Christmas	Christmas Swags Offer Interesting Weaving for Summer	Burlew, Margaret	√	√	H&C	13	3		Su 62	12
Holiday Weaving: Christmas	Combining Lace Weaves		√	√	WJ	4	2	14	Oc 79	14
Holiday Weaving: Christmas	Composition and Designing: Ideas for Christmas	Zielinski, S. A.; Robert Leclerc, ed.	√	>4	MWL	18			'51–'73	56
Holiday Weaving: Christmas	Creating Holiday Heirlooms		√	>4	SS&D	13	4	52	Fa 82	78
Holiday Weaving: Christmas	Handwoven Christmas Cards	Arnold, Ruth	√	>4	H&C	7	3		Su 56	7
Holiday Weaving: Christmas	Handwoven Trees	Wertenberger, Kathryn	√	>4	Hw	5	5		N/D 84	90
Holiday Weaving: Christmas	Heirloom Christmas, An		√	√	Hw	8	4		S/O 87	56
Holiday Weaving: Christmas	Here Comes Christmas	Lynn, Harriett W.	√	√	SS&D	2	4	8	Fa 71	16
Holiday Weaving: Christmas	Holiday Cheer				Hw	4	4		S/O 83	71
Holiday Weaving: Christmas	Holiday Greeting Cards		√	√	SS&D	14	4	56	Fa 83	68
Holiday Weaving: Christmas	Holiday Greeting Cards	Ridgeway, Terese	√	>4	SS&D	15	4	60	Fa 84	61
Holiday Weaving: Christmas	Holiday Tabard (Kathryn Wertenberger)		√	√	Hw	2	1		F-W 80	54, 59
Holiday Weaving: Christmas	Homespun Holidays		√		SS&D	12	4	48	Fa 81	69
Holiday weaving: Christmas	Joy to the World		√	√	WJ	6	2	22	Fa 81	59
Holiday Weaving: Christmas	Keep It Simple Christmas, A		√		Hw	7	4		S/O 86	34
Holiday Weaving: Christmas	Merry Christmas!	Barrett, Clotilde	√	>4	WJ	8	2	30	Fa 83	36
Holiday Weaving: Christmas	Merry Christmas—A Name Draft	Bliven, Jeanette; Norma Smayda	√	√	Hw	4	4		S/O 83	74
Holiday Weaving: Christmas	Merry Christmas, Handweavers	Tidball, Harriet	√	√	SCGM		10		63	1-30
Holiday Weaving: Christmas	Merry Christmas, Handweavers: Christmas Decorations and Novelties	Tidball, Harriet	√	>4	SCGM		10		63	18

SUBJECT	TITLE	AUTHOR	IL	INST	JOUR	VOL	NO	ISS	DATE	PAGE
Holiday Weaving: Christmas	Merry Christmas, Handweavers: Handwoven Christmas Cards	Tidball, Harriet	√	> 4	SCGM		10		63	1
Holiday Weaving: Christmas	Notes of a Pattern Weaver	Alvic, Philis	√	√	SS&D	15	1	57	Wi 83	74
Holiday Weaving: Christmas	Redwood Christmas Tree	Griswold, Irene T.	√		SS&D	3	1	9	Wi 71	12
Holiday Weaving: Christmas	"Santa" Stocking Stuffer	Sullivan, Donna	√	√	SS&D	15	4	60	Fa 84	64
Holiday Weaving: Christmas	Special Gifts		√		Hw	6	4		S/O 85	66
Holiday Weaving: Christmas	Stocking Stuffers		√		Hw	6	4		S/O 85	64
Holiday Weaving: Christmas	Suggestions for Christmas Gifts	Frey, Berta	√	> 4	H&C	16	4		Fa 65	18
Holiday Weaving: Christmas	Three and Four Harness Krokbragd (error-corrected PWC i4 83 p76)	Temple, Mary	√	√	PWC			3	Oc 82	56
Holiday Weaving: Christmas	Trifles: Christmas Ornaments (Pam Bolesta)		√	√	Hw	1	1		F-W 79	46
Holiday Weaving: Christmas	Weaving for the Holidays (error-corrected Hw v4 n4 83 p92)		√	> 4	Hw	3	5		N/D 82	78
Holiday Weaving: Christmas	Woven Christmas Greetings	Neher, Evelyn	√		H&C	2	3		Su 51	33
Holiday Weaving: Christmas Cards	Holiday Greetings (Carol Thilenius)		√	> 4	Hw	3	5		N/D 82	101
Holiday Weaving: Christmas Cards	Say it with a Card		√	√	Hw	2	1		F-W 80	81
Holiday Weaving: Christmas, Figures	Christmas Card, A		√	> 4	WJ	2	2	6	Oc 77	32
Holiday Weaving: Christmas, Ornaments	Idea for Gifts	Krasnoff, Julienne	√	> 4	H&C	21	3		Su 70	18
Holiday Weaving: Christmas, Yarn Novelties	Merry Christmas, Handweavers: Yarn Novelties	Tidball, Harriet	√		SCGM		10		63	29
Holiday Weaving: Easter	Easter Fun!		√	√	Hw	1	2		S-S 80	39
Holiday Weaving: Easter	Merry Christmas, Handweavers: Greeting Cards for Other Occasions	Tidball, Harriet	√	> 4	SCGM		10		63	17
Holiday Weaving: Thanksgiving	Cornucopia (Horn of Plenty)	Graser, Marie E.	√	√	WJ	7	2	26	Fa 82	52
Holiday Weaving: Valentine	Fantastic Finnweave, Part 2: Single-Thread Projects	Xenakis, Athanasios David	√	√	PWC			3	Oc 82	14
Holiday Weaving: Valentine	Merry Christmas, Handweavers: Greeting Cards for Other Occassions	Tidball, Harriet	√	√	SCGM		10		63	17
Holiday Weavings: Christmas	Holiday Runners	Skoy, Mary	√	> 4	WJ	12	2	46	Fa 87	22
Holland	Groupwork with Dutch Feltmaker Inge Evers	Clark, Sherry	√	√	SS&D	17	4	68	Fa 86	28
Holland	Lace Maker of Holland, Henk van der Zanden		√		H&C	17	2		Sp 66	15
Hollywood	Gilbert Adrian: Creating the Hollywood Dream Style	Kinsey, Susan Buchanan	√		Fa	14	3		M/J 87	49
Home	Theme Issue		√		Fa	8	3		M/J 81	
Home Furnishings: Handwoven	Home Weaving: Try Upholstery		√		Hw	1	1		F-W 79	42
Home Furnishings: Handwoven	Shades of a Desert Sunset		√		Hw	1	2		S-S 80	32
Home Furnishings: Handwoven	Weave Yourself A Special Place		√		Hw	1	1		F-W 79	36
Home Studio: Weaving	Home Studio?	Liebler, Barbara	√		Iw	5	2		Sp 80	56
Home Studio: Weaving	Home Studio: Some Practical Hints	Beschell, Lorraine	√		Iw	5	2		Sp 80	58
Honeycomb	Baby Bib (Margaretha Essén-Hedin)		√	√	Hw	8	2		M/A 87	44, I-7
Honeycomb	Corded Weaves — Four Harness Cross Cords		√	> 4	WJ	4	1	13	Jy 79	25
Honeycomb	Eight Shaft Warp Rep Honeycomb (Virginia West)		√	> 4	Hw	5	2		M/A 84	72, 95
Honeycomb	Fabric #4 Coverlet/Bedspread Fabric (Constance LaLena)		√	√	Hw	8	2		M/A 87	52, I-10
Honeycomb	Gang: Technical and Conceptual Applications to Loom Controlled Weave Structures	Towner, Naomi Whiting	√	> 4	AT	5			Ju 86	91
Honeycomb	Honeycomb: Curves Ahead	Alderman, Sharon D.	√	√	Hw	5	4		S/O 84	45
Honeycomb	Honeycomb Upholstery (Constance LaLena)		√	> 4	Hw	4	1		J/F 83	66, 91
Honeycomb	Rags to Riches: Honeycomb Bolero-Style Vest	Barrett, Phyllis K.	√	√	WJ	6	3	23	Wi 81	30

SUBJECT	TITLE	AUTHOR	IL	INST	JOUR	VOL	NO	ISS	DATE	PAGE
Honeycomb	Seat for All Seasons, A	Rasmussen, Peg	√	√	WJ	6	2	22	Fa 81	21
Honeycomb	Swatch #5, Silk Blouse Fabric (Lillian Whipple)		√	> 4	Hw	7	5		N/D 86	64, I-7
Honeycomb	Sweet Dreams Pillow Slips (Sharon D. Alderman)		√	√	Hw	5	4		S/O 84	45, 96
Honeycomb	Taste of Honey(comb), A	Rasmussen, Peg	√	√	SS&D	16	2	62	Sp 85	6
Honeycomb	Traditional Texture Weaves: Halkrus or Honeycomb	Zielinski, S. A.; Robert Leclerc, ed.	√	√	MWL	11			'51–'73	14
Honeycomb	Variations on an Overshot Threading	Lermond, Charles	√	√	WJ	12	2	46	Fa 87	25
Honeycomb and Weft Effects	Undulating Weft Effects (Honeycomb)	Tidball, Harriet	√	√	SCGM		9		63	1-25
Honeycomb, Brighton	Brighton Honeycomb	Muller, Donna	√	> 4	CW	5	3	15	My 84	12
Honeycomb, Turned	Take Advantage of Turned Drafts	Moes, Dini	√	> 4	SS&D	13	2	50	Sp 82	58
Honeycomb, Warp Rep	Eight Shaft Warp Rep Honeycomb (Virginia West)		√	> 4	Hw	5	2		M/A 84	72, 95
Hoods	Jacket for Hiking, A	Roth, Bettie G.	√	> 4	WJ	8	3	31	Wi 83	69
Hoods	Wymple in Tyme, A	Gibson-Roberts, Priscilla A.	√	√	Kn	3	4	8	Fa 87	56
Hooking	"American Hooked Rugs: 1850–1957" (Exhibit)	Scarborough, Jessica	√		Fa	8	6		N/D 81	68
Hooking	Anne W. Dickerson	Dickerson, Anne S.	√		Fa	14	5		N/D 87	12
Hooking	Chromatic Effervescence: The Hooked Surface As a Response to My Environment	Eyerman, Linda	√		Fa	10	2		M/A 83	22
Hooking	Dolphin Rug	Bahr, Ann	√	√	H&C	21	2		Sp 70	36
Hooking	Hooking Wild Horses (Zorach, Marguerite)		√		TM			10	A/M 87	88
Hooking	Rug Craftsmen	Olmsted, Anna W.	√		H&C	18	2		Sp 67	27
Hooking	Vera Grosowsky: Through the Surface	Paine, Frank	√		Fa	10	4		J/A 83	18
Hooking: Contemporary	Hooked on Texture: Unconventional Punch-Needle Rugs	Crouse, Gloria E.	√	√	TM			14	D/J 87	68
Hooking Handspun	Designs in Rughooking		√		H&C	23	3		M/J 72	51
Hooking Handspun	Rug for a Beginner	Holmes, Cora	√		S-O	10	1		Sp 86	24
Hooking: Latch	Fleecy Vest, A	Gilsdorf, Marilyn	√	√	WJ	8	4	32	Sp 84	9
Hooking: Locker	Locker Hooking	Rough, Joan Z.	√	√	SS&D	16	1	61	Wi 84	54
Hooking: Power Punch	Tapestry Gunner	Henry, Patti	√	√	TM			7	O/N 86	40
Hooking: Rags	Welcome to My World	Denton, Kay	√		Fa	8	3		M/J 81	52
Hooking: Technique	Traditional Rug Hooking with a Twist	Erickson, Janet Doub	√	√	TM			12	A/S 87	30
Hooking: Techniques	Hooked on Texture: Unconventional Punch-Needle Rugs	Crouse, Gloria E.	√	√	TM			14	D/J 87	68
Hooking: Techniques	Rug Hooking for Relaxation	Sizer, Theodore	√	√	H&C	17	2		Sp 66	8
Hooking: Techniques	Rug Hooking: The Flourishing of a Time-Honored Technique	Moshimer, Joan	√	√	Fa	7	5		S/O 80	37
Hooking Traditions: USA	Truth About American Hooking, The	Fallier, Jeanne H.	√	√	TM			14	D/J 87	20
Hopi Embroidery Weave	Hopi Embroidery Weave As a Technique for Tapestry	Atwood, Betty	√	√	WJ	5	1	17	Su 80	37
Hopi Embroidery Weave	Hopi Embroidery Weave, The	Atwood, Betty	√	√	SS&D	8	2	30	Sp 77	100
Hopsack Ground	Macro Plaid, Macro Twill	Xenakis, Athanasios David	√	> 4	PWC	3	1	7		55
Horse Accessories	Weaving on a Diamond Grid: Bedouin Style	Race, Mary E.	√	√	SS&D	12	1	45	Wi 80	20
Hound's Tooth	Resist Dyeing, Curiosities and Inventions: Hound's Tooth in Texture and Colour	Zielinski, S. A.; Robert Leclerc, ed.	√	√	MWL	17			'51–'73	68
Housing, Woven	Weaving in Africa	Cragholm, Lynn	√		H&C	23	1		J/F 72	18
Housing: Woven	Woven Houses of Thailand, The	Wilcox, Don	√		Fa	13	3		M/J 86	38
Huck	And Thereon Hangs a Towel		√	> 4	Hw	3	4		Se 82	58
Huck	Contemporary Approach to Traditional Weaves: M's and O's	Zielinski, S. A.; Robert Leclerc, ed.	√	√	MWL	8			'51–'73	75
Huck	Designed for Narrow Looms	Jennings, Lucy Anne	√	√	WJ	11	1	41	Su 86	26

SUBJECT	TITLE	AUTHOR	IL	INST	JOUR	VOL	NO	ISS	DATE	PAGE
Huck	Experiment in Group Study	Bryan, Dorothy	√	>4	H&C	10	3		Su 59	6
Huck	Huck and Huck Lace		√	>4	WJ	1	4	4	Ap 77	33
Huck	Huck Blouse (Jean Scorgie)		√	√	Hw	8	4		S/O 87	43, I-6
Huck	Huck for Mary Black	Moes, Dini	√	√	SS&D	16	2	62	Sp 85	52
Huck	Huck Lace Tray Cloth	Fishback, John S.	√	>4	H&C	11	2		Sp 60	62
Huck	Huckaback Lace	Jackson, Marguerite	√	√	H&C	14	2		Sp 63	20
Huck	Huckaback Lace, A Study of Fabric Structure	Needham, Bertha B.	√	>4	H&C	12	3		Su 61	26
Huck	Lacy Apron (Linda Ligon)		√	√	Hw	4	1		J/F 83	41, 81
Huck	Multi-Harness Huck: Learn About the Structure of This Family of Weaves and Design Your Own Variations	Barrett, Clotilde	√	>4	WJ	10	4	40	Sp 86	11
Huck	Name Draft Contest Winners		√	>4	WJ	11	4	44	Sp 87	46
Huck	Plaid Idea Notebook		√	√	Hw	4	5		N/D 83	41
Huck	Roller Towel (Mamie LaGrone)		√	√	Hw	1	2		S-S 80	27, 53
Huck	Sarah Fowler's Book of Drafts, Part 4	North, Lois	√	>4	SS&D	6	4	24	Fa 75	84
Huck	Shaker Towels: A Guild Devotes a Year of Study to Nineteenth Century Textiles (error-corrected WJ v11 n2 86 p68)	Eastlake, Sandy	√	>4	WJ	10	4	40	Sp 86	20
Huck	Silk & Linen Curtains		√	√	H&C	14	1		Wi 63	14
Huck	Three Adventures of a Wedding Dress	Chapin, Doloria	√	√	SS&D	4	3	15	Su 73	51
Huck	Variations on an Overshot Threading	Lermond, Charles	√	√	WJ	12	2	46	Fa 87	25
Huck	Weaver's Notebook: (Mildred Smith)		√	>4	SS&D	10	4	40	Fa 79	103
Huck	Weaving Table Linens	Eychaner, Barbara Smith	√	√	TM			11	J/J 87	52
Huck: 3-Shaft	White-on-White Huck Plaid Cloth (Margaretha Essén-Hedin)		√	√	Hw	4	5		N/D 83	60, 109
Huck: Companion	Shadow Weave Offers an Opportunity for Many Variations	Powell, Marian	√	√	H&C	12	3		Su 61	20
Huck: Corduroy Treadling	Composition and Designing Part 2: Variations on One Threading	Zielinski, S. A.; Robert Leclerc, ed.	√	√	MWL	19			'51–'73	7
Huck: Double Waffle Treadling	Composition and Designing Part 2: Variations on One Threading	Zielinski, S. A.; Robert Leclerc, ed.	√	√	MWL	19			'51–'73	7
Huck: Dropped Tabby Treadling	Composition and Designing Part 2: Variations on One Threading	Zielinski, S. A.; Robert Leclerc, ed.	√	√	MWL	19			'51–'73	7
Huck: Huckaback Lace Treadling	Composition and Designing Part 2: Variations on One Threading	Zielinski, S. A.; Robert Leclerc, ed.	√	√	MWL	19			'51–'73	7
Huck: Huckaback Turned Treadling	Composition and Designing Part 2: Variations on One Threading	Zielinski, S. A.; Robert Leclerc, ed.	√	√	MWL	19			'51–'73	7
Huck Lace	Eight Harness Huck Lace		√	>4	H&C	18	2		Sp 67	18
Huck Lace	Ella Bolster		√	>4	H&C	12	2		Sp 61	26
Huck Lace	Huck Lace from Eva Quinn		√	√	H&C	20	1		Wi 69	34
Huck Lace	Huckaback Lace	Jackson, Marguerite	√	√	H&C	14	2		Sp 63	20
Huck Lace	Huckaback Lace, A Study of Fabric Structure	Needham, Bertha B.	√	>4	H&C	12	3		Su 61	26
Huck, Lace	Lacey and Thin Fabrics		√	√	WJ	2	3	7	Ja 78	4
Huck Lace	Multi-Harness Huck: Learn About the Structure ofThis Family of Weaves and Design Your Own Variations	Barrett, Clotilde	√	>4	WJ	10	4	40	Sp 86	11
Huck Lace	Nubby and Nice Shawl (Roslyn Hahn)		√		Hw	7	5		N/D 86	30
Huck Lace	Swatch #1, Huck Lace for Blouse or Dress (Virginia West)		√	√	Hw	7	5		N/D 86	62, I-6
Huck Lace	Weaving As Drawn In — Classic Style, Part 2	Keasbey, Doramay	√	>4	SS&D	17	2	66	Sp 86	38
Huck Lace	Weaving Towels As a Means of Learning the Basic Four-Shaft Weaves	Barrett, Clotilde	√	√	WJ	8	2	30	Fa 83	11
Huck Lace	Weaving with Ramie		√	>4	WJ	8	2	30	Fa 83	80
Huck Lace	Woven Lace and Lacey Weaves: Huckaback Lace	Zielinski, S. A.; Robert Leclerc, ed.	√	>4	MWL	13			'51–'73	7

SUBJECT	TITLE	AUTHOR	IL	INST	JOUR	VOL	NO	ISS	DATE	PAGE
Huck Lace, Irregular	Woven Lace and Lacey Weaves: Swedish Lace	Zielinski, S. A.; Robert Leclerc, ed.	√	> 4	MWL	13			'51–'73	23
Huck Lace, Turned	Country Lace Cloth (Bryn Pinchin)		√	> 4	Hw	6	4		S/O 85	44, I-6
Huck Lace, Unsymmetrical	Woven Lace and Lacey Weaves: Swedish Lace	Zielinski, S. A.; Robert Leclerc, ed.	√	> 4	MWL	13			'51–'73	23
Huck: Multishaft System	Handloom Weaves: The Classification of Handloom Weaves, The Structural Group, The Grouped-Thread Class, Multi-Harness Huck System	Tidball, Harriet	√	> 4	SCGM		33		57	31
Huck: M's and O's Treadling	Composition and Designing Part 2: Variations on One Threading	Zielinski, S. A.; Robert Leclerc, ed.	√	√	MWL	19			'51–'73	7
Huck: M's and O's, Turned Treadling	Composition and Designing Part 2: Variations on One Threading	Zielinski, S. A.; Robert Leclerc, ed.	√	√	MWL	19			'51–'73	7
Huck: Overshot Treadling	Composition and Designing Part 2: Variations on One Threading	Zielinski, S. A.; Robert Leclerc, ed.	√	√	MWL	19			'51–'73	7
Huck: Shadow	Shadow Weave Offers an Opportunity for Many Variations	Powell, Marian	√	√	H&C	12	3		Su 61	20
Huck: Spot Weave Treadling	Composition and Designing Part 2: Variations on One Threading	Zielinski, S. A.; Robert Leclerc, ed.	√	√	MWL	19			'51–'73	7
Huck: Swivel Effect Treadling	Composition and Designing Part 2: Variations on One Threading	Zielinski, S. A.; Robert Leclerc, ed.	√	√	MWL	19			'51–'73	7
Huck System	Handloom Weaves: The Classification of Handloom Weaves, The Structural Group, The Grouped-Thread Class, Huck System	Tidball, Harriet	√	> 4	SCGM		33		57	30
Huck, Variation	Easy-weave, Soft and Absorbent Towel, An (Mary Ann Geers) (error-corrected Hw v6 n4 85 pI-2)		√	√	Hw	6	3		Su 85	84
Huck, Variation	Purple Haze Sweater Jacket (Mary Kay Stoehr)		√	> 4	Hw	6	1		J/F 85	40, I-13
Huck, Variation	Sachet for a Friend (Jane Patrick)		√	√	Hw	8	4		S/O 87	56, I-12
Huck, Variation	Wedding Dress Fabric (Sharon Condie)		√	√	Hw	4	3		M/J 83	55, 82
Huipils	Back Strap Weaving in Zacualpan Mexico	Cooper, Jane	√	√	SS&D	5	3	19	Su 74	13
Huipils	Guatemala Visited	Atwater, Mary Meigs	√	√	SCGM		15		65	24-36
Huipils	Guatemala Visited	Atwater, Mary Meigs	√		SCGM		15		65	45
Huipils	In Pursuit of the Elusive Huipil	Marks, Copeland	√		H&C	24	4		Au 73	6
Huipils	Weft-Wrap Openwork Techniques in Archaeological and Contemporary Textiles of Mexico	Johnson, Irmgard Weitlaner	√	√	TMJ	4	3		76	63
Huiple	Blue and Gold Huiple		√	√	Hw	1	2		S-S 80	69
Huiple	Red Huiple (Betty Davenport)		√	> 4	Hw	1	2		S-S 80	45, 68
Huiple	White Huiple (Betty Davenport)		√	√	Hw	1	2		S-S 80	45, 68
Humor	Confessions of a Handweaver's Husband	Brody, Eric	√		H&C	26	3		M/J 75	22
Humor: Lizard Coat	Power Fashion, The	Green Larry	√		TM			5	J/J 86	86
Humor: Philately	Tongue in Chic: The Postage Stamps of Isle de Haute Couture (error-corrected TM i9 87 p4)		√		TM			8	D/J 86	82
Humor: Purist Weaver	Peter Collingwood, His Weaves and Weaving: Weavers I Have Known by Peter D. Bunker	Collingwood, Peter; Harriet Tidball, ed.			SCGM		8		63	42
Hungarian Weaving	Hungarian Weaving	Allen, Jane Ingram	√	√	SS&D	10	3	39	Su 79	93
Hungary	Feltmaking in Hungary	Beede, Beth; Jill Garfunkel	√		Fa	13	4		J/A 86	6
Hungary	Zoltán Mihalkó: Hungarian Feltmaker	Beede, Beth; Jill Garfunkel	√	√	SS&D	17	4	68	Fa 86	12
Hydro Extracating	What a Handweaver Can Learn from the Scottish Weaving Industry (error-corrected WJ v2 n1 77 insert for vol. 1)	Barrett, Clotilde	√	√	WJ	1	3	3	Ja 77	11
I Cord	Garter Stitch Ribwarmer	Zimmermann, Elizabeth	√	√	Kn	3	1	5	F-W 86	46
Iceland	Contemporary Icelandic Weaving		√		Hw	8	3		M/J 87	63
Iceland	Fiber Art in Iceland	Hrafnhildur, Schram	√		Fa	9	6		N/D 82	68
Iceland	Glit — An Icelandic Inlay Technique	Heite, Louise B.	√	√	Hw	8	3		M/J 87	64

SUBJECT	TITLE	AUTHOR	IL	INST	JOUR	VOL	NO	ISS	DATE	PAGE
Iceland	High-Whorl Lap Spindle, The	Heite, Louise	√	√	S-O	10	1		Sp 86	36
Iceland	Icelandic Weaving: Saga in Wool	Hákonardóttir, Hildur	√		Hw	8	3		M/J 87	62
Ideas From Industry	Four Shaft Fascination	Gordon, Judith	√	√	Hw	6	1		J/F 85	12
Ideas From Industry	On Analyzing Commercial Fabrics	Gordon, Judith	√	√	Hw	6	2		M/A 85	89
Ideas From Industry	Spots or Stripes?	Gordon, Judith	√	>4	Hw	5	4		S/0 84	36
Ideas From Industry	Suitable Subtleties	Gordon, Judith	√	>4	Hw	5	3		Su 84	22
Ideas From Industry	Tisket, a Tasket, A	Gordon, Judith	√	>4	Hw	5	5		N/D 84	34
Ideas From Industry	Twill Plaid, A	Gordon, Judith	√	>4	Hw	5	2		M/A 84	41
Igolochkoy (Needle Punch)	Connie Lehman: Portable Secrets	Clurman, Irene	√		Fa	12	6		N/D 85	10
Ikat also see Dyes and Dyeing: Resist										
Ikat	Ann S. Epstein	Epstein, Ann S.	√		Fa	13	1		J/F 86	19
Ikat	Basic Ikat	Carlson, Estelle	√	√	Iw	5	3		Su 80	27
Ikat	Brushstrokes of Color	Bohannan, Ronnine	√	√	Hw	5	3		Su 84	56
Ikat	"Common Cord, The": Central Asian Textiles (Exhibit)	Prinzing, Debra	√		Fa	14	3		M/J 87	56
Ikat	Contemporary Satins: Chine and Ikat	Tidball, Harriet	√	√	SCGM		7		62	20
Ikat	Country Morning Table Runner (Patti Ball)		√	√	Hw	6	3		Su 85	82
Ikat	Designs in Sumba Textiles, Local Meanings and Foreign Influences	Adams, Monni	√		TMJ	3	2		De 71	28
Ikat	Evolution of an Artist: Morgan Clifford	Gue, Sandra	√		Fa	14	5		N/D 87	27
Ikat	"Fiber from the Marietta College Crafts National" (Exhibit)	Murray, Megan	√		Fa	11	2		M/A 84	76
Ikat	"Gaudy Ladies" (Exhibit)		√		Fa	8	4		J/A 81	44
Ikat	Handwoven Silk Garments: Ikat Dress	Schreiber, LaVonne	√	√	WJ	3	2	10	Oc 78	30
Ikat	Handwoven Silk Garments: Ikat Kimono	Barnett-Westfall, Lynn	√	√	WJ	3	2	10	Oc 78	30
Ikat	Handwoven Silk Garments: Ikat Shirt	Utzinger, Karen	√	√	WJ	3	2	10	Oc 78	29
Ikat	Ikat	Carlson, Estelle	√		Fa	5	1		J/F 78	41
Ikat	Ikat Notes: Nancy Belfer Talks About Her Recent Work	Belfer, Nancy	√		Fa	9	2		M/A 82	19
Ikat	Ikat Striped Ruana and Skirt	Colton, Mary Rawcliffe	√	√	Hw	5	4		S/0 84	60
Ikat	Ikat-Woven Images	Tacker, Sylvia	√	√	SS&D	18	1	69	Wi 86	68
Ikat	Ikats of Joan Hausrath: A Painterly Approach to Weaving, The	Dunn, Roger T.	√		Fa	8	6		N/D 81	48
Ikat	"Ikats of Orissa" (Exhibit)	De Bone, Mary	√		Fa	11	1		J/F 84	82
Ikat	In and on the Surface: The Tapestries of Judy Branfman	Mattera, Joanne	√		Fa	10	3		M/J 83	22
Ikat	Innovations in Indigo	Wada, Yoshiko Iwamoto	√		Fa	13	5		S/0 86	29
Ikat	"Jayn Thomas" (Exhibit)	Malarcher, Patricia	√		Fa	10	5		S/0 83	81
Ikat	Kasuri: A Japanese Textile	Dusenbury, Mary	√		TMJ	17			78	41
Ikat	Kasuri-Like-Effect Weaving	Akita, Mariko Olivia	√	√	WJ	6	2	22	Fa 81	18
Ikat	Keeping Tradition Alive	Wilcox, Don	√		Fa	14	1		J/F 87	44
Ikat	Learning the Ropes: Abaca	Coffman, Charlotte	√	√	S-O	7	4		Wi 83	40
Ikat	Mudmee: The Ikat Tradition in Thailand	McCauley, Susan L.	√		Fa	10	5		S/0 83	25
Ikat	Notes on Ikat Weaving	Schira, Cynthia	√	√	H&C	24	2		M/A 73	6
Ikat	Profile of a Thai Weaver	McCauley, Susan L.	√		Fa	10	5		S/0 83	26
Ikat	Revival of Ikat	Rushfelt, Joy M.	√	√	H&C	19	2		Sp 68	14
Ikat	Selected Batak Textiles: Technique and Function	Gittinger, Mattiebelle S.	√		TMJ	4	2		75	13
Ikat	Silk Production in Kohn Kaen	Marston, Ena			SS&D	7	3	27	Su 76	30
Ikat	Space Dyeing with Fiber-Reactive Dyes	Knutson, Linda	√	√	WJ	8	1	29	Su 83	89
Ikat	Stepping Out	Ridgeway, Terese	√		SS&D	18	1	69	Wi 86	82
Ikat	"Susan Goldin: Windows" (Exhibit)	Malarcher, Patricia	√		Fa	9	3		M/J 82	76
Ikat	Symbolic or Sacred? A Personal View	Lockwood, Diana W.	√	>4	WJ	9	3	35	Wi 85	45
Ikat	Table Dressing and Bedcovers		√		Fa	8	3		M/J 81	43

389

SUBJECT	TITLE	AUTHOR	IL	INST	JOUR	VOL	NO	ISS	DATE	PAGE
Ikat	Tapestry Effects in Boundweave Rugs	Ziebarth, Charlotte Molcar	√	√	Iw	5	1		Wi 79	23
Ikat	Textile Arts of India	Bernier, Ronald M.	√		WJ	2	1	5	Jy 77	31
Ikat	Traditional Ikats		√		H&C	24	3		M/J 73	38
Ikat	Variegated Ikat Spun Scarf		√	√	S-O	5			81	61
Ikat	Virginia Davis	Malarcher, Patricia	√		Fa	10	5		S/O 83	14
Ikat	Weavers of Bali	Hannon, Farrell	√		SS&D	18	4	72	Fa 87	46
Ikat	Wendy Shah: Subtle Rhythms	Mattera, Joanne	√		Fa	7	5		S/O 80	21
Ikat: Double	Additions to the Indonesian Collection	Gittinger, Mattiebelle S.	√		TMJ	4	3		76	43
Ikat: Double	Patolu and Its Techniques	De Bone, Mary Golden	√	√	TMJ	4	3		76	49
Ikat, Mock	Fiber Reactive Dyes	Ridgeway, Teresa	√	√	SS&D	13	1	49	Wi 81	34
Ikat: Pulled-Warp	New Technique for Pulled-Warp Ikat, A	Wu, Han-Lien	√	√	Iw	5	3		Su 80	29
Ikat: Spinning	Ikat-Spun Kimono, An	Lamb, Sara	√	√	S-O	8	4		Wi 84	16
Ikat: Technique	Balinese Ikat	Hannon, Farrell	√	√	WJ	5	1	17	Su 80	49
Ikat: Technique	Fullus: Ikat Blankets of Tarabuco, Bolivia	Meisch, Lynn A.	√	√	WJ	10	1	37	Su 85	54
Ikat, Velvet	Velvet Ikat	Stack, Lotus	√	>4	WJ	11	4	44	Sp 87	36
Ikat: Warp	Folk Textiles of Latin America	Kelemen, Pál	√		TMJ	1	4		De 65	2
Ikat, Warp	Gail McDonnell	Tacker, Sylvia	√		Fa	14	3		M/J 87	23
Ikat: Warp	Sumbanese Ikat	Hannon, Farrell	√	√	WJ	8	1	29	Su 83	38
Ikat: Warp	Tying Warp Ikat on the Loom	Hannon, Farrell	√	√	WJ	8	1	29	Su 83	41
Ikat, Warp	Velvet Ikat	Stack, Lotus	√	>4	WJ	11	4	44	Sp 87	36
Ikat: Warp	Warp Ikat	Reiss, Zenaide	√	√	SS&D	12	4	48	Fa 81	4
Ikat: Warp	Warp Ikat: Part 2: Quick Design Effects	Reiss, Zenaide	√	√	SS&D	13	1	49	Wi 81	16
Ikat: Weft, Technique	Weft Ikat: An Introduction	Burnlees, Dee	√	√	WJ	10	1	37	Su 85	62
Ikat, Weft: Technique	Weft Ikat for Rugs	Van Gelder, Lydia	√	√	WJ	5	4	20	Sp 81	31
Illustration	Francis Butler: "I Used to Be an Artist but I Couldn't Sit Still That Long"	Butler, Francis	√		Fa	5	5		S/O 78	40
Illustration: Fiber	Gloria Marconi: A Commercial Illustrator Mixes Her Media	Hecker, Carolyn A.	√		Fa	6	2		M/A 79	31
Illustration: Fiber	Jaki Ernst "Fibre Graphics and Soft Sculpture" (Exhibit)	Gilsenan, Nancy	√		Fa	7	6		N/D 80	69
Illustration: Fiber	Success of Susan Kittredge, The	Park, Betty	√		Fa	6	2		M/A 79	28
Images of the Southwest	Theme Issue		√		WJ	11	1	41	Su 86	
Importing	Consider Importing	Ziemke, Dene			SS&D	4	1	13	Wi 72	41
In-Lay	Kente: The Status Cloth of Ghana	Conklin, Sharon L.	√	√	SS&D	8	1	29	WI 76	18
In-Lay	Two-harness Weaves	Clark, Marion L.	√	√	H&C	14	2		Sp 63	17
Incentives	Things That Count	Ligon, Linda	√		Hw	8	4		S/O 87	99
Incidentals	Contemporary Approach to Traditional Weaves: Crackle Without Incidentals	Zielinski, S. A.; Robert Leclerc, ed.	√	√	MWL	8			'51–'73	30
Index to Drafts	Handweaver's Instruction Manual: Index of Drafts	Tidball, Harriet C. nee Douglas			SCGM		34		49	33
Indexes: Ciba Review	Ciba Review Index 1937–1974				Fa	9	6		N/D 82	52
Indexes: Complex Weavers	Complex Weavers Index Dec. 1979–Sept. 1983				CW	5	2	14	Ja 84	20
Indexes: Fiberarts	Fiberarts Index: 1976-1980				Fa	8	1		J/F 81	45
Indexes: Fiberarts	Fiberarts Index, 1983–1984		√		Fa	12	1		J/F 85	44
Indexes: Handweaver & Craftsman	H & C Index, 1950-1953, Vols. 1-5				H&C	5	3		Su 54	60
Indexes: Handweaver & Craftsman	H & C Index, 1954, Vol. 5				H&C	5	4		Fa 54	63
Indexes: Handweaver & Craftsman	H & C Index, 1955, Vol. 6				H&C	6	4		Fa 55	63
Indexes: Handweaver & Craftsman	H & C Index, 1956, Vol. 7				H&C	7	4		Fa 56	62
Indexes: Handweaver & Craftsman	H & C Index, 1957, Vol. 8				H&C	8	4		Fa 57	2
Indexes: Handweaver & Craftsman	H & C Index, 1958, Vol. 9				H&C	9	4		Fa 58	63

SUBJECT	TITLE	AUTHOR	IL	INST	JOUR	VOL	NO	ISS	DATE	PAGE
Indexes: Handweaver & Craftsman	H & C Index, 1959, Vol. 10				H&C	10	4		Fa 59	62
Indexes: Handweaver & Craftsman	H & C Index, 1960, Vol. 11				H&C	11	4		Fa 60	63
Indexes: Handweaver & Craftsman	H & C Index, 1961, Vol. 12				H&C	12	4		Fa 61	4
Indexes: Handweaver & Craftsman	H & C Index, 1962, Vol. 13				H&C	13	4		Fa 62	2
Indexes: Handweaver & Craftsman	H & C Index, 1963, Vol. 14				H&C	14	4		Fa 63	47
Indexes: Handweaver & Craftsman	H & C Index, 1964, Vol. 15				H&C	15	4		Fa 64	47
Indexes: Handweaver & Craftsman	H & C Index, 1965, Vol. 16				H&C	16	4		Fa 65	47
Indexes: Handweaver & Craftsman	H & C Index, 1966, Vol. 17				H&C	17	4		Fa 66	47
Indexes: Handweaver & Craftsman	H & C Index, 1967, Vol. 18				H&C	18	4		Fa 67	45
Indexes: Handweaver & Craftsman	H & C Index, 1968, Vol. 19				H&C	19	4		Fa 68	46
Indexes: Handweaver & Craftsman	H & C Index, 1969, Vol. 20				H&C	20	4		Fa 69	46
Indexes: Handweaver & Craftsman	H & C Index, 1970, Vol. 21				H&C	21	4		Fa 70	46
Indexes: Handweaver & Craftsman	H & C Index, 1972, Vol. 24				H&C	24	2		M/A 73	38
Indexes: Handwoven	Handwoven Index, 1979-1984				Hw	6	1		J/F 85	43
Indexes: Handwoven	Handwoven Index, 1982, Vol. III, Nos. 1-5				Hw	4	1		J/F 83	50A
Indexes: Handwoven	Handwoven Index, 1983, Vol. IV, Nos. 1-5				Hw	5	1		J/F 84	39
Indexes: Handwoven	Handwoven Index 1985, Vol. VI, Nos. 1-5				Hw	7	1		J/F 86	88
Indexes: Handwoven	Handwoven Index: 1986, Vol. VII, Nos. 1-5				Hw	8	1		J/F 87	54A
Indexes: Interweave	Interweave Index, 1975-1977, Vols. I-2				Iw	2	4		Su 77	32
Indexes: Interweave	Interweave Index, 1977-1978, Vol. III, Nos. 1—4				Iw	3	4		Su 78	47
Indexes: Interweave	Interweave Index, 1979, Vol. IV, Nos. 1-4				Iw	4	4		Fa 79	77
Indexes: Interweave	Interweave Index, 1980, Vol. V, Nos. 1—4				Iw	5	4		Fa 80	79
Indexes: Knitters	Knitters Index: Issues 1-6				Kn	3	3	7	Su 87	30
Indexes: Master Weaver Library	Weaving in the Past, Complete Index with Reference: Index	Zielinski, S. A.; Robert Leclerc, ed.			MWL	21 22			'51–'73	101
Indexes: Prairie Wool Companion	Prairie Wool Companion Index, Issues 1-4, Nov. 1981 – Oct. 1982	Black, Sue			PWC			4	Ja 83	72
Indexes: Prairie Wool Companion	Prairie Wool Companion Index, Issues 5-6, Spring and Summer 1983	Black, Sue			PWC	3	1	7		67
Indexes: Shuttle, Spindle & Dyepot	SS&D Index 1975, Issues 22-25				SS&D	7	1	25	Wi 75	81
Indexes: Shuttle, Spindle & Dyepot	SS&D Index 1976, Issues 26-29	Glowacki, Dorothy; Betty Shannon			SS&D	8	2	30	Sp 77	89
Indexes: Shuttle, Spindle & Dyepot	SS&D Index 1977, Issues 30-33	Glowacki, Dorothy; Betty Shannon			SS&D	9	2	34	Sp 78	72
Indexes: Shuttle, Spindle & Dyepot	SS&D Index 1978, Issues 34-37	Glowacki, Dorothy; Betty Shannon			SS&D	10	2	38	Sp 79	91
Indexes: Shuttle, Spindle & Dyepot	SS&D Index 1979, Issues 38-4l	Shannon, Betty; Dorothy Glowacki			SS&D	11	2	42	Sp 80	97
Indexes: Shuttle, Spindle & Dyepot	SS&D Index 1980, Issues 42-45	Glowacki, Dorothy; Betty Shannon			SS&D	12	2	46	Sp 81	59
Indexes: Shuttle, Spindle & Dyepot	SS&D Index 1981, Issues 46-49	Glowacki, Dorothy; Betty Shannon			SS&D	13	2	50	Sp 82	50
Indexes: Shuttle, Spindle & Dyepot	SS&D Index 1982, Issues 50-53	Glowacki, Dorothy; Betty Shannon			SS&D	14	2	54	Sp 83	26

SUBJECT	TITLE	AUTHOR	IL	INST	JOUR	VOL	NO	ISS	DATE	PAGE
Indexes: Shuttle, Spindle & Dyepot	SS&D Index 1983, Issues 54-57	Glowacki, Dorothy; Betty Shannon			SS&D	15	2	58	Sp 84	69
Indexes: Shuttle, Spindle & Dyepot	SS&D Index 1984, Issues 58-61	Glowacki, Dorothy; Betty Shannon			SS&D	16	2	62	Sp 85	74
Indexes: Shuttle, Spindle & Dyepot	SS&D Index 1985, Issues 62-65	Glowacki, Dorothy; Betty Shannon			SS&D	17	2	66	Sp 86	69
Indexes: Shuttle, Spindle & Dyepot	SS&D Index 1986, Issues 66-69	Glowacki, Dorothy; Betty Shannon			SS&D	18	2	70	Sp 87	35
Indexes: Spin-Off	Spin-Off Index, 1981, Vol. 5				S-O	6	4		82	8
Indexes: Spin-Off	Spin-Off Index, 1983, Vol. 7				S-O	8	1		Sp 84	54
Indexes: Spin-Off	Spin-Off Index, 1984, Vol. 8				S-O	9	1		Sp 85	46
Indexes: Spin-Off	Spin-Off Index, 1985, Vol. 9				S-O	10	1		Sp 86	49
Indexes: Spin-Off	Spin-Off Index 1986, Vol. 10, 1986				S-O	11	1		Sp 87	51
Indexes: The Textile Museum Journal	Textile Museum Journal Index, 1962-1967				TMJ	2	2		De 67	46
Indexes: The Weaver's Journal	Weaver's Journal Index and Errata Insert for Vol. I, July 1976—April 1977, The				WJ	2	1	5	Jy 77	30
Indexes: The Weaver's Journal	Weaver's Journal Index and Errata, The. Vol.V, Issues 17-20, July 1980-April 1981				WJ	6	1	21	Su 81	
Indexes: The Weaver's Journal	Weaver's Journal Index and Errata, The: Vol. VI, Issues 2I-24, July 1981-April 1982				WJ	7	1	25	Su 82	36a
Indexes: The Weaver's Journal	Weaver's Journal Index and Errata, The. Vol. VII, Issues 25-28, July 1982-April I983				WJ	8	1	29	Su 83	48
Indexes: The Weaver's Journal	Weaver's Journal Index and Errata, The. Vol. VIII, Issues 29-32, July 1983–April 1984				WJ	9	1	33	Su 84	65
Indexes: The Weaver's Journal	Weaver's Journal Index, The. Vol.IX, Issues 33-36, Summer 1984–Spring 1985				WJ	10	1	37	Su 85	74
Indexes: The Weaver's Journal	Weaver's Journal Index, The. Vol. X, Issues 37-40, July I985–April I986				WJ	11	1	41	Su 86	69
Indexes: The Weaver's Journal	Weaver's Journal Index, The. Vol. XI, Issues 4I-44, Summer 1986–Spring 1987				WJ	12	1	45	Su 87	62
Indexes: The Weaver's Journal	Weaver's Journal Index, Vol. IV, July 1979-April 1980, The				WJ	5	1	17	Su 80	28c
Indexes: Threads Magazine	Threads Magazine Index, Issues 1-6, O/N '85-A/S '86				TM			7	O/N 86	88
Indexes: Threads Magazine	Threads Magazine Index, Issues 7-12, O/N '86-A/S '87				TM			13	O/N 87	88
Indexing, Weaving Articles	Suggestions for Indexing	Jackson, Marguerite	√		H&C	14	4		Fa 63	23
India	All That Glitters: Shisha by Machine	Fanning, Robbie	√	√	TM			1	O/N 85	63
India	Banares Brocade	DuBois, Emily	√	> 4	AT	3			My 85	209
India	Bandhana (Tie Dye)	Westfall, Carol D.; Dipti Desai	√		AT	8			De 87	19
India	Bhotiya Woolens from India	Willis, Elizabeth Bayley	√		H&C	5	2		Sp 54	4
India	"Camel Belts from the Great Indian Desert" (Exhibit)	Janeiro, Jan	√		Fa	10	6		N/D 83	75
India	Costumes of Royal India	Levine, Betsy	√		TM			7	O/N 86	64
India	"Costumes of Royal India, The" (Exhibit)	McCann, Kathleen	√		Fa	13	1		J/F 86	58
India	Courtyard, Bazaar, Temple: Traditions in Indian Textile Expression		√		SS&D	13	4	52	Fa 82	44
India	Designer-Weaver in India, A	Sethna, Nelly H.	√		H&C	17	2		Sp 66	18
India	Dhabla Weaving in India	De Bone, Mary	√	√	SS&D	8	3	31	Su 77	9
India	Fabric Painting in India: The Kalamkaris of J. Gurappa Chetty	Lintault, M. Joan	√		Fa	9	1		J/F 82	64
India	Feltmaking in India: A Remnant of the Past	MacDougal, Marleah Drexler	√		Fa	6	6		N/D 79	10
India	Gujarati Embroidery	Westfall, Carol D.; Dipti Desai	√		AT	8			De 87	29

SUBJECT	TITLE	AUTHOR	IL	INST	JOUR	VOL	NO	ISS	DATE	PAGE
India	Handweaving in India Today	King, Edith B.; Earl L. King	√		H&C	7	4		Fa 56	10
India	"Ikats of Orissa" (Exhibit)	De Bone, Mary	√		Fa	11	1		J/F 84	82
India	Kantha	Westfall, Carol D.; Dipti Desai	√	√	AT	7			Ju 87	161
India	Kantha Cloths of Bengal: The Sari Transformed	Gupta, Asha	√		Fa	9	6		N/D 82	19
India	Kashmiri to Paisley: Evolution of the Paisley shawl	Larson-Fleming, Susan	√		WJ	11	3	43	Wi 87	37
India	Learning to See Pattern	Morrison, Skye	√	√	TM			2	D/J 85	44
India	"Master Dyers to the World" (Exhibit)	Sider, Sandra	√		Fa	11	1		J/F 84	83
India	Meaning of Folk Art in Rabari Life: A Closer Look at Mirrored Embroidery, The	Frater, Judy	√		TMJ	4	2		75	47
India	Modern Charkha, The		√		H&C	9	3		Su 58	23
India	Nek Chand's Fantasy Garden	Ziek, Bhakti	√		TM			3	F/M 86	88
India	Patolu and Its Techniques	De Bone, Mary Golden	√	√	TMJ	4	3		76	49
India	Phulkari	Westfall, Carol D.; Dipti Desai	√		AT	6			De 86	85
India	Preliminary Report on a Group of Important Mughal Textiles, A	Smart, Ellen S.	√		TMJ	25			86	5
India	Rabari Lodi: Creating a Fabric Through Social Alliance, The	Frater, Judy	√	√	WJ	10	1	37	Su 85	28
India	Rib Weaves from India, A Rich Source of Inspiration	Harvey, Virginia Isham	√	> 4	H&C	16	4		Fa 65	21
India	Scent of Flowers, Kishmir Shawls in the Collection of The Textile Museum, The	Mikosch, Elisabeth	√		TMJ	24			85	7
India	Second Type of Mughal Sash, A	Sonday, Milton; Nobuko Kajitani	√		TMJ	3	2		De 71	6
India	Sewing with Silk	Stoyer, Janet	√	√	TM			4	A/M 86	35
India	Spinning with Gandhi	Grant, Susan	√		S-O	2			78	15
India	St. Mary's Weavers		√		H&C	10	1		Wi 59	30
India	Textile Arts of India	Bernier, Ronald M.	√		WJ	2	1	5	Jy 77	31
India	Textiles from India		√		H&C	6	3		Su 55	9
India	Tie Dyeing in India (error-corrected H&C v14 n2 63 p46)	Arness, Judith Russell	√	√	H&C	14	1		Wi 63	6
India	Web of India, The	Malarcher, Patricia	√		SS&D	13	2	50	Sp 82	38
India	Weft Twining: History, The Nagas of Northeast India	Harvey, Virginia I.; Harriet Tidball	√		SCGM		28		69	11
Indians see Native Americans										
Indigo	African Artist in a Dying Trade, An	Kessler, Cristina	√	√	Fa	11	6		N/D 84	51
Indigo	Control Dyeing with Indigo	Taggart, Barbara		√	SS&D	5	3	19	Su 74	53
Indigo	Indigo	Weigle, Palmy	√	√	SS&D	8	3	31	Su 77	67
Indigo	Indigo, Discovery of Plants and Experiments in Dyeing	Gerber, Willi; Fred Gerber	√	√	H&C	19	4		Fa 68	4
Indigo	Indigo, Discovery of Plants and Experiments in Dyeing	Gerber, Willi; Fred Gerber	√	√	H&C	26	3		M/J 75	11
Indigo	Indigo Dyeing			√	TM			3	F/M 86	8
Indigo	Indigo Miscellany, An		√		Fa	13	5		S/O 86	25
Indigo	Indigo—The all Time Favorite Blue	Bliss, Anne	√	√	Hw	2	3		My 81	60
Indigo	Innovations in Indigo	Wada, Yoshiko Iwamoto	√		Fa	13	5		S/O 86	29
Indigo	Japanese Country Textiles (Exhibit)	Rowley, Kathleen	√		Fa	13	5		S/O 86	49
Indigo	Personal Exploration of Indigo, A	Miller, Dorothy	√	√	Fa	13	5		S/O 86	32
Indigo	Viditz-Ward Dyes in Evergreen; Students Still Blue	Ritchey, Janet	√		Iw	2	4		Su 77	13
Indigo	Wealth of Fiber: Nigeria's Adire Cloth, A	Ulrich, George	√		Fa	13	5		S/O 86	39
Indigo	Why Bother with Natural Dyeing?	Bulbach, Stanley	√	√	TM			5	J/J 86	32
Indigo: Blue-Pot Recipe	Fifty Years As a Coverlet Weaver	Bright, Harriett H.	√	√	WJ	6	2	22	Fa 81	54

SUBJECT	TITLE	AUTHOR	IL	INST	JOUR	VOL	NO	ISS	DATE	PAGE
Indigo: Crocking	Indigo Dyeing and the Problems of Crocking	Pendergrass, Mary	√	√	WJ	4	3	15	Ja 80	30
Indigo Dyeing	Miyako Jofu	Miller, Dorothy	√	√	AT	7			Ju 87	85
Indigo Dyers	Innovations in Indigo	Wada, Yoshiko Iwamoto	√		Fa	13	5		S/O 86	29
Indonesia	Additions to the Indonesian Collection	Gittinger, Mattiebelle S.	√		TMJ	4	3	76		43
Indonesia	Conversations with a Batik Master	Gittinger, Mattiebelle	√		TMJ	18		79		25
Indonesia	Designs in Sumba Textiles, Local Meanings and Foreign Influences	Adams, Monni	√		TMJ	3	2	De 71		28
Indonesia	Indonesian Textiles at The Textile Museum	Adams, Monni	√		TMJ	3	1	De 70		41
Indonesia	Selected Batak Textiles: Technique and Function	Gittinger, Mattiebelle S.	√		TMJ	4	2	75		13
Indonesia	Tapestries from Indonesia	Hitchcock, Michael	√	√	WJ	12	1	45	Su 87	55
Indonesia	"Textile Traditions of Indonesia" (Exhibit)	Dyer, Carolyn	√		Fa	5	1		J/F 78	15
Indonesia	Van Zuylen Batik, Pekalongan, Central Java (1890-1946)	de Raadt-Apell, M. J.	√		TMJ	19 20		80,81		75
Industry: Brocade Weaving	Banares Brocade	DuBois, Emily	√	>4	AT	3			My 85	209
Industry: Carpet, Anatolian	Carpet-Makers of Western Anatolia, 1750–1914, The	Quataert, Donald			TMJ	25		86		25
Industry: Cotton, (Britian)	Note on the Diffusion of the Automatic Loom Within the British Cotton Industry, A	Pourdeyhimi, B.; K. C. Jackson	√		AT	6			De 86	101
Industry: Fashion	Body as Canvas, The	Koda, Harold	√		TM			8	D/J 86	56
Industry: Hatting	Here Are the Last of the Hatters	Shufro, Cathy			TM			2	D/J 85	14
Industry: Loom Building	E.E. Gilmore, Loom Builder and Weaver	Watson, Aleta	√		H&C	23	5		S/O 72	24
Industry: Loom Building	LeClerc Loom Corporation, A Story of Three Generations, The	Holland, Nina	√		H&C	24	3		M/J 73	20
Industry: Sewing	Shirtmaker from a Small Planet	Coffin, David Page			TM			9	F/M 87	16
Industry: Sheep, Colonial America	Fleecing of the American Colonies, The	Liebler, Barbara	√		Iw	2	1	Fa 76		21
Industry: Silk	Silk City: Paterson, New Jersey	Malarcher, Patricia	√		Fa	13	1		J/F 86	31
Industry: Silk	Silk Makers, The		√		TM			4	A/M 86	14
Industry: Silk	Silk Production in Kohn Kaen	Marston, Ena			SS&D	7	3	27	Su 76	30
Industry: Silk	Silk Production of Lullingstone and Whitchurch, The	Rubbert, Toni	√		Hw	3	4		Se 82	27
Industry: Spinning, Littlewood Mill	Green Baize for Independence Hall from Penland Looms	Ford, Howard C.	√		H&C	7	2		Sp 56	14
Industry: Spinning/Weaving, Korea	Cheju Weavers, A New Industry Arises on a Korean Island	Ford, Howard C.	√		H&C	12	3		Su 61	11
Industry: Straw Hat	Peruvian Straw Hat: Documenting a Declining Industry, The	Zimmer, Roni	√		Fa	12	3		M/J 85	39
Industry: Textile	Behind the Scenes: A Fabric Printer	Lancaster, Zoe Woodruff	√		Fa	13	3		M/J 86	44
Industry: Textile	Behind the Scenes: A Textile Mill	Goodman, Deborah Lerme	√		Fa	13	3		M/J 86	40
Industry: Textile	Craftsmen in Industry				H&C	16	1		Wi 65	8
Industry: Textile	Denim Production: The Making of an American Staple	Rudich, Sally	√		Fa	13	5		S/O 86	11
Industry: Textile	Handweavers 1800—1840	Wilson, Kax	√		Iw	5	2		Sp 80	50
Industry: Textile	Handweaving for Industry: The Program of the Rhode Island School of Design	Heath, Howard	√		H&C	2	4		Fa 51	14
Industry, Textile	Handweaving in the Textile Industry	Hausner, Walter A.			H&C	9	1		Wi 57	28
Industry: Textile	I Was a Handweaver for the Textile Industry	Tergis, Marilyn	√	√	H&C	23	5		S/O 72	36
Industry: Textile	In the Gobelin Tradition: The Drouin Atelier	Gregg, Dorothy	√		SS&D	10	1	37	Wi 78	28
Industry: Textile	Jack Lenor Larsen	Znamierowski, Nell	√		H&C	22	3		Su 71	6
Industry: Textile	Jeans: The Inside Story	Goodman, Deborah Lerme	√	√	TM			3	F/M 86	27
Industry: Textile	Lee Company	Rudich, Sally	√		Fa	13	5		S/O 86	13
Industry: Textile	Levi Strauss & Co.	Scarborough, Jessica	√		Fa	13	5		S/O 86	17
Industry: Textile	Made by Machine: Textiles for the Eighties	Harris, Patricia; David Lyon	√		Fa	12	5		S/O 85	34

SUBJECT	TITLE	AUTHOR	IL	INST	JOUR	VOL	NO	ISS	DATE	PAGE
Industry: Textile	Michael Belangie Sees Common Problems for Hand and Power Weavers	Bryan, Dorothy			H&C	2	4		Fa 51	46
Industry: Textile	Mill Girls of 'Spindle City,' The	Rubbert, Toni Condon	√		S-O	10	1		Sp 86	16
Industry: Textile	Note on the Diffusion of the Automatic Loom Within the British Cotton Industry, A	Pourdeyhimi, B.; K. C. Jackson	√		AT	6			De 86	101
Industry: Textile	Opportunities for Handweavers in the Textile Industry		√		H&C	3	4		Fa 52	42
Industry: Textile	Opportunities for Handweavers in the Textile Industry				H&C	10	3		Su 59	13
Industry: Textile	OshKosh B'Gosh	Rudich, Sally	√		Fa	13	5		S/O 86	16
Industry: Textile	Slater Mill Historic Site, The	Rubbert, Toni Condon	√		S-O	8	2		Su 84	42
Industry: Textile	"Spindle City," Lowell, Massachusetts	Scarborough, Jessica	√		Fa	9	2		M/A 82	53
Industry: Textile	Technological Change and the Textile Industry: The Impact of the Industrial Revolution and the Computer Revolution	Thieme, Otto Charles	√		Fa	11	1		J/F 84	54
Industry: Textile	Tour Through Merrimack Valley Textile Museum, A	Britton, Nancy	√		Fa	9	2		M/A 82	52
Industry: Textile	Visit to a New Hampshire Mill				H&C	20	1		Wi 69	33
Industry: Textile	Weaving Along Sugar River	Adams, Eleanor	√		H&C	1	2		Su 50	28
Industry: Textile	Welsh Wool Yarn Factory Hires Disabled Veterans	Hetherington, E.	√		SS&D	5	1	17	Wi 73	28
Industry: Textile	What Ails the Apparel Industry?	Cannarella, Deborah			TM			1	O/N 85	16
Industry: Textile	William Morris, A Twentieth Century View of His Woven Textiles	Morris, Barbara J.	√		H&C	12	2		Sp 61	6
Industry: Textile	Wool from the Welsh Valleys	Rowe, Dilys	√		H&C	10	2		Sp 59	30
Industry: Textile	Working As a Handweaver; Some Reflections and Techniques	Bradley, Ann			SS&D	5	2	18	Sp 74	61
Industry: Textile	Woven Wood, Speciality of Robert Webb		√		H&C	16	2		Sp 65	19
Industry: Textile	Wrangler	Rudich, Sally	√		Fa	13	5		S/O 86	12
Industry: Textile, Brocade	Inside the Hangchow Brocade Factory: The Art and Craft of Mass Production	Drower, Sara	√		Fa	6	1		J/F 79	78
Industry: Textile, Design Management	Colour, Texture, Ornament, Line: A Question for Managers—Do You Know How Your Designers Think?	Willock, Jack			AT	4			De 85	97
Industry: Textile, Handlooms	Contemporary Fabrics from an Australia Handweaving Mill	Daniel, Robert	√		H&C	16	1		Wi 65	18
Industry: Textile, Ireland	Irish Weaving	Clement, Doris; Ted Clement	√		H&C	21	2		Sp 70	4
Industry: Textile, Jacquard Coverlets	Art of Indiana Coverlets, The	Gilfoy, Peggy S.	√		AT	2			De 84	69
Industry: Textile, Jacquard Coverlets	Ohio's Woven Coverlets: Textile Industry in a Rural Economy	Cunningham, Patricia A.	√		AT	2			De 84	165
Industry: Textile, Spinning	Bridging the Gap — Between Large Commercial Mills and Individual Handspinners		√		S-O	5			81	27
Industry: Weaving	Obi: The Textile Art of Nishijin	Donaldson, R. Alan	√		AT	1			De 83	115
Industry: Weaving, Cotton	Technical Progress and the Evolution of Wage Arrangements in the British Cotton Weaving Industry	Jackson, K. C.; B. Pourdeyhimi	√		AT	7			Ju 87	61
Industry: Weaving, Flow Chart	What a Handweaver Can Learn from the Scottish Weaving Industry (error-corrected WJ v2 n1 77 errata sheet for vol. 1)	Barrett, Clotilde	√	√	WJ	1	3	3	Ja 77	11
Industry: Wool	Appeal from the American Sheep Farmers, An	Painter, Ingrid			S-O	9	2		Su 85	7
Industry: Wool	Baa, Baa, Black Sheep, Have You Any Wool?	Bulbach, Stanley	√		S-O	9	2		Su 85	44
Industry: Wool	Emergence of a Specialty Wool Industry in the U.S., The	Donnelly, Robert			S-O	9	4		Wi 85	18
Industry: Wool	Mohair: A Multimillion Dollar Industry for Australia	Gray, Isabel			S-O	8	4		Wi 84	47
Industry: Wool	Visit to a New Hampshire Mill				H&C	20	1		Wi 69	33

SUBJECT	TITLE	AUTHOR	IL	INST	JOUR	VOL	NO	ISS	DATE	PAGE
Industry: Wool	Weaving in Wales	Kemp, Gwendoline	√		H&C	6	2		Sp 55	24
Industry: Wool	Wool as a Cottage Industry	Simmons, Paula	√		S-O	9	2		Su 85	42
Industry: Wool	Wool Forum: Growing and Working	Parker, Ron			S-O	11	2		Su 87	18
Industry: Wool	Wool Forum: Producers and Consumers vs Bureaucracy	Parker, Ron; Teresa Parker			S-O	10	4		Si 86	7
Industry: Wool	Wool—Most Versatile of Fibers, Part 1	Kiessling, Robert H.	√		H&C	2	3		Su 51	13
Industry: Wool	Wool—Most Versatile of Fibers, Part 2	Kiessling, Robert H.	√		H&C	2	4		Fa 51	25
Industry: Wool	Wool on a Small Scale: A Large Success	de la Cruz, Catherine Jacinta			S-O	9	4		Wi 85	21
Industry, Wool	Wool — That Wonderful Natural Fiber	Derr, Mary L.	√	√	WJ	2	2	6	Oc 77	2
Industry: Wool	Woolens and Tweeds: From Fleece to Woolen Yarn: Machine Processing	Tidball, Harriet	√		SCGM		4		61	11
Industry: Wool Production	Fuzzy Politics of Wool, The	Parker, Ron	√		TM			13	O/N 87	20
Industry: Workshops, Batik	Van Zuylen Batik, Pekalongan, Central Java (1890-1946)	de Raadt-Apell, M. J.	√		TMJ	19 20			80,81	75
Industry: Workshops, Felt Making	Felt-making Craftsmen of the Anatolian and Iranian Plateaux	Gervers, Michael; Veronika Gervers	√	√	TMJ	4	1		De 74	14
Industry: Yarn	U.S. Students Visit Danish Yarn Company				H&C	19	4		Fa 68	34
Industry/Artist: Finland	Artist and Industry — A Cooperative Effort		√		Hw	8	3		M/J 87	71
Ingrain Structure	Bolivian Highland Weaving, Part 1	Cason, Marjorie; Adele Cahlander	√		SS&D	6	2	22	Sp 75	4
Inkle Weaving see Band Weaving										
Inlay	Art and Tradition of Akwete Weaving, The	Lambrecht, Dora J.	√		SS&D	9	2	34	Sp 78	33
Inlay	Beyond the Fringe	Wertenberger, Kathryn	√	> 4	Hw	2	5		No 81	27
Inlay	Canvas Weave Elegance	Herring, Connie	√	> 4	PWC	4	1	11		23
Inlay	Contemporary Satins: Pick-Up and Inlay Damask	Tidball, Harriet	√	√	SCGM		7		62	16
Inlay	Daisy Dog Fur Coat (Betty Beard)		√	√	Hw	3	2		Mr 82	62, 87
Inlay	Decorative Weft on a Plain Weave Ground, Two Shaft Inlay and Brocade		√	√	WJ	5	4	20	Sp 81	15
Inlay	Design for a Lunch Cloth in Three Techniques	Redfield, Gail M.	√	√	H&C	19	3		Su 68	15
Inlay	Designed for Narrow Looms: A Summer Shirt Inspired by the Macedonian Chemise	Temple, Mary	√	√	WJ	10	1	37	Su 85	46
Inlay	Dunkagäng Ideas		√		Hw	7	2		M/A 86	44
Inlay	Dunkagäng, the Stuff of Hearts and Flowers	Alderman, Sharon	√	√	Hw	7	2		M/A 86	41
Inlay	Easy, Easier, Easiest Inlay		√	√	Hw	7	2		M/A 86	70
Inlay	Enchanted Vine Window Curtain (Carol Strickler)		√	√	Hw	3	1		Ja 82	38, 87
Inlay	Finnish Lace: a Leno Variation	Egen, Su	√	√	Hw	7	2		M/A 86	49
Inlay	Finnish Method of Weaving Transparent Inlay, A	Gray, Herbi	√	√	SS&D	17	1	65	Wi 85	14
Inlay	Flower Curtain	Xenakis, Athanasios David	√	√	PWC	4	1	11		32
Inlay	Four-Shaft Unbalanced Twill Braided Ribbon Inlay on Plain Weave Ground	Xenakis, Athanasios David	√	√	PWC	4	1	11		27
Inlay	Freedom of Laid-in Design, The	Neher, Evelyn	√	√	H&C	3	3		Su 52	18
Inlay	Gang: Technical and Conceptual Applications to Loom Controlled Weave Structures	Towner, Naomi Whiting	√	> 4	AT	5			Ju 86	91
Inlay	Glit — An Icelandic Inlay Technique	Heite, Louise B.	√	√	Hw	8	3		M/J 87	64
Inlay	How to Weave a Transparency	Keasbey, Doramay	√	√	Hw	4	1		J/F 83	27
Inlay	Inlay		√	√	Hw	3	1		Ja 82	36
Inlay	Inlay Techniques	Xenakis, Athanasios David			PWC	4	1	11		15
Inlay	Inlay We Trust, Part 1: Half Dukagång	Herring, Connie	√	√	PWC			5	Sp 83	59

SUBJECT	TITLE	AUTHOR	IL	INST	JOUR	VOL	NO	ISS	DATE	PAGE
Inlay	Isolated Overshot: Inlaid Runner	Xenakis, Athanasios David	√	√	PWC	3	2	8		31
Inlay	Lilies on an Antique Tray	Herring, Connie	√	√	PWC	4	1	11		30
Inlay	Loom Shaped Top with Dukagång Inlay	Searle, Karen	√	√	WJ	11	3	43	Wi 87	8
Inlay	Man's Shirt in Peruvian Inlay	Linder, Harry	√	> 4	WJ	4	2	14	Oc 79	8
Inlay	Moorman Inlay Technique, The	Searle, Karen	√	√	PWC	1	1		No 81	30
Inlay	Portfolio: Why I Work in Linen, A		√		Fa	14	2		M/A 87	39
Inlay	Simple Inlay on a Leno Ground	Xenakis, Athanasios David; Patti Sellon	√	√	PWC	4	1	11		18
Inlay	Simple Inlay on Sheer Plain Weave Ground	Xenakis, Athanasios David; Linda Lyon	√	√	PWC	4	1	11		16
Inlay	Strips & Stripes	Lewis, Lois	√	> 4	SS&D	14	2	54	Sp 83	60
Inlay	Summer and Winter and Other Two-Tie Unit Weaves: Methods for Weaving Two-Tie Units, Inlay	Tidball, Harriet	√	√	SCGM		19		66	51
Inlay	Tapestry Inlay for Fool-Proof Designing	Marquardt, Bertha	√	√	SS&D	6	1	21	Wi 74	38
Inlay	Traditional Dukagång for Contemporary Textiles		√	√	Hw	8	3		M/J 87	57
Inlay	Traditional Ways with Dunkagång	Post, Margaret	√	√	Hw	7	2		M/A 86	42
Inlay	Transparencies of Inger Harrison–Sheer Beauty, The	Keasbey, Doramay	√	√	Hw	3	1		Ja 82	40
Inlay	Two-tie Inlay	Xenakis, Athanasios David	√	√	PWC	4	1	11		19
Inlay	Versatile Inlay, Twill on Twill	Beard, Betty	√	√	SS&D	19	1	73	Wi 87	53
Inlay	Warp Boutonné	Lewis, Edward G.	√	√	WJ	7	2	26	Fa 82	64
Inlay	Why Not Try Embroidery Weaves?	Jones, Jeanetta L.	√	√	H&C	17	2		Sp 66	12
Inlay, Accidental	Resist Dyeing, Curiosities and Inventions: Accidental Inlay	Zielinski, S. A.; Robert Leclerc, ed.	√	√	MWL	17			'51–'73	73
Inlay, Greek	Inlay We Trust Part 3: Pillow Based on Greek Inlay Technique	Herring, Connie	√	√	PWC	3	4	10		44
Inlay, Loom-Controlled	Long Sweeping Evening Cape	Roth, Bettie G.	√	> 4	WJ	6	3	23	Wi 81	26
Inlay, Loom-Controlled	Loom-Controlled Inlay	Davenport, Betty	√	> 4	Hw	6	3		Su 85	11
Inlay, Loom-Controlled	Swivel Explored and Contradicted		√	√	WJ	3	4	12	Ap 79	5
Inlay, Loom-Controlled	Tulip Outfit with Loom Controlled Inlay (error-corrected WJ v6 n1 81 p28d)	Kuwabara, Nancy	√	> 4	WJ	5	3	19	Wi 81	28
Inlay, Loop	Immigrant Memories	Butcher-Younghans, Sherry	√		WJ	9	4	36	Sp 85	44
Inlay, Looped	Weaving in Quebec: Traditional Quebecois Weaving	Barrett, Clotilde	√	√	WJ	6	4	24	Sp 82	10
Inlay On Beiderwand	Inlay Techniques	Barrett, Clotilde	√	√	WJ	1	1	1	Jy 76	3
Inlay, Overshot	Creative Overshot: Laid-In Overshot	Windeknecht, Margaret B.	√	√	SCGM		31		78	52
Inlay, Plain Weave	Anemone Garden Transparency (Bobbie Irwin)		√	√	Hw	7	2		M/A 86	45, I-6
Inlay, Tabby	Guatemala Visited	Atwater, Mary Meigs	√	√	SCGM		15		65	13
Inlay, Tabby	Guatemala Visited	Atwater, Mary Meigs	√	√	SCGM		15		65	26
Inlay, Two- and Four-Shaft	Inlay Techniques	Barrett, Clotilde	√	√	WJ	1	1	1	Jy 76	3
Inlay, Variations	Transparencies		√	√	Hw	7	2		M/A 86	45
Inlay, Weft-Faced	Guatemala Visited	Atwater, Mary Meigs	√	√	SCGM		15		65	17
Inscriptions: Corner	Corner Inscriptions	Jarvis, Helen		√	PWC	5	2	16		19
Inscriptions: Pick-Up	Inscribing a Coverlet	Beevers, Sue	√	√	PWC	5	2	16		16
Inscriptions: Pick-up	Multishaft Overshot on Opposites	van der Hoogt, Madelyn	√	> 4	WJ	8	3	31	Wi 83	76
Inscriptions: Techniques	Inscribing a Coverlet	Beevers, Sue	√	√	PWC	5	2	16		16
Insect Repellents	Herbal Moth Repellents: Safeguard or Sentiment?	Buchanan, Rita			S-O	10	2		Su 86	25

SUBJECT	TITLE	AUTHOR	IL	INST	JOUR	VOL	NO	ISS	DATE	PAGE
Insect Repellents	Principles of Textile Conservation Science, No. 11. Requirements for Bulk Storage Protection Against Insect Damage	Rice, James W.	√	√	TMJ	2	4		De 69	31
Insects	Follow-Up on Silverfish and Firebrats			√	TM			5	J/J 86	8
Insects	Herbal Moth Repellents: Safeguard or Sentiment?	Buchanan, Rita			S-O	10	2		Su 86	25
Insects	Silverfish and Firebrats		√	√	TM			3	F/M 86	6
Insects: Clothes Moths	When Moths Fly Out of Your Closet	Hochberg, Bette	√	√	Iw	4	3		Su 79	50
Insects: Dye	Cochineal in Colorado: or, Is Your Local Cactus Bugged? (error-corrected Iw v1 n3 76 p25)	Bliss, Anne	√	√	Iw	1	2		Wi 76	20
Insects: Dye	Hooray, Hooray, The Cochineal	Arabian, Barbara		√	Iw	3	3		Sp 78	25
Insects: Dye	Insect Dyes	Gerber, Fred	√	√	Iw	3	3		Sp 78	23
Insects: Weaving Ants	Ants Weave, Too	Forel, Auguste	√		Iw	2	4		Su 77	15
Inspiration also see Designs and Designing: Sources										
Inspiration	A Weaver Ponders His, Craft Collection of Controversial Essays: Inspiration	Zielinski, S. A.; Robert Leclerc, ed.			MWL	21 22			'51–'73	43
Inspiration	Changing Seasons, The	Schomp, Halcyon; Hector Jaeger	√		Hw	5	5		N/D 84	61
Inspiration	Conversing with Gerhardt Knodel	Park, Betty	√		Fa	12	1		J/F 85	27
Inspiration	Courting the Muse	Liebler, Barbara	√		Hw	5	5		N/D 84	37
Inspiration	Crazy Quilt Wrap	Stoehr, Mary Kay	√		Hw	5	5		N/D 84	71
Inspiration	Cut, Paste, and Copy	Wolff, Colette	√	√	TM			8	D/J 86	52
Inspiration	Donna Martin: The Influence of the Southwest	D'Andrea, Patricia A.	√		Fa	14	5		N/D 87	18
Inspiration	Fall Foliage	Voiers, Leslie	√		Hw	5	5		N/D 84	69
Inspiration	Found Treasures	Jones, Janice	√		Hw	5	5		N/D 84	70
Inspiration	Handspun: Inspiration from Commercial Sources	Mintzer, Arlene	√		S-O	10	2		Su 86	33
Inspiration	Inspiration from the Past: Textile Treasures in the World of New York City Auctions	Sider, Sandra	√		Fa	11	6		N/D 84	62
Inspiration	Inspiration from Woven Samples of the Past or...a Bunch of Us Last Sunday	Bradley, Louise	√		Hw	5	5		N/D 84	50
Inspiration	Inspiring Words	Strickler, Carol	√		Hw	5	5		N/D 84	44
Inspiration	Lace & Flowers: Vintage Inspiration	George, Patrice	√	> 4	Hw	8	5		N/D 87	68
Inspiration	Maine Coast Memories	Jaeger, Hector; Halcyon Schomp	√		Hw	5	5		N/D 84	72
Inspiration	Music for Inspiration		√	√	Hw	4	2		M/A 83	51
Inspiration	Nature: A Color Source and Inspiration for Traditional Sweaters	Gibson-Roberts, Priscilla A.	√		S-O	9	3		Fa 85	42
Inspiration	Outrageous Colors	Wertenberger, Kathryn	√		Hw	5	5		N/D 84	68
Inspiration	Paisley-Inspired	Dobrovolny, Ardis	√		Hw	5	5		N/D 84	67
Inspiration	Shawl After Edgar Degas	Straight, Dixie	√		Hw	5	5		N/D 84	64
Inspiration	Sources of Inspiration: Bear River Migratory Bird Refuge	Williams, Terry Tempest	√		Hw	5	5		N/D 84	59
Inspiration	There's More to an Old Friar's Blanket than Monk's Belt	Centner, David J., OCD	√		Hw	5	5		N/D 84	41
Inspiration	Things That Count	Ligon, Linda	√		Hw	8	4		S/O 87	99
Inspiration	Thoughts from a New Zealander	Poore, Jenny			SS&D	9	3	35	Su 78	65
Inspiration	Thrums	Davenport, Betty	√		Hw	5	5		N/D 84	66
Inspiration	Time Capsules	White, Violet	√		Hw	8	1		J/F 87	75
Inspiration	Weaving Memories	Alderman, Sharon D.	√		Hw	5	5		N/D 84	57
Inspiration	Weaving, 'riting, and 'rithmetic	Tate, Blair	√		AT	6			De 86	57
Inspiration	Weddding Dress, My	Caliendo, Karen	√		Hw	5	5		N/D 84	76
Inspiration: African Strip Weaving	Ancient Awakenings		√		Hw	5	4		S/0 84	51

398

SUBJECT	TITLE	AUTHOR	IL	INST	JOUR	VOL	NO	ISS	DATE	PAGE
Inspiration: Basketry	Inspiration — Does it Come Before or After?	LaPlantz, Shereen	√		WJ	8	1	29	Su 83	54
Inspiration: Cotton Yarn	Inspiration for New Designs in Cotton	Hausner, Walter	√		H&C	3	4		Fa 52	23
Inspiration: Coverlets	Inspiration	Alvic, Philis	√		WJ	8	1	29	Su 83	65
Inspiration: Fiber	Inspired by Fiber: Textile Sensibility in Other Media	Malarcher, Patricia	√		Fa	10	6		N/D 83	33
Inspiration: Garment Form	Garment Form As Image, The	Koplos, Janet	√		Fa	10	6		N/D 83	66
Inspiration: Historical Garments	I Have This Fleece...Now What?	Adams, Brucie	√	√	Iw	5	4		Fa 80	62
Inspiration: Historical Textiles	On Eighteenth Century Flowered Silk Weaving as an Inspiration for Todays Complex Weavers	Fairbanks, Dale			CW	7	1	19	Se 85	8
Inspiration: Knitting	Knitters, Make a Trip to the Fabric Store	Guagliumi, Susan	√	√	TM			7	O/N 86	35
Inspiration: Native American Art	Terra Nova: Jack Lenor Larsen	Larson-Fleming, Susan	√		WJ	11	1	41	Su 86	49
Inspiration: Navajo Textiles	From Father Sky to Mother Earth: An Ethnic Inspiration	Bennett, Noël	√		WJ	8	1	29	Su 83	62
Inspiration: Sources	Inspiration	Dahl, E. E.			Hw	5	5		N/D 84	94
Inspiration: Sources	Inspirational Notes		√		Hw	5	5		N/D 84	92
Inspiration: Sources	"Sources of Inspiration" (Exhibit)		√		Fa	14	1		J/F 87	50
Inspiration: Southwest Landscape	Southwest Reflections: Fiber artists Inspired by the New Mexico Landscape	Colton, Mary Rawcliffe	√		WJ	11	1	41	Su 86	20
Inspiration: Textiles, Old	Something Old, Something New		√		S-O	9	3		Fa 85	13
Inspiration: Trees	Crochet Inspired by the Trees	Moon, Ellen	√	√	TM			11	J/J 87	56
Inspiration: Weaving	Ideas Are Where You Find Them	Breeze, Helen	√	> 4	H&C	3	2		Sp 52	22
Inspiration: Weaving, Museum Treasures	Museum Treasures Inspire Philadelphia Weavers		√		H&C	5	3		Su 54	19
Inspiration: West African Textiles	Woven Inspiration from West African Textiles	Renne, Elisha	√	√	WJ	10	4	40	Sp 86	60
Installing Exhibits	Textiles on Display: The Installation of Fiber Exhibitions	Rees, Linda	√	√	SS&D	17	4	68	Fa 86	38
Installing Textiles	Bringing Tapestry into the 20th Century	Mattera, Joanne	√	√	TM			1	O/N 85	52
Instructions: Handwoven Projects	General Instructions		√	√	Hw	8	5		N/D 87	I-1
Instructions: Projects	General Instructions		√	√	Hw	1	1		F-W 79	50
Instructions: Projects	General Instructions			√	Hw	1	2		S-S 80	50
Instructions: Projects	General Instructions			√	Hw	2	1		F-W 80	56
Instructions: Projects	General Instructions		√	√	Hw	6	1		J/F 85	I-1
Instructions: Projects	General Instructions		√	√	Hw	6	2		M/A 85	I-1
Instructions: Projects	General Instructions		√	√	Hw	6	3		Su 85	I-1
Instructions: Projects	General Instructions		√	√	Hw	6	4		S/O 85	I-1
Instructions: Projects	General Instructions		√	√	Hw	6	5		N/D 85	I-1
Instructions: Projects	General Instructions		√	√	Hw	7	2		M/A 86	I-1
Instructions: Projects	General Instructions		√	√	Hw	7	3		M/J 86	I-1
Instructions: Projects	General Instructions		√	√	Hw	7	4		S/O 86	I-1
Instructions: Projects	General Instructions		√	√	Hw	8	1		J/F 87	I-1
Instructions: Projects	General Instructions		√	√	Hw	8	2		M/A 87	I-3
Instructions: Projects	General Instructions		√	√	Hw	8	3		M/J 87	I-1
Instructions: Projects	General Instructions		√	√	Hw	8	4		S/O 87	I-1
Instructions: Projects	General Instructions and Yarn Chart		√		Hw	3	1		Ja 82	80
Instructions: Projects	General Instructions and Yarn Chart		√	√	Hw	3	2		Mr 82	76
Instructions: Projects	General Instructions and Yarn Chart		√		Hw	3	3		My 82	86
Instructions: Projects	General Instructions and Yarn Chart		√		Hw	3	5		N/D 82	84
Instructions: Projects	General Instructions and Yarn Chart		√		Hw	4	3		M/J 83	78
Instructions: Projects	General Instructions and Yarn Chart		√	√	Hw	4	5		N/D 83	92
Instructions: Projects	General Instructions and Yarn Chart		√	√	Hw	5	1		J/F 84	86
Instructions: Projects	General Instructions and Yarn Chart		√	√	Hw	5	2		M/A 84	92
Instructions: Projects	General Instructions and Yarn Chart		√	√	Hw	5	3		Su 84	91
Instructions: Projects	General Instructions and Yarn Chart		√	√	Hw	5	4		S/O 84	90

SUBJECT	TITLE	AUTHOR	IL	INST	JOUR	VOL	NO	ISS	DATE	PAGE
Instructions: Projects	General Instructions and Yarn Chart		√	√	Hw	5	5		N/D 84	I-1
Instructions: Projects	General Instructions and Yarn Chart		√	V	Hw	4	1		J/F 83	78
Instructions: Projects	General Instructions & Yarn Chart		√		Hw	2	2		Mr 81	68
Instructions: Projects	General Instructions & Yarn Chart		√		Hw	2	3		My 81	74
Instructions: Projects	General Instructions & Yarn Chart		√	√	Hw	2	4		Se 81	82
Instructions: Projects	General Instructions & Yarn Chart		√		Hw	2	5		No 81	78
Instructions: Projects	General Instructions & Yarn Chart		√		Hw	3	4		Se 82	80
Instructions: Projects	General Instructions & Yarn Chart		√		Hw	4	2		M/A 83	80
Instructions: Projects	General Instructions & Yarn Chart		√	√	Hw	4	4		S/O 83	91
Instructions: Projects	Instructions		√	√	Hw	7	1		J/F 86	I-1
Insulating: Window Coverings	Insulated Roman Shade — Doup Leno	Champion, Ellen	√	√	WJ	6	1	21	Su 81	24
Insulating: Window Coverings	Insulating Handwoven Shutters		√	>4	WJ	6	1	21	Su 81	20
Insulating: Window Coverings	Insulating Window Covering	Svenson, Mary Jane	√	√	WJ	6	1	21	Su 81	18
Intarsia	Knitting with Colors	Fassett, Kaffe	√	√	TM			3	F/M 86	68
Intarsia: Technique	Intarsia Technique	Rowley, Elaine		√	Kn	3	4	8	Fa 87	52
Integrated Drafts	All About Looms: Draw-Looms	Zielinski, S. A.; Robert Leclerc, ed.	√	>4	MWL	2			'51–'73	50
Integrated Structures	1 Fabric: 2 Faces	Moes, Dini	√	>4	SS&D	14	2	54	Sp 83	16
Integrated Weaves	Exploring the Textures: Another Texture Weave	Zielinski, S. A.; Robert Leclerc, ed.	√	√	MWL	11			'51–'73	87
Integrated Weaves, Balanced	Balanced Integrated Weaves	Marston, Ena	√	>4	SS&D	8	1	29	WI 76	10
Integrated Weaves, Unbalanced	More Integrated Weaves	Marston, Ena	√	>4	SS&D	8	2	30	Sp 77	20
Integrating Weaves: Technique	Notes on the Damask Weave	Ahrens, Jim		>4	CW	2	1	4	Oc 80	6
Interfacing: Fused	When a Fusing Fails	Coffin, David Page	√	√	TM			10	A/M 87	61
Interfacing: Hymo	Tailor's Logic	Hostek, Stanley	√	√	TM			14	D/J 87	42
Interfacings: Sources	Making Sense of Interfacing (error-corrected TM n12 p4)	Komives, Margaret Deck	√	√	TM			10	A/M 87	58
Interfacings: Types	Making Sense of Interfacing (error-corrected TM n12 p4)	Komives, Margaret Deck	√	√	TM			10	A/M 87	58
Interior	Rugs and Carpets — Their Importance in Interior Design		√		H&C	3	4		Fa 52	30
Interiors	April May: She Weaves Curtains with Images	Woelfle, Gretchen	√		Fa	7	6		N/D 80	28
Interiors	At Home		√		Hw	4	4		S/O 83	59
Interiors	Bridging the Gap Between Craft Artists and Interior Designers	Kraus, William	√		SS&D	16	4	64	Fa 85	37
Interiors	Chase Home	McCarthy, Bridget Beatty	√		SS&D	16	4	64	Fa 85	44
Interiors	Chase Home: Utah Arts Council	Burke, Dan E.	√		SS&D	16	4	64	Fa 85	40
Interiors	Considering Color		√		Hw	5	2		M/A 84	54
Interiors	Contemporary Handweaving for the Home, Memphis Guild Exhibition	Miller, Carolyn A.			H&C	10	2		Sp 59	20
Interiors	Cozy Retreat. A	LaLena, Constance	√		Hw	5	2		M/A 84	65
Interiors	Decorator's Use of Handwoven Fabrics, A	Storey, Walter Rendell	√		H&C	4	4		Fa 53	4
Interiors	Design for Interiors	Stewart-Pollack, Julie	√		Hw	5	2		M/A 84	52
Interiors	Designer Fabrics for Upholstery	West, Virginia	√		Hw	5	2		M/A 84	72
Interiors	Designing for an Interior: Notes of a Pattern Weaver	Alvic, Philis	√		WJ	9	4	36	Sp 85	69
Interiors	Fabrics for Interiors		√		Hw	5	2		M/A 84	63
Interiors	Fabrics for Interiors	VanSlyke, Gail Rutter		√	WJ	3	1	9	Jy 78	5
Interiors	Fiber and Architecture: John Ellis		√		Fa	3	3		M/J 76	17
Interiors	Fiberworks and Interior Decorating	Rau, Joanne	√		SS&D	13	1	49	Wi 81	45
Interiors	Handweaving in Effective Settings	Bryan, Dorothy	√		H&C	12	1		Wi 61	10
Interiors	Handweaving in Period and Contemporary Interiors	Bryan, Dorothy	√		H&C	4	4		Fa 53	16
Interiors	Handwoven Fabrics in the S. S. United States		√		H&C	4	1		Wi 52	15

SUBJECT	TITLE	AUTHOR	IL	INST	JOUR	VOL	NO	ISS	DATE	PAGE
Interiors	Historic Textiles for Contemporary Spaces	Lonier, Terri	√		Fa	12	1		J/F 85	64
Interiors	Home Comfort	Wertenberger, Kathryn	√		Hw	5	2		M/A 84	66
Interiors	Indigo and Cream		√		Hw	6	4		S/O 85	44
Interiors	Interiors Then and Now: 1850 — 1950, Rochester, New York		√		H&C	2	1		Wi 50	38
Interiors	Interview with Jack Lenor Larsen, An		√		WJ	7	1	25	Su 82	10
Interiors	"Joyce Kozloff" An Interior Decorated (Exhibit)	Greenberg, Blue	√		Fa	8	1		J/F 81	89
Interiors	Lever House Presents a Solution To A Unique Problem In Interior Design		√		H&C	4	3		Su 53	32
Interiors	Lines and Shapes in Interior Spaces		√		Hw	5	2		M/A 84	52
Interiors	"Maria" Rag Rug	Krook, Inga	√	√	Hw	6	3		Su 85	56
Interiors	Notes of a Pattern Weaver	Alvic, Philis	√		WJ	10	3	39	Wi 86	65
Interiors	Room from your Loom		√		H&C	26	2		Ap 75	25
Interiors	Rugs and Carpets, Their Importance in Interior Design		√		H&C	4	1		Wi 52	22
Interiors	Summer Dining		√		Hw	6	3		Su 85	60
Interiors	Summer Place, A		√		Hw	5	3		Su 84	72
Interiors	Sunday Tea		√		Hw	6	4		S/O 85	42
Interiors	Tapestry for Interiors	Harvey, Nancy	√		Hw	3	1		Ja 82	42
Interiors	Textiles in Nineteenth-Century America	Glaze, Mary	√		H&C	21	3		Su 70	4
Interiors	Textures for Interiors			√	Hw	5	2		M/A 84	56
Interiors	To Dress Your Room: Dress Your Loom	Shrauger, Carolyn	√		SS&D	7	3	27	Su 76	61
Interiors	Trends for Fashionable Interiors	Hick, Susan	√		WJ	7	1	25	Su 82	18
Interiors	Weave a Special Place		√		Hw	5	2		M/A 84	50
Interiors	Weaving for a Country Home		√		Hw	6	4		S/O 85	41
Interiors	Weavings for a Summer Home		√		Hw	6	3		Su 85	56
Interiors	Work with Style	Alderman, Sharon D.	√		Hw	5	2		M/A 84	68
Interlinking	After Emery: Further Considerations of Fabric Classification and Terminology	Rowe, Ann Pollard	√		TMJ	23			84	53
Interlocking Warp and Weft Structure	Interlocking Warp and Weft in the Nasca 2 Style	Rowe, Ann Pollard	√		TMJ	3	3		De 72	67
Interrelationship: Fabric Cross-Section/Interlacement Sequence	Multi-Layered Cloths: A Structured Approach	Hoskins, Janet A.	√	>4	AT	1			De 83	137
Interrelationship: Kaftan, Design/Weave Structure	Original Fabrics of Kaftan, The	El-Homossani, M. M.	√	>4	AT	1			De 83	263
Intertwining, Oblique, Variant	Nasca Sprang Tassels: Structure, Technique, and Order	Frame, Mary	√	√	TMJ	25			86	67
Interviews see People										
Iran	Kings, Heroes, Lovers: Pictorial Rugs from the Tribes and Villages of Iran	Goodman, Deborah Lerme	√		Fa	11	3		M/J 84	38
Iran	Little Gems of Ardebil, The	Ellis, Charles Grant	√		TMJ	1	3		De 64	18
Iran	Persian Legend in Silk		√		TM			14	D/J 87	92
Iran	Weavers in Iran, Thousands at Work on Primitive Looms	Leclerc, Robert	√		H&C	21	2		Sp 70	9
Ireland	Ballinskelligs Tapestry Works: Ancient Art/Modern Spirit, The	Burkhauser, Jude	√		Hw	3	1		Ja 82	55
Ireland	Elliot Weavers of Dublin	Burow, Nellie B.			SS&D	1	1	1	De 69	16
Ireland	Homespun Songs from Ireland's Clancy Brothers	Drake, Elizabeth A.	√		SS&D	16	4	64	Fa 85	62
Ireland	Irish Kinsale Cloak, The	Jones, Una	√	√	WJ	8	3	31	Wi 83	35
Ireland	Irish Weaving	Clement, Doris; Ted Clement	√		H&C	21	2		Sp 70	4
Ireland	Shepherds of Glenmore, The	Burkhauser, Jude	√		S-O	6	4		82	36
Ireland	There's a Lady Out Bantry Bay Way	Rubbert, Toni Condon	√		S-O	7	4		Wi 83	32
Ireland	Tweed Weavers of Glenmore, The	Burkhauser, Jude	√		Hw	3	3		My 82	56

401

SUBJECT	TITLE	AUTHOR	IL	INST	JOUR	VOL	NO	ISS	DATE	PAGE
Ireland	Weaving in Donegal (error-corrected H&C v23 n3 72 p11)	McNeill, Mary	√	√	H&C	23	2		M/A 72	35
Irish Tweed	Tweed Weavers of Glenmore, The	Burkhauser, Jude	√		Hw	3	3		My 82	56
Ironing	Pressing Need, Or the Ironing of It, A	Bradley, Louise	√	√	Hw	7	4		S/O 86	71
Ironing Boards	Irons, Boards, and Presses: A Survey of the Tools That Beautify Sewing	Coffin, David Page	√		TM			10	A/M 87	40
Irons: Malfunctions	VaporSimac Problems			√	TM			14	D/J 87	8
Irons: Selecting	Irons, Boards, and Presses: A Survey of the Tools That Beautify Sewing	Coffin, David Page	√		TM			10	A/M 87	40
Islamic Textiles	Group of Silk Islamic Banners, A	Denny, Walter B.	√		TMJ	4	1		De 74	67
Isle of Harris	Happy Weaver of the Isle of Harris, The	Ham, Phebe D.	√		SS&D	1	2	2	Mr 70	12
Israel	Fabrics from Israel	Keiner, Julia	√		H&C	5	4		Fa 54	30
Israel	Jews of Kurdistan, The	Meyerowitz, Carol Orlove	√	√	SS&D	14	2	54	Sp 83	23
Israel	Julia Keiner, Brings Fabrics from Israel		√		H&C	15	2		Sp 64	22
Israel	New Forms from Old Traditions	Amram, Hortense	√		H&C	3	1		Wi 51	27
Italy	Amazing Lace on Venetian Isle	Mattera, Joanna	√		TM			7	O/N 86	12
Italy	Gioanventura Rosetti and His Dye Book—1548 A. D.	Bliss, Anne	√		Iw	3	1		Fa 77	36
Italy	Italy at Work — Her Renaissance in Design Today		√		H&C	2	1		Wi 50	41
Italy	Marvelous Mezzaro, The	Wasiqullah, Alexandra	√		Fa	10	5		S/O 83	29
Italy	New Italian Renaissance Follows Liberation, A		√		H&C	3	1		Wi 51	10
Italy	Salute to Italy: Paola Besana		√		SS&D	16	2	62	Sp 85	25
Italy	Textile Sleuth Extraordinaire	Wasiqullah, Alexander	√		Fa	12	2		M/A 85	39
Italy	Traditional Weavers in Italy	Castaldi, Nora	√		H&C	2	4		Fa 51	20
Itinerant Craftsmen: Felt Makers	Felt-making Craftsmen of the Anatolian and Iranian Plateaux	Gervers, Michael; Veronika Gervers	√	√	TMJ	4	1		De 74	14
Itinerant: Weaving Teachers	Weaving in New Brunswick	Currey, Ruth Dunlop	√		H&C	12	1		Wi 61	29
Jackets	Adobe Jacket (Ronnine Bohannan)		√	√	Hw	7	3		M/J 86	49, I-11
Jackets	Autumn Bomber Jacket (Myrna Beeny)		√	√	Hw	3	4		Se 82	47, 83
Jackets	Autumn Pleasures Bog Jacket (Janice Jones)		√	√	Hw	5	4		S/0 84	76, 109
Jackets	Beautiful and Bold		√	√	Hw	1	2		S-S 80	42
Jackets	Bethlehem Jacket (Anita Mayer)		√	√	Hw	2	2		Mr 81	29, 79
Jackets	Beyond Rags: Fabric Strip Design	Larson-Fleming, Susan	√	√	WJ	9	4	36	Sp 85	47
Jackets	Blue Jacket (Jean Scorgie)		√	√	Hw	7	5		N/D 86	41, I-4
Jackets	Blue Medley Jacket (Dixie Straight)		√	√	Hw	6	1		J/F 85	31, I-5
Jackets	Bobbie L. Adelman's Jacket	Adelman, Bobbie L.	√	√	S-O	9	2		Su 85	15
Jackets	Boiled Wool (Mary Jane Hensley)	Adams, Brucie	√	√	Hw	5	3		Su 84	85
Jackets	Bolivian Milkmaid's Jacket (Susan Henrickson)		√	√	Hw	4	2		M/A 83	60, 97
Jackets	Boucle Jacket		√	√	S-O	7	3		Fa 83	59
Jackets	Bougainvillea Jacket (Barbara Smith Eychaner)		√	√	Hw	5	1		J/F 84	43, 110
Jackets	Boundweave Jacket (Jean Scorgie)		√	√	Hw	2	1		F-W 80	31, 74
Jackets	Bright Styles from the North	Kaplow, Roberta	√		SS&D	16	1	61	Wi 84	23
Jackets	Brown Jacket (Kathryn Wertenberger)		√	> 4	Hw	6	4		S/O 85	56, I-10
Jackets	Brown Jacket with Blue Edging	Keeler, Betty	√	√	S-O	10	1		Sp 86	21
Jackets	Butterfly Kimono Jacket	Bush, Carolyn	√	√	S-O	10	1		Sp 86	22
Jackets	Cannelé: Create a Sumptuous Fabric That Drapes Beautifully	Broughton, Cynthia	√	√	WJ	10	3	39	Wi 86	59
Jackets	Cardigan Jacket	Evans, Kerry	√	√	WJ	5	3	19	Wi 81	10
Jackets	Chanel Jacket	Ratigan, Dorothy	√	√	Kn	2	2	4	S-S 86	33
Jackets	Child's Play	Voiers, Leslie	√	√	SS&D	18	3	71	Su 87	22
Jackets	Child's Windcheater	Reekie, Stephanie	√	√	S-O	6	4		82	58

SUBJECT	TITLE	AUTHOR	IL	INST	JOUR	VOL	NO	ISS	DATE	PAGE
Jackets	Chiola Jacket (Jean Scorgie)		√	√	Hw	2	4		Se 81	54, 90
Jackets	Cocoon Wrap Jacket, The		√	√	WJ	5	3	19	Wi 81	18
Jackets	Complementary Crochet	Durston, Linda Moore	√	√	SS&D	15	1	57	Wi 83	68
Jackets	Cotton Jacket with Pleat	White, Jamie Leigh	√	√	WJ	7	3	27	Wi 82	68
Jackets	Crazy Quilt Bed Jacket (Mary Kay Stoehr)		√	√	Hw	5	5		N/D 84	71, I-13
Jackets	Dazzling Designs	Eagle, Elsie	√	√	SS&D	15	1	57	Wi 83	19
Jackets	Don's Jacket	Coulson, Louise	√	√	S-O	8	2		Su 84	49
Jackets	Double Weave Jacket, A	Scorgie, Jean	√	√	Hw	4	4		S/O 83	48
Jackets	Double-Breasted Jacket in Mosiac	Newton, Deborah	√	√	Kn	2	1	3	F-W 85	45, 8B
Jackets	Doubleweave Jacket: 4-Shaft Version (Jean Scorgie)		√	√	Hw	4	4		S/O 83	48, 99
Jackets	Doubleweave Jacket: 8-Shaft Version (Jean Scorgie)		√	>4	Hw	4	4		S/O 83	48, 99
Jackets	Embroidered Jacket (Carol Powalisz)		√	√	Hw	8	4		S/O 87	46, I-7
Jackets	Ethnic Inspired Jacket	Hurt, Doris	√	√	WJ	4	4	16	Ap 80	43
Jackets	Evolution of a Handspun Jacket	Gardner, Jean	√		S-O	9	1		Sp 85	28
Jackets	Fall Foliage Jacket (Leslie Voiers)		√	√	Hw	5	5		N/D 84	69, I-12
Jackets	Fashions by Linda Knutson and Lynn Daly		√	√	WJ	6	3	23	Wi 81	14
Jackets	Felted Fabric	Mayer, Anita Luvera	√	√	SS&D	15	3	59	Su 84	46
Jackets	Felted Jacket	Bennett, Siiri	√	>4	WJ	9	1	33	Su 84	49
Jackets	Feltmaking: Instant Delight	Green, Louise	√	√	Iw	3	4		Su 78	18
Jackets	Figured Piqué on a Ground of 2/2 Twill and 2/2 Hopsack	Xenakis, Athanasios David	√	>4	PWC	4	2	12		24
Jackets	Finnish Cotton Jacket (Kaino Leethem with Jean Scorgie)		√	√	Hw	5	3		Su 84	61, 106
Jackets	Free and Casual Look Wool Jacket, The	McGalliard, Lorraine	√	√	WJ	6	3	23	Wi 81	8
Jackets	From Sample to Finished Product	Keasbey, Doramay	√	>4	SS&D	15	3	59	Su 84	62
Jackets	Fulled Blazer	Newton, Deborah	√	√	Kn	3	1	5	F-W 86	38
Jackets	Fur Jacket (Ann Wittpenn)		√	√	Hw	4	1		J/F 83	33, 80
Jackets	Garments by Hanni Bureker		√	√	WJ	6	3	23	Wi 81	35
Jackets	Gray Jacket (Gilbert)			√	Hw	2	1		F-W 80	66
Jackets	Gray Plaid Jacket (Mary Kay Stoehr)		√	√	Hw	6	4		S/O 85	60, I-11
Jackets	Handspun, Handwoven Cocoon Jacket, A	Adams, Brucie	√	√	Hw	5	2		M/A 84	88
Jackets	Handspun Jacket		√	√	S-O	7	4		Wi 83	48
Jackets	Handweaves for Men's Wear		√		H&C	9	2		Sp 58	42
Jackets	Harris Tweed Jacket		√	√	Hw	2	5		No 81	49, 87
Jackets	Inkle Bands as Finishing Details on Garments	Brones, Britta	√	√	WJ	7	3	27	Wi 82	35
Jackets	Inside an Expensive Outfit	Galpin, Mary	√	√	TM			1	O/N 85	40
Jackets	Jacket and Camisole with Ikat Stripes (Ronnine Bohannan)		√	√	Hw	5	3		Su 84	56, 100
Jackets	Jacket for Hiking, A	Roth, Bettie G.	√	>4	WJ	8	3	31	Wi 83	69
Jackets	Jacket Inspired by West African Narrow Strip Weaving	Bradley, Louise	√	√	WJ	5	3	19	Wi 81	31
Jackets	Jacket (Nell Znamierowski)		√	>4	Hw	7	3		M/J 86	34, I-6
Jackets	Jacket of Handspun Samples, A	Fenner, Mary Sue	√	√	Hw	5	1		J/F 84	74
Jackets	Just an Idea	Beetem, Debra		√	Kn	3	1	5	F-W 86	37
Jackets	Kimono Jacket (Leslie Voiers)		√	√	Hw	8	4		S/O 87	41, I-5
Jackets	Knitting with Colors	Fassett, Kaffe	√	√	TM			3	F/M 86	68
Jackets	Lace Trilogy	Fauske, Carla	√	√	PWC			6	Su 83	52
Jackets	Lace Weave Skirt with Jacket and Top (Louise Bradley)		√	>4	Hw	5	3		Su 84	58, 104
Jackets	Loom Shaped—3 Ways (Ardis Dobrovolny) (error-corrected Hw v4 n3 83 p79)		√	√	Hw	3	2		Mr 82	46
Jackets	Man's Jacket: A Weaver's Challenge, A	Rasmussen, Peg	√	√	SS&D	15	2	58	Sp 84	58

SUBJECT	TITLE	AUTHOR	IL	INST	JOUR	VOL	NO	ISS	DATE	PAGE
Jackets	Mexican Motifs: The Mexican Men's Jacket	Tidball, Harriet	√	√	SCGM		6		62	20
Jackets	More Rags		√	√	Hw	2	3		My 81	49
Jackets	Oedipus Jacket, The	McClennen, Carol	√	√	S-O	7	4		Wi 83	31
Jackets	One Pattern, One Warp (Louise Bradley)		√	√	Hw	3	3		My 82	34, 97
Jackets	Peter Collingwood, His Weaves and Weaving: A Sleeved Jacket Made in Two Pieces	Collingwood, Peter; Harriet Tidball, ed.	√	√	SCGM		8		63	34
Jackets	Pins and Needles				TM			13	O/N 87	4
Jackets	Poppana Tapestry Jacket (Jean Scorgie)		√	√	Hw	4	3		M/J 83	48, 84
Jackets	Purple Haze Sweater Jacket (Mary Kay Stoehr)		√	> 4	Hw	6	1		J/F 85	40, I-13
Jackets	Rags At Work	Finch, Joan Freitag	√	√	SS&D	16	4	64	Fa 85	72
Jackets	Rags to Riches: Jackets from Rags	Brones, Britta	√	√	WJ	6	3	23	Wi 81	31
Jackets	Rainbow Jacket (Sara Lamb)		√	> 4	Hw	4	1		J/F 83	45, 84
Jackets	Recycling—Ragtime	Ligon, Linda	√	√	Iw	3	4		Su 78	22
Jackets	Red Wool Jacket (Linda Ligon)		√	√	Hw	2	5		No 81	51, 83
Jackets	Reversible Jacket in Double Weave, A	Evans, Jane	√	> 4	WJ	3	1	9	Jy 78	23
Jackets	Reversible Matelasse Jacket	Champion, Ellen	√	> 4	WJ	7	1	25	Su 82	41
Jackets	Ribbon Wefts	Sewell, Suzy	√	> 4	WJ	10	3	39	Wi 86	40
Jackets	Rose Jacket (Åse Blake)		√	> 4	Hw	8	3		M/J 87	56, I-9
Jackets	Safety-Pin Jacket (Mark Mahall)		√		TM			9	F/M 87	88
Jackets	Sahara Jacket (Eileen Ternullo)		√	√	Hw	8	2		M/A 87	56, I-11
Jackets	"Sand Dunes and Dune Grass": Two Garments from a Blended Draft (Ardis Dobrovolny)		√	√	Hw	6	2		M/A 85	57, I-14
Jackets	Save the Twist: Warping and Weaving with Overtwisted Yarns	Frame, Mary	√	√	S-O	11	2		Su 87	43
Jackets	Scandia Jacket		√	√	WJ	8	3	31	Wi 83	42
Jackets	Seersucker Blazer, A	Johannesen, Betty	√	√	WJ	8	3	31	Wi 83	22
Jackets	Shadow Weave Twill Jacket (Jean Scorgie)		√	√	Hw	8	4		S/O 87	43, I-6
Jackets	Sheep Jacket (Jean Scorgie)		√	√	Hw	7	2		M/A 86	70, I-13
Jackets	Silk Jacket (Jane Patrick)		√	> 4	Hw	4	1		J/F 83	50, 90
Jackets	Simply Natural	Linder, Harry	√	√	WJ	11	2	42	Fa 86	20
Jackets	Slightly Left of Center Jacket	Rowley, Elaine	√	√	PWC			6	Su 83	44
Jackets	Snakeskin Jacket (Mary Kay Stoehr)		√	√	Hw	5	4		S/O 84	54, 96
Jackets	Summer Harvest, Winter Jacket	O'Connor, Marina	√	√	S-O	11	2		Su 87	13
Jackets	Tailored Bog Jacket, A	Guy, Sallie T.	√	√	SS&D	17	1	65	Wi 85	26
Jackets	Tailored Bog Jacket (Revisited), A	Guy, Sallie T.	√	√	SS&D	18	1	69	Wi 86	60
Jackets	Tale of Two Knitters, A	Preen, Maureen	√		S-O	8	4		Wi 84	19
Jackets	Texture with Handspun	Page, Judy	√	√	WJ	6	2	22	Fa 81	20
Jackets	Textured Weave—An Alternative	Tanner, Virginia Leigh	√	√	WJ	7	3	27	Wi 82	58
Jackets	Three Color Progressions and Their Use in Sweater Jackets	Sylvan, Katherine	√	√	WJ	5	4	20	Sp 81	38
Jackets	Three Hand-Dyed Jackets (Sue Henrikson)		√	√	Hw	3	3		My 82	45, 96
Jackets	Try Shadow Weave Twill	Hewson, Betty	√	√	Hw	5	1		J/F 84	14
Jackets	Turned Overshot	Rowley, Elaine; Alexis Yiorgos Xenakis	√	> 4	PWC	3	2	8		53
Jackets	Tweed Jacket, Woven for TV		√		SS&D	6	1	21	Wi 74	14
Jackets	Vadmal Jacket (Janice Jones)		√	√	Hw	8	4		S/O 87	45, I-7
Jackets	Versatile Jacket, A	Hannah, Joyce	√	√	TM			1	O/N 85	44
Jackets	Warmth for a Cool Climate: Handspun Wool & Milkweed Down	Danielson, Esther	√	√	SS&D	17	4	68	Fa 86	24
Jackets	Wearing Handwovens with Style	Mayer, Anita	√	√	WJ	10	3	39	Wi 86	22
Jackets	Weave and Knit Suit		√	√	WJ	8	3	31	Wi 83	18

SUBJECT	TITLE	AUTHOR	IL	INST	JOUR	VOL	NO	ISS	DATE	PAGE
Jackets	Weaver Who Wastes Not, A	Porcella, Yvonne	√	√	SS&D	6	4	24	Fa 75	8
Jackets	Weaving and Tailoring Handspun Yardage	Simmons, Paula	√	√	S-O	2			78	48
Jackets	Weaving on a Board	Kappler, Erda	√	√	Hw	4	4		S/O 83	46
Jackets	Weaving with Handspuns: A Shepherd Jacket	Simmons, Paula	√	√	S-O	1			77	43
Jackets	What People Ask Before They Buy Handmade Fashions	Leslie, Victoria	√		TM			9	F/M 87	58
Jackets	White Jacket	Grange, Penny	√	√	WJ	8	3	31	Wi 83	16
Jackets	Why Be Needed by Pins?				TM			14	D/J 87	4
Jackets: Crochet	Crochet Inspired by the Trees	Moon, Ellen	√	√	TM			11	J/J 87	56
Jackets, Knitted	Rag Trade, The	Weissman, Julia	√		Kn	1	2	2	S-S 85	53
Jackets: Knitted	V-Neck Jacket	Upitis, Lizbeth	√	√	Kn	3	4	8	Fa 87	37
Jackets: Knitted	Windowpane Jacket: In Double Knit and Garter Stitch	Ellman, Norma	√	√	Kn	3	4	8	Fa 87	40
Jackets, Knitted	Winter Birches: The Jacket	Upitis, Lizbeth	√	√	Kn	1	2	2	S-S 85	44
Jacquard Weaving	Art of Indiana Coverlets, The	Gilfoy, Peggy S.	√		AT	2			De 84	69
Jacquard Weaving	Banares Brocade	DuBois, Emily	√	> 4	AT	3			My 85	209
Jacquard Weaving	Fabric About Fabric	Cannarella, Deborah	√		TM			1	O/N 85	72
Jacquard Weaving	Handweaver's Jacquard Loom, A	Mulkey, Philip O.	√		H&C	7	4		Fa 56	46
Jacquard Weaving	Inside the Hangchow Brocade Factory: The Art and Craft of Mass Production	Drower, Sara	√		Fa	6	1		J/F 79	78
Jacquard Weaving	Jacquard and Woven Silk Pictures, The	Adrosko, Rita J.	√		AT	1			De 83	9
Jacquard Weaving	Jacquard At the Brewery, The	Colwell, Ken	√		SS&D	7	2	26	Sp 76	14
Jacquard Weaving	Jacquard is Back	Lloyd, Ann	√		SS&D	18	4	72	Fa 87	10
Jacquard Weaving	Jacquard, Jacquard	Laing, K. M.	√		TM			3	F/M 86	10
Jacquard Weaving	Jacquard Loom: Where It Comes from, How It Works, The	Marcoux, Alice	√		Fa	9	2		M/A 82	34
Jacquard Weaving	Jacquard Loomed: Turn-of-the-Century Fabrics	Marcoux, Alice	√		Fa	9	2		M/A 82	35
Jacquard Weaving	Jacquard Pattern Reconstructions with Computer Spreadsheets	Carr, Margaret; Helen Jarvis; Gordon Jarvis	√	√	SS&D	17	3	67	Su 86	78
Jacquard Weaving	Jacquard Project: Selections from the Current Exhibition, The		√		Fa	9	2		M/A 82	36
Jacquard Weaving	Jacquard Tapestries of Boris Kroll, The		√		SS&D	12	2	46	Sp 81	47
Jacquard Weaving	Jacquard Weaving	Goldschmidt, Manfred			H&C	23	4		J/A 72	35
Jacquard Weaving	Jacquard Weaving in Huehuetenango	Anderson, Marilyn	√		Fa	9	2		M/A 82	31
Jacquard Weaving	Jacquard Weaving Part 1	Goldschmidt, Manfred	√		H&C	23	2		M/A 72	24
Jacquard Weaving	Kashmir or Paisley; Romance of the Shawl	Wilson, Kax	√		Iw	4	4		Fa 79	34
Jacquard Weaving	Obi: The Textile Art of Nishijin	Donaldson, R. Alan	√		AT	1			De 83	115
Jacquard Weaving	Ohio's Woven Coverlets: Textile Industry in a Rural Economy	Cunningham, Patricia A.	√		AT	2			De 84	165
Jacquard Weaving	Salut, Monsieur Jacquard	Carey, Joyce Marquess	√		Hw	2	3		My 81	57
Jacquard Weaving	Shelburne's Jacquard Loom: Is It a Computer? (error-corrected SS&D v17 n4 86 p10)	Vander Noordaa, Titia	√	√	SS&D	17	3	67	Su 86	34
Jacquard Weaving	Stars, Diamonds, Tables, and Sunrise: Motifs and Structures of Woven Coverlets	Cabeen, Lou	√	√	TM			14	D/J 87	32
Jacquard Weaving	Textile Arts of Multan, Pakistan	Shahzaman, Mahboob	√	> 4	SS&D	4	3	15	Su 73	8
Jacquard Weaving	Uncovering the Life and Weaving of John E. Schneider	Thieme, Otto Charles	√		SS&D	9	2	34	Sp 78	80
Jacquard Weaving	Unravelling the Mysteries of the Jacquard	Jirousek, Charlotte	√		WJ	9	1	33	Su 84	8
Jacquard Weaving	Weaving in the Austrian Tyrol		√		H&C	7	1		Wi 55	28
Japan	American Weaver in Japan		√		H&C	18	4		Fa 67	30
Japan	Ana Lisa Hedstrom: The Intuitive Language of Shibori	Scarborough, Jessica	√		Fa	13	1		J/F 86	26

SUBJECT	TITLE	AUTHOR	IL	INST	JOUR	VOL	NO	ISS	DATE	PAGE
Japan	Art of Stitched Shibori, The (error-corrected Fa v12 n3 85 p8)	Wada, Yoshiko; Mary Kellogg Rice, Jane Barton	√		Fa	12	2		M/A 85	55
Japan	Briading Technique Documented in an Early Nineteenth-Century Japanese Treatise, "Soshun Biko", A	Kinoshita, Masako	√	√	TMJ	25			86	47
Japan	Contemporary Tapestry in Japan: Individuality After Centuries of Textile Conformity	Lindenfeld, Lore	√		Fa	10	3		M/J 83	44
Japan	Culture & Costume in Edo Japan	Staples, Loretta	√		SS&D	12	1	45	Wi 80	26
Japan	Distant Mountains: The Influence of Funzo-e on the Tradition of Buddhist Clerical Robes in Japan	Lyman, Marie	√		TMJ	23			84	25
Japan	Divided Spaces: The Fences of Japan	Bess, Nancy Moore	√		Fa	14	4		S/O 87	28
Japan	Doncho for New York, A		√		H&C	15	4		Fa 64	12
Japan	D'Arcie Beytebiere: Windswept Designs In Pleated Silk	Tacker, Sylvia	√		Fa	13	1		J/F 86	28
Japan	Fingernail Weaving: The Crystallized Art of Patience	Kinoshita, Takeshi	√	√	SS&D	13	1	49	Wi 81	26
Japan	Fukumi Shimura: Japan's Colorist Supreme	Adachi, Barbara C.	√		Fa	12	4		J/A 85	28
Japan	"Fukusa: The Shojiro Nomura Collection" (Exhibit)	Janeiro, Jan	√		Fa	11	3		M/J 84	79
Japan	Fundraising Brings Kasuri Kimono Weaver to Nashville Workshop	Wilson, Sadye Tune	√		SS&D	9	2	34	Sp 78	4
Japan	Hiroko Ogawa: Keeping Alive the Art of Sashiko	Scarborough, Jessica	√		Fa	12	2		M/A 85	12
Japan	Japanese Country Textiles (Exhibit)	Rowley, Kathleen	√		Fa	13	5		S/O 86	49
Japan	Japanese Weaves Provide Ideas for Experiment	Freeman, Claire	√	√	H&C	21	1		Wi 70	4
Japan	Japanese Weaving Tools	Schreiber, LaVonne	√		WJ	9	2	34	Fa 84	47
Japan	Japan's Masterful Embroideries	Markrich, Lilo	√		TM			12	A/S 87	68
Japan	Kago-Uchi, The	Speiser, Noémi	√	√	AT	4			De 85	23
Japan	Kasuri: A Japanese Textile	Dusenbury, Mary	√		TMJ	17			78	41
Japan	Kasuri: The Japanese Ikat	Schrieber, La Vonne	√	√	SS&D	14	1	53	Wi 82	22
Japan	Katagami: Japanese Stencil Cutting	McCann, Kathleen	√		Fa	13	2		M/A 86	36
Japan	Kazuko Nishigaki Creates in Ancient Tradition	Major, Dana; John Major	√		SS&D	6	2	22	Sp 75	93
Japan	Kesa: Its Sacred and Secular Aspects	Kennedy, Alan	√		TMJ	22			83	67
Japan	Kudzu	Foster, Ann	√		S-O	3			79	23
Japan	Kumejima Kasuri: A Visit to a Remote Japanese Silk Center	Mitchell, Alison	√	√	WJ	10	1	37	Su 85	59
Japan	Kumihimo: The Art of Japanese Braiding	Moss, Helen E.	√		Fa	14	1		J/F 87	20
Japan	Learning to See Pattern	Morrison, Skye	√	√	TM			2	D/J 85	44
Japan	Learning to Weave in Japan	Schreiber, LaVonne	√		WJ	8	1	29	Su 83	79
Japan	Letter from Japan	Schrieber, Lavonne	√		WJ	12	1	45	Su 87	54
Japan	Living National Treasures of Japan, The	Adachi, Barbara Curtis	√		Fa	11	1		J/F 84	62
Japan	"Mingei — The Folk Arts of Japan" (Exhibit)	Meilach, Dona Z.	√		Fa	4	2		M/A 77	10
Japan	Miyako Jofu	Miller, Dorothy	√	√	AT	7			Ju 87	85
Japan	New Twist on Resist	Wada, Yoshiko Iwamoto; Shelley Karpilow	√	√	TM			8	D/J 86	20
Japan	Obi: The Textile Art of Nishijin	Donaldson, R. Alan	√		AT	1			De 83	115
Japan	Paper Clothing, East	Sahlstrand, Margaret	√	√	Fa	11	2		M/A 84	36
Japan	"Patterns" with a Look at Japanese Printing with Stencils (Exhibit)	Dyer, Carolyn	√		Fa	4	5		S/O 77	10
Japan	Personal Exploration of Indigo, A	Miller, Dorothy	√	√	Fa	13	5		S/O 86	32
Japan	Preparing Silk in Kumejima	Mitchell, Alison	√	√	WJ	10	2	38	Fa 85	53
Japan	Recent Gifts of Chinese and Japanese Textiles	Hays, Mary V.	√		TMJ	4	2		75	4

SUBJECT	TITLE	AUTHOR	IL	INST	JOUR	VOL	NO	ISS	DATE	PAGE
Japan	Ritual Fiber: Weaving Hope For The Future Into The Fabric Of Life	Wilcox, Don	√		Fa	13	6		N/D 86	7
Japan	Saganishiki	Karaki, Mihoko	√		SS&D	15	3	59	Su 84	50
Japan	Shinnosuke Seino: Innovator with Wool	Schreiber, Lavonne	√		WJ	12	2	46	Fa 87	34
Japan	Shokansai Iizuka: Bamboo Craftsman and Living National Treasure of Japan	Adachi, Barbara Curtis	√		Fa	11	1		J/F 84	59
Japan	Temari: Threads to the Past	Beall, Karen F.	√		Fa	14	2		M/A 87	7
Japan	Tenugui: Decorative Japanese Hand Towels		√		Fa	9	6		N/D 82	25
Japan	Tree-Bast Fiber Textiles of Japan	Dusenbury, Mary	√	√	S-O	10	3		Fa 86	35
Japan	Weaving in the Past: What Can We Learn From Japanese Weaving	Zielinski, S. A.; Robert Leclerc, ed.			MWL	21 22			'51–'73	91
Japan	Yuki Tsumugi, Kasuri Weaving of Yuki Japan	Thimann, Ann	√		SS&D	5	2	18	Sp 74	50
Japan: Textile Instruction Sources	Learning to Weave in Japan	Schrieber, LaVonne	√		WJ	8	1	29	Su 83	79
Jaspé also see Dyes and Dyeing: Resist										
Jaspé	Jaspe Process, The	Lopez, Beatriz	√	√	SS&D	8	3	31	Su 77	54
Jaspé	Jaspé Weaving	Young, Helen Daniels	√	√	H&C	5	3		Su 54	30
Java	Batik Making and the Royal Javanese Cemetery at Imogiri	Joseph, Rebecca M.	√		TMJ	24			85	83
Java	"Fabled Cloth: Batik from Java's North Coast" (Exhibit)	Goodman, Deborah Lerme	√		Fa	12	4		J/A 85	58
Java	Symbolic Scenes in Javanese Batik	Adams, Monni	√		TMJ	3	1		De 70	25
Jeans	From Rags to Riches: Artful Recycling	Loud, Dana	√		Fa	13	5		S/O 86	23
Jeans	Jeans: The Inside Story	Goodman, Deborah Lerme	√	√	TM			3	F/M 86	27
Jeans	Lee Company	Rudich, Sally	√		Fa	13	5		S/O 86	13
Jeans	Levi Strauss & Co.	Scarborough, Jessica	√		Fa	13	5		S/O 86	17
Jeans	Wrangler	Rudich, Sally	√		Fa	13	5		S/O 86	12
Jewelry: Contemporary	Good As Gold: Alternatives in American Jewelry		√		Fa	9	5		S/O 82	18
Jewelry: Fiber	Embroidered Neckpieces of Theodora Elston, The	Sacks, Star M.	√		Fa	6	3		M/J 79	51
Jewelry: Fiber	Fabulous Plumage of Mae Augarten, The	Forscey, Suzon	√		Fa	6	3		M/J 79	65
Jewelry: Fiber	"Tina Johnson-Depuy Soft Jewelry" (Exhibit)	Cardinale, Robert L.	√		Fa	6	3		M/J 79	81
Jewelry: Fiber/Metal	Timeless Knotted Jewelry: Marion Hunziker Meticulously Combines Fiber and Metalwork Techniques	Hunziker, Marion	√		Fa	8	4		J/A 81	19
Jewelry: Knitting	And a Necklace, Too	Upitis, Lizbeth	√	√	Kn	2	2	4	S-S 86	48
Jewelry: Textile	Ardyth Davis — Looking At Inkblots and Seeing Jewelry	Hecker, Carolyn A.	√		Fa	5	6		N/D 78	31
Jewelry: Woven	King's Ranson: Contest Rusults, A		√		WJ	10	1	37	Su 85	49
Jewelry: Woven	Soft Jewelry: A Different Adornment	Howell-Koehler, Nancy	√	√	SS&D	7	2	26	Sp 76	56
Jewelry: Woven, Necklaces	Woven Necklaces	Clement, Doris	√		H&C	21	4		Fa 70	8
Jisp	Notebook: Some Light Behind the Weave	Myers, Ruth Nordquist, ed.	√	> 4	SS&D	13	3	51	Su 82	16
Joining: Identical Fabrics	More About Fabrics: Identical Fabrics	Zielinski, S. A.; Robert Leclerc, ed.	√	√	MWL	20			'51–'73	69
Joinings	Afghans: Things to Consider and Finishes	Xenakis, Athanasios David	√	√	PWC	3	1	7		10
Joinings	Edges, Joinings, Trims, Embellishments, Closures…and More	Wilson, Jean	√	√	Hw	2	5		No 81	42
Joinings	Joinings, Edges and Trims	Wilson, Jean	√	√	SS&D	14	3	55	Su 83	50
Joinings: Inkle Bands	Weaving Inkle Bands: Joined Inkle Bands	Tidball, Harriet	√	√	SCGM		27		69	39
Joinings: Rag Strips	Hand Woven Rugs: Weaves, Plain Weave Rugs of Rag Stirps	Atwater, Mary Meigs	√	√	SCGM		29		48	3
Joinings: Strips	Peru, Textiles Unlimited: Textile Characteristics, Joined Strips	Tidball, Harriet	√		SCGM		25		68	20

SUBJECT	TITLE	AUTHOR	IL	INST	JOUR	VOL	NO	ISS	DATE	PAGE
Journals: Thomas Jackson	Thomas Jackson, Weaver: 17th and 18th Century Records	Tidball, Harriet	√		SCGM		13		64	1
Joy	Theme Issue		√		Fa	8	5		S/O 81	
Judaic Weaving	Jewish Textiles	Johnson, Faye	√		Hw	5	1		J/F 84	35
Judges and Judging also see Jurying										
Judges and Judging	Boulder Designer-Craftsmen 1971	Reitz, Don			SS&D	2	4	8	Fa 71	8
Judges and Judging	Criteria for Judging Handspun Yarn	Bliss, Anne			S-O	3			79	8
Judges and Judging	HGA Directors to Judge At Midwest				SS&D	4	2	14	Sp 73	55
Judges and Judging	Judging Handspun Wool	Blackman, Margery			SS&D	2	2	6	Sp 71	11
Judges and Judging	Spinning for a Finished Product Competition	Feldman-Wood, Florence			S-O	7	4		Wi 83	30
Judges and Judging	This Thing Called Judging	Schlegel, Lee-lee			SS&D	9	2	34	Sp 78	45
Judges and Judging: Point System	Philadelphia Guild Point System	Schlegel, Mary		√	SS&D	4	4	16	Fa 73	4
Jumpers	Blue Jumper (Louise Bradley)		√	√	Hw	6	4		S/O 85	52, I-8
Jumpers	Brown Wool Jumper	Buchanan, Rita	√	√	S-O	9	1		Sp 85	14
Jumpers	Tulip Outfit with Loom Controlled Inlay (error-corrected WJ v6 n1 81 p28d)	Kuwabara, Nancy	√	> 4	WJ	5	3	19	Wi 81	28
Jumpsuits	Jumpsuits, Anyone?	Fieldman, M. Lucille	√	> 4	SS&D	7	3	27	Su 76	60
Jurying also see Judges and Judging										
Jurying	Certificate of Excellence in Handweaving: The Jurying, The	White, Pat			SS&D	14	1	53	Wi 82	48
Jurying	Evening the Odds in Juried Competition	Williams, Ann			SS&D	17	3	67	Su 86	63
Jurying	Evolution of a Regional Juried Fiber Show: Fibers Unlimited, The	Rees, Linda			SS&D	17	3	67	Su 86	65
Jurying	Fibers Unlimited 1985	Tacker, Sylvia	√		SS&D	17	3	67	Su 86	68
Jurying	Jurying	Ligon, Linda	√		Iw	1	2		Wi 76	10
Jurying	Jurying by Point System	Shepps, Vincent C.		√	H&C	17	3		Su 66	7
Jurying	Look At the Juried Show: Jurors and Artists Talk About What It Takes, A	Malarcher, Patricia			Fa	9	5		S/O 82	53
Jurying	Making of an Exhibition: An Insider's Report, The	Wolff, Colette	√		Fa	12	3		M/J 85	46
Jurying	Nobody Likes to be Rejected	Brostoff, Laya			Hw	4	4		S/O 83	29
Jurying	Open Jurying in Pittsburg: Putting Your Work on the Line (Exhibit)	Myrinx, Elaine	√		Fa	6	2		M/A 79	23
Jurying	Supplementary Warp Patterning: Jurying Guild Exhibits	Tidball, Harriet			SCGM		17		66	46
Jurying	Tradition and Change: Fiber '79	Martin, Elaine	√		Iw	5	2		Sp 80	72
Jute	Plant Fibers: Hard Fibers		√	√	WJ	8	2	30	Fa 83	67
Jute	Survey of Leaf and Stem Fibers, A	Buchanan, Rita	√		S-O	10	3		Fa 86	24
Kaftan	Qotny & Alaga: Traditional Striped Fabrics for the Middle Eastern Kaftan	El-Homossani, M. M.	√	> 4	WJ	10	1	37	Su 85	33
Kaftan (Caftan)	Original Fabrics of Kaftan, The	El-Homossani, M. M.	√	> 4	AT	1			De 83	263
Kago-Uchi Weaving	Kago-Uchi, The	Speiser, Noémi	√	√	AT	4			De 85	23
Kantha	Kantha	Westfall, Carol D.; Dipti Desai	√	√	AT	7			Ju 87	161
Karakul	Know Your Fibers: Karakul	Ligon, Linda	√		Iw	2	3		Sp 77	12
Karellia	Karellian Red Pick	Howard, Miranda	√	√	Hw	2	5		No 81	36
Karellian Red Pick	Karellian Red Pick	Howard, Miranda	√	√	Hw	2	5		No 81	36
Karellian Red-Pick	Karelian Red-Picking	Ruchti, Willie Jager	√	> 4	WJ	5	2	18	Fa 80	34
Kashmir	Kashmir East and West	Mikosch, Elizabeth	√		TM			9	F/M 87	14
Kashmir	Kashmir or Paisley; Romance of the Shawl	Wilson, Kax	√		Iw	4	4		Fa 79	34
Kashmir	Paisley	Badone, Donalda	√		Hw	8	1		J/F 87	39
Kashmir	Scent of Flowers, Kashmir Shawls in the Collection of The Textile Museum, The	Mikosch, Elisabeth	√		TMJ	24			85	7

SUBJECT	TITLE	AUTHOR	IL	INST	JOUR	VOL	NO	ISS	DATE	PAGE
Kashmir	Textile Arts of India	Bernier, Ronald M.	√		WJ	2	1	5	Jy 77	31
Kashmir Shawls	Kashmiri to Paisley: Evolution of the Paisley shawl	Larson-Fleming, Susan	√		WJ	11	3	43	Wi 87	37
Kashmir Shawls	Paisley Shawls: A Democratic Fashion	Goodman, Deborah Lerme	√		Fa	12	3		M/J 85	52
Kashmir Shawls: Double-Woven	Catalogue of Kashmir Shawls in The Textile Museum	Mikosch, Elisabeth	√		TMJ	24			85	23
Kashmir Shawls: European	Scent of Flowers, Kishmir Shawls in the Collection of The Textile Museum, The	Mikosch, Elisabeth	√		TMJ	24			85	7
Kashmir Shawls: Twill-Woven	Catalogue of Kashmir Shawls in The Textile Museum	Mikosch, Elisabeth	√		TMJ	24			85	23
Kashmir Shawls: Woven and Embroidered	Catalogue of Kashmir Shawls in The Textile Museum	Mikosch, Elisabeth	√		TMJ	24			85	23
Kashmir Shawls: Woven and Embroidered	Scent of Flowers, Kishmir Shawls in the Collection of The Textile Museum, The	Mikosch, Elisabeth	√		TMJ	24			85	7
Kasuri also see Dyes and Dyeing: Resist										
Kasuri	Fundraising Brings Kasuri Kimono Weaver to Nashville Workshop	Wilson, Sadye Tune	√		SS&D	9	2	34	Sp 78	4
Kasuri	Kasuri: A Japanese Textile	Dusenbury, Mary	√		TMJ	17			78	41
Kasuri	Kasuri and I	Robinson, Irma	√		SS&D	1	2	2	Mr 70	19
Kasuri	Kasuri: The Japanese Ikat	Schrieber, La Vonne	√	√	SS&D	14	1	53	Wi 82	22
Kasuri	Kasuri-Like-Effect Weaving	Akita, Mariko Olivia	√	√	WJ	6	2	22	Fa 81	18
Kasuri	Kazuko Nishigaki Creates in Ancient Tradition	Major, Dana; John Major	√		SS&D	6	2	22	Sp 75	93
Kasuri	Kumejima Dorozome: The Vegetable Dye and Mud Mordanting Process of Silk Tsugumi	Miller, Dorothy	√	√	AT	5			Ju 86	131
Kasuri	Resist Dyeing, Curiosities and Inventions: Kasuri on Inkle Loom	Zielinski, S. A.; Robert Leclerc, ed.	√	√	MWL	17			'51–'73	38
Kasuri	Yuki Tsumugi, Kasuri Weaving of Yuki Japan	Thimann, Ann	√		SS&D	5	2	18	Sp 74	50
Kasuri: Technique, Kumejima	Kumejima Kasuri: A Visit to a Remote Japanese Silk Center	Mitchell, Alison	√	√	WJ	10	1	37	Su 85	59
Kasuri Techniques: Japan	Kasuri: A Japanese Textile	Dusenbury, Mary	√		TMJ	17			78	41
Kasuri Techniques: Ryukyu	Kasuri: A Japanese Textile	Dusenbury, Mary	√		TMJ	17			78	41
Katagami	Katagami: Japanese Stencil Cutting	McCann, Kathleen	√		Fa	13	2		M/A 86	36
Kenaf	Survey of Leaf and Stem Fibers, A	Buchanan, Rita	√		S-O	10	3		Fa 86	24
Kente Cloth	Ancient Awakenings		√		Hw	5	4		S/0 84	51
Kente Cloth	Kente on Four Harnesses	McCarthy, Catherine L.	√	√	SS&D	16	3	63	Su 85	6
Kente Cloth	Kente: The Status Cloth of Ghana	Conklin, Sharon L.	√	√	SS&D	8	1	29	WI 76	18
Kesa	Anne Wilson: Underlying Geometry	Koplos, Janet	√		Fa	10	3		M/J 83	62
Kesa	Recent Gifts of Chinese and Japanese Textiles	Hays, Mary V.	√		TMJ	4	2		75	4
Kesa: Sacred Aspects	Kesa: Its Sacred and Secular Aspects	Kennedy, Alan	√		TMJ	22			83	67
Kesa: Types	Distant Mountains: The Influence of Funzo-e on the Tradition of Buddhist Clerical Robes in Japan	Lyman, Marie	√		TMJ	23			84	25
Kesa: Types	Kesa: Its Sacred and Secular Aspects	Kennedy, Alan	√		TMJ	22			83	67
Key to Weaves	More About Fabrics: Key to Weaves	Zielinski, S. A.; Robert Leclerc, ed.		√	MWL	20			'51–'73	5
Khes	Textile Arts of Multan, Pakistan: Part 2	Shahzaman, Mahboob	√	> 4	SS&D	4	4	16	Fa 73	65
Kilts	Kilts	Branson, Branley Allan	√		Hw	4	5		N/D 83	34
Kilts	To Don a Kilt		√	√	Hw	4	5		N/D 83	39
Kilts	Weaver's Book of Scottish Tartans: The Scottish Tartans and Their Background: History of Tartans, The	Tidball, Harriet	√		SCGM		5		62	3
Kimono and Robes	Adinkra: Weft African Textile of Pride	Rex, Chris	√		Fa	9	6		N/D 82	36
Kimono and Robes	Balenciago: The Architect of Elegant Clothing	Koda, Harold	√		TM			11	J/J 87	20
Kimono and Robes	Bathrobe (Linda Ligon)		√	√	Hw	3	2		Mr 82	50, 91

SUBJECT	TITLE	AUTHOR	IL	INST	JOUR	VOL	NO	ISS	DATE	PAGE
Kimono and Robes	Butterfly Kimono Jacket	Bush, Carolyn	√	√	S-O	10	1		Sp 86	22
Kimono and Robes	Cardiac Algorithms or the Heart's Way of Inferring Meaning from Pattern	Courtney, Elizabeth	√		AT	5			Ju 86	51
Kimono and Robes	"Ch'ing Dynasty Court Robes, A Splendorous Sampling" (Exhibit)	Marcoux, Alice	√		Fa	11	2		M/A 84	78
Kimono and Robes	Culture & Costume in Edo Japan	Staples, Loretta	√		SS&D	12	1	45	Wi 80	26
Kimono and Robes	Distant Mountains: The Influence of Funzo-e on the Tradition of Buddhist Clerical Robes in Japan	Lyman, Marie	√		TMJ	23			84	25
Kimono and Robes	Fashion Show of Handwoven Garments		√	> 4	WJ	3	3	11	Ja 79	5
Kimono and Robes	Fleeting Fantasies: Julia Hill's Painting on Silk	Grover, Donald	√		Fa	6	4		J/A 79	12
Kimono and Robes	From English Handlooms Comes Royal Purple Velvet for Coronation Robe of Elizabeth II	Lee, Humphrey A.	√		H&C	4	2		Sp 53	17
Kimono and Robes	Fukumi Shimura: Japan's Colorist Supreme	Adachi, Barbara C.	√		Fa	12	4		J/A 85	28
Kimono and Robes	Fundraising Brings Kasuri Kimono Weaver to Nashville Workshop	Wilson, Sadye Tune	√		SS&D	9	2	34	Sp 78	4
Kimono and Robes	Handwoven Silk Garments: Ikat Kimono	Barnett-Westfall, Lynn	√	√	WJ	3	2	10	Oc 78	30
Kimono and Robes	Ikat Spun Lap Robe (Louise Bradley)	Bradley, Louise	√	√	Hw	2	4		Se 81	67
Kimono and Robes	Ikat-Spun Kimono, An	Lamb, Sara	√	√	S-O	8	4		Wi 84	16
Kimono and Robes	Kimono	Colton, Mary Rawcliffe	√	√	SS&D	15	1	57	Wi 83	30
Kimono and Robes	"Kimono As Art: Modern Textile Works by Kako Moriguchi, Rikizo Munehiro, and Fukumi Shimura" (Exhibit)	Koplos, Janet	√		Fa	13	1		J/F 86	60
Kimono and Robes	"Kimono East/Kimono West" (Exhibit)	Lusk, Jennie	√		Fa	7	5		S/O 80	71
Kimono and Robes	Kimono East/West	Wada, Yoshiko	√		Fa	9	1		J/F 82	19
Kimono and Robes	Kimono/Pants Ensemble, A	Selk, Karen	√	√	WJ	8	4	32	Sp 84	72
Kimono and Robes	Man's Robe (Jane Patrick) (error-corrected Hw v4 n3 83 p 79)		√	√	Hw	4	2		M/A 83	53, 86
Kimono and Robes	"Marika Contompasis: Pedestal and Wall Pieces" (Exhibits)	Dyer, Carolyn	√		Fa	9	4		J/A 82	73
Kimono and Robes	Miyako Jofu	Miller, Dorothy	√	√	AT	7			Ju 87	85
Kimono and Robes	Modular Clothing	Mayer, Anita	√	√	Hw	7	3		M/J 86	58
Kimono and Robes	Obi: The Textile Art of Nishijin	Donaldson, R. Alan	√		AT	1			De 83	115
Kimono and Robes	Pittsburg Artists Create Kimono Canvases		√		Fa	13	3		M/J 86	7
Kimono and Robes	Recent Gifts of Chinese and Japanese Textiles	Hays, Mary V.	√		TMJ	4	2		75	4
Kimono and Robes	Robes for Inspiration	Dyer, Carolyn	√		Fa	10	1		J/F 83	60
Kimono and Robes	Silk Kimono (Sharon Alderman)		√	> 4	Hw	1	2		S-S 80	28, 66
Kimono and Robes	Succeeding with the Knitting Machine	Mattera, Joanne	√		TM			2	D/J 85	50
Kimono and Robes	Textured Cottons: Dress and Sauna Robe	Henrikson, Sue	√	> 4	WJ	6	3	23	Wi 81	20
Kimono and Robes	Two Loom-Shaped Designs for Narrow Looms (Donna Gilbert)		√	√	Hw	2	1		F-W 80	28
Kimono and Robes	Visiting the Kimono School	Hannah, Joyce	√		TM			4	A/M 86	16
Kimono and Robes	What's in a Bale of Used Kimonos?	Marcus, Ruth-Claire			TM			7	O/N 86	16
Kimono Fabric	Japanese Weaves Provide Ideas for Experiment	Freeman, Claire	√	√	H&C	21	1		Wi 70	4
Kinujifu	Paper Clothing, East	Sahlstrand, Margaret	√	√	Fa	11	2		M/A 84	36
Kirman	Kirman's Heritage in Washington: Vase Rugs in The Textile Museum	Ellis, Charles Grant	√		TMJ	2	3		De 68	17
Kirman Vase Rugs	Kirman's Heritage in Washington: Vase Rugs in The Textile Museum	Ellis, Charles Grant	√		TMJ	2	3		De 68	17
Kites	Edinburg Tapestry Company		√		Fa	12	5		S/O 85	64
Kites	Making a Square Kite with a Long Tail	Morrison, Skye	√	√	Fa	5	4		J/A 78	40
Kites	"Shared Vision": A Gallery Tour with Two Artists: Jacque Parsley and Neisja Yenawine (Exhibit)	Arnow, Jan	√		Fa	8	4		J/A 81	28

SUBJECT	TITLE	AUTHOR	IL	INST	JOUR	VOL	NO	ISS	DATE	PAGE
Kites	Skye Morrison: Yours on a Kite String	Morrison, Skye	√	√	Fa	5	4		J/A 78	36
Kiwicraft	Kiwicraft	Horne, Beverley	√	√	S-O	3			79	52
Knee Rug	Two Prize-winning Canadian Projects		√	√	H&C	13	3		Su 62	32
Knit and Crochet	Theme Issue		√		Fa	5	3		M/J 78	
Knitted Fabric, Stitching	Marking and Sewing Intricate Shapes on Knits			√	TM			13	O/N 87	10
Knitters: Men	Manly Art of Knitting...What's Become of It, The	Weissman, Julia			Kn	3	2	6	Sp 87	15
Knitters: Men	Men Who Knit	Xenakis, Alexis Yiorgos	√		Kn	3	2	6	Sp 87	14
Knitting	Arctic Handknitted, One Hundred Per Cent Qiviut	Griffiths, Helen M.	√		H&C	22	2		Sp 71	6
Knitting	"Art to Wear" (Exhibit)	Murray, Megan	√		Fa	11	1		J/F 84	76
Knitting	Basic Knitting Machine, The	Guagliumi, Susan	√	√	TM			1	O/N 85	38
Knitting	Circular Knitting	Secretan, Hermine A.	√	√	SS&D	3	2	10	Sp 72	28
Knitting	Converting Images Into Sweaters	MacHenry, Rachel	√	√	TM			10	A/M 87	72
Knitting	Dazzling with Sequins	Kelsey, Barbara Shomer	√	√	TM			1	O/N 85	60
Knitting	Dione Christensen	Hutchinson, Amelia	√		Fa	5	3		M/J 78	57
Knitting	"Dione Christensen Fiberworks" (Exhibit)	Meyer, Florence	√		Fa	6	2		M/A 79	63
Knitting	Double Edge of Knitting, The	Mabee-Zust, Mariah	√		Fa	10	3		M/J 83	50
Knitting	Egmont Sweater, The	Zimmermann, Elizabeth	√	√	PWC			2	Ap 82	80
Knitting	Elaine's Knitted Top	Rowley, Elaine D.	√	√	PWC			2	Ap 82	89
Knitting	Exploring a Knitted Pattern	Bruzelius, Margaret	√	√	TM			6	A/S 86	35
Knitting	Fast Knitting on Pegs	Ellison, Nancy	√		S-O	5			81	18
Knitting	Ferne Cone — Knitting: The Stepchild of the Fiber Arts?	Nelson, Gladys	√		Fa	5	3		M/J 78	48
Knitting	Fleecy Vest, A	Gilsdorf, Marilyn	√	√	WJ	8	4	32	Sp 84	9
Knitting	Folk Textiles of Latin America	Kelemen, Pál	√		TMJ	1	4		De 65	2
Knitting	"Glorious Knits of Kaffe Fassett, The" (Exhibit)	McCann, Kathleen	√		Fa	13	2		M/A 86	53
Knitting	Hammock, The	Drooker, Penelope B.	√	√	TM			6	A/S 86	74
Knitting	Heathering	O'Connor, Marcie Archer	√	√	Kn	2	1	3	F-W 85	54
Knitting	"History of Knitting" (Exhibit)	Park, Betty	√		Fa	5	3		M/J 78	10
Knitting	Howard Zabler		√		Fa	5	3		M/J 78	54
Knitting	Instant Gratification: Susan Summa Tells How and Why She Learned to Love the Knitting Machine	Summa, Susan	√		Fa	8	5		S/O 81	56
Knitting	Jacqueline Fee's Sweater Workshop		√	√	Hw	4	3		M/J 83	74
Knitting	Kaffe Fassett: Dream Knitter (error-corrected Fa v5 n4 78 p63)		√		Fa	5	3		M/J 78	26
Knitting	Kay-O Wicks — The Habit of Knitting	Horton, Lucy	√		Fa	6	3		M/J 79	32
Knitting	Kiwicraft	Horne, Beverley	√	√	S-O	3			79	52
Knitting	Knitted Rugs	Austin, Carole	√		Fa	11	3		M/J 84	57
Knitting	Knitted Trifle Bag	Xenakis, Alexis Yiorgos	√	√	PWC	1	1		No 81	52
Knitting	Knitting Craft in Great Britain, The	Kinder, Kathleen	√		Fa	11	4		J/A 84	42
Knitting	Knitting from a Paper Pattern	Keeler, Betty	√	√	S-O	8	4		Wi 84	23
Knitting	Knitting from the Netherlands: Traditional Dutch Fishermen's Sweaters	Van der Klift-Tellegen, Henriette	√		Fa	12	4		J/A 85	45
Knitting	Knitting Odyssey, A	Dyett, Linda	√	√	TM			13	O/N 87	48
Knitting	Knitting with Colors	Fassett, Kaffe	√	√	TM			3	F/M 86	68
Knitting	Latvian Wedding Mittens	Upitis, Lizbeth	√	√	PWC			2	Ap 82	92
Knitting	Letting Knitting Happen	Edwards, Joyce	√		TM			10	A/M 87	86
Knitting	Llama Hat	Davidsohn, Marty	√	√	PWC			4	Ja 83	65
Knitting	Lots of Leg Warmers		√	√	PWC			4	Ja 83	67
Knitting	Martha Mahon: Tableaux	Fife, Lin	√		Fa	13	6		N/D 86	29
Knitting	Meg Swansen: A Conversation with Alexis Xenakis	Xenakis, Alexis Yiorgos	√		Kn	3	3	7	Su 87	26

SUBJECT	TITLE	AUTHOR	IL	INST	JOUR	VOL	NO	ISS	DATE	PAGE
Knitting	Methods for Multicolored Knitting	Righetti, Maggie	√	√	TM			6	A/S 86	40
Knitting	Mossy Bog, A	Rowley, Elaine	√	√	PWC			3	Oc 82	43
Knitting	Mother of Creative Knitting, The	Hecker, Carolyn	√		Fa	7	1		J/F 80	34
Knitting	My Knit Suit	Klinect, Ann W.	√		S-O	10	1		Sp 86	40
Knitting	Nonsagging Stockinette Stitch		√	√	TM			7	O/N 86	6
Knitting	Odyssey Knitting				TM			14	D/J 87	4
Knitting	Pencil Roving and the Navajo Ply	Adams, Brucie	√	√	Hw	6	1		J/F 85	75
Knitting	Peruvian Hat	Rowley, Elaine D.	√	√	PWC			4	Ja 83	65
Knitting	Peruvian Mittens	Xenakis, Alexis Yiorgos	√	√	PWC			4	Ja 83	62
Knitting	Portfolio of Contemporary Fiber Sculpture, A		√		Fa	11	4		J/A 84	34
Knitting	Qiviut Update	Griffiths, Helen M.	√		SS&D	7	4	28	Fa 76	60
Knitting	Recent Success of Carole Lubove-Klein: An Inspiring Yarn, The	McGuire, Patricia	√		Fa	9	5		S/O 82	20
Knitting	Romy's One-Shouldered Bodice	Klessen, Romy	√	√	PWC			2	Ap 82	87
Knitting	'Round and 'Round We Go, The Janet Sweater	Rowley, Elaine D.	√	√	PWC	1	1		No 81	50
Knitting	Ruby Brilliant: A Knitter Well-Named		√		Fa	10	1		J/F 83	19
Knitting	Shetland Lace Wedding Handkerchief, A (error-corrected TM n12 87 p4)	Korach, Alice	√	√	TM			11	J/J 87	42
Knitting	Spinners & Weavers in New Zealand Use Native Materials	Duncan, Molly	√		H&C	21	1		Wi 70	14
Knitting	Striped Knits and the Needlemaster			√	TM			7	O/N 86	8
Knitting	Teaching Children How to Knit	Baker, Ella			S-O	10	2		Su 86	42
Knitting	Two Styles of Buttonholes	Righetti, Maggie	√	√	TM			3	F/M 86	32
Knitting	Weave and Knit Pullover	Barrett, Clotilde	√	√	WJ	8	3	31	Wi 83	20
Knitting	Weave and Knit Suit		√	√	WJ	8	3	31	Wi 83	18
Knitting	Year of the Sweater, The	Katz, Ruth J.	√		Fa	7	1		J/F 80	39
Knitting: Abbreviations	School for Knitters		√	√	Kn	3	2	6	Sp 87	3
Knitting Accessories	Fast Knitting on Pegs	Ellison, Nancy	√		S-O	5			81	18
Knitting: Aran	Aran Knitting	Starmore, Alice	√	√	TM			14	D/J 87	50
Knitting Art	Mary Walker Phillips	Weissman, Julia	√		Kn	1	2	2	S-S 85	15
Knitting: Back Backwards	Confessions of a Backward Knitter	Swansen, Meg		√	Kn	3	3	7	Su 87	27
Knitting: Back-and-Forth	Back-and Forth Knitting			√	TM			6	A/S 86	12
Knitting: Backed	Weaving...On a Knitting Machine	Adams, Brucie	√	√	Hw	2	3		My 81	62
Knitting: Bias	Easy Striped Knits	Walker, Barbara G.	√	√	TM			4	A/M 86	54
Knitting: Bind Off	School for Knitters		√	√	Kn	3	2	6	Sp 87	3
Knitting: Brocade	Knit and Purl	Rowley, Elaine	√		Kn	1	1	1	F-W 84 CI	40 32
Knitting: Brocade	On Designing: Brocade Blouse	Newton, Deborah	√	√	Kn	1	1	1	F-W 84 CI	17 9
Knitting: Cast On	School for Knitters		√	√	Kn	3	2	6	Sp 87	3
Knitting: Cast On: Invisible	School for Knitters		√	√	Kn	3	2	6	Sp 87	3
Knitting: Cast-On, Double-Knit	Reversible Knitting		√	√	TM			14	D/J 87	6
Knitting: Casting-On, Invisible	Knitting Round on Straight Needles	Borssuck, Bee	√	√	TM			12	A/S 87	64
Knitting: Charting Paper	Charting Intarsia Designs	Guagliumi, Susan	√	√	TM			10	A/M 87	69
Knitting: Charting Paper	Knitting Machine Geometrics	Guagliumi, Susan	√	√	TM			10	A/M 87	66
Knitting: Circular	Cone of Aran Hats, A	Oakley, Helen	√	√	TM			13	O/N 87	27
Knitting: Circular, 2 Needles	Knitting Round on Straight Needles	Borssuck, Bee	√	√	TM			12	A/S 87	64
Knitting, Contemporary	Knitted Whimsey of Astrid Furnival, The	Elliott, Malinda	√		Fa	12	2		M/A 85	16
Knitting Cotton	Knitting with Cotton: Stitch Maneuvers Help Sweaters Stay in Shape	Dyett, Linda	√	√	TM			9	F/M 87	38
Knitting: Decrease	School for Knitters		√	√	Kn	3	2	6	Sp 87	3
Knitting: Decrease	To Narrow and to Fagot			√	TM			13	O/N 87	6
Knitting: Double-Strand, Double-Knit	Reversible Knitting		√	√	TM			14	D/J 87	6

SUBJECT	TITLE	AUTHOR	IL	INST	JOUR	VOL	NO	ISS	DATE	PAGE
Knitting: Elastic Thread	Coping with Elastic Thread			√	TM		12		A/S 87	10
Knitting: Finishes	Sampler of Knit Edgings and Applied Trims, A	Newton, Deborah	√	√	TM		12		A/S 87	38
Knitting: Finnknit	Finns Can Knit Too or How to Knit a Finn	Rowley, Elaine D.	√	√	PWC		2		Ap 82	76
Knitting: Flat	One-Row Stripes in Flat Knitting		√	√	TM		14		D/J 87	10
Knitting Gloves: Technique	Handknitting Gloves	Newton, Deborah	√	√	TM		14		D/J 87	24
Knitting: Graft, Garter Stitch	School for Knitters		√	√	Kn	3	2	6	Sp 87	3
Knitting: Graft, Stockinette	School for Knitters		√	√	Kn	3	2	6	Sp 87	3
Knitting Groups	Knitters Meet in Baltimore	Galpin, Mary	√	√	TM		3		F/M 86	32
Knitting Groups	Traveling Stitches	Camper, Dorothy			Kn	3	3	7	Su 87	24
Knitting Groups	Traveling Stitches	Camper, Dorothy			Kn	1	1	1	F-W 84 CI	62 52
Knitting Groups	Traveling Stitches	Camper, Dorothy			Kn	1	2	2	S-S 85	50
Knitting Groups	Traveling Stitches	Camper, Dorothy			Kn	2	1	3	F-W 85	74
Knitting Groups	Traveling Stitches	Camper, Dorothy			Kn	2	2	4	S-S 86	76
Knitting Groups	Traveling Stitches	Camper, Dorothy			Kn	3	1	5	F-W 86	66
Knitting Handspun	Almost McKinley Expedition Sweater, The	Kappeler, Erda	√		S-O	11	4		Wi 87	26
Knitting Handspun	Arans: A Saga in Wool (error-corrected S-O V4 80 p4)	Schlegel, Lee-lee	√	√	S-O	3			79	56
Knitting Handspun	Basic Boot Socks	Quinn, Celia	√		S-O	10	2		Su 86	13
Knitting Handspun	Bobbie L. Adelman's Jacket	Adelman, Bobbie L.	√	√	S-O	9	2		Su 85	15
Knitting Handspun	Bonnie Almond's Sweater	Almond, Bonnie	√	√	S-O	9	2		Su 85	13
Knitting Handspun	Brown Jacket with Blue Edging	Keeler, Betty	√	√	S-O	10	1		Sp 86	21
Knitting Handspun	Bye, Baby Bunting	Hayes, Beth	√		S-O	10	2		Su 86	19
Knitting Handspun	Cable-Ribbed Pullover Sweater		√	√	S-O	7	3		Fa 83	56
Knitting Handspun	Classic Alpaca Sweater, A (error-corrected S-O v9 n2 85 p61)	Reynolds, Donna	√	√	S-O	9	1		Sp 85	24
Knitting Handspun	Confessions of a Cotton Spinner	Clivio, Carol	√	√	S-O	10	4		Wi 86	38
Knitting Handspun	Confetti Sweater	Slaven, Pat	√	√	S-O	11	4		Wi 87	26
Knitting Handspun	Cowichan Country	Gibson-Roberts, Priscilla A.	√	√	Kn	3	1	5	F-W 86	61
Knitting Handspun	Crazy Gloves	Dugan, Judy	√	√	S-O	6	4		82	61
Knitting Handspun	Creative Knitwear		√		S-O	3			79	62
Knitting Handspun	Cross Country Ski Set	Chadwick, Louisa	√	√	S-O	11	4		Wi 87	34
Knitting Handspun	Dye Sampler Pullover, A	Van Sickle, Glenda	√	√	S-O	8	3		Fa 84	44
Knitting Handspun	Evolution of a Project	de Grassi, Laurel	√	√	S-O	10	4		Wi 86	21
Knitting Handspun	Exposition of the Epaulet Sweater	Zimmermann, Elizabeth	√	√	Hw	3	1		Ja 82	71
Knitting Handspun	Fair Isle Vest	Van Sickle, Glanda	√	√	S-O	8	3		Fa 84	45
Knitting Handspun	Fishperson's Earflap Hat	Sherrodd, Kristie	√	√	S-O	11	3		Fa 87	53
Knitting Handspun	Gansey in Handspun, The	Gibson-Roberts, Priscilla A.	√	√	Kn	1	1	1	F-W 84 CI	32,56B 24
Knitting Handspun	Guide to Ann's Knit Suit, A	Klinect, Ann W.		√	S-O	10	1		Sp 86	41
Knitting Handspun	Handspinner's Choice, The	Gibson-Roberts, Priscilla A.	√	√	Kn	1	2	2	S-S 85	56
Knitting Handspun	Handspun Angora Mittens	Rowe, Erica	√	√	S-O	8	1		Sp 84	51
Knitting Handspun	Handspun for Kaffe Fassett Sweaters	Adams, Brucie	√	√	S-O	11	4		Wi 87	32
Knitting Handspun	Handspun Knitwear That Lasts	Reynolds, Donna		√	S-O	7	2		Su 83	49
Knitting Handspun	Handspun Rainbow Sweater	Chilton, D. Lorraine	√	√	S-O	7	4		Wi 83	49
Knitting Handspun	Handspun Sampler Sweaters		√	√	S-O	5			81	62
Knitting Handspun	Hats, Hats, Hats	Martin, Jill			S-O	7	3		Fa 83	18
Knitting Handspun	Highlands Shawl	Bush, Nancy	√	√	Kn	4	1	9	Wi 87	40
Knitting Handspun	I Have This Fleece...Now What?	Adams, Brucie	√	√	Iw	5	4		Fa 80	62
Knitting Handspun	"Ice in Shadow" Sweater	Kluth, Liz	√	√	S-O	9	4		Wi 85	15
Knitting Handspun	Knit Tabard	Betts, Diane	√	√	S-O	9	2		Su 85	41

SUBJECT	TITLE	AUTHOR	IL	INST	JOUR	VOL	NO	ISS	DATE	PAGE
Knitting Handspun	Knit to Fit with Handspun	Adams, Brucie; Elizabeth Zimmermann	√		Hw	3	1		Ja 82	70
Knitting Handspun	Knitter's Puzzle: Damask Knitting with Your Handspun, A	Howard, Miranda	√	√	S-O	9	1		Sp 85	36
Knitting Handspun	Knitting with Handspun	O'Connor, Marcie Archer	√	√	Kn	1	1	1	F-W 84	55
									Cl	46
Knitting Handspun	Knitting with Handspun	O'Connor, Marcie Archer	√		Kn	1	2	2	S-S 85	54
Knitting Handspun	Lacy Mohair Vest, A	McPherson, Maggie	√	√	S-O	10	2		Su 86	18
Knitting Handspun	Linen Knits	Westerink, Claire; Erica Baker	√	√	S-O	10	3		Fa 86	17
Knitting Handspun	Llama Wool	Smith, Carolyn	√	√	S-O	11	2		Su 87	32
Knitting Handspun	Loving Touches: Handspinning for Babies	Hayes, Beth	√	√	S-O	11	2		Su 87	20
Knitting Handspun	Lynne Greaves' Sweater	Greaves, Lynne	√	√	S-O	9	2		Su 85	14
Knitting Handspun	Madeline Adkins' Sweater	Adkins, Madaline	√	√	S-O	9	2		Su 85	15
Knitting Handspun	Make It Yourself with Handwoven Wool	John, Sue	√		S-O	9	1		Sp 85	12
Knitting Handspun	Making Gloves That Fit	Buchanan, Rita	√	√	S-O	8	4		Wi 84	17
Knitting Handspun	Merino Pullover	Royce, Beverly	√	√	S-O	9	1		Sp 85	40
Knitting Handspun	Mittens	Rogers, Phyllis, Joan Holborn	√	√	S-O	4			80	61
Knitting Handspun	Mohair Sweater	Reynolds, Donna	√	√	S-O	8	2		Su 84	46
Knitting Handspun	Mohair Tam O'Shanter	Royce, Beverly; Florence Van Kleek	√	√	S-O	8	1		Sp 84	49
Knitting Handspun	Musk Ox, and Miscellaneous	Adams, Brucie	√	√	Iw	4	2		Sp 79	46
Knitting Handspun	Musk Ox Projects		√	√	S-O	7	1		Sp 83	23
Knitting Handspun	Nature: A Color Source and Inspiration for Traditional Sweaters	Gibson-Roberts, Priscilla A.	√		S-O	9	3		Fa 85	42
Knitting Handspun	Norwegian Luskofte	Gibson-Roberts, Priscilla A.	√	√	S-O	9	3		Fa 85	44
Knitting Handspun	Oedipus Jacket, The	McClennen, Carol	√	√	S-O	7	4		Wi 83	31
Knitting Handspun	Opinionated Knitter: Sheep to Shawl, The	Wright, Jenny	√		Kn	4	1	9	Wi 87	20
Knitting Handspun	Peruvian Hat	Ekstrom, Brenda	√	√	S-O	4			80	59
Knitting Handspun	Point of Departure	Ligon, Linda	√	√	S-O	10	2		Su 86	53
Knitting Handspun	Ramie	Cobb, Lorie	√		S-O	10	3		Fa 86	40
Knitting Handspun	Reversible Two-Faced Knitting	Thilenius, Carol	√	√	S-O	7	1		Sp 83	40
Knitting Handspun	Samplings	Mason, Lynn DeRose	√	√	S-O	11	2		Su 87	30
Knitting Handspun	Scarf and Cap	Switzer, Chris	√	√	S-O	4			80	58
Knitting Handspun	Spin for a Scarf		√		S-O	8	3		Fa 84	12
Knitting Handspun	Spin Your Own Lopi?	Gibson-Roberts, Priscilla A.	√	√	S-O	10	2		Su 86	40
Knitting Handspun	SPIN-OFF Book of World Records		√		S-O	4			80	20
Knitting Handspun	SPIN-OFF Book of World Records		√		S-O	7	3		Fa 83	11
Knitting Handspun	Spinners Explore Markets, Ideas	Bulbach, Stanley			TM			3	F/M 86	10
Knitting Handspun	Spinning with Down and Knitting with Feathers	von Ammon, Helen	√		S-O	10	4		Wi 86	15
Knitting Handspun	Spiral Tube Socks		√	√	S-O	11	1		Sp 87	22
Knitting Handspun	Stained Glass Vest	Shull, Paula	√	√	S-O	11	4		Wi 87	29
Knitting Handspun	Super Soft Sweater	Emerick, Patricia	√	√	S-O	11	1		Sp 87	16
Knitting Handspun	Sweater of Abundance	Chelsey, Randy	√	√	S-O	11	1		Sp 87	15
Knitting Handspun	Sweater of Many Colors, A	McIntee, Polly	√	√	S-O	11	2		Su 87	15
Knitting Handspun	Sweatshirt? Yes– A Sweatshirt with Options!, A	Klinect, Ann W.	√	√	S-O	7	1		Sp 83	43
Knitting Handspun	Tale of Two Knitters, A	Preen, Maureen	√		S-O	8	4		Wi 84	19
Knitting Handspun	Thirty-Button Classic	Gibson-Roberts, Priscilla A.	√	√	S-O	11	1		Sp 87	32
Knitting Handspun	Three-Ply Coat Sweater, A	Lacey, Sue	√	√	S-O	8	3		Fa 84	47
Knitting Handspun	Tips on Mittens	Martin, Jill	√	√	S-O	7	2		Su 83	51
Knitting Handspun	Triangular Shawl	Broad, Sue	√		WJ	7	3	27	Wi 82	11

SUBJECT	TITLE	AUTHOR	IL	INST	JOUR	VOL	NO	ISS	DATE	PAGE
Knitting Handspun	Turquoise Angora Pullover	Betts, Diane	√	√	S-O	9	4		Wi 85	36
Knitting Handspun	Two Blankets: Feather and Fan	Irwin, Marjorie	√		S-O	10	1		Sp 86	22
Knitting Handspun	Variations on a Midnight Rainbow	Raven, Lee	√	√	S-O	9	4		Wi 85	14
Knitting Handspun	Warm Wool Sweater, A	Livingston, Marilyn	√	√	S-O	10	4		Wi 86	40
Knitting Handspun	Woolen Socks		√	√	S-O	5			81	60
Knitting Handspun	Working with Lincoln Lamb's Wool	Betts, Diane	√	√	S-O	9	2		Su 85	41
Knitting Handspun: Machine	"Handspun on a Knitting Machine?" Sure!!	Adams, Brucie	√	√	Iw	6	1		Wi 80	60
Knitting: Increase	School for Knitters		√	√	Kn	3	2	6	Sp 87	3
Knitting Instructions: Accuracy	In Stone They Are not Writ	Righetti, Maggie			Kn	1	2	2	S-S 85	7
Knitting: Ireland	Homespun Songs from Ireland's Clancy Brothers	Drake, Elizabeth A.	√		SS&D	16	4	64	Fa 85	62
Knitting Linen	Linen Knits				S-O	10	3		Fa 86	16
Knitting: Loom	Susanna Lewis	Malarcher, Pat	√		Fa	5	3		M/J 78	52
Knitting: Machine	Intarsia Shawl	Lewis, Susanna	√	√	Kn	4	1	9	Wi 87	46
Knitting Machines	Basic Knitting Machine, The	Guagliumi, Susan	√	√	TM			1	O/N 85	34
Knitting Machines	Buyer's Guide to Knitting Machines, A	Weissman, Julia	√		Fa	9	2		M/A 82	43
Knitting Machines	In This Corner, Knitting Machines	Weissman, Julia	√		Kn	1	1	1	F-W 84 CI	64 50
Knitting Machines	Knitting Machine: A Creative Tool, The	Mendelson, Linda	√	√	Fa	5	3		M/J 78	32
Knitting Machines	Machine Knitters Meet in Seattle	Guagliumi, Susan			TM			12	A/S 87	16
Knitting Machines	Succeeding with the Knitting Machine	Mattera, Joanne	√		TM			2	D/J 85	50
Knitting Machines	Thread Weaving	Sample, Joan	√	√	TM			8	D/J 86	64
Knitting Machines	What Knitting Machine to Buy			√	TM			6	A/S 86	8
Knitting Machines: Power	Mechanical Marvels				TM			4	A/M 86	10
Knitting Machines: Power	Miracle Knitter				TM			4	A/M 86	6
Knitting: Make 1	School for Knitters		√	√	Kn	3	2	6	Sp 87	3
Knitting: Make 1 Raised Inc	School for Knitters		√	√	Kn	3	2	6	Sp 87	3
Knitting: Markers	Handknitting Markers			√	TM			12	A/S 87	10
Knitting: Markers	Yarn Markets			√	TM			4	A/M 86	8
Knitting Needles	All About Knitting Needles	Dyett, Linda	√		TM			4	A/M 86	30
Knitting Needles	Knitting In Close Quarters			√	TM			1	O/N 85	6
Knitting Needles	On Knitting Needles			√	TM			6	A/S 86	4
Knitting Needles	Tools				Kn	3	1	5	F-W 86	33
Knitting Needles: Circular	Circular Advice			√	TM			11	J/J 87	4
Knitting Needles: Circular	Taming Circular Needles			√	TM			12	A/S 87	4
Knitting: Number Knitting	Number Knitting — A New Way with an Old Art	Jarecka, Louise Llewellyn	√	√	H&C	2	1		Wi 50	22
Knitting: Pattern Adjusting	Special Fitting	Rowe, Mary	√	√	Kn	1	2	2	S-S 85	30
Knitting: Pattern Altering	Knitting for Petites			√	TM			12	A/S 87	6
Knitting: Patterns	Managing Knitting Patterns			√	TM			10	A/M 87	12
Knitting: Pick-Up	Afghan Jacket			√	TM			8	D/J 86	4
Knitting: Pick-Up	Follow-Up on Picking Up and Knitting			√	TM			5	J/J 86	8
Knitting: Pick-Up	How to Pick Up and Knit			√	TM			3	F/M 86	6
Knitting: Pleats	Perfect Pleats	Rowley, Elaine		√	Kn	3	2	6	Sp 87	24
Knitting: Reversible	Reversible Knitting		√	√	TM			14	D/J 87	6
Knitting: Ribbing, Cable	Knitting with Cotton: Stitch Maneuvers Help Sweaters Stay in Shape	Dyett, Linda	√	√	TM			9	F/M 87	38
Knitting Ribbon	Coronet, A	Clayton, Clare	√	√	Kn	3	2	6	Sp 87	32
Knitting: Ripping Out	Great Rip-Out, The	Sass, Millie	√	√	Kn	1	1	1	F-W 84 CI	5 3
Knitting: Seams, Reversible	Knitting Round on Straight Needles	Borssuck, Bee	√	√	TM			12	A/S 87	64
Knitting: Selvages	Don't Knit Selvages			√	TM			6	A/S 86	4
Knitting: Selvages	Edges of Knitting, The	Gaffey, Theresa	√	√	TM			5	J/J 86	54
Knitting: Short Rows, Improved	School for Knitters		√	√	Kn	3	2	6	Sp 87	3

SUBJECT	TITLE	AUTHOR	IL	INST	JOUR	VOL	NO	ISS	DATE	PAGE
Knitting Silk	Silk	Lawrence, Mary Jo	√	√	WJ	7	3	27	Wi 82	74
Knitting: Silk	Simple and Silk	Gibson-Roberts, Priscilla A.	√	√	Kn	2	2	4	S-S 86	54
Knitting: Socks	Shape of Socks, The	Gaffey, Theresa	√	√	TM			2	D/J 85	28
Knitting: SSD	School for Knitters		√	√	Kn	3	2	6	Sp 87	3
Knitting: SSK	School for Knitters		√	√	Kn	3	2	6	Sp 87	3
Knitting: Stitches	Knitting with Cotton: Stitch Maneuvers Help Sweaters Stay in Shape	Dyett, Linda	√	√	TM			9	F/M 87	38
Knitting: Stitches, Cross	Knitting with Cotton: Stitch Maneuvers Help Sweaters Stay in Shape	Dyett, Linda	√	√	TM			9	F/M 87	38
Knitting: Stitches, Eyelet	Knitted Yarn Over: This Simple Stitch Creates a Hole in the Fabric, The	MacNulty, Shirley W.	√	√	TM			10	A/M 87	38
Knitting: Stitches, Hopsac	One-Row Stripes in Flat Knitting		√	√	TM			14	D/J 87	10
Knitting: Stitches, Seed	Knitting with Cotton: Stitch Maneuvers Help Sweaters Stay in Shape	Dyett, Linda	√	√	TM			9	F/M 87	38
Knitting: Stitches, Stockinette	Knitting with Cotton: Stitch Maneuvers Help Sweaters Stay in Shape	Dyett, Linda	√	√	TM			9	F/M 87	38
Knitting: Stitches, Yarn Over	Knitted Yarn Over: This Simple Stitch Creates a Hole in the Fabric, The	MacNulty, Shirley W.	√	√	TM			10	A/M 87	38
Knitting: Symbols	School for Knitters		√	√	Kn	3	2	6	Sp 87	3
Knitting: Teaching Children	When Jeremy Learned to Knit	Hayes, Beth			TM			2	D/J 85	86
Knitting: Techniques	Confessions of a Backward Knitter	Swansen, Meg		√	Kn	3	3	7	Su 87	27
Knitting: Techniques	Fair Isle Knitting	Starmore, Alice	√	√	TM			8	D/J 86	44
Knitting: Techniques	Knitters Meet in Baltimore	Galpin, Mary	√	√	TM			3	F/M 86	32
Knitting: Techniques	School for Knitters		√	√	Kn	3	2	6	Sp 87	3
Knitting: Techniques	School for Knitters		√	√	Kn	3	3	7	Su 87	6
Knitting: Techniques	School for Knitters		√	√	Kn	3	4	8	Fa 87	3
Knitting: Techniques	School for Knitters		√	√	Kn	4	1	9	Wi 87	5
Knitting: Techniques	School for Knitters		√	√	Kn	1	1	1	F-W 84 CI	6 55
Knitting: Techniques	School for Knitters		√	√	Kn	1	2	2	S-S 85	8
Knitting: Techniques	School for Knitters		√	√	Kn	2	1	3	F-W 85	6
Knitting: Techniques	School for Knitters		√	√	Kn	2	2	4	S-S 86	28
Knitting: Techniques	School for Knitters		√	√	Kn	3	1	5	F-W 86	9
Knitting: Techniques, Circular	Knitting a Seamless Sweater	Zimmermann, Elizabeth	√	√	TM			7	O/N 86	47
Knitting: Theory	Knit and Purl	Rowley, Elaine	√		Kn	1	1	1	F-W 84 CI	40 32
Knitting Traditions: Guernsey Islands	Guernsey Tradition, The	Rowley, Elaine	√	√	Kn	1	1	1	F-W 84 CI	24 16
Knitting: Tubular	Knitting Round on Straight Needles	Borssuck, Bee	√	√	TM			12	A/S 87	64
Knitting: Twisting Yarn	Managing Twisted Knitting Yarns			√	TM			11	J/J 87	8
Knitting: Variegated	Variegated Knitting		√	√	TM			6	A/S 86	12
Knitting vs. Crochet	Knitting Vs. Crochet				TM			11	J/J 87	4
Knitting: Weave-Off, Invisible	Knitting Round on Straight Needles	Borssuck, Bee	√	√	TM			12	A/S 87	64
Knitting: Wisp	Wisp Knitting			√	TM			7	O/N 86	8
Knitting: Yarn Joins	Starting and Ending Yarns			√	TM			13	O/N 87	10
Knitting: Yarn Over	To Narrow and to Fagot			√	TM			13	O/N 87	6
Knitwear	Circular T	Upitis, Lizbeth	√	√	Kn	3	3	7	Su 87	15
Knitwear	Comfortable Cotton T's	Upitis, Lizbeth	√	√	Kn	3	3	7	Su 87	12
Knitwear	Coronet, A	Clayton, Clare	√	√	Kn	3	2	6	Sp 87	32
Knitwear	Fit to a T		√	√	Kn	3	3	7	Su 87	22
Knitwear	Heirloom Wedding Dress	Ellman, Norma	√	√	Kn	3	2	6	Sp 87	31
Knitwear	Lapsang Souchong	Upitis, Lizbeth	√	√	Kn	3	3	7	Su 87	16
Knitwear	Over the Shoulder T	Upitis, Lizbeth	√	√	Kn	3	3	7	Su 87	14
Knitwear	Sans Serif T	Rowley, Elaine	√	√	Kn	3	3	7	Su 87	22
Knitwear	Shirt for All Seasons, A	Rush, Helene	√	√	Kn	3	2	6	Sp 87	25

SUBJECT	TITLE	AUTHOR	IL	INST	JOUR	VOL	NO	ISS	DATE	PAGE
Knitwear	Shrinkage in Cotton Knits	Keele, Wendy	√	√	Kn	3	3	7	Su 87	3
Knitwear	Standard T.	Upitis, Lizbeth	√	√	Kn	3	3	7	Su 87	14
Knitwear	T in a Basket		√	√	Kn	3	3	7	Su 87	19
Knitwear	Tons of T's	Upitis, Lizbeth	√		Kn	3	3	7	Su 87	8
Knitwear: Signed	Signing Your Sweaters			√	TM			13	O/N 87	13
Knots and Knotting	And Knots	Clemner, Phyllis	√	√	SS&D	14	3	55	Su 83	26
Knots and Knotting	"Becky Clark Fiber" (Exhibit)	Farber, Deborah	√		Fa	6	1		J/F 79	89
Knots and Knotting	Before Heddles Were Invented	Bird, Junius B.	√		H&C	3	3		Su 52	5
Knots and Knotting	Diane Itter	Scheinman, Pam	√		Fa	5	2		M/A 78	20
Knots and Knotting	"Diane Itter: Recent Work" (Exhibit)	Park, Betty	√		Fa	8	5		S/O 81	68
Knots and Knotting	Easy Weaving for Easy Living		√	√	Hw	1	2		S-S 80	48
Knots and Knotting	Hammocks	Earth Guild	√	√	SS&D	14	3	55	Su 83	24
Knots and Knotting	High-Status Caps of the Kongo and Mbundu Peoples	Gibson, Gordon D.; Cecilia R. McGurk	√		TMJ	4	4		77	71
Knots and Knotting	"Infrastructure" (Exhibit)	Malarcher, Patricia	√		Fa	11	4		J/A 84	76
Knots and Knotting	Jimmie Benedict: Non-Stop Knotting	Pilsk, Adele	√		Fa	5	2		M/A 78	52
Knots and Knotting	Joan Michaels Paque		√		Fa	3	6		N/D 76	34
Knots and Knotting	Knotted Chinese Button	Baizerman, Suzanne	√	√	WJ	9	1	33	Su 84	7
Knots and Knotting	Leonardo's Knot	Austin, Carole	√		Fa	12	2		M/A 85	43
Knots and Knotting	Nelson Chang: Champion of Chinese Knotting	Westbrook, John R.,	√		Fa	14	3		M/J 87	6
Knots and Knotting	Renie Breskin Adams: Artist...Teacher...Self-Seeker	Sommer, Elyse	√		Fa	5	3		M/J 78	36
Knots and Knotting	Russ-Knotting from Sweden	Swenson, Astrid	√	√	SS&D	4	3	15	Su 73	24
Knots and Knotting	Secret Treasures of Tibet	Wiltsie-Vaniea, Anne	√		SS&D	18	3	71	Su 87	60
Knots and Knotting	Timeless Knotted Jewelry: Marion Hunziker Meticulously Combines Fiber and Metalwork Techniques	Hunziker, Marion	√		Fa	8	4		J/A 81	19
Knots and Knotting	"Tina Johnson-Depuy Soft Jewelry" (Exhibit)	Cardinale, Robert L.	√		Fa	6	3		M/J 79	81
Knots and Knotting	Why Knot?	Krantz, Hazel	√	√	Hw	5	4		S/0 84	24
Knots and Knotting: Clove Hitch	Traditional Berber Weaving in Central Morocco	Forelli, Sally; Jeanette Harries	√		TMJ	4	4		77	41
Knots and Knotting: Double Interlocking Knot	Peruvian Technique for Dimensional Knotting	Bravo, Monica	√	√	WJ	12	1	45	Su 87	17
Knots and Knotting: Ghiordes Knot	Traditional Berber Weaving in Central Morocco	Forelli, Sally; Jeanette Harries	√		TMJ	4	4		77	41
Knots and Knotting: Handweaving Knots	Peter Collingwood, His Weaves and Weaving: Knots Used in Handweaving	Collingwood, Peter; Harriet Tidball, ed.	√	√	SCGM		8		63	28
Knots and Knotting: Needle	Peruvian Technique for Dimensional Knotting	Bravo, Monica	√	√	WJ	12	1	45	Su 87	17
Knots and Knotting: Rya	Fabric #4: Accent Fabric (Constance LaLena)		√	√	Hw	6	3		Su 85	62, I-5
Knots and Knotting: Sewing	Neat Knots		√	√	TM			6	A/S 86	14
Knots and Knotting: Snitch Knot	Handweaver's Instruction Manual: Dressing the Loom, Loom Adjustments, Snitch Knot	Tidball, Harriet C. nee Douglas	√	√	SCGM		34		49	17
Knots and Knotting: Spanish Knot	Traditional Berber Weaving in Central Morocco	Forelli, Sally; Jeanette Harries	√		TMJ	4	4		77	41
Knots and Knotting: Spinner's Knot	Spinner's Knot, A	Raven, Lee	√	√	S-O	9	4		Wi 85	56
Knots and Knotting: Techniques	Peruvian Technique for Dimensional Knotting	Bravo, Monica	√	√	WJ	12	1	45	Su 87	17
Knots and Knotting: Weaver's Knot	Handweaver's Instruction Manual: Dressing the Loom, Correcting Errors, Weaver's Knot	Tidball, Harriet C. nee Douglas	√	√	SCGM		34		49	17
Knots and Knotting: Weaver's Knot	Weaver's Knot, The	Jarvis, P. R.	√	√	Iw	5	3		Su 80	63
Knots: Knitted	Lace and Knots	Newton, Deborah	√	√	Kn	3	4	8	Fa 87	20

417

SUBJECT	TITLE	AUTHOR	IL	INST	JOUR	VOL	NO	ISS	DATE	PAGE
Korea	Cheju Weavers, A New Industry Arises on a Korean Island	Ford, Howard C.	√		H&C	12	3		Su 61	11
Korea	Korean Journal	Blickenstaff, Maxine L.	√		SS&D	7	2	26	Sp 76	52
Krokbrågd	Boundweave: Learning from the Past	Waggoner, Phyllis	√	√	WJ	10	4	40	Sp 86	44
Krokbrågd	Christmas Miniatures, Part 2: Krokbragd Bellpulls (error-corrected PWC i4 83 p76)	Xenakis, Athanasios David	√	> 4	PWC			3	Oc 82	52
Krokbrågd	Double-faced, Double-woven, Three-harness Krokbragd	Holtzer, Marilyn Emerson	√	√	SS&D	14	4	56	Fa 83	46
Krokbrågd	How do I Krokbragd? Let me Count the Ways			√	Hw	2	4		Se 81	7
Krokbrågd	Krokbragd Rug (Lin Eppinger) (error-corrected Hw v2 n4 81 p22)		√	√	Hw	2	2		Mr 81	36
Krokbrågd	Mukluks (Bridget McNamara)		√	√	Hw	1	1		F-W 79	20, 54
Krokbrågd	Project in Krokbragd, A	Davenport, Betty	√	√	PWC			2	Ap 82	66
Krokbrågd	Rosemary R. Olmsted: Following Krokbragd's Crooked Path	Olmsted, Rosemary R.	√		Fa	11	3		M/J 84	28
Krokbrågd	Rugs in the Scandinavian Way		√	√	Hw	8	3		M/J 87	58
Krokbrågd	Summer and Winter Revisited, Part 2: I. On Designing with Krokbragd, Krokbragd Mug Rugs	Lyon, Linda	√	√	PWC			2	Ap 82	63
Krokbrågd	Summer and Winter Revisited, Part 2: II. Krokbragd on One, A Woolen Runner Project	Davenport, Betty	√	√	PWC			2	Ap 82	65
Krokbrågd	Three and Four Harness Krokbragd (error-corrected PWC i4 83 p76)	Temple, Mary	√	√	PWC			3	Oc 82	56
Krokbrågd	Weaving and Sheepskin, Naturally	Mason, Carole	√	√	WJ	5	3	19	Wi 81	46
Krokbrågd, Double-Faced	Double-Faced Krokbragd	Holtzer, Marilyn Emerson	√	> 4	WJ	9	4	36	Sp 85	59
Krokbrågd, Warp-Faced	Warp-Faced Krokbragd	Jensen, Gay; Donna Kaplan	√	> 4	WJ	12	2	46	Fa 87	62
Krubba	Why Not Try Embroidery Weaves?	Jones, Jeanetta L.	√	√	H&C	17	2		Sp 66	12
Kudzu	Kudzu	Foster, Ann	√		S-O	3			79	23
Kudzu	Kudzu: The Noxious Weed Transformed	Buchanan, Rita	√		Fa	14	2		M/A 87	48
Kumihimo	Briading Technique Documented in an Early Nineteenth-Century Japanese Treatise, "Soshun Biko", A	Kinoshita, Masako	√	√	TMJ	25			86	47
Kumihimo	Kago-Uchi, The	Speiser, Noémi	√	√	AT	4			De 85	23
Kumihimo	Kumihimo	Kinoshita, Masako	√	√	SS&D	11	3	43	Su 80	19
Kumihimo	Kumihimo (error-corrected SS&D v9 n2 78 p70)	Kinoshita, Masako	√	√	SS&D	9	1	33	Wi 77	117
Kumihimo	Kumihimo: The Art of Japanese Braiding	Moss, Helen E.	√		Fa	14	1		J/F 87	20
Kumihimo Braiding	Rainbow Jacket (Sara Lamb)		√	> 4	Hw	4	1		J/F 83	45, 84
Kurdistan	Jews of Kurdistan, The	Meyerowitz, Carol Orlove	√	√	SS&D	14	2	54	Sp 83	23
Labeling	Arianthé: Notes from a Production Weaver		√		Fa	5	5		S/O 78	32
Labeling	Care Labeling Rule of FTC			√	SS&D	4	1	13	Wi 72	42
Labeling	Developments in Man-made Fibers	Hausner, Walter			H&C	11	1		Wi 60	31
Labeling	Fair Isle Self-Labels		√	√	TM			8	D/J 86	8
Labeling	Laundry Care Labels Needed After July 3	Attix, George			SS&D	3	3	11	Su 72	10
Labeling	Tag End, The	Holland, Nina			H&C	23	6		N/D 72	40
Labeling	Uniform Label Law		√		SS&D	9	3	35	Su 78	76
Labeling	Wearables in the Market Place: Reporting on a Survey	Dunnewold, Jane	√		Fa	12	3		M/J 85	48
Labeling	What You Need to Know If You Make Fabric or Apparel for Wholesale or Retail Sale				Fa	9	1		J/F 82	52
Labeling: Laws	Fickle Feds Finger Fiber Felons	Rutovsky, Fran Cutrell			Fa	4	2		M/A 77	6
Labeling: Yarn	Send Along a Yarn Label			√	TM			11	J/J 87	6
Labels	Labels	Green, Marilyn	√		Hw	5	3		Su 84	14

SUBJECT	TITLE	AUTHOR	IL	INST	JOUR	VOL	NO	ISS	DATE	PAGE
Labels: Woven	Marks of Distinction: Woven Labels 1900–1940	Kluge, Chris	√		Fa	8	1		J/F 81	24
Lace also see Openwork Weaves										
Lace	Betty Boulez-Cuykx: Modern Lacemaker	de Backer, Lisette	√		Fa	13	3		M/J 86	23
Lace	"Historic Spanish Lace" (Exhibit)		√		Fa	14	1		J/F 87	54
Lace	Lace Constructions from Czechoslovakia				H&C	15	4		Fa 64	34
Lace	"Lace" (Exhibit)	Lo Presti, Louise	√		Fa	9	6		N/D 82	79
Lace	Lace Is My Career. Wire Is My Specialty		√		Fa	14	4		S/O 87	61
Lace	Lace-Weave Pullover Top (Elaine Rowley)		√	√	Hw	1	1		F-W 79	21, 56
Lace	New Skirts for Summer	Frey, Berta	√	> 4	H&C	4	1		Wi 52	33
Lace	Postal Service Celebrates Lace		√		TM			12	A/S 87	22
Lace	"Splendor of French Style, The" Textiles from Joan of Arc to Napoleon III (Exhibit)	Guagliumi, Susan	√		Fa	13	4		J/A 86	13
Lace	Stoles and Scarves		√	√	WJ	2	1	5	Jy 77	3
Lace	U.S. Postage Stamp Honors Lacemaking		√		Fa	14	2		M/A 87	30
Lace, Appropriate Yarn	Yarn for Lace?			√	TM			13	O/N 87	4
Lace, Atwater Bronson	Block Weaves Part 2, Atwater Bronson Lace		√	> 4	WJ	2	3	7	Ja 78	10
Lace, Atwater-Bronson	Atwater-Bronson Lace — Turned		√	√	WJ	2	4	8	Ap 78	20
Lace, Atwater-Bronson	Design and the Handweaver: Pattern	Atwater, Mary Meigs	√	> 4	SCGM		3		61	25
Lace, Atwater-Bronson	Hands to Work and Hearts to God	Erf, Mary Elva	√	√	WJ	8	1	29	Su 83	25
Lace, Atwater-Bronson	Home Weaving: Linen'n Lace	Xenaxis, Athanasios David	√	√	Hw	1	1		F-W 79	44
Lace, Atwater-Bronson	Imperial Tulip and Prairie Flower		√	√	PWC			5	Sp 83	15
Lace, Atwater-Bronson	Lace-Weave Tunic	Rowley, Elaine	√	√	PWC			5	Sp 83	18
Lace, Atwater-Bronson	Lacey and Thin Fabrics		√	√	WJ	2	3	7	Ja 78	4
Lace, Atwater-Bronson	Linen Tablerunner with Atwater Bronson Lace	Cyr, Gloria	√	> 4	WJ	7	2	26	Fa 82	37
Lace, Atwater-Bronson	Two-Tie Inlay	Xenakis, Athanasios David	√	√	PWC	4	1	11		19
Lace, Atwater-Bronson	Weaving Primer	Ingebretsen, Catherine	√	√	PWC			6	Su 83	4
Lace, Atwater-Bronson	Worsted Dress (Sharon Alderman)		√	√	Hw	3	4		Se 82	41, 95
Lace, Atwater-Bronson	Woven Lace, Part 1: The Bronson Systems — The Atwater-Bronson System	Xenakis, Athanasios David	√	√	PWC			5	Sp 83	12
Lace, Atwater-Bronson (Damask Effect)	Bronson Damask Effect, The		√	√	PWC			5	Sp 83	35
Lace, Atwater-Bronson (Damask Effect)	Orchid Shawl	Xenakis, Athanasios David	√	√	PWC			5	Sp 83	38
Lace, Atwater-Bronson (Damask Effect)	Two Placemats	Herring, Connie	√	√	PWC			5	Sp 83	36
Lace, Atwater-Bronson, Reversible	Weaving the Night Fantastic	Lyon, Linda	√	> 4	PWC			5	Sp 83	51
Lace, Atwater-Bronson System	Handloom Weaves: The Classification of Handloom Weaves, The Structural Group, Unit Class, Atwater-Bronson Lace System	Tidball, Harriet	√	> 4	SCGM		33		57	23
Lace, Atwater-Bronson, Variations	Woven Lace, Part 1: The Bronson Systems — 4-Thread and 8-Thread Atwater-Bronson	Xenakis, Athanasios David	√	√	PWC			5	Sp 83	13
Lace, Battenberg: Technique	Battenberg Lace: Making Lace with Woven Tape and a Needle	Kliot, Jules; Kaethe Kliot	√	√	TM			10	A/M 87	30
Lace, Belgian	"Belgian Lace" (Exhibit)		√		Fa	7	4		J/A 80	66
Lace, Bobbin	Kliots of Berkeley, The	Talley, Charles S.	√		Fa	7	4		J/A 80	44
Lace, Bronson	Bronson Lace Tablecloth and Napkins (Sallie T. Guy)		√	> 4	Hw	8	1		J/F 87	61, I-13
Lace, Bronson	Designing with Loom-Woven Open Weaves	Marston, Ena	√	√	SS&D	13	1	49	Wi 81	22
Lace, Bronson	Different Floats for Different Folks		√	√	PWC			5	Sp 83	31
Lace, Bronson	Flax	Miller, Suzanne	√	√	WJ	7	2	26	Fa 82	12

419

SUBJECT	TITLE	AUTHOR	IL	INST	JOUR	VOL	NO	ISS	DATE	PAGE
Lace, Bronson	Handspun/Handwoven Ramie Blouse	Champion, Ellen	√	> 4	WJ	9	2	34	Fa 84	52
Lace, Bronson	HGA Education Directory, 1984	Smayda, Norma	√	> 4	SS&D	15	4	60	Fa 84	6
Lace, Bronson	Kirschbaum Tablecloth (Julie Lawson)		√	√	Hw	8	1		J/F 87	58, I-10
Lace, Bronson	Lace Window Hanging with Plaid		√	√	PWC			5	Sp 83	27
Lace, Bronson	Linen Lace Blouse (Sharon Alderman)		√	√	Hw	1	2		S-S 80	45, 66
Lace, Bronson	Patterns Woven in Lace	Keasbey, Doramay	√	> 4	CW	3	2	8	Ja 82	11
Lace, Bronson	Projects with Cotton		√	√	WJ	4	2	14	Oc 79	28
Lace, Bronson	Red Lace Scarf (Betty Davenport)		√	√	Hw	7	1		J/F 86	63, I-13
Lace, Bronson	Silk	Sullivan, Donna	√	√	SS&D	16	2	62	Sp 85	42
Lace, Bronson	Some Loom-Woven Open Weaves (error-corrected SS&D v13 n1 81 p4)	Marston, Ena	√	√	SS&D	12	4	48	Fa 81	32
Lace, Bronson	Swatch #4, Linen Suit Fabric For Spring (Lillian Whipple)		√	√	Hw	7	5		N/D 86	64, I-7
Lace, Bronson	Upside-Down and Other Clever Tricks		√	> 4	PWC			5	Sp 83	29
Lace, Bronson	Victorian Garden (error-corrected PWC i8 p66)	Xenakis, Athanasios David	√	√	PWC	3	1	7		31
Lace, Bronson	Weaver's Challenge	Wertenberger, Kathryn	√	√	Hw	5	1		J/F 84	27
Lace, Bronson	Weaving Towels As a Means of Learning the Basic Four-Shaft Weaves	Barrett, Clotilde	√	√	WJ	8	2	30	Fa 83	11
Lace, Bronson	Whig Rose Study (continued)	Morgenstern, Marvin M.	√	√	WJ	7	3	27	Wi 82	23
Lace, Bronson	Woven Lace and Lacey Weaves: A Stronger Lace	Zielinski, S. A.; Robert Leclerc, ed.	√	√	MWL	13			'51–'73	60
Lace, Bronson	Woven Lace and Lacey Weaves: Bronson Lace	Zielinski, S. A.; Robert Leclerc, ed.	√	> 4	MWL	13			'51–'73	30
Lace, Bronson	Woven Lace and Lacey Weaves: Swedish Lace	Zielinski, S. A.; Robert Leclerc, ed.	√	> 4	MWL	13			'51–'73	17
Lace, Bronson	Woven Lace, Part 1: The Bronson Systems	Xenakis, Athanasios David	√	√	PWC			5	Sp 83	10
Lace, Bronson	Wrap Around Top (Betty Davenport)		√	√	Hw	6	2		M/A 85	18, I-3
Lace, Bronson Medallion	Weaving Primer	Ingebretsen, Catherine	√	√	PWC			6	Su 83	4
Lace, Bronson Spot	Translating Four-Harness Drafts for the Single Rigid Heddle Method		√	√	PWC			5	Sp 83	22
Lace, Bronson, Two-Block	Profile Drafting Lesson: Bronson Lace Towel (Sharon Alderman)		√	√	Hw	8	5		N/D 87	44, I-7
Lace, Bronson, Variations	Fun with Bronson Lace Variations	Davenport, Betty	√	√	PWC			5	Sp 83	46
Lace, Bronson, Variations	Two Silk Blouses (Amy Preckshot) (error-corrected Hw v7 n4 86 p I-16)		√	> 4	Hw	7	1		J/F 86	54, I-9
Lace, Brooks Bouquet	Brooks Lace and Weaving	Tod, Osma Gallinger	√		H&C	20	1		Wi 69	29
Lace, Brooks Bouquet	Weaving Primer	Ingebretsen, Catherine	√	√	PWC			6	Su 83	4
Lace, Brook's Bouquet	Finger Control: Or Getting the Most Out of Your Loom	Patrick, Jane	√	√	Hw	4	2		M/A 83	70
Lace, Classifications	Looking At Lace	Kliot, Jules; Kaethe Kliot	√		Fa	9	3		M/J 82	43
Lace, Contemporary	Contemporary Lace of Susan Wood, The	Darling, Drew	√		Fa	11	6		N/D 84	22
Lace, Contemporary	Lace and Cashmere		√		TM			8	D/J 86	12
Lace, Crochet	Lampshade Transfigured, A	Fauske, Carla	√	√	PWC	1	1		No 81	55
Lace, Danish Medallion	Designed for Narrow Looms: A Summer Shirt Inspired by the Macedonian Chemise	Temple, Mary	√	√	WJ	10	1	37	Su 85	46
Lace, Finnish	Finnish Lace	Howard, Miranda	√	> 4	Hw	5	3		Su 84	80
Lace, Finnish	Finnish Lace: a Leno Variation	Egen, Su	√	√	Hw	7	2		M/A 86	49
Lace, Finnish	Wear Your Best Apron	MacNutt, Dawn	√	√	SS&D	8	4	32	Fa 77	65
Lace, Finnish, Variation	Silk Blouse with Scarf (Sylvia Slater Berkowitz)		√	√	Hw	8	5		N/D 87	32, I-4
Lace, Hairpin	Creative Clothing: Surface Embellishment	Mayer, Anita Luvera	√	√	WJ	11	3	43	Wi 87	30
Lace, Handmade	Looking At Lace	Kliot, Jules; Kaethe Kliot	√		Fa	9	3		M/J 82	43
Lace, Knitted	Alpaca Vest	Newton, Deborah	√	√	Kn	3	4	8	Fa 87	21

SUBJECT	TITLE	AUTHOR	IL	INST	JOUR	VOL	NO	ISS	DATE	PAGE
Lace, Knitted	Arctic Handknitted, One Hundred Per Cent Qiviut	Griffiths, Helen M.	√		H&C	22	2		Sp 71	6
Lace, Knitted	Babushkas	Upitis, Lizbeth	√	√	Kn	4	1	9	Wi 87	48
Lace, Knitted	Basic Knitting Machine, The	Guagliumi, Susan	√	√	TM			1	O/N 85	38
Lace, Knitted	Bonnie Bonnet	Adams, Harriet	√	√	Kn	1	2	2	S-S 85	38
Lace, Knitted	Burra Lace Pullover	Bush, Nancy	√	√	Kn	3	4	8	Fa 87	26
Lace, Knitted	Faroese Shawls	Swansen, Meg	√	√	Kn	4	1	9	Wi 87	26
Lace, Knitted	Grandma's Checkerboard Lace	Yaksick, Karen	√	√	Kn	4	1	9	Wi 87	52
Lace, Knitted	Handspun into Lace	Fournier, Jane	√	√	SS&D	17	4	68	Fa 86	70
Lace, Knitted	Heirloom Wedding Dress	Ellman, Norma	√	√	Kn	3	2	6	Sp 87	31
Lace, Knitted	Knitter's Journey, A	Bush, Nancy	√		Kn	3	4	8	Fa 87	24
Lace, Knitted	Lace				Kn	1	2	2	S-S 85	20
Lace, Knitted	Lace and Knots	Newton, Deborah	√	√	Kn	3	4	8	Fa 87	20
Lace, Knitted	Lace and Legs	Upitis, Lizbeth	√		Kn	1	2	2	S-S 85	64
Lace, Knitted	Lace Collar	Drysdale, Rosemary	√	√	Kn	3	4	8	Fa 87	48
Lace, Knitted	Lace Curtains	Higginbotham, Charles	√	√	Kn	1	2	2	S-S 85	40
Lace, Knitted	Lace from Hand to Machine	Lewis, Susanna E.	√	√	Kn	1	2	2	S-S 85	71
Lace, Knitted	Lace Garland	Ocker, Emily	√	√	Kn	4	1	9	Wi 87	38
Lace, Knitted	Lace Shawl	Newton, Deborah	√	√	Kn	4	1	9	Wi 87	54
Lace, Knitted	Leaves and Trellises	Emerson, Rebecca	√	√	Kn	1	2	2	S-S 85	48, 72B
Lace, Knitted	Mr. Hunter's Lace	Yaksick, Karen	√	√	Kn	3	4	8	Fa 87	22
Lace, Knitted	On Designing in 2 Dimensions: Shawls and Scarves	Newton, Deborah	√	√	Kn	4	1	9	Wi 87	30
Lace, Knitted	On Designing with Lace	Newton, Deborah	√	√	Kn	1	2	2	S-S 85	21
Lace, Knitted	Ornamental and Functional	Rowley, Elaine			Kn	1	2	2	S-S 85	36
Lace, Knitted	Shawl in the English Tradition, A	Zimmermann, Elizabeth	√	√	Kn	1	2	2	S-S 85	59
Lace, Knitted	π Shawl, The	Zimmermann, Elizabeth	√	√	Kn	4	1	9	Wi 87	34
Lace, Knitted	Shetland Lace	Korach, Alice	√	√	TM			11	J/J 87	40
Lace, Knitted	Shetland Lace Wedding Handkerchief, A (error-corrected TM n12 87 p4)	Korach, Alice	√	√	TM			11	J/J 87	42
Lace, Knitted	Sidna's Shetland Shawl	Farley, Sidna	√	√	Kn	4	1	9	Wi 87	22
Lace, Knitted	Six Ways to Wear Your Lace	Beugler, Eugen	√	√	Kn	4	1	9	Wi 87	44
Lace, Knitted	Snowdrops and Snowflakes	George, Barbara	√	√	Kn	4	1	9	Wi 87	17
Lace, Knitted	Special Fittings: Tulips	Glover, Medrith J.	√	√	Kn	1	2	2	S-S 85	29, 72A
Lace, Knitted	Special Fittings: Valerie's Vest	August, Valerie	√	√	Kn	1	2	2	S-S 85	31
Lace, Knitted	Stitches from the Sea		√	√	Kn	3	4	8	Fa 87	49
Lace, Knitted	Stocking Basics	Upitis, Lizbeth	√	√	Kn	1	2	2	S-S 85	66
Lace, Knitted	Stonington Shawl	Zimmermann, Elizabeth	√	√	TM	1	2	2	S-S 85	60, 72B
Lace, Knitted	Summer Lace Sweater	Farley, Sidna	√	√	Kn	1	2	2	S-S 85	32, 72A
Lace, Knitted	T-Sweater	Rowley, Elaine	√	√	Kn	1	2	2	S-S 85	34, 72A
Lace, Knitted	Traditional Shetland Shawl, A	Zimmermann, Elizabeth	√	√	Kn	1	2	2	S-S 85	59
Lace, Knitted	Traditional Stockings: A Girl's Stocking (Lizbeth Upitis)		√	√	Kn	1	2	2	S-S 85	68
Lace, Knitted	Traditional Stockings: A Stocking from Rucava, Kurzeme, Latvia		√	√	Kn	1	2	2	S-S 85	69
Lace, Knitted	Traditional Stockings: A Stocking from Zemgale, Lativia (Elizeabete Zvirbulis)		√	√	Kn	1	2	2	S-S 85	69
Lace, Knitted	Traditional Stockings: Amish Baby Stockings (Mary Miller)		√	√	Kn	1	2	2	S-S 85	69
Lace, Knitted	Undies Revealed: Camisole	Upitis, Lizbeth	√	√	Kn	3	2	6	Sp 87	12
Lace, Knitted	Undies Revealed: Petticoat	Rowley, Elaine	√	√	Kn	3	2	6	Sp 87	13
Lace, Knitted	Winter Birches: The Blouse	Upitis, Lizbeth	√	√	Kn	1	2	2	S-S 85	46, 72B
Lace, Knitted	Winter Birches: The Jacket	Upitis, Lizbeth	√	√	Kn	1	2	2	S-S 85	44
Lace, Knitted	Wymple in Tyme, A	Gibson-Roberts, Priscilla A.	√	√	Kn	3	4	8	Fa 87	56

SUBJECT	TITLE	AUTHOR	IL	INST	JOUR	VOL	NO	ISS	DATE	PAGE
Lace, Knotted Looping	Windows to the Soul: The Lace Making of Luba Krejci	Kaminski, Vera E.	√	√	Fa	6	6		N/D 79	56
Lace, Leno	Figured Bead Leno Lace	Merritt, Elveana	√	√	WJ	6	1	21	Su 81	50
Lace, Leno	Lacy Triangular Stole of Handspun Wool, A	Kniskern, Edna Maki	√	√	WJ	6	2	22	Fa 81	48
Lace, Leno, Bead	Figured Bead Leno Lace	Merritt, Elveana	√	√	WJ	6	1	21	Su 81	50
Lace, Loom-Controlled	Gifts from Ancient Peru	Nass, Ulla	√	√	WJ	8	1	29	Su 83	32
Lace, Machine Made	Looking At Lace	Kliot, Jules; Kaethe Kliot	√		Fa	9	3		M/J 82	43
Lace, Macro	Bobbin Lace on a Grand Scale: When the Pillow Is a 12-ft. Pegboard	Lewis, Robin S.	√	√	TM			9	F/M 87	54
Lace Maker	Lace Maker of Holland, Henk van der Zanden			√	H&C	17	2		Sp 66	15
Lace Makers	Postal Service Celebrates Lace			√	TM			12	A/S 87	22
Lace Makers	To Be Not a Brute, Rousseau Made Lace	Hedrick, L. R.		√	TM			10	A/M 87	16
Lace Making	Amazing Lace on Venetian Isle	Mattera, Joanna		√	TM			7	O/N 86	12
Lace Making: Handspun	Lark Burger's Lacy Scarf			√	S-O	9	3		Fa 85	15
Lace, Myggtjall	Dress for Emily, A (Barbara Miller)		√	√	Hw	5	3		Su 84	50, 95
Lace, Needle	Contemporary Needle Lacers			√	TM			13	O/N 87	44
Lace, Needle	Needle Lace	Kaiser, Eunice	√	√	TM			13	O/N 87	40
Lace, Paper Spots	Patterns Woven in Lace	Keasbey, Doramay	√	> 4	CW	3	2	8	Ja 82	11
Lace, Pickets and Riddles	Woven Lace and Lacey Weaves: Pickets and Riddles for Four Harness Frames	Zielinski, S. A.; Robert Leclerc, ed.	√	√	MWL	13			'51–'73	71
Lace, Reticella	Story of Reticella, The	Cave, OEnone	√		H&C	11	3		Su 60	14
Lace, Searles, Free-Form	Freeform Twill & Freeform Searles Lace	Searles, Nancy	√	> 4	CW		23		Ja 87	10
Lace, Shetland	On Designing in 2 Dimensions: Shawls and Scarves	Newton, Deborah	√	√	Kn	4	1	9	Wi 87	30
Lace, Shetland	Shetland Lace	Korach, Alice	√	√	TM			11	J/J 87	40
Lace, Shetland	Yarns for Lace Knitting			√	TM			14	D/J 87	4
Lace, Spanish	Lina Hartman Silk Scarf (Louise Bradley)		√	√	Hw	5	5		N/D 84	53, I-7
Lace, Spanish	Linen Mats (Dixie Francis)		√	√	Hw	7	3		M/J 86	67, I-15
Lace, Spanish	Stoles and Scarves		√	√	WJ	2	1	5	Jy 77	3
Lace, Spanish Eyelet	Weaving Spanish Eyelet	Gubser, Elsie H.	√	√	H&C	10	1		Wi 59	48
Lace, Supplies	Battenberg Lace: Making Lace with Woven Tape and a Needle	Kliot, Jules; Kaethe Kliot	√	√	TM			10	A/M 87	30
Lace, Supplies	Bobbin Lace on a Grand Scale: When the Pillow Is a 12-ft. Pegboard	Lewis, Robin S.	√	√	TM			9	F/M 87	54
Lace, Swarthmore, Blocks	Swarthmore Lace Scarf (M. Linda Whitten)		√	√	Hw	7	1		J/F 86	69
Lace, Swedish	Gray Muffler (Janice Jones)		√	√	Hw	6	4		S/O 85	59, I-10
Lace, Swedish	Linen Lampshade (Robin Taylor Daugherty)		√	√	Hw	5	2		M/A 84	52, 97
Lace, Swedish	Napkins for a Box Lunch (Susan Feely) (error-corrected Hw v7 n4 86 p I-3)		√	√	Hw	7	3		M/J 86	75
Lace, Swedish	Projects with Cotton		√	√	WJ	4	2	14	Oc 79	28
Lace, Swedish	Silk Cocoon (Karen Smith) (error-corrected Hw v8 n4 87 p I-3)		√	√	Hw	8	2		M/A 87	57, I-15
Lace, Swedish	Some Loom-Woven Open Weaves (error-corrected SS&D v13 n1 81 p4)	Marston, Ena	√	√	SS&D	12	4	48	Fa 81	32
Lace, Swedish	Swedish Lace Napkins (Deborah Anthony)		√	√	Hw	8	1		J/F 87	57, I-10, Cover
Lace, Swedish	Weaving As Drawn In — Classic Style, Part 2	Keasbey, Doramay	√	> 4	SS&D	17	2	66	Sp 86	38
Lace, Swedish	White Bath Towel (Suzanne Urton)		√	√	Hw	4	3		M/J 83	52, 94
Lace, Swedish	Woven Lace and Lacey Weaves: A Stronger Lace	Zielinski, S. A.; Robert Leclerc, ed.	√	√	MWL	13			'51–'73	60
Lace, Swedish	Woven Lace and Lacey Weaves: Swedish Lace	Zielinski, S. A.; Robert Leclerc, ed.	√	> 4	MWL	13			'51–'73	17
Lace, Swedish (Mock Leno)	Casement Cloth (Constance LaLena)		√	√	Hw	3	4		Se 82	33, 84

SUBJECT	TITLE	AUTHOR	IL	INST	JOUR	VOL	NO	ISS	DATE	PAGE
Lace, Swedish System	Handloom Weaves: The Classification of Handloom Weaves, The Structural Group, The Grouped-Thread Class, Swedish Lace System	Tidball, Harriet	√	√	SCGM		33		57	31
Lace, Swedish, Turned Drafts	Woven Lace and Lacey Weaves: Swedish Lace	Zielinski, S. A.; Robert Leclerc, ed.	√	>4	MWL	13			'51–'73	17
Lace, Swedish, Turned Drafts	Woven Lace and Lacey Weaves: Turned Swedish Lace	Zielinski, S. A.; Robert Leclerc, ed.	√	>4	MWL	13			'51–'73	56
Lace, Swedish, Types	Three Swedish Weaves	af Kleen, Elizabeth	√		H&C	12	1		Wi 61	14
Lace, Tape	Battenberg Lace: Making Lace with Woven Tape and a Needle	Kliot, Jules; Kaethe Kliot	√	√	TM			10	A/M 87	30
Lace, Tarascan	Tarascan Lace		√	√	WJ	2	3	7	Ja 78	21
Lace, Tarascan	Tarascan Lace	Jenkins, Evelyn	√	√	H&C	11	1		Wi 60	12
Lace, Tarascan	Tarascan Lace (error-corrected WJ v9 n1 84 p70)	Thabet, Micheline	√	√	WJ	8	4	32	Sp 84	48
Lace, Tatted	Handspun into Lace	Fournier, Jane	√	√	SS&D	17	4	68	Fa 86	70
Lace, Techniques	Windows to the Soul: The Lace Making of Luba Krejci	Kaminski, Vera E.	√	√	Fa	6	6		N/D 79	56
Lace, Teneriffe	Teneriffe Lace — Brasilian Solo Lace	Kliot, Kaethe			SS&D	5	1	17	Wi 73	52
Lace, Teneriffe	Teneriffe Lace—Brazilian Point	Griffiths, Alice K.	√		SS&D	4	4	16	Fa 73	33
Lace, Teneriffe	Teneriffe Lace — Estonian Sun Lace	Kuisk, Harda		√	SS&D	5	1	17	Wi 73	52
Lace, Teneriffe	Teneriffe Lace — Legend of Nanduti, A Closely Related Lace	Ardita, Nessim	√		SS&D	5	1	17	Wi 73	53
Lace, Teneriffe	Teneriffe Lace — Making Nanduti	Robinson, Esther	√	√	SS&D	5	1	17	Wi 73	54
Lace, Teneriffe	Teneriffe Lace—Polka Spider Web	Galvin, Nellie L.	√		SS&D	4	4	16	Fa 73	33
Lace, Teneriffe	Teneriffe Lace — Sol or Sun Lace	Kaiser, Eunice			SS&D	5	1	17	Wi 73	52
Lace, Teneriffe	Teneriffe Lace—Spider Web Lace	Bolster, Ella S.	√		SS&D	4	4	16	Fa 73	33
Lace, Teneriffe	Teneriffe Lace—With Variations	Spencer, Elsie	√	√	SS&D	4	4	16	Fa 73	31
Lace, Teneriffe	Teneriffe Lace — With Variations, Part 2		√		SS&D	5	1	17	Wi 73	52
Lace, Turned Drafts	Woven Lace and Lacey Weaves: Projects in Turned Lace for Eight Shafts	Zielinski, S. A.; Robert Leclerc, ed.	√	>4	MWL	13			'51–'73	50
Lace, Turned Drafts	Woven Lace and Lacey Weaves: Turned Lace for Eight Shafts	Zielinski, S. A.; Robert Leclerc, ed.	√	>4	MWL	13			'51–'73	45
Lace, Turned Drafts	Woven Lace and Lacey Weaves: Turned Lace for Four Frames	Zielinski, S. A.; Robert Leclerc, ed.	√	√	MWL	13			'51–'73	12
Lace, Warp Bouquet (Brooks Lace)	Stoles and Scarves		√	√	WJ	2	1	5	Jy 77	3
Lace, Weft Bouquet (Danish Medallion)	Stoles and Scarves		√	√	WJ	2	1	5	Jy 77	3
Lace, Woven	Complex "Harness Lace"	Nass, Ulla	√	√	SS&D	9	3	35	Su 78	4
Lace, Woven	"Harness Lace:" A New Leno Set-Up	Nass, Ulla	√	√	SS&D	8	2	30	Sp 77	56
Lace, Woven	Lace Weaving: Toads and Cicadas	Gorski, Berni	√	√	SS&D	3	2	10	Sp 72	6
Lace, Woven	Rose-Beige Tablecloth (E. E. Gilmore)		√	>4	Hw	6	4		S/O 85	42, I-5
Lace, Woven	Town and Country Silk Scarves (Janice Jones)		√	√	Hw	5	4		S/0 84	72, 110
Lace, Woven	Two-harness Weaves	Clark, Marion L.	√	√	H&C	14	2		Sp 63	17
Lace, Woven	Weaver's Notebook		√	>4	SS&D	10	2	38	Sp 79	52
Lace, Woven	Weaver's Notebook (error-corrected SS&D v10 n3 79 p75)		√	>4	SS&D	10	2	38	Sp 79	53
Lace, Woven, Danish Medallion	Openwork Weaves	Marston, Ena	√	√	SS&D	10	2	38	Sp 79	18
Lace, Woven: Greek	How to Weave Your own Designs	Arnold, Ruth	√	√	H&C	11	3		Su 60	6
Lace, Woven, Spanish	Openwork Weaves	Marston, Ena	√	√	SS&D	10	2	38	Sp 79	18
Lambing	Sad Songs of Spring	Stevens, Velma	√		S-O	11	3		Fa 87	10
Lamé: Types	Lamé	Boyce, Ann	√		TM			8	D/J 86	32
Lampas, Double Cloth	David's Back...And Picks Up Where He Left Off	Xenakis, Athanasios David	√	>4	PWC	5	2	16		42
Lampas, Double Cloth	Lampas for Eight	Sullivan, Donna	√	>4	PWC	5	2	16		34
Lampas Ground	Introduction to Tied Unit Weaves, An	Kelly, Jacquie	√	>4	PWC	4	4	14		40

SUBJECT	TITLE	AUTHOR	IL	INST	JOUR	VOL	NO	ISS	DATE	PAGE
Lampas, Integrated Cloth	David's Back...And Picks Up Where He Left Off	Xenakis, Athanasios David	√	> 4	PWC	5	2	16		42
Lampas, Integrated Cloth	Lampas for Eight	Sullivan, Donna	√	> 4	PWC	5	2	16		34
Lampas, Pick-Up	David's Back...And Picks Up Where He Left Off	Xenakis, Athanasios David	√	> 4	PWC	5	2	16		42
Lampas, Pick-Up	Lampas for Eight	Sullivan, Donna	√	> 4	PWC	5	2	16		34
Lampas, Polychrome, Loom-Controlled	David's Back...And Picks Up Where He Left Off	Xenakis, Athanasios David	√	> 4	PWC	5	2	16		42
Lampas Weave	Chinese Brocades: Development of Supplementary Weft Patterning (error-corrected WJ v11 n4 87 p78)	Drooker, Penelope	√		WJ	11	3	43	Wi 87	47
Lampas Weave	Chinese Drawloom: A Study in Weave Structure, The	Sellin, Helen	√	> 4	WJ	9	2	34	Fa 84	6
Lampas Weave	Contrails Coverlet	Kelly, Jacquie	√	> 4	PWC	5	1	15		48
Lampas Weave	Lampas	Kelly, Jacquie	√	> 4	PWC	5	1	15		46
Lampas Weave	Ligetuhr Arbeit: A Seventeenth-Century Compound Mounting and a Family of Associated Weaves	Hilts, Patricia	√	> 4	AT	7			Ju 87	31
Lamps, Lampshades, Lanterns	Composition and Designing: Lamp Shades	Zielinski, S. A.; Robert Leclerc, ed.	√	√	MWL	18			'51–'73	85
Lamps, Lampshades, Lanterns	Designing Lamp Shades		√	√	H&C	8	4		Fa 57	24
Lamps, Lampshades, Lanterns	Hands to Work and Hearts to God	Erf, Mary Elva	√	√	WJ	8	1	29	Su 83	25
Lamps, Lampshades, Lanterns	Handweaving in the South Today	Ford, Toni	√		H&C	1	1		Ap 50	14
Lamps, Lampshades, Lanterns	Lampshade Transfigured, A	Fauske, Carla	√	√	PWC	1	1		No 81	55
Lamps, Lampshades, Lanterns	Lantern for a Craft Shop		√		SS&D	4	1	13	Wi 72	38
Lamps, Lampshades, Lanterns	Linen Lampshade (Robin Taylor Daugherty)		√	√	Hw	5	2		M/A 84	52, 97
Lamps, Lampshades, Lanterns	Magic Lanterns: Alice Ward's Handmade Paper Light/Shades	Holland, Nina	√		Fa	8	3		M/J 81	22
Lamps, Lampshades, Lanterns	Mood Lamp	Richards, Iris	√	√	WJ	3	2	10	Oc 78	44
Lamps, Lampshades, Lanterns	Shady Ladies	Scarborough, Jessica	√		Fa	11	3		M/J 84	12
Lampshades see Lamps, Lampshades, Lanterns										
Lancé	Brocade: The Lancé or Pick-Up Weaves	Tidball, Harriet	√	√	SCGM		22		67	38
Landes Hybrid Drafts	Turned Drafts in Double Two-Tie Unit Weave	van der Hoogt, Madelyn	√	> 4	WJ	9	2	34	Fa 84	13
Lanterns see Lamps, Lampshades, Lanterns										
Laos	Flourishing Art: USA Hmong Women Show How to Stitch Pa ndau, Their Flowery Cloth, A	Porter-Francis, Wendy	√	√	TM			9	F/M 87	33
Laos	"Hmong Art: Tradition and Change" (Exhibit)	Gordon, Beverly	√		Fa	12	6		N/D 85	36
Laos	Keeping Culture Alive with Needle and Thread	White, Virginia L.	√		Fa	9	3		M/J 82	40
Lap Robe	Custom Fabrics for a Classic Cadillac	Kelly, Jacquie	√	> 4	WJ	10	4	40	Sp 86	54
Lapels	Making Sense of Interfacing (error-corrected TM n12 p4)	Komives, Margaret Deck	√	√	TM			10	A/M 87	58
Lappet Weave	Little Known Weaves Worth Knowing Better: Lappet Weave	Zielinski, S. A.; Robert Leclerc, ed.	√	√	MWL	16			'51–'73	9
Latch-Hooking Handspun	Vera Tonrey's Latch Hook Rug		√		S-O	9	3		Fa 85	14
Latvia	Latvia	Upitis, Lizbeth	√		Kn	1	2	2	S-S 85	62
Latvia	Latvian Folk Costume Braids	Gulbis, Elina	√	√	SS&D	4	3	15	Su 73	46
Latvia	Mitten Miniatures	Upitis, Lizbeth	√	√	Kn	4	1	9	Wi 87	50
Lavender	Dyes from the Herb Garden	King, Helen	√	√	TM			6	A/S 86	58
Layered Textiles	Grau-Garriga: He Says It's Easy, But...	Brough, Hazel	√	√	SS&D	6	4	24	Fa 75	92
Layered Textiles	Layered Fabrics on Eight Harnesses	Marston, Ena	√	> 4	SS&D	6	4	24	Fa 75	50
Layered Textiles	Salmon Run: The Work of Northwest Artists Peggy Vanbianchi and Emily Standley	Hirschi, Ron	√		Fa	10	2		M/A 83	16

SUBJECT	TITLE	AUTHOR	IL	INST	JOUR	VOL	NO	ISS	DATE	PAGE
Layered Textiles	Tim Harding: Garments of Paradox	Theil, Linda	√		Fa	9	6		N/D 82	20
Layered Textiles: Stitched	Distant Mountains: The Influence of Funzo-e on the Tradition of Buddhist Clerical Robes in Japan	Lyman, Marie	√		TMJ	23			84	25
Learning	First Lessons	Ligon, Linda	√	√	Hw	7	5		N/D 86	106
Learning	Getting the Most Out of a Class	Chandler, Deborah			Hw	7	5		N/D 86	16
Learning	Learning Journey, A	Redding, Debbie	√		Hw	4	4		S/O 83	16
Learning	On Learning	Chandler, Deborah			Hw	7	4		S/O 86	20
Learning Disabilities	Creative Solutions	Chandler, Deborah		√	Hw	6	3		Su 85	28
Learning: Sample Weaving	Learning Journey Starts at Home, The	Redding, Debbie	√	√	Hw	4	2		M/A 83	18
Lease Rods	Examining the Shed	Koepp, William	√	√	WJ	10	4	40	Sp 86	76
Leather	Beading on Leather	Ellsworth, Wendy	√	√	TM			7	O/N 86	50
Leather	Chain Link Braid Made of Leather Forms a Round, Open Trimming	Sober, Marion	√	√	SS&D	4	4	16	Fa 73	50
Leather	Crochet—A Great Technique for Finishing Handwovens		√	> 4	WJ	7	3	27	Wi 82	18
Leather	Fashions by Linda Knutson and Lynn Daly		√	√	WJ	6	3	23	Wi 81	14
Leather	Handbags of Leather and Fabric	Emerson, Trudy	√	√	H&C	17	2		Sp 66	22
Leather	Leather Reliefs of Teruko Yamazaki, The	Koplos, Janet	√		Fa	14	4		S/O 87	12
Leather	Men's Clothing		√	> 4	WJ	2	3	7	Ja 78	32
Leather	Pine Tree Coat	Knollenberg, Barbara	√	> 4	WJ	1	2	2	Oc 76	32
Leather	"Skin Forms: Innovations in Leather" (Exhibit)	Mackin, Jeanne	√		Fa	7	2		M/A 80	67
Leather	These Toes Won't Drown in Tears of Clown	Montgomery, Larry	√		TM			11	J/J 87	14
Leather	Trimming the Southwestern Look	Chaudet, Annette	√	√	WJ	11	1	41	Su 86	35
Leather	Weaving with Leather	Termullo, Eileen	√	√	Hw	5	1		J/F 84	52
Leather, Flowers	Handwoven or Leather Flowers	Richards, Iris	√	√	WJ	4	1	13	Jy 79	34
Leather, Types	Binding Handwoven Garments with Leather	Knollenberg, Barbara	√	√	WJ	1	3	3	Ja 77	22
Leg Warmers	Lots of Leg Warmers		√	√	PWC			4	Ja 83	67
Legal	Copyright	LaLena, Constance		√	Hw	4	3		M/J 83	69
Legal: Contracts	Contracts: Olson	Olson, Pauline	√		Iw	1	3		Sp 76	22
Legends	Art and Tradition of Akwete Weaving, The	Lambrecht, Dora J.	√		SS&D	9	2	34	Sp 78	33
Legends	Legend of Maui and the Sun, The		√		SS&D	1	3	3	Ju 70	3
Legends	Persian Legend in Silk		√		TM			14	D/J 87	92
Legends	Purple in Antiquity	Davidson, Mary Frances			SS&D	2	1	5	De 70	26
Legends	Teneriffe Lace — Legend Of Nanduti, A Closely Related Lace	Ardita, Nessim	√		SS&D	5	1	17	Wi 73	53
Legends	Totems in Tapestry	Swingle, Daphne	√		H&C	22	2		Sp 71	5
Legislation: Craft/Arts	Proposed Federal Commission on the Arts of Interest to Craftsmen	Amram, Hortense			H&C	8	4		Fa 57	31
Leno	Don't Cry...Dye	Bliss, Anne	√	√	Hw	2	2		Mr 81	50
Leno	Finger Control: Or Getting the Most Out of Your Loom	Patrick, Jane	√	√	Hw	4	2		M/A 83	70
Leno	Guatemalan Gauze Weaves: A Description and Key to Identification	Pancake, Cherri M.; Suzanne Baizerman	√	√	TMJ	19 20			80,81	1
Leno	Leno Lace with One Shuttle	Deru, Crescent	√	√	H&C	11	4		Fa 60	46
Leno	Notes on Leno	Hausner, Walter	√	√	H&C	7	1		Wi 55	23
Leno	Old World Weavers at Work in the New	Kamola, Stephanie	√	> 4	H&C	7	2		Sp 56	24
Leno	Simple Inlay on a Leno Ground	Xenakis, Athanasios David; Patti Sellon	√	√	PWC	4	1	11		18
Leno	Three Ancient Peruvian Gauze Looms	Rowe, Ann Pollard; Junius B. Bird	√		TMJ	19,20			80,81	27
Leno	What is Leno?	Frey, Berta	√	> 4	H&C	6	2		Sp 55	4
Leno: 2-Shaft Loom	Weaving in Quebec: New Ideas and Techniques	Barrett, Clotilde	√	√	WJ	6	4	24	Sp 82	16

SUBJECT	TITLE	AUTHOR	IL	INST	JOUR	VOL	NO	ISS	DATE	PAGE
Leno: 3-Shaft Loom	Weaving in Quebec: New Ideas and Techniques	Barrett, Clotilde	√	√	WJ	6	4	24	Sp 82	16
Leno, Bead	Bead Leno	Davenport, Betty	√	√	PWC			6	Su 83	62
Leno, Bead	Bead Leno	DeRoy, Paul	√	> 4	WJ	1	2	2	Oc 76	36
Leno, Bead	Bead Leno	Wertenberger, Kathryn	√	> 4	Hw	8	2		M/A 87	88
Leno, Bead	Bead Leno Curtains (Sharon Alderman)		√	√	Hw	2	3		My 81	38, 82
Leno, Bead	Loom Controlled Bead Leno	Bardwell, Kathryn	√	√	SS&D	12	3	47	Su 81	50
Leno, Closed Shed	Pick-Up Leno, A Two-harness Loom Technique	Wallace, Meg	√	√	WJ	1	2	2	Oc 76	3
Leno, Distorted	Fabric Design, An Approach by a Young Weaver	Carson, Candace	√	√	H&C	20	1		Wi 69	16
Leno, Double Weave	Double Weaves: Leno in Double Weave on Four Shafts	Zielinski, S. A.; Robert Leclerc, ed.	√	√	MWL	15			'51–'73	72
Leno, Doup	Chenille Polo	Xenakis, Alexis Yiorgos	√	√	PWC			6	Su 83	34
Leno, Doup	"Cocoon" Hammock	Drooker, Penelope B.	√	> 4	WJ	5	4	20	Sp 81	46
Leno, Doup	Cotton Lace	Madden, Linda	√	√	WJ	11	2	42	Fa 86	25
Leno, Doup	Doup Leno	Skowronski, Hella; Sylvia Tacker	√	√	TM			4	A/M 86	56
Leno, Doup	Doup Leno	Skowronski, Hella; Sylvia Tacker	√		SCGM		32		80	1-46
Leno, Doup	Doup Leno (error-corrected WJ v3 n2 78 insert p38a)		√	√	WJ	3	2	10	Oc 78	32
Leno, Doup	Doup Leno: Introduction	Skowronski, Hella; Sylvia Tacker	√		SCGM		32		80	8
Leno, Doup	Doupe Leno for the Harness Loom	Xenakis, Alexis Yiorgos; Elaine Rowley	√	√	PWC			6	Su 83	10
Leno, Doup	Doupe Leno for the Rigid Heddle Loom	Xenakis, Athanasios David	√	√	PWC			6	Su 83	14
Leno, Doup	Experimenting with Leno Weaves	Chetwynd, Hilary	√	√	SS&D	5	3	19	Su 74	29
Leno, Doup	Exploring Doup Leno	Laughlin, Mary Elizabeth	√	> 4	CW	4	3	12	Ap 83	3
Leno, Doup	Inlay We Trust, Part 2: Leno Inlay	Herring, Connie	√	√	PWC			6	Su 83	48
Leno, Doup	Insulated Roman Shade — Doup Leno	Champion, Ellen	√	√	WJ	6	1	21	Su 81	24
Leno, Doup	Lace Trilogy	Fauske, Carla	√	√	PWC			6	Su 83	52
Leno, Doup	Leno Fabrics	Xenakis, Athanasios David	√	√	PWC			6	Su 83	18
Leno, Doup	Leno Vest	Lyon, Linda	√	√	PWC			6	Su 83	27
Leno, Doup	Leno with Doupes		√	√	H&C	26	2		Ap 75	18
Leno, Doup	Leno with Steel Doup Heddles	Barrett, Clotilde	√	√	WJ	6	3	23	Wi 81	48
Leno, Doup	Mexican Motifs: A Cotton Shawl in Leno or Gauze Weave	Tidball, Harriet	√	√	SCGM		6		62	16
Leno, Doup	Notes on Leno	Hausner, Walter	√	√	H&C	7	1		Wi 55	23
Leno, Doup	Peruvian Leno	Sayler, Mary	√	√	SS&D	3	3	11	Su 72	45
Leno, Doup	Pride of the Harvest Shawl	Davidsohn, Marty	√	√	PWC			6	Su 83	25
Leno, Doup	Slightly Left of Center Jacket	Rowley, Elaine	√	√	PWC			6	Su 83	44
Leno, Doup	Two String Sweaters	Brugger, Susan	√	√	PWC			6	Su 83	31
Leno, Doup	Ultimate T-Shirt, The	Xenakis, Alexis Yiorgos	√	√	PWC			6	Su 83	29
Leno, Doup	Weaving in Quebec: New Ideas and Techniques	Barrett, Clotilde	√	√	WJ	6	4	24	Sp 82	16
Leno, Doup	What is Leno?	Frey, Berta	√	> 4	H&C	6	2		Sp 55	4
Leno, Doup	Woven Fringes		√	> 4	WJ	3	3	11	Ja 79	14
Leno, Doup	Woven Lace and Lacey Weaves: Cross Weave	Zielinski, S. A.; Robert Leclerc, ed.	√	√	MWL	13			'51–'73	64
Leno, Doup	Yarn for the Weaving		√	√	PWC	3	1	7		21
Leno, Doup, Chenille	Super Rug: A Chenille "Twice-Woven" Rug	Champion, Ellen	√	√	WJ	6	4	24	Sp 82	26
Leno, Half-Heddle	Complex "Harness Lace"	Nass, Ulla	√	√	SS&D	9	3	35	Su 78	4
Leno, Half-Heddle	"Harness Lace:" A New Leno Set-Up	Nass, Ulla	√	√	SS&D	8	2	30	Sp 77	56
Leno in Double Weave	Woven Lace and Lacey Weaves: Leno in Double Weave	Zielinski, S. A.; Robert Leclerc, ed.	√	√	MWL	13			'51–'73	89

SUBJECT	TITLE	AUTHOR	IL	INST	JOUR	VOL	NO	ISS	DATE	PAGE
Leno, Loom-Controlled	Leno Sampler Wallhanging (Betty Davenport)		√	√	Hw	7	2		M/A 86	47, I-8
Leno, Loom-Controlled	Loom-Controlled Leno	Alderman, Sharon D.	√	√	Hw	2	3		My 81	38
Leno, Mexican, Antique	Pick-Up Leno, A Two-harness Loom Technique	Wallace, Meg	√	√	WJ	1	2	2	Oc 76	3
Leno, Milwaukee	Pick-Up Leno, A Two-harness Loom Technique	Wallace, Meg	√	√	WJ	1	2	2	Oc 76	3
Leno, Mock	Designing with Loom-Woven Open Weaves	Marston, Ena	√	√	SS&D	13	1	49	Wi 81	22
Leno, Mock	Lace & Flowers: Vintage Inspiration	George, Patrice	√	> 4	Hw	8	5		N/D 87	68
Leno, Mock	Mock-Leno Tablecloth		√	√	WJ	6	1	21	Su 81	12
Leno, Mock	Placemats	DeRoy, Paul	√	> 4	WJ	1	3	3	Ja 77	4
Leno, Mock	Roman Shades and Draw Draperies — Mock Leno		√	√	WJ	6	1	21	Su 81	22
Leno, Mock	Some Loom-Woven Open Weaves (error-corrected SS&D v13 n1 81 p4)	Marston, Ena	√	√	SS&D	12	4	48	Fa 81	32
Leno, Mock	Weaving with Ramie		√	> 4	WJ	8	2	30	Fa 83	80
Leno, Mock	Woven Lace and Lacey Weaves: Mock Leno	Zielinski, S. A.; Robert Leclerc, ed.	√	√	MWL	13			'51–'73	44
Leno, Mock	Woven Lace, Part 1: The Bronson Systems	Xenakis, Athanasios David	√	√	PWC			5	Sp 83	10
Leno, Norwegian	Pick-Up Leno, A Two-harness Loom Technique	Wallace, Meg	√	√	WJ	1	2	2	Oc 76	3
Leno, Open Shed	Pick-Up Leno, A Two-harness Loom Technique	Wallace, Meg	√	√	WJ	1	2	2	Oc 76	3
Leno, Patterned, System	Handloom Weaves: The Classification of Handloom Weaves, The Structural Group, The Gauze or Leno Class, Pattern Leno System	Tidball, Harriet	√	> 4	SCGM		33		57	38
Leno, Pick-Up	Fashion Show Of Handwoven Garments		√	> 4	WJ	3	3	11	Ja 79	5
Leno, Pick-Up	Lacy Triangular Stole of Handspun Wool, A	Kniskern, Edna Maki	√	√	WJ	6	2	22	Fa 81	48
Leno, Pick-Up	Leno Sampler Wallhanging (Betty Davenport)		√	√	Hw	7	2		M/A 86	47, I-8
Leno, Pick-Up	Pick-Up Leno: The Fine Linens of Ava Hessler		√	√	WJ	7	2	26	Fa 82	31
Leno, Pick-Up	Tablecloth and Runner Decorated with Overshot and Pick-Up Leno		√	√	WJ	6	1	21	Su 81	10
Leno, Pick-Up	Woven Fringes		√	> 4	WJ	3	3	11	Ja 79	14
Leno, Plain System	Handloom Weaves: The Classification of Handloom Weaves, The Structural Group, The Gauze or Leno Class, Plain Leno System	Tidball, Harriet	√	√	SCGM		33		57	38
Leno, Reverse Twist	Pick-Up Leno, A Two-harness Loom Technique	Wallace, Meg	√	√	WJ	1	2	2	Oc 76	3
Leno, Three-Thread	Complex "Harness Lace"	Nass, Ulla	√	√	SS&D	9	3	35	Su 78	4
Leno, Types	Leno		√		Hw	8	2		M/A 87	91
Liberia	Hammock, The	Drooker, Penelope B.	√	√	TM			6	A/S 86	74
Liberty Quilts	Liberty Quilts		√		TM			6	A/S 86	100
Libraries	Cataloging Your Home Library			√	SS&D	11	2	42	Sp 80	22
Libraries	Look Inside the HGA Library, A		√		SS&D	11	1	41	Wi 79	28
Libraries	Pattern for a Guild Library	LaFara, Betty	√		SS&D	2	1	5	De 70	12
Libraries	Using Libraries	Csipke, Steve		√	H&C	24	3		M/J 73	46
Libraries: American River College Textile Library	Textile Library Just for You, A	Roth, Bettie G.			CW	6	2	17	Ja 85	24
Libraries: Textile	Creating a Public Textile Library	Roth, Bettie G.		√	SS&D	9	3	35	Su 78	47
Libraries: Textile (Edna O. Healey)	Healey Collection				SS&D	9	3	35	Su 78	22
Library Skills	How to use a Weaving Book				H&C	26	2		Ap 75	22
License: Fancy Weaving Machines	Nineteenth Century License Agreements for Fancy Weaving Machines	Anderson, Clarita; Steven M. Spivak	√		AT	8			De 87	67

427

SUBJECT	TITLE	AUTHOR	IL	INST	JOUR	VOL	NO	ISS	DATE	PAGE
Lichens	Arctic Adventures with Qiviut	Hudson, Marjorie; Kathy Sparks	√	√	S-O	11	3		Fa 87	47
Lichens	Color Magic from Lichen Dyebaths	Casselman, Karen Leigh	√	√	SS&D	17	2	66	Sp 86	74
Lichens	Diverse Dyes	Bliss, Anne	√	√	Iw	3	2		Wi 78	30
Lichens	Dyeing with Lichens	Gerber, Willi; Fred Gerber	√	√	H&C	20	2		Sp 69	13
Lichens	Dyepot	Taggart, Barbara			SS&D	3	3	11	Su 72	40
Lichens	Lichens	Wipplinger, Michele	√	√	S-O	10	2		Su 86	34
Lichens	Lichens As Dyestuffs	Shaw, Lynn C.	√	√	SS&D	5	2	18	Sp 74	28
Lichens	Old Man's Beard, the Reindeer's Moss and the Stag's Horn, The	Bliss, Anne	√	√	Hw	7	2		M/A 86	72
Lichens	On Lichen Dyeing	Oakland, Amy		√	H&C	24	2		M/A 73	20
Lichens	Why Bother with Natural Dyeing?	Bulbach, Stanley	√	√	TM			5	J/J 86	32
Lifestyle	In Pursuit of a Lifestyle	Grant, Susan	√		Iw	5	2		Sp 80	32
Lifestyle	Jean Wilson	Rush, Beverly	√		Iw	5	2		Sp 80	43
Lifestyle	Lifestyle: A Roundtable Discussion	Ligon, Linda	√		Iw	5	2		Sp 80	22
Lifestyle	Mary Snyder	Pinchin, Bryn	√		Iw	5	2		Sp 80	47
Lifestyle	Weaving a Lifestyle: Cynthia Schira	Schira, Cynthia	√		Iw	5	2		Sp 80	27
Lifestyle	Weaving a Lifestyle: Malin Selander	West, Virginia	√		Iw	5	2		Sp 80	30
Lifestyle	Who Weaves?		√		Iw	5	2		Sp 80	34
Ligature Weaves, Beiderwand	Ligetuhr Arbeit: A Seventeenth-Century Compound Mounting and a Family of Associated Weaves	Hilts, Patricia	√	>4	AT	7			Ju 87	31
Ligature Weaves, Beiderwand, Tied	Ligetuhr Arbeit: A Seventeenth-Century Compound Mounting and a Family of Associated Weaves	Hilts, Patricia	√	>4	AT	7			Ju 87	31
Ligature Weaves, Crosson	Ligetuhr Arbeit: A Seventeenth-Century Compound Mounting and a Family of Associated Weaves	Hilts, Patricia	√	>4	AT	7			Ju 87	31
Ligature Weaves, Tied Lithuanian	Ligetuhr Arbeit: A Seventeenth-Century Compound Mounting and a Family of Associated Weaves	Hilts, Patricia	√	>4	AT	7			Ju 87	31
Ligetuhr	Lampas	Kelly, Jacquie	√	>4	PWC	5	1	15		46
Ligetuhr Arbeit Mounting	Ligetuhr Arbeit: A Seventeenth-Century Compound Mounting and a Family of Associated Weaves	Hilts, Patricia	√	>4	AT	7			Ju 87	31
Light	Play of Light: Susan Kelly Explains the Inner and Outer Workings of Her Tapestries, A	Kelly, Susan	√		Fa	8	5		S/O 81	54
Light	Presence of Light, The	Park, Betty	√		SS&D	15	4	60	Fa 84	36
Light	"Presence of Light, The" (Exhibit)	Talley, Charles	√		Fa	12	2		M/A 85	72
Light	Presence of Light: The Un-Traditional Quilts of Jan Myers, The	Gutcheon, Beth	√		Fa	8	3		M/J 81	60
Light	Revelations: Victoria Rivers' Neon and Fabric Constructions		√		Fa	8	5		S/O 81	50
Light-Testing: Yarn	Dyes from the Herb Garden	King, Helen	√	√	TM			6	A/S 86	58
Lightfastness	Considerations in the Selection and Application of Natural Dyes: Mordant Selection, Part 1	Crews, Patricia	√	√	SS&D	12	2	46	Sp 81	15
Lightfastness	Considerations in the Selection and Application of Natural Dyes: Dye-plant Selection (error-corrected SS&D v12 n4 81 p8)	Crews, Patricia	√	√	SS&D	12	3	47	Su 81	52
Lightfastness	How Fast is the Color?	Bliss, Anne	√	√	Hw	5	2		M/A 84	16
Lightfastness	Natural Dye Myth, The	Tillett, Leslie	√		Iw	4	2		Sp 79	55
Lightfastness	Tests for Desired Yarn Qualities	Koehler, Glory Dail		√	SS&D	7	2	26	Sp 76	68
Lightfastness	Why Bother with Natural Dyeing?	Bulbach, Stanley	√	√	TM			5	J/J 86	32
Lightfastness	Why Do Colors Flee the Light?	Goodman, Deborah Lerme	√		TM			1	O/N 85	8
Lightfastness: Natural Dyes	Ultraviolet Absorbers: A Treatment to Reduce Fading and Degradation of Textiles	Crews, Patricia Cox; Barbara M. Reagan			AT	8			De 87	43

SUBJECT	TITLE	AUTHOR	IL	INST	JOUR	VOL	NO	ISS	DATE	PAGE
Lightfastness Test	Fade Testing		√	√	TM			4	A/M 86	6
Lighting: Techniques	Weaving and Light: Creative Ideas and Techniques for Your Next Show	Hafermann, Candy Kreitlow	√	√	Iw	5	3		Su 80	34
Limitations: Power Loom	Beyond the Powerloom	Hausner, Walter			H&C	22	4		Fa 71	21
Linen	Art of Working with Linen, The		√		Fa	14	2		M/A 87	9
Linen	Chemical Dyeing of Linen	Gwynne, Elaine	√	√	WJ	7	2	26	Fa 82	23
Linen	Drawn Threadwork	Duroy, Marie-Pierre	√	√	TM			8	D/J 86	41
Linen	Handspun Linen Towels	Quinn, Celia	√	√	S-O	7	1		Sp 83	32
Linen	History of Linen, A	Mattera, Joanne	√	√	SS&D	8	3	31	Su 77	16
Linen	Learning the Flax of Life	Murrow, Romedy	√	√	S-O	9	3		Fa 85	49
Linen	Linen	Shaffer, Christine H.	√		H&C	12	2		Sp 61	29
Linen	Linen — A Luxury Fabric		√		H&C	26	2		Ap 75	14
Linen	Linen Facts		√		WJ	7	2	26	Fa 82	47
Linen	Linen Knits	Westerink, Claire; Erica Baker	√	√	S-O	10	3		Fa 86	17
Linen	Linen Lore	Goodman, Deborah Lerme	√		Fa	14	2		M/A 87	16
Linen	Linen Rug		√	√	Hw	2	3		My 81	50, 82
Linen	Linen: The Enduring Thread of History	Hoskins, Nancy Arthur	√		Fa	14	2		M/A 87	42
Linen	Linen Undergarments: A Proud Danish Heritage	Todd-Cope, Louise	√		Fa	14	2		M/A 87	51
Linen	My Linen Curtain	Handy, Virginia	√	√	S-O	10	3		Fa 86	23
Linen	Portfolio: Why I Work in Linen, A		√		Fa	14	2		M/A 87	38
Linen	Quinn's Spinning Notes	Quinn, Cecelia			S-O	5			81	55
Linen	Weaving of Linen, The	Chase, Mary A.	√	√	WJ	7	2	26	Fa 82	18
Linen	Weaving with Linen	Condit, Joan	√		H&C	6	3		Su 55	46
Linen	What the Well-Dressed Baby Will Wear This Season	Davis, Judy Green	√	√	S-O	10	4		Wi 86	14
Linen	Working with Linen: Barbara Eckhardt	Goodman, Deborah Lerme	√		Fa	14	2		M/A 87	35
Linen	Working with Linen: Karen Jenson Rutherford	Itter, Diane	√		Fa	14	2		M/A 87	34
Linen	Working with Linen: Shirley Ruth Elgot	Perry, Pamela	√		Fa	14	2		M/A 87	32
Linen	Working with Linen: Three Experiences		√		Fa	14	2		M/A 87	31
Linen	Yarns and Fibers: How Not to Weave Linen	Zielinski, S. A.; Robert Leclerc, ed.	√	√	MWL	4			'51–'73	19
Linen Handspun	Linen Knits				S-O	10	3		Fa 86	16
Linen, History	Linen: A Brief History				WJ	7	2	26	Fa 82	46
Linen, History	Yarns and Fibers: Linen	Zielinski, S. A.; Robert Leclerc, ed.			MWL	4			'51–'73	15
Linen, Tow	Sauna Towels	Freeberg, Judy	√	√	WJ	10	4	40	Sp 86	50
Linen Weaves	Handweaver's Instruction Manual: The Simple Linen Weaves	Tidball, Harriet C. nee Douglas		√	SCGM		34		49	31
Linen Weaving	Linen in Finland	Haglich, Sr. Bianca; Raija Ranne	√	√	SS&D	8	3	31	Su 77	84
Linen Weaving, Germany	Roses and Snowballs: The Development of Block Patterns in the German Linen-Weaving Tradition	Hilts, Patricia	√	>4	AT	5			Ju 86	167
Linens, 19th Century	Early American Linens	Gallagher, Constance	√	>4	H&C	15	3		Su 64	7
Linens, Household also see Specific Items										
Linens, Household	California Poppy Tablecloth and Napkins	Scorgie, Jean	√	√	Hw	6	3		Su 85	60
Linens, Household	Country Towel, City Towel		√		Hw	5	3		Su 84	70
Linens, Household	Early American Handwoven Linens	Gallagher, Constance D.			SS&D	1	1	1	De 69	12
Linens, Household	Edith Huntington Snow	Jarecka, Louise Llewellyn	√		H&C	1	1		Ap 50	7
Linens Household	Fantastic Finnweave, Part 3	Xenakis, Athanasios David	√	>4	PWC			4	Ja 83	17
Linens, Household	Great-Grandmother's Linens	Mattera, Joanne	√		TM			3	F/M 86	86
Linens, Household	Keep It Simple		√		Hw	7	3		M/J 86	73

SUBJECT	TITLE	AUTHOR	IL	INST	JOUR	VOL	NO	ISS	DATE	PAGE
Linens, Household	Linen and Waffle Weave: A Successful Marriage of Two Unlikely Elements		√		Hw	6	5		N/D 85	56
Linens, Household	Linens At Old Economy, The	Gallagher, Constance Dann	√	> 4	SS&D	7	3	27	Su 76	84
Linens, Household	L'Amour de Maman: The Acadian Textile Heritage	Rossetter, Tabitha Wilson	√		Fa	8	3		M/J 81	29
Linens, Household	On the Table		√		Hw	5	1		J/F 84	61
Linens, Household	One Warp, Many Projects		√		Hw	6	2		M/A 85	48
Linens, Household	Pennington Linens, Iowa Weaver Collects Old Designs		√		H&C	16	3		Su 65	14
Linens, Household	Pick-Up Leno: The Fine Linens of Ava Hessler		√	√	WJ	7	2	26	Fa 82	31
Linens, Household	Terrific Table Toppers		√	√	Hw	8	1		J/F 87	56
Linens, Household	Weave for a Summer Kitchen		√		Hw	1	2		S-S 80	26
Linens, Household	Weave for Your Kitchen		√		Hw	7	3		M/J 86	65
Linens, Household	Weave for Your Kitchen	Frey, Berta	√		H&C	1	2		Su 50	19
Linens, Household	Weaving a Fine Warp	Ligon, Linda	√	√	Hw	2	5		No 81	58
Lining: Rya	Lining the Overshot	Moes, Dini	√	√	SS&D	13	4	52	Fa 82	64
Linings	Basic Sewing Techniques in Handling Handwoven Fabrics for Garments	Knollenberg, Barbara	√	√	WJ	1	1	1	Jy 76	25
Linings	Finishes for Vadmal	Baizerman, Suzanne	√	√	WJ	10	3	39	Wi 86	30
Linings: Coat	Tailor's Logic	Hostek, Stanley	√	√	TM			14	D/J 87	42
Linsey-Woolsey	Eighteenth Century Mollie Costume	Spray, Kathy	√		WJ	6	3	23	Wi 81	38
Linsey-Woolsey	Linsey-Woolsey Using Handspun Yarns	Adams, Brucie	√	√	Hw	3	5		N/D 82	59
Linsey-Woolsey	Linsey-Woolseys at the Sheburne Museum, The (error-corrected SS&D v16 n3 85 p90)	Noordaa, Titia Vander	√		SS&D	16	2	62	Sp 85	59
Linsey-Woolsey	Notebook: Linsey-Woolsey (Ann Wedig)	Myers, Ruth, ed.	√	√	SS&D	12	3	47	Su 81	67
Literary Quotations	Distaffs: Scanning through History	Henzie, Susie	√		SS&D	9	4	36	Fa 78	56
Literary Quotations	Inspiring Words	Strickler, Carol	√		Hw	5	5		N/D 84	44
Literary Quotations: Art	Shuttle Power	Hanks, Nancy	√		SS&D	7	4	28	Fa 76	45
Literary Quotations: Art Works	Jane Lackey: A Vision Into Past and Future	Corwin, Nancy	√		Fa	13	6		N/D 86	18
Literary Quotations: Bath	Upfifting...Creative...Expansive...Comfortable Baths		√	√	Hw	3	2		Mr 82	50
Literary Quotations: Beauty	Double Edge of Knitting, The	Mabee-Zust, Mariah	√		Fa	10	3		M/J 83	50
Literary Quotations: Beauty	Rieke, Rieke — A Study in Beauty, Silence and Collaboration		√		Fa	5	6		N/D 78	35
Literary Quotations: Beauty	Who Weaves?		√		Iw	5	2		Sp 80	42
Literary Quotations: Brocades	Golden Brocades, The	Wilson, Kax	√		Iw	6	1		Wi 80	66
Literary Quotations: Color	Origins	Wilson, Kax			Iw	5	1		Wi 79	47
Literary Quotations: Color	Personal Approach to Color, A	Matlock, Ann	√		S-O	9	3		Fa 85	19
Literary Quotations: Commitment	Choosing a Focus of Study can Lead to New Growth, New Horizons, New Understanding	Chandler, Deborah			Hw	6	4		S/O 85	26
Literary Quotations: Contentment	In Pursuit of a Lifestyle	Grant, Susan	√		Iw	5	2		Sp 80	32
Literary Quotations: Crafts	Shepherds of Glenmore, The	Burkhauser, Jude	√		S-O	6	4		82	36
Literary Quotations: Creative Craftsman	"Art and Technics"	Mumford, Lewis			CW	2	1	4	Oc 80	4
Literary Quotations: Currants	Currants: Not Just for Eating	Bliss, Anne	√	√	Hw	7	4		S/O 86	74
Literary Quotations: Daisy	Daisy, Daisy, Give Me Your Color, Do	Bliss, Anne	√		Hw	6	4		S/O 85	80
Literary Quotations: Design	Composition and Designing: Introduction (from the classics)	Zielinski, S. A.; Robert Leclerc, ed.			MWL	18			'51–'73	5
Literary Quotations: Disorder	Tempting and Tempestuous	Upitis, Lizbeth	√		Kn	3	2	6	Sp 87	8
Literary Quotations: Dyeing	Why Bother with Natural Dyeing?	Bulbach, Stanley	√	√	TM			5	J/J 86	32
Literary Quotations: Dyes	Dyes of Early Tartans, The		√		Hw	4	5		N/D 83	75
Literary Quotations: Excellence	Excellence	Leggett, Dawn	√		S-O	10	2		Su 86	43
Literary Quotations: Exploration	Batwings and Butterflies	West, Virginia	√		Hw	6	2		M/A 85	41

SUBJECT	TITLE	AUTHOR	IL	INST	JOUR	VOL	NO	ISS	DATE	PAGE
Literary Quotations: Fashion	Revivified Past, A	Upitis, Lizbeth	√		Kn	3	1	5	F-W 86	12
Literary Quotations: Finances	Money Matters	Beschell, Lorraine	√		Fa	5	4		J/A 78	56
Literary Quotations: Fulling	Traditional Methods of Finishing Cloth by Hand	Gordon, Beverly	√	√	Iw	5	4		Fa 80	66
Literary Quotations: Goals	Setting Goals and Evaluating Priorities	LaLena, Constance	√	√	Iw	5	1		Wi 79	43
Literary Quotations: Heraldry	Banners		√	√	SS&D	11	4	44	Fa 80	47
Literary Quotations: Lace	Lace				Kn	1	2	2	S-S 85	20
Literary Quotations: Lichen	Lichens As Dyestuffs	Shaw, Lynn C.	√	√	SS&D	5	2	18	Sp 74	28
Literary Quotations: Lifestyle	In Pursuit of a Lifestyle	Grant, Susan	√		Iw	5	2		Sp 80	32
Literary Quotations: Linen, Processing	Yarns and Fibers: Linen	Zielinski, S. A.; Robert Leclerc, ed.		√	MWL	4			'51–'73	15
Literary Quotations: Madder	On Dyeing with Madder	Bliss, Anne	√	√	Iw	5	1		Wi 79	48
Literary Quotations: Mothproofing	Herbal Moth Repellents: Safeguard or Sentiment?	Buchanan, Rita			S-O	10	2		Su 86	25
Literary Quotations: Needlework	Darn That Hole	Markrich, Lilo	√	√	TM			5	J/J 86	38
Literary Quotations: Peace	Weaving Peace at Innisfree	Ohle, Carolyn	√		Hw	4	1		J/F 83	22
Literary Quotations: Plaids	Color It Plaid	Bliss, Anne		√	Hw	4	5		N/D 83	74
Literary Quotations: Scottish District Checks	Scottish District Checks	Snyder, Mary E.	√	√	H&C	16	2		Sp 65	9
Literary Quotations: Scottish Woolens	Woolens and Tweeds: Prologue or Afterthought	Tidball, Harriet			SCGM		4		61	46
Literary Quotations: Selvage	Catch It		√	√	Hw	6	1		J/F 85	63
Literary Quotations: Selvage	Wind It		√	√	Hw	6	1		J/F 85	66
Literary Quotations: Sharing	Stennett Heaton: He Finds Beauty in the Mini World		√		SS&D	7	1	25	Wi 75	8
Literary Quotations: Shawls	Ah, Shawls!	Upitis, Lizbeth	√		Kn	4	1	9	Wi 87	14
Literary Quotations: Sheep	Fabric of the Lake District: Herdwick Sheep	Humphries, Andrew B.	√		S-O	8	4		Wi 84	45
Literary Quotations: Sheep	Visit with Anne Blinks, A		√		Iw	3	3		Sp 78	15
Literary Quotations: Silk	Wild Silk	Kolander, Cheryl	√	√	Iw	2	3		Sp 77	8
Literary Quotations: Spindle Spinning	Back Strap Weaving in Zacualpan Mexico	Cooper, Jane	√	√	SS&D	5	3	19	Su 74	13
Literary Quotations: Spinning	Bernard Barton Spinning Wheel — 1766, The		√		S-O	7	4		Wi 83	16
Literary Quotations: Spinning	Betty Rodman, an Integrated Life	Staines, Barbara			S-O	4			80	19
Literary Quotations: Spinning	Dressing the Distaff	Henzie, Susie	√	√	SS&D	10	1	37	Wi 78	12
Literary Quotations: Spinning	Using the Fibers of Native Plants	Buchanan, Rita	√	√	S-O	9	4		Wi 85	29
Literary Quotations: Spinning	Women as Spinners: New England Spinsters	Gordon, Beverly	√		S-O	3			79	16
Literary Quotations: Spinning, Weaving	Cardiac Algorithms or the Heart's Way of Inferring Meaning from Pattern	Courtney, Elizabeth	√		AT	5			Ju 86	51
Literary Quotations: Stenciling	Stencils	Bliss, Anne	√	√	Hw	6	3		Su 85	86
Literary Quotations: Textiles	Tree-Bast Fiber Textiles of Japan	Dusenbury, Mary	√	√	S-O	10	3		Fa 86	35
Literary Quotations: Theory/Practice	Cynthia Laymon: Pleated Interplay	Michaels-Paque, Joan	√		Fa	12	5		S/O 85	12
Literary Quotations: Thistles	Thistles	Bliss, Anne	√	√	Hw	7	1		J/F 86	84
Literary Quotations: Truth	Elizabeth MacDonald: Finding the Ties That Bind Truth and Art	Reuter, Laurel	√		Fa	14	4		S/O 87	31
Literary Quotations: Tweeling	Versatile Twill, The		√		Hw	6	5		N/D 85	41
Literary Quotations: Weaver	Naomi Julian: Weaver	Vogt, Cy	√		Fa	5	6		N/D 78	28
Literary Quotations: Weaving	Bolivian Highland Weaving, Part 1	Cason, Marjorie; Adele Cahlander	√		SS&D	6	2	22	Sp 75	4
Literary Quotations: Weaving	Burls	Bogle, Michael			SS&D	11	4	44	Fa 80	35
Literary Quotations: Weaving	Composition and Designing: Art of Weaving (Quote from C.G.Gilroy)	Zielinski, S. A.; Robert Leclerc, ed.			MWL	18			'51–'73	91
Literary Quotations: Weaving	Design and the Handweaver: Color	Atwater, Mary Meigs		√	SCGM		3		61	15
Literary Quotations: Weaving	Exploring the Possibilities of Ancient Rose	Wells, Elizabeth	√	√	H&C	11	1		Wi 60	22

SUBJECT	TITLE	AUTHOR	IL	INST	JOUR	VOL	NO	ISS	DATE	PAGE
Literary Quotations: Weaving	Handweavers 1800—1840	Wilson, Kax	√		Iw	5	2		Sp 80	50
Literary Quotations: Weaving	Happy Weaving of Marriage Sheets	Bradley, Lavinia			SS&D	4	1	13	Wi 72	48
Literary Quotations: Weaving	Textile Arts of Multan, Pakistan	Shahzaman, Mahboob	√	> 4	SS&D	4	3	15	Su 73	8
Literary Quotations: Weaving	Tweed Weavers of Glenmore, The	Burkhauser, Jude	√		Hw	3	3		My 82	56
Literary Quotations: Weaving	Weaving Myths	Hively, Evelyn			Hw	3	2		Mr 82	10
Literary Quotations: Weaving/Spinning	Handweaving in Everyday Living	Green, Harry B.			H&C	10	4		Fa 59	24
Literary Quotations: Weeds	Lovely Dyes from Rank Weeds	Bliss, Anne	√		Iw	3	4		Su 78	38
Literary Quotations: Wind	Windworks: A Way of Working	Frasier, Debra			Fa	10	4		J/A 83	58
Literary References: Weaving	Happy Weaving of Marriage Sheets	Bradley, Lavinia			SS&D	4	1	13	Wi 72	48
Literature: Textile, Archeology	Peru, Textiles Unlimited: The Archaeological Literature	Tidball, Harriet			SCGM		25		68	7
Lithography	"Anni Albers: Current Work" (Exhibit)	Guyer, Niki	√		Fa	6	6		N/D 79	72
Lithuania	Lithuanian Pervarai: Producing a Twenty Shaft Pattern on a Twelve Shaft Loom	Meek, M. Kati	√	> 4	AT	1			De 83	159
Lithuania	Traditional Lithuanian Weaving in Chicago	Meek, M. Kati	√		SS&D	17	3	67	Su 86	50
Liturgical Weavings see Ecclesiastical/Liturgical Weavings										
Living	Double Lives: Can You Love Your "Work" When It's Your "Job"?	Mattera, Joanne	√		TM			10	A/M 87	62
Living National Treasures	Living National Treasures of Japan, The	Adachi, Barbara Curtis	√		Fa	11	1		J/F 84	62
Living National Treasures	Shokansai Iizuka: Bamboo Craftsman and Living National Treasure of Japan	Adachi, Barbara Curtis	√		Fa	11	1		J/F 84	59
Living National Treasures: Yanagi, Yoshitaki, Weaver	American Weaver in Japan		√		H&C	18	4		Fa 67	30
Llamas	Indian Textiles from Ecuador		√		H&C	10	1		Wi 59	19
Llamas	Llama Cape, The	Keeler, Betty			H&C	23	4		J/A 72	46
Llamas	Llama Wool	Smith, Carolyn	√	√	S-O	11	2		Su 87	32
Llamas	Llamas	Switzer, Chris	√	√	S-O	5			81	31
Llamas	My Wonderful Llamas and Their Wool	Thormahlen, Marian Oyen	√	√	S-O	8	4		Wi 84	29
Locked Wefts	Dhabla Weaving in India	De Bone, Mary	√	√	SS&D	8	3	31	Su 77	9
Locked Wefts	Resist Dyeing, Curiosities and Inventions: Clasped Wefts or Locked Weft	Zielinski, S. A.; Robert Leclerc, ed.	√	√	MWL	17			'51–'73	45
Locked Wefts: Pattern Weaves	Resist Dyeing, Curiosities and Inventions: Locked Wefts in Pattern Weaves	Zielinski, S. A.; Robert Leclerc, ed.	√	√	MWL	17			'51–'73	60
Locked Wefts: Swivel	Resist Dyeing, Curiosities and Inventions: Locked Wefts in Swivel	Zielinski, S. A.; Robert Leclerc, ed.	√	√	MWL	17			'51–'73	53
Lodi	Rabari Lodi: Creating a Fabric Through Social Alliance, The	Frater, Judy	√	√	WJ	10	1	37	Su 85	28
Log Cabin	Blue Rag Vest (Susan Snover)		√	√	Hw	2	3		My 81	50, 78
Log Cabin	Composition and Designing Part 2: Log Cabin	Zielinski, S. A.; Robert Leclerc, ed.	√	√	MWL	19			'51–'73	121
Log Cabin	Composition and Designing Part 2: Multiblock Log Cabin and Shadow Weave	Zielinski, S. A.; Robert Leclerc, ed.	√	> 4	MWL	19			'51–'73	126
Log Cabin	From Cotton Patch to Cotton Patches and Then Some	Linder, Olive	√	√	WJ	5	4	20	Sp 81	48
Log Cabin	Lincoln Log Placemats (Linda Ligon)		√	√	Hw	6	1		J/F 85	61, I-15
Log Cabin	Little Known Weaves Worth Knowing Better: Log Cabin	Zielinski, S. A.; Robert Leclerc, ed.	√	√	MWL	16			'51–'73	62
Log Cabin	Little Known Weaves Worth Knowing Better: Multiblock	Zielinski, S. A.; Robert Leclerc, ed.	√	√	MWL	16			'51–'73	68
Log Cabin	Log Cabin Effects for the Rigid Heddle Loom	Davenport, Betty Lynn	√	√	Hw	8	5		N/D 87	42
Log Cabin	Log Cabin Plaid		√	√	Hw	4	5		N/D 83	42
Log Cabin	Log Cabin Rag Rugs	Meany, Janet K.	√	√	WJ	9	4	36	Sp 85	50
Log Cabin	Notebook: Two-Harness Log Cabin (Betty LaFara)	Myers, Ruth, ed.	√	√	SS&D	12	2	46	Sp 81	28

SUBJECT	TITLE	AUTHOR	IL	INST	JOUR	VOL	NO	ISS	DATE	PAGE
Log Cabin	Rag Runner (Susan Snover) (error-corrected Hw v2 n4 81 p22)		√	√	Hw	2	3		My 81	50, 78
Log Cabin	Syncopated Log Cabin (Virginia West)		√	√	Hw	5	2		M/A 84	72, 94
Log Cabin	Two-Harness Textiles, The Loom-Controlled Weaves: Color-Effect Plain Weaves (Log Cabin)	Tidball, Harriet	√	√	SCGM		20		67	22
Log Cabin	Upholstery Fabric (Sharon Alderman)		√	√	Hw	1	1		F-W 79	42, 61
Log Cabin	Weaver's Notebook		√	√	SS&D	10	2	38	Sp 79	53
Log Cabin	Woodtones Log Cabin Afghan (Ardis Dobrovolny)		√	√	Hw	3	3		My 82	29, 88
Log Carrier	Card Woven Log Carrier		√	√	Hw	1	1		F-W 79	46, 61
Log Carrier	Weaving for the Holidays (Helen Jarvis) (error-corrected Hw v4 n4 83 p92)		√	>4	Hw	3	5		N/D 82	78
Log Carriers	Keep Warm! Log Carriers	Champion, Ellen	√	√	WJ	5	2	18	Fa 80	6
Logograms	One Guild's Story: From Founding an Organization to Building its Image	Piroch, Sigrid	√		WJ	12	2	46	Fa 87	30
Logwood	Why Bother with Natural Dyeing?	Bulbach, Stanley	√	√	TM			5	J/J 86	32
Long-Eyed Heddle Frame	Leno Fabrics	Xenakis, Athanasios David	√	√	PWC			6	Su 83	18
Long-Eyed Heddle Frame: Rigid Heddle	Red and Blue Canvas Weave Afghan	Xenakis, Athanasios David	√	√	PWC	3	1	7		22
Long-Eyed Heddles	Christmas Card, A		√	>4	WJ	2	2	6	Oc 77	32
Long-Eyed Heddles	Coverlet Weaves Using Two Ties	Barrett, Clotilde	√	>4	WJ	3	4	12	Ap 79	26
Long-Eyed Heddles	Damask with a Sword	Keasbey, Doramay	√	>4	CW	7	2	20	Ja 86	16
Long-Eyed Heddles	Double & Triple Harness Double-Cloth	Fabeck, Diane	√	>4	CW	7	3	21	My 86	7
Long-Eyed Heddles	Drawloom Basics	van der Hoogt, Madelyn	√	>4	Hw	7	2		M/A 86	61
Long-Eyed Heddles	Drawloom Special Harness for Double Weave	Malloy, Kim, OSB	√	>4	AT	1			De 83	77
Long-Eyed Heddles	Five Block Double Weave Using the Glimåkra Long Eyed Heddle Accessory	Tramba, Diane	√	>4	WJ	7	3	27	Wi 82	45
Long-Eyed Heddles	In Pursuit of Plakhta	Golay, Myrna	√	>4	WJ	11	3	43	Wi 87	34
Long-Eyed Heddles	Karelian Red-Picking	Ruchti, Willie Jager	√	>4	WJ	5	2	18	Fa 80	34
Long-Eyed Heddles	Layered Fabrics on Eight Harnesses	Marston, Ena	√	>4	SS&D	6	4	24	Fa 75	50
Long-Eyed Heddles	Ligetuhr Arbeit: A Seventeenth-Century Compound Mounting and a Family of Associated Weaves	Hilts, Patricia	√	>4	AT	7			Ju 87	31
Long-Eyed Heddles	Lithuanian Pervarai: Producing a Twenty Shaft Pattern on a Twelve Shaft Loom	Meek, M. Kati	√	>4	AT	1			De 83	159
Long-Eyed Heddles	Little Known Weaves Worth Knowing Better: Dropped Weaves	Zielinski, S. A.; Robert Leclerc, ed.	√	>4	MWL	16			'51–'73	18
Long-Eyed Heddles	Little Known Weaves Worth Knowing Better: Two-Harness Method	Zielinski, S. A.; Robert Leclerc, ed.	√	>4	MWL	16			'51–'73	23
Long-Eyed Heddles	Long Eyed Heddles	Ahrens, Jim	√	>4	CW	6	1	16	Se 84	3
Long-Eyed Heddles	Long-Eyed Heddles and Rising Shed Looms	Fabeck, Diane	√	>4	Iw	4	4		Fa 79	28
Long-Eyed Heddles	Notebook:"Someday" File, The (Maggie Weyers)	Myers, Ruth Nordquist, ed.			SS&D	15	3	59	Su 84	66
Long-Eyed Heddles	Oscar Knopf's Ingenious Invention	Miller, Ethel E.	√	>4	H&C	10	2		Sp 59	24
Long-Eyed Heddles	Satin and Long-Eyed Heddles	Hoskins, Janet A.; W. D. Hoskins	√	>4	WJ	6	1	21	Su 81	25
Long-Eyed Heddles	Scandinavian Designs for American Looms	Freeman, Claire	√		H&C	3	2		Sp 52	14
Long-Eyed Heddles	Skillbragd — A Decorative Pattern Weave		√	>4	Hw	8	3		M/J 87	60
Long-Eyed Heddles	Smalandsvav — Double Harness Weaving on an Ordinary Loom	Kelly, Jacquie	√	>4	CW	6	2	17	Ja 85	15
Long-Eyed Heddles	Some Additional Notes on the Damask—Threading the Pattern Harnesses	Ahrens, Jim	√	>4	CW	6	2	17	Ja 85	3
Long-Eyed Heddles	Ten-Harness Design for a Towel	Gubser, Elsie H.	√	>4	H&C	9	4		Fa 58	28
Long-Eyed Heddles	Three-Toned Blocks: Further Explorations with Long-Eyed Heddles	Broughton, Eve T.	√	>4	WJ	9	4	36	Sp 85	72

SUBJECT	TITLE	AUTHOR	IL	INST	JOUR	VOL	NO	ISS	DATE	PAGE
Long-Eyed Heddles	Three-Toned Blocks, Part 1: Simple Pattern	Broughton, Eve T.	√	>4	CW	6	1	16	Se 84	12
Long-Eyed Heddles	Three-Toned Blocks, Part 2: Reverses	Broughton, Eve T.	√	>4	CW	6	2	17	Ja 85	10
Long-Eyed Heddles	Three-Toned Blocks, Part 3: Alternating Designs	Broughton, Eve T.	√	>4	CW	6	3	18	My 85	10
Long-Eyed Heddles	Twill and Plain Weave Blocks with Long-Eyed Heddles	Broughton, Eve T.	√	>4	WJ	8	4	32	Sp 84	58
Long-Eyed Heddles	Upholstery and Bed Covering Fabric, Fabric #3 (Constance LaLena)		√	>4	Hw	7	2		M/A 86	64, I-12
Long-Eyed Heddles	Upphämta Display Towel		√	>4	Hw	8	3		M/J 87	42
Long-Eyed Heddles	Use of Long-Eyed Heddles for Patterned Double Weave, The	Howard, Ruth	√	>4	WJ	6	2	22	Fa 81	35
Long-Eyed Heddles	Weaving Damask	Arnold, Ruth	√	>4	H&C	6	3		Su 55	4
Long-Eyed Heddles	Weaving in Quebec: Traditional Quebecois Weaving	Barrett, Clotilde	√	√	WJ	6	4	24	Sp 82	10
Long-Eyed Heddles: Adjusting	Ups and Downs of the Long-Eyed Heddle	Swales, Lois	√	>4	CW	5	2	14	Ja 84	8
Long-Eyed Heddles: Calculating Shafts Required	Ups and Downs of the Long-Eyed Heddle	Swales, Lois	√	>4	CW	5	2	14	Ja 84	8
Long-Eyed Heddles: Countermarch Loom	Use Of Long-Eyed Heddles, The	Koob, Katherine; Barbara Keller; Ruth Howard	√	>4	CW	1	3	3	Ap 80	1
Long-Eyed Heddles: Drawloom	Use Of Long-Eyed Heddles, The	Koob, Katherine; Barbara Keller; Ruth Howard	√	>4	CW	1	3	3	Ap 80	1
Long-Eyed Heddles, Inverted	Long-Eyed Heddles and Rising Shed Looms	Fabeck, Diane	√	>4	Iw	4	4		Fa 79	28
Long-Eyed Heddles: Jack Loom	Double-Twill on a Jack Loom Using Two Sets of Ground Harnesses Equipped with Special Long-Eyed Heddles	Freimer, Betty	√	>4	CW	2	1	4	Oc 80	2
Long-Eyed Heddles: Jack Loom	Use Of Long-Eyed Heddles, The	Koob, Katherine; Barbara Keller; Ruth Howard	√	>4	CW	1	3	3	Ap 80	1
Long-Eyed Heddles: Threading, Treadling	Double-Twill on a Jack Loom Using Two Sets of Ground Harnesses Equipped with Special Long-Eyed Heddles	Freimer, Betty	√	>4	CW	2	1	4	Oc 80	2
Loom Accessories	Knotless Cords and Heddles on a Counter-march Loom (error-corrected SS&D v12 n3 81 p6)	Kinersly, Görel A. B.	√	√	SS&D	12	2	46	Sp 81	18
Loom Accessories: Heading Cords	Vertical Loom, The		√	√	WJ	1	3	3	Ja 77	16
Loom: Accessories, Long-Eyed Heddle Accessory	Five Block Double Weave Using the Glimåkra Long Eyed Heddle Accessory	Tramba, Diane	√	>4	WJ	7	3	27	Wi 82	45
Loom Accessories: Raddle	Dear Heddle			√	WJ	1	2	2	Oc 76	28
Loom Accessories: Raddle	System for Recording and Drafting Certain Types of Braids, A (error-corrected WJ v2 n1 77 insert for vol. 1)	Barrett, Clotilde; Ronnie Bohannan	√	√	WJ	1	2	2	Oc 76	20
Loom Accessories: Raddle	Very Special Raddle, A	Smayda, Norma	√		WJ	8	4	32	Sp 84	68
Loom Accessories: Tenter	Placemats	DeRoy, Paul	√	>4	WJ	1	3	3	Ja 77	4
Loom Adjustments	Handweaver's Instruction Manual: Dressing the Loom, Loom Adjustments	Tidball, Harriet C. nee Douglas			SCGM		34		49	17
Loom Builder	E.E. Gilmore, Loom Builder and Weaver	Watson, Aleta	√		H&C	23	5		S/O 72	24
Loom Cords: Knotless	Knotless Cords and Heddles on a Counter-march Loom (error-corrected SS&D v12 n3 81 p6)	Kinersly, Görel A. B.	√	√	SS&D	12	2	46	Sp 81	18
Loom Cords, Loop	Accurate, Knotless Tie-ups Using Loop Loom Cord	Kinersly, Gorel	√	√	WJ	5	1	17	Su 80	26
Loom: Knitting	Susanna Lewis	Malarcher, Pat	√		Fa	5	3		M/J 78	52
Loom Makers	Directory of Loom Makers				Hw	2	3		My 81	30
Loom Makers	McGarrs of Norwood, The				H&C	17	2		Sp 66	46
Loom Manufacturer	Fifty Years Ago in Handweaving: E. E. Gilmore, A Lifetime of Weaving		√		Hw	7	2		M/A 86	22
Loom-Controlled Design	Coverlet Weaves Using Two Ties	Barrett, Clotilde	√	>4	WJ	3	4	12	Ap 79	26

SUBJECT	TITLE	AUTHOR	IL	INST	JOUR	VOL	NO	ISS	DATE	PAGE
Loom-Controlled Design	Designing Rugs for Harness-Controlled Weaving		√	> 4	WJ	4	4	16	Ap 80	27
Loom-Controlled Design	Loom Controlled Designs		√	> 4	WJ	3	3	11	Ja 79	18
Loom-Controlled Design	Swivel Explored and Contradicted		√	√	WJ	3	4	12	Ap 79	5
Loom-Designed Garments	Wasteless, Waistless Dress. A	Holtzer, Marilyn F.	√	√	Hw	2	3		My 81	85
Loom-Shaped Garments	Bog Affair, A	Homme, Audrey	√	√	PWC			3	Oc 82	44
Loom-Shaped Garments	Bog Jacket, Basic Shaping	Davidsohn, Marty	√	√	PWC			3	Oc 82	35
Loom-Shaped Garments	Clothing from Rectangles	Liebler, Barbara	√	√	Iw	5	4		Fa 80	52
Loom-Shaped Garments	Mind Boggling Bogs	Herring, Connie	√	√	PWC			3	Oc 82	36
Loom-Shaped Weaving	Applying the Pulled Warp Technique to Loom-Shaped Clothing	Evans, Kerry	√	√	WJ	9	3	35	Wi 85	34
Loom-Shaped Weaving	Contemporary Costume, Strictly Handwoven: Warp and Weft Relationships in Loom-Shaped Edges	Tidball, Harriet	√	√	SCGM		24		68	3
Loom-Shaped Weaving	Cotton Shirts	Barnett-Westfall, Lynn	√	√	WJ	4	3	15	Ja 80	22
Loom-Shaped Weaving	Design a Dress--On the Loom	Holland, Nina	√	√	SS&D	6	2	22	Sp 75	37
Loom-Shaped Weaving	Fall Project: Loom Controlled Slacks (error-corrected H&C v26 n5 75 p45)	Roth, Mrs, Bettie G.	√	√	H&C	26	3		M/J 75	18
Loom-Shaped Weaving	Loom Shaped Top with Dukagång Inlay	Searle, Karen	√	√	WJ	11	3	43	Wi 87	8
Loom-Shaped Weaving	Peru, Textiles Unlimited: Textile Characteristics, Loom Shaping	Tidball, Harriet	√		SCGM		25		68	20
Loom-Shaped Weaving	Shaped Tapestry Bags from the Nazca-Ica Area of Peru	Bird, Junius B.	√		TMJ	1	3		De 64	2
Loom-Shaped Weaving	Weft Twining: Looms and Shaping	Harvey, Virginia I.; Harriet Tidball	√	√	SCGM		28		69	12
Looming Thoughts: American Textile/Apparel Industry	Looming Thoughts	Fannin, Allen			WJ	10	4	40	Sp 86	28
Looming Thoughts: Family/Weaving Integration	Looming Thoughts	Fannin, Allen			WJ	12	2	46	Fa 87	50
Looming Thoughts: Four "Multi" Shaft Illogic	Looming Thoughts	Fannin, Allen A.			WJ	11	4	44	Sp 87	7
Looming Thoughts: Handloom Weaving	Looming Thoughts	Fannin, Allen A.			WJ	9	2	34	Fa 84	22
Looming Thoughts: Handloom Weaving	Looming Thoughts	Fannin, Allen A.			WJ	8	3	31	Wi 83	61
Looming Thoughts: Handloom Weaving Movement	Looming Thoughts	Fannin, Allen	√		WJ	7	1	25	Su 82	26
Looming Thoughts: Handspinning	Looming Thoughts	Fannin, Allen	√		S-O	1			77	12
Looming Thoughts: Handspinning	Looming Thoughts	Fannin, Allen A.			WJ	9	2	34	Fa 84	22
Looming Thoughts: Handspinning Equipment	Looming Thoughts	Fannin, Allen A.			WJ	9	4	36	Sp 85	14
Looming Thoughts: Handspun/Handwoven	Looming Thoughts	Fannin, Allen A.			WJ	10	2	38	Fa 85	14
Looming Thoughts: Handweaving Equipment	Looming Thoughts	Fannin, Allen A.			WJ	9	4	36	Sp 85	14
Looming Thoughts: HGN Convergence '72	Looming Thoughts	Fannin, Allen; Dorothy Fannin			H&C	23	4		J/A 72	3
Looming Thoughts: Learning, Motivation	Looming Thoughts	Fannin, Allen A.			WJ	11	2	42	Fa 86	63
Looming Thoughts: Learning, Resources	Looming Thoughts	Fannin, Allen A.			WJ	11	2	42	Fa 86	63
Looming Thoughts: Misrepresentation, Craft World	Looming Thoughts	Fannin, Allen; Dorothy Fannin			H&C	24	3		M/J 73	17
Looms	All About Looms: Looms	Zielinski, S. A.; Robert Leclerc, ed.			MWL	2			'51–'73	7
Looms	Directory of Plans for Weaving and Spinning Equipment	Hammock, Noël			SS&D	6	2	22	Sp 75	27
Looms	Evolution of the Multi-Loom, The	Brokaw, Edith H., O.T.R.	√		H&C	3	4		Fa 52	9
Looms	Further Comments on Looms	Macomber, L. W.			H&C	5	3		Su 54	56
Looms	Loom May be a Piece of Furniture, A	Jackson, James J.	√		H&C	5	4		Fa 54	28

SUBJECT	TITLE	AUTHOR	IL	INST	JOUR	VOL	NO	ISS	DATE	PAGE
Looms: Accessories	Contemporary Tapestry: On Looms, Warping, Setting Up Tapestry Study Course — Part 1	O'Callaghan, Kate	√	√	WJ	4	3	15	Ja 80	41
Looms: Accessories	Shed Regulator for Counterbalance Looms, The	Koepp, William	√	√	WJ	10	3	39	Wi 86	67
Looms: Accessories, Stretcher	Simple but Effective: A Novel Stretcher	Beck, Ulrike	√	√	WJ	10	2	38	Fa 85	27
Looms: African Strip	Jacket Inspired by West African Narrow Strip Weaving	Bradley, Louise	√	√	WJ	5	3	19	Wi 81	31
Looms: Ancient	Ancient Peruvian Loom, An	Grossman, Ellin	√		H&C	9	2		Sp 58	20
Looms: Ancient	Ancient Peruvian Weaver	Clement, Doris W.	√		H&C	18	4		Fa 67	21
Looms: Antique	Reflection of the Past: Antique Looms, A	Saylor, Mary C.	√		SS&D	7	3	27	Su 76	26
Looms: Antique	Those Musty Old Looms	Ross, Nan	√		SS&D	8	2	30	Sp 77	43
Looms: Apron	Handweaver's Instruction Manual: The Loom, The Apron	Tidball, Harriet C. nee Douglas			SCGM		34		49	4
Looms: Aubusson Basse-Lisse	Contemporary Tapestry	Tidball, Harriet	√		SCGM		12		64	10
Looms: Automatic	All About Looms: The Best Loom	Zielinski, S. A.; Robert Leclerc, ed.	√		MWL	2			'51–'73	17
Looms: Automatic, Power	Development of Weaving Using Automatic Looms, The	Pourdeyhimi, B.; K. C. Jackson; K. Hepworth			AT	4			De 85	107
Looms: AVL	High-Tech Comes to Weaving: AVL Looms	Larson, Eden	√		Fa	14	4		S/O 87	36
Looms: AVL	Jim "The Legend" Ahrens	Xenakis, Alexis Yiorgos	√		PWC	4	4	14		6
Looms: Backstrap	Ancient Peruvian Loom, An	Grossman, Ellin	√		H&C	9	2		Sp 58	20
Looms: Backstrap	Art of Ixchel: Learning to Weave in Guatemala and Rhode Island, The	Schevill, Margot	√	√	WJ	8	1	29	Su 83	57
Looms: Backstrap	Back-Strap Looms in Bermuda		√		SS&D	4	2	14	Sp 73	22
Looms: Backstrap	Backstrap Looms	Conrad, Elvira	√		H&C	14	3		Su 63	17
Looms: Backstrap	Fixed-Heddle Looms to Make for Pennies Using Coffee Stirrers	Lee, Dr. Stanley H.	√	√	SS&D	5	1	17	Wi 73	21
Looms: Backstrap	Fundraising Brings Kasuri Kimono Weaver to Nashville Workshop	Wilson, Sadye Tune	√		SS&D	9	2	34	Sp 78	4
Looms: Backstrap	Guatemala Visited	Atwater, Mary Meigs	√		SCGM		15		65	43
Looms: Backstrap	Guatemala Weaver, The	Marks, Copeland A.	√		H&C	26	5		Oc 75	2
Looms: Backstrap	Guatemala Weaving Workshop	Kingsmill, Sally	√		H&C	26	3		M/J 75	28
Looms: Backstrap	Guatemalan Gauze Weaves: A Description and Key to Identification	Pancake, Cherri M.; Suzanne Baizerman	√	√	TMJ	19 20			80,81	1
Looms: Backstrap	Guatemalan Looms	Young, Helen Daniels	√		H&C	4	3		Su 53	16
Looms: Backstrap	Japanese Weaves Provide Ideas for Experiment	Freeman, Claire	√	√	H&C	21	1		Wi 70	4
Looms: Backstrap	Mexican Motifs: Mexico, Land of Contrasts	Tidball, Harriet	√		SCGM		6		62	1
Looms: Backstrap	Peru, Textiles Unlimited: Textile Characteristics, The Stick-Loom Set-Up	Tidball, Harriet	√		SCGM		25		68	20
Looms: Backstrap	Selected Batak Textiles: Technique and Function	Gittinger, Mattiebelle S.	√		TMJ	4	2		75	13
Looms: Backstrap	Understanding Some Complex Structures from Simple Andean Looms: Steps in Analysis and Reproduction	Cahlander, Adele	√	√	AT	1			De 83	181
Looms: Backstrap	Warping and Weaving Mitla Cloth on the Backstrap Loom	Knottenbelt, Maaike	√	√	TMJ	22			83	53
Looms: Backstrap	Weaving Processes in the Cuzco Area of Peru	Rowe, Ann Pollard	√	√	TMJ	4	2		75	30
Looms: Backstrap	Weaving with Rigid Heddle Backstrap Looms	Swanson, Karen	√	√	H&C	21	2		Sp 70	13
Looms: Backstrap	Weft Twining: Looms and Shaping	Harvey, Virginia I.; Harriet Tidball	√	√	SCGM		28		69	12
Looms: Backstrap, Source	Backstrap Looms			√	TM			11	J/J 87	11
Looms: Beater	Part 1, Build or Buy a Loom: Questions and Answers About Looms, Should Beater Be Adjustable?	Tidball, Harriet			SCGM		23		68	17

SUBJECT	TITLE	AUTHOR	IL	INST	JOUR	VOL	NO	ISS	DATE	PAGE
Looms: Board	Don't Cry...Dye	Bliss, Anne	√	√	Hw	2	2		Mr 81	50
Looms: Board	Off-Loom Child's Tabard		√	√	Hw	2	1		F-W 80	52, 69
Looms: Board	Textile Arts of Multan, Pakistan	Shahzaman, Mahboob	√	>4	SS&D	4	3	15	Su 73	8
Looms: Board	Weaving on a Board		√	√	H&C	7	3		Su 56	46
Looms: Board	Weaving on a Board	Kappler, Erda	√	√	Hw	4	4		S/O 83	46
Looms: Board, Shaped	Handwoven Cape on an Improvised Loom	Williams, Olive	√	√	H&C	22	3		Su 71	28
Looms: Cachi (Vertical Loom)	Cuna Cachi: A Study of Hammock Weaving Among the Cuna Indians of the San Blas Islands	Lambert, Anne M.	√	√	AT	5			Ju 86	105
Looms: Card Looms	Modern Loom from Medieval Sources, A	Cesari, Andrea	√	√	WJ	10	2	38	Fa 85	18
Looms: Cardboard	Cardboard Looms Help the Handicapped	Holmes, Margaret	√	√	SS&D	6	2	22	Sp 75	31
Looms: Cardboard	Puppets Challenge Ingenuity	Fowler, Mary Jean	√	√	SS&D	6	1	21	Wi 74	19
Looms: Cardboard, Shaped	Accessories: Hot Foot		√	√	WJ	2	4	8	Ap 78	9
Looms: Circular	Circular Loom, The	Cranston-Bennett, Mary Ellen	√	√	H&C	17	1		Wi 66	12
Looms: Circular	Handspuns for Tapestries	Szumski, Norma; Phyllis Clemmer; Clotilde Barrett	√		WJ	6	2	22	Fa 81	41
Looms: Circular	Round Rug Woven on a Hula Hoop, A	Pemberton, Mildred	√	√	H&C	20	3		Su 69	12
Looms: Circular	Teneriffe Lace — Wooden Disc Loom	Robinson, Esther	√	√	SS&D	5	1	17	Wi 73	52
Looms: Complex	Chinese Drawloom: A Study in Weave Structure, The	Sellin, Helen	√	>4	WJ	9	2	34	Fa 84	6
Looms: Complex	Is Complex Weaving for You?	Piroch, Sigrid	√		WJ	10	2	38	Fa 85	10
Looms: Complex	Three-Toned Blocks: Further Explorations with Long-Eyed Heddles	Broughton, Eve T.	√	>4	WJ	9	4	36	Sp 85	72
Looms: Complex	Unravelling the Mysteries of the Jacquard	Jirousek, Charlotte	√		WJ	9	1	33	Su 84	8
Looms: Complex	Use of the Dobby Loom for Multi-Harness Weave Manipulation, The	Renne, Elisha	√	>4	WJ	9	3	35	Wi 85	9
Looms: Compound Mounting, Divided Front Harness	Ligetuhr Arbeit: A Seventeenth-Century Compound Mounting and a Family of Associated Weaves	Hilts, Patricia	√	>4	AT	7			Ju 87	31
Looms: Compound Mounting (Ligetuhr Arbeit)	Ligetuhr Arbeit: A Seventeenth-Century Compound Mounting and a Family of Associated Weaves	Hilts, Patricia	√	>4	AT	7			Ju 87	31
Looms: Compu-Dobby	Skeleton Peg Plan for the Compu-Dobby, A	Gustafson, Susan			CW	6	3	18	My 85	24
Looms: Computer-Aided	Computers and Weavers: Software Is Just Another Tool in the Designer's Hand	Hoskins, Janet A.	√		TM			9	F/M 87	51
Looms: Computer-Controlled	Computer Control of Tie-ups and Treadling Sequence	Clement, Richard	√	√	WJ	8	3	31	Wi 83	32
Looms: Computer-Controlled	Interface	Ligon, Linda			Hw	4	3		M/J 83	76
Looms: Constructing and Adapting	Ahrens Looms, The	Bryan, Dorothy	√	√	H&C	6	3		Su 55	28
Looms: Constructing and Adapting	All About Looms: Draw-Looms	Zielinski, S. A.; Robert Leclerc, ed.	√	>4	MWL	2			'51–'73	55
Looms: Constructing and Adapting	All About Looms: How to Maintain and Improve a Weaving Loom	Zielinski, S. A.; Robert Leclerc, ed.	√	√	MWL	2			'51–'73	29
Looms: Constructing and Adapting	Barn Raising Experience, A	Bujnowski, Donald	√	√	SS&D	8	4	32	Fa 77	100
Looms: Constructing and Adapting	Build a Warp-Weighted Loom	Towner, Naomi Whiting	√	√	SS&D	6	3	23	Su 75	36
Looms: Constructing and Adapting	Build or Buy a Loom, Part 1 Patterns for Pick-Up and Brocade, Part 2	Tidball, Harriet	√	√	SCGM		23		68	1-38
Looms: Constructing and Adapting	Building an Extra Warp Beam		√	√	H&C	10	2		Sp 59	45
Looms: Constructing and Adapting	Cape-Able Garment	Hicks, C. Norman	√	√	SS&D	6	3	23	Su 75	18
Looms: Constructing and Adapting	Construct a Simple Shaft-Switching Device	Pickett, Alice	√	√	SS&D	16	3	63	Su 85	68
Looms: Constructing and Adapting	Constructing Front-Slung Treadles	Ziemke, Dene	√	√	SS&D	8	4	32	Fa 77	74
Looms: Constructing and Adapting	Contemporary Tapestry: On Looms, Warping, Setting Up Tapestry Study Course — Part 1	O'Callaghan, Kate	√	√	WJ	4	3	15	Ja 80	41
Looms: Constructing and Adapting	Converting the Vertical Pull AVL Flyshuttle to Horizontal Pull	Fry, Doug	√	√	CW		25		Se 87	18

SUBJECT	TITLE	AUTHOR	IL	INST	JOUR	VOL	NO	ISS	DATE	PAGE
Looms: Constructing and Adapting	Design for a One-Treadle Loom	Pariseau, George E., M.D.	√	√	H&C	3	3		Su 52	15
Looms: Constructing and Adapting	Doublejack or Sink the Floating Selvedge	Koepp, William	√	√	WJ	9	3	35	Wi 85	67
Looms: Constructing and Adapting	Draw Frame Device	Jansons, Ilga	√	√	SS&D	10	4	40	Fa 79	90
Looms: Constructing and Adapting	Drawloom Special Harness for Double Weave	Malloy, Kim, OSB	√	>4	AT	1			De 83	77
Looms: Constructing and Adapting	Easily Constructed Loom from Africa, An	Kren, Margo	√	√	SS&D	7	3	27	Su 76	19
Looms: Constructing and Adapting	Glimåkra Adaptations	Nicholson, Suzanne; Dick Nicholson		√	CW		24		My 87	11
Looms: Constructing and Adapting	Guatemalan Gauze Weaves: A Description and Key to Identification	Pancake, Cherri M.; Suzanne Baizerman	√	√	TMJ	19 20			80,81	1
Looms: Constructing and Adapting	Hand Woven Rugs: Weaves, Two-Warp Weave, Installing a Second Beam	Atwater, Mary Meigs	√	√	SCGM		29		48	21
Looms: Constructing and Adapting	Handweaver's Jacquard Loom, A	Mulkey, Philip O.	√		H&C	7	4		Fa 56	46
Looms: Constructing and Adapting	How to Build a Loom	Turnbull, Tom	√	√	H&C	23	3		M/J 72	3
Looms: Constructing and Adapting	How to Build a Loom	Turnbull, Tom	√	√	H&C	23	4		J/A 72	12
Looms: Constructing and Adapting	"I Wish I Had a Loom . . ."	Laine, Anna E.			WJ	9	4	36	Sp 85	57
Looms: Constructing and Adapting	Individualizing a Loom	Keasbey, Doramay			CW	4	1	10	Se 82	9
Looms: Constructing and Adapting	Iowa Student Builds her Loom	Will, Dorothy	√	√	H&C	6	4		Fa 55	20
Looms: Constructing and Adapting	Loom Bench	Ziemke, Dene			SS&D	8	3	31	Su 77	49
Looms: Constructing and Adapting	Loom Craft Studio		√		H&C	7	4		Fa 56	48
Looms: Constructing and Adapting	Loom for the Handicapped, A	Nicoll, Frances M.	√		H&C	7	3		Su 56	22
Looms: Constructing and Adapting	Loom in My Tote-Bag, The	Redman, Jane	√	√	SS&D	5	4	20	Fa 74	83
Looms: Constructing and Adapting	Loom May be a Piece of Furniture, A	Jackson, James J.	√		H&C	5	4		Fa 54	28
Looms: Constructing and Adapting	Loom with Removable Innards	Berglund, Hilma	√	√	SS&D	2	1	5	De 70	21
Looms: Constructing and Adapting	Low Budget Tapestry Loom, A	Gilstrap, Bill; Sara Gilstrap	√	√	WJ	5	4	20	Sp 81	42
Looms: Constructing and Adapting	Milwaukee Loom Builder		√		H&C	11	3		Su 60	57
Looms: Constructing and Adapting	Modification of the AVL Dobby Loom for Execution of Multi-Shaft Two-Tie Block Weaves	Gustafson, Susan L.	√	√	AT	1			De 83	235
Looms: Constructing and Adapting	New Freedom with a Counterbalance—Countermarch Loom	Hoyt, Peggy	√	>4	CW	5	3	15	My 84	3
Looms: Constructing and Adapting	Nine-Foot Loom for Rugs, A	Crowell, Ivan H.	√	√	H&C	7	4		Fa 56	14
Looms: Constructing and Adapting	One Man's Loom	Wight, James	√		Iw	4	4		Fa 79	22
Looms: Constructing and Adapting	Original Fabrics of Kaftan, The	El-Homossani, M. M.	√	>4	AT	1			De 83	263
Looms: Constructing and Adapting	Oscar Knopf's Ingenious Invention	Miller, Ethel E.	√	>4	H&C	10	2		Sp 59	24
Looms: Constructing and Adapting	Reflection of the Past: Antique Looms, A	Saylor, Mary C.	√		SS&D	7	3	27	Su 76	26
Looms: Constructing and Adapting	Remodeling a Loom	Ziemke, Dene			SS&D	8	2	30	Sp 77	94
Looms: Constructing and Adapting	Removable Sectional Beam Conversion Kit, A	Henneberger, Karel	√	√	SS&D	17	1	65	Wi 85	86
Looms: Constructing and Adapting	Retired Engineer Designs and Builds a Loom		√		H&C	16	2		Sp 65	40
Looms: Constructing and Adapting	Sectional Warp Beam	Russell, Harold W.; Fred J. Ahrens	√	√	SS&D	5	2	18	Sp 74	25
Looms: Constructing and Adapting	Setting Up a Tape Loom	Crawford, Grace Post	√	√	H&C	12	1		Wi 61	19
Looms: Constructing and Adapting	Shaft Switching, A Simple Method Usable for Finer Setts	Herring, Connie; Athanasios David Xenakis	√	√	PWC	3	3	9		29
Looms: Constructing and Adapting	Shaft Switching on a Jack Loom	Wilson, Sadye Tune	√	√	SS&D	10	1	37	Wi 78	70
Looms: Constructing and Adapting	Shaft-Switching Device of Richard Shultz		√	√	WJ	8	4	32	Sp 84	35
Looms: Constructing and Adapting	Shaft-Switching Device of William Koepp		√	√	WJ	8	4	32	Sp 84	32
Looms: Constructing and Adapting	Simple Selvage System, A	Koepp, William	√	√	SS&D	16	4	64	Fa 85	68
Looms: Constructing and Adapting	Spanish Colonial Loom: A Contemporary Loom-Maker Uses Traditional Tools to Construct a Replica for the Albuquerque Museum	Edwards, Jack	√	√	WJ	11	1	41	Su 86	16
Looms: Constructing and Adapting	Speed Up Tie-Up for the Counter March Loom	Gilmurray, Susan	√	√	SS&D	10	3	39	Su 79	50

SUBJECT	TITLE	AUTHOR	IL	INST	JOUR	VOL	NO	ISS	DATE	PAGE
Looms: Constructing and Adapting	Supplementary Warp Patterning: Adding an Extra Pattern Harness	Tidball, Harriet	√	√	SCGM		17		66	9
Looms: Constructing and Adapting	Those Musty Old Looms	Ross, Nan	√		SS&D	8	2	30	Sp 77	43
Looms: Constructing and Adapting	To Wind Bobbins Use Your Spinning Wheel	Stowell, Robert F.	√	√	H&C	7	4		Fa 56	17
Looms: Constructing and Adapting	Twenty-Harness Madness	Moore, Gen	√	> 4	SS&D	12	4	48	Fa 81	46
Looms: Constructing and Adapting	Variation of a Rigid Heddle Loom	Hoyt, Peggy	√	√	H&C	21	3		Su 70	6
Looms: Constructing and Adapting	Vertical Loom (continued) — Construction of a Warp Weighted Loom, The		√	√	WJ	1	4	4	Ap 77	27
Looms: Constructing and Adapting	Weaving His Way Back	Van Cleve, Kate	√		H&C	2	3		Su 51	11
Looms: Constructing and Adapting	Weaving in Therapy	Nicoll, Frances M., O.T.R.	√	√	H&C	11	3		Su 60	28
Looms: Constructing and Adapting, Disabled	Looms for the Handicapped	Gallinger, Osma C.	√		H&C	8	2		Sp 57	19
Looms: Constructing and Adapting, Drinking Straws	Children's Corner — A Woven Strap or Belt		√	√	WJ	3	4	12	Ap 79	38
Looms: Constructing and Adapting, Friction Brake	Arabesque	Herring, Connie	√	√	PWC	3	1	7		47
Looms: Counterbalance, 5-Shaft	Some Contemporary Textiles in Southern Asia	Hatch, David P.	√	√	H&C	11	3		Su 60	23
Looms: Counterbalance-Countermarch	New Freedom with a Counterbalance—Countermarch Loom	Hoyt, Peggy	√	> 4	CW	5	3	15	My 84	3
Looms: Counterbalanced	All About Looms: The Best Loom	Zielinski, S. A.; Robert Leclerc, ed.	√		MWL	2			'51–'73	14
Looms: Counterbalanced	Choosing a Floor Loom: Sinking vs. Rising Shed	Keasbey, Doramay	√	√	lw	5	3		Su 80	50
Looms: Counterbalanced	Handlooms in Use Today	Hausner, Walter	√		H&C	15	4		Fa 64	22
Looms: Counterbalanced	Iowa Student Builds her Loom	Will, Dorothy	√	√	H&C	6	4		Fa 55	20
Looms: Counterbalanced	Long Eyed Heddles	Ahrens, Jim	√	> 4	CW	6	1	16	Se 84	3
Looms: Counterbalanced	Part 1, Build or Buy a Loom: Loom Types, The Counter-Balanced Loom	Tidball, Harriet	√		SCGM		23		68	3
Looms: Countermarch	All About Looms: Double Tie-Up	Zielinski, S. A.; Robert Leclerc, ed.	√	√	MWL	2			'51–'73	40
Looms: Countermarch	All About Looms: The Best Loom	Zielinski, S. A.; Robert Leclerc, ed.	√		MWL	2			'51–'73	12
Looms: Countermarch	Choosing a Floor Loom: Sinking vs. Rising Shed	Keasbey, Doramay	√	√	lw	5	3		Su 80	50
Looms: Countermarch	Choosing a Loom, One Weaver's Experience with a Countermarch	Hoyt, Peggy	√	> 4	CW	4	1	10	Se 82	14
Looms: Countermarch	Countermarche: Pure and Simple	Tallarovic, Joanne	√	√	WJ	8	3	31	Wi 83	85
Looms: Countermarch	Countermarche Tie Up	van der Hoogt, Madelyn	√		CW	4	3	12	Ap 83	13
Looms: Countermarch	Damn That Barbara	Tewell, William H.			SS&D	9	3	35	Su 78	54
Looms: Countermarch	Experimental Countermarch	Gilmurray, Susan	√	√	SS&D	8	2	30	Sp 77	39
Looms: Countermarch	Handlooms in Use Today	Hausner, Walter	√		H&C	15	4		Fa 64	22
Looms: Countermarch	Knotless Cords and Heddles on a Counter-march Loom (error-corrected SS&D v12 n3 81 p6)	Kinersly, Görel A. B.	√	√	SS&D	12	2	46	Sp 81	18
Looms: Countermarch	Long Eyed Heddles	Ahrens, Jim	√	> 4	CW	6	1	16	Se 84	3
Looms: Countermarch	One Man's Loom	Wight, James	√		lw	4	4		Fa 79	22
Looms: Countermarch	Part 1, Build or Buy a Loom: The Counter-Marche Loom	Tidball, Harriet	√		SCGM		23		68	6
Looms: Countermarch	Peter Collingwood, His Weaves and Weaving: Tying-Up a Double Countermarch Loom	Collingwood, Peter; Harriet Tidball, ed.	√	√	SCGM		8		63	24
Looms: Countermarch	Speed Up Tie-Up for the Counter March Loom	Gilmurray, Susan	√	√	SS&D	10	3	39	Su 79	50
Looms: Countermarch	Universal Tie-Up for a 4-Shaft Countermarch Loom		√	√	WJ	6	3	23	Wi 81	47
Looms: Countermarch, Balance	Another Balancing Act for the Countermarch Loom	Koepp, William	√	√	CW	8	1	22	Se 86	9
Looms: Countermarch, Balance	Keeping the Glimakra Loom in Balance	Tidwell, Elmyra	√	√	CW	7	3	21	My 86	3

SUBJECT	TITLE	AUTHOR	IL	INST	JOUR	VOL	NO	ISS	DATE	PAGE
Looms: Countermarch, Tie-Up	Everything You've Always Wanted to Know About Tying Up a Countermarch Loom Without Really Trying...And with Perfect Success the First Time	van der Hoogt, Madelyn; Athanasios David Xenakis	√	√	PWC	4	2	12		44
Looms: Crossbar	Macroweave Effect, The (error-corrected SS&D v12 n3 81 p6)	Towne, Carroll A.	√	√	SS&D	12	2	46	Sp 81	16
Looms: Damask	Ahrens Looms, The	Bryan, Dorothy	√	√	H&C	6	3		Su 55	28
Looms: Damask	Penland's Damask Loom		√		H&C	6	3		Su 55	24
Looms: Damask	Weaving Damask	Arnold, Ruth	√	> 4	H&C	6	3		Su 55	4
Looms: Damask	Weaving Damask on a Damask Loom	Steele, Zella	√		H&C	21	4		Fa 70	4
Looms: Dobby	Ahrens Looms, The	Bryan, Dorothy	√	√	H&C	6	3		Su 55	28
Looms: Dobby	Dobby Loom: A Workbench Report, The	Bendich, Hilary	√		SS&D	11	4	44	Fa 80	79
Looms: Dobby	Dobby Loom Explained, The	Colwell, Ken	√	√	SS&D	11	4	44	Fa 80	7
Looms: Dobby	Handlooms in Use Today	Hausner, Walter	√		H&C	15	4		Fa 64	22
Looms: Dobby	Metamorphosis: Two-Tie Weaves and the Changeable Image	Carey, Joyce Marquess	√	> 4	AT	1			De 83	243
Looms: Dobby	Modification of the AVL Dobby Loom for Execution of Multi-Shaft Two-Tie Block Weaves	Gustafson, Susan L.	√	√	AT	1			De 83	235
Looms: Dobby	Use of the Dobby Loom for Multi-Harness Weave Manipulation, The	Renne, Elisha	√	> 4	WJ	9	3	35	Wi 85	9
Looms: Dobby	Witch Engine! The Machinations of the Dobby	Cutcher, Hal	√		Iw	2	4		Su 77	22
Looms: Dobby, Computer-Aided	Macomber's Designers Delight Dobby, A Report	Gordon, Judith	√		CW	4	1	10	Se 82	16
Looms: Dobby, Harness-Action	Long Eyed Heddles	Ahrens, Jim	√	> 4	CW	6	1	16	Se 84	3
Looms: Dobby, Microcomputer-Control System	Design of Interactive Systems for Real-Time Dobby Control	Hoskins, W. D.; J. A. Hoskins	√	√	AT	5			Ju 86	33
Looms: Double Tie-Up	All About Looms: Double Tie-Up	Zielinski, S. A.; Robert Leclerc, ed.	√	√	MWL	2			'51–'73	40
Looms: Double Tie-Up	All About Looms: Double Tie-Up Loom	Zielinski, S. A.; Robert Leclerc, ed.	√		MWL	2			'51–'73	21
Looms: Drawloom	Alice Hindson, Expert on the Draw-loom	Arnold, Ruth	√		H&C	10	4		Fa 59	12
Looms: Drawloom	All About Looms: Draw-Looms	Zielinski, S. A.; Robert Leclerc, ed.	√	> 4	MWL	2			'51–'73	46
Looms: Drawloom	All About Looms: The Best Loom	Zielinski, S. A.; Robert Leclerc, ed.	√		MWL	2			'51–'73	17
Looms: Drawloom	Chinese Artisans At Work	Goodman, Deborah Lerme	√		Fa	13	1		J/F 86	34
Looms: Drawloom	Chinese Drawloom: A Study in Weave Structure, The	Sellin, Helen	√	> 4	WJ	9	2	34	Fa 84	6
Looms: Drawloom	Damask on a Drawloom	Keasbey, Doramay	√	> 4	SS&D	8	1	29	WI 76	63
Looms: Drawloom	Double-Harness Techniques Employed in Egypt	El-Homossani, M. M.	√	> 4	AT	3			My 85	229
Looms: Drawloom	Drawloom Basics	van der Hoogt, Madelyn	√	> 4	Hw	7	2		M/A 86	61
Looms: Drawloom	Drawloom Magic	van der Hoogt, Madelyn	√	> 4	Hw	7	2		M/A 86	66
Looms: Drawloom	Drawloom Special Harness for Double Weave	Malloy, Kim, OSB	√	> 4	AT	1			De 83	77
Looms: Drawloom	Guatemala Visited	Atwater, Mary Meigs	√	√	SCGM		15		65	10
Looms: Drawloom	Handlooms in Use Today	Hausner, Walter	√		H&C	15	4		Fa 64	22
Looms: Drawloom	Multiple Shaft Weaving, Twill and Satin Blocks, Damask		√	> 4	WJ	5	4	20	Sp 81	10
Looms: Drawloom	Observations on a Chinese Drawloom	Sellin, Helen	√		WJ	8	2	30	Fa 83	6
Looms: Drawloom	On Eighteenth Century Flowered Silk Weaving as an Inspiration for Todays Complex Weavers	Fairbanks, Dale			CW	7	1	19	Se 85	8
Looms: Drawloom	Original Fabrics of Kaftan, The	El-Homossani, M. M.	√	> 4	AT	1			De 83	263
Looms: Drawloom	Oscar Knopf's Ingenious Invention	Miller, Ethel E.	√	> 4	H&C	10	2		Sp 59	24
Looms: Drawloom	Support System for Drawloom Weavers, A	van der Hoogt, Madelyn			CW	7	2	20	Ja 86	10
Looms: Drawloom, Damask	Some Additional Notes on the Damask—Threading the Pattern Harnesses	Ahrens, Jim	√	> 4	CW	6	2	17	Ja 85	3

SUBJECT	TITLE	AUTHOR	IL	INST	JOUR	VOL	NO	ISS	DATE	PAGE
Looms: Drawloom, Dobby	Ahrens Looms, The	Bryan, Dorothy	√	√	H&C	6	3		Su 55	28
Looms: Drawloom, Split-Harness	Split-Harness Drawloom, The	Malloy, Kim, OSB	√	>4	CW	2	1	4	Oc 80	3
Looms: East Asia	China and the Complexities of Weaving Technologies	Vollmer, John E.			AT	5			Ju 86	65
Looms: Ethnic	Ethnic Looms	Jorstad, Caroline	√		SS&D	13	4	52	Fa 82	40
Looms: Evaluating	All About Looms: How to Buy a Weaving Loom	Zielinski, S. A.; Robert Leclerc, ed.			MWL	2			'51–'73	19
Looms: Evaluating	Choosing a Loom, One Weaver's Experience with a Countermarch	Hoyt, Peggy	√	>4	CW	4	1	10	Se 82	14
Looms: Evaluating	Handweaver's Instruction Manual: The Loom, Standards for Judging	Tidball, Harriet C. nee Douglas			SCGM		34		49	4
Looms: Evaluating	It Isn't So Easy as It Sounds	Carter, Bill			H&C	4	1		Wi 52	56
Looms: Evaluating	On Buying Used Looms	Wertenberger, Kathryn			Hw	2	3		My 81	22
Looms: Evaluating	On Buying Your First Loom (and other torture)	Redding, Debbie	√	√	Hw	4	5		N/D 83	18
Looms: Evaluating	Part 1, Build or Buy a Loom: Basic Qualities Required of Any Loom	Tidball, Harriet			SCGM		23		68	11
Looms: Evaluating	Support System for Drawloom Weavers, A	van der Hoogt, Madelyn			CW	7	2	20	Ja 86	10
Looms: Evaluating	Those Musty Old Looms	Ross, Nan	√		SS&D	8	2	30	Sp 77	43
Looms: Evaluating	What Loom Shall I Buy?	Carter, Bill			H&C	5	1		Wi 53	40
Looms: Evaluating	What Loom Shall I Buy?	Carter, Bill	√		H&C	3	4		Fa 52	14
Looms: Evaluating, Guide	Are You Buying A Loom? Some Points to Consider	Muller, Ann	√	√	H&C	2	1		Wi 50	25
Looms: "Fancy Weaving"	Nineteenth Century License Agreements for Fancy Weaving Machines	Anderson, Clarita; Steven M. Spivak	√		AT	8			De 87	67
Looms: Finnish	Rag Rug Traditions	Meany, Janet K.	√		WJ	9	4	36	Sp 85	56
Looms: Finnish Tree	"I Wish I Had a Loom . . ."	Laine, Anna E.			WJ	9	4	36	Sp 85	57
Looms: Fixed Heddle, Vertical	Traditional Berber Weaving in Central Morocco	Forelli, Sally; Jeanette Harries	√		TMJ	4	4		77	41
Looms: Floor	1979 Fiberarts Equipment Directory: Looms, The		√		Fa	6	1		J/F 79	28
Looms: Floor	How to Buy a Floor Loom: A Primer (error-corrected Fa v6 n1 79 p60)	Packard, Rolfe	√		Fa	6	1		J/F 79	32
Looms: Floor	It's Exactly the Same (sort of)	Reddding, Debbie		√	Hw	3	2		Mr 82	26
Looms: Fly-Shuttle	Fly-Shutle Looms Enhance Weaving Pleasure	Brostoff, Laya	√		SS&D	6	2	22	Sp 75	74
Looms: Folding	Innovations in Looms	Weiner, A. N.	√		H&C	23	1		J/F 72	8
Looms: Frame	All About Looms: The Best Loom	Zielinski, S. A.; Robert Leclerc, ed.	√		MWL	2			'51–'73	18
Looms: Frame	Braiding on a Frame		√	√	WJ	2	4	8	Ap 78	22
Looms: Frame	Children's Corner: A Picture Frame Tapestry	Champion, Ellen	√	√	WJ	4	1	13	Jy 79	19
Looms: Frame	Contemporary Tapestry: On Looms, Warping, Setting Up Tapestry Study Course — Part 1	O'Callaghan, Kate	√	√	WJ	4	3	15	Ja 80	41
Looms: Frame	Delight the Youngsters with Handwoven Puppets	Richards, Iris	√	√	WJ	7	2	26	Fa 82	72
Looms: Frame	Loom in My Tote-Bag, The	Redman, Jane	√	√	SS&D	5	4	20	Fa 74	83
Looms: Frame	"Not a Child's Toy"	Cahlander, Adele W.	√	√	SS&D	3	3	11	Su 72	32
Looms: Frame	Vertical Loom (continued) Part 2, The Two-Beam Loom, The		√	√	WJ	2	1	5	Jy 77	8
Looms: Frame	Weaving on a Frame		√		H&C	2	4		Fa 51	54
Looms: Frame	Weft Twining: Looms and Shaping	Harvey, Virginia I.; Harriet Tidball	√	√	SCGM		28		69	12
Looms: Frame	Weft-Twined Weaving	Nichols, Evelyn C.	√	√	SS&D	16	3	63	Su 85	82
Looms: Gauze	Three Ancient Peruvian Gauze Looms	Rowe, Ann Pollard; Junius B. Bird	√		TMJ	19 20			80,81	27
Looms: Gobelins Haute-Lisse	Contemporary Tapestry	Tidball, Harriet	√		SCGM		12		64	10
Looms: Ground, Horizontal	Traditional Handlooms and Weavings of Tunisia	Reswick, Irmtraud H.	√		SS&D	12	2	46	Sp 81	21

SUBJECT	TITLE	AUTHOR	IL	INST	JOUR	VOL	NO	ISS	DATE	PAGE
Looms: Ground Stakes	Kurdish Kilim Weaving in the Van-Hakkari District of Eastern Turkey	Landreau, Anthony N.	√	√	TMJ	3	4		De 73	27
Looms: Ground Stakes, (Four)	Weaving Processes in the Cuzco Area of Peru	Rowe, Ann Pollard	√	√	TMJ	4	2		75	30
Looms: Ground Stakes, (Two)	Weaving Processes in the Cuzco Area of Peru	Rowe, Ann Pollard	√	√	TMJ	4	2		75	30
Looms: Handloom, Triaxial Weaving (Speculative)	Triaxial Weaves and Weaving: An Exploration for Hand Weavers	Mooney, David R.	√	√	AT	2			De 84	9
Looms: Heddles	Part 1, Build or Buy a Loom: Questions and Answers About Looms, String, Flat Steel, or Wire Heddles?	Tidball, Harriet			SCGM		23		68	16
Looms: Historic	Spanish Colonial Loom: A Contemporary Loom-Maker Uses Traditional Tools to Construct a Replica for the Albuquerque Museum	Edwards, Jack	√	√	WJ	11	1	41	Su 86	16
Looms: Historical	An English Lady's Loom	Alvic, Philis	√		CW	4	1	10	Se 82	12
Looms: Historical	Looms from the Past	Colwell, Ken	√		Hw	2	3		My 81	36
Looms: Horizontal Loom, Small Harnesses	Contemporary Tapestry	Tidball, Harriet	√		SCGM		12		64	11
Looms: Industrial, Triaxial Weaving	Triaxial Weaves and Weaving: An Exploration for Hand Weavers	Mooney, David R.	√	√	AT	2			De 84	9
Looms: Inkle	1979 Fiberarts Equipment Directory: Looms, Inkle, The		√		Fa	6	2		M/A 79	56
Looms: Inkle	Contemporary Tapestry	Tidball, Harriet			SCGM		12		64	11
Looms: Inkle	How to Warp and Weave on an Inkle Loom		√	√	Hw	7	3		M/J 86	43
Looms: Inkle	Little Known Weaves Worth Knowing Better: Inkle Drafts	Zielinski, S. A.; Robert Leclerc, ed.	√	√	MWL	16			'51–'73	114
Looms: Inkle	New, Functional Inkle Loom, A	Spencer, Edith L.	√	√	H&C	6	2		Sp 55	42
Looms: Inkle	Queensland Inkle Loom	Richardt, Ericka	√	√	SS&D	4	3	15	Su 73	15
Looms: Inkle	Weaving Inkle Bands: Inkle Looms	Tidball, Harriet			SCGM		27		69	1
Looms: Inkle	What and Why of "Inkle"	Atwater, Mary Meigs	√	√	H&C	3	2		Sp 52	18
Looms: Inkle, American	Weaving Inkle Bands: American Inkle Loom	Tidball, Harriet	√	√	SCGM		27		69	18
Looms: Inkle, Board Loom	Weaving Inkle Bands: The Board Loom for Inkle Weaving	Tidball, Harriet	√		SCGM		27		69	1
Looms: Inkle, English	Weaving Inkle Bands: Modern English Inkle Loom	Tidball, Harriet	√		SCGM		27		69	16
Looms: Inkle, Modern	Weaving Inkle Bands: Other Modern Inkle Looms	Tidball, Harriet			SCGM		27		69	21
Looms: Inkle, Primitive	Weaving Inkle Bands: Primitive Inkle Looms	Tidball, Harriet	√	√	SCGM		27		69	12
Looms: Innovations	Innovations in Looms	Weiner, A. N.	√		H&C	23	1		J/F 72	8
Looms: Izari-bata	Fundraising Brings Kasuri Kimono Weaver to Nashville Workshop	Wilson, Sadye Tune	√		SS&D	9	2	34	Sp 78	4
Looms: Izari-Bata	Kasuri: A Japanese Textile	Dusenbury, Mary	√		TMJ	17			78	41
Looms: Jack	All About Looms: The Best Loom	Zielinski, S. A.; Robert Leclerc, ed.	√		MWL	2			'51–'73	11
Looms: Jack	Handlooms in Use Today	Hausner, Walter	√		H&C	15	4		Fa 64	22
Looms: Jack	Part 1, Build or Buy a Loom: The Jack-Type Loom	Tidball, Harriet			SCGM		23		68	6
Looms: Jack	Part 1, Build or Buy a Loom: The Push-Up Harness Jack Loom	Tidball, Harriet	√		SCGM		23		68	8
Looms: Jack, Handcrafted	Retired Engineer Designs and Builds a Loom		√		H&C	16	2		Sp 65	40
Looms: Jack, Sheds	Part 1, Build or Buy a Loom: The Shed	Tidball, Harriet	√		SCGM		23		68	9
Looms: Jacquard	Handlooms in Use Today	Hausner, Walter	√		H&C	15	4		Fa 64	22
Looms: Jacquard	Handweaver's Jacquard Loom, A	Mulkey, Philip O.	√		H&C	7	4		Fa 56	46
Looms: Jacquard	Jacquard and Woven Silk Pictures, The	Adrosko, Rita J.	√		AT	1			De 83	9
Looms: Jacquard	Jacquard At the Brewery, The	Colwell, Ken	√		SS&D	7	2	26	Sp 76	14
Looms: Jacquard	Jacquard Demonstration		√		SS&D	2	3	7	Su 71	12
Looms: Jacquard	Jacquard Handlooms	Hausner, Walter			H&C	26	2		Ap 75	17

SUBJECT	TITLE	AUTHOR	IL	INST	JOUR	VOL	NO	ISS	DATE	PAGE
Looms: Jacquard	Jacquard Loom: Where It Comes from, How It Works, The	Marcoux, Alice	√		Fa	9	2		M/A 82	34
Looms: Jacquard	Restoring an Old Loom	Adrosko, Rita J.	√	√	H&C	15	3		Su 64	16
Looms: Jacquard	Shelburne's Jacquard Loom: Is It a Computer? (error-corrected SS&D v17 n4 86 p10)	Vander Noordaa, Titia	√	√	SS&D	17	3	67	Su 86	34
Looms: Jacquard	Unravelling the Mysteries of the Jacquard	Jirousek, Charlotte	√		WJ	9	1	33	Su 84	8
Looms: Jacquard	Weavers in Iran, Thousands at Work on Primitive Looms	Leclerc, Robert	√		H&C	21	2		Sp 70	9
Looms: Kago-Uchi (Rigid-Heddle)	Kago-Uchi, The	Speiser, Noémi	√	√	AT	4			De 85	23
Looms: Lap	Weaving on a Lap Loom	Lawson, Rosalie H.	√		H&C	5	3		Su 54	23
Looms: Louët	It's a Bird....It's a Plane	Crowder, Rachael	√		PWC	4	3	13		14
Looms: Low (Jibata)	Hanaori: An Okinawan Brocaded Textile	Miller, Dorothy	√	√	AT	1			De 83	173
Looms: Macomber	High-Tech Comes to Weaving: Macomber Looms	Henderson, Stew	√		Fa	14	4		S/O 87	35
Looms: Manufacturers	Ahrens and Violette		√		Hw	2	3		My 81	29
Looms: Manufacturers	Directory of Loom Makers				Hw	2	3		My 81	30
Looms: Manufacturers	Glimakra		√		Hw	2	3		My 81	29
Looms: Manufacturers	Hands that Make Your Looms, The				Hw	2	3		My 81	25
Looms: Manufacturers	LeClerc Loom Corporation, A Story of Three Generations, The	Holland, Nina	√		H&C	24	3		M/J 73	20
Looms: Manufacturers	Nilus LeClerc, Inc.		√		Hw	2	3		My 81	26
Looms: Manufacturers	Schacht Spindle Company		√		Hw	2	3		My 81	27
Looms: Manufacturers	Union Loom Works				Hw	2	3		My 81	28
Looms: Manufacturing	Equipment Forum				WJ	10	2	38	Fa 85	8
Looms: Market	Equipment Forum				WJ	10	2	38	Fa 85	8
Looms: MasterWeaver	MasterWeaver Loom: A New Concept in Hand-Weaving, The	El-Homossani, Dr. M. M.	√	√	WJ	8	4	32	Sp 84	54
Looms: Mirror	Ingenious Devices	Wachtel, Blanche	√		H&C	22	2		Sp 71	25
Looms: Multishaft	All About Looms: The Best Loom	Zielinski, S. A.; Robert Leclerc, ed.	√		MWL	2			'51–'73	15
Looms: Nadeau	I Say It's Easier Than It Sounds	Nadeau, Elphege	√	√	H&C	4	4		Fa 53	44
Looms: Narrow	Blankets and Afghans on a Narrow Loom	Davenport, Betty	√	√	PWC	3	1	7		14
Looms: Narrow	Narrow Loom Tablecloth		√		H&C	9	3		Su 58	45
Looms: Narrow	Project for a Very Narrow Loom: A Vest with Details Woven with Rug Yarn (error-corrected H&C v26 n5 75 p45)	Hendricks, Carolyn	√	√	H&C	26	3		M/J 75	16
Looms: Narrow	Russian Peasant Shirt Adaptation	Hendricks, Carolyn	√	√	SS&D	8	2	30	Sp 77	96
Looms: Narrow	Small Looms Offer a Wide Range for Experiment	Berglund, Hilma	√	√	H&C	12	2		Sp 61	22
Looms: Narrow	Two Loom-Shaped Designs for Narrow Looms (Donna Gilbert)		√	√	Hw	2	1		F-W 80	28
Looms: Narrow	Woolens from a 20-inch Loom	Skirm, Helen W.	√	√	H&C	9	1		Wi 57	26
Looms: Navajo	Contemporary Tapestry	Tidball, Harriet	√		SCGM		12		64	10
Looms: Navajo	Mable Morrow–Appreciation for Indian Arts, Part 1	Maxcy, Mabel E.	√		SS&D	5	1	17	Wi 73	29
Looms: Navajo	Navajo: Textiles, Blankets, Rugs, Tapestries	Morrow, Mable	√	√	SS&D	2	1	5	De 70	5
Looms: Navajo	On-loom Warping for Navajo Loom	Freilinger, Ida M.	√	√	SS&D	11	3	43	Su 80	8
Looms: Navajo	Vertical Loom (continued) Part 3, The Navajo Loom, The		√	√	WJ	2	2	6	Oc 77	23
Looms: One-Beam	Vertical Loom, The		√	√	WJ	1	3	3	Ja 77	16
Looms: One-Treadle	Design for a One-Treadle Loom	Pariseau, George E., M.D.	√	√	H&C	3	3		Su 52	15
Looms: Open-Heddle Reed	Queerest Loom I Ever Did See	Achorn, Leland J.	√		SS&D	1	4	4	Se 70	16
Looms: Open-Top Heddle/Reed	Development of a Loom by Dorothy Tow		√		H&C	20	4		Fa 69	17
Looms: Open-Top Heddles	New Loom, A	Tow, Dorothy	√		H&C	17	1		Wi 66	16
Looms: Opphämta	Ken Colwell on Opphämta				PWC	3	4	10		67

SUBJECT	TITLE	AUTHOR	IL	INST	JOUR	VOL	NO	ISS	DATE	PAGE
Looms: Other	1979 Fiberarts Equipment Directory: Looms, Other, The		√		Fa	6	1		J/F 79	57
Looms: Parts	Part 1, Build or Buy a Loom: Parts of the Loom	Tidball, Harriet	√		SCGM		23		68	5
Looms: Pattern, Laotian	Pattern Weaving, Laotian Style	Keasbey, Doramay	√	√	Hw	2	3		My 81	54
Looms: Peruvian	Three Ancient Peruvian Gauze Looms	Rowe, Ann Pollard; Junius B. Bird	√		TMJ	19 20			80,81	27
Looms: Pit	Banares Brocade	DuBois, Emily	√	>4	AT	3			My 85	209
Looms: Pit	Dhabla Weaving in India	De Bone, Mary	√	√	SS&D	8	3	31	Su 77	9
Looms: Pit	Rabari Lodi: Creating a Fabric Through Social Alliance, The	Frater, Judy	√	√	WJ	10	1	37	Su 85	28
Looms: Pit	Textile Arts of Multan, Pakistan	Shahzaman, Mahboob	√	>4	SS&D	4	3	15	Su 73	8
Looms: Portable	Part 1, Build or Buy a Loom: Special Loom Types, The Travel Loom	Tidball, Harriet			SCGM		23		68	12
Looms: Power	Beyond the Powerloom	Hausner, Walter			H&C	22	4		Fa 71	21
Looms: Power	Handweaver With Dobby-Powerloom	Goldschmidt, Manfred			CW	3	3	9	Ap 82	12
Looms: Power	Saga of a Fancy Woolen Loom, The	Gross, Laurence F.	√		SS&D	9	3	35	Su 78	25
Looms: Power, Types	Power Looms: The Effect of New Developments on Designers	Hausner, Walter	√		H&C	17	4		Fa 66	13
Looms: Primitive	African Textiles	Hempel, Toby Anne	√		SS&D	15	1	57	Wi 83	12
Looms: Primitive	African Textiles	Sieber, Roy	√		H&C	23	6		N/D 72	9
Looms: Primitive	All About Looms: Primitive Looms, Photographs	Zielinski, S. A.; Robert Leclerc, ed.	√		MWL	2			'51–'73	77
Looms: Primitive	Bolivian Highland Weaving, Part 1	Cason, Marjorie; Adele Cahlander	√		SS&D	6	2	22	Sp 75	4
Looms: Primitive	Contemporary Tapestry	Tidball, Harriet	√		SCGM		12		64	11
Looms: Primitive	Easily Constructed Loom from Africa, An	Kren, Margo	√	√	SS&D	7	3	27	Su 76	19
Looms: Primitive	Guatemala Visited	Atwater, Mary Meigs	√		SCGM		15		65	43
Looms: Primitive	Guatemalan Looms	Young, Helen Daniels	√		H&C	4	3		Su 53	16
Looms: Primitive	Highland Weavers in Asia	Hatch, David P.	√	√	H&C	11	1		Wi 60	6
Looms: Primitive	Jews of Kurdistan, The	Meyerowitz, Carol Orlove	√	√	SS&D	14	2	54	Sp 83	23
Looms: Primitive	Kente: The Status Cloth of Ghana	Conklin, Sharon L.	√	√	SS&D	8	1	29	WI 76	18
Looms: Primitive	Mexican Motifs: Mexico, Land of Contrasts	Tidball, Harriet	√		SCGM		6		62	1
Looms: Primitive	Mexico — Land of Weavers, Part 1	Hatch, David Porter	√		H&C	6	2		Sp 55	10
Looms: Primitive	Peru, Textiles Unlimited: Looms and Weaver's Tools	Tidball, Harriet	√		SCGM		25		68	5
Looms, Primitive	Ridge (Twill) Weave of the Hopi	Nelson, Nanci Neher	√	√	SS&D	14	2	54	Sp 83	52
Looms: Primitive	Secret Treasures of Tibet	Wiltsie-Vaniea, Anne	√		SS&D	18	3	71	Su 87	60
Looms: Primitive	Textiles and Looms from Guatemala & Mexico	Grossman, Ellin F.	√		H&C	7	1		Wi 55	6
Looms: Primitive	Weavers in Iran, Thousands at Work on Primitive Looms	Leclerc, Robert	√		H&C	21	2		Sp 70	9
Looms: Primitive	Weaving in the Desert: How Bedouin Women Make a Loom, Using Sticks and Rebars	Erickson, Janet Doub	√	√	TM			10	A/M 87	56
Looms: Primitive, Continuous Warp	Selected Batak Textiles: Technique and Function	Gittinger, Mattiebelle S.	√		TMJ	4	2		75	13
Looms: Primitive, Pit	Bhotiya Woolens from India	Willis, Elizabeth Bayley	√		H&C	5	2		Sp 54	4
Looms: Primitive, Treadle	Treadle Loom in the Peruvian Andes, The	Noble, Carol Rasmussen	√		SS&D	8	3	31	Su 77	46
Looms: Productivity Potential	Equipment for Production Efficiency: The Loom	LaLena, Constance			Hw	5	4		S/O 84	29
Looms: Reeds	Part 1, Build or Buy a Loom: Questions and Answers About Looms, What Reeds Are Most Useful?	Tidball, Harriet			SCGM		23		68	18
Looms: Repair and Maintenance	All About Looms: How to Maintain and Improve a Weaving Loom	Zielinski, S. A.; Robert Leclerc, ed.	√	√	MWL	2			'51–'73	29
Looms: Repair and Maintenance	Do-It-Yourself Maintenance	Redding, Eric		√	Hw	2	3		My 81	32
Looms: Repair and Maintenance	Loom Maintenance	Koepp, William	√		WJ	11	4	44	Sp 87	65

SUBJECT	TITLE	AUTHOR	IL	INST	JOUR	VOL	NO	ISS	DATE	PAGE
Looms: Repair and Maintenance	Technology of Handweaving: Taking Care of the Equipment	Zielinski, S. A.; Robert Leclerc, ed.		√	MWL	6			'51–'73	70
Looms: Reproduction, 17th Century	Spanish Colonial Loom: A Contemporary Loom-Maker Uses Traditional Tools to Construct a Replica for the Albuquerque Museum	Edwards, Jack	√	√	WJ	11	1	41	Su 86	16
Looms: Reproduction, 1800 Design	Reproduction of an 1800 Loom		√		H&C	19	3		Su 68	40
Looms: Restoration	Saga of a Fancy Woolen Loom, The	Gross, Laurence F.	√		SS&D	9	3	35	Su 78	25
Looms: Restoration and Repair	Restoring an Old Loom	Adrosko, Rita J.	√	√	H&C	15	3		Su 64	16
Looms: Rigid Heddle	Rigid Heddle Loom, The	Davenport, Betty	√	√	SS&D	13	1	49	Wi 81	72
Looms: Rigid-Heddle	1979 Fiberarts Equipment Directory: Rigid-Heddle Looms, The		√		Fa	6	1		J/F 79	56
Looms: Rigid-Heddle	Double Weave on a Rigid Heddle Loom	Gaston-Voûte, Suzanne	√	√	SS&D	8	3	31	Su 77	70
Looms: Rigid-Heddle	Erica: The new Rigid Heddle Loom	Cooper, Frayda	√		H&C	26	5		Oc 75	25
Looms: Rigid-Heddle	Essay: The Incredible, Flexible Rigid Heddle Loom	Rotert, Bette			PWC			2	Ap 82	60
Looms: Rigid-Heddle	Fixed-Heddle Looms to Make for Pennies Using Coffee Stirrers	Lee, Dr. Stanley H.	√	√	SS&D	5	1	17	Wi 73	21
Looms: Rigid-Heddle	New Look at the Rigid Heddle Loom, A	Davenport, Betty	√		Iw	4	4		Fa 79	41
Looms: Rigid-Heddle	Projects for a Six-Dent Rigid Heddle Backstrap Loom	Swanson, Karen	√	√	H&C	21	4		Fa 70	9
Looms: Rigid-Heddle	Rigid-Heddle Loom Warping	Davenport, Betty	√	√	Hw	3	3		My 82	73
Looms: Rigid-Heddle	Small Projects of Interest to Beginning Weavers	Freeman, Claire	√	√	H&C	20	4		Fa 69	9
Looms: Rigid-Heddle	Variation of a Rigid Heddle Loom	Hoyt, Peggy	√	√	H&C	21	3		Su 70	6
Looms: Rigid-Heddle	Weaving Inkle Bands: Rigid Heddle or Slot-And-Eye Heddle Looms	Tidball, Harriet	√	√	SCGM		27		69	15
Looms: Rigid-Heddle	Weaving with Rigid Heddle Backstrap Looms	Swanson, Karen	√	√	H&C	21	2		Sp 70	13
Looms: Rigid-Heddle, English	Weaving Inkle Bands: English Rigid Heddle Loom	Tidball, Harriet	√		SCGM		27		69	17
Looms: Rigid-Heddle, Folding	Part 1, Build or Buy a Loom: Questions and Answers About Looms, Rigid or Folding?	Tidball, Harriet	√		SCGM		23		68	13
Looms: Rigid-Heddle, Multiple-Heddle	Multiple Rigid Heddle Adventure, Part 1, The	Xenakis, Athanasios David	√	√	PWC	3	4	10		34
Looms: Rising Shed	Choosing a Floor Loom: Sinking vs. Rising Shed	Keasbey, Doramay	√	√	Iw	5	3		Su 80	50
Looms: Rocking-Beater	Weaving at Locust Grove	Lutz, Mrs. William C.	√		H&C	19	1		Wi 68	31
Looms: Round	Weaving on a Round Loom	Priest, Alice B.	√	√	H&C	19	2		Sp 68	35
Looms: Rug	Hand Woven Rugs: Equipment	Atwater, Mary Meigs			SCGM		29		48	2
Looms: Rug	Nine-Foot Loom for Rugs, A	Crowell, Ivan H.	√	√	H&C	7	4		Fa 56	14
Looms: Rug	Part 1, Build or Buy a Loom: Special Loom Types, The Rug Loom	Tidball, Harriet			SCGM		23		68	12
Looms: Salish	Fiber Heritage of the Salish	Whonnock Spinners & Weavers	√		WJ	9	2	34	Fa 84	65
Looms: Salish	Salish Weaving	Clark, Hilary	√	√	SS&D	3	2	10	Sp 72	12
Looms: Salish	Salish Weaving, Then and Now	Ling, Lorraine	√	√	Iw	4	1		Wi 78	38
Looms: Salish, Two-Bar	Vertical Loom (continued) Part 2, The Two-Beam Loom, The		√	√	WJ	2	1	5	Jy 77	8
Looms: Sample	Part 1, Build or Buy a Loom: Special Loom Types, The Sample Loom	Tidball, Harriet			SCGM		23		68	13
Looms: Selecting	Buying a Loom	Liebler, Barbara	√	√	Iw	2	3		Sp 77	26
Looms: Selecting	Choosing a Floor Loom: Sinking vs. Rising Shed	Keasbey, Doramay	√	√	Iw	5	3		Su 80	50
Looms: Selecting	How to Buy a Floor Loom: A Primer (error-corrected Fa v6 n1 79 p60)	Packard, Rolfe	√		Fa	6	1		J/F 79	32
Looms: Selecting	On Buying Your First Loom (and other torture)	Redding, Debbie	√	√	Hw	4	5		N/D 83	18

SUBJECT	TITLE	AUTHOR	IL	INST	JOUR	VOL	NO	ISS	DATE	PAGE
Looms: Setting-Up	All About Looms: Setting-Up the Loom	Zielinski, S. A.; Robert Leclerc, ed.		√	MWL	2			'51–'73	24
Looms: Shaft Assembly Space	Part 1, Build or Buy a Loom: Questions and Answers About Looms, Harness Assembly Space?	Tidball, Harriet			SCGM		23		68	14
Looms: Shafts	Part 1, Build or Buy a Loom: Questions and Answers About Looms, How Many Harnesses?	Tidball, Harriet			SCGM		23		68	14
Looms: Single Harness	Patolu and Its Techniques	De Bone, Mary Golden	√	√	TMJ	4	3		76	49
Looms: Slot-and-Eye	Contemporary Tapestry	Tidball, Harriet			SCGM		12		64	11
Looms: Slot-and-Eye	Weaving in Taiwan, An American Designer's Experience in Free China		√		H&C	13	1		Wi 62	10
Looms: Slot-and-Eye Heddle	Weaving Inkle Bands: Rigid Heddle or Slot-And-Eye Heddle Looms	Tidball, Harriet	√	√	SCGM		27		69	15
Looms: Squaw	Primitive Weaving, Rug Weaving on a Squaw Loom	Degenhart, Pearl C.	√		H&C	22	1		Wi 71	21
Looms: Stake	Back Strap Weaving in Zacualpan Mexico	Cooper, Jane	√	√	SS&D	5	3	19	Su 74	13
Looms: Stick	Costume and Weaving in Saraguro, Ecuador	Meisch, Lynn Ann	√		TMJ	19 20			80,81	55
Looms: Stick, Myan	Guatemalan Gauze Weaves: A Description and Key to Identification	Pancake, Cherri M.; Suzanne Baizerman	√	√	TMJ	19 20			80,81	1
Looms: Table	1979 Fiberarts Equipment Directory: Table Looms, The		√		Fa	6	1		J/F 79	46
Looms: Table	All About Looms: The Best Loom	Zielinski, S. A.; Robert Leclerc, ed.	√		MWL	2			'51–'73	18
Looms: Table	Doup Leno	Skowronski, Hella; Sylvia Tacker	√	√	TM			4	A/M 86	56
Looms: Table	Part 1, Build or Buy a Loom: Special Loom Types, The Table Loom	Tidball, Harriet			SCGM		23		68	12
Looms: Tape	Scintillating, Soft and Silent Seat, A	Chesley, Mariam Dolloff	√	√	Hw	5	2		M/A 84	27
Looms: Tape	Setting Up a Tape Loom	Crawford, Grace Post	√	√	H&C	12	1		Wi 61	19
Looms: Tape	Tape Loom — Then and Now, The	Chesley, Mariam Dolloff	√		Hw	3	5		N/D 82	56
Looms: Tape	Tape Looms	Van Artsdalen, Martha	√		SS&D	15	4	60	Fa 84	15
Looms: Tapestry	1979 Fiberarts Equipment Directory: Tapestry Looms, The		√		Fa	6	1		J/F 79	52
Looms: Tapestry	Bringing Tapestry into the 20th Century	Mattera, Joanne	√	√	TM			1	O/N 85	52
Looms: Tapestry	Contemporary Tapestry: On Looms, Warping, Setting Up Tapestry Study Course — Part 1	O'Callaghan, Kate	√	√	WJ	4	3	15	Ja 80	41
Looms: Tapestry	Grau-Garriga: He Says It's Easy, But...	Brough, Hazel	√	√	SS&D	6	4	24	Fa 75	92
Looms: Tapestry	Low Budget Tapestry Loom, A	Gilstrap, Bill; Sara Gilstrap	√	√	WJ	5	4	20	Sp 81	42
Looms: Tapestry	My Life	Weldon, Lynn L.	√	√	WJ	2	2	6	Oc 77	11
Looms: Tapestry	Scheuer Tapestry Studio: Applying Old Techniques to New Ideas, The	Scheuer, Ruth Tannenbaum	√		Fa	10	3		M/J 83	39
Looms: Tapestry, A-Frame	Contemporary Tapestry	Tidball, Harriet	√		SCGM		12		64	7
Looms: Tapestry, Frame	Contemporary Tapestry	Tidball, Harriet	√		SCGM		12		64	7
Looms: Tapestry, Frame, Rotating Shed Maker	Contemporary Tapestry	Tidball, Harriet	√		SCGM		12		64	7
Looms: Tapestry, Frame with Heddle Bar Rests	Contemporary Tapestry	Tidball, Harriet	√		SCGM		12		64	8
Looms: Tapestry, Frame with Tensioner	Contemporary Tapestry	Tidball, Harriet	√		SCGM		12		64	7
Looms: Tapestry, High-Warp	Barn Raising Experience, A	Bujnowski, Donald	√	√	SS&D	8	4	32	Fa 77	100
Looms: Tapestry, High-Warp	Commercial Establishment Discovers Fiber Arts, The	Jacopetti, Alexandra	√	√	SS&D	8	2	30	Sp 77	4
Looms: Tapestry, Low-Warp	French Tapestry Weaving in San Francisco	Tanenbaum, Ruth	√	√	SS&D	8	3	31	Su 77	12
Looms: Tapestry, Salish	Business Of Weaving — An Interview With Elaine P. Nixon, The	Derr, Mary	√		WJ	4	1	13	Jy 79	10
Looms: Tapestry, Types	Pile Weaves, Rugs and Tapestry: True Tapestry and Rugs	Zielinski, S. A.; Robert Leclerc, ed.		√	MWL	14			'51–'73	76

SUBJECT	TITLE	AUTHOR	IL	INST	JOUR	VOL	NO	ISS	DATE	PAGE
Looms: Tapestry, Upright, Sliding Harness	Contemporary Tapestry	Tidball, Harriet	√		SCGM		12		64	8
Looms: Tapestry, Vertical, Professional	Contemporary Tapestry	Tidball, Harriet	√		SCGM		12		64	9
Looms: Tapestry, Vertical, Treadle	Contemporary Tapestry	Tidball, Harriet	√		SCGM		12		64	9
Looms: Tatami	Weaving in Taiwan, An American Designer's Experience in Free China		√		H&C	13	1		Wi 62	10
Looms: Tensioning Systems	Vertical Loom (continued) Part 2, The Two-Beam Loom, The		√	√	WJ	2	1	5	Jy 77	8
Looms: Three-Shaft	Handweaver's Instruction Manual: Three Harness Weaves, Improvised 3-Harness Loom	Tidball, Harriet C. nee Douglas	√	√	SCGM		34		49	22
Looms: Tie-In Rods	Part 1, Build or Buy a Loom: Questions and Answers About Looms, Cord, Tape or Apron for Tie-In Rods?	Tidball, Harriet			SCGM		23		68	18
Looms: Tie-Ups	Part 1, Build or Buy a Loom: Questions and Answers About Looms, Cord or Wire Tie-Ups?	Tidball, Harriet			SCGM		23		68	15
Looms: Treadles	Part 1, Build or Buy a Loom: Questions and Answers About Looms, How Many Treadles?	Tidball, Harriet			SCGM		23		68	15
Looms: Treadling Ease	Part 1, Build or Buy a Loom: Questions and Answers About Looms, Threading Ease?	Tidball, Harriet			SCGM		23		68	17
Looms: Triangular	Weave a Mobius	Marquess, Joyce	√	√	SS&D	5	2	18	Sp 74	55
Looms: Triaxial Frame	Triaxial Weaves and Weaving: An Exploration for Hand Weavers	Mooney, David R.	√	√	AT	2			De 84	9
Looms: True-Shed (Drum Mechanism)	Fabrics from a New Type Multi-Harness Loom	Cory, Sue Armstrong	√	> 4	H&C	10	1		Wi 59	24
Looms: Twining	Band Loom Offers New Approach to Weft Twining	Tacker, Sylvia; Harold Tacker	√	√	SS&D	6	2	22	Sp 75	38
Looms: Twining Frame	Twining or Macrame Loom	Atkinson, Howard A.	√	√	SS&D	5	3	19	Su 74	24
Looms: Two-Beam	Vertical Loom (continued) Part 2, The Two-Beam Loom, The		√	√	WJ	2	1	5	Jy 77	8
Looms: Two-Harness (Sets)	All About Looms: Draw-Looms	Zielinski, S. A.; Robert Leclerc, ed.	√	> 4	MWL	2			'51–'73	46
Looms: Two-Harness (Sets)	All About Looms: The Best Loom	Zielinski, S. A.; Robert Leclerc, ed.	√		MWL	2			'51–'73	17
Looms: Two-Harness (Sets)	Five Block Double Weave Using the Glimåkra Long Eyed Heddle Accessory	Tramba, Diane	√	> 4	WJ	7	3	27	Wi 82	45
Looms: Two-Harness (Sets)	Supplementary Warp Patterning: Supplementary Warp Patterns on A Two-Harness Loom	Tidball, Harriet		√	SCGM		17		66	9
Looms: Two-Man	Weaving on a Two Man Loom	Kozikowski, Janusz	√		H&C	24	1		J/F 73	6
Looms: Two-Shaft	Brocade: Looms and Equipment	Tidball, Harriet	√		SCGM		22		67	7
Looms: Two-Shaft	Contemporary Project for Two-harness Looms, A	Brown, Harriette J.	√	√	H&C	7	3		Su 56	20
Looms: Two-Shaft	Don't Overlook Two Harness Looms	Brown, Harriette J.	√		H&C	5	3		Su 54	10
Looms: Types	Are You Buying a Loom? Some Points to Consider	Muller, Ann	√	√	H&C	2	1		Wi 50	25
Looms: Types	Handweaver's Instruction Manual: The Loom	Tidball, Harriet C. nee Douglas	√		SCGM		34		49	2
Looms: Types	Reflection of the Past: Antique Looms, A	Saylor, Mary C.	√		SS&D	7	3	27	Su 76	26
Looms: Unique	Highland Weavers in Asia	Hatch, David P.	√	√	H&C	11	1		Wi 60	6
Looms: Upright	Hand-Carved Color Harp		√		SS&D	6	1	21	Wi 74	46
Looms: Upright	Salish Weaving	Boxberger, Daniel L.	√		SS&D	13	4	52	Fa 82	30
Looms: Upright Poles	Mable Morrow—Collector, Scholar of Indian Arts, Part 2	Maxcy, Mabel E.	√		SS&D	5	2	18	Sp 74	33
Looms: Used	On Buying Used Looms	Wertenberger, Kathryn			Hw	2	3		My 81	22
Looms: Vertical	Traditional Handlooms and Weavings of Tunisia	Reswick, Irmtraud H.	√		SS&D	12	2	46	Sp 81	21
Looms: Vertical	Vertical Loom (continued) — Construction of a Warp Weighted Loom, The		√	√	WJ	1	4	4	Ap 77	27

SUBJECT	TITLE	AUTHOR	IL	INST	JOUR	VOL	NO	ISS	DATE	PAGE
Looms: Vertical	Vertical Loom (continued) Part 2, The Two-Beam Loom, The		√	√	WJ	2	1	5	Jy 77	8
Looms: Vertical	Vertical Loom (continued) Part 3, The Navajo Loom, The		√	√	WJ	2	2	6	Oc 77	23
Looms: Vertical	Vertical Loom, The		√	√	WJ	1	3	3	Ja 77	16
Looms: Vertical, Two-Bar, Suspended	Weaving a Cotton Saddlebag on the Santa Elena Peninsula of Ecuador	Hagino, Jane Parker; Karen E. Stothert	√	√	TMJ	22			83	19
Looms: Warp Beam, Sectional	Handweaver's Instruction Manual: The Loom, The Warp Beam	Tidball, Harriet C. nee Douglas	√		SCGM		34		49	4
Looms: Warp Beams	Part 1, Build or Buy a Loom: Questions and Answers About Looms, Sectional or Solid Warp Beam?	Tidball, Harriet			SCGM		23		68	17
Looms: Warp-Weighted	Build a Warp-Weighted Loom	Towner, Naomi Whiting	√	√	SS&D	6	3	23	Su 75	36
Looms: Warp-Weighted	Vertical Loom (continued) — Construction of a Warp Weighted Loom, The		√	√	WJ	1	4	4	Ap 77	27
Looms: Warp-Weighted	Vertical Loom, The		√	√	WJ	1	3	3	Ja 77	16
Looms: Weaving Space	Part 1, Build or Buy a Loom: Questions and Answers About Looms, How Wide the Weaving Space?	Tidball, Harriet			SCGM		23		68	16
Looms: Width	Part 1, Build or Buy a Loom: Questions and Answers About Looms, Loom Width?	Tidball, Harriet			SCGM		23		68	14
Looping	Janet Markarian: From Baskets to Bags, Containers Transformed	Koplos, Janet	√		Fa	11	1		J/F 84	16
Looping	Unique Technique for a Braided Strap from Colombia	Cahlander, Adele	√	√	WJ	7	1	25	Su 82	56
Looping Techniques	High-Status Caps of the Kongo and Mbundu Peoples	Gibson, Gordon D.; Cecilia R. McGurk	√		TMJ	4	4		77	71
Lopi	Spin Your Own Lopi?	Gibson-Roberts, Priscilla A.	√	√	S-O	10	2		Su 86	40
Lowell, Massachusetts	Mill Girls of 'Spindle City,' The	Rubbert, Toni Condon	√		S-O	10	1		Sp 86	16
M's and O's	Pattern and Structure in Handwoven Fabrics	Frey, Berta	√	√	H&C	6	4		Fa 55	4
Macedonia	Variation of the Macedonian Shirt	West, Virginia	√	√	WJ	7	2	26	Fa 82	50
Machine Knitting	All the News That's Fit to Knit	Hempel, Toby Ann	√		Fa	14	1		J/F 87	14
Machine Knitting	Argyle: The Transformation of a Classical Pattern Through the Design Process	Faust, Regine	√		Fa	9	4		J/A 82	24
Machine Knitting	Art to Wear — Three Innovators: Cate Fitt, Emma Vesey, Dina Schwartz Knapp		√		Fa	8	1		J/F 81	67
Machine Knitting	Be Your Own Designer	Lewis, Susanna	√	√	Kn	3	1	5	F-W 86	48
Machine Knitting	Bright Blouse	Lewis, Susanna	√	√	Kn	3	2	6	Sp 87	36
Machine Knitting	Dazzling with Sequins	Kelsey, Barbara Shomer	√	√	TM			1	O/N 85	60
Machine Knitting	Dubbelmossa	Adams, Harriet	√	√	Kn	2	1	3	F-W 85	50, 8B
Machine Knitting	Ellen Liss: Machine-Knit Wearables	Goodman, Deborah Lerme	√		Fa	11	4		J/A 84	16
Machine Knitting	From Harness Sheds to Double Beds	Guagliumi, Susan Fletcher	√		Fa	10	6		N/D 83	52
Machine Knitting	George Brett: Webs of a Mad Spider	McMillan, Sam	√		Fa	8	6		N/D 81	32
Machine Knitting	Gooden Gansey Sweaters	Gallagher, Marten	√		Fa	12	6		N/D 85	12
Machine Knitting	"Handspun on a Knitting Machine?" Sure!!	Adams, Brucie	√	√	Iw	6	1		Wi 80	60
Machine Knitting	Instant Gratification: Susan Summa Tells How and Why She Learned to Love the Knitting Machine	Summa, Susan	√		Fa	8	5		S/O 81	56
Machine Knitting	Knitted Palette of Brenda French, The	Pierce, Judith	√		Fa	13	2		M/A 86	43
Machine Knitting	Knitting Craft in Great Britain, The	Kinder, Kathleen	√		Fa	11	4		J/A 84	42
Machine Knitting	Knitting for a Living (error-corrected TM i6 A/S86 p6)	Guagliumi, Susan	√		TM			4	A/M 86	38
Machine Knitting	Knitting Machine: A Creative Tool, The	Mendelson, Linda	√	√	Fa	5	3		M/J 78	32
Machine Knitting	Lace from Hand to Machine	Lewis, Susanna E.	√	√	Kn	1	2	2	S-S 85	71
Machine Knitting	Machine Knit Ribbing for Woven Goods	Owens, Julie	√	√	Hw	6	2		M/A 85	30
Machine Knitting	Machine Knitters Meet in Seattle	Guagliumi, Susan			TM			12	A/S 87	16
Machine Knitting	Machine Knitting: The State of the Art		√		Fa	9	2		M/A 82	40

SUBJECT	TITLE	AUTHOR	IL	INST	JOUR	VOL	NO	ISS	DATE	PAGE
Machine Knitting	Machine Knitting with Handspun Yarn—Part 2	Adams, Brucie	√	√	Hw	4	4		S/O 83	76
Machine Knitting	Machine-Knit Popcorns	Guagliumi, Susan	√	√	TM			6	A/S 86	71
Machine Knitting	Rag Trade: Picture Postcard, The (Susanna Lewis)		√		Kn	3	1	5	F-W 86	68
Machine Knitting	Ropes and Braids	Lewis, Susanna E.	√	√	Kn	2	2	4	S-S 86	19
Machine Knitting	Striped Knits and the Needlemaster			√	TM			7	O/N 86	8
Machine Knitting	Succeeding with the Knitting Machine	Mattera, Joanne	√		T					
Machine Knitting	Susanna Lewis' "State of the Art" — A Lecture		√		Fa	9	2		M/A 82	47
Machine Knitting	Unlimited Possibilities of Machine Knitting: Charlotte Cain's Patterns of Infinity, The	Woelfle, Gretchen Erskine	√		Fa	6	4		J/A 79	58
Machine Knitting	Weaving...On a Knitting Machine	Adams, Brucie	√	√	Hw	2	3		My 81	62
Machine Knitting	Year of the Sweater, The	Katz, Ruth J.	√		Fa	7	1		J/F 80	39
Machine Knitting: Cables	Appropriate Designs for Short-Row and Slip Intarsia	Guagliumi, Susan	√	√	TM			10	A/M 87	70
Machine Knitting: Cables, Diagonal	Diagonal Cables: A Machine Knitter's Guide to Cabling Against the Grain	Guagliumi, Susan	√	√	TM			14	D/J 87	58
Machine Knitting: Diamonds	Appropriate Designs for Short-Row and Slip Intarsia	Guagliumi, Susan	√	√	TM			10	A/M 87	70
Machine Knitting: Ends Concealed	Machine-Knitting with No Loose Ends			√	TM			13	O/N 87	10
Machine Knitting: Fair Isle	Appropriate Designs for Short-Row and Slip Intarsia	Guagliumi, Susan	√	√	TM			10	A/M 87	70
Machine Knitting: Gadgets	Gadgets for Machine Knitters	Guagliumi, Susan		√	TM			13	O/N 87	14
Machine Knitting: Geometrics	Knitting Machine Geometrics	Guagliumi, Susan	√	√	TM			10	A/M 87	66
Machine Knitting Handspun	Cozy Afghan, A	Beetem, Debra	√	√	S-O	10	4		Wi 86	13
Machine Knitting Handspun	Handspinning for a Knitting Machine	Cartwright-Jones, Catherine			S-O	9	2		Su 85	20
Machine Knitting Handspun	Handspun for Kaffe Fassett Sweaters	Adams, Brucie	√	√	S-O	11	4		Wi 87	32
Machine Knitting Handspun	Machine Knitting with Handspun Cotton: First Experiments	Warren, Anne	√	√	S-O	11	2		Su 87	41
Machine Knitting Handspun	Machine Knitting with Handspun Yarn—Part 2	Adams, Brucie	√	√	Hw	4	4		S/O 83	76
Machine Knitting Handspun	Shepherd's Dancing Coat	Fleischer, Helen	√	√	S-O	11	1		Sp 87	17
Machine Knitting Handspun	Spinning to Machine Knit			√	TM			12	A/S 87	4
Machine Knitting Homespun	Machine-Knit Homespun			√	TM			10	A/M 87	4
Machine Knitting: Intarsia	Appropriate Designs for Short-Row and Slip Intarsia	Guagliumi, Susan	√	√	TM			10	A/M 87	70
Machine Knitting: Intarsia	Knitting Machine Geometrics	Guagliumi, Susan	√	√	TM			10	A/M 87	66
Machine Knitting: Knit-Purl	Appropriate Designs for Short-Row and Slip Intarsia	Guagliumi, Susan	√	√	TM			10	A/M 87	70
Machine Knitting: Knit-Weave	Thread Weaving	Sample, Joan	√	√	TM			8	D/J 86	64
Machine Knitting: Loop Control	No More Loops			√	TM			13	O/N 87	4
Machine Knitting: Metal	Arline M. Fisch	Fisch, Arline M.	√		Fa	13	1		J/F 86	18
Machine Knitting: Pleats	Appropriate Designs for Short-Row and Slip Intarsia	Guagliumi, Susan	√	√	TM			10	A/M 87	70
Machine Knitting: Short Row	Appropriate Designs for Short-Row and Slip Intarsia	Guagliumi, Susan	√	√	TM			10	A/M 87	70
Machine Knitting: Short Row	Knitting Machine Geometrics	Guagliumi, Susan	√	√	TM			10	A/M 87	66
Machine Knitting: Techniques	Basic Knitting Machine, The	Guagliumi, Susan	√	√	TM			1	O/N 85	34
Machine Knitting: Techniques	Knitters, Make a Trip to the Fabric Store	Guagliumi, Susan	√	√	TM			7	O/N 86	35
Machine Knitting: Vertical Joins	Appropriate Designs for Short-Row and Slip Intarsia	Guagliumi, Susan	√	√	TM			10	A/M 87	70
Machine Knitting: Weave Stitch	Weaving...On a Knitting Machine	Adams, Brucie	√	√	Hw	2	3		My 81	62
Machine Knitting: Wrapping On	Knitting Machine Geometrics	Guagliumi, Susan	√	√	TM			10	A/M 87	66
Machine Knitting: Yarn Ends	Managing Yarn Ends on the Knitting Machine			√	TM			9	F/M 87	10
Machine Lace	Schiffli Embroidery			√	Fa	9	3		M/J 82	49

SUBJECT	TITLE	AUTHOR	IL	INST	JOUR	VOL	NO	ISS	DATE	PAGE
Machine Quilting	Presence of Light: The Un-Traditional Quilts of Jan Myers, The	Gutcheon, Beth	√		Fa	8	3		M/J 81	60
Machine Stitching	So There Is a Use for Fancy Machine Stitches	Richter, Elizabeth Lee	√	√	TM			11	J/J 87	62
Macramé	Circular Macrame Form	Gilmurray, Susan	√	√	SS&D	5	2	18	Sp 74	52
Macramé	Clay and Cord		√		SS&D	2	1	5	De 70	15
Macramé	Guatamalan Finishes	Gotthoffer, Esther	√		H&C	22	1		Wi 71	18
Macramé	Macramé	Harvey, Virginia Isham	√	√	H&C	19	4		Fa 68	8
Macramé	Macramé, Ideal for Finishing Edges	Harvey, Virginia Isham	√	√	H&C	18	2		Sp 67	15
Macramé	Macramé, Knotting Can Add Pattern	Harvey, Virginia Isham	√	√	H&C	18	3		Su 67	13
Macramé	Macrame Popular At Murray State University		√		SS&D	4	3	15	Su 73	31
Macramé	Panel — A Statement of Unity, The	Zachofsky, Toni	√		H&C	22	4		Fa 71	20
Macramé	Rope Sculpture: Stanley Postek		√		H&C	26	5		Oc 75	9
Macramé	Stanley Postek, Who Learned Macramé At Sea		√	√	H&C	21	3		Su 70	8
Macramé	Ten Commandments of Fiber Manipulators	Pacque, Joan Michaels			SS&D	5	4	20	Fa 74	32
Macramé	Three Dimensional Macrame	Andes, Ellen; Gene Andes	√	√	H&C	23	3		M/J 72	43
Macramé	Three-Dimensional Macramé	Andes, Ellen; Gene Andes	√	√	H&C	23	5		S/O 72	18
Macramé	Tied Up in Knots	Mercer, Paul	√		H&C	22	2		Sp 71	9
Macramé	Why Macrame?	Paque, Joan Michaels	√		SS&D	3	3	11	Su 72	26
Macro-Gauze	Collingwood in Massachusetts, A	Brannen, Robert	√		SS&D	9	1	33	Wi 77	8
Macroweave	Macroweave Effect, The (error-corrected SS&D v12 n3 81 p6)	Towne, Carroll A.	√	√	SS&D	12	2	46	Sp 81	16
Madder Root	Diverse Dyes	Bliss, Anne	√	√	Iw	3	2		Wi 78	30
Madder Root	Madder Saga, The	Jones, Marilyn	√		SS&D	13	2	50	Sp 82	28
Madder Root	On Dyeing with Madder	Bliss, Anne	√	√	Iw	5	1		Wi 79	48
Madder Root	Reds and More Reds	Taggart, Barbara		√	SS&D	5	1	17	Wi 73	57
Madder Root, One-Pot Dyeing	SOAR Dyeworks	Bliss, Anne	√	√	S-O	10	2		Su 86	44
MadderRoot	Why Bother with Natural Dyeing?	Bulbach, Stanley	√	√	TM			5	J/J 86	32
Magazine Holders	Magazine Holder		√	√	WJ	6	4	24	Sp 82	21
Magnets: Draft Place Markers	Weaving with Magnets			√	TM			14	D/J 87	12
Maguey	Plant Fibers: Soft Fibers		√	√	WJ	8	2	30	Fa 83	67
Mai-Anju Knitters	Year of the Sweater, The	Katz, Ruth J.	√		Fa	7	1		J/F 80	39
Mailbag	Double Woven Mailbag with Name Tags	Verlinden, Lieve	√	√	WJ	7	1	25	Su 82	34
Maintenance Service: Textile	Evolution of an Artist: Michelle Lester	Malarcher, Pat	√		Fa	14	5		N/D 87	22
Management	Retailer's Rationale	Elkins, Arthur	√		SS&D	13	4	52	Fa 82	27
Management: Industry	Colour, Texture, Ornament, Line: A Question for Managers—Do You Know How Your Designers Think?	Willock, Jack			AT	4			De 85	97
Mandalas	Is the Mamluk Carpet a Mandala? A Speculation	Ellis, Charles Grant	√		TMJ	4	1		De 74	30
Mandalas	Katie Pasquini: Mandala Quilts	Pasquini, Katie	√		Fa	10	4		J/A 83	20
Mandalas, Lace	Fiber Mandalas: Doilies As Spiritual Art	Maines, Rachel	√		Fa	9	3		M/J 82	17
Mandarin Squares	Chinese Influence in Colonial Peruvian Tapestries	Cammann, Schuyler	√		TMJ	1	3		De 64	21
Mandarin Squares	Chinese Textile in Seventeenth Century Spain, A	Cammann, Schuyler	√		TMJ	1	4		De 65	57
Mandarin Squares	Recent Gifts of Chinese and Japanese Textiles	Hays, Mary V.	√		TMJ	4	2		75	4
Mandarin Squares: Ming	Ming Mandarin Squares	Cammann, Schuyler	√		TMJ	4	4		77	5
Manufacturers and Manufacturing: Braid	A. H. Rice Company: Maker of Silk Thread	Goodman, Deborah Lerme	√		Fa	13	1		J/F 86	54
Manufacturers and Manufacturing: Clothing	Surface Attraction	Mattera, Joanne	√		TM			7	O/N 86	20

SUBJECT	TITLE	AUTHOR	IL	INST	JOUR	VOL	NO	ISS	DATE	PAGE
Manufacturers and Manufacturing: Felt, Industrial	Manufacture of Industrial Felt, The	Goodman, Deborah Lerme	√	√	Fa	13	4		J/A 86	20
Manufacturers and Manufacturing: Looms	It's a Bird....It's a Plane	Crowder, Rachael	√		PWC	4	3	13		14
Manufacturers and Manufacturing: Looms	Jim "The Legend" Ahrens	Xenakis, Alexis Yiorgos	√		PWC	4	4	14		6
Manufacturers and Manufacturing: Polyester	Imitating the Silkworm	Stetson, G. Robert; Cathy Shufro; Dennis Danaher	√		TM			5	J/J 86	42
Manufacturers and Manufacturing: Spinning Wheels	It's a Bird....It's a Plane	Crowder, Rachael	√		PWC	4	3	13		14
Manufacturers and Manufacturing: Spinning Wheels	Personal History Involving the Spinning Wheel and One Man's Insatiable Curiosity, A	Mathews, Tom	√		Fa	6	2		M/A 79	18
Manufacturers and Manufacturing: Stetson Hats	Riding the Modern Range: Stetson Hats	Goodman, Deborah Lerme	√	√	Fa	13	4		J/A 86	8
Manufacturers and Manufacturing: Tuxedos	Tuxedo 100 Years Later, The	Shufro, Cathy	√		TM			7	O/N 86	54
Maori	Maori and Pakeha of New Zealand Use Wool and Phormium Tenax	Duncan, Molly	√	√	SS&D	5	1	17	Wi 73	65
Maori	Spinners & Weavers in New Zealand Use Native Materials	Duncan, Molly	√		H&C	21	1		Wi 70	14
Maori	Weaving with the Maoris of New Zealand	Giacchina, Polly Jacobs	√	√	Fa	11	3		M/J 84	48
Maori	Weft Twining: History, The Maori of New Zealand	Harvey, Virginia I.; Harriet Tidball	√		SCGM		28		69	7
Maps: Quilted, Sky	Nancy Smeltzer	Smeltzer, Nancy	√		Fa	13	5		S/O 86	19
Maps: Silk Road	Tracing the Silk Road	Dyer, Carolyn	√		Fa	13	1		J/F 86	22
Maquettes	Contemporary Navajo Weaving	Hedlund, Ann Lane	√		WJ	11	1	41	Su 86	30
Marbling	Marbling Cloth	Bliss, Anne	√	√	Hw	4	3		M/J 83	56
Marbling: Technique, Turkish	Turkish Marbling on Cloth or Paper	London, Rhoda	√	√	TM			11	J/J 87	66
Market, Handweavers'	Handweaver's Market				H&C	13	1		Wi 62	38
Marketing	Ann Bliss: Writing a Book About Her Friends		√		Fa	3	5		S/O 76	15
Marketing	Arianthé: Notes from a Production Weaver	Stettner, Arianthé	√		Fa	5	5		S/O 78	32
Marketing	Borrowing from the Bank	LaLena, Constance			Hw	6	3		Su 85	33
Marketing	Boston Guild Sales	Gallagher, Constance; Evelyn Bustead	√		H&C	11	4		Fa 60	49
Marketing	Bridging the Gap Between Craft Artists and Interior Designers	Kraus, William	√		SS&D	16	4	64	Fa 85	37
Marketing	Can a Weaver Earn a Living? Mais Certainement!	Ryall, Pierre	√		SS&D	7	3	27	Su 76	4
Marketing	Collection, The		√		WJ	3	3	11	Ja 79	30
Marketing	Come to the Fair				SS&D	1	3	3	Ju 70	11
Marketing	Commercial Establishment Discovers Fiber Arts, The	Jacopetti, Alexandra	√	√	SS&D	8	2	30	Sp 77	4
Marketing	Confluence: A Gallery	Ligon, Linda	√		Iw	2	3		Sp 77	10
Marketing	Connie LaLena: Colonial Textiles Today	Ligon, Linda	√		Iw	3	1		Fa 77	15
Marketing	Contemporary American Handweaving from an International Perspective	Alaniz, Leonore	√		WJ	11	3	43	Wi 87	26
Marketing	Deborah Ann Abbott: Power Loom Weaving on a New Hampshire Farm	Mattera, Joanne	√		Fa	9	1		J/F 82	35
Marketing	Designing the Line	Drooker, Penelope	√		SS&D	11	2	42	Sp 80	12
Marketing	Do You Want to Sell Your Weaving?	Redding, Winogene B.			H&C	5	1		Wi 53	30
Marketing	Does It Pay to Spin Your Own Yarn?	Hochberg, Bette			Iw	4	1		Wi 78	46
Marketing	Economics of Pricing, The	Cutcher, Hal			Fa	4	1		J/F 77	11
Marketing	Evaluating Your Work for the Market	Hoffmann, Jenet	√		SS&D	10	4	40	Fa 79	80
Marketing	From the Great Smokies to Rockefeller Center — The Southern Highland Handicraft Guild	Hart, Robert G.	√		H&C	2	3		Su 51	5

SUBJECT	TITLE	AUTHOR	IL	INST	JOUR	VOL	NO	ISS	DATE	PAGE
Marketing	Getting Your Work Into the Department Stores: Everything You Need to Know	Katz, Ruth J.			Fa	9	5		S/O 82	54
Marketing	Handweaving for Pleasure and Profit	Pasco, Henry H.			H&C	20	4		Fa 69	7
Marketing	Hobby or Business?	Smith, William L.	√		SS&D	18	4	72	Fa 87	44
Marketing	"How Much is That Spinner in the Window?"	Nicholas, Kristin	√		S-O	7	2		Su 83	42
Marketing	In Search of the Corporate Market	Koplos, Janet			Fa	9	5		S/O 82	52
Marketing	In the Market Place	Tillman, Jean E.			SS&D	2	2	6	Sp 71	5
Marketing	International Exposure Conference	Place, Jennifer	√		Fa	10	5		S/O 83	51
Marketing	It Still Can Be Beautiful: Although Utilitarian	Rutkovsky, Fran Cutrell	√	√	SS&D	7	3	27	Su 76	57
Marketing	Lee Carlin: Handweaving Entrepreneur	Ligon, Linda	√		Iw	3	1		Fa 77	26
Marketing	Making a Sales Call	LaLena, Constance		√	Hw	7	2		M/A 86	76
Marketing	Making Ends Meet At the Loom	Kosikowski, Janusz	√		SS&D	7	4	28	Fa 76	28
Marketing	Market Research: Know Your Customer	LaLena, Constance	√		Iw	6	1		Wi 80	58
Marketing	Market Research: Styles, Trends and Product Development	LaLena, Constance			Hw	2	2		Mr 81	63
Marketing	Marketing for Handweavers	Hart, Robert G.	√		H&C	1	2		Su 50	42
Marketing	Marketing Handwoven Fabric for Apparel & Interiors	Alaniz, Leonore	√		WJ	11	4	44	Sp 87	31
Marketing	Moneymakers for Weavers	Klessen, Romy	√	√	PWC	1	1		No 81	5
Marketing	Notes of a Pattern Weaver	Alvic, Philis	√		WJ	10	3	39	Wi 86	65
Marketing	On Selling Weaving	Phelps, Marie	√		H&C	11	1		Wi 60	53
Marketing	Own Your Own				SS&D	1	4	4	Se 70	13
Marketing	Paid Spinning Demonstrations	Hicks, C. Norman			SS&D	7	3	27	Su 76	46
Marketing	Personal Notes on a Dyeing Art	Lapin, Claudia	√		Fa	4	4		J/A 77	60
Marketing	Pricing for Profit 1. Keeping Essential Records	LaLena, Constance	√	√	Hw	2	5		No 81	75
Marketing	Pricing for Profit II: Pulling it all Together	LaLena, Constance		√	Hw	3	1		Ja 82	74
Marketing	Pricing the Craftsman's Products	Hart, Robert G.			H&C	1	3		Fa 50	58
Marketing	Pricing the Production Piece	La Lena, Constance J.	√	√	SS&D	10	2	38	Sp 79	10
Marketing	Production Spinning	Adams, Brucie			Iw	4	1		Wi 78	44
Marketing	Production Spinning	Simmons, Paula		√	Iw	4	4		Fa 79	61
Marketing	Production Weaving: A Feasibility Study				Hw	3	3		My 82	21
Marketing	Promoting the Craftsman's Product	Hart, Robert G.			H&C	2	1		Wi 50	48
Marketing	Promotional Methods	Egee, Dale			SS&D	15	2	58	Sp 84	4
Marketing	Quality or Charity? On What Basis Should Weaving Be Offered for Sale	The Gadred Weavers	√		H&C	1	2		Su 50	26
Marketing	Retailer's Rationale	Elkins, Arthur	√		SS&D	13	4	52	Fa 82	27
Marketing	Selling Through Galleries		√		Iw	1	3		Sp 76	20
Marketing	Setting the Right Price: A Workshop with Libby Platus (error-corrected Fa v13 n1 86 p5)	Caldwell, Rebecca	√		Fa	12	5		S/O 85	51
Marketing	She Sells Everything She Weaves	Knoizen, Frances	√		H&C	9	3		Su 58	22
Marketing	Shelburne Spinners: Pushing for Perfection	Cysewski, Catherine	√		Iw	3	1		Fa 77	22
Marketing	Shop One, A Unique Craftsmen's Venture in Rochester, N. Y.		√		H&C	5	3		Su 54	45
Marketing	Steps in Planning a Successful Sale	Webb, Mildred M.		√	SS&D	5	3	19	Su 74	50
Marketing	Story of Henry Reynolds, The		√		H&C	4	2		Sp 53	23
Marketing	Story of the Shuttle Shed, The		√		H&C	10	1		Wi 59	22
Marketing	Succeeding with the Knitting Machine	Mattera, Joanne	√		TM			2	D/J 85	50
Marketing	Sue Nechin of First Additions	Koplos, Janet	√		Fa	10	1		J/F 83	69
Marketing	Sven Scandinavian				Kn	1	1	1	F-W 84	58
									CI	48
Marketing	Taking It to the Streets: Marketing Your Multiples	Clark, Noel	√		Fa	5	5		S/O 78	26

SUBJECT	TITLE	AUTHOR	IL	INST	JOUR	VOL	NO	ISS	DATE	PAGE
Marketing	Tapestry: As a Business?	Harvey, Nancy	√	√	SS&D	15	3	59	Su 84	37
Marketing	Thoughts on Money, Art, and Spinning	Chelsey, Randy			S-O	11	1		Sp 87	14
Marketing	Tierra Wools Cooperative	Brown, Rachel	√	√	SS&D	18	2	70	Sp 87	62
Marketing	Toward a Professional Attitude in Weaving	Bradley, David H.			H&C	8	4		Fa 57	19
Marketing	Tying Up with Others		√		H&C	26	5		Oc 75	20
Marketing	Valhalla Weavers of North Carolina, The		√		H&C	4	2		Sp 53	48
Marketing	Vermont's Green Mountain Spinnery	Levinson, Nan	√		TM			7	O/N 86	61
Marketing	Wearables in the Market Place: Reporting on a Survey	Dunnewold, Jane	√		Fa	12	3		M/J 85	48
Marketing	Weaving Business, The	Cairns, Michael			SS&D	8	3	31	Su 77	6
Marketing	Weaving for a Livelihood	Hotchkiss, Ann			H&C	12	1		Wi 61	26
Marketing	Weaving for Sale	Kossick, Ebba	√		H&C	17	3		Su 66	23
Marketing	Weaving in the Marketplace	Morris, Betty			H&C	24	3		M/J 73	42
Marketing	Weaving that Pays	Cripps, Alice K.	√	√	H&C	12	3		Su 61	53
Marketing	What People Ask Before They Buy Handmade Fashions	Leslie, Victoria	√		TM			9	F/M 87	58
Marketing	When You Plan to Sell	af Kleen, Elisabeth; Nils af Kleen	√	√	H&C	14	3		Su 63	32
Marketing	Why Not "Tromp as Writ" Commercially?	Wilde, Ruth C.	√		H&C	2	2		Sp 51	22
Marketing: Agencies	South American Crafts		√		H&C	17	2		Sp 66	16
Marketing: Crafts	State Parks Feature Kentucky Crafts	Mellen, Patricia			H&C	26	3		M/J 75	9
Marketing: Galleries/Shops	Show Strategies (error-corrected SS&D v19 n1 87 p33)	Itter, Diane	√		SS&D	18	4	72	Fa 87	26
Marketing: Galleries/Shops	Show Strategies, Part 2	Itter, Diane	√		SS&D	19	1	73	Wi 87	28
Marketing: Manuscripts	Marketing: Selling How-To's	Lagan, Constance Hallinan			SS&D	16	3	63	Su 85	16
Marketing: Textile Industry	Colour, Texture, Ornament, Line: A Question for Managers—Do You Know How Your Designers Think?	Willock, Jack			AT	4			De 85	97
Marketing: Wholesale	Art-to-Wear Markets, The	Nechin, Sue			Fa	11	3		M/J 84	54
Markets, Native: Weaving	Peruvian Weaves of Contemporary Interest		√		H&C	12	4		Fa 61	31
Masks	"Art of African Masquerade, The" (Exhibit)	Dyer, Carolyn Price	√		Fa	13	3		M/J 86	56
Masks	"Felt and Papermaking" (Exhibit)	Harrison, Helen A.	√		Fa	11	2		M/A 84	79
Masks	Hope and Phillip Holtzman	Holtzman, Hope; Phillip Holtzman	√		Fa	14	2		M/A 87	23
Masks	Maskmaker Ralph Lee: Master Minding a Ghoulish Event	Murray, Megan	√		Fa	11	5		S/O 84	34
Masks	Masks At the Heart of Disguise	Koplos, Janet	√		Fa	11	5		S/O 84	32
Masks	Women Faces: A Triptych		√		Fa	12	5		S/O 85	66
Master Weaver Library	Master Weaver Library (Written '51–'73; Published by Nilus Leclerc, Inc., '79–'85)	Zielinski, S. A.; Robert Leclerc, ed.	√	√	MWL	1-20			'51–'73	
Master Weaver Library, Practical Projects	Master Weaver Library (Written '51–'73; Published by Nilus Leclerc, Inc., '79-'85)	Zielinski, S. A.; Robert Leclerc, ed.	√	√	MWL	1-20			'51–'73	
Matching Plaids	Evergreen	Alderman, Sharon	√	√	Hw	4	5		N/D 83	62
Matelassé	Magic of Matelassé, The	West, Virginia	√	> 4	PWC	4	3	13		44
Matelassé	Stitching Traditional Coverlet Weaves	Sellin, Helen G.	√	> 4	AT	1			De 83	289
Materials: Rug Weaving	Hand Woven Rugs: Warp and Weft Materials	Atwater, Mary Meigs			SCGM		29		48	1
Materials: Sources	Wearables in the Market Place: Reporting on a Survey	Dunnewold, Jane	√		Fa	12	3		M/J 85	48
Materials: Warp/Weft	Unusual Materials for Warp or Weft	Wertenberger, Kathryn	√	> 4	Hw	7	4		S/O 86	78
Materials: Weaving	What a Handweaver Can Learn from the Scottish Weaving Industry (error-corrected WJ v2 n1 77 insert for vol. 1)	Barrett, Clotilde	√	√	WJ	1	3	3	Ja 77	11
Mathematics: Coriolis Force, S and Z Twist	Mathematical Design Concepts Relative to Aesthetic Concerns	Michaels-Paque, J.	√		AT	8			De 87	155

SUBJECT	TITLE	AUTHOR	IL	INST	JOUR	VOL	NO	ISS	DATE	PAGE
Mathematics: Fibonacci Progression	Weaving, 'riting, and 'rithmetic	Tate, Blair	√		AT	6			De 86	57
Mathematics: Fibonacci Series	Bright & Bold		√	√	Hw	4	2		M/A 83	50
Mathematics: Fibonacci Series	Fibonacci Series, The		√	√	Hw	4	2		M/A 83	45
Mathematics: Fibonacci Series	Geometric Proportions As a Design Tool	Templeton, Peg	√	√	WJ	4	4	16	Ap 80	8
Mathematics: Fibonacci Series	Syllabus for Success	Michaels-Paque, Joan	√	√	SS&D	15	3	59	Su 84	11
Mathematics: Fibonacci Series, Spirals	Mathematical Design Concepts Relative to Aesthetic Concerns	Michaels-Paque, J.	√		AT	8			De 87	155
Mathematics: Formula, Determining Shaft Combinations	Satin and Long-Eyed Heddles	Hoskins, Janet A.; W. D. Hoskins	√	>4	WJ	6	1	21	Su 81	25
Mathematics: Formulas, Shrinkage and Weight	Choosing the Fiber for Feltmaking	Spark, Pat	√	√	SS&D	17	4	68	Fa 86	20
Mathematics: Geometric Progression	Acid Dyeing	Kormos, Antonia	√	√	SS&D	15	2	58	Sp 84	34
Mathematics: Geometric Progression	Weaving, 'riting, and 'rithmetic	Tate, Blair	√		AT	6			De 86	57
Mathematics: Geometry, Fabrics	Twillins, Color-Alternative Twills and Color-Alternate Twillins	Hoskins, Janet A.	√	>4	CW	2	3	6	Ap 81	1
Mathematics: Golden Mean	Composition and Designing: Proportions	Zielinski, S. A.; Robert Leclerc, ed.	√	√	MWL	18			'51–'73	48
Mathematics: Golden Section	Geometric Proportions As a Design Tool	Templeton, Peg	√	√	WJ	4	4	16	Ap 80	8
Mathematics: Knitting	π Shawl, The	Zimmermann, Elizabeth	√	√	Kn	4	1	9	Wi 87	34
Mathematics: Moebius	Mathematical Design Concepts Relative to Aesthetic Concerns	Michaels-Paque, J.	√		AT	8			De 87	155
Mathematics: Moebius	Moebius Vest, The	Homme, Audrey	√	√	WJ	11	4	44	Sp 87	48
Mathematics: Moebius	Syllabus for Success	Michaels-Paque, Joan	√	√	SS&D	15	3	59	Su 84	11
Mathematics: Number Progressions	Three Color Progressions and Their Use in Sweater Jackets	Sylvan, Katherine	√	√	WJ	5	4	20	Sp 81	38
Mathematics: Permutations (Formulas)	Composition and Designing Part 2: Pattern Variations: How to Find the Number	Zielinski, S. A.; Robert Leclerc, ed.		√	MWL	19			'51–'73	25
Mathematics: Ratios	Mathematical Design Concepts Relative to Aesthetic Concerns	Michaels-Paque, J.	√		AT	8			De 87	155
Mathematics: Sine Curve	Wedge Weave: A New Approach	Noble, Carol Rasmussen	√	√	WJ	5	2	18	Fa 80	49
Mathematics: Spinning, Twist	Plying a Balanced Yarn for Knitting	Quinn, Celia	√	√	S-O	11	4		Wi 87	30
Mathematics: Structural Textiles	New Look at Twills, A	Hoskins, Janet A.	√	>4	WJ	6	3	23	Wi 81	46
Mathematics: Weaving	Excerpt from Geometric Design in Weaving, An	Regensteiner, Else	√	√	WJ	11	4	44	Sp 87	13
Mathematics: Weaving	Flight Into Fantasy (error-corrected SS&D v12 n1 80 p6)	Hartford, Jane; Thom Hartford III	√		SS&D	11	4	44	Fa 80	57
Mathematics: Weaving	Opera Elegance	Sylvan, Katherine	√	√	SS&D	15	4	60	Fa 84	24
Mathematics: Weaving	Two Weavers in a Trailer		√	>4	H&C	4	2		Sp 53	20
Mathematics: Weaving	Variations on an Algebraic Equation	Redfield, Gail	√	>4	H&C	10	3		Su 59	46
Mathematics: Weaving, Algorithms	Automatic Analysis of Coloured Images	Hoskins, J. A.	√	√	AT	5			Ju 86	151
Mathematics: Weaving, Arithmetic Progression	Weaving, 'riting, and 'rithmetic	Tate, Blair	√		AT	6			De 86	57
Mathematics: Weaving, Multilayered Fabric Structures	Multi-Layered Cloths: A Structured Approach	Hoskins, Janet A.	√	>4	AT	1			De 83	137
Mathematics: Weaving, Shaft-Combinations	Double-faced, Double-woven, Three-harness Krokbragd	Holtzer, Marilyn Emerson	√	√	SS&D	14	4	56	Fa 83	46
Mats	Easy Striped Knits	Walker, Barbara G.	√	√	TM			4	A/M 86	54
Mats	Eight-Shaft Summer and Winter Towels (Berry Atwater Biehl)		√	>4	Hw	8	5		N/D 87	74
Mats	Miyako Jofu	Miller, Dorothy	√	√	AT	7			Ju 87	85
Mats	Table Mat (Janice Jones)		√	√	Hw	6	4		S/O 85	48, I-8
Mats	Three in One	Moes, Dini	√	√	SS&D	18	2	70	Sp 87	74
Mats, Floor	Child's Nap Mat (Louise Bradley)		√	√	Hw	8	2		M/A 87	48, I-7
Mats, Floor	Welcome Mat (Jane Patrick and Jean Anstine)		√	√	Hw	5	2		M/A 84	Cover, 96

SUBJECT	TITLE	AUTHOR	IL	INST	JOUR	VOL	NO	ISS	DATE	PAGE
Mats, Plant	Weft-Faced and Warp-Faced		√	√	PWC			5	Sp 83	34
Matting	Easy Weaving for Easy Living		√	√	Hw	1	2		S-S 80	48
Mattor	Cardwoven Mattor (Part 1)	Gray, Herbi	√	√	SS&D	14	4	56	Fa 83	64
Mattor	Hand Woven Rugs: Weaves, Plain Weave, Swedish "Matta" Technique	Atwater, Mary Meigs		√	SCGM		29		48	7
Mattor	Mattor (error-corrected WJ v2 n1 77 insert for vol. 1)	Dunham, Miriam	√	√	WJ	1	4	4	Ap 77	21
Mattor	Shadowweave, Part 2 — Unbalanced Shadowweave (error-corrected WJ v2 n1 77 insert for vol. 1)	Barrett, Clotilde	√	>4	WJ	1	2	2	Oc 76	14
Mattor	Textile Structure and Analysis, A Home Study Course in Twelve Lessons: Lessons in Weave Structure, 10. Shadow Weave and Mattor	Tidball, Harriet		>4	SCGM		18		66	29
Mattor System	Handloom Weaves: The Classification of Handloom Weaves, The Structural Group, The Rhythmic Weave Class, Mattor System (Matta, Ripsmattor)	Tidball, Harriet	√	>4	SCGM		33		57	36
Mawata	Preparing Silk in Kumejima	Mitchell, Alison	√	√	WJ	10	2	38	Fa 85	53
Mawata Caps	Novelty Silk Yarn from Bell Caps	Grayson, Persis	√	√	Hw	7	1		J/F 86	58
Mawata Flakes	Yuki Tsumugi	Urbanek, Karen	√	√	S-O	10	1		Sp 86	42
Meaning	Cardiac Algorithms or the Heart's Way of Inferring Meaning from Pattern	Courtney, Elizabeth	√		AT	5			Ju 86	51
Medallion Quilts	Medallion Quilting	Miller, Kristin	√	√	TM			14	D/J 87	60
Meet-and-Separate	Meet-and-Separate Technique	Martin, Mary	√	√	WJ	8	4	32	Sp 84	14
Meet-Cross-Separate	Meet, Cross, and Separate	Holtzer, Marilyn Emerson	√	√	SS&D	16	3	63	Su 85	17
Memorials: Atwater, Mary Meigs	Atwater Memorial				H&C	8	1		Wi 56	9
Memorials: Barbara Burke Lind Memorial Library	Memorial Library	Arness, Judith			H&C	18	2		Sp 67	17
Memorials: Berliner, Dr. Rudolf	Rudolf Berliner Memorial		√		TMJ	2	4		De 69	41
Memorials: House, Florence E.	Florence E. House Memorial				H&C	11	3		Su 60	21
Memorials: Smith, Mary Alice	Mary Alice Smith — A Memorial		√		H&C	22	1		Wi 71	3
Memorials: Wood, Lawson	Memorial Weaving Room, Tulsa		√		H&C	20	4		Fa 69	44
Memorium	In Memorium: Fiberworks Center for the Textile Arts 1973–1987	Talley, Charles	√		Fa	14	5		N/D 87	44
Memorium: Carl Schuster	In Memorium, Carl Schuster, Ph. D. (1904–1969)	Cammann, Schuyler			TMJ	3	3		De 72	2
Memorium: Carmichael, Leonard	In Memoriam: Leonard Carmichael, 1898-l973	Shapley, John	√		TMJ	3	4		De 73	3
Memorium: Frey, Berta	In Honor of Berta Frey	Johnson, Garnette			SS&D	3	2	10	Sp 72	4
Memorium: Frey, Berta	Tribute to Berta Frey	Carlisle, Nancy			SS&D	4	3	15	Su 73	37
Memorium: Liebes, Dorothy	Liebes Legend, The		√		H&C	23	6		N/D 72	6
Memorium: Matty, Norma	Rocky Mountain Memorial Book		√	>4	SS&D	3	1	9	Wi 71	40
Memorium: McMullan, Joseph V.	In Memoriam: Joseph V. McMullan, 1896–1973	Shapley, John	√		TMJ	3	4		De 73	3
Memorium: Smith, Mary Alice	Mary Alice Smith	Davenport, Martha	√		SS&D	2	1	5	De 70	4
Memorium: Tucker, Anna Gail	Memorial Craft Center for Florida Weaver		√		H&C	6	1		Wi 54	25
Memorium: Varela, Osmund L.	In Memoriam: Osmund Leonard Varela, 1891–1973		√		TMJ	3	4		De 73	3
Memory Stick	Hand Towels in Overshot Effect	Davenport, Betty	√	√	PWC	3	2	8		48
Men	Manly Art of Knitting...What's Become of It, The	Weissman, Julia			Kn	3	2	6	Sp 87	15
Men	Men Who Knit	Xenakis, Alexis Yiorgos	√		Kn	3	2	6	Sp 87	14
Mending	What a Handweaver Can Learn from the Scottish Weaving Industry (error-corrected WJ v2 n1 77 insert for vol. 1)	Barrett, Clotilde	√	√	WJ	1	3	3	Ja 77	11
Menswear	Handweaves for Men's Wear		√		H&C	9	2		Sp 58	42
Mentors: Textiles	Lucky Lessons from Two Grand Women	Dee, Constance			TM			11	J/J 87	16
Men's Clothing	Alpaca "Jerga" (Pam Bolesta)		√	√	Hw	1	1		F-W 79	22, 55

SUBJECT	TITLE	AUTHOR	IL	INST	JOUR	VOL	NO	ISS	DATE	PAGE
Men's Clothing	Handspun Plaid Shirt, A (Betty Keeler)		√		Hw	4	5		N/D 83	73
Men's Clothing	Man's Plaid Vest (Kathryn Wertenberger)		√	√	Hw	4	5		N/D 83	51, 98
Men's Clothing	Man's Robe (Jane Patrick) (error-corrected Hw v4 n3 83 p 79)		√	√	Hw	4	2		M/A 83	53, 86
Men's Clothing	Man's Shirt (Leslie Voiers)		√	√	Hw	4	4		S/O 83	43, 94
Men's Clothing	Man's Sport Coat (Kathryn Wertenberger)		√	√	Hw	5	1		J/F 84	47, 94
Men's Clothing	Man's Vest (Lou Cabeen)		√	√	Hw	5	4		S/0 84	43, 93
Men's Clothing	Masculine Element, The (Pam Bolesta)		√	√	Hw	2	1		F-W 80	34
Men's Clothing	Menswear		√		Hw	7	4		S/O 86	64
Men's Clothing	Michelin Man Sweater	Zimmermann, Elizabeth	√	√	Kn	2	2	4	S-S 86	72
Men's Clothing	Plaid Jacket in a Coarse Tweed Yarn for Autumn Comfort, A		√		Hw	6	4		S/O 85	56
Men's Clothing	Shirt for a Fellow Spinner, A	Gaustad, Stephenie	√	√	Hw	7	4		S/O 86	76
Men's Clothing	Wedding Shirt (Sharon Alderman)		√	√	Hw	1	2		S-S 80	34, 61
Mercerizing	Mercerizing: Not for Everyone	Amos, Alden	√		S-O	9	2		Su 85	30
Metal	American Inspiration		√		Fa	10	2		M/A 83	92
Metal	Arline M. Fisch	Fisch, Arline M.	√		Fa	13	1		J/F 86	18
Metal	Inspired by Fiber: Textile Sensibility in Other Media	Malarcher, Patricia	√		Fa	10	6		N/D 83	33
Metal: Gold	Threads of Gold	Austin, Carole	√		Fa	13	4		J/A 86	10
Metal Weaving	Molly Hart	Hart, Molly	√		Fa	14	2		M/A 87	23
Metallizing Textiles	Metallizing	Bayer, Jeffrey J.	√	√	SS&D	7	1	25	Wi 75	14
Metallizing Yarn	Yarns and Fibers: Metallizing	Zielinski, S. A.; Robert Leclerc, ed.	√	√	MWL	4			'51–'73	102
Mexican Codices	Heritage in Tapestry, A	Arvonio, John	√		H&C	23	4		J/A 72	9
Mexican Motifs	Mexican Motifs: Mexico, Land of Contrasts	Tidball, Harriet	√		SCGM		6		62	1-22
Mexican Weaving	Warping and Weaving Mitla Cloth on the Backstrap Loom	Knottenbelt, Maaike	√	√	TMJ	22			83	53
Mexico	Back Strap Weaving in Zacualpan Mexico	Cooper, Jane	√	√	SS&D	5	3	19	Su 74	13
Mexico	Backstrap Weaving in MesoAmerica	Baizerman, Suzanne; Karen Searle	√	√	Iw	5	4		Fa 80	38
Mexico	Bark Papermakers of San Pablito, The	Wilcox, Don	√	√	Fa	12	4		J/A 85	22
Mexico	Dyes of Mexico	Wipplinger, Michele	√	√	S-O	9	3		Fa 85	32
Mexico	Heritage in Tapestry, A	Arvonio, John	√		H&C	23	4		J/A 72	9
Mexico	Herminio Martinez: Tejedor		√		Fa	8	6		N/D 81	24
Mexico	Mayan Folk Textiles: Symbol of a Society	Dieterich, Mary	√		Hw	6	3		Su 85	64
Mexico	Mexican Motifs: The Oaxaca Belts	Tidball, Harriet	√	√	SCGM		6		62	19
Mexico	Mexican Travelogue, A	Hewitt, T. H.	√		H&C	3	3		Su 52	22
Mexico	Mexico — Land of Weavers, Part 1	Hatch, David Porter	√		H&C	6	2		Sp 55	10
Mexico	Mexico, Land of Weavers, Part 2	Hatch, David Porter	√		H&C	6	3		Su 55	13
Mexico	On Spinning Cotton	Ligon, Linda	√		Iw	1	4		Su 76	6
Mexico	Profitable Idea from Mexico, A		√	√	H&C	8	3		Su 57	46
Mexico	Robozos of Tenancingo	Hewitt, T. H.	√	√	H&C	8	3		Su 57	19
Mexico	Sisal for Hammocks	Hannah, Joyce	√		TM			6	A/S 86	18
Mexico	Study Opportunities: Mexican Tapestry Weaving in San Miguel	de la Garza, Phyllis	√		Hw	3	1		Ja 82	62
Mexico	Tarascan Lace	Jenkins, Evelyn	√	√	H&C	11	1		Wi 60	12
Mexico	Tarascan Lace (error-corrected WJ v9 n1 84 p70)	Thabet, Micheline	√	√	WJ	8	4	32	Sp 84	48
Mexico	Textiles and Looms from Guatemala & Mexico	Grossman, Ellin F.	√		H&C	7	1		Wi 55	6
Mexico	Two Weaves from Mexico	Gubser, Elsie H.	√	√	H&C	11	3		Su 60	26
Mexico	Uno Mas — The Secret of Mexican Tapestry	Hall, Joanne	√	√	SS&D	5	3	19	Su 74	88
Mexico	Vaquero Sweater & Quixquimtl	Frey, Berta	√	√	H&C	12	4		Fa 61	15

SUBJECT	TITLE	AUTHOR	IL	INST	JOUR	VOL	NO	ISS	DATE	PAGE
Mexico	Villanueva Tapestries		√		Fa	4	3		M/J 77	45
Mexico	Warping and Weaving Mitla Cloth on the Backstrap Loom	Knottenbelt, Maaike	√	√	TMJ	22			83	53
Mexico	Weft Looped Pile Fabrics from Mexico	Grossman, Ellin	√		H&C	8	2		Sp 57	6
Mexico	Weft-Wrap Openwork Techniques in Archaeological and Contemporary Textiles of Mexico	Johnson, Irmgard Weitlaner	√	√	TMJ	4	3		76	63
Mexico	Work of a Huave Indian Weaver in Oaxaca, Mexico: Complex Weave Structures Utilizing One Warp Set and Two Complementary Weft Sets, The	Connolly, Loris	√		AT	3			My 85	7
Microanalysis, Fiber	Fiber Analysis: The Thread of Fate	Porter, John	√		Fa	9	4		J/A 82	49
Microcomputer-Control System: Dobby Loom	Design of Interactive Systems for Real-Time Dobby Control	Hoskins, W. D.; J. A. Hoskins	√	√	AT	5			Ju 86	33
Microphotography	Scientific Research Suggests Ideas for Fabric Designs		√		H&C	15	3		Su 64	5
Middle East	Mystery of Pile Rugs, The	Austin, Carole	√		Fa	13	6		N/D 86	1
Middle East	Qotny & Alaga: Traditional Striped Fabrics for the Middle Eastern Kaftan	El-Homossani, M. M.	√	> 4	WJ	10	1	37	Su 85	33
Milling	What a Handweaver Can Learn from the Scottish Weaving Industry (error-corrected WJ v2 n1 77 insert for vol. 1)	Barrett, Clotilde	√	√	WJ	1	3	3	Ja 77	11
Mills: Spinning	Green Baize for Independence Hall from Penland Looms	Ford, Howard C.	√		H&C	7	2		Sp 56	14
Mills: Weaving (Fannin)	Determination and Innovation: A Successful Weaving Mill	Fago, D'Ann Calhoun	√		TM		14		D/J 87	14
Miniatures	Bookmarks: A Family Tradition	Isleib, Carol M.	√		Hw	3	4		Se 82	54
Miniatures	Carpets in Miniature		√		Fa	11	3		M/J 84	99
Miniatures	Christmas Miniatures, Part 1: Summer and Winter Coverlets	Lyon, Linda	√	√	PWC			3	Oc 82	50
Miniatures	Christmas Miniatures, Part 2: Krokbragd Bellpulls (error-corrected PWC i4 83 p76)	Xenakis, Athanasios David	√	> 4	PWC			3	Oc 82	52
Miniatures	Crocheted and Knitted "Precious Littles"	Rowley, Elaine D.	√	√	PWC			3	Oc 82	58
Miniatures	D. R. Wagner: 625 Stitches per Inch	Welty, Margaret	√		Fa	10	6		N/D 83	24
Miniatures	Decorative Miniatures in Silk by Jadwiga Rakowska		√		H&C	10	2		Sp 59	22
Miniatures	Dollhouse, The		√	√	SS&D	14	2	54	Sp 83	44
Miniatures	Ellen Krucker	Busby, Robert J.			H&C	20	1		Wi 69	44
Miniatures	"Fiber 82: Miniatures" (Exhibits)	Brown, Arleen Emery	√		Fa	9	4		J/A 82	72
Miniatures	Gift Project Shows Essence of Weaving in a Tiny Space	Bowen, Kernochan	√		SS&D	5	1	17	Wi 73	91
Miniatures	Heirloom Christmas, An		√	√	Hw	8	4		S/O 87	56
Miniatures	Historical American Weaving in Miniature	Strickler, Carol; Barbara Taggart	√	√	Iw	4	3		Su 79	48
Miniatures	Home Weaving: It's the Little Things that Count		√	√	Hw	1	1		F-W 79	38
Miniatures	Line As Movement: Adela Akers, The	Janeiro, Jan	√		Fa	8	2		M/A 81	70
Miniatures	Maggie Sciaretta-Potter: The Virtuosity of a Miniaturist	Talley, Charles	√		Fa	6	6		N/D 79	16
Miniatures	"Microfibers" (Exhibit)	McClelland, Elizabeth	√		Fa	8	2		M/A 81	66
Miniatures	"Mini Tapestry Exhibit" (Exhibit)	Bockelman, JoAnne	√		Fa	5	4		J/A 78	12
Miniatures	Miniature Cable Car from San Francisco	Ayer, Millie	√	> 4	SS&D	5	4	20	Fa 74	40
Miniatures	"Miniature Fibers" (Exhibit)	Vanderburg, Jan	√		Fa	7	1		J/F 80	65
Miniatures	Miniature Garments	Wood, Irene K.	√		SS&D	11	2	42	Sp 80	60
Miniatures	Miniature Musical Drafts	Newman, Margaret	√	√	SS&D	4	4	16	Fa 73	70
Miniatures	"Miniature Textiles: 4th International Exhibition" (Exhibit)	Talley, Charles S.	√		Fa	8	3		M/J 81	72
Miniatures	Miniature World, A	Piroch, Sigrid	√	> 4	PWC	5	2	16		26
Miniatures	Miniatures Adapted from Colonial Patterns	Gibbs, Emily	√	√	H&C	8	2		Sp 57	26

SUBJECT	TITLE	AUTHOR	IL	INST	JOUR	VOL	NO	ISS	DATE	PAGE
Miniatures	Miniatures, Fine Threads, Complex Weaves	Piroch, Sigrid		√	CW	7	2	20	Ja 86	3
Miniatures	Miniatures in Fiber: Working Small—An Exciting Challenge for the Contemporary Fiber Artist	Malarcher, Patricia	√		Fa	7	4		J/A 80	32
Miniatures	Mitten Miniatures	Upitis, Lizbeth	√	√	Kn	4	1	9	Wi 87	50
Miniatures	New HGA Name Draft: Miniature Coverlet in Overshot, A	Marston, Ena	√	√	SS&D	12	3	47	Su 81	12
Miniatures	Nineteenth Century Miniatures	Erf, Mary Elva Congleton	√		SS&D	16	1	61	Wi 84	60
Miniatures	Notes of a Pattern Weaver	Alvic, Philis	√		SS&D	13	4	52	Fa 82	76
Miniatures	Overshot Patterns: Emphasis on Miniatures	Marston, Ena	√	√	SS&D	11	1	41	Wi 79	40
Miniatures	Paradox of Perfection, The	Jenkins, Thomas W.	√		Fa	8	2		M/A 81	27
Miniatures	Riis, Mafong Collaborate in Thread & Silver		√		SS&D	5	1	17	Wi 73	4
Miniatures	Ruth Bilowus: Small and Precious Tapestries	Belfer, Nancy	√		Fa	7	2		M/A 80	15
Miniatures	She Likes to Do a Little Needlework (Esther Robertson)		√		TM			13	O/N 87	92
Miniatures	Small Endearments: 19th Century Quilts for Children and Dolls	Dyer, Carolyn	√		Fa	8	3		M/J 81	18
Miniatures	Small Expressions/Large Celebrations		√		SS&D	15	4	60	Fa 84	41
Miniatures	St. Mary's Weavers		√		H&C	10	1		Wi 59	30
Miniatures	Technicolor Tapestries of Teresa Graham Salt, The	Mathews, Kate	√		Fa	14	1		J/F 87	11
Miniatures	Textile Remains from a Late Temple in Egyptian Nubia	Adams, Nettie K.	√		AT	8			De 87	85
Miniatures	"Third International Exhibition of Miniature Textiles 1978" (Exhibit)	Spencer, Patricia	√		Fa	6	1		J/F 79	90
Miniatures	"Threads" (Exhibit)	Kurtz, Carol	√		Fa	10	4		J/A 83	62
Miniatures	To Weave a Tiny Tapestry	Marston, Ena	√	√	H&C	22	2		Sp 71	29
Miniatures	Traditional Teddy: Overshot in Miniature	Sullivan, Donna	√	√	PWC	5	2	16		14
Miniatures	Universe in a Shell, The		√		Fa	10	3		M/J 83	91
Miniatures	"Wisconsin Fiber Miniatures" (Exhibit)	Lowell-LaRoque, Jane V.	√		Fa	6	5		S/O 79	84
Miniatures	"Works in Miniature" (Exhibit)	Malarcher, Patricia	√		Fa	7	3		M/J 80	82
Miniatures	Woven and Other Textile Miniatures (error-corrected WJ v2 n1 77 insert for vol. 1)		√	√	WJ	1	4	4	Ap 77	16
Miniatures	Woven Miniatures		√	√	WJ	3	4	12	Ap 79	15
Miniatures: Knitted Garments	Barbara Walker Mosaic, The	Xenakis, Alexis Yiorgos	√		Kn	2	1	3	F-W 85	11
Miniatures: Tapestry	Tapestry Weaving Adapted to Miniature Scale	Clarke, Lois	√		H&C	13	4		Fa 62	10
Mistra	Mistra	Xenakis, Alexis Yiorgos	√		Kn	2	2	4	S-S 86	56
Mitering: Handwovens	Classy Corners	Bradley, Louise	√	√	Hw	6	1		J/F 85	86
Miters: Drawn Threadwork	Drawn Threadwork	Duroy, Marie-Pierre	√	√	TM			8	D/J 86	41
Miters: Knitting	Garter Stitch Ribwarmer	Zimmermann, Elizabeth	√	√	Kn	3	1	5	F-W 86	46
Miters: Knitting	Little Knowledge, A	Rowley, Elaine		√	Kn	3	1	5	F-W 86	41
Miters: Weaving	Mitered Corners for Identical Warp and Weft Patterns	Redfield, Gail M.	√	√	H&C	14	3		Su 63	21
Mitla Cloth	Warping and Weaving Mitla Cloth on the Backstrap Loom	Knottenbelt, Maaike	√	√	TMJ	22			83	53
Mittens and Gloves	Caps, Hats, Mittens, Gloves, Scarves, Socks Contest Winners				S-O	10	3		Fa 86	13
Mittens and Gloves	Crazy Gloves	Dugan, Judy	√	√	S-O	6	4		82	61
Mittens and Gloves	Cross Country Ski Set	Chadwick, Louisa	√	√	S-O	11	4		Wi 87	34
Mittens and Gloves	Felt Vest, Hat, Mittens	Betts, Diane	√	√	S-O	9	2		Su 85	39
Mittens and Gloves	Glen's Gloves: A Kaufman Retrospective	Lancaster, Zoe Woodruff	√		Fa	12	5		S/O 85	41
Mittens and Gloves	Hand-Felted Mittens (Sara Lamb)		√	√	Hw	4	5		N/D 83	84
Mittens and Gloves	Handknitting Gloves	Newton, Deborah	√	√	TM			14	D/J 87	24

SUBJECT	TITLE	AUTHOR	IL	INST	JOUR	VOL	NO	ISS	DATE	PAGE
Mittens and Gloves	Handspun Angora Mittens	Rowe, Erica	√	√	S-O	8	1		Sp 84	51
Mittens and Gloves	Handwoven Felt Mittens (Jane Kleinschmidt)		√	√	Hw	6	4		S/O 85	66, I-16
Mittens and Gloves	Latvian Wedding Mittens	Upitis, Lizbeth	√	√	PWC			2	Ap 82	92
Mittens and Gloves	Making Gloves that Fit	Buchanan, Rita	√	√	S-O	8	4		Wi 84	17
Mittens and Gloves	Mitten Miniatures	Upitis, Lizbeth	√	√	Kn	4	1	9	Wi 87	50
Mittens and Gloves	Mittens	Rogers, Phyllis, Joan Holborn	√	√	S-O	4			80	61
Mittens and Gloves	Peruvian Mittens	Xenakis, Alexis Yiorgos	√	√	PWC			4	Ja 83	62
Mittens and Gloves	Scandinavian Nålbinding: Needle Looped Fabric	Martinson, Kate	√	√	WJ	12	2	46	Fa 87	12
Mittens and Gloves	Scarf, Cap and Mittens Set (Marit Drenckhahn)		√	√	Hw	2	1		F-W 80	52, 78
Mittens and Gloves	SPIN-OFF Book of World Records		√		S-O	4			80	20
Mittens and Gloves	Tips on Mittens	Martin, Jill	√	√	S-O	7	2		Su 83	51
Mittens and Gloves	White and Red Mittens	Hansen, Shirley		√	Kn	3	1	5	F-W 86	35
Mittens and Gloves	Winning Woven Winter Warmers		√	> 4	Hw	7	1		J/F 86	32
Mittens and Gloves: Woven	Cut and Sew Mittens	Winchester, Nina	√	√	WJ	9	3	35	Wi 85	53
Miyako Island	Miyako Jofu	Miller, Dorothy	√	√	AT	7			Ju 87	85
Mobiles	Games Weavers Play		√		SS&D	10	4	40	Fa 79	56
Mobius	Weave a Mobius	Marquess, Joyce	√	√	SS&D	5	2	18	Sp 74	55
Mock Plain Weave	Twilight Dress (Mary Kay Stoehr)		√	√	Hw	7	3		M/J 86	51, I-12
Modern Art Movement	In the Shadow of Fame: Sophie Taeuber-Arp and Sonia Delaunay	Austin, Carol	√		Fa	12	5		S/O 85	50
Modules	Carol Hoffman: Research in Molecular Crochet		√		Fa	3	4		J/A 76	18
Modules	Designing with Modules	Sullivan, Donna	√	√	SS&D	16	4	64	Fa 85	54
Modules	Ken Weaver on Rep Weaving	Weaver, Ken	√		WJ	7	4	28	Sp 83	20
Modules	Module, a Basis for Textile Design, The	Justema, William	√	√	H&C	18	1		Wi 67	9
Modules	Weaving As an Olympic Event	Falls, Lynne Cowe	√		SS&D	19	1	73	Wi 87	10
Mohair	Angora Goats and Mohair	Chastant, Kathryn Ross	√	√	S-O	7	3		Fa 83	29
Mohair	Barbara's Blends		√		S-O	7	3		Fa 83	47
Mohair	Blending Mohair with Other Fibers	Bliss, Anne	√	√	S-O	7	3		Fa 83	43
Mohair	Designing the Warp: Parallel Considerations	Criscola, Jeanne	√	√	TM			1	O/N 85	66
Mohair	Dyeing Mohair and the Random Effect	Russell, Barbara	√	√	S-O	6	4		82	54
Mohair	Fiber Foray: Working with Kid Mohair	Quinn, Celia	√	√	S-O	10	1		Sp 86	44
Mohair	Finishing Mohair Yarns and Goods				S-O	7	3		Fa 83	62
Mohair	Lacy Mohair Vest, A	McPherson, Maggie	√	√	S-O	10	2		Su 86	18
Mohair	Making Felt with Mohair	Daugherty, Robin Taylor	√	√	S-O	7	3		Fa 83	48
Mohair	Mohair: A Multimillion Dollar Industry for Australia	Gray, Isabel			S-O	8	4		Wi 84	47
Mohair	Mohair Afghan/Great Shawl	Chastant, Kathryn Ross	√	√	S-O	6	4		82	57
Mohair	Mohair Council of America				S-O	7	3		Fa 83	60
Mohair	Mo's Have It, The	Pinchin, Bryn	√	√	S-O	7	3		Fa 83	23
Mohair	Ontario Mohair Company, The	Schaffernicht, Elisabeth	√		S-O	7	3		Fa 83	26
Mohair	Preparing, Spinning and Dyeing Mohair	Russell, Barbara		√	S-O	7	3		Fa 83	52
Mohair	Raising Angora Goats in Texas	Franklin, Sue			TM			8	D/J 86	12
Mohair	Soft Pink Throw, A	Keeler, Betty	√	√	S-O	8	4		Wi 84	31
Mohair	Spinning Mohair in Lesotho	Snieckus, Mary Ann	√		TM			8	D/J 86	66
Mohair	Weaving with Mohair		√	√	H&C	18	1		Wi 67	38
Mola: Techniques	Making Molas: Four Basic Techniques	Patera, Charlotte	√		Fa	8	5		S/O 81	38
Molas	"Art of the Cuna, The" (Exhibit)	Williams, Dai	√		Fa	10	4		J/A 83	64
Molas	Ethnic Textile Art at U.C.L.A. — "Yer Dailege: Kuna Women's Art" (Exhibit)	Dyer, Carolyn	√		Fa	8	2		M/A 81	59
Molas	Molas	La Pierre, Sharon	√		TM			14	D/J 87	48

SUBJECT	TITLE	AUTHOR	IL	INST	JOUR	VOL	NO	ISS	DATE	PAGE
Monk's Belt	Changing Seasons Hangings (Halcyon Schomp and Hector Jaeger)		√	√	Hw	5	5		N/D 84	61, I-15
Monk's Belt	Creative Monk's Belt	Windeknecht, Margaret B.	√	> 4	SS&D	9	1	33	Wi 77	28
Monk's Belt	Creative Monk's Belt: Introduction	Windeknecht, Margaret B.	√		SCGM		30		76	7
Monk's Belt	From the Collection of Anne Poussart		√	√	WJ	7	3	27	Wi 82	62
Monk's Belt	Macro Plaid, Macro Twill	Xenakis, Athanasios David	√	> 4	PWC	3	1	7		55
Monk's Belt	Monk's Belt	Moes, Dini	√	√	SS&D	18	4	72	Fa 87	52
Monk's Belt	Monk's Belt and Ways to Think of Blocks		√	> 4	Hw	8	5		N/D 87	57
Monk's Belt	Monk's Belt Bedspread (Anne Bliss)		√	√	Hw	3	2		Mr 82	56, 87
Monk's Belt	Monk's Belt Drapery (Constance LaLena)		√	√	Hw	5	2		M/A 84	64, 102
Monk's Belt	Monk's Belt Lap Robe (Louise Bradley)		√	√	Hw	8	5		N/D 87	56, I-14
Monk's Belt	Monk's Belt Placemats (Ritva MacLeod)		√	√	Hw	8	1		J/F 87	56, I-10
Monk's Belt	Munkabälte (Monk's Belt) (error-corrected Hw v8 n4 87 I-3)		√	√	Hw	8	3		M/J 87	37
Monk's Belt	Pillow Pair (Janice Jones)		√	√	Hw	7	4		S/O 86	52, I-12
Monk's Belt, Creative	Creative Monk's Belt	Windeknecht, Margaret B.	√	> 4	SCGM		30		76	1-40
Monk's Belt, Miniature	Miniature World, A	Piroch, Sigrid	√	> 4	PWC	5	2	16		26
Monk's Belt, Opposites	Creative Monk's Belt: Eight Harness Monk's Belt	Windeknecht, Margaret B.	√	> 4	SCGM		30		76	24
Monk's Belt, Opposites	Creative Monk's Belt: Four Harness Monk's Belt	Windeknecht, Margaret B.	√	√	SCGM		30		76	18
Monk's Belt, Opposites	Creative Monk's Belt: Opposites in Drafting and Weaving	Windeknecht, Margaret B.	√	√	SCGM		30		76	12
Monk's Belt, Opposites	Creative Monk's Belt: Using the Block Prinicple	Windeknecht, Margaret B.	√	√	SCGM		30		76	9
Monk's Belt, Opposites, Blocks Combined	Creative Monk's Belt: Putting the Blocks Together	Windeknecht, Margaret B.	√	> 4	SCGM		30		76	25
Monk's Belt, Opposites, Pick-Up	Creative Monk's Belt: Four Harness Monk's Belt	Windeknecht, Margaret B.	√	√	SCGM		30		76	18
Monk's Belt, Opposites, Thread Construction	Creative Monk's Belt: The Thread Construction	Windeknecht, Margaret B.	√	√	SCGM		30		76	16
Monk's Belt, Opposites, Variations	Creative Monk's Belt: Variations on Opposites	Windeknecht, Margaret B.	√	√	SCGM		30		76	14
Monk's Belt, Turned	Merry Christmas!	Barrett, Clotilde	√	> 4	WJ	8	2	30	Fa 83	36
Monk's Belt, Turned	Weaving Towels As a Means of Learning the Basic Four-Shaft Weaves	Barrett, Clotilde	√	√	WJ	8	2	30	Fa 83	11
Monk's Belt, Variation	Cushion (Margaretha Essén-Hedin)		√	√	Hw	5	3		Su 84	72, 118
Monogramming Machines	Monogramming Machines			√	TM			12	A/S 87	6
Monograms	Personal Touch, A		√	√	Hw	3	5		N/D 82	43
Moonlighting	Double Lives: Can You Love Your "Work" When It's Your "Job"?	Mattera, Joanne	√		TM			10	A/M 87	62
Moorman Technique	Inlay Techniques	Barrett, Clotilde	√	√	WJ	1	1	1	Jy 76	3
Moorman Technique	Jewel Dress (Betty Beard)		√	√	Hw	6	3		Su 85	46, I-8
Moorman Technique	Journey in Progress, A	Chittenden, Annie Curtis	√	√	SS&D	17	4	68	Fa 86	50
Moorman Technique	Kimono/Pants Ensemble, A	Selk, Karen	√	√	WJ	8	4	32	Sp 84	72
Moorman Technique	Lilies on an Antique Tray	Herring, Connie	√	√	PWC	4	1	11		30
Moorman Technique	Moorman Inlay Technique, The	Searle, Karen	√	√	PWC	1	1		No 81	30
Moorman Technique	Moorman Inspired Clothing	Durston, Linda Moore	√	√	SS&D	14	1	53	Wi 82	35
Moorman Technique	Moorman Technique		√		Hw	3	1		Ja 82	38
Moorman Technique	Moorman Technique: Applications	Ligon, Linda	√	√	Iw	1	4		Su 76	12
Moorman Technique	Moorman Weave Variations	Hoskins, Nancy Arthur	√	√	SS&D	13	1	49	Wi 81	6
Moorman Technique	Opera Elegance	Sylvan, Katherine	√	√	SS&D	15	4	60	Fa 84	24
Moorman Technique	Rainbow on the Table, A (Sharon Hakala, Carol Isleib, Carol Shabaz, Ruth Stump)	Isleib, Carol	√	√	Hw	5	3		Su 84	46
Moorman Technique	Rug Weaving: One Weaver's Approach	Hand, Barbara	√	> 4	WJ	7	4	28	Sp 83	32
Moorman Technique	Sara Gilfert	Gilfert, Sara	√		Fa	14	5		N/D 87	11

SUBJECT	TITLE	AUTHOR	IL	INST	JOUR	VOL	NO	ISS	DATE	PAGE
Moorman Technique	Theo Moorman: A Conversation with a Very Special Person		√		Fa	3	4		J/A 76	22
Moorman Technique	Theo Moorman, English Tapestry Weaver in San Francisco	Marston, Ena	√	√	H&C	20	1		Wi 69	12
Moorman Technique	Theo Moorman: Explorations	Bolster, Jane	√		SS&D	1	2	2	Mr 70	10
Moorman Technique	Twilight Dress (Mary Kay Stoehr)		√	√	Hw	7	3		M/J 86	51, I-12
Moorman Technique	Two Students of Theo Moorman: Hazel Maltby, Peg McNair		√		Fa	3	4		J/A 76	28
Moorman Technique, Variation	Handwoven Sweater. A	Hewson, Betty	√	√	Hw	4	4		S/O 83	85
Morocco	Traditional Berber Weaving in Central Morocco	Forelli, Sally; Jeanette Harries	√		TMJ	4	4		77	41
Mosaics: Feathers	Inca Feathers	Kwiatkowski, Ron	√	√	Iw	1	2		Wi 76	16
Mosiacs	"Joyce Kozloff" An Interior Decorated (Exhibit)	Greenberg, Blue	√		Fa	8	1		J/F 81	89
Mosiacs: Knitting	Barbara Walker Mosaic, The	Xenakis, Alexis Yiorgos	√		Kn	2	1	3	F-W 85	11
Mothproofing	Bugs in the Rugs and Grease in the Fleece		√		S-O	5			81	38
Mothproofing	Herbal Moth Repellents: Safeguard or Sentiment?	Buchanan, Rita			S-O	10	2		Su 86	25
Mothproofing	Moth Mix			√	SS&D	8	1	29	WI 76	96
Mothproofing	Mothproofing Techniques for Weavers and Spinners	Dezzany, Frances	√		Fa	7	1		J/F 80	44
Mothproofing	Techniques of Tapestry Weaves Part 3: Shading and Other Matters	O'Callaghan, Kate	√	√	WJ	5	1	17	Su 80	29
Mothproofing	When Moths Fly Out of Your Closet	Hochberg, Bette	√	√	Iw	4	3		Su 79	50
Mothproofing	Wool Dyeing and Mothproofing for the Handweaver	Mayer, Francis		√	WJ	2	3	7	Ja 78	41
Mothproofing: Products	Mothproofing Wool	Barrett, Clotilde transl.	√	√	WJ	8	2	30	Fa 83	59
Mothproofing: Wool	Mothproofing Wool	Barrett, Clotilde transl.	√	√	WJ	8	2	30	Fa 83	59
Motif Traditions: India	Rabari Lodi: Creating a Fabric Through Social Alliance, The	Frater, Judy	√	√	WJ	10	1	37	Su 85	28
Motifs: Decorative, Eagle	Use of Eagles as a Decorative and Symbolic Motif in 19th Century American Coverlets, The	Anderson, Clarita; Jo B. Paoletti	√		AT	3			My 85	173
Motivation	How to Succeed at Teaching (By Really Trying)	Redding, Debbie			Iw	4	4		Fa 79	48
Motivation	Motivation, Perspective, and Other Practical Philosophical Matters	Redding, Debbie			Hw	3	3		My 82	24
Mounting Textiles	Appendix II: Remounting of the Tapestry Cat. No. 1, (Katrina De Carbonnel)	Trilling, James			TMJ	21			82	109
Mounting Textiles	Contemporary Tapestry	Tidball, Harriet			SCGM		12		64	24
Mounting Textiles	Enlarged Patterns: A Fresh Look at Old Techniques	McClelland, Patricia Polett	√	> 4	WJ	7	4	28	Sp 83	68
Mounting Textiles	Fastening Alternative, A	Mattera, Joanne	√	√	SS&D	11	3	43	Su 80	27
Mounting Textiles	Healing Historical Textiles	Searle, Karen	√	√	SS&D	10	4	40	Fa 79	60
Mounting Textiles	Mounting the Rio Grande Exhibit	Pickens, Nora		√	SS&D	9	3	35	Su 78	58
Mounting Textiles	Myth, Music, and Magic: The Needlework of Pilar Coover	Schevill, Margot Blum	√	√	TM			14	D/J 87	30
Mounting Textiles	On Exhibiting: A Few Caveats	Rees, Linda		√	SS&D	7	1	25	Wi 75	60
Mounting Textiles	Ounce of Prevention: Methods for Mounting, An	Stack, Lotus; Mary Ann Butterfield	√	√	WJ	9	3	35	Wi 85	39
Mounting Textiles	Ounce of Prevention: Preventing Deterioration, An	Butterfield, Mary Ann; Lotus Stack	√	√	WJ	9	4	36	Sp 85	9
Mounting Textiles	Peru, Textiles Unlimited: Mounting and Care of Textiles	Tidball, Harriet	√		SCGM		25		68	18
Mounting Textiles	Roman Shades and Bedspread		√	√	WJ	3	1	9	Jy 78	32
Mounting Textiles	Stitches for Silk-and-Metal Embroidery (error-corrected TM I4 A/M 86 p4)	Payette, Lynn	√	√	TM			3	F/M 86	51
Mounting Textiles	Technical Features of a Middle Horizon Tapestry Shirt from Peru, The	Bird, Junius B.; Milica Dimitrijevic Skinner	√	√	TMJ	4	1		De 74	5

SUBJECT	TITLE	AUTHOR	IL	INST	JOUR	VOL	NO	ISS	DATE	PAGE
Mounting Textiles: Techniques	Textile Mounting	Palmai, Clarissa	√	√	TMJ	18			79	55
Mounting Window Coverings: Roman Shades	Insulating Window Covering	Svenson, Mary Jane	√	√	WJ	6	1	21	Su 81	18
Mounting Window Coverings: Shutters	Insulating Handwoven Shutters		√	>4	WJ	6	1	21	Su 81	20
Mounting Window Coverings: Tapestry	Handwoven Tapestries Become Practical	Nixon, Elaine P.	√		WJ	6	1	21	Su 81	15
Mounting/Framing Textiles	Color Blending in Needlepoint	Banks, Lloyd Walton	√	√	TM			10	A/M 87	24
Muffs	Timelessly Fashionable Turkish Coat, A	Xenakis, Alexis Yiorgos	√	√	PWC	1	1		No 81	43
Mug Rugs	Finns Can Knit Too or How to Knit a Finn	Rowley, Elaine D.	√	√	PWC			2	Ap 82	76
Mug Rugs	Mug Rugs and Table Runner (Jean Scorgie)		√	√	Hw	7	4		S/O 86	58, 59 I-10
Mug Rugs	Mug Rugs (Wendy Budde)		√	√	Hw	6	4		S/O 85	85
Mug Rugs	Summer and Winter Revisited, Part 2: I. On Designing with Krokbragd, Krokbragd Mug Rugs	Lyon, Linda	√	√	PWC			2	Ap 82	63
Mug Rugs	Weaving Primer	Parks, Deborah	√	√	PWC	3	4	10		4
Mulberry Cloth	Tree-Bast Fiber Textiles of Japan	Dusenbury, Mary	√	√	S-O	10	3		Fa 86	35
Multilayer Weaves	Warp Color Changes in Double and Multilayer Weaves	O'Connor, Paul	√	>4	WJ	12	2	46	Fa 87	55
Multilayered Cloth	Peruvian Multilayered Cloth	Schira, Cynthia	√	>4	H&C	18	3		Su 67	11
Multilayered Cloth: Quadruple	Quadruple Cloth, A Gauze Application	Edman, Larry E.	√	>4	PWC			2	Ap 82	72
Multilayered Cloth: Quadruple	Quadruple Cloth on the Rigid Heddle Loom, Editor's Note	Xenakis, Athanasios David	√	√	PWC			2	Ap 82	74
Multilayered Structures	Evolution of a Weaving, The	Kearney, Kathleen	√	√	SS&D	12	1	45	Wi 80	64
Multilayered Structures	Gang: Technical and Conceptual Applications to Loom Controlled Weave Structures	Towner, Naomi Whiting	√	>4	AT	5			Ju 86	91
Multilayered Structures	Layered Sculpture	Liebler, Barbara	√	>4	Iw	2	4		Su 77	16
Multilayered Structures	Multi-Layered Cloths: A Structured Approach	Hoskins, Janet A.	√	>4	AT	1			De 83	137
Multilayered Structures	Six-Harness Challenge: Triple Weave Pick-Up, A	Guagliumi, Susan	√	>4	SS&D	9	2	34	Sp 78	99
Multilayered Weaves: Quadruple	Double Weaves: Quadruple Fabrics on Eight Shafts	Zielinski, S. A.; Robert Leclerc, ed.	√	>4	MWL	15			'51–'73	156
Multiple-Harness (Sets) Weaving	Double & Triple Harness Double-Cloth	Fabeck, Diane	√	>4	CW	7	3	21	My 86	7
Multiple-Shaft Weaves	Multiple Shaft Weaving — Threading for 2-or-More-Tie Block Weaves		√	>4	WJ	6	2	22	Fa 81	42
Multiple-Shaft Weaves	Roses and Snowballs: The Development of Block Patterns in the German Linen-Weaving Tradition	Hilts, Patricia	√	>4	AT	5			Ju 86	167
Multiple-Shaft Weaving	Complex Weavers: A History of the Group, The	Best, Eleanor	√		SS&D	12	2	46	Sp 81	19
Multiple-Shaft Weaving	Four + Four: An Introduction to Those Extra Harnesses	Howard, Miranda	√	>4	Hw	3	4		Se 82	66
Multiple-Shaft Weaving	Lesley Shearer: Beyond the Limitations of the Four Harness Loom	Hunt, Elizabeth Ann	√		Fa	6	2		M/A 79	41
Multiple-Shaft Weaving	More Harnesses Make the Difference	Wertenberger, Kathryn	√	>4	Hw	2	3		My 81	40
Multiple-Shaft Weaving	Multiple Harness Weaving Course — Introduction (error-corrected WJ v5 n1 80 insert p28d)		√	>4	WJ	4	2	14	Oc 79	32
Multiple-Shaft Weaving	Multiple Harness Weaving Course — Part 2: Twills and Satins, With Contribution by Nancy Searles		√	>4	WJ	4	4	16	Ap 80	16
Multiple-Shaft Weaving	Multiple Harness Weaving Course Part 4: Twill Derivatives (cont'd)	Searles, Nancy M.	√	>4	WJ	5	2	18	Fa 80	19
Multiple-Shaft Weaving	"Painted Weavings" Lia Cook and Neda Al-Hilali (Exhibit)	Park, Betty	√		Fa	8	1		J/F 81	88
Multiple-Shaft Weaving	Twenty-Harness Madness	Moore, Gen	√	>4	SS&D	12	4	48	Fa 81	46
Multiple-Shaft Weaving	Why Multi-Harness Weaves for Clothing Fabrics	Hoskinson, Marian K.			CW	3	2	8	Ja 82	13
Multiple-Shaft Weaving	Working with Linen: Barbara Eckhardt	Goodman, Deborah Lerme	√		Fa	14	2		M/A 87	35

SUBJECT	TITLE	AUTHOR	IL	INST	JOUR	VOL	NO	ISS	DATE	PAGE
Multiple-Shaft Weaving: Uses	Multiple Harness Weaving Course — Part I (error-corrected WJ v4 n4 80 p16)		√	> 4	WJ	4	3	15	Ja 80	14
Mural, Fabric	Lucinda Sheets: A Quiltmaker's Mural is a Poem in Fabric	Richerson, Suzanne	√		Fa	10	2		M/A 83	15
Museum Textiles	Museum Textiles: How to Get at Them and Use Them	Gordon, Beverly	√		WJ	8	1	29	Su 83	14
Museum Villages: Old Sturbridge Village	Sturbridge Coverlet, A	Jarvis, Helen	√		PWC	5	2	16		20
Museums and Galleries	Behind the Scenes: A Museum Installation	Goodman, Deborah Lerme	√		Fa	13	3		M/J 86	42
Museums and Galleries	Boston Museum of Fine Arts Textile Collection				SS&D	1	1	1	De 69	15
Museums and Galleries	Collections and Recollections: The Textile Museum at Sixty		√		Fa	12	6		N/D 85	76
Museums and Galleries	Confluence: A Gallery	Ligon, Linda	√		Iw	2	3		Sp 77	10
Museums and Galleries	Contemporary Handweavers at the De Young Museum	Crockett, Candace	√		SS&D	2	2	6	Sp 71	4
Museums and Galleries	Cooper Union Museum, A Rich Source of Ideas for Designers and Weavers, The		√		H&C	13	3		Su 62	18
Museums and Galleries	Cooper-Hewitt Museum, The	Park, Betty	√		Fa	9	5		S/O 82	13
Museums and Galleries	Craft Today: The American Craft Museum (Exhibit)	Sider, Sandra	√		Fa	14	2		M/A 87	54
Museums and Galleries	Dard Hunter Paper Museum, The	Bard, Elizabeth A.	√		Fa	11	2		M/A 84	43
Museums and Galleries	Demonstrating at the Smithsonian	Bielenberg, Kristina	√		H&C	24	1		J/F 73	19
Museums and Galleries	Directory of Museums, Shops and Galleries in Arizona and New Mexico				WJ	11	1	41	Su 86	48
Museums and Galleries	Dr. Elisabeth Moses of the M. H. de Young Museum	Bryan, Dorothy	√		H&C	7	2		Sp 56	16
Museums and Galleries	Ethnic Costume		√		SS&D	12	1	45	Wi 80	16
Museums and Galleries	Fashion Tour		√		SS&D	12	1	45	Wi 80	48
Museums and Galleries	Fiber Lover's Guide to the San Francisco Bay Area, A	Scarborough, Jessica	√		Fa	11	3		M/J 84	43
Museums and Galleries	"Fibers" At Tactile Gallery		√	√	SS&D	6	2	22	Sp 75	14
Museums and Galleries	Five Thousand Fabrics: A Profile of the Kelsey Museum of Archeology		√		SS&D	11	4	44	Fa 80	33
Museums and Galleries	Getting Into the Galleries: Nine Dealers Tell How to Do It		√		Fa	9	5		S/O 82	43
Museums and Galleries	How a Textile Department Grew	Koplos, Janet	√		Fa	10	1		J/F 83	54
Museums and Galleries	Jacquard Demonstration		√		SS&D	2	3	7	Su 71	12
Museums and Galleries	Linsey-Woolseys at the Sheburne Museum, The (error-corrected SS&D v16 n3 85 p90)	Noordaa, Titia Vander	√		SS&D	16	2	62	Sp 85	59
Museums and Galleries	Looms from the Past	Colwell, Ken	√		Hw	2	3		My 81	36
Museums and Galleries	M.O.I.F.A.	Livingston, Lois; Marion Rinehart	√		SS&D	14	3	55	Su 83	46
Museums and Galleries	Memphis Guild Sponsors Textile Room		√		H&C	7	2		Sp 56	27
Museums and Galleries	Merrimack Valley Conservation Center		√		SS&D	11	3	43	Su 80	30
Museums and Galleries	Merrimack Valley Museum		√		H&C	17	3		Su 66	29
Museums and Galleries	Merrimack Valley Textile Museum	Rogers, Caroline S.	√		SS&D	1	1	1	De 69	14
Museums and Galleries	Mid-Twentieth Century Textures	Mailey, Jean E.	√		H&C	8	3		Su 57	6
Museums and Galleries	Mummery: Philadelphia's Happy New Year	Smeltzer, Nancy	√		Fa	14	3		M/J 87	39
Museums and Galleries	Museum of American Textile History	Saulson, Sarah Fusfeld	√		SS&D	17	4	68	Fa 86	80
Museums and Galleries	Museum Textiles: How to Get at Them and Use Them	Gordon, Beverly	√		WJ	8	1	29	Su 83	14
Museums and Galleries	New Craft Museum to Open in New York				H&C	7	1		Wi 55	27
Museums and Galleries	New Design Center in New York				H&C	9	4		Fa 58	31
Museums and Galleries	New England Weavers at Old Slater Mill		√		H&C	9	1		Wi 57	22
Museums and Galleries	New Learns from the Old: Treasures in Museums for Today's Weavers, The	Snow, Edith Huntington	√		H&C	3	1		Wi 51	18

SUBJECT	TITLE	AUTHOR	IL	INST	JOUR	VOL	NO	ISS	DATE	PAGE
Museums and Galleries	New York Handweavers at Cooper Union Museum		√		H&C	7	4		Fa 56	20
Museums and Galleries	Old Sturbridge Village		√		H&C	1	1		AP 50	16
Museums and Galleries	"Patch" by Ted Hallman, At the Smithsonian		√		SS&D	4	4	16	Fa 73	23
Museums and Galleries	Potomac Craftsmen Select a New Home	Keasbey, Doramay	√		SS&D	4	1	13	Wi 72	40
Museums and Galleries	Rare Textiles and Costumes in the Collection at the University of Washington	Harvey, Virginia I.	√		H&C	15	4		Fa 64	15
Museums and Galleries	Scottish Weaving Museum		√		H&C	7	1		Wi 55	63
Museums and Galleries	Selling Through Galleries		√		Iw	1	3		Sp 76	20
Museums and Galleries	Seminars on Early American Crafts	MacFarlane, Janet R.	√		H&C	2	2		Sp 51	29
Museums and Galleries	Shaker Textiles at the Met	Erf, Mary Elva	√	√	SS&D	14	1	53	Wi 82	61
Museums and Galleries	Shelburne's Jacquard Loom: Is It a Computer? (error-corrected SS&D v17 n4 86 p10)	Vander Noordaa, Titia	√	√	SS&D	17	3	67	Su 86	34
Museums and Galleries	Slave Shirt Woven for Booker T. Washington Museum		√		H&C	19	3		Su 68	21
Museums and Galleries	Tapestries at the Metropolitan Museum		√		H&C	26	2		Ap 75	4
Museums and Galleries	Tapestry Room from Croome Court, The		√		H&C	11	3		Su 60	30
Museums and Galleries	Textile Museum — 50th Anniversary, The		√		TMJ	4	1		De 74	4
Museums and Galleries	Textile Museum, 60th Anniversary 1925–1985, The				TMJ	24			85	4
Museums and Galleries	Textile Museum of Washington, D. C., Its Collections, Exhibitions, Research, Publications, Conservation, The		√		TMJ	2	2		De 67	37
Museums and Galleries	Textile Museum Offers World Famous Collections, The		√		H&C	16	4		Fa 65	10
Museums and Galleries	Textile Museum, The		√		Fa	8	6		N/D 81	67
Museums and Galleries	Textile Museum Turns Sixty, The	Goodman, Deborah Lerme	√		TM			1	O/N 85	12
Museums and Galleries	Textile Museum's White-Ground Rug, The		√		SS&D	8	4	32	Fa 77	45
Museums and Galleries	Textile Resources in Brooklyn Museum		√		H&C	11	4		Fa 60	21
Museums and Galleries	Textile Study Room: Metropolitan Museum, The	Murray, Megan	√		Fa	10	3		M/J 83	49
Museums and Galleries	Textile Treasures At the Met's Costume Institute	Lonier, Terri	√		Fa	11	5		S/O 84	37
Museums and Galleries	Textile Trends: Collecting in Chicago	Lonier, Terri	√		Fa	12	6		N/D 85	26
Museums and Galleries	Textile Trends: Collecting in New York	Sider, Sandra	√		Fa	12	6		N/D 85	24
Museums and Galleries	Textile Trends: Collecting in the San Francisco Area	Scarborough, Jessica	√		Fa	12	6		N/D 85	28
Museums and Galleries	Textile Trends: Collecting in the Southwest	Elliott, Malinda	√		Fa	12	6		N/D 85	27
Museums and Galleries	Textile Trends: Collecting in Washington, D.C.	Goodman, Deborah Lerme	√		Fa	12	6		N/D 85	25
Museums and Galleries	Textile Trends: The Museum Collection	Malarcher, Patricia	√		Fa	12	6		N/D 85	23
Museums and Galleries	Textiles At The Cooper Hewitt Museum	Fowler, Molly	√		SS&D	7	4	28	Fa 76	4
Museums and Galleries	Textiles from the Smithsonian's Collection	Adrosko, Rita	√		H&C	23	2		M/A 72	20
Museums and Galleries	Thousand Islands Museum Craft School	Barnes, Muriel			SS&D	1	3	3	Ju 70	4
Museums and Galleries	Toronto's "unMuseum" for Textiles	Talley, Charles	√		Fa	12	4		J/A 85	43
Museums and Galleries	Tour Through Merrimack Valley Textile Museum, A	Britton, Nancy	√		Fa	9	2		M/A 82	52
Museums and Galleries	Verbena Collection, The (error-corrected Fa v11 n1 84 p11)		√		Fa	10	5		S/O 83	64
Museums and Galleries	Washington Fiber	Mathews, Rich	√		Fa	3	5		S/O 76	9
Museums and Galleries	Way We Wore: San Francisco's Museum of Vintage Fashion, The	Scarborough, Jessica	√		Fa	14	5		N/D 87	5
Museums and Galleries	Weaving at Fort Hunter Museum	Meigs, Margaret Wister	√		H&C	4	2		Sp 53	26
Museums and Galleries	Weaving Classes in an Art Gallery	Holroyd, Ruth N.	√	√	H&C	22	4		Fa 71	12
Museums and Galleries	Weaving Courses at the Newark Museum	Reeve, Beatrice	√		H&C	4	4		Fa 53	33

SUBJECT	TITLE	AUTHOR	IL	INST	JOUR	VOL	NO	ISS	DATE	PAGE
Museums and Galleries	Whitney Museum of American Art, The (Exhibit)	Park, Betty	√		Fa	9	2		M/A 82	11
Museums and Galleries	Why Not Start Your Own Museum?	Amram, Hortense	√		H&C	4	3		Su 53	28
Museums and Galleries	Why Visit a Museum?	Reeve, Beatrice			H&C	8	4		Fa 57	9
Museums and Galleries	Winterthur Museum (error-corrected SS&D v13 n3 82 p4)	Sitko, Jane Bradley	√		SS&D	13	2	50	Sp 82	24
Museums and Galleries: Coverlets	Alling Museum, The	Rose, Kathy	√		Hw	3	5		N/D 82	33
Museums and Galleries: District of Columbia	Fiber in the Nation's Capital	Goodman, Deborah Lerme	√		Fa	11	6		N/D 84	48
Museums and Galleries: London	European Tapestry Collections: London's Victoria & Albert Museum	Downing, Marolyn			WJ	12	1	45	Su 87	21
Museums and Galleries: Looms and Equipment	On Eighteenth Century Flowered Silk Weaving as an Inspiration for Todays Complex Weavers	Fairbanks, Dale			CW	7	1	19	Se 85	8
Museums and Galleries: Old Slater Mill	Textile Fiber and Dye Garden		√		H&C	10	2		Sp 59	23
Museums and Galleries: Paris	European Textile Collections: Textile Research in Paris	Downing, Marolyn			WJ	11	2	42	Fa 86	53
Museums and Galleries: Smithsonian	Restoring an Old Loom	Adrosko, Rita J.	√	√	H&C	15	3		Su 64	16
Museums and Galleries: Textile	Thread City, Home for New Museum	Steinhagen, Janice			TM			12	A/S 87	22
Museums and Galleries: Textiles	On Eighteenth Century Flowered Silk Weaving as an Inspiration for Todays Complex Weavers	Fairbanks, Dale			CW	7	1	19	Se 85	8
Museums and Galleries: Windham Textile and History Museum	Thread City, Home for New Museum	Steinhagen, Janice			TM			12	A/S 87	22
Mushrooms	Dyes from Mushrooms: A Spectrum of Extraordinary Color	Rice, Miriam	√	√	TM			10	A/M 87	44
Mushrooms	Stalking the Wild Mushroom	Pepin, Yvonne	√	√	SS&D	16	4	64	Fa 85	22
Music	Homespun Songs from Ireland's Clancy Brothers	Drake, Elizabeth A.	√		SS&D	16	4	64	Fa 85	62
Music	Music for Inspiration		√	√	Hw	4	2		M/A 83	51
Music	Weaving Music	Henneberger, Karel	√	> 4	SS&D	16	4	64	Fa 85	6
Musk Ox	Arctic Adventures with Qiviut	Hudson, Marjorie; Kathy Sparks	√	√	S-O	11	3		Fa 87	47
Musk Ox	Arctic Handknitted, One Hundred Per Cent Qiviut	Griffiths, Helen M.	√		H&C	22	2		Sp 71	6
Musk Ox	Musk Ox, and Miscellaneous	Adams, Brucie	√	√	lw	4	2		Sp 79	46
Musk Ox	Musk Ox Projects		√	√	S-O	7	1		Sp 83	23
Musk Ox	Musk Ox, The	Howard, Helen Griffiths	√		S-O	7	1		Sp 83	16
Musk Ox	Qiviut: A Gift from the Musk Ox	Suval, Judy	√		SS&D	6	3	23	Su 75	15
Musk Ox	Qiviut from the Musk Ox		√		H&C	18	3		Su 67	5
Musk Ox	Qiviut — The Ultimate Luxury Fiber	Gibson-Roberts, Priscilla A.	√	√	Kn	3	4	8	Fa 87	58
Musk Ox	Qiviut Update	Griffiths, Helen M.	√		SS&D	7	4	28	Fa 76	60
Musk Ox	Quiviut	Huestis, Al			S-O	3			79	32
Musk Ox	Some Hints on Spinning Musk Ox Wool	Cornwall, E. Marguerite	√	√	S-O	7	1		Sp 83	20
Musk Ox	Summary of Wool Bureau Report on Musk Ox Fiber	Reed, Fran			S-O	7	1		Sp 83	42
Musk Ox Project	Arctic Handknitted, One Hundred Per Cent Qiviut	Griffiths, Helen M.	√		H&C	22	2		Sp 71	6
Musk Ox Project	Musk Ox, The	Howard, Helen Griffiths	√		S-O	7	1		Sp 83	16
Musk Ox Project	Qiviut: A Gift from the Musk Ox	Suval, Judy	√		SS&D	6	3	23	Su 75	15
Musk Ox Project	Qiviut from the Musk Ox		√		H&C	18	3		Su 67	5
Mythology	Ann Burian: Mythic Transformations	Hains, Maryellen	√		Fa	12	2		M/A 85	21
Mythology	Cotton: Legacy of Gods & Kings	Schmoller, Irene Laughing Cloud	√		WJ	11	2	42	Fa 86	11
Mythology	In the Web of Superstition: Myths and Folktales About Nets	Nappen, Barbara	√		Fa	9	3		M/J 82	30
Mythology	Linen: The Enduring Thread of History	Hoskins, Nancy Arthur	√		Fa	14	2		M/A 87	42

SUBJECT	TITLE	AUTHOR	IL	INST	JOUR	VOL	NO	ISS	DATE	PAGE
Mythology	Manly Art of Knitting...What's Become of It, The	Weissman, Julia			Kn	3	2	6	Sp 87	15
Mythology	Myth, Music, and Magic: The Needlework of Pilar Coover	Schevill, Margot Blum	√	√	TM			14	D/J 87	30
Mythology	Naomi Kark Schedl: A Concern with Empty Cradles	Richerson, Suzanne	√		Fa	6	6		N/D 79	20
Mythology	Peruvian Textile Fragment from the Beginning of the Middle Horizon	Conklin, William J	√		TMJ	3	1		De 70	15
Mythology	Selected Batak Textiles: Technique and Function	Gittinger, Mattiebelle S.	√		TMJ	4	2		75	13
Mythology	Silk Lore: The Myths of a Magical Fiber	Goodman, Deborah Lerme	√		Fa	13	1		J/F 86	42
Mythology	Spiders: Masters of Natural Textiles	Palmer, Jacqueline M.	√		Fa	14	4		S/O 87	33
Mythology	Tapestries from Egypt Influenced by Theatrical Performances	Berliner, Rudolf	√		TMJ	1	3		De 64	35
Mythology	Tapestry Roundel with Nilotic Scenes, A	Abdel-Malek, Laila	√		TMJ	25			86	33
Mythology	Tyrian Purple	Robinson, John P., Jr.	√		H&C	24	1		J/F 73	30
Mythology	Weaving Myths	Hively, Evelyn			Hw	3	2		Mr 82	10
Mythology: Mexico	Heritage in Tapestry, A	Arvonio, John	√		H&C	23	4		J/A 72	9
Mythology: Plains Indians	Margot Strand Jensen: Soft Painting	Singletary, Suzanne M.	√		Fa	11	1		J/F 84	18
M's and O's	Baby Blanket (Susan Ashley)		√	√	Hw	7	3		M/J 86	75
M's and O's	Computer Learns to Weave, The	Huff, Karen E.	√	√	SS&D	6	4	24	Fa 75	19
M's and O's	Contemporary Approach to Traditional Weaves: M's and O's	Zielinski, S. A.; Robert Leclerc, ed.	√	√	MWL	8			'51–'73	75
M's and O's	Early American Linens	Gallagher, Constance	√	> 4	H&C	15	3		Su 64	7
M's and O's	Eighteenth Century Weaving Puzzle, An	North, Lois	√	√	H&C	10	3		Su 59	14
M's and O's	Fashion Show of Handwoven Garments		√	> 4	WJ	3	3	11	Ja 79	5
M's and O's	Hands to Work and Hearts to God	Erf, Mary Elva	√	√	WJ	8	1	29	Su 83	25
M's and O's	Multiple Shaft Weaving — Threading for 2-or-More-Tie Block Weaves		√	> 4	WJ	6	2	22	Fa 81	42
M's and O's	Multiple Shaft Weaving — Tie-Ups for 2-or-More-Tie Block Weaves		√	> 4	WJ	6	3	23	Wi 81	41
M's and O's	M's and O's Blouse (Mary Kay Stoehr)		√	√	Hw	5	3		Su 84	65, 112
M's and O's	M's and O's "Popcorn" Sweater (Mary Kay Stoehr)		√	√	Hw	5	1		J/F 84	57, 98
M's and O's	Nineteenth Century Miniatures	Erf, Mary Elva Congleton	√	√	SS&D	16	1	61	Wi 84	60
M's and O's	Placemats	DeRoy, Paul	√	> 4	WJ	1	3	3	Ja 77	4
M's and O's	Practical Apron with M's and O's Border		√	√	WJ	7	2	26	Fa 82	29
M's and O's	Shaker Towel I (Sharon Alderman)		√	√	Hw	3	5		N/D 82	39, 90
M's and O's	Shaker Towel II (Sharon Alderman)		√	√	Hw	3	5		N/D 82	41, 90
M's and O's	Shaker Towels: A Guild Devotes a Year of Study to Nineteenth Century Textiles (error-corrected WJ v11 n2 86 p68)	Eastlake, Sandy	√	> 4	WJ	10	4	40	Sp 86	20
M's and O's	Simply Natural	Linder, Harry	√	√	WJ	11	2	42	Fa 86	20
M's and O's	Six-Harness M's and O's	Jackson, Marguerite	√	> 4	H&C	9	3		Su 58	15
M's and O's	Weaver's Challenge	Wertenberger, Kathryn	√	√	Hw	5	1		J/F 84	27
M's and O's	Weaving Towels As a Means of Learning the Basic Four-Shaft Weaves	Barrett, Clotilde	√	√	WJ	8	2	30	Fa 83	11
M's and O's	Weaving with Ramie		√	> 4	WJ	8	2	30	Fa 83	80
M's and O's, Multishaft System	Handloom Weaves: The Classification of Handloom Weaves, The Structural Group, The Grouped-Thread Class, Multiple-Harness M's and O's System	Tidball, Harriet	√	> 4	SCGM		33		57	32
M's and O's System	Handloom Weaves: The Classification of Handloom Weaves, The Structural Group, The Grouped-Thread Class, M's and O's System	Tidball, Harriet	√	√	SCGM		33		57	32
M's and O's, Turned	Take Advantage of Turned Drafts	Moes, Dini	√	> 4	SS&D	13	2	50	Sp 82	58
M's and O's, Two Foundation Shafts	Multiple Shaft Weaving: M's and O's with Two Foundation Shafts	Evans, Jane	√	> 4	WJ	6	1	21	Su 81	27

SUBJECT	TITLE	AUTHOR	IL	INST	JOUR	VOL	NO	ISS	DATE	PAGE
Name Tags	Miniature Cable Car from San Francisco	Ayer, Millie	√	>4	SS&D	5	4	20	Fa 74	40
Napkin Folding	Table Linen Artistry		√		Fa	14	2		M/A 87	77
Napkins	Bronson Lace Tablecloth and Napkins (Sallie T. Guy)		√	>4	Hw	8	1		J/F 87	61, I-13
Napkins	California Poppy Tablecloth and Napkins (Jean Scorgie)		√	√	Hw	6	3		Su 85	61, I-16
Napkins	Cotton Napkins (Barbara Smith Eychaner)		√	√	Hw	7	3		M/J 86	66, I-15
Napkins	Eight Harness Linen from Elizabeth Kackenmeister		√	>4	H&C	15	1		Wi 64	34
Napkins	Five Crackle Weave Projects	Macomber, Dorothea	√	√	H&C	9	3		Su 58	42
Napkins	Megablocks	Patrick, Jane	√	√	Hw	4	1		J/F 83	60
Napkins	Napkin (Henrietta Dyk)		√	√	Hw	5	1		J/F 84	61, 105
Napkins	Napkins and Bread Cloth (Barbara Smith Eychaner)		√	√	Hw	7	4		S/O 86	54, I-11
Napkins	Napkins for a Box Lunch (Susan Feely) (error-corrected Hw v7 n4 86 p I-3)		√	√	Hw	7	3		M/J 86	75
Napkins	Pastel Collection (Jane Patrick)		√	√	Hw	6	2		M/A 85	48, I-8
Napkins	Placemats and Napkins for a Found Treasure (Janice Jones)		√	√	Hw	5	5		N/D 84	70, I-12
Napkins	Plaid Basket Napkin (Robin Taylor Daugherty)		√	√	Hw	5	1		J/F 84	69, 103
Napkins	Quilted Placemat and Napkin (Henrietta Dyk)		√	>4	Hw	5	1		J/F 84	61, 104
Napkins	Rustic Napkins (Betty Davenport)		√	√	Hw	6	4		S/O 85	18, I-4
Napkins	Samantha Herbert Napkins (Louise Bradley)		√	√	Hw	5	5		N/D 84	51, I-6
Napkins	Satin Piqué	Morrison, Ruth	√	>4	PWC	4	3	13		34
Napkins	Swedish Lace Napkins (Deborah Anthony)		√	√	Hw	8	1		J/F 87	57, I-10, Cover
Napkins	Table Dressing and Bedcovers		√		Fa	8	3		M/J 81	43
Napkins	Tablecloth and Six Napkins in Two-Block Damask (Janet Carper)		√	>4	Hw	4	3		M/J 83	54, 94
Napkins	Tea Cozy, Mats and Napkins (Margaretha Essén-Hedin)		√	>4	Hw	4	3		M/J 83	41, 93
Napkins	Waffle Weave Table Linens (Hector Jaeger)		√	√	Hw	6	5		N/D 85	56, I-14
Napkins	Weaving Table Linens	Eychaner, Barbara Smith	√	√	TM			11	J/J 87	52
Napkins	Windowpane Checked Napkins (Beth Johnson)		√	√	Hw	3	3		My 82	49, 91
Napping	Irish Kinsale Cloak, The	Jones, Una	√	√	WJ	8	3	31	Wi 83	35
Napping	Teasels	Leadbeater, Eliza	√	√	Hw	2	5		No 81	54
Napping	Turkish Coat, A	Xenakis, Alexis Yiorgos	√	>4	Hw	2	2		Mr 81	39
Napping	Vadmal: A Study Group from the Frozen North Warms up to an Ancient Technique	Larson-Fleming, Susan	√	√	WJ	10	3	39	Wi 86	26
Napping	What a Handweaver Can Learn from the Scottish Weaving Industry (error-corrected WJ v2 n1 77 insert for vol. 1)	Barrett, Clotilde	√	√	WJ	1	3	3	Ja 77	11
Narrow-Loom Weaving	Big Work from Small Looms	Liebler, Barbara	√		Hw	2	2		Mr 81	61
Narrow-Loom Weaving	Designed for Narrow Looms	Jennings, Lucy Anne	√	√	WJ	11	1	41	Su 86	26
Narrow-Loom Weaving	Designed for Narrow Looms: A Summer Shirt Inspired by the Macedonian Chemise	Temple, Mary	√	√	WJ	10	1	37	Su 85	46
Narrow-Strip Weaving	Free and Casual Look Wool Jacket, The	McGalliard, Lorraine	√	√	WJ	6	3	23	Wi 81	8
Narrow-Strip Weaving	Jacket Inspired by West African Narrow Strip Weaving	Bradley, Louise	√	√	WJ	5	3	19	Wi 81	31
Narrow-Strip Weaving	Nigerian Weavers	Worsley, Marie	√		H&C	12	2		Sp 61	45
Narrow-Strip Weaving	Oval Cape	Sylvan, Katherine	√	√	WJ	5	3	19	Wi 81	36
Narrow-Strip Weaving	Woven Inspiration from West African Textiles	Renne, Elisha	√	√	WJ	10	4	40	Sp 86	60

467

SUBJECT	TITLE	AUTHOR	IL	INST	JOUR	VOL	NO	ISS	DATE	PAGE
National Endowment for the Arts	"National Crafts '81: Works by the 1981 National Endowment for the Arts Craft Fellows" (Exhibit)	Mattera, Joanne	√		Fa	9	1		J/F 82	82
National Endowment For The Arts	Shuttle Power	Hanks, Nancy	√		SS&D	7	4	28	Fa 76	45
National Industries for the Blind	Handspun Yarns Made by the Blind	Morgret, Eugene D.	√		H&C	1	3		Fa 50	17
Native American Textiles	Mable Morrow—Collector, Scholar of Indian Arts, Part 2	Maxcy, Mabel E.	√		SS&D	5	2	18	Sp 74	33
Native Americans	From Body Paint to Buffalo Hides	Bliss, Anne	√	√	Iw	4	1		Wi 78	42
Native Americans	From the Silverman Collection: Pueblo and Navajo Textiles	Coe, Kathryn	√		Fa	10	6		N/D 83	27
Native Americans	Indian Fingerweaving, Traditional Use for Ceremonial Sashes	White, John	√	√	H&C	19	3		Su 68	4
Native Americans	Indian Weavers and Contemporary Design		√		H&C	3	2		Sp 52	4
Native Americans	Mable Morrow–Appreciation for Indian Arts, Part 1	Maxcy, Mabel E.	√		SS&D	5	1	17	Wi 73	29
Native Americans	Spinning in the Southwest — Prehistoric, Historic, and Contemporary	Lawrence, Ramona Sakiestewa	√		S-O	1			77	8
Native Americans	Weaver Profile: Mahota Handwovens	Irwin, Bobbie	√		Hw	8	5		N/D 87	35
Native Americans: Akwesasne	"Baskets of Akwesasne" (Exhibit)	Doyle, Claire	√		Fa	11	1		J/F 84	77
Native Americans: Alabama-Coushatta	Mary E. Heickman, Texas Weaver and Teacher	Morse, Martha	√		H&C	17	3		Su 66	18
Native Americans: Aleut	Attu Basketry	McIver, Lucy	√	√	H&C	24	1		J/F 73	35
Native Americans: Anasazi	Ridge (Twill) Weave of the Hopi	Nelson, Nanci Neher	√	√	SS&D	14	2	54	Sp 83	52
Native Americans: Anasazi	Ring Basket of the Anasazi, The	Turnbaugh, Sarah Peabody	√		SS&D	9	1	33	Wi 77	101
Native Americans: Arawak	Unique Technique for a Braided Strap from Colombia	Cahlander, Adele	√	√	WJ	7	1	25	Su 82	56
Native Americans: Aymara	Bolivian Highland Weaving, Part 1	Cason, Marjorie; Adele Cahlander	√		SS&D	6	2	22	Sp 75	4
Native Americans: Aymara	Folk Textiles of Latin America	Kelemen, Pál	√		TMJ	1	4		De 65	2
Native Americans: Aztec	Folk Textiles of Latin America	Kelemen, Pál	√		TMJ	1	4		De 65	2
Native Americans: Basketry	Native American Basketry	Bernstein, Bruce	√		Fa	11	1		J/F 84	50
Native Americans: Basketry	Thinking About Historical Baskets	Rossbach, Ed	√		Fa	11	1		J/F 84	32
Native Americans: Cherokee	Cherokee Weavers Used Looms Over Two Hundred Years Ago	Coulter, Doris M.	√		H&C	18	3		Su 67	17
Native Americans: Cherokee	Doubleweave Basketry of the Cherokees	Ligon, Linda	√		Iw	4	1		Wi 78	28
Native Americans: Cherokee	Finger Weaving	Cooper, Karen Coody	√	√	TM			12	A/S 87	46
Native Americans: Cherokee	Finger Weaving Being Revived by Cherokees (error-corrected SS&D v5 n4 74 p69)	Coulter, Doris	√	√	SS&D	5	3	19	Su 74	55
Native Americans: Cherokee	Prehistoric Textiles Revealed by Potsherds	Kuttruff, Jenna Tedrick	√		SS&D	11	3	43	Su 80	40
Native Americans: Cherokee	Revival of Cherokee Arts and Crafts, The	Parris, John	√		H&C	4	2		Sp 53	9
Native Americans: Chilkat	Breath of Our Grandmothers	Samuel, Cheryl	√		WJ	8	1	29	Su 83	17
Native Americans: Chilkat	Chilkat Blanket: It Soon May Be No More, The	Eggleston, Phyllis	√	√	SS&D	7	1	25	Wi 75	44
Native Americans: Chilkat,	Chilkat Dancing Blanket, The	Samuel, Cheryl	√		SS&D	13	4	52	Fa 82	58
Native Americans: Chilkat	Chilkat Spinning	Samuel, Alena	√	√	TM			1	O/N 85	55
Native Americans: Chilkat	From Baskets to Blankets (error-corrected TM i7 O/N86 p5)	Samuel, Cheryl	√	√	TM			5	J/J 86	30
Native Americans: Chilkat	Temple of the Elelments, The	Samuel, Cheryl	√		SS&D	17	3	67	Su 86	10
Native Americans: Chilkat	Totems in Tapestry	Swingle, Daphne	√		H&C	22	2		Sp 71	5
Native Americans, Chilkat	Weft Twining: History, The Chilkat Blanket	Harvey, Virginia I.; Harriet Tidball	√		SCGM		28		69	5
Native Americans: Cowichan	Cowichan Country	Gibson-Roberts, Priscilla A.	√	√	Kn	3	1	5	F-W 86	61
Native Americans: Cuna	"Art of the Cuna, The" (Exhibit)	Williams, Dai	√		Fa	10	4		J/A 83	64
Native Americans: Cuna	Ethnic Textile Art at U.C.L.A. — "Yer Dailege: Kuna Women's Art" (Exhibit)	Dyer, Carolyn	√		Fa	8	2		M/A 81	59

SUBJECT	TITLE	AUTHOR	IL	INST	JOUR	VOL	NO	ISS	DATE	PAGE
Native Americans: Cuna	Making Molas: Four Basic Techniques	Patera, Charlotte	√		Fa	8	5		S/O 81	38
Native Americans: Cuna Indians	Cuna Cachi: A Study of Hammock Weaving Among the Cuna Indians of the San Blas Islands	Lambert, Anne M.	√	√	AT	5			Ju 86	105
Native Americans: Cuna Indians	Molas	La Pierre, Sharon	√		TM			14	D/J 87	48
Native Americans: Eastern Woodlands	Twined Bags and Pouches of the Eastern Woodlands	White, John Kennardh	√	√	H&C	20	3		Su 69	8
Native Americans: Ecuador	Indian Textiles from Ecuador		√		H&C	10	1		Wi 59	19
Native Americans: Eskimo	Arctic Handknitted, One Hundred Per Cent Qiviut	Griffiths, Helen M.	√		H&C	22	2		Sp 71	6
Native Americans: Eskimo	"Innerskins/Outerskins: Gut and Fishskin" (Exhibit)		√		TM			14	D/J 87	20
Native Americans: Eskimo	Patricia Bulitt: Gutsongs and Other Dances	Scarborough, Jessica	√		Fa	11	5		S/O 84	50
Native Americans: Guatemala	Guatemala Visited	Atwater, Mary Meigs	√		SCGM		15		65	1
Native Americans: Guatemalan Indians	Guatemala: Weaving, People	Frost, Gordon	√		Iw	5	4		Fa 80	30
Native Americans: Hopi	Braiding on a Frame		√	√	WJ	2	4	8	Ap 78	22
Native Americans: Hopi	Embellishments on the Rain Sash	Baizerman, Suzanne	√	√	WJ	11	2	42	Fa 86	22
Native Americans: Hopi	Folk Textiles of Latin America	Kelemen, Pál	√		TMJ	1	4		De 65	2
Native Americans: Hopi	Garments with Ethnic Flavor: Dress Inspired by the American Southwest		√	√	WJ	2	3	7	Ja 78	17
Native Americans: Hopi	Hopi Embroidery Weave As a Technique for Tapestry	Atwood, Betty	√	√	WJ	5	1	17	Su 80	37
Native Americans: Hopi	Hopi Embroidery Weave, The	Atwood, Betty	√	√	SS&D	8	2	30	Sp 77	100
Native Americans: Hopi	Hopi Woven Embroidery		√	√	WJ	2	3	7	Ja 78	24
Native Americans: Hopi	Pueblo Weaving: A Renaissance	Sakiestewa, Ramona	√		Iw	4	1		Wi 78	34
Native Americans: Hopi	Pueblo Weaving, An Ancient Art: Hopi Keep to Their Traditional Designs		√		H&C	19	1		Wi 68	5
Native Americans: Hopi	Ridge (Twill) Weave of the Hopi	Nelson, Nanci Neher	√	√	SS&D	14	2	54	Sp 83	52
Native Americans: Hopi	Ring Basket of the Anasazi, The	Turnbaugh, Sarah Peabody	√		SS&D	9	1	33	Wi 77	101
Native Americans: Huave Indians	Work of a Huave Indian Weaver in Oaxaca, Mexico: Complex Weave Structures Utilizing One Warp Set and Two Complementary Weft Sets, The	Connolly, Loris	√		AT	3			My 85	7
Native Americans: Inca	Folk Textiles of Latin America	Kelemen, Pál	√		TMJ	1	4		De 65	2
Native Americans: Inuit	Convergence '86 Preview: Pangnirtung Weavers	Stuart, Donald	√		SS&D	16	4	64	Fa 85	70
Native Americans: Inuit	Fiberscene		√		SS&D	15	2	58	Sp 84	56
Native Americans: Jívaro	Primitive Indian Designs Inspire Ecuador's Gift to United Nations		√		H&C	4	1		Wi 52	13
Native Americans: Lummi	Vestments by Indian Craftsmen: A Cooperative Enterprise of the Lummis, Navajos, and Sioux		√		H&C	18	1		Wi 67	6
Native Americans: Maya	Art of Ixchel: Learning to Weave in Guatemala and Rhode Island, The	Schevill, Margot	√	√	WJ	8	1	29	Su 83	57
Native Americans: Maya	Cristi — Sketch of a Guatemalan Weaver	Nash, Jeanne; Jeanne Schmelzer	√		Iw	5	4		Fa 80	28
Native Americans: Maya	Folk Textiles of Latin America	Kelemen, Pál	√		TMJ	1	4		De 65	2
Native Americans: Maya	Mayan Folk Textiles: Symbol of a Society	Dieterich, Mary	√		Hw	6	3		Su 85	64
Native Americans: Maya	Weavings of the Guatemalan Highland Maya	Marks, Copeland H.	√	√	SS&D	7	4	28	Fa 76	88
Native Americans: Mayoruna	Unique Finish from an Amazonian Bracelet, A	Thabet, Micheline	√	√	WJ	9	3	35	Wi 85	14
Native Americans: Miccosukee	Convergence Preview — Six Peaks, A		√		SS&D	11	2	42	Sp 80	47
Native Americans: Micmac	Basketry Traditions of Nova Scotia, The	Gordon, Joleen	√		SS&D	17	2	66	Sp 86	52
Native Americans: Nahuala	Nahuala Spinning	Linder, Harry; Olive Linder	√		S-O	2			78	23
Native Americans: Navajo	Auctioning Rugs Among the Navajos	Marcus, Ruth-Claire	√		TM			6	A/S 86	16
Native Americans: Navajo	Churro Sheep in the Navajo Tradition	McNeal, Dr. Lyle G.	√		WJ	10	2	38	Fa 85	31

SUBJECT	TITLE	AUTHOR	IL	INST	JOUR	VOL	NO	ISS	DATE	PAGE
Native Americans: Navajo	Commercial Materials in Modern Navajo Rugs	Hedlund, Ann Lane	√		TMJ	25			86	83
Native Americans: Navajo	Contemporary Navajo Weaving	Hedlund, Ann Lane	√		WJ	11	1	41	Su 86	30
Native Americans: Navajo	D. Y. Begay: A Navajo Weaver in New York City	Harvey, Nancy	√		SS&D	17	4	68	Fa 86	32
Native Americans: Navajo	Dyepot	Taggart, Barbara			SS&D	3	4	12	Fa 72	35
Native Americans: Navajo	Exploring a Tradition: Navajo Rugs, Classic and Contemporary	Elliott, Malinda	√		Fa	11	3		M/J 84	32
Native Americans: Navajo	"Eyedazzlers!" (Exhibit)	Lonier, Terri	√		Fa	11	3		M/J 84	77
Native Americans: Navajo	Folk Textiles of Latin America	Kelemen, Pál	√		TMJ	1	4		De 65	2
Native Americans: Navajo	From Father Sky to Mother Earth: An Ethnic Inspiration	Bennett, Noël	√		WJ	8	1	29	Su 83	62
Native Americans: Navajo	Hand Woven Rugs: Weaves, Four-Harness Overshot, Indian Saddle-Blanket Weave	Atwater, Mary Meigs	√	√	SCGM		29		48	18
Native Americans: Navajo	In the Spirit of the Navajo	Elliott, Malinda	√		SS&D	13	1	49	Wi 81	18
Native Americans: Navajo	Na´ashje´ii Asdzaa—Spider Woman		√		S-O	1			77	11
Native Americans: Navajo	Navajo Hip Spindle, Part 1	Hicks, C. Norman	√	√	SS&D	8	1	29	WI 76	95
Native Americans: Navajo	Navajo Hip Spindle, Part 2	Hicks, C. Norman		√	SS&D	8	2	30	Sp 77	41
Native Americans: Navajo	Navajo Inspired Rugs		√		Hw	6	2		M/A 85	58
Native Americans: Navajo	Navajo Inspired Rugs for Floor or Beast	Drooker, Penelope	√		Hw	6	2		M/A 85	60
Native Americans: Navajo	Navajo Saddle Blanket Patterns	Barrett, Clotilde	√	√	WJ	11	1	41	Su 86	56
Native Americans: Navajo	Navajo Saddle Blanket Patterns	Barrett, Clotilde	√	√	WJ	1	1	1	Jy 76	22
Native Americans: Navajo	Navajo Saddleblanket, The	Marquess, Joyce	√	> 4	SS&D	8	3	31	Su 77	25
Native Americans: Navajo	Navajo Tapestry	Keasbey, Doramay			SS&D	1	3	3	Ju 70	23
Native Americans: Navajo	Navajo: Textiles, Blankets, Rugs, Tapestries	Morrow, Mable	√	√	SS&D	1	4	4	Se 70	3
Native Americans: Navajo	Navajo: Textiles, Blankets, Rugs, Tapestries	Morrow, Mable	√	√	SS&D	2	1	5	De 70	5
Native Americans: Navajo	Navajo Three-Ply Method, The	Rossiter, Phyllis	√	√	SS&D	16	1	61	Wi 84	10
Native Americans: Navajo	Navajo Way, The	Esping, Mardel	√	√	Iw	2	2		Wi 77	30
Native Americans: Navajo	Navajo Way, The	Jolley, Ginger	√	√	S-O	11	4		Wi 87	38
Native Americans: Navajo	Navajo Weaving, Contemporary and Traditional		√		H&C	18	2		Sp 67	6
Native Americans: Navajo	Notes on Navajo Plying	Bateman, Wendy	√	√	S-O	9	2		Su 85	36
Native Americans: Navajo	Painted Rug Designs: Trader Hubbell's Influence on Navajo Weaving	Blue, Martha	√		Fa	14	5		N/D 87	5
Native Americans: Navajo	Pearl Sunrise: Weaving the "Old Way"	Sunrise, Pearl	√		Fa	11	3		M/J 84	34
Native Americans: Navajo	Pencil Roving and the Navajo Ply	Adams, Brucie	√	√	Hw	6	1		J/F 85	75
Native Americans: Navajo	Ramah Navajo Weavers, The	D'Andrea, Pat	√		WJ	12	1	45	Su 87	44
Native Americans: Navajo	Return of the Churro, The	Alderman, Sharon D.	√		S-O	8	1		Sp 84	46
Native Americans: Navajo	Ridge (Twill) Weave of the Hopi	Nelson, Nanci Neher	√	√	SS&D	14	2	54	Sp 83	52
Native Americans: Navajo	Rugs Woven on Summer and Winter Threading		√	> 4	WJ	3	1	9	Jy 78	12
Native Americans: Navajo	"Song of the Loom: New Traditions in Navajo Weaving, The" (Exhibit)		√		TM			11	J/J 87	18
Native Americans: Navajo	Spinning with Susie	Chacey, Ron	√	√	S-O	7	4		Wi 83	18
Native Americans: Navajo	Using the Navajo Saddle-Blanket Weave	Tergis, Marilyn	√	√	H&C	23	5		S/O 72	6
Native Americans: Navajo	Vertical Loom (continued) Part 3, The Navajo Loom, The		√	√	WJ	2	2	6	Oc 77	23
Native Americans: Navajo	Vestments by Indian Craftsmen: A Cooperative Enterprise of the Lummis, Navajos, and Sioux		√		H&C	18	1		Wi 67	6
Native Americans: Navajo	Weaving Brings Total Involvement with the Navajo	Bennett, Noël	√		SS&D	4	4	16	Fa 73	15
Native Americans: Navajo	Weaving the Navajo Way	Bighorse, Tiana; Noël Bennett	√		Iw	4	1		Wi 78	12
Native Americans: Nez Percé	Nez Percé Indian Art and Craft Revival	Connette, Ann	√	√	H&C	21	4		Fa 70	5

SUBJECT	TITLE	AUTHOR	IL	INST	JOUR	VOL	NO	ISS	DATE	PAGE
Native Americans: North America	Weft Twining: History, North American Indians	Harvey, Virginia I.; Harriet Tidball	√		SCGM		28		69	3
Native Americans: Otomi	Bark Papermakers of San Pablito, The	Wilcox, Don	√	√	Fa	12	4		J/A 85	22
Native Americans: Otomi	Weft Looped Pile Fabrics from Mexico	Grossman, Ellin	√		H&C	8	2		Sp 57	6
Native Americans: Otovala	Noble Tradition Preserved: An Ecuadorian Weaving Co-op, A	Llewellyn, Charles; Deborah Llewellyn	√		SS&D	11	3	43	Su 80	12
Native Americans: Penobscot	Inspiration — Does it Come Before or After?	LaPlantz, Shereen	√		WJ	8	1	29	Su 83	54
Native Americans: Pomo	Family Album of Pomo Baskets, A	Metzler, Sandra	√		Fa	11	1		J/F 84	63
Native Americans: Pueblo	Fragment, Pre-Columbian Cloth Found in Utah	Turner, Alta R.	√	√	H&C	22	1		Wi 71	20
Native Americans: Pueblo	Pueblo Weaving: A Renaissance	Sakiestewa, Ramona	√		Iw	4	1		Wi 78	34
Native Americans: Pueblo	Pueblo Weaving, An Ancient Art: Hopi Keep to Their Traditional Designs		√		H&C	19	1		Wi 68	5
Native Americans: Pueblo	Santa Fe Weaver Re-Creates Past	Ligon, Linda	√		Iw	1	1		Fa 75	4
Native Americans: Pueblo	Sweetgrass, Cedar & Sage: Portrait of a Southwestern Weaver	Schevill, Margot	√		WJ	10	1	37	Su 85	24
Native Americans: Pueblo, Southwest	Southwest Indian Twill Tapestry	Atwood, Betty	√		WJ	8	1	29	Su 83	35
Native Americans: Quechua (Peru)	Cultures to Meet in California	Rogers, Nora	√		Hw	6	1		J/F 85	18
Native Americans: Salish	Cowichan Country	Gibson-Roberts, Priscilla A.	√	√	Kn	3	1	5	F-W 86	61
Native Americans: Salish	Fiber Heritage of the Salish	Whonnock Spinners & Weavers	√		WJ	9	2	34	Fa 84	65
Native Americans: Salish	From Baskets to Blankets (error-corrected TM i7 O/N86 p5)	Samuel, Cheryl	√	√	TM			5	J/J 86	30
Native Americans: Salish	Salish Ladies	Froese, Louise	√		SS&D	3	2	10	Sp 72	13
Native Americans: Salish	Salish Weaving	Boxberger, Daniel L.	√		SS&D	13	4	52	Fa 82	30
Native Americans: Salish	Salish Weaving	Clark, Hilary	√	√	SS&D	3	2	10	Sp 72	12
Native Americans: Salish	Salish Weaving, Then and Now	Ling, Lorraine	√	√	Iw	4	1		Wi 78	38
Native Americans: Salish	Vertical Loom (continued) Part 2, The Two-Beam Loom, The		√	√	WJ	2	1	5	Jy 77	8
Native Americans: Seminole	In the Dark of the Swamp...Seminole Patchwork		√	√	Fa	4	3		M/J 77	38
Native Americans: Seminole	Method to Her Madness: Jane Lang Axtell's Seminole Patchwork, A	Buscho, Ann	√		Fa	8	1		J/F 81	31
Native Americans: Seminole	Seminole Patchwork	Ligon, Linda	√		Iw	1	2		Wi 76	8
Native Americans: Sioux	Painted Muslin Ghost Dance Costumes of the Sioux, C–1890	Wakeland, Robin	√		Fa	8	1		J/F 81	15
Native Americans: Sioux	Vestments by Indian Craftsmen: A Cooperative Enterprise of the Lummis, Navajos, and Sioux		√		H&C	18	1		Wi 67	6
Native Americans: Southeast (Prehistoric)	Prehistoric Twined Bag from Big Bone Cave, Tennessee: Manufacture, Repair, and Use, A	Kuttruff, Jenna Tedrick	√		AT	8			De 87	125
Native Americans: Tarascan	Tarascan Lace	Jenkins, Evelyn	√	√	H&C	11	1		Wi 60	12
Native Americans: Tarascan	Tarascan Lace (error-corrected WJ v9 n1 84 p70)	Thabet, Micheline	√	√	WJ	8	4	32	Sp 84	48
Native Americans: Tlingit	Chilkat Blanket: It Soon May Be No More, The	Eggleston, Phyllis	√	√	SS&D	7	1	25	Wi 75	44
Native Americans: Tlingit	Chilkat Dancing Blanket, The	Samuel, Cheryl	√		SS&D	13	4	52	Fa 82	58
Native Americans: Tlingit	Chilkat Spinning	Samuel, Alena	√	√	TM			1	O/N 85	55
Native Americans: Tlingit	Temple of the Elelments, The	Samuel, Cheryl	√		SS&D	17	3	67	Su 86	10
Native Americans: Weaving	Supplementary Warp Patterning: Native American Warp Pick-Up	Tidball, Harriet	√	√	SCGM		17		66	14
Native Americans: Weaving, Guatemala	Guatemala Visited	Atwater, Mary Meigs	√		SCGM		15		65	1-45
Native Americans: Woodland	Finger Weaving	Cooper, Karen Coody	√	√	TM			12	A/S 87	46
Native Americans: Woodland	Reviving the Lost Art of Woodland Indian Bag Weaving	King, Rod	√		Fa	13	2		M/A 86	27

SUBJECT	TITLE	AUTHOR	IL	INST	JOUR	VOL	NO	ISS	DATE	PAGE
Native Americans: Zuni	Pueblo Weaving, An Ancient Art: Hopi Keep to Their Traditional Designs		√		H&C	19	1		Wi 68	5
Nativity Scene: Handwoven	Joy to the World		√	√	WJ	6	2	22	Fa 81	59
Nativity Scene: Handwoven	Nativity Scene	Vargo, Bessie Mae	√	√	WJ	6	2	22	Fa 81	8
Natural Materials	Afro-American Sweetgrass Basketry	Johnson, Beth	√		Fa	9	5		S/O 82	23
Natural Materials	Baskets of Doug Elliot: Connecting with the Natural World, The	McMillan, Sue	√		Fa	11	1		J/F 84	71
Natural Materials	Design in Handwoven Screens, Part 1	Rossbach, Ed	√	√	H&C	6	1		Wi 54	16
Natural Materials	Design in Handwoven Screens Part 2	Rossbach, Ed	√		H&C	6	3		Su 55	16
Natural Materials	Dorothy Gill Barnes: Baskets from a Gathered Harvest	Fedders, Pat	√		Fa	11	1		J/F 84	24
Natural Materials	Doubleweave Basketry of the Cherokees	Ligon, Linda	√		Iw	4	1		Wi 78	28
Natural Materials	Easy Weaving for Easy Living		√	√	Hw	1	2		S-S 80	48
Natural Materials	Experience with Native Materials	Pratt, Lenora			H&C	13	4		Fa 62	8
Natural Materials	Milkweed and Balduinea in the Dyepot	Gerber, Fred; Willi Gerber	√	√	H&C	22	3		Su 71	23
Natural Materials	Natural Materials: A Challenge to the Weaver	Wilson, Patricia	√		H&C	23	1		J/F 72	14
Natural Materials	Nature's Baskets	Smith, Sue	√	√	Iw	2	4		Su 77	26
Natural Materials	Project Shared by Guild Members: Day Lily Basket		√	√	WJ	5	2	18	Fa 80	48
Natural Materials	Seaweed, A Practical Use by Oregon Weavers		√		H&C	19	4		Fa 68	14
Natural Materials	Shaker Technique: Part 1, Weaving with Wood, The	Gordon, Beverly	√		SS&D	7	4	28	Fa 76	32
Natural Materials	Weaving in Africa	Cragholm, Lynn	√		H&C	23	1		J/F 72	18
Natural Materials	What Makes a Basket a Basket?	Malarcher, Patricia	√		Fa	11	1		J/F 84	34
Natural Materials	Woven Houses of Thailand, The	Wilcox, Don	√		Fa	13	3		M/J 86	38
Natural Materials: Animal	Animal, Vegetable, Mineral: Grist for the Weaver's Loom	Wilson, Patricia			H&C	24	4		Au 73	23
Natural Materials: Aspen	Dyeing with Willows, Cottonwoods, Aspens and Poplars	Bliss, Anne	√	√	Iw	5	3		Su 80	54
Natural Materials: Bark	Twined Bags and Pouches of the Eastern Woodlands	White, John Kennardh	√	√	H&C	20	3		Su 69	8
Natural Materials: Bark, Cedar	Cedar Bark, A Versatile Natural Weaving Material	Wilson, Patricia	√	√	H&C	20	3		Su 69	7
Natural Materials: Cornhusk	Nez Percé Indian Art and Craft Revival	Connette, Ann	√	√	H&C	21	4		Fa 70	5
Natural Materials: Cottonwood	Dyeing with Willows, Cottonwoods, Aspens and Poplars	Bliss, Anne	√	√	Iw	5	3		Su 80	54
Natural Materials: Indian Hemp	Twined Bags and Pouches of the Eastern Woodlands	White, John Kennardh	√	√	H&C	20	3		Su 69	8
Natural Materials: Kola Nuts	African Artist in a Dying Trade, An	Kessler, Cristina	√	√	Fa	11	6		N/D 84	51
Natural Materials: Mineral	Animal, Vegetable, Mineral: Grist for the Weaver's Loom	Wilson, Patricia			H&C	24	4		Au 73	23
Natural Materials: Oak Splits	Appalachian Basketry	Overcast, Roy	√		Fa	4	1		J/F 77	20
Natural Materials: Pine Needles	Arlan Oftedahl: Pine Needle Basket Maker		√		Fa	4	1		J/F 77	31
Natural Materials: Plant	Basketry...A New Approach to an Old Art Form	Meilach, Dona	√	√	Fa	4	1		J/F 77	16
Natural Materials: Poplar	Dyeing with Willows, Cottonwoods, Aspens and Poplars	Bliss, Anne	√	√	Iw	5	3		Su 80	54
Natural Materials: Scouring	Pennyroyal Pick-up	Reedy, Dorrie		√	SS&D	15	1	57	Wi 83	79
Natural Materials, Unusual	Amazing Materials from Nature	Austin, Carole	√		Fa	14	3		M/J 87	24
Natural Materials: Vegetable	Animal, Vegetable, Mineral: Grist for the Weaver's Loom	Wilson, Patricia			H&C	24	4		Au 73	23
Natural Materials: Willow	Dyeing with Willows, Cottonwoods, Aspens and Poplars	Bliss, Anne	√	√	Iw	5	3		Su 80	54
Nature: Designs	Nature Designs		√		Hw	2	4		Se 81	56
Navajo Saddle Blanket Technique	Navajo Saddle Blanket Patterns	Barrett, Clotilde	√	√	WJ	1	1	1	Jy 76	22

SUBJECT	TITLE	AUTHOR	IL	INST	JOUR	VOL	NO	ISS	DATE	PAGE
Navajo Sheep Project	Navajo Sheep Project Update, A				S-O	8	2		Su 84	6
Navajo Sheep Project	Return of the Churro, The	Alderman, Sharon D.	√		S-O	8	1		Sp 84	46
Necklaces	Double-Woven Treasures from Old Peru	Cahlander, Adele	√	√	PWC			4	Ja 83	36
Necklines	Linen Shift: Plain Sewing Makes the Most of Your Fabric, A	Smith, Kathleen B.	√	√	TM			9	F/M 87	46
Necklines, Correcting	Correcting Shifting Necklines			√	TM			11	J/J 87	8
Neckpiece	Idea Notebook: A Workshop Necklace	Sheppard, Margaret	√	√	Hw	7	5		N/D 86	25
Neckpiece, Woven	Woven Pendant (Jane Patrick)		√	√	Hw	8	4		S/O 87	55, I-11
Neckpieces	Elmyra Tidwell	Tidwell, Elmyra	√		Fa	14	3		M/J 87	22
Neckpieces	Embroidered Neckpieces of Theodora Elston, The	Sacks, Star M.	√		Fa	6	3		M/J 79	51
Neckpieces	Fabulous Plumage of Mae Augarten, The	Forscey, Suzon	√		Fa	6	3		M/J 79	65
Neckpieces	Ruth Bilowus: Small and Precious Tapestries	Belfer, Nancy	√		Fa	7	2		M/A 80	15
Neckpieces	Very Special Craftswoman: Maria Consuelo Moya, A		√		Fa	3	2		M/A 76	32
Neckpieces	Warp-Faced Krokbragd	Jensen, Gay; Donna Kaplan	√	> 4	WJ	12	2	46	Fa 87	62
Neckpieces	Wearable Fine Thread Tapestries	Tidwell, Elmyra	√	√	WJ	10	3	39	Wi 86	34
Neckties	Accessories: Necktie		√	√	WJ	2	4	8	Ap 78	8
Neckties	Inkle Pattern for Belts and Neckties		√	√	WJ	4	4	16	Ap 80	21
Neckties	Knot of Ties, A (Janice Jones)		√	√	Hw	6	2		M/A 85	54, I-11
Neckties	Man's Sport Tie (Jane Patrick)		√	√	Hw	5	1		J/F 84	48, 89
Neckties	Off Set Twill Tie (Sharon Alderman)		√	> 4	Hw	7	4		S/O 86	65, I-16
Neckties	Profitable Idea from Mexico, A		√	√	H&C	8	3		Su 57	46
Neckties	Silk Necktie		√	√	Hw	2	1		F-W 80	55, 59
Neckties	Ties, Ties, Ties: A Good Idea Goes a Long Way		√		Hw	5	5		N/D 84	98
Neckties	Two Ties in Double Two-Tie (Amy Preckshot)		√	> 4	Hw	6	5		N/D 85	64, I-15
Neckties	Weaving Neckties on a Twenty-Inch Loom	Skirm, Helen W.	√	√	SS&D	1	4	4	Se 70	14
Needle Lace: Contemporary	Contemporary Needle Lacers		√		TM			13	O/N 87	44
Needle Lace: Techniques	Needle Lace	Kaiser, Eunice	√	√	TM			13	O/N 87	40
Needle Looping	Scandinavian Nålbinding: Needle Looped Fabric	Martinson, Kate	√	√	WJ	12	2	46	Fa 87	12
Needle Looping: Technique	Toothbrush Handle Rugs: Nålbinding with Rags	Nelson, Lila	√	√	WJ	12	2	46	Fa 87	16
Needle Looping: Technique	Toothbrush Rug Instructions		√	√	WJ	12	2	46	Fa 87	20
Needle Weaving	Cape-Able Garment	Hicks, C. Norman	√	√	SS&D	6	3	23	Su 75	18
Needle Weaving	Peruvian Technique for Dimensional Knotting	Bravo, Monica	√	√	WJ	12	1	45	Su 87	17
Needle Weaving	Scaffold Weaving: A Contemporary Garment Inspired by an Ancient Technique	Searle, Karen	√	√	WJ	10	2	38	Fa 85	65
Needlecases	Project by Guild Members		√	√	WJ	5	3	19	Wi 81	17
Needlepoint	Belinda Raab: Exploring an Interior World	Roberts, Kaki	√		Fa	14	2		M/A 87	14
Needlepoint	Color Blending in Needlepoint	Banks, Lloyd Walton	√	√	TM			10	A/M 87	24
Needlepoint	Evolution of an Artist: Lloyd Blanks	Blanks, Lloyd	√		Fa	14	5		N/D 87	30
Needlepoint	Jody House: Needlework Designer	Madison, Winifred	√		Fa	5	6		N/D 78	25
Needlepoint	"Linda Maxwell and Caroline Dahl: Terror Sampler and Other Dogs" (Exhibit)	Poon, Vivian	√		Fa	11	6		N/D 84	79
Needlepoint	Lushness of Nature: Jim Williams and His Needlepoint Art, The	Luddecke, Jane	√		Fa	6	4		J/A 79	50
Needlepoint	Needlepoint with Cardweaving	Porcella, Yvonne	√	√	SS&D	4	2	14	Sp 73	13
Needlepoint	Rita Maran, Executes Designs in Yarn for Artists		√		H&C	18	1		Wi 67	14
Needlepoint	She Likes to Do a Little Needlework (Esther Robertson)		√		TM			13	O/N 87	92

SUBJECT	TITLE	AUTHOR	IL	INST	JOUR	VOL	NO	ISS	DATE	PAGE
Needlepoint, Contemporary	Myth, Music, and Magic: The Needlework of Pilar Coover	Schevill, Margot Blum	√	√	TM			14	D/J 87	30
Needlepoint: Petit Point	D. R. Wagner: 625 Stitches per Inch	Welty, Margaret	√		Fa	10	6		N/D 83	24
Needlepoint, Woven	Shuttle	Marston, Ena	√	√	SS&D	2	4	8	Fa 71	14
Needles: Sewing, Types	Handsewing Stitches	Callaway, Grace	√	√	TM			12	A/S 87	53
Needles: Sticking	Unsticking Needles			√	TM			12	A/S 87	10
Needles: Threading	Knots in Threads			√	TM			8	D/J 86	4
Needles: Threading	Threading a Needle and Pulling It Through			√	TM			11	J/J 87	6
Needles: Threading	Threading Needles		√		TM			10	A/M 87	4
Needles: Threading	To Thread a Needle			√	TM			6	A/S 86	14
Needles: Threading	Twist Again			√	TM			12	A/S 87	4
Needlework	Artist's Need for Needlework, An	Benanti, Gigi	√		TM			9	F/M 87	20
Needlework	C.H.A.N. for Short: The Story of Rachel Maines	Alonso, Harriet	√		Fa	8	3		M/J 81	13
Needlework	Center for the History of American Needlework				Fa	9	3		M/J 82	18
Needlework	Handspinning for Needlework	Shurtleff, Chris Ann	√	√	S-O	7	2		Su 83	29
Needlework	Hobby of Queens, The	Rogers, Georgia M.			TM			3	F/M 86	12
Needlework	Hot Lips Houlihan Loves to Stitch		√		Fa	13	4		J/A 86	11
Needlework	Illuminated Tapestries of Amy Zerner, The	Daniels, Richard	√		Fa	9	3		M/J 82	22
Needlework	John Smith's Wonderful World		√		H&C	15	1		Wi 64	12
Needlework	"Needle Expressions '80" (Exhibit)		√		Fa	8	1		J/F 81	93
Needlework	"Needle Expressions '86" (Exhibit)	Reinsel, Susan J.	√		Fa	14	1		J/F 87	53
Needlework	"Needlework" (Exhibit)	Krueger, Glee	√		Fa	9	3		M/J 82	78
Needlework	Paracas Needle Technique, A	Hoskins, Nancy	√	√	Iw	5	4		Fa 80	34
Needlework	Peru, Textiles Unlimited: Textile Characteristics, Needlework	Tidball, Harriet	√		SCGM		25		68	20
Needlework	Right Out of History	Mattera, Joanne	√		Fa	9	3		M/J 82	55
Needlework	Traces of Time	Schimmel, Heidrun	√		Fa	9	3		M/J 82	70
Needlework	Yesterday's Necessity — Today's Choice	Goodrick, Gail L.			S-O	7	2		Su 83	30
Needlework Center	Center for the History of American Needlework				Fa	9	3		M/J 82	18
Needlework: Drawn Threadwork	Drawn Threadwork	Duroy, Marie-Pierre	√	√	TM			8	D/J 86	41
Needlework: Needle Punch	Connie Lehman: Portable Secrets	Clurman, Irene	√		Fa	12	6		N/D 85	10
Needlework: Technique	Old Time Fancy Work: Examples of Lesser Known Needlework Techniques	Maines, Rachel	√	√	Fa	8	3		M/J 81	16
Neon/Fabric	Revelations: Victoria Rivers' Neon and Fabric Constructions		√		Fa	8	5		S/O 81	50
Nepal	Nepal	Petrini, Marcy	√		SS&D	16	2	62	Sp 85	65
Net Weaves: Types	Woven Lace and Lacey Weaves: Net Weaves	Zielinski, S. A.; Robert Leclerc, ed.	√	√	MWL	13			'51–'73	75
Net Weaves: Whip Net	Woven Lace and Lacey Weaves: Net Weaves	Zielinski, S. A.; Robert Leclerc, ed.	√	√	MWL	13			'51–'73	85
Netherlands	Knitting from the Netherlands: Traditional Dutch Fishermen's Sweaters	Van der Klift-Tellegen, Henriette	√		Fa	12	4		J/A 85	45
Netherlands	Lace Maker of Holland, Henk van der Zanden		√		H&C	17	2		Sp 66	15
Netherlands, The	Listening to Threads	Reynders-Baas, Coby	√		WJ	11	4	44	Sp 87	21
Nets	"Barbara Shawcroft: Nets, Rope, And Cloth" (Exhibit)	Finucane, Brigid	√		Fa	12	4		J/A 85	68
Nets	Deborah Frederick: Rainbow Nets	Lansdell, Sarah	√		Fa	5	3		M/J 78	40
Nets	Here Today, Gone Tomorrow: The Transitory Sculpture of Virginia Gunter	Mattera, Joanne	√		Fa	8	2		M/A 81	18
Nets	In the Web of Superstition: Myths and Folktales About Nets	Nappen, Barbara	√		Fa	9	3		M/J 82	30
Nets	"Joanne Brandford: Recent Nets" (Exhibit)	Park, Betty	√		Fa	11	6		N/D 84	77

SUBJECT	TITLE	AUTHOR	IL	INST	JOUR	VOL	NO	ISS	DATE	PAGE
Nets	"Joanne Segal Brandford — Nets" (Exhibit)	Park, Betty	√		Fa	5	3		M/J 78	17
Nets	Kliots of Berkeley, The	Talley, Charles S.	√		Fa	7	4		J/A 80	44
Nets	Nets of Bernard Toale, The	Malarcher, Patricia	√		Fa	9	3		M/J 82	26
Nets, Lace, and Embroidery	Theme Issue		√		Fa	9	3		M/J 82	
Netting	Hamaca from Ecuador	Bowman, Susan	√	√	SS&D	10	3	39	Su 79	52
Netting	Using the Fibers of Native Plants	Buchanan, Rita	√	√	S-O	9	4		Wi 85	29
Netting: Handspun	Rita Buchanan's Knotted Net Onion Bag		√		S-O	9	3		Fa 85	15
Netting: Knotless	Conversation with Barbara Shawcroft, A		√		H&C	22	3		Su 71	21
Netting: Knotless	Conversation with Barbara Shawcroft: A Sculptor in Fiber, A	Mattera, Joanna	√		Fa	8	4		J/A 81	58
Netting: Knotless	Hops Strainers and Humouous Creatures	McNinch, Janet	√		SS&D	3	1	9	Wi 71	26
Netting: Knotless	Scandinavian Nålbinding: Needle Looped Fabric	Martinson, Kate	√	√	WJ	12	2	46	Fa 87	12
Netting: Knotless	"Show of Complements, A" (Exhibit)	Schevill, Margot Blum	√		Fa	13	4		J/A 86	50
Netting: Knotless	String Bags	Nunn, Robin; Alan West	√	√	SS&D	14	2	54	Sp 83	10
Netting: Knotted	And Knots	Clemner, Phyllis	√	√	SS&D	14	3	55	Su 83	26
Netting: Knotted	Hammocks	Earth Guild	√	√	SS&D	14	3	55	Su 83	24
Netting, Knotted	Knotted Netting Methods	Guagliumi, Susan	√	√	SS&D	10	3	39	Su 79	86
Netting: Knotted	Netted Hammock		√	√	WJ	4	1	13	Jy 79	43
Netting: Knotted	Rita Buchanan's Knotted Net Onion Bag		√		S-O	9	3		Fa 85	15
Nettles	Survey of Leaf and Stem Fibers, A	Buchanan, Rita	√		S-O	10	3		Fa 86	24
New Brunswick	Weaving in New Brunswick	Currey, Ruth Dunlop	√		H&C	12	1		Wi 61	29
New England	Women as Spinners: New England Spinsters	Gordon, Beverly	√		S-O	3			79	16
New Zealand	Excellence of Spinning, Vitality of Dyes Impress Visitor to 'Down Under'	Barker, Mary	√		SS&D	4	4	16	Fa 73	46
New Zealand	Fleece in the Hands of a New Zealand Spinner	Horne, Beverley	√		S-O	2			78	24
New Zealand	Fleece-to-Garment Competition in New Zealand	Ashford, Joy			SS&D	4	1	13	Wi 72	21
New Zealand	Kiwicraft	Horne, Beverley	√	√	S-O	3			79	52
New Zealand	Knitter's Journey: New Zealand, A	Zimmermann, Elizabeth	√		Kn	4	1	9	Wi 87	18
New Zealand	Maori and Pakeha of New Zealand Use Wool and Phormium Tenax	Duncan, Molly	√	√	SS&D	5	1	17	Wi 73	65
New Zealand	Mural Contest Winner from New Zealand		√		SS&D	4	1	13	Wi 72	30
New Zealand	New Zealand Interpretation of Compass and Double Square, A		√	√	H&C	8	4		Fa 57	20
New Zealand	New Zealand Spinners	Robinson, Margaret	√		H&C	10	3		Su 59	23
New Zealand	New Zealand Spinning	Ashford, Joy			SS&D	4	1	13	Wi 72	20
New Zealand	New Zealand Tapestry	Lough, Ida	√		H&C	19	3		Su 68	20
New Zealand	New Zealand Woolcrafts Festival	Guy, Sallie T.	√		SS&D	14	4	56	Fa 83	28
New Zealand	Rattle Your Dags	Swenson, Nancy	√		S-O	8	1		Sp 84	12
New Zealand	Spinners & Weavers in New Zealand Use Native Materials	Duncan, Molly	√		H&C	21	1		Wi 70	14
New Zealand	Spinning Down Under: What Are You Going to Do with the Yarn?	De Boer, Janet	√		S-O	1			77	23
New Zealand	Spinning in New Zealand	Ashford, Joy	√		H&C	21	3		Su 70	42
New Zealand	Thoughts from a New Zealander	Poore, Jenny			SS&D	9	3	35	Su 78	65
New Zealand	Three Crafts in New Zealand, The	Timlin, Jean			SS&D	1	2	2	Mr 70	18
New Zealand	Weaving with the Maoris of New Zealand	Giacchina, Polly Jacobs	√	√	Fa	11	3		M/J 84	48
New Zealand	Weft Twining: History, The Maori of New Zealand	Harvey, Virginia I.; Harriet Tidball	√		SCGM		28		69	7
Newsletters: Machine Knitting	Machine Knitters Meet in Seattle	Guagliumi, Susan			TM			12	A/S 87	16
Nicaragua	Nicaraguan Tapestries	Branfman, Judy	√		TM			8	D/J 86	14
Nigeria	Art and Tradition of Akwete Weaving, The	Lambrecht, Dora J.	√		SS&D	9	2	34	Sp 78	33

SUBJECT	TITLE	AUTHOR	IL	INST	JOUR	VOL	NO	ISS	DATE	PAGE
Nigeria	Nigerian Weavers	Worsley, Marie	√		H&C	12	2		Sp 61	45
Nishijin	Obi: The Textile Art of Nishijin	Donaldson, R. Alan	√		AT	1			De 83	115
Nomenclature: Colors	Centroid Colors, The	Bliss, Anne	√	√	Iw	5	4		Fa 80	56
Nonloom Weaving	West Indian Weaving, Nonloom Techniques of Interest	Schira, Cynthia	√		H&C	21	3		Su 70	17
Noppväv	Immigrant Memories	Butcher-Younghans, Sherry	√		WJ	9	4	36	Sp 85	44
Nordic Knitting	Methods for Multicolored Knitting	Righetti, Maggie	√	√	TM			6	A/S 86	40
North America	American Handweaving, A Mid-Century Viewpoint	Frey, Berta	√		H&C	1	1		Ap 50	5
North American Wool and Textile Small Industry Development	Robert Donnelly	de la Cruz, Catherine Jacinta	√		S-O	10	1		Sp 86	53
Norway	Aaklae Weaving	Mundal, Maria	√	√	H&C	5	1		Wi 53	20
Norway	Aklae: Norwegian Tapestry	Irlbeck, Sonja	√	√	WJ	8	1	29	Su 83	27
Norway	Card Woven Belt of East Telemark—An Adaptation of a Traditional Norwegian Technique	Nelson, Lila	√	√	WJ	9	1	33	Su 84	30
Norway	Finnweave in Norway: Yesterday and Today	Nelson, Lila	√		PWC			2	Ap 82	14
Norway	Firfletting Fringe Treatment from Norway	Searle, Karen	√	√	WJ	9	4	36	Sp 85	40
Norway	Modern Norwegian Tapestries	Longbers, Ingeborg	√		H&C	5	1		Wi 53	12
Norway	Nineteenth Century Tapestry in Billedvev, A	Nelson, Lila	√		WJ	10	2	38	Fa 85	26
Norway	Norwegian Luskofte	Gibson-Roberts, Priscilla A.	√	√	S-O	9	3		Fa 85	44
Norway	Norwegian Tapestries		√		H&C	10	4		Fa 59	46
Norway	Norwegian Tradition, The	Nelson, Lila	√		SS&D	7	4	28	Fa 76	6
Norway	Rugs in the Scandinavian Way		√	√	Hw	8	3		M/J 87	58
Norway	Scandinavian Nålbinding: Needle Looped Fabric	Martinson, Kate	√	√	WJ	12	2	46	Fa 87	12
Norway	Skillbragd — A Decorative Pattern Weave		√	> 4	Hw	8	3		M/J 87	60
Norway	Weaving in Rural Norway: A Living Tradition	Nelson, Lila	√		Hw	8	3		M/J 87	52
Notebook	Notebook: And the Threading is Easy	Myers, Ruth Nordquist	√	> 4	SS&D	13	4	52	Fa 82	12
Notebook	Notebook: Dusting Off the Inkle Loom	Myers, Ruth Nordquist	√	√	SS&D	14	1	53	Wi 82	44
Notebook: Stitchery	Texture Stitches for Needlepoint	Hamer, Rosalie	√	√	TM			5	J/J 86	62
Notebook: Tapestry	Tapestry		√	√	Hw	3	1		Ja 82	34
Notebook: Weaving	Virtuous Weaver and the Weaver's Notebook, The	Allen, Debbie			Hw	5	4		S/0 84	34
Nova Scotia	Basketmakers of Nova Scotia, The	Gordon, Joleen	√		SS&D	17	4	68	Fa 86	44
Nova Scotia	Basketry Traditions of Nova Scotia, The	Gordon, Joleen	√		SS&D	17	2	66	Sp 86	52
Nova Scotia	Nova Scotia Tartan, The	Black, Mary E.	√		H&C	6	2		Sp 55	26
Nova Scotia	Nova Scotia Weavers Arouse Interest in Wool	Major, Marjorie	√		H&C	5	1		Wi 53	28
Nova Scotia	Old Ways for the New	Gordon, Joleen	√		SS&D	17	4	68	Fa 86	48
Nova Scotia	Tapestry in Nova Scotia	Black, Mary E.	√	√	H&C	8	3		Su 57	24
Nova Scotia	Weaving in Nova Scotia — Yesterday and Today	Black, Mary E.	√		H&C	2	4		Fa 51	5
Numismatics	General Patterson's Tapestry	Sellschopp, Dr. E. A.	√		TMJ	2	4		De 69	2
Oak Galls	Dyes from Oak Galls	Bliss, Anne	√	√	Iw	6	1		Wi 80	64
Obi	Obi: The Textile Art of Nishijin	Donaldson, R. Alan	√		AT	1			De 83	115
Obituaries: Acton, Joseph D.	Joseph D. Acton				H&C	13	4		Fa 62	37
Obituaries: Aldrich, Mae	Aldrich, Mae				SS&D	5	1	17	Wi 73	16
Obituaries: Allen, Helen Louise	Helen Louise Allen				H&C	20	1		Wi 69	40
Obituaries: Amos, Mary Alice	Mary Alice Amos				H&C	19	4		Fa 68	40
Obituaries: Atwater, Mary Meigs	Mary Meigs Atwater				H&C	7	4		Fa 56	44
Obituaries: Barnes, Muriel	Muriel Barnes				SS&D	14	3	55	Su 83	79

SUBJECT	TITLE	AUTHOR	IL	INST	JOUR	VOL	NO	ISS	DATE	PAGE
Obituaries: Barrett, Earl W.	Earl Barrett , 1919–1983				WJ	8	2	30	Fa 83	4
Obituaries: Barrett, Earl W.	Earl W. Barrett				SS&D	15	1	57	Wi 83	91
Obituaries: Barrett, Helen S.	Helen S. Barrett				SS&D	18	2	70	Sp 87	60
Obituaries: Barrett, Phyllis J.	In Memorium				CW	7	3	21	My 86	7
Obituaries: Barrett, Phyllis Kachelhoffer	Phyllis Kachelhoffer Barrett				SS&D	17	2	66	Sp 86	6
Obituaries: Beck, Mrs. Robert C.	Mrs. Robert C. Beck				H&C	21	1		Wi 70	40
Obituaries: Bellinger, Louisa	Louisa Bellinger				H&C	20	1		Wi 69	40
Obituaries: Berliner, Dr. Rudolf P.	Rudolf P. Berliner, 1886–1967		√		TMJ	2	2		De 67	41
Obituaries: Bird, Junius Bouton	Junius Bouton Bird, 1907–1982		√		TMJ	21			82	i
Obituaries: Blumenau, Lili	Lili Blumenau				SS&D	8	1	29	WI 76	60
Obituaries: Bohm, Elaine	Elaine Bohm				H&C	21	3		Su 70	38
Obituaries: Boylan, Anne Mitchell	Anne Mitchell Boylan				H&C	21	1		Wi 70	40
Obituaries: Brenholts, Jeanne	Jeanne Brenholts				Fa	14	3		M/J 87	46
Obituaries: Brigham, Clara Rust	Mrs. Clara Rust Brigham				H&C	6	1		Wi 54	51
Obituaries: Burnham, Mrs. Nina	Mrs. Nina Burnham				H&C	13	4		Fa 62	47
Obituaries: Busse, Jane	Jane Busse				SS&D	18	4	72	Fa 87	7
Obituaries: Butterworth, Charles Y.	Charles Y. Butterworth				H&C	11	4		Fa 60	52
Obituaries: Campbell, David R.	David R. Campbell				H&C	14	3		Su 63	42
Obituaries: Cardarelle, Anthony	Anthony Cardarelle				H&C	22	1		Wi 71	40
Obituaries: Carpenter, Marian Powell	Marian Powell Carpenter				SS&D	17	2	66	Sp 86	8
Obituaries: Cate, Leslie	Leslie Cate				H&C	11	2		Sp 60	52
Obituaries: Choy, Katherine	Katherine Choy				H&C	9	3		Su 58	49
Obituaries: Churchill, David Carroll	David Carroll Churchill, Founder of Churchill Weavers				H&C	20	2		Sp 69	40
Obituaries: Clark, Eleanor	Eleanor Clark				H&C	9	3		Su 58	49
Obituaries: Cranch, Jeanette	Jeanette Cranch				H&C	15	3		Su 64	37
Obituaries: Crawford, Elizabeth	Elizabeth Crawford, 1910–1983				WJ	8	2	30	Fa 83	10
Obituaries: Crawford, Elizabeth "Libbie" Loar	Elizabeth "Libbie" Loar Crawford				SS&D	15	1	57	Wi 83	91
Obituaries: Cruickshank, Ronald	Ronald Cruickshank				H&C	21	1		Wi 70	40
Obituaries: Davis, Myra L.	Myra L. Davis				H&C	12	2		Sp 61	53
Obituaries: DeGraw, Evelyn	In Memory: Evelyn DeGraw				Hw	2	4		Se 81	23
Obituaries: Delauney, Sonia	Sonia Delauney 1885-1979		√		SS&D	11	4	44	Fa 80	21
Obituaries: Eaton, Allen H.	Allen H. Eaton				H&C	14	2		Sp 63	32
Obituaries: Emery, Irene	In Memory: Irene Emery				Hw	2	4		Se 81	23
Obituaries: Emery, Irene	Irene Emery, 1900–1981		√		TMJ	19 20			80,81	iii
Obituaries: Frey, Berta	Berta Frey				H&C	23	2		M/A 72	6
Obituaries: Frey, Marie	Marie Frey				H&C	20	1		Wi 69	38
Obituaries: Fuchs, Rudi	In Memoriam: Rudi Fuchs, 1905–1985				Hw	7	1		J/F 86	26
Obituaries: Fuchs, Rudolph A.	Rudolph A. Fuchs				SS&D	16	4	64	Fa 85	11
Obituaries: Gallinger, Milo	Milo Gallinger				H&C	7	4		Fa 56	44
Obituaries: Gardner, Jean	In Memory: Jean Gardner				Hw	8	2		M/A 87	4
Obituaries: Gardner, Jean	Jean Gardner				SS&D	18	2	70	Sp 87	59
Obituaries: Gonzales, Loraine	Loraine Gonzales				H&C	21	3		Su 70	38
Obituaries: Gravander, Axel	Axel Gravander				H&C	11	4		Fa 60	62
Obituaries: Grayson, Edwin	Edwin Grayson				SS&D	15	1	57	Wi 83	91
Obituaries: Guermonprez-Elsesser, Trude	Trude Elsesser				SS&D	7	3	27	Su 76	66
Obituaries: Harnden, Robert	Robert Harnden				H&C	16	2		Sp 65	32
Obituaries: Henderson, Ethel M.	Ethel M. Henderson				H&C	17	3		Su 66	37
Obituaries: Hickman, Elmer	Elmer Hickman				H&C	19	4		Fa 68	31

SUBJECT	TITLE	AUTHOR	IL	INST	JOUR	VOL	NO	ISS	DATE	PAGE
Obituaries: Hill, Helen	Helen Hill				H&C	13	1		Wi 62	47
Obituaries: Hopson, The Reverend Maurice	Reverend Maurice Hopson, The				SS&D	19	1	73	Wi 87	7
Obituaries: Hotchkiss, Clifford J.	Clifford J. Hotchkiss				H&C	20	2		Sp 69	39
Obituaries: Houle, Mrs. Edmund J.	Mrs. Edmund J. Houle				H&C	20	1		Wi 69	31
Obituaries: House, Florence E.	Florence E. House				H&C	9	1		Wi 57	50
Obituaries: Hulse, Dorothea M.	Dorothea M. Hulse				H&C	14	2		Sp 63	37
Obituaries: January, Garnett	Garnett January				H&C	19	1		Wi 68	18
Obituaries: January, Marjorie	Marjorie January				SS&D	8	1	29	WI 76	60
Obituaries: Johnson, Mrs. Nellie Sargent	Death of Mrs. Johnson				H&C	2	3		Su 51	43
Obituaries: Johnson, Mrs. Seth	Mrs. Seth Johnson				H&C	21	1		Wi 70	40
Obituaries: Kao, Ruth Lee	Ruth Lee Kao				Fa	12	6		N/D 85	8
Obituaries: Karasz, Mariska	Mariska Karasz				H&C	11	4		Fa 60	62
Obituaries: Kirby, Mary	Mary Kirby				H&C	14	2		Sp 63	32
Obituaries: Langevin, Carmen	Carmen Langevin				H&C	19	1		Wi 68	29
Obituaries: Lewis, Carolyn	Carolyn Lewis		√	√	H&C	22	1		Wi 71	40
Obituaries: Lytle, Edwina	Edwina Lytle				H&C	14	2		Sp 63	46
Obituaries: Marvin, Gerald L.	Gerald L. Marvin				H&C	18	4		Fa 67	22
Obituaries: Mason, William Cary	William Cary Mason				H&C	16	2		Sp 65	32
Obituaries: Millen, Roger	Roger Millen				H&C	7	2		Sp 56	19
Obituaries: Moses, Dr. Elisabeth	Dr. Elisabeth Moses				H&C	9	2		Sp 58	47
Obituaries: Nelson, William O.	William O. Nelson				H&C	12	1		Wi 61	45
Obituaries: Pariseau, George Emory	Major George Emory Pariseau				H&C	7	4		Fa 56	44
Obituaries: Parrott, Allen	Allen Parrott				Iw	4	2		Sp 79	6
Obituaries: Pennington, Fred A.	Fred A. Pennington				H&C	19	1		Wi 68	42
Obituaries: Peters, Rupert	Rupert Peters				H&C	12	2		Sp 61	52
Obituaries: Ringler, Aina	Aina Ringler				H&C	21	2		Sp 70	40
Obituaries: Romain, Grace Waffle	Grace Waffle Romain				SS&D	19	1	73	Wi 87	7
Obituaries: Ronin, Col. James Arthur, AF, ret.	Col. James Arthur Ronin, A.F., ret.		√		Hw	2	2		Mr 81	4
Obituaries: Ronin, Colonel James Arthur, ret.	In Memoriam: Colonel James Arthur Ronin, ret.				SS&D	12	2	46	Sp 81	90
Obituaries: Ross, Marjorie Ruth	In Memory: Marjorie Ruth Ross				Hw	2	4		Se 81	23
Obituaries: Schollenberger, Maude	Maude Schollenberger				H&C	14	1		Wi 63	45
Obituaries: Shepps, Dr. Vincent	Dr. Vincent Shepps				H&C	18	4		Fa 67	32
Obituaries: Smith, Mary Alice	Mary Alice Smith — A Memorial		√		H&C	22	1		Wi 71	3
Obituaries: Snow, Edith Huntington	Edith Huntington Snow				H&C	11	2		Sp 60	52
Obituaries: Snow, Edith Huntington	Edith Huntington Snow		√		H&C	11	3		Su 60	29
Obituaries: Spenser, Elsie H.	Elsie H. Spenser				SS&D	18	4	72	Fa 87	7
Obituaries: Talbot, Mrs. Arnold G.	Mrs. Arnold G. Talbot				H&C	12	2		Sp 61	52
Obituaries: Talbot, William R.	William R. Talbot				H&C	17	4		Fa 66	31
Obituaries: Talmage, Emily Terrel	Emily Terrel Talmage				SS&D	7	1	25	Wi 75	74
Obituaries: Tate-Bousman, Lou	Lou Tate Bousman				SS&D	10	4	40	Fa 79	84
Obituaries: TerLouw, Adrian	Adrian TerLouw				SS&D	18	3	71	Su 87	17
Obituaries: Thorsen, Mrs. Elizabeth	Mrs. Elizabeth Thorsen				H&C	13	1		Wi 62	42
Obituaries: Tidball, Harriet	Harriet Tidball				H&C	20	4		Fa 69	1
Obituaries: Tod, Osma Gallinger	Osma Gallinger Tod				SS&D	14	3	55	Su 83	79
Obituaries: Uhlmann, Ilse Etta	Ilse Etta Uhlmann				H&C	14	4		Fa 63	41
Obituaries: Van Cleve, Kate	Kate Van Cleve				H&C	18	4		Fa 67	16
Obituaries: Vogel, Edna	Edna Vogel, Noted Rugweaver		√		H&C	4	3		Su 53	7

SUBJECT	TITLE	AUTHOR	IL	INST	JOUR	VOL	NO	ISS	DATE	PAGE
Obituaries: Von Weise, Wenda	Wenda Von Weise				Fa	12	1		J/F 85	24
Obituaries: Wellman, Kathryn	Kathryn Wellman				H&C	9	2		Sp 58	31
Obituaries: Weston, Joseph	Joseph Weston				H&C	14	3		Su 63	48
Obituaries: Woody, Orlando	Orlando Woody, 1914–1968		√		TMJ	2	2		De 67	40
Observation: Public Fiber	Fabric Analysis "On the Road"	Drooker, P. B.	√		CW	5	2	14	Ja 84	6
Occupational Therapy see Therapy/Rehabilitation; Disabled										
Odd Weaves	More About Fabrics: Odd Weaves	Zielinski, S. A.; Robert Leclerc, ed.	√	√	MWL	20			'51–'73	41
Odd-Shaft Weaves	Why Always Four Harnesses?		√	> 4	H&C	10	2		Sp 59	6
Odd-Shaft Weaving	Why Always Four Harnesses?		√	> 4	H&C	10	2		Sp 59	6
Off-Loom Weaving	Fingerweaving: Two Perspectives, The Historic View	Turner, Alta R.	√	√	SS&D	6	4	24	Fa 75	44
Off-Loom Weaving	Fingerweaving: Two Perspectives, The Practical Lesson	Lee, Pamela	√	√	SS&D	6	4	24	Fa 75	44
Okinawa	Banana, Ramie, and Hemp in Okinawa (error-corrected Fa v14 n3 87 p4)	Miller, Dorothy	√		Fa	14	2		M/A 87	46
Okinawa	Hanaori: An Okinawan Brocaded Textile	Miller, Dorothy	√	√	AT	1			De 83	173
Okinawa	Kumejima Dorozome: The Vegetable Dye and Mud Mordanting Process of Silk Tsugumi	Miller, Dorothy	√	√	AT	5			Ju 86	131
Ondulé	Undulating Weft Effects: The Drafts, Ondulé	Tidball, Harriet	√		SCGM		9		63	18
Onion Skins	Dyeing Gold and Yellow	Blackburn, Edna	√	√	TM			1	O/N 85	28
Openwork Techniques: Cut-Fabric Work	Practical Definitions for Three Openwork Techniques		√		TMJ	4	4		77	35
Openwork Techniques: Deflected Element Embroidery	Practical Definitions for Three Openwork Techniques		√		TMJ	4	4		77	35
Openwork Techniques: Withdrawn Element Work	Practical Definitions for Three Openwork Techniques		√		TMJ	4	4		77	35
Openwork Weaves	Designing with Loom-Woven Open Weaves	Marston, Ena	√	√	SS&D	13	1	49	Wi 81	22
Openwork Weaves	Openwork Weaves	Marston, Ena	√	√	SS&D	10	2	38	Sp 79	18
Openwork Weaves	Some Loom-Woven Open Weaves (error-corrected SS&D v13 n1 81 p4)	Marston, Ena	√	√	SS&D	12	4	48	Fa 81	32
Openwork Weaves: Continuous Weft, Eyelet, Deviation	Two-Harness Textiles, The Open Work Weaves: Continuous Weft, Slit and Eyelet Weaves, An Eyelet Deviation	Tidball, Harriet	√	√	SCGM		21		67	10
Openwork Weaves: Continuous Weft, Eyelet, Rugs	Two-Harness Textiles, The Open Work Weaves: Continuous Weft, Slit and Eyelet Weaves, Eyelet Weave for Rugs	Tidball, Harriet	√	√	SCGM		21		67	11
Openwork Weaves: Continuous Weft, Eyelet, Single Direction	Two-Harness Textiles, The Open Work Weaves: Continuous Weft, Slit and Eyelet Weaves	Tidball, Harriet			SCGM		21		67	7
Openwork Weaves: Continuous Weft, Eyelet, Spanish	Two-Harness Textiles, The Open Work Weaves: Continuous Weft, Slit and Eyelet Weaves, Two Direction Eyelet or Spanish Eyelet	Tidball, Harriet	√	√	SCGM		21		67	8
Openwork Weaves: Continuous Weft, Eyelet, Split Single Direction	Two-Harness Textiles, The Open Work Weaves: Continuous Weft, Slit and Eyelet Weaves, Split Single-Direction Eyelet	Tidball, Harriet	√	√	SCGM		21		67	8
Openwork Weaves: Continuous Weft, Eyelet, Two-Direction	Two-Harness Textiles, The Open Work Weaves: Continuous Weft, Slit and Eyelet Weaves, Two Direction Eyelet or Spanish Eyelet	Tidball, Harriet	√	√	SCGM		21		67	8
Openwork Weaves: Continuous Weft, Eyelet, Two-Direction Split	Two-Harness Textiles, The Open Work Weaves: Continuous Weft, Slit and Eyelet Weaves, Two-Direction Split Eyelet	Tidball, Harriet	√	√	SCGM		21		67	9
Openwork Weaves: Continuous Weft, Slit, Single Direction	Two-Harness Textiles, The Open Work Weaves: Continuous Weft, Slit and Eyelet Weaves, Single Direction Eyelet	Tidball, Harriet	√	√	SCGM		21		67	8

SUBJECT	TITLE	AUTHOR	IL	INST	JOUR	VOL	NO	ISS	DATE	PAGE
Openwork Weaves: Crossed-Warp Weaves, Closed-Shed Gauze	Two-Harness Textiles, The Open Work Weaves: Gauze and Leno, The Crossed-Warp Weaves, Closed-Shed Gauze, Finnish Open Work	Tidball, Harriet	√	√	SCGM		21		67	28
Openwork Weaves: Crossed-Warp Weaves, Finnish Openwork	Two-Harness Textiles, The Open Work Weaves: Gauze and Leno, The Crossed-Warp Weaves, Closed-Shed Gauze, Finnish Open Work	Tidball, Harriet	√	√	SCGM		21		67	28
Openwork Weaves: Crossed-Warp Weaves, Gauze, Alternate Tabby Band	Two-Harness Textiles, The Open Work Weaves: Gauze and Leno, The Crossed-Warp Weaves, Alternate Gauze	Tidball, Harriet	√	√	SCGM		21		67	24
Openwork Weaves: Crossed-Warp Weaves, Gauze, Chinese	Two-Harness Textiles, The Open Work Weaves: Gauze and Leno, The Crossed-Warp Weaves, Tarascan, Peruvian, or Chinese Gauze	Tidball, Harriet	√	√	SCGM		21		67	34
Openwork Weaves: Crossed-Warp Weaves, Gauze, Group-Over-Group	Two-Harness Textiles, The Open Work Weaves: Gauze and Leno, The Crossed-Warp Weaves, Group-Over-Group Gauze	Tidball, Harriet	√	√	SCGM		21		67	24
Openwork Weaves: Crossed-Warp Weaves, Gauze, One-Over-One	Two-Harness Textiles, The Open Work Weaves: Gauze and Leno, The Crossed-Warp Weaves, One-Over-One Gauze	Tidball, Harriet	√	√	SCGM		21		67	21
Openwork Weaves: Crossed-Warp Weaves, Gauze, Peruvian	Two-Harness Textiles, The Open Work Weaves: Gauze and Leno, The Crossed-Warp Weaves, Tarascan, Peruvian, or Chinese Gauze	Tidball, Harriet	√	√	SCGM		21		67	34
Openwork Weaves: Crossed-Warp Weaves, Gauze, Tarascan	Two-Harness Textiles, The Open Work Weaves: Gauze and Leno, The Crossed-Warp Weaves, Tarascan, Peruvian, or Chinese Gauze	Tidball, Harriet	√	√	SCGM		21		67	34
Openwork Weaves: Crossed-Warp Weaves, Gauze, Two-Over-Two	Two-Harness Textiles, The Open Work Weaves: Gauze and Leno, The Crossed-Warp Weaves, Two-Over-Two Gauze	Tidball, Harriet	√	√	SCGM		21		67	23
Openwork Weaves: Crossed-Warp Weaves, Gauze, Two-Over-Two Split	Two-Harness Textiles, The Open Work Weaves: Gauze and Leno, The Crossed-Warp Weaves, Two-Over-Two Split Gauze	Tidball, Harriet	√	√	SCGM		21		67	23
Openwork Weaves: Crossed-Warp Weaves, Left and Right Gauze	Two-Harness Textiles, The Open Work Weaves: Gauze and Leno, The Crossed-Warp Weaves, Left-and-Right Gauze	Tidball, Harriet	√	√	SCGM		21		67	26
Openwork Weaves: Crossed-Warp Weaves, Left-Handed Gauze	Two-Harness Textiles, The Open Work Weaves: Gauze and Leno, The Crossed-Warp Weaves, Left-Handed Gauze	Tidball, Harriet	√	√	SCGM		21		67	25
Openwork Weaves: Crossed-Warp Weaves, Leno, Double-Weft	Two-Harness Textiles, The Open Work Weaves: Gauze and Leno, The Crossed-Warp Weaves, Double-Weft Leno	Tidball, Harriet	√	√	SCGM		21		67	32
Openwork Weaves: Crossed-Warp Weaves, Leno, Greek	Two-Harness Textiles, The Open Work Weaves: Gauze and Leno, The Crossed-Warp Weaves, Greek Leno	Tidball, Harriet	√	√	SCGM		21		67	33
Openwork Weaves: Crossed-Warp Weaves, Leno, Simple	Two-Harness Textiles, The Open Work Weaves: Gauze and Leno, The Crossed-Warp Weaves, Simple Leno	Tidball, Harriet	√	√	SCGM		21		67	29
Openwork Weaves: Crossed-Warp Weaves, One-Over-Two Gauze	Two-Harness Textiles, The Open Work Weaves: Gauze and Leno, The Crossed-Warp Weaves, One-Over-Two Gauze	Tidball, Harriet	√	√	SCGM		21		67	27
Openwork Weaves: Crossed-Warp Weaves, Two-Over-Four Gauze	Two-Harness Textiles, The Open Work Weaves: Gauze and Leno, The Crossed-Warp Weaves, Two-Over-Four Gauze	Tidball, Harriet	√	√	SCGM		21		67	27
Openwork Weaves: Extra-Weft Wrap, Techniques	Weft Wrap Openwork	Atwood, Betty	√	√	lw	4	1		Wi 78	20
Openwork Weaves: Floor Coverings: Rugs, Eyelet	Two-Harness Textiles, The Open Work Weaves: Continuous Weft, Slit and Eyelet Weaves, Eyelet Weave for Rugs	Tidball, Harriet	√	√	SCGM		21		67	11

SUBJECT	TITLE	AUTHOR	IL	INST	JOUR	VOL	NO	ISS	DATE	PAGE
Openwork Weaves: Interrupted Weft, Connected Slits	Two-Harness Textiles, The Open Work Weaves: Interrupted Weft, Slit and Eyelet Weaves: Connected Slits	Tidball, Harriet			SCGM		21		67	6
Openwork Weaves: Interrupted Weft, Dema-Desh	Two-Harness Textiles, The Open Work Weaves: Interrupted Weft, Slit and Eyelet Weaves: Dema-Desh	Tidball, Harriet			SCGM		21		67	6
Openwork Weaves: Interrupted Weft, Kelim	Two-Harness Textiles, The Open Work Weaves: Interrupted Weft, Slit and Eyelet Weaves: Kelim	Tidball, Harriet	√	√	SCGM		21		67	5
Openwork Weaves: Interrupted Weft, Peruvian Lattice	Two-Harness Textiles, The Open Work Weaves: Interrupted Weft, Slit and Eyelet Weaves: Peruvian Open Work	Tidball, Harriet			SCGM		21		67	6
Openwork Weaves: Interrupted Weft, Peruvian Lattice	Two-Harness Textiles, The Open Work Weaves: Interrupted Weft, Slit and Eyelet Weaves: Peruvian Lattice	Tidball, Harriet	√	√	SCGM		21		67	6
Openwork Weaves: Interrupted Weft, Slits	Two-Harness Textiles, The Open Work Weaves: Interrupted Weft, Slit and Eyelet Weaves: Slits	Tidball, Harriet	√	√	SCGM		21		67	5
Openwork Weaves: Interrupted Weft, Tapestry, Slit	Two-Harness Textiles, The Open Work Weaves: Interrupted Weft, Slit and Eyelet Weaves: Slit Tapestry	Tidball, Harriet	√	√	SCGM		21		67	5
Openwork Weaves: Interrupted Weft, Triangular Slits	Two-Harness Textiles, The Open Work Weaves: Interrupted Weft, Slit and Eyelet Weaves: Triangular Slits	Tidball, Harriet	√	√	SCGM		21		67	6
Openwork Weaves: Two-Shaft	Two-Harness Textiles, The Open Work Weaves	Tidball, Harriet	√	√	SCGM		21		67	1-34
Openwork Weaves: Warp and Weft Bouquets, Closed-Shed	Two-Harness Textiles, The Open Work Weaves: Closed-Shed Bouquets, Warp and Weft Closed-Shed Bouquets	Tidball, Harriet	√	√	SCGM		21		67	16
Openwork Weaves: Warp Bouquets, Brooks	Two-Harness Textiles, The Open Work Weaves: Warp Bouquets, Brooks Bouquet, An Open-Shed Bouquet	Tidball, Harriet	√	√	SCGM		21		67	13
Openwork Weaves: Warp Bouquets, Closed-Shed	Two-Harness Textiles, The Open Work Weaves: Closed-Shed Bouquets, Closed-Shed Warp Bouquet	Tidball, Harriet	√	√	SCGM		21		67	16
Openwork Weaves: Warp Bouquets, Closed-Shed, Brooks	Two-Harness Textiles, The Open Work Weaves: Closed-Shed Bouquets, Closed-Shed "Brooks" Bouquet	Tidball, Harriet	√	√	SCGM		21		67	16
Openwork Weaves: Warp Bouquets, Closed-Shed, Diagonal	Two-Harness Textiles, The Open Work Weaves: Closed-Shed Bouquets, Diagonal Closed-Shed Bouquet	Tidball, Harriet	√	√	SCGM		21		67	16
Openwork Weaves: Warp Bouquets, Open-Shed, Diagonal	Two-Harness Textiles, The Open Work Weaves: Warp Bouquets, Diagonal Open-Shed Bouquets	Tidball, Harriet	√	√	SCGM		21		67	15
Openwork Weaves: Warp Bouquets, Open-Shed, Large	Two-Harness Textiles, The Open Work Weaves: Warp Bouquets, Large Open-Shed Bouquets	Tidball, Harriet	√	√	SCGM		21		67	15
Openwork Weaves: Warp Bouquets, Staggered	Two-Harness Textiles, The Open Work Weaves: Warp Bouquets, Staggered Bouquets	Tidball, Harriet	√	√	SCGM		21		67	14
Openwork Weaves: Warp Bouquets, Variations	Two-Harness Textiles, The Open Work Weaves: Warp Bouquets, Bouquet Variations	Tidball, Harriet	√	√	SCGM		21		67	15
Openwork Weaves: Warp Tension	Two-Harness Textiles, The Open Work Weaves: Tensions	Tidball, Harriet	√	√	SCGM		21		67	4
Openwork Weaves: Weft Bouquets, Medallion, Danish	Two-Harness Textiles, The Open Work Weaves: Weft Bouquets, Danish Medallion	Tidball, Harriet	√	√	SCGM		21		67	17
Openwork Weaves: Weft Bouquets, Medallion, Spaced-Warp	Two-Harness Textiles, The Open Work Weaves: Weft Bouquets, Spaced-Warp Medallion	Tidball, Harriet	√	√	SCGM		21		67	19
Openwork Weaves: Weft Bouquets, Medallion, Stitch	Two-Harness Textiles, The Open Work Weaves: Weft Bouquets, Medallion Stitch	Tidball, Harriet	√	√	SCGM		21		67	19
Openwork Weaves: Wrapped Warps, Continuous-Weft	Two-Harness Textiles, The Open Work Weaves: Wrapped Warps, Continuous-Weft Wrapping	Tidball, Harriet	√	√	SCGM		21		67	12

SUBJECT	TITLE	AUTHOR	IL	INST	JOUR	VOL	NO	ISS	DATE	PAGE
Openwork Weaves: Wrapped Warps, Independent	Two-Harness Textiles, The Open Work Weaves: Wrapped Warps, Independent Warp Wrappings	Tidball, Harriet	√	√	SCGM		21		67	12
Openwork, Weft-Wrapped	Weft-Wrap Openwork Technique	Atwood, Betty	√	√	AT	3			My 85	65
Openwork, Weft-Wrapped	Weft-Wrap Openwork Techniques in Archaeological and Contemporary Textiles of Mexico	Johnson, Irmgard Weitlaner	√	√	TMJ	4	3		76	63
Openwork, Wrapped	Textile Remains from a Late Temple in Egyptian Nubia	Adams, Nettie K.	√		AT	8			De 87	85
Opphämta	In Pursuit of Plakhta	Golay, Myrna	√	>4	WJ	11	3	43	Wi 87	34
Opphämta	Upphämta Display Towel		√	>4	Hw	8	3		M/J 87	42
Opposites	Unharnessing the Summer and Winter Weave	Xenakis, Athanasios David	√		Iw	4	4		Fa 79	42
Opposites	Whig Rose Study (continued)	Morgenstern, Marvin M.	√	√	WJ	7	3	27	Wi 82	23
Opposites, Two-Block, Surface Interest	Surface Interest — Textiles of Today: Surface Interest Designs with Drafts, Group 3, Two-Surface Designs	Tidball, Harriet	√	>4	SCGM		2		61	13
Optical Art	Counterchange, A Device for Pattern Design	Justema, William	√		H&C	19	3		Su 68	8
Optical Art	Counterchange & New Color	Sonday, Milton	√		H&C	20	3		Su 69	23
Optical Art	Experiments in Design by an Ohio Weaver		√		H&C	17	3		Su 66	22
Optical Art	Fun with Optical Art		√	>4	H&C	17	1		Wi 66	23
Optical Art	Manipulated Warps or Having Fun with Controlled Distortion	Foster, Robert	√		H&C	16	2		Sp 65	12
Oregano	Dyes from the Herb Garden	King, Helen	√	√	TM			6	A/S 86	58
Organization	Organization Lets Creativity Flow	Shurtleff, Chris Ann	√		Hw	7	5		N/D 86	74
Organizations	National Standards Council of American Embroiderers	Waxler, Dorothy V.	√		Fa	9	3		M/J 82	56
Organizations	Women in Design International				Fa	9	4		J/A 82	48
Organizations: American Tapestry Alliance	American Tapestry Alliance, The	Rolingson, Beth	√		WJ	12	1	45	Su 87	32
Organizations: American Tapestry Alliance	Contemporary Tapestry: A Panoramic View (error-corrected SS&D v17 n3 86 p5)	Harvey, Nancy	√		SS&D	17	2	66	Sp 86	18
Organizations: Apprenticeship	National Council for Apprenticeship in Art and Craft				Fa	8	4		J/A 81	25
Organizations: Canada Council	Canada Council Art Bank, The	Kirby, William	√		AT	7			Ju 87	75
Organizations: Center for the History of American Needlework	C.H.A.N. for Short: The Story of Rachel Maines	Alonso, Harriet	√		Fa	8	3		M/J 81	13
Organizations: Complex Weavers	Complex Weavers: A History of the Group, The	Best, Eleanor	√		SS&D	12	2	46	Sp 81	19
Organizations: Domestic Premium-Wool Industry	Fuzzy Politics of Wool, The	Parker, Ron	√		TM			13	O/N 87	20
Organizations: Honorable Cordwainers' Company	Old Shoes Keeping Honourable Company	Clausen, Valerie	√		TM			11	J/J 87	16
Organizations: International Llama Association	Llama Wool	Smith, Carolyn	√	√	S-O	11	2		Su 87	32
Organizations: Lace	Postal Service Celebrates Lace		√		TM			12	A/S 87	22
Organizations: Mohair Council of America	Mohair Council of America				S-O	7	3		Fa 83	60
Organizations: Northwest Regional Spinners Association	Northwest Spinners: Success for Them, A Challenge for You	Molinari, Jean			S-O	11	2		Su 87	50
Organizations: Ramah Navajo Weavers	Ramah Navajo Weavers, The	D'Andrea, Pat	√		WJ	12	1	45	Su 87	44
Organizations: Salish Weavers	Salish Ladies	Froese, Louise	√		SS&D	3	2	10	Sp 72	13
Organizations: Spinning	Northwest Regional Spinning Association	Klinect, Ann W.			S-O	7	2		Su 83	8
Organizations: Tapestry West	Things to Come — Tapestry West				SS&D	1	4	4	Se 70	7
Organizations: The Complex Weavers	Complex Weavers, The				Fa	9	2		M/A 82	56
Organizations: Washington Hajji Baba Club	Washington Hajji Baba, The	Jones, H. McCoy	√		TMJ	2	2		De 67	35
Organizations: Wool Forum	Wool Forum: Growing and Working	Parker, Ron			S-O	11	2		Su 87	18

SUBJECT	TITLE	AUTHOR	IL	INST	JOUR	VOL	NO	ISS	DATE	PAGE
Organizations: World Craft Council	World Crafts Council		√		H&C	15	3		Su 64	22
Origami	Champion Promotion, A		√	√	Fa	14	1		J/F 87	7
Origami	Making Paper Cranes: A Hawaiian Wedding Ritual	Nakamura, Ann K.	√	√	Fa	13	6		N/D 86	9
Ornamentation see Embellishment										
Ottoman Turkish Textiles	Ottoman Turkish Textiles	Denny, Walter B.	√		TMJ	3	3		De 72	55
Outlining: Weaving	Peru, Textiles Unlimited, Part 2: Outlined Warp-Pattern Pick-Up	Tidball, Harriet	√	> 4	SCGM		26		69	24
Outlining: Weaving	Peru, Textiles Unlimited, Part 2: Supplementary Warp and Weft Outlines	Tidball, Harriet	√	> 4	SCGM		26		69	16
Overalls	OshKosh B'Gosh	Rudich, Sally	√		Fa	13	5		S/O 86	16
Overshot	All White Overshot Rug (error-corrected WJ v7 n1 82 p36b)	Kendahl, Connie	√	√	WJ	6	4	24	Sp 82	23
Overshot	And for Dessert				PWC	3	4	10		7
Overshot	Arabesque	Herring, Connie	√	√	PWC	3	1	7		47
Overshot	Blouse for Her — A Shirt for Him, A		√	√	WJ	4	3	15	Ja 80	4
Overshot	Bound Weave Rugs	Harrold, Yoko Tamari	√	√	WJ	2	1	5	Jy 77	20
Overshot	Boundweave Rug on an Overshot Threading	Kindahl, Connie	√	√	SS&D	17	3	67	Su 86	58
Overshot	Checkerboard Plaid		√	√	Hw	4	5		N/D 83	44
Overshot	Christmas Card, A		√	> 4	WJ	2	2	6	Oc 77	32
Overshot	Colonial Overshot, "Trompt as Writ"	Liebler, Barbara	√	√	Iw	1	2		Wi 76	14
Overshot	Computer Generated Overshot Variations	Velderman, Pat	√		H&C	22	4		Fa 71	10
Overshot	Contemporary Approach to Traditional Weaves: Overshot	Zielinski, S. A.; Robert Leclerc, ed.	√	√	MWL	7			'51–'73	9
Overshot	Contemporary Coverlet (Kathryn Wertenberger)		√	√	Hw	2	1		F-W 80	47, 70
Overshot	Contemporary Overshot Afghan (Lee-lee Schlegel)		√	√	Hw	3	3		My 82	29, 89
Overshot	Coverlet for Convergence 1988, A		√	√	SS&D	19	1	73	Wi 87	46
Overshot	Coverlet from Start to Finish, A	van der Hoogt, Madelyn	√	√	PWC	5	1	15		20
Overshot	Coverlet Weaves on a Rigid-Heddle (David Xenakis)		√	√	Hw	2	1		F-W 80	38
Overshot	Designing Rugs for Harness-Controlled Weaving		√	> 4	WJ	4	4	16	Ap 80	27
Overshot	Designs for Today from Great-Grandmother's Drafts	Riswold, Margaret	√	√	H&C	3	3		Su 52	20
Overshot	Different BUT Related	Smith, Dorothy N.	√	√	WJ	7	1	25	Su 82	32
Overshot	Display Towel (Carol Strickler)		√	> 4	Hw	8	3		M/J 87	43, I-4
Overshot	Double Corduroy Rug (error-corrected WJ v11 n3 87 p78)	Waggoner, Phyllis	√	√	WJ	11	2	42	Fa 86	42
Overshot	Dyed Cotton Rug in Overshot	Wright, Gilbert	√	√	WJ	7	4	28	Sp 83	81
Overshot	Fashion Show of Handwoven Garments		√	> 4	TMJ	3	3	11	Ja 79	5
Overshot	Fifty Years As a Coverlet Weaver	Bright, Harriett H.	√	√	WJ	6	2	22	Fa 81	54
Overshot	Figures in Boundweave	Waggoner, Phyllis	√	√	WJ	10	2	38	Fa 85	58
Overshot	Flamepoint Rugs for Everybody	Kirk, Betty Burian	√	√	WJ	8	4	32	Sp 84	12
Overshot	Four Place Mats (error-corrected WJ v6 n1 81 p28d)	Unger, Mary	√	√	WJ	5	2	18	Fa 80	52
Overshot	Free and Casual Look Wool Jacket, The	McGalliard, Lorraine	√	√	WJ	6	3	23	Wi 81	8
Overshot	Garments Made from Simple Patterns: Two Tabards		√	> 4	WJ	2	3	7	Ja 78	35
Overshot	Hand Woven Garments	Piper, Aris	√	> 4	WJ	5	3	19	Wi 81	24
Overshot	Handweaver's Instruction Manual: The Overshot Weave	Tidball, Harriet C. nee Douglas			SCGM		34		49	24
Overshot	Handweaver's Instruction Manual: The Overshot Weave, Weaving Overshot	Tidball, Harriet C. nee Douglas	√	√	SCGM		34		49	24
Overshot	Handwoven Flight Bags	Dickey, Helen F.	√	√	H&C	11	3		Su 60	46
Overshot	Heritage Project: Quilted Vest, A	King, Lorna J.	√	√	WJ	4	3	15	Ja 80	28

SUBJECT	TITLE	AUTHOR	IL	INST	JOUR	VOL	NO	ISS	DATE	PAGE
Overshot	Home Weaving: It's the Little Things that Count		√	√	Hw	1	1		F-W 79	38
Overshot	How One Weave Leads to Another	Barrett, Clotilde	√	>4	WJ	8	1	29	Su 83	75
Overshot	Isolated Overshot: Linen and Cotton Teacloth	Xenakis, Athanasios David	√	>4	PWC	3	2	8		36
Overshot	Isolated Overshot: Razzle-dazzle Placemats	Xenakis, Athanasios David	√	>4	PWC	3	2	8		40
Overshot	Keep Warm! Log Carriers	Champion, Ellen	√	√	WJ	5	2	18	Fa 80	6
Overshot	Lee's Surrender — to Sachets	Xenakis, Alexis Yiorgos	√	√	Hw	1	2		S-S 80	18
Overshot	Linen Kitchen Towel (Col. James Ronin) (error-corrected Hw v2 n1 80 p4)		√	√	Hw	1	2		S-S 80	27, 53
Overshot	Linen Placemats (Peg Templeton)		√	√	Hw	5	1		J/F 84	62, 107
Overshot	Lining the Overshot	Moes, Dini	√	√	SS&D	13	4	52	Fa 82	64
Overshot	Long Table Runners (Carol Klippenstein)		√	√	Hw	1	1		F-W 79	32, 59
Overshot	Luxury of Silk, The		√	√	Hw	1	2		S-S 80	28
Overshot	Merry Christmas—A Name Draft	Bliven, Jeanette; Norma Smayda	√	√	Hw	4	4		S/O 83	74
Overshot	Miniatures Adapted from Colonial Patterns	Gibbs, Emily	√	√	H&C	8	2		Sp 57	26
Overshot	Mitered Corners	Sullivan, Donna	√	>4	SS&D	15	3	59	Su 84	82
Overshot	Mitered Corners for Identical Warp and Weft Patterns	Redfield, Gail M.	√	√	H&C	14	3		Su 63	21
Overshot	Monk's Belt and Ways to Think of Blocks		√	>4	Hw	8	5		N/D 87	57
Overshot	Monk's Belt Bedspread (Anne Bliss)		√	√	Hw	3	2		Mr 82	56, 87
Overshot	Mood Lamp	Richards, Iris	√	√	WJ	3	2	10	Oc 78	44
Overshot	Multiple Harness Weaving Course Part 4: Twill Derivatives (cont'd)	Searles, Nancy M.	√	>4	WJ	5	2	18	Fa 80	19
Overshot	Name Draft (error-corrected WJ v8 n3 83 p68)		√	√	WJ	8	2	30	Fa 83	40
Overshot	Name Drafting	Mitchell, Peter	√	√	Hw	3	2		Mr 82	34
Overshot	New HGA Name Draft: Miniature Coverlet in Overshot, A	Marston, Ena	√	√	SS&D	12	3	47	Su 81	12
Overshot	Nineteenth Century Miniatures	Erf, Mary Elva Congleton	√	√	SS&D	16	1	61	Wi 84	60
Overshot	Norse Kjøkken	Rowley, Elaine	√	√	PWC	3	1	7		16
Overshot	Organize to Control Your Color	Templeton, Peg	√	√	Hw	2	4		Se 81	48
Overshot	Overshot	Liebler, Barbara	√	√	Hw	2	1		F-W 80	44
Overshot	Overshot Borders for Four Sides, Variations in Pattern and Plain Weave	Aldrich, Mae D.	√	>4	H&C	15	2		Sp 64	15
Overshot	Overshot: Contemporary Applications		√		Iw	1	3		Sp 76	14
Overshot	Overshot Derived from 2/2 Twill	Xenakis, Athanasios David	√	√	PWC	3	2	8		7
Overshot	Overshot Derived from 2/2 Twill: Apricot Accents	Lyon, Linda	√	√	PWC	3	2	8		21
Overshot	Overshot Derived from 2/2 Twill: Joanne's Runner	Christensen, Joanne	√	√	PWC	3	2	8		24
Overshot	Overshot Derived from 2/2 Twill: Ornamental Throw Rug in Overshot	Davidsohn, Marty	√	√	PWC	3	2	8		22
Overshot	Overshot Gamp, An	Strickler, Carol	√	√	Iw	3	2		Wi 78	35
Overshot	Overshot Part 2	Xenakis, Alexis Yiorgos			PWC	3	3	9		6
Overshot	Overshot Patterns	Marston, Ena	√	√	SS&D	4	2	14	Sp 73	20
Overshot	Overshot Patterns: Emphasis on Miniatures	Marston, Ena	√	√	SS&D	11	1	41	Wi 79	40
Overshot	Overshot Pillow (Sue Ellison)		√	√	Hw	1	1		F-W 79	36, 60
Overshot	Overshot Plaid		√	√	Hw	4	5		N/D 83	45
Overshot	Overshot: Rose Fashion	Liebler, Barbara	√	√	Iw	1	3		Sp 76	16
Overshot	Overshot Runner with Border (Lip Eppinger) (error-corrected Hw v5 n1 83 p88)		√	√	Hw	4	4		S/O 83	83, 109

SUBJECT	TITLE	AUTHOR	IL	INST	JOUR	VOL	NO	ISS	DATE	PAGE
Overshot	Overshot Sampler Bedspread for a Narrow Loom, An	Keasbey, Doramay	√	√	PWC	5	1	15		42
Overshot	Overshot: The Weave and the Designs	Marston, Ena	√	>4	SS&D	11	2	42	Sp 80	74
Overshot	Overshot Today, Updating a Tradition		√		Hw	4	1		J/F 83	55
Overshot	Overshot Treadling Sampler	Strickler, Carol	√	√	lw	3	3		Sp 78	45
Overshot	Overshot Upholstery (Sharon Alderman) (error-corrected Hw v3 n3 82 p87)		√	√	Hw	3	1		Ja 82	69, 82
Overshot	Pattern and Structure in Handwoven Fabrics	Frey, Berta	√	√	H&C	6	4		Fa 55	4
Overshot	Peter Stauffer — Early 19th Century Weaver	Rogers, Grace L.	√	>4	H&C	7	1		Wi 55	12
Overshot	Placemats	DeRoy, Paul	√	>4	WJ	1	3	3	Ja 77	4
Overshot	Planning for Threading and Treadling	Wertenberger, Kathryn	√	√	Hw	2	2		Mr 81	47
Overshot	Primary Patterns	Spoering, Kathy	√	√	WJ	9	1	33	Su 84	53
Overshot	Project by Guild Members		√	√	WJ	5	3	19	Wi 81	17
Overshot	Rag Rugs on Overshot Threading	Snover, Susan	√	√	WJ	5	4	20	Sp 81	22
Overshot	Rugs Woven on Summer and Winter Threading		√	>4	WJ	3	1	9	Jy 78	12
Overshot	Rustic Roundel	Lyon, Linda; Athanasios David Xenakis	√	>4	PWC	3	1	7		36
Overshot	Sarah Fowler's Book of Drafts, Part 1	North, Lois	√	>4	SS&D	6	1	21	Wi 74	8
Overshot	Sarah Fowler's Book of Drafts, Part 2		√	>4	SS&D	6	2	22	Sp 75	78
Overshot	Scented Sachets	Xenakis, Alexis Yiorgos	√	>4	PWC	3	2	8		56
Overshot	Shadow Weave	Evans, Jane	√	√	SS&D	15	4	60	Fa 84	57
Overshot	Skirt for the Wall, A		√	√	WJ	3	4	12	Ap 79	19
Overshot	Some Interpretations of Compass and Double Square		√	>4	H&C	4	4		Fa 53	18
Overshot	Stars, Diamonds, Tables, and Sunrise: Motifs and Structures of Woven Coverlets	Cabeen, Lou	√	√	TM			14	D/J 87	32
Overshot	Stars & Roses or Designing and Drafting Overshot	Marston, Ena	√	√	SS&D	4	3	15	Su 73	27
Overshot	Stitching Traditional Coverlet Weaves	Sellin, Helen G.	√	>4	AT	1			De 83	289
Overshot	Story of a Piece of Weaving		√	√	SS&D	6	1	21	Wi 74	85
Overshot	Swivel Variations for Four Harness Looms	James, Ona	√	√	H&C	14	4		Fa 63	11
Overshot	Tablecloth and Runner Decorated with Overshot and Pick-Up Leno		√	√	WJ	6	1	21	Su 81	10
Overshot	Tea Cozy, Mats and Napkins (Margaretha Essén-Hedin)		√	>4	Hw	4	3		M/J 83	41, 93
Overshot	Theme and Variations	Bress, Helene	√	√	Hw	6	2		M/A 85	62
Overshot	Traditional Coverlet (Marge Rohrer) (error-corrected Hw v2 n2 81 p68)		√	√	Hw	2	1		F-W 80	46, 73
Overshot	Treasury for Beginners: Overshot	Zielinski, S. A.; Robert Leclerc, ed.	√	√	MWL	1			'51–'73	100
Overshot	Variation of the Macedonian Shirt	West, Virginia	√	√	WJ	7	2	26	Fa 82	50
Overshot	Variations in the Honeysuckle Design	Frey, Berta	√	>4	H&C	1	3		Fa 50	26
Overshot	Variations on Whig Rose	Kaiser, Eunice Gifford	√	√	H&C	14	1		Wi 63	17
Overshot	Ways to Weave Overshot: Part 1	Marston, Ena	√	√	SS&D	11	3	43	Su 80	6
Overshot	Ways to Weave Overshot: Part 2	Marston, Ena	√	√	SS&D	12	1	45	Wi 80	36
Overshot	Ways to Weave Overshot: Part 3	Marston, Ena	√	√	SS&D	12	2	46	Sp 81	6
Overshot	Weaving As Drawn In—Classic Style, Part 1	Keasbey, Doramay	√	√	SS&D	17	1	65	Wi 85	28
Overshot	Weaving with Tabby: An Introduction to Overshot	Pettigrew, Dale	√	√	Hw	3	5		N/D 82	62
Overshot	White Coverlet (Carol Strickler)		√	√	Hw	3	5		N/D 82	49, 93
Overshot	White Shawl (Dale Pettigrew) (error-corrected Hw v4 n2 83 p80)		√	√	Hw	4	1		J/F 83	55, 90
Overshot	Why Explore Overshot?	Rupp, Michael E.			SS&D	7	2	26	Sp 76	66

SUBJECT	TITLE	AUTHOR	IL	INST	JOUR	VOL	NO	ISS	DATE	PAGE
Overshot	Windows: Kouverta	Xenaxis, Alexis Yiorgos	√	√	PWC	5	1	15		14
Overshot	Woven and Other Textile Miniatures (error-corrected WJ v2 n1 77 insert for vol. 1)		√	√	WJ	1	4	4	Ap 77	16
Overshot	Woven Miniatures		√	√	WJ	3	4	12	Ap 79	15
Overshot: 2-Tie, Double	Change of Heart and Other Progressive Ideas, A	Carey, Joyce Marquess	√	>4	PWC	3	3	9		18
Overshot: 2-Tie, Double	Floor's the Limit, The	Xenakis, Athanasios David	√	>4	PWC	3	3	9		12
Overshot: 2-Tie, Double	Handwoven American Coverlets of the Overshot Type	Carey, Joyce Marquess	√	>4	PWC	3	3	9		24
Overshot: 4-Shaft, Six-Block	Composition and Designing: Small Patterns	Zielinski, S. A.; Robert Leclerc, ed.	√	√	MWL	18			'51–'73	67
Overshot: 4-Shaft, Six-Block	Contemporary Approach to Traditional Weaves: 6-Block Overshot on Four Shafts	Zielinski, S. A.; Robert Leclerc, ed.	√	√	MWL	7			'51–'73	39
Overshot: 4-Shaft, Six-Block, Patterns	Contemporary Approach to Traditional Weaves: Patterns in 6-Block Overshot	Zielinski, S. A.; Robert Leclerc, ed.	√	√	MWL	7			'51–'73	46
Overshot: 4-Shaft, Twelve-Block	Contemporary Approach to Traditional Weaves: 12-Block Crackle and Overshot	Zielinski, S. A.; Robert Leclerc, ed.	√	√	MWL	7			'51–'73	75
Overshot: 6-Shaft	Contemporary Approach to Traditional Weaves: 6-Shaft Overshot	Zielinski, S. A.; Robert Leclerc, ed.	√	>4	MWL	7			'51–'73	60
Overshot: Adapting Patterns	Notebook: Adapting Large Overshot Patterns	Meyers, Ruth Nordquist,ed.	√	>4	SS&D	14	4	56	Fa 83	16
Overshot: Bound	Bound Overshot	Xenakis, Athanasios David	√	√	PWC	3	3	9		21
Overshot: Coded	Contemporary Approach to Traditional Weaves: Code in Overshot	Zielinski, S. A.; Robert Leclerc, ed.	√	√	MWL	7			'51–'73	83
Overshot: Creative	Creative Overshot	Windeknecht, Margaret B.	√	>4	SCGM		31		78	1-57
Overshot: Creative	Creative Overshot: Begin With A Line	Windeknecht, Margaret B.	√	√	SCGM		31		78	22
Overshot: Double Design	Freeform Design Technique	Searles, Nancy	√	>4	PWC	3	4	10		18
Overshot: Even-Tied	Blooming Leaf	Xenakis, Athanasios David	√	√	PWC	3	3	9		51
Overshot: Even-Tied	Even-Tied Overshot	Xenakis, Athanasios David	√	>4	PWC	3	3	9		40
Overshot: Even-Tied	Even-Tied Overshot on a Rigid Heddle Loom	Xenakis, Athanasios David	√	√	PWC	3	3	9		46
Overshot: Even-Tied	Even-Tied Overshot on Four Shafts with Shaft Switching	Herring, Connie; Athanasios David Xenakis	√	√	PWC	3	3	9		44
Overshot: Even-Tied	Quatrefoil	Xenakis, Athanasios David	√	√	PWC	3	3	9		53
Overshot: Even-Tied	Star and Diamond	Xenakis, Athanasios David	√	√	PWC	3	3	9		49
Overshot: Even-Tied	White on White	Lyon, Linda	√	√	PWC	3	3	9		60
Overshot: Expanded Twill	Creative Overshot: Expand a Twill	Windeknecht, Margaret B.	√	√	SCGM		31		78	15
Overshot: Experimental	Multi-Harness Overshot "Trials"	Deygout, Françoise	√	>4	CW		24		My 87	3
Overshot: Flamepoint	Carpet Bag Briefcase (Linda Ligon)		√	√	Hw	5	1		J/F 84	49, 91
Overshot: Floats of Six	Contemporary Approach to Traditional Weaves: Overshot with Floats of Six	Zielinski, S. A.; Robert Leclerc, ed.	√	√	MWL	7			'51–'73	56
Overshot: Honeysuckle	Variations on an Overshot Threading	Lermond, Charles	√	√	WJ	12	2	46	Fa 87	25
Overshot: Inlay	Creative Overshot: Laid-In Overshot	Windeknecht, Margaret B.	√	√	SCGM		31		78	52
Overshot: Inlay	Holiday Cheer (Janice Jones)		√	√	Hw	4	4		S/O 83	71
Overshot: Inlay	Isolated Overshot: Inlaid Runner	Xenakis, Athanasios David	√	√	PWC	3	2	8		31
Overshot: Introduction	Creative Overshot: Introduction	Windeknecht, Margaret B.	√		SCGM		31		78	10
Overshot: Locked Wefts	Resist Dyeing, Curiosities and Inventions: Locked Wefts in Pattern Weaves	Zielinski, S. A.; Robert Leclerc, ed.	√	√	MWL	17			'51–'73	60
Overshot: Miniature	Miniature World, A	Piroch, Sigrid	√	>4	PWC	5	2	16		26
Overshot: Miniature	Traditional Teddy: Overshot in Miniature	Sullivan, Donna	√	√	PWC	5	2	16		14

SUBJECT	TITLE	AUTHOR	IL	INST	JOUR	VOL	NO	ISS	DATE	PAGE
Overshot: Miniature	Weaving Towels As a Means of Learning the Basic Four-Shaft Weaves	Barrett, Clotilde	√	√	WJ	8	2	30	Fa 83	11
Overshot: Miniaturized, "Petit Point"	Petit Point Glasses Case (Janice Jones)		√	√	Hw	7	1		J/F 86	66, I-12
Overshot: Modern	Contemporary Approach to Traditional Weaves: Modern Overshot	Zielinski, S. A.; Robert Leclerc, ed.	√	√	MWL	7			'51–'73	17
Overshot: Modern	Modern Overshot (Frappé Moderne)	Collard, Agathe G.	√	√	WJ	5	4	20	Sp 81	28
Overshot: Multishaft	Contemporary Approach to Traditional Weaves: Multishaft Overshot	Zielinski, S. A.; Robert Leclerc, ed.	√	> 4	MWL	7			'51–'73	53
Overshot: Multishaft	Contemporary Approach to Traditional Weaves: Overshot Drafts on 8 Frames	Zielinski, S. A.; Robert Leclerc, ed.	√	> 4	MWL	7			'51–'73	23
Overshot: Multishaft	Creative Overshot: Eight-Harness Overshot	Windeknecht, Margaret B.	√	> 4	SCGM		31		78	54
Overshot: No tabby	Hand Woven Rugs: Weaves, Four-Harness Overshot, No-Tabby Technique	Atwater, Mary Meigs	√	√	SCGM		29		48	15
Overshot: On Opposites	Eight-Shaft Overshot on Opposites	van der Hoogt, Madelyn; Margaret Heller	√	> 4	PWC	4	4	14		34
Overshot: On Opposites	Overshot on Opposites	Xenakis, Athanasios David	√	√	PWC	3	2	8		26
Overshot: On Opposites	Overshot on Opposites: Linen Hand Towels	Xenakis, Athanasios David	√	√	PWC	3	2	8		29
Overshot: Opposites	Bags with Strong Handles	Foeley, Cora V.	√		H&C	16	2		Sp 65	33
Overshot: Opposites	Blanket Weave, The	Robitaille, Annette	√	> 4	WJ	8	4	32	Sp 84	62
Overshot: Opposites	Contemporary Approach to Traditional Weaves: Overshot on Opposites	Zielinski, S. A.; Robert Leclerc, ed.	√	√	MWL	7			'51–'73	25
Overshot: Opposites	Keep Warm! Colonial Comfort	Commings, Nancy	√	√	WJ	5	2	18	Fa 80	8
Overshot: Opposites	Monk's Belt	Moes, Dini	√	√	SS&D	18	4	72	Fa 87	52
Overshot: Opposites	Multishaft Overshot on Opposites	van der Hoogt, Madelyn	√	> 4	WJ	8	3	31	Wi 83	76
Overshot: Opposites	Variations on an Overshot Threading	Lermond, Charles	√	√	WJ	12	2	46	Fa 87	25
Overshot: Opposites, Multishaft	Contemporary Approach to Traditional Weaves: Multishaft Overshot on Opposites	Zielinski, S. A.; Robert Leclerc, ed.	√	> 4	MWL	7			'51–'73	66
Overshot: Opposites System	Handloom Weaves: The Classification of Handloom Weaves, The Structural Group, Twill Derivative Class, Opposites Overshot System	Tidball, Harriet	√	> 4	SCGM		33		57	18
Overshot: Overlay	Overshot Overlay for Ethnic Clothing	Marston, Ena	√		SS&D	9	3	35	Su 78	88
Overshot: Pattern Design	Creative Overshot: Create A Layout	Windeknecht, Margaret B.	√	√	SCGM		31		78	18
Overshot: "Petit Point"	Petit Point Evening Purse (Doramay Keasbey)		√	√	Hw	7	1		J/F 86	66, I-15
Overshot: Shaft-Switching	Blooming Leaf	Xenakis, Athanasios David	√	√	PWC	3	3	9		51
Overshot: Shaft-Switching	Quatrefoil	Xenakis, Athanasios David	√	√	PWC	3	3	9		53
Overshot: Shaft-Switching	Star and Diamond	Xenakis, Athanasios David	√	√	PWC	3	3	9		49
Overshot: Shaft-Switching	White on White	Lyon, Linda	√	√	PWC	3	3	9		60
Overshot: Shaft-Switching Technique	Even-Tied Overshot on Four Shafts with Shaft Switching	Herring, Connie; Athanasios David Xenakis	√	√	PWC	3	3	9		44
Overshot: Shaft-Switching Technique	In Timeless Form	Herring, Connie	√	√	PWC	3	3	9		35
Overshot: Shaft-Switching Technique	Tied Overshot Boundweave	Xenakis, Athanasios David	√	√	PWC	3	4	10		9
Overshot: Single Design	Freeform Design Technique	Searles, Nancy	√	> 4	PWC	3	4	10		18
Overshot: Swivel-Effect	Contemporary Approach to Traditional Weaves: Swivel Effect on Overshot Drafts	Zielinski, S. A.; Robert Leclerc, ed.	√	√	MWL	7			'51–'73	34
Overshot: System	Handloom Weaves: The Classification of Handloom Weaves, The Structural Group, Twill Derivative Class, Overshot System	Tidball, Harriet	√	> 4	SCGM		33		57	17
Overshot: Texture	Exploring the Textures: Texture Overshot	Zielinski, S. A.; Robert Leclerc, ed.	√	√	MWL	11			'51–'73	92

SUBJECT	TITLE	AUTHOR	IL	INST	JOUR	VOL	NO	ISS	DATE	PAGE
Overshot: Texture, Irregular	Exploring the Textures: Irregular Texture on Overshot Drafts	Zielinski, S. A.; Robert Leclerc, ed.	√	√	MWL	11			'51–'73	96
Overshot: Tied	Analysis of Star and Diamond Weave Structures, An (error-corrected SS&D v10 n1 78 p101)	Anderson, Clarita; Judith Gordon; Naomi Whiting Towner	√	>4	SS&D	9	4	36	Fa 78	71
Overshot: Tied	Double Two-Tie System Applied to Overshot	Xenakis, Athanasios David	√	>4	PWC	3	3	9		7
Overshot: Tied	Tied Overshot Boundweave	Xenakis, Athanasios David	√	√	PWC	3	4	10		9
Overshot: Treadling Variations	Creative Overshot: Additional Treadling Variations	Windeknecht, Margaret B.	√	√	SCGM		31		78	42
Overshot: Turned	Merry Christmas!	Barrett, Clotilde	√	>4	WJ	8	2	30	Fa 83	36
Overshot: Turned	Take Advantage of Turned Drafts	Moes, Dini	√	>4	SS&D	13	2	50	Sp 82	58
Overshot: Turned	Turned Drafts in Double Two-Tie Unit Weave	van der Hoogt, Madelyn	√	>4	WJ	9	2	34	Fa 84	13
Overshot: Turned	Turned Overshot	Rowley, Elaine; Alexis Yiorgos Xenakis	√	>4	PWC	3	2	8		53
Overshot: Turned	Weaver's Notebook		√	>4	SS&D	10	1	37	Wi 78	32
Overshot: Twill Derivative	Creative Overshot: Overshot as a Twill Derivative	Windeknecht, Margaret B.	√	√	SCGM		31		78	12
Overshot: Uneven-Tied	Freeform Design Technique	Searles, Nancy	√	>4	PWC	3	4	10		18
Overshot: Uneven-Tied	Uneven-Tied Overshot	Searles, Nancy	√	>4	PWC	3	4	10		14
Overshot: Uneven-Tied, Free-Form	Freeform Design Technique	Searles, Nancy	√	>4	PWC	3	4	10		18
Overshot: Variation	Double Corduroy Pillows (Pam Bolesta)		√	√	Hw	2	1		F-W 80	32, 60
Overshot: Variations	Pot Holders (Görel Kinersly)		√	√	Hw	6	4		S/O 85	65, I-14
Overshot: Warp	Supplementary Warp Patterns		√	>4	WJ	2	3	7	Ja 78	26
Overshot: Warp	Supplementary Warp Patterns		√	>4	WJ	2	3	7	Ja 78	26
Overshot: Warp-Faced	Whig Rose Study (continued)	Morgenstern, Marvin M.	√	√	WJ	7	3	27	Wi 82	23
Overshot: Warp/Weft	Supplementary Warp Patterns		√	>4	WJ	2	3	7	Ja 78	26
Overshot: Weft	Supplementary Warp Patterns		√	>4	WJ	2	3	7	Ja 78	26
Overshot: Whig Rose	Whig Rose Study	Morgenstern, Marvin M.	√	√	WJ	7	2	26	Fa 82	40
Overshot: Whig Rose	Whig Rose Study (continued)	Morgenstern, Marvin M.	√	√	WJ	7	3	27	Wi 82	23
Overtwist	Are You Ready to Collapse?	Frame, Mary	√	√	S-O	11	1		Sp 87	41
Overtwist	Checking the Twist	Gickie, John	√	√	S-O	11	1		Sp 87	27
Overtwist	Experimenting with Silk Crepe	Quinn, Celia	√	√	S-O	10	4		Wi 86	36
Overtwist	Irregularity in Handspun Part 2	Simmons, Paula	√	√	H&C	21	1		Wi 70	20
Overtwist	Overtwist, A Spinner's Problem	Simmons, Paula	√	√	H&C	19	1		Wi 68	37
Overtwist	Ringlets and Waves: Undulations from Overtwist	Frame, Mary	√	√	S-O	10	4		Wi 86	28
Overtwist	Save the Twist: Warping and Weaving with Overtwisted Yarns	Frame, Mary	√	√	S-O	11	2		Su 87	43
Overtwist	Vest with a Hidden Twist	Emerick, Patricia	√	√	S-O	11	4		Wi 87	36, I-46
Pacific Islands	"Patterns of Paradise: Tapa Cloth" (Exhibit)	Dyer, Carolyn	√		Fa	10	3		M/J 83	73
Packing/Shipping Textiles	Packing Recommendations for Textiles			√	SS&D	5	2	18	Sp 74	30
Packing/Shipping Textiles	Packing Textiles	Bolster, Ella S.		√	H&C	12	4		Fa 61	23
Padding	Four-Block Double Weave on Four Shafts	Barrett, Clotilde	√	√	WJ	8	1	29	Su 83	72
Padding	Horizontal Ribs & Vertical Cords	Moes, Dini	√	√	SS&D	17	4	68	Fa 86	84
Padding	Stitching Traditional Coverlet Weaves	Sellin, Helen G.	√	>4	AT	1			De 83	289
Padding: Wefts	Pick-Up Piqué (error-corrected SS&D v19 n1 87 p33)	Fletcher, Joyce	√	√	SS&D	18	4	72	Fa 87	60
Pageant	Backstage at the Miss Universe Pageant	Loper, Bobby Ann	√		Fa	13	3		M/J 86	12
Pageant	Plaited Pageantry		√		Fa	13	3		M/J 86	8
Pain	Happy Endings	Ligon, Linda	√	√	Hw	8	5		N/D 87	99
Pain	Weaving is a Pain in the...	Chandler, Deborah	√	√	Hw	6	2		M/A 85	26
Pain: Coping	Needlework Pain				TM		14		D/J 87	4

SUBJECT	TITLE	AUTHOR	IL	INST	JOUR	VOL	NO	ISS	DATE	PAGE
Pains	Yoga For Weavers	McCloud, Nena	√		Fa	5	2		M/A 78	40
Painted Paper	Painted Paper		√		Fa	11	2		M/A 84	51
Painted Textiles	"Painted Weavings" Lia Cook and Neda Al-Hilali (Exhibit)	Park, Betty	√		Fa	8	1		J/F 81	88
Painted Warp	Anna Zinsmeister	Zinsmeister, Anna	√		Fa	13	1		J/F 86	19
Painted Warp	Janislee Wiese: Painted Warps		√	√	Fa	5	1		J/F 78	63
Painted Warp	Portfolio: Why I Work in Linen, A		√		Fa	14	2		M/A 87	39
Painted Warps	Painted Warps	Marston, Ena			H&C	21	4		Fa 70	37
Painted Wefts	Technique: Painting Weft Threads for Tapestry	Colburn, Carol	√	√	Hw	3	1		Ja 82	58
Painting	"Thomasin Grim: New Work" (Exhibit)	Scarborough, Jessica	√		Fa	11	5		S/O 84	73
Painting: Fabric	Gloria Marconi: A Commercial Illustrator Mixes Her Media	Hecker, Carolyn A.	√		Fa	6	2		M/A 79	31
Painting: Fabric	Skye Morrison: Yours on a Kite String	Morrison, Skye	√	√	Fa	5	4		J/A 78	36
Painting: Fabric, Technique	Painted-Silk Clothing	Juve, Peggy	√	√	TM			12	A/S 87	24
Painting Silk: Technique	Painted Silk	Bliss, Anne	√	√	Hw	4	1		J/F 83	50
Painting: Silk, Wax Resist	Fleeting Fantasies: Julia Hill's Painting on Silk	Grover, Donald	√		Fa	6	4		J/A 79	12
Painting, Textile	Beyond Quilting	Dyett, Linda	√	√	TM			5	J/J 86	70
Painting, Textile	From White-on-White to Color	Currie, Meg	√		TM			3	F/M 86	39
Painting: Textile	Pie in the Sky: The Irreverent Art of Geraldine Serpa	Serpa, Geraldine	√		Fa	6	4		J/A 79	26
Paisley	Kashmir or Paisley; Romance of the Shawl	Wilson, Kax	√		Iw	4	4		Fa 79	34
Paisley	Kashmiri to Paisley: Evolution of the Paisley shawl	Larson-Fleming, Susan	√		WJ	11	3	43	Wi 87	37
Paisley	Paisley	Badone, Donalda	√		Hw	8	1		J/F 87	39
Paisley	Paisley Shawls: A Democratic Fashion	Goodman, Deborah Lerme	√		Fa	12	3		M/J 85	52
Pakeha	Maori and Pakeha of New Zealand Use Wool and Phormium Tenax	Duncan, Molly	√	√	SS&D	5	1	17	Wi 73	65
Pakistan	Christmas Embroidery in Pakistan	Garland, Mary	√		TM			14	D/J 87	90
Pakistan	Textile Arts of Multan, Pakistan	Shahzaman, Mahboob	√	> 4	SS&D	4	3	15	Su 73	8
Pakistan	Textile Arts of Multan, Pakistan: Part 2	Shahzaman, Mahboob	√	> 4	SS&D	4	4	16	Fa 73	65
Palestine	Seen Around the Country: Palestinian Costume Exhibit in New Mexico	Ulrich, Kenn	√		SS&D	9	4	36	Fa 78	84
Pandau	Flourishing Art: USA Hmong Women Show How to Stitch Pa ndau, Their Flowery Cloth, A	Porter-Francis, Wendy	√	√	TM			9	F/M 87	33
Panel Weaving	Weaving Primer	Parks, Deborah	√	√	PWC	4	2	12		36
Pants	Fall Project: Loom Controlled Slacks (error-corrected H&C v26 n5 75 p45)	Roth, Mrs, Bettie G.	√	√	H&C	26	3		M/J 75	18
Pants	Kimono/Pants Ensemble, A	Selk, Karen	√	√	WJ	8	4	32	Sp 84	72
Pants	Perfect Pair of Pants, A	Cowan, Sally	√	√	TM			7	O/N 86	26
Pants	Purple Pants (Jean Scorgie)		√	√	Hw	6	3		Su 85	53, I-12
Pants	Seattle Guild Garment Designs, Part 3, Skirts and Pants		√	√	SS&D	11	1	41	Wi 79	20
Pants: Harem	How Madame Grès Sculpts with Fabric	Cooper, Arlene	√	√	TM			10	A/M 87	50
Pants: Patterns	Simplifying Knit Pants Patterns			√	TM			12	A/S 87	10
Pants: Wraparounds	Quick and Elegant Wraparounds		√	√	TM			12	A/S 87	10
Paper and Papermaking	80 Papers: Only a 9' by 30' Store, But a Veritable U.N. Of Pulp	Mattera, Joanne	√		Fa	8	6		N/D 81	28
Paper and Papermaking	"Anne Flaten Pixley" (Exhibit)	Mattera, Joanne	√		Fa	6	6		N/D 79	68
Paper and Papermaking	Architectural Imagery Of Margery Freeman Appelbaum, The	McCann, Kathleen	√		Fa	13	1		J/F 86	12
Paper and Papermaking	"Assemblage: Wisconsin Paper" (Exhibit)	Bard, Elizabeth	√		Fa	11	1		J/F 84	78
Paper and Papermaking	Bark Papermakers of San Pablito, The	Wilcox, Don	√	√	Fa	12	4		J/A 85	22
Paper and Papermaking	"Basket and Paper Invitational Show" (Exhibit)	Howe, Cathe	√		Fa	12	3		M/J 85	71

SUBJECT	TITLE	AUTHOR	IL	INST	JOUR	VOL	NO	ISS	DATE	PAGE
Paper and Papermaking	Beth Ames Swartz: A Painter's Way With Paper	Krapes, Shelley	√		Fa	9	4		J/A 82	19
Paper and Papermaking	Carol Rosen: Paper Constructions	Scheinman, Pamela	√		Fa	11	2		M/A 84	16
Paper and Papermaking	Carole Beadle: The Artist and Her Work	Newby, Alice Bartholomew	√		Fa	9	4		J/A 82	44
Paper and Papermaking	Chris Craig	Craig, Chris	√		Fa	12	6		N/D 85	18
Paper and Papermaking	Claudia Hopf: Drawing With Scissors	Timmons, Christine	√		Fa	11	2		M/A 84	99
Paper and Papermaking	Claudie and Francis Hunzinger: Plants, Paper, and Poetry	Hunzinger, Claudie	√		Fa	11	4		J/A 84	10
Paper and Papermaking	Containers of Human Experience: Fragments from the Life of Lois Polansky	Muller, Marion	√		Fa	14	5		N/D 87	32
Paper and Papermaking	Cows in Fiber	Timmons, Chris	√		Fa	11	4		J/A 84	55
Paper and Papermaking	Crossing Over—Fiber in Print	Poon, Vivian	√		Fa	10	3		M/J 83	48
Paper and Papermaking	Dard Hunter Paper Museum, The	Bard, Elizabeth A.	√		Fa	11	2		M/A 84	43
Paper and Papermaking	Felt and Paper: A Portfolio		√		Fa	13	4		J/A 86	35
Paper and Papermaking	"Felt and Papermaking" (Exhibit)	Harrison, Helen A.	√		Fa	11	2		M/A 84	79
Paper and Papermaking	Felted Paper: A New Technique	Newby, Alice Bartholomew	√	√	Fa	9	4		J/A 82	42
Paper and Papermaking	Garment Form As Image, The	Koplos, Janet	√		Fa	10	6		N/D 83	66
Paper and Papermaking	Handmade Paper	Nicholas, Kristin	√	√	WJ	6	2	22	Fa 81	12
Paper and Papermaking	Homage to Hats: Handmade Paper Drawing/Collages Honor a Women's Tradition	Rusoff, Beverly	√		Fa	8	1		J/F 81	80
Paper and Papermaking	How Does Your Garden Grow? Plant Fibers and Handmade Paper	Plummer, Beverly	√		Fa	6	4		J/A 79	34
Paper and Papermaking	How to Make a Sheet of Paper	Toale, Bernard	√	√	Fa	9	4		J/A 82	39
Paper and Papermaking	Jody Klein's Paper Quilts		√		Fa	10	1		J/F 83	44
Paper and Papermaking	"Jody Klein's Paper Quilts" (Exhibit)	Storey, Isabelle B.	√		Fa	8	6		N/D 81	70
Paper and Papermaking	"Kathryn Lipke/Fiber-Paper-Pulp: Works in Handmade Paper" (Exhibit)	Piazza, Virginia	√		Fa	4	4		J/A 77	13
Paper and Papermaking	Learning Papermaking in Nantucket	Bach, Ann	√		Fa	11	2		M/A 84	47
Paper and Papermaking	"Made in Wisconsin: An Exhibition of Recent Works In-Of-and-On Handmade Paper" (Exhibit)	Hagemeister-Winzenz, Karon	√		Fa	5	4		J/A 78	19
Paper and Papermaking	Magic Lanterns: Alice Ward's Handmade Paper Light/Shades	Holland, Nina	√		Fa	8	3		M/J 81	22
Paper and Papermaking	Marcia Morse: A Collaboration with Paper	Rowley, Kathleen	√		Fa	11	2		M/A 84	20
Paper and Papermaking	"Meri Ann Walsh: Patterned Papers" (Exhibit)	Austin, Carole	√		Fa	8	6		N/D 81	65
Paper and Papermaking	Michele Tuegel's Paper Works	Marger, Mary Ann	√		Fa	13	4		J/A 86	30
Paper and Papermaking	Mindy Alper: Sculpting in Papier Mache	Saito, Shirley	√		Fa	11	4		J/A 84	18
Paper and Papermaking	"Nance O'Banion: Handmade Paper and Bamboo Painting" (Exhibit)	Janeiro, Jan	√		Fa	7	4		J/A 80	15
Paper and Papermaking	"Nance O'Banion: Painted Paper Skin Series" (Exhibits)	Rowley, Kathleen	√		Fa	9	4		J/A 82	70
Paper and Papermaking	Neda Al Hilali: An Interview	Park, Betty	√		Fa	6	4		J/A 79	40
Paper and Papermaking	"New American Paperworks" (Exhibit) (error-corrected Fa v13 n3 86 p5)	Shermeta, Margo	√		Fa	13	1		J/F 86	64
Paper and Papermaking	"New Dimensions in Handmade Paper" (Exhibit)	Koplos, Janet	√		Fa	8	5		S/O 81	72
Paper and Papermaking	Painted Paper		√		Fa	11	2		M/A 84	51
Paper and Papermaking	"Painted Weavings" Lia Cook and Neda Al-Hilali (Exhibit)	Park, Betty	√		Fa	8	1		J/F 81	88
Paper and Papermaking	Paper Abroad (Exhibit)	Waller, Irene	√		Fa	11	2		M/A 84	82
Paper and Papermaking	Paper and Fiber	Sousa, Jan	√	√	Iw	5	3		Su 80	32
Paper and Papermaking	Paper Art of Fritzi Huber Morrison, The	Kosta, Angela	√		Fa	11	2		M/A 84	22
Paper and Papermaking	Paper as Fiber	Morse, Marcia	√		SS&D	15	3	59	Su 84	20
Paper and Papermaking	Paper as object	Ligon, Linda	√	√	Iw	2	3		Sp 77	19
Paper and Papermaking	"Paper Clothing and More in San Francisco" (Exhibit)	Scarborough, Jessica	√		Fa	11	2		M/A 84	75

SUBJECT	TITLE	AUTHOR	IL	INST	JOUR	VOL	NO	ISS	DATE	PAGE
Paper and Papermaking	Paper Clothing, East	Sahlstrand, Margaret	√	√	Fa	11	2		M/A 84	36
Paper and Papermaking	"Paper" (Exhibit)	Toale, Bernard	√		Fa	7	5		S/O 80	69
Paper and Papermaking	Paper Palettes, A Profile of Kit Loney		√		SS&D	18	2	70	Sp 87	81
Paper and Papermaking	"Paper Sources" (Exhibit)	Papa, Nancy	√		Fa	5	4		J/A 78	16
Paper and Papermaking	Paper: Three Shows At the American Craft Museums (Exhibit)	Lonier, Terri	√		Fa	9	5		S/O 82	84
Paper and Papermaking	Paper Vessels of Sylvia Seventy, The	Stofflet, Mary	√		Fa	11	2		M/A 84	70
Paper and Papermaking	Paper Works of Kathryn Maxwell, The	Martin, Robert	√		Fa	14	2		M/A 87	8
Paper and Papermaking	Papermaking	O'Connor, Patricia	√	√	SS&D	14	3	55	Su 83	32
Paper and Papermaking	Papermaking as a Recycling Process: The Work of Frances Les	Les, Kathleen	√		Fa	6	4		J/A 79	18
Paper and Papermaking	Papermaking Classes and Workshops: A Selective List	Howe, Cathe	√		Fa	11	2		M/A 84	47
Paper and Papermaking	Papermaking in Chicago	Shermeta, Margo	√		Fa	11	2		M/A 84	54
Paper and Papermaking	Papermaking in the U.S.A.	Toale, Bernard	√		Fa	9	4		J/A 82	34
Paper and Papermaking	Papermaking: Where It's Coming From	Hughey, Michael W.	√	√	SS&D	10	4	40	Fa 79	45
Paper and Papermaking	Papermaking: Where It's Going	Pierucci, Louise	√	√	SS&D	10	4	40	Fa 79	47
Paper and Papermaking	Patricia T. Hetzler	Hetzler, Patricia T.	√		Fa	14	2		M/A 87	24
Paper and Papermaking	Peggy Conklin: Sculptured Paper	Tacker, Sylvia	√		Fa	13	3		M/J 86	25
Paper and Papermaking	Pioneer Paper Places: Pyramid Prints and Paperworks	Fife, Lin	√		Fa	13	4		J/A 86	24
Paper and Papermaking	Portfolio of Contemporary Fiber Sculpture, A		√		Fa	11	4		J/A 84	34
Paper and Papermaking	Rubber Stamp Acts: The Little Books of Marie Combs		√		Fa	8	5		S/O 81	18
Paper and Papermaking	Rugs: Lin Fife, Papermaker		√		Fa	9	2		M/A 82	61
Paper and Papermaking	Sanity, Madness and the Artist: The Work of Suzan Anson	Demoss, Virginia	√		Fa	6	2		M/A 79	36
Paper and Papermaking	Sculptural Paper: Foundations and Directions	Scarborough, Jessica	√		Fa	11	2		M/A 84	32
Paper and Papermaking	"Shared Vision": A Gallery Tour with Two Artists: Jacque Parsley and Neisja Yenawine (Exhibit)	Arnow, Jan	√		Fa	8	4		J/A 81	28
Paper and Papermaking	Thread of Continuity: Paper as Fabric, Craft as Art, and Other Ambiguities, The	Mattera, Joanne	√		Fa	6	4		J/A 79	31
Paper and Papermaking	Timeless Stitches: Myrna Shiras' Stitched Drawings	Schwartz, Joyce B.	√		Fa	8	3		M/J 81	65
Paper and Papermaking	Visual Language of Bella Feldman, The	Scarborough, Jessica	√		Fa	11	4		J/A 84	30
Paper and Papermaking	Wendy Shah: Subtle Rhythms	Mattera, Joanne	√		Fa	7	5		S/O 80	21
Paper and Papermaking	Words in Fiber	Rowley, Kathleen	√		Fa	11	2		M/A 84	66
Paper and Papermaking	"Works In, On, and Of Paper" (Exhibit)	Les, Kathleen	√		Fa	6	5		S/O 79	79
Paper and Papermaking: Kozo	Shifu: A Handwoven Paper Textile of Japan	Miller, Dorothy	√	√	AT	4			De 85	43
Paper and Papermaking: Technique	Shifu: A Handwoven Paper Textile of Japan	Miller, Dorothy	√	√	AT	4			De 85	43
Paper Clothing	Fashioned from Paper: Rosina Yue's "Clothing" Constructions	Scarborough, Jessica	√		Fa	8	1		J/F 81	76
Paper Clothing	"Paper Clothing and More in San Francisco" (Exhibit)	Scarborough, Jessica	√		Fa	11	2		M/A 84	75
Paper Clothing	Paper Clothing, East	Sahlstrand, Margaret	√	√	Fa	11	2		M/A 84	36
Paper Clothing	Paper Clothing: West	Koplos, Janet	√		Fa	11	2		M/A 84	39
Paper Doll Clothing	What a Doll! Provocative Paper Dolls, A Captivating Idea	Gould, Mary	√	√	Fa	8	1		J/F 81	78
Paper Weaving	Paper Weaving	Scanlin, Tommye McClure	√	√	Hw	7	4		S/O 86	28
Paper/Fiber	Paper and Fiber	Sousa, Jan	√	√	Iw	5	3		Su 80	32
Papercuts	Claudia Hopf: Drawing with Scissors	Timmons, Christine	√		Fa	11	2		M/A 84	99
Papermaking Traditions: Mexico	Bark Papermakers of San Pablito, The	Wilcox, Don	√	√	Fa	12	4		J/A 85	22
Papier Mâché	Mindy Alper: Sculpting in Papier Mache	Saito, Shirley	√		Fa	11	4		J/A 84	18

SUBJECT	TITLE	AUTHOR	IL	INST	JOUR	VOL	NO	ISS	DATE	PAGE
Paracas	Paracas Needle Technique, A	Hoskins, Nancy	√	√	Iw	5	4		Fa 80	34
Paraguay	Hammock, The	Drooker, Penelope B.	√	√	TM			6	A/S 86	74
Parkas	Hooded Parka (Susan Henrikson) (error-corrected Hw v5 n2 84 p93)		√	√	Hw	4	4		S/O 83	42, 93
Parkas	Parka (Betty Beard)		√	√	Hw	1	1		F-W 79	18, 53
Parkas	Weave Three--Cocktail Skirt, Coating, Parka	Snyder, Mary	√	> 4	SS&D	6	2	22	Sp 75	34
Parks' Bouquet	Parks' Bouquet	Parks, Deborah	√	√	PWC	4	1	11		36
Pascals Triangle	Flight Into Fantasy (error-corrected SS&D v12 n1 80 p6)	Hartford, Jane; Thom Hartford III	√		SS&D	11	4	44	Fa 80	57
Past/Future	Dialectic for Handweavers: or, on Looking Back (While Moving Forward), A	Fannin, Allen			Iw	3	3		Sp 78	39
Patches	Patches on Patches	Hahn, Kandra		√	TM			6	A/S 86	22
Patching	Prehistoric Twined Bag from Big Bone Cave, Tennessee: Manufacture, Repair, and Use, A	Kuttruff, Jenna Tedrick	√		AT	8			De 87	125
Patchwork	"Ann Trusty: Grid and Pattern" (Exhibit)	Stiles, David	√		Fa	9	1		J/F 82	79
Patchwork	Crazy Quilt for Babies Grand, A	Greenberg, Blue	√		Fa	8	2		M/A 81	31
Patchwork	Ethnic Textile Art at U.C.L.A. — "Afro-American Arts of the Suriname Rain Forest" (Exhibit)	Dyer, Carolyn	√		Fa	8	2		M/A 81	59
Patchwork	"Frank Gardner: Aleatory Works" (Exhibit)	Guagliumi, Susan	√		Fa	9	2		M/A 82	75
Patchwork	Handing Down More Than Just a Quilt	Hamilton, Carolyn	√		TM			12	A/S 87	86
Patchwork	Julie Berner	Berner, Julie	√		Fa	14	1		J/F 87	27
Patchwork	Patchwork Designs in Summer and Winter	Davenport, Betty	√	√	PWC	1	1		No 81	27
Patchwork	Patchwork Re-Ordered	Talley, Charles	√		Fa	7	1		J/F 80	24
Patchwork	Pieces of History	Meyers, Judith Philipp	√		Fa	14	5		N/D 87	54
Patchwork	Woven Garments	Henzie, Susie	√	√	WJ	3	4	12	Ap 79	44
Patchwork	Yvonne Porcella: A Modern Master of the Ethnic Clothing Tradition	Avery, Virginia	√		Fa	8	1		J/F 81	63
Patchwork	Zamani Soweto Sisters: A Patchwork of Lives		√		Fa	10	2		M/A 83	48
Patchwork: Interlocked Warp	Peru, Textiles Unlimited: Scaffold, Patchwork, or Interlocked Warp	Tidball, Harriet	√		SCGM		25		68	28
Patchwork, Medallion: Technique	Medallion Quilting	Miller, Kristin	√	√	TM			14	D/J 87	60
Patchwork, Miccosukee	Convergence Preview — Six Peaks, A		√		SS&D	11	2	42	Sp 80	47
Patchwork, Seminole	In the Dark of the Swamp...Seminole Patchwork		√	√	Fa	4	3		M/J 77	38
Patchwork: Seminole	Lamé	Boyce, Ann	√		TM			8	D/J 86	32
Patchwork: Seminole	Method to Her Madness: Jane Lang Axtell's Seminole Patchwork, A	Buscho, Ann	√		Fa	8	1		J/F 81	31
Patchwork: Seminole	Opera Elegance	Sylvan, Katherine	√	√	SS&D	15	4	60	Fa 84	24
Patchwork: Seminole	Seminole Patchwork	Ligon, Linda	√		Iw	1	2		Wi 76	8
Patchwork: Woven	Woven Patchwork	Marston, Ena	√	√	SS&D	4	1	13	Wi 72	18
Patent Satin	Lampas	Kelly, Jacquie	√	> 4	PWC	5	1	15		46
Patent Systems, Textile Machinery, American	Nineteenth Century License Agreements for Fancy Weaving Machines	Anderson, Clarita; Steven M. Spivak	√		AT	8			De 87	67
Pattern Boards: Tapa	Tapa-Making in Tonga	Raphael, Jenifer; Chad Raphael	√		Fa	13	6		N/D 86	24
Pattern Composition: Textile/Music	Cardiac Algorithms or the Heart's Way of Inferring Meaning from Pattern	Courtney, Elizabeth	√		AT	5			Ju 86	51
Pattern Continuity	Continuity of Patterning	Liebler, Barbara	√		Hw	6	1		J/F 85	92
Pattern Conversion: Knit—> Weave	Inspirations from Sweaters	Brewington, Judith	√	√	WJ	7	3	27	Wi 82	14
Pattern Design	Design and the Handweaver: Pattern	Atwater, Mary Meigs	√	√	SCGM		3		61	17
Pattern Drafts: Cuna Cachi	Cuna Cachi: A Study of Hammock Weaving Among the Cuna Indians of the San Blas Islands	Lambert, Anne M.	√	√	AT	5			Ju 86	105

SUBJECT	TITLE	AUTHOR	IL	INST	JOUR	VOL	NO	ISS	DATE	PAGE
Pattern: Evolution	From Simple Twills to Dobby Fantasies...A Progression	Marquess, Joyce	√	> 4	lw	4	4		Fa 79	38
Pattern: Ikat, Shifting	Tying Warp Ikat on the Loom	Hannon, Farrell	√	√	WJ	8	1	29	Su 83	41
Pattern: Layout	Accessories: Double Woven Bag		√	√	WJ	2	4	8	Ap 78	7
Pattern: Layout	Accessories: Drawstring Bag		√	√	WJ	2	4	8	Ap 78	5
Pattern: Layout	Accessories: Large Bags Made from Narrow Strips		√	√	WJ	2	4	8	Ap 78	6
Pattern: Layout	African Strip-Cloth Shirt Without Strips, An	O'Connor, Eileen	√	√	WJ	6	3	23	Wi 81	33
Pattern: Layout	Alexis' Favorite	Rowley, Elaine	√	√	Kn	1	1	1	F-W 84 CI	46,56B 48
Pattern: Layout	Alpaca Vest	Newton, Deborah	√	√	Kn	3	4	8	Fa 87	21
Pattern: Layout	Aran Knitting	Starmore, Alice	√	√	TM			14	D/J 87	50
Pattern: Layout	Art of Fashion Design: A Handweaver's Twill Cape, The	Johnson, Judith K.	√	√	WJ	7	3	27	Wi 82	12
Pattern: Layout	Autumn Sunset Cape (Leslie Voiers)		√	> 4	WJ	11	3	43	Wi 87	22
Pattern: Layout	Baby Jacket	Gibson-Roberts, Priscilla A.	√	√	Kn	3	2	6	Sp 87	42
Pattern: Layout	Beaded Sweater	Diven, Gail; Rosemary Drysdale	√	√	Kn	2	2	4	S-S 86	50
Pattern: Layout	Beginner's Hat and Scarf	Skoy, Mary Lonning	√	√	WJ	11	3	43	Wi 87	61
Pattern: Layout	Beginner's Tops	Legerski, Victoria	√	> 4	WJ	8	3	31	Wi 83	14
Pattern: Layout	Beginning with bands: Tablet woven garments and accessories	Holtzer, Marilyn Emerson	√	√	WJ	9	3	35	Wi 85	28
Pattern: Layout	Blouse for Her — A Shirt for Him, A		√	√	WJ	4	3	15	Ja 80	4
Pattern: Layout	Bog Affair, A	Homme, Audrey	√	√	PWC			3	Oc 82	44
Pattern: Layout	Bonnie Bonnet	Adams, Harriet	√	√	Kn	1	2	2	S-S 85	38
Pattern: Layout	Braid on the Bias (error-corrected Kn v3 n1 i5 f/w 86 p11)	Madden, Gail	√	√	Kn	2	2	4	S-S 86	35
Pattern: Layout	Bright Blouse	Lewis, Susanna	√	√	Kn	3	2	6	Sp 87	36
Pattern: Layout	Burra Lace Pullover	Bush, Nancy	√	√	Kn	3	4	8	Fa 87	26
Pattern: Layout	Cannelé: Create a Sumptuous Fabric That Drapes Beautifully	Broughton, Cynthia	√	√	WJ	10	3	39	Wi 86	59
Pattern: Layout	Cardigan Jacket	Evans, Kerry	√	√	WJ	5	3	19	Wi 81	10
Pattern: Layout	Carla's Zebra Top	Fauske, Carla	√	√	PWC			2	Ap 82	88
Pattern: Layout	Carnival Cable Pullover	Jensen, Candi	√	√	Kn	3	1	5	F-W 86	24
Pattern: Layout	Chanel Jacket	Ratigan, Dorothy	√	√	Kn	2	2	4	S-S 86	33
Pattern: Layout	Chenille Polo	Xenakis, Alexis Yiorgos	√	√	PWC			6	Su 83	34
Pattern: Layout	Child's Play	Voiers, Leslie	√	√	SS&D	18	3	71	Su 87	22
Pattern: Layout	Christmas Cards		√	> 4	WJ	7	2	26	Fa 82	54
Pattern: Layout	Classic, The	O'Connor, Pat	√	√	Kn	2	1	3	F-W 85	58
Pattern: Layout	Coat Couture	West, Virginia	√	> 4	SS&D	14	2	54	Sp 83	48
Pattern: Layout	Coat with Minimum Seams, The	Marston, Ena	√	√	SS&D	7	4	28	Fa 76	42
Pattern: Layout	Comfortable Cotton T's	Upitis, Lizbeth	√	√	Kn	3	3	7	Su 87	12
Pattern: Layout	Correct Sewing Methods in Tailoring	Bryan, Dorothy	√	√	H&C	10	3		Su 59	25
Pattern: Layout	Cotton Jacket with Pleat	White, Jamie Leigh	√	√	WJ	7	3	27	Wi 82	68
Pattern: Layout	Cotton Shirts	Barnett-Westfall, Lynn	√	√	WJ	4	3	15	Ja 80	22
Pattern: Layout	Cotton-Linen Garment in Basket Weave		√	√	WJ	7	3	27	Wi 82	32
Pattern: Layout	Couturier Fashion Design	West, Virginia	√	< 4	SS&D	13	4	52	Fa 82	34
Pattern: Layout	Creative Clothing: Surface Embellishment	Mayer, Anita Luvera	√	√	WJ	11	3	43	Wi 87	30
Pattern: Layout	Cut and Sew Mittens	Winchester, Nina	√	√	WJ	9	3	35	Wi 85	53
Pattern: Layout	Desert Tapestry Vest	Jennings, Lucy Anne	√	√	WJ	12	1	45	Su 87	52
Pattern: Layout	Designed for Narrow Looms	Jennings, Lucy Anne	√	√	WJ	11	1	41	Su 86	26
Pattern: Layout	Designed for Narrow Looms: A Summer Shirt Inspired by the Macedonian Chemise	Temple, Mary	√	√	WJ	10	1	37	Su 85	46
Pattern: Layout	Designing Handwoven Clothing	Thomason, Roger	√		SS&D	10	1	37	Wi 78	88

SUBJECT	TITLE	AUTHOR	IL	INST	JOUR	VOL	NO	ISS	DATE	PAGE
Pattern: Layout	Diamond Lattice Pullover	Frost, Jean	√	√	Kn	3	4	8	Fa 87	34
Pattern: Layout	Dimity Delight	Sullivan, Donna	√	> 4	PWC	5	1	15		17
Pattern: Layout	Double Woven House Boots	MacDonald, Margaret	√	> 4	WJ	6	4	24	Sp 82	44
Pattern: Layout	Dubbelmossa	Adams, Harriet	√	√	Kn	2	1	3	F-W 85	50, 8B
Pattern: Layout	Embroidery on the Loom	Drooker, Penelope B.	√	√	SS&D	9	3	35	Su 78	60
Pattern: Layout	Ethnic Inspired Jacket	Hurt, Doris	√	√	WJ	4	4	16	Ap 80	43
Pattern: Layout	Fair Isle in Natural Colors, The	Gibson-Roberts, Priscilla A.	√	√	Kn	2	1	3	F-W 85	34
Pattern: Layout	Fair Isle Knitting	Starmore, Alice	√	√	TM			8	D/J 86	44
Pattern: Layout	Fashion Show of Handwoven Garments		√	> 4	WJ	3	3	11	Ja 79	5
Pattern: Layout	Fashions by Linda Knutson and Lynn Daly		√	√	WJ	6	3	23	Wi 81	14
Pattern: Layout	Felted Fabric	Mayer, Anita Luvera	√	√	SS&D	15	3	59	Su 84	46
Pattern: Layout	Felted Jacket	Bennett, Siiri	√	> 4	WJ	9	1	33	Su 84	49
Pattern: Layout	Figured Piqué on a Ground of 2/2 Twill and 2/2 Hopsack	Xenakis, Athanasios David	√	> 4	PWC	4	2	12		24
Pattern: Layout	Fit to a T		√	√	Kn	3	3	7	Su 87	22
Pattern: Layout	Four-Block Double Weave on Four Shafts	Barrett, Clotilde	√	√	WJ	8	1	29	Su 83	72
Pattern: Layout	Four-Corner T-Shirt	Swansen, Meg	√	√	Kn	3	3	7	Su 87	28
Pattern: Layout	Four-Shaft Twill Neck Scarf	Kolling-Summers, Elizabeth	√	√	WJ	7	1	25	Su 82	29
Pattern: Layout	Free and Casual Look Wool Jacket, The	McGalliard, Lorraine	√	√	WJ	6	3	23	Wi 81	8
Pattern: Layout	From Elegance to Rag Weaving	Mick, Catherine	√	√	WJ	7	3	27	Wi 82	64
Pattern: Layout	From Sample to Finished Product	Keasbey, Doramay	√	> 4	SS&D	15	3	59	Su 84	62
Pattern: Layout	From the Collection of Anne Poussart		√	√	WJ	7	3	27	Wi 82	62
Pattern: Layout	Fulled Blazer	Newton, Deborah	√	√	Kn	3	1	5	F-W 86	38
Pattern: Layout	Gaffer's Gansey	Zimmermann, Elizabeth	√	√	Kn	1	1	1	F-W 84 CI	36,56B 28
Pattern: Layout	Gala Raincoat	Moes, Dini	√	√	WJ	6	3	23	Wi 81	12
Pattern: Layout	Galashiels Tweed Pullover	Bush, Nancy	√	√	Kn	4	1	9	Wi 87	42
Pattern: Layout	Gansey in Handspun, The	Gibson-Roberts, Priscilla A.	√	√	Kn	1	1	1	F-W 84 CI	32,56B 24
Pattern: Layout	Garden of Fair Isles, A	Rowe, Mary	√	√	Kn	2	1	3	F-W 85	40, 8B
Pattern: Layout	Garments by Hanni Bureker		√	√	WJ	6	3	23	Wi 81	35
Pattern: Layout	Garments Made from Simple Patterns: A Ruana		√	√	WJ	2	3	7	Ja 78	38
Pattern: Layout	Garments Made from Simple Patterns: Two Tabards		√	> 4	WJ	2	3	7	Ja 78	35
Pattern: Layout	Garments with Ethnic Flavor: Ethnic Dress with Supplementary Warp		√	√	WJ	2	3	7	Ja 78	14
Pattern: Layout	Glad Rags	Wroten, Barbara	√	√	SS&D	15	4	60	Fa 84	28
Pattern: Layout	Greek Chemises: Cut and Construction	Welters, Linda	√	√	WJ	10	1	37	Su 85	40
Pattern: Layout	Half Shawl Designed by Janet Checker		√	√	WJ	11	3	43	Wi 87	14
Pattern: Layout	Handcrafted Clothing Construction: Some Considerations	Peterson, Jill	√	√	Fa	3	5		S/O 76	32
Pattern: Layout	Handwoven Teddy Bear (Janice Jones)		√	√	Hw	6	4		S/O 85	63, I-12
Pattern: Layout	Happy Dress	Sprenger, Elserine	√	√	WJ	8	3	31	Wi 83	46
Pattern: Layout	Heirloom Wedding Dress	Ellman, Norma	√	√	Kn	3	2	6	Sp 87	31
Pattern: Layout	Hooded Rag Jacket (Jean Scorgie)		√	√	Hw	2	3		My 81	49, 81
Pattern: Layout	In the Dark of the Swamp...Seminole Patchwork		√	√	Fa	4	3		M/J 77	38
Pattern: Layout	Inlay We Trust, Part 2: Leno Inlay	Herring, Connie	√	√	PWC			6	Su 83	48
Pattern: Layout	Inspirations from Sweaters	Brewington, Judith	√	√	WJ	7	3	27	Wi 82	14
Pattern: Layout	Instructions for Weaving a Bog Shirt	Kinahan, Barbara	√	√	WJ	3	1	9	Jy 78	26
Pattern: Layout	Isolated Overshot: Linen and Cotton Teacloth	Xenakis, Athanasios David	√	> 4	PWC	3	2	8		36
Pattern: Layout	Jackie's Sweaters: Blouson, Dolman, Striped Silk	Kroeger, Jackie	√	√	Kn	1	1	1	F-W 84 CI	41 33

SUBJECT	TITLE	AUTHOR	IL	INST	JOUR	VOL	NO	ISS	DATE	PAGE
Pattern: Layout	Japanese Shopkeeper's Coat		√	√	WJ	3	3	11	Ja 79	40
Pattern: Layout	Josephina's Suit	Koopman, Albertje	√	> 4	WJ	4	4	16	Ap 80	50
Pattern: Layout	Josh's Gansey	Camper, Dorothy	√	√	Kn	1	1	1	F-W 84 CI	28 20
Pattern: Layout	Joy to the World		√	√	WJ	6	2	22	Fa 81	59
Pattern: Layout	Keep Warm! Colonial Comfort	Commings, Nancy	√	√	WJ	5	2	18	Fa 80	8
Pattern: Layout	Kimono/Pants Ensemble, A	Selk, Karen	√	√	WJ	8	4	32	Sp 84	72
Pattern: Layout	Knitting Odyssey, A	Dyett, Linda	√	√	TM			13	O/N 87	48
Pattern: Layout	Lace and Knots	Newton, Deborah	√	√	Kn	3	4	8	Fa 87	20
Pattern: Layout	Lace Trilogy	Fauske, Carla	√	√	PWC			6	Su 83	52
Pattern: Layout	Lace-Weave Tunic	Rowley, Elaine	√	√	PWC			5	Sp 83	18
Pattern: Layout	Leno Vest	Lyon, Linda	√	√	PWC			6	Su 83	27
Pattern Layout	Linen Undergarments: A Proud Danish Heritage	Todd-Cope, Louise	√	√	Fa	14	2		M/A 87	51
Pattern: Layout	Lining the Overshot	Moes, Dini	√	√	SS&D	13	4	52	Fa 82	64
Pattern: Layout	Little Knitting on the Side, A	Glover, Medrith	√	√	Kn	2	1	3	F-W 85	38
Pattern: Layout	Log Cabin Rag Rugs	Meany, Janet K.	√	√	WJ	9	4	36	Sp 85	50
Pattern: Layout	Long Sweeping Evening Cape	Roth, Bettie G.	√	> 4	WJ	6	3	23	Wi 81	26
Pattern: Layout	Loom Shaped Top with Dukagång Inlay	Searle, Karen	√	√	WJ	11	3	43	Wi 87	8
Pattern: Layout	Loom Woven Baskets	Bowman, Gloria	√	√	WJ	10	4	40	Sp 86	37
Pattern: Layout	Loom-Shaped Garment, A	Haynes, Albertje Koopman (see also Koopman)	√	√	SS&D	9	1	33	Wi 77	83
Pattern: Layout	Macedonian Shirt Design	Hoffman, Jenet	√	√	SS&D	8	2	30	Sp 77	97
Pattern: Layout	Man's Jacket: A Weaver's Challenge, A	Rasmussen, Peg	√	√	SS&D	15	2	58	Sp 84	58
Pattern: Layout	Margot Carter Blair		√	√	Fa	4	3		M/J 77	28
Pattern: Layout	Marvelous Mistake, A	Cramer, Pauline E.	√	√	SS&D	17	1	65	Wi 85	34
Pattern: Layout	Merry Christmas!	Barrett, Clotilde	√	> 4	WJ	8	2	30	Fa 83	36
Pattern: Layout	Mexican Motifs: A Mexican Quesquimitl	Tidball, Harriet	√	√	SCGM			6	62	13
Pattern: Layout	Mexican Motifs: The Mexican Men's Jacket	Tidball, Harriet	√	√	SCGM			6	62	20
Pattern: Layout	Michelin Man Sweater	Zimmermann, Elizabeth	√	√	Kn	2	2	4	S-S 86	72
Pattern: Layout	Mind Boggling Bogs	Herring, Connie	√	√	PWC			3	Oc 82	36
Pattern: Layout	Mind Boggling Bogs	Klessen, Romy	√	√	PWC			3	Oc 82	40
Pattern: Layout	Modern Interpretations of Ethnic Garments	Dickey, Enola	√	√	SS&D	9	2	34	Sp 78	28
Pattern: Layout	Moebius Vest, The	Homme, Audrey	√	√	WJ	11	4	44	Sp 87	48
Pattern: Layout	Moroccan Cocoon		√	√	WJ	8	3	31	Wi 83	10
Pattern: Layout	Mother and Daughter Bonnets	Clement, Doris	√	√	H&C	13	3		Su 62	36
Pattern: Layout	Mr. Hunter's Lace	Yaksick, Karen	√	√	Kn	3	4	8	Fa 87	22
Pattern: Layout	Nativity Scene	Vargo, Bessie Mae	√	√	WJ	6	2	22	Fa 81	8
Pattern: Layout	No-Sweat Sweatshirt, The	Glover, Medrith	√	√	Kn	3	1	5	F-W 86	28
Pattern: Layout	Now, That's a Cabled Sweater	Yaksick, Karen	√	√	Kn	3	1	5	F-W 86	30
Pattern: Layout	Olwen's Buffalo	MacGregor, Olwen	√	√	WJ	8	2	30	Fa 83	46
Pattern: Layout	On Designing: Brocade Blouse	Newton, Deborah	√	√	Kn	1	1	1	F-W 84 CI	17 9
Pattern: Layout	Particular Guernsey, A	Rowley, Elaine	√	√	Kn	1	1	1	F-W 84 CI	25,56A 17
Pattern: Layout	Pat White: The "Small Things" Are Her Signature	Park, Betty	√	√	SS&D	13	3	51	Su 82	58
Pattern: Layout	Pine Tree Coat	Knollenberg, Barbara	√	> 4	WJ	1	2	2	Oc 76	32
Pattern: Layout	Pleated Cardigan	Newton, Deborah	√	√	Kn	3	2	6	Sp 87	20
Pattern: Layout	Poncho	Hurt, Doris	√	> 4	WJ	3	3	11	Ja 79	44
Pattern: Layout	Poncho with Fringe Benefits, A	Epstein, Betty	√	√	H&C	23	1		J/F 72	28
Pattern: Layout	Project Notebook, A	Ligon, Linda	√	√	Iw	3	1		Fa 77	31
Pattern: Layout	Projects with Cotton		√	√	WJ	4	2	14	Oc 79	28

SUBJECT	TITLE	AUTHOR	IL	INST	JOUR	VOL	NO	ISS	DATE	PAGE
Pattern: Layout	Proportions of the Bog Shirt	Klessen, Romy	√	√	PWC			3	Oc 82	34
Pattern: Layout	Raglan Rectangles	Coifman, Lucienne	√	√	SS&D	18	1	69	Wi 86	10
Pattern: Layout	Rags At Work	Finch, Joan Freitag	√	√	SS&D	16	4	64	Fa 85	72
Pattern: Layout	Rags to Riches: Honeycomb Bolero-Style Vest	Barrett, Phyllis K.	√	√	WJ	6	3	23	Wi 81	30
Pattern: Layout	Rags to Riches: Jackets from Rags	Brones, Britta	√	√	WJ	6	3	23	Wi 81	31
Pattern: Layout	Rags to Riches: Ragstrip Vest	Scheirman, Pam	√	√	WJ	6	3	23	Wi 81	30
Pattern: Layout	Reversible Flamepoint Vest	Wittpenn, Ann	√	√	WJ	5	3	19	Wi 81	9
Pattern: Layout	Reversible Jacket in Double Weave, A	Evans, Jane	√	>4	WJ	3	1	9	Jy 78	23
Pattern: Layout	Ribbon Wefts	Sewell, Suzy	√	>4	WJ	10	3	39	Wi 86	40
Pattern: Layout	Ruched Blouse	Bruzelius, Margaret	√	√	Kn	2	2	4	S-S 86	40
Pattern: Layout	Russian Peasant Shirt Adaptation	Hendricks, Carolyn	√	√	SS&D	8	2	30	Sp 77	96
Pattern: Layout	Sans Serif T	Rowley, Elaine	√	√	Kn	3	3	7	Su 87	22
Pattern: Layout	Satin Weave Evening Bag	Lodge, Jean	√	>4	WJ	10	1	37	Su 85	39
Pattern: Layout	Scandia Jacket		√	√	WJ	8	3	31	Wi 83	42
Pattern: Layout	Scented Sachets	Xenakis, Alexis Yiorgos	√	>4	PWC	3	2	8		56
Pattern: Layout	Seattle Guild Garment Designs, Part 1	Noble, Judy	√	√	SS&D	10	3	39	Su 79	26
Pattern: Layout	Seattle Guild Garment Designs, Part 2: Completing the Top		√	√	SS&D	10	4	40	Fa 79	71
Pattern: Layout	Seattle Guild Garment Designs, Part 3, Skirts and Pants		√	√	SS&D	11	1	41	Wi 79	20
Pattern: Layout	Seattle Guild Garment Designs, Part 4: Edges, Closures, Capes and Dresses		√	√	SS&D	11	2	42	Sp 80	39
Pattern: Layout	Shawl in the English Tradition, A	Zimmermann, Elizabeth	√	√	Kn	1	2	2	S-S 85	59
Pattern: Layout	Sheep of a Sweater, A	Lambersten, Martha	√	√	Kn	3	4	8	Fa 87	51
Pattern: Layout	Silk	Lawrence, Mary Jo	√	√	WJ	7	3	27	Wi 82	74
Pattern: Layout	Simple and Silk	Gibson-Roberts, Priscilla A.	√	√	Kn	2	2	4	S-S 86	54
Pattern: Layout	Simple and Striped	Oakes, Nancy	√	√	Kn	3	1	5	F-W 86	44
Pattern: Layout	Simple Patterns for Handwoven Garments		√	√	WJ	3	3	11	Ja 79	24
Pattern: Layout	Simple Vests		√	√	WJ	5	3	19	Wi 81	41
Pattern: Layout	Simplest of all Tapestry Techniques Used in a Carrying Bag, The		√	√	WJ	7	3	27	Wi 82	37
Pattern: Layout	Skirt for the Wall, A		√	√	WJ	3	4	12	Ap 79	19
Pattern: Layout	Sky Celebration	Mayer, Anita Luvera	√	√	S-O	11	2		Su 87	36
Pattern: Layout	Sleeve Sweater	Rowley, Elaine	√	√	Kn	2	1	3	F-W 85	58
Pattern: Layout	Slightly Left of Center Jacket	Rowley, Elaine	√	√	PWC			6	Su 83	44
Pattern: Layout	Soft Sleeveless Blouse	Upitis, Lizbeth	√	√	Kn	3	4	8	Fa 87	37
Pattern: Layout	Special Summer Vest, A	Jennings, Lucy Anne	√	>4	WJ	9	3	35	Wi 85	42
Pattern: Layout	Spin-Weave-Wear		√	√	SS&D	16	1	61	Wi 84	70
Pattern: Layout	Sprang and Frame Plaiting for Garments		√	√	WJ	3	3	11	Ja 79	26
Pattern: Layout	Square Dance Skirts	Kaiser, Eunice	√	>4	H&C	7	1		Wi 55	46
Pattern: Layout	St. Ives Cardigan	Bush, Nancy	√	√	Kn	3	2	6	Sp 87	28
Pattern: Layout	Start with a Square	Shaw, Winifred	√		SS&D	16	3	63	Su 85	50
Pattern: Layout	Stitched Double Cloth Vest		√	√	WJ	7	1	25	Su 82	38
Pattern: Layout	Stonington Shawl	Zimmermann, Elizabeth	√	√	Kn	1	2	2	S-S 85	60, 72B
Pattern: Layout	Suited to Silk	Turner, Kathryn M.	√	√	SS&D	18	2	70	Sp 87	68
Pattern: Layout	Summer Blouse in Summer and Winter, A	Sullivan, Donna	√	√	PWC	4	4	14		18
Pattern: Layout	Summertime!	Coifman, Lucienne	√	√	SS&D	15	3	59	Su 84	74
Pattern: Layout	Symbolic or Sacred? A Personal View	Lockwood, Diana W.	√	>4	WJ	9	3	35	Wi 85	45
Pattern: Layout	T in a Basket		√	√	Kn	3	3	7	Su 87	19
Pattern: Layout	T-Sweater	Rowley, Elaine	√	√	Kn	1	2	2	S-S 85	34, 72A
Pattern: Layout	Tailored Bog Jacket, A	Guy, Sallie T.	√	√	SS&D	17	1	65	Wi 85	26
Pattern: Layout	Tailored Bog Jacket (Revisited), A	Guy, Sallie T.	√	√	SS&D	18	1	69	Wi 86	60
Pattern: Layout	Tailored Vest and Skirt, A	Arnold, Ruth	√	>4	WJ	9	3	35	Wi 85	56

SUBJECT	TITLE	AUTHOR	IL	INST	JOUR	VOL	NO	ISS	DATE	PAGE
Pattern: Layout	Tailoring a Suit Jacket	Bryan, Dorothy	√	√	H&C	11	1		Wi 60	28
Pattern: Layout	Tailoring a Suit Skirt	Bryan, Dorothy	√	√	H&C	10	4		Fa 59	28
Pattern: Layout	Tailoring Handwoven Fabrics	Bryan, Dorothy	√		H&C	10	2		Sp 59	17
Pattern: Layout	Tallis or Prayer Shawl, The	Derr, Mary	√	√	WJ	2	1	5	Jy 77	16
Pattern: Layout	Textiles of Coptic Egypt	Hoskins, Nancy Arthur	√	√	WJ	12	1	45	Su 87	58
Pattern: Layout	Textured Cottons: Dress and Sauna Robe	Henrikson, Sue	√	>4	WJ	6	3	23	Wi 81	20
Pattern: Layout	Textured Weave—An Alternative	Tanner, Virginia Leigh	√	√	WJ	7	3	27	Wi 82	58
Pattern: Layout	Thirty-Button Classic	Gibson-Roberts, Priscilla A.	√	√	S-O	11	1		Sp 87	32
Pattern: Layout	This Yoke's on You!	Glover, Medrith	√	√	Kn	3	2	6	Sp 87	35
Pattern: Layout	Three Color Progressions and Their Use in Sweater Jackets	Sylvan, Katherine	√	√	WJ	5	4	20	Sp 81	38
Pattern: Layout	Three in One	Moes, Dini	√	√	SS&D	18	2	70	Sp 87	74
Pattern: Layout	Three Personal Statements: Norma Minkowitz, Gillian Bull, Mardel Esping		√	√	Fa	3	5		S/O 76	22
Pattern: Layout	Tiffany's Gansey	Adams, Harriet	√	√	Kn	1	1	1	F-W 84 CI	29,56A 21
Pattern: Layout	Timelessly Fashionable Turkish Coat, A	Xenakis, Alexis Yiorgos	√	√	PWC	1	1		No 81	43
Pattern: Layout	Tool Kit from Inkle Bands, A	Hinson, Dolores M.	√	√	WJ	6	4	24	Sp 82	46
Pattern: Layout	Tote Bags with a Difference		√	>4	H&C	17	3		Su 66	20
Pattern: Layout	Traditional Fair Isle Sweater	Upitis, Lizbeth	√	√	Kn	2	1	3	F-W 85	26, 8B
Pattern: Layout	Traditional Shetland Shawl, A	Zimmermann, Elizabeth	√	√	Kn	1	2	2	S-S 85	59
Pattern: Layout	Traditional Teddy: Overshot in Miniature	Sullivan, Donna	√	√	PWC	5	2	16		14
Pattern: Layout	Travel Sweater	Upitis, Lizbeth	√	√	Kn	2	1	3	F-W 85	58
Pattern: Layout	Tunic Made from Narrow Strips	Barrett, Clotilde	√	√	WJ	4	3	15	Ja 80	9
Pattern: Layout	Turned Summer and Winter Jacket	Johnson, Melinda Raber	√	>4	WJ	8	3	31	Wi 83	58
Pattern: Layout	Twice Woven Bolero	Richards, Iris	√	√	WJ	4	3	15	Ja 80	24
Pattern: Layout	Two Prize-winning Canadian Projects		√	√	H&C	13	3		Su 62	32
Pattern: Layout	Two String Sweaters	Brugger, Susan	√	√	PWC			6	Su 83	31
Pattern: Layout	Two Unusual Multishaft Curtains	Xenakis, Athanasios David	√	>4	PWC	4	1	11		40
Pattern: Layout	Up, Up and Away in My Handwoven Balloon	Potter, Katie Forderhase	√	√	Hw	3	2		Mr 82	40
Pattern: Layout	V-Neck Jacket	Upitis, Lizbeth	√	√	Kn	3	4	8	Fa 87	37
Pattern: Layout	Vaquero Sweater & Quixquimtl	Frey, Berta	√	√	H&C	12	4		Fa 61	15
Pattern: Layout	Variation of the Macedonian Shirt	West, Virginia	√	√	WJ	7	2	26	Fa 82	50
Pattern: Layout	Variations on a Poncho Theme	d'Avila, Doris	√	√	WJ	2	3	7	Ja 78	30
Pattern: Layout	Veridian Green Cape	Barrett, Clotilde	√	>4	WJ	4	3	15	Ja 80	11
Pattern: Layout	Versatile Inlay, Twill on Twill	Beard, Betty	√	√	SS&D	19	1	73	Wi 87	53
Pattern: Layout	Versatile Vest and Matching Wrap Skirt, A	Dopps, Beth R.	√	√	WJ	7	3	27	Wi 82	21
Pattern: Layout	Violet Vestment	Hahn, Roslyn	√	>4	WJ	8	3	31	Wi 83	44
Pattern: Layout	Wear Your Best Apron	MacNutt, Dawn	√	√	SS&D	8	4	32	Fa 77	65
Pattern: Layout	Wearing Handwovens with Style	Mayer, Anita	√	√	WJ	10	3	39	Wi 86	22
Pattern: Layout	Weave and Knit Pullover	Barrett, Clotilde	√	√	WJ	8	3	31	Wi 83	20
Pattern: Layout	Weave and Knit Suit		√	√	WJ	8	3	31	Wi 83	18
Pattern: Layout	Weaver's Work Apron: A Project in Double Weave		√	√	WJ	7	2	26	Fa 82	27
Pattern: Layout	Weaving for Ethnic Clothing	Marston, Ena	√	√	SS&D	10	1	37	Wi 78	42
Pattern: Layout	Weaving in Quebec: Devotion to Garments	Barrett, Clotilde	√	√	WJ	6	4	24	Sp 82	18
Pattern: Layout	Weaving in Quebec: New Ideas and Techniques	Barrett, Clotilde	√	√	WJ	6	4	24	Sp 82	16
Pattern: Layout	White Circular Wrap	Richards, Iris	√	√	WJ	4	3	15	Ja 80	7
Pattern: Layout	Windowpane Jacket: In Double Knit and Garter Stitch	Ellman, Norma	√	√	Kn	3	4	8	Fa 87	40
Pattern: Layout	Winter Birches: The Blouse	Upitis, Lizbeth	√	√	Kn	1	2	2	S-S 85	46, 72B

SUBJECT	TITLE	AUTHOR	IL	INST	JOUR	VOL	NO	ISS	DATE	PAGE
Pattern: Layout	Winter Birches: The Jacket	Upitis, Lizbeth	√	√	Kn	1	2	2	S-S 85	44
Pattern: Layout	Winter Red: A Hand and Machine Knit Combination	Lewis, Susanna	√	√	Kn	3	4	8	Fa 87	28
Pattern: Layout	Win's Sweaters		√	√	WJ	8	3	31	Wi 83	12
Pattern: Layout	Woven Egmont Sweater	Klessen, Romy	√	√	PWC			2	Ap 82	83
Pattern: Layout	Woven Felted Boots		√	√	WJ	7	1	25	Su 82	28
Pattern: Layout	Woven Garments	Henzie, Susie	√	√	WJ	3	4	12	Ap 79	44
Pattern: Layout	Woven Skirt and Its Development, The	Poussart, Anne	√	√	WJ	8	3	31	Wi 83	39
Pattern: Layout	Wrist-to-Wrist Garment, The	Allen, Rose Mary	√	√	WJ	9	3	35	Wi 85	19
Pattern: Layout, Costume	Historical Components of Regional Costume in South-Eastern Europe, The	Gervers, Veronika			TMJ	4	2		75	61
Pattern Making	Make It Fit	Stoehr, Mary Kay	√	√	Hw	5	3		Su 84	64
Pattern Motifs: Coverlets	Stars, Diamonds, Tables, and Sunrise: Motifs and Structures of Woven Coverlets	Cabeen, Lou	√	√	TM			14	D/J 87	32
Pattern Selection: Handwoven Fabrics	Timelessness and Style ... Select a Pattern for Handwoven Fabric (error-corrected WJ v6 n1 81 p28d)	Davis, Helen B.	√		WJ	5	3	19	Wi 81	6
Pattern: Sewing	Basic Sewing Techniques in Handling Handwoven Fabrics for Garments	Knollenberg, Barbara	√	√	WJ	1	1	1	Jy 76	25
Pattern: Sketches	Irish Kinsale Cloak, The	Jones, Una	√	√	WJ	8	3	31	Wi 83	35
Pattern: Sketches	Jacket for Hiking, A	Roth, Bettie G.	√	> 4	WJ	8	3	31	Wi 83	69
Pattern: Tartans	Weaver's Book of Scottish Tartans: Tartan Patterns, The	Tidball, Harriet	√	√	SCGM		5		62	8
Pattern Weaves: Logical Development	Structure and Form in the Weaving of John Becker	Swannie, Suzanne	√		AT	6			De 86	173
Pattern Weaves, Warp-Stripe	Peru, Textiles Unlimited, Part 2: Opposites Warp-Stripe Patterns	Tidball, Harriet	√	> 4	SCGM		26		69	12
Pattern Weaves, Weft-Band	Peru, Textiles Unlimited, Part 2: A Structural Weft Pattern	Tidball, Harriet	√	√	SCGM		26		69	11
Pattern Weaves, Weft-Band	Peru, Textiles Unlimited, Part 2: Modern Weft-Pattern Bands	Tidball, Harriet	√	√	SCGM		26		69	12
Pattern Weaving	Changing Patterns in Midstream, Rethreading Made Unnecessary by New Device	Ziegler, Luise	√	√	H&C	13	2		Sp 62	12
Pattern Weaving	Pattern and Structure in Handwoven Fabrics	Frey, Berta	√	√	H&C	6	4		Fa 55	4
Pattern Weaving	Pattern Weaving	Barrett, Clotilde	√		WJ	4	4	16	Ap 80	6
Pattern-Ground Weaves	Baby Blanket (Margaretha Essén-Hedin)		√	> 4	Hw	8	2		M/A 87	45, I-7
Pattern-Ground Weaves	Chinese Drawloom: A Study in Weave Structure, The	Sellin, Helen	√	> 4	WJ	9	2	34	Fa 84	6
Pattern-Ground Weaves	Composition and Designing: Small Patterns	Zielinski, S. A.; Robert Leclerc, ed.	√	√	MWL	18			'51–'73	67
Pattern-Ground Weaves	Contrails Coverlet	Kelly, Jacquie	√	> 4	PWC	5	1	15		48
Pattern-Ground Weaves	Dal Dräll Table Runner (Nancy Klein)		√	> 4	Hw	1	2		S-S 80	25, 52
Pattern-Ground Weaves	David's Back...And Picks Up Where He Left Off	Xenakis, Athanasios David	√	> 4	PWC	5	2	16		42
Pattern-Ground Weaves	Double Two-Tie Twills and Basket Weave	Barrett, Clotilde	√	> 4	WJ	7	3	27	Wi 82	38
Pattern-Ground Weaves	Double-Twill on a Jack Loom Using Two Sets of Ground Harnesses Equipped with Special Long-Eyed Heddles	Freimer, Betty	√	> 4	CW	2	1	4	Oc 80	2
Pattern-Ground Weaves	Drawloom Special Harness for Double Weave	Malloy, Kim, OSB	√	> 4	AT	1			De 83	77
Pattern-Ground Weaves	Eight-Shaft Primer: Lampas for Eight	Sullivan, Donna	√	> 4	PWC	5	2	16		34
Pattern-Ground Weaves	Fantastic Finnweave, Part 3	Xenakis, Athanasios David	√	> 4	PWC			4	Ja 83	31
Pattern-Ground Weaves	Figured Piqué on a Ground of 2/2 Twill and 2/2 Hopsack	Xenakis, Athanasios David	√	> 4	PWC	4	2	12		24
Pattern-Ground Weaves	Finnish Lace: a Leno Variation	Egen, Su	√	√	Hw	7	2		M/A 86	49
Pattern-Ground Weaves	Five Block Double Weave Using the Glimåkra Long Eyed Heddle Accessory	Tramba, Diane	√	> 4	WJ	7	3	27	Wi 82	45

SUBJECT	TITLE	AUTHOR	IL	INST	JOUR	VOL	NO	ISS	DATE	PAGE
Pattern-Ground Weaves	Four + Four: An Introduction to Those Extra Harnesses	Howard, Miranda	√	>4	Hw	3	4		Se 82	66
Pattern-Ground Weaves	Gifts from Ancient Peru	Nass, Ulla	√	√	WJ	8	1	29	Su 83	32
Pattern-Ground Weaves	Glit — An Icelandic Inlay Technique	Heite, Louise B.	√	√	Hw	8	3		M/J 87	64
Pattern-Ground Weaves	Handwoven American Coverlets of the Overshot Type	Carey, Joyce Marquess	√	>4	PWC	3	3	9		24
Pattern-Ground Weaves	In My Country, It's Winter	Gagné-Collard, Agathe	√	>4	WJ	8	3	31	Wi 83	74
Pattern-Ground Weaves	In Pursuit of Plakhta	Golay, Myrna	√	>4	WJ	11	3	43	Wi 87	34
Pattern-Ground Weaves	Inlay Techniques	Barrett, Clotilde	√	√	WJ	1	1	1	Jy 76	3
Pattern-Ground Weaves	Introduction to Tied Unit Weaves, An	Kelly, Jacquie	√	>4	PWC	4	4	14		40
Pattern-Ground Weaves	Karelian Red-Picking	Ruchti, Willie Jager	√	>4	WJ	5	2	18	Fa 80	34
Pattern-Ground Weaves	Lampas	Kelly, Jacquie	√	>4	PWC	5	1	15		46
Pattern-Ground Weaves	Leonora Meek, Nebraska Weaver and Teacher		√	>4	H&C	15	2		Sp 64	23
Pattern-Ground Weaves	Little Known Weaves Worth Knowing Better: Broché	Zielinski, S. A.; Robert Leclerc, ed.	√	>4	MWL	16			'51–'73	84
Pattern-Ground Weaves	Little Known Weaves Worth Knowing Better: Turned Tufted Weave	Zielinski, S. A.; Robert Leclerc, ed.	√	√	MWL	16			'51–'73	103
Pattern-Ground Weaves	Long-Eyed Heddles and Rising Shed Looms	Fabeck, Diane	√	>4	Iw	4	4		Fa 79	28
Pattern-Ground Weaves	Macro Plaid, Macro Twill	Xenakis, Athanasios David	√	>4	PWC	3	1	7		55
Pattern-Ground Weaves	Multiple Shaft Weaving: M's and O's with Two Foundation Shafts	Evans, Jane	√	>4	WJ	6	1	21	Su 81	27
Pattern-Ground Weaves	Multiple Shaft Weaving, Twill and Satin Blocks, Damask		√	>4	WJ	5	4	20	Sp 81	10
Pattern-Ground Weaves	My Computer Designs a Bedspread	Salsbury, Nate	√	√	Hw	3	3		My 82	80
Pattern-Ground Weaves	Oscar Knopf's Ingenious Invention	Miller, Ethel E.	√	>4	H&C	10	2		Sp 59	24
Pattern-Ground Weaves	Pattern Weaving, Laotian Style	Keasbey, Doramay	√	√	Hw	2	3		My 81	54
Pattern-Ground Weaves	Pick-Up Patterned Double Weave	Keasbey, Doramay	√	√	Hw	5	2		M/A 84	80
Pattern-Ground Weaves	Pile Vest (Merja Winqvist)		√	√	Hw	8	3		M/J 87	73, I-15
Pattern-Ground Weaves	Skillbragd — A Decorative Pattern Weave		√	>4	Hw	8	3		M/J 87	60
Pattern-Ground Weaves	Spot Weaves — Old and New: Full Swivel	Zielinski, S. A.; Robert Leclerc, ed.	√	>4	MWL	12			'51–'73	85
Pattern-Ground Weaves	Spot Weaves — Old and New: Multi-Block Turned Swivel	Zielinski, S. A.; Robert Leclerc, ed.	√	>4	MWL	12			'51–'73	70
Pattern-Ground Weaves	Spot Weaves — Old and New: Multiple Spot-1	Zielinski, S. A.; Robert Leclerc, ed.	√	>4	MWL	12			'51–'73	41
Pattern-Ground Weaves	Spot Weaves — Old and New: Multiple Spot-2	Zielinski, S. A.; Robert Leclerc, ed.	√	>4	MWL	12			'51–'73	46
Pattern-Ground Weaves	Spot Weaves — Old and New: Plain Swivel	Zielinski, S. A.; Robert Leclerc, ed.	√	√	MWL	12			'51–'73	59
Pattern-Ground Weaves	Spot Weaves — Old and New: Swivel on Warp and Weft on Four Shafts	Zielinski, S. A.; Robert Leclerc, ed.	√	√	MWL	12			'51–'73	96
Pattern-Ground Weaves	Spot Weaves — Old and New: Triple Spot Weave	Zielinski, S. A.; Robert Leclerc, ed.	√	>4	MWL	12			'51–'73	52
Pattern-Ground Weaves	Spot Weaves — Old and New: Turned Swivel	Zielinski, S. A.; Robert Leclerc, ed.	√	√	MWL	12			'51–'73	65
Pattern-Ground Weaves	Supplementary Warp (Warp Brocade)	Wertenberger, Kathryn	√	>4	Hw	7	1		J/F 86	80
Pattern-Ground Weaves	Swatch #3 Skirt or Dress (Sharon Alderman)		√	>4	Hw	8	2		M/A 87	38, I-5
Pattern-Ground Weaves	Swatch #4 Vest (Sharon Alderman)		√	>4	Hw	8	2		M/A 87	38, I-5
Pattern-Ground Weaves	Three-Toned Blocks: Further Explorations with Long-Eyed Heddles	Broughton, Eve T.	√	>4	WJ	9	4	36	Sp 85	72
Pattern-Ground Weaves	"Tied Latvian" Weave, The (error-corrected CW n25 87 p31)	Evans, Jane A.	√	>4	CW		24		My 87	6
Pattern-Ground Weaves	Turned Drafts in Double Two-Tie Unit Weave	van der Hoogt, Madelyn	√	>4	WJ	9	2	34	Fa 84	13
Pattern-Ground Weaves	Twill and Plain Weave Blocks with Long-Eyed Heddles	Broughton, Eve T.	√	>4	WJ	8	4	32	Sp 84	58

SUBJECT	TITLE	AUTHOR	IL	INST	JOUR	VOL	NO	ISS	DATE	PAGE
Pattern-Ground Weaves	Unharnessing the Summer and Winter Weave	Xenakis, Athanasios David	√		Iw	4	4		Fa 79	42
Pattern-Ground Weaves	Upphämta Display Towel		√	>4	Hw	8	3		M/J 87	42
Pattern-Ground Weaves	Use Of Long-Eyed Heddles, The	Koob, Katherine; Barbara Keller; Ruth Howard	√	>4	CW	1	3	3	Ap 80	1
Pattern-Ground Weaves	Weaving with Ramie		√	>4	WJ	8	2	30	Fa 83	80
Pattern-Ground Weaves	Woven Lace and Lacey Weaves: Pickets and Riddles for Four Harness Frames	Zielinski, S. A.; Robert Leclerc, ed.	√	√	MWL	13			'51–'73	71
Pattern-Loom Mutualism	Structure and Form in the Weaving of John Becker	Swannie, Suzanne	√		AT	6			De 86	173
Pattern-Structure Weaves	Drawloom Basics	van der Hoogt, Madelyn	√	>4	Hw	7	2		M/A 86	61
Pattern-Structure Weaves	Drawloom Magic	van der Hoogt, Madelyn	√	>4	Hw	7	2		M/A 86	66
Patterns: Adjusting, Sewing	Perfect Pair of Pants, A	Cowan, Sally	√	√	TM			7	O/N 86	26
Patterns: Analysis	Learning to See Pattern	Morrison, Skye	√	√	TM			2	D/J 85	44
Patterns: Braiding	Unusual Braids Produced by Loop Manipulation	Speiser, Noémi	√	√	WJ	10	1	37	Su 85	15
Patterns: Brocade, Pick-Up	Part 2, Patterns for Pick-Up and Brocade	Tidball, Harriet	√		SCGM		23		68	26
Patterns: Construction, Sewing	Draping a Blouse	Sperry, Ellen	√	√	TM			3	F/M 86	46
Patterns: Coverlets	Art of Indiana Coverlets, The	Gilfoy, Peggy S.	√		AT	2			De 84	69
Patterns: Coverlets	Ohio's Woven Coverlets: Textile Industry in a Rural Economy	Cunningham, Patricia A.	√		AT	2			De 84	165
Patterns: Drafting	How to Draft a Half-Circle Skirt to Fit You		√	√	Hw	4	5		N/D 83	69
Patterns: Drafting Method	Drafter, The Draper, The Flat Patternmaker, The	Nebesar, Rebecca Lanxner	√	√	TM			11	J/J 87	33
Patterns: Dress Forms	Drafter, The Draper, The Flat Patternmaker, The	Nebesar, Rebecca Lanxner	√	√	TM			11	J/J 87	33
Patterns: Enlarged	Enlarged Patterns: A Fresh Look at Old Techniques	McClelland, Patricia Polett	√	>4	WJ	7	4	28	Sp 83	68
Patterns: Enlarging Techniques	Enlarging Patterns			√	TM			10	A/M 87	8
Patterns: Flat Method	Drafter, The Draper, The Flat Patternmaker, The	Nebesar, Rebecca Lanxner	√	√	TM			11	J/J 87	33
Patterns: Grist	Composition and Designing Part 2: Patterns in Grist	Zielinski, S. A.; Robert Leclerc, ed.	√	√	MWL	19			'51–'73	134
Patterns: Handwoven Accessories	Accessories: Bags and Slippers		√	√	WJ	5	3	19	Wi 81	42
Patterns: Handwoven Bags	Bags	Meiling, Nancy	√	√	WJ	6	3	23	Wi 81	40
Patterns: Handwoven Garments	Cardigan Jacket	Evans, Kerry	√	√	WJ	5	3	19	Wi 81	10
Patterns: Handwoven Garments	Cocoon Wrap Jacket, The		√	√	WJ	5	3	19	Wi 81	18
Patterns: Handwoven Garments	Eucharistic Vestments, The	Malloy, Kim, OSB	√	√	WJ	6	1	21	Su 81	37
Patterns: Handwoven Garments	Jacket Inspired by West African Narrow Strip Weaving	Bradley, Louise	√	√	WJ	5	3	19	Wi 81	31
Patterns: Handwoven Garments	Oval Cape	Sylvan, Katherine	√	√	WJ	5	3	19	Wi 81	36
Patterns: Handwoven Garments	Ruana	Sylvan, Katherine	√	√	WJ	5	3	19	Wi 81	34
Patterns: Handwoven Garments	Tale of a Talis, A	Sylvan, Katherine	√	√	WJ	6	1	21	Su 81	42
Patterns: Handwoven Garments	Tulip Outfit with Loom Controlled Inlay (error-corrected WJ v6 n1 81 p28d)	Kuwabara, Nancy	√	>4	WJ	5	3	19	Wi 81	28
Patterns: Handwoven Garments	Weaving Ecclesiastical Stoles and Chasubles	Reed, Kathy	√	√	WJ	6	1	21	Su 81	46
Patterns: Marking and Altering	Marking and Altering Patterns			√	TM			9	F/M 87	10
Patterns: Men's Clothing	Men's Patterns			√	TM			7	O/N 86	6
Patterns: Multisize, Tracing	Multisize Patterns			√	TM			13	O/N 87	4
Patterns: Muslin	New System for Getting an Ultra Fit, A	Lassiter, Betty			TM			12	A/S 87	22
Patterns: Navajo Rugs	Painted Rug Designs: Trader Hubbell's Influence on Navajo Weaving	Blue, Martha	√		Fa	14	5		N/D 87	5
Patterns: Overshot Coverlets	Ken Colwell on Coverlets	Colwell, Ken	√		PWC	3	3	9		56
Patterns: Plastic	Plastic Pattern Promises Perfect Fit, A	Fanning, Robbie			TM			12	A/S 87	20
Patterns: Publications	Drafter, The Draper, The Flat Patternmaker, The	Nebesar, Rebecca Lanxner	√	√	TM			11	J/J 87	33

SUBJECT	TITLE	AUTHOR	IL	INST	JOUR	VOL	NO	ISS	DATE	PAGE
Patterns: Quatrefoil	Quatrefoil	Xenakis, Athanasios David	√	√	PWC	3	3	9		53
Patterns: Repeat, Two-Dimension	Seventeen Pattern Types, A Study of Repeat Patterns in Two Dimensions	Elliott, Verda	√	> 4	CW		25		Se 87	23
Patterns: Sewing	Costume of a Plain People, The	Schiess, Kate	√	√	TM			5	J/J 86	65
Patterns: Sleeves, Dolmal	Drafter, The Draper, The Flat Patternmaker, The	Nebesar, Rebecca Lanxner	√	√	TM			11	J/J 87	33
Patterns: Slopers	Drafter, The Draper, The Flat Patternmaker, The	Nebesar, Rebecca Lanxner	√	√	TM			11	J/J 87	33
Patterns: Sources, Sweaters	Ultimate Sweater Pattern, The			√	TM			14	D/J 87	6
Patterns: Star and Diamond	Handwoven American Coverlets of the Overshot Type	Carey, Joyce Marquess	√	> 4	PWC	3	3	9		24
Patterns: Storage	Wrinkle-Free Patterns			√	TM			8	D/J 86	8
Patterns: Textile	Pattern...Pattern...Pattern	Park, Betty	√		Fa	9	1		J/F 82	11
Patterns: Twining, Split-Ply	Split-Ply Twining: Patterns of Three Camel Girths	Harvey, Virginia I.	√	√	TIAM		1		76	31
Patterns: Weaving, Brocade	Part 2, Patterns for Pick-Up and Brocade	Tidball, Harriet	√		SCGM		23		68	26
Patterns: Weaving, Supplementary Wefts	Brocade: Patterning on Plain-Weave Fabrics	Tidball, Harriet			SCGM		22		67	1
Peace Fleece	Spinning Fleece For Peace				TM			11	J/J 87	18
Peasant (European) Weaving	Supplementary Warp Patterning: Peasant Style Warp Pick-Up	Tidball, Harriet	√	√	SCGM		17		66	16
Pebble Weave	Bolivian Highland Weaving, Part 1	Cason, Marjorie; Adele Cahlander	√		SS&D	6	2	22	Sp 75	4
Pebble Weave	Bolivian Highland Weaving, Part 2	Cason, Marjorie; Adele Cahlander	√	√	SS&D	6	3	23	Su 75	65
Pebble Weave	Double-Woven Treasures from Old Peru	Cahlander, Adele	√	√	PWC			4	Ja 83	36
Pebble Weave, Double	Bolivian Highland Weaving, Part 1	Cason, Marjorie; Adele Cahlander	√		SS&D	6	2	22	Sp 75	4
Pebble Weave, Turned	Summer and Winter Revisited Part 4: Turned Pebble Weave	Xenakis, Athanasios David	√	√	PWC			4	Ja 83	52
Peg Plans	Design Decisions: Software Solutions	George, Patrice	√	> 4	Hw	5	5		N/D 84	47
Peg Plans	Metamorphosis: Two-Tie Weaves and the Changeable Image	Carey, Joyce Marquess	√	> 4	AT	1			De 83	243
Peg Plans	Modification of the AVL Dobby Loom for Execution of Multi-Shaft Two-Tie Block Weaves	Gustafson, Susan L.	√	√	AT	1			De 83	235
Peg Plans	Tie Ups, Pegplans & Drawdowns		√	> 4	CW	8	1	22	Se 86	27
Peg Plans	You Are Now Weaving Oakland	O'Hara, Sheila	√	> 4	AT	6			De 86	9
Penland School of Handicrafts	Penland's First 25 Years		√		H&C	5	2		Sp 54	8
Pens, Marking, Fabric	Marking Pens Reborn			√	TM			13	O/N 87	10
People: Aaron-Taylor, Susan	Speakers Bureau Presents		√		SS&D	7	3	27	Su 76	77
People: Abakanowicz, Magdalena	Abakanowicz		√		Fa	4	5		S/O 77	39
People: Abakanowicz, Magdalena	Corporate Collecting "Contemporary Tapestries" (Exhibit)	Dyer, Carolyn	√		Fa	4	5		S/O 77	16
People: Abakanowicz, Magdalena	"Fiber Art: Tapestries and Wall Hangings" (Exhibit)	Koplos, Janet	√		Fa	6	6		N/D 79	75
People: Abakanowicz, Magdalena	"Fiber Structures" Convergence '76 (Exhibit)	Mathews-Pulleyn, Kathryn	√		Fa	3	4		J/A 76	12
People: Abakanowicz, Magdalena	Interview with Mary Jane Jacob, An	Park, Betty	√		Fa	9	6		N/D 82	13
People: Abakanowicz, Magdalena	"Magdalena Abakanowicz" (Exhibit)	Koplos, Janet	√		Fa	10	2		M/A 83	66
People: Abakanowicz, Magdalena	Magdalena Abakanowicz Speaks	Park, Betty	√		Fa	10	2		M/A 83	11
People: Abakanowicz, Magdalena	"Ninth International Biennial of Tapestry" (Exhibit)	Pulleyn, Rob	√		Fa	6	4		J/A 79	62
People: Abakanowicz, Magdalena	When is Fiber Art "Art"?	Koplos, Janet	√		Fa	13	2		M/A 86	34
People: Abbott, Deborah Ann	Deborah Ann Abbott: Power Loom Weaving on a New Hampshire Farm	Mattera, Joanne	√		Fa	9	1		J/F 82	35
People: Abbott, Georgia Dille	Georgia Dille Abbott	Pauw, Alice Abbott			H&C	15	1		Wi 64	40
People: Abe, Eshiro	"Works In, On, and Of Paper" (Exhibit)	Les, Kathleen	√		Fa	6	5		S/O 79	79

SUBJECT	TITLE	AUTHOR	IL	INST	JOUR	VOL	NO	ISS	DATE	PAGE
People: Abroms, Harriet	Banners for Peace	Adels, Jill	√		Fa	12	4		J/A 85	36
People: Acton, Joseph D.	Diversity of Fabrics Comes from the Looms of Joseph D. Acton and Bret Carberry of Philadelphia, A		√		H&C	4	2		Sp 53	4
People: Adair, Arthur	Jurying	Ligon, Linda	√		Iw	1	2		Wi 76	10
People: Adams, B. J.	"Fibers" (Exhibit)	Meyer, Zach	√		Fa	4	4		J/A 77	11
People: Adams, B. J.	"Free Flow" (Exhibit)	Hecker, Carolyn	√		Fa	5	5		S/O 78	74
People: Adams, B. J.	Review/Discussion of Artspace's Innovative Yet Flawed "Fiber Freely Interpreted", A (Exhibit)		√		Fa	4	2		M/A 77	38
People: Adams, B. J.	Washington Fiber	Mathews, Rich	√		Fa	3	5		S/O 76	9
People: Adams, Barbara Jean	"Surface Design: Approaches '78" (Exhibit)	Arnow, Jan	√		Fa	6	2		M/A 79	67
People: Adams, Carol	Felt and Paper: A Portfolio		√		Fa	13	4		J/A 86	35
People: Adams, Eleanor	Livin' and Workin' on the Land: Fiber Art Outside the Mainstream	Talley, Charles S.	√		Fa	8	6		N/D 81	38
People: Adams, Mark	"Modern Aubusson Tapestry, The" (Exhibit)	Tanenbaum, Ruth	√		Fa	5	3		M/J 78	14
People: Adams, Mark	San Francisco Tapestry Workshop: A European-Style Atelier in the United States, The	Rowley, Kathleen	√		Fa	10	3		M/J 83	60
People: Adams, Mark	Weaving in San Francisco — Part 1	Prosser, Evelyn Bingham	√		WJ	6	2	22	Fa 81	44
People: Adams, Renie Breskin	"Currents"—Trends in Crafts (Exhibit)		√		Fa	13	5		S/O 86	53
People: Adams, Renie Breskin	"Needle Expressions '84" (Exhibit)	Koplos, Janet	√		Fa	12	2		M/A 85	74
People: Adams, Renie Breskin	Renie Breskin Adams: Artist...Teacher...Self-Seeker	Sommer, Elyse	√		Fa	5	3		M/J 78	36
People: Adams, Suzanne	Miniatures in Fiber: Working Small—An Exciting Challenge for the Contemporary Fiber Artist	Malarcher, Patricia	√		Fa	7	4		J/A 80	32
People: Adasko, Laura	"Landscapes" (Exhibit)	Clardy, Andrea	√		Fa	5	2		M/A 78	10
People: Adasko, Laura	"New Works in Batik by Laura Adasko" (Exhibit)	Gutcheon, Beth	√		Fa	5	3		M/J 78	12
People: Adcock, Carol	"Focus on Fiber" (Exhibit)	Hecker, Carolyn	√		Fa	6	3		M/J 79	83
People: Adcock, Carol	"Free Flow" (Exhibit)	Hecker, Carolyn	√		Fa	5	5		S/O 78	73
People: Adcock, Christine	"Basket and Paper Invitational Show" (Exhibit)	Howe, Cathe	√		Fa	12	3		M/J 85	71
People: Adelson, Laurie	Weaving Tradition in the Andes, A	Adelson, Laurie; Bruce Takami	√		Fa	6	4		J/A 79	22
People: Adrian, Gilbert	Gilbert Adrian: Creating the Hollywood Dream Style	Kinsey, Susan Buchanan	√		Fa	14	3		M/J 87	49
People: Afanasiev, Frances	American Handweaving 1960		√		H&C	11	2		Sp 60	10
People: Agano, Machiko	Eleventh International Biennial of Tapestry, The	Taylor, Elmer; Dianne Taylor	√		Fa	10	5		S/O 83	33
People: Ager, Lewa	Weaving Guilds—A Special Sharing		√		Iw	5	2		Sp 80	53
People: Ahlborn, Roxy Rehag	Surface Design and the Garment Form	Reith, Stephanie J.	√		Fa	8	1		J/F 81	34
People: Ahlskog, Sirkka	Sirkka Ahlskog — Versatile Craftsman		√		H&C	9	4		Fa 58	30
People: Ahrens, F. J.	Ahrens Looms, The	Bryan, Dorothy	√	√	H&C	6	3		Su 55	28
People: Ahrens, Jim	Jim "The Legend" Ahrens	Xenakis, Alexis Yiorgos	√		PWC	4	4	14		6
People: Ainsley, Sam	Edinburg Tapestry Company		√		Fa	12	5		S/O 85	64
People: Akers, Adela	Adela Akers, Designer-Weaver of Chicago		√		H&C	17	2		Sp 66	10
People: Akers, Adela	"Fiberworks" (Exhibit)	Park, Betty	√		Fa	4	6		N/D 77	10
People: Akers, Adela	Line As Movement: Adela Akers, The	Janeiro, Jan	√		Fa	8	2		M/A 81	70
People: Al Hilali, Neda	Sculptural Paper: Foundations and Directions	Scarborough, Jessica	√		Fa	11	2		M/A 84	32
People: Al-Hilali, Al	"Paper Sources" (Exhibit)	Papa, Nancy	√		Fa	5	4		J/A 78	16
People: Al-Hilali, Neda	"Art Fabric '77: the Contemporary American Tapestry" (Exhibit)	Papa, Nancy	√		Fa	4	4		J/A 77	12
People: Al-Hilali, Neda	Corporate Collecting "Contemporary Tapestries" (Exhibit)	Dyer, Carolyn	√		Fa	4	5		S/O 77	16

SUBJECT	TITLE	AUTHOR	IL	INST	JOUR	VOL	NO	ISS	DATE	PAGE
People: Al-Hilali, Neda	"Fiber R/Evolution" (Exhibit)	Rudich, Sally	√		Fa	13	4		J/A 86	45
People: Al-Hilali, Neda	"Fiber Works — Americas & Japan" (Exhibit)	Kato, Kuniko Lucy	√		Fa	5	1		J/F 78	10
People: Al-Hilali, Neda	Fiber Workspaces: A Room of Your Own	Bishop, Mara	√		Fa	4	4		J/A 77	38
People: Al-Hilali, Neda	"Four x Four, A Collaboration: A Special Environment " (Exhibit)	Welty, Margaret	√		Fa	7	1		J/F 80	69
People: Al-Hilali, Neda	Neda Al Hilali: An Interview	Park, Betty	√		Fa	6	4		J/A 79	40
People: Al-Hilali, Neda	"Neda Al Hilali" (Exhibit)	Janeiro, Jan	√		Fa	9	3		M/J 82	75
People: Al-Hilali, Neda	"Painted Weavings" Lia Cook and Neda Al-Hilali (Exhibit)	Park, Betty	√		Fa	8	1		J/F 81	88
People: Alaniz, Leonore	Contemporary American Handweaving from an International Perspective	Alaniz, Leonore	√		WJ	11	3	43	Wi 87	26
People: Alba, Lorraine	"Fiber Feelings" (Exhibit)	King, Dianne Hennessy	√		Fa	5	5		S/O 78	70
People: Albers, Anni	Anni Albers	Pettigrew, Dale	√		Hw	6	4		S/O 85	76
People: Albers, Anni	"Anni Albers: Current Work" (Exhibit)	Guyer, Niki	√		Fa	6	6		N/D 79	72
People: Albers, Anni	Anni Albers — Innovator in Textile Design		√		H&C	10	4		Fa 59	6
People: Albers, Anni	Sense of the Individual, The	Janeiro, Jan	√		Fa	11	2		M/A 84	52
People: Albers, Anni	Visit with Anni Albers, A	Margetts, Martina	√		TM			2	D/J 85	24
People: Albers, Anni	"Woven and Graphic Art of Anni Albers, The" (Exhibit)	Malarcher, Patricia	√		Fa	13	1		J/F 86	62
People: Albers, Annie	Behind the Scenes: A Museum Installation	Goodman, Deborah Lerme	√		Fa	13	3		M/J 86	42
People: Albertson, Nancy	"Left on the Loom" (Exhibit)	Dyer, Carolyn	√		Fa	5	2		M/A 78	16
People: Albertson, Nancy	"Paper and Felt Redefined" (Exhibit)	Ogden, Anne	√		Fa	5	2		M/A 78	17
People: Albin, Peggy Bass	"Revolution in Fiber Art" (Exhibit)		√		Fa	3	3		M/J 76	7
People: Albrecht, Jeanne	Arvada Project, The	Heath, Jennifer	√		Fa	5	4		J/A 78	45
People: Alexander, Bill	Jurying	Ligon, Linda	√		Iw	1	2		Wi 76	10
People: Alexander, Lynn	Open Tapestries by Lynn Alexander	Bryan, Dorothy	√		H&C	4	3		Su 53	30
People: Alexander, Marthann	Speakers Bureau Presents		√		SS&D	3	4	12	Fa 72	24
People: Allen, Barbara J.	Portfolio: Why I Work in Linen, A		√		Fa	14	2		M/A 87	38
People: Allen, Clarissa	Fiber on Martha's Vineyard	Erickson, Johanna	√		Fa	11	4		J/A 84	46
People: Allen, Helen Louise	Video Access to Textiles: The Helen L. Allen Textile Collection	Bard, Elizabeth A.	√		Fa	12	6		N/D 85	34
People: Allen, Laura	One Hundred Years Ago in Handweaving				Hw	7	3		M/J 86	27
People: Allen, Patsy	Double Lives: Can You Love Your "Work" When It's Your "Job"?	Mattera, Joanne	√		TM			10	A/M 87	62
People: Allen, Patsy	"Fabric Constructions: The Art Quilt" (Exhibit)	Klein, Jody	√		Fa	11	2		M/A 84	81
People: Allen, Patsy	"Quilts of Patsy Allen, The" (Exhibit)	Laymon, Cynthia	√		Fa	10	6		N/D 83	76
People: Allrich, Louise	Commissions: The Process, the Problems and the Prospects		√		Fa	6	5		S/O 79	45
People: Alonso, Harriet	"Stitcherhood Is Powerful" (Exhibit)	McGuire, Patricia	√		Fa	5	6		N/D 78	68
People: Alper, Mindy	Mindy Alper: Sculpting in Papier Mache	Saito, Shirley	√		Fa	11	4		J/A 84	18
People: Alvic, Philis	Variations on One Warp	Alvic, Philis	√		SS&D	12	4	48	Fa 81	70
People: Alvidres, Joseph	Joseph Alvidres	Alvidres, Joseph	√		Fa	13	2		M/A 86	15
People: Amaral, Olga	Olga Amaral, A Colombian Weaver's Year in the United States		√		H&C	18	4		Fa 67	20
People: Amat, Frederic	"Art Fabric: Mainstream, The" (Exhibit)	Janeiro, Jan	√		Fa	8	5		S/O 81	70
People: Amat, Frederic	Garment Form As Image, The	Koplos, Janet	√		Fa	10	6		N/D 83	66
People: Amat, Frederic	Papermaking in the U.S.A.	Toale, Bernard	√		Fa	9	4		J/A 82	34
People: Ames, Glen	Men Who Knit	Xenakis, Alexis Yiorgos	√		Kn	3	2	6	Sp 87	14
People: Ammann, Anneliese	Anneliese Ammann: Weaver	Kaspar, Patricia	√		Fa	5	6		N/D 78	20
People: Ammann, Anneliese	For Anneliese Ammann, Simplicity is Key to Woven Garments	Kaspar, Patricia	√		WJ	7	3	27	Wi 82	70
People: Amram, Hortense	American Handweaving 1960		√		H&C	11	2		Sp 60	13
People: Amram, Hortense	Hortense Amram, Designer and Weaver of Ceremonial Textiles		√	√	H&C	9	4		Fa 58	22

SUBJECT	TITLE	AUTHOR	IL	INST	JOUR	VOL	NO	ISS	DATE	PAGE
People: Anastasescu, Liliana	"Third International Exhibition of Miniature Textiles 1978" (Exhibit)	Spencer, Patricia	√		Fa	6	1		J/F 79	90
People: Anderson, Ann Stewart	"Ann Stewart Anderson: New Work" (Exhibit)	Arnow, Jan	√		Fa	7	1		J/F 80	64
People: Anderson, Ann Stewart	Hot Flash Fan, The		√		Fa	12	5		S/O 85	91
People: Anderson, Dona	Dona Anderson: Edging Towards the Unknown	Tacker, Sylvia	√		Fa	12	3		M/J 85	23
People: Anderson, Jan	"Fiber Departures" (Exhibit)	Dyer, Carolyn	√		Fa	4	3		M/J 77	9
People: Anderson, Jan	Scholarships '78		√		SS&D	9	4	36	Fa 78	44
People: Anderson, Lennart	Collaboration: A Vision of Unknown Territory	Parks, Betty	√		Fa	12	5		S/O 85	20
People: Anderson, Marilyn	"Four x Four, A Collaboration: A Special Environment " (Exhibit)	Welty, Margaret	√		Fa	7	1		J/F 80	69
People: Anderson, Ruth	Ruth Anderson, Custom Dyer	Kline, Michael	√		Fa	9	5		S/O 82	27
People: Anderson, Ruthadell	Commissions: The Process, the Problems and the Prospects		√		Fa	6	5		S/O 79	45
People: Anderson, Ruthadell	Legend of Maui and the Sun, The		√		SS&D	1	3	3	Ju 70	3
People: Anderson, Sally	Sally Anderson: Weaver		√		Fa	3	1		J/F 76	8
People: Anderson, Virginia	Livin' and Workin' on the Land: Fiber Art Outside the Mainstream	Talley, Charles S.	√		Fa	8	6		N/D 81	38
People: Andersson, Marja "Graset"	Portraits of Three Weavers: Sandra Ikse-Bergman, Marja "Graset" Andersson, Elisabet Hasselberg-Olsson	Talley, Charles S.	√		Fa	8	2		M/A 81	46
People: Andrews, Mary	Conversation with Mary Andrews, A	Pinchin, Bryn	√		Iw	5	4		Fa 80	24
People: Angelii, Elsa	Well-Worn Path to Where? A View of Contemporary Swedish Textiles, The	Talley, Charles S.	√		Fa	8	2		M/A 81	44
People: Angstadt, Jacob	In Search of Jacob Angstadt: A Master Weaver Lives Again		√		SS&D	7	2	26	Sp 76	27
People: Anliot, Sara Matsson	Sara Matsson Anliot	Bryan, Dorothy	√		H&C	11	3		Su 60	10
People: Anson, Suzan	Sanity, Madness and the Artist: The Work of Suzan Anson	Demoss, Virginia	√		Fa	6	2		M/A 79	36
People: Anthony, Janice	Janice Anthony's Contemporary Quilts	Henderson, Stew	√		Fa	13	4		J/A 86	22
People: Anthony, Janice	"Maine Coast Artists: Fabrications" (Exhibit)	Beem, Edgar Allen	√		Fa	11	4		J/A 84	80
People: Anttila, Eva	Contemporary Tapestry	Tidball, Harriet			SCGM		12		64	45
People: Anttila, Eva	Eva Anttila of Finland		√		H&C	15	1		Wi 64	16
People: Anvil, Eleen	Eleen Auvil, Versatile Designer Weaver		√		H&C	20	1		Wi 69	11
People: Appelbaum, Margery Freeman	Architectural Imagery of Margery Freeman Appelbaum, The	McCann, Kathleen	√		Fa	13	1		J/F 86	12
People: Arai, Junichi	Fabric About Fabric	Cannarella, Deborah	√		TM			1	O/N 85	72
People: Arai, Junichi	Made by Machine: Textiles for the Eighties	Harris, Patricia; David Lyon	√		Fa	12	5		S/O 85	34
People: Aralia, Elizabeth	Portfolio of Contemporary Fiber Sculpture, A		√		Fa	11	4		J/A 84	34
People: Arcadipone, Diana C.	"Fibrations" (Exhibit)	Silver, Elizabeth	√		Fa	6	5		S/O 79	85
People: Arcadipone, Diane	"Paper and Felt Redefined" (Exhibit)	Ogden, Anne	√		Fa	5	2		M/A 78	17
People: Archer, Sandra Brady	Boston Seven	Newman, Rochelle	√		SS&D	16	3	63	Su 85	71
People: Arianthe	"Mini Tapestry Exhibit" (Exhibit)	Bockelman, JoAnne	√		Fa	5	4		J/A 78	12
People: Arianthé	Two Weavers: A Business Association Which Works	LaLena, Constance	√		Hw	2	3		My 81	66
People: Arianthé (Stettner)	Arianthé: Notes from a Production Weaver	Stettner, Arianthé (see also Arianthé)	√		Fa	5	5		S/O 78	32
People: Arkenberg, Rebecca	Blueprinting on Fabric	Sider, Sandra	√	√	Fa	13	5		S/O 86	36
People: Armand-Delile, Diane	Quilting in France	Smeltzer, Nancy	√		Fa	13	2		M/A 86	49
People: Armstrong, Karen	"Karen Armstrong's Jungle Happening" (Exhibit)	Kerr, Connie	√		Fa	6	2		M/A 79	19
People: Aronoff, Jeffrey	From Canvas to Fabric...Jeffrey Aronoff 1980 Coty Award Winner		√		SS&D	11	4	44	Fa 80	50
People: Arouh, Leslie	Design by the Yard: Today's Fabric Innovators	Scarborough, Jessica	√		Fa	12	5		S/O 85	30

SUBJECT	TITLE	AUTHOR	IL	INST	JOUR	VOL	NO	ISS	DATE	PAGE
People: Arouh, Leslie	Interweavings, A Dance	Arouh, Leslie	√		Fa	7	1		J/F 80	16
People: Arp, Jean	Brief History of the International Biennial of Tapestry or "Watch Out for Women Who Knit", A	Taylor, Dianne	√		Fa	10	5		S/O 83	43
People: Arrizabalaga, Joan	Joan Arrizabalaga: Queen of the One-Armed Bandits		√		Fa	6	1		J/F 79	19
People: Asay, Roger	"Skin Forms: Innovations in Leather" (Exhibit)	Mackin, Jeanne	√		Fa	7	2		M/A 80	67
People: Attig, Charlotte	Charlotte Attig: Tassel Maker	Holst, Holly P.	√		Fa	9	6		N/D 82	26
People: Atwater, Mary Meigs	Mary Meigs Atwater: An Appreciation	Tidball, Harriet Douglas	√		H&C	4	1		Wi 52	18
People: Atwater, Mary Meigs	My Mother, The Weaver: Reminiscences About Mary Meigs Atwater	Biehl, Betty Atwater	√		SS&D	4	4	16	Fa 73	28
People: Atwater, Mary Meigs	Sense of the Individual, The	Janeiro, Jan	√		Fa	11	2		M/A 84	52
People: Atwater, Mary Miegs	Southern California Guild Honors Atwater	Brown, Barbara	√		SS&D	9	3	35	Su 78	38
People: Audunsdottir, Gudrun	Fiber Art in Iceland	Hrafnhildur, Schram	√		Fa	9	6		N/D 82	68
People: Auerkieff, Irena	Corporate Collecting "Contemporary Tapestries" (Exhibit)	Dyer, Carolyn	√		Fa	4	5		S/O 77	16
People: Augarten, Mae	Fabulous Plumage of Mae Augarten, The	Forscey, Suzon	√		Fa	6	3		M/J 79	65
People: Augusston, Augusta	"Contemporary Quilting: A Renaissance" (Exhibit)	Lauter, Estella	√		Fa	9	1		J/F 82	78
People: Aurdal, Synnove Anker	Contemporary Textile Art in Scandinavia	Talley, Charles S.	√		Fa	9	6		N/D 82	43
People: Aurel-Schneider, Jeanne	Paper Clothing: West	Koplos, Janet	√		Fa	11	2		M/A 84	39
People: Austin, Jean F.	"Basketworks": Visit to an Exhibition (Exhibit)		√		Fa	9	1		J/F 82	17
People: Austin, Joan	Teacher/Student Interface: Two Views of Education	Kosta, Angela	√		Fa	14	1		J/F 87	31
People: Aviks, Ilze	"Art of Crafts 1986" (Exhibit)		√		Fa	13	5		S/O 86	54
People: Axen, Gunila	Tiogruppen: When Working Together Works	Talley, Charles	√		Fa	11	6		N/D 84	41
People: Axtell, Jane Lang	Method to Her Madness: Jane Lang Axtell's Seminole Patchwork, A	Buscho, Ann	√		Fa	8	1		J/F 81	31
People: Aymon, Christine	"Miniature Textiles: 4th International Exhibition" (Exhibit)	Talley, Charles S.	√		Fa	8	3		M/J 81	72
People: Ayotte, Robert and Roberta	Weaving Together: The Ayottes of Center Sandwich, New Hampshire (Error-corrected WJ v11 n3 87 p78)	Elder, Shirley	√		WJ	11	2	42	Fa 86	30
People: Bacharach, David	Inspired by Fiber: Textile Sensibility in Other Media	Malarcher, Patricia	√		Fa	10	6		N/D 83	33
People: Bachman, Sally	Gallery (Tapestry)		√		Hw	3	1		Ja 82	52
People: Backlund, Agneta	Contemporary Textile Art in Scandinavia	Talley, Charles S.	√		Fa	9	6		N/D 82	43
People: Backus, Susan	Body as Canvas, The	Koda, Harold	√		TM			8	D/J 86	56
People: Badgley, Holly	Design by the Yard: Today's Fabric Innovators	Scarborough, Jessica	√		Fa	12	5		S/O 85	30
People: Baker, Carol	Fiber and Politics		√		Fa	13	3		M/J 86	20
People: Baker, Carol	"Fibrations" (Exhibit)	Silver, Elizabeth	√		Fa	6	5		S/O 79	85
People: Baker, Jan	Words in Fiber	Rowley, Kathleen	√		Fa	11	2		M/A 84	66
People: Baker, Kelley	Who Weaves?		√		Iw	5	2		Sp 80	41
People: Baker, Mary Winder	"Baker/Rapoport/Wick" in New York (Exhibit)	Park, Betty	√		Fa	4	5		S/O 77	15
People: Baker, Sheryl	"Show Biz" (Exhibit)	Scheinman, Pamela	√		Fa	7	4		J/A 80	69
People: Balazs, Iren	"Stitchery '79" (Exhibit)	Kerr, Connie	√		Fa	6	5		S/O 79	78
People: Baldwin, P. H.	Layne Goldsmith: Felted Worlds	Baldwin, P. H.	√		Fa	11	6		N/D 84	24
People: Balenciago, Christobal	Balenciago: The Architect of Elegant Clothing	Koda, Harold	√		TM			11	J/J 87	20
People: Ball, Sherry	"Fiber Structures" Convergence '76 (Exhibit)	Mathews-Pulleyn, Kathryn	√		Fa	3	4		J/A 76	12
People: Ballantyne, Margaret	Painted Surface, The (error-corrected Fa v9 n4 82 p9)		√		Fa	9	3		M/J 82	64
People: Ballard, Arthur J. (Pete)	Costumes on a Small Scale	Caldwell, Rebecca	√		Fa	11	5		S/O 84	87

SUBJECT	TITLE	AUTHOR	IL	INST	JOUR	VOL	NO	ISS	DATE	PAGE
People: Bally, Doris	Fiber Ten	McGuire, Patricia	√		Fa	4	6		N/D 77	26
People: Balone, Alice	Textile Trends: Collecting in the Southwest	Elliott, Malinda	√		Fa	12	6		N/D 85	27
People: Bardacke, Marge	Interview with Marge Bardacke, Basketmaker, An		√		Fa	4	1		J/F 77	34
People: Barker, Laurence	Paper Abroad (Exhibit)	Waller, Irene	√		Fa	11	2		M/A 84	82
People: Barker, Mary	Speakers Bureau Presents		√		SS&D	5	1	17	Wi 73	33
People: Barker, Phan Nguyen	Phan Nguyen Barker	Rulli, Linda	√		Fa	13	5		S/O 86	18
People: Barker, Sally	Pictorial Tapestry: A Portfolio of Contemporary Work	Goodman, Deborah Lerme	√		Fa	10	3		M/J 83	29
People: Barlow, Rick	Getting Into the Galleries: Nine Dealers Tell How to Do It		√		Fa	9	5		S/O 82	43
People: Barnard, Leonora Florian	Plastics in Fiber: A Persistent Presence	Malarcher, Patricia	√		Fa	12	1		J/F 85	56
People: Barnes, Dorothy	"Third International Exhibition of Miniature Textiles 1978" (Exhibit)	Spencer, Patricia	√		Fa	6	1		J/F 79	90
People: Barnes, Dorothy Gill	"Basketworks": Visit to an Exhibition (Exhibit)		√		Fa	9	1		J/F 82	17
People: Barnes, Dorothy Gill	Dorothy Gill Barnes: Baskets from a Gathered Harvest	Fedders, Pat	√		Fa	11	1		J/F 84	24
People: Barnes, Dorothy Gill	"Microfibers" (Exhibit)	McClelland, Elizabeth	√		Fa	8	2		M/A 81	66
People: Barnes, Francoise	Francoise Barnes: Contemporary Quilts	Canty, Judy	√		Fa	11	3		M/J 84	24
People: Barnes, Francoise	"Quilt National '79" (Exhibit)	Gutcheon, Beth	√		Fa	6	5		S/O 79	80
People: Barnes, Françoise	Quilt National on Tour		√		TM			13	O/N 87	14
People: Barnes, Jhane	Interview with Jhane Barnes: Designer, Weaver, Spinner, An	Lonier, Terri	√		Fa	10	4		J/A 83	55
People: Barnes, Jhane	Jhane Barnes		√		Hw	7	5		N/D 86	38
People: Barnes, Jhane	Jhane Barnes: A Convergence '88 Chicago Preview		√		SS&D	18	4	72	Fa 87	12
People: Barnett, Tina Takayanagi	"Fibers: From Function to Formalization" (Exhibit)	Scarborough, Jessica	√		Fa	9	1		J/F 82	76
People: Barrett, Clotilde	Clotilde Barrett: A Biographical Sketch		√		WJ	10	4	40	Sp 86	6
People: Barrett, Clotilde	Designers on Design		√		Fa	10	4		J/A 83	28
People: Barrett, Clotilde	Jurying	Ligon, Linda	√		Iw	1	2		Wi 76	10
People: Barrett, Clotilde	Speakers Bureau Presents		√		SS&D	6	4	24	Fa 75	63
People: Barrett, Helen	HGA Board of Directors Candidates		√		SS&D	11	2	42	Sp 80	26
People: Barrett, Phyllis	Certificate of Excellence in Handweaving: COE Holders, The	Drooker, Penelope B.	√		SS&D	14	1	53	Wi 82	49
People: Barrington, Sonya Lee	"Five Artists: Quilts" (Exhibit)	Scarborough, Jessica	√		Fa	13	5		S/O 86	47
People: Barron, Slater	Linted Palette of Slater Barron, The	Scarborough, Jessica	√		Fa	12	4		J/A 85	42
People: Barry, Flo	"Five Women from Texas" (Exhibit)	Leach, Vivian	√		Fa	6	1		J/F 79	86
People: Bartlett, Victoria	Sculpture Between Suggestion and Fact	Waller, Irene	√		Fa	9	3		M/J 82	100
People: Barton, Polly	Liturgical Vestment: A Contemporary Overview, The	Malarcher, Patricia	√		Fa	11	5		S/O 84	58
People: Bartsch-Treffkorn, Regine	Ballinskelligs Tapestry Works: Ancient Art/Modern Spirit, The	Burkhauser, Jude	√		Hw	3	1		Ja 82	55
People: Barzel, Dina	Dina Barzel		√		Fa	4	6		N/D 77	38
People: Barzel, Dina	People On Exhibit At Henry Gallery	Noble, Judy	√		SS&D	6	1	21	Wi 74	84
People: Bassler, James	"James Bassler" (Exhibit)	Malarcher, Patricia	√		Fa	8	6		N/D 81	71
People: Bassler, James	"Transformation: UCLA Alumnae in Fiber" (Exhibit)	Dyer, Carolyn	√		Fa	6	4		J/A 79	67
People: Bat-Zvi	Art Feeds the Hungry	Harel, Uri	√		Fa	13	4		J/A 86	11
People: Bataille, Nicholas	Imagery Is Personal in Tapestry Today	Clausen, Valerie	√		TM			9	F/M 87	66
People: Batchelor, Carolyn Prince	"Carolyn Prince Batchelor: Vessels" (Exhibit)	Lilligren, Ingrid	√		Fa	12	3		M/J 85	77
People: Batchelor, Carolyn Prince	Paper Clothing: West	Koplos, Janet	√		Fa	11	2		M/A 84	39
People: Bateman, Dr. William G.	Bateman Blend Weaves	Bateman, Dr. William G.; Virginia I. Harvey, ed.	√		SCGM		36		82	4

SUBJECT	TITLE	AUTHOR	IL	INST	JOUR	VOL	NO	ISS	DATE	PAGE
People: Bateman, Dr. William G.	Boulevard, Chevron, and Combination Weaves: Based on Dr. William G. Bateman's Manuscript	Bateman, Dr. William G.; Virginia I. Harvey, ed.	√	> 4	SCGM		38		87	1-93
People: Bateman, Dr. William G.	Multiple Tabby Weaves: Based on Dr. William G. Bateman's Manuscript	Bateman, Dr. William G.; Virginia I. Harvey, ed.			SCGM		35		81	1-92
People: Bateman, Dr. William G.	Park Weaves	Bateman, Dr. William G.; Virginia I. Harvey, ed.	√		SCGM		37		84	4
People: Bath, Virginia Churchill	Contemporary Needle Lacers		√		TM			13	O/N 87	44
People: Batson, Mary Jane	"Artists in Aprons" (Exhibit)	Alonzo, Harriet	√		Fa	6	3		M/J 79	76
People: Baugh, Deanna	"Theme Show in Utah, A" (Exhibit)	Alderman, Sharon D.	√		Fa	8	3		M/J 81	68
People: Beadle, Carole	Carole Beadle: The Artist and Her Work	Newby, Alice Bartholomew	√		Fa	9	4		J/A 82	44
People: Beadle, Carole	Felted Paper: A New Technique	Newby, Alice Bartholomew	√	√	Fa	9	4		J/A 82	42
People: Beadle, Carole	Jacquard Project: Selections from the Current Exhibition, The		√		Fa	9	2		M/A 82	36
People: Beadle, Carole	Pioneer Spirit of Carole Beadle: At the Frontier of Feltmaking, The	Howe, Cathe	√		Fa	6	6		N/D 79	36
People: Beadle, Carole	"Stitchery '77" (Exhibit)	Pierucci, Louise	√		Fa	4	3		M/J 77	11
People: Beauchemin, Micheline	"Third Montreal Tapestry Biennial, 1984" (Exhibit)	Duffy, Helen	√		Fa	12	3		M/J 85	79
+ People: Beaumont, Betty	"Fiber Works — Americas & Japan" (Exhibit)	Kato, Kuniko Lucy	√		Fa	5	1		J/F 78	10
People: Beaumont, Dorinda	"Art and Romance of Peasant Clothing, The" (Exhibit)	Dyer, Carolyn	√		Fa	5	3		M/J 78	16
People: Beck, Bobbi	"100% Wool" (Exhibit)	Goldin, Susan	√		Fa	4	6		N/D 77	18
People: Becker, John	Structure and Form in the Weaving of John Becker	Swannie, Suzanne	√		AT	6			De 86	173
People: Becker, Mary	Mary Becker		√		Fa	4	6		N/D 77	39
+ People: Becker, Pamela E.	Sampler of Surface Design, A	Westphal, Katherine	√		Fa	10	5		S/O 83	39
People: Becker, Robin	"Connections" (Exhibit)	Constantinides, Kathy	√		Fa	6	4		J/A 79	74
People: Becker, Robin	Hidden Sides, Hidden Lives: The Photo-Fiber Works of Robin Becker	Chressanthis, James	√		Fa	7	3		M/J 80	34
People: Becker, Robin	"Printed, Painted, and Dyed: The New Fabric Surface" (Exhibit)	Hecker, Carolyn	√		Fa	5	6		N/D 78	71
People: Becker, Robin	"Robin Becker and Joan Lintault: Visual Traces of the Past" (Exhibit)	Meloy, Margaret	√		Fa	11	1		J/F 84	80
People: Becker, Robin	"Survey of Illinois Fiber" (Exhibit)	Jensen, Janet	√		Fa	5	5		S/O 78	69
People: Becker, Robin	"Women of Fiber: Six Michigan Artists" (Exhibit)	Reid, Eve	√		Fa	8	5		S/O 81	74
People: Beckett, Susan	Protesting a Worldwide Danger		√		Fa	14	1		J/F 87	77
People: Beckett, Susan	Susan Beckett	Beckett, Susan	√		Fa	14	5		N/D 87	12
People: Beckwith, Carol	"Throbbing Needles II" (Exhibit)	Mattera, Joanne	√		Fa	7	2		M/A 80	71
People: Beede, Beth	Feltmaking Now: The Exciting Revival of an Ancient Technique	Gordon, Beverly	√		Fa	6	6		N/D 79	43
People: Begay, D. Y.	D. Y. Begay: A Navajo Weaver in New York City	Harvey, Nancy	√		SS&D	17	4	68	Fa 86	32
People: Begay, Mary Lee	Contemporary Navajo Weaving	Hedlund, Ann Lane	√		WJ	11	1	41	Su 86	30
People: Beinecke, Mary Ann	New Craft Program Will be Given on Nantucket Island		√		H&C	16	1		Wi 65	14
People: Beirich, Eileen	"Decade of Fibers, A" (Exhibit)	Franklin, Sue	√		Fa	5	1		J/F 78	17
People: Belangie, Michael	Michael Belangie Sees Common Problems for Hand and Power Weavers	Bryan, Dorothy			H&C	2	4		Fa 51	46
People: Belcher, Terry	When Prison Is Home: Challenging The Creative Spirit	Scarborough, Jessica	√		Fa	11	6		N/D 84	69
People: Belding, Emily	Emily Belding, Textile Designer		√		H&C	7	1		Wi 55	26
People: Belfer, Nancy	Ikat Notes: Nancy Belfer Talks About Her Recent Work	Belfer, Nancy	√		Fa	9	2		M/A 82	19
People: Bell, Lilian	Words in Fiber	Rowley, Kathleen	√		Fa	11	2		M/A 84	66
People: Bell, Lillian A.	Felt and Paper: A Portfolio		√		Fa	13	4		J/A 86	35
People: Ben-Haim, Zigi	Sculptural Paper: Foundations and Directions	Scarborough, Jessica	√		Fa	11	2		M/A 84	32

SUBJECT	TITLE	AUTHOR	IL	INST	JOUR	VOL	NO	ISS	DATE	PAGE
People: Benedict, Jimmie	"Fibers Southeast 1979" (Exhibit)	Johnson, Elma	√		Fa	6	2		M/A 79	68
People: Benedict, Jimmie	Jimmie Benedict: Non-Stop Knotting	Pilsk, Adele	√		Fa	5	2		M/A 78	52
People: Benedis, Sheila	"Basketry Today: And Quilts from the Collection of Phyllis Haders" (Exhibits)	von Weise, Wenda	√		Fa	9	4		J/A 82	75
People: Benedis, Sheila	What Makes a Basket a Basket?	Malarcher, Patricia	√		Fa	11	1		J/F 84	34
People: Benglis, Lynda	Whitney Museum of American Art, The (Exhibit)	Park, Betty	√		Fa	9	2		M/A 82	11
People: Benjamin-Fay, Joellen	Joellen Benjamin-Fay: Public Artist, Private Businesswoman	Strosnider, Ann	√	√	Fa	6	5		S/O 79	64
People: Benjamin-Murray, Betsy	Betsy Benjamin-Murray	Patton, Patti	√		Fa	4	3		M/J 77	43
People: Benjamin-Murray, Betsy	Sampler of Surface Design, A	Westphal, Katherine	√		Fa	10	5		S/O 83	39
People: Bennett, Kathleen M.	"Mini Tapestry Exhibit" (Exhibit)	Bockelman, JoAnne	√		Fa	5	4		J/A 78	12
People: Bennett, Mary Jane	Afro-American Sweetgrass Basketry	Johnson, Beth	√		Fa	9	5		S/O 82	23
People: Bennett, Noël	In the Spirit of the Navajo	Elliott, Malinda	√		SS&D	13	1	49	Wi 81	18
People: Bennett, Noël	Of Dreams and Transformations: An Interview with Noël Bennett		√		WJ	11	1	41	Su 86	7
People: Bennett, Noël	Weaving Brings Total Involvement with the Navajo	Bennett, Noël	√		SS&D	4	4	16	Fa 73	15
People: Berbas, Mary	Brief Creative Tale, A	Kosta, Angela	√		Fa	11	6		N/D 84	95
People: Berensohn, Paulus	Paulus Berensohn: A Potter Discovers Canvas Embroidery	Grover, Donald	√		Fa	6	5		S/O 79	28
People: Berezowska, Elizabeth	Tapestries of Elizabeth Berezowska, The	Carr, Diane	√		Fa	13	5		S/O 86	10
People: Berger-Fahrni, Maja	"Knowing the Ropes" (Exhibit)	Janeiro, Jan	√		Fa	6	4		J/A 79	72
People: Berglund, Hilma	American Handweaving 1960		√		H&C	11	2		Sp 60	14
People: Bergman, Agnes	One Hundred Sixty Years of Craftsmanship	Ligon, Linda	√		Iw	1	3		Sp 76	17
People: Bergman, Stephanie	"Fabric and Form: New Textile Art from Britain" (Exhibit)	Waller, Irene	√		Fa	9	6		N/D 82	80
People: Bergsteindottir, Steinunn	Fiber Art in Iceland	Hrafnhildur, Schram	√		Fa	9	6		N/D 82	68
People: Berlin, Rosalind	Contemporary Costume, Strictly Handwoven: Rosalind Berlin	Tidball, Harriet	√		SCGM		24		68	16
People: Berlin, Roz	Portfolio of Contemporary Fiber Sculpture, A		√		Fa	11	4		J/A 84	34
People: Berlin, Roz	Speakers Bureau Presents		√		SS&D	8	3	31	Su 77	83
People: Bernardi, Beatrice Boot	Four Seasons, Tapestries by Bernardi, The	Marston, Ena	√		H&C	20	2		Sp 69	8
People: Berner, Julie	Julie Berner	Berner, Julie	√		Fa	14	1		J/F 87	27
✦ People: Bero, Mary	Joyful Hieroglyphics: For Mary Bero Anything is Possible!		√		Fa	8	5		S/O 81	40
✦ People: Bero, Mary	Mary Bero	Weiss, Hedy	√		Fa	12	2		M/A 85	36
✦ People: Bero, Mary	"New Wisconsin Fiber": The First Group Show of American Fiber Art in Switzerland (Exhibit)	Bard, Elizabeth A.	√		Fa	10	6		N/D 83	43
People: Berrington, Claire L.	Open Jurying in Pittsburg: Putting Your Work on the Line (Exhibit)	Myrinx, Elaine	√		Fa	6	2		M/A 79	23
People: Berrish, Beverly	Paper Clothing: West	Koplos, Janet	√		Fa	11	2		M/A 84	39
People: Besana, Paola	Salute to Italy: Paola Besana		√		SS&D	16	2	62	Sp 85	25
✦ People: Bess, Nancy	"Works in Miniature" (Exhibit)	Malarcher, Patricia	√		Fa	7	3		M/J 80	82
✦ People: Bess, Nancy Moore	"Nancy Moore Bess: Baskets" (Exhibit)	Waller, Elsa	√		Fa	7	5		S/O 80	74
✦ People: Bess, Nancy Moore	Textile Study Group, The (Exhibit)	Guagliumi, Susan	√		Fa	13	3		M/J 86	54
People: Best, Eleanor	Certificate Holders: Now What?, The	Alderman, Sharon D.	√		SS&D	12	2	46	Sp 81	41
People: Bethel, Judith	Sculptural Paper: Foundations and Directions	Scarborough, Jessica	√		Fa	11	2		M/A 84	32
People: Beug, Doris	Dyeing in the Black Hills	Daly, Lynn	√		Iw	1	4		Su 76	18
People: Beugler, Eugen	Men Who Knit	Xenakis, Alexis Yiorgos	√		Kn	3	2	6	Sp 87	14
People: Beutlich, Tadek	"Fabric and Form: New Textile Art from Britain" (Exhibit)	Waller, Irene	√		Fa	9	6		N/D 82	80
People: Bewley, Deborah	Soft Sculpture: Old Forms, New Meanings	Gordon, Beverly	√		Fa	10	6		N/D 83	40

508

SUBJECT	TITLE	AUTHOR	IL	INST	JOUR	VOL	NO	ISS	DATE	PAGE
People: Beytebiere, D'Arcie	D'Arcie Beytebiere: Windswept Designs in Pleated Silk	Tacker, Sylvia	√		Fa	13	1		J/F 86	28
People: Bianchi, Ernestine	Weaving in San Francisco — Part 1	Prosser, Evelyn Bingham	√		WJ	6	2	22	Fa 81	44
People: Bierman, Bruce	Architect-Weaver and His Workaday World: Bruce Bierman's Business is Good Design, An	Malarcher, Patricia	√		Fa	7	6		N/D 80	60
People: Biggs, Marjorie	History in Stitches, A	Mattera, Joanne	√		Fa	7	3		M/J 80	37
People: Biggs, Marjorie	Judy Chicago's Dinner Party: A Review	Mattera, Joanne	√		Fa	7	3		M/J 80	16
People: Bighorse, Tiana	From Designing with the Wool	Bennett, Noël	√		Iw	4	1		Wi 78	17
People: Bighorse, Tiana	In the Spirit of the Navajo	Elliott, Malinda	√		SS&D	13	1	49	Wi 81	18
People: Bighorse, Tiana	Weaving the Navajo Way	Bighorse, Tiana; Noël Bennett	√		Iw	4	1		Wi 78	12
People: Billingsley, Mary	"Kari Lønning — Mary Billingsley" (Exhibit)	Beede, Beth	√		Fa	6	6		N/D 79	69
People: Bilowus, Ruth	Ruth Bilowus: Small and Precious Tapestries	Belfer, Nancy	√		Fa	7	2		M/A 80	15
People: Binford, Jacqui	"Textiles New Mexico 1976" (Exhibit)	Warner, Lucy Ann	√		Fa	3	2		M/A 76	12
People: Bisceglia, Therese	Felt and Paper: A Portfolio		√		Fa	13	4		J/A 86	35
People: Biscotto, Laura	Canadian Portfolio, A	Place, Jennifer	√		Fa	9	6		N/D 82	29
People: Bitar, Helen	Helen Bitar	Park, Betty	√		Fa	5	2		M/A 78	44
People: Bitar, Helen	Robert Pfannebecker: A Collector's Point of View	Park, Betty	√		Fa	5	4		J/A 78	42
People: Bitar, Helen	"Wearable Art" (Exhibit)	Hunt, E. Ann	√		Fa	6	3		M/J 79	78
People: Black, Glen	Glen Black, Handweaver of San Francisco		√		H&C	16	1		Wi 65	20
People: Black, Jappie King	Jappie King Black: The Siren and Other Tempting Crocheted Beings (error-corrected Fa v8 n2 81 p7)	West, Virginia	√		Fa	7	6		N/D 80	14
People: Black, Mary E.	Huck for Mary Black	Moes, Dini	√	√	SS&D	16	2	62	Sp 85	52
People: Black, Mary E.	Life and Times of Mary Black: A Visit with the Author of "The Key to Weaving", The	MacNutt, Dawn	√		Fa	8	4		J/A 81	63
People: Black, Robert, Jr.	Jacquard is Back	Lloyd, Ann	√		SS&D	18	4	72	Fa 87	10
People: Blackwell, Sarah	"Fibers '76" (Exhibit)		√		Fa	3	2		M/A 76	7
People: Bladholm, Cheri	Under Wraps		√		Fa	12	3		M/J 85	26
People: Blair, Margot Carter	Margot Carter Blair		√	√	Fa	4	3		M/J 77	28
People: Blake, Don	"Third Annual Fiber Show" (Exhibit)	Papa, Nancy	√		Fa	5	6		N/D 78	65
People: Blake, Maria Rose	Under Wraps		√		Fa	12	3		M/J 85	26
People: Blake, Nancy J.	"Fibers Unlimited 1979" (Exhibit)	Davidian, Robert	√		Fa	7	2		M/A 80	69
People: Blanks, Lloyd	Evolution of an Artist: Lloyd Blanks	Blanks, Lloyd	√		Fa	14	5		N/D 87	30
People: Blecher, Terry	History in Stitches, A	Mattera, Joanne	√		Fa	7	3		M/J 80	37
People: Blicharska, Honorata	"Honorata Blicharska" (Exhibit)		√		Fa	4	4		J/A 77	15
People: Blinks, Anne	Visit with Anne Blinks, A		√		Iw	3	3		Sp 78	15
People: Bliss, Ann	Ann Bliss: Writing a Book About Her Friends		√		Fa	3	5		S/O 76	15
People: Bliss, Anne	Publish Your Own Craft Book	Nell, Patti			Iw	1	2		Wi 76	18
People: Block, Sophia	Fiber on Martha's Vineyard	Erickson, Johanna	√		Fa	11	4		J/A 84	46
People: Blum, June	June Blum	Blum, June	√		Fa	13	2		M/A 86	14
People: Blumenthal, Betsy	"Works in Fiber" (Exhibit)	Arnow, Jan	√		Fa	8	2		M/A 81	61
People: Blumrich, Stephen	"Printed, Painted, and Dyed: The New Fabric Surface" (Exhibit)	Hecker, Carolyn	√		Fa	5	6		N/D 78	71
People: Bodine, Sarah	Designers on Design		√		Fa	10	4		J/A 83	28
People: Boeder, Caryl Kaiser	"100% Wool" (Exhibit)	Goldin, Susan	√		Fa	4	6		N/D 77	18
People: Boeder, Caryl Kaiser	"Young Americans: Fiber, Wood, Plastic, Leather" (Exhibit)	Malarcher, Patricia	√		Fa	4	6		N/D 77	14
People: Boguch, Janet	Alter Cloths and Shrines: The New Work of Janet Boguch	Tacker, Sylvia	√		Fa	14	5		N/D 87	6
People: Boguch, Janet	"Janet Boguch: Delivered Runes" (Exhibit)	Janeiro, Jan	√		Fa	6	5		S/O 79	83

SUBJECT	TITLE	AUTHOR	IL	INST	JOUR	VOL	NO	ISS	DATE	PAGE
People: Boguch, Janet	Memory, Metaphor, And Magic: The Art of Janet Boguch	Glowen, Ron	√		Fa	11	6		N/D 84	66
People: Bohannan, Ronnine	Designing Rep Weaves with the Aid of a Computer	Bohannan, Ronnine	√	√	WJ	7	4	28	Sp 83	24
People: Boland, Brian	Ballooning Art Form: The Making of a Hot Air Balloon Basket, A		√		SS&D	11	4	44	Fa 80	8
People: Bolder, Caryl Kaiser	1977 HGA Scholarships (error-corrected SS&D v9 n2 78 p70)		√		SS&D	9	1	33	Wi 77	46
People: Bolle, Ilsa	"Fiber Directions" (Exhibit)		√		Fa	14	1		J/F 87	70
People: Bolster, Ella	Ella Bolster		√	> 4	H&C	12	2		Sp 61	26
People: Bonner, June M.	"Microfibers" (Exhibit)	McClelland, Elizabeth	√		Fa	8	2		M/A 81	66
People: Booker, Cissy	Review/Discussion of Artspace's Innovative Yet Flawed "Fiber Freely Interpreted", A (Exhibit)		√		Fa	4	2		M/A 77	38
People: Boren, Peg	"Fibers '76" (Exhibit)		√		Fa	3	2		M/A 76	7
People: Bosscher, Madeleine	"Wall Hangings: The New Classicism" (Exhibit)	Grover, Donald	√		Fa	4	4		J/A 77	10
People: Bott, Peter	Fans and Fan Imagery	Howe, Katherine; Joanne Mattera	√		Fa	9	4		J/A 82	26
People: Bott, Peter	"Fiber/Fabric '81" (Exhibit)	Scarborough, Jessica	√		Fa	8	4		J/A 81	74
People: Boucher, Moisete	"Current Directions: Conseie des Arts Textiles du Quebec" (Exhibit)	Newman, Rochelle	√		Fa	12	1		J/F 85	74
People: Boulez-Cuykx, Betty	Betty Boulez-Cuykx: Modern Lacemaker	de Backer, Lisette	√		Fa	13	3		M/J 86	23
People: Bourget, Susan	"Art Couture '82" (Exhibit)	Guagliumi, Sasan	√		Fa	10	1		J/F 83	84
People: Boussard, Dana	Keeping Warm in Alaska		√		Fa	9	6		N/D 82	22
People: Boussard, Dana	"Landscapes" (Exhibit)	Clardy, Andrea	√		Fa	5	2		M/A 78	10
People: Boussard, Dana	"Wearable Art" (Exhibit)	Hunt, E. Ann	√		Fa	6	3		M/J 79	78
People: Boutinwald, Pat	Feltmaking Now: The Exciting Revival of an Ancient Technique	Gordon, Beverly	√		Fa	6	6		N/D 79	43
People: Bouton, Sheila	Pikes Peak Weavers Guild First Fibre Arts Festival (Exhibit)	Fife, Lin	√		Fa	3	5		S/O 76	6
People: Bowen, Gaza	Feltmaking Now: The Exciting Revival of an Ancient Technique	Gordon, Beverly	√		Fa	6	6		N/D 79	43
People: Bowen, Gaza	For the Body (error-corrected Fa v10 n2 83 p61)		√		Fa	10	1		J/F 83	32
People: Bowen, Gaza	Goody Twoshoes: Gaza Bowen, An Extraordinary Shoemaker		√		Fa	8	5		S/O 81	13
People: Bowen, Gaza	"Poetry for the Body, Clothing for the Spirit" (Exhibit)	Hickman, Pat	√		Fa	10	5		S/O 83	75
People: Bowers, Maryellen	"Festival of Weaving" (Exhibit)	Greenberg, Blue	√		Fa	7	4		J/A 80	71
People: Bowser, Josef	"Interweave '78" (Exhibit)	Yarnell, Grace	√		Fa	5	6		N/D 78	69
People: Boyd, Karen White	Miniatures in Fiber: Working Small—An Exciting Challenge for the Contemporary Fiber Artist	Malarcher, Patricia	√		Fa	7	4		J/A 80	32
People: Bradford, Bill	Commissions: The Process, the Problems and the Prospects		√		Fa	6	5		S/O 79	45
People: Bradley, David H.	American Handweaving 1960		√		H&C	11	2		Sp 60	48
People: Bradley, Sue	Knitting Craft in Great Britain, The	Kinder, Kathleen	√		Fa	11	4		J/A 84	42
People: Bramhall, Emily	Fiber on Martha's Vineyard	Erickson, Johanna	√		Fa	11	4		J/A 84	46
People: Bramhall, Pat and Butch	Pat and Butch Bramhall				SS&D	19	1	73	Wi 87	5
People: Brandford, Joanne	"Joanne Brandford: Recent Nets" (Exhibit)	Park, Betty	√		Fa	11	6		N/D 84	77
People: Brandford, Joanne Segal	"Beyond the Fringe" (Exhibit)	Einstein, Sylvia	√		Fa	7	2		M/A 80	70
People: Brandford, Joanne Segal	"Joanne Segal Brandford — Nets" (Exhibit)	Park, Betty	√		Fa	5	3		M/J 78	17
People: Brandford, Joanne Segal	"Landscapes" (Exhibit)	Clardy, Andrea	√		Fa	5	2		M/A 78	10
People: Brandford, Joanne Segal	"Show of Complements, A" (Exhibit)	Schevill, Margot Blum	√		Fa	13	4		J/A 86	50
People: Brandford, Joanne Segal	What Makes a Basket a Basket?	Malarcher, Patricia	√		Fa	11	1		J/F 84	34
People: Brandi, Giola and John	"Charms" (Exhibit)	Vander Lee, Jana	√		Fa	3	3		M/J 76	6

SUBJECT	TITLE	AUTHOR	IL	INST	JOUR	VOL	NO	ISS	DATE	PAGE
People: Brandon, Reiko	"Fiber from the Marietta College Crafts National" (Exhibit)	Murray, Megan	√		Fa	11	2		M/A 84	76
People: Brandon, Reiko Mochinaga	Reiko Mochinaga Brandon: Bridging Two Cultures	Moore, Marcia	√		Fa	13	6		N/D 86	16
People: Brandon, Sue	"Interweave 79" (Exhibit)	Constantinides, Kathy	√		Fa	7	1		J/F 80	66
People: Branfman, Judy	In and on the Surface: The Tapestries of Judy Branfman	Mattera, Joanne	√		Fa	10	3		M/J 83	22
People: Brathwaite, Trederick	Body as Canvas, The	Koda, Harold	√		TM			8	D/J 86	56
People: Braun-Reinitz, Janet	Garment Form As Image, The	Koplos, Janet	√		Fa	10	6		N/D 83	66
People: Breidfjord, Leifur	Fiber Art in Iceland	Hrafnhildur, Schram	√		Fa	9	6		N/D 82	68
People: Breitenbach, Cornelia	Art Consultants: Bridging the Gap Between Artist and Client	Goodman, Deborah Lerme	√		Fa	12	6		N/D 85	31
People: Breitenbach, Cornelia	"Surface Design: Approaches '78" (Exhibit)	Arnow, Jan	√		Fa	6	2		M/A 79	67
People: Brenholts, Jeanne	Fashionable Palette of Pittsburgh Paints, The	Brenholts, Jeanne	√		Fa	14	3		M/J 87	46
People: Brenholts, Jeanne	Pittsburg Artists Create Kimono Canvases		√		Fa	13	3		M/J 86	7
People: Brenholts, Jeanne	Sampler of Surface Design, A	Westphal, Katherine	√		Fa	10	5		S/O 83	39
People: Brenholts, Jeanne	Under Wraps		√		Fa	12	3		M/J 85	26
People: Brenholts, Jeanne	Words in Fiber	Rowley, Kathleen	√		Fa	11	2		M/A 84	66
People: Brennan, Archie	Edinburgh Tapestry Company: A Thriving Anachronism in Scotland, The	Soroka, Joanne	√		Fa	10	3		M/J 83	59
People: Brennan, Archie	Imagery Is Personal in Tapestry Today	Clausen, Valerie	√		TM			9	F/M 87	66
People: Brennan, Harold J.	American Handweaving 1960		√		H&C	11	2		Sp 60	9
People: Brennand-Wood, Michael	"Fabric and Form: New Textile Art from Britain" (Exhibit)	Waller, Irene	√		Fa	9	6		N/D 82	80
People: Brennand-Wood, Michael	Michael Brennand-Wood	Orlowsky, Dzvinia	√		Fa	14	1		J/F 87	26
People: Breskin-Adams, Renie	Liberated Embroidery		√		Fa	9	3		M/J 82	35
People: Brett, George	George Brett: Webs of a Mad Spider	McMillan, Sam	√		Fa	8	6		N/D 81	32
People: Bridwell, Betsy	Quilting For World Peace	Shufro, Cathy	√		TM			10	A/M 87	14
People: Bright, Harriett H.	Fifty Years As a Coverlet Weaver	Bright, Harriett H.	√	√	WJ	6	2	22	Fa 81	54
People: Brill, Glenn	"Glenn Brill: Recent Work" (Exhibit)	Rowley, Kathleen	√		Fa	12	1		J/F 85	72
People: Brilliant, Ruby	Ruby Brilliant: A Knitter Well-Named		√		Fa	10	1		J/F 83	19
People: Bringle, Edwina	Speakers Bureau Presents			√	SS&D	4	1	13	Wi 72	32
People: Brinkman, Alice	Guild in Focus: Fiber Artisans, A	Kline, Martha	√		Fa	11	5		S/O 84	47
People: Britt, Oscar	Men Who Knit	Xenakis, Alexis Yiorgos	√		Kn	3	2	6	Sp 87	14
People: Broaddus, John Eric	Conversing with Artist John Eric Broaddus	Stackel, I. M.	√		Fa	11	5		S/O 84	28
People: Broadwell, Sally	Sally Broadwell	Broadwell, Sally	√		Fa	14	4		S/O 87	19
People: Brock, M. Susan	Who Weaves?		√		Iw	5	2		Sp 80	34
People: Brod, Ruth	Crocheted Cream Puffs? What You See Is Not What You Get	Fedders, Pat	√		Fa	8	5		S/O 81	16
People: Brody, Laura	"Fiber Images" (Exhibit)	Park, Betty	√		Fa	13	2		M/A 86	54
People: Brody, Laura	Portfolio: Why I Work in Linen, A		√		Fa	14	2		M/A 87	39
People: Bromberg, Nancy	Cows in Fiber	Timmons, Chris	√		Fa	11	4		J/A 84	55
People: Bronson, Mary E.	Weave and Knit Suit		√	√	WJ	8	3	31	Wi 83	18
People: Brooke, Anne	Anne Brooke's Impeccable Woven Rugs	West, Virginia	√		Fa	6	6		N/D 79	24
People: Brooke, Anne	Result of Weaving Rugs, The	Brooke, Anne	√		WJ	7	4	28	Sp 83	39
People: Brooks, Marguerite	Brooks Lace and Weaving	Tod, Osma Gallinger	√		H&C	20	1		Wi 69	29
People: Brostoff, Laya	Dream—The Reality, The	Ligon, Linda	√		Iw	3	4		Su 78	12
People: Brown, Arleen Emery	On Working At Home	Brown, Arleen Emery	√		Fa	7	2		M/A 80	45
People: Brown, Barb	Fiber/Art Conditioned by Life: A Workshop with Sheila Hicks	Klein, Jody	√		Fa	12	5		S/O 85	58
People: Brown, Barbara	"Fabric and Form: New Textile Art from Britain" (Exhibit)	Waller, Irene	√		Fa	9	6		N/D 82	80
People: Brown, Corky	Return of the Rag, The	Basa, Lynn	√		Fa	14	3		M/J 87	29

SUBJECT	TITLE	AUTHOR	IL	INST	JOUR	VOL	NO	ISS	DATE	PAGE
People: Brown, Pat	Pat Brown	Brown, Pat	√		Fa	5	4		J/A 78	53
People: Brown, Rachel	Rachel Brown: Weaver At the Wheel	Daily, Laura	√		Fa	10	3		M/J 83	20
People: Brown, Sally	Sally Brown				SS&D	18	3	71	Su 87	5
People: Brown, Shannon	"Fibers Unlimited" (Exhibit)	Sherwood, Thomas	√		Fa	5	1		J/F 78	14
People: Brown, Tafi	Blues in the Light: Cyanotype on Fabric	Sider, Sandra	√		Fa	13	5		S/O 86	34
People: Brown, Tafi	"Quilt National '79" (Exhibit)	Gutcheon, Beth	√		Fa	6	5		S/O 79	80
People: Brown, William	Teaching At a Men's Prison	Plevin, Ann	√		Fa	14	1		J/F 87	36
People: Brownlee-Ramsdale, Sandra	Grrrhhhh: A Study of Social Patterns	Hickman, Deborah	√		Fa	14	4		S/O 87	23
People: Brownlee-Ramsdale, Sandra	Weaver of Images	Brownlee-Ramsdale, Sandra	√		AT	6			De 86	147
People: Bruzzese, Enzo	Tailor on Pressing, A	Hostek, Stanley	√	√	TM			10	A/M 87	43
People: Bryan, Dorothy	American Handweaving 1960		√		H&C	11	2		Sp 60	49
People: Bryan, Linda Nelson	Linda Nelson Bryan	Vozar, Linda	√		Fa	4	6		N/D 77	58
People: Bryant, Laura Militzer	Laura Militzer Bryant: Thought Process	Bryant, Laura Militzer	√		Fa	10	4		J/A 83	52
People: Bryant, Lois	Public Fiber: Looking At the Logistics	Koplos, Janet	√		Fa	12	1		J/F 85	32
People: Bryson, Janet Markarian	"Basketworks": Visit to an Exhibition (Exhibit)		√		Fa	9	1		J/F 82	17
People: Buadottir, Asgerdur	Contemporary Textile Art in Scandinavia	Talley, Charles S.	√		Fa	9	6		N/D 82	43
People: Buadottir, Asgerdur	Fiber Art in Iceland	Hrafnhildur, Schram	√		Fa	9	6		N/D 82	68
People: Buck, Virginia Knight	Family Album of Pomo Baskets, A	Metzler, Sandra	√		Fa	11	1		J/F 84	63
People: Buckman, Jan	"New Wisconsin Fiber": The First Group Show of American Fiber Art in Switzerland (Exhibit)	Bard, Elizabeth A.	√		Fa	10	6		N/D 83	43
People: Buderstadt, Bruce	"Houston Designer-Craftsmen 1976" (Exhibit)	Vander Lee, Jana	√		Fa	3	4		J/A 76	9
People: Buglund, Gail	Pikes Peak Weavers Guild First Fibre Arts Festival (Exhibit)	Fife, Lin	√		Fa	3	5		S/O 76	6
People: Buic, Jagoda	Enduring Art of Jagoda Buic, The	Mathews, Rich	√		Fa	11	4		J/A 84	64
People: Buic, Jagoda	"Fiberworks" (Exhibit)	Park, Betty	√		Fa	4	6		N/D 77	10
People: Buic, Jagoda	"Jagoda Buic" (Exhibit)	Mathews, Rich	√		Fa	4	5		S/O 77	13
People: Bujnowski, Don	Don Bujnowski		√		H&C	13	4		Fa 62	31
People: Bulbach, Stanley	Stanley Bulbach	McManus, Fran	√		S-O	8	2		Su 84	55
People: Bulbach, Stanley	Who Weaves?		√		Iw	5	2		Sp 80	36
People: Bulback, Stanley	Weaving in the Urban Tradition	Bulback, Stanley	√		SS&D	12	3	47	Su 81	7
People: Bulitt, Patricia	Patricia Bulitt: Gutsongs and Other Dances	Scarborough, Jessica	√		Fa	11	5		S/O 84	50
People: Bull, Gillian	Three Personal Statements: Norma Minkowitz, Gillian Bull, Mardel Esping		√		Fa	3	5		S/O 76	19
People: Bullington, Judy	"Forms and Surfaces" (Exhibit)		√		Fa	8	4		J/A 81	68
People: Bulow, Karen	Fabrics from Karen Bulow's Looms	Storey, Walter Rendell	√		H&C	5	1		Wi 53	14
People: Burbidge, Pauline	"Quilt National '83" (Exhibit)	Roe, Nancy	√		Fa	10	5		S/O 83	82
People: Burchard, Diane	Felt and Paper: A Portfolio		√		Fa	13	4		J/A 86	35
People: Bureker, Hanni	Garments by Hanni Bureker		√	√	WJ	6	3	23	Wi 81	35
People: Burg, Pam	Tangential Textiles: From Quiltmaking to Points Beyond	Rowley, Kristen Carlsen	√		Fa	9	2		M/A 82	22
People: Burhen, Jan	Speakers Bureau Presents		√		SS&D	7	4	28	Fa 76	99
People: Burian, Ann	Ann Burian: Mythic Transformations	Hains, Maryellen	√		Fa	12	2		M/A 85	21
People: Burian, Ann	"Ruth's Madcaps" (Exhibit)	Haynes, Maryellen	√		Fa	14	4		S/O 87	9
People: Burian, Ann	"Women of Fiber: Six Michigan Artists" (Exhibit)	Reid, Eve	√		Fa	8	5		S/O 81	74
People: Burke, Bill	Mummery: Philadelphia's Happy New Year	Smeltzer, Nancy	√		Fa	14	3		M/J 87	39
People: Burlew, Margaret	Focus on the HGA Board of Directors		√		SS&D	10	1	37	Wi 78	52
People: Burnham, Dorothy	Convergence '86 Preview: Keynote Speaker Dorothy Burnham	Dean, Ankaret	√		SS&D	16	3	63	Su 85	32
People: Burnham, Dorothy K.	Convergence '86 Preview: Toronto — A City in Transition	Baker, William R. M.	√		SS&D	17	1	65	Wi 85	42

SUBJECT	TITLE	AUTHOR	IL	INST	JOUR	VOL	NO	ISS	DATE	PAGE
People: Burnham, Dorothy K.	Making Weaving History	Xenakis, Alexis Yiorgos	√		PWC	4	3	13		6
People: Burningham, Charlene	Liturgical Vestment: A Contemporary Overview, The	Malarcher, Patricia	√		Fa	11	5		S/O 84	58
People: Burningham, Robert	Liturgical Vestment: A Contemporary Overview, The	Malarcher, Patricia	√		Fa	11	5		S/O 84	58
People: Burnside, Linda	"Fiber" (Exhibit)	Vander Lee, Jana	√		Fa	3	2		M/A 76	9
People: Burtt, Dick	Sheep Country Profiles: Dick Burtt	Gordon, Gerrie	√		Iw	1	4		Su 76	19
People: Busch, Elizabeth	Beyond Quilting	Dyett, Linda	√	√	TM			5	J/J 86	70
People: Bush, Birgitta	"Textiles New Mexico 1978" (Exhibit)	Tatum, Phyllis	√		Fa	5	4		J/A 78	10
People: Bush, Victor	Basketmakers of Nova Scotia, The	Gordon, Joleen	√		SS&D	17	4	68	Fa 86	44
People: Buskirk, Mary Balzer	Six Songs of Success	Meany, Janet K.	√		SS&D	18	3	71	Su 87	69
People: Butler, Francis	Francis Butler: "I Used to Be an Artist but I Couldn't Sit Still That Long"	Butler, Francis	√		Fa	5	5		S/O 78	40
People: Butler, Francis	On Fabric in the Southwest: Surface Design, A Bank, and Public Recognition	Brooks, Lois Ziff	√		Fa	6	5		S/O 79	54
People: Butler, Wayne P.	T-Shirts for Every Body: 20th Century Folkwear		√		Fa	8	6		N/D 81	22
People: Butrymowicz, Zofia	"Woven, Tied, and Knotted" (Exhibit)	Koplos, Janet	√		Fa	9	2		M/A 82	82
People: Buxton, Joanna	Three English Tapestry Weavers	Liebler, Barbara	√		Hw	3	1		Ja 82	61
People: Cacicedo, Jean	"Wearable Art" (Exhibit)	Hunt, E. Ann	√		Fa	6	3		M/J 79	78
People: Cacicedo, Jean Wlilliams	Machine Knitting: The State of the Art		√		Fa	9	2		M/A 82	40
People: Cain, Charlotte	Unlimited Possibilities of Machine Knitting: Charlotte Cain's Patterns of Infinity, The	Woelfle, Gretchen Erskine	√		Fa	6	4		J/A 79	58
People: Caldwell, Dorothy	Canadian Portfolio, A	Place, Jennifer	√		Fa	9	6		N/D 82	29
People: Caldwell, Dorothy	Dorothy Caldwell: Interacting with Image and Material	Duffy, Helen	√		Fa	13	6		N/D 86	22
People: Callanaupa, Nilda	Nilda Callanaupa	Franquemont, Ed	√		S-O	9	1		Sp 85	53
People: Camden, William	Few Observations on "Remains", A	Stanton, R. G.	√		AT	4			De 85	9
People: Cameron-Bell, Scott	Handwoven Clothing Today: The Couturier Touch	West, Virginia	√		Fa	8	1		J/F 81	39
People: Campbell, Christine	"North/South Carolina Fibers Competition" (Exhibit)	Laymon, Cynthia	√		Fa	10	4		J/A 83	68
People: Campbell, David R.	American Handweaving 1960		√		H&C	11	2		Sp 60	51
People: Campbell, Kay	Kay Campbell: The Shifting Balance of Order	Pencheff, Patricia	√		Fa	12	5		S/O 85	11
People: Campbell, Patricia	"Cloth Forms" (Exhibits)	Skudera, Gail	√		Fa	9	4		J/A 82	76
People: Campbell, Patricia	Eleventh International Biennial of Tapestry, The	Taylor, Elmer; Dianne Taylor	√		Fa	10	5		S/O 83	33
People: Campbell, Patricia	"Patricia Campbell: The Modular Form" (Exhibit)	Itter, Diane	√		Fa	11	3		M/J 84	75
People: Cann, Gwen	Profile of an HGA Rep		√		SS&D	16	2	62	Sp 85	58
People: Cannell, Susan	"Fabrications" (Exhibit)	Talley, Charles	√		Fa	6	4		J/A 79	76
People: Cantor, Meg	Feltmaking Now: The Exciting Revival of an Ancient Technique	Gordon, Beverly	√		Fa	6	6		N/D 79	43
People: Capo, Peter	Surface Attraction	Mattera, Joanne	√		TM			7	O/N 86	20
People: Carberry, Bret	Diversity of Fabrics Comes from the Looms of Joseph D. Acton and Bret Carberry of Philadelphia, A		√		H&C	4	2		Sp 53	4
People: Cardarelle, Anthony	Spinning Wheels from the Busy Workshop of Anthony Cardarelle	Martin, George	√		H&C	17	3		Su 66	6
People: Carl Schuster	In Memorium, Carl Schuster, Ph. D. (1904–1969)	Cammann, Schuyler			TMJ	3	3		De 72	2
People: Carlin, Lee	Lee Carlin: Handweaving Entrepreneur	Ligon, Linda	√		Iw	3	1		Fa 77	26
People: Carlson, Anne Marie	"Made in Wisconsin: An Exhibition of Recent Works In-Of-and-On Handmade Paper" (Exhibit)	Hagemeister-Winzenz, Karon	√		Fa	5	4		J/A 78	19
People: Carlson, Deborah	HGA Scholarships '79		√		SS&D	10	4	40	Fa 79	99
People: Carlson, Deborah Frazer	"Fiber National '86" (Exhibit)	Belfer, Nancy	√		Fa	14	1		J/F 87	51

SUBJECT	TITLE	AUTHOR	IL	INST	JOUR	VOL	NO	ISS	DATE	PAGE
People: Carlson, Estelle	Ikat	Carlson, Estelle	√		Fa	5	1		J/F 78	41
People: Carlson, Estelle	"Southern California Designer Crafts" (Exhibit)	Dyer, Carolyn	√		Fa	5	2		M/A 78	14
People: Carter, Margaret	Margaret Carter, A Weaver in Three States	Currey, Ruth Dunlop	√		H&C	21	4		Fa 70	12
People: Cassell, Martin	Coverlet for Convergence 1988, A		√	√	SS&D	19	1	73	Wi 87	46
People: Cate, Leslie L. and Mrs. Cate	Story of the Shuttle Shed, The		√		H&C	10	1		Wi 59	22
People: Cederblom, Aina	Career on Four Continents, A	Arndt, Jessie Ash	√		H&C	21	3		Su 70	15
People: Cerantola, Bandiera	"Third International Exhibition of Miniature Textiles 1978" (Exhibit)	Spencer, Patricia	√		Fa	6	1		J/F 79	90
People: Chaffee, Marilyn	"California Fibers: 11th Annual Show" (Exhibit)	Kosta, Angela	√		Fa	10	6		N/D 83	81
People: Chan, L.	Fabric of Creativity: Weaving Together Left– and Right–Brain Activites, The	Miles, Candice St. Jacques	√		Fa	11	6		N/D 84	44
People: Chand, Nek	Nek Chand's Fantasy Garden	Ziek, Bhakti	√		TM			3	F/M 86	88
People: Chanel, Gabrielle "Coco"	Knitting Odyssey, A	Dyett, Linda	√	√	TM			13	O/N 87	48
People: Chang, Nelson	Nelson Chang: Champion of Chinese Knotting	Westbrook, John R.,	√		Fa	14	3		M/J 87	6
People: Chapman, Charity	Tangential Textiles: From Quiltmaking to Points Beyond	Chapman, Charity	√		Fa	9	2		M/A 82	22
People: Chapman, Tana	"Ten Boston Fiber Artists" (Exhibit)	Serenyi, Peter	√		Fa	5	5		S/O 78	67
People: Chapnick, Karen	Canadian Portfolio, A	Place, Jennifer	√		Fa	9	6		N/D 82	29
People: Chapnick, Karen	"Fiber Departures" (Exhibit)	Dyer, Carolyn	√		Fa	4	3		M/J 77	9
People: Chapnick, Karen	"Fiber Structures and Fabric Surfaces" (Exhibit)	Itter, Diane	√		Fa	7	1		J/F 80	67
People: Chapnick, Karen	Karen Chapnick: Constructing Color	Green, Phyllis	√		Fa	13	2		M/A 86	12
People: Chapnick, Karen	"Ninth International Biennial of Tapestry" (Exhibit)	Pulleyn, Rob	√		Fa	6	4		J/A 79	62
People: Chapnick, Karen	Plastics in Fiber: A Persistent Presence	Malarcher, Patricia	√		Fa	12	1		J/F 85	56
People: Chappell, Nancy	Contemporary California Costume	Poon, Vivian	√		Fa	11	5		S/O 84	53
People: Chase, Debra	Debra Chase: Unwearable Wearables	Lonier, Terri	√		Fa	12	3		M/J 85	12
People: Chase, Patti	"Throbbing Needles II" (Exhibit)	Mattera, Joanne	√		Fa	7	2		M/A 80	71
People: Chatelain, Martha	Felt and Paper: A Portfolio		√		Fa	13	4		J/A 86	35
People: Chenevert, Melodie	Review/Discussion of Artspace's Innovative Yet Flawed "Fiber Freely Interpreted", A (Exhibit)		√		Fa	4	2		M/A 77	38
People: Cherepov, Klara	Klara Cherepov, A Career in Two Countries	Landis, Bruce	√		H&C	18	3		Su 67	19
People: Chesterfield, Mary	"Southern California Designer Crafts" (Exhibit)	Dyer, Carolyn	√		Fa	5	2		M/A 78	14
People: Chicago, Judy	"Birth Project, The" First Showing of Judy Chicago's New Work (Exhibit)	von Kreisler-Bomben, Kristin	√		Fa	10	1		J/F 83	81
People: Chicago, Judy	Hot Flash Fan, The		√		Fa	12	5		S/O 85	91
People: Chicago, Judy	Judy Chicago: The Second Decade	Keener, Terrah	√		SS&D	15	4	60	Fa 84	30
People: Chicago, Judy	Judy Chicago's Dinner Party: A Review	Mattera, Joanne	√		Fa	7	3		M/J 80	16
People: Chiesa, Wilfredo	Art Consultants: Bridging the Gap Between Artist and Client	Goodman, Deborah Lerme	√		Fa	12	6		N/D 85	31
People: Chisholm, Madeleine	"Fiber Works — Americas & Japan" (Exhibit)	Kato, Kuniko Lucy	√		Fa	5	1		J/F 78	10
People: Chittenden, Annie Curtis	Annie Curtis Chittenden	Chittenden, Annie Curtis	√		Fa	14	5		N/D 87	11
People: Chittenden, Annie Curtis	Journey in Progress, A	Chittenden, Annie Curtis	√	√	SS&D	17	4	68	Fa 86	50
People: Chmielewska, Monika	Old World Discipline — New World Markets	Chmielewska, Monika	√		SS&D	11	1	41	Wi 79	4
People: Chojnacka, Maria	"22 Polish Textile Artists" (Exhibit)	Park, Betty	√		Fa	4	5		S/O 77	8
People: Chown, Joyce	Joyce Chown's "Fabricated Structure: Weir"	Weir, Jean; Joyce Chown	√		Fa	11	4		J/A 84	39
People: Christensen, Deborah	Deborah Christensen	Ligon, Linda	√		Iw	2	2		Wi 77	16
People: Christensen, Dione	Dione Christensen	Hutchinson, Amelia	√		Fa	5	3		M/J 78	57

SUBJECT	TITLE	AUTHOR	IL	INST	JOUR	VOL	NO	ISS	DATE	PAGE
People: Christensen, Dione	"Dione Christensen Fiberworks" (Exhibit)	Meyer, Florence	√		Fa	6	2		M/A 79	63
People: Christjansen, Dorte	"Dorte Christjansen" (Exhibit)	Dyer, Carolyn	√		Fa	6	2		M/A 79	62
People: Christo	Christo: Running Fence Remembered	Woelfle, Gretchen	√		Fa	7	5		S/O 80	24
People: Christo	Gates: Project for Central Park, The		√		Fa	9	4		J/A 82	92
People: Christoph, Thom	Men Who Knit	Xenakis, Alexis Yiorgos	√		Kn	3	2	6	Sp 87	14
People: Chule	Chule's Wool Creations	Carter, Dianne	√		SS&D	17	4	68	Fa 86	30
People: Chule (Culevski), Dimitrije	Chule: Freedom to Weave		√		Iw	4	4		Fa 79	47
People: Chung, Eve Zweben	Tenth Annual Textile Exhibition, Olive Hyde Art Gallery (Exhibit)	Papa, Nancy	√		Fa	5	4		J/A 78	13
People: Chung, Zweben	"Fabrications" (Exhibit)	Talley, Charles	√		Fa	6	4		J/A 79	76
People: Cisek, Marsha	"Fiber Invitational" (Exhibit)	Bywater, William	√		Fa	7	2		M/A 80	66
People: Claessens, Jeanette	Eleventh International Biennial of Tapestry, The	Taylor, Elmer; Dianne Taylor	√		Fa	10	5		S/O 83	33
People: Clark, Barbara	Portfolio of Contemporary Fiber Sculpture, A		√		Fa	11	4		J/A 84	34
People: Clark, Grace Richey	Colorful Blinds and Fabrics from Texas		√		H&C	6	4		Fa 55	14
People: Clark, Kathryn	"New Dimensions in Handmade Paper" (Exhibit)	Koplos, Janet	√		Fa	8	5		S/O 81	72
People: Clark, Kathryn	"Paper and Felt Redefined" (Exhibit)	Ogden, Anne	√		Fa	5	2		M/A 78	17
People: Clark, Kathryn	Papermaking in the U.S.A.	Toale, Bernard	√		Fa	9	4		J/A 82	34
People: Clark, Ruth	Ruth Clark, Tapestry Weaver	Olson, Mabel C.	√	√	H&C	9	1		Wi 57	29
People: Clark, Sherry	Felt and Paper: A Portfolio		√		Fa	13	4		J/A 86	35
People: Clark, Sherry	Portfolio of Contemporary Fiber Sculpture, A		√		Fa	11	4		J/A 84	34
People: Clark, Thurid	Thurid Clark		√		Fa	3	6		N/D 76	8
People: Claybrook, Marjorie Walger	"Needle Expressions '80" (Exhibit)		√		Fa	8	1		J/F 81	93
People: Clayden, Marian	Art to Wear: Looking At the Movement	Scarborough, Jessica	√		Fa	12	3		M/J 85	56
People: Clayden, Marian	Marian Clayden: Fabric Dyer	Meilach, Dona Z.	√		Fa	5	1		J/F 78	43
People: Clayden, Marian	Marian Clayden's Clothing for Collectors	Park, Betty	√		Fa	6	3		M/J 79	55
People: Clayden, Marian	Passion for Elegance: Master Dyer Marian Clayden Creates Clothing by Listening to the Fabric, A	Levine, Betsy	√	√	TM			14	D/J 87	36
People: Clayton, Edith	Old Ways for the New	Gordon, Joleen	√		SS&D	17	4	68	Fa 86	48
People: Clifford, Morgan	Evolution of an Artist: Morgan Clifford	Gue, Sandra	√		Fa	14	5		N/D 87	27
People: Clifford, Morgan	Fiber in Minnesota: "Traditions/Transitions II" and "Art in Architecture" (Exhibit)	Stack, Lotus	√		Fa	11	3		M/J 84	80
People: Clifford, Morgan	International Invitational (Exhibit)		√		Fa	14	2		M/A 87	58
People: Clifford, Morgan	Morgan Clifford: New Directions in Brocades	Gue, Sandra	√		WJ	11	4	44	Sp 87	40
People: Clifton, Michelle	Cows in Fiber	Timmons, Chris	√		Fa	11	4		J/A 84	55
People: Cline, Barbara	Continuing Tradition, A		√		Fa	9	2		M/A 82	100
People: Clivio, Carol	Carol Clivio, Wizard of Spinning	Rossiter, Phyllis	√		S-O	8	4		Wi 84	53
People: Clodagh, Alison	There's a Lady Out Bantry Bay Way	Rubbert, Toni Condon	√		S-O	7	4		Wi 83	32
People: Close, Chuck	Pictorial Tapestry: A Portfolio of Contemporary Work	Goodman, Deborah Lerme	√		Fa	10	3		M/J 83	29
People: Clyne, Patricia	Not Necessarily Seventh Ave.	Dyett, Linda	√		TM			6	A/S 86	28
People: Coble, Richard W.	Good As Gold: Alternatives in American Jewelry		√		Fa	9	5		S/O 82	18
People: Cochran, Jane	Who Weaves?		√		Iw	5	2		Sp 80	34
People: Codling, David	Men Who Knit	Xenakis, Alexis Yiorgos	√		Kn	3	2	6	Sp 87	14
People: Coenens, Linda	"Wisconsin Fiber Miniatures" (Exhibit)	Lowell-LaRoque, Jane V.	√		Fa	6	5		S/O 79	84
People: Coffey, Marjorie	Marjorie Coffey	Coffey, Marjorie	√		Fa	4	6		N/D 77	40
People: Cohen, Rhoda	"Quilt National '79" (Exhibit)	Gutcheon, Beth	√		Fa	6	5		S/O 79	80
People: Cohen, Ronald R.	"Skin Forms: Innovations in Leather" (Exhibit)	Mackin, Jeanne	√		Fa	7	2		M/A 80	67

SUBJECT	TITLE	AUTHOR	IL	INST	JOUR	VOL	NO	ISS	DATE	PAGE
People: Coifman, Lucienne	Lucienne Coifman				SS&D	18	1	69	Wi 86	5
People: Coker, Alyce	"Seventh Annual Twin Ports Fibers Invitational" (Exhibit)	LaRoque, Jane V. Lowell	√		Fa	7	3		M/J 80	80
People: Coker, Sally	Fiber on Martha's Vineyard	Erickson, Johanna	√		Fa	11	4		J/A 84	46
People: Colaço, Madeleine	Embroidered Sambas of Madeleine Colaço, The	Mathews, Kate	√		Fa	14	5		N/D 87	34
People: Colaj, Eli	Art to Wear: Looking At the Movement	Scarborough, Jessica	√		Fa	12	3		M/J 85	56
People: Colburn, Carol	Technique: Painting Weft Threads for Tapestry	Colburn, Carol	√	√	Hw	3	1		Ja 82	58
People: Colby, Sas	Sas Colby	Talley, Charles	√		Fa	8	5		S/O 81	29
People: Cole, Candiss	Silken Gowns of Candiss Cole, The	Paqua, Al	√		Fa	6	3		M/J 79	41
People: Cole, Stephanie Kirsher	Stephanie Cole Kirsher	Vander Lee, Jana	√		Fa	3	6		N/D 76	11
People: Coleman, Bernice	Questions of Style: Contemporary Trends in the Fiber Arts	Howe-Echt, Katherine	√		Fa	7	2		M/A 80	38
People: Coleman, Elizabeth	Elizabeth Coleman and the Not-So-Homely Art of Sewing	Coleman, Elizabeth	√		Fa	6	3		M/J 79	29
People: Coleman, Marcia	"Toys and Games" (Exhibit)	Meilach, Dona Z.	√		Fa	4	1		J/F 77	7
People: Collingwood, Peter	Collingwood Connection, The		√		SS&D	14	4	56	Fa 83	38
People: Collingwood, Peter	Collingwood in Massachusetts, A	Brannen, Robert	√		SS&D	9	1	33	Wi 77	8
People: Collingwood, Peter	Peter Collingwood, English Rug Weaver		√		H&C	11	4		Fa 60	12
People: Collingwood, Peter	Peter Collingwood, His Weaves and Weaving: On Rug Designing	Collingwood, Peter; Harriet Tidball, ed.	√	√	SCGM		8		63	1-46
People: Collingwood, Peter	Peter Collingwood on Textile Structures	Levine, Betsy	√		TM			3	F/M 86	14
People: Collingwood, Peter	Self-supporting Workshop, A	Collingwood, Peter			H&C	15	4		Fa 64	7
People: Collingwood, Peter	Speakers Bureau Presents		√		SS&D	1	2	2	De 69	15
People: Collingwood, Peter	SS&D Interview: Peter Collingwood	Wilson, Sadye Tune	√		SS&D	10	4	40	Fa 79	4
People: Collingwood, Peter	Three British Weavers	Held, Shirley E.			H&C	23	6		N/D 72	33
People: Collins, Al	Behind the Scenes: A Fabric Printer	Lancaster, Zoe Woodruff	√		Fa	13	3		M/J 86	44
People: Collura, Vincene	Body as Canvas, The	Koda, Harold	√		TM			8	D/J 86	56
People: Colman, Bernice	"Southern California Designer Crafts" (Exhibit)	Dyer, Carolyn	√		Fa	5	2		M/A 78	14
People: Colony, John	Behind the Scenes: A Textile Mill	Goodman, Deborah Lerme	√		Fa	13	3		M/J 86	40
People: Colton, Mary Rawcliffe	Profile of an HGA Rep		√		SS&D	17	4	68	Fa 86	89
People: Colwell, Ken	Using a Computer: Four Views		√		Fa	13	5		S/O 86	7
People: Combs, Marie	"Entanglements" (Exhibit)	Markle, Marsha	√		Fa	4	2		M/A 77	16
People: Combs, Marie	"Images of the Moslem World" (Exhibit)		√		Fa	14	5		N/D 87	42
People: Combs, Marie	Marie Combs: Quilted Visions of Faraway Lands	Erbe, Pamela	√		Fa	12	1		J/F 85	16
People: Combs, Marie	Rubber Stamp Acts: The Little Books of Marie Combs		√		Fa	8	5		S/O 81	18
People: Combs, Marie	"Ruth's Madcaps" (Exhibit)	Haynes, Maryellen	√		Fa	14	4		S/O 87	9
People: Combs, Marie	"Women of Fiber: Six Michigan Artists" (Exhibit)	Reid, Eve	√		Fa	8	5		S/O 81	74
People: Comtomapasis, Maria	"Power Garments" (Exhibit)	Papa, Nancy	√		Fa	5	1		J/F 78	13
People: Condra, Nora	Quilts in Women's Lives	Mattera, Joanne	√		Fa	9	3		M/J 82	54
People: Cone, Ferne	Ferne Cone — Knitting: The Stepchild of the Fiber Arts?	Nelson, Gladys	√		Fa	5	3		M/J 78	48
People: Conklin, Peggy	Peggy Conklin: Sculptured Paper	Tacker, Sylvia	√		Fa	13	3		M/J 86	25
People: Connell, Julie	Selling through Galleries		√		Iw	1	3		Sp 76	20
People: Connelly, Karen Stevens	"Material/Culture" (Exhibit)	Ross, Douglas	√		Fa	14	2		M/A 87	55
People: Connelly, Karin	Karin Connelly: Analagous Structures	Connelly, Karin	√		Fa	12	1		J/F 85	90
People: Connelly, Karin S.	Paper Clothing: West	Koplos, Janet	√		Fa	11	2		M/A 84	39
People: Connolly, Loris	Who Weaves?		√		Iw	5	2		Sp 80	40
People: Connor, Maureen	On the Edge: Maureen Connor — Shaping a Response to the Past	Malarcher, Patricia	√		Fa	9	4		J/A 82	61
People: Conroy, Diana	Spinning—Australia	DeBoer, Janet			S-O	11	3		Fa 87	35
People: Constandse, Martha	Speakers Bureau Presents		√		SS&D	8	2	30	Sp 77	71

SUBJECT	TITLE	AUTHOR	IL	INST	JOUR	VOL	NO	ISS	DATE	PAGE
People: Constantine, Mildred	Conversation with Mildred Constantine	Park, Betty	√		Fa	8	6		N/D 81	14
People: Content, Judith	For the Body (error-corrected Fa v10 n2 83 p61)		√		Fa	10	1		J/F 83	32
People: Content, Judith	Silkworks	Goodman, Deborah Lerme	√		Fa	13	1		J/F 86	50
People: Content, Judith	Wall Hangings of Judith Content, The	Scarborough, Jessica	√		Fa	13	2		M/A 86	10
People: Contompasis, Marika	"Art to Wear" (Exhibit)	Murray, Megan	√		Fa	11	1		J/F 84	76
People: Contompasis, Marika	Art to Wear: Looking At the Movement	Scarborough, Jessica	√		Fa	12	3		M/J 85	56
People: Contompasis, Mirika	"Marika Contompasis: Pedestal and Wall Pieces" (Exhibits)	Dyer, Carolyn	√		Fa	9	4		J/A 82	73
People: Cook, Jan	Papermaking in the U.S.A.	Toale, Bernard	√		Fa	9	4		J/A 82	34
People: Cook, Lia	"California Women in Crafts" (Exhibit)	Dyer, Carolyn	√		Fa	4	2		M/A 77	10
People: Cook, Lia	Commissions: The Process, the Problems and the Prospects		√		Fa	6	5		S/O 79	45
People: Cook, Lia	"Fiber Departures" (Exhibit)	Dyer, Carolyn	√		Fa	4	3		M/J 77	9
People: Cook, Lia	"Fiber Structures and Fabric Surfaces" (Exhibit)	Itter, Diane	√		Fa	7	1		J/F 80	67
People: Cook, Lia	"Fiber Works — Americas & Japan" (Exhibit)	Kato, Kuniko Lucy	√		Fa	5	1		J/F 78	10
People: Cook, Lia	"Flexible Medium: Art Fabric from the Museum Collection, The" (Exhibit)	Goodman, Deborah Lerme	√		Fa	11	5		S/O 84	71
People: Cook, Lia	Lausanne Notebook: Our Special Report on the 8th Lausanne Biennial of Tapestry, A	Mathews, Rich	√		Fa	4	5		S/O 77	30
People: Cook, Lia	Lia Cook, An Interview	Papa, Nancy	√		Iw	4	4		Fa 79	24
People: Cook, Lia	"Lia Cook" (Exhibit)	Park, Betty	√		Fa	5	5		S/O 78	72
People: Cook, Lia	Lia Cook: Exploring the Territory Where Painting and Textiles Meet	Alexander, Judy	√		Fa	9	5		S/O 82	28
People: Cook, Lia	"Lia Cook: Shaped and Woven Constructions" (Exhibit)	Rowley, Kathleen	√		Fa	12	4		J/A 85	66
People: Cook, Lia	"Painted Weavings" Lia Cook and Neda Al-Hilali (Exhibit)	Park, Betty	√		Fa	8	1		J/F 81	88
People: Cook, Lia	Questions of Style: Contemporary Trends in the Fiber Arts	Howe-Echt, Katherine	√		Fa	7	2		M/A 80	38
People: Cook, Marie	Victorian Tapestry Workshop: A New Tradition in Australia, The	Newman, Rochelle	√		Fa	10	3		M/J 83	38
People: Cook, Myung-Sook	"Wisconsin Fiber Miniatures" (Exhibit)	Lowell-LaRoque, Jane V.	√		Fa	6	5		S/O 79	84
People: Cooke, Caren Eade	"Left on the Loom" (Exhibit)	Dyer, Carolyn	√		Fa	5	2		M/A 78	16
People: Cooney, Katy	"Ruth's Madcaps" (Exhibit)	Haynes, Maryellen	√		Fa	14	4		S/O 87	9
People: Cooper, Jennifer Finley	"Third Annual Fiber Show" (Exhibit)	Papa, Nancy	√		Fa	5	6		N/D 78	65
People: Cooper, Rochella	From Houston: Rochella Cooper, Anita Hickman	Vander Lee, Jana	√		Fa	3	3		M/J 76	10
People: Cooper, Rochella	"Houston Designer-Craftsmen 1976" (Exhibit)	Vander Lee, Jana	√		Fa	3	4		J/A 76	9
People: Cooperstein, Helen	Going Into Production: James Wight and Helen Cooperstein		√		Fa	3	1		J/F 76	15
People: Coover, Pilar	Myth, Music, and Magic: The Needlework of Pilar Coover	Schevill, Margot Blum	√	√	TM			14	D/J 87	30
People: Coover, Regan	Fiber At Artpark	MacDonald, Claudia	√		Fa	10	6		N/D 83	47
People: Cope, Louise Todd	Miniatures in Fiber: Working Small—An Exciting Challenge for the Contemporary Fiber Artist	Malarcher, Patricia	√		Fa	7	4		J/A 80	32
People: Corlett, Judy	"Art Couture '82" (Exhibit)	Guagliumi, Sasan	√		Fa	10	1		J/F 83	84
People: Corpier, Leslie	"Made in Wisconsin: An Exhibition of Recent Works In-Of-and-On Handmade Paper" (Exhibit)	Hagemeister-Winzenz, Karon	√		Fa	5	4		J/A 78	19
People: Corregan, Ruth	Guild in Focus: Fiber Artisans, A	Kline, Martha	√		Fa	11	5		S/O 84	47
People: Corsini, Deborah	"Deborah Corsini: Tapestries" (Exhibit)	Talley, Charles S.	√		Fa	7	5		S/O 80	68
People: Corsini, Deborah	T-Shirts for Every Body: 20th Century Folkwear		√		Fa	8	6		N/D 81	22
People: Cosgrove, Margery	"Fiber Techniques: The Weaver's Guild of Greater Cincinnati" (Exhibit)	Fedders, Pat	√		Fa	8	1		J/F 81	91

SUBJECT	TITLE	AUTHOR	IL	INST	JOUR	VOL	NO	ISS	DATE	PAGE
People: Cost-Peltz, Peggy	Profile of an HGA Rep		√		SS&D	16	1	61	Wi 84	9
People: Courtney, Esther	Spinning in Stehekin	Fridlund, Patricia	√		S-O	10	4		Wi 86	44
People: Covill, Tracy	"Houston Designer-Craftsmen 1976" (Exhibit)	Vander Lee, Jana	√		Fa	3	4		J/A 76	9
People: Cox, Ed, Sr.	Mummery: Philadelphia's Happy New Year	Smeltzer, Nancy	√		Fa	14	3		M/J 87	39
People: Cox, Jane	Jane Cox: Her Draft for Counterpins	Pinchin, C. B.	√	√	lw	4	3		Su 79	31
People: Craig, Chris	Chris Craig	Craig, Chris	√		Fa	12	6		N/D 85	18
People: Craig, Chris	"Felt and Papermaking" (Exhibit)	Harrison, Helen A.	√		Fa	11	2		M/A 84	79
People: Craig, Chris	"Fiberworks" (Exhibit)	Park, Betty	√		Fa	4	6		N/D 77	10
People: Craig, Natalie	Questions of Style: Contemporary Trends in the Fiber Arts	Howe-Echt, Katherine	√		Fa	7	2		M/A 80	38
People: Crain, Joyce	Joyce Crain: Walls of Light	Malarcher, Patricia	√		Fa	12	5		S/O 85	55
People: Crain, Joyce	Plastics in Fiber: A Persistent Presence	Malarcher, Patricia	√		Fa	12	1		J/F 85	56
People: Crain, Joyce	"Weaving Without Fiber" (Exhibit)	Hempel, Toby Anne	√		Fa	13	5		S/O 86	48
People: Cramer, Nancy Shaw	Country of Origin, USA: A Decade of Contemporary Rugs	Stevens, Rebeccah A. T.	√		Fa	11	3		M/J 84	60
People: Crane, Barbara	Barbara Crane	Crane, Barbara	√		Fa	13	4		J/A 86	27
People: Crane, Michael	Men Who Knit	Xenakis, Alexis Yiorgos	√		Kn	3	2	6	Sp 87	14
People: Crary, Sharon	Profile of an HGA Rep		√		SS&D	17	2	66	Sp 86	84
People: Crawford, Kathleen	Color Forecasting	Dyett, Linda	√		TM			3	F/M 86	22
People: Crawford, Kathleen	Not Necessarily Seventh Ave.	Dyett, Linda	√		TM			6	A/S 86	28
People: Creamer, Catherine	"Fiber from the Marietta College Crafts National" (Exhibit)	Murray, Megan	√		Fa	11	2		M/A 84	76
People: Creamer, Catherine	"With or Without a Loom" (Exhibit)	Rowley, Kristin Carlsen	√		Fa	8	5		S/O 81	67
People: Creamer, Catherine M.	Using a Computer: Four Views		√		Fa	13	5		S/O 86	7
People: Crisler, Carlye	Felt and Paper: A Portfolio		√		Fa	13	4		J/A 86	35
People: Cristi	Cristi — Sketch of a Guatemalan Weaver	Nash, Jeanne; Jeanne Schmelzer	√		lw	5	4		Fa 80	28
People: Crone-Coggins, Noreen	Dreaming, Drawing, Painting, and Stitching with Noreen Crone-Coggins	Crone-Coggins, Noreen	√		Fa	6	5		S/O 79	16
People: Crouse, Gloria	"For the Floor" (Exhibit)	Sider, Sandra	√		Fa	12	6		N/D 85	61
People: Crouse, Gloria E.	Country of Origin, USA: A Decade of Contemporary Rugs	Stevens, Rebeccah A. T.	√		Fa	11	3		M/J 84	60
People: Crow, Nancy	From Barn to Studio: On Moving to a Farm and Making a Workspace	Crow, Nancy	√		Fa	8	6		N/D 81	44
People: Crow, Nancy	"Quilt National '79" (Exhibit)	Gutcheon, Beth	√		Fa	6	5		S/O 79	80
People: Crow, Nancy	Textile Trends: Collecting in New York	Sider, Sandra	√		Fa	12	6		N/D 85	24
People: Cruickshank, Ronald	Ronald Cruickshank, Scottish Tapestry Weaver		√		H&C	13	2		Sp 62	18
People: Crump, Nancy	Nancy Crump		√		Fa	3	6		N/D 76	28
People: Culbertson, Ruth	Speakers Bureau Presents		√		SS&D	9	2	34	Sp 78	93
People: Cunha, Rhonda	"Fiber National '86" (Exhibit)	Belfer, Nancy	√		Fa	14	1		J/F 87	51
People: Cunningham, Beth	"Decade of Fibers, A" (Exhibit)	Franklin, Sue	√		Fa	5	1		J/F 78	17
People: Cunningham, Susan M.	"100% Wool" (Exhibit)	Goldin, Susan	√		Fa	4	6		N/D 77	18
People: Cunningham, Susanmarie	Susanmarie Cunningham: Wearable Soft Sculpture	Cunningham, Susanmarie	√		Fa	11	5		S/O 84	15
People: Curtis, Dolly	Dolly Curtis: Contrasts	Ligon, Linda	√		lw	3	4		Su 78	24
People: Curtis, Dolly	"Dolly Curtis Textile Graphics" (Exhibit)	Reed, Irene C.	√		Fa	6	2		M/A 79	70
People: Curtis, Dolly	Fiber Workspaces: A Room of Your Own	Bishop, Mara	√		Fa	4	4		J/A 77	38
People: Curtis, Sadie	Contemporary Navajo Weaving	Hedlund, Ann Lane	√		WJ	11	1	41	Su 86	30
People: Curtis, Sadie	Exploring a Tradition: Navajo Rugs, Classic and Contemporary	Elliott, Malinda	√		Fa	11	3		M/J 84	32
People: Curtis, Sadie	Textile Trends: Collecting in the Southwest	Elliott, Malinda	√		Fa	12	6		N/D 85	27
People: Cutcher, Elaine	Elaine Cutcher: Production Weaver		√		Fa	3	5		S/O 76	40
People: Cutcher, Hal and Elaine	Weaving on a Dobby Loom	Ligon, Linda	√		lw	1	4		Su 76	10

SUBJECT	TITLE	AUTHOR	IL	INST	JOUR	VOL	NO	ISS	DATE	PAGE
People: Cysarz, Jan	Introduction to Two Textilatelists, An	Allston, J. L.; J. A. Hoskins	√		AT	4			De 85	81
People: Czajkowska, Hannah	"Fiber in Focus" (Exhibit)	Skudera, Gail	√		Fa	10	6		N/D 83	82
People: da Conceicao, Maria	For the Body (error-corrected Fa v10 n2 83 p61)		√		Fa	10	1		J/F 83	32
People: da Conceicao, Maria	Maria da Conceicao: A Modern Romantic	Hecker, Carolyn	√		Fa	6	3		M/J 79	58
People: Dadey, Jane	CAD Quilts: The Computer As a Studio Tool	Dadey, Jane	√		Fa	14	4		S/O 87	38
People: Daehnert, Richard	"Fibers Southeast 1979" (Exhibit)	Johnson, Elma	√		Fa	6	2		M/A 79	68
People: Dahl, Caroline	Caroline Dahl	Dahl, Caroline	√		Fa	13	3		M/J 86	27
People: Dahl, Caroline	"Linda Maxwell and Caroline Dahl: Terror Sampler and Other Dogs" (Exhibit)	Poon, Vivian	√		Fa	11	6		N/D 84	79
People: Dahl, Carolyn A.	Felt and Paper: A Portfolio		√		Fa	13	4		J/A 86	35
People: Dalsgaard, Kristen	Dalsgaard Tapestries, The	Clement, Doris W.	√		H&C	17	1		Wi 66	6
People: Dalton, Kathleen	Contemporary Basketry		√		Fa	8	3		M/J 81	39
People: Dalton, Ken	Contemporary Basketry		√		Fa	8	3		M/J 81	39
People: Dalton, Suzanne	Public Fiber: Looking At the Logistics	Koplos, Janet	√		Fa	12	1		J/F 85	32
People: Daly, Lynn	Fashions by Linda Knutson and Lynn Daly		√	√	WJ	6	3	23	Wi 81	14
People: Damboritz, Ilka	Knitting Odyssey, A	Dyett, Linda	√	√	TM			13	O/N 87	48
People: Daniel, Susan	Improvs on Silk: The Fabric Painting of Susan Daniel	Fitt, Cate	√		Fa	8	5		S/O 81	45
People: Daniel, Susan	"Show Biz" (Exhibit)	Scheinman, Pamela	√		Fa	7	4		J/A 80	69
People: Daniels, Barton	Contemporary California Costume	Poon, Vivian	√		Fa	11	5		S/O 84	53
People: Darr-Hope, Heidi	Out of the Blue: Aerial Images		√		Fa	13	5		S/O 86	44
People: Darwall, Randall	Garments from the Loom: Handweaver Randall Darwall Focuses on the Cloth	Mattera, Joanne	√		Fa	10	1		J/F 83	20
People: Darwall, Randall	Portfolio: Randall Darwall		√		Hw	7	1		J/F 86	37
People: Darwall, Randall	Randall Darwall	Sayward, Jessica Lee	√		SS&D	15	2	58	Sp 84	48
People: Dashanko-Dobek, Anne	"100% Wool" (Exhibit)	Goldin, Susan	√		Fa	4	6		N/D 77	18
People: Davidian, Robert	Scholarships '78		√		SS&D	9	4	36	Fa 78	44
People: Davidson, Jeannie	Jeannie Davidson: Costuming for Shakespearean Theater	Rowley, Kathleen	√		Fa	11	5		S/O 84	66
People: Davidson, Mary Frances	Mary Frances Davidson: A Tribute	Pilsk, Adele	√		Fa	5	1		J/F 78	58
People: Davie, Lucretia	Sampler of Surface Design, A	Westphal, Katherine	√		Fa	10	5		S/O 83	39
People: Davies, Karen	"Connections" (Exhibit)	Constantinides, Kathy	√		Fa	6	4		J/A 79	74
People: Davis, Ann	Masks At the Heart of Disguise	Koplos, Janet	√		Fa	11	5		S/O 84	32
People: Davis, Ardyth	Ardyth Davis — Looking At Inkblots and Seeing Jewelry	Hecker, Carolyn A.	√		Fa	5	6		N/D 78	31
People: Davis, Ardyth	"Old Traditions/New Directions" (Exhibit)	West, Virginia	√		Fa	8	6		N/D 81	66
People: Davis, Ardyth	Washington Fiber	Mathews, Rich	√		Fa	3	5		S/O 76	9
People: Davis, Carol Martin	Hi-Tech Banner Sculptures	Polster, Nancy; Elsa Sreenivasam	√		Fa	12	3		M/J 85	42
People: Davis, Lenore	"Landscapes" (Exhibit)	Clardy, Andrea	√		Fa	5	2		M/A 78	10
People: Davis, Lenore	Lenore Davis: Dye Painted Soft Sculpture		√	√	Fa	5	1		J/F 78	68
People: Davis, Lenore	Lenore Davis: Figuring in Cloth	Frasier, Debra	√		Fa	10	5		S/O 83	10
People: Davis, Lenore	"Patchwork Garden, A" (Exhibit)	Hetzler, Patricia	√		Fa	8	5		S/O 81	73
People: Davis, Michael	Michael Davis	Davis, Michael	√		Fa	13	4		J/A 86	26
People: Davis, Michael	Portfolio of Contemporary Fiber Sculpture, A		√		Fa	11	4		J/A 84	34
People: Davis, Myra L.	Myra L. Davis, Master Weaver	Clement, Doris	√		H&C	12	1		Wi 61	24
People: Davis, Virginia	Design by the Yard: Today's Fabric Innovators	Scarborough, Jessica	√		Fa	12	5		S/O 85	30
People: Davis, Virginia	"Detailed Directions in Fiber" (Exhibit)	Van Gelder, Lydia	√		Fa	9	3		M/J 82	77
People: Davis, Virginia	Innovations in Indigo	Wada, Yoshiko Iwamoto	√		Fa	13	5		S/O 86	29
People: Davis, Virginia	Virginia Davis	Malarcher, Patricia	√		Fa	10	5		S/O 83	14
People: Davison, Marguerite Porter	Grouped Warp Threads	Davison, Marguerite Porter	√	√	H&C	26	3		M/J 75	24

SUBJECT	TITLE	AUTHOR	IL	INST	JOUR	VOL	NO	ISS	DATE	PAGE
People: Davison, Marguerite Porter	Heirloom Linens	Furniss, Frances	√		H&C	9	2		Sp 58	11
People: Day, Crane	Crane Day Designs	Colton, Mary Rawcliffe	√		SS&D	18	2	70	Sp 87	48
✝ People: de Amaral, Olga	Commissions: The Process, the Problems and the Prospects		√		Fa	6	5		S/O 79	45
✝ People: de Amaral, Olga	"Fiber Works — Americans & Japan" (Exhibit)	Kato, Kuniko Lucy	√		Fa	5	1		J/F 78	10
✝ People: de Amaral, Olga	Olga de Amaral		√		SS&D	5	2	18	Sp 74	4
✝ People: de Amaral, Olga	"Olga de Amaral" (Exhibit)	Grover, Donald	√		Fa	5	1		J/F 78	18
✝ People: de Amarol, Olga	Olga de Amarol: Toward a Language of Freedom	Scarborough, Jessica	√		Fa	12	4		J/A 85	51
People: de Castelbajac, Jean Charles	Paris Museum Surveys Fashion	Colton, Sarah	√		Fa	14	3		M/J 87	6
People: De Filippi, Diana	"Beyond the Fringe" (Exhibit)	Einstein, Sylvia	√		Fa	7	2		M/A 80	70
People: De La Rosa-Griffith, Lorie	"Left on the Loom" (Exhibit)	Dyer, Carolyn	√		Fa	5	2		M/A 78	16
People: De Luca, Angelina	Paper Clothing: West	Koplos, Janet	√		Fa	11	2		M/A 84	39
People: de Shabelsky, Natalie	Embroidery for the Goddess	Kelly, Mary B.	√		TM			11	J/J 87	26
People: de Vito, Patty	Everyday World of Fantasy, The	Smeltzer, Nancy	√		Fa	13	3		M/J 86	6
People: Deafenbaugh, Linda	Scholarship in Action		√		SS&D	7	4	28	Fa 76	108
People: Dean, Lina	"Interweave 79" (Exhibit)	Constantinides, Kathy	√		Fa	7	1		J/F 80	66
People: Debone, Anthony	Debones: Collaborative Art Works, The		√		Fa	5	2		M/A 78	55
People: Debone, Mary	Debones: Collaborative Art Works, The		√		Fa	5	2		M/A 78	55
People: DeCamillis, Nancy	Combine Techniques? Why not?	Derr, Mary L.	√		WJ	7	3	27	Wi 82	19
People: Deflor, Jeanne	"Fibers" (Exhibit)	Meyer, Zach	√		Fa	4	4		J/A 77	11
People: DeGraw, Evelyn	Kansas University, An Interview with Evelyn DeGraw (error-corrected H&C v22 n2 71 p4)	Lee, Jane	√		H&C	22	1		Wi 71	6
People: DeJoy, Karen	"Critters and Cohorts" (Exhibit)	Clark, Becky	√		Fa	4	6		N/D 77	13
People: Delaunay, Sonia	In the Shadow of Fame: Sophie Taeuber-Arp and Sonia Delaunay	Austin, Carol	√		Fa	12	5		S/O 85	50
People: Demane, Leslie Ann	Leslie Ann Demane		√		Fa	4	5		S/O 77	55
People: Demetrakas, Johanna	Right Out of History	Mattera, Joanne	√		Fa	9	3		M/J 82	55
People: Dempsey, Annie	Annie Dempsey: Sculptural Crochet (Exhibit)	Lindley, Susan	√		Fa	9	2		M/A 82	76
People: Denkin, Stephen	Glimakra Looms' N Yarns	Xenakis, Alexis Yiorgos	√		PWC	4	1	11		48
People: Denton, Kay	"Mini Tapestry Exhibit" (Exhibit)	Bockelman, JoAnne	√		Fa	5	4		J/A 78	12
People: Denton, Kay	Welcome to My World	Denton, Kay	√		Fa	8	3		M/J 81	52
People: Deny, Madeleine	"Third International Exhibition of Miniature Textiles 1978" (Exhibit)	Spencer, Patricia	√		Fa	6	1		J/F 79	90
People: Dessureau, Barbara	Profile of an HGA Rep		√		SS&D	16	3	63	Su 85	87
People: Dewey, Lilibet	Crossing Over—Fiber in Print	Poon, Vivian	√		Fa	10	3		M/J 83	48
People: Dey, Chris	"Art Fabric '77: the Contemporary American Tapestry" (Exhibit)	Papa, Nancy	√		Fa	4	4		J/A 77	12
People: Dey, Christine	"Fiber Departures" (Exhibit)	Dyer, Carolyn	√		Fa	4	3		M/J 77	9
People: Dey, Kris	"Fiber Structures and Fabric Surfaces" (Exhibit)	Itter, Diane	√		Fa	7	1		J/F 80	67
People: Dey, Kris	Fiber Workspaces: A Room of Your Own	Bishop, Mara	√		Fa	4	4		J/A 77	38
People: Dey, Kris	Questions of Style: Contemporary Trends in the Fiber Arts	Howe-Echt, Katherine	√		Fa	7	2		M/A 80	38
People: Dey, Kris	"Wall Hangings: The New Classicism" (Exhibit)	Grover, Donald	√		Fa	4	4		J/A 77	10
People: Dey, Kris	Words in Fiber	Rowley, Kathleen	√		Fa	11	2		M/A 84	66
People: Dezzany, Frances	Mothproofing Techniques for Weavers and Spinners	Dezzany, Frances	√		Fa	7	1		J/F 80	44
People: Di Mare, Dominic	"Dominic Di Mare" (Exhibit)	Park, Betty	√		Fa	4	3		M/J 77	8
People: Di Mare, Dominic	Interview with Dominic Di Mare: A Commitment to Forward Movement, An	Janeiro, Jan	√		Fa	13	1		J/F 86	55
People: Di Mare, Dominic	"Paper Sources" (Exhibit)	Papa, Nancy	√		Fa	5	4		J/A 78	16

SUBJECT	TITLE	AUTHOR	IL	INST	JOUR	VOL	NO	ISS	DATE	PAGE
People: Di Mare, Dominic	Robert Pfannebecker: A Collector's Point of View	Park, Betty	√		Fa	5	4		J/A 78	42
People: Di Nino, Lynn	If the Art Fits – Wear It! — Friends of the Rag	Strosnider, Ann	√		Fa	6	3		M/J 79	35
People: Dickerson, Anne W.	Anne W. Dickerson	Dickerson, Anne S.	√		Fa	14	5		N/D 87	12
People: Dickie, Nancy	"Fiber Feelings" (Exhibit)	King, Dianne Hennessy	√		Fa	5	5		S/O 78	70
People: Dickson, Ellen Fanger	Basket Inside Out: The Spiral Sculptures of Ellen Fanger Dickson, A	Dickson, Ellen Fanger	√		Fa	7	1		J/F 80	26
People: Diemoz, Bonita J.	"Fiber Structures" Convergence '76 (Exhibit)	Mathews-Pulleyn, Kathryn	√		Fa	3	4		J/A 76	12
People: Dieterich, Mary	Focus on the HGA Board of Directors			√	SS&D	10	3	39	Su 79	47
People: Dieterich, Mary	Gallery (Tapestry)			√	Hw	3	1		Ja 82	54
People: Diggs, Jo	Jo Diggs: An Interview with a Very Talented Woman			√	Fa	3	5		S/O 76	24
People: Diggs, Jo	"Textiles New Mexico 1976" (Exhibit)	Warner, Lucy Ann	√		Fa	3	2		M/A 76	12
People: Dill-Kocher, Laurie	Laurie Dill-Kocher	Dill-Kocher, Laurie	√		Fa	13	2		M/A 86	15
People: Dillon, Allester	Inspired by Fiber: Textile Sensibility in Other Media	Malarcher, Patricia	√		Fa	10	6		N/D 83	33
People: DiMare, Dominic	"Dominic DiMare: New Work" (Exhibit)	Janeiro, Jan	√		Fa	8	2		M/A 81	63
People: DiMare, Dominic	"Miniature Textiles: 4th International Exhibition" (Exhibit)	Talley, Charles S.	√		Fa	8	3		M/J 81	72
People: Dimond, Terry Jarrard	Ceremonial Structures of Terry Jarrard Dimond, The	Hyatt, Sharyn; Teresa Mangum	√		Fa	9	4		J/A 82	66
People: Dine, Jim	Garment Form As Image, The	Koplos, Janet	√		Fa	10	6		N/D 83	66
People: DiNino, Lynn	Lynn DiNino	Greer, Tyson	√		Fa	13	2		M/A 86	14
People: Ditson, Lea	Art to Wear: Looking At the Movement	Scarborough, Jessica	√		Fa	12	3		M/J 85	56
People: Dodge, Constance	"Constance Dodge: Mind Feelings" (Exhibit)	Flanagan, Jeanne	√		Fa	9	3		M/J 82	82
People: Dodge, Dorothy	Dorothy Dodge: Boldness in Fiber			√	SS&D	6	3	23	Su 75	4
People: Dodson, Anne	Felt and Paper: A Portfolio			√	Fa	13	4		J/A 86	35
People: Doherty, Allison	Felt and Paper: A Portfolio			√	Fa	13	4		J/A 86	35
People: Doherty, Rosemary	Rosemary Doherty			√	Fa	4	4		J/A 77	53
People: Donaldson, R. Alan	High Tech Meets High Touch: Pioneers in Art	Kaminski, Vera E.	√		Fa	13	5		S/O 86	6
People: Donnell, Radka	"Quilt National '79" (Exhibit)	Gutcheon, Beth	√		Fa	6	5		S/O 79	80
People: Donnell-Vogt, Radka	"Radka Donnell-Vogt: Patchwork Quilts" (Exhibit)	Chase, Pattie	√		Fa	7	5		S/O 80	76
People: Donnelly, Robert	Robert Donnelly	de la Cruz, Catherine Jacinta	√		S-O	10	1		Sp 86	53
People: Doria, Denis	Lausanne Notebook: Our Special Report on the 8th Lausanne Biennial of Tapestry, A	Mathews, Rich	√		Fa	4	5		S/O 77	30
People: Doria, Denis	"Third International Exhibition of Miniature Textiles 1978" (Exhibit)	Spencer, Patricia	√		Fa	6	1		J/F 79	90
People: Dougherty, Patrick	Portfolio of Contemporary Fiber Sculpture, A			√	Fa	11	4		J/A 84	34
People: Dove, Linda	Athens Tapestry Works	Many, Paul	√		Fa	5	4		J/A 78	51
People: Downs, Amy	Seamstress...Sorceress...Artist	Lowell-LaRoque, Jane	√		Fa	7	3		M/J 80	29
People: Dozier, Deborah S.	"Fiber National '84" (Exhibit)	Bard, Elizabeth A.	√		Fa	12	4		J/A 85	66
People: Draheim, Teliha	Contemporary California Costume	Poon, Vivian	√		Fa	11	5		S/O 84	53
People: Dreager, Jacqueline	"Works In, On, and Of Paper" (Exhibit)	Les, Kathleen	√		Fa	6	5		S/O 79	79
People: Dreher, Pat	Making a Living: Eight Fiber Artists Tell How They Do It	Rowley, Kathleen	√		Fa	9	5		S/O 82	38
People: Drizhal, Eva	Portfolio of Contemporary Fiber Sculpture, A			√	Fa	11	4		J/A 84	34
People: Droege, Carol	Advent Chasuble, An	Droege, Carol	√		SS&D	17	1	65	Wi 85	41
People: Drooker, Penelope	Certificate Holders: What Now? Part 3, The	Alderman, Sharon D.	√		SS&D	13	2	50	Sp 82	60

SUBJECT	TITLE	AUTHOR	IL	INST	JOUR	VOL	NO	ISS	DATE	PAGE
People: Drouin, Daniel and Denise	In the Gobelin Tradition: The Drouin Atelier	Gregg, Dorothy	√		SS&D	10	1	37	Wi 78	28
People: Drower: Sara	"Critters and Cohorts" (Exhibit)	Clark, Becky	√		Fa	4	6		N/D 77	13
People: Drower, Sara	"Fibers" (Exhibit)	Meyer, Zach	√		Fa	4	4		J/A 77	11
People: Drower, Sara	Review/Discussion of Artspace's Innovative Yet Flawed "Fiber Freely Interpreted", A (Exhibit)		√		Fa	4	2		M/A 77	38
People: Druding, Susan	American Yarn Shops: On the Endangered Species List?	Xenakis, Alexis Yiorgos	√		Kn	3	4	8	Fa 87	10
People: Drummond, Miss K. R.	London Bookshop	Clement, Doris	√		H&C	11	1		Wi 60	11
People: Drysdale, Rosemary	Swatching		√	√	Kn	3	4	8	Fa 87	42
People: Du Grenier, Robert	Inspired by Fiber: Textile Sensibility in Other Media	Malarcher, Patricia	√		Fa	10	6		N/D 83	33
People: DuBois, Emily	Design by the Yard: Today's Fabric Innovators	Scarborough, Jessica	√		Fa	12	5		S/O 85	30
People: Dubois, Emily	Emily Dubois	Packard, Myles	√		Fa	4	6		N/D 77	66
People: DuBois, Emily	"Introductions '80" Emily DuBois and Sylvia Seventy (Exhibit)	Janeiro, Jan	√		Fa	7	6		N/D 80	70
People: Dubois, Emily	More 1978 Scholarships		√		SS&D	10	1	37	Wi 78	107
People: DuBois, J.M.	San Francisco Tapestry Workshop: A European-Style Atelier in the United States, The	Rowley, Kathleen	√		Fa	10	3		M/J 83	60
People: duBois, Jan Marie	History in Stitches, A	Mattera, Joanne	√		Fa	7	3		M/J 80	37
People: Ducote, Camrose	Camrose Ducote's Menagerie: An Empathy with Animals	Redmond, Cheryl	√		Fa	10	3		M/J 83	27
People: Ducote, Camrose	Cows in Fiber	Timmons, Chris	√		Fa	11	4		J/A 84	55
People: Ducote, Camrose	Plastics In Fiber: A Persistent Presence	Malarcher, Patricia	√		Fa	12	1		J/F 85	56
People: Duffey, Judith	"Ceremonial Garments" (Exhibit)	Laymon, Cynthia	√		Fa	9	6		N/D 82	82
People: Duffy, Helen	Convergence '86 Preview: Toronto — A City in Transition	Baker, William R. M.	√		SS&D	17	1	65	Wi 85	43
People: Dukes, Phyllis	Ice Tapestries: The Environmental Art of Phyllis Dukes	Scarborough, Jessica	√		Fa	6	5		S/O 79	26
People: Dunatchik, Jean	Fiber Workspaces: A Room of Your Own	Bishop, Mara	√		Fa	4	4		J/A 77	38
People: Dunbar, Ann	Ann Dunbar		√		Fa	4	3		M/J 77	41
People: Duncan, Chris	Shady Ladies	Scarborough, Jessica	√		Fa	11	3		M/J 84	12
People: Duncan, Ligoa	Ligoa Duncan's Studio		√		H&C	8	4		Fa 57	18
People: Dunham, Miriam	Scholarship in Action		√		SS&D	7	4	28	Fa 76	108
People: Dunlap, Ralph and Rosalie Dunlap	Dunlaps: New Mexico to Tunisia, The	Gregg, Marcia			S-O	4			80	4
People: Dunlop, Valerie	Knitting Craft in Great Britain, The	Kinder, Kathleen	√		Fa	11	4		J/A 84	42
People: Dunnewold, Jane	Jane Dunnewold	Dunnewold, Jane	√		Fa	14	3		M/J 87	23
People: Dunwell, Anna	Tromping Through the Ages	Dunwell, Anna	√		Fa	9	2		M/A 82	26
People: Duplan, Alicia	Alicia Duplan: A Weaver in the Navajo Tradition	Erler, Mary	√		Fa	7	5		S/O 80	28
People: Duplan, Alicia	"Houston Designer-Craftsmen 1976" (Exhibit)	Vander Lee, Jana	√		Fa	3	4		J/A 76	9
People: Dushanko-Dobek, Ann	Lausanne Notebook: Our Special Report on the 8th Lausanne Biennial of Tapestry, A	Mathews, Rich	√		Fa	4	5		S/O 77	30
People: Dushanko-Dobek, Anne	Anne Dushanko-Dobek: Preserving Found Objects		√		Fa	5	3		M/J 78	44
People: Dushanko-Dobek, Anne	"Anne Dushanko-Dobek: Silent Voices" (Exhibit)	Scheinman, Pamela	√		Fa	11	4		J/A 84	77
People: Dutterer, Pauline	Pauline Dutterer, Designer and Weaver		√		H&C	3	2		Sp 52	28
People: Dyer, Carolyn	Fiber Workspaces: A Room of Your Own	Bishop, Mara	√		Fa	4	4		J/A 77	38
People: D'Agostino, Fernanda	"Fiber National '84" (Exhibit)	Bard, Elizabeth A.	√		Fa	12	4		J/A 85	66
People: Earl, Grace	Quilts in Women's Lives	Mattera, Joanne	√		Fa	9	3		M/J 82	54
People: Eckhardt, Barbara	Working with Linen: Barbara Eckhardt	Goodman, Deborah Lerme	√		Fa	14	2		M/A 87	35

522

SUBJECT	TITLE	AUTHOR	IL	INST	JOUR	VOL	NO	ISS	DATE	PAGE
People: Eckmann, Dorothy Fletcher	Country of Origin, USA: A Decade of Contemporary Rugs	Stevens, Rebeccah A. T.	√		Fa	11	3		M/J 84	60
People: Edelfsen, David	Plastics in Fiber: A Persistent Presence	Malarcher, Patricia	√		Fa	12	1		J/F 85	56
People: Edelmann, Yrjo	Painted Paper		√		Fa	11	2		M/A 84	51
People: Edens, Gerna	Gerna Edens: Textile Rhythms		√		Fa	10	4		J/A 83	14
People: Edgerton, Kate	Shroud, The		√		SS&D	12	1	45	Wi 80	15
People: Edman, Larry	Speakers Bureau Presents		√		SS&D	5	2	18	Sp 74	78
People: Edmonds, Chris Wolf	"Chris Wolf Edmonds" (Exhibit)	Brackman, Barbara	√		Fa	11	5		S/O 84	72
People: Eggers, Conni	Ecclesiastical Fiber	Eggers, Conni	√		Fa	4	6		N/D 77	36
People: Ehlin, Tina	Sampler of Surface Design, A	Westphal, Katherine	√		Fa	10	5		S/O 83	39
People: Ehni, Lari	"Five Women from Texas" (Exhibit)	Leach, Vivian	√		Fa	6	1		J/F 79	86
People: Ehni, Lari	"Revolution in Fiber Art" (Exhibit)		√		Fa	3	3		M/J 76	7
People: Ehrman, Marli	Marli Ehrman		√		H&C	11	2		Sp 60	25
People: Ehrmann, Marli	Marli-Weavers of Chicago, The	Uhlman, Ilse Etta	√		H&C	4	1		Wi 52	9
People: Ekengren, Kerstin	Kerstin Ekengren	af Kleen, Nils E.	√		H&C	15	2		Sp 64	18
People: Elgot, Shirley Ruth	"Microfibers" (Exhibit)	McClelland, Elizabeth	√		Fa	8	2		M/A 81	66
People: Elgot, Shirley Ruth	Working with Linen: Shirley Ruth Elgot	Perry, Pamela	√		Fa	14	2		M/A 87	32
People: Elgot, Shirley Ruth	Working with Linen: Three Experiences		√		Fa	14	2		M/A 87	31
People: Elliot, Beth	If the Art Fits – Wear It! — Friends of the Rag	Strosnider, Ann	√		Fa	6	3		M/J 79	35
People: Elliott, Doug	Baskets of Doug Elliot: Connecting with the Natural World, The	McMillan, Sue	√		Fa	11	1		J/F 84	71
People: Elliott, Lillian	Almost Roman Glass	Elliott, Lillian	√		Fa	10	6		N/D 83	20
People: Elliott, Lillian	"Basketworks": Visit to an Exhibition (Exhibit)		√		Fa	9	1		J/F 82	17
People: Elliott, Lillian	"Beyond the Fringe" (Exhibit)	Einstein, Sylvia	√		Fa	7	2		M/A 80	70
People: Elliott, Lillian	Conversation with Lillian Elliott, A	Janeiro, Jan	√		Fa	9	2		M/A 82	66
People: Elliott, Lillian	Lillian Elliott and Pat Hickman: The Pleasures and Problems of Collaboration		√		Fa	12	5		S/O 85	22
People: Elliott, Lillian	"Other Baskets" An Invitational Show in St. Louis (Exhibit)	Degener, Patricia	√		Fa	10	1		J/F 83	76
People: Elliott, Lillian	"Three Living Treasures From California" (Exhibit)	Brandford, Joanne Segal; Sandra Dickey Harner	√		Fa	12	5		S/O 85	70
People: Elliott, Lillian	What Makes a Basket a Basket?	Malarcher, Patricia	√		Fa	11	1		J/F 84	34
People: Elliott, Marny	History in Stitches, A	Mattera, Joanne	√		Fa	7	3		M/J 80	37
People: Elliott, Sally	Resemblance to Afghans; Crochet Rubbings?, A	Elliott, Sally	√		Fa	8	3		M/J 81	48
People: Ellis, John	Fiber and Architecture: John Ellis		√		Fa	3	3		M/J 76	17
People: Ellman, Norma	Swatching		√	√	Kn	3	4	8	Fa 87	42
People: Elston, Theodora	Embroidered Neckpieces of Theodora Elston, The	Sacks, Star M.	√		Fa	6	3		M/J 79	51
People: Emard, Kevin	Not Necessarily Seventh Ave.	Dyett, Linda	√		TM			6	A/S 86	28
People: Emery, Irene	Bouquets for Miss Irene Emery				TMJ	2	1		De 66	38
People: Endres, Linda Carollo	From a Family Album	Endres, Linda Carollo	√		Fa	7	3		M/J 80	70
People: Engel, Lauren	"Fabric/Nexus: New Connections" (Exhibit)	Moldovan, George	√		Fa	10	3		M/J 83	70
People: Enthoven, Jacqueline	Jacqueline Enthoven: Portrait of a Stitchery Teacher	Szajman, Rena	√		Fa	4	3		M/J 77	45
People: Enthoven, Jacqueline	Jacqueline Enthoven, Suggests Handwoven Fabrics for Embroidery		√		H&C	17	4		Fa 66	19
People: Epstein, Ann S.	Ann S. Epstein	Epstein, Ann S.	√		Fa	13	1		J/F 86	19
People: Epstein, Betty	Betty Epstein				SS&D	17	1	65	Wi 85	4
People: Epstein, Betty	Marvelous Mistake, A	Cramer, Pauline E.	√	√	SS&D	17	1	65	Wi 85	34
People: Epstein, Betty	Profile of a State Rep	Cramer, Pauline Ellis	√		SS&D	15	4	60	Fa 84	89
People: Erickson, Nancy	Fondness for Rabbits: Nancy Erickson's Quilts Deliver a Serious Message in a Soft Medium, A		√		Fa	8	6		N/D 81	17

SUBJECT	TITLE	AUTHOR	IL	INST	JOUR	VOL	NO	ISS	DATE	PAGE
People: Erickson, Nancy	"Needle Expressions '84" (Exhibit)	Koplos, Janet	√		Fa	12	2		M/A 85	74
People: Erickson, Nancy	Quiltmaker's Art, A	Mattera, Joanne	√		Fa	10	2		M/A 83	33
People: Ericson, Diane and Lois	Speakers Bureau Presents		√		SS&D	8	4	32	Fa 77	62
People: Erixon, Britta	Well-Worn Path to Where? A View of Contemporary Swedish Textiles, The	Talley, Charles S.	√		Fa	8	2		M/A 81	44
People: Ernst, Jaki	Jaki Ernst "Fibre Graphics and Soft Sculpture" (Exhibit)	Gilsenan, Nancy	√		Fa	7	6		N/D 80	69
People: Escola, Lea	"Scandinavian Touch, The" A Traveling Exhibit (Exhibit)	Mattera, Joanna	√		Fa	10	1		J/F 83	82
People: Eskind, Danica	Surface Design and the Garment Form	Reith, Stephanie J.	√		Fa	8	1		J/F 81	34
People: Esocoff, Phil	Textile-Inspired Architecture	Smeltzer, Nancy	√		Fa	14	4		S/O 87	5
People: Esping, Mardel	Three Personal Statements: Norma Minkowitz, Gillian Bull, Mardel Esping		√		Fa	3	5		S/O 76	19
People: Evans, Becky	Livin' and Workin' on the Land: Fiber Art Outside the Mainstream	Talley, Charles S.	√		Fa	8	6		N/D 81	38
People: Evans, Jane	Profile of an HGA Rep		√		SS&D	17	3	67	Su 86	84
People: Evans, Kerry	Handwoven Clothing Today: The Couturier Touch	West, Virginia	√		Fa	8	1		J/F 81	39
People: Evers, Inge	Groupwork with Dutch Feltmaker Inge Evers	Clark, Sherry	√	√	SS&D	17	4	68	Fa 86	28
People: Ewen, Phyllis	"Fibers: From Function to Formalization" (Exhibit)	Scarborough, Jessica	√		Fa	9	1		J/F 82	76
People: Eyerman, Linda	Chromatic Effervescence: The Hooked Surface As a Response to My Environment	Eyerman, Linda	√		Fa	10	2		M/A 83	22
People: Eyerman, Linda	Country of Origin, USA: A Decade of Contemporary Rugs	Stevens, Rebeccah A. T.	√		Fa	11	3		M/J 84	60
People: Eyerman, Linda	"Fiber Forms: Linda Eyerman, Jane Sauer" (Exhibit)	Degener, Patricia	√		Fa	8	3		M/J 81	73
People: Fabeck, Diane	Weaving Guilds—A Special Sharing		√		Iw	5	2		Sp 80	54
People: Fagan-Kennedy, Margo	Design by the Yard: Today's Fabric Innovators	Scarborough, Jessica	√		Fa	12	5		S/O 85	30
People: Fagelson, Pami Slatt	Quiltmaking: A Celebration of Life — Esther Parkhurst, Camille Shafer, Pami Slatt Fagelson		√		Fa	8	3		M/J 81	26
People: Faiola, Linda	Garments from the Loom: Handweaver Randall Darwall Focuses on the Cloth	Mattera, Joanne	√		Fa	10	1		J/F 83	20
People: Fair, Maurine	Maurine Fair	Ligon, Linda	√	√	Iw	2	2		Wi 77	20
People: Falkowska, Barbara	"22 Polish Textile Artists" (Exhibit)	Park, Betty	√		Fa	4	5		S/O 77	8
People: Fannin, Allen	Conversation with Allen Fannin				S-O	11	3		Fa 87	30
People: Fannin, Allen	Determination and Innovation: A Successful Weaving Mill	Fago, D'Ann Calhoun	√		TM			14	D/J 87	14
People: Fannin, Allen	Interview with Allen Fannin, An				WJ	6	2	22	Fa 81	28
People: Fannin, Dorothy	Determination and Innovation: A Successful Weaving Mill	Fago, D'Ann Calhoun	√		TM			14	D/J 87	14
People: Fannin, Dorothy	Interview with Allen Fannin, An				WJ	6	2	22	Fa 81	28
People: Farber, Deborah	"Critters and Cohorts" (Exhibit)	Clark, Becky	√		Fa	4	6		N/D 77	13
People: Farmer, Mary	Three English Tapestry Weavers	Liebler, Barbara	√		Hw	3	1		Ja 82	61
People: Farrell, Hannon	Hannon Farrell				SS&D	18	4	72	Fa 87	5
People: Farvolden, June	"Focus on Handwoven Fabric: Ontario Handweavers and Spinners" (Exhibits)	Place, Jennifer	√		Fa	9	4		J/A 82	74
People: Fash, Ruth	Under Wraps		√		Fa	12	3		M/J 85	26
People: Fassett, Kaffe	"Glorious Knits of Kaffe Fassett, The" (Exhibit)	McCann, Kathleen	√		Fa	13	2		M/A 86	53
People: Fassett, Kaffe	Kaffe Fassett		√		Kn	2	2	4	S-S 86	14
People: Fassett, Kaffe	Kaffe Fassett: Dream Knitter (error-corrected Fa v5 n4 78 p63)		√		Fa	5	3		M/J 78	26
People: Fassett, Kaffe	Possessed by Color	Miller, Irene Preston	√		TM			3	F/M 86	71
People: Fawkes, Judith Poxson	"Crafts Northwest, Circa 1980" (Exhibit)	Evans, Rojean; Louise Klemperer	√		Fa	7	5		S/O 80	75

SUBJECT	TITLE	AUTHOR	IL	INST	JOUR	VOL	NO	ISS	DATE	PAGE
People: FeBland, Harriet	"100% Wool" (Exhibit)	Goldin, Susan	√		Fa	4	6		N/D 77	18
People: Fechter, Anita	"Art of Basketry, The" (Exhibit)	Park, Betty	√		Fa	4	2		M/A 77	9
People: Feldblum, Jane	"Mini Tapestry Exhibit" (Exhibit)	Bockelman, JoAnne	√		Fa	5	4		J/A 78	12
People: Feldman, Bella	Plastics in Fiber: A Persistent Presence	Malarcher, Patricia	√		Fa	12	1		J/F 85	56
People: Feldman, Bella	Visual Language of Bella Feldman, The	Scarborough, Jessica	√		Fa	11	4		J/A 84	30
People: Feldman, Bella Tabak	"Bella Tabak Feldman: Recent Sculpture" (Exhibit)	Scarborough, Jessica	√		Fa	10	2		M/A 83	70
People: Felgar, Judy	"Fiber Structures" Convergence '76 (Exhibit)	Mathews-Pulleyn, Kathryn	√		Fa	3	4		J/A 76	12
People: Felix, Deborah J.	Deborah J. Felix	Bard, Elizabeth	√		Fa	12	2		M/A 85	34
People: Fender, Tom	"Art Fabric '77: the Contemporary American Tapestry" (Exhibit)	Papa, Nancy	√		Fa	4	4		J/A 77	12
People: Fender, Tom	Corporate Collecting "Contemporary Tapestries" (Exhibit)	Dyer, Carolyn	√		Fa	4	5		S/O 77	16
People: Fender, Tom	"Fiber Works — Americas & Japan" (Exhibit)	Kato, Kuniko Lucy	√		Fa	5	1		J/F 78	10
People: Fender, Tom	Fiber Workspaces: A Room of Your Own	Bishop, Mara	√		Fa	4	4		J/A 77	38
People: Fender, Tom	"Paper Sources" (Exhibit)	Papa, Nancy	√		Fa	5	4		J/A 78	16
People: Fender, Tom	"Transformation: UCLA Alumnae in Fiber" (Exhibit)	Dyer, Carolyn	√		Fa	6	4		J/A 79	67
People: Ferandell, Michele	Crossing Over—Fiber in Print	Poon, Vivian	√		Fa	10	3		M/J 83	48
People: Ferguson, Bette Mankin	Portfolio of Contemporary Fiber Sculpture, A		√		Fa	11	4		J/A 84	34
People: Ferguson, Catherine	"Beds, Sweet Dreams, and Other Things" (Exhibit)	Bissell, June	√		Fa	6	4		J/A 79	70
People: Fernandez, Gil	Gil Fernandez: Light and Color	Ligon, Linda	√		Iw	2	1		Fa 76	8
People: Ferree, Maralyce	Maralyce Ferree: Dual-Purpose Weavings	Mimoso, Sophie	√		Fa	7	2		M/A 80	12
People: Ferrero, Pat	Quilts in Women's Lives	Mattera, Joanne	√		Fa	9	3		M/J 82	54
People: Fidler, Ellie	"Ellie Fidler — Tapestries" (Exhibit)	Tanenbaum, Ruth	√		Fa	5	4		J/A 78	14
People: Fidler, Ellie	Ellie Fidler: The Power of Concentration	Cooke, Leslie	√		Fa	7	2		M/A 80	48
People: Field, Jacqueline	Gallery (Tapestry)		√		Hw	3	1		Ja 82	51
People: Fife, Lin	"Contemporary Directions in Fiber" (Exhibit)	Meloy, Margaret	√		Fa	14	4		S/O 87	42
People: Fife, Lin	Lin Fife: Products of Passion (error-corrected Fa v12 n1 85 p24)	Fife, Lin	√		Fa	11	5		S/O 84	12
People: Fife, Lin	"Patterns" (Exhibit)	Malarcher, Patricia	√		Fa	10	2		M/A 83	76
People: Fife, Lin	Rugs: Lin Fife, Papermaker		√		Fa	9	2		M/A 82	61
People: Fike, Philip	Good As Gold: Alternatives in American Jewelry		√		Fa	9	5		S/O 82	18
People: Filliger-Nolte, Pia	Under Wraps		√		Fa	12	3		M/J 85	26
People: Finch-Hurley, Jerri	Cows in Fiber	Timmons, Chris	√		Fa	11	4		J/A 84	55
People: Finch-Hurley, Jerri	Jerri Finch-Hurley	Finch-Hurley, Jerri	√		Fa	13	1		J/F 86	18
People: Finch-Hurley, Jerri	Jerri Finch-Hurley: Quilted Paintings	Wonder, Danny	√		Fa	11	2		M/A 84	27
People: Fink, Shirley	"Ten Boston Fiber Artists" (Exhibit)	Serenyi, Peter	√		Fa	5	5		S/O 78	67
People: Fiore, Linda Vargo	Touch of Whimsy, A	Gonder, Pamela	√		SS&D	7	3	27	Su 76	86
People: Fiore, Rose	"Throbbing Needles II" (Exhibit)	Mattera, Joanne	√		Fa	7	2		M/A 80	71
People: First, Deborah	"North/South Carolina Fibers Competition" (Exhibit)	Laymon, Cynthia	√		Fa	10	4		J/A 83	68
People: Fisch, Arline	Inspired by Fiber: Textile Sensibility in Other Media	Malarcher, Patricia	√		Fa	10	6		N/D 83	33
People: Fisch, Arline	Teacher/Student Interface: Two Views of Education	Kosta, Angela	√		Fa	14	1		J/F 87	31
People: Fisch, Arline M.	Arline M. Fisch	Fisch, Arline M.	√		Fa	13	1		J/F 86	18
People: Fisch, Olga Anhalzar	Primitive Indian Designs Inspire Ecuador's Gift to United Nations		√		H&C	4	1		Wi 52	13
People: Fischer, Gail Marie	Color Xerography and the Fiber Artist	Theil, Linda	√		Fa	8	5		S/O 81	59
People: Fischer, Mildred	Papermaking in the U.S.A.	Toale, Bernard	√		Fa	9	4		J/A 82	34
People: Fischer, Nancy	"Mini Tapestry Exhibit" (Exhibit)	Bockelman, JoAnne	√		Fa	5	4		J/A 78	12

SUBJECT	TITLE	AUTHOR	IL	INST	JOUR	VOL	NO	ISS	DATE	PAGE
People: Fisk, Elizabeth	Elizabeth Fisk, Early 20th Century Vermont Weaver	Atwood, Betty	√		H&C	19	3		Su 68	18
People: Fitt, Cate	Art to Wear — Three Innovators: Cate Fitt, Emma Vesey, Dina Schwartz Knapp		√		Fa	8	1		J/F 81	67
People: Fitt, Cate	For the Body (error-corrected Fa v10 n2 83 p61)		√		Fa	10	1		J/F 83	32
People: Fitzgerald, Veronica	"Quilt National '85": A Proving Ground (Exhibit)	Roe, Nancy	√		Fa	12	6		N/D 85	58
People: Flavin, Sonja	Sonja Flavin: Weaving for the Classics	Sobieszek, Robert A.	√		Fa	11	3		M/J 84	70
People: Flemming, John	Masks At the Heart of Disguise	Koplos, Janet	√		Fa	11	5		S/O 84	32
People: Floor, Marcia	Soft Sculpture: Old Forms, New Meanings	Gordon, Beverly	√		Fa	10	6		N/D 83	40
People: Fohn-Hansen, Lydia	Musk Ox, The	Howard, Helen Griffiths	√		S-O	7	1		Sp 83	16
People: Foley, Pat	Fiber Workspaces: A Room of Your Own	Bishop, Mara	√		Fa	4	4		J/A 77	38
People: Foley, Pat	"Statements in Fibre" (Exhibit)	Wagner, Liz	√		Fa	6	1		J/F 79	88
People: Ford, Margaret	Inspired by Fiber: Textile Sensibility in Other Media	Malarcher, Patricia	√		Fa	10	6		N/D 83	33
People: Ford-Pohlmann, Marjorie	Marjorie Ford-Pohlmann: Fiber Design Professional	LaLena, Constance	√		Hw	5	3		Su 84	82
People: Fornari, Cindy	Cindy Fornari: Painted Warps		√		Fa	3	5		S/O 76	30
People: Fortuny, Mariano	Paris Museum Surveys Fashion	Colton, Sarah	√		Fa	14	3		M/J 87	6
People: Fortuny, Mariano	Pleats, Pleats, Pleats: For Sculptural Garments and Sculpture Itself		√		Fa	9	1		J/F 82	40
People: Foster, Karen	"Art and Romance of Peasant Clothing, The" (Exhibit)	Dyer, Carolyn	√		Fa	5	3		M/J 78	16
People: Fournier, Jane	Handspun into Lace	Fournier, Jane	√	√	SS&D	17	4	68	Fa 86	70
People: Fowler, Molly	Portraits by a Weaver		√		SS&D	8	4	32	Fa 77	38
People: Fowler, Molly R.—M.,	Felt and Paper: A Portfolio		√		Fa	13	4		J/A 86	35
People: Fowler, Shelly	Fantasy Figures: Shelly Fowler's Fabric Dolls	Place, Jennifer	√		Fa	10	1		J/F 83	16
People: Fox, Sandi	Small Endearments: 19th Century Quilts for Children and Dolls	Dyer, Carolyn	√		Fa	8	3		M/J 81	18
People: Fox, Sandi	"Southern California Designer Crafts" (Exhibit)	Dyer, Carolyn	√		Fa	5	2		M/A 78	14
People: Fox, Sheila	1977 HGA Scholarships (error-corrected SS&D v9 n2 78 p70)		√		SS&D	9	1	33	Wi 77	46
People: Fox, Sheila	"Contemporary Fiber Art" (Exhibit)	Guyer, Niki	√		Fa	5	6		N/D 78	66
People: Fox, Sheila	Sheila Fox: Three-Dimensional Plaiting	Malarcher, Pat	√		Fa	6	5		S/O 79	22
People: Fox, Sheila	"Woven Works: Tradition And Innovation" (Exhibit)	White, Patrick E.	√		Fa	12	6		N/D 85	60
People: Fraas, Gayle	Fraas—Slade: Painted Views	Reith, Stephanie	√		Fa	8	5		S/O 81	32
People: Fraas, Gayle	"Maine Coast Artists: Fabrications" (Exhibit)	Beem, Edgar Allen	√		Fa	11	4		J/A 84	80
People: Fraas/Slade	For the Body (error-corrected Fa v10 n2 83 p61)		√		Fa	10	1		J/F 83	32
People: Frank, May	Shadow Weave Vest (error-corrected WJ v9 n2 84 p82)		√	> 4	WJ	8	3	31	Wi 83	81
People: Franklin, Lois	Knitting Craft in Great Britain, The	Kinder, Kathleen	√		Fa	11	4		J/A 84	42
People: Franzel-Annett, Linda	Women Faces: A Triptych		√		Fa	12	5		S/O 85	66
People: Frasier, Debra	Windworks: A Way of Working	Frasier, Debra	√		Fa	10	4		J/A 83	58
People: Frazer, Patti	Fiber Artists Find New Showcase in San Diego (Exhibit)	Meilach, Dona	√		Fa	3	4		J/A 76	8
People: Frederick, Deborah	Deborah Frederick: Rainbow Nets	Lansdell, Sarah	√		Fa	5	3		M/J 78	40
People: Frederick, Deborah	"Stitchery '79" (Exhibit)	Kerr, Connie	√		Fa	6	5		S/O 79	78
People: Frederick, Helen C.	Pioneer Paper Places: Pyramid Prints and Paperworks	Fife, Lin	√		Fa	13	4		J/A 86	24
People: Freeman, Susie	Knitting Craft in Great Britain, The	Kinder, Kathleen	√		Fa	11	4		J/A 84	42
People: French, Brenda	Knitted Palette of Brenda French, The	Pierce, Judith	√		Fa	13	2		M/A 86	43
People: French, Mrs. H. Palmer	One Hundred-Year Old Weaver, A		√		H&C	12	1		Wi 61	56
People: Freund, Helga	"Structures in Fiber" (Exhibit)	Padin, Carmen	√		Fa	5	6		N/D 78	70

SUBJECT	TITLE	AUTHOR	IL	INST	JOUR	VOL	NO	ISS	DATE	PAGE
People: Frey, Berta	American Handweaving 1960		√		H&C	11	2		Sp 60	5
People: Frey, Berta	New Woodstock Studio for Berta Frey				H&C	9	1		Wi 57	24
People: Frey, Hey	Yurt in Artpark, The	Brennan, Joan	√		Fa	9	3		M/J 82	19
People: Frickinger, Johann	Eighteenth Century German Court Weaver: Johann Michael Frickinger, An	Hilts, Patricia	√		SS&D	11	4	44	Fa 80	16
People: Fried, Penelope	"Power Garments" (Exhibit)	Papa, Nancy	√		Fa	5	1		J/F 78	13
People: Friedlander, Bilge	Paper: Three Shows At the American Craft Museums (Exhibit)	Lonier, Terri	√		Fa	9	5		S/O 82	84
People: Friedman, Donna Coats	Hi-Tech Banner Sculptures	Polster, Nancy; Elsa Sreenivasam	√		Fa	12	3		M/J 85	42
People: Friedman, Jan	"Fiber Invitational" (Exhibit)	Richerson, Suzanne	√		Fa	8	4		J/A 81	76
People: Fry, Gladys	Slave Quilts: Threads of History	Grabiner, Dana M.	√		Fa	13	5		S/O 86	22
People: Fuchs, Douglas	Basketmaker's Year "Down Under", A	Malarcher, Patricia	√		Fa	8	4		J/A 81	47
People: Fuchs, Douglas	"Forms in Fiber" (Exhibit)	Brown, Arleen Emery	√		Fa	7	5		S/O 80	73
People: Fuchs, Douglas	What Makes a Basket a Basket?	Malarcher, Patricia	√		Fa	11	1		J/F 84	34
People: Fuchs, Douglas	"Works in Miniature" (Exhibit)	Malarcher, Patricia	√		Fa	7	3		M/J 80	82
People: Fuchs, Douglas Eric	Scholarship Report: Fuchs At Varpapuu	Fuchs, Douglas Eric	√		SS&D	7	1	25	Wi 75	92
People: Fuchs, Douglas Eric	Scholarship Winner Has Impressive Credentials				SS&D	6	3	23	Su 75	72
People: Fukotomi, Sachi	Tailor's Logic	Hostek, Stanley	√	√	TM			14	D/J 87	42
People: Fukumoto, Shigeki	Shigeki and Shihoko Fukumoto: Balancing Art and Function	Lancaster, Zöe Woodruff	√		Fa	13	6		N/D 86	5
✳ People: Fukumoto, Shihoko	Innovations in Indigo	Wada, Yoshiko Iwamoto	√		Fa	13	5		S/O 86	29
✦ People: Fukumoto, Shihoko	Shigeki and Shihoko Fukumoto: Balancing Art and Function	Lancaster, Zöe Woodruff	√		Fa	13	6		N/D 86	5
People: Fuller, Leslie	Leslie Fuller: Pan-Creative Quiltmaker	Horton, Lucy	√		Fa	7	5		S/O 80	19
People: Fuller, Leslie	Quiltmaker's Art, A	Mattera, Joanne	√		Fa	10	2		M/A 83	33
People: Fuller, Lucy	Few Words About Feet, Shoes and Other Things We Walk On, A	Katz, Ruth J.	√		Fa	6	3		M/J 79	53
People: Fulleylove, Madge	From Portraits to Textile Designs		√	> 4	H&C	11	1		Wi 60	20
People: Funk, Charlotte	Progression of Ideas, or The Shortest Distance Between 2 Ideas is a Diagonal Line, A		√		Iw	6	1		Wi 80	35
People: Funk, Charlotte	Twills of Charlotte Funk, The	Patrick, Jane	√		Hw	6	5		N/D 85	36
People: Furch, Rue	Rue Furch		√		Fa	4	3		M/J 77	42
People: Furioso, Giorgio	Why Sew Those Lines? An Interview with Giorgio Furioso and Carolyn Thomas	Paca, Al	√		Fa	7	4		J/A 80	25
People: Furnival, Astrid	Knitted Whimsey of Astrid Furnival, The	Elliott, Malinda	√		Fa	12	2		M/A 85	16
People: Gagné, Nicole	Canadian Portfolio, A	Place, Jennifer	√		Fa	9	6		N/D 82	29
People: Gale-Nosek, Cynthia	Cynthia Gale-Nosek: Searching for the Limits of Crochet	Gale-Nosek, Cynthia	√		Fa	11	4		J/A 84	49
People: Gallinger, Osma C.	American Handweaving 1960		√		H&C	11	2		Sp 60	15
People: Gallo, Frank	Felt and Paper: A Portfolio		√		Fa	13	4		J/A 86	35
People: Galloway, Bertha	Weaving Guilds—A Special Sharing		√		Iw	5	2		Sp 80	54
People: Galvin, Bob	Mummery: Philadelphia's Happy New Year	Smeltzer, Nancy	√		Fa	14	3		M/J 87	39
People: Gamache, Elene	"Current Directions: Conseie des Arts Textiles du Quebec" (Exhibit)	Newman, Rochelle	√		Fa	12	1		J/F 85	74
People: Ganda	Profile of a Thai Weaver	McCauley, Susan L.	√		Fa	10	5		S/O 83	26
People: Gandhi, Mahatma	Craftsman and Social Conscience, Part 2: Mahatma Gandhi, The	Hepburn, Ian			Hw	5	5		N/D 84	22
People: Gandhi, Mahatma	Spinning with Gandhi	Grant, Susan	√		S-O	2			78	15
People: Gano, Laurie	Tapestry Weaver's Answers, A		√		TM			10	A/M 87	18
People: Garabedian, Charles	"Artists' Quilts" (Exhibit)	Woelfle, Gretchen	√		Fa	8	4		J/A 81	70
People: Gardner, Frank	"Frank Gardner: Aleatory Works" (Exhibit)	Guagliumi, Susan	√		Fa	9	2		M/A 82	75
People: Gardner, Lisa	Lisa Gardner: Cultural Perspectives	Poon, Vivian	√		Fa	12	1		J/F 85	14
People: Garrett, Cay	Cay Garrett of San Francisco		√		H&C	18	4		Fa 67	29
People: Garrett, Howard	Canadian Portfolio, A	Place, Jennifer	√		Fa	9	6		N/D 82	29

527

SUBJECT	TITLE	AUTHOR	IL	INST	JOUR	VOL	NO	ISS	DATE	PAGE
People: Garrett, John	"Basketry: Tradition in New Form" (Exhibit)	Scarborough, Jessica	√		Fa	9	3		M/J 82	83
People: Garrett, John	Baskets of John Garrett: A Mesh of Ideas and Materials, The	Garrett, John	√		Fa	11	1		J/F 84	26
People: Garrett, John	"Four x Four, A Collaboration: A Special Environment " (Exhibit)	Welty, Margaret	√		Fa	7	1		J/F 80	69
People: Garrett, John	"Tangents: Art in Fiber" (Exhibit)	Krinn, Linda	√		Fa	14	3		M/J 87	55
People: Garrett, Nancy	"Textiles New Mexico 1976" (Exhibit)	Warner, Lucy Ann	√		Fa	3	2		M/A 76	12
People: Garrido, Luis	Garrido, Contemporary Spanish Tapestry Weaver		√		H&C	16	1		Wi 65	12
People: Garver, Elizabeth	For the Body (error-corrected Fa v10 n2 83 p61)		√		Fa	10	1		J/F 83	32
People: Garvey, Barbara	Folkwear: In the Company of Some Friends		√		Fa	3	5		S/O 76	36
People: Gaston-Voûte, Suzanne	Camera Strap in Double-Weave Pick-Up	Gaston-Voûte, Suzanne	√	√	PWC			2	Ap 82	10
People: Geary, Kay	Kay Geary	Bryan, Dorothy	√		H&C	3	2		Sp 52	26
People: Geiger, Judith	Felt and Paper: A Portfolio		√		Fa	13	4		J/A 86	35
People: Geiger, Judith	Sampler of Surface Design, A	Westphal, Katherine	√		Fa	10	5		S/O 83	39
People: Gemzoe, Jette	"Scandinavian Touch, The" A Traveling Exhibit (Exhibit)	Mattera, Joanna	√		Fa	10	1		J/F 83	82
People: Geneslaw, Ruth	"Contemporary Fiber Art" (Exhibit)	Guyer, Niki	√		Fa	5	6		N/D 78	66
People: Geneslaw, Ruth	"Landscapes" (Exhibit)	Clardy, Andrea	√		Fa	5	2		M/A 78	10
People: Geneslaw, Ruth	Miniatures in Fiber: Working Small—An Exciting Challenge for the Contemporary Fiber Artist	Malarcher, Patricia	√		Fa	7	4		J/A 80	32
People: Geneslaw, Ruth	Portfolio of Contemporary Fiber Sculpture, A		√		Fa	11	4		J/A 84	34
People: Geneslaw, Ruth	Public Fiber: Looking At the Logistics	Koplos, Janet	√		Fa	12	1		J/F 85	32
People: Geneslaw, Ruth	"Ruth Geneslaw/Pat Malarcher" (Exhibit)	Guyar, Niki	√		Fa	6	4		J/A 79	66
People: Geneslaw, Ruth	"Works in Miniature" (Exhibit)	Malarcher, Patricia	√		Fa	7	3		M/J 80	82
People: Gentille, Terry A.	Printed Fabric: Another View		√		Fa	9	1		J/F 82	100
People: Gerber Family	Dye and Spin Workshops on Nantucket	Beinecke, Mary Ann	√	√	SS&D	4	1	13	Wi 72	12
People: Gerber, Fred	Lifestyle: A Roundtable Discussion	Ligon, Linda	√		Iw	5	2		Sp 80	22
People: Gerber, Fred and Willi	Speakers Bureau Presents				SS&D	2	2	6	Sp 71	18
People: Gibson, Kathryn	Country of Origin, USA: A Decade of Contemporary Rugs	Stevens, Rebeccah A. T.	√		Fa	11	3		M/J 84	60
People: Gibson, Kathryn	Cows in Fiber	Timmons, Chris	√		Fa	11	4		J/A 84	55
People: Gibson-Roberts, Priscilla A.	Like the Ad Says: "We've Come a Long Way"	Gibson-Roberts, Priscilla A.			S-O	11	3		Fa 87	26
People: Gibson-Roberts, Priscilla A.	Swatching		√	√	Kn	3	4	8	Fa 87	42
People: Gilbert, James	Spatial Transitions	Gilbert, James	√		SS&D	9	3	35	Su 78	12
People: Gilbert, James R.	Plastics in Fiber: A Persistent Presence	Malarcher, Patricia	√		Fa	12	1		J/F 85	56
People: Gilbert, James R.	Portfolio of Contemporary Fiber Sculpture, A		√		Fa	11	4		J/A 84	34
People: Gilbert, Linda	Linda Gilbert	Gilbert, Linda	√		Fa	5	5		S/O 78	16
People: Gilfallan, Joan	Joan Gilfallan	Gilfallan, Joan	√		Fa	7	5		S/O 80	43
People: Gilfert, Sally	Athens Tapestry Works	Many, Paul	√		Fa	5	4		J/A 78	51
People: Gilfert, Sara	Sara Gilfert	Gilfert, Sara	√		Fa	14	5		N/D 87	11
People: Gilmor, Jane Ellen	"Soft Art" (Exhibit)	Richerson, Suzanne	√		Fa	4	4		J/A 77	16
People: Gilmore, E. E.	E.E. Gilmore, Loom Builder and Weaver	Watson, Aleta	√		H&C	23	5		S/O 72	24
People: Gilmore, E. E.	Fifty Years Ago in Handweaving: E. E. Gilmore, A Lifetime of Weaving		√		Hw	7	2		M/A 86	22
People: Gilmore, Lily	"Textile Works: Lily Gilmore, Judith Moir, Sheila O'Hara" (Exhibit)	Mazur, Carole	√		Fa	8	2		M/A 81	67
People: Gilmore, Susan	"Third Annual Fiber Show" (Exhibit)	Papa, Nancy	√		Fa	5	6		N/D 78	65
People: Gilmurray, Sue	Fiber Ten	McGuire, Patricia	√		Fa	4	6		N/D 77	26
People: Ginsberg-Place, Ruth	Boston Seven	Newman, Rochelle	√		SS&D	16	3	63	Su 85	71

SUBJECT	TITLE	AUTHOR	IL	INST	JOUR	VOL	NO	ISS	DATE	PAGE
People: Ginsberg-Place, Ruth	"Boston Seven: A Fiber Show, The" (Exhibit)	Goldman, Judy Ann	√		Fa	6	3		M/J 79	73
People: Ginsberg-Place, Ruth	Cycle of Growth, A	Mattera, Joanne	√		Fa	7	2		M/A 80	24
People: Ginsberg-Place, Ruth	Weaving — A Delicate Balance	Ginsberg-Place, Ruth	√		H&C	23	4		J/A 72	43
People: Ginstrom, Roy	Roy Ginstrom, Versatile Handweaver and Designer of Fabrics for Power Looms		√		H&C	13	3		Su 62	6
People: Gioello, Debi	New System for Getting an Ultra Fit, A	Lassiter, Betty			TM			12	A/S 87	22
People: Giordano, Jo Ann	Rugs: Jo Ann Giordano, Silk Screener		√		Fa	9	2		M/A 82	60
People: Giordano, JoAnn	Fiber At Artpark	MacDonald, Claudia	√		Fa	10	6		N/D 83	47
People: Giordano, JoAnn	JoAnn Giordano: A Modern Mythology	Malarcher, Patricia	√		Fa	13	6		N/D 86	13
People: Giordano, JoAnn	Silkworks	Goodman, Deborah Lerme	√		Fa	13	1		J/F 86	50
People: Giordono, JoAnn	Country of Origin, USA: A Decade of Contemporary Rugs	Stevens, Rebeccah A. T.	√		Fa	11	3		M/J 84	60
People: Gipple, Nancy	Fans and Fan Imagery	Howe, Katherine; Joanne Mattera	√		Fa	9	4		J/A 82	26
People: Gipple, Nancy	Quiltmaker's Art, A	Mattera, Joanne	√		Fa	10	2		M/A 83	33
People: Girardin, Juanita	What People Ask Before They Buy Handmade Fashions	Leslie, Victoria	√		TM			9	F/M 87	58
People: Glantz, Mary Ann	"Four x Four, A Collaboration: A Special Environment " (Exhibit)	Welty, Margaret	√		Fa	7	1		J/F 80	69
People: Glantz, Mary Ann	Lifestyle: A Roundtable Discussion	Ligon, Linda	√		Iw	5	2		Sp 80	22
People: Glantz, Mary Ann	Questions of Style: Contemporary Trends in the Fiber Arts	Howe-Echt, Katherine	√		Fa	7	2		M/A 80	38
People: Glashausser, Suellen	"Art of Basketry, The" (Exhibit)	Park, Betty	√		Fa	4	2		M/A 77	9
People: Glashausser, Suellen	Liberated Embroidery		√		Fa	9	3		M/J 82	35
People: Glashausser, Suellen	Questions of Style: Contemporary Trends in the Fiber Arts	Howe-Echt, Katherine	√		Fa	7	2		M/A 80	38
People: Glashausser, Suellen	Sculptural Paper: Foundations and Directions	Scarborough, Jessica	√		Fa	11	2		M/A 84	32
People: Glashausser, Suellen	"Suellen Glashausser — Fences" (Exhibit)	Malarcher, Pat	√		Fa	6	3		M/J 79	77
People: Glashausser, Suellen	"Women Artists: Clay, Fiber, Metal" (Exhibit)	Malarcher, Patricia	√		Fa	5	2		M/A 78	11
People: Glaves, Jeannine	Portfolio: Jeannine Glaves		√		Hw	7	1		J/F 86	38
People: Glazer, Patti	"Patti Glazer, Woven Tapestry" (error-corrected Fa v3 n5 76 p2) (Exhibit)	Mathews, Richard	√		Fa	3	4		J/A 76	6
People: Glenn, Jeff	Jeff Glenn	Glenn, Jeff	√		Fa	14	1		J/F 87	26
People: Glenn, Jeff	Jeff Glenn: Software for a High-Tech World	Poon, Vivian	√		Fa	12	4		J/A 85	9
People: Glover, Elvira	Profile of an HGA Rep	Keen, Annette	√		SS&D	19	1	73	Wi 87	49
People: Glowacki, Martha	Good As Gold: Alternatives in American Jewelry		√		Fa	9	5		S/O 82	18
People: Glowen, Kathy	Country of Origin, USA: A Decade of Contemporary Rugs	Stevens, Rebeccah A. T.	√		Fa	11	3		M/J 84	60
People: Godfrey, Bill	Fashionable Palette of Pittsburgh Paints, The	Brenholts, Jeanne	√		Fa	14	3		M/J 87	46
People: Godfrey, Bill	Pittsburg Artists Create Kimono Canvases		√		Fa	13	3		M/J 86	7
People: Goetemann, Judith	Verbena Collection, The (error-corrected Fa v11 n1 84 p11)		√		Fa	10	5		S/O 83	64
People: Goffigan, Dale	Dale Goffigan: Textile Designer		√		Fa	12	3		M/J 85	66
People: Gold, Rae	Open Jurying in Pittsburg: Putting Your Work on the Line (Exhibit)	Myrinx, Elaine	√		Fa	6	2		M/A 79	23
People: Goldberg, Jean	Contemporary Needle Lacers		√		TM			13	O/N 87	44
People: Goldberg, Susan B.	Susan B. Goldberg		√		H&C	16	4		Fa 65	12
People: Golder, Stuart	Inspired by Fiber: Textile Sensibility in Other Media	Malarcher, Patricia	√		Fa	10	6		N/D 83	33
People: Goldin, Susan	Miniatures in Fiber: Working Small—An Exciting Challenge for the Contemporary Fiber Artist	Malarcher, Patricia	√		Fa	7	4		J/A 80	32

SUBJECT	TITLE	AUTHOR	IL	INST	JOUR	VOL	NO	ISS	DATE	PAGE
People: Goldin, Susan	"Susan Goldin: Windows" (Exhibit)	Malarcher, Patricia	√		Fa	9	3		M/J 82	76
People: Goldschmidt, Manfred	Manfred Goldschmidt		√		H&C	11	3		Su 60	20
People: Goldsmith, Layne	Felt and Paper: A Portfolio		√		Fa	13	4		J/A 86	35
People: Goldsmith, Layne	"Felt and Papermaking" (Exhibit)	Harrison, Helen A.	√		Fa	11	2		M/A 84	79
People: Goldsmith, Layne	"Felting" (Exhibit)	Park, Betty	√		Fa	7	6		N/D 80	71
People: Goldstein, Marna	"Beds, Sweet Dreams, and Other Things" (Exhibit)	Bissell, June	√		Fa	6	4		J/A 79	70
People: Goo, Jane	Hawaiian Quilt, The	White-Hansen, Sue Ellen	√	√	TM			13	O/N 87	22
People: Goodman, Eva	Not Necessarily Seventh Ave.	Dyett, Linda	√		TM			6	A/S 86	28
People: Goodman, Ron	Ron Goodman		√		Fa	3	6		N/D 76	40
People: Goodman, Ronald	Speakers Bureau Presents		√		SS&D	1	4	4	Se 70	7
People: Gordon, Claudia	"Textiles New Mexico 1976" (Exhibit)	Warner, Lucy Ann	√		Fa	3	2		M/A 76	12
People: Gordon, Coco	Paper: Three Shows At the American Craft Museums (Exhibit)	Lonier, Terri	√		Fa	9	5		S/O 82	84
People: Gordon, John Charles	John Charles Gordon		√		Fa	4	4		J/A 77	32
People: Gordon, John Charles	John Charles Gordon, An Explorer in Materials		√		H&C	20	1		Wi 69	19
People: Gordon, John Charles	Public Fiber: Looking At the Logistics	Koplos, Janet	√		Fa	12	1		J/F 85	32
People: Gordon, Joleen	Old Ways for the New	Gordon, Joleen	√		SS&D	17	4	68	Fa 86	48
People: Gordon, Lida	"Fiber Forms '78" (Exhibit)	Patton, Ellen	√		Fa	5	5		S/O 78	66
People: Gordon, Lida	Lida Gordon	Meloy, Margaret	√		Fa	13	5		S/O 86	19
People: Gordon, Lida	Lida Gordon: An Interview	Arnow, Jan	√		Fa	6	2		M/A 79	50
People: Gordon, Lida	"Lida Gordon: Recent Works" (Exhibit)	Meloy, Margaret	√		Fa	10	4		J/A 83	63
People: Gordon, Mildred and Carlton	Gordons, Weavers at Greenbrier Art Colony, The		√	> 4	H&C	16	3		Su 65	18
People: Gordon, Mr. Carlton R. and Mrs. Gordon	Gordons of Bucks County, The		√		H&C	10	1		Wi 59	27
People: Goss-Garland, Carol	"Basketry: Tradition in New Form" (Exhibit)	Scarborough, Jessica	√		Fa	9	3		M/J 82	83
People: Gothard, Lark	Lark Gothard	Gothard, Lark	√		Fa	12	6		N/D 85	18
People: Goto, Naomi	Under Wraps		√		Fa	12	3		M/J 85	26
People: Gottdiener, Jennifer	"Jennifer Gottdiener: Installation — Thread as Volume" (Exhibit)	Welty, Margaret	√		Fa	7	5		S/O 80	70
People: Gotthoffer, Mrs. Nathan R.	Experiments in Design by an Ohio Weaver		√		H&C	17	3		Su 66	22
People: Gould, Mary	Masks At the Heart of Disguise	Koplos, Janet	√		Fa	11	5		S/O 84	32
People: Gould, Mary	What A Doll! Provocative Paper Dolls, A Captivating Idea	Gould, Mary	√	√	Fa	8	1		J/F 81	78
People: Gowell, Ruth	Washington Fiber	Mathews, Rich	√		Fa	3	5		S/O 76	9
People: Grade, Thomas	"Assemblage: Wisconsin Paper" (Exhibit)	Bard, Elizabeth	√		Fa	11	1		J/F 84	78
People: Grade, Thomas E.	"New Wisconsin Fiber": The First Group Show of American Fiber Art in Switzerland (Exhibit)	Bard, Elizabeth A.	√		Fa	10	6		N/D 83	43
People: Grae, Ida	Ida Grae—A Totally Textural Experience	Kaplan, Suzan	√		SS&D	5	4	20	Fa 74	4
People: Grae, Ida Dean	Ida Dean Grae				H&C	14	3		Su 63	4
People: Grae, Ida Dean	Ida Dean Grae — Imaginative Teacher	Brayn, Dorothy	√		H&C	6	2		Sp 55	16
People: Graff, Junia	Who Weaves?		√		Iw	5	2		Sp 80	35
People: Graff, Marv	Year of the Sweater, The	Katz, Ruth J.	√		Fa	7	1		J/F 80	39
People: Graffin, Daniel	"Daniel Graffin: Traces" (Exhibit)	Janeiro, Jan	√		Fa	7	2		M/A 80	73
People: Graffin, Daniel	Innovations in Indigo	Wada, Yoshiko Iwamoto	√		Fa	13	5		S/O 86	29
People: Graffin, Daniel	Twelfth International Biennial of Tapestry	Taylor, Dianne; Elmer Taylor	√		Fa	12	6		N/D 85	50
People: Graham, Mary Long	Mary Long Graham: Resolving Chaos and Order	Goodman, Deborah Lerme	√		Fa	13	3		M/J 86	24
People: Grange, Penny	Moroccan Cocoon		√	√	WJ	8	3	31	Wi 83	10
People: Grant, Susan	In Pursuit of a Lifestyle	Grant, Susan	√		Iw	5	2		Sp 80	32

SUBJECT	TITLE	AUTHOR	IL	INST	JOUR	VOL	NO	ISS	DATE	PAGE
People: Granville, Marianne	Marianne Granville, Designer with Old World Background	Harvey, Jane	√		H&C	16	4		Fa 65	16
People: Grashow, Jim	Jim Grashow: Inspired by Architecture		√		Fa	12	1		J/F 85	62
People: Grau-Garriga, Josef	Grau-Garriga: He Says It's Easy, But...	Brough, Hazel	√	√	SS&D	6	4	24	Fa 75	92
People: Grau-Garriga, Josef	"Josef Grau-Garriga" (Exhibit)	Grover, Donald	√		Fa	5	2		M/A 78	13
People: Grau-Garriga, Josep	Commissions: The Process, the Problems and the Prospects		√		Fa	6	5		S/O 79	45
People: Grau-Garriga, Josep	"Fiberworks" (Exhibit)	Park, Betty	√		Fa	4	6		N/D 77	10
People: Grau-Garriga, Josep	Grau-Garriga: An Interview	Nelson, Susan Venable; Valerie Bechtol	√		Fa	5	4		J/A 78	32
People: Grau-Garriga, Josep	Talk with Josep Grau-Garriga, A	Kurtz, Carol; B. J. Adams	√		SS&D	9	4	36	Fa 78	4
People: Grau-Garriga, Josep	Tradition and Change: Fiber '79	Martin, Elaine	√		Iw	5	2		Sp 80	72
People: Grau-Garriga, Joseph	Dirk Holger and Grau-Garriga: The Legacy of Lurçat	Broderson, Jan	√		H&C	22	3		Su 71	10
People: Gravander, Valborg (Mama)	"Mama" Gravander	Bryan, Dorothy	√		H&C	5	4		Fa 54	4
People: Graves, Ka	Fabric of Creativity: Weaving Together Left– and Right–Brain Activites, The	Miles, Candice St. Jacques	√		Fa	11	6		N/D 84	44
People: Graves, Michael	Collaboration: A Vision of Unknown Territory	Parks, Betty	√		Fa	12	5		S/O 85	20
People: Gray, Nancy	"Ten Boston Fiber Artists" (Exhibit)	Serenyi, Peter	√		Fa	5	5		S/O 78	67
People: Gray, Robert W.	American Handweaving 1960		√		H&C	11	2		Sp 60	17
People: Grayson, Persis Dwinell	Persis Grayson, Weaver & Spinner	Amos, Mary Alice	√		H&C	19	1		Wi 68	10
People: Greaver, Nancy	Nancy Greaver		√		Fa	4	4		J/A 77	51
People: Greaver, Nancy	"Textiles New Mexico 1976" (Exhibit)	Warner, Lucy Ann	√		Fa	3	2		M/A 76	12
People: Greedy, Allan	"Fiber Invitational" (Exhibit)	Richerson, Suzanne	√		Fa	8	4		J/A 81	76
People: Green, Julie	Julie Green: The World of Fiber	Lyon, David	√		Fa	14	1		J/F 87	40
People: Green, Louise and Bill	Setting Up Shop	Ligon, Linda	√		Iw	2	4		Su 77	18
People: Greenfelder, Gayle	"Contemporary Quilting: A Renaissance" (Exhibit)	Lauter, Estella	√		Fa	9	1		J/F 82	78
People: Greenwald, Caroline	"New American Paperworks" (Exhibit) (error-corrected Fa v13 n3 86 p5)	Shermeta, Margo	√		Fa	13	1		J/F 86	64
People: Greenwald, Caroline	Sculptural Paper: Foundations and Directions	Scarborough, Jessica	√		Fa	11	2		M/A 84	32
People: Greer, Dorothy	Publish Your Own Craft Book	Nell, Patti			Iw	1	2		Wi 76	18
People: Greer, Nancy Osborne	One Hundred Years Ago in Handweaving				Hw	7	3		M/J 86	27
People: Gregor, Helen Frances	Convergence '86 Preview: Toronto — A City in Transition	Baker, William R. M.	√		SS&D	17	1	65	Wi 85	43
People: Gregor, Helen Frances	"Fiber Works — Americas & Japan" (Exhibit)	Kato, Kuniko Lucy	√		Fa	5	1		J/F 78	10
People: Grelle, Marilyn	"Fiber in the Service of Art: The Work of Wilma King and Marilyn Grelle" (Exhibit)	Mathews, Rich	√		Fa	4	2		M/A 77	18
People: Grelle, Marilyn	Washington Fiber	Mathews, Rich	√		Fa	3	5		S/O 76	9
People: Greneslaw, Ruth	Masks At the Heart of Disguise	Koplos, Janet	√		Fa	11	5		S/O 84	32
People: Greneslaw, Ruth	Silkworks	Goodman, Deborah Lerme	√		Fa	13	1		J/F 86	50
People: Grès Alix	How Madame Grès Sculpts with Fabric	Cooper, Arlene	√	√	TM			10	A/M 87	50
People: Grey, Lisa	Designer: Grey, Lisa				SS&D	11	2	42	Sp 80	95
People: Griffey, Margaret	Why Do I Weave Tapestries? An Exploration of Color Theory and Tapestry Design (error-corrected Fa v7 n6 80 p8)	Griffey, Margaret	√		Fa	7	4		J/A 80	55
People: Griffin, Elizabeth	Canadian Portfolio, A	Place, Jennifer	√		Fa	9	6		N/D 82	29
People: Griffin, Elizabeth	Public Fiber: Looking At the Logistics	Koplos, Janet	√		Fa	12	1		J/F 85	32
People: Griffin, Gertrude	Gertrude Griffin Comes from Ireland to Canada	Clement, Doris W.	√		H&C	19	1		Wi 68	17
People: Grim, Thomasin	"Thomasin Grim: New Work" (Exhibit)	Scarborough, Jessica	√		Fa	11	5		S/O 84	73
People: Grim, Thomasin	"Threads" (Exhibit)	Kurtz, Carol	√		Fa	10	4		J/A 83	62
People: Grim, Thomasin	"Three Weavers: Thomasin Grim, Jane Lackey, Bhakti Ziek" (Exhibit)	Rowley, Kathleen	√		Fa	9	6		N/D 82	82

SUBJECT	TITLE	AUTHOR	IL	INST	JOUR	VOL	NO	ISS	DATE	PAGE
People: Grinberg, Alan	Design by the Yard: Today's Fabric Innovators	Scarborough, Jessica	√		Fa	12	5		S/O 85	30
People: Grisham, Marilyn	Secrets of the Land	Bladow, Suzanne	√		Fa	7	1		J/F 80	48
People: Grosen, Francoise	"Fiberworks" (Exhibit)	Park, Betty	√		Fa	4	6		N/D 77	10
People: Grosowsky, Vera	Vera Grosowsky: Through the Surface	Paine, Frank	√		Fa	10	4		J/A 83	18
People: Gross, Judith	Review/Discussion of Artspace's Innovative Yet Flawed "Fiber Freely Interpreted", A (Exhibit)		√		Fa	4	2		M/A 77	38
People: Gross, Laurie	Liturgical Vestment: A Contemporary Overview, The	Malarcher, Patricia	√		Fa	11	5		S/O 84	58
People: Grossen, Francois	Fiber in Minnesota: "Traditions/Transitions II" and "Art in Architecture" (Exhibit)	Stack, Lotus	√		Fa	11	3		M/J 84	80
People: Grossen, Francoise	"Fiber Art: Tapestries and Wall Hangings" (Exhibit)	Koplos, Janet	√		Fa	6	6		N/D 79	75
People: Grossen, Francoise	Hangups		√		Fa	3	6		N/D 76	6
People: Grossen, Francoise	"Transformation: UCLA Alumnae in Fiber" (Exhibit)	Dyer, Carolyn	√		Fa	6	4		J/A 79	67
People: Grossen, Francoise	"Woven, Tied, and Knotted" (Exhibit)	Koplos, Janet	√		Fa	9	2		M/A 82	82
People: Grummet, Pat	Pleats, Pleats, Pleats: For Sculptural Garments and Sculpture Itself		√		Fa	9	1		J/F 82	40
People: Grummitt, Patricia	Bobbin Lace: An Exquisite Labor of Love	McIlvain, Myra Hargrave	√		Fa	13	3		M/J 86	14
People: Grzelak-Malerich, Lee	Liberated Embroidery		√		Fa	9	3		M/J 82	35
People: Guagliumi, Susan	Eye of a Photographer, Hand of a Weaver: An Artist Combines Two Art Forms	Guagliumi, Susan	√		Fa	8	6		N/D 81	35
People: Guardino, Donna	Felt and Paper: A Portfolio		√		Fa	13	4		J/A 86	35
People: Guay, Nancy	Double Lives: Can You Love Your "Work" When It's Your "Job"?	Mattera, Joanne	√		TM			10	A/M 87	62
People: Guay, Nancy	"Fiber Art: An Uncommon Thread" (Exhibit)	Park, Betty	√		Fa	9	2		M/A 82	78
People: Gubser, Elsie	Elsie Gubser: Weaving Pioneer		√		Iw	4	3		Su 79	44
People: Guermonprez, Trude	"Tapestries of Trude Guermonprez: A Retrospective, The" (Exhibit)	Rowley, Kathleen	√		Fa	10	3		M/J 83	68
People: Guermonprez, Trude	Trude Guermonprez	Bryan, Dorothy	√		H&C	11	2		Sp 60	30
People: Guermonprez, Trude	Words in Fiber	Rowley, Kathleen	√		Fa	11	2		M/A 84	66
People: Guest, John	Yurt in Artpark, The	Brennan, Joan	√		Fa	9	3		M/J 82	19
People: Gunter, Virginia	Here Today, Gone Tomorrow: The Transitory Sculpture of Virginia Gunter	Mattera, Joanne	√		Fa	8	2		M/A 81	18
People: Gurrier, Elizabeth	Elizabeth Gurrier Multiples	King, A. J.	√		Fa	4	6		N/D 77	30
People: Gurrier, Elizabeth	"Great American Foot, The" (Exhibit)	Grover, Donald	√		Fa	5	4		J/A 78	15
People: Gurrier, Elizabeth	"Needle and Cloth: Ten Years Later" (Exhibit)	Hulbert, Elizabeth McKey	√		Fa	10	3		M/J 83	72
People: Gusber, Elsie H.	American Handweaving 1960		√		H&C	11	2		Sp 60	13
People: Gushee, Helen	Rag Rugs: Helen Gushee Helps Keep a Tradition Alive	Woelfle, Gretchen	√		Fa	7	5		S/O 80	31
People: Guy, Sallie T.	Speakers Bureau Presents		√		SS&D	6	1	21	Wi 74	75
People: Haddow, Deloris	"Left on the Loom" (Exhibit)	Dyer, Carolyn	√		Fa	5	2		M/A 78	16
People: Haeseler, John	Pikes Peak Weavers Guild First Fibre Arts Festival (Exhibit)	Fife, Lin	√		Fa	3	5		S/O 76	6
People: Hagemeister-Winzenz, Karon	"Assemblage: Wisconsin Paper" (Exhibit)	Bard, Elizabeth	√		Fa	11	1		J/F 84	78
People: Hagemeister-Winzenz, Karon	"New Wisconsin Fiber": The First Group Show of American Fiber Art in Switzerland (Exhibit)	Bard, Elizabeth A.	√		Fa	10	6		N/D 83	43
People: Hagen, Betty	Review/Discussion of Artspace's Innovative Yet Flawed "Fiber Freely Interpreted", A (Exhibit)		√		Fa	4	2		M/A 77	38
People: Hagen, Chad Alice	Chad Alice Hagen's Felt Work	Bard, Elizabeth A.	√		Fa	13	4		J/A 86	30
People: Hagen-Liddle, Nance	Scholarship in Action		√		SS&D	7	4	28	Fa 76	108
People: Hagerty, Martha	Spinning Fleece for Peace				TM			11	J/J 87	18

SUBJECT	TITLE	AUTHOR	IL	INST	JOUR	VOL	NO	ISS	DATE	PAGE
People: Hagerty, Peter	Spinning Fleece for Peace				TM			11	J/J 87	18
People: Haigh-Neal, Marian	"Other Baskets" An Invitational Show in St. Louis (Exhibit)	Degener, Patricia	√		Fa	10	1		J/F 83	76
People: Haines, Maryellen	"Ruth's Madcaps" (Exhibit)	Haynes, Maryellen	√		Fa	14	4		S/O 87	9
People: Hains, Maryellen	Fiber At Artpark	MacDonald, Claudia	√		Fa	10	6		N/D 83	47
People: Haire, Bill	Year of the Sweater, The	Katz, Ruth J.	√		Fa	7	1		J/F 80	39
People: Hakala, Lahja	Dyes from Mushrooms: A Spectrum of Extraordinary Color	Rice, Miriam	√	√	TM			10	A/M 87	44
People: Hall, Catherine	"Show Biz" (Exhibit)	Scheinman, Pamela	√		Fa	7	4		J/A 80	69
People: Hall, Joanne	Tapestry in Twill: A Free Approach	Hall, Joanne	√	√	Hw	3	1		Ja 82	46
People: Hall, Lynn	"Lynn Hall: Figure and Furniture" (Exhibit)	Shermeta, Margo	√		Fa	12	1		J/F 85	73
People: Hall, Martha	Who Weaves?		√		Iw	5	2		Sp 80	42
People: Hallet, Henry	Fiber Ten	McGuire, Patricia	√		Fa	4	6		N/D 77	26
People: Hallett, Henry	Tapestry Gallery		√		Iw	4	2		Sp 79	28
People: Hallman, H. Theodore	Convergence Preview — Six Peaks, A		√		SS&D	11	2	42	Sp 80	47
People: Hallman, Ted	"Patch" by Ted Hallman, At the Smithsonian		√		SS&D	4	4	16	Fa 73	23
People: Hallman, Ted	Sunrise Titles and Twills		√		Iw	6	1		Wi 80	38
People: Hallman, Ted	Ted Hallman at Ottawa		√		SS&D	3	1	9	Wi 71	29
People: Halpern, Nancy	"New England Images" (Exhibit)	Harris, Patricia; David Lyon	√		Fa	10	6		N/D 83	78
People: Halpern, Nancy	"Quilt National '79" (Exhibit)	Gutcheon, Beth	√		Fa	6	5		S/O 79	80
People: Halpern, Nancy	Quiltmaker's Art, A	Mattera, Joanne	√		Fa	10	2		M/A 83	33
People: Hamaker, Barbara	You Are Unique — There is No Competition!	Hamaker, Barbara	√		WJ	6	4	24	Sp 82	37
People: Hamatani, Akio	Lausanne Notebook: Our Special Report on the 8th Lausanne Biennial of Tapestry, A	Mathews, Rich	√		Fa	4	5		S/O 77	30
People: Hambidge, Mary Crovatt	Mary Crovatt Hambidge	Schaller, Karin	√		Fa	11	5		S/O 84	24
People: Hambidge, Mary Crovatt	Weavers of Rabun, The		√		H&C	7	2		Sp 56	6
People: Hamelecourt, Juliette	Embroidered Life, An (error-corrected Fa v7 n4 80 p6)	Alonso, Harriet	√		Fa	7	3		M/J 80	66
People: Hamilton, Ann	"Tangents: Art in Fiber" (Exhibit)	Krinn, Linda	√		Fa	14	3		M/J 87	55
People: Hammock, Noël	HGA Board Candidates: Vote for Three		√		SS&D	10	2	38	Sp 79	48
People: Hammond, Harmony	On the Edge: Harmony Hammond — Collecting, Reclaiming, Connecting	Willard, Janice	√		Fa	9	4		J/A 82	58
People: Hampton, Suzy	Setting Up Shop	Ligon, Linda	√		Iw	2	4		Su 77	18
People: Hancock, Carol Rae	Art Consultants: Bridging the Gap Between Artist and Client	Goodman, Deborah Lerme	√		Fa	12	6		N/D 85	31
People: Hand, Barbara	Rug Weaving: One Weaver's Approach	Hand, Barbara	√	> 4	WJ	7	4	28	Sp 83	32
People: Handler, Gloria Welniak	"Wisconsin Fiber Miniatures" (Exhibit)	Lowell-LaRoque, Jane V.	√		Fa	6	5		S/O 79	84
People: Handy, Virginia	Focus on Flax: From Flax to Fabric with Virginia Handy	Christian, Donna Allgaier	√		S-O	10	3		Fa 86	22
People: Haney, Lynn	Lynn Haney		√		Fa	4	1		J/F 77	38
People: Hanks, Nancy	Shuttle Power	Hanks, Nancy	√		SS&D	7	4	28	Fa 76	45
People: Hansen, Birgette	Labor Banners of Australia	Mancini, Anne	√		Fa	14	5		N/D 87	36
People: Hansen, Brita	"German Wearable Textiles" (Exhibit)	Van Til, Reinder	√		Fa	12	6		N/D 85	59
People: Haputli, Ellen	For the Body (error-corrected Fa v10 n2 83 p61)		√		Fa	10	1		J/F 83	32
People: Hardesty, Steve	Weaver of Scotland's Past	Quigley, Edward T.	√		Hw	4	5		N/D 83	35
People: Harding, Tim	Tim Harding: Garments of Paradox	Theil, Linda	√		Fa	9	6		N/D 82	20
People: Harding, Tim	Under Wraps		√		Fa	12	3		M/J 85	26
People: Hardjonagors, R. T.	Conversations with a Batik Master	Gittinger, Mattiebelle S.	√		TMJ	18			79	25
People: Haring, Keith	Body as Canvas, The	Koda, Harold	√		TM			8	D/J 86	56
People: Harkinson, Gordon	If the Art Fits – Wear It! — Friends of the Rag	Strosnider, Ann	√		Fa	6	3		M/J 79	35
People: Harnden, Robert	Robert Harnden — Diplomat & Weaver	Schobinger, Helen J.	√		H&C	11	1		Wi 60	16

SUBJECT	TITLE	AUTHOR	IL	INST	JOUR	VOL	NO	ISS	DATE	PAGE
People: Harp, Holly	On Fabric in the Southwest: Surface Design, A Bank, and Public Recognition	Brooks, Lois Ziff	√		Fa	6	5		S/O 79	54
People: Harris, John	"Softworks" (Exhibit)		√		Fa	3	6		N/D 76	10
People: Harrison, Diana	"Fabric and Form: New Textile Art from Britain" (Exhibit)	Waller, Irene	√		Fa	9	6		N/D 82	80
People: Harrison, Inger	Transparencies of Inger Harrison–Sheer Beauty, The	Keasbey, Doramay	√	√	Hw	3	1		Ja 82	40
People: Harrison, Paul	Collegiate Fashion Show Highlights Textile Program	Belfer, Nancy	√		Fa	14	1		J/F 87	6
People: Hart, Carol	Art That Functions	Lønning, Kari	√		Fa	8	3		M/J 81	40
People: Hart, Carol G.	What Makes a Basket a Basket?	Malarcher, Patricia	√		Fa	11	1		J/F 84	34
People: Hart, Molly	Molly Hart	Hart, Molly	√		Fa	14	2		M/A 87	23
People: Hart, Rick	High-Tech Comes to Weaving: Macomber Looms	Henderson, Stew	√		Fa	14	4		S/O 87	35
People: Hart, Robert G.	American Handweaving 1960		√		H&C	11	2		Sp 60	14
People: Hartford, Jane	HGA Board Candidates: Vote for Three		√		SS&D	10	2	38	Sp 79	48
People: Hartford, Jane	HGA Board of Directors Candidates		√		SS&D	11	2	42	Sp 80	26
People: Hartford, Jane	"Theme Show in Utah, A" (Exhibit)	Alderman, Sharon D.	√		Fa	8	3		M/J 81	68
People: Harvey, Nancy	Tapestry for Interiors	Harvey, Nancy	√		Hw	3	1		Ja 82	42
People: Harvey, Nancy	Who Weaves?		√		Iw	5	2		Sp 80	35
People: Haskell, Vicki	Scholarships '78		√		SS&D	9	4	36	Fa 78	44
People: Hasse, Carol	Piecing Cloth to Harness the Wind	Montgomery, Larry	√	√	TM			11	J/J 87	48
People: Hasselberg, Stina	Picture Lace	Larson-Fleming, Susan	√		WJ	9	4	36	Sp 85	42
People: Hasselberg-Olsson, Elisabet	Contemporary Swedish Weaving		√		Hw	8	3		M/J 87	35
People: Hasselberg-Olsson, Elisabet	Contemporary Textile Art in Scandinavia	Talley, Charles S.	√		Fa	9	6		N/D 82	43
People: Hasselberg-Olsson, Elisabet	Portraits of Three Weavers: Sandra Ikse-Bergman, Marja "Graset" Andersson, Elisabet Hasselberg-Olsson	Talley, Charles S.	√		Fa	8	2		M/A 81	46
People: Hasselberg-Olsson, Elisabet	"Scandinavian Touch, The" A Traveling Exhibit (Exhibit)	Mattera, Joanna	√		Fa	10	1		J/F 83	82
People: Hasselgren, Inger	Contemporary Textile Art in Scandinavia	Talley, Charles S.	√		Fa	9	6		N/D 82	43
People: Hauptli, Ellen	Ellen Hauptli's Pleats	Levine, Betsy	√		TM			5	J/J 86	48
People: Hauptli, Ellen	"Maximum Coverage: Wearables by Contemporary American Artists" (Exhibit)	Risseeuw, Mary	√		Fa	8	1		J/F 81	93
People: Hauptli, Ellen	Pleats, Pleats, Pleats: For Sculptural Garments and Sculpture Itself		√		Fa	9	1		J/F 82	40
People: Hausner, Walter	American Handweaving 1960		√		H&C	11	2		Sp 60	13
People: Hausrath, Joan	Ikats of Joan Hausrath: A Painterly Approach to Weaving, The	Dunn, Roger T.	√		Fa	8	6		N/D 81	48
People: Hawthorne, John	It's Like a Hobby	Fitt, Cate	√		Fa	8	2		M/A 81	38
People: Hayashi, Arawana	Fabric of Movement, The	Lyon, David	√		Fa	13	3		M/J 86	76
People: Hayes, Margaret	Portfolio of Contemporary Fiber Sculpture, A		√		Fa	11	4		J/A 84	34
People: Hazlett, Paula	Masks At the Heart of Disguise	Koplos, Janet	√		Fa	11	5		S/O 84	32
People: Healy, Sherry	Papermaking in Chicago	Shermeta, Margo	√		Fa	11	2		M/A 84	54
People: Heap, Jessica	Australian Spinner Raises Profitable Flock of Goats	Berger, Charles	√		H&C	17	3		Su 66	11
People: Hearn, Mary Alice	Certificate Holders: What Now? Part 3, The	Alderman, Sharon D.	√		SS&D	13	2	50	Sp 82	60
People: Hedges, Sharon	"Art to Wear" (Exhibit)	Murray, Megan	√		Fa	11	1		J/F 84	76
People: Hedges, Sharon	Sharon Hedges	Malarcher, Pat	√		Fa	5	3		M/J 78	56
People: Hedstrom, Ana Lisa	Ana Lisa Hedstrom: The Intuitive Language of Shibori	Scarborough, Jessica	√		Fa	13	1		J/F 86	26
People: Hedstrom, Ana Lisa	Art to Wear: Looking At the Movement	Scarborough, Jessica	√		Fa	12	3		M/J 85	56
People: Hedstrom, Ana Lisa	Artwear '87				TM			10	A/M 87	22
People: Hedstrom, Ana Lisa	"Poetry for the Body, Clothing for the Spirit" (Exhibit)	Hickman, Pat	√		Fa	10	5		S/O 83	75

SUBJECT	TITLE	AUTHOR	IL	INST	JOUR	VOL	NO	ISS	DATE	PAGE
People: Hedstrom, Ana Lisa	Surface Design and the Garment Form	Reith, Stephanie J.	√		Fa	8	1		J/F 81	34
People: Hedstrom, Lisa	"Printed, Painted, and Dyed: The New Fabric Surface" (Exhibit)	Hecker, Carolyn	√		Fa	5	6		N/D 78	71
People: Hedstrom, Lisa	Tenth Annual Textile Exhibition, Olive Hyde Art Gallery (Exhibit)	Papa, Nancy	√		Fa	5	4		J/A 78	13
People: Hedsttrom, Ana Lisa	Surface Design Conference in Kansas City	Craig-Linenberger, Gerry	√		TM			12	A/S 87	20
People: Hege, Orpha M.	"Focus on Fiber" (Exhibit)	Hecker, Carolyn	√		Fa	6	3		M/J 79	83
People: Heggtveit, Mandy	"Focus on Handwoven Fabric: Ontario Handweavers and Spinners" (Exhibits)	Place, Jennifer	√		Fa	9	4		J/A 82	74
People: Heickman, Mary E.	Mary E. Heickman, Texas Weaver and Teacher	Morse, Martha	√		H&C	17	3		Su 66	18
People: Heikes, Grete	Grete Heikes: Weaver	Schneider, Paul	√		Fa	6	1		J/F 79	14
People: Heilmann-Levine, Barbara	"Barbara Heilmann-Levine: Tapestries and Paintings" (Exhibit)	Pasquine, Ruth	√		Fa	10	2		M/A 83	69
People: Heimann, Anne	"100% Wool" (Exhibit)	Goldin, Susan	√		Fa	4	6		N/D 77	18
People: Hein, Jennifer	HGA Scholarship Award —Jennifer Hein		√		SS&D	18	4	72	Fa 87	50
People: Heisler, Marcia	Masks At the Heart of Disguise	Koplos, Janet	√		Fa	11	5		S/O 84	32
People: Helbing-Muecke, Marion	Under Wraps		√		Fa	12	3		M/J 85	26
People: Helfman, Muriel Nezhnie	"Fiber Forms '78" (Exhibit)	Patton, Ellen	√		Fa	5	5		S/O 78	66
People: Helfman, Muriel Nezhnie	Tapestries of Muriel Nezhnie Helfman	Salter, Deborah	√		H&C	23	5		S/O 72	43
People: Helfman, Muriel Nezhnie	Tapestry Gallery		√		lw	4	2		Sp 79	30
People: Heller, Barbara	Sacred Places: Barbara Heller Weaves Landscapes Where Spirits Might Dwell, Places of Meditation (error-corrected Fa v7 n5 80 p5)	Redmond, Cheryl A.	√		Fa	7	3		M/J 80	58
People: Heller, Barbara	Spirit Tracings of Barbara Heller, The	Strong, Ruth	√		Fa	13	4		J/A 86	15
People: Heller, Barbara	Stones & Symbols	McGillveray, Brenda	√		SS&D	18	1	69	Wi 86	71
People: Heller, Jennifer	"Distilling the Essence of Basketry" (Exhibit)	Anderson, Ann Stewart	√		Fa	13	2		M/A 86	52
People: Hemenway, Nancy	"Nancy Hemenway: Aqua Lapis" (Exhibit)	Skudera, Gail	√		Fa	11	5		S/O 84	72
People: Hempel, Marcella	Spinning—Australia	DeBoer, Janet			S-O	11	3		Fa 87	35
People: Henderson, Helen	American Handweaving 1960		√		H&C	11	2		Sp 60	15
People: Hendricks, Carolyn	Sampler of Surface Design, A	Westphal, Katherine	√		Fa	10	5		S/O 83	39
People: Hendricks, Linda	Washington Fiber	Mathews, Rich	√		Fa	3	5		S/O 76	9
People: Henegar, Susan Hart	San Francisco Tapestry Workshop: A European-Style Atelier in the United States, The	Rowley, Kathleen	√		Fa	10	3		M/J 83	60
People: Henion, Dee	Interview with Dee Henion, An		√		Fa	3	2		M/A 76	17
People: Hennix, Kirsten	Well-Worn Path to Where? A View of Contemporary Swedish Textiles, The	Talley, Charles S.	√		Fa	8	2		M/A 81	44
People: Henry, Gerry	Art That Functions	Lønning, Kari	√		Fa	8	3		M/J 81	40
People: Henzie, Susie	Who Weaves?		√		lw	5	2		Sp 80	41/42
People: Herman, Nancy	Banners for Peace	Adels, Jill	√		Fa	12	4		J/A 85	36
People: Herman, Nancy	Songs in Fabric: Quiltmaker Nancy Herman Is an Unusual Musician	Rowland, Amy Zaffarano	√		Fa	9	4		J/A 82	22
People: Herman, Scholton	Brief History of the International Biennial of Tapestry or "Watch Out for Women Who Knit", A	Taylor, Dianne	√		Fa	10	5		S/O 83	43
People: Hernmarck, Helena	"Art in Craft Media" (Exhibit)		√		Fa	13	4		J/A 86	58
People: Hernmarck, Helena	Helena Hernmarck: An Interview		√		Fa	5	2		M/A 78	32
People: Hernmarck, Helena	"Old Traditions/New Directions" (Exhibit)	West, Virginia	√		Fa	8	6		N/D 81	66
People: Hernmarck, Helena	Questions of Style: Contemporary Trends in the Fiber Arts	Howe-Echt, Katherine	√		Fa	7	2		M/A 80	38
People: Herpich, Hanns	"Third International Exhibition of Miniature Textiles 1978" (Exhibit)	Spencer, Patricia	√		Fa	6	1		J/F 79	90
People: Herrick, Laurie	Laurie Herrick		√		Fa	4	6		N/D 77	43
People: Herrick, Laurie	Laurie Herrick, Contemporary Weaver and Teacher	Furniss, Frances	√		H&C	18	4		Fa 67	10

SUBJECT	TITLE	AUTHOR	IL	INST	JOUR	VOL	NO	ISS	DATE	PAGE
People: Herring, Connie	sere-chrysalis-seer		√		PWC	4	2	12		34
People: Herron, Ruth	Weaving Guilds—A Special Sharing		√		lw	5	2		Sp 80	52
People: Herschel, Caroline	History in Stitches, A	Mattera, Joanne	√		Fa	7	3		M/J 80	37
People: Hertenstein, Bonnie	Papermaking in Chicago	Shermeta, Margo	√		Fa	11	2		M/A 84	54
People: Hessler, Ava	Pick-Up Leno: The Fine Linens of Ava Hessler		√	√	WJ	7	2	26	Fa 82	31
People: Hetzler, Patricia T.	Patricia T. Hetzler	Hetzler, Patricia T.	√		Fa	14	2		M/A 87	24
People: Hewes, Jean	"Fabric Constructions: The Art Quilt" (Exhibit)	Klein, Jody	√		Fa	11	2		M/A 84	81
People: Hewitt, Barbara	Blues in the Light: Cyanotype on Fabric	Sider, Sandra	√		Fa	13	5		S/O 86	34
People: Heyden, Silvia	"Festival of Weaving" (Exhibit)	Greenberg, Blue	√		Fa	7	4		J/A 80	71
People: Heyden, Silvia	"Fiber Forms '78" (Exhibit)	Patton, Ellen	√		Fa	5	5		S/O 78	66
People: Heyden, Silvia	Silvia Heyden: I think of the Weft as a Violin Bow	Heyman, Dorothy	√		Fa	6	2		M/A 79	46
People: Heyden, Sylvia	Sylvia Heyden		√		SS&D	14	4	56	Fa 83	42
People: Heyman, Dorothy	"Festival of Weaving" (Exhibit)	Greenberg, Blue	√		Fa	7	4		J/A 80	71
People: Heywood, Vivian	"Soft Art" (Exhibit)	Richerson, Suzanne	√		Fa	4	4		J/A 77	16
People: Hickman, Anita	From Houston: Rochella Cooper, Anita Hickman	Vander Lee, Jana	√		Fa	3	3		M/J 76	10
People: Hickman, Anita	"Houston Designer-Craftsmen 1976" (Exhibit)	Vander Lee, Jana	√		Fa	3	4		J/A 76	9
People: Hickman, Annie	Annie Hickman: Populating an Insect World	Hempel, Toby Anne	√		Fa	14	3		M/J 87	32
People: Hickman, Pat	Almost Roman Glass	Elliott, Lillian	√		Fa	10	6		N/D 83	20
People: Hickman, Pat	"Beyond the Fringe" (Exhibit)	Einstein, Sylvia	√		Fa	7	2		M/A 80	70
People: Hickman, Pat	"Contemporary Quilting: A Renaissance" (Exhibit)	Lauter, Estella	√		Fa	9	1		J/F 82	78
People: Hickman, Pat	Garment Form As Image, The	Koplos, Janet	√		Fa	10	6		N/D 83	66
People: Hickman, Pat	Lillian Elliott and Pat Hickman: The Pleasures and Problems of Collaboration		√		Fa	12	5		S/O 85	22
People: Hickman, Pat	"Other Baskets" An Invitational Show in St. Louis (Exhibit)	Degener, Patricia	√		Fa	10	1		J/F 83	76
People: Hickman, Pat	What Makes a Basket a Basket?	Malarcher, Patricia	√		Fa	11	1		J/F 84	34
People: Hickok, Cindy	Cindy Hickok: Stuffed Characters	Fowler, Mary Jean	√		Fa	5	5		S/O 78	22
People: Hickok, Cindy	"Decade of Fibers, A" (Exhibit)	Franklin, Sue	√		Fa	5	1		J/F 78	17
People: Hickok, Cindy	"Five Women From Texas" (Exhibit)	Leach, Vivian	√		Fa	6	1		J/F 79	86
People: Hickok, Cindy	Soft Sculpture: Old Forms, New Meanings	Gordon, Beverly	√		Fa	10	6		N/D 83	40
People: Hicks, Sheila	Brief History of the International Biennial of Tapestry or "Watch Out for Women Who Knit", A	Taylor, Dianne	√		Fa	10	5		S/O 83	43
People: Hicks, Sheila	Commissions: The Process, the Problems and the Prospects		√		Fa	6	5		S/O 79	45
People: Hicks, Sheila	Fiber/Art Conditioned by Life: A Workshop with Sheila Hicks	Klein, Jody	√		Fa	12	5		S/O 85	58
People: Hicks, Sheila	"Fiberworks" (Exhibit)	Park, Betty	√		Fa	4	6		N/D 77	10
People: Hicks, Sheila	Lausanne Notebook: Our Special Report on the 8th Lausanne Biennial of Tapestry, A	Mathews, Rich	√		Fa	4	5		S/O 77	30
People: Hicks, Sheila	Made by Machine: Textiles for the Eighties	Harris, Patricia; David Lyon	√		Fa	12	5		S/O 85	34
People: Hicks, Sheila	Sheila Hicks: An Affinity for Architecture	Koenigsberg, Nancy	√		Fa	12	5		S/O 85	60
People: Hiebel, Kaye	Sampler of Surface Design, A	Westphal, Katherine	√		Fa	10	5		S/O 83	39
People: Hiebel, Kaye	"Wildlife Physics" (Exhibit)	Kitzman, Betty Lou	√		Fa	12	2		M/A 85	72
People: Higby, Kristy	Feltmaking Now: The Exciting Revival of an Ancient Technique	Gordon, Beverly	√		Fa	6	6		N/D 79	43
People: Higby, Kristy L.	"Connections" (Exhibit)	Constantinides, Kathy	√		Fa	6	4		J/A 79	74
People: Higby, Sha Sha	Fabric of Sha Sha Higby's Imagination, The	Wheater, Kathleen	√		Fa	14	3		M/J 87	35
People: Higginbotham, Charles	Men Who Knit	Xenakis, Alexis Yiorgos	√		Kn	3	2	6	Sp 87	14

SUBJECT	TITLE	AUTHOR	IL	INST	JOUR	VOL	NO	ISS	DATE	PAGE
People: Higgins, Janet	Janet Higgins: Soft Sculpture in Motion	Marquess, Joyce	√		Fa	7	2		M/A 80	62
People: Hilger, Chuck	Papermaking in Chicago	Shermeta, Margo	√		Fa	11	2		M/A 84	54
People: Hilger, Chuck	Sculptural Paper: Foundations and Directions	Scarborough, Jessica	√		Fa	11	2		M/A 84	32
People: Hill, Clinton	Paper: Three Shows At the American Craft Museums (Exhibit)	Lonier, Terri	√		Fa	9	5		S/O 82	84
People: Hill, Julia	Fleeting Fantasies: Julia Hill's Painting on Silk	Grover, Donald	√		Fa	6	4		J/A 79	12
People: Hill, Julia	Julia Hill: Art And Textile Lab	Lancaster, Zöe Woodruff	√		Fa	12	3		M/J 85	11
People: Hill, Julia	"Kimono East/Kimono West" (Exhibit)	Lusk, Jennie	√		Fa	7	5		S/O 80	71
People: Hill, Julia	Kimono East/West	Wada, Yoshiko	√		Fa	9	1		J/F 82	19
People: Hill, Susan	History in Stitches, A	Mattera, Joanne	√		Fa	7	3		M/J 80	37
People: Hill, Susan	When Prison Is Home: Challenging the Creative Spirit	Scarborough, Jessica	√		Fa	11	6		N/D 84	69
People: Hillyer, June	Handwoven Clothing Today: The Couturier Touch	West, Virginia	√		Fa	8	1		J/F 81	39
People: Hilty, Lucy	Quilts in Women's Lives	Mattera, Joanne	√		Fa	9	3		M/J 82	54
People: Hindson, Alice	Alice Hindson, Expert on the Draw-loom	Arnold, Ruth	√		H&C	10	4		Fa 59	12
People: Hirshfield, Deborah L.	"Survey of Illinois Fiber" (Exhibit)	Jensen, Janet	√		Fa	5	5		S/O 78	69
People: Hjelholt, Berit	"Fiber Structures" Convergence '76 (Exhibit)	Mathews-Pulleyn, Kathryn	√		Fa	3	4		J/A 76	12
People: Hochberg, Bernard	Country of Origin, USA: A Decade of Contemporary Rugs	Stevens, Rebeccah A. T.	√		Fa	11	3		M/J 84	60
People: Hochstrasser, Marie	"Forms and Surfaces" (Exhibit)		√		Fa	8	4		J/A 81	68
People: Hock, Leni	Leni Hoch: "...To Hell with These Loom-Shaped Garments"	Grant, Susan	√		Fa	5	5		S/O 78	46
People: Hodge, William	Convergence '86 Preview: Toronto — A City in Transition	Baker, William R. M.	√		SS&D	17	1	65	Wi 85	43
People: Hoff, Carleigh	Costume for Dance: The Living Sculpture of Carleigh Hoff	Parshall, Priscilla	√		Fa	8	1		J/F 81	28
People: Hoff, Carleigh	On Fabric in the Southwest: Surface Design, A Bank, and Public Recognition	Brooks, Lois Ziff	√		Fa	6	5		S/O 79	54
People: Hoffman, Carol	Carol Hoffman: Research in Molecular Crochet		√		Fa	3	4		J/A 76	18
People: Hoffmann, Jenet	"Works in Miniature" (Exhibit)	Malarcher, Patricia	√		Fa	7	3		M/J 80	82
People: Hofman, Elisabeth	Certificate of Excellence in Handweaving: COE Holders, The	Drooker, Penelope B.	√		SS&D	14	1	53	Wi 82	49
People: Hoke, Ann-Mari	Versatile Swedish Weaver, Ann-Mari Hoke, A		√		H&C	8	2		Sp 57	20
People: Holbourne, David	David Holbourne	Holbourne, David	√		SS&D	3	4	12	Fa 72	50
People: Holbourne, David	Three British Weavers	Held, Shirley E.			H&C	23	6		N/D 72	33
People: Holder, Tina Fung	Craft Today: The American Craft Museum (Exhibit)	Sider, Sandra	√		Fa	14	2		M/A 87	54
People: Holger, Dirk	Dirk Holger and Grau-Garriga: The Legacy of Lurçat	Broderson, Jan	√		H&C	22	3		Su 71	10
People: Holland, Nina	Country of Origin, USA: A Decade of Contemporary Rugs	Stevens, Rebeccah A. T.	√		Fa	11	3		M/J 84	60
People: Holland, Nina	Floorcloths: A New Look at an Old Technique	Holland, Nina	√		Fa	7	5		S/O 80	34
People: Holland, Nina	"Nina Holland: Bound Weave Rugs/Hangings" (Exhibit)	Bess, Nancy Moore	√		Fa	9	1		J/F 82	83
People: Holmer, Martie	"Beyond the Fringe" (Exhibit)	Einstein, Sylvia	√		Fa	7	2		M/A 80	70
People: Holmes, Mimi	Mimi Holmes: Treasure Troves of Human Conflict	Lamberson, Peggy	√		Fa	13	6		N/D 86	20
People: Holoien, Merry	Merry Holoien: A Harmony of Color and Sound	Ormseth, Laurie	√		Fa	13	2		M/A 86	6
People: Holroyd, Ruth	Speakers Bureau Presents		√		SS&D	5	3	19	Su 74	67
✦ People: Holsenbeck, Bryant	Art That Functions	Lønning, Kari	√		Fa	8	3		M/J 81	40
✦ People: Holsenbeck, Bryant	Brookfield Basketry Institute, The	Smith, Sue M.	√		Fa	12	2		M/A 85	46

SUBJECT	TITLE	AUTHOR	IL	INST	JOUR	VOL	NO	ISS	DATE	PAGE
* People: Holsenbeck, Bryant	For the Body (error-corrected Fa v10 n2 83 p61)		√		Fa	10	1		J/F 83	32
People: Holtzer, Marilyn F.	Who Weaves?		√		Iw	5	2		Sp 80	37
People: Holtzman, Hope	Hope and Phillip Holtzman	Holtzman, Hope; Phillip Holtzman	√		Fa	14	2		M/A 87	23
People: Holtzman, Phillip	Hope and Phillip Holtzman	Holtzman, Hope; Phillip Holtzman	√		Fa	14	2		M/A 87	23
People: Holwek, Oskar	Paper Abroad (Exhibit)	Waller, Irene	√		Fa	11	2		M/A 84	82
People: Holzknecht, Katherine	1977 HGA Scholarships (error-corrected SS&D v9 n2 78 p70)		√		SS&D	9	1	33	Wi 77	46
People: Holzknecht, Katherine	Gridworks	Tacker, Sylvia	√		SS&D	16	4	64	Fa 85	30
People: Holzknecht, Katherine	Hi-Tech Banner Sculptures	Polster, Nancy; Elsa Sreenivasam	√		Fa	12	3		M/J 85	42
People: Holzman, Sandra	Sandra Holzman: Marbleized Fabrics	Piucci, Joanna	√		Fa	10	5		S/O 83	21
People: Hooper, Luther	Alice Hindson, Expert on the Draw-loom	Arnold, Ruth	√		H&C	10	4		Fa 59	12
People: Hoops, Elizabeth	"Fiber Techniques: The Weaver's Guild of Greater Cincinnati" (Exhibit)	Fedders, Pat	√		Fa	8	1		J/F 81	91
People: Hoover, Doris	Doris Hoover: Quiltmaker and Folk Artist	Papa, Nancy	√		Fa	6	1		J/F 79	16
People: Hoover, Doris	"Patchwork Garden, A" (Exhibit)	Hetzler, Patricia	√		Fa	8	5		S/O 81	73
People: Hoover, Susan	Gallery (Tapestry)		√		Hw	3	1		Ja 82	49
People: Hoover, Susan	"Miniature Fibers" (Exhibit)	Vanderburg, Jan	√		Fa	7	1		J/F 80	65
People: Hoover, Susan	Paradox of Perfection, The	Jenkins, Thomas W.	√		Fa	8	2		M/A 81	27
People: Hopf, Claudia	Claudia Hopf: Drawing with Scissors	Timmons, Christine	√		Fa	11	2		M/A 84	99
People: Hopkins, Andrea	Livin' and Workin' on the Land: Fiber Art Outside the Mainstream	Talley, Charles S.	√		Fa	8	6		N/D 81	38
People: Hornell, Lori	Fiber Ten	McGuire, Patricia	√		Fa	4	6		N/D 77	26
People: Horton, Lucy	Crochet as a Madness	Horton, Lucy	√		Fa	5	3		M/J 78	22
People: Hoskin, Sharla Jean	"Forms and Surfaces" (Exhibit)		√		Fa	8	4		J/A 81	68
People: Hoskinson, Marian	Focus on the HGA Board of Directors		√		SS&D	10	3	39	Su 79	46
People: Hostek, Stanley	Tailor's Logic	Hostek, Stanley	√	√	TM			14	D/J 87	42
People: Houlihan, Elena Hiatt	Design by the Yard: Today's Fabric Innovators	Scarborough, Jessica	√		Fa	12	5		S/O 85	30
People: House, Jody	Jody House: Needlework Designer	Madison, Winifred	√		Fa	5	6		N/D 78	25
People: Hovius, Dorothea	"Ten Boston Fiber Artists" (Exhibit)	Serenyi, Peter	√		Fa	5	5		S/O 78	67
People: Howard, Constance	Workshop with Needle Artist Constance Howard, A	Hearst, Kate	√		TM			14	D/J 87	18
People: Howard, Margaret	Speakers Bureau Presents		√		SS&D	4	4	16	Fa 73	14
People: Howe, Cathe	Contemporary California Costume	Poon, Vivian	√		Fa	11	5		S/O 84	53
People: Howe, Ed	Fabric of Movement, The	Lyon, David	√		Fa	13	3		M/J 86	76
People: Howe, Katherine	Fans and Fan Imagery	Howe, Katherine; Joanne Mattera	√		Fa	9	4		J/A 82	26
People: Howe, Katherine	Katherine Howe "Color Card Series" Woven Paintings (Exhibit)	Dyer, Carolyn	√		Fa	7	4		J/A 80	72
People: Howe, Katherine	Painted Surface, The (error-corrected Fa v9 n4 82 p9)		√		Fa	9	3		M/J 82	64
People: Howell, Douglass Morse	Paper: Three Shows At the American Craft Museums (Exhibit)	Lonier, Terri	√		Fa	9	5		S/O 82	84
People: Howell, James and Marie	James and Marie Howell, Designers		√		H&C	10	2		Sp 59	11
People: Howell, Marie	Modern Church Textiles	Howell, Marie	√		H&C	13	3		Su 62	20
People: Howell, Marie and James A.	Ark Curtain	Howell, Marie	√		H&C	15	2		Sp 64	37
People: Howenstein, Drea	"Fiber Invitational" (Exhibit)	Bywater, William	√		Fa	7	2		M/A 80	66
People: Howie, Andrew J.	American Handweaving 1960		√		H&C	11	2		Sp 60	50
People: Hoyer, Kathryn	1977 HGA Scholarships (error-corrected SS&D v9 n2 78 p70)		√		SS&D	9	1	33	Wi 77	46
People: Hu, Mary Lee	Good As Gold: Alternatives in American Jewelry		√		Fa	9	5		S/O 82	18

SUBJECT	TITLE	AUTHOR	IL	INST	JOUR	VOL	NO	ISS	DATE	PAGE
People: Hu, Mary Lee	Inspired by Fiber: Textile Sensibility in Other Media	Malarcher, Patricia	√		Fa	10	6		N/D 83	33
People: Hu, Mary Lee	"Other Baskets" An Invitational Show in St. Louis (Exhibit)	Degener, Patricia	√		Fa	10	1		J/F 83	76
People: Hubbard, Suzanne F.	Country of Origin, USA: A Decade of Contemporary Rugs	Stevens, Rebeccah A. T.	√		Fa	11	3		M/J 84	60
People: Hubbell, J. L.	Painted Rug Designs: Trader Hubbell's Influence on Navajo Weaving	Blue, Martha	√		Fa	14	5		N/D 87	5
People: Hudson, David	Men Who Knit	Xenakis, Alexis Yiorgos	√		Kn	3	2	6	Sp 87	14
People: Huebner, Marianne	Marianne Huebner Solves Many Problems in Restoring Textiles		√		H&C	16	2		Sp 65	13
People: Hughes, Betty	Knitting for a Living (error-corrected TM i6 A/S86 p6)	Guagliumi, Susan	√		TM			4	A/M 86	38
People: Hughto, Margie	Fans and Fan Imagery	Howe, Katherine; Joanne Mattera	√		Fa	9	4		J/A 82	26
People: Hulse, Dorothea	American Handweaving 1960:		√		H&C	11	2		Sp 60	14
People: Hulse, Dorothea	Circuit Riding Weavers		√		H&C	10	1		Wi 59	11
People: Hungerland, Buff	Sampler of Surface Design, A	Westphal, Katherine	√		Fa	10	5		S/O 83	39
People: Hunt, Betty	Pikes Peak Weavers Guild First Fibre Arts Festival (Exhibit)	Fife, Lin	√		Fa	3	5		S/O 76	6
People: Hunt, Zoe	Kaffe Fassett: Dream Knitter (error-corrected Fa v5 n4 78 p63)		√		Fa	5	3		M/J 78	26
People: Hunter, Carol S.	"Private Spaces, Private Lives" A Juried Fiber Show (Exhibit)	Hunt, Elizabeth Ann	√		Fa	7	6		N/D 80	75
People: Hunter, Dard	Dard Hunter Paper Museum, The	Bard, Elizabeth A.	√		Fa	11	2		M/A 84	43
People: Hunter, Lissa	Contemporary Archeology: The Baskets of Lissa Hunter	Scarborough, Jessica	√		Fa	9	5		S/O 82	25
People: Huntington, Madge	Fabric Speaks	Huntington, Madge	√		Fa	7	2		M/A 80	31
People: Hunziker, Marion	Timeless Knotted Jewelry: Marion Hunziker Meticulously Combines Fiber and Metalwork Techniques	Hunziker, Marion	√		Fa	8	4		J/A 81	19
People: Hunzinger, Claudie	Claudie and Francis Hunzinger: Plants, Paper, and Poetry	Hunzinger, Claudie	√		Fa	11	4		J/A 84	10
People: Hunzinger, Francis	Claudie and Francis Hunzinger: Plants, Paper, and Poetry	Hunzinger, Claudie	√		Fa	11	4		J/A 84	10
People: Husong, Trudonna	"Fibers '76" (Exhibit)		√		Fa	3	2		M/A 76	7
People: Hutton, Holly	Blues in the Light: Cyanotype on Fabric	Sider, Sandra	√		Fa	13	5		S/O 86	34
People: Hyland, Rebecca	"Fibers Unlimited 1979" (Exhibit)	Davidian, Robert	√		Fa	7	2		M/A 80	69
People: Hyland, Rebecca	"Fibers Unlimited" (Exhibit)	Sherwood, Thomas	√		Fa	5	1		J/F 78	14
People: Hyman, Ann Williamson	"Artwear '87" (Exhibit)		√		Fa	14	2		M/A 87	58
People: Ikse, Sandra	Contemporary Textile Art in Scandinavia	Talley, Charles S.	√		Fa	9	6		N/D 82	43
People: Ikse-Bergman, Sandra	Portraits of Three Weavers: Sandra Ikse-Bergman, Marja "Graset" Andersson, Elisabet Hasselberg-Olsson	Talley, Charles S.	√		Fa	8	2		M/A 81	46
People: Ingram, Judith	Portfolio of Contemporary Fiber Sculpture, A		√		Fa	11	4		J/A 84	34
People: Iranpour, Sharon	Who Weaves?		√		Iw	5	2		Sp 80	42
People: Ireland, Elaine	San Francisco Tapestry Workshop: A European-Style Atelier in the United States, The	Rowley, Kathleen	√		Fa	10	3		M/J 83	60
People: Irwin, Kim	Banff Experience: A Personal View of Fibre Interchange 1980, The	Irwin, Kim	√		Fa	8	4		J/A 81	35
People: Isaacs, Ron	Garment Form As Image, The	Koplos, Janet	√		Fa	10	6		N/D 83	66
People: Ishikawa, Adele	"Microfibers" (Exhibit)	McClelland, Elizabeth	√		Fa	8	2		M/A 81	66
People: Isobe, Harumi	"Third International Exhibition of Miniature Textiles 1978" (Exhibit)	Spencer, Patricia	√		Fa	6	1		J/F 79	90
People: Itter, Diane	Art of Working with Linen, The		√		Fa	14	2		M/A 87	9
People: Itter, Diane	Designers on Design		√		Fa	10	4		J/A 83	28
People: Itter, Diane	Diane Itter	Scheinman, Pam	√		Fa	5	2		M/A 78	20
People: Itter, Diane	"Diane Itter: Recent Work" (Exhibit)	Park, Betty	√		Fa	8	5		S/O 81	68

SUBJECT	TITLE	AUTHOR	IL	INST	JOUR	VOL	NO	ISS	DATE	PAGE
⁺ People: Itter, Diane	Fans and Fan Imagery	Howe, Katherine; Joanne Mattera	√		Fa	9	4		J/A 82	26
⁻ People: Itter, Diane	Jacquard Project: Selections from the Current Exhibition, The		√		Fa	9	2		M/A 82	36
⁺ People: Itter, Diane	"Miniature Fibers" (Exhibit)	Vanderburg, Jan	√		Fa	7	1		J/F 80	65
⁺ People: Itter, Diane	Miniatures in Fiber: Working Small—An Exciting Challenge for the Contemporary Fiber Artist	Malarcher, Patricia	√		Fa	7	4		J/A 80	32
⁺ People: Itter, Diane	Textile Trends: The Museum Collection	Malarcher, Patricia	√		Fa	12	6		N/D 85	23
⁺ People: Itter, Diane	"Threads" (Exhibit)	Kurtz, Carol	√		Fa	10	4		J/A 83	62
⁺ People: Itter, Diane	"Young Americans: Fiber, Wood, Plastic, Leather" (Exhibit)	Malarcher, Patricia	√		Fa	4	6		N/D 77	14
People: Iverson, Susan	Susan Iverson: With Both Feet Firmly Planted (error-corrected Fa v3 n5 76 p2)		√		Fa	3	4		J/A 76	14
People: Iverson, Virginia	Fiber on Martha's Vineyard	Erickson, Johanna	√		Fa	11	4		J/A 84	46
People: Ives, Peggy	Peggy Ives Retires — Long Established Business to C. S. Bourgeois		√		H&C	6	2		Sp 55	28
⁺ People: Iwata, Kiyomi	Kiyomi Iwata: A Singularity of Vision	Park, Betty	√		Fa	13	1		J/F 86	10
⁺ People: Iwata, Kiyomi	"Kiyomi Iwata: Works in Fiber" (Exhibit)	Malarcher, Patricia	√		Fa	9	2		M/A 82	77
↓ People: Iwata, Kiyomi	Rapport with Fabric and Dye: Kiyomi Iwata, A	Malarcher, Pat	√		Fa	7	1		J/F 80	28
People: Jackson, Elizabeth Browning	Exuberant Art of Elizabeth Browning Jackson, The	Place, Jennifer	√		Fa	10	6		N/D 83	12
People: Jackson, Margaret	Fabrics from A Desert Weaver	Kirkpatrick, Isabell; Pat Kirkpatrick	√		H&C	7	3		Su 56	27
People: Jackson, Thomas	Thomas Jackson, Weaver: 17th and 18th Century Records	Tidball, Harriet	√	√	SCGM		13		64	1-37
People: Jacob, Mary Jane	Interview with Mary Jane Jacob, An	Park, Betty	√		Fa	9	6		N/D 82	13
People: Jacobi, Peter	Collaboration: Peter and Ritzi Jacobi (error-corrected Fa v13 n1 86 p6)	Corpier, Leslee	√		Fa	12	5		S/O 85	27
People: Jacobi, Peter	"Ritzi and Peter Jacobi" (Exhibit)	Mathews, Rich	√		Fa	4	5		S/O 77	12
People: Jacobi, Peter and Ritzi	"Fiber Structures" Convergence '76 (Exhibit)	Mathews-Pulleyn, Kathryn	√		Fa	3	4		J/A 76	12
People: Jacobi, Ritzi	Collaboration: Peter and Ritzi Jacobi (error-corrected Fa v13 n1 86 p6)	Corpier, Leslee	√		Fa	12	5		S/O 85	27
People: Jacobi, Ritzi	"Miniature Textiles: 4th International Exhibition" (Exhibit)	Talley, Charles S.	√		Fa	8	3		M/J 81	72
People: Jacobi, Ritzi	"Ritzi and Peter Jacobi" (Exhibit)	Mathews, Rich	√		Fa	4	5		S/O 77	12
People: Jacobi, Ritzi and Peter	"Ninth International Biennial of Tapestry" (Exhibit)	Pulleyn, Rob	√		Fa	6	4		J/A 79	62
People: Jacobi, Ritzi and Peter	Ritzi and Peter Jacobi: Conversation	Paca Al, ed.	√		Fa	8	4		J/A 81	50
People: Jacobs, Ferne	Ferne Jacobs		√		Fa	4	1		J/F 77	24
People: Jacobs, Ferne	Ferne Jacobs: A Study in 3-Dimensional Order	Brown, Arleen Emery	√		SS&D	11	4	44	Fa 80	80
People: Jacobs, Ferne	"Ferne Jacobs: New Works" (Exhibit)	Park, Betty	√		Fa	6	1		J/F 79	84
People: Jacobs, Ferne	What Makes a Basket a Basket?	Malarcher, Patricia	√		Fa	11	1		J/F 84	34
People: Jacobs, Virginia	Building on Experience: Virginia Jacobs' Fabric Constructions	Rowland, Amy Zaffarano	√		Fa	7	4		J/A 80	39
People: Jacobsen, Lolli	Livin' and Workin' on the Land: Fiber Art Outside the Mainstream	Talley, Charles S.	√		Fa	8	6		N/D 81	38
People: Jacobsen, Lollie	Textile Apprenticeship in Northern California	Montgomery, Larry			TM		9		F/M 87	20
People: Jacobson, Gail	Textile Life, The	Jacobson, Gail	√		Fa	14	3		M/J 87	5
People: Jacoby, Victor	Livin' and Workin' on the Land: Fiber Art Outside the Mainstream	Talley, Charles S.	√		Fa	8	6		N/D 81	38
People: Jacoby, Victor	Pictorial Tapestry: A Portfolio of Contemporary Work	Goodman, Deborah Lerme	√		Fa	10	3		M/J 83	29
People: Jacoby, Victor	Tapestry (Part 3): An Inside View	Harvey, Nancy	√	√	SS&D	15	2	58	Sp 84	20
People: Jacoby, Victor	Victor Jacoby: Rich Colors and Bold Designs	Kahn, Kathy; Susan Larson-Fleming	√		WJ	12	1	45	Su 87	36

SUBJECT	TITLE	AUTHOR	IL	INST	JOUR	VOL	NO	ISS	DATE	PAGE
People: Jacopetti, Alexandra	Folkwear: In the Company of Some Friends		√		Fa	3	5		S/O 76	36
People: Jacopetti, Alexandra	"Seven Sonoma County Fibre Artists" (Exhibit)	Robinson, Sharon	√		Fa	3	4		J/A 76	6
People: Jacopetti, Alexandria	"Art and Romance of Peasant Clothing, The" (Exhibit)	Dyer, Carolyn	√		Fa	5	3		M/J 78	16
People: Jacquard, Joseph Marie	Jacquard and Woven Silk Pictures, The	Adrosko, Rita J.	√		AT	1			De 83	9
People: Jaffe, Joanne	"Fantasy Clothes/Fantastic Costumes" (Exhibit)	Dyer, Carolyn	√		Fa	4	2		M/A 77	11
People: Jaffie, H. R.	Hand-Painted Silk	Jaffie, H. R.	√		Fa	10	5		S/O 83	17
People: Jagodyinski, J. V.	"Mini Tapestry Exhibit" (Exhibit)	Bockelman, JoAnne	√		Fa	5	4		J/A 78	12
People: James, Michael	"Michael James: A Ten-Year Retrospective" (Exhibit)	Klein, Jody	√		Fa	11	2		M/A 84	80
People: James, Michael	Quiltmaker's Art, A	Mattera, Joanne	√		Fa	10	2		M/A 83	33
People: James, Michael	"Redefining the American Quilt" (Exhibit)		√		Fa	14	4		S/O 87	43
People: Jamet, Louise	"Fiberous": Fiber as a Source of Inspiration (Exhibit)	Willard, Janice	√		Fa	10	1		J/F 83	80
People: Janeiro, Jan	"Fiber from the Marietta College Crafts National" (Exhibit)	Murray, Megan	√		Fa	11	2		M/A 84	76
People: Janeiro, Jan	"Infrastructure" (Exhibit)	Malarcher, Patricia	√		Fa	11	4		J/A 84	76
People: Janeiro, Jan	"Jan Janeiro: Recent Textiles" (Exhibit)	Talley, Charles S.	√		Fa	8	2		M/A 81	65
People: Janeiro, Jan	Making a Living: Eight Fiber Artists Tell How They Do It	Rowley, Kathleen	√		Fa	9	5		S/O 82	38
People: Janeirós, Jan	Ongoing Feather: Jan Janeirós Search for a Personal Metaphor, The	Talley, Charles	√		Fa	6	4		J/A 79	46
People: Jansen, Catherine	Soft Sculpture: Old Forms, New Meanings	Gordon, Beverly	√		Fa	10	6		N/D 83	40
People: January, Marjorie	Januarys of Wilmington Ohio, The		√		H&C	5	3		Su 54	26
People: January, Marjorie and Garnett	Chasubles from Marjorie January's Looms		√		H&C	19	1		Wi 68	18
People: Jarmain, Susan	Canadian Classic, A	Baker, William R. M.	√		SS&D	18	3	71	Su 87	52
People: Jefferies, William	Imagery Is Personal in Tapestry Today	Clausen, Valerie	√		TM			9	F/M 87	66
People: Jeffery, Sharon	"New England Images" (Exhibit)	Harris, Patricia; David Lyon	√		Fa	10	6		N/D 83	78
People: Jenkins, Dennis	Fiber and Architecture: Dennis Jenkins		√		Fa	3	3		M/J 76	35
People: Jenny, Harriet	Portfolio: Harriet Jenny		√		Hw	7	1		J/F 86	36
People: Jensen, Margot Strand	Cut from the Same Cloth	Andrews, Kathy Boals	√		Fa	13	3		M/J 86	21
People: Jensen, Margot Strand	Margot Strand Jensen: Soft Painting	Singletary, Suzanne M.	√		Fa	11	1		J/F 84	18
People: Jensen, Margot Strand	Under Wraps		√		Fa	12	3		M/J 85	26
People: Jenuwine, Kim	Sampler of Surface Design, A	Westphal, Katherine	√		Fa	10	5		S/O 83	39
People: Jerger, Lieve	Lace Is My Career. Wire Is My Specialty		√		Fa	14	4		S/O 87	61
People: Johannsdottir, Sigridur	Fiber Art in Iceland	Hrafnhildur, Schram	√		Fa	9	6		N/D 82	68
People: Johansen, Marg	Marg Johansen, An American Represented in International Tapestry Show		√		H&C	17	1		Wi 66	20
People: Johansen, Wailani	Wailani Johansen, Quiltmaker: Sharing the Tradition of the Hawaiian Quilt	Rex, Chris	√		Fa	9	3		M/J 82	60
People: Johns, Dean	Pictorial Tapestry: A Portfolio of Contemporary Work	Goodman, Deborah Lerme	√		Fa	10	3		M/J 83	29
People: Johns, Dean	Words in Fiber	Rowley, Kathleen	√		Fa	11	2		M/A 84	66
People: Johns, Kay	"Surface Design South Central" (Exhibit)	Erhler, Mary	√		Fa	6	4		J/A 79	75
People: Johnson, Barbara	Fibre Interchange At the Banff Centre	Corpier, Leslee	√		Fa	12	4		J/A 85	40
People: Johnson, Beth	Table Dressing and Bedcovers		√		Fa	8	3		M/J 81	43
People: Johnson, Beth	Three Production Weavers: Beth Johnson		√		Hw	3	3		My 82	48
People: Johnson, David	David Johnson and Geary Jones	Rudick, Sally	√		Fa	12	5		S/O 85	18
People: Johnson, Helga	Log Cabin Rag Rugs	Meany, Janet K.	√	√	WJ	9	4	36	Sp 85	50
People: Johnson Klara	Klara Johnson: A Weaver's Vision Realized	Magoffin, Connie	√	√	WJ	11	4	44	Sp 87	62

SUBJECT	TITLE	AUTHOR	IL	INST	JOUR	VOL	NO	ISS	DATE	PAGE
People: Johnson, Leslie	T-Shirts for Every Body: 20th Century Folkwear		√		Fa	8	6		N/D 81	22
People: Johnson, Melinda Raber	Summer and Winter Garments (Melinda Raber Johnson)		√	√	WJ	11	3	43	Wi 87	44
People: Johnson, Pamela Gustavson	"Pamela Gustavson Johnson: Constructivist Quilts" (Exhibit)	Brackman, Barbara	√		Fa	10	2		M/A 83	68
People: Johnson, Sandra McMorris	Clothesline Palette: Three Hundred Yards of Color		√		Fa	9	1		J/F 82	22
People: Johnson-Depuy, Tina	"Tina Johnson-Depuy Soft Jewelry" (Exhibit)	Cardinale, Robert L.	√		Fa	6	3		M/J 79	81
People: Jolley, Ginger	Ginger Jolley: Inspired by Navajo Weaving	Jolley, Ginger	√		Fa	11	3		M/J 84	36
People: Jones, Allen	Influence from the East: Textiles and Textile Patterns in Western Art	Park, Betty	√		Fa	12	2		M/A 85	22
People: Jones, Ellen	Ellen Jones		√		Fa	4	1		J/F 77	38
People: Jones, Gary	Publish Your Own Craft Book	Nell, Patti			Iw	1	2		Wi 76	18
People: Jones, Geary	David Johnson and Geary Jones	Rudick, Sally	√		Fa	12	5		S/O 85	18
People: Jones, Laura	Felt and Paper: A Portfolio		√		Fa	13	4		J/A 86	35
People: Jones, Marilyn and Gary	Raising a Spinner's Flock	Ligon, Linda	√	√	Iw	2	3		Sp 77	14
People: Jones, Martha	Weaver (A Poem for Martha Jones)	Smith, Anna Deavere	√		SS&D	16	3	63	Su 85	38
People: Jones, Ruth	Imagery Is Personal in Tapestry Today	Clausen, Valerie	√		TM			9	F/M 87	66
People: Jones-Henderson, Napoleon	"Contemporary African American Crafts" (Exhibit)	Pilsk, Adele	√		Fa	6	6		N/D 79	74
People: Juelin, Becky	Setting Up Shop	Ligon, Linda	√		Iw	2	4		Su 77	18
People: Julian, Alexander	Alexander Julian		√		Hw	7	5		N/D 86	39
People: Julian, Alexander	Alexander Julian: Cut of a Different Cloth	De Leon, Sherry	√		Fa	12	3		M/J 85	64
People: Julian, Alexander	Alexander Julian's Foundation for Aesthetic Understanding	Lancaster, Zöe Woodruff	√		Fa	14	1		J/F 87	24
People: Julian, Naomi	Naomi Julian: Weaver	Vogt, Cy	√		Fa	5	6		N/D 78	28
People: Jung, Dora	Artist and Industry — A Cooperative Effort		√		Hw	8	3		M/J 87	71
People: Jung, Dora	Dora Jung, Distinguished Finnish Weaver		√		H&C	10	2		Sp 59	14
People: Jung, Dora	Dora Jung: The Artist and the Person	Talley, Charles	√		Fa	12	1		J/F 85	39
People: Junichi, Arai	Fabric About Fabric	Cannarella, Deborah	√		TM			1	O/N 85	72
People: Junker, Holly	Out of the Blue: Aerial Images		√		Fa	13	5		S/O 86	44
People: Jupena, Urban	Shaped Sculptured Rugs — A Workshop with Urban Jupena		√	√	WJ	4	1	13	Jy 79	5
People: Juul-Hansen, Kjeld	Kjeld Juul-Hansen		√		H&C	9	2		Sp 58	29
People: Juve, Peggy	Art Wear of Peggy Juve, The	Tacker, Sylvia	√		Fa	14	1		J/F 87	25
People: Juve, Peggy	Sampler of Surface Design, A	Westphal, Katherine	√		Fa	10	5		S/O 83	39
People: Kagoshima, E'Wao	"Great American Foot, The" (Exhibit)	Grover, Donald	√		Fa	5	4		J/A 78	15
People: Kahn, Dennery	Inspired by Fiber: Textile Sensibility in Other Media	Malarcher, Patricia	√		Fa	10	6		N/D 83	33
People: Kahn, Erika	Garment Form As Image, The	Koplos, Janet	√		Fa	10	6		N/D 83	66
People: Kahn, Erika	"Works In, On, and Of Paper" (Exhibit)	Les, Kathleen	√		Fa	6	5		S/O 79	79
People: Kahn, Lydia	Two-Harness Designs	Bryan, Dorothy	√		H&C	9	3		Su 58	28
People: Kakalia, Deborah Kepola	Hawaiian Quilt, The	White-Hansen, Sue Ellen	√	√	TM			13	O/N 87	22
People: Kamola, Stephanie and Teofil	Old World Weavers at Work in the New	Kamola, Stephanie	√	√	H&C	7	2		Sp 56	24
People: Kandinsky, Vasily	Textiles and the Art of Kandinsky	Parks, Betty	√		Fa	9	4		J/A 82	11
People: Kanter, Jodi	Portfolio: Why I Work in Linen, A		√		Fa	14	2		M/A 87	40
People: Kao, Ruth	"Fiber R/Evolution" (Exhibit)	Rudich, Sally	√		Fa	13	4		J/A 86	45
People: Kao, Ruth	"Ruth Kao: Silk Sense" (Exhibit)	Sider, Sandra	√		Fa	12	1		J/F 85	72
People: Kapan, Cynthia	Blues in the Light: Cyanotype on Fabric	Sider, Sandra	√		Fa	13	5		S/O 86	34
People: Kaplan, Annette	Commissions: The Process, the Problems and the Prospects		√		Fa	6	5		S/O 79	45
People: Kaplow, Roberta	Bright Styles from the North	Kaplow, Roberta	√		SS&D	16	1	61	Wi 84	23

SUBJECT	TITLE	AUTHOR	IL	INST	JOUR	VOL	NO	ISS	DATE	PAGE
People: Karkosh, Clayton	Fiber as Set Design: The Work of Clayton Karkosh and Associates		√		Fa	3	4		J/A 76	34
People: Karvinen, Annikki	Annikki Karvinen: Finnish Designer of Wovens	Talley, Charles	√		Fa	13	4		J/A 86	16
People: Kary, Marshall	"Works In, On, and Of Paper" (Exhibit)	Les, Kathleen	√		Fa	6	5		S/O 79	79
People: Kashiwa, Wendy	"Old Traditions/New Directions" (Exhibit)	West, Virginia	√		Fa	8	6		N/D 81	66
People: Kasmiersky, Terri	"Fiber" (Exhibit)	Vander Lee, Jana	√		Fa	3	2		M/A 76	9
People: Kasten, Sam	Nantucket Looms and Sam Kasten	Erickson, Johanna	√		SS&D	17	3	67	Su 86	70
People: Katsaros, Maria	Teacher/**Student** Interface: Two Views of Education		√		Fa	14	1		J/F 87	34
People: Katsiaficias, Diane	Papermaking in the U.S.A.	Toale, Bernard	√		Fa	9	4		J/A 82	34
People: Katz, Ruth	Few Words About Feet, Shoes and Other Things We Walk On, A	Katz, Ruth J.	√		Fa	6	3		M/J 79	53
People: Kaufman, Annie	Santa Fe Weaving Center, The	Elliott, Malinda	√		Fa	9	5		S/O 82	32
People: Kaufman, Deborah	Feltmaking Now: The Exciting Revival of an Ancient Technique	Gordon, Beverly	√		Fa	6	6		N/D 79	43
People: Kaufman, Deborah	More Than Just a Fling	Kaufman, Deborah	√		Fa	7	3		M/J 80	54
People: Kaufman, Deborah	"Paper and Felt Redefined" (Exhibit)	Ogden, Anne	√		Fa	5	2		M/A 78	17
People: Kaufman, Glen	"Fibers Southeast 1979" (Exhibit)	Johnson, Elma	√		Fa	6	2		M/A 79	68
People: Kaufman, Glen	Garment Form As Image, The	Koplos, Janet	√		Fa	10	6		N/D 83	66
People: Kaufman, Glen	Glen's Gloves: A Kaufman Retrospective	Lancaster, Zoe Woodruff	√		Fa	12	5		S/O 85	41
People: Kaufman, Glen	Miniatures in Fiber: Working Small—An Exciting Challenge for the Contemporary Fiber Artist	Malarcher, Patricia	√		Fa	7	4		J/A 80	32
People: Kaufman, Glen	Scientific Research Suggests Ideas for Fabric Designs		√		H&C	15	3		Su 64	5
People: Kauppi, Sten	Sten Kauppi		√		H&C	5	1		Wi 53	48
People: Kaur, Nirmal	"Crafts Northwest, Circa 1980" (Exhibit)	Evans, Rojean; Louise Klemperer	√		Fa	7	5		S/O 80	75
People: Kaur, Nirmal	"Wearable Art" (Exhibit)	Hunt, E. Ann	√		Fa	6	3		M/J 79	78
People: Kaye, David H.	"Fiber Works — Americas & Japan" (Exhibit)	Kato, Kuniko Lucy	√		Fa	5	1		J/F 78	10
People: Kaye, David H.	"Interweave 79" (Exhibit)	Constantinides, Kathy	√		Fa	7	1		J/F 80	66
People: Kaye, David H.	Portfolio: Why I Work in Linen, A		√		Fa	14	2		M/A 87	41
People: Kearney, Annette	"Statements in Fibre" (Exhibit)	Wagner, Liz	√		Fa	6	1		J/F 79	88
People: Keasbey, Doramay	Weaving Guilds—A Special Sharing		√		Iw	5	2		Sp 80	55
People: Keen, Annette	Profile of an HGA Rep		√		SS&D	18	4	72	Fa 87	73
People: Keene, Susan Warner	Canadian Portfolio, A	Place, Jennifer	√		Fa	9	6		N/D 82	29
People: Keene, Susan Warner	Convergence '86 Preview: Toronto — A City in Transition	Baker, William R. M.	√		SS&D	17	1	65	Wi 85	43
People: Keene, Susan Warner	Felt and Paper: A Portfolio		√		Fa	13	4		J/A 86	35
People: Keiner, Julia	Fabrics from Israel	Keiner, Julia	√		H&C	5	4		Fa 54	30
People: Keiner, Julia	Julia Keiner, Brings Fabrics from Israel		√		H&C	15	2		Sp 64	22
People: Kele, Judit	Judit Kele: The Sound of the Way It Feels	Colton, Sarah	√		Fa	14	3		M/J 87	42
People: Kelley, Helen	Quilting by the Lake in Central New York	Wright, Yolanda	√		Fa	10	2		M/A 83	50
People: Kelly, Linda	Stitched Double Cloth—Matelassé		√		WJ	7	1	25	Su 82	37
People: Kelly, Mary Ann	"Boston Seven: A Fiber Show, The" (Exhibit)	Goldman, Judy Ann	√		Fa	6	3		M/J 79	73
People: Kelly, Rose	"Rose Kelly: Printed, Painted and Woven Textiles" (Exhibit)	Small, Deborah	√		Fa	9	6		N/D 82	84
People: Kelly, Rose	Sampler of Surface Design, A	Westphal, Katherine	√		Fa	10	5		S/O 83	39
People: Kelly, Susan	Play of Light: Susan Kelly Explains the Inner and Outer Workings of Her Tapestries, A	Kelly, Susan	√		Fa	8	5		S/O 81	54
People: Kelm, Kathy	"Surface Design: Approaches '78" (Exhibit)	Arnow, Jan	√		Fa	6	2		M/A 79	67
People: Kemble, Julie	Canadian Portfolio, A	Place, Jennifer	√		Fa	9	6		N/D 82	29
People: Kennedy, Janet	Public Fiber: Looking At the Logistics	Koplos, Janet	√		Fa	12	1		J/F 85	32

SUBJECT	TITLE	AUTHOR	IL	INST	JOUR	VOL	NO	ISS	DATE	PAGE
People: Kennedy, Norman	Four Posts of Poverty, The	Xenaxis, Alexis Yiorgos	√		PWC	5	1	15		6
People: Kennedy, Norman	Norman Kennedy — Weaver at Williamsburg	Slater, Deborah	√		H&C	23	1		J/F 72	23
People: Kent, Kate Peck	Kate Peck Kent: An Anthropologist's Lifetime Involvement with Textiles	Schevill, Margot Blum	√		WJ	11	1	41	Su 86	11
People: Kent, Margi	Costuming for Rock Music Videos	Pierce, Judith	√		Fa	14	3		M/J 87	51
People: Kern, Marilyn	Surface Attraction	Mattera, Joanne	√		TM			7	O/N 86	20
People: Kern, Mary Sue	Mary Sue Kern: Embodied Dualities	Logiudice, JoEL	√		Fa	13	5		S/O 86	26
People: Kerr, Connie	Open Jurying in Pittsburg: Putting Your Work on the Line (Exhibit)	Myrinx, Elaine	√		Fa	6	2		M/A 79	23
People: Kerr, Connie	Speakers Bureau Presents		√		SS&D	9	3	35	Su 78	82
People: Kerr, Mollie	"Southern California Designer Crafts" (Exhibit)	Dyer, Carolyn	√		Fa	5	2		M/A 78	14
People: Kessenich, Loraine	Weaving Guilds—A Special Sharing		√		Iw	5	2		Sp 80	53
People: Khank, Emmanuelle	Paris Museum Surveys Fashion	Colton, Sarah	√		Fa	14	3		M/J 87	6
People: Kidd, Jane	Concerns and Influences in My Work	Kidd, Jane	√		AT	6			De 86	135
People: Kidd, Robert L.	Profile: Robert L. Kidd	Fleming, Ray Frost	√		H&C	23	5		S/O 72	9
People: Kilgore, Katherine	Tapestry (Part 3): An Inside View	Harvey, Nancy	√	√	SS&D	15	2	58	Sp 84	20
People: Kimmel, Melissa	"Works in Fiber" (Exhibit)	Arnow, Jan	√		Fa	8	2		M/A 81	61
People: Kimura, Aya	"Ladders and Windows" (Exhibit)	Kester, Bernard	√		Fa	13	4		J/A 86	52
People: Kindahl, Connie	Connie Kindahl	French, Elizabeth	√		SS&D	17	3	67	Su 86	56
People: King, Bucky	Contemporary Needle Lacers		√		TM			13	O/N 87	44
People: King, Wilma	"Fiber in the Service of Art: The Work of Wilma King and Marilyn Grelle" (Exhibit)	Mathews, Rich	√		Fa	4	2		M/A 77	18
People: Kinsella, Pat	Artist/Designer: Two Approaches to Fabric	Kinsella, Pat	√		AT	3			My 85	57
People: Kinsella, Pat	Double Lives: Can You Love Your "Work" When It's Your "Job"?	Mattera, Joanne	√		TM			10	A/M 87	62
People: Kinsella, Pat	"Textiles by Pat Kinsella and Sheila O'Hara" (Exhibit)	Janeiro, Jan	√		Fa	6	3		M/J 79	72
People: Kinsella, Pat	"Vibrant Structures" (Exhibit)	Shermeta, Margo	√		Fa	11	6		N/D 84	75
People: Kipp, Maria	American Handweaving 1960		√		H&C	11	2		Sp 60	11
People: Kipp, Maria	Maria Kipp — Her Career as a Weaver	Bryan, Dorothy	√		H&C	3	1		Wi 51	15
People: Kirch, Ingrid	Under Wraps		√		Fa	12	3		M/J 85	26
People: Kirkland, Larry	Eleventh International Biennial of Tapestry, The	Taylor, Elmer; Dianne Taylor	√		Fa	10	5		S/O 83	33
People: Kirkland, Lawrence	"National Crafts '81: Works by the 1981 National Endowment for the Arts Craft Fellows" (Exhibit)	Mattera, Joanne	√		Fa	9	1		J/F 82	82
People: Kirmeyer, Maxine	"Third Annual Fiber Show" (Exhibit)	Papa, Nancy	√		Fa	5	6		N/D 78	65
People: Kittay, Harriet	American Inspiration		√		Fa	10	2		M/A 83	92
People: Kittredge, Susan	Success of Susan Kittredge, The	Park, Betty	√		Fa	6	2		M/A 79	28
People: Kittredge, Susan Bird	Masks At the Heart of Disguise	Koplos, Janet	√		Fa	11	5		S/O 84	32
People: Kjelland, Suzanne	Color Theory for Handweavers Part 3: Visual Illusions with Color	Wald, Pat Boutin	√	√	WJ	10	4	40	Sp 86	40
People: Klebanoff, Susan	Interview with Susan Klebanoff, An		√		SS&D	13	3	51	Su 82	34
People: Klebanoff, Susan	Multilayered Tapestries of Susan Klebanoff, The	Brien, Elise	√		Fa	14	3		M/J 87	21
People: Kleibacker, Charles	Techniques of Haute Couture (error-corrected TM i7 O/N86 p5)	Rhodes, Elizabeth A.	√	√	TM			6	A/S 86	52
People: Klein, Jody	Artifact...Image...Art		√		Fa	7	3		M/J 80	19
People: Klein, Jody	Cows in Fiber	Timmons, Chris	√		Fa	11	4		J/A 84	55
People: Klein, Jody	Jody Klein: Quilted Constructions	Perry, Pamela	√		Fa	12	2		M/A 85	18
People: Klein, Jody	Jody Klein's Paper Quilts		√		Fa	10	1		J/F 83	44
People: Klein, Jody	"Jody Klein's Paper Quilts" (Exhibit)	Storey, Isabelle B.	√		Fa	8	6		N/D 81	70
People: Kline, Franz	"Modern Aubusson Tapestry, The" (Exhibit)	Tanenbaum, Ruth	√		Fa	5	3		M/J 78	14
People: Kline, Kathy	"Soft Art" (Exhibit)	Richerson, Suzanne	√		Fa	4	4		J/A 77	16

SUBJECT	TITLE	AUTHOR	IL	INST	JOUR	VOL	NO	ISS	DATE	PAGE
+ People: Kling, Candace	Twentieth Century Ribbon Sculptress Candace Kling	Betzina, Sandra	√		TM			12	A/S 87	62
+ People: Kling, Kandace	Contemporary California Costume	Poon, Vivian	√		Fa	11	5		S/O 84	53
People: Kliot, Jules	Kliots of Berkeley, The	Talley, Charles S.	√		Fa	7	4		J/A 80	44
People: Kliot, Kaethe	Kliots of Berkeley, The	Talley, Charles S.	√		Fa	7	4		J/A 80	44
People: Klippenstein, Carol	Carol Klippenstein		√		Fa	4	4		J/A 77	48
People: Knapp, Dina	For the Body (error-corrected Fa v10 n2 83 p61)		√		Fa	10	1		J/F 83	32
People: Knapp, Dina Schwartz	Art to Wear — Three Innovators: Cate Fitt, Emma Vesey, Dina Schwartz Knapp		√		Fa	8	1		J/F 81	67
People: Knauer, Katherine	Funeral	Knauer, Katherine	√		Fa	13	6		N/D 86	30
People: Knauss, Lewis	"Contemporary Fiber Art" (Exhibit)	Guyer, Niki	√		Fa	5	6		N/D 78	66
People: Knauss, Lewis	Lewis Knauss: New Work	Park, Betty	√		Fa	9	3		M/J 82	11
People: Knauss, Lewis	"Macungie Notes — Lewis Knauss" (Exhibit)	Park, Betty	√		Fa	5	2		M/A 78	15
People: Knauss, Lewis	"Young Americans: Fiber, Wood, Plastic, Leather" (Exhibit)	Malarcher, Patricia	√		Fa	4	6		N/D 77	14
People: Knodel, Gerhardt	"Art Fabric '77: the Contemporary American Tapestry" (Exhibit)	Papa, Nancy	√		Fa	4	4		J/A 77	12
People: Knodel, Gerhardt	"Art Fabric: Mainstream, The" (Exhibit)	Janeiro, Jan	√		Fa	8	5		S/O 81	70
People: Knodel, Gerhardt	Conversing with Gerhardt Knodel	Park, Betty	√		Fa	12	1		J/F 85	27
People: Knodel, Gerhardt	Designers on Design		√		Fa	10	4		J/A 83	28
People: Knodel, Gerhardt	Gerhardt Knodel	Olendorf, Donna	√		Fa	5	6		N/D 78	44
People: Knodel, Gerhardt	"Gerhardt Knodel—Makes Places to Be" (Exhibit)	Livingstone, Joan	√		Fa	10	3		M/J 83	71
People: Knodel, Gerhardt	Jacquard Project: Selections from the Current Exhibition, The		√		Fa	9	2		M/A 82	36
People: Knodel, Gerhardt	Keynote in Chicago: Knodel	Livingstone, Joan	√		SS&D	18	3	71	Su 87	37
People: Knodel, Gerhardt	Lausanne Notebook: Our Special Report on the 8th Lausanne Biennial of Tapestry, A	Mathews, Rich	√		Fa	4	5		S/O 77	30
People: Knodel, Gerhardt	"Miniature Textiles: 4th International Exhibition" (Exhibit)	Talley, Charles S.	√		Fa	8	3		M/J 81	72
People: Knodel, Gerhardt G.	"Fiberworks" (Exhibit)	Park, Betty	√		Fa	4	6		N/D 77	10
People: Knoll, Florence	Knoll Textiles		√		H&C	9	3		Su 58	12
People: Knollenberg, Barbara	Barbara Knollenberg, Fashion Designer, A Personal Story		√		WJ	6	3	23	Wi 81	10
People: Knollenberg, Barbara	Handwoven Clothing Today: The Couturier Touch	West, Virginia	√		Fa	8	1		J/F 81	39
People: Knopf, Oscar	Oscar Knopf's Ingenious Invention	Miller, Ethel E.	√	> 4	H&C	10	2		Sp 59	24
People: Knutson, Linda	Fashions by Linda Knutson and Lynn Daly		√	√	WJ	6	3	23	Wi 81	14
People: Kobayashi, Masakazu	Commissions: The Process, the Problems and the Prospects		√		Fa	6	5		S/O 79	45
People: Kobayashi, Masakazu	"Contemporary Japanese Tapestry, The" (Exhibit)	Glass, Laurie H.	√		Fa	4	6		N/D 77	22
People: Kobayashi, Masakazu	Contemporary Tapestry in Japan: Individuality After Centuries of Textile Conformity	Lindenfeld, Lore	√		Fa	10	3		M/J 83	44
People: Kobayashi, Masakazu	"Fiberworks" (Exhibit)	Park, Betty	√		Fa	4	6		N/D 77	10
People: Kobayashi, Masakazu	Lausanne Notebook: Our Special Report on the 8th Lausanne Biennial of Tapestry, A	Mathews, Rich	√		Fa	4	5		S/O 77	30
People: Kobayashi, Masakazu	"Third International Exhibition of Miniature Textiles 1978" (Exhibit)	Spencer, Patricia	√		Fa	6	1		J/F 79	90
People: Kobayaski, Naomi	Lausanne Notebook: Our Special Report on the 8th Lausanne Biennial of Tapestry, A	Mathews, Rich	√		Fa	4	5		S/O 77	30
People: Kocher, Robert	"Soft Art" (Exhibit)	Richerson, Suzanne	√		Fa	4	4		J/A 77	16
People: Kodaini, Mia	"Show Biz" (Exhibit)	Scheinman, Pamela	√		Fa	7	4		J/A 80	69
People: Koenigsberg, Nancy	Fiber/Art Conditioned by Life: A Workshop with Sheila Hicks	Klein, Jody	√		Fa	12	5		S/O 85	58

SUBJECT	TITLE	AUTHOR	IL	INST	JOUR	VOL	NO	ISS	DATE	PAGE
People: Koepp, William	Shaft-Switching Device of William Koepp		√	√	WJ	8	4	32	Sp 84	32
People: Koike, Janet	Quiltmaker's Art, A	Mattera, Joanne	√		Fa	10	2		M/A 83	33
People: Konijn, Nelleke	Twelfth International Biennial Of Tapestry	Taylor, Dianne; Elmer Taylor	√		Fa	12	6		N/D 85	50
People: Koopman, Alberje	Alberje Koopman		√		SS&D	16	1	61	Wi 84	4
People: Koopman, Albertje	Albertje Koopman		√		Hw	4	1		J/F 83	56
People: Koopman, Albertje	Interview with Albertje Koopman, An	LaLena, Constance	√		Hw	7	3		M/J 86	89
People: Koopman, Albertje	Who Weaves?		√		Iw	5	2		Sp 80	42
People: Kopecek, Vera Wainar	Vera Wainar Kopecek: Her Work Stands Alone	Hunt, Elizabeth Ann	√		Fa	7	2		M/A 80	55
People: Korczak, Ewa	To the Walls: The 13th Lausanne Biennial (Exhibit)	Zepeda, Susan G.	√		Fa	14	4		S/O 87	41
People: Koretsky, Donna	"New Dimensions in Handmade Paper" (Exhibit)	Koplos, Janet	√		Fa	8	5		S/O 81	72
People: Kormos, Antonia	Applicant #029: Antonia Kormos	Wertheimer, Sheila	√		SS&D	10	2	38	Sp 79	68
People: Kors, Michael	Diary of a Collection	Mattera, Joanne	√		TM			13	O/N 87	36
People: Kortland, Hannie	Eleventh International Biennial of Tapestry, The	Taylor, Elmer; Dianne Taylor	√		Fa	10	5		S/O 83	33
People: Kotani, Akiko	"Akiko Kotani" (Exhibit)	Malarcher, Patricia	√		Fa	8	4		J/A 81	73
People: Kotani, Akiko	"Fiber Art: An Uncommon Thread" (Exhibit)	Park, Betty	√		Fa	9	2		M/A 82	78
People: Kott, Jerry	Few Words About Feet, Shoes and Other Things We Walk On, A	Katz, Ruth J.	√		Fa	6	3		M/J 79	53
People: Koumoutseas, Kathe	Handwoven Clothing Today: The Couturier Touch	West, Virginia	√		Fa	8	1		J/F 81	39
People: Kovach, Janet	Who Weaves?		√		Iw	5	2		Sp 80	34
People: Kowalski, Libby	"Fiber in Focus" (Exhibit)	Skudera, Gail	√		Fa	10	6		N/D 83	82
People: Kozel, Ina	"Maximum Coverage: Wearables by Contemporary American Artists" (Exhibit)	Risseeuw, Mary	√		Fa	8	1		J/F 81	93
People: Kozikowski, Janusz	Janusz Kozikowski	Kozikowski, Janusz	√		Fa	7	5		S/O 80	43
People: Kozikowski, Janusz	Tapestries of Nancy and Janusz Kozikowski, The	Elliott, Malinda	√		Fa	13	2		M/A 86	23
People: Kozikowski, Janusz and Nancy	Fiber and Architecture: Janusz and Nancy Kozikowski		√		Fa	3	3		M/J 76	28
People: Kozikowski, Nancy	Tapestries of Nancy and Janusz Kozikowski, The	Elliott, Malinda	√		Fa	13	2		M/A 86	23
People: Kozikowski, Nancy	"Textiles New Mexico 1978" (Exhibit)	Tatum, Phyllis	√		Fa	5	4		J/A 78	10
People: Kozikowski, Nancy and Janusz	Ghost Rugs	Kozikowski, Janusz; Nancy Kozikowski	√		Iw	4	1		Wi 78	24
People: Kozikowski, Nancy and Janusz	Spirit of New Mexico: It Comes Alive in Weaving, The		√		SS&D	7	2	26	Sp 76	4
People: Kozikowski, Nancy and Janusz	Weaving on a Two Man Loom	Kozikowski, Janusz	√		H&C	24	1		J/F 73	6
People: Kozloff, Joyce	"Joyce Kozloff" An Interior Decorated (Exhibit)	Greenberg, Blue	√		Fa	8	1		J/F 81	89
People: Kraber, Penelope	"Art and Romance of Peasant Clothing, The" (Exhibit)	Dyer, Carolyn	√		Fa	5	3		M/J 78	16
People: Kraft, Grace	Grace Kraft: Charting a Private World	Summar, Polly	√		Fa	14	3		M/J 87	16
People: Kraft, Grace	Grace Kraft: Not Just Another Piece of Cloth from the Factory	Vozar, Linda	√	√	Fa	5	5		S/O 78	36
People: Kraft, Kathy	"Seven Sonoma County Fibre Artists" (Exhibit)	Robinson, Sharon	√		Fa	3	4		J/A 76	6
People: Kramer, Helen	Adapting Handwoven Fabrics to Interior Design	Storey, Walter Rendell	√		H&C	4	3		Su 53	8
People: Kramer, Helen	Studies in Color and Texture through Fabric	Kramer, Helen	√		H&C	6	1		Wi 54	13
People: Kramer, Helen Kroll	American Handweaving 1960		√		H&C	11	2		Sp 60	13
People: Krank, Wolfram	"Textiles New Mexico 1976" (Exhibit)	Warner, Lucy Ann	√		Fa	3	2		M/A 76	12
People: Krasnoff, Julienne	Focus on the HGA Board of Directors		√		SS&D	10	3	39	Su 79	46
People: Kraynek, Fran	"Basket-Maker's Art, The" (Exhibit)	Grover, Donald	√		Fa	6	6		N/D 79	73

SUBJECT	TITLE	AUTHOR	IL	INST	JOUR	VOL	NO	ISS	DATE	PAGE
People: Kraynek, Fran	"Forms in Fiber" (Exhibit)	Brown, Arleen Emery	√		Fa	7	5		S/O 80	73
People: Kraynek-Prince, Fran	Craft Today: The American Craft Museum (Exhibit)	Sider, Sandra	√		Fa	14	2		M/A 87	54
People: Kraynek-Prince, Fran	Fran Kraynek-Prince and Neil Prince	Scarborough, Jessica	√		Fa	12	5		S/O 85	19
People: Kreckel, Ann	Handwoven Clothing Today: The Couturier Touch	West, Virginia	√		Fa	8	1		J/F 81	39
People: Kregloe, Liz	Liz Kregloe: A Collage of Interior Spaces	Weinstein, Ann	√		Fa	13	3		M/J 86	28
People: Krejci, Luba	"Fiberworks" (Exhibit)	Park, Betty	√		Fa	4	6		N/D 77	10
People: Krejci, Luba	Windows to the Soul: The Lace Making of Luba Krejci	Kaminski, Vera E.	√	√	Fa	6	6		N/D 79	56
People: Krell, Paul	Masks At the Heart of Disguise	Koplos, Janet	√		Fa	11	5		S/O 84	32
People: Kremer, Roberta	"New Wisconsin Fiber": The First Group Show of American Fiber Art in Switzerland (Exhibit)	Bard, Elizabeth A.	√		Fa	10	6		N/D 83	43
People: Kremer, Roberta	Roberta Kremer: A Dialogue with Fiber	Bard, Elizabeth A.	√		Fa	11	4		J/A 84	24
People: Kristjansdottir, Asrun	Fiber Art in Iceland	Hrafnhildur, Schram	√		Fa	9	6		N/D 82	68
People: Kristoferson, Susan	Kimono East/West	Wada, Yoshiko	√		Fa	9	1		J/F 82	19
People: Kroeger, Nicole	"Fiber" (Exhibit)	Vander Lee, Jana	√		Fa	3	2		M/A 76	9
People: Kroetsch, Glenn	Conflict Resolved: The Hows and Whys of Hand-Dyed Relief Painting, A	Kroetsch, Glenn	√		Fa	8	4		J/A 81	13
People: Kroll, Boris	Jacquard Tapestries of Boris Kroll, The		√		SS&D	12	2	46	Sp 81	47
People: Krondahl, Hans	Hans Krondahl		√		SS&D	5	3	19	Su 74	4
People: Krondahl, Hans	Hans Krondahl's "Homage to Garbo" (Exhibit)	Talley, Charles	√		Fa	11	4		J/A 84	79
People: Krout, Jonathan	"National Crafts '81: Works by the 1981 National Endowment for the Arts Craft Fellows" (Exhibit)	Mattera, Joanne	√		Fa	9	1		J/F 82	82
People: Krucker, Ellen	Ellen Krucker, Designer of Miniatures	Busby, Robert J.	√		H&C	20	1		Wi 69	44
People: Kubota, Shigeo	Contemporary Tapestry in Japan: Individuality After Centuries of Textile Conformity	Lindenfeld, Lore	√		Fa	10	3		M/J 83	44
People: Kubota, Shigeo	Lausanne Notebook: Our Special Report on the 8th Lausanne Biennial of Tapestry, A	Mathews, Rich	√		Fa	4	5		S/O 77	30
People: Kuchma, Jaroslava Lialia	Pictorial Tapestry: A Portfolio of Contemporary Work	Goodman, Deborah Lerme	√		Fa	10	3		M/J 83	29
People: Kuchta, Clara	"Swiss Tapestries" (Exhibit)	Talley, Charles S.	√		Fa	7	6		N/D 80	74
People: Kuhre, Carol	Athens Tapestry Works	Many, Paul	√		Fa	5	4		J/A 78	51
People: Kukkasjärvi, Irma	Reinterpreting Rya: Irma Kukkasjärvi Energizes an Ancient Technique	Ojala, Liisa Kanning	√		WJ	9	4	36	Sp 85	26
People: Kukkasjarvi, Irma	"Scandinavian Touch, The" A Traveling Exhibit (Exhibit)	Mattera, Joanna	√		Fa	10	1		J/F 83	82
People: Kundel, Alice	Handwoven Clothing Today: The Couturier Touch	West, Virginia	√		Fa	8	1		J/F 81	39
People: Kuno, Toshihiro	Twelfth International Biennial of Tapestry	Taylor, Dianne; Elmer Taylor	√		Fa	12	6		N/D 85	50
People: Kurosu, Reiko	"Fiber As Art" An Exhibition in the Philippines (Exhibit)		√		Fa	7	6		N/D 80	76
People: Kuryluk, Ewa	Ewa Kuryluk: Distillations in Fiber	Scarborough, Jessica	√		Fa	12	2		M/A 85	14
People: Kusama, Tetsuo	"Contemporary Japanese Tapestry, The" (Exhibit)	Glass, Laurie H.	√		Fa	4	6		N/D 77	22
People: Kusama, Tetsuo	Contemporary Tapestry in Japan: Individuality After Centuries of Textile Conformity	Lindenfeld, Lore	√		Fa	10	3		M/J 83	44
People: Kusama, Tetsuo	"Fiber Works — Americas & Japan" (Exhibit)	Kato, Kuniko Lucy	√		Fa	5	1		J/F 78	10
People: Kusama, Tetsuo	Lausanne Notebook: Our Special Report on the 8th Lausanne Biennial of Tapestry, A	Mathews, Rich	√		Fa	4	5		S/O 77	30
People: Kushner, Robert	Pattern...Pattern...Pattern	Park, Betty	√		Fa	9	1		J/F 82	11
People: Kuter, Leslie	Textile Trends: Collecting in Washington, D.C.	Goodman, Deborah Lerme	√		Fa	12	6		N/D 85	25

SUBJECT	TITLE	AUTHOR	IL	INST	JOUR	VOL	NO	ISS	DATE	PAGE
People: Kuwarbara, Nancy	Handwoven Clothing Today: The Couturier Touch	West, Virginia	√		Fa	8	1		J/F 81	39
People: Kwiatkowski, Ron	Jurying	Ligon, Linda	√		Iw	1	2		Wi 76	10
People: La France, Linda Fox	Linda Fox La France: Designer — Tapestry Weaver	Hunt, Elizabeth Ann	√		Iw	4	2		Sp 79	36
People: La Palma	"Wearables" (Exhibit)	Grover, Donald	√		Fa	6	6		N/D 79	76
People: La Pierre, Sharon	Sharon La Pierre		√		Fa	4	1		J/F 77	28
People: Labarthe, Caroll	Fashionable Palette of Pittsburgh Paints, The	Brenholts, Jeanne	√		Fa	14	3		M/J 87	46
People: Labbens, Soizik	Quilting in France	Smeltzer, Nancy	√		Fa	13	2		M/A 86	49
People: Lackey, Elaine	Textile Apprenticeship in Northern California	Montgomery, Larry			TM			9	F/M 87	20
People: Lackey, Jane	Jane Lackey: A Vision Into Past and Future	Corwin, Nancy	√		Fa	13	6		N/D 86	18
People: Lackey, Jane	"Three Weavers: Thomasin Grim, Jane Lackey, Bhakti Ziek" (Exhibit)	Rowley, Kathleen	√		Fa	9	6		N/D 82	82
People: Lagerfeld, Karl	Knitting Odyssey, A	Dyett, Linda	√	√	TM			13	O/N 87	48
People: Lagerfeld, Karl	When Is Art Fashion and Fashion Art?	Martin, Richard	√		TM			11	J/J 87	12
People: Lahaussois, Betsy	Machine Knitting: The State of the Art		√		Fa	9	2		M/A 82	40
People: Laky, Gyöngy	Convergence Preview — Six Peaks, A		√		SS&D	11	2	42	Sp 80	47
People: Laky, Gyöngy	Gyöngy Laky: Experimental Thinking in Textiles	Scarborough, Jessica	√		Fa	11	1		J/F 84	21
People: Laky, Gyöngy	Gyongy Laky's Transformations (Exhibit)		√		Fa	13	4		J/A 86	54
People: Laky, Gyöngy	Interview ith Gyöngy Laky, An		√		Fa	4	2		M/A 77	24
People: Lala, Susan	Profile of an HGA Rep		√		SS&D	16	4	64	Fa 85	87
People: LaLena, Constance	By the Yard	Mattera, Joanne	√		TM			5	J/J 86	50
People: LaLena, Constance	Connie LaLena: Colonial Textiles Today	Ligon, Linda	√		Iw	3	1		Fa 77	15
People: LaLena, Constance	Three Production Weavers: Constance LaLena		√		Hw	3	3		My 82	52
People: Laman, Jean	"Houston Designer-Craftsmen 1976" (Exhibit)	Vander Lee, Jana	√		Fa	3	4		J/A 76	9
People: Lamb, Lisa	"With or Without a Loom" (Exhibit)	Rowley, Kristin Carlsen	√		Fa	8	5		S/O 81	67
People: Lamb, Liza	Liza Lamb	Rowley, Kristin	√		Fa	13	5		S/O 86	18
People: Lambert, Barbara	Metamorphosis in Maine: The Art of Barbara Lambert	Levy, Beverly Sauer	√		Fa	11	3		M/J 84	20
People: Lambert, Ed	"Fiber As Art" An Exhibition in the Philippines (Exhibit)		√		Fa	7	6		N/D 80	76
People: Lambert, Ed	Silks of Ed Lambert: In Pursuit of the Moving Image, The	Whittaker, Lynn	√		Fa	9	5		S/O 82	60
People: Lampe, Eia	Eia Lampe Advocates Classical Weaving Techniques For Today		√		H&C	17	2		Sp 66	6
People: Lancaster, Zoe Woodroof	Design by the Yard: Today's Fabric Innovators	Scarborough, Jessica	√		Fa	12	5		S/O 85	30
People: Lancaster, Zoe Woodruff	Silkworks	Goodman, Deborah Lerme	√		Fa	13	1		J/F 86	50
People: Landers, Deborah	"Works in Fiber" (Exhibit)	Arnow, Jan	√		Fa	8	2		M/A 81	61
People: Landis, Lucille	Projects from a Connecticut Weaver	Krasnoff, Julienne	√	> 4	H&C	21	1		Wi 70	16
People: Landis, Lucille	"Weaving with Lucille Landis" (Exhibit)	Hartman, Shirley G.	√		Fa	9	2		M/A 82	76
People: Landis, Richard	"Fiber Works — Americas & Japan" (Exhibit)	Kato, Kuniko Lucy	√		Fa	5	1		J/F 78	10
People: Landis, Richard	"Wall Hangings: The New Classicism" (Exhibit)	Grover, Donald	√		Fa	4	4		J/A 77	10
People: Lange, Susan	Felt and Paper: A Portfolio		√		Fa	13	4		J/A 86	35
People: Langer, Joan	Pikes Peak Weavers Guild First Fibre Arts Festival (Exhibit)	Fife, Lin	√		Fa	3	5		S/O 76	6
People: Langlet, Ragnhild	"California Women in Crafts" (Exhibit)	Dyer, Carolyn	√		Fa	4	2		M/A 77	10
People: Langlet, Ragnhild	"Three Living Treasures from California" (Exhibit)	Brandford, Joanne Segal; Sandra Dickey Harner	√		Fa	12	5		S/O 85	70
People: Langlet, Ragnild	"Fiberworks 1976" (Exhibit)	Papa, Nancy	√		Fa	4	1		J/F 77	9

SUBJECT	TITLE	AUTHOR	IL	INST	JOUR	VOL	NO	ISS	DATE	PAGE
People: Langlet, Ranghild	On Fabric in the Southwest: Surface Design, A Bank, and Public Recognition	Brooks, Lois Ziff	√		Fa	6	5		S/O 79	54
People: Lapin, Claudia	Fixing to Dye: Confessions of a Silk Addict	Lapin, Claudia	√	√	Fa	5	1		J/F 78	30
People: LaPlantz, Shereen	"Basketry Today: And Quilts from the Collection of Phyllis Haders" (Exhibits)	von Weise, Wenda	√		Fa	9	4		J/A 82	75
People: LaPlantz, Shereen	Day in the Life of a Basketmaker: The Very Personal Approach of Shereen LaPlantz, A	LaPlantz, Shereen	√		Fa	6	6		N/D 79	6
People: LaPlantz, Shereen	What Makes a Basket a Basket?	Malarcher, Patricia	√		Fa	11	1		J/F 84	34
People: Larcade, Margaret	"Houston Designer-Craftsmen 1976" (Exhibit)	Vander Lee, Jana	√		Fa	3	4		J/A 76	9
People: Larkin, Anya	Fabric Painting in New York	Katz, Ruth J.	√		Fa	9	1		J/F 82	61
People: Larkin, Christina	Contemporary Needle Lacers		√		TM			13	O/N 87	44
People: Larochette, Jean Pierre	San Francisco Tapestry Workshop: A European-Style Atelier in the United States, The	Rowley, Kathleen	√		Fa	10	3		M/J 83	60
People: Larochette, Jean Pierre	Weaving in San Francisco — Part 1	Prosser, Evelyn Bingham	√		WJ	6	2	22	Fa 81	44
People: Larochette, Jean-Pierre	Aubusson Tapestry	Larochette, Jean-Pierre	√		SS&D	13	4	52	Fa 82	5
People: Larochette, Jean-Pierre	Imagery Is Personal in Tapestry Today	Clausen, Valerie	√		TM			9	F/M 87	66
People: Larochette, Jean-Pierre	Yael Lurie — Other Places, Other Visions	Tannenbaum, Ruth	√		Fa	5	6		N/D 78	40
People: LaRoque, Jane V. Lowell	Pictorial Tapestry: A Portfolio of Contemporary Work	Goodman, Deborah Lerme	√		Fa	10	3		M/J 83	29
People: Larsen, Jack Lenor	Exhibition by Larsen and Riegger Indicates Broadening Field of Craft Cooperation		√		H&C	2	2		Sp 51	32
People: Larsen, Jack Lenor	Interview with Jack Lenor Larsen, An		√		WJ	7	1	25	Su 82	10
People: Larsen, Jack Lenor	Jack Lenor Larsen		√		SS&D	15	4	60	Fa 84	22
People: Larsen, Jack Lenor	Jack Lenor Larsen		√		H&C	11	2		Sp 60	22
People: Larsen, Jack Lenor	Jack Lenor Larsen				Iw	4	3		Su 79	24
People: Larsen, Jack Lenor	Jack Lenor Larsen	Znamierowski, Nell	√		H&C	22	3		Su 71	6
People: Larsen, Jack Lenor	"Jack Lenor Larsen: 30 Years of Creative Textiles" (Exhibit)	Zoppetti, Patti	√		Fa	9	5		S/O 82	82
People: Larsen, Jack Lenor	Jack Lenor Larsen: Convergence '76 Keynoter		√		SS&D	7	1	25	Wi 75	4
People: Larsen, Jack Lenor	Made by Machine: Textiles for the Eighties	Harris, Patricia; David Lyon	√		Fa	12	5		S/O 85	34
People: Larsen, Jack Lenor	Talk with Jack Lenor Larsen, A		√		SS&D	12	2	46	Sp 81	11
People: Larsen, Jack Lenor	Taproot: Jack Lenor Larsen	Goldin, Susan	√		Iw	4	3		Su 79	17
People: Larsen, Jack Lenor	Terra Nova: Jack Lenor Larsen	Larson-Fleming, Susan	√		WJ	11	1	41	Su 86	49
People: Larson, Jack Lenor	Designers on Design		√		Fa	10	4		J/A 83	28
People: Larson, Lois	Design Exercises for Inspitarion and Fun	McNair, Peg	√	√	Fa	14	1		J/F 87	47
People: Larzelere, Judith Ann	"Quilt National '87" (Exhibit)		√		Fa	14	3		M/J 87	62
People: Lasseau, Benjie	"Fibers: From Function to Formalization" (Exhibit)	Scarborough, Jessica	√		Fa	9	1		J/F 82	76
People: Latkowska-Zychska, Ewa	Lausanne Notebook: Our Special Report on the 8th Lausanne Biennial of Tapestry, A	Mathews, Rich	√		Fa	4	5		S/O 77	30
People: Laurell, Karl	Fabrics from the Looms of Karl Laurell		√		H&C	2	4		Fa 51	9
People: Lauretano, Janet	"100% Wool" (Exhibit)	Goldin, Susan	√		Fa	4	6		N/D 77	18
People: Laury, Jean Ray	"Jean Ray Laury — Exhibit of Stitchery" (Exhibit)	Gutcheon, Beth	√		Fa	6	2		M/A 79	66
People: Laury, Jean Ray	"Jean Ray Laury: Quilted Work" (Exhibit)	Sprague, Mary	√		Fa	9	1		J/F 82	84
People: Lautz, Lynn	Liturgical Vestment: A Contemporary Overview, The	Malarcher, Patricia	√		Fa	11	5		S/O 84	58
People: Lavonen, Maija	Contemporary Textile Art in Scandinavia	Talley, Charles S.	√		Fa	9	6		N/D 82	43
People: Law, Rachael Nash	"Basketworks": Visit to an Exhibition (Exhibit)		√		Fa	9	1		J/F 82	17
People: Lawty, Sue	Imagery Is Personal in Tapestry Today	Clausen, Valerie	√		TM			9	F/M 87	66

SUBJECT	TITLE	AUTHOR	IL	INST	JOUR	VOL	NO	ISS	DATE	PAGE
People: Lawty, Sue	Sue Lawty: Journeying in Tapestry	Dunwell, Anna	√		Fa	11	2		M/A 84	12
People: Layman, Marie	"Marie Lyman: Liturgical Vestments" (Exhibit)	Griffin, Rachel	√		Fa	7	3		M/J 80	77
People: Laymon, Cynthia	"Cynthia Laymon: Fiber/Paper Constructions" (Exhibits)	Syverson, Gilda Morina	√		Fa	9	4		J/A 82	71
People: Laymon, Cynthia	Cynthia Laymon: Pleated Interplay	Michaels-Paque, Joan	√		Fa	12	5		S/O 85	12
People: Laymon, Cynthia	Public Fiber: Looking At the Logistics	Koplos, Janet	√		Fa	12	1		J/F 85	32
People: Laymon, Cynthia	"Survey of Illinois Fiber" (Exhibit)	Jensen, Janet	√		Fa	5	5		S/O 78	69
People: LeClerc, Alfred	LeClerc Loom Corporation, A Story of Three Generations, The	Holland, Nina	√		H&C	24	3		M/J 73	20
People: Leduc, Isabelle	"Third Montreal Tapestry Biennial, 1984" (Exhibit)	Duffy, Helen	√		Fa	12	3		M/J 85	79
People: Lee, Anong	Fiber At Artpark	MacDonald, Claudia	√		Fa	10	6		N/D 83	47
People: Lee, Dong Chun	"Partners in Art: Brushwork by Lee, Dong Chun and Embroidery by Yu, Chug Hee" (Exhibit)	Backer, Ellen	√		Fa	4	3		M/J 77	16
People: Lee, Mary	Exploring a Tradition: Navajo Rugs, Classic and Contemporary	Elliott, Malinda	√		Fa	11	3		M/J 84	32
People: Lee, Ralph	Maskmaker Ralph Lee: Master Minding a Ghoulish Event	Murray, Megan	√		Fa	11	5		S/O 84	34
People: Leeds, Alice Whitman	Extra, Extra!!		√		Fa	13	4		J/A 86	73
People: Leffingwell, Jeanne	Keeping Warm in Alaska		√		Fa	9	6		N/D 82	22
People: Leffingwell, Jeanne	Sky Curtain (Jeanne Leffingwell)		√		TM			2	D/J 85	88
People: Legge, Jean	"Decade of Fibers, A" (Exhibit)	Franklin, Sue	√		Fa	5	1		J/F 78	17
People: Legrand, Didier	Didier Legrand: Magic Afoot	Monico, Michele	√		Fa	12	4		J/A 85	12
People: Legrand, Didier	Under Wraps		√		Fa	12	3		M/J 85	26
People: Lehman, Connie	Connie Lehman: Portable Secrets	Clurman, Irene	√		Fa	12	6		N/D 85	10
People: Lehman, Connie McEntire	Connie McEntire Lehman's Side Glances from Drawings Into Dye-Painted Hangings	Clurman, Irene	√		Fa	8	5		S/O 81	26
People: Lehrer, Warren	Grrrhhhh: A Study of Social Patterns	Hickman, Deborah	√		Fa	14	4		S/O 87	23
People: Lein, Greta	Greta Lein, Young Norweigan Designer-Weaver	Nygards-Kers, Ingrid	√		H&C	14	1		Wi 63	15
People: LeLena, Constance	Production Weaving: From Nature-Inspired Warps to Linsey-Woolsey	Ligon, Linda	√		Iw	1	2		Wi 76	6
People: LeMar, Christine	Who Weaves?		√		Iw	5	2		Sp 80	35/42
People: Leogrande, Rene	More 1978 Scholarships		√		SS&D	10	1	37	Wi 78	107
People: Leppick, Mary	Everyday World of Fantasy, The	Smeltzer, Nancy	√		Fa	13	3		M/J 86	6
People: Les, Frances	Papermaking as a Recycling Process: The Work of Frances Les	Les, Kathleen	√		Fa	6	4		J/A 79	18
People: Lesch, Alma	"Web of Kentucky Thread, A" (Exhibit)	Meloy, Margaret	√		Fa	12	5		S/O 85	72
People: Lessman-Moss, Janice	Janice Lessman-Moss: Fiber Structures and Cultivated Contrasts	McClelland, Elizabeth	√		Fa	11	6		N/D 84	18
People: Lester, Michelle	Evolution of an Artist: Michelle Lester	Malarcher, Pat	√		Fa	14	5		N/D 87	22
People: Lester, Michelle	Michelle Lester	Preston, P. K.	√		Fa	5	2		M/A 78	48
People: Lester, Michelle	"Michelle Lester: New Tapestries" (Exhibit)	Park, Betty	√		Fa	6	1		J/F 79	85
People: Lester, Michelle	"Mini Tapestry Exhibit" (Exhibit)	Bockelman, JoAnne	√		Fa	5	4		J/A 78	12
People: Lester, Michelle	Questions of Style: Contemporary Trends in the Fiber Arts	Howe-Echt, Katherine	√		Fa	7	2		M/A 80	38
People: Lester, Michelle	Speakers Bureau Presents		√		SS&D	5	4	20	Fa 74	65
People: Lester, Michelle	Tapestry Gallery		√		Iw	4	2		Sp 79	34
People: Levin, Linda	Linda Levin: Quilted Impressions	Goodman, Deborah Lerme	√		Fa	14	2		M/A 87	13
People: Levittoux-Swiderska, Barbara	"22 Polish Textile Artists" (Exhibit)	Park, Betty	√		Fa	4	5		S/O 77	8
People: Levy, Abigail Jurist	Abigail Jurist Levy: Dyed Paper and Silk Assemblages	Goodman, Deborah Lerme	√		Fa	12	4		J/A 85	16
People: Lewbell, Lynne	"Seven Sonoma County Fibre Artists" (Exhibit)	Robinson, Sharon	√		Fa	3	4		J/A 76	6
People: Lewis, Robin	Big Bobbin Lace	Scanlin, Tommye McClure	√		Fa	13	2		M/A 86	32

SUBJECT	TITLE	AUTHOR	IL	INST	JOUR	VOL	NO	ISS	DATE	PAGE
People: Lewis, Susanna	Designers on Design		√		Fa	10	4		J/A 83	28
People: Lewis, Susanna	Machine Knitting: The State of the Art		√		Fa	9	2		M/A 82	40
People: Lewis, Susanna	Susanna Lewis	Malarcher, Pat	√		Fa	5	3		M/J 78	52
People: Lewis, Susanna	Susanna Lewis' "State of the Art" — A Lecture		√		Fa	9	2		M/A 82	47
People: Lewis, Susanna	Swatching		√	√	Kn	3	4	8	Fa 87	42
People: Libes, Sharon	"Patterns" (Exhibit)	Malarcher, Patricia	√		Fa	10	2		M/A 83	76
People: Licea, Erica	"Fiber/Fabric '81" (Exhibit)	Scarborough, Jessica	√		Fa	8	4		J/A 81	74
People: Licea-Kane, Erica	Out of the Blue: Aerial Images		√		Fa	13	5		S/O 86	44
People: Lichtenstein, Roy	"Modern Aubusson Tapestry, The" (Exhibit)	Tanenbaum, Ruth	√		Fa	5	3		M/J 78	14
People: Lichterman, Heidi	Handwoven Clothing Today: The Couturier Touch	West, Virginia	√		Fa	8	1		J/F 81	39
People: Lieberman, Louis	Papermaking in the U.S.A.	Toale, Bernard	√		Fa	9	4		J/A 82	34
People: Liebes, Dorothy	Dorothy Liebes		√		H&C	11	2		Sp 60	18
People: Liebes, Dorothy	Sense of the Individual, The	Janeiro, Jan	√		Fa	11	2		M/A 84	52
People: Liebes, Dorothy Wright	Legacy of Color and Texture: Dorothy Liebes, 1899-1972, A	Weltge, Sigrid	√		lw	4	3		Su 79	25
People: Liebes, Dorothy Wright	Liebes Legacy, The	Roth, Bettie G.	√		SS&D	13	2	50	Sp 82	18
People: Lind, Amy Jo	Fiber and Architecture: Amy Jo Lind and Maggie Nicholson		√		Fa	3	3		M/J 76	16
People: Lindao de Cruz, Doña Isabela	Weaving a Cotton Saddlebag on the Santa Elena Peninsula of Ecuador	Hagino, Jane Parker; Karen E. Stothert	√	√	TMJ	22			83	19
People: Lindgren, Jill	Jill Lindgren: Costuming for Opera	Elliott, Malinda	√		Fa	11	5		S/O 84	62
People: Lindquist, Ona	Plastics in Fiber: A Persistent Presence	Malarcher, Patricia	√		Fa	12	1		J/F 85	56
People: Lindsay, Kate	Contemporary California Costume	Poon, Vivian	√		Fa	11	5		S/O 84	53
People: Lindsay, R. H.	Know Your Supplier				S-O	11	3		Fa 87	41
People: Linfault, Joan	"Frontiers of Contemporary Weaving" (Exhibit)	Clark, Barbara	√		Fa	4	1		J/F 77	6
People: Lingwood, Rex	"Skin Forms: Innovations in Leather" (Exhibit)	Mackin, Jeanne	√		Fa	7	2		M/A 80	67
People: Lintault, Joan	Color Xerography and the Fiber Artist	Theil, Linda	√		Fa	8	5		S/O 81	59
People: Lintault, Joan	"Printed, Painted, and Dyed: The New Fabric Surface" (Exhibit)	Hecker, Carolyn	√		Fa	5	6		N/D 78	71
People: Lintault, Joan	"Robin Becker and Joan Lintault: Visual Traces of the Past" (Exhibit)	Meloy, Margaret	√		Fa	11	1		J/F 84	80
People: Lintault, M. Joan	"Beds, Sweet Dreams, and Other Things" (Exhibit)	Bissell, June	√		Fa	6	4		J/A 79	70
People: Lipetz, Lin	"Basket and Paper Invitational Show" (Exhibit)	Howe, Cathe	√		Fa	12	3		M/J 85	71
People: Lipke, Kathryn	"Kathryn Lipke/Fiber-Paper-Pulp: Works in Handmade Paper" (Exhibit)	Piazza, Virginia	√		Fa	4	4		J/A 77	13
People: Lipke, Kathryn	Sculptural Paper: Foundations and Directions	Scarborough, Jessica	√		Fa	11	2		M/A 84	32
People: Lipkin, Janet	Art to Wear: Looking At the Movement	Scarborough, Jessica	√		Fa	12	3		M/J 85	56
People: Lipkin, Janet	Artwear '87				TM			10	A/M 87	22
People: Lipkin, Janet	Under Wraps		√		Fa	12	3		M/J 85	26
People: Lippold, Carol	"Detailed Directions in Fiber" (Exhibit)	Van Gelder, Lydia	√		Fa	9	3		M/J 82	77
People: Lippold, Larry	"Fiber R/Evolution" (Exhibit)	Rudich, Sally	√		Fa	13	4		J/A 86	45
People: Lippold, Larry	Fragil Landscape	Akamine, Estelle	√		TM			5	J/J 86	88
People: Lipshie, Amy	"Amy Lipshie: Tapestries" (Exhibit)	Park, Betty	√		Fa	12	3		M/J 85	76
People: Lipson, Michelle	"Printed, Painted, and Dyed: The New Fabric Surface" (Exhibit)	Hecker, Carolyn	√		Fa	5	6		N/D 78	71
People: Liss, Ellen	Ellen Liss: Machine-Knit Wearables	Goodman, Deborah Lerme	√		Fa	11	4		J/A 84	16
People: Liss, Ellen	Under Wraps		√		Fa	12	3		M/J 85	26
People: Littlefield, Pat	Felt and Paper: A Portfolio		√		Fa	13	4		J/A 86	35
People: Litvak, Gale	Who Weaves?		√		lw	5	2		Sp 80	40

SUBJECT	TITLE	AUTHOR	IL	INST	JOUR	VOL	NO	ISS	DATE	PAGE
People: Livingstone, Joan	Feltmaking Now: The Exciting Revival of an Ancient Technique	Gordon, Beverly	√		Fa	6	6		N/D 79	43
People: Livingstone, Joan	"Fiber Works — Americas & Japan" (Exhibit)	Kato, Kuniko Lucy	√		Fa	5	1		J/F 78	10
People: Livingstone, Joan	"Joan Livingstone: Lamia Lemures" (Exhibit)	Malarcher, Patricia	√		Fa	7	4		J/A 80	67
People: Livingstone, Joan	"Joan Livingstone/Recent Work: Felt/Wood" (Exhibit)	Park, Betty	√		Fa	4	4		J/A 77	14
People: Livingstone, Joan	Twelfth International Biennial of Tapestry	Taylor, Dianne; Elmer Taylor	√		Fa	12	6		N/D 85	50
People: Livingstone, Karen	Tailor's Logic	Hostek, Stanley	√	√	TM			14	D/J 87	42
People: Lizon, Tana Krizova	"Fiber 82: Miniatures" (Exhibits)	Brown, Arleen Emery	√		Fa	9	4		J/A 82	72
People: Lloyd, Marcia	"Skin Forms: Innovations in Leather" (Exhibit)	Mackin, Jeanne	√		Fa	7	2		M/A 80	67
People: Lochmiller, Linda	"Ceremonial Garments" (Exhibit)	Laymon, Cynthia	√		Fa	9	6		N/D 82	82
People: Lockwood, Diana	Ecclesiastical Weavings of Diana Lockwood, The		√	> 4	WJ	4	3	15	Ja 80	18
People: Logsdon, Woody	Photoweavings of Woody Logsdon, The	Logsdon, Anne	√		Fa	14	4		S/O 87	26
People: Lohmann, Pat	"Soft Art" (Exhibit)	Richerson, Suzanne	√		Fa	4	4		J/A 77	16
People: Lohnes, Albert	Albert Lohnes		√		Fa	5	3		M/J 78	53
People: Loney, Kit	Paper Palettes, A Profile of Kit Loney		√		SS&D	18	2	70	Sp 87	81
People: Long, Mary Ellen	Felt and Paper: A Portfolio		√		Fa	13	4		J/A 86	35
People: Lønning, Kari	Art That Functions	Lønning, Kari	√		Fa	8	3		M/J 81	40
People: Lønning, Kari	Kari Lønning		√		Fa	4	4		J/A 77	49
People: Lønning, Kari	Kari Lønning: Exploring Color and Form in Rattan	Lønning, Kari	√	√	Fa	11	1		J/F 84	12
People: Lønning, Kari	"Kari Lønning — Mary Billingsley" (Exhibit)	Beede, Beth	√		Fa	6	6		N/D 79	69
People: Look, Dona	Fiber in the Nation's Capital	Goodman, Deborah Lerme	√		Fa	11	6		N/D 84	48
People: Loud, Dana	Two Dimensions in a 3-D Disguise		√		Fa	14	3		M/J 87	75
People: Lowe, Connie	"Connections" (Exhibit)	Constantinides, Kathy	√		Fa	6	4		J/A 79	74
People: Lowell, Carol	Under Wraps		√		Fa	12	3		M/J 85	26
People: Lowell, Joan	Pikes Peak Weavers Guild First Fibre Arts Festival (Exhibit)	Fife, Lin	√		Fa	3	5		S/O 76	6
People: Lozano, Matias	Matias Lozano, Designer Weaver		√		H&C	10	1		Wi 59	28
People: Lubove-Klein, Carole	Fiber Ten	McGuire, Patricia	√		Fa	4	6		N/D 77	26
People: Lubove-Klein, Carole	Recent Success of Carole Lubove-Klein: An Inspiring Yarn, The	McGuire, Patricia	√		Fa	9	5		S/O 82	20
People: Luchessa, Gayle	"Contemporary Directions in Fiber" (Exhibit)	Meloy, Margaret	√		Fa	14	4		S/O 87	42
People: Luchessa, Gayle	"Felting" (Exhibit)	Park, Betty	√		Fa	7	6		N/D 80	71
People: Luchessa, Gayle	Gayle Luchessa	Papa, Nancy	√		Fa	4	5		S/O 77	56
People: Luksus, Tzaims	Tzaims Luksus		√		H&C	14	1		Wi 63	12
People: Lundberg, Thomas	Liberated Embroidery		√		Fa	9	3		M/J 82	35
People: Lundberg, Thomas	"Thomas Lundberg" (Exhibit)	Itter, Diane	√		Fa	10	4		J/A 83	67
People: Lundgren, Jorjanna	Fiber Artists Find New Showcase in San Diego (Exhibit)	Meilach, Dona	√		Fa	3	4		J/A 76	8
People: Lurçat, Jean	Brief History of the International Biennial of Tapestry or "Watch Out for Women Who Knit", A	Taylor, Dianne	√		Fa	10	5		S/O 83	43
People: Lurçat, Jean	Imagery Is Personal in Tapestry Today	Clausen, Valerie	√		TM			9	F/M 87	66
People: Lurie, Amanda	Amanda Lurie: One Weaver's Path	Lurie, Amanda	√		Fa	10	4		J/A 83	16
People: Lurie, Yael	Imagery Is Personal in Tapestry Today	Clausen, Valerie	√		TM			9	F/M 87	66
People: Lurie, Yael	San Francisco Tapestry Workshop: A European-Style Atelier in the United States, The	Rowley, Kathleen	√		Fa	10	3		M/J 83	60
People: Lurie, Yael	Yael Lurie — Other Places, Other Visions	Tannenbaum, Ruth	√		Fa	5	6		N/D 78	40
People: Lust, Scarlatina	T-Shirts for Every Body: 20th Century Folkwear		√		Fa	8	6		N/D 81	22

552

SUBJECT	TITLE	AUTHOR	IL	INST	JOUR	VOL	NO	ISS	DATE	PAGE
People: Lustig, Marlena	Getting Into the Galleries: Nine Dealers Tell How to Do It		√		Fa	9	5		S/O 82	43
People: Luttikhuizen, Esther	Stitched, Stuffed, and Painted: The Art of Esther Luttikhuizen	Acosta, Dan	√		Fa	12	2		M/A 85	61
People: Lyman, Constance	Papermaking in Chicago	Shermeta, Margo	√		Fa	11	2		M/A 84	54
People: Lyman, Lucy	Knitting for a Living (error-corrected TM i6 A/S86 p6)	Guagliumi, Susan	√		TM			4	A/M 86	38
People: Lyman, Susan	"Basket-Maker's Art, The" (Exhibit)	Grover, Donald	√		Fa	6	6		N/D 79	73
People: Lyman, Susan	Papermaking in the U.S.A.	Toale, Bernard	√		Fa	9	4		J/A 82	34
People: Lyman, Susan	"Susan Lyman's Paper Structures" (Exhibit)	Roberts, Stephen	√		Fa	8	5		S/O 81	69
People: Lyman, Susan	"Terminal": Drawing in Three Dimensions	Lyman, Susan	√		Fa	11	4		J/A 84	60
People: Lyon, Nancy	Crackle Weave, Part 1	Lyon, Nancy	√	√	SS&D	19	1	73	Wi 87	21
People: Lyon, Nancy	Designer Nancy Lyon				SS&D	11	2	42	Sp 80	16
People: Måås-Fjetterström, Märta	Harts and Flowers: Sweden's Märta Måås-Fjetterstrom's Designs Inspired a Textile Renaissance	Selkurt, Claire	√		WJ	9	4	36	Sp 85	30
People: Mabee-Zust, Mariah	Double Edge of Knitting, The	Mabee-Zust, Mariah	√		Fa	10	3		M/J 83	50
People: Mabry, Gwenyth	Fiber and Architecture: Gwenyth Mabry		√		Fa	3	3		M/J 76	24
People: MacCallum, Barbara	Barbara MacCallum	Gordon, Lida	√		Fa	14	3		M/J 87	22
People: MacCallum, Barbara	"Barbara MacCallum: Recent Work" (Exhibit)	Schedl, Naomi Kark	√		Fa	12	4		J/A 85	68
People: MacCallum, Barbara	"Interweave '78" (Exhibit)	Yarnell, Grace	√		Fa	5	6		N/D 78	69
People: MacCallum, Barbara	Plastics in Fiber: A Persistent Presence	Malarcher, Patricia	√		Fa	12	1		J/F 85	56
People: MacCallum, Barbara	Structure and Surface: The Work of Barbara MacCallum	Koplos, Janet	√		Fa	10	2		M/A 83	62
People: MacDonald, Elizabeth	Elizabeth MacDonald: Finding the Ties That Bind Truth and Art	Reuter, Laurel	√		Fa	14	4		S/O 87	31
People: MacDonald, Linda	"Five Artists: Quilts" (Exhibit)	Scarborough, Jessica	√		Fa	13	5		S/O 86	47
People: MacDongal, Marleah	"Free Flow" (Exhibit)	Hecker, Carolyn	√		Fa	5	5		S/O 78	74
People: Mack-Pachler, Ilona	Textile Study Group, The (Exhibit)	Guagliumi, Susan	√		Fa	13	3		M/J 86	54
People: MacKenzie, Clinton	HGA Board Candidates: Vote for Three		√		SS&D	10	2	38	Sp 79	49
People: MacKenzie, Clinton	Questions of Style: Contemporary Trends in the Fiber Arts	Howe-Echt, Katherine	√		Fa	7	2		M/A 80	38
People: MacLeod, Sondra	Watercolors in Fiber: The Flower Tapestries of Sondra MacLeod	LeMaistre, Margaret	√		SS&D	17	3	67	Su 86	21
People: MacNutt, Dawn	Dawn MacNutt: Sculptural Weaver	LeMaistre, Margaret	√		SS&D	17	2	66	Sp 86	48
People: MacNutt, Dawn	"Trees and Other Things" (Exhibit)	Hillis, Anne	√		Fa	5	4		J/A 78	17
People: Macrorie, Joyce	"Entanglements" (Exhibit)	Markle, Marsha	√		Fa	4	2		M/A 77	16
People: Madsen, Britta	Contemporary Textile Art in Scandinavia	Talley, Charles S.	√		Fa	9	6		N/D 82	43
People: Mafong, Richard	Riis, Mafong Collaborate in Thread & Silver		√		SS&D	5	1	17	Wi 73	4
People: Mahall, Mark	Safety-Pin Jacket (Mark Mahall)		√		TM			9	F/M 87	88
People: Mahon, Martha	Martha Mahon: Tableaux	Fife, Lin	√		Fa	13	6		N/D 86	29
People: Mahoney, Leanne	Leanne Mahoney: Costuming for Ballet	Tejeda, Christina	√		Fa	11	5		S/O 84	64
People: Mailes, Gene	Dream—The Reality, The	Ligon, Linda	√		Iw	3	4		Su 78	12
People: Mailey, Jean	American Handweaving 1960		√		H&C	11	2		Sp 60	8
People: Maines, Rachel	C.H.A.N. for Short: The Story of Rachel Maines	Alonso, Harriet	√		Fa	8	3		M/J 81	13
People: Mairet, Ethel	"Weaver's Life, Ethel Mairet, 1872–1952, A" (Exhibit)	Waller, Irene	√		Fa	11	4		J/A 84	78
People: Malarcher, Pat	"Ruth Geneslaw/Pat Malarcher" (Exhibit)	Guyar, Niki	√		Fa	6	4		J/A 79	66
People: Malarcher, Patricia	"Patricia Malarcher: Pieced Reflections" (Exhibit)	Scheinman, Pamela	√		Fa	11	2		M/A 84	77
People: Malarcher, Patricia	Silkworks	Goodman, Deborah Lerme	√		Fa	13	1		J/F 86	50
People: Malarcher, Patricia	"Weaving Without Fiber" (Exhibit)	Hempel, Toby Anne	√		Fa	13	5		S/O 86	48
People: Malerich, Lee A.	Lee A. Malerich	Malerich, Lee A.	√		Fa	14	1		J/F 87	27
People: Malmberg, Lars	Glimakra Looms' N Yarns	Xenakis, Alexis Yiorgos	√		PWC	4	1	11		48

SUBJECT	TITLE	AUTHOR	IL	INST	JOUR	VOL	NO	ISS	DATE	PAGE
People: Maltby, Hazel	Two Students of Theo Moorman: Hazel Maltby, Peg McNair		√		Fa	3	4		J/A 76	28
People: Mandell, Elizabeth	Getting Into the Galleries: Nine Dealers Tell How to Do It		√		Fa	9	5		S/O 82	43
People: Mangat, Terri	"Contemporary Quilts" (Exhibit)		√		Fa	8	3		M/J 81	74
People: Mangat, Terri	Creative Process: Terri Mangat, The	Mangat, Terri	√		Fa	11	6		N/D 84	36
People: Mangat, Terrie Hancock	"Quilt National '83" (Exhibit)	Roe, Nancy	√		Fa	10	5		S/O 83	82
People: Manger, Barbara	"Fiber R/Evolution" (Exhibit)	Rudich, Sally	√		Fa	13	4		J/A 86	45
People: Manger, Barbara	"New Wisconsin Fiber": The First Group Show of American Fiber Art in Switzerland (Exhibit)	Bard, Elizabeth A.	√		Fa	10	6		N/D 83	43
People: Maniates, Cynthia	McDonnell Douglas		√		Fa	12	5		S/O 85	65
People: Mannes, Eve	Getting Into the Galleries: Nine Dealers Tell How to Do It		√		Fa	9	5		S/O 82	43
People: Manno, Angela	Angela Manno	Manno, Angela	√		Fa	12	5		S/O 85	18
People: Manno, Angela	Verbena Collection, The (error-corrected Fa v11 n1 84 p11)		√		Fa	10	5		S/O 83	64
People: Mansfield, Pat	"Critters and Cohorts" (Exhibit)	Clark, Becky	√		Fa	4	6		N/D 77	13
People: Manual, K. Lee	Contemporary California Costume	Poon, Vivian	√		Fa	11	5		S/O 84	53
People: Manuel, K. Lee	Artwear '87				TM			10	A/M 87	22
People: Manuel, K. Lee	K. Lee Manuel: Wearable Dreams		√		Fa	3	5		S/O 76	12
People: Manuila-Howell, Sanda	Return of the Rag, The	Basa, Lynn	√		Fa	14	3		M/J 87	29
People: Marchi, Mary	Review/Discussion of Artspace's Innovative Yet Flawed "Fiber Freely Interpreted", A (Exhibit)		√		Fa	4	2		M/A 77	38
People: Marconi, Gloria	Gloria Marconi: A Commercial Illustrator Mixes Her Media	Hecker, Carolyn A.	√		Fa	6	2		M/A 79	31
People: Marcoux, Alice	Jacquard Project: Selections from the Current Exhibition, The		√		Fa	9	2		M/A 82	36
People: Marcus, Sharon	"Crafts Northwest, Circa 1980" (Exhibit)	Evans, Rojean; Louise Klemperer	√		Fa	7	5		S/O 80	75
People: Marcus, Sharon	Gallery (Tapestry)		√		Hw	3	1		Ja 82	48
People: Marcus, Sharon	International Tapestry (Exhibit)		√		Fa	13	4		J/A 86	59
People: Marcus, Sharon	Sharon Marcus	Marcus, Sharon	√		Fa	13	6		N/D 86	2
People: Marcus, Sharon	Sharon Marcus: Designing for Tapestry, One Approach to the Creative Process	Marcus, Sharon	√		Fa	11	6		N/D 84	26
People: Marcus, Sharon	"Woven Works: Tradition and Innovation" (Exhibit)	White, Patrick E.	√		Fa	12	6		N/D 85	60
People: Markarian	"Janet Markarian" (Exhibit)	Skudera, Gail	√		Fa	13	4		J/A 86	53
People: Markarian, Janet	Janet Markarian: From Baskets to Bags, Containers Transformed	Koplos, Janet	√		Fa	11	1		J/F 84	16
People: Markham, Gervase	Some Remarks on the Work of Markham	Stanton, R. G.; J. L. Allston	√	√	AT	2			De 84	95
People: Marois, Marcel	Imagery and Structure: The Tapestries of Marcel Marois	Russell, Elfleda	√		Fa	8	6		N/D 81	57
People: Marsh, Edith	Weaving Guilds—A Special Sharing		√		Iw	5	2		Sp 80	55
People: Marshall, Andrea	Warping It Up with Andrea	Duffy, Joe	√		SS&D	17	1	65	Wi 85	49
People: Marshall, John	Under Wraps		√		Fa	12	3		M/J 85	26
People: Martens, Chris	Miniatures in Fiber: Working Small—An Exciting Challenge for the Contemporary Fiber Artist	Malarcher, Patricia	√		Fa	7	4		J/A 80	32
People: Martens, Chris	"Women Artists: Clay, Fiber, Metal" (Exhibit)	Malarcher, Patricia	√		Fa	5	2		M/A 78	11
People: Martens, Christine	Liturgical Vestment: A Contemporary Overview, The	Malarcher, Patricia	√		Fa	11	5		S/O 84	58
People: Martens, Christine	"Voyage Continued" An Illuminating Experience (Exhibit)	Malarcher, Patricia	√		Fa	8	2		M/A 81	16
People: Martin, Donna	Donna Martin: The Influence of the Southwest	D'Andrea, Patricia A.	√		Fa	14	5		N/D 87	18
People: Martin, Edna	Contemporary Textile Art in Scandinavia	Talley, Charles S.	√		Fa	9	6		N/D 82	43

SUBJECT	TITLE	AUTHOR	IL	INST	JOUR	VOL	NO	ISS	DATE	PAGE
People: Martin, Kay	Junque Quilts	Murray, Clare	√		Fa	14	4		S/O 87	6
People: Martinez, Herminio	Herminio Martinez: Tejedor		√		Fa	8	6		N/D 81	24
People: Marto, Diana	Paper Clothing: West	Koplos, Janet	√		Fa	11	2		M/A 84	39
People: Marty, Kathleen	1977 HGA Scholarships (error-corrected SS&D v9 n2 78 p70)		√		SS&D	9	1	33	Wi 77	46
People: Marvin, Grace	Grace Marvin, Her Ideas on Making Clothing from Handwoven Fabrics		√	√	H&C	13	3		Su 62	14
People: Marvin, Grace	HGA Board of Directors Candidates		√		SS&D	11	2	42	Sp 80	26
People: Masafumi, Yamagishi	Lausanne Notebook: Our Special Report on the 8th Lausanne Biennial of Tapestry, A	Mathews, Rich	√		Fa	4	5		S/O 77	30
People: Mason, Ernest	Personal History Involving the Spinning Wheel and One Man's Insatiable Curiosity, A	Mathews, Tom	√		Fa	6	2		M/A 79	18
People: Mason, Kimberly	"Fibrations" (Exhibit)	Silver, Elizabeth	√		Fa	6	5		S/O 79	85
People: Masseau, Jean Carlson	Quilted Gardens of Jean Carlson Masseau, The	Pellegrino, Mary C.	√		Fa	13	2		M/A 86	9
People: Masseaw, Jean Carlson	Cows in Fiber	Timmons, Chris	√		Fa	11	4		J/A 84	55
People: Mather, Fran	By the Yard	Mattera, Joanne	√		TM			5	J/J 86	50
People: Mather, Fran	Fran Mather: Handweaving in Asheville, North Carolina	Mattera, Joanne	√		Fa	9	1		J/F 82	38
People: Mather, Fran	Handwoven Clothing Today: The Couturier Touch	West, Virginia	√		Fa	8	1		J/F 81	39
People: Mathews, Richard	Richard Mathews: Fiber Sculptor		√		Fa	3	1		J/F 76	12
People: Mathison, Fiona	Edinburgh Tapestry Company: A Thriving Anachronism in Scotland, The	Soroka, Joanne	√		Fa	10	3		M/J 83	59
People: Matiosian, Pamela	Mixed Media Vocabulary of Pamela Matiosian, The	Yovovich, Noël	√		Fa	13	6		N/D 86	6
People: Matlock, Ann	Ann Matlock	Erler, Mary	√		Fa	6	3		M/J 79	46
People: Matsubara, Fuyuko	"Show of Complements, A" (Exhibit)	Schevill, Margot Blum	√		Fa	13	4		J/A 86	50
People: Mattera, Joanne	"Fiber Drawings: Works in Thread on Paper" (Exhibit)	Krapes, Shelley	√		Fa	5	5		S/O 78	65
People: Mattera, Joanne	"Paper" (Exhibit)	Toale, Bernard	√		Fa	7	5		S/O 80	69
People: Mattera, Joanne	Thread of Continuity: Paper as Fabric, Craft as Art, and Other Ambiguities, The	Mattera, Joanne	√		Fa	6	4		J/A 79	31
People: Matthews, Martha	"Martha Matthews: Tapestry" (Exhibit)	Laymon, Cynthia	√		Fa	9	1		J/F 82	85
People: Matthews, Martha	Pictorial Tapestry: A Portfolio of Contemporary Work	Goodman, Deborah Lerme	√		Fa	10	3		M/J 83	29
People: Matzger, Lucy	Cylaine Handwoven Designs: Arlene Wohl and Lucy Matzger		√		WJ	7	3	27	Wi 82	8
People: Maxwell, Kathryn	Paper Works of Kathryn Maxwell, The	Martin, Robert	√		Fa	14	2		M/A 87	8
People: Maxwell, Linda	"Linda Maxwell and Caroline Dahl: Terror Sampler and Other Dogs" (Exhibit)	Poon, Vivian	√		Fa	11	6		N/D 84	79
People: Maxwell, Ruth	Postal Service Celebrates Lace		√		TM			12	A/S 87	22
People: Maxwell, Virginia	Washington Fiber	Mathews, Rich	√		Fa	3	5		S/O 76	9
People: May, April	April May: She Weaves Curtains with Images	Woelfle, Gretchen	√		Fa	7	6		N/D 80	28
People: May, April	April May: Visions of Space	May, April	√		Fa	10	6		N/D 83	22
People: May, April D.	Inner Visions	May, April D.	√		SS&D	15	3	59	Su 84	57
People: May, Therese	"Fiber Feelings" (Exhibit)	King, Dianne Hennessy	√		Fa	5	5		S/O 78	70
People: May, Therese	Therese May: Moving Freely from Fabric to Paint and Back Again	Huffaker, Katherine	√		Fa	9	1		J/F 82	26
People: May, Therese	Therese May: Risking to Grow	Scarborough, Jessica	√		Fa	12	4		J/A 85	15
People: Mayer, Anita	Anita Mayer	Wilson, Jean	√		Hw	2	2		Mr 81	28
People: Mayer, Francisca	Francisca Mayer, Designer-Weaver in the Peruvian Highland	Boyer, Ruth McDonald	√		H&C	19	2		Sp 68	18
People: Mayhew, Lewis	Lewis Mayhew, Versatile Northwest Weaver		√		H&C	14	3		Su 63	9
People: Maynard, Michele	Words in Fiber	Rowley, Kathleen	√		Fa	11	2		M/A 84	66

SUBJECT	TITLE	AUTHOR	IL	INST	JOUR	VOL	NO	ISS	DATE	PAGE
People: McAfee, Phoebe	Weaving in San Francisco — Part 1	Prosser, Evelyn Bingham	√		WJ	6	2	22	Fa 81	44
People: McAllister, Christine	Shady Ladies	Scarborough, Jessica	√		Fa	11	3		M/J 84	12
People: McCall, Philena	"Artists in Aprons" (Exhibit)	Alonzo, Harriet	√		Fa	6	3		M/J 79	76
People: McCandlish, Joan	Joan McCandlish	McCandlish, Joan	√		Fa	14	4		S/O 87	18
People: McClain, Patti Parks	Way We Wore: San Francisco's Museum of Vintage Fashion, The	Scarborough, Jessica	√		Fa	14	5		N/D 87	5
People: McClelland, Alice	Alice McClelland	Heath, Jennifer	√		Fa	5	4		J/A 78	50
People: McClelland, Patricia	"Patricia McClelland: Woven Work" (Exhibit)	MacNutt, Dawn	√		Fa	7	5		S/O 80	74
People: McClendon, Maxine	"Houston Designer-Craftsmen 1976" (Exhibit)	Vander Lee, Jana	√		Fa	3	4		J/A 76	9
People: McConahay, Shirley	"Fibers" (Exhibit)	Meyer, Zach	√		Fa	4	4		J/A 77	11
People: McCormick-Snyder, Maria	Quilting by the Lake in Central New York	Wright, Yolanda	√		Fa	10	2		M/A 83	50
People: McCowan, Michael	Livin' and Workin' on the Land: Fiber Art Outside the Mainstream	Talley, Charles S.	√		Fa	8	6		N/D 81	38
People: McDaniel, Claribel	Midwest Tapestry Weaver	Wallace, Lysbeth	√		H&C	11	1		Wi 60	18
People: McDonnell, Gail	Gail McDonnell	Tacker, Sylvia	√		Fa	14	3		M/J 87	23
People: McDougall, Elsie	Textiles and Looms from Guatemala & Mexico	Grossman, Ellin F.	√		H&C	7	1		Wi 55	6
People: McDowell, Ruth	"New England Images" (Exhibit)	Harris, Patricia; David Lyon	√		Fa	10	6		N/D 83	78
People: McElroy, Jane	Soft Boxes: Ritual For Our Common Life	McElroy, Jane	√		Fa	10	2		M/A 83	21
People: McGarr, Mr. and Mrs. Wallace	McGarrs of Norwood, The				H&C	17	2		Sp 66	46
People: McGeary, Gay	Open Jurying in Pittsburg: Putting Your Work on the Line (Exhibit)	Myrinx, Elaine	√		Fa	6	2		M/A 79	23
People: McIlrath, Tim	Tim McIlrath	Ligon, Linda	√		Iw	2	2		Wi 77	18
People: McIntyre, Walter and Lorna	Time Warp on the Coldstream	McIntyre, Walter	√		SS&D	15	4	60	Fa 84	50
People: McKee, John	Men Who Knit	Xenakis, Alexis Yiorgos	√		Kn	3	2	6	Sp 87	14
People: McLeod, Christine	Ordinary Weaver and Her Extraordinary Rugs, An	Xenakis, Alexis Yiorgos	√		PWC	4	2	12		4
People: McMorran, Tina	Tina McMorran	Chalmers, Marjorie	√		SS&D	3	3	11	Su 72	23
People: McMorran, Tina	Tina McMorran	Stevens, Bernice A.	√		H&C	15	3		Su 64	14
People: McNair, Peg	Color Theory for Handweavers Part 3: Visual Illusions with Color	Wald, Pat Boutin	√	√	WJ	10	4	40	Sp 86	40
People: McNair, Peg	Evolution of an Artist: Peg McNair	McNair, Peg	√		Fa	14	5		N/D 87	19
People: McNair, Peg	"Peg McNair/Tapestries" (Exhibit)	Petersen, Jill	√		Fa	4	3		M/J 77	12
People: McNair, Peg	"Textiles New Mexico 1976" (Exhibit)	Warner, Lucy Ann	√		Fa	3	2		M/A 76	12
People: McNair, Peg	Two Students of Theo Moorman: Hazel Maltby, Peg McNair		√		Fa	3	4		J/A 76	28
People: McNally-Warner, Judith	Gallery (Tapestry)		√		Hw	3	1		Ja 82	50
People: McNally-Warner, Judith	Who Weaves?		√		Iw	5	2		Sp 80	38/42
People: McPeek, Mary	Postal Service Celebrates Lace		√		TM			12	A/S 87	22
People: McQueen, John	"Fiber R/Evolution" (Exhibit)	Rudich, Sally	√		Fa	13	4		J/A 86	45
People: McQueen, John	"Fiber Works — Americas & Japan" (Exhibit)	Kato, Kuniko Lucy	√		Fa	5	1		J/F 78	10
People: McQueen John	"Interlacing: The Elemental Fabric" (Exhibit)		√		Fa	14	3		M/J 87	62
People: McQueen, John	John McQueen: An Interview	Park, Betty	√		Fa	6	1		J/F 79	21
People: McQueen, John	"John McQueen" (Exhibit)		√		Fa	4	4		J/A 77	14
People: McQueen, John	"Other Baskets" An Invitational Show in St. Louis (Exhibit)	Degener, Patricia	√		Fa	10	1		J/F 83	76
People: McQueen, John	Robert Pfannebecker: A Collector's Point of View	Park, Betty	√		Fa	5	4		J/A 78	42
People: McQueen, John	What Makes a Basket a Basket?	Malarcher, Patricia	√		Fa	11	1		J/F 84	34
People: McQueen, John	When is Fiber Art "Art"?	Koplos, Janet	√		Fa	13	2		M/A 86	34

SUBJECT	TITLE	AUTHOR	IL	INST	JOUR	VOL	NO	ISS	DATE	PAGE
People: Mead, Constance	Fine Art of Collecting Baskets, The (error-corrected TM i14 '87 p4)	Bowers, Sandra W.		√	TM			13	O/N 87	16
People: Meany, Janet	Profile of an HGA Rep	Meany, Janet	√		SS&D	17	1	65	Wi 85	89
People: Mears, Ellen	Scholarships '78		√		SS&D	9	4	36	Fa 78	44
People: Mears, Ellen Savage	"Felt: A Rich Tradition and Current Involvements" (Exhibit)	Constantinides, Kathy	√		Fa	6	3		M/J 79	74
People: Mecagni, Carol	Boston Seven	Newman, Rochelle	√		SS&D	16	3	63	Su 85	71
People: Mecagni, Carol	"Boston Seven: A Fiber Show, The" (Exhibit)	Goldman, Judy Ann	√		Fa	6	3		M/J 79	73
People: Mecagni, Carol	"Carol Mecagni: Illuminated Tapestries" (Exhibit)	Newman, Rochelle	√		Fa	9	2		M/A 82	79
People: Meckler, Marsha	"Fabrications" (Exhibit)	Talley, Charles	√		Fa	6	4		J/A 79	76
People: Medel, Rebecca	Twelfth International Biennial of Tapestry	Taylor, Dianne; Elmer Taylor	√		Fa	12	6		N/D 85	50
People: Meek, Leonora	Leonora Meek, Nebraska Weaver and Teacher		√	> 4	H&C	15	2		Sp 64	23
People: Meikle, Margaret	HGA Scholarships '79		√		SS&D	10	4	40	Fa 79	99
People: Meixner, Leann	"Felt: A Rich Tradition and Current Involvements" (Exhibit)	Constantinides, Kathy	√		Fa	6	3		M/J 79	74
People: Melander, Karin	Weaving Guilds—A Special Sharing		√		Iw	5	2		Sp 80	54
People: Melton, Jean	"Festival of Weaving" (Exhibit)	Greenberg, Blue	√		Fa	7	4		J/A 80	71
People: Meltzer, Bonnie	Crocheter Gets Wired, A	Carlton, Bronwyn	√		Fa	7	1		J/F 80	31
People: Meltzer, Bonnie	"Wearable Art" (Exhibit)	Hunt, E. Ann	√		Fa	6	3		M/J 79	78
People: Meltzer, Marilyn	Fiber Ten	McGuire, Patricia	√		Fa	4	6		N/D 77	26
People: Mendelson, Linda	Knitting Machine: A Creative Tool, The	Mendelson, Linda	√	√	Fa	5	3		M/J 78	32
People: Merkel, Sidonie	"With or Without a Loom" (Exhibit)	Rowley, Kristin Carlsen	√		Fa	8	5		S/O 81	67
People: Merrill, Eleanor	"Eleanor Merrill" (Exhibit)	Vander Lee, Jana	√		Fa	4	1		J/F 77	8
People: Merritt, Francis S.	American Handweaving 1960		√		H&C	11	2		Sp 60	9
People: Merritt, Nancy	"Works in Miniature" (Exhibit)	Malarcher, Patricia	√		Fa	7	3		M/J 80	82
People: Mertz, Jonathan	Livin' and Workin' on the Land: Fiber Art Outside the Mainstream	Talley, Charles S.	√		Fa	8	6		N/D 81	38
People: Mesarch, Christine	"Throbbing Needles II" (Exhibit)	Mattera, Joanne	√		Fa	7	2		M/A 80	71
People: Messinesi, Aristide	Tribute to a Famous Weaver	Wilkinson, Dorothy	√		H&C	17	4		Fa 66	32
People: Metcalf, Nancy	Get Into a Good Book: Public Art for Kids	Covel, John	√		Fa	6	5		S/O 79	33
People: Meteyer, Seth	"Power Garments" (Exhibit)	Papa, Nancy	√		Fa	5	1		J/F 78	13
People: Metz, Barbara	Papermaking in Chicago	Shermeta, Margo	√		Fa	11	2		M/A 84	54
People: Metzler, Bonnie	Speakers Bureau Presents		√		SS&D	3	1	9	Wi 71	10
People: Meyer, Elspeth	Verbena Collection, The (error-corrected Fa v11 n1 84 p11)		√		Fa	10	5		S/O 83	64
People: Meyers, Christine	Muslin Ladies: Trapunto Drawings of Christine Meyers	Rowland, Amy Zaffarano	√		Fa	10	3		M/J 83	19
People: Meyers, Judith Philipp	Pieces of History	Meyers, Judith Philipp	√		Fa	14	5		N/D 87	54
✦ People: Michaels-Paque, Joan	Public Fiber: Looking At the Logistics	Koplos, Janet	√		Fa	12	1		J/F 85	32
People: Mickelson, Joan	Folklore of Puppeteer Joan Mickelson, The	Van Til, Reinder	√		Fa	13	1		J/F 86	14
People: Mickey, Alice	Sampler of Surface Design, A	Westphal, Katherine	√		Fa	10	5		S/O 83	39
People: Mihalko, Zoltan	Feltmaking in Hungary	Beede, Beth; Jill Garfunkel	√		Fa	13	4		J/A 86	6
People: Mihalkó, Zoltán	Zoltán Mihalkó: Hungarian Feltmaker	Beede, Beth; Jill Garfunkel	√	√	SS&D	17	4	68	Fa 86	12
People: Mike, Rose	Textile Trends: Collecting in the Southwest	Elliott, Malinda	√		Fa	12	6		N/D 85	27
People: Miller, Chelsea	"Infrastructure" (Exhibit)	Malarcher, Patricia	√		Fa	11	4		J/A 84	76
People: Miller, Chelsea	"Material/Culture" (Exhibit)	Ross, Douglas	√		Fa	14	2		M/A 87	55
People: Miller, Christine	Quilts in Women's Lives	Mattera, Joanne	√		Fa	9	3		M/J 82	54
People: Miller, Constance	Felt and Paper: A Portfolio		√		Fa	13	4		J/A 86	35
People: Miller, Dorothy	Personal Exploration of Indigo, A	Miller, Dorothy	√	√	Fa	13	5		S/O 86	32

SUBJECT	TITLE	AUTHOR	IL	INST	JOUR	VOL	NO	ISS	DATE	PAGE
People: Miller, Dottie	"Textiles New Mexico 1976" (Exhibit)	Warner, Lucy Ann	√		Fa	3	2		M/A 76	12
People: Miller, Gammy	For the Body (error-corrected Fa v10 n2 83 p61)		√		Fa	10	1		J/F 83	32
People: Miller, Gammy	Gammy Miller: Coiled Poems	Miller, Gammy	√		Fa	11	6		N/D 84	16
People: Miller, Hortense	Quilts in Women's Lives	Mattera, Joanne	√		Fa	9	3		M/J 82	54
People: Miller, Jennifer	Design Exercises for Inspitarion and Fun	McNair, Peg	√	√	Fa	14	1		J/F 87	47
People: Miller, Kitt	Kitt Miller: Art Among Friends	Wolfe, Gregory	√		Fa	14	3		M/J 87	10
People: Miller, Lea Van Puymbroeck	Lea Van Puymbroeck Miller, Innovator in Handweaving	Boyer, Ruth M.	√		H&C	20	2		Sp 69	15
People: Miller, Linda	Art That Functions	Lønning, Kari	√		Fa	8	3		M/J 81	40
People: Miller, Linda	HGA Scholarship Award	Braun, Suzan G.	√		SS&D	16	3	63	Su 85	62
People: Miller, Linda	Linda Miller: Textile Constructions	Goodman, Deborah Lerme	√		Fa	12	3		M/J 85	17
People: Miller, Margaret J.	"California Fibers: 11th Annual Show" (Exhibit)	Kosta, Angela	√		Fa	10	6		N/D 83	81
People: Miller, Martin	Everyday World of Fantasy, The	Smeltzer, Nancy	√		Fa	13	3		M/J 86	6
People: Millette, Alice	"Fiber Techniques: The Weaver's Guild of Greater Cincinnati" (Exhibit)	Fedders, Pat	√		Fa	8	1		J/F 81	91
People: Mills, Ann Newdigate	Imagery Is Personal in Tapestry Today	Clausen, Valerie	√		TM			9	F/M 87	66
People: Mills, Laura Strand	Complex Surfaces of Laura Strand Mills, The	Lancaster, Zoë Woodruff	√		Fa	14	2		M/A 87	29
People: Mills, Laura Strand	"Local Options: The Work of Laura Strand Mills and Jo Peterson" (Exhibit)	Ferguson, Tom	√		Fa	10	3		M/J 83	69
People: Mincer, Kathy	Kathy Mincer: In Pursuit of Excellence	Linder, Olive	√		SS&D	13	2	50	Sp 82	31
People: Minkowitz, Norma	"Great American Foot, The" (Exhibit)	Grover, Donald	√		Fa	5	4		J/A 78	15
People: Minkowitz, Norma	Miniatures in Fiber: Working Small—An Exciting Challenge for the Contemporary Fiber Artist	Malarcher, Patricia	√		Fa	7	4		J/A 80	32
People: Minkowitz, Norma	Norma Minkowitz	Minkowitz, Norma	√		Fa	13	3		M/J 86	26
People: Minkowitz, Norma	"Norma Minkowitz" (Exhibit)	Grover, Donald	√		Fa	6	5		S/O 79	77
People: Minkowitz, Norma	On the Other Foot: The Shoe Sculptures of Norma Minkowitz		√		Fa	10	1		J/F 83	13
People: Minkowitz, Norma	"Poetry for the Body, Clothing for the Spirit" (Exhibit)	Hickman, Pat	√		Fa	10	5		S/O 83	75
People: Minkowitz, Norma	Portfolio of Contemporary Fiber Sculpture, A		√		Fa	11	4		J/A 84	34
People: Minkowitz, Norma	Soft Sculpture: Old Forms, New Meanings	Gordon, Beverly	√		Fa	10	6		N/D 83	40
People: Minkowitz, Norma	Three Personal Statements: Norma Minkowitz, Gillian Bull, Mardel Esping		√		Fa	3	5		S/O 76	19
People: Minor, Edna	Edna Minor of the Craft Students League		√		H&C	4	3		Su 53	4
People: Minsky-Jackson, Debra	Debra Minsky-Jackson: Renaissance Visions in Fiber	Grunberg, Liane	√		Fa	11	4		J/A 84	68
People: Mitchell, Ann	Ann Mitchell: Tapestry-Maker	Dishongh, Suzanne	√		Fa	5	2		M/A 78	53
People: Mitchell, Emily	Country of Origin, USA: A Decade of Contemporary Rugs	Stevens, Rebeccah A. T.	√		Fa	11	3		M/J 84	60
People: Mitchell, Julia	Fiber on Martha's Vineyard	Erickson, Johanna	√		Fa	11	4		J/A 84	46
People: Mitchell, Julia	"Julia Mitchell: Landscape Tapestries" (Exhibit)	Poon, Vivian	√		Fa	10	6		N/D 83	80
People: Mitchell, Julia	Julia Mitchell: On Martha's Vineyard	Erickson, Johanna	√		SS&D	15	3	59	Su 84	60
People: Mitchell, Julia	Pictorial Tapestry: A Portfolio of Contemporary Work	Goodman, Deborah Lerme	√		Fa	10	3		M/J 83	29
People: Mitchem, Patti	"Patti Mitchem: Rep Weave Hangings" (Exhibit)	Barnett-Westfall, Lynn	√		Fa	8	3		M/J 81	67
People: Miyake, Issey	"Issey Miyake: Fashion Without Taboos" (Exhibit)	Mathews, Cleve	√		Fa	12	3		M/J 85	70
People: Miyake, Issey	"Paper Clothing and More in San Francisco" (Exhibit)	Scarborough, Jessica	√		Fa	11	2		M/A 84	75
People: Miyake, Issey	Paper Clothing: West	Koplos, Janet	√		Fa	11	2		M/A 84	39
People: Moes, Dini	"Focus on Handwoven Fabric: Ontario Handweavers and Spinners" (Exhibits)	Place, Jennifer	√		Fa	9	4		J/A 82	74

SUBJECT	TITLE	AUTHOR	IL	INST	JOUR	VOL	NO	ISS	DATE	PAGE
People: Moholy-Nagy	Marli-Weavers of Chicago, The	Uhlman, Ilse Etta	√		H&C	4	1		Wi 52	9
People: Moir, Judith	"Textile Works: Lily Gilmore, Judith Moir, Sheila O'Hara" (Exhibit)	Mazur, Carole	√		Fa	8	2		M/A 81	67
People: Mondt, Carol	"California Women in Crafts" (Exhibit)	Dyer, Carolyn	√		Fa	4	2		M/A 77	10
People: Monick-Isenberg, Lynda	Portfolio: Why I Work in Linen, A		√		Fa	14	2		M/A 87	38
People: Monsen, Ragnhild	Contemporary Textile Art in Scandinavia	Talley, Charles S.	√		Fa	9	6		N/D 82	43
People: Monte, Cedrus	Sensuous Silk: Cedrus Monte's Painted Silk Garments	Gilliland, David	√		Fa	8	1		J/F 81	17
People: Moon, Ellen	Under Wraps		√		Fa	12	3		M/J 85	26
People: Mooney, David	Triaxial Weaving of David Mooney, The	Goodman, Deborah Lerme	√	√	Fa	13	3		M/J 86	34
People: Mooney, David R.	Pictorial Tapestry: A Portfolio of Contemporary Work	Goodman, Deborah Lerme	√		Fa	10	3		M/J 83	29
People: Moore, Beatrice	Life of a Country Weaver, The	Day, Jim	√		Fa	7	1		J/F 80	55
People: Moore, Henry	Henry Moore: A New Dimension: The Translation of Watercolors from Paper to Tapestry	Goodman, Deborah Lerme	√		Fa	11	2		M/A 84	62
People: Moore, Iris	"Fabrications" (Exhibit)	Talley, Charles	√		Fa	6	4		J/A 79	76
People: Moore, Janet	1977 HGA Scholarships (error-corrected SS&D v9 n2 78 p70)		√		SS&D	9	1	33	Wi 77	46
People: Moore, Margaret Marbanian	"Stitchery '77" (Exhibit)	Pierucci, Louise	√		Fa	4	3		M/J 77	11
People: Moore, Thomas	To the Walls: The 13th Lausanne Biennial (Exhibit)	Zepeda, Susan G.	√		Fa	14	4		S/O 87	41
People: Moorman, Theo	Personal Comment, A	McNair, Peg	√		Fa	3	4		J/A 76	32
People: Moorman, Theo	Theo Moorman	Waller, Irene	√		SS&D	17	4	68	Fa 86	60
People: Moorman, Theo	Theo Moorman: A Conversation with a Very Special Person		√		Fa	3	4		J/A 76	22
People: Moorman, Theo	Theo Moorman, English Tapestry Weaver in San Francisco	Marston, Ena	√	√	H&C	20	1		Wi 69	12
People: Moorman, Theo	"Theo Moorman: Experiments in Weaving" (Exhibit)	Dunwell, Anna	√		Fa	9	5		S/O 82	80
People: Moorman, Theo	Theo Moorman: Explorations	Bolster, Jane	√		SS&D	1	2	2	Mr 70	10
People: Moorman, Theo	Theo Moorman: Poet on the Loom				SS&D	6	4	24	Fa 75	15
People: Moran, Susan	Design by the Yard: Today's Fabric Innovators	Scarborough, Jessica	√		Fa	12	5		S/O 85	30
People: Morgan, Lucy	Penland School of Handicrafts		√		H&C	23	2		M/A 72	8
People: Morgan, Lucy C.	Penland's First 25 Years		√		H&C	5	2		Sp 54	8
People: Morias, Jane	Transferring Feelings to Fabric: Jane Morias	Park, Betty	√		Fa	5	1		J/F 78	52
People: Moriguchi, Kako	"Kimono As Art: Modern Textile Works by Kako Moriguchi, Rikizo Munehiro, and Fukumi Shimura" (Exhibit)	Koplos, Janet	√		Fa	13	1		J/F 86	60
People: Moriguchi, Kunihiko	Kimono East/West	Wada, Yoshiko	√		Fa	9	1		J/F 82	19
People: Morris, Michelle	"Interweave 79" (Exhibit)	Constantinides, Kathy	√		Fa	7	1		J/F 80	66
People: Morris, Michelle	"Michelle Morris: Tapestries and Related Work" (Exhibit)	Fitt, Cate	√		Fa	7	4		J/A 80	65
People: Morris, Michelle	Pictorial Tapestry: A Portfolio of Contemporary Work	Goodman, Deborah Lerme	√		Fa	10	3		M/J 83	29
People: Morris, William	Craftsman and Social Conscience: William Morris, The	Hepburn, Ian			Hw	5	4		S/O 84	26
People: Morris, William	Imagery Is Personal in Tapestry Today	Clausen, Valerie	√		TM			9	F/M 87	66
People: Morris, William	William Morris, A Twentieth Century View of His Woven Textiles	Morris, Barbara J.	√		H&C	12	2		Sp 61	6
People: Morris, William	William Morris: The Sanford and Helen Berger Collection	Austin, Carole	√		Fa	12	3		M/J 85	47
People: Morrison, Connie	"Fine Focus" (Exhibit)	Rice, Nancy Newman	√		Fa	12	2		M/A 85	74
People: Morrison, Fritzi Huber	Felt and Paper: A Portfolio		√		Fa	13	4		J/A 86	35
People: Morrison, Fritzi Huber	Paper Art of Fritzi Huber Morrison, The	Kosta, Angela	√		Fa	11	2		M/A 84	22
People: Morrison, Lois	Limited Editions: The Wearable Books of Lois Morrison	Rudich, Sally	√		Fa	12	3		M/J 85	91

SUBJECT	TITLE	AUTHOR	IL	INST	JOUR	VOL	NO	ISS	DATE	PAGE
People: Morrison, Ruth	Portfolio: Ruth Morrison		√		Hw	7	1		J/F 86	38
People: Morrison, Skye	Canadian Portfolio, A	Place, Jennifer	√		Fa	9	6		N/D 82	29
People: Morrison, Skye	Skye Morrison: Yours on a Kite String	Morrison, Skye	√	√	Fa	5	4		J/A 78	36
People: Morrow, Mable	Mable Morrow–Appreciation for Indian Arts, Part 1	Maxcy, Mabel E.	√		SS&D	5	1	17	Wi 73	29
People: Morrow, Mable	Mable Morrow—Collector, Scholar of Indian Arts, Part 2	Maxcy, Mabel E.	√		SS&D	5	2	18	Sp 74	33
People: Morse, Marcia	Making a Living: Eight Fiber Artists Tell How They Do It	Rowley, Kathleen	√		Fa	9	5		S/O 82	38
People: Morse, Marcia	Marcia Morse: A Collaboration with Paper	Rowley, Kathleen	√		Fa	11	2		M/A 84	20
People: Moscinski, Dave	Mummery: Philadelphia's Happy New Year	Smeltzer, Nancy	√		Fa	14	3		M/J 87	39
People: Moseley, Kathy	Setting Up Shop	Ligon, Linda	√		Iw	2	4		Su 77	18
People: Moses, Cherie	Canadian Portfolio, A	Place, Jennifer	√		Fa	9	6		N/D 82	29
People: Moses, Dr. Elisabeth	Dr. Elisabeth Moses of the M. H. de Young Museum	Bryan, Dorothy	√		H&C	7	2		Sp 56	16
People: Moshimer, Joan	Rug Hooking: The Flourishing of a Time-Honored Technique	Moshimer, Joan	√	√	Fa	7	5		S/O 80	37
People: Moss, Janice Lessman	HGA Scholarships '79		√		SS&D	10	4	40	Fa 79	100
People: Mossman, Bernard	Basketmakers of Nova Scotia, The	Gordon, Joleen	√		SS&D	17	4	68	Fa 86	44
People: Motti, Mary	Masks At the Heart of Disguise	Koplos, Janet	√		Fa	11	5		S/O 84	32
People: Moulton, Peggy	Color Xerography and the Fiber Artist	Theil, Linda	√		Fa	8	5		S/O 81	59
People: Moulton, Peggy	"Stitchery '79" (Exhibit)	Kerr, Connie	√		Fa	6	5		S/O 79	78
People: Moya, Maria Consuelo	"Textiles New Mexico 1976" (Exhibit)	Warner, Lucy Ann	√		Fa	3	2		M/A 76	12
People: Moya, Maria Consuelo	Very Special Craftswoman: Maria Consuelo Moya, A		√		Fa	3	2		M/A 76	32
People: Moya, Sam	Sam Moya	Ligon, Linda	√		Iw	2	2		Wi 77	14
People: Moya, Sam	Who Weaves?		√		Iw	5	2		Sp 80	41/42
People: Moyer, Gisela	"Assemblage: Wisconsin Paper" (Exhibit)	Bard, Elizabeth	√		Fa	11	1		J/F 84	78
People: Moyer, Gisela Magdalena	Felt and Paper: A Portfolio		√		Fa	13	4		J/A 86	35
People: Mphuthi, Johanna	Zamani Soweto Sisters: A Patchwork of Lives		√		Fa	10	2		M/A 83	48
People: Muerdter, Catharine	Table Dressing and Bedcovers		√		Fa	8	3		M/J 81	43
People: Mufson, Phyllis	San Francisco School of Fabric Arts, The	Papa, Nancy	√		Fa	6	1		J/F 79	13
People: Muir, Kathie	Labor Banners of Australia	Mancini, Anne	√		Fa	14	5		N/D 87	36
People: Mulders, Lydia	Woven Murals	Mulders, Lydia	√		H&C	13	2		Sp 62	22
People: Mundal, Maria	Maria Mundal, Tapestry Weaver		√		H&C	12	3		Su 61	44
People: Mundal, Maria	Maria Mundal — Visualized Melodies		√		SS&D	2	3	7	Su 71	20
People: Mundal, Maria	Weaver from Norway — Maria Mundal		√		H&C	2	2		Sp 51	57
People: Munehiro, Rikizo	"Kimono As Art: Modern Textile Works by Kako Moriguchi, Rikizo Munehiro, and Fukumi Shimura" (Exhibit)	Koplos, Janet	√		Fa	13	1		J/F 86	60
People: Muñoz, Aurelia	"Aurelia Muñoz" (Exhibit)	Park, Betty	√		Fa	4	6		N/D 77	21
People: Munoz, Aurelia	Lausanne Notebook: Our Special Report on the 8th Lausanne Biennial of Tapestry, A	Mathews, Rich	√		Fa	4	5		S/O 77	30
People: Munro, Rebecca	Rebecca Munro: But It Turned Out All Right	Erler, Mary	√		Fa	6	6		N/D 79	28
People: Munson, Howard	Through the Camera's Eye: Howard Munson's Body Coverings	Akamine, Estelle	√		Fa	14	3		M/J 87	44
People: Muraoka, Rebecca	Hawaiian Quilt, The	White-Hansen, Sue Ellen	√	√	TM			13	O/N 87	22
People: Murashima, Kumiko	Kumiko Murashima: The East and West of Weaving	Balassa, Eva	√		Fa	6	1		J/F 79	17
People: Murphy, Maggy	Appalachian Basketry	Overcast, Roy	√		Fa	4	1		J/F 77	20
People: Murphy, Michael	If the Art Fits – Wear It! — Friends of the Rag	Strosnider, Ann	√		Fa	6	3		M/J 79	35
People: Murphy, Susan	Fiber In Minnesota: "Traditions/Transitions II" and "Art in Architecture" (Exhibit)	Stack, Lotus	√		Fa	11	3		M/J 84	80

SUBJECT	TITLE	AUTHOR	IL	INST	JOUR	VOL	NO	ISS	DATE	PAGE
People: Murray, Clare M.	Clare M. Murray	Murray, Clare M.	√		Fa	13	6		N/D 86	2
People: Murray, Jeff	If the Art Fits – Wear It! — Friends of the Rag	Strosnider, Ann	√		Fa	6	3		M/J 79	35
People: Murray, Michelle	What People Ask Before They Buy Handmade Fashions	Leslie, Victoria	√		TM			9	F/M 87	58
People: Musick, Deborah Boggio	Livin' and Workin' on the Land: Fiber Art Outside the Mainstream	Talley, Charles S.	√		Fa	8	6		N/D 81	38
People: Musk, Denise	Knitting Craft in Great Britain, The	Kinder, Kathleen	√		Fa	11	4		J/A 84	42
People: Muszynska, Teresa	"22 Polish Textile Artists" (Exhibit)	Park, Betty	√		Fa	4	5		S/O 77	8
People: Myatt, Ted	Men Who Knit	Xenakis, Alexis Yiorgos	√		Kn	3	2	6	Sp 87	14
People: Myers, Deuse	"Baskets in La Jolla" (Exhibit)	Blaylock, Mary P.	√		Fa	11	1		J/F 84	79
People: Myers, George Hewitt	Dedication to George Hewitt Myers		√		TMJ	24			85	4
People: Myers, George Hewitt, Mr. and Mrs.	Textile Museum — 50th Anniversary, The		√		TMJ	4	1		De 74	4
People: Myers, Jan	Presence of Light: The Un-Traditional Quilts of Jan Myers, The	Gutcheon, Beth	√		Fa	8	3		M/J 81	60
People: Myers, Jan	Quiltmaker's Art, A	Mattera, Joanne	√		Fa	10	2		M/A 83	33
People: Myers, Ruth Nordquist	Coverlet for Convergence 1988, A		√	√	SS&D	19	1	73	Wi 87	46
People: Myrvold, Pia	"Fourth Nordic Textiltriennale" (Exhibit)	Talley, Charles	√		Fa	13	3		M/J 86	51
People: M'Kasibe, Florence	Zamani Soweto Sisters: A Patchwork of Lives		√		Fa	10	2		M/A 83	48
People: Nabors-Pearson, Tomijann	"100% Wool" (Exhibit)	Goldin, Susan	√		Fa	4	6		N/D 77	18
People: Nabors-Pearson, Tomijann	"Textiles New Mexico 1976" (Exhibit)	Warner, Lucy Ann	√		Fa	3	2		M/A 76	12
People: Nagin, Rise	"Needle Expressions '86" (Exhibit)	Reinsel, Susan J.	√		Fa	14	1		J/F 87	53
People: Nagin, Rise Rice	"Wearables" (Exhibit)	Grover, Donald	√		Fa	6	6		N/D 79	76
People: Naito, Hideharu	Innovations in Indigo	Wada, Yoshiko Iwamoto	√		Fa	13	5		S/O 86	29
People: Nakamura, Earlene	Hair As a Sculptor's Medium	Akamine, Estelle	√		Fa	14	3		M/J 87	24
People: Nash, Dominie	Out of the Blue: Aerial Images		√		Fa	13	5		S/O 86	44
People: Nawir, Ferril	Verbena Collection, The (error-corrected Fa v11 n1 84 p11)		√		Fa	10	5		S/O 83	64
People: Naylor, Randy	"Fourth Nordic Textiltriennale" (Exhibit)	Talley, Charles	√		Fa	13	3		M/J 86	51
People: Nchang, Lillian	Zamani Soweto Sisters: A Patchwork of Lives		√		Fa	10	2		M/A 83	48
People: Nechin, Sue	Sue Nechin of First Additions	Koplos, Janet	√		Fa	10	1		J/F 83	69
People: Nechvatal, Mary Bero	"Wisconsin Fiber Miniatures" (Exhibit)	Lowell-LaRoque, Jane V.	√		Fa	6	5		S/O 79	84
People: Needham, Julia	Quilts at Arrowmont (Exhibit)		√		Fa	13	3		M/J 86	53
People: Neeson, John	Victorian Tapestry Workshop: A New Tradition in Australia, The	Newman, Rochelle	√		Fa	10	3		M/J 83	38
People: Neff, Ilene	Banners for Peace	Adels, Jill	√		Fa	12	4		J/A 85	36
People: Nelson, Judith	"Fiber Structure National" (Exhibit)	Dyer, Carolyn	√		Fa	8	5		S/O 81	75
People: Nelson, Lila	Weaving Guilds—A Special Sharing		√		Iw	5	2		Sp 80	54
People: Nelson, Robert	On Fabric in the Southwest: Surface Design, A Bank, and Public Recognition	Brooks, Lois Ziff	√		Fa	6	5		S/O 79	54
People: Nelson, Susan Venable	Portfolio of Contemporary Fiber Sculpture, A		√		Fa	11	4		J/A 84	34
People: Nelson, Susan Venable	"Weaving Without Fiber" (Exhibit)	Hempel, Toby Anne	√		Fa	13	5		S/O 86	48
People: Neri, Manuel	Sculptural Paper: Foundations and Directions	Scarborough, Jessica	√		Fa	11	2		M/A 84	32
People: Nettles, Margareta	Margareta Nettles — Weaver, Designer	Slater, Deborah	√		H&C	23	1		J/F 72	22
People: Nevers, Jette	"Scandinavian Touch, The" A Traveling Exhibit (Exhibit)	Mattera, Joanna	√		Fa	10	1		J/F 83	82
People: Newbill, Elizabeth	"Quilts—Innovation and Tradition" (Exhibit)	Barnard, Eileen Wolford	√		Fa	10	3		M/J 83	72
People: Newman, Barbara Johansen	"Needle and Cloth: Ten Years Later" (Exhibit)	Hulbert, Elizabeth McKey	√		Fa	10	3		M/J 83	72
People: Newman, Rochelle	Boston Seven	Newman, Rochelle	√		SS&D	16	3	63	Su 85	71

SUBJECT	TITLE	AUTHOR	IL	INST	JOUR	VOL	NO	ISS	DATE	PAGE
People: Nezhnie, Muriel	Weaving the Horror of the Holocaust	Townsend, William D.	√		SS&D	15	3	59	Su 84	16
People: Ngcobo, Elizabeth	Zamani Soweto Sisters: A Patchwork of Lives		√		Fa	10	2		M/A 83	48
People: Nicholson, Laura Foster	"Fiber R/Evolution" (Exhibit)	Rudich, Sally	√		Fa	13	4		J/A 86	45
People: Nicholson, Maggie	Fiber and Architecture: Amy Jo Lind and Maggie Nicholson		√		Fa	3	3		M/J 76	16
People: Nickolson, Ann McKenzie	Just Playing in Space: Ann McKenzie Nickolson's Textile Artwork	Koplos, Janet	√		Fa	8	2		M/A 81	34
People: Nickolson, Anne McKenzie	Anne McKenzie Nickolson	Nickolson, Anne McKenzie	√		Fa	12	6		N/D 85	20
People: Nielson, Dawn	"Left on the Loom" (Exhibit)	Dyer, Carolyn	√		Fa	5	2		M/A 78	16
People: Nininger, Susan	Contemporary California Costume	Poon, Vivian	√		Fa	11	5		S/O 84	53
People: Nininger, Susan	Conversation with Costumer Susan Nininger, A	Lonier, Terri	√		Fa	10	6		N/D 83	63
People: Nininger, Susan	Costuming for Rock Music Videos	Pierce, Judith	√		Fa	14	3		M/J 87	51
People: Nininger, Susan	"Fibers" (Exhibit)	Meyer, Zach	√		Fa	4	4		J/A 77	11
People: Nininger, Susan	If the Art Fits – Wear It! — Friends of the Rag	Strosnider, Ann	√		Fa	6	3		M/J 79	35
People: Nininger, Susan	"Wearable Art" (Exhibit)	Hunt, E. Ann	√		Fa	6	3		M/J 79	78
People: Nisbet, Jacquetta	Jacquetta Nisbet to Give Workshop on Peruvian Pebble Weave (error-corrected SS&D v5 n1 73 p93)	Black, Mary	√		SS&D	4	4	16	Fa 73	76
People: Nishio, Eizo	Twelfth International Biennial of Tapestry	Taylor, Dianne; Elmer Taylor	√		Fa	12	6		N/D 85	50
People: Nivola, Ruth	Good As Gold: Alternatives in American Jewelry		√		Fa	9	5		S/O 82	18
People: Nix, Nick	Body as Canvas, The	Koda, Harold	√		TM			8	D/J 86	56
People: Nixon, Elaine P.	Business of Weaving — An Interview with Elaine P. Nixon, The	Derr, Mary	√		WJ	4	1	13	Jy 79	10
People: Noguchi, Isamu	"Modern Aubusson Tapestry, The" (Exhibit)	Tanenbaum, Ruth	√		Fa	5	3		M/J 78	14
People: Noland, Kenneth	Contemporary Navajo Weaving	Hedlund, Ann Lane	√		WJ	11	1	41	Su 86	30
People: Nomura, Shojiro	"Fukusa: The Shojiro Nomura Collection" (Exhibit)	Janeiro, Jan	√		Fa	11	3		M/J 84	79
People: Nomura, Teresa	Return of the Rag, The	Basa, Lynn	√		Fa	14	3		M/J 87	29
People: Nomura, Teresa	Teresa Nomura: Fabric and Fantasy	Sage, Jan	√		Fa	11	5		S/O 84	20
People: Nordgren, Elizabeth	Designer: Nordgren, Elizabeth				SS&D	11	2	42	Sp 80	93
People: Nordstrom, Lisa Merton	Country of Origin, USA: A Decade of Contemporary Rugs	Stevens, Rebeccah A. T.	√		Fa	11	3		M/J 84	60
People: Norgaard, Inge	Tapestries of Inge Norgaard, The	Byers, Helen	√		Fa	11	4		J/A 84	22
People: Nottingham, Walter	Convergence Preview — Six Peaks, A		√		SS&D	11	2	42	Sp 80	47
People: Nottingham, Walter	"Filaments of the Imagination" (Exhibit)	Morse, Marcia	√		Fa	8	4		J/A 81	69
People: Nottingham, Walter	"Works in Miniature" (Exhibit)	Malarcher, Patricia	√		Fa	7	3		M/J 80	82
People: Nottingham, Walter G.	"Fiberworks" (Exhibit)	Park, Betty	√		Fa	4	6		N/D 77	10
People: Novak, Anne	Certificate Success	Drooker, Penelope	√		SS&D	16	1	61	Wi 84	66
People: Nugent, Bob	"Paper" (Exhibit)	Toale, Bernard	√		Fa	7	5		S/O 80	69
People: Nugent, Bob	Sculptural Paper: Foundations and Directions	Scarborough, Jessica	√		Fa	11	2		M/A 84	32
People: Nugent, Catherine Siri	Felt and Paper: A Portfolio		√		Fa	13	4		J/A 86	35
People: Nushawg, Mickey	Machine Knitting: The State of the Art		√		Fa	9	2		M/A 82	40
People: Nushawg, Mickey	Succeeding with the Knitting Machine	Mattera, Joanne	√		TM			2	D/J 85	50
People: Nyquist, Jan	HGA Board of Directors Candidates		√		SS&D	11	2	42	Sp 80	26
People: Nyquist, Janet	Janet Nyquist, Custom Weaver of Apparel Fabrics		√	√	H&C	16	1		Wi 65	16
People: Oakroot, Melody	Melody Oakroot-Cedar Weaver	London, Bill	√	√	S-O	10	3		Fa 86	45
People: Oberg, Mandelina	Mandelina Oberg	Herman, Mary R.	√		H&C	8	4		Fa 57	48
People: Obermeyer, Lindsay	Teacher/**Student** Interface: Two Views of Education		√		Fa	14	1		J/F 87	34

SUBJECT	TITLE	AUTHOR	IL	INST	JOUR	VOL	NO	ISS	DATE	PAGE
People: Obole, Teri	"Left on the Loom" (Exhibit)	Dyer, Carolyn	√		Fa	5	2		M/A 78	16
People: Oda, Hiromi	"Transformation: UCLA Alumnae in Fiber" (Exhibit)	Dyer, Carolyn	√		Fa	6	4		J/A 79	67
People: Oftedahl, Arlan	Arlan Oftedahl: Pine Needle Basket Maker		√		Fa	4	1		J/F 77	31
People: Ogawa, Hiroko	Hiroko Ogawa: Keeping Alive the Art of Sashiko	Scarborough, Jessica	√		Fa	12	2		M/A 85	12
People: O'Hara, Sheila	Sheila O'Hara's Geometrics	Rowley, Kathleen M.	√		SS&D	12	4	48	Fa 81	20
People: Ohberg, Margareta	Margareta Ohberg, From Sweden to a Long Career in America		√		H&C	12	3		Su 61	17
People: Oldenberg, Betty	Perfect Balance, A	LaLena, Constance	√		Hw	3	4		Se 82	77
People: Olds, Mrs.	My Friend, Mrs. Olds	Barker, Irene	√		S-O	9	4		Wi 85	47
People: Oleszko, Pat	Altered Ego: An Interview with Pat Oleszko	Lonier, Terri	√		Fa	10	1		J/F 83	26
People: Oliver, Augusta	Weaving Guilds—A Special Sharing		√		Iw	5	2		Sp 80	55
People: Olmsted, Rosemary R.	Rosemary R. Olmsted: Following Krokbragd's Crooked Path	Olmsted, Rosemary R.	√		Fa	11	3		M/J 84	28
People: Olsen, Christine Evelyn	"Fibers Unlimited 1979" (Exhibit)	Davidian, Robert	√		Fa	7	2		M/A 80	69
People: Olson, Pauline	Arvada Project, The	Heath, Jennifer	√		Fa	5	4		J/A 78	45
People: Olszewski, Michael	"Michael Olszewski: Pleated and Stitched Silk" (Exhibit)	Poon, Vivian	√		Fa	11	3		M/J 84	78
People: Oltchick, Ellen	"Pin Rugs of Ellen Oltchick, The" (Exhibit)	Poon, Vivian	√		Fa	10	6		N/D 83	74
People: Onagi, Yoichi	"Fiber Works — Americas & Japan" (Exhibit)	Kato, Kuniko Lucy	√		Fa	5	1		J/F 78	10
People: Onagi, Yoichi	Lausanne Notebook: Our Special Report on the 8th Lausanne Biennial of Tapestry, A	Mathews, Rich	√		Fa	4	5		S/O 77	30
People: Opdahl, Martha	Martha Opdahl	Opdahl, Martha	√		Fa	13	4		J/A 86	27
People: Opdahl, Martha	Tufted Rugs of Martha Opdahl, The	Piucci, Joanna A.	√		Fa	11	3		M/J 84	15
People: Oppenheimer, Ed	Conversation with Ed Oppenheimer, A	Pulleyn, Rob	√		Fa	4	4		J/A 77	24
People: Oppenheimer, Ed	Country of Origin, USA: A Decade of Contemporary Rugs	Stevens, Rebeccah A. T.	√		Fa	11	3		M/J 84	60
People: Oppenheimer, Ed	Ed Oppenheimer: Rugs	Ligon, Linda	√		Iw	5	1		Wi 79	31
People: Oren, Lynda Lowe	"Felt: A Rich Tradition and Current Involvements" (Exhibit)	Constantinides, Kathy	√		Fa	6	3		M/J 79	74
People: Oren, Lynda Lowe	Feltmaking Now: The Exciting Revival of an Ancient Technique	Gordon, Beverly	√		Fa	6	6		N/D 79	43
People: Orr, Leah	Fiber World of Leah Orr, The	Orr, Leah	√		SS&D	9	3	35	Su 78	8
People: Otsuka, Sueko	Visiting the Kimono School	Hannah, Joyce	√		TM			4	A/M 86	16
People: Outremont, Gilda	"Fiberous": Fiber as a Source of Inspiration (Exhibit)	Willard, Janice	√		Fa	10	1		J/F 83	80
People: Owen, Irene	Tapestry: Its Limitations Challenge Individual Creativity	Harvey, Nancy	√		SS&D	17	1	65	Wi 85	57
People: Owens, Rose	Contemporary Navajo Weaving	Hedlund, Ann Lane	√		WJ	11	1	41	Su 86	30
People: Owings, Cindy	Cindy Owings: Applying Dyes with an Airbrush		√	√	Fa	5	1		J/F 78	66
People: O'Banion, Nance	Craft Today: The American Craft Museum (Exhibit)	Sider, Sandra	√		Fa	14	2		M/A 87	54
People: O'Banion, Nance	"Fiberworks 1976" (Exhibit)	Papa, Nancy	√		Fa	4	1		J/F 77	9
People: O'Banion, Nance	Making a Living: Eight Fiber Artists Tell How They Do It	Rowley, Kathleen	√		Fa	9	5		S/O 82	38
People: O'Banion, Nance	"Nance O'Banion: Handmade Paper and Bamboo Painting" (Exhibit)	Janeiro, Jan	√		Fa	7	4		J/A 80	15
People: O'Banion, Nance	"Nance O'Banion: Painted Paper Skin Series" (Exhibits)	Rowley, Kathleen	√		Fa	9	4		J/A 82	70
People: O'Banion, Nance	"Nance O'Banion: Rocks, Curtains, Windows, and Walls" (Exhibit)	Talley, Charles	√		Fa	12	5		S/O 85	69
People: O'Banion, Nance	"Paper Sources" (Exhibit)	Papa, Nancy	√		Fa	5	4		J/A 78	16
People: O'Banion, Nance	Questions of Style: Contemporary Trends in the Fiber Arts	Howe-Echt, Katherine	√		Fa	7	2		M/A 80	38

SUBJECT	TITLE	AUTHOR	IL	INST	JOUR	VOL	NO	ISS	DATE	PAGE
People: O'Banion, Nance	Sculptural Paper: Foundations and Directions	Scarborough, Jessica	√		Fa	11	2		M/A 84	32
People: O'Callaghan, Kate	Statement of My Ideas	O'Callaghan, Kate	√		WJ	5	4	20	Sp 81	35
People: O'Connell, Celia	"Surface Design South Central" (Exhibit)	Erhler, Mary	√		Fa	6	4		J/A 79	75
People: O'Connell, Chris	Interview with Chris O'Connell, An	Durstan, Linda Moore	√		Hw	6	1		J/F 85	76
People: O'Connor, Marcie Archer	Spinner's Specialty: Heathered Yarns, A	Searle, Karen	√	√	WJ	9	2	34	Fa 84	56
People: O'Connor, P. R.	Fiber in Minnesota: "Traditions/Transitions II" and "Art in Architecture" (Exhibit)	Stack, Lotus	√		Fa	11	3		M/J 84	80
People: O'Connor, Sudie Lea	"Beds, Sweet Dreams, and Other Things" (Exhibit)	Bissell, June	√		Fa	6	4		J/A 79	70
People: O'Hara, Sheila	Making a Living: Eight Fiber Artists Tell How They Do It	Rowley, Kathleen	√		Fa	9	5		S/O 82	38
People: O'Hara, Sheila	Sheila O'Hara	O'Hara, Sheila	√		Fa	13	3		M/J 86	26
People: O'Hara, Sheila	Sheila O'Hara: Wry Humor and Virtuoso Weaving	Park, Betty	√		Fa	10	1		J/F 83	64
People: O'Hara, Sheila	"Textile Works: Lily Gilmore, Judith Moir, Sheila O'Hara" (Exhibit)	Mazur, Carole	√		Fa	8	2		M/A 81	67
People: O'Hara, Sheila	"Textiles by Pat Kinsella and Sheila O'Hara" (Exhibit)	Janeiro, Jan	√		Fa	6	3		M/J 79	72
People: O'Hara, Sheila	Using a Computer: Four Views		√		Fa	13	5		S/O 86	7
People: O'Hara, Sheila	You Are Now Weaving Oakland	O'Hara, Sheila	√	> 4	AT	6			De 86	9
People: O'Hara, Shelia	Shelia O'Hara: Triangles, Squares and Other Landmarks	Draheim, Teliha	√		Iw	6	1		Wi 80	42
People: O'Rourke, Robbie	"New England Images" (Exhibit)	Harris, Patricia; David Lyon	√		Fa	10	6		N/D 83	78
People: O'Shea, Mary Lynn	"Art Couture/Haute Couture" (Exhibit)	McGuire, Patricia	√		Fa	9	1		J/F 82	86
People: O'Shea, Mary Lynn	Flowers, Beautiful Flowers: Ronna Riebman, Batik: Mary Lynn O'Shea, Tapestry		√		Fa	8	3		M/J 81	35
People: O'Shea, Mary Lynn	For the Body (error-corrected Fa v10 n2 83 p61)		√		Fa	10	1		J/F 83	32
People: Paccione, Vicki	Sampler of Surface Design, A	Westphal, Katherine	√		Fa	10	5		S/O 83	39
People: Paccione, Vicki	Words in Fiber	Rowley, Kathleen	√		Fa	11	2		M/A 84	66
People: Painter, Hal	Hal Painter, Weaver of Tapestries and Rugs		√		H&C	16	3		Su 65	10
People: Painter, Hal	Speakers Bureau Presents		√		SS&D	7	2	26	Sp 76	78
People: Painter, Hal	Tapestry (Part 3): An Inside View	Harvey, Nancy	√	√	SS&D	15	2	58	Sp 84	20
People: Painter, Hal	Tapestry Today as Seen By Hal Painter				H&C	20	2		Sp 69	20
People: Painter, Hal	Who Weaves?		√		Iw	5	2		Sp 80	36
People: Palau, Marta	"Fiber Works — Americas & Japan" (Exhibit)	Kato, Kuniko Lucy	√		Fa	5	1		J/F 78	10
People: Pannucci, Cunthia	For the Body (error-corrected Fa v10 n2 83 p61)		√		Fa	10	1		J/F 83	32
People: Pannucci, Cynthia	Cynthia Pannucci: Relocating, Creating, Connecting	Mattera, Joanne	√		Fa	9	3		M/J 82	23
People: Panzarella, Genna	"Poetry for the Body, Clothing for the Spirit" (Exhibit)	Hickman, Pat	√		Fa	10	5		S/O 83	75
People: Papa, Nancy	Santa Fe Weaving Center, The	Elliott, Malinda	√		Fa	9	5		S/O 82	32
✝ People: Paque, Joan Michaels	Joan Michaels Paque		√		Fa	3	6		N/D 76	34
✝ People: Paque, Joan Michaels	Review/Discussion of Artspace's Innovative Yet Flawed "Fiber Freely Interpreted", A (Exhibit)		√		Fa	4	2		M/A 77	38
✝ People: Paque, Joan Michaels	Speakers Bureau Presents		√		SS&D	2	1	5	De 70	17
People: Pardington, Joyce	"Textiles New Mexico 1976" (Exhibit)	Warner, Lucy Ann	√		Fa	3	2		M/A 76	12
People: Park, Claire Campbell	Claire Campbell Park: Celebrating Color, Light, and Energy	Kerlin, Thomas J.	√		Fa	14	3		M/J 87	15
People: Parker, Gertrude	Gertrude Parker: Metamorphosing a Humble Material	Haney, Jeanna T.	√		Fa	14	4		S/O 87	8
People: Parker, Loni	Bringing Freedom to Fibers: Loni Parker	Brough, Hazel	√		SS&D	7	3	27	Su 76	44

ALSO SEE MICHAELS-PAQUE

SUBJECT	TITLE	AUTHOR	IL	INST	JOUR	VOL	NO	ISS	DATE	PAGE
People: Parker, Sharron	Felt and Paper: A Portfolio		√		Fa	13	4		J/A 86	35
People: Parkhurst, Esther	Esther Parkhurst	Sider, Sandra	√		Fa	12	6		N/D 85	17
People: Parkhurst, Esther	Quiltmaking: A Celebration of Life — Esther Parkhurst, Camille Shafer, Pami Slatt Fagelson		√		Fa	8	3		M/J 81	26
People: Parkhurst, Esther	"Southern California Designer Crafts" (Exhibit)	Dyer, Carolyn	√		Fa	5	2		M/A 78	14
People: Parriaud, Cosabeth	Quilting in France	Smeltzer, Nancy	√		Fa	13	2		M/A 86	49
People: Parrish, Sandra	Captured Shadows	Ligon, Linda	√		Iw	1	2		Wi 76	12
People: Parrott, Alice	Alice Parrott	Davis, Mary Woodard	√		Iw	2	1		Fa 76	6
People: Parsley, Jacque	Fans and Fan Imagery	Howe, Katherine; Joanne Mattera	√		Fa	9	4		J/A 82	26
People: Parsley, Jacque	"Jacque Parsley: Avallon Series" (Exhibit)	Anderson, Ann Stewart	√		Fa	9	5		S/O 82	82
People: Parsley, Jacque	"Jacque Parsley: Collage, A New Direction" (Exhibit)	Meloy, Margaret	√		Fa	11	6		N/D 84	76
People: Parsley, Jacque	"Shared Vision": A Gallery Tour with Two Artists: Jacque Parsley and Neisja Yenawine (Exhibit)	Arnow, Jan	√		Fa	8	4		J/A 81	28
People: Parsley, Jacque	"Web of Kentucky Thread, A" (Exhibit)	Meloy, Margaret	√		Fa	12	5		S/O 85	72
People: Parslow, Virginia D.	American Handweaving 1960		√		H&C	11	2		Sp 60	11
People: Pasco, Henry	Focus on the HGA Board of Directors		√		SS&D	10	1	37	Wi 78	52
People: Pasquini, Katie	Katie Pasquini: Mandala Quilts	Pasquini, Katie	√		Fa	10	4		J/A 83	20
People: Patrie, Pam	Pam Patrie: Tapestry, Imagery, Artistry	Carlton, Bronwyn	√		Fa	6	6		N/D 79	60
People: Pattera, Charlotte	"Needle Expressions '80" (Exhibit)		√		Fa	8	1		J/F 81	93
People: Patti, Francine	Portfolio: Why I Work in Linen, A		√		Fa	14	2		M/A 87	40
People: Patton, Joan	Contemporary Basketry		√		Fa	8	3		M/J 81	39
People: Paul, Dianne	Who Weaves?		√		Iw	5	2		Sp 80	39
People: Pcturczyn	"Space Sails: American Banners" (Exhibit)	Deyo, Diane	√		Fa	9	5		S/O 82	82
People: Pearlstein, Pillip	"Modern Aubusson Tapestry, The" (Exhibit)	Tanenbaum, Ruth	√		Fa	5	3		M/J 78	14
People: Peavy, Martin	Martin Peavy: An Improvisational Approach to Rugs	Peavy, Martin	√		Fa	11	3		M/J 84	22
People: Peleg, Rina	"National Crafts '81: Works by the 1981 National Endowment for the Arts Craft Fellows" (Exhibit)	Mattera, Joanne	√		Fa	9	1		J/F 82	82
People: Peleg, Rina	"Other Baskets" An Invitational Show in St. Louis (Exhibit)	Degener, Patricia	√		Fa	10	1		J/F 83	76
People: Peleg, Rina	Rina Peleg: Plaiting in Clay	Peleg, Rina	√		Fa	10	6		N/D 83	16
People: Pelz, Ruth	If the Art Fits – Wear It! — Friends of the Rag	Strosnider, Ann	√		Fa	6	3		M/J 79	35
People: Penages, Melissa	Art to Wear: Looking At the Movement	Scarborough, Jessica	√		Fa	12	3		M/J 85	56
People: Penalba, Alicia	"Fiberworks" (Exhibit)	Park, Betty	√		Fa	4	6		N/D 77	10
People: Pendleton, Mary	Arizona Arts Center at Sedona Offers Program Year Around	Warren, Hamilton	√		H&C	13	1		Wi 62	16
People: Pendleton, Mary	Ohio Weaving Venture, An	Pendleton, Mary	√		H&C	4	4		Fa 53	23
People: Pennington, Fred A.	Pennington Linens, Iowa Weaver Collects Old Designs		√		H&C	16	3		Su 65	14
People: Pennington, Lora	Garment Form As Image, The	Koplos, Janet	√		Fa	10	6		N/D 83	66
People: Pennington, Lora	Sculptural Paper: Foundations and Directions	Scarborough, Jessica	√		Fa	11	2		M/A 84	32
People: Pepper, David	Masks At the Heart of Disguise	Koplos, Janet	√		Fa	11	5		S/O 84	32
People: Percival, Sande	"Felting" (Exhibit)	Park, Betty	√		Fa	7	6		N/D 80	71
People: Perez, Sheila	"Wearables" (Exhibit)	Grover, Donald	√		Fa	6	6		N/D 79	76
People: Perry, Pamela	Country of Origin, USA: A Decade of Contemporary Rugs	Stevens, Rebeccah A. T.	√		Fa	11	3		M/J 84	60
People: Perry, Pamela	"Show of Fans, A" (Exhibit)	Goodman, Deborah Lerme	√		Fa	12	6		N/D 85	56
People: Perry, Pamela Vea	Fans and Fan Imagery	Howe, Katherine; Joanne Mattera	√		Fa	9	4		J/A 82	26

SUBJECT	TITLE	AUTHOR	IL	INST	JOUR	VOL	NO	ISS	DATE	PAGE
People: Pertegato, Francesco	Textile Sleuth Extraordinaire	Wasiqullah, Alexander	√		Fa	12	2		M/A 85	39
People: Peters, George	"Space Sails: American Banners" (Exhibit)	Deyo, Diane	√		Fa	9	5		S/O 82	82
People: Peterson, Barbara	Guild in Focus: Fiber Artisans, A	Kline, Martha	√		Fa	11	5		S/O 84	47
People: Peterson, Jo	"Local Options: The Work of Laura Strand Mills and Jo Peterson" (Exhibit)	Ferguson, Tom	√		Fa	10	3		M/J 83	69
People: Peterson, Jo	Public Fiber: Looking At the Logistics	Koplos, Janet	√		Fa	12	1		J/F 85	32
People: Petrich, Nora	Piecing Cloth to Harness the Wind	Montgomery, Larry	√	√	TM			11	J/J 87	48
People: Petrini, Marcy	Computers Don't Weave (error-corrected SS&D v14 n4 83 p4)	Petrini, Marcy	√		SS&D	14	3	55	Su 83	62
People: Petrini, Marcy F.	Profile of an HGA Rep		√		SS&D	18	1	69	Wi 86	37
People: Pfannebecker, Robert	Robert Pfannebecker: A Collector's Point of View	Park, Betty	√		Fa	5	4		J/A 78	42
People: Pfeiffer, Judy	Good Hope Farm	Sitko, Jane Bradley	√		SS&D	18	2	70	Sp 87	40
People: Pfeiffer, Judy	Judy Pfeiffer				SS&D	18	2	70	Sp 87	5
People: Phillips, Ellen	Felt and Paper: A Portfolio		√		Fa	13	4		J/A 86	35
People: Phillips, Mary Walker	Mary Walker Phillips	Weissman, Julia	√		Kn	1	2	2	S-S 85	15
People: Phillips, Mary Walker	Mary Walker Phillips, Her New Approach to Knitting		√		H&C	16	2		Sp 65	17
People: Phillips, Mary Walker	"Mary Walker Phillips — Wall Hangings" (Exhibit)	Mathews, Richard; Joan Burton	√		Fa	3	4		J/A 76	8
People: Phillips, Mary Walker	Mother of Creative Knitting, The	Hecker, Carolyn	√		Fa	7	1		J/F 80	34
People: Phillips, Ossie	Ossie Phillips: A Tradition of Mountain Weaving	Sheward, Cynthia M.	√		Fa	14	2		M/A 87	25
People: Pickett, Alice	Alice Pickett: Rugmaker	Pickett, Alice	√		Fa	7	5		S/O 80	55
People: Pickett, Alice	Country of Origin, USA: A Decade of Contemporary Rugs	Stevens, Rebeccah A. T.	√		Fa	11	3		M/J 84	60
People: Pickett, Barbara Setsu	Feltmaking Now: The Exciting Revival of an Ancient Technique	Gordon, Beverly	√		Fa	6	6		N/D 79	43
People: Pickett, Barbara Setsu	Handwoven Velvet of Barbara Pickett, The	Cohn, Lisa	√	√	Hw	8	1		J/F 87	20
People: Pierce, Lynn	Lynn Pierce	Pierce, Lynn	√		Fa	14	4		S/O 87	18
People: Pierce, Sue	Art Consultants: Bridging the Gap Between Artist and Client	Goodman, Deborah Lerme	√		Fa	12	6		N/D 85	31
People: Pierruci, Louise	Fiber Ten	McGuire, Patricia	√		Fa	4	6		N/D 77	26
People: Pierucci, Louise	Louise Pierucci: A Triumph of Tenacity	McGuire, Patricia	√		SS&D	6	4	24	Fa 75	41
People: Pierucci, Louise	Papermaking: Where It's Going	Pierucci, Louise	√	√	SS&D	10	4	40	Fa 79	47
People: Pierucci, Louise Holeman	Open Jurying in Pittsburg: Putting Your Work on the Line (Exhibit)	Myrinx, Elaine	√		Fa	6	2		M/A 79	23
People: Pierucci-Holeman, Louise	Convergence Preview — Six Peaks, A		√		SS&D	11	2	42	Sp 80	47
People: Pieters, Edward	"Works In, On, and Of Paper" (Exhibit)	Les, Kathleen	√		Fa	6	5		S/O 79	79
People: Pintor, V. A.	Papermaking in Chicago	Shermeta, Margo	√		Fa	11	2		M/A 84	54
People: Pitman, Louise L.	American Handweaving 1960		√		H&C	11	2		Sp 60	11
People: Pixley, Anne Flaten	"Anne Flaten Pixley" (Exhibit)	Mattera, Joanne	√		Fa	6	6		N/D 79	68
People: Pixley, Anne Flaten	"Ninth International Biennial of Tapestry" (Exhibit)	Pulleyn, Rob	√		Fa	6	4		J/A 79	62
People: Plaisted, Mary Bridget	Mary Bridget Plaisted, Colorado Weaver		√	√	H&C	22	1		Wi 71	15
People: Plaisted, Mary Bridget	One Hundred Sixty Years of Craftsmanship	Ligon, Linda	√		Iw	1	3		Sp 76	17
People: Plato, Geraldine	Under Wraps		√		Fa	12	3		M/J 85	26
People: Platus, Libby	Fiber Workspaces: A Room of Your Own	Bishop, Mara	√		Fa	4	4		J/A 77	38
People: Platus, Libby	Libby Platus: Heroic Fiber Sculpture		√		SS&D	6	4	24	Fa 75	4
People: Plewka-Schmidt, Urszula	"Ninth International Biennial of Tapestry" (Exhibit)	Pulleyn, Rob	√		Fa	6	4		J/A 79	62
People: Plotner, Judith	Masks At the Heart of Disguise	Koplos, Janet	√		Fa	11	5		S/O 84	32
People: Plummer, Beverly	How Does Your Garden Grow? Plant Fibers and Handmade Paper	Plummer, Beverly	√		Fa	6	4		J/A 79	34
People: Plummer, Beverly	Papermaking in the U.S.A.	Toale, Bernard	√		Fa	9	4		J/A 82	34

SUBJECT	TITLE	AUTHOR	IL	INST	JOUR	VOL	NO	ISS	DATE	PAGE
People: Pohlman, Marjorie	Marjorie Pohlman		√		Fa	4	6		N/D 77	45
People: Pohlmann, Marj	Focus on the HGA Board of Directors		√		SS&D	10	1	37	Wi 78	52
People: Poisson, R.	Imagery Is Personal in Tapestry Today	Clausen, Valerie	√		TM			9	F/M 87	66
People: Polansky, Lois	Containers of Human Experience: Fragments from the Life of Lois Polansky	Muller, Marion	√		Fa	14	5		N/D 87	32
People: Polansky, Lois	Garment Form As Image, The	Koplos, Janet	√		Fa	10	6		N/D 83	66
People: Polansky, Lois	"Show of Fans, A" (Exhibit)	Goodman, Deborah Lerme	√		Fa	12	6		N/D 85	56
People: Pollack, Junco Sato	"Contemporary Shibori" (Exhibit)	Howe, Cathe	√		Fa	11	3		M/J 84	82
People: Pollack, Junco Sato	Junco Sato Pollack: Seashells of Silk	Norton, Deborah	√		Fa	12	3		M/J 85	18
People: Pollack, Junco Sato	Sericulture in Upstate New York	Bard, Elizabeth A.	√		Fa	13	1		J/F 86	36
People: Pollack, Junco Sato	"Soft As Silk" (Exhibit)	Guagliumi, Susan	√		Fa	10	1		J/F 83	78
People: Pollack, Mark	"Interlacing: The Elemental Fabric" (Exhibit)		√		Fa	14	3		M/J 87	62
People: Pollack, Mark C.	Made by Machine: Textiles for the Eighties	Harris, Patricia; David Lyon	√		Fa	12	5		S/O 85	34
People: Pollen, J.	Surface Designers Meet in Nantucket	Northup, Wendy			TM			9	F/M 87	16
People: Pollock, Junco Sato	Surface Designers Meet in Nantucket	Northup, Wendy			TM			9	F/M 87	16
People: Pollock, Martha	Martha Pollock	Bryan, Dorothy	√		H&C	7	4		Fa 56	7
People: Poon, Vivian	Vivian Poon: Exposing Facades	Rowley, Kathleen	√		Fa	13	4		J/A 86	12
People: Pope, Bill	Pope of Lightship Baskets, The	Hoppe, Flo	√		SS&D	18	1	69	Wi 86	30
People: Popenoe, Laura K.	Felt and Paper: A Portfolio		√		Fa	13	4		J/A 86	35
People: Poplawski, Stefan	Lausanne Notebook: Our Special Report on the 8th Lausanne Biennial of Tapestry, A	Mathews, Rich	√		Fa	4	5		S/O 77	30
People: Porcella, Yvonne	"Five Artists: Quilts" (Exhibit)	Scarborough, Jessica	√		Fa	13	5		S/O 86	47
People: Porcella, Yvonne	For the Body (error-corrected Fa v10 n2 83 p61)		√		Fa	10	1		J/F 83	32
People: Porcella, Yvonne	Silkworks	Goodman, Deborah Lerme	√		Fa	13	1		J/F 86	50
People: Porcella, Yvonne	Yvonne Porcella		√		Fa	4	5		S/O 77	52
People: Porcella, Yvonne	Yvonne Porcella	Porcella, Yvonne	√		Fa	13	6		N/D 86	3
People: Porcella, Yvonne	Yvonne Porcella: A Modern Master of the Ethnic Clothing Tradition	Avery, Virginia	√		Fa	8	1		J/F 81	63
People: Portela, Carmo	Carmo Portela, Portuguese Tapestry Weaver	Portela, Carmo	√		SS&D	17	4	68	Fa 86	35
People: Porter, Allan	Tapestry by Allan Porter		√		H&C	14	2		Sp 63	13
People: Porter, Faith	"Fantasy Clothes/Fantastic Costumes" (Exhibit)	Dyer, Carolyn	√		Fa	4	2		M/A 77	11
People: Porter, Faith	"Great American Foot, The" (Exhibit)	Grover, Donald	√		Fa	5	4		J/A 78	15
People: Porter, Phil	Liturgical Vestment: A Contemporary Overview, The	Malarcher, Patricia	√		Fa	11	5		S/O 84	58
People: Posin, Mitchell	Fiber on Martha's Vineyard	Erickson, Johanna	√		Fa	11	4		J/A 84	46
People: Post, Linda R.	"Stitchery '79" (Exhibit)	Kerr, Connie	√		Fa	6	5		S/O 79	78
People: Postek, Stanley	Rope Sculpture: Stanley Postek		√		H&C	26	5		Oc 75	9
People: Postek, Stanley	Stanley Postek, Who Learned Macramé At Sea		√	√	H&C	21	3		Su 70	8
People: Potter, Maggie	HGA Scholarships '79		√		SS&D	10	4	40	Fa 79	100
People: Poussart, Anne	From the Collection of Anne Poussart		√	√	WJ	7	3	27	Wi 82	62
People: Powell, Carolyn	Bottom Line, The	Weissman, Julia	√		Kn	3	4	8	Fa 87	11
People: Power-Kleiner, Jacquelyn	Return of the Rag, The	Basa, Lynn	√		Fa	14	3		M/J 87	29
People: Poxson-Fawkes, Judith	Conversion of Sorts: Judith Poxson Fawkes—A Background in Painting, A Present in Weaving, A	Griffin, Rachael	√		Fa	7	6		N/D 80	52
People: Prager, Gail Reed	Patchwork Re-Ordered	Talley, Charles	√		Fa	7	1		J/F 80	24
People: Preckshot, Amy	Handwoven Clothing Today: The Couturier Touch	West, Virginia	√		Fa	8	1		J/F 81	39
People: Preston, Jan	"Fiber As Art" An Exhibition in the Philippines (Exhibit)		√		Fa	7	6		N/D 80	76
People: Price, Ken	"Artists' Quilts" (Exhibit)	Woelfle, Gretchen	√		Fa	8	4		J/A 81	70

SUBJECT	TITLE	AUTHOR	IL	INST	JOUR	VOL	NO	ISS	DATE	PAGE
People: Prichard, Nancy	Felt and Paper: A Portfolio		√		Fa	13	4		J/A 86	35
People: Prince, Neil	"Forms in Fiber" (Exhibit)	Brown, Arleen Emery	√		Fa	7	5		S/O 80	73
People: Prince, Neil	Fran Kraynek-Prince and Neil Prince	Scarborough, Jessica	√		Fa	12	5		S/O 85	19
People: Priscilla, Lil	Junque Quilts	Murray, Clare	√		Fa	14	4		S/O 87	6
People: Proust, Geoffrey	Continuing Tradition, A		√		Fa	9	2		M/A 82	100
People: Pujol, Elliott	"Basketry: Tradition in New Form" (Exhibit)	Scarborough, Jessica	√		Fa	9	3		M/J 82	83
People: Pulleyn, Robert	"Textiles New Mexico 1976" (Exhibit)	Warner, Lucy Ann	√		Fa	3	2		M/A 76	12
People: Purdom, Lois	"Seven Sonoma County Fibre Artists" (Exhibit)	Robinson, Sharon	√		Fa	3	4		J/A 76	6
People: Puryear, Marjorie Durko	Marjorie Durko Puryear	Puryear, Marjorie Durko	√		Fa	14	4		S/O 87	19
People: Quambusch-Rapaud, Anne	Under Wraps		√		Fa	12	3		M/J 85	26
People: Quargnali, Enza	Enza Quargnali: Batiker		√		Fa	4	2		M/A 77	34
People: Quigley, Viola-Joyce	Handweaving in Memphis	Hansen, Helen; Meade Nichol	√		H&C	8	1		Wi 56	19
People: Raab, Belinda	Belinda Raab: Exploring an Interior World	Roberts, Kaki	√		Fa	14	2		M/A 87	14
People: Rabinowe, Eve	Fiber Workspaces: A Room of Your Own	Bishop, Mara	√		Fa	4	4		J/A 77	38
People: Rabinowe, Victoria	Lifestyle: A Roundtable Discussion	Ligon, Linda	√		Iw	5	2		Sp 80	22
People: Rabinowe, Victoria	Santa Fe Weaving Center, The	Elliott, Malinda	√		Fa	9	5		S/O 82	32
People: Rabinowe, Victoria	Victoria Rabinowe		√		Fa	3	6		N/D 76	18
People: Rademacher, Jane	Jane Rademacher: A Working Weaver in Rural Wisconsin	Lowell-LaRoque, Jane V.	√		Fa	6	2		M/A 79	21
People: Rademacher, Jane	"Seventh Annual Twin Ports Fibers Invitational" (Exhibit)	LaRoque, Jane V. Lowell	√		Fa	7	3		M/J 80	80
People: Rahoult, Lena	"Scandinavian Touch, The" A Traveling Exhibit (Exhibit)	Mattera, Joanna	√		Fa	10	1		J/F 83	82
People: Rajch, Andrzej	"Fifth Lodz Triennale, The" (Exhibit)	Ravarra, Patricia	√		Fa	13	3		M/J 86	50
People: Rajnai, John	Tailor on Pressing, A	Hostek, Stanley	√	√	TM			10	A/M 87	43
People: Rake, Jane	Jane Rake's Crochet	Dunn, Katherine	√		Fa	6	3		M/J 79	62
People: Rakowska, Jadwiga	Decorative Miniatures in Silk by Jadwiga Rakowska		√		H&C	10	2		Sp 59	22
People: Randles, Virginia	"Quilt National '79" (Exhibit)	Gutcheon, Beth	√		Fa	6	5		S/O 79	80
People: Rankin, Ann	"Stitchery '79" (Exhibit)	Kerr, Connie	√		Fa	6	5		S/O 79	78
People: Ranney, Diane	Fabric of Creativity: Weaving Together Left– and Right–Brain Activites, The	Miles, Candice St. Jacques	√		Fa	11	6		N/D 84	44
People: Rapoport, Debra	"Baker/Rapoport/Wick" in New York (Exhibit)	Park, Betty	√		Fa	4	5		S/O 77	15
People: Rapport, Debra	Creative Process: Debra Rapport, The	Rapport, Debra	√		Fa	11	6		N/D 84	34
People: Ray, Carolyn	Fabric Painting in New York	Katz, Ruth J.	√		Fa	9	1		J/F 82	61
People: Raynor, Penny	Sampler of Surface Design, A	Westphal, Katherine	√		Fa	10	5		S/O 83	39
People: Reagles, Shirley	"California Fibers: 11th Annual Show" (Exhibit)	Kosta, Angela	√		Fa	10	6		N/D 83	81
People: Reckewell, Sabine	"Fiber Structures and Fabric Surfaces" (Exhibit)	Itter, Diane	√		Fa	7	1		J/F 80	67
People: Redding, Debbie and Eric	Setting Up Shop	Ligon, Linda	√		Iw	2	4		Su 77	18
People: Redding, Noreen	Athens Tapestry Works	Many, Paul	√		Fa	5	4		J/A 78	51
People: Redding, Winogene	Sixty Years of Weaving At Arrowmont	Johnson, Debbie	√		Fa	12	5		S/O 85	39
People: Redding, Winogene B.	Do You Want to Sell Your Weaving?	Redding, Winogene B.			H&C	5	1		Wi 53	30
People: Redfield, Sarah	"Beyond the Fringe" (Exhibit)	Einstein, Sylvia	√		Fa	7	2		M/A 80	70
People: Reed, Irene C.	Good As Gold: Alternatives in American Jewelry		√		Fa	9	5		S/O 82	18
People: Reed, Joanna	Crewel Gardens	Cunningham, Anne S.	√		TM			6	A/S 86	48
People: Rees, Linda E.	"Fibers Unlimited" (Exhibit)	Sherwood, Thomas	√		Fa	5	1		J/F 78	14
People: Reese, Karen	Karen Reese		√		Fa	4	3		M/J 77	32
People: Reeve, Catharine	Papermaking in Chicago	Shermeta, Margo	√		Fa	11	2		M/A 84	54
People: Reeve, Jay	Men Who Knit	Xenakis, Alexis Yiorgos	√		Kn	3	2	6	Sp 87	14

SUBJECT	TITLE	AUTHOR	IL	INST	JOUR	VOL	NO	ISS	DATE	PAGE
People: Reeves, Jane	"Quilts by Jane Reeves" (Exhibit)		√		Fa	14	1		J/F 87	71
People: Regensteiner, Else	American Handweaving 1960		√		H&C	11	2		Sp 60	9
People: Regensteiner, Else	SS&D Interview: Else Regensteiner	Towner, Naomi Whiting	√		SS&D	10	2	38	Sp 79	4
People: Reichel, Myra	Handwoven Clothing Today: The Couturier Touch	West, Virginia	√		Fa	8	1		J/F 81	39
People: Reike, Gail	It's All It Can Be: The Work of Gail Reike		√		Fa	3	2		M/A 76	20
People: Reis, Christine Olsen	Beaded Fish (Christine Olsen Reis)		√		TM			11	J/J 87	84
People: Renee, Paula	Paula Renee	Renee, Paula	√		Fa	13	6		N/D 86	3
People: Renee, Paula	Tree of Life	Renee, Paula	√		SS&D	17	2	66	Sp 86	80
People: Renne, Elisha	Table Dressing and Bedcovers		√		Fa	8	3		M/J 81	43
People: Renne, Joan	Dream Weaver: Joan Renne		√		WJ	12	1	45	Su 87	40
People: Replinger, Dot	Review/Discussion of Artspace's Innovative Yet Flawed "Fiber Freely Interpreted", A (Exhibit)		√		Fa	4	2		M/A 77	38
People: Resen, Gail J.	Portfolio of Contemporary Fiber Sculpture, A		√		Fa	11	4		J/A 84	34
People: Resen, Gail Johnson	Poetry in Fiber: Gail Johnson Resen Talks About Her Work	Resen, Gail Johnson	√		Fa	7	4		J/A 80	20
People: Restieaux, Mary	"Gaudy Ladies" (Exhibit)		√		Fa	8	4		J/A 81	44
People: Reve	If the Art Fits – Wear It! — Friends of the Rag	Strosnider, Ann	√		Fa	6	3		M/J 79	35
People: Rex, Chris	Speakers Bureau Presents				SS&D	8	1	29	WI 76	60
People: Reynolds, Henry	Story of Henry Reynolds, The		√		H&C	4	2		Sp 53	23
People: Rhein, Eric	For the Body (error-corrected Fa v10 n2 83 p61)		√		Fa	10	1		J/F 83	32
People: Rhein, Margaret	HGA Scholarship Winners Challenge the Future		√		SS&D	6	4	24	Fa 75	43
People: Rhodes, Tonya	Contemporary Costume, Strictly Handwoven: Tonya Rhodes	Tidball, Harriet	√		SCGM		24		68	26
People: Riccardi, Mary Elinor Steinbaugh	Speakers Bureau Presents		√		SS&D	9	1	33	Wi 77	51
People: Rice, Miriam	Mushroom Dyes	Meltzer-Smith, Sandra Jo	√		SS&D	11	3	43	Su 80	53
People: Rice, Mirian C.	Stalking the Wild Mushroom	Pepin, Yvonne	√	√	SS&D	16	4	64	Fa 85	22
People: Rich, Florence	Traditional Rug Hooking with a Twist	Erickson, Janet Doub	√	√	TM			12	A/S 87	30
People: Richards-Watson, Linda	Linda Richards-Watson: Finding the Eclectic	Rowley, Kathleen	√		Fa	10	4		J/A 83	12
People: Riebman, Ronna	Flowers, Beautiful Flowers: Ronna Riebman, Batik: Mary Lynn O'Shea, Tapestry		√		Fa	8	3		M/J 81	35
People: Riedl, Fritz	Tapestries by Fritz Riedl		√		H&C	18	3		Su 67	42
People: Riegger, Hal	Exhibition by Larsen and Riegger Indicates Broadening Field of Craft Cooperation		√		H&C	2	2		Sp 51	32
People: Riegler, Maggie	Maggie Riegler Exhibit Tours USA		√		SS&D	4	1	13	Wi 72	32
People: Riegler, Maggie	Three British Weavers	Held, Shirley E.			H&C	23	6		N/D 72	33
People: Rieke, Gail	"Textiles New Mexico 1978" (Exhibit)	Tatum, Phyllis	√		Fa	5	4		J/A 78	10
People: Rieke, Gail and Zachariah	Rieke, Rieke — A Study in Beauty, Silence and Collaboration		√		Fa	5	6		N/D 78	35
People: Rieke, Zachariah	"Textiles New Mexico 1978" (Exhibit)	Tatum, Phyllis	√		Fa	5	4		J/A 78	10
People: Riis, John	Commissions: The Process, the Problems and the Prospects		√		Fa	6	5		S/O 79	45
People: Riis, John Eric	Speakers Bureau Presents		√		SS&D	4	3	15	Su 73	19
People: Riis, Jon Eric	Riis, Mafong Collaborate in Thread & Silver		√		SS&D	5	1	17	Wi 73	4
People: Rinaldi, Zorine	"Interweave 79" (Exhibit)	Constantinides, Kathy	√		Fa	7	1		J/F 80	66
People: Ringgold, Faith	Woman on a Pedestal and Other Everyday Folks	Guyer, Niki	√		Fa	8	2		M/A 81	22
People: Ripps, Rodney	Whitney Museum of American Art, The (Exhibit)	Park, Betty	√		Fa	9	2		M/A 82	11

SUBJECT	TITLE	AUTHOR	IL	INST	JOUR	VOL	NO	ISS	DATE	PAGE
People: Rivers, Victoria	"Beds, Sweet Dreams, and Other Things" (Exhibit)	Bissell, June	√		Fa	6	4		J/A 79	70
People: Rivers, Victoria	Revelations: Victoria Rivers' Neon and Fabric Constructions		√		Fa	8	5		S/O 81	50
People: Rivers, Victoria	Victoria Rivers: Sculpting in Fiber and Neon	Scarborough, Jessica	√		Fa	12	1		J/F 85	22
People: Robberts, Lea	"Decade of Fibers, A" (Exhibit)	Franklin, Sue	√		Fa	5	1		J/F 78	17
People: Robbins, Louise	"Decade of Fibers, A" (Exhibit)	Franklin, Sue	√		Fa	5	1		J/F 78	17
People: Robbins, Louise	Louise Robbins	Vander Lee, Jana	√		Fa	3	2		M/A 76	26
People: Roberti, Marilyn	Sampler of Surface Design, A	Westphal, Katherine	√		Fa	10	5		S/O 83	39
People: Roberts, Cliff	"Fiber Departures" (Exhibit)	Dyer, Carolyn	√		Fa	4	3		M/J 77	9
People: Roberts, Louis	American Handweaving 1960		√		H&C	11	2		Sp 60	11
People: Roberts, Miriam Nathan	"Emerging Quiltmakers" (Exhibit)	McMorris, Penny	√		Fa	12	1		J/F 85	75
People: Roberts, Trudi	California Rags	Saulson, Sarah F.	√	√	SS&D	18	1	69	Wi 86	44
People: Robertsdottir, Ragna	Fiber Art in Iceland	Hrafnhildur, Schram	√		Fa	9	6		N/D 82	68
People: Robertson, Bill	She Likes to Do a Little Needlework (Esther Robertson)		√		TM			13	O/N 87	92
People: Robertson, Esther	She Likes to Do a Little Needlework (Esther Robertson)		√		TM			13	O/N 87	92
People: Robinson, Irma	American Handweaving 1960		√		H&C	11	2		Sp 60	48
People: Robinson, Irma	Color Theory for Handweavers Part 2: Visual Mix	Boutin-Wald, Pat	√	√	WJ	10	3	39	Wi 86	47
People: Robinson, Joyce	Pikes Peak Weavers Guild First Fibre Arts Festival (Exhibit)	Fife, Lin	√		Fa	3	5		S/O 76	6
People: Robinson, Sharon	Army of Softies: An Artist Talks About Her Delightfully Peculiar Obsession, An	Robinson, Sharon	√		Fa	8	6		N/D 81	25
People: Robinson, Sharon	For the Body (error-corrected Fa v10 n2 83 p61)		√		Fa	10	1		J/F 83	32
People: Roche, Kevin	Everyday World of Fantasy, The	Smeltzer, Nancy	√		Fa	13	3		M/J 86	6
People: Rockwell, Svetlana	Getting Into the Galleries: Nine Dealers Tell How to Do It		√		Fa	9	5		S/O 82	43
People: Rodman, Betty	Betty Rodman, an Integrated Life	Staines, Barbara			S-O	4			80	19
People: Rodriguez, Maria	Maria Rodriguez		√		Hw	7	5		N/D 86	37
People: Roesch-Sanchez, Jacquelyn	Art to Wear: Looking At the Movement	Scarborough, Jessica	√		Fa	12	3		M/J 85	56
People: Roesch-Sanchez, Jacquelyn	Machine Knitting: The State of the Art		√		Fa	9	2		M/A 82	40
People: Roesch-Sanchez, Jacquelyn	Succeeding with the Knitting Machine	Mattera, Joanne	√		TM			2	D/J 85	50
People: Rogers, Sally	Quilting for World Peace	Shufro, Cathy	√		TM			10	A/M 87	14
People: Rogoyska, Marta	"Gaudy Ladies" (Exhibit)		√		Fa	8	4		J/A 81	44
People: Rogoyska, Marta	Imagery Is Personal in Tapestry Today	Clausen, Valerie	√		TM			9	F/M 87	66
People: Rogoyska, Marta	Three English Tapestry Weavers	Liebler, Barbara	√		Hw	3	1		Ja 82	61
People: Rolstad, Koryn	Bannerworks	Strosnider, Ann	√		Fa	10	5		S/O 83	66
People: Romeis, Dana	Dana Romeis: Spatial Problem-Solving	Detter, Jan	√		Fa	14	1		J/F 87	18
People: Romesberg, Gail	"Textiles New Mexico 1976" (Exhibit)	Warner, Lucy Ann	√		Fa	3	2		M/A 76	12
People: Rommerts, Joke	"Third International Exhibition of Miniature Textiles 1978" (Exhibit)	Spencer, Patricia	√		Fa	6	1		J/F 79	90
People: Ronin, Col. James Arthur	Colonel Ronin, Spinning Flyer	Ligon, Linda	√		Iw	2	4		Su 77	25
People: Rose, Elsie	Weaver Rose — A New Perspective	Kaye, Alda Ganze	√		SS&D	8	2	30	Sp 77	8
People: Rose, Sally	Portfolio of Contemporary Fiber Sculpture, A		√		Fa	11	4		J/A 84	34
People: Rose, Sally	"Private Spaces, Private Lives" A Juried Fiber Show (Exhibit)	Hunt, Elizabeth Ann	√		Fa	7	6		N/D 80	75
People: Rose, William Henry Harrison	HGA Education Directory, 1984		√	> 4	SS&D	15	4	60	Fa 84	6
People: Rose, William Henry Harrison	One Hundred Years Ago in Handweaving				Hw	7	3		M/J 86	27

SUBJECT	TITLE	AUTHOR	IL	INST	JOUR	VOL	NO	ISS	DATE	PAGE
People: Rose, William Henry Harrison	Weaver Rose — A New Perspective	Kaye, Alda Ganze	√		SS&D	8	2	30	Sp 77	8
People: Rose, William Henry Harrison (Weaver Rose)	Weaver Rose of Rhode Island 1839–1913	Pariseau, George E., M.D.	√		H&C	6	1		Wi 54	4
People: Rosen, Carol	Carol Rosen: Paper Constructions	Scheinman, Pamela	√		Fa	11	2		M/A 84	16
People: Rosen, Carol	Paper and Wood Constructions (Exhibit)		√		Fa	13	5		S/O 86	54
People: Rosen, Evie	American Yarn Shops: On the Endangered Species List?	Xenakis, Alexis Yiorgos	√		Kn	3	4	8	Fa 87	10
People: Rosen, Norma	For the Body (error-corrected Fa v10 n2 83 p61)		√		Fa	10	1		J/F 83	32
People: Rosen, Norma	Norma Rosen: A Printmaker Turns to Fabrics	Cornett, James	√		Fa	7	4		J/A 80	23
People: Rosen-Queralt, Jann	Jann Rosen-Queralt: An Architecture Of Indirection	Rubin, Jean	√		Fa	12	2		M/A 85	47
People: Rosenbaum, Gail	Certificate Holders: What Now? Part 3, The	Alderman, Sharon D.	√		SS&D	13	2	50	Sp 82	60
People: Rosenberg, Bettina	"Textiles New Mexico 1976" (Exhibit)	Warner, Lucy Ann	√		Fa	3	2		M/A 76	12
People: Rosenberg, Kay	Boston Seven	Newman, Rochelle	√		SS&D	16	3	63	Su 85	71
People: Rosetti, Gioanventura	Gioanventura Rosetti and His Dye Book—1548 A. D.	Bliss, Anne	√		Iw	3	1		Fa 77	36
People: Ross, Gloria	Contemporary Navajo Weaving	Hedlund, Ann Lane	√		WJ	11	1	41	Su 86	30
People: Ross, Mabel	Mabel Ross	Raven, Lee	√		S-O	9	2		Su 85	55
People: Rossbach, Ed	"Art Fabric: Mainstream, The" (Exhibit)	Janeiro, Jan	√		Fa	8	5		S/O 81	70
People: Rossbach, Ed	Designers on Design		√		Fa	10	4		J/A 83	28
People: Rossbach, Ed	Ed Rossbach	Rossbach, Ed	√		Fa	11	6		N/D 84	60
People: Rossbach, Ed	Ed Rossbach: Embracing the Fabric of Art	West, Virginia	√		Fa	9	1		J/F 82	31
People: Rossbach, Ed	"Fiber R/Evolution" (Exhibit)	Rudich, Sally	√		Fa	13	4		J/A 86	45
People: Rossbach, Ed	"Three Living Treasures from California" (Exhibit)	Brandford, Joanne Segal; Sandra Dickey Harner	√		Fa	12	5		S/O 85	70
People: Rossbach, Ed	What Makes a Basket a Basket?	Malarcher, Patricia	√		Fa	11	1		J/F 84	34
People: Rossbach, Ed	Words in Fiber	Rowley, Kathleen	√		Fa	11	2		M/A 84	66
People: Rossell, Ana	Ana Rossell: Weaving with Flair for C. A. R. E.	Ligon, Linda	√		Iw	3	1		Fa 77	18
People: Rossen, Lee	Design Exercises for Inspitarion and Fun	McNair, Peg	√	√	Fa	14	1		J/F 87	47
People: Rossiter, Prudence Punderson	"Artists in Aprons" (Exhibit)	Alonzo, Harriet	√		Fa	6	3		M/J 79	76
People: Rost, Inez	Weaving Guilds—A Special Sharing		√		Iw	5	2		Sp 80	52
People: Rothrock, Lynn	Lynn Rothrock: Disturbing Creatures, Menacing Devil Dolls	Wiley, Lois	√		Fa	6	1		J/F 79	75
People: Roush, Jack	Selling through Galleries		√		Iw	1	3		Sp 76	20
People: Rousseau, Jean-Jacque	To Be Not a Brute, Rousseau Made Lace	Hedrick, L. R.	√		TM			10	A/M 87	16
People: Rousseau-Vermette, Mariette	"Fiber Works — Americas & Japan" (Exhibit)	Kato, Kuniko Lucy	√		Fa	5	1		J/F 78	10
People: Rowley, Kathleen	Making a Living: Eight Fiber Artists Tell How They Do It	Rowley, Kathleen	√		Fa	9	5		S/O 82	38
People: Rowley, Kristin	Country of Origin, USA: A Decade of Contemporary Rugs	Stevens, Rebeccah A. T.	√		Fa	11	3		M/J 84	60
People: Rowley, Kristin Carlsen	Kristin Carlsen Rowley: Rugmaker	Rowley, Kristin Carlsen	√		Fa	7	5		S/O 80	52
People: Rubel, Sandy	Fashionable Threads		√		SS&D	8	4	32	Fa 77	70
People: Rubin, Deann Joy	Pictorial Tapestry: A Portfolio of Contemporary Work	Goodman, Deborah Lerme	√		Fa	10	3		M/J 83	29
People: Rubin, Deann Joy	Self-Portrait	Rubin, Deann Joy	√		SS&D	15	1	57	Wi 83	72
People: Rubottom, Sibyl	Floats of Fancy	Woelfle, Gretchen	√		Fa	8	2		M/A 81	52
People: Ruddick, Dorothy	"Art Fabric: Mainstream, The" (Exhibit)	Janeiro, Jan	√		Fa	8	5		S/O 81	70
People: Ruffner, Trenna	Postal Service Celebrates Lace		√		TM			12	A/S 87	22
People: Ruge, Jane	"Kimono East/Kimono West" (Exhibit)	Lusk, Jennie	√		Fa	7	5		S/O 80	71
People: Rundel, Wayne	Contemporary Basketry		√		Fa	8	3		M/J 81	39
People: Rupley, Penny	Penny Rupley	Ragland, Marla	√		Fa	5	4		J/A 78	52

SUBJECT	TITLE	AUTHOR	IL	INST	JOUR	VOL	NO	ISS	DATE	PAGE
People: Rupp, Clarice	Pikes Peak Weavers Guild First Fibre Arts Festival (Exhibit)	Fife, Lin	√		Fa	3	5		S/O 76	6
People: Ruskin, John	Story of Reticella, The	Cave, OEnone	√		H&C	11	3		Su 60	14
People: Rusoff, Beverly	Homage to Hats: Handmade Paper Drawing/Collages Honor a Women's Tradition	Rusoff, Beverly	√		Fa	8	1		J/F 81	80
People: Russell, Joan	Fiber Ten	McGuire, Patricia	√		Fa	4	6		N/D 77	26
People: Russell, Joan	Joan Russell: Space Series	McGuire, Patricia	√		Fa	12	4		J/A 85	18
People: Russell, Kate	Kate Russell: Weaving the Structure of Life	Russell, Kate	√		Fa	12	4		J/A 85	11
People: Ruszczynska-Szafranska, Agnieska	"Fiber Art: Tapestries and Wall Hangings" (Exhibit)	Koplos, Janet	√		Fa	6	6		N/D 79	75
People: Rutherford, Karen	"Fiber Structure National" (Exhibit)	Dyer, Carolyn	√		Fa	8	5		S/O 81	75
People: Rutherford, Karen Jenson	"Karen Jenson Rutherford: Wall Hangings" (Exhibit)	Towner, Naomi Whiting	√		Fa	7	6		N/D 80	72
People: Rutherford, Karen Jenson	Working with Linen: Karen Jenson Rutherford	Itter, Diane	√		Fa	14	2		M/A 87	34
People: Rutkowsky, Fran Cutrell	It Still Can Be Beautiful: Although Utilitarian	Rutkovsky, Fran Cutrell	√	√	SS&D	7	3	27	Su 76	57
People: Rutledge, Pat	"Pat Rutledge: Batiks" (Exhibit)	Ellis, Betty	√		Fa	9	1		J/F 82	77
People: Rutt, Richard	Bishop of Leicester, The	Rutt, Richard	√		Kn	4	1	9	Wi 87	10
People: Ruz, Otilia	Knitting Odyssey, A	Dyett, Linda	√	√	TM			13	O/N 87	48
People: Ryan, Catherine	Crazy Quilt for Babies Grand, A	Greenberg, Blue	√		Fa	8	2		M/A 81	31
People: Ryan, Maggy	"Five Women from Texas" (Exhibit)	Leach, Vivian	√		Fa	6	1		J/F 79	86
People: Ryan, Sally	Sampler of Surface Design, A	Westphal, Katherine	√		Fa	10	5		S/O 83	39
People: Saar, Betye	On the Edge: Betye Saar — Personal Time Travels	Woelfle, Gretchen Erskine	√		Fa	9	4		J/A 82	56
People: Saari, Leslie	Postal Service Celebrates Lace		√		TM			12	A/S 87	22
People: Sabiston, Carole	Carol Sabiston's Sails: An Expression of the Interaction of Sea and Land	Bellerby, Greg	√		Fa	10	3		M/J 83	16
People: Sacks, Star	Getting Into the Galleries: Nine Dealers Tell How to Do It		√		Fa	9	5		S/O 82	43
People: Sage, Priscilla	"In the Garden of Strange Gods" (Exhibit)	McDonald, Julie Jensen	√		Fa	14	4		S/O 87	41
People: Sage, Priscilla	Plastics in Fiber: A Persistent Presence	Malarcher, Patricia	√		Fa	12	1		J/F 85	56
People: Sage, Priscilla	Priscilla Sage	Clardy, Andrea	√		Fa	5	2		M/A 78	26
People: Sage, Priscilla	"Priscilla Sage: Small Paintings and Fiber Sculpture" (Exhibit)	Richerson, Suzanne	√		Fa	8	3		M/J 81	69
People: Sage, Priscilla	"Soft Art" (Exhibit)	Richerson, Suzanne	√		Fa	4	4		J/A 77	16
People: Sahlstrand, Margaret	Paper Clothing: West	Koplos, Janet	√		Fa	11	2		M/A 84	39
People: Sailors, Robert D.	Robert D. Sailors		√		H&C	16	4		Fa 65	6
People: Saint Laurent, Yves	"Yves Saint Laurent: 25 Years of Design" (Exhibit)	Lonier, Terri	√		Fa	12	1		J/F 85	76
People: Sakiestewa, Ramona	Contemporary Navajo Weaving	Hedlund, Ann Lane	√		WJ	11	1	41	Su 86	30
People: Sakiestewa, Ramona	Sweetgrass, Cedar & Sage: Portrait of a Southwestern Weaver	Schevill, Margot	√		WJ	10	1	37	Su 85	24
People: Sakurai, Sadako	Paper Clothing, East	Sahlstrand, Margaret	√	√	Fa	11	2		M/A 84	36
People: Salomon, Marjorie Scott	Making of a Weaver, The	Drooker, Penelope B.	√		SS&D	14	3	55	Su 83	28
People: Salomon, Moocho Scott	Woven World of Moocho Scott Salomon, The	Drooker, Penelope	√		Fa	11	5		S/O 84	22
People: Salt, Teresa Graham	Technicolor Tapestries of Teresa Graham Salt, The	Mathews, Kate	√		Fa	14	1		J/F 87	11
People: Salt, Theresa Graham	"North/South Carolina Fibers Competition" (Exhibit)	Laymon, Cynthia	√		Fa	10	4		J/A 83	68
People: Salvi Family	Patolu and Its Techniques	De Bone, Mary Golden	√	√	TMJ	4	3		76	49
People: Salzmann, Myra	"Fiber Structure National" (Exhibit)	Dyer, Carolyn	√		Fa	8	5		S/O 81	75
People: Samaras, Lucas	"Cloth Forms" (Exhibits)	Skudera, Gail	√		Fa	9	4		J/A 82	76
People: Sander, Florence	Weaving Guilds—A Special Sharing		√		Iw	5	2		Sp 80	53

SUBJECT	TITLE	AUTHOR	IL	INST	JOUR	VOL	NO	ISS	DATE	PAGE
People: Sanders, James	"Frontiers of Contemporary Weaving" (Exhibit)	Clark, Barbara	√		Fa	4	1		J/F 77	6
People: Sandiford, Margaret	Spinning—Australia	DeBoer, Janet			S-O	11	3		Fa 87	35
People: Sandoval, Alonzo Arturo	Lausanne Notebook: Our Special Report on the 8th Lausanne Biennial of Tapestry, A	Mathews, Rich	√		Fa	4	5		S/O 77	30
People: Sandoval, Arturo	Woven Collages of Arturo Sandoval, The	Park, Betty	√		Fa	6	5		S/O 79	70
People: Sandoval, Arturo Alonzo	Arturo Alonzo Sandoval	Sandoval, Arturo Alonzo	√		Fa	11	6		N/D 84	58
People: Sandoval, Arturo Alonzo	"Contemporary Directions in Fiber" (Exhibit)	Meloy, Margaret	√		Fa	14	4		S/O 87	42
People: Sandoval, Arturo Alonzo	"Forms and Surfaces" (Exhibit)		√		Fa	8	4		J/A 81	68
People: Sandoval, Arturo Alonzo	Plastics in Fiber: A Persistent Presence	Malarcher, Patricia	√		Fa	12	1		J/F 85	56
People: Sandoval, Arturo Alonzo	Silkworks	Goodman, Deborah Lerme	√		Fa	13	1		J/F 86	50
People: Santistevan, Maria	Pikes Peak Weavers Guild First Fibre Arts Festival (Exhibit)	Fife, Lin	√		Fa	3	5		S/O 76	6
People: Sarchielli, Judith	Judith Sarchielli: Mukluk Maker	Sarchielli, Judith	√		Fa	5	6		N/D 78	23
People: Sargent, Lori	Tapestry: Its Limitations Challenge Individual Creativity	Harvey, Nancy	√		SS&D	17	1	65	Wi 85	57
People: Sato, Wataru	Paper Clothing, East	Sahlstrand, Margaret	√	√	Fa	11	2		M/A 84	36
People: Sauer, Dick	New Images from the Loom: An Interview with Dick Sauer	Powis-Turner, Margaret	√		SS&D	6	4	24	Fa 75	56
People: Sauer, Jane	"Basketry Today: And Quilts from the Collection of Phyllis Haders" (Exhibits)	von Weise, Wenda	√		Fa	9	4		J/A 82	75
People: Sauer, Jane	"Fiber Forms: Linda Eyerman, Jane Sauer" (Exhibit)	Degener, Patricia	√		Fa	8	3		M/J 81	73
People: Sauer, Jane	Knotted Sculpture of Jane Sauer, The	Falconer, Crisa Meahl	√		Fa	13	3		M/J 86	31
People: Sauer, Jane	What Makes a Basket a Basket?	Malarcher, Patricia	√		Fa	11	1		J/F 84	34
People: Saupe, Deborah O'Brien	Deborah O'Brien Saupe: The Search for Balance	Gaynor, Katherine A.	√		Fa	13	5		S/O 86	24
People: Savaglau, Anne E.	"Miniature Fibers" (Exhibit)	Vanderburg, Jan	√		Fa	7	1		J/F 80	65
People: Saville, Joy	"Joy Saville: Contemporary Quilting" (Exhibits)	Park, Betty	√		Fa	9	4		J/A 82	72
People: Sayed, Ahmed	Contemporary Egyptian Childern's Tapestries		√		Fa	4	6		N/D 77	65
People: Sayler, Mary	Focus on the HGA Board of Directors		√		SS&D	10	3	39	Su 79	47
People: Scarborough, Jessica	Earth Batik: Jessica Scarborough Buries Her Art in the Earth	Scarborough, Jessica	√		Fa	7	6		N/D 80	41
People: Schaeffer, Bertha	Decorator's Use of Handwoven Fabrics, A	Storey, Walter Rendell	√		H&C	4	4		Fa 53	4
People: Schafler, Julie	Getting Into the Galleries: Nine Dealers Tell How to Do It		√		Fa	9	5		S/O 82	43
People: Schapiro, Miriam	Fans and Fan Imagery	Howe, Katherine; Joanne Mattera	√		Fa	9	4		J/A 82	26
People: Schapiro, Miriam	Garment Form As Image, The	Koplos, Janet	√		Fa	10	6		N/D 83	66
People: Scharf, Kenny	Body as Canvas, The	Koda, Harold	√		TM			8	D/J 86	56
People: Schattschneider, Ellen	More 1978 Scholarships		√		SS&D	10	1	37	Wi 78	107
People: Schedl, Naomi	"Material/Culture" (Exhibit)	Ross, Douglas	√		Fa	14	2		M/A 87	55
People: Schedl, Naomi	"Naomi Kark Schedl: Coverings, Enclosures, and Pathways" (Exhibit)	Richerson, Suzanne	√		Fa	11	4		J/A 84	73
People: Schedl, Naomi Kark	Naomi Kark Schedl: A Concern with Empty Cradles	Richerson, Suzanne	√		Fa	6	6		N/D 79	20
People: Schedl, Naomi Kark	Plastics in Fiber: A Persistent Presence	Malarcher, Patricia	√		Fa	12	1		J/F 85	56
People: Schedl, Naomi Kark	"Soft Art" (Exhibit)	Richerson, Suzanne	√		Fa	4	4		J/A 77	16
People: Scheinman, Pam	Casting Shadows: The Work of Pam Scheinman	Scheinman, Pam	√		Fa	5	1		J/F 78	60
People: Scheinman, Pam	Pleats, Pleats, Pleats: For Sculptural Garments and Sculpture Itself		√		Fa	9	1		J/F 82	40
People: Schell, Dennis	HGA Scholarship Winners Challenge the Future		√		SS&D	6	4	24	Fa 75	43
People: Scherer, Deidre	Portraits of Aging (Exhibit)		√		Fa	13	4		J/A 86	54

SUBJECT	TITLE	AUTHOR	IL	INST	JOUR	VOL	NO	ISS	DATE	PAGE
People: Schettino, Janet	Tenth Annual Textile Exhibition, Olive Hyde Art Gallery (Exhibit)	Papa, Nancy	√		Fa	5	4		J/A 78	13
People: Scheu, Georgia	Under Wraps		√		Fa	12	3		M/J 85	26
People: Scheuer, Ruth	"From American Looms: Scheuer Tapestry Studio" (Exhibit) (error-corrected Fa v12 n6 85 p9)	Park, Betty	√		Fa	12	5		S/O 85	76
People: Scheuer, Ruth Tannenbaum	Scheuer Tapestry Studio: Applying Old Techniques to New Ideas, The	Scheuer, Ruth Tannenbaum	√		Fa	10	3		M/J 83	39
People: Scheuer, Ruth Tannenbaum	Universe in a Shell, The		√		Fa	10	3		M/J 83	91
People: Schiele, Moik	Lausanne Notebook: Our Special Report on the 8th Lausanne Biennial of Tapestry, A	Mathews, Rich	√		Fa	4	5		S/O 77	30
People: Schimmel, Heidrun	Traces of Time	Schimmel, Heidrun	√		Fa	9	3		M/J 82	70
People: Schira, Cynthia	"Cynthia Schira" (Exhibit)	Park, Betty	√		Fa	5	3		M/J 78	13
People: Schira, Cynthia	"Cynthia Schira" (Exhibit)	Zopetti, Patti	√		Fa	6	4		J/A 79	73
People: Schira, Cynthia	Jacquard Project: Selections from the Current Exhibition, The		√		Fa	9	2		M/A 82	36
People: Schira, Cynthia	Lausanne Notebook: Our Special Report on the 8th Lausanne Biennial of Tapestry, A	Mathews, Rich	√		Fa	4	5		S/O 77	30
People: Schira, Cynthia	"Old Traditions/New Directions" (Exhibit)	West, Virginia	√		Fa	8	6		N/D 81	66
People: Schira, Cynthia	Selling through Galleries		√		lw	1	3		Sp 76	20
People: Schira, Cynthia	SS&D Interview: Cynthia Schira (error-corrected SS&D v10 n2 79 p56)	Park, Betty	√		SS&D	10	1	37	Wi 78	4
People: Schira, Cynthia	Textile Trends: The Museum Collection	Malarcher, Patricia	√		Fa	12	6		N/D 85	23
People: Schira, Cynthia	Time and Vision: The Work of Cynthia Schira	Janeiro, Jan	√		Fa	9	5		S/O 82	68
People: Schira, Cynthia	Using a Computer: Four Views		√		Fa	13	5		S/O 86	7
People: Schira, Cynthia	Weaving a Lifestyle: Cynthia Schira	Schira, Cynthia	√		lw	5	2		Sp 80	27
People: Schloss, Julia	Textile Trends: Collecting in Washington, D.C.	Goodman, Deborah Lerme	√		Fa	12	6		N/D 85	25
People: Schmidt, Sherry Conrad	"Baskets in La Jolla" (Exhibit)	Blaylock, Mary P.	√		Fa	11	1		J/F 84	79
People: Schmidt, Sherry Conrad	"Fiber Structure National" (Exhibit)	Dyer, Carolyn	√		Fa	8	5		S/O 81	75
People: Schmidtke, Margrit	Margrit Schmidtke: An Evolving Artist	Schmidtke, Sheila	√		Fa	13	5		S/O 86	42
People: Schneider, Charlotte	"Fibers Unlimited" (Exhibit)	Sherwood, Thomas	√		Fa	5	1		J/F 78	14
People: Schneider, John E.	Uncovering the Life and Weaving of John E. Schneider	Thieme, Otto Charles	√		SS&D	9	2	34	Sp 78	80
People: Schneider, Terri	Sampler of Surface Design, A	Westphal, Katherine	√		Fa	10	5		S/O 83	39
People: Schoettle, Marian	"Conceptual Clothing" (Exhibit)	Waller, Irene	√		Fa	14	3		M/J 87	62
People: Schofield, Barb	Everyday World of Fantasy, The	Smeltzer, Nancy	√		Fa	13	3		M/J 86	6
People: Schott, Lorelei	Weaving-Drawing-Painting-Paper, A Profile of Lorelei Schott		√		WJ	6	1	21	Su 81	13
People: Schroeder, Philis	Speakers Bureau Presents		√		SS&D	3	2	10	Sp 72	8
People: Schroeder, Philis (see also Alvic)	Philis Schroeder: No Room for Error		√		SS&D	6	3	23	Su 75	5
People: Schroeder, Susan	Quiltmaker's Art, A	Mattera, Joanne	√		Fa	10	2		M/A 83	33
People: Schulman, Barbara	"Private Spaces, Private Lives" A Juried Fiber Show (Exhibit)	Hunt, Elizabeth Ann	√		Fa	7	6		N/D 80	75
People: Schultz, Judith B.	"Focus on Fiber" (Exhibit)	Hecker, Carolyn	√		Fa	6	3		M/J 79	83
People: Schulze, Joan	"Joan Schulze" (Exhibit)	Papa, Nancy	√		Fa	4	3		M/J 77	17
People: Schulze, Joan	Making a Living: Eight Fiber Artists Tell How They Do It	Rowley, Kathleen	√		Fa	9	5		S/O 82	38
People: Schulze, Joan	Sampler of Surface Design, A	Westphal, Katherine	√		Fa	10	5		S/O 83	39
People: Schulze, Joan	Tenth Annual Textile Exhibition, Olive Hyde Art Gallery (Exhibit)	Papa, Nancy	√		Fa	5	4		J/A 78	13
People: Schumacher, E. F.	Craftsman and Social Conscience: E. F. Schumacher, The	Hepburn, Ian			Hw	6	1		J/F 85	20
People: Schumacher, E. F.	Dream—The Reality, The	Ligon, Linda	√		lw	3	4		Su 78	12

SUBJECT	TITLE	AUTHOR	IL	INST	JOUR	VOL	NO	ISS	DATE	PAGE
People: Schussheim, Rowen	Portfolio of Contemporary Fiber Sculpture, A		√		Fa	11	4		J/A 84	34
People: Schuster, Sherri	Inspired by Fiber: Textile Sensibility in Other Media	Malarcher, Patricia	√		Fa	10	6		N/D 83	33
People: Schwartzott, Carol Ann	"100% Wool" (Exhibit)	Goldin, Susan	√		Fa	4	6		N/D 77	18
People: Schweizer, Kerstin	Certificate Holders: Now What? Part 2, The	Alderman, Sharon D.	√		SS&D	12	4	48	Fa 81	52
People: Schwinn, Sylvia	"Seven Sonoma County Fibre Artists" (Exhibit)	Robinson, Sharon	√		Fa	3	4		J/A 76	6
People: Sciaretta-Potter, Maggie	Maggie Sciaretta-Potter: The Virtuosity of a Miniaturist	Talley, Charles	√		Fa	6	6		N/D 79	16
People: Sciarretta-Potter, Maggie	"Third Annual Fiber Show" (Exhibit)	Papa, Nancy	√		Fa	5	6		N/D 78	65
People: Scofield, Karen	Fashionable Palette of Pittsburgh Paints, The	Brenholts, Jeanne	√		Fa	14	3		M/J 87	46
People: Scott, Isabel	Isabel Scott Fabrics		√		H&C	9	1		Wi 57	8
People: Scott, Isabel	Isabel Scott, Handweaver and Designer	Storey, Walter Rendell	√		H&C	4	2		Sp 53	14
✛ People: Scott, Joyce J.	Good As Gold: Alternatives in American Jewelry		√		Fa	9	5		S/O 82	18
People: Scott, Lorelei	"Private Spaces, Private Lives" A Juried Fiber Show (Exhibit)	Hunt, Elizabeth Ann	√		Fa	7	6		N/D 80	75
People: Scott, Nell	Contemporary Costume, Strictly Handwoven: Nell Scott Originals	Tidball, Harriet	√		SCGM		24		68	1
People: Scott, Sue	Sue Scott		√		Fa	4	5		S/O 77	53
People: Sebastiane	"Conceptual Clothing" (Exhibit)	Waller, Irene	√		Fa	14	3		M/J 87	62
People: Sebert, Carol	Canadian Portfolio, A	Place, Jennifer	√		Fa	9	6		N/D 82	29
People: Seeks, Rosalie	Rosalie Seeks: Cascading Dream Garden	Richerson, Suzanne	√		Fa	12	1		J/F 85	21
People: Seeks, Rosalie	"Soft Art" (Exhibit)	Richerson, Suzanne	√		Fa	4	4		J/A 77	16
People: Seeks, Rosalie	"Women Artists: Clay, Fiber, Metal" (Exhibit)	Malarcher, Patricia	√		Fa	5	2		M/A 78	11
People: Seelig, Warren	Fans and Fan Imagery	Howe, Katherine; Joanne Mattera	√		Fa	9	4		J/A 82	26
People: Seelig, Warren	"Old Traditions/New Directions" (Exhibit)	West, Virginia	√		Fa	8	6		N/D 81	66
People: Seelig, Warren	Paper as Object	Ligon, Linda	√	√	Iw	2	3		Sp 77	19
People: Seelig, Warren	Questions of Style: Contemporary Trends in the Fiber Arts	Howe-Echt, Katherine	√		Fa	7	2		M/A 80	38
People: Seelig, Warren	"Vibrant Structures" (Exhibit)	Shermeta, Margo	√		Fa	11	6		N/D 84	75
People: Seelig, Warren	Warren Seelig	Park, Betty	√		Fa	7	5		S/O 80	59
People: Seelig, Warren	Warren Seelig: A Conversation	Ligon, Linda	√		Iw	3	2		Wi 78	20
People: Segal, Joanne	"Infrastructure" (Exhibit)	Malarcher, Patricia	√		Fa	11	4		J/A 84	76
People: Segunda, David	Ruth and David Segunda		√		Fa	4	6		N/D 77	62
People: Segunda, Ruth	Ruth and David Segunda		√		Fa	4	6		N/D 77	62
People: Seibert, Janet Behrens	Hi-Tech Banner Sculptures	Polster, Nancy; Elsa Sreenivasam	√		Fa	12	3		M/J 85	42
People: Seino, Shinnosuke	Shinnosuke Seino: Innovator with Wool	Schreiber, Lavonne	√		WJ	12	2	46	Fa 87	34
People: Sekijima, Hisako	"Basket-Maker's Art, The" (Exhibit)	Grover, Donald	√		Fa	6	6		N/D 79	73
People: Sekijima, Hisako	"Distilling the Essence of Basketry" (Exhibit)	Anderson, Ann Stewart	√		Fa	13	2		M/A 86	52
People: Sekijima, Hisako	Hisako Sekijima, Basketmaker	Koplos, Janet	√		Fa	13	5		S/O 86	14
People: Sekijima, Hisako	What Makes a Basket a Basket?	Malarcher, Patricia	√		Fa	11	1		J/F 84	34
✛ People: Sekimachi, Kay	"Fiberworks 1976" (Exhibit)	Papa, Nancy	√		Fa	4	1		J/F 77	9
✛ People: Sekimachi, Kay	"Infrastructure" (Exhibit)	Malarcher, Patricia	√		Fa	11	4		J/A 84	76
✛ People: Sekimachi, Kay	Kay Sekimachi: Successful on Her Own Terms	Talley, Charles	√		Fa	9	5		S/O 82	72
✛ People: Sekimachi, Kay	"Miniature Fibers" (Exhibit)	Vanderburg, Jan	√		Fa	7	1		J/F 80	65
✛ People: Sekimachi, Kay	Two Textile Artists Honored		√		TM			1	O/N 85	10
People: Selander, Malin	Designer Collection: Malin Selander		√	√	Hw	7	5		N/D 86	60
People: Selander, Malin	Malin Selander	Cromstedt, Cathrine	√		H&C	17	1		Wi 66	22
People: Selander, Malin	Swedish Workshop		√	√	H&C	12	4		Fa 61	12

SUBJECT	TITLE	AUTHOR	IL	INST	JOUR	VOL	NO	ISS	DATE	PAGE
People: Selander, Malin	Weaving a Lifestyle: Malin Selander	West, Virginia	√		lw	5	2		Sp 80	30
People: Self, Lois	Certificate Holders: Now What?, The	Alderman, Sharon D.	√		SS&D	12	2	46	Sp 81	41
People: Selfe, Jenny	Gooden Gansey Sweaters	Gallagher, Marten	√		Fa	12	6		N/D 85	12
People: Selfe, Pat	Gooden Gansey Sweaters	Gallagher, Marten	√		Fa	12	6		N/D 85	12
People: Selfridge, Gail	Knitting Machine Geometrics	Guagliumi, Susan	√	√	TM			10	A/M 87	66
People: Semmens, Beverly J.	"Fiber Forms '78" (Exhibit)	Patton, Ellen	√		Fa	5	5		S/O 78	66
People: Senger, Emma	Emma & Felix Senger		√		Fa	4	6		N/D 77	44
People: Senger, Felix	Emma & Felix Senger		√		Fa	4	6		N/D 77	44
People: Senner, Eileen	Miniatures in Fiber: Working Small—An Exciting Challenge for the Contemporary Fiber Artist	Malarcher, Patricia	√		Fa	7	4		J/A 80	32
People: Serff, Abraham	Designs from Serff Patterns	Abel, Isabel I.	√	> 4	H&C	11	4		Fa 60	6
People: Serpa, Geraldine	Pie in the Sky: The Irreverent Art of Geraldine Serpa	Serpa, Geraldine	√		Fa	6	4		J/A 79	26
People: Service, Jeff	Jeff Service		√		Fa	3	6		N/D 76	22
People: Sethna, Nelly H.	Designer-Weaver in India, A	Sethna, Nelly H.	√		H&C	17	2		Sp 66	18
People: Seventy, Sylvia	"Introductions '80" Emily DuBois and Sylvia Seventy (Exhibit)	Janeiro, Jan	√		Fa	7	6		N/D 80	70
People: Seventy, Sylvia	Making a Living: Eight Fiber Artists Tell How They Do It	Rowley, Kathleen	√		Fa	9	5		S/O 82	38
People: Seventy, Sylvia	Paper Vessels of Sylvia Seventy, The	Stofflet, Mary	√		Fa	11	2		M/A 84	70
People: Seventy, Sylvia	What Makes a Basket a Basket?	Malarcher, Patricia	√		Fa	11	1		J/F 84	34
People: Sewell, Elizabeth	HGA Scholarship Winners Challenge the Future		√		SS&D	6	4	24	Fa 75	43
People: Sewell, Suzy	Beyond Rags: Fabric Strip Design	Larson-Fleming, Susan	√	√	WJ	9	4	36	Sp 85	47
People: Shafer, Camille	Quiltmaking: A Celebration of Life — Esther Parkhurst, Camille Shafer, Pami Slatt Fagelson		√		Fa	8	3		M/J 81	26
People: Shah, Wendy	Wendy Shah: Subtle Rhythms	Mattera, Joanne	√		Fa	7	5		S/O 80	21
People: Shahzaman, Mahboob	Textile Arts of Multan, Pakistan	Shahzaman, Mahboob	√	> 4	SS&D	4	3	15	Su 73	8
People: Shannon, Betty	Focus on the HGA Board of Directors		√		SS&D	10	3	39	Su 79	46
People: Sharifi, Puri	Knitting Craft in Great Britain, The	Kinder, Kathleen	√		Fa	11	4		J/A 84	42
People: Sharpe, Susan	Images in Sharpe Focus: Susan Sharpe's Quilts Are Drawn, Painted and Stitched	Jernigan, Bonnie	√		Fa	10	2		M/A 83	19
People: Sharples, Genevah	HGA Board of Directors Candidates		√		SS&D	11	2	42	Sp 80	26
People: Shaw, Winifred	Winifred Shaw				SS&D	16	3	63	Su 85	4
People: Shaw, Winifred Clark	Win's Sweaters		√	√	WJ	8	3	31	Wi 83	12
People: Shaw-Sutton, Carol	Rites of Passage: Carol Shaw-Sutton's Twig and Thread Constructions	Park, Betty	√		Fa	7	6		N/D 80	49
People: Shaw-Sutton, Carol	Twelfth International Biennial of Tapestry	Taylor, Dianne; Elmer Taylor	√		Fa	12	6		N/D 85	50
People: Shaw-Sutton, Carol	"Works in Miniature" (Exhibit)	Malarcher, Patricia	√		Fa	7	3		M/J 80	82
People: Shaw-Sutton, Carol	"Young Americans: Fiber, Wood, Plastic, Leather" (Exhibit)	Malarcher, Patricia	√		Fa	4	6		N/D 77	14
People: Shawcroft, Barbara	Barbara Shawcroft	Shawcroft, Barbara	√		SS&D	3	1	9	Wi 71	25
People: Shawcroft, Barbara	"Barbara Shawcroft: Nets, Rope, and Cloth" (Exhibit)	Finucane, Brigid	√		Fa	12	4		J/A 85	68
People: Shawcroft, Barbara	Conversation with Barbara Shawcroft, A		√		H&C	22	3		Su 71	21
People: Shawcroft, Barbara	Conversation with Barbara Shawcroft: A Sculptor in Fiber, A	Mattera, Joanna	√		Fa	8	4		J/A 81	58
People: Shawcroft, Barbara	"Fiber Works — Americas & Japan" (Exhibit)	Kato, Kuniko Lucy	√		Fa	5	1		J/F 78	10
People: Shawcroft, Barbara	Public Fiber: The Long-Range Problem of Conservation	Austin, Carole	√		Fa	14	5		N/D 87	13
People: Shea, Judith	Garment Form As Image, The	Koplos, Janet	√		Fa	10	6		N/D 83	66
People: Shea, Judith	Paper Clothing: West	Koplos, Janet	√		Fa	11	2		M/A 84	39
People: Shea, Judith	Whitney Museum of American Art, The (Exhibit)	Park, Betty	√		Fa	9	2		M/A 82	11

SUBJECT	TITLE	AUTHOR	IL	INST	JOUR	VOL	NO	ISS	DATE	PAGE
People: Shea, Susan	Fiber on Martha's Vineyard	Erickson, Johanna	√		Fa	11	4		J/A 84	46
People: Shearer, Lesley	Lesley Shearer: Beyond the Limitations of the Four Harness Loom	Hunt, Elizabeth Ann	√		Fa	6	2		M/A 79	41
People: Shearer, Lesley	Lesley Shearer: Creation with Control	Ligon, Linda	√		Iw	2	4		Su 77	10
People: Sheehan, Diane	"Fiber R/Evolution" (Exhibit)	Rudich, Sally	√		Fa	13	4		J/A 86	45
People: Sheehan, Diane	"Filaments of the Imagination" (Exhibit)	Morse, Marcia	√		Fa	8	4		J/A 81	69
People: Sheehan, Diane	What Makes a Basket a Basket?	Malarcher, Patricia	√		Fa	11	1		J/F 84	34
People: Sheets, Lucinda	Lucinda Sheets: A Quiltmaker's Mural is a Poem In Fabric	Richerson, Suzanne	√		Fa	10	2		M/A 83	15
People: Sheets, Lucinda	Warm Quilt — Look Again!, A	Woelfle, Gretchen Erskine	√		Fa	7	3		M/J 80	62
People: Shefrin, Jessie	"Fiber R/Evolution" (Exhibit)	Rudich, Sally	√		Fa	13	4		J/A 86	45
People: Sherwin, Sarina	"Left on the Loom" (Exhibit)	Dyer, Carolyn	√		Fa	5	2		M/A 78	16
People: Sherwin, Serina	Serina Sherwin: Interview	Meilach, Dona Z.	√		Fa	4	6		N/D 77	49
People: Sherwood, Lillie	Danish Twined Rag Rugs: Lillie Sherwood's Legacy	Irwin, Bobbie	√	√	WJ	10	4	40	Sp 86	32
People: Shields, Alan	"Cloth Forms" (Exhibits)	Skudera, Gail	√		Fa	9	4		J/A 82	76
People: Shimura, Fukumi	Fukumi Shimura: Japan's Colorist Supreme	Adachi, Barbara C.	√		Fa	12	4		J/A 85	28
People: Shimura, Fukumi	"Kimono As Art: Modern Textile Works by Kako Moriguchi, Rikizo Munehiro, and Fukumi Shimura" (Exhibit)	Koplos, Janet	√		Fa	13	1		J/F 86	60
People: Shinn, Carol	Carol Shinn: The Conscious and the Unconscious	Brien, D. Elise	√		Fa	14	5		N/D 87	17
People: Shinn, Carol	Fabric of Creativity: Weaving Together Left– and Right–Brain Activites, The	Miles, Candice St. Jacques	√		Fa	11	6		N/D 84	44
People: Shipman, Frank	Under Wraps		√		Fa	12	3		M/J 85	26
People: Shiras, Myrna	Timeless Stitches: Myrna Shiras' Stitched Drawings	Schwartz, Joyce B.	√		Fa	8	3		M/J 81	65
People: Shirley, Roz	Freeform Felt	Shirley, Roz	√	√	SS&D	18	3	71	Su 87	81
People: Shirley, Roz	Portfolio of Contemporary Fiber Sculpture, A		√		Fa	11	4		J/A 84	34
People: Shoemaker, George	"Fiber Invitational" (Exhibit)	Bywater, William	√		Fa	7	2		M/A 80	66
People: Shokansai, Lizuka	Shokansai Iizuka: Bamboo Craftsman and Living National Treasure of Japan	Adachi, Barbara Curtis	√		Fa	11	1		J/F 84	59
People: Shox, Lari	Body as Canvas, The	Koda, Harold	√		TM			8	D/J 86	56
People: Shull, Mildred	Who Weaves?		√		Iw	5	2		Sp 80	38
People: Shultz, Richard	Shaft-Switching Device of Richard Shultz		√	√	WJ	8	4	32	Sp 84	35
People: Sibley, Betsy	Sampler of Surface Design, A	Westphal, Katherine	√		Fa	10	5		S/O 83	39
People: Sider, Sandra	Blues in the Light: Cyanotype on Fabric	Sider, Sandra	√		Fa	13	5		S/O 86	34
People: Sidore, Micala	"Micala Sidore: Sign Language" (Exhibit)	Temple, Nancy	√		Fa	12	3		M/J 85	72
People: Siegel, Ellen	Ellen Siegel, Designer for the Handloom and Power Loom		√		H&C	15	1		Wi 64	6
People: Silber, Julie	Julie Silber: Exploring the Art and History of Quilts	Scarborough, Jessica	√		Fa	12	6		N/D 85	14
People: Silberkleit, Amy	Amy Silberkleit: Bringing Gothic Tales to Life	Grunberg, Liane	√		Fa	13	1		J/F 86	17
People: Silva, Jude	Paper Clothing: West	Koplos, Janet	√		Fa	11	2		M/A 84	39
People: Siminoff, Frances	Siminoff	Weigle, Palmy			SS&D	1	3	3	Ju 70	20
People: Siminoff, Frances	Siminoff Textiles	Trayer, Blanche C.	√		H&C	9	1		Wi 57	18
People: Simkin, Phil	All the News That's Fit to Knit	Hempel, Toby Ann	√		Fa	14	1		J/F 87	14
People: Simmons, Lisa	Fabric Painting in New York	Katz, Ruth J.	√		Fa	9	1		J/F 82	61
People: Simmons, Paula	Lifestyle: A Roundtable Discussion	Ligon, Linda	√		Iw	5	2		Sp 80	22
People: Simon, Sidney	Tree of Life	Renee, Paula	√		SS&D	17	2	66	Sp 86	80
People: Simpson, Rona E.	"Contemporary African American Crafts" (Exhibit)	Pilsk, Adele	√		Fa	6	6		N/D 79	74
People: Sinton, Carol	Soft Sculpture: Old Forms, New Meanings	Gordon, Beverly	√		Fa	10	6		N/D 83	40
People: Siska, Sissi	Telling Stories with Color and Pattern	Behrens, Ahn	√		Fa	13	2		M/A 86	68
People: Sitter-Liver, Beatrix	Books Without Words	Gore, Ann	√		Fa	9	4		J/A 82	21

SUBJECT	TITLE	AUTHOR	IL	INST	JOUR	VOL	NO	ISS	DATE	PAGE
People: Sizemore, Sandra	"Fibrations" (Exhibit)	Silver, Elizabeth	√		Fa	6	5		S/O 79	85
People: Skogman, Susan	"Soft Art" (Exhibit)	Richerson, Suzanne	√		Fa	4	4		J/A 77	16
People: Skowronski, Hella	Doup Leno	Skowronski, Hella; Sylvia Tacker	√	√	TM			4	A/M 86	56
People: Skowronski, Hella	Hella Skowronski		√		H&C	11	4		Fa 60	18
People: Skowronski, Hella	Hella Skowronski Experiments with Sprang		√		H&C	20	1		Wi 69	4
People: Skudera, Gail	"Gail Skudera: Textile Paintings" (Exhibit)	Koplos, Janet	√		Fa	9	6		N/D 82	84
People: Skudera, Gail	"Sources of Inspiration" (Exhibit)		√		Fa	14	1		J/F 87	50
People: Skycraft, Peggy	"Crafts Northwest, Circa 1980" (Exhibit)	Evans, Rojean; Louise Klemperer	√		Fa	7	5		S/O 80	75
People: Slade, Duncan	Fraas—Slade: Painted Views	Reith, Stephanie	√		Fa	8	5		S/O 81	32
People: Slade, Duncan	"Maine Coast Artists: Fabrications" (Exhibit)	Beem, Edgar Allen	√		Fa	11	4		J/A 84	80
People: Slater, Carmon	Controlled Chaos: The Floorcloths of Carmon Slater	Fife, Lin	√		Fa	12	5		S/O 85	16
People: Slavit, Ann	"Great American Foot, The" (Exhibit)	Grover, Donald	√		Fa	5	4		J/A 78	15
People: Slivka, Rose	Designers on Design		√		Fa	10	4		J/A 83	28
People: Small, Kay	Scandia Jacket		√	√	WJ	8	3	31	Wi 83	42
People: Smayda, Norma	Profile of an HGA Rep	Smayda, Susan	√		SS&D	15	2	58	Sp 84	39
People: Smeltzer, Nancy	Nancy Smeltzer	Smeltzer, Nancy	√		Fa	13	5		S/O 86	19
People: Smith, Barbara	Barbara Smith: Views from Within	Lucas, Jane	√		Fa	10	5		S/O 83	18
People: Smith, Barbara Lee	Textile Trends: Collecting in Chicago	Lonier, Terri	√		Fa	12	6		N/D 85	26
People: Smith, Bell	Quilt National on Tour		√		TM			13	O/N 87	14
People: Smith, Elly	"Needle Expressions '86" (Exhibit)	Reinsel, Susan J.	√		Fa	14	1		J/F 87	53
People: Smith, Eunice	Double Two-Tie Twills and Basket Weave	Barrett, Clotilde	√	> 4	WJ	7	3	27	Wi 82	38
People: Smith, J. Weldon	Designers on Design		√		Fa	10	4		J/A 83	28
People: Smith, Jack D.	"Fiber Invitational" (Exhibit)	Bywater, William	√		Fa	7	2		M/A 80	66
People: Smith, Jennifer	If the Art Fits – Wear It! — Friends of the Rag	Strosnider, Ann	√		Fa	6	3		M/J 79	35
People: Smith, John	Tapestries in Rope	Smith, John	√	√	H&C	17	1		Wi 66	10
People: Smith, Katherine Todd	Few Words About Feet, Shoes and Other Things We Walk On, A	Katz, Ruth J.	√		Fa	6	3		M/J 79	53
People: Smith, Mary Ruth	"Five Women from Texas" (Exhibit)	Leach, Vivian	√		Fa	6	1		J/F 79	86
People: Smith, Mary Ruth	Mary Ruth Smith: Stitcher	Vander Lee, Jana	√		Fa	3	1		J/F 76	6
People: Smith, Noel	Basketmakers of Nova Scotia, The	Gordon, Joleen	√		SS&D	17	4	68	Fa 86	44
People: Smith, Richard	"Fabric and Form: New Textile Art from Britain" (Exhibit)	Waller, Irene	√		Fa	9	6		N/D 82	80
People: Smith, Sherri	Commissions: The Process, the Problems and the Prospects		√		Fa	6	5		S/O 79	45
People: Smith, Sherri	Designers on Design		√		Fa	10	4		J/A 83	28
People: Smith, Sherri	"Fiberworks" (Exhibit)	Park, Betty	√		Fa	4	6		N/D 77	10
People: Smith, Sherri	"Frontiers of Contemporary Weaving" (Exhibit)	Clark, Barbara	√		Fa	4	1		J/F 77	6
People: Smith, Sherri	"Sherri Smith: New Works" (Exhibit)	Malarcher, Pat	√		Fa	5	5		S/O 78	75
People: Smith, Sherri	"Sherri Smith: Recent Work" (Exhibit)	Kirkland, Lawrence P.	√		Fa	7	4		J/A 80	63
People: Smith, Sherrie	Sherrie Smith	Ligon, Linda	√		Iw	2	1		Fa 76	10
People: Smith, Wilcke	Contemporary Needle Lacers		√		TM			13	O/N 87	44
People: Smith, Wilcke	Fiber and Architecture: Wilcke Smith		√		Fa	3	3		M/J 76	18
People: Smith, Wilcke	"Stitchery '79" (Exhibit)	Kerr, Connie	√		Fa	6	5		S/O 79	78
People: Snodgrass, Cindy	Cindy Snodgrass: Wind Sculptures	Wilson, Karen	√		Fa	6	5		S/O 79	56
People: Snodgrass, Cindy	"Cloth Forms" (Exhibits)	Skudera, Gail	√		Fa	9	4		J/A 82	76
People: Snodgrass, Cindy	Creative Process: Cindy Snodgrass, The	Snodgrass, Cindy	√		Fa	11	6		N/D 84	38
People: Snow, Edith Huntington	Edith Huntington Snow	Jarecka, Louise Llewellyn	√		H&C	1	1		Ap 50	7
People: Snow, Edith Huntington	Edith Huntington Snow, Weaver, Artist, Craftsman (Reprint)	Jarecka, Louise Llewellyn	√		H&C	26	2		Ap 75	10

SUBJECT	TITLE	AUTHOR	IL	INST	JOUR	VOL	NO	ISS	DATE	PAGE
People: Snow, Lee Erlin	"Southern California Designer Crafts" (Exhibit)	Dyer, Carolyn	√		Fa	5	2		M/A 78	14
People: Snyder, Maria McCormick	"Quilt National '79" (Exhibit)	Gutcheon, Beth	√		Fa	6	5		S/O 79	80
People: Snyder, Mary	Mary Snyder	Pinchin, Bryn	√		lw	5	2		Sp 80	47
People: Snyder, Mary E.	Circuit Riding Weavers		√		H&C	10	1		Wi 59	11
People: Solaris, Maria "Willie"	Hand-Carved Color Harp		√		SS&D	6	1	21	Wi 74	46
People: Someroski, James Mel	Convergence Preview — Six Peaks, A		√		SS&D	11	2	42	Sp 80	47
People: Sonju, Unn	Contemporary Textile Art in Scandinavia	Talley, Charles S.	√		Fa	9	6		N/D 82	43
People: Sonnemann, Nell Booker	Applique Art of Nell Booker Sonnemann, The	Malarcher, Patricia	√		Fa	7	3		M/J 80	24
People: Sorkin, Linda	Paper Clothing: West	Koplos, Janet	√		Fa	11	2		M/A 84	39
People: Sorkin, Linda	Papermaking in Chicago	Shermeta, Margo	√		Fa	11	2		M/A 84	54
People: Soule, Dianne E.	Dianne E. Soule: Batik Portraits	Bard, Elizabeth A.	√		Fa	12	6		N/D 85	11
People: Sousa, Jan	"Miniature Fibers" (Exhibit)	Vanderburg, Jan	√		Fa	7	1		J/F 80	65
People: Spark, Patricia	"Mini Tapestry Exhibit" (Exhibit)	Bockelman, JoAnne	√		Fa	5	4		J/A 78	12
People: Sparks, Barbara	Succeeding with the Knitting Machine	Mattera, Joanne	√		TM			2	D/J 85	50
People: Sparks, Rebecca	Machine Knitting: The State of the Art		√		Fa	9	2		M/A 82	40
People: Speer, Andrew	"Paper and Felt Redefined" (Exhibit)	Ogden, Anne	√		Fa	5	2		M/A 78	17
People: Spencer, Patricia	"Seventh Annual Twin Ports Fibers Invitational" (Exhibit)	LaRoque, Jane V. Lowell	√		Fa	7	3		M/J 80	80
People: Spiegel, Raoul	"Art Couture/Haute Couture" (Exhibit)	McGuire, Patricia	√		Fa	9	1		J/F 82	86
People: St. Germain, Patrick	"Wildlife Physics" (Exhibit)	Kitzman, Betty Lou	√		Fa	12	2		M/A 85	72
People: Stack, Lotus	How a Textile Department Grew	Koplos, Janet	√		Fa	10	1		J/F 83	54
People: Stahlecker, Karen	Felt and Paper: A Portfolio		√		Fa	13	4		J/A 86	35
People: Stahlecker, Karen	"Karen Stahlecker" (Exhibit)	Shermeta, Margo	√		Fa	10	5		S/O 83	80
People: Stahlecker, Karen	Paper Clothing: West	Koplos, Janet	√		Fa	11	2		M/A 84	39
People: Stahlecker, Karen	Papermaking in Chicago	Shermeta, Margo	√		Fa	11	2		M/A 84	54
People: Stalin, Julie	Fiber Ten	McGuire, Patricia	√		Fa	4	6		N/D 77	26
People: Stalnaker, Budd	"Paper and Felt Redefined" (Exhibit)	Ogden, Anne	√		Fa	5	2		M/A 78	17
People: Stalnaker, Budd	"Works in Fiber" (Exhibit)	Arnow, Jan	√		Fa	8	2		M/A 81	61
People: Stamsta, Jean	Jean Stamsta	Stamsta, Jean	√		SS&D	3	3	11	Su 72	15
People: Stamsta, Jean	"Jean Stamsta: Great Lake Series" (Exhibit)	Bard, Elizabeth A.	√		Fa	10	2		M/A 83	70
People: Stamsta, Jean	Jean Stamsta: Weaver		√		Fa	4	2		M/A 77	30
People: Stamsta, Jean	"Women Artists: Clay, Fiber, Metal" (Exhibit)	Malarcher, Patricia	√		Fa	5	2		M/A 78	11
People: Standley, Emily	Salmon Run: The Work of Northwest Artists Peggy Vanbianchi and Emily Standley	Hirschi, Ron	√		Fa	10	2		M/A 83	16
People: Standley, Emily	"Unsettled Images: Peggy Vanbianchi & Emily Standley" (Exhibit)	Rowlands-Tarbox, Jean L.	√		Fa	12	5		S/O 85	71
People: Staniszkis, Joanna	Canadian Portfolio, A	Place, Jennifer	√		Fa	9	6		N/D 82	29
People: Stanley, Martha	Livin' and Workin' on the Land: Fiber Art Outside the Mainstream	Talley, Charles S.	√		Fa	8	6		N/D 81	38
People: States, Diantha	Certificate of Excellence in Handweaving: COE Holders, The	Drooker, Penelope B.	√		SS&D	14	1	53	Wi 82	49
People: Stauffer, Peter	Peter Stauffer — Early 19th Century Weaver	Rogers, Grace L.	√	> 4	H&C	7	1		Wi 55	12
People: Stavitsky, Ellen	"Paper" (Exhibit)	Toale, Bernard	√		Fa	7	5		S/O 80	69
People: Stedman, Jan	"Paper Sources" (Exhibit)	Papa, Nancy	√		Fa	5	4		J/A 78	16
People: Steele, Lois	She Sells Everything She Weaves	Knoizen, Frances	√		H&C	9	3		Su 58	22
People: Steenberg, Marilyn	"Revolution in Fiber Art" (Exhibit)		√		Fa	3	3		M/J 76	7
People: Stefl, Jerry	Jerry Stefl: Fantasy, Beads, and Fiber	Matthews, Marianne R.	√		Fa	11	2		M/A 84	24
People: Stefl, Jerry	"Stitchery '77" (Exhibit)	Pierucci, Louise	√		Fa	4	3		M/J 77	11
People: Stegmier, Georgia	"100% Wool" (Exhibit)	Goldin, Susan	√		Fa	4	6		N/D 77	18
People: Steiger, Harwood	Southwestern Rhythms of Harwood Steiger Fabrics, The	Beeaff, Dianne Ebertt	√		Fa	13	2		M/A 86	29

SUBJECT	TITLE	AUTHOR	IL	INST	JOUR	VOL	NO	ISS	DATE	PAGE
People: Stein, Annabelle	Under Wraps		√		Fa	12	3		M/J 85	26
People: Stein, Ethel	"Dyer's Art: Ikat, Batik, Plangi, The" (Exhibit)	Dyer, Carolyn	√		Fa	5	4		J/A 78	11
People: Stein, Judith	For the Body (error-corrected Fa v10 n2 83 p61)		√		Fa	10	1		J/F 83	32
People: Stein, Martha	"Mini Tapestry Exhibit" (Exhibit)	Bockelman, JoAnne	√		Fa	5	4		J/A 78	12
People: Steiner, Joan	"Joan Steiner: Hats/New Sculpture" (Exhibit)	Katz, Ruth J.	√		Fa	7	5		S/O 80	72
People: Steiner, Lois	"Fiber Departures" (Exhibit)	Dyer, Carolyn	√		Fa	4	3		M/J 77	9
People: Stephenson, Jim	Inspired by Fiber: Textile Sensibility in Other Media	Malarcher, Patricia	√		Fa	10	6		N/D 83	33
People: Stern-Straeter, Dorle	Quiltmaker's Art, A	Mattera, Joanne	√		Fa	10	2		M/A 83	33
People: Sterrenberg, Jean	Inspired by Fiber: Textile Sensibility in Other Media	Malarcher, Patricia	√		Fa	10	6		N/D 83	33
People: Sterrenburg, Joan	"Paper and Felt Redefined" (Exhibit)	Ogden, Anne	√		Fa	5	2		M/A 78	17
People: Sterrenburg, Joan	Papermaking in the U.S.A.	Toale, Bernard	√		Fa	9	4		J/A 82	34
People: Sterrenburg, Joan	"Stitchery '77" (Exhibit)	Pierucci, Louise	√		Fa	4	3		M/J 77	11
People: Sterrenburg, Joan	"Works in Fiber" (Exhibit)	Arnow, Jan	√		Fa	8	2		M/A 81	61
People: Stettner, Arianthé	Arianthé: Notes from a Production Weaver	Stettner, Arianthé	√		Fa	5	5		S/O 78	32
People: Stettner, Arianthe	Who Weaves?		√		Iw	5	2		Sp 80	37
People: Stevens, Mary	Fiber on Martha's Vineyard	Erickson, Johanna	√		Fa	11	4		J/A 84	46
People: Stevens, Missy	Missy Stevens: Connecting Art and Fabric	Mallinckrodt, Casey	√		Fa	14	4		S/O 87	20
People: Stevens, Thomas	Jacquard and Woven Silk Pictures, The	Adrosko, Rita J.	√		AT	1			De 83	9
People: Stewart, Leora	"Leora Stewart: New Works—Deborah Warner: Four Corners Journal" (Exhibit)	Malarcher, Patricia	√		Fa	6	6		N/D 79	71
People: Stewart, Leora K.	Leora K. Stewart: Form in Three-Dimensional Space		√		SS&D	1	4	4	Se 70	5
People: Stewart, Marion	Marion Stewart		√		H&C	13	4		Fa 62	17
People: Stewart, Wendy	80 Papers: Only a 9' by 30' Store, But a Veritable U.N. of Pulp	Mattera, Joanne	√		Fa	8	6		N/D 81	28
People: Stimson, Paris Ann	HGA Scholarships '79		√		SS&D	10	4	40	Fa 79	100
People: Stinson, Dilys	Dilys Stinson: Tapestry Maker	Mathews-Pulleyn, Kathryn	√		Fa	4	5		S/O 77	22
People: Stinson, Dilys	Tapestries of Dilys Stinson, The	Harris, Patricia; David Lyon	√		Fa	13	2		M/A 86	18
People: Stocksdale, Joy	Art to Wear: Looking At the Movement	Scarborough, Jessica	√		Fa	12	3		M/J 85	56
People: Stocksdale, Joy	"Young Americans: Fiber, Wood, Plastic, Leather" (Exhibit)	Malarcher, Patricia	√		Fa	4	6		N/D 77	14
People: Stoller, Karen	Karen Stoller		√		SS&D	11	4	44	Fa 80	79
People: Stoller, Karen	"Karen Stoller: Fiber" (Exhibit)	Reese, Ralph Henry	√		Fa	8	1		J/F 81	96
People: Stone, Molly	Inspired by Fiber: Textile Sensibility in Other Media	Malarcher, Patricia	√		Fa	10	6		N/D 83	33
People: Stoner, Gabriel	"Art Couture VII" (Exhibit)	Guagliumi, Susan Fletcher	√		Fa	12	3		M/J 85	78
People: Straus, Peter	High-Tech Comes to Weaving: AVL Looms	Larson, Eden	√		Fa	14	4		S/O 87	36
People: Strauss, Meredith	Made by Machine: Textiles for the Eighties	Harris, Patricia; David Lyon	√		Fa	12	5		S/O 85	34
People: Strauss, Meredith	Plastics in Fiber: A Persistent Presence	Malarcher, Patricia	√		Fa	12	1		J/F 85	56
People: Strengell, Marianne	American Handweaving 1960		√		H&C	11	2		Sp 60	11
People: Strengell, Marianne	Marianne Strengell		√		H&C	13	4		Fa 62	14
People: Strengell, Marianne	Marianne Strengell, Textile Consultant to Architects	Bemis, Marion Holden	√		H&C	8	1		Wi 56	6
People: Strengell, Marianne	New Philippine Textiles	Gele, Emilé	√		H&C	5	3		Su 54	14
People: Strengell, Marianne	Two Textile Artists Honored		√		TM			1	O/N 85	10
People: Strickler, Darius	Sculptural Paper: Foundations and Directions	Scarborough, Jessica	√		Fa	11	2		M/A 84	32
People: Strommen, Kim	"Fiber R/Evolution" (Exhibit)	Rudich, Sally	√		Fa	13	4		J/A 86	45

SUBJECT	TITLE	AUTHOR	IL	INST	JOUR	VOL	NO	ISS	DATE	PAGE
People: Stuart, Alice	Alice Stuart	Turner, Alta R.	√		H&C	12	1		Wi 61	16
People: Studstill, Pam	"Quilt National '83" (Exhibit)	Roe, Nancy	√		Fa	10	5		S/O 83	82
People: Studstill, Pamela	Pamela Studstill	Solon, Marcia Goren	√		Fa	12	2		M/A 85	32
People: Stump, Patricia	"Houston Designer-Craftsmen 1976" (Exhibit)	Vander Lee, Jana	√		Fa	3	4		J/A 76	9
People: Stumpf, Patricia	Verbena Collection, The (error-corrected Fa v11 n1 84 p11)		√		Fa	10	5		S/O 83	64
People: Stumpff, Linda Moon	"Textiles New Mexico 1976" (Exhibit)	Warner, Lucy Ann	√		Fa	3	2		M/A 76	12
People: Suino, Dorothea	Kimono East/West	Wada, Yoshiko	√		Fa	9	1		J/F 82	19
People: Suino, Dorothy	"Kimono East/Kimono West" (Exhibit)	Lusk, Jennie	√		Fa	7	5		S/O 80	71
People: Sulikowski, June	Knitting for a Living (error-corrected TM i6 A/S86 p6)	Guagliumi, Susan	√		TM			4	A/M 86	38
People: Sullivan, Donna	Certificate Success	Drooker, Penelope	√		SS&D	16	1	61	Wi 84	66
People: Sullivan, Donna	COE Diary, A	Drooker, Penelope			SS&D	16	2	62	Sp 85	30
People: Sullivan, Mary Elizabeth	Thirty Interesting Years	Sullivan, Mary Elizabeth	√		H&C	8	1		Wi 56	16
People: Summa, Susan	For the Body (error-corrected Fa v10 n2 83 p61)		√		Fa	10	1		J/F 83	32
People: Summa, Susan	Instant Gratification: Susan Summa Tells How and Why She Learned to Love the Knitting Machine	Summa, Susan	√		Fa	8	5		S/O 81	56
People: Summa, Susan	Machine Knitting: The State of the Art		√		Fa	9	2		M/A 82	40
People: Summa, Susan	Succeeding with the Knitting Machine	Mattera, Joanne	√		TM			2	D/J 85	50
People: Sundberg, Kerstin Åsling	Contemporary Swedish Weaving		√		Hw	8	3		M/J 87	35
People: Sunrise, Pearl	Pearl Sunrise: Weaving the "Old Way"	Sunrise, Pearl	√		Fa	11	3		M/J 84	34
People: Suntrader, Cid	Cid Suntrader: Weaving with Glass	Suntrader, Cid	√		Fa	14	4		S/O 87	5
People: Sutter, Winston H.	Textiles Designed for Contemporary Furniture		√		H&C	12	2		Sp 61	17
People: Sutton, Carol Shaw	"National Crafts '81: Works by the 1981 National Endowment for the Arts Craft Fellows" (Exhibit)	Mattera, Joanne	√		Fa	9	1		J/F 82	82
People: Sutton, Sara	Year of the Sweater, The	Katz, Ruth J.	√		Fa	7	1		J/F 80	39
People: Svensson, Inez	Tiogruppen: When Working Together Works	Talley, Charles	√		Fa	11	6		N/D 84	41
People: Swain, Bessie	Weaving Guilds—A Special Sharing		√		Iw	5	2		Sp 80	53
People: Swann, Anne	Anne Swann	Packard, Myles	√		Fa	4	3		M/J 77	22
People: Swanson, Janet	Janet Swanson	Swanson, Janet	√		Fa	7	5		S/O 80	43
People: Swanson, Karen	"Karen Swanson" (Exhibit)	Sunshine, Joanna	√		Fa	4	2		M/A 77	13
People: Swanson, Meg	Meg Swansen: A Conversation with Alexis Xenakis	Xenakis, Alexis Yiorgos	√		Kn	3	3	7	Su 87	26
People: Swanson, Susan	"Contemporary Shibori" (Exhibit)	Howe, Cathe	√		Fa	11	3		M/J 84	82
People: Sward, Marilyn	Papermaking in Chicago	Shermeta, Margo	√		Fa	11	2		M/A 84	54
People: Swartz, Beth Ames	Beth Ames Swartz: A Painter's Way with Paper	Krapes, Shelley	√		Fa	9	4		J/A 82	19
People: Swendeman, Dorothy	Tapestry (Part 3): An Inside View	Harvey, Nancy	√	√	SS&D	15	2	58	Sp 84	20
People: Swenson, Astrid	Pattern Sticks, Invention of Astrid Swenson of Queens College		√	√	H&C	19	4		Fa 68	21
People: Swickard, Nancy	Sampler of Surface Design, A	Westphal, Katherine	√		Fa	10	5		S/O 83	39
People: Swim, Laurie	Laurie Swim: A Contemporary Quiltmaker with Roots in the Past	Himel, Susan	√		Fa	7	4		J/A 80	18
People: Swit, Loretta	Hot Lips Houlihan Loves to Stitch		√		Fa	13	4		J/A 86	11
People: Switzer, Chris	Setting Up Shop	Ligon, Linda	√		Iw	2	4		Su 77	18
People: Sykes, Barbara	"Ideas and Capabilities: Barbara Sykes' Fiber Constructions" (Exhibit)	Blakely, Deborah	√		Fa	8	1		J/F 81	94
People: Sylvan, Katherine	Katherine Sylvan				SS&D	15	4	60	Fa 84	4
People: Sylvan, Kathy	Who Weaves?		√		Iw	5	2		Sp 80	39
People: Sylvester, Donna	Felt and Paper: A Portfolio		√		Fa	13	4		J/A 86	35
People: Szilvitzky, Margit	"Third International Exhibition of Miniature Textiles 1978" (Exhibit)	Spencer, Patricia	√		Fa	6	1		J/F 79	90

SUBJECT	TITLE	AUTHOR	IL	INST	JOUR	VOL	NO	ISS	DATE	PAGE
People: Szumski, Norma J.	China: Fiber Arts in the People's Republic	Szumski, Norma J.	√		SS&D	15	1	57	Wi 83	47
People: Tabak, Bella	"Tangents: Art in Fiber" (Exhibit)	Krinn, Linda	√		Fa	14	3		M/J 87	55
People: Taeuber-Arp, Sophie	In the Shadow of Fame: Sophie Taeuber-Arp and Sonia Delaunay	Austin, Carol	√		Fa	12	5		S/O 85	50
People: Takagi, Toshiko	Contemporary Tapestry in Japan: Individuality After Centuries of Textile Conformity	Lindenfeld, Lore	√		Fa	10	3		M/J 83	44
People: Takami, Bruce	Weaving Tradition in the Andes, A	Adelson, Laurie; Bruce Takami	√		Fa	6	4		J/A 79	22
People: Takeda, Sharon	"Transformation: UCLA Alumnae In Fiber" (Exhibit)	Dyer, Carolyn	√		Fa	6	4		J/A 79	67
People: Talbot, Arnold G. and Mrs. Talbot	Talbot Weavers' Golden Anniversary (error-corrected H&C v5 n4 54 p43)		√		H&C	5	3		Su 54	4
People: Tallarovic, Joanne	Countermarche: Pure and Simple	Tallarovic, Joanne	√	√	WJ	8	3	31	Wi 83	85
People: Talley, Charles	1977 HGA Scholarships (error-corrected SS&D v9 n2 78 p70)		√		SS&D	9	1	33	Wi 77	46
People: Talley, Charles	Charles Talley: A Candid Account of a Passionate Weaver and How He Got That Way	Talley, Charles	√		Fa	6	2		M/A 79	25
People: Tamosaitis, Anastazija	Anastazija Tamosaitis	Matranga, Victoria	√		SS&D	17	3	67	Su 86	54
People: Tamura, Shuji	Spirit Exits Through the Embroiderer's Hands, The	Colwell, Katherine	√	√	TM			12	A/S 87	18
People: Tanenbaum, Ruth	Weaving in San Francisco — Part 1	Prosser, Evelyn Bingham	√		WJ	6	2	22	Fa 81	44
People: Tanji, Lydia	Contemporary California Costume	Poon, Vivian	√		Fa	11	5		S/O 84	53
People: Tannenbaum, Anne	Sampler of Surface Design, A	Westphal, Katherine	√		Fa	10	5		S/O 83	39
People: Taryan, Hedi	"Hedi Taryan: The Infinity of Small Things" (Exhibit)	Chamish, Barry	√		Fa	10	5		S/O 83	79
People: Tate, Blair	Miniatures in Fiber: Working Small—An Exciting Challenge for the Contemporary Fiber Artist	Malarcher, Patricia	√		Fa	7	4		J/A 80	32
People: Tate, Blair	RISD Faculty Show (Exhibit)		√		Fa	13	4		J/A 86	59
People: Taute, Ginny	"Revolution in Fiber Art" (Exhibit)		√		Fa	3	3		M/J 76	7
People: Tawney, Lenore	Commissions: The Process, the Problems and the Prospects		√		Fa	6	5		S/O 79	45
People: Tawney, Lenore	"Fiber Art: An Uncommon Thread" (Exhibit)	Park, Betty	√		Fa	9	2		M/A 82	78
People: Tawney, Lenore	"Fiber R/Evolution" (Exhibit)	Rudich, Sally	√		Fa	13	4		J/A 86	45
People: Tawney, Lenore	"Fiberworks" (Exhibit)	Park, Betty	√		Fa	4	6		N/D 77	10
People: Tawney, Lenore	Lenore Tawney		√		H&C	13	2		Sp 62	6
People: Taylor, Dean	"Seven Sonoma County Fibre Artists" (Exhibit)	Robinson, Sharon	√		Fa	3	4		J/A 76	6
People: Taylor, Janet	"Tapestries by Janet Taylor" (Exhibit)	Malarcher, Patricia	√		Fa	9	5		S/O 82	81
People: Taylor, Janet	"Women Artists: Clay, Fiber, Metal" (Exhibit)	Malarcher, Patricia	√		Fa	5	2		M/A 78	11
People: Taylor-Brown, Cameron	Cameron Taylor-Brown	Taylor-Brown, Cameron	√		Fa	14	2		M/A 87	24
People: Taylor-Brown, Cameron	Public Fiber: Looking At the Logistics	Koplos, Janet	√		Fa	12	1		J/F 85	32
People: TerBeest, Char	Char TerBeest: Basket Builder	TerBeest, Char	√		Fa	9	4		J/A 82	17
People: TerLouw, Betty	HGA Board Candidates: Vote for Three		√		SS&D	10	2	38	Sp 79	49
People: Thalaker, Don	Commissions: The Process, the Problems and the Prospects		√		Fa	6	5		S/O 79	45
People: Thibado, Theo	Weaving Guilds—A Special Sharing		√		Iw	5	2		Sp 80	55
People: Thibado, Theo	Who Weaves?		√		Iw	5	2		Sp 80	39
People: Thiel, Alice Jean	More 1978 Scholarships		√		SS&D	10	1	37	Wi 78	107
People: Thielen, William H.	"Needle Expressions '80" (Exhibit)		√		Fa	8	1		J/F 81	93
People: Thieme, Otto	"Wisconsin Fiber Miniatures" (Exhibit)	Lowell-LaRoque, Jane V.	√		Fa	6	5		S/O 79	84
People: Thilenius, Carol	Certificate Holders: Now What? Part 2, The	Alderman, Sharon D.	√		SS&D	12	4	48	Fa 81	52
People: Thomas, Carolyn	Athens Tapestry Works	Many, Paul	√		Fa	5	4		J/A 78	51

SUBJECT	TITLE	AUTHOR	IL	INST	JOUR	VOL	NO	ISS	DATE	PAGE
People: Thomas, Carolyn	Why Sew Those Lines? An Interview with Giorgio Furioso and Carolyn Thomas	Paca, Al	√		Fa	7	4		J/A 80	25
People: Thomas, Jayn	"Fiber/Fabric '81" (Exhibit)	Scarborough, Jessica	√		Fa	8	4		J/A 81	74
People: Thomas, Jayn	HGA Scholarships '79		√		SS&D	10	4	40	Fa 79	100
People: Thomas, Jayn	"Jayn Thomas" (Exhibit)	Malarcher, Patricia	√		Fa	10	5		S/O 83	81
People: Thomas, Jayn	Wefts of Light: Jayn Thomas' Fabric Hangings	Scarborough, Jessica	√		Fa	9	1		J/F 82	23
People: Thomas, Nedalee	Quilted Autograph Collection, A	Pierce, Judith	√		Fa	14	3		M/J 87	5
People: Thomason, Roger	HGA Board Candidates: Vote for Three		√		SS&D	10	2	38	Sp 79	48
People: Thompson, Carolyn	Tapestry Gallery		√		Iw	4	2		Sp 79	32
People: Thompson, Elizabeth	"Baskets of Akwesasne" (Exhibit)	Doyle, Claire	√		Fa	11	1		J/F 84	77
People: Thompson, Rena	HGA Scholarships '79		√		SS&D	10	4	40	Fa 79	100
People: Thompson, Rena	Rena Thompson: Echoes of Intuitive Truths	Park, Betty	√		Fa	13	2		M/A 86	46
People: Thomson, Madeleine	"Throbbing Needles II" (Exhibit)	Mattera, Joanne	√		Fa	7	2		M/A 80	71
People: Thordardottir, Thorbjoerg	Culture That Supports Culture, A		√		Fa	10	4		J/A 83	84
People: Thorkelsdottir, Gudrun	Fiber Art in Iceland	Hrafnhildur, Schram	√		Fa	9	6		N/D 82	68
People: Thorne, Richard	Men Who Knit	Xenakis, Alexis Yiorgos	√		Kn	3	2	6	Sp 87	14
People: Thornton, Julietta	Whose Zoo? Julietta Thornton's Incredible Fiber Sculptures	Kennett, Don	√		Fa	8	5		S/O 81	20
People:Thorpe, Azalea	American Handweaving 1960		√		H&C	11	2		Sp 60	48
People: Thorpe, Jane	Art to Wear: Looking At the Movement	Scarborough, Jessica	√		Fa	12	3		M/J 85	56
People: Thurston, Stephen	Speakers Bureau Presents		√		SS&D	7	1	25	Wi 75	63
People: Tidball, Harriet	Double-Warp Weaving from Harriet Tidball's Looms	Bryan, Dorothy	√	√	H&C	5	4		Fa 54	15
People: Tidball, Harriet	Harriet Tidball	Harvey, Virginia I.; Sylvia Tacker	√		SS&D	8	4	32	Fa 77	4
People: Tidwell, Elmyra	Elmyra Tidwell	Tidwell, Elmyra	√		Fa	14	3		M/J 87	22
People: Tidwell, Elmyra	Wearable Fine Thread Tapestries	Tidwell, Elmyra	√	√	WJ	10	3	39	Wi 86	34
People: Tifft, Jennifer	Review/Discussion of Artspace's Innovative Yet Flawed "Fiber Freely Interpreted", A (Exhibit)		√		Fa	4	2		M/A 77	38
People: Tikkanen, Maisa	"Scandinavian Touch, The" A Traveling Exhibit (Exhibit)	Mattera, Joanna	√		Fa	10	1		J/F 83	82
People: Tippett, Leonard Henry Caleb	Work of L. H. C. Tippett, The	Stanton, R. G.	√		AT	7			Ju 87	179
People: Tissari, Mirja	Contemporary Textile Art in Scandinavia	Talley, Charles S.	√		Fa	9	6		N/D 82	43
People: Titelman, Ingrid Peterson	Well-Worn Path to Where? A View of Contemporary Swedish Textiles, The	Talley, Charles S.	√		Fa	8	2		M/A 81	44
People: Toale, Bernard	"Bernard Toale: Works in Fiber" (Exhibit)	Malarcher, Patricia	√		Fa	7	2		M/A 80	65
People: Toale, Bernard	Nets of Bernard Toale, The	Malarcher, Patricia	√		Fa	9	3		M/J 82	26
People: Tobacco, Leah	Zamani Soweto Sisters: A Patchwork of Lives		√		Fa	10	2		M/A 83	48
People: Todacheeny, Stella	"Song of the Loom: New Traditions in Navajo Weaving, The" (Exhibit)		√		TM			11	J/J 87	18
People: Tomayko, Vicki	"Connections" (Exhibit)	Constantinides, Kathy	√		Fa	6	4		J/A 79	74
People: Tomita, Jun	Rugs: Jun Tomita, Weaver		√		Fa	9	2		M/A 82	61
People: Tomito, Jun and Noriko	Letter from Japan	Schrieber, Lavonne	√		WJ	12	1	45	Su 87	54
People: Tomlinson, Kerry	Verbena Collection, The (error-corrected Fa v11 n1 84 p11)		√		Fa	10	5		S/O 83	64
People: Toplitz, Susan	Year of the Sweater, The	Katz, Ruth J.	√		Fa	7	1		J/F 80	39
People: Towner, Mary	Country of Origin, USA: A Decade of Contemporary Rugs	Stevens, Rebeccah A. T.	√		Fa	11	3		M/J 84	60
People: Towner, Mary	Felt and Paper: A Portfolio		√		Fa	13	4		J/A 86	35
People: Towner, Naomi	Focus on the HGA Board of Directors		√		SS&D	10	1	37	Wi 78	52
People: Towner, Naomi	Naomi Towner	Towner, George	√		SS&D	3	1	9	Wi 71	6
People: Towner, Naomi W.	Naomi W. Towner: Hangings & Coverings		√		SS&D	5	2	18	Sp 74	92

SUBJECT	TITLE	AUTHOR	IL	INST	JOUR	VOL	NO	ISS	DATE	PAGE
People: Tracy, William	Painted Surface, The (error-corrected Fa v9 n4 82 p9)		√		Fa	9	3		M/J 82	64
People: Train, Elizabeth	"Frontiers of Contemporary Weaving" (Exhibit)	Clark, Barbara	√		Fa	4	1		J/F 77	6
People: Trentham, Gary	"Fibers Southeast 1979" (Exhibit)	Johnson, Elma	√		Fa	6	2		M/A 79	68
People: Trentham, Gary	Gary Trentham's Objets d'Art: An Interview	West, Virginia	√		SS&D	11	3	43	Su 80	70
People: Trentham, Gary	Robert Pfannebecker: A Collector's Point of View	Park, Betty	√		Fa	5	4		J/A 78	42
People: Trentham, Gary	What Makes a Basket a Basket?	Malarcher, Patricia	√		Fa	11	1		J/F 84	34
People: Trien, May Rolstad	Miniatures in Fiber: Working Small—An Exciting Challenge for the Contemporary Fiber Artist	Malarcher, Patricia	√		Fa	7	4		J/A 80	32
People: Trilling, JoEllen	JoEllen Trilling: Contemporary Pied Piper	Backer, Ellen	√		Fa	5	4		J/A 78	24
People: Trujillo, Jacob O.	Chimayó—A Town of Weavers	Trujillo, Lisa Rockwood	√		WJ	11	1	41	Su 86	60
People: Trusty, Ann	"Ann Trusty: Grid and Pattern" (Exhibit)	Stiles, David	√		Fa	9	1		J/F 82	79
People: Tsosie, Juanita	Exploring a Tradition: Navajo Rugs, Classic and Contemporary	Elliott, Malinda	√		Fa	11	3		M/J 84	32
People: Tsuchiya, Sonoko	Making Fabric Flowers	Ritch, Diane; Yoshiko Iwamoto Wada	√	√	TM			13	O/N 87	68
People: Tsumugi, Yuki	Yuki Tsumugi	Urbanek, Karen	√	√	S-O	10	1		Sp 86	42
People: Tsutsumi, Toshiko	Lausanne Notebook: Our Special Report on the 8th Lausanne Biennial of Tapestry, A	Mathews, Rich	√		Fa	4	5		S/O 77	30
People: Tuegel, Michele	Michele Tuegel's Paper Works	Marger, Mary Ann	√		Fa	13	4		J/A 86	30
People: Tufts, Susan	Susan Tufts		√		Fa	4	3		M/J 77	44
People: Turczyn, Pam	Evolution of an Artist: Pam Turczyn	Turczyn, Pam	√		Fa	14	5		N/D 87	24
People: Turgeon, Lulu	Production Weaving in Quebec	Turgeon, Lulu	√		Hw	3	3		My 82	54
People: Turner, Alta R.	Designs from a Weaving Teacher's Studio		√		H&C	12	4		Fa 61	22
People: Turner, Jocelyn	For the Body (error-corrected Fa v10 n2 83 p61)		√		Fa	10	1		J/F 83	32
People: Turner, Kathryn	Profile of an HGA Rep		√		SS&D	18	2	70	Sp 87	39
People: Turner, Katy	Certificate Holders: Now What?, The	Alderman, Sharon D.	√		SS&D	12	2	46	Sp 81	41
People: Turnley, Ann	"Paper" (Exhibit)	Toale, Bernard	√		Fa	7	5		S/O 80	69
People: Tuttle, Elizabeth	Elizabeth Tuttle: Pointillist Crochet	Demske, Barbara	√		Fa	7	4		J/A 80	48
People: Tuttle, Elizabeth	"Threads" (Exhibit)	Kurtz, Carol	√		Fa	10	4		J/A 83	62
People: Tworek-Pierzgaiska, Janina	"22 Polish Textile Artists" (Exhibit)	Park, Betty	√		Fa	4	5		S/O 77	8
People: Twycross-Reed, Pamela	"Landscapes" (Exhibit)	Clardy, Andrea	√		Fa	5	2		M/A 78	10
People: Tyiska, Stephanie	More 1978 Scholarships		√		SS&D	10	1	37	Wi 78	107
People: Tyler, Mary	"Entanglements" (Exhibit)	Markle, Marsha	√		Fa	4	2		M/A 77	16
People: Tyler, Pat D.	Felt and Paper: A Portfolio		√		Fa	13	4		J/A 86	35
People: Tyrrell, Lilian	"Lilian Tyrrell: Tapestries" (Exhibit)	McClelland, Elizabeth	√		Fa	11	6		N/D 84	76
People: Udall, Dorothy	Maridadi West: A Fort Collins, Colorado Fabric Design Studio with Its Roots in East Africa	Mattera, Joanne	√		Fa	9	2		M/A 82	24
People: Ungar, Fred	Ready for the Needle	Coffin, David Page	√	√	TM			12	A/S 87	43
People: Unruh, Ione	Ione Unruh		√		Fa	4	6		N/D 77	63
People: Unruh, Joyce	"Fantasy Clothes/Fantastic Costumes" (Exhibit)	Dyer, Carolyn	√		Fa	4	2		M/A 77	11
People: Unser, Marion	One Hundred Sixty Years of Craftsmanship	Ligon, Linda	√		Iw	1	3		Sp 76	17
People: Upitis, Lizbeth	Latvian Wedding Mittens	Upitis, Lizbeth	√	√	PWC			2	Ap 82	92
People: Upitis, Lizbeth	Swatching		√	√	Kn	3	4	8	Fa 87	42
People: Uravich, Andrea V.	Soft Sculpture: Old Forms, New Meanings	Gordon, Beverly	√		Fa	10	6		N/D 83	40
People: Uravitch, Andrea	Andrea Uravitch		√		Fa	3	6		N/D 76	14
People: Uravitch, Andrea V.	Andrea V. Uravitch, "Wild and Domestic" (Exhibit)	Stevens, Rebecca A. T.	√		Fa	10	2		M/A 83	71

SUBJECT	TITLE	AUTHOR	IL	INST	JOUR	VOL	NO	ISS	DATE	PAGE
People: Uravitch, Andrea V.	Cows in Fiber	Timmons, Chris	√		Fa	11	4		J/A 84	55
People: Urbonas, Chris	Two Weavers: A Business Association Which Works	LaLena, Constance	√		Hw	2	3		My 81	66
People: Urruty, Jean	Sheep Country Profiles: Jean Urruty	Gordon, Gerrie	√		Iw	2	3		Sp 77	25
People: Utterback, Connie	"Presence of Light, The" (Exhibit)	Talley, Charles	√		Fa	12	2		M/A 85	72
People: Uyemura, Ken J.	Speakers Bureau Presents		√		SS&D	2	3	7	Su 71	24
People: Uyemura, Kenneth J.	Kenneth J. Uyemura: A Feeling of Relatedness		√		SS&D	4	3	15	Su 73	45
People: Valentino, Richard	San Francisco School of Fabric Arts, The	Papa, Nancy	√		Fa	6	1		J/F 79	13
People: Valinski, Dennis	"Cloth Forms" (Exhibits)	Skudera, Gail	√		Fa	9	4		J/A 82	76
People: Valinski, Dennis	Dionysian Spirits: Dennis Valinski's Sculptures of Life	Snodgrass, Cindy	√		Fa	8	5		S/O 81	48
People: Van Buskirk, Libby	"Ten Boston Fiber Artists" (Exhibit)	Serenyi, Peter	√		Fa	5	5		S/O 78	67
People: Van Cleve, Kate	American Handweaving 1960		√		H&C	11	2		Sp 60	12
People: Van Cleve, Kate	Kate Van Cleve — Master Weaver	Clement, Doris Wilcox	√		H&C	9	3		Su 58	30
People: van der Hoogt, Madelyn	Weaving Places	Xenakis, Alexis Yiorgos	√		PWC	4	2	12		28
People: van der Zanden, Henk	Lace Maker of Holland, Henk van der Zanden		√		H&C	17	2		Sp 66	15
People: Van Derpool, Karen	"Felting" (Exhibit)	Park, Betty	√		Fa	7	6		N/D 80	71
People: Van Derpool, Karen	"Paper and Felt Redefined" (Exhibit)	Ogden, Anne	√		Fa	5	2		M/A 78	17
People: Van Dommelen, David B.	Speakers Bureau Presents		√		SS&D	2	4	8	Fa 71	24
People: Van Gelder, Lydia	"Seven Sonoma County Fibre Artists" (Exhibit)	Robinson, Sharon	√		Fa	3	4		J/A 76	6
People: Van Ginhoven, Anke	"Anke Van Ginhoven: Tapestries 1977" (Exhibit)	Cantieni, Graham	√		Fa	5	1		J/F 78	21
People: van Hall, Frances	Frances van Hall	Bryan, Dorothy	√		H&C	11	2		Sp 60	43
People: van Reesema, Elizabeth Siewertsz	Listening to Threads	Reynders-Baas, Coby	√		WJ	11	4	44	Sp 87	21
People: Van Stralen, Trudy	Three Production Weavers: Trudy Van Stralen		√		Hw	3	3		My 82	50
People: Van Zant, Charlotte	Keeping Warm in Alaska		√		Fa	9	6		N/D 82	22
People: Van Zuylen, Eliza	Van Zuylen Batik, Pekalongan, Central Java (1890-1946)	de Raadt-Apell, M. J.	√		TMJ	19 20			80,81	75
People: Vanbianchi, Peggy	Salmon Run: The Work of Northwest Artists Peggy Vanbianchi and Emily Standley	Hirschi, Ron	√		Fa	10	2		M/A 83	16
People: Vanbianchi, Peggy	"Unsettled Images: Peggy Vanbianchi & Emily Standley" (Exhibit)	Rowlands-Tarbox, Jean L.	√		Fa	12	5		S/O 85	71
People: Vander Lee, Jana	"Common Threads Shared" (Exhibit)	Dishough, Susanne	√		Fa	4	6		N/D 77	16
People: Vander Meer, Kerry	Fans and Fan Imagery	Howe, Katherine; Joanne Mattera	√		Fa	9	4		J/A 82	26
People: Vander Meer, Kerry	Paper Clothing: West	Koplos, Janet	√		Fa	11	2		M/A 84	39
People: Vander Meer, Kerry	Public Fiber: Looking At the Logistics	Koplos, Janet	√		Fa	12	1		J/F 85	32
People: VanSlyke, Gail Rutter	Gail Rutter VanSlyke: A Weaver's Commitment	Hunt, Ann	√		Fa	6	5		S/O 79	40
People: Vargo, Diane	Fiber Ten	McGuire, Patricia	√		Fa	4	6		N/D 77	26
People: Vargo, Diane	Open Jurying in Pittsburg: Putting Your Work on the Line (Exhibit)	Myrinx, Elaine	√		Fa	6	2		M/A 79	23
People: Vaughn, Vivien Leigh	"Baskets in La Jolla" (Exhibit)	Blaylock, Mary P.	√		Fa	11	1		J/F 84	79
People: Vaughn, Vivien Leigh	"Fiber Structure National" (Exhibit)	Dyer, Carolyn	√		Fa	8	5		S/O 81	75
People: Vavra, Georgia	"Art Couture '82" (Exhibit)	Guagliumi, Sasan	√		Fa	10	1		J/F 83	84
People: Vavra, Rudy	"Houston Designer-Craftsmen 1976" (Exhibit)	Vander Lee, Jana	√		Fa	3	4		J/A 76	9
People: Veness, Tim	Notes on Designing for Drape	Veness, Tim	√		Hw	7	5		N/D 86	76
People: Veren, Boris	Boris Veren's Offers a Rare Book Service	Howie, Andrew	√		H&C	16	2		Sp 65	15
People: Vernon, Diana	Knitting Craft in Great Britain, The	Kinder, Kathleen	√		Fa	11	4		J/A 84	42
People: Veselka, Aldona	Traditional Lithuanian Weaving in Chicago	Meek, M. Kati	√		SS&D	17	3	67	Su 86	50

SUBJECT	TITLE	AUTHOR	IL	INST	JOUR	VOL	NO	ISS	DATE	PAGE
People: Vesey, Emma	Art to Wear — Three Innovators: Cate Fitt, Emma Vesey, Dina Schwartz Knapp		√		Fa	8	1		J/F 81	67
People: Vesey, Emma	Machine Knitting: The State of the Art		√		Fa	9	2		M/A 82	40
People: Vetter, Vesta	Handweaver Plans an Interior, A	Bryan, Dorothy	√		H&C	6	1		Wi 54	8
People: Vetters, Vesta	Designing Satisfactory Upholstery Fabrics		√		H&C	4	1		Wi 52	20
People: Viani, Emma	Spindle and Distaff	Florentine, Gemma	√	√	TM			2	D/J 85	33
People: Vidak, Istvan	Feltmaking in Hungary	Beede, Beth; Jill Garfunkel	√		Fa	13	4		J/A 86	6
People: Viditz-Ward, Anton	Viditz-Ward Dyes in Evergreen; Students Still Blue	Ritchey, Janet	√		Iw	2	4		Su 77	13
People: Vilhelmsdottir, Eva	Fiber Art in Iceland	Hrafnhildur, Schram	√		Fa	9	6		N/D 82	68
People: Virgils, Katherine	Katherine Virgils	Waller, Irene	√		Fa	10	5		S/O 83	12
People: Voiers, Leslie	Leslie Voiers				SS&D	18	3	71	Su 87	5
People: von Godin, Wilhelmine	Modern Handweaver Restores Famous Tapestries, A		√	√	H&C	3	2		Sp 52	9
People: von Kleeck, Caroline	Feltmaking Now: The Exciting Revival of an Ancient Technique	Gordon, Beverly	√		Fa	6	6		N/D 79	43
People: von Ladau, Jackie	Jackie von Ladau, Versatile Weaver	Clement, Doris	√	√	H&C	10	3		Su 59	20
People: von Weise, Wenda	"Fiber Invitational" (Exhibit)	Bywater, William	√		Fa	7	2		M/A 80	66
People: von Weise, Wenda F.	"Quilt National '79" (Exhibit)	Gutcheon, Beth	√		Fa	6	5		S/O 79	80
People: Vowles, Christine	"Fibers Unlimited 1979" (Exhibit)	Davidian, Robert	√		Fa	7	2		M/A 80	69
People: V'Soske, Stanislav	V'Soske Rugs Through the Years	V'Soske, Vesta S.	√		H&C	5	4		Fa 54	8
People: Wada, Yoshiko	"Dyer's Art: Ikat, Batik, Plangi, The" (Exhibit)	Dyer, Carolyn	√		Fa	5	4		J/A 78	11
People: Wada, Yoshiko Iwamoto	Innovations in Indigo	Wada, Yoshiko Iwamoto	√		Fa	13	5		S/O 86	29
People: Wagner, D. R.	D. R. Wagner: 625 Stitches per Inch	Welty, Margaret	√		Fa	10	6		N/D 83	24
People: Wagner, D. R.	"Ritual Narratives" (Exhibit)		√		Fa	13	3		M/J 86	57
People: Wagner, Daniel	"Interweave '78" (Exhibit)	Yarnell, Grace	√		Fa	5	6		N/D 78	69
People: Wagstaff, Jan	"Frontiers of Contemporary Weaving" (Exhibit)	Clark, Barbara	√		Fa	4	1		J/F 77	6
People: Wagstaff, Jan	"Jan Wagstaff: Woven and Painted Canvas" (Exhibit)	Malarcher, Patricia	√		Fa	8	6		N/D 81	64
People: Wahling, Jon B.	"Fiber Forms '78" (Exhibit)	Patton, Ellen	√		Fa	5	5		S/O 78	66
People: Wainwright, Ann	Folkwear: In the Company of Some Friends		√		Fa	3	5		S/O 76	36
People: Walker, Barbara	Barbara Walker Mosaic, The	Xenakis, Alexis Yiorgos	√		Kn	2	1	3	F-W 85	11
People: Walker, Linda Berry	Interview with Linda Berry Walker...A Spinning and Dyeing Business, An	Horton, Lucy	√		Fa	4	5		S/O 77	26
People: Walker, Sally McKenna	Sally McKenna Walker's Sculpture: Tension Resolved Through Balance	Miles, Candice St. Jacques	√		Fa	11	4		J/A 84	14
People: Wallace, Lysbeth	Lysbeth Wallace Discusses Teaching Methods		√		H&C	15	1		Wi 64	18
People: Waller, Elsa	"Recent Work by Elsa Waller" (Exhibit)	Harrington, Elaine	√		Fa	8	4		J/A 81	71
People: Waller, Irene	In Retrospect, Irene Waller	Waller, Irene	√		SS&D	12	4	48	Fa 81	10
People: Waller, Irene	Irene Waller		√		SS&D	4	2	14	Sp 73	56
People: Waller, Irene	Speakers Bureau Presents		√		SS&D	4	2	14	Sp 73	55
People: Wallman, Agneta	Tapestry Gallery		√		Iw	4	2		Sp 79	33
People: Walsh, Gloriah	"Art Couture VII" (Exhibit)	Guagliumi, Susan Fletcher	√		Fa	12	3		M/J 85	78
People: Walsh, Joan	Body as Canvas, The	Koda, Harold	√		TM			8	D/J 86	56
People: Walsh, John	Body as Canvas, The	Koda, Harold	√		TM			8	D/J 86	56
People: Walsh, Meri Ann	"Meri Ann Walsh: Patterned Papers" (Exhibit)	Austin, Carole	√		Fa	8	6		N/D 81	65
People: Walters, Kai	Kai Walters	Pilsk, Adele	√		Fa	4	6		N/D 77	42
People: Walters, Marge	Fiber and Architecture: Marge Walters		√		Fa	3	3		M/J 76	33
People: Wantz, Justine	Papermaking in Chicago	Shermeta, Margo	√		Fa	11	2		M/A 84	54
People: Ward, Alice	Magic Lanterns: Alice Ward's Handmade Paper Light/Shades	Holland, Nina	√		Fa	8	3		M/J 81	22

SUBJECT	TITLE	AUTHOR	IL	INST	JOUR	VOL	NO	ISS	DATE	PAGE
People: Ward, Barbara	Soft Sculpture of Barbara Ward, The	Harris, Patricia; David Lyon	√		Fa	14	1		J/F 87	10
People: Ward, Sandra	"Fabric/Nexus: New Connections" (Exhibit)	Moldovan, George	√		Fa	10	3		M/J 83	70
People: Warner, Debbie	"Women Artists: Clay, Fiber, Metal" (Exhibit)	Malarcher, Patricia	√		Fa	5	2		M/A 78	11
People: Warner, Deborah	"Deborah Warner's Visual Journal" (Exhibit)	Poon, Vivian	√		Fa	10	6		N/D 83	76
People: Warner, Deborah	"Leora Stewart: New Works—Deborah Warner: Four Corners Journal" (Exhibit)	Malarcher, Patricia	√		Fa	6	6		N/D 79	71
People: Warner, Deborah Courtney	"Contemporary Fiber Art" (Exhibit)	Guyer, Niki	√		Fa	5	6		N/D 78	66
People: Warren, Judi	Paper Clothing: West	Koplos, Janet	√		Fa	11	2		M/A 84	39
People: Warren, Judy	Quilting by the Lake in Central New York	Wright, Yolanda	√		Fa	10	2		M/A 83	50
People: Warren, Verina	Verina Warren	Scarborough, Jessica	√		Fa	13	4		J/A 86	26
People: Washington, Misti	Art That Functions	Lønning, Kari	√		Fa	8	3		M/J 81	40
People: Washington, Misti	Misti Washington				SS&D	16	4	64	Fa 85	4
People: Wassef, Rames Wissa	Tapping the Artist Within: The Wissa Wassef Tapestries			√	H&C	26	3		M/J 75	5
People: Watanabe, Akiko	Fundraising Brings Kasuri Kimono Weaver to Nashville Workshop	Wilson, Sadye Tune	√		SS&D	9	2	34	Sp 78	4
People: Watanabe, Hiroko	Lausanne Notebook: Our Special Report on the 8th Lausanne Biennial of Tapestry, A	Mathews, Rich	√		Fa	4	5		S/O 77	30
People: Watkins, Lois	One Hundred Sixty Years of Craftsmanship	Ligon, Linda	√		Iw	1	3		Sp 76	17
People: Watson, Ann	Country of Origin, USA: A Decade of Contemporary Rugs	Stevens, Rebeccah A. T.	√		Fa	11	3		M/J 84	60
People: Watson, Susan	Canadian Portfolio, A	Place, Jennifer	√		Fa	9	6		N/D 82	29
People: Watts, Bill	Soft Sculpture Set for Albee's "Seascape"		√		Fa	4	2		M/A 77	29
People: Weaver, Ken	Ken Weaver on Rep Weaving	Weaver, Ken	√		WJ	7	4	28	Sp 83	20
People: Webb, Mrs. Vanderbilt	American Handweaving 1960		√		H&C	11	2		Sp 60	7
People: Webb, Olive	Weaving Guilds—A Special Sharing		√		Iw	5	2		Sp 80	52
People: Webber, Helen	Collaborations II: Let's Do Business		√		Fa	12	5		S/O 85	66
People: Webster, Joan	"Beds, Sweet Dreams, and Other Things" (Exhibit)	Bissell, June	√		Fa	6	4		J/A 79	70
People: Wechsler, Susan	"Women Artists: Clay, Fiber, Metal" (Exhibit)	Malarcher, Patricia	√		Fa	5	2		M/A 78	11
People: Wederquist, Lisa	Pikes Peak Weavers Guild First Fibre Arts Festival (Exhibit)	Fife, Lin	√		Fa	3	5		S/O 76	6
People: Weege, Bill	"Made in Wisconsin: An Exhibition of Recent Works In-Of-And-On Handmade Paper" (Exhibit)	Hagemeister-Winzenz, Karon	√		Fa	5	4		J/A 78	19
People: Weghorst, Linda	Linda Weghorst: Portraits in Fiber		√		Fa	4	4		J/A 77	44
People: Wegner, Wendy L.	"Works in Fiber" (Exhibit)	Arnow, Jan	√		Fa	8	2		M/A 81	61
People: Weichsel, Lynn	"Show of Fans, A" (Exhibit)	Goodman, Deborah Lerme	√		Fa	12	6		N/D 85	56
People: Weiler, Melody	Wear an Original Painting: Melody Weiler's Airbrushed Shirtscapes	Speight, Jerry	√	√	Fa	8	1		J/F 81	13
People: Weir, Jane	"Festival of Weaving" (Exhibit)	Greenberg, Blue	√		Fa	7	4		J/A 80	71
People: Weisbord, Ellen	Country of Origin, USA: A Decade of Contemporary Rugs	Stevens, Rebeccah A. T.	√		Fa	11	3		M/J 84	60
People: Weisman, Sandy	Boston Seven	Newman, Rochelle	√		SS&D	16	3	63	Su 85	71
People: Welch, Ann	Verbena Collection, The (error-corrected Fa v11 n1 84 p11)		√		Fa	10	5		S/O 83	64
People: Weller, Catherine	Sampler of Surface Design, A	Westphal, Katherine	√		Fa	10	5		S/O 83	39
People: Wellner, Linda	"Needle Expressions '80" (Exhibit)		√		Fa	8	1		J/F 81	93
People: Welsh-May, Denise	Touch of the Poet: Wearables by Denise Welsh-May, A	Park, Betty	√		Fa	6	6		N/D 79	52
People: Welte, Jennifer	Collegiate Fashion Show Highlights Textile Program	Belfer, Nancy	√		Fa	14	1		J/F 87	6

SUBJECT	TITLE	AUTHOR	IL	INST	JOUR	VOL	NO	ISS	DATE	PAGE
People: Welty, Margaret	"Left on the Loom" (Exhibit)	Dyer, Carolyn	√		Fa	5	2		M/A 78	16
People: Welty, Margaret	Margaret Welty: Minimalist Weaver	Les, Kathleen	√		Fa	5	4		J/A 78	28
People: Welty, Margaret	Questions of Style: Contemporary Trends in the Fiber Arts	Howe-Echt, Katherine	√		Fa	7	2		M/A 80	38
People: Wendt, Kath	"Left on the Loom" (Exhibit)	Dyer, Carolyn	√		Fa	5	2		M/A 78	16
People: Wertenberger, Kathryn	Handwoven Clothing Today: The Couturier Touch	West, Virginia	√		Fa	8	1		J/F 81	39
People: Wertenberger, Kathryn	Jurying	Ligon, Linda	√		Iw	1	2		Wi 76	10
People: Weslien, Katharina	"Fiber Structure National" (Exhibit)	Dyer, Carolyn	√		Fa	8	5		S/O 81	75
People: Weslien, Katrina	"Felt: A Rich Tradition and Current Involvements" (Exhibit)	Constantinides, Kathy	√		Fa	6	3		M/J 79	74
People: West, Virginia	Designer Collection: Virginia West		√	√	Hw	7	5		N/D 86	62
People: Westerink, Claire	Portfolio: Why I Work in Linen, A		√		Fa	14	2		M/A 87	41
People: Westerman, Marie	Portfolio: Why I Work in Linen, A		√		Fa	14	2		M/A 87	39
People: Westfall, Carol	Carol Westfall: Adapting Dye Transfer Methods	Park, Betty	√		Fa	5	1		J/F 78	64
People: Westfall, Carol	Miniatures in Fiber: Working Small—An Exciting Challenge for the Contemporary Fiber Artist	Malarcher, Patricia	√		Fa	7	4		J/A 80	32
People: Westfall, Carol	"Women Artists: Clay, Fiber, Metal" (Exhibit)	Malarcher, Patricia	√		Fa	5	2		M/A 78	11
People: Westfall, Carol D.	"100% Wool" (Exhibit)	Goldin, Susan	√		Fa	4	6		N/D 77	18
People: Weston, Joseph	Rugs by an Architect		√	√	H&C	13	4		Fa 62	6
People: Westphal, Katherine	Creative Process: Katherine Westphal, The	Westphal, Katherine	√		Fa	11	6		N/D 84	32
People: Westphal, Katherine	Designers on Design		√		Fa	10	4		J/A 83	28
People: Westphal, Katherine	"Fiberworks 1976" (Exhibit)	Papa, Nancy	√		Fa	4	1		J/F 77	9
People: Westphal, Katherine	Liturgical Vestment: A Contemporary Overview, The	Malarcher, Patricia	√		Fa	11	5		S/O 84	58
People: Westphal, Katherine	"Paper Clothing and More in San Francisco" (Exhibit)	Scarborough, Jessica	√		Fa	11	2		M/A 84	75
People: Westphal, Katherine	Paper Clothing: West	Koplos, Janet	√		Fa	11	2		M/A 84	39
People: Westphal, Katherine	Way of Working: Katherine Westphal and the Creative Process, A	Janeiro, Jan	√		Fa	7	6		N/D 80	35
People: Wetherbee, Martha	Shaker Baskets Today	Wetherbee, Martha	√		SS&D	19	1	73	Wi 87	60
People: Wheeler, Barbara	Know Your Supplier				S-O	11	3		Fa 87	41
People: Wheeler, Margaret Roach	Weaver Profile: Mahota Handwovens	Irwin, Bobbie	√		Hw	8	5		N/D 87	35
People: Wheelock, Warren	American Yarn Shops: On the Endangered Species List?	Xenakis, Alexis Yiorgos	√		Kn	3	4	8	Fa 87	10
People: Whipple, Lillian	Designer Collection: Lillian Whipple		√	√	Hw	7	5		N/D 86	64
People: White, Dondi	Body as Canvas, The	Koda, Harold	√		TM			8	D/J 86	56
People: White, Fifi	Surface Design Conference in Kansas City	Craig-Linenberger, Gerry	√		TM			12	A/S 87	20
People: White, Pat	Pat White: The "Small Things" Are Her Signature	Park, Betty	√	√	SS&D	10	3	51	Su 82	58
People: White, Patricia	"Art Couture/Haute Couture" (Exhibit)	McGuire, Patricia	√		Fa	9	1		J/F 82	86
People: White, Patricia	Handwoven Clothing Today: The Couturier Touch	West, Virginia	√		Fa	8	1		J/F 81	39
People: White, Patricia	"New Elegance: Contemporary Wearable Art, The" (Exhibit)	Malarcher, Patricia	√		Fa	12	4		J/A 85	44
People: Whitham, Franklin	Franklin Whitham	King, Bucky	√		Iw	2	2		Wi 77	13
People: Whitmire, Jane	"Embroiderer's Guild Of America, 11th Biennial Exhibition" (Exhibit)	Itter, Diane	√		Fa	12	2		M/A 85	76
People: Whitten, Paul	Nantucket Lightship Baskets: A Sailor's Pastime Revisited	Lucas, Eleanor L.	√		Fa	5	5		S/O 78	52
People: Whitten, Robin	Designer: Linekin Bay Fabrics				SS&D	11	2	42	Sp 80	93
People: Whitten, Robin	Linekin Bay Fabrics: Handweaving in a Maine Production Studio	Mattera, Joanne	√		Fa	9	1		J/F 82	39

SUBJECT	TITLE	AUTHOR	IL	INST	JOUR	VOL	NO	ISS	DATE	PAGE
People: Wick, Susan	"Baker/Rapoport/Wick" in New York (Exhibit)	Park, Betty	√		Fa	4	5		S/O 77	15
People: Wicks, Kay-O	Kay-O Wicks — The Habit of Knitting	Horton, Lucy	√		Fa	6	3		M/J 79	32
People: Wiersba, Diane	Diane Wiersba	Gilfoy, Peggy S.	√		H&C	15	3		Su 64	19
People: Wiese, Janislee	Janislee Wiese: Painted Warps		√	√	Fa	5	1		J/F 78	63
People: Wight, James	Going Into Production: James Wight and Helen Cooperstein		√		Fa	3	1		J/F 76	15
People: Wikoff, Naj	"Cloth Forms" (Exhibits)	Skudera, Gail	√		Fa	9	4		J/A 82	76
People: Wilce, Leroy	"Leroy Wilce: Adobe Walls" (Exhibit)	Dyer, Carolyn	√		Fa	4	4		J/A 77	17
People: Wilce, Letitia	On Fabric in the Southwest: Surface Design, A Bank, and Public Recognition	Brooks, Lois Ziff	√		Fa	6	5		S/O 79	54
People: Wilcox, Leslie	"Fibers: From Function to Formalization" (Exhibit)	Scarborough, Jessica	√		Fa	9	1		J/F 82	76
People: Wilcox, Leslie	Leslie Wilcox	Wilcox, Leslie	√		Fa	12	5		S/O 85	19
People: Wiley, Pamela	Sampler of Surface Design, A	Westphal, Katherine	√		Fa	10	5		S/O 83	39
People: Wilkerson, Joyce	Joyce Wilkerson: Silk Screening a Warp		√	√	Fa	5	1		J/F 78	65
People: Wilkinson, Dorothy	Miss Wilkinson of London Visits America				H&C	16	1		Wi 65	11
People: Willard, Dennis	Athens Tapestry Works	Many, Paul	√		Fa	5	4		J/A 78	51
People: Williams, Betty	Betty Williams: Colors of the Earth	Robbins, Judy	√		SS&D	18	4	72	Fa 87	57
People: Williams, Jim	Lushness of Nature: Jim Williams and His Needlepoint Art, The	Luddecke, Jane	√		Fa	6	4		J/A 79	50
People: Williams, Pat	"Interweave '78" (Exhibit)	Yarnell, Grace	√		Fa	5	6		N/D 78	69
People: Williams, Pat	"Paper and Felt Redefined" (Exhibit)	Ogden, Anne	√		Fa	5	2		M/A 78	17
People: Williams-Cacicedo, Jean	Art to Wear: Looking At the Movement	Scarborough, Jessica	√		Fa	12	3		M/J 85	56
People: Williamson, Ann	Under Wraps		√		Fa	12	3		M/J 85	26
People: Willis, Bonnie	American Handweaving 1960		√		H&C	11	2		Sp 60	47
People: Willock, Jack	Introduction to Two Textilatelists, An	Allston, J. L.; J. A. Hoskins	√		AT	4			De 85	81
People: Willson, Gayle and Paul	Getting Into the Galleries: Nine Dealers Tell How to Do It		√		Fa	9	5		S/O 82	43
People: Wilson, Anne	"Anne Wilson: Grid Constructions" (Exhibit)	Finkel, Marilyn	√		Fa	6	2		M/A 79	65
People: Wilson, Anne	"Anne Wilson: Recent Work" (Exhibit)	Arajs, Ilze	√		Fa	11	4		J/A 84	75
People: Wilson, Anne	Anne Wilson: Underlying Geometry	Koplos, Janet	√		Fa	10	3		M/J 83	62
People: Wilson, Anne	Questions of Style: Contemporary Trends in the Fiber Arts	Howe-Echt, Katherine	√		Fa	7	2		M/A 80	38
People: Wilson, Anne	"Tangents: Art in Fiber" (Exhibit)	Krinn, Linda	√		Fa	14	3		M/J 87	55
People: Wilson, Anne	Textile Trends: Collecting in Chicago	Lonier, Terri	√		Fa	12	6		N/D 85	26
People: Wilson, Clare	Fiber Workspaces: A Room of Your Own	Bishop, Mara	√		Fa	4	4		J/A 77	38
People: Wilson, Jay	Patience and Planning	Wilson, Jay	√		Fa	8	2		M/A 81	29
People: Wilson, Jean	Jean Wilson	Rush, Beverly	√		Iw	5	2		Sp 80	43
People: Wilson, Marcia	Masks At the Heart of Disguise	Koplos, Janet	√		Fa	11	5		S/O 84	32
People: Wilson, Sadye Tune	One-Woman Publishing Show, A	Xenakis, Alexis Yiorgos	√		PWC	5	2	16		6
People: Windeknecht, Margaret	Margaret and Tom Windeknecht: Computer Drafts	Pilsk, Adele	√		Fa	5	5		S/O 78	18
People: Windeknecht, Margaret and Tom	Time to Revitalize, A	Xenakis, Alexis Yiorgos	√		PWC	4	1	11		10
People: Windeknecht, Tom	Margaret and Tom Windeknecht: Computer Drafts	Pilsk, Adele	√		Fa	5	5		S/O 78	18
People: Winsor, Jackie	"Jackie Winsor" (Exhibit)	Malarcher, Pat	√		Fa	6	4		J/A 79	68
People: Winzenz, Karon Hagemeister	Karon Hagemeister Winzenz: Fusing Fiber, Time, and Ritual	Bard, Elizabeth A.	√		Fa	12	1		J/F 85	10
People: Wise, Susan	"California Women in Crafts" (Exhibit)	Dyer, Carolyn	√		Fa	4	2		M/A 77	10
People: Wissa-Wassef, Ramses	Contemporary Egyptian Childern's Tapestries		√		Fa	4	6		N/D 77	65
People: Witsell, Rebecca Rogers	Fiber and Architecture: Rebecca Rogers Witsell		√		Fa	3	3		M/J 76	23
People: Wittenberg, Barbara	Speakers Bureau Presents		√		SS&D	6	3	23	Su 75	59

SUBJECT	TITLE	AUTHOR	IL	INST	JOUR	VOL	NO	ISS	DATE	PAGE
People: Wittenberg, Barbara	Weaving Workshop with Barbara Wittenberg: Sharing is Pervasive, A	Aikin, Patti	√		Fa	8	4		J/A 81	21
People: Woell, Kathy	Kathy Woell Original, A	Sitko, Jane Bradley	√		SS&D	19	1	73	Wi 87	36
People: Wohl, Arlene	Cylaine Handwoven Designs: Arlene Wohl and Lucy Matzger		√		WJ	7	3	27	Wi 82	8
People: Wojtyna-Drouet, Krystyna	"22 Polish Textile Artists" (Exhibit)	Park, Betty	√		Fa	4	5		S/O 77	8
People: Wolfe, Leslie	"Critters and Cohorts" (Exhibit)	Clark, Becky	√		Fa	4	6		N/D 77	13
People: Wolfer, Joan	"Needle Expressions '86" (Exhibit)	Reinsel, Susan J.	√		Fa	14	1		J/F 87	53
People: Wolfson, Emily Wilson	Speakers Bureau Presents		√		SS&D	6	2	22	Sp 75	70
People: Womersley, Richard	Kaffe Fassett: Dream Knitter (error-corrected Fa v5 n4 78 p63)		√		Fa	5	3		M/J 78	26
People: Wong, Paul	"Made in Wisconsin: An Exhibition of Recent Works In-Of-and-On Handmade Paper" (Exhibit)	Hagemeister-Winzenz, Karon	√		Fa	5	4		J/A 78	19
People: Wong, Paul	Papermaking in the U.S.A.	Toale, Bernard	√		Fa	9	4		J/A 82	34
People: Wong, Paul	Sculptural Paper: Foundations and Directions	Scarborough, Jessica	√		Fa	11	2		M/A 84	32
People: Wood, Susan	Contemporary Lace of Susan Wood, The	Darling, Drew	√		Fa	11	6		N/D 84	22
People: Woodbury, Jo	"Made in Wisconsin: An Exhibition of Recent Works In-Of-and-On Handmade Paper" (Exhibit)	Hagemeister-Winzenz, Karon	√		Fa	5	4		J/A 78	19
People: Woolstenhulme, Kate	Kate Woolstenhulme: A Sense of Place	Walters, Roberta	√		Fa	10	2		M/A 83	56
People: Worst, Edward F.	Edward F. Worst: Craftsman and Educator	Pettigrew, Dale	√		Hw	6	5		N/D 85	73
People: Worthen, Richard	Fiber and Architecture: Richard Worthen		√		Fa	3	3		M/J 76	32
People: Wright, Nancy	"Textiles New Mexico 1978" (Exhibit)	Tatum, Phyllis	√		Fa	5	4		J/A 78	10
People: Wright, Sandi	Santa Fe Weaving Center, The	Elliott, Malinda	√		Fa	9	5		S/O 82	32
People: Wright, Sandi	"Textiles New Mexico 1978" (Exhibit)	Tatum, Phyllis	√		Fa	5	4		J/A 78	10
People: Wulke, Joy	Working with the Wall ... A Community Garden		√		SS&D	10	4	40	Fa 79	8
People: Yacopino, Phyllis	Speakers Bureau Presents		√		SS&D	3	3	11	Su 72	17
People: Yagi, Mariyo	"Fiberworks" (Exhibit)	Park, Betty	√		Fa	4	6		N/D 77	10
People: Yagi, Mariyo	"Mariyo Yagi" (Exhibit)	Park, Betty	√		Fa	5	1		J/F 78	19
People: Yamaguchi, Keiko	Mysterious Figurines of Keiko Yamaguchi, The	Hempel, Toby Anne	√		Fa	14	4		S/O 87	16
People: Yamamoto, Mitsue	What People Ask Before They Buy Handmade Fashions	Leslie, Victoria	√		TM			9	F/M 87	58
People: Yamazaki, Teruko	Leather Reliefs of Teruko Yamazaki, The	Koplos, Janet	√		Fa	14	4		S/O 87	12
People: Yao, C. J.	Silk Reflections of C. J. Yao, The	Nicoli, Antony	√		Fa	13	1		J/F 86	47
People: Yardley, Valerie	Who Weaves?		√		Iw	5	2		Sp 80	38
People: Yarmolinsky, Sirpa	"New American Paperworks" (Exhibit) (error-corrected Fa v13 n3 86 p5)	Shermeta, Margo	√		Fa	13	1		J/F 86	64
People: Yarmolinsky, Sirpa	Paper Reliefs of Sirpa Yarmolinsky, The	Goodman, Deborah Lerme	√		Fa	12	5		S/O 85	17
People: Yarmolinsky, Sirpa	"Sirpa Yarmolinsky: Paper and Linen Constructions" (Exhibit)	Malarcher, Patricia	√		Fa	9	1		J/F 82	84
People: Yatsko, Jan	Jan Yatsko's Bird's Nest Baskets		√		Fa	11	1		J/F 84	57
People: Yazzi, Susie	Spinning with Susie	Chacey, Ron	√	√	S-O	7	4		Wi 83	18
People: Yelland, Robert	Livin' and Workin' on the Land: Fiber Art Outside the Mainstream	Talley, Charles S.	√		Fa	8	6		N/D 81	38
People: Yenawine, Neisja	"Shared Vision": A Gallery Tour with Two Artists: Jacque Parsley and Neisja Yenawine (Exhibit)	Arnow, Jan	√		Fa	8	4		J/A 81	28
People: Yesley, Irene	Country of Origin, USA: A Decade of Contemporary Rugs	Stevens, Rebeccah A. T.	√		Fa	11	3		M/J 84	60
People: Yeung, Jing	Collegiate Fashion Show Highlights Textile Program	Belfer, Nancy	√		Fa	14	1		J/F 87	6
People: Yoors, Jan	American Handweaving 1960		√		H&C	11	2		Sp 60	16
People: Yoors, Jan	New Directions for Jan Yoors: Tapestry Weaver Now Known as Author and Photographer		√		H&C	18	4		Fa 67	6

SUBJECT	TITLE	AUTHOR	IL	INST	JOUR	VOL	NO	ISS	DATE	PAGE
People: Yoors, Jan	Tapestries	Yoors, Jan	√		H&C	5	1		Wi 53	18
People: Yori, Polly	Polly Yori (error-corrected H&C v21 n3 70 p45)	Marston, Ena	√	> 4	H&C	21	1		Wi 70	19
People: Yorko, Aloyse	Quilting by the Lake in Central New York	Wright, Yolanda	√		Fa	10	2		M/A 83	50
People: Yoshida, Kazumi	Made by Machine: Textiles for the Eighties	Harris, Patricia; David Lyon	√		Fa	12	5		S/O 85	34
People: Yost, Erma Martin	"Ceremonial Works" (Exhibit)		√		Fa	13	2		M/A 86	56
People: Youdelman, Nancy	"Nancy Youdelman: Shattered Glass" (Exhibit)	Woelfle, Gretchen	√		Fa	7	3		M/J 80	74
People: Yovan, Susan	"Fiber Techniques: The Weaver's Guild of Greater Cincinnati" (Exhibit)	Fedders, Pat	√		Fa	8	1		J/F 81	91
People: Yow, Susan B.	"Young Americans: Fiber, Wood, Plastic, Leather" (Exhibit)	Malarcher, Patricia	√		Fa	4	6		N/D 77	14
People: Yowell, Susanne	Around the World and Home Again	Greenberg, Blue	√		Fa	9	6		N/D 82	99
People: Yowell, Susanne	Fans and Fan Imagery	Howe, Katherine; Joanne Mattera	√		Fa	9	4		J/A 82	26
People: Yowell, Susanne	"Fibers Southeast 1979" (Exhibit)	Johnson, Elma	√		Fa	6	2		M/A 79	68
People: Yowell, Susanne K.	"Young Americans: Fiber, Wood, Plastic, Leather" (Exhibit)	Malarcher, Patricia	√		Fa	4	6		N/D 77	14
People: Yu, Chug Hee	"Partners in Art: Brushwork by Lee, Dong Chun and Embroidery by Yu, Chug Hee" (Exhibit)	Backer, Ellen	√		Fa	4	3		M/J 77	16
People: Yue, Rosina	Creative Process: Rosina Yue, The	Yue, Rosina	√		Fa	11	6		N/D 84	40
People: Yue, Rosina	Fashioned from Paper: Rosina Yue's "Clothing" Constructions	Scarborough, Jessica	√		Fa	8	1		J/F 81	76
People: Yue, Rosina	Paper Clothing: West	Koplos, Janet	√		Fa	11	2		M/A 84	39
People: Zabler, Howard	Howard Zabler		√		Fa	5	3		M/J 78	54
People: Zahorec, Ellen	"Patterns" (Exhibit)	Malarcher, Patricia	√		Fa	10	2		M/A 83	76
People: Zahorec, Ellen	Saved Threads: Ellen Zahorec Explores Layers of Time		√		Fa	8	5		S/O 81	42
People: Zehner, Leonoor M.	Fashionable Palette of Pittsburgh Paints, The	Brenholts, Jeanne	√		Fa	14	3		M/J 87	46
People: Zeisler, Claire	Artist's Collection: Claire Zeisler, An	Lonier, Terri	√		Fa	12	6		N/D 85	29
People: Zeisler, Claire	Claire Zeisler	Uhlmann, Etta	√		H&C	13	4		Fa 62	34
People: Zeisler, Claire	"Claire Zeisler" (Exhibit)	Mathews, Rich	√		Fa	4	1		J/F 77	12
People: Zeisler, Claire	"Claire Zeisler" (Exhibit)	Richerson, Suzanne	√		Fa	6	4		J/A 79	69
People: Zeisler, Claire	Conversation with Claire Zeisler, A	Koplos, Janet	√		Fa	10	4		J/A 83	25
People: Zeisler, Claire	"Fiber R/Evolution" (Exhibit)	Rudich, Sally	√		Fa	13	4		J/A 86	45
People: Zeisler, Claire	"Fiber Works — Americas & Japan" (Exhibit)	Kato, Kuniko Lucy	√		Fa	5	1		J/F 78	10
People: Zeisler, Claire	"Sculpture of Claire Zeisler" (Exhibit)	Malarcher, Patricia	√		Fa	12	6		N/D 85	57
People: Zeisler, Claire	"Women Artists: Clay, Fiber, Metal" (Exhibit)	Malarcher, Patricia	√		Fa	5	2		M/A 78	11
People: Zemsky, Leslie	Collegiate Fashion Show Highlights Textile Program	Belfer, Nancy	√		Fa	14	1		J/F 87	6
People: Zerner, Amy	Fabric Collages (Exhibit)	Zerner, Amy	√		Fa	14	3		M/J 87	64
People: Zerner, Amy	Illuminated Tapestries of Amy Zerner, The	Daniels, Richard	√		Fa	9	3		M/J 82	22
People: Zerobnick, Alan	These Toes Won't Drown in Tears of Clown	Montgomery, Larry	√		TM			11	J/J 87	14
People: Ziek, Bhakti	Bhakti Ziek	Ziek, Bhakti	√		Fa	13	3		M/J 86	27
People: Ziek, Bhakti	"Three Weavers: Thomasin Grim, Jane Lackey, Bhakti Ziek" (Exhibit)	Rowley, Kathleen	√		Fa	9	6		N/D 82	82
People: Zielinski, Stanislaw A.	Master Weaver: Stanislaw A. Zielinski, The	Zielinski, Miwa	√		SS&D	10	3	39	Su 79	62
People: Ziemba, Wanda	"Felting" (Exhibit)	Park, Betty	√		Fa	7	6		N/D 80	71
People: Zimmermann, Elizabeth	Afternoon with Elizabeth, An	Xenakis, Alexis Yiorgos	√		Kn	1	1	1	F-W 84 CI	10 4
People: Zimmermann, Elizabeth	Sampler of Knit Edgings and Applied Trims, A	Newton, Deborah	√	√	TM			12	A/S 87	38

SUBJECT	TITLE	AUTHOR	IL	INST	JOUR	VOL	NO	ISS	DATE	PAGE
People: Zinsmeister, Anna	Anna Zinsmeister	Zinsmeister, Anna	√		Fa	13	1		J/F 86	19
People: Zipperer, Joyce	Art of Unweaving, The		√		Fa	10	6		N/D 83	99
People: Znamierowski, Nell	Designers on Design		√		Fa	10	4		J/A 83	28
People: Znamierowski, Nell	Nell Znamierowski: Color & Design	Liebler, Barbara	√		Hw	2	4		Se 81	40
People: Znamierowski, Nellie	Rya Rugs		√		H&C	10	4		Fa 59	10
People: Zorach, Marguerite	Hooking Wild Horses (Zorach, Marguerite)		√		TM			10	A/M 87	88
People: Zotto-Beltz, Mary Ann	Fiber Workspaces: A Room of Your Own	Bishop, Mara	√		Fa	4	4		J/A 77	38
Peppervine	Diverse Dyes	Bliss, Anne	√	√	Iw	3	2		Wi 78	30
Periodicals	Ars Textrina				CW	5	2	14	Ja 84	19
Periodicals	Ars Textrina	Stanton, R. G., ed.			PWC	5	1	15		52
Periodicals	Ars Textrina (Textile Journal)	Stanton, Ralph, ed; Janet Hoskins, mg. ed.			Hw	7	5		N/D 86	11
Periodicals	Ars Textrina, Vol. I				Hw	5	3		Su 84	18
Periodicals	Color Trends				Hw	5	5		N/D 84	13
Periodicals	Heddle				Hw	5	3		Su 84	18
Periodicals	Home Fashions Textiles				Hw	6	4		S/O 85	35
Periodicals	Knitters				Hw	5	5		N/D 84	13
Periodicals	Linens Domestic and Bath Products				Hw	6	4		S/O 85	35
Periodicals	Teaching for Learning				Hw	5	5		N/D 84	13
Periodicals	Threads Magazine	Tauntom Press, Inc.	√		WJ	10	3	39	Wi 86	73
Periodicals	Warp and Weft	Robin and Russ Handweavers			SS&D	3	3	11	Su 72	13
Periodicals, Basketry	Three Basketry Journals				TM			3	F/M 86	16
Periodicals, Color	Foreseeing Colors				TM			3	F/M 86	16
Periodicals, Fashion	Matter of Style, A	Ligon, Linda	√		Hw	4	5		N/D 83	12
Periodicals, Foreign	Australian Hand Weaver and Spinner, The				WJ	7	3	27	Wi 82	52
Periodicals, Foreign	Deutsches Textilforum				WJ	7	2	26	Fa 82	62
Periodicals, Foreign	En Bref (French)	Association des Tisserands d'Ici, Quebec	√		WJ	11	3	43	Wi 87	64
Periodicals, Foreign	Fiber Forum (Australia)				Hw	3	5		N/D 82	12
Periodicals, Foreign	Fibre Forum				WJ	7	2	26	Fa 82	61
Periodicals, Foreign	Goed Handwerk				WJ	7	1	25	Su 82	66
Periodicals, Foreign	Haandarbejdets Fremme				WJ	7	1	25	Su 82	66
Periodicals, Foreign	Hali (Rugs)				Hw	3	5		N/D 82	14
Periodicals, Foreign	Hali — The International Journal of Oriental Carpets and Textiles				WJ	6	1	21	Su 81	54
Periodicals, Foreign	Heddle (Canada)				Hw	5	5		N/D 84	12
Periodicals, Foreign	Heimatwerk				WJ	7	1	25	Su 82	66
Periodicals, Foreign	Hemslojden				WJ	7	1	25	Su 82	66
Periodicals, Foreign	Kotiteollisuus				WJ	7	1	25	Su 82	66
Periodicals, Foreign	Kunst & Handwerk (Arts & Crafts) (West Germany)				WJ	7	1	25	Su 82	64
Periodicals, Foreign	La Navette				WJ	7	2	26	Fa 82	62
Periodicals, Foreign	Landsforeningen Stoftrykken—&Vaever Lauget				WJ	7	1	25	Su 82	66
Periodicals, Foreign	L'Atelier Des Metiers D'Art				WJ	7	2	26	Fa 82	62
Periodicals, Foreign	Ontario Crafts and Craft News				WJ	7	2	26	Fa 82	61
Periodicals, Foreign	Quarterly Journal of the Hand Weavers' and Spinners' Guild of Australia				SS&D	4	3	15	Su 73	53
Periodicals, Foreign	Texilforum (West Germany)				Hw	3	5		N/D 82	12
Periodicals, Foreign	Textile History (England)				WJ	7	2	26	Fa 82	61
Periodicals, Foreign	Textile/Art				WJ	7	2	26	Fa 82	62
Periodicals, Foreign	Textiles Para El Hogar				WJ	7	1	25	Su 82	67
Periodicals, Foreign	Textilkunst				WJ	7	1	25	Su 82	66
Periodicals, Foreign	Vav Magasinet				WJ	7	3	27	Wi 82	52

SUBJECT	TITLE	AUTHOR	IL	INST	JOUR	VOL	NO	ISS	DATE	PAGE
Periodicals, Foreign	Väv Magazinet (Sweden)				Hw	3	5		N/D 82	12
Periodicals, Foreign	Vävmagazinet	Johansson, Lillemor, ed.	√		PWC			6	Su 83	66
Periodicals, Foreign	Weavers Journal (Great Britain), The				WJ	7	3	27	Wi 82	52
Periodicals, Foreign	Web, Quarterly Journal of the New Zealand Spinning, Weaving & Woolcrafts Council, The				SS&D	3	1	9	Wi 71	38
Periodicals, Foreign	Web, The				WJ	7	2	26	Fa 82	61
Periodicals, Foreign	Webe Mit				WJ	7	1	25	Su 82	66
Periodicals, Textiles	Removing Stains				TM			3	F/M 86	16
Periodicals, The Master Weaver	Master Weaver: Stanislaw A. Zielinski, The	Zielinski, Miwa	√		SS&D	10	3	39	Su 79	62
Periodicals, Weaving	All About Twills				TM			3	F/M 86	16
Persia	Gifts from Kashan to Cairo	Ellis, Charles Grant	√		TMJ	1	1		No 62	33
Persia	Historic Persian Handiwork at the Textile Museum (Exhibit)	Dyer, Carolyn Price	√		Fa	14	5		N/D 87	42
Persia	Persian Handcrafted Items	Brockway, Edith	√		H&C	26	5		Oc 75	16
Persia	Weaving in the Past: The Romance of Persian Weaving	Zielinski, S. A.; Robert Leclerc, ed.			MWL	21 22			'51–'73	85
Peru	Ancient Peruvian Loom, An	Grossman, Ellin	√		H&C	9	2		Sp 58	20
Peru	Andean Spinning	Franquemont, Ed	√		S-O	9	1		Sp 85	54
Peru	Andes Tradition, An	McConnell, Kathleen	√	√	SS&D	18	2	70	Sp 87	29
Peru	Archeological Rags	Hickman, Pat	√		Fa	9	1		J/F 82	70
Peru	Before Heddles Were Invented	Bird, Junius B.	√		H&C	3	3		Su 52	5
Peru	Chavin Textiles and the Origins of Peruvian Weaving	Conklin, William J	√		TMJ	3	2		De 71	13
Peru	Color and Design in Andean Warp-Faced Fabrics	Femenias, Blenda	√		WJ	12	2	46	Fa 87	44
Peru	Cultures to Meet in California	Rogers, Nora	√		Hw	6	1		J/F 85	18
Peru	Francisca Mayer, Designer-Weaver in the Peruvian Highland	Boyer, Ruth McDonald	√		H&C	19	2		Sp 68	18
Peru	From Peru, Gods Eyes on a Stick	Atwood, Betty	√	√	SS&D	5	1	17	Wi 73	8
Peru	Gifts from Ancient Peru	Nass, Ulla	√	√	WJ	8	1	29	Su 83	32
Peru	Identifying Hands at Work on a Paracas Mantle	Paul, Anne; Susan A. Niles	√		TMJ	23			84	5
Peru	Inca Feathers	Kwiatkowski, Ron	√	√	Iw	1	2		Wi 76	16
Peru	Indigenous Weft-Faced Garments of Peru	Noble, Carol Rasmussen	√		SS&D	13	3	51	Su 82	44
Peru	Interlocking Warp and Weft in the Nasca 2 Style	Rowe, Ann Pollard	√		TMJ	3	3		De 72	67
Peru	Kindred Spirits of Peru	Glaves, Jeannine	√		S-O	8	1		Sp 84	22
Peru	Lenten Curtains from Colonial Peru	Kelemen, Pál	√		TMJ	3	1		De 70	5
Peru	Man's Shirt in Peruvian Inlay	Linder, Harry	√	> 4	WJ	4	2	14	Oc 79	8
Peru	Nasca Sprang Tassels: Structure, Technique, and Order	Frame, Mary	√	√	TMJ	25			86	67
Peru	Nilda Callanaupa	Franquemont, Ed	√		S-O	9	1		Sp 85	53
Peru	Notes on Plaiting in the Upper Amazon Basin, Peru	Blinks, Anne	√	√	Iw	5	4		Fa 80	51
Peru	Paracas Needle Technique, A	Hoskins, Nancy	√	√	Iw	5	4		Fa 80	34
Peru	Peru, Textiles Unlimited: Ancient Peru	Tidball, Harriet	√		SCGM		25		68	1
Peru	Peru, Textiles Unlimited, Part 2	Tidball, Harriet	√	√	SCGM		26		69	1
Peru	Peruvian Crossed-Warp Weave, A	Castle, Nancy	√	√	TMJ	4	4		77	61
Peru	Peruvian Journey	Regensteiner, Else			H&C	17	1		Wi 66	34
Peru	Peruvian Multilayered Cloth	Schira, Cynthia	√	> 4	H&C	18	3		Su 67	11
Peru	Peruvian Slings: Their Uses and Regional Variations	Noble, Carol Rasmussen	√		WJ	6	4	24	Sp 82	53
Peru	Peruvian Straw Hat: Documenting a Declining Industry, The	Zimmer, Roni	√		Fa	12	3		M/J 85	39
Peru	Peruvian Technique for Dimensional Knotting	Bravo, Monica	√	√	WJ	12	1	45	Su 87	17

593

SUBJECT	TITLE	AUTHOR	IL	INST	JOUR	VOL	NO	ISS	DATE	PAGE
Peru	Peruvian Textile Fragment from the Beginning of the Middle Horizon	Conklin, William J	√		TMJ	3	1		De 70	15
Peru	Peruvian Weaves of Contemporary Interest		√		H&C	12	4		Fa 61	31
Peru	Pre-Incan Weavers of Peru, The	Blumenau, Lili	√		H&C	3	3		Su 52	12
Peru	Rare Peruvian Textiles		√		H&C	9	2		Sp 58	18
Peru	Re-Establishing Provenience of Two Paracas Mantles	Paul, Anne			TMJ	19 20			80,81	35
Peru	Shaped Tapestry Bags from the Nazca-Ica Area of Peru	Bird, Junius B.	√		TMJ	1	3		De 64	2
Peru	Sling Braiding in the Macusani Area of Peru	Zorn, Elayne	√	√	TMJ	19 20			80,81	41
Peru	Spaced-Weft Twining of Ancient Peru: A Contemporary Interpretation	Rogers, Nora	√	√	Iw	5	4		Fa 80	42
Peru	Spinners of Chijnaya, Alpaca Yarns from Peruvian Village	Cloney, Gordon	√		H&C	16	4		Fa 65	15
Peru	Spinners of Taquile	Coker, Sharon	√		S-O	8	1		Sp 84	24
Peru	Study of Andean Spinning in the Cuzco Region, A	Goodell, Miss Grace	√	√	TMJ	2	3		De 68	2
Peru	Tapices Of San Pedro de Cajas, Peru, The	Thornton, Sandra K.	√	√	WJ	12	1	45	Su 87	23
Peru	Technical Features of a Middle Horizon Tapestry Shirt from Peru, The	Bird, Junius B.; Milica Dimitrijevic Skinner	√		TMJ	4	1		De 74	5
Peru	Technical Features of Inca Tapestry Tunics	Rowe, Ann Pollard	√		TMJ	17			78	5
Peru	Textile Evidence for Huari Music	Rowe, Ann Pollard	√		TMJ	18			79	5
Peru	Three Ancient Peruvian Gauze Looms	Rowe, Ann Pollard; Junius B. Bird	√		TMJ	19,20			80,81	27
Peru	Tiahuanaco Tapestry Design	Sawyer, Alan R.	√		TMJ	1	2		De 63	27
Peru	Treadle Loom in the Peruvian Andes, The	Noble, Carol Rasmussen	√		SS&D	8	3	31	Su 77	46
Peru	Unique Finish from an Amazonian Bracelet, A	Thabet, Micheline	√	√	WJ	9	3	35	Wi 85	14
Peru	Vignettes from Peru	Wilson, Kax	√		Iw	5	4		Fa 80	46
Peru	Visit to Peru	Fife, Lin	√		Fa	9	6		N/D 82	60
Peru	Weaving Processes in the Cuzco Area of Peru	Rowe, Ann Pollard	√	√	TMJ	4	2		75	30
Peru	Weft Twining: History, Peru	Harvey, Virginia I.; Harriet Tidball			SCGM		28		69	2
Peru	World Crafts Council, An American Spinner Meets Peruvian Craftsmen	Reade, Dorothy	√		H&C	20	1		Wi 69	8
Peruvian Slings	Peruvian Slings: Their Uses and Regional Variations	Noble, Carol Rasmussen	√		WJ	6	4	24	Sp 82	53
Peruvian Textile Studies: History/Trends	Brief History of the Study of Ancient Peruvian Textiles, A	King, Mary Elizabeth	√		TMJ	2	1		De 66	39
Peruvian Textiles	Chinese Influence in Colonial Peruvian Tapestries	Cammann, Schuyler	√		TMJ	1	3		De 64	21
Peruvian Textiles	Peru: Textiles Unlimited	Tidball, Harriet	√		SCGM		25		68	1-36
Peruvian Textiles	Peruvian Journey	Regensteiner, Else			H&C	17	1		Wi 66	34
Peruvian Textiles	Shaped Tapestry Bags from the Nazca-Ica Area of Peru	Bird, Junius B.	√		TMJ	1	3		De 64	2
Peruvian Textiles	Tapestry: Technique and Tradition	Scott, Gail R.	√		H&C	22	3		Su 71	16
Peruvian Textiles	Tiahuanaco Tapestry Design	Sawyer, Alan R.	√		TMJ	1	2		De 63	27
Peruvian Textiles: Structures, Common and Uncommon	Peru, Textiles Unlimited: Conclusions	Tidball, Harriet			SCGM		25		68	33
Peruvian Textiles: Techniques	Peru, Textiles Unlimited, Part 2:	Tidball, Harriet	√	√	SCGM		26		69	1-46
Peruvian Textiles: Techniques	Peru, Textiles Unlimited, Part 2: Plain Weave Stripes	Tidball, Harriet	√	√	SCGM		26		69	2
Peruvian Textiles: Today	Peru, Textiles Unlimited: Textiles and Peru Today	Tidball, Harriet	√		SCGM		25		68	12

SUBJECT	TITLE	AUTHOR	IL	INST	JOUR	VOL	NO	ISS	DATE	PAGE
Peruvian Weaving	Jacquetta Nisbet to Give Workshop on Peruvian Pebble Weave (error-corrected SS&D v5 n1 73 p93)	Black, Mary	√		SS&D	4	4	16	Fa 73	76
Peruvian Weaving	Peru, Textiles Unlimited, Part 2: Plain Weave Stripes	Tidball, Harriet	√	√	SCGM		26		69	2
Peruvian Weaving	Peruvian Weft Twining	Schira, Cynthia	√	√	H&C	17	3		Su 66	14
Peruvian Weaving	Weaving Processes in the Cuzco Area of Peru	Rowe, Ann Pollard	√	√	TMJ	4	2		75	30
Peruvian Weaving Techniques	Peruvian Leno	Sayler, Mary	√	√	SS&D	3	3	11	Su 72	45
Pervarai	Lithuanian Pervarai: Producing a Twenty Shaft Pattern on a Twelve Shaft Loom	Meek, M. Kati	√	> 4	AT	1			De 83	159
Petit Point	"Ritual Narratives" (Exhibit)		√		Fa	13	3		M/J 86	57
Petit Point	Variations on an Overshot Threading	Lermond, Charles	√	√	WJ	12	2	46	Fa 87	25
Petit Point Treadling	Delicate Dots...Petit Point Treadling	Keasbey, Doramay	√	√	Hw	7	1		J/F 86	66
Petticoats	Making Swirly Skirts	Callaway, Grace	√	√	TM			10	A/M 87	35
Ph Chart	Principles of Textile Conservation Science, No. 5. The Characteristics of Soils and Stains Encountered on Historic Textiles	Rice, James W.	√	√	TMJ	1	3		De 64	8
Ph System	Principles of Textile Conservation Science, No. 6. The Wonders of Water in Wetcleaning	Rice, James W.	√	√	TMJ	2	1		De 66	15
Philately	Costumes Through the Ages Stamp Collecting Kit	Smeltzer, Nancy	√		Fa	13	3		M/J 86	29
Philately	U.S. Postage Stamp Honors Lacemaking		√		Fa	14	2		M/A 87	30
Philately: Lace	Postal Service Celebrates Lace		√		TM			12	A/S 87	22
Philately: Textile Theme	Comparison of Some Varied Themes	Stanton, R. G.; J. L. Allston	√		AT	2			De 84	217
Philately: Textile Theme	From Fibre to Haute Coutoure on World Postage Stamps	Cysarz, J. M.	√		AT	4			De 85	89
Philately: Textile Theme	Introduction to Two Textilatelists, An	Allston, J. L.; J. A. Hoskins	√		AT	4			De 85	81
Philately: Textiles	Mail Art: The Romance of Textiles on Stamps	Schuessler, Raymond	√		Fa	12	4		J/A 85	26
Philippine Islands	New Philippine Textiles	Gele, Emilé	√		H&C	5	3		Su 54	14
Philippine Islands	Three Faces of the Eight-Pointed Star Motif (error-corrected SS&D v14 n4 83 p4)	Coffman, Charlotte	√	√	SS&D	14	3	55	Su 83	56
Philippines	Backstrap Weaving in the Philippines	Ng, Mary	√		SS&D	9	1	33	Wi 77	18
Philippines	Learning the Ropes: Abaca	Coffman, Charlotte	√	√	S-O	7	4		Wi 83	40
Philippines	Piña	Wallace, Lysbeth	√		WJ	8	2	30	Fa 83	77
Philosophy	Dream—The Reality, The	Ligon, Linda	√		Iw	3	4		Su 78	12
Philosophy	Journey in Progress, A	Chittenden, Annie Curtis	√	√	SS&D	17	4	68	Fa 86	50
Philosophy	On Weaving, Life and Art	Liebler, Barbara	√		Iw	4	4		Fa 79	19
Philosophy	Setting Goals and Evaluating Priorities	LaLena, Constance	√	√	Iw	5	1		Wi 79	43
Philosophy	Taproot: Jack Lenor Larsen	Goldin, Susan	√		Iw	4	3		Su 79	17
Philosophy	Today's Conscious Aesthetic Philosophy 'Asks Us to Rationalize the Non-Rational'	McCarthy, Judy; Sue Ferguson	√		SS&D	4	4	16	Fa 73	54
Philosophy: Art/Craft	Forum	Cummings, Mimi			Hw	2	4		Se 81	10
Philosophy: Art/Craft	Forum	Hochberg, Bette			Hw	2	2		Mr 81	12
Philosophy: Art/Craft	Forum	Liebler, Barbara			Hw	2	2		Mr 81	21
Philosophy: Art/Craft	Notes of a Pattern Weaver	Alvic, Philis			SS&D	14	1	53	Wi 82	32
Philosophy: Art/Craft	Working with Material	Albers, Anni			Iw	3	2		Wi 78	12
Philosophy: Constructivism	Concerns and Influences in My Work	Kidd, Jane	√		AT	6			De 86	135
Philosophy: Creative Craftsmen/Knowledge of Craft	A Weaver Ponders His Craft, Collection of Controversial Essays: Problems	Zielinski, S. A.; Robert Leclerc, ed.			MWL	21 22			'51–'73	51
Philosophy: Design	Marianne Strengell's Approach to Design	Bryan, Dorothy	√		H&C	11	4		Fa 60	29
Philosophy: Design	Warren Seelig: A Conversation	Ligon, Linda	√		Iw	3	2		Wi 78	20
Philosophy: Handloom Weaving	Dialectic for Handweavers: or, on Looking Back (While Moving Forward), A	Fannin, Allen			Iw	3	3		Sp 78	39

SUBJECT	TITLE	AUTHOR	IL	INST	JOUR	VOL	NO	ISS	DATE	PAGE
Philosophy: Modern Weaving	A Weaver Ponders His Craft, Collection of Controversial Essays: Modern Weaving	Zielinski, S. A.; Robert Leclerc, ed.			MWL	21 22			'51–'73	57
Philosophy: Moorman, Theo	Toward Abstraction and Simplicity	Moorman, Theo	√		SS&D	3	1	9	Wi 71	30
Philosophy: Navajo Weaving	Weaving the Navajo Way	Bighorse, Tiana; Noël Bennett	√		Iw	4	1		Wi 78	12
Philosophy: Spinning	Handspinning as Art	Walker, Linda Berry	√		S-O	2			78	56
Philosophy: Spinning	Handspinning Project, The	Keefe, Carolyn	√		S-O	3			79	32
Philosophy: Spinning	Handspun Yarn as Art	Burkhauser, Jude			S-O	3			79	22
Philosophy: Spinning	Spinning in the Abbey	Liggett, Brother Mark, OFM			S-O	6	4		82	4
Philosophy: Spinning	Spinning with Gandhi	Grant, Susan	√		S-O	2			78	15
Philosophy: Spinning	Woolworth: Experiments in Spinning	Lorance, Marilyn			S-O	3			79	38
Philosophy: Tapestry	Approach to Tapestry Weaving, An	Brostoff, Laya	√		Iw	4	2		Sp 79	27
Philosophy: Textile Arts, Ancient/Modern	Peru, Textiles Unlimited: Reflections on Styles	Tidball, Harriet	√		SCGM		25		68	25
Philosophy: Textiles/Design/Symbolism	Keynote in Chicago: Knodel	Livingstone, Joan	√		SS&D	18	3	71	Su 87	37
Philosophy: Weaving	Choosing a Focus of Study Can Lead to New Growth, New Horizons, New Understanding	Chandler, Deborah			Hw	6	4		S/O 85	26
Philosophy: Weaving	Roy Ginstrom, Versatile Handweaver and Designer of Fabrics for Power Looms		√		H&C	13	3		Su 62	6
Philosophy: Weaving	SS&D Interview: Peter Collingwood	Wilson, Sadye Tune	√		SS&D	10	4	40	Fa 79	4
Philosophy: Weaving	Theo Moorman: Poet on the Loom				SS&D	6	4	24	Fa 75	15
Philosophy: Weaving	Weaving — Better Than Bridge	Chandler, Deborah	√		Hw	8	3		M/J 87	18
Philosophy: Weaving	Weaving on the Left Side of the Brain	Allen, Debbie	√		Hw	6	4		S/O 85	12
Philosophy: Weaving	Weaving Out of One's Own Tradition	Centner, David			Iw	5	4		Fa 80	32
Philosophy: Weaving	What's Wrong with Being a Weaver?	Kniskern, Verne B.	√		Hw	8	2		M/A 87	10
Philosophy: Weaving, "Easy" Fallacy	A Weaver Ponders His Craft, Collection of Controversial Essays: Handweaving Made Easy	Zielinski, S. A.; Robert Leclerc, ed.			MWL	21 22			'51–'73	65
Philosophy: Weaving/Art	Weaving as Art	Centner, Rev. David J., OCD	√		Iw	3	1		Fa 77	11
Philosophy: Weaving/Work	Determination and Innovation: A Successful Weaving Mill	Fago, D'Ann Calhoun	√		TM			14	D/J 87	14
Photocopying: Textile	Photocopying Textiles			√	TM			9	F/M 87	12
Photographer	New Directions for Jan Yoors: Tapestry Weaver Now Known as Author and Photographer		√		H&C	18	4		Fa 67	6
Photographic Processes: Cyanotype	Blueprinting on Fabric	Sider, Sandra	√	√	Fa	13	5		S/O 86	36
Photographic Processes: Cyanotype	Blues in the Light: Cyanotype on Fabric	Sider, Sandra	√		Fa	13	5		S/O 86	34
Photographing Textiles: Equipment	Photographing Textiles for a Museum	Varela, Osmund Leonard	√	√	TMJ	1	1		No 62	23
Photographing Textiles: Techniques	Photographing Textiles for a Museum	Varela, Osmund Leonard	√	√	TMJ	1	1		No 62	23
Photography	Behind the Scenes: Your Own Studio	Rudich, Sally	√		Fa	13	3		M/J 86	47
Photography	Focus on Textiles	Turner, Lew	√	√	SS&D	13	3	51	Su 82	22
Photography	Photograph Your Weaving	Hansen, Pauline M.	√	√	SS&D	5	2	18	Sp 74	79
Photography	Photographer at Convergence, The	Brown, Carolyn		√	SS&D	17	2	66	Sp 86	61
Photography	Photographing Your Fiber Art	Meltzer, Steve	√	√	Fa	10	4		J/A 83	35
Photography	Photographing Your Fiber Work	Long, Doug	√	√	Fa	4	5		S/O 77	45
Photography	Photographing Your Fiber Work — Two Common Problems and Their Solutions	Hamamura, John	√	√	SS&D	9	4	36	Fa 78	20
Photography	Representing Fiber Work Through Photography	Itter, Diane	√	√	SS&D	17	3	67	Su 86	42
Photography	Surface Design and the Garment Form	Reith, Stephanie J.	√		Fa	8	1		J/F 81	34
Photography	Through the Camera's Eye: Howard Munson's Body Coverings	Akamine, Estelle	√		Fa	14	3		M/J 87	44

SUBJECT	TITLE	AUTHOR	IL	INST	JOUR	VOL	NO	ISS	DATE	PAGE
Photography: Black and White	Photographing Textiles, Part 1, Black and White	Krasnoff, Julienne	√	√	SS&D	7	1	25	Wi 75	86
Photography: Color	Photographing Textiles, Part 2, Color	Krasnoff, Julienne	√	√	SS&D	7	2	26	Sp 76	48
Photography: Micro	Stennett Heaton: He Finds Beauty in the Mini World		√		SS&D	7	1	25	Wi 75	8
Photography: Record Keeping	Photographing Textiles for a Museum	Varela, Osmund Leonard	√	√	TMJ	1	1		No 62	23
Photography: Textile	More About Fabrics: Photography of Textiles	Zielinski, S. A.; Robert Leclerc, ed.		√	MWL	20			'51–'73	61
Photomicrography	Fibers	Abrahams, Howard	√		Iw	1	3		Sp 76	8
Photoprinting: Textile	Captured Shadows	Ligon, Linda	√		Iw	1	2		Wi 76	12
Photoprinting: Textile	Hidden Sides, Hidden Lives: The Photo-Fiber Works of Robin Becker	Chressanthis, James	√		Fa	7	3		M/J 80	34
Photoprinting: Textile	Portrait of a Village	Becker, Robin; James Chressanthis	√		Fa	9	6		N/D 82	40
Photoprinting: Textile, Kodalith	Eye of a Photographer, Hand of a Weaver: An Artist Combines Two Art Forms	Guagliumi, Susan	√		Fa	8	6		N/D 81	35
Photoprinting: Textiles, Silk-Screen	Photographic Processes for Textiles	Ligon, Linda	√	√	Iw	2	2		Wi 77	21
Photoweaving	Photoweavings of Woody Logsdon, The	Logsdon, Anne	√		Fa	14	4		S/O 87	26
Phulkari	Phulkari	Westfall, Carol D.; Dipti Desai	√		AT	6			De 86	85
Picasso	Picasso, The Weaver		√		SS&D	11	4	44	Fa 80	15
Pick-and-Pick	Anatomy of a Quilted Counterpane (page revised WJ v9 n1 84 p70)	Adrosko, Rita J.	√		WJ	8	4	32	Sp 84	42
Pick-and-Pick	Shadowweave, Part 1 (error-corrected WJ v2 n1 77 insert for vol. 1)	Barrett, Clotilde	√	> 4	WJ	1	1	1	Jy 76	13
Pick-Up	Adaptations of Primitive Warp-Pattern Weaves	Landreau, Tony	√	√	H&C	8	1		Wi 56	25
Pick-Up	Alternative Summer and Winter Pickup Technique, An	Salsbury, Nate	√	√	Iw	5	4		Fa 80	69
Pick-Up	Autumn Leaves, A Design in Summer-and-Winter	Arnold, Ruth	√	√	H&C	14	3		Su 63	14
Pick-Up	Backstrap Weaving for Penance and Profit	Coffman, Charlotte	√	√	WJ	7	1	25	Su 82	60
Pick-Up	Beiderwand Made Easy: An Old Weave Adapts to Four-Harness (revision SS&D v7 n4 76 p27)	Gordon, Judith	√	√	SS&D	7	3	27	Su 76	68
Pick-Up	Bolivian Highland Weaving, Part 1	Cason, Marjorie; Adele Cahlander	√		SS&D	6	2	22	Sp 75	4
Pick-Up	Bolivian Highland Weaving, Part 2	Cason, Marjorie; Adele Cahlander	√	√	SS&D	6	3	23	Su 75	65
Pick-Up	Cardwoven Double Weave, Part 2	Gray, Herbi	√	√	SS&D	15	1	57	Wi 83	92
Pick-Up	Cardwoven Mattor (Part 1)	Gray, Herbi	√	√	SS&D	14	4	56	Fa 83	64
Pick-Up	Colonial Coverlets, Part 4: Doubleweave	Liebler, Barbara	√	√	Iw	2	1		Fa 76	29
Pick-Up	Complex "Harness Lace"	Nass, Ulla	√	√	SS&D	9	3	35	Su 78	4
Pick-Up	Complimentary-Weft Plain Weave — A Pick-up Technique (error-corrected WJ v5 n1 80 p28d)	Hanley, Janet	√	√	WJ	4	4	16	Ap 80	22
Pick-Up	Corner Inscriptions	Jarvis, Helen		√	PWC	5	2	16		19
Pick-Up	Damask	Mudge, Christine	√	> 4	Iw	6	1		Wi 80	46
Pick-Up	Decorative Miniatures in Silk by Jadwiga Rakowska		√		H&C	10	2		Sp 59	22
Pick-Up	Decorative Weft on a Plain Weave Ground, Two Shaft Inlay and Brocade		√	√	WJ	5	4	20	Sp 81	15
Pick-Up	Designing for Warp-face	Sullivan, Donna	√	√	SS&D	19	1	73	Wi 87	15
Pick-Up	Double Weave, Finnweave and Mexican Variations	Frey, Berta	√	√	H&C	12	2		Sp 61	12
Pick-Up	Double Weave Pick-Up with Straight Diagonal Lines	Wolter, Edith L.	√	√	WJ	7	4	28	Sp 83	61
Pick-Up	Double-Weave Pick-Up	Neely, Cynthia H.	√	√	TM			8	D/J 86	36

SUBJECT	TITLE	AUTHOR	IL	INST	JOUR	VOL	NO	ISS	DATE	PAGE
Pick-Up	Drawloom Basics	van der Hoogt, Madelyn	√	> 4	Hw	7	2		M/A 86	61
Pick-Up	Embroidery on the Loom	Drooker, Penelope B.	√	√	SS&D	9	3	35	Su 78	60
Pick-Up	Evolution of a Weaving, The	Kearney, Kathleen	√	√	SS&D	12	1	45	Wi 80	64
Pick-Up	Fashion Show of Handwoven Garments		√	> 4	WJ	3	3	11	Ja 79	5
Pick-Up	Finnish Techniques	Tanner, Kersten	√		SS&D	6	3	23	Su 75	45
Pick-Up	Finnweave	Barrett, Clotilde	√	> 4	WJ	11	4	44	Sp 87	25
Pick-Up	First Prize for the Holders of Hot Pots Show	Champion, Ellen	√	√	WJ	2	4	8	Ap 78	41
Pick-Up	Four Harness Damask — A Pick-up Weave	Merritt, Elveana	√	√	WJ	5	1	17	Su 80	20
Pick-Up	Four-Harness Damask	Foster, Frances A.	√	√	H&C	9	1		Wi 57	23
Pick-Up	Go Adventuring with Your Pick-Up Stick (error-corrected H&C v2 n4 51 p64)	Roberts, Elizabeth	√	√	H&C	2	2		Sp 51	28
Pick-Up	Graphic Weave for a Special Occasion (Carrie Rogers)		√	√	Hw	1	2		S-S 80	38
Pick-Up	Guatemala Visited	Atwater, Mary Meigs	√	> 4	SCGM		15		65	19
Pick-Up	Guatemalan Belt Weave	Christensen, Evelyn	√	√	Hw	7	2		M/A 86	68
Pick-Up	Handbag in Finnweave		√	√	H&C	16	1		Wi 65	33
Pick-Up	Huckaback Lace	Jackson, Marguerite	√	√	H&C	14	2		Sp 63	20
Pick-Up	Inscribing a Coverlet	Beevers, Sue	√	√	PWC	5	2	16		16
Pick-Up	Instructions: Pick-Up Figured Piqué (error-corrected PWC v4 n3 i13 p4)	Xenakis, Athanasios David	√	√	PWC	4	2	12		39
Pick-Up	Karelian Red-Picking	Ruchti, Willie Jager	√	> 4	WJ	5	2	18	Fa 80	34
Pick-Up	Karellian Red Pick Dress (Miranda Howard)		√	√	Hw	2	5		No 81	36, 90
Pick-Up	Keep Warm! Foot Cozy	Barrett, Clotilde	√	√	WJ	5	2	18	Fa 80	12
Pick-Up	Lacy Triangular Stole of Handspun Wool, A	Kniskern, Edna Maki	√	√	WJ	6	2	22	Fa 81	48
Pick-Up	Leno Lace with One Shuttle	Deru, Crescent	√	√	H&C	11	4		Fa 60	46
Pick-Up	Mexican Motifs: The Oaxaca Belts	Tidball, Harriet	√	√	SCGM		6		62	19
Pick-Up	New Pick-Up Weave, A	Deru, Crescent B.	√	> 4	H&C	10	4		Fa 59	26
Pick-Up	Old & New Uses for Double Weave	Macomber, Dorothea	√	√	H&C	8	4		Fa 57	16
Pick-Up	Patterned Double Weave		√	√	Hw	7	2		M/A 86	56
Pick-Up	Pick-Up Damask	Drooker, Penelope B.	√	> 4	SS&D	11	1	41	Wi 79	38
Pick-Up	Pick-Up Leno, A Two-harness Loom Technique	Wallace, Meg	√	√	WJ	1	2	2	Oc 76	3
Pick-Up	Pick-Up Leno: The Fine Linens of Ava Hessler		√	√	WJ	7	2	26	Fa 82	31
Pick-Up	Pick-Up Piqué (error-corrected SS&D v19 n1 87 p33)	Fletcher, Joyce	√	√	SS&D	18	4	72	Fa 87	60
Pick-Up	Pictures in Summer & Winter Pick-up	Griffin, Gertrude	√	√	Hw	7	2		M/A 86	54
Pick-Up	Portable Weaving: A Band of Ideas for Bands	Bradley, Louise; Jean Anstine	√	√	Hw	7	3		M/J 86	40
Pick-Up	Practical Weave for Rugs (Reprint), A	Atwater, Mary Meigs	√	> 4	H&C	26	1		J/F 75	7
Pick-Up	Sandstone Pillows (Janice Jones)		√	√	Hw	5	2		M/A 84	59, 99
Pick-Up	Simple Matelasse by the Pick-Up Method		√	√	WJ	7	1	25	Su 82	40
Pick-Up	Simple Method for Weaving Deflected Warps	Frey, Berta	√	√	H&C	20	4		Fa 69	4
Pick-Up	Six-Harness Challenge: Triple Weave Pick-Up, A	Guagliumi, Susan	√	> 4	SS&D	9	2	34	Sp 78	99
Pick-Up	Stoles and Scarves		√	√	WJ	2	1	5	Jy 77	3
Pick-Up	Summer and Winter and Other Two-Tie Unit Weaves: Methods for Weaving Two-Tie Units, Pick-Up	Tidball, Harriet	√	√	SCGM		19		66	50
Pick-Up	Summer-and-Winter Pick-up Weave	Brouwer, Martha	√	√	SS&D	8	3	31	Su 77	58
Pick-Up	Tablecloth and Runner Decorated with Overshot and Pick-Up Leno		√	√	WJ	6	1	21	Su 81	10

SUBJECT	TITLE	AUTHOR	IL	INST	JOUR	VOL	NO	ISS	DATE	PAGE
Pick-Up	Tarascan Lace		√	√	WJ	2	3	7	Ja 78	21
Pick-Up	Two Weaves from Mexico	Gubser, Elsie H.	√	√	H&C	11	3		Su 60	26
Pick-Up	Two-harness Weaves	Clark, Marion L.	√	√	H&C	14	2		Sp 63	17
Pick-Up	Upphämta Display Towel		√	> 4	Hw	8	3		M/J 87	42
Pick-Up	Vestment Variations: A Weaver From the Netherlands Creates Garments for the Ecclesiastical Calendar	Jansen, Netty	√	> 4	WJ	10	3	39	Wi 86	53
Pick-Up	Warp Boutonné	Lewis, Edward G.	√	√	WJ	7	2	26	Fa 82	64
Pick-Up	Warp-Faced Double Cloth: Adaptation of an Andean Technique for the Treadle Loom	Cahlander, Adele	√	√	WJ	10	4	40	Sp 86	72
Pick-Up	Weaving a City Skyline	Wennerstrom, Ann K.	√	√	WJ	7	1	25	Su 82	30
Pick-Up	Weaving on a Diamond Grid: Bedouin Style	Race, Mary E.	√	√	SS&D	12	1	45	Wi 80	20
Pick-Up	Weaving Processes in the Cuzco Area of Peru	Rowe, Ann Pollard	√	√	TMJ	4	2		75	30
Pick-Up	Weaving the Girdle of Rameses	Hilts, Patricia	√	> 4	WJ	9	1	33	Su 84	22
Pick-Up	Woven Fringes		√	> 4	WJ	3	3	11	Ja 79	14
Pick-Up, Chancay	Peru, Textiles Unlimited, Part 2: The Chancay Pick-Up Weave	Tidball, Harriet	√	√	SCGM		26		69	22
Pick-Up, Cross-Barred	Peru, Textiles Unlimited, Part 2: The Cross-Barred Pick-Up	Tidball, Harriet	√	√	SCGM		26		69	23
Pick-Up, Damask	Damask with a Sword	Keasbey, Doramay	√	> 4	CW	7	2	20	Ja 86	16
Pick-Up (Lancé) Weaves: Technique	Brocade: The Lancé or Pick-Up Weaves	Tidball, Harriet	√	√	SCGM		22		67	38
Pick-Up, Loom-Controlled	Loom-Controlled Adaptation of a Mexican Pick-Up Pattern Technique	Keasbey, Doramay	√	> 4	CW	6	2	17	Ja 85	19
Pick-Up, Mexican	Garments with Ethnic Flavor: Mexican Motif Skirt		√	√	WJ	2	3	7	Ja 78	13
Pick-Up, One-Skip Technique	Guatemala Visited	Atwater, Mary Meigs	√	√	SCGM		15		65	24
Pick-Up, Piqué	Double Piqué, Double Weave (error-corrected PWC v4 n4 i14 p33)	van der Hoogt, Madelyn	√	> 4	PWC	4	3	13		40
Pick-Up, Piqué	Pick Up Pick-Up Piqué		√	√	PWC	4	3	13		23
Pick-Up, Skip Technique	Guatemala Visited	Atwater, Mary Meigs	√	√	SCGM		15		65	24
Pick-Up, Tabby Shed	Guatemala Visited	Atwater, Mary Meigs	√	√	SCGM		15		65	24
Pick-Up Thimble	Treasury for Beginners: Pick-Up Thimble	Zielinski, S. A.; Robert Leclerc, ed.	√	√	MWL	1			'51–'73	34
Pick-Up, Warp-Faced	Guatemala Visited	Atwater, Mary Meigs	√	√	SCGM		15		65	17
Pick-Up Weaves, Atwater-Bronson	Brocade: Pick-Up Atwater-Bronson	Tidball, Harriet	√	√	SCGM		22		67	39
Pick-Up Weaves, Combination	Brocade: Combination Pick-Up	Tidball, Harriet	√	√	SCGM		22		67	44
Pick-Up Weaves, Methods	Brocade: Pick-Up Methods	Tidball, Harriet		√	SCGM		22		67	40
Pick-Up Weaves, Overlay, No Tabby	Brocade: Overlay No-Tabby Pick-Up	Tidball, Harriet	√	√	SCGM		22		67	45
Pick-Up Weaves, Overlay with Tabby	Brocade: Overlay Pick-Up with Tabby	Tidball, Harriet	√	√	SCGM		22		67	42
Pick-Up Weaves, Overlay with Tabby, Single	Brocade: An Overlay Pick-Up with Single Tabby	Tidball, Harriet	√	√	SCGM		22		67	44
Pick-Up Weaves, Overlay/Underlay, Closed-Shed	Brocade: Overlay-Underlay Closed-Shed Pick-Up	Tidball, Harriet	√	√	SCGM		22		67	43
Pick-Up Weaves, Structural Diagrams	Brocade: Structural Diagrams for Pick-Up Weaves	Tidball, Harriet	√		SCGM		22		67	50
Pick-Up Weaves, Underlay	Brocade: Underlay Pick-Up	Tidball, Harriet	√	√	SCGM		22		67	46
Pick-Up Weaves, Variables	Brocade: Variables in Pick-Up Weaves	Tidball, Harriet			SCGM		22		67	41
Picker, Fibers	Devices to Aid in Wool Processing	Adams, Brucie	√		Hw	3	4		Se 82	69
Picnic Blanket	Sunny Skies		√		Hw	5	3		Su 84	69
Picnic Cloth	On-the-Beach Cloth (Miranda Howard)		√	> 4	Hw	3	4		Se 82	67, 89
Pictorial Fiber	"Frank Gardner: Aleatory Works" (Exhibit)	Guagliumi, Susan	√		Fa	9	2		M/A 82	75

SUBJECT	TITLE	AUTHOR	IL	INST	JOUR	VOL	NO	ISS	DATE	PAGE
Pictorial Fiber	Portraits of Aging (Exhibit)		√		Fa	13	4		J/A 86	54
Pictorial Fiber	Telling Stories with Color and Pattern	Behrens, Ahn	√		Fa	13	2		M/A 86	68
Pictorial Fiber	Therese May: Moving Freely from Fabric to Paint and Back Again	Huffaker, Katherine	√		Fa	9	1		J/F 82	26
Pictorial Fiber: Quilted	Fraas—Slade: Painted Views	Reith, Stephanie	√		Fa	8	5		S/O 81	32
Pictorial Tapestry	Pictorial Tapestry: A Portfolio of Contemporary Work	Goodman, Deborah Lerme	√		Fa	10	3		M/J 83	29
Pictorial Textiles	JoAnn Giordano: A Modern Mythology	Malarcher, Patricia	√		Fa	13	6		N/D 86	13
Pictorial Weaving	Dunkagäng Ideas		√		Hw	7	2		M/A 86	44
Pictorial Weaving	Dunkagäng, the Stuff of Hearts and Flowers	Alderman, Sharon	√	√	Hw	7	2		M/A 86	41
Pictorial Weaving	Inside the Hangchow Brocade Factory: The Art and Craft of Mass Production	Drower, Sara	√		Fa	6	1		J/F 79	78
Pictorial Weaving	Inspiration in Boundweave	Strauss, Lynn	√	> 4	Hw	7	2		M/A 86	38
Pictorial Weaving	Inspired Double Weave		√		Hw	7	2		M/A 86	58
Pictorial Weaving	Kings, Heroes, Lovers: Pictorial Rugs From the Tribes and Villages of Iran	Goodman, Deborah Lerme	√		Fa	11	3		M/J 84	38
Pictorial Weaving	Patterned Double Weave		√	√	Hw	7	2		M/A 86	56
Pictorial Weaving	Pictures in Summer & Winter Pick-up	Griffin, Gertrude	√	√	Hw	7	2		M/A 86	54
Pictorial Weaving	Salut, Monsieur Jacquard	Carey, Joyce Marquess	√		Hw	2	3		My 81	57
Pictorial Weaving	Silk Reflections of C. J. Yao, The	Nicoli, Antony	√		Fa	13	1		J/F 86	47
Pictorial Weaving	Storytelling in Boundweave	Strauss, Lynn	√	√	Hw	7	2		M/A 86	35
Pictorial Weaving	Traditional Ways with Dunkagäng	Post, Margaret	√	√	Hw	7	2		M/A 86	42
Pictorial Weavings	Jacquard and Woven Silk Pictures, The	Adrosko, Rita J.	√		AT	1			De 83	9
Piecing Quilts: Crazy	Guilding the Lily: Embroidery Stitches in Victorian Crazy Quilts	Horton, Margaret	√	√	TM			10	A/M 87	48
Pigments: 18th Century	Where Did All the Silver Go? Identifying Eighteenth-Century Chinese Painted and Printed Silks	Lee-Whitman, Leanna; Maruta Skelton	√		TMJ	22			83	33
Pile	Cotton String Rug (Jean Bendon)		√	√	Hw	3	2		Mr 82	51, 90
Pile, Corduroy	Amazing Color-Pattern Corduroy Rug		√	> 4	PWC	3	4	10		22
Pile, Corduroy	Corde du Roi	Wilson, Kax	√		Iw	5	3		Su 80	49
Pile, Corduroy	Corduroy Vest/Jacket Fabric (Sharon Alderman)		√	> 4	Hw	4	4		S/O 83	52, 98
Pile, Corduroy	Diagonal Corduroy	Xenakis, Athanasios David	√	> 4	PWC	3	4	10		51
Pile, Cut	Extra-Warp Woven-Pile	Sullivan, Donna	√	√	SS&D	17	1	65	Wi 85	19
Pile, Cut	Gifts from Kashan to Cairo	Ellis, Charles Grant	√		TMJ	1	1		No 62	33
Pile, Cut	Kurdish Kilim Weaving in the Van-Hakkari District of Eastern Turkey	Landreau, Anthony N.	√	√	TMJ	3	4		De 73	27
Pile, Cut	Little Gems of Ardebil, The	Ellis, Charles Grant	√		TMJ	1	3		De 64	18
Pile , Cut	Some Compartment Designs for Carpets, and Herat	Ellis, Charles Grant	√		TMJ	1	4		De 65	42
Pile, Cut	Textiles Come Alive with Pile Weaves	Wilson, Jean	√		SS&D	5	3	19	Su 74	93
Pile, Cut	Three in One	Moes, Dini	√	√	SS&D	18	2	70	Sp 87	74
Pile, Cut/Uncut	Corduroy: An Account of Discovery	Alderman, Sharon D.	√	> 4	Hw	4	4		S/O 83	54
Pile Cutting	Diagonal Corduroy	Xenakis, Athanasios David	√	> 4	PWC	3	4	10		51
Pile, Double Corduroy	Color Related Decorating Textiles Rugs, Draperies, Upholstery: Double Corduroy Pile Rugs	Rhodes, Tonya Stalons; Harriet Tidball, ed.			SCGM		14		65	1
Pile, Double Corduroy	Double Corduroy	Lyon, Linda	√	√	PWC	3	1	7		51
Pile, Double Corduroy	Double Corduroy Pillows (Pam Bolesta)		√	√	Hw	2	1		F-W 80	32, 60
Pile, Double Corduroy	Double Corduroy Rug (Marilyn Dillard)		√	√	Hw	7	4		S/O 86	45, I-9
Pile, Double Corduroy	Double Corduroy with Varied Pile	Collingwood, Peter	√	√	Hw	7	4		S/O 86	47
Pile, Double Corduroy	Making the Most of Your Weave	Barnes, Muriel	√	> 4	H&C	19	4		Fa 68	15
Pile, Extra-Warp	Extra-Warp Woven-Pile	Sullivan, Donna	√	√	SS&D	17	1	65	Wi 85	19

SUBJECT	TITLE	AUTHOR	IL	INST	JOUR	VOL	NO	ISS	DATE	PAGE
Pile, Fabric Strip	Double Corduroy Rug (error-corrected WJ v11 n3 87 p78)	Waggoner, Phyllis	√	√	WJ	11	2	42	Fa 86	42
Pile, Ghiordes Knots	Fleece Rug	Hochberg, Bette	√	√	Hw	2	2		Mr 81	52
Pile, Ghiordes Knots	Fleece Rug (Elizabeth Ligon)		√	√	Hw	2	2		Mr 81	52, 80
Pile , Knotted	How Much Yarn for the Job? Rya and Flossa	Towner, Naomi W.	√	√	SS&D	8	4	32	Fa 77	14
Pile, Knotted, Ghiordes	Kazak Rugs	Tschebull, Raoul	√		TMJ	3	2		De 71	2
Pile, Knotted, Ghiordes	Turkish Carpet with Spots and Stripes, A	Mackie, Louise W.	√		TMJ	4	3		76	4
Pile, Knotted, Rya	Reinterpreting Rya: Irma Kukkasjärvi Energizes An Ancient Technique	Ojala, Liisa Kanning	√		WJ	9	4	36	Sp 85	26
Pile, Knotted, Senna Knot	Kirman's Heritage in Washington: Vase Rugs in The Textile Museum	Ellis, Charles Grant	√		TMJ	2	3		De 68	17
Pile, Knotted, Silk	Silk Reflections of C. J. Yao, The	Nicoli, Antony	√		Fa	13	1		J/F 86	47
Pile, Knotted, Spanish Knot	Two Remarkable Fifteenth Century Carpets from Spain	Mackie, Louise W.	√		TMJ	4	4		77	15
Pile, Knotted, Swedish	Hand Woven Rugs: Weaves, Plain Weave, Rugs with Knotted Pile	Atwater, Mary Meigs	√	√	SCGM		29		48	10
Pile, Loop, Cut	Double Two-Tie Twills and Basket Weave	Barrett, Clotilde	√	> 4	WJ	7	3	27	Wi 82	38
Pile, Looped, Weft	Weft Looped Pile Fabrics from Mexico	Grossman, Ellin	√		H&C	8	2		Sp 57	6
Pile, Rya Knots	Ahka Peacock Coat (Anita Mayer)		√	√	Hw	2	2		Mr 81	29, 79
Pile, Silk	Ottoman Prayer Rugs, The	Ellis, Charles Grant	√		TMJ	2	4		De 69	5
Pile, Tufts	Notebook: Floats on the Surface (Helen Cronk, Susan Orr)	Meyers, Ruth Nordquist, ed.	√	√	SS&D	14	3	55	Su 83	90
Pile, Velvet	Corded Rep Weave and Velvet Rugs	Proulx, Bibiane April	√	√	SS&D	17	3	67	Su 86	80
Pile, Velvet	Handwoven Velvet of Barbara Pickett, The	Cohn, Lisa	√	√	Hw	8	1		J/F 87	20
Pile, Velvet	Ottoman Turkish Textiles	Denny, Walter B.	√		TMJ	3	3		De 72	55
Pile, Velvet	Preliminary Report on a Group of Important Mughal Textiles, A	Smart, Ellen S.	√		TMJ	25			86	5
Pile, Velvet, Silk	From English Handlooms Comes Royal Purple Velvet for Coronation Robe of Elizabeth II	Lee, Humphrey A.	√		H&C	4	2		Sp 53	17
Pile, Warp	Velvet Ikat	Stack, Lotus	√	> 4	WJ	11	4	44	Sp 87	36
Pile, Warp-Loop	Custom Fabrics for a Classic Cadillac	Kelly, Jacquie	√	> 4	WJ	10	4	40	Sp 86	54
Pile Weaves	Josephina's Suit	Koopman, Albertje	√	> 4	WJ	4	4	16	Ap 80	50
Pile Weaves	Ordinary Weaver and Her Extraordinary Rugs, An	Xenakis, Alexis Yiorgos	√		PWC	4	2	12		4
Pile Weaves	Pile Weaves, Rugs and Tapestry: Colours in Corduroy	Zielinski, S. A.; Robert Leclerc, ed.	√	√	MWL	14			'51–'73	16
Pile Weaves	Pile Weaves, Rugs and Tapestry: Corduroy	Zielinski, S. A.; Robert Leclerc, ed.	√	√	MWL	14			'51–'73	7
Pile Weaves	Pile Weaves, Rugs and Tapestry: Handwoven Furcoat	Zielinski, S. A.; Robert Leclerc, ed.	√	> 4	MWL	14			'51–'73	21
Pile Weaves	Shaped Sculptured Rugs — A Workshop with Urban Jupena		√	√	WJ	4	1	13	Jy 79	5
Pile Weaves	Summer and Winter and Other Two-Tie Unit Weaves: Methods for Weaving Two-Tie Units, Pile Weaves	Tidball, Harriet	√	> 4	SCGM		19		66	49
Pile Weaves	Weaving in Quebec: New Traditions	Barrett, Clotilde	√	√	WJ	6	4	24	Sp 82	14
Pile Weaves	Wooly Afghan in Summer and Winter Pile Techniques	Champion, Ellen	√	√	WJ	4	4	16	Ap 80	14
Pile Weaves, Chenille	Pile Weaves, Rugs and Tapestry: Chenille	Zielinski, S. A.; Robert Leclerc, ed.	√	√	MWL	14			'51–'73	26
Pile Weaves, Chenille	Pile Weaves, Rugs and Tapestry: Free Patterns in Chenille	Zielinski, S. A.; Robert Leclerc, ed.	√	√	MWL	14			'51–'73	43
Pile Weaves, Double Corduroy	Peter Collingwood, His Weaves and Weaving: Double Corduroy Pile Rugs	Collingwood, Peter; Harriet Tidball, ed.	√	√	SCGM		8		63	3
Pile Weaves, Patterned	Pile Weaves, Rugs and Tapestry: Patterns in Velvet Rugs	Zielinski, S. A.; Robert Leclerc, ed.	√	√	MWL	14			'51–'73	70
Pile Weaves, Turned	Little Known Weaves Worth Knowing Better: Turned Tufted Weave	Zielinski, S. A.; Robert Leclerc, ed.	√	√	MWL	16			'51–'73	103

SUBJECT	TITLE	AUTHOR	IL	INST	JOUR	VOL	NO	ISS	DATE	PAGE
Pile Weaves, Turned, Terry	Little Known Weaves Worth Knowing Better: Turned Tufted Weave	Zielinski, S. A.; Robert Leclerc, ed.	√	√	MWL	16			'51–'73	103
Pile Weaves, Velvet	Pile Weaves, Rugs and Tapestry: Velvet Rugs	Zielinski, S. A.; Robert Leclerc, ed.	√	√	MWL	14			'51–'73	65
Pile, Weft Loop	Textile Remains from a Late Temple in Egyptian Nubia	Adams, Nettie K.	√		AT	8			De 87	85
Pile Weft-Loop	Textiles with Patterns in Weft-Loop Pile	Trilling, James	√		TMJ	21			82	93
Pile, Weft-Looped	Immigrant Memories	Butcher-Younghans, Sherry	√		WJ	9	4	36	Sp 85	44
Pillar Cover	Chinese Rugs	Ellis, Charles Grant	√		TMJ	2	3		De 68	35
Pilling	Rx: Pills	Leggett, Dawn	√	√	S-O	8	4		Wi 84	35
Pilling	Whither Pills?	Zimmermann, Elizabeth			S-O	8	4		Wi 84	38
Pilling: Removal	De-Pilling Woolens			√	TM		10		A/M 87	12
Pillow Covers	Easy Striped Knits	Walker, Barbara G.	√	√	TM		4		A/M 86	54
Pillow Covers	Pillows		√	√	Hw	5	2		M/A 84	59
Pillow Covers	Silken Dreams of Faraway Lands	Rudich, Sally	√		Fa	12	4		J/A 85	80
Pillow Covers	Sweet Dreams Pillow Slips (Sharon D. Alderman)		√	√	Hw	5	4		S/O 84	45, 96
Pillow Covers	Table Tapestries	Barrett, Clotilde	√	>4	WJ	7	4	28	Sp 83	73
Pillow-also see Cushions and Pillows										
Pillowcases	Baby Pillow Case (Sigrid Piroch)		√	√	Hw	8	2		M/A 87	50, I-8
Pillowcases	Dimity Delight	Sullivan, Donna	√	>4	PWC	5	1	15		17
Pillowcases	Heirloom Pillowcases (Sharon Alderman)		√	>4	Hw	8	4		S/O 87	57, I-13
Pillowcases	Lacy Linen Pillowcase (Linda Ligon)		√	√	Hw	2	5		No 81	58, 81
Pillowcases	Sweet Dreams Pillow Slips (Sharon D. Alderman)		√	√	Hw	5	4		S/O 84	45, 96
Pillowcases	Tailored Pillowcase (Linda Ligon)		√	√	Hw	2	5		No 81	58, 80
Pin Cushions	Tetrahedron (Carol Strickler)		√	√	Hw	6	4		S/O 85	64, I-15
Piña	Plant Fibers: Hard Fibers		√	√	WJ	8	2	30	Fa 83	67
Piña	Survey of Leaf and Stem Fibers, A	Buchanan, Rita	√		S-O	10	3		Fa 86	24
Piña, Pineapple Fiber	Piña	Wallace, Lysbeth	√		WJ	8	2	30	Fa 83	77
Pinafores	Rosepath Pinafore (Janice Jones)		√	√	Hw	7	2		M/A 86	60, I-4
Pioneers: Fiber Art	Conversation with Claire Zeisler, A	Koplos, Janet	√		Fa	10	4		J/A 83	25
Pioneers: Handweaving	Alice Stuart	Turner, Alta R.	√		H&C	12	1		Wi 61	16
Pioneers: Handweaving	Anni Albers	Pettigrew, Dale	√		Hw	6	4		S/O 85	76
Pioneers: Handweaving	Anni Albers — Innovator in Textile Design		√		H&C	10	4		Fa 59	6
Pioneers: Handweaving	Edward F. Worst: Craftsman and Educator	Pettigrew, Dale	√		Hw	6	5		N/D 85	73
Pioneers: Handweaving	Elizabeth Fisk, Early 20th Century Vermont Weaver	Atwood, Betty	√		H&C	19	3		Su 68	18
Pioneers: Handweaving	Elsie Gubser: Weaving Pioneer		√		Iw	4	3		Su 79	44
Pioneers: Handweaving	Legacy of Color and Texture: Dorothy Liebes, 1899-1972, A	Weltge, Sigrid	√		Iw	4	3		Su 79	25
Pioneers: Handweaving	Liebes Legacy, The	Roth, Bettie G.	√		SS&D	13	2	50	Sp 82	18
Pioneers: Handweaving	Life and Times of Mary Black: A Visit with the Author of "The Key to Weaving", The	MacNutt, Dawn	√		Fa	8	4		J/A 81	63
Pioneers: Handweaving	Mary Crovatt Hambidge	Schaller, Karin	√		Fa	11	5		S/O 84	24
Pioneers: Handweaving	Mary Meigs Atwater		√		Hw	3	5		N/D 82	50
Pioneers: Handweaving	Mary Meigs Atwater: An Appreciation	Tidball, Harriet Douglas	√		H&C	4	1		Wi 52	18
Pioneers: Handweaving	Myra L. Davis, Master Weaver	Clement, Doris	√		H&C	12	1		Wi 61	24
Pioneers: Handweaving	One Hundred Sixty Years of Craftsmanship	Ligon, Linda	√		Iw	1	3		Sp 76	17
Pioneers: Handweaving	Quarter Century of Handweavers' Progress, A	Atwater, Mary Meigs	√		H&C	2	2		Sp 51	5
Pioneers: Handweaving	Weavers in Cleveland	Rial, Katherine	√		H&C	6	3		Su 55	26

SUBJECT	TITLE	AUTHOR	IL	INST	JOUR	VOL	NO	ISS	DATE	PAGE
Pioneers: Handweaving	"Weaver's Life, Ethel Mairet, 1872–1952, A" (Exhibit)	Waller, Irene	√		Fa	11	4		J/A 84	78
Pioneers: Handweaving	"Woven and Graphic Art of Anni Albers, The" (Exhibit)	Malarcher, Patricia	√		Fa	13	1		J/F 86	62
Pioneers: Handweaving, Grace Richey Clark	Colorful Blinds and Fabrics from Texas		√		H&C	6	4		Fa 55	14
Pioneers: Loom Manufacturing	Fifty Years Ago in Handweaving: E. E. Gilmore, A Lifetime of Weaving		√		Hw	7	2		M/A 86	22
Piqué	Figured Piqué	Xenakis, Athanasios David	√	√	PWC	4	2	12		12
Piqué	Figured Piqué Patterning with the Double Two-Tie System (error-corrected PWC v4 n3 i13 p4)	Xenakis, Athanasios David; Patti Sellon	√	> 4	PWC	4	2	12		20
Piqué	Library of Loom-Controlled Patterns in Figured Piqué, A	Sellon, Patti; Athanasios David Xenakis	√	√	PWC	4	2	12		18
Piqué	Peculiar Piqué Pillow	Lyon, Linda	√	> 4	PWC	4	2	12		30
Piqué	Pique (A Brief Synopsis)	Schneider, Mary	√	> 4	CW	7	22	20	Ja 86	22
Piqué	Piqued by Piqué				PWC	4	3	13		33
Piqué	Planning Figured Piqué Designs on Pre-Marked Graph Paper	Xenakis, Athanasios David	√	> 4	PWC	4	2	12		16
Piqué	Ribbed Piqué	Sullivan, Donna	√	√	SS&D	18	3	71	Su 87	30
Piqué	Weaving Classes Show Growth at San Jose State College	Hatch, David P.	√	> 4	H&C	13	2		Sp 62	23
Piqué	What Is Piqué...And How is It Like Beiderwand? (error-corrected PWC v4 n3 i13 p4)	van der Hoogt, Madelyn	√	√	PWC	4	2	12		7
Piqué, Backed	Four Is Not Always Enough	Sullivan, Donna	√	> 4	PWC	4	3	13		18
Piqué, Backed	What Is Piqué...And How Is It Like Beiderwand? (error-corrected PWC v4 n3 i13 p4)	van der Hoogt, Madelyn	√	√	PWC	4	2	12		7
Piqué, Bedford Cord	Bedford Cord Piqué	Xenakis, Athanasios David; Madelyn van der Hoogt	√	> 4	PWC	4	3	13		42
Piqué, Double, Patterned	Double Piqué, Double Weave (error-corrected PWC v4 n4 i14 '87 p33)	van der Hoogt, Madelyn	√	> 4	PWC	4	3	13		40
Piqué, Figured	Figured Piqué	Xenakis, Athanasios David	√	√	PWC	4	2	12		12
Piqué, Figured	Figured Piqué on a Ground of 2/2 Twill and 2/2 Hopsack	Xenakis, Athanasios David	√	> 4	PWC	4	2	12		24
Piqué, Figured	Figured Piqué Patterning with the Double Two-Tie System (error-corrected PWC v4 n3 i13 p4)	Xenakis, Athanasios David; Patti Sellon	√	> 4	PWC	4	2	12		20
Piqué, Figured	Pick-Up Piqué (error-corrected SS&D v19 n1 87 p33)	Fletcher, Joyce	√	√	SS&D	18	4	72	Fa 87	60
Piqué, Figured	Weaving Figured Piqué on a Loom with One Warp Beam	Xenakis, Athanasios David	√	√	PWC	4	2	12		14
Piqué, Figured, Loom-Controlled	Stitcher Designer Hints for Loom-Controlled Figured Piqué	van der Hoogt, Madelyn	√	> 4	PWC	4	3	13		48
Piqué, Figured, Pick-Up	Instructions: Pick-Up Figured Piqué (error-corrected PWC v4 n3 i13 p4)	Xenakis, Athanasios David	√	√	PWC	4	2	12		39
Piqué, Figured, Wadded and Backed	Celtic Knot (error-corrected PWC v4 n4 i14 p33)	Xenakis, Athanasios David	√	√	PWC	4	3	13		24
Piqué, Figured, Wadded and Backed	Designing for Piqué (error-corrected PWC v4 n4 i14 '87 p33)	Sullivan, Donna	√	> 4	PWC	4	3	13		28
Piqué, Figured, Wadded and Backed	Lynn's Pillows	Tedder, Lynn	√	√	PWC	4	3	13		25
Piqué, Figured, Wadded and Backed	Potholders by Design	Keasbey, Doramay	√	> 4	PWC	4	3	13		50
Piqué, Figured, Wadded and Backed	Pretty, Piqué & Pink	Keasbey, Doramay	√	> 4	PWC	4	3	13		47

SUBJECT	TITLE	AUTHOR	IL	INST	JOUR	VOL	NO	ISS	DATE	PAGE
Piqué, Not Backed	What Is Piqué...And How Is It Like Beiderwand? (error-corrected PWC v4 n3 i13 p4)	van der Hoogt, Madelyn	√	√	PWC	4	2	12		7
Piqué, Pick-Up	Four Is Not Always Enough	Sullivan, Donna	√	> 4	PWC	4	3	13		18
Piqué, Pick-Up, 4-Shaft	Pick Up Pick-Up Piqué (error-corrected PWC v4 n4 i14 '87 p33)		√	√	PWC	4	3	13		23
Piqué, Plain	Four Is Not Always Enough	Sullivan, Donna	√	> 4	PWC	4	3	13		18
Piqué, Satin	Satin Piqué	Morrison, Ruth	√	> 4	PWC	4	3	13		34
Piqué, Twill Diaper	Twill Diaper Piqué (error-corrected PWC v4 n4 i14 p33)	Xenakis, Athanasios David; Madelyn van der Hoogt	√	> 4	PWC	4	3	13		36
Piqué, Wadded and Backed	Four Is Not Always Enough	Sullivan, Donna	√	> 4	PWC	4	3	13		18
Piqué, Wadded and Backed	What Is Piqué...And How Is It Like Beiderwand? (error-corrected PWC v4 n3 i13 p4)	van der Hoogt, Madelyn	√	√	PWC	4	2	12		7
Piqué, Wadded, Not Backed	What Is Piqué...And How Is It Like Beiderwand? (error-corrected PWC v4 n3 i13 p4)	van der Hoogt, Madelyn	√	√	PWC	4	2	12		7
Piqué, Waved	Designing for Piqué (error-corrected PWC v4 n4 i14 '87 p33)	Sullivan, Donna	√	> 4	PWC	4	3	13		28
Piqué, Waved	Four Is Not Always Enough	Sullivan, Donna	√	> 4	PWC	4	3	13		18
Place Mats	Clasped Weft Mats		√	√	Hw	3	1		Ja 82	35, 84
Place Mats	Colonial Mats (Pat Epstein)		√	√	Hw	3	5		N/D 82	46, 94
Place Mats	Contemporary Project for Two-harness Looms, A	Brown, Harriette J.	√	√	H&C	7	3		Su 56	20
Place Mats	Continuation School Program, A	Bryan, Dorothy	√	√	H&C	6	4		Fa 55	23
Place Mats	Corded Rep Weave and Velvet Rugs	Proulx, Bibiane April	√	√	SS&D	17	3	67	Su 86	80
Place Mats	Corkscrew Weave	Barrett, Clotilde	√	> 4	WJ	5	1	17	Su 80	16
Place Mats	Cotton Placemat (Martha Hall)		√	√	Hw	1	2		S-S 80	30, 56
Place Mats	Country Harvest Placemats (Linda Ligon)		√	√	Hw	5	4		S/O 84	48, 95
Place Mats	Crackle		√	√	WJ	3	3	11	Ja 79	32
Place Mats	Designing Rep Weave	Ridgeway, Terese		> 4	SS&D	16	3	63	Su 85	28
Place Mats	Eight-Shaft Overshot on Opposites	van der Hoogt, Madelyn; Margaret Heller	√	> 4	PWC	4	4	14		34
Place Mats	Experimenting with Color and Two-Tie Weaving on the Rigid Heddle	Niekrasz, Jennifer	√	√	PWC	4	4	14		21
Place Mats	Five Crackle Weave Projects	Macomber, Dorothea	√	√	H&C	9	3		Su 58	42
Place Mats	Four Place Mats (error-corrected WJ v6 n1 81 p28d)	Unger, Mary	√	√	WJ	5	2	18	Fa 80	52
Place Mats	Four Projects from Mrs. Elsie H. Gubser	Gubser, Elsie H.	√	√	H&C	6	3		Su 55	49
Place Mats	From Rags to Riches	Krook, Inga	√	√	Hw	4	3		M/J 83	32
Place Mats	Handweaving in the South Today	Ford, Toni	√		H&C	1	1		Ap 50	14
Place Mats	How One Weave Leads to Another	Barrett, Clotilde	√	> 4	WJ	8	1	29	Su 83	75
Place Mats	How to Weave Your own Designs	Arnold, Ruth	√	√	H&C	11	3		Su 60	6
Place Mats	Huck Lace Tray Cloth	Fishback, John S.	√	> 4	H&C	11	2		Sp 60	62
Place Mats	Irish Linen Placemat		√	√	H&C	21	2		Sp 70	38
Place Mats	Isolated Overshot: Razzle-dazzle Placemats	Xenakis, Athanasios David	√	> 4	PWC	3	2	8		40
Place Mats	Lincoln Log Placemats (Linda Ligon)		√	√	Hw	6	1		J/F 85	61, I-15
Place Mats	Linen Blend Placemats (Pam Bartl)		√	√	Hw	1	2		S-S 80	30, 56
Place Mats	Linen Mats (Dixie Francis)		√	√	Hw	7	3		M/J 86	67, I-15
Place Mats	Linen Placemats (Peg Templeton)		√	√	Hw	5	1		J/F 84	62, 107
Place Mats	Mats from Plastic Vegetable Bags		√		H&C	9	1		Wi 57	24
Place Mats	Monk's Belt Placemats (Ritva MacLeod)		√	√	Hw	8	1		J/F 87	56, I-10
Place Mats	More About Fabrics: Practical Projects in Tabby	Zielinski, S. A.; Robert Leclerc, ed.	√	√	MWL	20			'51–'73	29
Place Mats	More About Fabrics: Projects in Coarse Fibers Sisal Mats	Zielinski, S. A.; Robert Leclerc, ed.	√	√	MWL	20			'51–'73	51

SUBJECT	TITLE	AUTHOR	IL	INST	JOUR	VOL	NO	ISS	DATE	PAGE
Place Mats	Multiple Shaft Weaving — 2-Tie Four-End Block Drafts (Gladys Riehl)		√	> 4	WJ	6	4	24	Sp 82	48
Place Mats	Multiple Shaft Weaving: M's and O's with Two Foundation Shafts	Evans, Jane	√	> 4	WJ	6	1	21	Su 81	27
Place Mats	Name Drafting	Mitchell, Peter	√	√	Hw	3	2		Mr 82	34
Place Mats	New Design for Place Mats	Frey, Berta	√	> 4	H&C	6	4		Fa 55	28
Place Mats	New Projects for Four Harness Looms	Frey, Berta	√	√	H&C	8	2		Sp 57	49
Place Mats	Nylon Mats	Speckert, Gene K., OTR	√	√	SS&D	4	3	15	Su 73	29
Place Mats	Overshot	Liebler, Barbara	√	√	Hw	2	1		F-W 80	44
Place Mats	Paired-Thread Finnweave Projects: Five Placemats Based on a Chinese Lattice Design, The	Xenakis, Athanasios David	√	√	PWC			2	Ap 82	34
Place Mats	Pastel Collection (Jane Patrick)		√	√	Hw	6	2		M/A 85	48, I-8
Place Mats	Patchwork Designs in Summer and Winter	Davenport, Betty	√	√	PWC	1	1		No 81	27
Place Mats	Place Mat by Carolyn Lewis		√	√	H&C	13	4		Fa 62	46
Place Mats	Place Mats for the Governor's Mansion		√	√	H&C	11	3		Su 60	43
Place Mats	Placemats	DeRoy, Paul	√	> 4	WJ	1	3	3	Ja 77	4
Place Mats	Placemats and Napkins for a Found Treasure (Janice Jones)		√	√	Hw	5	5		N/D 84	70, I-12
Place Mats	Placemats and Runner (Mary Skoy)		√	√	Hw	8	2		M/A 87	83, I-16
Place Mats	Placemats (Bridget McNamara) (error-corrected Hw v1 n2 80 p64)		√	√	Hw	1	1		F-W 79	33, 54
Place Mats	Planning for Threading and Treadling	Wertenberger, Kathryn	√	√	Hw	2	2		Mr 81	47
Place Mats	Plastic Tote Bag	Speckert, Gene K., OTR	√	√	SS&D	4	2	14	Sp 73	57
Place Mats	Prize Place Mat		√	> 4	H&C	19	4		Fa 68	33
Place Mats	Production-Wise Placemats (error-corrected WJ v9 n2 84 p82)	Hall, Nancy Terrell	√	√	WJ	9	1	33	Su 84	44
Place Mats	Projects for a Six-Dent Rigid Heddle Backstrap Loom	Swanson, Karen	√	√	H&C	21	4		Fa 70	9
Place Mats	Quilted Placemat and Napkin (Henrietta Dyk)		√	> 4	Hw	5	1		J/F 84	61, 104
Place Mats	Rag Placemat		√	√	Hw	2	3		My 81	50, 78
Place Mats	Rainbow on the Table, A (Sharon Hakala, Carol Isleib, Carol Shabaz, Ruth Stump)	Isleib, Carol	√	√	Hw	5	3		Su 84	46
Place Mats	Recycling Plastic Bags	Ager, Lewa	√	√	SS&D	5	4	20	Fa 74	22
Place Mats	Rio Grande Placemats (Betty Davenport)		√	√	Hw	7	4		S/O 86	57, I-11
Place Mats	Rustic Placemats (Betty Davenport)		√	√	Hw	6	4		S/O 85	18, I-3
Place Mats	Satin Piqué	Morrison, Ruth	√	> 4	PWC	4	3	13		34
Place Mats	Shadowweave, Part 1 (error-corrected WJ v2 n1 77 insert for vol. 1)	Barrett, Clotilde	√	> 4	WJ	1	1	1	Jy 76	13
Place Mats	Smålands Weave on Eight Shafts	Shannon, Eileen	√	> 4	WJ	9	1	33	Su 84	47
Place Mats	Some Linen Weavers of New England (error-corrected H&C v2 n3 51 p54)		√	√	H&C	2	1		Wi 50	47
Place Mats	Stitched Double Cloth—Matelassé		√		WJ	7	1	25	Su 82	37
Place Mats	Striped Cotton Placemats (Sharon Alderman)		√	√	Hw	4	2		M/A 83	41, 84
Place Mats	Striped Placemats (Susan Feely)		√	√	Hw	8	1		J/F 87	59, I-9
Place Mats	Summer and Winter Poppana Table Mat (Janice Jones)		√	√	Hw	8	5		N/D 87	87, I-16
Place Mats	Supplementary Warp Placemats (Betty Davenport)		√	> 4	Hw	3	3		My 82	75, 98
Place Mats	Tea Cozy, Mats and Napkins (Margaretha Essén-Hedin)		√	> 4	Hw	4	3		M/J 83	41, 93
Place Mats	Three-Tie Unit Twill Mats (Carol Powalisz)		√	> 4	Hw	8	5		N/D 87	47, I-8
Place Mats	Tied-Unit Table Mats (Carol Strickler, Janice Jones)		√	√	Hw	8	5		N/D 87	54, I-12
Place Mats	Twill Placemats (Dian Stanley)		√	√	Hw	8	2		M/A 87	81, I-16
Place Mats	Two Placemats	Herring, Connie	√	√	PWC			5	Sp 83	36

SUBJECT	TITLE	AUTHOR	IL	INST	JOUR	VOL	NO	ISS	DATE	PAGE
Place Mats	Two-harness Weaves	Freeman, Claire	√	√	H&C	11	4		Fa 60	40
Place Mats	Variety in Place Mats — Fran K. Mason		√	√	H&C	14	2		Sp 63	14
Place Mats	Waffle Weave Table Linens (Hector Jaeger)		√	√	Hw	6	5		N/D 85	56, I-14
Place Mats	Weaving in Quebec: Traditional Quebecois Weaving	Barrett, Clotilde	√	√	WJ	6	4	24	Sp 82	10
Place Mats	Weaving Primer	Ingebretsen, Catherine	√	√	PWC			6	Su 83	4
Place Mats	Weaving Table Linens	Eychaner, Barbara Smith	√	√	TM			11	J/J 87	52
Place Mats	Weaving with Ramie		√	> 4	WJ	8	2	30	Fa 83	80
Place Mats	Weaving with Tabby: An Introduction to Overshot	Pettigrew, Dale	√	√	Hw	3	5		N/D 82	62
Place Mats	Woven Reed Placemats	Ingebretsen, Cathy	√	√	PWC	3	2	8		4
Plaids see Checks, Plaids, Tartans										
Plain Weave	Meet, Cross, and Separate	Holtzer, Marilyn Emerson	√	√	SS&D	16	3	63	Su 85	17
Plain Weave	Patolu and Its Techniques	De Bone, Mary Golden	√	√	TMJ	4	3		76	49
Plain Weave	Pattern and Structure in Handwoven Fabrics	Frey, Berta	√	√	H&C	6	4		Fa 55	4
Plain Weave	Tabby Weave, Ways to Make It More Interesting	Hausner, Walter	√		H&C	12	4		Fa 61	6
Plain Weave	Textile Structure and Analysis, A Home Study Course in Twelve Lessons: Lessons in Weave Structure, 1. Plain Weave	Tidball, Harriet		√	SCGM		18		66	23
Plain Weave, Balanced (Tabby)	Two-Harness Textiles, The Loom-Controlled Weaves: Balanced Plain Weave (Tabby)	Tidball, Harriet	√	√	SCGM		20		67	5
Plain Weave, Basket Weave System	Handloom Weaves: The Classification of Handloom Weaves, The Structural Group, Plain Weave Class, Basket System	Tidball, Harriet	√	√	SCGM		33		57	11
Plain Weave, Denting Variations	Swatch #3, Cotton Dress Fabric for Summer (Lillian Whipple)		√	√	Hw	7	5		N/D 86	64, I-7
Plain Weave, Double-Faced	Simple Damask-Like Effects Using Element Diameter Differential and Element Tension Differential	Xenakis, Athanasios David	√	> 4	AT	1			De 83	317
Plain Weave, Giant Warp/Weft	World's Wildest Weaving, The	Herring, Connie	√		PWC	1	1		No 81	41
Plain Weave, Grouped Warps	Four-Harness Woolen Curtain (Sharon Alderman) (error-corrected Hw v2 n2 81 p68)		√	√	Hw	2	1		F-W 80	68
Plain Weave, Grouped Warps/Wefts	What If...Vest (Betty Davenport)		√	√	Hw	5	4		S/O 84	74, 108
Plain Weave, Haircord	Skirt/Slacks Fabric #4 (Sharon D. Alderman)		√	√	Hw	5	3		Su 84	62, 109
Plain Weave, Inlay	Christmas Transparencies (Görel Kinersly)		√	√	Hw	6	4		S/O 85	66, I-16
Plain Weave, Inlay	Glit Coat (Louise B. Heite)		√	√	Hw	8	3		M/J 87	65, I-14
Plain Weave, Inlay	Inlaid Blouse and Scarf (Jean Scorgie)		√	> 4	Hw	8	2		M/A 87	58, I-12
Plain Weave, Inlay	Swatch #3, Jacket Fabric (Malin Salander)		√	√	Hw	7	5		N/D 86	60, I-5
Plain Weave, Inlay	Swatch Collection #11: Fabrics 1- 5 (Sharon Alderman)		√	> 4	Hw	6	2		M/A 85	46, I-5
Plain Weave, Locked Wefts	Two-Harness Textiles, The Loom-Controlled Weaves: Special Effects for Plain Weaves, Locked Wefts (Clasped Weft Weave)	Tidball, Harriet	√	√	SCGM		20		67	27
Plain Weave, Log Cabin System	Handloom Weaves: The Classification of Handloom Weaves, The Structural Group, Plain Weave Class, Log Cabin System	Tidball, Harriet	√	√	SCGM		33		57	12
Plain Weave, Overcheck	Skirt/Dress Fabric #2 & #3 (Sharon D. Alderman)		√	√	Hw	5	3		Su 84	62, 108
Plain Weave, Rib Overplaid	Fabrics That Go Bump (error-corrected PWC i4 83 p76)	Xenakis, Athanasios David	√	√	PWC			3	Oc 82	18

SUBJECT	TITLE	AUTHOR	IL	INST	JOUR	VOL	NO	ISS	DATE	PAGE
Plain Weave, Rib Overplaid	Killarney	Xenakis, Athanasios David	√	>4	PWC	3	1	7		25
Plain Weave, Spaced Warp and Weft	Two-Harness Textiles, The Loom-Controlled Weaves: Spaced Structures, Spaced Warp and Weft Plain Weave	Tidball, Harriet	√	√	SCGM		20		67	13
Plain Weave, Spaced-Warp	Blouse (Sharon Alderman)		√	√	Hw	1	2		S-S 80	41, 60
Plain Weave, Spaced-Warp	Two-Harness Textiles, The Loom-Controlled Weaves: Spaced Structures, Spaced-Warp Plain Weave	Tidball, Harriet	√	√	SCGM		20		67	12
Plain Weave, Spaced-Weave System	Handloom Weaves: The Classification of Handloom Weaves, The Structural Group, Plain Weave Class, Spaced Weave System	Tidball, Harriet	√	√	SCGM		33		57	12
Plain Weave, Spaced-Weft	Two-Harness Textiles, The Loom-Controlled Weaves: Spaced Structures, Spaced-Weft Plain Weave	Tidball, Harriet	√	√	SCGM		20		67	13
Plain Weave, Stripes	Peru, Textiles Unlimited, Part 2: Patterned Stripes on Plain Weave	Tidball, Harriet	√	√	SCGM		26		69	7
Plain Weave, Stripes	Peru, Textiles Unlimited, Part 2: Plain Weave Stripes	Tidball, Harriet	√	√	SCGM		26		69	2
Plain Weave, Supplementary Threads	Two-Harness Textiles, The Loom-Controlled Weaves: Special Effects for Plain Weaves, Supplementary Threads	Tidball, Harriet	√	√	SCGM		20		67	26
Plain Weave, Surface Interest	Surface Interest — Textiles of Today: Surface Interest Designs with Drafts, Group 1, Accented Designs	Tidball, Harriet	√	√	SCGM		2		61	8
Plain Weave, Tabby System	Handloom Weaves: The Classification of Handloom Weaves, The Structural Group, Plain Weave Class	Tidball, Harriet	√	√	SCGM		33		57	10
Plain Weave, Tie-Dye Wefts	Two-Harness Textiles, The Loom-Controlled Weaves: Decorating Plain-Weave Webs, Tie-Dye Wefts (Jaspé, Kasuri, Ikat, Bandhana)	Tidball, Harriet	√	√	SCGM		20		67	29
Plain Weave, Twisted Wefts	Two-Harness Textiles, The Loom-Controlled Weaves: Special Effects for Plain Weaves, Twisted Wefts	Tidball, Harriet	√	√	SCGM		20		67	27
Plain Weave, Uneven Beat	Weaving Primer, Part 2	Lyon, Linda	√	>4	PWC	4	1	11		45
Plain Weave, Variations	Plain Weave Variations		√		H&C	20	3		Su 69	34
Plain Weave, Warp and Weft Floats	Swatch #5, Medallions for Jacket or Coat (Virginia West)		√	>4	Hw	7	5		N/D 86	62, I-6
Plain Weave, Warp Emphasis	Two-Harness Textiles, The Loom-Controlled Weaves: Warp Emphasis Plain Weave	Tidball, Harriet	√	√	SCGM		20		67	9
Plain Weave, Warp Emphasis	Wedding Shirt (Sharon Alderman)		√	√	Hw	1	2		S-S 80	34, 61
Plain Weave, Warp Rep System	Handloom Weaves: The Classification of Handloom Weaves, The Structural Group, Plain Weave Class, Warp Rep System	Tidball, Harriet	√	√	SCGM		33		57	11
Plain Weave, Warp-Emphasis System	Handloom Weaves: The Classification of Handloom Weaves, The Structural Group, Plain Weave Class, Tabby System	Tidball, Harriet	√	√	SCGM		33		57	10
Plain Weave, Warp-Faced	Designing for Warp-face	Sullivan, Donna	√	√	SS&D	19	1	73	Wi 87	15
Plain Weave, Warp-Faced	Flat-Woven Structures Found in Nomadic and Village Weavings from the Near East and Central Asia	Wertime, John T.	√		TMJ	18			79	33
Plain Weave, Warp-Faced	Handloom Weaves: The Classification of Handloom Weaves, The Structural Group, Plain Weave Class, Warp Emphasis System	Tidball, Harriet	√	√	SCGM		33		57	10
Plain Weave, Warp-Faced	Weaving a Cotton Saddlebag on the Santa Elena Peninsula of Ecuador	Hagino, Jane Parker; Karen E. Stothert	√	√	TMJ	22			83	19
Plain Weave, Warp-Faced Cord Weaves	Two-Harness Textiles, The Loom-Controlled Weaves: Warp-Face Plain Weave (Rep, Weft Cord)	Tidball, Harriet	√	√	SCGM		20		67	6

SUBJECT	TITLE	AUTHOR	IL	INST	JOUR	VOL	NO	ISS	DATE	PAGE
Plain Weave, Warp-Faced Rep	Two-Harness Textiles, The Loom-Controlled Weaves: Warp-Face Plain Weave (Rep, Weft Cord)	Tidball, Harriet	√	√	SCGM		20		67	6
Plain Weave, Weft Emphasis	Two-Harness Textiles, The Loom-Controlled Weaves: Weft-Emphasis Plain Weave	Tidball, Harriet	√	√	SCGM		20		67	11
Plain Weave, Weft Floats	Swatch #1, Blouse Fabric (Malin Salander)		√	√	Hw	7	5		N/D 86	60, I-5
Plain Weave, Weft Floats	Swatch #3, Striped Fabric for Blouse (Virginia West)		√	√	Hw	7	5		N/D 86	62, I-6
Plain Weave, Weft Floats	Swatch #4, Skirt Fabric (Malin Salander)		√	√	Hw	7	5		N/D 86	60, I-6
Plain Weave, Weft Rep System	Handloom Weaves: The Classification of Handloom Weaves, The Structural Group, Plain Weave Class, Weft Rep System	Tidball, Harriet	√	√	SCGM		33		57	11
Plain Weave, Weft-Faced	Classical Greek Textiles from Nymphaeum	Wild, John Peter	√		TMJ	4	4		77	33
Plain Weave, Weft-Faced	Handloom Weaves: The Classification of Handloom Weaves, The Structural Group, Plain Weave Class, Weft Emphasis System	Tidball, Harriet	√	√	SCGM		33		57	11
Plain Weave, Weft-Faced	Inspired Bedspread (Anne-Mette Holm)		√	√	Hw	8	3		M/J 87	49, I-7, Cover
Plain Weave, Weft-Faced	Peru, Textiles Unlimited, Part 2: Weft Face Plain Weave	Tidball, Harriet	√	√	SCGM		26		69	5
Plain Weave, Weft-Faced	Rug, Fabric #1 (Constance LaLena)		√	√	Hw	8	4		S/O 87	36, I-3
Plain Weave, Weft-Faced	Two-Harness Textiles, The Loom-Controlled Weaves: Weft-Face Plain Weave (Tapestry)	Tidball, Harriet	√	√	SCGM		20		67	9
Plaiting	Basketry Technics, Part 2	Harvey, Virginia	√		SS&D	6	3	23	Su 75	30
Plaiting	Baskets and Curls	LaPlantz, Shereen	√	√	SS&D	13	1	49	Wi 81	38
Plaiting	Baskets of John Garrett: A Mesh of Ideas and Materials, The	Garrett, John	√		Fa	11	1		J/F 84	26
Plaiting	Coiled Hexagonal Plaiting	LaPlantz, Shereen	√	√	SS&D	18	2	70	Sp 87	17
Plaiting	Double Woven Bag Inspired by a South American Bag, A	Barrett, Clotilde	√	√	WJ	1	2	2	Oc 76	29
Plaiting	Hexagonal Plaiting (error-corrected SS&D v10 n2 79 p56)	Westfall, Carol D.	√	√	SS&D	9	4	36	Fa 78	40
Plaiting	Man-Made Fibers: Season's Greetings		√	√	WJ	5	2	18	Fa 80	46
Plaiting	Notes on Plaiting in the Upper Amazon Basin, Peru	Blinks, Anne	√	√	Iw	5	4		Fa 80	51
Plaiting	Plaited Silk: Myrna Wacknov	Fox, Judy Kellar	√		SS&D	16	2	62	Sp 85	44
Plaiting	Plaiting: Non-Loom Weaving	Laky, Gyöngy	√	√	SS&D	12	2	46	Sp 81	33
Plaiting	Plaiting with Recycled Materials	Westfall, Carol	√	√	SS&D	8	4	32	Fa 77	87
Plaiting	Sheila Fox: Three-Dimensional Plaiting	Malarcher, Pat	√		Fa	6	5		S/O 79	22
Plaiting	Technology of Basketry: North American Roots and Relations to Cloth, The	Turnbaugh, Sarah Peabody	√	√	SS&D	8	1	29	WI 76	32
Plaiting	What Makes a Basket a Basket?	Malarcher, Patricia	√		Fa	11	1		J/F 84	34
Plaiting: Baskets, Technique	Plaited Basket, The	LaPlantz, Shereen	√	√	Hw	7	3		M/J 86	76
Plaiting: Bias	Bias Plaiting	LaPlantz, Shereen	√	√	Hw	7	3		M/J 86	81
Plaiting Ceremonial: Maypole	Plaited Pageantry		√		Fa	13	3		M/J 86	8
Plaiting Clay	Rina Peleg: Plaiting in Clay	Peleg, Rina	√		Fa	10	6		N/D 83	16
Plaiting: Frame	Sprang and Frame Plaiting for Garments		√	√	WJ	3	3	11	Ja 79	26
Plaiting: Metal	Barbara MacCallum	Gordon, Lida	√		Fa	14	3		M/J 87	22
Plaiting: Straight	Straight Plaiting	LaPlantz, Shereen	√	√	Hw	7	3		M/J 86	81
Plaiting: Techniques	Plaiting, Possibilities for Use with Weaving	Schira, Cynthia	√	√	H&C	21	1		Wi 70	8
Plakhta	In Pursuit of Plakhta	Golay, Myrna	√	> 4	WJ	11	3	43	Wi 87	34
Plangi also see Dyes and Dyeing: Resist										
Plangi	Textile Arts of India	Bernier, Ronald M.	√		WJ	2	1	5	Jy 77	31
Planning: Conferences	Planning a Regional Spinner's Gathering	Franc, Marilyn			S-O	11	4		Wi 87	16

SUBJECT	TITLE	AUTHOR	IL	INST	JOUR	VOL	NO	ISS	DATE	PAGE
Planning: Events	Planning to Conclusion	LaLena, Constance			Hw	8	4		S/O 87	19
Planning: Large Projects	Guide to Undertaking a Large Project, A	Ranill, Jane		√	Hw	8	4		S/O 87	87
Planning: Large Projects	Start with a Room-Sized Rug and Work Up	Johnston, Coleen	√		Hw	8	4		S/O 87	85
Planning: Large Projects	Weaving a Bedspread — A Case Study	McKay, Wendy	√	√	Hw	8	4		S/O 87	89
Planning: Workshops	How to Sponsor a Workshop, Part 1: The Basics of Organizing a Workshop	Amos, Alden		√	Hw	8	2		M/A 87	75
Planning: Workshops	How to Sponsor a Workshop Part 2: The Workshop Begins	Amos, Alden			Hw	8	4		S/O 87	73
Plans also see Construction Plans										
Plans: Flyer, Spindle, Arm Assembly	"Workbench" Wheel and Reel		√	√	SS&D	4	1	13	Wi 72	24
Plans: Workshop Space	Shared Work Space May Be Just What You're Looking For, A	Levy, Julie	√	√	TM			9	F/M 87	42
Plant Fibers	Claudie and Francis Hunzinger: Plants, Paper, and Poetry	Hunzinger, Claudie	√		Fa	11	4		J/A 84	10
Plant Fibers	How Does Your Garden Grow? Plant Fibers and Handmade Paper	Plummer, Beverly	√		Fa	6	4		J/A 79	34
Plant Materials	Adventures in Dyeing Wood and Bark (error-corrected SS&D v9 n4 78 p34)	Hearne, Gladys	√	√	SS&D	9	3	35	Su 78	20
Plant Materials	African Textiles	Sieber, Roy	√		H&C	23	6		N/D 72	9
Plant Materials	Basketmakers of Nova Scotia, The	Gordon, Joleen	√		SS&D	17	4	68	Fa 86	44
Plant Materials	Exotic Woods for the Dyepot	Held, Shirley E.	√	√	SS&D	9	4	36	Fa 78	48
Plant Materials	Florida Weaver's Use of Native Materials, A	Ames, Helen B.	√	√	H&C	4	2		Sp 53	50
Plant Materials	Hearth Brooms (Anne Bliss)		√	√	Hw	1	2		S-S 80	27, 57
Plant Materials	Making an Open-Weave Willow Basket	Hart, Carol	√	√	TM			4	A/M 86	24
Plant Materials	Milkweed and Balduinea in the Dyepot	Gerber, Fred; Willi Gerber	√	√	H&C	22	3		Su 71	23
Plant Materials	Milkweed and Balduinea in the Dyepot (Reprint)	Gerber, Fred; Willi Gerber	√	√	H&C	26	1		J/F 75	19
Plant Materials	Nature's Colors, Naturally	Lorance, Marilyn	√		SS&D	10	1	37	Wi 78	49
Plant Materials	Pine Needle Basketry	Washington, Misti	√	√	SS&D	16	4	64	Fa 85	46
Plant Materials	Plaiting, Possibilities for Use with Weaving	Schira, Cynthia	√	√	H&C	21	1		Wi 70	8
Plant Materials	Twining with Leaves and Corn Husks (error-corrected SS&D v14 n4 83 p4)	Jensen, Elizabeth Jane	√	√	SS&D	14	3	55	Su 83	10
Plant Materials	Uncommon Dyewood: Manzanita—From the Chaparral, An	Hall, Joanne Arvidson	√	√	SS&D	7	3	27	Su 76	55
Plant Materials	Weaving with Florida's Native Materials	Henderson, Helen	√	√	H&C	9	2		Sp 58	7
Plant Materials	West Indian Weaving, Nonloom Techniques of Interest	Schira, Cynthia	√		H&C	21	3		Su 70	17
Plant Materials: Beach Rye Grass	Attu Basketry	McIver, Lucy	√	√	H&C	24	1		J/F 73	35
Plant Materials: Paper Mulberry	Shifu: A Handwoven Paper Textile of Japan	Miller, Dorothy	√	√	AT	4			De 85	43
Plant Materials: Spanish Moss	Mary E. Heickman, Texas Weaver and Teacher	Morse, Martha	√		H&C	17	3		Su 66	18
Plastics	Working with Plastic				WJ	10	4	40	Sp 86	78
Plastics/Fiber	Plastics in Fiber: A Persistent Presence	Malarcher, Patricia	√		Fa	12	1		J/F 85	56
Pleats	Ana Lisa Hedstrom: The Intuitive Language Of Shibori	Scarborough, Jessica	√		Fa	13	1		J/F 86	26
Pleats	Double Lives: Can You Love Your "Work" When It's Your "Job"?	Mattera, Joanne	√		TM			10	A/M 87	62
Pleats	Double Weave: Plain and Patterned: Pleats and Tucks, The	Tidball, Harriet	√	> 4	SCGM		1		60	32
Pleats	D'Arcie Beytebiere: Windswept Designs In Pleated Silk	Tacker, Sylvia	√		Fa	13	1		J/F 86	28
Pleats	Ellen Hauptli's Pleats	Levine, Betsy	√		TM			5	J/J 86	48
Pleats	How Madame Grès Sculpts with Fabric	Cooper, Arlene	√	√	TM			10	A/M 87	50
Pleats	"Michael Olszewski: Pleated and Stitched Silk" (Exhibit)	Poon, Vivian	√		Fa	11	3		M/J 84	78

SUBJECT	TITLE	AUTHOR	IL	INST	JOUR	VOL	NO	ISS	DATE	PAGE
Pleats	Pleats, Pleats, Pleats: For Sculptural Garments and Sculpture Itself		√		Fa	9	1		J/F 82	40
Pleats	Textural Approach to Arashi Shibori, A	Beytebiere, D'Arcie	√	√	TM			8	D/J 86	24
Pleats	Wall Hangings of Judith Content, The	Scarborough, Jessica	√		Fa	13	2		M/A 86	10
Pleats: Hand	Pleating by Hand	Mattera, Joanne	√		Fa	9	1		J/F 82	60
Pleats: Industrial	Industrial Pleating	Katz, Ruth J.	√		Fa	9	1		J/F 82	60
Pleats: Knitted	Perfect Pleats	Rowley, Elaine		√	Kn	3	2	6	Sp 87	24
Pleats: Knitted	Pleated Cardigan	Newton, Deborah	√	√	Kn	3	2	6	Sp 87	20
Pleats: Knitted	Pleats in Hand-Knit Fabrics	Newton, Deborah	√	√	Kn	3	2	6	Sp 87	23
Pleats, "Permanent"	Pleated Curtain (Kathryn Wertenberger)		√	√	Hw	5	2		M/A 84	67, 104
Plying	Irregularity in Handspun Part 2	Simmons, Paula	√	√	H&C	21	1		Wi 70	20
Plying	Navajo Three-Ply Method, The	Rossiter, Phyllis	√	√	SS&D	16	1	61	Wi 84	10
Plying	Notes on Navajo Plying	Bateman, Wendy	√	√	S-O	9	2		Su 85	36
Plying	Pencil Roving and the Navajo Ply	Adams, Brucie	√	√	Hw	6	1		J/F 85	75
Plying	Plying a Balanced Yarn for Knitting	Quinn, Celia	√	√	S-O	11	4		Wi 87	30
Plying	Spinning in Bolivia	Meisch, Lynn A.	√	√	S-O	10	1		Sp 86	25
Plying	Three Spun Threads	Royce, Beverly	√	√	S-O	9	1		Sp 85	39
Plying	Two Heads Are Better Than One, or A Story with a Good Twist	Kirschner, Lee	√	√	S-O	8	4		Wi 84	42
Plying	Using Your Mistakes	Martin, Jill			S-O	8	1		Sp 84	52
Plying: Drop Spindle	Faster Drop Spindle Plying	Hitchcock, Helen Hull	√	√	SS&D	8	4	32	Fa 77	94
Pocket Weave, Two-Thread	Antique Stripe Evening Bag (Sigrid Piroch)		√	> 4	Hw	6	1		J/F 85	36, I-10
Pocket Weave, Two-Thread	Aurora Borealis Evening Clutch Bag (Sigrid Piroch)		√	> 4	Hw	6	1		J/F 85	37, I-10
Pockets	Lining Patch Pockets		√	√	TM			2	D/J 85	6
Pockets	Pockets in a Reversible Fabric		√	√	TM			4	A/M 86	6
Pockets	Tailor's Logic	Hostek, Stanley	√	√	TM			14	D/J 87	42
Pockets: Cargo	Making Pockets	Faiola, Linda	√	√	TM			13	O/N 87	30
Pockets: Construction	Making Pockets	Faiola, Linda	√	√	TM			13	O/N 87	30
Pockets: Construction	Perfecting the Pocket	Coffin, David Page	√	√	TM			8	D/J 86	28
Pockets: Double Weave	Double Weaves: Pattern in Double Weaves	Zielinski, S. A.; Robert Leclerc, ed.	√	> 4	MWL	15			'51–'73	104
Pockets: Indian	Making Pockets	Faiola, Linda	√	√	TM			13	O/N 87	30
Pockets: Inseam	Making Pockets	Faiola, Linda	√	√	TM			13	O/N 87	30
Pockets: Repair	Repairing Pants Pockets		√	√	TM			9	F/M 87	6
Pockets: Techniques	Patch Pocket Without Top Stitching		√	√	TM			8	D/J 86	8
Pockets: Tubular Weave	Vertical Pockets	Krasnoff, Julienne Hallen	√	√	H&C	21	1		Wi 70	21
Pockets: Woven	Planning Pockets	Krasnoff, Julienne Hallen	√	√	H&C	20	4		Fa 69	15
Poetry	Answer Me In Wool Baby	Coverdale, Joan	√		SS&D	11	2	42	Sp 80	33
Poetry	Apollo's Legacy or "A Dyer's Vision"	Martin, Jill			Hw	3	3		My 82	9
Poetry	Caterpillar and The Butterfly, The	Masten, Ric			Iw	5	2		Sp 80	39
Poetry	Celebrations of Life	Koopman, Albertje	√		Hw	4	1		J/F 83	59
Poetry	Complaint of the Weaving Wife	Hung-tu, Tung			Hw	7	1		J/F 86	50
Poetry	"Crow Quilt"	Halpern, Nancy	√		Fa	8	3		M/J 81	24
Poetry	Fleece Power	Coverdale, Joan	√		SS&D	11	2	42	Sp 80	33
Poetry	From Paint to Fiber	Siewert-Miller, Elisabet	√		SS&D	3	2	10	Sp 72	18
Poetry	Hopi Apocalypse	Schnur, Susan	√		Fa	7	2		M/A 80	46
Poetry	I Am a Weaver	Strong, Gladys			Hw	7	3		M/J 86	10
Poetry	I Dust and Arrange My Tools	Towner, Naomi Whiting			Fa	9	3		M/J 82	9
Poetry	Leona at Her Quilt Frame	Lehrman, Stevanne Ruth			Fa	7	3		M/J 80	40
Poetry	Linen: The Enduring Thread of History	Hoskins, Nancy Arthur	√		Fa	14	2		M/A 87	42
Poetry	"Midnight, May 30"	Schoeberlein, Liz	√		Fa	8	3		M/J 81	24
Poetry	Mindspinning	Sousa, Jan			Iw	5	4		Fa 80	10

SUBJECT	TITLE	AUTHOR	IL	INST	JOUR	VOL	NO	ISS	DATE	PAGE
Poetry	Navajo Legend	Bennett, Noël	√		WJ	8	1	29	Su 83	62
Poetry	Ode to My Socks	Neruda, Pablo	√		Fa	10	1		J/F 83	15
Poetry	Ode to the Other Side of Barn Sides				Fa	6	6		N/D 79	8
Poetry	Onion Gold	Kolander, Cheryl	√	√	S-O	9	3		Fa 85	40
Poetry	"Quilt, The"	Smith, Corless	√		Fa	8	3		M/J 81	25
Poetry	Saga of Gyöngh Laky, The	Block, Joyce	√		Fa	11	1		J/F 84	22
Poetry	Screen for All Seasons, A	Ridgeway, Terese	√	√	SS&D	16	4	64	Fa 85	52
Poetry	Sheep	Keel, Betty			S-O	2			78	5
Poetry	Song of the Bobbin	Nelson, Lois	√		SS&D	4	3	15	Su 73	42
Poetry	Song of the Sky Loom (A Poem)		√		WJ	7	1	25	Su 82	71
Poetry	Summer Into Fall	Sheets, Lucinda	√		Fa	10	2		M/A 83	15
Poetry	Tarry 'oo				Hw	5	2		M/A 84	8
Poetry	This I Ask of Ye...	Kolander, Cheryl	√		Hw	3	2		Mr 82	14
Poetry	Thought Patterns	Baetke, Fern			S-O	7	4		Wi 83	4
Poetry	To Clothe a Weary World in Song	Clement, Robbie	√		Hw	4	4		S/O 83	10
Poetry	Weaver (A Poem for Martha Jones)	Smith, Anna Deavere	√		SS&D	16	3	63	Su 85	38
Poetry	Weaver Looks at Sweden, A	Swenson, Astrid			SS&D	3	2	10	Sp 72	36
Poetry	Weaver, The	Drouillard, Judith			Hw	5	5		N/D 84	10
Poetry	Weaver, The	Solberg, Jeanne Bingham			Iw	5	1		Wi 79	11
Poetry	Weaving	Robson, Deborah	√		Fa	10	4		J/A 83	43
Poetry	Who Can Figure It	Van Winckel, Nance			Hw	8	5		N/D 87	30
Poetry	Who Weaves?		√		Iw	5	2		Sp 80	39
Poetry	Whole Cloth	Dolan, Anne			Hw	7	3		M/J 86	10
Poetry	Windhover, The	Hopkins, Gerard Manley			WJ	8	4	32	Sp 84	16
Poetry	Word Weaver	Krueger, Susan			Hw	3	4		Se 82	10
Poetry	Yarns	Peterson, Edel J.			Hw	6	1		J/F 85	4
Poetry	Young Man in a T	Xenakis, Benjamin	√	√	Kn	3	3	7	Su 87	15
Poetry: Silkworm Cycle	Raising the Silkworm in a Northern Climate	Szpakowski, Marceline		√	AT	2			De 84	157
Points: Turning	Handy Point Turner			√	TM			12	A/S 87	10
Poisons: Dye Plants	Poisonous Dye Plants	Ellis, Jennie Faye		√	SS&D	4	2	14	Sp 73	46
Poland	"22 Polish Textile Artists" (Exhibit)	Park, Betty	√		Fa	4	5		S/O 77	8
Poland	Contemporary Polish Weaving	Jarecka, Louise Llewellyn	√		H&C	1	2		Su 50	15
Poland	Old World Discipline — New World Markets	Chmielewska, Monika	√		SS&D	11	1	41	Wi 79	4
Poland	Polish Art Weaving 1960-1976		√		SS&D	9	1	33	Wi 77	120
Poland	Technique & History of the Polish Double-weave, The	Wimmer, Gayle	√		H&C	24	3		M/J 73	8
Polychrome	Bound Weaving	Turner, Alta R.	√	√	H&C	15	3		Su 64	10
Polychrome	Bound Weaving	Turner, Alta R.	√	> 4	H&C	15	4		Fa 64	19
Polychrome	Chinese Brocades: Development of Supplementary Weft Patterning (error-corrected WJ v11 n4 87 p78)	Drooker, Penelope	√		WJ	11	3	43	Wi 87	47
Polychrome	Double Weave: Plain and Patterned: Double Weave Polychrome, The	Tidball, Harriet	√	> 4	SCGM		1		60	33
Polychrome	Fantastic Finnweave, Part 3	Xenakis, Athanasios David	√	> 4	PWC			4	Ja 83	25
Polychrome	Figures in Boundweave	Waggoner, Phyllis	√	√	WJ	10	2	38	Fa 85	58
Polychrome	Kuvikas	Schoenfeld, Klara	√	> 4	H&C	12	2		Sp 61	20
Polychrome	Multiple Shaft Weaving — 2-Tie Four-End Block Drafts		√	> 4	WJ	6	4	24	Sp 82	48
Polychrome	Navajo Saddle Blanket Patterns	Barrett, Clotilde	√	√	WJ	11	1	41	Su 86	56
Polychrome	Polychrome Double Weave (error-corrected SS&D v7 n1 75 p64)	Marston, Ena	√	> 4	SS&D	7	1	25	Wi 75	52
Polychrome	Summer and Winter and Other Two-Tie Unit Weaves: Methods for Weaving Two-Tie Units, Polychrome Weave	Tidball, Harriet	√	> 4	SCGM		19		66	38

SUBJECT	TITLE	AUTHOR	IL	INST	JOUR	VOL	NO	ISS	DATE	PAGE
Polychrome	Summer and Winter — Part 1		√	>4	WJ	2	4	8	Ap 78	28
Polychrome	Supplementary Warp Patterning: Multi-Polychrome Supplementary Warps	Tidball, Harriet	√	>4	SCGM		17		66	21
Polychrome	Unharnessing the Summer and Winter Weave	Xenakis, Athanasios David	√		lw	4	4		Fa 79	42
Polychrome	Using the Navajo Saddle-Blanket Weave	Tergis, Marilyn	√	√	H&C	23	5		S/O 72	6
Polynesia	Tapa-Making in Tonga	Raphael, Jenifer; Chad Raphael	√		Fa	13	6		N/D 86	24
Ponchos	Adventures in Dyeing Wood and Bark (error-corrected SS&D v9 n4 78 p34)	Hearne, Gladys	√	√	SS&D	9	3	35	Su 78	20
Ponchos	Bag, Hat and Quesquemitl	Thorne, Sylvia; June Segermark	√	√	SS&D	3	1	9	Wi 71	18
Ponchos	Composition and Designing: Ponchos	Zielinski, S. A.; Robert Leclerc, ed.	√	√	MWL	18			'51–'73	81
Ponchos	Contemporary Costume, Strictly Handwoven: An Oval Poncho	Tidball, Harriet	√	√	SCGM		24		68	18
Ponchos	Contemporary Costume, Strictly Handwoven: The Nell Scott Poncho	Tidball, Harriet	√	√	SCGM		24		68	6
Ponchos	Erica: The new Rigid Heddle Loom	Cooper, Frayda	√		H&C	26	5		Oc 75	25
Ponchos	Garments Made from Simple Patterns: Blanket Poncho		√	√	WJ	2	3	7	Ja 78	38
Ponchos	Garments Made from Simple Patterns: Loom Shaped Poncho		√	√	WJ	2	3	7	Ja 78	39
Ponchos	Goldenrod Poncho Wins HGA Award	Hunter, Frances	√	√	SS&D	5	4	20	Fa 74	95
Ponchos	Handspun Yarn Production Rates in the Cuzco Region of Peru	Bird, Junius B.	√		TMJ	2	3		De 68	9
Ponchos	Indian Paintbrush Poncho (Betty Davenport)		√	√	Hw	2	4		Se 81	57, 93
Ponchos	Instant Gratification: Susan Summa Tells How and Why She Learned to Love the Knitting Machine	Summa, Susan	√		Fa	8	5		S/O 81	56
Ponchos	Mary Bridget Plaisted, Colorado Weaver		√	√	H&C	22	1		Wi 71	15
Ponchos	Novel Ski Poncho	Marvin, Grace	√	√	H&C	14	4		Fa 63	34
Ponchos	Poncho	Hurt, Doris	√	>4	WJ	3	3	11	Ja 79	44
Ponchos	Poncho with Fringe Benefits, A	Epstein, Betty	√	√	H&C	23	1		J/F 72	28
Ponchos	Project Notebook, A	Ligon, Linda	√	√	lw	3	1		Fa 77	31
Ponchos	Projects At Chautauqua Summer School	Snyder, Mary E.	√	√	H&C	23	3		M/J 72	14
Ponchos	Rag Trade: Picture Postcard, The (Susanna Lewis)	Weissman, Julia	√		Kn	3	1	5	F-W 86	68
Ponchos	Stadium Poncho (Carol Klippenstein)		√	√	Hw	1	1		F-W 79	28, 58
Ponchos	Variations on a Poncho Theme	d'Avilla, Doris	√	√	WJ	2	3	7	Ja 78	30
Ponchos	Wool Poncho (Bridget McNamara)		√	√	Hw	1	1		F-W 79	18, 52
Ponchos	Wrapped in Style: Poncho Cape (Betty Beard)		√	√	Hw	6	1		J/F 85	41, I-14
Popcorn Weave	Notebook: Popcorn Weave (Sigrid Piroch)	Myers, Ruth, ed.	√	√	SS&D	12	3	47	Su 81	66
Poppana	Annikki Karvinen: Finnish Designer of Wovens	Talley, Charles	√		Fa	13	4		J/A 86	16
Poppana	No More Hot Hands—A Handwoven Skillet Holder!		√	√	Hw	8	3		M/J 87	23
Poppana	Poppana!		√	√	Hw	8	3		M/J 87	74
Poppana	Poppana Runner (Janice Jones)		√	√	Hw	4	2		M/A 83	50, 88
Poppana	Poppana Tapestry Jacket (Jean Scorgie)		√	√	Hw	4	3		M/J 83	48, 84
Popular Taste	Changes in Weaving	LaLena, Constance			Hw	8	1		J/F 87	24
Portfolios	Portfolio: Fashion Designers		√		Hw	7	5		N/D 86	37
Portfolios	Professional Portfolio	LaLena, Constance			Hw	5	2		M/A 84	38
Portraits	Dianne E. Soule: Batik Portraits	Bard, Elizabeth A.	√		Fa	12	6		N/D 85	11
Portraits	From a Family Album	Endres, Linda Carollo	√		Fa	7	3		M/J 80	70
Portraits Embroidery	Japan's Masterful Embroideries	Markrich, Lilo	√		TM			12	A/S 87	68
Portraits, Fiber	Linda Weghorst: Portraits in Fiber		√		Fa	4	4		J/A 77	44

SUBJECT	TITLE	AUTHOR	IL	INST	JOUR	VOL	NO	ISS	DATE	PAGE
Portraits, Fiber	Stitched, Stuffed, and Painted: The Art of Esther Luttikhuizen	Acosta, Dan	√		Fa	12	2		M/A 85	61
Portraits, Tapestry	"Honorata Blicharska" (Exhibit)		√		Fa	4	4		J/A 77	15
Portraits, Tapestry	Sharon La Pierre		√		Fa	4	1		J/F 77	28
Portraits Woven	Jacquard and Woven Silk Pictures, The	Adrosko, Rita J.	√		AT	1			De 83	9
Portraits Woven	Portraits by a Weaver		√		SS&D	8	4	32	Fa 77	38
Portraits, Woven	Portraits in Double Weave	Strickler, Carol	√	√	WJ	1	3	3	Ja 77	30
Portugal	Carmo Portela, Portuguese Tapestry Weaver	Portela, Carmo	√		SS&D	17	4	68	Fa 86	35
Portugal	Weaving Through Portugal	Papa, Nancy	√		SS&D	6	3	23	Su 75	89
Potholders	Hotpots		√		WJ	3	2	10	Oc 78	5
Potholders	Pot Holders (Görel Kinersly)		√	√	Hw	6	4		S/O 85	65, I-14
Potholders	Potholders by Design	Keasbey, Doramay	√	> 4	PWC	4	3	13		50
Potholders	Weaver's Work Apron: A Project in Double Weave		√	√	WJ	7	2	26	Fa 82	27
Powder Puffs	Powder Puffs (Lila Alexander)		√	√	Hw	6	4		S/O 85	64, I-14
Power-Loom Weaving	Deborah Ann Abbott: Power Loom Weaving on a New Hampshire Farm	Mattera, Joanne	√		Fa	9	1		J/F 82	35
Power-Loom Weaving	Made by Machine: Textiles for the Eighties	Harris, Patricia; David Lyon	√		Fa	12	5		S/O 85	34
Power-Loom Weaving	Tromping Through the Ages	Dunwell, Anna	√		Fa	9	2		M/A 82	26
Prehistoric Textiles: Bag, Utilitarian	Prehistoric Twined Bag from Big Bone Cave, Tennessee: Manufacture, Repair, and Use, A	Kuttruff, Jenna Tedrick	√		AT	8			De 87	125
Prehistoric Textiles: Southeastern United States	Prehistoric Textiles Revealed by Potsherds	Kuttruff, Jenna Tedrick	√		SS&D	11	3	43	Su 80	40
Preservation: Textiles	Current Trends in Textiles Conservation and Preservation	Block, Ira			AT	8			De 87	9
Preservation: Textiles	Ounce of Prevention: Preservation and Storage, An	Butterfield, Mary Ann; Lotus Stack	√	√	WJ	10	1	37	Su 85	7
Preshrinking: Fabrics	Ready for the Needle	Coffin, David Page	√	√	TM			12	A/S 87	43
Preshrinking: Wool Yardage	Preshrinking Wool Yardage			√	TM			14	D/J 87	10
Presses	Irons, Boards, and Presses: A Survey of the Tools That Beautify Sewing	Coffin, David Page	√		TM			10	A/M 87	40
Pressing	Irons, Boards, and Presses: A Survey of the Tools That Beautify Sewing	Coffin, David Page	√		TM			10	A/M 87	40
Pressing: Beaters	Irons, Boards, and Presses: A Survey of the Tools That Beautify Sewing	Coffin, David Page	√		TM			10	A/M 87	40
Pressing: Sources	Irons, Boards, and Presses: A Survey of the Tools That Beautify Sewing	Coffin, David Page	√		TM			10	A/M 87	40
Pricing	Double Lives: Can You Love Your "Work" When It's Your "Job"?	Mattera, Joanne	√		TM			10	A/M 87	62
Pricing	Personal Notes on a Dyeing Art	Lapin, Claudia	√		Fa	4	4		J/A 77	60
Prickly Pear	Diverse Dyes	Bliss, Anne	√	√	Iw	3	2		Wi 78	30
Primitive Design	Color Symbolism in Primitive Societies (error-corrected Fa v13 n4 86 p5)	Janeiro, Jan	√		Fa	13	2		M/A 86	30
Primitive Weaving	Adventures with Guatemalan Weaving	Young, Helen Daniels	√		H&C	4	1		Wi 52	26
Primitive Weaving	Highland Weavers in Asia	Hatch, David P.	√	√	H&C	11	1		Wi 60	6
Primitive Weaving	Kente: The Status Cloth of Ghana	Conklin, Sharon L.	√	√	SS&D	8	1	29	WI 76	18
Primitive Weaving	Nigerian Weavers	Worsley, Marie	√		H&C	12	2		Sp 61	45
Primitive Weaving	Primitive Weaving, Rug Weaving on a Squaw Loom	Degenhart, Pearl C.	√		H&C	22	1		Wi 71	21
Primitive Weaving: Mexico	Mexican Motifs: A Cotton Shawl in Leno or Gauze Weave	Tidball, Harriet	√	√	SCGM		6		62	16
Primitive Weaving: Mexico	Mexican Motifs: A Fine Cotton Warp-Pattern Fabric	Tidball, Harriet	√	√	SCGM		6		62	18
Primitive Weaving: Mexico	Mexican Motifs: A Mexican Quesquimitl	Tidball, Harriet	√	√	SCGM		6		62	13
Primitive Weaving: Mexico	Mexican Motifs: The Mexican Men's Jacket	Tidball, Harriet	√	√	SCGM		6		62	20

SUBJECT	TITLE	AUTHOR	IL	INST	JOUR	VOL	NO	ISS	DATE	PAGE
Primitive Weaving: Mexico	Mexican Motifs: The Oaxaca Belts	Tidball, Harriet	√	√	SCGM		6		62	19
Printers, Computer	Printers: Characteristics and Functions	Strickler, Stewart; Carol Strickler		√	Hw	7	3		M/J 86	30
Printing Fabric	Leaf Printing	Ligon, Linda	√	√	Hw	4	3		M/J 83	60
Printing Fabric	Norma Rosen: A Printmaker Turns to Fabrics	Cornett, James	√		Fa	7	4		J/A 80	23
Printing Fabric: Cyanotype	Blueprinting on Fabric	Sider, Sandra	√	√	Fa	13	5		S/O 86	36
Printing Fabric: Cyanotype	Blues in the Light: Cyanotype on Fabric	Sider, Sandra	√		Fa	13	5		S/O 86	34
Printmaker	"Woven and Graphic Art of Anni Albers, The" (Exhibit)	Malarcher, Patricia	√		Fa	13	1		J/F 86	62
Prison Projects: Quilt	When Prison Is Home: Challenging the Creative Spirit	Scarborough, Jessica	√		Fa	11	6		N/D 84	69
Problems: Creative Drafting	Composition and Designing Part 2: Traps in Creative Drafting	Zielinski, S. A.; Robert Leclerc, ed.	√	√	MWL	19			'51–'73	138
Problems: Designing, Satin	Contemporary Satins: Technical Problems	Tidball, Harriet		√	SCGM		7		62	21
Problems: Double Weave, Double-Width	Double Weaves: Practice in Double Width Fabrics	Zielinski, S. A.; Robert Leclerc, ed.			MWL	15			'51–'73	132
Problems: Double Weave, Stitching	Double Weaves: Problems in Double Weaves Stitching	Zielinski, S. A.; Robert Leclerc, ed.	√	> 4	MWL	15			'51–'73	141
Problems: Dyeing	Problem Solving	Bliss, Anne; with Margaret Emerson		√	Iw	3	3		Sp 78	34
Problems: Spinning	Problems with Your Flyer and Bobbin Wheel Spinning	Raven, Lee	√	√	S-O	11	4		Wi 87	23
Problems: Tie-Downs, Table Looms	Solving a Problem in Multi-Harness	Jackson, Marguerite		√	H&C	13	4		Fa 62	19
Problems: Weaving	Contemporary Costume, Strictly Handwoven: References and Special Problems	Tidball, Harriet			SCGM		24		68	44
Problems: Weaving	Weaver's Bag of Tricks, A	Liebler, Barbara	√		Iw	1	3		Sp 76	30
Problems: Weaving, Satin	Contemporary Satins: Technical Problems	Tidball, Harriet		√	SCGM		7		62	21
Processing: Natural Materials	Pine Needle Basketry	Washington, Misti	√	√	SS&D	16	4	64	Fa 85	46
Processing: Natural Materials, Pine Needles	Pine Needle Basketry	Clark, June	√	√	WJ	5	1	17	Su 80	10
Procrastination	How to Succeed At Failure	Rhodes, Donna M.	√		Fa	7	6		N/D 80	32
Producing Multiples	Theme Issue		√		Fa	5	5		S/O 78	
Production Basketry	Kari Lønning: Exploring Color and Form in Rattan	Lønning, Kari	√	√	Fa	11	1		J/F 84	12
Production Control: Carpet	Carpet-Makers of Western Anatolia, 1750–1914, The	Quataert, Donald			TMJ	25			86	25
Production Drafts	Contemporary Approach to Traditional Weaves: Production Drafts	Zielinski, S. A.; Robert Leclerc, ed.	√	> 4	MWL	7			'51–'73	121
Production Dyeing	Interview with Linda Berry Walker...A Spinning and Dyeing Business, An	Horton, Lucy	√		Fa	4	5		S/O 77	26
Production Dyeing	Production Dyeing with Natural Dyes	Van Stralen, Trudy	√	√	S-O	11	4		Wi 87	57
Production Dyeing	Ruth Anderson, Custom Dyer	Kline, Michael	√		Fa	9	5		S/O 82	27
Production Fabric Printing	Francis Butler: "I Used to Be an Artist but I Couldn't Sit Still That Long"	Butler, Francis	√		Fa	5	5		S/O 78	40
Production Fabric Printing	Grace Kraft: Not Just Another Piece of Cloth from the Factory	Vozar, Linda	√	√	Fa	5	5		S/O 78	36
Production Knitting	Knitting for a Living (error-corrected TM i6 A/S86 p6)	Guagliumi, Susan	√		TM			4	A/M 86	38
Production Knitting	Succeeding with the Knitting Machine	Mattera, Joanne	√		TM			2	D/J 85	50
Production Spinning	Conversation with Allen Fannin				S-O	11	3		Fa 87	30
Production Spinning	Does It Pay to Spin Your Own Yarn?	Hochberg, Bette			Iw	4	1		Wi 78	46
Production Spinning	Door Closes for Shelburne Spinners, The	Clark, Katherine	√		SS&D	9	3	35	Su 78	34
Production Spinning	Handspinning as Art	Walker, Linda Berry	√		S-O	2			78	56
Production Spinning	Interview with Linda Berry Walker...A Spinning and Dyeing Business, An	Horton, Lucy	√		Fa	4	5		S/O 77	26
Production Spinning	Lee Carlin: Handweaving Entrepreneur	Ligon, Linda	√		Iw	3	1		Fa 77	26

SUBJECT	TITLE	AUTHOR	IL	INST	JOUR	VOL	NO	ISS	DATE	PAGE
Production Spinning	Musk Ox, and Miscellaneous	Adams, Brucie	√	√	Iw	4	2		Sp 79	46
Production Spinning	Production Handspinning	Carlin, Lee J.	√		S-O	1			77	50
Production Spinning	Production Spinning	Adams, Brucie			Iw	4	1		Wi 78	44
Production Spinning	Production Spinning	Simmons, Paula		√	Iw	4	4		Fa 79	61
Production Spinning	Rachel Brown: Weaver At the Wheel	Daily, Laura	√		Fa	10	3		M/J 83	20
Production Spinning	Shelburne Spinners: Pushing for Perfection	Cysewski, Catherine	√		Iw	3	1		Fa 77	22
Production Spinning	Speed Spinning	Thompson, Nancy	√	√	Iw	4	1		Wi 78	46
Production Spinning	Spinners of Chijnaya, Alpaca Yarns from Peruvian Village	Cloney, Gordon	√		H&C	16	4		Fa 65	15
Production Spinning/Knitting	Recent Success of Carole Lubove-Klein: An Inspiring Yarn, The	McGuire, Patricia	√		Fa	9	5		S/O 82	20
Production Weaving	Adapting Handwoven Fabrics to Interior Design	Storey, Walter Rendell	√		H&C	4	3		Su 53	8
Production Weaving	Ahrens Looms, The	Bryan, Dorothy	√	√	H&C	6	3		Su 55	28
Production Weaving	Alice Parrott	Davis, Mary Woodard	√		Iw	2	1		Fa 76	6
Production Weaving	Ana Rossell: Weaving with Flair for C. A. R. E.	Ligon, Linda	√		Iw	3	1		Fa 77	18
Production Weaving	Architect-Weaver and His Workaday World: Bruce Bierman's Business is Good Design, An	Malarcher, Patricia	√		Fa	7	6		N/D 80	60
Production Weaving	Arianthé: Notes from a Production Weaver	Stettner, Arianthé	√		Fa	5	5		S/O 78	32
Production Weaving	Arrowcraft: Tennessee Cottage Industry	Pilsk, Adele	√		Fa	5	5		S/O 78	20
Production Weaving	Artist/Designer: Two Approaches to Fabric	Kinsella, Pat	√		AT	3			My 85	57
Production Weaving	Blocks in Production	LaLena, Constance	√	√	Hw	8	5		N/D 87	22
Production Weaving	Bright Styles from the North	Kaplow, Roberta	√		SS&D	16	1	61	Wi 84	23
Production Weaving	By the Yard	Mattera, Joanne	√		TM			5	J/J 86	50
Production Weaving	Can a Weaver Earn a Living? Mais Certainement!	Ryall, Pierre	√		SS&D	7	3	27	Su 76	4
Production Weaving	Chule: Freedom to Weave		√		Iw	4	4		Fa 79	47
Production Weaving	Commitment	LaLena, Constance			Hw	2	4		Se 81	76
Production Weaving	Connie LaLena: Colonial Textiles Today	Ligon, Linda	√		Iw	3	1		Fa 77	15
Production Weaving	Conversation with Ed Oppenheimer, A	Pulleyn, Rob	√		Fa	4	4		J/A 77	24
Production Weaving	Conversation with Mary Andrews, A	Pinchin, Bryn	√		Iw	5	4		Fa 80	24
Production Weaving	Deborah Ann Abbott: Power Loom Weaving on a New Hampshire Farm	Mattera, Joanne	√		Fa	9	1		J/F 82	35
Production Weaving	Denmark's Vaeveboden	Hill, Patricia C.	√	> 4	H&C	5	2		Sp 54	16
Production Weaving	Design by the Yard: Today's Fabric Innovators	Scarborough, Jessica	√		Fa	12	5		S/O 85	30
Production Weaving	Design Decisions: Software Solutions	George, Patrice	√	> 4	Hw	5	5		N/D 84	47
Production Weaving	Designer: Grey, Lisa			SS&D	11	2	42	Sp 80	95
Production Weaving	Designer: Nancy Lyon			SS&D	11	2	42	Sp 80	16
Production Weaving	Designer: Nordgren, Elizabeth			SS&D	11	2	42	Sp 80	93
Production Weaving	Designing the Line	Drooker, Penelope	√		SS&D	11	2	42	Sp 80	12
Production Weaving	Determination and Innovation: A Successful Weaving Mill	Fago, D'Ann Calhoun	√		TM			14	D/J 87	14
Production Weaving	Dream—The Reality, The	Ligon, Linda	√		Iw	3	4		Su 78	12
Production Weaving	Dyeing to Order	Henrikson, Sue	√		Hw	3	3		My 82	45
Production Weaving	Ed Oppenheimer: Rugs	Ligon, Linda	√		Iw	5	1		Wi 79	31
Production Weaving	Elaine Cutcher: Production Weaver		√		Fa	3	5		S/O 76	40
Production Weaving	Elizabeth Fisk, Early 20th Century Vermont Weaver	Atwood, Betty	√		H&C	19	3		Su 68	18
Production Weaving	Ellen Siegel, Designer for the Handloom and Power Loom		√		H&C	15	1		Wi 64	6
Production Weaving	Equipment for Production Efficiency: Other Helpful Equipment	LaLena, Constance	√		Hw	5	5		N/D 84	79

SUBJECT	TITLE	AUTHOR	IL	INST	JOUR	VOL	NO	ISS	DATE	PAGE
Production Weaving	Equipment for Production Efficiency: The Loom	LaLena, Constance			Hw	5	4		S/O 84	29
Production Weaving	Evaluating Your Work for the Market	Hoffmann, Jenet	√		SS&D	10	4	40	Fa 79	80
Production Weaving	Evolution of an Artist: Michelle Lester	Malarcher, Pat	√		Fa	14	5		N/D 87	22
Production Weaving	Fabrics from a Desert Weaver	Kirkpatrick, Isabell; Pat Kirkpatrick	√		H&C	7	3		Su 56	27
Production Weaving	Fabrics from Karen Bulow's Looms	Storey, Walter Rendell	√		H&C	5	1		Wi 53	14
Production Weaving	Fabrics from the Looms of Karl Laurell		√		H&C	2	4		Fa 51	9
Production Weaving	Farmcraft Story, The	Whittemore, A. P., Jr.	√		H&C	7	4		Fa 56	27
Production Weaving	Fashionable Threads		√		SS&D	8	4	32	Fa 77	70
Production Weaving	Fiber World of Leah Orr, The	Orr, Leah	√		SS&D	9	3	35	Su 78	8
Production Weaving	Financial Statements: An Aid to Financial Management	LaLena, Constance	√	√	Hw	6	2		M/A 85	33
Production Weaving	Five Pillows from One Warp	Alderman, Sharon D.	√		Hw	3	3		My 82	38
Production Weaving	Following a Family Pattern		√	√	H&C	8	4		Fa 57	15
Production Weaving	Fran Mather: Handweaving in Asheville, North Carolina	Mattera, Joanne	√		Fa	9	1		J/F 82	38
Production Weaving	Francisca Mayer, Designer-Weaver in the Peruvian Highland	Boyer, Ruth McDonald	√		H&C	19	2		Sp 68	18
Production Weaving	Glen Black Handweaver of San Francisco		√		H&C	16	1		Wi 65	20
Production Weaving	Going Into Production: James Wight and Helen Cooperstein		√		Fa	3	1		J/F 76	15
Production Weaving	Gordons of Bucks County, The		√		H&C	10	1		Wi 59	27
Production Weaving	Handweaving for a Living — How Feasible?	Carlin, Lee			SS&D	6	4	24	Fa 75	33
Production Weaving	Handwoven Fabrics on the High Seas	Ames, Helen B.	√		H&C	2	2		Sp 51	9
Production Weaving	Help in the Studio I: Evaluating Your Needs	LaLena, Constance	√		Hw	3	5		N/D 82	81
Production Weaving	Help in the Studio II: Hiring a Permanent Staff	LaLena, Constance		√	Hw	4	1		J/F 83	74
Production Weaving	In Production? Rug Weaving	Fawkes, Judith Poxson	√		Iw	5	1		Wi 79	36
Production Weaving	Interview with Allen Fannin, An				WJ	6	2	22	Fa 81	28
Production Weaving	It Still Can Be Beautiful: Although Utilitarian	Rutkovsky, Fran Cutrell	√	√	SS&D	7	3	27	Su 76	57
Production Weaving	Jackie von Ladau, Versatile Weaver	Clement, Doris	√	√	H&C	10	3		Su 59	20
Production Weaving	Klara Cherepov, A Career in Two Countries	Landis, Bruce	√		H&C	18	3		Su 67	19
Production Weaving	Lee Carlin: Handweaving Entrepreneur	Ligon, Linda	√		Iw	3	1		Fa 77	26
Production Weaving	Leni Hoch: "...To Hell with These Loom-Shaped Garments"	Grant, Susan	√		Fa	5	5		S/O 78	46
Production Weaving	Linekin Bay Fabrics: Handweaving in a Maine Production Studio	Mattera, Joanne	√		Fa	9	1		J/F 82	39
Production Weaving	Lord, Let My Words Be Pleasant Today for Tomorrow I May Have to Eat Them	Redding, Debbie	√	√	Hw	5	5		N/D 84	26
Production Weaving	Making Ends Meet At the Loom	Kosikowski, Janusz	√		SS&D	7	4	28	Fa 76	28
Production Weaving	Market Research: Styles, Trends and Product Development	LaLena, Constance			Hw	2	2		Mr 81	63
Production Weaving	Martha Pollock	Bryan, Dorothy	√		H&C	7	4		Fa 56	7
Production Weaving	Mary Crovatt Hambidge	Schaller, Karin	√		Fa	11	5		S/O 84	24
Production Weaving	Michael Belangie Sees Common Problems for Hand and Power Weavers	Bryan, Dorothy			H&C	2	4		Fa 51	46
Production Weaving	Nantucket Looms, Versatile Uses For Island Fabrics		√		H&C	20	2		Sp 69	18
Production Weaving	Ohio Weaving Venture, An	Pendleton, Mary	√		H&C	4	4		Fa 53	23
Production Weaving	Olga Amaral, A Colombian Weaver's Year in the United States		√		H&C	18	4		Fa 67	20
Production Weaving	One Warp, Many Fabrics	Liebler, Barbara	√	> 4	Iw	3	1		Fa 77	28
Production Weaving	One Warp, One Pattern, Five Garments	Bradley, Louise	√		Hw	3	3		My 82	34
Production Weaving	Pauline Dutterer, Designer and Weaver		√		H&C	3	2		Sp 52	28

SUBJECT	TITLE	AUTHOR	IL	INST	JOUR	VOL	NO	ISS	DATE	PAGE
Production Weaving	Peggy Ives Retires — Long Established Business to C. S. Bourgeois		√		H&C	6	2		Sp 55	28
Production Weaving	Planning Your Studio Space	LaLena, Constance		√	Hw	4	2		M/A 83	76
Production Weaving	Portfolio: Randall Darwall		√		Hw	7	1		J/F 86	37
Production Weaving	Pricing the Production Piece	La Lena, Constance J.	√	√	SS&D	10	2	38	Sp 79	10
Production Weaving	Problems in Designing for Hand and Power Looms	Hausner, Walter	√		H&C	3	1		Wi 51	33
Production Weaving	Production Weaving: A Feasibility Study				Hw	3	3		My 82	21
Production Weaving	Production Weaving: from Nature-Inspired Warps to Linsey-Woolsey	Ligon, Linda	√		Iw	1	2		Wi 76	6
Production Weaving	Production Weaving in Quebec	Turgeon, Lulu	√		Hw	3	3		My 82	54
Production Weaving	Production-Wise Placemats (error-corrected WJ v9 n2 84 p82)	Hall, Nancy Terrell	√	√	WJ	9	1	33	Su 84	44
Production Weaving	Profile: Robert L. Kidd	Fleming, Ray Frost	√		H&C	23	5		S/O 72	9
Production Weaving	Randall Darwall	Sayward, Jessica Lee	√		SS&D	15	2	58	Sp 84	48
Production Weaving	Result of Weaving Rugs, The	Brooke, Anne	√		WJ	7	4	28	Sp 83	39
Production Weaving	Rug Weaving: One Weaver's Approach	Hand, Barbara	√	> 4	WJ	7	4	28	Sp 83	32
Production Weaving	Santa Fe Weaving Center, The	Elliott, Malinda	√		Fa	9	5		S/O 82	32
Production Weaving	Self-supporting Workshop, A	Collingwood, Peter			H&C	15	4		Fa 64	7
Production Weaving	Setting Goals and Evaluating Priorities	LaLena, Constance	√	√	Iw	5	1		Wi 79	43
Production Weaving	She Sells Everything She Weaves	Knoizen, Frances	√		H&C	9	3		Su 58	22
Production Weaving	Sheila O'Hara: Wry Humor and Virtuoso Weaving	Park, Betty	√		Fa	10	1		J/F 83	64
Production Weaving	SS&D Interview: Peter Collingwood	Wilson, Sadye Tune	√		SS&D	10	4	40	Fa 79	4
Production Weaving	Story of Henry Reynolds, The		√		H&C	4	2		Sp 53	23
Production Weaving	Story of the Johnson Rugs, The	Gallinger, Osma Couch	√		H&C	7	2		Sp 56	28
Production Weaving	Story of the Shuttle Shed, The		√		H&C	10	1		Wi 59	22
Production Weaving	Talk with Jack Lenor Larsen, A		√		SS&D	12	2	46	Sp 81	11
Production Weaving	Taproot: Jack Lenor Larsen	Goldin, Susan	√		Iw	4	3		Su 79	17
Production Weaving	Three Production Weavers: Beth Johnson		√		Hw	3	3		My 82	48
Production Weaving	Three Production Weavers: Constance LaLena		√		Hw	3	3		My 82	52
Production Weaving	Three Production Weavers: Trudy Van Stralen		√		Hw	3	3		My 82	50
Production Weaving	Toward Professionalism in Weaving	Bradley, David H.			H&C	8	4		Fa 57	19
Production Weaving	Truchas Becomes a Weaving Center	Ehly, Jean	√		H&C	24	4		Au 73	40
Production Weaving	Tweed Weavers of Glenmore, The	Burkhauser, Jude	√		Hw	3	3		My 82	56
Production Weaving	Two Weavers: A Business Association Which Works	LaLena, Constance	√		Hw	2	3		My 81	66
Production Weaving	Warp-Faced Weaving, Part 1	Jensen, Gay	√	√	Hw	3	3		My 82	42
Production Weaving	Weaver-Designer Plans a Fabric, The	Blumenau, Lili	√		H&C	3	1		Wi 51	8
Production Weaving	Weaving a Lifestyle: Malin Selander	West, Virginia	√		Iw	5	2		Sp 80	30
Production Weaving	Weaving as a Professional: Production Weaving/Designing	Checker, Janet	√		WJ	6	3	23	Wi 81	29
Production Weaving	Weaving for Sale	Kossick, Ebba	√		H&C	17	3		Su 66	23
Production Weaving	Weaving on a Two Man Loom	Kozikowski, Janusz	√		H&C	24	1		J/F 73	6
Production Weaving	Weaving that Pays	Cripps, Alice K.	√	√	H&C	12	3		Su 61	53
Production Weaving	Western German Weavers	Abbott, Edith E.	√		H&C	8	4		Fa 57	22
Production Weaving	Women in Weaving	LaLena, Constance	√		Iw	4	4		Fa 79	54
Production Weaving: Power Looms	Roy Ginstrom, Versatile Handweaver and Designer of Fabrics for Power Looms		√		H&C	13	3		Su 62	6
Production Weaving: Tapestry	Bringing Tapestry into the 20th Century	Mattera, Joanne	√		TM			1	O/N 85	48
Production Weaving: Test Samples	I Was a Handweaver for the Textile Industry	Tergis, Marilyn	√	√	H&C	23	5		S/O 72	36
Professional Craftsman	Edward F. Worst: Craftsman and Educator	Pettigrew, Dale	√		Hw	6	5		N/D 85	73
Professional Craftsman	Interview with Chris O'Connell, An	Durstan, Linda Moore	√		Hw	6	1		J/F 85	76

SUBJECT	TITLE	AUTHOR	IL	INST	JOUR	VOL	NO	ISS	DATE	PAGE
Professional Craftsmen	Anni Albers	Pettigrew, Dale	√		Hw	6	4		S/O 85	76
Professionalism	Being Professional	Dunwell, Anna	√		Fa	10	4		J/A 83	40
Professionalism	Changes in Weaving	LaLena, Constance			Hw	8	1		J/F 87	24
Professionalism	Commitment	LaLena, Constance			Hw	2	4		Se 81	76
Professionalism	Consideration of Professionalism, A	Reynolds, Donna			S-O	7	1		Sp 83	12
Professionalism	Evening the Odds in Juried Competition	Williams, Ann			SS&D	17	3	67	Su 86	63
Professionalism	Personal Notes on a Dyeing Art	Lapin, Claudia	√		Fa	4	4		J/A 77	60
Professionalism	Toward a Professional Attitude in Weaving	Bradley, David H.			H&C	8	4		Fa 57	19
Professionalism	Women in Weaving	LaLena, Constance	√		Iw	4	4		Fa 79	54
Professionals also see People										
Professionals, Fiber	Kay Sekimachi: Successful on Her Own Terms	Talley, Charles	√		Fa	9	5		S/O 82	72
Professionals, Fiber	Silks of Ed Lambert: In Pursuit of the Moving Image, The	Whittaker, Lynn	√		Fa	9	5		S/O 82	60
Professionals, Fiber	Time and Vision: The Work of Cynthia Schira	Janeiro, Jan	√		Fa	9	5		S/O 82	68
Profiles see People										
Project Planning: Weaving	Planning a Project	Redding, Debbie		√	Hw	3	1		Ja 82	23
Projects: Aid To Artisans	Christmas Embroidery in Pakistan	Garland, Mary	√		TM			14	D/J 87	90
Projects: ARTSearch	Video Access to Textiles: The Helen L. Allen Textile Collection	Bard, Elizabeth A.	√		Fa	12	6		N/D 85	34
Projects: Binders	Handwoven Specialties: 62 Articles for the Handweaver to Make	Tidball, Harriet	√	√	SCGM		11		64	31
Projects: Block Printing	Classroom Block Printing Project, A	Green, Julie	√	√	Fa	14	1		J/F 87	41
Projects: Book Boxes	Handwoven Specialties: 62 Articles for the Handweaver to Make	Tidball, Harriet	√	√	SCGM		11		64	32
Projects: Bookmarks	Handwoven Specialties: 62 Articles for the Handweaver to Make	Tidball, Harriet	√	√	SCGM		11		64	21
Projects: Braids and Braiding	System for Recording and Drafting Certain Types of Braids, A (error-corrected WJ v2 n1 77 insert for vol. 1)	Barrett, Clotilde; Ronnie Bohannan	√	√	WJ	1	2	2	Oc 76	20
Projects: Cases	Handwoven Specialties: 62 Articles for the Handweaver to Make	Tidball, Harriet	√	√	SCGM		11		64	12
Projects: Casserole Holder	Handwoven Specialties: 62 Articles for the Handweaver to Make	Tidball, Harriet	√	√	SCGM		11		64	18
Projects: Casual Book Covers	Handwoven Specialties: 62 Articles for the Handweaver to Make	Tidball, Harriet	√	√	SCGM		11		64	28
Projects: Closet Boxes	Handwoven Specialties: 62 Articles for the Handweaver to Make	Tidball, Harriet		√	SCGM		11		64	38
Projects: Coasters	Handwoven Specialties: 62 Articles for the Handweaver to Make	Tidball, Harriet		√	SCGM		11		64	22
Projects: Covered Boxes	Handwoven Specialties: 62 Articles for the Handweaver to Make	Tidball, Harriet	√	√	SCGM		11		64	34
Projects: Covered Button Earrings	Handwoven Specialties: 62 Articles for the Handweaver to Make	Tidball, Harriet			SCGM		11		64	9
Projects: Covered Buttons	Handwoven Specialties: 62 Articles for the Handweaver to Make	Tidball, Harriet			SCGM		11		64	9
Projects: Covered Match Boxes	Handwoven Specialties: 62 Articles for the Handweaver to Make	Tidball, Harriet		√	SCGM		11		64	22
Projects: Covered Metal Cans	Handwoven Specialties: 62 Articles for the Handweaver to Make	Tidball, Harriet	√	√	SCGM		11		64	35
Projects: Covered Panel	Handwoven Specialties: 62 Articles for the Handweaver to Make	Tidball, Harriet	√	√	SCGM		11		64	26
Projects: Cushions	Handwoven Specialties: 62 Articles for the Handweaver to Make	Tidball, Harriet	√	√	SCGM		11		64	2
Projects: Desk Accessories	Handwoven Specialties: 62 Articles for the Handweaver to Make	Tidball, Harriet	√	√	SCGM		11		64	38
Projects Desk Set	Handwoven Specialties: 62 Articles for the Handweaver to Make	Tidball, Harriet	√	√	SCGM		11		64	36

SUBJECT	TITLE	AUTHOR	IL	INST	JOUR	VOL	NO	ISS	DATE	PAGE
Projects: Ear Cosy	Handwoven Specialties: 62 Articles for the Handweaver to Make	Tidball, Harriet	√	√	SCGM		11		64	8
Projects: Flags, Civil War	Civil War History Preserved: The Pennsylvania Flag Project	Ashton, Mary	√		Fa	14	5		N/D 87	10
Projects: Four-Shaft Looms	New Projects for Four Harness Looms	Frey, Berta	√	√	H&C	8	2		Sp 57	49
Projects: Golf Club Socks	Handwoven Specialties: 62 Articles for the Handweaver to Make	Tidball, Harriet	√	√	SCGM		11		64	7
Projects: Handicraft Promotion	Weaving in Taiwan, An American Designer's Experience in Free China		√		H&C	13	1		Wi 62	10
Projects: Hangers	Handwoven Specialties: 62 Articles for the Handweaver to Make	Tidball, Harriet		√	SCGM		11		64	38
Projects: Hinged Notebook	Handwoven Specialties: 62 Articles for the Handweaver to Make	Tidball, Harriet	√	√	SCGM		11		64	29
Projects: Hot Dish Pad	Handwoven Specialties: 62 Articles for the Handweaver to Make	Tidball, Harriet	√	√	SCGM		11		64	18
Projects: Household Files	Handwoven Specialties: 62 Articles for the Handweaver to Make	Tidball, Harriet	√	√	SCGM		11		64	28
Projects: Jacquard	Jacquard Project: Selections from the Current Exhibition, The		√		Fa	9	2		M/A 82	36
Projects: Japanese Accordion Book	Handwoven Specialties: 62 Articles for the Handweaver to Make	Tidball, Harriet	√	√	SCGM		11		64	27
Projects: Jewelry Cases	Handwoven Specialties: 62 Articles for the Handweaver to Make	Tidball, Harriet	√	√	SCGM		11		64	11
Projects: Large	Guide to Undertaking a Large Project, A	Ranill, Jane		√	Hw	8	4		S/O 87	87
Projects: Large	Start with a Room-Sized Rug and Work Up	Johnston, Coleen	√		Hw	8	4		S/O 87	85
Projects: Laundry Bag	Handwoven Specialties: 62 Articles for the Handweaver to Make	Tidball, Harriet	√	√	SCGM		11		64	13
Projects: Lingerie Cases	Handwoven Specialties: 62 Articles for the Handweaver to Make	Tidball, Harriet	√	√	SCGM		11		64	11
Projects: Log Carrier	Handwoven Specialties: 62 Articles for the Handweaver to Make	Tidball, Harriet	√	√	SCGM		11		64	13
Projects: Make-It-Yourself Kits	Handwoven Specialties: 62 Articles for the Handweaver to Make	Tidball, Harriet	√	√	SCGM		11		64	23
Projects: Motorist's Caddy	Handwoven Specialties: 62 Articles for the Handweaver to Make	Tidball, Harriet	√	√	SCGM		11		64	15
Projects: Napkin Case	Handwoven Specialties: 62 Articles for the Handweaver to Make	Tidball, Harriet	√	√	SCGM		11		64	33
Projects: Narrow Loom	Small Looms Offer a Wide Range for Experiment	Berglund, Hilma	√	√	H&C	12	2		Sp 61	22
Projects: Party Candle Holder	Handwoven Specialties: 62 Articles for the Handweaver to Make	Tidball, Harriet	√	√	SCGM		11		64	23
Projects: Peace	Ribbon Project: Miles of Banners for Peace, The		√		Fa	12	5		S/O 85	49
Projects: Pin Wheel Cushion	Handwoven Specialties: 62 Articles for the Handweaver to Make	Tidball, Harriet	√	√	SCGM		11		64	5
Projects: Place Mat Cases	Handwoven Specialties: 62 Articles for the Handweaver to Make	Tidball, Harriet		√	SCGM		11		64	28
Projects: Pot Holder	Handwoven Specialties: 62 Articles for the Handweaver to Make	Tidball, Harriet	√	√	SCGM		11		64	18
Projects: Pot-Holder Mitt	Handwoven Specialties: 62 Articles for the Handweaver to Make	Tidball, Harriet	√	√	SCGM		11		64	19
Projects: Primitive Loom	Handwoven Specialties: 62 Articles for the Handweaver to Make	Tidball, Harriet	√	√	SCGM		11		64	22
Projects: Quilt	"Kentucky Quilt Project: 1800–1900, The" (Exhibit)		√		Fa	10	2		M/A 83	51
Projects: Quilt	Quilted Childhood Visions	Oberlink, Peter	√		Fa	14	1		J/F 87	6
Projects: Re-Covering a Book	Handwoven Specialties: 62 Articles for the Handweaver to Make	Tidball, Harriet	√	√	SCGM		11		64	33
Projects: Saddle Bag	Handwoven Specialties: 62 Articles for the Handweaver to Make	Tidball, Harriet		√	SCGM		11		64	14
Projects: Saddle Shoe-Carrier	Handwoven Specialties: 62 Articles for the Handweaver to Make	Tidball, Harriet	√	√	SCGM		11		64	14
Projects: Scrap Weaving	From Scraps to Wall Hangings	Niemeier, Eileen			H&C	10	3		Su 59	19

SUBJECT	TITLE	AUTHOR	IL	INST	JOUR	VOL	NO	ISS	DATE	PAGE
Projects: Sheep	Churro Sheep in the Navajo Tradition	McNeal, Dr. Lyle G.	√		WJ	10	2	38	Fa 85	31
Projects: Shoe Bags	Handwoven Specialties: 62 Articles for the Handweaver to Make	Tidball, Harriet	√	√	SCGM		11		64	9
Projects: Shoe Forms	Handwoven Specialties: 62 Articles for the Handweaver to Make	Tidball, Harriet	√	√	SCGM		11		64	10
Projects: Silkworks	Silkworks	Goodman, Deborah Lerme	√		Fa	13	1		J/F 86	50
Projects: Simple	Keep It Simple		√		Hw	7	3		M/J 86	73
Projects: Simple	Keep it Simple		√	√	Hw	8	2		M/A 87	83
Projects: Simple	Keep It Simple	Patrick, June			Hw	6	3		Su 85	82
Projects: Simple, Weaving	Keep It Simple		√	√	Hw	8	4		S/O 87	35
Projects: Simple, Weaving	Keep It Simple		√	√	Hw	8	5		N/D 87	32
Projects: Slip Covers for Pillows	Handwoven Specialties: 62 Articles for the Handweaver to Make	Tidball, Harriet	√	√	SCGM		11		64	4
Projects: Sofa Throws	Handwoven Specialties: 62 Articles for the Handweaver to Make	Tidball, Harriet	√	√	SCGM		11		64	2
Projects: Spinning	Handspun Yarns for Weavers	Burnlees, Dee	√	√	WJ	8	2	30	Fa 83	21
Projects: Spinning, Dyeing, Weaving	Weaving a Route to the Future: An Income-Generating Fiber Project in the West Indies	Clark, Sherry	√		Fa	12	2		M/A 85	48
Projects: Square Bag, Round Bag	Handwoven Specialties: 62 Articles for the Handweaver to Make	Tidball, Harriet	√	√	SCGM		11		64	17
Projects: Sun Shield	Handwoven Specialties: 62 Articles for the Handweaver to Make	Tidball, Harriet	√	√	SCGM		11		64	36
Projects: Tatting	Tatting	Suter, Betty	√	√	TM			6	A/S 86	64
Projects: Telephone Book Cover	Handwoven Specialties: 62 Articles for the Handweaver to Make	Tidball, Harriet	√	√	SCGM		11		64	31
Projects: Thai Bag	Handwoven Specialties: 62 Articles for the Handweaver to Make	Tidball, Harriet	√	√	SCGM		11		64	16
Projects: Tray Holder	Handwoven Specialties: 62 Articles for the Handweaver to Make	Tidball, Harriet	√	√	SCGM		11		64	6
Projects: Typewriter Cover	Handwoven Specialties: 62 Articles for the Handweaver to Make	Tidball, Harriet		√	SCGM		11		64	20
Projects: Umbrella Cover	Handwoven Specialties: 62 Articles for the Handweaver to Make	Tidball, Harriet	√	√	SCGM		11		64	9
Projects: Weaving	Handwoven Specialties: 62 Articles for the Handweaver to Make	Tidball, Harriet	√	√	SCGM		11		64	1-38
Projects: Weaving, Casements	Color Related Decorating Textiles; Rugs, Draperies, Upholstery: The Textile Designs, Yellow Casements	Rhodes, Tonya Stalons; Harriet Tidball, ed.	√	> 4	SCGM		14		65	20
Projects: Weaving, Damask	Contemporary Satins: An Alphabet of Satin Designs	Tidball, Harriet	√	> 4	SCGM		7		62	22
Projects: Weaving, Drapery	Color Related Decorating Textiles; Rugs, Draperies, Upholstery: The Textile Designs, Blue Draperies	Rhodes, Tonya Stalons; Harriet Tidball, ed.	√	√	SCGM		14		65	13
Projects: Weaving, Drapery	Color Related Decorating Textiles; Rugs, Draperies, Upholstery: The Textile Designs, Green Drapery	Rhodes, Tonya Stalons; Harriet Tidball, ed.	√	> 4	SCGM		14		65	26
Projects: Weaving, Drapery	Color Related Decorating Textiles; Rugs, Draperies, Upholstery: The Textile Designs, Red Drapery	Rhodes, Tonya Stalons; Harriet Tidball, ed.	√	> 4	SCGM		14		65	32
Projects: Weaving, Guatemalan Textiles	Guatemala Visited	Atwater, Mary Meigs	√	√	SCGM		15		65	17-41
Projects: Weaving, Rugs, Pile	Color Related Decorating Textiles; Rugs, Draperies, Upholstery: Double Corduroy Pile Rugs	Rhodes, Tonya Stalons; Harriet Tidball, ed.	√	√	SCGM		14		65	4
Projects: Weaving, Sachets	Handwoven Specialties: 62 Articles for the Handweaver to Make	Tidball, Harriet	√	√	SCGM		11		64	20
Projects: Weaving, Satin	Contemporary Satins: An Alphabet of Satin Designs	Tidball, Harriet	√	> 4	SCGM		7		62	22
Projects: Weaving, Satin	More About Fabrics: Projects in Satin	Zielinski, S. A.; Robert Leclerc, ed.	√	> 4	MWL	20			'51–'73	17

SUBJECT	TITLE	AUTHOR	IL	INST	JOUR	VOL	NO	ISS	DATE	PAGE
Projects: Weaving, Upholstery	Color Related Decorating Textiles; Rugs, Draperies, Upholstery: The Textile Designs, Blue Upholstrey	Rhodes, Tonya Stalons; Harriet Tidball, ed.	√	√	SCGM		14		65	10
Projects: Weaving, Upholstery	Color Related Decorating Textiles; Rugs, Draperies, Upholstery: The Textile Designs, Green Upholstery	Rhodes, Tonya Stalons; Harriet Tidball, ed.	√	>4	SCGM		14		65	23
Projects: Weaving, Upholstery	Color Related Decorating Textiles; Rugs, Draperies, Upholstery: The Textile Designs, Red Upholstery	Rhodes, Tonya Stalons; Harriet Tidball, ed.	√	>4	SCGM		14		65	29
Projects: Weaving, Upholstrey	Color Related Decorating Textiles; Rugs, Draperies, Upholstery: The Textile Designs, Yellow Upholstrey	Rhodes, Tonya Stalons; Harriet Tidball, ed.	√	>4	SCGM		14		65	17
Projects: Weaving, Yardage	Handspun Yarns for Weavers	Burnlees, Dee	√	√	WJ	8	2	30	Fa 83	21
Projects: Yardstick or Ruler Holder	Handwoven Specialties: 62 Articles for the Handweaver to Make	Tidball, Harriet	√	√	SCGM		11		64	21
Promotion	Champion Promotion, A		√	√	Fa	14	1		J/F 87	7
Proportion	Body in Question, The	Rowley, Elaine			Kn	3	2	6	Sp 87	54
Prose Poem	Creative Process: Debra Rapport, The	Rapport, Debra	√		Fa	11	6		N/D 84	34
Protest Quilt	Protesting a Worldwide Danger		√		Fa	14	1		J/F 87	77
Provenience: Archeological Textiles	Re-Establishing Provenience of Two Paracas Mantles	Paul, Anne			TMJ	19 20			80,81	35
Proverb: Tradition	Obi: The Textile Art of Nishijin	Donaldson, R. Alan	√		AT	1			De 83	115
Psychology: Color	Composition and Designing: Subjective Colours	Zielinski, S. A.; Robert Leclerc, ed.		√	MWL	18			'51–'73	38
Psychology: Color	Feeling for Color, A	Vinroot, Sally	√		Hw	2	4		Se 81	47
Psychology: Color and Weaving	Color and Dyeing: Observations on the Effect of Color on the Handweaver	Tidball, Harriet	√		SCGM		16		65	11
Psychology: Self-Fulfillment	You Are Unique — There is No Competition!	Hamaker, Barbara	√		WJ	6	4	24	Sp 82	37
Psychology: Visual Stimuli	Shine On	Liebler, Barbara			Hw	7	1		J/F 86	75
Psychology: Weaving	A Weaver Ponders His Craft, Collection of Controversial Essays: Psychology of Handweaving	Zielinski, S. A.; Robert Leclerc, ed.			MWL	21 22			'51–'73	7
Public Art	Get Into a Good Book: Public Art for Kids	Covel, John	√		Fa	6	5		S/O 79	33
Public Art	Woven Collages of Arturo Sandoval, The	Park, Betty	√		Fa	6	5		S/O 79	70
Public Fiber	Big Bobbin Lace	Scanlin, Tommye McClure	√		Fa	13	2		M/A 86	32
Public Fiber	Christo: Running Fence Remembered	Woelfle, Gretchen	√		Fa	7	5		S/O 80	24
Public Fiber	Cindy Snodgrass: Wind Sculptures	Wilson, Karen	√		Fa	6	5		S/O 79	56
Public Fiber	Conversing with Gerhardt Knodel	Park, Betty	√		Fa	12	1		J/F 85	27
Public Fiber	Fiber and Architecture	Stanford, Shirley	√		Fa	3	3		M/J 76	14
Public Fiber	Gail Rutter VanSlyke: A Weaver's Commitment	Hunt, Ann	√		Fa	6	5		S/O 79	40
Public Fiber	Hammock, The	Drooker, Penelope B.	√	√	TM			6	A/S 86	74
Public Fiber	Handweaver at the HemisFair, A	White, Ruth W.			H&C	19	3		Su 68	12
Public Fiber	"Ideas and Capabilities: Barbara Sykes' Fiber Constructions" (Exhibit)	Blakely, Deborah	√		Fa	8	1		J/F 81	94
Public Fiber	Joellen Benjamin-Fay: Public Artist, Private Businesswoman	Strosnider, Ann	√	√	Fa	6	5		S/O 79	64
Public Fiber	Kliots of Berkeley, The	Talley, Charles S.	√		Fa	7	4		J/A 80	44
Public Fiber	Lisa Gardner: Cultural Perspectives	Poon, Vivian	√		Fa	12	1		J/F 85	14
Public Fiber	On Fabric in the Southwest: Surface Design, A Bank, and Public Recognition	Brooks, Lois Ziff	√		Fa	6	5		S/O 79	54
Public Fiber	Public Fiber: Looking At the Logistics	Koplos, Janet	√		Fa	12	1		J/F 85	32
Public Fiber	Public Fiber: The Long-Range Problem of Conservation	Austin, Carole	√		Fa	14	5		N/D 87	13
Public Fiber	Rosalie Seeks: Cascading Dream Garden	Richerson, Suzanne	√		Fa	12	1		J/F 85	21
Public Fiber	Theme Issue		√		Fa	6	5		S/O 79	
Publications: Carl Schuster	Publications: Carl Schuster				TMJ	3	3		De 72	3
Publicity	Organizing a Major Textile Show	Papa, Nancy		√	SS&D	8	1	29	WI 76	28

SUBJECT	TITLE	AUTHOR	IL	INST	JOUR	VOL	NO	ISS	DATE	PAGE
Publicity	Publicity: The Press Release	LaLena, Constance			Hw	7	1		J/F 86	73
Publishing	Ann Bliss: Writing a Book About Her Friends		√		Fa	3	5		S/O 76	15
Publishing	One-Woman Publishing Show, A	Xenakis, Alexis Yiorgos	√		PWC	5	2	16		6
Publishing	Publish Your Own Craft Book	Nell, Patti; Linda Ligon			Iw	1	2		Wi 76	18
Pulled Warps and Wefts	Weaving Primer, Part 3	Xenakis, Athanasios David	√	> 4	PWC	4	1	11		46
Pulled-Warp Technique	Applying the Pulled Warp Technique to Loom-Shaped Clothing	Evans, Kerry	√	√	WJ	9	3	35	Wi 85	34
Pulled-Warp Technique	Handspun Yarn for a Pulled Warp Vest	Adams, Brucie	√	√	Hw	7	1		J/F 86	78
Pulled-Warp Technique	Shaping with the Warp	Bowman, Gloria	√	√	SS&D	11	1	41	Wi 79	26
Pullovers	Autumn Oak Pullover (Ardis Dobrovolny)		√	√	Hw	3	4		Se 82	49, 91
Pullovers	Bittersweet Pullover (Ardis Dobrovolny)		√	√	Hw	3	4		Se 82	48, 90
Pullovers	Wooly Woolens	Thilenius, Carol; Marion Simpson	√	√	Hw	3	4		Se 82	44
Puppets	Amy Silberkleit: Bringing Gothic Tales to Life	Grunberg, Liane	√		Fa	13	1		J/F 86	17
Puppets	Delight the Youngsters with Handwoven Puppets	Richards, Iris	√	√	WJ	7	2	26	Fa 82	72
Puppets	Folklore of Puppeteer Joan Mickelson, The	Van Til, Reinder	√		Fa	13	1		J/F 86	14
Puppets	Games Weavers Play		√		SS&D	10	4	40	Fa 79	56
Puppets	Puppets Challenge Ingenuity	Fowler, Mary Jean	√	√	SS&D	6	1	21	Wi 74	19
Puppets	Toys and Other Fun Stuff	Ligon, Linda	√	√	Iw	2	1		Fa 76	13
Puppets	Victoria Rabinowe		√		Fa	3	6		N/D 76	18
Purchasing Practices: Guilds	Purchasing Materials	Gisler, Jim			H&C	24	3		M/J 73	13
Puzzels and Games	Leaf and Bast Fibers Crossword, A	Gaustad, Stephenie	√		S-O	10	3		Fa 86	47
Puzzels and Games	Let's Go for a Spin	Byerly, Lillian			S-O	9	2		Su 85	6
Puzzels and Games	Let's Go for a Spin	Byerly, Lillian			S-O	9	3		Fa 85	3
Puzzels and Games	Weaver's Puzzle, A		√		Hw	7	5		N/D 86	34
Puzzles and Games	Games Weavers Play		√		SS&D	10	4	40	Fa 79	56
Puzzles and Games	Time Out				Kn	3	2	6	Sp 87	5
Puzzles and Games: Checker Board	Checker Board (Julia Hanan)		√	√	Hw	2	1		F-W 80	55, 69
Pyjamas	Contemporary Costume, Strictly Handwoven: Dress Pyjamas	Tidball, Harriet	√	√	SCGM		24		68	35
Qiviut see Musk Ox										
Qotny (Silk and Cotton)	Original Fabrics of Kaftan, The	El-Homossani, M. M.	√	> 4	AT	1			De 83	263
Quadruple Cloth	Double Weaves: Quadruple Fabrics on Eight Shafts	Zielinski, S. A.; Robert Leclerc, ed.	√	> 4	MWL	15			'51–'73	156
Quadruple Cloth	Quadruple Cloth, A Gauze Application	Edman, Larry E.	√	> 4	PWC			2	Ap 82	72
Quadruple Cloth	Quadruple Cloth on the Rigid Heddle Loom, Editor's Note	Xenakis, Athanasios David	√	√	PWC			2	Ap 82	74
Quality	Point to Ponder, A (Daniel Yankelovich)				Hw	2	5		No 81	23
Quality: Dyes and Dyeing	Importance of Quality in the Art of Dyeing, The	McManus, Fran			S-O	7	2		Su 83	10
Quality: Fabrics	On Making Good Cloth	Darwall, Randall	√		Hw	7	5		N/D 86	22
Quality: Handspinning	Consideration of Professionalism, A	Reynolds, Donna			S-O	7	1		Sp 83	12
Quality: Handspinning	Tropos — Part 3	Bulback, Stanley			S-O	7	1		Sp 83	10
Quebec	Imagery and Structure: The Tapestries of Marcel Marois	Russell, Elfleda	√		Fa	8	6		N/D 81	57
Quebec	Production Weaving in Quebec	Turgeon, Lulu	√		Hw	3	3		My 82	54
Quebec	Weaving in Quebec	Barrett, Clotilde	√	√	WJ	6	4	24	Sp 82	8
Quebec	Weaving in Quebec: Devotion to Garments	Barrett, Clotilde	√	√	WJ	6	4	24	Sp 82	18
Quebec	Weaving in Quebec: New Ideas and Techniques	Barrett, Clotilde	√	√	WJ	6	4	24	Sp 82	16

SUBJECT	TITLE	AUTHOR	IL	INST	JOUR	VOL	NO	ISS	DATE	PAGE
Quebec	Weaving in Quebec: New Traditions	Barrett, Clotilde	√	√	WJ	6	4	24	Sp 82	14
Quebec	Weaving in Quebec: Traditional Quebecois Weaving	Barrett, Clotilde	√	√	WJ	6	4	24	Sp 82	10
Questionnaire Responces: Weaving Interests	Update of CW Questionnaire	Laughlin, Mary Elizabeth	√		CW		24		My 87	27
Questionnaire Responses: Drawlooms	Support System for Drawloom Weavers, A	van der Hoogt, Madelyn			CW	7	2	20	Ja 86	10
Questionnaire Responses: Looms	The Looms We Use	van der Hoogt, Madelyn			CW	4	1	10	Se 82	6
Questionnaire Responses: Weaving Interests	Weaving Interests of CW Members Questionnaire Results	Laughlin, Mary Elizabeth			CW	6	3	18	My 85	15
Quilt Batting: Wool	Wool Quilt Batting		√	√	TM			8	D/J 86	7
Quilt Pieces, Marking	Marking Quilt Pieces			√	TM			14	D/J 87	12
Quilted Constructions	Jody Klein: Quilted Constructions	Perry, Pamela	√		Fa	12	2		M/A 85	18
Quilters	Deborah Christensen	Ligon, Linda	√		Iw	2	2		Wi 77	16
Quilters	Franklin Whitham	King, Bucky	√		Iw	2	2		Wi 77	13
Quilters	Quilts in Women's Lives	Mattera, Joanne	√		Fa	9	3		M/J 82	54
Quilters	Sam Moya	Ligon, Linda	√		Iw	2	2		Wi 77	14
Quilters	Tim McIlrath	Ligon, Linda	√		Iw	2	2		Wi 77	18
Quilting	Beyond Quilting	Dyett, Linda	√	√	TM			5	J/J 86	70
Quilting	Cows in Fiber	Timmons, Chris	√		Fa	11	4		J/A 84	55
Quilting	Quilted Vest (Susan Henrickson)		√	√	Hw	4	2		M/A 83	61, 96
Quilting	Quilting by Machine		√	√	TM			7	O/N 86	8
Quilting	Wall Hangings of Judith Content, The	Scarborough, Jessica	√		Fa	13	2		M/A 86	10
Quilting, Contemporary	"Art to Wear" (Exhibit)	Murray, Megan	√		Fa	11	1		J/F 84	76
Quilting, Contemporary	Sue Pierce: Quilted Vessels	Goodman, Deborah Lerme	√		Fa	11	1		J/F 84	100
Quilting, Hand	Heritage Project: Quilted Vest, A	King, Lorna J.	√	√	WJ	4	3	15	Ja 80	28
Quilting, Handwoven Fabrics	Maurine Fair	Ligon, Linda	√	√	Iw	2	2		Wi 77	20
Quilting, Hints	Taping a Straight Line			√	TM			1	O/N 85	6
Quilting, Kantha	Kantha	Westfall, Carol D.; Dipti Desai	√	√	AT	7			Ju 87	161
Quilting, Strip	Strip-Quilted Rounds			√	TM			8	D/J 86	8
Quilting Techniques	Hawaiian Quilt, The	White-Hansen, Sue Ellen	√	√	TM			13	O/N 87	22
Quilting Techniques	Ins and Outs of Hand Quilting, The	Giganti, Maria; Carol Clyne	√	√	TM			2	D/J 85	64
Quilting Techniques	Pine Tree Coat	Knollenberg, Barbara	√	>4	WJ	1	2	2	Oc 76	32
Quilting Techniques	Punch and Poke Quilting Without Thimbles	Millett, Sandra	√	√	TM			7	ON 86	32
Quilting Techniques	Quilting by the Lake in Central New York	Wright, Yolanda	√		Fa	10	2		M/A 83	50
Quilting Techniques: Loom-Controlled	Loom Controlled Quilted Fabrics	Bardwell, Kathryn	√	√	WJ	7	1	25	Su 82	39
Quilting Techniques: Loom-Controlled	Matelasse Double Cloth Stitched to Form the Design	Kelly, Linda	√	>4	WJ	7	1	25	Su 82	43
Quilting Techniques: Loom-Controlled	Reversible Matelasse Jacket	Champion, Ellen	√	>4	WJ	7	1	25	Su 82	41
Quilting Techniques, On-Loom	Stitching Traditional Coverlet Weaves	Sellin, Helen G.	√	>4	AT	1			De 83	289
Quilts also see Bed Coverings										
Quilts	Impressions of an Exposition	Levy, Julie			TM			8	D/J 86	12
Quilts, Amish	Amish Quilts	Fox, Judy Kellar	√		Fa	10	2		M/A 83	28
Quilts, Children's Art	Quilted Childhood Visions	Oberlink, Peter	√		Fa	14	1		J/F 87	6
Quilts, Contemporary	Amish Quilts	Fox, Judy Kellar	√		Fa	10	2		M/A 83	28
Quilts, Contemporary	"Ann Trusty: Grid and Pattern" (Exhibit)	Stiles, David	√		Fa	9	1		J/F 82	79
Quilts, Contemporary	"Art Quilt, The" (Exhibit)	McMorris, Penny; Kile, Michael	√		TM			7	O/N 86	30
Quilts, Contemporary	"Artists' Quilts" (Exhibit)	Woelfle, Gretchen	√		Fa	8	4		J/A 81	70
Quilts, Contemporary	Barbara Crane	Crane, Barbara	√		Fa	13	4		J/A 86	27
Quilts, Contemporary	"Barbara MacCallum: Recent Work" (Exhibit)	Schedl, Naomi Kark	√		Fa	12	4		J/A 85	68

SUBJECT	TITLE	AUTHOR	IL	INST	JOUR	VOL	NO	ISS	DATE	PAGE
Quilts, Contemporary	Beyond Quilting	Dyett, Linda	√	√	TM			5	J/J 86	70
Quilts, Contemporary	CAD Quilts: The Computer As a Studio Tool	Dadey, Jane	√		Fa	14	4		S/O 87	38
Quilts, Contemporary	"Chris Wolf Edmonds" (Exhibit)	Brackman, Barbara	√		Fa	11	5		S/O 84	72
Quilts, Contemporary	Clare M. Murray	Murray, Clare M.	√		Fa	13	6		N/D 86	2
Quilts, Contemporary	Connie McEntire Lehman's Side Glances from Drawings Into Dye-Painted Hangings	Clurman, Irene	√		Fa	8	5		S/O 81	26
Quilts, Contemporary	"Contemporary Quilting: A Renaissance" (Exhibit)	Lauter, Estella	√		Fa	9	1		J/F 82	78
Quilts, Contemporary	"Contemporary Quilts" (Exhibit)		√		Fa	8	3		M/J 81	74
Quilts, Contemporary	Crazy Quilt for Babies Grand, A	Greenberg, Blue	√		Fa	8	2		M/A 81	31
Quilts, Contemporary	Creative Process: Terri Mangat, The	Mangat, Terri	√		Fa	11	6		N/D 84	36
Quilts, Contemporary	Cut from the Same Cloth	Andrews, Kathy Boals	√		Fa	13	3		M/J 86	21
Quilts, Contemporary	Deborah Christensen	Ligon, Linda	√		Iw	2	2		Wi 77	16
Quilts, Contemporary	Debra Minsky-Jackson: Renaissance Visions in Fiber	Grunberg, Liane	√		Fa	11	4		J/A 84	68
Quilts, Contemporary	Doris Hoover: Quiltmaker and Folk Artist	Papa, Nancy	√		Fa	6	1		J/F 79	16
Quilts, Contemporary	Double Lives: Can You Love Your "Work" When It's Your "Job"?	Mattera, Joanne	√		TM			10	A/M 87	62
Quilts, Contemporary	"Emerging Quiltmakers" (Exhibit)	McMorris, Penny	√		Fa	12	1		J/F 85	75
Quilts, Contemporary	Esther Parkhurst	Sider, Sandra	√		Fa	12	6		N/D 85	17
Quilts, Contemporary	"Fabric Constructions: The Art Quilt" (Exhibit)	Klein, Jody	√		Fa	11	2		M/A 84	81
Quilts, Contemporary	"Five Artists: Quilts" (Exhibit)	Scarborough, Jessica	√		Fa	13	5		S/O 86	47
Quilts, Contemporary	Flourishing Art: USA Hmong Women Show How to Stitch Pa ndau, Their Flowery Cloth, A	Porter-Francis, Wendy	√	√	TM			9	F/M 87	33
Quilts, Contemporary	Fondness for Rabbits: Nancy Erickson's Quilts Deliver a Serious Message in a Soft Medium, A		√		Fa	8	6		N/D 81	17
Quilts, Contemporary	Francoise Barnes: Contemporary Quilts	Canty, Judy	√		Fa	11	3		M/J 84	24
Quilts, Contemporary	From White-on-White to Color	Currie, Meg	√		TM			3	F/M 86	39
Quilts, Contemporary	Funeral	Knauer, Katherine	√		Fa	13	6		N/D 86	30
Quilts, Contemporary	Further Thoughts on "The Artist & The Quilt"	Dunnewold, Jane			Fa	11	2		M/A 84	56
Quilts, Contemporary	Heritage Quilt, The	Greenberg, Blue	√		Fa	12	2		M/A 85	90
Quilts, Contemporary	Hey, Sailor, Let Me Shorten Your Sleeve	Violante, Elizabeth	√		TM			6	A/S 86	98
Quilts, Contemporary	Images in Sharpe Focus: Susan Sharpe's Quilts Are Drawn, Painted and Stitched	Jernigan, Bonnie	√		Fa	10	2		M/A 83	19
Quilts, Contemporary	"Images of the Moslem World" (Exhibit)		√		Fa	14	5		N/D 87	42
Quilts, Contemporary	Ins and Outs of Hand Quilting, The	Giganti, Maria; Carol Clyne	√	√	TM			2	D/J 85	64
Quilts, Contemporary	Janice Anthony's Contemporary Quilts	Henderson, Stew	√		Fa	13	4		J/A 86	22
Quilts, Contemporary	"Jean Ray Laury: Quilted Work" (Exhibit)	Sprague, Mary	√		Fa	9	1		J/F 82	84
Quilts, Contemporary	Jerri Finch-Hurley	Finch-Hurley, Jerri	√		Fa	13	1		J/F 86	18
Quilts, Contemporary	Jerri Finch-Hurley: Quilted Paintings	Wonder, Danny	√		Fa	11	2		M/A 84	27
Quilts, Contemporary	"Joy Saville: Contemporary Quilting" (Exhibits)	Park, Betty	√		Fa	9	4		J/A 82	72
Quilts, Contemporary	Joyful Hieroglyphics: For Mary Bero Anything is Possible!		√		Fa	8	5		S/O 81	40
Quilts, Contemporary	Julie Berner	Berner, Julie	√		Fa	14	1		J/F 87	27
Quilts, Contemporary	Junque Quilts	Murray, Clare	√		Fa	14	4		S/O 87	6
Quilts, Contemporary	Katie Pasquini: Mandala Quilts	Pasquini, Katie	√		Fa	10	4		J/A 83	20
Quilts, Contemporary	Keeping Warm in Alaska		√		Fa	9	6		N/D 82	22
Quilts, Contemporary	Laurie Swim: A Contemporary Quiltmaker with Roots in the Past	Himel, Susan	√		Fa	7	4		J/A 80	18
Quilts, Contemporary	Leslie Fuller: Pan-Creative Quiltmaker	Horton, Lucy	√		Fa	7	5		S/O 80	19
Quilts, Contemporary	Liberty Quilts		√		TM			6	A/S 86	100

SUBJECT	TITLE	AUTHOR	IL	INST	JOUR	VOL	NO	ISS	DATE	PAGE
Quilts, Contemporary	Linda Levin: Quilted Impressions	Goodman, Deborah Lerme	√		Fa	14	2		M/A 87	13
Quilts, Contemporary	Log Cabins	Larzelere, Judith Ann	√	√	TM			3	F/M 86	58
Quilts, Contemporary	Lucinda Sheets: A Quiltmaker's Mural is a Poem in Fabric	Richerson, Suzanne	√		Fa	10	2		M/A 83	15
Quilts, Contemporary	"Maine Coast Artists: Fabrications" (Exhibit)	Beem, Edgar Allen	√		Fa	11	4		J/A 84	80
Quilts, Contemporary	Margot Strand Jensen: Soft Painting	Singletary, Suzanne M.	√		Fa	11	1		J/F 84	18
Quilts, Contemporary	Marie Combs: Quilted Visions of Faraway Lands	Erbe, Pamela	√		Fa	12	1		J/F 85	16
Quilts, Contemporary	Medallion Quilting	Miller, Kristin	√	√	TM			14	D/J 87	60
Quilts, Contemporary	"Michael James: A Ten-Year Retrospective" (Exhibit)	Klein, Jody	√		Fa	11	2		M/A 84	80
Quilts, Contemporary	Nancy Smeltzer	Smeltzer, Nancy	√		Fa	13	5		S/O 86	19
Quilts, Contemporary	"New England Images" (Exhibit)	Harris, Patricia; David Lyon	√		Fa	10	6		N/D 83	78
Quilts, Contemporary	"Pamela Gustavson Johnson: Constructivist Quilts" (Exhibit)	Brackman, Barbara	√		Fa	10	2		M/A 83	68
Quilts, Contemporary	Pamela Studstill	Solon, Marcia Goren	√		Fa	12	2		M/A 85	32
Quilts, Contemporary	"Patchwork Garden, A" (Exhibit)	Hetzler, Patricia	√		Fa	8	5		S/O 81	73
Quilts, Contemporary	Patchwork Re-Ordered	Talley, Charles	√		Fa	7	1		J/F 80	24
Quilts, Contemporary	"Patricia Malarcher: Pieced Reflections" (Exhibit)	Scheinman, Pamela	√		Fa	11	2		M/A 84	77
Quilts Contemporary	Pieces of History	Meyers, Judith Philipp	√		Fa	14	5		N/D 87	54
Quilts, Contemporary	Presence of Light: The Un-Traditional Quilts of Jan Myers, The	Gutcheon, Beth	√		Fa	8	3		M/J 81	60
Quilts, Contemporary	"Quilt National '79" (Exhibit)	Gutcheon, Beth	√		Fa	6	5		S/O 79	80
Quilts, Contemporary	Quilt National '85	Levine, Betsy	√		TM			2	D/J 85	10
Quilts, Contemporary	"Quilt National '85": A Proving Ground (Exhibit)	Roe, Nancy	√		Fa	12	6		N/D 85	58
Quilts, Contemporary	"Quilt National '87" (Exhibit)		√		Fa	14	3		M/J 87	62
Quilts, Contemporary	Quilted Autograph Collection, A	Pierce, Judith	√		Fa	14	3		M/J 87	5
Quilts, Contemporary	Quilted Gardens of Jean Carlson Masseau, The	Pellegrino, Mary C.	√		Fa	13	2		M/A 86	9
Quilts, Contemporary	Quilting in France	Smeltzer, Nancy	√		Fa	13	2		M/A 86	49
Quilts, Contemporary	Quiltmaker's Art, A	Mattera, Joanne	√		Fa	10	2		M/A 83	33
Quilts, Contemporary	Quiltmaking: A Celebration of Life — Esther Parkhurst, Camille Shafer, Pami Slatt Fagelson		√		Fa	8	3		M/J 81	26
Quilts, Contemporary	"Quilts as Textile Art: Collection of Mary Woodard Davis" (Exhibit)		√		Fa	3	2		M/A 76	8
Quilts, Contemporary	Quilts at Arrowmont (Exhibit)		√		Fa	13	3		M/J 86	53
Quilts, Contemporary	"Quilts by Jane Reeves" (Exhibit)		√		Fa	14	1		J/F 87	71
Quilts, Contemporary	"Quilts—Innovation and Tradition" (Exhibit)	Barnard, Eileen Wolford	√		Fa	10	3		M/J 83	72
Quilts, Contemporary	"Quilts of Patsy Allen, The" (Exhibit)	Laymon, Cynthia	√		Fa	10	6		N/D 83	76
Quilts, Contemporary	"Radka Donnell-Vogt: Patchwork Quilts" (Exhibit)	Chase, Pattie	√		Fa	7	5		S/O 80	76
Quilts, Contemporary	"Redefining the American Quilt" (Exhibit)		√		Fa	14	4		S/O 87	43
Quilts, Contemporary	Rochester Honor Quilt: Celebrating Surface Design, The		√		Fa	10	5		S/O 83	98
Quilts, Contemporary	Sam Moya	Ligon, Linda	√		Iw	2	2		Wi 77	14
Quilts, Contemporary	Songs in Fabric: Quiltmaker Nancy Herman Is an Unusual Musician	Rowland, Amy Zaffarano	√		Fa	9	4		J/A 82	22
Quilts, Contemporary	Spinning Fleece for Peace				TM			11	J/J 87	18
Quilts, Contemporary	Tangential Textiles: From Quiltmaking to Points Beyond	Chapman, Charity	√		Fa	9	2		M/A 82	22
Quilts, Contemporary	Tangential Textiles: From Quiltmaking to Points Beyond	Rowley, Kristen Carlsen	√		Fa	9	2		M/A 82	22

SUBJECT	TITLE	AUTHOR	IL	INST	JOUR	VOL	NO	ISS	DATE	PAGE
Quilts, Contemporary	Therese May: Moving Freely from Fabric to Paint and Back Again	Huffaker, Katherine	√		Fa	9	1		J/F 82	26
Quilts, Contemporary	Therese May: Risking to Grow	Scarborough, Jessica	√		Fa	12	4		J/A 85	15
Quilts, Contemporary	Tim McIlrath	Ligon, Linda	√		Iw	2	2		Wi 77	18
Quilts, Contemporary	Tons of Quilts at Liberty Festival	Wolff, Colette	√		TM			6	A/S 86	22
Quilts, Contemporary	Wailani Johansen, Quiltmaker: Sharing the Tradition of the Hawaiian Quilt	Rex, Chris	√		Fa	9	3		M/J 82	60
Quilts, Contemporary	Warm Quilt — Look Again!, A	Woelfle, Gretchen Erskine	√		Fa	7	3		M/J 80	62
Quilts, Contemporary	When Prison Is Home: Challenging The Creative Spirit	Scarborough, Jessica	√		Fa	11	6		N/D 84	69
Quilts, Contemporary	Yvonne Porcella	Porcella, Yvonne	√		Fa	13	6		N/D 86	3
Quilts, Contemporary, Curved Pieces	Shapely Curves	Anthony, Janice	√	√	TM			11	J/J 87	30
Quilts, Contemporary, Map	Around the World and Home Again	Greenberg, Blue	√		Fa	9	6		N/D 82	99
Quilts, Contemporary, Paper	"Jody Klein's Paper Quilts" (Exhibit)	Storey, Isabelle B.	√		Fa	8	6		N/D 81	70
Quilts, Crazy	Guilding the Lily: Embroidery Stitches in Victorian Crazy Quilts	Horton, Margaret	√	√	TM			10	A/M 87	48
Quilts, Geometric	Double Lives: Can You Love Your "Work" When It's Your "Job"?	Mattera, Joanne	√		TM			10	A/M 87	62
Quilts, Marking Tops	Marking Quilt Top			√	TM			11	J/J 87	6
Quilts, Metal	American Inspiration		√		Fa	10	2		M/A 83	92
Quilts, Paper	Jody Klein's Paper Quilts		√		Fa	10	1		J/F 83	44
Quilts, Pattern Making	Shapely Curves	Anthony, Janice	√	√	TM			11	J/J 87	30
Quilts, Peace	Quilting for World Peace	Shufro, Cathy	√		TM			10	A/M 87	14
Quilts, Piecing	Medallion Quilting	Miller, Kristin	√	√	TM			14	D/J 87	60
Quixquimtl	Vaquero Sweater & Quixquimtl	Frey, Berta	√	√	H&C	12	4		Fa 61	15
Quiz: Overshot	Contemporary Approach to Traditional Weaves: Quizz in Overshot	Zielinski, S. A.; Robert Leclerc, ed.	√	√	MWL	7			'51–'73	88
Quotations: Art/Craft	Notes of a Pattern Weaver	Alvic, Philis			SS&D	14	1	53	Wi 82	32
Quotations: Tapestry Cartoon Transfer	Contemporary Tapestry	Tidball, Harriet	√	√	SCGM		12			64	27
Raanu	Fashions by Linda Knutson and Lynn Daly		√	√	WJ	6	3	23	Wi 81	14
Raanu	Finnish Techniques	Tanner, Kersten	√		SS&D	6	3	23	Su 75	45
Raanu	Ryijy Plus Raanu		√		SS&D	4	2	14	Sp 73	12
Rabari	Rabari Lodi: Creating a Fabric Through Social Alliance, The	Frater, Judy	√	√	WJ	10	1	37	Su 85	28
Raffia	African Textiles	Sieber, Roy	√		H&C	23	6		N/D 72	9
Raffia	Hal Painter Explores the Possibilities of Raffia		√		H&C	3	4		Fa 52	28
Raffia	Raffia Tapestries	Del Deo, Josephine	√	√	H&C	9	1		Wi 57	20
Rags: Bias-Strip Preparation	Rotary Rags for Rugs		√	√	TM			13	O/N 87	10
Rags: Hooking	Welcome to My World	Denton, Kay	√		Fa	8	3		M/J 81	52
Rags: Knitting	Rags At Work	Finch, Joan Freitag	√	√	SS&D	16	4	64	Fa 85	72
Rags: Knitting	Rags to Riches	Upitis, Lizbeth	√	√	Kn	3	1	5	F-W 86	56
Rags: Looping	Toothbrush Handle Rugs: Nålbinding with Rags	Nelson, Lila	√	√	WJ	12	2	46	Fa 87	16
Rags: Preparation	From Rags to Riches	Krook, Inga	√	√	Hw	4	3		M/J 83	32
Rags: Preparation	Rag Prep	Roberts, Diane	√	√	Hw	2	3		My 81	53
Rags: Preparation	Story of My Dining Room Rug, The	Rogers, Carrie M.	√	√	WJ	6	4	24	Sp 82	24
Rags: Twining	Danish Twined Rag Rugs: Lillie Sherwood's Legacy	Irwin, Bobbie	√	√	WJ	10	4	40	Sp 86	32
Rags: Weaving	Barefoot Comfort Rag Rug (Linda Ligon)		√	√	Hw	5	4		S/O 84	70, 105
Rags: Weaving	Blue Rag Vest (Susan Snover)		√	√	Hw	2	3		My 81	50, 78
Rags: Weaving	California Rags	Saulson, Sarah F.	√	√	SS&D	18	1	69	Wi 86	44
Rags: Weaving	Country Rags for a City Apartment	LaLena, Constance	√		Hw	6	3		Su 85	62
Rags: Weaving	Double Corduroy Rug (error-corrected WJ v11 n3 87 p78)	Waggoner, Phyllis	√	√	WJ	11	2	42	Fa 86	42

SUBJECT	TITLE	AUTHOR	IL	INST	JOUR	VOL	NO	ISS	DATE	PAGE
Rags: Weaving	Four Place Mats (error-corrected WJ v6 n1 81 p28d)	Unger, Mary	√	√	WJ	5	2	18	Fa 80	52
Rags: Weaving	From Cotton Patch to Cotton Patches and Then Some	Linder, Olive	√	√	WJ	5	4	20	Sp 81	48
Rags: Weaving	From Elegance to Rag Weaving	Mick, Catherine	√	√	WJ	7	3	27	Wi 82	64
Rags: Weaving	From Rags to Riches	Krook, Inga	√	√	Hw	4	3		M/J 83	32
Rags: Weaving	From Rags to Riches: Artful Recycling	Loud, Dana	√		Fa	13	5		S/O 86	23
Rags: Weaving	Glad Rags		√		Hw	2	3		My 81	50
Rags: Weaving	Glad Rags: The Designs of Rose Jurisich		√	√	Hw	2	3		My 81	46
Rags: Weaving	Hand Woven Rugs: Weaves, Plain Weave, Rugs of Rag Stirps	Atwater, Mary Meigs	√	√	SCGM		29		48	3
Rags: Weaving	Home Weaving: It's the Little Things that Count		√	√	Hw	1	1		F-W 79	38
Rags: Weaving	If You Have Four Harnesses		√	√	H&C	24	4		Au 73	39
Rags: Weaving	Log Cabin Rag Rugs	Meany, Janet K.	√	√	WJ	9	4	36	Sp 85	50
Rags: Weaving	"Maria" Rag Rug	Krook, Inga	√	√	Hw	6	3		Su 85	56
Rags: Weaving	More Rags		√	√	Hw	2	3		My 81	49
Rags: Weaving	Mystery Sun Rug	Oles, Jery	√	> 4	WJ	8	4	32	Sp 84	10
Rags: Weaving	Overshot 'n Rags (Jane Patrick)		√	√	Hw	5	2		M/A 84	108
Rags: Weaving	Pile Weaves, Rugs and Tapestry: Catalogne or Plain Rag Rugs	Zielinski, S. A.; Robert Leclerc, ed.		√	MWL	14			'51–'73	74
Rags: Weaving	Poppana!		√	√	Hw	8	3		M/J 87	74
Rags: Weaving	Pushing the Limits with Rags	Linder, Olive	√	√	Hw	2	3		My 81	51
Rags: Weaving	Rag Bag (Connie Farnbach)		√	√	Hw	2	3		My 81	50, 79
Rags: Weaving	Rag Placemat		√	√	Hw	2	3		My 81	50, 78
Rags: Weaving	Rag Rug Traditions	Meany, Janet K.	√		WJ	9	4	36	Sp 85	56
Rags: Weaving	Rag Rugs		√	√	WJ	4	1	13	Jy 79	22
Rags: Weaving	Rag Rugs	Michaelis, Aimida	√		SS&D	2	4	8	Fa 71	25
Rags: Weaving	Rag Rugs, Not Always Made from Rags	Erickson, Johanna	√	√	TM			3	F/M 86	40
Rags: Weaving	Rag Rugs on Overshot Threading	Snover, Susan	√	√	WJ	5	4	20	Sp 81	22
Rags: Weaving	Rag Rugs with Overlapping Weft Ends	White, Ruth	√	√	WJ	6	4	24	Sp 82	28
Rags: Weaving	Rag Runner (Susan Snover) (error-corrected Hw v2 n4 81 p22)		√	√	Hw	2	3		My 81	50, 78
Rags: Weaving	Rag Table Runner (Inga Krook)		√	√	Hw	8	3		M/J 87	39, I-5
Rags: Weaving	Rag Vest (Susan Snover)		√	√	Hw	4	1		J/F 83	44, 86
Rags: Weaving	Rag Weaving: A History of Necessity		√		Hw	8	3		M/J 87	38
Rags: Weaving	Rags At Work	Finch, Joan Freitag	√	√	SS&D	16	4	64	Fa 85	72
Rags: Weaving	Rags (Susan Snover)		√	√	Hw	2	3		My 81	43
Rags: Weaving	Rags to Riches: Ragstrip Vest	Scheirman, Pam	√	√	WJ	6	3	23	Wi 81	30
Rags: Weaving	Rags to Rugs (error-corrected H&C v14 n1 63 p46)	Shaver, Bee	√	√	H&C	13	4		Fa 62	40
Rags: Weaving	Rags Unlimited	Evans, Jane A.	√	> 4	Hw	2	3		My 81	44
Rags: Weaving	Ragtime	Erickson, Johanna	√	√	SS&D	14	3	55	Su 83	41
Rags: Weaving	Recycling—Ragtime	Ligon, Linda	√	√	Iw	3	4		Su 78	22
Rags: Weaving	Ripsmatta Rug (Diane Tramba) (error-corrected Hw v2 n4 81 p22)		√	> 4	Hw	2	3		My 81	45, 83
Rags: Weaving	Rugs in the American Tradition, Ruth Place Finds a Continuing Demand		√		H&C	19	2		Sp 68	20
Rags: Weaving	Shaker Technique: Part 2, Rag Rugs, The	Gordon, Beverly	√	√	SS&D	8	1	29	WI 76	83
Rags: Weaving	Sock Top Bathmat (Paula Pfaff)		√	√	WJ	10	4	40	Sp 86	49
Rags: Weaving	Start With a Room-Sized Rug and Work Up	Johnston, Coleen	√		Hw	8	4		S/O 87	85
Rags, Weaving	Stenciled Rag Rug (Betty Oldenberg)		√	√	Hw	5	3		Su 84	74
Rags: Weaving	Story of My Dining Room Rug, The	Rogers, Carrie M.	√	√	WJ	6	4	24	Sp 82	24
Rags: Weaving	Twill Wool Rag Rug (Mary Kay Stoehr)		√	> 4	Hw	5	2		M/A 84	57, 95

SUBJECT	TITLE	AUTHOR	IL	INST	JOUR	VOL	NO	ISS	DATE	PAGE
Rags: Weaving	Weaving in Quebec: Traditional Quebecois Weaving	Barrett, Clotilde	√	√	WJ	6	4	24	Sp 82	10
Rags: Weaving	Weaving with Rags			√	Hw	2	3		My 81	80
Ramie	Backstrap Weaving in the Philippines	Ng, Mary	√		SS&D	9	1	33	Wi 77	18
Ramie	Banana, Ramie, and Hemp in Okinawa (error-corrected Fa v14 n3 87 p4)	Miller, Dorothy	√		Fa	14	2		M/A 87	46
Ramie	Florida Weaver's Use of Native Materials, A	Ames, Helen B.	√	√	H&C	4	2		Sp 53	50
Ramie	From Ramie Top to Ramie Top	Knishern, Edna Maki	√	√	SS&D	9	2	34	Sp 78	78
Ramie	Handspun/Handwoven Ramie Blouse	Champion, Ellen	√	>4	WJ	9	2	34	Fa 84	52
Ramie	Miyako Jofu	Miller, Dorothy	√	√	AT	7			Ju 87	85
Ramie	Plant Fibers: Hard Fibers		√	√	WJ	8	2	30	Fa 83	67
Ramie	Ramie	Cobb, Lorie	√		S-O	10	3		Fa 86	40
Ramie	Ramie	Quinn, Celia	√	√	S-O	8	4		Wi 84	50
Ramie	Survey of Leaf and Stem Fibers, A	Buchanan, Rita	√		S-O	10	3		Fa 86	24
Ramie	Weaving with Ramie		√	>4	WJ	8	2	30	Fa 83	80
Random Patterns	Composition and Designing Part 2: Random Patterns	Zielinski, S. A.; Robert Leclerc, ed.	√	>4	MWL	19			'51–'73	102
Random Patterns	Composition and Designing Part 2: Random Patterns and Colours	Zielinski, S. A.; Robert Leclerc, ed.	√	√	MWL	19			'51–'73	115
Random Patterns, Twill	Composition and Designing Part 2: Random Patterns in Twills	Zielinski, S. A.; Robert Leclerc, ed.	√	>4	MWL	19			'51–'73	108
Rank Insignia Textiles: Mandarin Squares	Chinese Influence in Colonial Peruvian Tapestries	Cammann, Schuyler	√		TMJ	1	3		De 64	21
Rank Insignia Textiles: Mandarin Squares	Chinese Textile in Seventeenth Century Spain, A	Cammann, Schuyler	√		TMJ	1	4		De 65	57
Ratings: Weaving	Master Looks At Ratings, A	Hausner, Walter			SS&D	3	4	12	Fa 72	32
Ratings: Weaving	Master Weaver	Ridgeway, Terese	√		SS&D	15	2	58	Sp 84	66
Ratings: Weaving	Member Answers Walter Hausner, A				SS&D	4	1	13	Wi 72	21
Ratings: Weaving	Rating System of Boston Guild	Beck, Dorothy			H&C	12	2		Sp 61	50
Ratings: Weaving	Ratings for Experimental Weavers?				SS&D	3	1	9	Wi 71	42
Ratings: Weaving Efficiency	How Do You Rate Your Weaving Efficiency?	Larsen, Jack Lenor	√		H&C	3	1		Wi 51	25
Rayon	Colorful Scarves	Waggoner, Phyllis	√	√	WJ	12	2	46	Fa 87	48
Rearranged Treadling	Creative Drafting and Analysis: Analysis Developed - 3	Zielinski, S. A.; Robert Leclerc, ed.	√	√	MWL	3			'51–'73	104
Rebozos	Mexican Motifs: Mexico, Land of Contrasts	Tidball, Harriet	√		SCGM		6		62	1
Rebozos	Robozos of Tenancingo	Hewitt, T. H.	√	√	H&C	8	3		Su 57	19
Recipes	Home Cooking		√	√	Hw	1	1		F-W 79	33
Recipes	Main Weavers Wild Blueberry Pie		√	√	SS&D	11	4	44	Fa 80	37
Recipes: Flaxseed Muffins	From Warp to Muffins				Hw	5	1		J/F 84	11
Recipes: Indigo Blue-Pot	Fifty Years As a Coverlet Weaver	Bright, Harriett H.	√	√	WJ	6	2	22	Fa 81	54
Recipes: Soap	Recipe for a Neutral Soap	Walsh, Joan Lee		√	WJ	3	3	11	Ja 79	17
Recipes: Tanning Fur	Recipe for Tanning Rabbit Fur	Clemmer, Phyllis	√	√	WJ	8	3	31	Wi 83	16
Records	What a Handweaver Can Learn from the Scottish Weaving Industry (error-corrected WJ v2 n1 77 insert for vol. 1)	Barrett, Clotilde	√	√	WJ	1	3	3	Ja 77	11
Records: Business	Computers for the Fiber Professional	LaLena, Constance		√	Hw	3	2		Mr 82	72
Records: Business	Pricing for Profit 1. Keeping Essential Records	LaLena, Constance	√	√	Hw	2	5		No 81	75
Records: Business	Pricing for Profit II: Pulling it all Together	LaLena, Constance		√	Hw	3	1		Ja 82	74
Records: Business	Production Efficiency: Working Smart	LaLena, Constance		√	Hw	3	3		My 82	78
Records: Weaving	Treasury for Beginners: Organizing Materials	Zielinski, S. A.; Robert Leclerc, ed.	√	√	MWL	1			'51–'73	120
Recreational Weaving	Weaving for Recreation	Dupire, Jean	√		H&C	8	4		Fa 57	43

SUBJECT	TITLE	AUTHOR	IL	INST	JOUR	VOL	NO	ISS	DATE	PAGE
Recreational Weaving	Weaving Program at the Guild for the Jewish Blind		√		H&C	10	2		Sp 59	29
Recycling	Plaiting with Recycled Materials	Westfall, Carol	√	√	SS&D	8	4	32	Fa 77	87
Recycling	Recycling Plastic Bags	Ager, Lewa	√	√	SS&D	5	4	20	Fa 74	22
Recycling: Fabrics	Anatomy of a Quilted Counterpane (page revised WJ v9 n1 84 p70)	Adrosko, Rita J.	√		WJ	8	4	32	Sp 84	42
Recycling: Fur	Recycling—Ragtime	Ligon, Linda	√	√	Iw	3	4		Su 78	22
Recycling: Hmong Remnants	Keeping Tradition Alive	Wilcox, Don	√		Fa	14	1		J/F 87	44
Recycling: Jeans	From Rags to Riches: Artful Recycling	Loud, Dana	√		Fa	13	5		S/O 86	23
Recycling Materials	Roberta Kremer: A Dialogue with Fiber	Bard, Elizabeth A.	√		Fa	11	4		J/A 84	24
Recycling Materials	Something Out of Nothing	Spencer, Edith L.	√	√	H&C	8	3		Su 57	14
Recycling: Paper	Papermaking as a Recycling Process: The Work of Frances Les	Les, Kathleen	√		Fa	6	4		J/A 79	18
Recycling: Rags	Danish Twined Rag Rugs: Lillie Sherwood's Legacy	Irwin, Bobbie	√	√	WJ	10	4	40	Sp 86	32
Recycling: Rags	Four Place Mats (error-corrected WJ v6 n1 81 p28d)	Unger, Mary	√	√	WJ	5	2	18	Fa 80	52
Recycling: Rags	From Cotton Patch to Cotton Patches and Then Some	Linder, Olive	√	√	WJ	5	4	20	Sp 81	48
Recycling: Rags	From Elegance to Rag Weaving	Mick, Catherine	√	√	WJ	7	3	27	Wi 82	64
Recycling: Rags	From Rags to Riches	Krook, Inga	√	√	Hw	4	3		M/J 83	32
Recycling: Rags	Glad Rags: The Designs of Rose Jurisich		√	√	Hw	2	3		My 81	46
Recycling Rags	Log Cabin Rag Rugs	Meany, Janet K.	√	√	WJ	9	4	36	Sp 85	50
Recycling: Rags	"Maria" Rag Rug	Krook, Inga	√	√	Hw	6	3		Su 85	56
Recycling: Rags	Mystery Sun Rug	Oles, Jery	√	> 4	WJ	8	4	32	Sp 84	10
Recycling: Rags	Pushing the Limits with Rags	Linder, Olive	√	√	Hw	2	3		My 81	51
Recycling: Rags	Rag Rugs		√	√	WJ	4	1	13	Jy 79	22
Recycling: Rags	Rag Rugs on Overshot Threading	Snover, Susan	√	√	WJ	5	4	20	Sp 81	22
Recycling: Rags	Rag Rugs with Overlapping Weft Ends	White, Ruth	√	√	WJ	6	4	24	Sp 82	28
Recycling: Rags	Rags (Susan Snover)		√	√	Hw	2	3		My 81	43
Recycling: Rags	Rags to Riches: Ragstrip Vest	Scheirman, Pam	√	√	WJ	6	3	23	Wi 81	30
Recycling: Rags	Rags Unlimited	Evans, Jane A.	√	> 4	Hw	2	3		My 81	44
Recycling: Rags	Recycling—Ragtime	Ligon, Linda	√	√	Iw	3	4		Su 78	22
Recycling: Rags	Sock Top Bathmat (Paula Pfaff)		√	√	WJ	10	4	40	Sp 86	49
Recycling: Rags	Start With a Room-Sized Rug and Work Up	Johnston, Coleen	√		Hw	8	4		S/O 87	85
Recycling: Rags	Story of My Dining Room Rug, The	Rogers, Carrie M.	√	√	WJ	6	4	24	Sp 82	24
Recycling: Rags	Toothbrush Handle Rugs: Nålbinding with Rags	Nelson, Lila	√	√	WJ	12	2	46	Fa 87	16
Recycling: Rags	Weaving in Quebec: Traditional Quebecois Weaving	Barrett, Clotilde	√	√	WJ	6	4	24	Sp 82	10
Recycling: Synthetics	Gala Raincoat	Moes, Dini	√	√	WJ	6	3	23	Wi 81	12
Recycling: Yarn	Minor Miracles — New Life for Old Yarn	Bliss, Anne	√	√	Hw	8	4		S/O 87	68
Reed	Florida Weaver's Use of Native Materials, A	Ames, Helen B.	√	√	H&C	4	2		Sp 53	50
Reinforcements: Stitched	Reinforcements	Bradley, Louise	√	√	Hw	8	4		S/O 87	22
Relationship: Twill Diagonal and Yarn Twist	Fascination of Twills (Fourshafts): High Quality in Twill Yardage	Zielinski, S. A.; Robert Leclerc, ed.	√	√	MWL	9			'51–'73	95
Reliefs	Conflict Resolved: The Hows and Whys of Hand-Dyed Relief Painting, A	Kroetsch, Glenn	√		Fa	8	4		J/A 81	13
Reliefs	Conflict Resolved: The Hows and Whys of Hand-Dyed Relief Painting, A	Kroetsch, Glenn	√		Fa	8	4		J/A 81	13
Reliefs	"Jan Janeiro: Recent Textiles" (Exhibit)	Talley, Charles S.	√		Fa	8	2		M/A 81	65
Reliefs	"Jarmila Machova: Fibers" (Exhibit)	Dyer, Carolyn	√		Fa	9	1		J/F 82	75
Reliefs	"Theo Moorman: Experiments in Weaving" (Exhibit)	Dunwell, Anna	√		Fa	9	5		S/O 82	80
Reliefs, Leather	Leather Reliefs of Teruko Yamazaki, The	Koplos, Janet	√		Fa	14	4		S/O 87	12

SUBJECT	TITLE	AUTHOR	IL	INST	JOUR	VOL	NO	ISS	DATE	PAGE
Religious Communities	Abbey of Regina Laudis, O.S.B. from Notes of the Abbey Community		√		SS&D	16	3	63	Su 85	42
Religious Communities: Amish	Amish Quilts	Fox, Judy Kellar	√		Fa	10	2		M/A 83	28
Religious Communities: Harmonist	"Harmonist Needlework and Textiles" (Exhibit)	Thomas, Kay	√		Fa	7	6		N/D 80	68
Religious Communities: Shaker	Hands to Work and Hearts to God	Erf, Mary Elva	√	√	WJ	8	1	29	Su 83	25
Religious Communities: Shaker	Shaker Textiles	Hillenburg, Nancy	√	√	WJ	8	1	29	Su 83	22
Religous Communities: Shaker	Shaker Towels: A Guild Devotes a Year of Study to Nineteenth Century Textiles (error-corrected WJ v11 n2 86 p68)	Eastlake, Sandy	√	> 4	WJ	10	4	40	Sp 86	20
Reminiscences: Weaving	Thirty Interesting Years	Sullivan, Mary Elizabeth	√		H&C	8	1		Wi 56	16
Rep, Corded, Warp-Faced	Corded Rep Weave and Velvet Rugs	Proulx, Bibiane April	√	√	SS&D	17	3	67	Su 86	80
Rep, Ripsmatta	Ripsmatta Rug (Diane Tramba, Marianne Goddard, Joanne Tallarovie)		√	> 4	Hw	2	3		My 81	45, 83
Rep, Warp	New Pick-Up Weave, A	Deru, Crescent B.	√	> 4	H&C	10	4		Fa 59	26
Rep, Warp	Seat and Back for Director's Chairs (Constance LaLena)		√	√	Hw	4	3		M/J 83	50, 85
Rep Weaves	Designing Rep Weave	Ridgeway, Terese	√	> 4	SS&D	16	3	63	Su 85	28
Rep Weaves	Designing Rep Weaves with the Aid of a Computer	Bohannan, Ronnine	√	√	WJ	7	4	28	Sp 83	24
Rep Weaves	Four-Block Warp Rep (error-corrected WJ v8 n1 83 p50)	Robitaille, Annette	√	> 4	WJ	7	4	28	Sp 83	16
Rep Weaves	Four-Shaft, Two-Block Warp-Faced Rep Floor Covering	Kolling-Summers, Elizabeth	√	√	WJ	7	4	28	Sp 83	15
Rep Weaves	Ikats of Joan Hausrath: A Painterly Approach to Weaving, The	Dunn, Roger T.	√		Fa	8	6		N/D 81	48
Rep Weaves	Ken Weaver on Rep Weaving	Weaver, Ken	√		WJ	7	4	28	Sp 83	20
Rep Weaves	Magazine Holder		√	√	WJ	6	4	24	Sp 82	21
Rep Weaves	"Patti Mitchem: Rep Weave Hangings" (Exhibit)	Barnett-Westfall, Lynn	√		Fa	8	3		M/J 81	67
Rep Weaves	Rep Weaves	Proulx, Bibiane April	√	> 4	WJ	7	4	28	Sp 83	10
Rep Weaves	Rep Weaves: Introduction	Barrett, Clotilde	√		WJ	7	4	28	Sp 83	8
Rep Weaves	Traditional Texture Weaves: Rep	Zielinski, S. A.; Robert Leclerc, ed.	√	> 4	MWL	11			'51–'73	7
Rep Weaves	Weaver's Commission Workshop	Meany, Janet	√		SS&D	10	3	39	Su 79	40
Rep Weaves	Weaving in Quebec: New Traditions	Barrett, Clotilde	√	√	WJ	6	4	24	Sp 82	14
Rep Weaves, Tied	Rep Weaves	Proulx, Bibiane April	√	> 4	WJ	7	4	28	Sp 83	10
Rep Weaves, Two-Way Rep Cord	Peru, Textiles Unlimited, Part 2: Two-Way Rep Cord	Tidball, Harriet	√	√	SCGM		26		69	6
Rep Weaves, Warp-Faced	Mattor (error-corrected WJ v2 n1 77 insert for vol. 1)	Dunham, Miriam	√	√	WJ	1	4	4	Ap 77	21
Repair see Restoration and Repair										
Reproductions: Colonial Textiles	Connie LaLena: Colonial Textiles Today	Ligon, Linda	√		Iw	3	1		Fa 77	15
Reproductions: Colonial Textiles	Production Weaving: From Nature-Inspired Warps to Linsey-Woolsey	Ligon, Linda	√		Iw	1	2		Wi 76	6
Reproductions: Early American Fabrics	Early American Linens	Gallagher, Constance	√	> 4	H&C	15	3		Su 64	7
Reproductions: Early American Textiles, Linens	Pennington Linens, Iowa Weaver Collects Old Designs		√		H&C	16	3		Su 65	14
Reproductions: Early American Textiles, Rug	Carpets for a Historic Philadelphia House	Scott, Chester M.	√	√	H&C	16	3		Su 65	13
Reproductions: Fabrics, 18th Century	Williamsburg Weaving	Brown, Bonnie	√		H&C	12	2		Sp 61	30
Reproductions: Fabrics, Period	New Craft Program Will be Given on Nantucket Island		√		H&C	16	1		Wi 65	14
Reproductions: Historic Fabrics	Green Baize for Independence Hall from Penland Looms	Ford, Howard C.	√		H&C	7	2		Sp 56	14
Reproductions: Historic Fabrics	Shroud, The		√		SS&D	12	1	45	Wi 80	15
Reproductions: Historic Fabrics	"The Robe," is Woven on a California Handloom	Marshall, Bertha	√		H&C	4	3		Su 53	14

SUBJECT	TITLE	AUTHOR	IL	INST	JOUR	VOL	NO	ISS	DATE	PAGE
Reproductions: Historic Textiles	Designs in Old Linen Tablecloths	Gubser, Elsie H.	√	> 4	H&C	9	3		Su 58	21
Reproductions: Historic Textiles	Sturbridge Coverlet, A	Jarvis, Helen	√		PWC	5	2	16		20
Reproductions: Historical Costume	Costume from the Adams Period, A	di Franco, Toni Lee	√	√	SS&D	8	1	29	WI 76	43
Reproductions: Historical Costumes	Making Clothes in Colonial Style	Morris, Gitta	√		TM			6	A/S 86	20
Reproductions: Historical Fabrics	Notebook:"Someday" File, The (Maxine Bickenstaff)	Myers, Ruth Nordquist, ed.			SS&D	15	3	59	Su 84	66
Reproductions: Historical Fabrics	Warping It Up with Andrea	Duffy, Joe	√		SS&D	17	1	65	Wi 85	49
Reproductions: Historical Textiles	Gift to My Country: Lincoln Bedroom Coverlet, A	Jarvis, Helen N.	√	√	SS&D	9	4	36	Fa 78	17
Reproductions: Historical Textiles	Shaker Textiles at the Met	Erf, Mary Elva	√	√	SS&D	14	1	53	Wi 82	61
Reproductions: Loom, 17th Century	Spanish Colonial Loom: A Contemporary Loom-Maker Uses Traditional Tools to Construct a Replica for the Albuquerque Museum	Edwards, Jack	√	√	WJ	11	1	41	Su 86	16
Reproductions: Period Textiles	Unraveling Textile History		√		Fa	12	1		J/F 85	67
Research: Brocade	Chinese Brocades: Development of Supplementary Weft Patterning (error-corrected WJ v11 n4 87 p78)	Drooker, Penelope	√		WJ	11	3	43	Wi 87	47
Research: Cotton	In Search of Colored Cotton	Fox, Sally	√	√	S-O	11	4		Wi 87	48
Research: Cotton	Naturally Colored Cottons	Fox, Sally	√		S-O	11	1		Sp 87	29
Research: Historical Textiles	European Textile Collections: Textile Research in Paris	Downing, Marolyn			WJ	11	2	42	Fa 86	53
Research: Methods, Weaving	A Weaver Ponders His Craft, Collection of Controversial Essays: Research	Zielinski, S. A.; Robert Leclerc, ed.		√	MWL	21 22			'51–'73	35
Research: Needs, Weaving	A Weaver Ponders His Craf, Collection of Controversial Essays: Research	Zielinski, S. A.; Robert Leclerc, ed.		√	MWL	21 22			'51–'73	35
Research: Plant Fibers	New Philippine Textiles	Gele, Emilé	√		H&C	5	3		Su 54	14
Research: Textile	Kate Peck Kent: An Anthropologist's Lifetime Involvement with Textiles	Schevill, Margot Blum	√		WJ	11	1	41	Su 86	11
Research: Textile	Mastering the Art of Research	Austin, Carole			Fa	13	5		S/O 86	21
Research: Textile, State of Research	Coptic Tapestry of Byzantine Style, A	Berliner, Rudolf	√		TMJ	1	1		No 62	3
Research: Textile Study Room	Textile Study Room: Metropolitan Museum, The	Murray, Megan	√		Fa	10	3		M/J 83	49
Research: Textile, Ultraviolet Absorbers/Fading and Degradation	Ultraviolet Absorbers: A Treatment to Reduce Fading and Degradation of Textiles	Crews, Patricia Cox; Barbara M. Reagan			AT	8			De 87	43
Research: Theory and Methodology	Anatolian Rugs: An Essay on Method	Denny, Walter B.	√		TMJ	3	4		De 73	7
Resource Guide: Nordic Countries	Textile Resource Guide to the Nordic Countries, A	Talley, Charles	√		Hw	8	3		M/J 87	77
Resources: Blueprinting, Fabric	Blueprinting on Fabric	Sider, Sandra	√	√	Fa	13	5		S/O 86	36
Resources: Indigo	Indigo Miscellany, An		√		Fa	13	5		S/O 86	25
Resources: Paper	Pioneer Paper Places: Pyramid Prints and Paperworks	Fife, Lin	√		Fa	13	4		J/A 86	24
Resources: Quilt	Quilt Resource Sampler		√		Fa	8	3		M/J 81	10
Resources: Rubber Stamp Printing	Rubber Stamping on Fabric	Goodman, Deborah Lerme	√		Fa	13	2		M/A 86	38
Resources: Twill	Twill Resources				Hw	6	5		N/D 85	42
Restoration and Repair	Civil War History Preserved: The Pennsylvania Flag Project	Ashton, Mary	√		Fa	14	5		N/D 87	10
Restoration and Repair	Giving New Life to Antique Wedding Gowns	Mandell, Patricia	√		Fa	14	3		M/J 87	18
Restoration and Repair	Textile Sleuth Extraordinaire	Wasiqullah, Alexander	√		Fa	12	2		M/A 85	39
Restoration and Repair: Costume	Debra Minsky-Jackson: Renaissance Visions in Fiber	Grunberg, Liane	√		Fa	11	4		J/A 84	68
Restoration and Repair: Historical Tapestries	Modern Handweaver Restores Famous Tapestries, A		√	√	H&C	3	2		Sp 52	9

SUBJECT	TITLE	AUTHOR	IL	INST	JOUR	VOL	NO	ISS	DATE	PAGE
Restoration and Repair: Silk, Sun-Damaged	Repairing Sun-Damaged Silk			√	TM			11	J/J 87	10
Restoration and Repair: Textile	In the Spirit of the Navajo	Elliott, Malinda	√		SS&D	13	1	49	Wi 81	18
Restoration and Repair: Textile	Marianne Huebner Solves Many Problems in Restoring Textiles		√		H&C	16	2		Sp 65	13
Restoration and Repair: Textile	Restoring a Crocheted Tablecloth			√	TM			14	D/J 87	6
Restoration and Repair: Textiles	Handweaving in Spain	Arnold, Ruth	√		H&C	8	4		Fa 57	10
Restoration and Repair: Textiles	Noël Bennett: The Delicate Art of Restoration	Elliott, Malinda	√	√	Fa	9	1		J/F 82	44
Revival Traditional Crafts	Handspinning in New Hampshire	Brackett, Thelma	√		H&C	17	1		Wi 66	18
Revival Traditional Crafts	Revival of Stitchery, Appliqué, and Collage	Belfer, Nancy	√		H&C	18	1		Wi 67	21
Revival Traditional Crafts: India	Tie Dyeing in India (error-corrected H&C v14 n2 63 p46)	Arness, Judith Russell	√	√	H&C	14	1		Wi 63	6
Rhythmic Weave Class	Handloom Weaves: The Classification of Handloom Weaves, The Structural Group, The Rhythmic Weave Class	Tidball, Harriet			SCGM		33		57	35
Rhythmic Weave Class, Balanced	Handloom Weaves: The Classification of Handloom Weaves, The Structural Group, The Rhythmic Weave Class, Balanced Texture-Complex System	Tidball, Harriet			SCGM		33		57	35
Rhythmic Weave Class, Unbalanced	Handloom Weaves: The Classification of Handloom Weaves, The Structural Group, The Rhythmic Weave Class, Unbalanced Texture-Complex System	Tidball, Harriet	√		SCGM		33		57	35
Rib, Warp	Qotny & Alaga: Traditional Striped Fabrics for the Middle Eastern Kaftan	El-Homossani, M. M.	√	>4	WJ	10	1	37	Su 85	33
Rib Weave	Horizontal Ribs & Vertical Cords	Moes, Dini	√	√	SS&D	17	4	68	Fa 86	84
Rib Weave	Rep Weaves	Proulx, Bibiane April	√	>4	WJ	7	4	28	Sp 83	10
Rib Weave	Rib Weave		√		Hw	3	1		Ja 82	37
Rib Weave	Rib Weaves from India, A Rich Source of Inspiration	Harvey, Virginia Isham	√	>4	H&C	16	4		Fa 65	21
Rib Weave	Silk Jacket (Jane Patrick)		√	>4	Hw	4	1		J/F 83	50, 90
Rib Weave	Warp-Faced Tablerunner in Rib Weave	Kolling-Summers, Elizabeth	√	√	WJ	7	4	28	Sp 83	14
Rib Weave, Double-Faced	Multiple Rigid Heddle Adventure, Part 1, The	Xenakis, Athanasios David	√	√	PWC	3	4	10		34
Rib Weave, Double-Faced	Two Alpaca and Wool Scarves	Xenakis, Athanasios David	√	>4	PWC	3	4	10		40
Rib Weave, Double-Faced	Weaving Primer	Parks, Deborah	√	√	PWC	3	3	9		4
Rib Weave, Weft-Faced	Rib Weave Rug (Mary Veercamp) (error-corrected Hw v4 n4 83 p92)		√	√	Hw	4	2		M/A 83	47, 84
Ribbing: Neck Down, Technique	Zippers in Knits, Perfect Ribs			√	TM			13	O/N 87	8
Ribbing: Single-Pointed Needles	Ribbing on Single-Pointed Needles			√	TM			13	O/N 87	13
Ribbing: Tubular	Knitting Round on Straight Needles	Borssuck, Bee	√	√	TM			12	A/S 87	64
Ribbon	Rapt with Ribbons	Nager, Sandra	√		TM			12	A/S 87	14
Ribbon	Yarns and Fibers: Unusual Yarns - 2	Zielinski, S. A.; Robert Leclerc, ed.		√	MWL	4			'51–'73	85
Ribbon: Control	Managing Ribbon Yarn			√	TM			11	J/J 87	6
Ribbon: Knitting	Coronet, A	Clayton, Clare	√	√	Kn	3	2	6	Sp 87	32
Ribbon Project	After the Ribbon	Fanning, Robbie			TM			2	D/J 85	12
Ribbon, The	Ribbon: A Celebration of Life, The	Pettigrew, Dale	√		Hw	6	5		N/D 85	70
Ribbon Weaving	Colorful Scarves	Waggoner, Phyllis	√	√	WJ	12	2	46	Fa 87	48
Ribbon Weaving	Ribbon in the Warp	Allen, Ernestine	√	√	H&C	21	4		Fa 70	15
Ribbon Weaving	Ribbon Wefts	Sewell, Suzy	√	>4	WJ	10	3	39	Wi 86	40
Ribbon Work: Techniques	Decorative Ribbon Work	Kling, Candace	√	√	TM			12	A/S 87	58
Ribbons: Card Woven	Mind Boggling Bogs	Herring, Connie	√	√	PWC			3	Oc 82	36
Ribbons: Jacquard, Pictorial	Jacquard and Woven Silk Pictures, The	Adrosko, Rita J.	√		AT	1			De 83	9
Ribwarmers	Be Your Own Designer	Lewis, Susanna	√	√	Kn	3	1	5	F-W 86	48

SUBJECT	TITLE	AUTHOR	IL	INST	JOUR	VOL	NO	ISS	DATE	PAGE
Ribwarmers	Garter Stitch Ribwarmer	Zimmermann, Elizabeth	√	√	Kn	3	1	5	F-W 86	46
Ricksha	Painted Cloth Gardens on Wheels	Wilcox, Don	√		TM			9	F/M 87	18
Ridge (Twill) Weave	Ridge (Twill) Weave of the Hopi	Nelson, Nanci Neher	√	√	SS&D	14	2	54	Sp 83	52
Rigid-Heddle Weaving	Analagous Color Scheme Scarf #3 (Ardis Dolbrovolny)		√	√	Hw	2	4		Se 81	33, 93
Rigid-Heddle Weaving	Baby Blanket	Ingebretsen, Cathy	√	√	PWC	3	1	7		6
Rigid-Heddle Weaving	Beginner's Hat and Scarf	Skoy, Mary Lonning	√	√	WJ	11	3	43	Wi 87	61
Rigid-Heddle Weaving	Beyond the Fringe	Wertenberger, Kathryn	√	> 4	Hw	2	5		No 81	27
Rigid-Heddle Weaving	Bittersweet Pullover (Ardis Dobrovolny)		√	√	Hw	3	4		Se 82	48, 90
Rigid-Heddle Weaving	Blankets and Afghans on a Narrow Loom	Davenport, Betty	√	√	PWC	3	1	7		14
Rigid-Heddle Weaving	Bog Jacket, Basic Shaping	Davidsohn, Marty	√	√	PWC			3	Oc 82	35
Rigid-Heddle Weaving	Bolivian Milkmaid's Jacket (Susan Henrickson)		√	√	Hw	4	2		M/A 83	60, 97
Rigid-Heddle Weaving	Bougainvillea Jacket (Barbara Smith Eychaner)		√	√	Hw	5	1		J/F 84	43, 110
Rigid-Heddle Weaving	Chenille Polo	Xenakis, Alexis Yiorgos	√	√	PWC			6	Su 83	34
Rigid-Heddle Weaving	Clasped Weft Mats		√	√	Hw	3	1		Ja 82	35, 84
Rigid-Heddle Weaving	Complementary Scarf #6 (Ardis Dobrovolny)		√	√	Hw	2	4		Se 81	33, 93
Rigid-Heddle Weaving	Complementary Scarf #7 (Ardis Dobrovolny)		√	√	Hw	2	4		Se 81	33, 93
Rigid-Heddle Weaving	Complementary Scarf #8 (Ardis Dobrovolny)		√	√	Hw	2	4		Se 81	33, 93
Rigid-Heddle Weaving	Cotton Wrap (Sharon Alderman)		√	√	Hw	4	3		M/J 83	44, 81
Rigid-Heddle Weaving	Country Casual Afghan (Morris Percelay)		√	√	Hw	3	3		My 82	29, 88
Rigid-Heddle Weaving	Country Silk Top (Betty Davenport)		√	√	Hw	5	3		Su 84	59, 102
Rigid-Heddle Weaving	Dolman Top (Elaine Rowley)		√	√	Hw	1	2		S-S 80	45, 67
Rigid-Heddle Weaving	Double Weave on a Rigid Heddle Loom	Gaston-Voûte, Suzanne	√	√	SS&D	8	3	31	Su 77	70
Rigid-Heddle Weaving	Drapery Fabric (Constance LaLena)		√	√	Hw	3	4		Se 82	33, 84
Rigid-Heddle Weaving	Essay: The Incredible, Flexible Rigid Heddle Loom	Rotert, Bette			PWC			2	Ap 82	60
Rigid-Heddle Weaving	Fireside Throw and Pillow (Betty Davenport)		√	√	Hw	8	1		J/F 87	72, I-13
Rigid-Heddle Weaving	Fleece Rug (Elizabeth Ligon)		√	√	Hw	2	2		Mr 81	52, 80
Rigid-Heddle Weaving	Graphic Weave for a Special Occasion (Carrie Rogers)		√	√	Hw	1	2		S-S 80	38
Rigid-Heddle Weaving	Gray Jacket (Gilbert)			√	Hw	2	1		F-W 80	66
Rigid-Heddle Weaving	Guatemalan Blouse (Betty Davenport)		√	√	Hw	4	2		M/A 83	55, 94
Rigid-Heddle Weaving	Guatemalan Vest (Betty Davenport)		√	√	Hw	4	2		M/A 83	56, 93
Rigid-Heddle Weaving	Harris Tweed Jacket		√	√	Hw	2	5		No 81	49, 87
Rigid-Heddle Weaving	Indian Paintbrush Poncho (Betty Davenport)		√	√	Hw	2	4		Se 81	57, 93
Rigid-Heddle Weaving	Inkle Tape for Vest (Betty Davenport)		√	√	Hw	4	2		M/A 83	56, 93
Rigid-Heddle Weaving	Inlay We Trust Part 3: Pillow Based on Greek Inlay Technique	Herring, Connie	√	√	PWC	3	4	10		44
Rigid-Heddle Weaving	Jacket in Horizontal Cord Weave, A	Duncan, Nadine	√	√	PWC			2	Ap 82	59
Rigid-Heddle Weaving	"Karen Swanson" (Exhibit)	Sunshine, Joanna	√		Fa	4	2		M/A 77	13
Rigid-Heddle Weaving	Lace-Weave Tunic	Rowley, Elaine	√	√	PWC			5	Sp 83	18
Rigid-Heddle Weaving	Leno Vest	Lyon, Linda	√	√	PWC			6	Su 83	27
Rigid-Heddle Weaving	Log Cabin Runner (Betty Davenport)		√	√	Hw	8	5		N/D 87	42, I-4
Rigid-Heddle Weaving	Loom Shaped Top with Dukagång Inlay	Searle, Karen	√	√	WJ	11	3	43	Wi 87	8
Rigid-Heddle Weaving	Loopy Shawls (Halcyon)		√	√	Hw	1	1		F-W 79	20, 52
Rigid-Heddle Weaving	More Creative Two Harness Weaving	Liebler, Barbara	√		Iw	5	1		Wi 79	46
Rigid-Heddle Weaving	One Heddle Two-Tie Weaving	Xenakis, Athanasios David	√	√	PWC	1	1		No 81	24
Rigid-Heddle Weaving	Patterns from the Weaver's Guild		√	√	H&C	26	5		Oc 75	29
Rigid-Heddle Weaving	Poppana Runner (Janice Jones)		√	√	Hw	4	2		M/A 83	50, 88

SUBJECT	TITLE	AUTHOR	IL	INST	JOUR	VOL	NO	ISS	DATE	PAGE
Rigid-Heddle Weaving	Pride of the Harvest Shawl	Davidsohn, Marty	√	√	PWC		6		Su 83	25
Rigid-Heddle Weaving	Project in Krokbragd, A	Davenport, Betty	√	√	PWC		2		Ap 82	66
Rigid-Heddle Weaving	Quilted Vest (Susan Henrickson)		√	√	Hw	4	2		M/A 83	61, 96
Rigid-Heddle Weaving	Rainbow Heather Shawl (Pat Colony)		√	√	Hw	2	5		No 81	52, 88
Rigid-Heddle Weaving	Refreshingly Simple Runner (Betty Davenport)		√	> 4	Hw	6	3		Su 85	11, I-3
Rigid-Heddle Weaving	Ribbon Blouse (Grace Hirsch)		√	√	Hw	4	1		J/F 83	44, 88
Rigid-Heddle Weaving	Ribweave Dress Fabric (Julia Green)		√	√	Hw	3	1		Ja 82	37, 87
Rigid-Heddle Weaving	Rigid Heddle Loom, The	Davenport, Betty	√	√	SS&D	13	1	49	Wi 81	72
Rigid-Heddle Weaving	Rigid-Heddle Weaving: How to Weave More Ends per Inch	Davenport, Betty	√	√	Hw	7	3		M/J 86	68
Rigid-Heddle Weaving	Roggeband	Blinks, Anne	√	√	Iw	3	3		Sp 78	16
Rigid-Heddle Weaving	Rustic Napkins (Betty Davenport)		√	√	Hw	6	4		S/O 85	18, I-4
Rigid-Heddle Weaving	Rustic Placemats (Betty Davenport)		√	√	Hw	6	4		S/O 85	18, I-3
Rigid-Heddle Weaving	Samples—Quick & Easy!	Davenport, Betty	√	√	Hw	7	5		N/D 86	78
Rigid-Heddle Weaving	Shadow Scarves (Judy Steinkoenig)		√	√	Hw	3	4		Se 82	73
Rigid-Heddle Weaving	Shrug/Shannon Sweater/Shawl Fabric (Sharon Alderman)		√	√	Hw	2	3		My 81	87, 89
Rigid-Heddle Weaving	Small Table Runner (Betty Davenport)		√	√	Hw	1	1		F-W 79	32, 59
Rigid-Heddle Weaving	Southwest Sunrise Top (Ardis Dobrovolny)		√	√	Hw	6	3		Su 85	42, I-7
Rigid-Heddle Weaving	Split-Complementary Scarf #1 (Ardis Dobrovolny)		√	√	Hw	2	4		Se 81	33, 93
Rigid-Heddle Weaving	Split-Complementary Scarf #2 (Ardis Dobrovolny)		√	√	Hw	2	4		Se 81	33, 93
Rigid-Heddle Weaving	Stole		√	√	Hw	2	3		My 81	88, 79
Rigid-Heddle Weaving	Supplementary Warp Placemats (Betty Davenport)		√	> 4	Hw	3	3		My 82	75, 98
Rigid-Heddle Weaving	Sweater-Coat (Linda Urquhart)		√	√	Hw	4	4		S/O 83	41, 109
Rigid-Heddle Weaving	Triadic Color Scheme Scarf #4 (Ardis Dobrovolny)		√	√	Hw	2	4		Se 81	33, 93
Rigid-Heddle Weaving	Triadic Color Scheme Scarf #5 (Ardis Dobrovolny)		√	√	Hw	2	4		Se 81	33, 93
Rigid-Heddle Weaving	Two Loom-Shaped Designs for Narrow Looms (Donna Gilbert)		√	√	Hw	2	1		F-W 80	28
Rigid-Heddle Weaving	Two String Sweaters	Brugger, Susan	√	√	PWC		6		Su 83	31
Rigid-Heddle Weaving	Ultimate T-Shirt, The	Xenakis, Alexis Yiorgos	√	√	PWC		6		Su 83	29
Rigid-Heddle Weaving	Upholstery Fabric 1 (Constance LaLena)		√	√	Hw	3	4		Se 82	33, 84
Rigid-Heddle Weaving	Weaving Figured Piqué on a Loom with One Warp Beam	Xenakis, Athanasios David	√	√	PWC	4	2	12		14
Rigid-Heddle Weaving	Weaving Primer	Parks, Deborah	√	√	PWC	4	2	12		36
Rigid-Heddle Weaving	Weaving Primer	Parks, Deborah	√	√	PWC	3	4	10		4
Rigid-Heddle Weaving	Weaving Primer, Part 1	Parks, Deborah	√	√	PWC	4	1	11		44
Rigid-Heddle Weaving	Weaving Primer, Part 2	Lyon, Linda	√	> 4	PWC	4	1	11		45
Rigid-Heddle Weaving	Weaving Primer, Part 3	Xenakis, Athanasios David	√	> 4	PWC	4	1	11		46
Rigid-Heddle Weaving	What If...Vest (Betty Davenport)		√	√	Hw	5	4		S/0 84	74, 108
Rigid-Heddle Weaving	Window Pane Delivery Blanket	Mueller, Cynthia	√	√	PWC	3	1	7		8
Rigid-Heddle Weaving	Woodtones Log Cabin Afghan (Ardis Dobrovolny)		√	√	Hw	3	3		My 82	29, 88
Rigid-Heddle Weaving	Woolen Scarf	Ingebretsen, Cathy	√	√	PWC	3	1	7		7
Rigid-Heddle Weaving	Woven Reed Placemats	Ingebretsen, Cathy	√	√	PWC	3	2	8		4
Rigid-Heddle Weaving	Wrap Around Shawl (Nell Znamierowski)		√	√	Hw	2	5		No 81	50, 86
Rigid-Heddle Weaving	Yarn for the Weaving		√	√	PWC	3	1	7		21
Rigid-Heddle Weaving: Backstrap	Weaving with Rigid Heddle Backstrap Looms	Swanson, Karen	√	√	H&C	21	2		Sp 70	13
Rigid-Heddle Weaving: Block	Multiple Rigid Heddle Adventure, Part 1, The	Xenakis, Athanasios David	√	√	PWC	3	4	10		34

SUBJECT	TITLE	AUTHOR	IL	INST	JOUR	VOL	NO	ISS	DATE	PAGE
Rigid-Heddle Weaving: Block Techniques	Two Alpaca and Wool Scarves	Xenakis, Athanasios David	√	√	PWC	3	4	10		40
Rigid-Heddle Weaving: Jackets	Inlay We Trust, Part 2: Leno Inlay	Herring, Connie	√	√	PWC			6	Su 83	48
Rigid-Heddle Weaving: Linen	Woven Lace, Part 1: The Bronson Systems — Tips on Weaving with Linen, Rigid Heddle Loom	Xenakis, Athanasios David	√	√	PWC			5	Sp 83	14
Rigid-Heddle Weaving: Multiple-Heddle	Double Corduroy	Lyon, Linda	√	√	PWC	3	1	7		51
Rigid-Heddle Weaving: Multiple-Heddle	Fiesta Plaid	Xenakis, Athanasios David	√	√	PWC	3	1	7		39
Rigid-Heddle Weaving: Multiple-Heddle	Incredible Five-Color, Two-Tie Afghan for a Super Kid, The	Xenakis, Athanasios David	√	√	PWC	1	1		No 81	35
Rigid-Heddle Weaving: Multiple-Heddle	Isolated Overshot: Inlaid Runner	Xenakis, Athanasios David	√	√	PWC	3	2	8		31
Rigid-Heddle Weaving: Multiple-Heddle	Killarney	Xenakis, Athanasios David	√	> 4	PWC	3	1	7		25
Rigid-Heddle Weaving: Multiple-Heddle	Mind Boggling Bogs	Herring, Connie	√	√	PWC			3	Oc 82	36
Rigid-Heddle Weaving: Multiple-Heddle	More Moneymakers for Weavers	Klessen, Romy	√	√	PWC			2	Ap 82	9
Rigid-Heddle Weaving: Multiple-Heddle	Overshot Derived from 2/2 Twill	Xenakis, Athanasios David	√	√	PWC	3	2	8		7
Rigid-Heddle Weaving: Multiple-Heddle	Overshot Derived from 2/2 Twill: Apricot Accents	Lyon, Linda	√	√	PWC	3	2	8		21
Rigid-Heddle Weaving: Multiple-Heddle	Overshot Derived from 2/2 Twill: Joanne's Runner	Christensen, Joanne	√	√	PWC	3	2	8		24
Rigid-Heddle Weaving: Multiple-Heddle	Overshot Derived from 2/2 Twill: Ornamental Throw Rug in Overshot	Davidsohn, Marty	√	√	PWC	3	2	8		22
Rigid-Heddle Weaving: Multiple-Heddle	Overshot on Opposites: Linen Hand Towels	Xenakis, Athanasios David	√	√	PWC	3	2	8		29
Rigid-Heddle Weaving: Multiple-Heddle	Summer and Winter Revisited, Part 1: Two-Heddle Double Cloth	Xenakis, Athanasios David	√	√	PWC			2	Ap 82	61
Rigid-Heddle Weaving: Multiple-Heddle	Summer and Winter Revisited, Part 2: I. On Designing with Krokbragd, Krokbragd Mug Rugs	Lyon, Linda	√	√	PWC			2	Ap 82	63
Rigid-Heddle Weaving: Multiple-Heddle	Threading Two Rigid Heddles		√	√	Hw	7	3		M/J 86	71
Rigid-Heddle Weaving: Multiple-Heddle	Timelessly Fashionable Turkish Coat, A	Xenakis, Alexis Yiorgos	√	√	PWC	1	1		No 81	43
Rigid-Heddle Weaving: Multiple-Heddle	'Twill Skirt the Issue	Xenakis, Athanasios David	√	√	PWC	1	1		No 81	49
Rigid-Heddle Weaving: Multiple-Heddle	Woven Egmont Sweater	Klessen, Romy	√	√	PWC			2	Ap 82	83
Rigid-Heddle Weaving: Multiple-Heddle, Doup Stick	Lynn's Pillows	Tedder, Lynn	√	√	PWC	4	3	13		25
Rigid-Heddle Weaving: Multiple-Heddle, Pick-Up	Bath Towel Set, A	Xenakis, Athanasios David	√	√	PWC	1	1		No 81	24
Rigid-Heddle Weaving: Multiple-Heddle, Pick-Up	Blooming Leaf	Xenakis, Athanasios David	√	√	PWC	3	3	9		51
Rigid-Heddle Weaving: Multiple-Heddle, Pick-Up	Celtic Knot (error-corrected PWC v4 n4 i14 p33)	Xenakis, Athanasios David	√	√	PWC	4	3	13		24
Rigid-Heddle Weaving: Multiple-Heddle, Pick-Up	Christmas Miniatures, Part 1: Summer and Winter Coverlets	Lyon, Linda	√	√	PWC			3	Oc 82	50
Rigid-Heddle Weaving: Multiple-Heddle, Pick-Up	Christmas Miniatures, Part 2: Krokbragd Bellpulls (error-corrected PWC i4 83 p76)	Xenakis, Athanasios David	√	√	PWC			3	Oc 82	52
Rigid-Heddle Weaving: Multiple-Heddle, Pick-Up	Cotton Hanging — on a Chinese Folk Motif	Xenakis, Athanasios David	√	√	PWC	1	1		No 81	39

SUBJECT	TITLE	AUTHOR	IL	INST	JOUR	VOL	NO	ISS	DATE	PAGE
Rigid-Heddle Weaving: Multiple-Heddle, Pick-Up	Double Two-Tie Unit Weave: An Expansion of Options for Rigid Heddle Weaving, The	Xenakis, Athanasios David	√	√	Iw	5	1		Wi 79	39
Rigid-Heddle Weaving: Multiple-Heddle, Pick-Up	Even-Tied Overshot on a Rigid Heddle Loom	Xenakis, Athanasios David	√	√	PWC	3	3	9		46
Rigid-Heddle Weaving: Multiple-Heddle, Pick-Up	Experimenting with Color and Two-Tie Weaving on the Rigid Heddle	Niekrasz, Jennifer	√	√	PWC	4	4	14		21
Rigid-Heddle Weaving: Multiple-Heddle, Pick-Up	Fabrics That Go Bump (error-corrected PWC i4 83 p76)	Xenakis, Athanasios David	√	√	PWC			3	Oc 82	18
Rigid-Heddle Weaving: Multiple-Heddle, Pick-Up	Fantastic Finnweave, Part 1	Xenakis, Athanasios David	√	√	PWC			2	Ap 82	18
Rigid-Heddle Weaving: Multiple-Heddle, Pick-Up	Fantastic Finnweave, Part 2	Xenakis, Athanasios David	√	√	PWC			3	Oc 82	10
Rigid-Heddle Weaving: Multiple-Heddle, Pick-Up	Fantastic Finnweave, Part 3	Xenakis, Athanasios David	√	√	PWC			4	Ja 83	10
Rigid-Heddle Weaving: Multiple-Heddle, Pick-Up	Halfghan	Xenakis, Athanasios David	√	√	PWC	3	1	7		34
Rigid-Heddle Weaving: Multiple-Heddle, Pick-Up	Instructions: Pick-Up Figured Piqué (error-corrected PWC v4 n3 i13 p4)	Xenakis, Athanasios David	√	√	PWC	4	2	12		39
Rigid-Heddle Weaving: Multiple-Heddle, Pick-Up	Lynn's Pillows	Tedder, Lynn	√	√	PWC	4	3	13		25
Rigid-Heddle Weaving: Multiple-Heddle, Pick-Up	Moorman Inlay Technique, The	Searle, Karen	√	√	PWC	1	1		No 81	30
Rigid-Heddle Weaving: Multiple-Heddle, Pick-Up	Norse Kjøkken	Rowley, Elaine	√	√	PWC	3	1	7		16
Rigid-Heddle Weaving: Multiple-Heddle, Pick-Up	Paired-Thread Finnweave Projects: Five Placemats Based on a Chinese Lattice Design, The	Xenakis, Athanasios David	√	√	PWC			2	Ap 82	34
Rigid-Heddle Weaving: Multiple-Heddle, Pick-Up	Patchwork Designs in Summer and Winter	Davenport, Betty	√	√	PWC	1	1		No 81	27
Rigid-Heddle Weaving: Multiple-Heddle, Pick-Up	Pillow and Table Runner in Summer and Winter Weave	Xenakis, Athanasios David	√	√	PWC	1	1		No 81	21
Rigid-Heddle Weaving: Multiple-Heddle, Pick-Up	Quadruple Cloth on the Rigid Heddle Loom	Xenakis, Athanasios David	√	√	PWC			2	Ap 82	74
Rigid-Heddle Weaving: Multiple-Heddle, Pick-Up	Quatrefoil	Xenakis, Athanasios David	√	√	PWC	3	3	9		53
Rigid-Heddle Weaving: Multiple-Heddle, Pick-Up	Red and Blue Canvas Weave Afghan	Xenakis, Athanasios David	√	√	PWC	3	1	7		22
Rigid-Heddle Weaving: Multiple-Heddle, Pick-Up	Splendor of a Folk Warp, A (Joanne Christensen)		√	√	Hw	2	1		F-W 80	48
Rigid-Heddle Weaving: Multiple-Heddle, Pick-Up	Star and Diamond	Xenakis, Athanasios David	√	√	PWC	3	3	9		49
Rigid-Heddle Weaving: Multiple-Heddle, Pick-Up	Summer and Winter Revisited Part 4: Turned Pebble Weave	Xenakis, Athanasios David	√	√	PWC			4	Ja 83	52
Rigid-Heddle Weaving: Multiple-Heddle, Pick-Up	Summer and Winter Unharnessed	Xenakis, Athanasios David	√	√	PWC	1	1		No 81	10
Rigid-Heddle Weaving: Multiple-Heddle, Pick-Up	Tablecloth in Summer and Winter	Xenakis, Athanasios David	√	√	PWC	1	1		No 81	16
Rigid-Heddle Weaving: Multiple-Heddle, Pick-Up	Tied Overshot Boundweave	Xenakis, Athanasios David	√	√	PWC	3	4	10		9

SUBJECT	TITLE	AUTHOR	IL	INST	JOUR	VOL	NO	ISS	DATE	PAGE
Rigid-Heddle Weaving: Multiple-Heddle, Pick-Up	Two Floor Pillows for the Rigid Heddle Loom	Christensen, Joanne	√	√	Hw	2	2		Mr 81	56
Rigid-Heddle Weaving: Multiple-Heddle, Pick-Up	Unharnessing the Summer and Winter Weave	Xenakis, Athanasios David	√		Iw	4	4		Fa 79	42
Rigid-Heddle Weaving: Multiple-Heddle, Pick-Up	Waffle Pillows (David Xenakis)		√	√	Hw	1	2		S-S 80	70
Rigid-Heddle Weaving: Multiple-Heddle, Pick-Up	White on White	Lyon, Linda	√	√	PWC	3	3	9		60
Rigid-Heddle Weaving: Pick-Up	All Around — Year Around Shawl	Herring, Connie	√	√	PWC			2	Ap 82	70
Rigid-Heddle Weaving: Pick-Up	Autumn Oak Pullover (Ardis Dobrovolny)		√	√	Hw	3	4		Se 82	49, 91
Rigid-Heddle Weaving: Pick-Up	Bead Leno	Davenport, Betty	√	√	PWC			6	Su 83	62
Rigid-Heddle Weaving: Pick-Up	Blue and Gold Huiple		√	√	Hw	1	2		S-S 80	69
Rigid-Heddle Weaving: Pick-Up	Blue and White Stole (Betty Davenport) (error-corrected Hw v1 n2 80 p64)		√	√	Hw	1	1		F-W 79	36, 60
Rigid-Heddle Weaving: Pick-Up	Blue Scarf (Suzanne Gaston-Voute)		√	√	Hw	7	1		J/F 86	64, I-14
Rigid-Heddle Weaving: Pick-Up	Bronson Damask Effect, The		√	√	PWC			5	Sp 83	35
Rigid-Heddle Weaving: Pick-Up	Bronson Spot Weave System, The		√	√	PWC			5	Sp 83	20
Rigid-Heddle Weaving: Pick-Up	Camera Strap in Double-Weave Pick-Up	Gaston-Voûte, Suzanne	√	√	PWC			2	Ap 82	10
Rigid-Heddle Weaving: Pick-Up	Celtic Knot Box Cushion	Xenakis, Athanasios David	√	√	PWC	3	4	10		60
Rigid-Heddle Weaving: Pick-Up	Children's Chair Seat & Back Rest (Andrea McCormack)		√	√	Hw	3	1		Ja 82	28, 81
Rigid-Heddle Weaving: Pick-Up	Children's Weft-Face Rug (Mary Skoy)		√	√	Hw	3	1		Ja 82	28, 81
Rigid-Heddle Weaving: Pick-Up	"Chiola" India Top (Betty Davenport)		√	√	Hw	2	2		Mr 81	54, 74
Rigid-Heddle Weaving: Pick-Up	Cotton Top (Betty Davenport)		√	> 4	Hw	7	3		M/J 86	68, I-16
Rigid-Heddle Weaving: Pick-Up	Coverlet Weaves on a Rigid-Heddle (David Xenakis)		√	√	Hw	2	1		F-W 80	38
Rigid-Heddle Weaving: Pick-Up	Crocus Shawl (Betty Davenport)		√	√	Hw	2	4		Se 81	56, 84
Rigid-Heddle Weaving: Pick-Up	Delicate Dots...Petit Point Treadling	Keasbey, Doramay	√	√	Hw	7	1		J/F 86	66
Rigid-Heddle Weaving: Pick-Up	Designing Inkle Bands	Davenport, Betty	√	√	PWC			4	Ja 83	56
Rigid-Heddle Weaving: Pick-Up	Diagonal Corduroy	Xenakis, Athanasios David	√	> 4	PWC	3	4	10		51
Rigid-Heddle Weaving: Pick-Up	Different Floats for Different Folks		√	√	PWC			5	Sp 83	31
Rigid-Heddle Weaving: Pick-Up	Double Woven Mailbag with Name Tags	Verlinden, Lieve	√	√	WJ	7	1	25	Su 82	34
Rigid-Heddle Weaving: Pick-Up	Doupe Leno for the Rigid Heddle Loom	Xenakis, Athanasios David	√	√	PWC			6	Su 83	14
Rigid-Heddle Weaving: Pick-Up	Dress Yoke and Cuffs (Linda Ligon)		√	√	Hw	3	1		Ja 82	27, 87
Rigid-Heddle Weaving: Pick-Up	Fantastic Finnweave, Part 2: Single-Thread Projects	Xenakis, Athanasios David	√	√	PWC			3	Oc 82	14
Rigid-Heddle Weaving: Pick-Up	Fun with Bronson Lace Variations	Davenport, Betty	√	√	PWC			5	Sp 83	46
Rigid-Heddle Weaving: Pick-Up	Guatemalan Shirt (Betty Davenport)		√	√	Hw	2	2		Mr 81	54, 72
Rigid-Heddle Weaving: Pick-Up	Hand Towels in Overshot Effect	Davenport, Betty	√	√	PWC	3	2	8		48
Rigid-Heddle Weaving: Pick-Up	Holiday Runners	Skoy, Mary	√	√	WJ	12	2	46	Fa 87	22
Rigid-Heddle Weaving: Pick-Up	Home Weaving: Linen'n Lace	Xenaxis, Athanasios David	√	√	Hw	1	1		F-W 79	44
Rigid-Heddle Weaving: Pick-Up	Imperial Tulip and Prairie Flower		√	√	PWC			5	Sp 83	15
Rigid-Heddle Weaving: Pick-Up	Inlay We Trust, Part 1: Half Dukagång	Herring, Connie	√	√	PWC			5	Sp 83	59
Rigid-Heddle Weaving: Pick-Up	Lace Trilogy	Fauske, Carla	√	√	PWC			6	Su 83	52
Rigid-Heddle Weaving: Pick-Up	Lace Window Hanging with Plaid		√	√	PWC			5	Sp 83	27
Rigid-Heddle Weaving: Pick-Up	Lace-Weave Pullover Top (Elaine Rowley)		√	√	Hw	1	1		F-W 79	21, 56
Rigid-Heddle Weaving: Pick-Up	Leno Fabrics	Xenakis, Athanasios David	√	√	PWC			6	Su 83	18
Rigid-Heddle Weaving: Pick-Up	Leno Sampler Wallhanging (Betty Davenport)		√	√	Hw	7	2		M/A 86	47, I-8
Rigid-Heddle Weaving: Pick-Up	Lilies on an Antique Tray	Herring, Connie	√	√	PWC	4	1	11		30
Rigid-Heddle Weaving: Pick-Up	New Look at the Rigid Heddle Loom, A	Davenport, Betty	√		Iw	4	4		Fa 79	41

SUBJECT	TITLE	AUTHOR	IL	INST	JOUR	VOL	NO	ISS	DATE	PAGE
Rigid-Heddle Weaving: Pick-Up	Orchid Shawl	Xenakis, Athanasios David	√	√	PWC			5	Sp 83	38
Rigid-Heddle Weaving: Pick-Up	Parks' Bouquet	Parks, Deborah	√	√	PWC	4	1	11		36
Rigid-Heddle Weaving: Pick-Up	Red Huiple (Betty Davenport)		√	√	Hw	1	2		S-S 80	45, 68
Rigid-Heddle Weaving: Pick-Up	Red Lace Scarf (Betty Davenport)		√	√	Hw	7	1		J/F 86	63, I-13
Rigid-Heddle Weaving: Pick-Up	Rigid Heddle Wool Curtain (Betty Davenport)		√	√	Hw	2	1		F-W 80	Cover, 72
Rigid-Heddle Weaving: Pick-Up	Rio Grande Placemats (Betty Davenport)		√	√	Hw	7	4		S/O 86	57, I-11
Rigid-Heddle Weaving: Pick-Up	Shaped Silk Sheath	Xenakis, Athanasios David; Alexis Yiorgos Xenakis	√	√	PWC			6	Su 83	39
Rigid-Heddle Weaving: Pick-Up	Slightly Left of Center Jacket	Rowley, Elaine	√	√	PWC			6	Su 83	44
Rigid-Heddle Weaving: Pick-Up	Small Table Runner (Betty Davenport)		√	√	Hw	1	1		F-W 79	32, 59
Rigid-Heddle Weaving: Pick-Up	Spice Up Plain Weave with Warp Floats	Davenport, Betty	√	√	Hw	7	4		S/O 86	56
Rigid-Heddle Weaving: Pick-Up	Supplementary Warp Top (Betty Davenport)		√	√	Hw	6	1		J/F 85	34, I-8
Rigid-Heddle Weaving: Pick-Up	Table Runner in Linen		√	√	PWC			5	Sp 83	25
Rigid-Heddle Weaving: Pick-Up	Thrum Pillows (Betty Davenport)		√	√	Hw	5	5		N/D 84	66, I-10
Rigid-Heddle Weaving: Pick-Up	Translating Four-Harness Drafts for the Single Rigid Heddle Method		√	√	PWC			5	Sp 83	22
Rigid-Heddle Weaving: Pick-Up	Tulip Blouse (Betty Davenport)		√	√	Hw	8	2		M/A 87	61, I-14
Rigid-Heddle Weaving: Pick-Up	Two Alpaca and Wool Scarves	Xenakis, Athanasios David	√	√	PWC	3	4	10		40
Rigid-Heddle Weaving: Pick-Up	Two Placemats	Herring, Connie	√	√	PWC			5	Sp 83	36
Rigid-Heddle Weaving: Pick-Up	Two Tote Bags (Betty Davenport)		√	√	Hw	6	5		N/D 85	12, I-4
Rigid-Heddle Weaving: Pick-Up	Two-Tie Inlay	Xenakis, Athanasios David	√	√	PWC	4	1	11		19
Rigid-Heddle Weaving: Pick-Up	Upside-Down and Other Clever Tricks		√	> 4	PWC			5	Sp 83	29
Rigid-Heddle Weaving: Pick-Up	V-Neck Top with Lace Bands (Betty Davenport)		√	√	Hw	3	2		Mr 82	44, 80
Rigid-Heddle Weaving: Pick-Up	Variegated Scarf (Betty Davenport)		√	√	Hw	7	1		J/F 86	63, I-14
Rigid-Heddle Weaving: Pick-Up	Victorian Garden (error-corrected PWC i8 p66)	Xenakis, Athanasios David	√	√	PWC	3	1	7		31
Rigid-Heddle Weaving, Pick-Up	Waffle Weave Wool Top (Betty Davenport)		√	√	Hw	1	1		F-W 79	21, 55
Rigid-Heddle Weaving: Pick-Up	Weaving Primer	Ingebretsen, Catherine	√	√	PWC			6	Su 83	4
Rigid-Heddle Weaving: Pick-Up	Weaving Primer	Parks, Deborah	√	√	PWC	3	3	9		4
Rigid-Heddle Weaving: Pick-Up	Weaving the Night Fantastic	Lyon, Linda	√	> 4	PWC			5	Sp 83	51
Rigid-Heddle Weaving: Pick-Up	Weft Faced Pillows (Jane Patrick)		√	√	Hw	4	2		M/A 83	66, 98
Rigid-Heddle Weaving: Pick-Up	Weft-Faced and Warp-Faced		√	√	PWC			5	Sp 83	34
Rigid-Heddle Weaving: Pick-Up	White Huiple (Betty Davenport)		√	√	Hw	1	2		S-S 80	45, 68
Rigid-Heddle Weaving: Pick-Up	Wool Skirt and Shawl	Crosby, Roberta	√	√	PWC			5	Sp 83	55
Rigid-Heddle Weaving: Pick-Up	Woven Lace, Part 1: The Bronson Systems	Xenakis, Athanasios David	√	√	PWC			5	Sp 83	10
Rigid-Heddle Weaving: Pick-Up	Woven Lace, Part 1: The Bronson Systems — 4-Thread and 8-Thread Atwater-Bronson	Xenakis, Athanasios David	√	√	PWC			5	Sp 83	13
Rigid-Heddle Weaving: Pick-Up	Woven Lace, Part 1: The Bronson Systems — The Atwater-Bronson System	Xenakis, Athanasios David	√	√	PWC			5	Sp 83	12
Rigid-Heddle Weaving: Pick-Up	Wrap Around Top (Betty Davenport)		√	√	Hw	6	2		M/A 85	18, I-3
Rigid-Heddle Weaving (Two Looms)	Double Ecology Shawl	Lyon, Linda; Connie Herring; Athanasios David Xenakis	√	√	PWC	3	4	10		64
Rigid-Heddle Worksheet	Hand Towels in Overshot Effect	Davenport, Betty	√	√	PWC	3	2	8		48
Ring Shawls	Spinning a Gossamer Web	Gibson-Roberts, Priscilla A.	√	√	Kn	4	1	9	Wi 87	62
Rinktiné	Lithuanian Pervarai: Producing a Twenty Shaft Pattern on a Twelve Shaft Loom	Meek, M. Kati	√	> 4	AT	1			De 83	159

SUBJECT	TITLE	AUTHOR	IL	INST	JOUR	VOL	NO	ISS	DATE	PAGE
Ripple Weave	Weaving Ripples and Curves	Irvine, Marie M.	√	√	SS&D	12	1	45	Wi 80	52
Rippsmatta	Shadowweave, Part 2 — Unbalanced Shadowweave (error-corrected WJ v2 n1 77 insert for vol. 1)	Barrett, Clotilde	√	> 4	WJ	1	2	2	Oc 76	14
Ripsmatta	Ripsmatta Table Runner (Jean Scorgie, Dixie Straight-Allen)		√	√	Hw	8	5		N/D 87	60, I-15
Ripsmattor, Warp-Faced	Ripsmattor Table Runner (Gloria Martin)		√	√	Hw	4	3		M/J 83	Cover, 90
Ritual	Funeral	Knauer, Katherine	√		Fa	13	6		N/D 86	30
Ritual Art	Ritual and Art in Traditional Societies	Janeiro, Jan	√		Fa	13	6		N/D 86	4
Ritual Fiber	Dorothy Caldwell: Interacting with Image and Material	Duffy, Helen	√		Fa	13	6		N/D 86	22
Ritual Fiber	Haitian Voodoo Banners: Dazzling Invitations to the Spirits	Lorenzo, Lauri	√		Fa	13	6		N/D 86	11
Ritual Fiber	Jane Lackey: A Vision Into Past and Future	Corwin, Nancy	√		Fa	13	6		N/D 86	18
Ritual Fiber	Mimi Holmes: Treasure Troves of Human Conflict	Lamberson, Peggy	√		Fa	13	6		N/D 86	20
Ritual Fiber	Reiko Mochinaga Brandon: Bridging Two Cultures	Moore, Marcia	√		Fa	13	6		N/D 86	16
Ritual Fiber	Ritual Fiber: Weaving Hope for the Future Into the Fabric of Life	Wilcox, Don	√		Fa	13	6		N/D 86	7
Ritual Textiles: Chasuble	Reflections on the Chasuble	Centner, The Rev. David J., O.C.D.	√		Hw	5	1		J/F 84	36
Ritual Textiles: Ukrainian	Embroidery for the Goddess	Kelly, Mary B.	√		TM			11	J/J 87	26
Rlitual Traditions: Hawaii	Making Paper Cranes: A Hawaiian Wedding Ritual	Nakamura, Ann K.	√	√	Fa	13	6		N/D 86	9
"Robe, The"	"The Robe," is Woven on a California Handloom	Marshall, Bertha	√		H&C	4	3		Su 53	14
Robes see Kimono and Robes										
Robotic Sewing System	Robots Can Sew Too	Goodman, Deborah Lerme	√		TM			8	D/J 86	14
Rocks, Embellished	Claire Zeisler's Fragments and Dashes	Levine, Betsy	√		TM			1	O/N 85	84
Roggeband	Roggeband	Blinks, Anne	√	√	Iw	3	3		Sp 78	16
Roman (Late) Textiles	Appendix I: The Development of Interlace and Related Patterns	Trilling, James	√		TMJ	21			82	104
Roman (Late) Textiles	Drawloom Textiles in Wool and Silk (with a Structural Analysis by Ann Pollard Rowe)	Trilling, James	√		TMJ	21			82	96
Roman (Late) Textiles	Resist-Dyed Textiles	Trilling, James	√		TMJ	21			82	102
Roman (Late) Textiles	Tapestries	Trilling, James	√		TMJ	21			82	29
Roman (Late) Textiles	Textiles with Patterns in Weft-Loop Pile	Trilling, James	√		TMJ	21			82	93
Roman Textiles (England)	Roman Textiles from Vindolanda, Hexham, England	Wild, John Peter	√		TMJ	18			79	19
Romania	"Romanian Folk Textiles" (Exhibit)	Dyer, Carolyn	√		Fa	5	3		M/J 78	11
Romania	Romanian Housewife Spins a Yarn	Jones, Peter	√		S-O	8	1		Sp 84	40
Rooing	Spinning a Gossamer Web	Gibson-Roberts, Priscilla A.	√	√	Kn	4	1	9	Wi 87	62
Room Divider	Inlay Techniques	Barrett, Clotilde	√	> 4	WJ	1	1	1	Jy 76	3
Room Dividers see Blinds and Screens										
Ropes and Rope Making	Contemporary Uses for an Ancient Fiber: Spanish Moss	Elliott, Douglas B.	√	√	SS&D	9	2	34	Sp 78	51
Ropes and Rope Making	Ropes for Every Use	Piroch, Sigrid	√	√	Hw	7	4		S/O 86	14
Ropes and Rope Making	Tapestries in Rope	Smith, John	√	√	H&C	17	1		Wi 66	10
Rose Fashion see Treadling										
Rosemary	Dyes from the Herb Garden	King, Helen	√	√	TM			6	A/S 86	58
Roving	Enhance with Unspuns	Fowler, Mary Jean	√		SS&D	7	3	27	Su 76	33
Roving	"Harness Lace:" A New Leno Set-Up	Nass, Ulla	√	√	SS&D	8	2	30	Sp 77	56
Roving, Linen	Linen Rug		√	√	Hw	2	3		My 81	50, 82
Roving, Pencil	Pencil Roving		√	√	Hw	6	1		J/F 85	74
Roving, Pencil	Pencil Roving and the Navajo Ply	Adams, Brucie	√	√	Hw	6	1		J/F 85	75

SUBJECT	TITLE	AUTHOR	IL	INST	JOUR	VOL	NO	ISS	DATE	PAGE
Royalty: Needlework	Hobby of Queens, The	Rogers, Georgia M.			TM			3	F/M 86	12
Ruana	Antique Bronze Ruana (Jean Scorgie)		√	√	Hw	7	5		N/D 86	45, I-3
Ruana	Fingerwoven Ruana (Linda Ligon)		√	√	Hw	1	1		F-W 79	18, 52
Ruaña	Garments Made from Simple Patterns: A Ruana		√	√	WJ	2	3	7	Ja 78	38
Ruana	Ikat Striped Ruana and Skirt	Colton, Mary Rawcliffe	√	√	Hw	5	4		S/0 84	60
Ruaña	Ruana	Sylvan, Katherine	√	√	WJ	5	3	19	Wi 81	34
Ruana	Ruana for Beginners, A	Rose, Violet	√	√	Hw	8	4		S/O 87	48
Ruana	Ruana (Kathryn Wertenberger)		√	√	Hw	2	2		Mr 81	53, 77
Ruana	Warped-Faced Ruana	D'Ambrosio, Gina	√	√	S-O	10	2		Su 86	17
Rubber Stamp Printing	Jody Klein's Paper Quilts		√		Fa	10	1		J/F 83	44
Rubber Stamp Printing	Making a Good Impression: A Guide to Rubber Stamp Printing	Rosen, Norma	√		Fa	10	1		J/F 83	43
Rubber Stamp Printing	Words in Fiber	Rowley, Kathleen	√		Fa	11	2		M/A 84	66
Rubber Stamps	Rubber Stamp Acts: The Little Books of Marie Combs		√		Fa	8	5		S/O 81	18
Rubber Stamps	Rubber Stamping on Fabric	Goodman, Deborah Lerme	√		Fa	13	2		M/A 86	38
Rubbings: Crochet	Resemblance to Afghans; Crochet Rubbings?, A	Elliott, Sally	√		Fa	8	3		M/J 81	48
Ruching	Ruched Blouse	Bruzelius, Margaret	√	√	Kn	2	2	4	S-S 86	40
Rue	Why Bother with Natural Dyeing?	Bulbach, Stanley	√	√	TM			5	J/J 86	32
Ruffling	Vadmal: A Study Group from the Frozen North Warms up to an Ancient Technique	Larson-Fleming, Susan	√	√	WJ	10	3	39	Wi 86	26
Rugs see Floor Coverings										
Rug Weavers	Afghan Carpet Weavers		√		H&C	24	3		M/J 73	27
Rug Weavers	Alice Pickett: Rugmaker	Pickett, Alice	√		Fa	7	5		S/O 80	55
Rug Weavers	Exploring a Tradition: Navajo Rugs, Classic and Contemporary	Elliott, Malinda	√		Fa	11	3		M/J 84	32
Rug Weavers	Ginger Jolley: Inspired by Navajo Weaving	Jolley, Ginger	√		Fa	11	3		M/J 84	36
Rug Weavers	Janet Swanson	Swanson, Janet	√		Fa	7	5		S/O 80	43
Rug Weavers	Janusz Kozikowski	Kozikowski, Janusz	√		Fa	7	5		S/O 80	43
Rug Weavers	Joan Gilfallan	Gilfallan, Joan	√		Fa	7	5		S/O 80	43
Rug Weavers	Kristin Carlsen Rowley: Rugmaker	Rowley, Kristin Carlsen	√		Fa	7	5		S/O 80	52
Rug Weavers	Pearl Sunrise: Weaving the "Old Way"	Sunrise, Pearl	√		Fa	11	3		M/J 84	34
Rug Weavers	Rag Rugs: Helen Gushee Helps Keep a Tradition Alive	Woelfle, Gretchen	√		Fa	7	5		S/O 80	31
Rug Weavers	Self-supporting Workshop, A	Collingwood, Peter			H&C	15	4		Fa 64	7
Rug Weavers: Navajo	Weaving the Navajo Way	Bighorse, Tiana; Noël Bennett	√		Iw	4	1		Wi 78	12
Rug Weaving	Structure and Form in the Weaving of John Becker	Swannie, Suzanne	√		AT	6			De 86	173
Rug Weaving: Commercial	Kurdish Kilim Weaving in the Van-Hakkari District of Eastern Turkey	Landreau, Anthony N.	√	√	TMJ	3	4		De 73	27
Rug Weaving Hints	Hints on Weaving and Finishing Rugs		√	√	WJ	2	2	6	Oc 77	16
Runner	Warp-Face Runner (Gay Jensen)			√	Hw	3	3		My 82	Cover 93
Russia	Karelian Red-Picking	Ruchti, Willie Jager	√	> 4	WJ	5	2	18	Fa 80	34
Russia	Russian Costumes At The Metropolitan Museum		√		SS&D	8	3	31	Su 77	88
Rya also see Floor Coverings										
Rya	Finnish Ryijy (Rya)		√	√	Hw	8	3		M/J 87	72
Rya	How Much Yarn for the Job? Rya and Flossa	Towner, Naomi W.	√	√	SS&D	8	4	32	Fa 77	14
Rya	Reinterpreting Rya: Irma Kukkasjärvi Energizes an Ancient Technique	Ojala, Liisa Kanning	√		WJ	9	4	36	Sp 85	26
Rya	Ryijy Plus Raanu		√		SS&D	4	2	14	Sp 73	12
Ryss Technique	Why Not Try Embroidery Weaves?	Jones, Jeanetta L.	√	√	H&C	17	2		Sp 66	12

SUBJECT	TITLE	AUTHOR	IL	INST	JOUR	VOL	NO	ISS	DATE	PAGE
Sachets	Sachet for a Friend (Jane Patrick)		√	√	Hw	8	4		S/O 87	56, I-12
Sachets	Scented Sachets	Xenakis, Alexis Yiorgos	√	>4	PWC	3	2	8		56
Sachets	Six Little Sachets (Dixie Straight)		√	√	Hw	6	4		S/O 85	64, I-14
Sachets	Tetrahedron (Carol Strickler)		√	√	Hw	6	4		S/O 85	64, I-15
Sachets: Knitted	Sachets	Ellman, Norma	√	√	Kn	3	2	6	Sp 87	32
Saddle Blanket Weave, Navajo	Using the Navajo Saddle-Blanket Weave	Tergis, Marilyn	√	√	H&C	23	5		S/O 72	6
Saddle Blankets	Handspun, Handwoven Saddle Blanket, A	Newsted, Jean	√	√	WJ	8	2	30	Fa 83	22
Saddle Blankets	Navajo Saddle Blanket Patterns	Barrett, Clotilde	√	√	WJ	11	1	41	Su 86	56
Saddle Blankets	Navajo Saddle Blanket Patterns	Barrett, Clotilde	√	√	WJ	1	1	1	Jy 76	22
Saddle Blankets	Navajo Saddleblanket, The	Marquess, Joyce	√	>4	SS&D	8	3	31	Su 77	25
Saddle Blankets	New Method for Pile Weave, A	Deru, Crescent	√	>4	H&C	8	3		Su 57	16
Saddle Blankets	Saddle Blanket	Corsini, Gale	√	√	WJ	6	4	24	Sp 82	29
Saddle Blankets	Saddle Blanket (Halcyon)		√	√	Hw	2	1		F-W 80	35, 58
Saddle Blankets	Traditional Berber Weaving in Central Morocco	Forelli, Sally; Jeanette Harries	√		TMJ	4	4		77	41
Saddle Cover	Chinese Rugs	Ellis, Charles Grant	√		TMJ	2	3		De 68	35
Saddle-Blanket Weave	Hand Woven Rugs: Weaves, Four-Harness Overshot, Indian Saddle-Blanket Weave	Atwater, Mary Meigs	√	√	SCGM		29		48	18
Saddlebags	Saddlebags		√	√	S-O	5			81	58
Saddlebags	Sprang and Frame Plaiting for Garments		√	√	WJ	3	3	11	Ja 79	26
Saddlebags	Tagari: A Greek Saddlebag of Handspun Wools, The	Koster, Joan Boura	√	√	WJ	6	2	22	Fa 81	24
Saganishiki	Saganishiki	Karaki, Mihoko	√		SS&D	15	3	59	Su 84	50
Sage	Dyes from the Herb Garden	King, Helen	√	√	TM			6	A/S 86	58
Sailmaking	Piecing Cloth to Harness the Wind	Montgomery, Larry	√	√	TM			11	J/J 87	48
Sails	Carol Sabiston's Sails: An Expression of the Interaction of Sea and Land	Bellerby, Greg	√		Fa	10	3		M/J 83	16
Sails	Piecing Cloth to Harness the Wind	Montgomery, Larry	√	√	TM			11	J/J 87	48
Sails	"Space Sails: American Banners" (Exhibit)	Deyo, Diane	√		Fa	9	5		S/O 82	82
Sails, Port Townsend	Piecing Cloth to Harness the Wind	Montgomery, Larry	√	√	TM			11	J/J 87	48
Salish Weaving	Salish Weaving	Boxberger, Daniel L.	√		SS&D	13	4	52	Fa 82	30
Salish Weaving	Salish Weaving	Clark, Hilary	√	√	SS&D	3	2	10	Sp 72	12
Salish Weaving	Salish Weaving, Then and Now	Ling, Lorraine	√	√	Iw	4	1		Wi 78	38
Salt Bag	Bags	Meiling, Nancy	√	√	WJ	6	3	23	Wi 81	40
Salvaging	Minimizing Water Damage	Ziemke, Dene		√	SS&D	9	2	34	Sp 78	56
Sampler Library: Lampas Weaves	Lampas Library	Sullivan, Donna	√		PWC	5	2	16		38
Sampler Library: Piqué	Library of Loom-Controlled Patterns in Figured Piqué, A	Sellon, Patti; Athanasios David Xenakis	√	√	PWC	4	2	12		18
Samplers amd Sampling: Twill	Twill Derivative and Unit Classes	Wilson, Patricia	√	√	SS&D	3	3	11	Su 72	38
Samplers amd Sampling: Unit Weaves	Twill Derivative and Unit Classes	Wilson, Patricia	√	√	SS&D	3	3	11	Su 72	38
Samplers and Sampling	Applicant 3-86	Sullivan, Donna	√		SS&D	18	4	72	Fa 87	32
Samplers and Sampling	Beginning Weavers, More Than One Answer to Many Questions	Frey, Berta		√	H&C	14	1		Wi 63	9
Samplers and Sampling	Challenge of One Technique	Wilson, Jean	√		SS&D	3	4	12	Fa 72	36
Samplers and Sampling	Choosing the Fiber for Feltmaking	Spark, Pat	√	√	SS&D	17	4	68	Fa 86	20
Samplers and Sampling	Designing Drafts	Kurtz, Carol	√	√	SS&D	10	4	40	Fa 79	28
Samplers and Sampling	Drafting with Color	Kurtz, Carol	√	√	SS&D	11	1	41	Wi 79	10
Samplers and Sampling	If You Have Four Harnesses	Hagarty, Harriet May		√	H&C	23	5		S/O 72	16
Samplers and Sampling	Learning from the Learning Exchange	Petrini, Marcy	√	>4	SS&D	18	1	69	Wi 86	62
Samplers and Sampling	Learning Journey Starts at Home, The	Redding, Debbie	√	√	Hw	4	2		M/A 83	18
Samplers and Sampling	Mini-Course—Maxi-Success	Ziemke, Dene	√		SS&D	6	2	22	Sp 75	88
Samplers and Sampling	On the Value of Making Samples	Wertenberger, Kathryn	√		Hw	1	2		S-S 80	12
Samplers and Sampling	Sampler to Aid in Designing Fabrics, A		√	√	H&C	5	4		Fa 54	22

SUBJECT	TITLE	AUTHOR	IL	INST	JOUR	VOL	NO	ISS	DATE	PAGE
Samplers and Sampling	Sampling Draft	Wilson, Particia		√	SS&D	2	2	6	Sp 71	12
Samplers and Sampling	Sett and the Hand of the Fabric	Roth, Bettie G.	√	√	SS&D	12	3	47	Su 81	16
Samplers and Sampling	Suggestions for the Beginning Weaver	Gulick, Evelyn M.	√	√	H&C	19	1		Wi 68	12
Samplers and Sampling	Swedish Workshop		√	√	H&C	12	4		Fa 61	12
Samplers and Sampling	Theme and Variations	Bress, Helene	√	√	Hw	6	2		M/A 85	62
Samplers and Sampling: Andean Tubular Trim	Special Andean Tubular Trim—Woven Without Heddles, A	Cahlander, Adele; Ed Franquemont; Barbara Bergman	√	√	WJ	6	3	23	Wi 81	54
Samplers and Sampling: Bedspread Fabric	Bedspread Fabric	Skreko, Margaret	√	>4	CW	1	3	3	Ap 80	8
Samplers and Sampling: Bobbin Lace	Bobbin Lace — Just Twist, Cross, and Throw	Southard, Doris	√	√	SS&D	5	3	19	Su 74	77
Samplers and Sampling: Bound Weave	Boundweave	Evans, Jane	√	√	WJ	1	4	4	Ap 77	3
Samplers and Sampling: Bound Weave	Small Project in Bound Weave for Beginners, A	Krasnoff, Julienne H.	√	√	H&C	20	3		Su 69	13
Samplers and Sampling: Bound Weave	Studies in Boundweave	Mershon, Janis	√	√	SS&D	12	2	46	Sp 81	50
Samplers and Sampling: Brocade	Decorative Weft on a Plain Weave Ground, Two Shaft Inlay and Brocade		√	√	WJ	5	4	20	Sp 81	15
Samplers and Sampling: Brocade	Supplementary Warp (Warp Brocade)	Wertenberger, Kathryn	√	>4	Hw	7	1		J/F 86	80
Samplers and Sampling: Checks and Plaids	Woolens and Tweeds: Designing Woolen Fabrics: New Designs for Woolens	Tidball, Harriet	√	√	SCGM		4		61	38
Samplers and Sampling: Color and 2-Tie Weaving	Experimenting with Color and Two-Tie Weaving on the Rigid Heddle	Niekrasz, Jennifer	√	√	PWC	4	4	14		21
Samplers and Sampling: Color and Weave Effects	Color and Weave Effects with Four Harness Summer and Winter		√	√	WJ	5	2	18	Fa 80	24
Samplers and Sampling: Color and Weave Effects	Color-and-Weave Effects	Wertenberger, Kathryn	√	>4	Hw	5	2		M/A 84	36
Samplers and Sampling: Color Gamp	Color-Order Gamp	Strickler, Carol	√	√	lw	2	4		Su 77	24
Samplers and Sampling: Color Gamp	Sampling	Strickler, Carol	√	√	lw	2	3		Sp 77	24
Samplers and Sampling: Color Gamp	Weave Color: A Color Sampler (Carol Strickler)		√	√	Hw	1	1		F-W 79	8
Samplers and Sampling: Color Sampler	Primary Patterns	Spoering, Kathy	√	√	WJ	9	1	33	Su 84	53
Samplers and Sampling: Combined Structures	Four Harness Straight Draw and Combination Weaves		√	>4	WJ	4	2	14	Oc 79	22
Samplers and Sampling: Coverlet Patterns	Overshot Sampler Bedspread for a Narrow Loom, An	Keasbey, Doramay	√	√	PWC	5	1	15		42
Samplers and Sampling: Coverlets	Coverlet Weaving	Williams, Ann	√	√	SS&D	14	4	56	Fa 83	32
Samplers and Sampling: Crackle	Crackle		√	√	WJ	3	3	11	Ja 79	32
Samplers and Sampling: Crackle Weave	Crackle Weave and Its Possible Variations	Snyder, Mary E.	√	>4	H&C	13	1		Wi 62	13
Samplers and Sampling: Crackle Weave	Multiple Harness Crackle		√	>4	WJ	4	1	13	Jy 79	15
Samplers and Sampling: District Checks	Scottish District Checks	Snyder, Mary E.	√	√	H&C	16	2		Sp 65	9
Samplers and Sampling: Diversified Plain Weave	Diversified Plain Weave	Wertenberger, Kathryn	√	>4	Hw	8	5		N/D 87	62
Samplers and Sampling: Double Weave	Double Weave, Finnweave and Mexican Variations	Frey, Berta	√	√	H&C	12	2		Sp 61	12
Samplers and Sampling: Double Weave	Double Weave, First Steps in Development	Hausner, Walter	√	>4	H&C	15	2		Sp 64	10
Samplers and Sampling: Double Weave	Double Weaves	Zielinski, S. A.; Robert Leclerc, ed.	√	√	MWL	15			'51–'73	9
Samplers and Sampling: Double Weave	Double-Weave Pick-Up	Neely, Cynthia H.	√	√	TM			8	D/J 86	36
Samplers and Sampling: Double Weave	Four Harness Double Width Weaving	Frey, Berta	√	√	H&C	12	1		Wi 61	6

SUBJECT	TITLE	AUTHOR	IL	INST	JOUR	VOL	NO	ISS	DATE	PAGE
Samplers and Sampling: Drawn Threadwork	Drawn Threadwork	Duroy, Marie-Pierre	√	√	TM			8	D/J 86	41
Samplers and Sampling: Exchange	Sample Exchange		√	√	H&C	17	3		Su 66	12
Samplers and Sampling: Fabric Structures	Color Related Decorating Textiles; Rugs, Draperies, Upholstery: Upholstery Fabrics, Fabric Structure	Rhodes, Tonya Stalons; Harriet Tidball, ed.		√	SCGM		14		65	7
Samplers and Sampling: Fabrics, Upholstery	Color Related Decorating Textiles; Rugs, Draperies, Upholstery: Upholstery Fabrics, Upholstery Samples	Rhodes, Tonya Stalons; Harriet Tidball, ed.		√	SCGM		14		65	6
Samplers and Sampling: Finger-Controlled Weaves	Finger Control: Or Getting the Most Out of Your Loom	Patrick, Jane	√	√	Hw	4	2		M/A 83	70
Samplers and Sampling: Finishing	Finishing Notes		√		Hw	2	5		No 81	53
Samplers and Sampling: Finnish Lace	Finnish Lace: a Leno Variation	Egen, Su	√	√	Hw	7	2		M/A 86	49
Samplers and Sampling: Finnweave	Fantastic Finnweave, Part 1	Xenakis, Athanasios David	√	√	PWC			2	Ap 82	18
Samplers and Sampling: Finnweave	Finnweave	Barrett, Clotilde	√	>4	WJ	11	4	44	Sp 87	25
Samplers and Sampling: Huck	Sampler in 8-Harness Huck		√	>4	H&C	12	2		Sp 61	49
Samplers and Sampling: Knitted Finishes	Sampler of Knit Edgings and Applied Trims, A	Newton, Deborah	√	√	TM			12	A/S 87	38
Samplers and Sampling: Lace, Leno	Figured Bead Leno Lace	Merritt, Elveana	√	√	WJ	6	1	21	Su 81	50
Samplers and Sampling: Lace Weaves	Lace Medley	Drooker, Penelope	√		Hw	5	3		Su 84	78
Samplers and Sampling: Lampas	David's Back...And Picks Up Where He Left Off	Xenakis, Athanasios David	√	>4	PWC	5	2	16		42
Samplers and Sampling: Lampas	Lampas for Eight	Sullivan, Donna	√	>4	PWC	5	2	16		34
Samplers and Sampling: Leno	Pick-Up Leno, A Two-harness Loom Technique	Wallace, Meg	√	√	WJ	1	2	2	Oc 76	3
Samplers and Sampling: Leno	Unusual Ways with Leno	Davenport, Betty	√	√	Hw	7	2		M/A 86	46
Samplers and Sampling: Leno, Bead	Bead Leno	Wertenberger, Kathryn	√	>4	Hw	8	2		M/A 87	88
Samplers and Sampling: Leno, Doup	Doup Leno: Drafts for Multiple Harness Looms	Skowronski, Hella; Sylvia Tacker	√	>4	SCGM		32		80	36
Samplers and Sampling: Leno, Doup	Doup Leno (error-corrected WJ v3 n2 78 insert p38a)		√	√	WJ	3	2	10	Oc 78	32
Samplers and Sampling: Leno, Doup	Doup Leno: Sample Project	Skowronski, Hella; Sylvia Tacker	√	√	SCGM		32		80	16
Samplers and Sampling: Log Cabin	Log Cabin Effects for the Rigid Heddle Loom	Davenport, Betty Lynn	√	√	Hw	8	5		N/D 87	42
Samplers and Sampling: Overshot	Overshot Treadling Sampler	Strickler, Carol	√	√	Iw	3	3		Sp 78	45
Samplers and Sampling: Overshot Gamp	Overshot Gamp, An	Strickler, Carol	√	√	Iw	3	2		Wi 78	35
Samplers and Sampling: Pebble Weave	Double-Woven Treasures from Old Peru	Cahlander, Adele	√	√	PWC			4	Ja 83	36
Samplers and Sampling: Plaids	Plaids (error-corrected Hw v5 n1 84 p7)	Wertenberger, Kathryn	√	√	Hw	4	5		N/D 83	50
Samplers and Sampling: Pleats, Knitted	Pleats in Hand-Knit Fabrics	Newton, Deborah	√	√	Kn	3	2	6	Sp 87	23
Samplers and Sampling: Preparing Cards	Textile Structure and Analysis, A Home Study Course in Twelve Lessons: Woven Diagrams, Materials and Equipment	Tidball, Harriet		√	SCGM		18		66	3
Samplers and Sampling: Preparing Cards	Textile Structure and Analysis, A Home Study Course in Twelve Lessons: Preparing Card for the Woven Diagram	Tidball, Harriet		√	SCGM		18		66	6
Samplers and Sampling: Rigid-Heddle Weaving	Rigid-Heddle Weaving: How to Weave More Ends per Inch	Davenport, Betty	√	√	Hw	7	3		M/J 86	68
Samplers and Sampling: Rigid-Heddle Weaving	Samples—Quick & Easy!	Davenport, Betty	√	√	Hw	7	5		N/D 86	78
Samplers and Sampling: Rigid-Heddle Weaving	Weaving with Rigid Heddle Backstrap Looms	Swanson, Karen	√	√	H&C	21	2		Sp 70	13

SUBJECT	TITLE	AUTHOR	IL	INST	JOUR	VOL	NO	ISS	DATE	PAGE
Samplers and Sampling: Rug Techniques	Another Loom Another Tote Bag, Rug Sampler Project for Beginners	Krasnoff, Julienne	√	√	H&C	22	1		Wi 71	32
Samplers and Sampling: Rugs	Make a Basic Rug Sampler	Karlin, Edith	√	√	SS&D	3	3	11	Su 72	30
Samplers and Sampling: Rugs	Rugweaving: Teaching on Two Harnesses	Mattera, Joanne	√	√	lw	5	1		Wi 79	27
Samplers and Sampling: Rugs, Pile	Color Related Decorating Textiles; Rugs, Draperies, Upholstery: Double Corduroy Pile Rugs, Set-Up and Weaving	Rhodes, Tonya Stalons; Harriet Tidball, ed.	√	√	SCGM		14		65	2
Samplers and Sampling: Shadow Weave	Shadow Weave	Wertenberger, Kathryn	√	>4	Hw	8	1		J/F 87	76
Samplers and Sampling: Shadow Weave	Shadow Weave Offers an Opportunity for Many Variations	Powell, Marian	√	√	H&C	12	3		Su 61	20
Samplers and Sampling: Shaft-Switching	Shaft-Switching on 3-end Drafts: Striped Patterns, Part 2		√	√	WJ	6	2	22	Fa 81	16
Samplers and Sampling: Soumak	Make a Soumak Sampler Into a Tote Bag		√	√	WJ	2	2	6	Oc 77	28
Samplers and Sampling: Stitchery	Sampler of Contemporary Stitchery, A		√		Fa	12	2		M/A 85	31
Samplers and Sampling: Stitchery	Stitch in Time, A	Harris, Patricia; David Lyon	√		Fa	12	2		M/A 85	27
Samplers and Sampling: Stripes	Stripe Study Group, A		√	√	Hw	4	2		M/A 83	24
Samplers and Sampling: Summer and Winter	Rugs Woven on Summer and Winter Threading		√	>4	WJ	3	1	9	Jy 78	12
Samplers and Sampling: Summer and Winter	Summer and Winter on More Than Four Shafts		√	>4	Hw	8	5		N/D 87	88
Samplers and Sampling: Summer and Winter	Summer and Winter Treadling Gamp, A	Strickler, Carol	√	√	lw	3	4		Su 78	43
Samplers and Sampling: Summer and Winter	Summer and Winter Unharnessed	Xenakis, Athanasios David	√	√	PWC	1	1		No 81	10
Samplers and Sampling: Supplementary Warp Patterning	Supplementary Warp Patterning: The Experimental Method	Tidball, Harriet	√	>4	SCGM		17		66	20
Samplers and Sampling: Swap	Yankee Weavers		√	√	SS&D	1	1	1	De 69	5
Samplers and Sampling: Tapestry	Introduction to Tapestry, An (error-corrected SS&D v8 n2 77 p51)	Pierucci, Louise	√	√	SS&D	7	4	28	Fa 76	69
Samplers and Sampling: Tapestry	Introduction to Tapestry, Part 2, An	Pierucci, Louise	√	√	SS&D	8	1	29	WI 76	73
Samplers and Sampling: Tapestry	Techniques of Tapestry Weaves Part 2: Making a Sampler	O'Callaghan, Kate	√	√	WJ	4	4	16	Ap 80	45
Samplers and Sampling: Tapestry	Techniques of Tapestry Weaves Part 3: Shading and Other Matters	O'Callaghan, Kate	√	√	WJ	5	1	17	Su 80	29
Samplers and Sampling: Tapestry, Coptic	Textiles of Coptic Egypt	Hoskins, Nancy Arthur	√	√	WJ	12	1	45	Su 87	58
Samplers and Sampling: Tapestry, Norwegian	Aklae: Norwegian Tapestry	Irlbeck, Sonja	√	√	WJ	8	1	29	Su 83	27
Samplers and Sampling: Tapestry/Tabby	Textiles of Coptic Egypt	Hoskins, Nancy Arthur	√	√	WJ	12	1	45	Su 87	58
Samplers and Sampling: Texture	First Step in Designing Textures, A	Hausner, Walter	√	√	H&C	9	2		Sp 58	14
Samplers and Sampling: Twill	Eight-Shaft Twill Sampler, An	Strickler, Carol	√	>4	lw	6	1		Wi 80	52
Samplers and Sampling: Twill	Multiple Harness Weaving Course — Part 2: Twills and Satins, With Contribution by Nancy Searles		√	>4	WJ	4	4	16	Ap 80	16
Samplers and Sampling: Twill	Techniques for Better Weaving (error-corrected TM i9 D/J 86 p4)	Osterkamp, Peggy	√	√	TM			7	O/N 86	42
Samplers and Sampling: Twill	Twill "Sampler" to Wear, A	Bohannan, Ronnine	√		Hw	6	5		N/D 85	44
Samplers and Sampling: Twill	Variations on a Twill Theme: No. 1	Marston, Ena	√	√	SS&D	5	1	17	Wi 73	34
Samplers and Sampling: Twill Derivatives	Multiple Harness Weaving Course Part 4: Twill Derivatives (cont'd)	Searles, Nancy M.	√	>4	WJ	5	2	18	Fa 80	19
Samplers and Sampling: Twill Gamp	Sampling	Strickler, Carol	√	√	lw	3	1		Fa 77	43
Samplers and Sampling: Twills, Plaited	Plaited twills		√	>4	WJ	7	4	28	Sp 83	76
Samplers and Sampling: Twining	Danish Twined Rag Rugs: Lillie Sherwood's Legacy	Irwin, Bobbie	√	√	WJ	10	4	40	Sp 86	32
Samplers and Sampling: Twining	Peruvian Weft Twining	Schira, Cynthia	√	√	H&C	17	3		Su 66	14
Samplers and Sampling: Two-Shaft Weaves	Two-harness Weaves	Clark, Marion L.	√	√	H&C	14	2		Sp 63	17

SUBJECT	TITLE	AUTHOR	IL	INST	JOUR	VOL	NO	ISS	DATE	PAGE
Samplers and Sampling: Unusual Materials	Unusual Materials for Warp or Weft	Wertenberger, Kathryn	√	>4	Hw	7	4		S/O 86	78
Samplers and Sampling: Waffle Weave	Waffle Weave	Wertenberger, Kathryn	√	>4	Hw	8	4		S/O 87	83
Samplers and Sampling: Warping Cards	Textile Structure and Analysis, A Home Study Course in Twelve Lessons: Warping the Cards	Tidball, Harriet	√	√	SCGM		18		66	7
Samplers and Sampling: Warping Cards, Special Projects	Textile Structure and Analysis, A Home Study Course in Twelve Lessons: Warping for Special Problems	Tidball, Harriet	√	√	SCGM		18		66	8
Samplers and Sampling: Weaving	From Sample to Finished Product	Keasbey, Doramay	√	>4	SS&D	15	3	59	Su 84	62
Samplers and Sampling: Weaving	Importance of Samples, The	Frey, Berta	√	√	H&C	7	3		Su 56	13
Samplers and Sampling: Weaving	Woven Samplers	Spencer, Elsie H.	√	>4	H&C	17	4		Fa 66	16
Samplers and Sampling: Weaving, Brocade	Brocade: Sampling and Designing	Tidball, Harriet	√	√	SCGM		22		67	13
Samplers and Sampling: Weaving the Cards	Textile Structure and Analysis, A Home Study Course in Twelve Lessons: Weaving the Cards	Tidball, Harriet	√	√	SCGM		18		66	11
Samplers and Sampling: Weaving, Yarn-Twist Variations	Composition and Designing: Patterns in Twist	Zielinski, S. A.; Robert Leclerc, ed.	√	√	MWL	18			'51–'73	75
San Blas Islands	Cuna Cachi: A Study of Hammock Weaving Among the Cuna Indians of the San Blas Islands	Lambert, Anne M.	√	√	AT	5			Ju 86	105
San Blas Islands	Ethnic Textile Art at U.C.L.A. — "Yer Dailege: Kuna Women's Art" (Exhibit)	Dyer, Carolyn	√		Fa	8	2		M/A 81	59
San Blas Islands	Making Molas: Four Basic Techniques	Patera, Charlotte	√		Fa	8	5		S/O 81	38
San Blas Islands	Molas	La Pierre, Sharon	√		TM			14	D/J 87	48
San Francisco Tapestry Workshop	San Francisco Tapestry Workshop: A European-Style Atelier in the United States, The	Rowley, Kathleen	√		Fa	10	3		M/J 83	60
Sansevieria (Bowstring Hemp)	Survey of Leaf and Stem Fibers, A	Buchanan, Rita	√		S-O	10	3		Fa 86	24
Sardinia	Design Award to Isabel Scott Fabrics for Exclusive Sardinian Import		√		H&C	13	2		Sp 62	16
Sardinia	Sardinian Debut, Colorful Tapestries and Rugs Interest American Weavers	Balkin, Emanuel	√		H&C	13	1		Wi 62	21
Sari	Banares Brocade	DuBois, Emily	√	>4	AT	3			My 85	209
Sari	Textile Arts of India	Bernier, Ronald M.	√		WJ	2	1	5	Jy 77	31
Sari	Web of India, The	Malarcher, Patricia	√		SS&D	13	2	50	Sp 82	38
Sari (Patolu, Wedding Sari)	Patolu and Its Techniques	De Bone, Mary Golden	√	√	TMJ	4	3		76	49
Sarongs	Van Zuylen Batik, Pekalongan, Central Java (1890-1946)	de Raadt-Apell, M. J.	√		TMJ	19 20			80,81	75
Sashes see Bands, Belts, Sashes										
Sashiko	Hiroko Ogawa: Keeping Alive the Art of Sashiko	Scarborough, Jessica	√		Fa	12	2		M/A 85	12
Sateen	More About Fabrics: Satins and Sateens	Zielinski, S. A.; Robert Leclerc, ed.	√	>4	MWL	20			'51–'73	11
Satin	Composition and Designing Part 2: Random Satins	Zielinski, S. A.; Robert Leclerc, ed.	√	>4	MWL	19			'51–'73	83
Satin	Contemporary Satins: The Satin Interval	Tidball, Harriet	√	>4	SCGM		7		62	2
Satin	Damask	Nyquist, Jan	√	>4	CW	8	1	22	Se 86	3
Satin	Designing Damask	Nyquist, Jan	√	>4	SS&D	10	4	40	Fa 79	16
Satin	Felted Jacket	Bennett, Siiri	√	>4	WJ	9	1	33	Su 84	49
Satin	Long Eyed Heddles	Ahrens, Jim	√	>4	CW	6	1	16	Se 84	3
Satin	Moneymakers for Weavers	Klessen, Romy	√	√	PWC	1	1		No 81	5
Satin	More About Fabrics: Satins and Sateens	Zielinski, S. A.; Robert Leclerc, ed.	√	>4	MWL	20			'51–'73	11
Satin	Multiple Harness Weaving Course — Part 2: Twills and Satins, With Contribution by Nancy Searles		√	>4	WJ	4	4	16	Ap 80	16
Satin	Multiple Shaft Weaving, Twill and Satin Blocks, Damask		√	>4	WJ	5	4	20	Sp 81	10

SUBJECT	TITLE	AUTHOR	IL	INST	JOUR	VOL	NO	ISS	DATE	PAGE
Satin	Qotny & Alaga: Traditional Striped Fabrics for the Middle Eastern Kaftan	El-Homossani, M. M.	√	>4	WJ	10	1	37	Su 85	33
Satin	Satin — The Designer Weave	Nyquist, Jan	√	>4	CW	7	3	21	My 86	15
Satin	Satin — The Designer Weave (error-corrected SS&D v10 n4 79 p66)	Nyquist, Janet	√	>4	SS&D	10	3	39	Su 79	77
Satin	Satin Weave Evening Bag	Lodge, Jean	√	>4	WJ	10	1	37	Su 85	39
Satin	Satin--On Four	Howard, Miranda	√	√	Hw	2	3		My 81	34
Satin	Slipcover Fabric #1 (Constance LaLena)		√	>4	Hw	4	3		M/J 83	50, 85
Satin	Textile Structure and Analysis, A Home Study Course in Twelve Lessons: Lessons in Weave Structure, 4. Satin	Tidball, Harriet		>4	SCGM		18		66	25
Satin	Verticals	O'Shaughnessy, Marjorie	√	>4	SS&D	15	1	57	Wi 83	8
Satin	Vestment Variations: A Weaver From the Netherlands Creates Garments for the Ecclesiastical Calendar	Jansen, Netty	√	>4	WJ	10	3	39	Wi 86	53
Satin, Compound	Contemporary Satins: Compound Satin	Tidball, Harriet	√	>4	SCGM		7		62	9
Satin, Contemporary	Contemporary Satins: History	Tidball, Harriet	√	√	SCGM		7		62	1-33
Satin, Contemporary	Contemporary Satins: Technical Problems	Tidball, Harriet		√	SCGM		7		62	21
Satin, Damask	Roller Shade for Window, Fabric #1 (Constance LaLena)		√	>4	Hw	7	2		M/A 86	64, I-12
Satin, Damask	Upholstery and Bed Covering Fabric, Fabric #3 (Constance LaLena)		√	>4	Hw	7	2		M/A 86	64, I-12
Satin, Damask	Upholstery Fabric, Fabric #2 (Constance LaLena)		√	>4	Hw	7	2		M/A 86	64, I-12
Satin, Damask, Mock	Gang: Technical and Conceptual Applications to Loom Controlled Weave Structures	Towner, Naomi Whiting	√	>4	AT	5			Ju 86	91
Satin, Derivatives	Satin — The Designer Weave	Nyquist, Jan	√	>4	CW	7	3	21	My 86	15
Satin, Double	Contemporary Satins: Double Satin	Tidball, Harriet	√	>4	SCGM		7		62	10
Satin, False	Horizon Striped Tunic (Mary Martinez)		√	√	Hw	3	4		Se 82	65, 92
Satin, Half-	Introduction to Tied Unit Weaves, An	Kelly, Jacquie	√	>4	PWC	4	4	14		40
Satin, Half-	Splendor of a Folk Warp, A (Joanne Christensen)		√	√	Hw	2	1		F-W 80	48
Satin, Half-, System	Handloom Weaves: The Classification of Handloom Weaves, The Structural Group, Unit Class, Half-Satin System	Tidball, Harriet	√	>4	SCGM		33		57	24
Satin, Irregular	Contemporary Satins: Irregular Satin	Tidball, Harriet	√	>4	SCGM		7		62	11
Satin, Long-Eyed Heddles	Satin and Long-Eyed Heddles	Hoskins, Janet A.; W. D. Hoskins	√	>4	WJ	6	1	21	Su 81	25
Satin, Stitching Sequence Order	Simple Methods for Deriving Satin Stitching Sequences and Damask Tie-Ups	Xenakis, A. David	√	>4	CW	6	1	16	Se 84	19
Satin, Surface Interest	Surface Interest — Textiles of Today: Surface Interest Designs with Drafts, Group 3, Two-Surface Designs	Tidball, Harriet	√	>4	SCGM		2		61	13
Satin-Base Weave	Original Fabrics of Kaftan, The	El-Homossani, M. M.	√	>4	AT	1			De 83	263
Satin-Sateen: Pick-Up	Painting and Brocading on the Loom	Ziek, Bhakti	√	√	TM		6		A/S 86	42
Satin/Sateen	Computers and Weavers: Software Is Just Another Tool in the Designer's Hand	Hoskins, Janet A.	√		TM		9		F/M 87	51
Satinet	More About Fabrics: Satins and Sateens	Zielinski, S. A.; Robert Leclerc, ed.	√	>4	MWL	20			'51–'73	11
Satinet Technique	Fascination of Twills (Fourshafts): Broken Twill and Satinet	Zielinski, S. A.; Robert Leclerc, ed.	√	√	MWL	9			'51–'73	89
Saudi Arabia	Weaving of Saudi Arabia		√		SS&D	14	2	54	Sp 83	20
Savory	Dyes from the Herb Garden	King, Helen	√	√	TM		6		A/S 86	58
Scaffold Weaving	Peru, Textiles Unlimited: Scaffold, Patchwork, or Interlocked Warp	Tidball, Harriet	√		SCGM		25		68	28
Scaffold Weaving	Peru, Textiles Unlimited: Scaffold, Patchwork, or Interlocked Warp	Tidball, Harriet	√		SCGM		25		68	28

SUBJECT	TITLE	AUTHOR	IL	INST	JOUR	VOL	NO	ISS	DATE	PAGE
Scaffold Weaving	Scaffold Weaving: A Contemporary Garment Inspired by an Ancient Technique	Searle, Karen	√	√	WJ	10	2	38	Fa 85	65
Scaffolding	Archeological Rags	Hickman, Pat	√		Fa	9	1		J/F 82	70
Scaffolding Technique	Interlocking Warp and Weft in the Nasca 2 Style	Rowe, Ann Pollard	√		TMJ	3	3		De 72	67
Scandinavia	Card Woven Belt of East Telemark—An Adaptation of a Traditional Norwegian Technique	Nelson, Lila	√	√	WJ	9	1	33	Su 84	30
Scandinavia	Contemporary Textile Art in Scandinavia	Talley, Charles S.	√		Fa	9	6		N/D 82	43
Scandinavia	Harts and Flowers: Sweden's Märta Määs-Fjetterstrom's Designs Inspired a Textile Renaissance	Selkurt, Claire	√		WJ	9	4	36	Sp 85	30
Scandinavia	Immigrant Memories	Butcher-Younghans, Sherry	√		WJ	9	4	36	Sp 85	44
Scandinavia	Krossvefnadur (rölakan) _ A Nordic Tapestry Technique		√	√	Hw	8	3		M/J 87	66
Scandinavia	Mystery of Pile Rugs, The	Austin, Carole	√		Fa	13	6		N/D 86	1
Scandinavia	Peripatetic Weaver, The	Schobinger, Helen J.	√		H&C	1	1		Ap 50	12
Scandinavia	Picture Lace	Larson-Fleming, Susan	√		WJ	9	4	36	Sp 85	42
Scandinavia	Reinterpreting Rya: Irma Kukkasjärvi Energizes an Ancient Technique	Ojala, Liisa Kanning	√		WJ	9	4	36	Sp 85	26
Scandinavia	Revival of Double Weave in Scandinavia	Schrum, Louaine M.	√	√	H&C	8	1		Wi 56	22
Scandinavia	Scandinavia Revisited: Reflections on the Weaver's Art	Talley, Charles	√		Hw	8	3		M/J 87	32
Scandinavia	Scandinavian Designs for American Looms	Freeman, Claire	√		H&C	3	2		Sp 52	14
Scandinavia	Scandinavian Nålbinding: Needle Looped Fabric	Martinson, Kate	√	√	WJ	12	2	46	Fa 87	12
Scandinavia	"Scandinavian Touch, The" A Traveling Exhibit (Exhibit)	Mattera, Joanna	√		Fa	10	1		J/F 83	82
Scandinavia	Textile Resource Guide to the Nordic Countries, A	Talley, Charles	√		Hw	8	3		M/J 87	77
Scandinavia	Toothbrush Handle Rugs: Nålbinding with Rags	Nelson, Lila	√	√	WJ	12	2	46	Fa 87	16
Scandinavian	Firfletting Fringe Treatment from Norway	Searle, Karen	√	√	WJ	9	4	36	Sp 85	40
Scarves, Shawls, Stoles	Accessories: Children's Scarves		√	√	WJ	2	4	8	Ap 78	5
Scarves, Shawls, Stoles	Accessories: Man's Scarf		√	√	WJ	4	3	15	Ja 80	40
Scarves, Shawls, Stoles	All Around — Year Around Shawl	Herring, Connie	√	> 4	PWC			2	Ap 82	70
Scarves, Shawls, Stoles	Alpaca Stripe Scarf (Chris Switzer) (error-corrected Hw v2 n2 81 p68)		√	√	Hw	2	1		F-W 80	55, 80
Scarves, Shawls, Stoles	Analagous Color Scheme Scarf #3 (Ardis Dolbrovolny)		√	√	Hw	2	4		Se 81	33, 93
Scarves, Shawls, Stoles	Arctic Handknitted, One Hundred Per Cent Qiviut	Griffiths, Helen M.	√		H&C	22	2		Sp 71	6
Scarves, Shawls, Stoles	Baby Camel Down and Tussah Scarf		√	√	Hw	7	4		S/O 86	67, I-13
Scarves, Shawls, Stoles	Balenciago: The Architect of Elegant Clothing	Koda, Harold	√		TM			11	J/J 87	20
Scarves, Shawls, Stoles	Bead Leno	Davenport, Betty	√	√	PWC			6	Su 83	62
Scarves, Shawls, Stoles	Beginner's Hat and Scarf	Skoy, Mary Lonning	√	√	WJ	11	3	43	Wi 87	61
Scarves, Shawls, Stoles	Blue and Maroon Alpaca Plaid		√	√	Hw	4	5		N/D 83	46, 98
Scarves, Shawls, Stoles	Blue and White Stole (Betty Davenport) (error-corrected Hw v1 n2 80 p64)		√	√	Hw	1	1		F-W 79	36, 60
Scarves, Shawls, Stoles	Blue Scarf (Suzanne Gaston-Voute)		√	√	Hw	7	1		J/F 86	64, I-14
Scarves, Shawls, Stoles	Blue/Green Brushed Mohair		√	√	Hw	4	5		N/D 83	46, 96
Scarves, Shawls, Stoles	Bouquet of Shawls, A	Templeton, Peg	√	√	Hw	5	3		Su 84	75
Scarves, Shawls, Stoles	Boxed Rainbows: What to Do with a Dye Kit	Bliss, Anne	√	√	Hw	4	2		M/A 83	68
Scarves, Shawls, Stoles	Brushed Neutrals		√	√	Hw	4	5		N/D 83	46, 96
Scarves, Shawls, Stoles	Caps, Hats, Mittens, Gloves, Scarves, Socks Contest Winners				S-O	10	3		Fa 86	13

SUBJECT	TITLE	AUTHOR	IL	INST	JOUR	VOL	NO	ISS	DATE	PAGE
Scarves, Shawls, Stoles	Cashmere Challenge, The	Urbanek, Karen	√	√	S-O	10	1		Sp 86	37
Scarves, Shawls, Stoles	Casual But Chic		√	> 4	WJ	8	4	32	Sp 84	70
Scarves, Shawls, Stoles	Catalogue of Kashmir Shawls in The Textile Museum	Mikosch, Elisabeth	√		TMJ	24			85	23
Scarves, Shawls, Stoles	Chaos in the Kitchen: Part 1	Gerber, Willi; Fred Gerber	√	√	SS&D	5	3	19	Su 74	70
Scarves, Shawls, Stoles	Chevron Twill Scarf (M. Linda Whitten)		√	√	Hw	7	4		S/O 86	35, I-5
Scarves, Shawls, Stoles	Cluster of Scarves, A		√		Hw	6	2		M/A 85	50
Scarves, Shawls, Stoles	Cluster of Scarves, A (Dixie Straight)		√	√	Hw	6	2		M/A 85	51, I-10
Scarves, Shawls, Stoles	Colonial Stole (Gladys Strong)		√	> 4	Hw	3	5		N/D 82	50, 89
Scarves, Shawls, Stoles	Color and Design in Andean Warp-Faced Fabrics	Femenias, Blenda	√		WJ	12	2	46	Fa 87	44
Scarves, Shawls, Stoles	Color Blanket Shawl & Top (Priscilla Plate)		√	√	Hw	2	4		Se 81	50, 89
Scarves, Shawls, Stoles	Color Blended Scarves		√	√	S-O	11	1		Sp 87	23
Scarves, Shawls, Stoles	Color Wheel Scarves (Ardis Dobrovolny)		√	√	Hw	2	4		Se 81	33, 93
Scarves, Shawls, Stoles	Colorful Scarves	Waggoner, Phyllis	√	√	WJ	12	2	46	Fa 87	48
Scarves, Shawls, Stoles	Complementary Scarf #6 (Ardis Dobrovolny)		√	√	Hw	2	4		Se 81	33, 93
Scarves, Shawls, Stoles	Complementary Scarf #7 (Ardis Dobrovolny)		√	√	Hw	2	4		Se 81	33, 93
Scarves, Shawls, Stoles	Complementary Scarf #8 (Ardis Dobrovolny)		√	√	Hw	2	4		Se 81	33, 93
Scarves, Shawls, Stoles	Contemporary Satins: An Alphabet of Satin Designs	Tidball, Harriet	√	> 4	SCGM		7		62	22
Scarves, Shawls, Stoles	Cotton Lace	Madden, Linda	√	√	WJ	11	2	42	Fa 86	25
Scarves, Shawls, Stoles	Cotton Wrap (Sharon Alderman)		√	√	Hw	4	3		M/J 83	44, 81
Scarves, Shawls, Stoles	Crackle Stole and Pillow (Nell Znamierowski)		√	√	Hw	8	5		N/D 87	49, I-9
Scarves, Shawls, Stoles	Crocus Shawl (Betty Davenport)		√	√	Hw	2	4		Se 81	56, 84
Scarves, Shawls, Stoles	Designing for the Opphämta Loom	Johns, Greg	√	> 4	PWC	3	4	10		68
Scarves, Shawls, Stoles	Donegal Tweed Scarf (Linda Hardison)		√	√	Hw	7	1		J/F 86	71
Scarves, Shawls, Stoles	Double Ecology Shawl	Lyon, Linda; Connie Herring; Athanasios David Xenakis	√	√	PWC	3	4	10		64
Scarves, Shawls, Stoles	Double Weave Project for the Beginner	Krasnoff, Julienne	√	√	H&C	21	4		Fa 70	11
Scarves, Shawls, Stoles	Doup Leno (error-corrected WJ v3 n2 78 insert p38a)		√	√	WJ	3	2	10	Oc 78	32
Scarves, Shawls, Stoles	Elegant Plaid Shawl, An	Kolling-Summers, Elizabeth	√	√	WJ	7	3	27	Wi 82	69
Scarves, Shawls, Stoles	Erica: The new Rigid Heddle Loom	Cooper, Frayda	√		H&C	26	5		Oc 75	25
Scarves, Shawls, Stoles	Even Beat, An	Ligon, Linda	√	√	Hw	7	4		S/O 86	98
Scarves, Shawls, Stoles	Evolution of an Idea: Olive and Harry Develop Some New Angles on Weaving a Stole, The	Linder, Olive; Harry Linder	√	> 4	Hw	5	1		J/F 84	66
Scarves, Shawls, Stoles	Experimenting with Silk Crepe	Quinn, Celia	√	√	S-O	10	4		Wi 86	36
Scarves, Shawls, Stoles	Fiber Foray: Color Exercises for the Beginner	Quinn, Celia	√	√	S-O	9	3		Fa 85	36
Scarves, Shawls, Stoles	Fine Lace Shawl, A	Quinn, Celia	√		S-O	8	4		Wi 84	14
Scarves, Shawls, Stoles	Floating Selvedges	Ligon, Linda	√	√	Hw	7	3		M/J 86	92
Scarves, Shawls, Stoles	Folk Textiles of Latin America	Kelemen, Pál	√		TMJ	1	4		De 65	2
Scarves, Shawls, Stoles	Four-Season Stole (Lynn Tedder)		√	√	Hw	8	4		S/O 87	35, I-3
Scarves, Shawls, Stoles	Four-Shaft Twill Neck Scarf	Kolling-Summers, Elizabeth	√	√	WJ	7	1	25	Su 82	29
Scarves, Shawls, Stoles	From Sheep to Shawl	Van Ord, Kay; Stewart Van Ord	√	√	WJ	6	2	22	Fa 81	57
Scarves, Shawls, Stoles	From Sheep to Skirt In Five Days	Copestick, Myrtis Gorst	√	√	H&C	3	3		Su 52	25
Scarves, Shawls, Stoles	Frosted Pastel Cashmere Scarf, A	Quinn, Celia	√	√	S-O	9	3		Fa 85	41
Scarves, Shawls, Stoles	Fun with Bronson Lace Variations	Davenport, Betty	√	√	PWC			5	Sp 83	46

SUBJECT	TITLE	AUTHOR	IL	INST	JOUR	VOL	NO	ISS	DATE	PAGE
Scarves, Shawls, Stoles	Garments from the Loom: Handweaver Randall Darwall Focuses on the Cloth	Mattera, Joanne	√		Fa	10	1		J/F 83	20
Scarves, Shawls, Stoles	Gilded Forest Scarf (Linda Ligon)		√	√	Hw	2	5		No 81	4, 83
Scarves, Shawls, Stoles	Glowing Embers Scarf (Leslie Voiers)		√	√	Hw	6	5		N/D 85	43, I-5
Scarves, Shawls, Stoles	Good Hope Farm	Sitko, Jane Bradley	√		SS&D	18	2	70	Sp 87	40
Scarves, Shawls, Stoles	Gray Muffler (Janice Jones)		√	√	Hw	6	4		S/O 85	59, I-10
Scarves, Shawls, Stoles	Green Plaid Blanket or Scarf (Diane Tramba)			>4	Hw	2	1		F-W 80	27, 64
Scarves, Shawls, Stoles	Half Shawl Designed by Janet Checker		√	√	WJ	11	3	43	Wi 87	14
Scarves, Shawls, Stoles	Hand Woven Garments	Piper, Aris	√	>4	WJ	5	3	19	Wi 81	24
Scarves, Shawls, Stoles	Hand-Dyed Angora Bunny Scarf	Hart, Jacque	√	√	S-O	11	4		Wi 87	26
Scarves, Shawls, Stoles	Houndstooth Scarf (Sharon Alderman)		√	√	Hw	2	1		F-W 80	51, 57
Scarves, Shawls, Stoles	How to Weave a Plaid Triangular Shawl	Elich-McCall, Charoltte	√	√	Hw	4	5		N/D 83	54
Scarves, Shawls, Stoles	Ikat Spun Shrug (Louise Bradley)	Bradley, Louise	√	√	Hw	2	4		Se 81	67
Scarves, Shawls, Stoles	In My Country, It's Winter	Gagné-Collard, Agathe	√	>4	WJ	8	3	31	Wi 83	74
Scarves, Shawls, Stoles	Indigo/Claret Silky Rayon		√	√	Hw	4	5		N/D 83	46, 98
Scarves, Shawls, Stoles	Inlaid Blouse and Scarf (Jean Scorgie)		√	>4	Hw	8	2		M/A 87	58, I-12
Scarves, Shawls, Stoles	Instant Color! Paint a Garden on Your Warp	Colburn, Carol	√	√	Hw	1	2		S-S 80	44
Scarves, Shawls, Stoles	Jacqueline Fee's Sweater Workshop		√	√	Hw	4	3		M/J 83	74
Scarves, Shawls, Stoles	Jaspé Shawl (Linda Ligon)		√	√	Hw	5	4		S/0 84	63, 100
Scarves, Shawls, Stoles	Jean Newsted's Angora Scarf		√		S-O	9	3		Fa 85	13
Scarves, Shawls, Stoles	Kashmir East and West	Mikosch, Elizabeth	√		TM			9	F/M 87	14
Scarves, Shawls, Stoles	Kashmir or Paisley; Romance of the Shawl	Wilson, Kax	√		Iw	4	4		Fa 79	34
Scarves, Shawls, Stoles	Kashmiri to Paisley: Evolution of the Paisley shawl	Larson-Fleming, Susan	√		WJ	11	3	43	Wi 87	37
Scarves, Shawls, Stoles	Keep Warm! Large Rectangular Shawl	Sylvan, Katherine	√	>4	WJ	5	2	18	Fa 80	10
Scarves, Shawls, Stoles	Keeping Track	Ligon, Linda	√	√	Hw	8	1		J/F 87	90
Scarves, Shawls, Stoles	Knitter's Journey, A	Bush, Nancy	√		Kn	3	4	8	Fa 87	24
Scarves, Shawls, Stoles	Lacy Triangular Stole of Handspun Wool, A	Kniskern, Edna Maki	√	√	WJ	6	2	22	Fa 81	48
Scarves, Shawls, Stoles	Large Shawl (Halcyon)		√	√	Hw	2	1		F-W 80	33, 60
Scarves, Shawls, Stoles	Lark Burger's Lacy Scarf		√		S-O	9	3		Fa 85	15
Scarves, Shawls, Stoles	Last Word, The		√	√	Hw	4	2		M/A 83	67
Scarves, Shawls, Stoles	Lighter Weight Wool Scarf	Fitch, Marjorie	√	√	H&C	11	3		Su 60	22
Scarves, Shawls, Stoles	Lina Hartman Silk Scarf (Louise Bradley)		√	√	Hw	5	5		N/D 84	53, I-7
Scarves, Shawls, Stoles	Liquid Shimmer Scarf (Linda Ligon)		√	√	Hw	8	4		S/O 87	54, I-10
Scarves, Shawls, Stoles	Loopy Shawls (Halcyon)		√	√	Hw	1	1		F-W 79	20, 52
Scarves, Shawls, Stoles	Making Gloves That Fit	Buchanan, Rita	√	√	S-O	8	4		Wi 84	17
Scarves, Shawls, Stoles	Mending Warps	Ligon, Linda	√	√	Hw	7	1		J/F 86	34
Scarves, Shawls, Stoles	Merino Scarf with Pastel Highlights	Quinn, Celia	√	√	S-O	9	3		Fa 85	37
Scarves, Shawls, Stoles	Mexican Motifs: A Cotton Shawl in Leno or Gauze Weave	Tidball, Harriet	√	√	SCGM		6		62	16
Scarves, Shawls, Stoles	Mexican Motifs: A Mexican Quesquimitl	Tidball, Harriet	√	√	SCGM		6		62	13
Scarves, Shawls, Stoles	Mexican Motifs: Mexico, Land of Contrasts	Tidball, Harriet	√		SCGM		6		62	1
Scarves, Shawls, Stoles	More About Fabrics: Practical Projects in Tabby	Zielinski, S. A.; Robert Leclerc, ed.	√	√	MWL	20			'51–'73	29
Scarves, Shawls, Stoles	Musk Ox Projects		√	√	S-O	7	1		Sp 83	23
Scarves, Shawls, Stoles	Nubby and Nice Shawl (Roslyn Hahn)		√		Hw	7	5		N/D 86	30
Scarves, Shawls, Stoles	Number Knitting — A New Way with an Old Art	Jarecka, Louise Llewellyn	√	√	H&C	2	1		Wi 50	22
Scarves, Shawls, Stoles	One-Warp Boutique		√		Hw	6	2		M/A 85	53
Scarves, Shawls, Stoles	Orchid Shawl	Xenakis, Athanasios David	√	√	PWC			5	Sp 83	38

SUBJECT	TITLE	AUTHOR	IL	INST	JOUR	VOL	NO	ISS	DATE	PAGE
Scarves, Shawls, Stoles	'Outrageous' Scarf #1 (Kathryn Wertenberger)		√	>4	Hw	5	5		N/D 84	68, I-7
Scarves, Shawls, Stoles	'Outrageous' Scarf #2 (Kathryn Wertenberger)		√	√	Hw	5	5		N/D 84	68, I-8
Scarves, Shawls, Stoles	'Outrageous' Scarf #3 (Kathryn Wertenberger)		√	√	Hw	5	5		N/D 84	68, I-8
Scarves, Shawls, Stoles	Paisley	Badone, Donalda	√		Hw	8	1		J/F 87	39
Scarves, Shawls, Stoles	Paisley Shawls: A Democratic Fashion	Goodman, Deborah Lerme	√		Fa	12	3		M/J 85	52
Scarves, Shawls, Stoles	Periwinkle Scarf (Linda Ligon)		√	√	Hw	8	1		J/F 87	90, I-8
Scarves, Shawls, Stoles	Pink/Orange Wool Plaid		√	√	Hw	4	5		N/D 83	46, 96
Scarves, Shawls, Stoles	Plaid Shawl (Jean Scorgie)		√	√	Hw	6	4		S/O 85	58, I-12
Scarves, Shawls, Stoles	Prayer Shawls	Bercey, Lee	√	√	H&C	20	1		Wi 69	20
Scarves, Shawls, Stoles	Pride of the Harvest Shawl	Davidsohn, Marty	√	√	PWC			6	Su 83	25
Scarves, Shawls, Stoles	Project Notebook, A	Ligon, Linda	√	√	Iw	3	1		Fa 77	31
Scarves, Shawls, Stoles	Projects for a Six-Dent Rigid Heddle Backstrap Loom	Swanson, Karen	√	√	H&C	21	4		Fa 70	9
Scarves, Shawls, Stoles	Projects with Cotton		√	√	WJ	4	2	14	Oc 79	28
Scarves, Shawls, Stoles	Quatrefoil	Xenakis, Athanasios David	√	√	PWC	3	3	9		53
Scarves, Shawls, Stoles	Rainbow Heather Shawl (Pat Colony)		√	√	Hw	2	5		No 81	52, 88
Scarves, Shawls, Stoles	Rainbow Scarf (Lynne Giles)		√	>4	Hw	8	4		S/O 87	63, I-14
Scarves, Shawls, Stoles	Red Lace Scarf (Betty Davenport)		√	√	Hw	7	1		J/F 86	63, I-13
Scarves, Shawls, Stoles	Ribbon Scarf or Sash (Margery Wilder)		√	√	Hw	7	2		M/A 86	32
Scarves, Shawls, Stoles	Scarf and Cap	Switzer, Chris	√	√	S-O	4			80	58
Scarves, Shawls, Stoles	Scarf and Hat Set (Janice Jones)		√	√	Hw	4	4		S/O 83	44, 94
Scarves, Shawls, Stoles	Scarf, Cap and Mittens Set (Marit Drenckhahn)		√	√	Hw	2	1		F-W 80	52, 78
Scarves, Shawls, Stoles	Scarf (Nell Znamierowski)		√	>4	Hw	7	3		M/J 86	34, I-6
Scarves, Shawls, Stoles	Scarves in Variegated Yarns	Irwin, Bobbie	√	√	S-O	11	4		Wi 87	53
Scarves, Shawls, Stoles	Scent of Flowers, Kishmir Shawls in the Collection of The Textile Museum, The	Mikosch, Elisabeth	√		TMJ	24			85	7
Scarves, Shawls, Stoles	Shadow Scarves (Judy Steinkoenig)		√	√	Hw	3	4		Se 82	73
Scarves, Shawls, Stoles	Shawl in the English Tradition, A	Zimmermann, Elizabeth	√	√	Kn	1	2	2	S-S 85	59
Scarves, Shawls, Stoles	Shawl Inspired by Edgar Degas' "Ballet Seen from a Box, 1885" (Dixie Straight)		√	√	Hw	5	5		N/D 84	64, I-9
Scarves, Shawls, Stoles	Shawls without Seams	Pfeiffer, Judy	√	√	SS&D	18	2	70	Sp 87	43
Scarves, Shawls, Stoles	Sheaf of Shawls, Sashes and Scarves, A (Susan Snover)		√	√	Hw	6	2		M/A 85	52, I-9
Scarves, Shawls, Stoles	Shetland Lace	Korach, Alice	√	√	TM			11	J/J 87	40
Scarves, Shawls, Stoles	Silk	Sullivan, Donna	√	√	SS&D	16	2	62	Sp 85	42
Scarves, Shawls, Stoles	Silk Blouse with Scarf (Sylvia Slater Berkowitz)		√	√	Hw	8	5		N/D 87	32, I-4
Scarves, Shawls, Stoles	Silk Scarf (Halcyon Schomp)		√	√	Hw	3	5		N/D 82	45, 86
Scarves, Shawls, Stoles	Silk Scarf (Hector Jaeger)		√	√	Hw	7	1		J/F 86	57, I-12
Scarves, Shawls, Stoles	Silk Scarf (Sharon Alderman)		√	>4	Hw	4	1		J/F 83	43, 82
Scarves, Shawls, Stoles	Silk Shawl	Glaves, Jeannine; Ruth Morrison	√	√	S-O	9	4		Wi 85	16
Scarves, Shawls, Stoles	Simple Scarf, Simple Luxury (error-corrected Hw v5 n1 83 p88)	Alderman, Sharon	√	√	Hw	4	4		S/O 83	64
Scarves, Shawls, Stoles	Simple Skirt and Matching Shawl, A	Hewson, Betty	√	√	Hw	4	5		N/D 83	24
Scarves, Shawls, Stoles	Skirt and Stole (Mary Pendergrass)		√	√	Hw	1	1		F-W 79	23, 56
Scarves, Shawls, Stoles	Spin a Tartan—Naturally	Adams, Brucie	√	√	Hw	4	5		N/D 83	72
Scarves, Shawls, Stoles	Spin for a Scarf		√		S-O	8	3		Fa 84	12
Scarves, Shawls, Stoles	Spinning a Gossamer Web	Gibson-Roberts, Priscilla A.	√	√	Kn	4	1	9	Wi 87	62
Scarves, Shawls, Stoles	Splendor of a Folk Warp, A (Joanne Christensen)		√	√	Hw	2	1		F-W 80	48

SUBJECT	TITLE	AUTHOR	IL	INST	JOUR	VOL	NO	ISS	DATE	PAGE
Scarves, Shawls, Stoles	Split-Complementary Scarf #1 (Ardis Dobrovolny)		√	√	Hw	2	4		Se 81	33, 93
Scarves, Shawls, Stoles	Split-Complementary Scarf #2 (Ardis Dobrovolny)		√	√	Hw	2	4		Se 81	33, 93
Scarves, Shawls, Stoles	Sprang and Frame Plaiting for Garments		√	√	WJ	3	3	11	Ja 79	26
Scarves, Shawls, Stoles	Square Shawl (Sharon Alderman)		√	√	Hw	6	4		S/O 85	31, I-4
Scarves, Shawls, Stoles	Stole		√	√	Hw	2	3		My 81	88, 79
Scarves, Shawls, Stoles	Stoles and Scarves		√	√	WJ	2	1	5	Jy 77	3
Scarves, Shawls, Stoles	Stonington Shawl	Zimmermann, Elizabeth	√	√	Kn	1	2	2	S-S 85	60, 72B
Scarves, Shawls, Stoles	Summer and Winter Stole (Nell Znamierowski)		√	√	Hw	8	5		N/D 87	51, I-10
Scarves, Shawls, Stoles	Super Scarf	Herring, Connie	√	> 4	PWC	3	1	7		28
Scarves, Shawls, Stoles	Swarthmore Lace Scarf (M. Linda Whitten)		√	√	Hw	7	1		J/F 86	69
Scarves, Shawls, Stoles	Tallis or Prayer Shawl, The	Derr, Mary	√	√	WJ	2	1	5	Jy 77	16
Scarves, Shawls, Stoles	Tarascan Lace (error-corrected WJ v9 n1 84 p70)	Thabet, Micheline	√	√	WJ	8	4	32	Sp 84	48
Scarves, Shawls, Stoles	Textile Arts of India	Bernier, Ronald M.	√		WJ	2	1	5	Jy 77	31
Scarves, Shawls, Stoles	Tinsel Trimmed Scarf (Linda Ligon)		√	√	Hw	2	5		No 81	4, 82
Scarves, Shawls, Stoles	Town and Country Silk Scarves (Janice Jones)		√	√	Hw	5	4		S/0 84	72, 110
Scarves, Shawls, Stoles	Traditional Berber Weaving in Central Morocco	Forelli, Sally; Jeanette Harries	√		TMJ	4	4		77	41
Scarves, Shawls, Stoles	Traditional Shetland Shawl, A	Zimmermann, Elizabeth	√	√	Kn	1	2	2	S-S 85	59
Scarves, Shawls, Stoles	Triadic Color Scheme Scarf #4 (Ardis Dobrovolny)		√	√	Hw	2	4		Se 81	33, 93
Scarves, Shawls, Stoles	Triadic Color Scheme Scarf #5 (Ardis Dobrovolny)		√	√	Hw	2	4		Se 81	33, 93
Scarves, Shawls, Stoles	Triangular Shawl	Broad, Sue	√		WJ	7	3	27	Wi 82	11
Scarves, Shawls, Stoles	Twill Scarf (Sharon Alderman)		√	> 4	Hw	2	1		F-W 80	51, 57
Scarves, Shawls, Stoles	Twill Stoll	Harding, Patricia	√	√	S-O	4			80	61
Scarves, Shawls, Stoles	Two Alpaca and Wool Scarves	Xenakis, Athanasios David	√	> 4	PWC	3	4	10		40
Scarves, Shawls, Stoles	Variegated Ikat Spun Scarf		√	√	S-O	5			81	61
Scarves, Shawls, Stoles	Variegated Scarf (Betty Davenport)		√	√	Hw	7	1		J/F 86	63, I-14
Scarves, Shawls, Stoles	Very Fine Scarf, A	Buchanan, Steve	√	√	S-O	10	2		Su 86	20
Scarves, Shawls, Stoles	Warm and Wooly: For Texture		√	√	Hw	1	1		F-W 79	24
Scarves, Shawls, Stoles	Weavers Demonstrate for Mrs. Johnson		√	√	H&C	19	4		Fa 68	11
Scarves, Shawls, Stoles	Weaving Handspun Yarn: Triangular Shawl	Ellison, Nancy	√	√	WJ	12	2	46	Fa 87	42
Scarves, Shawls, Stoles	Weaving in Quebec: Devotion to Garments	Barrett, Clotilde	√	√	WJ	6	4	24	Sp 82	18
Scarves, Shawls, Stoles	Weaving Primer	Parks, Deborah	√	√	PWC	3	3	9		4
Scarves, Shawls, Stoles	Weaving with Mohair		√	√	H&C	18	1		Wi 67	38
Scarves, Shawls, Stoles	What People Ask Before They Buy Handmade Fashions	Leslie, Victoria	√		TM			9	F/M 87	58
Scarves, Shawls, Stoles	White on White	Lyon, Linda	√	√	PWC	3	3	9		60
Scarves, Shawls, Stoles	White on White Shawl (Polly Scott)		√	√	Hw	7	5		N/D 86	31
Scarves, Shawls, Stoles	White Shawl (Dale Pettigrew) (error-corrected Hw v4 n2 83 p80)		√	√	Hw	4	1		J/F 83	55, 90
Scarves, Shawls, Stoles	Windowpane Scarf/Belt (Louise Bradley)		√	√	Hw	8	4		S/O 87	54, I-11
Scarves, Shawls, Stoles	Winning Woven Winter Warmers		√	> 4	Hw	7	1		J/F 86	32
Scarves, Shawls, Stoles	Winter Elegance	Linder, Olive	√		S-O	9	4		Wi 85	38
Scarves, Shawls, Stoles	Wintertime Warmer, A	Steiner, Betty	√	√	SS&D	8	4	32	Fa 77	97
Scarves, Shawls, Stoles	Wool Shawl (Kim Naver)		√	√	Hw	8	3		M/J 87	51, I-8
Scarves, Shawls, Stoles	Wool Skirt and Shawl	Crosby, Roberta	√	√	PWC			5	Sp 83	55
Scarves, Shawls, Stoles	Woolen Scarf	Ingebretsen, Cathy	√	√	PWC	3	1	7		7

SUBJECT	TITLE	AUTHOR	IL	INST	JOUR	VOL	NO	ISS	DATE	PAGE
Scarves, Shawls, Stoles	Woven Reed Placemats	Ingebretsen, Cathy	√	√	PWC	3	2	8		4
Scarves, Shawls, Stoles	Woven Structures of European Shawls in The Textile Museum Collection, The	Rowe, Ann Pollard			TMJ	24			85	55
Scarves, Shawls, Stoles	Wrap Around Shawl (Nell Znamierowski)		√	√	Hw	2	5		No 81	50, 86
Scarves, Shawls, Stoles: Knitted	Ah, Shawls!	Upitis, Lizbeth	√		Kn	4	1	9	Wi 87	14
Scarves, Shawls, Stoles: Knitted	Babushkas	Upitis, Lizbeth	√	√	Kn	4	1	9	Wi 87	48
Scarves, Shawls, Stoles: Knitted	Beginnings...	Rowley, Elaine	√	√	Kn	4	1	9	Wi 87	25
Scarves, Shawls, Stoles: Knitted	Faroese Shawls	Swansen, Meg	√	√	Kn	4	1	9	Wi 87	26
Scarves, Shawls, Stoles: Knitted	Grandma's Checkerboard Lace	Yaksick, Karen	√	√	Kn	4	1	9	Wi 87	52
Scarves, Shawls, Stoles: Knitted	Highlands Shawl	Bush, Nancy	√	√	Kn	4	1	9	Wi 87	40
Scarves, Shawls, Stoles: Knitted	Intarsia Shawl	Lewis, Susanna	√	√	Kn	4	1	9	Wi 87	46
Scarves, Shawls, Stoles: Knitted	Lace Garland	Ocker, Emily	√	√	Kn	4	1	9	Wi 87	38
Scarves, Shawls, Stoles: Knitted	Lace Shawl	Newton, Deborah	√	√	Kn	4	1	9	Wi 87	54
Scarves, Shawls, Stoles: Knitted	On Designing in 2 Dimensions: Shawls and Scarves	Newton, Deborah	√	√	Kn	4	1	9	Wi 87	30
Scarves, Shawls, Stoles: Knitted	Opinionated Knitter: Sheep to Shawl, The	Wright, Jenny	√		Kn	4	1	9	Wi 87	20
Scarves, Shawls, Stoles: Knitted	π Shawl, The	Zimmermann, Elizabeth	√	√	Kn	4	1	9	Wi 87	34
Scarves, Shawls, Stoles: Knitted	Sidna's Shetland Shawl	Farley, Sidna	√	√	Kn	4	1	9	Wi 87	22
Scarves, Shawls, Stoles: Knitted	Six Ways to Wear Your Lace	Beugler, Eugen	√	√	Kn	4	1	9	Wi 87	44
Scarves, Shawls, Stoles: Knitted	Snowdrops and Snowflakes	George, Barbara	√	√	Kn	4	1	9	Wi 87	17
Scarves, Shawls, Stoles: Knitted	Summer Harvest, Winter Jacket	O'Connor, Marina	√	√	S-O	11	2		Su 87	13
Scarves, Shawls, Stoles: Knitted	Your Yarn Shop			√	Kn	4	1	9	Wi 87	9
Scheuer Tapestry Studio	Bringing Tapestry into the 20th Century	Mattera, Joanne	√	√	TM			1	O/N 85	52
Scheuer Tapestry Studio	Imagery Is Personal in Tapestry Today	Clausen, Valerie	√		TM			9	F/M 87	66
Scheuer Tapestry Studio	Scheuer Tapestry Studio: Applying Old Techniques to New Ideas, The	Scheuer, Ruth Tannenbaum	√		Fa	10	3		M/J 83	39
Scholarships see HGA Scholarships										
Schools see Education										
Scotland	Dovecot Studios	Soroka, Joanne	√		SS&D	12	4	48	Fa 81	36
Scotland	Edinburgh Tapestry Company: A Thriving Anachronism in Scotland, The	Soroka, Joanne	√		Fa	10	3		M/J 83	59
Scotland	Kashmiri to Paisley: Evolution of the Paisley shawl	Larson-Fleming, Susan	√		WJ	11	3	43	Wi 87	37
Scotland	Kilts	Branson, Branley Allan	√		Hw	4	5		N/D 83	34
Scotland	Paisley	Badone, Donalda	√		Hw	8	1		J/F 87	39
Scotland	Ronald Cruickshank, Scottish Tapestry Weaver		√		H&C	13	2		Sp 62	18
Scotland	Scotland	Torphy, Helen	√		SS&D	15	4	60	Fa 84	10
Scotland	Scottish Weaving Museum		√		H&C	7	1		Wi 55	63
Scotland	Tapestry Weavers of Edinburgh, The	Lister, John A.	√		H&C	12	1		Wi 61	22
Scotland	Tweed	Wilson, Kax	√		Iw	5	2		Sp 80	59
Scotland	Woolens and Tweeds: Designing Woolen Fabrics: Scottish Woolens	Tidball, Harriet	√	√	SCGM		4		61	28
Scotland	Woolens and Tweeds: Designing Woolen Fabrics: The District Checks	Tidball, Harriet	√	√	SCGM		4		61	29
Scouring	Another Look at Wool Scouring: Ingredients, Problems, and Techniques	Raven, Lee		√	S-O	9	4		Wi 85	25
Scouring	Fibre Preparation	Fraser, Victoria Keller	√		H&C	24	3		M/J 73	32
Scouring: Cloth	What a Handweaver Can Learn from the Scottish Weaving Industry (error-corrected WJ v2 n1 77 insert for vol. 1)	Barrett, Clotilde	√	√	WJ	1	3	3	Ja 77	11
Scouring: Fiber, Wool	Scouring a Fleece	Wallace, Meg		√	WJ	1	2	2	Oc 76	18
Scouring: Fibers	Some Preliminary Chemistry for Dyers	Viditz-Ward, Anton	√	√	Iw	3	3		Sp 78	29
Scouring: Fleece	Preparing a Columbia Fleece for Handweaving	Wilson, Helen		√	WJ	2	2	6	Oc 77	22

SUBJECT	TITLE	AUTHOR	IL	INST	JOUR	VOL	NO	ISS	DATE	PAGE
Scouring: Fleeces	Pennyroyal Pick-up	Reedy, Dorrie		√	SS&D	15	1	57	Wi 83	79
Scouring: Silk	How to Scour Silk	Bromberg, Kay	√	√	WJ	4	4	16	Ap 80	40
Scouring: Silk	Silk Dyeing		√	√	WJ	3	2	10	Oc 78	21
Scouring Wool	Washing Greasy Wool			√	TM			14	D/J 87	10
Scouring: Yarn	What a Handweaver Can Learn from the Scottish Weaving Industry (error-corrected WJ v2 n1 77 insert for vol. 1)	Barrett, Clotilde	√	√	WJ	1	3	3	Ja 77	11
Scrambled Drafts	Contemporary Approach to Traditional Weaves: New Patterns in Traditional Weaves	Zielinski, S. A.; Robert Leclerc, ed.	√	>4	MWL	8			'51–'73	86
Scrambled Drafts	Creative Drafting and Analysis: Scrambled Drafts	Zielinski, S. A.; Robert Leclerc, ed.	√	>4	MWL	3			'51–'73	77
Screen-Printing Process	Limited-Edition Vests	Stocksdale, Joy	√	√	TM			4	A/M 86	60
Screens see Blinds and Screens										
Scrimshaw	Nantucket Lightship Baskets: A Sailor's Pastime Revisited	Lucas, Eleanor L.	√		Fa	5	5		S/O 78	52
Sculptural/Conceptual Fiber	"K18–Stoffwechsel": A Report on the Exhibition and Symposium Held in Kassel, West Germany (Exhibit)	Vander Lee, Jana	√		Fa	10	1		J/F 83	52
Sculpture	Andrea V. Uravitc "Wild and Domestic" (Exhibit)	Stevens, Rebecca A. T.	√		Fa	10	2		M/A 83	71
Sculpture	Annie Dempsey: Sculptural Crochet (Exhibit)	Lindley, Susan	√		Fa	9	2		M/A 82	76
Sculpture	Architectural Imagery of Margery Freeman Appelbaum, The	McCann, Kathleen	√		Fa	13	1		J/F 86	12
Sculpture	Banff Experience: A Personal View of Fibre Interchange 1980, The	Irwin, Kim	√		Fa	8	4		J/A 81	35
Sculpture	"Bella Tabak Feldman: Recent Sculpture" (Exhibit)	Scarborough, Jessica	√		Fa	10	2		M/A 83	70
Sculpture	"Carolyn Prince Batchelor: Vessels" (Exhibit)	Lilligren, Ingrid	√		Fa	12	3		M/J 85	77
Sculpture	Ceremonial Structures of Terry Jarrard Dimond, The	Hyatt, Sharyn; Teresa Mangum	√		Fa	9	4		J/A 82	66
Sculpture	Collaboration: Peter and Ritzi Jacobi (error-corrected Fa v13 n1 86 p6)	Corpier, Leslee	√		Fa	12	5		S/O 85	27
Sculpture	"Constance Dodge: Mind Feelings" (Exhibit)	Flanagan, Jeanne	√		Fa	9	3		M/J 82	82
Sculpture	Crocheted Cream Puffs? What You See Is Not What You Get	Fedders, Pat	√		Fa	8	5		S/O 81	16
Sculpture	Dionysian Spirits: Dennis Valinski's Sculptures of Life	Snodgrass, Cindy	√		Fa	8	5		S/O 81	48
Sculpture	"Dominic DiMare: New Work" (Exhibit)	Janeiro, Jan	√		Fa	8	2		M/A 81	63
Sculpture	Exuberant Art of Elizabeth Browning Jackson, The	Place, Jennifer	√		Fa	10	6		N/D 83	12
Sculpture	Fabric of Sha Sha Higby's Imagination, The	Wheater, Kathleen	√		Fa	14	3		M/J 87	35
Sculpture	"Flexible Medium: Art Fabric from the Museum Collection, The" (Exhibit)	Goodman, Deborah Lerme	√		Fa	11	5		S/O 84	71
Sculpture	"Frank Lincoln Viner–Fantaisie: Constructions and Objects" (Exhibit)	Malarcher, Pat	√		Fa	7	1		J/F 80	73
Sculpture	George Brett: Webs of a Mad Spider	McMillan, Sam	√		Fa	8	6		N/D 81	32
Sculpture	Get Into a Good Book: Public Art for Kids	Covel, John	√		Fa	6	5		S/O 79	33
Sculpture	Girls Who Wear Cactus	Akamine, Estelle	√		TM			4	A/M 86	66
Sculpture	Hangups		√		Fa	3	6		N/D 76	6
Sculpture	Here Today, Gone Tomorrow: The Transitory Sculpture of Virginia Gunter	Mattera, Joanne	√		Fa	8	2		M/A 81	18
Sculpture	Hi-Tech Banner Sculptures	Polster, Nancy; Elsa Sreenivasam	√		Fa	12	3		M/J 85	42
Sculpture	"In the Garden of Strange Gods" (Exhibit)	McDonald, Julie Jensen	√		Fa	14	4		S/O 87	41
Sculpture	"Infrastructure" (Exhibit)	Malarcher, Patricia	√		Fa	11	4		J/A 84	76

SUBJECT	TITLE	AUTHOR	IL	INST	JOUR	VOL	NO	ISS	DATE	PAGE
Sculpture	Interview with Dominic Di Mare: A Commitment to Forward Movement, An	Janeiro, Jan	√		Fa	13	1		J/F 86	55
Sculpture	It's Like a Hobby	Fitt, Cate	√		Fa	8	2		M/A 81	38
Sculpture	Jann Rosen-Queralt: An Architecture of Indirection	Rubin, Jean	√		Fa	12	2		M/A 85	47
Sculpture	Jim Grashow: Inspired by Architecture		√		Fa	12	1		J/F 85	62
Sculpture	"Karen Stahlecker" (Exhibit)	Shermeta, Margo	√		Fa	10	5		S/O 83	80
Sculpture	Kiyomi Iwata: A Singularity of Vision	Park, Betty	√		Fa	13	1		J/F 86	10
Sculpture	"Kiyomi Iwata: Works in Fiber" (Exhibit)	Malarcher, Patricia	√		Fa	9	2		M/A 82	77
Sculpture	Knotted Sculpture of Jane Sauer, The	Falconer, Crisa Meahl	√		Fa	13	3		M/J 86	31
Sculpture	Lynn DiNino	Greer, Tyson	√		Fa	13	2		M/A 86	14
Sculpture	"Lynn Hall: Figure and Furniture" (Exhibit)	Shermeta, Margo	√		Fa	12	1		J/F 85	73
Sculpture	"Magdalena Abakanowicz" (Exhibit)	Koplos, Janet	√		Fa	10	2		M/A 83	66
Sculpture	"Maine Coast Artists: Fabrications" (Exhibit)	Beem, Edgar Allen	√		Fa	11	4		J/A 84	80
Sculpture	"Marika Contompasis: Pedestal and Wall Pieces" (Exhibits)	Dyer, Carolyn	√		Fa	9	4		J/A 82	73
Sculpture	"Nance O'Banion: Rocks, Curtains, Windows, and Walls" (Exhibit)	Talley, Charles	√		Fa	12	5		S/O 85	69
Sculpture	"Naomi Kark Schedl: Coverings, Enclosures, and Pathways" (Exhibit)	Richerson, Suzanne	√		Fa	11	4		J/A 84	73
Sculpture	"Neda Al Hilali" (Exhibit)	Janeiro, Jan	√		Fa	9	3		M/J 82	75
Sculpture	On the Edge: Harmony Hammond — Collecting, Reclaiming, Connecting	Willard, Janice	√		Fa	9	4		J/A 82	58
Sculpture	On the Edge: Maureen Connor — Shaping a Response to the Past	Malarcher, Patricia	√		Fa	9	4		J/A 82	61
Sculpture	On the Other Foot: The Shoe Sculptures of Norma Minkowitz		√		Fa	10	1		J/F 83	13
Sculpture	Papermaking in the U.S.A.	Toale, Bernard	√		Fa	9	4		J/A 82	34
Sculpture	"Patricia Campbell: The Modular Form" (Exhibit)	Itter, Diane	√		Fa	11	3		M/J 84	75
Sculpture	"Patricia Malarcher: Pieced Reflections" (Exhibit)	Scheinman, Pamela	√		Fa	11	2		M/A 84	77
Sculpture	Rina Peleg: Plaiting in Clay	Peleg, Rina	√		Fa	10	6		N/D 83	16
Sculpture	Ritzi and Peter Jacobi: Conversation	Paca Al, ed.	√		Fa	8	4		J/A 81	50
Sculpture	Sculpture Between Suggestion and Fact	Waller, Irene	√		Fa	9	3		M/J 82	100
Sculpture	"Sculpture of Claire Zeisler" (Exhibit)	Malarcher, Patricia	√		Fa	12	6		N/D 85	57
Sculpture	"Shared Vision": A Gallery Tour with Two Artists: Jacque Parsley and Neisja Yenawine (Exhibit)	Arnow, Jan	√		Fa	8	4		J/A 81	28
Sculpture	"Sirpa Yarmolinsky: Paper and Linen Constructions" (Exhibit)	Malarcher, Patricia	√		Fa	9	1		J/F 82	84
Sculpture	Soft Sculpture: Old Forms, New Meanings	Gordon, Beverly	√		Fa	10	6		N/D 83	40
Sculpture	"Space Sails" Soar (Exhibit)	Reid, Eve	√		Fa	13	4		J/A 86	51
Sculpture	"Susan Lyman's Paper Structures" (Exhibit)	Roberts, Stephen	√		Fa	8	5		S/O 81	69
Sculpture	"Terminal": Drawing in Three Dimensions	Lyman, Susan	√		Fa	11	4		J/A 84	60
Sculpture	Twelfth International Biennial of Tapestry	Taylor, Dianne; Elmer Taylor	√		Fa	12	6		N/D 85	50
Sculpture	Visual Language of Bella Feldman, The	Scarborough, Jessica	√		Fa	11	4		J/A 84	30
Sculpture	"Voyage Continued" An Illuminating Experience (Exhibit)	Malarcher, Patricia	√		Fa	8	2		M/A 81	16
Sculpture	Whitney Museum of American Art, The (Exhibit)	Park, Betty	√		Fa	9	2		M/A 82	11
Sculpture	"With or Without a Loom" (Exhibit)	Rowley, Kristin Carlsen	√		Fa	8	5		S/O 81	67
Sculpture	"Woven, Tied, and Knotted" (Exhibit)	Koplos, Janet	√		Fa	9	2		M/A 82	82
Sculpture	Yurt in Artpark, The	Brennan, Joan	√		Fa	9	3		M/J 82	19
Sculpture: Basketry	Basket Inside Out: The Spiral Sculptures of Ellen Fanger Dickson, A	Dickson, Ellen Fanger	√		Fa	7	1		J/F 80	26

SUBJECT	TITLE	AUTHOR	IL	INST	JOUR	VOL	NO	ISS	DATE	PAGE
Sculpture: Basketry	"Ferne Jacobs: New Works" (Exhibit)	Park, Betty	√		Fa	6	1		J/F 79	84
Sculpture: Basketry	Michael Davis	Davis, Michael	√		Fa	13	4		J/A 86	26
Sculpture: Basketry	New Direction for the Art of Basketry, A	La Pierre, Sharon	√		WJ	8	3	31	Wi 83	54
Sculpture: Basketry	Rites of Passage: Carol Shaw-Sutton's Twig and Thread Constructions	Park, Betty	√		Fa	7	6		N/D 80	49
Sculpture: Fabric	Artifact...Image...Art		√		Fa	7	3		M/J 80	19
Sculpture: Felt	Shinnosuke Seino: Innovator with Wool	Schreiber, Lavonne	√		WJ	12	2	46	Fa 87	34
Sculpture: Fiber	Anne Dushanko-Dobek: Preserving Found Objects		√		Fa	5	3		M/J 78	44
Sculpture: Fiber	Christo: Running Fence Remembered	Woelfle, Gretchen	√		Fa	7	5		S/O 80	24
Sculpture: Fiber	Conflict Resolved: The Hows and Whys of Hand-Dyed Relief Painting, A	Kroetsch, Glenn	√		Fa	8	4		J/A 81	13
Sculpture: Fiber	Conversation with Barbara Shawcroft: A Sculptor in Fiber, A	Mattera, Joanna	√		Fa	8	4		J/A 81	58
Sculpture: Fiber	Cows in Fiber	Timmons, Chris	√		Fa	11	4		J/A 84	55
Sculpture: Fiber	Cynthia Gale-Nosek: Searching for the Limits of Crochet	Gale-Nosek, Cynthia	√		Fa	11	4		J/A 84	49
Sculpture: Fiber	Enduring Art of Jagoda Buic, The	Mathews, Rich	√		Fa	11	4		J/A 84	64
Sculpture: Fiber	Ewa Kuryluk: Distillations in Fiber	Scarborough, Jessica	√		Fa	12	2		M/A 85	14
Sculpture: Fiber	"Fiber Forms: Linda Eyerman, Jane Sauer" (Exhibit)	Degener, Patricia	√		Fa	8	3		M/J 81	73
Sculpture: Fiber	"Fiber R/Evolution" (Exhibit)	Rudich, Sally	√		Fa	13	4		J/A 86	45
Sculpture: Fiber	Gyongy Laky's Transformations (Exhibit)		√		Fa	13	4		J/A 86	54
Sculpture: Fiber	Manipulated Rope	Meilach, Dona Z.	√		Fa	5	1		J/F 78	46
Sculpture: Fiber	Naomi Kark Schedl: A Concern with Empty Cradles	Richerson, Suzanne	√		Fa	6	6		N/D 79	20
Sculpture: Fiber	Poetry in Fiber: Gail Johnson Resen Talks About Her Work	Resen, Gail Johnson	√		Fa	7	4		J/A 80	20
Sculpture: Fiber	Portfolio of Contemporary Fiber Sculpture, A		√		Fa	11	4		J/A 84	34
Sculpture: Fiber	"Priscilla Sage: Small Paintings and Fiber Sculpture" (Exhibit)	Richerson, Suzanne	√		Fa	8	3		M/J 81	69
Sculpture: Fiber	"Recent Work by Elsa Waller" (Exhibit)	Harrington, Elaine	√		Fa	8	4		J/A 81	71
Sculpture: Fiber	Reiko Mochinaga Brandon: Bridging Two Cultures	Moore, Marcia	√		Fa	13	6		N/D 86	16
Sculpture: Fiber	Sally McKenna Walker's Sculpture: Tension Resolved Through Balance	Miles, Candice St. Jacques	√		Fa	11	4		J/A 84	14
Sculpture: Fiber	Sheila O'Hara	O'Hara, Sheila	√		Fa	13	3		M/J 86	26
Sculpture: Fiber	Why Sew Those Lines? An Interview with Giorgio Furioso and Carolyn Thomas	Paca, Al	√		Fa	7	4		J/A 80	25
Sculpture: Fiber, Animals	Whose Zoo? Julietta Thornton's Incredible Fiber Sculptures	Kennett, Don	√		Fa	8	5		S/O 81	20
Sculpture: Fiber/Neon	Victoria Rivers: Sculpting in Fiber and Neon	Scarborough, Jessica	√		Fa	12	1		J/F 85	22
Sculpture: Figures	Lenore Davis: Figuring in Cloth	Frasier, Debra	√		Fa	10	5		S/O 83	10
Sculpture: Hats	"Joan Steiner: Hats/New Sculpture" (Exhibit)	Katz, Ruth J.	√		Fa	7	5		S/O 80	72
Sculpture: Knitted	Martha Mahon: Tableaux	Fife, Lin	√		Fa	13	6		N/D 86	29
Sculpture: Linen	Working with Linen: Shirley Ruth Elgot	Perry, Pamela	√		Fa	14	2		M/A 87	32
Sculpture: Living	Costume for Dance: The Living Sculpture of Carleigh Hoff	Parshall, Priscilla	√		Fa	8	1		J/F 81	28
Sculpture: Low-Relief	Fragil Landscape	Akamine, Estelle	√		TM			5	J/J 86	88
Sculpture: Low-Relief	Paper Reliefs Of Sirpa Yarmolinsky, The	Goodman, Deborah Lerme	√		Fa	12	5		S/O 85	17
Sculpture: Metal	American Inspiration		√		Fa	10	2		M/A 83	92
Sculpture: Mixed Media	Camrose Ducote's Menagerie: An Empathy with Animals	Redmond, Cheryl	√		Fa	10	3		M/J 83	27
Sculpture: Mixed Media	Karin Connelly: Analagous Structures	Connelly, Karin	√		Fa	12	1		J/F 85	90
Sculpture: Mixed Media	Leslie Wilcox	Wilcox, Leslie	√		Fa	12	5		S/O 85	19

SUBJECT	TITLE	AUTHOR	IL	INST	JOUR	VOL	NO	ISS	DATE	PAGE
Sculpture: Mixed Media	Mimi Holmes: Treasure Troves of Human Conflict	Lamberson, Peggy	√		Fa	13	6		N/D 86	20
Sculpture: Mixed Media	Mysterious Figurines of Keiko Yamaguchi, The	Hempel, Toby Anne	√		Fa	14	4		S/O 87	16
Sculpture: Mud	Meaning of Folk Art in Rabari Life: A Closer Look at Mirrored Embroidery, The	Frater, Judy	√		TMJ	4	2		75	47
Sculpture: Paper	Architectural Imagery of Margery Freeman Appelbaum, The	McCann, Kathleen	√		Fa	13	1		J/F 86	12
Sculpture: Paper	"Introductions '80" Emily DuBois and Sylvia Seventy (Exhibit)	Janeiro, Jan	√		Fa	7	6		N/D 80	70
Sculpture: Paper	Peggy Conklin: Sculptured Paper	Tacker, Sylvia	√		Fa	13	3		M/J 86	25
Sculpture: Paper	Sculptural Paper: Foundations and Directions	Scarborough, Jessica	√		Fa	11	2		M/A 84	32
Sculpture: Paper/Mixed Media	Paper Vessels of Sylvia Seventy, The	Stofflet, Mary	√		Fa	11	2		M/A 84	70
Sculpture: Papier Mâché	Mindy Alper: Sculpting in Papier Mache	Saito, Shirley	√		Fa	11	4		J/A 84	18
Sculpture: Relief	Lida Gordon	Meloy, Margaret	√		Fa	13	5		S/O 86	19
Sculpture: Ribbon	Candy's Sampler (Candace Kling)				TM			12	A/S 87	88
Sculpture: Ribbon	Twentieth Century Ribbon Sculptress Candace Kling	Betzina, Sandra	√		TM			12	A/S 87	62
Sculpture: Silk, Moulded	Junco Sato Pollack: Seashells Of Silk	Norton, Deborah	√		Fa	12	3		M/J 85	18
Sculpture: Textile	Abakanowicz		√		Fa	4	5		S/O 77	39
Sculpture: Textile	Ancient Peruvian Weaver	Clement, Doris W.	√		H&C	18	4		Fa 67	21
Sculpture: Textile	"Aurelia Muñoz" (Exhibit)	Park, Betty	√		Fa	4	6		N/D 77	21
Sculpture: Textile	Carol Hoffman: Research in Molecular Crochet		√		Fa	3	4		J/A 76	18
Sculpture: Textile	Carol Sabiston's Sails: An Expression of the Interaction of Sea and Land	Bellerby, Greg	√		Fa	10	3		M/J 83	16
Sculpture: Textile	Cindy Snodgrass: Wind Sculptures	Wilson, Karen	√		Fa	6	5		S/O 79	56
Sculpture, Textile	"Claire Zeisler" (Exhibit)	Mathews, Rich	√		Fa	4	1		J/F 77	12
Sculpture: Textile	"Claire Zeisler" (Exhibit)	Richerson, Suzanne	√		Fa	6	4		J/A 79	69
Sculpture: Textile	Concerns and Influences in My Work	Kidd, Jane	√		AT	6			De 86	135
Sculpture: Textile	Dawn MacNutt: Sculptural Weaver	LeMaistre, Margaret	√		SS&D	17	2	66	Sp 86	48
Sculpture, Textile	"Dominic Di Mare" (Exhibit)	Park, Betty	√		Fa	4	3		M/J 77	8
Sculpture: Textile	Feltmaking: Instant Delight	Green, Louise	√	√	Iw	3	4		Su 78	18
Sculpture: Textile	Figure-in-the-Round, A Caricature	Lebovitz, Connie	√	√	SS&D	6	1	21	Wi 74	5
Sculpture: Textile	Freeform Felt	Shirley, Roz	√	√	SS&D	18	3	71	Su 87	81
Sculpture: Textile	Industrial Fabric & the Woven Form	Zausner, Judith	√		H&C	23	6		N/D 72	43
Sculpture: Textile	Interview with Gyöngy Laky, An		√		Fa	4	2		M/A 77	24
Sculpture: Textile	"Jackie Winsor" (Exhibit)	Malarcher, Pat	√		Fa	6	4		J/A 79	68
Sculpture: Textile	"Jagoda Buic" (Exhibit)	Mathews, Rich	√		Fa	4	5		S/O 77	13
Sculpture: Textile	Jean Stamsta	Stamsta, Jean	√		SS&D	3	3	11	Su 72	15
Sculpture: Textile	Jean Stamsta: Weaver		√		Fa	4	2		M/A 77	30
Sculpture: Textile	Joan Michaels Paque		√		Fa	3	6		N/D 76	34
Sculpture: Textile	John Charles Gordon, An Explorer in Materials		√		H&C	20	1		Wi 69	19
Sculpture: Textile	June Blum	Blum, June	√		Fa	13	2		M/A 86	14
Sculpture: Textile	K. Lee Manuel: Wearable Dreams		√		Fa	3	5		S/O 76	12
Sculpture: Textile	Ken Weaver on Rep Weaving	Weaver, Ken	√		WJ	7	4	28	Sp 83	20
Sculpture: Textile	Layered Sculpture	Liebler, Barbara	√	> 4	Iw	2	4		Su 77	16
Sculpture: Textile	Leora K. Stewart: Form in Three-Dimensional Space		√		SS&D	1	4	4	Se 70	5
Sculpture: Textile	Libby Platus: Heroic Fiber Sculpture		√		SS&D	6	4	24	Fa 75	4
Sculpture: Textile	Magdalena Abakanowicz Speaks	Park, Betty	√		Fa	10	2		M/A 83	11
Sculpture: Textile	"Mariyo Yagi" (Exhibit)	Park, Betty	√		Fa	5	1		J/F 78	19
Sculpture: Textile	More About Fabrics: Textile Sculpture	Zielinski, S. A.; Robert Leclerc, ed.		√	MWL	20			'51–'73	85
Sculpture: Textile	Mushrooms Sprout on Stereo Cabinet	Crowley, Alice M.	√		SS&D	5	4	20	Fa 74	24

SUBJECT	TITLE	AUTHOR	IL	INST	JOUR	VOL	NO	ISS	DATE	PAGE
Sculpture: Textile	Obsession with Trees, An	MacNutt, Dawn	√	√	SS&D	9	4	36	Fa 78	88
Sculpture: Textile	Olwen's Buffalo	MacGregor, Olwen	√	√	WJ	8	2	30	Fa 83	46
Sculpture: Textile	On Weaving, Life and Art	Liebler, Barbara	√		Iw	4	4		Fa 79	19
Sculpture: Textile	Plain Weave — Plane Weave	Carey, Joyce Marquess	√	√	PWC	3	4	10		56
Sculpture: Textile	Pleats, Pleats, Pleats: For Sculptural Garments and Sculpture Itself		√		Fa	9	1		J/F 82	40
Sculpture: Textile	Protest in Hawaii		√		SS&D	2	3	7	Su 71	10
Sculpture: Textile	Richard Mathews: Fiber Sculptor		√		Fa	3	1		J/F 76	12
Sculpture: Textile	Ron Goodman		√		Fa	3	6		N/D 76	40
Sculpture: Textile	"Sculpture in Fiber"		√		H&C	23	2		M/A 72	10
Sculpture: Textile	Serina Sherwin: Interview	Meilach, Dona Z.	√		Fa	4	6		N/D 77	49
Sculpture: Textile	Shaping with the Warp	Bowman, Gloria	√	√	SS&D	11	1	41	Wi 79	26
Sculpture: Textile	Sheila Fox: Three-Dimensional Plaiting	Malarcher, Pat	√		Fa	6	5		S/O 79	22
Sculpture: Textile	Stepping Out (Lenore Davis)		√		TM			8	D/J 86	84
Sculpture: Textile	Students Learn Creating with Fiber	Thomason, Roger	√		SS&D	6	1	21	Wi 74	4, 10
Sculpture: Textile	"Stuffings" Exhibited At Pittsburgh	Thomas, Kay	√		SS&D	5	1	17	Wi 73	83
Sculpture: Textile	Touch of Whimsy, A	Gonder, Pamela	√		SS&D	7	3	27	Su 76	86
Sculpture: Textile	Twelfth International Tapestry Biennale, The	Coifman, Lucienne	√		SS&D	17	2	66	Sp 86	45
Sculpture: Textile	Twelfth International Tapestry Biennale, The	Waller, Irene	√		SS&D	17	2	66	Sp 86	42
Sculpture: Textile	Weaving As an Olympic Event	Falls, Lynne Cowe	√		SS&D	19	1	73	Wi 87	10
Sculpture: Textile	Wool Worker's Flock	Waltner, Willard; Elma Waltner	√	√	Hw	4	4		S/O 83	75
Sculpture: Textile	Woven Circles and Cones	Henzie, Susie	√	√	SS&D	10	4	40	Fa 79	58
Sculpture: Textile, Bands, Tablet-Woven	Too Late for the Book	Collingwood, Peter	√	√	PWC	3	4	10		29
Sculpture: Textile, Furniture	Fiber and Architecture: Dennis Jenkins		√		Fa	3	3		M/J 76	35
Sculpture: Textile, Rope	Rope Sculpture: Stanley Postek		√		H&C	26	5		Oc 75	9
Sculpture: Textile, Triaxial Weaves	Braiding Triaxial Weaves: Enhancements and Design for Artworks	Mooney, David R.	√	√	AT	5			Ju 86	9
Sculpture: Textile (Wall)	Seaforms in Spokane	Proctor, Geri	√	√	Hw	3	4		Se 82	14
Sculpture: Textile/Metal	Riis, Mafong Collaborate in Thread & Silver		√		SS&D	5	1	17	Wi 73	4
Sculpture: Twining, Split-Plt	Split-Ply Twining: Three-Dimensional Designs	Harvey, Virginia I.	√	√	TIAM		1		76	37
Sculpture: Wall	"Nancy Hemenway: Aqua Lapis" (Exhibit)	Skudera, Gail	√		Fa	11	5		S/O 84	72
Sculpture: Woven	Kay Sekimachi: Successful on Her Own Terms	Talley, Charles	√		Fa	9	5		S/O 82	72
Sculpture: Woven	Magical Menagerie (Lael Diehm)	Groesbeck, Kaye	√	√	Hw	6	5		N/D 85	34
Seam Bulk	Basic Sewing Techniques in Handling Handwoven Fabrics for Garments	Knollenberg, Barbara	√	√	WJ	1	1	1	Jy 76	25
Seam: Rolls	Irons, Boards, and Presses: A Survey of the Tools That Beautify Sewing	Coffin, David Page	√		TM			10	A/M 87	40
Seaming	Seaming and Finishing	Thompson, Chris	√	√	PWC			3	Oc 82	46
Seams	Stitching in the Ditch		√	√	TM			5	J/J 86	10
Seams: Automatic-Stitched	Construction Details with Automatic Stitches	Richter, Elizabeth Lee	√	√	TM			11	J/J 87	64
Seams: Flat-Fell	Linen Shift: Plain Sewing Makes the Most of Your Fabric, A	Smith, Kathleen B.	√	√	TM			9	F/M 87	46
Seams: Interfacing	Making Sense of Interfacing (error-corrected TM n12 p4)	Komives, Margaret Deck	√	√	TM			10	A/M 87	58
Seams: Knitted	Putting Knitted Pieces Together	Guagliumi, Susan	√	√	TM			11	J/J 87	45
Seams: Ripping	No-Nip Seam Ripper			√	TM			12	A/S 87	10
Seams: Selvage-Join	Linen Shift: Plain Sewing Makes the Most of Your Fabric, A	Smith, Kathleen B.	√	√	TM			9	F/M 87	46
Seams: Types	Basic Sewing Techniques in Handling Handwoven Fabrics for Garments	Knollenberg, Barbara	√	√	WJ	1	1	1	Jy 76	25

SUBJECT	TITLE	AUTHOR	IL	INST	JOUR	VOL	NO	ISS	DATE	PAGE
Seaweed	Seaweed, A Practical Use by Oregon Weavers		√		H&C	19	4		Fa 68	14
Seersucker	Origins	Wilson, Kax	√		Iw	4	4		Fa 79	51
Seersucker	Seersucker	Linder, Olive	√	√	Hw	2	2		Mr 81	37
Seersucker	Seersucker Blazer, A	Johannesen, Betty	√	√	WJ	8	3	31	Wi 83	22
Seersucker	Seersucker Dress (Sharon Alderman)		√	√	Hw	4	3		M/J 83	42, 79
Seersucker	Seersucker for Caftan (Sharon Alderman)		√	√	Hw	1	2		S-S 80	41, 60
Seersucker	Summer Seersucker		√	√	Hw	4	3		M/J 83	42
Self-Confidence	My Success is Absolutely Assured	Chandler, Deborah	√		Hw	7	1		J/F 86	23
Selvages	Catch It		√	√	Hw	6	1		J/F 85	63
Selvages	Cover It	Raymond, Nish	√	√	Hw	6	1		J/F 85	64
Selvages	Design It		√		Hw	6	1		J/F 85	61
Selvages	Don't Float Past This			√	Hw	6	5		N/D 85	47
Selvages	Doublejack or Sink the Floating Selvedge	Koepp, William	√	√	WJ	9	3	35	Wi 85	67
Selvages	Flaunt It		√	√	Hw	6	1		J/F 85	65
Selvages	Make Your Selvages Talk	Gulick, Evelyn M.	√	√	H&C	5	2		Sp 54	12
Selvages	Rug Weaving: How to Avoid Drawing-in of the Warp	Stanley, Martha	√	√	WJ	6	2	22	Fa 81	10
Selvages	Salvaging the Selvedge		√	√	Hw	4	5		N/D 83	22
Selvages	Second Week, The	Redding, Debbie	√	√	Hw	5	3		Su 84	28
Selvages	Selvages	Marston, Ena	√	√	SS&D	10	4	40	Fa 79	26
Selvages	Selvedge Notes	Ligon, Linda			Hw	6	1		J/F 85	62
Selvages	Selvedges, Selveges, Salvages	Chandler, Deborah	√	√	Hw	8	4		S/O 87	26
Selvages	Shadowweave, Part 2 — Unbalanced Shadowweave (error-corrected WJ v2 n1 77 insert for vol. 1)	Barrett, Clotilde	√	> 4	WJ	1	2	2	Oc 76	14
Selvages	Simple Selvage System, A	Koepp, William	√	√	SS&D	16	4	64	Fa 85	68
Selvages	Stitching Traditional Coverlet Weaves	Sellin, Helen G.	√	> 4	AT	1			De 83	289
Selvages	Summer and Winter Revisited, Part 2: III. Selvedges for Krokbragd and Other Weft-Faced Cloths	Ingebretsen, Catherine	√	√	PWC		2		Ap 82	68
Selvages	Treasury for Beginners: Curving of Selvedges	Zielinski, S. A.; Robert Leclerc, ed.	√	√	MWL	1			'51–'73	94
Selvages	Treasury for Beginners: Selvedges	Zielinski, S. A.; Robert Leclerc, ed.	√	√	MWL	1			'51–'73	88
Selvages	Two Placemats	Herring, Connie	√	√	PWC		5		Sp 83	36
Selvages	Wind It		√	√	Hw	6	1		J/F 85	66
Selvages	Woolens and Tweeds: Weaving Woolens: Selvages	Tidball, Harriet		√	SCGM		4		61	18
Selvages	Your Selvage is Showing!	Carter, Bill	√		H&C	3	1		Wi 51	21
Selvages: Card Woven	Cardwoven Selvedge for Weft-Faced Rugs, A	Stanley, Martha	√	√	WJ	7	1	25	Su 82	48
Selvages: Floating	Basic Sewing Techniques in Handling Handwoven Fabrics for Garments	Knollenberg, Barbara	√	√	WJ	1	1	1	Jy 76	25
Selvages: Floating	Double-faced, Double-woven, Three-harness Krokbragd	Holtzer, Marilyn Emerson	√	√	SS&D	14	4	56	Fa 83	46
Selvages: Floating	Floating Selvedges	Ligon, Linda	√	√	Hw	7	3		M/J 86	92
Selvages: Floating	Hints on Weaving and Finishing Rugs		√	√	WJ	2	2	6	Oc 77	16
Selvages: Floating	Navajo Saddle Blanket Patterns	Barrett, Clotilde	√	√	WJ	1	1	1	Jy 76	22
Selvages: Floating	Weaving with Handspun Yarns: Suggestions for Beginning Spinners	Simmons, Paula	√	√	H&C	17	4		Fa 66	4
Selvages: Four	Peru, Textiles Unlimited: Textile Characteristics, End Selvages	Tidball, Harriet	√		SCGM		25		68	20
Selvages: Four	Weaving Processes in the Cuzco Area of Peru	Rowe, Ann Pollard	√	√	TMJ	4	2		75	30
Selvages: Knitting	Don't Knit Selvages			√	TM		6		A/S 86	4
Selvages: Knitting	Edges of Knitting, The	Gaffey, Theresa	√	√	TM		5		J/J 86	54
Selvages: Loops	Linen Mats (Dixie Francis)		√	√	Hw	7	3		M/J 86	67, I-15

SUBJECT	TITLE	AUTHOR	IL	INST	JOUR	VOL	NO	ISS	DATE	PAGE
Selvages: Picot	Picot Trimmed Top (Eileen O'Connor)		√	√	Hw	6	1		J/F 85	65, I-16
Selvages: Plain Weave	What a Handweaver Can Learn from the Scottish Weaving Industry (error-corrected WJ v2 n1 77 insert for vol. 1)	Barrett, Clotilde	√	√	WJ	1	3	3	Ja 77	11
Selvages: Problems/Solutions	Selvedge Gremlins (and what to do about them)	Centner, Dave	√	√	Hw	6	1		J/F 85	59
Selvages: Techniques	Edges of Knitting, The	Gaffey, Theresa	√	√	TM			5	J/J 86	54
Selvages: Twined, Technique	Vertical Loom (continued) Part 3, The Navajo Loom, The		√	√	WJ	2	2	6	Oc 77	23
Seminars see Conferences										
Senior Citizens: Fiber	Teaching Fiber to the Elderly: A Personal Experience	Bryan, Linda Nelson	√		Fa	4	6		N/D 77	60
Senior Citizens: Weaving	Draperies for a Synagogue		√		H&C	9	4		Fa 58	45
Senior Citizens: Weaving	Draperies for a Synagogue		√		H&C	9	4		Fa 58	45
Senior Citizens: Weaving	One Hundred-Year Old Weaver, A		√		H&C	12	1		Wi 61	56
Senior Citizens: Weaving Programs	Weaving for the Senior Set	Dodge, Doris	√		H&C	7	1		Wi 55	16
Senior Citizens: Weaving/Spinning	Guilds Aid Disabled, Aged with Weaving Lessons and Projects	Edwards, Lois			SS&D	5	1	17	Wi 73	5
Sequins	Dazzling with Sequins	Kelsey, Barbara Shomer	√	√	TM			1	O/N 85	60
Sericulture	China and the Complexities of Weaving Technologies	Vollmer, John E.			AT	5			Ju 86	65
Sericulture	Growing Silkworms at Home	Fenner, Monica	√	√	SS&D	9	3	35	Su 78	100
Sericulture	Guide to Raising Silk, A	Fleming, Barbara	√	√	Iw	3	1		Fa 77	34
Sericulture	History of Silk, A	Mattera, Joanne	√	√	SS&D	8	2	30	Sp 77	24
Sericulture	Introduction to Silk Dyeing, An	Walsh, Joan Lea		√	WJ	3	2	10	Oc 78	14
Sericulture	Keeping Silkworms: The Art of Sericulture	Fenner, Monnie	√	√	S-O	8	1		Sp 84	28
Sericulture	Keeping Silkworms: The Art of Sericulture	Fenner, Monnie	√	√	S-O	8	2		Su 84	29
Sericulture	Preparing Silk in Kumejima	Mitchell, Alison	√	√	WJ	10	2	38	Fa 85	53
Sericulture	Raising Silkworms, The Glenna Harris Guild's Project	Pentler, Fumiko	√	√	H&C	20	1		Wi 69	14
Sericulture	Raising the Silkworm in a Northern Climate	Szpakowski, Marceline		√	AT	2			De 84	157
Sericulture	Raw Silk for the Handweaver	Wehrlin, Max	√		H&C	6	2		Sp 55	22
Sericulture	Saints and the Silkworms, The	Alderman, Sharon	√	√	Iw	3	4		Su 78	15
Sericulture	Sericulture in Upstate New York	Bard, Elizabeth A.	√		Fa	13	1		J/F 86	36
Sericulture	Silk	Chadwick, A.	√	√	WJ	3	2	10	Oc 78	6
Sericulture	Silk Culture Comments	Lukens, Petronel	√	√	H&C	22	2		Sp 71	15
Sericulture	Silk Makers, The		√		TM			4	A/M 86	14
Sericulture	Silk Production of Lullingstone and Whitchurch, The	Rubbert, Toni	√		Hw	3	4		Se 82	27
Sericulture	Silk, the Story of a Culture	Drooker, Penelope	√		Hw	7	1		J/F 86	49
Service	"How is Cloth Made?"	Edgren, Esther			SS&D	1	2	2	Mr 70	15
Service	Weavers Are Needed	Biehl, Betty Atwater			SS&D	3	3	11	Su 72	29
Service, Community	Guilds Aid Disabled, Aged with Weaving Lessons and Projects	Edwards, Lois			SS&D	5	1	17	Wi 73	5
Service, Community	Service Through Weaving				SS&D	2	4	8	Fa 71	31
Servietta	Guatemala Visited	Atwater, Mary Meigs	√	√	SCGM		15		65	38
Set Design	Fiber as Set Design: The Work of Clayton Karkosh and Associates		√		Fa	3	4		J/A 76	34
Set Design	Ione Unruh		√		Fa	4	6		N/D 77	63
Set Design	John Charles Gordon		√		Fa	4	4		J/A 77	32
Set Design	Soft Sculpture Set for Albee's "Seascape"		√		Fa	4	2		M/A 77	29
Sett	Abelard's Advice	Hilts, Pat	√	√	Hw	4	4		S/O 83	20
Sett	Basic Guide to Sett, Woolen Yarn (error-ccorrected H&C v18 n4 67 p45)	Russell, Harold W.	√	√	H&C	18	3		Su 67	32
Sett	Brocade: Warp and Weft Densities	Tidball, Harriet			SCGM		22		67	11

SUBJECT	TITLE	AUTHOR	IL	INST	JOUR	VOL	NO	ISS	DATE	PAGE
Sett	Choosing the Right Reed		√	√	Hw	7	4		S/O 86	85
Sett	Getting Sett	Liebler, Barbara	√	√	lw	2	4		Su 77	30
Sett	Handloom Weaves: Warp and Weft	Tidball, Harriet			SCGM		33		57	8
Sett	How Many Ends to the Inch?	Frey, Berta	√		H&C	3	3		Su 52	11
Sett	Sett and the Hand of the Fabric	Roth, Bettie G.	√	√	SS&D	12	3	47	Su 81	16
Sett	Sett Chart				Hw	7	5		N/D 86	I-8
Sett	Thomas Jackson, Weaver: 17th and 18th Century Records	Tidball, Harriet	√	√	SCGM		13		64	35
Sett	Treasury for Beginners: Compound Sleying	Zielinski, S. A.; Robert Leclerc, ed.	√	√	MWL	1			'51–'73	68
Sett	Woolens and Tweeds: Weaving Woolens: Warp Setts	Tidball, Harriet		√	SCGM		4		61	15
Sett	Yarns and Fibers: The Yarn and the Sett of Warp	Zielinski, S. A.; Robert Leclerc, ed.	√	√	MWL	4			'51–'73	34
Sett, Calculations	Everything a Weaver Should Know About Warps and Warping: Sett of Warp for a Perfect Fabric	Zielinski, S. A.; Robert Leclerc, ed.	√	√	MWL	5			'51–'73	45
Sett, Calculations	Techniques for Better Weaving (error-corrected TM i9 D/J 86 p4)	Osterkamp, Peggy	√	√	TM			7	O/N 86	42
Sett, Calculations, Atypical Sett	Everything a Weaver Should Know About Warps and Warping: Extreme Setts of Warp	Zielinski, S. A.; Robert Leclerc, ed.		√	MWL	5			'51–'73	53
Sett, Calculations, Heavy Yarns	Everything a Weaver Should Know About Warps and Warping: Sett of Warp for Heavy Yarns	Zielinski, S. A.; Robert Leclerc, ed.		√	MWL	5			'51–'73	51
Sett, Calculations, Sett Indicator	Everything a Weaver Should Know About Warps and Warping: Sett Indicator	Zielinski, S. A.; Robert Leclerc, ed.	√	√	MWL	5			'51–'73	59
Sett, Chart	Sett Chart		√		Hw	8	5		N/D 87	I-5
Sett, Cotton	Handweaver's Instruction Manual: The Yarns, Warp Settings, Cotton	Tidball, Harriet C. nee Douglas		√	SCGM		34		49	8
Sett, Heavy Yarns, Chart	Everything a Weaver Should Know About Warps and Warping: Table for Heavy Sett of Yarns	Zielinski, S. A.; Robert Leclerc, ed.	√		MWL	5			'51–'73	100
Sett, Linen	Handweaver's Instruction Manual: The Yarns, Warp Settings, Linen	Tidball, Harriet C. nee Douglas		√	SCGM		34		49	8
Sett, Shaft-Switching	Shaft Switching, A Simple Method Usable for Finer Setts	Herring, Connie; Athanasios David Xenakis	√	√	PWC	3	3	9		29
Sett, Wool	Handweaver's Instruction Manual: The Yarns, Warp Settings, Wool	Tidball, Harriet C. nee Douglas		√	SCGM		34		49	8
Setting Formula: Plain Weave	Determining Maximum Sett				CW		23		Ja 87	28
Setting Formula: Satin Weave	Determining Maximum Sett				CW		23		Ja 87	28
Setting Formula: Twill, 2/2	Determining Maximum Sett				CW		23		Ja 87	28
Seventeen Pattern Types	Seventeen Pattern Types, A Study of Repeat Patterns in Two Dimensions	Elliott, Verda	√	>4	CW		25		Se 87	23
Severus, Saint	Saint Severus: Parton Saint of Weavers	Moes, Dini	√		SS&D	16	2	62	Sp 85	58
Sewing	Biased Toward Bias	Bradley, Louise	√	√	Hw	6	3		Su 85	24
Sewing	Classy Corners	Bradley, Louise	√	√	Hw	6	1		J/F 85	86
Sewing	Elizabeth Coleman and the Not-So-Homely Art of Sewing	Coleman, Elizabeth	√		Fa	6	3		M/J 79	29
Sewing	Why Sewing Is Sagging	Galpin, Mary			TM			7	O/N 86	16
Sewing: 18th Century	Linen Shift: Plain Sewing Makes the Most of Your Fabric, A	Smith, Kathleen B.	√	√	TM			9	F/M 87	46
Sewing Bird	Linen Shift: Plain Sewing Makes the Most of Your Fabric, A	Smith, Kathleen B.	√	√	TM			9	F/M 87	46
Sewing Bird: Source	Sewing Bird			√	TM			11	J/J 87	11
Sewing: Hand, French	Coudre a Main: Costumes by Hand	Tacker, Sylvia	√		Fa	12	2		M/A 85	49
Sewing: Handwoven Fabrics	Basic Sewing Techniques in Handling Handwoven Fabrics for Garments	Knollenberg, Barbara	√	√	WJ	1	1	1	Jy 76	25
Sewing: Handwoven Fabrics	Sewing What You Weave	Shaeffer, Claire	√	√	Hw	7	5		N/D 86	46
Sewing: Handwovens	Sewing Handwovens	Betzina, Sandra	√	√	TM			2	D/J 85	20
Sewing Kit	Compact Sewing Kit Made from Thrums	Secretan, Hermine	√	√	SS&D	5	2	18	Sp 74	62

SUBJECT	TITLE	AUTHOR	IL	INST	JOUR	VOL	NO	ISS	DATE	PAGE
Sewing Machines	Buyer's Guide to Sewing Machines, A	Piucci, Joanna	√		Fa	10	2		M/A 83	39
Sewing Machines	Sewing Without Singer	Galpin, Mary			TM			5	J/J 86	20
Sewing Machines	Silicon Sewing Machine, The	Fanning, Robbie			TM			1	O/N 85	14
Sewing Machines	What Sewing Machine to Buy			√	TM			6	A/S 86	8
Sewing Machines: Computerized	Computer Sewing Corrections			√	TM			14	D/J 87	4
Sewing Machines: Computerized	Microchips in the Sewing Room, The	Fanning, Robbie	√	√	TM			12	A/S 87	34
Sewing Machines: Foot Pedals, Scotching	Wrestling Foot Pedals to the Mat			√	TM			14	D/J 87	10
Sewing Machines: Industrial	Industrial Sewing Machines At Home			√	TM			10	A/M 87	6
Sewing Machines: Leatherwork	These Toes Won't Drown in Tears of Clown	Montgomery, Larry	√		TM			11	J/J 87	14
Sewing Machines: Overlock	Needles, Loopers, and Knives	Fanning, Robbie	√	√	TM			3	F/M 86	42
Sewing Order	Drafter, The Draper, The Flat Patternmaker, The	Nebesar, Rebecca Lanxner	√	√	TM			11	J/J 87	33
Sewing: Pattern Construction	Draping a Blouse	Sperry, Ellen	√	√	TM			3	F/M 86	46
Sewing: Silk	Sewing with Silk	Stoyer, Janet	√	√	TM			4	A/M 86	35
Sewing: Supplies	Proper Sewing Equipment	Betzina, Sandra	√		Hw	7	5		N/D 86	72
Sewing: Techniques	Cutting, a Moment of Truth	Bradley, Louise	√	√	Hw	7	2		M/A 86	27
Sewing: Techniques	Fine & Fancy: Good Sewing Techniques for Good Cloth	Bliss, Anne		√	Hw	4	1		J/F 83	38
Sewing: Techniques	Getting it Straight	Bradley, Louise	√	√	Hw	6	5		N/D 85	23
Sewing: Techniques	Let's Face It!	Bradley, Louise	√	√	Hw	8	1		J/F 87	34
Sewing: Techniques	Reinforcements	Bradley, Louise	√	√	Hw	8	4		S/O 87	22
Sewing: Techniques	Sewing What You Weave	Shaeffer, Claire	√	√	Hw	7	5		N/D 86	46
Sewing: Techniques	Techniques of Haute Couture (error-corrected TM i7 O/N86 p5)	Rhodes, Elizabeth A.	√	√	TM			6	A/S 86	52
Shadow Weave	A. Meder Inspired Belt (Louise Bradley)		√	√	Hw	5	5		N/D 84	52, I-4
Shadow Weave	Coat with Cape Sleeves (Leslie Voiers)		√	√	Hw	6	4		S/O 85	54, I-9
Shadow Weave	Fascination with Form, A	Richardson, Pat	√	>4	SS&D	12	3	47	Su 81	54
Shadow Weave	Liquid Shimmer Scarf (Linda Ligon)		√	√	Hw	8	4		S/O 87	54, I-10
Shadow Weave	Magnified Twill Throw (Sharon Alderman)		√	√	Hw	6	5		N/D 85	53, I-12
Shadow Weave	More Moneymakers for Weavers	Klessen, Romy	√	√	PWC			2	Ap 82	9
Shadow Weave	Olive Dress (Jean Scorgie)		√	>4	Hw	7	5		N/D 86	44, I-3
Shadow Weave	Shadow Weave		√	√	Hw	6	5		N/D 85	51
Shadow Weave	Shadow Weave		√	√	Hw	8	5		N/D 87	51
Shadow Weave	Shadow Weave	Evans, Jane	√	√	SS&D	15	4	60	Fa 84	57
Shadow Weave	Shadow Weave	Wertenberger, Kathryn	√	>4	Hw	8	1		J/F 87	76
Shadow Weave	Shadow Weave Cape (Pat Richardson)		√	√	Hw	8	5		N/D 87	51, I-10
Shadow Weave	Shadow Weave Offers an Opportunity for Many Variations	Powell, Marian	√	√	H&C	12	3		Su 61	20
Shadow Weave	Shadow Weave — Part 4. The Relationship Between Shadow Weave and Corkscrew Weave		√	>4	WJ	1	4	4	Ap 77	30
Shadow Weave	Shadow Weave Purse (Jane Patrick)		√	√	Hw	6	5		N/D 85	50, I-9
Shadow Weave	Shadow Weave Rug on Four Harnesses		√	√	WJ	4	4	16	Ap 80	24
Shadow Weave	Shadow Weave Twill Jacket (Jean Scorgie)		√	√	Hw	8	4		S/O 87	43, I-6
Shadow Weave	Shadow Weave Vest (error-corrected WJ v9 n2 84 p82)		√	>4	WJ	8	3	31	Wi 83	81
Shadow Weave	Simple Damask-Like Effects Using Element Diameter Differential and Element Tension Differential	Xenakis, Athanasios David	√	>4	AT	1			De 83	317
Shadow Weave	Textile Structure and Analysis, A Home Study Course in Twelve Lessons: Lessons in Weave Structure, 10. Shadow Weave and Mattor	Tidball, Harriet		>4	SCGM		18		66	29
Shadow Weave	Variations on an Overshot Threading	Lermond, Charles	√	√	WJ	12	2	46	Fa 87	25

SUBJECT	TITLE	AUTHOR	IL	INST	JOUR	VOL	NO	ISS	DATE	PAGE
Shadow Weave	Vestment Variations: A Weaver From the Netherlands Creates Garments for the Ecclesiastical Calendar	Jansen, Netty	√	>4	WJ	10	3	39	Wi 86	53
Shadow Weave	Warp-Patterned Rug (Ronnine Bohannan) (error-corrected Hw v8 n4 87 p I-3)		√	>4	Hw	7	4		S/O 86	41, I-7
Shadow Weave	Weaver's Notebook		√	√	SS&D	10	2	38	Sp 79	52
Shadow Weave	Weaving the Color Patterns of Shadow Weave		√		Hw	6	5		N/D 85	51
Shadow Weave Conversion	Shadowweave, Part 3 — Marian Powell's Shadow Weave Conversion	Barrett, Clotilde	√	>4	WJ	1	3	3	Ja 77	25
Shadow Weave, Multiblock	Composition and Designing Part 2: Multiblock Log Cabin and Shadow Weave	Zielinski, S. A.; Robert Leclerc, ed.	√	>4	MWL	19			'51–'73	126
Shadow Weave, Multiblock	Little Known Weaves Worth Knowing Better: Multiblock	Zielinski, S. A.; Robert Leclerc, ed.	√	>4	MWL	16			'51–'73	68
Shadow Weave System	Handloom Weaves: The Classification of Handloom Weaves, The Structural Group, The Rhythmic Weave Class, Shadow Weave System	Tidball, Harriet	√	>4	SCGM		33		57	36
Shadow Weave, Unbalanced	Shadowweave, Part 2 — Unbalanced Shadowweave (error-corrected WJ v2 n1 77 insert for vol. 1)	Barrett, Clotilde	√	>4	WJ	1	2	2	Oc 76	14
Shaft Limitations: Weave Structure Possibilities	Composition and Designing Part 2: The Limit of Four Shafts	Zielinski, S. A.; Robert Leclerc, ed.	√	√	MWL	19			'51–'73	34
Shaft Requirements: Various Weave Structures	Composition and Designing Part 2: Too Many Frames? What to do with It	Zielinski, S. A.; Robert Leclerc, ed.	√	>4	MWL	19			'51–'73	27
Shaft-Switching	Amazing Color-Pattern Corduroy Rug		√	>4	PWC	3	4	10		22
Shaft-Switching	Blooming Leaf	Xenakis, Athanasios David	√	√	PWC	3	3	9		51
Shaft-Switching	Construct A Simple Shaft-Switching Device	Pickett, Alice	√	√	SS&D	16	3	63	Su 85	68
Shaft-Switching	Double Two-tie System Applied to Overshot	Xenakis, Athanasios David	√	>4	PWC	3	3	9		7
Shaft-Switching	Even-Tied Overshot on Four Shafts with Shaft Switching	Herring, Connie; Athanasios David Xenakis	√	√	PWC	3	3	9		44
Shaft-Switching	How Shaft-Switching Began	Collingwood, Peter	√	√	WJ	6	2	22	Fa 81	14
Shaft-Switching	In Production? Rug Weaving	Fawkes, Judith Poxson	√		Iw	5	1		Wi 79	36
Shaft-Switching	In Timeless Form	Herring, Connie	√	√	PWC	3	3	9		35
Shaft-Switching	Quatrefoil	Xenakis, Athanasios David	√	√	PWC	3	3	9		53
Shaft-Switching	Rug Weaving: One Weaver's Approach	Hand, Barbara	√	>4	WJ	7	4	28	Sp 83	32
Shaft-Switching	Rugs for Interiors	Roach, Dianne Carol	√		SS&D	16	4	64	Fa 85	18
Shaft-Switching	Shaft Switch Technique (error-corrected WJ v6 n1 81 p28d)		√	√	WJ	5	1	17	Su 80	5
Shaft-Switching	Shaft Switch Techniques (error-corrected WJ v5 n1 80 p5)	Busse, Jane	√	√	WJ	4	4	16	Ap 80	11
Shaft-Switching	Shaft Switching, A Simple Method Usable for Finer Setts	Herring, Connie; Athanasios David Xenakis	√	√	PWC	3	3	9		29
Shaft-Switching	Shaft Switching on Boundweave (Nancy Kraushaar)		√	√	WJ	5	3	19	Wi 81	38
Shaft-Switching	Shaft-Switch Rugs with Pinstripe Pattern Areas		√	√	WJ	5	2	18	Fa 80	28
Shaft-Switching	Shaft-Switching	Barrett, Clotilde	√	√	WJ	8	4	32	Sp 84	28
Shaft-Switching	Shaft-Switching Device of Richard Shultz		√	√	WJ	8	4	32	Sp 84	35
Shaft-Switching	Shaft-Switching Device of William Koepp		√	√	WJ	8	4	32	Sp 84	32
Shaft-Switching	Shaft-Switching on 3-End Drafts		√	√	WJ	5	4	20	Sp 81	24
Shaft-Switching	Shaft-Switching on 3-End Drafts: Striped Patterns, Part 1		√	√	WJ	6	1	21	Su 81	7
Shaft-Switching	Shaft-Switching on 3-end Drafts: Striped Patterns, Part 2		√	√	WJ	6	2	22	Fa 81	16
Shaft-Switching	Shaft-Switching on a Jack Loom	Wilson, Sadye Tune	√	√	SS&D	10	1	37	Wi 78	70
Shaft-Switching	Shaft-Switching on Rising Shed Looms Using Weighted Floating Heddles	Harse, Crys	√	√	WJ	9	4	36	Sp 85	63

SUBJECT	TITLE	AUTHOR	IL	INST	JOUR	VOL	NO	ISS	DATE	PAGE
Shaft-Switching	Star and Diamond	Xenakis, Athanasios David	√	√	PWC	3	3	9		49
Shaft-Switching	Three-Color, Weft-Faced Block Weave	Neely, Cynthia H.	√	>4	SS&D	15	2	58	Sp 84	74
Shaft-Switching	Warp Stuffer Weave with Shaft Switching Applications	Evans, Jane A.	√	>4	Hw	4	3		M/J 83	72
Shaft-Switching	White on White	Lyon, Linda	√	√	PWC	3	3	9		60
Shaft-Switching: Designs	Shaft-Switching	Barrett, Clotilde	√	√	WJ	8	4	32	Sp 84	28
Shaft-Switching: Devices	Shaft-Switching	Barrett, Clotilde	√	√	WJ	8	4	32	Sp 84	28
Shaft-Switching: Devices	Shaft-Switching Device of Richard Shultz		√	√	WJ	8	4	32	Sp 84	35
Shaft-Switching: Devices	Shaft-Switching Device of William Koepp		√	√	WJ	8	4	32	Sp 84	32
Shaft-Switching: Devices	Shaft-Switching on a Jack Loom	Wilson, Sadye Tune	√	√	SS&D	10	1	37	Wi 78	70
Shaft-Switching: Devices	Shaft-Switching on Rising Shed Looms Using Weighted Floating Heddles	Harse, Crys	√	√	WJ	9	4	36	Sp 85	63
Shaft-Switching, Double	Shaft-Switching to Create Tapestry Effects	Green, Andrea	√	√	WJ	8	4	32	Sp 84	36
Shaft-Switching: Drafting	Shaft-Switching	Barrett, Clotilde	√	√	WJ	8	4	32	Sp 84	28
Shaker Angel	Hands to Work and Hearts to God	Erf, Mary Elva	√	√	WJ	8	1	29	Su 83	25
Shaker: Tape Chair Seats	Chair Seats Woven of Tape and Ash Splints	Sober, Marion Burr	√	√	H&C	19	3		Su 68	13
Shaker Textiles	Hands to Work and Hearts to God	Erf, Mary Elva	√	√	WJ	8	1	29	Su 83	25
Shaker Textiles	Shaker Textiles	Hillenburg, Nancy	√	√	WJ	8	1	29	Su 83	22
Shaker Textiles	Simple Gifts	Alderman, Sharon	√		Hw	3	5		N/D 82	39
Shakers	Shaker Technique: Part 1, Weaving with Wood, The	Gordon, Beverly	√		SS&D	7	4	28	Fa 76	32
Shakers	Shaker Technique: Part 2, Rag Rugs, The	Gordon, Beverly	√	√	SS&D	8	1	29	WI 76	83
Shakers	Shaker Textiles at the Met	Erf, Mary Elva	√	√	SS&D	14	1	53	Wi 82	61
Shakers: Eastlake	Shaker Towels: A Guild Devotes a Year of Study to Nineteenth Century Textiles (error-corrected WJ v11 n2 86 p68)	Eastlake, Sandy	√	>4	WJ	10	4	40	Sp 86	20
Shawls see Scarves, Shawls, Stoles										
Shearing Sheep	Rattle Your Dags	Swenson, Nancy	√		S-O	8	1		Sp 84	12
Shearing Sheep	Shearing the Sheep	Goodman, Deborah Lerme			TM			1	O/N 85	10
Shearing Sheep	Sheep Shearing Robots	Sector, Bob			S-O	8	1		Sp 84	16
Shearing Sheep	To Shear Or Not to Shear?	Ciesiel, Marihelen			S-O	11	4		Wi 87	11
Shearing Sheep: Australian Technique	There's More Than One Way to Shear a Sheep	Parker, Ron; Teresa Parker	√	√	TM			13	O/N 87	61
Shed Rods	Examining the Shed	Koepp, William	√	√	WJ	10	4	40	Sp 86	76
Sheds	Examining the Shed	Koepp, William	√	√	WJ	10	4	40	Sp 86	76
Sheds: Pattern-Ground Weaving	Ups and Downs of the Long-Eyed Heddle	Swales, Lois	√	>4	CW	5	2	14	Ja 84	8
Sheds: Problems/Solutions	Rx: Shed Corrections	Guy, Sallie T.	√	√	Hw	3	1		Ja 82	78
Sheds: Regulator	Shed Regulator for Counterbalance Looms, The	Koepp, William	√	√	WJ	10	3	39	Wi 86	67
Sheds: Techniques	Highland Weavers in Asia	Hatch, David P.	√	√	H&C	11	1		Wi 60	6
Sheep and Sheep Breeds	Amazing Basques and Their Sheep, The	Dayton, Rita	√		S-O	3			79	19
Sheep and Sheep Breeds	Beverley Royce's "Recipe" for Merino	Royce, Beverly	√	√	S-O	5			81	49
Sheep and Sheep Breeds	Breeds of Sheep	Blackburn, Edna	√		SS&D	3	2	10	Sp 72	35
Sheep and Sheep Breeds	Choosing the Fiber for Feltmaking	Spark, Pat	√	√	SS&D	17	4	68	Fa 86	20
Sheep and Sheep Breeds	Fleece in the Hands of a New Zealand Spinner	Horne, Beverley	√		S-O	2			78	24
Sheep and Sheep Breeds	Good Hope Farm	Sitko, Jane Bradley	√		SS&D	18	2	70	Sp 87	40
Sheep and Sheep Breeds	Handspun Yarns from Black Sheep Wool	Simmons, Paula	√	√	H&C	14	3		Su 63	6
Sheep and Sheep Breeds	How to Raise Sheep, Advice For Ambitious Spinners	Simmons, Paula	√		H&C	22	2		Sp 71	24
Sheep and Sheep Breeds	If You Want to Work with the Best Wool Yarns, Spin Them Yourself	Bulback, Stanley	√	√	TM			13	O/N 87	56
Sheep and Sheep Breeds	Native British Sheep: The Rare Breeds	Leadbeater, Eliza	√		S-O	3			79	19

SUBJECT	TITLE	AUTHOR	IL	INST	JOUR	VOL	NO	ISS	DATE	PAGE
Sheep and Sheep Breeds	Navajo Sheep Project Update, A				S-O	8	2		Su 84	6
Sheep and Sheep Breeds	Novelty Yarns: Creation in Color and Texture	Dick, Barbara Ann	√	√	SS&D	12	3	47	Su 81	32
Sheep and Sheep Breeds	Number 7140, The Controversial Sheep In Plaid Clothing		√		SS&D	5	1	17	Wi 73	40
Sheep and Sheep Breeds	Polycerate Sheep	Painter, Ingrid	√		SS&D	13	3	51	Su 82	46
Sheep and Sheep Breeds	Premium Wool—A Producer's Perspective	Parker, Ron			S-O	11	3		Fa 87	39
Sheep and Sheep Breeds	Return of the Churro, The	Alderman, Sharon D.	√		S-O	8	1		Sp 84	46
Sheep and Sheep Breeds	Scotland	Torphy, Helen	√		SS&D	15	4	60	Fa 84	10
Sheep and Sheep Breeds	Selecting Wool for Handspinning (error-corrected SS&D v13 n1 81 p4)	Fleet, Malcolm		√	SS&D	12	4	48	Fa 81	66
Sheep and Sheep Breeds	So You Want to Buy Some Sheep	Ekstrom, Brenda	√		S-O	4			80	34
Sheep and Sheep Breeds	Some Physical Characteristics of Wool of Interest to Handspinners	Adams, Brucie	√		S-O	1			77	28
Sheep and Sheep Breeds	Spin Your Own Lopi?	Gibson-Roberts, Priscilla A.	√	√	S-O	10	2		Su 86	40
Sheep and Sheep Breeds	Spinning Down Under: What Are You Going to Do with the Yarn?	De Boer, Janet	√		S-O	1			77	23
Sheep and Sheep Breeds	There's a Lady Out Bantry Bay Way	Rubbert, Toni Condon	√		S-O	7	4		Wi 83	32
Sheep and Sheep Breeds	Villa de Cordero Negro: "Country Home of the Black Lamb"	Pepin, Yvonne	√		SS&D	17	3	67	Su 86	30
Sheep and Sheep Breeds	What Kind of Wool Is It?	Bulback, Stanley			TM			13	O/N 87	20
Sheep and Sheep Breeds	Wild Sheep	Decker, Eugene	√		S-O	3			79	26
Sheep and Sheep Breeds	Wonderful Worsted	Dozer, Iris	√	√	S-O	7	2		Su 83	32
Sheep and Sheep Breeds	Wool — Most Versatile of Fibers, Part 1	Kiessling, Robert H.	√		H&C	2	3		Su 51	13
Sheep and Sheep Breeds	Wool Production from Small Flocks of Sheep	Nicholas, Kristin	√		S-O	7	2		Su 83	39
Sheep and Sheep Breeds	Wool — That Wonderful Natural Fiber	Derr, Mary L.	√	√	WJ	2	2	6	Oc 77	2
Sheep and Sheep Breeds	Woolens and Tweeds: Sheep, Distribution and Breeds	Tidball, Harriet			SCGM		4		61	2
Sheep and Sheep Breeds	Wools of Britain, The	Seagroatt, Margaret	√		H&C	24	2		M/A 73	33
Sheep and Sheep Breeds: Black Welsh	Black Welsh Mountain Sheep	Moroney, Anne-Marie	√	√	S-O	11	4		Wi 87	51
Sheep and Sheep Breeds: Border Leicester	Border Leicester	Walker, Linda Berry	√	√	Hw	2	3		My 81	64
Sheep and Sheep Breeds: Cheviot, Border	Border Cheviot	Walker, Linda Berry	√	√	Hw	4	1		J/F 83	63
Sheep and Sheep Breeds: Cheviot, North Country	North Country Cheviot	Walker, Linda Berry	√	√	Hw	4	1		J/F 83	63
Sheep and Sheep Breeds: Churro	Churro Sheep in the Navajo Tradition	McNeal, Dr. Lyle G.	√		WJ	10	2	38	Fa 85	31
Sheep and Sheep Breeds: Churro	Commercial Materials in Modern Navajo Rugs	Hedlund, Ann Lane	√		TMJ	25			86	83
Sheep and Sheep Breeds: Clun Forest	Clun Forest	Walker, Linda Berry	√		Iw	6	1		Wi 80	62
Sheep and Sheep Breeds: Columbia	Columbia, The	Adams, Brucie	√		Iw	3	4		Su 78	36
Sheep and Sheep Breeds: Corriedale	Breeds of Sheep for Spinners: Corriedale	Nickerson, Signe	√	√	S-O	10	4		Wi 86	18
Sheep and Sheep Breeds: Corriedale	Corriedale	Walker, Linda Berry	√		Hw	3	1		Ja 82	73
Sheep and Sheep Breeds: Cotswold	Cotswold	Murray, Gwen B.	√		S-O	11	1		Sp 87	47
Sheep and Sheep Breeds: Cotswold	Cotswold	Walker, Linda Berry	√	√	Hw	3	4		Se 82	71
Sheep and Sheep Breeds: Herdwick	Fabric of the Lake District: Herdwick Sheep	Humphries, Andrew B.	√		S-O	8	4		Wi 84	45
Sheep and Sheep Breeds: Icelandic	Spinning with Icelandic Wool	Heite, Louise	√	√	S-O	10	1		Sp 86	33
Sheep and Sheep Breeds: Jacob	Jacob	Walker, Linda Berry	√	√	Iw	5	4		Fa 80	64
Sheep and Sheep Breeds: Jacob	Jacob Wool — A Handspinner's Delight	Thormahlen, Marian Oyen	√	√	WJ	11	3	43	Wi 87	57

SUBJECT	TITLE	AUTHOR	IL	INST	JOUR	VOL	NO	ISS	DATE	PAGE
Sheep and Sheep Breeds: Jacob	Spotting a Good Jacob	Painter, Ingrid	√		S-O	7	2		Su 83	18
Sheep and Sheep Breeds: Karakul	Karakul	Walker, Linda Berry	√		Hw	3	2		Mr 82	60
Sheep and Sheep Breeds: Karakul	Know Your Fibers: Karakul	Ligon, Linda	√		Iw	2	3		Sp 77	12
Sheep and Sheep Breeds: Lincoln	Lincoln	Walker, Linda Berry	√	√	Iw	5	1		Wi 79	52
Sheep and Sheep Breeds: Merino	Experiments with Merino	Adams, Brucie	√	√	Iw	5	1		Wi 79	50
Sheep and Sheep Breeds: Merino	Merino	Walker, Linda Berry	√	√	Iw	5	3		Su 80	59
Sheep and Sheep Breeds: Navajo	Saving the Navajo Sheep	Timmons, Chris	√		Fa	11	3		M/J 84	54
Sheep and Sheep Breeds: Perendale	Perendale	Walker, Linda Berry	√	√	Hw	2	4		Se 81	69
Sheep and Sheep Breeds: Rambouillet	Rambouillet	Walker, Linda Berry	√	√	Iw	4	3		Su 79	55
Sheep and Sheep Breeds: Romney	Romney	Walker, Linda Berry	√		Iw	5	2		Sp 80	63
Sheep and Sheep Breeds: Scottish Blackface	Scottish Blackface	Walker, Linda Berry	√	√	Iw	4	4		Fa 79	60
Sheep and Sheep Raising	Yarn Starts Here, Photo Essay, The	Babb, Lou	√		SS&D	7	3	27	Su 76	31
Sheep Industry: Navajo	Churro Sheep in the Navajo Tradition	McNeal, Dr. Lyle G.	√		WJ	10	2	38	Fa 85	31
Sheep Raising	Allen Farm Sheep and Wool Company	Erickson, Johanna	√		SS&D	17	3	67	Su 86	25
Sheep Raising	Appeal from the American Sheep Farmers, An	Painter, Ingrid			S-O	9	2		Su 85	7
Sheep Raising	Good Hope Farm	Sitko, Jane Bradley	√		SS&D	18	2	70	Sp 87	40
Sheep Raising	How to Raise Sheep, Advice For Ambitious Spinners	Simmons, Paula	√		H&C	22	2		Sp 71	24
Sheep Raising	How to Raise Sheep: Advice for Ambitious Spinners, Part 2	Simmons, Paula	√	√	H&C	22	3		Su 71	19
Sheep Raising	I Think I'll Get a Sheep	Green, Louise			SS&D	1	2	2	Mr 70	5
Sheep Raising	Raising a Spinner's Flock	Ligon, Linda	√	√	Iw	2	3		Sp 77	14
Sheep Raising	Roggeband	Blinks, Anne	√	√	Iw	3	3		Sp 78	16
Sheep Raising	Villa de Cordero Negro: "Country Home of the Black Lamb"	Pepin, Yvonne	√		SS&D	17	3	67	Su 86	30
Sheep-to-Shawl	Ewe Can't Win This Wrestling Match	Byers, Patricia			TM			10	A/M 87	18
Sheep-to-Shawl	From Sheep to Shawl	Thorne, Sylvia	√		H&C	17	1		Wi 66	36
Sheep-To-Shawl	From Sheep to Shawl	Van Ord, Kay; Stewart Van Ord	√	√	WJ	6	2	22	Fa 81	57
Sheep-to-Shawl	From Sheep to Shawl in Four Hours	Lockwood, Sheri	√		S-O	8	2		Su 84	43
Sheep-to-Shawl	Grandadddy of Sheep-To-Shawls: The Newberry Coat 1811, The				S-O	6	4		82	20
Sheep-to-Shawl	Opinionated Knitter: Sheep to Shawl, The	Wright, Jenny	√		Kn	4	1	9	Wi 87	20
Sheep-to-Shawl	Shear to Share	Best, Eleanor	√	√	SS&D	15	1	57	Wi 83	28
Sheep-to-Shawl	Sheep to Shawl	Thorne, Sylvia	√		SS&D	3	2	10	Sp 72	33
Sheep-to-Shawl	Sheep to Shawl: A Wonderful Show	Steinberg, Natali	√		S-O	6	4		82	41
Sheep-to-Shawl	Sheep to Shawl in Albuquerque		√		Iw	1	2		Wi 76	23
Sheep-To-Shawl	Utah Guild Sheep to Shawl	Hartford, Jane	√		SS&D	8	2	30	Sp 77	23
Sheep-to-Shawl	Weavers Demonstrate for Mrs. Johnson		√		H&C	19	4		Fa 68	11
Sheepherding	Sheep Country Profiles: Jean Urruty	Gordon, Gerrie	√		Iw	2	3		Sp 77	25
Sheepherding Traditions: Ireland	Shepherds of Glenmore, The	Burkhauser, Jude	√		S-O	6	4		82	36
Shelters: Felted	Shelters and Symbols	Gordon, Beverly	√	√	SS&D	11	1	41	Wi 79	53
Shelters: Woven	It's Really Only an Inverted Basket	Hoelter, Jane	√	√	SS&D	9	4	36	Fa 78	26
Shelters: Woven	Turkoman Yurt, The		√	√	SS&D	10	1	37	Wi 78	24
Shetland Islands	Double Edge of Knitting, The	Mabee-Zust, Mariah	√		Fa	10	3		M/J 83	50
Shetland Islands	Knitter's Journey, A	Bush, Nancy	√		Kn	3	4	8	Fa 87	24
Shetland Islands	Shetlands, The	Bush, Nancy	√		Kn	1	2	2	S-S 85	62
Shetland Islands	Spinning a Gossamer Web	Gibson-Roberts, Priscilla A.	√	√	Kn	4	1	9	Wi 87	62
Shibori	Ana Lisa Hedstrom: The Intuitive Language of Shibori	Scarborough, Jessica	√		Fa	13	1		J/F 86	26

SUBJECT	TITLE	AUTHOR	IL	INST	JOUR	VOL	NO	ISS	DATE	PAGE
Shibori	Art of Stitched Shibori, The (error-corrected Fa v12 n3 85 p8)	Wada, Yoshiko; Mary Kellogg Rice, Jane Barton	√		Fa	12	2		M/A 85	55
Shibori	"Contemporary Shibori" (Exhibit)	Howe, Cathe	√		Fa	11	3		M/J 84	82
Shibori	Innovations in Indigo	Wada, Yoshiko Iwamoto	√		Fa	13	5		S/O 86	29
Shibori	Resist Dyeing, Curiosities and Inventions: Shibori	Zielinski, S. A.; Robert Leclerc, ed.	√	√	MWL	17			'51–'73	10
Shibori	Shihoko Fukumoto (Exhibit)		√		Fa	14	2		M/A 87	61
Shibori, Arashi	Shibori Tip		√	√	TM		9		F/M 87	10
Shibori: Technique	D'Arcie Beytebiere: Windswept Designs in Pleated Silk	Tacker, Sylvia	√		Fa	13	1		J/F 86	28
Shibori: Techniques	Stitched Shibori Techniques: A Sampling	Wada, Yoshiko; Mary Kellogg Rice, Jane Barton	√	√	Fa	12	2		M/A 85	58
Shifts	Linen Shift: Plain Sewing Makes the Most of Your Fabric, A	Smith, Kathleen B.	√	√	TM		9		F/M 87	46
Shifu	Kazuko Nishigaki Creates in Ancient Tradition	Major, Dana; John Major	√		SS&D	6	2	22	Sp 75	93
Shifu	Paper Clothing, East	Sahlstrand, Margaret	√	√	Fa	11	2		M/A 84	36
Shifu	Shifu: A Handwoven Paper Textile of Japan	Miller, Dorothy	√	√	AT	4			De 85	43
Shifu: Technique	Shifu: A Handwoven Paper Textile	Miller, Dorothy	√	√	Hw	6	3		Su 85	69
Shininess	Shine On	Liebler, Barbara			Hw	7	1		J/F 86	75
Shirts: Interfacing	Making Sense of Interfacing (error-corrected TM n12 p4)	Komives, Margaret Deck	√	√	TM		10		A/M 87	58
Shirts see Blouses, Shirts, Tops										
Shisha Mirror Embroidery	All That Glitters: Shisha by Machine	Fanning, Robbie	√	√	TM		1		O/N 85	63
Shisha Mirror Embroidery	Gujarati Embroidery	Westfall, Carol D.; Dipti Desai	√		AT	8			De 87	29
Shoelaces	Lace Up in Style, Handwoven Shoelaces (Kathy Rug)		√	√	Hw	8	2		M/A 87	17
Shoelaces: Card Weaving	Preppy Look is in the Cards, The	Xenakis, Athanasios David	√	√	PWC	1	1		No 81	6
Shoemaking	Shoemaker's Art, The	Bowen, Gaza	√	√	TM		5		J/J 86	56
Shoulder Pads	Custom-Fit Shoulder Pads		√	√	TM		4		A/M 86	8
Shoulder Pads	Pleated Shoulder Pads		√	√	TM		9		F/M 87	10
Shoulder Pads	Preventing Shoulder-Pad Show-Through		√	√	TM		14		D/J 87	12
Shoulder Pads	Tailor's Logic	Hostek, Stanley	√	√	TM		14		D/J 87	42
Shows: Costumed Lamb	Number 7140, The Controversial Sheep In Plaid Clothing		√		SS&D	5	1	17	Wi 73	40
Shows: Trade	Design Supermarket	Northup, Wendy			TM		7		O/N 86	10
Shows: Trade	New "Trade" Shows	Fanning, Robbie			TM		1		O/N 85	14
Shrinkage	Designing the Warp: Parallel Considerations	Criscola, Jeanne	√	√	TM		1		O/N 85	66
Shrinkage	Shrinkage in Cotton Knits	Keele, Wendy	√	√	Kn	3	3	7	Su 87	3
Shrinkage	Superwash Wool	Donnelly, Robert	√		S-O	10	2		Su 86	49
Shrinkage Differential: Cotton/Wool	Pretty, Piqué & Pink	Keasbey, Doramay	√	> 4	PWC	4	3	13		47
Shrinkage: Fabrics	Ready for the Needle	Coffin, David Page	√	√	TM		12		A/S 87	43
Shroud of Turin	Shroud, The		√		SS&D	12	1	45	Wi 80	15
Shuttle Rotation Technique	Boundweave Rug on an Overshot Threading	Kindahl, Connie	√	√	SS&D	17	3	67	Su 86	58
Siam	Silks from Siam	Woodward, Carol H.	√		H&C	2	3		Su 51	23
Silesia	Tailor's Logic	Hostek, Stanley	√	√	TM		14		D/J 87	42
Silk	A. H. Rice Company: Maker of Silk Thread	Goodman, Deborah Lerme	√		Fa	13	1		J/F 86	54
Silk	Ana Lisa Hedstrom: The Intuitive Language of Shibori	Scarborough, Jessica	√		Fa	13	1		J/F 86	26
Silk	Art of Silk Dyeing, The (Photo-corrections WJ v10 n3 86 p6)	Wipplinger, Michelle	√	√	WJ	10	2	38	Fa 85	46

SUBJECT	TITLE	AUTHOR	IL	INST	JOUR	VOL	NO	ISS	DATE	PAGE
Silk	Availability of Silk to the Fiber Craftsman				WJ	3	2	10	Oc 78	12
Silk	China and the Complexities of Weaving Technologies	Vollmer, John E.			AT	5			Ju 86	65
Silk	Designs in Ancient Figured Silks	Blumenau, Lili	√		H&C	2	1		Wi 50	5
Silk	D'Arcie Beytebiere: Windswept Designs in Pleated Silk	Tacker, Sylvia	√		Fa	13	1		J/F 86	28
Silk	Experimenting with Silk Crepe	Quinn, Celia	√	√	S-O	10	4		Wi 86	36
Silk	Guide to Raising Silk, A	Fleming, Barbara	√	√	Iw	3	1		Fa 77	34
Silk	Handweaving with Silk	Derr, Mary		√	WJ	3	2	10	Oc 78	40
Silk	Handwoven Silk Garments: A Wedding Dress	Best, Eleanor	√	√	WJ	3	2	10	Oc 78	28
Silk	Handwoven Silk Garments: Blue Silk Dress	Alvic, Philis	√	> 4	WJ	3	2	10	Oc 78	27
Silk	Handwoven Silk Garments: Ikat Dress	Schreiber, LaVonne	√	√	WJ	3	2	10	Oc 78	30
Silk	Handwoven Silk Garments: Ikat Kimono	Barnett-Westfall, Lynn	√	√	WJ	3	2	10	Oc 78	30
Silk	Handwoven Silk Garments: Ikat Shirt	Utzinger, Karen	√	√	WJ	3	2	10	Oc 78	29
Silk	History of Silk, A	Mattera, Joanne	√	√	SS&D	8	2	30	Sp 77	24
Silk	How to Scour Silk	Bromberg, Kay	√	√	WJ	4	4	16	Ap 80	40
Silk	Introduction fo Silk Dyeing, An	Walsh, Joan Lea		√	WJ	3	2	10	Oc 78	14
Silk	Junco Sato Pollack: Seashells of Silk	Norton, Deborah	√		Fa	12	3		M/J 85	18
Silk	Kiyomi Iwata: A Singularity of Vision	Park, Betty	√		Fa	13	1		J/F 86	10
Silk	Kumejima Dorozome: The Vegetable Dye and Mud Mordanting Process of Silk Tsugumi	Miller, Dorothy	√	√	AT	5			Ju 86	131
Silk	Kumejima Kasuri: A Visit to a Remote Japanese Silk Center	Mitchell, Alison	√	√	WJ	10	1	37	Su 85	59
Silk	Making Sense of Interfacing (error-corrected TM n12 p4)	Komives, Margaret Deck	√	√	TM			10	A/M 87	58
Silk	Mistra	Xenakis, Alexis Yiorgos	√		Kn	2	2	4	S-S 86	56
Silk	Novelty Silk Yarn from Bell Caps	Grayson, Persis	√	√	Hw	7	1		J/F 86	58
Silk	Plaited Silk: Myrna Wacknov	Fox, Judy Kellar	√		SS&D	16	2	62	Sp 85	44
Silk	Preparing Silk in Kumejima	Mitchell, Alison	√	√	WJ	10	2	38	Fa 85	53
Silk	Quinn's Spinning Notes	Quinn, Cecelia			S-O	5			81	55
Silk	Randall Darwall	Sayward, Jessica Lee	√		SS&D	15	2	58	Sp 84	48
Silk	Raw Silk for the Handweaver	Wehrlin, Max	√		H&C	6	2		Sp 55	22
Silk	Raw Silk Reeling: How to Do It Yourself	Derr, Mary		√	WJ	3	3	11	Ja 79	12
Silk	Saints and the Silkworms, The	Alderman, Sharon	√	√	Iw	3	4		Su 78	15
Silk	Sericulture in Upstate New York	Bard, Elizabeth A.	√		Fa	13	1		J/F 86	36
Silk	Sewing with Silk	Stoyer, Janet	√	√	TM			4	A/M 86	35
Silk	Silk		√		S-O	1			77	34
Silk	Silk	Chadwick, A.	√	√	WJ	3	2	10	Oc 78	6
Silk	Silk	Lawrence, Mary Jo	√	√	WJ	7	3	27	Wi 82	74
Silk	Silk	Sullivan, Donna	√	√	SS&D	16	2	62	Sp 85	42
Silk	Silk: A Fiber of Many Faces	Quinn, Celia	√	√	S-O	8	3		Fa 84	30
Silk	Silk and Fiber Reactive Dyes		√	√	WJ	3	2	10	Oc 78	24
Silk	Silk City: Paterson, New Jersey	Malarcher, Patricia	√		Fa	13	1		J/F 86	31
Silk	Silk Dyeing		√	√	WJ	3	2	10	Oc 78	21
Silk	Silk Lore: The Myths of a Magical Fiber	Goodman, Deborah Lerme	√		Fa	13	1		J/F 86	42
Silk	Silk Production in Kohn Kaen	Marston, Ena			SS&D	7	3	27	Su 76	30
Silk	Silk Reflections of C. J. Yao, The	Nicoli, Antony	√		Fa	13	1		J/F 86	47
Silk	Silk Retrospective	Marston, Ena			SS&D	14	1	53	Wi 82	34
Silk	"Silk Roads/China Ships" (Exhibit)	Sider, Sandra	√		Fa	11	4		J/A 84	74
Silk	Silk: Spinner's Luxury		√	√	Hw	5	4		S/O 84	85
Silk	Silk, the Story of a Culture	Drooker, Penelope	√		Hw	7	1		J/F 86	49
Silk	Silk Trivia: Miscellaneous Facts About a Versatile Fiber	Goodman, Deborah Lerme	√		Fa	13	1		J/F 86	44

SUBJECT	TITLE	AUTHOR	IL	INST	JOUR	VOL	NO	ISS	DATE	PAGE
Silk	Silk: Working with Reeled, Spun, and Mawata		√	√	S-O	5			81	46
Silk	"Silken Threads and Silent Needles" (Exhibit)	Dunnewold, Jane	√		Fa	11	6		N/D 84	78
Silk	Silks from Siam	Woodward, Carol H.	√		H&C	2	3		Su 51	23
Silk	Silkworks	Goodman, Deborah Lerme	√		Fa	13	1		J/F 86	50
Silk	"Soft As Silk" (Exhibit)	Guagliumi, Susan	√		Fa	10	1		J/F 83	78
Silk	Suited to Silk	Turner, Kathryn M.	√	√	SS&D	18	2	70	Sp 87	68
Silk	Theme Issue		√		Fa	13	1		J/F 86	
Silk	Tips for Dyeing Silk	Bliss, Anne		√	Hw	7	1		J/F 86	61
Silk	Tracing the Silk Road	Dyer, Carolyn	√		Fa	13	1		J/F 86	22
Silk	Yarns and Fibers: Facts About Silk	Zielinski, S. A.; Robert Leclerc, ed.			MWL	4			'51–'73	43
Silk	Yarns and Fibers: How to Weave Silk	Zielinski, S. A.; Robert Leclerc, ed.	√	√	MWL	4			'51–'73	46
Silk	Yarns and Fibers: Silk and Rayon	Zielinski, S. A.; Robert Leclerc, ed.			MWL	4			'51–'73	57
Silk	Yarns and Fibers: Weaving of Fine Silk	Zielinski, S. A.; Robert Leclerc, ed.		√	MWL	4			'51–'73	61
Silk	Yuki Tsumugi	Urbanek, Karen	√	√	S-O	10	1		Sp 86	42
Silk Box	Silk Box	Barrett, Clotilde	√		WJ	3	2	10	Oc 78	13
Silk: Embroidery	Persian Legend in Silk		√		TM			14	D/J 87	92
Silk Fabric: Types	Painted-Silk Clothing	Juve, Peggy	√	√	TM			12	A/S 87	24
Silk Moth	Wild Silk	Kolander, Cheryl	√	√	Iw	2	3		Sp 77	8
Silk, Painted	Silks of Ed Lambert: In Pursuit of the Moving Image, The	Whittaker, Lynn	√		Fa	9	5		S/O 82	60
Silk, Painted	Telling Stories with Color and Pattern	Behrens, Ahn	√		Fa	13	2		M/A 86	68
Silk Picture Weaving	Jacquard and Woven Silk Pictures, The	Adrosko, Rita J.	√		AT	1			De 83	9
Silk Picture Weaving	Salut, Monsieur Jacquard	Carey, Joyce Marquess	√		Hw	2	3		My 81	57
Silk Pile: Kirman Rugs	Kirman's Heritage in Washington: Vase Rugs in The Textile Museum	Ellis, Charles Grant	√		TMJ	2	3		De 68	17
Silk Production	Silk Production of Lullingstone and Whitchurch, The	Rubbert, Toni	√		Hw	3	4		Se 82	27
Silk: Properties	Therapeutic Aspects of Silk, The	Kolander, Cheryl			Fa	13	1		J/F 86	76
Silk Reeling	Ontario Handspinning Seminar	Johnston, Constance	√	√	H&C	23	5		S/O 72	23
Silk Reeling	Raw Silk Reeling: How to Do It Yourself	Derr, Mary		√	WJ	3	3	11	Ja 79	12
Silk Reeling	Silk	Chadwick, A.	√	√	WJ	3	2	10	Oc 78	6
Silk Road	Tracing the Silk Road	Dyer, Carolyn	√		Fa	13	1		J/F 86	22
Silk Roads: China-Roman World	Some Early Silk Finds in Northwest Europe	Wild, John-Peter	√		TMJ	23			84	17
Silk Screen	Casting Shadows: the Work of Pam Scheinman	Scheinman, Pam	√		Fa	5	1		J/F 78	60
Silk Screen	Dyeing with Fiber Reactive Dyes on Cotton	Read, Kay	√	√	WJ	4	2	14	Oc 79	42
Silk Screen	Francis Butler: "I Used To Be An Artist but I Couldn't Sit Still That Long"	Butler, Francis	√		Fa	5	5		S/O 78	40
Silk Screen	Grace Kraft: Charting A Private World	Summar, Polly	√		Fa	14	3		M/J 87	16
Silk Screen	JoAnn Giordano: A Modern Mythology	Malarcher, Patricia	√		Fa	13	6		N/D 86	13
Silk Screen	Joyce Wilkerson: Silk Screening a Warp		√	√	Fa	5	1		J/F 78	65
Silk Screen	Photographic Processes for Textiles	Ligon, Linda	√	√	Iw	2	2		Wi 77	21
Silk Screen	Resist Dyeing, Curiosities and Inventions: Batik 2	Zielinski, S. A.; Robert Leclerc, ed.	√	√	MWL	17			'51–'73	30
Silk Screen	Rugs: Jo Ann Giordano, Silk Screener		√		Fa	9	2		M/A 82	60
Silk Screen	Southwestern Rhythms of Harwood Steiger Fabrics, The	Beeaff, Dianne Ebertt	√		Fa	13	2		M/A 86	29
Silk Screen: Technique	Grace Kraft: Not Just Another Piece of Cloth from the Factory	Vozar, Linda	√	√	Fa	5	5		S/O 78	36
Silk: Spider Sacs	Spiders: Masters of Natural Textiles	Palmer, Jacqueline M.	√		Fa	14	4		S/O 87	33

SUBJECT	TITLE	AUTHOR	IL	INST	JOUR	VOL	NO	ISS	DATE	PAGE
Silk: Starching	How to Dye and Starch Silk	Bromberg, Kay	√	√	WJ	5	1	17	Su 80	43
Silk: Sun-Damaged	Repairing Sun-Damaged Silk			√	TM			11	J/J 87	10
Silk: Therapeutic Aspects	Therapeutic Aspects of Silk, The	Kolander, Cheryl	√		Fa	13	1		J/F 86	76
Silk Trade Routes: China to Mexico	Chinese Influence in Colonial Peruvian Tapestries	Cammann, Schuyler	√		TMJ	1	3		De 64	21
Silk: Types	On Eighteenth Century Flowered Silk Weaving as an Inspiration for Todays Complex Weavers	Fairbanks, Dale			CW	7	1	19	Se 85	8
Silk: Types	Sensuous Silk	West, Virginia	√		Hw	7	1		J/F 86	52
Silk Weaving	Banares Brocade	DuBois, Emily	√	>4	AT	3			My 85	209
Silk Weaving	Jacquard and Woven Silk Pictures, The	Adrosko, Rita J.	√		AT	1			De 83	9
Silk Weaving Centers	Jacquard and Woven Silk Pictures, The	Adrosko, Rita J.	√		AT	1			De 83	9
Silk Weaving: Drawloom	Tribute to a Famous Weaver	Wilkinson, Dorothy	√		H&C	17	4		Fa 66	32
Silk: Wild	Wild Silk	Kolander, Cheryl	√	√	Iw	2	3		Sp 77	8
Silkworms see Sericulture										
Silver: Painted Outlines and Accents	Where Did All the Silver Go? Identifying Eighteenth-Century Chinese Painted and Printed Silks	Lee-Whitman, Leanna; Maruta Skelton	√		TMJ	22			83	33
Singing	Four Posts of Poverty, The	Xenaxis, Alexis Yiorgos	√		PWC	5	1	15		6
Single-Thread Harness Pattern Weaving	Single Thread Harness Pattern Weaving	Fry, Laura	√	>4	CW	5	1	13	Se 83	14
Sisal	More About Fabrics: Projects in Coarse Fibers Sisal Mats	Zielinski, S. A.; Robert Leclerc, ed.	√	√	MWL	20			'51–'73	51
Sisal	Sisal for Hammocks	Hannah, Joyce	√		TM			6	A/S 86	18
Sisal	Sisal Production in Highland Guatemala	Ventura, Carol	√		Fa	14	2		M/A 87	44
Sisal	Survey of Leaf and Stem Fibers, A	Buchanan, Rita	√		S-O	10	3		Fa 86	24
Sizing	Vest with a Hidden Twist	Emerick, Patricia	√	√	S-O	11	4		Wi 87	36, I-46
Sizing: Cotton	Spinning Cotton with the Linders	Linder, Olive; Harry Linder	√	√	WJ	11	2	42	Fa 86	14
Sizing: Handspun	Weaving with Handspun Linen Yarn	Fannin, Allen A.	√	√	H&C	19	2		Sp 68	10
Sizing: Handspun Warps	Weaving with Handspun Yarns: Suggestions for Beginning Spinners	Simmons, Paula	√	√	H&C	17	4		Fa 66	4
Sizing: Silk	Embossed Silk (Jane Patrick)		√	√	Hw	3	5		N/D 82	30, 98
Sizing: Warps	Handspun, Handwoven Cocoon Jacket, A	Adams, Brucie	√	√	Hw	5	2		M/A 84	88
Sizing: Warps	Warp Sizing	Adams, Brucie		√	Hw	6	3		Su 85	79
Skewing	Plying a Balanced Yarn for Knitting	Quinn, Celia	√	√	S-O	11	4		Wi 87	30
Skillbragd	Skillbragd — A Decorative Pattern Weave		√	>4	Hw	8	3		M/J 87	60
Skills: Weaving	Treasury for Beginners: Skills in Handweaving	Zielinski, S. A.; Robert Leclerc, ed.		√	MWL	1			'51–'73	126
Skip Plain Weave	Complimentary-Weft Plain Weave — A Pick-up Technique (error-corrected WJ v5 n1 80 p28d)	Hanley, Janet	√	√	WJ	4	4	16	Ap 80	22
Skip Plain Weave	Traditional Berber Weaving in Central Morocco	Forelli, Sally; Jeanette Harries	√		TMJ	4	4		77	41
Skip Plain Weave, Inlay	Dolman Top (Sharon Alderman)		√	√	Hw	6	2		M/A 85	47, I-7
Skirts	Beginning with bands: Tablet Woven Garments and Accessories	Holtzer, Marilyn Emerson	√	√	WJ	9	3	35	Wi 85	28
Skirts	Bias Striped Skirt (Sharon Alderman)		√	√	Hw	5	1		J/F 84	45, 88
Skirts	Blanket Weave, The	Robitaille, Annette	√	>4	WJ	8	4	32	Sp 84	62
Skirts	Color and Design in Andean Warp-Faced Fabrics	Femenias, Blenda	√		WJ	12	2	46	Fa 87	44
Skirts	Colorful Cotton Coordinates (Pat Short) (error-corrected WJ v11 n3 87 p78)		√	√	WJ	11	2	42	Fa 86	40
Skirts	Cotton Skirt and Blouse	Gant, Helen Mosely	√	√	S-O	6	4		82	63
Skirts	Crochet—A Great Technique for Finishing Handwovens		√	>4	WJ	7	3	27	Wi 82	18
Skirts	District Check Wrap Skirt (Stephenie Gaustad)		√	√	Hw	4	5		N/D 83	68, 108
Skirts	Fashion Show of Handwoven Garments		√	>4	WJ	3	3	11	Ja 79	5

SUBJECT	TITLE	AUTHOR	IL	INST	JOUR	VOL	NO	ISS	DATE	PAGE
Skirts	From Elsie H. Gubser's Studio		√	> 4	H&C	7	3		Su 56	24
Skirts	From Sheep to Skirt in Five Days	Copestick, Myrtis Gorst	√	√	H&C	3	3		Su 52	25
Skirts	Garments Win At 1974 Midwest Conference		√	√	SS&D	6	2	22	Sp 75	92
Skirts	Garments with Ethnic Flavor: Mexican Motif Skirt		√	√	WJ	2	3	7	Ja 78	13
Skirts	Glad Rags: the designs of Rose Jurisich		√	√	Hw	2	3		My 81	46
Skirts	Greek Chemises: Cut and Construction	Welters, Linda	√	√	WJ	10	1	37	Su 85	40
Skirts	Hand Woven Garments	Piper, Aris	√	> 4	WJ	5	3	19	Wi 81	24
Skirts	Ikat Striped Ruana and Skirt	Colton, Mary Rawcliffe	√	√	Hw	5	4		S/O 84	60
Skirts	In Pursuit of Plakhta	Golay, Myrna	√	> 4	WJ	11	3	43	Wi 87	34
Skirts	Inside an Expensive Outfit	Galpin, Mary	√	√	TM			1	O/N 85	40
Skirts	Knitted Palette of Brenda French, The	Pierce, Judith	√		Fa	13	2		M/A 86	43
Skirts	Lace Trilogy	Fauske, Carla	√	√	PWC			6	Su 83	52
Skirts	Lace Weave Skirt with Jacket and Top (Louise Bradley)		√	> 4	Hw	5	3		Su 84	58, 104
Skirts	Make It Yourself with Handwoven Wool	John, Sue	√		S-O	9	1		Sp 85	12
Skirts	Make It Yourself with Handwoven Wool	Zawistoski, Patsy	√		S-O	9	1		Sp 85	12
Skirts	Maurine Fair	Ligon, Linda	√	√	lw	2	2		Wi 77	20
Skirts	Musical Skirt, A	Wood, Geraldine	√	√	H&C	14	4		Fa 63	39
Skirts	New Skirts for Summer	Frey, Berta	√	> 4	H&C	4	1		Wi 52	33
Skirts	Project Notebook, A	Ligon, Linda	√	√	lw	3	1		Fa 77	31
Skirts	Rags At Work	Finch, Joan Freitag	√	√	SS&D	16	4	64	Fa 85	72
Skirts	Seattle Guild Garment Designs, Part 3, Skirts and Pants		√	√	SS&D	11	1	41	Wi 79	20
Skirts	Silk Blouse and Skirt (Jean Sullivan)		√	√	Hw	7	3		M/J 86	52, I-14
Skirts	Silky Dress-Up: Skirt (C. Bryn Pinchin)		√	√	Hw	6	1		J/F 85	38, I-11
Skirts	Simple Skirt and Matching Shawl, A	Hewson, Betty	√	√	Hw	4	5		N/D 83	24
Skirts	Skirt and Child's Dress (Halcyon Schomp) (error-corrected Hw v4 n4 83 p92)		√	√	Hw	4	3		M/J 83	46, 87
Skirts	Skirt and Stole (Mary Pendergrass)		√	√	Hw	1	1		F-W 79	23, 56
Skirts	Skirt for the Wall, A		√	√	WJ	3	4	12	Ap 79	19
Skirts	Skirt (Nell Znamierowski)		√	√	Hw	7	3		M/J 86	34, I-7
Skirts	Skirt with Warp Stripe Pattern	Frey, Berta	√	√	H&C	14	2		Sp 63	38
Skirts	Special Tie-Up for Skirt Designed by Berta Frey		√	> 4	H&C	4	3		Su 53	54
Skirts	Sprang and Frame Plaiting for Garments		√	√	WJ	3	3	11	Ja 79	26
Skirts	Spring Ensemble (Ronnine Bohannan)		√	√	Hw	6	2		M/A 85	56, I-13
Skirts	Square Dance Skirts	Kaiser, Eunice	√	> 4	H&C	7	1		Wi 55	46
Skirts	Succeeding with the Knitting Machine	Mattera, Joanne	√		TM			2	D/J 85	50
Skirts	Tailored Vest and Skirt, A	Arnold, Ruth	√	> 4	WJ	9	3	35	Wi 85	56
Skirts	Tailoring a Suit Skirt	Bryan, Dorothy	√	√	H&C	10	4		Fa 59	28
Skirts	Turned Overshot	Rowley, Elaine; Alexis Yiorgos Xenakis	√	> 4	PWC	3	2	8		53
Skirts	Tweed Skirt (Leslie Voiers)		√	√	Hw	8	1		J/F 87	53, I-7
Skirts	'Twill Skirt the Issue	Xenakis, Athanasios David	√	√	PWC	1	1		No 81	49
Skirts	Utilitarian Hang-up	Nelson, Ruthe	√	√	WJ	3	3	11	Ja 79	11
Skirts	Variations on a Midnight Rainbow	Ligon, Linda	√	√	S-O	9	4		Wi 85	14
Skirts	Versatile Vest and Matching Wrap Skirt, A	Dopps, Beth R.	√	√	WJ	7	3	27	Wi 82	21
Skirts	Wear Your Wall Hanging	West, Virginia	√	√	SS&D	4	2	14	Sp 73	11
Skirts	Weave and Knit Suit		√	√	WJ	8	3	31	Wi 83	18
Skirts	Weave Three--Cocktail Skirt, Coating, Parka	Snyder, Mary	√	> 4	SS&D	6	2	22	Sp 75	34
Skirts	Weaver's Notebook		√	> 4	SS&D	10	1	37	Wi 78	33

SUBJECT	TITLE	AUTHOR	IL	INST	JOUR	VOL	NO	ISS	DATE	PAGE
Skirts	Weaving in Quebec: Devotion to Garments	Barrett, Clotilde	√	√	WJ	6	4	24	Sp 82	18
Skirts	Weaving Skirts	Wood, Gerry	√	> 4	H&C	9	4		Fa 58	18
Skirts	What People Ask Before They Buy Handmade Fashions	Leslie, Victoria	√		TM			9	F/M 87	58
Skirts	Wool Skirt and Shawl	Crosby, Roberta	√	√	PWC			5	Sp 83	55
Skirts	Woven Skirt and Its Development, The	Poussart, Anne	√	√	WJ	8	3	31	Wi 83	39
Skirts	Wrap Skirt (Anne Bliss)		√	√	Hw	7	1		J/F 86	55, I-11
Skirts: Circular	Making Swirly Skirts	Callaway, Grace	√	√	TM			10	A/M 87	35
Skirts, Evening	Contemporary Costume, Strictly Handwoven: An Evening Skirt	Tidball, Harriet	√	√	SCGM		24		68	34
Skirts: Pattern	Plastic Pattern Promises Perfect Fit, A	Fanning, Robbie			TM			12	A/S 87	20
Skirts: Sags	Making Swirly Skirts	Callaway, Grace	√	√	TM			10	A/M 87	35
Slack-Tension Weaving	Origins	Wilson, Kax	√		Iw	4	4		Fa 79	51
Slave Quilts	Slave Quilts: Threads of History	Grabiner, Dana M.	√		Fa	13	5		S/O 86	22
Sleeve Boards	Irons, Boards, and Presses: A Survey of the Tools That Beautify Sewing	Coffin, David Page	√		TM			10	A/M 87	40
Sleeves	Batwings and Butterflies	West, Virginia	√		Hw	6	2		M/A 85	41
Sleeves	Linen Shift: Plain Sewing Makes the Most of Your Fabric, A	Smith, Kathleen B.	√	√	TM			9	F/M 87	46
Sleeves	More About Sleeves			√	TM			11	J/J 87	4
Sleeves	Sleeves That Won't Twist		√	√	TM			2	D/J 85	6
Sleeves: Altering	Fitting the Fitted Sleeve	Nebesar, Rebecca Lanxner	√	√	TM			9	F/M 87	28
Sleeves: Cap	Poetry of Sleeves: Shaping and Sewing Cloth to Fit the Arm, The	Nebesar, Rebecca Lanxner	√	√	TM			9	F/M 87	24
Sleeves: Crochet	Crochet Inspired by the Trees	Moon, Ellen	√	√	TM			11	J/J 87	56
Sleeves: Fitting	Fitting the Fitted Sleeve	Nebesar, Rebecca Lanxner	√	√	TM			9	F/M 87	28
Sleeves: Knitted	Setting in Knitted Sleeves		√	√	TM			4	A/M 86	8
Sleeves: Set-In	Machine-Eased Sleeve Caps		√	√	TM			10	A/M 87	12
Sleeves: Set-In	Sewing a Set-In Sleeve	Nebesar, Rebecca Lanxner	√	√	TM			9	F/M 87	27
Sleeves: Sewing	Poetry of Sleeves: Shaping and Sewing Cloth to Fit the Arm, The	Nebesar, Rebecca Lanxner	√	√	TM			9	F/M 87	24
Sleying and Threading	Doup Leno: Sample Project, Threading the Loom	Skowronski, Hella; Sylvia Tacker	√	√	SCGM		32		80	17
Sleying and Threading	Techniques for Better Weaving (error-corrected TM i9 D/J 86 p4)	Osterkamp, Peggy	√	√	TM			7	O/N 86	42
Sleying, Compound	Treasury for Beginners: Compound Sleying	Zielinski, S. A.; Robert Leclerc, ed.	√	√	MWL	1			'51–'73	68
Slide Library: Complex Weaves	Isolation	Fry, Laura			CW	5	1	13	Se 83	15
Slides	Representing Fiber Work Through Photography	Itter, Diane	√	√	SS&D	17	3	67	Su 86	42
Slides: Quilts	Fashionable Quilts	Wolff, Colette	√		TM			10	A/M 87	16
Slings	Peruvian Slings: Their Uses and Regional Variations	Noble, Carol Rasmussen	√		WJ	6	4	24	Sp 82	53
Slings: Dance	Sling Braiding in the Macusani Area of Peru	Zorn, Elayne	√	√	TMJ	19 20			80,81	41
Slings: Herding	Sling Braiding in the Macusani Area of Peru	Zorn, Elayne	√	√	TMJ	19 20			80,81	41
Slippage: Design Technique	More About Fabrics: Slippage	Zielinski, S. A.; Robert Leclerc, ed.	√	√	MWL	20			'51–'73	73
Slits and Tabs	Jacket for Hiking, A	Roth, Bettie G.	√	> 4	WJ	8	3	31	Wi 83	69
Slits and Tabs	Moebius Vest, The	Homme, Audrey	√	√	WJ	11	4	44	Sp 87	48
Slits and Tabs	More Creative Two Harness Weaving	Liebler, Barbara	√		Iw	5	1		Wi 79	46
Slits and Tabs	Utilitarian Hang-up	Nelson, Ruthe	√	√	WJ	3	3	11	Ja 79	11

SUBJECT	TITLE	AUTHOR	IL	INST	JOUR	VOL	NO	ISS	DATE	PAGE
Slits and Tabs	Weft-Wrap Openwork Techniques in Archaeological and Contemporary Textiles of Mexico	Johnson, Irmgard Weitlaner	√	√	TMJ	4	3		76	63
Slits, Horizontal	Skirt for the Wall, A		√	√	WJ	3	4	12	Ap 79	19
Smålands Weave	Smålands Weave on Eight Shafts	Shannon, Eileen	√	> 4	WJ	9	1	33	Su 84	47
Smocking	Smocked Blouse (Melba Ellis Short)		√	√	Hw	5	3		Su 84	66, 114
Smocking	Smocking	English, Trudy	√	√	SS&D	14	1	53	Wi 82	38
Smocking	Transfer Dots for Smocking			√	TM			5	J/J 86	10
Smocking: Technique	Handwoven Smocks	Short, Melba Ellis	√	√	Hw	5	3		Su 84	66
Snowflakes	Fantastic Finnweave, Part 2: Single-Thread Projects	Xenakis, Athanasios David	√	√	PWC			3	Oc 82	14
Soaps	Recipe for a Neutral Soap	Walsh, Joan Lee		√	WJ	3	3	11	Ja 79	17
Soaps: Molecular Structure and Characteristics	Principles of Textile Conservation Science, No. 7. Characteristics of Detergents for Cleaning Historic Textiles	Rice, James W.	√	√	TMJ	2	1		De 66	23
Social Conscience and Craftsman	Craftsman and Social Conscience: E. F. Schumacher, The	Hepburn, Ian			Hw	6	1		J/F 85	20
Social Conscience and Craftsman	Craftsman and Social Conscience, The Part 2: Mahatma Gandhi	Hepburn, Ian			Hw	5	5		N/D 84	22
Social Conscience and Craftsman	Craftsman and Social Conscience: William Morris, The	Hepburn, Ian			Hw	5	4		S/O 84	26
Sociology	Amazing Basques and Their Sheep, The	Dayton, Rita	√		S-O	3			79	19
Sociology	Women as Spinners: New England Spinsters	Gordon, Beverly	√		S-O	3			79	16
Sociology: Weaving	Looming Thoughts	Fannin, Allen; Dorothy Fannin			H&C	23	3		M/J 72	12
Socks	Cross Country Ski Set	Chadwick, Louisa	√	√	S-O	11	4		Wi 87	34
Socks	Spiral Tube Socks		√	√	S-O	11	1		Sp 87	22
Socks	Woolen Socks		√	√	S-O	5			81	60
Socks and Stockings	Basic Boot Socks	Quinn, Celia	√		S-O	10	2		Su 86	13
Socks and Stockings	Crocheted Socks		√	√	TM			12	A/S 87	8
Socks and Stockings	Evolution of a Project	de Grassi, Laurel	√	√	S-O	10	4		Wi 86	21
Socks and Stockings	Knit Socks for Survival			√	TM			8	D/J 86	4
Socks and Stockings	Lace and Legs	Upitis, Lizbeth	√		Kn	1	2	2	S-S 85	64
Socks and Stockings	Shape of Socks, The	Gaffey, Theresa	√	√	TM			2	D/J 85	28
Socks and Stockings	Stocking Basics	Upitis, Lizbeth	√	√	Kn	1	2	2	S-S 85	66
Socks and Stockings	Traditional Stockings: A Girl's Stocking (Lizbeth Upitis)		√	√	Kn	1	2	2	S-S 85	68
Socks and Stockings	Traditional Stockings: A Stocking from Rucava, Kurzeme, Latvia		√	√	Kn	1	2	2	S-S 85	69
Socks and Stockings	Traditional Stockings: A Stocking from Zemgale, Lativia (Elizeabete Zvirbulis)		√	√	Kn	1	2	2	S-S 85	69
Socks and Stockings	Traditional Stockings: Amish Baby Stockings (Mary Miller)		√	√	Kn	1	2	2	S-S 85	69
Soft Sculpture	Altered Ego: An Interview with Pat Oleszko	Lonier, Terri	√		Fa	10	1		J/F 83	26
Soft Sculpture	Ann Burian: Mythic Transformations	Hains, Maryellen	√		Fa	12	2		M/A 85	21
Soft Sculpture	Ann Dunbar		√		Fa	4	3		M/J 77	41
Soft Sculpture	Anne Swann	Packard, Myles	√		Fa	4	3		M/J 77	22
Soft Sculpture	Army of Softies: An Artist Talks About Her Delightfully Peculiar Obsession, An	Robinson, Sharon	√		Fa	8	6		N/D 81	25
Soft Sculpture	Cindy Hickok: Stuffed Characters	Fowler, Mary Jean	√		Fa	5	5		S/O 78	22
Soft Sculpture	Debra Minsky-Jackson: Renaissance Visions in Fiber	Grunberg, Liane	√		Fa	11	4		J/A 84	68
Soft Sculpture	Elizabeth Gurrier Multiples	King, A. J.	√		Fa	4	6		N/D 77	30
Soft Sculpture	Fantasy Figures: Shelly Fowler's Fabric Dolls	Place, Jennifer	√		Fa	10	1		J/F 83	16
Soft Sculpture	Fiber and Architecture: Dennis Jenkins		√		Fa	3	3		M/J 76	35

SUBJECT	TITLE	AUTHOR	IL	INST	JOUR	VOL	NO	ISS	DATE	PAGE
Soft Sculpture	Jaki Ernst "Fibre Graphics and Soft Sculpture" (Exhibit)	Gilsenan, Nancy	√		Fa	7	6		N/D 80	69
Soft Sculpture	Janet Higgins: Soft Sculpture in Motion	Marquess, Joyce	√		Fa	7	2		M/A 80	62
Soft Sculpture	Jerri Finch-Hurley: Quilted Paintings	Wonder, Danny	√		Fa	11	2		M/A 84	27
Soft Sculpture	Joan Arrizabalaga: Queen of the One-Armed Bandits		√		Fa	6	1		J/F 79	19
Soft Sculpture	JoEllen Trilling: Contemporary Pied Piper	Backer, Ellen	√		Fa	5	4		J/A 78	24
Soft Sculpture	Karen Reese		√		Fa	4	3		M/J 77	32
Soft Sculpture	Lenore Davis: Dye Painted Soft Sculpture		√	√	Fa	5	1		J/F 78	68
Soft Sculpture	Linda Nelson Bryan	Vozar, Linda	√		Fa	4	6		N/D 77	58
Soft Sculpture	Lynn Rothrock: Disturbing Creatures, Menacing Devil Dolls	Wiley, Lois	√		Fa	6	1		J/F 79	75
Soft Sculpture	Marjorie Ford-Pohlmann: Fiber Design Professional	LaLena, Constance	√		Hw	5	3		Su 84	82
Soft Sculpture	Metamorphosis in Maine: The Art of Barbara Lambert	Levy, Beverly Sauer	√		Fa	11	3		M/J 84	20
Soft Sculpture	Muslin Ladies: Trapunto Drawings of Christine Meyers	Rowland, Amy Zaffarano	√		Fa	10	3		M/J 83	19
Soft Sculpture	Nancy Greaver		√		Fa	4	4		J/A 77	51
Soft Sculpture	"Patricia Malarcher: Pieced Reflections" (Exhibit)	Scheinman, Pamela	√		Fa	11	2		M/A 84	77
Soft Sculpture	Pie in the Sky: The Irreverent Art of Geraldine Serpa	Serpa, Geraldine	√		Fa	6	4		J/A 79	26
Soft Sculpture	Portfolio of Contemporary Fiber Sculpture, A		√		Fa	11	4		J/A 84	34
Soft Sculpture	Priscilla Sage	Clardy, Andrea	√		Fa	5	2		M/A 78	26
Soft Sculpture	"Robin Becker and Joan Lintault: Visual Traces of the Past" (Exhibit)	Meloy, Margaret	√		Fa	11	1		J/F 84	80
Soft Sculpture	Sanity, Madness and the Artist: The Work of Suzan Anson	Demoss, Virginia	√		Fa	6	2		M/A 79	36
Soft Sculpture	Soft Boxes: Ritual for Our Common Life	McElroy, Jane	√		Fa	10	2		M/A 83	21
Soft Sculpture	Soft Sculpture of Barbara Ward, The	Harris, Patricia; David Lyon	√		Fa	14	1		J/F 87	10
Soft Sculpture	Soft Sculpture: Old Forms, New Meanings	Gordon, Beverly	√		Fa	10	6		N/D 83	40
Soft Sculpture	Soft Sculpture Set For Albee's "Seascape"		√		Fa	4	2		M/A 77	29
Soft Sculpture	"Softworks" (Exhibit)		√		Fa	3	6		N/D 76	10
Soft Sculpture	Stitched, Stuffed, and Painted: The Art of Esther Luttikhuizen	Acosta, Dan	√		Fa	12	2		M/A 85	61
Soft Sculpture	Susanmarie Cunningham: Wearable Soft Sculpture	Cunningham, Susanmarie	√		Fa	11	5		S/O 84	15
Soft Sculpture	Transferring Feelings to Fabric: Jane Morias	Park, Betty	√		Fa	5	1		J/F 78	52
Soft Sculpture	Woman on a Pedestal and Other Everyday Folks	Guyer, Niki	√		Fa	8	2		M/A 81	22
Soils/Stains: Nonsoluable	Principles of Textile Conservation Science, No. 7. Characteristics of Detergents for Cleaning Historic Textiles	Rice, James W.	√	√	TMJ	2	1		De 66	23
Soils/Stains: Soluable	Principles of Textile Conservation Science, No. 6. The Wonders of Water in Wetcleaning	Rice, James W.	√	√	TMJ	2	1		De 66	15
Songs	Homespun Songs from Ireland's Clancy Brothers	Drake, Elizabeth A.	√		SS&D	16	4	64	Fa 85	62
Songs	Linen Lore	Goodman, Deborah Lerme	√		Fa	14	2		M/A 87	16
Songs	Love-Spinning Farewell in Hawaii	McCarty, Carole	√		SS&D	6	1	21	Wi 74	41
Songs	"Mood Indigo"	Ellington, Duke			Fa	13	5		S/O 86	75
Songs	Spinning with Icelandic Wool	Heite, Louise	√	√	S-O	10	1		Sp 86	33
Songs	There's An Old Spinning Wheel in the Parlor	Rossiter, Phyllis	√		S-O	9	1		Sp 85	31
Songs	Weaver Is a Rose, A	Kozikowski, Janusz			Fa	5	5		S/O 78	13
Songs	"Woad Song"				Iw	3	1		Fa 77	4

SUBJECT	TITLE	AUTHOR	IL	INST	JOUR	VOL	NO	ISS	DATE	PAGE
Songs: Fabric	Songs in Fabric: Quiltmaker Nancy Herman Is an Unusual Musician	Rowland, Amy Zaffarano	√		Fa	9	4		J/A 82	22
Songs: Weaving/Spinning	Burls	Bogle, Michael	√		SS&D	12	1	45	Wi 80	31
Soumak	Finger Control: Or Getting the Most Out of Your Loom	Patrick, Jane	√	√	Hw	4	2		M/A 83	70
Soumak	Guatemala Visited	Atwater, Mary Meigs	√	√	SCGM		15		65	24
Soumak	Guatemala Visited	Atwater, Mary Meigs	√	√	SCGM		15		65	30
Soumak	Hand Woven Rugs: Weaves, Plain Weave, Soumak Technique	Atwater, Mary Meigs	√	√	SCGM		29		48	11
Soumak	Painting and Brocading on the Loom	Ziek, Bhakti	√	√	TM			6	A/S 86	42
Soumak	Peruvian Accented Mexican Blouse: Analyze—Then Improvise	Lawrence, Margaret	√	√	SS&D	7	1	25	Wi 75	40
Soumak	Soumak Rug (Jean Scorgie)		√	√	Hw	6	4		S/O 85	41, I-4
Soumak	Soumak-Woven Rug in a 15th Century International Sytle, A	Ellis, Charles Grant	√		TMJ	1	2		De 63	3
Soumak: Techniques	Make a Soumak Sampler into a Tote Bag		√	√	WJ	2	2	6	Oc 77	28
Sources: Dyes	Color Specialists, The		√		Kn	2	1	3	F-W 85	64
Sources: Yarn	Color Specialists, The		√		Kn	2	1	3	F-W 85	64
South America	South American Crafts		√		H&C	17	2		Sp 66	16
Southern Highland Handicraft Guild	From the Great Smokies to Rockefeller Center-The Southern Highland Handicraft Guild	Hart, Robert G.	√		H&C	2	3		Su 51	5
Southwest, U. S. A.	Churro Sheep in the Navajo Tradition	McNeal, Dr. Lyle G.	√		WJ	10	2	38	Fa 85	31
Southwest, U. S. A.	Sweetgrass, Cedar & Sage: Portrait of a Southwestern Weaver	Schevill, Margot	√		WJ	10	1	37	Su 85	24
Southwest, USA	Spinning in the Southwest — Prehistoric, Historic, and Contemporary	Lawrence, Ramona Sakiestewa	√		S-O	1			77	8
Space	Divided Spaces: The Fences of Japan	Bess, Nancy Moore	√		Fa	14	4		S/O 87	28
Space-Age Textiles	From Handloom to Missile				H&C	13	4		Fa 62	30
Spaced Denting	More About Fabrics: Spaced Fabrics	Zielinski, S. A.; Robert Leclerc, ed.	√	√	MWL	20			'51–'73	45
Spaced Warps	More About Fabrics: Spaced Fabrics	Zielinski, S. A.; Robert Leclerc, ed.	√	√	MWL	20			'51–'73	45
Spaced Wefts	More About Fabrics: Spaced Fabrics	Zielinski, S. A.; Robert Leclerc, ed.	√	√	MWL	20			'51–'73	45
Spain	Contemporary Alpujarra Rugs	Lorton, Henni	√		H&C	4	4		Fa 53	28
Spain	Garrido, Contemporary Spanish Tapestry Weaver		√		H&C	16	1		Wi 65	12
Spain	Handweaving in Spain	Arnold, Ruth	√		H&C	8	4		Fa 57	10
Spain	On Foreign Soil But Common Ground, Textile Assembly Meets in Spain	Mailey, Jean	√		H&C	21	1		Wi 70	18
Spanish Moss	Contemporary Uses for an Ancient Fiber: Spanish Moss	Elliott, Douglas B.	√	√	SS&D	9	2	34	Sp 78	51
Spanish Weave	Pick-Up Leno, A Two-harness Loom Technique	Wallace, Meg	√	√	WJ	1	2	2	Oc 76	3
Spanish-American Textiles	Southwestern Spanish Textiles (error-corrected SS&D v9 n4 78 p34)	Spillman, Trish; Marion Rinehart	√		SS&D	9	3	35	Su 78	56
Spanish-American Weaving	Truchas Becomes a Weaving Center	Ehly, Jean	√		H&C	24	4		Au 73	40
Special Olympics	Fiber is "Special"	Jackson, Mary Lynn; Cheryl McWilliams	√		SS&D	15	2	58	Sp 84	13
Speed: Weaving	From the Weaver's Bench	Elam, E. T.			H&C	23	4		J/A 72	33
Spider Silk	Spiders: Masters of Natural Textiles	Palmer, Jacqueline M.	√		Fa	14	4		S/O 87	33
Spider Weave	Tunic with Ribbons (Carol Powalisz)		√	√	Hw	8	1		J/F 87	52, I-8
Spider Weave	Woven Woolen Whimseys		√	√	WJ	2	2	6	Oc 77	14
Spider Weave, Linear Zigzag	Swatch #5 Blouse (Sharon Alderman) (error-corrected Hw v8 n4 87 p I-3)		√	√	Hw	8	2		M/A 87	38, I-5
Spin-Off Autumn Retreat (SOAR)	From SOAR to Rendezvous	Pettigrew, Dale			S-O	10	4		Wi 86	35
Spin-Off Autumn Retreat (SOAR)	Second Spin-Off Autumn Retreat, The		√		S-O	9	1		Sp 85	44

SUBJECT	TITLE	AUTHOR	IL	INST	JOUR	VOL	NO	ISS	DATE	PAGE
Spin-Off Autumn Retreat (SOAR)	SOAR 1985: Some Observations and Asides	Bulbach, Stanley			S-O	10	2		Su 86	16
Spin-Off Autumn Retreat (SOAR)	SOAR: A High Time	Pettigrew, Dale	√		S-O	8	1		Sp 84	6
Spin-Off Autumn Retreat (SOAR)	SOAR Sampler, A				S-O	10	2		Su 86	33
Spin-Off Magazine	Way We Were...The Way We're Going, The	Ligon, Linda	√		S-O	11	3		Fa 87	27
Spin-Ply Joins	Tree-Bast Fiber Textiles of Japan	Dusenbury, Mary	√	√	S-O	10	3		Fa 86	35
Spindlemuff	Spindlemuff is a Mythical Beast, The	Seifert, Walter	√	√	H&C	24	2		M/A 73	36
Spindles	High Whorl Spindle, The	Hochberg, Bette	√	√	SS&D	11	1	41	Wi 79	12
Spindles	Spinning with a Bead Whorl Spindle	Hochberg, Bette	√	√	SS&D	10	2	38	Sp 79	22
Spindles, Drop	Spindle	Chesley, Zina Mae		√	SS&D	2	2	6	Sp 71	22
Spindles, Hip	Navajo Hip Spindle, Part 1	Hicks, C. Norman	√	√	SS&D	8	1	29	WI 76	95
Spindles, Hip	Navajo Hip Spindle, Part 2	Hicks, C. Norman		√	SS&D	8	2	30	Sp 77	41
Spindles, Supported	Spindle	Chesley, Zina Mae		√	SS&D	2	2	6	Sp 71	22
Spinners	Like the Ad Says: "We've Come a Long Way"	Gibson-Roberts, Priscilla A.			S-O	11	3		Fa 87	26
Spinners	Northwest Spinners: Success for Them, A Challenge for You	Molinari, Jean			S-O	11	2		Su 87	50
Spinners	Portrait of a Spinner	Grayson, Persis			S-O	11	3		Fa 87	24
Spinners	Way We Were...The Way We're Going, The	Ligon, Linda	√		S-O	11	3		Fa 87	27
Spinning	Before Heddles Were Invented	Bird, Junius B.	√		H&C	3	3		Su 52	5
Spinning	Betty Rodman, an Integrated Life	Staines, Barbara			S-O	4			80	19
Spinning	Certificate of Excellence in Handspinning				SS&D	12	2	46	Sp 81	13
Spinning	Certificate of Excellence in Handspinning, The	Shaffer-Meyer, Rima; Arlene M. Stein			SS&D	13	2	50	Sp 82	35
Spinning	COE in Handspinning, The	Shaffer-Meyer, Rima			SS&D	15	2	58	Sp 84	25
Spinning	Colonel Ronin, Spinning Flyer	Ligon, Linda	√		Iw	2	4		Su 77	25
Spinning	Color in Spinning	Adams, Brucie		√	Iw	3	2		Wi 78	34
Spinning	Controlling the Size and Texture of Handspun Yarn	Hochberg, Bette	√	√	SS&D	9	4	36	Fa 78	31
Spinning	Coverlets: A Spinner's Challenge			√	S-O	6	4		82	25
Spinning	Demonstration Do's and Don'ts	Dokka, Margaret		√	SS&D	7	3	27	Su 76	64
Spinning	Des Moines Weavers Learn to Spin	Seeburger, Marze Marvin	√		H&C	6	1		Wi 54	56
Spinning	Distaffs: Scanning through History	Henzie, Susie	√		SS&D	9	4	36	Fa 78	56
Spinning	Does It Pay to Spin Your Own Yarn?	Hochberg, Bette			Iw	4	1		Wi 78	46
Spinning	Dressing the Distaff	Henzie, Susie	√	√	SS&D	10	1	37	Wi 78	12
Spinning	Eugene Spinners, The	Reade, Dorothy	√		H&C	18	3		Su 67	20
Spinning	Excellence of Spinning, Vitality of Dyes Impress Visitor to 'Down Under'	Barker, Mary	√		SS&D	4	4	16	Fa 73	46
Spinning	Fair Isle in Natural Colors, The	Gibson-Roberts, Priscilla A.	√	√	Kn	2	1	3	F-W 85	34
Spinning	Fibers for Spinning		√		WJ	9	2	34	Fa 84	42
Spinning	Fleece-to-Garment Competition in New Zealand	Ashford, Joy			SS&D	4	1	13	Wi 72	21
Spinning	From Sheep to Shawl	Van Ord, Kay; Stewart Van Ord	√	√	WJ	6	2	22	Fa 81	57
Spinning	Fur Fashions	Lucas, Jerie	√	√	SS&D	15	2	58	Sp 84	26
Spinning	Gravander Spinners, Raising Funds to Buy a Camel, The	McKinley, Esther D.	√		H&C	18	2		Sp 67	12
Spinning	Handspinning in New Hampshire	Brackett, Thelma	√		H&C	17	1		Wi 66	18
Spinning	Handspinning, Why Not Enjoy It	Senders, Diane	√		H&C	22	2		Sp 71	13
Spinning	Handspun, Handwoven Saddle Blanket, A	Newsted, Jean	√	√	WJ	8	2	30	Fa 83	22
Spinning	Handspun into Lace	Fournier, Jane	√	√	SS&D	17	4	68	Fa 86	70
Spinning	Handspun Yarn for a Pulled Warp Vest	Adams, Brucie	√	√	Hw	7	1		J/F 86	78
Spinning	Handspun/Handwoven Ramie Blouse	Champion, Ellen	√	> 4	WJ	9	2	34	Fa 84	52
Spinning	High Whorl Spindle, The	Hochberg, Bette	√	√	SS&D	11	1	41	Wi 79	12

SUBJECT	TITLE	AUTHOR	IL	INST	JOUR	VOL	NO	ISS	DATE	PAGE
Spinning	Home Built Box Spinner	Barrow, Cynthia	√	√	WJ	2	4	8	Ap 78	43
Spinning	I Have This Fleece...Now What?	Adams, Brucie	√	√	Iw	5	4		Fa 80	62
Spinning	Interview with Linda Berry Walker...A Spinning and Dyeing Business, An	Horton, Lucy	√		Fa	4	5		S/O 77	26
Spinning	Irish Kinsale Cloak, The	Jones, Una	√	√	WJ	8	3	31	Wi 83	35
Spinning	It Started with Two Rams				SS&D	1	1	1	De 69	16
Spinning	It's Time to Rock	Thorne, Sylvia			SS&D	3	1	9	Wi 71	28
Spinning	Kathy Mincer: In Pursuit of Excellence	Linder, Olive	√		SS&D	13	2	50	Sp 82	31
Spinning	Knitting with Handspun	O'Connor, Marcie Archer	√		Kn	1	2	2	S-S 85	54
Spinning	Learn to Spin on Our Sheep Farm	Jones, Mrs. Gary	√		SS&D	2	3	7	Su 71	18
Spinning	Lions and Tigers and.....Sheep?	Johnson, Ginger R.	√		S-O	8	2		Su 84	24
Spinning	Looking at Distaffs	Hochberg, Bette	√		Iw	3	3		Sp 78	43
Spinning	Love-Spinning Farewell in Hawaii	McCarty, Carole	√		SS&D	6	1	21	Wi 74	41
Spinning	Musk Ox, and Miscellaneous	Adams, Brucie	√	√	Iw	4	2		Sp 79	46
Spinning	Navajo Three-Ply Method, The	Rossiter, Phyllis	√	√	SS&D	16	1	61	Wi 84	10
Spinning	New Zealand Spinning	Ashford, Joy			SS&D	4	1	13	Wi 72	20
Spinning	Novelty Yarns: Creation in Color and Texture	Dick, Barbara Ann	√	√	SS&D	12	3	47	Su 81	32
Spinning	Ontario Handspinning Seminar	Johnston, Constance	√	√	H&C	23	5		S/O 72	23
Spinning	Overtwist, A Spinner's Problem	Simmons, Paula	√	√	H&C	19	1		Wi 68	37
Spinning	Paid Spinning Demonstrations	Hicks, C. Norman			SS&D	7	3	27	Su 76	46
Spinning	Precise Control of Size and Quality in Handspun Yarn, Part 1, The	Ross, Mabel	√	√	SS&D	16	3	63	Su 85	12
Spinning	Precise Control of Twist in Handspun Yarn, Part 2, The	Ross, Mabel	√	√	SS&D	16	4	64	Fa 85	26
Spinning	Production Spinning	Adams, Brucie			Iw	4	1		Wi 78	44
Spinning	Rachel Brown: Weaver At the Wheel	Daily, Laura	√		Fa	10	3		M/J 83	20
Spinning	Recent Success of Carole Lubove-Klein: an Inspiring Yarn, The	McGuire, Patricia	√		Fa	9	5		S/O 82	20
Spinning	Song of the Bobbin	Nelson, Lois	√		SS&D	4	3	15	Su 73	42
Spinning	Spin-in Bean-Fest				SS&D	1	1	1	De 69	14
Spinning	Spinner's Specialty: Heathered Yarns, A	Searle, Karen	√	√	WJ	9	2	34	Fa 84	56
Spinning	Spinning—Australia	DeBoer, Janet			S-O	11	3		Fa 87	35
Spinning	Spinning Bulky Yarns	Kronenberg, Bud	√	√	SS&D	13	1	49	Wi 81	78
Spinning	Spinning Demonstrations	Sumpter, Frances R.			SS&D	3	4	12	Fa 72	31
Spinning	Spinning Down Under: What Are You Going to Do with the Yarn?	De Boer, Janet	√		S-O	1			77	23
Spinning	Spinning Fine Yarn (It'a Method, not Magic)	Hochberg, Bette	√	√	Iw	5	3		Su 80	56
Spinning	Spinning for a Finished Product Competition	Feldman-Wood, Florence			S-O	7	4		Wi 83	30
Spinning	Spinning for an Ombré Project	Adams, Brucie	√	√	Hw	4	2		M/A 83	78
Spinning	Spinning in a Special Climate	Allen, Marian			S-O	11	3		Fa 87	50
Spinning	Spinning in Bolivia	Meisch, Lynn A.	√	√	S-O	10	1		Sp 86	25
Spinning	Spinning in New Zealand	Ashford, Joy	√		H&C	21	3		Su 70	42
Spinning	Spinning in Stehekin	Fridlund, Patricia	√		S-O	10	4		Wi 86	44
Spinning	Spinning Novelty Yarns	d'Avila, Doris	√	√	Iw	4	4		Fa 79	58
Spinning	Spinning Questions and Answers	Hicks, C. Norman		√	SS&D	8	4	32	Fa 77	81
Spinning	Spinning Wheels	Rizner, Constance	√		SS&D	14	3	55	Su 83	16
Spinning	Structuring a Bulky Yarn	Bartl, Pam	√	√	Iw	5	2		Sp 80	62
Spinning	Sweater's Tale, A	Owens, Julie	√	√	Hw	6	4		S/O 85	82
Spinning	Teaching the Blind to Spin: A Group Session	Gonzales, Carolyn	√		SS&D	10	3	39	Su 79	90
Spinning	Teaching the Blind to Spin: An Impromptu Lesson	Chapin, Doloria		√	SS&D	10	3	39	Su 79	91
Spinning	Texas State Spinning Bee		√		Fa	3	6		N/D 76	12

SUBJECT	TITLE	AUTHOR	IL	INST	JOUR	VOL	NO	ISS	DATE	PAGE
Spinning	Textile Arts of Multan, Pakistan	Shahzaman, Mahboob	√	> 4	SS&D	4	3	15	Su 73	8
Spinning	Texture in Spinning	O'Connor, Marcie Archer	√	√	Kn	2	2	4	S-S 86	53
Spinning	Thoughts on Money, Art, and Spinning	Chelsey, Randy			S-O	11	1		Sp 87	14
Spinning	Thoughts on the Certificate of Excellence in Handspinning	Dozer, Iris	√		SS&D	17	4	68	Fa 86	67
Spinning	Three Crafts in New Zealand, The	Timlin, Jean			SS&D	1	2	2	Mr 70	18
Spinning	Through the "Almanack" Office Window	Parr, Rowena			S-O	11	3		Fa 87	36
Spinning	We Dyed in the Woods	Castino, Ruth	√	√	SS&D	4	3	15	Su 73	22
Spinning	"Weaver's Life, Ethel Mairet, 1872–1952, A" (Exhibit)	Waller, Irene	√		Fa	11	4		J/A 84	78
Spinning	Wheels Turn for French Revolution		√		Iw	1	1		Fa 75	14
Spinning	Wyoming Holds Golden Fleece Spinning Contest	Adams, Brucie	√		SS&D	5	4	20	Fa 74	10
Spinning	Wyoming Spinners Create with Wool	Adams, Brucie	√		Iw	1	1		Fa 75	10
Spinning	Yarn Design: The Fine Points in Black and White	Meyer, Peggy Frost	√	√	WJ	12	2	46	Fa 87	38
Spinning	Zoo Story	Sermon, Margaret	√		SS&D	2	4	8	Fa 71	10
Spinning: 17th Century	Some Remarks on the Work of Markham	Stanton, R. G.; J. L. Allston	√	√	AT	2			De 84	95
Spinning: 18th Century	Handweaving and the Powerloom in 18th Century America	Cooper, Grace Rogers	√		H&C	22	4		Fa 71	5
Spinning Angora	Angora: A Spinner's Delight	Howard, Miranda	√	√	S-O	6	4		82	43
Spinning Angora	More About Angora			√	TM			7	O/N 86	4
Spinning Angora	Mo's Have It, The	Pinchin, Bryn	√	√	S-O	7	3		Fa 83	23
Spinning Animal Fibers	Angora Goats and Mohair	Chastant, Kathryn Ross	√	√	S-O	7	3		Fa 83	29
Spinning Animal Fibers	Guide to Spinning Other Fibers, A	Hochberg, Bette	√		S-O	1			77	15
Spinning Animal Fibers	My Wonderful Llamas and Their Wool	Thormahlen, Marian Oyen	√	√	S-O	8	4		Wi 84	29
Spinning Animal Fibers	Pet Yarn	Kroll, Carol	√		S-O	1			77	18
Spinning Animal Fibers	Study of Andean Spinning in the Cuzco Region, A	Goodell, Miss Grace	√	√	TMJ	2	3		De 68	2
Spinning Animal Fibers	Weaving with Handspun Alpaca	Anderson, J.	√		H&C	17	2		Sp 66	20
Spinning Bark	Chilkat Spinning	Samuel, Alena	√	√	TM			1	O/N 85	55
Spinning, Beginning	Easing the Beginner's Fears	Irwin, Bobbie		√	S-O	10	4		Wi 86	24
Spinning, Beginning	Handspinning in New Hampshire	Brackett, Thelma	√		H&C	17	1		Wi 66	18
Spinning, Beginning	Smart (Dumb)-Head Spinning	Norton, Becky			S-O	8	2		Su 84	44
Spinning, Beginning	When You Begin to Spin	Simmons, Paula	√	√	H&C	17	3		Su 66	8
Spinning: Beginning	Words of Wisdom for Beginning Spinners				S-O	11	3		Fa 87	38
Spinning: Bulk	Bulk Spinning	Benson, Sallyann	√	√	SS&D	14	2	54	Sp 83	36
Spinning Caribou Hair	New Fiber for Spinners: Caribou, A	Goodfellow, Robin; Keith Slater	√		S-O	10	4		Wi 86	46
Spinning Cashgora	Closer Look at Cashgora, A	Presser, Fran	√	√	S-O	10	4		Wi 86	49
Spinning Cashgora	From the Woolcombers Bench: Cashgora	Dozer, Iris		√	S-O	10	2		Su 86	39
Spinning Cedar	Melody Oakroot-Cedar Weaver	London, Bill	√	√	S-O	10	3		Fa 86	45
Spinning Cellulose Fibers	Spinning Fibers for Crochet	Linder, Harry P.	√	√	S-O	10	1		Sp 86	30
Spinning, Commercial	Vermont's Green Mountain Spinnery	Levinson, Nan	√		TM			7	O/N 86	61
Spinning Cotton	Acadian Brown Cotton	Exner, Beatrice B.	√		H&C	11	4		Fa 60	22
Spinning Cotton	Acadian Cotton Spinning	Schiller, Elaine Z.	√	√	SS&D	5	3	19	Su 74	75
Spinning Cotton	Back Strap Weaving in Zacualpan Mexico	Cooper, Jane	√	√	SS&D	5	3	19	Su 74	13
Spinning Cotton	Confessions of a Brave New Cotton Spinner	Hammett-Bregger, Frieda			S-O	3			79	15
Spinning Cotton	Confessions of a Cotton Spinner	Clivio, Carol	√	√	S-O	10	4		Wi 86	38
Spinning Cotton	Cotton, Cool and Comfy	Gibson-Roberts, Priscilla A.	√	√	Kn	3	2	6	Sp 87	48
Spinning Cotton	Croatian Shirt, A	Gaustad, Stephenie	√	√	S-O	9	2		Su 85	28
Spinning Cotton	Discover Cotton Spinning	Ajeman, Norma; Irene Laughing Cloud Schmoller	√	√	WJ	8	3	31	Wi 83	49

SUBJECT	TITLE	AUTHOR	IL	INST	JOUR	VOL	NO	ISS	DATE	PAGE
Spinning Cotton	Fiber Foray: Ginned Cotton	Quinn, Celia	√	√	S-O	9	2		Su 85	26
Spinning Cotton	Have Spindle Will Travel	Ruane, Joan	√	√	S-O	7	4		Wi 83	38
Spinning Cotton	King Cotton Is Back	Linder, Olive; Harry Linder	√		SS&D	5	2	18	Sp 74	65
Spinning Cotton	L'Amour de Maman: The Acadian Textile Heritage	Rossetter, Tabitha Wilson	√		Fa	8	3		M/J 81	29
Spinning Cotton	Machine Knitting with Handspun Cotton: First Experiments	Warren, Anne	√	√	S-O	11	2		Su 87	41
Spinning Cotton	Modern Charkha, The		√		H&C	9	3		Su 58	23
Spinning Cotton	More on....Charkha Techniques	Shepard, Mark	√	√	S-O	8	2		Su 84	36
Spinning Cotton	My Affair with King Cotton	Franklin, Sue	√	√	TM			9	F/M 87	39
Spinning Cotton	Quinn's Spinning Notes	Quinn, Cecelia			S-O	5			81	55
Spinning Cotton	Spinning Cotton with the Linders	Linder, Olive; Harry Linder	√	√	WJ	11	2	42	Fa 86	14
Spinning Cotton	Sunrise Handspun Basket	Burditt, Larry	√	√	S-O	11	1		Sp 87	18
Spinning Cotton	Why Spin Cotton?	Baker, Ella	√	√	S-O	9	2		Su 85	31
Spinning Cotton Lint	Dyeing and Spinning Cotton Lint	Linder, Harry; Olive Linder	√	√	SS&D	10	2	38	Sp 79	62
Spinning Cotton: Mexican Technique	On Spinning Cotton	Ligon, Linda	√		Iw	1	4		Su 76	6
Spinning Dog Hair	Dealing with Dog Hair	Murrow, Romedy	√		S-O	8	1		Sp 84	36
Spinning Dog Hair	Hair of the Dog, The	Adams, Brucie	√	√	Hw	3	2		Mr 82	62
Spinning Dog Hair	Spinning and Use of Dog's Hair, The	Pubols, Dorothy M.	√	√	WJ	4	1	13	Jy 79	36
Spinning: Dog Hair	Spinning Doghair	Barrett, Clotilde	√	√	WJ	1	1	1	Jy 76	27
Spinning Down	Spinning with Down and Knitting with Feathers	von Ammon, Helen	√		S-O	10	4		Wi 86	15
Spinning Exotic Fibers (Camel)	Super Soft Sweater	Emerick, Patricia	√	√	S-O	11	1		Sp 87	16
Spinning Exotic Fibers (Camel)	Sweater of Abundance	Chelsey, Randy	√	√	S-O	11	1		Sp 87	15
Spinning Flax	Continuous Thread, Part 3: From Flax Seed to Linen Cloth, The	Calhoun, Wheeler; Lee Kirschner	√	√	S-O	7	4		Wi 83	35
Spinning Flax	Fiber Foray: Getting Started with Line Flax	Quinn, Celia	√	√	S-O	9	4		Wi 85	46
Spinning Flax	Flax	Miller, Suzanne	√	√	WJ	7	2	26	Fa 82	12
Spinning Flax	Florida Spinner, Richard Butler, Chooses Flax	Tod, Osma G.	√		H&C	18	1		Wi 67	16
Spinning Flax	History of Linen, A	Mattera, Joanne	√	√	SS&D	8	3	31	Su 77	16
Spinning Flax	Impatient Spinner's Way to Spin Flax, The	Gordon, Carol	√	√	S-O	10	4		Wi 86	42
Spinning Flax	Learning to Spin	Parslow, Virginia D.	√	√	H&C	8	1		Wi 56	10
Spinning Flax	Line Flax Spinning	Heyl, Maxine; Linda Wilson	√	√	WJ	7	2	26	Fa 82	20
Spinning Flax	Spinning at the Smithsonian	Epskamp, Sally	√		S-O	5			81	35
Spinning Flax	Spinning Flax	Fannin, Allen A.	√	√	H&C	18	2		Sp 67	21
Spinning Flax (New Zealand)	Spinners & Weavers in New Zealand Use Native Materials	Duncan, Molly	√		H&C	21	1		Wi 70	14
Spinning: "Frotte Yarn" (Variegated)	Kasuri-Like-Effect Weaving	Akita, Mariko Olivia	√	√	WJ	6	2	22	Fa 81	18
Spinning Ikat	Handspun Ikat	Bradley, Louise	√	√	Hw	2	4		Se 81	65
Spinning Ikat	Ikat Spun Lap Robe (Louise Bradley)	Bradley, Louise	√	√	Hw	2	4		Se 81	67
Spinning Ikat	Ikat Spun Shrug (Louise Bradley)	Bradley, Louise	√	√	Hw	2	4		Se 81	67
Spinning Ikat	Ikat Spun Vest (Debbie Redding)	Bradley, Louise	√	√	Hw	2	4		Se 81	67
Spinning Ikat	Ikat-Spun Kimono, An	Lamb, Sara	√	√	S-O	8	4		Wi 84	16
Spinning Jenny	Spinning Jenny: A Modern Application of the Circular Spinner, The	Goody, Rabbit	√		S-O	8	1		Sp 84	26
Spinning Linen	Quinn's Spinning Notes	Quinn, Cecelia			S-O	5			81	55
Spinning Llama Wool	Llama Wool	Smith, Carolyn	√	√	S-O	11	2		Su 87	32
Spinning Lore	Study of Andean Spinning in the Cuzco Region, A	Goodell, Miss Grace	√	√	TMJ	2	3		De 68	2
Spinning Mohair	Are You Ready to Collapse?	Frame, Mary	√	√	S-O	11	1		Sp 87	41

SUBJECT	TITLE	AUTHOR	IL	INST	JOUR	VOL	NO	ISS	DATE	PAGE
Spinning Mohair	Lesotho Mohair				TM			10	A/M 87	4
Spinning Mohair	Preparing, Spinning and Dyeing Mohair	Russell, Barbara		√	S-O	7	3		Fa 83	52
Spinning Mohair	Spinning Mohair in Lesotho	Snieckus, Mary Ann	√		TM			8	D/J 86	66
Spinning Musk Ox Wool	Some Hints on Spinning Musk Ox Wool	Cornwall, E. Marguerite	√	√	S-O	7	1		Sp 83	20
Spinning: One-Hand	Spinning for Softness & Speed	Simmons, Paula	√	√	SS&D	14	1	53	Wi 82	66
Spinning Paper	Paper Clothing, East	Sahlstrand, Margaret	√	√	Fa	11	2		M/A 84	36
Spinning Paper	Shifu: A Handwoven Paper Textile	Miller, Dorothy	√	√	Hw	6	3		Su 85	69
Spinning Paper	Shifu: A Handwoven Paper Textile of Japan	Miller, Dorothy	√	√	AT	4			De 85	43
Spinning Pencil Roving	Pencil Roving		√	√	Hw	6	1		J/F 85	74
Spinning Plant Fibers	Contemporary Uses for an Ancient Fiber: Spanish Moss	Elliott, Douglas B.	√	√	SS&D	9	2	34	Sp 78	51
Spinning Plant Fibers	Corn Silk Challenge, The	Gherity, Delle		√	SS&D	7	3	27	Su 76	9
Spinning Plant Fibers	Guide to Spinning Other Fibers, A	Hochberg, Bette	√		S-O	1			77	15
Spinning Plant Fibers	Kudzu	Foster, Ann	√		S-O	3			79	23
Spinning Qiviut (Musk Ox)	Arctic Adventures with Qiviut	Hudson, Marjorie; Kathy Sparks	√	√	S-O	11	3		Fa 87	47
Spinning Qiviut (Musk Ox)	Qiviut — The Ultimate Luxury Fiber	Gibson-Roberts, Priscilla A.	√	√	Kn	3	4	8	Fa 87	58
Spinning, Rainbow Dyed Fleece	Rainbow Dyeing	Rowe, Erica	√	√	WJ	8	2	30	Fa 83	31
Spinning Ramie	Backstrap Weaving in the Philippines	Ng, Mary	√		SS&D	9	1	33	Wi 77	18
Spinning Ramie	From Ramie Top to Ramie Top	Knishern, Edna Maki	√	√	SS&D	9	2	34	Sp 78	78
Spinning Ramie	Miyako Jofu	Miller, Dorothy	√	√	AT	7			Ju 87	85
Spinning Ramie	Sunrise Handspun Basket	Burditt, Larry	√	√	S-O	11	1		Sp 87	18
Spinning Revival	Conversation with Allen Fannin				S-O	11	3		Fa 87	30
Spinning Revival	Like the Ad Says: "We've Come a Long Way"	Gibson-Roberts, Priscilla A.			S-O	11	3		Fa 87	26
Spinning Revival	Portrait of a Spinner	Grayson, Persis			S-O	11	3		Fa 87	24
Spinning Revival	Through the "Almanack" Office Window	Parr, Rowena			S-O	11	3		Fa 87	36
Spinning Revival	Way We Were...The Way We're Going, The	Ligon, Linda	√		S-O	11	3		Fa 87	27
Spinning Silk	Fiber Foray: Spinning Silk Cap and Mawata	Quinn, Celia	√	√	S-O	8	3		Fa 84	49
Spinning Silk	Fiber Foray: Spinning Silk Cocoons	Quinn, Celia	√	√	S-O	8	2		Su 84	27
Spinning Silk	Keeping Silkworms: The Art of Sericulture	Fenner, Monnie	√	√	S-O	8	2		Su 84	29
Spinning Silk	Novelty Silk Yarn from Bell Caps	Grayson, Persis	√	√	Hw	7	1		J/F 86	58
Spinning Silk	Quinn's Spinning Notes	Quinn, Cecilia			S-O	5			81	55
Spinning Silk	Shiny and Un	Gibson-Roberts, Priscilla A.	√		Kn	2	2	4	S-S 86	58
Spinning Silk	Silk		√		S-O	1			77	34
Spinning Silk	Silk	Chadwick, A.	√	√	WJ	3	2	10	Oc 78	6
Spinning Silk	Silk: Spinner's Luxury		√	√	Hw	5	4		S/0 84	85
Spinning Silk	Spinning Silk	Sullivan, Donna	√	√	SS&D	16	2	62	Sp 85	39
Spinning Silk	Yuki Tsumugi	Urbanek, Karen	√	√	S-O	10	1		Sp 86	42
Spinning Sisal	Sisal Production in Highland Guatemala	Ventura, Carol	√	√	Fa	14	2		M/A 87	44
Spinning Spanish Moss	Mary E. Heickman, Texas Weaver and Teacher	Morse, Martha	√	√	H&C	17	3		Su 66	18
Spinning: Spindle	Basic Spindle Spinning	Vernon, Jeanne			SS&D	4	3	15	Su 73	41
Spinning Techniques	Six of One, Half a Dozen of the Other (a roundtable discussion with six spinners)		√		S-O	5			81	51
Spinning Techniques: Acadian	Acadian Cotton Spinning	Schiller, Elaine Z.	√	√	SS&D	5	3	19	Su 74	75
Spinning Techniques: Charkha	More on....Charkha Techniques	Shepard, Mark	√	√	S-O	8	2		Su 84	36
Spinning Techniques: Charkha	Spinning on the Charkha	Raven, Lee	√	√	S-O	7	1		Sp 83	24
Spinning Techniques: Drop Spindle	Andean Spinning	Franquemont, Ed	√		S-O	9	1		Sp 85	54
Spinning Techniques: Drop Spindle	Beginning Spinning with Minimal Equipment	Ellison, Nancy	√	√	S-O	4			80	37

SUBJECT	TITLE	AUTHOR	IL	INST	JOUR	VOL	NO	ISS	DATE	PAGE
Spinning Techniques: Drop Spindle	Bulk Spinning	Benson, Sallyann	√	√	SS&D	14	2	54	Sp 83	36
Spinning Techniques: Drop Spindle	Handspun Yarn Production Rates in the Cuzco Region of Peru	Bird, Junius B.	√		TMJ	2	3		De 68	9
Spinning Techniques: Drop Spindle	Kurdish Kilim Weaving in the Van-Hakkari District of Eastern Turkey	Landreau, Anthony N.	√	√	TMJ	3	4		De 73	27
Spinning Techniques: Drop Spindle	Nahuala Spinning	Linder, Harry; Olive Linder	√		S-O	2			78	23
Spinning Techniques: Drop Spindle	Spindle and Distaff	Florentine, Gemma	√	√	TM			2	D/J 85	33
Spinning Techniques: Drop Spindle	Spindle Spinning with Sheep Wool	Cagnoni, Mary		√	SS&D	2	4	8	Fa 71	23
Spinning Techniques: Drop Spindle	Spinners of Chijnaya, Alpaca Yarns from Peruvian Village	Cloney, Gordon	√		H&C	16	4		Fa 65	15
Spinning Techniques: Drop Spindle	Spinning Lesson, A	Muller, Ann	√	√	H&C	2	3		Su 51	17
Spinning Techniques: Drop Spindle	Study of Andean Spinning in the Cuzco Region, A	Goodell, Miss Grace	√	√	TMJ	2	3		De 68	2
Spinning Techniques: Drop Spindle	Traditional Berber Weaving in Central Morocco	Forelli, Sally; Jeanette Harries	√		TMJ	4	4		77	41
Spinning Techniques: Drop Spindle	Using a Drop Spindle	Hicks, C. Norman		√	SS&D	5	4	20	Fa 74	79
Spinning Techniques: Drop Spindle	Using a Drop Spinkle, Part 2 (error-corrected SS&D v6 n2 75 p61)	Hicks, C. Norman		√	SS&D	6	1	21	Wi 74	48
Spinning Techniques: Drop Spindle	Weavers of Cyprus	Macdonald, Elizabeth	√		H&C	5	4		Fa 54	24
Spinning Techniques: Drop Spindle, High Whorl	High Whorl Spindle, The	Hochberg, Bette	√	√	SS&D	11	1	41	Wi 79	12
Spinning Techniques: Hip Spindle	Navajo Hip Spindle, Part 1	Hicks, C. Norman	√	√	SS&D	8	1	29	WI 76	95
Spinning Techniques: Hip Spindle	Navajo Hip Spindle, Part 2	Hicks, C. Norman		√	SS&D	8	2	30	Sp 77	41
Spinning Techniques: Hip Spindle	Navajo Way, The	Jolley, Ginger	√	√	S-O	11	4		Wi 87	38
Spinning Techniques: Hip Spindle	Spinning with Susie	Chacey, Ron	√	√	S-O	7	4		Wi 83	18
Spinning Techniques: Navajo Spindle	Navajo: Textiles, Blankets, Rugs, Tapestries	Morrow, Mable	√	√	SS&D	2	1	5	De 70	5
Spinning Techniques: Power Spinning	From Bobbin Flyer to Electric Spinner	Holborn, Joan	√	√	S-O	3			79	44
Spinning Techniques: Power Spinning	Vermont's Green Mountain Spinnery	Levinson, Nan	√		TM			7	O/N 86	61
Spinning Techniques: Spindle	Cuna Cachi: A Study of Hammock Weaving Among the Cuna Indians of the San Blas Islands	Lambert, Anne M.	√	√	AT	5			Ju 86	105
Spinning Techniques: Stick Spindle	Sling Braiding in the Macusani Area of Peru	Zorn, Elayne	√	√	TMJ	19 20			80,81	41
Spinning Techniques: Supported Spindle	Back Strap Weaving in Zacualpan Mexico	Cooper, Jane	√	√	SS&D	5	3	19	Su 74	13
Spinning Techniques: Supported Spindle	Costume and Weaving in Saraguro, Ecuador	Meisch, Lynn Ann	√		TMJ	19 20			80,81	55
Spinning Techniques: Supported Spindle	Discover Cotton Spinning	Ajeman, Norma; Irene Laughing Cloud Schmoller	√	√	WJ	8	3	31	Wi 83	49
Spinning Techniques: Supported Spindle	Fiber Foray: Ginned Cotton	Quinn, Celia	√	√	S-O	9	2		Su 85	26
Spinning Techniques: Supported Spindle	Have Spindle Will Travel	Ruane, Joan	√	√	S-O	7	4		Wi 83	38
Spinning Techniques: Supported Spindle	High-Whorl Lap Spindle, The	Heite, Louise	√	√	S-O	10	1		Sp 86	36
Spinning Techniques: Supported Spindle	Hooked Stick	Quinn, Celia	√	√	S-O	9	2		Su 85	34
Spinning Techniques: Supported Spindle	Spinning Cotton with the Linders	Linder, Olive; Harry Linder	√	√	WJ	11	2	42	Fa 86	14
Spinning Techniques: Supported Spindle	Spinning in Ecuador	Meisch, Lynn Ann	√	√	S-O	4			80	24

SUBJECT	TITLE	AUTHOR	IL	INST	JOUR	VOL	NO	ISS	DATE	PAGE
Spinning Techniques: Supported Spindle	Spinning with a Bead Whorl Spindle	Hochberg, Bette	√	√	SS&D	10	2	38	Sp 79	22
Spinning Techniques: Supported Spindle	Weaving a Cotton Saddlebag on the Santa Elena Peninsula of Ecuador	Hagino, Jane Parker; Karen E. Stothert	√	√	TMJ	22			83	19
Spinning Techniques: Thigh Spinning	Chilkat Spinning	Samuel, Alena	√	√	TM			1	O/N 85	55
Spinning Techniques: Thigh Spinning	Melody Oakroot-Cedar Weaver	London, Bill	√	√	S-O	10	3		Fa 86	45
Spinning Techniques: Thigh Spinning	Using the Fibers of Native Plants	Buchanan, Rita	√	√	S-O	9	4		Wi 85	29
Spinning Techniques: Wheel	Add a New Twist to Your Spinning	Hochberg, Bette	√	√	S-O	5			81	42
Spinning Techniques: Wheel	Angora Fiber Spinning	Betts, Diane		√	S-O	9	4		Wi 85	35
Spinning Techniques: Wheel	Beyond the Machine (The creative uses of imprecision)	d'Avila, Doris	√	√	S-O	4			80	50
Spinning Techniques: Wheel	Confessions of a Cotton Spinner	Clivio, Carol	√	√	S-O	10	4		Wi 86	38
Spinning Techniques: Wheel	Confessions of a Mad Spinner	de la Garza, Phyllis			S-O	5			81	15
Spinning Techniques: Wheel	Controlled Spinning	Ronin, Col. James A.		√	SS&D	3	3	11	Su 72	36
Spinning Techniques: Wheel	Coverlets: A Spinner's Challenge			√	S-O	6	4		82	25
Spinning Techniques: Wheel	Designer Yarns: Slubs and Spirals	Chapin, Doloria	√	√	S-O	3			79	54
Spinning Techniques: Wheel	Discover Cotton Spinning	Ajeman, Norma; Irene Laughing Cloud Schmoller	√	√	WJ	8	3	31	Wi 83	49
Spinning Techniques: Wheel	Fiber Foray: Spinning Combed Alpaca	Quinn, Celia	√	√	S-O	9	1		Sp 85	26
Spinning Techniques: Wheel	From Bobbin Flyer to Electric Spinner	Holborn, Joan	√	√	S-O	3			79	44
Spinning Techniques: Wheel	From the Woolcombers Bench: Cashgora	Dozer, Iris		√	S-O	10	2		Su 86	39
Spinning Techniques: Wheel	Great Wheel, The	Hicks, C. Norman	√	√	SS&D	4	2	14	Sp 73	38
Spinning Techniques: Wheel	Great Wheel, The	Turner, Katy	√	√	S-O	3			79	46
Spinning Techniques: Wheel	Handspinning Technique	Rees, Linda E.	√		H&C	24	3		M/J 73	32
Spinning Techniques: Wheel	Impatient Spinner's Way to Spin Flax, The	Gordon, Carol	√	√	S-O	10	4		Wi 86	42
Spinning Techniques: Wheel	"Indian Spinner" or Large Orifice Spinning Wheels	Hicks, C. Norman	√	√	SS&D	9	1	33	Wi 77	31
Spinning Techniques: Wheel	Irregularity in Handspun	Simmons, Paula	√	√	H&C	20	4		Fa 69	13
Spinning Techniques: Wheel	Learning to Spin	Parslow, Virginia D.	√	√	H&C	8	1		Wi 56	10
Spinning Techniques: Wheel	Practical Approach to the Great Wheel, A	Reynolds, Donna	√	√	S-O	8	4		Wi 84	39
Spinning Techniques: Wheel	Rx: Pills	Leggett, Dawn	√	√	S-O	8	4		Wi 84	35
Spinning Techniques: Wheel	Speed Spinning	Thompson, Nancy	√	√	Iw	4	1		Wi 78	46
Spinning Techniques: Wheel	Spinning a Fine Yarn	Plowman, Judith	√	√	S-O	4			80	47
Spinning Techniques: Wheel	Spinning Australian Cashmere and Cashgora	Feldman-Wood, Florence	√	√	S-O	9	4		Wi 85	40
Spinning Techniques: Wheel	Spinning Fancy Yarns	Metchette, Glenna	√	√	SS&D	14	1	53	Wi 82	16
Spinning Techniques: Wheel	Spinning for Softness & Speed	Simmons, Paula	√	√	SS&D	14	1	53	Wi 82	66
Spinning Techniques: Wheel	Spinning in Ecuador	Meisch, Lynn Ann	√	√	S-O	4			80	24
Spinning Techniques: Wheel	Spinning in the Grease	Ekstrom, Brenda	√	√	S-O	3			79	50
Spinning Techniques: Wheel	Spinning Lesson, A	Muller, Ann	√	√	H&C	2	3		Su 51	17
Spinning Techniques: Wheel	Spinning on a Saxony or Castle Wheel	Hicks, C. Norman	√	√	SS&D	7	4	28	Fa 76	51
Spinning Techniques: Wheel	Spinning Unique and Useable Yarns	Donohue, Sandra	√	√	S-O	8	4		Wi 84	33
Spinning Techniques: Wheel	Spinning: Where to Begin	Rossiter, Phyllis	√	√	SS&D	16	2	62	Sp 85	10
Spinning Techniques: Wheel	Twist Demystified	Clark, Marlyn	√	√	S-O	7	2		Su 83	25
Spinning Techniques: Wheel	Two-Flyer Spinning Wheel, The	Ronin, Col. James A. ret.	√	√	S-O	1			77	40
Spinning Techniques: Wheel	Weavers of Cyprus	Macdonald, Elizabeth	√		H&C	5	4		Fa 54	24
Spinning Techniques: Wheel	Worsted Spinning	Zoller, Mary	√	√	S-O	7	4		Wi 83	26
Spinning Techniques: Wheel, Bulk Spinner	Bulk Spinning	Benson, Sallyann	√	√	SS&D	14	2	54	Sp 83	36
Spinning Techniques: Wheel, Single-Drive-Band	Reining in Baby Huey	Centner, Dave, O.C.D.		√	S-O	11	4		Wi 87	18

681

SUBJECT	TITLE	AUTHOR	IL	INST	JOUR	VOL	NO	ISS	DATE	PAGE
Spinning: War-Effort	New Zealand Spinners	Robinson, Margaret	√		H&C	10	3		Su 59	23
Spinning Warp	Navajo Way, The	Jolley, Ginger	√	√	S-O	11	4		Wi 87	38
Spinning: Warp/Weft	Tagari: A Greek Saddlebag of Handspun Wools, The	Koster, Joan Boura	√	√	WJ	6	2	22	Fa 81	24
Spinning Weft	Navajo Way, The	Jolley, Ginger	√	√	S-O	11	4		Wi 87	38
Spinning Wheel Makers	Spinning Wheels from the Busy Workshop of Anthony Cardarelle	Martin, George	√		H&C	17	3		Su 66	6
Spinning Wheels	Collection of Spinning Wheels, A	Cummer, Joan	√		S-O	7	2		Su 83	22
Spinning Wheels	Colonial Equipment	Pennington, David; Michael Taylor	√		S-O	2			78	40
Spinning Wheels	Great Wheel, The	Hicks, C. Norman	√	√	SS&D	4	2	14	Sp 73	38
Spinning Wheels	Great Wheel, The	Turner, Katy	√	√	S-O	3			79	46
Spinning Wheels	Great Wool Wheel, The	Vernon, Jeanne	√	√	SS&D	5	1	17	Wi 73	45
Spinning Wheels	Mechanization of the Bobbin-Flyer Spinning Wheel, The	Ronin, Col. James A. ret.	√	√	S-O	2			78	44
Spinning Wheels	New Approach to a Traditional Design	Ziegler, Luise	√	√	H&C	14	3		Su 63	11
Spinning Wheels	Personal History Involving the Spinning Wheel and One Man's Insatiable Curiosity, A	Mathews, Tom	√		Fa	6	2		M/A 79	18
Spinning Wheels	Practical Approach to the Great Wheel, A	Reynolds, Donna	√	√	S-O	8	4		Wi 84	39
Spinning Wheels	Short History of the Spinning Wheel, A	Swenson, Astrid	√		SS&D	7	3	27	Su 76	40
Spinning Wheels	Singer Spinning Wheel, The	Rossiter, Phyllis J.	√	√	S-O	8	2		Su 84	34
Spinning Wheels	Spindle	Chesley, Zina Mae	√	√	SS&D	2	4	8	Fa 71	23
Spinning Wheels	Spinning Wheels	Parslow, Virginia D.	√	√	H&C	7	2		Sp 56	20
Spinning Wheels	Spinning Wheels	Rizner, Constance	√		SS&D	14	3	55	Su 83	16
Spinning Wheels	Spinning Wheels from the Busy Workshop of Anthony Cardarelle	Martin, George	√		H&C	17	3		Su 66	6
Spinning Wheels	Spinning: Where to Begin	Rossiter, Phyllis	√	√	SS&D	16	2	62	Sp 85	10
Spinning Wheels	Spinning with Gandhi	Grant, Susan	√		S-O	2			78	15
Spinning Wheels	There's An Old Spinning Wheel in the Parlor	Rossiter, Phyllis	√		S-O	9	1		Sp 85	31
Spinning Wheels	Three Big T's	Eldridge, Lois A.			S-O	8	2		Su 84	40
Spinning Wheels	Two-Flyer Spinning Wheel, The	Ronin, Col. James A. ret.	√	√	S-O	1			77	40
Spinning Wheels: 19th Century	Sanford Wheel		√		SS&D	2	3	7	Su 71	22
Spinning Wheels: Adjusting Bands	Learning to Adjust the Bands That Govern the Flyer and Bobbin	Quinn, Celia	√	√	S-O	11	2		Su 87	25
Spinning Wheels: Antique	Aurora Colony Antique Spinning Wheel Showcase	Cobb, Lorie	√		S-O	10	3		Fa 86	43
Spinning Wheels: Antique	Old Spinning Wheels			√	TM			7	O/N 86	4
Spinning Wheels: Castle	1979 Fiberarts Equipment Directory: Spinning Wheels, Castle, The		√		Fa	6	1		J/F 79	60
Spinning Wheels: Charkha	Modern Charkha, The		√		H&C	9	3		Su 58	23
Spinning Wheels: Charkha	More on....Charkha Techniques	Shepard, Mark	√	√	S-O	8	2		Su 84	36
Spinning Wheels: Charkha	Spinning on the Charkha	Raven, Lee	√	√	S-O	7	1		Sp 83	24
Spinning Wheels: Constructing and Adapting	Colonel Ronin, Spinning Flyer	Ligon, Linda	√		Iw	2	4		Su 77	25
Spinning Wheels: Constructing and Adapting	Converting the Ashford Wheel	Hicks, C. Norman		√	SS&D	8	3	31	Su 77	52
Spinning Wheels: Constructing and Adapting	Fast Ashford Wheel, The	Hayes, Jan	√	√	SS&D	9	1	33	Wi 77	81
Spinning Wheels: Constructing and Adapting	Having an Inventor-Husband	Oliver, Olga	√		SS&D	3	4	12	Fa 72	15
Spinning Wheels: Constructing and Adapting	Ideal Spinning Wheel, The	Kronenberg, Bud			SS&D	12	1	45	Wi 80	12
Spinning Wheels: Constructing and Adapting	Iron and Steel Spinning Wheel: Reconstructed Treadle Sewing Machine, An	Whitaker, James H.	√	√	SS&D	8	4	32	Fa 77	60
Spinning Wheels: Constructing and Adapting	New Approach to a Traditional Design	Ziegler, Luise	√	√	H&C	14	3		Su 63	11

SUBJECT	TITLE	AUTHOR	IL	INST	JOUR	VOL	NO	ISS	DATE	PAGE
Spinning Wheels: Constructing and Adapting	Spindle	Hicks, C. Norman	√	√	SS&D	6	3	23	Su 75	63
Spinning Wheels: Constructing and Adapting	To Wind Bobbins Use Your Spinning Wheel	Stowell, Robert F.	√	√	H&C	7	4		Fa 56	17
Spinning Wheels: Constructing and Adapting	Twenty-two Spinning Wheels	Heintz, Dr. Kenneth; Dr. Henry Thomas	√		SS&D	5	4	20	Fa 74	60
Spinning Wheels: Construction and Adapting	Spindle	Hicks, C. Norman			SS&D	6	4	24	Fa 75	55
Spinning Wheels: Construction and Adapting	Spinning Bulky Yarns	Kronenberg, Bud	√	√	SS&D	13	1	49	Wi 81	78
Spinning Wheels: Construction and Adapting	Working Drawings for Tyrolese Type Spinning Wheel	Heintz, Kenneth G.	√	√	SS&D	4	4	16	Fa 73	61
Spinning Wheels: Evaluating	Antique Spinning Wheels	Goodman, Deborah Lerme	√		TM			6	A/S 86	61
Spinning Wheels: Evaluating	Buyer's Guide to Spinning Wheel Design	Amos, Alden	√		S-O	4			80	40
Spinning Wheels: Evaluating	Buying an Old Spinning Wheel	Edgerton, Kate	√		SS&D	1	1	1	De 69	10
Spinning Wheels: Evaluating	Collecting Spinning Wheels	Ralph, William	√	√	H&C	24	1		J/F 73	16
Spinning Wheels: Evaluating	Misunderstood Spinning Wheel, The	Kronenberg, Bud	√	√	SS&D	12	3	47	Su 81	11
Spinning Wheels: Evaluating	Practical Approach to the Great Wheel, A	Reynolds, Donna	√	√	S-O	8	4		Wi 84	39
Spinning Wheels: Evaluating	Will It Work? A Guide to Evaluating a Spinning Wheel	Pauli, Karen	√		S-O	4			80	43
Spinning Wheels: Horizontal	Bernard Barton Spinning Wheel — 1766, The		√		S-O	7	4		Wi 83	16
Spinning Wheels: Kachi Rabari	Rabari Lodi: Creating a Fabric Through Social Alliance, The	Frater, Judy	√	√	WJ	10	1	37	Su 85	28
Spinning Wheels: Large Orifice	"Indian Spinner" or Large Orifice Spinning Wheels	Hicks, C. Norman	√	√	SS&D	9	1	33	Wi 77	31
Spinning Wheels: Louët	It's a Bird....It's a Plane	Crowder, Rachael	√		PWC	4	3	13		14
Spinning Wheels: Mechanical Principles	Spinning Wheel, The	Matheison, Ian			H&C	23	4		J/A 72	4
Spinning Wheels: Mechanical Principles	Spinning Wheel, The	Mathieson, Ian			H&C	23	1		J/F 72	10
Spinning Wheels: Misconceptions	Misunderstood Spinning Wheel, The	Kronenberg, Bud	√	√	SS&D	12	3	47	Su 81	11
Spinning Wheels: Other	1979 Fiberarts Equipment Directory: Spinning Wheels, Other, The		√		Fa	6	1		J/F 79	67
Spinning Wheels: Patent Pendulum	Patent Pendulum Spinning Wheel, The		√		H&C	20	3		Su 69	33
Spinning Wheels: Repair and Maintenance	Old Wheel Spins Again, An	Wetter, Cora M.			H&C	5	3		Su 54	31
Spinning Wheels: Repair and Maintenance	On Repairing Spinning Wheels	Fannin, Allen A.			H&C	18	4		Fa 67	33
Spinning Wheels: Repair and Maintenance	Reconditioning Wheels	Edgerton, Kate	√	√	SS&D	1	3	3	Ju 70	19
Spinning Wheels: Repair and Maintenance	Antique Spinning Wheels	Goodman, Deborah Lerme	√		TM			6	A/S 86	61
Spinning Wheels: Repair and Maintenance	Simple Repairs on a Saxony	Edgerton, Kate	√	√	SS&D	1	2	2	Mr 70	20
Spinning Wheels: Saxony	1979 Fiberarts Equipment Directory: Spinning Wheels, Saxony, The (error-corrected Fa v6 n2 79 p60)		√		Fa	6	1		J/F 79	65
Spinning Wheels: Single-Drive-Band	Reining in Baby Huey	Centner, Dave, O.C.D.		√	S-O	11	4		Wi 87	18
Spinning Wheels: Tension	Double-Belt And Scotch Tension	Hoering, Martha	√	√	SS&D	5	2	18	Sp 74	59
Spinning Wheels: Two-Treadle	Two Treadle Spinning Wheels	Houston, Jourdan	√		H&C	24	4		Au 73	32
Spinning Wool	Beverley Royce's "Recipe" for Merino	Royce, Beverly	√	√	S-O	5			81	49
Spinning Wool	Bhotiya Woolens from India	Willis, Elizabeth Bayley	√		H&C	5	2		Sp 54	4
Spinning Wool	Border Leicester	Walker, Linda Berry	√	√	Hw	2	3		My 81	64
Spinning Wool	Clun Forest	Walker, Linda Berry	√		Iw	6	1		Wi 80	62
Spinning Wool	Corriedale	Walker, Linda Berry	√		Hw	3	1		Ja 82	73
Spinning Wool	Cowichan Country	Gibson-Roberts, Priscilla A.	√	√	Kn	3	1	5	F-W 86	61
Spinning Wool	Experiments with Merino	Adams, Brucie	√	√	Iw	5	1		Wi 79	50

SUBJECT	TITLE	AUTHOR	IL	INST	JOUR	VOL	NO	ISS	DATE	PAGE
Spinning Wool	Great Wool Wheel, The	Vernon, Jeanne	√	√	SS&D	5	1	17	Wi 73	45
Spinning Wool	Handspun Plaid Shirt, A (Betty Keeler)		√		Hw	4	5		N/D 83	73
Spinning Wool	Handspun Yarns from Black Sheep Wool	Simmons, Paula	√	√	H&C	14	3		Su 63	6
Spinning Wool	If You Want to Work with the Best Wool Yarns, Spin Them Yourself	Bulback, Stanley	√	√	TM			13	O/N 87	56
Spinning Wool	Irregularity in Handspun, Part 3	Simmons, Paula		√	H&C	21	2		Sp 70	20
Spinning Wool	Jacob	Walker, Linda Berry	√		Iw	5	4		Fa 80	64
Spinning Wool	Karakul	Walker, Linda Berry	√		Hw	3	2		Mr 82	60
Spinning Wool	Learning to Spin	Parslow, Virginia D.	√	√	H&C	8	1		Wi 56	10
Spinning Wool	Llamas	Switzer, Chris	√	√	S-O	5			81	31
Spinning Wool	Loving Touches: Handspinning for Babies	Hayes, Beth	√	√	S-O	11	2		Su 87	20
Spinning Wool	Merino	Walker, Linda Berry	√	√	Iw	5	3		Su 80	59
Spinning Wool	Navajo Way, The	Jolley, Ginger	√	√	S-O	11	4		Wi 87	38
Spinning Wool	New Zealand Spinners	Robinson, Margaret	√		H&C	10	3		Su 59	23
Spinning Wool	Perendale	Walker, Linda Berry	√	√	Hw	2	4		Se 81	69
Spinning Wool	Point of Departure	Ligon, Linda	√	√	S-O	10	2		Su 86	53
Spinning Wool	Quinn's Spinning Notes	Quinn, Cecelia			S-O	5			81	55
Spinning Wool	Romney	Walker, Linda Berry	√		Iw	5	2		Sp 80	63
Spinning Wool	Selecting Wool for Handspinning (error-corrected SS&D v13 n1 81 p4)	Fleet, Malcolm		√	SS&D	12	4	48	Fa 81	66
Spinning Wool	Spin a Tartan—Naturally	Adams, Brucie	√	√	Hw	4	5		N/D 83	72
Spinning Wool	SPIN-OFF Book of World Records				S-O	3			79	14
Spinning Wool	Spinning a Fine Yarn	Plowman, Judith	√	√	S-O	4			80	47
Spinning Wool	Spinning a Gossamer Web	Gibson-Roberts, Priscilla A.	√	√	Kn	4	1	9	Wi 87	62
Spinning Wool	Spinning Lesson, A	Muller, Ann	√	√	H&C	2	3		Su 51	17
Spinning Wool	Spinning Traditional Knitting Yarns for Ethnic Sweaters	Gibson-Roberts, Priscilla A.	√	√	S-O	8	4		Wi 84	26
Spinning Wool	Spinning with Icelandic Wool	Heite, Louise	√	√	S-O	10	1		Sp 86	33
Spinning Wool	Triangular Shawl	Broad, Sue	√		WJ	7	3	27	Wi 82	11
Spinning Wool	Weaving on a Board	Kappler, Erda	√	√	Hw	4	4		S/O 83	46
Spinning Wool	Wonderful Worsted	Dozer, Iris L.	√	√	SS&D	15	3	59	Su 84	26
Spinning Wool	Wool: From Fleece to Knitting Yarn	Gibson-Roberts, Priscilla A.	√	√	S-O	8	3		Fa 84	27
Spinning Wool	Woolens and Tweeds: From Fleece to Woolen Yarn: Spinning	Tidball, Harriet	√	√	SCGM		4		61	9
Spinning Wool: Cheviot, Border	Border Cheviot	Walker, Linda Berry	√	√	Hw	4	1		J/F 83	63
Spinning Wool: Cheviot, North Country	North Country Cheviot	Walker, Linda Berry	√	√	Hw	4	1		J/F 83	63
Spinning Wool: Corriedale	Corriedale	Walker, Linda Berry	√		Hw	3	1		Ja 82	73
Spinning Wool: Cotswold	Cotswold	Walker, Linda Berry	√	√	Hw	3	4		Se 82	71
Spinning Wool: Fine Spinning	Aussie Augments	George, Barbara	√	√	Kn	4	1	9	Wi 87	62
Spinning Wool: Jacob	Jacob Wool — A Handspinner's Delight	Thormahlen, Marian Oyen	√	√	WJ	11	3	43	Wi 87	57
Spinning Wool: Llama	Llama Cape, The	Keeler, Betty			H&C	23	4		J/A 72	46
Spinning: Worsted	If You Want to Work with the Best Wool Yarns, Spin Them Yourself	Bulback, Stanley	√	√	TM			13	O/N 87	56
Spinning Yarn: Soviet and American Fleeces	Spinning Fleece for Peace				TM			11	J/J 87	18
Splicing	Splicing from Central America	Sober, Marion B.	√	√	H&C	22	4		Fa 71	18
Splintwork	Basketry Technics, Part 2	Harvey, Virginia	√		SS&D	6	3	23	Su 75	30
Split-Ply Twining	Split-Ply Twining	Harvey, Virginia I.	√	√	TIAM		1		76	1-40
Sportswear	Where's the Sport in Sportswear?	McComb, Richard	√		TM			2	D/J 85	36
Spot, Bronson	Bronson Spot Weave System, The		√	√	PWC			5	Sp 83	20
Spot, Bronson	Dress/Blouse Fabric (Sharon Alderman)		√	√	Hw	3	2		Mr 82	9, 79
Spot, Bronson	Early American Linens	Gallagher, Constance	√	>4	H&C	15	3		Su 64	7
Spot, Bronson	Ice Blue Blouse (Jean Scorgie)		√	>4	Hw	7	5		N/D 86	42, I-3

SUBJECT	TITLE	AUTHOR	IL	INST	JOUR	VOL	NO	ISS	DATE	PAGE
Spot, Bronson	Kirschbaum Tablecloth (Julie Lawson)		√	√	Hw	8	1		J/F 87	58, I-10
Spot, Bronson	New Skirts for Summer	Frey, Berta	√	> 4	H&C	4	1		Wi 52	33
Spot, Bronson	Notebook: Some Light Behind the Weave (Manasota Weavers)	Myers, Ruth Nordquist, ed.	√	> 4	SS&D	13	3	51	Su 82	16
Spot, Bronson	Reflections on 7560 Weft Picks	Ligon, Linda	√	> 4	Hw	8	3		M/J 87	98
Spot, Bronson	Silk Purse (Sharon Alderman)		√	√	Hw	4	1		J/F 83	43, 83
Spot, Bronson	Simple Damask-Like Effects Using Element Diameter Differential and Element Tension Differential	Xenakis, Athanasios David	√	> 4	AT	1			De 83	317
Spot, Bronson	Special Tie-Up for Skirt Designed By Berta Frey		√	> 4	H&C	4	3		Su 53	54
Spot, Bronson	Spot Bronson (Virginia West)		√	√	Hw	5	2		M/A 84	74, 94
Spot Bronson	Spot Weave Rug	Hanley, Janet	√	√	WJ	3	4	12	Ap 79	40
Spot, Bronson	Spot Weaving, Four Harnesses Offer Many Possibilities for Design	Burlew, Margaret	√	√	H&C	16	2		Sp 65	7
Spot, Bronson	Swivel Variations for Four Harness Looms	James, Ona	√	√	H&C	14	4		Fa 63	11
Spot, Bronson System	Handloom Weaves: The Classification of Handloom Weaves, The Structural Group, The Grouped-Thread Class, Spot Bronson System	Tidball, Harriet	√	> 4	SCGM		33		57	30
Spot Weaves	Designs in Old Linen Tablecloths	Gubser, Elsie H.	√	> 4	H&C	9	3		Su 58	21
Spot Weaves	Eight Harness Drapery from the Loom of Doris Cochran		√	> 4	H&C	13	2		Sp 62	11
Spot Weaves	More About Larch Trees	The Gadred Weavers	√	> 4	H&C	2	3		Su 51	28
Spot Weaves	Slipcover Fabric #2 (Constance LaLena)		√	> 4	Hw	4	3		M/J 83	50, 85
Spot Weaves	Spot Weaves — Old and New: Multiple Spot-2	Zielinski, S. A.; Robert Leclerc, ed.	√	> 4	MWL	12			'51–'73	46
Spot Weaves	Spots or Stripes?	Gordon, Judith	√	> 4	Hw	5	4		S/0 84	36
Spot Weaves, Multiple Spot	Spot Weaves — Old and New: Multiple Spot-1	Zielinski, S. A.; Robert Leclerc, ed.	√	> 4	MWL	12			'51–'73	41
Spot Weaves, Triple	Spot Weaves — Old and New: Triple Spot Weave	Zielinski, S. A.; Robert Leclerc, ed.	√	> 4	MWL	12			'51–'73	52
Spot Weaves, Variations	Spot Weaves — Old and New: Spot Weaves	Zielinski, S. A.; Robert Leclerc, ed.	√	> 4	MWL	12			'51–'73	7
Spots	Spots or Stripes?	Gordon, Judith	√	> 4	Hw	5	4		S/0 84	36
Sprang	Concrete and Grace, Fiber Allusions (error-corrected SS&D v6 n2 75 p44)	Kliot, Jules; Kaethe Kliot; Jenifer Kaufman	√		SS&D	6	1	21	Wi 74	33
Sprang	Easy Weaving for Easy Living		√	√	Hw	1	2		S-S 80	48
Sprang	Embellishments on the Rain Sash	Baizerman, Suzanne	√	√	WJ	11	2	42	Fa 86	22
Sprang	Fantastic Finnweave, Part 3	Xenakis, Athanasios David	√	> 4	PWC			4	Ja 83	33
Sprang	Hammock, The	Drooker, Penelope B.	√	√	TM			6	A/S 86	74
Sprang	Hella Skowronski Experiments with Sprang		√		H&C	20	1		Wi 69	4
Sprang	Listening to Threads	Reynders-Baas, Coby	√		WJ	11	4	44	Sp 87	21
Sprang	Nasca Sprang Tassels: Structure, Technique, and Order	Frame, Mary	√	√	TMJ	25			86	67
Sprang	Sprang a New Way	Reddy, Mary; Hella Skowronski	√	√	SS&D	6	2	22	Sp 75	22
Sprang	Sprang and Frame Plaiting for Garments		√	√	WJ	3	3	11	Ja 79	26
Sprang	Sprang and Weaving	Skowronski, Hella; Mary Reddy	√	√	SS&D	7	3	27	Su 76	79
Sprang	Sprang, Revival of an Ancient Technique	Collingwood, Peter	√	√	H&C	15	2		Sp 64	6
Sprang	Sprang Time	Linder, Olive			SS&D	10	3	39	Su 79	88
Sprang	World of Ancient and Modern Sprang, The	Collingwood, Peter	√	√	SS&D	5	1	17	Wi 73	90
Sprang: On-Loom	Sprang on the Loom	Searle, Karen	√	√	WJ	11	4	44	Sp 87	24
St. Augustine Weave	Two Weaves from Mexico	Gubser, Elsie H.	√	√	H&C	11	3		Su 60	26
Stain Removal: Blood	Removing Bloodstains			√	TM			10	A/M 87	10

SUBJECT	TITLE	AUTHOR	IL	INST	JOUR	VOL	NO	ISS	DATE	PAGE
Stains, Age Spots, Quilts	Age Spots			√	TM			9	F/M 87	8
Stair Carpet	Boundweave Stair Carpet, A		√		Hw	5	2		M/A 84	47
Stamp Collecting see Philately										
Standardization: Groups	Toward Standardizing the Language of the Hand Loom Designer Weaver	Daniels, Parmely Clark			H&C	24	4		Au 73	14
Standardization: Terminology, Weaving	Toward Standardizing the Language of the Hand Loom Designer Weaver	Daniels, Parmely Clark			H&C	24	4		Au 73	14
Standards	In Search of Excellence	Dieterich, Mary			SS&D	9	4	36	Fa 78	102
Standards: Color	Centroid Colors, The	Bliss, Anne	√	√	Iw	5	4		Fa 80	56
Standards: Fabrics	Weaving Weights and Qualities	Blumenau, Lili			H&C	8	2		Sp 57	9
Standards: Fleeces	Handspinner's Guide to Fleece Selection and Evaluation, A	Hiersch, Vicki			S-O	7	4		Wi 83	50
Standards: Jurying	Jurying by Point System	Shepps, Vincent C.		√	H&C	17	3		Su 66	7
Standards: Spinning	Criteria for Judging Handspun Yarn	Bliss, Anne			S-O	3			79	8
Standards: Spinning	Excellence	Leggett, Dawn	√		S-O	10	2		Su 86	43
Standards: Spinning	Musk Ox, and Miscellaneous	Adams, Brucie	√	√	Iw	4	2		Sp 79	46
Standards: Spinning	Sixteenth Century Labor Day, A	Amos, Alden	√		S-O	5			81	8
Standards: Spinning, Wool	Judging Handspun Wool	Blackman, Margery			SS&D	2	2	6	Sp 71	11
Standards: Weaving	A Weaver Ponders His Craft, Collection of Controversial Essays: Standards	Zielinski, S. A.; Robert Leclerc, ed.			MWL	21 22			'51–'73	61
Standards: Weaving	Looming Thoughts	Fannin, Allen; Dorothy Fannin			H&C	24	1		J/F 73	13
Standards: Weaving	Looming Thoughts	Fannin, Allen; Dorothy Fannin			H&C	24	2		M/A 73	17
Standards: Weaving	Quality or Charity? On What Basis Should Weaving Be Offered for Sale	The Gadred Weavers	√		H&C	1	2		Su 50	26
Star and Diamond Weaves	Analysis of Star and Diamond Weave Structures, An (error-corrected SS&D v10 n1 78 p101)	Anderson, Clarita; Judith Gordon; Naomi Whiting Towner	√	> 4	SS&D	9	4	36	Fa 78	71
Star-Fashion see Treadling										
Starching	How to Dye and Starch Silk	Bromberg, Kay	√	√	WJ	5	1	17	Su 80	43
Statement: Weaving	Involvement in What Is to Be	Bassler, Jim			SS&D	3	1	9	Wi 71	25
Statements: Fiber	Lisa Gardner: Cultural Perspectives	Poon, Vivian	√		Fa	12	1		J/F 85	14
Statements: Political	Fiber and Politics		√		Fa	13	3		M/J 86	20
Statements: Shawcroft, Barbara	Barbara Shawcroft	Shawcroft, Barbara	√		SS&D	3	1	9	Wi 71	25
Statements: Tapestry	Statement of My Ideas	O'Callaghan, Kate	√		WJ	5	4	20	Sp 81	35
Statements: Weaving Guilds	Are We Becoming Workshop Junkies?	Brostoff, Laya			SS&D	10	2	38	Sp 79	33
Statistical Procedures: Textile Industry	Work of L. H. C. Tippett, The	Stanton, R. G.	√		AT	7			Ju 87	179
Statistics: Technological Application	Work of L. H. C. Tippett, The	Stanton, R. G.	√		AT	7			Ju 87	179
Statue of Liberty Poncho	Rag Trade: Picture Postcard, The (Susanna Lewis)		√		Kn	3	1	5	F-W 86	68
Steeks Technique	Fair Isle Knitting	Starmore, Alice	√	√	TM			8	D/J 86	44
Stehekin, Washington	Spinning in Stehekin	Fridlund, Patricia	√		S-O	10	4		Wi 86	44
Stenciling	Fragil Landscape	Akamine, Estelle	√		TM			5	J/J 86	88
Stenciling	Katagami: Japanese Stencil Cutting	McCann, Kathleen	√		Fa	13	2		M/A 86	36
Stenciling	Stenciled Rag Rug (Betty Oldenberg)		√	√	Hw	5	3		Su 84	74
Stenciling	Stencils	Bliss, Anne	√	√	Hw	6	3		Su 85	86
Stenciling	Wear an Original Painting: Melody Weiler's Airbrushed Shirtscapes	Speight, Jerry	√	√	Fa	8	1		J/F 81	13
Stencils: Antique Japanese	"Patterns" with a Look at Japanese Printing with Stencils (Exhibit)	Dyer, Carolyn	√		Fa	4	5		S/O 77	10
Sterilization: Fibers	Anthrax Sterilization Methods and Their Effects on Fibers	Towner, Naomi Whiting; Helen Cushman		√	SS&D	7	3	27	Su 76	94
Stevengraphs	Jacquard and Woven Silk Pictures, The	Adrosko, Rita J.	√		AT	1			De 83	9
Stitched Drawings	Timeless Stitches: Myrna Shiras' Stitched Drawings	Schwartz, Joyce B.	√		Fa	8	3		M/J 81	65

SUBJECT	TITLE	AUTHOR	IL	INST	JOUR	VOL	NO	ISS	DATE	PAGE
Stitchery	Backgrounds for Stitchery	Marston, Ena		√	SS&D	3	1	9	Wi 71	13
Stitchery	Coat from a Blanket, A	Denecke, Gerlinda	√	√	TM			2	D/J 85	41
Stitchery	Crazy Quilt for Babies Grand, A	Greenberg, Blue	√		Fa	8	2		M/A 81	31
Stitchery	Crocheted Cream Puffs? What You See Is Not What You Get	Fedders, Pat	√		Fa	8	5		S/O 81	16
Stitchery	D. R. Wagner: 625 Stitches per Inch	Welty, Margaret	√		Fa	10	6		N/D 83	24
Stitchery	Fiber and Architecture: Wilcke Smith		√		Fa	3	3		M/J 76	18
Stitchery	Flourishing Art: China, Guizhou Women Continue to Embroider Their Legends, A	Rossi, Gail	√		TM			9	F/M 87	30
Stitchery	Flourishing Art: USA Hmong Women Show How to Stitch Pa ndau, Their Flowery Cloth, A	Porter-Francis, Wendy	√	√	TM			9	F/M 87	33
Stitchery	Folk Textiles of Latin America	Kelemen, Pál	√		TMJ	1	4		De 65	2
Stitchery	Goody Twoshoes: Gaza Bowen, An Extraordinary Shoemaker		√		Fa	8	5		S/O 81	13
Stitchery	Guatamalan Finishes	Gotthoffer, Esther	√		H&C	22	1		Wi 71	18
Stitchery	Helen Bitar	Park, Betty	√		Fa	5	2		M/A 78	44
Stitchery	History in Stitches, A	Mattera, Joanne	√		Fa	7	3		M/J 80	37
Stitchery	Jacqueline Enthoven: Portrait of a Stitchery Teacher	Szajman, Rena	√		Fa	4	3		M/J 77	45
Stitchery	Jan Orr				H&C	19	2		Sp 68	26
Stitchery	"Jean Ray Laury — Exhibit of Stitchery" (Exhibit)	Gutcheon, Beth	√		Fa	6	2		M/A 79	66
Stitchery	Jerri Finch-Hurley: Quilted Paintings	Wonder, Danny	√		Fa	11	2		M/A 84	27
Stitchery	Joyful Hieroglyphics: For Mary Bero Anything is Possible!		√		Fa	8	5		S/O 81	40
Stitchery	Knotting Stitches for Weavers	Hoskins, Nancy Arthur	√	√	SS&D	15	3	59	Su 84	6
Stitchery	Making Molas: Four Basic Techniques	Patera, Charlotte	√		Fa	8	5		S/O 81	38
Stitchery	Mary Ruth Smith: Stitcher	Vander Lee, Jana	√		Fa	3	1		J/F 76	6
Stitchery	"Michael Olszewski: Pleated and Stitched Silk" (Exhibit)	Poon, Vivian	√		Fa	11	3		M/J 84	78
Stitchery	M's and O's "Popcorn" Sweater (Mary Kay Stoehr)		√	√	Hw	5	1		J/F 84	57, 98
Stitchery	"Needle Expressions '84" (Exhibit)	Koplos, Janet	√		Fa	12	2		M/A 85	74
Stitchery	Parks' Bouquet	Parks, Deborah	√	√	PWC	4	1	11		36
Stitchery	"Patricia Malarcher: Pieced Reflections" (Exhibit)	Scheinman, Pamela	√		Fa	11	2		M/A 84	77
Stitchery	Reinforcements	Bradley, Louise	√	√	Hw	8	4		S/O 87	22
Stitchery	Revival of Stitchery, Appliqué, and Collage	Belfer, Nancy	√		H&C	18	1		Wi 67	21
Stitchery	Sas Colby	Talley, Charles	√		Fa	8	5		S/O 81	29
Stitchery	Saved Threads: Ellen Zahorec Explores Layers of Time		√		Fa	8	5		S/O 81	42
Stitchery	Stitch in Time, A	Harris, Patricia; David Lyon	√		Fa	12	2		M/A 85	27
Stitchery	"Stitcherhood Is Powerful" (Exhibit)	McGuire, Patricia	√		Fa	5	6		N/D 78	68
Stitchery	"Stitchery '77" (Exhibit)	Pierucci, Louise	√		Fa	4	3		M/J 77	11
Stitchery	"Stitchery '79" (Exhibit)	Kerr, Connie	√		Fa	6	5		S/O 79	78
Stitchery	Stitches	Wilson, Jean	√	√	SS&D	15	4	60	Fa 84	67
Stitchery	Susan Tufts		√		Fa	4	3		M/J 77	44
Stitchery	Theme Issue		√		Fa	4	3		M/J 77	
Stitchery	Threads of Gold	Austin, Carole	√		Fa	13	4		J/A 86	10
Stitchery	Timeless Stitches: Myrna Shiras' Stitched Drawings	Schwartz, Joyce B.	√		Fa	8	3		M/J 81	65
Stitchery	Tina McMorran	Stevens, Bernice A.	√		H&C	15	3		Su 64	14
Stitchery	Versatile Inlay, Twill on Twill	Beard, Betty	√	√	SS&D	19	1	73	Wi 87	53
Stitchery	Very Special Craftswoman: Maria Consuelo Moya, A		√		Fa	3	2		M/A 76	32

SUBJECT	TITLE	AUTHOR	IL	INST	JOUR	VOL	NO	ISS	DATE	PAGE
Stitchery	Villanueva Tapestries		√		Fa	4	3		M/J 77	45
Stitchery	Weaving, Applique and Stitchery	Belfer, Nancy	√		Iw	5	3		Su 80	41
Stitchery: Accessory Stitching	Paracas Needle Technique, A	Hoskins, Nancy	√	√	Iw	5	4		Fa 80	34
Stitchery: Braid Stitch	Nose to the Grindstone	Phillips, Constance	√	√	TM			7	O/N 86	90
Stitchery: Constructional Stitching	Paracas Needle Technique, A	Hoskins, Nancy	√	√	Iw	5	4		Fa 80	34
Stitchery, Contemporary	Mary Bero	Weiss, Hedy	√		Fa	12	2		M/A 85	36
Stitchery: Crewel	Crewel Gardens	Cunningham, Anne S.	√		TM			6	A/S 86	48
Stitchery: Gros Point	Totems in Tapestry	Swingle, Daphne	√		H&C	22	2		Sp 71	5
Stitchery: On-Loom	Sauna Towel (Phyllis Griffith)		√	√	Hw	1	2		S-S 80	47, 54
Stitchery: Perching	What a Handweaver Can Learn from the Scottish Weaving Industry (error-corrected WJ v2 n1 77 insert for vol. 1)	Barrett, Clotilde	√	√	WJ	1	3	3	Ja 77	11
Stitchery: Peruvian Needle Stitch	Finish Your Work	Stoehr, Mary Kay	√	√	Hw	5	1		J/F 84	54
Stitchery: Satin Stitch	Phulkari	Westfall, Carol D.; Dipti Desai	√		AT	6			De 86	85
Stitchery: Shisha Embroidery	Gujarati Embroidery	Westfall, Carol D.; Dipti Desai	√		AT	8			De 87	29
Stitchery: Techniques	Stitched Finishes in the Guatemalan Tradition	Pancake, Cherri; Karen Searle; Sue Baizerman	√	√	Hw	2	5		No 81	29
Stitchery: Techniques	Stitchery in Its Many Forms		√	√	Fa	4	3		M/J 77	20
Stitchery: Techniques	Stitches for Silk-and-Metal Embroidery (error-corrected TM I4 A/M 86 p4)	Payette, Lynn	√	√	TM			3	F/M 86	51
Stitchery: Techniques	Texture Stitches for Needlepoint	Hamer, Rosalie	√	√	TM			5	J/J 86	62
Stitchery Yarn, Handspun	Norwegian Luskofte	Gibson-Roberts, Priscilla A.	√	√	S-O	9	3		Fa 85	44
Stitches: Back	Handsewing Stitches	Callaway, Grace	√	√	TM			12	A/S 87	53
Stitches: Baseball	Piecing Cloth to Harness the Wind	Montgomery, Larry	√	√	TM			11	J/J 87	48
Stitches: Basting	Handsewing Stitches	Callaway, Grace	√	√	TM			12	A/S 87	53
Stitches: Buttonhole	Needle Lace	Kaiser, Eunice	√	√	TM			13	O/N 87	40
Stitches: Hemstitches	Handsewing Stitches	Callaway, Grace	√	√	TM			12	A/S 87	53
Stitches: Overcast	Handsewing Stitches	Callaway, Grace	√	√	TM			12	A/S 87	53
Stitches: Round	Piecing Cloth to Harness the Wind	Montgomery, Larry	√	√	TM			11	J/J 87	48
Stitches: Saddler	Piecing Cloth to Harness the Wind	Montgomery, Larry	√	√	TM			11	J/J 87	48
Stitches: Tacking	Handsewing Stitches	Callaway, Grace	√	√	TM			12	A/S 87	53
Stitching Point Edges	Getting a Handle on Sewing Details			√	TM			13	O/N 87	13
Stitching Treadle, Double Weave	Double Weaves: Drafts for Double Weaves	Zielinski, S. A.; Robert Leclerc, ed.	√	>4	MWL	15			'51–'73	89
Stoles see Scarves, Shawls, Stoles										
Storage: Animal Fibers	Bugs in the Rugs and Grease in the Fleece		√		S-O	5			81	38
Storage: Animal Fibers	Fleece in the Hands of a New Zealand Spinner	Horne, Beverley	√		S-O	2			78	24
Storage: Animal Fibers	Herbal Moth Repellents: Safeguard or Sentiment?	Buchanan, Rita			S-O	10	2		Su 86	25
Storage: Interfacing	Storing Interfacing			√	TM			12	A/S 87	10
Storage: Space	Weaving in the Urban Tradition	Bulback, Stanley	√		SS&D	12	3	47	Su 81	7
Storage Techniques: Textiles	Principles of Textile Conservation Science, No. 9. How Humidity May Affect Rug, Tapestry, and Other Textile Collections	Rice, James W.	√	√	TMJ	2	3		De 68	53
Storage: Textiles	Current Trends in Textiles Conservation and Preservation	Block, Ira			AT	8			De 87	9
Storage: Textiles	Ounce of Prevention: Preservation and Storage, An	Butterfield, Mary Ann; Lotus Stack	√	√	WJ	10	1	37	Su 85	7

SUBJECT	TITLE	AUTHOR	IL	INST	JOUR	VOL	NO	ISS	DATE	PAGE
Storage: Textiles	Principles of Textile Conservation Science, No. 11. Requirements for Bulk Storage Protection Against Insect Damage	Rice, James W.	√	√	TMJ	2	4		De 69	31
Storage: Weaving Materials	Suggestions for Storage	Crosson, Janet Gray		√	H&C	15	4		Fa 64	21
Storage: Yarn	Knitters Need Baggies			√	TM			10	A/M 87	10
Storage: Yarn	What a Handweaver Can Learn from the Scottish Weaving Industry (error-corrected WJ v2 n1 77 errata sheet for vol. 1)	Barrett, Clotilde	√	√	WJ	1	3	3	Ja 77	11
Storage: Yarn	Yarn Storage Trees	Keasbey, Doramay	√	√	SS&D	10	2	38	Sp 79	86
Storytelling	Four Posts of Poverty, The	Xenaxis, Alexis Yiorgos	√		PWC	5	1	15		6
Storytelling: Weaving	Inspiration in Boundweave	Strauss, Lynn	√	> 4	Hw	7	2		M/A 86	38
Storytelling: Weaving	Storytelling in Boundweave	Strauss, Lynn	√		Hw	7	2		M/A 86	35
Straps, Spaghetti	Quick Spaghetti Straps		√	√	TM			11	J/J 87	8
Straps, Spaghetti	Quick Spaghetti Straps			√	TM			14	D/J 87	12
Strip Weaving	Adinkra: Weft African Textile of Pride	Rex, Chris	√		Fa	9	6		N/D 82	36
Strip Weaving	African Textiles	Sieber, Roy	√		H&C	23	6		N/D 72	9
Strip Weaving	Blankets and Afghans on a Narrow Loom	Davenport, Betty	√	√	PWC	3	1	7		14
Strip Weaving	Kente on Four Harnesses	McCarthy, Catherine L.	√	√	SS&D	16	3	63	Su 85	6
Strip Weaving	Kente: The Status Cloth of Ghana	Conklin, Sharon L.	√	√	SS&D	8	1	29	WI 76	18
Strip Weaving	Modular Clothing	Mayer, Anita	√	√	Hw	7	3		M/J 86	58
Strip Weaving	My African Shirt	Linder, Harry	√		Iw	1	4		Su 76	8
Strip Weaving	Put It Together: Large Cloths from Small Looms	Davenport, Betty	√	√	Hw	8	1		J/F 87	73
Strip Weaving	Strips & Stripes	Lewis, Lois	√	> 4	SS&D	14	2	54	Sp 83	60
Strip Weaving	Weavers in Iran, Thousands at Work on Primitive Looms	Leclerc, Robert	√		H&C	21	2		Sp 70	9
Stripes	Boxed Rainbows: What to Do with a Dye Kit	Bliss, Anne	√	√	Hw	4	2		M/A 83	68
Stripes	Bright & Bold		√	√	Hw	4	2		M/A 83	50
Stripes	Bright, Breezy Stripes	Leethem, Kaino	√		Hw	5	3		Su 84	60
Stripes	Color and Design in Andean Warp-Faced Fabrics	Femenias, Blenda	√		WJ	12	2	46	Fa 87	44
Stripes	Color Rotation Trick, A		√	√	Hw	4	2		M/A 83	40
Stripes	Composition and Designing: Stripes	Zielinski, S. A.; Robert Leclerc, ed.	√	√	MWL	18			'51–'73	72
Stripes	Cool and Casual Cotton		√		Hw	6	3		Su 85	42
Stripes	Critique: Una Flor Morada, A		√	√	Hw	4	2		M/A 83	44
Stripes	Fall Foliage Jacket (Leslie Voiers)		√	√	Hw	5	5		N/D 84	69, I-12
Stripes	Fibonacci Series, The		√	√	Hw	4	2		M/A 83	45
Stripes	Finger Control: Or Getting the Most Out of Your Loom	Patrick, Jane	√	√	Hw	4	2		M/A 83	70
Stripes	Garments with Ethnic Flavor: Blue and White Twill Dress		√	√	WJ	2	3	7	Ja 78	18
Stripes	Glossary of Stripes, A				Hw	4	2		M/A 83	48
Stripes	Guatemalan Stripes	Davenport, Betty	√	√	Hw	4	2		M/A 83	54
Stripes	How to Warp a Stripe			√	Hw	2	1		F-W 80	57
Stripes	Jacket Fabric #3 (Sharon D. Alderman)		√	√	Hw	5	4		S/O 84	56, 102
Stripes	Last Word, The		√	√	Hw	4	2		M/A 83	67
Stripes	Little Dye Makes the Difference, A	Henrikson, Susan	√	√	Hw	4	2		M/A 83	60
Stripes	Look of Bands, The		√		Hw	7	3		M/J 86	44
Stripes	Master's Palette, A		√	√	Hw	4	2		M/A 83	49
Stripes	Modular Design Applied: A Man's Robe		√	√	Hw	4	2		M/A 83	52
Stripes	Original Fabrics of Kaftan, The	El-Homossani, M. M.	√	> 4	AT	1			De 83	263
Stripes	Peru, Textiles Unlimited, Part 2: Patterned Stripes on Plain Weave	Tidball, Harriet	√	√	SCGM		26		69	7

SUBJECT	TITLE	AUTHOR	IL	INST	JOUR	VOL	NO	ISS	DATE	PAGE
Stripes	Peru, Textiles Unlimited, Part 2: Plain Weave Stripes	Tidball, Harriet	√	√	SCGM		26		69	2
Stripes	Planning and Weaving New Stripes	Blumenau, Lili	√	√	H&C	4	4		Fa 53	9
Stripes	Planning Stripes	McDonald, Pat	√	√	Hw	2	4		Se 81	30
Stripes	Prism Pleasure Blanket	Jaeger, Hector	√		Hw	6	3		Su 85	58
Stripes	Qotny & Alaga: Traditional Striped Fabrics for the Middle Eastern Kaftan	El-Homossani, M. M.	√	> 4	WJ	10	1	37	Su 85	33
Stripes	Repetition Repetition Repetition		√	√	Hw	4	2		M/A 83	49
Stripes	Rugs of Mary Veerkamp, The		√	√	Hw	4	2		M/A 83	46
Stripes	Seersucker Blazer, A	Johannesen, Betty	√	√	WJ	8	3	31	Wi 83	22
Stripes	Sequence of Dominance	Davis, Helen	√	√	Hw	4	2		M/A 83	42
Stripes	Shadowweave, Part 1 (error-corrected WJ v2 n1 77 insert for vol. 1)	Barrett, Clotilde	√	> 4	WJ	1	1	1	Jy 76	13
Stripes	Skirt Fabric #5 (Sharon D. Alderman)		√	√	Hw	5	4		S/O 84	56, 102
Stripes	Skirt/Dress Fabric #1 (Sharon D. Alderman)		√	√	Hw	5	3		Su 84	62, 108
Stripes	Sling Chair	Alderman, Sharon	√		Hw	6	3		Su 85	58
Stripes	Spots or Stripes?	Gordon, Judith	√	> 4	Hw	5	4		S/O 84	36
Stripes	Stripe as a Design Module, The	Liebler, Barbara	√	√	Hw	4	2		M/A 83	52
Stripes	Stripe Study Group, A		√	√	Hw	4	2		M/A 83	24
Stripes	Striped Placemats (Susan Feely)		√	√	Hw	8	1		J/F 87	59, I-9
Stripes	Striped Upholstery, Fabric #3 (Constance LaLena)		√	√	Hw	8	4		S/O 87	36, I-4
Stripes	Stripes		√	√	Hw	4	2		M/A 83	40
Stripes	Strips & Stripes	Lewis, Lois	√	> 4	SS&D	14	2	54	Sp 83	60
Stripes	Summer Stripes		√		Hw	6	3		Su 85	58
Stripes	Swatch Collection #7	Alderman, Sharon	√		Hw	4	2		M/A 83	58
Stripes	Thomas Jackson, Weaver: 17th and 18th Century Records	Tidball, Harriet	√	√	SCGM		13		64	35
Stripes	Tucked Dresses	Wertenberger, Kathryn; Nancy Kuwabara	√	√	Hw	4	2		M/A 83	63
Stripes	Warping for Stripes	Davenport, Betty	√	√	Hw	6	4		S/O 85	18
Stripes	Wrap Skirt (Anne Bliss)		√	√	Hw	7	1		J/F 86	55, I-11
Stripes	Wrapping Your Stripes		√	√	Hw	4	2		M/A 83	48
Stripes and Bands	Two-Harness Textiles, The Loom-Controlled Weaves: Stripes and Bands	Tidball, Harriet	√	√	SCGM		20		67	15
Stripes, Plain Weave	Leno with Steel Doup Heddles	Barrett, Clotilde	√	√	WJ	6	3	23	Wi 81	48
Stripes, Texture	Texture as Stripe		√	√	Hw	4	2		M/A 83	66
Stripes, Vertical	Composition and Designing Part 2: Vertical Stripes in Texture and Colour	Zielinski, S. A.; Robert Leclerc, ed.	√	> 4	MWL	19			'51–'73	58
Stripes, Warp	Peru, Textiles Unlimited, Part 2: Opposites Warp-Stripe Patterns	Tidball, Harriet	√	> 4	SCGM		26		69	12
Stripes, Warp-Patterned	Peru, Textiles Unlimited, Part 2: Structural Warp-Stripe Patterns	Tidball, Harriet	√	√	SCGM		26		69	10
Stripes, Weft Pattern	Woven Skirt and Its Development, The	Poussart, Anne	√	√	WJ	8	3	31	Wi 83	39
Structures: Fiber	Anne Wilson: Underlying Geometry	Koplos, Janet	√		Fa	10	3		M/J 83	62
Structures: Fiber	Janice Lessman-Moss: Fiber Structures And Cultivated Contrasts	McClelland, Elizabeth	√		Fa	11	6		N/D 84	18
Structures: Fiber	"Lenore Tawney: A Personal World" (Exhibit)	Malarcher, Pat	√		Fa	5	6		N/D 78	63
Structures: Fiber/Metal	Mary Sue Kern: Embodied Dualities	Logiudice, JoEL	√		Fa	13	5		S/O 86	26
Structures: Mixed Media	Deborah O'Brien Saupe: The Search for Balance	Gaynor, Katherine A.	√		Fa	13	5		S/O 86	24
Structures, Mixed Media	"Janet Markarian" (Exhibit)	Skudera, Gail	√		Fa	13	4		J/A 86	53
Structures: Mixed Media	Kay Campbell: The Shifting Balance of Order	Pencheff, Patricia	√		Fa	12	5		S/O 85	11
Structures: Mixed Media	"Ladders and Windows" (Exhibit)	Kester, Bernard	√		Fa	13	4		J/A 86	52

SUBJECT	TITLE	AUTHOR	IL	INST	JOUR	VOL	NO	ISS	DATE	PAGE
Structures: Mixed Media	Lisa Gardner: Cultural Perspectives	Poon, Vivian	√		Fa	12	1		J/F 85	14
Structures: Mixed Media	Mixed Media Vocabulary of Pamela Matiosian, The	Yovovich, Noël	√		Fa	13	6		N/D 86	6
Structures: Mixed Media	"Weaving Without Fiber" (Exhibit)	Hempel, Toby Anne	√		Fa	13	5		S/O 86	48
Structures: Mixed-Media	Conversation with Lillian Elliott, A	Janeiro, Jan	√		Fa	9	2		M/A 82	66
Structures: Mixed-Media	On the Edge: Harmony Hammond — Collecting, Reclaiming, Connecting	Willard, Janice	√		Fa	9	4		J/A 82	58
Structures: Textile	Margrit Schmidtke: An Evolving Artist	Schmidtke, Sheila	√		Fa	13	5		S/O 86	42
Student Industries	Berea College Fireside Industries Now Employ Sixty Weavers	Stahl, Sam	√		H&C	19	2		Sp 68	5
Studio Workshop	Self-supporting Workshop, A	Collingwood, Peter			H&C	15	4		Fa 64	7
Studios	Acton Opens New Studio and Shop				H&C	7	4		Fa 56	51
Studios	Anne Wilson: Underlying Geometry	Koplos, Janet	√		Fa	10	3		M/J 83	62
Studios	Bringing Tapestry into the 20th Century	Mattera, Joanne	√	√	TM			1	O/N 85	52
Studios	Colorful Blinds and Fabrics from Texas		√		H&C	6	4		Fa 55	14
Studios	Dovecot Studios	Soroka, Joanne	√		SS&D	12	4	48	Fa 81	36
Studios	Fiber Workspaces: A Room of Your Own	Bishop, Mara	√		Fa	4	4		J/A 77	38
Studios	Five Ateliers: A Tour of Weaving Studios in Australia, France, Scotland, Sweden, and the U.S.A.		√		Fa	10	3		M/J 83	36
Studios	From Barn to Studio: On Moving to a Farm and Making a Workspace	Crow, Nancy	√		Fa	8	6		N/D 81	44
Studios	Home Studio?	Liebler, Barbara	√		Iw	5	2		Sp 80	56
Studios	Home Studio: Some Practical Hints	Beschell, Lorraine	√		Iw	5	2		Sp 80	58
Studios	Ligoa Duncan's Studio		√		H&C	8	4		Fa 57	18
Studios	Maridadi West: A Fort Collins, Colorado Fabric Design Studio with Its Roots in East Africa	Mattera, Joanne	√		Fa	9	2		M/A 82	24
Studios	New Woodstock Studio for Berta Frey				H&C	9	1		Wi 57	24
Studios	Plymouth Hoe	Bates, Wynne	√		SS&D	3	2	10	Sp 72	43
Studios	Scheuer Tapestry Studio: Applying Old Techniques to New Ideas, The	Scheuer, Ruth Tannenbaum	√		Fa	10	3		M/J 83	39
Studios	Tapestries of Nancy and Janusz Kozikowski, The	Elliott, Malinda	√		Fa	13	2		M/A 86	23
Studios	Weaving in the Urban Tradition	Bulback, Stanley	√		SS&D	12	3	47	Su 81	7
Studios	Workspaces		√		Fa	7	5		S/O 80	16
Studios	Workspaces		√		Fa	7	6		N/D 80	10
Studios: Ballinskelligs Tapestry Works	Ballinskelligs Tapestry Works: Ancient Art/Modern Spirit, The	Burkhauser, Jude	√		Hw	3	1		Ja 82	55
Studios: Construction	Down on the Farm: An Unusual Insulation Technique		√		Fa	8	6		N/D 81	46
Studios: Dyeing	Ultimate Dyeing Studio, The			√	Fa	5	1		J/F 78	37
Studios: Home	On Working At Home	Brown, Arleen Emery	√		Fa	7	2		M/A 80	45
Studios: Papermaking	Pioneer Paper Places: Pyramid Prints and Paperworks	Fife, Lin	√		Fa	13	4		J/A 86	24
Studios: Photography	Behind the Scenes: Your Own Studio	Rudich, Sally	√		Fa	13	3		M/J 86	47
Studios: Quilting	Quilting in France	Smeltzer, Nancy	√		Fa	13	2		M/A 86	49
Studios: Space	Planning Your Studio Space	LaLena, Constance		√	Hw	4	2		M/A 83	76
Studios: Surface-Design	Shared Work Space May Be Just What You're Looking For, A	Levy, Julie	√	√	TM			9	F/M 87	42
Studios: Tapestry	West Dean and the Tapestry Studio	Sarginson, Peter			Fa	11	2		M/A 84	65
Studios: Weaving, Bastad, Sweden	Harts and Flowers: Sweden's Märta Mäas-Fjetterstrom's Designs Inspired a Textile Renaissance	Selkurt, Claire	√		WJ	9	4	36	Sp 85	30
Study Groups: Complex Weavers	Study Groups				CW		24		My 87	14
Study Groups: Complex Weavers (Additions)	Study Groups				CW		25		Se 87	14
Study Groups see Education										

SUBJECT	TITLE	AUTHOR	IL	INST	JOUR	VOL	NO	ISS	DATE	PAGE
Stuffer Warps	Rugs Woven on Summer and Winter Threading		√	> 4	WJ	3	1	9	Jy 78	12
Stuffer Weave, Double-Faced	Practical Weave for Rugs, A	Atwater, Mary Meigs	√	> 4	H&C	5	2		Sp 54	24
Stuffer Weft	Jacket in Horizontal Cord Weave, A	Duncan, Nadine	√	√	PWC			2	Ap 82	59
Stuffer Wefts	Corded Weaves — Four Harness Cross Cords		√	> 4	WJ	4	1	13	Jy 79	25
Stuffing: Materials	Stuff: Precedents and Alternatives to Polyester	Mattera, Joanne	√		Iw	5	3		Su 80	46
Stumpwork	Stumpwork		√	√	TM			10	A/M 87	8
Style	Matter of Style, A	Ligon, Linda	√		Hw	4	1		J/F 83	14
Style	Wearing Handwovens with Style	Mayer, Anita	√	√	WJ	10	3	39	Wi 86	22
Style Trends	Market Research: Styles, Trends and Product Development	LaLena, Constance			Hw	2	2		Mr 81	63
Suits	Block Twill and Plain Weave Suit (Leslie Voiers, Phyllis Tichy)		√	> 4	Hw	8	5		N/D 87	53, I-12
Suits	Contemporary Costume, Strictly Handwoven: The Bolero Suit	Tidball, Harriet	√	√	SCGM		24		68	40
Suits	Glad Rags	Wroten, Barbara	√	√	SS&D	15	4	60	Fa 84	28
Suits	Guide to Ann's Knit Suit, A	Klinect, Ann W.		√	S-O	10	1		Sp 86	41
Suits	Prize-Winning Suit, A	Karsten, Phyllis	√	√	S-O	8	4		Wi 84	15
Suits	Suited to Silk	Turner, Kathryn M.	√	√	SS&D	18	2	70	Sp 87	68
Suits: Boxy, 1950's	Balenciago: The Architect of Elegant Clothing	Koda, Harold	√		TM			11	J/J 87	20
Suits: Chanel-Style, Knitted	Odyssey Knitting				TM			14	D/J 87	4
Suits: Custom Tailored	Tailor's Logic	Hostek, Stanley	√	√	TM			14	D/J 87	42
Sumba	Sumbanese Ikat	Hannon, Farrell	√	√	WJ	8	1	29	Su 83	38
Sumba	Tiedyeing An Art on the Island of Sumba	Adams, Moni	√	√	H&C	22	1		Wi 71	9
Summer and Winter	Alternative Summer and Winter Pickup Technique, An	Salsbury, Nate	√	√	Iw	5	4		Fa 80	69
Summer and Winter	Autumn Leaves, A Design in Summer-and-Winter	Arnold, Ruth	√	√	H&C	14	3		Su 63	14
Summer and Winter	Building on a Tradition	Alvic, Philis	√		Iw	4	3		Su 79	45
Summer and Winter	But What's the Tie-Up?	van der Hoogt, Madelyn	√	> 4	PWC	5	1	15		36
Summer and Winter	Checker Board (Julia Hanan)		√	√	Hw	2	1		F-W 80	55, 69
Summer and Winter	Christmas Gretings from the Weaver's Journal Staff		√	> 4	WJ	3	2	10	Oc 78	41
Summer and Winter	Christmas Miniatures, Part 1: Summer and Winter Coverlets	Lyon, Linda	√	√	PWC			3	Oc 82	50
Summer and Winter	Colonial Coverlets, Part 3: Summer and Winter	Liebler, Barbara	√	√	Iw	1	4		Su 76	24
Summer and Winter	Color and Weave Effects with Four Harness Summer and Winter		√	√	WJ	5	2	18	Fa 80	24
Summer and Winter	Color in Summer and Winter	Alvic, Philis	√	√	WJ	7	4	28	Sp 83	64
Summer and Winter	Colorful Cotton Coordinates (Pat Short) (error-corrected WJ v11 n3 87 p78)		√	√	WJ	11	2	42	Fa 86	40
Summer and Winter	Constellations: A Summer and Winter Weave on Ten Harnesses	Bergman, Margaret	√	> 4	CW	5	3	15	My 84	20
Summer and Winter	Contemporary Approach to Traditional Weaves: Summer and Winter	Zielinski, S. A.; Robert Leclerc, ed.	√	> 4	MWL	7			'51–'73	93
Summer and Winter	Coverlet Weaves Using Two Ties	Barrett, Clotilde	√	> 4	WJ	3	4	12	Ap 79	26
Summer and Winter	Designing Rugs for Harness-Controlled Weaving		√	> 4	WJ	4	4	16	Ap 80	27
Summer and Winter	Designs in Summer-and-Winter	Barrett, Ruth L.	√	> 4	H&C	12	4		Fa 61	34
Summer and Winter	Drafting: A Personal Approach, Part 2	Alvic, Philis	√	> 4	SS&D	13	2	50	Sp 82	46
Summer and Winter	Early American Coverlet of The Summer and Winter Type		√	> 4	WJ	3	4	12	Ap 79	35
Summer and Winter	Ecclesiastical Weavings of Diana Lockwood, The		√	> 4	WJ	4	3	15	Ja 80	18

SUBJECT	TITLE	AUTHOR	IL	INST	JOUR	VOL	NO	ISS	DATE	PAGE
Summer and Winter	Even-Tied Overshot	Xenakis, Athanasios David	√	> 4	PWC	3	3	9		40
Summer and Winter	Fabrics from a New Type Multi-Harness Loom	Cory, Sue Armstrong	√	> 4	H&C	10	1		Wi 59	24
Summer and Winter	Four-End Block Draft or Summer and Winter	McClanathan, Barbara	√	√	WJ	8	4	32	Sp 84	22
Summer and Winter	Garments Made from Simple Patterns: Two Tabards		√	> 4	WJ	2	3	7	Ja 78	35
Summer and Winter	Garments with Ethnic Flavor: Pine Tree Cape		√	> 4	WJ	2	3	7	Ja 78	16
Summer and Winter	Guatemala Visited	Atwater, Mary Meigs	√	√	SCGM		15		65	24
Summer and Winter	Guatemala Visited	Atwater, Mary Meigs	√	√	SCGM		15		65	37
Summer and Winter	Hand Woven Rugs: Weaves, Summer and Winter	Atwater, Mary Meigs		√	SCGM		29		48	21
Summer and Winter	Handbag by Muriel Barnes (error-corrected H&C v14 n1 63 p46)		√	> 4	H&C	13	4		Fa 62	42
Summer and Winter	Handweaver's Instruction Manual: The Summer and Winter Weave	Tidball, Harriet C. nee Douglas	√	√	SCGM		34		49	29
Summer and Winter	Handwoven Silk Garments: Blue Silk Dress	Alvic, Philis	√	> 4	WJ	3	2	10	Oc 78	27
Summer and Winter	Introduction to Tied Unit Weaves, An	Kelly, Jacquie	√	> 4	PWC	4	4	14		40
Summer and Winter	Josephina's Suit	Koopman, Albertje	√	> 4	WJ	4	4	16	Ap 80	50
Summer and Winter	Kuvikas	Schoenfeld, Klara	√	> 4	H&C	12	2		Sp 61	20
Summer and Winter	Long Sweeping Evening Cape	Roth, Bettie G.	√	> 4	WJ	6	3	23	Wi 81	26
Summer and Winter	Loom Controlled Designs		√	> 4	WJ	3	3	11	Ja 79	18
Summer and Winter	Man-Made Fibers: Baby Blankets		√	√	WJ	5	2	18	Fa 80	43
Summer and Winter	Megablocks	Patrick, Jane	√	√	Hw	4	1		J/F 83	60
Summer and Winter	More Harnesses Make the Difference	Wertenberger, Kathryn	√	> 4	Hw	2	3		My 81	40
Summer and Winter	Multiple Shaft Weaving — 2-Tie Four-End Block Drafts		√	> 4	WJ	6	4	24	Sp 82	48
Summer and Winter	New Method for Pile Weave, A	Deru, Crescent	√	> 4	H&C	8	3		Su 57	16
Summer and Winter	Nineteenth Century Miniatures	Erf, Mary Elva Congleton	√	> 4	SS&D	16	1	61	Wi 84	60
Summer and Winter	Notes from a Rugweaver's Journal	Schomp, Halcyon; Hector Jaeger	√	√	Hw	3	4		Se 82	35
Summer and Winter	Notes of a Pattern Weaver	Alvic, Philis	√	> 4	SS&D	14	4	56	Fa 83	82
Summer and Winter	Nubby Upholstery (Kathryn Wertenberger)		√	> 4	Hw	5	2		M/A 84	66, 103
Summer and Winter	Patchwork Designs in Summer and Winter	Davenport, Betty	√	√	PWC	1	1		No 81	27
Summer and Winter	Pattern and Structure in Handwoven Fabrics	Frey, Berta	√	√	H&C	6	4		Fa 55	4
Summer and Winter	Pictures in Summer & Winter Pick-up	Griffin, Gertrude	√	√	Hw	7	2		M/A 86	54
Summer and Winter	Pillow and Table Runner in Summer and Winter Weave	Xenakis, Athanasios David	√	√	PWC	1	1		No 81	21
Summer and Winter	Pine Tree Coat	Knollenberg, Barbara	√	> 4	WJ	1	2	2	Oc 76	32
Summer and Winter	Production-Wise Placemats (error-corrected WJ v9 n2 84 p82)	Hall, Nancy Terrell	√	√	WJ	9	1	33	Su 84	44
Summer and Winter	Profile Drafting Lesson: Summer and Winter Towel (Sharon Alderman)		√	√	Hw	8	5		N/D 87	44, I-6
Summer and Winter	Quick Thick Rug, A		√	√	WJ	7	4	28	Sp 83	43
Summer and Winter	Roman Shades and Bedspread		√	√	WJ	3	1	9	Jy 78	32
Summer and Winter	Rugs for Interiors	Roach, Dianne Carol	√		SS&D	16	4	64	Fa 85	18
Summer and Winter	Rugs Woven on Summer and Winter Threading		√	> 4	WJ	3	1	9	Jy 78	12
Summer and Winter	Shaft Switch Technique (error-corrected WJ v6 n1 81 p28d)		√	√	WJ	5	1	17	Su 80	5
Summer and Winter	Shaft-Switching Combined with Harness Control	Barrett, Clotilde	√	> 4	WJ	9	1	33	Su 84	37
Summer and Winter	Split-Harness Drawloom, The	Malloy, Kim, OSB	√	> 4	CW	2	1	4	Oc 80	3

693

SUBJECT	TITLE	AUTHOR	IL	INST	JOUR	VOL	NO	ISS	DATE	PAGE
Summer and Winter	Stars, Diamonds, Tables, and Sunrise: Motifs and Structures of Woven Coverlets	Cabeen, Lou	√	√	TM			14	D/J 87	32
Summer and Winter	Stitching Traditional Coverlet Weaves	Sellin, Helen G.	√	>4	AT	1			De 83	289
Summer and Winter	Stripes in Summer and Winter Weave	Parker, Ella W.	√		H&C	4	3		Su 53	19
Summer and Winter	Summer and Winter — A Stock of Options	Minard, Juanita	√	√	SS&D	10	3	39	Su 79	42
Summer and Winter	Summer and Winter, A Unit Weave	Marston, Ena			SS&D	4	4	16	Fa 73	25
Summer and Winter	Summer and Winter Accent (Kathryn Wertenberger)		√	>4	Hw	5	2		M/A 84	66, 104
Summer and Winter	Summer and Winter and Other Two-Tie Unit Weaves	Tidball, Harriet	√	√	SCGM		19		66	1-58
Summer and Winter	Summer and Winter for Four Shafts	Allen, Debbie	√	√	Hw	8	5		N/D 87	86
Summer and Winter	Summer and Winter Garments (Melinda Raber Johnson)		√	√	WJ	11	3	43	Wi 87	44
Summer and Winter	Summer and Winter Kitchen Towels (Beth Johnson Brewin) (error-corrected Hw v8 n3 87 pl-3) (error-corrected Hw v8 n1 87 p I-3)		√	√	Hw	7	3		M/J 86	65, I-13
Summer and Winter	Summer and Winter on More Than Four Shafts		√	>4	Hw	8	5		N/D 87	88
Summer and Winter	Summer and Winter — Part 1		√	>4	WJ	2	4	8	Ap 78	28
Summer and Winter	Summer and Winter Poppana Table Mat (Janice Jones)		√	√	Hw	8	5		N/D 87	87, I-16
Summer and Winter	Summer and Winter Rug (Jean Anstine) (error-corrected Hw v4 n2 83 p80)		√	√	Hw	3	5		N/D 82	48, 87
Summer and Winter	Summer and Winter Stole (Nell Znamierowski)		√	√	Hw	8	5		N/D 87	51, I-10
Summer and Winter	Summer and Winter Suiting	Upson, Frieda	√	>4	SS&D	12	1	45	Wi 80	62
Summer and Winter	Summer and Winter Treadling Gamp, A	Strickler, Carol	√	√	Iw	3	4		Su 78	43
Summer and Winter	Summer-and-Winter as Developed in the Nineties	Frey, Berta	√	√	H&C	21	2		Sp 70	11
Summer and Winter	Summer-and-Winter, Experiments with Four Blocks on Four Harnesses	Aldrich, Mae D.	√	√	H&C	17	4		Fa 66	21
Summer and Winter	Summer-and-Winter Pick-up Weave	Brouwer, Martha	√	√	SS&D	8	3	31	Su 77	58
Summer and Winter	Summer/Winter	Flugg, Barbara Gentry	√	>4	Iw	2	1		Fa 76	12
Summer and Winter	Swivel Variations for Four Harness Looms	James, Ona	√	√	H&C	14	4		Fa 63	11
Summer and Winter	Tablecloth in Summer and Winter	Xenakis, Athanasios David	√	√	PWC	1	1		No 81	16
Summer and Winter	Textile Structure and Analysis, A Home Study Course in Twelve Lessons: Lessons in Weave Structure, 6. Summer and Winter	Tidball, Harriet		√	SCGM		18		66	26
Summer and Winter	Turned Drafts in Double Two-Tie Unit Weave	van der Hoogt, Madelyn	√	>4	WJ	9	2	34	Fa 84	13
Summer and Winter	Two-Tie Unit for Rugs: Part 1, The Double-Faced Stuffer Weave and Summer-and-Winter, The	Windeknecht, Margaret	√	>4	SS&D	16	1	61	Wi 84	82
Summer and Winter	Two-Tie Unit for Rugs: Part 2 Warping and Weaving Methods, The	Windeknecht, Margaret	√	>4	SS&D	16	2	62	Sp 85	34
Summer and Winter	Unharnessing the Summer and Winter Weave	Xenakis, Athanasios David	√		Iw	4	4		Fa 79	42
Summer and Winter	Variation on a Finnish Weave by a Texas Weaver (error-corrected H&C v17 n2 66 p48)	Sheppard, Margaret	√	>4	H&C	16	3		Su 65	20
Summer and Winter	Warp Stuffer Weave with Shaft Switching Applications	Evans, Jane A.	√	>4	Hw	4	3		M/J 83	72
Summer and Winter	Weaver's Notebook		√	√	SS&D	9	4	36	Fa 78	101
Summer and Winter	Weaving As Drawn In—Classic Style, Part 1	Keasbey, Doramay	√	√	SS&D	17	1	65	Wi 85	28
Summer and Winter	Weaving for the Holidays (error-corrected Hw v4 n4 83 p92)		√	>4	Hw	3	5		N/D 82	78
Summer and Winter	Workshop at Home, Weaving Summer and Winter	Arnold, Ruth	√	√	H&C	9	3		Su 58	6

SUBJECT	TITLE	AUTHOR	IL	INST	JOUR	VOL	NO	ISS	DATE	PAGE
Summer and Winter, 4-Block, 4-Shaft	Four-Shaft Primer: Tie Talk	Sullivan, Donna	√	> 4	PWC	4	4	14		14
Summer and Winter, 4-Block, 4-Shaft	S&W Wrapper	Sullivan, Donna	√	√	SS&D	15	1	57	Wi 83	24
Summer and Winter, 4-Block, 4-Shaft	Summer Blouse in Summer and Winter, A	Sullivan, Donna	√	√	PWC	4	4	14		18
Summer and Winter, 4-Block, 4-Shaft Method	Summer and Winter and Other Two-Tie Unit Weaves: Methods for Weaving Two-Tie Units, Four Block, Four-Harness, Summer and Winter	Tidball, Harriet	√	> 4	SCGM		19		66	54
Summer and Winter, Color Placement	Contemporary Approach to Traditional Weaves: Colours in Summer and Winter	Zielinski, S. A.; Robert Leclerc, ed.	√	> 4	MWL	7			'51–'73	119
Summer and Winter, Double	Coverlet Weaves Using Two Ties	Barrett, Clotilde	√	> 4	WJ	3	4	12	Ap 79	26
Summer and Winter, Double	Designing Rugs for Harness-Controlled Weaving		√	> 4	WJ	4	4	16	Ap 80	27
Summer and Winter, Double	Introduction to Tied Unit Weaves, An	Kelly, Jacquie	√	> 4	PWC	4	4	14		40
Summer and Winter, Double	Multiple Shaft Weaving — 2-Tie Four-End Block Drafts		√	> 4	WJ	6	4	24	Sp 82	48
Summer and Winter, Double	Rainbow Blankets	Sullivan, Donna	√	> 4	PWC	4	4	14		27
Summer and Winter, Double, System	Handloom Weaves: The Classification of Handloom Weaves, The Structural Group, Unit Class, Double Summer and Winter System	Tidball, Harriet	√	> 4	SCGM		33		57	22
Summer and Winter, Miniature	Miniature World, A	Piroch, Sigrid	√	> 4	PWC	5	2	16		26
Summer and Winter, Modern	Contemporary Approach to Traditional Weaves: Modern Summer and Winter	Zielinski, S. A.; Robert Leclerc, ed.	√	> 4	MWL	7			'51–'73	101
Summer and Winter, One-Block	Notebook: Warmables (Judy Healey)	Meyers, Ruth Nordquist, ed.	√	√	SS&D	15	1	57	Wi 83	80
Summer and Winter, Opposites, Weft-Faced	Woven Pendant (Jane Patrick)		√	√	Hw	8	4		S/O 87	55, I-11
Summer and Winter, Pile	Wooly Afghan in Summer and Winter Pile Techniques	Champion, Ellen	√	√	WJ	4	4	16	Ap 80	14
Summer and Winter, Production Drafts	Contemporary Approach to Traditional Weaves: Production Drafts	Zielinski, S. A.; Robert Leclerc, ed.	√	> 4	MWL	7			'51–'73	121
Summer and Winter, Surface Interest	Surface Interest — Textiles of Today: Surface Interest Designs with Drafts, Group 3, Two-Surface Designs	Tidball, Harriet	√	> 4	SCGM		2		61	13
Summer and Winter System	Handloom Weaves: The Classification of Handloom Weaves, The Structural Group, Unit Class, Summer and Winter System	Tidball, Harriet	√	> 4	SCGM		33		57	21
Summer and Winter, Tabby Ground, 4-Shaft	Contemporary Approach to Traditional Weaves: Summer and Winter with Tabby Ground	Zielinski, S. A.; Robert Leclerc, ed.	√	√	MWL	7			'51–'73	109
Summer and Winter, Tabby Ground, 8-Shaft	Contemporary Approach to Traditional Weaves: Summer and Winter with Tabby Ground	Zielinski, S. A.; Robert Leclerc, ed.	√	> 4	MWL	7			'51–'73	109
Summer and Winter, Turned	Turned Summer and Winter Jacket	Johnson, Melinda Raber	√	> 4	WJ	8	3	31	Wi 83	58
Summer and Winter, Turned	Weaving Towels As a Means of Learning the Basic Four-Shaft Weaves	Barrett, Clotilde	√	√	WJ	8	2	30	Fa 83	11
Summer and Winter, Two-Harness (Sets)	Little Known Weaves Worth Knowing Better: Two-Harness Method	Zielinski, S. A.; Robert Leclerc, ed.	√	> 4	MWL	16			'51–'73	36
Summer and Winter, Variations	Summer and Winter Unharnessed	Xenakis, Athanasios David	√	√	PWC	1	1		No 81	10
Summer and Winter, Weaving Methods	Summer and Winter and Other Two-Tie Unit Weaves: Summer and Winter Weaving Methods	Tidball, Harriet	√	√	SCGM		19		66	11
Superstitions: Textile Related	Black Cats and Green Stitches	Phillips, Constance	√		TM			13	O/N 87	90
Supplementary Warps	Bolivian Highland Weaving, Part 1	Cason, Marjorie; Adele Cahlander	√		SS&D	6	2	22	Sp 75	4
Supplementary Warps	Coat for Handwoven Yardage, A	Roth, Bettie G.	√	> 4	WJ	7	3	27	Wi 82	6
Supplementary Warps	Garments Made from Simple Patterns: Loom Shaped Poncho		√	√	WJ	2	3	7	Ja 78	39
Supplementary Warps	Garments with Ethnic Flavor: Ethnic Dress with Supplementary Warp		√	√	WJ	2	3	7	Ja 78	14

SUBJECT	TITLE	AUTHOR	IL	INST	JOUR	VOL	NO	ISS	DATE	PAGE
Supplementary Warps	Man's Shirt In Peruvian Inlay	Linder, Harry	√	> 4	WJ	4	2	14	Oc 79	8
Supplementary Warps	Supplementary Warp Placemats (Betty Davenport)		√	> 4	Hw	3	3		My 82	75, 98
Supplementary Warps	Supplementary Warps: The One-Shuttle Solution (error-corrected SS&D v19 n1 87 p33)	Mortensen, Diane L.	√	√	SS&D	18	4	72	Fa 87	66
Supplementary Warps	Velvet Ikat	Stack, Lotus	√	> 4	WJ	11	4	44	Sp 87	36
Supplementary Warps	Verticals	O'Shaughnessy, Marjorie	√	> 4	SS&D	15	1	57	Wi 83	8
Supplementary Warps	Weaver's Notebook: (Merritt, Elveana)		√	√	SS&D	10	4	40	Fa 79	102
Supplementary Warps and Wefts	Peculiar Piqué Pillow	Lyon, Linda	√	> 4	PWC	4	2	12		30
Supplementary Warps, Warp-Weft Overshot Border	Supplementary Warp Patterning: Warp-Weft Overshot Rose Border	Tidball, Harriet	√	> 4	SCGM		17		66	27
Supplementary Warps, Warp-Weft Patterning	Supplementary Warp Patterning: Coordinated Supplementary Warp-Weft Patterns	Tidball, Harriet	√	> 4	SCGM		17		66	25
Supplementary Warps, Warp-Weft Rosepath	Supplementary Warp Patterning: Warp-Weft Rosepath	Tidball, Harriet	√	> 4	SCGM		17		66	26
Supplementary Warps-to-Wefts	Linen Lattice Towel (Linda Ligon)		√	√	Hw	5	3		Su 84	70, 105
Supplementary Wefts	Autumn Oak Pullover (Ardis Dobrovolny)		√	√	Hw	3	4		Se 82	49, 91
Supplementary Wefts	Chinese Drawloom: A Study in Weave Structure, The	Sellin, Helen	√	> 4	WJ	9	2	34	Fa 84	6
Supplementary Wefts	Coat for Handwoven Yardage, A	Roth, Bettie G.	√	> 4	WJ	7	3	27	Wi 82	6
Supplementary Wefts	Decorative Weft on a Plain Weave Ground, Two Shaft Inlay and Brocade		√	√	WJ	5	4	20	Sp 81	15
Supplementary Wefts	Garments with Ethnic Flavor: Ethnic Dress with Supplementary Warp		√	√	WJ	2	3	7	Ja 78	14
Supplementary Wefts	Grrrhhhh: A Study of Social Patterns	Hickman, Deborah	√		Fa	14	4		S/O 87	23
Supplementary Wefts	Hanaori: An Okinawan Brocaded Textile	Miller, Dorothy	√	√	AT	1			De 83	173
Supplementary Wefts	In Pursuit of Plakhta	Golay, Myrna	√	> 4	WJ	11	3	43	Wi 87	34
Supplementary Wefts	Inlay Techniques	Barrett, Clotilde	√	√	WJ	1	1	1	Jy 76	3
Supplementary Wefts	Lithuanian Pervarai: Producing a Twenty Shaft Pattern on a Twelve Shaft Loom	Meek, M. Kati	√	> 4	AT	1			De 83	159
Supplementary Wefts	Macro Plaid, Macro Twill	Xenakis, Athanasios David	√	> 4	PWC	3	1	7		55
Supplementary Wefts	Morgan Clifford: New Directions in Brocades	Gue, Sandra	√		WJ	11	4	44	Sp 87	40
Supplementary Wefts	Smålands Weave on Eight Shafts	Shannon, Eileen	√	> 4	WJ	9	1	33	Su 84	47
Supplementary Wefts	Supplementary Warp Patterns		√	> 4	WJ	2	3	7	Ja 78	26
Supplementary Wefts	Supplementary Weft Float Patterning	Marston, Ena	√	√	SS&D	9	4	36	Fa 78	63
Supplementary Wefts	Three Faces of the Eight-Pointed Star Motif (error-corrected SS&D v14 n4 83 p4)	Coffman, Charlotte	√	√	SS&D	14	3	55	Su 83	56
Supplementary Wefts	Versatile Inlay, Twill on Twill	Beard, Betty	√	√	SS&D	19	1	73	Wi 87	53
Supplementary Wefts	Woven Inspiration from West African Textiles	Renne, Elisha	√	√	WJ	10	4	40	Sp 86	60
Supplementary-Warp	Macro Plaid, Macro Twill	Xenakis, Athanasios David	√	> 4	PWC	3	1	7		55
Supplementary-Warp Accents	Peru, Textiles Unlimited, Part 2: Supplementary Warp Accents	Tidball, Harriet	√	√	SCGM		26		69	8
Supplementary-Warp and -Weft Outlines	Peru, Textiles Unlimited, Part 2: Supplementary Warp and Weft Outlines	Tidball, Harriet	√	> 4	SCGM		26		69	16
Supplementary-Warp Brocade	Supplementary Warp (Warp Brocade)	Wertenberger, Kathryn	√	> 4	Hw	7	1		J/F 86	80
Supplementary-Warp, Deflection	Simple Method for Weaving Deflected Warps	Frey, Berta	√	√	H&C	20	4		Fa 69	4
Supplementary-Warp Looping	Warp Boutonné	Lewis, Edward G.	√	√	WJ	7	2	26	Fa 82	64
Supplementary-Warp Patterning	Egyptian Shirt (Kathryn Wertenberger)		√	√	Hw	2	2		Mr 81	54, 70
Supplementary-Warp Patterning	Peru, Textiles Unlimited, Part 2: Supplementary Warp Patterning	Tidball, Harriet	√	√	SCGM		26		69	9

SUBJECT	TITLE	AUTHOR	IL	INST	JOUR	VOL	NO	ISS	DATE	PAGE
Supplementary-Warp Patterning	Supplementary Warp Patterning: Dresses Styled From Warp Pattern Fabrics	Tidball, Harriet	√	> 4	SCGM		17		66	31
Supplementary-Warp Patterning	Supplementary Warp Patterning: Introduction	Tidball, Harriet	√	√	SCGM		17		66	1-46
Supplementary-Warp Patterning	Veridian Green Cape	Barrett, Clotilde	√	> 4	WJ	4	3	15	Ja 80	11
Supplementary-Warp Patterning	Weaving Processes in the Cuzco Area of Peru	Rowe, Ann Pollard	√	√	TMJ	4	2		75	30
Supplementary-Warp Patterning, Classic	Supplementary Warp Patterning: Classic Patterns in Supplementary Warp	Tidball, Harriet	√	> 4	SCGM		17		66	23
Supplementary-Warp Patterning, Contemporary	Supplementary Warp Patterning: Contemporary Draperies in Supplementary Warp	Tidball, Harriet	√		SCGM		17		66	28
Supplementary-Warp Patterning, Loom-Controlled	Holiday Greetings (Carol Thilenius)		√	> 4	Hw	3	5		N/D 82	101
Supplementary-Warp Patterning, Pick-Up	Weaving Processes in the Cuzco Area of Peru	Rowe, Ann Pollard	√	√	TMJ	4	2		75	30
Supplementary-Warp Patterning, Structure	Supplementary Warp Patterning: Structure	Tidball, Harriet			SCGM		17		66	2
Supplementary-Warp Patterning, Two-Harness (Sets) Loom	Supplementary Warp Patterning: Supplementary Warp Patterns on A Two-Harness Loom	Tidball, Harriet		√	SCGM		17		66	9
Supplementary-Warp Pick-Up	Supplementary Warp Patterning: Native American Warp Pick-Up	Tidball, Harriet	√	√	SCGM		17		66	14
Supplementary-Warp Pick-Up	Supplementary Warp Patterning: Supplementary Warp Pick-Ups	Tidball, Harriet	√	√	SCGM		17		66	13
Supplementary-Warp Pick-Up, Peasant Style	Supplementary Warp Patterning: Peasant Style Warp Pick-Up	Tidball, Harriet	√	√	SCGM		17		1966	16
Supplementary-Warp Weaves	Parks' Bouquet	Parks, Deborah	√	√	PWC	4	1	11		36
Supplementary-Warp Weaves	Summer and Winter and Other Two-Tie Unit Weaves: Methods for Weaving Two-Tie Units, Supplementary Warp Method	Tidball, Harriet	√	√	SCGM		19		66	46
Supplementary-Warp Weaves	Textile Structure and Analysis, A Home Study Course in Twelve Lessons: Lessons in Weave Structure, 7. Supplementary Warp Weaves	Tidball, Harriet		> 4	SCGM		18		66	27
Supplementary-Warp Weaves	Two Unusual Multishaft Curtains	Xenakis, Athanasios David	√	> 4	PWC	4	1	11		40
Supplementary-Warps, Deflected	Peru, Textiles Unlimited, Part 2: Deflected Supplementary Warps	Tidball, Harriet	√	√	SCGM		26		69	18
Supplementary-Warps, Distorted	Supplementary Warp Patterning: Distorted Supplementary Warps	Tidball, Harriet	√	√	SCGM		17		66	11
Supplementary-Warps, Diverted	Supplementary Warp Patterning: Diverted Supplementary Warps	Tidball, Harriet	√	√	SCGM		17		66	10
Supplementary-Warps, Fringes	Supplementary Warp Patterning: Supplementary Warp Fringes	Tidball, Harriet	√	√	SCGM		17		66	13
Supplementary-Warps, Pattern Harness Weaving	Supplementary Warp Patterning: A Sash from Chiapas	Tidball, Harriet	√	√	SCGM		17		66	17
Supplementary-Warps, Polychrome	Supplementary Warp Patterning: Multi-Polychrome Supplementary Warps	Tidball, Harriet	√	> 4	SCGM		17		66	21
Supplementary-Warps, Turned, Warp-Wefts	Supplementary Warp Patterning: Turned Supplementary Warp-Wefts	Tidball, Harriet	√	√	SCGM		17		66	12
Supplementary-Weft Brocade	Bath Towel Set, A	Xenakis, Athanasios David	√	> 4	PWC	1	1		No 81	24
Supplementary-Weft Patterning	Chinese Brocades: Development of Supplementary Weft Patterning (error-corrected WJ v11 n4 87 p78)	Drooker, Penelope	√		WJ	11	3	43	Wi 87	47
Supplementary-Weft Patterning	Designs in Sumba Textiles, Local Meanings and Foreign Influences	Adams, Monni	√		TMJ	3	2		De 71	28
Supplementary-Weft Patterning	Flat-Woven Structures Found in Nomadic and Village Weavings from the Near East and Central Asia	Wertime, John T.	√		TMJ	18			79	33
Supplementary-Weft Patterning	Peru, Textiles Unlimited, Part 2: Supplementary Weft Patterning, Style I	Tidball, Harriet	√	√	SCGM		26		69	20

SUBJECT	TITLE	AUTHOR	IL	INST	JOUR	VOL	NO	ISS	DATE	PAGE
Supplementary-Weft Patterning	Peru, Textiles Unlimited, Part 2: Supplementary Weft Patterning, Style II	Tidball, Harriet	√	>4	SCGM		26		69	21
Supplementary-Weft Patterning	Selected Batak Textiles: Technique and Function	Gittinger, Mattiebelle S.	√		TMJ	4	2		75	13
Supplementary-Weft Patterning	Skillbragd Runner (Myrna Golay)		√	>4	Hw	8	3		M/J 87	61, I-12
Supplementary-Weft Patterning	Thrum Pillows (Betty Davenport)		√	√	Hw	5	5		N/D 84	66, I-10
Supplementary-Weft, Pick-Up	Peru, Textiles Unlimited, Part 2: Supplementary Weft Pick-Up	Tidball, Harriet	√	√	SCGM		26		69	27
Supplementary-Weft, Polychrome, Pick-Up	Peru, Textiles Unlimited, Part 2: Polychrome Weft Pick-Up	Tidball, Harriet	√	√	SCGM		26		69	28
Supplementary-Weft Weaves	Two Unusual Multishaft Curtains	Xenakis, Athanasios David	√	>4	PWC	4	1	11		40
Suppliers: Silk	Availability of Silk to the Fiber Craftsman				WJ	3	2	10	Oc 78	12
Suppliers: Wool	Know Your Supplier				S-O	11	3		Fa 87	41
Supply: Sources	Knitting Machine Geometrics	Guagliumi, Susan	√	√	TM			10	A/M 87	66
Surface Decoration	"Forms and Surfaces" (Exhibit)		√		Fa	8	4		J/A 81	68
Surface Decoration	Structure and Surface: The Work of Barbara MacCallum	Koplos, Janet	√		Fa	10	2		M/A 83	62
Surface Decoration: Techniques	Fabric Ornamentation	Kaufman, Glen	√		H&C	17	1		Wi 66	14
Surface Design	"Ann Trusty: Grid and Pattern" (Exhibit)	Stiles, David	√		Fa	9	1		J/F 82	79
Surface Design	Art to Wear — Three Innovators: Cate Fitt, Emma Vesey, Dina Schwartz Knapp		√		Fa	8	1		J/F 81	67
Surface Design	Artist in Focus, The	Goldberg, Barbara B.	√		Fa	11	3		M/J 84	52
Surface Design	Color Xerography and the Fiber Artist	Theil, Linda	√		Fa	8	5		S/O 81	59
Surface Design	Cynthia Pannucci: Relocating, Creating, Connecting	Mattera, Joanne	√		Fa	9	3		M/J 82	23
Surface Design	Exploration of Caustic Soda, An	Bissell, June M.	√		Fa	7	6		N/D 80	43
Surface Design	"Fabric/Nexus: New Connections" (Exhibit)	Moldovan, George	√		Fa	10	3		M/J 83	70
Surface Design	Hand-Painted Silk	Jaffie, H. R.	√		Fa	10	5		S/O 83	17
Surface Design	Improvs on Silk: The Fabric Painting of Susan Daniel	Fitt, Cate	√		Fa	8	5		S/O 81	45
Surface Design	"James Bassler" (Exhibit)	Malarcher, Patricia	√		Fa	8	6		N/D 81	71
Surface Design	Just Playing in Space: Ann McKenzie Nickolson's Textile Artwork	Koplos, Janet	√		Fa	8	2		M/A 81	34
Surface Design	Katherine Virgils	Waller, Irene	√		Fa	10	5		S/O 83	12
Surface Design	Learning to See Pattern	Morrison, Skye	√	√	TM			2	D/J 85	44
Surface Design	Lenore Davis: Figuring in Cloth	Frasier, Debra	√		Fa	10	5		S/O 83	10
Surface Design	On Fabric in the Southwest: Surface Design, A Bank, and Public Recognition	Brooks, Lois Ziff	√		Fa	6	5		S/O 79	54
Surface Design	Print and Dye Works	Goldberg, Barbara; Antoinette Minichiello-Winters	√		Fa	9	3		M/J 82	25
Surface Design	Revelations: Victoria Rivers' Neon and Fabric Constructions		√		Fa	8	5		S/O 81	50
Surface Design	Rochester Honor Quilt: Celebrating Surface Design, The		√		Fa	10	5		S/O 83	98
Surface Design	Rugs: Jo Ann Giordano, Silk Screener		√		Fa	9	2		M/A 82	60
Surface Design	Sampler of Surface Design, A	Westphal, Katherine	√		Fa	10	5		S/O 83	39
Surface Design	Sandra Holzman: Marbleized Fabrics	Piucci, Joanna	√		Fa	10	5		S/O 83	21
Surface Design	"Shared Vision": A Gallery Tour with Two Artists: Jacque Parsley and Neisja Yenawine (Exhibit)	Arnow, Jan	√		Fa	8	4		J/A 81	28
Surface Design	Stretching Fabric in Small Spaces	Levy, Julie	√	√	TM			3	F/M 86	34
Surface Design	Surface Design and the Garment Form	Reith, Stephanie J.	√		Fa	8	1		J/F 81	34
Surface Design	Surface Design Association's Southeast Regional Conference	Mattera, Joanne	√		Fa	9	1		J/F 82	54
Surface Design	Surface Design Conference 1985	Scarborough, Jessica	√		Fa	12	5		S/O 85	46

SUBJECT	TITLE	AUTHOR	IL	INST	JOUR	VOL	NO	ISS	DATE	PAGE
Surface Design	Surface Design Conference in Kansas City	Craig-Linenberger, Gerry	√		TM			12	A/S 87	20
Surface Design	Surface Designers Meet in Nantucket	Northup, Wendy			TM			9	F/M 87	16
Surface Design	Theme Issue		√		Fa	10	5		S/O 83	
Surface Design	Turkish Marbling on Cloth or Paper	London, Rhoda	√	√	TM			11	J/J 87	66
Surface Design	Verbena Collection, The (error-corrected Fa v11 n1 84 p11)		√		Fa	10	5		S/O 83	64
Surface Design	Words in Fiber	Rowley, Kathleen	√		Fa	11	2		M/A 84	66
Surface Design: Techniques	Surface Design Techniques — The Basics	Bliss, Anne	√	√	Hw	8	1		J/F 87	78
Surface Interest	Surface Interest Has Become a Favorite for Apparel Fabrics	Slason, Helen	√	> 4	H&C	18	3		Su 67	22
Surface Interest	Surface Interest — Textiles of Today	Tidball, Harriet	√		SCGM		2		61	1-22
Surface Interest	Weaver's Notebook		√	√	SS&D	9	4	36	Fa 78	100
Surface Interest: Double-Faced Weaves	Surface Interest — Textiles of Today: Surface Interest Designs with Drafts, Group 4, Double-Faced Designs	Tidball, Harriet	√	> 4	SCGM		2		61	16
Surface Interest: Variations	Summer and Winter and Other Two-Tie Unit Weaves: Methods for Weaving Two-Tie Units, Surface Interest Variations	Tidball, Harriet	√	√	SCGM		19		66	47
Surface Interest: Weaving	Surface Interest — Textiles of Today: Surface Interest Designs with Drafts, Group 1, Accented Designs	Tidball, Harriet			SCGM		2		61	7
Surface Interest: Weaving, Accented Designs	Surface Interest — Textiles of Today: Surface Interest Designs with Drafts, Group 1, Accented Designs	Tidball, Harriet	√	√	SCGM		2		61	8
Surface Interest: Weaving, Backed-Fabric Designs	Surface Interest — Textiles of Today: Surface Interest Designs with Drafts, Group 5, Backed-Fabric Designs	Tidball, Harriet	√	> 4	SCGM		2		61	18
Surface Interest: Weaving, Reinforced Designs	Surface Interest — Textiles of Today: Surface Interest Designs with Drafts, Group 2, Reinforced Designs	Tidball, Harriet	√	> 4	SCGM		2		61	10
Surface Interest: Weaving, Two-Surface Designs	Surface Interest — Textiles of Today: Surface Interest Designs with Drafts, Group 3, Two-Surface Designs	Tidball, Harriet	√	> 4	SCGM		2		61	13
Surrealism	"Fashion and Surrealism" (Exhibit)		√		TM			14	D/J 87	16
Survey Results: Wool Availability, America	Survey on the Availability of American Wool, A	Derr, Mary L.			WJ	2	2	6	Oc 77	36
Surveys	Getting Acquainted: A Survey Report	Patrick, Jane			Hw	3	1		Ja 82	16
Surveys	Interweave Readers Unique, Poll Shows	Ellison, Sue			Iw	4	3		Su 79	8
Surveys	PWC Reader Survey, The				PWC	3	2	8		73
Surveys	Spin-Off Survey				S-O	10	3		Fa 86	15
Surveys	Wearables in the Market Place: Reporting on a Survey	Dunnewold, Jane	√		Fa	12	3		M/J 85	48
Surveys: Drawloom Weavers	Drawlooms	Hoyt, Peggy			CW	6	2	17	Ja 85	27
Swaddling Clothes	Nativity Scene	Vargo, Bessie Mae	√	√	WJ	6	2	22	Fa 81	8
Swaddling Clothes	Swaddling Clothes	Marston, Ena	√		SS&D	4	1	13	Wi 72	23
Swatch Collections	Handwoven Swatch Collection #1	Alderman, Sharon	√		Hw	1	2		S-S 80	41
Swatch Collections	Making of a Swatch Collection, The	Alderman, Sharon D.	√	√	Hw	2	4		Se 81	36
Swatch Collections	Matter of Style: Swatch Collection #5, A	Alderman, Sharon	√		Hw	3	2		Mr 82	8
Swatch Collections	Swatch Collection #15	Alderman, Sharon	√	√	Hw	8	2		M/A 87	38, I-4
Swatch Collections	Swatch Collection #6: Followup		√		Hw	4	1		J/F 83	68
Swatch Collections: Fabric, Apparel	Diana Sanderson Swatch Collection				Hw	7	5		N/D 86	46, I-4
Swatch Collections: Fabric, Apparel	Handwoven Swatch Collection #2	Alderman, Sharon	√		Hw	2	1		F-W 80	50
Swatch Collections: Fabric, Apparel	Handwoven Swatch Collection #3 (Sharon Alderman)		√		Hw	2	3		My 81	87
Swatch Collections: Fabric, Apparel	Lillian Whipple Swatch Collection				Hw	7	5		N/D 86	64, I-7

SUBJECT	TITLE	AUTHOR	IL	INST	JOUR	VOL	NO	ISS	DATE	PAGE
Swatch Collections: Fabric, Apparel	Malin Salander Swatch Collection				Hw	7	5		N/D 86	60, I-5
Swatch Collections: Fabric, Apparel	Swatch Collection #10	Alderman, Sharon D.	√		Hw	5	4		S/O 84	56
Swatch Collections: Fabric, Apparel	Swatch Collection #11	Alderman, Sharon	√		Hw	6	2		M/A 85	46
Swatch Collections: Fabric, Apparel	Swatch Collection #14	Alderman, Sharon	√	> 4	Hw	7	4		S/O 86	24
Swatch Collections: Fabric, Apparel	Swatch Collection #16: Fabrics for Fall '87	Alderman, Sharon	√	√	Hw	8	4		S/O 87	52
Swatch Collections: Fabric, Apparel	Swatch Collection #6	Alderman, Sharon	√		Hw	3	4		Se 82	41
Swatch Collections: Fabric, Apparel	Swatch Collection #7	Alderman, Sharon	√		Hw	4	2		M/A 83	58
Swatch Collections: Fabric, Apparel	Swatch Collection #8	Alderman, Sharon	√		Hw	4	4		S/O 83	52
Swatch Collections: Fabric, Apparel	Swatch Collection #9	Alderman, Sharon D.	√		Hw	5	3		Su 84	62
Swatch Collections: Fabric, Apparel	Swatch Collection, #I4	Alderman, Sharon	√	√	Hw	7	4		S/O 86	24
Swatch Collections: Fabric, Apparel	Virginia West Swatch Collection		√		Hw	7	5		N/D 86	62, I-6
Swatch Collections: Fashion Fabric	Swatch Collection #13	Alderman, Sharon	√		Hw	7	3		M/J 86	28
Swatch Collections: Fashion Fabrics	Swatch Collection #12: Classic Fabrics for City Fashions	Alderman, Sharon D.	√	√	Hw	6	5		N/D 85	48
Swatch Collections: Fashion Institute of Technology	Lace & Flowers: Vintage Inspiration	George, Patrice	√	> 4	Hw	8	5		N/D 87	68
Swatch Collections: Techniques	Making of Swatch Collection #6, The	Alderman, Sharon	√	√	Hw	3	4		Se 82	42
Swatches	Handspun Swatches 1986		√		S-O	10	3		Fa 86	14
Swatches	SPIN-OFF Book of World Records		√		S-O	7	3		Fa 83	11
Swatches	Swatches		√		S-O	8	3		Fa 84	16
Swatches	Swatches and Fine Threads		√		S-O	9	3		Fa 85	16
Swatches: Double Weave	Double Weave	Wertenberger, Kathryn	√	> 4	Hw	5	4		S/O 84	81
Swatches: Fabric Industry	Millions of Swatches at FIT	Kennedy, Alan			TM			11	J/J 87	18
Swatches: Historical Fabrics	Fine Fabrics: A Continuing Tradition		√		Hw	3	5		N/D 82	30
Swatches: Knitting	Hands On	Elkins, Barbara	√	√	Kn	3	4	8	Fa 87	46
Swatches: Knitting	Mill End Mystery	Upitis, Lizbeth	√		Kn	3	4	8	Fa 87	36
Swatches: Knitting	Opinionated Knitter, The	Zimmermann, Elizabeth		√	Kn	3	4	8	Fa 87	45
Swatches: Knitting	Swatching		√	√	Kn	3	4	8	Fa 87	42
Swatches: Machine Knitting	Machine Knitting with Handspun Cotton: First Experiments	Warren, Anne	√	√	S-O	11	2		Su 87	41
Swatches: Woolens and Tweeds	Woolens and Tweeds: Portfolio Analysis	Tidball, Harriet	√	√	SCGM		4		61	42
Sweater-Coat	Sweater-Coat (Linda Urquhart)		√	√	Hw	4	4		S/O 83	41, 109
Sweaters	Alexis' Favorite	Rowley, Elaine	√	√	Kn	1	1	1	F-W 84	46,56B CI 38
Sweaters	Almost McKinley Expedition Sweater, The	Kappeler, Erda	√		S-O	11	4		Wi 87	26
Sweaters	Arans: A Saga in Wool (error-corrected S-O V4 80 p4)	Schlegel, Lee-lee	√	√	S-O	3			79	56
Sweaters	Basic Knitting Machine, The	Guagliumi, Susan	√	√	TM			1	O/N 85	38
Sweaters	Beaded Sweater	Drysdale, Rosemary; Gail Diven	√	√	Kn	2	2	4	S-S 86	50
Sweaters	Block Sweater	Morris, Sandy	√	√	Kn	2	1	3	F-W 85	56
Sweaters	Bonnie Almond's Sweater	Almond, Bonnie	√	√	S-O	9	2		Su 85	13
Sweaters	Burra Lace Pullover	Bush, Nancy	√	√	Kn	3	4	8	Fa 87	26
Sweaters	Cable-Ribbed Pullover Sweater		√	√	S-O	7	3		Fa 83	56
Sweaters	Carnival Cable Pullover	Jensen, Candi	√	√	Kn	3	1	5	F-W 86	24
Sweaters	Child's Cardigan Sweater (Elizabeth Millard)		√	√	Hw	5	3		Su 84	49, 93

SUBJECT	TITLE	AUTHOR	IL	INST	JOUR	VOL	NO	ISS	DATE	PAGE
Sweaters	Child's Play	Voiers, Leslie	√	√	SS&D	18	3	71	Su 87	22
Sweaters	Classic Alpaca Sweater, A (error-corrected S-O v9 n2 85 p61)	Reynolds, Donna	√	√	S-O	9	1		Sp 85	24
Sweaters	Classic, The	O'Connor, Pat	√	√	Kn	2	1	3	F-W 85	58
Sweaters	Color Games	Berent, Mary, et al.	√	√	S-O	11	1		Sp 87	21
Sweaters	Colorful Cotton Coordinates (Pat Short) (error-corrected WJ v11 n3 87 p78)		√	√	WJ	11	2	42	Fa 86	40
Sweaters	Confessions of a Cotton Spinner	Clivio, Carol	√	√	S-O	10	4		Wi 86	38
Sweaters	Confetti Sweater	Slaven, Pat	√	√	S-O	11	4		Wi 87	26
Sweaters	Converting Images Into Sweaters	MacHenry, Rachel	√	√	TM			10	A/M 87	72
Sweaters	Cowichan Country	Gibson-Roberts, Priscilla A.	√	√	Kn	3	1	5	F-W 86	61
Sweaters	Designing with Ribs	Newton, Deborah	√	√	Kn	2	2	4	S-S 86	62
Sweaters	Diamond Lattice Pullover	Frost, Jean	√	√	Kn	3	4	8	Fa 87	34
Sweaters	Double Two-Tie Twills and Basket Weave	Barrett, Clotilde	√	> 4	WJ	7	3	27	Wi 82	38
Sweaters	Dye Sampler Pullover, A	Van Sickle, Glenda	√	√	S-O	8	3		Fa 84	44
Sweaters	Egmont Sweater, The	Zimmermann, Elizabeth	√	√	PWC			2	Ap 82	80
Sweaters	Evolution of a Project	de Grassi, Laurel	√	√	S-O	10	4		Wi 86	21
Sweaters	Exploring a Knitted Pattern	Bruzelius, Margaret	√	√	TM			6	A/S 86	35
Sweaters	Exposition of the Epaulet Sweater	Zimmermann, Elizabeth	√	√	Hw	3	1		Ja 82	71
Sweaters	Fair Isle in Natural Colors, The	Gibson-Roberts, Priscilla A.	√	√	Kn	2	1	3	F-W 85	34
Sweaters	Fair Isle Knitting	Starmore, Alice	√	√	TM			8	D/J 86	44
Sweaters	Finish Your Work	Stoehr, Mary Kay	√	√	Hw	5	1		J/F 84	54
Sweaters	Fleece-to-Garment Competition in New Zealand	Ashford, Joy		√	SS&D	4	1	13	Wi 72	21
Sweaters	Fur Fashions	Lucas, Jerie	√	√	SS&D	15	2	58	Sp 84	26
Sweaters	Gaffer's Gansey	Zimmermann, Elizabeth	√	√	Kn	1	1	1	F-W 84 CI	36,56B 28
Sweaters	Galashiels Tweed Pullover	Bush, Nancy	√	√	Kn	4	1	9	Wi 87	42
Sweaters	Gansey in Handspun, The	Gibson-Roberts, Priscilla A.	√	√	Kn	1	1	1	F-W 84 CI	32,56B 24
Sweaters	Gansey with Yoke	Farley, Sidna	√	√	Kn	3	2	6	Sp 87	27
Sweaters	Garden of Fair Isles, A	Rowe, Mary	√	√	Kn	2	1	3	F-W 85	40, 8B
Sweaters	Gooden Gansey Sweaters	Gallagher, Marten	√		Fa	12	6		N/D 85	12
Sweaters	Great American Sweater, A	Newton, Deborah	√	√	Kn	2	2	4	S-S 86	64
Sweaters	Handspun for Kaffe Fassett Sweaters	Adams, Brucie	√	√	S-O	11	4		Wi 87	32
Sweaters	Handspun Rainbow Sweater	Chilton, D. Lorraine	√	√	S-O	7	4		Wi 83	49
Sweaters	Handspun Sampler Sweaters		√	√	S-O	5			81	62
Sweaters	Handwoven Sweater, A	Hewson, Betty	√	√	Hw	4	4		S/O 83	85
Sweaters	"Ice in Shadow" Sweater	Kluth, Liz	√	√	S-O	9	4		Wi 85	15
Sweaters	Jackie's Sweaters: Blouson, Dolman, Striped Silk	Kroeger, Jackie	√	√	Kn	1	1	1	F-W 84 CI	41 33
Sweaters	Josh's Gansey	Camper, Dorothy	√	√	Kn	1	1	1	F-W 84 CI	28 20
Sweaters	Kay-O Wicks — The Habit of Knitting	Horton, Lucy	√		Fa	6	3		M/J 79	32
Sweaters	Knitted Palette of Brenda French, The	Pierce, Judith	√		Fa	13	2		M/A 86	43
Sweaters	Knitter's Puzzle: Damask Knitting with Your Handspun, A	Howard, Miranda	√	√	S-O	9	1		Sp 85	36
Sweaters	Knitting a Seamless Sweater	Zimmermann, Elizabeth	√	√	TM			7	O/N 86	47
Sweaters	Knitting with Colors	Fassett, Kaffe	√	√	TM			3	F/M 86	68
Sweaters	Knitting from the Netherlands: Traditional Dutch Fishermen's Sweaters	Van der Klift-Tellegen, Henriette	√		Fa	12	4		J/A 85	45
Sweaters	Lace and Knots	Newton, Deborah	√	√	Kn	3	4	8	Fa 87	20
Sweaters	Lace Trilogy	Fauske, Carla	√	√	PWC			6	Su 83	52
Sweaters	Little Knitting on the Side, A	Glover, Medrith	√	√	Kn	2	1	3	F-W 85	38

SUBJECT	TITLE	AUTHOR	IL	INST	JOUR	VOL	NO	ISS	DATE	PAGE
Sweaters	Llama Wool	Smith, Carolyn	√	√	S-O	11	2		Su 87	32
Sweaters	Lynne Greaves' Sweater	Greaves, Lynne	√	√	S-O	9	2		Su 85	14
Sweaters	Machine Knitting with Handspun Yarn—Part 2	Adams, Brucie	√	√	Hw	4	4		S/O 83	76
Sweaters	Machine-Knit Popcorns	Guagliumi, Susan	√	√	TM			6	A/S 86	71
Sweaters	Madeline Adkins' Sweater	Adkins, Madaline	√	√	S-O	9	2		Su 85	15
Sweaters	Make It Yourself with Handwoven Wool	John, Sue	√		S-O	9	1		Sp 85	12
Sweaters	Merino Pullover	Royce, Beverly	√	√	S-O	9	1		Sp 85	40
Sweaters	Michelin Man Sweater	Zimmermann, Elizabeth	√	√	Kn	2	2	4	S-S 86	72
Sweaters	Modular Clothing	Mayer, Anita	√	√	Hw	7	3		M/J 86	58
Sweaters	Mohair Sweater	Reynolds, Donna	√	√	S-O	8	2		Su 84	46
Sweaters	Mr. Hunter's Lace	Yaksick, Karen	√	√	Kn	3	4	8	Fa 87	22
Sweaters	Nature: A Color Source and Inspiration for Traditional Sweaters	Gibson-Roberts, Priscilla A.	√		S-O	9	3		Fa 85	42
Sweaters	No-Sweat Sweatshirt, The	Glover, Medrith	√	√	Kn	3	1	5	F-W 86	28
Sweaters	Notes of a Textile Sleuth	Upitis, Lizbeth	√	√	Kn	2	1	3	F-W 85	22
Sweaters	Now, That's a Cabled Sweater	Yaksick, Karen	√	√	Kn	3	1	5	F-W 86	30
Sweaters	On Designing: Brocade Blouse	Newton, Deborah	√	√	Kn	1	1	1	F-W 84 CI	17 9
Sweaters	On Designing with Slip Stitch Bands	Newton, Deborah	√	√	Kn	3	1	5	F-W 86	21
Sweaters	Opinionated Knitter, The	Zimmermann, Elizabeth			Kn	2	1	3	F-W 85	8
Sweaters	Particular Guernsey, A	Rowley, Elaine	√	√	Kn	1	1	1	F-W 84 CI	25,56A 17
Sweaters	Patchwork Sweaters (Ronnine Bohannan)		√	> 4	Hw	6	5		N/D 85	45, I-6
Sweaters	Pleated Cardigan	Newton, Deborah	√	√	Kn	3	2	6	Sp 87	20
Sweaters	Rag Trade, The	Weissman, Julia	√		Kn	1	1	1	F-W 84 CI	70 53
Sweaters	Rag Trade, The	Weissman, Julia	√		Kn	2	2	4	S-S 86	59
Sweaters	Rag Trade, The	Weissman, Julia	√		Kn	2	1	3	F-W 85	76
Sweaters	Recent Success of Carole Lubove-Klein: An Inspiring Yarn, The	McGuire, Patricia	√		Fa	9	5		S/O 82	20
Sweaters	Reversible Two-Faced Knitting	Thilenius, Carol	√	√	S-O	7	1		Sp 83	40
Sweaters	Roomie Sweater	Rowley, Elaine	√	√	Kn	3	4	8	Fa 87	47
Sweaters	'Round and 'Round We Go, The Janet Sweater	Rowley, Elaine D.	√	√	PWC	1	1		No 81	50
Sweaters	Ruby Brilliant: A Knitter Well-Named		√		Fa	10	1		J/F 83	19
Sweaters	Sheep of a Sweater, A	Lambersten, Martha	√	√	Kn	3	4	8	Fa 87	51
Sweaters	Shirt for All Seasons, A	Rush, Helene	√	√	Kn	3	2	6	Sp 87	25
Sweaters	Simple and Striped	Oakes, Nancy	√	√	Kn	3	1	5	F-W 86	44
Sweaters	Sleeve Sweater	Rowley, Elaine	√	√	Kn	2	1	3	F-W 85	58
Sweaters	Special Fittings: Tulips	Glover, Medrith J.	√	√	Kn	1	2	2	S-S 85	29, 72A
Sweaters	St. Ives Cardigan	Bush, Nancy	√	√	Kn	3	2	6	Sp 87	28
Sweaters	Stardust Medallion Sweater	Hayes, Beth	√	√	S-O	11	2		Su 87	24
Sweaters	Succeeding with the Knitting Machine	Mattera, Joanne	√		TM			2	D/J 85	50
Sweaters	Summer Lace Sweater	Farley, Sidna	√	√	Kn	1	2	2	S-S 85	32, 72A
Sweaters	Super Soft Sweater	Emerick, Patricia	√	√	S-O	11	1		Sp 87	16
Sweaters	Sweater (Betty Beard)		√	√	Hw	1	1		F-W 79	24, 57
Sweaters	Sweater of Abundance	Chelsey, Randy	√	√	S-O	11	1		Sp 87	15
Sweaters	Sweater of Many Colors, A	McIntee, Polly	√	√	S-O	11	2		Su 87	15
Sweaters	Sweater's Tale, A	Owens, Julie	√	√	Hw	6	4		S/O 85	82
Sweaters	Sweatshirt? Yes– A Sweatshirt with Options!, A	Klinect, Ann W.	√	√	S-O	7	1		Sp 83	43
Sweaters	T-Sweater	Rowley, Elaine	√	√	Kn	1	2	2	S-S 85	34, 72A
Sweaters	Thirty-Button Classic	Gibson-Roberts, Priscilla A.	√	√	S-O	11	1		Sp 87	32
Sweaters	Thoughts on Sweater Design	Dewees, Libby	√		S-O	9	3		Fa 85	47

SUBJECT	TITLE	AUTHOR	IL	INST	JOUR	VOL	NO	ISS	DATE	PAGE
Sweaters	Three-Ply Coat Sweater, A	Lacey, Sue	√	√	S-O	8	3		Fa 84	47
Sweaters	Tiffany's Gansey	Adams, Harriet	√	√	Kn	1	1	1	F-W 84 CI	29,56A 21
Sweaters	Traditional Fair Isle Sweater	Upitis, Lizbeth	√	√	Kn	2	1	3	F-W 85	26, 8B
Sweaters	Travel Sweater	Upitis, Lizbeth	√	√	Kn	2	1	3	F-W 85	58
Sweaters	Turquoise Angora Pullover	Betts, Diane	√	√	S-O	9	4		Wi 85	36
Sweaters	Two String Sweaters	Brugger, Susan	√	√	PWC			6	Su 83	31
Sweaters	Versatile Inlay, Twill on Twill	Beard, Betty	√	√	SS&D	19	1	73	Wi 87	53
Sweaters	Warm Wool Sweater, A	Livingston, Marilyn	√	√	S-O	10	4		Wi 86	40
Sweaters	Weave and Knit Pullover	Barrett, Clotilde	√	√	WJ	8	3	31	Wi 83	20
Sweaters	Welts and Bobbles: Crop Top	Dana, Zelda	√	√	Kn	2	2	4	S-S 86	38
Sweaters	What People Ask Before They Buy Handmade Fashions	Leslie, Victoria	√		TM			9	F/M 87	58
Sweaters	Winter Colors	Beeny, Merna	√	√	Hw	4	1		J/F 83	64
Sweaters	Woven Egmont Sweater	Klessen, Romy	√	√	PWC			2	Ap 82	83
Sweaters	Wrist-to-Wrist Garment, The	Allen, Rose Mary	√	√	WJ	9	3	35	Wi 85	19
Sweaters	Year of the Sweater, The	Katz, Ruth J.	√		Fa	7	1		J/F 80	39
Sweaters	Your Ski Jumper	Filson, Alice	√	√	SS&D	2	3	7	Su 71	19
Sweaters: Aran	Aran Knitting	Starmore, Alice	√	√	TM			14	D/J 87	50
Sweaters: Bohus	Norwegian Luskofte	Gibson-Roberts, Priscilla A.	√	√	S-O	9	3		Fa 85	44
Sweaters: Crochet	Crochet Inspired by the Trees	Moon, Ellen	√	√	TM			11	J/J 87	56
Sweaters: Crochet	Crocheting Wearable Fabric	McGoveran, Mary	√	√	TM			9	F/M 87	62
Sweaters: Drying	Hanging Sweaters and Yarns		√	√	TM			8	D/J 86	8
Sweaters: Front Bands	Cardigan Front Bands			√	TM			8	D/J 86	6
Sweaters: Handwoven	Inspirations from Sweaters	Brewington, Judith	√	√	WJ	7	3	27	Wi 82	14
Sweaters: In-The-Round	Sweaters in the Round Without Steeks			√	TM			10	A/M 87	10
Sweaters: Lengthening	Lengthening a Finished Sweater		√	√	TM			9	F/M 87	6
Sweaters: Luskofte	Norwegian Luskofte	Gibson-Roberts, Priscilla A.	√	√	S-O	9	3		Fa 85	44
Sweaters: Muslin Patterns	Making Sweater "Muslins"			√	TM			9	F/M 87	12
Sweaters: Panel Designs	Fine Yarns: Special and Accessible	Newton, Deborah	√	√	Kn	3	4	8	Fa 87	16
Sweaters: Pattern Sources	Ultimate Sweater Pattern, The			√	TM			14	D/J 87	6
Sweaters: Washing	Washing Cotton Sweaters			√	TM			10	A/M 87	8
Sweaters: Woven	Branding Iron Sweater (Ardis Dobrovolny)		√	√	Hw	7	4		S/O 86	68, I-14
Sweaters: Woven	Contemporary Costume, Strictly Handwoven: The Nell Scott Sweater	Tidball, Harriet	√	√	SCGM		24		68	8
Sweaters: Woven	M's and O's "Popcorn" Sweater (Mary Kay Stoehr)		√	√	Hw	5	1		J/F 84	57, 98
Sweaters: Woven	Raglan Rectangles	Coifman, Lucienne	√	√	SS&D	18	1	69	Wi 86	10
Sweaters: Woven	Vaquero Sweater & Quixquimtl	Frey, Berta	√	√	H&C	12	4		Fa 61	15
Sweaters: Woven	Win's Sweaters		√	√	WJ	8	3	31	Wi 83	12
Sweden	Bogus Bohus	Bush, Nancy	√	√	Kn	2	1	3	F-W 85	49
Sweden	Contemporary Swedish Weaving		√		Hw	8	3		M/J 87	35
Sweden	Exploring a Knitted Pattern	Bruzelius, Margaret	√	√	TM			6	A/S 86	35
Sweden	From Hand to Hand: Swedish Weaving Today	Krondahl, Hans	√		Hw	8	3		M/J 87	34
Sweden	From Mexico to Rumania to Sweden	Landreau, Anthony N.	√		TMJ	2	4		De 69	37
Sweden	Handarbetets vanner: Artists and Craftsmakers Collaborate in Sweden	Talley, Charles	√		Fa	10	3		M/J 83	56
Sweden	Harts and Flowers: Sweden's Märta Määs-Fjetterstrom's Designs Inspired a Textile Renaissance	Selkurt, Claire	√		WJ	9	4	36	Sp 85	30
Sweden	Immigrant Memories	Butcher-Younghans, Sherry	√		WJ	9	4	36	Sp 85	44
Sweden	Kerstin Ekengren	af Kleen, Nils E.	√		H&C	15	2		Sp 64	18

SUBJECT	TITLE	AUTHOR	IL	INST	JOUR	VOL	NO	ISS	DATE	PAGE
Sweden	Learning to Weave in Sweden	Chase, Mary A.	√		H&C	24	3		M/J 73	7
Sweden	"Mama" Gravander	Bryan, Dorothy	√		H&C	5	4		Fa 54	4
Sweden	Picture Lace	Larson-Fleming, Susan	√		WJ	9	4	36	Sp 85	42
Sweden	Portraits of Three Weavers: Sandra Ikse-Bergman, Marja "Graset" Andersson, Elisabet Hasselberg-Olsson	Talley, Charles S.	√		Fa	8	2		M/A 81	46
Sweden	Rag Weaving: A History of Necessity		√		Hw	8	3		M/J 87	38
Sweden	Reinterpreting Old Weaves for Today and Tomorrow	Essén-Hedin, Margaretha	√		Hw	8	3		M/J 87	40
Sweden	Russ-Knotting from Sweden	Swenson, Astrid	√	√	SS&D	4	3	15	Su 73	24
Sweden	Sara Matsson Anliot	Bryan, Dorothy	√		H&C	11	3		Su 60	10
Sweden	Sätergläntan School in Sweden, Landmark in the History of Handweaving, The	Longbers, Ingeborg	√		H&C	1	3		Fa 50	4
Sweden	Sätergläntan School in Sweden, Landmark in the History of Handweaving, The	Longbers, Ingeborg	√		H&C	1	3		Fa 50	4
Sweden	Smålands Weave on Eight Shafts	Shannon, Eileen	√	> 4	WJ	9	1	33	Su 84	47
Sweden	Summer Study in Sweden	Schobinger, Helen J.	√		H&C	9	3		Su 58	24
Sweden	Swedish Design	Krondahl, Hans	√		Hw	4	2		M/A 83	30
Sweden	Swedish Textile Art Today	Widman, Dag	√		H&C	24	1		J/F 73	32
Sweden	Swedish Textiles Today: A Rich Tradition, A Supportive Society	Talley, Charles S.	√		Fa	8	2		M/A 81	42
Sweden	Swedish Touch, The		√		SS&D	4	1	13	Wi 72	22
Sweden	Swedish Workshop		√	√	H&C	12	4		Fa 61	12
Sweden	Tiogruppen: When Working Together Works	Talley, Charles	√		Fa	11	6		N/D 84	41
Sweden	Upphämta Display Towel		√	> 4	Hw	8	3		M/J 87	42
Sweden	Vadmal: A Study Group from the Frozen North Warms up to an Ancient Technique	Larson-Fleming, Susan	√	√	WJ	10	3	39	Wi 86	26
Sweden	Weaver Looks at Sweden, A	Swenson, Astrid			SS&D	3	2	10	Sp 72	36
Sweden	Well-Worn Path to Where? A View of Contemporary Swedish Textiles, The	Talley, Charles S.	√		Fa	8	2		M/A 81	44
Sweden	Woolens and Tweeds: Designing Woolen Fabrics: Swedish Woolens	Tidball, Harriet			SCGM		4		61	26
Sweden	Workshop Tour to Sweden	Young, Dorothy M.	√		SS&D	4	2	14	Sp 73	41
Swedish Language	Glossary Swedish Weaving Terms				Hw	4	2		M/A 83	102
Swedish Language	Reading Swedish: A Crash Course		√		Hw	4	2		M/A 83	33
Swedish-American	Immigrant Memories	Butcher-Younghans, Sherry	√		WJ	9	4	36	Sp 85	44
Swimwear	Sewing Swimsuits	Callaway, Grace	√	√	TM			5	J/J 86	24
Swimwear, Men	Sewing Swimsuits	Callaway, Grace	√	√	TM			5	J/J 86	24
Swivel	Contemporary Approach to Traditional Weaves: Swivel Effect on Overshot Drafts	Zielinski, S. A.; Robert Leclerc, ed.	√	√	MWL	7			'51–'73	34
Swivel	Notebook: Swivel, A Method of Treadling	Myers, Ruth Nordquist, ed.	√	√	SS&D	14	2	54	Sp 83	8
Swivel	Novel Ski Poncho	Marvin, Grace	√	√	H&C	14	4		Fa 63	34
Swivel	Silk Purse (Sharon Alderman)		√	√	Hw	4	1		J/F 83	43, 83
Swivel	Swivel Explored and Contradicted		√	√	WJ	3	4	12	Ap 79	5
Swivel	Swivel Treadled Runner (Mary Anderson)		√	√	Hw	3	5		N/D 82	55, 97
Swivel	Swivel Variations for Four Harness Looms	James, Ona	√	√	H&C	14	4		Fa 63	11
Swivel	Variations on an Overshot Threading	Lermond, Charles	√	√	WJ	12	2	46	Fa 87	25
Swivel	Whig Rose Study (continued)	Morgenstern, Marvin M.	√	√	WJ	7	3	27	Wi 82	23
Swivel	White Dress (Sharon Alderman)		√	> 4	Hw	2	3		My 81	88
Swivel Effect on Overshot: Locked Wefts	Resist Dyeing, Curiosities and Inventions: Locked Wefts in Pattern Weaves	Zielinski, S. A.; Robert Leclerc, ed.	√	√	MWL	17			'51–'73	60
Swivel: Full Swivel	Spot Weaves — Old and New: Full Swivel	Zielinski, S. A.; Robert Leclerc, ed.	√	> 4	MWL	12			'51–'73	85

SUBJECT	TITLE	AUTHOR	IL	INST	JOUR	VOL	NO	ISS	DATE	PAGE
Swivel: Locked Wefts	Resist Dyeing, Curiosities and Inventions: Locked Wefts in Pattern Weaves	Zielinski, S. A.; Robert Leclerc, ed.	√	√	MWL	17			'51–'73	60
Swivel: Locked Wefts	Resist Dyeing, Curiosities and Inventions: Locked Wefts in Swivel	Zielinski, S. A.; Robert Leclerc, ed.	√	√	MWL	17			'51–'73	53
Swivel: Miniature	Miniature World, A	Piroch, Sigrid	√	> 4	PWC	5	2	16		26
Swivel: On Warp and Weft	Spot Weaves — Old and New: Swivel on Warp and Weft on Four Shafts	Zielinski, S. A.; Robert Leclerc, ed.	√	√	MWL	12			'51–'73	96
Swivel: Plain	Spot Weaves — Old and New: Plain Swivel	Zielinski, S. A.; Robert Leclerc, ed.	√	√	MWL	12			'51–'73	59
Swivel: Polychrome	Spot Weaves — Old and New: Polychrone Swivel	Zielinski, S. A.; Robert Leclerc, ed.	√	> 4	MWL	12			'51–'73	79
Swivel: Turned	Spot Weaves — Old and New: Turned Swivel	Zielinski, S. A.; Robert Leclerc, ed.	√	√	MWL	12			'51–'73	65
Swivel: Turned, Multiblock	Spot Weaves — Old and New: Multi-Block Turned Swivel	Zielinski, S. A.; Robert Leclerc, ed.	√	> 4	MWL	12			'51–'73	70
Swivel: Two-Harness (Sets)	Little Known Weaves Worth Knowing Better: Two-Harness Method	Zielinski, S. A.; Robert Leclerc, ed.	√	> 4	MWL	16			'51–'73	36
Swivel: Weft-Faced	Spot Weaves — Old and New: Weft Face Swivel	Zielinski, S. A.; Robert Leclerc, ed.	√	√	MWL	12			'51–'73	93
Symbolic Motifs: Eagle	Use of Eagles as a Decorative and Symbolic Motif in 19th Century American Coverlets, The	Anderson, Clarita; Jo B. Paoletti	√		AT	3			My 85	173
Symbolism	Adinkra: Weft African Textile of Pride	Rex, Chris	√		Fa	9	6		N/D 82	36
Symbolism	Alter Cloths and Shrines: The New Work of Janet Boguch	Tacker, Sylvia	√		Fa	14	5		N/D 87	6
Symbolism	"Birth Symbol in Traditional Women's Art, The" (Exhibit)	Vanco, John	√		Fa	13	3		M/J 86	52
Symbolism	Chinese Influence in Colonial Peruvian Tapestries	Cammann, Schuyler	√		TMJ	1	3		De 64	21
Symbolism	Fiber Mandalas: Doilies As Spiritual Art	Maines, Rachel	√		Fa	9	3		M/J 82	17
Symbolism	Floral Symbolism: The Western Rose	Austin, Carole	√		Fa	13	2		M/A 86	42
Symbolism	Flourishing Art: USA Hmong Women Show How to Stitch Pa ndau, Their Flowery Cloth, A	Porter-Francis, Wendy	√	√	TM			9	F/M 87	33
Symbolism	Fukusa: The Art of Giving	Lancaster, Deborah Lerme	√		Fa	13	6		N/D 86	27
Symbolism	Funeral	Knauer, Katherine	√		Fa	13	6		N/D 86	30
Symbolism	Guatemala Visited	Atwater, Mary Meigs	√	√	SCGM		15		65	40
Symbolism	Haitian Voodoo Banners: Dazzling Invitations to the Spirits	Lorenzo, Lauri	√		Fa	13	6		N/D 86	11
Symbolism	Jane Lackey: A Vision Into Past and Future	Corwin, Nancy	√		Fa	13	6		N/D 86	18
Symbolism	JoAnn Giordano: A Modern Mythology	Malarcher, Patricia	√		Fa	13	6		N/D 86	13
Symbolism	Kantha	Westfall, Carol D.; Dipti Desai	√	√	AT	7			Ju 87	161
Symbolism	Labor Banners of Australia	Mancini, Anne	√		Fa	14	5		N/D 87	36
Symbolism	Making Paper Cranes: A Hawaiian Wedding Ritual	Nakamura, Ann K.	√	√	Fa	13	6		N/D 86	9
Symbolism	Meaning of Folk Art in Rabari Life: A Closer Look at Mirrored Embroidery, The	Frater, Judy	√		TMJ	4	2		75	47
Symbolism	Mimi Holmes: Treasure Troves of Human Conflict	Lamberson, Peggy	√		Fa	13	6		N/D 86	20
Symbolism	My Life	Weldon, Lynn L.	√	√	WJ	2	2	6	Oc 77	11
Symbolism	Ritual Fiber: Weaving Hope for the Future Into the Fabric of Life	Wilcox, Don	√		Fa	13	6		N/D 86	7
Symbolism	Secret Treasures of Tibet	Wiltsie-Vaniea, Anne	√		SS&D	18	3	71	Su 87	60
Symbolism	Spirit Tracings of Barbara Heller, The	Strong, Ruth	√		Fa	13	4		J/A 86	15
Symbolism	Symbolic Scenes in Javanese Batik	Adams, Monni	√		TMJ	3	1		De 70	25
Symbolism: Abstract	Symbolic Meanings in Oriental Rug Patterns: Part 1	Cammann, Schuyler V.R.	√		TMJ	3	3		De 72	5
Symbolism: Anatolian Rugs	Anatolian Rugs: An Essay on Method	Denny, Walter B.	√		TMJ	3	4		De 73	7

SUBJECT	TITLE	AUTHOR	IL	INST	JOUR	VOL	NO	ISS	DATE	PAGE
Symbolism: Batak Textiles	Selected Batak Textiles: Technique and Function	Gittinger, Mattiebelle S.	√		TMJ	4	2		75	13
Symbolism: Carpets, Mamluk	Is the Mamluk Carpet a Mandala? A Speculation	Ellis, Charles Grant	√		TMJ	4	1		De 74	30
Symbolism: Carpets, Persian, Five-Medallion	Symbolic Meanings in Oriental Rug Patterns: Part 3	Cammann, Schuyler V.R.	√		TMJ	3	3		De 72	42
Symbolism, Color	Color Symbolism in Primitive Societies (error-corrected Fa v13 n4 86 p5)	Janeiro, Jan	√		Fa	13	2		M/A 86	30
Symbolism: Coptic Textiles	Tapestry Roundel with Nilotic Scenes, A	Abdel-Malek, Laila	√		TMJ	25			86	33
Symbolism: Dress, Southeast Asia	Dress and Design in Highland Southeast Asia: The Hmong (Miao) and the Yao	Adams, Monni	√		TMJ	4	1		De 74	51
Symbolism: Ecclesiastical	Weaving for the Church—A Challenge	Hahan, Roslyn J.	√		Hw	5	1		J/F 84	32
Symbolism: Egyptian Carpets, Mameluks	Symbolic Meanings in Oriental Rug Patterns: Part 3	Cammann, Schuyler V.R.	√		TMJ	3	3		De 72	42
Symbolism: Folk Art, Peru	General Patterson's Tapestry	Sellschopp, Dr. E. A.	√		TMJ	2	4		De 69	2
Symbolism: Islamic Banners	Group of Silk Islamic Banners, A	Denny, Walter B.	√		TMJ	4	1		De 74	67
Symbolism: Islamic Rugs	Symbolic Meanings in Oriental Rug Patterns: Part 1	Cammann, Schuyler V.R.	√		TMJ	3	3		De 72	5
Symbolism: Kasuri	Kasuri: A Japanese Textile	Dusenbury, Mary	√		TMJ	17			78	41
Symbolism: Mandarin Squares	Ming Mandarin Squares	Cammann, Schuyler	√		TMJ	4	4		77	5
Symbolism: Music	Textile Evidence for Huari Music	Rowe, Ann Pollard	√		TMJ	18			79	5
Symbolism: Music, Peruvian Tunics	Textile Evidence for Huari Music	Rowe, Ann Pollard	√		TMJ	18			79	5
Symbolism: Persian Carpets, Chinese Influence	Symbolic Meanings in Oriental Rug Patterns: Part 2	Cammann, Schuyler V.R.	√		TMJ	3	3		De 72	22
Symbolism: Persian Carpets, Chinese Influence	Symbolic Meanings in Oriental Rug Patterns: Part 3	Cammann, Schuyler V.R.	√		TMJ	3	3		De 72	42
Symbolism: Phulkari	Phulkari	Westfall, Carol D.; Dipti Desai	√		AT	6			De 86	85
Symbolism: Rugs, Middle Eastern	Iconography of Everyday Life in Nineteenth-Century Middle Eastern Rugs, The	Paquin, Gerard A.	√		TMJ	22			83	5
Symbolism: Ukrainian	Embroidery for the Goddess	Kelly, Mary B.	√		TM			11	J/J 87	26
Symbols: Knitting	Symbols				Kn	1	2	2	S-S 85	36
Symbols: Status	High-Status Caps of the Kongo and Mbundu Peoples	Gibson, Gordon D.; Cecilia R. McGurk	√		TMJ	4	4		77	71
Symmetry Operations: Seventeen Pattern Types	Seventeen Pattern Types, A Study of Repeat Patterns in Two Dimensions	Elliott, Verda	√	>4	CW		25		Se 87	23
Symposium	Symposium on Contemporary Textile Art	West, Virginia	√		Fa	5	4		J/A 78	18
Symposium: Art/Architecture	Art and Architecture	Janeiro, Jan	√		Fa	9	3		M/J 82	52
Symposium: Costume Society of England	English Costume Society Symposium	Shep, R. L.			TM			7	O/N 86	16
Symposium: Wearable Art	Roots of Wearables, The	Creager, Clara			TM			14	D/J 87	16
Synthetic Materials	Baskets of John Garrett: A Mesh of Ideas and Materials, The	Garrett, John	√		Fa	11	1		J/F 84	26
Synthetics	What Is a Synthetic?	Neidig, Dorothy A.			SS&D	2	4	8	Fa 71	31
Synthetics: Mylar	Man-Made Fibers: Season's Greetings		√	√	WJ	5	2	18	Fa 80	46
Synthetics: Polyester	Imitating the Silkworm	Stetson, G. Robert; Cathy Shufro; Dennis Danaher	√		TM			5	J/J 86	42
Synthetics: Polyester	Polyester in Japan	Wasserman, Andrea Stix	√		TM			5	J/J 86	20
Synthetics: Saran Weft	Gala Raincoat	Moes, Dini	√	√	WJ	6	3	23	Wi 81	12
T-Shirts also see Blouses, Shirts, Tops										
T–Shirts	Circular T	Upitis, Lizbeth	√	√	Kn	3	3	7	Su 87	15
T–Shirts	Comfortable Cotton T's	Upitis, Lizbeth	√	√	Kn	3	3	7	Su 87	12
T–Shirts	Fit to a T		√	√	Kn	3	3	7	Su 87	22
T–Shirts	Four-Corner T-Shirt	Swansen, Meg	√	√	Kn	3	3	7	Su 87	28
T–Shirts	Lapsang Souchong	Upitis, Lizbeth	√	√	Kn	3	3	7	Su 87	16

SUBJECT	TITLE	AUTHOR	IL	INST	JOUR	VOL	NO	ISS	DATE	PAGE
T–Shirts	Over the Shoulder T	Upitis, Lizbeth	√	√	Kn	3	3	7	Su 87	14
T–Shirts	Sans Serif T	Rowley, Elaine	√	√	Kn	3	3	7	Su 87	22
T–Shirts	Standard T.	Upitis, Lizbeth	√	√	Kn	3	3	7	Su 87	14
T–Shirts	T in a Basket		√	√	Kn	3	3	7	Su 87	19
T–Shirts	Tons of T's	Upitis, Lizbeth	√		Kn	3	3	7	Su 87	8
T-Shirts	T-Shirts for Every Body: 20th Century Folkwear		√		Fa	8	6		N/D 81	22
Taaniko	Maori and Pakeha of New Zealand Use Wool and Phormium Tenax	Duncan, Molly	√	√	SS&D	5	1	17	Wi 73	65
Taaniko	Spinners & Weavers in New Zealand Use Native Materials	Duncan, Molly	√		H&C	21	1		Wi 70	14
Taaniko	Weft Twining: History, The Maori of New Zealand	Harvey, Virginia I.; Harriet Tidball	√		SCGM		28		69	7
Taaniko	Weft Twining: The Structures of Weft Twining, Taaniko	Harvey, Virginia I.; Harriet Tidball	√	√	SCGM		28		69	36
Taaniko: Techniques	Weft Twining	Smith, Joyce Ronald	√	√	TM			2	D/J 85	69
Tabards	Easy Tabard, An	Davenport, Betty	√	√	Hw	5	1		J/F 84	50
Tabards	Garments Made from Simple Patterns: Two Tabards		√	> 4	WJ	2	3	7	Ja 78	35
Tabards	Holiday Tabard (Kathryn Wertenberger)		√	√	Hw	2	1		F-W 80	54, 59
Tabards	Knit Tabard	Betts, Diane	√	√	S-O	9	2		Su 85	41
Tabards	Rag Trade, The	Weissman, Julia	√		Kn	1	2	2	S-S 85	53
Tabards	Simple and Striped	Oakes, Nancy	√	√	Kn	3	1	5	F-W 86	44
Tabards	Working with Lincoln Lamb's Wool	Betts, Diane	√	√	S-O	9	2		Su 85	41
Tabby	More About Fabrics: Practical Projects in Tabby	Zielinski, S. A.; Robert Leclerc, ed.	√	√	MWL	20			'51–'73	29
Tabby	More About Fabrics: Tabby	Zielinski, S. A.; Robert Leclerc, ed.	√	√	MWL	20			'51–'73	19
Tabby	Tabby Color	Alvic, Philis	√	√	SS&D	15	2	58	Sp 84	91
Tabby	Treasury for Beginners: Basic Weave	Zielinski, S. A.; Robert Leclerc, ed.	√	√	MWL	1			'51–'73	96
Tabby, Alternate (Italian Style)	Variations on an Overshot Threading	Lermond, Charles	√	√	WJ	12	2	46	Fa 87	25
Tabby, Compound, Warp-Faced	Chinese Brocades: Development of Supplementary Weft Patterning (error-corrected WJ v11 n4 87 p78)	Drooker, Penelope	√		WJ	11	3	43	Wi 87	47
Tabby, Variations	Variety is the Spice of Life, or Tabby Tricks	Redding, Debbie	√	√	Hw	2	5		No 81	73
Tabby, Weft-Effect	Basic Designs for Every Weaver's File	Hausner, Walter	√	√	H&C	14	4		Fa 63	22
Table Coverings	Eight Harness Linen from Elizabeth Kackenmeister		√	> 4	H&C	15	1		Wi 64	34
Table Coverings	Florida Spinner, Richard Butler, Chooses Flax	Tod, Osma G.	√		H&C	18	1		Wi 67	16
Table Coverings	Georgia Dille Abbott	Pauw, Alice Abbott			H&C	15	1		Wi 64	40
Table Coverings	History of Table Linens, A				Hw	8	3		M/J 87	40
Table Coverings	New Zealand Interpretation of Compass and Double Square, A		√	√	H&C	8	4		Fa 57	20
Table Coverings	Thomas Jackson, Weaver: 17th and 18th Century Records	Tidball, Harriet	√	> 4	SCGM		13		64	25
Table Coverings: Credence Cloth	Credence Cloth (Kathleen French)		√	√	Hw	5	1		J/F 84	33, 92
Table Coverings: Lunch Cloth	Design for a Lunch Cloth in Three Techniques	Redfield, Gail M.	√	√	H&C	19	3		Su 68	15
Table Coverings: Luncheon Cloth	Crackle Weave Luncheon Cloth (Gladys Strong)		√	√	Hw	3	5		N/D 82	51, 95
Table Coverings: Mats	Linen Table Mat (Janice Jones)		√	√	Hw	5	2		M/A 84	53, 98
Table Coverings: Picnic Cloth	Simple Summer Linens		√	√	Hw	1	2		S-S 80	30
Table Coverings: Runners	Blooming Leaf	Xenakis, Athanasios David	√	√	PWC	3	3	9		51
Table Coverings: Runners	Christman Runner (Deborah Dobbs) (error-corrected Hw v8 n1 87 p I-16)		√	√	Hw	7	4		S/O 86	34, I-6

SUBJECT	TITLE	AUTHOR	IL	INST	JOUR	VOL	NO	ISS	DATE	PAGE
Table Coverings: Runners	Cotton Table Runner, A (Lynette Theodore)		√	√	Hw	6	4		S/O 85	84
Table Coverings: Runners	Country Morning Table Runner (Patti Ball)		√	√	Hw	6	3		Su 85	82
Table Coverings: Runners	Coverlet Weaves on a Rigid-Heddle (David Xenakis)		√	√	Hw	2	1		F-W 80	38
Table Coverings: Runners	Crackle Christmas Runner (Jean Scorgie)		√	√	Hw	8	4		S/O 87	58, I-13
Table Coverings: Runners	Dal Dräll Table Runner (Nancy Klein)		√	>4	Hw	1	2		S-S 80	25, 52
Table Coverings: Runners	Double Weave Runner (Jean Scorgie, Kathe Fletcher)		√	√	Hw	7	2		M/A 86	57, I-10
Table Coverings: Runners	Double Weave Runner (Miranda Howard)		√	>4	Hw	6	3		Su 85	36, I-16
Table Coverings: Runners	Double Weave Table Runner (Robert P. Owen)		√	>4	Hw	8	5		N/D 87	41, 76
Table Coverings: Runners	Eight-Shaft Summer and Winter Towels (Debbie Allen)		√	>4	Hw	8	5		N/D 87	74
Table Coverings: Runners	Figured Bead Leno Lace	Merritt, Elveana	√	√	WJ	6	1	21	Su 81	50
Table Coverings: Runners	Finnish Lace	Howard, Miranda	√	>4	Hw	5	3		Su 84	80
Table Coverings: Runners	Four-Block Double Weave on Four Shafts	Barrett, Clotilde	√	√	WJ	8	1	29	Su 83	72
Table Coverings: Runners	Four-Block Warp Rep (error-corrected WJ v8 n1 83 p50)	Robitaille, Annette	√	>4	WJ	7	4	28	Sp 83	16
Table Coverings: Runners	Ikat with Ease	Bliss, Anne	√	√	Hw	2	4		Se 81	60
Table Coverings: Runners	Isolated Overshot: Inlaid Runner	Xenakis, Athanasios David	√	√	PWC	3	2	8		31
Table Coverings: Runners	Karen Braun's Table Runner and Tray Covering		√		S-O	9	3		Fa 85	14
Table Coverings: Runners	Lace & Flowers: Vintage Inspiration	George, Patrice	√	>4	Hw	8	5		N/D 87	68
Table Coverings: Runners	Linen Tablerunner with Atwater Bronson Lace	Cyr, Gloria	√	>4	WJ	7	2	26	Fa 82	37
Table Coverings: Runners	Log Cabin Runner (Betty Davenport)		√	√	Hw	8	5		N/D 87	42, I-4
Table Coverings: Runners	Long Table Runners (Carol Klippenstein)		√	√	Hw	1	1		F-W 79	32, 59
Table Coverings: Runners	Man-Made Fibers: Table Runner		√	>4	WJ	5	2	18	Fa 80	45
Table Coverings: Runners	Mug Rugs and Table Runner (Jean Scorgie)		√	√	Hw	7	4		S/O 86	58, 59 I-10
Table Coverings: Runners	Multiple Shaft Weaving — 2-Tie Four-End Block Drafts (Myrna L. Golay)		√	>4	WJ	6	4	24	Sp 82	48
Table Coverings: Runners	Name Draft Contest Winners (Kathryn Turner)		√	>4	WJ	11	4	44	Sp 87	46
Table Coverings: Runners	Name Draft Contest Winners (Sister Joan Marie Lovett, OSB)		√	>4	WJ	11	4	44	Sp 87	46
Table Coverings: Runners	Overshot Derived from 2/2 Twill: Joanne's Runner	Christensen, Joanne	√	√	PWC	3	2	8		24
Table Coverings: Runners	Overshot Runner with Border (Lip Eppinger) (error-corrected Hw v5 n1 83 p88)		√	√	Hw	4	4		S/O 83	83, 109
Table Coverings: Runners	Penny-wise Table Runner (Linda Ligon)		√	√	Hw	5	4		S/O 84	73, 109
Table Coverings: Runners	Picture Lace	Larson-Fleming, Susan	√		WJ	9	4	36	Sp 85	42
Table Coverings: Runners	Pillow and Table Runner in Summer and Winter Weave	Xenakis, Athanasios David	√	√	PWC	1	1		No 81	21
Table Coverings: Runners	Placemats	DeRoy, Paul	√	>4	WJ	1	3	3	Ja 77	4
Table Coverings: Runners	Placemats and Runner (Mary Skoy)		√	√	Hw	8	2		M/A 87	83, I-16
Table Coverings: Runners	Poppana Runner (Janice Jones)		√	√	Hw	4	2		M/A 83	50, 88
Table Coverings: Runners	Rag Runner (Susan Snover) (error-corrected Hw v2 n4 81 p22)		√	√	Hw	2	3		My 81	50, 78
Table Coverings: Runners	Rag Table Runner (Inga Krook)		√	√	Hw	8	3		M/J 87	39, I-5
Table Coverings: Runners	Rainbow on the Table, A (Sharon Hakala, Carol Isleib, Carol Shabaz, Ruth Stump)	Isleib, Carol	√	√	Hw	5	3		Su 84	46
Table Coverings: Runners	Red, Brown and Ecru Mat (Gloria Martin)		√	√	Hw	6	3		Su 85	38, I-15
Table Coverings: Runners	Refreshingly Simple Runner (Betty Davenport)		√	>4	Hw	6	3		Su 85	11, I-3
Table Coverings: Runners	Ripsmatta Table Runner (Jean Scorgie, Dixie Straight-Allen)		√	√	Hw	8	5		N/D 87	60, I-15

SUBJECT	TITLE	AUTHOR	IL	INST	JOUR	VOL	NO	ISS	DATE	PAGE
Table Coverings: Runners	Ripsmattor Table Runner (Gloria Martin)		√	√	Hw	4	3		M/J 83	Cover, 90
Table Coverings: Runners	Small Table Runner (Betty Davenport)		√	√	Hw	1	1		F-W 79	32, 59
Table Coverings: Runners	Star and Diamond	Xenakis, Athanasios David	√	√	PWC	3	3	9		49
Table Coverings: Runners	Summer and Winter Revisited, Part 2: II. Krokbragd on One, A Woolen Runner Project	Davenport, Betty	√	√	PWC			2	Ap 82	65
Table Coverings: Runners	Swivel Treadled Runner (Mary Anderson)		√	√	Hw	3	5		N/D 82	55, 97
Table Coverings: Runners	Table Runner		√	√	H&C	10	3		Su 59	44
Table Coverings: Runners	Table Runner in Linen		√	√	PWC			5	Sp 83	25
Table Coverings: Runners	Table Turned , The(error-corrected Hw v5 n3 84 p92)	Dobrovolny, Ardis	√	> 4	Hw	5	1		J/F 84	64
Table Coverings: Runners	Tablecloth and Runner Decorated with Overshot and Pick-Up Leno		√	√	WJ	6	1	21	Su 81	10
Table Coverings: Runners	Touch the Earth Table Runner (Robin Taylor Daugherty)		√	√	Hw	5	4		S/0 84	64, 100
Table Coverings: Runners	Twill with a Twist	Keasbey, Doramay	√	> 4	Hw	6	5		N/D 85	31
Table Coverings: Runners	Warp-Faced Tablerunner in Rib Weave	Kolling-Summers, Elizabeth	√	√	WJ	7	4	28	Sp 83	14
Table Coverings: Runners	Weaving for the Holidays (Kaino Leethem) (error-corrected Hw v4 n4 83 p92)		√	> 4	Hw	3	5		N/D 82	78
Table Coverings: Runners	Weaving Table Linens	Eychaner, Barbara Smith	√	√	TM			11	J/J 87	52
Table Coverings: Table Tapestry	Table Tapestries	Barrett, Clotilde	√	> 4	WJ	7	4	28	Sp 83	73
Table Coverings: Tablecloths	Anniversary Tablecloth, An		√		Hw	8	4		S/0 87	86
Table Coverings: Tablecloths	Bronson Lace Tablecloth and Napkins (Sallie T. Guy)		√	> 4	Hw	8	1		J/F 87	61, I-13
Table Coverings: Tablecloths	California Poppy Tablecloth and Napkins (Jean Scorgie)		√	√	Hw	6	3		Su 85	61, I-16
Table Coverings: Tablecloths	Color Gamp Tablecloth and Napkins (Carrie Lee Seachord)		√	√	Hw	5	3		Su 84	77, 117
Table Coverings: Tablecloths	Contemporary Satins: A Damask Table Cloth Pattern	Tidball, Harriet	√	√	SCGM		7		62	15
Table Coverings: Tablecloths	Country Kitchen Checked Cloth (Margaretha Essén-Hedin) (error-corrected Hw v5 n2 84 p93) (error-corrected Hw v8 n1 87 pI-16)		√	> 4	Hw	4	5		N/D 83	58, 106
Table Coverings: Tablecloths	Ella Bolster		√	> 4	H&C	12	2		Sp 61	26
Table Coverings: Tablecloths	Evergreen Plaid Tablecloth (Sharon Alderman)		√	√	Hw	4	5		N/D 83	62, 108
Table Coverings: Tablecloths	Heritage Tablecloth (Margaretha Essén-Hedin)		√	√	Hw	8	3		M/J 87	41, I-7
Table Coverings: Tablecloths	Kirschbaum Tablecloth (Julie Lawson)		√	√	Hw	8	1		J/F 87	58, I-10
Table Coverings: Tablecloths	Lace Weave Gamp Tablecloth (Penelope Drooker)		√	> 4	Hw	5	3		Su 84	78, 110
Table Coverings: Tablecloths	Mock-Leno Tablecloth		√	√	WJ	6	1	21	Su 81	12
Table Coverings: Tablecloths	Narrow Loom Tablecloth		√		H&C	9	3		Su 58	45
Table Coverings: Tablecloths	Nutmeg Tablecloth		√	√	WJ	6	1	21	Su 81	9
Table Coverings: Tablecloths	Restoring a Crocheted Tablecloth			√	TM			14	D/J 87	6
Table Coverings: Tablecloths	Rose-Beige Tablecloth (E. E. Gilmore)		√	> 4	Hw	6	4		S/O 85	42, I-5
Table Coverings: Tablecloths	Swedish Curtains and Tablecloth Fabrics (Kerstin Eberhardson)		√	√	Hw	4	2		M/A 83	29, 82
Table Coverings: Tablecloths	Table Dressing and Bedcovers		√		Fa	8	3		M/J 81	43
Table Coverings: Tablecloths	Tablecloth and Runner Decorated with Overshot and Pick-Up Leno		√	√	WJ	6	1	21	Su 81	10
Table Coverings: Tablecloths	Tablecloth and Six Napkins in Two-Block Damask (Janet Carper)		√	> 4	Hw	4	3		M/J 83	54, 94
Table Coverings: Tablecloths	Tablecloth in Bergman Weave	Morrison, Ruth	√	> 4	PWC	4	4	14		38
Table Coverings: Tablecloths	Tablecloth in Double Weave, A	Robinson, Irma	√	> 4	H&C	8	4		Fa 57	44
Table Coverings: Tablecloths	Tablecloth in Summer and Winter	Xenakis, Athanasios David	√	√	PWC	1	1		No 81	16

SUBJECT	TITLE	AUTHOR	IL	INST	JOUR	VOL	NO	ISS	DATE	PAGE
Table Coverings: Tablecloths	Weaving Table Linens	Eychaner, Barbara Smith	√	√	TM			11	J/J 87	52
Table Coverings: Tablecloths	White-on-White Huck Plaid Cloth (Margaretha Essén-Hedin)		√	√	Hw	4	5		N/D 83	60, 109
Table Coverings: Teacloths	Isolated Overshot: Linen and Cotton Teacloth	Xenakis, Athanasios David	√	>4	PWC	3	2	8		36
Table Coverings: Teacloths	Tea Cloth (Sharon Alderman)		√	√	Hw	2	1		F-W 80	43, 76
Table Linens	Contemporary Satins: An Alphabet of Satin Designs	Tidball, Harriet	√	>4	SCGM		7		62	22
Tablet Weaving see Band Weaving										
Taffeta	Origins	Wilson, Kax			Iw	5	1		Wi 79	47
Tag System	Handloom Weaves: The Classification of Handloom Weaves, The Structural Group, Unit Class, Tag System	Tidball, Harriet	√	>4	SCGM		33		57	26
Tailoring also see Clothing Construction										
Tailoring	Hemming Ways	Wroten, Barbara	√	√	SS&D	18	3	71	Su 87	74
Tailoring	Not Necessarily Seventh Ave.	Dyett, Linda	√		TM			6	A/S 86	28
Tailoring	Simple Skirt and Matching Shawl, A	Hewson, Betty	√	√	Hw	4	5		N/D 83	24
Tailoring: Custom	Tailor's Logic	Hostek, Stanley	√	√	TM			14	D/J 87	42
Tailoring: Fit	Perfect Fit	Allen, Alice	√	√	TM			12	A/S 87	71
Tailoring: Handspun	Suggestions for Tailoring Material Woven of Handspun Yarns	Simmons, Paula	√	√	H&C	18	4		Fa 67	17
Tailoring: Handspun	Weaving and Tailoring Handspun Yardage	Simmons, Paula	√	√	S-O	2			78	48
Tailoring: Handspun	Weaving with Handspuns: A Shepherd Jacket	Simmons, Paula	√	√	S-O	1			77	43
Tailoring: Handwoven Fabric	Calm and Cool...Sewing Handwoven Fabric	Krantz, Hazel	√	√	Hw	4	3		M/J 83	29
Tailoring: Handwoven Fabrics	Basic Sewing Techniques in Handling Handwoven Fabrics for Garments	Knollenberg, Barbara	√	√	WJ	1	1	1	Jy 76	25
Tailoring: Handwoven Fabrics	Beautiful Fabric Is Not Enough	Lommen, Sandy	√	√	SS&D	15	2	58	Sp 84	40
Tailoring: Handwoven Fabrics	Bits and Pieces	Knollenberg, Barbara	√	√	WJ	1	4	4	Ap 77	11
Tailoring: Handwoven Fabrics	Handwoven Fabric: Beginnings, A Fitting Start	Wertenberger, Kathryn	√		Hw	3	2		Mr 82	32
Tailoring: Handwoven Fabrics	Macedonian Shirt Design	Hoffman, Jenet	√	√	SS&D	8	2	30	Sp 77	97
Tailoring: Handwoven Fabrics	Man's Jacket: A Weaver's Challenge, A	Rasmussen, Peg	√	√	SS&D	15	2	58	Sp 84	58
Tailoring: Handwoven Fabrics	Pine Tree Coat	Knollenberg, Barbara	√	>4	WJ	1	2	2	Oc 76	32
Tailoring: Handwoven Fabrics	Planning Fabrics to Meet Tailors' Requirements	Bryan, Dorothy		√	H&C	10	1		Wi 59	18
Tailoring: Handwoven Fabrics	Russian Peasant Shirt Adaptation	Hendricks, Carolyn	√	√	SS&D	8	2	30	Sp 77	96
Tailoring: Handwoven Fabrics	Tailored Bog Jacket, A	Guy, Sallie T.	√	√	SS&D	17	1	65	Wi 85	26
Tailoring: Handwoven Fabrics	Tailoring a Suit Jacket	Bryan, Dorothy	√	√	H&C	11	1		Wi 60	28
Tailoring: Handwoven Fabrics	Tailoring a Suit Skirt	Bryan, Dorothy	√	√	H&C	10	4		Fa 59	28
Tailoring: Handwoven Fabrics	Tailoring Handwoven Fabrics	Bryan, Dorothy	√		H&C	10	2		Sp 59	17
Tailoring: Handwoven Fabrics	Tailoring Handwoven Fabrics	Smith, Jane Raven	√	√	H&C	8	1		Wi 56	48
Tailoring: Handwoven/Handspun	Contemporary Gown, Traditional Flavor	Linder, Olive	√	>4	SS&D	6	3	23	Su 75	51
Tailoring: Handwoven/Handspun	Warmth for a Cool Climate: Handspun Wool & Milkweed Down	Danielson, Esther	√	√	SS&D	17	4	68	Fa 86	24
Tailoring: Linings	Knitting Odyssey, A	Dyett, Linda	√	√	TM			13	O/N 87	48
Tailoring: Piqué	Notes from the Tailor	Kussube, Kay; Alexis Yiorgos Xenakis		√	PWC	4	2	12		27
Tailoring: Techniques	Basic Sewing Techniques in Handling Handwoven Fabrics for Garments	Knollenberg, Barbara	√	√	WJ	1	1	1	Jy 76	25
Tailoring: Techniques	Correct Sewing Methods in Tailoring	Bryan, Dorothy	√	√	H&C	10	3		Su 59	25
Tailoring: Techniques	Inside an Expensive Outfit	Galpin, Mary	√	√	TM			1	O/N 85	40
Tailoring: Techniques	Playing with Darts	Abbott, Deborah	√	√	TM			14	D/J 87	64
Tailoring: Techniques	Reversible Jacket in Double Weave, A	Evans, Jane	√	>4	WJ	3	1	9	Jy 78	23
Tailoring: Techniques	Seattle Guild Garment Designs, Part 2: Completing the Top		√	√	SS&D	10	4	40	Fa 79	71

SUBJECT	TITLE	AUTHOR	IL	INST	JOUR	VOL	NO	ISS	DATE	PAGE
Tailoring: Techniques	Seattle Guild Garment Designs, Part 3, Skirts and Pants		√	√	SS&D	11	1	41	Wi 79	20
Tailoring: Techniques	Sewing Handwovens	Betzina, Sandra	√	√	TM			2	D/J 85	20
Tailoring: Techniques	Sewing with Silk	Stoyer, Janet	√	√	TM			4	A/M 86	35
Tailoring: Techniques	Suggestions for Tailoring Material Woven of Handspun Yarns	Simmons, Paula	√	√	H&C	18	4		Fa 67	17
Tailoring: Techniques	Tailoring Handwoven Fabrics	Bryan, Dorothy	√		H&C	10	2		Sp 59	17
Tailoring: Techniques	Tailor's Logic	Hostek, Stanley	√	√	TM			14	D/J 87	42
Tailoring: Techniques	Techniques of Haute Couture (error-corrected TM i7 O/N86 p5)	Rhodes, Elizabeth A.	√	√	TM			6	A/S 86	52
Tailoring Tools: Pressing	Tailor's Pressing Tools			√	TM			13	O/N 87	10
Tailor's Board	Irons, Boards, and Presses: A Survey of the Tools That Beautify Sewing	Coffin, David Page	√		TM			10	A/M 87	40
Tailor's Chalk	Following Up			√	TM			9	F/M 87	8
Taiwan	Weaving in Taiwan, An American Designer's Experience in Free China		√		H&C	13	1		Wi 62	10
Talis	Tale of a Talis, A	Sylvan, Katherine	√	√	WJ	6	1	21	Su 81	42
Tallit	Tallit (Faye Johnson)		√	√	Hw	5	1		J/F 84	35, 91
Tallit	Weaver's Story of Two Prayer Shawls, Garments Used in Jewish Ritual, A	Schlein, Alice	√	> 4	CW	3	3	9	Ap 82	6
Tamba Weaving	Kazuko Nishigaki Creates in Ancient Tradition	Major, Dana; John Major	√		SS&D	6	2	22	Sp 75	93
Tanning	Recipe for Tanning Rabbit Fur	Clemmer, Phyllis	√	√	WJ	8	3	31	Wi 83	16
Tansy	Dyes from the Herb Garden	King, Helen	√	√	TM			6	A/S 86	58
Tapa Cloth	Tapa-Making in Tonga	Raphael, Jenifer; Chad Raphael	√		Fa	13	6		N/D 86	24
Tapa Cloth: Technique	Tapa-Making Process, The	Raphael, Jenifer; Chad Raphael	√	√	Fa	13	6		N/D 86	25
Tape Weaving	Inkle Tape for Vest (Betty Davenport)		√	√	Hw	4	2		M/A 83	56, 93
Tape Weaving	Scintillating, Soft and Silent Seat, A	Chesley, Mariam Dolloff	√	√	Hw	5	2		M/A 84	27
Tape-Recordings: Weaving Lessons	Weaving Lessons by a Tape Recorder				H&C	10	4		Fa 59	21
Tapestries	"Amy Lipshie: Tapestries" (Exhibit)	Park, Betty	√		Fa	12	3		M/J 85	76
Tapestries	"Anke Van Ginhoven: Tapestries 1977" (Exhibit)	Cantieni, Graham	√		Fa	5	1		J/F 78	21
Tapestries	"Barbara Heilmann-Levine: Tapestries and Paintings" (Exhibit)	Pasquine, Ruth	√		Fa	10	2		M/A 83	69
Tapestries	"Deborah Corsini: Tapestries" (Exhibit)	Talley, Charles S.	√		Fa	7	5		S/O 80	68
Tapestry	"Akiko Kotani" (Exhibit)	Malarcher, Patricia	√		Fa	8	4		J/A 81	73
Tapestry	Alicia Duplan: A Weaver in the Navajo Tradition	Erler, Mary	√		Fa	7	5		S/O 80	28
Tapestry	American Tapestry Alliance, The	Rolingson, Beth	√		WJ	12	1	45	Su 87	32
Tapestry	Appendix I: The Development of Interlace and Related Patterns	Trilling, James	√		TMJ	21			82	104
Tapestry	April May: Visions of Space	May, April	√		Fa	10	6		N/D 83	22
Tapestry	Athens Tapestry Works	Many, Paul	√		Fa	5	4		J/A 78	51
Tapestry	Barberini Tapestries		√		H&C	17	1		Wi 66	33
Tapestry	Bicentennial Tapestry, A	Howard, Margaret	√		SS&D	7	1	25	Wi 75	30
Tapestry	But Is It Tapestry?	Meltzer, Marilyn	√		SS&D	5	3	19	Su 74	39
Tapestry	"Carol Mecagni: Illuminated Tapestries" (Exhibit)	Newman, Rochelle	√		Fa	9	2		M/A 82	79
Tapestry	Carol Shinn: The Conscious and the Unconscious	Brien, D. Elise	√		Fa	14	5		N/D 87	17
Tapestry	Charles Talley: A Candid Account of a Passionate Weaver and How He Got That Way	Talley, Charles	√		Fa	6	2		M/A 79	25
Tapestry	Children's Chair Seat & Back Rest (Andrea McCormack)		√	√	Hw	3	1		Ja 82	28, 81
Tapestry	"Claire Zeisler" (Exhibit)	Mathews, Rich	√		Fa	4	1		J/F 77	12

SUBJECT	TITLE	AUTHOR	IL	INST	JOUR	VOL	NO	ISS	DATE	PAGE
Tapestry	Comminicating Through Craft	de Mar, Lola	√		Fa	14	1		J/F 87	38
Tapestry	Conference Sampler		√		SS&D	14	4	56	Fa 83	44
Tapestry	Contemporary Egyptian Childern's Tapestries		√		Fa	4	6		N/D 77	65
Tapestry	Convergence '74, Hurschler Collection	Hurschler, Paul; Flora Hurschler	√		SS&D	5	3	19	Su 74	43
Tapestry	Conversation with Lillian Elliott, A	Janeiro, Jan	√		Fa	9	2		M/A 82	66
Tapestry	Coventry Tapestry, The Largest Woven in Modern Times, The		√		H&C	14	1		Wi 63	18
Tapestry	Critics Choice		√		SS&D	1	3	3	Ju 70	11
Tapestry	Cross-Weave Tapestry (Aslaug Sverrisdóttir)		√	√	Hw	8	3		M/J 87	67, I-15
Tapestry	Cycle of Growth, A	Mattera, Joanne	√		Fa	7	2		M/A 80	24
Tapestry	D. R. Wagner: 625 Stitches per Inch	Welty, Margaret	√		Fa	10	6		N/D 83	24
Tapestry	David Johnson and Geary Jones	Rudick, Sally	√		Fa	12	5		S/O 85	18
Tapestry	Diamond Odyssey		√		SS&D	14	4	56	Fa 83	40
Tapestry	Donna Martin: The Influence of the Southwest	D'Andrea, Patricia A.	√		Fa	14	5		N/D 87	18
Tapestry	Dyeing: A Personal Palette for Tapestry	Bliss, Anne	√	√	Hw	3	1		Ja 82	66
Tapestry	Ecclesiastical Tapestries		√		H&C	8	3		Su 57	50
Tapestry	Edinburg Tapestry Company		√		Fa	12	5		S/O 85	64
Tapestry	Eleventh International Biennial of Tapestry, The	Taylor, Elmer; Dianne Taylor	√		Fa	10	5		S/O 83	33
Tapestry	Elmyra Tidwell	Tidwell, Elmyra	√		Fa	14	3		M/J 87	22
Tapestry	Evolution of an Artist: Michelle Lester	Malarcher, Pat	√		Fa	14	5		N/D 87	22
Tapestry	Evolution of an Artist: Peg McNair	McNair, Peg	√		Fa	14	5		N/D 87	19
Tapestry	Eye of a Photographer, Hand of a Weaver: An Artist Combines Two Art Forms	Guagliumi, Susan	√		Fa	8	6		N/D 81	35
Tapestry	Fiber and Architecture: Janusz and Nancy Kozikowski		√		Fa	3	3		M/J 76	28
Tapestry	"Fiber Art: Tapestries and Wall Hangings" (Exhibit)	Koplos, Janet	√		Fa	6	6		N/D 79	75
Tapestry	"Fiber from the Marietta College Crafts National" (Exhibit)	Murray, Megan	√		Fa	11	2		M/A 84	76
Tapestry	"Fiber in Focus" (Exhibit)	Skudera, Gail	√		Fa	10	6		N/D 83	82
Tapestry	Five Ateliers: A Tour of Weaving Studios in Australia, France, Scotland, Sweden, and the U.S.A.		√		Fa	10	3		M/J 83	36
Tapestry	"Flemish Tapestries of Willem De Kempeneer" (Exhibit)	Vander Lee, Jana	√		Fa	3	5		S/O 76	7
Tapestry	"Flexible Medium: Art Fabric from the Museum Collection, The" (Exhibit)	Goodman, Deborah Lerme	√		Fa	11	5		S/O 84	71
Tapestry	Flowers, Beautiful Flowers: Ronna Riebman, Batik: Mary Lynn O'Shea, Tapestry		√		Fa	8	3		M/J 81	35
Tapestry	Folk Textiles of Latin America	Kelemen, Pál	√		TMJ	1	4		De 65	2
Tapestry	From a Family Album	Endres, Linda Carollo	√		Fa	7	3		M/J 80	70
Tapestry	"From American Looms: Scheuer Tapestry Studio" (Exhibit) (error-corrected Fa v12 n6 85 p9)	Park, Betty	√		Fa	12	5		S/O 85	76
Tapestry	"Gaudy Ladies" (Exhibit)		√		Fa	8	4		J/A 81	44
Tapestry	Ghost Rugs	Kozikowski, Janusz; Nancy Kozikowski	√		Iw	4	1		Wi 78	24
Tapestry	Guatemala Visited	Atwater, Mary Meigs	√	√	SCGM		15		65	24
Tapestry	Guatemala Visited	Atwater, Mary Meigs	√	√	SCGM		15		65	23
Tapestry	Handweaving in Spain	Arnold, Ruth	√		H&C	8	4		Fa 57	10
Tapestry	Handwoven Tapestries Chosen As Governor's Awards in the Arts		√		SS&D	2	2	6	Sp 71	13

SUBJECT	TITLE	AUTHOR	IL	INST	JOUR	VOL	NO	ISS	DATE	PAGE
Tapestry	Hans Krondahl's "Homage to Garbo" (Exhibit)	Talley, Charles	√		Fa	11	4		J/A 84	79
Tapestry	"Hedi Taryan: The Infinity of Small Things" (Exhibit)	Chamish, Barry	√		Fa	10	5		S/O 83	79
Tapestry	Herminio Martinez: Tejedor		√		Fa	8	6		N/D 81	24
Tapestry	"Honorata Blicharska" (Exhibit)		√		Fa	4	4		J/A 77	15
Tapestry	How Much Yarn for the Job? Tapestry	Towner, Naomi W.	√	√	SS&D	9	1	33	Wi 77	73
Tapestry	"Ideas and Capabilities: Barbara Sykes' Fiber Constructions" (Exhibit)	Blakely, Deborah	√		Fa	8	1		J/F 81	94
Tapestry	Illuminated Tapestries of Amy Zerner, The	Daniels, Richard	√		Fa	9	3		M/J 82	22
Tapestry	Imagery and Structure: The Tapestries of Marcel Marois	Russell, Elfleda	√		Fa	8	6		N/D 81	57
Tapestry	In and On the Surface: The Tapestries of Judy Branfman	Mattera, Joanne	√		Fa	10	3		M/J 83	22
Tapestry	International Tapestry (Exhibit)		√		Fa	13	4		J/A 86	59
Tapestry	Interview with Dee Henion, An		√		Fa	3	2		M/A 76	17
Tapestry	It's All It Can Be: The Work of Gail Reike		√		Fa	3	2		M/A 76	20
Tapestry	Jeff Glenn	Glenn, Jeff	√		Fa	14	1		J/F 87	26
Tapestry	Jeff Glenn: Software for a High-Tech World	Poon, Vivian	√		Fa	12	4		J/A 85	9
Tapestry	Joan Russell: Space Series	McGuire, Patricia	√		Fa	12	4		J/A 85	18
Tapestry	"Julia Mitchell: Landscape Tapestries" (Exhibit)	Poon, Vivian	√		Fa	10	6		N/D 83	80
Tapestry	Kai Walters	Pilsk, Adele	√		Fa	4	6		N/D 77	42
Tapestry	"Karen Swanson" (Exhibit)	Sunshine, Joanna	√		Fa	4	2		M/A 77	13
Tapestry	Kate Russell: Weaving the Structure of Life	Russell, Kate	√		Fa	12	4		J/A 85	11
Tapestry	Keeping Warm in Alaska		√		Fa	9	6		N/D 82	22
Tapestry	Laurie Dill-Kocher	Dill-Kocher, Laurie	√		Fa	13	2		M/A 86	15
Tapestry	Laurie Herrick		√		Fa	4	6		N/D 77	43
Tapestry	Letter from Japan	Schrieber, Lavonne	√		WJ	12	1	45	Su 87	54
Tapestry	Life of a Country Weaver, The	Day, Jim	√		Fa	7	1		J/F 80	55
Tapestry	"Lilian Tyrrell: Tapestries" (Exhibit)	McClelland, Elizabeth	√		Fa	11	6		N/D 84	76
Tapestry	Linda Gilbert	Gilbert, Linda	√		Fa	5	5		S/O 78	16
Tapestry	Linda Weghorst: Portraits in Fiber		√		Fa	4	4		J/A 77	44
Tapestry	Line As Movement: Adela Akers, The	Janeiro, Jan	√		Fa	8	2		M/A 81	70
Tapestry	"Martha Matthews: Tapestry" (Exhibit)	Laymon, Cynthia	√		Fa	9	1		J/F 82	85
Tapestry	"Micala Sidore: Sign Language" (Exhibit)	Temple, Nancy	√		Fa	12	3		M/J 85	72
Tapestry	"Michelle Lester: New Tapestries" (Exhibit)	Park, Betty	√		Fa	6	1		J/F 79	85
Tapestry	"Michelle Morris: Tapestries and Related Work" (Exhibit)	Fitt, Cate	√		Fa	7	4		J/A 80	65
Tapestry	Modern Handweaver Restores Famous Tapestries, A		√	√	H&C	3	2		Sp 52	9
Tapestry	Modular Clothing	Mayer, Anita	√	√	Hw	7	3		M/J 86	58
Tapestry	Multilayered Tapestries of Susan Klebanoff, The	Brien, Elise	√		Fa	14	3		M/J 87	21
Tapestry	Nancy Crump		√		Fa	3	6		N/D 76	28
Tapestry	National Mini Tapestry Exhibit	Cameron, Carolyn W.	√		SS&D	9	3	35	Su 78	48
Tapestry	Native Craftsmen Produce for Nile Hilton Hotel		√		H&C	11	3		Su 60	54
Tapestry	Navajo Weaving, Contemporary and Traditional		√		H&C	18	2		Sp 67	6
Tapestry	Nineteenth Century Tapestry in Billedvev, A	Nelson, Lila	√		WJ	10	2	38	Fa 85	26
Tapestry	Norwegian Tapestries		√		H&C	10	4		Fa 59	46
Tapestry	Pam Patrie: Tapestry, Imagery, Artistry	Carlton, Bronwyn	√		Fa	6	6		N/D 79	60
Tapestry	Paradox of Perfection, The	Jenkins, Thomas W.	√		Fa	8	2		M/A 81	27

SUBJECT	TITLE	AUTHOR	IL	INST	JOUR	VOL	NO	ISS	DATE	PAGE
Tapestry	Patience and Planning	Wilson, Jay	√		Fa	8	2		M/A 81	29
Tapestry	"Peg McNair/Tapestries" (Exhibit)	Petersen, Jill	√		Fa	4	3		M/J 77	12
Tapestry	Peru, Textiles Unlimited, Part 2: Tapestry	Tidball, Harriet	√	√	SCGM		26		69	38
Tapestry	Play of Light: Susan Kelly Explains the Inner and Outer Workings of Her Tapestries, A	Kelly, Susan	√		Fa	8	5		S/O 81	54
Tapestry	Portfolio of Contemporary Fiber Sculpture, A		√		Fa	11	4		J/A 84	34
Tapestry	Portraits of Three Weavers: Sandra Ikse-Bergman, Marja "Graset" Andersson, Elisabet Hasselberg-Olsson	Talley, Charles S.	√		Fa	8	2		M/A 81	46
Tapestry	Raffia Tapestries	Del Deo, Josephine	√	√	H&C	9	1		Wi 57	20
Tapestry	Rieke, Rieke — A Study in Beauty, Silence and Collaboration		√		Fa	5	6		N/D 78	35
Tapestry	Ritzi and Peter Jacobi: Conversation	Paca Al, ed.	√		Fa	8	4		J/A 81	50
Tapestry	"Roman Heritage: Textiles from Egypt and the Eastern Mediterranean, 300–600 A.D., The" (Exhibit)		√		Fa	9	4		J/A 82	32
Tapestry	"Ruth Kao: Silk Sense" (Exhibit)	Sider, Sandra	√		Fa	12	1		J/F 85	72
Tapestry	Sacred Places: Barbara Heller Weaves Landscapes Where Spirits Might Dwell, Places of Meditation (error-corrected Fa v7 n5 80 p5)	Redmond, Cheryl A.	√		Fa	7	3		M/J 80	58
Tapestry	Scheuer Tapestry Studio: Applying Old Techniques to New Ideas, The	Scheuer, Ruth Tannenbaum	√		Fa	10	3		M/J 83	39
Tapestry	Scientific Research Suggests Ideas for Fabric Designs		√		H&C	15	3		Su 64	5
Tapestry	Secrets of the Land	Bladow, Suzanne	√		Fa	7	1		J/F 80	48
Tapestry	Seventh Lausanne Biennial, The		√		SS&D	7	2	26	Sp 76	41
Tapestry	Sharon La Pierre		√		Fa	4	1		J/F 77	28
Tapestry	Sharon Marcus	Marcus, Sharon	√		Fa	13	6		N/D 86	2
Tapestry	Sharon Marcus: Designing for Tapestry, One Approach to the Creative Process	Marcus, Sharon	√		Fa	11	6		N/D 84	26
Tapestry	Silk Reflections of C. J. Yao, The	Nicoli, Antony	√		Fa	13	1		J/F 86	47
Tapestry	Six Songs of Success	Meany, Janet K.	√		SS&D	18	3	71	Su 87	69
Tapestry	Southwest Reflections: Fiber artists Inspired by the New Mexico Landscape	Colton, Mary Rawcliffe	√		WJ	11	1	41	Su 86	20
Tapestry	Special Piece—A Special Place, A	Harvey, Nancy	√		WJ	8	1	29	Su 83	67
Tapestry	Spirit of New Mexico: It Comes Alive in Weaving, The		√		SS&D	7	2	26	Sp 76	4
Tapestry	Spirit Tracings of Barbara Heller, The	Strong, Ruth	√		Fa	13	4		J/A 86	15
Tapestry	Sue Lawty: Journeying in Tapestry	Dunwell, Anna	√		Fa	11	2		M/A 84	12
Tapestry	Susan Beckett	Beckett, Susan	√		Fa	14	5		N/D 87	12
Tapestry	"Swiss Tapestries" (Exhibit)	Talley, Charles S.	√		Fa	7	6		N/D 80	74
Tapestry	Tapestries at Temple Emanu-El	Golub, Ina	√		SS&D	14	1	53	Wi 82	41
Tapestry	Tapestries at the Metropolitan Museum		√		H&C	26	2		Ap 75	4
Tapestry	Tapestries by Fritz Riedl		√		H&C	18	3		Su 67	42
Tapestry	"Tapestries by Janet Taylor" (Exhibit)	Malarcher, Patricia	√		Fa	9	5		S/O 82	81
Tapestry	Tapestries from Indonesia	Hitchcock, Michael	√	√	WJ	12	1	45	Su 87	55
Tapestry	Tapestries of Coptic Egypt, The	Hoskins, Nancy Arthur	√		AT	6			De 86	211
Tapestry	Tapestries of Dilys Stinson, The	Harris, Patricia; David Lyon	√		Fa	13	2		M/A 86	18
Tapestry	Tapestries of Elizabeth Berezowska, The	Carr, Diane	√		Fa	13	5		S/O 86	10
Tapestry	Tapestries of Inge Norgaard, The	Byers, Helen	√		Fa	11	4		J/A 84	22
Tapestry	Tapestries of Muriel Nezhnie Helfman	Salter, Deborah	√		H&C	23	5		S/O 72	43
Tapestry	Tapestries of Nancy and Janusz Kozikowski, The	Elliott, Malinda	√		Fa	13	2		M/A 86	23
Tapestry	"Tapestries of Trude Guermonprez: A Retrospective, The" (Exhibit)	Rowley, Kathleen	√		Fa	10	3		M/J 83	68

SUBJECT	TITLE	AUTHOR	IL	INST	JOUR	VOL	NO	ISS	DATE	PAGE
Tapestry	Tapestry: A Brief Overview	Bliss, Anne	√		Iw	4	2		Sp 79	15
Tapestry	Tapestry and Embroidery	Drooker, Penelope B.	√		Iw	5	3		Su 80	37
Tapestry	Tapestry by Allan Porter		√		H&C	14	2		Sp 63	13
Tapestry	Tapestry, Dwight D. Eisenhower Library		√		H&C	15	1		Wi 64	31
Tapestry	Tapestry Effects in Boundweave Rugs	Ziebarth, Charlotte Molcar	√	√	Iw	5	1		Wi 79	23
Tapestry	Tapestry for a Midwest Chapel	Helfman, Muriel Nezhnie	√		H&C	21	2		Sp 70	8
Tapestry	Tapices of San Pedro de Cajas, Peru, The	Thornton, Sandra K.	√	√	WJ	12	1	45	Su 87	23
Tapestry	Technicolor Tapestries of Teresa Graham Salt, The	Mathews, Kate	√		Fa	14	1		J/F 87	11
Tapestry	Temple of the Elelments, The	Samuel, Cheryl	√		SS&D	17	3	67	Su 86	10
Tapestry	"Tenth International Biennial of Tapestry: Four Views" (Exhibit)	Shawcroft, Barbara	√		Fa	8	6		N/D 81	52
Tapestry	Textile Remains from a Late Temple in Egyptian Nubia	Adams, Nettie K.	√		AT	8			De 87	85
Tapestry	Theme Issue		√		WJ	12	1	45	Su 87	
Tapestry	Theme Issue		√		Fa	7	2		M/A 80	
Tapestry	Theme Issue		√		Fa	10	3		M/J 83	
Tapestry	Things to Come — Tapestry West				SS&D	1	4	4	Se 70	7
Tapestry	Time and Vision: The Work of Cynthia Schira	Janeiro, Jan	√		Fa	9	5		S/O 82	68
Tapestry	To the Walls: The 13th Lausanne Biennial (Exhibit)	Zepeda, Susan G.	√		Fa	14	4		S/O 87	41
Tapestry	Twelfth International Tapestry Biennale, The	Coifman, Lucienne	√		SS&D	17	2	66	Sp 86	45
Tapestry	Twelfth International Tapestry Biennale, The	Waller, Irene	√		SS&D	17	2	66	Sp 86	42
Tapestry	Twelve Part Harmony: Taos Tapestry Collective		√		WJ	12	1	45	Su 87	48
Tapestry	Two Dimensions in A 3-D Disguise		√		Fa	14	3		M/J 87	75
Tapestry	Two-Harness Textiles, The Loom-Controlled Weaves: Weft-Face Plain Weave (Tapestry)	Tidball, Harriet	√	√	SCGM		20		67	9
Tapestry	Universe in a Shell, The		√		Fa	10	3		M/J 83	91
Tapestry	Victor Jacoby: Rich Colors and Bold Designs	Kahn, Kathy; Susan Larson-Fleming	√		WJ	12	1	45	Su 87	36
Tapestry	Victorian Tapestry Workshop: A New Tradition in Australia, The	Newman, Rochelle	√		Fa	10	3		M/J 83	38
Tapestry	Villanueva Tapestries		√		Fa	4	3		M/J 77	45
Tapestry	Visions of Space	May, April	√		SS&D	14	1	53	Wi 82	14
Tapestry	Wearable Fine Thread Tapestries	Tidwell, Elmyra	√	√	WJ	10	3	39	Wi 86	34
Tapestry	Weaving a Lifestyle: Cynthia Schira	Schira, Cynthia	√		Iw	5	2		Sp 80	27
Tapestry	Weaving the Horror of the Holocaust	Townsend, William D.	√		SS&D	15	3	59	Su 84	16
Tapestry	Welcome to My World	Denton, Kay	√		Fa	8	3		M/J 81	52
Tapestry	Well-Worn Path to Where? A View of Contemporary Swedish Textiles, The	Talley, Charles S.	√		Fa	8	2		M/A 81	44
Tapestry	"Wildfire" Wins Best-in-Show		√		SS&D	4	1	13	Wi 72	39
Tapestry	William Morris, His Designs for Carpets & Tapestries	Morris, Barbara J.	√		H&C	12	4		Fa 61	18
Tapestry	Words in Fiber	Rowley, Kathleen	√		Fa	11	2		M/A 84	66
Tapestry	Woven Murals	Mulders, Lydia	√		H&C	13	2		Sp 62	22
Tapestry	"Woven, Tied, and Knotted" (Exhibit)	Koplos, Janet	√		Fa	9	2		M/A 82	82
Tapestry	Woven Woolen Whimseys		√	√	WJ	2	2	6	Oc 77	14
Tapestry: Aaklae	Rugs by an Architect		√	√	H&C	13	4		Fa 62	6
Tapestry, Aubusson	Aubusson Tapestry	Larochette, Jean-Pierre	√		SS&D	13	4	52	Fa 82	5
Tapestry: Aubusson	Aubussons on Tour		√		H&C	13	4		Fa 62	20
Tapestry: Aubusson	Bringing Tapestry into the 20th Century	Mattera, Joanne	√		TM			1	O/N 85	48
Tapestry: Aubusson	French Tapestry Weaving in San Francisco	Tanenbaum, Ruth	√	√	SS&D	8	3	31	Su 77	12

SUBJECT	TITLE	AUTHOR	IL	INST	JOUR	VOL	NO	ISS	DATE	PAGE
Tapestry: Aubusson	"Modern Aubusson Tapestry, The" (Exhibit)	Tanenbaum, Ruth	√		Fa	5	3		M/J 78	14
Tapestry: Aubusson	Painters at the Loom		√		H&C	5	4		Fa 54	19
Tapestry: Aubusson	Twentieth Century Aubusson Tapestries		√		H&C	1	2		Su 50	10
Tapestry: Aubusson	Weaving in San Francisco — Part 1	Prosser, Evelyn Bingham	√		WJ	6	2	22	Fa 81	44
Tapestry: Aubusson Style	San Francisco Tapestry Workshop: A European-Style Atelier in the United States, The	Rowley, Kathleen	√		Fa	10	3		M/J 83	60
Tapestry Bags	Shaped Tapestry Bags from the Nazca-Ica Area of Peru	Bird, Junius B.	√		TMJ	1	3		De 64	2
Tapestry Center: San Francisco Tapestry Workshop	Weaving in San Francisco — Part 1	Prosser, Evelyn Bingham	√		WJ	6	2	22	Fa 81	44
Tapestry: Contemporary	Aaklae Weaving	Mundal, Maria	√	√	H&C	5	1		Wi 53	20
Tapestry, Contemporary	American Tapestry Alliance, The	Rolingson, Beth	√		WJ	12	1	45	Su 87	32
Tapestry: Contemporary	Anastazija Tamosaitis	Matranga, Victoria	√		SS&D	17	3	67	Su 86	54
Tapestry, Contemporary	Ann Mitchell: Tapestry-Maker	Dishongh, Suzanne	√		Fa	5	2		M/A 78	53
Tapestry: Contemporary	Betty Williams: Colors of the Earth	Robbins, Judy	√		SS&D	18	4	72	Fa 87	57
Tapestry: Contemporary	Carmo Portela, Portuguese Tapestry Weaver	Portela, Carmo	√		SS&D	17	4	68	Fa 86	35
Tapestry: Contemporary	"Contemporary Japanese Tapestry, The" (Exhibit)	Glass, Laurie H.	√		Fa	4	6		N/D 77	22
Tapestry: Contemporary	Contemporary Navajo Weaving	Hedlund, Ann Lane	√		WJ	11	1	41	Su 86	30
Tapestry: Contemporary	Contemporary Tapestries, A Midwest Designer's Approach	McDaniel, Claribel	√		H&C	13	1		Wi 62	9
Tapestry: Contemporary	Contemporary Tapestry	Byers, Pat	√		TM			6	A/S 86	24
Tapestry: Contemporary	Contemporary Tapestry	Tidball, Harriet	√	√	SCGM		12		64	1-46
Tapestry: Contemporary	Contemporary Tapestry	Tidball, Harriet	√	√	SCGM		12		64	30
Tapestry: Contemporary	Contemporary Tapestry: A Panoramic View (error-corrected SS&D v17 n3 86 p5)	Harvey, Nancy	√		SS&D	17	2	66	Sp 86	18
Tapestry: Contemporary	Contemporary Tapestry in Japan: Individuality After Centuries of Textile Conformity	Lindenfeld, Lore	√		Fa	10	3		M/J 83	44
Tapestry: Contemporary	Contemporary Tapestry: On Looms, Warping, Setting Up Tapestry Study Course — Part 1	O'Callaghan, Kate	√	√	WJ	4	3	15	Ja 80	41
Tapestry, Contemporary	Corporate Collecting "Contemporary Tapestries" (Exhibit)	Dyer, Carolyn	√		Fa	4	5		S/O 77	16
Tapestry: Contemporary	Corporate Commission, The	Creager, Clara	√	√	SS&D	16	1	61	Wi 84	38
Tapestry, Contemporary	"Cynthia Schira" (Exhibit)	Park, Betty	√		Fa	5	3		M/J 78	13
Tapestry, Contemporary	Dilys Stinson: Tapestry Maker	Mathews-Pulleyn, Kathryn	√		Fa	4	5		S/O 77	22
Tapestry: Contemporary	Dovecot Studios	Soroka, Joanne	√		SS&D	12	4	48	Fa 81	36
Tapestry, Contemporary	Dream Weaver: Joan Renne		√		WJ	12	1	45	Su 87	40
Tapestry, Contemporary	"Ellie Fidler — Tapestries" (Exhibit)	Tanenbaum, Ruth	√		Fa	5	4		J/A 78	14
Tapestry: Contemporary	Eva Anttila of Finland		√		H&C	15	1		Wi 64	16
Tapestry: Contemporary	Garrido, Contemporary Spanish Tapestry Weaver		√		H&C	16	1		Wi 65	12
Tapestry, Contemporary	Handwoven Tapestries Become Practical	Nixon, Elaine P.	√		WJ	6	1	21	Su 81	15
Tapestry, Contemporary	Helena Hernmarck: An Interview		√		Fa	5	2		M/A 78	32
Tapestry, Contemporary	Ice Tapestries: The Environmental Art of Phyllis Dukes	Scarborough, Jessica	√		Fa	6	5		S/O 79	26
Tapestry, Contemporary	Imagery Is Personal in Tapestry Today	Clausen, Valerie	√		TM			9	F/M 87	66
Tapestry, Contemporary	Jacquard Tapestries of Boris Kroll, The		√		SS&D	12	2	46	Sp 81	47
Tapestry, Contemporary	Letter from Japan	Schrieber, Lavonne	√		WJ	12	1	45	Su 87	54
Tapestry, Contemporary	Michelle Lester	Preston, P. K.	√		Fa	5	2		M/A 78	48
Tapestry: Contemporary	Modern Norwegian Tapestries	Longbers, Ingeborg	√		H&C	5	1		Wi 53	12
Tapestry: Contemporary	Modern Tapestry on the New S. S. Andrea Doria	Storey, Walter Rendell	√		H&C	4	3		Su 53	35
Tapestry: Contemporary	Nicaraguan Tapestries	Branfman, Judy	√		TM			8	D/J 86	14

SUBJECT	TITLE	AUTHOR	IL	INST	JOUR	VOL	NO	ISS	DATE	PAGE
Tapestry: Contemporary	Open Tapestries by Lynn Alexander	Bryan, Dorothy	√		H&C	4	3		Su 53	30
Tapestry: Contemporary	Painters at the Loom		√		H&C	5	4		Fa 54	19
Tapestry: Contemporary	Picasso, The Weaver		√		SS&D	11	4	44	Fa 80	15
Tapestry: Contemporary	Pictorial Tapestry: A Portfolio of Contemporary Work	Goodman, Deborah Lerme	√		Fa	10	3		M/J 83	29
Tapestry, Contemporary	Polish Art Weaving 1960-1976		√		SS&D	9	1	33	Wi 77	120
Tapestry, Contemporary	Ramah Navajo Weavers, The	D'Andrea, Pat	√		WJ	12	1	45	Su 87	44
Tapestry: Contemporary	Rubik Reworked	Reesor, Tracy	√		SS&D	14	3	55	Su 83	98
Tapestry: Contemporary	Sheila Hicks	Holtzer, Marilyn Emerson	√		SS&D	16	1	61	Wi 84	43
Tapestry, Contemporary	Statement of My Ideas	O'Callaghan, Kate	√		WJ	5	4	20	Sp 81	35
Tapestry: Contemporary	Stones & Symbols	McGillveray, Brenda	√		SS&D	18	1	69	Wi 86	71
Tapestry: Contemporary	Tapestries	Yoors, Jan	√		H&C	5	1		Wi 53	18
Tapestry: Contemporary	Tapestry and Today's Weavers		√	√	H&C	5	1		Wi 53	4
Tapestry: Contemporary	Tapestry (Part 3): An Inside View	Harvey, Nancy	√	√	SS&D	15	2	58	Sp 84	20
Tapestry: Contemporary	Tapestry Today as Seen by Hal Painter				H&C	20	2		Sp 69	20
Tapestry: Contemporary	Tree of Life	Renee, Paula	√		SS&D	17	2	66	Sp 86	80
Tapestry, Contemporary	Twelve Part Harmony: Taos Tapestry Collective		√		WJ	12	1	45	Su 87	48
Tapestry: Contemporary	Twentieth Century Aubusson Tapestries		√		H&C	1	2		Su 50	10
Tapestry, Contemporary	Victor Jacoby: Rich Colors and Bold Designs	Kahn, Kathy; Susan Larson-Fleming	√		WJ	12	1	45	Su 87	36
Tapestry: Contemporary	Watercolors in Fiber: The Flower Tapestries of Sondra MacLeod	LeMaistre, Margaret	√		SS&D	17	3	67	Su 86	21
Tapestry: Contemporary	Weaving As an Olympic Event	Falls, Lynne Cowe	√		SS&D	19	1	73	Wi 87	10
Tapestry, Contemporary	Yosemite Dress Inspired by Snow and Sugar Pines	Durr, Judy	√		SS&D	5	3	19	Su 74	20
Tapestry: Coptic	Coptic Tapestry of Byzantine Style, A	Berliner, Rudolf	√		TMJ	1	1		No 62	3
Tapestry: Coptic	Remarks on Some Tapestries from Egypt	Berliner, Rudolf	√		TMJ	1	4		De 65	20
Tapestry: Cross-Weave	Cross-Weave Tapestry (Aslaug Sverrisdóttir)		√	√	Hw	8	3		M/J 87	67, I-15
Tapestry: Egypt	Tapestries from Egypt Influenced by Theatrical Performances	Berliner, Rudolf	√		TMJ	1	3		De 64	35
Tapestry, Embroidered	Embroidered Life, An (error-corrected Fa v7 n4 80 p6)	Alonso, Harriet	√		Fa	7	3		M/J 80	66
Tapestry: French	Weaving in San Francisco — Part 2	Prosser, Evelyn Bingham	√	√	WJ	6	3	23	Wi 81	50
Tapestry: Gobelins	Bringing Tapestry into the 20th Century	Mattera, Joanne	√		TM			1	O/N 85	48
Tapestry: Gobelins	Contemporary Tapestry	Tidball, Harriet			SCGM		12		64	27
Tapestry: Gobelins	Gobelin Tapestries	Frech, Mary L.	√		H&C	26	1		J/F 75	12
Tapestry: Gobelins	Gobelins Royal Tapestry Works: Tradition and Change in France	Rex, Chris	√		Fa	10	3		M/J 83	58
Tapestry: Gobelins	In the Gobelin Tradition: The Drouin Atelier	Gregg, Dorothy	√		SS&D	10	1	37	Wi 78	28
Tapestry: Gobelins	Painters at the Loom		√		H&C	5	4		Fa 54	19
Tapestry: Gobelins	Scheuer Tapestry Studio: Applying Old Techniques to New Ideas, The	Scheuer, Ruth Tannenbaum	√		Fa	10	3		M/J 83	39
Tapestry: Gobelins	Tapestry, Dwight D. Eisenhower Library		√		H&C	15	1		Wi 64	31
Tapestry: Gobelins	Tapestry Room from Croome Court, The		√		H&C	11	3		Su 60	30
Tapestry: Gobelins	Two Weeks In The South of France: At a Gobelins Tapestry Workshop	Lucas, Mary	√		Fa	8	4		J/A 81	38
Tapestry: Gobelins	Weaving in San Francisco — Part 1	Prosser, Evelyn Bingham	√		WJ	6	2	22	Fa 81	44
Tapestry: Gros Point	Totems in Tapestry	Swingle, Daphne	√		H&C	22	2		Sp 71	5
Tapestry, Henry Moore	Henry Moore: A New Dimension: The Translation of Watercolors from Paper to Tapestry	Goodman, Deborah Lerme	√		Fa	11	2		M/A 84	62
Tapestry, Henry Moore	Weaving the Tapestries, A First-Person Account	Stinson, Dilys	√		Fa	11	2		M/A 84	64
Tapestry, Henry Moore	West Dean and the Tapestry Studio	Sarginson, Peter			Fa	11	2		M/A 84	65
Tapestry: Hooked	Vera Grosowsky: Through the Surface	Paine, Frank	√		Fa	10	4		J/A 83	18

717

SUBJECT	TITLE	AUTHOR	IL	INST	JOUR	VOL	NO	ISS	DATE	PAGE
Tapestry: Islamic-Style Development	More About the Developing Islamic Style in Tapestries	Berliner, Rudolf	√		TMJ	2	1		De 66	3
Tapestry: Linen	Portfolio: Why I Work in Linen, A		√		Fa	14	2		M/A 87	38
Tapestry: Materials	Contemporary Tapestry	Tidball, Harriet		√	SCGM		12		64	4
Tapestry, Medieval, Unicorn	Tapestry Masterpieces		√		SS&D	5	2	18	Sp 74	93
Tapestry: Mexico	Heritage in Tapestry, A	Arvonio, John	√		H&C	23	4		J/A 72	9
Tapestry, Mini	"Mini Tapestry Exhibit" (Exhibit)	Bockelman, JoAnne	√		Fa	5	4		J/A 78	12
Tapestry, Miniature	Riis, Mafong Collaborate in Thread & Silver		√		SS&D	5	1	17	Wi 73	4
Tapestry: Navajo	Navajo Tapestry	Keasbey, Doramay			SS&D	1	3	3	Ju 70	23
Tapestry: Navajo	Navajo: Textiles, Blankets, Rugs, Tapestries	Morrow, Mable	√	√	SS&D	1	4	4	Se 70	3
Tapestry: Needlework	Embroidered Sambas of Madeleine Colaço, The	Mathews, Kate	√		Fa	14	5		N/D 87	34
Tapestry, Nicaraguan	Political Arguing				TM			10	A/M 87	4
Tapestry: Peruvian	Chinese Influence in Colonial Peruvian Tapestries	Cammann, Schuyler	√		TMJ	1	3		De 64	21
Tapestry: Peruvian	General Patterson's Tapestry	Sellschopp, Dr. E. A.	√		TMJ	2	4		De 69	2
Tapestry: Peruvian	Tiahuanaco Tapestry Design	Sawyer, Alan R.	√		TMJ	1	2		De 63	27
Tapestry: Portraits	Portraits by a Weaver		√		SS&D	8	4	32	Fa 77	38
Tapestry: Rag	Ragtime	Erickson, Johanna	√	√	SS&D	14	3	55	Su 83	41
Tapestry: Roman	Tapestries	Trilling, James	√		TMJ	21			82	29
Tapestry Roundel	Tapestry Roundel with Nilotic Scenes, A	Abdel-Malek, Laila	√		TMJ	25			86	33
Tapestry Roundels, Coptic	Horsemen in Tapestry Roundels Found in Egypt	Berliner, Rudolf	√		TMJ	1	2		De 63	39
Tapestry: Rugs	Hand Woven Rugs: Weaves, Plain Weave, Tapestry Techniques	Atwater, Mary Meigs	√	√	SCGM		29		48	11
Tapestry: Supplies	Weaving in San Francisco — Part 2	Prosser, Evelyn Bingham	√	√	WJ	6	3	23	Wi 81	50
Tapestry Techniques	Helena Hernmarck: An Interview		√		Fa	5	2		M/A 78	32
Tapestry Techniques	Aklae: Norwegian Tapestry	Irlbeck, Sonja	√	√	WJ	8	1	29	Su 83	27
Tapestry Techniques	Blue-Bleak Embers	Colton, Mary Rawcliffe	√	√	WJ	8	4	32	Sp 84	16
Tapestry Techniques	Bringing Tapestry into the 20th Century	Mattera, Joanne	√	√	TM			1	O/N 85	52
Tapestry Techniques	Clasped Weft, or "Meet-and-Separate"		√		Hw	3	1		Ja 82	35
Tapestry Techniques	Contemporary Tapestry	Tidball, Harriet	√	√	SCGM		12		64	19
Tapestry Techniques	Contemporary Tapestry	Tidball, Harriet	√	√	SCGM		12		64	30
Tapestry Techniques	Experimenting in Tapestry and Wall Hanging Techniques	Blumenau, Lili	√	√	H&C	14	3		Su 63	18
Tapestry Techniques	Exploring Wedge Weave	Mattera, Joanne	√	√	Iw	3	2		Wi 78	24
Tapestry Techniques	Fingernail Weaving: The Crystallized Art of Patience	Kinoshita, Takeshi	√	√	SS&D	13	1	49	Wi 81	26
Tapestry Techniques	Hopi Embroidery Weave As a Technique for Tapestry	Atwood, Betty	√	√	WJ	5	1	17	Su 80	37
Tapestry Techniques	Idea Notebook, An	Ligon, Linda	√	√	Iw	4	2		Sp 79	38
Tapestry Techniques	Introduction to Tapestry, An (error-corrected SS&D v8 n2 77 p51)	Pierucci, Louise	√	√	SS&D	7	4	28	Fa 76	69
Tapestry Techniques	Introduction to Tapestry, Part 2, An	Pierucci, Louise	√	√	SS&D	8	1	29	WI 76	73
Tapestry Techniques	Krossvefnadur (rölakan) – A Nordic Tapestry Technique		√	√	Hw	8	3		M/J 87	66
Tapestry Techniques	Meet-and-Separate Technique	Martin, Mary	√	√	WJ	8	4	32	Sp 84	14
Tapestry Techniques	New Zealand Tapestry	Lough, Ida	√		H&C	19	3		Su 68	20
Tapestry Techniques	Painters at the Loom		√		H&C	5	4		Fa 54	19
Tapestry Techniques	Pile Weaves, Rugs and Tapestry: True Tapestry and Rugs	Zielinski, S. A.; Robert Leclerc, ed.		√	MWL	14			'51–'73	76
Tapestry Techniques	Ruth Clark, Tapestry Weaver	Olson, Mabel C.	√	√	H&C	9	1		Wi 57	29
Tapestry Techniques	Solving the Circle	Mattera, Joanne	√	√	SS&D	7	1	25	Wi 75	67
Tapestry Techniques	Tapestries from Indonesia	Hitchcock, Michael	√	√	WJ	12	1	45	Su 87	55
Tapestry Techniques	Tapestry		√	√	Hw	3	1		Ja 82	34

SUBJECT	TITLE	AUTHOR	IL	INST	JOUR	VOL	NO	ISS	DATE	PAGE
Tapestry Techniques	Tapestry	Harvey, Nancy	√	√	SS&D	14	3	55	Su 83	20
Tapestry Techniques	Tapestry and Today's Weavers		√	√	H&C	5	1		Wi 53	4
Tapestry: Techniques	Tapestry Gunner	Henry, Patti	√	√	TM			7	O/N 86	40
Tapestry Techniques	Tapestry Tips—Part 1	Harvey, Nancy	√	√	WJ	12	1	45	Su 87	13
Tapestry Techniques	Tapestry Tips, Part 2	Harvey, Nancy	√	√	WJ	12	2	46	Fa 87	9
Tapestry Techniques	Tapestry Weaving with Unspun Flax	Westerink, Claire	√	√	WJ	11	2	42	Fa 86	49
Tapestry Techniques	Techniques of Tapestry Weaves Part 2: Making a Sampler	O'Callaghan, Kate	√	√	WJ	4	4	16	Ap 80	45
Tapestry Techniques	Techniques of Tapestry Weaves Part 3: Shading and Other Matters	O'Callaghan, Kate	√	√	WJ	5	1	17	Su 80	29
Tapestry Techniques	Techniques of Tapestry Weaves Part 4: Developing Design for Tapestry	O'Callaghan, Kate	√	√	WJ	5	2	18	Fa 80	15
Tapestry Techniques	Textiles of Coptic Egypt	Hoskins, Nancy Arthur	√	√	WJ	12	1	45	Su 87	58
Tapestry Techniques	Variations On A Landes Theme	Coutts, Lucele	√	√	WJ	8	4	32	Sp 84	24
Tapestry Techniques	Weaving in San Francisco — Part 2	Prosser, Evelyn Bingham	√	√	WJ	6	3	23	Wi 81	50
Tapestry Techniques	Why Do I Weave Tapestries? An Exploration of Color Theory and Tapestry Design (error-corrected Fa v7 n6 80 p8)	Griffey, Margaret	√		Fa	7	4		J/A 80	55
Tapestry Techniques: Dovetail	Shaped Tapestry Bags from the Nazca-Ica Area of Peru	Bird, Junius B.	√		TMJ	1	3		De 64	2
Tapestry Techniques: Gobelins	Tapestry by Allan Porter		√		H&C	14	2		Sp 63	13
Tapestry Techniques: Hatching	Hatching	Marston, Ena	√	√	SS&D	10	3	39	Su 79	56
Tapestry Techniques: Interlocked	Technical Features of a Middle Horizon Tapestry Shirt from Peru, The	Bird, Junius B.; Milica Dimitrijevic Skinner	√		TMJ	4	1		De 74	5
Tapestry Techniques: Interlocked	Textile Evidence for Huari Music	Rowe, Ann Pollard	√		TMJ	18			79	5
Tapestry Techniques: Interlocked, Discontinuous Wefts	Technical Features of Inca Tapestry Tunics	Rowe, Ann Pollard	√		TMJ	17			78	5
Tapestry Techniques: Mexican	Study Opportunities: Mexican Tapestry Weaving in San Miguel	de la Garza, Phyllis	√		Hw	3	1		Ja 82	62
Tapestry Techniques: Pile Weave	Techniques of Tapestry Weaves Part 2: Making a Sampler	O'Callaghan, Kate	√	√	WJ	4	4	16	Ap 80	45
Tapestry Techniques: Rolag	Pile Weaves, Rugs and Tapestry: Rolag Tapestry	Zielinski, S. A.; Robert Leclerc, ed.		√	MWL	14			'51–'73	83
Tapestry Techniques: Slit	Techniques of Tapestry Weaves Part 2: Making a Sampler	O'Callaghan, Kate	√	√	WJ	4	4	16	Ap 80	45
Tapestry Techniques: Slit	Vest With Slits Made of Five Tapestry Strips	De Bone, Mary	√	√	SS&D	5	2	18	Sp 74	83
Tapestry Techniques: Slit-Tapestry	Kurdish Kilim Weaving in the Van-Hakkari District of Eastern Turkey	Landreau, Anthony N.	√	√	TMJ	3	4		De 73	27
Tapestry Techniques: Slopes	Techniques of Tapestry Weaves Part 2: Making a Sampler	O'Callaghan, Kate	√	√	WJ	4	4	16	Ap 80	45
Tapestry Techniques: Tabby	Techniques of Tapestry Weaves Part 2: Making a Sampler	O'Callaghan, Kate	√	√	WJ	4	4	16	Ap 80	45
Tapestry Techniques: Wedge Weave	Techniques of Tapestry Weaves Part 2: Making a Sampler	O'Callaghan, Kate	√	√	WJ	4	4	16	Ap 80	45
Tapestry Techniques: Wedge Weave	Wedge Weave: A New Approach	Noble, Carol Rasmussen	√	√	WJ	5	2	18	Fa 80	49
Tapestry Traditions: Ireland	Ballinskelligs Tapestry Works: Ancient Art/Modern Spirit, The	Burkhauser, Jude	√		Hw	3	1		Ja 82	55
Tapestry: Twill	Progression of Ideas, or The Shortest Distance Between 2 Ideas is a Diagonal Line, A		√		Iw	6	1		Wi 80	35
Tapestry: Twill	Sunrise Titles and Twills		√		Iw	6	1		Wi 80	38
Tapestry: Uses	Idea Notebook, An	Ligon, Linda	√	√	Iw	4	2		Sp 79	38
Tapestry: Warp-Faced, Stuffed	Commercial Establishment Discovers Fiber Arts, The	Jacopetti, Alexandra	√	√	SS&D	8	2	30	Sp 77	4
Tapestry Wearables	Tapestries to Wear	Mayer, Anita Luvera	√	√	Hw	5	5		N/D 84	54
Tapestry Weaver	Aubusson Tapestry	Larochette, Jean-Pierre	√		SS&D	13	4	52	Fa 82	5
Tapestry Weaver	Kumiko Murashima: The East and West of Weaving	Balassa, Eva	√		Fa	6	1		J/F 79	17
Tapestry Weaver	Legend of Maui and the Sun, The		√		SS&D	1	3	3	Ju 70	3

SUBJECT	TITLE	AUTHOR	IL	INST	JOUR	VOL	NO	ISS	DATE	PAGE
Tapestry Weaver	Maria Mundal — Visualized Melodies		√		SS&D	2	3	7	Su 71	20
Tapestry Weaver	Old World Discipline — New World Markets	Chmielewska, Monika	√		SS&D	11	1	41	Wi 79	4
Tapestry Weavers	Acadians Honor Tapestry Master	Whitney, Gladys	√		SS&D	6	4	24	Fa 75	7
Tapestry Weavers	Alice Parrott	Davis, Mary Woodard	√		Iw	2	1		Fa 76	6
Tapestry Weavers	Dalsgaard Tapestries, The	Clement, Doris W.	√		H&C	17	1		Wi 66	6
Tapestry Weavers	Dream Weaver: Joan Renne		√		WJ	12	1	45	Su 87	40
Tapestry Weavers	Eia Lampe Advocates Classical Weaving Techniques for Today		√		H&C	17	2		Sp 66	6
Tapestry Weavers	Eva Anttila of Finland		√		H&C	15	1		Wi 64	16
Tapestry Weavers	Four Seasons, Tapestries by Bernardi, The	Marston, Ena	√		H&C	20	2		Sp 69	8
Tapestry Weavers	Garrido, Contemporary Spanish Tapestry Weaver		√		H&C	16	1		Wi 65	12
Tapestry Weavers	Gil Fernandez: Light and Color	Ligon, Linda	√		Iw	2	1		Fa 76	8
Tapestry Weavers	Letter from Japan	Schrieber, Lavonne	√		WJ	12	1	45	Su 87	54
Tapestry Weavers	Linda Fox La France: Designer — Tapestry Weaver	Hunt, Elizabeth Ann	√		Iw	4	2		Sp 79	36
Tapestry Weavers	Marg Johansen, An American Represented in International Tapestry Show		√		H&C	17	1		Wi 66	20
Tapestry Weavers	Maria Mundal, Tapestry Weaver		√		H&C	12	3		Su 61	44
Tapestry Weavers	Midwest Tapestry Weaver	Wallace, Lysbeth	√		H&C	11	1		Wi 60	18
Tapestry Weavers	New Directions for Jan Yoors: Tapestry Weaver Now Known as Author and Photographer		√		H&C	18	4		Fa 67	6
Tapestry Weavers	Olga Amaral, A Colombian Weaver's Year in the United States		√		H&C	18	4		Fa 67	20
Tapestry Weavers	Ronald Cruickshank, Scottish Tapestry Weaver		√		H&C	13	2		Sp 62	18
Tapestry Weavers	Spirit of New Mexico: It Comes Alive in Weaving, The		√		SS&D	7	2	26	Sp 76	4
Tapestry Weavers	Tapestries of Muriel Nezhnie Helfman	Salter, Deborah	√		H&C	23	5		S/O 72	43
Tapestry Weavers	Tapestry Gallery		√		Iw	4	2		Sp 79	28
Tapestry Weavers	Tapestry (Part 3): An Inside View	Harvey, Nancy	√	√	SS&D	15	2	58	Sp 84	20
Tapestry Weavers	Tapestry Weavers of Edinburgh, The	Lister, John A.	√		H&C	12	1		Wi 61	22
Tapestry Weavers	Twelve Part Harmony: Taos Tapestry Collective		√		WJ	12	1	45	Su 87	48
Tapestry Weavers	Victor Jacoby: Rich Colors and Bold Designs	Kahn, Kathy; Susan Larson-Fleming	√		WJ	12	1	45	Su 87	36
Tapestry Weavers	Woven Murals	Mulders, Lydia	√		H&C	13	2		Sp 62	22
Tapestry Weaving	Africa Inspires a Weaver	Gawne, Arlene	√		SS&D	16	3	63	Su 85	46
Tapestry Weaving	Approach to Tapestry Weaving, An	Brostoff, Laya	√		Iw	4	2		Sp 79	27
Tapestry Weaving	Ballinskelligs Tapestry Works: Ancient Art/Modern Spirit, The	Burkhauser, Jude	√		Hw	3	1		Ja 82	55
Tapestry Weaving	Barn Raising Experience, A	Bujnowski, Donald	√	√	SS&D	8	4	32	Fa 77	100
Tapestry Weaving	Boston Seven	Newman, Rochelle	√		SS&D	16	3	63	Su 85	71
Tapestry Weaving	Bright Styles from the North	Kaplow, Roberta	√		SS&D	16	1	61	Wi 84	23
Tapestry Weaving	Cartoon, The	Brostoff, Laya	√	√	Hw	3	1		Ja 82	26
Tapestry Weaving	Children's Corner: A Picture Frame Tapestry	Champion, Ellen	√	√	WJ	4	1	13	Jy 79	19
Tapestry Weaving	Circular Loom, The	Cranston-Bennett, Mary Ellen	√	√	H&C	17	1		Wi 66	12
Tapestry Weaving	Clasped Weft Mats		√	√	Hw	3	1		Ja 82	35, 84
Tapestry Weaving	Contemporary Tapestry	Tidball, Harriet	√	√	SCGM		12		64	16
Tapestry Weaving	Cushion Creations	Speth, Lottie	√	√	SS&D	15	1	57	Wi 83	38
Tapestry Weaving	Desert Tapestry Vest	Jennings, Lucy Anne	√	√	WJ	12	1	45	Su 87	52
Tapestry Weaving	Desert Triptych: Three Tapestry Pillows (Carol Kampert)		√	√	Hw	3	1		Ja 82	Cover, 89

SUBJECT	TITLE	AUTHOR	IL	INST	JOUR	VOL	NO	ISS	DATE	PAGE
Tapestry Weaving	Dirk Holger and Grau-Garriga: The Legacy of Lurçat	Broderson, Jan	√		H&C	22	3		Su 71	10
Tapestry Weaving	Distort, Rearrange, Combine	Crockett, Candace	√		SS&D	5	2	18	Sp 74	20
Tapestry Weaving	Dovecot Studios	Soroka, Joanne	√		SS&D	12	4	48	Fa 81	36
Tapestry Weaving	Dream Weaver: Joan Renne		√		WJ	12	1	45	Su 87	40
Tapestry Weaving	Dress Yoke and Cuffs (Linda Ligon)		√	√	Hw	3	1		Ja 82	27, 87
Tapestry Weaving	Egyptian Tapestries By the Children of Harrania	Davis, Peter	√		H&C	14	4		Fa 63	9
Tapestry Weaving	Ellie Fidler: The Power of Concentration	Cooke, Leslie	√		Fa	7	2		M/A 80	48
Tapestry Weaving	Flat Tapestry Cartoon — Ready to Go, A	Swendeman, Dorothy	√	√	Hw	3	1		Ja 82	30
Tapestry Weaving	Gifts from Ancient Peru	Nass, Ulla	√	√	WJ	8	1	29	Su 83	32
Tapestry Weaving	Hal Painter, Weaver of Tapestries and Rugs		√		H&C	16	3		Su 65	10
Tapestry Weaving	Handspuns for Tapestries	Szumski, Norma; Phyllis Clemmer; Clotilde Barrett	√		WJ	6	2	22	Fa 81	41
Tapestry Weaving	Happy Dress	Sprenger, Elserine	√	√	WJ	8	3	31	Wi 83	46
Tapestry Weaving	Harmony by Contrast	Newman, Rochelle	√		SS&D	14	3	55	Su 83	92
Tapestry Weaving	Harts and Flowers: Sweden's Märta Määs-Fjetterstrom's Designs Inspired a Textile Renaissance	Selkurt, Claire	√		WJ	9	4	36	Sp 85	30
Tapestry Weaving	Home Weaving: A Trio of Rugs		√	√	Hw	1	1		F-W 79	30
Tapestry Weaving	In the Gobelin Tradition: The Drouin Atelier	Gregg, Dorothy	√		SS&D	10	1	37	Wi 78	28
Tapestry Weaving	Indian Textiles from Ecuador		√		H&C	10	1		Wi 59	19
Tapestry Weaving	Inlay Techniques	Barrett, Clotilde	√	√	WJ	1	1	1	Jy 76	3
Tapestry Weaving	Inner Visions	May, April D.	√		SS&D	15	3	59	Su 84	57
Tapestry Weaving	Introduction to Tapestry, An (error-corrected SS&D v8 n2 77 p51)	Pierucci, Louise	√	√	SS&D	7	4	28	Fa 76	69
Tapestry Weaving	Introduction to Tapestry, Part 2, An	Pierucci, Louise	√	√	SS&D	8	1	29	WI 76	73
Tapestry Weaving	Journey in Progress, A	Chittenden, Annie Curtis	√	√	SS&D	17	4	68	Fa 86	50
Tapestry Weaving	Julia Mitchell: On Martha's Vineyard	Erickson, Johanna	√		SS&D	15	3	59	Su 84	60
Tapestry Weaving	Kente: The Status Cloth of Ghana	Conklin, Sharon L.	√	√	SS&D	8	1	29	WI 76	18
Tapestry Weaving	Los Tejedorcitos De San Isidro		√		SS&D	6	1	21	Wi 74	80
Tapestry Weaving	Low Budget Tapestry Loom, A	Gilstrap, Bill; Sara Gilstrap	√	√	WJ	5	4	20	Sp 81	42
Tapestry Weaving	Margareta Ohberg, From Sweden to a Long Career in America		√		H&C	12	3		Su 61	17
Tapestry Weaving	Maria Mundal, Tapestry Weaver		√		H&C	12	3		Su 61	44
Tapestry Weaving	My Life	Weldon, Lynn L.	√	√	WJ	2	2	6	Oc 77	11
Tapestry Weaving	Notes for a Potential Tapestry Weaver	Schira, Cynthia	√	√	H&C	19	4		Fa 68	12
Tapestry Weaving	Plain Weave — Plane Weave	Carey, Joyce Marquess	√	√	PWC	3	4	10		56
Tapestry Weaving	Planting Seeds	Greene, Susan	√		Hw	5	3		Su 84	40
Tapestry Weaving	Poppana Tapestry Jacket (Jean Scorgie)		√	√	Hw	4	3		M/J 83	48, 84
Tapestry Weaving	Reinterpreting Rya: Irma Kukkasjärvi Energizes an Ancient Technique	Ojala, Liisa Kanning	√		WJ	9	4	36	Sp 85	26
Tapestry Weaving	Return to Basic Disciplines	Stark, Ruthellen	√		SS&D	2	1	5	De 70	10
Tapestry Weaving	Roman Textiles from Vindolanda, Hexham, England	Wild, John Peter	√		TMJ	18			79	19
Tapestry Weaving	Ronald Cruickshank, Scottish Tapestry Weaver		√		H&C	13	2		Sp 62	18
Tapestry Weaving	Ruth Bilowus: Small and Precious Tapestries	Belfer, Nancy	√		Fa	7	2		M/A 80	15
Tapestry Weaving	Self-Portrait	Rubin, Deann Joy	√		SS&D	15	1	57	Wi 83	72
Tapestry Weaving	Shaped Sculptured Rugs — A Workshop with Urban Jupena		√	√	WJ	4	1	13	Jy 79	5
Tapestry Weaving	Silvia Heyden: I Think of the Weft as a Violin Bow	Heyman, Dorothy	√		Fa	6	2		M/A 79	46

SUBJECT	TITLE	AUTHOR	IL	INST	JOUR	VOL	NO	ISS	DATE	PAGE
Tapestry Weaving	Sirkka Ahlskog — Versatile Craftsman		√		H&C	9	4		Fa 58	30
Tapestry Weaving	Stones & Symbols	McGillveray, Brenda	√		SS&D	18	1	69	Wi 86	71
Tapestry Weaving	Sylvia Heyden		√		SS&D	14	4	56	Fa 83	42
Tapestry Weaving	Talk with Josep Grau-Garriga, A	Kurtz, Carol; B. J. Adams	√		SS&D	9	4	36	Fa 78	4
Tapestry Weaving	Tapestries	Trilling, James	√		TMJ	21			82	29
Tapestry Weaving	Tapestries in Rope	Smith, John	√	√	H&C	17	1		Wi 66	10
Tapestry Weaving	Tapestry	Harvey, Nancy	√	√	SS&D	14	3	55	Su 83	20
Tapestry Weaving	Tapestry: As a Business?	Harvey, Nancy	√	√	SS&D	15	3	59	Su 84	37
Tapestry Weaving	Tapestry Backpack		√	√	WJ	2	2	6	Oc 77	9
Tapestry Weaving	Tapestry (Carol Klippenstein)		√	√	Hw	1	1		F-W 79	23, 55
Tapestry Weaving	Tapestry Face Pillows (Sharon La Pierre)		√	√	SS&D	4	2	14	Sp 73	9
Tapestry Weaving	Tapestry for Interiors	Harvey, Nancy	√		Hw	3	1		Ja 82	42
Tapestry Weaving	Tapestry in Nova Scotia	Black, Mary E.	√	√	H&C	8	3		Su 57	24
Tapestry Weaving	Tapestry in Twill: A Free Approach	Hall, Joanne	√	√	Hw	3	1		Ja 82	46
Tapestry Weaving	Tapestry Inlay for Fool-Proof Designing	Marquardt, Bertha	√	√	SS&D	6	1	21	Wi 74	38
Tapestry Weaving	Tapestry: Its Limitations Challenge Individual Creativity	Harvey, Nancy	√		SS&D	17	1	65	Wi 85	57
Tapestry Weaving	Tapestry: Part 2—The Dreaded Circle	Harvey, Nancy	√	√	SS&D	14	4	56	Fa 83	8
Tapestry Weaving	Tapestry Weaver's Answers, A		√		TM			10	A/M 87	18
Tapestry Weaving	Tapestry Weaving and Design	Crump, Nancy	√	√	Iw	4	2		Sp 79	24
Tapestry Weaving	Tapices of San Pedro de Cajas, Peru, The	Thornton, Sandra K.	√	√	WJ	12	1	45	Su 87	23
Tapestry Weaving	Technique: Painting Weft Threads for Tapestry	Colburn, Carol	√	√	Hw	3	1		Ja 82	58
Tapestry Weaving	Temple Tapestry	Rapp, Sylvia	√		SS&D	15	2	58	Sp 84	24
Tapestry Weaving	Think Big	Lovell-Cooper, Sylvia	√		SS&D	3	1	9	Wi 71	41
Tapestry Weaving	Three English Tapestry Weavers	Liebler, Barbara	√		Hw	3	1		Ja 82	61
Tapestry Weaving	Tina McMorran	Stevens, Bernice A.	√		H&C	15	3		Su 64	14
Tapestry Weaving	Unicorn	Bogdan, Janet	√		SS&D	6	2	22	Sp 75	97
Tapestry Weaving	Uno Mas — The Secret of Mexican Tapestry	Hall, Joanne	√	√	SS&D	5	3	19	Su 74	88
Tapestry Weaving	Variations on a Theme of Marigolds (Görel Kinersly)		√	√	Hw	5	1		J/F 84	81
Tapestry Weaving	Vera Wainar Kopecek: Her Work Stands Alone	Hunt, Elizabeth Ann	√		Fa	7	2		M/A 80	55
Tapestry Weaving	Weaver of Images	Brownlee-Ramsdale, Sandra	√		AT	6			De 86	147
Tapestry Weaving	Weaving in San Francisco — Part 1	Prosser, Evelyn Bingham	√		WJ	6	2	22	Fa 81	44
Tapestry Weaving	Weaving in San Francisco — Part 2	Prosser, Evelyn Bingham	√	√	WJ	6	3	23	Wi 81	50
Tapestry Weaving	Weaving the Tapestries, A First-Person Account	Stinson, Dilys	√		Fa	11	2		M/A 84	64
Tapestry Weaving	West Dean and the Tapestry Studio	Sarginson, Peter			Fa	11	2		M/A 84	65
Tapestry Weaving: Arras	Edinburgh Tapestry Company: A Thriving Anachronism in Scotland, The	Soroka, Joanne	√		Fa	10	3		M/J 83	59
Tapestry Weaving: Aubusson-Style	Yael Lurie — Other Places, Other Visions	Tannenbaum, Ruth	√		Fa	5	6		N/D 78	40
Tapestry Weaving: China	Ko-Ssu	Wilson, Kay	√		H&C	24	4		Au 73	42
Tapestry Weaving: Gobelins	Concerns and Influences in My Work	Kidd, Jane	√		AT	6			De 86	135
Tapestry Weaving: Mexican	Uno Mas — The Secret of Mexican Tapestry	Hall, Joanne	√	√	SS&D	5	3	19	Su 74	88
Tapestry Weaving: Mexico	Study Opportunities: Mexican Tapestry Weaving in San Miguel	de la Garza, Phyllis	√		Hw	3	1		Ja 82	62
Tapestry Weaving: Miniatures	Tapestry Weaving Adapted to Miniature Scale	Clarke, Lois	√		H&C	13	4		Fa 62	10
Tapestry Weaving: Miniatures	To Weave a Tiny Tapestry	Marston, Ena	√	√	H&C	22	2		Sp 71	29
Tapestry Weaving: Twill	Southwest Indian Twill Tapestry	Atwood, Betty	√		WJ	8	1	29	Su 83	35
Tapestry, Weft-Faced	Black & White Rug (Jette Kai)		√	√	Hw	8	3		M/J 87	50, I-8

SUBJECT	TITLE	AUTHOR	IL	INST	JOUR	VOL	NO	ISS	DATE	PAGE
Tapestry, Weft-Faced	Tin & Tapestry Hanging (Elisabeth La Cour)		√	√	Hw	8	3		M/J 87	48, I-9
Tapestry: Wissa Wassef	Tapping the Artist Within: The Wissa Wassef Tapestries		√		H&C	26	3		M/J 75	5
Tappet (Hessian Weave)	Contemporary Fabrics from an Australia Handweaving Mill	Daniel, Robert	√		H&C	16	1		Wi 65	18
Tartan Profiles: Color Sequence	Weaver's Book of Scottish Tartans: The Tartan Profiles, Diagrams of Setts, The	Tidball, Harriet	√	√	SCGM		5		62	26
Tartan Profiles: Sett Diagrams	Weaver's Book of Scottish Tartans: The Tartan Profiles, Diagrams of Setts, The	Tidball, Harriet	√	√	SCGM		5		62	26
Tartan see Checks, Plaids, Tartans										
Tartan Setts	Weaver's Book of Scottish Tartans: The Tartan Setts, Listing of 260 Tartan Setts, The	Tidball, Harriet	√	√	SCGM		5		62	13
Tassels and Tassel Making	Charlotte Attig: Tassel Maker	Holst, Holly P.	√		Fa	9	6		N/D 82	26
Tassels and Tassel Making	Dubbelmossa	Adams, Harriet	√	√	Kn	2	1	3	F-W 85	50, 8B
Tassels and Tassel Making	Guatamalan Finishes	Gotthoffer, Esther	√		H&C	22	1		Wi 71	18
Tassels and Tassel Making	Making Tassels		√	√	TM			3	F/M 86	6
Tassels and Tassel Making	Nasca Sprang Tassels: Structure, Technique, and Order	Frame, Mary	√	√	TMJ	25			86	67
Tassels and Tassel Making	Peru, Textiles Unlimited, Part 2: Tassels	Tidball, Harriet	√	√	SCGM		26		69	43
Tassels and Tassel Making	Splicing from Central America	Sober, Marion B.	√	√	H&C	22	4		Fa 71	18
Tassels and Tassel Making: Tzitzis	Tallis or Prayer Shawl, The	Derr, Mary	√	√	WJ	2	1	5	Jy 77	16
Tassels and Tasselmaking	Tassel Making	Welch, Nancy; Doris Hoover	√	√	Fa	5	6		N/D 78	22
Tatting	Lacy Linen Pillowcase (Linda Ligon)		√	√	Hw	2	5		No 81	58, 81
Tatting	Tatting	Tooker, Dorothy	√		SS&D	17	4	68	Fa 86	74
Tatting Techniques	Tatting	Suter, Betty	√	√	TM			6	A/S 86	64
Taxes	Hobby Businesses in 1986	Battersby, Mark E.	√		Fa	13	3		M/J 86	17
Taxes	Hobby or Business?	Smith, William L.	√		SS&D	18	4	72	Fa 87	44
Taxes	Income Tax for the Craftsman	Illsley, Ednah	√		Iw	2	2		Wi 77	10
Taxes	Tax Tips-Education and Convention Expenses	Smith, William L.	√		SS&D	19	1	73	Wi 87	8
Taxes: Income	Deductions	Ashe, Alan W.			SS&D	2	1	5	De 70	19
Taxes: Income	Deductions When Home Is Used for Business	Ashe, Alan W.			SS&D	1	4	4	Se 70	6
Tea Cosy	Double Woven Tea Cosy		√	> 4	WJ	2	1	5	Jy 77	15
Tea Cozy	Hotpots		√		WJ	3	2	10	Oc 78	5
Tea Cozy	Table Dressing and Bedcovers		√		Fa	8	3		M/J 81	43
Tea Cozy	Tea Cozy, Mats and Napkins (Margaretha Essén-Hedin)		√	> 4	Hw	4	3		M/J 83	41, 93
Tea Cozy	Two for Tea (Sharon Alderman)		√	√	Hw	2	1		F-W 80	42
Teaching see Education: Teaching										
Teasels	Dipsacus Fullonum: Fuller's Teasel		√		WJ	8	2	30	Fa 83	58
Teasels	Hand Teasels and Shears		√		SS&D	2	2	6	Sp 71	18
Teasels	Noble Tradition Preserved: An Ecuadorian Weaving Co-op, A	Llewellyn, Charles; Deborah Llewellyn	√		SS&D	11	3	43	Su 80	12
Teasels	Tämä on Ihana!	Scorgie, Jean	√		Hw	7	1		J/F 86	45
Teasels	Teasel Industry in New York State, The	Jarvis, Helen			SS&D	8	4	32	Fa 77	71
Teasels	Teasel Tools	Antuñez de Mayolo, Kay	√	√	SS&D	13	4	52	Fa 82	10
Teasels	Teasels	Leadbeater, Eliza	√	√	Hw	2	5		No 81	54
Technique Analyses: Illustrations	Handweaver's Instruction Manual: Technique Analyses	Tidball, Harriet C. nee Douglas	√		SCGM		34		49	41
Technology: Color-Copy Machines	Incredible Color Copy Machine, The	Redding, Debbie	√		Hw	2	4		Se 81	74
Technology: Finishing Wool	Superwash Wool	Donnelly, Robert	√		S-O	10	2		Su 86	49
Technology: Man-Made Fibers	Man-Made Fibers	Hausner, Walter	√		WJ	9	3	35	Wi 85	61

SUBJECT	TITLE	AUTHOR	IL	INST	JOUR	VOL	NO	ISS	DATE	PAGE
Technology: Socio-Cultural Aspects	Technological Change and the Textile Industry: The Impact of the Industrial Revolution and the Computer Revolution	Thieme, Otto Charles	√		Fa	11	1		J/F 84	54
Technology: Spinning	Bridging the Gap — Between Large Commercial Mills and Individual Handspinners		√		S-O	5			81	27
Technology: Spinning	Leonardo Da Vinci's Ideas on the Mechanization of Spinning	Born, W.			S-O	2			78	47
Technology: Spinning	Processes of Woollen Thread Construction, The		√		S-O	5			81	30
Technology: Spinning Wheels	Reining in Baby Huey	Centner, Dave, O.C.D.		√	S-O	11	4		Wi 87	18
Technology: Textile Conservation	Techniques in Textile Conservation	Brown, Geoffrey I.	√	√	S-O	10	2		Su 86	45
Technology: Textile Industry	Technological Change and the Textile Industry: The Impact of the Industrial Revolution and the Computer Revolution	Thieme, Otto Charles	√		Fa	11	1		J/F 84	54
Technology: Weaving	High-Tech Comes to Weaving: AVL Looms	Larson, Eden	√		Fa	14	4		S/O 87	36
Technology: Weaving	High-Tech Comes to Weaving: Macomber Looms	Henderson, Stew	√		Fa	14	4		S/O 87	35
Technology: Weaving, China	China and the Complexities of Weaving Technologies	Vollmer, John E.			AT	5			Ju 86	65
Technology: Weaving, Progress	Technical Progress and the Evolution of Wage Arrangements in the British Cotton Weaving Industry	Jackson, K. C.; B. Pourdeyhimi	√		AT	7			Ju 87	61
Templates: Sewing	Perfecting the Pocket	Coffin, David Page	√	√	TM			8	D/J 86	28
Tennessee	Prehistoric Twined Bag from Big Bone Cave, Tennessee: Manufacture, Repair, and Use, A	Kuttruff, Jenna Tedrick	√		AT	8			De 87	125
Tents	Some Unusual Turkish Embroideries of the Early Eighteenth Century	Johnstone, Pauline	√		TMJ	24			85	75
Tents	Tents in History	Austin, Carole	√		Fa	12	4		J/A 85	47
Tents	Traditional Berber Weaving in Central Morocco	Forelli, Sally; Jeanette Harries	√		TMJ	4	4		77	41
Terminology: Embroidery	Perspective on Embroidery: In Answer to Emery, A	From, Dot	√		AT	6			De 86	195
Terminology: Knitting	Knits, Knuckles and Knots	Wolfe, Susan			Kn	2	2	4	S-S 86	4
Terminology: Obsolete, Translating	Weaving in the Past Complete: Old Books — How to Read Them	Zielinski, S. A.; Robert Leclerc, ed.			MWL	21 22			'51–'73	95
Terminology: Sticks, Swords, Battens	Five, Six, Pick-up Sticks		√	√	Hw	7	2		M/A 86	53
Terminology: Twill	Twill Basics		√	√	Hw	6	5		N/D 85	57
Terminology: Weaving	Let's Pull Together	Barrett, Clotilde	√	√	WJ	8	1	29	Su 83	85
Terminology: Weaving	Understanding Weaving Terms	Tidball, Harriet Douglas	√		H&C	2	2		Sp 51	20
Terminology: Weaving	What's in a Name? or: Sticks and Stones Can Break My Bones, but Names Can Sure Confuse Me	Redding, Debbie			Hw	2	2		Mr 81	22
Terminology: Weaving, Hand-Loom, Standardization	Toward Standardizing the Language of the Hand Loom Designer Weaver	Daniels, Parmely Clark			H&C	24	4		Au 73	14
Terry Weave	Terry Weave, or Turkish Towelling	Nyquist, Janet	√	√	SS&D	1	2	2	Mr 70	17
Testing: Fibers	Creative Drafting and Analysis: Analysis of Yarns	Zielinski, S. A.; Robert Leclerc, ed.		√	MWL	3			'51–'73	92
Testing: Fibers	Designing the Warp: Parallel Considerations	Criscola, Jeanne	√	√	TM			1	O/N 85	66
Testing: Fibers	Yarns and Fibers: Analysis of Yarns	Zielinski, S. A.; Robert Leclerc, ed.		√	MWL	4			'51–'73	109
Testing: Fibers	Yarns and Fibers: Yarns for Specialized Production	Zielinski, S. A.; Robert Leclerc, ed.			MWL	4			'51–'73	63
Testing: Fibers, Musk Ox	Summary of Wool Bureau Report on Musk Ox Fiber	Reed, Fran			S-O	7	1		Sp 83	42
Testing: Washfastness	Testing Washfastness		√	√	TM			7	O/N 86	6
Textilatelists	Introduction to Two Textilatelists, An	Allston, J. L.; J. A. Hoskins	√		AT	4			De 85	81

SUBJECT	TITLE	AUTHOR	IL	INST	JOUR	VOL	NO	ISS	DATE	PAGE
Textilately	Comparison of Some Varied Themes	Stanton, R. G.; J. L. Allston	√		AT	2			De 84	217
Textilately	From Fibre to Haute Coutoure on World Postage Stamps	Cysarz, J. M.	√		AT	4			De 85	89
Textilately	Introduction to Two Textilatelists, An	Allston, J. L.; J. A. Hoskins	√		AT	4			De 85	81
Textile Analysis/Classification: Roman Textiles (England)	Roman Textiles from Vindolanda, Hexham, England	Wild, John Peter	√		TMJ	18			79	19
Textile Arts: Denmark	At Home in a Changing World	Talley, Charles	√		Hw	8	3		M/J 87	44
Textile Arts Movement: America	Sense of the Individual, The	Janeiro, Jan	√		Fa	11	2		M/A 84	52
Textile Chronology: Peru	Peru, Textiles Unlimited: Textile Chronology	Tidball, Harriet	√		SCGM		25		68	8
Textile Design, Industrial	Made by Machine: Textiles for the Eighties	Harris, Patricia; David Lyon	√		Fa	12	5		S/O 85	34
Textile Designer	Evolution of an Artist: Pam Turczyn	Turczyn, Pam	√		Fa	14	5		N/D 87	24
Textile Designers	Surface Attraction	Mattera, Joanne	√		TM			7	O/N 86	20
Textile Exhibit Catalogues	Architectures 85: La Tapisserie En France 1945–1985				Hw	7	4		S/O 86	11
Textile Exhibit Catalogues	Courtyard, Bazaar, Temple: Traditions of Textile Expression in India	Hacker, Katherine F.; Krista Jensen Turnbull			Hw	7	4		S/O 86	11
Textile Exhibit Catalogues	Fabrics in Celebration From the Collection of the Indianapolis Museum of Art	Gilfoy, Peggy Stoltz	√		Hw	7	4		S/O 86	11
Textile Exhibit Catalogues	Fibres Art 85 (France)				Hw	7	4		S/O 86	11
Textile Exhibit Catalogues	From the Tree Where the Bark Grows...North American Basket Treasures from the Peabody Museum, Harvard University	Brandford, Joanne Segal	√		Hw	7	4		S/O 86	11
Textile Heritage: Past/Future	Reinterpreting Old Weaves for Today and Tomorrow	Essén-Hedin, Margaretha	√		Hw	8	3		M/J 87	40
Textile Mills: Harrisville Designs	Behind the Scenes: A Textile Mill	Goodman, Deborah Lerme	√		Fa	13	3		M/J 86	40
Textile Painting	Peru, Textiles Unlimited: Tie-Dye, Ikat, Painting	Tidball, Harriet	√		SCGM		25		68	32
Textile Traditions: Acadia	L'Amour de Maman: The Acadian Textile Heritage	Rossetter, Tabitha Wilson	√		Fa	8	3		M/J 81	29
Textile Traditions: Acadians	Acadian Brown Cotton	Exner, Beatrice B.	√		H&C	11	4		Fa 60	22
Textile Traditions: Afghanistan	Afghan Carpets	Spooner, Brian	√		SS&D	5	2	18	Sp 74	41
Textile Traditions: Afghanistan	Yurts (Not Your Average Dwelling)	Landess, Susan	√		Fa	5	6		N/D 78	26
Textile Traditions: Africa	Adinkra: Weft African Textile of Pride	Rex, Chris	√		Fa	9	6		N/D 82	36
Textile Traditions: Africa	African American Thread Fare	White, Marcia	√		Fa	9	6		N/D 82	56
Textile Traditions: Africa	African Artist in a Dying Trade, An	Kessler, Cristina	√	√	Fa	11	6		N/D 84	51
Textile Traditions: Africa	African Textiles	Hempel, Toby Anne	√		SS&D	15	1	57	Wi 83	12
Textile Traditions: Africa	African Textiles	Sieber, Roy	√		H&C	23	6		N/D 72	9
Textile Traditions: Africa	American Sojourn of African Textiles, An	Lonier, Terri	√		Fa	11	1		J/F 84	66
Textile Traditions: Africa	"In Praise of Heroes" (Exhibit)	Malarcher, Patricia	√		Fa	10	1		J/F 83	78
Textile Traditions: Africa	Kente: The Status Cloth of Ghana	Conklin, Sharon L.	√	√	SS&D	8	1	29	WI 76	18
Textile Traditions: Africa	Maridadi West: A Fort Collins, Colorado Fabric Design Studio with Its Roots in East Africa	Mattera, Joanne	√		Fa	9	2		M/A 82	24
Textile Traditions: Africa	Pelete Bite: Kalabari Cut-Thread Cloth	Thieme, Otto Charles	√		Fa	10	5		S/O 83	46
Textile Traditions: Africa	Wealth of Fiber: Nigeria's Adire Cloth , A	Ulrich, George	√		Fa	13	5		S/O 86	39
Textile Traditions: Africa	Weaving in Africa	Cragholm, Lynn	√		H&C	23	1		J/F 72	18
Textile Traditions: Africa	Woven Inspiration from West African Textiles	Renne, Elisha	√	√	WJ	10	4	40	Sp 86	60
Textile Traditions: Africa	Zamani Soweto Sisters: A Patchwork of Lives		√		Fa	10	2		M/A 83	48
Textile Traditions: Afro-American	Ethnic Textile Art at U.C.L.A. — "Afro-American Arts of the Suriname Rain Forest" (Exhibit)	Dyer, Carolyn	√		Fa	8	2		M/A 81	59
Textile Traditions: Akwesasne	"Baskets of Akwesasne" (Exhibit)	Doyle, Claire	√		Fa	11	1		J/F 84	77

SUBJECT	TITLE	AUTHOR	IL	INST	JOUR	VOL	NO	ISS	DATE	PAGE
Textile Traditions: America	American Heritage: Three Rugmaking Traditions, An	Woelfle, Gretchen	√		Fa	7	5		S/O 80	31
Textile Traditions: America	Weaver Rose of Rhode Island 1839–1913	Pariseau, George E., M.D.	√		H&C	6	1		Wi 54	4
Textile Traditions: America, 19th Century	Textiles in Nineteenth-Century America	Glaze, Mary	√		H&C	21	3		Su 70	4
Textile Traditions: Amish	Amish Quilts	Fox, Judy Kellar	√		Fa	10	2		M/A 83	28
Textile Traditions: Amish	Costume of a Plain People, The	Schiess, Kate	√	√	TM			5	J/J 86	65
Textile Traditions: Anasazi	Ridge (Twill) Weave of the Hopi	Nelson, Nanci Neher	√	√	SS&D	14	2	54	Sp 83	52
Textile Traditions: Andes	Color and Design in Andean Warp-Faced Fabrics	Femenias, Blenda	√		WJ	12	2	46	Fa 87	44
Textile Traditions: Andes	Special Andean Tubular Trim—Woven Without Heddles, A	Cahlander, Adele; Ed Franquemont; Barbara Bergman	√	√	WJ	6	3	23	Wi 81	54
Textile Traditions: Andes	Understanding Some Complex Structures from Simple Andean Looms: Steps in Analysis and Reproduction	Cahlander, Adele	√	√	AT	1			De 83	181
Textile Traditions: Andes	Warp-Faced Double Cloth: Adaptation of an Andean Technique for the Treadle Loom	Cahlander, Adele	√	√	WJ	10	4	40	Sp 86	72
Textile Traditions: Andes	Weaving Tradition in the Andes, A	Adelson, Laurie; Bruce Takami	√		Fa	6	4		J/A 79	22
Textile Traditions: Andes, Colombia	Unique Technique for a Braided Strap from Colombia	Cahlander, Adele	√	√	WJ	7	1	25	Su 82	56
Textile Traditions: Antebellum South	Slave Quilts: Threads of History	Grabiner, Dana M.	√		Fa	13	5		S/O 86	22
Textile Traditions: Arab	Original Fabrics of Kaftan, The	El-Homossani, M. M.	√	> 4	AT	1			De 83	263
Textile Traditions: Armenia	Behind the Scenes: A "Missing" Tradition	Goodman, Deborah Lerme	√		Fa	13	3		M/J 86	46
Textile Traditions: Asia	"Common Cord, The": Central Asian Textiles (Exhibit)	Prinzing, Debra	√		Fa	14	3		M/J 87	56
Textile Traditions: Asia	Highland Weavers in Asia	Hatch, David P.	√	√	H&C	11	1		Wi 60	6
Textile Traditions: Asia	Some Contemporary Textiles in Southern Asia	Hatch, David P.	√	√	H&C	11	3		Su 60	23
Textile Traditions: Asia	Weaving in Southeast Asia (addition SS&D v7 n4 76 p27)	Marston, Ena			SS&D	7	2	26	Sp 76	30
Textile Traditions: Basketry	Basketry Techniques: A Sampler (from a 1902 Book)	Mason, Otis Tufton	√		Iw	4	1		Wi 78	26
Textile Traditions: Bedouin	Weaving in the Desert: How Bedouin Women Make a Loom, Using Sticks and Rebars	Erickson, Janet Doub	√	√	TM			10	A/M 87	56
Textile Traditions: Bengal	Kantha	Westfall, Carol D.; Dipti Desai	√	√	AT	7			Ju 87	161
Textile Traditions: Berber	Traditional Berber Weaving in Central Morocco	Forelli, Sally; Jeanette Harries	√		TMJ	4	4		77	41
Textile Traditions: Bolivia	Detective Story: Unravelling the Mystery of a 7-Loop Braid, A	Cahlander, Adele	√	√	WJ	10	1	37	Su 85	12
Textile Traditions: Bolivia	"Fabled Fabrics: Bolivian Fabrics from the Hill Collection" (Exhibit)	Dyer, Carolyn	√		Fa	9	6		N/D 82	84
Textile Traditions: Bolivia	Fullus: Ikat Blankets of Tarabuco, Bolivia	Meisch, Lynn A.	√	√	WJ	10	1	37	Su 85	54
Textile Traditions: Borneo	"Heads and Tales: Traditional Art of Borneo" (Exhibit)	Dyer, Carolyn Price	√		Fa	11	4		J/A 84	74
Textile Traditions: Carpets	London Carpeted in Oriental Gardens: The 4th International Conference on Oriental Carpets	Dyer, Carolyn Price	√		Fa	11	3		M/J 84	66
Textile Traditions: Cherokee	Cherokee Weavers Used Looms Over Two Hundred Years Ago	Coulter, Doris M.	√		H&C	18	3		Su 67	17
Textile Traditions: Cherokee	Doubleweave Basketry of the Cherokees	Ligon, Linda	√		Iw	4	1		Wi 78	28
Textile Traditions: Cherokee	Revival of Cherokee Arts and Crafts, The	Parris, John	√		H&C	4	2		Sp 53	9
Textile Traditions: Chilkat	Breath of Our Grandmothers, The	Samuel, Cheryl	√		WJ	8	1	29	Su 83	17
Textile Traditions: China	China and the Complexities of Weaving Technologies	Vollmer, John E.			AT	5			Ju 86	65
Textile Traditions: China	China: Fiber Arts in the People's Republic	Szumski, Norma J.	√		SS&D	15	1	57	Wi 83	47
Textile Traditions: China	Chinese Artisans At Work	Goodman, Deborah Lerme	√		Fa	13	1		J/F 86	34

SUBJECT	TITLE	AUTHOR	IL	INST	JOUR	VOL	NO	ISS	DATE	PAGE
Textile Traditions: China	"Ch'ing Dynasty Court Robes, A Splendorous Sampling" (Exhibit)	Marcoux, Alice	√		Fa	11	2		M/A 84	78
Textile Traditions: China	Flourishing Art: China, Guizhou Women Continue to Embroider Their Legends, A	Rossi, Gail	√		TM			9	F/M 87	30
Textile Traditions: China	Guizhou Textiles	Rossi, Gail	√		SS&D	18	1	69	Wi 86	39
Textile Traditions: China	Ming Mandarin Squares	Cammann, Schuyler	√		TMJ	4	4		77	5
Textile Traditions: China	Nelson Chang: Champion of Chinese Knotting	Westbrook, John R.,	√		Fa	14	3		M/J 87	6
Textile Traditions: China	Sericulture in Upstate New York	Bard, Elizabeth A.	√		Fa	13	1		J/F 86	36
Textile Traditions: China	"Silk as Ceremony: The Dress of China in the Late Ch'ing Dynasty Period (1759–1911)" (Exhibit)	Mattera, Joanne	√		Fa	8	3		M/J 81	75
Textile Traditions: China	Silk Lore: The Myths of a Magical Fiber	Goodman, Deborah Lerme	√		Fa	13	1		J/F 86	42
Textile Traditions: China	"Silk Roads/China Ships" (Exhibit)	Sider, Sandra	√		Fa	11	4		J/A 84	74
Textile Traditions: Colonial America	Dearest Daughter	Strickler, Carol	√		Hw	3	5		N/D 82	36
Textile Traditions: Coptic Tapestries	Tapestries of Coptic Egypt, The	Hoskins, Nancy Arthur	√		AT	6			De 86	211
Textile Traditions: Crete	Weaving in Crete	Znamierowski, Nell	√		H&C	15	4		Fa 64	8
Textile Traditions: Cuna Indians	Cuna Cachi: A Study of Hammock Weaving Among the Cuna Indians of the San Blas Islands	Lambert, Anne M.	√	√	AT	5			Ju 86	105
Textile Traditions: Cuzco	Weaving Processes in the Cuzco Area of Peru	Rowe, Ann Pollard	√	√	TMJ	4	2		75	30
Textile Traditions: Cyprus	Weavers of Cyprus	Macdonald, Elizabeth	√		H&C	5	4		Fa 54	24
Textile Traditions: Denmark	At Home in a Changing World	Talley, Charles	√		Hw	8	3		M/J 87	44
Textile Traditions: Denmark	Linen Undergarments: A Proud Danish Heritage	Todd-Cope, Louise	√		Fa	14	2		M/A 87	51
Textile Traditions: Ecuador	Indian Textiles from Ecuador		√		H&C	10	1		Wi 59	19
Textile Traditions: Ecuador	Janet Markarian: From Baskets to Bags, Containers Transformed	Koplos, Janet	√		Fa	11	1		J/F 84	16
Textile Traditions: Egypt	Double-Harness Techniques Employed in Egypt	El-Homossani, M. M.	√	> 4	AT	3			My 85	229
Textile Traditions: Egypt	Kohl Bags	Austin, Carole	√		Fa	11	4		J/A 84	48
Textile Traditions: Egypt	Tapestries of Coptic Egypt, The	Hoskins, Nancy Arthur	√		AT	6			De 86	211
Textile Traditions: Egypt	Textiles of Coptic Egypt	Hoskins, Nancy Arthur	√	√	WJ	12	1	45	Su 87	58
Textile Traditions: England	English Textiles Referred to by Celia Fiennes	Stewart, Imogen	√		AT	4			De 85	67
Textile Traditions: England	Few Observations on "Remains", A	Stanton, R. G.	√		AT	4			De 85	9
Textile Traditions: England	Some Remarks on the Work of Markham	Stanton, R. G.; J. L. Allston	√	√	AT	2			De 84	98
Textile Traditions: Eskimo	Gutwork	Hickman, Pat	√		Fa	7	6		N/D 80	46
Textile Traditions: Eskimo	Patricia Bulitt: Gutsongs and Other Dances	Scarborough, Jessica	√		Fa	11	5		S/O 84	50
Textile Traditions: Fair Isle	Notes of a Textile Sleuth	Upitis, Lizbeth	√	√	Kn	2	1	3	F-W 85	22
Textile Traditions: Far East	"Birth Symbol in Traditional Women's Art, The" (Exhibit)	Vanco, John	√		Fa	13	3		M/J 86	52
Textile Traditions: Faroe Islands	Faroese Shawls	Swansen, Meg	√	√	Kn	4	1	9	Wi 87	26
Textile Traditions: Finland	Annikki Karvinen: Finnish Designer of Wovens	Talley, Charles	√		Fa	13	4		J/A 86	16
Textile Traditions: Finland	Finnish Textile Art: From Byzantine to Bauhaus	Rantanen, Kristi	√		Hw	8	3		M/J 87	68
Textile Traditions: Finland	Reinterpreting Rya: Irma Kukkasjärvi Energizes an Ancient Technique	Ojala, Liisa Kanning	√		WJ	9	4	36	Sp 85	26
Textile Traditions: Floor Coverings	From Straw Mats to Hooked Rugs: Floor Coverings of the 19th Century	Thieme, Otto Charles	√		Fa	11	3		M/J 84	55
Textile Traditions: France	"Splendor of French Style, The" Textiles from Joan of Arc to Napoleon III (Exhibit)	Guagliumi, Susan	√		Fa	13	4		J/A 86	13
Textile Traditions: France	Two Weeks in the South of France: At a Gobelins Tapestry Workshop	Lucas, Mary	√		Fa	8	4		J/A 81	38
Textile Traditions: Garments	Shapes of Garments, The (Reprint)	Burnham, Dorothy K.			TM			9	F/M 87	50

SUBJECT	TITLE	AUTHOR	IL	INST	JOUR	VOL	NO	ISS	DATE	PAGE
Textile Traditions: German Linen Weaves	Roses and Snowballs: The Development of Block Patterns in the German Linen-Weaving Tradition	Hilts, Patricia	√	>4	AT	5			Ju 86	167
Textile Traditions: German Linen Weaves	Seventeenth and Eighteenth Century Twills: The German Linen Tradition	Hilts, Patricia	√	>4	AT	3			My 85	139
Textile Traditions: Germany	Post-War Influences in West German Weaving	Reiser, Bertl	√		H&C	4	3		Su 53	11
Textile Traditions: Germany	Western German Weavers	Abbott, Edith E.	√		H&C	8	4		Fa 57	22
Textile Traditions: Germany, 17th Century	Ligetuhr Arbeit: A Seventeenth-Century Compound Mounting and a Family of Associated Weaves	Hilts, Patricia	√	>4	AT	7			Ju 87	31
Textile Traditions: Ghana	"Arts of Ghana" (Exhibit)	Dyer, Carolyn	√		Fa	5	1		J/F 78	19
Textile Traditions: Greece	Arachne's Children	Koster, Joan Bouza	√	√	SS&D	9	3	35	Su 78	16
Textile Traditions: Greece	Greek Craft Summer: The American Farm School	Regensteiner, Else	√		SS&D	7	3	27	Su 76	100
Textile Traditions: Greece	Greek Dower Sheet, A	Xenakis, Alexis Yiorgos	√		Hw	1	2		S-S 80	36
Textile Traditions: Greece	Handwoven Flocati of Epirus, The	Gans, Naomi Beth; Catherine Haywood	√	√	SS&D	12	3	47	Su 81	35
Textile Traditions: Greece	Inlay We Trust Part 3: Pillow Based on Greek Inlay Technique	Herring, Connie	√	√	PWC	3	4	10		44
Textile Traditions: Greece	Journey Through Greece, Two Americans in Search of Native Weaving	Znamierowski, Nell	√		H&C	14	2		Sp 63	8
Textile Traditions: Greece	Portrait of a Village	Becker, Robin; James Chressanthis	√		Fa	9	6		N/D 82	40
Textile Traditions: Greece	Search for Handweaving in Greece, A (error-corrected H&C v21 n3 70 p42)	Turner, Alta R.	√		H&C	21	2		Sp 70	16
Textile Traditions: Greece	Spinners and Weavers of Modern Greece		√		H&C	1	2		Su 50	30
Textile Traditions: Greece	Tagari: A Greek Saddlebag of Handspun Wools, The	Koster, Joan Boura	√	√	WJ	6	2	22	Fa 81	24
Textile Traditions: Greece	Windows: Kouverta	Xenaxis, Alexis Yiorgos	√	√	PWC	5	1	15		14
Textile Traditions: Guatemala	Adventures with Guatemalan Weaving	Young, Helen Daniels	√		H&C	4	1		Wi 52	26
Textile Traditions: Guatemala	Art of Ixchel: Learning to Weave in Guatemala and Rhode Island, The	Schevill, Margot	√	√	WJ	8	1	29	Su 83	57
Textile Traditions: Guatemala	"Century of Change in Guatemalan Textiles, A" (Exhibit)	Brown, Arleen Emery	√		Fa	9	3		M/J 82	79
Textile Traditions: Guatemala	Divide . . . and Conquer	Baizerman, Suzanne	√		WJ	9	2	34	Fa 84	61
Textile Traditions: Guatemala	Guatemala Visited	Atwater, Mary Meigs	√		SCGM		15		65	1-46
Textile Traditions: Guatemala	Guatemala Weaver, The	Marks, Copeland A.	√		H&C	26	5		Oc 75	2
Textile Traditions: Guatemala	Guatemala: Weaving, People	Frost, Gordon	√		Iw	5	4		Fa 80	30
Textile Traditions: Guatemala	In Pursuit of the Elusive Huipil	Marks, Copeland	√		H&C	24	4		Au 73	6
Textile Traditions: Guatemala	Jacquard Weaving in Huehuetenango	Anderson, Marilyn	√		Fa	9	2		M/A 82	31
Textile Traditions: Guatemala	Sisal Production in Highland Guatemala	Ventura, Carol	√		Fa	14	2		M/A 87	44
Textile Traditions: Guatemala	Stitched Finishes in the Guatemalan Tradition	Pancake, Cherri; Karen Searle; Sue Baizerman	√	√	Hw	2	5		No 81	29
Textile Traditions: Guatemala	Textiles and Looms from Guatemala & Mexico	Grossman, Ellin F.	√		H&C	7	1		Wi 55	6
Textile Traditions: Guatemala	"Weavers of the Jade Needle" An Exhibition of Highland Guatemalan Textiles (Exhibit)	Stout, Carol	√		Fa	3	2		M/A 76	30
Textile Traditions: Guatemala	Weavings of the Guatemalan Highland Maya	Marks, Copeland H.	√	√	SS&D	7	4	28	Fa 76	88
Textile Traditions: Gullah	Afro-American Sweetgrass Basketry	Johnson, Beth	√		Fa	9	5		S/O 82	23
Textile Traditions: Haiti	Haitian Voodoo Banners: Dazzling Invitations to the Spirits	Lorenzo, Lauri	√		Fa	13	6		N/D 86	11
Textile Traditions: Hawaii	Hawaiian Quilt, The	White-Hansen, Sue Ellen	√	√	TM			13	O/N 87	22
Textile Traditions: Hawaii	Hawaiian Quilting: Tradition Through Change	Akana, Elizabeth A.	√		Fa	9	3		M/J 82	62
Textile Traditions: Hawaii	Wailani Johansen, Quiltmaker: Sharing the Tradition of the Hawaiian Quilt	Rex, Chris	√		Fa	9	3		M/J 82	60
Textile Traditions: High Andes	From the High Andes to New York		√		H&C	12	1		Wi 61	53

728

SUBJECT	TITLE	AUTHOR	IL	INST	JOUR	VOL	NO	ISS	DATE	PAGE
Textile Traditions: Hispanic-American	Blankets of New Mexico	Kozikowski, Janusz	√		SS&D	10	1	37	Wi 78	60
Textile Traditions: Hmong, Laos	"Hmong Art: Tradition and Change" (Exhibit)	Gordon, Beverly	√		Fa	12	6		N/D 85	36
Textile Traditions: Hmong, Laos	Keeping Culture Alive with Needle and Thread	White, Virginia L.	√		Fa	9	3		M/J 82	40
Textile Traditions: Hopi	Pueblo Weaving, An Ancient Art: Hopi Keep to Their Traditional Designs		√		H&C	19	1		Wi 68	5
Textile Traditions: Hungary	Feltmaking in Hungary	Beede, Beth; Jill Garfunkel	√		Fa	13	4		J/A 86	6
Textile Traditions: Hungary	Zoltán Mihalkó: Hungarian Feltmaker	Beede, Beth; Jill Garfunkel	√	√	SS&D	17	4	68	Fa 86	12
Textile Traditions: Iceland	Icelandic Weaving: Saga In Wool	Hákonardóttir, Hildur	√		Hw	8	3		M/J 87	62
Textile Traditions: India	All That Glitters: Shisha by Machine	Fanning, Robbie	√	√	TM			1	O/N 85	63
Textile Traditions: India	Banares Brocade	DuBois, Emily	√	> 4	AT	3			My 85	209
Textile Traditions: India	Bandhana (Tie Dye)	Westfall, Carol D.; Dipti Desai	√		AT	8			De 87	19
Textile Traditions: India	Bhotiya Woolens from India	Willis, Elizabeth Bayley	√		H&C	5	2		Sp 54	4
Textile Traditions: India	"Camel Belts from the Great Indian Desert" (Exhibit)	Janeiro, Jan	√		Fa	10	6		N/D 83	75
Textile Traditions: India	Costumes of Royal India	Levine, Betsy	√		TM			7	O/N 86	64
Textile Traditions: India	Courtyard, Bazaar, Temple: Traditions in Indian Textile Expression		√		SS&D	13	4	52	Fa 82	44
Textile Traditions: India	Dhabla Weaving in India	De Bone, Mary	√	√	SS&D	8	3	31	Su 77	9
Textile Traditions: India	"Dowries from Kutch: A Women's Folk Art Tradition in India" (Exhibit)	Dyer, Carolyn	√		Fa	7	1		J/F 80	70
Textile Traditions: India	Fabric Painting in India: The Kalamkaris of J. Gurappa Chetty	Lintault, M. Joan	√		Fa	9	1		J/F 82	64
Textile Traditions: India	Feltmaking In India: A Remnant of the Past	MacDougal, Marleah Drexler	√		Fa	6	6		N/D 79	10
Textile Traditions: India	Gujarati Embroidery	Westfall, Carol D.; Dipti Desai	√		AT	8			De 87	29
Textile Traditions: India	Handweaving in India Today	King, Edith B.; Earl L. King	√		H&C	7	4		Fa 56	10
Textile Traditions: India	"Ikats of Orissa" (Exhibit)	De Bone, Mary	√		Fa	11	1		J/F 84	82
Textile Traditions: India	Kantha Cloths of Bengal: The Sari Transformed	Gupta, Asha	√		Fa	9	6		N/D 82	19
Textile Traditions: India	Kashmiri to Paisley: Evolution of the Paisley shawl	Larson-Fleming, Susan	√		WJ	11	3	43	Wi 87	37
Textile Traditions: India	"Master Dyers to the World" (Exhibit)	Sider, Sandra	√		Fa	11	1		J/F 84	83
Textile Traditions: India	Patolu and Its Techniques	De Bone, Mary Golden	√	√	TMJ	4	3	76		49
Textile Traditions: India	Phulkari	Westfall, Carol D.; Dipti Desai	√		AT	6			De 86	85
Textile Traditions: India	Rabari Lodi: Creating a Fabric Through Social Alliance, The	Frater, Judy	√	√	WJ	10	1	37	Su 85	28
Textile Traditions: India	Rib Weaves from India, A Rich Source of Inspiration	Harvey, Virginia Isham	√	> 4	H&C	16	4		Fa 65	21
Textile Traditions: India	Textile Arts of India	Bernier, Ronald M.	√		WJ	2	1	5	Jy 77	31
Textile Traditions: India	Textiles from India		√		H&C	6	3		Su 55	9
Textile Traditions: India	Tie Dyeing in India (error-corrected H&C v14 n2 63 p46)	Arness, Judith Russell	√	√	H&C	14	1		Wi 63	6
Textile Traditions: India	Web of India, The	Malarcher, Patricia	√		SS&D	13	2	50	Sp 82	38
Textile Traditions: Indian Asia	"Arts of Indian Asia: The Joy of Artistic Expression, The" (Exhibit)	Dyer, Carolyn	√		Fa	5	5		S/O 78	64
Textile Traditions: Indonesia	"Indonesia: The Fabled Islands of Spice" (Exhibit)	Dyer, Carolyn	√		Fa	6	2		M/A 79	71
Textile Traditions: Indonesia	Sumbanese Ikat	Hannon, Farrell	√	√	WJ	8	1	29	Su 83	38
Textile Traditions: Indonesia	Tapestries from Indonesia	Hitchcock, Michael	√	√	WJ	12	1	45	Su 87	55
Textile Traditions: Indonesia	"Textile Traditions of Indonesia" (Exhibit)	Dyer, Carolyn	√		Fa	5	1		J/F 78	15
Textile Traditions: Indonesia	Weavers of Bali	Hannon, Farrell	√		SS&D	18	4	72	Fa 87	46

SUBJECT	TITLE	AUTHOR	IL	INST	JOUR	VOL	NO	ISS	DATE	PAGE
Textile Traditions: Iran	Kings, Heroes, Lovers: Pictorial Rugs from the Tribes and Villages of Iran	Goodman, Deborah Lerme	√		Fa	11	3		M/J 84	38
Textile Traditions: Iran	Weavers in Iran, Thousands at Work on Primitive Looms	Leclerc, Robert	√		H&C	21	2		Sp 70	9
Textile Traditions: Ireland	Homespun Songs from Ireland's Clancy Brothers	Drake, Elizabeth A.	√		SS&D	16	4	64	Fa 85	62
Textile Traditions: Ireland	Irish Kinsale Cloak, The	Jones, Una	√	√	WJ	8	3	31	Wi 83	35
Textile Traditions: Ireland	Irish Weaving	Clement, Doris; Ted Clement	√		H&C	21	2		Sp 70	4
Textile Traditions: Ireland	Tweed Weavers of Glenmore,The	Burkhauser, Jude	√		Hw	3	3		My 82	56
Textile Traditions: Israel	New Forms from Old Traditions	Amram, Hortense	√		H&C	3	1		Wi 51	27
Textile Traditions: Italy	Italian Textiles (Exhibit)		√		Fa	14	1		J/F 87	69
Textile Traditions: Italy	Marvelous Mezzaro, The	Wasiqullah, Alexandra	√		Fa	10	5		S/O 83	29
Textile Traditions: Italy	Textile Sleuth Extraordinaire	Wasiqullah, Alexander	√		Fa	12	2		M/A 85	39
Textile Traditions: Italy	Traditional Weavers in Italy	Castaldi, Nora	√		H&C	2	4		Fa 51	20
Textile Traditions: Japan	Ana Lisa Hedstrom: The Intuitive Language of Shibori	Scarborough, Jessica	√		Fa	13	1		J/F 86	26
Textile Traditions: Japan	Art of Stitched Shibori, The (error-corrected Fa v12 n3 85 p8)	Wada, Yoshiko; Mary Kellogg Rice, Jane Barton	√		Fa	12	2		M/A 85	55
Textile Traditions: Japan	Culture & Costume in Edo Japan	Staples, Loretta	√		SS&D	12	1	45	Wi 80	26
Textile Traditions: Japan	D'Arcie Beytebiere: Windswept Designs In Pleated Silk	Tacker, Sylvia	√		Fa	13	1		J/F 86	28
Textile Traditions: Japan	Fukumi Shimura: Japan's Colorist Supreme	Adachi, Barbara C.	√		Fa	12	4		J/A 85	28
Textile Traditions: Japan	Fukusa: The Art of Giving	Lancaster, Deborah Lerme	√		Fa	13	6		N/D 86	27
Textile Traditions: Japan	"Fukusa: The Shojiro Nomura Collection" (Exhibit)	Janeiro, Jan	√		Fa	11	3		M/J 84	79
Textile Traditions: Japan	Innovations in Indigo	Wada, Yoshiko Iwamoto	√		Fa	13	5		S/O 86	29
Textile Traditions: Japan	Japanese Country Textiles (Exhibit)	Rowley, Kathleen	√		Fa	13	5		S/O 86	49
Textile Traditions: Japan	Japanese Weaves Provide Ideas for Experiment	Freeman, Claire	√	√	H&C	21	1		Wi 70	4
Textile Traditions: Japan	Japan's Masterful Embroideries	Markrich, Lilo	√		TM			12	A/S 87	68
Textile Traditions: Japan	Katagami: Japanese Stencil Cutting	McCann, Kathleen	√		Fa	13	2		M/A 86	36
Textile Traditions: Japan	Kazuko Nishigaki Creates in Ancient Tradition	Major, Dana; John Major	√		SS&D	6	2	22	Sp 75	93
Textile Traditions: Japan	Kumejima Kasuri: A Visit to a Remote Japanese Silk Center	Mitchell, Alison	√	√	WJ	10	1	37	Su 85	59
Textile Traditions: Japan	Living National Treasures of Japan, The	Adachi, Barbara Curtis	√		Fa	11	1		J/F 84	62
Textile Traditions: Japan	New Twist on Resist	Wada, Yoshiko Iwamoto; Shelley Karpilow	√	√	TM			8	D/J 86	20
Textile Traditions: Japan	Paper Clothing, East	Sahlstrand, Margaret	√	√	Fa	11	2		M/A 84	36
Textile Traditions: Japan	Preparing Silk in Kumejima	Mitchell, Alison	√	√	WJ	10	2	38	Fa 85	53
Textile Traditions: Japan	Shokansai Iizuka: Bamboo Craftsman and Living National Treasure of Japan	Adachi, Barbara Curtis	√		Fa	11	1		J/F 84	59
Textile Traditions: Japan	Temari: Threads to the Past	Beall, Karen F.	√		Fa	14	2		M/A 87	7
Textile Traditions: Japan	Tenugui: Decorative Japanese Hand Towels		√		Fa	9	6		N/D 82	25
Textile Traditions: Japan	"Traditional Japanese Designs: The Tom and Frances Blakemore Collection of Textiles Stencils and Costumes" (Exhibit)	Dyer, Carolyn	√		Fa	7	3		M/J 80	81
Textile Traditions: Japan	Weaving in the Past: What Can We Learn From Japanese Weaving	Zielinski, S. A.; Robert Leclerc, ed.			MWL	21 22			'51–'73	91
Textile Traditions: Java	"Fabled Cloth: Batik from Java's North Coast" (Exhibit)	Goodman, Deborah Lerme	√		Fa	12	4		J/A 85	58
Textile Traditions: Judaic	Jewish Textiles	Johnson, Faye	√		Hw	5	1		J/F 84	35
Textile Traditions: Korea	Korean Journal	Blickenstaff, Maxine L.	√		SS&D	7	2	26	Sp 76	52
Textile Traditions: Kurdistan	Jews of Kurdistan, The	Meyerowitz, Carol Orlove	√	√	SS&D	14	2	54	Sp 83	23

SUBJECT	TITLE	AUTHOR	IL	INST	JOUR	VOL	NO	ISS	DATE	PAGE
Textile Traditions: Laos	Flourishing Art: USA Hmong Women Show How to Stitch Pa ndau, Their Flowery Cloth, A	Porter-Francis, Wendy	√	√	TM			9	F/M 87	33
Textile Traditions: Laos	Pattern Weaving, Laotian Style	Keasbey, Doramay	√	√	Hw	2	3		My 81	54
Textile Traditions: Latin America	Folk Textiles of Latin America	Kelemen, Pál	√		TMJ	1	4		De 65	2
Textile Traditions: Latvia	Latvian Wedding Mittens	Upitis, Lizbeth	√	√	PWC			2	Ap 82	92
Textile Traditions: Lithuania	Anastazija Tamosaitis	Matranga, Victoria	√		SS&D	17	3	67	Su 86	54
Textile Traditions: Lithuania	Lithuanian Pervarai: Producing a Twenty Shaft Pattern on a Twelve Shaft Loom	Meek, M. Kati	√	> 4	AT	1			De 83	159
Textile Traditions: Lithuania	Traditional Lithuanian Weaving in Chicago	Meek, M. Kati	√		SS&D	17	3	67	Su 86	50
Textile Traditions: Maori	Weaving with the Maoris of New Zealand	Giacchina, Polly Jacobs	√	√	Fa	11	3		M/J 84	48
Textile Traditions: Mayan	Mayan Folk Textiles: Symbol of a Society	Dieterich, Mary	√		Hw	6	3		Su 85	64
Textile Traditions: Mesoamerica	Backstrap Weaving in MesoAmerica	Baizerman, Suzanne; Karen Searle	√	√	Iw	5	4		Fa 80	38
Textile Traditions: Mexico	Mexican Motifs: Mexico, Land of Contrasts	Tidball, Harriet	√	√	SCGM		6		62	1
Textile Traditions: Mexico	Mexico — Land of Weavers, Part 1	Hatch, David Porter	√		H&C	6	2		Sp 55	10
Textile Traditions: Mexico	Mexico, Land of Weavers, Part 2	Hatch, David Porter	√		H&C	6	3		Su 55	13
Textile Traditions: Mexico	Robozos of Tenancingo	Hewitt, T. H.	√	√	H&C	8	3		Su 57	19
Textile Traditions: Mexico	Textiles and Looms from Guatemala & Mexico	Grossman, Ellin F.	√		H&C	7	1		Wi 55	6
Textile Traditions: Mexico	Work of a Huave Indian Weaver in Oaxaca, Mexico: Complex Weave Structures Utilizing One Warp Set and Two Complementary Weft Sets, The	Connolly, Loris	√		AT	3			My 85	7
Textile Traditions: Middle East	Qotny & Alaga: Traditional Striped Fabrics for the Middle Eastern Kaftan	El-Homossani, M. M.	√	> 4	WJ	10	1	37	Su 85	33
Textile Traditions: Miyako (Jofu)	Miyako Jofu	Miller, Dorothy	√	√	AT	7			Ju 87	85
Textile Traditions: Morocco	From the Far West: Carpets and Textiles of Morocco	West, Virginia	√		Hw	2	3		My 81	14
Textile Traditions: Native Americans	Indian Weavers and Contemporary Design		√		H&C	3	2		Sp 52	4
Textile Traditions: Native Americans	Thinking About Historical Baskets	Rossbach, Ed	√		Fa	11	1		J/F 84	32
Textile Traditions: Navajo	Churro Sheep in the Navajo Tradition	McNeal, Dr. Lyle G.	√		WJ	10	2	38	Fa 85	31
Textile Traditions: Navajo	"Eyedazzlers!" (Exhibit)	Lonier, Terri	√		Fa	11	3		M/J 84	77
Textile Traditions: Navajo	From Father Sky to Mother Earth: An Ethnic Inspiration	Bennett, Noël	√		WJ	8	1	29	Su 83	62
Textile Traditions: Navajo	From the Silverman Collection: Pueblo and Navajo Textiles	Coe, Kathryn	√		Fa	10	6		N/D 83	27
Textile Traditions: Navajo	Navajo: Textiles, Blankets, Rugs, Tapestries	Morrow, Mable	√	√	SS&D	1	4	4	Se 70	3
Textile Traditions: Navajo	Navajo: Textiles, Blankets, Rugs, Tapestries	Morrow, Mable	√	√	SS&D	2	1	5	De 70	5
Textile Traditions: Navajo	Navajo Weaving, Contemporary and Traditional		√		H&C	18	2		Sp 67	6
Textile Traditions: Navajo	"Patterns and Sources of Navajo Weaving" (Exhibit)	Mattera, Joanne	√		Fa	7	4		J/A 80	68
Textile Traditions: Navajo	Ramah Navajo Weavers, The	D'Andrea, Pat	√		WJ	12	1	45	Su 87	44
Textile Traditions: Navajo	"Song of The Loom: New Traditions In Navajo Weaving, The" (Exhibit)		√		TM			11	J/J 87	18
Textile Traditions: Navajo	Weaving the Navajo Way	Bighorse, Tiana; Noël Bennett	√		Iw	4	1		Wi 78	12
Textile Traditions: Nepal	Nepal	Petrini, Marcy	√		SS&D	16	2	62	Sp 85	65
Textile Traditions: New Guinea, Gilbert Islands	Basketry Armor	Austin, Carole	√		Fa	14	1		J/F 87	28
Textile Traditions: New Mexico	Blankets of New Mexico	Kozikowski, Janusz	√		SS&D	10	1	37	Wi 78	60
Textile Traditions: Nez Percé	Nez Percé Indian Art and Craft Revival	Connette, Ann	√	√	H&C	21	4		Fa 70	5
Textile Traditions: Nigeria	Art and Tradition of Akwete Weaving, The	Lambrecht, Dora J.	√		SS&D	9	2	34	Sp 78	33
Textile Traditions: Nigeria	Nigerian Weavers	Worsley, Marie	√		H&C	12	2		Sp 61	45

SUBJECT	TITLE	AUTHOR	IL	INST	JOUR	VOL	NO	ISS	DATE	PAGE
Textile Traditions: Nordic	Krossvefnadur (rölakan) _ A Nordic Tapestry Technique		√	√	Hw	8	3		M/J 87	66
Textile Traditions: North America	Tromping Through the Ages	Dunwell, Anna	√		Fa	9	2		M/A 82	26
Textile Traditions: North America, Pattern	Pattern...Pattern...Pattern	Park, Betty	√		Fa	9	1		J/F 82	11
Textile Traditions: North America, Quilts	"Baltimore Album Quilts" (Exhibit)	Park, Betty	√		Fa	8	6		N/D 81	69
Textile Traditions: North America, Rugs	"American Hooked Rugs: 1850–1957" (Exhibit)	Scarborough, Jessica	√		Fa	8	6		N/D 81	68
Textile Traditions: Norway	Aklae: Norwegian Tapestry	Irlbeck, Sonja	√	√	WJ	8	1	29	Su 83	27
Textile Traditions: Norway	Finnweave in Norway: Yesterday and Today	Nelson, Lila	√		PWC			2	Ap 82	14
Textile Traditions: Norway	Firfletting Fringe Treatment from Norway	Searle, Karen	√	√	WJ	9	4	36	Sp 85	40
Textile Traditions: Norway	Krokbragd	Alderman, Sharon D.	√	√	Hw	2	2		Mr 81	33
Textile Traditions: Norway	Nineteenth Century Tapestry in Billedvev, A	Nelson, Lila	√		WJ	10	2	38	Fa 85	26
Textile Traditions: Norway	Norwegian Tradition, The	Nelson, Lila	√		SS&D	7	4	28	Fa 76	6
Textile Traditions: Norway	Scandinavian Nålbinding: Needle Looped Fabric	Martinson, Kate	√	√	WJ	12	2	46	Fa 87	12
Textile Traditions: Norway	Weaving in Rural Norway: A Living Tradition	Nelson, Lila	√		Hw	8	3		M/J 87	52
Textile Traditions: Nova Scotia	Weaving in Nova Scotia — Yesterday and Today	Black, Mary E.	√		H&C	2	4		Fa 51	5
Textile Traditions: Okinawa	Banana, Ramie, and Hemp in Okinawa (error-corrected Fa v14 n3 87 p4)	Miller, Dorothy	√		Fa	14	2		M/A 87	46
Textile Traditions: Pakistan	Textile Arts of Multan, Pakistan	Shahzaman, Mahboob	√	> 4	SS&D	4	3	15	Su 73	8
Textile Traditions: Pakistan	Textile Arts of Multan, Pakistan: Part 2	Shahzaman, Mahboob	√	> 4	SS&D	4	4	16	Fa 73	65
Textile Traditions: Papercuts	Claudia Hopf: Drawing with Scissors	Timmons, Christine	√		Fa	11	2		M/A 84	99
Textile Traditions: Persia	Weaving in the Past: The Romance of Persian Weaving	Zielinski, S. A.; Robert Leclerc, ed.			MWL	21 22			'51–'73	85
Textile Traditions: Peru	Andes Tradition, An	McConnell, Kathleen	√	√	SS&D	18	2	70	Sp 87	29
Textile Traditions: Peru	Archeological Rags	Hickman, Pat	√		Fa	9	1		J/F 82	70
Textile Traditions: Peru	Double-Woven Treasures from Old Peru	Cahlander, Adele	√	√	PWC			4	Ja 83	36
Textile Traditions: Peru	Francisca Mayer, Designer-Weaver in the Peruvian Highland	Boyer, Ruth McDonald	√		H&C	19	2		Sp 68	18
Textile Traditions: Peru	Handspun Yarn Production Rates in the Cuzco Region of Peru	Bird, Junius B.	√		TMJ	2	3		De 68	9
Textile Traditions: Peru	Inca Feathers	Kwiatkowski, Ron	√	√	Iw	1	2		Wi 76	16
Textile Traditions: Peru	Kindred Spirits of Peru	Glaves, Jeannine	√		S-O	8	1		Sp 84	22
Textile Traditions: Peru	Notes on Plaiting in the Upper Amazon Basin, Peru	Blinks, Anne	√	√	Iw	5	4		Fa 80	51
Textile Traditions: Peru	Paracas Needle Technique, A	Hoskins, Nancy	√	√	Iw	5	4		Fa 80	34
Textile Traditions: Peru	Peru, Textiles Unlimited: Textile Chronology	Tidball, Harriet	√		SCGM		25		68	8
Textile Traditions: Peru	Peruvian Multilayered Cloth	Schira, Cynthia	√	> 4	H&C	18	3		Su 67	11
Textile Traditions: Peru	Peruvian Straw Hat: Documenting a Declining Industry, The	Zimmer, Roni	√		Fa	12	3		M/J 85	39
Textile Traditions: Peru	Peruvian Technique for Dimensional Knotting	Bravo, Monica	√	√	WJ	12	1	45	Su 87	17
Textile Traditions: Peru	Peruvian Weaves of Contemporary Interest		√		H&C	12	4		Fa 61	31
Textile Traditions: Peru	Spaced-Weft Twining of Ancient Peru: A Contemporary Interpretation	Rogers, Nora	√	√	Iw	5	4		Fa 80	42
Textile Traditions: Peru	Spinners of Taquile	Coker, Sharon	√		S-O	8	1		Sp 84	24
Textile Traditions: Peru	Study of Andean Spinning in the Cuzco Region, A	Goodell, Miss Grace	√	√	TMJ	2	3		De 68	2
Textile Traditions: Peru	Tapices of San Pedro de Cajas, Peru, The	Thornton, Sandra K.	√	√	WJ	12	1	45	Su 87	23
Textile Traditions: Peru	Unique Finish from an Amazonian Bracelet, A	Thabet, Micheline	√	√	WJ	9	3	35	Wi 85	14
Textile Traditions: Peru	Visit to Peru	Fife, Lin	√		Fa	9	6		N/D 82	60

SUBJECT	TITLE	AUTHOR	IL	INST	JOUR	VOL	NO	ISS	DATE	PAGE
Textile Traditions: Peru	World Crafts Council, An American Spinner Meets Peruvian Craftsmen	Reade, Dorothy	√		H&C	20	1		Wi 69	8
Textile Traditions: Peru (Costa)	Vignettes from Peru	Wilson, Kax	√		Iw	5	4		Fa 80	46
Textile Traditions: Peru (Selva)	Vignettes from Peru	Wilson, Kax	√		Iw	5	4		Fa 80	46
Textile Traditions: Peru (Sierra)	Vignettes from Peru	Wilson, Kax	√		Iw	5	4		Fa 80	46
Textile Traditions: Peru, Spanish-Colonial Period	Lenten Curtains from Colonial Peru	Kelemen, Pál	√		TMJ	3	1		De 70	5
Textile Traditions: Philippines	Backstrap Weaving in the Philippines	Ng, Mary	√		SS&D	9	1	33	Wi 77	18
Textile Traditions: Philippines	"People and Art of the Philippines, The" (Exhibit)	Dyer, Carolyn	√		Fa	9	3		M/J 82	84
Textile Traditions: Polynesia	Tapa-Making in Tonga	Raphael, Jenifer; Chad Raphael	√		Fa	13	6		N/D 86	24
Textile Traditions: Pomo	Family Album of Pomo Baskets, A	Metzler, Sandra	√		Fa	11	1		J/F 84	63
Textile Traditions: Pueblo	From the Silverman Collection: Pueblo and Navajo Textiles	Coe, Kathryn	√		Fa	10	6		N/D 83	27
Textile Traditions: Pueblo	Pueblo Weaving: A Renaissance	Sakiestewa, Ramona	√		Iw	4	1		Wi 78	34
Textile Traditions: Pueblo	Pueblo Weaving, An Ancient Art: Hopi Keep to Their Traditional Designs		√		H&C	19	1		Wi 68	5
Textile Traditions: Pueblo	Santa Fe Weaver Re-Creates Past	Ligon, Linda	√		Iw	1	1		Fa 75	4
Textile Traditions: Pueblo, Southwest	Southwest Indian Twill Tapestry	Atwood, Betty	√		WJ	8	1	29	Su 83	35
Textile Traditions: Quebec	Weaving in Quebec	Barrett, Clotilde	√	√	WJ	6	4	24	Sp 82	8
Textile Traditions: Quebec	Weaving in Quebec: Traditional Quebecois Weaving	Barrett, Clotilde	√	√	WJ	6	4	24	Sp 82	10
Textile Traditions: Quilts	"Quilts: A Tradition of Variations" (Exhibit)	Rowley, Kathleen	√		Fa	10	2		M/A 83	68
Textile Traditions: Rag Rugs	Rag Rug Traditions	Meany, Janet K.	√		WJ	9	4	36	Sp 85	56
Textile Traditions: Roman	"Roman Heritage: Textiles from Egypt and the Eastern Mediterranean, 300–600 A.D., The" (Exhibit)		√		Fa	9	4		J/A 82	32
Textile Traditions: Romania	"Romanian Folk Textiles" (Exhibit)	Dyer, Carolyn	√		Fa	5	3		M/J 78	11
Textile Traditions: Romania	Romanian Housewife Spins a Yarn	Jones, Peter	√		S-O	8	1		Sp 84	40
Textile Traditions: Rural	Weaving in the Urban Tradition	Bulback, Stanley	√		SS&D	12	3	47	Su 81	7
Textile Traditions: Salish	Fiber Heritage of the Salish	Whonnock Spinners & Weavers	√		WJ	9	2	34	Fa 84	65
Textile Traditions: Salish	Salish Weaving, Then and Now	Ling, Lorraine	√	√	Iw	4	1		Wi 78	38
Textile Traditions: San Blas Islands	Ethnic Textile Art at U.C.L.A. — "Yer Dailege: Kuna Women's Art" (Exhibit)	Dyer, Carolyn	√		Fa	8	2		M/A 81	59
Textile Traditions: San Luis Valley	Las Artistas Del Valle: Images of Everyday Life in Colorado's San Luis Valley	Reith, Stephanie J.	√		Fa	10	3		M/J 83	24
Textile Traditions: Sardinia	Sardinian Debut, Colorful Tapestries and Rugs Interest American Weavers	Balkin, Emanuel	√		H&C	13	1		Wi 62	21
Textile Traditions: Saudi Arabia	Weaving of Saudi Arabia		√		SS&D	14	2	54	Sp 83	20
Textile Traditions: Scandinavia	Scandinavia Revisited: Reflections on the Weaver's Art	Talley, Charles	√		Hw	8	3		M/J 87	32
Textile Traditions: Scandinavia	Scandinavian Designs for American Looms	Freeman, Claire	√		H&C	3	2		Sp 52	14
Textile Traditions: Scandinavia	Scandinavian Traditions		√		WJ	9	4	36	Sp 85	24
Textile Traditions: Scotland	Four Posts of Poverty, The	Xenaxis, Alexis Yiorgos	√		PWC	5	1	15		6
Textile Traditions: Scotland	Kashmiri to Paisley: Evolution of the Paisley shawl	Larson-Fleming, Susan	√		WJ	11	3	43	Wi 87	37
Textile Traditions: Scotland	Waulking Tweeds at the Marshfield School of Weaving	Gallagher, Kate	√		Hw	6	4		S/O 85	10
Textile Traditions: Seminole	In the Dark of the Swamp...Seminole Patchwork		√	√	Fa	4	3		M/J 77	38
Textile Traditions: Shaker	Hands to Work and Hearts to God	Erf, Mary Elva	√	√	WJ	8	1	29	Su 83	25
Textile Traditions: Shaker	Shaker Textiles	Hillenburg, Nancy	√	√	WJ	8	1	29	Su 83	22
Textile Traditions: Shaker	Shaker Towels: A Guild Devotes a Year of Study to Nineteenth Century Textiles (error-corrected WJ v11 n2 86 p68)	Eastlake, Sandy	√	> 4	WJ	10	4	40	Sp 86	20

SUBJECT	TITLE	AUTHOR	IL	INST	JOUR	VOL	NO	ISS	DATE	PAGE
Textile Traditions: Shetland Islands	Knitter's Journey, A	Bush, Nancy	√		Kn	3	4	8	Fa 87	24
Textile Traditions: Shetland Islands	Stitches from the Sea		√	√	Kn	3	4	8	Fa 87	49
Textile Traditions: Slavic Countries	"Our Shining Heritage: Textile Arts of the Slavs and Their Neighbors" (Exhibit)	Mackin, Jeanne	√		Fa	8	4		J/A 81	75
Textile Traditions: Southwest U. S. A.	Sweetgrass, Cedar & Sage: Portrait of a Southwestern Weaver	Schevill, Margot	√		WJ	10	1	37	Su 85	24
Textile Traditions: Southwestern U. S. A.	Weft Wrap Openwork	Atwood, Betty	√	√	Iw	4	1		Wi 78	20
Textile Traditions: Spain	Handweaving in Spain	Arnold, Ruth	√		H&C	8	4		Fa 57	10
Textile Traditions: Spanish (Southwest USA)	Jerga: A Twill in Harmony with its Heritage	Wilson, Kax	√		Hw	6	5		N/D 85	60
Textile Traditions: Sumba	Tiedyeing An Art on the Island of Sumba	Adams, Moni	√	√	H&C	22	1		Wi 71	9
Textile Traditions: Sweden	Boundweave: Learning from the Past	Waggoner, Phyllis	√	√	WJ	10	4	40	Sp 86	44
Textile Traditions: Sweden	From Hand to Hand: Swedish Weaving Today	Krondahl, Hans	√		Hw	8	3		M/J 87	34
Textile Traditions: Sweden	Harts and Flowers: Sweden's Märta Mäas-Fjetterstrom's Designs Inspired a Textile Renaissance	Selkurt, Claire	√		WJ	9	4	36	Sp 85	30
Textile Traditions: Sweden	Immigrant Memories	Butcher-Younghans, Sherry	√		WJ	9	4	36	Sp 85	44
Textile Traditions: Sweden	Picture Lace	Larson-Fleming, Susan	√		WJ	9	4	36	Sp 85	42
Textile Traditions: Sweden	Smålands Weave on Eight Shafts	Shannon, Eileen	√	> 4	WJ	9	1	33	Su 84	47
Textile Traditions: Sweden	Upphämta Display Towel		√	> 4	Hw	8	3		M/J 87	42
Textile Traditions: Tennessee	One-Woman Publishing Show, A	Xenakis, Alexis Yiorgos	√		PWC	5	2	16		6
Textile Traditions: Thailand	Keeping Tradition Alive	Wilcox, Don	√		Fa	14	1		J/F 87	44
Textile Traditions: Thailand	Mudmee: The Ikat Tradition in Thailand	McCauley, Susan L.	√		Fa	10	5		S/O 83	25
Textile Traditions: Thailand	Thailand	Lala, Susan	√		SS&D	18	4	72	Fa 87	74
Textile Traditions: Thailand	Woven Houses of Thailand, The	Wilcox, Don	√		Fa	13	3		M/J 86	38
Textile Traditions: Tibet	Secret Treasures of Tibet	Wiltsie-Vaniea, Anne	√		SS&D	18	3	71	Su 87	60
Textile Traditions: Tunisia	Traditional Handlooms and Weavings of Tunisia	Reswick, Irmtraud H.	√		SS&D	12	2	46	Sp 81	21
Textile Traditions: Turkey	"At The Edge of Asia: Five Centuries of Turkish Textiles" (Exhibit)	Dyer, Carolyn Price	√		Fa	10	4		J/A 83	65
Textile Traditions: Turkey	Kaleidoscopic Tour of Turkey, A	Dyer, Carol; Carel Bertram	√		Fa	7	5		S/O 80	48
Textile Traditions: Turkey	Traditional Felt Rugmaking in Turkey	Ispay, Francis	√	√	Fa	13	4		J/A 86	18
Textile Traditions: Turkey	Turkish Carpet with Spots and Stripes, A	Mackie, Louise W.	√		TMJ	4	3		76	4
Textile Traditions: Turkmen	"Turkmen: Tribal Carpets and Traditions" (Exhibit)	Dyer, Carol	√		Fa	8	3		M/J 81	70
Textile Traditions: Ukraine	In Pursuit of Plakhta	Golay, Myrna	√	> 4	WJ	11	3	43	Wi 87	34
Textile Traditions: Urban	Weaving in the Urban Tradition	Bulback, Stanley	√		SS&D	12	3	47	Su 81	7
Textile Traditions: USA	"American Quilts: A Handmade Legacy" (Exhibit)	Janeiro, Jan	√		Fa	8	4		J/A 81	72
Textile Traditions: USA	Table Dressing and Bedcovers		√		Fa	8	3		M/J 81	43
Textile Traditions: West Indies	West Indian Weaving, Nonloom Techniques of Interest	Schira, Cynthia	√		H&C	21	3		Su 70	17
Textile Traditions: Yoruk	"Flowers of the Yayla: Yoruk Weaving of the Toros Mountains" (Exhibit)	Bloom, Mary Jane	√		Fa	11	3		M/J 84	76
Textile Traditions: Yugoslavia	Brief Survey of Textile Traditions of Yugoslavia, A	Dittmar, Ana	√		S-O	8	1		Sp 84	41
Textile Traditions: Zuni	Pueblo Weaving, An Ancient Art: Hopi Keep to Their Traditional Designs		√		H&C	19	1		Wi 68	5
Textiles: Finland	Stacks And Racks of Handwovens in Finland		√		SS&D	5	2	18	Sp 74	91
Textiles, Interiors	Color Related Decorating Textiles Rugs, Draperies, Upholstery	Rhodes, Tonya Stalons; Harriet Tidball, ed.	√	√	SCGM		14		65	35
Textiles: Mixed-Media	Tangential Textiles: From Quiltmaking to Points Beyond	Chapman, Charity	√		Fa	9	2		M/A 82	22

SUBJECT	TITLE	AUTHOR	IL	INST	JOUR	VOL	NO	ISS	DATE	PAGE
Textiles: Tobacco-Related	Silken Dreams of Faraway Lands	Rudich, Sally	√		Fa	12	4		J/A 85	80
Textiles: Undulating Wefts, Functional Uses	Undulating Weft Effects: (Honeycomb), Functional Uses	Tidball, Harriet	√		SCGM		9		63	4
Texture	Block Weaves as Color and Texture Effects	Znamierowski, Nell	√	√	Hw	8	5		N/D 87	48
Texture	Blue Jumper (Louise Bradley)		√	√	Hw	6	4		S/O 85	52, I-8
Texture	Composition and Designing Part 2: Patterns in Grist	Zielinski, S. A.; Robert Leclerc, ed.	√	√	MWL	19			'51–'73	134
Texture	Design and the Handweaver: Texture	Atwater, Mary Meigs		√	SCGM		3		61	9
Texture	Hooked on Texture: Unconventional Punch-Needle Rugs	Crouse, Gloria E.	√	√	TM			14	D/J 87	68
Texture	Of Treasures & Textures	Liebler, Barbara			Hw	8	2		M/A 87	22
Texture	Plaid Idea Notebook		√	√	Hw	4	5		N/D 83	41
Texture	Spice Up Plain Weave with Warp Floats	Davenport, Betty	√	√	Hw	7	4		S/O 86	56
Texture	Textural Approach to Arashi Shibori, A	Beytebiere, D'Arcie	√	√	TM			8	D/J 86	24
Texture	Textured Rugs from the Pacific Coast		√		H&C	3	3		Su 52	37
Texture: Double Weave	Double Weave: Plain and Patterned: Texture Variations in Two Block Double Weave, The	Tidball, Harriet	√	>4	SCGM		1		60	22
Texture: Knitting	Contrasting Textures	Rowley, Elaine			Kn	2	2	4	S-S 86	67
Texture: Knitting	Simple and Silk	Gibson-Roberts, Priscilla A.	√	√	Kn	2	2	4	S-S 86	54
Texture: Piqué	Designing for Piqué (error-corrected PWC v4 n4 i14 p33)	Sullivan, Donna	√	>4	PWC	4	3	13		28
Texture: Spinning	Texture in Spinning	O'Connor, Marcie Archer	√	√	Kn	2	2	4	S-S 86	53
Texture: Stripes	Texture as Stripe		√	√	Hw	4	2		M/A 83	66
Texture: Tied Units	Texture Possibilities of the Three-Tie Unit Weaves	Xenakis, Athanasios David	√	>4	PWC	4	4	14		49
Texture: Warp Stripe	Handloom Weaves: The Classification of Handloom Weaves, The Structural Group, The Rhythmic Weave Class, Warp Stripe Texture System	Tidball, Harriet	√	>4	SCGM		33		57	37
Texture: Weaving	Chained Weft for Surface Texture	Malbin, Rosemary S.	√	√	SS&D	11	4	44	Fa 80	26
Texture: Weaving	Design in Cotton	Bishop, Mrs. Carlton T.	√	>4	H&C	6	4		Fa 55	11
Texture: Weaving	Design Variations in Simple Textures	Hausner, Walter	√	√	H&C	8	1		Wi 56	12
Texture: Weaving	Effective Weave for Rugs, An		√	√	H&C	11	1		Wi 60	26
Texture: Weaving	Exploring the Textures: Accidental Weaves	Zielinski, S. A.; Robert Leclerc, ed.	√	>4	MWL	11			'51–'73	79
Texture: Weaving	Exploring the Textures: Another Texture Weave	Zielinski, S. A.; Robert Leclerc, ed.	√	√	MWL	11			'51–'73	87
Texture: Weaving	Exploring the Textures: Designing the Texture	Zielinski, S. A.; Robert Leclerc, ed.	√	√4	MWL	11			'51–'73	74
Texture: Weaving	Exploring the Textures: Irregular Texture on Overshot Drafts	Zielinski, S. A.; Robert Leclerc, ed.	√	√	MWL	11			'51–'73	96
Texture: Weaving	Exploring the Textures: More Textures on Four Shafts	Zielinski, S. A.; Robert Leclerc, ed.	√	√	MWL	11			'51–'73	110
Texture: Weaving	Exploring the Textures: Patterns in Texture on Four Shafts	Zielinski, S. A.; Robert Leclerc, ed.	√	√	MWL	11			'51–'73	102
Texture: Weaving	Exploring the Textures: Projects in Texture	Zielinski, S. A.; Robert Leclerc, ed.	√	√	MWL	11			'51–'73	124
Texture: Weaving	Exploring the Textures: Texture Effects in Fine Yarns	Zielinski, S. A.; Robert Leclerc, ed.	√	√	MWL	11			'51–'73	106
Texture: Weaving	Exploring the Textures: Texture Overshot	Zielinski, S. A.; Robert Leclerc, ed.	√	√	MWL	11			'51–'73	92
Texture: Weaving	Exploring the Textures: The Third Dimension	Zielinski, S. A.; Robert Leclerc, ed.	√	>4	MWL	11			'51–'73	60
Texture: Weaving	Exploring the Textures: What About Texture?	Zielinski, S. A.; Robert Leclerc, ed.			MWL	11			'51–'73	55
Texture: Weaving	Fabrics That Go Bump (error-corrected PWC i4 83 p76)	Xenakis, Athanasios David	√	√	PWC			3	Oc 82	18
Texture: Weaving	First Step in Designing Textures, A	Hausner, Walter	√	√	H&C	9	2		Sp 58	14

SUBJECT	TITLE	AUTHOR	IL	INST	JOUR	VOL	NO	ISS	DATE	PAGE
Texture: Weaving	Mid-Twentieth Century Textures	Mailey, Jean E.	√		H&C	8	3		Su 57	6
Texture: Weaving	More About Fabrics: Ideas for New Textures Without Weft	Zielinski, S. A.; Robert Leclerc, ed.		√	MWL	20			'51–'73	91
Texture: Weaving	Notes of a Pattern Weaver	Alvic, Philis	√		SS&D	14	3	55	Su 83	66
Texture: Weaving	On Textures — Notes of a Contemporary Weaver	Blumenau, Lili	√		H&C	1	2		Su 50	8
Texture: Weaving	Resist Dyeing, Curiosities and Inventions: Hound's Tooth in Texture and Colour	Zielinski, S. A.; Robert Leclerc, ed.	√	√	MWL	17			'51–'73	68
Texture: Weaving	Studies in Color and Texture through Fabric	Kramer, Helen	√		H&C	6	1		Wi 54	13
Texture: Weaving	Texture Weaving — What and Why	Atwater, Mary M.	√		H&C	2	1		Wi 50	33
Texture: Weaving	Texture with Handspun	Page, Judy	√	√	WJ	6	2	22	Fa 81	20
Texture: Weaving	Textured Cottons	Henrikson, Sue	√	> 4	WJ	6	3	23	Wi 81	20
Texture: Weaving	Textured Cottons: Dress and Sauna Robe	Henrikson, Sue	√	> 4	WJ	6	3	23	Wi 81	20
Texture: Weaving	Textured Weave—An Alternative	Tanner, Virginia Leigh	√	√	WJ	7	3	27	Wi 82	58
Texture: Weaving	Traditional Texture Weaves: Basket	Zielinski, S. A.; Robert Leclerc, ed.	√	√	MWL	11			'51–'73	36
Texture: Weaving	Traditional Texture Weaves: Better Waffle	Zielinski, S. A.; Robert Leclerc, ed.	√	√	MWL	11			'51–'73	32
Texture: Weaving	Traditional Texture Weaves: Half-Waffle	Zielinski, S. A.; Robert Leclerc, ed.	√	√	MWL	11			'51–'73	21
Texture: Weaving	Traditional Texture Weaves: Halkrus or Honeycomb	Zielinski, S. A.; Robert Leclerc, ed.	√	√	MWL	11			'51–'73	14
Texture: Weaving	Traditional Texture Weaves: In Search of a Better Waffle	Zielinski, S. A.; Robert Leclerc, ed.	√	> 4	MWL	11			'51–'73	25
Texture: Weaving	Traditional Texture Weaves: Rep	Zielinski, S. A.; Robert Leclerc, ed.	√	> 4	MWL	11			'51–'73	7
Texture: Weaving	Traditional Texture Weaves: Stitched Basket	Zielinski, S. A.; Robert Leclerc, ed.	√	√	MWL	11			'51–'73	39
Texture: Weaving	Traditional Texture Weaves: Traditional Textures on Four Shafts	Zielinski, S. A.; Robert Leclerc, ed.	√	√	MWL	11			'51–'73	46
Texture: Weaving	Traditional Texture Weaves: Waffle Weaves	Zielinski, S. A.; Robert Leclerc, ed.	√	> 4	MWL	11			'51–'73	18
Texture: Weaving, 4-Shaft	Traditional Texture Weaves: Traditional Textures on Four Shafts	Zielinski, S. A.; Robert Leclerc, ed.	√	√	MWL	11			'51–'73	46
Texture: Weaving, Multishaft	Exploring the Textures: Multishaft Textures	Zielinski, S. A.; Robert Leclerc, ed.	√	> 4	MWL	11			'51–'73	116
Texture: Weaving, Multishaft, Irregular	Exploring the Textures: Irregular Textures on Eight Shafts	Zielinski, S. A.; Robert Leclerc, ed.	√	> 4	MWL	11			'51–'73	121
Texture: Weaving, Tracking	Exploring the Textures: Crepe	Zielinski, S. A.; Robert Leclerc, ed.	√	> 4	MWL	11			'51–'73	68
Thailand	Keeping Tradition Alive	Wilcox, Don	√		Fa	14	1		J/F 87	44
Thailand	Mudmee: The Ikat Tradition in Thailand	McCauley, Susan L.	√		Fa	10	5		S/O 83	25
Thailand	Profile of a Thai Weaver	McCauley, Susan L.	√		Fa	10	5		S/O 83	26
Thailand	Silk Production in Kohn Kaen	Marston, Ena			SS&D	7	3	27	Su 76	30
Thailand	Silks from Siam	Woodward, Carol H.	√		H&C	2	3		Su 51	23
Thailand	Thailand	Lala, Susan	√		SS&D	18	4	72	Fa 87	74
Thailand	Tours of Thailand				TM			14	D/J 87	16
Thailand	Woven Houses of Thailand, The	Wilcox, Don	√		Fa	13	3		M/J 86	38
Thatch	Woven Houses of Thailand, The	Wilcox, Don	√		Fa	13	3		M/J 86	38
Theater	"Show Biz" (Exhibit)	Scheinman, Pamela	√		Fa	7	4		J/A 80	69
Theater Costume	"Diaghilev—Costumes and Designs of the Ballets Russes" (Exhibit)	Grover, Donald	√		Fa	6	3		M/J 79	79
Theater Textiles	Altered Ego: An Interview with Pat Oleszko	Lonier, Terri	√		Fa	10	1		J/F 83	26
Theater Textiles	Dorothy Liebes Designs Fabrics for U.S. Theatre at the Brussels World's Fair		√		H&C	9	2		Sp 58	26
Theater Textiles	Fiber as Set Design: The Work of Clayton Karkosh and Associates		√		Fa	3	4		J/A 76	34

SUBJECT	TITLE	AUTHOR	IL	INST	JOUR	VOL	NO	ISS	DATE	PAGE
Theater Textiles	Ione Unruh		√		Fa	4	6		N/D 77	63
Theater Textiles	Reiko Mochinaga Brandon: Bridging Two Cultures	Moore, Marcia	√		Fa	13	6		N/D 86	16
Theater Textiles	Soft Sculpture Set for Albee's "Seascape"		√		Fa	4	2		M/A 77	29
Theater Textiles: Stage Curtain (Japanese Doncho)	Doncho for New York, A		√		H&C	15	4		Fa 64	12
Theme Weaving	Back to School in Style		√		Hw	2	1		F-W 80	52
Theme Weaving	Christmas		√		Hw	2	1		F-W 80	54
Theme Weaving	Home Weaving		√		Hw	1	1		F-W 79	32
Theme Weaving	Russet, Shades of Fall		√		Hw	2	1		F-W 80	32
Theme Weaving	Summer Weave		√		Hw	1	2		S-S 80	25
Theme Weaving	Summertime		√		Hw	4	3		M/J 83	41
Theme Weaving	Warm and Wooly		√		Hw	1	1		F-W 79	18
Theme Weaving	Weaving the Blues		√		Hw	3	4		Se 82	65
Theme Weaving	Winter Weaving		√		Hw	2	1		F-W 80	27
Theory: Knitting	Knit and Purl	Rowley, Elaine	√		Kn	1	1	1	F-W 84 CI	40 32
Therapy/Rehabilitation also see Disabled; Occupational Therapy										
Therapy/Rehabilitation	Adapting Handwoven Fabrics to Interior Design	Storey, Walter Rendell	√		H&C	4	3		Su 53	8
Therapy/Rehabilitation	Betty Rodman, an Integrated Life	Staines, Barbara			S-O	4			80	19
Therapy/Rehabilitation	Braille Pattern Board Developed for Wasinger	Tope, Carolyn	√		SS&D	4	3	15	Su 73	18
Therapy/Rehabilitation	Cabrillo College Stroke Center (error-corrected Hw v2 n4 81 p22)	McKay, Wendy: Ann Thiamann, Lynn Giles	√		Hw	2	3		My 81	12
Therapy/Rehabilitation	Cardboard Looms Help the Handicapped	Holmes, Margaret	√	√	SS&D	6	2	22	Sp 75	31
Therapy/Rehabilitation	Design Courses Precede Weaving at the University of Kansas	Fitzgerald, Jeanne			H&C	4	2		Sp 53	34
Therapy/Rehabilitation	Do's and Don'ts	Biehl, Mary Atwater			SS&D	4	1	13	Wi 72	19
Therapy/Rehabilitation	Edith Huntington Snow, Weaver, Artist, Craftsman (Reprint)	Jarecka, Louise Llewellyn	√		H&C	26	2		Ap 75	10
Therapy/Rehabilitation	Evolution of the Multi-Loom, The	Brokaw, Edith H., O.T.R.	√		H&C	3	4		Fa 52	9
Therapy/Rehabilitation	Fabrics from A Desert Weaver	Kirkpatrick, Isabell; Pat Kirkpatrick	√		H&C	7	3		Su 56	27
Therapy/Rehabilitation	Guilds Aid Disabled, Aged with Weaving Lessons and Projects	Edwards, Lois			SS&D	5	1	17	Wi 73	5
Therapy/Rehabilitation	Handweaving in a Naval Hospital	Ames, Helen B.	√		H&C	4	1		Wi 52	52
Therapy/Rehabilitation	Haptic Visions	Brubaker, Paul			WJ	11	4	44	Sp 87	59
Therapy/Rehabilitation	"How is Cloth Made?"	Edgren, Esther			SS&D	1	2	2	Mr 70	15
Therapy/Rehabilitation	Klara Johnson: A Weaver's Vision Realized	Magoffin, Connie	√	√	WJ	11	4	44	Sp 87	62
Therapy/Rehabilitation	Loom for the Handicapped, A	Nicoll, Frances M.	√		H&C	7	3		Su 56	22
Therapy/Rehabilitation	Looms for the Handicapped	Gallinger, Osma C.	√		H&C	8	2		Sp 57	19
Therapy/Rehabilitation	Mills College Weavers	Byran, Dorothy	√		H&C	8	3		Su 57	22
Therapy/Rehabilitation	Most Gratifying Work Is with Children, The	Keatley, Kathy			SS&D	2	3	7	Su 71	16
Therapy/Rehabilitation	Myra L. Davis, Master Weaver	Clement, Doris	√		H&C	12	1		Wi 61	24
Therapy/Rehabilitation	New York University's Annual Spring Conference on Industrial Arts	Ames, Helen B.	√		H&C	1	2		Su 50	13
Therapy/Rehabilitation	Pioneer in a New Profession — The Boston School of Occupational Therapy	Van Cleve, Kate	√		H&C	1	3		Fa 50	33
Therapy/Rehabilitation	Prescription — Weaving	Anderson, Betty	√		H&C	6	1		Wi 54	24
Therapy/Rehabilitation	School Psychologist Finds Weaving Valuable	Griswold, Irene T.			SS&D	5	1	17	Wi 73	73
Therapy/Rehabilitation	St. Mary's Weavers		√		H&C	10	1		Wi 59	30
Therapy/Rehabilitation	Successful Volunteer Project, A	Bryan, Dorothy	√		H&C	5	2		Sp 54	19
Therapy/Rehabilitation	Therapy in Weaving	Sober, Marion Burr, ORT	√		SS&D	1	1	1	De 69	3

SUBJECT	TITLE	AUTHOR	IL	INST	JOUR	VOL	NO	ISS	DATE	PAGE
Therapy/Rehabilitation	Weavers Are Needed	Biehl, Betty Atwater			SS&D	3	3	11	Su 72	29
Therapy/Rehabilitation	Weaving as an Occupational Therapy	Waagen, Alice K.	√		Hw	5	5		N/D 84	18
Therapy/Rehabilitation	Weaving at La Villita, School and Shop in Restored Village	Reed, J. H.	√		H&C	14	2		Sp 63	16
Therapy/Rehabilitation	Weaving His Way Back	Van Cleve, Kate	√		H&C	2	3		Su 51	11
Therapy/Rehabilitation	Weaving in New York City's Hospital Program	Ames, Helen B.	√		H&C	1	3		Fa 50	15
Therapy/Rehabilitation	Weaving in Therapy	Nicoll, Frances M., O.T.R.	√	√	H&C	11	3		Su 60	28
Therapy/Rehabilitation	Weaving in Therapy, Your Patients Teach You the Best Methods	Reding, Sgt. Lucy Frances	√	√	H&C	14	1		Wi 63	20
Therapy/Rehabilitation: Blind	Handspun Yarns Made by the Blind	Morgret, Eugene D.	√		H&C	1	3		Fa 50	17
Therapy/Rehabilitation: Blind	Teaching the Blind to Weave	Bradford, Eileen			H&C	6	1		Wi 54	26
Therapy/Rehabilitation: Blind	Weaving for the Blind	Lees, Maureen V.	√	√	H&C	8	2		Sp 57	22
Therapy/Rehabilitation: Community Weavery	Weaving Peace at Innisfree	Ohle, Carolyn	√		Hw	4	1		J/F 83	22
Therapy/Rehabilitation: Seniors	Draperies for a Synagogue		√		H&C	9	4		Fa 58	45
Third Hand: Sewing Machine	Handy Third Hand		√	√	TM			14	D/J 87	10
Thread: Elastic-Covered	Putting Knitted Pieces Together	Guagliumi, Susan	√	√	TM			11	J/J 87	45
Thread: Knotless	Knots in Threads			√	TM			8	D/J 86	4
Thread: Metallic	Threads of Gold	Austin, Carole	√		Fa	13	4		J/A 86	10
Thread: Organizer	Bread-Rag Thread Snag		√	√	TM			12	A/S 87	10
Thread: Silk	A. H. Rice Company: Maker of Silk Thread	Goodman, Deborah Lerme	√		Fa	13	1		J/F 86	54
Thread: Sizes	Handsewing Stitches	Callaway, Grace	√	√	TM			12	A/S 87	53
Threading also see Drafts and Drafting										
Threading and Sleying	Can You Use Comfort, Sley & Thread in the Same Sentence?	Gustafson, Susan L.	√	√	CW	8	1	22	Se 86	11
Threading and Sleying	Color Coding Helps Avoid Threading Errors		√	√	CW	1	1	1	De 79	2
Threading and Sleying	Designing in the Reed	Hausner, Walter	√	√	H&C	8	2		Sp 57	10
Threading and Sleying	Doup Leno (error-corrected WJ v3 n2 78 insert p38a)		√	√	WJ	3	2	10	Oc 78	32
Threading and Sleying	Planning and Weaving New Stripes	Blumenau, Lili	√	√	H&C	4	4		Fa 53	9
Threading and Sleying	Treasury for Beginners: Threading and Sleying	Zielinski, S. A.; Robert Leclerc, ed.	√	√	MWL	1			'51–'73	19
Threading and Sleying: Continuous Warp	New Loom, A	Tow, Dorothy	√		H&C	17	1		Wi 66	16
Threading and Sleying: Double Weave, Four-Color	Double Weave in Four Colors Part 1	Broughton, Eve	√	>4	CW		23		Ja 87	3
Threading and Sleying: Straight Draw	Four Harness Straight Draw and Combination Weaves		√	>4	WJ	4	2	14	Oc 79	22
Threading and Sleying: Supplementary Warps	Supplementary Warp Patterning: Threading and Sleying	Tidball, Harriet			SCGM		17		66	5
Threading and Sleying: Technique	Enjoy Threading Your Loom	Barrett, Clotilde	√	√	WJ	7	4	28	Sp 83	66
Threading and Sleying: Transposed Warps	Supplementary Warp Patterning: Mobile Warps	Tidball, Harriet		√	SCGM		17		66	10
Threading and Sleying: Without Cross	Warping with a Horizontal Reel	Tidball, Harriet	√	√	H&C	10	4		Fa 59	16
Threading: Balancing Patterns	Overshot Sampler Bedspread for a Narrow Loom, An	Keasbey, Doramay	√	√	PWC	5	1	15		42
Threading: Basic Weaves	Basic Weaves, Tool to Develop Fabric Structures (error-corrected H&C v20 n4 69 p43)	Hausner, Walter	√	√	H&C	20	3		Su 69	4
Threading: Blocks, Overshot	Coverlet: Make Someday Today, Start a Coverlet, A	van der Hoogt, Madelyn	√	√	PWC	5	1	15		24
Threading, Double Weave, Four-Color	Double Weave in Four Colors Part 2	Broughton, Eve	√	>4	CW		24		My 87	17
Threading: Elements, Doup Leno (Photograph Only)	Doup Leno: Sample Project, Threading the Loom	Skowronski, Hella; Sylvia Tacker	√		SCGM		32		80	18
Threading: Lampas, Variations	Eight-Shaft Primer: Lampas for Eight	Sullivan, Donna	√	>4	PWC	5	2	16		34

SUBJECT	TITLE	AUTHOR	IL	INST	JOUR	VOL	NO	ISS	DATE	PAGE
Threading: Pattern Harness	Some Additional Notes on the Damask—Threading the Pattern Harnesses	Ahrens, Jim	√	> 4	CW	6	2	17	Ja 85	3
Threading: Pattern-Ground Shafts	Use of Long-Eyed Heddles for Patterned Double Weave, The	Howard, Ruth	√	> 4	WJ	6	2	22	Fa 81	35
Threading: Profile Draft Technique	Miniature World, A	Piroch, Sigrid	√	> 4	PWC	5	2	16		26
Threading: Rigid-Heddles	Threading Two Rigid Heddles		√	√	Hw	7	3		M/J 86	71
Threading: Straight Draw	Drafts		√	√	WJ	1	1	1	Jy 76	12
Threading: Systems	Handloom Weaves: Threading Systems and Weaving Methods	Tidball, Harriet			SCGM		33		57	9
Threading: Technique	Threading Without Error	Keeler, Betty	√	√	Hw	8	5	.	N/D 87	85
Threading: Variations	Designing Four-Shaft Double Weaves	Muller, Donna	√	√	WJ	7	4	28	Sp 83	56
Threading: Variations	Overshot: The Weave and the Designs	Marston, Ena	√	> 4	SS&D	11	2	42	Sp 80	74
Threading: Woolens	Woolens and Tweeds: Weaving Woolens: Threadings for Woolens	Tidball, Harriet		√	SCGM		4		61	17
Three-Shaft Weaving	Fragment, Pre-Columbian Cloth Found In Utah	Turner, Alta R.	√	√	H&C	22	1		Wi 71	20
Three-Shaft Weaving	Handweaver's Instruction Manual: Three Harness Weaves, The Three-Harness Weaves	Tidball, Harriet C. nee Douglas		√	SCGM		34		49	22
Three-Shaft Weaving	Little Known Weaves Worth Knowing Better: Three-Shaft Weaves	Zielinski, S. A.; Robert Leclerc, ed.	√	√	MWL	16			'51–'73	47
Three-Shaft Weaving	Patterns from the Weaver's Guild		√	√	H&C	26	5		Oc 75	29
Three-Shaft Weaving	Simple Method for Weaving Deflected Warps	Frey, Berta	√	√	H&C	20	4		Fa 69	4
Three-Shaft Weaving	Story of My Dining Room Rug, The	Rogers, Carrie M.	√	√	WJ	6	4	24	Sp 82	24
Three-Shaft Weaving	Three Harness Weaving from the Cross Country Weavers		√	√	H&C	19	1		Wi 68	20
Three-Shaft Weaving: Backstrap Loom	Mexican Motifs: A Mexican Quesquimitl	Tidball, Harriet	√	√	SCGM		6		62	13
Thrift: Weaving	Sheepskate Weaving	Ligon, Linda	√		Hw	5	4		S/O 84	69
Throckmorton Coat	Ravensthorpe: A Festival of Wool	Walker, Pauline; Carol Taylor	√		S-O	7	2		Su 83	17
Throws see Afghans, Blankets, Throws										
Thrums	Last Word, The		√	√	Hw	4	2		M/A 83	67
Thrums	Rug from Thrums, A	Kaleda, Ruth	√	√	H&C	13	3		Su 62	41
Thrums	Thrum Basketry	Coutts, Lucele	√	√	SS&D	8	3	31	Su 77	43
Thrums	Thrums Up		√	√	Hw	5	3		Su 84	20
Tibet	Secret Treasures of Tibet	Wiltsie-Vaniea, Anne	√		SS&D	18	3	71	Su 87	60
Tick Weave	Harris Tweed Jacket		√	√	Hw	2	5		No 81	49, 87
Tick Weave	Tickweave Upholstery (Sharon D. Alderman)		√	√	Hw	5	2		M/A 84	68, 105
Ticking	Weaving Table Linens	Eychaner, Barbara Smith	√	√	TM			11	J/J 87	52
Tie-Down Shafts	Four-Shaft Primer: Tie Talk	Sullivan, Donna	√	> 4	PWC	4	4	14		14
Tie-Down Warps	Four-Shaft Primer: Tie Talk	Sullivan, Donna	√	> 4	PWC	4	4	14		14
Tie-Downs, Table Looms, Problems	Solving A Problem in Multi-Harness	Jackson, Marguerite		√	H&C	13	4		Fa 62	19
Tie-Dye also see Dyes and Dyeing: Resist										
Tie-Ups also see Drafts and Drafting										
Tie-Ups	Accurate, Knotless Tie-ups Using Loop Loom Cord	Kinersly, Gorel	√	√	WJ	5	1	17	Su 80	26
Tie-Ups	Designing from the Tie-Up, A Multiharness Tool (error-corrected Iw v5 n1 79 p10)	Alderman, Sharon D.	√	> 4	Iw	4	4		Fa 79	30
Tie-Ups	Metamorphosis: Two-Tie Weaves and the Changeable Image	Carey, Joyce Marquess	√	> 4	AT	1			De 83	243
Tie-Ups	Peter Collingwood, His Weaves and Weaving: Tying-Up a Double Countermarch Loom	Collingwood, Peter; Harriet Tidball, ed.	√	√	SCGM		8		63	24

SUBJECT	TITLE	AUTHOR	IL	INST	JOUR	VOL	NO	ISS	DATE	PAGE
Tie-Ups	Special Tie-Up for Skirt Designed By Berta Frey		√	>4	H&C	4	3		Su 53	54
Tie-Ups	Speed Up Tie-Up for the Counter March Loom	Gilmurray, Susan	√	√	SS&D	10	3	39	Su 79	50
Tie-Ups	Thomas Jackson, Weaver: 17th and 18th Century Records	Tidball, Harriet		√	SCGM		13		64	15
Tie-Ups	Tie Ups, Pegplans & Drawdowns		√	>4	CW	8	1	22	Se 86	27
Tie-Ups	Tie-Up Made Easy	Heintz, Kenneth	√	√	SS&D	5	3	19	Su 74	68
Tie-Ups	Treasury for Beginners: Rhythm and Tie-Up	Zielinski, S. A.; Robert Leclerc, ed.	√	>4	MWL	1			'51–'73	35
Tie-Ups: Block Weaves, Simplified	Use of Long-Eyed Heddles for Patterned Double Weave, The	Howard, Ruth	√	>4	WJ	6	2	22	Fa 81	35
Tie-Ups: Complex	"Adding" Treadles for a Complex Weave	Windeknecht, Margaret	√	>4	CW	3	3	9	Ap 82	4
Tie-Ups: Countermarch	Constellations: A Summer and Winter Weave on Ten Harnesses	Bergman, Margaret	√	>4	CW	5	3	15	My 84	20
Tie-Ups: Countermarch	Countermarche: Pure and Simple	Tallarovic, Joanne	√	√	WJ	8	3	31	Wi 83	85
Tie-Ups: Countermarch	Countermarche Tie Up	van der Hoogt, Madelyn	√		CW	4	3	12	Ap 83	13
Tie-Ups: Countermarch	Experimental Countermarch	Gilmurray, Susan	√	√	SS&D	8	2	30	Sp 77	39
Tie-Ups: Countermarch	Universal Tie-Up for a 4-Shaft Countermarch Loom		√	√	WJ	6	3	23	Wi 81	47
Tie-Ups: Countermarch Loom	Everything You've Always Wanted to Know About Tying Up a Countermarch Loom Without Really Trying...And with Perfect Success the First Time	van der Hoogt, Madelyn; Athanasios David Xenakis	√	√	PWC	4	2	12		44
Tie-Ups: Damask	Simple Methods for Deriving Satin Stitching Sequences and Damask Tie-Ups	Xenakis, A. David	√	>4	CW	6	1	16	Se 84	19
Tie-Ups: Designing	Warp Up Your Loom All Ye Fearful Ones!		√	>4	CW	1	1	1	De 79	2
Tie-Ups: Direct	Drafts		√	√	WJ	1	1	1	Jy 76	12
Tie-Ups: Double Weave, Four-Color	Double Weave in Four Colors Part 1	Broughton, Eve	√	>4	CW		23		Ja 87	3
Tie-Ups: Double Weave, Four-Color	Double Weave in Four Colors Part 2	Broughton, Eve	√	>4	CW		24		My 87	17
Tie-Ups: Huck, Multiple-Harness	Multi-Harness Huck: Learn About the Structure of This Family of Weaves and Design Your Own Variations	Barrett, Clotilde	√	>4	WJ	10	4	40	Sp 86	11
Tie-Ups: In-Progress Changes	Metamorphosis: Two-Tie Weaves and the Changeable Image	Carey, Joyce Marquess	√	>4	AT	1			De 83	243
Tie-Ups: Pattern-Ground System	Three-Toned Blocks, Part 1: Simple Pattern	Broughton, Eve T.	√	>4	CW	6	1	16	Se 84	12
Tie-Ups: Profile Draft Technique	Miniature World, A	Piroch, Sigrid	√	>4	PWC	5	2	16		26
Tie-Ups: Profile System	But What's the Tie-Up?	van der Hoogt, Madelyn	√	>4	PWC	5	1	15		36
Tie-Ups: Skeleton	Little Known Weaves Worth Knowing Better: Skeleton Tie-Ups	Zielinski, S. A.; Robert Leclerc, ed.	√	>4	MWL	16			'51–'73	89
Tie-Ups: Skeleton, Lampas	Lampas for Eight	Sullivan, Donna	√	>4	PWC	5	2	16		34
Tie-Ups: Standard Twill	Drafts		√	√	WJ	1	1	1	Jy 76	12
Tie-Ups: Supplementary Warps	Supplementary Warp Patterning: Tie-Up and Treadling	Tidball, Harriet	√		SCGM		17		66	5
Tie-Ups: Technique	Loom-Controlled Adaptation of a Mexican Pick-Up Pattern Technique	Keasbey, Doramay	√	>4	CW	6	2	17	Ja 85	19
Tie-Ups: Tied Block Weaves	Multiple Shaft Weaving — Tie-Ups for 2-or-More-Tie Block Weaves		√	>4	WJ	6	3	23	Wi 81	41
Tie-Ups: Turned Drafts	Turned Drafts in Double Two-Tie Unit Weave	van der Hoogt, Madelyn	√	>4	WJ	9	2	34	Fa 84	13
Tie-Ups: Twill	From Simple Twills to Dobby Fantasies...A Progression	Marquess, Joyce	√	>4	Iw	4	4		Fa 79	38
Tie-Ups: Variations	Use of the Dobby Loom for Multi-Harness Weave Manipulation, The	Renne, Elisha	√	>4	WJ	9	3	35	Wi 85	9
Tie-Ups: Variations	Variations on an Overshot Threading	Lermond, Charles	√	√	WJ	12	2	46	Fa 87	25
Tie-Ups: Variations	Whig Rose Study (continued)	Morgenstern, Marvin M.	√	√	WJ	7	3	27	Wi 82	23
Tie-Ups: Variations, Whig Rose	Whig Rose Study	Morgenstern, Marvin M.	√	√	WJ	7	2	26	Fa 82	40

SUBJECT	TITLE	AUTHOR	IL	INST	JOUR	VOL	NO	ISS	DATE	PAGE
Tied Latvian, Traditional	"Tied Latvian" Weave, The (error-corrected CW n25 87 p31)	Evans, Jane A.	√	>4	CW		24		My 87	6
Tied Latvian, Variations	"Tied Latvian" Weave, The (error-corrected CW n25 87 p31)	Evans, Jane A.	√	>4	CW		24		My 87	6
Tied Lithuanian	Borders: Notes of a Pattern Weaver	Alvic, Philis	√	>4	WJ	11	2	42	Fa 86	55
Tied Lithuanian	Dimai or Tied Lithuanian (Computer Drafts-Eleanor Best)	Petraitis, Ada	√	>4	CW	4	2	11	Ja 83	16
Tied Lithuanian	Drafting: A Personal Approach, Part 2	Alvic, Philis	√	>4	SS&D	13	2	50	Sp 82	46
Tied Lithuanian	Lithuanian Pervarai: Producing a Twenty Shaft Pattern on a Twelve Shaft Loom	Meek, M. Kati	√	>4	AT	1			De 83	159
Tied Lithuanian	Notes of a Pattern Weaver	Alvic, Philis	√		SS&D	13	4	52	Fa 82	76
Tied Lithuanian	Point Block Progression: Notes of a Pattern Weaver	Alvic, Philis	√	>4	WJ	10	4	40	Sp 86	67
Tied Lithuanian	Tied Lithuanian	Alvic, Philis	√	>4	CW	3	3	9	Ap 82	7
Tied Lithuanian	Tied Lithuanian: Notes of a Pattern Weaver	Alvic, Philis	√	>4	WJ	9	3	35	Wi 85	50
Tied Lithuanian	Turned Drafts in Double Two-Tie Unit Weave	van der Hoogt, Madelyn	√	>4	WJ	9	2	34	Fa 84	13
Tied Weaves see Unit Structure										
Time	Reflections on 7560 Weft Picks	Ligon, Linda	√	>4	Hw	8	3		M/J 87	98
Time: Efficient Use	Pricing the Production Piece	La Lena, Constance J.	√	√	SS&D	10	2	38	Sp 79	10
Time Line: Peruvian Civilization	Vignettes from Peru	Wilson, Kax	√		Iw	5	4		Fa 80	46
Time: Management	How to Weave When you Don't Have Time to Weave	Butterfield, Ann	√		Hw	3	2		Mr 82	38
Time: Management	Managing Your Time, Part 1	LaLena, Constance	√	√	Iw	5	2		Sp 80	64
Time: Management	Managing Your Time, Part 2	LaLena, Constance		√	Iw	5	3		Su 80	60
Time Samples: Braiding	Sling Braiding in the Macusani Area of Peru	Zorn, Elayne	√	√	TMJ	19 20			80,81	41
Time Samples: Production Rate: Poncho, Fiber-to-Fabric	Handspun Yarn Production Rates in the Cuzco Region of Peru	Bird, Junius B.	√		TMJ	2	3		De 68	9
Time Samples: Production Rate, Spinning Yarn	Handspun Yarn Production Rates in the Cuzco Region of Peru	Bird, Junius B.	√		TMJ	2	3		De 68	9
Time Samples: Production Rate, Weaving	Weaving a Cotton Saddlebag on the Santa Elena Peninsula of Ecuador	Hagino, Jane Parker; Karen E. Stothert	√	√	TMJ	22			83	19
Time Samples: Spinning Yarn	Study of Andean Spinning in the Cuzco Region, A	Goodell, Miss Grace	√	√	TMJ	2	3		De 68	2
Time-Line: Weaving	Thread That Runs So True — A Weaving Time Line	Strickler, Carol	√		Hw	3	5		N/D 82	45
Tips and Timesavers: Weaving	Tips and Timesavers	Keasbey, Doramay	√	√	PWC	5	2	16		22
Titles	Plight of the Untitled, The	Kniskern, Edna Maki	√		Fa	8	4		J/A 81	32
Tool Kit	Tool Kit from Inkle Bands, A	Hinson, Dolores M.	√	√	WJ	6	4	24	Sp 82	46
Tools	McMorran Yarn Balance				TM		1		O/N 85	78
Tools: Basketry	Making an Open-Weave Willow Basket	Hart, Carol	√	√	TM		4		A/M 86	24
Tools: Bobbins, Antique	Antique Fiber Tools		√		WJ	9	2	34	Fa 84	35
Tools: Color	Tools: Color Planning Devices		√		Hw	2	4		Se 81	73
Tools: Combs, Weaver's	Antique Fiber Tools		√		WJ	9	2	34	Fa 84	36
Tools: Cotton, Antique	Antique Fiber Tools		√		WJ	9	2	34	Fa 84	32
Tools: Darning	Darn That Hole	Markrich, Lilo	√	√	TM		5		J/J 86	38
Tools: Feltmaking	Felt-making Craftsmen of the Anatolian and Iranian Plateaux	Gervers, Michael; Veronika Gervers	√	√	TMJ	4	1		De 74	14
Tools: Fiber, Antique	Antique Fiber Tools		√		WJ	9	2	34	Fa 84	29
Tools: Flax, Antique	Antique Fiber Tools		√		WJ	9	2	34	Fa 84	32
Tools: Hebedo Guage	Battenberg Lace: Making Lace with Woven Tape and a Needle	Kliot, Jules; Kaethe Kliot	√	√	TM		10		A/M 87	30
Tools: Hooking	Tapestry Gunner	Henry, Patti	√	√	TM		7		O/N 86	40
Tools: Knitting	Tools	Swansen, Meg	√	√	Kn	1	2	2	S-S 85	10
Tools: Knitting, Ball Winder	Tools	Swansen, Meg	√		Kn	1	1	1	F-W 84	54
										CI

SUBJECT	TITLE	AUTHOR	IL	INST	JOUR	VOL	NO	ISS	DATE	PAGE
Tools: Knitting, Umbrella Swift	Tools	Swansen, Meg	√		Kn	1	1	1	F-W 84 CI	54
Tools: Pressing	Irons, Boards, and Presses: A Survey of the Tools That Beautify Sewing	Coffin, David Page	√		TM			10	A/M 87	40
Tools: Sewing	Making a Great Shirt Collar	Coffin, David Page	√	√	TM			4	A/M 86	42
Tools: Shuttles, Antique	Antique Fiber Tools		√		WJ	9	2	34	Fa 84	36
Tools: Sleying	Reed-Sleying Hooks			√	TM			4	A/M 86	8
Tools: Swifts and Winders, Antique	Antique Fiber Tools		√		WJ	9	2	34	Fa 84	36
Tools: Tailoring	Tailor's Pressing Tools			√	TM			13	O/N 87	10
Tools: Tapestry	Contemporary Tapestry	Tidball, Harriet	√		SCGM		12		64	12
Tools: Weaving	Teasel Tools	Antuñez de Mayolo, Kay	√	√	SS&D	13	4	52	Fa 82	10
Tools: Weaving	Two-Harness Textiles, The Open Work Weaves: Tools	Tidball, Harriet	√		SCGM		21		67	1
Tools: Weaving, Antique	Antique Fiber Tools		√		WJ	9	2	34	Fa 84	33/38
Tools: Weaving, Japanese	Japanese Weaving Tools	Schreiber, LaVonne	√		WJ	9	2	34	Fa 84	47
Tools: Wool, Antique	Antique Fiber Tools		√		WJ	9	2	34	Fa 84	30
Tools: Yarn Winding	Tools		√		Kn	3	4	8	Fa 87	8
Tops see Blouses, Shirts, Tops										
Totes see Bags, Purses, Totes										
Totonicapan Weave	Guatemala Visited	Atwater, Mary Meigs	√		SCGM		15		65	24
Towels	Apron and Kitchen Towels		√	√	Hw	1	2		S-S 80	26, 53
Towels	Bath Towel (Jane Patrick) (error-corrected Hw v3 n4 82 p81)		√	> 4	Hw	3	2		Mr 82	50, 90
Towels	Bath Towel Set, A	Xenakis, Athanasios David	√	√	PWC	1	1		No 81	24
Towels	Checked Towels (Margaretha Essén-Hedin)		√	√	Hw	8	5		N/D 87	55, I-13
Towels	Cheery Checked Towels (Barbara Eychener)		√	> 4	Hw	3	4		Se 82	59, 82
Towels	Chenille Bath Towel (Phyllis Ronin)		√	√	Hw	1	2		S-S 80	29, 54
Towels	Crisp and Colorful Linen Towels		√	√	WJ	7	2	26	Fa 82	30
Towels	Demystifying Complex Weaves: A Step-by-Step Exploration from Four to Sixteen Harnesses	Piroch, Sigrid	√	> 4	WJ	10	3	39	Wi 86	8
Towels	Display Towel (Astrid Sonesson)		√	> 4	Hw	8	3		M/J 87	43, I-4
Towels	Dunkagäng Guest Towels (Sharon Alderman)		√	√	Hw	7	2		M/A 86	I-5
Towels	Easy-weave, Soft and Absorbent Towel, An (Mary Ann Geers) (error-corrected Hw v6 n4 85 p I-2)		√	√	Hw	6	3		Su 85	84
Towels	Eight-Shaft Summer and Winter Towels (Georgean Curran)		√	> 4	Hw	8	5		N/D 87	74
Towels	Embroidery for the Goddess	Kelly, Mary B.	√		TM			11	J/J 87	26
Towels	Finger Tip Towel (James Ronin)		√	> 4	Hw	1	2		S-S 80	29, 67
Towels	Hand Towels in Overshot Effect	Davenport, Betty	√	√	PWC	3	2	8		48
Towels	Hand Towels (Inger Mattson)		√	√	Hw	4	2		M/A 83	31, 83
Towels	Hands to Work and Hearts to God	Erf, Mary Elva	√	√	WJ	8	1	29	Su 83	25
Towels	Handspun Linen Towels	Quinn, Celia	√	√	S-O	7	1		Sp 83	32
Towels	Heap of Linen Towels, A (Linda Ligon)		√	√	Hw	6	2		M/A 85	54, I-12
Towels	Hemstitch in Time, A	Ligon, Linda	√	√	Hw	8	2		M/A 87	98
Towels	Linen Bath Towels (Beth Johnson Brewin)		√	√	Hw	5	3		Su 84	70, 105
Towels	Linen Kitchen Towel (Col. James Ronin) (error-corrected Hw v2 n1 80 p4)		√	√	Hw	1	2		S-S 80	27, 53
Towels	Linen Lattice Towel (Linda Ligon)		√	√	Hw	5	3		Su 84	70, 105
Towels	Linen Towels		√	√	H&C	21	1		Wi 70	13
Towels	Linen Towels	Frey, Berta	√	√	H&C	14	3		Su 63	13
Towels	Luxury of Silk, The		√	√	Hw	1	2		S-S 80	28

SUBJECT	TITLE	AUTHOR	IL	INST	JOUR	VOL	NO	ISS	DATE	PAGE
Towels	Nineteenth Century Miniatures	Erf, Mary Elva Congleton	√		SS&D	16	1	61	Wi 84	60
Towels	Overshot on Opposites: Linen Hand Towels	Xenakis, Athanasios David	√	√	PWC	3	2	8		29
Towels	Pastel Collection (Jane Patrick)		√	√	Hw	6	2		M/A 85	48, I-8
Towels	Plaited twills		√	> 4	WJ	7	4	28	Sp 83	76
Towels	Poinsettia Finger Towels (Phyllis Mullin)		√	> 4	Hw	1	2		S-S 80	29, 56
Towels	Profile Drafting Lesson: Bronson Lace Towel (Sharon Alderman)		√	√	Hw	8	5		N/D 87	44, I-7
Towels	Profile Drafting Lesson: Summer and Winter Towel (Sharon Alderman)		√	√	Hw	8	5		N/D 87	44, I-6
Towels	Profile Drafting Lesson: Twill Towel (Sharon Alderman)		√	> 4	Hw	8	5		N/D 87	44, I-7
Towels	Roller Towel (Mamie LaGrone)		√	√	Hw	1	2		S-S 80	27, 53
Towels	Sauna Towel (Phyllis Griffith)		√	√	Hw	1	2		S-S 80	47, 54
Towels	Sauna Towels	Freeberg, Judy	√	√	WJ	10	4	40	Sp 86	50
Towels	Shaker Towel I (Sharon Alderman)		√	√	Hw	3	5		N/D 82	39, 90
Towels	Shaker Towel II (Sharon Alderman)		√	√	Hw	3	5		N/D 82	41, 90
Towels	Shaker Towel III (Sharon Alderman)		√	√	Hw	3	5		N/D 82	41, 91
Towels	Shaker Towel IV (Sharon Alderman)		√	√	Hw	3	5		N/D 82	39, 92
Towels	Shaker Towel V (Sharon Alderman)		√	> 4	Hw	3	5		N/D 82	41, 92
Towels	Shaker Towels: A Guild Devotes a Year of Study to Nineteenth Century Textiles (error-corrected WJ v11 n2 86 p68)	Eastlake, Sandy	√	> 4	WJ	10	4	40	Sp 86	20
Towels	Soft Surprise Guest Towels (Matilda MacGeorge)		√	√	Hw	6	4		S/O 85	86
Towels	Some Unusual Turkish Embroideries of the Early Eighteenth Century	Johnstone, Pauline	√		TMJ	24			85	75
Towels	Stars Finger Towels		√	> 4	Hw	1	2		S-S 80	55
Towels	Summer and Winter Kitchen Towels (Beth Johnson Brewin) (error-corrected Hw v8 n3 87 p I-3) (error-corrected Hw v8 n1 87 p I-3)		√	√	Hw	7	3		M/J 86	65, I-13
Towels	Ten-Harness Design for a Towel	Gubser, Elsie H.	√	> 4	H&C	9	4		Fa 58	28
Towels	Tenugui: Decorative Japanese Hand Towels		√		Fa	9	6		N/D 82	25
Towels	Towel for a Summer Day		√		Hw	4	3		M/J 83	52
Towels	Twilled Cottolin Towels	Waggoner, Phyllis	√	√	WJ	11	1	41	Su 86	42
Towels	Weave for Your Kitchen	Frey, Berta	√		H&C	1	2		Su 50	19
Towels	Weaving Spanish Eyelet	Gubser, Elsie H.	√	√	H&C	10	1		Wi 59	48
Towels	Weaving Table Linens	Eychaner, Barbara Smith	√	√	TM			11	J/J 87	52
Towels	Weaving Towels As a Means of Learning the Basic Four-Shaft Weaves	Barrett, Clotilde	√	√	WJ	8	2	30	Fa 83	11
Towels	White Bath Towel (Suzanne Urton)		√	√	Hw	4	3		M/J 83	52, 94
Towels, Kitchen	And Thereon Hangs a Towel		√	> 4	Hw	3	4		Se 82	58
Towels, Shaker	Simple Gifts	Alderman, Sharon	√		Hw	3	5		N/D 82	39
Toys	Handwoven Teddy Bear (Janice Jones)		√	√	Hw	6	4		S/O 85	63, I-12
Toys	Idea Notebook: Carefree Cats		√	√	Hw	7	5		N/D 86	21
Toys	Tetrahedron (Carol Strickler)		√	√	Hw	6	4		S/O 85	64, I-15
Toys	Them Little Mousies	Gickie, John	√	√	S-O	9	1		Sp 85	21
Toys	Toy Chick (Sally Decker)		√	√	Hw	1	2		S-S 80	39, 63
Toys	Toys and Other Fun Stuff	Ligon, Linda	√	√	Iw	2	1		Fa 76	13
Toys	Weaving in Donegal (error-corrected H&C v23 n3 72 p11)	McNeill, Mary	√	√	H&C	23	2		M/A 72	35
Toys	Wool Worker's Flock	Waltner, Willard; Elma Waltner	√	√	Hw	4	4		S/O 83	75
Toys, Handwoven	Olwen's Buffalo	MacGregor, Olwen	√	√	WJ	8	2	30	Fa 83	46
Toys: Teddy Bear	Traditional Teddy: Overshot in Miniature	Sullivan, Donna	√	√	PWC	5	2	16		14
Tracking	Are You Ready to Collapse?	Frame, Mary	√	√	S-O	11	1		Sp 87	41

SUBJECT	TITLE	AUTHOR	IL	INST	JOUR	VOL	NO	ISS	DATE	PAGE
Tracking	Cool and Casual Cotton		√		Hw	6	3		Su 85	42
Tracking	Exploring the Textures: Crepe	Zielinski, S. A.; Robert Leclerc, ed.	√	> 4	MWL	11			'51–'73	68
Tracking	Finishing Handwoven Materials	Thilenius, Carol	√	√	Iw	2	3		Sp 77	16
Tracking	Handspun Plaid Shirt, A (Betty Keeler)		√		Hw	4	5		N/D 83	73
Tracking	Keep It Simple		√	√	Hw	8	4		S/O 87	35
Tracking	Ringlets and Waves: Undulations from Overtwist	Frame, Mary	√	√	S-O	10	4		Wi 86	28
Tracking	Save the Twist: Warping and Weaving with Overtwisted Yarns	Frame, Mary	√	√	S-O	11	2		Su 87	43
Tracking	Tracking, the Mystery of the Crinkling Cloth	Alderman, Sharon	√	√	Hw	6	4		S/O 85	31
Trade Materials: Weaving	Commercial Materials in Modern Navajo Rugs	Hedlund, Ann Lane	√		TMJ	25			86	83
Trade Regulations	Care Labeling Rule Of FTC			√	SS&D	4	1	13	Wi 72	42
Trade Regulations	Laundry Care Labels Needed After July 3	Attix, George			SS&D	3	3	11	Su 72	10
Trade Shows: Admission Policies	Wants to See Show				TM			13	O/N 87	4
Trade Shows: Hobby	One Who Dies with the Most Stuff Wins!, The	Guagliumi, Susan			TM			11	J/J 87	15
Trade Shows: Industrial Sewing	Shirtmaker from a Small Planet	Coffin, David Page			TM			9	F/M 87	16
Trade Shows: Needlework	One Who Dies with the Most Stuff Wins!, The	Guagliumi, Susan			TM			11	J/J 87	15
Trade Shows: Sewing Machine Dealers	Latest Stuff in Sewing, The	Fanning, Robbie		√	TM			14	D/J 87	20
Trade Shows: Textile	Surface Attraction	Mattera, Joanne	√		TM			7	O/N 86	20
Trade Unions: Textile Industry	Technical Progress and the Evolution of Wage Arrangements in the British Cotton Weaving Industry	Jackson, K. C.; B. Pourdeyhimi	√		AT	7			Ju 87	61
Trading Posts	Contemporary Navajo Weaving	Hedlund, Ann Lane	√		WJ	11	1	41	Su 86	30
Traditional Weaving: Berea College Fireside Industries	Berea College Fireside Industries Now Employ Sixty Weavers	Stahl, Sam	√		H&C	19	2		Sp 68	5
Transcribing: Block Patterns	Composition and Designing Part 2: Transcribing	Zielinski, S. A.; Robert Leclerc, ed.	√	> 4	MWL	19			'51–'73	44
Transparent Textiles	April May: She Weaves Curtains with Images	Woelfle, Gretchen	√		Fa	7	6		N/D 80	28
Transparent Textiles	Betty Williams: Colors of the Earth	Robbins, Judy	√		SS&D	18	4	72	Fa 87	57
Transparent Textiles	Border Squares Curtain (Sharon D. Alderman)		√	> 4	Hw	5	2		M/A 84	69, 106
Transparent Textiles	Canvas Weave Elegance	Herring, Connie	√	> 4	PWC	4	1	11		23
Transparent Textiles	Doup Leno	Skowronski, Hella; Sylvia Tacker	√	√	TM			4	A/M 86	56
Transparent Textiles	Finnish Method of Weaving Transparent Inlay, A	Gray, Herbi	√	√	SS&D	17	1	65	Wi 85	14
Transparent Textiles	Flower Curtain	Xenakis, Athanasios David	√	√	PWC	4	1	11		32
Transparent Textiles	Four-Shaft Unbalanced Twill Braided Ribbon Inlay on Plain Weave Ground	Xenakis, Athanasios David	√	√	PWC	4	1	11		27
Transparent Textiles	Home Weaving: Linen'n Lace	Xenaxis, Athanasios David	√	√	Hw	1	1		F-W 79	44
Transparent Textiles	How to Weave a Transparency	Keasbey, Doramay	√	√	Hw	4	1		J/F 83	27
Transparent Textiles	Lilies on an Antique Tray	Herring, Connie	√	√	PWC	4	1	11		30
Transparent Textiles	Moorman Technique		√		Hw	3	1		Ja 82	38
Transparent Textiles	Parks' Bouquet	Parks, Deborah	√	√	PWC	4	1	11		36
Transparent Textiles	Rigid Heddle Wool Curtain (Betty Davenport)		√	√	Hw	2	1		F-W 80	Cover, 72
Transparent Textiles	Screen for All Seasons, A	Ridgeway, Terese	√	√	SS&D	16	4	64	Fa 85	52
Transparent Textiles	Season's End Transparency (Görel Kinersly)		√	√	Hw	5	4		S/0 84	69, 105
Transparent Textiles	Simple Inlay on a Leno Ground	Xenakis, Athanasios David; Patti Sellon	√	√	PWC	4	1	11		18

744

SUBJECT	TITLE	AUTHOR	IL	INST	JOUR	VOL	NO	ISS	DATE	PAGE
Transparent Textiles	Simple Inlay on Sheer Plain Weave Ground	Xenakis, Athanasios David; Linda Lyon	√	√	PWC	4	1	11		16
Transparent Textiles	Traces of Time	Schimmel, Heidrun	√		Fa	9	3		M/J 82	70
Transparent Textiles	Transparencies		√	√	Hw	7	2		M/A 86	45
Transparent Textiles	Transparencies of Inger Harrison–Sheer Beauty, The	Keasbey, Doramay	√	√	Hw	3	1		Ja 82	40
Transparent Textiles	Transparency Notes		√	√	Hw	6	4		S/O 85	67
Transparent Textiles	Transparent Textiles	Burlew, Margaret	√	√	SS&D	17	1	65	Wi 85	10
Transparent Textiles	Transparent Weaving with Handspun Cotton Weft	Green, Andrea	√	√	WJ	8	2	30	Fa 83	44
Transparent Textiles	Two Unusual Multishaft Curtains	Xenakis, Athanasios David	√	> 4	PWC	4	1	11		40
Transparent Textiles	Two-Tie Inlay	Xenakis, Athanasios David	√	√	PWC	4	1	11		19
Transparent Textiles	Using Light as a Design Element	Liebler, Barbara	√		Hw	5	3		Su 84	88
Transparent Textiles	Weaving Primer, Part 1	Parks, Deborah	√	√	PWC	4	1	11		44
Transparent Textiles	Weaving Primer, Part 2	Lyon, Linda	√	> 4	PWC	4	1	11		45
Transparent Textiles	Weaving Primer, Part 3	Xenakis, Athanasios David	√	> 4	PWC	4	1	11		46
Transparent Textiles	Windows: Sendoni Curtains	Xenakis, Alexis Yiorgos	√	> 4	PWC	4	1	11		4
Transparent Textiles: Techniques, Finnish	Finnish Transparent Weaving	Utzinger, Karin	√	√	WJ	5	1	17	Su 80	34
Trapunto	Ann Dunbar		√		Fa	4	3		M/J 77	41
Trapunto	Fantastic Finnweave, Part 3	Xenakis, Athanasios David	√	> 4	PWC			4	Ja 83	24
Trapunto	Janet Higgins: Soft Sculpture in Motion	Marquess, Joyce	√		Fa	7	2		M/A 80	62
Trapunto	Karen Reese		√		Fa	4	3		M/J 77	32
Trapunto	Linda Nelson Bryan	Vozar, Linda	√		Fa	4	6		N/D 77	58
Trapunto	Muslin Ladies: Trapunto Drawings of Christine Meyers	Rowland, Amy Zaffarano	√		Fa	10	3		M/J 83	19
Trapunto: Layered, Technique	Layered Trapunto	Morrison, Lois	√	√	TM			12	A/S 87	50
Travail à La Planche	Weaving in Quebec: Traditional Quebecois Weaving	Barrett, Clotilde	√	√	WJ	6	4	24	Sp 82	10
Travel	Adventures in Pursuit of Yarns	Gallagher, Constance	√		H&C	12	3		Su 61	51
Travel	American Weaver in Japan		√		H&C	18	4		Fa 67	30
Travel	British Versatility	Leek, Yvonne B.			SS&D	6	3	23	Su 75	41
Travel	Dorothy Meredith in Asia	Stamsta, Jean			H&C	16	3		Su 65	29
Travel	Mexican Travelogue, A	Hewitt, T. H.	√		H&C	3	3		Su 52	22
Travel	Peripatetic Weaver, The	Schobinger, Helen J.	√		H&C	1	1		Ap 50	12
Travel	Peruvian Journey	Regensteiner, Else			H&C	17	1		Wi 66	34
Travel	Tips for Traveling Weavers	Coffman, Charlotte	√	√	SS&D	13	2	50	Sp 82	22
Travel	Tours of Thailand				TM			14	D/J 87	16
Travel	Travel Tidbits: Great Smoky Mountain National Park	Switzer, Chris	√		Hw	7	4		S/O 86	38
Travel	Travel Tidbits: Yellowstone Park Area	Switzer, Chris	√		Hw	7	3		M/J 86	21
Travel	Weaver's Journey, A	Gonzalez, Loraine			H&C	15	2		Sp 64	33
Travel	Weaving Through Portugal	Papa, Nancy	√		SS&D	6	3	23	Su 75	89
Travel	Workshop Tour to Sweden	Young, Dorothy M.	√		SS&D	4	2	14	Sp 73	41
Travel: British Isles	Weaving Tour of British Isles				H&C	18	2		Sp 67	34
Travel: British Isles, France, Greece	Ken Colwell: Travels with Ken	Colwell, Ken	√		PWC	4	2	12		31
Travel: Craft Tours	European Craft Tour, A	Polaski, Lois	√		H&C	23	1		J/F 72	16
Travel: Craft Tours	Handweaver & Craftsman Tour of Europe, 1972	Polaski, Lois	√		H&C	23	2		M/A 72	13
Travel: U.S.A.	Weaver's Wanderlust, A	Redding, Debbie			Hw	3	4		Se 82	18
Travel: Weaving Tour	Wool Gathering in Wales	Clement, Doris; Ted Clement	√		H&C	23	1		J/F 72	26

SUBJECT	TITLE	AUTHOR	IL	INST	JOUR	VOL	NO	ISS	DATE	PAGE
Tray Cloth	Lilies on an Antique Tray	Herring, Connie	√	√	PWC	4	1	11		30
Treadling also see Drafts and Drafting										
Treadling	From the Weaver's Bench: Full Width Projects	Elam, E. T.		√	H&C	23	5		S/O 72	30
Treadling	Thomas Jackson, Weaver: 17th and 18th Century Records	Tidball, Harriet		√	SCGM		13		64	15
Treadling: As-Drawn-In	Colonial Overshot, "Trompt as Writ"	Liebler, Barbara	√	√	Iw	1	2		Wi 76	14
Treadling: As-Drawn-In	Composition and Designing Part 2: Four Shaft Random Drafts Woven-As-Drawn-In	Zielinski, S. A.; Robert Leclerc, ed.	√	√	MWL	19			'51–'73	98
Treadling: As-Drawn-In	Coverlet: Make Someday Today, Start a Coverlet, A	van der Hoogt, Madelyn	√	√	PWC	5	1	15		24
Treadling: As-Drawn-In	Drafts		√	√	WJ	1	1	1	Jy 76	12
Treadling: As-Drawn-In	Little Known Weaves Worth Knowing Better: Tromp-As-Writ	Zielinski, S. A.; Robert Leclerc, ed.	√	√	MWL	16			'51–'73	94
Treadling: As-Drawn-In	Mitered Corners for Identical Warp and Weft Patterns	Redfield, Gail M.	√	√	H&C	14	3		Su 63	21
Treadling: As-Drawn-In	Multiple Harness Weaving Course Part 4: Twill Derivatives (cont'd)	Searles, Nancy M.	√	> 4	WJ	5	2	18	Fa 80	19
Treadling: As-Drawn-In	Treadle as Drawn In	Frey, Berta	√	> 4	H&C	5	3		Su 54	24
Treadling: As-Drawn-In	Weaving As Drawn In—Classic Style, Part 1	Keasbey, Doramay	√	√	SS&D	17	1	65	Wi 85	28
Treadling: As-Drawn-In	Weaving As Drawn In—Classic Style, Part 2	Keasbey, Doramay	√	> 4	SS&D	17	2	66	Sp 86	38
Treadling: As-Drawn-In, (Blocks)	Miniature World, A	Piroch, Sigrid	√	> 4	PWC	5	2	16		26
Treadling: As-Drawn-In, Overshot	Handweaver's Instruction Manual: The Overshot Weave, Weaving As-Drawn-In	Tidball, Harriet C. nee Douglas		√	SCGM		34		49	25
Treadling: Block Sequences on Overshot	Ways to Weave Overshot: Part 3	Marston, Ena	√	√	SS&D	12	2	46	Sp 81	6
Treadling: Boundweave on Overshot	Ways to Weave Overshot: Part 2	Marston, Ena	√	√	SS&D	12	1	45	Wi 80	36
Treadling: Compound	Little Known Weaves Worth Knowing Better: Skeleton Tie-Ups	Zielinski, S. A.; Robert Leclerc, ed.	√	> 4	MWL	16			'51–'73	89
Treadling: Double Weave, Four-Color	Double Weave in Four Colors Part 1	Broughton, Eve	√	> 4	CW		23		Ja 87	3
Treadling: Double Weave, Four-Color	Double Weave in Four Colors Part 2	Broughton, Eve	√	> 4	CW		24		My 87	17
Treadling: Double Weave, Patterned	Use of Long-Eyed Heddles for Patterned Double Weave, The	Howard, Ruth	√	> 4	WJ	6	2	22	Fa 81	35
Treadling: Honeycomb Fashion	Ways to Weave Overshot: Part 1	Marston, Ena	√	√	SS&D	11	3	43	Su 80	6
Treadling: Huck, Multiple-Harness	Multi-Harness Huck: Learn About the Structure of This Family of Weaves and Design Your Own Variations	Barrett, Clotilde	√	> 4	WJ	10	4	40	Sp 86	11
Treadling: Italian Fashion	Ways to Weave Overshot: Part 1	Marston, Ena	√	√	SS&D	11	3	43	Su 80	6
Treadling: Keeping Track	Keeping Track	Ligon, Linda	√	√	Hw	8	1		J/F 87	90
Treadling: Lace, Bronson on Overshot	Ways to Weave Overshot: Part 3	Marston, Ena	√	√	SS&D	12	2	46	Sp 81	6
Treadling: Long-Eyed Heddle System	Some Additional Notes on the Damask—Threading the Pattern Harnesses	Ahrens, Jim	√	> 4	CW	6	2	17	Ja 85	3
Treadling: Mattor, Variations	Mattor (error-corrected WJ v2 n1 77 insert for vol. 1)	Dunham, Miriam	√	√	WJ	1	4	4	Ap 77	21
Treadling: Opposites	Ways to Weave Overshot: Part 1	Marston, Ena	√	√	SS&D	11	3	43	Su 80	6
Treadling: Overshot, As-Drawn-In	Creative Overshot: Traditional Treadling	Windeknecht, Margaret B.	√	√	SCGM		31		78	31
Treadling: Overshot, Bound Weave Method	Creative Overshot: Additional Treadling Variations	Windeknecht, Margaret B.	√	√	SCGM		31		78	42
Treadling: Overshot, Feather Stitch Method	Creative Overshot: Additional Treadling Variations	Windeknecht, Margaret B.	√	√	SCGM		31		78	42
Treadling: Overshot, Honeycomb Method	Creative Overshot: Additional Treadling Variations	Windeknecht, Margaret B.	√	√	SCGM		31		78	42
Treadling: Overshot, Lace and Texture Method	Creative Overshot: Additional Treadling Variations	Windeknecht, Margaret B.	√	√	SCGM		31		78	42

SUBJECT	TITLE	AUTHOR	IL	INST	JOUR	VOL	NO	ISS	DATE	PAGE
Treadling: Overshot, M's and O's Method	Creative Overshot: Additional Treadling Variations	Windeknecht, Margaret B.	√	√	SCGM		31		78	42
Treadling: Overshot, No-Tabby Method	Creative Overshot: Additional Treadling Variations	Windeknecht, Margaret B.	√	√	SCGM		31		78	42
Treadling: Overshot, Opposite	Handweaver's Instruction Manual: The Overshot Weave, Weaving "Opposite" Drafts	Tidball, Harriet C. nee Douglas		√	SCGM		34		49	27
Treadling: Overshot, Opposites	Creative Overshot: Traditional Treadling	Windeknecht, Margaret B.	√	√	SCGM		31		78	31
Treadling: Overshot, Petit Point Method	Creative Overshot: Additional Treadling Variations	Windeknecht, Margaret B.	√	√	SCGM		31		78	42
Treadling: Overshot, Polychrome Method	Creative Overshot: Additional Treadling Variations	Windeknecht, Margaret B.	√	√	SCGM		31		78	42
Treadling: Overshot, Rose Fashion	Creative Overshot: Traditional Treadling	Windeknecht, Margaret B.	√	√	SCGM		31		78	31
Treadling: Overshot, Shadow Method	Creative Overshot: Additional Treadling Variations	Windeknecht, Margaret B.	√	√	SCGM		31		78	42
Treadling: Overshot, Swivel Method	Creative Overshot: Additional Treadling Variations	Windeknecht, Margaret B.	√	√	SCGM		31		78	42
Treadling: Overshot, Undulating	Creative Overshot: Undulate the Treadling	Windeknecht, Margaret B.	√	√	SCGM		31		78	36
Treadling: Overshot, Variations	Creative Overshot: Additional Treadling Variations	Windeknecht, Margaret B.	√	√	SCGM		31		78	42
Treadling: Overshot Variations	Ways to Weave Overshot: Part 1	Marston, Ena	√	√	SS&D	11	3	43	Su 80	6
Treadling: Overshot Variations	Ways to Weave Overshot: Part 2	Marston, Ena	√	√	SS&D	12	1	45	Wi 80	36
Treadling: Overshot Variations	Ways to Weave Overshot: Part 3	Marston, Ena	√	√	SS&D	12	2	46	Sp 81	6
Treadling: Petit Point	Delicate Dots...Petit Point Treadling	Keasbey, Doramay	√	√	Hw	7	1		J/F 86	66
Treadling: Problems/Solutions	Rx: Warp End Breakage and Treadling Errors	Guy, Sallie T.	√	√	Hw	3	4		Se 82	22
Treadling: Profile Draft Technique	Miniature World, A	Piroch, Sigrid	√	> 4	PWC	5	2	16		26
Treadling: Rose Fashion	Coverlet: Make Someday Today, Start a Coverlet, A	van der Hoogt, Madelyn	√	√	PWC	5	1	15		24
Treadling: Rose Fashion	Little Known Weaves Worth Knowing Better: A Rose Is a Rose	Zielinski, S. A.; Robert Leclerc, ed.	√	√	MWL	16			'51–'73	99
Treadling: Rose Fashion	Mitered Corners for Identical Warp and Weft Patterns	Redfield, Gail M.	√	√	H&C	14	3		Su 63	21
Treadling: Rose Fashion	Overshot Patterns: Emphasis on Miniatures	Marston, Ena	√	√	SS&D	11	1	41	Wi 79	40
Treadling: Rose Fashion	Overshot: Rose Fashion	Liebler, Barbara	√	√	Iw	1	3		Sp 76	16
Treadling: Rose Fashion	Ways to Weave Overshot: Part 1	Marston, Ena	√	√	SS&D	11	3	43	Su 80	6
Treadling: Rose Fashion	Ways to Weave Overshot: Part 3	Marston, Ena	√	√	SS&D	12	2	46	Sp 81	6
Treadling: Rose Fashion	Weaving As Drawn In—Classic Style, Part 1	Keasbey, Doramay	√	√	SS&D	17	1	65	Wi 85	28
Treadling: Rose Fashion, Overshot	Handweaver's Instruction Manual: The Overshot Weave, Weaving Rose Fashion	Tidball, Harriet C. nee Douglas	√	√	SCGM		34		49	26
Treadling: Satin	Contemporary Satins: Treadling Satins	Tidball, Harriet	√	> 4	SCGM		7		62	8
Treadling: Shadow Weave	Ways to Weave Overshot: Part 1	Marston, Ena	√	√	SS&D	11	3	43	Su 80	6
Treadling: Star Fashion	Overshot Patterns: Emphasis on Miniatures	Marston, Ena	√	√	SS&D	11	1	41	Wi 79	40
Treadling: Star Fashion	Ways to Weave Overshot: Part 1	Marston, Ena	√	√	SS&D	11	3	43	Su 80	6
Treadling: Star Fashion	Weaving As Drawn In—Classic Style, Part 1	Keasbey, Doramay	√	√	SS&D	17	1	65	Wi 85	28
Treadling: Straight and Reverse	Multiple Harness Weaving Course Part 4: Twill Derivatives (cont'd)	Searles, Nancy M.	√	> 4	WJ	5	2	18	Fa 80	19
Treadling: Straight Draw	Four Harness Straight Draw and Combination Weaves		√	> 4	WJ	4	2	14	Oc 79	22
Treadling: Swivel on Overshot	Notebook: Swivel, A Method of Treadling	Myers, Ruth Nordquist, ed.	√	√	SS&D	14	2	54	Sp 83	8
Treadling: Swivel on Overshot	Ways to Weave Overshot: Part 2	Marston, Ena	√	√	SS&D	12	1	45	Wi 80	36
Treadling: Swivel on Spot Bronson	Notebook: Swivel, A Method of Treadling	Myers, Ruth Nordquist, ed.	√	√	SS&D	14	2	54	Sp 83	8
Treadling: Swivel on Summer and Winter	Notebook: Swivel, A Method of Treadling	Myers, Ruth Nordquist, ed.	√	√	SS&D	14	2	54	Sp 83	8

SUBJECT	TITLE	AUTHOR	IL	INST	JOUR	VOL	NO	ISS	DATE	PAGE
Treadling: Tied Block Weaves	Multiple Shaft Weaving — Tie-Ups for 2-or-More-Tie Block Weaves		√	> 4	WJ	6	3	23	Wi 81	41
Treadling: Tromp-As-Writ	Little Known Weaves Worth Knowing Better: Tromp-As-Writ	Zielinski, S. A.; Robert Leclerc, ed.	√	√	MWL	16			'51–'73	94
Treadling: Turned	White Bath Towel (Suzanne Urton)		√	√	Hw	4	3		M/J 83	52, 94
Treadling: Turned Drafts	Turned Drafts in Double Two-Tie Unit Weave	van der Hoogt, Madelyn	√	> 4	WJ	9	2	34	Fa 84	13
Treadling: Turned Drafts	Weaver's Challenge	Wertenberger, Kathryn	√	√	Hw	5	1		J/F 84	27
Treadling: Twill	Fascination of Twills (Fourshafts): More About Twills	Zielinski, S. A.; Robert Leclerc, ed.	√	√	MWL	9			'51–'73	92
Treadling: Twill	Patterns from the Weaver's Guild		√	√	H&C	26	5		Oc 75	29
Treadling: Variations	Basic Weaves, Tool to Develop Fabric Structures (error-corrected H&C v20 n4 69 p43)	Hausner, Walter	√	√	H&C	20	3		Su 69	4
Treadling: Variations	Couturier Fashions: Part 1, Couturier Fabric Design	West, Virginia	√	√	SS&D	13	3	51	Su 82	8
Treadling: Variations	Crackle		√	√	WJ	3	3	11	Ja 79	32
Treadling: Variations	Crackle Weave, Part 1	Lyon, Nancy	√	√	SS&D	19	1	73	Wi 87	21
Treadling: Variations	Designing Four-Shaft Double Weaves	Muller, Donna	√	√	WJ	7	4	28	Sp 83	56
Treadling: Variations	Doup Leno: Sample Project, Treadling and Variations	Skowronski, Hella; Sylvia Tacker		√	SCGM		32		80	22
Treadling: Variations	Drafting: A Personal Approach, Part 2	Alvic, Philis	√	> 4	SS&D	13	2	50	Sp 82	46
Treadling: Variations	Exploring the Possibilities of Ancient Rose	Wells, Elizabeth	√	√	H&C	11	1		Wi 60	22
Treadling: Variations	New Ways with Old Drafts (error-corrected H&C v2 n4 F51 p64)	Frey, Berta	√	√	H&C	2	3		Su 51	8
Treadling: Variations	One Warp, Many Fabrics	Liebler, Barbara	√	> 4	Iw	3	1		Fa 77	28
Treadling: Variations	Overshot: The Weave and the Designs	Marston, Ena	√	> 4	SS&D	11	2	42	Sp 80	74
Treadling: Variations	Overshot Treadling Sampler	Strickler, Carol	√	√	Iw	3	3		Sp 78	45
Treadling: Variations	Personal Approach to Drafting, A	Alvic, Philis	√	> 4	SS&D	13	1	49	Wi 81	32
Treadling: Variations	Rugs Based on Four Harness Twills (error-corrected WJ v2 n2 77 insert for vol. 2)		√	√	WJ	2	1	5	Jy 77	23
Treadling: Variations	Studies in Boundweave	Mershon, Janis	√	√	SS&D	12	2	46	Sp 81	50
Treadling: Variations	Summer and Winter Treadling Gamp, A	Strickler, Carol	√	√	Iw	3	4		Su 78	43
Treadling: Variations	Theme and Variations	Bress, Helene	√	√	Hw	6	2		M/A 85	62
Treadling: Variations	Variations on an Overshot Threading	Lermond, Charles	√	√	WJ	12	2	46	Fa 87	25
Treadling: Variations	Variations on One Warp	Alvic, Philis	√		SS&D	12	4	48	Fa 81	70
Treadling: Variations	Variations on Whig Rose	Kaiser, Eunice Gifford	√	√	H&C	14	1		Wi 63	17
Treadling: Variations	Whig Rose Study	Morgenstern, Marvin M.	√	√	WJ	7	2	26	Fa 82	40
Treadling: Variations	Whig Rose Study (continued)	Morgenstern, Marvin M.	√	√	WJ	7	3	27	Wi 82	23
Treadling: Variations on Huck	Composition and Designing Part 2: Variations on One Threading	Zielinski, S. A.; Robert Leclerc, ed.	√	√	MWL	19			'51–'73	7
Treadling: Woolens	Woolens and Tweeds: Weaving Woolens: Treadlings	Tidball, Harriet	√	√	SCGM		4		61	19
Trends: Handcrafts	Changes in Weaving	LaLena, Constance			Hw	8	1		J/F 87	24
Triangular Weaving	How to Weave a Plaid Triangular Shawl	Elich-McCall, Charoltte	√	√	Hw	4	5		N/D 83	54
Triangular Weaving	Lacy Triangular Stole of Handspun Wool, A	Kniskern, Edna Maki	√	√	WJ	6	2	22	Fa 81	48
Triangular Weaving	Simple Skirt and Matching Shawl, A	Hewson, Betty	√	√	Hw	4	5		N/D 83	24
Triangular Weaving	Triangular Shawl	Broad, Sue	√		WJ	7	3	27	Wi 82	11
Triangular Weaving	Weaving Handspun Yarn: Triangular Shawl	Ellison, Nancy	√	√	WJ	12	2	46	Fa 87	42
Triangular Weaving: Technique	On the Angle	Davenport, Betty; Suzanne Gaston-Voute	√	√	Hw	7	1		J/F 86	62
Triaxial Weaves	Triaxial Weaves and Weaving: An Exploration for Hand Weavers	Mooney, David R.	√	√	AT	2			De 84	9
Triaxial Weaving	Triaxial Weaving of David Mooney, The	Goodman, Deborah Lerme	√	√	Fa	13	3		M/J 86	34

SUBJECT	TITLE	AUTHOR	IL	INST	JOUR	VOL	NO	ISS	DATE	PAGE
Triaxial Weaving: Basic	Triaxial Weaves and Weaving: An Exploration for Hand Weavers	Mooney, David R.	√	√	AT	2			De 84	9
Triaxial Weaving: Basic, Variations	Triaxial Weaves and Weaving: An Exploration for Hand Weavers	Mooney, David R.	√	√	AT	2			De 84	9
Triaxial Weaving: Basketry	Triaxial Weaves and Weaving: An Exploration for Hand Weavers	Mooney, David R.	√	√	AT	2			De 84	9
Triaxial Weaving: Braiding Techniques	Braiding Triaxial Weaves: Enhancements and Design for Artworks	Mooney, David R.	√	√	AT	5			Ju 86	9
Triaxial Weaving: Braiding Techniques	Handweaving Triaxial Weaves with Braiding Techniques: Triaxial Braiding	Mooney, David R.	√	√	AT	3			My 85	99
Triaxial Weaving: Plaits, Duplicate	Triaxial Weaves and Weaving: An Exploration for Hand Weavers	Mooney, David R.	√	√	AT	2			De 84	9
Triaxial Weaving: Plaits, Triplicate	Triaxial Weaves and Weaving: An Exploration for Hand Weavers	Mooney, David R.	√	√	AT	2			De 84	9
Triaxial Weaving: Twill Patterns	Triaxial Weaves and Weaving: An Exploration for Hand Weavers	Mooney, David R.	√	√	AT	2			De 84	9
Tricot	Have You Tried Tricot?	Nyquist, Janet		> 4	SS&D	1	3	3	Ju 70	17
Triple Cloth	Polly Yori (error-corrected H&C v21 n3 70 p45)	Marston, Ena	√	> 4	H&C	21	1		Wi 70	19
Triple Weave, Pick-Up	Inspired Double Weave		√		Hw	7	2		M/A 86	58
Tubular Bands, Woven	Peru, Textiles Unlimited, Part 2: Tubular Tapes	Tidball, Harriet	√	√	SCGM		26		69	37
Tubular Edge-Binding	Andean Crossed-Warp Techniques for Decorative Trims, Part 2 — Tubular Bands (error-corrected WJ v3 n1 insert for vol.2)	Cahlander, Adele	√	√	WJ	3	1	9	Jy 78	38
Tubular Edge-Binding	Tubular Edge-Binding from Bolivia, A	Cahlander, Adele; Marjorie Cason	√	√	WJ	1	4	4	Ap 77	13
Tubular Knitting	Knitting Round on Straight Needles	Borssuck, Bee	√	√	TM			12	A/S 87	64
Tubular Weaving	Andean Crossed-Warp Techniques for Decorative Trims, Part 1 — Flat Bands	Cahlander, Adele	√	√	WJ	2	4	8	Ap 78	10
Tubular Weaving	Andean Crossed-Warp Techniques for Decorative Trims, Part 2 — Tubular Bands (error-corrected WJ v3 n1 insert for vol. 2)	Cahlander, Adele	√	√	WJ	3	1	9	Jy 78	38
Tubular Weaving: Piping	On the Edge		√	√	Hw	4	4		S/O 83	34
Tucks	Double Weave: Plain and Patterned: Pleats and Tucks, The	Tidball, Harriet	√	> 4	SCGM		1		60	32
Tucks	Michigan Weaving, Third Conference at Hartland Shows Wide Variety		√	√	H&C	13	1		Wi 62	18
Tucks	Tale of Tucks, A (error-corrected SS&D v7 n1 75 p63)	Guagliumi, Susan	√	> 4	SS&D	7	1	25	Wi 75	56
Tucks	Tuck Tactics	Speth, Lottie	√	√	SS&D	15	3	59	Su 84	80
Tucks	Tuck Weaving	Frey, Berta	√	√	H&C	9	4		Fa 58	11
Tucks	Tucked Dresses	Wertenberger, Kathryn; Nancy Kuwabara	√	√	Hw	4	2		M/A 83	63
Tufting, Pick-Up	Hand Woven Rugs: Weaves, Plain Weave, Picked-Up Tufting	Atwater, Mary Meigs	√	√	SCGM		29		48	7
Tumeric	Why Bother with Natural Dyeing?	Bulbach, Stanley	√	√	TM			5	J/J 86	32
Tunics	Blouse for Her — A Shirt for Him, A		√	√	WJ	4	3	15	Ja 80	4
Tunics	Contemporary Costume, Strictly Handwoven: The Tunic	Tidball, Harriet	√	√	SCGM		24		68	28
Tunics	Easy Striped Knits	Walker, Barbara G.	√	√	TM			4	A/M 86	54
Tunics	Embroidery on the Loom	Drooker, Penelope B.	√	√	SS&D	9	3	35	Su 78	60
Tunics	Fashion Show of Handwoven Garments		√	> 4	WJ	3	3	11	Ja 79	5
Tunics	Fashions by Linda Knutson and Lynn Daly		√	√	WJ	6	3	23	Wi 81	14
Tunics	From the Collection of Anne Poussart		√	√	WJ	7	3	27	Wi 82	62
Tunics	Greek Chemises: Cut and Construction	Welters, Linda	√	√	WJ	10	1	37	Su 85	40
Tunics	Horizon Striped Tunic (Mary Martinez)		√	√	Hw	3	4		Se 82	65, 92
Tunics	Lace-Weave Tunic	Rowley, Elaine	√	√	PWC			5	Sp 83	18
Tunics	Medieval Textiles from the Tellem Caves in Central Mali, West Africa	Bedaux, Rogier M. A.; Rita Bolland	√		TMJ	19 20			80,81	65
Tunics	Painted-Silk Clothing	Juve, Peggy	√	√	TM			12	A/S 87	24

SUBJECT	TITLE	AUTHOR	IL	INST	JOUR	VOL	NO	ISS	DATE	PAGE
Tunics	Projects with Cotton		√	√	WJ	4	2	14	Oc 79	28
Tunics	Silk Tunic (Anne Bliss)		√	√	Hw	4	1		J/F 83	49, 92
Tunics	Southwest Reflections: Fiber artists Inspired by the New Mexico Landscape	Colton, Mary Rawcliffe	√		WJ	11	1	41	Su 86	20
Tunics	Succeeding with the Knitting Machine	Mattera, Joanne	√		TM			2	D/J 85	50
Tunics	Summertime!	Coifman, Lucienne	√	√	SS&D	15	3	59	Su 84	74
Tunics	Tapestries	Trilling, James	√		TMJ	21			82	29
Tunics	Tapestries of Coptic Egypt, The	Hoskins, Nancy Arthur	√		AT	6			De 86	211
Tunics	Textiles of Coptic Egypt	Hoskins, Nancy Arthur	√	√	WJ	12	1	45	Su 87	58
Tunics	Textured Cottons: Dress and Sauna Robe	Henrikson, Sue	√	> 4	WJ	6	3	23	Wi 81	20
Tunics	Tunic Made from Narrow Strips	Barrett, Clotilde	√	√	WJ	4	3	15	Ja 80	9
Tunics	Tunic with Ribbons (Carol Powalisz)		√	√	Hw	8	1		J/F 87	52, I-8
Tunics	Waffle Weave Tunic (Sharon Alderman)		√	√	Hw	3	2		Mr 82	45, 82
Tunics: 1950's	Balenciago: The Architect of Elegant Clothing	Koda, Harold	√		TM			11	J/J 87	20
Tunics: Inca, Colonial	Technical Features of Inca Tapestry Tunics	Rowe, Ann Pollard	√		TMJ	17			78	5
Tunics: Inca, Provincial	Technical Features of Inca Tapestry Tunics	Rowe, Ann Pollard	√		TMJ	17			78	5
Tunics: Musician, Peru	Textile Evidence for Huari Music	Rowe, Ann Pollard	√		TMJ	18			79	5
Tunisia	Dunlaps: New Mexico to Tunisia, The	Gregg, Marcia			S-O	4			80	4
Tunisia	Traditional Handlooms and Weavings of Tunisia	Reswick, Irmtraud H.	√		SS&D	12	2	46	Sp 81	21
Turkey	"At the Edge of Asia: Five Centuries of Turkish Textiles" (Exhibit)	Dyer, Carolyn Price	√		Fa	10	4		J/A 83	65
Turkey	Felt-making Craftsmen of the Anatolian and Iranian Plateaux	Gervers, Michael; Veronika Gervers	√	√	TMJ	4	1		De 74	14
Turkey	Feltmaking	Wald, Pat Boutin	√	√	S-O	1			77	46
Turkey	Kaleidoscopic Tour of Turkey, A	Dyer, Carol; Carel Bertram	√		Fa	7	5		S/O 80	48
Turkey	Some Unusual Turkish Embroideries of the Early Eighteenth Century	Johnstone, Pauline	√		TMJ	24			85	75
Turkey	Textile Museum's White-Ground Rug, The		√		SS&D	8	4	32	Fa 77	45
Turkey	Traditional Felt Rugmaking in Turkey	Ispay, Francis	√	√	Fa	13	4		J/A 86	18
Turkey Feather Blanket	Sweetgrass, Cedar & Sage: Portrait of a Southwestern Weaver	Schevill, Margot	√		WJ	10	1	37	Su 85	24
Turned Drafts	Contemporary Approach to Traditional Weaves: Modern Damask and Other Turned Twills	Zielinski, S. A.; Robert Leclerc, ed.	√	> 4	MWL	8			'51–'73	83
Turned Drafts	Skirt with Warp Stripe Pattern	Frey, Berta	√	√	H&C	14	2		Sp 63	38
Turned Drafts	Some Experiments with Turned Drafts	Carter, Helen H.	√	> 4	CW	5	2	14	Ja 84	3
Turned Drafts, Summer and Winter	Contemporary Approach to Traditional Weaves: Production Drafts	Zielinski, S. A.; Robert Leclerc, ed.	√	> 4	MWL	7			'51–'73	121
Turned Tufted Weave	Little Known Weaves Worth Knowing Better: Turned Tufted Weave	Zielinski, S. A.; Robert Leclerc, ed.	√	√	MWL	16			'51–'73	103
Turned Twills	Fascination of Twills (Multishafts): Turned Twills-Two Harness Method-2	Zielinski, S. A.; Robert Leclerc, ed.	√	> 4	MWL	10			'51–'73	31
Turned Warps	Peter Collingwood, His Weaves and Weaving: A Sleeved Jacket Made in Two Pieces	Collingwood, Peter; Harriet Tidball, ed.	√	√	SCGM		8		63	34
Turned Weaves	Summer and Winter Revisited Part 4: Turned Pebble Weave	Xenakis, Athanasios David	√	√	PWC			4	Ja 83	52
Turned Weaves, Warp-Float Face/Weft-Float Face	Peru, Textiles Unlimited, Part 2: Two-Way Rep Cord	Tidball, Harriet	√	√	SCGM		26		69	6
Tuxedos	Tuxedo 100 Years Later, The	Shufro, Cathy	√		TM			7	O/N 86	54
Tweed	Handweaver's Instruction Manual: Twill Weaves	Tidball, Harriet C. nee Douglas			SCGM		34		49	23
Tweed	Handweaver's Instruction Manual: Twill Weaves, Weaving Tweeds	Tidball, Harriet C. nee Douglas		√	SCGM		34		49	23
Tweed	Happy Weaver of the Isle of Harris, The	Ham, Phebe D.	√		SS&D	1	2	2	Mr 70	12

SUBJECT	TITLE	AUTHOR	IL	INST	JOUR	VOL	NO	ISS	DATE	PAGE
Tweed	Homespun Songs from Ireland's Clancy Brothers	Drake, Elizabeth A.	√		SS&D	16	4	64	Fa 85	62
Tweed	Some Interpretations of Compass and Double Square		√	> 4	H&C	4	4		Fa 53	18
Tweed	Swatch #6: Blue-Red Tweed (Sharon Alderman)		√	√	Hw	6	5		N/D 85	48, I-11
Tweed	Tweed	Wilson, Kax	√		Iw	5	2		Sp 80	59
Tweed	Tweed Jacket, Woven for TV		√		SS&D	6	1	21	Wi 74	14
Tweed	Tweed Skirt (Leslie Voiers)		√	√	Hw	8	1		J/F 87	53, I-7
Tweed	Tweed Weavers of Glenmore, The	Burkhauser, Jude	√		Hw	3	3		My 82	56
Tweed	Waulking Tweeds at the Marshfield School of Weaving	Gallagher, Kate	√		Hw	6	4		S/O 85	10
Tweed	Weaving Tweeds	Hotchkiss, Clifford; Ann Hotchkiss		√	H&C	13	2		Sp 62	14
Tweed	Welsh Wool Yarn Factory Hires Disabled Veterans	Hetherington, E.	√		SS&D	5	1	17	Wi 73	28
Tweed	Why Not Tweeds?	Redding, Winogene	√	√	H&C	1	3		Fa 50	30
Tweed, Harris	Tweed of Harris, The	Johnson, Beth	√		Hw	2	5		No 81	47
Tweeling	More About Fabrics: Tweeling	Zielinski, S. A.; Robert Leclerc, ed.	√	> 4	MWL	20			'51–'73	108
Twice Woven	Martin Peavy: An Improvisational Approach to Rugs	Peavy, Martin	√		Fa	11	3		M/J 84	22
Twice-Woven Chenille	Doup Leno (error-corrected WJ v3 n2 78 insert p38a)		√	√	WJ	3	2	10	Oc 78	32
Twice-Woven Rug	Super Rug: A Chenille "Twice-Woven" Rug	Champion, Ellen	√	√	WJ	6	4	24	Sp 82	26
Twice-Woven Technique	Hand Woven Rugs: Weaves, Plain Weave, Twice-Woven Rugs	Atwater, Mary Meigs	√	√	SCGM		29		48	5
Twice-Woven Technique	Jeff Glenn	Glenn, Jeff	√		Fa	14	1		J/F 87	26
Twice-Woven Technique	"Show of Complements, A" (Exhibit)	Schevill, Margot Blum	√		Fa	13	4		J/A 86	50
Twice-Woven Techniques	Twice Woven Bolero	Richards, Iris	√	√	WJ	4	3	15	Ja 80	24
Twill	Abelard's Advice	Hilts, Pat	√	√	Hw	4	4		S/O 83	20
Twill	Accessories: Large Bags Made from Narrow Strips		√	√	WJ	2	4	8	Ap 78	6
Twill	Accessories: Necktie		√	√	WJ	2	4	8	Ap 78	8
Twill	Art of Fashion Design: A Handweaver's Twill Cape, The	Johnson, Judith K.	√	√	WJ	7	3	27	Wi 82	12
Twill	Bag for all Seasons (Barbara Grace), A		√	√	Hw	3	2		Mr 82	67
Twill	Bath Towel (Jane Patrick) (error-corrected Hw v3 n4 82 p81)		√	> 4	Hw	3	2		Mr 82	50, 90
Twill	Beach Bag (Sharon Alderman)		√	√	Hw	4	3		M/J 83	43, 80
Twill	Beginner's Tops	Legerski, Victoria	√	> 4	WJ	8	3	31	Wi 83	14
Twill	Beyond Rags: Fabric Strip Design	Larson-Fleming, Susan	√	√	WJ	9	4	36	Sp 85	47
Twill	Blue/Green Brushed Mohair		√	√	Hw	4	5		N/D 83	46, 96
Twill	Bolivian Highland Weaving, Part 1	Cason, Marjorie; Adele Cahlander	√		SS&D	6	2	22	Sp 75	4
Twill	Changing the Angle of the Twill Diagonal Line	Laughlin, Elizabeth	√	> 4	SS&D	7	4	28	Fa 76	11
Twill	Cherry Vest (Marie Lebair O'Brient)		√	√	Hw	7	1		J/F 86	71
Twill	Child's Dress Pattern	Deygout, Françoise	√	> 4	CW		24		My 87	13
Twill	Cloud and Sky Brushed Afghan (Jean Scorgie)		√	√	Hw	7	1		J/F 86	I-7
Twill	Cocoon Wrap Jacket, The		√	√	WJ	5	3	19	Wi 81	18
Twill	Color and Weave Effects	Poulton, Jim	√	> 4	WJ	5	3	19	Wi 81	14
Twill	Colorful Linen Draperies Designed and Woven by Marie Phelps		√	√	H&C	1	1		Ap 50	18
Twill	Contemporary Approach to Traditional Weaves: Crackle and Twill	Zielinski, S. A.; Robert Leclerc, ed.	√	√	MWL	8			'51–'73	17
Twill	Corded Weaves — Four Harness Cross Cords		√	> 4	WJ	4	1	13	Jy 79	25

SUBJECT	TITLE	AUTHOR	IL	INST	JOUR	VOL	NO	ISS	DATE	PAGE
Twill	Cotton Shirt and Children's Dresses Fabric (Lillemor Johansson and Astrid Linderoth)		√	√	Hw	4	2		M/A 83	32, 82
Twill	Couturier Fashion Design	West, Virginia	√	> 4	SS&D	13	4	52	Fa 82	34
Twill	Coverlet or Bedspread (Constance LaLena)		√	√	Hw	4	5		N/D 83	70, 102
Twill	District Check Wrap Skirt (Stephenie Gaustad)		√	√	Hw	4	5		N/D 83	68, 108
Twill	Don't Float Past This			√	Hw	6	5		N/D 85	47
Twill	Double Chenille Vest (Lucy Anne Jennings)		√	√	Hw	7	3		M/J 86	44, I-10
Twill	Double-faced, Double-woven, Three-harness Krokbragd	Holtzer, Marilyn Emerson	√	√	SS&D	14	4	56	Fa 83	46
Twill	Drafts		√	√	WJ	1	1	1	Jy 76	12
Twill	Early American Linens	Gallagher, Constance	√	> 4	H&C	15	3		Su 64	7
Twill	Embroidered Jacket (Carol Powalisz)		√	√	Hw	8	4		S/O 87	46, I-7
Twill	Enlarged Patterns: A Fresh Look at Old Techniques	McClelland, Patricia Polett	√	> 4	WJ	7	4	28	Sp 83	68
Twill	Even Beat, An	Ligon, Linda	√	√	Hw	7	4		S/O 86	98
Twill	Fantastic Finnweave, Part 3	Xenakis, Athanasios David	√	> 4	PWC			4	Ja 83	22
Twill	Fashion Show of Handwoven Garments		√	> 4	WJ	3	3	11	Ja 79	5
Twill	Fashions by Linda Knutson and Lynn Daly		√	√	WJ	6	3	23	Wi 81	14
Twill	Five Pillows on One Warp (Sharon D. Alderman)		√	> 4	Hw	3	3		My 82	38, 93
Twill	Flat-Woven Structures Found in Nomadic and Village Weavings from the Near East and Central Asia	Wertime, John T.	√		TMJ	18			79	33
Twill	Fleecy Vest, A	Gilsdorf, Marilyn	√	√	WJ	8	4	32	Sp 84	9
Twill	Four Shaft Fascination	Gordon, Judith	√	√	Hw	6	1		J/F 85	12
Twill	Four-Shaft Twill Neck Scarf	Kolling-Summers, Elizabeth	√	√	WJ	7	1	25	Su 82	29
Twill	From Sample to Finished Product	Keasbey, Doramay	√	> 4	SS&D	15	3	59	Su 84	62
Twill	From Simple Twills to Dobby Fantasies...A Progression	Marquess, Joyce	√	> 4	Iw	4	4		Fa 79	38
Twill	From the Collection of Anne Poussart		√	√	WJ	7	3	27	Wi 82	62
Twill	Garments by Hanni Bureker		√	√	WJ	6	3	23	Wi 81	35
Twill	Garments Made from Simple Patterns: A Vest		√	√	WJ	2	3	7	Ja 78	37
Twill	Garments with Ethnic Flavor: Desert Dusk Coat		√		WJ	2	3	7	Ja 78	16
Twill	Gunclub Checks (Judy Steinkoenig)		√	√	Hw	4	5		N/D 83	66, 106
Twill	Handspun, Handwoven Saddle Blanket, A	Newsted, Jean	√	√	WJ	8	2	30	Fa 83	22
Twill	Handweaver's Instruction Manual: Twill Weaves, Simple Twills	Tidball, Harriet C. nee Douglas	√	√	SCGM		34		49	23
Twill	Handwoven Teddy Bear (Janice Jones)		√	√	Hw	6	4		S/O 85	63, I-12
Twill	Heap of Linen Towels, A (Linda Ligon)		√	√	Hw	6	2		M/A 85	54, I-12
Twill	Home Weaving: A Happy Plaid (Halcyon)		√	√	Hw	1	1		F-W 79	40
Twill	If You Have Four Harnesses	Hagerty, Harriet May	√	√	H&C	26	1		J/F 75	24
Twill	Ikat Spun Vest (Debbie Redding)	Bradley, Louise	√	√	Hw	2	4		Se 81	67
Twill	Inspirations from Sweaters	Brewington, Judith	√	√	WJ	7	3	27	Wi 82	14
Twill	Jacket for Hiking, A	Roth, Bettie G.	√	> 4	WJ	8	3	31	Wi 83	69
Twill	Jacket or Coat (Sharon Alderman)		√	√	Hw	2	4		Se 81	36, 86
Twill	Jacket (Sharon Alderman)		√	> 4	Hw	2	1		F-W 80	50, 62
Twill	Jerga: A Twill in Harmony with its Heritage	Wilson, Kax	√		Hw	6	5		N/D 85	60
Twill	Kate Woolstenhulme: A Sense of Place	Walters, Roberta	√		Fa	10	2		M/A 83	56
Twill	Lesson in Cut and Sewn Handwoven Garments, A (error-corrected Hw v2 n2 81 p68)	Wertenberger, Katheryn	√	√	Hw	2	1		F-W 80	36

SUBJECT	TITLE	AUTHOR	IL	INST	JOUR	VOL	NO	ISS	DATE	PAGE
Twill	Linen Bath Towels (Beth Johnson Brewin)		√	√	Hw	5	3		Su 84	70, 105
Twill	Longest Warp in the World or, The Double Two-Tie Unit Threading System	Miller, Mary Ann	√	> 4	CW	3	3	9	Ap 82	2
Twill	MacCallum Tartan Afghan (Jane Merryman)		√	√	Hw	4	5		N/D 83	Cover, 96
Twill	Man-Made Fibers: Baby Blankets		√	√	WJ	5	2	18	Fa 80	43
Twill	Man-Made Fibers: Table Runner		√	> 4	WJ	5	2	18	Fa 80	45
Twill	Mending Warps	Ligon, Linda	√	√	Hw	7	1		J/F 86	34
Twill	More About Fabrics: Practical Projects for Basket and Twill	Zielinski, S. A.; Robert Leclerc, ed.	√	√	MWL	20			'51–'73	35
Twill	More About Fabrics: Tweeling	Zielinski, S. A.; Robert Leclerc, ed.	√	> 4	MWL	20			'51–'73	108
Twill	More Logical Method of Drafting, A	Hoyt, Peggy	√	> 4	CW	5	3	15	My 84	22
Twill	Multiple Harness Weaving Course — Part 2: Twills and Satins, With Contribution by Nancy Searles		√	> 4	WJ	4	4	16	Ap 80	16
Twill	Mystery Sun Rug	Oles, Jery	√	> 4	WJ	8	4	32	Sp 84	10
Twill	Natural Colors Wool Throw (Sharon Alderman)		√	√	Hw	2	1		F-W 80	Cover, 65
Twill	New Look at Twills, A	Hoskins, Janet A.	√	> 4	WJ	6	3	23	Wi 81	46
Twill	Nineteenth Century Miniatures	Erf, Mary Elva Congleton	√	√	SS&D	16	1	61	Wi 84	60
Twill	Notebook: And the Threading is Easy	Myers, Ruth Nordquist, ed.	√	> 4	SS&D	13	4	52	Fa 82	12
Twill	Notebook: Some Light Behind the Weave (Lucile Landis)	Myers, Ruth Nordquist, ed.	√	> 4	SS&D	13	3	51	Su 82	16
Twill	Notebook: Tartans	Myers, Ruth Nordquist, ed.	√	√	SS&D	13	1	49	Wi 81	24
Twill	Off the Hook: Bosnian Crochet (Charlotte Winston)		√	√	Hw	2	5		No 81	45
Twill	One Pattern, One Warp (Louise Bradley)		√	√	Hw	3	3		My 82	34, 97
Twill	'Outrageous' Scarf #1 (Kathryn Wertenberger)		√	> 4	Hw	5	5		N/D 84	68, I-7
Twill	'Outrageous' Scarf #2 (Kathryn Wertenberger)		√	> 4	Hw	5	5		N/D 84	68, I-7
Twill	'Outrageous' Scarf #3 (Kathryn Wertenberger)		√	> 4	Hw	5	5		N/D 84	68, I-7
Twill	Oval Cape	Sylvan, Katherine	√	√	WJ	5	3	19	Wi 81	36
Twill	Overshot Patterns	Marston, Ena	√	√	SS&D	4	2	14	Sp 73	20
Twill	Pattern and Structure in Handwoven Fabrics	Frey, Berta	√	√	H&C	6	4		Fa 55	4
Twill	Peru, Textiles Unlimited, Part 2: Twills	Tidball, Harriet	√	> 4	SCGM		26		69	30
Twill	Placemats	DeRoy, Paul	√	> 4	WJ	1	3	3	Ja 77	4
Twill	Placemats (Bridget McNamara) (error-corrected Hw v1 n2 80 p64)		√	√	Hw	1	1		F-W 79	33, 54
Twill	Plaid Afghan (Lynette Theodore)		√	√	Hw	6	5		N/D 85	58
Twill	Plum Special Sherpa Coat (Betty Beard)		√	√	Hw	3	1		Ja 82	36, 84
Twill	Point Twill 125 Years Old	Stuart, Helen C.	√	√	SS&D	3	4	12	Fa 72	41
Twill	Prism Pleasure Blanket (Hector Jaeger)		√	√	Hw	6	3		Su 85	58, I-13
Twill	Progression of Ideas, or The Shortest Distance Between 2 Ideas is a Diagonal Line, A		√		Iw	6	1		Wi 80	35
Twill	Queen Anne's Pattern	Wood, Gerry	√	> 4	H&C	10	4		Fa 59	15
Twill	Rainbow Blankets	Sullivan, Donna	√	> 4	PWC	4	4	14		27
Twill	Reversible Coat (Eileen O'Connor)		√	√	Hw	6	5		N/D 85	46, I-8
Twill	Ribbon Scarf or Sash (Margery Wilder)		√	√	Hw	7	2		M/A 86	32
Twill	Roman Textiles from Vindolanda, Hexham, England	Wild, John Peter	√		TMJ	18			79	19
Twill	Rose Jacket (Åse Blake)		√	> 4	Hw	8	3		M/J 87	56, I-9
Twill	Sarah Fowler's Book of Drafts, Part 2		√	> 4	SS&D	6	2	22	Sp 75	78
Twill	Sarah Fowler's Book of Drafts, Part 4	North, Lois	√	> 4	SS&D	6	4	24	Fa 75	84

SUBJECT	TITLE	AUTHOR	IL	INST	JOUR	VOL	NO	ISS	DATE	PAGE
Twill	Sauna Towels	Freeberg, Judy	√	√	WJ	10	4	40	Sp 86	50
Twill	Scandia Jacket		√	√	WJ	8	3	31	Wi 83	42
Twill	Shades of Fall Lap Robe (Leslie Voiers)		√	√	Hw	5	4		S/O 84	71, 106
Twill	Shirt for a Fellow Spinner, A	Gaustad, Stephenie	√	√	Hw	7	4		S/O 86	76
Twill	Skirt (Sharon Alderman)		√	√	Hw	2	1		F-W 80	50, 62
Twill	Sky Celebration	Mayer, Anita Luvera	√	√	S-O	11	2		Su 87	36
Twill	Southwest Indian Twill Tapestry	Atwood, Betty	√		WJ	8	1	29	Su 83	35
Twill	Spring Ensemble (Ronnine Bohannan)		√	√	Hw	6	2		M/A 85	56, I-13
Twill	Stoles and Scarves		√	√	WJ	2	1	5	Jy 77	3
Twill	Summer and Winter and Other Two-Tie Unit Weaves: Methods for Weaving Two-Tie Units, Two-Element Weaves, Twill Sequence	Tidball, Harriet	√	> 4	SCGM		19		66	41
Twill	Sunny Skies Picnic Blanket (Halcyon Schomp and Hector Jaeger)		√	√	Hw	5	3		Su 84	69, 106
Twill	Sunrise Titles and Twills		√		Iw	6	1		Wi 80	38
Twill	Super Rug: A Chenille "Twice-Woven" Rug	Champion, Ellen	√	√	WJ	6	4	24	Sp 82	26
Twill	Swatch #1, Wool Coat Fabric for Winter (Lillian Whipple)		√	√	Hw	7	5		N/D 86	64, I-7
Twill	Swatch #2: Plain Twill Blue Tweed for Skirt (Sharon Alderman)		√	√	Hw	6	5		N/D 85	48, I-10
Twill	Swatch #3, Twill (Diana Sanderson)		√	√	Hw	7	5		N/D 86	46, I-4
Twill	Swatch #4, Twill (Diana Sanderson)		√	√	Hw	7	5		N/D 86	46, I-5
Twill	Swatch #5, Twill (Diana Sanderson)		√	√	Hw	7	5		N/D 86	46, I-5
Twill	Swatch Collection Skirt (Sharon Alderman)		√	√	Hw	4	1		J/F 83	68, 94
Twill	Symbolic or Sacred? A Personal View	Lockwood, Diana W.	√	> 4	WJ	9	3	35	Wi 85	45
Twill	Tapestry in Twill: A Free Approach	Hall, Joanne	√	√	Hw	3	1		Ja 82	46
Twill	Techniques for Better Weaving (error-corrected TM i9 D/J 86 p4)	Osterkamp, Peggy	√	√	TM			7	O/N 86	42
Twill	Textile Structure and Analysis, A Home Study Course in Twelve Lessons: Lessons in Weave Structure, 2. Twill	Tidball, Harriet		√	SCGM		18		66	24
Twill	Three Color Progressions and Their Use in Sweater Jackets	Sylvan, Katherine	√	√	WJ	5	4	20	Sp 81	38
Twill	Three-Toned Blocks: Further Explorations with Long-Eyed Heddles	Broughton, Eve T.	√	> 4	WJ	9	4	36	Sp 85	72
Twill	Timelessly Fashionable Turkish Coat, A	Xenakis, Alexis Yiorgos	√	√	PWC	1	1		No 81	43
Twill	Treasury for Beginners: More About Twills	Zielinski, S. A.; Robert Leclerc, ed.	√	√	MWL	1			'51–'73	110
Twill	Treasury for Beginners: Twills	Zielinski, S. A.; Robert Leclerc, ed.	√	√	MWL	1			'51–'73	108
Twill	Twill Basics		√	√	Hw	6	5		N/D 85	57
Twill	Twill Color and Weave Effects...From the Computer	O'Connor, Paul	√	> 4	Iw	6	1		Wi 80	28
Twill	Twill Plaid		√	√	Hw	4	5		N/D 83	43
Twill	Twill Scarf (Sharon Alderman)		√	> 4	Hw	2	1		F-W 80	51, 57
Twill	'Twill Skirt the Issue	Xenakis, Athanasios David	√	√	PWC	1	1		No 81	49
Twill	Twill Striped Blouse (Mary Kay Stoehr)		√	√	Hw	5	3		Su 84	64, 113
Twill	Twill Wool Rag Rug (Mary Kay Stoehr)		√	> 4	Hw	5	2		M/A 84	57, 95
Twill	Twills, Another Look	Chandler, Deborah	√	> 4	Hw	6	5		N/D 85	26
Twill	Two Pastel Throws (Sharon Alderman)		√	√	Hw	3	4		Se 82	34, 82
Twill	Up, Up and Away in my Handwoven Balloon	Potter, Katie Forderhase	√	√	Hw	3	2		Mr 82	40
Twill	Upholstery Fabric (Constance LaLena)		√	√	Hw	4	5		N/D 83	70, 102
Twill	Versatile Inlay, Twill on Twill	Beard, Betty	√	√	SS&D	19	1	73	Wi 87	53
Twill	Versatile Twill, The		√		Hw	6	5		N/D 85	41

SUBJECT	TITLE	AUTHOR	IL	INST	JOUR	VOL	NO	ISS	DATE	PAGE
Twill	Versatility of Four-shaft Twill, The		√	√	WJ	8	3	31	Wi 83	82
Twill	Warm and Wooly: Bright and Soft		√		Hw	1	1		F-W 79	28
Twill	Warmth for a Cool Climate: Handspun Wool & Milkweed Down	Danielson, Esther	√	√	SS&D	17	4	68	Fa 86	24
Twill	Warping and Weaving Mitla Cloth on the Backstrap Loom	Knottenbelt, Maaike	√	√	TMJ	22			83	53
Twill	Weave and Knit Suit		√	√	WJ	8	3	31	Wi 83	18
Twill	Weave Color: A Color Sampler (Carol Strickler)		√	√	Hw	1	1		F-W 79	8
Twill	Weaving As Drawn In — Classic Style, Part 2	Keasbey, Doramay	√	> 4	SS&D	17	2	66	Sp 86	38
Twill	Weaving of the Plaid, The	Freilinger, Ida M.	√	√	SS&D	12	1	45	Wi 80	59
Twill	White Crib Blanket (Linda Ligon)		√	√	Hw	3	5		N/D 82	47, 86
Twill	Winter Wrap-Ups Revisited	Deschaines, Sybil	√	> 4	SS&D	16	1	61	Wi 84	26
Twill	Wool and Mohair Throw (Pat Sheret)		√	√	Hw	6	5		N/D 85	59
Twill	Wool Poncho (Bridget McNamara)		√	√	Hw	1	1		F-W 79	18, 52
Twill	Working with the Bias	West, Virginia	√	> 4	WJ	12	1	45	Su 87	9
Twill	Worsted Skirt (Sharon Alderman)		√	√	Hw	3	4		Se 82	41, 94
Twill	Woven Structures of European Shawls in The Textile Museum Collection, The	Rowe, Ann Pollard			TMJ	24			85	55
Twill	Yardage (Constance LaLena)		√	√	Hw	4	5		N/D 83	70, 102
Twill	Yarn Twist and Twills			√	Hw	6	5		N/D 85	44
Twill, 2-Tie, 4-End Block	Multiple Shaft Weaving — 2-Tie Four-End Block Drafts		√	> 4	WJ	6	4	24	Sp 82	48
Twill, 2-Tie, Double	Double Two-Tie Twills and Basket Weave	Barrett, Clotilde	√	> 4	WJ	7	3	27	Wi 82	38
Twill, 2-Tie, Double	Twills in Double Two-Tie Unit Weave	van der Hoogt, Madelyn	√	> 4	Hw	6	5		N/D 85	64
Twill, 2-Tie, Double	Two Ties in Double Two-Tie (Amy Preckshot)		√	> 4	Hw	6	5		N/D 85	64, I-15
Twill, 3-Shaft	Blue and White Bed Ticking (Jane Patrick)		√	√	Hw	3	5		N/D 82	30, 99
Twill, 3-Shaft	Mukluks (Bridget McNamara)		√	√	Hw	1	1		F-W 79	20, 54
Twill, 3-Tie Unit	Three-Tie Unit Twill Mats (Carol Powalisz)		√	> 4	Hw	8	5		N/D 87	47, I-8
Twill, Angle Variations	Fascination of Twills (Fourshafts): Twills-2	Zielinski, S. A.; Robert Leclerc, ed.	√	√	MWL	9			'51–'73	12
Twill, Block	Box-Pleated Blouse (Maury Young)		√	√	Hw	8	2		M/A 87	62, I-14
Twill, Block	Plaid Blanket and Pillow (Margaretha Essén-Hedin)		√	> 4	Hw	8	1		J/F 87	71, I-14
Twill, Block	Twill Block and Stripe Pillows (Pam Pawl)		√	> 4	Hw	6	5		N/D 85	52, I-11
Twill, Block	Weaving Block Twills		√	> 4	Hw	8	5		N/D 87	52
Twill, Block System	Handloom Weaves: The Classification of Handloom Weaves, The Structural Group, Unit Class, Twill-Block System	Tidball, Harriet	√	> 4	SCGM		33		57	25
Twill, Braided	Braided Twill Purse Organizer and Card Case (Sharon Alderman)		√	> 4	Hw	5	1		J/F 84	49, 94
Twill, Broken	And Thereon Hangs a Towel		√	> 4	Hw	3	4		Se 82	58
Twill, Broken	Autumn Bomber Jacket (Myrna Beeny)		√	√	Hw	3	4		Se 82	47, 83
Twill, Broken	Broken Twill Rug (Halcyon)		√	√	Hw	1	1		F-W 79	31, 58
Twill, Broken	Brushed Wool Wrap Coat (Jean Scorgie and Kaino Leethem)		√	√	Hw	4	1		J/F 83	46, 88
Twill, Broken	Daisy Dog Fur Coat (Betty Beard)		√	√	Hw	3	2		Mr 82	62, 87
Twill, Broken	Elegant Plaid Shawl, An	Kolling-Summers, Elizabeth	√	√	WJ	7	3	27	Wi 82	69
Twill, Broken	Fascination of Twills (Fourshafts): Broken Twill and Satinet	Zielinski, S. A.; Robert Leclerc, ed.	√	√	MWL	9			'51–'73	89
Twill, Broken	Finnish Cotton Jacket (Kaino Leethem with Jean Scorgie)		√	√	Hw	5	3		Su 84	61, 106
Twill, Broken	King Size Bound Bouclé Blanket (Halcyon)		√	√	Hw	4	4		S/O 83	62, 106
Twill, Broken	Man's Robe (Jane Patrick)		√	√	Hw	4	2		M/A 83	53, 86

SUBJECT	TITLE	AUTHOR	IL	INST	JOUR	VOL	NO	ISS	DATE	PAGE
Twill, Broken	Peaches and Cream Bouclé Throw (Halcyon)		√	√	Hw	4	4		S/O 83	62, 108
Twill, Broken	Plum Wooly Jacket (Linda Ligon)		√	√	Hw	5	1		J/F 84	46, 108
Twill, Broken	Rainbow Jacket (Sara Lamb)		√	>4	Hw	4	1		J/F 83	45, 84
Twill, Broken	Shawl Inspired by Edgar Degas' "Ballet Seen from a Box, 1885" (Dixie Straight)		√	√	Hw	5	5		N/D 84	64, I-9
Twill, Broken	Silk Tunic (Anne Bliss)		√	√	Hw	4	1		J/F 83	49, 92
Twill, Broken	Summer Harvest, Winter Jacket	O'Connor, Marina	√	√	S-O	11	2		Su 87	13
Twill, Broken	Swatch #2, Lightweight Wool Suit Fabric for Fall (Lillian Whipple)		√	>4	Hw	7	5		N/D 86	64, I-7
Twill, Broken	Swatch #3: Granite Weave Tweed (Sharon Alderman)		√	√	Hw	6	5		N/D 85	48, I-10
Twill, Broken	Swatch Collection #11: Fabrics 3 (Sharon Alderman)		√	>4	Hw	6	2		M/A 85	46, I-5
Twill, Broken	Technical Information for Cape Fabric (Sharon Alderman)		√	√	Hw	5	5		N/D 84	60, I-14
Twill, Broken	Touch the Earth Table Runner (Robin Taylor Daugherty)		√	√	Hw	5	4		S/O 84	64, 100
Twill, Broken	Twilled Cottolin Towels	Waggoner, Phyllis	√	√	WJ	11	1	41	Su 86	42
Twill, Broken	Winter Colors	Beeny, Merna	√	√	Hw	4	1		J/F 83	64
Twill, Broken Double-Faced, 3/1	Double-Faced 3/1 Broken Twill Woven on Tablets	Collingwood, Peter	√	√	AT	1			De 83	91
Twill, Broken (False Damask)	Bedspread (Marilyn Dillard)		√	√	Hw	4	4		S/O 83	60, 105
Twill, Broken (Satinet)	Fascination of Twills (Fourshafts): Broken Twill and Satinet	Zielinski, S. A.; Robert Leclerc, ed.	√	√	MWL	9			'51–'73	89
Twill, Broken, Turned	Fascination of Twills (Multishafts): Turned Twills-4-Group B: Broken Twills	Zielinski, S. A.; Robert Leclerc, ed.	√	>4	MWL	10			'51–'73	46
Twill, Broken Twill System	Handloom Weaves: The Classification of Handloom Weaves, The Structural Group, Twill Class, Broken Twill System	Tidball, Harriet	√	>4	SCGM		33		57	15
Twill, Broken (Two-Block)	Jacket Fabric #6 (Sharon D. Alderman)		√	>4	Hw	5	3		Su 84	62, 109
Twill, Broken, Weft-Faced	Hooded Russet Coat (Carol Thilenius)		√	√	Hw	3	4		Se 82	45, 86
Twill Class	Handloom Weaves: The Classification of Handloom Weaves, The Structural Group, Twill Class	Tidball, Harriet	√	√	SCGM		33		57	13
Twill, Color	Fascination of Twills (Fourshafts): Colour Effects in Twills	Zielinski, S. A.; Robert Leclerc, ed.	√	√	MWL	9			'51–'73	80
Twill, Color	Fascination of Twills (Fourshafts): More on Colours in Twills	Zielinski, S. A.; Robert Leclerc, ed.	√	>4	MWL	9			'51–'73	85
Twill, Compound, Weft-Faced	Chinese Brocades: Development of Supplementary Weft Patterning (error-corrected WJ v11 n4 87 p78)	Drooker, Penelope	√		WJ	11	3	43	Wi 87	47
Twill, Compound, Weft-Faced	Newly Excavated Caftan from the Northern Caucasus, A	Riboud, Krishna	√		TMJ	4	3		76	21
Twill, Computer-Aided	Computers and Weavers: Software Is Just Another Tool in the Designer's Hand	Hoskins, Janet A.	√		TM			9	F/M 87	51
Twill, Corkscrew	Corkscrew Weave	Barrett, Clotilde	√	>4	WJ	5	1	17	Su 80	16
Twill, Corkscrew	Hat Band (Barbara Elkins)		√	√	Hw	2	1		F-W 80	35, 69
Twill, Corkscrew	Off Set Twill Tie (Sharon Alderman)		√	>4	Hw	7	4		S/O 86	65, I-16
Twill, Corkscrew	Shadow Weave — Part 4. The Relationship Between Shadow Weave and Corkscrew Weave		√	>4	WJ	1	4	4	Ap 77	30
Twill, Crazy (Irregular)	Fascination of Twills (Fourshafts): Crazy Twills	Zielinski, S. A.; Robert Leclerc, ed.	√	√	MWL	9			'51–'73	46
Twill Damask	Multiple Shaft Weaving, Twill and Satin Blocks, Damask		√	>4	WJ	5	4	20	Sp 81	10
Twill, Damask, Turned	Fascination of Twills (Multishafts): Modern Damask and Other Turned Twills	Zielinski, S. A.; Robert Leclerc, ed.	√	>4	MWL	10			'51–'73	65
Twill, Damask, Turned	Fascination of Twills (Multishafts): Turned Twills-1-The "D" Class: Dimity, Diaper, Dornick, Damask	Zielinski, S. A.; Robert Leclerc, ed.	√	>4	MWL	10			'51–'73	35

SUBJECT	TITLE	AUTHOR	IL	INST	JOUR	VOL	NO	ISS	DATE	PAGE
Twill, Damask, Turned	Fascination of Twills (Multishafts): Turned Twills-5-Group B: Damask	Zielinski, S. A.; Robert Leclerc, ed.	√	>4	MWL	10			'51–'73	49
Twill, Damask, Turned, Problems	Fascination of Twills (Multishafts): Turned Twills-6-Problems in Damask	Zielinski, S. A.; Robert Leclerc, ed.	√	>4	MWL	10			'51–'73	52
Twill Derivative Class	Handloom Weaves: The Classification of Handloom Weaves, The Structural Group, Twill Derivative Class	Tidball, Harriet			SCGM		33		57	17
Twill, Derivatives	Crackle Weave		√	√	Hw	8	5		N/D 87	48
Twill, Derivatives	Multiple Harness Weaving Course — Part 3: Twill Derivatives		√	>4	WJ	5	1	17	Su 80	40
Twill Derivatives	Multiple Harness Weaving Course Part 4: Twill Derivatives (cont'd)	Searles, Nancy M.	√	>4	WJ	5	2	18	Fa 80	19
Twill Derivatives	Multiple Harness Weaving Course Part 5. Twill Derivatives (continued)		√	>4	WJ	5	3	19	Wi 81	12
Twill, Derivatives	Overshot Derived from 2/2 Twill	Xenakis, Athanasios David	√	√	PWC	3	2	8		7
Twill Derivatives, Goose-Foot	Keep Warm! Large Rectangular Shawl	Sylvan, Katherine	√	>4	WJ	5	2	18	Fa 80	10
Twill, Diamond	Fascination of Twills (Fourshafts): Diamond Twill for Production	Zielinski, S. A.; Robert Leclerc, ed.	√	√	MWL	9			'51–'73	62
Twill, Diamond	Roman Textiles from Vindolanda, Hexham, England	Wild, John Peter	√		TMJ	18			79	19
Twill, Diamond	Warping and Weaving Mitla Cloth on the Backstrap Loom	Knottenbelt, Maaike	√	√	TMJ	22			83	53
Twill, Diamond, 12-Shaft	Fascination of Twills (Multishafts): Twelve-Shaft Diamond Twill	Zielinski, S. A.; Robert Leclerc, ed.	√	>4	MWL	10			'51–'73	80
Twill, Diamond, 6- and 8-Shaft	Fascination of Twills (Multishafts): How to Design Diamond Twills on Six and Eight Shafts	Zielinski, S. A.; Robert Leclerc, ed.	√	>4	MWL	10			'51–'73	72
Twill, Diamond, Higher, 4-Shaft	Fascination of Twills (Fourshafts): Higher Diamond Twills on Four Shafts	Zielinski, S. A.; Robert Leclerc, ed.	√	√	MWL	9			'51–'73	68
Twill, Diamond, Higher, Projects	Fascination of Twills (Fourshafts): Higher Diamonds-Practical Projects	Zielinski, S. A.; Robert Leclerc, ed.	√	√	MWL	9			'51–'73	76
Twill, Diamond, Unsymmetrical	Fascination of Twills (Fourshafts): Modern Unsymmetric Diamond Twill	Zielinski, S. A.; Robert Leclerc, ed.	√	√	MWL	9			'51–'73	41
Twill, Diaper, Turned	But What's the Tie-Up?	van der Hoogt, Madelyn	√	>4	PWC	5	1	15		36
Twill, Diaper, Turned	Drafting: A Personal Approach, Part 3	Alvic, Philis	√	>4	SS&D	13	3	51	Su 82	40
Twill, Diaper, Turned	Fascination of Twills (Multishafts): Turned Twills-1-The "D" Class: Dimity, Diaper, Dornick, Damask	Zielinski, S. A.; Robert Leclerc, ed.	√	>4	MWL	10			'51–'73	35
Twill, Dimity	Fascination of Twills (Fourshafts): Dimity	Zielinski, S. A.; Robert Leclerc, ed.	√	√	MWL	9			'51–'73	24
Twill, Dimity, Turned	Fascination of Twills (Multishafts): Turned Twills-1-The "D" Class: Dimity, Diaper, Dornick, Damask	Zielinski, S. A.; Robert Leclerc, ed.	√	>4	MWL	10			'51–'73	35
Twill, Dornick	Antique Bronze Ruana (Jean Scorgie)		√	√	Hw	7	5		N/D 86	45, I-3
Twill, Dornick	Fascination of Twills (Fourshafts): Twills-3	Zielinski, S. A.; Robert Leclerc, ed.	√	>4	MWL	9			'51–'73	17
Twill, Dornick	Glowing Embers Scarf (Leslie Voiers)		√	√	Hw	6	5		N/D 85	43, I-5
Twill, Dornick	Swatch #1: Reversing Twill Warp and Weft (Sharon Alderman)		√	√	Hw	6	5		N/D 85	48, I-9
Twill, Dornick	Swatch #4: Dark Blue Dornick Twill with Silk Stripes (Sharon Alderman)		√	√	Hw	6	5		N/D 85	48, I-10
Twill, Dornick, Patterned	Fascination of Twills (Fourshafts): Four Shaft Patterns in Dornick	Zielinski, S. A.; Robert Leclerc, ed.	√	√	MWL	9			'51–'73	34
Twill, Dornick, Turned	Fascination of Twills (Multishafts): Turned Twills Dornick-3	Zielinski, S. A.; Robert Leclerc, ed.	√	>4	MWL	10			'51–'73	43
Twill, Dornick, Turned	Fascination of Twills (Multishafts): Turned Twills-1-The "D' Class: Dimity, Diaper, Dornick, Damask	Zielinski, S. A.; Robert Leclerc, ed.	√	>4	MWL	10			'51–'73	35
Twill, Dornik	Cotton/Linen Jacket (Sharon Alderman)		√	√	Hw	4	2		M/A 83	58, 92
Twill, Dornik	Jacket or Vest Fabric (Sharon Alderman)		√	√	Hw	3	2		Mr 82	9, 78
Twill, Dornik	Man's Jacket: A Weaver's Challenge, A	Rasmussen, Peg	√	√	SS&D	15	2	58	Sp 84	58
Twill, Dornik	Man's Sport Coat (Kathryn Wertenberger)		√	√	Hw	5	1		J/F 84	47, 94

SUBJECT	TITLE	AUTHOR	IL	INST	JOUR	VOL	NO	ISS	DATE	PAGE
Twill, Double	Double-Twill on a Jack Loom Using Two Sets of Ground Harnesses Equipped with Special Long-Eyed Heddles	Freimer, Betty	√	>4	CW	2	1	4	Oc 80	2
Twill, Double Diagonal	Fascination of Twills (Fourshafts): Twills with Double Diagonal	Zielinski, S. A.; Robert Leclerc, ed.	√	√	MWL	9			'51–'73	20
Twill, Double Diagonal	Fascination of Twills (Multishafts): Double Diagonal Twill for 6 and 8 Frames	Zielinski, S. A.; Robert Leclerc, ed.	√	>4	MWL	10			'51–'73	25
Twill, Double, System	Handloom Weaves: The Classification of Handloom Weaves, The Structural Group, Unit Class, Double-Twill System	Tidball, Harriet	√	>4	SCGM		33		57	27
Twill, Double-Broken (False Damask) System	Handloom Weaves: The Classification of Handloom Weaves, The Structural Group, Unit Class, Double-Broken-Twill System	Tidball, Harriet	√	>4	SCGM		33		57	27
Twill Double-Faced	Designing Damask	Nyquist, Jan	√	>4	SS&D	10	4	40	Fa 79	16
Twill, Double-Faced	Double-Faced Fabric (Sharon Alderman)		√	>4	Hw	3	4		Se 82	41, 95
Twill, Double-Faced	Doubleface Twill (Constance LaLena)		√	>4	Hw	5	2		M/A 84	64, 102
Twill, Double-Faced	Eight Harness Linen from Elizabeth Kackenmeister		√	>4	H&C	15	1		Wi 64	34
Twill, Double-Faced	Kimono Jacket (Leslie Voiers)		√	√	Hw	8	4		S/O 87	41, I-5
Twill, Double-Faced	Swatch Collection Vest (Sharon Alderman)		√	>4	Hw	4	1		J/F 83	68, 94
Twill, Double-Faced, Surface Interest	Surface Interest — Textiles of Today: Surface Interest Designs with Drafts, Group 4, Double-Faced Designs	Tidball, Harriet	√	>4	SCGM		2		61	16
Twill, Expanded	Versatile Twill	Liebler, Barbara	√	>4	Iw	6	1		Wi 80	26
Twill, Extended	Computer Learns to Weave, The	Huff, Karen E.	√	√	SS&D	6	4	24	Fa 75	19
Twill, Extended Point, Twill System	Handloom Weaves: The Classification of Handloom Weaves, The Structural Group, Twill Class, Extended Point Twill System	Tidball, Harriet	√	>4	SCGM		33		57	15
Twill, Fancy	Designing Fancy Twills in Double Two-Tie Unit Weave	Kelly, Jacquie	√	>4	Iw	6	1		Wi 80	49
Twill, Fancy	Multiple Harness Weaving Course Part 5. Twill Derivatives (continued)		√	>4	WJ	5	3	19	Wi 81	12
Twill, Float Ratio	Fraction of the Twill Story, A		√	√	Hw	6	5		N/D 85	46
Twill, Free-Form	Freeform Twill & Freeform Searles Lace	Searles, Nancy	√	>4	CW		23		Ja 87	10
Twill, Goose-Eye	Goose-eye Twill (Constance LaLena)		√	√	Hw	5	2		M/A 84	63, 100
Twill, Ground	Introduction to Tied Unit Weaves, An	Kelly, Jacquie	√	>4	PWC	4	4	14		40
Twill, Half-Basket	Samantha Herbert Napkins (Louise Bradley)		√	√	Hw	5	5		N/D 84	51, I-6
Twill, Herringbone	Colorful Scarves	Waggoner, Phyllis	√	√	WJ	12	2	46	Fa 87	48
Twill, Herringbone	Man's Sport Jacket/Woman's Blazer (Sharon Alderman)		√	√	Hw	2	1		F-W 80	50, 63
Twill, Herringbone	Ruana (Kathryn Wertenberger)		√	√	Hw	2	2		Mr 81	53, 77
Twill, Herringbone	Twill Upholstery Fabric (Constance LaLena)		√	√	Hw	4	1		J/F 83	66, 91
Twill, Herringbone	Warping and Weaving Mitla Cloth on the Backstrap Loom	Knottenbelt, Maaike	√	√	TMJ	22			83	53
Twill, Herringbone, Undulating	Snakeskin Jacket (Mary Kay Stoehr)		√	√	Hw	5	4		S/O 84	54, 96
Twill, Herringbone, Warp-Faced	Chevron Twill Belt (Gay Jensen)		√	√	Hw	3	4		Se 82	50, 85
Twill, High, As-Drawn-In	Fascination of Twills (Multishafts): High Twills-1	Zielinski, S. A.; Robert Leclerc, ed.	√	>4	MWL	10			'51–'73	7
Twill, High, Enlarging	Fascination of Twills (Multishafts): High Twills-4	Zielinski, S. A.; Robert Leclerc, ed.	√	>4	MWL	10			'51–'73	21
Twill, High, Fancy	Fascination of Twills (Multishafts): High Twills-3	Zielinski, S. A.; Robert Leclerc, ed.	√	>4	MWL	10			'51–'73	16
Twill, High, Rose Fashion	Fascination of Twills (Multishafts): High Twills-2	Zielinski, S. A.; Robert Leclerc, ed.	√	>4	MWL	10			'51–'73	12
Twill, Higher, 4-Shaft	Fascination of Twills (Fourshafts): Higher Twills for Four Shafts	Zielinski, S. A.; Robert Leclerc, ed.	√	√	MWL	9			'51–'73	56
Twill, Houndstooth	Houndstooth Scarf (Sharon Alderman)		√	√	Hw	2	1		F-W 80	51, 57
Twill, Huck Lace	Fascination of Twills (Multishafts): Multishafts Twill or Huck Lace	Zielinski, S. A.; Robert Leclerc, ed.	√	>4	MWL	10			'51–'73	68

SUBJECT	TITLE	AUTHOR	IL	INST	JOUR	VOL	NO	ISS	DATE	PAGE
Twill, Inlay	Twills of Charlotte Funk, The	Patrick, Jane	√		Hw	6	5		N/D 85	36
Twill, Inlay	Wrapped in Style: Poncho Cape (Betty Beard)		√	√	Hw	6	1		J/F 85	41, I-14
Twill, Integrated	Exploring the Textures: Another Texture Weave	Zielinski, S. A.; Robert Leclerc, ed.	√	√	MWL	11			'51–'73	87
Twill, Interlocking	Multiple Harness Weaving Course — Part 3: Twill Derivatives		√	> 4	WJ	5	1	17	Su 80	40
Twill, Interlocking	Shadow Weave — Part 4. The Relationship Between Shadow Weave and Corkscrew Weave		√	> 4	WJ	1	4	4	Ap 77	30
Twill, Jeans	Ikat Spun Lap Robe (Louise Bradley)	Bradley, Louise	√	√	Hw	2	4		Se 81	67
Twill, Jeans	Ikat Spun Shrug (Louise Bradley)	Bradley, Louise	√	√	Hw	2	4		Se 81	67
Twill, Jeans	Patterns from the Weaver's Guild		√	√	H&C	26	5		Oc 75	29
Twill, Lace	Fascination of Twills (Fourshafts): Twill Lace	Zielinski, S. A.; Robert Leclerc, ed.	√	√	MWL	9			'51–'73	38
Twill, Macro	Macro Plaid, Macro Twill	Xenakis, Athanasios David	√	> 4	PWC	3	1	7		55
Twill, Manifold	Custom Fabrics for a Classic Cadillac	Kelly, Jacquie	√	> 4	WJ	10	4	40	Sp 86	54
Twill, Manifold	Manifold Twills—Unlimited Opportunity for Experimentation	Redfield, Gail	√	√	SS&D	5	4	20	Fa 74	72
Twill, Modified	Autumn Pleasures Bog Jacket (Janice Jones)		√	√	Hw	5	4		S/O 84	76, 109
Twill, Multiple-Layered	Shelia O'Hara: Triangles, Squares and Other Landmarks	Draheim, Teliha	√		Iw	6	1		Wi 80	42
Twill, Multiple-Shaft	Textile Structure and Analysis, A Home Study Course in Twelve Lessons: Lessons in Weave Structure, 11. Multiple-Harness Twills	Tidball, Harriet		> 4	SCGM		18		66	29
Twill, Opposites	Twill Rugs (Marilyn Dillard)		√	√	Hw	6	5		N/D 85	Cover, I-5
Twill, Opposites, Rosepath	Boundweave Coat (Jean Scorgie)		√	√	Hw	2	1		F-W 80	31, 75
Twill, Optic	Optic Twill (Constance LaLena)		√	√	Hw	5	2		M/A 84	64, 100
Twill, Overshot System, Hybrid	Handloom Weaves: The Classification of Handloom Weaves, The Structural Group, Twill Derivative Class, Hybrid (Twill-Overshot) System	Tidball, Harriet	√	> 4	SCGM		33		57	18
Twill, Pattern, Random	Fascination of Twills (Multishafts): Practical Projects for Random Twills	Zielinski, S. A.; Robert Leclerc, ed.	√	√	MWL	10			'51–'73	64
Twill, Pattern, Random	Fascination of Twills (Multishafts): Random Patterns in Twills	Zielinski, S. A.; Robert Leclerc, ed.	√	> 4	MWL	10			'51–'73	59
Twill, Pattern, Turned	Fascination of Twills (Multishafts): Turned Twills-7-Group C: Turned Pattern Twills	Zielinski, S. A.; Robert Leclerc, ed.	√	> 4	MWL	10			'51–'73	55
Twill, Patterned	Fascination of Twills (Fourshafts): Patterns in 1:2 Twill on Four Shafts	Zielinski, S. A.; Robert Leclerc, ed.	√	√	MWL	9			'51–'73	30
Twill, Pick-Up	Mary Atwater Wallhanging (Gertrude Griffin)		√	√	Hw	7	2		M/A 86	55, I-9
Twill, Plaid	Jacket/Coat, Fabric #1 (Sharon Alderman)		√	√	Hw	8	4		S/O 87	52, I-8
Twill, Plain	Wooly Woolens	Thilenius, Carol; Marion Simpson	√	√	Hw	3	4		Se 82	44
Twill, Plain Twill System	Handloom Weaves: The Classification of Handloom Weaves, The Structural Group, Twill Class, Plain Twill System	Tidball, Harriet	√	> 4	SCGM		33		57	14
Twill, Plaited	Casual But Chic		√	> 4	WJ	8	4	32	Sp 84	70
Twill, Plaited	Plaited Twill Projects: Notes of A Pattern Weaver	Alvic, Philis	√	> 4	WJ	11	4	44	Sp 87	55
Twill, Plaited	Twills in Double Two-Tie Unit Weave	van der Hoogt, Madelyn	√	> 4	Hw	6	5		N/D 85	64
Twill, Plaited	Two Ties in Double Two-Tie (Amy Preckshot)		√	> 4	Hw	6	5		N/D 85	64, I-15
Twill, Point	And Thereon Hangs a Towel		√	> 4	Hw	3	4		Se 82	58
Twill, Point	Barefoot Comfort Rag Rug (Linda Ligon)		√	√	Hw	5	4		S/O 84	70, 105
Twill, Point	Bedspread Fabric	Skreko, Margaret	√	> 4	CW	1	3	3	Ap 80	8
Twill, Point	Book That's Bound to Please, A	Ligon, Linda	√	√	Hw	4	4		S/O 83	67

SUBJECT	TITLE	AUTHOR	IL	INST	JOUR	VOL	NO	ISS	DATE	PAGE
Twill, Point	Chevron Twill Scarf (M. Linda Whitten)		√	√	Hw	7	4		S/O 86	35, I-5
Twill, Point	Christmas Card	Nyquist, Janet	√	> 4	CW	1	2	2	Fe 80	11
Twill, Point	Christmas Cards		√	> 4	WJ	7	2	26	Fa 82	54
Twill, Point	Couturier Fashions: Part 1, Couturier Fabric Design	West, Virginia	√	√	SS&D	13	3	51	Su 82	8
Twill, Point	Demystifying Complex Weaves: A Step-by-Step Exploration from Four to Sixteen Harnesses	Piroch, Sigrid	√	> 4	WJ	10	3	39	Wi 86	8
Twill, Point	Different Boundweave on Six Harnesses, A (error-corrected WJ v3 n1 insert for vol. 2)	Strickler, Carol	√	> 4	WJ	2	4	8	Ap 78	36
Twill, Point	Donegal Tweed Scarf (Linda Hardison)		√	√	Hw	7	1		J/F 86	71
Twill, Point	Ethnic Inspired Jacket	Hurt, Doris	√	√	WJ	4	4	16	Ap 80	43
Twill, Point	Figures in Boundweave	Waggoner, Phyllis	√	√	WJ	10	2	38	Fa 85	58
Twill, Point	Garments with Ethnic Flavor: Blue and White Twill Dress		√	√	WJ	2	3	7	Ja 78	18
Twill, Point	Hand Towels (Inger Mattson)		√	√	Hw	4	2		M/A 83	31, 83
Twill, Point	Hand Woven Garments	Piper, Aris	√	> 4	WJ	5	3	19	Wi 81	24
Twill, Point	In Pursuit of Plakhta	Golay, Myrna	√	> 4	WJ	11	3	43	Wi 87	34
Twill, Point	Mug Rugs (Wendy Budde)		√	√	Hw	6	4		S/O 85	85
Twill, Point	Navajo Saddle Blanket Patterns	Barrett, Clotilde	√	√	WJ	11	1	41	Su 86	56
Twill, Point	Olwen's Buffalo	MacGregor, Olwen	√	√	WJ	8	2	30	Fa 83	46
Twill, Point	Patchwork Sweaters (Ronnine Bohannan)		√	> 4	Hw	6	5		N/D 85	45, I-6
Twill, Point	Ruana	Sylvan, Katherine	√	√	WJ	5	3	19	Wi 81	34
Twill, Point	Rugs Based on Four Harness Twills (error-corrected WJ v2 n2 77 insert for vol. 2)		√	√	WJ	2	1	5	Jy 77	23
Twill, Point	Saddle Blanket (Halcyon)		√	√	Hw	2	1		F-W 80	35, 58
Twill, Point	Shadowweave, Part 1 (error-corrected WJ v2 n1 77 insert for vol. 1)	Barrett, Clotilde	√	> 4	WJ	1	1	1	Jy 76	13
Twill, Point	Special Summer Vest, A	Jennings, Lucy Anne	√	> 4	WJ	9	3	35	Wi 85	42
Twill, Point	Suitable Subtleties	Gordon, Judith	√	> 4	Hw	5	3		Su 84	22
Twill, Point	Summer and Winter — Part 1		√	> 4	WJ	2	4	8	Ap 78	28
Twill, Point	Table Tapestries	Barrett, Clotilde	√	> 4	WJ	7	4	28	Sp 83	73
Twill, Point	Upholstery or Cushion, Fabric #2 (Constance LaLena)		√	√	Hw	8	4		S/O 87	36, I-3
Twill, Point	Variations on a Poncho Theme	d'Avilla, Doris	√	√	WJ	2	3	7	Ja 78	30
Twill, Point	Waffle Weave	Wertenberger, Kathryn	√	> 4	Hw	8	4		S/O 87	83
Twill, Point	Weaving Towels As a Means of Learning the Basic Four-Shaft Weaves	Barrett, Clotilde	√	√	WJ	8	2	30	Fa 83	11
Twill, Point	Woven Fringes		√	> 4	WJ	3	3	11	Ja 79	14
Twill, Point	Woven Reed Placemats	Ingebretsen, Cathy	√	√	PWC	3	2	8		4
Twill, Point	Wrist-to-Wrist Garment, The	Allen, Rose Mary	√	√	WJ	9	3	35	Wi 85	19
Twill, Point, 3-Shaft	Krokbragd Rug (Lin Eppinger) (error-corrected Hw v2 n4 81 p22)		√	√	Hw	2	2		Mr 81	36
Twill, Point, Expanded, Opposites	Expanded Point Twill	McCeary, Gay	√	> 4	Iw	4	3		Su 79	37
Twill, Point, Expanded, Opposites Modified	Expanded Point Twill	McCeary, Gay	√	> 4	Iw	4	3		Su 79	37
Twill, Point, Extended	Rugs Based on Four Harness Twills (error-corrected WJ v2 n2 77 insert for vol. 2)		√	√	WJ	2	1	5	Jy 77	23
Twill, Point, Extended	Shadowweave, Part 2 — Unbalanced Shadowweave (error-corrected WJ v2 n1 77 insert for vol. 1)	Barrett, Clotilde	√	> 4	WJ	1	2	2	Oc 76	14
Twill, Point, Extended	White Jacket	Grange, Penny	√	√	WJ	8	3	31	Wi 83	16
Twill, Point Twill System	Handloom Weaves: The Classification of Handloom Weaves, The Structural Group, Twill Class, Point Twill System	Tidball, Harriet	√	> 4	SCGM		33		57	14
Twill, Point, Variation	Dress Fabric (Sharon Alderman)		√	> 4	Hw	1	2		S-S 80	41, 61

SUBJECT	TITLE	AUTHOR	IL	INST	JOUR	VOL	NO	ISS	DATE	PAGE
Twill, Point, Variation	Floating Selvedges	Ligon, Linda	√	√	Hw	7	3		M/J 86	92
Twill, Point, Weft-Faced	Mexican Motifs: The Mexican Men's Jacket	Tidball, Harriet	√	√	SCGM		6		62	20
Twill, Random Pattern	Composition and Designing Part 2: Random Patterns in Twills	Zielinski, S. A.; Robert Leclerc, ed.	√	>4	MWL	19			'51–'73	108
Twill, Reversed	Tunic Made from Narrow Strips	Barrett, Clotilde	√	√	WJ	4	3	15	Ja 80	9
Twill, Reversed	Versatile Twill	Liebler, Barbara	√	√	Iw	6	1		Wi 80	26
Twill, Reversing	Twill Accent Fabrics (Sharon D. Alderman)		√	>4	Hw	5	2		M/A 84	69, 107
Twill, Rosepath	Boundweave: Learning from the Past	Waggoner, Phyllis	√	√	WJ	10	4	40	Sp 86	44
Twill, Rosepath	Christmas Boot or After Ski Boot (Jean Scorgie)		√	√	Hw	4	4		S/O 83	72, 100
Twill, Rosepath	Color-and-Weave on Rosepath	Windeknecht, Margaret; Thomas Windeknecht	√	√	SS&D	13	2	50	Sp 82	8
Twill, Rosepath	Each One Picked a Color—4th and 5th Graders Weave a Blanket	Hanna, Linda	√		WJ	9	1	33	Su 84	34
Twill, Rosepath	Figures in Boundweave	Waggoner, Phyllis	√	√	WJ	10	2	38	Fa 85	58
Twill, Rosepath	Half Shawl Designed by Janet Checker		√	√	WJ	11	3	43	Wi 87	14
Twill, Rosepath	Holiday Runners	Skoy, Mary	√	>4	WJ	12	2	46	Fa 87	22
Twill, Rosepath	Lina Hartman Silk Scarf (Louise Bradley)		√	√	Hw	5	5		N/D 84	53, I-7
Twill, Rosepath	Rags to Riches: Jackets from Rags	Brones, Britta	√	√	WJ	6	3	23	Wi 81	31
Twill, Rosepath	Reversible Flamepoint Vest	Wittpenn, Ann	√	√	WJ	5	3	19	Wi 81	9
Twill, Rosepath	Rugs In the Scandinavian Way		√	√	Hw	8	3		M/J 87	58
Twill, Rosepath Opposites	Boundweave Jacket (Jean Scorgie)		√	√	Hw	2	1		F-W 80	31, 74
Twill, Rosepath, Swedish	Cut and Sew Mittens	Winchester, Nina	√	√	WJ	9	3	35	Wi 85	53
Twill, Rosepath, Variations	Knot of Ties, A (Janice Jones)		√	√	Hw	6	2		M/A 85	54, I-11
Twill, Rosepath, Variations	Pastel Collection (Jane Patrick)		√	√	Hw	6	2		M/A 85	48, I-8
Twill, Rosepath, Variations	Scarf, Cap and Mittens Set (Marit Drenckhahn)		√	√	Hw	2	1		F-W 80	52, 78
Twill, Rosepath, Weft Loops	Powder Puffs (Lila Alexander)		√	√	Hw	6	4		S/O 85	64, I-14
Twill, Rosepath, Weft-Faced	Bound Rosepath Rug (Phyllis Waggoner)		√	√	Hw	8	3		M/J 87	59, I-11
Twill, Satin System	Handloom Weaves: The Classification of Handloom Weaves, The Structural Group, Twill Class, Satin System	Tidball, Harriet	√	>4	SCGM		33		57	16
Twill, Skip, Weft-Faced	Rug (Marilyn Dillard)		√	√	Hw	4	4		S/O 83	60, 105
Twill, Steep	Multiple Harness Weaving Course — Part 3: Twill Derivatives		√	>4	WJ	5	1	17	Su 80	40
Twill, Step	Fascination of Twills (Fourshafts): 12-Step Twills	Zielinski, S. A.; Robert Leclerc, ed.	√	√	MWL	9			'51–'73	52
Twill, Straight	Alpaca "Jerga" (Pam Bolesta)		√	√	Hw	1	1		F-W 79	22, 55
Twill, Straight	Garments with Ethnic Flavor: Blue and White Twill Dress		√	√	WJ	2	3	7	Ja 78	18
Twill, Straight	On Handwoven Upholstery	Ligon, Linda	√	>4	Hw	3	2		Mr 82	58
Twill, Straight	Patchwork Sweaters (Ronnine Bohannan)		√	>4	Hw	6	5		N/D 85	45, I-6
Twill, Straight	Red Wool Jacket (Linda Ligon)		√	√	Hw	2	5		No 81	51, 83
Twill, Straight	Ribbon Wefts	Sewell, Suzy	√	>4	WJ	10	3	39	Wi 86	40
Twill, Straight	Rug Based on 3-Shaft Striaght Twill		√	√	WJ	5	4	20	Sp 81	20
Twill, Straight	Stadium Poncho (Carol Klippenstein)		√	√	Hw	1	1		F-W 79	28, 58
Twill, Straight	Twill Accent Fabrics (Sharon D. Alderman)		√	>4	Hw	5	2		M/A 84	69, 107
Twill, Straight	Twill Plaid, A	Gordon, Judith	√	>4	Hw	5	2		M/A 84	41
Twill, Straight	Twilled Cottolin Towels	Waggoner, Phyllis	√	√	WJ	11	1	41	Su 86	42
Twill, Straight	Vestment Variations: A Weaver From the Netherlands Creates Garments for the Ecclesiastical Calendar	Jansen, Netty	√	>4	WJ	10	3	39	Wi 86	53
Twill, Straight and Broken	Ducky Sacque and Bonnet (Cara L. Bernhauser)		√	√	Hw	5	3		Su 84	51, 94
Twill, Straight Draw	One Warp, Many Fabrics	Liebler, Barbara	√	>4	Iw	3	1		Fa 77	28

SUBJECT	TITLE	AUTHOR	IL	INST	JOUR	VOL	NO	ISS	DATE	PAGE
Twill, Straight Draw	Rugs Based on Four Harness Twills (error-corrected WJ v2 n2 77 insert for vol. 2)		√	√	WJ	2	1	5	Jy 77	23
Twill, Straight Draw	Table Tapestries	Barrett, Clotilde	√	> 4	WJ	7	4	28	Sp 83	73
Twill, Stripe	Heirloom Pillowcases (Sharon Alderman)		√	> 4	Hw	8	4		S/O 87	57, I-13
Twill, Striped	Skirt or Suit, Fabric #5 (Sharon Alderman)		√	√	Hw	8	4		S/O 87	52, I-9
Twill, Surface Interest	Surface Interest — Textiles of Today: Surface Interest Designs with Drafts, Group 1, Accented Designs	Tidball, Harriet	√	√	SCGM		2		61	8
Twill, Surface Interest	Surface Interest — Textiles of Today: Surface Interest Designs with Drafts, Group 2, Reinforced Deisngs	Tidball, Harriet	√	> 4	SCGM		2		61	10
Twill, Texture	Exploring the Textures: More Textures on Four Shafts	Zielinski, S. A.; Robert Leclerc, ed.	√	√	MWL	11			'51–'73	110
Twill Traditions: Scandinavia	Rose Jacket in Twill		√	> 4	Hw	8	3		M/J 87	56
Twill, Triple-Warp	You Are Now Weaving Oakland	O'Hara, Sheila	√	> 4	AT	6			De 86	9
Twill, Turned	Contemporary Approach to Traditional Weaves: Modern Damask and Other Turned Twills	Zielinski, S. A.; Robert Leclerc, ed.	√	> 4	MWL	8			'51–'73	83
Twill, Turned	Dimity Delight	Sullivan, Donna	√	> 4	PWC	5	1	15		17
Twill, Turned	Twill Diaper Piqué (error-corrected PWC v4 n4 i14 '87 p33)	Xenakis, Athanasios David; Madelyn van der Hoogt	√	> 4	PWC	4	3	13		36
Twill, Turned, Tie-Up	Fascination of Twills (Multishafts): Turned Twills-2-The Tie-Up	Zielinski, S. A.; Robert Leclerc, ed.	√	> 4	MWL	10			'51–'73	39
Twill, Turned, Two-Harness (Sets)	Little Known Weaves Worth Knowing Better: Two-Harness Method	Zielinski, S. A.; Robert Leclerc, ed.	√	> 4	MWL	16			'51–'73	31
Twill, Turned, Two-Harness (Sets) Method	Fascination of Twills (Multishafts): Turned Twills-Two Harness Method-2	Zielinski, S. A.; Robert Leclerc, ed.	√	> 4	MWL	10			'51–'73	31
Twill, Two-Block	Profile Drafting Lesson: Twill Towel (Sharon Alderman)		√	> 4	Hw	8	5		N/D 87	44, I-7
Twill, Two-Faced	Notebook: One Fabric — Two Faces	Myers, Ruth Nordquist, ed.	√	> 4	SS&D	13	2	50	Sp 82	16
Twill, Two-Tie	Plaited Twills		√	> 4	WJ	7	4	28	Sp 83	76
Twill, Types	Multiple Harness Weaving Course — Part I (error-corrected WJ v4 n4 80 p16)		√	> 4	WJ	4	3	15	Ja 80	14
Twill, Unbalanced	Brown Jacket (Kathryn Wertenberger)		√	> 4	Hw	6	4		S/O 85	56, I-10
Twill, Unbalanced	Four-Shaft Unbalanced Twill Braided Ribbon Inlay on Plain Weave Ground	Xenakis, Athanasios David	√	√	PWC	4	1	11		27
Twill, Unbalanced	Sheila O'Hara's Geometrics	Rowley, Kathleen M.	√		SS&D	12	4	48	Fa 81	20
Twill, Unbalanced	Swatch #5: Bluish-red Warp-striped Worsted (Sharon Alderman)		√	> 4	Hw	6	5		N/D 85	48, I-10
Twill, Undulating	Fascination of Twills (Fourshafts): Twills-2	Zielinski, S. A.; Robert Leclerc, ed.	√	√	MWL	9			'51–'73	12
Twill, Undulating	Garments Made from Simple Patterns: Blanket Poncho		√	√	WJ	2	3	7	Ja 78	38
Twill, Undulating	Men's Clothing		√	> 4	WJ	2	3	7	Ja 78	32
Twill, Undulating	Shadow Weave Vest (error-corrected WJ v9 n2 84 p82)		√	> 4	WJ	8	3	31	Wi 83	81
Twill, Undulating	Symbolic or Sacred? A Personal View	Lockwood, Diana W.	√	> 4	WJ	9	3	35	Wi 85	45
Twill, Undulating	Trifles: Silk Purse, About the Size of a Sow's Ear (Linda Ligon)		√	√	Hw	1	1		F-W 79	47
Twill, Undulating	Twill with a Twist	Keasbey, Doramay	√	> 4	Hw	6	5		N/D 85	31
Twill, Undulating	Undulating Twill Upholstery (Sharon Alderman)		√	√	Hw	3	1		Ja 82	69, 82
Twill, Undulating	Undulating Twills	Carey, Joyce Marquess	√	> 4	Iw	6	1		Wi 80	31
Twill, Undulating	Undulating Warps and Wefts	Wertenberger, Kathryn	√	> 4	Hw	6	4		S/O 85	90
Twill, Undulating	Versatile Twill	Liebler, Barbara	√	√	Iw	6	1		Wi 80	26
Twill, Undulating Twill System	Handloom Weaves: The Classification of Handloom Weaves, The Structural Group, Twill Class, Undulating Twill System	Tidball, Harriet	√	> 4	SCGM		33		57	16
Twill, Uneven	Two Faces of Uneven Twill, The		√		Hw	6	5		N/D 85	47

762

SUBJECT	TITLE	AUTHOR	IL	INST	JOUR	VOL	NO	ISS	DATE	PAGE
Twill, Variation	Crazy Quilt Bed Jacket (Mary Kay Stoehr)		√	√	Hw	5	5		N/D 84	71, I-13
Twill, Variation	Design Decisions: Software Solutions	George, Patrice	√	>4	Hw	5	5		N/D 84	47
Twill, Variation	Hemstitch in Time, A	Ligon, Linda	√	√	Hw	8	2		M/A 87	98
Twill, Variation	Sampling	Strickler, Carol	√	√	Iw	3	1		Fa 77	43
Twill, Variation	Twill Placemats (Dian Stanley)		√	√	Hw	8	2		M/A 87	81, I-16
Twill, Variation	You Are Now Weaving Oakland	O'Hara, Sheila	√	>4	AT	6			De 86	9
Twill, Variations	Notebook: Baby Blankets and Afghans	Myers, Ruth Nordquist, ed.	√	>4	SS&D	12	4	48	Fa 81	50
Twill, Variations	Variations on a Twill Theme: No. 1	Marston, Ena	√	√	SS&D	5	1	17	Wi 73	34
Twill, Variations	Variations on a Twill Theme, No. 2	Marston, Ena	√	>4	SS&D	5	3	19	Su 74	34
Twill, Variations	Weaving Table Linens	Eychaner, Barbara Smith	√	√	TM			11	J/J 87	52
Twill, Warp, Unbalanced	Nutmeg Tablecloth		√	√	WJ	6	1	21	Su 81	9
Twill, Warp-Faced	Fascination of Twills (Fourshafts): Twills-1	Zielinski, S. A.; Robert Leclerc, ed.	√	>4	MWL	9			'51–'73	7
Twill, Warp-Faced	Warp-Faced 2/2 Twill: Part 2	Jensen, Gay	√	√	Hw	3	4		Se 82	50
Twill, Weft-Faced	Fascination of Twills (Fourshafts): Twills-1	Zielinski, S. A.; Robert Leclerc, ed.	√	>4	MWL	9			'51–'73	7
Twill, Weft-Faced	Jacket (Sharon Alderman)		√	√	Hw	1	2		S-S 80	41, 61
Twill, Weft-Faced	Navajo Inspired Rugs (Penelope Drooker)		√	√	Hw	6	2		M/A 85	58, I-16
Twill, Weft-Faced	Navajo Saddleblanket, The	Marquess, Joyce	√	>4	SS&D	8	3	31	Su 77	25
Twill, Weft-Faced	Striped Cotton Placemats (Sharon Alderman)		√	√	Hw	4	2		M/A 83	41, 84
Twill, Whipcord	Upholstery Fabric 2 (Constance LaLena)		√	>4	Hw	3	4		Se 82	33, 84
Twill, Yardage	Fascination of Twills (Fourshafts): High Quality in Twill Yardage	Zielinski, S. A.; Robert Leclerc, ed.	√	√	MWL	9			'51–'73	95
Twill-Tapestry Technique	Kashmir East and West	Mikosch, Elizabeth	√		TM			9	F/M 87	14
Twillin	New Look at Twills, A	Hoskins, Janet A.	√	>4	WJ	6	3	23	Wi 81	46
Twillins	Twillins, Color-Alternative Twills and Color-Alternate Twillins	Hoskins, Janet A.	√	>4	CW	2	3	6	Ap 81	1
Twillins, Color-Alternate	Twillins, Color-Alternative Twills and Color-Alternate Twillins	Hoskins, Janet A.	√	>4	CW	2	3	6	Ap 81	1
Twills	Notes on the Damask Weave	Ahrens, Jim		>4	CW	2	1	4	Oc 80	6
Twills, Color-Alternate	Twillins, Color-Alternative Twills and Color-Alternate Twillins	Hoskins, Janet A.	√	>4	CW	2	3	6	Ap 81	1
Twine Making	Spinning for Survival — Making Twine		√		S-O	1			77	53
Twining	Band Loom Offers New Approach to Weft Twining	Tacker, Sylvia; Harold Tacker	√	√	SS&D	6	2	22	Sp 75	38
Twining	Before Heddles Were Invented	Bird, Junius B.	√		H&C	3	3		Su 52	5
Twining	Breath of Our Grandmothers, The	Samuel, Cheryl	√		WJ	8	1	29	Su 83	17
Twining	Chilkat Blanket: It Soon May Be No More, The	Eggleston, Phyllis	√	√	SS&D	7	1	25	Wi 75	44
Twining	Chilkat Spinning	Samuel, Alena	√	√	TM			1	O/N 85	55
Twining	From Baskets to Blankets (error-corrected TM i7 O/N86 p5)	Samuel, Cheryl	√	√	TM			5	J/J 86	30
Twining	Hearth Brooms (Anne Bliss)		√	√	Hw	1	2		S-S 80	27, 57
Twining	Hungarian Weaving	Allen, Jane Ingram	√	√	SS&D	10	3	39	Su 79	93
Twining	Indian Fingerweaving, Traditional Use for Ceremonial Sashes	White, John	√	√	H&C	19	3		Su 68	4
Twining	Maori and Pakeha of New Zealand Use Wool and Phormium Tenax	Duncan, Molly	√	√	SS&D	5	1	17	Wi 73	65
Twining	Nez Percé Indian Art and Craft Revival	Connette, Ann	√	√	H&C	21	4		Fa 70	5
Twining	No Weavers Nearby? Form a Beginning Class—And a Guild	Zorick, Jean	√		SS&D	5	4	20	Fa 74	87
Twining	Prehistoric Twined Bag from Big Bone Cave, Tennessee: Manufacture, Repair, and Use, A	Kuttruff, Jenna Tedrick	√		AT	8			De 87	125
Twining	Reviving the Lost Art of Woodland Indian Bag Weaving	King, Rod	√		Fa	13	2		M/A 86	27
Twining	Students Learn Creating with Fiber	Thomason, Roger	√		SS&D	6	1	21	Wi 74	4, 10

SUBJECT	TITLE	AUTHOR	IL	INST	JOUR	VOL	NO	ISS	DATE	PAGE
Twining	Technology of Basketry: North American Roots and Relations to Cloth, The	Turnbaugh, Sarah Peabody	√	√	SS&D	8	1	29	WI 76	32
Twining	Temple of the Elelments, The	Samuel, Cheryl	√		SS&D	17	3	67	Su 86	10
Twining	Twined Bags and Pouches of the Eastern Woodlands	White, John Kennardh	√	√	H&C	20	3		Su 69	8
Twining	Twining Trick, A	Hoskins, Nancy Arthur	√	√	SS&D	18	4	72	Fa 87	8
Twining	Twining Variations	Reiss, Zenaide	√	√	SS&D	4	1	13	Wi 72	43
Twining	Twining with Leaves and Corn Husks (error-corrected SS&D v14 n4 83 p4)	Jensen, Elizabeth Jane	√	√	SS&D	14	3	55	Su 83	10
Twining	Variations on a Landes Theme	Coutts, Lucele	√	√	WJ	8	4	32	Sp 84	24
Twining	Weft-Twined Weaving	Nichols, Evelyn C.	√	√	SS&D	16	3	63	Su 85	82
Twining, Basketry	Twine a Basket! (Mary Pendergrass)		√	√	Hw	1	1		F-W 79	34
Twining Frame	Twined Bag, A		√	√	WJ	1	3	3	Ja 77	27
Twining, Primitive: Maori	Weft Twining: History, The Maori of New Zealand	Harvey, Virginia I.; Harriet Tidball	√		SCGM		28		69	7
Twining, Primitive: Nagas	Weft Twining: History, The Nagas of Northeast India	Harvey, Virginia I.; Harriet Tidball	√		SCGM		28		69	11
Twining, Spilt-Ply: Introduction	Split-Ply Twining	Harvey, Virginia I.	√		TIAM		1		76	4
Twining, Split-Ply: Basic Structural Changes	Split-Ply Twining: A Sample Showing the Two Basic Structural Changes	Harvey, Virginia I.	√	√	TIAM		1		76	14
Twining, Split-Ply: Materials	Split-Ply Twining: Materials	Harvey, Virginia I.	√	√	TIAM		1		76	8
Twining, Split-Ply: Open Structures	Split-Ply Twining: Open Structures	Harvey, Virginia I.	√	√	TIAM		1		76	36
Twining, Split-Ply: Penetrations Plies	Split-Ply Twining: The Various Penetrations of the Plies	Harvey, Virginia I.	√	√	TIAM		1		76	26
Twining, Split-Ply: Structure	Split-Ply Twining: The Structure	Harvey, Virginia I.	√	√	TIAM		1		76	7
Twining, Split-Ply: Substituting, Adding, Subtracting Cords	Split-Ply Twining: Substituting, Adding and Subtracting Cords	Harvey, Virginia I.	√	√	TIAM		1		76	42
Twining, Split-Ply: Technique	Split-Ply Twining: Some Beginnings and Methods of Weaving	Harvey, Virginia I.	√	√	TIAM		1		76	12
Twining, Split-Ply: Vertical Intersection	Split-Ply Twining: A Sample with a Vertical Intersection	Harvey, Virginia I.	√	√	TIAM		1		76	20
Twining, Techniques	Modern Twined Bags for Weaving Without a Loom	Spencer, Elsie H.	√	√	H&C	21	1		Wi 70	12
Twining, Techniques	Spaced-Weft Twining of Ancient Peru: A Contemporary Interpretation	Rogers, Nora	√	√	Iw	5	4		Fa 80	42
Twining Techniques	Twined Bag, A		√	√	WJ	1	3	3	Ja 77	27
Twining: Versatility	Weft Twining: The Versatility of Twining	Harvey, Virginia I.; Harriet Tidball	√		SCGM		28		69	16
Twining, Warp	Cardweaving Without Cards	Tacker, Sylvia	√	√	SS&D	13	2	50	Sp 82	42
Twining, Warp	Christmas Project, A	Richards, Iris	√	√	WJ	1	2	2	Oc 76	12
Twining, Warp Spacing	Weft Twining: Twining for Spacing	Harvey, Virginia I.; Harriet Tidball	√		SCGM		28		69	15
Twining, Warp-Patterned	Spaced-Weft Twining of Ancient Peru: A Contemporary Interpretation	Rogers, Nora	√	√	Iw	5	4		Fa 80	42
Twining, Weft	Danish Twined Rag Rugs: Lillie Sherwood's Legacy	Irwin, Bobbie	√	√	WJ	10	4	40	Sp 86	32
Twining, Weft	Hammock, The	Drooker, Penelope B.	√	√	TM			6	A/S 86	74
Twining, Weft	Peruvian Weft Twining	Schira, Cynthia	√	√	H&C	17	3		Su 66	14
Twining, Weft	Weft Twining	Harvey, Virginia I.; Harriet Tidball			SCGM		28		69	1-39
Twining, Weft	Weft Twining	Smith, Joyce Ronald	√	√	TM			2	D/J 85	69
Twining, Weft	Weft Twining	Harvey, Virginia I.; Harriet Tidball	√	√	SCGM		28		69	21
Twining, Weft	Weft Twining: The Structures of Weft Twining	Harvey, Virginia I.; Harriet Tidball								
Twining, Weft	Weft-Twined Weaving	Nichols, Evelyn C.	√	√	SS&D	16	3	63	Su 85	82
Twining, Weft: Braiding	Weft Twining: The Structures of Weft Twining, Braiding	Harvey, Virginia I.; Harriet Tidball	√	√	SCGM		28		69	30
Twining, Weft: Braiding, Turns	Weft Twining: The Structures of Weft Twining, Braided Turns	Harvey, Virginia I.; Harriet Tidball	√	√	SCGM		28		69	31

SUBJECT	TITLE	AUTHOR	IL	INST	JOUR	VOL	NO	ISS	DATE	PAGE
Twining, Weft: Chaining	Weft Twining: The Structures of Weft Twining, Chaining	Harvey, Virginia I.; Harriet Tidball	√	√	SCGM		28		69	37
Twining, Weft: Countered, Turns	Weft Twining: The Structures of Weft Twining, Plain and Countered Twining Turns	Harvey, Virginia I.; Harriet Tidball	√	√	SCGM		28		69	27
Twining, Weft: Countered, Two-Colors	Weft Twining: The Structures of Weft Twining, Countered Twining with Two Colors	Harvey, Virginia I.; Harriet Tidball	√	√	SCGM		28		69	26
Twining, Weft: Diverted Warps	Weft Twining: The Structures of Weft Twining, Other Variations of Twining	Harvey, Virginia I.; Harriet Tidball	√	√	SCGM		28		69	25
Twining, Weft: Looped	Weft Twining: The Structures of Weft Twining, Loops of a Twined Ground	Harvey, Virginia I.; Harriet Tidball	√	√	SCGM		28		69	33
Twining, Weft: Outlining	Weft Twining: The Structures of Weft Twining, Twined Outlining	Harvey, Virginia I.; Harriet Tidball	√	√	SCGM		28		69	32
Twining, Weft: Plain, Turns	Weft Twining: The Structures of Weft Twining, Plain and Countered Twining Turns	Harvey, Virginia I.; Harriet Tidball	√	√	SCGM		28		69	27
Twining, Weft: Simple, Variations	Weft Twining: The Structures of Weft Twining, Variations of Simple Twining	Harvey, Virginia I.; Harriet Tidball	√	√	SCGM		28		69	22
Twining, Weft: Spaced	Spaced-Weft Twining of Ancient Peru: A Contemporary Interpretation	Rogers, Nora	√	√	Iw	5	4		Fa 80	42
Twining, Weft: Taaniko	Weft Twining: The Structures of Weft Twining, Taaniko	Harvey, Virginia I.; Harriet Tidball	√	√	SCGM		28		69	36
Twining, Weft: Three-Colors	Weft Twining: The Structures of Weft Twining, Twining with Three Color	Harvey, Virginia I.; Harriet Tidball	√	√	SCGM		28		69	29
Twining, Weft: Two-Colors	Weft Twining: The Structures of Weft Twining, Twining with Two Colors	Harvey, Virginia I.; Harriet Tidball	√	√	SCGM		28		69	24
Twining, Weft: Variations	Weft Twining: The Structures of Weft Twining, Other Variations of Twining	Harvey, Virginia I.; Harriet Tidball	√	√	SCGM		28		69	25
Twining, Weft: Yarn Embellishments	Weft Twining: The Structures of Weft Twining, Surface Yarns Added to Twining	Harvey, Virginia I.; Harriet Tidball	√	√	SCGM		28		69	34
Two-Faced Weaves	Complimentary-Weft Plain Weave — A Pick-up Technique (error-corrected WJ v5 n1 80 p28d)	Hanley, Janet	√	√	WJ	4	4	16	Ap 80	22
Two-Faced Weaves	Backed Cloth on Four Harnesses		√	√	WJ	4	1	13	Jy 79	30
Two-Faced Weaves	Work of a Huave Indian Weaver in Oaxaca, Mexico: Complex Weave Structures Utilizing One Warp Set and Two Complementary Weft Sets, The	Connolly, Loris	√		AT	3			My 85	7
Two-Faced Weaves	You are Now Weaving Oakland	O'Hara, Sheila	√	>4	AT	6			De 86	9
Two-Harness (Sets) System	Long Eyed Heddles	Ahrens, Jim	√	>4	CW	6	1	16	Se 84	3
Two-Harness (Sets) Weaving	Banares Brocade	DuBois, Emily	√	>4	AT	3			My 85	209
Two-Harness (Sets) Weaving	Chinese Drawloom: A Study in Weave Structure, The	Sellin, Helen	√	>4	WJ	9	2	34	Fa 84	6
Two-Harness (Sets) Weaving	Christmas Card, A		√	>4	WJ	2	2	6	Oc 77	32
Two-Harness (Sets) Weaving	Double & Triple Harness Double-Cloth	Fabeck, Diane	√	>4	CW	7	3	21	My 86	7
Two-Harness (Sets) Weaving	Double-Twill on a Jack Loom Using Two Sets of Ground Harnesses Equipped with Special Long-Eyed Heddles	Freimer, Betty	√	>4	CW	2	1	4	Oc 80	2
Two-Harness (Sets) Weaving	Drawloom Basics	van der Hoogt, Madelyn	√	>4	Hw	7	2		M/A 86	61
Two-Harness (Sets) Weaving	Drawloom Magic	van der Hoogt, Madelyn	√	>4	Hw	7	2		M/A 86	66
Two-Harness (Sets) Weaving	Fascination of Twills (Multishafts): Turned Twills-Two Harness Method-2	Zielinski, S. A.; Robert Leclerc, ed.	√	>4	MWL	10			'51–'73	31
Two-Harness (Sets) Weaving	In Pursuit of Plakhta	Golay, Myrna	√	>4	WJ	11	3	43	Wi 87	34
Two-Harness (Sets) Weaving	Karelian Red-Picking	Ruchti, Willie Jager	√	>4	WJ	5	2	18	Fa 80	34
Two-Harness (Sets) Weaving	Ken Colwell on Opphämta				PWC	3	4	10		67
Two-Harness (Sets) Weaving	Layered Fabrics on Eight Harnesses	Marston, Ena	√	>4	SS&D	6	4	24	Fa 75	50
Two-Harness (Sets) Weaving	Little Known Weaves Worth Knowing Better: Two-Harness Method	Zielinski, S. A.; Robert Leclerc, ed.	√	>4	MWL	16			'51–'73	23
Two-Harness (Sets) Weaving	Long-Eyed Heddles and Rising Shed Looms	Fabeck, Diane	√	>4	Iw	4	4		Fa 79	28
Two-Harness (Sets) Weaving	Smalandsvav—Double Harness Weaving on an Ordinary Loom	Kelly, Jacquie	√	>4	CW	6	2	17	Ja 85	15

SUBJECT	TITLE	AUTHOR	IL	INST	JOUR	VOL	NO	ISS	DATE	PAGE
Two-Harness (Sets) Weaving	Three-Toned Blocks, Part 1: Simple Pattern	Broughton, Eve T.	√	>4	CW	6	1	16	Se 84	12
Two-Harness (Sets) Weaving	Three-Toned Blocks, Part 2: Reverses	Broughton, Eve T.	√	>4	CW	6	2	17	Ja 85	10
Two-Harness (Sets) Weaving	Three-Toned Blocks, Part 3: Alternating Designs	Broughton, Eve T.	√	>4	CW	6	3	18	My 85	10
Two-Harness (Sets) Weaving	Twill and Plain Weave Blocks with Long-Eyed Heddles	Broughton, Eve T.	√	>4	WJ	8	4	32	Sp 84	58
Two-Harness (Sets) Weaving	Use Of Long-Eyed Heddles, The	Koob, Katherine; Barbara Keller; Ruth Howard	√	>4	CW	1	3	3	Ap 80	1
Two-Harness (Sets) Weaving: Egypt	Double-Harness Techniques Employed in Egypt	El-Homossani, M. M.	√	>4	AT	3			My 85	229
Two-Harness (Sets) Weaving: Method	Drawloom Special Harness for Double Weave	Malloy, Kim, OSB	√	>4	AT	1			De 83	77
Two-Harness (Sets) Weaving: Method	Lithuanian Pervarai: Producing a Twenty Shaft Pattern on a Twelve Shaft Loom	Meek, M. Kati	√	>4	AT	1			De 83	159
Two-Shaft Looms	Two-Harness Rugs	Van Cleve, Kate	√		H&C	4	2		Sp 53	53
Two-Shaft Weaves	Two-Harness Textiles, The Loom-Controlled Weaves: Two-Harness Textiles	Tidball, Harriet			SCGM		20		67	1
Two-Shaft Weaves: Basket Weave	Handweaver's Instruction Manual: Two-Harness Weaves, Basket Weave	Tidball, Harriet C. nee Douglas		√	SCGM		34		49	21
Two-Shaft Weaves: Checks, Plaids, Tartans	Handweaver's Instruction Manual: Two-Harness Weaves, Stripes and Plaids	Tidball, Harriet C. nee Douglas		√	SCGM		34		49	21
Two-Shaft Weaves: Drafts	Little Known Weaves Worth Knowing Better: Drafts for Two Shafts	Zielinski, S. A.; Robert Leclerc, ed.	√	√	MWL	16			'51–'73	38
Two-Shaft Weaves: Leno	Handweaver's Instruction Manual: Two-Harness Weaves, Leno Twist Open Work	Tidball, Harriet C. nee Douglas	√	√	SCGM		34		49	22
Two-Shaft Weaves: Loom-Controlled Techniques	Two-Harness Textiles, The Loom-Controlled Weaves	Tidball, Harriet	√	√	SCGM		20		67	1-30
Two-Shaft Weaves: Rep Weaves	Handweaver's Instruction Manual: Two-Harness Weaves, Color-Pattern Reps	Tidball, Harriet C. nee Douglas		√	SCGM		34		49	21
Two-Shaft Weaves: Stripes	Handweaver's Instruction Manual: Two-Harness Weaves, Stripes and Plaids	Tidball, Harriet C. nee Douglas		√	SCGM		34		49	21
Two-Shaft Weaves: Tabby	Handweaver's Instruction Manual: Two-Harness Weaves, Tabby	Tidball, Harriet C. nee Douglas		√	SCGM		34		49	21
Two-Shaft Weaving	Creative Two Harness Weaving	Liebler, Barbara	√	√	lw	4	4		Fa 79	64
Two-Shaft Weaving	More Creative Two Harness Weaving	Liebler, Barbara	√		lw	5	1		Wi 79	46
Two-Shaft Weaving	Rugweaving: Teaching on Two Harnesses	Mattera, Joanne	√	√	lw	5	1		Wi 79	27
Two-Shaft Weaving	Two Harness Weaves by Draft & Shuttle Guild		√		H&C	13	2		Sp 62	30
Two-Shaft Weaving	Two Weaves from Mexico	Gubser, Elsie H.	√	√	H&C	11	3		Su 60	26
Two-Shaft Weaving	Two-Harness Designs	Bryan, Dorothy	√		H&C	9	3		Su 58	28
Two-Shaft Weaving	Two-harness Weaves	Clark, Marion L.	√	√	H&C	14	2		Sp 63	17
Two-Shaft Weaving	Two-harness Weaves	Freeman, Claire	√	√	H&C	11	4		Fa 60	40
Two-Shuttle Technique	Technology of Handweaving: Weaving With Two Shuttles	Zielinski, S. A.; Robert Leclerc, ed.		√	MWL	6			'51–'73	65
Two-Surface Weaves, Surface Interest	Surface Interest — Textiles of Today: Surface Interest Designs with Drafts, Group 3, Two-Surface Designs	Tidball, Harriet	√	>4	SCGM		2		61	13
Two-Tie Weaves see Unit Structure										
Two-Warp Pick-Up Technique	Hand Woven Rugs: Weaves, Two-Warp Weave, Pick-Up Method	Atwater, Mary Meigs	√	√	SCGM		29		48	26
Two-Warp Technique	Tuck Weaving	Frey, Berta	√	√	H&C	9	4		Fa 58	11
Two-Warp Weaves	More About Fabrics: Two-Warp Weaves	Zielinski, S. A.; Robert Leclerc, ed.	√	√	MWL	20			'51–'73	55
Two-Warp Weaves	Practical Weave for Rugs, A	Atwater, Mary Meigs	√	>4	H&C	5	2		Sp 54	24
Tying-In	Treasury for Beginners: Tying-In	Zielinski, S. A.; Robert Leclerc, ed.		√	MWL	1			'51–'73	21

SUBJECT	TITLE	AUTHOR	IL	INST	JOUR	VOL	NO	ISS	DATE	PAGE
Tzutes	Guatemala Visited	Atwater, Mary Meigs	√	√	SCGM		15		65	38
U S A, Southern	Handweaving in the South Today	Ford, Toni	√		H&C	1	1		Ap 50	14
Ultrasuede	Beyond Rags: Fabric Strip Design	Larson-Fleming, Susan	√	√	WJ	9	4	36	Sp 85	47
Ultrasuede	Japanese Shopkeeper's Coat		√	√	WJ	3	3	11	Ja 79	40
Ultrasuede	Stitched Double Cloth Vest		√	√	WJ	7	1	25	Su 82	38
Ultraviolet Absorbers: Types	Ultraviolet Absorbers: A Treatment to Reduce Fading and Degradation of Textiles	Crews, Patricia Cox; Barbara M. Reagan			AT	8			De 87	43
Undergarments	Tempting and Tempestuous	Upitis, Lizbeth	√		Kn	3	2	6	Sp 87	8
Undergarments: Knitted	Undies Revealed: Petticoat	Rowley, Elaine	√	√	Kn	3	2	6	Sp 87	13
Undergarments: Linen	Linen Undergarments: A Proud Danish Heritage	Todd-Cope, Louise	√		Fa	14	2		M/A 87	51
Undergraments: Knitted	Undies Revealed: Camisole	Upitis, Lizbeth	√	√	Kn	3	2	6	Sp 87	12
Underwear	Underneath it All: A Brief History of Underwear and Fashion's Changing Silhouette	Singletary, Suzanne	√		Fa	11	5		S/O 84	44
Undulating Overshot	Creative Overshot: Undulate the Treadling	Windeknecht, Margaret B.	√	√	SCGM		31		78	36
Undulating-Weft Effects	Undulating Weft Effects: (Honeycomb), Characteristics	Tidball, Harriet	√		SCGM		9		63	3
Undulating-Weft Effects, Characteristics	Undulating Weft Effects: (Honeycomb), Characteristics	Tidball, Harriet	√		SCGM		9		63	3
Undulating-Weft Textiles: Beating	Undulating Weft Effects: Designing Undulating Weft Textiles, The Beat	Tidball, Harriet		√	SCGM		9		63	5
Undulating-Weft Textiles: Cell Outlining	Undulating Weft Effects: Designing Undulating Weft Textiles, Choice of Styles	Tidball, Harriet		√	SCGM		9		63	7
Undulating-Weft Textiles: Take-Up	Undulating Weft Effects: Designing Undulating Weft Textiles, Take-Up	Tidball, Harriet		√	SCGM		9		63	5
Undulating-Weft Textiles: Threading	Undulating Weft Effects: Designing Undulating Weft Textiles, Threadings	Tidball, Harriet	√	√	SCGM		9		63	5
Undulating-Weft Textiles: Tie-Ups	Undulating Weft Effects: Designing Undulating Weft Textiles, Tie-Ups	Tidball, Harriet		√	SCGM		9		63	6
Undulating-Weft Textiles: Treadling	Undulating Weft Effects: Designing Undulating Weft Textiles, Treadling Orders	Tidball, Harriet	√	√	SCGM		9		63	6
Undulating-Weft Textiles: Warp	Undulating Weft Effects: Designing Undulating Weft Textiles, The Warp	Tidball, Harriet		√	SCGM		9		63	4
Undulating-Weft Textiles, Warp Tension	Undulating Weft Effects: Designing Undulating Weft Textiles, Warp Tension	Tidball, Harriet		√	SCGM		9		63	5
Undulating-Weft Textiles: Weft Control	Undulating Weft Effects: Designing Undulating Weft Textiles, Weft Control	Tidball, Harriet		√	SCGM		9		63	5
Undulating-Weft Textiles: Wefts	Undulating Weft Effects: Designing Undulating Weft Textiles, The Weft	Tidball, Harriet		√	SCGM		9		63	4
Undulating-Weft Weaves	Summer and Winter and Other Two-Tie Unit Weaves: Methods for Weaving Two-Tie Units, Undulating Weft Weaves	Tidball, Harriet	√	√	SCGM		19		66	45
Undulation: Warps and Wefts	Undulating Warps and Wefts	Wertenberger, Kathryn	√	>4	Hw	6	4		S/O 85	90
Uniforms	Where's the Sport in Sportswear?	McComb, Richard	√		TM			2	D/J 85	36
Unit Class Weaves	Handloom Weaves: The Classification of Handloom Weaves, The Structural Group, Unit Class	Tidball, Harriet	√	√	SCGM		33		57	20
Unit Sructure, 2-Tie, Twill Sequence Method	Summer and Winter and Other Two-Tie Unit Weaves: Methods for Weaving Two-Tie Units, Two-Element Weaves, Twill Sequence	Tidball, Harriet	√	>4	SCGM		19		66	41
Unit Structure: 1-2-1 Tie, 10-End Block, Boulevard Weave	Bateman Boulevard, Chevron, and Combination Weaves: Boulevard Structures, Division 2	Bateman, Dr. William G.; Virginia I. Harvey, ed.	√	>4	SCGM		38		87	48
Unit Structure: 1-2-1 Tie, 12-End Block, Boulevard Weave	Bateman Boulevard, Chevron, and Combination Weaves: Boulevard Structures, Division 3	Bateman, Dr. William G.; Virginia I. Harvey, ed.	√	>4	SCGM		38		87	54

SUBJECT	TITLE	AUTHOR	IL	INST	JOUR	VOL	NO	ISS	DATE	PAGE
Unit Structure: 1-2-1 Tie, 6-End Block, Boulevard Weave	Bateman Boulevard, Chevron, and Combination Weaves: Boulevard Structures, Division 1	Bateman, Dr. William G.; Virginia I. Harvey, ed.	√	>4	SCGM		38		87	17
Unit Structure: 1-2-1 Tie, 8-End Block, Boulevard Weave	Bateman Boulevard, Chevron, and Combination Weaves: Boulevard Structures, Division 2	Bateman, Dr. William G.; Virginia I. Harvey, ed.	√	>4	SCGM		38		87	37
Unit Structure: 1-2-3-2-1 Tie, 10-End Block, Bateman Chevron Weaves	Bateman Boulevard, Chevron, and Combination Weaves: Chevron Structures, Division 1	Bateman, Dr. William G.; Virginia I. Harvey, ed.	√	>4	SCGM		38		87	59
Unit Structure: 1-2-3-2-1 Tie, 12-End Block, Bateman Chevron Weaves	Bateman Boulevard, Chevron, and Combination Weaves: Chevron Structures, Division 2	Bateman, Dr. William G.; Virginia I. Harvey, ed.	√	>4	SCGM		38		87	62
Unit Structure: 1-2-3-2-1 Tie, 14-End Block, Bateman Chevron Weaves	Bateman Boulevard, Chevron, and Combination Weaves: Chevron Structures, Division 3	Bateman, Dr. William G.; Virginia I. Harvey, ed.	√	>4	SCGM		38		87	69
Unit Structure: 1-2-3-2-1 Tie, 16-End Block, Bateman Chevron Weaves	Bateman Boulevard, Chevron, and Combination Weaves: Chevron Structures, Division 4	Bateman, Dr. William G.; Virginia I. Harvey, ed.	√	>4	SCGM		38		87	72
Unit Structure: 1-2-3-2-1 Tie, 20-End Block, Bateman Chevron Weaves	Bateman Boulevard, Chevron, and Combination Weaves: Chevron Structures, Division 5	Bateman, Dr. William G.; Virginia I. Harvey, ed.	√	>4	SCGM		38		87	80
Unit Structure: 1-Tie	Block Weaves Part 2, Atwater Bronson Lace		√	>4	WJ	2	3	7	Ja 78	10
Unit Structure: 1-Tie	Lines, Squares, Rectangles	Marston, Ena	√	√	SS&D	14	3	55	Su 83	72
Unit Structure: 1-Tie	Single-Tied Unit Weave		√	>4	Hw	8	5		N/D 87	54
Unit Structure: 1-Tie, 4-End Block	Extending Dr. Bateman's Park Weaves	Harvey, Virginia I.	√	>4	CW	6	3	18	My 85	3
Unit Structure: 1-Tie, 5-End Block	Modern Overshot (Frappé Moderne)	Collard, Agathe G.	√	√	WJ	5	4	20	Sp 81	28
Unit Structure: 1-Tie, 6-End Block	Tied-Unit Table Mats (Carol Strickler, Janice Jones)		√	√	Hw	8	5		N/D 87	54, I-12
Unit Structure: 1-Tie, 7-End Block	Modern Overshot (Frappé Moderne)	Collard, Agathe G.	√	√	WJ	5	4	20	Sp 81	28
Unit Structure: 2-or-More-Tie Block	Multiple Shaft Weaving — Tie-Ups for 2-or-More-Tie Block Weaves		√	>4	WJ	6	3	23	Wi 81	41
Unit Structure: 2-Tie	Coverlet Weaves Using Two Ties	Barrett, Clotilde	√	>4	WJ	3	4	12	Ap 79	26
Unit Structure: 2-Tie	Expanded Point Twill	McCeary, Gay	√	>4	Iw	4	3		Su 79	37
Unit Structure: 2-Tie	Experimenting with Color and Two-Tie Weaving on the Rigid Heddle	Niekrasz, Jennifer	√	√	PWC	4	4	14		21
Unit Structure: 2-Tie	Incredible Five-Color, Two-Tie Afghan for a Super Kid, The	Xenakis, Athanasios David	√	√	PWC	1	1		No 81	35
Unit Structure: 2-Tie	Inlay Techniques	Barrett, Clotilde	√	√	WJ	1	1	1	Jy 76	3
Unit Structure: 2-Tie	Kuvikas	Schoenfeld, Klara	√	>4	H&C	12	2		Sp 61	20
Unit Structure: 2-Tie	Landes Hybrid	Strickler, Carol	√	>4	Iw	1	3		Sp 76	11
Unit Structure: 2-Tie	Lines, Squares, Rectangles	Marston, Ena	√	√	SS&D	14	3	55	Su 83	72
Unit Structure: 2-Tie	Moorman Inlay Technique, The	Searle, Karen	√	√	PWC	1	1		No 81	30
Unit Structure: 2-Tie	More Harnesses Make the Difference	Wertenberger, Kathryn	√	>4	Hw	2	3		My 81	40
Unit Structure: 2-Tie	One Heddle Two-Tie Weaving	Xenakis, Athanasios David	√	√	PWC	1	1		No 81	24
Unit Structure: 2-Tie	Pillow and Table Runner in Summer and Winter Weave	Xenakis, Athanasios David	√	√	PWC	1	1		No 81	21
Unit Structure: 2-Tie	Simple Damask-Like Effects Using Element Diameter Differential and Element Tension Differential	Xenakis, Athanasios David	√	>4	AT	1			De 83	317
Unit Structure: 2-Tie	Summer and Winter, A Unit Weave	Marston, Ena			SS&D	4	4	16	Fa 73	25
Unit Structure: 2-Tie	Summer and Winter and Other Two-Tie Unit Weaves	Tidball, Harriet			SCGM		19		66	1
Unit Structure: 2-Tie	Summer and Winter Revisited Part 4: Turned Pebble Weave	Xenakis, Athanasios David	√	√	PWC			4	Ja 83	52
Unit Structure: 2-Tie	Summer and Winter Unharnessed	Xenakis, Athanasios David	√	√	PWC	1	1		No 81	10
Unit Structure: 2-Tie	Summer Blouse in Summer and Winter, A	Sullivan, Donna	√	√	PWC	4	4	14		18
Unit Structure: 2-Tie	Tablecloth in Summer and Winter	Xenakis, Athanasios David	√	√	PWC	1	1		No 81	16
Unit Structure: 2-Tie	Three-Color, Weft-Faced Block Weave	Neely, Cynthia H.	√	>4	SS&D	15	2	58	Sp 84	74

SUBJECT	TITLE	AUTHOR	IL	INST	JOUR	VOL	NO	ISS	DATE	PAGE
Unit Structure: 2-Tie	Unharnessing the Summer and Winter Weave	Xenakis, Athanasios David	√		Iw	4	4		Fa 79	42
Unit Structure: 2-Tie, 3-End Block	Fabric #2: Upholstery Fabric (Constance LaLena)		√	√	Hw	6	3		Su 85	62, I-4
Unit Structure: 2-Tie, 3-End Block	Multiple Shaft Weaving — Threading for 2-or-more-tie Block Weaves		√	>4	WJ	6	2	22	Fa 81	42
Unit Structure: 2-Tie, 3-End Block	Rugs on a Three-End Block Draft	Kindahl, Connie	√	√	WJ	8	4	32	Sp 84	19
Unit Structure: 2-Tie, 3-End Block	Shaft-Switching on 3-End Drafts		√	√	WJ	5	4	20	Sp 81	24
Unit Structure: 2-Tie, 3-End Block	Shaft-Switching on 3-End Drafts: Striped Patterns, Part 1		√	√	WJ	6	1	21	Su 81	7
Unit Structure: 2-Tie, 3-End Block	Shaft-Switching to Create Tapestry Effects	Green, Andrea	√	√	WJ	8	4	32	Sp 84	36
Unit Structure: 2-Tie, 3-End Block	Two Block Rug in Boundweave	Waggoner, Phyllis	√	√	WJ	12	1	45	Su 87	26
Unit Structure: 2-Tie, 4-Block, 4-Shaft, Summer and Winter Method	Summer and Winter and Other Two-Tie Unit Weaves: Methods for Weaving Two-Tie Units, Four Block, Four-Harness, Summer and Winter	Tidball, Harriet	√	>4	SCGM		19		66	54
Unit Structure: 2-Tie, 4-End Block	"Adding" Treadles for a Complex Weave	Windeknecht, Margaret	√	>4	CW	3	3	9	Ap 82	4
Unit Structure: 2-Tie, 4-End Block	Casual But Chic		√	>4	WJ	8	4	32	Sp 84	70
Unit Structure: 2-Tie, 4-End Block	Four-End Block Draft or Summer and Winter	McClanathan, Barbara	√	√	WJ	8	4	32	Sp 84	22
Unit Structure: 2-Tie, 4-End Block	Long Sweeping Evening Cape	Roth, Bettie G.	√	>4	WJ	6	3	23	Wi 81	26
Unit Structure: 2-Tie, 4-End Block	Multiple Shaft Weaving — 2-Tie Four-End Block Drafts		√	>4	WJ	6	4	24	Sp 82	48
Unit Structure: 2-Tie, 4-End Block	Multiple Shaft Weaving — Threading for 2-or-more-tie Block Weaves		√	>4	WJ	6	2	22	Fa 81	42
Unit Structure: 2-Tie, 4-End Block	Production-Wise Placemats (error-corrected WJ v9 n2 84 p82)	Hall, Nancy Terrell	√	√	WJ	9	1	33	Su 84	44
Unit Structure: 2-Tie, 4-End Block	Shaft Switch Technique (error-corrected WJ v6 n1 81 p28d)		√	√	WJ	5	1	17	Su 80	5
Unit Structure: 2-Tie, 4-End Block	Shaft Switching on Boundweave (Nancy Kraushaar)		√	√	WJ	5	3	19	Wi 81	38
Unit Structure: 2-Tie, 4-End Block	Shaft-Switch Rugs with Pinstripe Pattern Areas		√	√	WJ	5	2	18	Fa 80	28
Unit Structure: 2-Tie, 4-End Block	Shaft-Switching Combined with Harness Control	Barrett, Clotilde	√	>4	WJ	9	1	33	Su 84	37
Unit Structure: 2-Tie, 4-End Block	Shaft-Switching on Rising Shed Looms Using Weighted Floating Heddles	Harse, Crys	√	√	WJ	9	4	36	Sp 85	63
Unit Structure: 2-Tie, 6- to 10-End Block	Bateman Blend Weaves Extended Beyond Eight Harnesses, Part 1	Harvey, Virginia I.	√	>4	CW	4	3	12	Ap 83	9
Unit Structure: 2-Tie, 6-End Block	Multiple Shaft Weaving — Threading for 2-or-More-Tie Block Weaves		√	>4	WJ	6	2	22	Fa 81	42
Unit Structure: 2-Tie, 6-End Block	Observations on the Six-End Block Draft for Rug Weaving	Schlein, Alice	√	√	WJ	6	4	24	Sp 82	30
Unit Structure: 2-Tie, 6-End Block	"Tied Latvian" Weave, The (error-corrected CW n25 87 p31)	Evans, Jane A.	√	>4	CW		24		My 87	6
Unit Structure: 2-Tie, Contemporary Treatment	Summer and Winter and Other Two-Tie Unit Weaves: Methods for Weaving Two-Tie Units, Contemporary Treatments	Tidball, Harriet	√	√	SCGM		19		66	48
Unit Structure: 2-Tie, Crackle Weave Method	Summer and Winter and Other Two-Tie Unit Weaves: Methods for Weaving Two-Tie Units, Crackle Weave Method	Tidball, Harriet	√	>4	SCGM		19		66	34
Unit Structure: 2-Tie, Double	Braided Twill Purse Organizer and Card Case (Sharon Alderman)		√	>4	Hw	5	1		J/F 84	49, 94
Unit Structure: 2-Tie, Double	Change Of Heart and Other Progressive Ideas, A	Carey, Joyce Marquess	√	>4	PWC	3	3	9		18
Unit Structure: 2-Tie, Double	Contemporary Approach to Traditional Weaves: Modern Summer and Winter	Zielinski, S. A.; Robert Leclerc, ed.	√	>4	MWL	7			'51–'73	101
Unit Structure: 2-Tie, Double	Coverlet Weaves Using Two Ties	Barrett, Clotilde	√	>4	WJ	3	4	12	Ap 79	26
Unit Structure: 2-Tie, Double	Designs from Serff Patterns	Abel, Isabel I.	√	>4	H&C	11	4		Fa 60	6
Unit Structure: 2-Tie, Double	Dimai or Tied Lithuanian (Computer Drafts-Eleanor Best)	Petraitis, Ada	√	>4	CW	4	2	11	Ja 83	16

SUBJECT	TITLE	AUTHOR	IL	INST	JOUR	VOL	NO	ISS	DATE	PAGE
Unit Structure: 2-Tie, Double	Double Two-tie System Applied to Overshot	Xenakis, Athanasios David	√	>4	PWC	3	3	9		7
Unit Structure: 2-Tie, Double	Double Two-Tie Unit Weave: An Expansion of Options for Rigid Heddle Weaving, The	Xenakis, Athanasios David	√	√	lw	5	1		Wi 79	39
Unit Structure: 2-Tie, Double	Floor's the Limit, The	Xenakis, Athanasios David	√	>4	PWC	3	3	9		12
Unit Structure: 2-Tie, Double	Four-Shaft Primer: Tie Talk	Sullivan, Donna	√	>4	PWC	4	4	14		14
Unit Structure: 2-Tie, Double	Handwoven American Coverlets of the Overshot Type	Carey, Joyce Marquess	√	>4	PWC	3	3	9		24
Unit Structure: 2-Tie, Double	Introduction to Tied Unit Weaves, An	Kelly, Jacquie	√	>4	PWC	4	4	14		40
Unit Structure: 2-Tie, Double	Two-Tie Inlay	Xenakis, Athanasios David	√	√	PWC	4	1	11		19
Unit Structure: 2-Tie, Double	Weaver's Notebook (error-corrected SS&D v10 n1 78 p98)		√	>4	SS&D	9	4	36	Fa 78	101
Unit structure: 2-Tie, Double, 10-End Block	Tied Lithuanian	Alvic, Philis	√	>4	CW	3	3	9	Ap 82	7
Unit Structure: 2-Tie, Double, 4-End Block	Designing Fancy Twills in Double Two-Tie Unit Weave	Kelly, Jacquie	√	>4	lw	6	1		Wi 80	49
Unit Structure: 2-Tie, Double, 4-End Block	Double Two-Tie Twills and Basket Weave	Barrett, Clotilde	√	>4	WJ	7	3	27	Wi 82	38
Unit Structure: 2-Tie, Double, 4-End Block	Plaited Twill Projects: Notes of A Pattern Weaver	Alvic, Philis	√	>4	WJ	11	4	44	Sp 87	55
Unit Structure: 2-Tie, Double, 4-End Block	Plaited twills		√	>4	WJ	7	4	28	Sp 83	76
Unit Structure: 2-Tie Double, 4-End Block	The Longest Warp in the World or, The Double Two-Tie Unit Threading System	Miller, Mary Ann	√	>4	CW	3	3	9	Ap 82	2
Unit Structure: 2-Tie, Double, 4-End Block	Turned Drafts in Double Two-Tie Unit Weave	van der Hoogt, Madelyn	√	>4	WJ	9	2	34	Fa 84	13
Unit Structure: 2-Tie, Double, 4-End Block	Twills in Double Two-Tie Unit Weave	van der Hoogt, Madelyn	√	>4	Hw	6	5		N/D 85	64
Unit Structure: 2-Tie, Double, 4-End Block	Two Ties in Double Two-Tie (Amy Preckshot)		√	>4	Hw	6	5		N/D 85	64, I-15
Unit Structure: 2-Tie, Double, 5-End Block	Rags Unlimited	Evans, Jane A.	√	>4	Hw	2	3		My 81	44
Unit Structure: 2-Tie, Double, 6-End Block	Dimai	Petraitis, Ada	√	>4	CW	5	3	15	My 84	5
Unit Structure: 2-Tie, Double, 6-End Block	In My Country, It's Winter	Gagné-Collard, Agathe	√	>4	WJ	8	3	31	Wi 83	74
Unit Structure: 2-Tie, Double Summer and Winter and Twill	Summer and Winter and Other Two-Tie Unit Weaves: Methods for Weaving Two-Tie Units, Double-Summer and Winter-Twill	Tidball, Harriet	√	>4	SCGM		19		66	56
Unit Structure: 2-Tie, Double-Faced Stuffer Weave	Summer and Winter and Other Two-Tie Unit Weaves: Methods for Weaving Two-Tie Units, Double-Faced Stuffer Weave	Tidball, Harriet	√	>4	SCGM		19		66	52
Unit Structure: 2-Tie, Inlay Method	Summer and Winter and Other Two-Tie Unit Weaves: Methods for Weaving Two-Tie Units, Inlay	Tidball, Harriet	√	√	SCGM		19		66	51
Unit Structure: 2-Tie, Multishaft	Metamorphosis: Two-Tie Weaves and the Changeable Image	Carey, Joyce Marquess	√	>4	AT	1			De 83	243
Unit Structure: 2-Tie, Multishaft	Modification of the AVL Dobby Loom for Execution of Multi-Shaft Two-Tie Block Weaves	Gustafson, Susan L.	√	√	AT	1			De 83	235
Unit Structure: 2-Tie, Opposites Method	Summer and Winter and Other Two-Tie Unit Weaves: Methods for Weaving Two-Tie Units, Opposites Method	Tidball, Harriet	√	>4	SCGM		19		66	35
Unit Structure: 2-Tie, Pick-Up Method	Summer and Winter and Other Two-Tie Unit Weaves: Methods for Weaving Two-Tie Units, Pick-Up	Tidball, Harriet	√	√	SCGM		19		66	50
Unit Structure: 2-Tie, Pile Weaves	Summer and Winter and Other Two-Tie Unit Weaves: Methods for Weaving Two-Tie Units, Pile Weaves	Tidball, Harriet	√	>4	SCGM		19		66	49

SUBJECT	TITLE	AUTHOR	IL	INST	JOUR	VOL	NO	ISS	DATE	PAGE
Unit Structure: 2-Tie, Polychrome Method	Summer and Winter and Other Two-Tie Unit Weaves: Methods for Weaving Two-Tie Units, Polychrome Weave	Tidball, Harriet	√	>4	SCGM		19		66	38
Unit Structure: 2-Tie, Single	Taking Charge of Your Design	West, Virginia	√	>4	Hw	8	5		N/D 87	46
Unit Structure: 2-Tie, Single, 3-End Block	Block Weave Rug (Jean Scorgie, Janice Jones)		√	√	Hw	8	5		N/D 87	58, I-14
Unit Structure: 2-Tie, Straight-Draw	Metamorphosis: Two-Tie Weaves and the Changeable Image	Carey, Joyce Marquess	√	>4	AT	1			De 83	243
Unit Structure: 2-Tie, Supplementary-Warp Method	Summer and Winter and Other Two-Tie Unit Weaves: Methods for Weaving Two-Tie Units, Supplementary Warp Method	Tidball, Harriet	√	√	SCGM		19		66	46
Unit Structure: 2-Tie, Surface Interest Variations	Summer and Winter and Other Two-Tie Unit Weaves: Methods for Weaving Two-Tie Units, Surface Interest Variations	Tidball, Harriet	√	√	SCGM		19		66	47
Unit Structure: 2-Tie, Undulating Weft Weaves	Summer and Winter and Other Two-Tie Unit Weaves: Methods for Weaving Two-Tie Units, Undulating Weft Weaves	Tidball, Harriet	√	√	SCGM		19		66	45
Unit Structure: 3-Tie	Leonora Meek, Nebraska Weaver and Teacher		√	>4	H&C	15	2		Sp 64	23
Unit Structure: 3-Tie	Simple Damask-Like Effects Using Element Diameter Differential and Element Tension Differential	Xenakis, Athanasios David	√	>4	AT	1			De 83	317
Unit Structure: 3-Tie	Texture Possibilities of the Three-Tie Unit Weaves	Xenakis, Athanasios David	√	>4	PWC	4	4	14		49
Unit Structure: 3-Tie, 16-End Block	Bergman	Alvic, Philis	√	>4	CW	2	1	4	Oc 80	10
Unit Structure: 3-Tie, 16-End Block	Bergman: Notes of a Pattern Weaver	Alvic, Philis	√	>4	WJ	10	1	37	Su 85	64
Unit Structure: 3-Tie, 6-End Block	Three-Tie Unit Twill Mats (Carol Powalisz)		√	>4	Hw	8	5		N/D 87	47, I-8
Unit Structure: 3-Tie, 8- to 30-End Block	Bateman Blend Weaves Extended Beyond Eight Harnesses, Part 2	Harvey, Virginia I.	√	>4	CW	5	1	13	Se 83	3
Unit Structure: 3-Tie, Opposites	Variation on a Finnish Weave by a Texas Weaver (error-corrected H&C v17 n2 66 p48)	Sheppard, Margaret	√	>4	H&C	16	3		Su 65	20
Unit Structure: 4-Tie, 10- to 36-End Block	Bateman Blend Weaves Extended Beyond Eight Harnesses, Part 2	Harvey, Virginia I.	√	>4	CW	5	1	13	Se 83	3
Unit Structure: 4-Tie, 10-End Block	Christmas Miniatures, Part 2: Krokbragd Bellpulls (error-corrected PWC i4 83 p76)	Xenakis, Athanasios David	√	>4	PWC			3	Oc 82	52
Unit Structure: 6-End Block, Huck	Multi-Harness Huck: Learn About the Structure of This Family of Weaves and Design Your Own Variations	Barrett, Clotilde	√	>4	WJ	10	4	40	Sp 86	11
Unit Structure: Multiple-Tie Drafts	Multiple Shaft Weaving — Threading for 2-or-more-tie Block Weaves		√	>4	WJ	6	2	22	Fa 81	42
Unit Structure: Tied	Analysis of Star and Diamond Weave Structures, An (error-corrected SS&D v10 n1 78 p101)	Anderson, Clarita; Judith Gordon; Naomi Whiting Towner	√	>4	SS&D	9	4	36	Fa 78	71
Unit Structure: Tied	Overshot: The Weave and the Designs	Marston, Ena	√	>4	SS&D	11	2	42	Sp 80	74
Unit Structure: Tied	Shaft-Switching	Barrett, Clotilde	√	√	WJ	8	4	32	Sp 84	28
Unit Structure: Tied, 3-End Block	Shaft-Switching on 3-end Drafts: Striped Patterns, Part 2		√	√	WJ	6	2	22	Fa 81	16
Unit Structure: Tied, 4-End Draft	Shaft Switch Technique (error-corrected WJ v6 n1 81 p28d)		√	√	WJ	5	1	17	Su 80	5
Unit Structure: Tied, Bateman Blend	Notes from a Beginning Complex Weaver	McKee, Marguerite	√	>4	CW		25		Se 87	3
Unit System see Unit Structure										
Unit Weave see Unit Structure										
Unraveling Seams: Serged	Unraveling Serged Seams		√	√	TM			14	D/J 87	6
Upholstering	Notes on Uphlstering the Chair	Wertenberger, Kathryn		√	Hw	5	2		M/A 84	110
Upholstery	Desk Chair with Subtle Plaid Pattern	Lohse, Joyce	√	√	WJ	7	1	25	Su 82	24
Upholstery	Upholstery	Wendler, Maxine	√	√	WJ	7	1	25	Su 82	22
Upphämta, Sword	Display Towel (Astrid Sonesson)		√	>4	Hw	8	3		M/J 87	43, I-4

SUBJECT	TITLE	AUTHOR	IL	INST	JOUR	VOL	NO	ISS	DATE	PAGE
Vadmal	Fall Wrap Up — Weaves and Fabrics for Classic Garments		√	√	Hw	8	4		S/O 87	40
Vadmal	Finishes for Vadmal	Baizerman, Suzanne	√	√	WJ	10	3	39	Wi 86	30
Vadmal	Vadmal: A Study Group from the Frozen North Warms up to an Ancient Technique	Larson-Fleming, Susan	√	√	WJ	10	3	39	Wi 86	26
Valentine see Holiday Weavings										
Velcro	Fastening Alternative, A	Mattera, Joanne	√		SS&D	11	3	43	Su 80	27
Velvet, Patterned	Pile Weaves, Rugs and Tapestry: Patterns in Velvet Rugs	Zielinski, S. A.; Robert Leclerc, ed.	√	√	MWL	14			'51–'73	70
Velvet Weaving	Velvet Ikat	Stack, Lotus	√	> 4	WJ	11	4	44	Sp 87	36
Venezuela	Hammock, The	Drooker, Penelope B.	√	√	TM			6	A/S 86	74
Vests	Alpaca Vest	Newton, Deborah	√	√	Kn	3	4	8	Fa 87	21
Vests	Applying the Pulled Warp Technique to Loom-Shaped Clothing	Evans, Kerry	√	√	WJ	9	3	35	Wi 85	34
Vests	Bedford Cord Vests (Sharon Alderman)		√	√	Hw	6	1		J/F 85	27, I-4
Vests	Beginning with Bands: Tablet Woven Garments and Accessories	Holtzer, Marilyn Emerson	√	√	WJ	9	3	35	Wi 85	28
Vests	Blue Rag Vest (Susan Snover)		√	√	Hw	2	3		My 81	50, 78
Vests	Boiled Wool	Smith, Mary	√	√	TM			13	O/N 87	63
Vests	Cherry Vest (Marie Lebair O'Brient)		√	√	Hw	7	1		J/F 86	71
Vests	Christmas Vest (Yvonne Stahl)		√	> 4	Hw	4	4		S/O 83	71, 101
Vests	Colorful Waistcoats Woven by Elsie H. Gubser		√	√	H&C	18	1		Wi 67	18
Vests	Creative Clothing: Surface Embellishment	Mayer, Anita Luvera	√	√	WJ	11	3	43	Wi 87	30
Vests	Demystifying Complex Weaves: A Step-by-Step Exploration from Four to Sixteen Harnesses	Piroch, Sigrid	√	> 4	WJ	10	3	39	Wi 86	8
Vests	Desert Tapestry Vest	Jennings, Lucy Anne	√	√	WJ	12	1	45	Su 87	52
Vests	Designing for Piqué (error-corrected PWC v4 n4 i14 '87 p33)	Sullivan, Donna	√	> 4	PWC	4	3	13		28
Vests	Double Chenille Vest (Lucy Anne Jennings)		√	√	Hw	7	3		M/J 86	44, I-10
Vests	Double Two-Tie Twills and Basket Weave	Barrett, Clotilde	√	> 4	WJ	7	3	27	Wi 82	38
Vests	Double Woven Quilted Vest (Yvone Stahl)		√	√	Hw	5	1		J/F 84	54, 97
Vests	Double Woven Vest (Betty Beard)		√	√	Hw	1	1		F-W 79	24, 57
Vests	Fair Isle Vest	Van Sickle, Glanda	√	√	S-O	8	3		Fa 84	45
Vests	Fashion Show of Handwoven Garments		√	> 4	WJ	3	3	11	Ja 79	5
Vests	Felt Vest, Hat, Mittens	Betts, Diane	√	√	S-O	9	2		Su 85	39
Vests	Finns Can Knit Too or How to Knit a Finn	Rowley, Elaine D.	√	√	PWC			2	Ap 82	76
Vests	Fleecy Vest, A	Gilsdorf, Marilyn	√	√	WJ	8	4	32	Sp 84	9
Vests	From the Collection of Anne Poussart		√	√	WJ	7	3	27	Wi 82	62
Vests	Fur Vest (Ann Wittpenn)		√	√	Hw	4	1		J/F 83	35, 80
Vests	Garments by Hanni Bureker		√	√	SS&D	6	3	23	Wi 81	35
Vests	Garments Made from Simple Patterns: A Vest		√	√	WJ	2	3	7	Ja 78	37
Vests	Girl's Vest	Howard, Miranda	√	√	S-O	6	4		82	59
Vests	Glad Rags: The Designs of Rose Jurisich		√	√	Hw	2	3		My 81	46
Vests	Go For It!	Eldridge, Lois A.	√	√	S-O	7	4		Wi 83	45
Vests	Guatemalan Vest (Betty Davenport)		√	√	Hw	4	2		M/A 83	56, 93
Vests	Handspun Yarn for a Pulled Warp Vest	Adams, Brucie	√	√	Hw	7	1		J/F 86	78
Vests	Heritage Project: Quilted Vest, A	King, Lorna J.	√	√	WJ	4	3	15	Ja 80	28
Vests	Hollow Oak Vest	Rush, Helene	√	√	Kn	2	2	4	S-S 86	30
Vests	Horizontal Ribs & Vertical Cords	Moes, Dini	√	√	SS&D	17	4	68	Fa 86	84
Vests	If the Vest Fits...	Upitis, Lizbeth	√	√	Kn	3	2	6	Sp 87	40
Vests	Ikat Spun Vest (Debbie Redding)	Bradley, Louise	√	√	Hw	2	4		Se 81	67
Vests	Knitting with Colors	Fassett, Kaffe	√	√	TM			3	F/M 86	68

SUBJECT	TITLE	AUTHOR	IL	INST	JOUR	VOL	NO	ISS	DATE	PAGE
Vests	Lacy Mohair Vest, A	McPherson, Maggie	√	√	S-O	10	2		Su 86	18
Vests	Leaves and Trellises	Emerson, Rebecca	√	√	Kn	1	2	2	S-S 85	48, 72B
Vests	Leno Vest	Lyon, Linda	√	√	PWC			6	Su 83	27
Vests	Lesson in Cut and Sewn Handwoven Garments, A (error-corrected Hw v2 n2 81 p68)	Wertenberger, Kathryn	√	√	Hw	2	1		F-W 80	36
Vests	Limited-Edition Vests	Stocksdale, Joy	√	√	TM			4	A/M 86	60
Vests	Linen Knits	Westerink, Claire; Erica Baker	√	√	S-O	10	3		Fa 86	17
Vests	Linen Knits (Claire Westerink)				S-O	10	3		Fa 86	16
Vests	Linen Knits (Erica Baker)				S-O	10	3		Fa 86	16
Vests	Lining the Overshot	Moes, Dini	√	√	SS&D	13	4	52	Fa 82	64
Vests	Make It Yourself with Handwoven Wool	Zawistoski, Patsy	√		S-O	9	1		Sp 85	12
Vests	Man's Plaid Vest (Kathryn Wertenberger)		√	√	Hw	4	5		N/D 83	51, 98
Vests	Man's Vest (Lou Cabeen)		√	√	Hw	5	4		S/O 84	43, 93
Vests	Masculine Element, The (Pam Bolesta)		√	√	Hw	2	1		F-W 80	34
Vests	Modular Clothing	Mayer, Anita	√	√	Hw	7	3		M/J 86	58
Vests	Moebius Vest, The	Homme, Audrey	√	√	WJ	11	4	44	Sp 87	48
Vests	More Moneymakers for Weavers	Klessen, Romy	√	√	PWC			2	Ap 82	9
Vests	One Pattern, One Warp (Louise Bradley)		√	√	Hw	3	3		My 82	34, 97
Vests	Pair of Vests (Anne Bliss)		√	√	Hw	6	1		J/F 85	72, I-16
Vests	Paisley Inspired Vest (Ardis Dobrovolny)		√	√	Hw	5	5		N/D 84	67, I-11
Vests	Pick-Up Piqué (error-corrected SS&D v19 n1 87 p33)	Fletcher, Joyce	√	√	SS&D	18	4	72	Fa 87	60
Vests	Pile Vest (Merja Winqvist)		√	√	Hw	8	3		M/J 87	73, I-15
Vests	Practical Handwoven Vests		√	√	H&C	8	4		Fa 57	46
Vests	Pretty, Piqué & Pink	Keasbey, Doramay	√	> 4	PWC	4	3	13		47
Vests	Project for a Very Narrow Loom: A Vest with Details Woven with Rug Yarn (error-corrected H&C v26 n5 75 p45)	Hendricks, Carolyn	√	√	H&C	26	3		M/J 75	16
Vests	Project for a Very Narrow Loom: A Vest with Details Woven with Rug Yarn (error-corrected H&C v26 n5 75 p45)	Hendricks, Carolyn	√	√	H&C	26	3		M/J 75	16
Vests	Quilted Vest (Susan Henrickson)		√	√	Hw	4	2		M/A 83	61, 96
Vests	Rag Vest (Susan Snover)		√	√	Hw	4	1		J/F 83	44, 86
Vests	Rags to Riches: Honeycomb Bolero-Style Vest	Barrett, Phyllis K.	√	√	WJ	6	3	23	Wi 81	30
Vests	Rags to Riches: Ragstrip Vest	Scheirman, Pam	√	√	WJ	6	3	23	Wi 81	30
Vests	Reversible Felted Wool Vest (Pam Bolesta)		√	√	Hw	1	1		F-W 79	20, 54
Vests	Reversible Flamepoint Vest	Wittpenn, Ann	√	√	WJ	5	3	19	Wi 81	9
Vests	Reversible Vest		√	√	S-O	7	3		Fa 83	58
Vests	Reversible Vest (Jean Scorgie)		√	√	Hw	7	4		S/O 86	66, I-13
Vests	Samples—Quick & Easy!	Davenport, Betty	√	√	Hw	7	5		N/D 86	78
Vests	Shadow Weave Vest (error-corrected WJ v9 n2 84 p82)		√	> 4	WJ	8	3	31	Wi 83	81
Vests	Silky Dress-Up: Vest (C. Bryn Pinchin)		√	> 4	Hw	6	1		J/F 85	38, I-11
Vests	Simple and Silk	Gibson-Roberts, Priscilla A.	√	√	Kn	2	2	4	S-S 86	54
Vests	Simple and Striped	Oakes, Nancy	√	√	Kn	3	1	5	F-W 86	44
Vests	Simple Vests		√	√	WJ	5	3	19	Wi 81	41
Vests	Ski Vest (Pam Bolesta)		√	√	Hw	2	1		F-W 80	34, 61
Vests	Special Fittings: Valerie's Vest	August, Valerie	√	√	Kn	1	2	2	S-S 85	31
Vests	Special Summer Vest, A	Jennings, Lucy Anne	√	> 4	WJ	9	3	35	Wi 85	42
Vests	Square-rigged Vests	Swansen, Meg	√	√	Kn	2	1	3	F-W 85	62
Vests	Stained Glass Vest	Shull, Paula	√	√	S-O	11	4		Wi 87	29
Vests	Stitched Double Cloth Vest		√	√	WJ	7	1	25	Su 82	38

SUBJECT	TITLE	AUTHOR	IL	INST	JOUR	VOL	NO	ISS	DATE	PAGE
Vests	Tailored Vest and Skirt, A	Arnold, Ruth	√	>4	WJ	9	3	35	Wi 85	56
Vests	Textured Cottons	Henrikson, Sue	√	>4	WJ	6	3	23	Wi 81	20
Vests	Tubular Weave Vest and Hat (Sharon Lappin Lumsden)		√	√	Hw	8	1		J/F 87	48, I-6
Vests	Twice Woven Bolero	Richards, Iris	√	√	WJ	4	3	15	Ja 80	24
Vests	Variations on a Midnight Rainbow	Raven, Lee	√	√	S-O	9	4		Wi 85	14
Vests	Versatile Vest and Matching Wrap Skirt, A	Dopps, Beth R.	√	√	WJ	7	3	27	Wi 82	21
Vests	Vest with a Hidden Twist	Emerick, Patricia	√	√	S-O	11	4		Wi 87	36, I-46
Vests	Vest with Slits Made of Five Tapestry Strips	De Bone, Mary	√	√	SS&D	5	2	18	Sp 74	83
Vests	Vests	Lamb, Sara	√	√	S-O	9	1		Sp 85	16
Vests	Warmth for a Cool Climate: Handspun Wool & Milkweed Down	Danielson, Esther	√	√	SS&D	17	4	68	Fa 86	24
Vests	Wearing Handwovens with Style	Mayer, Anita	√	√	WJ	10	3	39	Wi 86	22
Vests	Weaving and Sheepskin, Naturally	Mason, Carole	√	√	WJ	5	3	19	Wi 81	46
Vests	Weaving in Quebec: New Ideas and Techniques	Barrett, Clotilde	√	√	WJ	6	4	24	Sp 82	16
Vests	What If...Vest (Betty Davenport)		√	√	Hw	5	4		S/O 84	74, 108
Vests	What People Ask Before They Buy Handmade Fashions	Leslie, Victoria	√		TM			9	F/M 87	58
Vests	Woven Garments	Henzie, Susie	√	√	WJ	3	4	12	Ap 79	44
Victorian Tapestry Workshop	Victorian Tapestry Workshop: A New Tradition in Australia, The	Newman, Rochelle	√		Fa	10	3		M/J 83	38
Vicuna	Indian Textiles from Ecuador		√		H&C	10	1		Wi 59	19
Vicuna	Paco-Vicuna: An Endangered Species		√		S-O	5			81	34
Video	Costuming for Rock Music Videos	Pierce, Judith	√		Fa	14	3		M/J 87	51
Video	Video Access to Textiles: The Helen L. Allen Textile Collection	Bard, Elizabeth A.	√		Fa	12	6		N/D 85	34
Video: Fitting Skirts	New System for Getting an Ultra Fit, A	Lassiter, Betty			TM			12	A/S 87	22
Video: Fitting Sleeves	New System for Getting an Ultra Fit, A	Lassiter, Betty			TM			12	A/S 87	22
Video Review	Fundamentals of Handspinning	Brown, Rachael			S-O	11	2		Su 87	12
Video Reviews	Tapestry Weaving—Level I	Harvey, Nancy			WJ	10	4	40	Sp 86	83
Video Reviews	Tapestry Weaving — Level I	Harvey, Nancy, inst.	√		PWC	4	1	11		55
Video Reviews	Tapestry Weaving—Level II	Harvey, Nancy			WJ	12	1	45	Su 87	71
Video Reviews	Traditional New England Basketmaking (John McGuire)	Brookfield Craft Center			WJ	12	2	46	Fa 87	68
Video Tape	Tapestry Weaving – Level 1	Harvey, Nancy (Instructor)			Hw	7	4		S/O 86	10
Video-Computer System: Textile Design	From Image to Woven Structure: A Video-Computer System for Textile Designers	Peterson, Lisa Lee	√	√	AT	7			Ju 87	109
Videos: Knitting	Knitting Video, The	Xenakis, Alexis Yiorgos; Elaine Rowley			Kn	1	2	2	S-S 85	74
Vincian Knot	Leonardo's Knot	Austin, Carole	√		Fa	12	2		M/A 85	43
Vintage Costume	Linen Shift: Plain Sewing Makes the Most of Your Fabric, A	Smith, Kathleen B.	√	√	TM			9	F/M 87	46
Vintage Costume	Where's the Sport in Sportswear?	McComb, Richard	√		TM			2	D/J 85	36
Volunteers	Healing Historical Textiles	Searle, Karen	√	√	SS&D	10	4	40	Fa 79	60
Volunteers	Successful Volunteer Project, A	Bryan, Dorothy	√		H&C	5	2		Sp 54	19
Wadding: Warp and Weft	Bedford Cord Piqué	Xenakis, Athanasios David; Madelyn van der Hoogt	√	>4	PWC	4	3	13		42
Waffle, Half-	Traditional Texture Weaves: Half-Waffle	Zielinski, S. A.; Robert Leclerc, ed.	√	√	MWL	11			'51–'73	21
Waffle Weave	Afghan and Pillow Set	D'Ambrosio, Gina	√	√	S-O	11	2		Su 87	14
Waffle Weave	Computer Learns to Weave, The	Huff, Karen E.	√	√	SS&D	6	4	24	Fa 75	19
Waffle Weave	Enlarged Patterns: A Fresh Look at Old Techniques	McClelland, Patricia Polett	√	>4	WJ	7	4	28	Sp 83	68
Waffle Weave	Insulating Handwoven Shutters		√	>4	WJ	6	1	21	Su 81	20

SUBJECT	TITLE	AUTHOR	IL	INST	JOUR	VOL	NO	ISS	DATE	PAGE
Waffle Weave	Special Summer Vest, A	Jennings, Lucy Anne	√	> 4	WJ	9	3	35	Wi 85	42
Waffle Weave	Traditional Texture Weaves: Better Waffle	Zielinski, S. A.; Robert Leclerc, ed.	√	√	MWL	11			'51–'73	32
Waffle Weave	Traditional Texture Weaves: In Search of a Better Waffle	Zielinski, S. A.; Robert Leclerc, ed.	√	> 4	MWL	11			'51–'73	25
Waffle Weave	Traditional Texture Weaves: Waffle Weaves	Zielinski, S. A.; Robert Leclerc, ed.	√	> 4	MWL	11			'51–'73	18
Waffle Weave	Tunic/Loose Vest Fabric (Sharon Alderman)		√	> 4	Hw	3	2		Mr 82	9, 78
Waffle Weave	Waffle Weave	Wertenberger, Kathryn	√	> 4	Hw	8	4		S/O 87	83
Waffle Weave	Waffle Weave Table Linens (Hector Jaeger)		√	√	Hw	6	5		N/D 85	56, I-14
Waffle Weave	Waffle Weave Throw (Hector Jaeger)		√	√	Hw	6	5		N/D 85	54, I-13
Waffle Weave	Waffle Weave: Twill in 3-D		√	> 4	Hw	6	5		N/D 85	55
Waffle Weave	Waffle Weave Wool Top (Betty Davenport)		√	√	Hw	1	1		F-W 79	21, 55
Waffle Weave	Waffle-Weave		√	√	SS&D	12	1	45	Wi 80	62
Waffle Weave	Weaver's Notebook		√	> 4	SS&D	10	2	38	Sp 79	52
Waffle Weave	Weaver's Notebook: (Bettie Jo Conrad) (error-corrected SS&D v11 n2 80 p18)		√	√	SS&D	10	4	40	Fa 79	103
Waistbands	Perfect Waistbands		√	√	TM			8	D/J 86	6
Waistbands, Elastic	Waistband Elastic		√	√	TM			11	J/J 87	10
Waistbands: Recycled Elastic	Ready-Made Waistband Elastic			√	TM			11	J/J 87	8
Wales	Weaving in Wales	Kemp, Gwendoline	√		H&C	6	2		Sp 55	24
Wales	Welsh Wool Yarn Factory Hires Disabled Veterans	Hetherington, E.	√		SS&D	5	1	17	Wi 73	28
Wales	Wool from the Welsh Valleys	Rowe, Dilys	√		H&C	10	2		Sp 59	30
Wales	Wool Gathering in Wales	Clement, Doris; Ted Clement	√		H&C	23	1		J/F 72	26
Wall Coverings: Fabric	Fabrics for Interiors	VanSlyke, Gail Rutter		√	WJ	3	1	9	Jy 78	5
Wall Hangings	Aklae: Norwegian Tapestry	Irlbeck, Sonja	√	√	WJ	8	1	29	Su 83	27
Wall Hangings	Batik Plus Handweaving	D'Angelo, Anne A.; Margaret B. Windeknecht	√		SS&D	4	3	15	Su 73	57
Wall Hangings	Bergman: Notes of a Pattern Weaver	Alvic, Philis	√	> 4	WJ	10	1	37	Su 85	64
Wall Hangings	Betty Williams: Colors of the Earth	Robbins, Judy	√		SS&D	18	4	72	Fa 87	57
Wall Hangings	Bhakti Ziek	Ziek, Bhakti	√		Fa	13	3		M/J 86	27
Wall Hangings	Black Rope and Straw Form	Kuemmerlein, Janet	√		SS&D	4	3	15	Su 73	49
Wall Hangings	"Blue Chest of Drawers" Hanging (Kerstin Åsling-Sundberg)		√	> 4	Hw	8	3		M/J 87	37, I-6
Wall Hangings	Boston Seven	Newman, Rochelle	√		SS&D	16	3	63	Su 85	71
Wall Hangings	Boundweave: Learning from the Past	Waggoner, Phyllis	√	√	WJ	10	4	40	Sp 86	44
Wall Hangings	Breath of Our Grandmothers, The	Samuel, Cheryl	√		WJ	8	1	29	Su 83	17
Wall Hangings	Bringing Freedom to Fibers: Loni Parker	Brough, Hazel	√		SS&D	7	3	27	Su 76	44
Wall Hangings	Building on a Tradition	Alvic, Philis	√		Iw	4	3		Su 79	45
Wall Hangings	Business of Weaving — An Interview with Elaine P. Nixon, The	Derr, Mary	√		WJ	4	1	13	Jy 79	10
Wall Hangings	Cameron Taylor-Brown	Taylor-Brown, Cameron	√		Fa	14	2		M/A 87	24
Wall Hangings	Celtic Knot (error-corrected PWC v4 n4 i14 '87 p33)	Zenakis, Athanasios David	√	√	PWC	4	3	13		24
Wall Hangings	Change of Heart and Other Progressive Ideas, A	Carey, Joyce Marquess	√	> 4	PWC	3	3	9		18
Wall Hangings	Changing Seasons Hangings (Halcyon Schomp and Hector Jaeger)		√	√	Hw	5	5		N/D 84	61, I-15
Wall Hangings	Claire Zeisler	Uhlmann, Etta	√		H&C	13	4		Fa 62	34
Wall Hangings	Collingwood Connection, The		√		SS&D	14	4	56	Fa 83	38
Wall Hangings	Collingwood in Massachusetts, A	Brannen, Robert	√		SS&D	9	1	33	Wi 77	8
Wall Hangings	Color in Summer and Winter	Alvic, Philis	√	√	WJ	7	4	28	Sp 83	64

SUBJECT	TITLE	AUTHOR	IL	INST	JOUR	VOL	NO	ISS	DATE	PAGE
Wall Hangings	Complimentary-Weft Plain Weave — A Pick-up Technique (error-corrected WJ v5 n1 80 p28d)	Hanley, Janet	√	√	WJ	4	4	16	Ap 80	22
Wall Hangings	Connie McEntire Lehman's Side Glances from Drawings Into Dye-Painted Hangings	Clurman, Irene	√		Fa	8	5		S/O 81	26
Wall Hangings	Contemporary Use of Traditional Damask, A	Lalena, Constance	√		WJ	8	1	29	Su 83	69
Wall Hangings	Conversion of Sorts: Judith Poxson Fawkes—A Background in Painting, A Present in Weaving, A	Griffin, Rachael	√		Fa	7	6		N/D 80	52
Wall Hangings	Corded Weaves: Four Harness Cords for Upholstery Fabric, Drapery Material and Wallhangings		√	√	WJ	3	1	9	Jy 78	28
Wall Hangings	Corkscrew Weave	Barrett, Clotilde	√	> 4	WJ	5	1	17	Su 80	16
Wall Hangings	Cotton: An Invitation	Hagan, Kathleen	√		WJ	4	2	14	Oc 79	12
Wall Hangings	Cotton Hanging — on a Chinese Folk Motif	Xenakis, Athanasios David	√	√	PWC	1	1		No 81	39
Wall Hangings	Designing for an Interior: Notes of a Pattern Weaver	Alvic, Philis	√		WJ	9	4	36	Sp 85	69
Wall Hangings	Distort, Rearrange, Combine	Crockett, Candace	√		SS&D	5	2	18	Sp 74	20
Wall Hangings	Double-Woven Treasures from Old Peru	Cahlander, Adele	√	√	PWC			4	Ja 83	36
Wall Hangings	Drafting: A Personal Approach, Part 2	Alvic, Philis	√	> 4	SS&D	13	2	50	Sp 82	46
Wall Hangings	Drafting: A Personal Approach, Part 3	Alvic, Philis	√	> 4	SS&D	13	3	51	Su 82	40
Wall Hangings	Enlarged Patterns: A Fresh Look at Old Techniques	McClelland, Patricia Polett	√	> 4	WJ	7	4	28	Sp 83	68
Wall Hangings	Exciting Endeavor, An	Schira, Cynthia	√		SS&D	2	4	8	Fa 71	12
Wall Hangings	Fantastic Finnweave, Part 1	Xenakis, Athanasios David	√	√	PWC			2	Ap 82	18
Wall Hangings	Fantastic Finnweave, Part 3	Xenakis, Athanasios David	√	> 4	PWC			4	Ja 83	10
Wall Hangings	Farmer and His Wife, Figure Boundweave, A	Pissowotski, Inge	√	√	WJ	5	4	20	Sp 81	8
Wall Hangings	Fascination with Form, A	Richardson, Pat	√	> 4	SS&D	12	3	47	Su 81	54
Wall Hangings	Feltmaking: Instant Delight	Green, Louise	√	√	Iw	3	4		Su 78	18
Wall Hangings	Fiber and Architecture: Marge Walters		√		Fa	3	3		M/J 76	33
Wall Hangings	"Fiber Art: Tapestries and Wall Hangings" (Exhibit)	Koplos, Janet	√		Fa	6	6		N/D 79	75
Wall Hangings	"Fiber Invitational" (Exhibit)	Richerson, Suzanne	√		Fa	8	4		J/A 81	76
Wall Hangings	Finnish Method of Weaving Transparent Inlay, A	Gray, Herbi	√	√	SS&D	17	1	65	Wi 85	14
Wall Hangings	Four-Shaft Unbalanced Twill Braided Ribbon Inlay on Plain Weave Ground	Xenakis, Athanasios David	√	√	PWC	4	1	11		27
Wall Hangings	From Field and Garden	Williams, Betty	√		SS&D	2	3	7	Su 71	6
Wall Hangings	From Paint to Fiber	Siewert-Miller, Elisabet	√		SS&D	3	2	10	Sp 72	18
Wall Hangings	From Scraps to Wall Hangings	Niemeier, Eileen			H&C	10	3		Su 59	19
Wall Hangings	Fun with Optical Art		√	> 4	H&C	17	1		Wi 66	23
Wall Hangings	Gold Arabesque Decorates New HGA Headquarters	Pocock, Sylvia	√		SS&D	5	4	20	Fa 74	77
Wall Hangings	Graphic Weave for a Special Occasion (Carrie Rogers)		√	√	Hw	1	2		S-S 80	38
Wall Hangings	Gridworks	Tacker, Sylvia	√		SS&D	16	4	64	Fa 85	30
Wall Hangings	Handspuns for Tapestries	Szumski, Norma; Phyllis Clemmer; Clotilde Barrett	√		WJ	6	2	22	Fa 81	41
Wall Hangings	Hanging Based on HGA Name Draft to Decorate New Offices	Fuchs, Rudolph	√	√	SS&D	5	4	20	Fa 74	14
Wall Hangings	Happy Birthday, U.S.A. — Weavers Salute Bicentennial (Esther Gotthoffer)		√		SS&D	7	4	28	Fa 76	53
Wall Hangings	Harts and Flowers: Sweden's Märta Määs-Fjetterstrom's Designs Inspired a Textile Renaissance	Selkurt, Claire	√		WJ	9	4	36	Sp 85	30

SUBJECT	TITLE	AUTHOR	IL	INST	JOUR	VOL	NO	ISS	DATE	PAGE
Wall Hangings	Holiday Cheer (Janice Jones)		√	√	Hw	4	4		S/O 83	71
Wall Hangings	Huguenot Coverlets	Strickler, Carol	√	> 4	WJ	1	2	2	Oc 76	8
Wall Hangings	I Ching	Meaney, Elaine	√		SS&D	3	2	10	Sp 72	22
Wall Hangings	Ikat-Woven Images	Tacker, Sylvia	√	√	SS&D	18	1	69	Wi 86	68
Wall Hangings	In Timeless Form	Herring, Connie	√	√	PWC	3	3	9		35
Wall Hangings	Inlay We Trust, Part 1: Half Dukagång	Herring, Connie	√	√	PWC			5	Sp 83	59
Wall Hangings	Inspiration	Alvic, Philis	√		WJ	8	1	29	Su 83	65
Wall Hangings	Inspired Double Weave		√		Hw	7	2		M/A 86	58
Wall Hangings	Interface: A Wire Weaving	Sullivan, Donna	√	√	WJ	7	1	25	Su 82	20
Wall Hangings	JoAnn Giordano: A Modern Mythology	Malarcher, Patricia	√		Fa	13	6		N/D 86	13
Wall Hangings	John Smith's Wonderful World		√		H&C	15	1		Wi 64	12
Wall Hangings	Joyful Hieroglyphics: For Mary Bero Anything is Possible!		√		Fa	8	5		S/O 81	40
Wall Hangings	"Kari Lønning — Mary Billingsley" (Exhibit)	Beede, Beth	√		Fa	6	6		N/D 79	69
Wall Hangings	Ken Weaver on Rep Weaving	Weaver, Ken	√		WJ	7	4	28	Sp 83	20
Wall Hangings	Kerstin Ekengren	af Kleen, Nils E.	√		H&C	15	2		Sp 64	18
Wall Hangings	Las Artistas Del Valle: Images of Everyday Life in Colorado's San Luis Valley	Reith, Stephanie J.	√		Fa	10	3		M/J 83	24
Wall Hangings	Laughing Gulls of St. Petersburg	Aldrich, Mae	√		SS&D	5	4	20	Fa 74	75
Wall Hangings	Leno Sampler Wallhanging (Betty Davenport)		√	√	Hw	7	2		M/A 86	47, I-8
Wall Hangings	Lenore Tawney		√		H&C	13	2		Sp 62	6
Wall Hangings	Loom Controlled Designs		√	> 4	WJ	3	3	11	Ja 79	18
Wall Hangings	Macrame Popular At Murray State University		√		SS&D	4	3	15	Su 73	31
Wall Hangings	Marketable Weed Holders	Lindbergh, Susie	√	√	SS&D	4	2	14	Sp 73	16
Wall Hangings	Mary Atwater Wallhanging (Gertrude Griffin)		√	√	Hw	7	2		M/A 86	55, I-9
Wall Hangings	Mary Bero	Weiss, Hedy	√		Fa	12	2		M/A 85	36
Wall Hangings	Modular Weaves to Be Stuffed on the Loom	Russell, Joan	√	√	SS&D	5	4	20	Fa 74	97
Wall Hangings	Moorman Weave Variations	Hoskins, Nancy Arthur	√	√	SS&D	13	1	49	Wi 81	6
Wall Hangings	Naomi W. Towner: Hangings & Coverings		√		SS&D	5	2	18	Sp 74	92
Wall Hangings	Notes of a Pattern Weaver	Alvic, Philis	√		SS&D	13	4	52	Fa 82	76
Wall Hangings	On Weaving, Life and Art	Liebler, Barbara	√		Iw	4	4		Fa 79	19
Wall Hangings	Organize to Control Your Color	Templeton, Peg	√	√	Hw	2	4		Se 81	48
Wall Hangings	Overshot: Contemporary Applications		√		Iw	1	3		Sp 76	14
Wall Hangings	Overshot 'n Rags (Jane Patrick)		√	√	Hw	5	2		M/A 84	108
Wall Hangings	Overshot Wall Piece (Janice Jones) (error-corrected Hw v8 n1 87 p I-16)		√	√	Hw	6	4		S/O 85	50, I-7
Wall Hangings	Paired-Thread Finnweave Projects: Lynn's Zebra, The	Xenakis, Athanasios David	√	√	PWC			2	Ap 82	36
Wall Hangings	Paired-Thread Finnweave Projects: Medusa, the Gorgeous Gorgon, The	Xenakis, Athanasios David	√	√	PWC			2	Ap 82	43
Wall Hangings	Personal Approach to Drafting, A	Alvic, Philis	√	> 4	SS&D	13	1	49	Wi 81	32
Wall Hangings	Pick-Up Patterned Double Weave	Keasbey, Doramay	√	√	Hw	5	2		M/A 84	80
Wall Hangings	Preliminary Report on a Group of Important Mughal Textiles, A	Smart, Ellen S.	√		TMJ	25			86	5
Wall Hangings	Primary Patterns	Spoering, Kathy	√	√	WJ	9	1	33	Su 84	53
Wall Hangings	Progression from Meticulous Yardage to Grand Commissions	Bernard-Boone, Ann	√		SS&D	5	1	17	Wi 73	71
Wall Hangings	Progression of Ideas, or The Shortest Distance Between 2 Ideas is a Diagonal Line, A		√		Iw	6	1		Wi 80	35
Wall Hangings	Reinterpreting Rya: Irma Kukkasjärvi Energizes an Ancient Technique	Ojala, Liisa Kanning	√		WJ	9	4	36	Sp 85	26

SUBJECT	TITLE	AUTHOR	IL	INST	JOUR	VOL	NO	ISS	DATE	PAGE
Wall Hangings	Remove the Reed (error-corrected SS&D v5 n3 i19 74 p65)	Garrett, Cay	√	√	SS&D	5	1	17	Wi 73	88
Wall Hangings	Rena Thompson: Echoes of Intuitive Truths	Park, Betty	√		Fa	13	2		M/A 86	46
Wall Hangings	Rita Maran, Executes Designs in Yarn for Artists		√		H&C	18	1		Wi 67	14
Wall Hangings	Rubik Reworked	Reesor, Tracy	√		SS&D	14	3	55	Su 83	98
Wall Hangings	Rug Weaving: One Weaver's Approach	Hand, Barbara	√	> 4	WJ	7	4	28	Sp 83	32
Wall Hangings	Rugs Woven on Summer and Winter Threading		√	> 4	WJ	3	1	9	Jy 78	12
Wall Hangings	Salmon Derby (Lynn Strauss)		√	> 4	Hw	7	2		M/A 86	37, I-4
Wall Hangings	School of the Art Institute	Regensteiner, Else	√		SS&D	3	1	9	Wi 71	27
Wall Hangings	Sheila Hicks	Holtzer, Marilyn Emerson	√		SS&D	16	1	61	Wi 84	43
Wall Hangings	Sheila O'Hara's Geometrics	Rowley, Kathleen M.	√		SS&D	12	4	48	Fa 81	20
Wall Hangings	"Sherri Smith: Recent Work" (Exhibit)	Kirkland, Lawrence P.	√		Fa	7	4		J/A 80	63
Wall Hangings	Simple Inlay on Sheer Plain Weave Ground	Xenakis, Athanasios David; Linda Lyon	√	√	PWC	4	1	11		16
Wall Hangings	Six Songs of Success	Meany, Janet K.	√		SS&D	18	3	71	Su 87	69
Wall Hangings	Skirt for the Wall, A		√	√	WJ	3	4	12	Ap 79	19
Wall Hangings	Southwest Reflections: Fiber artists Inspired by the New Mexico Landscape	Colton, Mary Rawcliffe	√		WJ	11	1	41	Su 86	20
Wall Hangings	"Spiders" on the Wall		√		SS&D	1	1	1	De 69	17
Wall Hangings	Spinning Doghair	Barrett, Clotilde	√	√	WJ	1	1	1	Jy 76	27
Wall Hangings	SS&D Interview: Cynthia Schira (error-corrected SS&D v10 n2 79 p56)	Park, Betty	√		SS&D	10	1	37	Wi 78	4
Wall Hangings	Stepping Out	Ridgeway, Terese	√		SS&D	18	1	69	Wi 86	82
Wall Hangings	Summer and Winter — Part 1		√	> 4	WJ	2	4	8	Ap 78	28
Wall Hangings	Summer and Winter Revisited Part 4: Turned Pebble Weave	Xenakis, Athanasios David	√	√	PWC			4	Ja 83	52
Wall Hangings	Sunrise Titles and Twills		√		Iw	6	1		Wi 80	38
Wall Hangings	Tapestry and Embroidery	Drooker, Penelope B.	√		Iw	5	3		Su 80	37
Wall Hangings	"Textile Works: Lily Gilmore, Judith Moir, Sheila O'Hara" (Exhibit)	Mazur, Carole	√		Fa	8	2		M/A 81	67
Wall Hangings	"Theo Moorman: Experiments in Weaving" (Exhibit)	Dunwell, Anna	√		Fa	9	5		S/O 82	80
Wall Hangings	Think Big	Lovell-Cooper, Sylvia	√		SS&D	3	1	9	Wi 71	41
Wall Hangings	Tied Lithuanian: Notes of a Pattern Weaver	Alvic, Philis	√	> 4	WJ	9	3	35	Wi 85	50
Wall Hangings	Tied Overshot Boundweave	Xenakis, Athanasios David	√	√	PWC	3	4	10		9
Wall Hangings	Tin & Tapestry Hanging (Elisabeth La Cour)		√	√	Hw	8	3		M/J 87	48, I-9
Wall Hangings	Tina McMorran	Stevens, Bernice A.	√		H&C	15	3		Su 64	14
Wall Hangings	Transparencies of Inger Harrison–Sheer Beauty, The	Keasbey, Doramay	√	√	Hw	3	1		Ja 82	40
Wall Hangings	Twill Diaper Piqué (error-corrected PWC v4 n4 i14 p33)	Xenakis, Athanasios David; Madelyn van der Hoogt	√	> 4	PWC	4	3	13		36
Wall Hangings	Two Tubes in Double Weave (error-corrected SS&D v5 n4 74 p69)	Neale, Mary Beth	√	> 4	SS&D	5	3	19	Su 74	8
Wall Hangings	Unusual Ways with Leno	Davenport, Betty	√	√	Hw	7	2		M/A 86	46
Wall Hangings	Utilitarian Hang-up	Nelson, Ruthe	√	√	WJ	3	3	11	Ja 79	11
Wall Hangings	Variations on One Warp	Alvic, Philis	√		SS&D	12	4	48	Fa 81	70
Wall Hangings	Wall Hanging with a Story	Cripps, Alice K.	√	√	H&C	17	1		Wi 66	47
Wall Hangings	Wall Hangings of Judith Content, The	Scarborough, Jessica	√		Fa	13	2		M/A 86	10
Wall Hangings	Warp Color Changes in Double and Multilayer Weaves	O'Connor, Paul	√	> 4	WJ	12	2	46	Fa 87	55
Wall Hangings	Wear Your Wall Hanging	West, Virginia	√	√	SS&D	4	2	14	Sp 73	11

SUBJECT	TITLE	AUTHOR	IL	INST	JOUR	VOL	NO	ISS	DATE	PAGE
Wall Hangings	Weaver's Commission Workshop	Meany, Janet	√		SS&D	10	3	39	Su 79	40
Wall Hangings	Weaving A City Skyline	Wennerstrom, Ann K.	√	√	WJ	7	1	25	Su 82	30
Wall Hangings	Weaving a Wall Hanging	Collingwood, Peter	√	√	H&C	11	4		Fa 60	15
Wall Hangings	Weaving and Felt	Swendeman, Dorothy	√	√	Iw	5	3		Su 80	43
Wall Hangings	Weaving and Felt: Laminated Wefts		√		Iw	5	3		Su 80	45
Wall Hangings	Weaving, Applique and Stitchery	Belfer, Nancy	√		Iw	5	3		Su 80	41
Wall Hangings	Weaving the Girdle of Rameses	Hilts, Patricia	√	> 4	WJ	9	1	33	Su 84	22
Wall Hangings	Weaving-Drawing-Painting-Paper, A Profile of Lorelei Schott		√		WJ	6	1	21	Su 81	13
Wall Hangings	Wefts of Light: Jayn Thomas' Fabric Hangings	Scarborough, Jessica	√		Fa	9	1		J/F 82	23
Wall Hangings	Wire Your Wall Hangings	Adams, Carol; Patricia L. Magee	√	√	SS&D	15	1	57	Wi 83	100
Wall Hangings	Working with the Wall ... A Community Garden		√		SS&D	10	4	40	Fa 79	8
Wall Hangings	Woven Image, The	Ginsberg, Ruth L.	√		SS&D	2	4	8	Fa 71	6
Wall Hangings	Woven World of Moocho Scott Salomon, The	Drooker, Penelope	√		Fa	11	5		S/O 84	22
Wall Hangings: Skirt	Skirt for the Wall, A		√	√	WJ	3	4	12	Ap 79	19
Wall Hangings: Skirt	Utilitarian Hang-up	Nelson, Ruthe	√	√	WJ	3	3	11	Ja 79	11
Wall Relief	Building on Experience: Virginia Jacobs' Fabric Constructions	Rowland, Amy Zaffarano	√		Fa	7	4		J/A 80	39
Wall Relief	"Fiber in the Service of Art: The Work of Wilma King and Marilyn Grelle" (Exhibit)	Mathews, Rich	√		Fa	4	2		M/A 77	18
Wall Relief	"Leroy Wilce: Adobe Walls" (Exhibit)	Dyer, Carolyn	√		Fa	4	4		J/A 77	17
Wall Relief	"Macungie Notes — Lewis Knauss" (Exhibit)	Park, Betty	√		Fa	5	2		M/A 78	15
Wall Relief	Margaret Welty: Minimalist Weaver	Les, Kathleen	√		Fa	5	4		J/A 78	28
Wall Relief	Mary Ruth Smith: Stitcher	Vander Lee, Jana	√		Fa	3	1		J/F 76	6
Wall Relief	Poetry in Fiber: Gail Johnson Resen Talks About Her Work	Resen, Gail Johnson	√		Fa	7	4		J/A 80	20
Wall Relief	"Ritzi and Peter Jacobi" (Exhibit)	Mathews, Rich	√		Fa	4	5		S/O 77	12
Wall Relief	Rosemary Doherty		√		Fa	4	4		J/A 77	53
Wall Relief	Sally Anderson: Weaver		√		Fa	3	1		J/F 76	8
Wall Relief	Sue Scott		√		Fa	4	5		S/O 77	53
Wall Relief	Thurid Clark		√		Fa	3	6		N/D 76	8
Wall Relief, Multilayered	Multilayered Tapestries of Susan Klebanoff, The	Brien, Elise	√		Fa	14	3		M/J 87	21
Walnut, Black	Why Bother with Natural Dyeing?	Bulbach, Stanley	√	√	TM			5	J/J 86	32
War-Effort: Spinning	New Zealand Spinners	Robinson, Margaret	√		H&C	10	3		Su 59	23
Warp and Weft Effect Contrasts	Simple Damask-Like Effects Using Element Diameter Differential and Element Tension Differential	Xenakis, Athanasios David	√	> 4	AT	1			De 83	317
Warp and Weft Substitutions	Flat-Woven Structures Found in Nomadic and Village Weavings from the Near East and Central Asia	Wertime, John T.	√		TMJ	18			79	33
Warp Beams, Double	Building an Extra Warp Beam		√	√	H&C	10	2		Sp 59	45
Warp Beams, Double	Practical Weave for Rugs, A	Atwater, Mary Meigs	√	> 4	H&C	5	2		Sp 54	24
Warp Beams, Double	Supplementary Warp Patterning: Handling Two Warps, Two-Beam Warping	Tidball, Harriet		√	SCGM		17		66	6
Warp Beams, Double	Why an Extra Beam?	Xenakis, Athanasios David			PWC	1	1		No 81	34
Warp Beams, Hanging	Supplementary Warp Patterning: Handling Two Warps, A Hanging Beam	Tidball, Harriet		√	SCGM		17		66	6
Warp Beams, Number	Everything a Weaver Should Know About Warps and Warping: How to Save on the Number of Warp Beams	Zielinski, S. A.; Robert Leclerc, ed.	√	√	MWL	5			'51–'73	69
Warp Beams, Sectional	Everything a Weaver Should Know About Warps and Warping: Sectional Warp Beam	Zielinski, S. A.; Robert Leclerc, ed.	√	√	MWL	5			'51–'73	32

SUBJECT	TITLE	AUTHOR	IL	INST	JOUR	VOL	NO	ISS	DATE	PAGE
Warp Beams, Two	Case for Two Warp Beams, The	Batchelder, Joy			CW	7	1	19	Se 85	5
Warp Calculation	Treasury for Beginners: The Warp	Zielinski, S. A.; Robert Leclerc, ed.		√	MWL	1			'51–'73	73
Warp: Corkscrew	Original Fabrics of Kaftan, The	El-Homossani, M. M.	√	> 4	AT	1			De 83	263
Warp Draw-In	Rug Weaving: How to Avoid Drawing-in of the Warp	Stanley, Martha	√	√	WJ	6	2	22	Fa 81	10
Warp Dyeing	Random Warp Dyeing: A Spontaneous Steam Dye Process	D'Ambrosio, Gina	√	√	WJ	10	3	39	Wi 86	42
Warp End Breakage: Problems/Solutions	Rx: Warp End Breakage and Treadling Errors	Guy, Sallie T.	√	√	Hw	3	4		Se 82	22
Warp Fringe	Gala Raincoat	Moes, Dini	√	√	WJ	6	3	23	Wi 81	12
Warp Painting	Cindy Fornari: Painted Warps		√		Fa	3	5		S/O 76	30
Warp Painting	Dyes for Painting Warps	Bliss, Anne	√	√	Hw	5	4		S/0 84	65
Warp Painting	Fashion Show of Handwoven Garments		√	> 4	WJ	3	3	11	Ja 79	5
Warp Painting	Fiber Reactive Dyes	Ridgeway, Teresa	√	√	SS&D	13	1	49	Wi 81	34
Warp Painting	Handwoven Silk Garments: Ikat Dress	Schreiber, LaVonne	√	√	WJ	3	2	10	Oc 78	30
Warp Painting	Instant Color! Paint a Garden on your Warp	Colburn, Carol	√	√	Hw	1	2		S-S 80	44
Warp Painting	Moorman Inspired Clothing	Durston, Linda Moore	√	√	SS&D	14	1	53	Wi 82	35
Warp Painting	Painting and Brocading on the Loom	Ziek, Bhakti	√	√	TM			6	A/S 86	42
Warp Painting	Silk and Fiber Reactive Dyes		√	√	WJ	3	2	10	Oc 78	24
Warp Painting	Silk Dyeing		√	√	WJ	3	2	10	Oc 78	21
Warp Painting	Symbolic or Sacred? A Personal View	Lockwood, Diana W.	√	> 4	WJ	9	3	35	Wi 85	45
Warp Painting	Two-Harness Textiles, The Loom-Controlled Weaves: Decorating Plain-Weave Webs, Chiné (Warp Painting:	Tidball, Harriet	√	√	SCGM		20		67	30
Warp Painting: Chiné	Contemporary Satins: Chine and Ikat	Tidball, Harriet	√	√	SCGM		7		62	20
Warp Painting: Inkle	Warp-Painting on the Inkle Loom			√	Hw	7	3		M/J 86	46
Warp Sett: Variations	Whig Rose Study (continued)	Morgenstern, Marvin M.	√	√	WJ	7	3	27	Wi 82	23
Warp Sett: Variations, Whig Rose	Whig Rose Study	Morgenstern, Marvin M.	√	√	WJ	7	2	26	Fa 82	40
Warp Stripe Texture System	Handloom Weaves: The Classification of Handloom Weaves, The Structural Group, The Rhythmic Weave Class, Warp Stripe Texture System	Tidball, Harriet	√	> 4	SCGM		33		57	37
Warp Tension: Problems/Solutions	Rx: Uneven Warp Tension	Guy, Sallie T.	√	√	Hw	3	3		My 82	84
Warp-Dominant Weave	Beechwood Throw (Judy Steinkoenig)		√	√	Hw	5	2		M/A 84	58, 97
Warp-Emphasis Weave	Color Gamp Tablecloth and Napkins (Carrie Lee Seachord)		√	√	Hw	5	3		Su 84	77, 117
Warp-Emphasis Weave	Jacket and Camisole with Ikat Stripes (Ronnine Bohannan)		√	√	Hw	5	3		Su 84	56, 100
Warp-Faced Ground	Chinese Drawloom: A Study in Weave Structure, The	Sellin, Helen	√	> 4	WJ	9	2	34	Fa 84	6
Warp-Faced, Pattern Weave, Pick-Up	Calendar in Guatemalan Belt Weave (Evelyn Christensen)		√	√	Hw	7	2		M/A 86	69, I-14
Warp-Faced Weaves	Adobe Jacket (Ronnine Bohannan)		√	√	Hw	7	3		M/J 86	49, I-11
Warp-Faced Weaves	Backstrap Weaving for Penance and Profit	Coffman, Charlotte	√	√	WJ	7	1	25	Su 82	60
Warp-Faced Weaves	Band Bag (Jane Patrick) (error-corrected Hw v4 n3 83 p79)		√	√	Hw	4	2		M/A 83	Cover, 5I, 89
Warp-Faced Weaves	Blocks and Warp-Faced Weaving			√	Hw	8	5		N/D 87	61
Warp-Faced Weaves	Brushed Wool Wrap Coat (Jean Scorgie and Kaino Leethem)		√	√	Hw	4	1		J/F 83	46, 88
Warp-Faced Weaves	Card Weaving, Patterns Translated to a Handloom	Priest, Alice R.	√	√	H&C	12	2		Sp 61	15
Warp-Faced Weaves	Christmas Project, A	Richards, Iris	√	√	WJ	1	2	2	Oc 76	12
Warp-Faced Weaves	Colonial Mats (Pat Epstein)		√	√	Hw	3	5		N/D 82	46, 94
Warp-Faced Weaves	Composition and Designing: Pattern in Warp	Zielinski, S. A.; Robert Leclerc, ed.	√	√	MWL	18			'51–'73	79

SUBJECT	TITLE	AUTHOR	IL	INST	JOUR	VOL	NO	ISS	DATE	PAGE
Warp-Faced Weaves	Cuna Cachi: A Study of Hammock Weaving Among the Cuna Indians of the San Blas Islands	Lambert, Anne M.	√	√	AT	5			Ju 86	105
Warp-Faced Weaves	Four-Shaft, Two-Block Warp-Faced Rep Floor Covering	Kolling-Summers, Elizabeth	√	√	WJ	7	4	28	Sp 83	15
Warp-Faced Weaves	Incredible Five-Color, Two-Tie Afghan for a Super Kid, The	Xenakis, Athanasios David	√	√	PWC	1	1		No 81	35
Warp-Faced Weaves	Kente: The Status Cloth of Ghana	Conklin, Sharon L.	√	√	SS&D	8	1	29	WI 76	18
Warp-Faced Weaves	Kurdish Kilim Weaving in the Van-Hakkari District of Eastern Turkey	Landreau, Anthony N.	√	√	TMJ	3	4		De 73	27
Warp-Faced Weaves	Mattor (error-corrected WJ v2 n1 77 insert for vol. 1)	Dunham, Miriam	√	√	WJ	1	4	4	Ap 77	21
Warp-Faced Weaves	Shadowweave, Part 2 — Unbalanced Shadowweave (error-corrected WJ v2 n1 77 insert for vol. 1)	Barrett, Clotilde	√	> 4	WJ	1	2	2	Oc 76	14
Warp-Faced Weaves	Sling Chair (Sharon Alderman)		√	√	Hw	6	3		Su 85	58, I-15
Warp-Faced Weaves	Tow Linen Shades (Robin Taylor Daugherty)		√	√	Hw	5	2		M/A 84	55, 96
Warp-Faced Weaves	Two Unusual Multishaft Curtains	Xenakis, Athanasios David	√	> 4	PWC	4	1	11		40
Warp-Faced Weaves	Warp Faced Patterning	Riccardi, Mary Elinor Steinbaugh	√	√	SS&D	10	2	38	Sp 79	40
Warp-Faced Weaves	Warp-Faced 2/2 Twill: Part 2	Jensen, Gay	√	√	Hw	3	4		Se 82	50
Warp-Faced Weaves	Warp-Faced Krokbragd	Jensen, Gay; Donna Kaplan	√	> 4	WJ	12	2	46	Fa 87	62
Warp-Faced Weaves	Warp-Faced Tablerunner in Rib Weave	Kolling-Summers, Elizabeth	√	√	WJ	7	4	28	Sp 83	14
Warp-Faced Weaves	Warp-Faced Weaving, Part 1	Jensen, Gay	√	√	Hw	3	3		My 82	42
Warp-Faced Weaves	Weaving the Girdle of Rameses	Hilts, Patricia	√	> 4	WJ	9	1	33	Su 84	22
Warp-Faced Weaving	Portable Weaving: A Band of Ideas for Bands	Bradley, Louise; Jean Anstine	√	√	Hw	7	3		M/J 86	40
Warp-Float Blocks	Linen Mats (Dixie Francis)		√	√	Hw	7	3		M/J 86	67, I-15
Warp-Pattern System	Handloom Weaves: The Classification of Handloom Weaves, The Structural Group, Unit Class, Warp Pattern System	Tidball, Harriet	√	> 4	SCGM		33		57	29
Warp-Pattern Weaves	Adaptations of Primitive Warp-Pattern Weaves	Landreau, Tony	√	√	H&C	8	1		Wi 56	25
Warp-Pattern Weaves	Bolivian Highland Weaving, Part 1	Cason, Marjorie; Adele Cahlander	√		SS&D	6	2	22	Sp 75	4
Warp-Pattern Weaves	Mexican Caprice	Snyder, Mary E.	√	> 4	CW	2	2	5	Ja 81	7
Warp-Pattern Weaves	Mexican Motifs: A Fine Cotton Warp-Pattern Fabric	Tidball, Harriet	√	√	SCGM		6		62	18
Warp-Pattern Weaves	Peru, Textiles Unlimited, Part 2: A Warp Pattern Weave	Tidball, Harriet	√	> 4	SCGM		26		69	19
Warp-Pattern Weaves	Turned Drafts in Double Two-Tie Unit Weave	van der Hoogt, Madelyn	√	> 4	WJ	9	2	34	Fa 84	13
Warp-Pattern Weaves	Understanding Some Complex Structures from Simple Andean Looms: Steps in Analysis and Reproduction	Cahlander, Adele	√	√	AT	1			De 83	181
Warp-Pattern Weaves	Warp Pattern Weaves	Dudley, Barbara	√	> 4	H&C	17	4		Fa 66	30
Warp-Pattern Weaves	Warp-pattern Weaving	Frey, Berta	√	√	H&C	10	3		Su 59	9
Warp-Pattern Weaves	Weaving the Girdle of Rameses on Nine Harnesses	Parkinson, Alberta	√	> 4	CW	3	2	8	Ja 82	1
Warp-Pattern Weaves, Double-Faced, Opposites	Peru, Textiles Unlimited, Part 2: An Opposites Warp-Pattern Weave	Tidball, Harriet	√	√	SCGM		26		69	14
Warp-Patterning, Pick-Up	Peru, Textiles Unlimited, Part 2: Outlined Warp-Pattern Pick-Up	Tidball, Harriet	√	> 4	SCGM		26		69	24
Warp-Patterning, Pick-Up, Contrasting Ground	Peru, Textiles Unlimited, Part 2: Warp Pick-Up With Contrasting Ground	Tidball, Harriet	√	> 4	SCGM		26		69	25
Warp-Patterning, Pick-Up, Three-Color	Peru, Textiles Unlimited, Part 2: Three-Color Warp-Pattern Pick-Up	Tidball, Harriet	√	> 4	SCGM		26		69	26
Warp-Rib Weaves	Original Fabrics of Kaftan, The	El-Homossani, M. M.	√	> 4	AT	1			De 83	263

SUBJECT	TITLE	AUTHOR	IL	INST	JOUR	VOL	NO	ISS	DATE	PAGE
Warp-Stuffer System	Handloom Weaves: The Classification of Handloom Weaves, The Structural Group, Unit Class, Warp Stuffer System	Tidball, Harriet	√	> 4	SCGM		33		57	28
Warp-Stuffer Weave	Warp Stuffer Weave with Shaft Switching Applications	Evans, Jane A.	√	> 4	Hw	4	3		M/J 83	72
Warp-Tension Devices	Weighty Matters		√		PWC	4	3	13		32
Warp/Weft Calculations	Creative Solutions	Chandler, Deborah		√	Hw	6	3		Su 85	28
Warp/Weft, Discontinuous	Interlocking Warp and Weft in the Nasca 2 Style	Rowe, Ann Pollard	√		TMJ	3	3		De 72	67
Warped-Faced Weaves	Warp-Face Runner (Gay Jensen)		√	√	Hw	3	3		My 82	Cover 93
Warped-Faced Weaves	Warped-Faced Ruana	D'Ambrosio, Gina	√	√	S-O	10	2		Su 86	17
Warping Reel, Horizontal	Piña	Wallace, Lysbeth	√		WJ	8	2	30	Fa 83	77
Warps and Warping	Absolutely Impossible Warp, The	Stumbough, Virginia			Hw	5	1		J/F 84	16
Warps and Warping	Adapting Inkle Patterns to Wider Widths	Carlson, Estelle	√	√	SS&D	8	1	29	WI 76	87
Warps and Warping	Angel Sticks, An Aid to Warping	Walrath, E. K.	√	√	H&C	20	3		Su 69	15
Warps and Warping	Assertiveness Training for Beginning Weavers	Chandler, Deborah	√	√	Hw	7	3		M/J 86	24
Warps and Warping	Bands to Broadloom: Converting Card Weaving Designs to a Four-Harness Loom	De Peaux, Barbara; Mary Tyler	√	√	SS&D	8	1	29	WI 76	86
Warps and Warping	Contemporary Tapestry: On Looms, Warping, Setting Up Tapestry Study Course — Part 1	O'Callaghan, Kate	√	√	WJ	4	3	15	Ja 80	41
Warps and Warping	Coverlet Weaving	Williams, Ann	√	√	SS&D	14	4	56	Fa 83	32
Warps and Warping	Designing for Warp-face	Sullivan, Donna	√	√	SS&D	19	1	73	Wi 87	15
Warps and Warping	Designing the Warp: Parallel Considerations	Criscola, Jeanne	√	√	TM			1	O/N 85	66
Warps and Warping	Efficient Warping	Larsen, Jack Lenor	√		H&C	3	3		Su 52	32
Warps and Warping	Exploring Doup Leno	Laughlin, Mary Elizabeth	√	> 4	CW	4	3	12	Ap 83	3
Warps and Warping	French Tapestry Weaving in San Francisco	Tanenbaum, Ruth	√	√	SS&D	8	3	31	Su 77	12
Warps and Warping	Handloom Weaves: Warp and Weft	Tidball, Harriet			SCGM		33		57	8
Warps and Warping	Handwoven Cape on an Improvised Loom	Williams, Olive	√	√	H&C	22	3		Su 71	28
Warps and Warping	How to Tie on a New Warp	Thomas, Mrs. Tollie			SS&D	2	2	6	Sp 71	30
Warps and Warping	How to Warp with a Paddle—Beam Without Paper, Part 1	Landis, Lucille	√	√	SS&D	16	1	61	Wi 84	72
Warps and Warping	I Was a Handweaver for the Textile Industry	Tergis, Marilyn	√	√	H&C	23	5		S/O 72	36
Warps and Warping	In Order to Weave you Must be Warped!	Redding, Debbie	√	√	Hw	1	2		S-S 80	6
Warps and Warping	Inlay Techniques	Barrett, Clotilde	√	√	WJ	1	1	1	Jy 76	3
Warps and Warping	Kasuri: The Japanese Ikat	Schrieber, La Vonne	√	√	SS&D	14	1	53	Wi 82	22
Warps and Warping	Kurdish Kilim Weaving in the Van-Hakkari District of Eastern Turkey	Landreau, Anthony N.	√	√	TMJ	3	4		De 73	27
Warps and Warping	Long Warps	Scorgie, Jean	√	√	Hw	6	2		M/A 85	43
Warps and Warping	Miyako Jofu	Miller, Dorothy	√	√	AT	7			Ju 87	85
Warps and Warping	Navajo: Textiles, Blankets, Rugs, Tapestries	Morrow, Mable	√	√	SS&D	2	1	5	De 70	5
Warps and Warping	New Aid to Warping, A		√		H&C	5	1		Wi 53	50
Warps and Warping	New Method of Warping, A	Irey, Margaret	√	√	H&C	4	3		Su 53	50
Warps and Warping	Notes for Beginning Weavers: Warping the Most Interesting Part of Weaving	Frey, Berta		√	H&C	16	2		Sp 65	20
Warps and Warping	One Warp, Many Projects		√		Hw	6	2		M/A 85	48
Warps and Warping	Original Fabrics of Kaftan, The	El-Homossani, M. M.	√	> 4	AT	1			De 83	263
Warps and Warping	Preparing a Warp	Peters, Rupert	√	√	H&C	5	2		Sp 54	20
Warps and Warping	Ribbon in the Warp	Allen, Ernestine	√	√	H&C	21	4		Fa 70	15
Warps and Warping	Ridge (Twill) Weave of the Hopi	Nelson, Nanci Neher	√	√	SS&D	14	2	54	Sp 83	52
Warps and Warping	Sky Celebration	Mayer, Anita Luvera	√	√	S-O	11	2		Su 87	36
Warps and Warping	Space-Dented Warp	Fry, Laura	√	√	WJ	4	3	15	Ja 80	26
Warps and Warping	Supplementary Warp for Novelty Yarns	Davenport, Betty	√	√	Hw	6	1		J/F 85	34

SUBJECT	TITLE	AUTHOR	IL	INST	JOUR	VOL	NO	ISS	DATE	PAGE
Warps and Warping	Supplementary Warp (Warp Brocade)	Wertenberger, Kathryn	√	>4	Hw	7	1		J/F 86	80
Warps and Warping	Supplementary Warps: The One-Shuttle Solution (error-corrected SS&D v19 n1 87 p33)	Mortensen, Diane L.	√	√	SS&D	18	4	72	Fa 87	66
Warps and Warping	Techniques for Better Weaving (error-corrected TM i9 D/J 86 p4)	Osterkamp, Peggy	√	√	TM			7	O/N 86	42
Warps and Warping	Theme and Variations	Bress, Helene	√	√	Hw	6	2		M/A 85	62
Warps and Warping	Tie-Dyed Warp	Weintraub, Fran	√	√	SS&D	4	1	13	Wi 72	38
Warps and Warping	Unusual Materials for Warp or Weft	Wertenberger, Kathryn	√	>4	Hw	7	4		S/O 86	78
Warps and Warping	Vertical Loom (continued) Part 3, The Navajo Loom, The		√	√	WJ	2	2	6	Oc 77	23
Warps and Warping	Warping Adaptations for Fine Warps	MacFarlane, Rosemary	√	√	SS&D	12	4	48	Fa 81	16
Warps and Warping	Warping for Stripes	Davenport, Betty	√	√	Hw	6	4		S/O 85	18
Warps and Warping	Warping in Color	Moes, Dini	√	√	SS&D	14	4	56	Fa 83	24
Warps and Warping	Wrap Up Your Warp	Voiers, Leslie	√	>4	SS&D	18	1	69	Wi 86	49
Warps and Warping: Accuracy Check Points	Doup Leno: Sample Project, Check Points	Skowronski, Hella; Sylvia Tacker			SCGM		32		80	23
Warps and Warping: Adding Warps	Solving a Difficult Warping Problem	Greer, Gertrude G.	√	√	H&C	2	3		Su 51	44
Warps and Warping: Backing in Warp	Everything a Weaver Should Know About Warps and Warping: Backing in Warp	Zielinski, S. A.; Robert Leclerc, ed.	√	√	MWL	5			'51–'73	92
Warps and Warping: Backstrap Loom	Backstrap Weaving in the Philippines	Ng, Mary	√		SS&D	9	1	33	Wi 77	18
Warps and Warping: Beaming	Everything a Weaver Should Know About Warps and Warping: Beaming	Zielinski, S. A.; Robert Leclerc, ed.		√	MWL	5			'51–'73	73
Warps and Warping: Beaming	Handweaver's Instruction Manual: Dressing the Loom, Chain Warping, Beaming	Tidball, Harriet C. nee Douglas		√	SCGM		34		49	15
Warps and Warping: Beaming	How to Warp with a Paddle — Beam Without Paper, Part 2	Landis, Lucille	√	√	SS&D	6	4	24	Fa 75	72
Warps and Warping: Beaming	How to Warp with a Paddle—Beam without Paper, Part 2	Landis, Lucille	√	√	SS&D	16	2	62	Sp 85	70
Warps and Warping: Beaming	Treasury for Beginners: Beaming	Zielinski, S. A.; Robert Leclerc, ed.		√	MWL	1			'51–'73	15
Warps and Warping: Beaming, Double	Tuck Tactics	Speth, Lottie	√	√	SS&D	15	3	59	Su 84	80
Warps and Warping: Board Loom	Weaving on a Board	Kappler, Erda	√	√	Hw	4	4		S/O 83	46
Warps and Warping: Card Weaving	Card Weaving	Frey, Berta	√	√	H&C	18	3		Su 67	8
Warps and Warping: Cards	How to Warp and Weave Cards		√	√	Hw	7	3		M/J 86	45
Warps and Warping: Chaining	Handweaver's Instruction Manual: Dressing the Loom, Chain Warping	Tidball, Harriet C. nee Douglas	√	√	SCGM		34		49	13
Warps and Warping: Chains, Dark-Light	Fantastic Finnweave, Part 1	Xenakis, Athanasios David	√	√	PWC			2	Ap 82	18
Warps and Warping: Circular	Pin-Warp Collar	Porcella, Yvonne	√	√	SS&D	4	3	15	Su 73	56
Warps and Warping: Continuous	Secret Treasures of Tibet	Wiltsie-Vaniea, Anne	√		SS&D	18	3	71	Su 87	60
Warps and Warping: Continuous	Weaving a Cotton Saddlebag on the Santa Elena Peninsula of Ecuador	Hagino, Jane Parker; Karen E. Stothert	√	√	TMJ	22			83	19
Warps and Warping: Continuous, Extended and Integrated	Selected Batak Textiles: Technique and Function	Gittinger, Mattiebelle S.	√		TMJ	4	2		75	13
Warps and Warping: Continuous Techniques	Weaving Processes in the Cuzco Area of Peru	Rowe, Ann Pollard	√	√	TMJ	4	2		75	30
Warps and Warping: Continuous Warp, On-Loom	Cuna Cachi: A Study of Hammock Weaving Among the Cuna Indians of the San Blas Islands	Lambert, Anne M.	√	√	AT	5			Ju 86	105
Warps and Warping: Correcting Errors	Handweaver's Instruction Manual: Dressing the Loom, Correcting Errors	Tidball, Harriet C. nee Douglas	√	√	SCGM		34		49	16
Warps and Warping: Counting Threads	Handweaver's Instruction Manual: Dressing the Loom, Chain Warping, Counting Threads	Tidball, Harriet C. nee Douglas		√	SCGM		34		49	13
Warps and Warping: Crowded-Warp Patterning	Peru, Textiles Unlimited, Part 2: Crowded-Warp Patterning	Tidball, Harriet	√	√	SCGM		26		69	13
Warps and Warping: Double Beams	Tale of Tucks, A (error-corrected SS&D v7 n1 75 p63)	Guagliumi, Susan	√	>4	SS&D	7	1	25	Wi 75	56

SUBJECT	TITLE	AUTHOR	IL	INST	JOUR	VOL	NO	ISS	DATE	PAGE
Warps and Warping: Double Warp	Seersucker	Linder, Olive	√	√	Hw	2	2		Mr 81	37
Warps and Warping: Double Warp	Warp Pattern Weaves	Dudley, Barbara	√	>4	H&C	17	4		Fa 66	30
Warps and Warping: Drawloom	Drawloom Magic	van der Hoogt, Madelyn	√	>4	Hw	7	2		M/A 86	66
Warps and Warping: Dummy	Warping: A Compleat Guide	Patrick, Jane	√	√	Hw	3	3		My 82	70
Warps and Warping: Dummy Warps	Short Cuts in Weaving		√	√	H&C	26	2		Ap 75	34
Warps and Warping: Figure-Eight	Andean Crossed-Warp Techniques for Decorative Trims, Part 2 — Tubular Bands (error-corrected WJ v3 n1 insert for vol.2)	Cahlander, Adele	√	√	WJ	3	1	9	Jy 78	38
Warps and Warping: Figure-of-Eight	On-loom Warping for Navajo Loom	Freilinger, Ida M.	√	√	SS&D	11	3	43	Su 80	8
Warps and Warping: Floating Warp	Five Harness Pattern on a Four Harness Loom, A	Thilenius, Carol	√	√	Iw	4	3		Su 79	34
Warps and Warping: Floating Warps	Double-faced, Double-woven, Three-harness Krokbragd	Holtzer, Marilyn Emerson	√	√	SS&D	14	4	56	Fa 83	46
Warps and Warping: Full Size Warp	Everything A Weaver Should Know About Warps and Warping: Full Size Warps	Zielinski, S. A.; Robert Leclerc, ed.	√	√	MWL	5			'51–'73	83
Warps and Warping: Grouped Warp Threads	Grouped Warp Threads	Davison, Marguerite Porter	√	√	H&C	26	3		M/J 75	24
Warps and Warping: Handspun	Weaving with Handspun Linen Yarn	Fannin, Allen A.	√	√	H&C	19	2		Sp 68	10
Warps and Warping: Handspun	Weaving with Handspun Yarns: Suggestions for Beginning Spinners	Simmons, Paula	√	√	H&C	17	4		Fa 66	4
Warps and Warping: Handspun, Overtwist	Save the Twist: Warping and Weaving with Overtwisted Yarns	Frame, Mary	√	√	S-O	11	2		Su 87	43
Warps and Warping: Hanging Warp System	Everything A Weaver Should Know About Warps and Warping: Hanging Warp System	Zielinski, S. A.; Robert Leclerc, ed.	√	√	MWL	5			'51–'73	95
Warps and Warping: High-Warp	Commercial Establishment Discovers Fiber Arts, The	Jacopetti, Alexandra	√	√	SS&D	8	2	30	Sp 77	4
Warps and Warping: High-Warp Loom	Commercial Establishment Discovers Fiber Arts, The	Jacopetti, Alexandra	√	√	SS&D	8	2	30	Sp 77	4
Warps and Warping: Ikat	Patolu and Its Techniques	De Bone, Mary Golden	√	√	TMJ	4	3		76	49
Warps and Warping: Ikat	Tying Warp Ikat on the Loom	Hannon, Farrell	√	√	WJ	8	1	29	Su 83	41
Warps and Warping: Inkle	New, Functional Inkle Loom, A	Spencer, Edith L.	√	√	H&C	6	2		Sp 55	42
Warps and Warping: Inkle, Board Loom	Weaving Inkle Bands: Preparing the Board Loom and Weaving, Warping	Tidball, Harriet	√	√	SCGM		27		69	4
Warps and Warping: Inkle Loom	How to Warp and Weave on an Inkle Loom		√	√	Hw	7	3		M/J 86	43
Warps and Warping: Interlocked Warps	Peru, Textiles Unlimited: Scaffold, Patchwork, or Interlocked Warp	Tidball, Harriet	√		SCGM		25		68	28
Warps and Warping: Interlooping	Evolution of a Weaving, The	Kearney, Kathleen	√	√	SS&D	12	1	45	Wi 80	64
Warps and Warping: Lease	Technology of Handweaving: The Lease and the Lease Rods	Zielinski, S. A.; Robert Leclerc, ed.	√	√	MWL	6			'51–'73	17
Warps and Warping: Leash Cross	Handweaver's Instruction Manual: Dressing the Loom, Chain Warping, The Leash	Tidball, Harriet C. nee Douglas	√	√	SCGM		34		49	14
Warps and Warping: Linen	From Warp to Muffins				Hw	5	1		J/F 84	11
Warps and Warping: Linen	Yarns and Fibers: How Not to Weave Linen	Zielinski, S. A.; Robert Leclerc, ed.	√	√	MWL	4			'51–'73	19
Warps and Warping: Long-Eyed Heddle System	Some Additional Notes on the Damask—Threading the Pattern Harnesses	Ahrens, Jim	√	>4	CW	6	2	17	Ja 85	3
Warps and Warping: Mitla Cloth	Warping and Weaving Mitla Cloth on the Backstrap Loom	Knottenbelt, Maaike	√	√	TMJ	22			83	53
Warps and Warping: Multiple Thread	Have You Tried Multiple Thread Warping?	Currey, Ruth Dunlop	√	√	H&C	5	3		Su 54	28
Warps and Warping: Multiple Warps	Everything A Weaver Should Know About Warps and Warping: Multiple Warps	Zielinski, S. A.; Robert Leclerc, ed.	√	√	MWL	5			'51–'73	62
Warps and Warping: Multiple Warps	You are Now Weaving Oakland	O'Hara, Sheila	√	>4	AT	6			De 86	9
Warps and Warping: Orlon	New Man-Made Fiber Developed for Handweavers, A	Laurell, Karl	√	√	H&C	5	1		Wi 53	27

784

SUBJECT	TITLE	AUTHOR	IL	INST	JOUR	VOL	NO	ISS	DATE	PAGE
Warps and Warping: Paddle	How to Warp with a Paddle — Beam Without Paper	Landis, Lucille	√	√	SS&D	6	3	23	Su 75	83
Warps and Warping: Paddle	Paddle Warping — One Weaver Tells Why	Ryan, Shirley	√	√	Hw	3	3		My 82	68
Warps and Warping: Paddle	Warping: A Compleat Guide	Patrick, Jane	√	√	Hw	3	3		My 82	68
Warps and Warping: Pattern in Warp	Everything A Weaver Should Know About Warps and Warping: Patterns in Warp	Zielinski, S. A.; Robert Leclerc, ed.	√	√	MWL	5			'51–'73	90
Warps and Warping: Problems, Vibrations	Everything A Weaver Should Know About Warps and Warping: Vibrations	Zielinski, S. A.; Robert Leclerc, ed.	√	√	MWL	5			'51–'73	41
Warps and Warping: Problems/Solutions	Dog on the Loom, The	Allen, Debbie	√		Hw	5	2		M/A 84	20
Warps and Warping: Problems/Solutions	Mending Warps	Ligon, Linda	√	√	Hw	7	1		J/F 86	34
Warps and Warping: Problems/Solutions	Problems in Warping (error-corrected H&C v2 n3 51 p54)	Frey, Berta	√	√	H&C	2	1		Wi 50	29
Warps and Warping: Problems/Solutions	Second Week, The	Redding, Debbie	√	√	Hw	5	3		Su 84	28
Warps and Warping: Problems/Solutions	Solving a Difficult Warping Problem	Greer, Gertrude G.	√	√	H&C	2	3		Su 51	44
Warps and Warping: Reel, Horizontal	Warping with a Horizontal Reel	Tidball, Harriet	√	√	H&C	10	4		Fa 59	16
Warps and Warping: Rigid-Heddle Loom	Rigid-Heddle Loom Warping	Davenport, Betty	√	√	Hw	3	3		My 82	73
Warps and Warping: Sectional	Engineers Approach to Sectional Warping, An	Groth, Paul E.	√	√	Hw	7	4		S/O 86	16
Warps and Warping: Sectional	Sectional Warp Beam	Russell, Harold W.; Fred J. Ahrens	√	√	SS&D	5	2	18	Sp 74	25
Warps and Warping: Sectional	Sectional Warping Simplified	Granberg, Carol	√	√	H&C	6	1		Wi 54	49
Warps and Warping: Sectional	Sectional Warping Without Spools	Gubser, Elsie H.	√	√	H&C	8	1		Wi 56	50
Warps and Warping: Sectional	Solving a Warping Problem	Nunnelly, Gordon M., M. D.	√		H&C	9	4		Fa 58	29
Warps and Warping: Sectional Beam	Method for Warping a Sectional Beam	Karlin, Edith	√	√	SS&D	5	3	19	Su 74	59
Warps and Warping: Sectional Warping	Everything A Weaver Should Know About Warps and Warping: Sectional Warping	Zielinski, S. A.; Robert Leclerc, ed.		√	MWL	5			'51–'73	29
Warps and Warping: Sectional Warping	Handweaver's Instruction Manual: Dressing the Loom, Sectional Warping	Tidball, Harriet C. nee Douglas	√	√	SCGM		34		49	15
Warps and Warping: Sectional Warping	Treasury for Beginners: Sectional Warping	Zielinski, S. A.; Robert Leclerc, ed.		√	MWL	1			'51–'73	12
Warps and Warping: Silk	Handweaving with Silk	Derr, Mary		√	WJ	3	2	10	Oc 78	40
Warps and Warping: Silk	Sensuous Silk	West, Virginia	√		Hw	7	1		J/F 86	52
Warps and Warping: Sizing	Warp Sizing	Adams, Brucie		√	Hw	6	3		Su 85	79
Warps and Warping: Sleying	Handweaver's Instruction Manual: Dressing the Loom, Chain Warping, Sleying	Tidball, Harriet C. nee Douglas		√	SCGM		34		49	14
Warps and Warping: Spaced Warp	Notebook: Plain Weave on Spaced Warp (Alice Johnson)	Myers, Ruth, ed.	√	√	SS&D	12	3	47	Su 81	67
Warps and Warping: Spaced Warp	Two Unusual Multishaft Curtains	Xenakis, Athanasios David	√	>4	PWC	4	1	11		40
Warps and Warping: Spools	Farmcraft Story, The	Whittemore, A. P., Jr.	√		H&C	7	4		Fa 56	27
Warps and Warping: Stripes	How to Warp a Stripe			√	Hw	2	1		F-W 80	57
Warps and Warping: Stuffer Warp	Two-Tie Unit for Rugs: Part 2 Warping and Weaving Methods, The	Windeknecht, Margaret	√	>4	SS&D	16	2	62	Sp 85	34
Warps and Warping: Stuffer Warps	Hand Woven Rugs: Weaves, Two-Warp Weave	Atwater, Mary Meigs			SCGM		29		48	21
Warps and Warping: Supplementary Warp	Supplementary Warp Patterns		√	>4	WJ	2	3	7	Ja 78	26
Warps and Warping: Supplementary Warps	If You Have 4 Harnesses	Hagarty, Harriet May		√	H&C	24	2		M/A 73	44
Warps and Warping: Syncopation Method	Verticals	O'Shaughnessy, Marjorie	√	>4	SS&D	15	1	57	Wi 83	8
Warps and Warping: Tape Loom	Setting Up a Tape Loom	Crawford, Grace Post	√	√	H&C	12	1		Wi 61	19
Warps and Warping: Tapestry Loom	Contemporary Tapestry	Tidball, Harriet	√	√	SCGM		12		64	13

SUBJECT	TITLE	AUTHOR	IL	INST	JOUR	VOL	NO	ISS	DATE	PAGE
Warps and Warping: Technique	Webschule Sindelfingen	McKeown, Alice	√	√	SS&D	6	3	23	Su 75	8
Warps and Warping: Techniques	Easy Warping Without a Cross	Best, Eleanor	√	√	SS&D	15	1	57	Wi 83	15
Warps and Warping: Techniques	Everything A Weaver Should Know About Warps and Warping: Warping & Warping Equipment	Zielinski, S. A.; Robert Leclerc, ed.	√	√	MWL	5			'51–'73	7
Warps and Warping: Techniques	Everything A Weaver Should Know About Warps and Warping: Warps Without Equipment	Zielinski, S. A.; Robert Leclerc, ed.	√	√	MWL	5			'51–'73	77
Warps and Warping: Techniques	Great Warping War, The	Sullivan, Donna; Madelyn van der Hoogt	√		PWC	5	2	16		12
Warps and Warping: Techniques	Integrated Approach to Warping, An	Schulz, Peter		√	Hw	3	3		My 82	30
Warps and Warping: Techniques	Loom Set Up for Sample and Short Warps, A	Blumenau, Lili	√	√	H&C	7	3		Su 56	30
Warps and Warping: Techniques	Ruana for Beginners, A	Rose, Violet	√	√	Hw	8	4		S/O 87	48
Warps and Warping: Techniques	Treasury for Beginners: More About Warping	Zielinski, S. A.; Robert Leclerc, ed.		√	MWL	1			'51–'73	78
Warps and Warping: Techniques	Unique Method of Warping, A	Frey, Berta	√	√	H&C	6	1		Wi 54	60
Warps and Warping: Techniques	Warping: A Compleat Guide	Patrick, Jane	√	√	Hw	3	3		My 82	64
Warps and Warping: Techniques, Double-Warp	Double-Warp Weaving from Harriet Tidball's Looms	Bryan, Dorothy	√	√	H&C	5	4		Fa 54	15
Warps and Warping: Tension	Second Week, The	Redding, Debbie	√	√	Hw	5	3		Su 84	28
Warps and Warping: Tension	Tension	Chandler, Deborah			Hw	7	2		M/A 86	21
Warps and Warping: Tension Control	Doup Leno: Sample Project, Jumpers	Skowronski, Hella; Sylvia Tacker	√	√	SCGM		32		80	19
Warps and Warping: Tension Problems	Supplementary Warp Patterning: Tension Problems	Tidball, Harriet	√	√	SCGM		17		66	7
Warps and Warping: Threading	Handweaver's Instruction Manual: Dressing the Loom, Chain Warping, Threading	Tidball, Harriet C. nee Douglas		√	SCGM		34		49	14
Warps and Warping: Tie-Downs	Touch of Fur, A	Dickey, Enola	√	√	SS&D	8	4	32	Fa 77	85
Warps and Warping: Tie-In	Handweaver's Instruction Manual: Dressing the Loom, Chain Warping, The Tie-In	Tidball, Harriet C. nee Douglas	√	√	SCGM		34		49	15
Warps and Warping: Tricks	Warping: A Compleat Guide	Patrick, Jane	√	√	Hw	3	3		My 82	71
Warps and Warping: Triple Warp	Sheila O'Hara: Triangles, Squares and Other Landmarks	Draheim, Teliha	√		Iw	6	1		Wi 80	42
Warps and Warping: Triple Warp	Sheila O'Hara's Geometrics	Rowley, Kathleen M.	√		SS&D	12	4	48	Fa 81	20
Warps and Warping: Triple Warp Tensions	Bedford Cord Piqué	Xenakis, Athanasios David; Madelyn van der Hoogt	√	>4	PWC	4	3	13		42
Warps and Warping: Tubular Project	Textured Cottons: Seamless, No-Sweat Shirt	Rasmussen, Peg	√	√	WJ	6	3	23	Wi 81	25
Warps and Warping: Two Warps, Two Tensions	Figured Piqué	Xenakis, Athanasios David	√	√	PWC	4	2	12		12
Warps and Warping: Two-Warp Technique	Hand Woven Rugs: Weaves, Two-Warp Weave	Atwater, Mary Meigs			SCGM		29		48	21
Warps and Warping: Two-Warp Technique, Hanging Beam	Supplementary Warp Patterning: Handling Two Warps, A Hanging Beam	Tidball, Harriet		√	SCGM		17		66	6
Warps and Warping: Two-Warp Technique, Simultaneous	Supplementary Warp Patterning: Handling Two Warps, Simultaneous Warping	Tidball, Harriet		√	SCGM		17		66	6
Warps and Warping: Two-Warp Technique, Two Beams	Supplementary Warp Patterning: Handling Two Warps, Two-Beam Warping	Tidball, Harriet		√	SCGM		17		66	6
Warps and Warping: Two-Warp Technique, Weighted Chains	Supplementary Warp Patterning: Handling Two Warps, Weighted Chains	Tidball, Harriet	√	√	SCGM		17		66	6
Warps and Warping: Two-Warp Technique, Weighted Threads	Supplementary Warp Patterning: Handling Two Warps, Weighted Threads	Tidball, Harriet		√	SCGM		17		66	6
Warps and Warping: Two-Warps, One Beam	Weaving Figured Piqué on a Loom with One Warp Beam	Xenakis, Athanasios David	√	√	PWC	4	2	12		14
Warps and Warping: Variations	One Warp, Many Fabrics	Liebler, Barbara	√	>4	Iw	3	1		Fa 77	28
Warps and Warping: Variegated Yarn	Party Ensemble with Style		√	√	Hw	6	3		Su 85	44

SUBJECT	TITLE	AUTHOR	IL	INST	JOUR	VOL	NO	ISS	DATE	PAGE
Warps and Warping: Warp, Weighted	Beiderwand Made Easy: An Old Weave Adapts to Four-Harness (revision SS&D v7 n4 76 p27)	Gordon, Judith	√	√	SS&D	7	3	27	Su 76	68
Warps and Warping: Winding Warp	Handweaver's Instruction Manual: Dressing the Loom, Chain Warping, Winding the Warp	Tidball, Harriet C. nee Douglas		√	SCGM		34		49	13
Warps: Painted	Painted Warps	Marston, Ena			H&C	21	4		Fa 70	37
Warps: Pulled	Weaving Primer, Part 3	Xenakis, Athanasios David	√	>4	PWC	4	1	11		46
Warps: Variations	Variations on One Warp	Alvic, Philis	√		SS&D	12	4	48	Fa 81	70
Warps: Weighted	More Creative Two Harness Weaving	Liebler, Barbara	√		Iw	5	1		Wi 79	46
Warps: Weighted	Seersucker Blazer, A	Johannesen, Betty	√	√	WJ	8	3	31	Wi 83	22
Warps: Weighted	Supplementary Warp Patterns		√	>4	WJ	2	3	7	Ja 78	26
Warps/Wefts: Distorted	Manipulated Warps or Having Fun with Controlled Distortion	Foster, Robert	√		H&C	16	2		Sp 65	12
Washfastness	Testing Washfastness		√	√	TM			7	O/N 86	6
Washing: Knitting	Putting Knitted Pieces Together	Guagliumi, Susan	√	√	TM			11	J/J 87	45
Washing: Silk	Sensuous Silk	West, Virginia	√		Hw	7	1		J/F 86	52
Water: Chemical and Physical Properties	Principles of Textile Conservation Science, No. 6. The Wonders of Water in Wetcleaning	Rice, James W.	√	√	TMJ	2	1		De 66	15
Watteau Paintings: Fashion Inspiration	When Is Art Fashion and Fashion Art?	Martin, Richard	√		TM			11	J/J 87	12
Waulking	Waulking Tweeds at the Marshfield School of Weaving	Gallagher, Kate	√		Hw	6	4		S/O 85	10
Wax: Removal	Wax Removal			√	TM			5	J/J 86	10
Wearable Art	Ana Lisa Hedstrom: The Intuitive Language of Shibori	Scarborough, Jessica	√		Fa	13	1		J/F 86	26
Wearable Art	Art As Clothing: Clothing As Art		√		SS&D	12	1	45	Wi 80	85
Wearable Art	"Art to Wear" (Exhibit)	Murray, Megan	√		Fa	11	1		J/F 84	76
Wearable Art	Art to Wear: Looking At the Movement	Scarborough, Jessica	√		Fa	12	3		M/J 85	56
Wearable Art	Art Wear of Peggy Juve, The	Tacker, Sylvia	√		Fa	14	1		J/F 87	25
Wearable Art	"Artwear '87" (Exhibit)		√		Fa	14	2		M/A 87	58
Wearable Art	Collegiate Fashion Show Highlights Textile Program	Belfer, Nancy	√		Fa	14	1		J/F 87	6
Wearable Art	For the Body (error-corrected Fa v10 n2 83 p61)		√		Fa	10	1		J/F 83	32
Wearable Art	"German Wearable Textiles" (Exhibit)	Van Til, Reinder	√		Fa	12	6		N/D 85	59
Wearable Art	New Elegance: Contemporary Art Wear, The	Van Artsdalen, Martha	√		SS&D	16	1	61	Wi 84	50
Wearable Art	"New Elegance: Contemporary Wearable Art, The" (Exhibit)	Malarcher, Patricia	√		Fa	12	4		J/A 85	44
Wearable Art	Painted-Silk Clothing	Juve, Peggy	√	√	TM			12	A/S 87	24
Wearable Art	Rag Trade, The	Weissman, Julia	√		Kn	1	2	2	S-S 85	53
Wearable Art	Return of the Rag, The	Basa, Lynn	√		Fa	14	3		M/J 87	29
Wearable Art	Roots of Wearables, The	Creager, Clara			TM			14	D/J 87	16
Wearable Art	Tapestries to Wear	Mayer, Anita Luvera	√	√	Hw	5	5		N/D 84	54
Wearable Art	Theme Issue		√		Fa	12	3		M/J 85	
Wearable Art	Under Wraps		√		Fa	12	3		M/J 85	26
Wearable Art	Wearable Art at P. S. 152	Wallach, Nancy	√		Fa	7	6		N/D 80	25
Wearable Art	"Wearable Art" (Exhibit)	Hunt, E. Ann	√		Fa	6	3		M/J 79	78
Wearable Art	Wearable Fine Thread Tapestries	Tidwell, Elmyra	√	√	WJ	10	3	39	Wi 86	34
Wearable Art	Weaver Profile: Mahota Handwovens	Irwin, Bobbie	√		Hw	8	5		N/D 87	35
Wearable Art: Buttons	Buttons: Wearable Art in Miniature	Epstein, Diana	√		Fa	12	3		M/J 85	61
Wearable Books	Limited Editions: The Wearable Books of Lois Morrison	Rudich, Sally	√		Fa	12	3		M/J 85	91
Wearable Folk Art	"Wearable Folk Art" (Exhibit)	Dyer, Carolyn	√		Fa	6	3		M/J 79	82
Wearables	Adinkra: Weft African Textile of Pride	Rex, Chris	√		Fa	9	6		N/D 82	36

SUBJECT	TITLE	AUTHOR	IL	INST	JOUR	VOL	NO	ISS	DATE	PAGE
Wearables	Ann Matlock	Erler, Mary	√		Fa	6	3		M/J 79	46
Wearables	"Art Couture '82" (Exhibit)	Guagliumi, Sasan	√		Fa	10	1		J/F 83	84
Wearables	"Art Couture VII" (Exhibit)	Guagliumi, Susan Fletcher	√		Fa	12	3		M/J 85	78
Wearables	"Art Couture/Haute Couture" (Exhibit)	McGuire, Patricia	√		Fa	9	1		J/F 82	86
Wearables	Art to Wear — Three Innovators: Cate Fitt, Emma Vesey, Dina Schwartz Knapp		√		Fa	8	1		J/F 81	67
Wearables	Carol Klippenstein		√		Fa	4	4		J/A 77	48
Wearables	"Ch'ing Dynasty Court Robes, A Splendorous Sampling" (Exhibit)	Marcoux, Alice	√		Fa	11	2		M/A 84	78
Wearables	Cindy Fornari: Painted Warps		√		Fa	3	5		S/O 76	30
Wearables	Contemporary California Costume	Poon, Vivian	√		Fa	11	5		S/O 84	53
Wearables	Conversing with Artist John Eric Broaddus	Stackel, I. M.	√		Fa	11	5		S/O 84	28
Wearables	Creative Process: Katherine Westphal, The	Westphal, Katherine	√		Fa	11	6		N/D 84	32
Wearables	Cynthia Pannucci: Relocating, Creating, Connecting	Mattera, Joanne	√		Fa	9	3		M/J 82	23
Wearables	Elizabeth Coleman and the Not-So-Homely Art of Sewing	Coleman, Elizabeth	√		Fa	6	3		M/J 79	29
Wearables	"Fabric/Nexus: New Connections" (Exhibit)	Moldovan, George	√		Fa	10	3		M/J 83	70
Wearables	"Fantasy Clothes/Fantastic Costumes" (Exhibit)	Dyer, Carolyn	√		Fa	4	2		M/A 77	11
Wearables	"Felt and Papermaking" (Exhibit)	Harrison, Helen A.	√		Fa	11	2		M/A 84	79
Wearables	"Fiber from the Marietta College Crafts National" (Exhibit)	Murray, Megan	√		Fa	11	2		M/A 84	76
Wearables	Folkwear: In the Company of Some Friends		√		Fa	3	5		S/O 76	36
Wearables	Garment Form As Image, The	Koplos, Janet	√		Fa	10	6		N/D 83	66
Wearables	Garments from the Loom: Handweaver Randall Darwall Focuses on the Cloth	Mattera, Joanne	√		Fa	10	1		J/F 83	20
Wearables	Handcrafted Clothing Construction: Some Considerations	Peterson, Jill	√		Fa	3	5		S/O 76	32
Wearables	If the Art Fits – Wear It! — Friends of the Rag	Strosnider, Ann	√		Fa	6	3		M/J 79	35
Wearables	Instant Gratification: Susan Summa Tells How and Why She Learned to Love the Knitting Machine	Summa, Susan	√		Fa	8	5		S/O 81	56
Wearables	Interview with Jhane Barnes: Designer, Weaver, Spinner, An	Lonier, Terri	√		Fa	10	4		J/A 83	55
Wearables	Jane Rake's Crochet	Dunn, Katherine	√		Fa	6	3		M/J 79	62
Wearables	Janet Higgins: Soft Sculpture in Motion	Marquess, Joyce	√		Fa	7	2		M/A 80	62
Wearables	Jo Diggs: An Interview with a Very Talented Woman		√		Fa	3	5		S/O 76	24
Wearables	"Joan Steiner: Hats/New Sculpture" (Exhibit)	Katz, Ruth J.	√		Fa	7	5		S/O 80	72
Wearables	K. Lee Manuel: Wearable Dreams		√		Fa	3	5		S/O 76	12
Wearables	Knitting Craft in Great Britain, The	Kinder, Kathleen	√		Fa	11	4		J/A 84	42
Wearables	Maralyce Ferree: Dual-Purpose Weavings	Mimoso, Sophie	√		Fa	7	2		M/A 80	12
Wearables	Margot Carter Blair		√	√	Fa	4	3		M/J 77	28
Wearables	Maria da Conceicao: A Modern Romantic	Hecker, Carolyn	√		Fa	6	3		M/J 79	58
Wearables	Marian Clayden's Clothing for Collectors	Park, Betty	√		Fa	6	3		M/J 79	55
Wearables	Marvelous Mezzaro, The	Wasiqullah, Alexandra	√		Fa	10	5		S/O 83	29
Wearables	"Maximum Coverage: Wearables by Contemporary American Artists" (Exhibit)	Risseeuw, Mary	√		Fa	8	1		J/F 81	93
Wearables	Method to Her Madness: Jane Lang Axtell's Seminole Patchwork, A	Buscho, Ann	√		Fa	8	1		J/F 81	31
Wearables	"Paper Clothing and More in San Francisco" (Exhibit)	Scarborough, Jessica	√		Fa	11	2		M/A 84	75
Wearables	Paper Clothing, East	Sahlstrand, Margaret	√	√	Fa	11	2		M/A 84	36

SUBJECT	TITLE	AUTHOR	IL	INST	JOUR	VOL	NO	ISS	DATE	PAGE
Wearables	Paper Clothing: West	Koplos, Janet	√		Fa	11	2		M/A 84	39
Wearables	Pleats, Pleats, Pleats: For Sculptural Garments and Sculpture Itself		√		Fa	9	1		J/F 82	40
Wearables	"Poetry for the Body, Clothing for the Spirit" (Exhibit)	Hickman, Pat	√		Fa	10	5		S/O 83	75
Wearables	"Power Garments" (Exhibit)	Papa, Nancy	√		Fa	5	1		J/F 78	13
Wearables	Recent Success of Carole Lubove-Klein: An Inspiring Yarn, The	McGuire, Patricia	√		Fa	9	5		S/O 82	20
Wearables	Robes for Inspiration	Dyer, Carolyn	√		Fa	10	1		J/F 83	60
Wearables	Ruth and David Segunda		√		Fa	4	6		N/D 77	62
Wearables	"Salute to California: Fifty Years of Fashion, 1930–1980" (Exhibit)	Dyer, Carolyn	√		Fa	8	1		J/F 81	95
Wearables	Sampler of Surface Design, A	Westphal, Katherine	√		Fa	10	5		S/O 83	39
Wearables	Santa Fe Weaving Center, The	Elliott, Malinda	√		Fa	9	5		S/O 82	32
Wearables	Seamstress...Sorceress...Artist	Lowell-LaRoque, Jane	√		Fa	7	3		M/J 80	29
Wearables	Sensuous Silk: Cedrus Monte's Painted Silk Garments	Gilliland, David	√		Fa	8	1		J/F 81	17
Wearables	Silken Gowns of Candiss Cole, The	Paqua, Al	√		Fa	6	3		M/J 79	41
Wearables	Sue Nechin of First Additions	Koplos, Janet	√		Fa	10	1		J/F 83	69
Wearables	Surface Design and the Garment Form	Reith, Stephanie J.	√		Fa	8	1		J/F 81	34
Wearables	T-Shirts for Every Body: 20th Century Folkwear		√		Fa	8	6		N/D 81	22
Wearables	Teresa Nomura: Fabric and Fantasy	Sage, Jan	√		Fa	11	5		S/O 84	20
Wearables	Theme Issue		√		Fa	6	3		M/J 79	
Wearables	Theme Issue		√		Fa	8	1		J/F 81	
Wearables	Three Personal Statements: Norma Minkowitz, Gillian Bull, Mardel Esping		√		Fa	3	5		S/O 76	19
Wearables	Tim Harding: Garments of Paradox	Theil, Linda	√		Fa	9	6		N/D 82	20
Wearables	Touch of the Poet: Wearables by Denise Welsh-May, A	Park, Betty	√		Fa	6	6		N/D 79	52
Wearables	Very Special Craftswoman: Maria Consuelo Moya, A		√		Fa	3	2		M/A 76	32
Wearables	Wear an Original Painting: Melody Weiler's Airbrushed Shirtscapes	Speight, Jerry	√	√	Fa	8	1		J/F 81	13
Wearables	Wearables	Luddecke, Jane	√		Fa	6	3		M/J 79	27
Wearables	"Wearables" (Exhibit)	Grover, Donald	√		Fa	6	6		N/D 79	76
Wearables	Wearables in the Market Place: Reporting on a Survey	Dunnewold, Jane	√		Fa	12	3		M/J 85	48
Wearables	Weaving Workshop with Barbara Wittenberg: Sharing is Pervasive, A	Aikin, Patti	√		Fa	8	4		J/A 81	21
Wearables	Who, How, What, and When of Wearables, The	Grover, Donald	√		Fa	6	3		M/J 79	66
Wearables	Words in Fiber	Rowley, Kathleen	√		Fa	11	2		M/A 84	66
Wearables	Yvonne Porcella		√		Fa	4	5		S/O 77	52
Wearables	Yvonne Porcella: A Modern Master of the Ethnic Clothing Tradition	Avery, Virginia	√		Fa	8	1		J/F 81	63
Wearables: Abstract	Abstracted Wearables (Exhibit)				Fa	14	2		M/A 87	61
Wearables: Crochet	Crocheting Wearable Fabric	McGoveran, Mary	√	√	TM			9	F/M 87	62
Wearables: Handwoven	Handwoven Clothing Today: The Couturier Touch	West, Virginia	√		Fa	8	1		J/F 81	39
Wearables: Machine-Knit	Ellen Liss: Machine-Knit Wearables	Goodman, Deborah Lerme	√		Fa	11	4		J/A 84	16
Wearables: Painted Silk	Painted-Silk Clothing	Juve, Peggy	√	√	TM			12	A/S 87	24
Wearables: Pattern Sources	Who, How, What, and When of Wearables, The	Grover, Donald	√		Fa	6	3		M/J 79	66
Wearables: Quilted	Fashionable Quilts	Wolff, Colette	√		TM			10	A/M 87	16
Wearables: Soft Sculpture	Susanmarie Cunningham: Wearable Soft Sculpture	Cunningham, Susanmarie	√		Fa	11	5		S/O 84	15
Wearables, Tapestry	Wearable Fine Thread Tapestries	Tidwell, Elmyra	√	√	WJ	10	3	39	Wi 86	34

SUBJECT	TITLE	AUTHOR	IL	INST	JOUR	VOL	NO	ISS	DATE	PAGE
Wearables: Unwearable, Screen	Debra Chase: Unwearable Wearables	Lonier, Terri	√		Fa	12	3		M/J 85	12
Weave Classifications	Exploring Weaving Techniques	Larsen, Jack Lenor	√		H&C	3	4		Fa 52	4
Weave Classifications	Handloom Weaves: Classification of Handloom Weaves	Tidball, Harriet			SCGM		33		57	3
Weave Classifications: Introduction	Handloom Weaves: Introduction to the Classification	Tidball, Harriet			SCGM		33		57	2
Weave Identification Key	More About Fabrics: Key to Weaves	Zielinski, S. A.; Robert Leclerc, ed.		√	MWL	20			'51–'73	5
Weave Patterns: Ancient Rose	Exploring the Possibilities of Ancient Rose	Wells, Elizabeth	√	√	H&C	11	1		Wi 60	22
Weave Patterns: Blooming Leaf	Blooming Leaf	Xenakis, Athanasios David	√	√	PWC	3	3	9		51
Weave Patterns: Blooming Leaf of Mexico	Blouse for Her — A Shirt for Him, A		√	√	WJ	4	3	15	Ja 80	4
Weave Patterns: Bound Weave	Christmas Card, A		√	> 4	WJ	2	2	6	Oc 77	32
Weave Patterns: Compass and Double Square	New Zealand Interpretation of Compass and Double Square, A		√	√	H&C	8	4		Fa 57	20
Weave Patterns: Double Chariot Wheel	Coverlet: Make Someday Today, Start a Coverlet, A	van der Hoogt, Madelyn	√	√	PWC	5	1	15		24
Weave Patterns: Eight-Pointed Star	Three Faces of the Eight-Pointed Star Motif (error-corrected SS&D v14 n4 83 p4)	Coffman, Charlotte	√	√	SS&D	14	3	55	Su 83	56
Weave Patterns: Goose-Foot	Keep Warm! Large Rectangular Shawl	Sylvan, Katherine	√	> 4	WJ	5	2	18	Fa 80	10
Weave Patterns: Honeysuckle	Garments with Ethnic Flavor: Ethnic Dress with Supplementary Warp		√	√	WJ	2	3	7	Ja 78	14
Weave Patterns: Honeysuckle	Mood Lamp	Richards, Iris	√	√	WJ	3	2	10	Oc 78	44
Weave Patterns: Honeysuckle	Supplementary Warp Patterns		√	> 4	WJ	2	3	7	Ja 78	26
Weave Patterns: Honeysuckle	Variations in the Honeysuckle Design	Frey, Berta	√	> 4	H&C	1	3		Fa 50	26
Weave Patterns: Krokbrågd Figures	Three and Four Harness Krokbragd (error-corrected PWC i4 83 p76)	Temple, Mary	√	√	PWC			3	Oc 82	56
Weave Patterns: Monk's Belt	Supplementary Warp Patterns		√	> 4	WJ	2	3	7	Ja 78	26
Weave Patterns: Queen Anne's Pattern	Queen Anne's Pattern	Wood, Gerry	√	> 4	H&C	10	4		Fa 59	15
Weave Patterns: Rosepath	Accessories: Large Bags Made from Narrow Strips		√	√	WJ	2	4	8	Ap 78	6
Weave Patterns: Rosepath	From Elsie H. Gubser's Studio		√	> 4	H&C	7	3		Su 56	24
Weave Patterns: Rosepath	Garments Made from Simple Patterns: Two Tabards		√	> 4	WJ	2	3	7	Ja 78	35
Weave Patterns: Rosepath	Rosepath		√		Hw	7	2		M/A 86	60
Weave Patterns: Rosepath	Versatile Rosepath		√		Hw	6	2		M/A 85	54
Weave Patterns: Rosepath	Weaving Skirts	Wood, Gerry	√	> 4	H&C	9	4		Fa 58	18
Weave Patterns: Rosepath, Variations	Drafting Plans for 4-Harness Rosepath Motifs	Strickler, Carol	√	√	SS&D	5	1	17	Wi 73	58
Weave Patterns: Rosepath, Vertical	Midwest Conference Presents Sources of Inspiration for Color		√	> 4	H&C	13	4		Fa 62	18
Weave Patterns: Rosepath, Vertical	Three Swedish Weaves	af Kleen, Elizabeth	√		H&C	12	1		Wi 61	14
Weave Patterns: Sewing	Sewing Swimsuits	Callaway, Grace	√	√	TM			5	J/J 86	24
Weave Patterns: Star and Diamond	Designs from Serff Patterns	Abel, Isabel I.	√	> 4	H&C	11	4		Fa 60	6
Weave Patterns: Star and Diamond	Peter Stauffer — Early 19th Century Weaver	Rogers, Grace L.	√	> 4	H&C	7	1		Wi 55	12
Weave Patterns: Star and Diamond	Star and Diamond	Xenakis, Athanasios David	√	√	PWC	3	3	9		49
Weave Patterns: Star Patterns	Coverlet Weaves Using Two Ties	Barrett, Clotilde	√	> 4	WJ	3	4	12	Ap 79	26
Weave Patterns: Wheel of Fortune	Designing Rugs for Harness-Controlled Weaving		√	> 4	WJ	4	4	16	Ap 80	27
Weave Patterns: Whig Rose	Variations on Whig Rose	Kaiser, Eunice Gifford	√	√	H&C	14	1		Wi 63	17
Weave Structure also see Combined Structures; Specific Structures										

SUBJECT	TITLE	AUTHOR	IL	INST	JOUR	VOL	NO	ISS	DATE	PAGE
Weave Structures	Designing the Warp: Parallel Considerations	Criscola, Jeanne	√	√	TM			1	O/N 85	66
Weaver Bird Nest	Weaver Bird Nest—Ploceidae Family	Romey, Lucretia	√		SS&D	6	3	23	Su 75	7
"Weaver Rose"	One Hundred Years Ago in Handweaving				Hw	7	3		M/J 86	27
Weaver Rose (see Rose, William Henry Harrison)										
Weaver/Designer	Marianne Granville, Designer with Old World Background	Harvey, Jane	√		H&C	16	4		Fa 65	16
Weaver/Designer	Weaving a Lifestyle: Cynthia Schira	Schira, Cynthia	√		Iw	5	2		Sp 80	27
Weaver/Designer	Weaving a Lifestyle: Malin Selander	West, Virginia	√		Iw	5	2		Sp 80	30
Weaver/Spinner	Persis Grayson, Weaver & Spinner	Amos, Mary Alice	√		H&C	19	1		Wi 68	10
Weaver/Teacher	Conversation with Mary Andrews, A	Pinchin, Bryn	√		Iw	5	4		Fa 80	24
Weaver/Teacher	Mary Snyder	Pinchin, Bryn	√		Iw	5	2		Sp 80	47
Weaver/Writer	Jean Wilson	Rush, Beverly	√		Iw	5	2		Sp 80	43
Weavers	What's Wrong with Being a Weaver?	Kniskern, Verne B.	√		Hw	8	2		M/A 87	10
Weavers: 18th Century	Eighteenth Century German Court Weaver: Johann Michael Frickinger, An	Hilts, Patricia	√		SS&D	11	4	44	Fa 80	16
Weavers: 18th Century	In Search of Jacob Angstadt: A Master Weaver Lives Again		√		SS&D	7	2	26	Sp 76	27
Weavers: 19th Century	Designs from Serff Patterns	Abel, Isabel I.	√	> 4	H&C	11	4		Fa 60	6
Weavers: 19th Century	Peter Stauffer — Early 19th Century Weaver	Rogers, Grace L.	√	> 4	H&C	7	1		Wi 55	12
Weavers: Blind	Haptic Visions	Brubaker, Paul			WJ	11	4	44	Sp 87	59
Weavers: Blind	Klara Johnson: A Weaver's Vision Realized	Magoffin, Connie	√	√	WJ	11	4	44	Sp 87	62
Weavers: Contemporary	Some Contemporary Weavers in Northern California	Bryan, Dorothy	√		H&C	1	3		Fa 50	9
Weavers: Contemporary	Weaver Craftsman in the Contemporary Scene, The	Blumenau, Lili	√		H&C	1	1		Ap 50	13
Weavers: Differences	Looming Thoughts	Fannin, Allen; Dorothy Fannin			H&C	23	5		S/O 72	5
Weavers in Literature	Burls	Bogle, Michael			SS&D	11	4	44	Fa 80	35
Weavers of Rabun	Mary Crovatt Hambidge	Schaller, Karin	√		Fa	11	5		S/O 84	24
Weavers of Rabun	Weavers of Rabun, The		√		H&C	7	2		Sp 56	6
Weavers' School, The	Weaving Places	Xenakis, Alexis Yiorgos	√		PWC	4	2	12		28
Weavers: Serious	Looming Thoughts	Fannin, Allen; Dorothy Fannin			H&C	23	6		N/D 72	37
Weaver's Knot	Handweaver's Instruction Manual: Dressing the Loom, Correcting Errors, Weaver's Knot	Tidball, Harriet C. nee Douglas	√	√	SCGM		34		49	17
Weaver's Knot	Weaver's Knot, The	Jarvis, P. R.	√	√	Iw	5	3		Su 80	63
Weaving	Complete Pleasure of Weaving, The	MacInnes, Ginger	√		H&C	7	2		Sp 56	13
Weaving	Weaving — A Delicate Balance	Ginsberg-Place, Ruth	√		H&C	23	4		J/A 72	43
Weaving	Why Do You Want to Weave?	Frey, Berta			H&C	3	4		Fa 52	16
Weaving: 17th Century	Some Remarks on the Work of Markham	Stanton, R. G.; J. L. Allston	√	√	AT	2			De 84	95
Weaving: 19th Century	Weaver Rose — A New Perspective	Kaye, Alda Ganze	√		SS&D	8	2	30	Sp 77	8
Weaving: Abroad	Weaving Abroad II	Huebner, Marianne	√		H&C	21	4		Fa 70	21
Weaving, America, 18th Century	Handweaving and the Powerloom in 18th Century America	Cooper, Grace Rogers	√		H&C	22	4		Fa 71	5
Weaving: Bedouin	Weaving in the Desert: How Bedouin Women Make a Loom, Using Sticks and Rebars	Erickson, Janet Doub	√	√	TM			10	A/M 87	56
Weaving, Beginning	Another Loom Another Tote Bag, Rug Sampler Project for Beginners	Krasnoff, Julienne	√	√	H&C	22	1		Wi 71	32
Weaving, Beginning	Beginning Weavers, More Than One Answer to Many Questions	Frey, Berta		√	H&C	14	1		Wi 63	9
Weaving, Beginning	For Beginning Weavers — What Yarns Can I Use?	Frey, Berta	√	√	H&C	17	2		Sp 66	17

SUBJECT	TITLE	AUTHOR	IL	INST	JOUR	VOL	NO	ISS	DATE	PAGE
Weaving, Beginning	Notes for Beginning Weavers: A Teacher Offers Suggestions for Avoiding Errors	Frey, Berta			H&C	16	1		Wi 65	21
Weaving, Beginning	Notes for Beginning Weavers: Learning to Invent Your Own Shortcuts	Frey, Berta			H&C	16	3		Su 65	22
Weaving, Beginning	Notes for Beginning Weavers: Warping the Most Interesting Part of Weaving	Frey, Berta		√	H&C	16	2		Sp 65	20
Weaving: Beginning	Sampling Draft	Wilson, Particia		√	SS&D	2	2	6	Sp 71	12
Weaving, Beginning	Small Project in Bound Weave for Beginners, A	Krasnoff, Julienne H.	√	√	H&C	20	3		Su 69	13
Weaving, Beginning	Small Projects of Interest To Beginning Weavers	Freeman, Claire	√	√	H&C	20	4		Fa 69	9
Weaving, Beginning	Suggestions for the Beginning Weaver	Gulick, Evelyn M.	√	√	H&C	19	1		Wi 68	12
Weaving, Beginning	Treasury for Beginners: Weaves for Beginners	Zielinski, S. A.; Robert Leclerc, ed.		√	MWL	1			'51–'73	95
Weaving, Beginning	Weaving on a Frame		√		H&C	2	4		Fa 51	54
Weaving, Beginning	Weaving Primer	Ingebretsen, Catherine	√	√	PWC			6	Su 83	4
Weaving, Beginning	Woven Reed Placemats	Ingebretsen, Cathy	√	√	PWC	3	2	8		4
Weaving Centers	Allied Arts Guild	Bryan, Dorothy	√		H&C	8	1		Wi 56	20
Weaving Centers	Denmark's Vaeveboden	Hill, Patricia C.	√	> 4	H&C	5	2		Sp 54	16
Weaving Centers	Egyptian Tapestries by the Children of Harrania	Davis, Peter	√		H&C	14	4		Fa 63	9
Weaving Centers	Indian Textiles from Ecuador		√		H&C	10	1		Wi 59	19
Weaving Centers	Los Tejidos Nortenos	Ligon, Linda	√		Iw	1	4		Su 76	15
Weaving Centers	Nantucket Looms, Fabrics by Island Weavers in Restored Inn	Chesrown, Melva A.	√		H&C	14	4		Fa 63	6
Weaving Centers	Nantucket Looms, Versatile Uses for Island Fabrics		√		H&C	20	2		Sp 69	18
Weaving Centers	New Craft Program Will be Given on Nantucket Island		√		H&C	16	1		Wi 65	14
Weaving Centers	Plymouth Colony Farms		√		H&C	1	1		Ap 50	38
Weaving Centers	San Francisco's Yarn Depot		√		H&C	8	1		Wi 56	31
Weaving Centers	St. Mary's Weavers		√		H&C	10	1		Wi 59	30
Weaving Centers	Talbot Weavers' Golden Anniversary (error-corrected H&C v5 n4 54 p43)		√		H&C	5	3		Su 54	4
Weaving Centers	Two Weavers in a Trailer		√	> 4	H&C	4	2		Sp 53	20
Weaving Centers	Two Weavers in Washington	Arndt, Jessie Ash			H&C	20	4		Fa 69	20
Weaving Centers	Weavers of Rabun, The		√		H&C	7	2		Sp 56	6
Weaving Centers	Weaving at La Villita, School and Shop in Restored Village	Reed, J. H.	√		H&C	14	2		Sp 63	16
Weaving Centers	Weaving Center for Pasadena Girls	Barrett, Katharine A.	√		H&C	9	2		Sp 58	22
Weaving Centers	Yarn Depot, The		√		SS&D	1	1	1	De 69	9
Weaving Centers	Young Weavers in Kentucky		√		H&C	14	3		Su 63	45
Weaving Centers: Community	"Weave Ye Not In"		√		SS&D	4	2	14	Sp 73	10
Weaving Centers: Home	Planning a Home Weaving Center	Tidball, Harriet	√		H&C	6	4		Fa 55	18
Weaving Centers: Iran	Persian Handcrafted Items	Brockway, Edith	√		H&C	26	5		Oc 75	16
Weaving Centers: The Shuttle-Craft Guild	Weaving in the Far West		√		H&C	1	1		Ap 50	20
Weaving Centers: Truchas Weavers	Truchas Becomes a Weaving Center	Ehly, Jean	√		H&C	24	4		Au 73	40
Weaving Centers: Weavers of Rabun	Mary Crovatt Hambidge	Schaller, Karin	√		Fa	11	5		S/O 84	24
Weaving Chenille	Double Chenille Vest (Lucy Anne Jennings)		√	√	Hw	7	3		M/J 86	44, I-10
Weaving Chenille	Pile Weaves, Rugs and Tapestry: Chenille	Zielinski, S. A.; Robert Leclerc, ed.	√	√	MWL	14			'51–'73	26
Weaving Chenille	Pile Weaves, Rugs and Tapestry: The Ultimate in Chenille	Zielinski, S. A.; Robert Leclerc, ed.	√	√	MWL	14			'51–'73	49
Weaving: Chilkat	Totems in Tapestry	Swingle, Daphne	√		H&C	22	2		Sp 71	5
Weaving: Coded	Busy Signal	Krasnoff, Julienne	√	> 4	SS&D	2	4	8	Fa 71	9

SUBJECT	TITLE	AUTHOR	IL	INST	JOUR	VOL	NO	ISS	DATE	PAGE
Weaving: Coded	Contemporary Approach to Traditional Weaves: Code in Overshot	Zielinski, S. A.; Robert Leclerc, ed.	√	√	MWL	7			'51–'73	83
Weaving: Coded	Hanging Based on HGA Name Draft to Decorate New Offices	Fuchs, Rudolph	√	√	SS&D	5	4	20	Fa 74	14
Weaving: Coded	Linbogarn Shirt	Scorgie, Jean	√	√	WJ	7	1	25	Su 82	53
Weaving: Coded	Merry Christmas—A Name Draft	Bliven, Jeanette; Norma Smayda	√	√	Hw	4	4		S/O 83	74
Weaving: Coded	Miniature Musical Drafts	Newman, Margaret	√	√	SS&D	4	4	16	Fa 73	70
Weaving: Coded	Name Drafting	Mitchell, Peter	√	√	Hw	3	2		Mr 82	34
Weaving: Coded	Resist Dyeing, Curiosities and Inventions: Coded Weaving	Zielinski, S. A.; Robert Leclerc, ed.	√	√	MWL	17			'51–'73	65
Weaving: Coded	Weaving Music	Henneberger, Karel	√	> 4	SS&D	16	4	64	Fa 85	6
Weaving: Coded	What's in a Name? Name Drafts Drawn by Hand or Computer	Mansfield, Susan	√	√	WJ	10	3	39	Wi 86	15
Weaving: Coded, Name Drafts	Name Draft (error-corrected WJ v8 n3 83 p68)		√	√	WJ	8	2	30	Fa 83	40
Weaving: Coded, Numerical	Composition and Designing Part 2: Numerical Patterns	Zielinski, S. A.; Robert Leclerc, ed.	√	√	MWL	19			'51–'73	40
Weaving: Coded, Random Numbers	Composition and Designing Part 2: Four Shaft Random Drafts Woven-As-Drawn-In	Zielinski, S. A.; Robert Leclerc, ed.	√	√	MWL	19			'51–'73	98
Weaving: Coded, Random Numbers	Composition and Designing Part 2: Random Drafts	Zielinski, S. A.; Robert Leclerc, ed.	√	√	MWL	19			'51–'73	79
Weaving: Coded, Random Numbers	Composition and Designing Part 2: Random Patterns	Zielinski, S. A.; Robert Leclerc, ed.	√	> 4	MWL	19			'51–'73	102
Weaving: Coded, Random Numbers	Composition and Designing Part 2: Random Patterns and Colours	Zielinski, S. A.; Robert Leclerc, ed.	√	√	MWL	19			'51–'73	115
Weaving: Coded, Random Numbers	Composition and Designing Part 2: Random Patterns in Twills	Zielinski, S. A.; Robert Leclerc, ed.	√	> 4	MWL	19			'51–'73	108
Weaving Collapse Fabric	Save the Twist: Warping and Weaving with Overtwisted Yarns	Frame, Mary	√	√	S-O	11	2		Su 87	43
Weaving: Commercial	British Revival in Handweaving, The	Hall, Wendy	√		H&C	4	3		Su 53	21
Weaving: Commercial	Diversity of Fabrics Comes from the Looms of Joseph D. Acton and Bret Carberry of Philadelphia, A		√		H&C	4	2		Sp 53	4
Weaving: Commercial	Dorothy Liebes Studio				H&C	5	1		Wi 53	35
Weaving: Commercial	Guatemala Visited	Atwater, Mary Meigs			SCGM		15		65	24
Weaving: Commercial	Handweaver's Place in the U. S. Textile Market, The	Kaufmann, Edgar, Jr.	√		H&C	5	4		Fa 54	11
Weaving: Commercial	Handweaving in the Textile Industry	Hausner, Walter A.			H&C	9	1		Wi 57	28
Weaving: Commercial	Interview with Jack Lenor Larsen, An		√		WJ	7	1	25	Su 82	10
Weaving: Commercial	Isabel Scott Fabrics		√		H&C	9	1		Wi 57	8
Weaving: Commercial	Isabel Scott, Handweaver and Designer	Storey, Walter Rendell	√		H&C	4	2		Sp 53	14
Weaving: Commercial	Jacquard is Back	Lloyd, Ann	√		SS&D	18	4	72	Fa 87	10
Weaving: Commercial	Knoll Textiles		√		H&C	9	3		Su 58	12
Weaving: Commercial	Maria Kipp — Her Career as a Weaver	Bryan, Dorothy	√		H&C	3	1		Wi 51	15
Weaving: Commercial	Nantucket Looms and Sam Kasten	Erickson, Johanna	√		SS&D	17	3	67	Su 86	70
Weaving: Commercial	Old World Weavers at Work in the New	Kamola, Stephanie	√	√	H&C	7	2		Sp 56	24
Weaving: Commercial	Pueblo Deco	Sitko, Jane Bradley	√		SS&D	18	4	72	Fa 87	40
Weaving, Commercial	Rancocas Fabrics		√		H&C	8	2		Sp 57	41
Weaving, Commercial	Weaving Along Sugar River	Adams, Eleanor	√		H&C	1	2		Su 50	28
Weaving, Commercial	Weaving for the Wholesale Market—Bane or Boon?	Holland, Nina	√		SS&D	5	3	19	Su 74	81
Weaving, Commercial	Weaving in the Marketplace	Morris, Betty			H&C	24	3		M/J 73	42
Weaving, Commercial	Why Not "Tromp as Writ" Commercially?	Wilde, Ruth C.	√		H&C	2	2		Sp 51	22
Weaving: Contemporary	Contemporary Polish Weaving	Jarecka, Louise Llewellyn	√		H&C	1	2		Su 50	15
Weaving Cotton	Acadian Brown Cotton	Exner, Beatrice B.	√		H&C	11	4		Fa 60	22
Weaving Cotton	Design in Cotton	Bishop, Mrs. Carlton T.	√	> 4	H&C	6	4		Fa 55	11
Weaving: Coverlets	Coverlet: Weaving and Finishing Hints, A	van der Hoogt, Madelyn	√	√	PWC	5	1	15		34

SUBJECT	TITLE	AUTHOR	IL	INST	JOUR	VOL	NO	ISS	DATE	PAGE
Weaving: Crete	Weaving in Crete	Znamierowski, Nell	√		H&C	15	4		Fa 64	8
Weaving Doup Leno: Counterbalanced Loom	Doup Leno: Weaving Doup Leno on a Counter Balance Loom	Skowronski, Hella; Sylvia Tacker	√	√	SCGM		32		80	45
Weaving: Eighteenth Century	Norman Kennedy — Weaver at Williamsburg	Slater, Deborah	√		H&C	23	1		J/F 72	23
Weaving: Europe, Contemporary	Weaving Abroad	Huebner, Marianne A.	√		H&C	21	3		Su 70	10
Weaving Flax Tow	Slave Shirt Woven for Booker T. Washington Museum		√		H&C	19	3		Su 68	21
Weaving: France	French Weaving 1972	Watt, Ruth	√		H&C	23	6		N/D 72	48
Weaving Fur	Discarded Fur Pieces for Rugs and Pillows	Cook, Bonny	√	√	SS&D	4	3	15	Su 73	20
Weaving Fur	Furry Pillow	Cox, Dorothy	√	√	WJ	7	2	26	Fa 82	56
Weaving Fur	Touch of Fur, A	Dickey, Enola	√	√	SS&D	8	4	32	Fa 77	85
Weaving Fur	Weaving in the Fur Weft	Patrick, Jane; Ann Wittpenn	√	√	Hw	4	1		J/F 83	33
Weaving Groups	Shuttle	Marston, Ena			SS&D	2	3	7	Su 71	11
Weaving: Guilt/Self-Worth	Unweaving Faulty Fabric	Redding, Debbie	√		Hw	5	2		M/A 84	22
Weaving Handspun	Afghan and Pillow Set	D'Ambrosio, Gina	√	√	S-O	11	2		Su 87	14
Weaving Handspun	Baa, Baa, Black Sheep, Have You Any Wool?	Bulbach, Stanley	√		S-O	9	2		Su 85	44
Weaving Handspun	Bedside Runner		√	√	S-O	7	3		Fa 83	57
Weaving Handspun	Boucle Jacket		√	√	S-O	7	3		Fa 83	59
Weaving Handspun	Brown Wool Jumper	Buchanan, Rita	√	√	S-O	9	1		Sp 85	14
Weaving Handspun	Butterfly Kimono Jacket	Bush, Carolyn	√	√	S-O	10	1		Sp 86	22
Weaving Handspun	Cashmere Challenge, The	Urbanek, Karen	√	√	S-O	10	1		Sp 86	37
Weaving Handspun	Child's Windcheater	Reekie, Stephanie	√	√	S-O	6	4		82	58
Weaving Handspun	Christening Blanket	Nathans, Barbara	√	√	S-O	4			80	60
Weaving Handspun	Color Blended Scarves		√	√	S-O	11	1		Sp 87	23
Weaving Handspun	Cotton Skirt and Blouse	Gant, Helen Mosely	√	√	S-O	6	4		82	63
Weaving Handspun	Croatian Shirt, A	Gaustad, Stephenie	√	√	S-O	9	2		Su 85	28
Weaving Handspun	Don's Jacket	Coulson, Louise	√	√	S-O	8	2		Su 84	49
Weaving Handspun	Evening Cocoon		√	√	S-O	5			81	56
Weaving Handspun	Evolution of a Handspun Jacket	Gardner, Jean	√		S-O	9	1		Sp 85	28
Weaving Handspun	Experimenting with Silk Crepe	Quinn, Celia	√	√	S-O	10	4		Wi 86	36
Weaving Handspun	From Sheep to Shawl	Van Ord, Kay; Stewart Van Ord	√	√	WJ	6	2	22	Fa 81	57
Weaving Handspun	Frosted Pastel Cashmere Scarf, A	Quinn, Celia	√	√	S-O	9	3		Fa 85	41
Weaving Handspun	Girl's Vest	Howard, Miranda	√	√	S-O	6	4		82	59
Weaving Handspun	Go For It!	Eldridge, Lois A.	√	√	S-O	7	4		Wi 83	45
Weaving Handspun	Gray Topcoat	Buchanan, Rita; Steve Buchanan	√	√	S-O	9	4		Wi 85	13
Weaving Handspun	Hand-Dyed Angora Bunny Scarf	Hart, Jacque	√	√	S-O	11	4		Wi 87	26
Weaving Handspun	Handspun, Handwoven Cocoon Jacket, A	Adams, Brucie	√	√	Hw	5	2		M/A 84	88
Weaving Handspun	Handspun, Handwoven Saddle Blanket, A	Newsted, Jean	√	√	WJ	8	2	30	Fa 83	22
Weaving Handspun	Handspun Jacket		√	√	S-O	7	4		Wi 83	48
Weaving Handspun	Handspun Linen Towels	Quinn, Celia	√	√	S-O	7	1		Sp 83	32
Weaving Handspun	Handspun Plaid Shirt, A (Betty Keeler)		√		Hw	4	5		N/D 83	73
Weaving Handspun	Handspun Wedding Gown, A	Anderson, Arlene	√	√	S-O	8	4		Wi 84	13
Weaving Handspun	Handspun Yarns from Black Sheep Wool	Simmons, Paula	√	√	H&C	14	3		Su 63	6
Weaving Handspun	Handspuns for Tapestries	Szumski, Norma; Phyllis Clemmer; Clotilde Barrett	√		WJ	6	2	22	Fa 81	41
Weaving Handspun	I Have This Fleece...Now What?	Adams, Brucie	√	√	Iw	5	4		Fa 80	62
Weaving Handspun	Ikat-Spun Kimono, An	Lamb, Sara	√	√	S-O	8	4		Wi 84	16
Weaving Handspun	Jacket of Handspun Samples, A	Fenner, Mary Sue	√	√	Hw	5	1		J/F 84	74

SUBJECT	TITLE	AUTHOR	IL	INST	JOUR	VOL	NO	ISS	DATE	PAGE
Weaving Handspun	Karen Braun's Table Runner and Tray Covering		√		S-O	9	3		Fa 85	14
Weaving Handspun	Kasuri-Like-Effect Weaving	Akita, Mariko Olivia	√	√	WJ	6	2	22	Fa 81	18
Weaving Handspun	Kinsale Cloak	Adams, Brucie	√	√	S-O	4			80	56
Weaving Handspun	Lacy Triangular Stole of Handspun Wool, A	Kniskern, Edna Maki	√	√	WJ	6	2	22	Fa 81	48
Weaving Handspun	Linsey-Woolsey Using Handspun Yarns	Adams, Brucie	√	√	Hw	3	5		N/D 82	59
Weaving Handspun	Make It Yourself with Handwoven Wool	Zawistoski, Patsy	√		S-O	9	1		Sp 85	12
Weaving Handspun	Man's Shirt		√	√	S-O	5			81	58
Weaving Handspun	Martin's Creek Settlement: A Pictorial Weaving	Thompson, Kathleen; Alice Tipton	√		S-O	9	3		Fa 85	39
Weaving Handspun	Melody Oakroot-Cedar Weaver	London, Bill	√	√	S-O	10	3		Fa 86	45
Weaving Handspun	Merino Scarf with Pastel Highlights	Quinn, Celia	√	√	S-O	9	3		Fa 85	37
Weaving Handspun	Mohair Afghan/Great Shawl	Chastant, Kathryn Ross	√	√	S-O	6	4		82	57
Weaving Handspun	Morning Glory	Bulbach, Stanley	√	√	S-O	9	1		Sp 85	15
Weaving Handspun	My Linen Curtain	Handy, Virginia	√	√	S-O	10	3		Fa 86	23
Weaving Handspun	My Wonderful Llamas and Their Wool	Thormahlen, Marian Oyen	√	√	S-O	8	4		Wi 84	29
Weaving Handspun	Needlework Tool Case	Reese, Sharron	√	√	S-O	10	3		Fa 86	21
Weaving Handspun	Prize-Winning Suit, A	Karsten, Phyllis	√	√	S-O	8	4		Wi 84	15
Weaving Handspun	Reversible Vest		√	√	S-O	7	3		Fa 83	58
Weaving Handspun	Ringlets and Waves: Undulations from Overtwist	Frame, Mary	√	√	S-O	10	4		Wi 86	28
Weaving Handspun	Saddlebags		√	√	S-O	5			81	58
Weaving Handspun	Scarf and Cap	Switzer, Chris	√	√	S-O	4			80	58
Weaving Handspun	Scarves in Variegated Yarns	Irwin, Bobbie	√	√	S-O	11	4		Wi 87	53
Weaving Handspun	Seat for All Seasons, A	Rasmussen, Peg	√	√	WJ	6	2	22	Fa 81	21
Weaving Handspun	Silk and Cotton Shirt, A	Daugherty, Robin	√	√	S-O	6	4		82	60
Weaving Handspun	Silk Shawl	Glaves, Jeannine; Ruth Morrison	√	√	S-O	9	4		Wi 85	16
Weaving Handspun	Silk Top		√	√	S-O	5			81	59
Weaving Handspun	Sky Celebration	Mayer, Anita Luvera	√	√	S-O	11	2		Su 87	36
Weaving Handspun	Soft Pink Throw, A	Keeler, Betty	√	√	S-O	8	4		Wi 84	31
Weaving Handspun	Spin a Tartan—Naturally	Adams, Brucie	√	√	Hw	4	5		N/D 83	72
Weaving Handspun	SPIN-OFF Book of World Records		√		S-O	7	3		Fa 83	11
Weaving Handspun	Stanley Bulbach	McManus, Fran	√		S-O	8	2		Su 84	55
Weaving Handspun	Summer Harvest, Winter Jacket	O'Connor, Marina	√	√	S-O	11	2		Su 87	13
Weaving Handspun	Swatches		√		S-O	8	3		Fa 84	16
Weaving Handspun	Tagari: A Greek Saddlebag of Handspun Wools, The	Koster, Joan Boura	√	√	WJ	6	2	22	Fa 81	24
Weaving Handspun	Texture With Handspun	Page, Judy	√	√	WJ	6	2	22	Fa 81	20
Weaving Handspun	Transparent Weaving with Handspun Cotton Weft	Green, Andrea	√	√	WJ	8	2	30	Fa 83	44
Weaving Handspun	Twill Stoll	Harding, Patricia	√	√	S-O	4			80	61
Weaving Handspun	Variations on a Midnight Rainbow	Ligon, Linda	√	√	S-O	9	4		Wi 85	14
Weaving Handspun	Variegated Ikat Spun Scarf		√	√	S-O	5			81	61
Weaving Handspun	Very Fine Scarf, A	Buchanan, Steve	√	√	S-O	10	2		Su 86	20
Weaving Handspun	Vests	Lamb, Sara	√	√	S-O	9	1		Sp 85	16
Weaving Handspun	Warped-Faced Ruana	D'Ambrosio, Gina	√	√	S-O	10	2		Su 86	17
Weaving Handspun	Weaving and Tailoring Handspun Yardage	Simmons, Paula	√	√	S-O	2			78	48
Weaving Handspun	Weaving Handspun Yarn: Triangular Shawl	Ellison, Nancy	√	√	WJ	12	2	46	Fa 87	42
Weaving Handspun	Weaving with Handspun Alpaca	Anderson, J.	√		H&C	17	2		Sp 66	20
Weaving Handspun	Weaving with Handspun Wools	Ingraham, Harold	√		H&C	1	3		Fa 50	18
Weaving Handspun	Weaving with Handspun Yarns: Suggestions for Beginning Spinners	Simmons, Paula	√	√	H&C	17	4		Fa 66	4

SUBJECT	TITLE	AUTHOR	IL	INST	JOUR	VOL	NO	ISS	DATE	PAGE
Weaving Handspun	Weaving with Handspuns: A Shepherd Jacket	Simmons, Paula	√	√	S-O	1			77	43
Weaving Handspun	Wool Blanket	Goony, Elaine	√	√	S-O	6	4		82	62
Weaving Handspun	Your Ski Jumper	Filson, Alice	√	√	SS&D	2	3	7	Su 71	19
Weaving Handspun: Cotton	Simply Natural	Linder, Harry	√	√	WJ	11	2	42	Fa 86	20
Weaving Handspun Linen	Weaving with Handspun Linen Yarn	Fannin, Allen A.	√	√	H&C	19	2		Sp 68	10
Weaving Handspun, Overtwist	Save the Twist: Warping and Weaving with Overtwisted Yarns	Frame, Mary	√	√	S-O	11	2		Su 87	43
Weaving Ikat	Balinese Ikat	Hannon, Farrell	√	√	WJ	5	1	17	Su 80	49
Weaving Ikat, Double	Patolu and Its Techniques	De Bone, Mary Golden	√	√	TMJ	4	3		76	49
Weaving: Ireland	Weaving in Donegal (error-corrected H&C v23 n3 72 p11)	McNeill, Mary	√	√	H&C	23	2		M/A 72	35
Weaving Kudzu Fibers	Kudzu: The Noxious Weed Transformed	Buchanan, Rita	√		Fa	14	2		M/A 87	48
Weaving Leather	Weaving with Leather	Termullo, Eileen	√	√	Hw	5	1		J/F 84	52
Weaving Lessons	First Lessons	Ligon, Linda	√	√	Hw	7	5		N/D 86	106
Weaving Linen	Flax	Miller, Suzanne	√	√	WJ	7	2	26	Fa 82	12
Weaving Linen	Linen Towels	Frey, Berta	√	√	H&C	14	3		Su 63	13
Weaving Linen	Some Linen Weavers of New England (error-corrected H&C v2 n3 51 p54)		√	√	H&C	2	1		Wi 50	47
Weaving Linen	Three Adventures of a Wedding Dress	Chapin, Doloria	√	√	SS&D	4	3	15	Su 73	51
Weaving Linen	Tips on Weaving Linen on the Rigid Heddle Loom	Xenakis, Athanasios David		√	PWC	1	1		No 81	20
Weaving Linen	Weaving a Fine Warp	Ligon, Linda	√	√	Hw	2	5		No 81	58
Weaving Linen	Weaving of Linen, The	Chase, Mary A.	√	√	WJ	7	2	26	Fa 82	18
Weaving Linen	Weaving with Linen	Condit, Joan	√		H&C	6	3		Su 55	46
Weaving Linen	Woven Lace, Part 1: The Bronson Systems — Tips on Weaving with Linen, Rigid Heddle Loom	Xenakis, Athanasios David	√	√	PWC			5	Sp 83	14
Weaving Linen	Yarns and Fibers: How Not to Weave Linen	Zielinski, S. A.; Robert Leclerc, ed.	√	√	MWL	4			'51–'73	19
Weaving: Loom Shaped	Textured Cottons: Seamless, No-Sweat Shirt	Rasmussen, Peg	√	√	WJ	6	3	23	Wi 81	25
Weaving: Loom-Shaped	African Strip-Cloth Shirt Without Strips, An	O'Connor, Eileen	√	√	WJ	6	3	23	Wi 81	33
Weaving: Loom-Shaped	Cardigan Jacket	Evans, Kerry	√	√	WJ	5	3	19	Wi 81	10
Weaving: Loom-Shaped	Classic Dress, The	Hewson, Betty	√	√	Hw	5	3		Su 84	24
Weaving: Loom-Shaped	Color Wheels and Color Blankets: Tools of the Designer	Wertenberger, Kathryn	√	√	Hw	2	4		Se 81	50
Weaving: Loom-Shaped	Costumes of Royal India	Levine, Betsy	√		TM			7	O/N 86	64
Weaving: Loom-Shaped	Dress (size 14) Shaped on Loom (size 24")	Roth, Bettie	√	√	SS&D	3	1	9	Wi 71	17
Weaving: Loom-Shaped	Embroidery on the Loom	Drooker, Penelope B.	√	√	SS&D	9	3	35	Su 78	60
Weaving: Loom-Shaped	Finish Your Work	Stoehr, Mary Kay	√	√	Hw	5	1		J/F 84	54
Weaving: Loom-Shaped	Garments Made from Simple Patterns: Loom Shaped Poncho		√	√	WJ	2	3	7	Ja 78	39
Weaving: Loom-Shaped	Garments Made from Simple Patterns: Two Tabards		√	> 4	WJ	2	3	7	Ja 78	35
Weaving: Loom-Shaped	Gray on Gray with Loom-shaped Ease		√		Hw	6	4		S/O 85	60
Weaving: Loom-Shaped	Handwoven Sweater, A	Hewson, Betty	√	√	Hw	4	4		S/O 83	85
Weaving: Loom-Shaped	Loom Designed Garments	Thomason, Roger	√		SS&D	1	3	3	Ju 70	10
Weaving: Loom-Shaped	Loom Shaped—3 Ways (error-corrected Hw v4 n3 83 p79)		√	√	Hw	3	2		Mr 82	44
Weaving: Loom-Shaped	Loom-Shaped Garment, A	Haynes, Albertje Koopman	√	√	SS&D	9	1	33	Wi 77	83
Weaving: Loom-Shaped	Make It Fit	Stoehr, Mary Kay	√	√	Hw	5	3		Su 84	64
Weaving: Loom-Shaped	Shaping with the Warp	Bowman, Gloria	√	√	SS&D	11	1	41	Wi 79	26
Weaving: Loom-Shaped	Three in One	Moes, Dini	√	√	SS&D	18	2	70	Sp 87	74
Weaving: Loom-Shaped	Weaving Ripples and Curves	Irvine, Marie M.	√	√	SS&D	12	1	45	Wi 80	52

796

SUBJECT	TITLE	AUTHOR	IL	INST	JOUR	VOL	NO	ISS	DATE	PAGE
Weaving: Loom-Shaped	Weaving with Handspuns: A Shepherd Jacket	Simmons, Paula	√	√	S-O	1			77	43
Weaving: Loom-Shaped (Triangular Shawl)	How to Weave a Plaid Triangular Shawl	Elich-McCall, Charoltte	√	√	Hw	4	5		N/D 83	54
Weaving: Loom-Shaped (Triangular Shawl)	Simple Skirt and Matching Shawl, A	Hewson, Betty	√	√	Hw	4	5		N/D 83	24
Weaving Metal	Interface: A Wire Weaving	Sullivan, Donna	√	√	WJ	7	1	25	Su 82	20
Weaving Metal	Molly Hart	Hart, Molly	√		Fa	14	2		M/A 87	23
Weaving Metal	Silver and Gold	Bramhall, Pat; Butch Bramhall	√	√	SS&D	19	1	73	Wi 87	40
Weaving Monk's Belt	Creative Monk's Belt: The Finished Product	Windeknecht, Margaret B.	√	√	SCGM		30		76	37
Weaving: Mt. Vernon	Martha Washington's Inaugural Gown	Reams, Dorothy E.	√		SS&D	7	3	27	Su 76	15
Weaving: Natural Materials	Dogbones from Trees?	Jackson, Mariechen	√		SS&D	2	1	5	De 70	18
Weaving: Natural Materials	From Field and Garden	Williams, Betty	√		SS&D	2	3	7	Su 71	6
Weaving: Natural Materials	New Philippine Textiles	Gele, Emilé	√		H&C	5	3		Su 54	14
Weaving: Natural Materials	Weaving in Hawaii	Robinson, Hester A.	√		H&C	3	4		Fa 52	12
Weaving: Natural Materials	Weaving Materials from the Sea	Wilson, Patricia	√		SS&D	2	1	5	De 70	3
Weaving: Natural Materials	Weaving with Native Materials	Fuchs, Rudolph	√		H&C	2	4		Fa 51	21
Weaving: Off-Loom	Fabric Design, An Approach by a Young Weaver	Carson, Candace	√	√	H&C	20	1		Wi 69	16
Weaving: Off-Loom	Woven Woolen Whimseys		√	√	WJ	2	2	6	Oc 77	14
Weaving On-Opposites	Creative Monk's Belt	Windeknecht, Margaret B.	√	>4	SS&D	9	1	33	Wi 77	28
Weaving: On-Opposites	Mexican Motifs: The Mexican Men's Jacket	Tidball, Harriet	√	√	SCGM		6		62	20
Weaving: On-Opposites	Overshot on Opposites	Xenakis, Athanasios David	√	√	PWC	3	2	8		26
Weaving Orlon	New Man-Made Fiber Developed for Handweavers, A	Laurell, Karl	√	√	H&C	5	1		Wi 53	27
Weaving Overshot	Weaving with Tabby: An Introduction to Overshot	Pettigrew, Dale	√	√	Hw	3	5		N/D 82	62
Weaving Painted Paper	Weaving-Drawing-Painting-Paper, A Profile of Lorelei Schott		√		WJ	6	1	21	Su 81	13
Weaving Paper	Paper as Fiber	Morse, Marcia	√		SS&D	15	3	59	Su 84	20
Weaving Paper	Paper Clothing, East	Sahlstrand, Margaret	√	√	Fa	11	2		M/A 84	36
Weaving Paper	Paper Weaving	Scanlin, Tommye McClure	√	√	Hw	7	4		S/O 86	28
Weaving Paper	Shifu: A Handwoven Paper Textile	Miller, Dorothy	√	√	Hw	6	3		Su 85	69
Weaving Paper	Shifu: A Handwoven Paper Textile of Japan	Miller, Dorothy	√	√	AT	4			De 85	43
Weaving Patterns: Bird's Eye	Sarah Fowler's Book of Drafts, Part 1	North, Lois	√	>4	SS&D	6	1	21	Wi 74	8
Weaving Patterns: Bird's Eye	Sarah Fowler's Book of Drafts, Part 4	North, Lois	√	>4	SS&D	6	4	24	Fa 75	84
Weaving Patterns: Diamond Diaper	Sarah Fowler's Book of Drafts, Part 2		√	>4	SS&D	6	2	22	Sp 75	78
Weaving Patterns: Diamond Diaper	Sarah Fowler's Book of Drafts, Part 4	North, Lois	√	>4	SS&D	6	4	24	Fa 75	84
Weaving Patterns: Dutch Diaper	Sarah Fowler's Book of Drafts, Part 3	North, Lois	√	>4	SS&D	6	3	23	Su 75	74
Weaving Patterns: Lee's Surrender	"Lee's Surrender"	Ashwell, Eleanor V.	√	√	SS&D	6	2	22	Sp 75	85
Weaving Patterns: Nine Snowballs	Sarah Fowler's Book of Drafts, Part 1	North, Lois	√	>4	SS&D	6	1	21	Wi 74	8
Weaving Patterns: Primrose Diaper	Sarah Fowler's Book of Drafts, Part 1	North, Lois	√	>4	SS&D	6	1	21	Wi 74	8
Weaving Patterns: Queen's Delight	Sarah Fowler's Book of Drafts, Part 1	North, Lois	√	>4	SS&D	6	1	21	Wi 74	8
Weaving Patterns: Rose Diaper	Sarah Fowler's Book of Drafts, Part 3	North, Lois	√	>4	SS&D	6	3	23	Su 75	74
Weaving Patterns: Royal Beauty	Sarah Fowler's Book of Drafts, Part 2		√	>4	SS&D	6	2	22	Sp 75	78
Weaving Patterns: Russian Diamond	Sarah Fowler's Book of Drafts, Part 2		√	>4	SS&D	6	2	22	Sp 75	78
Weaving Patterns: Spring and Fall	Sarah Fowler's Book of Drafts, Part 2		√	>4	SS&D	6	2	22	Sp 75	78

SUBJECT	TITLE	AUTHOR	IL	INST	JOUR	VOL	NO	ISS	DATE	PAGE
Weaving Patterns: Westfield Diaper	Sarah Fowler's Book of Drafts, Part 3	North, Lois	√	>4	SS&D	6	3	23	Su 75	74
Weaving: Personal Meaning	Weaving — Better Than Bridge	Chandler, Deborah	√		Hw	8	3		M/J 87	18
Weaving Piña	Piña	Wallace, Lysbeth	√		WJ	8	2	30	Fa 83	77
Weaving Polychrome	Peru, Textiles Unlimited, Part 2: Polychrome Weft Pick-Up	Tidball, Harriet	√	√	SCGM		26		69	28
Weaving Practices, Efficient	Haptic Visions	Brubaker, Paul			WJ	11	4	44	Sp 87	59
Weaving Process	From Elsie H. Gubser's Studio		√	>4	H&C	7	3		Su 56	24
Weaving Process	Textile Arts of Multan, Pakistan	Shahzaman, Mahboob	√	>4	SS&D	4	3	15	Su 73	8
Weaving Process	Treasury for Beginners: How to Weave Easier and Faster	Zielinski, S. A.; Robert Leclerc, ed.			MWL	1			'51–'73	9
Weaving Process: Beating	Even Beat, An	Ligon, Linda	√	√	Hw	7	4		S/O 86	98
Weaving Process: Beating	From the Weaver's Bench: Full Width Projects	Elam, E. T.		√	H&C	23	5		S/O 72	30
Weaving Process: Beating	Handweaver's Instruction Manual: Weaving, The Beat	Tidball, Harriet C. nee Douglas		√	SCGM		34		49	18
Weaving Process: Beating	Notebook: Some Light Behind the Weave	Myers, Ruth Nordquist, ed.	√	>4	SS&D	13	3	51	Su 82	16
Weaving Process: Beating	Two-Harness Textiles, The Open Work Weaves: Beating	Tidball, Harriet	√	√	SCGM		21		67	4
Weaving Process: Beating Weft	Problems of Beating in Weft, The		√	√	Hw	5	2		M/A 84	14
Weaving Process: Cutting-Off	Handweaver's Instruction Manual: Weaving, Cutting the Warp	Tidball, Harriet C. nee Douglas	√	√	SCGM		34		49	20
Weaving Process: Design Variables	Characteristics of Handweaves	Howell, Marie	√		H&C	12	1		Wi 61	18
Weaving Process: Double Beating	Treasury for Beginners: Double Beating	Zielinski, S. A.; Robert Leclerc, ed.		√	MWL	1			'51–'73	42
Weaving Process: Edges	Treasury for Beginners: Edges	Zielinski, S. A.; Robert Leclerc, ed.		√	MWL	1			'51–'73	92
Weaving Process: Fastening Weft Ends	Handweaver's Instruction Manual: Weaving, Fastening Weft Ends	Tidball, Harriet C. nee Douglas		√	SCGM		34		49	19
Weaving Process: Finishes, On-Loom	Handweaver's Instruction Manual: Weaving, End Finishes	Tidball, Harriet C. nee Douglas	√	√	SCGM		34		49	20
Weaving Process: Motion Sequences, Continuous Warp Looms	Weaving Processes in the Cuzco Area of Peru	Rowe, Ann Pollard	√	√	TMJ	4	2		75	30
Weaving Process: Rhythm	Treasury for Beginners: Rhythm	Zielinski, S. A.; Robert Leclerc, ed.		√	MWL	1			'51–'73	31
Weaving Process: Rhythm	Treasury for Beginners: Rhythm and Tie-Up	Zielinski, S. A.; Robert Leclerc, ed.		>4	MWL	1			'51–'73	35
Weaving Process: Selvages	Handweaver's Instruction Manual: Weaving, Selvages	Tidball, Harriet C. nee Douglas		√	SCGM		34		49	19
Weaving Process: Treadling	Handweaver's Instruction Manual: Weaving, Treadling	Tidball, Harriet C. nee Douglas		√	SCGM		34		49	18
Weaving Process: Two-Shuttle Weaving	Handweaver's Instruction Manual: Weaving, Two-Shuttle Weaving	Tidball, Harriet C. nee Douglas		√	SCGM		34		49	18
Weaving Programs see Education										
Weaving Ramie	Miyako Jofu	Miller, Dorothy	√	√	AT	7			Ju 87	85
Weaving Ramie	Weaving with Ramie		√	>4	WJ	8	2	30	Fa 83	80
Weaving: Reed Removed	Remove the Reed (error-corrected SS&D v5 n3 i19 74 p65)	Garrett, Cay	√	√	SS&D	5	1	17	Wi 73	88
Weaving Ribbon	Tunic with Ribbons (Carol Powalisz)		√	√	Hw	8	1		J/F 87	52, I-8
Weaving Ribbon	Yarns and Fibers: Unusual Yarns - 2	Zielinski, S. A.; Robert Leclerc, ed.		√	MWL	4			'51–'73	85
Weaving: Scope	Else Regensteiner Explores Weaving's Great Scope		√		SS&D	6	4	24	Fa 75	52
Weaving Silk	Chinese Artisans At Work	Goodman, Deborah Lerme	√		Fa	13	1		J/F 86	34
Weaving Silk	Decorative Miniatures in Silk by Jadwiga Rakowska		√		H&C	10	2		Sp 59	22
Weaving Silk	Handweaving with Silk	Derr, Mary		√	WJ	3	2	10	Oc 78	40
Weaving Silk	Handwoven Silk Garments: A Wedding Dress	Best, Eleanor	√	√	WJ	3	2	10	Oc 78	28

SUBJECT	TITLE	AUTHOR	IL	INST	JOUR	VOL	NO	ISS	DATE	PAGE
Weaving Silk	Handwoven Silk Garments: Blue Silk Dress	Alvic, Philis	√	>4	WJ	3	2	10	Oc 78	27
Weaving Silk	Handwoven Silk Garments: Ikat Dress	Schreiber, LaVonne	√	√	WJ	3	2	10	Oc 78	30
Weaving Silk	Handwoven Silk Garments: Ikat Kimono	Barnett-Westfall, Lynn	√	√	WJ	3	2	10	Oc 78	30
Weaving Silk	Handwoven Silk Garments: Ikat Shirt	Utzinger, Karen	√	√	WJ	3	2	10	Oc 78	29
Weaving Silk	Sensuous Silk	West, Virginia	√		Hw	7	1		J/F 86	52
Weaving Silk	Silk: Spinner's Luxury		√	√	Hw	5	4		S/O 84	85
Weaving Silk	Weavers in Iran, Thousands at Work on Primitive Looms	Leclerc, Robert	√		H&C	21	2		Sp 70	9
Weaving Silk	Yarns and Fibers: How to Weave Silk	Zielinski, S. A.; Robert Leclerc, ed.	√	√	MWL	4			'51–'73	46
Weaving Silk	Yarns and Fibers: Weaving of Fine Silk	Zielinski, S. A.; Robert Leclerc, ed.		√	MWL	4			'51–'73	61
Weaving Spanish Moss	Mary E. Heickman, Texas Weaver and Teacher	Morse, Martha	√	√	H&C	17	3		Su 66	18
Weaving: Speed	From the Weaver's Bench	Elam, E. T.			H&C	23	4		J/A 72	33
Weaving Tabby	More About Fabrics: Tabby	Zielinski, S. A.; Robert Leclerc, ed.	√	√	MWL	20			'51–'73	19
Weaving: Tartans	Weaver's Book of Scottish Tartans: The Weaving of Tartans, The	Tidball, Harriet		√	SCGM		5		62	10
Weaving Technique also see Combined Techniques; Specific Technique										
Weaving Techniques	Exploring Weaving Techniques	Larsen, Jack Lenor	√		H&C	3	4		Fa 52	4
Weaving Techniques	Handloom Weaves: Threading Systems and Weaving Methods	Tidball, Harriet			SCGM		33		57	9
Weaving Techniques: Neglected	Forgotten Weaving Techniques	Hausner, Walter			H&C	24	3		M/J 73	14
Weaving Techniques: Shaft-Switching	Anne Brooke's Impeccable Woven Rugs	West, Virginia	√		Fa	6	6		N/D 79	24
Weaving Tips: Tools and Methods	Tipsa and Timesavers	Keasbey, Doramay	√	√	PWC	5	2	16		22
Weaving: Trade Materials	Commercial Materials in Modern Navajo Rugs	Hedlund, Ann Lane	√		TMJ	25			86	83
Weaving: Traditional/Contemporary	Fiber Horizons	LaLena, Constance			Hw	4	5		N/D 83	26
Weaving: Variations	Making the Most of Your Weave	Barnes, Muriel	√	>4	H&C	19	4		Fa 68	15
Weaving Velvet	Pile Weaves, Rugs and Tapestry: Velvet Rugs	Zielinski, S. A.; Robert Leclerc, ed.	√	√	MWL	14			'51–'73	65
Weaving Wood	Yarns and Fibers: Unusual Yarns - Partitions	Zielinski, S. A.; Robert Leclerc, ed.		√	MWL	4			'51–'73	89
Weaving Wood: Poplar	Shaker Technique: Part 1, Weaving with Wood, The	Gordon, Beverly	√		SS&D	7	4	28	Fa 76	32
Weaving Wool	Woolens and Tweeds: Weaving Woolens	Tidball, Harriet		√	SCGM		4		61	15
Weaving Wool	Working with Wool	Healey, Edna O.	√	√	SS&D	2	4	8	Fa 71	15
Weaving: Wool/Copper	Double Lives: Can You Love Your "Work" When It's Your "Job"?	Mattera, Joanne	√		TM			10	A/M 87	62
Weavings, Celebratory	Amanda Lurie: One Weaver's Path	Lurie, Amanda	√		Fa	10	4		J/A 83	16
Weavings: Dual-Purpose	Maralyce Ferree: Dual-Purpose Weavings	Mimoso, Sophie	√		Fa	7	2		M/A 80	12
Wedge Weave	Exploring Wedge Weave	Mattera, Joanne	√	√	Iw	3	2		Wi 78	24
Wedge Weave	Wedge Weave: A New Approach	Noble, Carol Rasmussen	√	√	WJ	5	2	18	Fa 80	49
Weekend Weaver: Projects, Weaving	Double Corduroy Rug (error-corrected WJ v11 n3 87 p78)	Waggoner, Phyllis	√	√	WJ	11	2	42	Fa 86	42
Weekend Weaver: Projects, Weaving	Holiday Runners	Skoy, Mary	√	>4	WJ	12	2	46	Fa 87	22
Weekend Weaver: Projects, Weaving	Loom Shaped Top with Dukagång Inlay	Searle, Karen	√	√	WJ	11	3	43	Wi 87	8
Weekend Weaver: Projects, Weaving	Moebius Vest, The	Homme, Audrey	√	√	WJ	11	4	44	Sp 87	48
Weekend Weaver: Projects, Weaving	Twilled Cottolin Towels	Waggoner, Phyllis	√	√	WJ	11	1	41	Su 86	42
Weekend Weaver: Projects, Weaving	Two Block Rug in Boundweave	Waggoner, Phyllis	√	√	WJ	12	1	45	Su 87	26

SUBJECT	TITLE	AUTHOR	IL	INST	JOUR	VOL	NO	ISS	DATE	PAGE
Weft: Beating	Problems of Beating in Weft, The		√	√	Hw	5	2		M/A 84	14
Weft: Synthetic, Dry Cleaner Bag	Gala Raincoat	Moes, Dini	√	√	WJ	6	3	23	Wi 81	12
Weft Wrapping, Knotted	Peru, Textiles Unlimited, Part 2: Filet	Tidball, Harriet	√	√	SCGM		26		69	46
Weft Wrapping, Soumak	Hopi Woven Embroidery		√	√	WJ	2	3	7	Ja 78	24
Weft Wrapping, Soumak	Make a Soumak Sampler Into a Tote Bag		√	√	WJ	2	2	6	Oc 77	28
Weft Wrapping, Soumak	Peruvian Accented Mexican Blouse: Analyze—Then Improvise	Lawrence, Margaret	√	√	SS&D	7	1	25	Wi 75	40
Weft-Faced Pattern Weaves	Weft-Faced and Warp-Faced		√	√	PWC			5	Sp 83	34
Weft-Faced Patterning	Chinese Drawloom: A Study in Weave Structure, The	Sellin, Helen	√	> 4	WJ	9	2	34	Fa 84	6
Weft-Faced Patterning	More Rags		√	√	Hw	2	3		My 81	49
Weft-Faced Weaves	Accessories: Drawstring Bag		√	√	WJ	2	4	8	Ap 78	5
Weft-Faced Weaves	Block Weave Rug (Jean Scorgie, Janice Jones)		√	√	Hw	8	5		N/D 87	58, I-14
Weft-Faced Weaves	Composition and Designing: Pattern in Warp	Zielinski, S. A.; Robert Leclerc, ed.	√	√	MWL	18			'51–'73	79
Weft-Faced Weaves	Desert Sunset Rugs (Hector and Halcyon)		√	√	Hw	1	2		S-S 80	32, 58
Weft-Faced Weaves	Double Chenille Vest (Lucy Anne Jennings)		√	√	Hw	7	3		M/J 86	44, I-10
Weft-Faced Weaves	Farmer and His Wife, Figure Boundweave, A	Pissowotski, Inge	√	√	WJ	5	4	20	Sp 81	8
Weft-Faced Weaves	Kente: The Status Cloth of Ghana	Conklin, Sharon L.	√	√	SS&D	8	1	29	WI 76	18
Weft-Faced Weaves	Kurdish Kilim Weaving in the Van-Hakkari District of Eastern Turkey	Landreau, Anthony N.	√	√	TMJ	3	4		De 73	27
Weft-Faced Weaves	Maine Coast Rug (Halcyon Schomp and Hector Jaeger)		√	√	Hw	5	5		N/D 84	72, I-14
Weft-Faced Weaves	Mexican Motifs: The Mexican Men's Jacket	Tidball, Harriet	√	√	SCGM		6		62	20
Weft-Faced Weaves	Observations on the Six-End Block Draft for Rug Weaving	Schlein, Alice	√	√	WJ	6	4	24	Sp 82	30
Weft-Faced Weaves	Poppana Runner (Janice Jones)		√	√	Hw	4	2		M/A 83	50, 88
Weft-Faced Weaves	Saddle Blanket	Corsini, Gale	√	√	WJ	6	4	24	Sp 82	29
Weft-Faced Weaves	Shadowweave, Part 2 — Unbalanced Shadowweave (error-corrected WJ v2 n1 77 insert for vol. 1)	Barrett, Clotilde	√	> 4	WJ	1	2	2	Oc 76	14
Weft-Faced Weaves	Shaft Switching on Boundweave (Nancy Kraushaar)		√	√	WJ	5	3	19	Wi 81	38
Weft-Faced Weaves	Techniques Used in a Carrying Bag, The		√	√	WJ	7	3	27	Wi 82	37
Weft-Faced Weaves	Three-Toned Blocks: Further Explorations with Long-Eyed Heddles	Broughton, Eve T.	√	> 4	WJ	9	4	36	Sp 85	72
Weft-Faced Weaves	Two Tote Bags (Betty Davenport)		√	√	Hw	6	5		N/D 85	12, I-4
Weft-Faced Weaves	Two Unusual Multishaft Curtains	Xenakis, Athanasios David	√	> 4	PWC	4	1	11		40
Weft-Faced Weaves	Weaving and Sheepskin, Naturally	Mason, Carole	√	√	WJ	5	3	19	Wi 81	46
Weft-Faced Weaves	Weft-Faced Weaving of Block Weaves		√	√	Hw	8	5		N/D 87	59
Wefts	Unusual Materials for Warp or Weft	Wertenberger, Kathryn	√	> 4	Hw	7	4		S/O 86	78
Wefts	Unusual Upholstery from Discarded Stockings	Ross, Marjorie Ruth	√	√	H&C	8	2		Sp 57	47
Wefts	Woolens and Tweeds: Weaving Woolens: Weft Relationships	Tidball, Harriet		√	SCGM		4		61	16
Wefts: Chained	Chained Weft for Surface Texture	Malbin, Rosemary S.	√	√	SS&D	11	4	44	Fa 80	26
Wefts: Discontinuous	Corner Inscriptions	Jarvis, Helen		√	PWC	5	2	16		19
Wefts: Flax, Unspun	Tapestry Weaving with Unspun Flax	Westerink, Claire	√	√	WJ	11	2	42	Fa 86	49
Wefts: Interrupted	Designing Block Weaves	Kurtz, Carol	√	> 4	SS&D	11	2	42	Sp 80	5
Wefts: Natural Material, Reed	Woven Reed Placemats	Ingebretsen, Cathy	√	√	PWC	3	2	8		4
Wefts: Pattern, Discontinuous	Corner Inscriptions	Jarvis, Helen		√	PWC	5	2	16		19
Wefts: Pulled	Weaving Primer, Part 3	Xenakis, Athanasios David	√	> 4	PWC	4	1	11		46

SUBJECT	TITLE	AUTHOR	IL	INST	JOUR	VOL	NO	ISS	DATE	PAGE
Wefts: Rigid	Macroweave Effect, The (error-corrected SS&D v12 n3 81 p6)	Towne, Carroll A.	√	√	SS&D	12	2	46	Sp 81	16
Wefts: Spaced	Colonial Stole (Gladys Strong)		√	> 4	Hw	3	5		N/D 82	50, 89
Wefts: Twisted	Shaker Textiles	Hillenburg, Nancy	√	√	WJ	8	1	29	Su 83	22
Wefts: Variations	Variations on One Warp	Alvic, Philis	√		SS&D	12	4	48	Fa 81	70
Weighted Warps	Weaving Figured Piqué on a Loom with One Warp Beam	Xenakis, Athanasios David	√	√	PWC	4	2	12		14
Weld	Ancient Yellow Goes Modern, An	Bliss, Anne	√	√	Iw	4	2		Sp 79	44
West Indies	Plaiting, Possibilities for Use with Weaving	Schira, Cynthia	√	√	H&C	21	1		Wi 70	8
West Indies	Weaving a Route to the Future: An Income-Generating Fiber Project in the West Indies	Clark, Sherry	√		Fa	12	2		M/A 85	48
West Indies	West Indian Weaving, Nonloom Techniques of Interest	Schira, Cynthia	√		H&C	21	3		Su 70	17
Whig Rose Study	Whig Rose Study	Morgenstern, Marvin M.	√	√	WJ	7	2	26	Fa 82	40
Whig Rose Study	Whig Rose Study (continued)	Morgenstern, Marvin M.	√	√	WJ	7	3	27	Wi 82	23
White House, The	Gift to My Country: Lincoln Bedroom Coverlet, A	Jarvis, Helen N.	√	√	SS&D	9	4	36	Fa 78	17
Wickerwork	Basketry Technics, Part 2	Harvey, Virginia	√		SS&D	6	3	23	Su 75	30
Wickerwork	British Revival in Handweaving, The	Hall, Wendy	√		H&C	4	3		Su 53	21
Wickerwork	Technology of Basketry: North American Roots and Relations to Cloth, The	Turnbaugh, Sarah Peabody	√	√	SS&D	8	1	29	WI 76	32
Wickerwork	Wickerwork Basket Weaving in Four-Strand Designs (error-corrected SS&D v14 n1 82 p6)	Jensen, Elizabeth Jane	√	√	SS&D	13	4	52	Fa 82	20
Wigan	Tailor's Logic	Hostek, Stanley	√	√	TM			14	D/J 87	42
Willow	Basket Willow: Cultivating and Gathering the Withy	Hart, Carol	√	√	TM			3	F/M 86	63
Willow	Making an Open-Weave Willow Basket	Hart, Carol	√	√	TM			4	A/M 86	24
Window Coverings	Feltmaking: Instant Delight	Green, Louise	√	√	Iw	3	4		Su 78	18
Window Coverings	Transparent Weaving with Handspun Cotton Weft	Green, Andrea	√	√	WJ	8	2	30	Fa 83	44
Window Coverings: Casements	Fabrics for Interiors	VanSlyke, Gail Rutter		√	WJ	3	1	9	Jy 78	5
Window Coverings: Casements	Open Weave Casement	Cronk, Helen H.	√	> 4	H&C	13	2		Sp 62	32
Window Coverings: Casements	Transparent Textiles	Burlew, Margaret	√	√	SS&D	17	1	65	Wi 85	10
Window Coverings: Curtains	April May: She Weaves Curtains with Images	Woelfle, Gretchen	√		Fa	7	6		N/D 80	28
Window Coverings: Curtains	Border Squares Curtain (Sharon D. Alderman)		√	> 4	Hw	5	2		M/A 84	69, 106
Window Coverings: Curtains	Canvas Weave Elegance	Herring, Connie	√	> 4	PWC	4	1	11		23
Window Coverings: Curtains	Crewel Gardens	Cunningham, Anne S.	√		TM			6	A/S 86	48
Window Coverings: Curtains	Enchanted Vine Window Curtain (Carol Strickler)		√	√	Hw	3	1		Ja 82	38, 87
Window Coverings: Curtains	Flower Curtain	Xenakis, Athanasios David	√	√	PWC	4	1	11		32
Window Coverings: Curtains	Four-Harness Woolen Curtain (Sharon Alderman) (error-corrected Hw v2 n2 81 p68)		√	√	Hw	2	1		F-W 80	68
Window Coverings: Curtains	Kitchen Curtains for a Restored 18th Century Homestead		√	√	H&C	19	3		Su 68	28
Window Coverings: Curtains	Lace Curtains	Higginbotham, Charles	√	√	Kn	1	2	2	S-S 85	40
Window Coverings: Curtains	My Linen Curtain	Handy, Virginia	√	√	S-O	10	3		Fa 86	23
Window Coverings: Curtains	Parks' Bouquet	Parks, Deborah	√	√	PWC	4	1	11		36
Window Coverings: Curtains	Rigid Heddle Wool Curtain (Betty Davenport)		√	√	Hw	2	1		F-W 80	Cover, 72
Window Coverings: Curtains	Silk & Linen Curtains		√	√	H&C	14	1		Wi 63	14
Window Coverings: Curtains	Springtime Curtains (Margaretha Essén-Hedin)		√	√	Hw	5	3		Su 84	72, 117

SUBJECT	TITLE	AUTHOR	IL	INST	JOUR	VOL	NO	ISS	DATE	PAGE
Window Coverings: Curtains	Swedish Curtains and Tablecloth Fabrics (Kerstin Eberhardson)		√	√	Hw	4	2		M/A 83	29, 82
Window Coverings: Curtains	Two Unusual Multishaft Curtains	Xenakis, Athanasios David	√	> 4	PWC	4	1	11		40
Window Coverings: Curtains	Two-Tie Inlay	Xenakis, Athanasios David	√	√	PWC	4	1	11		19
Window Coverings: Curtains	Weaving Primer, Part 1	Parks, Deborah	√	√	PWC	4	1	11		44
Window Coverings: Curtains	Weaving Primer, Part 3	Xenakis, Athanasios David	√	> 4	PWC	4	1	11		46
Window Coverings: Curtains	Windows: Sendoni Curtains	Xenakis, Alexis Yiorgos	√	> 4	PWC	4	1	11		4
Window Coverings: Draperies	Colorful Linen Draperies Designed and Woven by Marie Phelps		√	√	H&C	1	1		Ap 50	18
Window Coverings: Draperies	Corded Weaves: Four Harness Cords for Upholstery Fabric, Drapery Material and Wallhangings		√	√	WJ	3	1	9	Jy 78	28
Window Coverings: Draperies	Handwoven Curtains for Headquarters	Spencer, Elsie	√	√	SS&D	6	1	21	Wi 74	22
Window Coverings: Draperies	Linen and Silk Drapery		√	√	H&C	18	3		Su 67	10
Window Coverings: Draperies	Roman Shades and Draw Draperies — Mock Leno		√	√	WJ	6	1	21	Su 81	22
Window Coverings: Draperies	Saga of My Draperies, The	Strickler, Carol	√		Hw	5	2		M/A 84	71
Window Coverings: Hanging	Lace Window Hanging with Plaid		√	√	PWC			5	Sp 83	27
Window Coverings: Roman Shades	Insulated Roman Shade — Doup Leno	Champion, Ellen	√	√	WJ	6	1	21	Su 81	24
Window Coverings: Roman Shades	Insulating Window Covering	Svenson, Mary Jane	√	√	WJ	6	1	21	Su 81	18
Window Coverings: Roman Shades	Roman Shades and Draw Draperies — Mock Leno		√	√	WJ	6	1	21	Su 81	22
Window Coverings: Roman Shades, Technique	Roman Shades and Bedspread		√	√	WJ	3	1	9	Jy 78	32
Window Coverings: Shades	Tow Linen Shades (Robin Taylor Daugherty)		√	√	Hw	5	2		M/A 84	55, 96
Window Coverings: Shutters	Insulating Handwoven Shutters		√	> 4	WJ	6	1	21	Su 81	20
Window Coverings: Tapestry	Handwoven Tapestries Become Practical	Nixon, Elaine P.	√		WJ	6	1	21	Su 81	15
Window Shades see Window Coverings										
Wisteria	Tree-Bast Fiber Textiles of Japan	Dusenbury, Mary	√	√	S-O	10	3		Fa 86	35
Woad	Woad: A Medieval Dye	Austin, Carol	√		Fa	13	3		M/J 86	29
Women: Weavers	Women in Weaving	LaLena, Constance	√		Iw	4	4		Fa 79	54
Women/Design	Shaping the World Through Design	Welty, Margaret	√		Fa	9	4		J/A 82	48
Women/Fiber	"Birth Symbol in Traditional Women's Art, The" (Exhibit)	Vanco, John	√		Fa	13	3		M/J 86	52
Women/Fiber	Quilts in Women's Lives	Mattera, Joanne	√		Fa	9	3		M/J 82	54
Women/Fiber	"Women of Fiber: Six Michigan Artists" (Exhibit)	Reid, Eve	√		Fa	8	5		S/O 81	74
Women/Fiber Statements	Vivian Poon: Exposing Facades	Rowley, Kathleen	√		Fa	13	4		J/A 86	12
Wood: Woven	Woven Wood, Speciality of Robert Webb		√		H&C	16	2		Sp 65	19
Wool	Beverley Royce's "Recipe" for Merino	Royce, Beverly	√	√	S-O	5			81	49
Wool	Bhotiya Woolens from India	Willis, Elizabeth Bayley	√		H&C	5	2		Sp 54	4
Wool	From Lamb to Rack: Wool	Hodges, Eva			Hw	4	2		M/A 83	101
Wool	If You Want to Work with the Best Wool Yarns, Spin Them Yourself	Bulback, Stanley	√	√	TM			13	O/N 87	56
Wool	Make It with Wool		√		Hw	6	2		M/A 85	10
Wool	New Zealand Woolcrafts Festival	Guy, Sallie T.	√		SS&D	14	4	56	Fa 83	28
Wool	Nova Scotia Weavers Arouse Interest in Wool	Major, Marjorie	√		H&C	5	1		Wi 53	28
Wool	Opinionated Knitter: Thoughts on Wool, The	Zimmermann, Elizabeth			Kn	1	1	1	F-W 84 CI	39 31
Wool	Quinn's Spinning Notes	Quinn, Cecelia			S-O	5			81	55
Wool	Sheep Country Profiles: Dick Burtt	Gordon, Gerrie	√		Iw	1	4		Su 76	19

SUBJECT	TITLE	AUTHOR	IL	INST	JOUR	VOL	NO	ISS	DATE	PAGE
Wool	Why Wool Felts	Mattera, Joanne	√		Fa	6	6		N/D 79	48
Wool	Wool: Choosing a Domestic Fleece	Walker, Linda Berry	√		S-O	8	3		Fa 84	21
Wool	Wool Fibre Structure	Australian Wool Board	√		SS&D	4	3	15	Su 73	60
Wool	Wool Forum: Producers and Consumers vs Bureaucracy	Parker, Ron; Teresa Parker			S-O	10	4		Si 86	7
Wool	Wool: Mill-Prepared for Handspinners	Wheeler, Barbara R.	√		S-O	8	3		Fa 84	23
Wool	Wool: Selecting British Fleeces	Leadbeater, Eliza			S-O	8	3		Fa 84	25
Wool	Wool — That Wonderful Natural Fiber	Derr, Mary L.	√	√	WJ	2	2	6	Oc 77	2
Wool	Wools of Britain, The	Seagroatt, Margaret	√		H&C	24	2		M/A 73	33
Wool	Yarns and Fibers: Wool	Zielinski, S. A.; Robert Leclerc, ed.			MWL	4			'51–'73	29
Wool, Boiled	Boiled Wool	Adams, Brucie	√	√	Hw	5	3		Su 84	85
Wool Characteristics	Characteristics of Wool	Boyd, Ruth	√		H&C	26	5		Oc 75	43
Wool Characteristics	Choosing the Fiber for Feltmaking	Spark, Pat	√	√	SS&D	17	4	68	Fa 86	20
Wool Characteristics	Fleece in the Hands of a New Zealand Spinner	Horne, Beverley	√		S-O	2			78	24
Wool, Characteristics	If You Want to Work with the Best Wool Yarns, Spin Them Yourself	Bulback, Stanley	√	√	TM			13	O/N 87	56
Wool Characteristics	Native British Sheep: The Rare Breeds	Leadbeater, Eliza	√		S-O	3			79	19
Wool Characteristics	Selecting Wool for Handspinning (error-corrected SS&D v13 n1 81 p4)	Fleet, Malcolm		√	SS&D	12	4	48	Fa 81	66
Wool Characteristics	Some Physical Characteristics of Wool of Interest to Handspinners	Adams, Brucie	√		S-O	1			77	28
Wool Characteristics	Wool — Most Versatile of Fibers, Part 1	Kiessling, Robert H.	√		H&C	2	3		Su 51	13
Wool Characteristics	Wool on the Hoof	Lis, Mary Jane	√	√	SS&D	12	4	48	Fa 81	64
Wool Characteristics	Woolens and Tweeds: Woolen and Worsted Yarns: The Wool Fiber	Tidball, Harriet	√		SCGM		4		61	6
Wool Characteristics, Merino	Experiments with Merino	Adams, Brucie	√	√	Iw	5	1		Wi 79	50
Wool Combs and Combing also see Worsted										
Wool Combs and Combing	Wonderful Worsted	Dozer, Iris L.	√	√	SS&D	15	3	59	Su 84	26
Wool Combs and Combing	Woolcombing	Adams, Brucie	√	√	Iw	3	3		Sp 78	41
Wool: Drying	Drying Wool			√	TM			9	F/M 87	4
Wool: Grades	Raw Wool Values, How They Determine the End Use	Innes, J. Alisdair		√	H&C	15	1		Wi 64	15
Wool: Icelandic	Spin Your Own Lopi?	Gibson-Roberts, Priscilla A.	√	√	S-O	10	2		Su 86	40
Wool: Icelandic	Spinning with Icelandic Wool	Heite, Louise	√	√	S-O	10	1		Sp 86	33
Wool: Identification	What Kind Of Wool Is It?	Bulback, Stanley			TM			13	O/N 87	20
Wool: New Zealand	Maori and Pakeha of New Zealand Use Wool and Phormium Tenax	Duncan, Molly	√	√	SS&D	5	1	17	Wi 73	65
Wool: Processed Commercially	Commercial Materials in Modern Navajo Rugs	Hedlund, Ann Lane	√		TMJ	25			86	83
Wool: Softening Rinse	To Soften and Itchy Sweater			√	TM			6	A/S 86	14
Woolen	Wool — Most Versatile of Fibers, Part 2	Kiessling, Robert H.	√		H&C	2	4		Fa 51	25
Woolen	Woolens and Tweeds: Woolen and Worsted Yarns	Tidball, Harriet	√		SCGM		4		61	4
Woolens and Tweeds	Woolens and Tweeds	Tidball, Harriet	√	√	SCGM		4		61	1-46
Woolens: Scottish	Woolens and Tweeds: Designing Woolen Fabrics: Scottish Woolens	Tidball, Harriet	√	√	SCGM		4		61	28
Woolens: Swedish	Woolens and Tweeds: Designing Woolen Fabrics: Swedish Woolens	Tidball, Harriet			SCGM		4		61	26
Woolens: Welsh	Wool Gathering in Wales	Clement, Doris; Ted Clement	√		H&C	23	1		J/F 72	26
Words/Fiber	Words in Fiber	Rowley, Kathleen	√		Fa	11	2		M/A 84	66
Work Kits, Weaving Study Course	Textile Structure and Analysis, A Home Study Course in Twelve Lessons: Work Kits for the Lessons in Textile Structure	Tidball, Harriet			SCGM		18		66	5

SUBJECT	TITLE	AUTHOR	IL	INST	JOUR	VOL	NO	ISS	DATE	PAGE
Work Practices	Determination and Innovation: A Successful Weaving Mill	Fago, D'Ann Calhoun	√		TM			14	D/J 87	14
Work Practices	Identifying Hands at Work on a Paracas Mantle	Paul, Anne; Susan A. Niles	√		TMJ	23			84	5
Work Practices	Setting Goals and Evaluating Priorities	LaLena, Constance	√	√	Iw	5	1		Wi 79	43
Work Practices: Efficiency	Production Efficiency: Working Smart	LaLena, Constance		√	Hw	3	3		My 82	78
Work Practices: Weaving	One Weaver's Viewpoint	Freeman, Claire			H&C	11	1		Wi 60	10
Work Skills	Identifying Hands at Work on a Paracas Mantle	Paul, Anne; Susan A. Niles	√		TMJ	23			84	5
Workshop Tours	Planning a Workshop Tour	LaPlantz, Shereen	√	√	SS&D	13	4	52	Fa 82	46
Workshop/Studio: Fabric	Fabric Workshop: A Philadelphia Environment Where Experimentation Reigns, The	Park, Betty	√		Fa	9	1		J/F 82	21
Workshops also see Education: Workshops										
Workshops	Approaching the Workshop: A Teacher's Perspective	Merrill, Ruth			S-O	7	2		Su 83	52
Workshops	Are We Becoming Workshop Junkies?	Brostoff, Laya			SS&D	10	2	38	Sp 79	33
Workshops	How to Sponsor a Workshop Part 2: The Workshop Begins	Amos, Alden			Hw	8	4		S/O 87	73
Workshops	Individual/Artistic Development: A Workshop by Francoise Grossen	Lilligren, Ingrid	√		Fa	11	3		M/J 84	45
Workshops	Weaver's Commission Workshop	Meany, Janet	√		SS&D	10	3	39	Su 79	40
Workshops	Workshops	Harvey, Nancy			Hw	7	1		J/F 86	13
Workshops: Disabled	Arbutus Crafts				SS&D	2	1	5	De 70	17
Workshops: Dyeing	We Dyed in the Woods	Castino, Ruth	√	√	SS&D	4	3	15	Su 73	22
Workshops: Embroidery, Japanese	Spirit Exits Through the Embroiderer's Hands, The	Colwell, Katherine	√	√	TM			12	A/S 87	18
Workshops: Experimental Fiber	New Brunswick Craft School: Hosting A Workshop by Barbara MacCallum, The	Bauer, Nancy	√		Fa	11	5		S/O 84	40
Workshops: Fiber	Fiber/Art Conditioned by Life: A Workshop with Sheila Hicks	Klein, Jody	√		Fa	12	5		S/O 85	58
Workshops: Organization	How to Sponsor a Workshop, Part 1: The Basics of Organizing a Workshop	Amos, Alden		√	Hw	8	2		M/A 87	75
Workshops, Organizing	Good Leadership Is Prerequisite for Good Workshop	Entner, Betty C.			SS&D	5	4	20	Fa 74	37
Workshops: Planning	"Dye-In" in Detail: For Novices in Nova Scotia, A	Lock, Carolyn		√	SS&D	7	2	26	Sp 76	36
Workshops: Print and Dye Works	Shared Work Space May Be Just What You're Looking For, A	Levy, Julie	√	√	TM			9	F/M 87	42
Workshops: Selling	Setting the Right Price: A Workshop with Libby Platus (error-corrected Fa v13 n1 86 p5)	Caldwell, Rebecca	√		Fa	12	5		S/O 85	51
World Crafts Council	Crafts, Wine Gardens and World Friendship	Dyer, Carolyn	√		Fa	8	2		M/A 81	24
World's Fair: Brussels	Dorothy Liebes Designs Fabrics for U.S. Theatre at the Brussels World's Fair		√		H&C	9	2		Sp 58	26
Worsted	From the Woolcombers Bench: Cashgora	Dozer, Iris		√	S-O	10	2		Su 86	39
Worsted	Handspun Jacket		√	√	S-O	7	4		Wi 83	48
Worsted	Tagari: A Greek Saddlebag of Handspun Wools, The	Koster, Joan Boura	√	√	WJ	6	2	22	Fa 81	24
Worsted	Wonderful Worsted	Dozer, Iris	√	√	S-O	7	2		Su 83	32
Worsted	Wonderful Worsted	Dozer, Iris L.	√	√	SS&D	15	3	59	Su 84	26
Worsted	Wonderful Worsted II: Alternate Methods of Woolcombing	Dozier, Iris	√	√	S-O	7	4		Wi 83	21
Worsted	Wool — Most Versatile of Fibers, Part 2	Kiessling, Robert H.	√		H&C	2	4		Fa 51	25
Worsted	Woolens and Tweeds: Woolen and Worsted Yarns	Tidball, Harriet	√		SCGM		4		61	4
Worsted	Worsted Spinning	Zoller, Mary	√	√	S-O	7	4		Wi 83	26
Woven Fashion	Theme Issue		√		WJ	11	3	43	Wi 87	

SUBJECT	TITLE	AUTHOR	IL	INST	JOUR	VOL	NO	ISS	DATE	PAGE
WPA Weaving	Colorful Blinds and Fabrics from Texas		√		H&C	6	4		Fa 55	14
Wrapping	"Becky Clark Fiber" (Exhibit)	Farber, Deborah	√		Fa	6	1		J/F 79	89
Wrapping	Hearth Brooms (Anne Bliss)		√	√	Hw	1	2		S-S 80	27, 57
Wrapping, Extra-Weft	Hopi Embroidery Weave As a Technique for Tapestry	Atwood, Betty	√	√	WJ	5	1	17	Su 80	37
Wrapping, Extra-Weft	Shaped Sculptured Rugs — A Workshop with Urban Jupena		√	√	WJ	4	1	13	Jy 79	5
Wrapping, Extra-Weft	Weft Wrap Openwork	Atwood, Betty	√	√	Iw	4	1		Wi 78	20
Wrapping, Knitting	Egmont Sweater, The	Xenakis, Athanasios David	√	√	PWC			2	Ap 82	82
Wrapping: Techniques	Wrapping Techniques	Ericson, Lois	√	√	SS&D	2	1	5	De 70	27
Wrapping, Warp	Chavin Textiles and the Origins of Peruvian Weaving	Conklin, William J	√		TMJ	3	2		De 71	13
Wrapping, Weft	Painting and Brocading on the Loom	Ziek, Bhakti	√	√	TM			6	A/S 86	42
Wrapping, Weft	Soumak Rug (Jean Scorgie)		√	√	Hw	6	4		S/O 85	41, I-4
Wrapping, Weft	Weft-Wrap Openwork Technique	Atwood, Betty	√	√	AT	3			My 85	65
Wristlets: Plaited	Notes on Plaiting in the Upper Amazon Basin, Peru	Blinks, Anne	√	√	Iw	5	4		Fa 80	51
Xerography	Angela Manno	Manno, Angela	√		Fa	12	5		S/O 85	18
Xerography	"Robin Becker and Joan Lintault: Visual Traces of the Past" (Exhibit)	Meloy, Margaret	√		Fa	11	1		J/F 84	80
Xerography: Color	Color Xerography and the Fiber Artist	Theil, Linda	√		Fa	8	5		S/O 81	59
Xerography, Color	Incredible Color Copy Machine, The	Redding, Debbie	√		Hw	2	4		Se 81	74
Xerography: Technique	Color Xerox Transfer Process			√	Fa	8	5		S/O 81	63
Xerography: Textiles	Salmon Run: The Work of Northwest Artists Peggy Vanbianchi and Emily Standley	Hirschi, Ron	√		Fa	10	2		M/A 83	16
Yardage	Basic Sewing Techniques in Handling Handwoven Fabrics for Garments	Knollenberg, Barbara	√	√	WJ	1	1	1	Jy 76	25
Yardage	Coat for Handwoven Yardage, A	Roth, Bettie G.	√	> 4	WJ	7	3	27	Wi 82	6
Yardage	Crackle		√	√	WJ	3	3	11	Ja 79	32
Yardage	Garments with Ethnic Flavor: Mexican Embroidery Combined with Handwoven Yardage		√	> 4	WJ	2	3	7	Ja 78	17
Yardage	Handspun Yarns for Weavers	Burnlees, Dee	√	√	WJ	8	2	30	Fa 83	21
Yardage	One Weaver's Approach to Designing Yardage	Alderman, Sharon	√	√	Iw	3	2		Wi 78	22
Yardage	Projects with Cotton		√	√	WJ	4	2	14	Oc 79	28
Yardage	Shadowweave, Part 1 (error-corrected WJ v2 n1 77 insert for vol. 1)	Barrett, Clotilde	√	> 4	WJ	1	1	1	Jy 76	13
Yardage	Space-Dented Warp	Fry, Laura	√	√	WJ	4	3	15	Ja 80	26
Yardage, Silk	Moneymakers for Weavers	Klessen, Romy	√	√	PWC	1	1		No 81	5
Yardage, Twill	Fascination of Twills (Fourshafts): High Quality in Twill Yardage	Zielinski, S. A.; Robert Leclerc, ed.	√	√	MWL	9			'51–'73	95
Yardage, Wool	Moneymakers for Weavers	Klessen, Romy	√	> 4	PWC	1	1		No 81	5
Yarn	Fiberarts Special: All About Yarn	Mattera, Joanne	√		Fa	7	1		J/F 80	Insert
Yarn	Theme Issue		√		Fa	7	1		J/F 80	
Yarn, Analysis	Handspun Yarn Production Rates in the Cuzco Region of Peru	Bird, Junius B.	√		TMJ	2	3		De 68	9
Yarn, Balling	Managing Balls of Yarn				TM			8	D/J 86	8
Yarn, Calculating Yardage Requirements	Computerized Weaving Calculations (error-corrected SS&D v12 n4 81 p8)	Jarvis, Helen		√	SS&D	12	3	47	Su 81	46
Yarn, Calculating Yardage Requirements	Coverlet: Make Someday Today, Start a Coverlet, A	van der Hoogt, Madelyn	√	√	PWC	5	1	15		24
Yarn, Calculating Yardage Requirements	Designing the Warp: Parallel Considerations	Criscola, Jeanne	√	√	TM			1	O/N 85	66
Yarn, Calculating Yardage Requirements	Handweaver's Instruction Manual: Thread Requirements	Tidball, Harriet C. nee Douglas		√	SCGM		34		49	9

SUBJECT	TITLE	AUTHOR	IL	INST	JOUR	VOL	NO	ISS	DATE	PAGE
Yarn, Calculating Yardage Requirements	How Much Yarn for the Job?	Towner, Naomi Whiting		√	SS&D	6	4	24	Fa 75	36
Yarn, Calculating Yardage Requirements	How Much Yarn for the Job? Rya and Flossa	Towner, Naomi W.	√	√	SS&D	8	4	32	Fa 77	14
Yarn, Calculating Yardage Requirements	How Much Yarn for the Job? Tapestry	Towner, Naomi W.	√	√	SS&D	9	1	33	Wi 77	73
Yarn, Calculating Yardage Requirements	Planning a Project	Redding, Debbie		√	Hw	3	1		Ja 82	23
Yarn, Calculating Yardage Requirements	Treasury for Beginners: The Warp	Zielinski, S. A.; Robert Leclerc, ed.		√	MWL	1			'51–'73	73
Yarn, Calculating Yardage Requirements	Yarn Shop Dilemma, The	Liebler, Barbara	√	√	Iw	1	1		Fa 75	16
Yarn, Combinations: Wool and Man Made Fibers	Baby Blanket	Ingebretsen, Cathy	√	√	PWC	3	1	7		6
Yarn, Commercial	Behind the Scenes: A Textile Mill	Goodman, Deborah Lerme	√		Fa	13	3		M/J 86	40
Yarn, Commercial	Commercial Materials in Modern Navajo Rugs	Hedlund, Ann Lane	√		TMJ	25			86	83
Yarn, Commercial	Fine Cottons Offer Wide Possibilities		√		H&C	5	3		Su 54	27
Yarn, Commercial	Handspun: Inspiration from Commercial Sources	Mintzer, Arlene	√		S-O	10	2		Su 86	33
Yarn, Commercial	Mill End Yarns	Wertenberger, Kathryn			Hw	5	4		S/O 84	77
Yarn, Commercial	Superwash Wool	Donnelly, Robert	√		S-O	10	2		Su 86	49
Yarn, Commercial	Yarns		√		Kn	1	2	2	S-S 85	37
Yarn, Commercial	Yarns	Elkins, Barbara	√		Kn	1	1	1	F-W 84 CI	52 44
Yarn, Commercial	Yarns and Fibers: Yarns: Commercial Specifications	Zielinski, S. A.; Robert Leclerc, ed.			MWL	4			'51–'73	70
Yarn, Commercial	Yarns and Fibers: Yarns for Specialized Production	Zielinski, S. A.; Robert Leclerc, ed.			MWL	4			'51–'73	63
Yarn, Cotton	Commercial Materials in Modern Navajo Rugs	Hedlund, Ann Lane	√		TMJ	25			86	83
Yarn, Cotton	Fine Cottons Offer Wide Possibilities		√		H&C	5	3		Su 54	27
Yarn, Cotton	Knitting with Cotton: Stitch Maneuvers Help Sweaters Stay in Shape	Dyett, Linda	√	√	TM			9	F/M 87	38
Yarn, Cotton: Types	Understanding Cotton Fiber & Yarns	Ayotte, Robert; Roberta Ayotte	√		WJ	11	2	42	Fa 86	27
Yarn Count Systems	Fleece in the Hands of a New Zealand Spinner	Horne, Beverley	√		S-O	2			78	24
Yarn Count Systems	History of Linen, A	Mattera, Joanne	√	√	SS&D	8	3	31	Su 77	16
Yarn Count Systems	Understanding Cotton Fiber & Yarns	Ayotte, Robert; Roberta Ayotte	√		WJ	11	2	42	Fa 86	27
Yarn Count Systems	Weaving with Linen	Condit, Joan	√		H&C	6	3		Su 55	46
Yarn Count Systems	Wool — Most Versatile of Fibers, Part 2	Kiessling, Robert H.	√		H&C	2	4		Fa 51	25
Yarn Count Systems	Woolens and Tweeds: From Fleece to Woolen Yarn: Woolen Yarn Sizes	Tidball, Harriet	√	√	SCGM		4		61	13
Yarn Count Systems	Yarn Count or Number	Hausner, Walter			H&C	9	3		Su 58	31
Yarn Count Systems	Yarn Count Systems				WJ	6	3	23	Wi 81	28
Yarn Count Systems	Yarn Counts				S-O	1			77	4
Yarn Count Systems	Yarn Counts	Hausner, Walter			WJ	8	2	30	Fa 83	52
Yarn Count Systems	Yarns and Fibers: Modern Count of Yarn	Zielinski, S. A.; Robert Leclerc, ed.		√	MWL	4			'51–'73	39
Yarn Count Systems	Yarns and Fibers: Tex System	Zielinski, S. A.; Robert Leclerc, ed.	√		MWL	4			'51–'73	114
Yarn, Creative Uses	Using the Yarn You've Got	Giles, Lynne	√	√	Hw	8	4		S/O 87	63
Yarn, Crepe	Vest with a Hidden Twist	Emerick, Patricia	√	√	S-O	11	4		Wi 87	36, I-46
Yarn, Design	Designer Yarn — A Use for Acid Dyes	Omer, Martha			S-O	6	4		82	56
Yarn, Design	Designer Yarns: Slubs and Spirals	Chapin, Doloria	√	√	S-O	3			79	54
Yarn, Design	Designing Yarn	Noble, Judith G.	√		S-O	2			78	53

SUBJECT	TITLE	AUTHOR	IL	INST	JOUR	VOL	NO	ISS	DATE	PAGE
Yarn, Design	Discover Cotton Spinning	Ajeman, Norma; Irene Laughing Cloud Schmoller	√	√	WJ	8	3	31	Wi 83	49
Yarn, Design	Elements of Yarn Structure	Quinn, Celia	√	√	S-O	6	4		82	46
Yarn, Design	Flax: Yarn Design Determines Choice	Leadbeater, Eliza	√	√	S-O	8	3		Fa 84	34
Yarn, Design	Handspinning as Art	Walker, Linda Berry	√		S-O	2			78	56
Yarn, Design	Inspiration for New Designs in Cotton	Hausner, Walter	√		H&C	3	4		Fa 52	23
Yarn, Design	Jacob Wool — A Handspinner's Delight	Thormahlen, Marian Oyen	√	√	WJ	11	3	43	Wi 87	57
Yarn, Design	Personal Approach to Color, A	Matlock, Ann	√		S-O	9	3		Fa 85	19
Yarn, Design	Precise Control of Size and Quality in Handspun Yarn, Part 1, The	Ross, Mabel	√	√	SS&D	16	3	63	Su 85	12
Yarn, Design	Precise Control of Twist in Handspun Yarn, Part 2, The	Ross, Mabel	√	√	SS&D	16	4	64	Fa 85	26
Yarn, Design	Six of One, Half a Dozen of the Other (a roundtable discussion with six spinners)		√		S-O	5			81	51
Yarn, Design	What to do with a Rainbow	Klinect, Ann W.	√		S-O	9	3		Fa 85	26
Yarn, Design	Yarn Design: The Fine Points in Black and White	Meyer, Peggy Frost	√	√	WJ	12	2	46	Fa 87	38
Yarn, Design, Twist	Composition and Designing: Patterns in Twist	Zielinski, S. A.; Robert Leclerc, ed.	√	√	MWL	18			'51–'73	75
Yarn, Difficult in Weaving	Yarns and Fibers: Difficult Yarns	Zielinski, S. A.; Robert Leclerc, ed.		√	MWL	4			'51–'73	93
Yarn, Embroidery	Stitches for Silk-and-Metal Embroidery (error-corrected TM I4 A/M 86 p4)	Payette, Lynn	√	√	TM			3	F/M 86	51
Yarn, Evaluation, Twist	Checking the Twist	Gickie, John	√	√	S-O	11	1		Sp 87	27
Yarn, Handling: Silk	Yarn Handling (Cheryl Kolander)		√	√	Hw	7	1		J/F 86	60
Yarn, Handspun	Adventures in Pursuit of Yarns	Gallagher, Constance	√		H&C	12	3		Su 61	51
Yarn, Handspun	Alaskan Yarns on Tour				H&C	19	4		Fa 68	11
Yarn, Handspun	Confetti Sweater	Slaven, Pat	√	√	S-O	11	4		Wi 87	26
Yarn, Handspun	Controlling the Size and Texture of Handspun Yarn	Hochberg, Bette	√	√	SS&D	9	4	36	Fa 78	31
Yarn, Handspun	Cotton, Cool and Comfy	Gibson-Roberts, Priscilla A.	√	√	Kn	3	2	6	Sp 87	48
Yarn, Handspun	Cotton Shirts	Barnett-Westfall, Lynn	√	√	WJ	4	3	15	Ja 80	22
Yarn, Handspun	Creative Knitwear		√		S-O	3			79	62
Yarn, Handspun	Cross Country Ski Set	Chadwick, Louisa	√	√	S-O	11	4		Wi 87	34
Yarn, Handspun	Fair Isle in Natural Colors, The	Gibson-Roberts, Priscilla A.	√	√	Kn	2	1	3	F-W 85	34
Yarn, Handspun	Fine, Finer, Finest	Raven, Lee		√	S-O	9	4		Wi 85	24
Yarn, Handspun	Finest Thread		√		S-O	8	3		Fa 84	17
Yarn, Handspun	Finishing a Woolen Knitting Yarn	Gibson-Roberts, Priscilla A.			S-O	9	2		Su 85	38
Yarn, Handspun	Garments by Hanni Bureker		√	√	WJ	6	3	23	Wi 81	35
Yarn, Handspun	Handspinning for Needlework	Shurtleff, Chris Ann	√	√	S-O	7	2		Su 83	29
Yarn, Handspun	Handspun for Kaffe Fassett Sweaters	Adams, Brucie	√	√	S-O	11	4		Wi 87	32
Yarn, Handspun	Handspun, Handwoven Saddle Blanket, A	Newsted, Jean	√	√	WJ	8	2	30	Fa 83	22
Yarn, Handspun	Handspun: Inspiration from Commercial Sources	Mintzer, Arlene	√		S-O	10	2		Su 86	33
Yarn, Handspun	Handspun into Lace	Fournier, Jane	√	√	SS&D	17	4	68	Fa 86	70
Yarn, Handspun	Handspun Yarn as Art	Burkhauser, Jude			S-O	3			79	22
Yarn, Handspun	Handspun Yarn for a Pulled Warp Vest	Adams, Brucie	√	√	Hw	7	1		J/F 86	78
Yarn, Handspun	Handspun Yarn Production Rates in the Cuzco Region of Peru	Bird, Junius B.	√		TMJ	2	3		De 68	9
Yarn, Handspun	Handspun Yarns for Weavers	Burnlees, Dee	√	√	WJ	8	2	30	Fa 83	21
Yarn, Handspun	Handspun Yarns from Black Sheep Wool	Simmons, Paula	√	√	H&C	14	3		Su 63	6
Yarn, Handspun	Handspun Yarns Made by the Blind	Morgret, Eugene D.	√		H&C	1	3		Fa 50	17

SUBJECT	TITLE	AUTHOR	IL	INST	JOUR	VOL	NO	ISS	DATE	PAGE
Yarn, Handspun	Handspuns for Tapestries	Szumski, Norma; Phyllis Clemmer; Clotilde Barrett	√		WJ	6	2	22	Fa 81	41
Yarn, Handspun	Heathering	O'Connor, Marcie Archer	√	√	Kn	2	1	3	F-W 85	54
Yarn, Handspun	Irish Kinsale Cloak, The	Jones, Una	√	√	WJ	8	3	31	Wi 83	35
Yarn, Handspun	Irregularity in Handspun	Simmons, Paula	√	√	H&C	20	4		Fa 69	13
Yarn, Handspun	Irregularity in Handspun, Part 2	Simmons, Paula	√	√	H&C	21	1		Wi 70	20
Yarn, Handspun	Jacob Wool — A Handspinner's Delight	Thormahlen, Marian Oyen	√	√	WJ	11	3	43	Wi 87	57
Yarn, Handspun	Kasuri-Like-Effect Weaving	Akita, Mariko Olivia	√	√	WJ	6	2	22	Fa 81	18
Yarn, Handspun	Knitting with Handspun	O'Connor, Marcie Archer	√	√	Kn	1	1	1	F-W 84 CI	55 46
Yarn, Handspun	Knitting with Handspun	O'Connor, Marcie Archer	√		Kn	1	2	2	S-S 85	54
Yarn, Handspun	Lacy Triangular Stole of Handspun Wool, A	Kniskern, Edna Maki	√	√	WJ	6	2	22	Fa 81	48
Yarn, Handspun	Nature: A Color Source and Inspiration for Traditional Sweaters	Gibson-Roberts, Priscilla A.	√		S-O	9	3		Fa 85	42
Yarn, Handspun	Noils Using Handspun Yarns	Conover, Jean	√		SS&D	12	1	45	Wi 80	63
Yarn, Handspun	Novelty Yarns: Creation in Color and Texture	Dick, Barbara Ann	√	√	SS&D	12	3	47	Su 81	32
Yarn, Handspun	One Hundred Yard Rule	Gibson-Roberts, Priscilla A.	√	√	Kn	1	2	2	S-S 85	58
Yarn, Handspun	Precise Control of Size and Quality in Handspun Yarn, Part 1, The	Ross, Mabel	√	√	SS&D	16	3	63	Su 85	12
Yarn, Handspun	Precise Control of Twist in Handspun Yarn, Part 2, The	Ross, Mabel	√	√	SS&D	16	4	64	Fa 85	26
Yarn, Handspun	Recent Success of Carole Lubove-Klein: An Inspiring Yarn, The	McGuire, Patricia	√		Fa	9	5		S/O 82	20
Yarn, Handspun	Scarves in Variegated Yarns	Irwin, Bobbie	√	√	S-O	11	4		Wi 87	53
Yarn, Handspun	Seat for All Seasons, A	Rasmussen, Peg	√	√	WJ	6	2	22	Fa 81	21
Yarn, Handspun	Shirt for a Fellow Spinner, A	Gaustad, Stephenie	√	√	Hw	7	4		S/O 86	76
Yarn, Handspun	Six of One, Half a Dozen of the Other (a roundtable discussion with six spinners)		√		S-O	5			81	51
Yarn, Handspun	Spinning Traditional Knitting Yarns for Ethnic Sweaters	Gibson-Roberts, Priscilla A.	√	√	S-O	8	4		Wi 84	26
Yarn, Handspun	Spinning Unique and Useable Yarns	Donohue, Sandra	√	√	S-O	8	4		Wi 84	33
Yarn, Handspun	Study of Andean Spinning in the Cuzco Region, A	Goodell, Miss Grace	√	√	TMJ	2	3		De 68	2
Yarn, Handspun	Sweater's Tale, A	Owens, Julie	√	√	Hw	6	4		S/O 85	82
Yarn, Handspun	Tagari: A Greek Saddlebag of Handspun Wools, The	Koster, Joan Boura	√	√	WJ	6	2	22	Fa 81	24
Yarn, Handspun	Texture in Spinning	O'Connor, Marcie Archer	√	√	Kn	2	2	4	S-S 86	53
Yarn, Handspun	Texture with Handspun	Page, Judy	√	√	WJ	6	2	22	Fa 81	20
Yarn, Handspun	Three Spun Threads	Royce, Beverly	√	√	S-O	9	1		Sp 85	39
Yarn, Handspun	Transparent Weaving with Handspun Cotton Weft	Green, Andrea	√	√	WJ	8	2	30	Fa 83	44
Yarn, Handspun	Using Unplanned Yarn in a Planned Project	Chandler, Deborah	√		Hw	8	2		M/A 87	24
Yarn, Handspun	What to do with a Rainbow	Klinect, Ann W.	√		S-O	9	3		Fa 85	26
Yarn, Handspun	Wool: From Fleece to Knitting Yarn	Gibson-Roberts, Priscilla A.	√	√	S-O	8	3		Fa 84	27
Yarn, Heathered	Spinner's Specialty: Heathered Yarns, A	Searle, Karen	√	√	WJ	9	2	34	Fa 84	56
Yarn, Inventory	Effective Yarn Storage and Inventory Control	Keasbey, Doramay		√	Hw	8	4		S/O 87	67
Yarn, Knitting	Yarns		√		Kn	3	2	6	Sp 87	47
Yarn, Knitting	Yarns		√		Kn	3	3	7	Su 87	39
Yarn, Knitting	Yarns		√		Kn	3	4	8	Fa 87	5
Yarn, Knitting	Yarns		√		Kn	4	1	9	Wi 87	21
Yarn, Knitting	Yarns		√		Kn	2	1	3	F-W 85	30
Yarn, Knitting	Yarns		√		Kn	2	2	4	S-S 86	60

SUBJECT	TITLE	AUTHOR	IL	INST	JOUR	VOL	NO	ISS	DATE	PAGE
Yarn, Knitting	Yarns		√		Kn	3	1	5	F-W 86	6
Yarn, Knitting	Yarns	Elkins, Barbara	√		Kn	1	1	1	F-W 84	52
									CI	42
Yarn, Lace Knitting	Shetland Lace	Korach, Alice	√	√	TM			11	J/J 87	40
Yarn, Lace Knitting	Yarns for Lace Knitting			√	TM			14	D/J 87	4
Yarn, Laminated	Yarns and Fibers: Metallic Yarns	Zielinski, S. A.; Robert Leclerc, ed.			MWL	4			'51–'73	98
Yarn, Man-Made	Current Developments in Man-made Yarns and Fibers	Hausner, Walter			H&C	9	3		Su 58	41
Yarn, Man-Made	Fiberglas Designs		√		H&C	19	3		Su 68	32
Yarn, Manufacturing	What a Handweaver Can Learn from the Scottish Weaving Industry (error-corrected WJ v2 n1 77 insert for vol. 1)	Barrett, Clotilde	√	√	WJ	1	3	3	Ja 77	11
Yarn, Metallic	Back to the Gold Standard	Siminoff	√		H&C	1	3		Fa 50	24
Yarn, Metallic	Costumes of Royal India	Levine, Betsy	√		TM			7	O/N 86	64
Yarn, Metallic	Handwoven Wedding Chuppa	Horger, Millicent	√	√	WJ	7	4	28	Sp 83	50
Yarn, Metallic	Metallic Yarns		√		H&C	7	2		Sp 56	48
Yarn, Metallic	Metallic Yarns	Wertenberger, Kathryn			Hw	6	1		J/F 85	89
Yarn, Metallic	Notes on Using Metallic Yarn	Piroch, Sigrid	√	√	Hw	6	1		J/F 85	I-9
Yarn, Metallic	Stitches for Silk-and-Metal Embroidery (error-corrected TM I4 A/M 86 p4)	Payette, Lynn	√	√	TM			3	F/M 86	51
Yarn, Metallic	Weave and Knit Pullover	Barrett, Clotilde	√	√	WJ	8	3	31	Wi 83	20
Yarn, Metallic	Yarns and Fibers: Metallic Yarns	Zielinski, S. A.; Robert Leclerc, ed.			MWL	4			'51–'73	98
Yarn, Mill-End	Mill End Mystery	Upitis, Lizbeth	√		Kn	3	4	8	Fa 87	36
Yarn, Mixed Fibers	Caribou Hair and the Creation of a New Fabric	Goodfellow, Robin	√		AT	6			De 86	119
Yarn, Natural Fibers, Plant	Yarns and Fibers: Unusual Yarns - 1	Zielinski, S. A.; Robert Leclerc, ed.		√	MWL	4			'51–'73	79
Yarn, Natural Materials, Wood	Yarns and Fibers: Unusual Yarns - Partitions	Zielinski, S. A.; Robert Leclerc, ed.		√	MWL	4			'51–'73	89
Yarn, Novelty	Beyond the Machine (The creative uses of imprecision)	d'Avila, Doris	√	√	S-O	4			80	50
Yarn, Novelty	Catch It		√	√	Hw	6	1		J/F 85	63
Yarn, Novelty	City Couture		√		Hw	6	1		J/F 85	40
Yarn, Novelty	Designer Yarns: Slubs and Spirals	Chapin, Doloria	√	√	S-O	3			79	54
Yarn, Novelty	Designing the Warp: Parallel Considerations	Criscola, Jeanne	√	√	TM			1	O/N 85	66
Yarn, Novelty	Evening Bags that Shine with Flash & Glitter	Piroch, Sigrid	√	√	Hw	6	1		J/F 85	36
Yarn, Novelty	Exploring the Fun & Fantasy of Novelties		√		Hw	6	1		J/F 85	31
Yarn, Novelty	Irregularity in Handspun, Part 3	Simmons, Paula		√	H&C	21	2		Sp 70	20
Yarn, Novelty	Jacob Wool — A Handspinner's Delight	Thormahlen, Marian Oyen	√	√	WJ	11	3	43	Wi 87	57
Yarn, Novelty	More Than Four can Double Your Fun	Pinchin, C. Bryn	√	>4	Hw	6	1		J/F 85	38
Yarn, Novelty	Novelty Silk Yarn from Bell Caps	Grayson, Persis	√	√	Hw	7	1		J/F 86	58
Yarn, Novelty	Novelty Yarns: Creation in Color and Texture	Dick, Barbara Ann	√	√	SS&D	12	3	47	Su 81	32
Yarn, Novelty	Quiet Elegance		√		Hw	6	1		J/F 85	32
Yarn, Novelty	Spinning Bulky Yarns	Kronenberg, Bud	√	√	SS&D	13	1	49	Wi 81	78
Yarn, Novelty	Spinning Fancy Yarns	Metchette, Glenna	√	√	SS&D	14	1	53	Wi 82	16
Yarn, Novelty	Spinning Novelty Yarns	d'Avila, Doris	√	√	Iw	4	4		Fa 79	58
Yarn, Novelty	Structuring a Bulky Yarn	Bartl, Pam	√	√	Iw	5	2		Sp 80	62
Yarn, Novelty	Supplementary Warp for Novelty Yarns	Davenport, Betty	√	√	Hw	6	1		J/F 85	34
Yarn, Novelty	Use of Novelty Yarns in Weaving, The	Blumenau, Lili	√		H&C	3	2		Sp 52	16
Yarn, Novelty	Yarn Design: The Fine Points in Black and White	Meyer, Peggy Frost	√	√	WJ	12	2	46	Fa 87	38
Yarn, Novelty	Yarn for the Weaving		√	√	PWC	3	1	7		21

SUBJECT	TITLE	AUTHOR	IL	INST	JOUR	VOL	NO	ISS	DATE	PAGE
Yarn, Novelty	Yarns and Fibers: Unusual Yarns - 2	Zielinski, S. A.; Robert Leclerc, ed.		√	MWL	4			'51–'73	85
Yarn, Organization System	Floss-Organizing System, A		√	√	TM			13	O/N 87	10
Yarn, Production Rate, Drop Spindle	Handspun Yarn Production Rates in the Cuzco Region of Peru	Bird, Junius B.	√		TMJ	2	3		De 68	9
Yarn, Production Rate, Drop Spindle	Study of Andean Spinning in the Cuzco Region, A	Goodell, Miss Grace	√	√	TMJ	2	3		De 68	2
Yarn, Resources	Yarn Resource Page: A Guide to Specified Yarns and How to Make Substitutions				PWC			2	Ap 82	7
Yarn, Ribbon	Coronet, A	Clayton, Clare	√	√	Kn	3	2	6	Sp 87	32
Yarn, Selection	Choosing Yarns	Redding, Debbie	√	√	Hw	1	1		F–W 79	48
Yarn, Selection	Color Related Decorating Textiles Rugs, Draperies, Upholstery: Drapery and Casement Fabrics, Choosing the Proper Yarns	Rhodes, Tonya Stalons; Harriet Tidball, ed.			SCGM		14		65	8
Yarn, Selection	Doup Leno: Warp and Weft Yarns	Skowronski, Hella; Sylvia Tacker	√		SCGM		32		80	15
Yarn, Selection	Handloom Weaves: Warp and Weft	Tidball, Harriet			SCGM		33		57	8
Yarn, Selection	Handweaver's Instruction Manual: The Yarns, Thread Size Standards	Tidball, Harriet C. nee Douglas		√	SCGM		34		49	7
Yarn, Selection	On Buying Yarn	Krasnoff, Julienne			H&C	21	3		Su 70	45
Yarn, Selection	Rug Weaving: Rug Yarns	Stanley, Martha	√		WJ	6	3	23	Wi 81	44
Yarn, Selection	Summer and Winter and Other Two-Tie Unit Weaves: Balance and Yarns	Tidball, Harriet	√	√	SCGM		19		66	14
Yarn, Selection	Treasury for Beginners: Yarns for Beginners	Zielinski, S. A.; Robert Leclerc, ed.		√	MWL	1			'51–'73	71
Yarn, Selection	Two-Harness Textiles, The Open Work Weaves: Materials	Tidball, Harriet			SCGM		21		67	3
Yarn, Selection	Weaving Inkle Bands: Yarns for Inkle Weaving	Tidball, Harriet	√		SCGM		27		69	21
Yarn, Selection	Weaving with Linen	Condit, Joan	√		H&C	6	3		Su 55	46
Yarn, Selection	What Kinds of Yarns for Handweaving?	Brown, Myrtle A.	√		H&C	1	2		Su 50	22
Yarn, Shrinkage	Boiled Wool	Adams, Brucie	√	√	Hw	5	3		Su 84	85
Yarn, Silk	Stitches for Silk-and-Metal Embroidery (error-corrected TM I4 A/M 86 p4)	Payette, Lynn	√	√	TM			3	F/M 86	51
Yarn, Sources	Peter Collingwood, His Weaves and Weaving: Addresses and Miscellaneous Information	Tidball, Harriet			SCGM		8		63	46
Yarn, Sources	Yarns and Fibers: List of Dealers or Manufacturers of Yarns	Zielinski, S. A.; Robert Leclerc, ed.			MWL	4			'51–'73	117
Yarn, Space-Dyed	Space-Dyed or Variegated?				Hw	7	3		M/J 86	55
Yarn, Space-Dyed	Space-dyed Stripes Ensemble (Kathryn Wertenberger)		√	√	Hw	6	3		Su 85	44, I-8
Yarn, Space-Dyed	Special Warp Effects with Space-Dyed Yarn	Bohannan, Ronnine	√	√	Hw	7	3		M/J 86	50
Yarn, Space-Dyed	Suggestions for Using Space-Dyed Yarns			√	Hw	7	3		M/J 86	54
Yarn, Space-Dyed	Unlocking the Secret of Space-Dyed Yarn for a Weft-Wise Design	Stoehr, Mary Kay	√	√	Hw	7	3		M/J 86	52
Yarn, Space-Dyed	Weaving with Space-Dyed Yarns		√		Hw	7	3		M/J 86	49
Yarn, Splicing	How to Splice Yarn		√	√	TM			10	A/M 87	10
Yarn, Standards	Handweaver's Instruction Manual: The Yarns, Thread Size Standards	Tidball, Harriet C. nee Douglas	√	√	SCGM		34		49	7
Yarn, Standards: Grist	How Much Twist Do I Need?	Amos, Alden		√	S-O	11	1		Sp 87	25
Yarn, Standards: Ramie/Linen	How Much Twist Do I Need?	Amos, Alden		√	S-O	11	1		Sp 87	25
Yarn, Standards: Silk/Cotton	How Much Twist Do I Need?	Amos, Alden		√	S-O	11	1		Sp 87	25
Yarn, Standards: Twist	How Much Twist Do I Need?	Amos, Alden		√	S-O	11	1		Sp 87	25
Yarn, Storage	Effective Yarn Storage and Inventory Control	Keasbey, Doramay		√	Hw	8	4		S/O 87	67
Yarn, Structure	Add a New Twist to Your Spinning	Hochberg, Bette	√	√	S-O	5			81	42
Yarn, Structure	Are You Ready to Collapse?	Frame, Mary	√	√	S-O	11	1		Sp 87	41

SUBJECT	TITLE	AUTHOR	IL	INST	JOUR	VOL	NO	ISS	DATE	PAGE
Yarn, Structure	Before Heddles Were Invented	Bird, Junius B.	√		H&C	3	3		Su 52	5
Yarn, Structure	Checking the Twist	Gickie, John	√	√	S-O	11	1		Sp 87	27
Yarn, Structure	Controlling the Size and Texture of Handspun Yarn	Hochberg, Bette	√	√	SS&D	9	4	36	Fa 78	31
Yarn, Structure	Designer Yarns: Slubs and Spirals	Chapin, Doloria	√	√	S-O	3			79	54
Yarn, Structure	Elements of Yarn Structure	Quinn, Celia	√	√	S-O	6	4		82	46
Yarn, Structure	Experimenting with Silk Crepe	Quinn, Celia	√	√	S-O	10	4		Wi 86	36
Yarn, Structure	Exploring the Textures: Crepe	Zielinski, S. A.; Robert Leclerc, ed.	√	> 4	MWL	11			'51–'73	68
Yarn, Structure	Handspun Yarn Production Rates in the Cuzco Region of Peru	Bird, Junius B.	√		TMJ	2	3		De 68	9
Yarn, Structure	How Much Twist Do I Need?	Amos, Alden		√	S-O	11	1		Sp 87	25
Yarn, Structure	Irregularity in Handspun, Part 3	Simmons, Paula		√	H&C	21	2		Sp 70	20
Yarn, Structure	Knitting with Handspun	O'Connor, Marcie Archer	√		Kn	1	2	2	S-S 85	54
Yarn, Structure	Precise Control of Size and Quality in Handspun Yarn, Part 1, The	Ross, Mabel	√	√	SS&D	16	3	63	Su 85	12
Yarn, Structure	Precise Control of Twist in Handspun Yarn, Part 2, The	Ross, Mabel	√	√	SS&D	16	4	64	Fa 85	26
Yarn, Structure	Ringlets and Waves: Undulations from Overtwist	Frame, Mary	√	√	S-O	10	4		Wi 86	28
Yarn, Structure	Roman Textiles from Vindolanda, Hexham, England	Wild, John Peter	√		TMJ	18			79	19
Yarn, Structure	S and Z Twist	Hausner, Walter	√		H&C	14	2		Sp 63	37
Yarn, Structure	Save the Twist: Warping and Weaving with Overtwisted Yarns	Frame, Mary	√	√	S-O	11	2		Su 87	43
Yarn, Structure	Spinning Fine Yarn (It'a Method, not Magic)	Hochberg, Bette	√	√	Iw	5	3		Su 80	56
Yarn, Structure	Study of Andean Spinning in the Cuzco Region, A	Goodell, Miss Grace	√	√	TMJ	2	3		De 68	2
Yarn, Structure	Texture in Spinning	O'Connor, Marcie Archer	√	√	Kn	2	2	4	S-S 86	53
Yarn, Structure	Threading Needles		√		TM			10	A/M 87	4
Yarn, Structure	Twist Demystified	Clark, Marlyn	√	√	S-O	7	2		Su 83	25
Yarn, Structure	Weaving with Lofty Yarns	Frey, Berta	√	√	H&C	18	2		Sp 67	35
Yarn, Structure	Yarn Twist and Twills			√	Hw	6	5		N/D 85	44
Yarn, Structure Considerations	Using the Yarn You've Got	Giles, Lynne	√	√	Hw	8	4		S/O 87	63
Yarn, Structure: Twist	Woolens and Tweeds: Designing Woolen Fabrics: Influence of Twist Upon Fabric	Tidball, Harriet	√		SCGM		4		61	41
Yarn, Structure	Inspiration for New Designs in Cotton	Hausner, Walter	√		H&C	3	4		Fa 52	23
Yarn, Synthetic	Characteristics of Man-made Yarns	Hausner, Walter	√		H&C	6	3		Su 55	19
Yarn, Synthetic	Commercial Materials in Modern Navajo Rugs	Hedlund, Ann Lane	√		TMJ	25			86	83
Yarn, Synthetic	Designing the Warp: Parallel Considerations	Criscola, Jeanne	√	√	TM			1	O/N 85	66
Yarn, Synthetic	Yarns and Fibers: Synthetic Yarns	Zielinski, S. A.; Robert Leclerc, ed.			MWL	4			'51–'73	54
Yarn, Tangles	Untangling Yarn Bobbins			√	TM			9	F/M 87	12
Yarn, Twist: Tabby Weave	More About Fabrics: Tabby	Zielinski, S. A.; Robert Leclerc, ed.	√	√	MWL	20			'51–'73	19
Yarn, Types	Fiberarts Yarn Chart		√		Fa	7	1		J/F 80	Insert
Yarn, Types	For Beginning Weavers — What Yarns Can I Use?	Frey, Berta	√	√	H&C	17	2		Sp 66	17
Yarn, Types	Understanding Yarns	Redding, Debbie	√		Hw	5	1		J/F 84	18
Yarn, Types: Woolen	Woolens and Tweeds: From Fleece to Woolen Yarn: Types of Woolen Yarn	Tidball, Harriet		√	SCGM		4		61	14
Yarn, Unspun	Enhance with Unspuns	Fowler, Mary Jean	√		SS&D	7	3	27	Su 76	33
Yarn, Variations	Whig Rose Study (continued)	Morgenstern, Marvin M.	√	√	WJ	7	3	27	Wi 82	23
Yarn, Variegated	Kasuri-Like-Effect Weaving	Akita, Mariko Olivia	√	√	WJ	6	2	22	Fa 81	18
Yarn, Variegated	Space Dyeing with Fiber-Reactive Dyes	Knutson, Linda	√	√	WJ	8	1	29	Su 83	89

SUBJECT	TITLE	AUTHOR	IL	INST	JOUR	VOL	NO	ISS	DATE	PAGE
Yarn, Warp Considerations	Using the Yarn You've Got	Giles, Lynne	√	√	Hw	8	4		S/O 87	63
Yarn, Warp Considerations	Yarns and Fibers: The Yarn and the Sett of Warp	Zielinski, S. A.; Robert Leclerc, ed.	√	√	MWL	4			'51–'73	34
Yarn, Weft Considerations	Using the Yarn You've Got	Giles, Lynne	√	√	Hw	8	4		S/O 87	63
Yarn, Weight	Weighty Matters	Elkins, Barbara		√	Kn	3	4	8	Fa 87	46
Yarn, Winding	How to Wind Yarn Loosely			√	TM			11	J/J 87	6
Yarn, Woven (Chenille)	Yarn for the Weaving		√	√	PWC	3	1	7		21
Yarn, Yardage	One Hundred Yard Rule	Gibson-Roberts, Priscilla A.	√	√	Kn	1	2	2	S-S 85	58
Yoga	Yoga For Weavers	McCloud, Nena	√		Fa	5	2		M/A 78	40
Yokes see Collars, Cuffs, Yokes										
Yugoslavia	Brief Survey of Textile Traditions of Yugoslavia, A	Dittmar, Ana	√		S-O	8	1		Sp 84	41
Yurts	Shelters and Symbols	Gordon, Beverly	√	√	SS&D	11	1	41	Wi 79	53
Yurts	Yurt in Artpark, The	Brennan, Joan	√		Fa	9	3		M/J 82	19
Yurts	Yurts (Not Your Average Dwelling)	Landess, Susan	√		Fa	5	6		N/D 78	26
Yurts: Turkoman	Turkoman Yurt, The		√	√	SS&D	10	1	37	Wi 78	24
Zippers: Hand-Stitched	Zippers in Knits, Perfect Ribs			√	TM			13	O/N 87	8

author index

AUTHOR	TITLE	JOUR	VOL	NO	ISS	DATE	PAGE
Aarnio, Rauha	Beautiful Rugs	H&C	11	2		Sp 60	60
Aarnio, Rauha	New Rugs & Ryijys	H&C	11	2		Sp 60	60
Abakanowicz, Magdalena	see Jacob, Mary Jane	Fa	10	5		S/O 83	58
Abbey, Barbara	Complete Book of Knitting, The	Kn	1	2	2	S-S 85	79
Abbey, Barbara	Complete Book of Knitting, The	TM			9	F/M 87	76
Abbey, Barbara	Knitting Lace	Kn	1	2	2	S-S 85	79
Abbey, Barbara	Knitting Lace	TM			9	F/M 87	76
Abbot Hall Art Gallery Catalogue	Turcoman of Iran, The	TMJ	3	3		72	80
Abbott, Deborah	Buttons	TM		2		D/J 85	56
Abbott, Deborah	Playing with Darts	TM			14	D/J 87	64
Abbott, Edith E.	Western German Weavers	H&C	8	4		Fa 57	22
Abdel-Malek, Laila	Tapestry Roundel with Nilotic Scenes, A	TMJ	25			86	33
Abel, Isabel	Multiple Harness Patterns from the Early 1700's	Iw	5	1		Wi 79	65
Abel, Isabel I.	Designs from Serff Patterns	H&C	11	4		Fa 60	6
Abel, Isabel I.	Multiple Harness Patterns from the Early 1700's — The Snavely Patterns	SS&D	11	2	42	Sp 80	82
Abel, Isabel I.	Multiple Harness Patterns from the Early 1700's, The Snavely Patterns	WJ	4	3	15	Ja 80	46
Abrahams, Howard	Fibers	Iw	1	3		Sp 76	8
Abrahamsson, Greta	Cross Stitch Patterns	H&C	3	3		Su 52	64
Acar, Belkis	Kilim Ve Düz Dokuma Yaygilar	TMJ	4	3		76	75
Achorn, Leland J.	Queerest Loom I Ever Did See	SS&D	1	4	4	Se 70	16
Acosta, Dan	Stitched, Stuffed, and Painted: The Art of Esther Luttikhuizen	Fa	12	2		M/A 85	61
Adachi, Barbara C.	Fukumi Shimura: Japan's Colorist Supreme	Fa	12	4		J/A 85	28
Adachi, Barbara Curtis	Living National Treasures of Japan, The	Fa	11	1		J/F 84	62
Adachi, Barbara Curtis	Shokansai Iizuka: Bamboo Craftsman and Living National Treasure of Japan	Fa	11	1		J/F 84	59
Adams, B. J.	see Kurtz, Carol	SS&D	9	4	36	Fa 78	4
Adams, Brucie	Boiled Wool	Hw	5	3		Su 84	85
Adams, Brucie	Boiled Wool (Mary Jane Hensley)	Hw	5	3		Su 84	85
Adams, Brucie	Carding Machines	Iw	4	3		Su 79	54
Adams, Brucie	Color in Spinning	Iw	3	2		Wi 78	34
Adams, Brucie	Columbia, The	Iw	3	4		Su 78	36
Adams, Brucie	Devices to Aid in Wool Processing	Hw	3	4		Se 82	69
Adams, Brucie	Experiments with Merino	Iw	5	1		Wi 79	50
Adams, Brucie	Hair of the Dog, The	Hw	3	2		Mr 82	62
Adams, Brucie	Handspun for Kaffe Fassett Sweaters	S-O	11	4		Wi 87	32
Adams, Brucie	Handspun, Handwoven Cocoon Jacket, A	Hw	5	2		M/A 84	88
Adams, Brucie	"Handspun on a Knitting Machine?" Sure!!	Iw	6	1		Wi 80	60
Adams, Brucie	Handspun Yarn for a Pulled Warp Vest	Hw	7	1		J/F 86	78
Adams, Brucie	I Have This Fleece...Now What?	Iw	5	4		Fa 80	62
Adams, Brucie	Kinsale Cloak	S-O	4			80	56
Adams, Brucie	Linsey-Woolsey Using Handspun Yarns	Hw	3	5		N/D 82	59
Adams, Brucie	Machine Knitting with Handspun Yarn—Part 2	Hw	4	4		S/O 83	76
Adams, Brucie	Musk Ox, and Miscellaneous	Iw	4	2		Sp 79	46
Adams, Brucie	Pencil Roving and the Navajo Ply	Hw	6	1		J/F 85	75
Adams, Brucie	Prepared Fibers: A Sourcelist	Hw	2	5		No 81	71
Adams, Brucie	Production Spinning	Iw	4	1		Wi 78	44
Adams, Brucie	Some Physical Characteristics of Wool of Interest to Handspinners	S-O	1			77	28
Adams, Brucie	Spin a Tartan—Naturally	Hw	4	5		N/D 83	72
Adams, Brucie	Spinning and Weaving in a Country School	Iw	1	3		Sp 76	29
Adams, Brucie	Spinning for an Ombré Project	Hw	4	2		M/A 83	78
Adams, Brucie	Warp Sizing	Hw	6	3		Su 85	79
Adams, Brucie	Weaving...On a Knitting Machine	Hw	2	3		My 81	62
Adams, Brucie	Woolcombing	Iw	3	3		Sp 78	41

AUTHOR	TITLE	JOUR	VOL	NO	ISS	DATE	PAGE
Adams, Brucie	Wyoming Holds Golden Fleece Spinning Contest	SS&D	5	4	20	Fa 74	10
Adams, Brucie	Wyoming Spinners Create with Wool	Iw	1	1		Fa 75	10
Adams, Brucie; Elizabeth Zimmermann	Knit to Fit with Handspun	Hw	3	1		Ja 82	70
Adams, Carol; Patricia L. Magee	Wire Your Wall Hangings	SS&D	15	1	57	Wi 83	100
Adams, Eleanor	Weaving Along Sugar River	H&C	1	2		Su 50	28
Adams, Harriet	Bonnie Bonnet	Kn	1	2	2	S-S 85	38
Adams, Harriet	Dubbelmossa	Kn	2	1	3	F-W 85	50, 8B
Adams, Harriet	Tiffany's Gansey	Kn	1	1	1	F-W 84 CI	29,56A 21
Adams, Moni	Tiedyeing An Art on the Island of Sumba	H&C	22	1		Wi 71	9
Adams, Monni	Designs in Sumba Textiles, Local Meanings and Foreign Influences	TMJ	3	2		De 71	28
Adams, Monni	Dress and Design in Highland Southeast Asia: The Hmong (Miao) and the Yao	TMJ	4	1		De 74	51
Adams, Monni	Indonesian Textiles at the Textile Museum	TMJ	3	1		De 70	41
Adams, Monni	Symbolic Scenes in Javanese Batik	TMJ	3	1		De 70	25
Adams, Nettie K.	Textile Remains from a Late Temple in Egyptian Nubia	AT	8			De 87	85
Adams, Renie	see Sommer, Elyse	Iw	3	4		Su 78	45
Adams, Sally	Weavers in the Southeast	H&C	20	2		Sp 69	6
Adasko, Laura; Alice Huberman	Batik In Many Forms	SS&D	7	1	25	Wi 75	34
Adelman, Bobbie L.	Bobbie L. Adelman's Jacket	S-O	9	2		Su 85	15
Adels, Jill	Banners For Peace	Fa	12	4		J/A 85	36
Adelson, Laurie; Arthur Tracht	Aymara Weavings: Ceremonial Textiles of Colonial and 19th Century Bolivia	WJ	10	1	37	Su 85	84
Adelson, Laurie; Bruce Takami	Weaving Tradition in the Andes, A	Fa	6	4		J/A 79	22
Adkins, Madaline	Madeline Adkins' Sweater	S-O	9	2		Su 85	15
Adrosko, Rita	Textiles from the Smithsonian's Collection	H&C	23	2		M/A 72	20
Adrosko, Rita J.	Anatomy of a Quilted Counterpane (page revised WJ v9 n1 84 p70)	WJ	8	4	32	Sp 84	42
Adrosko, Rita J.	Natural Dyes in the United States	SS&D	1	2	2	Mr 70	23
Adrosko, Rita J.	Natural Dyes in the United States	H&C	20	2		Sp 69	41
Adrosko, Rita J.	Restoring an Old Loom	H&C	15	3		Su 64	16
Adrosko, Rita J.	see Partridge, Virginia Parslow	Fa	13	4		J/A 86	61
Adrosko, Rita J.	The Jacquard and Woven Silk Pictures	AT	1			De 83	9
af Kleen, Elisabeth; Nils af Kleen	When You Plan to Sell	H&C	14	3		Su 63	32
af Kleen, Elizabeth	Three Swedish Weaves	H&C	12	1		Wi 61	14
af Kleen, Elizabeth	Weaving Rya and Flossa Rugs	H&C	13	3		Su 62	29
af Kleen, Nils	see af Kleen, Elisabeth	H&C	14	3		Su 63	32
af Kleen, Nils E.	Kerstin Ekengren	H&C	15	2		Sp 64	18
Ager, Lewa	Recycling Plastic Bags	SS&D	5	4	20	Fa 74	22
Ahrens, Fred J.	see Russell, Harold W.	SS&D	5	2	18	Sp 74	25
Ahrens, Jim	Long Eyed Heddles	CW	6	1	16	Se 84	3
Ahrens, Jim	Notes on the Damask Weave	CW	2	1	4	Oc 80	6
Ahrens, Jim	Some Additional Notes on the Damask—Threading the Pattern Harnesses	CW	6	2	17	Ja 85	3
Aiken, Joyce	see Laury, Jean Ray	SS&D	6	4	24	Fa 75	30
Aikin, Patti	Happy Anniversary, Too	SS&D	16	1	61	Wi 84	45
Aikin, Patti	Weaving Workshop with Barbara Wittenberg: Sharing is Pervasive, A	Fa	8	4		J/A 81	21
Ajeman, Norma; Irene Laughing Cloud Schmoller	Discover Cotton Spinning	WJ	8	3	31	Wi 83	49
Akamine, Estelle	Fragil Landscape	TM			5	J/J 86	88
Akamine, Estelle	Girls Who Wear Cactus	TM			4	A/M 86	66

AUTHOR	TITLE	JOUR	VOL	NO	ISS	DATE	PAGE
Akamine, Estelle	Hair As a Sculptor's Medium	Fa	14	3		M/J 87	24
Akamine, Estelle	Through the Camera's Eye: Howard Munson's Body Coverings	Fa	14	3		M/J 87	44
Akana, Elizabeth A.	Hawaiian Quilting: Tradition Through Change	Fa	9	3		M/J 82	62
Akita, Mariko Olivia	Kasuri-Like-Effect Weaving	WJ	6	2	22	Fa 81	18
Alaniz, Leonore	Contemporary American Handweaving from an International Perspective	WJ	11	3	43	Wi 87	26
Alaniz, Leonore	Marketing Handwoven Fabric for Apparel & Interiors	WJ	11	4	44	Sp 87	31
Albers, Anni	Anni Albers: On Design	H&C	13	3		Su 62	43
Albers, Anni	Anni Albers: On Designing	H&C	11	2		Sp 60	60
Albers, Anni	Anni Albers: On Weaving	H&C	16	4		Fa 65	43
Albers, Anni	Working with Material	Iw	3	2		Wi 78	12
Alderman, Sharon	Double-Faced Cloth: One Cloth, Two Appearances	Hw	3	4		Se 82	61
Alderman, Sharon	Dunkagäng, the Stuff of Hearts and Flowers	Hw	7	2		M/A 86	41
Alderman, Sharon	Evergreen	Hw	4	5		N/D 83	62
Alderman, Sharon	Handwoven Fabric: Beginnings, Decision Making	Hw	3	2		Mr 82	31
Alderman, Sharon	Handwoven Swatch Collection 1	Hw	1	2		S-S 80	41
Alderman, Sharon	Handwoven Swatch Collection 2	Hw	2	1		F-W 80	50
Alderman, Sharon	Magnified Twill Blanket	Hw	6	5		N/D 85	53
Alderman, Sharon	Matter of Style: Swatch Collection 5, A	Hw	3	2		Mr 82	8
Alderman, Sharon	One Weaver's Approach to Designing Yardage	Iw	3	2		Wi 78	22
Alderman, Sharon	Profile Drafting: Getting the Big Picture	Hw	8	5		N/D 87	44
Alderman, Sharon	Saints and the Silkworms, The	Iw	3	4		Su 78	15
Alderman, Sharon	Secret of a Corrugated Surface: Bedford Cord, The (error-corrected Hw v6 n3 85 p I-2)	Hw	6	1		J/F 85	27
Alderman, Sharon	Simple Gifts	Hw	3	5		N/D 82	39
Alderman, Sharon	Simple Scarf, Simple Luxury (error-corrected Hw v5 n1 83 p88)	Hw	4	4		S/O 83	64
Alderman, Sharon	Sling Chair	Hw	6	3		Su 85	58
Alderman, Sharon	Swatch Collection 11	Hw	6	2		M/A 85	46
Alderman, Sharon	Swatch Collection 13	Hw	7	3		M/J 86	28
Alderman, Sharon	Swatch Collection 14	Hw	7	4		S/O 86	24
Alderman, Sharon	Swatch Collection 15	Hw	8	2		M/A 87	38
Alderman, Sharon	Swatch Collection 16: Fabrics for Fall '87	Hw	8	4		S/O 87	52
Alderman, Sharon	Swatch Collection 6	Hw	3	4		Se 82	41
Alderman, Sharon	Swatch Collection 7	Hw	4	2		M/A 83	58
Alderman, Sharon	Swatch Collection 8	Hw	4	4		S/O 83	52
Alderman, Sharon	The Making of Swatch Collection 6	Hw	3	4		Se 82	42
Alderman, Sharon	Tracking, the Mystery of the Crinkling Cloth	Hw	6	4		S/O 85	31
Alderman, Sharon D.	Avoiding and Repairing Weaving Errors	Hw	2	5		No 81	60
Alderman, Sharon D.	Bias Striped Skirt, A	Hw	5	1		J/F 84	45
Alderman, Sharon D.	But What Do I Do With It?	Hw	7	5		N/D 86	50
Alderman, Sharon D.	Certificate Holders: Now What? Part 2, The	SS&D	12	4	48	Fa 81	52
Alderman, Sharon D.	Certificate Holders: Now What?, The	SS&D	12	2	46	Sp 81	41
Alderman, Sharon D.	Certificate Holders: What Now? Part 3, The	SS&D	13	2	50	Sp 82	60
Alderman, Sharon D.	Corduroy: An Account of Discovery	Hw	4	4		S/O 83	54
Alderman, Sharon D.	Design In Weaving: Tailoring an Overshot	Hw	3	1		Ja 82	68
Alderman, Sharon D.	Designing from the Tie-Up, A Multiharness Tool (error-corrected Iw v5 n1 79 p10)	Iw	4	4		Fa 79	30
Alderman, Sharon D.	Finishing Handwoven Fabrics	SS&D	9	1	33	Wi 77	13
Alderman, Sharon D.	Five Pillows from One Warp	Hw	3	3		My 82	38
Alderman, Sharon D.	Honeycomb: Curves Ahead	Hw	5	4		S/O 84	45
Alderman, Sharon D.	Krokbragd	Hw	2	2		Mr 81	33
Alderman, Sharon D.	Loom-Controlled Leno	Hw	2	3		My 81	38
Alderman, Sharon D.	Making of a Swatch Collection, The	Hw	2	4		Se 81	36
Alderman, Sharon D.	Return of the Churro, The	S-O	8	1		Sp 84	46

AUTHOR	TITLE	JOUR	VOL	NO	ISS	DATE	PAGE
Alderman, Sharon D.	Swatch Collection 10	Hw	5	4		S/O 84	56
Alderman, Sharon D.	Swatch Collection 12: Classic Fabrics for City Fashions	Hw	6	5		N/D 85	48
Alderman, Sharon D.	Swatch Collection 9	Hw	5	3		Su 84	62
Alderman, Sharon D.	"Theme Show In Utah, A" (Exhibit)	Fa	8	3		M/J 81	68
Alderman, Sharon D.	Very Special Cape, A	Hw	2	4		Se 81	46
Alderman, Sharon D.	Weaving Memories	Hw	5	5		N/D 84	57
Alderman, Sharon D.	Work with Style	Hw	5	2		M/A 84	68
Alderman, Sharon D.; Kathryn Wertenberger	Handwoven, Tailormade	Fa	10	1		J/F 83	58
Alderman, Sharon D.; Kathryn Wertenberger	Handwoven, Tailormade, A Tandem Guide to Fabric Designing, Weaving, Sewing and Tailoring	WJ	7	3	27	Wi 82	49
Aldrich, Mae	Laughing Gulls of St. Petersburg	SS&D	5	4	20	Fa 74	75
Aldrich, Mae D.	Overshot Borders for Four Sides, Variations in Pattern and Plain Weave	H&C	15	2		Sp 64	15
Aldrich, Mae D.	Pinellas Weavers	H&C	20	2		Sp 69	12
Aldrich, Mae D.	Summer-and-Winter, Experiments with Four Blocks on Four Harnesses	H&C	17	4		Fa 66	21
Alexander, Judy	Lia Cook: Exploring the Territory Where Painting and Textiles Meet	Fa	9	5		S/O 82	28
Alexander, Marthann	Simple Weaving	SS&D	1	2	2	Mr 70	23
Alexander, Marthann	Simple Weaving	H&C	20	4		Fa 69	42
Alexander, Marthann	Teaching Children to Weave, Need for Simple Techniques and Devices	H&C	14	1		Wi 63	19
Alexander, Marthann	Weaving Handcraft	H&C	5	4		Fa 54	43
Alexander, Marthann	Weaving Handcraft — 15 Simple Ways to Weave	H&C	10	2		Sp 59	60
Alexander, Peter; Robert Hudson	Wool, Its Chemistry and Physics	H&C	6	1		Wi 54	61
Allan, G. Ernestine	Fish Provide the Ideas for a Series of Colorful Bookmarks	H&C	16	4		Fa 65	17
Allard, Mary	Rug Making — Techniques and Design	H&C	14	4		Fa 63	43
Allen, Alice	Perfect Fit	TM			12	A/S 87	71
Allen, Debbie	Dog on the Loom, The	Hw	5	2		M/A 84	20
Allen, Debbie	Summer and Winter for Four Shafts	Hw	8	5		N/D 87	86
Allen, Debbie	Virtuous Weaver and the Weaver's Notebook, The	Hw	5	4		S/O 84	34
Allen, Debbie	Weaving on the Left Side of the Brain	Hw	6	4		S/O 85	12
Allen, Ernestine	Ribbon in the Warp	H&C	21	4		Fa 70	15
Allen, Jane Ingram	Hungarian Weaving	SS&D	10	3	39	Su 79	93
Allen, Jeanne	Designer's Guide To Color 3	SS&D	18	3	71	Su 87	73
Allen, Marian	Spinning in a Special Climate	S-O	11	3		Fa 87	50
Allen, Rose Mary	Wrist-to-Wrist Garment, The	WJ	9	3	35	Wi 85	19
Aller, Doris	Handmade Rugs	H&C	5	2		Sp 54	15
Allston, J. L.	see Stanton, R. G.	AT	2			De 84	95
Allston, J. L.	see Stanton, R. G.	AT	2			De 84	217
Allston, J. L.; J. A. Hoskins	An Introduction to Two Textilatelists	AT	4			De 85	81
Almond, Bonnie	Bonnie Almond's Sweater	S-O	9	2		Su 85	13
Almond, Bonnie H.	Report on the ARBA Convention	S-O	8	2		Su 84	21
Alonso, Harriet	C.H.A.N. for Short: The Story of Rachel Maines	Fa	8	3		M/J 81	13
Alonso, Harriet	Embroidered Life, An (error-corrected Fa v7 n4 80 p6)	Fa	7	3		M/J 80	66
Alonso, Harriet	"Hawaiian Quilts: Treasures of an Island Folk Art" (Exhibit)	Fa	6	6		N/D 79	77
Alonzo, Harriet	"Artists in Aprons" (Exhibit)	Fa	6	3		M/J 79	76
Alonzo, Harriet	"Hair" (Exhibit)	Fa	7	6		N/D 80	73
Altpeter, Dorothy; Corinne Anderson; Margaret Thostesen	How to Make Braided Rugs	H&C	2	1		Wi 50	62
Alvic, Philis	An English Lady's Loom	CW	4	1	10	Se 82	12
Alvic, Philis	Bergman	CW	2	1	4	Oc 80	10
Alvic, Philis	Bergman: Notes of a Pattern Weaver	WJ	10	1	37	Su 85	64
Alvic, Philis	Borders: Notes of a Pattern Weaver	WJ	11	2	42	Fa 86	55
Alvic, Philis	Building on a Tradition	Iw	4	3		Su 79	45

AUTHOR	TITLE	JOUR	VOL	NO	ISS	DATE	PAGE
Alvic, Philis	Color in Summer and Winter	WJ	7	4	28	Sp 83	64
Alvic, Philis	Designing for an Interior: Notes of a Pattern Weaver	WJ	9	4	36	Sp 85	69
Alvic, Philis	Drafting: A Personal Approach, Part 2	SS&D	13	2	50	Sp 82	46
Alvic, Philis	Drafting: A Personal Approach, Part 3	SS&D	13	3	51	Su 82	40
Alvic, Philis	Handwoven Silk Garments: Blue Silk Dress	WJ	3	2	10	Oc 78	27
Alvic, Philis	Inspiration	WJ	8	1	29	Su 83	65
Alvic, Philis	Notes of a Pattern Weaver	SS&D	13	4	52	Fa 82	76
Alvic, Philis	Notes of a Pattern Weaver	SS&D	14	1	53	Wi 82	32
Alvic, Philis	Notes of a Pattern Weaver	WJ	10	3	39	Wi 86	65
Alvic, Philis	Notes of a Pattern Weaver	SS&D	14	2	54	Sp 83	76
Alvic, Philis	Notes of a Pattern Weaver	SS&D	14	3	55	Su 83	66
Alvic, Philis	Notes of a Pattern Weaver	SS&D	14	4	56	Fa 83	82
Alvic, Philis	Notes of a Pattern Weaver	SS&D	15	1	57	Wi 83	74
Alvic, Philis	One-of-a-kind Garment in Beiderwand, A	WJ	9	1	33	Su 84	51
Alvic, Philis	Personal Approach to Drafting, A	SS&D	13	1	49	Wi 81	32
Alvic, Philis	Plaited Twill Projects: Notes of a Pattern Weaver	WJ	11	4	44	Sp 87	55
Alvic, Philis	Point Block Progression: Notes of a Pattern Weaver	WJ	10	4	40	Sp 86	67
Alvic, Philis	Tabby Color	SS&D	15	2	58	Sp 84	91
Alvic, Philis	Tied Lithuanian	CW	3	3	9	Ap 82	7
Alvic, Philis	Tied Lithuanian: Notes of a Pattern Weaver	WJ	9	3	35	Wi 85	50
Alvic, Philis	Variations on One Warp	SS&D	12	4	48	Fa 81	70
Alvidres, Joseph	Joseph Alvidres	Fa	13	2		M/A 86	15
American Craft Museum Catalogue	For the Floor: An International Exhibition of Contemporary Handmade Rugs	WJ	9	4	36	Sp 85	78
American River College	American River College Textile Collection Bibliography	Hw	7	1		J/F 86	21
American Wool Council	Sidney Sheep	Iw	2	1		Fa 76	32
American Wool Council	Spinning Your Own Wool Yarn	S-O	4			80	15
American Wool Council	Weaving—A Timeless Craft	Iw	3	2		Wi 78	41
Ames, Helen B.	Florida Weaver's Use of Native Materials, A	H&C	4	2		Sp 53	50
Ames, Helen B.	Handweaving in a Naval Hospital	H&C	4	1		Wi 52	52
Ames, Helen B.	Handwoven Fabrics on the High Seas	H&C	2	2		Sp 51	9
Ames, Helen B.	New York University's Annual Spring Conference on Industrial Arts	H&C	1	2		Su 50	13
Ames, Helen B.	Weaving in New York City's Hospital Program	H&C	1	3		Fa 50	15
Amini, Majid	Oriental Rugs Care and Repair	WJ	6	4	24	Sp 82	57
Amir, M. K. Zephyr	Supreme Persian Carpets	SS&D	5	2	18	Sp 74	68
Amon, Martha; Ruth Rawson	Handcraft Simplified	H&C	12	3		Su 61	61
Amos, Alden	Buyer's Guide to Spinning Wheel Design	S-O	4			80	40
Amos, Alden	Carded Rainbow Batts	S-O	9	1		Sp 85	19
Amos, Alden	How Much Twist Do I Need?	S-O	11	1		Sp 87	25
Amos, Alden	How to Sponsor a Workshop, Part 1: The Basics of Organizing a Workshop	Hw	8	2		M/A 87	75
Amos, Alden	How to Sponsor a Workshop Part 2: The Workshop Begins	Hw	8	4		S/O 87	73
Amos, Alden	Mercerizing: Not for Everyone	S-O	9	2		Su 85	30
Amos, Alden	Sixteeneth Century Labor Day, A	S-O	5			81	8
Amos, Alden	So You Want to Weave Tartan?	Hw	4	5		N/D 83	37
Amos, Alden	Spinning Wheel Primer	Iw	2	3		Sp 77	33
Amos, Alden, et al.	Hundred and One Questions for Spinners, A	Iw	4	1		Wi 78	54
Amos, Mary Alice	Persis Grayson, Weaver & Spinner	H&C	19	1		Wi 68	10
Amram, Hortense	Cooperative Weaving Project, A	H&C	5	4		Fa 54	31
Amram, Hortense	New Forms from Old Traditions	H&C	3	1		Wi 51	27
Amram, Hortense	Proposed Federal Commission on the Arts of Interest to Craftsmen	H&C	8	4		Fa 57	31
Amram, Hortense	Why Not Start Your Own Museum?	H&C	4	3		Su 53	28

AUTHOR	TITLE	JOUR	VOL	NO	ISS	DATE	PAGE
Amsden, Charles Avery	Navaho Weaving: Its Technic and History	SS&D	5	3	19	Su 74	62
Anavian, George	see Anavian, Rahim	TMJ	4	4		77	97
Anavian, Rahim; George Anavian	Royal Persian and Kashmir Brocades	TMJ	4	4		77	97
Anawalt, Patricia Rieff	Indian Clothing Before Cortes	Fa	9	6		N/D 82	58
Anders, Eunice	South of the Border Down Canada Way	SS&D	3	3	11	Su 72	6
Anderson, Ann Stewart	"Distilling the Essence of Basketry" (Exhibit)	Fa	13	2		M/A 86	52
Anderson, Ann Stewart	"Jacque Parsley: Avallon Series" (Exhibit)	Fa	9	5		S/O 82	82
Anderson, Arlene	Handspun Wedding Gown, A	S-O	8	4		Wi 84	13
Anderson, Barbara	Stylish No-Sew Hat	WJ	6	3	23	Wi 81	39
Anderson, Beryl	Creative Spinning, Weaving and Plant Dyeing	H&C	24	3		M/J 73	6
Anderson, Betty	Prescription — Weaving	H&C	6	1		Wi 54	24
Anderson, Clarita	Artifacts Don't "Lie"	AT	7			Ju 87	9
Anderson, Clarita	Coverlet Bibliography	AT	2			De 84	203
Anderson, Clarita	see Ulasewicz, Connie	AT	2			De 84	113
Anderson, Clarita; Jo B. Paoletti	The Use of Eagles As a Decorative and Symbolic Motif in 19th Century American Coverlets	AT	3			My 85	173
Anderson, Clarita; Judith Gordon; Naomi Whiting Towner	Analysis of Star and Diamond Weave Structures, An (error-corrected SS&D v10 n1 78 p101)	SS&D	9	4	36	Fa 78	71
Anderson, Clarita; Steven M. Spivak	Nineteenth Century License Agreements for Fancy Weaving Machines	AT	8			De 87	67
Anderson, Corinne	see Altpeter, Dorothy	H&C	2	1		Wi 50	62
Anderson, Donald	Elements of Design	H&C	21	3		Su 70	39
Anderson, J.	Weaving Demonstrations	H&C	15	4		Fa 64	14
Anderson, J.	Weaving with Handspun Alpaca	H&C	17	2		Sp 66	20
Anderson, Marcile	Galloon — A French Braid with Two Wefts	SS&D	5	3	19	Su 74	83
Anderson, Marcile	Inkle Weaving, Fun and Challenge	SS&D	5	4	20	Fa 74	29
Anderson, Marilyn	Guatemalan Textiles Today	Iw	3	4		Su 78	45
Anderson, Marilyn	Guatemalan Textiles Today	WJ	8	1	29	Su 83	52
Anderson, Marilyn	Jacquard Weaving in Huehuetenango	Fa	9	2		M/A 82	31
Anderson, Marilyn	see Taber, Barbara	SS&D	7	1	25	Wi 75	34
Anderson, Marilyn	see Taber, Barbara	WJ	8	1	29	Su 83	52
Anderson, Ruth Matilda	Hispanic Costume 1450-1530	WJ	8	3	31	Wi 83	64
Anderson, Ruth Matilda	Spanish Costume Extremadura	H&C	3	2		Sp 52	61
Andes, Ellen; Gene Andes	Three Dimensional Macrame	H&C	23	3		M/J 72	43
Andes, Ellen; Gene Andes	Three-Dimensional Macramé	H&C	23	5		S/O 72	18
Andes, Ellen; Penelope Drooker; Gene Andes	Weave and Wear It	WJ	4	4	16	Ap 80	26
Andes, Gene	see Andes, Ellen	H&C	23	3		M/J 72	43
Andes, Gene	see Andes, Ellen	H&C	23	5		S/O 72	18
Andes, Gene	see Andes, Ellen	WJ	4	4	16	Ap 80	26
Andrews, Kathy Boals	Cut from the Same Cloth	Fa	13	3		M/J 86	21
Angelil, Muriel	Roman Heritage, The	SS&D	13	3	51	Su 82	69
Anita, Sister M.	We Like Weaving	H&C	22	1		Wi 71	17
Anstine, Jean	see Bradley, Louise	Hw	7	3		M/J 86	40
Anthony, Janice	Shapely Curves	TM			11	J/J 87	30
Anton, F.; F. J. Dockstoder	Pre-Columbian Art & Later Indian Tribal Arts	H&C	20	1		Wi 69	43
Antuñez de Mayolo, Kay	Teasel Tools	SS&D	13	4	52	Fa 82	10
Appalshop Films	Oaksie. A 16mm Color Film	SS&D	11	4	44	Fa 80	67
Appleton, LeRoy H.	Indian Art of the Americas	H&C	1	3		Fa 50	60
April-Proulx, Bibiane	French-English Weaving Glossary	WJ	8	4	32	Sp 84	67

AUTHOR	TITLE	JOUR	VOL	NO	ISS	DATE	PAGE
Arabian, Barbara	Hooray, Hooray, The Cochineal	Iw	3	3		Sp 78	25
Arajs, Ilze	"Anne Wilson: Recent Work" (Exhibit)	Fa	11	4		J/A 84	75
Ardita, Nessim	Teneriffe Lace — Legend of Nanduti, A Closely Related Lace	SS&D	5	1	17	Wi 73	53
Arensberg, Susan MacMillan	Javanese Batiks	WJ	8	2	30	Fa 83	65
Argente, Philip P.	Costumes of Chios. Their Development from the XVth to the XXth Century, The	H&C	4	3		Su 53	61
Arndt, Jessie Ash	Career on Four Continents, A	H&C	21	3		Su 70	15
Arndt, Jessie Ash	Two Weavers in Washington	H&C	20	4		Fa 69	20
Arness, Judidth R.	Potomac Craftsmen	H&C	15	4		Fa 64	18
Arness, Judith	Memorial Library	H&C	18	2		Sp 67	17
Arness, Judith Russell	Tie Dyeing in India (error-corrected H&C v14 n2 63 p46)	H&C	14	1		Wi 63	6
Arnold, Kari	Fiber-Mix Dyeing of Textiles	SS&D	16	2	62	Sp 85	46
Arnold, Kari Ann	Weave Design	SS&D	15	1	57	Wi 83	94
Arnold, Ruth	Alice Hindson, Expert on the Draw-loom	H&C	10	4		Fa 59	12
Arnold, Ruth	Autumn Leaves, A Design in Summer-and-Winter	H&C	14	3		Su 63	14
Arnold, Ruth	Handweaving in Spain	H&C	8	4		Fa 57	10
Arnold, Ruth	Handwoven Christmas Cards	H&C	7	3		Su 56	7
Arnold, Ruth	How to Weave Your own Designs	H&C	11	3		Su 60	6
Arnold, Ruth	Methods of Finishing Handwoven Fabrics: Finishing Linen	H&C	8	4		Fa 57	27
Arnold, Ruth	Tailored Vest and Skirt, A	WJ	9	3	35	Wi 85	56
Arnold, Ruth	Weaving Damask	H&C	6	3		Su 55	4
Arnold, Ruth	Weaving on a Draw-Loom	H&C	7	3		Su 56	59
Arnold, Ruth	Workshop at Home, Weaving Summer and Winter	H&C	9	3		Su 58	6
Arnow, Jan	"Ann Stewart Anderson: New Work" (Exhibit)	Fa	7	1		J/F 80	64
Arnow, Jan	Lida Gordon: An Interview	Fa	6	2		M/A 79	50
Arnow, Jan	"Shared Vision": A Gallery Tour with Two Artists: Jacque Parsley and Neisja Yenawine (Exhibit)	Fa	8	4		J/A 81	28
Arnow, Jan	"Surface Design: Approaches '78" (Exhibit)	Fa	6	2		M/A 79	67
Arnow, Jan	"Works in Fiber" (Exhibit)	Fa	8	2		M/A 81	61
Aronson, Joseph	Furniture and Decoration	H&C	4	2		Sp 53	62
Arouh, Leslie	Interweavings, A Dance	Fa	7	1		J/F 80	16
Arts Council of Great Britain	Islamic Carpets from the Joseph V. McMullan Collection	TMJ	3	4		De 73	46
Arvonio, John	Heritage in Tapestry, A	H&C	23	4		J/A 72	9
Ascher, Marcia; Robert Ascher	Code of the Quipu	Fa	9	2		M/A 82	58
Ascher, Robert	see Ascher, Marcia	Fa	9	2		M/A 82	58
Ash, Beryl; Anthony Dyson	Introducing Dyeing and Printing	SS&D	5	1	17	Wi 73	77
Ashe, Alan W.	Deductions	SS&D	2	1	5	De 70	19
Ashe, Alan W.	Deductions When Home Is Used for Business	SS&D	1	4	4	Se 70	6
Ashford, Joy	Fleece-to-Garment Competition in New Zealand	SS&D	4	1	13	Wi 72	21
Ashford, Joy	New Zealand Spinning	SS&D	4	1	13	Wi 72	20
Ashford, Joy	Spinning in New Zealand	H&C	21	3		Su 70	42
Ashley, Clifford	Ashley Book of Knots, The	H&C	21	3		Su 70	39
Ashton, Mary	Civil War History Preserved: The Pennsylvania Flag Project	Fa	14	5		N/D 87	10
Ashwell, Eleanor V.	"Lee's Surrender"	SS&D	6	2	22	Sp 75	85
Ashwell, Eleanor V.	What Makes a Good Guild?	SS&D	2	1	5	De 70	7
Askenfors, Gunilla	Felting	WJ	6	1	21	Su 81	31
Asman, Ann	Alpaca in the Raw	S-O	9	2		Su 85	24
Aspell, Amy	Cookbook Weaving I	SS&D	9	4	36	Fa 78	81
Association des Tisserands d'Ici, Quebec	En Bref (French)	WJ	11	3	43	Wi 87	64
Association des Tisserands d'Ici, Quebec	Grain d'Orge (French)	WJ	11	3	43	Wi 87	64
Atkinson, Howard A.	Twining or Macrame Loom	SS&D	5	3	19	Su 74	24
Atkinson, R. R.	Jute, Fibre to Yarn	H&C	16	3		Su 65	44

AUTHOR	TITLE	JOUR	VOL	NO	ISS	DATE	PAGE
Attix, George	Laundry Care Labels Needed After July 3	SS&D	3	3	11	Su 72	10
Atwater, Mary M.	Guatemala Visited, Shuttle Craft Bulletin #15, Reprint	H&C	16	3		Su 65	45
Atwater, Mary M.	Texture Weaving — What and Why	H&C	2	1		Wi 50	33
Atwater, Mary Meigs	Byways in Handweaving	H&C	5	1		Wi 53	59
Atwater, Mary Meigs	Design and the Handweaver	SCGM		3		61	1-26
Atwater, Mary Meigs	Design and the Handweaver, Shuttle Craft Guild Monograph No. 3	H&C	12	3		Su 61	60
Atwater, Mary Meigs	Guatemala Visited	SCGM		15		65	1-46
Atwater, Mary Meigs	Hand Woven Rugs	SCGM		29		48	1-28
Atwater, Mary Meigs	Practical Weave for Rugs, A	H&C	5	2		Sp 54	24
Atwater, Mary Meigs	Practical Weave for Rugs (Reprint), A	H&C	26	1		J/F 75	7
Atwater, Mary Meigs	Quarter Century of Handweavers' Progress, A	H&C	2	2		Sp 51	5
Atwater, Mary Meigs	Shuttle-Craft Book of American Hand-weaving, The	H&C	17	4		Fa 66	43
Atwater, Mary Meigs	Shuttle-Craft Book of American Hand-Weaving, The	H&C	2	2		Sp 51	64
Atwater, Mary Meigs	Shuttle-Craft Book of American Hand-Weaving, The	Hw	7	4		S/O 86	12
Atwater, Mary Meigs	Shuttle-Craft Book of American Hand-Weaving, The	TM			11	J/J 87	72
Atwater, Mary Meigs	Shuttle-Craft Book of American Hand-Weaving, The	PWC	4	3	13		52
Atwater, Mary Meigs	Shuttle-Craft Book Of American Handweaving, The	WJ	11	3	43	Wi 87	63
Atwater, Mary Meigs	What and Why of "Inkle"	H&C	3	2		Sp 52	18
Atwood, Betty	Elizabeth Fisk, Early 20th Century Vermont Weaver	H&C	19	3		Su 68	18
Atwood, Betty	From Peru, Gods Eyes on a Stick	SS&D	5	1	17	Wi 73	8
Atwood, Betty	Hopi Embroidery Weave As a Technique for Tapestry	WJ	5	1	17	Su 80	37
Atwood, Betty	Hopi Embroidery Weave, The	SS&D	8	2	30	Sp 77	100
Atwood, Betty	Southwest Indian Twill Tapestry	WJ	8	1	29	Su 83	35
Atwood, Betty	Weft Wrap Openwork	Iw	4	1		Wi 78	20
Atwood, Betty	Weft-Wrap Openwork Technique	AT	3			My 85	65
Auger, Shirley Venit	Wearable Paintings	H&C	24	4		Au 73	34
August, Valerie	Special Fittings: Valerie's Vest	Kn	1	2	2	S-S 85	31
Auld, Rhoda L.	Molas	Fa	4	3		M/J 77	54
Austin, Carol	Common Sense and Good Housekeeping: A Basic Guide to Textile Conservation (Clarification Fa v9 n2 82 p7)	Fa	9	1		J/F 82	43
Austin, Carol	In the Shadow of Fame: Sophie Taeuber-Arp and Sonia Delaunay	Fa	12	5		S/O 85	50
Austin, Carol	Shopping Foreign Flea Markets	Fa	12	6		N/D 85	45
Austin, Carol	Woad: A Medieval Dye	Fa	13	3		M/J 86	29
Austin, Carole	Amazing Materials from Nature	Fa	14	3		M/J 87	24
Austin, Carole	Basketry Armor	Fa	14	1		J/F 87	28
Austin, Carole	Early Christian Church Curtains	Fa	14	2		M/A 87	28
Austin, Carole	Floral Symbolism: The Western Rose	Fa	13	2		M/A 86	42
Austin, Carole	Handkerchiefs and Politics	Fa	12	3		M/J 85	51
Austin, Carole	Knitted Rugs	Fa	11	3		M/J 84	57
Austin, Carole	Kohl Bags	Fa	11	4		J/A 84	48
Austin, Carole	Leonardo's Knot	Fa	12	2		M/A 85	43
Austin, Carole	Mastering the Art of Research	Fa	13	5		S/O 86	21
Austin, Carole	"Meri Ann Walsh: Patterned Papers" (Exhibit)	Fa	8	6		N/D 81	65
Austin, Carole	Mystery of Pile Rugs, The	Fa	13	6		N/D 86	1
Austin, Carole	Probing the Creative Process: A Book List to Begin With	Fa	11	6		N/D 84	53
Austin, Carole	Public Fiber: The Long-Range Problem of Conservation	Fa	14	5		N/D 87	13
Austin, Carole	Tents in History	Fa	12	4		J/A 85	47
Austin, Carole	Threads of Gold	Fa	13	4		J/A 86	10
Austin, Carole	Whence the Tutu?	Fa	11	5		S/O 84	46
Austin, Carole	William Morris: The Sanford and Helen Berger Collection	Fa	12	3		M/J 85	47
Australian Wool Board	Wool Fibre Structure	SS&D	4	3	15	Su 73	60
Australian Wool Corporation	Traditional Knitting with Wool	Kn	2	1	3	F-W 85	79
Avery, Virginia	Quilts to Wear	Fa	10	6		N/D 83	58

AUTHOR	TITLE	JOUR	VOL	NO	ISS	DATE	PAGE
Avery, Virginia	Yvonne Porcella: A Modern Master of the Ethnic Clothing Tradition	Fa	8	1		J/F 81	63
Axelsson, Astrid	see Trotzig, Liv	SS&D	6	3	23	Su 75	49
Axford, Lavonne Brady	Weaving, Spinning, and Dyeing	Iw	1	2		Wi 76	28
Ayer, Millie	Miniature Cable Car from San Francisco	SS&D	5	4	20	Fa 74	40
Ayotte, Robert; Roberta Ayotte	Understanding Cotton Fiber & Yarns	WJ	11	2	42	Fa 86	27
Ayotte, Roberta	see Ayotte, Robert	WJ	11	2	42	Fa 86	27
Aytes, Barbara	Adventures in Knitting	TM			9	F/M 87	76
Azaad, Meyer	Half For You	Iw	2	1		Fa 76	32
Babb, Lou	Yarn Starts Here, Photo Essay, The	SS&D	7	3	27	Su 76	31
Bach, Ann	Learning Papermaking in Nantucket	Fa	11	2		M/A 84	47
Bach, Pieter, ed.	Textiles, Costume and Doll Collections: in the United States and Canada	WJ	6	4	24	Sp 82	57
Bacharach, Jere L.; Irene A. Bierman, ed.	Warp and Weft of Islam: Oriental Carpets and Weavings from Pacific Northwest Collections, The	SS&D	9	4	36	Fa 78	81
Bachman, Sally	Creative Dyeing	Iw	3	3		Sp 78	26
Backer, Ellen	JoEllen Trilling: Contemporary Pied Piper	Fa	5	4		J/A 78	24
Backer, Ellen	"Partners in Art: Brushwork by Lee, Dong Chun and Embroidery by Yu, Chug Hee" (Exhibit)	Fa	4	3		M/J 77	16
Backlin-Landman, Hedy	Textiles Related to Wallpapers	H&C	16	3		Su 65	16
Badone, Donalda	Paisley	Hw	8	1		J/F 87	39
Baetke, Fern	Thought Patterns	S-O	7	4		Wi 83	4
Bahr, Ann	Dolphin Rug	H&C	21	2		Sp 70	36
Baines, Patricia	Spinning Wheels, Spinners and Spinning	SS&D	9	4	36	Fa 78	80
Baines, Patricia	Spinning Wheels, Spinners and Spinning	Iw	3	3		Sp 78	50
Baines, Patricia	Spinning Wheels, Spinners and Spinning	S-O	7	2		Su 83	15
Baines, Patricia	Spinning Wheels, Spinners and Spinning	SS&D	17	3	67	Su 86	87
Bair, Fred; James E. Norris	Practical Business and Tax Guide for the Craftsperson, A (Secong Edition)	Hw	8	4		S/O 87	12
Baity, Elizabeth Chesley	Man is a Weaver	H&C	2	1		Wi 50	61
Baizerman, Sue	see Pancake, Cherri	Hw	2	5		No 81	29
Baizerman, Suzanne	Divide . . . and Conquer	WJ	9	2	34	Fa 84	61
Baizerman, Suzanne	Embellishments on the Rain Sash	WJ	11	2	42	Fa 86	22
Baizerman, Suzanne	Finishes for Vadmal	WJ	10	3	39	Wi 86	30
Baizerman, Suzanne	Hemstitching for Linens	WJ	10	4	40	Sp 86	25
Baizerman, Suzanne	Knotted Chinese Button	WJ	9	1	33	Su 84	7
Baizerman, Suzanne	see Cahlander, Adele	Hw	8	4		S/O 87	12
Baizerman, Suzanne	see Cahlander, Adele	PWC	4	2	12		51
Baizerman, Suzanne	see Pancake, Cherri M.	TMJ	19 20			80,81	1
Baizerman, Suzanne; Karen Searle	Backstrap Weaving in MesoAmerica	Iw	5	4		Fa 80	38
Baizerman, Suzanne; Karen Searle	Finishes in the Ethnic Tradition	SS&D	10	2	38	Sp 79	74
Baizerman, Suzanne; Karen Searle	Finishes in the Ethnic Tradition	Iw	3	4		Su 78	45
Baizerman, Suzanne; Karen Searle	Finishes in the Ethnic Tradition	WJ	3	3	11	Ja 79	42
Baizerman, Suzanne; Karen Searle	Finishes in the Ethnic Tradition	Fa	8	4		J/A 81	34
Baizerman, Suzanne; Karen Searle	Latin American Brocades: Explorations in Supplementary Weft Techniques	SS&D	8	2	30	Sp 77	37
Baizerman, Suzanne; Karen Searle	Latin American Brocades: Explorations in Supplementary Weft Techniques	Iw	3	2		Wi 78	42
Baizerman, Suzanne; Karen Searle	Latin American Brocades: Explorations in Supplementary Weft Techniques	WJ	6	4	24	Sp 82	57
Baker, Ella	Cotton in the Natural Dyepot	S-O	9	3		Fa 85	29
Baker, Ella	Teaching Children How to Knit	S-O	10	2		Su 86	42

AUTHOR	TITLE	JOUR	VOL	NO	ISS	DATE	PAGE
Baker, Ella	Why Spin Cotton?	S-O	9	2		Su 85	31
Baker, Erica	see Westerink, Claire	S-O	10	3		Fa 86	17
Baker, June	Decorative Braiding and Weaving	H&C	24	3		M/J 73	6
Baker, Muriel	Stumpwork, The Art of Raised Embroidery	Fa	6	4		J/A 79	17
Baker, Muriel L.	Handbook of American Crewel Embroidery, A	WJ	8	1	29	Su 83	53
Baker, William R. M.	Canadian Classic, A	SS&D	18	3	71	Su 87	52
Baker, William R. M.	Convergence '86 Preview: Toronto — A City in Transition	SS&D	17	1	65	Wi 85	42
Baker, Wilma S. V.	Silk Pictures of Thomas Stevens, The	H&C	9	2		Sp 58	61
Balassa, Eva	Kumiko Murashima: The East and West of Weaving	Fa	6	1		J/F 79	17
Baldwin, Ed; Stevie Baldwin	Scrap Fabric Crafts	WJ	7	3	27	Wi 82	48
Baldwin, P. H.	Layne Goldsmith: Felted Worlds	Fa	11	6		N/D 84	24
Baldwin, Stevie	see Baldwin, Ed	WJ	7	3	27	Wi 82	48
Balkin, Emanuel	Sardinian Debut, Colorful Tapestries and Rugs Interest American Weavers	H&C	13	1		Wi 62	21
Ball, Margaret	Color and Weave Effects for Four-Harness Twills	SS&D	8	1	29	WI 76	71
Ballarian, Anna	Fabric Collage	WJ	3	1	9	Jy 78	37
Bane, Allyne	Tailoring (Out of Print)	TM			7	O/N 86	74
Banks, Lloyd Walton	Color Blending in Needlepoint	TM			10	A/M 87	24
Bard, Elizabeth	"Assemblage: Wisconsin Paper" (Exhibit)	Fa	11	1		J/F 84	78
Bard, Elizabeth	Deborah J. Felix	Fa	12	2		M/A 85	34
Bard, Elizabeth A.	Chad Alice Hagen's Felt Work	Fa	13	4		J/A 86	30
Bard, Elizabeth A.	Dard Hunter Paper Museum, The	Fa	11	2		M/A 84	43
Bard, Elizabeth A.	Dianne E. Soule: Batik Portraits	Fa	12	6		N/D 85	11
Bard, Elizabeth A.	"Fiber National '84" (Exhibit)	Fa	12	4		J/A 85	66
Bard, Elizabeth A.	"Jean Stamsta: Great Lake Series" (Exhibit)	Fa	10	2		M/A 83	70
Bard, Elizabeth A.	Karon Hagemeister Winzenz: Fusing Fiber, Time, and Ritual	Fa	12	1		J/F 85	10
Bard, Elizabeth A.	"New Wisconsin Fiber": The First Group Show of American Fiber Art in Switzerland (Exhibit)	Fa	10	6		N/D 83	43
Bard, Elizabeth A.	Roberta Kremer: A Dialogue with Fiber	Fa	11	4		J/A 84	24
Bard, Elizabeth A.	Sericulture in Upstate New York	Fa	13	1		J/F 86	36
Bard, Elizabeth A.	Video Access to Textiles: The Helen L. Allen Textile Collection	Fa	12	6		N/D 85	34
Bardwell, Kathryn	Loom Controlled Bead Leno	SS&D	12	3	47	Su 81	50
Bardwell, Kathryn	Loom Controlled Quilted Fabrics	WJ	7	1	25	Su 82	39
Barker, Irene	My Friend, Mrs. Olds	S-O	9	4		Wi 85	47
Barker, Mary	Excellence of Spinning, Vitality of Dyes Impress Visitor to 'Down Under'	SS&D	4	4	16	Fa 73	46
Barnard, Eileen Wolford	"Quilts—Innovation and Tradition" (Exhibit)	Fa	10	3		M/J 83	72
Barnes, Galer	Conversion Factor, The	Kn	3	1	5	F-W 86	54
Barnes, Muriel	Making the Most of Your Weave	H&C	19	4		Fa 68	15
Barnes, Muriel	Thousand Islands Museum Craft School	SS&D	1	3	3	Ju 70	4
Barnett, Linda Lowman	Group of Quilters Fit Ideas to Theme of Gift	TM			7	O/N 86	33
Barnett-Westfall, Lynn	Cotton Shirts	WJ	4	3	15	Ja 80	22
Barnett-Westfall, Lynn	Handwoven Silk Garments: Ikat Kimono	WJ	3	2	10	Oc 78	30
Barnett-Westfall, Lynn	"Patti Mitchem: Rep Weave Hangings" (Exhibit)	Fa	8	3		M/J 81	67
Barrett, Clotilde	Boundweave	Hw	4	2		M/A 83	15
Barrett, Clotilde	Boundweave	WJ	7	4	28	Sp 83	49
Barrett, Clotilde	Boundweave	SS&D	15	3	59	Su 84	35
Barrett, Clotilde	Computer Weaving	WJ	4	3	15	Ja 80	35
Barrett, Clotilde	Corkscrew Weave	WJ	5	1	17	Su 80	16
Barrett, Clotilde	Coverlet Weaves Using Two Ties	WJ	3	4	12	Ap 79	26
Barrett, Clotilde	Double Two-Tie Twills and Basket Weave	WJ	7	3	27	Wi 82	38
Barrett, Clotilde	Double Woven Bag Inspired by a South American Bag, A	WJ	1	2	2	Oc 76	29
Barrett, Clotilde	Enjoy Threading Your Loom	WJ	7	4	28	Sp 83	66

AUTHOR	TITLE	JOUR	VOL	NO	ISS	DATE	PAGE
Barrett, Clotilde	Finnweave	WJ	11	4	44	Sp 87	25
Barrett, Clotilde	Four-Block Double Weave on Four Shafts	WJ	8	1	29	Su 83	72
Barrett, Clotilde	How One Weave Leads to Another	WJ	8	1	29	Su 83	75
Barrett, Clotilde	Inlay Techniques	WJ	1	1	1	Jy 76	3
Barrett, Clotilde	Keep Warm! Foot Cozy	WJ	5	2	18	Fa 80	12
Barrett, Clotilde	Keep Warm! Woolen Throw	WJ	5	2	18	Fa 80	14
Barrett, Clotilde	Leno with Steel Doup Heddles	WJ	6	3	23	Wi 81	48
Barrett, Clotilde	Let's Pull Together	WJ	8	1	29	Su 83	85
Barrett, Clotilde	Merry Christmas!	WJ	8	2	30	Fa 83	36
Barrett, Clotilde	Multi-Harness Huck: Learn About the Structure of This Family of Weaves and Design Your Own Variations	WJ	10	4	40	Sp 86	11
Barrett, Clotilde	Navajo Saddle Blanket Patterns	WJ	1	1	1	Jy 76	22
Barrett, Clotilde	Navajo Saddle Blanket Patterns	WJ	11	1	41	Su 86	56
Barrett, Clotilde	Pattern Weaving	WJ	4	4	16	Ap 80	6
Barrett, Clotilde	Rep Weaves: Introduction	WJ	7	4	28	Sp 83	8
Barrett, Clotilde	see Szumski, Norma	WJ	6	2	22	Fa 81	41
Barrett, Clotilde	Seen Around the Country: Threads Unlimited IV	SS&D	10	1	37	Wi 78	84
Barrett, Clotilde	Shadow Weave and Corkscrew Weave	Iw	5	3		Su 80	71
Barrett, Clotilde	Shadowweave, Part 1 (error-corrected WJ v2 n1 77 insert for vol. 1)	WJ	1	1	1	Jy 76	13
Barrett, Clotilde	Shadowweave, Part 2 — Unbalanced Shadowweave (error-corrected WJ v2 n1 77 insert for vol. 1)	WJ	1	2	2	Oc 76	14
Barrett, Clotilde	Shadowweave, Part 3 — Marian Powell's Shadow Weave Conversion	WJ	1	3	3	Ja 77	25
Barrett, Clotilde	Shaft-Switching	WJ	8	4	32	Sp 84	28
Barrett, Clotilde	Shaft-Switching Combined with Harness Control	WJ	9	1	33	Su 84	37
Barrett, Clotilde	Silk Box	WJ	3	2	10	Oc 78	13
Barrett, Clotilde	Spinning Doghair	WJ	1	1	1	Jy 76	27
Barrett, Clotilde	Summer and Winter and Beyond	Iw	5	1		Wi 79	65
Barrett, Clotilde	Summer & Winter and Beyond	WJ	7	3	27	Wi 82	51
Barrett, Clotilde	Table Tapestries	WJ	7	4	28	Sp 83	73
Barrett, Clotilde	Tunic Made from Narrow Strips	WJ	4	3	15	Ja 80	9
Barrett, Clotilde	Veridian Green Cape	WJ	4	3	15	Ja 80	11
Barrett, Clotilde	Weave and Knit Pullover	WJ	8	3	31	Wi 83	20
Barrett, Clotilde	Weaving in Quebec	WJ	6	4	24	Sp 82	8
Barrett, Clotilde	Weaving in Quebec: Devotion to Garments	WJ	6	4	24	Sp 82	18
Barrett, Clotilde	Weaving in Quebec: New Ideas and Techniques	WJ	6	4	24	Sp 82	16
Barrett, Clotilde	Weaving in Quebec: New Traditions	WJ	6	4	24	Sp 82	14
Barrett, Clotilde	Weaving in Quebec: Traditional Quebecois Weaving	WJ	6	4	24	Sp 82	10
Barrett, Clotilde	Weaving Towels As a Means of Learning the Basic Four-Shaft Weaves	WJ	8	2	30	Fa 83	11
Barrett, Clotilde	What a Handweaver Can Learn from the Scottish Weaving Industry (error-corrected WJ v2 n1 77 insert for vol. 1)	WJ	1	3	3	Ja 77	11
Barrett, Clotilde; Eunice Smith	Double Two-Tie Unit Weave	Hw	5	5		N/D 84	12
Barrett, Clotilde; Ronnie Bohannan	System for Recording and Drafting Certain Types of Braids, A (error-corrected WJ v2 n1 77 insert for vol. 1)	WJ	1	2	2	Oc 76	20
Barrett, Clotilde transl.	Mothproofing Wool	WJ	8	2	30	Fa 83	59
Barrett, Earl	Short and Sweet Drawdown Program for Computers, A (error-corrected WJ v7 n1 82 p36b)	WJ	6	3	23	Wi 81	42
Barrett, Earl W.	Electric Drill Becomes a Quill Spinner and a Bobbin Winder, An	WJ	1	1	1	Jy 76	19
Barrett, Earl W.	Introduction to Computers for Weavers, An	WJ	7	4	28	Sp 83	25
Barrett, Earl W.	Introduction to Computers for Weavers, An—Part 2: What's Inside the Box?	WJ	8	1	29	Su 83	45
Barrett, Earl W.	Introduction to Computers for Weavers—Part 3: What's Inside the Box? (cont'd); More On I/O	WJ	8	2	30	Fa 83	24
Barrett, Katharine A.	Southern California Guild Conference	H&C	9	1		Wi 57	15
Barrett, Katharine A.	Weaving Center for Pasadena Girls	H&C	9	2		Sp 58	22

AUTHOR	TITLE	JOUR	VOL	NO	ISS	DATE	PAGE
Barrett, Phyllis K.	Rags to Riches: Honeycomb Bolero-Style Vest	WJ	6	3	23	Wi 81	30
Barrett, Ruth L.	Designs in Summer-and-Winter	H&C	12	4		Fa 61	34
Barrett, Timothy	Japanese Papermaking: Traditions, Tools and Techniques	Fa	13	1		J/F 86	45
Barrios, Lina E.	Hierba, Montaña y El Arbol de la Vida en San Pedro Sacatepequez, Guatemala	WJ	9	2	34	Fa 84	78
Barrow, Cynthia	Home Built Box Spinner	WJ	2	4	8	Ap 78	43
Barss, Peter	Older Ways — Traditional Nova Scotian Craftsmen	WJ	6	2	22	Fa 81	40
Bartl, Pam	Structuring a Bulky Yarn	lw	5	2		Sp 80	62
Barton, Jane	see Wada, Yoshiko	Hw	6	3		Su 85	14
Barton, Jane	see Wada, Yoshiko	Fa	11	6		N/D 84	56
Barton, Jane	see Wada, Yoshiko	Fa	12	2		M/A 85	55
Barton, Jane	see Wada, Yoshiko	Fa	12	2		M/A 85	58
Barton, Jane; et al.	Itchiku Kubota: Kimono in the Tsujigahana Tradition (catalogue)	Hw	6	3		Su 85	14
Basa, Lynn	Return of the Rag, The	Fa	14	3		M/J 87	29
Bassler, Jim	Involvement in What Is to Be	SS&D	3	1	9	Wi 71	25
Batchelder, Helen Tilton	Handicraft Club of Rhode Island, The	H&C	7	1		Wi 55	15
Batchelder, Joy	Case for Two Warp Beams, The	CW	7	1	19	Se 85	5
Bateman, Dr. William G.; Virginia I. Harvey, ed.	Bateman Blend Weaves, Based on Dr. William G. Bateman's Manuscript	SCGM		36		82	1-144
Bateman, Dr. William G.; Virginia I. Harvey, ed.	Boulevard, Chevron, and Combination Weaves, Based on Dr. William G. Bateman's Manuscript	SCGM		38		87	1-93
Bateman, Dr. William G.; Virginia I. Harvey, ed.	Multiple Tabby Weaves, Based on Dr. William G. Bateman's Manuscript	SCGM		35		81	1-92
Bateman, Dr. William G.; Virginia I, Harvey, ed.	Park Weaves, Based on Dr. William G. Bateman's Manuscript	SCGM		37		84	1-96
Bateman, Wendy	Notes on Navajo Plying	S-O	9	2		Su 85	36
Bates, Wynne	Plymouth Hoe	SS&D	3	2	10	Sp 72	43
Bateson, Vivienne	Woven Fashion	Hw	6	2		M/A 85	72
Bateson, Vivienne	Woven Fashion	SS&D	16	3	63	Su 85	8
Bath, Virginia Churchill	Lace	SS&D	11	1	41	Wi 79	32
Battenfield, Jackie	Ikat Technique	SS&D	10	2	38	Sp 79	72
Battenfield, Jackie	Ikat Technique	Fa	5	5		S/O 78	82
Battersby, Mark E.	Hobby Businesses in 1986	Fa	13	3		M/J 86	17
Bauer, Nancy	New Brunswick Craft School: Hosting a Workshop by Barbara MacCallum, The	Fa	11	5		S/O 84	40
Baumann, Agnes	Selling Handcraft for Profit — A Directory for Skilled Craftsmen Who Have Products to sell	H&C	6	4		Fa 55	59
Bayer, Herbert; Walter Gropius; Ise Gropius, eds.	Bauhaus 1919 — 1928	H&C	3	3		Su 52	64
Bayer, Jeffrey J.	Metallizing	SS&D	7	1	25	Wi 75	14
Beall, Karen F.	Temari: Threads to the Past	Fa	14	2		M/A 87	7
Beard, Betty	Versatile Inlay, Twill on Twill	SS&D	19	1	73	Wi 87	53
Beattie, May H.	Some Weft-Float Brocaded Rugs of the Bergama-Ezine Region	TMJ	3	2		De 71	20
Beattie, May H.	Thyssen-Bornemisza Collection of Oriental Rugs, The	TMJ	3	4		De 73	46
Beattie, May H.	Thyssen-Bornemisza Collection of Oriental Tugs, The	TMJ	4	1		De 74	85
Becher, Lotte	Handweaving: Designs and Instructions	H&C	6	2		Sp 55	61
Bechtol, Valerie	see Nelson, Susan Venable	Fa	5	4		J/A 78	32
Beck, Dorothy	Rating System of Boston Guild	H&C	12	2		Sp 61	50
Beck, Dorothy; Hazel Chase	Handwoven Embroidery Weaves	SS&D	2	1	5	De 70	31
Beck, Dorothy; Hazel Chase	Handwoven Embroidery Weaves	H&C	16	3		Su 65	43
Beck, Dorothy; Hazel Chase	Weavers Answer Book	SS&D	2	1	5	De 70	31
Beck, Dorothy; Hazel Chase	Weavers Answer Book	H&C	14	1		Wi 63	43

AUTHOR	TITLE	JOUR	VOL	NO	ISS	DATE	PAGE
Beck, Ulrike	Simple But Effective: A Novel Stretcher	WJ	10	2	38	Fa 85	27
Becker, Mary Lamb	Mittens to Knit	Kn	3	1	5	F-W 86	69
Becker, Robin; James Chressanthis	Portrait of a Village	Fa	9	6		N/D 82	40
Beckett, Susan	Susan Beckett	Fa	14	5		N/D 87	12
Becklake, Vera L.	Antique Spinning Chairs	WJ	11	2	42	Fa 86	58
Bedaux, Rogier M. A.; Rita Bolland	Medieval Textiles from the Tellem Caves in Central Mali, West Africa	TMJ	19 20			80,81	65
Beeaff, Dianne Ebertt	Southwestern Rhythms of Harwood Steiger Fabrics, The	Fa	13	2		M/A 86	29
Beebee, Dorothy	see Rice, Miriam	WJ	5	2	18	Fa 80	31
Beebee, Dorothy	see Rice, Miriam	Hw	2	3		My 81	70
Beecher, Helen Carls	Tabby and Twill — Wool and Worsted	H&C	4	4		Fa 53	59
Beede, Beth	"Kari Lønning — Mary Billingsley" (Exhibit)	Fa	6	6		N/D 79	69
Beede, Beth; Jill Garfunkel	Feltmaking in Hungary	Fa	13	4		J/A 86	6
Beede, Beth; Jill Garfunkel	Zoltán Mihalkó: Hungarian Feltmaker	SS&D	17	4	68	Fa 86	12
Beem, Edgar Allen	"Maine Coast Artists: Fabrications" (Exhibit)	Fa	11	4		J/A 84	80
Beeny, Merna	Autumn Colors	Hw	3	4		Se 82	47
Beeny, Merna	Spring and Summer Colors	Hw	4	3		M/J 83	95
Beeny, Merna	Winter Colors	Hw	4	1		J/F 83	64
Beetem, Debra	Cozy Afghan, A	S-O	10	4		Wi 86	13
Beetem, Debra	Just an Idea	Kn	3	1	5	F-W 86	37
Beevers, Sue	Inscribing a Coverlet	PWC	5	2	16		16
Behrens, Ahn	Telling Stories with Color and Pattern	Fa	13	2		M/A 86	68
Beinecke, Mary Ann	Dye and Spin Workshops on Nantucket	SS&D	4	1	13	Wi 72	12
Belash, Constantine A.	Braiding and Knotting for Amateurs	H&C	3	4		Fa 52	62
Belfer, Nancy	Collegiate Fashion Show Highlights Textile Program	Fa	14	1		J/F 87	6
Belfer, Nancy	Collegiate Weavers: Buffalo, New York	SS&D	9	3	35	Su 78	85
Belfer, Nancy	Designing in Batik and Tie Dye	H&C	23	4		J/A 72	26
Belfer, Nancy	"Fiber National '86" (Exhibit)	Fa	14	1		J/F 87	51
Belfer, Nancy	Ikat Notes: Nancy Belfer Talks About Her Recent Work	Fa	9	2		M/A 82	19
Belfer, Nancy	Revival of Stitchery, Appliqué, and Collage	H&C	18	1		Wi 67	21
Belfer, Nancy	Ruth Bilowus: Small and Precious Tapestries	Fa	7	2		M/A 80	15
Belfer, Nancy	Weaving, Applique and Stitchery	Iw	5	3		Su 80	41
Belfer, Nancy	Weaving: Design and Expression	SS&D	7	1	25	Wi 75	34
Belfer, Nancy	Weaving — Design and Expression	WJ	2	1	5	Jy 77	29
Bell, Lilian A.	Papyrus, Tapa, Amate & Rice Paper	Fa	13	2		M/A 86	41
Bell, Lilian A.	Plant Fibers for Papermaking	Fa	13	2		M/A 86	41
Bellamy, Virginia Woods	Number Knitting	H&C	3	4		Fa 52	61
Bellerby, Greg	Carol Sabiston's Sails: An Expression of the Interaction of Sea and Land	Fa	10	3		M/J 83	16
Bellinger, Louisa	see Bird, Junius	H&C	6	3		Su 55	61
Bellinger, Louisa	see Kuhnel, Ernest	H&C	4	4		Fa 53	59
Bellinger, Louisa	Workshop Notes: Craft Habits Part 1(#19) Loom Types Suggested by Weaving Details	H&C	11	2		Sp 60	60
Bellinger, Louisa	Workshop Notes: Craft Habits Part 2 (#20) Spinning Fibers in Warp Yarns	H&C	11	2		Sp 60	60
Bemis, Elijah	Dyer's Companion, The	SS&D	6	1	21	Wi 74	32
Bemis, Marion Holden	Marianne Strengell, Textile Consultant to Architects	H&C	8	1		Wi 56	6
Benanti, Gigi	Artist's Need for Needlework, An	TM			9	F/M 87	20
Bendich, Hilary	Dobby Loom: A Workbench Report, The	SS&D	11	4	44	Fa 80	79
Bennet, Anna G.	Five Centuries of Tapestry	SS&D	8	3	31	Su 77	62
Bennett, Anna G.; Ruth Berson	Fans in Fashion	Fa	9	4		J/A 82	53
Bennett, H., ed.	Concise Chemical and Technical Dictionary	H&C	14	2		Sp 63	44

AUTHOR	TITLE	JOUR	VOL	NO	ISS	DATE	PAGE
Bennett, Jennifer	Part-Time Challenge: When Textile Art Plays a Secondary Role in One's Life, The	Fa	10	3		M/J 83	51
Bennett, Noël	Designing with the Wool	Iw	4	3		Su 79	66
Bennett, Noël	From Designing with the Wool	Iw	4	1		Wi 78	17
Bennett, Noël	From Father Sky to Mother Earth: An Ethnic Inspiration	WJ	8	1	29	Su 83	62
Bennett, Noël	Navajo Legend	WJ	8	1	29	Su 83	62
Bennett, Noël	see Bighorse, Tiana	Iw	4	1		Wi 78	12
Bennett, Noël	Weaving Brings Total Involvement with the Navajo	SS&D	4	4	16	Fa 73	15
Bennett, Noël; Tiana Bighorse	Working with the Wool	H&C	24	2		M/A 73	5
Bennett, Noël; Tiana Bighorse	Working with the Wool: How to Weave a Navajo Rug	SS&D	5	2	18	Sp 74	68
Bennett, Paul	Artist Craftsman!	H&C	24	3		M/J 73	22
Bennett, Siiri	Felted Jacket	WJ	9	1	33	Su 84	49
Bennett, Wendell C.	Ancient Arts of the Andes	H&C	5	3		Su 54	57
Benson, Elizabeth P.	see Rowe, Ann P.	Iw	5	4		Fa 80	75
Benson, Elizabeth P., ed.	see Rowe, Anne Pollard, ed.	Fa	7	6		N/D 80	59
Benson, Oscar H.	see Gallinger, Osma Couch	H&C	2	1		Wi 50	59
Benson, Oscar H.	see Tod, Osma Gallinger	SS&D	7	1	25	Wi 75	34
Benson, Sallyann	Bulk Spinning	SS&D	14	2	54	Sp 83	36
Bercey, Lee	Prayer Shawls	H&C	20	1		Wi 69	20
Berdinka, Regine	Weaving & Felting	SS&D	15	2	58	Sp 84	10
Berent, Mary, et al.	Color Games	S-O	11	1		Sp 87	21
Berger, Charles	Australian Spinner Raises Profitable Flock of Goats	H&C	17	3		Su 66	11
Berger, Florence S.	Cincinnati Celebrates '76	SS&D	8	2	30	Sp 77	60
Berger, René	"Tenth International Biennial of Tapestry: A Juror" (Exhibit)	Fa	8	6		N/D 81	55
Berglund, Hilma	Design in Weaving	H&C	8	4		Fa 57	13
Berglund, Hilma	Loom with Removable Innards	SS&D	2	1	5	De 70	21
Berglund, Hilma	Small Looms Offer a Wide Range for Experiment	H&C	12	2		Sp 61	22
Bergman, Barbara	see Cahlander, Adele	WJ	6	3	23	Wi 81	54
Bergman, Margaret	Constellations: A Summer and Winter Weave on Ten Harnesses	CW	5	3	15	My 84	20
Berlant, Anthony	see Kahlenberg, Mary Hunt	TMJ	3	4		De 73	47
Berlant, Anthony; Mary Hunt Kahlenberg	Walk in Beauty: The Navajo and Their Blankets	SS&D	9	2	34	Sp 78	47
Berliner, Rudolf	Coptic Tapestry of Byzantine Style, A	TMJ	1	1		No 62	3
Berliner, Rudolf	Horsemen in Tapestry Roundels Found in Egypt	TMJ	1	2		De 63	39
Berliner, Rudolf	More About the Developing Islamic Style in Tapestries	TMJ	2	1		De 66	3
Berliner, Rudolf	Remarks on Some Tapestries from Egypt	TMJ	1	4		De 65	20
Berliner, Rudolf	Tapestries from Egypt Influenced by Theatrical Performances	TMJ	1	3		De 64	35
Bernal, Susan Scott	Slentre Braiding	SS&D	9	2	34	Sp 78	63
Bernard-Boone, Ann	Progression from Meticulous Yardage to Grand Commissions	SS&D	5	1	17	Wi 73	71
Berner, Julie	Julie Berner	Fa	14	1		J/F 87	27
Bernier, Ronald M.	Textile Arts of India	WJ	2	1	5	Jy 77	31
Bernstein, Betty	see Mies, Mary	SS&D	11	3	43	Su 80	9
Bernstein, Bruce	Native American Basketry	Fa	11	1		J/F 84	50
Bernstein, Bruce	Other Ethnological Collections	Fa	11	1		J/F 84	50
Bernstein, Marion H.	Off-Loom Weaving	SS&D	3	2	10	Sp 72	39
Berson, Ruth	see Bennett, Anna G.	Fa	9	4		J/A 82	53
Bertram, Carel	see Dyer, Carol	Fa	7	5		S/O 80	48
Beschell, Lorraine	Home Studio: Some Practical Hints	Iw	5	2		Sp 80	58
Beschell, Lorraine	Money Matters	Fa	5	4		J/A 78	56
Beschell, Lorraine	Professional Finishing: Hints for Beginners, Reminders for Old Hands	Fa	5	6		N/D 78	54
Beschell, Lorraine	That First Solo Show	Iw	5	1		Wi 79	53
Beskow, Elsa	Pelle's New Suit	Iw	2	1		Fa 76	32

AUTHOR	TITLE	JOUR	VOL	NO	ISS	DATE	PAGE
+ Bess, Nancy	see Gilman, Rachel Seidel	SS&D	10	1	37	Wi 78	77
+ Bess, Nancy Moore	Divided Spaces: The Fences of Japan	Fa	14	4		S/O 87	28
+ Bess, Nancy Moore	"Nina Holland: Bound Weave Rugs/Hangings" (Exhibit)	Fa	9	1		J/F 82	83
Best, Eleanor	Are You Pegging, Tyeing-Up or Punching the Computer?	CW	3	2	8	Ja 82	8
Best, Eleanor	Complex Weavers: A History of the Group, The	SS&D	12	2	46	Sp 81	19
Best, Eleanor	Easy Warping Without a Cross	SS&D	15	1	57	Wi 83	15
Best, Eleanor	Handwoven Silk Garments: A Wedding Dress	WJ	3	2	10	Oc 78	28
Best, Eleanor	Shear to Share	SS&D	15	1	57	Wi 83	28
Best, Eleanor	Weavers' Friendship Coverlet	Hw	3	5		N/D 82	68
Best, Eleanor	Weaves: A Design Handbook	CW		25		Se 87	17
Best, Eleanor	Weaves: A Design Handbook	PWC	5	2	16		54
Bethe, Monica	see Stinchecum, Amanda Mayer	Hw	6	3		Su 85	14
Betts, Diane	Angora Fiber Spinning	S-O	9	4		Wi 85	35
Betts, Diane	Felt Vest, Hat, Mittens	S-O	9	2		Su 85	39
Betts, Diane	Feltmaking Experience, A	S-O	9	2		Su 85	39
Betts, Diane	Knit Tabard	S-O	9	2		Su 85	41
Betts, Diane	Turquoise Angora Pullover	S-O	9	4		Wi 85	36
Betts, Diane	Working with Lincoln Lamb's Wool	S-O	9	2		Su 85	41
Betzina, Sandra	Power Sewing: New Ways to Make Fine Clothes Fast	Hw	7	5		N/D 86	12
Betzina, Sandra	Proper Sewing Equipment	Hw	7	5		N/D 86	72
Betzina, Sandra	Sewing Handwovens	TM			2	D/J 85	20
Betzina, Sandra	Twentieth Century Ribbon Sculptress Candace Kling	TM			12	A/S 87	62
Beugler, Eugen	Six Ways to Wear Your Lace	Kn	4	1	9	Wi 87	44
Beukers, Henriette	Velten—Valkning—Felting	Hw	4	5		N/D 83	80
Beutlich, Tadek	Technique of Woven Tapestry, The	H&C	18	3		Su 67	44
Beveridge, June H.	Warp/Weft/Set. A Reference Manual for Handweavers	WJ	6	4	24	Sp 82	59
Beveridge, June H.	Warp/Weft/Sett	SS&D	12	2	46	Sp 81	71
Beveridge, June H.	Warp/Weft/Sett, A Reference Manual for Handweavers	Iw	6	1		Wi 80	69
Beveridge, June H.	Warp/Weft/Sett: A Reference Manual for Handweavers	Fa	8	4		J/A 81	41
Beytebiere, D'Arcie	A Textural Approach to Arashi Shibori	TM			8	D/J 86	24
Bick, Georgie	Preparation and the Tapestry, The	SS&D	2	2	6	Sp 71	6
Bieck, Doris Spath	Art of Spinning in the Grease, The Pioneer Way, The	WJ	8	2	30	Fa 83	62
Biehl, Betty Atwater	My Mother, The Weaver: Reminiscences About Mary Meigs Atwater	SS&D	4	4	16	Fa 73	28
Biehl, Betty Atwater	Weavers Are Needed	SS&D	3	3	11	Su 72	29
Biehl, Mary Atwater	Do's and Don'ts	SS&D	4	1	13	Wi 72	19
Bielenberg, Kristina	Demonstrating at the Smithsonian	H&C	24	1		J/F 73	19
Bierman, Irene A., ed.	see Bacharach, Jere L.	SS&D	9	4	36	Fa 78	81
Bighorse, Tiana	see Bennett, Noël	SS&D	5	2	18	Sp 74	68
Bighorse, Tiana	see Bennett, Noël	H&C	24	2		M/A 73	5
Bighorse, Tiana; Noël Bennett	Weaving the Navajo Way	Iw	4	1		Wi 78	12
Bird, Adren J.; Steven Goldsberry; J. Puninani Kaneloa Bird	Craft of Hawaiian Lauhala Weaving, The	WJ	8	2	30	Fa 83	63
Bird, Junius B.	Before Heddles Were Invented	H&C	3	3		Su 52	5
Bird, Junius B.	Handspun Yarn Production Rates in the Cuzco Region of Peru	TMJ	2	3		De 68	9
Bird, Junius B.	see Rowe, Ann Pollard	TMJ	19 20			80,81	27
Bird, Junius B.	Shaped Tapestry Bags from the Nazca-Ica Area of Peru	TMJ	1	3		De 64	2
Bird, Junius B.; Milica Dimitrijevic Skinner	Technical Features of a Middle Horizon Tapestry Shirt from Peru, The	TMJ	4	1		De 74	5
Bird, Junius; Louisa Bellinger	Paracas Fabrics and Nazca Needlework	H&C	6	3		Su 55	61
Birrell, Verda	Textile Arts — A Handbook of Fabric Structure and Design, The	H&C	10	2		Sp 59	59
Birren, Faber	New Horizons in Color	H&C	10	3		Su 59	60

AUTHOR	TITLE	JOUR	VOL	NO	ISS	DATE	PAGE
Birren, Faber	Textile Colorist, The	WJ	6	1	21	Su 81	53
Birren, Faber	Textile Colorist, The	Fa	9	4		J/A 82	52
Birrin, Faber	Textile Colorist, The	Hw	2	4		Se 81	78
Bishop, Mara	Fiber Workspaces: A Room of Your Own	Fa	4	4		J/A 77	38
Bishop, Mrs. Carlton T.	Design in Cotton	H&C	6	4		Fa 55	11
Bishop, Robert	see Safford, Carleton L.	TMJ	3	4		De 73	47
Bishop, Robert; Elizabeth Safanda	Gallery of Amish Quilts, Design Diversity from a Plain People, A	Fa	7	1		J/F 80	15
Bissell, June	"Beds, Sweet Dreams, and Other Things" (Exhibit)	Fa	6	4		J/A 79	70
Bissell, June M.	Exploration of Caustic Soda, An	Fa	7	6		N/D 80	43
Bjerregaard, Lena	Techniques of Guatemalan Weaving	SS&D	9	4	36	Fa 78	80
Bjerregaard, Lena	Techniques of Guatemalan Weaving	lw	3	2		Wi 78	41
Bjerregaard, Lena	Techniques of Guatemalan Weaving	WJ	2	4	8	Ap 78	40
Black, Elizabeth	see Wipplinger, Michelle	Hw	3	2		Mr 82	22
Black, Mary	Jacquetta Nisbet to Give Workshop on Peruvian Pebble Weave (error-corrected SS&D v5 n1 73 p93)	SS&D	4	4	16	Fa 73	76
Black, Mary E.	Key to Weaving	H&C	1	1		Ap 50	49
Black, Mary E.	New Key to Weaving	H&C	9	2		Sp 58	59
Black, Mary E.	New Key to Weaving	Fa	3	1		J/F 76	4
Black, Mary E.	Nova Scotia Tartan, The	H&C	6	2		Sp 55	26
Black, Mary E.	see Chown, M. Joyce	H&C	11	4		Fa 60	59
Black, Mary E.	Sett and Weaving of Tartans, The	H&C	10	2		Sp 59	59
Black, Mary E.	Tapestry in Nova Scotia	H&C	8	3		Su 57	24
Black, Mary E.	Weaving for Beginners	H&C	6	1		Wi 54	61
Black, Mary E.	Weaving in Nova Scotia — Yesterday and Today	H&C	2	4		Fa 51	5
Black, Mary E.; Bessie R. Murray	You Can Weave	SS&D	6	3	23	Su 75	50
Black, Mary E.; M. Joyce Chown	Ready Reference Tables for Handweavers	H&C	11	4		Fa 60	59
Black, Mary E.; M. Joyce Chown	Thread Guide for Handweavers	H&C	11	4		Fa 60	59
Black, Sue	Prairie Wool Companion Index, Issues 5-6, Spring and Summer 1983	PWC	3	1	7		67
Black, Sue	Prairie Wool Companion Index, Issues l-4, Nov. 1981 – Oct. 1982	PWC			4	Ja 83	72
Blackburn, Edna	Breeds of Sheep	SS&D	3	2	10	Sp 72	35
Blackburn, Edna	Dyeing Gold and Yellow	TM			1	O/N 85	28
Blackburn, Edna	From Canada to China and Back Again (Edna Blackburn)	S-O	6	4		82	31
Blackman, Margery	Judging Handspun Wool	SS&D	2	2	6	Sp 71	11
Bladow, Suzanne	Secrets of the Land	Fa	7	1		J/F 80	48
Blakely, Deborah	"Ideas and Capabilities: Barbara Sykes' Fiber Constructions" (Exhibit)	Fa	8	1		J/F 81	94
Blanks, Lloyd	Evolution of an Artist: Lloyd Blanks	Fa	14	5		N/D 87	30
Blaylock, Mary P.	"Baskets in La Jolla" (Exhibit)	Fa	11	1		J/F 84	79
Blickenstaff, Maxine L.	Korean Journal	SS&D	7	2	26	Sp 76	52
Blinks, Anne	Notes on Plaiting in the Upper Amazon Basin, Peru	lw	5	4		Fa 80	51
Blinks, Anne	Roggeband	lw	3	3		Sp 78	16
Bliss, Anne	Ancient Yellow Goes Modern, An	lw	4	2		Sp 79	44
Bliss, Anne	Annatto: Color for Complexions, Cheese and Cloth	Hw	5	5		N/D 84	82
Bliss, Anne	Bindweeds	Hw	6	5		N/D 85	86
Bliss, Anne	Blending Mohair with Other Fibers	S-O	7	3		Fa 83	43
Bliss, Anne	Boxed Rainbows: What to Do with a Dye Kit	Hw	4	2		M/A 83	68
Bliss, Anne	Centroid Colors, The	lw	5	4		Fa 80	56
Bliss, Anne	Cochineal in Colorado: or, Is Your Local Cactus Bugged? (error-corrected lw v1 n3 76 p25)	lw	1	2		Wi 76	20
Bliss, Anne	Color It Plaid	Hw	4	5		N/D 83	74
Bliss, Anne	Color Variations: Uses for Mordants and Additives	Hw	5	1		J/F 84	80
Bliss, Anne	Cracked, Pots, Snaggled Skeins and Other Dyeing Dilemmas	Hw	2	5		No 81	68

AUTHOR	TITLE	JOUR	VOL	NO	ISS	DATE	PAGE
Bliss, Anne	Criteria for Judging Handspun Yarn	S-O	3			79	8
Bliss, Anne	Currants: Not Just for Eating	Hw	7	4		S/O 86	74
Bliss, Anne	Daisy, Daisy, Give Me Your Color, Do	Hw	6	4		S/O 85	80
Bliss, Anne	Dandelion Dye and Other Delights	Iw	2	3		Sp 77	22
Bliss, Anne	Diverse Dyes	Iw	3	2		Wi 78	30
Bliss, Anne	Do It Yourself Guide to Space-Dyed Yarn	Hw	7	3		M/J 86	55
Bliss, Anne	Don't Cry...Dye	Hw	2	2		Mr 81	50
Bliss, Anne	Dye a Bundle	Hw	5	3		Su 84	87
Bliss, Anne	Dyeing: A Personal Palette for Tapestry	Hw	3	1		Ja 82	66
Bliss, Anne	Dyeing by the Yard	Iw	5	2		Sp 80	60
Bliss, Anne	Dyeing in the Rockies	SS&D	8	1	29	WI 76	14
Bliss, Anne	Dyeing with the Synthetics	Hw	6	1		J/F 85	69
Bliss, Anne	Dyeing with Willows, Cottonwoods, Aspens and Poplars	Iw	5	3		Su 80	54
Bliss, Anne	Dyes for Handspuns: Fiber to Yarn	S-O	6	4		82	52
Bliss, Anne	Dyes for Painting Warps	Hw	5	4		S/0 84	65
Bliss, Anne	Dyes from Oak Galls	Iw	6	1		Wi 80	64
Bliss, Anne	Fine & Fancy: Good Sewing Techniques for Good Cloth	Hw	4	1		J/F 83	38
Bliss, Anne	From Body Paint to Buffalo Hides	Iw	4	1		Wi 78	42
Bliss, Anne	Get Some Razzle Dazzle—Try "Brazzle"	Iw	2	4		Su 77	28
Bliss, Anne	Getting Woaded for Winter	Iw	2	1		Fa 76	22
Bliss, Anne	Gioanventura Rosetti and His Dye Book—1548 A. D.	Iw	3	1		Fa 77	36
Bliss, Anne	Handbook of Dyes from Natural Materials, A	SS&D	13	2	50	Sp 82	63
Bliss, Anne	Handbook of Dyes from Natural Materials, A	Hw	2	4		Se 81	79
Bliss, Anne	Handbook of Dyes from Natural Materials, A	Fa	9	4		J/A 82	52
Bliss, Anne	Hints for Dyeing	S-O	9	3		Fa 85	53
Bliss, Anne	How Fast is the Color?	Hw	5	2		M/A 84	16
Bliss, Anne	How Much Dye Can a Dyebath Dye If a Dyebath Can Dye Dye?	Hw	6	2		M/A 85	85
Bliss, Anne	Ikat with Ease	Hw	2	4		Se 81	60
Bliss, Anne	Indigo—The all Time Favorite Blue	Hw	2	3		My 81	60
Bliss, Anne	Juicy Fruits and Nut Hulls: (is it a dye or a stain?)	Hw	4	4		S/O 83	80
Bliss, Anne	Last Species: Osage Orange, Bois d'Arc, Horse Apple, Hedge Apple, The	Iw	1	3		Sp 76	24
Bliss, Anne	Lovely Dyes from Rank Weeds	Iw	3	4		Su 78	38
Bliss, Anne	Marbling Cloth	Hw	4	3		M/J 83	56
Bliss, Anne	Minor Miracles — New Life for Old Yarn	Hw	8	4		S/O 87	68
Bliss, Anne	North American Dye Plants	Hw	7	4		S/O 86	12
Bliss, Anne	Old Man's Beard, the Reindeer's Moss and the Stag's Horn, The	Hw	7	2		M/A 86	72
Bliss, Anne	On Dyeing with Madder	Iw	5	1		Wi 79	48
Bliss, Anne	Painted Silk	Hw	4	1		J/F 83	50
Bliss, Anne	Pastel	Hw	5	3		Su 84	86
Bliss, Anne	Prairie Plants: Natives and Immigrants	Hw	3	4		Se 82	74
Bliss, Anne	Putting the King in the Pot	Iw	1	4		Su 76	20
Bliss, Anne	SOAR Dyeworks	S-O	10	2		Su 86	44
Bliss, Anne	Solar Dyeing: A New Look At Fermentation	Iw	1	1		Fa 75	12
Bliss, Anne	Spring Greens (make more than green!)	Hw	3	2		Mr 82	69
Bliss, Anne	Stencils	Hw	6	3		Su 85	86
Bliss, Anne	Surface Design Techniques — The Basics	Hw	8	1		J/F 87	78
Bliss, Anne	Tapestry: A Brief Overview	Iw	4	2		Sp 79	15
Bliss, Anne	This Year, Plan and Plant a Dye Patch	Iw	2	2		Wi 77	28
Bliss, Anne	Thistles	Hw	7	1		J/F 86	84
Bliss, Anne	Tie-Dye...Naturally	Iw	4	3		Su 79	58
Bliss, Anne	Tips for Dyeing Silk	Hw	7	1		J/F 86	61
Bliss, Anne	Using Natural Dyes	S-O	8	3		Fa 84	42

AUTHOR	TITLE	JOUR	VOL	NO	ISS	DATE	PAGE
Bliss, Anne	Weeds: A Guide for Dyers and Herbalists	SS&D	10	4	40	Fa 79	64
Bliss, Anne	Weeds: A Guide for Dyers and Herbalists	Iw	3	4		Su 78	45
Bliss, Anne	Weeds — A Guide for Dyers and Herbalists	WJ	3	2	10	Oc 78	45
Bliss, Anne; with Margaret Emerson	Problem Solving	Iw	3	3		Sp 78	34
Bliven, Jeanette; Norma Smayda	Merry Christmas—A Name Draft	Hw	4	4		S/O 83	74
Block, Ira	Current Trends in Textiles Conservation and Preservation	AT	8			De 87	9
Block, Joyce	Saga of Gyöngh Laky, The	Fa	11	1		J/F 84	22
Block, Mary	Den Stroa Vavboken	H&C	3	4		Fa 52	61
Bloedel, Linda	Second Look at Soft Drink Mix Dyes, A	WJ	9	2	34	Fa 84	24
Bloom, Mary Jane	"Flowers of the Yayla: Yoruk Weaving of the Toros Mountains" (Exhibit)	Fa	11	3		M/J 84	76
Blue, Martha	Painted Rug Designs: Trader Hubbell's Influence on Navajo Weaving	Fa	14	5		N/D 87	5
Blue, Martha	see Davidson, Marion	Iw	5	1		Wi 79	63
Blue, Martha	see Davidson, Marion	Fa	6	6		N/D 79	51
Blue Mountain Crafts Council	Joy of Crafts	Iw	1	1		Fa 75	20
Blum, Grace D.	Functional Overshot — Basic Sources for Modern Fabric Design	H&C	11	2		Sp 60	59
Blum, June	June Blum	Fa	13	2		M/A 86	14
Blumenau, Lili	Art and Craft of Hand Weaving, Including Fabric Design, The	H&C	14	2		Sp 63	44
Blumenau, Lili	Art and Craft of Hand Weaving, The	H&C	6	3		Su 55	62
Blumenau, Lili	Art Education in the United States Today	H&C	2	3		Su 51	30
Blumenau, Lili	Creative Design in Wall Hangings	H&C	19	1		Wi 68	43
Blumenau, Lili	Designs in Ancient Figured Silks	H&C	2	1		Wi 50	5
Blumenau, Lili	Experimenting in Tapestry and Wall Hanging Techniques	H&C	14	3		Su 63	18
Blumenau, Lili	Loom Set Up for Sample and Short Warps, A	H&C	7	3		Su 56	30
Blumenau, Lili	On Textures — Notes of a Contemporary Weaver	H&C	1	2		Su 50	8
Blumenau, Lili	Planning and Weaving New Stripes	H&C	4	4		Fa 53	9
Blumenau, Lili	Pre-Incan Weavers of Peru, The	H&C	3	3		Su 52	12
Blumenau, Lili	Second Craftsmen's Conference	H&C	9	4		Fa 58	14
Blumenau, Lili	Textiles in the United Nations Buildings	H&C	4	1		Wi 52	10
Blumenau, Lili	Use of Novelty Yarns in Weaving, The	H&C	3	2		Sp 52	16
Blumenau, Lili	Weaver Craftsman in the Contemporary Scene, The	H&C	1	1		Ap 50	13
Blumenau, Lili	Weaver-Designer Plans a Fabric, The	H&C	3	1		Wi 51	8
Blumenau, Lili	Weaves in Figured Silks	H&C	2	2		Sp 51	25
Blumenau, Lili	Weaving Weights and Qualities	H&C	8	2		Sp 57	9
Blythe, LeGetta	Gift from the Hills	H&C	9	3		Su 58	59
Boaz, Franz	Primitive Art	H&C	4	3		Su 53	63
Bockelman, JoAnne	"Mini Tapestry Exhibit" (Exhibit)	Fa	5	4		J/A 78	12
Bogdan, Janet	Unicorn	SS&D	6	2	22	Sp 75	97
Bogdanor, Lura Jim	Collingwood Rug Workshop	SS&D	1	4	4	Se 70	11
Bogdanor, Lura Jim	To the Finish	Hw	8	3		M/J 87	16
Bogdanor, Lura Jim	To the Finish	WJ	11	1	41	Su 86	80
Bogdanor, Lura Jim	To the Finish	SS&D	17	4	68	Fa 86	88
Bogdonoff, Nancy Dick	Handwoven Textiles of Early New England: The Legacy of a Rural People 1640-1880	SS&D	7	1	25	Wi 75	34
Bogle, Michael	Burls	SS&D	11	4	44	Fa 80	35
Bogle, Michael	Burls	SS&D	12	1	45	Wi 80	31
Bogolyubov, Andrei Andreyevich	Carpets of Central Asia	TMJ	4	1		De 74	85
Bohannan, Ronnie	see Barrett, Clotilde	WJ	1	2	2	Oc 76	20
Bohannan, Ronnine	Brushstrokes of Color	Hw	5	3		Su 84	56
Bohannan, Ronnine	Designing Rep Weaves with the Aid of a Computer	WJ	7	4	28	Sp 83	24
Bohannan, Ronnine	Special Warp Effects with Space-Dyed Yarn	Hw	7	3		M/J 86	50
Bohannan, Ronnine	Twill "Sampler" to Wear, A	Hw	6	5		N/D 85	44

AUTHOR	TITLE	JOUR	VOL	NO	ISS	DATE	PAGE
Boland, Loay C.	Seen Around the Country: Colorado Fibers	SS&D	10	1	37	Wi 78	84
Bolland, Rita	see Bedaux, Rogier M. A.	TMJ	19 20			80,81	65
Bolster, Ella S.	Packing Textiles	H&C	12	4		Fa 61	23
Bolster, Ella S.	Teneriffe Lace—Spider Web Lace	SS&D	4	4	16	Fa 73	33
Bolster, Jane	Theo Moorman: Explorations	SS&D	1	2	2	Mr 70	10
Bolton, Eileen	Lichens for Vegetable Dyeing	H&C	24	1		J/F 73	28
Bolton, Eileen M.	Lichens for Vegetable Dyeing	H&C	12	1		Wi 61	59
Booth, J. E.	Principles of Textile Testing	H&C	19	2		Sp 68	47
Borgatti, Jean	Cloth As a Metaphor: Nigerian Textiles from the Museum of Cultural History	WJ	8	3	31	Wi 83	68
Borghetty, Hector C., translator	see Edelstein, Sidney M., translator	SS&D	3	4	12	Fa 72	47
Born, W.	Leonardo Da Vinci's Ideas on the Mechanization of Spinning	S-O	2			78	47
Borssuck, B.	Ninety-seven Needlepoint Alphabets	Iw	1	1		Fa 75	20
Borssuck, Bee	Knitting Round on Straight Needles	TM			12	A/S 87	64
Bossert, Helmuth	Folk Art of Europe	H&C	5	1		Wi 53	60
Boston Weaver's Guild Publications	Weaver's Wisdon, 250 Aids to Happier Weaving	WJ	5	2	18	Fa 80	31
Boutin-Wald, Pat	Color Theory for Handweavers Part 2: Visual Mix	WJ	10	3	39	Wi 86	47
Bowden, Peter	Wool Trade in Tudor and Stuart England, The	H&C	16	3		Su 65	44
Bowen, Gaza	The Shoemaker's Art	TM			5	J/J 86	56
Bowen, Godfrey	Wool Away	H&C	26	2		Ap 75	21
Bowen, Godfrey	Wool Away–The Art and Technique of Shearing	SS&D	7	1	25	Wi 75	35
Bowen, Godfrey	Wool Away-The Art and Technique of Shearing	Iw	1	2		Wi 76	28
Bowen, Kernochan	Four-Harness Weaving	Iw	3	4		Su 78	44
Bowen, Kernochan	Four-Harness Weaving, The Complete Guide to Warping and Weaving on a Four-Harness Loom	SS&D	10	1	37	Wi 78	77
Bowen, Kernochan	Gift Project Shows Essence of Weaving in a Tiny Space	SS&D	5	1	17	Wi 73	91
Bowers, Sandra W.	Fine Art of Collecting Baskets, The (error-corrected TM i14 '87 p4)	TM			13	O/N 87	16
Bowman, Cora	Craft to College Credit	S-O	9	2		Su 85	48
Bowman, Gloria	Loom Woven Baskets	WJ	10	4	40	Sp 86	37
Bowman, Gloria	Shaping with the Warp	SS&D	11	1	41	Wi 79	26
Bowman, Susan	Hamaca from Ecuador	SS&D	10	3	39	Su 79	52
Bowman, Susan; Susan Guagliumi; Olive Linder	Hammocks — A Swing Story	SS&D	10	3	39	Su 79	52
Boxberger, Daniel L.	Salish Weaving	SS&D	13	4	52	Fa 82	30
Boyce, Ann	Lamé	TM			8	D/J 86	32
Boyd, Doris	Eight Harness Patterned Double Weave Clothing	Iw	5	3		Su 80	71
Boyd, Doris	Tabby is Terrific!	Iw	5	3		Su 80	71
Boyd, E.	Popular Arts of Spanish New Mexico	TMJ	4	2		75	79
Boyd, Ruth	Characteristics of Wool	H&C	26	5		Oc 75	43
Boydston, Kay	Successful Experiment. Michigan Group Explores Natural Dyes	H&C	14	1		Wi 63	11
Boyer, Ruth M.	Lea Van Puymbroeck Miller, Innovator in Handweaving	H&C	20	2		Sp 69	15
Boyer, Ruth McDonald	Francisca Mayer, Designer-Weaver in the Peruvian Highland	H&C	19	2		Sp 68	18
Brabec, Barbara	Creative Cash	Iw	5	1		Wi 79	65
Brabec, Barbara	Creative Cash — How to Sell Your Crafts, Needlework, Designs and Know-How	WJ	4	3	15	Ja 80	46
Brabec, Barbara	Homemade Money	Hw	6	2		M/A 85	72
Brackett, Thelma	Handspinning in New Hampshire	H&C	17	1		Wi 66	18
Brackman, Barbara	"Chris Wolf Edmonds" (Exhibit)	Fa	11	5		S/O 84	72
Brackman, Barbara	"Pamela Gustavson Johnson: Constructivist Quilts" (Exhibit)	Fa	10	2		M/A 83	68
Bradbury, Francis M.	English Crewel Designs, Sixteenth to Eighteenth Centuries	WJ	8	3	31	Wi 83	67
Bradbury, Katherine	Simplified Warping for Cardweaving	SS&D	5	1	17	Wi 73	84
Bradbury, Mary Louise	Bradbury Hit-and-Miss System	SS&D	3	2	10	Sp 72	27
Bradford, Eileen	Teaching the Blind to Weave	H&C	6	1		Wi 54	26

AUTHOR	TITLE	JOUR	VOL	NO	ISS	DATE	PAGE
Bradley, Ann	Working As a Handweaver; Some Reflections and Techniques	SS&D	5	2	18	Sp 74	61
Bradley, David H.	Toward Professionalism in Weaving	H&C	8	4		Fa 57	19
Bradley, Lavinia	Happy Weaving of Marriage Sheets	SS&D	4	1	13	Wi 72	48
Bradley, Lavinia	Inkle Weaving	Hw	4	4		S/O 83	24
Bradley, Lavinia	Inkle Weaving	WJ	8	3	31	Wi 83	67
Bradley, Lavinia	Inkle Weaving	PWC			4	Ja 83	69
Bradley, Louise	Biased Toward Bias	Hw	6	3		Su 85	24
Bradley, Louise	But Why Does it Spin?	S-O	5			81	10
Bradley, Louise	Classy Corners	Hw	6	1		J/F 85	86
Bradley, Louise	Cutting, a Moment of Truth	Hw	7	2		M/A 86	27
Bradley, Louise	Fringe Elements	Hw	5	4		S/O 84	22
Bradley, Louise	Getting It Straight	Hw	6	5		N/D 85	23
Bradley, Louise	Handspun Ikat	Hw	2	4		Se 81	65
Bradley, Louise	Ikat Spun Bog Jacket (Louise Bradley)	Hw	2	4		Se 81	67
Bradley, Louise	Ikat Spun Lap Robe (Louise Bradley)	Hw	2	4		Se 81	67
Bradley, Louise	Ikat Spun Shrug (Louise Bradley)	Hw	2	4		Se 81	67
Bradley, Louise	Ikat Spun Vest (Debbie Redding)	Hw	2	4		Se 81	67
Bradley, Louise	Inspiration from Woven Samples of the Past or...a Bunch of Us Last Sunday	Hw	5	5		N/D 84	50
Bradley, Louise	Jacket Inspired by West African Narrow Strip Weaving	WJ	5	3	19	Wi 81	31
Bradley, Louise	Let's Face It!	Hw	8	1		J/F 87	34
Bradley, Louise	One Warp, One Pattern, Five Garments	Hw	3	3		My 82	34
Bradley, Louise	Pressing Need, Or the Ironing of It, A	Hw	7	4		S/O 86	71
Bradley, Louise	Reinforcements	Hw	8	4		S/O 87	22
Bradley, Louise	Tacky–to–Tasteful—Finishing Touches for Household Linens	Hw	8	3		M/J 87	27
Bradley, Louise; Jean Anstine	Portable Weaving: A Band of Ideas for Bands	Hw	7	3		M/J 86	40
Bradley, Sue	Stitches in Time	Kn	3	2	6	Sp 87	51
Bradshaw, Susan	Reversible Cardwoven Hanging	S-O	10	4		Wi 86	16
Bramhall, Butch	see Bramhall, Pat	SS&D	19	1	73	Wi 87	40
Bramhall, Pat; Butch Bramhall	Silver and Gold	SS&D	19	1	73	Wi 87	40
Brandford, Joanne Segal	From the Tree Where the Bark Grows...North American Basket Treasures from the Peabody Museum, Harvard University	Hw	7	4		S/O 86	11
Brandford, Joanne Segal; Sandra Dickey Harner	"Three Living Treasures from California" (Exhibit)	Fa	12	5		S/O 85	70
Branfman, Judy	Nicaraguan Tapestries	TM			8	D/J 86	14
Brannen, Robert	Collingwood in Massachusetts, A	SS&D	9	1	33	Wi 77	8
Branson, Branley Allan	Kilts	Hw	4	5		N/D 83	34
Braun, Susan G.	HGA Scholarship	SS&D	18	1	69	Wi 86	9
Braun, Suzan G.	HGA Scholarship Award	SS&D	16	3	63	Su 85	62
Bravo, Monica	Peruvian Technique for Dimensional Knotting	WJ	12	1	45	Su 87	17
Brayn, Dorothy	Ida Dean Grae — Imaginative Teacher	H&C	6	2		Sp 55	16
Breeze, Helen	Ideas Are Where You Find Them	H&C	3	2		Sp 52	22
Brenholts, Jeanne	Fashionable Palette of Pittsburgh Paints, The	Fa	14	3		M/J 87	46
Brennan, Harold J.	Craft Arts in Education, The	H&C	6	1		Wi 54	12
Brennan, Harold J.	Crafts in Education, Part 2, The	H&C	6	2		Sp 55	15
Brennan, Harold J.	Education of the Creative Craftsman	H&C	11	3		Su 60	13
Brennan, Joan	Yurt in Artpark, The	Fa	9	3		M/J 82	19
Bress, Helene	Inkle Weaving	H&C	26	5		Oc 75	14
Bress, Helene	Inkle Weaving	SS&D	7	2	26	Sp 76	34
Bress, Helene	Macrame Book, The	SS&D	4	2	14	Sp 73	44
Bress, Helene	Theme and Variations	Hw	6	2		M/A 85	62
Bress, Helene	Weaving Book, Patterns and Ideas, The	SS&D	13	1	49	Wi 81	90

AUTHOR	TITLE	JOUR	VOL	NO	ISS	DATE	PAGE
Bress, Helene	Weaving Book, The	Hw	2	5		No 81	93
Bress, Helene	Weaving Book, The	WJ	6	3	23	Wi 81	60
Bress, Helene	Weaving Book, The	Fa	9	2		M/A 82	58
Brett, K. B.	Ontario Handwoven Textiles	H&C	7	2		Sp 56	63
Brett, Katherine B.	English Embroidery in the Royal Ontario Museum	TMJ	3	4		De 73	46
Brewer, Helen	Norwegian Double Weave Pick Up...Directions and Designs	Hw	3	5		N/D 82	12
Brewer, Helen	Norwegian Double Weave Pick-Up. Directions and Designs	WJ	7	1	25	Su 82	64
Brewington, Judith	Inspirations from Sweaters	WJ	7	3	27	Wi 82	14
Bridenbaugh, Carl	Colonial Craftsman, The	H&C	1	3		Fa 50	60
Brien, D. Elise	Carol Shinn: The Conscious and the Unconscious	Fa	14	5		N/D 87	17
Brien, Elise	Multilayered Tapestries of Susan Klebanoff, The	Fa	14	3		M/J 87	21
Bright, Harriett H.	Fifty Years As a Coverlet Weaver	WJ	6	2	22	Fa 81	54
Britton, Nancy	Tour Through Merrimack Valley Textile Museum, A	Fa	9	2		M/A 82	52
Broad, Sue	Triangular Shawl	WJ	7	3	27	Wi 82	11
Broadwell, Sally	Sally Broadwell	Fa	14	4		S/O 87	19
Broby-Johansen, R.	Body and Clothes: An Illustrated History of Costume	H&C	20	2		Sp 69	43
Brockway, Edith	Persian Handcrafted Items	H&C	26	5		Oc 75	16
Broderson, Jan	Dirk Holger and Grau-Garriga: The Legacy of Lurçat	H&C	22	3		Su 71	10
Brody, Eric	Confessions of a Handweaver's Husband	H&C	26	3		M/J 75	22
Brokaw, Edith H., O.T.R.	Evolution of the Multi-Loom, The	H&C	3	4		Fa 52	9
Bromberg, Kay	How to Dye and Starch Silk	WJ	5	1	17	Su 80	43
Bromberg, Kay	How to Scour Silk	WJ	4	4	16	Ap 80	40
Brones, Britta	Inkle Bands as Finishing Details on Garments	WJ	7	3	27	Wi 82	35
Brones, Britta	Rags to Riches: Jackets from Rags	WJ	6	3	23	Wi 81	31
Bronson, J.; R. Bronson	Domestic Manufacturer's Assistant, The	H&C	1	1		Ap 50	49
Bronson, J.; R. Bronson	Early American Weaving and Dyeing	SS&D	9	3	35	Su 78	96
Bronson, J.; R. Bronson	Early American Weaving and Dyeing — The Domestic Manufacturer's Assistant and Family Directory in the Arts of Weaving and Dyeing	WJ	3	1	9	Jy 78	37
Bronson, R.	see Bronson, J.	SS&D	9	3	35	Su 78	96
Bronson, R.	see Bronson, J.	H&C	1	1		Ap 50	49
Bronson, R.	see Bronson, J.	WJ	3	1	9	Jy 78	37
Brooke, Anne	Result of Weaving Rugs, The	WJ	7	4	28	Sp 83	39
Brookfield Craft Center	Traditional New England Basketmaking (John McGuire)	WJ	12	2	46	Fa 87	68
Brooklyn Botanic Garden	Dye Plants and Dyeing — A Handbook	Fa	5	1		J/F 78	40
Brooklyn Botanic Garden; Palmy Weigle, guest ed.	Natural Plant Dyeing	SS&D	5	3	19	Su 74	62
Brooklyn Botanic Gardens	Dye Plants and Dyeing — A Handbook	H&C	16	1		Wi 65	44
Brooklyn Museum	Late Egyptian and Coptic Art	H&C	4	1		Wi 52	62
Brooks, Lois Ziff	On Fabric in the Southwest: Surface Design, A Bank, And Public Recognition	Fa	6	5		S/O 79	54
Brooks, Marguerite G.	Fringes from Warp Ends	H&C	6	1		Wi 54	46
Brophil, Gladys Rogers	Handweaving from Many Countries at the International Trade Fair	H&C	1	3		Fa 50	31
Brophil, Gladys Rogers	More Textiles Shown in "Good Design" 1951	H&C	2	2		Sp 51	38
Brostoff, Laya	Approach to Tapestry Weaving, An	Iw	4	2		Sp 79	27
Brostoff, Laya	Are We Becoming Workshop Junkies?	SS&D	10	2	38	Sp 79	33
Brostoff, Laya	Cartoon, The	Hw	3	1		Ja 82	26
Brostoff, Laya	Fly-Shutle Looms Enhance Weaving Pleasure	SS&D	6	2	22	Sp 75	74
Brostoff, Laya	Nobody Likes to Be Rejected	Hw	4	4		S/O 83	29
Brostoff, Laya	Professional Handweaving on the Fly-Shuttle Loom	Iw	4	1		Wi 78	54
Brostoff, Laya	Professional Handweaving on the Fly-Shuttle Loom	WJ	3	3	11	Ja 79	42
Brostoff, Laya	Professional Weaving on the Fly Shuttle Loom	SS&D	10	3	39	Su 79	36
Brostoff, Laya	Weaving a Tapestry	WJ	7	3	27	Wi 82	50

AUTHOR	TITLE	JOUR	VOL	NO	ISS	DATE	PAGE
Brostoff, Laya	Weaving with a Strong Back	Hw	3	3		My 82	41
Brostoff, Laya	Winding a Bobbin	SS&D	8	1	29	WI 76	39
Brostrom, Ethel; Harry Marinsky	How to Make Draperies and Slipcovers	H&C	2	3		Su 51	63
Brotherton, Germaine	Rush and Leafcraft	Iw	3	2		Wi 78	42
Broudy, Eric	Book of Looms: A History of the Handloom from Ancient Times to the Present, The	SS&D	11	1	41	Wi 79	32
Broudy, Eric	Book of Looms: A History of the Handloom from Ancient Times to the Present, The	Iw	4	4		Fa 79	70
Broudy, Eric	Book of Looms, The	WJ	5	4	20	Sp 81	44
Brough, Hazel	Are Those Colors Really from Plants?	SS&D	8	4	32	Fa 77	67
Brough, Hazel	Bringing Freedom to Fibers: Loni Parker	SS&D	7	3	27	Su 76	44
Brough, Hazel	Grau-Garriga: He Says It's Easy, But...	SS&D	6	4	24	Fa 75	92
Broughton, Cynthia	Cannelé: Create a Sumptuous Fabric That Drapes Beautifully	WJ	10	3	39	Wi 86	59
Broughton, Eve	Double Weave in Four Colors Part 1	CW		23		Ja 87	3
Broughton, Eve	Double Weave in Four Colors Part 2	CW		24		My 87	17
Broughton, Eve T.	Three-Toned Blocks: Further Explorations with Long-Eyed Heddles	WJ	9	4	36	Sp 85	72
Broughton, Eve T.	Three-Toned Blocks, Part 1: Simple Pattern	CW	6	1	16	Se 84	12
Broughton, Eve T.	Three-Toned Blocks, Part 2: Reverses	CW	6	2	17	Ja 85	10
Broughton, Eve T.	Three-Toned Blocks, Part 3: Alternating Designs	CW	6	3	18	My 85	10
Broughton, Eve T.	Twill and Plain Weave Blocks with Long-Eyed Heddles	WJ	8	4	32	Sp 84	58
Brouwer, Martha	Summer-and-Winter Pick-up Weave	SS&D	8	3	31	Su 77	58
Brown, Arleen Emery	"Century Of Change in Guatemalan Textiles, A" (Exhibit)	Fa	9	3		M/J 82	79
Brown, Arleen Emery	Ferne Jacobs: A Study in 3-Dimensional Order	SS&D	11	4	44	Fa 80	80
Brown, Arleen Emery	"Fiber 82: Miniatures" (Exhibit)	Fa	9	4		J/A 82	72
Brown, Arleen Emery	"Forms in Fiber" (Exhibit)	Fa	7	5		S/O 80	73
Brown, Arleen Emery	On Working At Home	Fa	7	2		M/A 80	45
Brown, Barbara	Southern California Guild Honors Atwater	SS&D	9	3	35	Su 78	38
Brown, Bonnie	Williamsburg Weaving	H&C	12	2		Sp 61	30
Brown, Carolyn	Photographer at Convergence, The	SS&D	17	2	66	Sp 86	61
Brown, Geoffrey I.	Techniques in Textile Conservation	S-O	10	2		Su 86	45
Brown, Harriette J.	Contemporary Project for Two-harness Looms, A	H&C	7	3		Su 56	20
Brown, Harriette J.	Don't Overlook Two Harness Looms	H&C	5	3		Su 54	10
Brown, Harriette J.	Hand Weaving for Pleasure and Profit	H&C	3	3		Su 52	61
Brown, Melissa J.	Plumage in the Dyepot	SS&D	9	1	33	Wi 77	103
Brown, Myrtle A.	What Kinds of Yarns for Handweaving?	H&C	1	2		Su 50	22
Brown, Pat	Pat Brown	Fa	5	4		J/A 78	53
Brown, Pauline, ed.	Embroidery: A Complete Course in Embroidery Design and Technique	TM			13	O/N 87	76
Brown, Rachael	Fundamentals of Handspinning	S-O	11	2		Su 87	12
Brown, Rachel	Tierra Wools Cooperative	SS&D	18	2	70	Sp 87	62
Brown, Rachel	Weaving, Spinning and Dyeing Book, The	SS&D	11	3	43	Su 80	75
Brown, Rachel	Weaving, Spinning, and Dyeing Book, The	Iw	3	4		Su 78	44
Brown, Rachel	Weaving, Spinning and Dyeing Book, The	WJ	3	2	10	Oc 78	45
Brown, Sally	Confetti Basketry	SS&D	18	3	71	Su 87	9
Brown, William J.	Penland School of Crafts, The	H&C	16	3		Su 65	21
Brownell, Effielee E.	Southern California Hand Weavers Guild, The	H&C	6	2		Sp 55	30
Brownlee-Ramsdale, Sandra	Weaver of Images	AT	6			De 86	147
Bruandet, Pierre	Painting on Silk	WJ	7	3	27	Wi 82	50
Brubaker, Paul	Haptic Visions	WJ	11	4	44	Sp 87	59
Brubaker, Paul	Weaving Texts Recorded For the Blind	Fa	3	5		S/O 76	35
Brugger, Susan	Two String Sweaters	PWC			6	Su 83	31
Bruzelius, Margaret	Exploring a Knitted Pattern	TM			6	A/S 86	35
Bruzelius, Margaret	Ruched Blouse	Kn	2	2	4	S-S 86	40

AUTHOR	TITLE	JOUR	VOL	NO	ISS	DATE	PAGE
Bryan, Dorothy	Ahrens Looms, The	H&C	6	3		Su 55	28
Bryan, Dorothy	Allied Arts Guild	H&C	8	1		Wi 56	20
Bryan, Dorothy	California Designed	H&C	7	1		Wi 55	30
Bryan, Dorothy	California State-wide Conference	H&C	6	4		Fa 55	30
Bryan, Dorothy	Chenille Rugs from California	H&C	2	3		Su 51	22
Bryan, Dorothy	Contemporary Religious Art in California	H&C	4	1		Wi 52	7
Bryan, Dorothy	Continuation School Program, A	H&C	6	4		Fa 55	23
Bryan, Dorothy	Correct Sewing Methods in Tailoring	H&C	10	3		Su 59	25
Bryan, Dorothy	Double-Warp Weaving from Harriet Tidball's Looms	H&C	5	4		Fa 54	15
Bryan, Dorothy	Dr. Elisabeth Moses of the M. H. de Young Museum	H&C	7	2		Sp 56	16
Bryan, Dorothy	Experiment in Group Study	H&C	10	3		Su 59	6
Bryan, Dorothy	Frances van Hall	H&C	11	2		Sp 60	43
Bryan, Dorothy	From California, Double Woven Fabrics for Varied Uses	H&C	12	3		Su 61	6
Bryan, Dorothy	Handweaver Plans an Interior, A	H&C	6	1		Wi 54	8
Bryan, Dorothy	Handweaving in Effective Settings	H&C	12	1		Wi 61	10
Bryan, Dorothy	Handweaving in Period and Contemporary Interiors	H&C	4	4		Fa 53	16
Bryan, Dorothy	High Fashion in Handweaving	H&C	2	1		Wi 50	20
Bryan, Dorothy	Kay Geary	H&C	3	2		Sp 52	26
Bryan, Dorothy	Knotted and Tufted Rugs	H&C	9	1		Wi 57	4
Bryan, Dorothy	Living Color, Northern California Conference Theme	H&C	10	4		Fa 59	22
Bryan, Dorothy	"Mama" Gravander	H&C	5	4		Fa 54	4
Bryan, Dorothy	Maria Kipp — Her Career as a Weaver	H&C	3	1		Wi 51	15
Bryan, Dorothy	Marianne Strengell's Approach to Design	H&C	11	4		Fa 60	29
Bryan, Dorothy	Martha Pollock	H&C	7	4		Fa 56	7
Bryan, Dorothy	Michael Belangie Sees Common Problems for Hand and Power Weavers	H&C	2	4		Fa 51	46
Bryan, Dorothy	Modern Danish Textiles	H&C	9	2		Sp 58	40
Bryan, Dorothy	Northern California Conference	H&C	8	4		Fa 57	28
Bryan, Dorothy	Northern California Conference	H&C	11	4		Fa 60	26
Bryan, Dorothy	Northern California Handweavers Conference	H&C	7	3		Su 56	62
Bryan, Dorothy	Northern California Handweaving Conference	H&C	9	4		Fa 58	24
Bryan, Dorothy	Open Tapestries by Lynn Alexander	H&C	4	3		Su 53	30
Bryan, Dorothy	Planning Fabrics to Meet Tailors' Requirements	H&C	10	1		Wi 59	18
Bryan, Dorothy	Richmond Art Center, A Unique Adventure, The	H&C	3	3		Su 52	34
Bryan, Dorothy	Sara Matsson Anliot	H&C	11	3		Su 60	10
Bryan, Dorothy	Some Contemporary Weavers in Northern California	H&C	1	3		Fa 50	9
Bryan, Dorothy	Successful Volunteer Project, A	H&C	5	2		Sp 54	19
Bryan, Dorothy	Tailoring a Suit Jacket	H&C	11	1		Wi 60	28
Bryan, Dorothy	Tailoring a Suit Skirt	H&C	10	4		Fa 59	28
Bryan, Dorothy	Tailoring Handwoven Fabrics	H&C	10	2		Sp 59	17
Bryan, Dorothy	Training in Handweaving Offered on the Pacific Coast	H&C	2	2		Sp 51	16
Bryan, Dorothy	Trude Guermonprez	H&C	11	2		Sp 60	30
Bryan, Dorothy	Two-Harness Designs	H&C	9	3		Su 58	28
Bryan, Dorothy	West Coast Weaving in Modern Interiors	H&C	3	4		Fa 52	7
Bryan, Dorothy	Western Handweaving 1957	H&C	8	4		Fa 57	6
Bryan, Dorothy	Woven Bell Pulls	H&C	11	1		Wi 60	46
Bryan, Dorothy	Woven Telephone Book Covers	H&C	8	3		Su 57	26
Bryan, Linda Nelson	Teaching Fiber to the Elderly: A Personal Experience	Fa	4	6		N/D 77	60
Bryant, Laura Militzer	Laura Militzer Bryant: Thought Process	Fa	10	4		J/A 83	52
Buchanan, Rita	Brown Wool Jumper	S-O	9	1		Sp 85	14
Buchanan, Rita	Grow Your Own Colors: Plant a Dye Garden (error-corrected S-O v11 n2 '87 p7)	S-O	11	1		Sp 87	35
Buchanan, Rita	Herbal Moth Repellents: Safeguard or Sentiment?	S-O	10	2		Su 86	25
Buchanan, Rita	Kudzu: The Noxious Weed Transformed	Fa	14	2		M/A 87	48

AUTHOR	TITLE	JOUR	VOL	NO	ISS	DATE	PAGE
Buchanan, Rita	Making Gloves That Fit	S-O	8	4		Wi 84	17
Buchanan, Rita	Survey of Leaf and Stem Fibers, A	S-O	10	3		Fa 86	24
Buchanan, Rita	Using the Fibers of Native Plants	S-O	9	4		Wi 85	29
Buchanan, Rita	Weaver's Garden, A	SS&D	19	1	73	Wi 87	51
Buchanan, Rita	Weaving the Family Tartan	S-O	10	2		Su 86	36
Buchanan, Rita; Steve Buchanan	Gray Topcoat	S-O	9	4		Wi 85	13
Buchanan, Steve	see Buchanan, Rita	S-O	9	4		Wi 85	13
Buchanan, Steve	Very Fine Scarf, A	S-O	10	2		Su 86	20
Budgey, Elfriede	Nova Scotia Designer Craftsmen: Profile '81	SS&D	13	1	49	Wi 81	30
Buferd, Norma Bradley	see Cooper, Patricia	lw	2	4		Su 77	35
Buferd, Norma Bradley	see Cooper, Patricia	Fa	7	6		N/D 80	58
Buhler, Alfred	see Larsen, Jack Lenor	Fa	5	1		J/F 78	40
Bujnowski, Donald	Barn Raising Experience, A	SS&D	8	4	32	Fa 77	100
Bulbach, Stanley	Baa, Baa, Black Sheep, Have You Any Wool?	S-O	9	2		Su 85	44
Bulbach, Stanley	Morning Glory	S-O	9	1		Sp 85	15
Bulbach, Stanley	SOAR 1985: Some Observations and Asides	S-O	10	2		Su 86	16
Bulbach, Stanley	Spinners Explore Markets, Ideas	TM			3	F/M 86	10
Bulbach, Stanley	Why Bother with Natural Dyeing?	TM			5	J/J 86	32
Bulback, Stanley	If You Want to Work with the Best Wool Yarns, Spin Them Yourself	TM			13	O/N 87	56
Bulback, Stanley	Tropos — Part 3	S-O	7	1		Sp 83	10
Bulback, Stanley	Weaving in the Urban Tradition	SS&D	12	3	47	Su 81	7
Bulback, Stanley	What Kind of Wool Is It?	TM			13	O/N 87	20
Bunch, Roger	see Bunch, Roland	SS&D	9	3	35	Su 78	96
Bunch, Roland; Roger Bunch	Highland Maya: Patterns of Life and Clothing in Indian Guatemala, The	SS&D	9	3	35	Su 78	96
Burbridge, Pauline	Making Patchwork for Pleasure and Profit	TM			3	F/M 86	78
Burditt, Larry	Sunrise Handspun Basket	S-O	11	1		Sp 87	18
Burgess, Leslie	Little Shaping Story, A	Hw	4	3		M/J 83	26
Burhen, Jan	see Wilson, Jean	SS&D	5	2	18	Sp 74	68
Burke, Dan E.	Chase Home: Utah Arts Council	SS&D	16	4	64	Fa 85	40
Burkett, M. E.	Art of the Felt Maker, The	WJ	6	3	23	Wi 81	59
Burkhauser, Jude	Ballinskelligs Tapestry Works: Ancient Art/Modern Spirit, The	Hw	3	1		Ja 82	55
Burkhauser, Jude	Handspun Yarn as Art	S-O	3			79	22
Burkhauser, Jude	Shepherds of Glenmore, The	S-O	6	4		82	36
Burkhauser, Jude	Tweed Weavers of Glenmore, The	Hw	3	3		My 82	56
Burks, Arthur J.	see Underhill, Vera Bisbee	H&C	3	1		Wi 51	61
Burlew, Margaret	Christmas Swags Offer Interesting Weaving for Summer	H&C	13	3		Su 62	12
Burlew, Margaret	Spot Weaving, Four Harnesses Offer Many Possibilities for Design	H&C	16	2		Sp 65	7
Burlew, Margaret	Transparent Textiles	SS&D	17	1	65	Wi 85	10
Burlew, Margaret	Weavers Bag — From Montana to Convergence '74, The	SS&D	5	1	17	Wi 73	39
Burnham, Dorothy K.	Comfortable Arts, The	WJ	7	1	25	Su 82	63
Burnham, Dorothy K.	Cut My Cote	SS&D	5	1	17	Wi 73	77
Burnham, Dorothy K.	Cut My Cote	Fa	6	3		M/J 79	16
Burnham, Dorothy K.	see Burnham, Harold B.	SS&D	4	2	14	Sp 73	44
Burnham, Dorothy K.	see Burnham, Harold B.	H&C	24	1		J/F 73	28
Burnham, Dorothy K.	see Burnham, Harold B.	TMJ	3	4		De 73	46
Burnham, Dorothy K.	Shapes of Garments, The (Reprint)	TM			9	F/M 87	50
Burnham, Dorothy K.	Unlike the Lilies: Doukhobor Textile Traditions in Canada	Hw	8	3		M/J 87	14
Burnham, Dorothy K.	Unlike the Lilies: Doukhobor Textile Traditions in Canada	WJ	11	2	42	Fa 86	75
Burnham, Dorothy K.	Unlike the Lilies: Doukhobor Textile Traditions in Canada	TM			11	J/J 87	72
Burnham, Dorothy K.	Unlike the Lilies, Doukhobor Textile Traditions in Canada	PWC	4	3	13		52
Burnham, Dorothy K.	Warp and Weft: A Textile Terminology	SS&D	12	2	46	Sp 81	70

AUTHOR	TITLE	JOUR	VOL	NO	ISS	DATE	PAGE
Burnham, Dorothy K.	Warp and Weft: A Textile Terminology	Iw	5	4		Fa 80	76
Burnham, Dorothy K.	Warp and Weft, A Textile Terminology	WJ	5	2	18	Fa 80	31
Burnham, Dorothy K.	Warp and Weft, A Textile Terminology	Fa	7	6		N/D 80	34
Burnham, Harold B.; Dorothy K. Burnham	Keep Me Warm One Night	SS&D	4	2	14	Sp 73	44
Burnham, Harold B.; Dorothy K. Burnham	Keep Me Warm One Night: Early Handweaving in Eastern Canada	H&C	24	1		J/F 73	28
Burnham, Harold B.; Dorothy K. Burnham	'Keep Me Warm One Night,' Early Handweaving in Eastern Canada	TMJ	3	4		De 73	46
Burnlees, Dee	Handspun Yarns for Weavers	WJ	8	2	30	Fa 83	21
Burnlees, Dee	Weft Ikat: An Introduction	WJ	10	1	37	Su 85	62
Burow, Nellie B.	Elliot Weavers of Dublin	SS&D	1	1	1	De 69	16
Burress, John	Punkin Summer	H&C	9	4		Fa 58	60
Burton, Dorothy S.	Versatile Bronson	Hw	5	4		S/O 84	14
Burton, Joan	see Mathews, Richard	Fa	3	4		J/A 76	8
Busby, Robert J.	Ellen Krucker	H&C	20	1		Wi 69	44
Busby, Robert J.	Ellen Krucker, Designer of Miniatures	H&C	20	1		Wi 69	44
Busch, Akiko	For the Floor: The World at Our Feet	SS&D	16	3	63	Su 85	54
Buscho, Ann	Method to Her Madness: Jane Lang Axtell's Seminole Patchwork, A	Fa	8	1		J/F 81	31
Bush, Carolyn	Butterfly Kimono Jacket	S-O	10	1		Sp 86	22
Bush, Nancy	Bogus Bohus	Kn	2	1	3	F-W 85	49
Bush, Nancy	Burra Lace Pullover	Kn	3	4	8	Fa 87	26
Bush, Nancy	Galashiels Tweed Pullover	Kn	4	1	9	Wi 87	42
Bush, Nancy	Highlands Shawl	Kn	4	1	9	Wi 87	40
Bush, Nancy	Knitter's Journey, A	Kn	3	4	8	Fa 87	24
Bush, Nancy	Shetlands, The	Kn	1	2	2	S-S 85	62
Bush, Nancy	St. Ives Cardigan	Kn	3	2	6	Sp 87	28
Bushnell, G. H. S.	Ancient People and Places — Peru	H&C	9	1		Wi 57	60
Busse, Jane	Shaft Switch Techniques (error-corrected WJ v5 n1 80 p5)	WJ	4	4	16	Ap 80	11
Bustead, Evelyn	see Gallagher, Constance	H&C	11	4		Fa 60	49
Butcher-Younghans, Sherry	Immigrant Memories	WJ	9	4	36	Sp 85	44
Butler, Anne	Arco Encyclopedia of Embroidery Stitches, The	Iw	5	4		Fa 80	77
Butler, Francis	Francis Butler: "I Used to Be an Artist But I Couldn't Sit Still That Long"	Fa	5	5		S/O 78	40
Butterfield, Ann	How to Weave When You Don't Have Time to Weave	Hw	3	2		Mr 82	38
Butterfield, Mary Ann	see Stack, Lotus	WJ	9	3	35	Wi 85	39
Butterfield, Mary Ann; Lotus Stack	Ounce of Prevention: Avoiding the Immediate Need for Textile Conservation, An	WJ	9	2	34	Fa 84	39
Butterfield, Mary Ann; Lotus Stack	Ounce of Prevention: Preservation and Storage, An	WJ	10	1	37	Su 85	7
Butterfield, Mary Ann; Lotus Stack	Ounce of Prevention: Preventing Deterioration, An	WJ	9	4	36	Sp 85	9
Buxton-Keenlyside, Judith	Selected Canadian Spinning Wheels in Perspective: An Analytical Approach	SS&D	12	2	46	Sp 81	71
Buxton-Keenlyside, Judith	Selected Canadian Spinning Wheels in Perspective: An Analytical Approach	S-O	4			80	15
Byerly, Lillian	Let's Go for a Spin	S-O	9	2		Su 85	6
Byerly, Lillian	Let's Go for a Spin	S-O	9	3		Fa 85	3
Byers, Helen	Tapestries of Inge Norgaard, The	Fa	11	4		J/A 84	22
Byers, Pat	Contemporary Tapestry	TM			6	A/S 86	24
Byers, Pat	On Designing Fabric for Suits	TM			6	A/S 86	24
Byers, Patricia	Ewe Can't Win This Wrestling Match	TM			10	A/M 87	18
Byers, Patricia	Plucking Angora Rabbits	TM			5	J/J 86	18
Byran, Dorothy	Mills College Weavers	H&C	8	3		Su 57	22
Bywater, William	"Fiber Invitational" (Exhibit)	Fa	7	2		M/A 80	66
Cabeen, Lou	Stars, Diamonds, Tables, and Sunrise: Motifs and Structures of Woven Coverlets	TM			14	D/J 87	32

AUTHOR	TITLE	JOUR	VOL	NO	ISS	DATE	PAGE
Cabrera, Roberto; Patricia Flaherty	Classic Tailoring Techniques: A Construction Guide for Men's Wear	TM			7	O/N 86	72
Cabrera, Roberto; Patricia Flaherty Meyers	Classic Tailoring Techniques: A Construction Guide for Women' Wear	TM			7	O/N 86	72
Cagnoni, Mary	Spindle Spinning with Sheep Wool	SS&D	2	4	8	Fa 71	23
Cahlander, Adele	Andean Crossed-Warp Techniques For Decorative Trims, Part 1 — Flat Bands	WJ	2	4	8	Ap 78	10
Cahlander, Adele	Andean Crossed-Warp Techniques For Decorative Trims, Part 2 — Tubular Bands (error-corrected WJ v3 n1 insert for vol. 2)	WJ	3	1	9	Jy 78	38
Cahlander, Adele	Bolivian Tubular Edging and Crossed-Warp Techniques	lw	3	4		Su 78	46
Cahlander, Adele	Detective Story: Unravelling the Mystery of a 7-Loop Braid, A	WJ	10	1	37	Su 85	12
Cahlander, Adele	Double-woven Treasures from Old Peru	PWC			4	Ja 83	36
Cahlander, Adele`	Doubleweave: Some Ideas for Conserving Yarn	PWC			2	Ap 82	46
Cahlander, Adele	see Cason, Marjorie	SS&D	6	2	22	Sp 75	4
Cahlander, Adele	see Cason, Marjorie	SS&D	6	3	23	Su 75	65
Cahlander, Adele	see Cason, Marjorie	SS&D	8	3	31	Su 77	61
Cahlander, Adele	see Cason, Marjorie	lw	2	2		Wi 77	32
Cahlander, Adele	see Cason, Marjorie	WJ	1	4	4	Ap 77	25
Cahlander, Adele	see Cason, Marjorie	Fa	4	4		J/A 77	62
Cahlander, Adele	Understanding Some Complex Structures from Simple Andean Looms: Steps in Analysis and Reproduction	AT	1			De 83	181
Cahlander, Adele	Unique Technique for a Braided Strap from Colombia	WJ	7	1	25	Su 82	56
Cahlander, Adele	Warp-Faced Double Cloth: Adaptation of an Andean Technique for the Treadle Loom	WJ	10	4	40	Sp 86	72
Cahlander, Adele; Ed Franquemont; Barbara Bergman	Special Andean Tubular Trim—Woven Without Heddles, A	WJ	6	3	23	Wi 81	54
Cahlander, Adele; Elayne Zorn; Ann Pollard Rowe	Sling Braiding of the Andes; Weaver's Journal Monograph IV	WJ	5	4	20	Sp 81	45
Cahlander, Adele; Marjorie Cason	Tubular Edge-Binding from Bolivia, A	WJ	1	4	4	Ap 77	13
Cahlander, Adele; Suzanne Baizerman	Double-Woven Treasures from Old Peru	Hw	8	4		S/O 87	12
Cahlander, Adele; Suzanne Baizerman	Double-Woven Treasures from Old Peru	PWC	4	2	12		51
Cahlander, Adele W.	"Not a Child's Toy"	SS&D	3	3	11	Su 72	32
Cain, Lois	Weavers of Spokane	H&C	6	4		Fa 55	26
Cairns, Michael	Weaving Business, The	SS&D	8	3	31	Su 77	6
Caldwell, Rebecca	Advisers Guide to Costume Resources, An (error-corrected Fa v12 n1 85 p24)	Fa	11	5		S/O 84	48
Caldwell, Rebecca	Costumes on a Small Scale	Fa	11	5		S/O 84	87
Caldwell, Rebecca	Setting The Right Price: A Workshop with Libby Platus (error-corrected Fa v13 n1 86 p5)	Fa	12	5		S/O 85	51
Calhoun, Wheeler; Lee Kirschner	Continuous Thread: From Flax Seed to Linen Cloth, The	S-O	7	1		Sp 83	28
Calhoun, Wheeler; Lee Kirschner	Continuous Thread, Part 2: From Flax Seed to Linen Cloth, The	S-O	7	2		Su 83	44
Calhoun, Wheeler; Lee Kirschner	Continuous Thread, Part 3: From Flax Seed to Linen Cloth, The	S-O	7	4		Wi 83	35
Caliendo, Karen	Weddding Dress, My	Hw	5	5		N/D 84	76
Callaway, Grace	Handsewing Stitches	TM			12	A/S 87	53
Callaway, Grace	Making Swirly Skirts	TM			10	A/M 87	35
Callaway, Grace	Sewing Swimsuits	TM			5	J/J 86	24
Callister, J. Herbert	see Warren, William L.	TMJ	3	4		De 73	47
Cameron, Carolyn W.	National Mini Tapestry Exhibit	SS&D	9	3	35	Su 78	48
Cammann, Schuyler	Chinese Influence in Colonial Peruvian Tapestries	TMJ	1	3		De 64	21
Cammann, Schuyler	Chinese Textile in Seventeenth Century Spain, A	TMJ	1	4		De 65	57
Cammann, Schuyler	In Memorium, Carl Schuster, Ph. D. (1904–1969)	TMJ	3	3		De 72	2

AUTHOR	TITLE	JOUR	VOL	NO	ISS	DATE	PAGE
Cammann, Schuyler	Ming Mandarin Squares	TMJ	4	4		77	5
Cammann, Schuyler V.R.	Symbolic Meanings in Oriental Rug Patterns: Part 1	TMJ	3	3		De 72	5
Cammann, Schuyler V.R.	Symbolic Meanings in Oriental Rug Patterns: Part 2	TMJ	3	3		De 72	22
Cammann, Schuyler V.R.	Symbolic Meanings in Oriental Rug Patterns: Part 3	TMJ	3	3		De 72	42
Campbell, John; Susan Campbell	Cotton of a Different Color	WJ	4	2	14	Oc 79	20
Campbell, Susan	see Campbell, John	WJ	4	2	14	Oc 79	20
Camper, Dorothy	Josh's Gansey	Kn	1	1	1	F-W 84 CI	28 20
Camper, Dorothy	Traveling Stitches	Kn	1	1	1	F-W 84 CI	62 52
Camper, Dorothy	Traveling Stitches	Kn	1	2	2	S-S 85	50
Camper, Dorothy	Traveling Stitches	Kn	2	1	3	F-W 85	74
Camper, Dorothy	Traveling Stitches	Kn	2	2	4	S-S 86	76
Camper, Dorothy	Traveling Stitches	Kn	3	1	5	F-W 86	66
Camper, Dorothy	Traveling Stitches	Kn	3	3	7	Su 87	24
Cannarella, Deborah	Crochet Pattern for Pinwheel Spread	TM			7	O/N 86	18
Cannarella, Deborah	Fabric About Fabric	TM			1	O/N 85	72
Cannarella, Deborah	Ten Years and Ten Pounds of Crochet	TM			1	O/N 85	80
Cannarella, Deborah	What Ails the Apparel Industry?	TM			1	O/N 85	16
Canongate Publishing Ltd., publ.	Master Weavers/Tapestry from the Dovecot Studios 1912–1980	WJ	7	2	26	Fa 82	57
Cantieni, Graham	"Anke Van Ginhoven: Tapestries 1977" (Exhibit)	Fa	5	1		J/F 78	21
Canty, Judy	Francoise Barnes: Contemporary Quilts	Fa	11	3		M/J 84	24
Caplin, Lee Evan, ed.	Business of Art, The	Hw	5	3		Su 84	16
Caplin, Lee Evan, ed.	Business of Art, The	WJ	8	3	31	Wi 83	66
Caraway, Caren	Mola Design Coloring Book, The	WJ	8	3	31	Wi 83	67
Caraway, Caren	Peruvian Textile Designs	WJ	8	3	31	Wi 83	67
Carbee, Gail	Textiles 101/102, You're Looking Good	Fa	3	3		M/J 76	42
Cardinale, Robert L.	"Tina Johnson-Depuy Soft Jewelry" (Exhibit)	Fa	6	3		M/J 79	81
✝ Carey, Joyce Marquess	Blocks and Profiles	WJ	7	2	26	Fa 82	33
✝ Carey, Joyce Marquess	Change of Heart and Other Progressive Ideas, A	PWC	3	3	9		18
✝ Carey, Joyce Marquess	Computer Imagery: True Confessions from a "Graph Paper Addict"	Fa	9	2		M/A 82	17
✝ Carey, Joyce Marquess	Handwoven American Coverlets of the Overshot Type	PWC	3	3	9		24
✝ Carey, Joyce Marquess	Metamorphosis: Two-Tie Weaves and the Changeable Image	AT	1			De 83	243
✝ Carey, Joyce Marquess	Plain Weave — Plane Weave	PWC	3	4	10		56
✝ Carey, Joyce Marquess	Salut, Monsieur Jacquard	Hw	2	3		My 81	57
✝ Carey, Joyce Marquess	Undulating Twills	Iw	6	1		Wi 80	31
✝ Carey, Joyce Marquess	Very Basics of Weaving Drafting: Two and Three Shafts, The	WJ	6	2	22	Fa 81	50
✝ Carey, Joyce Marquess	Weave Analysis	WJ	7	1	25	Su 82	45
Carlano, Marianne; Larry Salmon, eds.	French Textiles from the Middle Ages through the Second Empire	Hw	8	5		N/D 87	13
Carlin, Lee	Handweaving for a Living —How Feasible?	SS&D	6	4	24	Fa 75	33
Carlin, Lee J.	Production Handspinning	S-O	1			77	50
Carlisle, Nancy	Tribute to Berta Frey	SS&D	4	3	15	Su 73	37
Carlson, Estelle	Adapting Inkle Patterns to Wider Widths	SS&D	8	1	29	WI 76	87
Carlson, Estelle	Basic Ikat	Iw	5	3		Su 80	27
Carlson, Estelle	Ikat	Fa	5	1		J/F 78	41
Carlson, Estelle	Technique Sources Sparse—So Weaver Innovates	SS&D	7	1	25	Wi 75	89
Carlstedt, Catherina; Ylva Kongback	Rep: A Guide to Swedish Warp-faced Rep	PWC	5	2	16		53
Carlton, Bronwyn	Crocheter Gets Wired, A	Fa	7	1		J/F 80	31
Carlton, Bronwyn	Pam Patrie: Tapestry, Imagery, Artistry	Fa	6	6		N/D 79	60
Carpenter, Marie; Anne Wallace	From Swatches to Sweater: A Simple Method of Sweater Design (2 vols.)	TM			12	A/S 87	76

AUTHOR	TITLE	JOUR	VOL	NO	ISS	DATE	PAGE
Carpenter, Marie; Anne Wallace	From Swatches to Sweaters	Kn	3	4	8	Fa 87	63
Carr, Diane	Tapestries of Elizabeth Berezowska, The	Fa	13	5		S/O 86	10
Carr, Margaret; Helen Jarvis; Gordon Jarvis	Jacquard Pattern Reconstructions with Computer Spreadsheets	SS&D	17	3	67	Su 86	78
Carr, Richard	see Sutton, Ann	Hw	8	3		M/J 87	17
Carr, Richard	see Sutton, Ann	SS&D	16	3	63	Su 85	9
Carr, Sandy, ed.	The Elle Knitting Book: 50 Exclusive Designs from France	TM			2	D/J 85	76
Carroll, Amy, ed.	Sweater Book, The	Kn	2	2	4	S-S 86	78
Carson, Candace	Fabric Design, An Approach by a Young Weaver	H&C	20	1		Wi 69	16
Carter, Bill	It Isn't So Easy As It Sounds	H&C	4	1		Wi 52	56
Carter, Bill	Knowledge of Shuttles Is Important	H&C	2	3		Su 51	31
Carter, Bill	What Loom Shall I Buy?	H&C	3	4		Fa 52	14
Carter, Bill	What Loom Shall I Buy?	H&C	5	1		Wi 53	40
Carter, Bill	Your Selvage Is Showing!	H&C	3	1		Wi 51	21
Carter, Dianne	Chule's Wool Creations	SS&D	17	4	68	Fa 86	30
Carter, Fern	Braided Rug Book	H&C	4	3		Su 53	63
Carter, Helen H.	Some Experiments with Turned Drafts	CW	5	2	14	Ja 84	3
Carter, Michael	Crafts of China	SS&D	9	4	36	Fa 78	82
Cartwright-Jones, Catherine	Handspinning for a Knitting Machine	S-O	9	2		Su 85	20
Cartwright-Jones, Rhys	Professional Spinner	S-O	11	2		Su 87	16
Cary, Mara	Useful Baskets	Iw	3	2		Wi 78	42
Cason, Marjorie	see Cahlander, Adele	WJ	1	4	4	Ap 77	13
Cason, Marjorie; Adele Cahlander	Art of Bolivian Highland Weaving, The	Iw	2	2		Wi 77	32
Cason, Marjorie; Adele Cahlander	Art of Bolivian Highland Weaving, The	WJ	1	4	4	Ap 77	25
Cason, Marjorie; Adele Cahlander	Art of Bolivian Highland Weaving, The	Fa	4	4		J/A 77	62
Cason, Marjorie; Adele Cahlander	Art of Bolivian Highland Weaving: Unique, Traditional Techniques for the Modern Weaver, The	SS&D	8	3	31	Su 77	61
Cason, Marjorie; Adele Cahlander	Bolivian Highland Weaving, Part 1	SS&D	6	2	22	Sp 75	4
Cason, Marjorie; Adele Cahlander	Bolivian Highland Weaving, Part 2	SS&D	6	3	23	Su 75	65
Casselman, Karen L.	Winter Dyeing with Umbilicate Lichens (error-corrected SS&D v9 n4 78 p34)	SS&D	9	2	34	Sp 78	8
Casselman, Karen Leigh	Color Magic from Lichen Dyebaths	SS&D	17	2	66	Sp 86	74
Casselman, Karen Leigh	Craft of the Dyer: Colour from Plants and Lichens of the Northeast	SS&D	12	2	46	Sp 81	70
Casselman, Karen Leigh	Craft of the Dyer: Colour from Plants and Lichens of the Northeast	Hw	2	4		Se 81	80
Casselman, Karen Leigh	Craft of the Dyer: Colour from Plants and Lichens of the Northeast	WJ	5	3	19	Wi 81	51
Castaldi, Nora	Traditional Weavers in Italy	H&C	2	4		Fa 51	20
Castino, Ruth	Spinning and Dyeing the Natural Way	SS&D	6	3	23	Su 75	50
Castino, Ruth	Spinning and Dyeing the Natural Way	Iw	1	2		Wi 76	28
Castino, Ruth	Spinning and Dyeing the Natural Way	Iw	2	3		Sp 77	32
Castino, Ruth	We Dyed in the Woods	SS&D	4	3	15	Su 73	22
Castle, Nancy	Peruvian Crossed-Warp Weave, A	TMJ	4	4		77	61
Cate, Katharine F.	Methods of Finishing Handwoven Fabrics: Finishing Woolens	H&C	8	4		Fa 57	26
Catling, Dorothy; John Grayson	Identification of Vegetable Fibres	WJ	8	3	31	Wi 83	67
Cave, OEnone	Story of Reticella, The	H&C	11	3		Su 60	14
Centner, Dave	Selvedge Gremlins (and what to do about them)	Hw	6	1		J/F 85	59
Centner, Dave, O.C.D.	Reining in Baby Huey	S-O	11	4		Wi 87	18
Centner, David	Weaving Out of One's Own Tradition	Iw	5	4		Fa 80	32
Centner, David J., O.C.D.	Craft As Contemplative Encounter	Iw	4	3		Su 79	60

AUTHOR	TITLE	JOUR	VOL	NO	ISS	DATE	PAGE
Centner, David J., OCD	There's More to an Old Friar's Blanket than Monk's Belt	Hw	5	5		N/D 84	41
Centner, Rev. David J., OCD	Weaving as Art	Iw	3	1		Fa 77	11
Centner, The Rev. David J., O.C.D.	Reflections on the Chasuble	Hw	5	1		J/F 84	36
Cesari, Andrea	Modern Loom from Medieval Sources, A	WJ	10	2	38	Fa 85	18
Chacey, Ron	Spinning with Susie	S-O	7	4		Wi 83	18
Chadwick, A.	Silk	WJ	3	2	10	Oc 78	6
Chadwick, Eileen	Craft of Hand Spinning, The	Iw	5	3		Su 80	70
Chadwick, Eileen	Craft of Handspinning, The	SS&D	12	1	45	Wi 80	82
Chadwick, Louisa	Cross Country Ski Set	S-O	11	4		Wi 87	34
Chalmers, Marjorie	Tina McMorran	SS&D	3	3	11	Su 72	23
Chamberlain, Marcia; Candace Crockett	Beyond Weaving	SS&D	6	3	23	Su 75	49
Chamish, Barry	"Hedi Taryan: The Infinity of Small Things" (Exhibit)	Fa	10	5		S/O 83	79
Champion, Ellen	Certificate of Excellence in Handspinning	S-O	11	3		Fa 87	28
Champion, Ellen	Children's Corner: A Picture Frame Tapestry	WJ	4	1	13	Jy 79	19
Champion, Ellen	First Prize For the Holders of Hot Pots Show	WJ	2	4	8	Ap 78	41
Champion, Ellen	Handspun/Handwoven Ramie Blouse	WJ	9	2	34	Fa 84	52
Champion, Ellen	Insulated Roman Shade — Doup Leno	WJ	6	1	21	Su 81	24
Champion, Ellen	Keep Warm! Log Carriers	WJ	5	2	18	Fa 80	6
Champion, Ellen	Ojo de Dios	WJ	4	2	14	Oc 79	40
Champion, Ellen	Reversible Matelasse Jacket	WJ	7	1	25	Su 82	41
Champion, Ellen	Super Rug: A Chenille "Twice-Woven" Rug	WJ	6	4	24	Sp 82	26
Champion, Ellen	Wooly Afghan in Summer and Winter Pile Techniques	WJ	4	4	16	Ap 80	14
Chandler, Deborah	Alphabet Soup	Hw	8	5		N/D 87	90
Chandler, Deborah	Assertiveness Training for Beginning Weavers	Hw	7	3		M/J 86	24
Chandler, Deborah	Choosing a Focus of Study Can Lead to New Growth, New Horizons, New Understanding	Hw	6	4		S/O 85	26
Chandler, Deborah	Creative Solutions	Hw	6	3		Su 85	28
Chandler, Deborah	Getting the Most Out of a Class	Hw	7	5		N/D 86	16
Chandler, Deborah	My Success is Absolutely Assured	Hw	7	1		J/F 86	23
Chandler, Deborah	On Learning	Hw	7	4		S/O 86	20
Chandler, Deborah	Selvedges, Selveges, Selvages	Hw	8	4		S/O 87	26
Chandler, Deborah	Spinning Teachers Extraordinaire	S-O	10	4		Wi 86	10
Chandler, Deborah	Tension	Hw	7	2		M/A 86	21
Chandler, Deborah	Tools of the Trade	Hw	6	1		J/F 85	23
Chandler, Deborah	Twills, Another Look	Hw	6	5		N/D 85	26
Chandler, Deborah	Using Unplanned Yarn in a Planned Project	Hw	8	2		M/A 87	24
Chandler, Deborah	Weaving — Better Than Bridge	Hw	8	3		M/J 87	18
Chandler, Deborah	Weaving is a Pain in the...	Hw	6	2		M/A 85	26
Channing, Marion	Magic of Spinning, The	H&C	17	2		Sp 66	45
Chapin, Doloria	Designer Yarns: Slubs and Spirals	S-O	3			79	54
Chapin, Doloria	Let's Go Spinning: International Handspinning Directory and Handbook, 1971	H&C	22	3		Su 71	41
Chapin, Doloria	Teaching the Blind to Spin: An Impromptu Lesson	SS&D	10	3	39	Su 79	91
Chapin, Doloria	Three Adventures of a Wedding Dress	SS&D	4	3	15	Su 73	51
Chapin, Doloria, ed.	International Handspinning Directory and Handbook 1971	SS&D	2	2	6	Sp 71	34
Chapman, S. D., ed.	see Pointing, K. G., ed.	WJ	6	3	23	Wi 81	60
Chapman, Suzanne E.	Early American Design Motifs	SS&D	6	4	24	Fa 75	30
Chapman, Suzanne E.	Early American Design Motifs	H&C	4	1		Wi 52	60
Charles E. Tuttle Co., Inc. distr.	Knitting & Crocheting Fun	WJ	8	1	29	Su 83	53
Chase, Hazel	see Beck, Dorothy	SS&D	2	1	5	De 70	31
Chase, Hazel	see Beck, Dorothy	SS&D	2	1	5	De 70	31
Chase, Hazel	see Beck, Dorothy	H&C	14	1		Wi 63	43

AUTHOR	TITLE	JOUR	VOL	NO	ISS	DATE	PAGE
Chase, Hazel	see Beck, Dorothy	H&C	16	3		Su 65	43
Chase, Judith Wragg	Afro-American Art & Craft	SS&D	4	1	13	Wi 72	34
Chase, Mary A.	Flax Processing	WJ	7	2	26	Fa 82	5
Chase, Mary A.	Learning to Weave in Sweden	H&C	24	3		M/J 73	7
Chase, Mary A.	Weaving of Linen, The	WJ	7	2	26	Fa 82	18
Chase, Patti; with Mimi Dolbier	Contemporary Quilt: New American Quilts and Fabric Art, The	Iw	4	2		Sp 79	63
Chase, Pattie	"Radka Donnell-Vogt: Patchwork Quilts" (Exhibit)	Fa	7	5		S/O 80	76
Chastant, Kathryn Ross	Angora Goats and Mohair	S-O	7	3		Fa 83	29
Chastant, Kathryn Ross	Mohair Afghan/Great Shawl	S-O	6	4		82	57
Chattapadhyaya, Kamaladevi	Carpets and Floor Coverings of India	H&C	22	3		Su 71	44
Chaudet, Annette	Trimming the Southwestern Look	WJ	11	1	41	Su 86	35
Checker, Janet	Weaving as a Professional: Production Weaving/Designing	WJ	6	3	23	Wi 81	29
Checkowy, Edna	Working Weaver—Reeds: Increasing Their Efficiency	SS&D	16	4	64	Fa 85	12
Chelsey, Randy	Sweater of Abundance	S-O	11	1		Sp 87	15
Chelsey, Randy	Thoughts on Money, Art, and Spinning	S-O	11	1		Sp 87	14
Chen, Lydia; Editors of Echo Books	Chinese Knotting	WJ	8	1	29	Su 83	53
Chesley, Mariam Dolloff	Scintillating, Soft and Silent Seat, A	Hw	5	2		M/A 84	27
Chesley, Mariam Dolloff	Tape Loom — Then and Now, The	Hw	3	5		N/D 82	56
Chesley, Zina Mae	Hand-Carding by Machine	SS&D	1	3	3	Ju 70	18
Chesley, Zina Mae	Spindle	SS&D	2	4	8	Fa 71	23
Chesley, Zina Mae	Spindle	SS&D	1	2	2	Mr 70	20
Chesley, Zina Mae	Spindle	SS&D	2	1	5	De 70	16
Chesley, Zina Mae	Spindle	SS&D	2	2	6	Sp 71	22
Chesrown, Melva A.	Nantucket Looms, Fabrics by Island Weavers in Restored Inn	H&C	14	4		Fa 63	6
Chesterman, John	see Marten, Michael	Iw	4	2		Sp 79	64
Chetwynd, Hilary	Experimenting with Leno Weaves	SS&D	5	3	19	Su 74	29
Chetwynd, Hilary	Simple Weaving	H&C	20	4		Fa 69	42
Chevreul, M. E.	Principles of Harmony & Contrast of Colors & Their Application to the Arts, The	H&C	19	2		Sp 68	43
Chicago, Judy; Susan Hill	Embroidering Our Heritage: The Dinner Party Needlework	Fa	9	3		M/J 82	58
Chilton, D. Lorraine	Handspun Rainbow Sweater	S-O	7	4		Wi 83	49
Chittenden, Annie Curtis	Annie Curtis Chittenden	Fa	14	5		N/D 87	11
Chittenden, Annie Curtis	Journey in Progress, A	SS&D	17	4	68	Fa 86	50
Chmielewska, Monika	Old World Discipline — New World Markets	SS&D	11	1	41	Wi 79	4
Chown, Joyce	see Weir, Jean	Fa	11	4		J/A 84	39
Chown, M. Joyce	see Black, Mary E.	H&C	11	4		Fa 60	59
Chown, M. Joyce	see Black, Mary E.	H&C	11	4		Fa 60	59
Chown, M. Joyce; Mary E. Black	Color Guide for Handweavers	H&C	11	4		Fa 60	59
Chressanthis, James	Hidden Sides, Hidden Lives: The Photo-Fiber Works of Robin Becker	Fa	7	3		M/J 80	34
Chressanthis, James	see Becker, Robin	Fa	9	6		N/D 82	40
Christensen, Erwin O.	Index of American Design, The	H&C	2	1		Wi 50	59
Christensen, Erwin O.	Index of American Design, The	H&C	10	2		Sp 59	60
Christensen, Evelyn	Guatemalan Belt Weave	Hw	7	2		M/A 86	68
Christensen, Joanne	Overshot Derived from 2/2 Twill: Joanne's Runner	PWC	3	2	8		24
Christensen, Joanne	Two Floor Pillows for the Rigid Heddle Loom	Hw	2	2		Mr 81	56
Christian, Donna Allgaier	Focus on Flax: From Flax to Fabric with Virginia Handy	S-O	10	3		Fa 86	22
Christopher, F. J.	Hand Loom Weaving	H&C	7	2		Sp 56	64
Chung, Young Y.	Art of Oriental Embroidery: History, Aesthetics, and Technique, The	Fa	7	4		J/A 80	75
Cie des Editions de l'alma	Mon Tricot 1500 Patterns	TM			9	F/M 87	74
Ciesiel, Marihelen	To Shear or Not to Shear?	S-O	11	4		Wi 87	11

AUTHOR	TITLE	JOUR	VOL	NO	ISS	DATE	PAGE
Clack Handcrafts	How to Weave	H&C	3	1		Wi 51	61
Clardy, Andrea	"Landscapes" (Exhibit)	Fa	5	2		M/A 78	10
Clardy, Andrea	Priscilla Sage	Fa	5	2		M/A 78	26
Clark, Barbara	"Frontiers of Contemporary Weaving" (Exhibit)	Fa	4	1		J/F 77	6
Clark, Becky	"Critters and Cohorts" (Exhibit)	Fa	4	6		N/D 77	13
Clark, Eleanor W.	Weavers' Seminar in Massachusetts	H&C	6	4		Fa 55	9
Clark, Hazel	Fibers to Fabrics	SS&D	17	3	67	Su 86	86
Clark, Hazel	Fibres to Fabrics: Techniques and Projects for Handspinners	TM			13	O/N 87	76
Clark, Hilary	Salish Weaving	SS&D	3	2	10	Sp 72	12
Clark, June	Pine Needle Basketry	WJ	5	1	17	Su 80	10
Clark, Katherine	Door Closes for Shelburne Spinners, The	SS&D	9	3	35	Su 78	34
Clark, Leta W.	How to Make Money with Your Crafts	SS&D	5	2	18	Sp 74	68
Clark, Marion L.	Two-harness Weaves	H&C	14	2		Sp 63	17
Clark, Marlyn	Twist Demystified	S-O	7	2		Su 83	25
Clark, Nancy, et al.	Ventilation, A Practical Guide	Hw	7	4		S/O 86	12
Clark, Noel	Taking It to the Streets: Marketing Your Multiples	Fa	5	5		S/O 78	26
Clark, Sherry	Groupwork with Dutch Feltmaker Inge Evers	SS&D	17	4	68	Fa 86	28
Clark, Sherry	Weaving a Route to the Future: An Income-Generating Fiber Project in the West Indies	Fa	12	2		M/A 85	48
Clarke, Leslie	Craftsman in Textiles, The	H&C	19	4		Fa 68	44
Clarke, Lois	Tapestry Weaving Adapted to Miniature Scale	H&C	13	4		Fa 62	10
Clausen, Valerie	Imagery Is Personal in Tapestry Today	TM			9	F/M 87	66
Clausen, Valerie	Old Shoes Keeping Honourable Company	TM			11	J/J 87	16
Clayton, Clare	Coronet, A	Kn	3	2	6	Sp 87	32
Clement, Doris	Christmas Cards	H&C	15	2		Sp 64	20
Clement, Doris	Coverlet from Museum Collection	H&C	15	1		Wi 64	36
Clement, Doris	Handloom in the Automobile Industry, The	H&C	10	3		Su 59	61
Clement, Doris	Jackie von Ladau, Versatile Weaver	H&C	10	3		Su 59	20
Clement, Doris	London Bookshop	H&C	11	1		Wi 60	11
Clement, Doris	Mother and Daughter Bonnets	H&C	13	3		Su 62	36
Clement, Doris	Myra L. Davis, Master Weaver	H&C	12	1		Wi 61	24
Clement, Doris	Rochester Weavers, New York Guild Sponsors Variety of Projects (error-corrected H&C v14 n1 63 p46)	H&C	13	4		Fa 62	12
Clement, Doris	Woven Necklaces	H&C	21	4		Fa 70	8
Clement, Doris; Ted Clement	Irish Weaving	H&C	21	2		Sp 70	4
Clement, Doris; Ted Clement	Wool Gathering in Wales	H&C	23	1		J/F 72	26
Clement, Doris W.	Ancient Peruvian Weaver	H&C	18	4		Fa 67	21
Clement, Doris W.	Dalsgaard Tapestries, The	H&C	17	1		Wi 66	6
Clement, Doris W.	Gertrude Griffin Comes from Ireland to Canada	H&C	19	1		Wi 68	17
Clement, Doris Wilcox	Kate Van Cleve — Master Weaver	H&C	9	3		Su 58	30
Clement, Richard	Computer Control of Tie-ups and Treadling Sequence	WJ	8	3	31	Wi 83	32
Clement, Robbie	To Clothe a Weary World in Song	Hw	4	4		S/O 83	10
Clement, Ted	see Clement, Doris	H&C	21	2		Sp 70	4
Clement, Ted	see Clement, Doris	H&C	23	1		J/F 72	26
Clemmer, Phyllis	Recipe for Tanning Rabbit Fur	WJ	8	3	31	Wi 83	16
Clemmer, Phyllis	see Szumski, Norma	WJ	6	2	22	Fa 81	41
Clemner, Phyllis	And Knots	SS&D	14	3	55	Su 83	26
Clivio, Carol	Confessions of a Cotton Spinner	S-O	10	4		Wi 86	38
Cloney, Gordon	Spinners of Chijnaya, Alpaca Yarns from Peruvian Village	H&C	16	4		Fa 65	15
Close, Eunice	How to Make Gloves	H&C	2	1		Wi 50	62
Clurman, Irene	Connie Lehman: Portable Secrets	Fa	12	6		N/D 85	10

AUTHOR	TITLE	JOUR	VOL	NO	ISS	DATE	PAGE
Clurman, Irene	Connie McEntire Lehman's Side Glances from Drawings Into Dye-Painted Hangings	Fa	8	5		S/O 81	26
Clyne, Carol	see Giganti, Maria	TM			2	D/J 85	64
Coats and Clark	One Hundred Embroidery Stitches	Iw	5	4		Fa 80	77
Coatts, Margot	Weaver's Life: Ethel Mairet 1872–1952, A	Hw	5	3		Su 84	16
Cobb, Lorie	Aurora Colony Antique Spinning Wheel Showcase	S-O	10	3		Fa 86	43
Cobb, Lorie	Ramie	S-O	10	3		Fa 86	40
Cochran, Doris M.	Weavers Were Founders of Potomac Craftsmen	H&C	6	2		Sp 55	48
Cochrane, Diane	This Business of Art	Iw	4	4		Fa 79	72
Coe, Kathryn	From the Silverman Collection: Pueblo and Navajo Textiles	Fa	10	6		N/D 83	27
Coe, Ralph T.	Lost and Found Traditions: Native American Art 1965–1985	Hw	8	5		N/D 87	12
Coe, Ralph T.	Lost and Found Traditions: Native American Art 1965-1985	SS&D	19	1	73	Wi 87	52
Coffey, Marjorie	Marjorie Coffey	Fa	4	6		N/D 77	40
Coffin, David Page	Irons, Boards, and Presses: A Survey of the Tools That Beautify Sewing	TM			10	A/M 87	40
Coffin, David Page	Making a Great Shirt Collar	TM			4	A/M 86	42
Coffin, David Page	Perfecting the Pocket	TM			8	D/J 86	28
Coffin, David Page	Ready for the Needle	TM			12	A/S 87	43
Coffin, David Page	Shirtmaker from a Small Planet	TM			9	F/M 87	16
Coffin, David Page	When a Fusing Fails	TM			10	A/M 87	61
Coffinet, Julien; Maurice Pianzola	Tapestry	H&C	23	5		S/O 72	34
Coffinet, Julien; Maurice Pianzola	Tapestry: Craft and Art	SS&D	5	4	20	Fa 74	64
Coffman, Charlotte	Backstrap Weaving for Penance and Profit	WJ	7	1	25	Su 82	60
Coffman, Charlotte	Complementary-Warp Weave (error-corrected WJ v7 n4 83 p4)	WJ	7	3	27	Wi 82	53
Coffman, Charlotte	Learning the Ropes: Abaca	S-O	7	4		Wi 83	40
Coffman, Charlotte	Three Faces of the Eight-Pointed Star Motif (error-corrected SS&D v14 n4 83 p4)	SS&D	14	3	55	Su 83	56
Coffman, Charlotte	Tips for Traveling Weavers	SS&D	13	2	50	Sp 82	22
Cogar, Kathryn	Cache Valley Winter Blues: Felted Coat	SS&D	17	4	68	Fa 86	16
Cohen, Arthur	Sonia Delaunay	Fa	8	1		J/F 81	20
Cohen, Eve	see Erickson, Mary Anne	TM			14	D/J 87	76
Cohn, Lisa	Handwoven Velvet of Barbara Pickett, The	Hw	8	1		J/F 87	20
Coifman, Lucienne	Biennale/Another View, The	SS&D	15	1	57	Wi 83	76
Coifman, Lucienne	Raglan Rectangles	SS&D	18	1	69	Wi 86	10
Coifman, Lucienne	Summertime!	SS&D	15	3	59	Su 84	74
Coker, Sharon	Spinners of Taquile	S-O	8	1		Sp 84	24
Colburn, Carol	Instant Color! Paint a Garden on Your Warp	Hw	1	2		S-S 80	44
Colburn, Carol	Technique: Painting Weft Threads for Tapestry	Hw	3	1		Ja 82	58
Colby, Averil	Quilting	H&C	23	4		J/A 72	26
Coleman, Elizabeth	Elizabeth Coleman and the Not-So-Homely Art of Sewing	Fa	6	3		M/J 79	29
Collacott, Margaret C.	Textile Arts Club of Cleveland, Ohio	H&C	6	3		Su 55	25
Collard, Agathe G.	Modern Overshot (Frappé Moderne)	WJ	5	4	20	Sp 81	28
Collingwood, Peter	Double Corduroy with Varied Pile	Hw	7	4		S/O 86	47
Collingwood, Peter	Double-Faced 3/1 Broken Twill Woven on Tablets	AT	1			De 83	91
Collingwood, Peter	How Shaft-Switching Began	WJ	6	2	22	Fa 81	14
Collingwood, Peter	Maker's Hand: A Close Look at Textile Structures, The	WJ	12	2	46	Fa 87	66
Collingwood, Peter	Maker's Hand: A Close Look at Textile Structures, The	TM			11	J/J 87	72
Collingwood, Peter	Maker's Hand: A Close Look at Textile Structures, The	PWC	5	1	15		52
Collingwood, Peter	see Sutton, Ann	Hw	8	2		M/A 87	15
Collingwood, Peter	Self-supporting Workshop, A	H&C	15	4		Fa 64	7
Collingwood, Peter	Sprang, Revival of an Ancient Technique	H&C	15	2		Sp 64	6
Collingwood, Peter	Techniques of Rug Weaving, The	H&C	20	1		Wi 69	41
Collingwood, Peter	Techniques of Sprang: Plaiting on Stretched Threads, The	TMJ	4	2		75	79

AUTHOR	TITLE	JOUR	VOL	NO	ISS	DATE	PAGE
Collingwood, Peter	Techniques of Sprang, The	SS&D	5	2	18	Sp 74	69
Collingwood, Peter	Techniques of Tablet Weaving, The	Hw	4	2		M/A 83	15
Collingwood, Peter	Techniques of Tablet Weaving, The	WJ	7	3	27	Wi 82	48
Collingwood, Peter	Techniques of Tablet Weaving, The	Fa	10	4		J/A 83	49
Collingwood, Peter	Techniques of Tablet Weaving, The	SS&D	14	2	54	Sp 83	63
Collingwood, Peter	Techniques of Tablet Weaving, The	PWC			4	Ja 83	68
Collingwood, Peter	Too Late for the Book	PWC	3	4	10		29
Collingwood, Peter	Weaving a Wall Hanging	H&C	11	4		Fa 60	15
Collingwood, Peter	World of Ancient and Modern Sprang, The	SS&D	5	1	17	Wi 73	90
Collingwood, Peter; Harriet Tidball, ed.	Peter Collingwood: His Weaves and Weaving	SCGM		8		63	1-46
Colque, Juan Cutipa	see Zorn, Elayne	S-O	9	2		Su 85	21
Colson, Lois	Lingonberries in the Pot	SS&D	3	1	9	Wi 71	33
Colton, Mary Rawcliffe	Blue-Bleak Embers	WJ	8	4	32	Sp 84	16
Colton, Mary Rawcliffe	Crane Day Designs	SS&D	18	2	70	Sp 87	48
Colton, Mary Rawcliffe	Ikat Striped Ruana and Skirt	Hw	5	4		S/0 84	60
Colton, Mary Rawcliffe	Kimono	SS&D	15	1	57	Wi 83	30
Colton, Mary Rawcliffe	Southwest Reflections: Fiber Artists Inspired by the New Mexico Landscape	WJ	11	1	41	Su 86	20
Colton, Sarah	Judit Kele: The Sound of the Way It Feels	Fa	14	3		M/J 87	42
Colton, Sarah	Paris Museum Surveys Fashion	Fa	14	3		M/J 87	6
Columbus, Joseph Vincent	Conservation Notes: A Specialized Vacuum Device for Fragil Textiles	TMJ	1	1		No 62	56
Colwell, Katherine	Spirit Exits Through the Embroiderer's Hands, The	TM			12	A/S 87	18
Colwell, Ken	Books on Overshot: A Bibliography	PWC	3	2	8		43
Colwell, Ken	Computers—Is It Still Handweaving?	PWC	4	1	11		51
Colwell, Ken	Dobby Loom Explained, The	SS&D	11	4	44	Fa 80	7
Colwell, Ken	Doubleweave: A Popular Technique of the 19th Century Coverlet Weaver	PWC			2	Ap 82	53
Colwell, Ken	Jacquard at the Brewery, The	SS&D	7	2	26	Sp 76	14
Colwell, Ken	Ken Colwell on Collecting	PWC	4	4	14		5
Colwell, Ken	Ken Colwell on Coverlets	PWC	3	3	9		56
Colwell, Ken	Ken Colwell on Weaving	PWC	4	3	13		17
Colwell, Ken	Ken Colwell: Travels with Ken	PWC	4	2	12		31
Colwell, Ken	Looms from the Past	Hw	2	3		My 81	36
Colwell, Ken	New Items for Complex Weavers	CW	2	3	6	Ap 81	5
Comings, Marian	Arizona Guild Weaves for the Govenor	H&C	7	2		Sp 56	44
Commings, Nancy	Keep Warm! Colonial Comfort	WJ	5	2	18	Fa 80	8
Compton, Rae	Complete Book of Traditional Knitting, The	Kn	1	2	2	S-S 85	79
Compton, Rae	Complete Book of Traditional Knitting, The	Kn	2	1	3	F-W 85	78
Con, J. M.	Carpets from the Orient	H&C	18	2		Sp 67	43
Condit, Joan	Weaving with Linen	H&C	6	3		Su 55	46
Cone, Ferne Geller	Knit Art	Fa	5	3		M/J 78	59
Conklin, Sharon L.	Kente: The Status Cloth of Ghana	SS&D	8	1	29	WI 76	18
Conklin, William J	Chavin Textiles and the Origins of Peruvian Weaving	TMJ	3	2		De 71	13
Conklin, William J	Peruvian Textile Fragment from the Beginning of the Middle Horizon	TMJ	3	1		De 70	15
Conn, Richard	Robes of White Shell and Sunrise: Personal Decorative Arts of the Native American	TMJ	4	2		75	79
Connelly, Karin	Karin Connelly: Analagous Structures	Fa	12	1		J/F 85	90
Connette, Ann	Nez Percé Indian Art and Craft Revival	H&C	21	4		Fa 70	5
Connolly, Loris	The Work of a Huave Indian Weaver in Oaxaca, Mexico: Complex Weave Structures Utilizing One Warp Set and Two Complementary Weft Sets	AT	3			My 85	7
Connors, Carol	Gauge Revisor, The	Kn	3	1	5	F-W 86	54
Conover, Jean	Noils Using Handspun Yarns	SS&D	12	1	45	Wi 80	63
Conrad, Elvira	Backstrap Looms	H&C	14	3		Su 63	17
Conroy, Mary	Complete Book of Crazy Patchwork, The	Fa	14	2		M/A 87	61

AUTHOR	TITLE	JOUR	VOL	NO	ISS	DATE	PAGE
Constantine, Mildred; Jack Lenor Larsen	Art Fabric: Mainstream, The	Hw	2	4		Se 81	79
Constantine, Mildred; Jack Lenor Larsen	Art Fabric: Mainstream, The	Hw	7	5		N/D 86	14
Constantine, Mildred; Jack Lenor Larsen	Art Fabric: Mainstream, The	WJ	7	2	26	Fa 82	59
Constantine, Mildred; Jack Lenor Larsen	Art Fabric: Mainstream, The	WJ	12	2	46	Fa 87	66
Constantine, Mildred; Jack Lenor Larsen	Art Fabric: Mainstream, The	Fa	8	6		N/D 81	62
Constantine, Mildred; Jack Lenor Larsen	Beyond Craft: The Art Fabric	SS&D	6	4	24	Fa 75	29
Constantine, Mildred; Jack Lenor Larsen	Beyond Craft: The Art Fabric	Hw	7	5		N/D 86	14
Constantine, Mildred; Jack Lenor Larsen	Beyond Craft: The Art Fabric	WJ	12	2	46	Fa 87	66
Constantine, Mildred; Jack Lenor Larsen	Beyond Craft: The Art Fabric	TMJ	4	2		75	79
Constantinides, Kathy	"Artist Collects: Historic Fabrics from the Collection of Gerhardt Krodel, An" (Exhibit) (error-corrected Fa v7 n4 80 p6)	Fa	7	3		M/J 80	78
Constantinides, Kathy	"Connections" (Exhibit)	Fa	6	4		J/A 79	74
Constantinides, Kathy	Coptic Textiles: The Art of the Ancient Weaver	Fa	7	6		N/D 80	19
Constantinides, Kathy	"Felt: A Rich Tradition and Current Involvements" (Exhibit)	Fa	6	3		M/J 79	74
Constantinides, Kathy	"Interweave 79" (Exhibit)	Fa	7	1		J/F 80	66
Conte, Christine	Maya Culture & Costume: A Catalogue of the Taylor Museum's E. B. Ricketson Collection of Guatemalan Textiles	WJ	10	1	37	Su 85	86
Cook, Bonny	Discarded Fur Pieces for Rugs and Pillows	SS&D	4	3	15	Su 73	20
Cook, Bonny	Weaving with Antique (Second Hand) Fur	SS&D	3	2	10	Sp 72	38
Cooke, Leslie	Ellie Fidler: The Power of Concentration	Fa	7	2		M/A 80	48
Cooley, Theodore R.	Practical Dyeing Method for the Fabric Conservator, A	TMJ	2	4		De 69	23
Cooper, Arlene	How Madame Grès Sculpts with Fabric	TM		10		A/M 87	50
Cooper, Frayda	Erica: The New Rigid Heddle Loom	H&C	26	5		Oc 75	25
Cooper, Grace Rogers	Handweaving and the Powerloom in 18th Century America	H&C	22	4		Fa 71	5
Cooper, Jane	Back Strap Weaving in Zacualpan Mexico	SS&D	5	3	19	Su 74	13
Cooper, Karen Coody	Finger Weaving	TM		12		A/S 87	46
Cooper, Patricia; Norma Bradley Buferd	Quilters, The	Iw	2	4		Su 77	35
Cooper, Patricia; Norma Bradley Buferd	Quilters, Women and Domestic Art, The	Fa	7	6		N/D 80	58
Copestick, Myrtis Gorst	From Sheep to Skirt in Five Days	H&C	3	3		Su 52	25
Cordry, Donald; Dorothy Cordry	Mexican Indian Costumes	H&C	20	3		Su 69	41
Cordry, Donald; Dorothy Cordry	Mexican Indian Costumes	TMJ	3	4		De 73	46
Cordry, Dorothy	see Cordry, Donald	H&C	20	3		Su 69	41
Cordry, Dorothy	see Cordry, Donald	TMJ	3	4		De 73	46
Corey, Rosita	De Cordova Exhibit	SS&D	3	4	12	Fa 72	46
Corey, Rosita, ed.	see Weavers' Guild of Boston	SS&D	11	4	44	Fa 80	66
Cornett, James	Norma Rosen: A Printmaker Turns to Fabrics	Fa	7	4		J/A 80	23
Cornwall, E. Marguerite	Some Hints on Spinning Musk Ox Wool	S-O	7	1		Sp 83	20
Corpier, Leslee	Collaboration: Peter and Ritzi Jacobi (error-corrected Fa v13 n1 86 p6)	Fa	12	5		S/O 85	27
Corpier, Leslee	Fibre Interchange at the Banff Centre	Fa	12	4		J/A 85	40
Corrie, Rebecca Wells	see Pauly, Sarah Buie	TMJ	4	2		75	80
Corsini, Gale	Saddle Blanket	WJ	6	4	24	Sp 82	29
Corwin, Nancy	Jane Lackey: A Vision Into Past and Future	Fa	13	6		N/D 86	18
Cory, Sue Armstrong	Fabrics from a New Type Multi-Harness Loom	H&C	10	1		Wi 59	24
Cosh, Sylvia	Crochet Sweater Book, The	TM		11		J/J 87	73
Couch, Jo-Alice	Income for the Handicapped — A Philadelphia Story	H&C	2	4		Fa 51	28

AUTHOR	TITLE	JOUR	VOL	NO	ISS	DATE	PAGE
Coulson, Louise	Don's Jacket	S-O	8	2		Su 84	49
Coulter, Doris	Finger Weaving Being Revived by Cherokees (error-corrected SS&D v5 n4 74 p69)	SS&D	5	3	19	Su 74	55
Coulter, Doris M.	Cherokee Weavers Used Looms Over Two Hundred Years Ago	H&C	18	3		Su 67	17
Countess of Wilton	Book of Costume, The	TM			11	J/J 87	72
Courtney, Elizabeth	Cardiac Algorithms or the Heart's Way of Inferring Meaning from Pattern	AT	5			Ju 86	51
Coutts, Lucele	Basketry Drop Spindle	SS&D	11	4	44	Fa 80	49
Coutts, Lucele	Baskets and Beyond	SS&D	9	3	35	Su 78	96
Coutts, Lucele	Baskets and Beyond	Iw	3	2		Wi 78	42
Coutts, Lucele	Baskets and Beyond	Fa	5	4		J/A 78	59
Coutts, Lucele	Thrum Basketry	SS&D	8	3	31	Su 77	43
Coutts, Lucele	Variations on a Landes Theme	WJ	8	4	32	Sp 84	24
Covel, John	Get Into a Good Book: Public Art for Kids	Fa	6	5		S/O 79	33
Coverdale, Joan	Answer Me in Wool Baby	SS&D	11	2	42	Sp 80	33
Coverdale, Joan	Fleece Power	SS&D	11	2	42	Sp 80	33
Cowan, Sally	A Perfect Pair of Pants	TM			7	O/N 86	26
Cox, Doris; Barbara Warren	Creative Hands	H&C	2	4		Fa 51	62
Cox, Dorothy	Furry Pillow	WJ	7	2	26	Fa 82	56
Cox, Penni	Fleece to Fibers At Museum of Man	SS&D	5	4	20	Fa 74	50
Cox, Truda	Beginning Spinning	SS&D	4	1	13	Wi 72	34
Cox-Chapman, Mally	Aid to Artisans	TM			13	O/N 87	14
Craft and Folk Art Museum, Los Angles, CA	Craft International	PWC			5	Sp 83	68
Craft Course Publishers	Easy to Weave Wall Decorations	WJ	3	3	11	Ja 79	43
Craft Course Publishers	Soft and Simple Weaving	WJ	3	3	11	Ja 79	43
Craft Course Publishers	Weaving on Driftwood Looms	WJ	3	3	11	Ja 79	43
Cragholm, Lynn	Weaving in Africa	H&C	23	1		J/F 72	18
Craig, Chris	Chris Craig	Fa	12	6		N/D 85	18
Craig-Linenberger, Gerry	Surface Design Conference in Kansas City	TM			12	A/S 87	20
Cramer, Edith	Handbook of Early American Decoration	H&C	2	2		Sp 51	60
Cramer, Pauline E.	Marvelous Mistake, A	SS&D	17	1	65	Wi 85	34
Cramer, Pauline Ellis	Profile of a State Rep	SS&D	15	4	60	Fa 84	89
Cranbrook Academy of Art Museum	Gerhardt Knodel Makes Places to Be	WJ	7	4	28	Sp 83	49
Cranch, George E.	Unusual Colors from Experiments with Vegetable Dyes	H&C	13	3		Su 62	13
Crane, Barbara	Barbara Crane	Fa	13	4		J/A 86	27
Cranston-Bennett, Mary Ellen	Circular Loom, The	H&C	17	1		Wi 66	12
Crawford, Grace Post	Setting Up a Tape Loom	H&C	12	1		Wi 61	19
Crawford, Libby	Snow White and a Seven-Yard Warp	SS&D	2	1	5	De 70	11
Creager, Clara	All About Weaving	Hw	6	1		J/F 85	17
Creager, Clara	Corporate Commission, The	SS&D	16	1	61	Wi 84	38
Creager, Clara	Roots of Wearables, The	TM			14	D/J 87	16
Creager, Clara	Weaving: A Creative Approach for Beginners	Fa	3	3		M/J 76	7
Creager, Clara	Weaving: Creative Approach for Beginners	SS&D	6	2	22	Sp 75	64
Creekmore, Betsey	Traditional American Crafts	H&C	20	3		Su 69	41
Crews, Particia Cox; Barbara M. Reagan	Ultraviolet Absorbers: A Treatment to Reduce Fading and Degradation of Textiles	AT	8			De 87	43
Crews, Patricia	Considerations in the Selection and Application of Natural Dyes: Mordant Selection, Part 1	SS&D	12	2	46	Sp 81	15
Crews, Patricia	Considerations in the Selection and Application of Natural Dyes: Dye-plant Selection (error-corrected SS&D v12 n4 81 p8)	SS&D	12	3	47	Su 81	52
Cripps, Alice K.	Adventures in Weaving on a 2 Harness Loom	H&C	1	3		Fa 50	62
Cripps, Alice K.	Wall Hanging with a Story	H&C	17	1		Wi 66	47
Cripps, Alice K.	Weaving That Pays	H&C	12	3		Su 61	53
Criscola, Jeanne	Designing the Warp: Parallel Considerations	TM			1	O/N 85	66

AUTHOR	TITLE	JOUR	VOL	NO	ISS	DATE	PAGE
Criscola, Jeanne	Designing the Warp: Parallel Considerations	TM			1	O/N 85	66
Crockett, Candace	Card Weaving	SS&D	5	3	19	Su 74	62
Crockett, Candace	Complete Spinning Book, The	SS&D	9	3	35	Su 78	97
Crockett, Candace	Complete Spinning Book, The	lw	3	2		Wi 78	40
Crockett, Candace	Complete Spinning Book, The	WJ	8	2	30	Fa 83	62
Crockett, Candace	Complete Spinning Book, The	Fa	5	4		J/A 78	59
Crockett, Candace	Considering Cardweaving	H&C	22	3		Su 71	13
Crockett, Candace	Contemporary Handweavers at the De Young Museum	SS&D	2	2	6	Sp 71	4
Crockett, Candace	Distort, Rearrange, Combine	SS&D	5	2	18	Sp 74	20
Crockett, Candace	New Approaches to Cardweaving	SS&D	4	4	16	Fa 73	72
Crockett, Candace	see Chamberlain, Marcia	SS&D	6	3	23	Su 75	49
Crockett, S. R.; K. A. Hilton	Basic Chemistry of Textile Colouring & Finishing	H&C	7	4		Fa 56	60
Crockett, S. R.; K. A. Hilton	Basic Chemistry of Textile Preparation	H&C	7	4		Fa 56	59
Cromstedt, Cathrine	Malin Selander	H&C	17	1		Wi 66	22
Crone-Coggins, Noreen	Dreaming, Drawing, Painting, and Stitching with Noreen Crone-Coggins	Fa	6	5		S/O 79	16
Cronk, Helen H.	Open Weave Casement	H&C	13	2		Sp 62	32
Crosby, Roberta	Wool Skirt and Shawl	PWC		5		Sp 83	55
Crossman, Catherine	University of Wisconsin Holds Conference for School Teachers	SS&D	5	1	17	Wi 73	60
Crosson, Janet Gray	Let's Get Technical: An Overview of Handwoven Pennsylvania Jacquard Coverlets: 1830-1860	SS&D	11	1	41	Wi 79	33
Crosson, Janet Gray	Suggestions for Storage	H&C	15	4		Fa 64	21
Crosson, Janet Gray	Weaving Drafts and Diaper Twills in Lancaster County	lw	4	3		Su 79	40
Crouse, Gloria E.	Hooked on Texture: Unconventional Punch-Needle Rugs	TM			14	D/J 87	68
Crow, Nancy	From Barn to Studio: On Moving to a Farm and Making a Workspace	Fa	8	6		N/D 81	44
Crowder, Jennie	see Vinroot, Sally	Fa	9	4		J/A 82	53
Crowder, Rachael	It's a Bird....It's a Plane	PWC	4	3	13		14
Crowell, Ivan H.	Nine-Foot Loom for Rugs, A	H&C	7	4		Fa 56	14
Crowley, Alice M.	Mushrooms Sprout on Stereo Cabinet	SS&D	5	4	20	Fa 74	24
Crump, Nancy	Tapestry Weaving and Design	lw	4	2		Sp 79	24
Csipke, Steve	Using Libraries	H&C	24	3		M/J 73	46
Culhane, Isabel	Camp Culhane, It's All in the Family	SS&D	6	3	23	Su 75	23
CUM-Leclerc	Scandinavian Handweaving and Rya	SS&D	5	4	20	Fa 74	64
Cummer, Joan	Collection of Spinning Wheels, A	S-O	7	2		Su 83	22
Cummings, Mimi	Forum	Hw	2	4		Se 81	10
Cunningham, Anne S.	Crewel Gardens	TM			6	A/S 86	48
Cunningham, Patricia A.	Ohio's Woven Coverlets: Textile Industry in a Rural Economy	AT	2			De 84	165
Cunningham, Susanmarie	Susanmarie Cunningham: Wearable Soft Sculpture	Fa	11	5		S/O 84	15
Currey, Ruth	Experimental Workshop Tests New Approaches to Weaving	H&C	21	4		Fa 70	19
Currey, Ruth Dunlop	Handweaves for the Well-Dressed Baby	H&C	2	3		Su 51	52
Currey, Ruth Dunlop	Have You Tried Multiple Thread Warping?	H&C	5	3		Su 54	28
Currey, Ruth Dunlop	Margaret Carter, A Weaver in Three States	H&C	21	4		Fa 70	12
Currey, Ruth Dunlop	New England Crafts at Worcester	H&C	7	1		Wi 55	18
Currey, Ruth Dunlop	Strawbery Banke, A Restored New England Village	H&C	22	2		Sp 71	14
Currey, Ruth Dunlop	Weaving in New Brunswick	H&C	12	1		Wi 61	29
Currie, Meg	From White-on-White to Color	TM			3	F/M 86	39
Curtis, Dolly	State Grant — A Two-Way Street, The	SS&D	8	4	32	Fa 77	8
Cushman, Helen	see Towner, Naomi Whiting	SS&D	7	3	27	Su 76	94
Cutcher, Elaine	see Cutcher, Hal	Fa	3	4		J/A 76	40
Cutcher, Hal	Economics of Pricing, The	Fa	4	1		J/F 77	11
Cutcher, Hal	Witch Engine! The Machinations of the Dobby	lw	2	4		Su 77	22
Cutcher, Hal; Elaine Cutcher	Cutcher's Corner	Fa	3	4		J/A 76	40

AUTHOR	TITLE	JOUR	VOL	NO	ISS	DATE	PAGE
Cutter, Thomas	see Clark, Nancy	Hw	7	4		S/O 86	12
Cyr, Gloria	Linen Tablerunner with Atwater Bronson Lace	WJ	7	2	26	Fa 82	37
Cyrus-Zetterström, Ulla	Manual of Swedish Handweaving	WJ	2	4	8	Ap 78	39
Cyrus-Zetterström, Ulla	Manual of Swedish Handweaving	WJ	9	1	33	Su 84	60
Cyrus-Zetterström, Ulla	Manual of Swedish Handweaving	SS&D	16	1	61	Wi 84	21
Cyrus-Zetterström, Ulla	Manual of Swedish Handweaving	PWC	3	2	8		62
Cyrus-Zetterström, Ulla	Manual of Swedish Handweaving, The	Hw	5	3		Su 84	18
Cysarz, J. M.	From Fibre to Haute Coutoure on World Postage Stamps	AT	4			De 85	89
Cysewski, Catherine	Shelburne Spinners: Pushing for Perfection	Iw	3	1		Fa 77	22
D'Angelo, Anne A.; Margaret B. Windeknecht	Batik Handbook: A Color Guide to Procion Dyes	SS&D	4	2	14	Sp 73	44
D'Angelo, Anne A.; Margaret B. Windeknecht	Batik Plus Handweaving	SS&D	4	3	15	Su 73	57
d'Avila, Doris	Beyond the Machine (The creative uses of imprecision)	S-O	4			80	50
da Conceicao, Maria	Wearable Art	Fa	7	4		J/A 80	14
Dadey, Jane	CAD Quilts: The Computer As a Studio Tool	Fa	14	4		S/O 87	38
Dahl, Caroline	Caroline Dahl	Fa	13	3		M/J 86	27
Dahl, Caroline	Freestyle Embroidery: New Images with Traditional Stitches	TM			1	O/N 85	22
Dahl, E. E.	Inspiration	Hw	5	5		N/D 84	94
Dailey, Linda	Convergence '84: Dallas	SS&D	15	4	60	Fa 84	38
Daily, Laura	Rachel Brown: Weaver At the Wheel	Fa	10	3		M/J 83	20
Dalby, Gill	Natural Dyes, Fast or Fugitive	Hw	6	4		S/O 85	22
Dale, Julie Schafler	Art to Wear	TM			9	F/M 87	74
Daley, Billie	see Hewitt, Furze	Kn	4	1	9	Wi 87	61
Daly, Lynn	Dyeing in the Black Hills	Iw	1	4		Su 76	18
Dana, Mrs. William Starr	How to Know the Wild Flowers	H&C	22	3		Su 71	43
Dana, Zelda	Welts and Bobbles: Crop Top	Kn	2	2	4	S-S 86	38
Danaher, Dennis	see Stetson, G. Robert	TM			5	J/J 86	42
Danieko, Norm	Norm's Professional Yarn Finder	TM			1	O/N 85	78
Daniel, Robert	Contemporary Fabrics from An Australia Handweaving Mill	H&C	16	1		Wi 65	18
Daniels, Parmely Clark	Toward Standardizing the Language of the Hand Loom Designer Weaver	H&C	24	4		Au 73	14
Daniels, Richard	Illuminated Tapestries of Amy Zerner, The	Fa	9	3		M/J 82	22
Danielson, Esther	Warmth for a Cool Climate: Handspun Wool & Milkweed Down	SS&D	17	4	68	Fa 86	24
Darling, Drew	Contemporary Lace of Susan Wood, The	Fa	11	6		N/D 84	22
Darwall, Randall	On Making Good Cloth	Hw	7	5		N/D 86	22
Daugherty, Robin	Silk and Cotton Shirt, A	S-O	6	4		82	60
Daugherty, Robin Taylor	Heart Basket, The	Hw	8	1		J/F 87	62
Daugherty, Robin Taylor	Making Felt with Mohair	S-O	7	3		Fa 83	48
Daugherty, Robin Taylor	Twill Woven Market Basket	Hw	6	1		J/F 85	80
Davenport, Betty	Bead Leno	PWC			6	Su 83	62
Davenport, Betty	Blankets and Afghans on a Narrow Loom	PWC	3	1	7		14
Davenport, Betty	Color Effects in Weft-faced Plain Weave (error-corrected Hw v7 n1 86 pl-3)	Hw	6	5		N/D 85	12
Davenport, Betty	Designing Inkle Bands	PWC			4	Ja 83	56
Davenport, Betty	Easy Tabard, An	Hw	5	1		J/F 84	50
Davenport, Betty	Experiments in Color and Weave with Floats	Hw	8	2		M/A 87	60
Davenport, Betty	Fun with Bronson Lace Variations	PWC			5	Sp 83	46
Davenport, Betty	Garments from Narrow Fabrics	Hw	6	2		M/A 85	18
Davenport, Betty	Guatemalan Stripes	Hw	4	2		M/A 83	54
Davenport, Betty	Hand Towels in Overshot Effect	PWC	3	2	8		48
Davenport, Betty	Hands on Rigid Heddle Weaving	PWC	5	1	15		55
Davenport, Betty	Loom-Controlled Inlay	Hw	6	3		Su 85	11
Davenport, Betty	New Look at the Rigid Heddle Loom, A	Iw	4	4		Fa 79	41

AUTHOR	TITLE	JOUR	VOL	NO	ISS	DATE	PAGE
Davenport, Betty	Patchwork Designs in Summer and Winter	PWC	1	1		No 81	27
Davenport, Betty	Project in Krokbragd, A	PWC		2		Ap 82	66
Davenport, Betty	Put It Together: Large Cloths from Small Looms	Hw	8	1		J/F 87	73
Davenport, Betty	Rigid Heddle Loom, The	SS&D	13	1	49	Wi 81	72
Davenport, Betty	Rigid-Heddle Loom Warping	Hw	3	3		My 82	73
Davenport, Betty	Rigid-Heddle Weaving: How to Weave More Ends per Inch	Hw	7	3		M/J 86	68
Davenport, Betty	Samples—Quick & Easy!	Hw	7	5		N/D 86	78
Davenport, Betty	Spice Up Plain Weave with Warp Floats	Hw	7	4		S/O 86	56
Davenport, Betty	Summer and Winter Revisited, Part 2: II. Krokbragd on One, A Woolen Runner Project	PWC		2		Ap 82	65
Davenport, Betty	Supplementary Warp for Novelty Yarns	Hw	6	1		J/F 85	34
Davenport, Betty	Textures and Patterns for the Rigid Heddle Loom	Hw	2	1		F-W 80	21
Davenport, Betty	Thrums	Hw	5	5		N/D 84	66
Davenport, Betty	Unusual Ways with Leno	Hw	7	2		M/A 86	46
Davenport, Betty	Value of Value, The	Hw	2	4		Se 81	70
Davenport, Betty	Warping for Stripes	Hw	6	4		S/O 85	18
Davenport, Betty	What if...Vest	Hw	5	4		S/0 84	75
Davenport, Betty Linn	Textures and Patterns for the Rigid Heddle Loom	WJ	5	3	19	Wi 81	51
Davenport, Betty Lynn	Log Cabin Effects for the Rigid Heddle Loom	Hw	8	5		N/D 87	42
Davenport, Betty; Suzanne Gaston-Voute	On the Angle	Hw	7	1		J/F 86	62
Davenport, Elsie	Your Handspinning	Iw	2	3		Sp 77	31
Davenport, Elsie	Your Yarn Dyeing — A Book for Handweavers and Spinners	H&C	6	4		Fa 55	61
Davenport, Elsie G.	Your Handspinning	SS&D	2	1	5	De 70	31
Davenport, Elsie G.	Your Handspinning	H&C	4	4		Fa 53	60
Davenport, Elsie G.	Your Handspinning	H&C	15	4		Fa 64	43
Davenport, Elsie G.	Your Handweaving	H&C	4	2		Sp 53	62
Davenport, Elsie G.	Your Yarn Dyeing	SS&D	4	3	15	Su 73	53
Davenport, Martha	Mary Alice Smith	SS&D	2	1	5	De 70	4
Davenport, Martha P.	Two Crafts, Weaving & Stitchery Combine Well	H&C	21	3		Su 70	34
Davidian, Robert	"Fibers Unlimited 1979" (Exhibit)	Fa	7	2		M/A 80	69
Davidsohn, Marty	Bog Jacket, Basic Shaping	PWC		3		Oc 82	35
Davidsohn, Marty	Llama Hat	PWC		4		Ja 83	65
Davidsohn, Marty	Overshot Derived from 2/2 Twill: Ornamental Throw Rug in Overshot	PWC	3	2	8		22
Davidsohn, Marty	Pride of the Harvest Shawl	PWC		6		Su 83	25
Davidson, Marion; Martha Blue	Making It Legal: A Law Primer for the Craftmaker, Visual Artist, and Writer	Iw	5	1		Wi 79	63
Davidson, Marion; Martha Blue	Making It Legal: A Law Primer for the Craftmaker, Visual Artist, and Writer	Fa	6	6		N/D 79	51
Davidson, Mary Frances	Dye-Pot, The	SS&D	6	1	21	Wi 74	32
Davidson, Mary Frances	Dye-Pot, The	H&C	1	3		Fa 50	64
Davidson, Mary Frances	Purple in Antiquity	SS&D	2	1	5	De 70	26
Davis, Helen	Sequence of Dominance	Hw	4	2		M/A 83	42
Davis, Helen B.	Timelessness and Style ... Select a Pattern for Handwoven Fabric (error-corrected WJ v6 n1 81 p28d)	WJ	5	3	19	Wi 81	6
Davis, Judy Green	What the Well-Dressed Baby Will Wear This Season	S-O	10	4		Wi 86	14
Davis, Kathy	Northern California Handweavers Conference	H&C	24	4		Au 73	36
Davis, Mary Kay	Needlework Doctor: How to Solve Every Kind of Needlework Problem, The	Fa	11	6		N/D 84	56
Davis, Mary Woodard	Alice Parrott	Iw	2	1		Fa 76	6
Davis, Michael	Abundance of Baskets, An	SS&D	17	1	65	Wi 85	6
Davis, Michael	Michael Davis	Fa	13	4		J/A 86	26
Davis, Nancy, ed.	McCall's Guide — Interchangeable Yarns for Knit and Crochet Revised	TM			1	O/N 85	76
Davis, Peter	Egyptian Tapestries by the Children of Harrania	H&C	14	4		Fa 63	9

AUTHOR	TITLE	JOUR	VOL	NO	ISS	DATE	PAGE
Davis, Sally Ann	National Directory of Shops, Galleries, Shows, Fairs: Where to Exhibit and Sell Your Work, 1982/1983.	SS&D	14	2	54	Sp 83	63
Davison, Marguerite P.	Handweaver's Pattern Book, A	Fa	3	1		J/F 76	4
Davison, Marguerite Porter	Grouped Warp Threads	H&C	26	3		M/J 75	24
Davison, Marguerite Porter, ed.	Handweaver's Source Book, A	H&C	5	1		Wi 53	60
Davison, Mildred; Christa C. Mayer-Thurman	Coverlets	TMJ	3	4		De 73	46
Dawson, Amy	Bobbin Lacemaking for Beginners	SS&D	10	1	37	Wi 78	78
Day, Cyrus L.	Knots and Splices	H&C	5	1		Wi 53	60
Day, Jim	Life of a Country Weaver, The	Fa	7	1		J/F 80	55
Dayan, Ruth; Wilburt Feinberg	Crafts of Israel	SS&D	6	2	22	Sp 75	63
Dayton, Rita	Amazing Basques and Their Sheep, The	S-O	3			79	19
de Backer, Lisette	Betty Boulez-Cuykx: Modern Lacemaker	Fa	13	3		M/J 86	23
de Barrios, Linda Asturias	see de Castellanos, Guisela Mayer	WJ	11	3	43	Wi 87	65
de Barrios, Linda Asturias; et al.	Comalapa: Native Dress and Its Significance	WJ	11	3	43	Wi 87	65
De Bone, Mary	Dhabla Weaving in India	SS&D	8	3	31	Su 77	9
De Bone, Mary	"Ikats of Orissa" (Exhibit)	Fa	11	1		J/F 84	82
De Bone, Mary	Vest with Slits Made of Five Tapestry Strips	SS&D	5	2	18	Sp 74	83
De Bone, Mary Golden	Patolu and Its Techniques	TMJ	4	3		76	49
de Castellanos, Guisela Mayer; et al.	Tzute y Jerarquia en Sololá Multipurpose Cloths and Hierarchy in Sololá	WJ	11	3	43	Wi 87	65
de Dillmont, Therese	Complete Encyclopedia of Needlework, The	WJ	7	1	25	Su 82	63
de Dillmont, Therese	Les Dentelles Aux Fuseaux Bobbin Lace (English Translation)	SS&D	6	4	24	Fa 75	30
de Grassi, Laurel	Evolution of a Project	S-O	10	4		Wi 86	21
de la Cruz, Catherine Jacinta	Robert Donnelly	S-O	10	1		Sp 86	53
de la Cruz, Catherine Jacinta	Wool on a Small Scale: A Large Success	S-O	9	4		Wi 85	21
de la Garza, Phyllis	Confessions of a Mad Spinner	S-O	5			81	15
de la Garza, Phyllis	Study Opportunities: Mexican Tapestry Weaving in San Miguel	Hw	3	1		Ja 82	62
De Leon, Sherry	Alexander Julian: Cut of a Different Cloth	Fa	12	3		M/J 85	64
de Mar, Lola	Comminicating Through Craft	Fa	14	1		J/F 87	38
de Paola, Tomie	Charles Needs a Cloak	Iw	2	1		Fa 76	32
De Peaux, Barbara; Mary Tyler	Bands to Broadloom: Converting Card Weaving Designs to a Four-Harness Loom	SS&D	8	1	29	WI 76	86
de Raadt-Apell, M. J.	Van Zuylen Batik, Pekalongan, Central Java (1890-1946)	TMJ	19 20			80,81	75
de Rodas, Idalma Mejía	see de Barrios, Linda Asturias	WJ	11	3	43	Wi 87	57
de Rodas, Idalma Mejía	see de Castellanos, Guisela Mayer	WJ	11	3	43	Wi 87	65
de Rodriguez, Judy Ziek; Nona M. Ziek	Weaving on a Backstrap Loom: Pattern Designs from Guatemala	SS&D	10	3	39	Su 79	34
de Saint-Aubin, Charles Germain	Art of the Embroiderer	Fa	10	6		N/D 83	58
Dean, Ankaret	Convergence '86 Fashions	SS&D	18	1	69	Wi 86	16
Dean, Ankaret	Convergence '86 Preview: Keynote Speaker Dorothy Burnham	SS&D	16	3	63	Su 85	32
Dean, Ankaret	Five Fibre Pieces	SS&D	18	2	70	Sp 87	8
Dean, Ankaret	Weave Your Wardrobe	Hw	2	5		No 81	94
Dean, Beryl	Ecclesiastical Embroidery	H&C	10	1		Wi 59	59
Dean, Ida	Dressing the Loom	H&C	4	4		Fa 53	59
DeBoer, Janet	Spinning—Australia	S-O	11	3		Fa 87	35
DeBoer, Janet	Spinning Down Under: What Are You Going to Do with the Yarn?	S-O	1			77	23
DeBoer, Janet, ed.	Dyeing for Fibers and Fabrics	Hw	6	3		Su 85	20
DeBoer, Janet, ed.	Dyeing for Fibres and Fabrics	WJ	10	2	38	Fa 85	82
DeBoy, Kathleen, ed.	Fiberarts Design Book, The	Hw	2	2		Mr 81	67
Decker, Eugene	Wild Sheep	S-O	3			79	26
Dedekam, Phyllis	Air Robe	SS&D	18	3	71	Su 87	47
Dedera, Don	Navajo Rugs, How to Find, Evaluate, Buy and Care for Them	SS&D	7	3	27	Su 76	34

AUTHOR	TITLE	JOUR	VOL	NO	ISS	DATE	PAGE
Dedra, Don	Navajo Rugs — How to Find, Evaluate, Buy and Care for Them	WJ	3	3	11	Ja 79	41
Dee, Anne Patterson, ed.	Art & Craft Periodicals 85: A Guide to Art, Craft, Needlecraft, Crafts, Marketing, Home Business & Related Magazines, Newspapers & Newsletters	Hw	7	5		N/D 86	14
Dee, Constance	Lucky Lessons from Two Grand Women	TM			11	J/J 87	16
Deems, Flo	Pointillist Color Effects in Spinning: A Study Program	S-O	4			80	53
Degener, Patricia	"Fiber Forms: Linda Eyerman, Jane Sauer" (Exhibit)	Fa	8	3		M/J 81	73
Degener, Patricia	"Other Baskets" An Invitational Show in St. Louis (Exhibit)	Fa	10	1		J/F 83	76
Degenhart, Pearl C.	Primitive Weaving, Rug Weaving on a Squaw Loom	H&C	22	1		Wi 71	21
Del Deo, Josephine	Raffia Tapestries	H&C	9	1		Wi 57	20
Del Deo, Josephine	see Gallinger, Osma	H&C	9	1		Wi 57	59
Del Deo, Josephine	see Tod, Osma	H&C	17	3		Su 66	43
Dembeck, Adeline	Guidebook to Man-made Textile Fibers	H&C	21	1		Wi 70	43
Demoss, Virginia	Sanity, Madness and the Artist: The Work of Suzan Anson	Fa	6	2		M/A 79	36
Demske, Barbara	Elizabeth Tuttle: Pointillist Crochet	Fa	7	4		J/A 80	48
Dendel, Esther	Designing from Nature	WJ	4	2	14	Oc 79	38
Dendel, Esther	see Marston, Ena	SS&D	9	1	33	Wi 77	4
Dendel, Esther Warner	African Fabric Crafts, Sources of African Design and Technique	H&C	26	3		M/J 75	30
Dendel, Esther Warner	Aftican Fabric Crafts	SS&D	6	3	23	Su 75	50
Dendel, Esther Warner	Basic Book of Twining, The	SS&D	10	2	38	Sp 79	72
Dendel, Esther Warner	Basic Book of Twining, The	Iw	4	1		Wi 78	54
Denecke, Gerlinda	A Coat from a Blanket	TM			2	D/J 85	41
Denny, Grace	Fabrics. Eight Edition	H&C	14	2		Sp 63	43
Denny, Grace	Fabrics. Seventh Revised Edition	H&C	4	3		Su 53	61
Denny, Walter B.	Anatolian Rugs: An Essay on Method	TMJ	3	4		De 73	7
Denny, Walter B.	Group of Silk Islamic Banners, A	TMJ	4	1		De 74	67
Denny, Walter B.	Ottoman Turkish Textiles	TMJ	3	3		De 72	55
Denton, Kay	Welcome to My World	Fa	8	3		M/J 81	52
Denwood, Philip	Tibetan Carpet, The	TMJ	4	2		75	79
Depas, Spencer	Macrame, Weaving & Tapestry: Art in Fiber	SS&D	5	1	17	Wi 73	77
DeRoy, Paul	Bead Leno	WJ	1	2	2	Oc 76	36
DeRoy, Paul	Placemats	WJ	1	3	3	Ja 77	4
Derr, Mary	Business of Weaving — An Interview with Elaine P. Nixon, The	WJ	4	1	13	Jy 79	10
Derr, Mary	Handweaving with Silk	WJ	3	2	10	Oc 78	40
Derr, Mary	Raw Silk Reeling: How to Do It Yourself	WJ	3	3	11	Ja 79	12
Derr, Mary	Tallis or Prayer Shawl, The	WJ	2	1	5	Jy 77	16
Derr, Mary L.	Combine Techniques? Why Not?	WJ	7	3	27	Wi 82	19
Derr, Mary L.	Survey on the Availability of American Wool, A	WJ	2	2	6	Oc 77	36
Derr, Mary L.	Wool — That Wonderful Natural Fiber	WJ	2	2	6	Oc 77	2
Deru, Crescent	Leno Lace with One Shuttle	H&C	11	4		Fa 60	46
Deru, Crescent	New Method for Pile Weave, A	H&C	8	3		Su 57	16
Deru, Crescent B.	New Pick-Up Weave, A	H&C	10	4		Fa 59	26
Desai, Dipti	see Westfall, Carol D.	AT	6			De 86	85
Desai, Dipti	see Westfall, Carol D.	AT	7			Ju 87	161
Desai, Dipti	see Westfall, Carol D.	AT	8			De 87	19
Desai, Dipti	see Westfall, Carol D.	AT	8			De 87	29
Deschaines, Sybil	Winter Wrap-Ups Revisited	SS&D	16	1	61	Wi 84	26
Deschamps, Kalli	Procion M: The Thick and the Thin	Iw	3	4		Su 78	40
Deschamps, Kalli	Weaving As Art At Hellgate High	Iw	1	2		Wi 76	25
Detter, Jan	Dana Romeis: Spatial Problem-Solving	Fa	14	1		J/F 87	18
Deuss, Krystyna	Indian Costumes from Guatemala	WJ	9	2	34	Fa 84	78
Dewees, Libby	Thoughts on Sweater Design	S-O	9	3		Fa 85	47
Dexter, Janetta	see Hansen, Robin	Kn	3	1	5	F-W 86	69

AUTHOR	TITLE	JOUR	VOL	NO	ISS	DATE	PAGE
Deygout, Françoise	Child's Dress Pattern	CW		24		My 87	13
Deygout, Françoise	Multi-Harness Overshot "Trials"	CW		24		My 87	3
Deyo, Diane	"Space Sails: American Banners" (Exhibit)	Fa	9	5		S/O 82	82
Dezzany, Frances	Mothproofing Techniques for Weavers and Spinners	Fa	7	1		J/F 80	44
di Franco, Toni Lee	Costume from the Adams Period, A	SS&D	8	1	29	WI 76	43
Dick, Barbara Ann	Novelty Yarns: Creation in Color and Texture	SS&D	12	3	47	Su 81	32
Dickerson, Anne S.	Anne W. Dickerson	Fa	14	5		N/D 87	12
Dickey, Enola	Modern Interpretations of Ethnic Garments	SS&D	9	2	34	Sp 78	28
Dickey, Enola	Touch of Fur, A	SS&D	8	4	32	Fa 77	85
Dickey, Helen F.	Handwoven Flight Bags	H&C	11	3		Su 60	46
Dickinson, Hattie K.	Orange Gown Has Brass Trim	SS&D	3	4	12	Fa 72	33
Dickson, Ellen Fanger	Basket Inside Out: The Spiral Sculptures of Ellen Fanger Dickson, A	Fa	7	1		J/F 80	26
Dieseldorff, Dr. Herbert Quirin	X Balam Q'ué, El Pájaro Sol: El Traje Regional De Cobán	WJ	10	1	37	Su 85	85
Dieterich, Mary	In Search of Excellence	SS&D	9	4	36	Fa 78	102
Dieterich, Mary	Mayan Folk Textiles: Symbol of a Society	Hw	6	3		Su 85	64
Dieterich, Mary	National Crafts Planning Project: A Report to the HGA Membership	SS&D	12	4	48	Fa 81	75
Dill-Kocher, Laurie	Laurie Dill-Kocher	Fa	13	2		M/A 86	15
Dimand, M. S.; Jean Mailey	Oriental Rugs in The Metropolitan Muesum of Art	TMJ	4	1		De 74	85
Dirks, Katherine	How to Care for Your Antique Textiles	H&C	24	1		J/F 73	40
Dishongh, Suzanne	Ann Mitchell: Tapestry-Maker	Fa	5	2		M/A 78	53
Dishough, Susanne	"Common Threads Shared" (Exhibit)	Fa	4	6		N/D 77	16
Disney, Jean	Handwoven Rugs from the Northwest	H&C	6	4		Fa 55	42
Dittmar, Ana	Brief Survey of Textile Traditions of Yugoslavia, A	S-O	8	1		Sp 84	41
Dittrick, Mark	Hard Crochet	Fa	5	3		M/J 78	59
Diurson, Vera	see Sampe-Hultberg, Astrid	H&C	3	3		Su 52	62
Diven, Gail	see Drysdale, Rosemary	Kn	2	2	4	S-S 86	50
Diven, Gail; Rosemary Drysdale	Beaded Sweater	Kn	2	2	4	S-S 86	50
Dobrovolny, Ardis	Color Theory Applied	Hw	2	4		Se 81	33
Dobrovolny, Ardis	Paisley-Inspired	Hw	5	5		N/D 84	67
Dobrovolny, Ardis	Table Turned, The (error-corrected Hw v5 n3 84 p92)	Hw	5	1		J/F 84	64
Dobsevage, David	Little Blue Dress, A	TM			7	O/N 86	58
Dockstader, Frederick J.	Song of the Loom: New Traditions In Navajo Weaving, The	WJ	12	2	46	Fa 87	67
Dockstader, Frederick J.	Weaving Arts of the North American Indians	Iw	4	4		Fa 79	74
Dockstoder, F. J.	see Anton, F.	H&C	20	1		Wi 69	43
Doczi, György	Power of Limits: Proportional Harmonies in Nature, Art and Architecture, The	PWC			4	Ja 83	70
Dodd, Gerald R.	Managements Workbooks for Self-Employed People	Hw	7	1		J/F 86	18
Dodge, Doris	Weaving for the Senior Set	H&C	7	1		Wi 55	16
Dodge, Dorothy	Bauhaus Weaving	H&C	22	4		Fa 71	17
Dokka, Margaret	Demonstration Do's and Don'ts	SS&D	7	3	27	Su 76	64
Dolan, Anne	Whole Cloth	Hw	7	3		M/J 86	10
Dolbier, Mimi	see Chase, Patti	Iw	4	2		Sp 79	63
Doleman, Paul	New Way to Draft Double-Twist/Double-Turn Tablet Weaving, A	SS&D	11	4	44	Fa 80	42
Don, Sarah	Art of Shetland Lace, The	Kn	1	2	2	S-S 85	78
Don, Sarah	Fair Isle Knitting	Kn	2	1	3	F-W 85	78
Donahue, Leo O.	Encyclopedia of Batik Designs	Fa	10	4		J/A 83	50
Donahue, Patric	Fair at the Top	H&C	21	4		Fa 70	18
Donaldson, R. Alan	Obi: The Textile Art of Nishijin	AT	1			De 83	115
Donkin, R. A.	Spanish Red: an Ethnogeographical Study of Cochineal and the Opuntia Cactus	SS&D	10	3	39	Su 79	34
Donnelly, Robert	Emergence of a Specialty Wool Industry in the U.S., The	S-O	9	4		Wi 85	18
Donnelly, Robert	Superwash Wool	S-O	10	2		Su 86	49

AUTHOR	TITLE	JOUR	VOL	NO	ISS	DATE	PAGE
Donohue, Sandra	Spinning Unique and Useable Yarns	S-O	8	4		Wi 84	33
Dooling, D. M., ed.	Way of Working, A	Iw	4	3		Su 79	60
Dooling, D. M., ed.	Way of Working, A	WJ	4	1	13	Jy 79	41
Dopps, Beth R.	Versatile Vest and Matching Wrap Skirt, A	WJ	7	3	27	Wi 82	21
Doran, Pat	see Goldring, Marc	Hw	6	4		S/O 85	20
Dougherty, Robin Taylor	Appalachian Twin Bottomed Egg Basket	Hw	5	1		J/F 84	69
Dowd, Merle	How to Make More Money from Your Crafts	Iw	1	4		Su 76	29
Downer, Marion	Discovering Design	H&C	4	2		Sp 53	62
Downing, Marolyn	European Tapestry Collections: London's Victoria & Albert Museum	WJ	12	1	45	Su 87	21
Downing, Marolyn	European Textile Collections: Textile Research in Paris	WJ	11	2	42	Fa 86	53
Downs, Joseph, ed.	American Furniture, Queen Anne and Chippendale Periods in the Henry Francis du Pont Winterthur Museum	H&C	3	3		Su 52	61
Doyle, Claire	"Baskets of Akwesasne" (Exhibit)	Fa	11	1		J/F 84	77
Dozer, Iris	From the Woolcombers Bench: Cashgora	S-O	10	2		Su 86	39
Dozer, Iris	Guild Life Crisis	S-O	10	1		Sp 86	18
Dozer, Iris	Thoughts on the Certificate of Excellence in Handspinning	SS&D	17	4	68	Fa 86	67
Dozer, Iris	Wonderful Worsted	S-O	7	2		Su 83	32
Dozer, Iris L.	Wonderful Worsted	SS&D	15	3	59	Su 84	26
Dozier, Iris	Wonderful Worsted II: Alternate Methods of Woolcombing	S-O	7	4		Wi 83	21
Draheim, Teliha	Sheila O'Hara: Triangles, Squares and Other Landmarks	Iw	6	1		Wi 80	42
Drake, Elizabeth A.	Homespun Songs from Ireland's Clancy Brothers	SS&D	16	4	64	Fa 85	62
Droege, Carol	Advent Chasuble, An	SS&D	17	1	65	Wi 85	41
Drooker, P. B.	Fabric Analysis "On the Road"	CW	5	2	14	Ja 84	6
Drooker, Penelope	Certificate Success	SS&D	16	1	61	Wi 84	66
Drooker, Penelope	Chinese Brocades: Development of Supplementary Weft Patterning (error-corrected WJ v11 n4 87 p78)	WJ	11	3	43	Wi 87	47
Drooker, Penelope	COE Diary, A	SS&D	16	2	62	Sp 85	30
Drooker, Penelope	COE Retrospective	SS&D	15	4	60	Fa 84	19
Drooker, Penelope	Crate Expectations	SS&D	16	1	61	Wi 84	69
Drooker, Penelope	Designing the Line	SS&D	11	2	42	Sp 80	12
Drooker, Penelope	Hammock Making Techniques	Hw	3	5		N/D 82	12
Drooker, Penelope	Hammock Making Techniques	WJ	6	4	24	Sp 82	60
Drooker, Penelope	Lace Medley	Hw	5	3		Su 84	78
Drooker, Penelope	Navajo Inspired Rugs for Floor or Beast	Hw	6	2		M/A 85	60
Drooker, Penelope	see Andes, Ellen	WJ	4	4	16	Ap 80	26
Drooker, Penelope	Silk, the Story of a Culture	Hw	7	1		J/F 86	49
Drooker, Penelope	Woven World of Moocho Scott Salomon, The	Fa	11	5		S/O 84	22
Drooker, Penelope B.	Certificate of Excellence in Handweaving: COE Holders, The	SS&D	14	1	53	Wi 82	49
Drooker, Penelope B.	"Cocoon" Hammock	WJ	5	4	20	Sp 81	46
Drooker, Penelope B.	Embroidering with the Loom	SS&D	11	2	42	Sp 80	83
Drooker, Penelope B.	Embroidering with the Loom: Creative Combinations of Weaving and Stitchery	Iw	4	3		Su 79	65
Drooker, Penelope B.	Embroidery on the Loom	SS&D	9	3	35	Su 78	60
Drooker, Penelope B.	Hammock, The	TM			6	A/S 86	74
Drooker, Penelope B.	League of New Hampshire Craftsmen	SS&D	9	1	33	Wi 77	42
Drooker, Penelope B.	Making of a Weaver, The	SS&D	14	3	55	Su 83	28
Drooker, Penelope B.	Pick-Up Damask	SS&D	11	1	41	Wi 79	38
Drooker, Penelope B.	Samplers You Can Use	Fa	13	2		M/A 86	41
Drooker, Penelope B.	Tapestry and Embroidery	Iw	5	3		Su 80	37
Droop, Joan	Rugmaking	H&C	23	1		J/F 72	33
Drouillard, Judith	Weaver, The	Hw	5	5		N/D 84	10
Drower, Sara	Inside the Hangchow Brocade Factory: The Art and Craft of Mass Production	Fa	6	1		J/F 79	78
Druding, Susan	see Amos, Alden	Iw	4	1		Wi 78	54

AUTHOR	TITLE	JOUR	VOL	NO	ISS	DATE	PAGE
Drysdale, Rosemary	Lace Collar	Kn	3	4	8	Fa 87	48
Drysdale, Rosemary	see Diven, Gail	Kn	2	2	4	S-S 86	50
Drysdale, Rosemary; Gail Diven	Beaded Sweater	Kn	2	2	4	S-S 86	50
du Halde, Pere Jean-Baptiste	Cotton and Silk Making in Manchu China	Iw	6	1		Wi 80	70
DuBoff, Leonard D.	Business Forms and Contracts (in Plain English) for Craftspeople	Hw	8	4		S/O 87	14
DuBoff, Leonard D.	Business Forms and Contracts (In Plain English) for Craftspeople	WJ	11	4	44	Sp 87	74
DuBoff, Leonard D.	Law (In Plain English) for Craftspeople, The	WJ	9	3	35	Wi 85	84
DuBoff, Leonard D.	The Law (In Plain English) for Craftspeople	Hw	6	2		M/A 85	71
DuBoff, Leonard D.; Michael Scott, ed.	Law (In Plain English) for Craftspeople, The	Fa	12	2		M/A 85	54
DuBois, Emily	Banares Brocade	AT	3			My 85	209
Duchemin, Mad	Hand Weaving	Iw	1	2		Wi 76	28
Duchemin, Mad	Hand Weaving: An Introduction to Weaving on 2, 3 And 4 Harnesses	SS&D	7	4	28	Fa 76	66
Duchemin, Mad	Handweaving, An Introduction to Weaving on 2, 3, 4 Harnesses	Fa	3	1		J/F 76	6
Dudley, Barbara	Warp Pattern Weaves	H&C	17	4		Fa 66	30
Duffy, Helen	Dorothy Caldwell: Interacting with Image and Material	Fa	13	6		N/D 86	22
Duffy, Helen	"Third Montreal Tapestry Biennial, 1984" (Exhibit)	Fa	12	3		M/J 85	79
Duffy, Joe	Warping It Up with Andrea	SS&D	17	1	65	Wi 85	49
Dugan, Judy	Crazy Gloves	S-O	6	4		82	61
Duncan, Ida Riley	Knit to Fit — A Comprehensive Guide to Hand and Machine Knitting	H&C	14	3		Su 63	44
Duncan, Molly	Creative Crafts with Wool and Flax	SS&D	3	1	9	Wi 71	38
Duncan, Molly	Maori and Pakeha of New Zealand Use Wool and Phormium Tenax	SS&D	5	1	17	Wi 73	65
Duncan, Molly	Spin, Dye and Weave Your Own Wool	H&C	24	3		M/J 73	6
Duncan, Molly	Spin, Dye & Weave Your Own Wool	SS&D	4	3	15	Su 73	53
Duncan, Molly	Spin Your Own Wool	H&C	19	4		Fa 68	41
Duncan, Molly	Spin Your Own Wool	H&C	23	3		M/J 72	27
Duncan, Molly	Spinners & Weavers in New Zealand Use Native Materials	H&C	21	1		Wi 70	14
Duncan, Nadine	Jacket in Horizontal Cord Weave, A	PWC			2	Ap 82	59
Dunham, Miriam	Mattor (error-corrected WJ v2 n1 77 insert for vol. 1)	WJ	1	4	4	Ap 77	21
Dunn, Katherine	Jane Rake's Crochet	Fa	6	3		M/J 79	62
Dunn, Roger T.	Ikats of Joan Hausrath: A Painterly Approach to Weaving, The	Fa	8	6		N/D 81	48
Dunnewold, Jane	Further Thoughts on "The Artist & The Quilt"	Fa	11	2		M/A 84	56
Dunnewold, Jane	Jane Dunnewold	Fa	14	3		M/J 87	23
Dunnewold, Jane	"Silken Threads and Silent Needles" (Exhibit)	Fa	11	6		N/D 84	78
Dunnewold, Jane	Wearables in the Market Place: Reporting on a Survey	Fa	12	3		M/J 85	48
Dunwell, Anna	Being Professional	Fa	10	4		J/A 83	40
Dunwell, Anna	Sue Lawty: Journeying in Tapestry	Fa	11	2		M/A 84	12
Dunwell, Anna	"Theo Moorman: Experiments in Weaving" (Exhibit)	Fa	9	5		S/O 82	80
Dunwell, Anna	Thinking About the Business of Art	Fa	11	2		M/A 84	57
Dunwell, Anna	Tromping Through the Ages	Fa	9	2		M/A 82	26
Dupire, Jean	Weaving for Recreation	H&C	8	4		Fa 57	43
DuPuy, Edward L.	Artisans of the Appalachians	H&C	19	1		Wi 68	43
Durand, Dianne	Complete Book of Smocking	Hw	4	1		J/F 83	18
Duroy, Marie-Pierre	Drawn Threadwork	TM			8	D/J 86	41
Durr, Judy	Yosemite Dress Inspired by Snow and Sugar Pines	SS&D	5	3	19	Su 74	20
Durstan, Linda Moore	Interview with Chris O'Connell, An	Hw	6	1		J/F 85	76
Durston, Linda Moore	Complementary Crochet	SS&D	15	1	57	Wi 83	68
Durston, Linda Moore	Moorman Inspired Clothing	SS&D	14	1	53	Wi 82	35
Dusenbury, Mary	Kasuri: A Japanese Textile	TMJ	17			78	41
Dusenbury, Mary	Tree-Bast Fiber Textiles of Japan	S-O	10	3		Fa 86	35
Dwyer, Peggy	see Berent, Mary	S-O	11	1		Sp 87	21
Dyer, Anne	Dyes from Natural Sources	SS&D	8	3	31	Su 77	63

AUTHOR	TITLE	JOUR	VOL	NO	ISS	DATE	PAGE
Dyer, Carol	"Turkmen: Tribal Carpets and Traditions" (Exhibit)	Fa	8	3		M/J 81	70
Dyer, Carol; Carel Bertram	Kaleidoscopic Tour of Turkey, A	Fa	7	5		S/O 80	48
Dyer, Carolyn	"Art and Romance of Peasant Clothing, The" (Exhibit)	Fa	5	3		M/J 78	16
Dyer, Carolyn	"Arts of Ghana" (Exhibit)	Fa	5	1		J/F 78	19
Dyer, Carolyn	"Arts of Indian Asia: The Joy of Artistic Expression, The" (Exhibit)	Fa	5	5		S/O 78	64
Dyer, Carolyn	"California Women in Crafts" (Exhibit)	Fa	4	2		M/A 77	10
Dyer, Carolyn	Corporate Collecting "Contemporary Tapestries" (Exhibit)	Fa	4	5		S/O 77	16
Dyer, Carolyn	Crafts, Wine Gardens and World Friendship	Fa	8	2		M/A 81	24
Dyer, Carolyn	"Dorte Christjansen" (Exhibit)	Fa	6	2		M/A 79	62
Dyer, Carolyn	"Dowries from Kutch: A Women's Folk Art Tradition in India" (Exhibit)	Fa	7	1		J/F 80	70
Dyer, Carolyn	"Dyer's Art: Ikat, Batik, Plangi, The" (Exhibit)	Fa	5	4		J/A 78	11
Dyer, Carolyn	Ethnic Textile Art at U.C.L.A. — "Afro-American Arts of the Suriname Rain Forest" (Exhibit)	Fa	8	2		M/A 81	59
Dyer, Carolyn	Ethnic Textile Art at U.C.L.A. — "Yer Dailege: Kuna Women's Art" (Exhibit)	Fa	8	2		M/A 81	59
Dyer, Carolyn	"Fabled Fabrics: Bolivian Fabrics from the Hill Collection" (Exhibit)	Fa	9	6		N/D 82	84
Dyer, Carolyn	"Fantasy Clothes/Fantastic Costumes" (Exhibit)	Fa	4	2		M/A 77	11
Dyer, Carolyn	"Fiber Departures" (Exhibit)	Fa	4	3		M/J 77	9
Dyer, Carolyn	"Fiber Structure National" (Exhibit)	Fa	8	5		S/O 81	75
Dyer, Carolyn	"Grass" (Exhibit)	Fa	4	1		J/F 77	5
Dyer, Carolyn	"Indonesia: The Fabled Islands of Spice" (Exhibit)	Fa	6	2		M/A 79	71
Dyer, Carolyn	"Jarmila Machova: Fibers" (Exhibit)	Fa	9	1		J/F 82	75
Dyer, Carolyn	Katherine Howe "Color Card Series" Woven Paintings (Exhibit)	Fa	7	4		J/A 80	72
Dyer, Carolyn	"Left on the Loom" (Exhibit)	Fa	5	2		M/A 78	16
Dyer, Carolyn	"Leroy Wilce: Adobe Walls" (Exhibit)	Fa	4	4		J/A 77	17
Dyer, Carolyn	"Loom, the Needle, and the Dye Pot, The" (Exhibit)	Fa	5	1		J/F 78	20
Dyer, Carolyn	"Marika Contompasis: Pedestal and Wall Pieces" (Exhibits)	Fa	9	4		J/A 82	73
Dyer, Carolyn	"Patterns of Paradise: Tapa Cloth" (Exhibit)	Fa	10	3		M/J 83	73
Dyer, Carolyn	"Patterns" with a Look at Japanese Printing with Stencils (Exhibit)	Fa	4	5		S/O 77	10
Dyer, Carolyn	"People and Art of the Philippines, The" (Exhibit)	Fa	9	3		M/J 82	84
Dyer, Carolyn	"Renaissance Costume and Textiles: 1450–1620" (Exhibit)	Fa	6	6		N/D 79	70
Dyer, Carolyn	Robes for Inspiration	Fa	10	1		J/F 83	60
Dyer, Carolyn	"Romanian Folk Textiles" (Exhibit)	Fa	5	3		M/J 78	11
Dyer, Carolyn	"Salute to California: Fifty Years of Fashion, 1930–1980" (Exhibit)	Fa	8	1		J/F 81	95
Dyer, Carolyn	Small Endearments: 19th Century Quilts for Children and Dolls	Fa	8	3		M/J 81	18
Dyer, Carolyn	"Southern California Designer Crafts" (Exhibit)	Fa	5	2		M/A 78	14
Dyer, Carolyn	"Textile Traditions of Indonesia" (Exhibit)	Fa	5	1		J/F 78	15
Dyer, Carolyn	Tracing the Silk Road	Fa	13	1		J/F 86	22
Dyer, Carolyn	"Traditional Japanese Designs: The Tom and Frances Blakemore Collection of Textiles Stencils and Costumes" (Exhibit)	Fa	7	3		M/J 80	81
Dyer, Carolyn	"Transformation: UCLA Alumnae in Fiber" (Exhibit)	Fa	6	4		J/A 79	67
Dyer, Carolyn	"Wearable Folk Art" (Exhibit)	Fa	6	3		M/J 79	82
Dyer, Carolyn Price	"Art of African Masquerade, The" (Exhibit)	Fa	13	3		M/J 86	56
Dyer, Carolyn Price	"At the Edge of Asia: Five Centuries of Turkish Textiles" (Exhibit)	Fa	10	4		J/A 83	65
Dyer, Carolyn Price	"Elegant Art: Fantasy and Fashion in the Eighteenth Century, An" (Exhibit)	Fa	10	4		J/A 83	66
Dyer, Carolyn Price	"Heads and Tales: Traditional Art of Borneo" (Exhibit)	Fa	11	4		J/A 84	74
Dyer, Carolyn Price	Historic Persian Handiwork at the Textile Museum (Exhibit)	Fa	14	5		N/D 87	42
Dyer, Carolyn Price	International Carpet Extravaganza	Fa	14	1		J/F 87	52
Dyer, Carolyn Price	London Carpeted in Oriental Gardens: The 4th International Conference on Oriental Carpets	Fa	11	3		M/J 84	66
Dyett, Linda	All About Knitting Needles	TM			4	A/M 86	30
Dyett, Linda	Beyond Quilting	TM			5	J/J 86	70
Dyett, Linda	Color Forecasting	TM			3	F/M 86	22

AUTHOR	TITLE	JOUR	VOL	NO	ISS	DATE	PAGE
Dyett, Linda	Knitting Odyssey, A	TM		13		O/N 87	48
Dyett, Linda	Knitting with Cotton: Stitch Maneuvers Help Sweaters Stay in Shape	TM		9		F/M 87	38
Dyett, Linda	Not Necessarily Seventh Ave.	TM		6		A/S 86	28
Dyson, Anthony	see Ash, Beryl	SS&D	5	1	17	Wi 73	77
Dzervitis, Aleksandra; Lilija Treimanis	Latviesu Jostas (Latvian Sashes, Belts and Bands)	SS&D	14	1	53	Wi 82	65
Dzervitis, Aleksandra; Lilija Treimanis	Latviesu Jostas/Latvian Sashes, Belts and Bands	Hw	4	3		M/J 83	12
Dzevitis, Alexandra; Lilija Treimanis	Latvian Sashes, Belts And Bands	WJ	7	3	27	Wi 82	49
D'Ambrosio, Gina	Afghan and Pillow Set	S-O	11	2		Su 87	14
D'Ambrosio, Gina	Random Warp Dyeing: A Spontaneous Steam Dye Process	WJ	10	3	39	Wi 86	42
D'Ambrosio, Gina	Warped-Faced Ruana	S-O	10	2		Su 86	17
D'Andrea, Pat	Ramah Navajo Weavers, The	WJ	12	1	45	Su 87	44
D'Andrea, Patricia A.	Donna Martin: The Influence of the Southwest	Fa	14	5		N/D 87	18
d'Avila, Doris	Spinning Novelty Yarns	Iw	4	4		Fa 79	58
d'Avilla, Doris	Variations on a Poncho Theme	WJ	2	3	7	Ja 78	30
D'Harcourt, Raoul	Textiles of Ancient Peru and Their Techniques	SS&D	5	4	20	Fa 74	66
D'Harcourt, Raoul	Textiles of Ancient Peru and Their Techniques	H&C	14	1		Wi 63	43
Eades, B. G.	Painted Warps	H&C	15	4		Fa 64	43
Eagle, Elsie	Dazzling Designs	SS&D	15	1	57	Wi 83	19
Earnshaw, Pat	Bobbin and Needle Laces: Identification and Care	SS&D	17	1	65	Wi 85	90
Earth Guild	Hammocks	SS&D	14	3	55	Su 83	24
Eastlake, Sandy	Shaker Towels: A Guild Devotes a Year of Study to Nineteenth Century Textiles (error-corrected WJ v11 n2 86 p68)	WJ	10	4	40	Sp 86	20
Eaton, Allen	Beauty Behind Barbed Wire	H&C	3	2		Sp 52	62
Eaton, Allen H.	Handicrafts of New England	H&C	1	1		Ap 50	52
Eberhardt, Margaret	Use of Native Craft Materials	H&C	4	2		Sp 53	63
Edberg, Ragnar	see Hoppe, Elisabeth	SS&D	7	3	27	Su 76	34
Edberg, Ragnar	see Hoppe, Elizabeth	Iw	2	1		Fa 76	33
Edelstein, Sidney M.; Hector C. Borghetty, translators	Plictho of Gioanventura Rosetti, The	SS&D	3	4	12	Fa 72	47
Edgerton, Kate	Buying an Old Spinning Wheel	SS&D	1	1	1	De 69	10
Edgerton, Kate	Reconditioning Wheels	SS&D	1	3	3	Ju 70	19
Edgerton, Kate	Simple Repairs on a Saxony	SS&D	1	2	2	Mr 70	20
Edgren, Esther	"How is Cloth Made?"	SS&D	1	2	2	Mr 70	15
Editors of American Fabrics Magazine	Encyclopedia of Textiles	H&C	12	2		Sp 61	59
Editors of Echo Books	see Chen, Lydia	WJ	8	1	29	Su 83	53
Editors of Fiberarts Magazine	Fiberarts Design Book, The	WJ	6	2	22	Fa 81	40
Editors of House and Garden	House and Garden Complete Guide to Interior Decoration, Fifth Edition	H&C	5	1		Wi 53	59
Editors Of Sunset Magazine	Weaving Techniques and Projects	SS&D	6	3	23	Su 75	49
Edman, Larry E.	Quadruple Cloth, A Gauze Application	PWC		2		Ap 82	72
Edson, Julie Green	Timeless Togs for Tiny Tots	Hw	3	2		Mr 82	54
Edson, Nicki Hitz; Arlene Stimmel	Creative Crochet	Fa	5	3		M/J 78	59
Edson, Nicki Hitz; Arlene Stimmel	Creative Crochet	TM		4		A/M 86	74
Edwards, Jack	Spanish Colonial Loom: A Contemporary Loom-Maker Uses Traditional Tools to Construct a Replica for the Albuquerque Museum	WJ	11	1	41	Su 86	16
Edwards, Joyce	Letting Knitting Happen	TM		10		A/M 87	86
Edwards, Lois	Guilds Aid Disabled, Aged with Weaving Lessons and Projects	SS&D	5	1	17	Wi 73	5
Egee, Dale	Promotional Methods	SS&D	15	2	58	Sp 84	4
Egen, Su	Finnish Lace: A Leno Variation	Hw	7	2		M/A 86	49
Eggers, Conni	Ecclesiastical Fiber	Fa	4	6		N/D 77	36
Eggleston, Phyllis	Chilkat Blanket: It Soon May Be No More, The	SS&D	7	1	25	Wi 75	44

AUTHOR	TITLE	JOUR	VOL	NO	ISS	DATE	PAGE
Ehly, Jean	Truchas Becomes a Weaving Center	H&C	24	4		Au 73	40
Eicher, Joanne Bulolz	Nigerian Handcrafted Textiles	WJ	6	4	24	Sp 82	59
Eiland, Murray	Chinese and Exotic Rugs	Hw	3	5		N/D 82	14
Eiland, Murray	Oriental Rugs: A New Comprehensive Guide, Third Ed.	Hw	3	5		N/D 82	12
Eiland, Murray L.	Oriental Rugs, A Comprehensive Guide	TMJ	4	1		De 74	85
Einstein, Sylvia	"Beyond the Fringe" (Exhibit)	Fa	7	2		M/A 80	70
Eircher, Joanne B., et al.	African Dress II	WJ	11	3	43	Wi 87	64
Eisema, Alberta; Nicole Eisema	Gift from a Sheep	Iw	5	1		Wi 79	65
Eisema, Nicole	see Eisema, Alberta	Iw	5	1		Wi 79	65
Eiseman, Alberta; Nicole Eiseman	Gift from a Sheep: The Story Of How Wool Is Made	SS&D	12	1	45	Wi 80	83
Eiseman, Nicole	see Eiseman, Alberta	SS&D	12	1	45	Wi 80	83
Eisman, Leatrice	Alive with Color	Kn	2	1	3	F-W 85	73
Ekert, Marianne	Handmade Felt	Hw	6	3		Su 85	20
Ekert, Marianne	Handmade Felt	WJ	10	2	38	Fa 85	82
Ekstrom, Brenda	Peruvian Hat	S-O	4			80	59
Ekstrom, Brenda	So You Want to Buy Some Sheep	S-O	4			80	34
Ekstrom, Brenda	Spinning in the Grease	S-O	3			79	50
El-Homossani, Dr. M. M.	MasterWeaver Loom: A New Concept in Hand-Weaving, The	WJ	8	4	32	Sp 84	54
El-Homossani, M. M.	Double-Harness Techniques Employed in Egypt	AT	3			My 85	229
El-Homossani, M. M.	Qotny & Alaga: Traditional Striped Fabrics for the Middle Eastern Kaftan	WJ	10	1	37	Su 85	33
El-Homossani, M. M.	The Original Fabrics of Kaftan	AT	1			De 83	263
Elalouf, Sion	Knitting Architect, The	TM			12	A/S 87	76
Elam, E. T.	From the Weaver's Bench	H&C	23	4		J/A 72	33
Elam, E. T.	From the Weaver's Bench: Full Width Projects	H&C	23	5		S/O 72	30
Elder, Shirley	Weaving Together: The Ayottes of Center Sandwich, New Hampshire (Error-corrected WJ v11 n3 87 p78)	WJ	11	2	42	Fa 86	30
Eldridge, Lois A.	Go For It!	S-O	7	4		Wi 83	45
Eldridge, Lois A.	Three Big T's	S-O	8	2		Su 84	40
Elich-McCall, Charoltte	How to Weave a Plaid Triangular Shawl	Hw	4	5		N/D 83	54
Elkins, Arthur	Retailer's Rationale	SS&D	13	4	52	Fa 82	27
Elkins, Barbara	Hands On	Kn	3	4	8	Fa 87	46
Elkins, Barbara	Weighty Matters	Kn	3	4	8	Fa 87	46
Elkins, Barbara	Yarns	Kn	1	1	1	F-W 84 CI	52 42
Ellington, Duke	"Mood Indigo"	Fa	13	5		S/O 86	75
Elliott, Blanche E.	Northwest Arkansas Guild	H&C	7	1		Wi 55	50
Elliott, Douglas B.	Contemporary Uses for an Ancient Fiber: Spanish Moss	SS&D	9	2	34	Sp 78	51
Elliott, Lillian	Almost Roman Glass	Fa	10	6		N/D 83	20
Elliott, Malinda	Exploring a Tradition: Navajo Rugs, Classic and Contemporary	Fa	11	3		M/J 84	32
Elliott, Malinda	In the Spirit of the Navajo	SS&D	13	1	49	Wi 81	18
Elliott, Malinda	Jill Lindgren: Costuming for Opera	Fa	11	5		S/O 84	62
Elliott, Malinda	Knitted Whimsey of Astrid Furnival, The	Fa	12	2		M/A 85	16
Elliott, Malinda	Noël Bennett: The Delicate Art of Restoration	Fa	9	1		J/F 82	44
Elliott, Malinda	Santa Fe Weaving Center, The	Fa	9	5		S/O 82	32
Elliott, Malinda	Tapestries of Nancy and Janusz Kozikowski, The	Fa	13	2		M/A 86	23
Elliott, Malinda	Textile Trends: Collecting in the Southwest	Fa	12	6		N/D 85	27
Elliott, Malinda, ed.	see Fisher, Nora, ed.	WJ	9	2	34	Fa 84	78
Elliott, Sally	Resemblance to Afghans; Crochet Rubbings?, A	Fa	8	3		M/J 81	48
Elliott, Verda	Seventeen Pattern Types, A Study of Repeat Patterns in Two Dimensions	CW		25		Se 87	23
Ellis, Betty	"Pat Rutledge: Batiks" (Exhibit)	Fa	9	1		J/F 82	77
Ellis, Charles Grant	Carpet Collections of the Philadelphia Museum of Art	TMJ	17			78	29

AUTHOR	TITLE	JOUR	VOL	NO	ISS	DATE	PAGE
Ellis, Charles Grant	Chinese Rugs	TMJ	2	3		De 68	35
Ellis, Charles Grant	Gifts from Kashan to Cairo	TMJ	1	1		No 62	33
Ellis, Charles Grant	Is the Mamluk Carpet a Mandala? A Speculation	TMJ	4	1		De 74	30
Ellis, Charles Grant	Kirman's Heritage in Washington: Vase Rugs in the Textile Museum	TMJ	2	3		De 68	17
Ellis, Charles Grant	Little Gems of Ardebil, The	TMJ	1	3		De 64	18
Ellis, Charles Grant	Mysteries of the Misplaced Mamluks	TMJ	2	2		De 67	2
Ellis, Charles Grant	Ottoman Prayer Rugs, The	TMJ	2	4		De 69	5
Ellis, Charles Grant	Some Compartment Designs for Carpets, and Herat	TMJ	1	4		De 65	42
Ellis, Charles Grant	Soumak-Woven Rug in a 15th Century International Sytle, A	TMJ	1	2		De 63	3
Ellis, Charles Grant	Strengths of The Textile Museum's Oriental Carpet Collection, The	TMJ	24			85	61
Ellis, Jennie Faye	Poisonous Dye Plants	SS&D	4	2	14	Sp 73	46
Ellison, Nancy	Beginning Spinning with Minimal Equipment	S-O	4			80	37
Ellison, Nancy	Fast Knitting on Pegs	S-O	5			81	18
Ellison, Nancy	Weaving Handspun Yarn: Triangular Shawl	WJ	12	2	46	Fa 87	42
Ellison, Sue	Interweave Readers Unique, Poll Shows	Iw	4	3		Su 79	8
Ellman, Norma	Heirloom Wedding Dress	Kn	3	2	6	Sp 87	31
Ellman, Norma	Sachets	Kn	3	2	6	Sp 87	32
Ellman, Norma	Windowpane Jacket: In Double Knit and Garter Stitch	Kn	3	4	8	Fa 87	40
Ellsworth, Wendy	Beading on Leather	TM			7	O/N 86	50
Elvehjem Art Center, University Of Wisconsin	American Coverlets	SS&D	6	2	22	Sp 75	63
Emerick, Patricia	Super Soft Sweater	S-O	11	1		Sp 87	16
Emerick, Patricia	Vest with a Hidden Twist	S-O	11	4		Wi 87	36, I-46
Emerson, Margaret	see Bliss, Anne	Iw	3	3		Sp 78	34
Emerson, Rebecca	Leaves and Trellises	Kn	1	2	2	S-S 85	48, 72B
Emerson, Trudy	Handbags of Leather and Fabric	H&C	17	2		Sp 66	22
Emery, Irene	Primary Structures of Fabrics — An Illustrated Classification, The	H&C	17	3		Su 66	43
Enciso, Jorge	Design Motifs of Ancient Mexico	H&C	5	1		Wi 53	61
Endres, Linda Carollo	From a Family Album	Fa	7	3		M/J 80	70
English, Trudy	Smocking	SS&D	14	1	53	Wi 82	38
Enright, Elizabeth	Tatsinda	Iw	2	1		Fa 76	32
Enthoven, Jacqueline	Stitches of Creative Embroidery, The	H&C	15	4		Fa 64	44
Entner, Betty C.	Good Leadership Is Prerequisite for Good Workshop	SS&D	5	4	20	Fa 74	37
Epskamp, Sally	Spinning at the Smithsonian	S-O	5			81	35
Epstein, Ann S.	Ann S. Epstein	Fa	13	1		J/F 86	19
Epstein, Betty	Poncho with Fringe Benefits, A	H&C	23	1		J/F 72	28
Epstein, Diana	Buttons: Wearable Art in Miniature	Fa	12	3		M/J 85	61
Erbe, Pamela	Marie Combs: Quilted Visions of Faraway Lands	Fa	12	1		J/F 85	16
Erdmann, Kurt	Seven Hundred Years of Oriental Carpets	TMJ	3	2		De 71	42
Erf, Mary Elva	Christmas Is Coming: An Advent Calendar	SS&D	7	4	28	Fa 76	20
Erf, Mary Elva	Hands to Work and Hearts to God	WJ	8	1	29	Su 83	25
Erf, Mary Elva	Shaker Textiles at the Met	SS&D	14	1	53	Wi 82	61
Erf, Mary Elva Congleton	Nineteenth Century Miniatures	SS&D	16	1	61	Wi 84	60
Erhler, Mary	"Surface Design South Central" (Exhibit)	Fa	6	4		J/A 79	75
Erickson, Janet Doub	Traditional Rug Hooking with a Twist	TM			12	A/S 87	30
Erickson, Janet Doub	Weaving in the Desert: How Bedouin Women Make a Loom, Using Sticks and Rebars	TM			10	A/M 87	56
Erickson, Johanna	Allen Farm Sheep and Wool Company	SS&D	17	3	67	Su 86	25
Erickson, Johanna	Fiber on Martha's Vineyard	Fa	11	4		J/A 84	46
Erickson, Johanna	Julia Mitchell: On Martha's Vineyard	SS&D	15	3	59	Su 84	60
Erickson, Johanna	Nantucket Looms and Sam Kasten	SS&D	17	3	67	Su 86	70
Erickson, Johanna	Rag Rugs, Not Always Made from Rags	TM			3	F/M 86	40
Erickson, Johanna	Ragtime	SS&D	14	3	55	Su 83	41

AUTHOR	TITLE	JOUR	VOL	NO	ISS	DATE	PAGE
Erickson, Johanna	Rya Rugs	SS&D	13	3	51	Su 82	36
Erickson, Mary Anne; Eve Cohen	Knitting by Design	TM		14		D/J 87	76
Ericson, Lois	see Krevitsky, Nik	SS&D	6	3	23	Su 75	49
Ericson, Lois	Wrapping Techniques	SS&D	2	1	5	De 70	27
Ericson, Lois; Diane Ericson Frode	Design & Sew It Yourself, A Work Book for Creative Clothing	WJ	8	3	31	Wi 83	68
Ericson, Virginia D.	Your Spinning Teacher	S-O	1			77	36
Erler, Mary	Alicia Duplan: A Weaver in the Navajo Tradition	Fa	7	5		S/O 80	28
Erler, Mary	Ann Matlock	Fa	6	3		M/J 79	46
Erler, Mary	Rebecca Munro: But It Turned Out All Right	Fa	6	6		N/D 79	28
Esping, Mardel	Navajo Way, The	Iw	2	2		Wi 77	30
Essén-Hedin, Margaretha	Reinterpreting Old Weaves for Today and Tomorrow	Hw	8	3		M/J 87	40
Estes, Josephine E.	Original Miniature Patterns for Hand Weaving, Part 2	H&C	9	3		Su 58	63
Evans, Jane	Boundweave	WJ	1	4	4	Ap 77	3
Evans, Jane	Multiple Shaft Weaving: M's and O's with Two Foundation Shafts	WJ	6	1	21	Su 81	27
Evans, Jane	Reversible Jacket in Double Weave, A	WJ	3	1	9	Jy 78	23
Evans, Jane	Shadow Weave	SS&D	15	4	60	Fa 84	57
Evans, Jane A.	Rags Unlimited	Hw	2	3		My 81	44
Evans, Jane A.	Tartan or Plaid?	Hw	4	5		N/D 83	33
Evans, Jane A.	"Tied Latvian" Weave, The (error-corrected CW n25 87 p31)	CW		24		My 87	6
Evans, Jane A.	Warp Stuffer Weave with Shaft Switching Applications	Hw	4	3		M/J 83	72
Evans, Kerry	Applying the Pulled Warp Technique to Loom-Shaped Clothing	Hw	7	1		J/F 86	21
Evans, Kerry	Applying the Pulled Warp Technique to Loom-Shaped Clothing	WJ	9	2	34	Fa 84	79
Evans, Kerry	Applying the Pulled Warp Technique to Loom-Shaped Clothing	WJ	9	3	35	Wi 85	34
Evans, Kerry	Cardigan Jacket	WJ	5	3	19	Wi 81	10
Evans, Kerry	Treadled Togs	SS&D	13	3	51	Su 82	78
Evans, Kerry	Treadled Togs. A Pattern Book of Loom-Fashion Clothing	WJ	6	2	22	Fa 81	39
Evans, Kerry	Treadled Togs: A Pattern Book of Loom-Fashioned Clothing	Hw	2	5		No 81	93
Evans, Rojean; Louise Klemperer	"Crafts Northwest, Circa 1980" (Exhibit)	Fa	7	5		S/O 80	75
Everett, Marion	Fringe Using a Gold Knubby Rayon	WJ	5	2	18	Fa 80	42
Exner, Beatrice B.	Acadian Brown Cotton	H&C	11	4		Fa 60	22
Eychaner, Barbara Smith	Weaving Table Linens	TM		11		J/J 87	52
Eyerman, Linda	Chromatic Effervescence: The Hooked Surface As a Response to My Environment	Fa	10	2		M/A 83	22
Fabeck, Diane	Double & Triple Harness Double-Cloth	CW	7	3	21	My 86	7
Fabeck, Diane	Long-Eyed Heddles and Rising Shed Looms	Iw	4	4		Fa 79	28
Fabri, Ralph	Color: A Complete Guide for Artists	H&C	18	4		Fa 67	45
Fago, D'Ann Calhoun	Determination and Innovation: A Successful Weaving Mill	TM		14		D/J 87	14
Fahnestock, Ann	Early Home Textile Production in Chautauqua County, New York	S-O	6	4		82	32
Faiola, Linda	Making Pockets	TM		13		O/N 87	30
Fair, Maurine	For Good Health and Long Life	SS&D	3	1	9	Wi 71	34
Fair, Maurine	Prize-Winning Gown and Coat	SS&D	2	2	6	Sp 71	16
Fairbairn, J. E.	Romance of Harris Tweeds, The	H&C	2	3		Su 51	21
Fairbanks, Dale	On Eighteenth Century Flowered Silk Weaving as an Inspiration for Todays Complex Weavers	CW	7	1	19	Se 85	8
Fairservis, Walter A., Jr.	Research Survey on the History of Wool, A	H&C	6	3		Su 55	61
Falconer, Crisa Meahl	Knotted Sculpture of Jane Sauer, The	Fa	13	3		M/J 86	31
Fallier, Jeanne H.	Truth About American Hooking, The	TM		14		D/J 87	20
Falls, Lynne Cowe	Weaving As An Olympic Event	SS&D	19	1	73	Wi 87	10
Fanderl, Liesl	Bauerliches Stricken	Kn	1	2	2	S-S 85	79
Fanderl, Liesl	Stricken 3	Kn	1	2	2	S-S 85	79
Fanderl, Lisl	Bäuerliches Stricken 1	TM		9		F/M 87	76

AUTHOR	TITLE	JOUR	VOL	NO	ISS	DATE	PAGE
Fanderl, Lisl	Bäuerliches Stricken 2	TM			9	F/M 87	76
Fanderl, Lisl	Bäuerliches Stricken 3	TM			9	F/M 87	76
Fannin, Allen	Dialectic for Handweavers: or, on Looking Back (While Moving Forward), A	Iw	3	3		Sp 78	39
Fannin, Allen	Handspinning: Art and Technique	SS&D	2	2	6	Sp 71	34
Fannin, Allen	Handspinning: Art and Technique	H&C	23	6		N/D 72	41
Fannin, Allen	Handspinning: Art and Technique	Iw	2	3		Sp 77	31
Fannin, Allen	Handspinning: Art & Technique	H&C	22	2		Sp 71	45
Fannin, Allen	Handspinning: Art & Technique	WJ	6	4	24	Sp 82	59
Fannin, Allen	Handspinning: The Unexamined Life	S-O	10	2		Su 86	35
Fannin, Allen	Looming Thoughts	S-O	1			77	12
Fannin, Allen	Looming Thoughts	WJ	7	1	25	Su 82	26
Fannin, Allen	Looming Thoughts	WJ	10	4	40	Sp 86	28
Fannin, Allen	Looming Thoughts	WJ	12	2	46	Fa 87	50
Fannin, Allen A.	Handloom Weaving Technology	Iw	5	1		Wi 79	58
Fannin, Allen A.	Handloom Weaving Technology	WJ	5	4	20	Sp 81	44
Fannin, Allen A.	Handloom Weaving Technology	Fa	7	6		N/D 80	65
Fannin, Allen A.	Looming Thoughts	WJ	8	3	31	Wi 83	61
Fannin, Allen A.	Looming Thoughts	WJ	9	2	34	Fa 84	22
Fannin, Allen A.	Looming Thoughts	WJ	9	4	36	Sp 85	14
Fannin, Allen A.	Looming Thoughts	WJ	10	2	38	Fa 85	14
Fannin, Allen A.	Looming Thoughts	WJ	11	2	42	Fa 86	63
Fannin, Allen A.	Looming Thoughts	WJ	11	4	44	Sp 87	7
Fannin, Allen A.	On Repairing Spinning Wheels	H&C	18	4		Fa 67	33
Fannin, Allen A.	Proper Preparation of Fibers for Spinners	H&C	20	3		Su 69	19
Fannin, Allen A.	Spinning Flax	H&C	18	2		Sp 67	21
Fannin, Allen A.	Weaving with Handspun Linen Yarn	H&C	19	2		Sp 68	10
Fannin, Allen; Dorothy Fannin	Looming Thoughts	H&C	23	3		M/J 72	12
Fannin, Allen; Dorothy Fannin	Looming Thoughts	H&C	23	4		J/A 72	3
Fannin, Allen; Dorothy Fannin	Looming Thoughts	H&C	23	5		S/O 72	5
Fannin, Allen; Dorothy Fannin	Looming Thoughts	H&C	23	6		N/D 72	37
Fannin, Allen; Dorothy Fannin	Looming Thoughts	H&C	24	1		J/F 73	13
Fannin, Allen; Dorothy Fannin	Looming Thoughts	H&C	24	2		M/A 73	17
Fannin, Allen; Dorothy Fannin	Looming Thoughts	H&C	24	3		M/J 73	17
Fannin, Allen; Dorothy Fannin	Looming Thoughts	H&C	24	4		Au 73	17
Fannin, Dorothy	see Fannin, Allen	H&C	23	3		M/J 72	12
Fannin, Dorothy	see Fannin, Allen	H&C	23	4		J/A 72	3
Fannin, Dorothy	see Fannin, Allen	H&C	23	5		S/O 72	5
Fannin, Dorothy	see Fannin, Allen	H&C	23	6		N/D 72	37
Fannin, Dorothy	see Fannin, Allen	H&C	24	1		J/F 73	13
Fannin, Dorothy	see Fannin, Allen	H&C	24	2		M/A 73	17
Fannin, Dorothy	see Fannin, Allen	H&C	24	3		M/J 73	17
Fannin, Dorothy	see Fannin, Allen	H&C	24	4		Au 73	17
Fanning, Robbie	After the Ribbon	TM			2	D/J 85	12
Fanning, Robbie	All That Glitters: Shisha by Machine	TM			1	O/N 85	63
Fanning, Robbie	Fear of Weaving	Hw	1	1		F-W 79	10
Fanning, Robbie	Latest Stuff in Sewing, The	TM			14	D/J 87	20
Fanning, Robbie	Microchips in the Sewing Room, The	TM			12	A/S 87	34

AUTHOR	TITLE	JOUR	VOL	NO	ISS	DATE	PAGE
Fanning, Robbie	Needles, Loopers, and Knives	TM			3	F/M 86	42
Fanning, Robbie	New "Trade" Shows	TM			1	O/N 85	14
Fanning, Robbie	Plastic Pattern Promises Perfect Fit, A	TM			12	A/S 87	20
Fanning, Robbie	Silicon Sewing Machine, The	TM			1	O/N 85	14
Farber, Deborah	"Becky Clark Fiber" (Exhibit)	Fa	6	1		J/F 79	89
Farley, Sidna	Gansey with Yoke	Kn	3	2	6	Sp 87	27
Farley, Sidna	Sidna's Shetland Shawl	Kn	4	1	9	Wi 87	22
Farley, Sidna	Summer Lace Sweater	Kn	1	2	2	S-S 85	32, 72A
Fassett, Kaffe	Glorious Knits	Kn	2	2	4	S-S 86	78
Fassett, Kaffe	Glorious Knits	Hw	7	2		M/A 86	88
Fassett, Kaffe	Glorious Knits: Thirty-Five Designs for Sweaters, Dresses, Vests, and Shawls	SS&D	17	3	67	Su 86	85
Fassett, Kaffe	Knitting with Colors	TM			3	F/M 86	68
Fauske, Carla	Carla's Zebra Top	PWC			2	Ap 82	88
Fauske, Carla	Lace Trilogy	PWC			6	Su 83	52
Fauske, Carla	Lampshade Transfigured, A	PWC	1	1		No 81	55
Fauske, Clara	Bogs	PWC			3	Oc 82	39
Faust, Regine	Argyle: The Transformation of a Classical Pattern Through the Design Process	Fa	9	4		J/A 82	24
Fawkes, Judith Poxson	In Production? Rug Weaving	Iw	5	1		Wi 79	36
Fedders, Pat	Crocheted Cream Puffs? What You See Is not What You Get	Fa	8	5		S/O 81	16
Fedders, Pat	Dorothy Gill Barnes: Baskets from a Gathered Harvest	Fa	11	1		J/F 84	24
Fedders, Pat	"Fiber Techniques: The Weaver's Guild of Greater Cincinnati" (Exhibit)	Fa	8	1		J/F 81	91
Fee, Jacqueline	Sweater Workshop, The	Hw	4	3		M/J 83	13
Fee, Jacqueline	Sweater Workshop, The	WJ	8	2	30	Fa 83	62
Fee, Jacqueline	Sweater Workshop, The	TM			12	A/S 87	76
Feeley, Helen	Complete Book of Rug Braiding, The	H&C	9	2		Sp 58	53
Feinberg, Wilburt	see Dayan, Ruth	SS&D	6	2	22	Sp 75	63
Feldman, Annette	Fun with Felt	WJ	6	2	22	Fa 81	40
Feldman, Betty Suter	Lace and Lectures	TM			10	A/M 87	20
Feldman-Wood, Florence	Australian Cashmere and Cashgora	S-O	9	1		Sp 85	42
Feldman-Wood, Florence	First International Cashmere Seminar	S-O	10	1		Sp 86	39
Feldman-Wood, Florence	Spinning Australian Cashmere and Cashgora	S-O	9	4		Wi 85	40
Feldman-Wood, Florence	Spinning for a Finished Product Competition	S-O	7	4		Wi 83	30
Femenias, Blenda	Color and Design in Andean Warp-Faced Fabrics	WJ	12	2	46	Fa 87	44
Fenner, Mary Sue	Jacket of Handspun Samples, A	Hw	5	1		J/F 84	74
Fenner, Monica	Growing Silkworms at Home	SS&D	9	3	35	Su 78	100
Fenner, Monnie	Keeping Silkworms: The Art of Sericulture	S-O	8	1		Sp 84	28
Fenner, Monnie	Keeping Silkworms: The Art of Sericulture	S-O	8	2		Su 84	29
Ferguson, Sue	see McCarthy, Judy	SS&D	4	4	16	Fa 73	54
Ferguson, Tom	"Local Options: The Work of Laura Strand Mills and Jo Peterson" (Exhibit)	Fa	10	3		M/J 83	69
Field, Anne	Ashford Book of Spinning, The	Hw	8	3		M/J 87	15
Field, Anne	Ashford Book of Spinning, The	WJ	12	2	46	Fa 87	65
Field, Anne	Ashford Book of Spinning, The	SS&D	18	4	72	Fa 87	56
Fieldman, M. Lucille	Jumpsuits, Anyone?	SS&D	7	3	27	Su 76	60
Fife, Lin	Controlled Chaos: The Floorcloths of Carmon Slater	Fa	12	5		S/O 85	16
Fife, Lin	Lin Fife: Products of Passion (error-corrected Fa v12 n1 85 p24)	Fa	11	5		S/O 84	12
Fife, Lin	Martha Mahon: Tableaux	Fa	13	6		N/D 86	29
Fife, Lin	Pikes Peak Weavers Guild First Fibre Arts Festival (Exhibit)	Fa	3	5		S/O 76	6
Fife, Lin	Pioneer Paper Places: Pyramid Prints and Paperworks	Fa	13	4		J/A 86	24
Fife, Lin	Visit to Peru	Fa	9	6		N/D 82	60
Filson, Alice	Your Ski Jumper	SS&D	2	3	7	Su 71	19

AUTHOR	TITLE	JOUR	VOL	NO	ISS	DATE	PAGE
Finch, Joan Freitag	Rags At Work	SS&D	16	4	64	Fa 85	72
Finch, Karen; Greta Putnam	Care & Preservation of Textiles, The	Hw	7	3		M/J 86	14
Finch, Karen, O.B.E.; Greta Putman	Caring for Textiles	SS&D	9	2	34	Sp 78	49
Finch-Hurley, Jerri	Jerri Finch-Hurley	Fa	13	1		J/F 86	18
Finkel, Marilyn	"Anne Wilson: Grid Constructions" (Exhibit)	Fa	6	2		M/A 79	65
Finnish Consulate General of New York	Finland's Rya Rugs	SS&D	13	4	52	Fa 82	54
Finucane, Brigid	"Barbara Shawcroft: Nets, Rope, and Cloth" (Exhibit)	Fa	12	4		J/A 85	68
Fisch, Arline M.	Arline M. Fisch	Fa	13	1		J/F 86	18
Fisch, Arline M.	Textile Techniques in Metal for Jewelers, Sculptors, and Textile Artists	SS&D	7	3	27	Su 76	34
Fisch, Arline M.	Textile Techniques in Metal for Jewelers, Sculptors and Textile Artists	Fa	5	4		J/A 78	59
Fischer, Ernst; Gertrud Ingers	Flamskvavnad — Flemish Weaving	H&C	12	3		Su 61	61
Fishback, John S.	Huck Lace Tray Cloth	H&C	11	2		Sp 60	62
Fishback, John S.	Sixteen-Harness Design for Draperies, A	H&C	11	1		Wi 60	24
Fisher, Abby Sue	Clothing Change Through Contact: Traditional Guatemalan Dress	WJ	10	3	39	Wi 86	60
Fisher, Judy, ed.	Angora Handbook	S-O	11	2		Su 87	12
Fisher, Nora; Malinda Elliott, eds.	Beyond Boundaries: Highland Maya Dress at the Museum of International Folk Art	WJ	9	2	34	Fa 84	78
Fisher, Pat	Rug Weaving with Natural Dyed Yarns	SS&D	2	2	6	Sp 71	28
Fitch, Betsy	Floppy Dolls (error-corrected SS&D v9 n2 78 p70)	SS&D	9	1	33	Wi 77	22
Fitch, Marjorie	Belts Are Interesting Projects	H&C	4	4		Fa 53	14
Fitch, Marjorie	Lighter Weight Wool Scarf	H&C	11	3		Su 60	22
Fitt, Cate	Improvs on Silk: The Fabric Painting of Susan Daniel	Fa	8	5		S/O 81	45
Fitt, Cate	It's Like a Hobby	Fa	8	2		M/A 81	38
Fitt, Cate	"Michelle Morris: Tapestries and Related Work" (Exhibit)	Fa	7	4		J/A 80	65
Fitzgerald, Jeanne	Design Courses Precede Weaving at the University of Kansas	H&C	4	2		Sp 53	34
Flaherty, Patricia	see Cabrera, Roberto	TM			7	O/N 86	72
Flanagan, Jane	Action in Appalachia: A Community Craft Center Bustles	SS&D	7	3	27	Su 76	96
Flanagan, Jeanne	"Constance Dodge: Mind Feelings" (Exhibit)	Fa	9	3		M/J 82	82
Flanders, John	Craftsman's Way, Canadian Expressions, The	Hw	3	4		Se 82	16
Fleet, Malcolm	Selecting Wool for Handspinning (error-corrected SS&D v13 n1 81 p4)	SS&D	12	4	48	Fa 81	66
Fleischer, Helen	Shepherd's Dancing Coat	S-O	11	1		Sp 87	17
Fleming, Barbara	Guide to Raising Silk, A	Iw	3	1		Fa 77	34
Fleming, Ray Frost	Profile: Robert L. Kidd	H&C	23	5		S/O 72	9
Flemming, Ernst	see Jaques, Renate	H&C	9	3		Su 58	60
Fletcher, Joyce	Pick-Up Piqué (error-corrected SS&D v19 n1 87 p33)	SS&D	18	4	72	Fa 87	60
Florentine, Gemma	Spindle and Distaff	TM			2	D/J 85	33
Florisoone, Michel	see Verlet, Pierre	SS&D	10	2	38	Sp 79	73
Florisoone, Michel	see Verlet, Pierre	Iw	4	4		Fa 79	72
Flugg, Barbara Gentry	Summer/Winter	Iw	2	1		Fa 76	12
Foale, Marion	Marion Foale's Classic Knitwear	Kn	3	4	8	Fa 87	62
Foeley, Cora V.	Bags with Strong Handles	H&C	16	2		Sp 65	33
Foeley, Cora V.	Woven Rag Doll, A	H&C	17	3		Su 66	17
Fohn-Hansen, Lydia	Weaving in Alaska	H&C	4	3		Su 53	27
Foley, D. J.	see Lord, P. S.	H&C	22	1		Wi 71	41
Folts, Teresa	Inkle Path to Weaving, The	WJ	2	3	7	Ja 78	34
Folts, Teressa	Inkle Path to Weaving, The	SS&D	9	3	35	Su 78	94
Folts, Teressa; David Mathieson	Warping the Loom Alone	H&C	24	2		M/A 73	5
Ford, Alice	Pictorial Folk Art	H&C	4	3		Su 53	62
Ford, Howard C.	Cheju Weavers, A New Industry Arises on a Korean Island	H&C	12	3		Su 61	11
Ford, Howard C.	Green Baize for Independence Hall from Penland Looms	H&C	7	2		Sp 56	14

AUTHOR	TITLE	JOUR	VOL	NO	ISS	DATE	PAGE
Ford, Toni	Common Denominator of the Handicrafts, The	H&C	3	1		Wi 51	23
Ford, Toni	Handweaving in the South Today	H&C	1	1		Ap 50	14
Ford, Toni	Preparing Plant Fibers for Handweaving	H&C	2	1		Wi 50	10
Forel, Auguste	Ants Weave, Too	Iw	2	4		Su 77	15
Forelli, Sally; Jeanette Harries	Traditional Berber Weaving in Central Morocco	TMJ	4	4		77	41
Forman, B.	see Wassef, Ramses Wissa	H&C	14	4		Fa 63	43
Forman, W.	see Wassef, Ramses Wissa	H&C	14	4		Fa 63	43
Forscey, Suzon	Fabulous Plumage of Mae Augarten, The	Fa	6	3		M/J 79	65
Foster, Ann	Kudzu	S-O	3			79	23
Foster, Frances A.	Four-Harness Damask	H&C	9	1		Wi 57	23
Foster, Robert	Manipulated Warps or Having Fun with Controlled Distortion	H&C	16	2		Sp 65	12
Foster, Vanda	Bags and Purses	WJ	9	1	33	Su 84	61
Fougner, Dave	Manly Art of Knitting, The	Fa	5	3		M/J 78	59
Fournier, Jane	Handspun into Lace	SS&D	17	4	68	Fa 86	70
Fowler, Mary Jean	Cindy Hickok: Stuffed Characters	Fa	5	5		S/O 78	22
Fowler, Mary Jean	Enhance with Unspuns	SS&D	7	3	27	Su 76	33
Fowler, Mary Jean	Puppets Challenge Ingenuity	SS&D	6	1	21	Wi 74	19
Fowler, Molly	Textiles At The Cooper Hewitt Museum	SS&D	7	4	28	Fa 76	4
Fox, Byrdann	Wall Clothing/Wag-Hraegel	Iw	5	2		Sp 80	77
Fox, Judy Kellar	A Quilting Bee Among the Amish	TM		4		A/M 86	12
Fox, Judy Kellar	Amish Quilts	Fa	10	2		M/A 83	28
Fox, Judy Kellar	Plaited Silk: Myrna Wacknov	SS&D	16	2	62	Sp 85	44
Fox, Nancy	Pueblo Weaving and Textile Arts	SS&D	10	3	39	Su 79	34
Fox, Nancy	Pueblo Weaving and Textile Arts	Iw	4	1		Wi 78	53
Fox, Nancy	Pueblo Weaving and Textile Arts	WJ	4	2	14	Oc 79	39
Fox, Sally	In Search of Colored Cotton	S-O	11	4		Wi 87	48
Fox, Sally	Naturally Colored Cottons	S-O	11	1		Sp 87	29
Fraas, Gayle; Duncan Slade	Personal Flags of Everyday Life	Fa	10	1		J/F 83	99
Frame, Mary	Are You Ready to Collapse?	S-O	11	1		Sp 87	41
Frame, Mary	Nasca Sprang Tassels: Structure, Technique, and Order	TMJ	25			86	67
Frame, Mary	Ringlets and Waves: Undulations from Overtwist	S-O	10	4		Wi 86	28
Frame, Mary	Save the Twist: Warping and Weaving with Overtwisted Yarns	S-O	11	2		Su 87	43
Franc, Marilyn	Planning a Regional Spinner's Gathering	S-O	11	4		Wi 87	16
Frank, Elizabeth	Designing for the Custom Trade	H&C	3	1		Wi 51	44
Franklin, Sue	"Decade of Fibers, A" (Exhibit)	Fa	5	1		J/F 78	17
Franklin, Sue	My Affair with King Cotton	TM		9		F/M 87	39
Franklin, Sue	Raising Angora Goats in Texas	TM		8		D/J 86	12
Franquemont, Ed	Andean Spinning	S-O	9	1		Sp 85	54
Franquemont, Ed	Nilda Callanaupa	S-O	9	1		Sp 85	53
Franquemont, Ed	see Cahlander, Adele	WJ	6	3	23	Wi 81	54
Fraser, Douglas	Primitive Art	H&C	14	1		Wi 63	45
Fraser, Kennedy	Fashionable Mind, The	Fa	10	5		S/O 83	57
Fraser, Victoria Keller	Fibre Preparation	H&C	24	3		M/J 73	32
Frasier, Debra	Lenore Davis: Figuring in Cloth	Fa	10	5		S/O 83	10
Frasier, Debra	Windworks: A Way of Working	Fa	10	4		J/A 83	58
Frater, Judy	Meaning of Folk Art in Rabari Life: A Closer Look at Mirrored Embroidery, The	TMJ	4	2		75	47
Frater, Judy	Rabari Lodi: Creating a Fabric Through Social Alliance, The	WJ	10	1	37	Su 85	28
Frech, Mary L.	Gobelin Tapestries	H&C	26	1		J/F 75	12
Fredlund, Jane; Birgit Wiberg	Rag Rug Weaves: Patterns from Sweden	WJ	11	2	42	Fa 86	74

AUTHOR	TITLE	JOUR	VOL	NO	ISS	DATE	PAGE
Fredlund, Jane; Birgit Wiberg	Rag Rug Weaves: Patterns from Sweden	Fa	13	5		S/O 86	60
Fredlund, Jane; Birgit Wiberg	Rag Rug Weaves: Patterns from Sweden	SS&D	18	2	70	Sp 87	38
Freeberg, Judy	Sauna Towels	WJ	10	4	40	Sp 86	50
Freeborn, Mary-Eleanor	Dyeing for Beginners	SS&D	3	2	10	Sp 72	39
Freeman, Charles	Pillow Lace in the East Midlands	H&C	10	3		Su 59	59
Freeman, Claire	Japanese Weaves Provide Ideas for Experiment	H&C	21	1		Wi 70	4
Freeman, Claire	One Weaver's Viewpoint	H&C	11	1		Wi 60	10
Freeman, Claire	Scandinavian Designs for American Looms	H&C	3	2		Sp 52	14
Freeman, Claire	Small Projects of Interest to Beginning Weavers	H&C	20	4		Fa 69	9
Freeman, Claire	Two-harness Weaves	H&C	11	4		Fa 60	40
Freilinger, Ida M.	On-loom Warping for Navajo Loom	SS&D	11	3	43	Su 80	8
Freilinger, Ida M.	Weaving of the Plaid, The	SS&D	12	1	45	Wi 80	59
Freimer, Betty	Double-Twill on a Jack Loom Using Two Sets of Ground Harnesses Equipped with Special Long-Eyed Heddles	CW	2	1	4	Oc 80	2
French, Elizabeth	Connie Kindahl	SS&D	17	3	67	Su 86	56
French, Thomas; Charles Vierck	Manual of Engineering Drawing, A	H&C	5	4		Fa 54	57
Freudenheim, Betty	see Larsen, Jack Lenor	WJ	12	2	46	Fa 87	66
Frey, Berta	Adjusting the Draft	H&C	10	1		Wi 59	14
Frey, Berta	American Handweaving, A Mid-Century Viewpoint	H&C	1	1		Ap 50	5
Frey, Berta	Beginning Weavers, More Than One Answer to Many Questions	H&C	14	1		Wi 63	9
Frey, Berta	Card Weaving	H&C	18	3		Su 67	8
Frey, Berta	Cloth Analysis — The Draft from the Fabric	H&C	2	4		Fa 51	11
Frey, Berta	Designing and Drafting for Handweavers	H&C	26	5		Oc 75	12
Frey, Berta	Designing and Drafting for Handweavers	SS&D	7	1	25	Wi 75	35
Frey, Berta	Designing and Drafting for Handweavers, Basic Principles of Cloth Construction	H&C	9	3		Su 58	60
Frey, Berta	Designing Bedspreads for Use in Modern Interiors	H&C	13	3		Su 62	9
Frey, Berta	Double Weave, Finnweave and Mexican Variations	H&C	12	2		Sp 61	12
Frey, Berta	Double Weave on Eight Harnesses for Patterned Fabrics	H&C	12	3		Su 61	23
Frey, Berta	End and Selvage Borders	H&C	9	2		Sp 58	46
Frey, Berta	Experiences in Organizing School Weaving Departments	H&C	5	4		Fa 54	26
Frey, Berta	Feather Cape, After the One Pocahontas Took to England	H&C	21	4		Fa 70	22
Frey, Berta	For Beginning Weavers — What Yarns Can I Use?	H&C	17	2		Sp 66	17
Frey, Berta	Four Harness Double Width Weaving	H&C	12	1		Wi 61	6
Frey, Berta	Four Harness Weaving	SS&D	3	4	12	Fa 72	47
Frey, Berta	Handweaving 1965	H&C	16	2		Sp 65	6
Frey, Berta	How Many Ends to the Inch?	H&C	3	3		Su 52	11
Frey, Berta	Importance of Samples, The	H&C	7	3		Su 56	13
Frey, Berta	Linen Towels	H&C	14	3		Su 63	13
Frey, Berta	New Design for Place Mats	H&C	6	4		Fa 55	28
Frey, Berta	New Projects for Four Harness Looms	H&C	8	2		Sp 57	49
Frey, Berta	New Skirts for Summer	H&C	4	1		Wi 52	33
Frey, Berta	New Ways with Old Drafts (error-corrected H&C v2 n4 51 p64)	H&C	2	3		Su 51	8
Frey, Berta	Notes for Beginning Weavers: A Teacher Offers Suggestions for Avoiding Errors	H&C	16	1		Wi 65	21
Frey, Berta	Notes for Beginning Weavers: Learning to Invent Your Own Shortcuts	H&C	16	3		Su 65	22
Frey, Berta	Notes for Beginning Weavers: Warping the Most Interesting Part of Weaving	H&C	16	2		Sp 65	20
Frey, Berta	Pattern and Structure in Handwoven Fabrics	H&C	6	4		Fa 55	4
Frey, Berta	Pattern Blocks, Basic Tool for Design	H&C	19	2		Sp 68	8
Frey, Berta	Problems in Warping (error-corrected H&C v2 n3 51 p54)	H&C	2	1		Wi 50	29
Frey, Berta	Program Suggestions for Weavers' Guilds	H&C	7	1		Wi 55	29

AUTHOR	TITLE	JOUR	VOL	NO	ISS	DATE	PAGE
Frey, Berta	Quilted Fabrics, A Method of Draft Writing for Individual Designs	H&C	14	4		Fa 63	17
Frey, Berta	Seven Projects in Rosepath	SS&D	7	2	26	Sp 76	34
Frey, Berta	Seven Projects in Rosepath	H&C	2	1		Wi 50	59
Frey, Berta	Simple Method for Weaving Deflected Warps	H&C	20	4		Fa 69	4
Frey, Berta	Skirt with Warp Stripe Pattern	H&C	14	2		Sp 63	38
Frey, Berta	Suggestions for Christmas Gifts	H&C	16	4		Fa 65	18
Frey, Berta	Summer-and-Winter as Developed in the Nineties	H&C	21	2		Sp 70	11
Frey, Berta	Treadle as Drawn In	H&C	5	3		Su 54	24
Frey, Berta	Tuck Weaving	H&C	9	4		Fa 58	11
Frey, Berta	Unique Method of Warping, A	H&C	6	1		Wi 54	60
Frey, Berta	Vaquero Sweater & Quixquimtl	H&C	12	4		Fa 61	15
Frey, Berta	Variations in the Honeysuckle Design	H&C	1	3		Fa 50	26
Frey, Berta	Warp-pattern Weaving	H&C	10	3		Su 59	9
Frey, Berta	Weave for Your Kitchen	H&C	1	2		Su 50	19
Frey, Berta	Weaving with Lofty Yarns	H&C	18	2		Sp 67	35
Frey, Berta	What is a Draft?	H&C	9	1		Wi 57	11
Frey, Berta	What is Leno?	H&C	6	2		Sp 55	4
Frey, Berta	Why Do You Want to Weave?	H&C	3	4		Fa 52	16
Frey, Berta	Wool for Sheer Draperies and Upholstery	H&C	2	4		Fa 51	44
Fridlund, Patricia	Spinning in Stehekin	S-O	10	4		Wi 86	44
Frode, Diane Ericson	see Ericson, Lois	WJ	8	3	31	Wi 83	68
Froese, Louise	Salish Ladies	SS&D	3	2	10	Sp 72	13
From, Dot	A Perspective on Embroidery: In Answer to Emery	AT	6			De 86	195
Frost, Gordon	Guatemala: Weaving, People	Iw	5	4		Fa 80	30
Frost, Jean	Diamond Lattice Pullover	Kn	3	4	8	Fa 87	34
Fry, Doug	Converting the Vertical Pull AVL Flyshuttle to Horizontal Pull	CW		25		Se 87	18
Fry, Eric C.	Book of Knots and Ropework, The	WJ	8	1	29	Su 83	52
Fry, Eric C.	Book of Knots and Ropework, The (Practical and Decorative)	Hw	4	4		S/O 83	24
Fry, Laura	Finishing Fabric	CW	7	1	19	Se 85	18
Fry, Laura	Isolation	CW	5	1	13	Se 83	15
Fry, Laura	Report from Pacific Northwest	CW		25		Se 87	20
Fry, Laura	Single Thread Harness Pattern Weaving	CW	5	1	13	Se 83	14
Fry, Laura	Space-Dented Warp	WJ	4	3	15	Ja 80	26
Fry, Mary G.	see Lambert, Patricia	WJ	12	1	45	Su 87	69
Fry, Mary G.	see Lambert, Patricia	TM			13	O/N 87	76
Fry, Mary G.	see Lambert, Patricia	PWC	4	4	14		53
Frye, Melinda Young	Non-Native American Basketry	Fa	11	1		J/F 84	51
Fuchs, Douglas Eric	Scholarship Report: Fuchs At Varpapuu	SS&D	7	1	25	Wi 75	92
Fuchs, Rudolph	Handweaving at North Texas State College	H&C	2	2		Sp 51	14
Fuchs, Rudolph	Hanging Based on HGA Name Draft to Decorate New Offices	SS&D	5	4	20	Fa 74	14
Fuchs, Rudolph	Weaving with Native Materials	H&C	2	4		Fa 51	21
Fuhrmann, Brigitta	Bobbin Lace, A Contemporary Approach	SS&D	8	3	31	Su 77	62
Furniss, Frances	Heirloom Linens	H&C	9	2		Sp 58	11
Furniss, Frances	Laurie Herrick, Contemporary Weaver and Teacher	H&C	18	4		Fa 67	10
Furry, Margaret S.; Bess M. Viemont	Home Dyeing with Natural Dyes	SS&D	5	2	18	Sp 74	68
Gadney, Alan	How to Enter and Win Fabric and Fiber Crafts Contests	Fa	10	4		J/A 83	49
Gadred Weavers	Color and Structure	H&C	1	3		Fa 50	21
Gadred Weavers	More About Larch Trees	H&C	2	3		Su 51	28
Gadred Weavers	On Time, Tools, and Techniques	H&C	2	4		Fa 51	18
Gadred Weavers	Quality or Charity? On What Basis Should Weaving Be Offered for Sale	H&C	1	2		Su 50	26
Gadred Weavers	System in Symbols, A	H&C	2	1		Wi 50	16
Gaffey, Theresa	The Edges of Knitting	TM			5	J/J 86	54

AUTHOR	TITLE	JOUR	VOL	NO	ISS	DATE	PAGE
Gaffey, Theresa	The Shape of Socks	TM			2	D/J 85	28
Gagné-Collard, Agathe	In My Country, It's Winter	WJ	8	3	31	Wi 83	74
Gale, Elizabeth	From Fibers to Fabrics	SS&D	4	1	13	Wi 72	34
Gale, Elizabeth	From Fibres to Fabrics	H&C	23	6		N/D 72	41
Gale-Nosek, Cynthia	Cynthia Gale-Nosek: Searching for the Limits of Crochet	Fa	11	4		J/A 84	49
Gallagher, Constance	Adventures in Pursuit of Yarns	H&C	12	3		Su 61	51
Gallagher, Constance	Early American Linens	H&C	15	3		Su 64	7
Gallagher, Constance	More Linen Heirlooms	Hw	5	5		N/D 84	14
Gallagher, Constance D.	Early American Handwoven Linens	SS&D	1	1	1	De 69	12
Gallagher, Constance D.	More Linen Heirlooms	SS&D	14	3	55	Su 83	61
Gallagher, Constance D.	Pattern Analysis	H&C	19	4		Fa 68	6
Gallagher, Constance D. N.	Linen Heirlooms	H&C	20	2		Sp 69	41
Gallagher, Constance D. N.	Linen Heirlooms	WJ	8	1	29	Su 83	51
Gallagher, Constance Dann	Linens At Old Economy, The	SS&D	7	3	27	Su 76	84
Gallagher, Constance; Evelyn Bustead	Boston Guild Sales	H&C	11	4		Fa 60	49
Gallagher, Kate	Waulking Tweeds at the Marshfield School of Weaving	Hw	6	4		S/O 85	10
Gallagher, Marten	Gooden Gansey Sweaters	Fa	12	6		N/D 85	12
Galligher, Constance D.	More Linen Heirlooms	WJ	7	4	28	Sp 83	48
Gallinger, Osma	Joy of Handweaving, The	H&C	1	1		Ap 50	52
Gallinger, Osma C.	Looms for the Handicapped	H&C	8	2		Sp 57	19
Gallinger, Osma Couch	Basket Pioneering, A Complete Study of Round Basketry Materials, Revised Edition	H&C	7	2		Sp 56	59
Gallinger, Osma Couch	Joy of Handweaving, The	H&C	1	3		Fa 50	62
Gallinger, Osma Couch	Story of the Johnson Rugs, The	H&C	7	2		Sp 56	28
Gallinger, Osma Couch; Oscar H. Benson	Hand Weaving with Reeds and Fibers	H&C	2	1		Wi 50	59
Gallinger, Osma; Josephine Del Deo	Rug Weaving for Everyone	H&C	9	1		Wi 57	59
Galpin, Mary	Inside an Expensive Outfit	TM			1	O/N 85	40
Galpin, Mary	Knitters Meet in Baltimore	TM			3	F/M 86	32
Galpin, Mary	Sewing Without Singer	TM			5	J/J 86	20
Galpin, Mary	Why Sewing Is Sagging	TM			7	O/N 86	16
Galvin, Nellie L.	Teneriffe Lace—Polka Spider Web	SS&D	4	4	16	Fa 73	33
Galvin, Nellie L., ed.	German Weaver's Pattern Book 1784-1810, A	H&C	12	4		Fa 61	43
Gandi, Rene	African Crafts and Craftsmen	SS&D	3	3	11	Su 72	13
Gans, Naomi Beth; Catherine Haywood	Handwoven Flocati of Epirus, The	SS&D	12	3	47	Su 81	35
Gans-Ruedin, E.	Caucasian Carpets	TM			11	J/J 87	72
Gans-Ruedin, Erwin	Splendor of Persian Carpets, The	Iw	5	1		Wi 79	59
Gans-Ruedin, Erwin	Splendor of Persian Carpets, The	Iw	5	3		Su 80	70
Gant, Helen Mosely	Cotton Skirt and Blouse	S-O	6	4		82	63
Gardi, René	African Crafts & Craftsmen	H&C	22	2		Sp 71	44
Gardner, George	Costume in the Streets of New York: A Photo Essay	Fa	11	5		S/O 84	42
Gardner, Jean	Evolution of a Handspun Jacket	S-O	9	1		Sp 85	28
Garfunkel, Jill	see Beede, Beth	Fa	13	4		J/A 86	6
Garfunkel, Jill	see Beede, Beth	SS&D	17	4	68	Fa 86	12
Garland, Mary	Christmas Embroidery in Pakistan	TM			14	D/J 87	90
Garoutte, Sally, ed.	Uncoverings 1985, Volume 6 of the Research Papers of American Quilt Study Group	TM			11	J/J 87	73
Garrett, Cay	Remove the Reed (error-corrected SS&D v5 n3 i19 74 p65)	SS&D	5	1	17	Wi 73	88
Garrett, Cay	Warping All by Yourself	SS&D	5	4	20	Fa 74	64
Garrett, Cay	Warping All by Yourself	H&C	26	2		Ap 75	24
Garrett, Cay	Warping All by Yourself	Hw	2	1		F-W 80	21
Garrett, Cay	Warping All by Yourself	Hw	4	3		M/J 83	13

AUTHOR	TITLE	JOUR	VOL	NO	ISS	DATE	PAGE
Garrett, John	Baskets of John Garrett: A Mesh of Ideas and Materials, The	Fa	11	1		J/F 84	26
Gaston-Voûte, Suzanne	Camera Strap in Double-Weave Pick-Up	PWC		2		Ap 82	10
Gaston-Voûte, Suzanne	Double Weave on a Rigid Heddle Loom	SS&D	8	3	31	Su 77	70
Gaston-Voûte, Suzanne	see Davenport, Betty	Hw	7	1		J/F 86	62
Gaudy, Betty	Installation Ceremony of Guild Officers, Verde Valley	Hw	7	5		N/D 86	15
Gaustad, Stephenie	Croatian Shirt, A	S-O	9	2		Su 85	28
Gaustad, Stephenie	Leaf and Bast Fibers Crossword, A	S-O	10	3		Fa 86	47
Gaustad, Stephenie	Shirt for a Fellow Spinner, A	Hw	7	4		S/O 86	76
Gaustad, Stephenie	Tale of a Skirt	Hw	4	5		N/D 83	68
Gawne, Arlene	Africa Inspires a Weaver	SS&D	16	3	63	Su 85	46
Gaworski, Michael	see Warming, Wanda	Fa	9	6		N/D 82	58
Gaynor, Katherine A.	Deborah O'Brien Saupe: The Search for Balance	Fa	13	5		S/O 86	24
Geehr, Peg	Mannings — A Weavers Paradise, The	H&C	26	1		J/F 75	15
Gehret, Ellen J.	Rural Pennsylvania Clothing	SS&D	8	3	31	Su 77	61
Geijer, Agnes	History of Textile Art, A	WJ	7	1	25	Su 82	63
Geijer, Agnes	Oriental Textiles in Sweden	H&C	3	2		Sp 52	61
Geijer, Agnes	Oriental Textiles in Sweden	TMJ	3	2		De 71	38
Gele, Emilé	New Philippine Textiles	H&C	5	3		Su 54	14
Genfan, Herb; Lyn Taetzsch	How to Start Your Own Craft Business	H&C	26	1		J/F 75	28
Gentille, Terry	Printed Textiles: A Guide to Creative Design Fundamentals	Fa	10	3		M/J 83	52
Gentry, Barbara	see Ligon, Linda	Iw	3	4		Su 78	28
George, Barbara	Aussie Augments	Kn	4	1	9	Wi 87	62
George, Barbara	Snowdrops and Snowflakes	Kn	4	1	9	Wi 87	17
George, Patrice	Design Decisions: Software Solutions	Hw	5	5		N/D 84	47
George, Patrice	Lace & Flowers: Vintage Inspiration	Hw	8	5		N/D 87	68
Gerber, Fred	Cochineal and the Insect Dyes	Iw	3	4		Su 78	46
Gerber, Fred	Insect Dyes	Iw	3	3		Sp 78	23
Gerber, Fred	Investigative Method—A Tool for Study, Part 1	SS&D	6	1	21	Wi 74	62
Gerber, Fred	Investigative Method—A Tool for Study, Part 2	SS&D	6	2	22	Sp 75	53
Gerber, Fred	Investigative Method of Natural Dyeing, The	Iw	3	4		Su 78	45
Gerber, Fred	see Gerber, Willi	SS&D	5	1	17	Wi 73	25
Gerber, Fred	see Gerber, Willi	SS&D	5	2	18	Sp 74	87
Gerber, Fred	see Gerber, Willi	SS&D	5	3	19	Su 74	70
Gerber, Fred	see Gerber, Willi	SS&D	5	4	20	Fa 74	92
Gerber, Fred	see Gerber, Willi	H&C	19	4		Fa 68	4
Gerber, Fred	see Gerber, Willi	H&C	20	2		Sp 69	13
Gerber, Fred	see Gerber, Willi	H&C	23	6		N/D 72	16
Gerber, Fred	see Gerber, Willi	H&C	26	3		M/J 75	11
Gerber, Fred; Juanita Gerber	Investigative Method — A Tool for Study, Part 3	SS&D	6	4	24	Fa 75	69
Gerber, Fred; Willi Gerber	Milkweed and Balduinea in the Dyepot	H&C	22	3		Su 71	23
Gerber, Fred; Willi Gerber	Milkweed and Balduinea in the Dyepot (Reprint)	H&C	26	1		J/F 75	19
Gerber, Fred; Willi Gerber	Notes on Vegetalbe Dyeing	H&C	23	3		M/J 72	28
Gerber, Frederick	Alkanet	Iw	5	3		Su 80	66
Gerber, Frederick H.	Cochineal and the Insect Dyes	SS&D	10	1	37	Wi 78	78
Gerber, Frederick H.	Cochineal and the Insect Dyes	WJ	3	2	10	Oc 78	46
Gerber, Frederick H.	Indigo and the Antiquity of Dyeing	SS&D	9	1	33	Wi 77	40
Gerber, Frederick H.	Indigo and the Antiquity of Dyeing	Iw	3	2		Wi 78	43
Gerber, Frederick H.	Indigo and the Antiquity of Dyeing	WJ	2	2	6	Oc 77	34
Gerber, Frederick H.	Investigative Method of Natural Dyeing, The	WJ	3	3	11	Ja 79	42

AUTHOR	TITLE	JOUR	VOL	NO	ISS	DATE	PAGE
Gerber, Juanita	see Gerber, Fred	SS&D	6	4	24	Fa 75	69
Gerber, Willi	see Gerber, Fred	H&C	22	3		Su 71	23
Gerber, Willi	see Gerber, Fred	H&C	23	3		M/J 72	28
Gerber, Willi	see Gerber, Fred	H&C	26	1		J/F 75	19
Gerber, Willi; Fred Gerber	Chaos in the Kitchen: Part 1	SS&D	5	3	19	Su 74	70
Gerber, Willi; Fred Gerber	Chaos in the Kitchen, Part 2	SS&D	5	4	20	Fa 74	92
Gerber, Willi; Fred Gerber	Cochineal as a Domestic Dyestuff	H&C	23	6		N/D 72	16
Gerber, Willi; Fred Gerber	Dyeing with Lichens	H&C	20	2		Sp 69	13
Gerber, Willi; Fred Gerber	Indigo, Discovery of Plants and Experiments in Dyeing	H&C	19	4		Fa 68	4
Gerber, Willi; Fred Gerber	Indigo, Discovery of Plants and Experiments in Dyeing	H&C	26	3		M/J 75	11
Gerber, Willi; Fred Gerber	Quercitron, The Forgotten Dyestuff, Producer of Clear, Bright Colors	SS&D	5	1	17	Wi 73	25
Gerber, Willi; Fred Gerber	Quercitron, The Forgotten Dyestuffs, Producer of Clear, Bright Colors: Part 2	SS&D	5	2	18	Sp 74	87
Gervers, Michael; Veronika Gervers	Felt-making Craftsmen of the Anatolian and Iranian Plateaux	TMJ	4	1		De 74	14
Gervers, Veronika	Historical Components of Regional Costume in South-Eastern Europe, The	TMJ	4	2		75	61
Gervers, Veronika	Influence of Ottoman Turkish Textiles and Costume in Eastern Europe, The	Fa	10	5		S/O 83	57
Gervers, Veronika	Influence of Ottoman Turkish Textiles and Costumes in Eastern Europe, The	WJ	8	2	30	Fa 83	65
Gervers, Veronika	see Gervers, Michael	TMJ	4	1		De 74	14
Gervers, Veronika, ed.	Studies in Textile History: In Memory of Harold B. Burnham	SS&D	9	3	35	Su 78	94
Getty, Nilda C. Fernandez	Contemporary Crafts of the Americas	Iw	1	1		Fa 75	20
Gherity, Delle	Corn Silk Challenge, The	SS&D	7	3	27	Su 76	9
Giacchina, Polly Jacobs	Weaving with the Maoris of New Zealand	Fa	11	3		M/J 84	48
Gibbs, Emily	Miniatures Adapted from Colonial Patterns	H&C	8	2		Sp 57	26
Gibson, Gordon D.; Cecilia R. McGurk	High-Status Caps of the Kongo and Mbundu Peoples	TMJ	4	4		77	71
Gibson-Roberts, Priscilla A.	Baby Jacket	Kn	3	2	6	Sp 87	42
Gibson-Roberts, Priscilla A.	Cotton, Cool and Comfy	Kn	3	2	6	Sp 87	48
Gibson-Roberts, Priscilla A.	Cowichan Country	Kn	3	1	5	F-W 86	61
Gibson-Roberts, Priscilla A.	Fair Isle in Natural Colors, The	Kn	2	1	3	F-W 85	34
Gibson-Roberts, Priscilla A.	Finishing a Woolen Knitting Yarn	S-O	9	2		Su 85	38
Gibson-Roberts, Priscilla A.	Gansey in Handspun, The	Kn	1	1	1	F-W 84 CI	32,56B 24
Gibson-Roberts, Priscilla A.	Handspinner's Choice, The	Kn	1	2	2	S-S 85	56
Gibson-Roberts, Priscilla A.	Knitting in the Old Way	SS&D	17	3	67	Su 86	85
Gibson-Roberts, Priscilla A.	Like the Ad Says: "We've Come a Long Way"	S-O	11	3		Fa 87	26
Gibson-Roberts, Priscilla A.	Nature: A Color Source and Inspiration for Traditional Sweaters	S-O	9	3		Fa 85	42
Gibson-Roberts, Priscilla A.	Norwegian Luskofte	S-O	9	3		Fa 85	44
Gibson-Roberts, Priscilla A.	One Hundred Yard Rule	Kn	1	2	2	S-S 85	58
Gibson-Roberts, Priscilla A.	Qiviut — The Ultimate Luxury Fiber	Kn	3	4	8	Fa 87	58
Gibson-Roberts, Priscilla A.	Shiny and Un	Kn	2	2	4	S-S 86	58
Gibson-Roberts, Priscilla A.	Simple and Silk	Kn	2	2	4	S-S 86	54
Gibson-Roberts, Priscilla A.	Spin Your Own Lopi?	S-O	10	2		Su 86	40
Gibson-Roberts, Priscilla A.	Spinning a Gossamer Web	Kn	4	1	9	Wi 87	62
Gibson-Roberts, Priscilla A.	Spinning Traditional Knitting Yarns for Ethnic Sweaters	S-O	8	4		Wi 84	26
Gibson-Roberts, Priscilla A.	Thirty-Button Classic	S-O	11	1		Sp 87	32
Gibson-Roberts, Priscilla A.	Tips on Spinning a Wool Embroidery Yarn	S-O	9	3		Fa 85	46

AUTHOR	TITLE	JOUR	VOL	NO	ISS	DATE	PAGE
Gibson-Roberts, Priscilla A.	Wool: From Fleece to Knitting Yarn	S-O	8	3		Fa 84	27
Gibson-Roberts, Priscilla A.	Wymple in Tyme, A	Kn	3	4	8	Fa 87	56
Gickie, John	Checking the Twist	S-O	11	1		Sp 87	27
Gickie, John	Them Little Mousies	S-O	9	1		Sp 85	21
Giganti, Maria; Carol Clyne	Ins and Outs of Hand Quilting, The	TM			2	D/J 85	64
Gilbert, Donna Lee	Baby's First Hang-Up	SS&D	11	4	44	Fa 80	26
Gilbert, James	Spatial Transitions	SS&D	9	3	35	Su 78	12
Gilbert, Linda	Linda Gilbert	Fa	5	5		S/O 78	16
Gilbreath, Alice	Fun with Weaving	SS&D	8	4	32	Fa 77	72
Gilby, Myriam	Free Weaving	SS&D	7	4	28	Fa 76	66
Giles, Lynn	see McKay, Wendy	Hw	2	3		My 81	12
Giles, Lynne	Art/Culture/Future: American Craft '86	Hw	7	5		N/D 86	91
Giles, Lynne	Using the Yarn You've Got	Hw	8	4		S/O 87	63
Giles, Lynne	Warp-Faced Rugs	Hw	7	4		S/O 86	40
Gilfallan, Joan	Joan Gilfallan	Fa	7	5		S/O 80	43
Gilfert, Sara	Sara Gilfert	Fa	14	5		N/D 87	11
Gilfoy, Peggy S.	Art of Indiana Coverlets, The	AT	2			De 84	69
Gilfoy, Peggy S.	Diane Wiersba	H&C	15	3		Su 64	19
Gilfoy, Peggy Stoltz	Fabrics in Celebration from the Collection of the Indianapolis Museum of Art	Hw	7	4		S/O 86	11
Gilfoy, Peggy Stoltz	Fabrics in Celebration: From the Collection of the Indianapolis Museum of Art	SS&D	16	3	63	Su 85	8
Gilliland, David	Sensuous Silk: Cedrus Monte's Painted Silk Garments	Fa	8	1		J/F 81	17
Gillis, Myrtle Lovell	Take One Spinning Wheel	H&C	7	2		Sp 56	59
Gillispie, Charles, ed.	Diderot Pictorial Encyclopedia of Trades and Industry, A	H&C	10	3		Su 59	59
Gilman, Rachel Seidel; Nancy Bess	Step by Step Basketry	SS&D	10	1	37	Wi 78	77
Gilmurray, Susan	Circular Macrame Form	SS&D	5	2	18	Sp 74	52
Gilmurray, Susan	Experimental Countermarch	SS&D	8	2	30	Sp 77	39
Gilmurray, Susan	Speed Up Tie-Up for the Counter March Loom	SS&D	10	3	39	Su 79	50
Gilmurray, Susan	Weaving Tricks	Hw	2	3		My 81	70
Gilmurray, Susan	Weaving Tricks	WJ	6	1	21	Su 81	53
Gilmurray, Susan	Weaving Tricks	Fa	9	4		J/A 82	53
Gilmurray, Susan W.	see King, Bucky	SS&D	3	4	12	Fa 72	28
Gilpin, Elizabeth	Tour and Shop	H&C	4	1		Wi 52	61
Gilsdorf, Marilyn	Fleecy Vest, A	WJ	8	4	32	Sp 84	9
Gilsdorf, Marilyn	Safe Dye for Children, A	WJ	8	4	32	Sp 84	47
Gilsenan, Nancy	Jaki Ernst "Fibre Graphics and Soft Sculpture" (Exhibit)	Fa	7	6		N/D 80	69
Gilstrap, Bill; Sara Gilstrap	Low Budget Tapestry Loom, A	WJ	5	4	20	Sp 81	42
Gilstrap, Sara	see Gilstrap, Bill	WJ	5	4	20	Sp 81	42
Ginsberg, Ruth L.	Woven Image, The	SS&D	2	4	8	Fa 71	6
Ginsberg-Place, Ruth	Weaving — A Delicate Balance	H&C	23	4		J/A 72	43
Ginsburg, Madeleine	Victorian Dress in Photographs	Fa	11	4		J/A 84	54
Girault, Louis	Textiles Boliviens, Région de Charazani, Catalogues du Musée l'Homme	TMJ	3	3		De 72	79
Gisler, Jim	Purchasing Materials	H&C	24	3		M/J 73	13
Gittinger, Mattiebelle	Conversations with a Batik Master	TMJ	18			79	25
Gittinger, Mattiebelle	Master Dyers to the World—Techniques and Trade in Early Indian Dyed Cotton Textiles	WJ	7	4	28	Sp 83	48
Gittinger, Mattiebelle S.	Additions to the Indonesian Collection	TMJ	4	3		76	43
Gittinger, Mattiebelle S.	Selected Batak Textiles: Technique and Function	TMJ	4	2		75	13
Glantz, Mary Ann	Weaver Dyes, A	SS&D	2	3	7	Su 71	23
Glaser, Liana J.	Art of Simple Batik, The	WJ	5	3	19	Wi 81	52

AUTHOR	TITLE	JOUR	VOL	NO	ISS	DATE	PAGE
Glashausser, Suellen; Carol Westfall	Plaiting Step-by-Step	SS&D	9	2	34	Sp 78	49
Glass, Laurie H.	"Contemporary Japanese Tapestry, The" (Exhibit)	Fa	4	6		N/D 77	22
Glauco, Reali; Adelchi Meneghini; Mario Trevisan	Bachicoltura Moderna	Hw	7	1		J/F 86	18
Glaves, Jeannine	Kindred Spirits of Peru	S-O	8	1		Sp 84	22
Glaves, Jeannine; Ruth Morrison	Silk Shawl	S-O	9	4		Wi 85	16
Glaze, Mary	Textiles in Nineteenth-Century America	H&C	21	3		Su 70	4
Glenn, Jeff	Jeff Glenn	Fa	14	1		J/F 87	26
Glover, Medrith	Little Knitting on the Side, A	Kn	2	1	3	F-W 85	38
Glover, Medrith	No-Sweat Sweatshirt, The	Kn	3	1	5	F-W 86	28
Glover, Medrith	This Yoke's on You!	Kn	3	2	6	Sp 87	35
Glover, Medrith J.	Special Fittings: Tulips	Kn	1	2	2	S-S 85	29, 72A
Glowacki, Dorothy	see Shannon, Betty	SS&D	11	2	42	Sp 80	97
Glowacki, Dorothy; Betty Shannon	SS&D Index 1976, Issues 26-29	SS&D	8	2	30	Sp 77	89
Glowacki, Dorothy; Betty Shannon	SS&D Index 1977, Issues 30-33	SS&D	9	2	34	Sp 78	72
Glowacki, Dorothy; Betty Shannon	SS&D Index 1978, Issues 34-37	SS&D	10	2	38	Sp 79	91
Glowacki, Dorothy; Betty Shannon	SS&D Index 1980, Issues 42-45	SS&D	12	2	46	Sp 81	59
Glowacki, Dorothy; Betty Shannon	SS&D Index 1981, Issues 46-49	SS&D	13	2	50	Sp 82	50
Glowacki, Dorothy; Betty Shannon	SS&D Index 1982, Issues 50-53	SS&D	14	2	54	Sp 83	26
Glowacki, Dorothy; Betty Shannon	SS&D Index 1983, Issues 54-57	SS&D	15	2	58	Sp 84	69
Glowacki, Dorothy; Betty Shannon	SS&D Index 1984, Issues 58-61	SS&D	16	2	62	Sp 85	74
Glowacki, Dorothy; Betty Shannon	SS&D Index 1985, Issues 62-65	SS&D	17	2	66	Sp 86	69
Glowacki, Dorothy; Betty Shannon	SS&D Index 1986, Issues 66-69	SS&D	18	2	70	Sp 87	35
Glowen, Ron	Memory, Metaphor, and Magic: The Art of Janet Boguch	Fa	11	6		N/D 84	66
Gnatkowski, Janice	One Hundred Sixty-seven International Sheep Breeds	S-O	3			79	10
Goerdeler, Pearl Pomeroy	Yarn Animals You Can Make	H&C	2	3		Su 51	62
Golay, Myrna	In Pursuit of Plakhta	WJ	11	3	43	Wi 87	34
Goldberg, Barbara; Antoinette Minichiello-Winters	Print and Dye Works	Fa	9	3		M/J 82	25
Goldberg, Barbara B.	Artist in Focus, The	Fa	11	3		M/J 84	52
Goldin, Susan	"100% Wool" (Exhibit)	Fa	4	6		N/D 77	18
Goldin, Susan	Taproot: Jack Lenor Larsen	Iw	4	3		Su 79	17
Goldin, Susan	Thoughts on the New Basketry	Iw	3	3		Sp 78	11
Goldman, Judy Ann	"Boston Seven: A Fiber Show, The" (Exhibit)	Fa	6	3		M/J 79	73
Goldring, Marc; Pat Doran; Thomas Wolf	Computers & Crafts: A Practical Guide	Hw	6	4		S/O 85	20
Goldsberry, Steven	see Bird, Adren J.	WJ	8	2	30	Fa 83	63
Goldschmidt, Manfred	Handweaver with Dobby-Powerloom	CW	3	3	9	Ap 82	12
Goldschmidt, Manfred	Jacquard Weaving	H&C	23	4		J/A 72	35
Goldschmidt, Manfred	Jacquard Weaving Part 1	H&C	23	2		M/A 72	24
Goldstein, Barbara	All Sweaters in Every Gauge	Kn	1	1	1	F-W 84	15
Goldstein, Rosalie, ed.	Fiber R/Evolution	Hw	8	2		M/A 87	12
Golub, Ina	Tapestries at Temple Emanu-El	SS&D	14	1	53	Wi 82	41
Gonder, Pamela	Touch of Whimsy, A	SS&D	7	3	27	Su 76	86

AUTHOR	TITLE	JOUR	VOL	NO	ISS	DATE	PAGE
Gonsalve, Alyson Smith, ed.	Weaving Techniques and Projects	Fa	3	2		M/A 76	25
Gonsalves, Alyson Smith	Weaving Techniques and Projects	SS&D	5	3	19	Su 74	62
Gonzales, Carolyn	Teaching the Blind to Spin: A Group Session	SS&D	10	3	39	Su 79	90
Gonzalez, Loraine	Weaver's Journey, A	H&C	15	2		Sp 64	33
Gooch, Peter H.	Ideas for Fabric Printing and Dyeing	SS&D	7	1	25	Wi 75	35
Goodell, Miss Grace	Study of Andean Spinning in the Cuzco Region, A	TMJ	2	3		De 68	2
Goodfellow, Robin	Caribou Hair and the Creation of a New Fabric	AT	6			De 86	119
Goodfellow, Robin; Keith Slater	New Fiber for Spinners: Caribou, A	S-O	10	4		Wi 86	46
Goodloe, William H.	Coconut Palm Frond Weaving	H&C	23	6		N/D 72	41
Goodloe, William H.	Coconut Palm Frond Weaving	WJ	8	2	30	Fa 83	65
Goodloe, William H.	Coconut Palm Weaving	SS&D	4	1	13	Wi 72	35
Goodman, Deborah Lerme	A. H. Rice Company: Maker of Silk Thread	Fa	13	1		J/F 86	54
Goodman, Deborah Lerme	Abigail Jurist Levy: Dyed Paper and Silk Assemblages	Fa	12	4		J/A 85	16
Goodman, Deborah Lerme	Antique Spinning Wheels	TM			6	A/S 86	61
Goodman, Deborah Lerme	Art Consultants: Bridging the Gap Between Artist and Client	Fa	12	6		N/D 85	31
Goodman, Deborah Lerme	Behind the Scenes: A "Missing" Tradition	Fa	13	3		M/J 86	46
Goodman, Deborah Lerme	Behind the Scenes: A Museum Installation	Fa	13	3		M/J 86	42
Goodman, Deborah Lerme	Behind the Scenes: A Textile Mill	Fa	13	3		M/J 86	40
Goodman, Deborah Lerme	Chinese Artisans at Work	Fa	13	1		J/F 86	34
Goodman, Deborah Lerme	Craft Fairs: To Show Or Not to Show	Fa	12	2		M/A 85	50
Goodman, Deborah Lerme	Ellen Liss: Machine-Knit Wearables	Fa	11	4		J/A 84	16
Goodman, Deborah Lerme	"Fabled Cloth: Batik from Java's North Coast" (Exhibit)	Fa	12	4		J/A 85	58
Goodman, Deborah Lerme	Fiber Conversations, Scandinavian/American-Style	Fa	10	6		N/D 83	53
Goodman, Deborah Lerme	Fiber in the Nation's Capital	Fa	11	6		N/D 84	48
Goodman, Deborah Lerme	"Flexible Medium: Art Fabric from the Museum Collection, The" (Exhibit)	Fa	11	5		S/O 84	71
Goodman, Deborah Lerme	Henry Moore: A New Dimension: The Translation of Watercolors from Paper to Tapestry	Fa	11	2		M/A 84	62
Goodman, Deborah Lerme	Jeans: The Inside Story	TM			3	F/M 86	27
Goodman, Deborah Lerme	Kings, Heroes, Lovers: Pictorial Rugs from the Tribes and Villages of Iran	Fa	11	3		M/J 84	38
Goodman, Deborah Lerme	Linda Levin: Quilted Impressions	Fa	14	2		M/A 87	13
Goodman, Deborah Lerme	Linda Miller: Textile Constructions	Fa	12	3		M/J 85	17
Goodman, Deborah Lerme	Linen Lore	Fa	14	2		M/A 87	16
Goodman, Deborah Lerme	Manufacture of Industrial Felt, The	Fa	13	4		J/A 86	20
Goodman, Deborah Lerme	Mary Long Graham: Resolving Chaos and Order	Fa	13	3		M/J 86	24
Goodman, Deborah Lerme	Paisley Shawls: A Democratic Fashion	Fa	12	3		M/J 85	52
Goodman, Deborah Lerme	Paper Reliefs of Sirpa Yarmolinsky, The	Fa	12	5		S/O 85	17
Goodman, Deborah Lerme	Pictorial Tapestry: A Portfolio of Contemporary Work	Fa	10	3		M/J 83	29
Goodman, Deborah Lerme	Riding the Modern Range: Stetson Hats	Fa	13	4		J/A 86	8
Goodman, Deborah Lerme	Robots Can Sew Too	TM			8	D/J 86	14
Goodman, Deborah Lerme	Rubber Stamping on Fabric	Fa	13	2		M/A 86	38
Goodman, Deborah Lerme	Shearing the Sheep	TM			1	O/N 85	10
Goodman, Deborah Lerme	"Show of Fans, A" (Exhibit)	Fa	12	6		N/D 85	56
Goodman, Deborah Lerme	Silk Lore: The Myths of a Magical Fiber	Fa	13	1		J/F 86	42
Goodman, Deborah Lerme	Silk Trivia: Miscellaneous Facts About a Versatile Fiber	Fa	13	1		J/F 86	44
Goodman, Deborah Lerme	Silkworks	Fa	13	1		J/F 86	50
Goodman, Deborah Lerme	Sue Pierce: Quilted Vessels	Fa	11	1		J/F 84	100
Goodman, Deborah Lerme	Textile Museum Turns Sixty, The	TM			1	O/N 85	12
Goodman, Deborah Lerme	Textile Trends: Collecting in Washington, D.C.	Fa	12	6		N/D 85	25
Goodman, Deborah Lerme	Triaxial Weaving of David Mooney, The	Fa	13	3		M/J 86	34
Goodman, Deborah Lerme	Why Do Colors Flee the Light?	TM			1	O/N 85	8
Goodman, Deborah Lerme	Working with Linen: Barbara Eckhardt	Fa	14	2		M/A 87	35
Goodman, Deborah Lorme	Magic Shuttle, The	WJ	8	3	31	Wi 83	65

AUTHOR	TITLE	JOUR	VOL	NO	ISS	DATE	PAGE
Goodrick, Gail L.	Yesterday's Necessity — Today's Choice	S-O	7	2		Su 83	30
Goodwin, Jill	Dyer's Manual, A	WJ	8	3	31	Wi 83	66
Goodwin, Jill	Dyer's Manual, A	PWC	3	1	7		61
Goody, Esther N. ed.	From Craft to Industry: The Ethnography of Proto-Industrial Cloth Production	WJ	9	3	35	Wi 85	85
Goody, Rabbit	Spinning Jenny: A Modern Application of the Circular Spinner, The	S-O	8	1		Sp 84	26
Goodyear, Carmen	Sheep Book, The	Iw	2	1		Fa 76	32
Goodyear, Nancy L.	Hazards Faced by Weavers	SS&D	13	3	51	Su 82	15
Goony, Elaine	Wool Blanket	S-O	6	4		82	62
Gordon, Beverly	Domestic American Textiles: A Bibliographic Sourcebook	SS&D	10	2	38	Sp 79	73
Gordon, Beverly	Domestic American Textiles: "A Bibliographic Sourcebook"	Hw	5	4		S/0 84	15
Gordon, Beverly	Domestic American Textiles; A Bibliographic Sourcebook	WJ	9	2	34	Fa 84	79
Gordon, Beverly	Feltmaking Now: The Exciting Revival of an Ancient Technique	Fa	6	6		N/D 79	43
Gordon, Beverly	Feltmaking—Traditions, Techniques, and Contemporary Explorations	WJ	5	3	19	Wi 81	52
Gordon, Beverly	Final Step. Traditional Methods and Contemporary Applications for Finishing Cloth by Hand, The	WJ	7	2	26	Fa 82	57
Gordon, Beverly	Final Steps: Traditional Methods and Contemporary Applications for Finishing Cloth by Hand, The	Fa	10	1		J/F 83	57
Gordon, Beverly	"Hmong Art: Tradition and Change" (Exhibit)	Fa	12	6		N/D 85	36
Gordon, Beverly	Museum Textiles: How to Get at Them and Use Them	WJ	8	1	29	Su 83	14
Gordon, Beverly	Shaker Technique: Part 1, Weaving with Wood, The	SS&D	7	4	28	Fa 76	32
Gordon, Beverly	Shaker Technique: Part 2, Rag Rugs, The	SS&D	8	1	29	WI 76	83
Gordon, Beverly	Shaker Textile Arts	SS&D	12	1	45	Wi 80	82
Gordon, Beverly	Shaker Textile Arts	Iw	6	1		Wi 80	73
Gordon, Beverly	Shaker Textile Arts	Fa	7	4		J/A 80	22
Gordon, Beverly	Shelters and Symbols	SS&D	11	1	41	Wi 79	53
Gordon, Beverly	Soft Sculpture: Old Forms, New Meanings	Fa	10	6		N/D 83	40
Gordon, Beverly	Traditional Methods of Finishing Cloth by Hand	Iw	5	4		Fa 80	66
Gordon, Beverly	Women as Spinners: New England Spinsters	S-O	3			79	16
Gordon, Carol	Impatient Spinner's Way to Spin Flax, The	S-O	10	4		Wi 86	42
Gordon, Flo Ann	Nature's Dyes	SS&D	4	3	15	Su 73	53
Gordon, Gerrie	Sheep Country Profiles: Dick Burtt	Iw	1	4		Su 76	19
Gordon, Gerrie	Sheep Country Profiles: Jean Urruty	Iw	2	3		Sp 77	25
Gordon, Jean	Pageant of the Rose	H&C	4	4		Fa 53	61
Gordon, Joleen	Basketmakers of Nova Scotia, The	SS&D	17	4	68	Fa 86	44
Gordon, Joleen	Basketry Traditions of Nova Scotia, The	SS&D	17	2	66	Sp 86	52
Gordon, Joleen	Old Ways for the New	SS&D	17	4	68	Fa 86	48
Gordon, Judith	Beiderwand	CW	1	2	2	Fe 80	1
Gordon, Judith	Beiderwand Made Easy: An Old Weave Adapts to Four-Harness (revision SS&D v7 n4 76 p27)	SS&D	7	3	27	Su 76	68
Gordon, Judith	Convergence '88	CW		25		Se 87	10
Gordon, Judith	Four Shaft Fascination	Hw	6	1		J/F 85	12
Gordon, Judith	Macomber's Designers Delight Dobby, A Report	CW	4	1	10	Se 82	16
Gordon, Judith	On Analyzing Commercial Fabrics	Hw	6	2		M/A 85	89
Gordon, Judith	Problem of Twist, A	SS&D	12	4	48	Fa 81	28
Gordon, Judith	see Anderson, Clarita	SS&D	9	4	36	Fa 78	71
Gordon, Judith	Spots or Stripes?	Hw	5	4		S/0 84	36
Gordon, Judith	Suitable Subtleties	Hw	5	3		Su 84	22
Gordon, Judith	Tisket, a Tasket, A	Hw	5	5		N/D 84	34
Gordon, Judith	Twill Plaid, A	Hw	5	2		M/A 84	41
Gordon, Judith	Weave Master and Weave Master Plus, A Report (error-corrected CW v5 n3 84 p25)	CW	5	1	13	Se 83	7
Gordon, Lida	Barbara MacCallum	Fa	14	3		M/J 87	22
Gore, Ann	Books Without Words	Fa	9	4		J/A 82	21

AUTHOR	TITLE	JOUR	VOL	NO	ISS	DATE	PAGE
Gorski, Berni	Lace Weaving: Toads and Cicadas	SS&D	3	2	10	Sp 72	6
Gostelow, Mary	Complete International Book of Embroidery, The	SS&D	10	1	37	Wi 78	78
Gostelow, Mary	Embroidery of All of Russia	Fa	5	5		S/O 78	62
Gothard, Lark	Lark Gothard	Fa	12	6		N/D 85	18
Gottdiener, Jennifer	Toward a Standard Drafting System	H&C	24	2		M/A 73	12
Gottfridsson, Inger; Ingrid Gottfridsson	Swedish Mitten Book, Traditional Patterns from Gotlan, The	Kn	3	1	5	F-W 86	69
Gottfridsson, Inger; Ingrid Gottfridsson	The Swedish Mitten Book: Traditional Patterns from Gotland	TM			6	A/S 86	84
Gottfridsson, Ingrid	see Gottfridsson, Inger	Kn	3	1	5	F-W 86	69
Gottfridsson, Ingrid	see Gottfridsson, Inger	TM			6	A/S 86	28
Gotthoffer, Esther	Contemporary Hangings at Brookfield	SS&D	1	1	1	De 69	2
Gotthoffer, Esther	Guatamalan Finishes	H&C	22	1		Wi 71	18
Gould, Mary	What a Doll! Provocative Paper Dolls, a Captivating Idea	Fa	8	1		J/F 81	78
Goutmann, Marylyn	Fabric Structures—Basic Weave Design	WJ	5	3	19	Wi 81	51
Grabiner, Dana M.	Slave Quilts: Threads of History	Fa	13	5		S/O 86	22
Grace, Leslie	Bit of Rope Turns Cloth Into a Dancer's Costume, A	TM			10	A/M 87	20
Grae, Ida	Nature's Colors	SS&D	6	2	22	Sp 75	63
Grae, Ida	Nature's Colors: Dyes from Plants	H&C	26	1		J/F 75	30
Granberg, Carol	Sectional Warping Simplified	H&C	6	1		Wi 54	49
Grange, Penny	White Jacket	WJ	8	3	31	Wi 83	16
Grant, Jay S.	Family Hobby Becomes a Family Business	H&C	7	4		Fa 56	49
Grant, Susan	Bibliography of Children's Textile Literature, A	Iw	4	4		Fa 79	66
Grant, Susan	In Pursuit of a Lifestyle	Iw	5	2		Sp 80	32
Grant, Susan	Leni Hoch: "...To Hell with These Loom-Shaped Garments"	Fa	5	5		S/O 78	46
Grant, Susan	Spinning with Gandhi	S-O	2			78	15
Grant, Susan	Unnatural Acts with Natural Dyes or How I Learned to Love the Weed	Fa	5	1		J/F 78	48
Graser, Marie E.	Cornucopia (Horn of Plenty)	WJ	7	2	26	Fa 82	52
Graser, Marie E.	Double Handled Melon Basket (error-corrected WJ v7 n1 82 p36b)	WJ	6	4	24	Sp 82	42
Graser, Marie E.	Onion Basket	WJ	8	2	30	Fa 83	48
Graves, John; Susan Graves	Simple Ways to Hang a Weaving	WJ	10	4	40	Sp 86	69
Graves, Susan	see Graves, John	WJ	10	4	40	Sp 86	69
Gray, Herbi	Cardwoven Double Weave, Part 2	SS&D	15	1	57	Wi 83	92
Gray, Herbi	Cardwoven Gauze	PWC			6	Su 83	57
Gray, Herbi	Cardwoven Mattor (Part 1)	SS&D	14	4	56	Fa 83	64
Gray, Herbi	Finnish Method of Weaving Transparent Inlay, A	SS&D	17	1	65	Wi 85	14
Gray, Herbi	On-Loom Card Weaving: A Modern Extension of an Ancient Craft	SS&D	14	2	54	Sp 83	62
Gray, Herbi	On-Loom Cardweaving: "A Modern Extension of an Ancient Craft"	Hw	5	4		S/O 84	14
Gray, Herbi	On-Loom Cardweaving, A Modern Extension of an Ancient Craft	WJ	7	2	26	Fa 82	60
Gray, Herbi	On-Loom Cardweaving: A Modern Extension of an Ancient Craft	Fa	10	3		M/J 83	54
Gray, Isabel	Mohair: A Multimillion Dollar Industry for Australia	S-O	8	4		Wi 84	47
Gray, Verdelle	Looms! For Us!	SS&D	4	1	13	Wi 72	15
Grayson, John	see Catling, Dorothy	WJ	8	3	31	Wi 83	67
Grayson, Persis	Novelty Silk Yarn from Bell Caps	Hw	7	1		J/F 86	58
Grayson, Persis	Portrait of a Spinner	S-O	11	3		Fa 87	24
Grayson, Persis	Teacher's Tricks	S-O	10	1		Sp 86	10
Greaves, Lynne	Lynne Greaves' Sweater	S-O	9	2		Su 85	14
Green, Andrea	Shaft-Switching to Create Tapestry Effects	WJ	8	4	32	Sp 84	36
Green, Andrea	Transparent Weaving with Handspun Cotton Weft	WJ	8	2	30	Fa 83	44
Green, Harry B.	Handweaving in Everyday Living	H&C	10	4		Fa 59	24
Green, Jennifer	Self-Sufficient Weaver, The	WJ	8	3	31	Wi 83	68
Green, Judy	Natural Dyes from the Northwest	SS&D	7	2	26	Sp 76	34

AUTHOR	TITLE	JOUR	VOL	NO	ISS	DATE	PAGE
Green, Julie	Classroom Block Printing Project, A	Fa	14	1		J/F 87	41
Green, Larry	Power Fashion, The	TM		5		J/J 86	86
Green, Louise	Felt Making for the Artist	WJ	3	1	9	Jy 78	36
Green, Louise	Felt Making for the Fiber Artist	SS&D	10	1	37	Wi 78	78
Green, Louise	Felt Making for the Fiber Artist	Iw	3	3		Sp 78	50
Green, Louise	Feltmaking: Instant Delight	Iw	3	4		Su 78	18
Green, Louise	Free and Easy Speed Weaving	Iw	3	3		Sp 78	50
Green, Louise	Free and Easy Speed Weaving	WJ	3	1	9	Jy 78	36
Green, Louise	I Think I'll Get a Sheep	SS&D	1	2	2	Mr 70	5
Green, Louise; Debbie Redding	Weaving on Simple Looms	Hw	2	1		F-W 80	21
Green, Louise; Deborah Redding	Weaving on Simple Looms	Iw	2	4		Su 77	36
Green, Marilyn	Beads, Buttons & Findings	Hw	7	5		N/D 86	84
Green, Marilyn	Cataloging Your Needlework Library	Hw	5	5		N/D 84	14
Green, Marilyn	Labels	Hw	5	3		Su 84	14
Green, Phyllis	Karen Chapnick: Constructing Color	Fa	13	2		M/A 86	12
Green, Renah E.	Gift Box Covered with Handwoven Fabrics, A	H&C	17	4		Fa 66	12
Greenberg, Blue	Around the World and Home Again	Fa	9	6		N/D 82	99
Greenberg, Blue	Crazy Quilt for Babies Grand, A	Fa	8	2		M/A 81	31
Greenberg, Blue	"Festival of Weaving" (Exhibit)	Fa	7	4		J/A 80	71
Greenberg, Blue	Heritage Quilt, The	Fa	12	2		M/A 85	90
Greenberg, Blue	"Joyce Kozloff" An Interior Decorated (Exhibit)	Fa	8	1		J/F 81	89
Greene, Susan	Planting Seeds	Hw	5	3		Su 84	40
Greer, Gertrude G.	Adventures in Weaving	H&C	2	1		Wi 50	60
Greer, Gertrude G.	Adventures in Weaving	H&C	2	3		Su 51	61
Greer, Gertrude G.	Solving a Difficult Warping Problem	H&C	2	3		Su 51	44
Greer, Gertrude G.	Weaver At Five, A	H&C	2	2		Sp 51	49
Greer, Tyson	Lynn DiNino	Fa	13	2		M/A 86	14
Gregg, Dorothy	In the Gobelin Tradition: The Drouin Atelier	SS&D	10	1	37	Wi 78	28
Gregg, Marcia	Dunlaps: New Mexico to Tunisia, The	S-O	4			80	4
Grey	Using Procion Fiber Reactive Dyes for Batik, Fabric Printing and Tie-Dye	Fa	5	1		J/F 78	40
Grey, Herbi	On-Loom Card Weaving	PWC		3		Oc 82	63
Grey, Robin	Robin Grey's Batiker's Guide	Fa	4	2		M/A 77	41
Griffey, Margaret	Why Do I Weave Tapestries? An Exploration of Color Theory and Tapestry Design (error-corrected Fa v7 n6 80 p8)	Fa	7	4		J/A 80	55
Griffin, Gertrude	From a Dyer's Diary	SS&D	1	3	3	Ju 70	21
Griffin, Gertrude	From a Dyer's Diary	SS&D	4	1	13	Wi 72	11
Griffin, Gertrude	Japanese Tote—The Furoshiki, A	SS&D	6	1	21	Wi 74	78
Griffin, Gertrude	Pictures in Summer & Winter Pick-up	Hw	7	2		M/A 86	54
Griffin, Rachael	Conversion of Sorts: Judith Poxson Fawkes—A Background in Painting, A Present in Weaving, A	Fa	7	6		N/D 80	52
Griffin, Rachel	"Marie Lyman: Liturgical Vestments" (Exhibit)	Fa	7	3		M/J 80	77
Griffiths, Alice K.	Teneriffe Lace—Brazilian Point	SS&D	4	4	16	Fa 73	33
Griffiths, Helen M.	Arctic Handknitted, One Hundred Per Cent Qiviut	H&C	22	2		Sp 71	6
Griffiths, Helen M.	Qiviut Update	SS&D	7	4	28	Fa 76	60
Griswold, Irene T.	Redwood Christmas Tree	SS&D	3	1	9	Wi 71	12
Griswold, Irene T.	School Psychologist Finds Weaving Valuable	SS&D	5	1	17	Wi 73	73
Griswold, Kathleen	see Griswold, Lester	H&C	24	2		M/A 73	5
Griswold, Lester; Kathleen Griswold	New Handicraft Processes and Projects, 10th Edition, The	H&C	24	2		M/A 73	5
Groesbeck, Kaye	Magical Menagerie (Lael Diehm)	Hw	6	5		N/D 85	34
Groff, Russell E.	Card Weaving or Tablet Weaving	SS&D	3	4	12	Fa 72	47
Groff, Russell E.	Card Weaving or Tablet Weaving	H&C	12	2		Sp 61	59

AUTHOR	TITLE	JOUR	VOL	NO	ISS	DATE	PAGE
Gropius, Ise, ed.	see Bayer, Herbert, ed.	H&C	3	3		Su 52	64
Gropius, Walter, ed.	see Bayer, Herbert, ed.	H&C	3	3		Su 52	64
Gross, Laurence F.	Saga of a Fancy Woolen Loom, The	SS&D	9	3	35	Su 78	25
Grossman, Ellin	Ancient Peruvian Loom, An	H&C	9	2		Sp 58	20
Grossman, Ellin	Weft Looped Pile Fabrics from Mexico	H&C	8	2		Sp 57	6
Grossman, Ellin F.	Textiles and Looms from Guatemala & Mexico	H&C	7	1		Wi 55	6
Groth, Paul E.	Engineers Approach to Sectional Warping, An	Hw	7	4		S/O 86	16
Grover, Donald	"Basket-Maker's Art, The" (Exhibit)	Fa	6	6		N/D 79	73
Grover, Donald	"Diaghilev—Costumes and Designs of the Ballets Russes" (Exhibit)	Fa	6	3		M/J 79	79
Grover, Donald	"Embroidery Through the Ages" (Exhibit)	Fa	5	6		N/D 78	62
Grover, Donald	Fleeting Fantasies: Julia Hill's Painting on Silk	Fa	6	4		J/A 79	12
Grover, Donald	"Great American Foot, The" (Exhibit)	Fa	5	4		J/A 78	15
Grover, Donald	"Josef Grau-Garriga" (Exhibit)	Fa	5	2		M/A 78	13
Grover, Donald	"Norma Minkowitz" (Exhibit)	Fa	6	5		S/O 79	77
Grover, Donald	"Olga de Amaral" (Exhibit)	Fa	5	1		J/F 78	18
Grover, Donald	Paulus Berensohn: A Potter Discovers Canvas Embroidery	Fa	6	5		S/O 79	28
Grover, Donald	"Wall Hangings: The New Classicism" (Exhibit)	Fa	4	4		J/A 77	10
Grover, Donald	"Wearables" (Exhibit)	Fa	6	6		N/D 79	76
Grover, Donald	Who, How, What, and When of Wearables, The	Fa	6	3		M/J 79	66
Grunberg, Liane	Amy Silberkleit: Bringing Gothic Tales to Life	Fa	13	1		J/F 86	17
Grunberg, Liane	Debra Minsky-Jackson: Renaissance Visions in Fiber	Fa	11	4		J/A 84	68
Grünig, Erika Deletaz	Apprenons a Tisser	WJ	9	1	33	Su 84	59
Guagliumi, Sasan	"Art Couture '82" (Exhibit)	Fa	10	1		J/F 83	84
Guagliumi, Susan	Appropriate Designs for Short-Row and Slip Intarsia	TM			10	A/M 87	70
Guagliumi, Susan	Basic Knitting Machine, The	TM			1	O/N 85	34
Guagliumi, Susan	Charting Intarsia Designs	TM			10	A/M 87	69
Guagliumi, Susan	Diagonal Cables: A Machine Knitter's Guide to Cabling Against the Grain	TM			14	D/J 87	58
Guagliumi, Susan	Drafting Primer	WJ	5	2	18	Fa 80	33
Guagliumi, Susan	Drafting Primer	Hw	2	3		My 81	70
Guagliumi, Susan	Eye of a Photographer, Hand of a Weaver: An Artist Combines Two Art Forms	Fa	8	6		N/D 81	35
Guagliumi, Susan	"Frank Gardner: Aleatory Works" (Exhibit)	Fa	9	2		M/A 82	75
Guagliumi, Susan	Gadgets for Machine Knitters	TM			13	O/N 87	14
Guagliumi, Susan	Handwoven	SS&D	8	2	30	Sp 77	38
Guagliumi, Susan	Handwoven	WJ	1	3	3	Ja 77	32
Guagliumi, Susan	Knitters, Make a Trip to the Fabric Store	TM			7	O/N 86	35
Guagliumi, Susan	Knitting for a Living (error-corrected TM i6 A/S86 p6)	TM			4	A/M 86	38
Guagliumi, Susan	Knitting Machine Geometrics	TM			10	A/M 87	66
Guagliumi, Susan	Knotted Netting Methods	SS&D	10	3	39	Su 79	86
Guagliumi, Susan	Machine Knitters Meet in Seattle	TM			12	A/S 87	16
Guagliumi, Susan	Machine-Knit Popcorns	TM			6	A/S 86	71
Guagliumi, Susan	One Who Dies with the Most Stuff Wins!, The	TM			11	J/J 87	15
Guagliumi, Susan	Putting Knitted Pieces Together	TM			11	J/J 87	45
Guagliumi, Susan	see Bowman, Susan	SS&D	10	3	39	Su 79	52
Guagliumi, Susan	Six-Harness Challenge: Triple Weave Pick-Up, A	SS&D	9	2	34	Sp 78	99
Guagliumi, Susan	"Soft As Silk" (Exhibit)	Fa	10	1		J/F 83	78
Guagliumi, Susan	"Splendor of French Style, The" Textiles from Joan of Arc to Napoleon III (Exhibit)	Fa	13	4		J/A 86	13
Guagliumi, Susan	Tale of Tucks, A (error-corrected SS&D v7 n1 75 p63)	SS&D	7	1	25	Wi 75	56
Guagliumi, Susan	Textile Study Group, The (Exhibit)	Fa	13	3		M/J 86	54
Guagliumi, Susan Fletcher	"Art Couture VII" (Exhibit)	Fa	12	3		M/J 85	78
Guagliumi, Susan Fletcher	From Harness Sheds to Double Beds	Fa	10	6		N/D 83	52
Guagliumi, Susan Fletcher	Tapestry Washings at the Wadsworth Atheneum	Hw	5	2		M/A 84	18

AUTHOR	TITLE	JOUR	VOL	NO	ISS	DATE	PAGE
Gubser, Elsie H.	Bobbin Lace	H&C	17	4		Fa 66	45
Gubser, Elsie H.	Designs in Old Linen Tablecloths	H&C	9	3		Su 58	21
Gubser, Elsie H.	Four Projects from Mrs. Elsie H. Gubser	H&C	6	3		Su 55	49
Gubser, Elsie H.	Sectional Warping Without Spools	H&C	8	1		Wi 56	50
Gubser, Elsie H.	Ten-Harness Design for a Towel	H&C	9	4		Fa 58	28
Gubser, Elsie H.	Tricks of the Trade	H&C	6	4		Fa 55	29
Gubser, Elsie H.	Two Weaves from Mexico	H&C	11	3		Su 60	26
Gubser, Elsie H.	Weaving Spanish Eyelet	H&C	10	1		Wi 59	48
Gue, Sandra	Evolution of An Artist: Morgan Clifford	Fa	14	5		N/D 87	27
Gue, Sandra	Morgan Clifford: New Dircetions in Brocades	WJ	11	4	44	Sp 87	40
Gulbis, Elina	Latvian Folk Costume Braids	SS&D	4	3	15	Su 73	46
Gulick, Evelyn M.	Make Your Selvages Talk	H&C	5	2		Sp 54	12
Gulick, Evelyn M.	Suggestions for the Beginning Weaver	H&C	19	1		Wi 68	12
Gupta, Asha	Kantha Cloths of Bengal: The Sari Transformed	Fa	9	6		N/D 82	19
Gustafson, Paula	Salis Weaving	Hw	2	4		Se 81	80
Gustafson, Paula	Salish Weaving	WJ	6	3	23	Wi 81	59
Gustafson, Susan	Skeleton Peg Plan for the Compu-Dobby, A	CW	6	3	18	My 85	24
Gustafson, Susan	Weaver's Spreadsheet Template	CW	6	3	18	My 85	21
Gustafson, Susan L.	Can You Use Comfort, Sley & Thread in the Same Sentence?	CW	8	1	22	Se 86	11
Gustafson, Susan L.	Modification of the AVL Dobby Loom for Execution of Multi-Shaft Two-Tie Block Weaves	AT	1			De 83	235
Gustafsson & Saarto	Pellavasta Kudottua (Flax Weaving)	H&C	10	1		Wi 59	60
Gutcheon, Beth	"Jean Ray Laury — Exhibit of Stitchery" (Exhibit)	Fa	6	2		M/A 79	66
Gutcheon, Beth	"New Works in Batik by Laura Adasko" (Exhibit)	Fa	5	3		M/J 78	12
Gutcheon, Beth	Presence of Light: The Un-Traditional Quilts of Jan Myers, The	Fa	8	3		M/J 81	60
Gutcheon, Beth	"Quilt National '79" (Exhibit)	Fa	6	5		S/O 79	80
Guy, Sallie T.	Accent on Napkins	Hw	8	1		J/F 87	60
Guy, Sallie T.	Coverlet Tradition in Kentucky, The	Iw	4	3		Su 79	35
Guy, Sallie T.	Demonstrating How Cloth Is Made	SS&D	6	2	22	Sp 75	24
Guy, Sallie T.	Double Width Weaving: Dealing with the Fold	CW	5	3	15	My 84	17
Guy, Sallie T.	New Zealand Woolcrafts Festival	SS&D	14	4	56	Fa 83	28
Guy, Sallie T.	Quicksand Craft Center: A New Way of Life for Kentucky Mountain Women	Hw	2	4		Se 81	16
Guy, Sallie T.	Rx: Shed Corrections	Hw	3	1		Ja 82	78
Guy, Sallie T.	Rx: Uneven Warp Tension	Hw	3	3		My 82	84
Guy, Sallie T.	Rx: Warp End Breakage and Treadling Errors	Hw	3	4		Se 82	22
Guy, Sallie T.	Rx: Winding and Threading Errors	Hw	2	5		No 81	66
Guy, Sallie T.	Tailored Bog Jacket, A	SS&D	17	1	65	Wi 85	26
Guy, Sallie T.	Tailored Bog Jacket (Revisited), A	SS&D	18	1	69	Wi 86	60
Guy, Sallie T.	twill ^ 2 = Double Width Afghans	SS&D	15	1	57	Wi 83	34
Guyar, Niki	"Ruth Geneslaw/Pat Malarcher" (Exhibit)	Fa	6	4		J/A 79	66
Guyer, Niki	"Anni Albers: Current Work" (Exhibit)	Fa	6	6		N/D 79	72
Guyer, Niki	"Contemporary Fiber Art" (Exhibit)	Fa	5	6		N/D 78	66
Guyer, Niki	Woman on a Pedestal and Other Everyday Folks	Fa	8	2		M/A 81	22
Guyler, Vivian Varney	Design in Nature	SS&D	3	2	10	Sp 72	38
Gwynne, Elaine	Chemical Dyeing of Linen	WJ	7	2	26	Fa 82	23
Hacker, Katherine F.; Krista Jensen Turnbull	Courtyard, Bazaar, Temple: Traditions of Textile Expression in India	Hw	7	4		S/O 86	11
Hafermann, Candy Kreitlow	Weaving and Light: Creative Ideas and Techniques for Your Next Show	Iw	5	3		Su 80	34
Hagan, Kathleen	Cotton: An Invitation	WJ	4	2	14	Oc 79	12
Hagarty, Harriet May	If You Have 4 Harnesses	H&C	24	2		M/A 73	44
Hagarty, Harriet May	If You Have Four Harnesses	H&C	23	5		S/O 72	16
Hagarty, Harriet May	If You Have Four Harnesses	H&C	23	6		N/D 72	32

AUTHOR	TITLE	JOUR	VOL	NO	ISS	DATE	PAGE
Hagarty, Harriet May	If You Have Four Harnesses	H&C	24	3		M/J 73	30
Hagarty, Harriet May	If You Have Four Harnesses	H&C	24	1		J/F 73	11
Hagarty, Harriet May	If You Have Four Harnesses	H&C	26	1		J/F 75	24
Hagemeister-Winzenz, Karon	"Made in Wisconsin: An Exhibition of Recent Works In-Of-And-On Handmade Paper" (Exhibit)	Fa	5	4		J/A 78	19
Hagino, Jane Parker; Karen E. Stothert	Weaving a Cotton Saddlebag on the Santa Elena Peninsula of Ecuador	TMJ	22			83	19
Haglich, Sr. Bianca; Raija Ranne	Linen in Finland	SS&D	8	3	31	Su 77	84
Hahn, Kandra	Patches on Patches	TM			6	A/S 86	22
Hahn, Roslyn	Textiles for Today's Church: A Guide to Creating Fiber Art	Hw	6	3		Su 85	20
Hahn, Roslyn	Violet Vestment	WJ	8	3	31	Wi 83	44
Hahn, Roslyn J.	Weaving for the Church—A Challenge	Hw	5	1		J/F 84	32
Haight, Barbara M.	see Merrill, Ruth R.!	SS&D	7	2	26	Sp 76	34
Hains, Maryellen	Ann Burian: Mythic Transformations	Fa	12	2		M/A 85	21
Hákonardóttir, Hildur	Icelandic Weaving: Saga In Wool	Hw	8	3		M/J 87	62
Hald, Margrethe	Ancient Danish Textiles from Bogs and Burials, A Comparative Study of Costume and Iron Age Textiles	SS&D	13	2	50	Sp 82	62
Hald, Margrethe	Ancient Danish Textiles from Bogs and Burials—A Comparative Study of Costume and Iron Age Textiles	WJ	6	4	24	Sp 82	58
Hall, A. R., ed.	see Singer, Charles, ed.	H&C	8	2		Sp 57	59
Hall, A. S.	Standard Handbook of Textiles, The	H&C	17	1		Wi 66	45
Hall, Carolyn	Sewing Machine Craft Book, The	Fa	8	4		J/A 81	62
Hall, Carolyn Vosburg	Design By Decision: A Practical Approach to the Creative Process	Fa	8	2		M/A 81	13
Hall, Carolyn Vosburg	Give and Take of Apprenticeship in the Fiber Arts: A Master's View, The (error-noted but uncorrected Fa v8 n5 81 p6)	Fa	8	4		J/A 81	24
Hall, Eliza Calvert	Book of Hand-Woven Coverlets, A	H&C	18	1		Wi 67	43
Hall, Joanne	Mexican Tapestry Weaving	SS&D	8	3	31	Su 77	61
Hall, Joanne	Mexican Tapestry Weaving	WJ	1	4	4	Ap 77	26
Hall, Joanne	Mexican Tapestry Weaving	Fa	4	4		J/A 77	62
Hall, Joanne	Tapestry in Twill: A Free Approach	Hw	3	1		Ja 82	46
Hall, Joanne	Uno Mas — The Secret Of Mexican Tapestry	SS&D	5	3	19	Su 74	88
Hall, Joanne Arvidson	Uncommon Dyewood: Manzanita—From the Chaparral, An	SS&D	7	3	27	Su 76	55
Hall, Julie	Tradition and Change—The New American Craftsman	SS&D	9	3	35	Su 78	95
Hall, Margaret	see Irwin, John	TMJ	3	4		De 73	46
Hall, Margaret	see Irwin, John	TMJ	4	2		75	80
Hall, Nancy Terrell	Production-wise Placemats (error-corrected WJ v9 n2 84 p82)	WJ	9	1	33	Su 84	44
Hall, Wendy	British Revival in Handweaving, The	H&C	4	3		Su 53	21
Haller, Jean M.	Tartan Book: A Study Group Project, The	Hw	4	5		N/D 83	31
Halpern, Nancy	"Crow Quilt"	Fa	8	3		M/J 81	24
Halsey, Mark	Double Cloth (on four-shaft looms) Monograph 2	SS&D	11	1	41	Wi 79	34
Halsy, Mike; Lore Youngmark	Foundations of Weaving	Fa	3	2		M/A 76	25
Ham, Phebe D.	Happy Weaver of the Isle of Harris, The	SS&D	1	2	2	Mr 70	12
Hamaker, Barbara	Clothing: A Handwoven Approach	SS&D	10	3	39	Su 79	35
Hamaker, Barbara	Clothing: A Handwoven Approach	Iw	4	2		Sp 79	62
Hamaker, Barbara	Clothing: A Handwoven Approach	WJ	4	3	15	Ja 80	45
Hamaker, Barbara	Clothing: A Handwoven Approach	Hw	1	2		S-S 80	14
Hamaker, Barbara	You Are Unique — There is No Competition!	WJ	6	4	24	Sp 82	37
Hamamura, John	Photographing Your Fiber Work — Two Common Problems and Their Solutions	SS&D	9	4	36	Fa 78	20
Hamamura, John; Susan Hamamura	Woven Works	SS&D	10	3	39	Su 79	35
Hamamura, John; Susan Hamamura	Woven Works	Iw	4	3		Su 79	64

AUTHOR	TITLE	JOUR	VOL	NO	ISS	DATE	PAGE
Hamamura, John; Susan Hamamura	Woven Works	WJ	3	3	11	Ja 79	43
Hamamura, John; Susan Hamamura	Woven Works	Fa	5	6		N/D 78	73
Hamamura, Susan	see Hamamura, John	SS&D	10	3	39	Su 79	35
Hamamura, Susan	see Hamamura, John	Iw	4	3		Su 79	64
Hamamura, Susan	see Hamamura, John	WJ	3	3	11	Ja 79	43
Hamamura, Susan	see Hamamura, John	Fa	5	6		N/D 78	73
Hambidge, Jay	Elements of Dynamic Symmetry, The	H&C	19	3		Su 68	42
Hambidge, Jay	Practical Applications of Dynamic Symmetry	H&C	19	3		Su 68	41
Hamelin, Véronique	Le Flêché Authentique Du Québec	WJ	8	2	30	Fa 83	63
Hamer, Rosalie	Texture Stitches for Needlepoint	TM			5	J/J 86	62
Hamilton, Carolyn	Handing Down More Than Just a Quilt	TM			12	A/S 87	86
Hamilton, Eva B.	North Shore Weavers Guild	H&C	20	4		Fa 69	33
Hamilton, Stephen	Aritst's Suggestions for More Effective Display of Handweaving, An	H&C	13	2		Sp 62	10
Hammett-Bregger, Frieda	Confessions of a Brave New Cotton Spinner	S-O	3			79	15
Hammock, Noël	Directory of Plans for Weaving and Spinning Equipment	SS&D	6	2	22	Sp 75	27
Hammond, Joyce D.	Tifaifai and Quilts of Polynesia	Fa	14	2		M/A 87	61
Hammond, Joyce D.	Tifaifai and Quilts of Polynesia	TM			13	O/N 87	78
Hamre, Ida; Hanne Meedam	Making Simple Clothes	WJ	6	4	24	Sp 82	58
Hancock, Charlene	Rainbow of Color At MLH Conference	SS&D	1	4	4	Se 70	21
Hand, Barbara	Rug Weaving: One Weaver's Approach	WJ	7	4	28	Sp 83	32
Handweavers and Spinners Guild of Victoria	Wool and Beyond: First Australian Fibre Conference	SS&D	14	2	54	Sp 83	62
Handweavers Guild of Boston	Processing and Finishing Handwoven Textiles	SS&D	12	4	48	Fa 81	63
Handy, Virginia	My Linen Curtain	S-O	10	3		Fa 86	23
Handy, Virginia	Virginia's Handy Tips for Flax Growing	S-O	10	3		Fa 86	44
Handy-Marchello, Barbara	Mother-Wit and the Dyepot	WJ	9	2	34	Fa 84	25
Haney, Jeanna T.	Gertrude Parker: Metamorphosing a Humble Material	Fa	14	4		S/O 87	8
Hanks, Nancy	Shuttle Power	SS&D	7	4	28	Fa 76	45
Hanley, Janet	Complimentary-Weft Plain Weave — A Pick-up Technique (error-corrected WJ v5 n1 80 p28d)	WJ	4	4	16	Ap 80	22
Hanley, Janet	Spot Weave Rug	WJ	3	4	12	Ap 79	40
Hanna, Linda	Each One Picked a Color—4th and 5th Graders Weave a Blanket	WJ	9	1	33	Su 84	34
Hannah, Joyce	Sisal for Hammocks	TM			6	A/S 86	18
Hannah, Joyce	Versatile Jacket, A	TM			1	O/N 85	44
Hannah, Joyce	Visiting the Kimono School	TM			4	A/M 86	16
Hannon, Farrell	Balinese Ikat	WJ	5	1	17	Su 80	49
Hannon, Farrell	Sumbanese Ikat	WJ	8	1	29	Su 83	38
Hannon, Farrell	Tying Warp Ikat on the Loom	WJ	8	1	29	Su 83	41
Hannon, Farrell	Weavers of Bali	SS&D	18	4	72	Fa 87	46
Hansen, Debby; Betty Morris	Basketry Workshop & Show at the Fairtree Gallery, A	H&C	24	3		M/J 73	43
Hansen, Helen; Meade Nichol	Handweaving in Memphis	H&C	8	1		Wi 56	19
Hansen, Pauline M.	Photograph Your Weaving	SS&D	5	2	18	Sp 74	79
Hansen, Robin	Fox & Geese & Fences	Kn	3	1	5	F-W 86	69
Hansen, Robin; Janetta Dexter	Flying Geese & Partidge Feet, More Mittens from Up North and Down East	Kn	3	1	5	F-W 86	69
Hansen, Shirley	White and Red Mittens	Kn	3	1	5	F-W 86	35
Hanson, Lori	see Amos, Alden	Iw	4	1		Wi 78	54
Hardin, Noma	International Textile Exhibition, The	H&C	6	1		Wi 54	28
Harding, Patricia	Twill Stoll	S-O	4			80	61
Hardt, Blanche	Texas Fabrics	H&C	8	3		Su 57	31
Harel, Uri	Art Feeds the Hungry	Fa	13	4		J/A 86	11

AUTHOR	TITLE	JOUR	VOL	NO	ISS	DATE	PAGE
Hargrove, John	Weavers Draft Book and Clothiers Assistant, The	SS&D	10	4	40	Fa 79	64
Hargrove, John	Weavers Draft Book and Clothiers Assistant, The	WJ	7	1	25	Su 82	63
Hargrove, John (Compiler)	Weavers Draft Book and Clothiers Assistant, The	Iw	4	3		Su 79	66
Harner, Sandra Dickey	see Brandford, Joanne Segal	Fa	12	5		S/O 85	70
Haroutunian, Judith	Covered Things	WJ	8	1	29	Su 83	53
Harries, Jeanette	see Forelli, Sally	TMJ	4	4		77	41
Harrington, Elaine	"Recent Work by Elsa Waller" (Exhibit)	Fa	8	4		J/A 81	71
Harris, Moira F.	see Eircher, Joanne B.	WJ	11	3	43	Wi 87	64
Harris, Pat	"Show-Off" Bobbin Lace	SS&D	6	3	23	Su 75	21
Harris, Patricia; David Lyon	Made By Machine: Textiles for the Eighties	Fa	12	5		S/O 85	34
Harris, Patricia; David Lyon	"New England Images" (Exhibit)	Fa	10	6		N/D 83	78
Harris, Patricia; David Lyon	Soft Sculpture of Barbara Ward, The	Fa	14	1		J/F 87	10
Harris, Patricia; David Lyon	Stitch in Time, A	Fa	12	2		M/A 85	27
Harris, Patricia; David Lyon	Tapestries of Dilys Stinson, The	Fa	13	2		M/A 86	18
Harrison, Helen A.	"Felt and Papermaking" (Exhibit)	Fa	11	2		M/A 84	79
Harrisville Designs	Fabric Book, The	Iw	6	1		Wi 80	69
Harrold, Yoko Tamari	Bound Weave Rugs	WJ	2	1	5	Jy 77	20
Harse, Crys	Shaft-Switching on Rising Shed Looms Using Weighted Floating Heddles	WJ	9	4	36	Sp 85	63
Hart, Carol	Basket Willow: Cultivating and Gathering the Withy	TM			3	F/M 86	63
Hart, Carol	Making an Open-Weave Willow Basket	TM			4	A/M 86	24
Hart, Carol; Dan Hart	Natural Basketry	SS&D	8	1	29	Wi 76	70
Hart, Carol; Dan Hart	Natural Basketry	Fa	4	1		J/F 77	43
Hart, Dan	see Hart, Carol	SS&D	8	1	29	Wi 76	70
Hart, Dan	see Hart, Carol	Fa	4	1		J/F 77	43
Hart, Jacque	Hand-Dyed Angora Bunny Scarf	S-O	11	4		Wi 87	26
Hart, Molly	Molly Hart	Fa	14	2		M/A 87	23
Hart, Robert G.	From the Great Smokies to Rockefeller Center — The Southern Highland Handicraft Guild	H&C	2	3		Su 51	5
Hart, Robert G.	How to Sell Your Handicraft	H&C	5	1		Wi 53	59
Hart, Robert G.	Marketing for Handweavers	H&C	1	2		Su 50	42
Hart, Robert G.	Pricing the Craftsman's Products	H&C	1	3		Fa 50	58
Hart, Robert G.	Promoting the Craftsman's Product	H&C	2	1		Wi 50	48
Hart, Rosana	Living with Llamas: Adventures, Photos, and a Practical Guide	Fa	13	5		S/O 86	57
Harter, Jim, selector	Animals: 1419 Copyrightfree Illustrations	Fa	7	4		J/A 80	22
Hartford, Jane	Fashion Ballet	SS&D	6	1	21	Wi 74	85
Hartford, Jane	Utah Guild Sheep to Shawl	SS&D	8	2	30	Sp 77	23
Hartford, Jane; Thom Hartford III	Flight Into Fantasy (error-corrected SS&D v12 n1 80 p6)	SS&D	11	4	44	Fa 80	57
Hartford, Thom III	see Hartford, Jane	SS&D	11	4	44	Fa 80	57
Hartman, Shirley G.	"Weaving with Lucille Landis" (Exhibit)	Fa	9	2		M/A 82	76
Hartung, Rolf	Creative Textile Design—Color and Texture	SS&D	3	4	12	Fa 72	47
Hartung, Rolf	Creative Textile Design—Thread and Fabric	SS&D	3	4	12	Fa 72	47
Hartung, Rolf	Creative Textile Design — Thread and Fabric	H&C	16	1		Wi 65	43
Hartung, Rolf	More Creative Textile Design — Color and Texture	H&C	16	4		Fa 65	44
Harvey, Jane	Marianne Granville, Designer with Old World Background	H&C	16	4		Fa 65	16
Harvey, Nancy	Contemporary Tapestry: A Panoramic View (error-corrected SS&D v17 n3 86 p5)	SS&D	17	2	66	Sp 86	18
Harvey, Nancy	D. Y. Begay: A Navajo Weaver in New York City	SS&D	17	4	68	Fa 86	32
Harvey, Nancy	Guide to Successful Tapestry Weaving, The	WJ	6	2	22	Fa 81	39

AUTHOR	TITLE	JOUR	VOL	NO	ISS	DATE	PAGE
Harvey, Nancy	Guide to Successful Tapestry Weaving, The	WJ	12	1	45	Su 87	69
Harvey, Nancy	Guide to Successful Tapestry Weaving, The	PWC		3		Oc 82	63
Harvey, Nancy	Patterns for Tapestry Weaving: Projects and Techniques	Hw	6	1		J/F 85	16
Harvey, Nancy	Patterns for Tapestry Weaving—Projects and Techniques	WJ	12	1	45	Su 87	69
Harvey, Nancy	Special Piece—A Special Place, A	WJ	8	1	29	Su 83	67
Harvey, Nancy	Tapestry	SS&D	14	3	55	Su 83	20
Harvey, Nancy	Tapestry: As a Business?	SS&D	15	3	59	Su 84	37
Harvey, Nancy	Tapestry for Interiors	Hw	3	1		Ja 82	42
Harvey, Nancy	Tapestry: Its Limitations Challenge Individual Creativity	SS&D	17	1	65	Wi 85	57
Harvey, Nancy	Tapestry: Part 2—The Dreaded Circle	SS&D	14	4	56	Fa 83	8
Harvey, Nancy	Tapestry (Part 3): An Inside View	SS&D	15	2	58	Sp 84	20
Harvey, Nancy	Tapestry Tips—Part 1	WJ	12	1	45	Su 87	13
Harvey, Nancy	Tapestry Tips, Part 2	WJ	12	2	46	Fa 87	9
Harvey, Nancy	Tapestry Weaving – Level 1	Hw	7	4		S/O 86	10
Harvey, Nancy	Tapestry Weaving—Level 1	WJ	10	4	40	Sp 86	83
Harvey, Nancy	Tapestry Weaving — Level 1	PWC	4	1	11		55
Harvey, Nancy	Tapestry Weaving—Level 2	WJ	12	1	45	Su 87	71
Harvey, Nancy	Workshops	Hw	7	1		J/F 86	13
Harvey, Virginia	Basketry Technics, Part 1	SS&D	6	2	22	Sp 75	12
Harvey, Virginia	Basketry Technics, Part 2	SS&D	6	3	23	Su 75	30
Harvey, Virginia	Bateman Legacy, The	PWC	4	4	14		50
Harvey, Virginia	Color and Design in Macrame	SS&D	3	2	10	Sp 72	38
Harvey, Virginia	Techniques of Basketry, The	SS&D	6	2	22	Sp 75	64
Harvey, Virginia	Techniques of Basketry, The	Fa	4	1		J/F 77	43
Harvey, Virginia	Threads in Action	SS&D	1	3	3	Ju 70	22
Harvey, Virginia	Threads in Action Monograph, Vols.1 & 2	H&C	21	2		Sp 70	41
Harvey, Virginia; Harriet Tidball	Weft Twining, Shuttle Craft Guild Monograph Twenty-Eight, 1969	H&C	21	1		Wi 70	42
Harvey, Virginia I.	Bateman Blend Weaves Extended Beyond Eight Harnesses, Part 1	CW	4	3	12	Ap 83	9
Harvey, Virginia I.	Bateman Blend Weaves Extended Beyond Eight Harnesses, Part 2	CW	5	1	13	Se 83	3
Harvey, Virginia I.	Color and Design in Macrame	H&C	22	4		Fa 71	26
Harvey, Virginia I.	Extending Dr. Bateman's Park Weaves	CW	6	3	18	My 85	3
Harvey, Virginia I.	Extending Dr. William G. Bateman's Multiple Tabby Weaves Beyond Eight Harnesses (error-corrected CW v4 n3 83 p12)	CW	4	2	11	Ja 83	4
Harvey, Virginia I.	Macramé: The Art of Creative Knotting	H&C	18	3		Su 67	43
Harvey, Virginia I.	Rare Textiles and Costumes in the Collection at the University of Washington	H&C	15	4		Fa 64	15
Harvey, Virginia I.	see Tidball, Harriet	PWC	4	1	11		54
Harvey, Virginia I.	Split-Ply Twining	SS&D	7	3	27	Su 76	34
Harvey, Virginia I.	Split-Ply Twining	TIAM		1		76	1-46
Harvey, Virginia I., ed.	Bateman Blend Weaves	PWC	3	1	7		62
Harvey, Virginia I., ed.	Bateman Blend Weaves: Based on Dr. William Bateman's Manuscript	WJ	7	2	26	Fa 82	59
Harvey, Virginia I., ed.	Bateman Blend Weaves: Based on Dr. William G. Bateman's Manuscript	Hw	4	1		J/F 83	18
Harvey, Virginia I., ed.	Bateman Blend Weaves: Based on Dr. William G. Bateman's Unpublished Manuscript, Papers, Samples	SS&D	14	4	56	Fa 83	74
Harvey, Virginia I., ed.	Multiple Tabby Weaves, Based on Dr. William G. Bateman's Manuscript	SS&D	13	2	50	Sp 82	63
Harvey, Virginia I., ed.	Multiple Tabby Weaves. Based On Dr. William G. Bateman's Manuscript	WJ	6	2	22	Fa 81	39
Harvey, Virginia I., ed.	Multiple Tabby Weaves - Based on Dr. William G. Bateman's Manuscript	PWC		5		Sp 83	68
Harvey, Virginia I., ed.	Park Weaves	Hw	6	3		Su 85	20
Harvey, Virginia I., ed.	Park Weaves Based on Dr. William G. Bateman's Manuscript	WJ	10	2	38	Fa 85	81
Harvey, Virginia I., ed.	Park Weaves Based on Dr. William G. Batemen's Manuscript	PWC	4	1	11		53
Harvey, Virginia I., ed.	Park Weaves Based on Dr. William G. Batemen's Unpublished Manuscript	SS&D	17	2	66	Sp 86	85
Harvey, Virginia I., ed.	see Bateman, Dr. William G.	SCGM		35		81	1-92

AUTHOR	TITLE	JOUR	VOL	NO	ISS	DATE	PAGE
Harvey, Virginia I., ed.	see Bateman, Dr. William G.	SCGM		36		82	1-144
Harvey, Virginia I., ed.	see Bateman, Dr. William G.	SCGM		37		84	1-96
Harvey, Virginia I., ed.	see Bateman, Dr. William G.	SCGM		38		87	1-93
Harvey, Virginia I.; Harriet Tidball	Weft Twining	SCGM		28		69	1-39
Harvey, Virginia I.; Sylvia Tacker	Harriet Tidball	SS&D	8	4	32	Fa 77	4
Harvey, Virginia Isham	Macramé	H&C	19	4		Fa 68	8
Harvey, Virginia Isham	Macramé, Ideal for Finishing Edges	H&C	18	2		Sp 67	15
Harvey, Virginia Isham	Macramé, Knotting Can Add Pattern	H&C	18	3		Su 67	13
Harvey, Virginia Isham	Rib Weaves from India, A Rich Source of Inspiration	H&C	16	4		Fa 65	21
Hatch, David P.	Highland Weavers in Asia	H&C	11	1		Wi 60	6
Hatch, David P.	Some Contemporary Textiles in Southern Asia	H&C	11	3		Su 60	23
Hatch, David P.	Weaving Classes Show Growth at San Jose State College	H&C	13	2		Sp 62	23
Hatch, David Porter	Mexico — Land of Weavers, Part 1	H&C	6	2		Sp 55	10
Hatch, David Porter	Mexico, Land of Weavers, Part 2	H&C	6	3		Su 55	13
Hausner, Walter	Basic Designs for Every Weaver's File	H&C	14	4		Fa 63	22
Hausner, Walter	Basic Weaves, Tool to Develop Fabric Structures (error-corrected H&C v20 n4 69 p43)	H&C	20	3		Su 69	4
Hausner, Walter	Beyond the Powerloom	H&C	22	4		Fa 71	21
Hausner, Walter	Characteristics of Man-made Yarns	H&C	6	3		Su 55	19
Hausner, Walter	Co-ordinated Fabrics	H&C	12	3		Su 61	9
Hausner, Walter	Cotton Plays a Vital Role	H&C	3	3		Su 52	8
Hausner, Walter	Current Developments in Man-made Yarns and Fibers	H&C	9	3		Su 58	41
Hausner, Walter	Design for Hand & Power Loom	H&C	21	1		Wi 70	11
Hausner, Walter	Design Variations in Simple Textures	H&C	8	1		Wi 56	12
Hausner, Walter	Designing in the Reed	H&C	8	2		Sp 57	10
Hausner, Walter	Developments in Man-made Fibers	H&C	11	1		Wi 60	31
Hausner, Walter	Developments in Man-made Fibers	H&C	12	1		Wi 61	13
Hausner, Walter	Dip Dyeing	H&C	22	2		Sp 71	12
Hausner, Walter	Double Weave, First Steps in Development	H&C	15	2		Sp 64	10
Hausner, Walter	Fabric Analysis	H&C	23	1		J/F 72	12
Hausner, Walter	First Step in Designing Textures, A	H&C	9	2		Sp 58	14
Hausner, Walter	Forgotten Weaving Techniques	H&C	24	3		M/J 73	14
Hausner, Walter	Handlooms in Use Today	H&C	15	4		Fa 64	22
Hausner, Walter	Inspiration for New Designs in Cotton	H&C	3	4		Fa 52	23
Hausner, Walter	Jacquard Handlooms	H&C	26	2		Ap 75	17
Hausner, Walter	Man-made Fibers	WJ	9	3	35	Wi 85	61
Hausner, Walter	Master Looks At Ratings, A	SS&D	3	4	12	Fa 72	32
Hausner, Walter	New Developments in Man-made Fibers	H&C	7	3		Su 56	12
Hausner, Walter	Notes on Color Fastness	H&C	10	2		Sp 59	46
Hausner, Walter	Notes on Leno	H&C	7	1		Wi 55	23
Hausner, Walter	On Weaving Chenille Rugs	H&C	3	2		Sp 52	59
Hausner, Walter	Power Looms: The Effect of New Developments on Designers	H&C	17	4		Fa 66	13
Hausner, Walter	Problems in Designing for Hand and Power Looms	H&C	3	1		Wi 51	33
Hausner, Walter	Reed as a Design Element, The	H&C	21	4		Fa 70	20
Hausner, Walter	S and Z Twist	H&C	14	2		Sp 63	37
Hausner, Walter	Suggestions for Finishing Handwoven Fabrics	H&C	10	4		Fa 59	9
Hausner, Walter	Tabby Weave, Ways to Make It More Interesting	H&C	12	4		Fa 61	6
Hausner, Walter	Yarn Count or Number	H&C	9	3		Su 58	31
Hausner, Walter	Yarn Counts	WJ	8	2	30	Fa 83	52
Hausner, Walter A.	Handweaving in the Textile Industry	H&C	9	1		Wi 57	28
Hayes, Beth	Bye, Baby Bunting	S-O	10	2		Su 86	19

AUTHOR	TITLE	JOUR	VOL	NO	ISS	DATE	PAGE
Hayes, Beth	Loving Touches: Handspinning for Babies	S-O	11	2		Su 87	20
Hayes, Beth	Stardust Medallion Sweater	S-O	11	2		Su 87	24
Hayes, Beth	When Jeremy Learned to Knit	TM			2	D/J 85	86
Hayes, Jan	Fast Ashford Wheel, The	SS&D	9	1	33	Wi 77	81
Hayes, Marie	Swedish-English Weaving Glossary	H&C	24	4		Au 73	5
Hayes, Marie C.	Swedish-English Weaving Glossary	SS&D	4	4	16	Fa 73	63
Hayfield, Jesse	California Workshop	H&C	10	4		Fa 59	40
Haynes, Albertje Koopman (see also Koopman)	Loom-Shaped Garment, A	SS&D	9	1	33	Wi 77	83
Haynes, Maryellen	"Ruth's Madcaps" (Exhibit)	Fa	14	4		S/O 87	9
Hays, Mary V.	Recent Gifts of Chinese and Japanese Textiles	TMJ	4	2		75	4
Haywood, Catherine	see Gans, Naomi Beth	SS&D	12	3	47	Su 81	35
Hazen, Gale Grigg	Sew Sane: A Common Sense Approach to Making Your Sewing Machine Work for You	TM			8	D/J 86	74
Hazlett, Paula Renee	Governors' Conference Features Fiber	SS&D	13	1	49	Wi 81	14
Healey, Edna O.	Working with Wool	SS&D	2	4	8	Fa 71	15
Hearne, Gladys	Adventures in Dyeing Wood and Bark (error-corrected SS&D v9 n4 78 p34)	SS&D	9	3	35	Su 78	20
Hearst, Kate	Getting Away Close to Home	TM			7	O/N 86	14
Hearst, Kate	Workshop with Needle Artist Constance Howard, A	TM			14	D/J 87	18
Heartz, Robert F.	Hand Woven Place Mats	H&C	6	1		Wi 54	61
Heartz, Robert F.	Ties for the Handweaver	H&C	6	1		Wi 54	61
Heath, Howard	Handweaving for Industry: The Program at the Rhode Island School of Design	H&C	2	4		Fa 51	14
Heath, Jennifer	Alice McClelland	Fa	5	4		J/A 78	50
Heath, Jennifer	Arvada Project, The	Fa	5	4		J/A 78	45
Hecker, Carolyn	"Focus on Fiber" (Exhibit)	Fa	6	3		M/J 79	83
Hecker, Carolyn	"Free Flow" (Exhibit)	Fa	5	5		S/O 78	73
Hecker, Carolyn	Maria da Conceicao: A Modern Romantic	Fa	6	3		M/J 79	58
Hecker, Carolyn	Mother of Creative Knitting, The	Fa	7	1		J/F 80	34
Hecker, Carolyn	"Printed, Painted, and Dyed: The New Fabric Surface" (Exhibit)	Fa	5	6		N/D 78	71
Hecker, Carolyn A.	Ardyth Davis — Looking At Inkblots and Seeing Jewelry	Fa	5	6		N/D 78	31
Hecker, Carolyn A.	Gloria Marconi: A Commercial Illustrator Mixes Her Media	Fa	6	2		M/A 79	31
Hedlund, Ann Lane	Commercial Materials in Modern Navajo Rugs	TMJ	25			86	83
Hedlund, Ann Lane	Contemporary Navajo Weaving	WJ	11	1	41	Su 86	30
Hedrick, L. R.	To Be Not a Brute, Rousseau Made Lace	TM			10	A/M 87	16
Heimstedt, Leslie	How a "Secret" Spread	SS&D	11	1	41	Wi 79	50
Heintz, Dr. Kenneth; Dr. Henry Thomas	Twenty-two Spinning Wheels	SS&D	5	4	20	Fa 74	60
Heintz, Dr. Kenneth G.	Satisfactory Repair Heddles	SS&D	4	3	15	Su 73	43
Heintz, Kenneth	Tie-Up Made Easy	SS&D	5	3	19	Su 74	68
Heintz, Kenneth G.	see Jackie, Erma	SS&D	4	4	16	Fa 73	53
Heintz, Kenneth G.	Working Drawings for Tyrolese Type Spinning Wheel	SS&D	4	4	16	Fa 73	61
Heisey, John W.	Checklist of American Coverlet Weavers, A	SS&D	10	1	37	Wi 78	77
Heisey, John W. (Compiler)	Checklist of American Coverlet Weavers, A	Iw	4	3		Su 79	66
Heite, Louise	High-Whorl Lap Spindle, The	S-O	10	1		Sp 86	36
Heite, Louise	Spinning with Icelandic Wool	S-O	10	1		Sp 86	33
Heite, Louise B.	Glit — An Icelandic Inlay Technique	Hw	8	3		M/J 87	64
Held, Shirley	Dyeing with Tree Blossoms	SS&D	8	4	32	Fa 77	41
Held, Shirley	Weaving: A Handbook for Fiber Craftsmen	Fa	3	3		M/J 76	40
Held, Shirley E.	Exotic Woods for the Dyepot	SS&D	9	4	36	Fa 78	48
Held, Shirley E.	see Marston, Ena	SS&D	9	1	33	Wi 77	4
Held, Shirley E.	Three British Weavers	H&C	23	6		N/D 72	33
Helfman, Muriel Nezhnie	Tapestry for a Midwest Chapel	H&C	21	2		Sp 70	8

AUTHOR	TITLE	JOUR	VOL	NO	ISS	DATE	PAGE
Helleloid, Richard	Tax Reliever, The	SS&D	10	4	40	Fa 79	64
Heller, K. J.	Craftworker's Marketing Directory	Hw	7	5		N/D 86	14
Heller, Margaret	see van der Hoogt, Madelyn	PWC	4	4	14		34
Hempel, Toby Anne	African Textiles	SS&D	15	1	57	Wi 83	12
Hempel, Toby Anne	All the News That's Fit to Knit	Fa	14	1		J/F 87	14
Hempel, Toby Anne	Annie Hickman: Populating An Insect World	Fa	14	3		M/J 87	32
Hempel, Toby Anne	Mysterious Figurines of Keiko Yamaguchi, The	Fa	14	4		S/O 87	16
Hempel, Toby Anne	"Weaving Without Fiber" (Exhibit)	Fa	13	5		S/O 86	48
Henderson, Helen	Weaving with Florida's Native Materials	H&C	9	2		Sp 58	7
Henderson, Philip	William Morris: His Life, Work and Friends	H&C	19	1		Wi 68	43
Henderson, Philip, ed.	Letters of William Morris to His Family and Friends, The	H&C	2	3		Su 51	61
Henderson, Stew	High-Tech Comes to Weaving: Macomber Looms	Fa	14	4		S/O 87	35
Henderson, Stew	Janice Anthony's Contemporary Quilts	Fa	13	4		J/A 86	22
Hendricks, Carolyn	Project for a Very Narrow Loom: A Vest with Details Woven with Rug Yarn (error-corrected H&C v26 n5 75 p45)	H&C	26	3		M/J 75	16
Hendricks, Carolyn	Russian Peasant Shirt Adaptation	SS&D	8	2	30	Sp 77	96
Henneberger, Karel	Removable Sectional Beam Conversion Kit, A	SS&D	17	1	65	Wi 85	86
Henneberger, Karel	Weaving Music	SS&D	16	4	64	Fa 85	6
Henrikson, Sue	Dyeing to Order	Hw	3	3		My 82	45
Henrikson, Sue	Textured Cottons	WJ	6	3	23	Wi 81	20
Henrikson, Sue	Textured Cottons: Dress and Sauna Robe	WJ	6	3	23	Wi 81	20
Henrikson, Susan	Little Dye Makes the Difference, A	Hw	4	2		M/A 83	60
Henrikson, Susan	Multi-Color, One Pot Dyeing	WJ	8	4	32	Sp 84	39
Henrikson, Susan	see Kampert, Carol	Hw	2	4		Se 81	79
Henrikson, Susan	"Union" Dyes and Another Look at a "Rainbow" Pot	S-O	6	4		82	16
Henry Niles, publ.	Art and Craft Catalyst 1983	WJ	8	2	30	Fa 83	65
Henry, Patti	Tapestry Gunner	TM			7	O/N 86	40
Henzie, Susie	Appraisal of Convergence '72, An	SS&D	3	4	12	Fa 72	41
Henzie, Susie	Distaffs: Scanning Through History	SS&D	9	4	36	Fa 78	56
Henzie, Susie	Dressing the Distaff	SS&D	10	1	37	Wi 78	12
Henzie, Susie	Entanglements	SS&D	3	2	10	Sp 72	45
Henzie, Susie	First Fifteen Years, The	SS&D	16	1	61	Wi 84	44
Henzie, Susie	Woven Circles and Cones	SS&D	10	4	40	Fa 79	58
Henzie, Susie	Woven Garments	WJ	3	4	12	Ap 79	44
Henzie, Suzie	Distaff, The	WJ	7	2	26	Fa 82	10
Hepburn, Ian	Craftsman and Social Conscience: E. F. Schumacher, The	Hw	6	1		J/F 85	20
Hepburn, Ian	Craftsman and Social Conscience, Part 2: Mahatma Gandhi, The	Hw	5	5		N/D 84	22
Hepburn, Ian	Craftsman and Social Conscience: William Morris, The	Hw	5	4		S/0 84	26
Hepworth, K.	see Pourdeyhimi, B.	AT	4			De 85	107
Herman, Mary R.	Mandelina Oberg	H&C	8	4		Fa 57	48
Herold, Joyce	see McKee, Barbara	TMJ	4	2		75	80
Herring, Connie	All Around — Year Around Shawl	PWC			2	Ap 82	70
Herring, Connie	Arabesque	PWC	3	1	7		47
Herring, Connie	Canvas Weave Elegance	PWC	4	1	11		23
Herring, Connie	In Timeless Form	PWC	3	3	9		35
Herring, Connie	Inlay We Trust, Part 1: Half Dukagång	PWC			5	Sp 83	59
Herring, Connie	Inlay We Trust, Part 2: Leno Inlay	PWC			6	Su 83	48
Herring, Connie	Inlay We Trust Part 3: Pillow Based on Greek Inlay Technique	PWC	3	4	10		44
Herring, Connie	Lilies on An Antique Tray	PWC	4	1	11		30
Herring, Connie	Mind Boggling Bogs	PWC			3	Oc 82	36
Herring, Connie	see Lyon, Linda	PWC	3	4	10		64
Herring, Connie	Super Scarf	PWC	3	1	7		28
Herring, Connie	Two Placemats	PWC			5	Sp 83	36

AUTHOR	TITLE	JOUR	VOL	NO	ISS	DATE	PAGE
Herring, Connie	World's Wildest Weaving, The	PWC	1	1		No 81	41
Herring, Connie; Athanasios David Xenakis	Even-Tied Overshot on Four Shafts with Shaft Switching	PWC	3	3	9		44
Herring, Connie; Athanasios David Xenakis	Shaft Switching, A Simple Method Usable for Finer Setts	PWC	3	3	9		29
Herring, Ruth; Karen Manners	Knitting Masterpieces	Kn	3	4	8	Fa 87	63
Herring, Ruth; Karen Manners	Knitting Masterpieces	TM			14	D/J 87	76
Hesketh, Christian	Tartans	H&C	13	1		Wi 62	43
Hessler, Jean	Two Easy Dye Methods	Hw	8	2		M/A 87	86
Hetherington, E.	Welsh Wool Yarn Factory Hires Disabled Veterans	SS&D	5	1	17	Wi 73	28
Hetzler, Patricia	"Patchwork Garden, A" (Exhibit)	Fa	8	5		S/O 81	73
Hetzler, Patricia T.	Patricia T. Hetzler	Fa	14	2		M/A 87	24
Hewitt, Furze; Billie Daley	Classic Knitted Cotton Edgings	Kn	4	1	9	Wi 87	61
Hewitt, T. H.	Mexican Travelogue, A	H&C	3	3		Su 52	22
Hewitt, T. H.	Robozos of Tenancingo	H&C	8	3		Su 57	19
Hewson, Betty	Classic Dress, The	Hw	5	3		Su 84	24
Hewson, Betty	Handwoven Sweater, A	Hw	4	4		S/O 83	85
Hewson, Betty	Simple Skirt and Matching Shawl, A	Hw	4	5		N/D 83	24
Hewson, Betty	Try Shadow Weave Twill	Hw	5	1		J/F 84	14
Heyl, Maxine; Linda Wilson	Line Flax Spinning	WJ	7	2	26	Fa 82	20
Heyman, Dorothy	Silvia Heyden: I think of the Weft as a Violin Bow	Fa	6	2		M/A 79	46
Hick, Susan	Fashion Trends	WJ	7	2	26	Fa 82	16
Hick, Susan	Fashion Trends	WJ	7	3	27	Wi 82	16
Hick, Susan	Fashion Trends	WJ	7	4	28	Sp 83	40
Hick, Susan	Fashion Trends	WJ	8	2	30	Fa 83	28
Hick, Susan	Fashion Trends	WJ	8	3	31	Wi 83	26
Hick, Susan	Fashion Trends	WJ	8	4	32	Sp 84	56
Hick, Susan	Fashion Trends	WJ	9	1	33	Su 84	12
Hick, Susan	Fashion Trends	WJ	9	2	34	Fa 84	10
Hick, Susan	Fashion Trends: Fall	WJ	10	1	37	Su 85	20
Hick, Susan	Fashion Trends: Fall	WJ	11	1	41	Su 86	54
Hick, Susan	Fashion Trends: Spring	WJ	10	3	39	Wi 86	38
Hick, Susan	Fashion Trends: Summer	WJ	9	4	36	Sp 85	20
Hick, Susan	Fashion Trends: Summer	WJ	10	4	40	Sp 86	52
Hick, Susan	Fashion Trends: Winter	WJ	10	2	38	Fa 85	24
Hick, Susan	see Nelipovitch, Kate	WJ	6	3	23	Wi 81	6
Hick, Susan	Trends for Fashionable Interiors	WJ	7	1	25	Su 82	18
Hickman, Deborah	Grrrhhhh: A Study of Social Patterns	Fa	14	4		S/O 87	23
Hickman, Pat	Archeological Rags	Fa	9	1		J/F 82	70
Hickman, Pat	Gutwork	Fa	7	6		N/D 80	46
Hickman, Pat	"Poetry for the Body, Clothing for the Spirit" (Exhibit)	Fa	10	5		S/O 83	75
Hicks, C. Norman	Alternates to Hand Carding	SS&D	7	1	25	Wi 75	74
Hicks, C. Norman	Bench Carding	SS&D	7	2	26	Sp 76	60
Hicks, C. Norman	Cape-Able Garment	SS&D	6	3	23	Su 75	18
Hicks, C. Norman	Carding, Part 3	SS&D	6	2	22	Sp 75	60
Hicks, C. Norman	Converting the Ashford Wheel	SS&D	8	3	31	Su 77	52
Hicks, C. Norman	Great Wheel, The	SS&D	4	2	14	Sp 73	38
Hicks, C. Norman	"Indian Spinner" or Large Orifice Spinning Wheels	SS&D	9	1	33	Wi 77	31
Hicks, C. Norman	Navajo Hip Spindle, Part 1	SS&D	8	1	29	WI 76	95
Hicks, C. Norman	Navajo Hip Spindle, Part 2	SS&D	8	2	30	Sp 77	41
Hicks, C. Norman	Paid Spinning Demonstrations	SS&D	7	3	27	Su 76	46

AUTHOR	TITLE	JOUR	VOL	NO	ISS	DATE	PAGE
Hicks, C. Norman	Spindle	SS&D	6	3	23	Su 75	63
Hicks, C. Norman	Spindle	SS&D	6	4	24	Fa 75	55
Hicks, C. Norman	Spinning on a Saxony or Castle Wheel	SS&D	7	4	28	Fa 76	51
Hicks, C. Norman	Spinning Questions and Answers	SS&D	8	4	32	Fa 77	81
Hicks, C. Norman	Using a Drop Spindle	SS&D	5	4	20	Fa 74	79
Hicks, C. Norman	Using a Drop Spinkle, Part 2 (error-corrected SS&D v6 n2 75 p61)	SS&D	6	1	21	Wi 74	48
⊹ Hicks, Shelia, ed.	American Fabrics and Fashions Magazine	Hw	2	4		Se 81	79
Hiersch, Vicki	Handspinner's Guide to Fleece Selection and Evaluation, A	S-O	7	4		Wi 83	50
Higginbotham, Charles	Lace Curtains	Kn	1	2	2	S-S 85	40
Hill, Johathan	see Wasserman, Tamara E.	WJ	6	3	23	Wi 81	60
Hill, Jonathan S.	see Wasserman, Tamara E.	Hw	3	2		Mr 82	22
Hill, Jonathan S.	see Wasserman, Tamara E.	Fa	9	6		N/D 82	58
Hill, Patricia C.	Denmark's Vaeveboden	H&C	5	2		Sp 54	16
Hill, Susan	see Chicago, Judy	Fa	9	3		M/J 82	58
Hillenburg, Nancy	Shaker Textiles	WJ	8	1	29	Su 83	22
Hillis, Anne	"Trees and Other Things" (Exhibit)	Fa	5	4		J/A 78	17
Hilton, K. A.	see Crockett, S. R.	H&C	7	4		Fa 56	59
Hilton, K. A.	see Crockett, S. R.	H&C	7	4		Fa 56	60
Hilts, Pat	Abelard's Advice	Hw	4	4		S/O 83	20
Hilts, Patricia	Eighteenth Century German Court Weaver: Johann Michael Frickinger, An	SS&D	11	4	44	Fa 80	16
Hilts, Patricia	Ligetuhr Arbeit: A Seventeenth-Century Compound Mounting and a Family of Associated Weaves	AT	7			Ju 87	31
Hilts, Patricia	List of Early Published German Weaving Books (1677–1840)	AT	5			Ju 86	192
Hilts, Patricia	Roses and Snowballs: The Development of Block Patterns in the German Linen-Weaving Tradition	AT	5			Ju 86	167
Hilts, Patricia	Seventeenth and Eighteenth Century Twills: The German Linen Tradition	AT	3			My 85	139
Hilts, Patricia	Weaving the Girdle of Rameses	WJ	9	1	33	Su 84	22
Himel, Susan	Laurie Swim: A Contemporary Quiltmaker with Roots in the Past	Fa	7	4		J/A 80	18
Hindmarsh, Lorna	Notebook for Kenyan Dyers, A	WJ	9	1	33	Su 84	59
Hindson, Alice	Designer's Drawloom	H&C	9	3		Su 58	59
Hinson, Dolores M.	Tool Kit from Inkle Bands, A	WJ	6	4	24	Sp 82	46
Hinz, Bill	see Meilach, Dona Z.	SS&D	6	4	24	Fa 75	31
Hinz, Jay	see Meilach, Dona Z.	SS&D	6	4	24	Fa 75	31
Hirschi, Ron	Salmon Run: The Work of Northwest Artists Peggy Vanbianchi and Emily Standley	Fa	10	2		M/A 83	16
Hitchcock, Helen Hull	Faster Drop Spindle Plying	SS&D	8	4	32	Fa 77	94
Hitchcock, Michael	Tapestries from Indonesia	WJ	12	1	45	Su 87	55
Hively, Evelyn	Weaving Myths	Hw	3	2		Mr 82	10
Hjert, Jeri; Paul Von Rosensteil	Loom Construction	SS&D	10	2	38	Sp 79	74
Hjert, Jeri; Paul Von Rosenstiel	Loom Construction	Iw	4	1		Wi 78	55
Hjert, Jeri; Paul Von Rosenstiel	Loom Construction	WJ	3	3	11	Ja 79	42
Hjert, Jeri; Paul Von Rosenstiel	Loom Construction	Fa	6	3		M/J 79	16
Hochberg, Bette	Add a New Twist to Your Spinning	S-O	5			81	42
Hochberg, Bette	Carders: Hand or Drum	S-O	3			79	40
Hochberg, Bette	Controlling the Size and Texture of Handspun Yarn	SS&D	9	4	36	Fa 78	31
Hochberg, Bette	Does It Pay to Spin Your Own Yarn?	Iw	4	1		Wi 78	46
Hochberg, Bette	Events in Textile History	Fa	10	2		M/A 83	52
Hochberg, Bette	Fiber Facts for Finishing Fabrics	Hw	2	5		No 81	62
Hochberg, Bette	Fibre Facts	WJ	6	4	24	Sp 82	60
Hochberg, Bette	Fibre Facts	Fa	9	1		J/F 82	58

AUTHOR	TITLE	JOUR	VOL	NO	ISS	DATE	PAGE
Hochberg, Bette	Fibre Properties That Affect Weaving	SS&D	13	2	50	Sp 82	72
Hochberg, Bette	Fleece Rug	Hw	2	2		Mr 81	52
Hochberg, Bette	Forum	Hw	2	2		Mr 81	12
Hochberg, Bette	Guide to Spinning Other Fibers, A	S-O	1			77	15
Hochberg, Bette	Handspindles	SS&D	9	1	33	Wi 77	41
Hochberg, Bette	Handspindles	WJ	1	4	4	Ap 77	26
Hochberg, Bette	Handspindles	WJ	5	2	18	Fa 80	32
Hochberg, Bette	Handspindles	S-O	4			80	15
Hochberg, Bette	Handspinners Handbook	Fa	4	2		M/A 77	41
Hochberg, Bette	Handspinner's Handbook	SS&D	8	2	30	Sp 77	38
Hochberg, Bette	High Whorl Spindle, The	SS&D	11	1	41	Wi 79	12
Hochberg, Bette	Looking at Distaffs	Iw	3	3		Sp 78	43
Hochberg, Bette	Reprints of Bette Hochberg's Textile Articles	WJ	7	1	25	Su 82	64
Hochberg, Bette	see Amos, Alden	Iw	4	1		Wi 78	54
Hochberg, Bette	Spin Span Spun: Fact and Folklore for Spinners	SS&D	11	2	42	Sp 80	82
Hochberg, Bette	Spin Span Spun: Fact and Folklore for Spinners	WJ	4	3	15	Ja 80	45
Hochberg, Bette	Spin Span Spun: Fact and Folklore for Spinners	S-O	3			79	10
Hochberg, Bette	Spin Span Spun: Fact and Folklore for Spinners	Fa	7	2		M/A 80	22
Hochberg, Bette	Spinning Fine Yarn (It's Method, not Magic)	Iw	5	3		Su 80	56
Hochberg, Bette	Spinning with a Bead Whorl Spindle	SS&D	10	2	38	Sp 79	22
Hochberg, Bette	When Moths Fly Out of Your Closet	Iw	4	3		Su 79	50
Hockberg, Bette	Handspindles	Iw	2	3		Sp 77	32
Hockberg, Bette	Handspinner's Handbook	Iw	2	3		Sp 77	32
Hodges, Eva	From Lamb to Rack: Wool	Hw	4	2		M/A 83	101
Hoelter, Jane	It's Really Only an Inverted Basket	SS&D	9	4	36	Fa 78	26
Hoering, Martha	Double-Belt and Scotch Tension	SS&D	5	2	18	Sp 74	59
Hoff, Anne	Simple Book of Belt-Weaving, A	SS&D	4	2	14	Sp 73	44
Hoffman, Henry	Weaving on Paper or Draw-Down Made Easy	H&C	11	1		Wi 60	59
Hoffman, Jenet	Macedonian Shirt Design	SS&D	8	2	30	Sp 77	97
Hoffman, Marta	Warp-Weighted Loom, The	Hw	4	4		S/O 83	27
Hoffmann, Jenet	Evaluating Your Work for the Market	SS&D	10	4	40	Fa 79	80
Hoffmann, Marta	Warp-Weighted Loom: Studies in the History and Technology of an Ancient Implement, The	Hw	5	1		J/F 84	22
Hoffmann, Marta	Warp-Weighted Loom, Studies in the History & Technology of an Ancient Implement, The	H&C	17	1		Wi 66	45
Hoffmeister, Adolf	see Verlet, Pierre	SS&D	10	2	38	Sp 79	73
Hoffmeister, Adolf	see Verlet, Pierre	Iw	4	4		Fa 79	72
Hofstrom, Juanita	Twentieth Century Rug	H&C	22	1		Wi 71	16
Hoisington, Gladys	Princeton Weavers Guild	H&C	16	2		Sp 65	41
Holborn, Joan	From Bobbin Flyer to Electric Spinner	S-O	3			79	44
Holbourne, David	Basic Book of Machine Knitting, The	SS&D	11	3	43	Su 80	75
Holbourne, David	Book of Machine Knitting, The	TM			5	J/J 86	12
Holbourne, David	David Holbourne	SS&D	3	4	12	Fa 72	50
Holcombe, Elizabeth	Respectfully Submitted	SS&D	2	3	7	Su 71	4
Holderness, Esther R.	Peasant Chic	SS&D	9	4	36	Fa 78	82
Holdgate, Charles	Net Making	H&C	24	1		J/F 73	29
Holland, Nina	Design a Dress—On the Loom	SS&D	6	2	22	Sp 75	37
Holland, Nina	Floorcloths: A New Look at an Old Technique	Fa	7	5		S/O 80	34
Holland, Nina	Inkle Loom Weaving	SS&D	5	2	18	Sp 74	68
Holland, Nina	LeClerc Loom Corporation, A Story of Three Generations, The	H&C	24	3		M/J 73	20
Holland, Nina	Magic Lanterns: Alice Ward's Handmade Paper Light/Shades	Fa	8	3		M/J 81	22
Holland, Nina	Tag End, The	H&C	23	6		N/D 72	40
Holland, Nina	Weaving for the Wholesale Market—Bane Or Boon?	SS&D	5	3	19	Su 74	81

AUTHOR	TITLE	JOUR	VOL	NO	ISS	DATE	PAGE
Holland, Nina	Weaving Primer, The	Iw	4	2		Sp 79	60
Hollen, Norma; Jane Saddler	Textiles	H&C	19	4		Fa 68	44
Hollen, Norma; Jane Saddler	Textiles	H&C	7	1		Wi 55	59
Hollen, Norma; Jane Saddler	Textiles (Second Edition)	H&C	16	4		Fa 65	44
Hollen, Norma R.	Pattern Making by the Flat-Pattern Method	WJ	6	4	24	Sp 82	60
Hollingworth, Shelagh	Complete Book of Traditional Aran Knitting, The	TM			6	A/S 86	84
Holm, Bill	Northwest Coast Indian Art: An Analysis of Form	H&C	22	3		Su 71	42
Holmes, Cora	Rug for a Beginner	S-O	10	1		Sp 86	24
Holmes, James	Manuscript Notes on Weaving	Hw	8	2		M/A 87	13
Holmes, James, M.S.A.	Manuscript Notes on Weaving	PWC	4	2	12		50
Holmes, Margaret	Cardboard Looms Help the Handicapped	SS&D	6	2	22	Sp 75	31
Holmyard, E. J., ed.	see Singer, Charles, ed.	H&C	8	2		Sp 57	59
Holroyd, Ruth N.	Future Weavers	SS&D	2	3	7	Su 71	13
Holroyd, Ruth N.	Weaving Classes in An Art Gallery	H&C	22	4		Fa 71	12
Holroyd, Ruth N., ed	Jacob Angstadt Designs Drawn from His Weavers Patron Book	SS&D	7	4	28	Fa 76	65
Holroyd, Ruth N., ed	Jacob Angstadt—His Weavers Patron Book	SS&D	7	4	28	Fa 76	65
Holst, Holly P.	Charlotte Attig: Tassel Maker	Fa	9	6		N/D 82	26
Holtz-Carter, Nancy Merle	Cottage Crafts & Fibers; A Reference Book	WJ	9	4	36	Sp 85	78
Holtzer, Marilyn	Chemical Eye Injuries and Contact Lenses: A Dangerous Combination	SS&D	12	1	45	Wi 80	7
Holtzer, Marilyn	Diagonal Triple-turn Cardweaving	SS&D	11	2	42	Sp 80	100
Holtzer, Marilyn Emerson	Beginning with Bands: Tablet Woven Garments and Accessories	WJ	9	3	35	Wi 85	28
Holtzer, Marilyn Emerson	Blouse of Cards	SS&D	16	3	63	Su 85	20
Holtzer, Marilyn Emerson	Double-faced, Double-woven, Three-harness Krokbragd	SS&D	14	4	56	Fa 83	46
Holtzer, Marilyn Emerson	Double-Faced Krokbragd	WJ	9	4	36	Sp 85	59
Holtzer, Marilyn Emerson	Meet, Cross, and Separate	SS&D	16	3	63	Su 85	17
Holtzer, Marilyn Emerson	Sheila Hicks	SS&D	16	1	61	Wi 84	43
Holtzer, Marilyn F.	Double- and Double-Faced Cloth on Six-Hole Cards	Iw	5	2		Sp 80	66
Holtzer, Marilyn F.	Wasteless, Waistless Dress, A	Hw	2	3		My 81	85
Holtzman, Hope; Phillip Holtzman	Hope and Phillip Holtzman	Fa	14	2		M/A 87	23
Holtzman, Phillip	see Holtzman, Hope	Fa	14	2		M/A 87	23
Holz, Loretta	How to Sell Your Art and Crafts	Iw	2	4		Su 77	34
Holz, Loretta	How to Sell Your Arts and Crafts: A Marketing Guide for Creative People	SS&D	9	2	34	Sp 78	49
Homme, Audrey	Bog Affair, A	PWC			3	Oc 82	44
Homme, Audrey	Moebius Vest, The	WJ	11	4	44	Sp 87	48
Hooper, Luther	Hand-Loom Weaving	H&C	2	4		Fa 51	61
Hooper, Luther	Hand-Loom Weaving	WJ	5	1	17	Su 80	47
Hoover, Doris	see Welch, Nancy	Fa	5	6		N/D 78	22
Hoover, Doris; Nancy Welch	Tassels	WJ	7	1	25	Su 82	64
Hopa, Ngapara	Art of Piupiu Making, The	SS&D	4	1	13	Wi 72	34
Hope, Thomas	Costumes of the Greeks and Romans	WJ	4	3	15	Ja 80	45
Hopkins, Gerard Manley	Windhover, The	WJ	8	4	32	Sp 84	16
Hopkins, Giles E.	Wool as an Apparel Fibre	H&C	5	1		Wi 53	59
Hoppe, E.; E. Ostlund; L. Melen	Free Weaving on Frame and Loom	SS&D	6	3	23	Su 75	49
Hoppe, Elisabeth; Ragnar Edberg	Carding, Spinning, Dyeing, An Introduction to the Traditional Wool and Flax Crafts	SS&D	7	3	27	Su 76	34
Hoppe, Elizabeth; Ragnar Edberg	Carding, Spinning, Dyeing	Iw	2	1		Fa 76	33
Hoppe, Flo	Color in the Woven Basket	SS&D	16	3	63	Su 85	22
Hoppe, Flo	Pope of Lightship Baskets, The	SS&D	18	1	69	Wi 86	30

AUTHOR	TITLE	JOUR	VOL	NO	ISS	DATE	PAGE
Hoppe, Ostlund, Melen	Free Weaving on Frame and Loom	H&C	26	3		M/J 75	30
Horger, Millicent	Handwoven Wedding Chuppa, A	WJ	7	4	28	Sp 83	50
Horne, Beverley	Fleece in the Hands of a New Zealand Spinner	S-O	2			78	24
Horne, Beverley	Fleece in Your Hands	Iw	2	3		Sp 77	32
Horne, Beverley	Fleece in Your Hands	S-O	3			79	11
Horne, Beverley	Kiwicraft	S-O	3			79	52
Hornung, Clarence P.	Handbook of Designs and Devices	H&C	3	4		Fa 52	62
Horton, Lucy	Crochet as a Madness	Fa	5	3		M/J 78	22
Horton, Lucy	Interview with Linda Berry Walker...A Spinning and Dyeing Business, An	Fa	4	5		S/O 77	26
Horton, Lucy	Kay-O Wicks — The Habit of Knitting	Fa	6	3		M/J 79	32
Horton, Lucy	Leslie Fuller: Pan-Creative Quiltmaker	Fa	7	5		S/O 80	19
Horton, Margaret	Guilding the Lily: Embroidery Stitches in Victorian Crazy Quilts	TM			10	A/M 87	48
Horton, Susan	Living the Craftsman's Gospel	H&C	24	2		M/A 73	46
Hoskins, J. A.	Automatic Analysis of Coloured Images	AT	5			Ju 86	151
Hoskins, J. A.	see Allston, J. L.	AT	4			De 85	81
Hoskins, J. A.	see Hoskins, W. D.	AT	5			Ju 86	33
Hoskins, Janet	Pattern Master III (Software)	Hw	5	3		Su 84	18
Hoskins, Janet A.	Computerized Analysis of the Drawdown (addendum SS&D v13 n1 81 p4)	SS&D	13	1	49	Wi 81	76
Hoskins, Janet A.	Computerized Fabric Analysis (error-corrected SS&D v14 n2 83 p4)	SS&D	14	1	53	Wi 82	26
Hoskins, Janet A.	Computers and Weavers: Software Is Just Another Tool in the Designer's Hand	TM			9	F/M 87	51
Hoskins, Janet A.	Multi-Layered Cloths: A Structured Approach	AT	1			De 83	137
Hoskins, Janet A.	New Look at Twills, A	WJ	6	3	23	Wi 81	46
Hoskins, Janet A.	Stitched Doublecloths	CW	3	1	7	Se 81	1
Hoskins, Janet A.	Twillins, Color-Alternative Twills and Color-Alternate Twillins	CW	2	3	6	Ap 81	1
Hoskins, Janet A.; W. D. Hoskins	Satin and Long-Eyed Heddles	WJ	6	1	21	Su 81	25
Hoskins, Janet, mg. ed.	see Stanton, Ralph, ed.	Hw	7	5		N/D 86	11
Hoskins, Nancy	Paracas Needle Technique, A	Iw	5	4		Fa 80	34
Hoskins, Nancy Arthur	Knotting Stitches for Weavers	SS&D	15	3	59	Su 84	6
Hoskins, Nancy Arthur	Linen: The Enduring Thread of History	Fa	14	2		M/A 87	42
Hoskins, Nancy Arthur	Moorman Weave Variations	SS&D	13	1	49	Wi 81	6
Hoskins, Nancy Arthur	Textiles of Coptic Egypt	WJ	12	1	45	Su 87	58
Hoskins, Nancy Arthur	The Tapestries of Coptic Egypt	AT	6			De 86	211
Hoskins, Nancy Arthur	Twining Trick, A	SS&D	18	4	72	Fa 87	8
Hoskins, Nancy Arthur	Universal Stitches for Weaving, Embroidery and Other Fiber Arts	Hw	4	3		M/J 83	12
Hoskins, Nancy Arthur	Universal Stitches for Weaving, Embroidery and Other Fiber Arts	WJ	7	2	26	Fa 82	57
Hoskins, Nancy Arthur	Universal Stitches for Weaving, Embroidery, and Other Fiber Arts	SS&D	14	2	54	Sp 83	64
Hoskins, Nancy Arthur	Universal Stitches for Weaving, Embroidery and Other Fiber Arts	PWC	3	2	8		61
Hoskins, W. D.	see Hoskins, Janet A.	WJ	6	1	21	Su 81	25
Hoskins, W. D.; J. A. Hoskins	Design of Interactive Systems for Real-Time Dobby Control	AT	5			Ju 86	33
Hoskinson, Marian K.	Sixteen-Harness Beiderwand Coverlet	SS&D	14	4	56	Fa 83	19
Hoskinson, Marian K.	Why Multi-Harness Weaves for Clothing Fabrics	CW	3	2	8	Ja 82	13
Hostek, Stanley	Hand Stitches for the Fine Custom Tailored Garment	TM			7	O/N 86	72
Hostek, Stanley	Men's Custom Tailored Coats	TM			7	O/N 86	72
Hostek, Stanley	Men's Custom Tailored Pants	TM			7	O/N 86	72
Hostek, Stanley	Men's Custom Tailored Vests	TM			7	O/N 86	72
Hostek, Stanley	Stanley Hostek on Darts	TM			14	D/J 87	67
Hostek, Stanley	Tailor on Pressing, A	TM			10	A/M 87	43
Hostek, Stanley	Tailor's Logic	TM			14	D/J 87	42
Hotchkiss, Ann	see Hotchkiss, Clifford	H&C	13	2		Sp 62	14
Hotchkiss, Ann	Weaving for a Livelihood	H&C	12	1		Wi 61	26

AUTHOR	TITLE	JOUR	VOL	NO	ISS	DATE	PAGE
Hotchkiss, Clifford; Ann Hotchkiss	Weaving Tweeds	H&C	13	2		Sp 62	14
House, Florence E.	Notes on Weaving Techniques	H&C	18	1		Wi 67	43
House, Florence E.	Notes on Weaving Techniques	H&C	2	3		Su 51	62
Housego, Jenny	Tribal Rugs: An Introduction to the Weaving of the Tribes of Iran	Iw	4	2		Sp 79	64
Houston, Jourdan	Two Treadle Spinning Wheels	H&C	24	4		Au 73	32
Howard, Constance	Embroidery and Color	Fa	4	3		M/J 77	54
Howard, Constance, ed.	Textile Crafts	SS&D	10	4	40	Fa 79	63
Howard, Constance, ed.	Textile Crafts	Iw	3	4		Su 78	45
Howard, Helen Griffiths	Musk Ox, The	S-O	7	1		Sp 83	16
Howard, Margaret	Analysis Based on Warp Threads	SS&D	3	2	10	Sp 72	15
Howard, Margaret	Bicentennial Tapestry, A	SS&D	7	1	25	Wi 75	30
Howard, Margaret F.	Basic Woven Fabric	SS&D	5	3	19	Su 74	63
Howard, Miranda	Angora: A Spinner's Delight	S-O	6	4		82	43
Howard, Miranda	Double Weave Blocks on Eight	Hw	6	3		Su 85	36
Howard, Miranda	Finnish Lace	Hw	5	3		Su 84	80
Howard, Miranda	Four + Four: An Introduction to Those Extra Harnesses	Hw	3	4		Se 82	66
Howard, Miranda	Girl's Vest	S-O	6	4		82	59
Howard, Miranda	Karellian Red Pick	Hw	2	5		No 81	36
Howard, Miranda	Knitter's Puzzle: Damask Knitting with Your Handspun, A	S-O	9	1		Sp 85	36
Howard, Miranda	Satin--On Four	Hw	2	3		My 81	34
Howard, Ruth	see Koob, Katherine	CW	1	3	3	Ap 80	1
Howard, Ruth	Tie-Ups: The Key to Multiharness Weaving	Hw	7	5		N/D 86	13
Howard, Ruth	Use of Long-Eyed Heddles for Patterned Double Weave, The	WJ	6	2	22	Fa 81	35
Howe, Cathe	"Basket and Paper Invitational Show" (Exhibit)	Fa	12	3		M/J 85	71
Howe, Cathe	Blocked, A First-Person Account	Fa	11	6		N/D 84	55
Howe, Cathe	"Contemporary Shibori" (Exhibit)	Fa	11	3		M/J 84	82
Howe, Cathe	Papermaking Classes and Workshops: A Selective List	Fa	11	2		M/A 84	47
Howe, Cathe	Pioneer Spirit of Carole Beadle: At the Frontier of Feltmaking, The	Fa	6	6		N/D 79	36
Howe, Katherine; Joanne Mattera	Fans and Fan Imagery	Fa	9	4		J/A 82	26
Howe-Echt, Katherine	Questions of Style: Contemporary Trends in the Fiber Arts	Fa	7	2		M/A 80	38
Howell, Marie	Ark Curtain	H&C	15	2		Sp 64	37
Howell, Marie	Characteristics of Handweaves	H&C	12	1		Wi 61	18
Howell, Marie	Modern Church Textiles	H&C	13	3		Su 62	20
Howell-Koehler, Nancy	Soft Jewelry: A Different Adornment	SS&D	7	2	26	Sp 76	56
Hower, Virginia G.	Weaving, Spinning, & Dyeing: A Beginner's Manual	SS&D	7	4	28	Fa 76	65
Howie, Andrew	Boris Veren's Offers a Rare Book Service	H&C	16	2		Sp 65	15
Howie, Andrew J.	Southern California Conference	H&C	13	3		Su 62	21
Howie, Andrew J.	Twenty-Five Weavers, California Study Group Has Varied Programs, The	H&C	13	2		Sp 62	21
Hoyt, Peggy	Choosing a Loom, One Weaver's Experience with a Countermarch	CW	4	1	10	Se 82	14
Hoyt, Peggy	Converting a 10-Shaft Drawloom to 25 Shafts	CW	7	1	19	Se 85	3
Hoyt, Peggy	Drawlooms	CW	6	2	17	Ja 85	27
Hoyt, Peggy	More Logical Method of Drafting, A	CW	5	3	15	My 84	22
Hoyt, Peggy	New Freedom with a Counterbalance— Countermarch Loom	CW	5	3	15	My 84	3
Hoyt, Peggy	see Sellin, Helen	PWC	5	2	16		33
Hoyt, Peggy	Variation of a Rigid Heddle Loom	H&C	21	3		Su 70	6
Hrafnhildur, Schram	Fiber Art in Iceland	Fa	9	6		N/D 82	68
Hubel, Reinhard G.	Book of Carpets, The	TMJ	3	2		De 71	44
Huberman, Alice	see Adasko, Laura	SS&D	7	1	25	Wi 75	34
Hudson, Marjorie; Kathy Sparks	Arctic Adventures with Qiviut	S-O	11	3		Fa 87	47
Hudson, Robert	see Alexander, Peter	H&C	6	1		Wi 54	61

AUTHOR	TITLE	JOUR	VOL	NO	ISS	DATE	PAGE
Huebner, Marianne	Weaving Abroad II	H&C	21	4		Fa 70	21
Huebner, Marianne A.	Weaving Abroad	H&C	21	3		Su 70	10
Huestis, Al	Quiviut	S-O	3			79	32
Huey, Carol	Graduate School...Is It Right for You?	Iw	5	4		Fa 80	71
Huff, Karen E.	Computer Learns to Weave, The	SS&D	6	4	24	Fa 75	19
Huffaker, Katherine	Therese May: Moving Freely from Fabric to Paint and Back Again	Fa	9	1		J/F 82	26
Hughes, G. Bernard	Living Crafts	H&C	6	1		Wi 54	63
Hughes, Sukey	Washi, The World of Japanese Paper	Fa	6	4		J/A 79	14
Hughey, Michael W.	Papermaking: Where It's Coming From	SS&D	10	4	40	Fa 79	45
Hugues, Patricia	Le Langage Du Tissu	WJ	8	3	31	Wi 83	65
Hulbert, Elizabeth McKey	"Needle and Cloth: Ten Years Later" (Exhibit)	Fa	10	3		M/J 83	72
Huldt, Ake	see Stavenow, Ake	H&C	14	1		Wi 63	44
Hull, Raymond	see Naumann, Rose	SS&D	4	4	16	Fa 73	63
Hulquist, Kay	see Thoeming, Bette	Hw	8	5		N/D 87	70
Humphery, Laney	Creativity	Hw	6	3		Su 85	22
Humphries, Andrew B.	Fabric of the Lake District: Herdwick Sheep	S-O	8	4		Wi 84	45
Humphries, Mary; Carol Outram	If Fashion Starts in the Fabric, Where Are Our Fabric Designers?	CW	3	1	7	Se 81	4
Hung-tu, Tung	Complaint of the Weaving Wife	Hw	7	1		J/F 86	50
Hunt, Ann	Gail Rutter VanSlyke: A Weaver's Commitment	Fa	6	5		S/O 79	40
Hunt, Antony	Textile Design	H&C	4	4		Fa 53	61
Hunt, E. Ann	"Wearable Art" (Exhibit)	Fa	6	3		M/J 79	78
Hunt, Elizabeth Ann	Lesley Shearer: Beyond the Limitations of the Four Harness Loom	Fa	6	2		M/A 79	41
Hunt, Elizabeth Ann	Linda Fox La France: Designer — Tapestry Weaver	Iw	4	2		Sp 79	36
Hunt, Elizabeth Ann	"Private Spaces, Private Lives" a Juried Fiber Show (Exhibit)	Fa	7	6		N/D 80	75
Hunt, Elizabeth Ann	Vera Wainar Kopecek: Her Work Stands Alone	Fa	7	2		M/A 80	55
Hunter, Andrew	see McGreevy, Susan Brown	WJ	11	1	41	Su 86	14
Hunter, Frances	Goldenrod Poncho Wins HGA Award	SS&D	5	4	20	Fa 74	95
Huntington, Madge	Fabric Speaks	Fa	7	2		M/A 80	31
Hunziker, Marion	Timeless Knotted Jewelry: Marion Hunziker Meticulously Combines Fiber and Metalwork Techniques	Fa	8	4		J/A 81	19
Hunzinger, Claudie	Claudie and Francis Hunzinger: Plants, Paper, and Poetry	Fa	11	4		J/A 84	10
Hurry, Gaynel	Tips on Home Dyeing	H&C	22	4		Fa 71	19
Hurschler, Flora	see Hurschler, Paul	SS&D	5	3	19	Su 74	43
Hurschler, Paul; Flora Hurschler	Convergence '74, Hurschler Collection	SS&D	5	3	19	Su 74	43
Hurt, Doris	Ethnic Inspired Jacket	WJ	4	4	16	Ap 80	43
Hurt, Doris	Poncho	WJ	3	3	11	Ja 79	44
Hutchins, Jane K.	Protecting Your Collection: Textile Conservation	Fa	12	6		N/D 85	40
Hutchins, Jeane, ed.	Fiberarts Design Book II, The	WJ	8	4	32	Sp 84	65
Hutchinson, Amelia	Dione Christensen	Fa	5	3		M/J 78	57
Hutton, Helen	see Lewes, Klares	H&C	13	3		Su 62	43
Hutton, Helen	see Lewes, Klares	H&C	13	4		Fa 62	43
Hutton, Jessie	Singer Fashion Tailoring (Out of Print)	TM			7	O/N 86	74
Hyatt, Sharyn; Teresa Mangum	Ceremonial Structures of Terry Jarrard Dimond, The	Fa	9	4		J/A 82	66
Ickes, Marguerite	Weaving as a Hobby	SS&D	1	2	2	Mr 70	23
Ickis, Marguerite	Braided Rugs for Fun and Profit	H&C	2	4		Fa 51	62
Ickis, Marguerite	Folk Arts and Crafts	H&C	9	2		Sp 58	59
Ickis, Marguerite	Weaving as a Hobby	H&C	20	3		Su 69	41
Illsley, Ednah	Income Tax for the Craftsman	Iw	2	2		Wi 77	10
Illsley, Ednah	Spinners' Potluck	Iw	3	4		Su 78	46
Ingebretsen, Catherine	Summer and Winter Revisited, Part 2: III. Selvedges for Krokbragd and Other Weft-Faced Cloths	PWC			2	Ap 82	68

AUTHOR	TITLE	JOUR	VOL	NO	ISS	DATE	PAGE
Ingebretsen, Catherine	Weaving Primer	PWC			6	Su 83	4
Ingebretsen, Cathy	Baby Blanket	PWC	3	1	7		6
Ingebretsen, Cathy	Woolen Scarf	PWC	3	1	7		7
Ingebretsen, Cathy	Woven Reed Placemats	PWC	3	2	8		4
Ingenthron, Walter W., Jr.	see Russell, Harold W.	SS&D	2	4	8	Fa 71	33
Ingers, Gertrud	Flamskvävnad	H&C	20	3		Su 69	43
Ingers, Gertrud	Flemish Weaving	H&C	23	4		J/A 72	26
Ingers, Gertrud	Flemish Weaving, A Guide to Tapestry Technique	SS&D	3	3	11	Su 72	13
Ingers, Gertrud	Nya Mattor	H&C	10	4		Fa 59	59
Ingers, Gertrud	see Fischer, Ernst	H&C	12	3		Su 61	61
Ingraham, Harold	Weaving with Handspun Wools	H&C	1	3		Fa 50	18
Innes, J. Alisdair	Raw Wool Values, How They Determine the End Use	H&C	15	1		Wi 64	15
Ireland, Marion P.	Textile Art in the Church — Vestments, Paraments, and Hangings in Contemporary Worship, Art, and Architecture	H&C	22	4		Fa 71	26
Ireland, Marion P.	Textile Art in the Church — Vestments, Paraments, and Hangings in Contemporary Worship, Art and Architecture	WJ	4	3	15	Ja 80	46
Irey, Margaret	New Method of Warping, A	H&C	4	3		Su 53	50
Irlbeck, Sonja	Aklae: Norwegian Tapestry	WJ	8	1	29	Su 83	27
Irvine, Marie M.	Weaving Ripples and Curves	SS&D	12	1	45	Wi 80	52
Irwin, Bobbie	Danish Twined Rag Rugs: Lillie Sherwood's Legacy	WJ	10	4	40	Sp 86	32
Irwin, Bobbie	Easing the Beginner's Fears	S-O	10	4		Wi 86	24
Irwin, Bobbie	Scarves in Variegated Yarns	S-O	11	4		Wi 87	53
Irwin, Bobbie	Weaver Profile: Mahota Handwovens	Hw	8	5		N/D 87	35
Irwin, John; Margaret Hall	Indian Embroideries, Vol.II	TMJ	4	2		75	80
Irwin, John; Margaret Hall	Indian Painted and Printed Fabrics	TMJ	3	4		De 73	46
Irwin, John Rice	Baskets and Basket Makers in Southern Appalachia	SS&D	14	4	56	Fa 83	75
Irwin, Kim	Banff Experience: A Personal View of Fibre Interchange 1980, The	Fa	8	4		J/A 81	35
Irwin, Marjorie	Two Blankets: Feather and Fan	S-O	10	1		Sp 86	22
Isleib, Carol	Rainbow on the Table, A (Sharon Hakala, Carol Isleib, Carol Shabaz, Ruth Stump)	Hw	5	3		Su 84	46
Isleib, Carol M.	Bookmarks: A Family Tradition	Hw	3	4		Se 82	54
Ispay, Francis	Traditional Felt Rugmaking in Turkey	Fa	13	4		J/A 86	18
Ito, Toshiko	Tsujigahana, the Flower of Japanese Textile Arts	Hw	6	3		Su 85	14
Itten, Johannes	Design and Form — The Basic Course at the Bauhaus	H&C	15	3		Su 64	44
Itter, Diane	"Embroiderer's Guild of America, 11th Biennial Exhibition" (Exhibit)	Fa	12	2		M/A 85	76
Itter, Diane	"Fiber Structures and Fabric Surfaces" (Exhibit)	Fa	7	1		J/F 80	67
Itter, Diane	Grant Fellowships for the Fiber Artist	Fa	11	4		J/A 84	50
Itter, Diane	"Patricia Campbell: The Modular Form" (Exhibit)	Fa	11	3		M/J 84	75
Itter, Diane	Representing Fiber Work Through Photography	SS&D	17	3	67	Su 86	42
Itter, Diane	Show Strategies (error-corrected SS&D v19 n1 87 p33)	SS&D	18	4	72	Fa 87	26
Itter, Diane	Show Strategies, Part 2	SS&D	19	1	73	Wi 87	28
Itter, Diane	"Thomas Lundberg" (Exhibit)	Fa	10	4		J/A 83	67
Itter, Diane	Working with Linen: Karen Jenson Rutherford	Fa	14	2		M/A 87	34
Jackie, Erma; Kenneth G. Heintz	Mini-Session Increases Weaving Program 4-Fold	SS&D	4	4	16	Fa 73	53
Jackson, Constance; Judith Plowman	Three Bags Full: Spinning, Weaving and Woolcraft	S-O	4			80	15
Jackson, Constance; Judith Plowman	Woolcraft Book, Spinning, Dyeing, Weaving, The	S-O	6	4		82	10
Jackson, Constance; Judith Plowman	Woolcraft Book, Spinning, Dyeing, Weaving, The	WJ	6	4	24	Sp 82	59
Jackson, James J.	Loom May be a Piece of Furniture, A	H&C	5	4		Fa 54	28
Jackson, K. C.	see Pourdeyhimi, B.	AT	6			De 86	101
Jackson, K. C.	see Pourdeyhimi, B.	AT	4			De 85	107

AUTHOR	TITLE	JOUR	VOL	NO	ISS	DATE	PAGE
Jackson, K. C.; B. Pourdeyhimi	Technical Progress and the Evolution of Wage Arrangements in the British Cotton Weaving Industry	AT	7			Ju 87	61
Jackson, Lloyd H.	Yarn and Cloth Calculations	H&C	3	1		Wi 51	61
Jackson, Marguerite	Huckaback Lace	H&C	14	2		Sp 63	20
Jackson, Marguerite	Six-Harness M's and O's	H&C	9	3		Su 58	15
Jackson, Marguerite	Solving a Problem in Multi-Harness	H&C	13	4		Fa 62	19
Jackson, Marguerite	Suggestions for Indexing	H&C	14	4		Fa 63	23
Jackson, Mariechen	Dogbones from Trees?	SS&D	2	1	5	De 70	18
Jackson, Mary Lynn; Cheryl McWilliams	Fiber is "Special"	SS&D	15	2	58	Sp 84	13
Jacob, Mary Jane; Magdalena Abakanowicz; Jasia Reichardt	Magdalena Abakanowicz	Fa	10	5		S/O 83	58
Jacobs, Betty E. M.	Growing Herbs and Plants for Dyeing	Iw	3	1		Fa 77	44
Jacobs, Betty E. M.	Growing Herbs and Plants for Dyeing	WJ	3	1	9	Jy 78	36
Jacobs, E. M.	Growing Herbs and Plants for Dyeing	SS&D	9	4	36	Fa 78	81
Jacobson, Gail	Textile Life, The	Fa	14	3		M/J 87	5
Jacoby, Heinrich	How to Know Oriental Carpets & Rugs	H&C	5	4		Fa 54	59
Jacopetti, Alexandra	Commercial Establishment Discovers Fiber Arts, The	SS&D	8	2	30	Sp 77	4
Jacopin, Armand J.	Some Practical Suggestions for Making Ecclesiastical Vesture	H&C	9	3		Su 58	18
Jaeger, Hector	Prism Pleasure Blanket	Hw	6	3		Su 85	58
Jaeger, Hector	see Schomp, Halcyon	Hw	3	4		Se 82	35
Jaeger, Hector	see Schomp, Halcyon	Hw	5	5		N/D 84	61
Jaeger, Hector; Halcyon Schomp	Maine Coast Memories	Hw	5	5		N/D 84	72
Jaffie, H. R.	Hand-Painted Silk	Fa	10	5		S/O 83	17
James, Esther	Michigan Guild Project: A Four-Panel Folding Screen	SS&D	9	1	33	Wi 77	114
James, George Wharton	Indian Blankets and Their Makers: The Navaho	SS&D	6	2	22	Sp 75	64
James, Ona	Swivel Variations for Four Harness Looms	H&C	14	4		Fa 63	11
Janeiro, Jan	"American Quilts: A Handmade Legacy" (Exhibit)	Fa	8	4		J/A 81	72
Janeiro, Jan	Art and Architecture	Fa	9	3		M/J 82	52
Janeiro, Jan	"Art Fabric: Mainstream, The" (Exhibit)	Fa	8	5		S/O 81	70
Janeiro, Jan	"Camel Belts from the Great Indian Desert" (Exhibit)	Fa	10	6		N/D 83	75
Janeiro, Jan	Color Symbolism in Primitive Societies (error-corrected Fa v13 n4 86 p5)	Fa	13	2		M/A 86	30
Janeiro, Jan	Conversation with Lillian Elliott, A	Fa	9	2		M/A 82	66
Janeiro, Jan	"Daniel Graffin: Traces" (Exhibit)	Fa	7	2		M/A 80	73
Janeiro, Jan	"Dominic DiMare: New Work" (Exhibit)	Fa	8	2		M/A 81	63
Janeiro, Jan	"Fukusa: The Shojiro Nomura Collection" (Exhibit)	Fa	11	3		M/J 84	79
Janeiro, Jan	Interview with Dominic Di Mare: A Commitment to Forward Movement, An	Fa	13	1		J/F 86	55
Janeiro, Jan	"Introductions '80" Emily DuBois and Sylvia Seventy (Exhibit)	Fa	7	6		N/D 80	70
Janeiro, Jan	"Janet Boguch: Delivered Runes" (Exhibit)	Fa	6	5		S/O 79	83
Janeiro, Jan	"Knowing the Ropes" (Exhibit)	Fa	6	4		J/A 79	72
Janeiro, Jan	Line As Movement: Adela Akers, The	Fa	8	2		M/A 81	70
Janeiro, Jan	"Nance O'Banion: Handmade Paper and Bamboo Painting" (Exhibit)	Fa	7	4		J/A 80	15
Janeiro, Jan	"Neda Al Hilali" (Exhibit)	Fa	9	3		M/J 82	75
Janeiro, Jan	Ritual and Art in Traditional Societies	Fa	13	6		N/D 86	4
Janeiro, Jan	Sense of the Individual, The	Fa	11	2		M/A 84	52
Janeiro, Jan	Sources: A.K.A. the Muse	Fa	11	6		N/D 84	52
Janeiro, Jan	"Textiles by Pat Kinsella and Sheila O'Hara" (Exhibit)	Fa	6	3		M/J 79	72
Janeiro, Jan	Time and Vision: The Work of Cynthia Schira	Fa	9	5		S/O 82	68
Janeiro, Jan	Way of Working: Katherine Westphal and the Creative Process, A	Fa	7	6		N/D 80	35
Jansen, Netty	Vestment Variations: A Weaver from the Netherlands Creates Garments for the Ecclesiastical Calendar	WJ	10	3	39	Wi 86	53
Jansons, Ilga	Draw Frame Device	SS&D	10	4	40	Fa 79	90
Jaques, Renate	Deutsche Textilkunst	H&C	5	1		Wi 53	59

AUTHOR	TITLE	JOUR	VOL	NO	ISS	DATE	PAGE
Jaques, Renate; Ernst Flemming	Encyclopedia of Textiles	H&C	9	3		Su 58	60
Jarecka, Louise Llewellyn	Contemporary Polish Weaving	H&C	1	2		Su 50	15
Jarecka, Louise Llewellyn	Edith Huntington Snow	H&C	1	1		Ap 50	7
Jarecka, Louise Llewellyn	Edith Huntington Snow, Weaver, Artist, Craftsman (Reprint)	H&C	26	2		Ap 75	10
Jarecka, Louise Llewellyn	Made in Poland	H&C	1	3		Fa 50	64
Jarecka, Louise Llewellyn	Number Knitting — A New Way with an Old Art	H&C	2	1		Wi 50	22
Jarvis, Gordon	see Carr, Margaret	SS&D	17	3	67	Su 86	78
Jarvis, Helen	Computerized Weaving Calculations (error-corrected SS&D v12 n4 81 p8)	SS&D	12	3	47	Su 81	46
Jarvis, Helen	Corner Inscriptions	PWC	5	2	16		19
Jarvis, Helen	see Carr, Margaret	SS&D	17	3	67	Su 86	78
Jarvis, Helen	Sturbridge Coverlet, A	PWC	5	2	16		20
Jarvis, Helen	Teasel Industry in New York State, The	SS&D	8	4	32	Fa 77	71
Jarvis, Helen N.	Gift to My Country: Lincoln Bedroom Coverlet, A	SS&D	9	4	36	Fa 78	17
Jarvis, P. R.	Weaver's Knot, The	Iw	5	3		Su 80	63
Jefferson, Annis Lee	Summer and Winter: Technique and Variations	Iw	2	4		Su 77	36
Jefferson, Brian	Profitable Crafts Marketing: A Complete Guide to Successful Selling	Hw	7	4		S/O 86	8
Jefferson, Brian T.	Profitable Crafts Marketing	WJ	12	2	46	Fa 87	68
Jeffs, Angela, ed.	Wild Knitting	Fa	7	4		J/A 80	14
Jeklin, Mrs. Lewis	Tacoma Weavers Guild	H&C	9	1		Wi 57	14
Jenkins, Evelyn	Tarascan Lace	H&C	11	1		Wi 60	12
Jenkins, Evelyn L.	Nineteen Forty-eight Cardwoven Belt Still in Frequent Use	SS&D	5	1	17	Wi 73	74
Jenkins, Thomas W.	Paradox of Perfection, The	Fa	8	2		M/A 81	27
Jennings, Lucy Anne	Desert Tapestry Vest	WJ	12	1	45	Su 87	52
Jennings, Lucy Anne	Designed for Narrow Looms	WJ	11	1	41	Su 86	26
Jennings, Lucy Anne	Special Summer Vest, A	WJ	9	3	35	Wi 85	42
Jensen, Candi	Carnival Cable Pullover	Kn	3	1	5	F-W 86	24
Jensen, Elizabeth Jane	Twining with Leaves and Corn Husks (error-corrected SS&D v14 n4 83 p4)	SS&D	14	3	55	Su 83	10
Jensen, Elizabeth Jane	Wickerwork Basket Weaving in Four-Strand Designs (error-corrected SS&D v14 n1 82 p6)	SS&D	13	4	52	Fa 82	20
Jensen, Gay	Warp-Faced 2/2 Twill: Part 2	Hw	3	4		Se 82	50
Jensen, Gay	Warp-Faced Weaving, Part 1	Hw	3	3		My 82	42
Jensen, Gay; Donna Kaplan	Warp-Faced Krokbragd	WJ	12	2	46	Fa 87	62
Jensen, Janet	"Survey of Illinois Fiber" (Exhibit)	Fa	5	5		S/O 78	69
Jernigan, Bonnie	Images in Sharpe Focus: Susan Sharpe's Quilts Are Drawn, Painted and Stitched	Fa	10	2		M/A 83	19
Jevnikar, Jana	Careers in the Arts: A Resource Guide	Fa	10	3		M/J 83	54
Jewish Museum, New York	Danzig 1939: Treasures of a Destroyed Community	SS&D	11	4	44	Fa 80	67
Jiangsu Handicraft Art Society	Treasures of Suzhow Embroidery	AT	8			De 87	61
Jirousek, Charlotte	Unravelling the Mysteries of the Jacquard	WJ	9	1	33	Su 84	8
Jobé, Joseph, ed.	Great Tapestries: The Web of History from the 12th to the 20th Century	H&C	19	2		Sp 68	43
Johannesen, Betty	Seersucker Blazer, A	WJ	8	3	31	Wi 83	22
Johansen, Marg	Developing Career Weavers	SS&D	6	2	22	Sp 75	46
Johansson, Lillemor	Damask and Opphamta with Weaving Sword or Drawloom	Hw	5	4		S/O 84	13
Johansson, Lillemor	Damask and Opphamta with Weaving Sword or Drawloom	WJ	9	3	35	Wi 85	84
Johansson, Lillemor	Damask and Opphamta with Weaving Sword or Drawloom	SS&D	16	1	61	Wi 84	22
Johansson, Lillemor	Damask and Opphamta with Weaving Sword or Drawloom	PWC	3	3	9		66
Johansson, Lillemor	Opphämta Och Damast Med Skälblad Eller Dragvävstol	WJ	8	2	30	Fa 83	66
Johansson, Lillemor, ed.	Vävmagazinet	PWC			6	Su 83	66
John, Edith	Experimental Embroidery	Fa	4	3		M/J 77	54
John, Sue	Make It Yourself with Handwoven Wool	S-O	9	1		Sp 85	12
Johns, Greg	Designing for the Opphämta Loom	PWC	3	4	10		68

AUTHOR	TITLE	JOUR	VOL	NO	ISS	DATE	PAGE
Johnson, Astrid; Sylvia Mellqvist-Johansson; Eva-Lisa Nordin	Vackra Tras Mattor och Andra Vävar (Beautiful Rag Rugs and Other Weaving)	Hw	5	2		M/A 84	13
Johnson, Beth	Afro-American Sweetgrass Basketry	Fa	9	5		S/O 82	23
Johnson, Beth	Tweed of Harris, The	Hw	2	5		No 81	47
Johnson, Debbie	Sixty Years of Weaving At Arrowmont	Fa	12	5		S/O 85	39
Johnson, Elma	"Fibers Southeast 1979" (Exhibit)	Fa	6	2		M/A 79	68
Johnson, Faye	Jewish Textiles	Hw	5	1		J/F 84	35
Johnson, Garnette	In Honor of Berta Frey	SS&D	3	2	10	Sp 72	4
Johnson, Geraldine Niva	Weaving Rag Rugs: A Women's Craft in Western Maryland	Hw	7	3		M/J 86	12
Johnson, Geraldine Niva	Weaving Rag Rugs: A Women's Craft in Western Maryland	WJ	11	2	42	Fa 86	74
Johnson, Ginger R.	Lions and Tigers and.....Sheep?	S-O	8	2		Su 84	24
Johnson, Irmgard Weitlaner	Weft-Wrap Openwork Techniques in Archaeological and Contemporary Textiles of Mexico	TMJ	4	3		76	63
Johnson, Judith K.	Art of Fashion Design: A Handweaver's Twill Cape, The	WJ	7	3	27	Wi 82	12
Johnson, Meda; Glen Kaufman	Design on Fabrics	H&C	18	4		Fa 67	39
Johnson, Meda Parker	see Kaufman, Glen	Fa	8	6		N/D 81	73
Johnson, Melinda Raber	Turned Summer and Winter Jacket	WJ	8	3	31	Wi 83	58
Johnson, Nellie Sargent	Learn to Weave	H&C	1	1		Ap 50	52
Johnson, Pauline	Creative Bookbinding	Fa	6	4		J/A 79	15
Johnston, Coleen	Start with a Room-Sized Rug and Work Up	Hw	8	4		S/O 87	85
Johnston, Constance	Ontario Handspinning Seminar	H&C	23	5		S/O 72	23
Johnston, Dr. Robert N.	School for American Craftsmen	H&C	23	2		M/A 72	17
Johnston, Ralph	see Johnston, Ruth	SS&D	17	3	67	Su 86	85
Johnston, Ruth; Ralph Johnston	Sashes, Straps and Bands: Original Patterns in Warp-Faced Twill for the Four-Harness Loom	SS&D	17	3	67	Su 86	85
Johnstone, Pauline	Some Unusual Turkish Embroideries of the Early Eighteenth Century	TMJ	24			85	75
Johnstone, Pauline	Turkish Embroidery	Hw	8	5		N/D 87	14
Jolley, Ginger	Ginger Jolley: Inspired by Navajo Weaving	Fa	11	3		M/J 84	36
Jolley, Ginger	Navajo Way, The	S-O	11	4		Wi 87	38
Jones, Alice Varney	Weaving Fabrics for Men's Wear	H&C	1	1		Ap 50	40
Jones, H. McCoy	Washington Hajji Baba, The	TMJ	2	2		De 67	35
Jones, Janice	Found Treasures	Hw	5	5		N/D 84	70
Jones, Jeanetta L.	Why Not Try Embroidery Weaves?	H&C	17	2		Sp 66	12
Jones, Marilyn	Madder Saga, The	SS&D	13	2	50	Sp 82	28
Jones, Mrs. Gary	Learn to Spin on Our Sheep Farm	SS&D	2	3	7	Su 71	18
Jones, Peter	Romanian Housewife Spins a Yarn	S-O	8	1		Sp 84	40
Jones, Sachiye, ed.	Black Sheep Newsletter Companion: Writings for the Shepherd and Handspinner, Vol. 1	SS&D	17	2	66	Sp 86	86
Jones, Suzi	Pacific Basket Makers, A Living Tradition	WJ	8	3	31	Wi 83	67
Jones, Una	Irish Kinsale Cloak, The	WJ	8	3	31	Wi 83	35
Jorstad, Caroline	Ethnic Looms	SS&D	13	4	52	Fa 82	40
Joseph, Rebecca M.	Batik Making and the Royal Javanese Cemetery at Imogiri	TMJ	24			85	83
Joyce, Carol	Designing for Printed Textiles: A Guide to Studio and Free-lance Work	Fa	10	3		M/J 83	52
Judd, Eva Marie	Hui Mea Hana of Honolulu	H&C	8	4		Fa 57	51
Justema, Doris	see Justema, William	SS&D	3	1	9	Wi 71	38
Justema, Doris	see Justema, William	H&C	22	4		Fa 71	37
Justema, William	Color Game	SS&D	3	1	9	Wi 71	11
Justema, William	Counterchange, A Device for Pattern Design	H&C	19	3		Su 68	8
Justema, William	Documents & Design	H&C	21	4		Fa 70	40
Justema, William	Module, A Basis for Textile Design, The	H&C	18	1		Wi 67	9
Justema, William	Pleasures of Pattern, The	H&C	20	2		Sp 69	43
Justema, William	Textile Designs from Wallpaper	H&C	16	1		Wi 65	5

AUTHOR	TITLE	JOUR	VOL	NO	ISS	DATE	PAGE
Justema, William; Doris Justema	Weaving and Needlecraft Color Course	H&C	22	4		Fa 71	37
Justema, William; Doris Justema	Weaving & Needlecraft Color Course	SS&D	3	1	9	Wi 71	38
Justin, Valerie Sharaf	Flat-Woven Rugs of the World	Fa	7	6		N/D 80	34
Juve, Peggy	Painted-Silk Clothing	TM			12	A/S 87	24
Juve, Peggy	Panel Dress, A	TM			12	A/S 87	29
Kackenmeister, Elizabeth	Hemstitched Finish	H&C	16	2		Sp 65	37
Kafka, Francis	Hand Decoration of Fabrics, The	H&C	10	2		Sp 59	54
Kagan, Sasha	Sasha Kagan Sweater Book, The	Kn	2	2	4	S-S 86	78
Kahlenberg, Mary Hunt	see Berlant, Anthony	SS&D	9	2	34	Sp 78	47
Kahlenberg, Mary Hunt; Anthony Berlant	Navajo Blanket, The	TMJ	3	4		De 73	47
Kahn, Deborah, ed.	Handspun Project Book, The	Iw	4	2		Sp 79	61
Kahn, Debra, ed.	Handspun Project Book, The	S-O	8	4		Wi 84	11
Kahn, Kathy; Susan Larson-Fleming	Victor Jacoby: Rich Colors and Bold Designs	WJ	12	1	45	Su 87	36
Kaiser, Eunice	Needle Lace	TM			13	O/N 87	40
Kaiser, Eunice	Square Dance Skirts	H&C	7	1		Wi 55	46
Kaiser, Eunice	Teneriffe Lace — Sol or Sun Lace	SS&D	5	1	17	Wi 73	52
Kaiser, Eunice Gifford	Variations on Whig Rose	H&C	14	1		Wi 63	17
Kajitani, Nobuko	see Sonday, Milton	TMJ	3	1		De 70	45
Kajitani, Nobuko	see Sonday, Milton	TMJ	3	2		De 71	6
Kaleda, Ruth	Rug from Thrums, A	H&C	13	3		Su 62	41
Kaminski, Vera E.	High Tech Meets High Touch: Pioneers in Art	Fa	13	5		S/O 86	6
Kaminski, Vera E.	Windows to the Soul: The Lace Making of Luba Krejci	Fa	6	6		N/D 79	56
Kamola, Stephanie	Old World Weavers at Work in the New	H&C	7	2		Sp 56	24
Kampert, Carol; Susan Henrickson	Guide to Using Cushing Dyes	Hw	2	4		Se 81	79
Kaneloa, J. Puninani	see Bird, Adren J.	WJ	8	2	30	Fa 83	63
Kaplan, Donna	see Jensen, Gay	WJ	12	2	46	Fa 87	62
Kaplan, Susan	Fabric Encounter	H&C	24	4		Au 73	19
Kaplan, Suzan	Ida Grae—A Totally Textural Experience	SS&D	5	4	20	Fa 74	4
Kaplow, Roberta	Bright Styles from the North	SS&D	16	1	61	Wi 84	23
Kappeler, Erda	Almost McKinley Expedition Sweater, The	S-O	11	4		Wi 87	26
Kappler, Erda	Weaving on a Board	Hw	4	4		S/O 83	46
Karaki, Mihoko	Saganishiki	SS&D	15	3	59	Su 84	50
Karjala, Beth	Bevy of Belts, A	Hw	8	1		J/F 87	46
Karlin, Edith	Make a Basic Rug Sampler	SS&D	3	3	11	Su 72	30
Karlin, Edith	Method for Warping a Sectional Beam	SS&D	5	3	19	Su 74	59
Karpilow, Shelley	see Wada, Yoshiko Iwamoto	TM			8	D/J 86	20
Karpilow, Shelley	Working Method for the Home, A	TM			8	D/J 86	22
Karsten, Phyllis	Prize-Winning Suit, A	S-O	8	4		Wi 84	15
Kaspar, Patricia	Anneliese Ammann: Weaver	Fa	5	6		N/D 78	20
Kaspar, Patricia	For Anneliese Ammann, Simplicity is Key to Woven Garments	WJ	7	3	27	Wi 82	70
Kasper, Susan; Roslyn Logsdon	Seen Around the Country: Fiber at the Torpedo Factory	SS&D	9	4	36	Fa 78	86
Kaswell, Ernest	Textile Fibres, Yarns, and Fabrics	H&C	4	3		Su 53	62
Katchen, Carole	Promoting and Selling Your Art	Iw	4	4		Fa 79	72
Kato, Kuniko Lucy	"Fiber Works — Americas & Japan" (Exhibit)	Fa	5	1		J/F 78	10
Katsaros, Maria	see Obeymeyer, Lindsay	Fa	14	1		J/F 87	34
Katz, Ruth	Card Weaving	WJ	2	1	5	Jy 77	30
Katz, Ruth	Footwear, Shoes & Socks You Can Make Yourself	SS&D	11	2	42	Sp 80	83
Katz, Ruth J.	Fabric Painting in New York	Fa	9	1		J/F 82	61
Katz, Ruth J.	Few Words About Feet, Shoes and Other Things We Walk On, A	Fa	6	3		M/J 79	53

AUTHOR	TITLE	JOUR	VOL	NO	ISS	DATE	PAGE
Katz, Ruth J.	Getting Your Work Into the Department Stores: Everything You Need to Know	Fa	9	5		S/O 82	54
Katz, Ruth J.	Industrial Pleating	Fa	9	1		J/F 82	60
Katz, Ruth J.	"Joan Steiner: Hats/New Sculpture" (Exhibit)	Fa	7	5		S/O 80	72
Katz, Ruth J.	Year of the Sweater, The	Fa	7	1		J/F 80	39
Kauffman, Henry	Pennsylvania Dutch, American Folk Art	H&C	4	2		Sp 53	63
Kaufman, Alice; Christopher Selser	Navajo Weaving Tradition: 1650 to the Present, The	WJ	11	1	41	Su 86	14
Kaufman, Deborah	More Than Just a Fling	Fa	7	3		M/J 80	54
Kaufman, Glen	Fabric Ornamentation	H&C	17	1		Wi 66	14
Kaufman, Glen	see Johnson, Meda	H&C	18	4		Fa 67	39
Kaufman, Glen; Meda Parker Johnson	Design on Fabrics, 2nd ed.	Fa	8	6		N/D 81	73
Kaufman, Jenifer	see Kliot, Jules	SS&D	6	1	21	Wi 74	33
Kaufmann, Edgar, Jr.	Handweaver's Place in the U. S. Textile Market, The	H&C	5	4		Fa 54	11
Kaufmann, Ruth	New American Tapestry, The	H&C	19	3		Su 68	41
Kaye, Alda Ganze	Weaver Rose — A New Perspective	SS&D	8	2	30	Sp 77	8
Keall, E. J.	see Vollmer, John E.	WJ	8	4	32	Sp 84	66
Kearney, Kathleen	Evolution of a Weaving, The	SS&D	12	1	45	Wi 80	64
Keasbey, Doramay	Adventures of a Computer Convert (Computer Programming By A Novice)	WJ	8	3	31	Wi 83	28
Keasbey, Doramay	Choosing a Floor Loom: Sinking vs. Rising Shed	Iw	5	3		Su 80	50
Keasbey, Doramay	Damask on a Drawloom	SS&D	8	1	29	WI 76	63
Keasbey, Doramay	Damask with a Sword	CW	7	2	20	Ja 86	16
Keasbey, Doramay	Deciphering Drafts	PWC	4	4	14		30
Keasbey, Doramay	Delicate Dots...Petit Point Treadling	Hw	7	1		J/F 86	66
Keasbey, Doramay	Discerning the Pattern	SS&D	7	2	26	Sp 76	84
Keasbey, Doramay	Effective Yarn Storage and Inventory Control	Hw	8	4		S/O 87	67
Keasbey, Doramay	From Sample to Finished Product	SS&D	15	3	59	Su 84	62
Keasbey, Doramay	How to Weave a Transparency	Hw	4	1		J/F 83	27
Keasbey, Doramay	Individualizing a Loom	CW	4	1	10	Se 82	9
Keasbey, Doramay	Loom-Controlled Adaptation of a Mexican Pick-Up Pattern Technique	CW	6	2	17	Ja 85	19
Keasbey, Doramay	Navajo Tapestry	SS&D	1	3	3	Ju 70	23
Keasbey, Doramay	Overshot Sampler Bedspread for a Narrow Loom, An	PWC	5	1	15		42
Keasbey, Doramay	Pattern Devices for Handweavers	Hw	3	4		Se 82	16
Keasbey, Doramay	Pattern Devices for Handweavers	WJ	6	4	24	Sp 82	57
Keasbey, Doramay	Pattern Devices for Handweavers	SS&D	14	4	56	Fa 83	74
Keasbey, Doramay	Pattern Weaving, Laotian Style	Hw	2	3		My 81	54
Keasbey, Doramay	Patterns Woven in Lace	CW	3	2	8	Ja 82	11
Keasbey, Doramay	Pick-Up Patterned Double Weave	Hw	5	2		M/A 84	80
Keasbey, Doramay	Potholders by Design	PWC	4	3	13		50
Keasbey, Doramay	Potomac Craftsmen Select a New Home	SS&D	4	1	13	Wi 72	40
Keasbey, Doramay	Pretty, Piqué & Pink	PWC	4	3	13		47
Keasbey, Doramay	Tips and Timesavers	PWC	5	2	16		22
Keasbey, Doramay	Transparencies of Inger Harrison–Sheer Beauty, The	Hw	3	1		Ja 82	40
Keasbey, Doramay	Twill with a Twist	Hw	6	5		N/D 85	31
Keasbey, Doramay	Weaving As Drawn In—Classic Style, Part 1	SS&D	17	1	65	Wi 85	28
Keasbey, Doramay	Weaving As Drawn In — Classic Style, Part 2	SS&D	17	2	66	Sp 86	38
Keasbey, Doramay	Yarn Storage Trees	SS&D	10	2	38	Sp 79	86
Keatley, Kathy	Most Gratifying Work Is with Children, The	SS&D	2	3	7	Su 71	16
Keefe, Carolyn	Handspinning Project, The	S-O	3			79	32
Keel, Betty	Sheep	S-O	2			78	5
Keele, Wendy	Shrinkage in Cotton Knits	Kn	3	3	7	Su 87	3
Keeler, Betty	Brown Jacket with Blue Edging	S-O	10	1		Sp 86	21

AUTHOR	TITLE	JOUR	VOL	NO	ISS	DATE	PAGE
Keeler, Betty	Knitting from a Paper Pattern	S-O	8	4		Wi 84	23
Keeler, Betty	Llama Cape, The	H&C	23	4		J/A 72	46
Keeler, Betty	Making of a Coat, The	H&C	23	1		J/F 72	20
Keeler, Betty	Soft Pink Throw, A	S-O	8	4		Wi 84	31
Keeler, Betty	Threading Without Error	Hw	8	5		N/D 87	85
Keeler, Betty	Weaving with Fur for a Bag	H&C	26	1		J/F 75	22
Keen, Annette	Profile of an HGA Rep	SS&D	19	1	73	Wi 87	49
Keener, Terrah	Judy Chicago: The Second Decade	SS&D	15	4	60	Fa 84	30
Keiner, Julia	Fabrics from Israel	H&C	5	4		Fa 54	30
Kelemen, Pál	Folk Textiles of Latin America	TMJ	1	4		De 65	2
Kelemen, Pál	Lenten Curtains from Colonial Peru	TMJ	3	1		De 70	5
Kelemen, Pál	Medieval American Art — Masterpieces of the New World Before Columbus	H&C	9	3		Su 58	60
Keller, Barbara	see Knob, Katherine	CW	1	3	3	Ap 80	1
Keller, Ika	Batik: The Art & Craft	H&C	18	1		Wi 67	45
Keller, Ila	Batik	SS&D	4	4	16	Fa 73	63
Keller, Ila	Batik, The Art and Craft	WJ	8	2	30	Fa 83	65
Kellett, Althea	Ontario Workshop	SS&D	3	1	9	Wi 71	12
Kelly, Jacquie	Contrails Coverlet	PWC	5	1	15		48
Kelly, Jacquie	Custom Fabrics for a Classic Cadillac	WJ	10	4	40	Sp 86	54
Kelly, Jacquie	Designing Fancy Twills in Double Two-Tie Unit Weave	Iw	6	1		Wi 80	49
Kelly, Jacquie	Introduction to Tied Unit Weaves, An	PWC	4	4	14		40
Kelly, Jacquie	Lampas	PWC	5	1	15		46
Kelly, Jacquie	Smalandsvav — Double Harness Weaving on an Ordinary Loom	CW	6	2	17	Ja 85	15
Kelly, Jacquie	Tied Weave Glossary	PWC	4	4	14		44
Kelly, Linda	Matelasse Double Cloth Stitched to Form the Design	WJ	7	1	25	Su 82	43
Kelly, Mary B.	Embroidery for the Goddess	TM			11	J/J 87	26
Kelly, Susan	Play of Light: Susan Kelly Explains the Inner and Outer Workings of Her Tapestries, A	Fa	8	5		S/O 81	54
Kelsey, Barbara Shomer	Dazzling with Sequins	TM			1	O/N 85	60
Kelsey Museum of Archaeology	Art of the Ancient Weaver: Textiles from Egypt (4th-12th century, A. D.), The	SS&D	11	4	44	Fa 80	66
Kemp, Gwendoline	Weaving in Wales	H&C	6	2		Sp 55	24
Kendahl, Connie	All White Overshot Rug (error-corrected WJ v7 n1 82 p36b)	WJ	6	4	24	Sp 82	23
Kennedy, Alan	Kesa: Its Sacred and Secular Aspects	TMJ	22			83	67
Kennedy, Alan	Millions of Swatches at FIT	TM			11	J/J 87	18
Kennedy, Doris Finch	see Wilson, Sadye Tune	Hw	5	2		M/A 84	13
Kennedy, Doris Finch	see Wilson, Sadye Tune	WJ	8	4	32	Sp 84	65
Kennedy, Doris Finch	see Wilson, Sadye Tune	Fa	12	6		N/D 85	46
Kennedy, Doris Finch	see Wilson, Sadye Tune	SS&D	14	4	56	Fa 83	34
Kennedy, Doris Finch	see Wilson, Sadye Tune	SS&D	15	3	59	Su 84	36
Kennedy, Doris Finch	see Wilson, Sadye Tune	PWC	3	2	8		60
Kennelly, Martha Mullan	Northern California Handweavers Conference	H&C	22	3		Su 71	32
Kennett, Don	Whose Zoo? Julietta Thornton's Incredible Fiber Sculptures	Fa	8	5		S/O 81	20
Kent, Kate P.	West African Cloth	SS&D	4	1	13	Wi 72	34
Kent, Kate Peck	Cultivation and Weaving of Cotton in the Prehistoric Southwest United States, The	H&C	9	1		Wi 57	63
Kent, Kate Peck	Navajo Weaving, Three Centuries of Change	Hw	7	2		M/A 86	88
Kent, Kate Peck	Navajo Weaving: Three Centuries of Change	WJ	11	1	41	Su 86	15
Kent, Kate Peck	Navajo Weaving: Three Centuries of Change	SS&D	18	4	72	Fa 87	55
Kent, Kate Peck	Prehistoric Textiles of the Southwest	Hw	4	4		S/O 83	25
Kent, Kate Peck	Prehistoric Textiles of the Southwest	WJ	8	4	32	Sp 84	66
Kent, Kate Peck	Prehistoric Textiles of the Southwest	Fa	10	5		S/O 83	57
Kent, Kate Peck	Prehistoric Textiles of the Southwest	SS&D	14	4	56	Fa 83	74

AUTHOR	TITLE	JOUR	VOL	NO	ISS	DATE	PAGE
Kent, Kate Peck	Prehistoric Textiles of the Southwest	PWC			6	Su 83	68
Kent, Kate Peck	Pueblo Indian Textiles—A Living Tradition	WJ	9	1	33	Su 84	60
Kent, Kate Peck	Pueblo Indian Textiles: A Living Tradition	Fa	11	5		S/O 84	52
Kerimov, Lyatif	Folk Designs from the Caucasus for Weaving and Needlework	SS&D	6	4	24	Fa 75	31
Kerlin, Thomas J.	Claire Campbell Park: Celebrating Color, Light, and Energy	Fa	14	3		M/J 87	15
Kerr, Connie	Exhibition Spaces	SS&D	14	3	55	Su 83	8
Kerr, Connie	"Karen Armstrong's Jungle Happening" (Exhibit)	Fa	6	2		M/A 79	19
Kerr, Connie	"Stitchery '79" (Exhibit)	Fa	6	5		S/O 79	78
Kessenich, Loraine	Anyone Can Blend	H&C	7	1		Wi 55	22
Kessenich, Loraine	What is Fabric Analysis?	H&C	18	1		Wi 67	15
Kessler, Cristina	African Artist in a Dying Trade, An	Fa	11	6		N/D 84	51
Kester, Bernard	"Ladders and Windows" (Exhibit)	Fa	13	4		J/A 86	52
Kidd, Jane	Concerns and Influences in My Work	AT	6			De 86	135
Kierstead, Sallie Pease	Natural Dyes	SS&D	4	3	15	Su 73	53
Kiessling, Robert H.	Wool—Most Versatile of Fibers, Part 1	H&C	2	3		Su 51	13
Kiessling, Robert H.	Wool—Most Versatile of Fibers, Part 2	H&C	2	4		Fa 51	25
Kille, Eleanor C., O.T.R.	Weaving for the Mentally Handicapped	H&C	4	4		Fa 53	26
Kinahan, Barbara	Instructions for Weaving a Bog Shirt	WJ	3	1	9	Jy 78	26
Kindahl, Connie	Boundweave Rug on an Overshot Threading	SS&D	17	3	67	Su 86	58
Kindahl, Connie	Rugs on a Three-End Block Draft	WJ	8	4	32	Sp 84	19
Kinder, Kathleen	Knitting Craft in Great Britain, The	Fa	11	4		J/A 84	42
Kinersly, Gorel	Accurate, Knotless Tie-ups Using Loop Loom Cord	WJ	5	1	17	Su 80	26
Kinersly, Görel A. B.	Knotless Cords and Heddles on a Counter-march Loom (error-corrected SS&D v12 n3 81 p6)	SS&D	12	2	46	Sp 81	18
King, A. J.	Elizabeth Gurrier Multiples	Fa	4	6		N/D 77	30
King, Bucky	Ecclesiastical Weaving	WJ	6	1	21	Su 81	35
King, Bucky	Franklin Whitham	Iw	2	2		Wi 77	13
King, Bucky	Stitchery '66	H&C	18	1		Wi 67	25
King, Bucky	Weaving as Related to Embroidery	SS&D	1	2	2	Mr 70	6
King, Bucky; Jude Martin	Ecclesiastical Crafts	SS&D	10	4	40	Fa 79	63
King, Bucky; Susan W. Gilmurray	Finishes and Embellishments	SS&D	3	4	12	Fa 72	28
King, Dianne Hennessy	"Fiber Feelings" (Exhibit)	Fa	5	5		S/O 78	70
King, Earl L.	see King, Edith B	H&C	7	4		Fa 56	10
King, Edith B.; Earl L. King	Handweaving in India Today	H&C	7	4		Fa 56	10
King, Helen	Dyes from the Herb Garden	TM			6	A/S 86	58
King, Lorna J.	Heritage Project: Quilted Vest, A	WJ	4	3	15	Ja 80	28
King, Mary Elizabeth	Brief History of the Study of Ancient Peruvian Textiles, A	TMJ	2	1		De 66	39
King, Rod	Reviving the Lost Art of Woodland Indian Bag Weaving	Fa	13	2		M/A 86	27
King, William A.	Warp and Weft from Tibet	SS&D	4	4	16	Fa 73	64
King, William A.	Warp and Weft from Tibet	H&C	17	4		Fa 66	45
King, William A.	Warp and Weft from Tibet	H&C	9	4		Fa 58	60
Kingsmill, Sally	Guatemala Weaving Workshop	H&C	26	3		M/J 75	28
Kinney, Ralph Parsons	Complete Book of Furniture Repair and Refinishing, The	H&C	2	1		Wi 50	62
Kinoshita, Masako	Briading Technique Documented in an Early Nineteenth-Century Japanese Treatise, "Soshun Biko", A	TMJ	25			86	47
Kinoshita, Masako	Kumihimo	SS&D	11	3	43	Su 80	19
Kinoshita, Masako	Kumihimo (error-corrected SS&D v9 n2 78 p70)	SS&D	9	1	33	Wi 77	117
Kinoshita, Takeshi	Fingernail Weaving: The Crystallized Art of Patience	SS&D	13	1	49	Wi 81	26
Kinsella, Pat	Artist/Designer: Two Approaches to Fabric	AT	3			My 85	57
Kinsey, Susan Buchanan	Gilbert Adrian: Creating the Hollywood Dream Style	Fa	14	3		M/J 87	49
Kinzel, Marianne	First Book of Modern Lace Knitting, The	Kn	1	2	2	S-S 85	78

AUTHOR	TITLE	JOUR	VOL	NO	ISS	DATE	PAGE
Kinzel, Marianne	Second Book of Modern Lace Knitting, The	Kn	1	2	2	S-S 85	78
Kirby, Mary	Designing on the Loom	SS&D	5	2	18	Sp 74	68
Kirby, Mary	Designing on the Loom	H&C	6	4		Fa 55	59
Kirby, Mary	Designing on the Loom	Fa	3	1		J/F 76	4
Kirby, William	Canada Council Art Bank, The	AT	7			Ju 87	75
Kircher, Ursula	Schopferisches Weben—Creative Weaving	SS&D	6	3	23	Su 75	49
Kirk, Betty Burian	Flamepoint Rugs for Everybody	WJ	8	4	32	Sp 84	12
Kirk, Ray	Second Annual Handcrafted Wool Showcase	S-O	3			79	6
Kirkland, Lawrence P.	"Sherri Smith: Recent Work" (Exhibit)	Fa	7	4		J/A 80	63
Kirkpatrick, Isabell; Pat Kirkpatrick	Fabrics from a Desert Weaver	H&C	7	3		Su 56	27
Kirkpatrick, Pat	see Kirkpatrick, Isabell	H&C	7	3		Su 56	27
Kirschner, Lee	see Calhoun, Wheeler	S-O	7	1		Sp 83	28
Kirschner, Lee	see Calhoun, Wheeler	S-O	7	2		Su 83	44
Kirschner, Lee	see Calhoun, Wheeler	S-O	7	4		Wi 83	35
Kirschner, Lee	Two Heads Are Better Than One, or A Story with a Good Twist	S-O	8	4		Wi 84	42
Kiser, Charlotte E.	Westchester County Crafts Program	H&C	3	1		Wi 51	38
Kitamura, Tetsuro	see Barton, Jane	Hw	6	3		Su 85	14
Kitzman, Betty Lou	"Wildlife Physics" (Exhibit)	Fa	12	2		M/A 85	72
Klein, Chuck	Ojos De Dios	H&C	24	1		J/F 73	28
Klein, Jody	"Fabric Constructions: The Art Quilt" (Exhibit)	Fa	11	2		M/A 84	81
Klein, Jody	Fiber/Art Conditioned by Life: A Workshop with Sheila Hicks	Fa	12	5		S/O 85	58
Klein, Jody	"Michael James: A Ten-Year Retrospective" (Exhibit)	Fa	11	2		M/A 84	80
Kleinberg, Eliot	Vexillology? Call the ABC Flag Company	Fa	12	4		J/A 85	41
Klemperer, Louise	see Evans, Rojean	Fa	7	5		S/O 80	75
Klessen, Romy	Mind Boggling Bogs	PWC			3	Oc 82	40
Klessen, Romy	Moneymakers for Weavers	PWC	1	1		No 81	5
Klessen, Romy	More Moneymakers for Weavers	PWC			2	Ap 82	9
Klessen, Romy	Proportions of the Bog Shirt	PWC			3	Oc 82	34
Klessen, Romy	Romy's One-Shouldered Bodice	PWC			2	Ap 82	87
Klessen, Romy	Romy's Soapbox	PWC			2	Ap 82	88
Klessen, Romy	Three Color Basket in Single Crochet	PWC			4	Ja 83	60
Klessen, Romy	Woven Egmont Sweater	PWC			2	Ap 82	83
Kline, Martha	Guild in Focus: Fiber Artisans, A	Fa	11	5		S/O 84	47
Kline, Michael	Ruth Anderson, Custom Dyer	Fa	9	5		S/O 82	27
Kline, Morris	Mathematics in Western Culture	H&C	5	1		Wi 53	60
Klinect, Ann W.	Guide to Ann's Knit Suit, A	S-O	10	1		Sp 86	41
Klinect, Ann W.	My Knit Suit	S-O	10	1		Sp 86	40
Klinect, Ann W.	Northwest Regional Spinning Association	S-O	7	2		Su 83	8
Klinect, Ann W.	Sweatshirt? Yes– A Sweatshirt with Options!, A	S-O	7	1		Sp 83	43
Klinect, Ann W.	What to do with a Rainbow	S-O	9	3		Fa 85	26
Kling, Candace	Decorative Ribbon Work	TM			12	A/S 87	58
Kling, Mary Nell	Making Narrow Looms Do Big Jobs	H&C	2	1		Wi 50	13
Kliot, Jules	Sprang: Language and Techniques	SS&D	5	3	19	Su 74	63
Kliot, Jules	Sprang: Language and Techniques	SS&D	6	3	23	Su 75	49
Kliot, Jules	Sprang — Language & Technique	WJ	3	1	9	Jy 78	35
Kliot, Jules	Tapestry Loom Techniques	WJ	3	1	9	Jy 78	35
Kliot, Jules	Vertical Loom — Principles and Construction, The	WJ	3	1	9	Jy 78	35
Kliot, Jules; Kaethe Kliot	Battenberg Lace: Making Lace with Woven Tape and a Needle	TM			10	A/M 87	30
Kliot, Jules; Kaethe Kliot	Bobbin Lace & the Linen Stitch	H&C	24	2		M/A 73	39
Kliot, Jules; Kaethe Kliot	Kume Himo Techniques of Japanese Plaiting	WJ	3	1	9	Jy 78	35

AUTHOR	TITLE	JOUR	VOL	NO	ISS	DATE	PAGE
Kliot, Jules; Kaethe Kliot	Looking At Lace	Fa	9	3		M/J 82	43
Kliot, Jules; Kaethe Kliot	Stitches of Bobbin Lace: Structure and Classification	SS&D	5	3	19	Su 74	62
Kliot, Jules; Kaethe Kliot	Tatting — Designs from Victorian Lace Craft	SS&D	11	1	41	Wi 79	32
Kliot, Jules; Kaethe Kliot	Tatting: Designs from Victorian Lace Craft	Iw	4	3		Su 79	66
Kliot, Jules; Kaethe Kliot, eds.	Battenberg and Point Lace — Techniques, Stitches and Designs from Victorian Needlework	SS&D	10	3	39	Su 79	36
Kliot, Jules; Kaethe Kliot, eds.	Battenberg and Point Lace Techniques, Stitches and Designs from Victorian Needlework	WJ	3	1	9	Jy 78	35
Kliot, Jules; Kaethe Kliot, eds.	Irish Crocheted Lace	WJ	5	1	17	Su 80	47
Kliot, Jules; Kaethe Kliot; Jenifer Kaufman	Concrete and Grace, Fiber Allusions (error-corrected SS&D v6 n2 75 p44)	SS&D	6	1	21	Wi 74	33
Kliot, Kaethe	see Kliot, Jules	H&C	24	2		M/A 73	39
Kliot, Kaethe	see Kliot, Jules	SS&D	6	1	21	Wi 74	33
Kliot, Kaethe	see Kliot, Jules	SS&D	11	1	41	Wi 79	32
Kliot, Kaethe	see Kliot, Jules	Iw	4	3		Su 79	66
Kliot, Kaethe	see Kliot, Jules	WJ	3	1	9	Jy 78	35
Kliot, Kaethe	see Kliot, Jules	Fa	9	3		M/J 82	43
Kliot, Kaethe	see Kliot, Jules	TM			10	A/M 87	30
Kliot, Kaethe	see Kliot, Jules	SS&D	5	3	19	Su 74	62
Kliot, Kaethe	Teneriffe Lace — Brasilian Solo Lace	SS&D	5	1	17	Wi 73	52
Kliot, Kaethe, ed.	see Kliot, Jules, ed.	SS&D	10	3	39	Fa 79	36
Kliot, Kaethe, ed.	see Kliot, Jules, ed.	WJ	3	1	9	Jy 78	35
Kliot, Kaethe, ed.	see Kliot, Jules, ed.	WJ	5	1	17	Su 80	47
Kluge, Chris	Marks of Distinction: Woven Labels 1900–1940	Fa	8	1		J/F 81	24
Kluge, Gini	From Spinner to Weaver	S-O	8	1		Sp 84	43
Kluger, Marilyn	Joy of Spinning, The	SS&D	3	1	9	Wi 71	38
Kluger, Marilyn	Joy of Spinning, The	H&C	23	1		J/F 72	32
Kluger, Marilyn	Joy of Spinning, The	Iw	2	3		Sp 77	32
Kluth, Liz	"Ice in Shadow" Sweater	S-O	9	4		Wi 85	15
Knauer, Katherine	Funeral	Fa	13	6		N/D 86	30
Knight, Brian	Rug Weaving, Technique and Design	WJ	6	3	23	Wi 81	60
Knight, Martha R.	Weaving Program for Children, A	H&C	2	3		Su 51	58
Knishern, Edna Maki	From Ramie Top to Ramie Top	SS&D	9	2	34	Sp 78	78
Kniskern, Edna Maki	Lacy Triangular Stole of Handspun Wool, A	WJ	6	2	22	Fa 81	48
Kniskern, Edna Maki	Plight of the Untitled, The	Fa	8	4		J/A 81	32
Kniskern, Verne B.	New Twist in Making Fringe, A	Hw	6	1		J/F 85	7
Kniskern, Verne B.	What's Wrong with Being A Weaver?	Hw	8	2		M/A 87	10
Knoizen, Frances	She Sells Everything She Weaves	H&C	9	3		Su 58	22
Knollenberg, Barbara	Basic Sewing Techniques in Handling Handwoven Fabrics for Garments.	WJ	1	1	1	Jy 76	25
Knollenberg, Barbara	Binding Handwoven Garments with Leather	WJ	1	3	3	Ja 77	22
Knollenberg, Barbara	Bits and Pieces	WJ	1	4	4	Ap 77	11
Knollenberg, Barbara	Designing Borders on Clothing	WJ	2	1	5	Jy 77	12
Knollenberg, Barbara	Pine Tree Coat	WJ	1	2	2	Oc 76	32
Knottenbelt, Maaike	Warping and Weaving Mitla Cloth on the Backstrap Loom	TMJ	22			83	53
Knox, Patty	New Directions in Fair Isle Knitting	Kn	2	1	3	F-W 85	79
Knutson, Linda	Getting Started with Chemical Dyes	S-O	8	3		Fa 84	39
Knutson, Linda	Space Dyeing with Fiber-Reactive Dyes	WJ	8	1	29	Su 83	89
Knutson, Linda	Synthetic Dyes for Natural Fibers	Hw	4	1		J/F 83	18
Knutson, Linda	Synthetic Dyes for Natural Fibers	WJ	7	2	26	Fa 82	58
Knutson, Linda	Synthetic Dyes for Natural Fibers	Fa	10	1		J/F 83	57

AUTHOR	TITLE	JOUR	VOL	NO	ISS	DATE	PAGE
Kobler, Virginia	Bellevue Fair	H&C	18	1		Wi 67	26
Koblo, Martin	World of Color — An Introduction to the Theory and Use of Color in Art	H&C	14	4		Fa 63	43
Koda, Harold	Balenciago: The Architect of Elegant Clothing	TM			11	J/J 87	20
Koda, Harold	Body as Canvas, The	TM			8	D/J 86	56
Koehler, Glory Dail	Acid Dyes, Part 1, The	SS&D	6	3	23	Su 75	53
Koehler, Glory Dail	Acid Dyes, Part 2, The	SS&D	6	4	24	Fa 75	78
Koehler, Glory Dail	Chemical Dyeing, Part 2	SS&D	6	2	22	Sp 75	59
Koehler, Glory Dail	Chemical Dyeing: Preparation, Part 1	SS&D	6	1	21	Wi 74	70
Koehler, Glory Dail	Direct Dyes	SS&D	7	3	27	Su 76	88
Koehler, Glory Dail	Dyepot	SS&D	7	4	28	Fa 76	58
Koehler, Glory Dail	Stock Solution, The	SS&D	7	1	25	Wi 75	76
Koehler, Glory Dail	Tests for Desired Yarn Qualities	SS&D	7	2	26	Sp 76	68
Koehler, Glory Dail	Vat Dyes	SS&D	8	1	29	WI 76	37
Koehler, Nancy J.	Macramé Workshop	H&C	21	4		Fa 70	28
Koenig, Marion; Gill Speirs	Making Rugs for Pleasure and Profit	WJ	6	4	24	Sp 82	60
Koenigsberg, Nancy	Sheila Hicks: An Affinity for Architecture	Fa	12	5		S/O 85	60
Koepp, William	Another Balancing Act for the Countermarch Loom	CW	8	1	22	Se 86	9
Koepp, William	Doublejack or Sink the floating selvedge	WJ	9	3	35	Wi 85	67
Koepp, William	Examining the Shed	WJ	10	4	40	Sp 86	76
Koepp, William	Loom Maintenance	WJ	11	4	44	Sp 87	65
Koepp, William	Shed Regulator for Counterbalance Looms, The	WJ	10	3	39	Wi 86	67
Koepp, William	Simple Selvage System, A	SS&D	16	4	64	Fa 85	68
Koepp, William A.	Doublejack	SS&D	14	1	53	Wi 82	7
Kolander, Cheryl	Natural Dyeing of Silk Fiber	SS&D	9	2	34	Sp 78	58
Kolander, Cheryl	Onion Gold	S-O	9	3		Fa 85	40
Kolander, Cheryl	Silk Worker's Notebook, A	SS&D	12	1	45	Wi 80	83
Kolander, Cheryl	Silk Worker's Notebook, A	Iw	5	1		Wi 79	60
Kolander, Cheryl	Silk Worker's Notebook, A	WJ	10	4	40	Sp 86	82
Kolander, Cheryl	Silk Worker's Notebook, A	Fa	13	1		J/F 86	45
Kolander, Cheryl	Silk Worker's Notebook, A	TM			5	J/J 86	12
Kolander, Cheryl	Therapeutic Aspects of Silk, The	Fa	13	1		J/F 86	76
Kolander, Cheryl	This I Ask of Ye...	Hw	3	2		Mr 82	14
Kolander, Cheryl	Wild Silk	Iw	2	3		Sp 77	8
Kolling-Summers, Elizabeth	Elegant Plaid Shawl, An	WJ	7	3	27	Wi 82	69
Kolling-Summers, Elizabeth	Four-Shaft Twill Neck Scarf	WJ	7	1	25	Su 82	29
Kolling-Summers, Elizabeth	Four-Shaft, Two-Block Warp-Faced Rep Floor Covering	WJ	7	4	28	Sp 83	15
Kolling-Summers, Elizabeth	Warp-Faced Tablerunner in Rib Weave	WJ	7	4	28	Sp 83	14
Komives, Margaret Deck	Making Sense of Interfacing (error-corrected TM n12 p4)	TM			10	A/M 87	58
Kongback, Ylva	see Carlstedt, Catherina	PWC	5	2	16		53
Konieczny, M. G.	Textiles of Baluchistan	WJ	6	1	21	Su 81	54
Koob, Katherine; Barbara Keller; Ruth Howard	Use of Long-Eyed Heddles, The	CW	1	3	3	Ap 80	1
Kooijman, Simon	Tapa in Polynesia	TMJ	4	2		75	80
Koopman, Albertje	Celebrations of Life	Hw	4	1		J/F 83	59
Koopman, Albertje	Fashioning a Workshop	SS&D	16	1	61	Wi 84	29
Koopman, Albertje	Josephina's Suit	WJ	4	4	16	Ap 80	50
Kopette, Linda	Simple Pillow, A	SS&D	4	1	13	Wi 72	36
Koplos, Janet	Anne Wilson: Underlying Geometry	Fa	10	3		M/J 83	62
Koplos, Janet	Conversation with Claire Zeisler, A	Fa	10	4		J/A 83	25
Koplos, Janet	"Fiber Art: Tapestries and Wall Hangings" (Exhibit)	Fa	6	6		N/D 79	75
Koplos, Janet	"Gail Skudera: Textile Paintings" (Exhibit)	Fa	9	6		N/D 82	84

AUTHOR	TITLE	JOUR	VOL	NO	ISS	DATE	PAGE
Koplos, Janet	Garment Form As Image, The	Fa	10	6		N/D 83	66
Koplos, Janet	Hisako Sekijima, Basketmaker	Fa	13	5		S/O 86	14
Koplos, Janet	How a Textile Department Grew	Fa	10	1		J/F 83	54
Koplos, Janet	In Search of the Corporate Market	Fa	9	5		S/O 82	52
Koplos, Janet	Janet Markarian: From Baskets to Bags, Containers Transformed	Fa	11	1		J/F 84	16
Koplos, Janet	Just Playing in Space: Ann McKenzie Nickolson's Textile Artwork	Fa	8	2		M/A 81	34
Koplos, Janet	"Kimono As Art: Modern Textile Works by Kako Moriguchi, Rikizo Munehiro, and Fukumi Shimura" (Exhibit)	Fa	13	1		J/F 86	60
Koplos, Janet	Leather Reliefs of Teruko Yamazaki, The	Fa	14	4		S/O 87	12
Koplos, Janet	"Magdalena Abakanowicz" (Exhibit)	Fa	10	2		M/A 83	66
Koplos, Janet	Masks At the Heart of Disguise	Fa	11	5		S/O 84	32
Koplos, Janet	"Needle Expressions '84" (Exhibit)	Fa	12	2		M/A 85	74
Koplos, Janet	"New Dimensions in Handmade Paper" (Exhibit)	Fa	8	5		S/O 81	72
Koplos, Janet	Paper Clothing: West	Fa	11	2		M/A 84	39
Koplos, Janet	Public Fiber: Looking At the Logistics	Fa	12	1		J/F 85	32
Koplos, Janet	Structure and Surface: The Work of Barbara MacCallum	Fa	10	2		M/A 83	62
Koplos, Janet	Sue Nechin of First Additions	Fa	10	1		J/F 83	69
Koplos, Janet	When is Fiber Art "Art"?	Fa	13	2		M/A 86	34
Koplos, Janet	"Woven, Tied, and Knotted" (Exhibit)	Fa	9	2		M/A 82	82
Kopycinski, Joseph V.	Textile Industry—Information Sources	SS&D	6	1	21	Wi 74	32
Korach, Alice	Shetland Lace	TM			11	J/J 87	40
Korach, Alice	Shetland Lace Wedding Handkerchief, A (error-corrected TM n12 p4)	TM			11	J/J 87	42
Kormos, Antonia	Acid Dyeing	SS&D	15	2	58	Sp 84	34
Kosikowski, Janusz	Making Ends Meet At the Loom	SS&D	7	4	28	Fa 76	28
Kossick, Ebba	Weaving for Sale	H&C	17	3		Su 66	23
Kosta, Angela	Brief Creative Tale, A	Fa	11	6		N/D 84	95
Kosta, Angela	"California Fibers: 11th Annual Show" (Exhibit)	Fa	10	6		N/D 83	81
Kosta, Angela	Paper Art of Fritzi Huber Morrison, The	Fa	11	2		M/A 84	22
Kosta, Angela	**Teacher**/Student Interface: Two Views of Education	Fa	14	1		J/F 87	31
Koster, Joan	Handloom Construction: A Practical Guide for the Non-Expert	Iw	5	3		Su 80	71
Koster, Joan Boura	Tagari: A Greek Saddlebag of Handspun Wools, The	WJ	6	2	22	Fa 81	24
Koster, Joan Bouza	Arachne's Children	SS&D	9	3	35	Su 78	16
Koster, Joan Bouza	Carding Box, The	SS&D	10	4	40	Fa 79	24
Koster, Joan Bouza	Summer Shades	SS&D	18	3	71	Su 87	40
Kozikowski, Janusz	Blankets of New Mexico	SS&D	10	1	37	Wi 78	60
Kozikowski, Janusz	Janusz Kozikowski	Fa	7	5		S/O 80	43
Kozikowski, Janusz	Weaver Is a Rose, A	Fa	5	5		S/O 78	13
Kozikowski, Janusz	Weaving on a Two Man Loom	H&C	24	1		J/F 73	6
Kozikowski, Janusz; Nancy Kozikowski	Ghost Rugs	Iw	4	1		Wi 78	24
Kozikowski, Nancy	see Kozikowski, Janusz	Iw	4	1		Wi 78	24
Kramer, Helen	Studies in Color and Texture Through Fabric	H&C	6	1		Wi 54	13
Kramer, Jack	Dyer's Garden Is Feature of Landscape Plan	SS&D	4	4	16	Fa 73	35
Krantz, Hazel	Calm and Cool...Sewing Handwoven Fabric	Hw	4	3		M/J 83	29
Krantz, Hazel	Why Knot?	Hw	5	4		S/O 84	24
Krapes, Shelley	Beth Ames Swartz: A Painter's Way with Paper	Fa	9	4		J/A 82	19
Krapes, Shelley	"Fiber Drawings: Works in Thread on Paper" (Exhibit)	Fa	5	5		S/O 78	65
Krasnoff, Julienne	Another Loom Another Tote Bag, Rug Sampler Project for Beginners	H&C	22	1		Wi 71	32
Krasnoff, Julienne	Busy Signal	SS&D	2	4	8	Fa 71	9
Krasnoff, Julienne	Double Weave Project for the Beginner	H&C	21	4		Fa 70	11
Krasnoff, Julienne	Idea for Gifts	H&C	21	3		Su 70	18
Krasnoff, Julienne	On Buying Yarn	H&C	21	3		Su 70	45
Krasnoff, Julienne	Photographing Textiles, Part 1, Black and White	SS&D	7	1	25	Wi 75	86

AUTHOR	TITLE	JOUR	VOL	NO	ISS	DATE	PAGE
Krasnoff, Julienne	Photographing Textiles, Part 2, Color	SS&D	7	2	26	Sp 76	48
Krasnoff, Julienne	Projects from a Connecticut Weaver	H&C	21	1		Wi 70	16
Krasnoff, Julienne	see Lewis, Alfred Allan	SS&D	7	4	28	Fa 76	65
Krasnoff, Julienne	Try Something Different	H&C	21	2		Sp 70	19
Krasnoff, Julienne H.	Small Project in Bound Weave for Beginners, A	H&C	20	3		Su 69	13
Krasnoff, Julienne Hallen	Planning Pockets	H&C	20	4		Fa 69	15
Krasnoff, Julienne Hallen	Vertical Pockets	H&C	21	1		Wi 70	21
Kraus, William	Bridging the Gap Between Craft Artists and Interior Designers	SS&D	16	4	64	Fa 85	37
Kren, Margo	Easily Constructed Loom from Africa, An	SS&D	7	3	27	Su 76	19
Krevitsky, Nik	Batik — Art and Craft	H&C	15	3		Su 64	45
Krevitsky, Nik; Lois Ericson	Shaped Weaving	SS&D	6	3	23	Su 75	49
Krinn, Linda	"Tangents: Art in Fiber" (Exhibit)	Fa	14	3		M/J 87	55
Kroeger, Jackie	Jackie's Sweaters: Blouson, Dolman, Striped Silk	Kn	1	1	1	F-W 84 CI	41 33
Kroetsch, Glenn	Conflict Resolved: The Hows and Whys of Hand-Dyed Relief Painting, A	Fa	8	4		J/A 81	13
Krohn, Val Frieling	Hawaii Dye Plants and Dye Recipes	WJ	8	2	30	Fa 83	65
Krohn, Val Frieling	Hawaii Dye Plants and Dye Recipes	Fa	9	4		J/A 82	52
Kroll, Carol	Pet Yarn	S-O	1			77	18
Kroll, Carol	Putting on the Dog	SS&D	8	2	30	Sp 77	38
Kroll, Carol	Putting on the Dog	Iw	1	4		Su 76	29
Kroll, Carol	Whole Craft of Spinning—From Raw Materials to the Finished Yarn, The	WJ	8	1	29	Su 83	53
Kroncke, Grete	Mounting Handicraft	SS&D	4	2	14	Sp 73	44
Kroncke, Grete	Mounting Handicraft: Ideas and Instructuins for Assembling and Finishing	H&C	22	2		Sp 71	46
Kroncke, Grete	Simple Weaving	SS&D	4	4	16	Fa 73	63
Krondahl, Hans	From Hand to Hand: Swedish Weaving Today	Hw	8	3		M/J 87	34
Krondahl, Hans	Swedish Design	Hw	4	2		M/A 83	29
Kronenberg, Bud	Ideal Spinning Wheel, The	SS&D	12	1	45	Wi 80	12
Kronenberg, Bud	Misunderstood Spinning Wheel, The	SS&D	12	3	47	Su 81	11
Kronenberg, Bud	Spinning Bulky Yarns	SS&D	13	1	49	Wi 81	78
Kronenberg, Bud	Spinning Wheel Building and Restoration	SS&D	12	4	48	Fa 81	63
Kronke, Grete	Weaving with Cane and Reed: Modern Basketry	H&C	19	3		Su 68	41
Kronkright, Dale	see Odegaard, Nancy	Fa	11	1		J/F 84	43
Krook, Inga	From Rags to Riches	Hw	4	3		M/J 83	32
Krook, Inga	"Maria" Rag Rug	Hw	6	3		Su 85	56
Krueger, Glee	"Needlework" (Exhibit)	Fa	9	3		M/J 82	78
Krueger, Susan	Word Weaver	Hw	3	4		Se 82	10
Kubota, Itchiku	see Barton, Jane	Hw	6	3		Su 85	14
Kuemmerlein, Janet	Black Rope and Straw Form	SS&D	4	3	15	Su 73	49
Kuhnel, Ernest; Louisa Bellinger	Catalogue of Spanish Rugs	H&C	4	4		Fa 53	59
Kuhnel, Ernst	Cairene Rugs, 15 C. — 17 C. Technical Analysis by Louisa Bellinger	H&C	9	2		Sp 58	59
Kuhnel, Ernst	Dated Tiraz Fabrics	H&C	4	1		Wi 52	60
Kuhnel, Ernst	see van Bode, Wilhelm	H&C	10	1		Wi 59	60
Kuisk, Harda	Teneriffe Lace — Estonian Sun Lace	SS&D	5	1	17	Wi 73	52
Kuo, Susanna	Nexus: A Collaboration in Textile Art	Iw	5	3		Su 80	22
Kurtz, Carol	Basic Drafting	SS&D	10	3	39	Su 79	18
Kurtz, Carol	Color Use in Patterned Weaves	SS&D	11	3	43	Su 80	22
Kurtz, Carol	Designing Block Weaves	SS&D	11	2	42	Sp 80	5
Kurtz, Carol	Designing Drafts	SS&D	10	4	40	Fa 79	28
Kurtz, Carol	Drafting with Color	SS&D	11	1	41	Wi 79	10
Kurtz, Carol	"Threads" (Exhibit)	Fa	10	4		J/A 83	62

AUTHOR	TITLE	JOUR	VOL	NO	ISS	DATE	PAGE
Kurtz, Carol; B. J. Adams	Talk with Josep Grau-Garriga, A	SS&D	9	4	36	Fa 78	4
Kurtz, Carol S.	Design for Weaving: A Study Guide for Drafting, Design and Color	Hw	3	3		My 82	14
Kurtz, Carol S.	Designing for Weaving: A Study Guide for Drafting, Design and Color	SS&D	13	4	52	Fa 82	66
Kurtz, Carol S.	Designing for Weaving: A Study Guide for Drafting, Design and Color	WJ	6	4	24	Sp 82	60
Kurtz, Carol S.	Designing for Weaving: A Study Guide for Drafting, Design and Color	WJ	11	4	44	Sp 87	74
Kurtz, Carol S.	Designing for Weaving: A Study Guide for Drafting, Design and Color	Fa	9	3		M/J 82	58
Kussube, Kay; Alexis Yiorgos Xenakis	Notes from the Tailor	PWC	4	2	12		27
Kuttruff, Jenna Tedrick	Prehistoric Textiles Revealed by Potsherds	SS&D	11	3	43	Su 80	40
Kuttruff, Jenna Tedrick	Prehistoric Twined Bag from Big Bone Cave, Tennessee: Manufacture, Repair, and Use, A	AT	8			De 87	125
Kuwabara, Nancy	Experiences in History	SS&D	9	1	33	Wi 77	106
Kuwabara, Nancy	see Wertenberger, Kathryn	Hw	4	2		M/A 83	63
Kuwabara, Nancy	Tulip Outfit with Loom Controlled Inlay (error-corrected WJ v6 n1 81 p28d)	WJ	5	3	19	Wi 81	28
Kwiatkowski, Ron	Hawaiian Feather Techniques	Iw	1	4		Su 76	16
Kwiatkowski, Ron	Inca Feathers	Iw	1	2		Wi 76	16
Kybal, Antonin	Modern Textile Designer: Antonin Kybal	H&C	15	2		Sp 64	43
Kybalova, Ludmilla	Contemporary Tapestries from Czechoslovakia	H&C	17	1		Wi 66	43
La Pierre, Sharon	Effective Designing	SS&D	11	3	43	Su 80	36
La Pierre, Sharon	Exploring Basketry in China Today	Fa	12	4		J/A 85	54
La Pierre, Sharon	Molas	TM			14	D/J 87	48
La Pierre, Sharon	New Direction for the Art of Basketry, A	WJ	8	3	31	Wi 83	54
La Pierre, Sharon	You Can Design, An Adventure in Creating	WJ	8	3	31	Wi 83	67
La Pierre, Sharon	You Can Design: An Adventure in Creating	SS&D	15	3	59	Su 84	34
LaBranche, Carol	Dear Yarn Shop	Kn	3	4	8	Fa 87	10
Lacey, Sue	Selected Bibliography for Handspinners, A	S-O	8	3		Fa 84	11
Lacey, Sue	Selected Bibliography for Handspinners, A	S-O	9	2		Su 85	49
Lacey, Sue	Three-Ply Coat Sweater, A	S-O	8	3		Fa 84	47
Ladbury, Ann	Dressmaker's Dictionary, The	Fa	10	1		J/F 83	58
LaFara, Betty	Pattern for a Guild Library	SS&D	2	1	5	De 70	12
Lagan, Constance Hallinan	Marketing: Selling How-To's	SS&D	16	3	63	Su 85	16
Laine, Anna E.	"I Wish I Had a Loom . . ."	WJ	9	4	36	Sp 85	57
Laing, Ellen Johnston	Oriental Rug of A. D. 1280, An	TMJ	4	1		De 74	82
Laing, K. M.	Jacquard, Jacquard	TM			3	F/M 86	10
Laky, Gyöngy	Plaiting: Non-Loom Weaving	SS&D	12	2	46	Sp 81	33
Lala, Susan	Thailand	SS&D	18	4	72	Fa 87	74
LaLena, Connie	Personal Color System for Dyers, A	Iw	3	3		Sp 78	20
LaLena, Constance	Blocks in Production	Hw	8	5		N/D 87	22
LaLena, Constance	Borrowing from the Bank	Hw	6	3		Su 85	33
LaLena, Constance	Break-Even Analysis	Hw	7	4		S/O 86	60
LaLena, Constance	Changes in Weaving	Hw	8	1		J/F 87	24
LaLena, Constance	Commitment	Hw	2	4		Se 81	76
LaLena, Constance	Computers for the Fiber Professional	Hw	3	2		Mr 82	72
Lalena, Constance	Contemporary Use of Traditional Damask, A	WJ	8	1	29	Su 83	69
LaLena, Constance	Copyright	Hw	4	3		M/J 83	69
LaLena, Constance	Country Rags for a City Apartment	Hw	6	3		Su 85	62
LaLena, Constance	Cozy Retreat, A	Hw	5	2		M/A 84	65
LaLena, Constance	Defining Your Business	Iw	5	4		Fa 80	58
LaLena, Constance	Designer Notes on Fabrics for Interiors	Hw	3	4		Se 82	34
LaLena, Constance	Equipment for Production Efficiency: Other Helpful Equipment	Hw	5	5		N/D 84	79
LaLena, Constance	Equipment for Production Efficiency: The Loom	Hw	5	4		S/O 84	29
LaLena, Constance	Fabrics for a Country Kitchen	Hw	6	4		S/O 85	46

AUTHOR	TITLE	JOUR	VOL	NO	ISS	DATE	PAGE
LaLena, Constance	Fabrics for Interiors 1	Hw	3	4		Se 82	33
LaLena, Constance	Fabrics for Interiors 10	Hw	8	2		M/A 87	52
LaLena, Constance	Fabrics for Interiors 2	Hw	4	1		J/F 83	66
LaLena, Constance	Fabrics for Interiors 3	Hw	4	3		M/J 83	50
LaLena, Constance	Fabrics for Interiors 4: Tartan for a Child's Room	Hw	4	5		N/D 83	70
LaLena, Constance	Fabrics for Interiors 6	Hw	5	5		N/D 84	32
LaLena, Constance	Fabrics for Interiors 7	Hw	6	3		Su 85	62
LaLena, Constance	Fabrics for Interiors 8	Hw	6	4		S/O 85	46
LaLena, Constance	Fabrics for Interiors 9	Hw	7	2		M/A 86	64, I-12
LaLena, Constance	Fabrics for Interiors 9: Contemporary Damask Fabrics for a Bedroom	Hw	7	2		M/A 86	64
LaLena, Constance	Fiber Horizons	Hw	4	5		N/D 83	26
LaLena, Constance	Financial Statements: An Aid to Financial Management	Hw	6	2		M/A 85	33
LaLena, Constance	Guild Show or Sale, A	Hw	6	4		S/O 85	72
LaLena, Constance	Health and Safety Hazards in the Fiber Studio	Hw	4	5		N/D 83	79
LaLena, Constance	Help in the Studio I: Evaluating your Needs	Hw	3	5		N/D 82	81
LaLena, Constance	Help in the Studio II: Hiring a Permanent Staff	Hw	4	1		J/F 83	74
LaLena, Constance	Interview with Albertje Koopman, An	Hw	7	3		M/J 86	89
LaLena, Constance	Keeping Books	Hw	8	2		M/A 87	28
LaLena, Constance	Making a Sales Call	Hw	7	2		M/A 86	76
LaLena, Constance	Managing Your Time, Part 1	Iw	5	2		Sp 80	64
LaLena, Constance	Managing Your Time, Part 2	Iw	5	3		Su 80	60
LaLena, Constance	Marjorie Ford-Pohlmann: Fiber Design Professional	Hw	5	3		Su 84	82
LaLena, Constance	Market Research: Know Your Customer	Iw	6	1		Wi 80	58
LaLena, Constance	Market Research: Styles, Trends and Product Development	Hw	2	2		Mr 81	63
LaLena, Constance	Perfect Balance, A	Hw	3	4		Se 82	77
LaLena Constance	Planning for the Future	Hw	5	1		J/F 84	77
LaLena, Constance	Planning to Conclusion	Hw	8	4		S/O 87	19
LaLena, Constance	Planning Your Studio Space	Hw	4	2		M/A 83	76
LaLena, Constance	Pricing for Profit 1. Keeping Essential Records	Hw	2	5		No 81	75
LaLena, Constance	Pricing for Profit II: Pulling it all Together	Hw	3	1		Ja 82	74
LaLena, Constance	Production Efficiency: Working Smart	Hw	3	3		My 82	78
LaLena, Constance	Professional Portfolio	Hw	5	2		M/A 84	38
LaLena, Constance	Publicity: The Press Release	Hw	7	1		J/F 86	73
LaLena, Constance	Sales Brochures	Hw	6	5		N/D 85	80
LaLena, Constance	Setting Goals and Evaluating Priorities	Iw	5	1		Wi 79	43
LaLena, Constance	Simple Rustic Fabrics for a Den	Hw	5	5		N/D 84	33
LaLena, Constance	Summer Whites	Hw	4	3		M/J 83	51
LaLena, Constance	Two Weavers: A Business Association Which Works	Hw	2	3		My 81	66
LaLena, Constance	Women in Weaving	Iw	4	4		Fa 79	54
LaLena, Constance J.	Fabrics for Interiors 11: The Southwest Collection	Hw	8	4		S/O 87	36
LaLena, Constance J.	Pricing the Production Piece	SS&D	10	2	38	Sp 79	10
Laliberte, Norman	Banners and Hangings — Design and Construction	H&C	17	3		Su 66	43
Lamb, Sara	Ikat-Spun Kimono, An	S-O	8	4		Wi 84	16
Lamb, Sara	Vests	S-O	9	1		Sp 85	16
Lamberson, Peggy	Mimi Holmes: Treasure Troves of Human Conflict	Fa	13	6		N/D 86	20
Lambersten, Martha	Sheep of a Sweater, A	Kn	3	4	8	Fa 87	51
Lambert, Anne M.	Cuna Cachi: A Study of Hammock Weaving Among the Cuna Indians of the San Blas Islands	AT	5			Ju 86	105
Lambert, Patricia; Barbara Staepelaere; Mary G. Fry	Color and Fiber	WJ	12	1	45	Su 87	69
Lambert, Patricia; Barbara Staepelaere; Mary G. Fry	Color and Fiber	TM			13	O/N 87	76

AUTHOR	TITLE	JOUR	VOL	NO	ISS	DATE	PAGE
Lambert, Patricia; Barbara Staepelaere; Mary G. Fry	Color and Fiber	PWC	4	4	14		53
Lambrecht, Dora J.	Art and Tradition of Akwete Weaving, The	SS&D	9	2	34	Sp 78	33
Lancaster, Deborah Lerme	Fukusa: The Art of Giving	Fa	13	6		N/D 86	27
Lancaster, Don	Incredible Secret Money Machine, The	Iw	4	1		Wi 78	54
Lancaster, Zöe Woodruff	Alexander Julian's Foundation for Aesthetic Understanding	Fa	14	1		J/F 87	24
Lancaster, Zöe Woodruff	Behind the Scenes: A Fabric Printer	Fa	13	3		M/J 86	44
Lancaster, Zöe Woodruff	Complex Surfaces of Laura Strand Mills, The	Fa	14	2		M/A 87	29
Lancaster, Zöe Woodruff	Glen's Gloves: A Kaufman Retrospective	Fa	12	5		S/O 85	41
Lancaster, Zöe Woodruff	Julia Hill: Art and Textile Lab	Fa	12	3		M/J 85	11
Lancaster, Zöe Woodruff	Shigeki and Shihoko Fukumoto: Balancing Art and Function	Fa	13	6		N/D 86	5
Landes, John	Book of Patterns for Handweaving, A	WJ	3	1	9	Jy 78	36
Landess, Susan	Yurts (Not Your Average Dwelling)	Fa	5	6		N/D 78	26
Landis, Bruce	Klara Cherepov, A Career in Two Countries	H&C	18	3		Su 67	19
Landis, Lucille	How to Warp with a Paddle — Beam Without Paper	SS&D	6	3	23	Su 75	83
Landis, Lucille	How to Warp with a Paddle—Beam Without Paper, Part 1	SS&D	16	1	61	Wi 84	72
Landis, Lucille	How to Warp with a Paddle — Beam Without Paper, Part 2	SS&D	6	4	24	Fa 75	72
Landis, Lucille	How to Warp with a Paddle—Beam without Paper, Part 2	SS&D	16	2	62	Sp 85	70
Landis, Lucille	Twills and Twill Derivatives	SS&D	9	1	33	Wi 77	40
Landis, Lucille	Warp with a Paddle and Beam Without Paper	WJ	10	3	39	Wi 86	72
Landreau, Anthony N.	From Mexico to Rumania to Sweden	TMJ	2	4		De 69	37
Landreau, Anthony N.	Kurdish Kilim Weaving in the Van-Hakkari District of Eastern Turkey	TMJ	3	4		De 73	27
Landreau, Anthony; W. R. Pickering	From the Bosporus to Samarkand: Flat-Woven Rugs	H&C	20	3		Su 69	43
Landreau, Tony	Adaptations of Primitive Warp-Pattern Weaves	H&C	8	1		Wi 56	25
Lang, Elizabeth; Erica Dakin Voolich	Parallel Shadow Weave	PWC	5	1	15		52
Lang, John	Geometric Designs for Artists and Craftsmen	H&C	10	3		Su 59	60
Langton, Janet F.	Home Dyeing with Native Plants Provides Wide Range of Colors	H&C	19	3		Su 68	16
Lanier, Mildred B.	English and Oriental Carpets at Williamsburg	TMJ	4	2		75	80
Lann, Carol K.	Producing Hand-Woven Clothing on a Small Scale	WJ	7	4	28	Sp 83	48
Lansdell, Sarah	Deborah Frederick: Rainbow Nets	Fa	5	3		M/J 78	40
Lansing, Linda	see Ledbetter, Marie	TM			7	O/N 86	74
Lapin, Claudia	Fixing to Dye: Confessions of a Silk Addict	Fa	5	1		J/F 78	30
Lapin, Claudia	Personal Notes on a Dyeing Art	Fa	4	4		J/A 77	60
Lapin, Lynne; Betsy Wanes, eds.	Arts and Crafts Market, l978 (error-corrected WJ v2 n4 78 insert for sheet vol. 2)	WJ	2	3	7	Ja 78	34
Lapin, Lynne, ed.	Craft Worker's Market, 1980	WJ	4	3	15	Ja 80	46
Lapin, Lynne, ed.	Craftsworker's Market, 1979	W.I	3	4	12	Ap 79	46
Lapin, Lynne, ed.	Craftworker's Market, l979	Iw	4	2		Sp 79	62
LaPlantz, Shereen	Baskets and Curls	SS&D	13	1	49	Wi 81	38
LaPlantz, Shereen	Bias Plaiting	Hw	7	3		M/J 86	81
LaPlantz, Shereen	Coiled Hexagonal Plaiting	SS&D	18	2	70	Sp 87	17
LaPlantz, Shereen	Day in the Life of a Basketmaker: The Very Personal Approach of Shereen LaPlantz, A	Fa	6	6		N/D 79	6
LaPlantz, Shereen	Inspiration — Does it Come Before or After?	WJ	8	1	29	Su 83	54
LaPlantz, Shereen	Mad Weave Book, The	Hw	6	5		N/D 85	20
LaPlantz, Shereen	Mad Weave Book, The	WJ	10	2	38	Fa 85	82
LaPlantz, Shereen	Mad Weave Book, The	TM			2	D/J 85	76
LaPlantz, Shereen	Plaited Basket, The	Hw	7	3		M/J 86	76
LaPlantz, Shereen	Plaited Basketry: The Woven Form	Hw	4	3		M/J 83	14
LaPlantz, Shereen	Plaited Basketry: The Woven Form	WJ	7	3	27	Wi 82	49
LaPlantz, Shereen	Plaited Basketry: The Woven Form	Fa	10	1		J/F 83	58
LaPlantz, Shereen	Planning a Workshop Tour	SS&D	13	4	52	Fa 82	46

AUTHOR	TITLE	JOUR	VOL	NO	ISS	DATE	PAGE
LaPlantz, Shereen	Straight Plaiting	Hw	7	3		M/J 86	81
LaPlantz, Shereen	Wandering with My Hands	WJ	3	4	12	Ap 79	23
Lark Book Staff; Marianne Philbin, eds.	Ribbon, The	Hw	6	5		N/D 85	18
Larochette, Jean-Pierre	Aubusson Tapestry	SS&D	13	4	52	Fa 82	5
LaRoque, Jane V. Lowell	"Seventh Annual Twin Ports Fibers Invitational" (Exhibit)	Fa	7	3		M/J 80	80
Larsen, Jack Lenor	At the Cranbrook Academy of Art	H&C	3	2		Sp 52	24
Larsen, Jack Lenor	Efficient Warping	H&C	3	3		Su 52	32
Larsen, Jack Lenor	Exploring Weaving Techniques	H&C	3	4		Fa 52	4
Larsen, Jack Lenor	How Do You Rate Your Weaving Efficiency?	H&C	3	1		Wi 51	25
Larsen, Jack Lenor	International Textile Exhibition, The	H&C	4	1		Wi 52	30
Larsen, Jack Lenor	see Constantine, Mildred	SS&D	6	4	24	Fa 75	29
Larsen, Jack Lenor	see Constantine, Mildred	Hw	2	4		Se 81	79
Larsen, Jack Lenor	see Constantine, Mildred	Hw	7	5		N/D 86	14
Larsen, Jack Lenor	see Constantine, Mildred	Hw	7	5		N/D 86	14
Larsen, Jack Lenor	see Constantine, Mildred	WJ	7	2	26	Fa 82	59
Larsen, Jack Lenor	see Constantine, Mildred	WJ	12	2	46	Fa 87	66
Larsen, Jack Lenor	see Constantine, Mildred	WJ	12	2	46	Fa 87	66
Larsen, Jack Lenor	see Constantine, Mildred	Fa	8	6		N/D 81	62
Larsen, Jack Lenor	see Constantine, Mildred	TMJ	4	2		75	79
Larsen, Jack Lenor	see Thorpe, Azalea Stuart	H&C	18	4		Fa 67	39
Larsen, Jack Lenor	see Thorpe, Azalea Stuart	Iw	3	4		Su 78	44
Larsen, Jack Lenor; Betty Freudenheim	Interlacing: The Elemental Fabric	WJ	12	2	46	Fa 87	66
Larsen, Jack Lenor, et al.	Dyer's Art, Ikat, Batik, Plangi, The	SS&D	8	4	32	Fa 77	72
Larsen, Jack Lenor; Jeanne Weeks	Fabrics for Interiors	SS&D	7	3	27	Su 76	34
Larsen, Jack Lenor with Alfred Buhler, Bronwen Solyom, Garrett Solyom	Dyer's Art: Ikat, Batik, Plangi, The	Fa	5	1		J/F 78	40
Larsen, Jack Lenore; Jeanne Weeks	Fabrics for Interiors: A Guide for Architects, Designers, and Consumers	Fa	3	5		S/O 76	39
Larson, Eden	High-Tech Comes to Weaving: AVL Looms	Fa	14	4		S/O 87	36
Larson, Knut	Rugs and Carpets of the Orient	H&C	18	4		Fa 67	39
Larson, Lois	Software for Weavers...A Resource	Hw	7	4		S/O 86	12
Larson, Lois	Software for Weavers . . . A Resource	WJ	11	2	42	Fa 86	75
Larson, Lois	Software for Weavers: A Resource	SS&D	17	3	67	Su 86	86
Larson-Fleming, Susan	Beyond Rags: Fabric Strip Design	WJ	9	4	36	Sp 85	47
Larson-Fleming, Susan	Kashmiri to Paisley: Evolution of the Paisley Shawl	WJ	11	3	43	Wi 87	37
Larson-Fleming, Susan	Picture Lace	WJ	9	4	36	Sp 85	42
Larson-Fleming, Susan	see Kahn, Kathy	WJ	12	1	45	Su 87	36
Larson-Fleming, Susan	Terra Nova: Jack Lenor Larsen	WJ	11	1	41	Su 86	49
Larson-Fleming, Susan	Vadmal: A Study Group from the Frozen North Warms Up to an Ancient Technique	WJ	10	3	39	Wi 86	26
Larzelere, Judith Ann	Log Cabins	TM			3	F/M 86	58
Las Aranas Spinners and Weavers Guild	Dyeing with Natural Materials	SS&D	4	3	15	Su 73	53
Lasansky, Jeannette	Willow, Oak and Rye	SS&D	10	4	40	Fa 79	63
Lasansky, Jeannette	Willow, Oak and Rye	Fa	7	6		N/D 80	65
Lasansky, Jeannette, ed.	In the Heart of Pennsylvania	TM			3	F/M 86	78
Lassiter, Betty	New System for Getting an Ultra Fit, A	TM			12	A/S 87	22
Lathrop, Nornan M.	1983 Index to How to Do It Information	Hw	7	5		N/D 86	14
Laue, Dietmar, ed.	see Sterk, Beatrijs, ed.	Hw	7	4		S/O 86	10
Laughlin, Elizabeth	Changing the Angle of the Twill Diagonal Line	SS&D	7	4	28	Fa 76	11
Laughlin, Mary Elizabeth	Exploring Doup Leno	CW	4	3	12	Ap 83	3
Laughlin, Mary Elizabeth	More Than Four	SS&D	8	3	31	Su 77	61
Laughlin, Mary Elizabeth	More Than Four	Iw	2	4		Su 77	35

AUTHOR	TITLE	JOUR	VOL	NO	ISS	DATE	PAGE
Laughlin, Mary Elizabeth	More Then Four	WJ	3	3	11	Ja 79	41
Laughlin, Mary Elizabeth	Update of CW Questionnaire	CW		24		My 87	27
Laughlin, Mary Elizabeth	Weaving Interests of CW Members Questionnaire Results	CW	6	3	18	My 85	15
Laurell, Karl	New Man-Made Fiber Developed for Handweavers, A	H&C	5	1		Wi 53	27
Laurell, Karl	Review of Handweaving, A	H&C	15	1		Wi 64	14
Laurell, Karl	School for American Craftsmen Observes Its Tenth Anniversary, The	H&C	4	4		Fa 53	12
Laury, Jean Ray	Creative Woman's Getting-It-All-Together (At Home) Handbook, The	Iw	3	2		Wi 78	40
Laury, Jean Ray	Creative Woman's Getting-It-All-Together At Home Handbook, The	Fa	5	5		S/O 78	62
Laury, Jean Ray	Dolls: Knitted and Woven	H&C	26	5		Oc 75	36
Laury, Jean Ray	Quilted Clothing	Fa	11	1		J/F 84	58
Laury, Jean Ray; Joyce Aiken	Creative Body Coverings	SS&D	6	4	24	Fa 75	30
Lauter, Estella	"Contemporary Quilting: A Renaissance" (Exhibit)	Fa	9	1		J/F 82	78
Lawless, Dorothy	Rug Hooking and Braiding	H&C	4	3		Su 53	62
Lawrence, Ellen	Bobbin Lace: Designs and Instructions	SS&D	11	1	41	Wi 79	32
Lawrence, Margaret	Peruvian Accented Mexican Blouse: Analyze—Then Improvise	SS&D	7	1	25	Wi 75	40
Lawrence, Mary Jo	Silk	WJ	7	3	27	Wi 82	74
Lawrence, Ramona Sakiestewa	Spinning in the Southwest — Prehistoric, Historic, and Contemporary	S-O	1			77	8
Lawson, Rosalie H.	Weaving on a Lap Loom	H&C	5	3		Su 54	23
Laymon, Cynthia	"Ceremonial Garments" (Exhibit)	Fa	9	6		N/D 82	82
Laymon, Cynthia	"Martha Matthews: Tapestry" (Exhibit)	Fa	9	1		J/F 82	85
Laymon, Cynthia	"North/South Carolina Fibers Competition" (Exhibit)	Fa	10	4		J/A 83	68
Laymon, Cynthia	"Quilts of Patsy Allen, The" (Exhibit)	Fa	10	6		N/D 83	76
Leach, Vivian	"Five Women from Texas" (Exhibit)	Fa	6	1		J/F 79	86
Leadbeater, Eliza	Flax (error-corrected S-O V3 79 p11)	S-O	2			78	18
Leadbeater, Eliza	Flax: Yarn Design Determines Choice	S-O	8	3		Fa 84	34
Leadbeater, Eliza	Handspinning	SS&D	7	4	28	Fa 76	65
Leadbeater, Eliza	Handspinning	Iw	2	3		Sp 77	32
Leadbeater, Eliza	Native British Sheep: The Rare Breeds	S-O	3			79	19
Leadbeater, Eliza	Spinning and Spinning Wheels	S-O	3			79	10
Leadbeater, Eliza	Teasels	Hw	2	5		No 81	54
Leadbeater, Eliza	Wool: Selecting British Fleeces	S-O	8	3		Fa 84	25
Leavitt, Jean	Making a Round Cord	TM			1	O/N 85	6
Lebovitz, Connie	Figure-in-the-Round, A Caricature	SS&D	6	1	21	Wi 74	5
Lebovitz, Constance	Design for Torah Cover Based on 'Torah is Truth' and 'Tree of Life'	SS&D	4	4	16	Fa 73	18
Lebovitz, Constance	Weaving in High School	SS&D	7	4	28	Fa 76	19
LeClerc, Robert	Warp and Weave	SS&D	2	4	8	Fa 71	35
Leclerc, Robert	Weavers in Iran, Thousands at Work on Primitive Looms	H&C	21	2		Sp 70	9
Leclerc, Robert, ed.	see Zielinski, S. A.	MWL	1			'51–'73	
Leclerc, Robert, ed.	see Zielinski, S. A.	MWL	2			'51–'73	11
Leclerc, Robert, ed.	see Zielinski, S. A.	MWL	3			'51–'73	
Leclerc, Robert, ed.	see Zielinski, S. A.	MWL	4			'51–'73	15
Leclerc, Robert, ed.	see Zielinski, S. A.	MWL	5			'51–'73	
Leclerc, Robert, ed.	see Zielinski, S. A.	MWL	6			'51–'73	
Leclerc, Robert, ed.	see Zielinski, S. A.	MWL	7			'51–'73	
Leclerc, Robert, ed.	see Zielinski, S. A.	MWL	8			'51–'73	
Leclerc, Robert, ed.	see Zielinski, S. A.	MWL	9			'51–'73	
Leclerc, Robert, ed.	see Zielinski, S. A.	MWL	10			'51–'73	
Leclerc, Robert, ed.	see Zielinski, S. A.	MWL	11			'51–'73	
Leclerc, Robert, ed.	see Zielinski, S. A.	MWL	12			'51–'73	
Leclerc, Robert, ed.	see Zielinski, S. A.	MWL	13			'51–'73	
Leclerc, Robert, ed.	see Zielinski, S. A.	MWL	14			'51–'73	
Leclerc, Robert, ed.	see Zielinski, S. A.	MWL	15			'51–'73	

AUTHOR	TITLE	JOUR	VOL	NO	ISS	DATE	PAGE
Leclerc, Robert, ed.	see Zielinski, S. A.	MWL	16			'51–'73	
Leclerc, Robert, ed.	see Zielinski, S. A.	MWL	17			'51–'73	
Leclerc, Robert, ed.	see Zielinski, S. A.	MWL	18			'51–'73	
Leclerc, Robert, ed.	see Zielinski, S. A.	MWL	19			'51–'73	
Leclerc, Robert, ed.	see Zielinski, S. A.	MWL	20			'51–'73	
Leclerc, Robert, ed.	see Zielinski, S. A.	MWL	21 22			'51–'73	
Ledbetter, Marie; Linda Lansing	Tailoring: Traditional and Contemporary Techniques	TM		7		O/N 86	74
Lee, Dr. Stanley H.	Fixed-Heddle Looms to Make for Pennies Using Coffee Stirrers	SS&D	5	1	17	Wi 73	21
Lee, Humphrey A.	From English Handlooms Comes Royal Purple Velvet for Coronation Robe of Elizabeth II	H&C	4	2		Sp 53	17
Lee, Jane	Kansas University, An Interview with Evelyn DeGraw (error-corrected H&C v22 n2 71 p4)	H&C	22	1		Wi 71	6
Lee, Pamela	Fingerweaving: Two Perspectives, The Practical Lesson	SS&D	6	4	24	Fa 75	44
Lee-Whitman, Leanna; Maruta Skelton	Where Did All the Silver Go? Identifying Eighteenth-Century Chinese Painted and Printed Silks	TMJ	22			83	33
Leek, Yvonne B.	British Versatility	SS&D	6	3	23	Su 75	41
Leeming, Joseph	Fun with String	SS&D	6	4	24	Fa 75	30
Leene, J. E., ed.	Textile Conservation	SS&D	4	1	13	Wi 72	34
Leene, Jentina E., ed.	Textile Conservation	H&C	23	6		N/D 72	41
Leene, Jentina E., ed.	Textile Conservation	TMJ	3	4		De 73	47
Lees, Maureen V.	Weaving for the Blind	H&C	8	2		Sp 57	22
Leethem, Kaino	Bright, Breezy Stripes	Hw	5	3		Su 84	60
Leffmann, Theo Claire	Commissions: Challenge and Discipline	SS&D	3	3	11	Su 72	18
Legerski, Victoria	Beginner's Tops	WJ	8	3	31	Wi 83	14
Leggett, Dawn	Excellence	S-O	10	2		Su 86	43
Leggett, Dawn	Rx: Pills	S-O	8	4		Wi 84	35
Lehman, Sue	see Berent, Mary	S-O	11	1		Sp 87	21
Lehner, Ernst; Johanna Lehner	Folklore and Symbolism of Flowers, Plants and Trees	H&C	12	3		Su 61	61
Lehner, Johanna	see Lehner, Ernst	H&C	12	3		Su 61	61
Lehrman, Stevanne Ruth	Leona at Her Quilt Frame	Fa	7	3		M/J 80	40
Leibler, Barbara	Impressionistic Use of Color	Hw	4	5		N/D 83	90
Leinonen, Virpi	Kaunista Kangaspuilla	Hw	6	4		S/O 85	24
LeMaistre, Margaret	Dawn MacNutt: Sculptural Weaver	SS&D	17	2	66	Sp 86	48
LeMaistre, Margaret	Watercolors in Fiber: The Flower Tapestries of Sondra MacLeod	SS&D	17	3	67	Su 86	21
Lenderman, Max	Textile Students Take Looms Outdoors At RIT	SS&D	5	4	20	Fa 74	8
Lep, Annette	New Look At Crochet, A	TM		9		F/M 87	86
Lepper, Arthur Alden	see Myers, Diana K.	Fa	13	2		M/A 86	41
Lermond, Charles	Variations on an Overshot Threading	WJ	12	2	46	Fa 87	25
Les, Kathleen	Margaret Welty: Minimalist Weaver	Fa	5	4		J/A 78	28
Les, Kathleen	Papermaking as a Recycling Process: The Work of Frances Les	Fa	6	4		J/A 79	18
Les, Kathleen	"Works In, On, and Of Paper" (Exhibit)	Fa	6	5		S/O 79	79
Les Tisserands-Créateurs de Québec	Boutonne D'Hier Et D'Aujourdhui	WJ	8	3	31	Wi 83	66
Lesch, Alma	Vegetable Dyeing	SS&D	2	4	8	Fa 71	35
Lesch, Alma	Vegetable Dyeing	H&C	22	2		Sp 71	44
Lesch, Alma	Vegetable Dyeing	H&C	23	6		N/D 72	41
Leslie, Victoria	What People Ask Before They Buy Handmade Fashions	TM		9		F/M 87	58
Levine, Betsy	Claire Zeisler's Fragments and Dashes	TM		1		O/N 85	84
Levine, Betsy	Costumes of Royal India	TM		7		O/N 86	64
Levine, Betsy	Ellen Hauptli's Pleats	TM		5		J/J 86	48
Levine, Betsy	"Fiber R/Evolution" (Exhibit)	TM		5		J/J 86	16
Levine, Betsy	Passion for Elegance: Master Dyer Marian Clayden Creates Clothing by Listening to the Fabric, A	TM		14		D/J 87	36

AUTHOR	TITLE	JOUR	VOL	NO	ISS	DATE	PAGE
Levine, Betsy	Peter Collingwood on Textile Structures	TM			3	F/M 86	14
Levine, Betsy	Quilt National '85	TM			2	D/J 85	10
Levine, Betsy	"The Flexible Medium: 20th Cnetury American Art Fabric" (Seminar)	TM			1	O/N 85	12
Levine, Betty	Software Choices for Weavers and Designers	TM			9	F/M 87	53
Levinson, Nan	Vermont's Green Mountain Spinnery	TM			7	O/N 86	61
Levy, Beverly Sauer	Metamorphosis in Maine: The Art of Barbara Lambert	Fa	11	3		M/J 84	20
Levy, Julie	Impressions of an Exposition	TM			8	D/J 86	12
Levy, Julie	Shared Work Space May be Just What You're Looking For, A	TM			9	F/M 87	42
Levy, Julie	Stretching Fabric in Small Spaces	TM			3	F/M 86	34
Lew, Jennifer F.	see Proctor, Richard	Hw	7	1		J/F 86	18
Lew, Jennifer F.	see Proctor, Richard M.	WJ	10	2	38	Fa 85	82
Lew, Jennifer F.	see Proctor, Richard M.	TM			2	D/J 85	78
Lewes, Klares; Helen Hutton	Rug Weaving	H&C	13	3		Su 62	43
Lewes, Klares; Helen Hutton	Rug Weaving	H&C	13	4		Fa 62	43
Lewis, Alfred Allan: Julienne Krasnoff	Everybody's Weaving Book	SS&D	7	4	28	Fa 76	65
Lewis, Edward G.	Warp Boutonné	WJ	7	2	26	Fa 82	64
Lewis, Elsie M.	Weavers Guild of Greater Cincinnati	H&C	3	3		Su 52	44
Lewis, Ethel	Romance of Textiles, The Story of Design in Weaing, The	H&C	5	2		Sp 54	61
Lewis, Lois	Strips & Stripes	SS&D	14	2	54	Sp 83	60
Lewis, Robin S.	Bobbin Lace on a Grand Scale: When the Pillow Is a 12-ft. Pegboard	TM			9	F/M 87	54
Lewis, Roger	Weaving	H&C	5	3		Su 54	57
Lewis, Susanna	Be Your Own Designer	Kn	3	1	5	F-W 86	48
Lewis, Susanna	Bright Blouse	Kn	3	2	6	Sp 87	36
Lewis, Susanna	Intarsia Shawl	Kn	4	1	9	Wi 87	46
Lewis, Susanna	Winter Red: A Hand and Machine Knit Combination	Kn	3	4	8	Fa 87	28
Lewis, Susanna E.	Lace from Hand to Machine	Kn	1	2	2	S-S 85	71
Lewis, Susanna E.	Ropes and Braids	Kn	2	2	4	S-S 86	19
Lewis, Susanna E.	Simple Crossings for Hand Knitters	Kn	2	2	4	S-S 86	21
Lewis, Susanna E.; Julia Weissman	Machine Knitter's Guide to Creating Fabrics, A	TM			5	J/J 86	12
Lewis, Susanna E.; Julia Weissman	Machine Knitter's Guide to Creating Fabrics: Jacquard, Lace, Intarsia, Ripple and More, A	Kn	3	1	5	F-W 86	71
Lewis, Susanna E.; Julia Weissman	Machine Knitter's Guide to Creating Fabrics, Jacquard, Lace, Intarsia, Ripple and More, A	PWC	4	2	12		53
Liberty, J. E.	Practical Tailoring	TM			7	O/N 86	72
Lichten, Frances	Decorative Art of Victoria's Era	H&C	1	3		Fa 50	64
Lichten, Frances	Folk Art of Rural Pennsylvania	H&C	14	4		Fa 63	44
Liebler, Barbara	Adapting a Weave to Your Purpose	Iw	4	3		Su 79	52
Liebler, Barbara	Big Work from Small Looms	Hw	2	2		Mr 81	61
Liebler, Barbara	Buying a Loom	Iw	2	3		Sp 77	26
Liebler, Barbara	Care Enough	Iw	4	2		Sp 79	42
Liebler, Barbara	Challenge of the Ugly Color, The	Hw	8	4		S/O 87	70
Liebler, Barbara	Clothing from Rectangles	Iw	5	4		Fa 80	52
Liebler, Barbara	Colonial Coverlets, Part 3: Summer and Winter	Iw	1	4		Su 76	24
Liebler, Barbara	Colonial Coverlets, Part 4: Doubleweave	Iw	2	1		Fa 76	29
Liebler, Barbara	Colonial Overshot, "Trompt as Writ"	Iw	1	2		Wi 76	14
Liebler, Barbara	Color Excitement	Hw	6	2		M/A 85	80
Liebler, Barbara	Color Scheming	Hw	5	4		S/0 84	88
Liebler, Barbara	Color—Something Worth Dyeing For	Iw	3	3		Sp 78	36
Liebler, Barbara	Continuity of Patterning	Hw	6	1		J/F 85	92
Liebler, Barbara	Courting the Muse	Hw	5	5		N/D 84	37
Liebler, Barbara	Creative Two Harness Weaving	Iw	4	4		Fa 79	64

AUTHOR	TITLE	JOUR	VOL	NO	ISS	DATE	PAGE
Liebler, Barbara	Design Concept, The	Iw	3	2		Wi 78	28
Liebler, Barbara	Design Placement for Garments	Hw	7	5		N/D 86	26
Liebler, Barbara	Dynamic Design	Hw	6	5		N/D 85	89
Liebler, Barbara	Fleecing of the American Colonies, The	Iw	2	1		Fa 76	21
Liebler, Barbara	Focal Point Through Color Contrast	Hw	4	4		S/O 83	82
Liebler, Barbara	Forum	Hw	2	2		Mr 81	21
Liebler, Barbara	Functional or Decorative Design	Hw	8	1		J/F 87	12
Liebler, Barbara	Getting Sett	Iw	2	4		Su 77	30
Liebler, Barbara	Hands on Weaving	TM			11	J/J 87	72
Liebler, Barbara	Happy Ending, A	Iw	1	4		Su 76	22
Liebler, Barbara	Happy Ending, II, A	Iw	2	1		Fa 76	24
Liebler, Barbara	Home Studio?	Iw	5	2		Sp 80	56
Liebler, Barbara	Improving Your Concentration	Hw	6	4		S/O 85	68
Liebler, Barbara	Layered Sculpture	Iw	2	4		Su 77	16
Liebler, Barbara	More Creative Two Harness Weaving	Iw	5	1		Wi 79	46
Liebler, Barbara	Nell Znamierowski: Color & Design	Hw	2	4		Se 81	40
Liebler, Barbara	Of Treasures & Textures	Hw	8	2		M/A 87	22
Liebler, Barbara	On Weaving, Life and Art	Iw	4	4		Fa 79	19
Liebler, Barbara	One Warp, Many Fabrics	Iw	3	1		Fa 77	28
Liebler, Barbara	Overshot	Hw	2	1		F-W 80	44
Liebler, Barbara	Overshot: Rose Fashion	Iw	1	3		Sp 76	16
Liebler, Barbara	Personality of Color, The	Hw	7	4		S/O 86	80
Liebler, Barbara	Relative Scale	Hw	5	2		M/A 84	78
Liebler, Barbara	Repetition	Hw	6	3		Su 85	92
Liebler, Barbara	Representational Space	Hw	7	3		M/J 86	62
Liebler, Barbara	Sculptor's Approach to Clothing Design, A	Hw	5	1		J/F 84	76
Liebler, Barbara	Shine On	Hw	7	1		J/F 86	75
Liebler, Barbara	Spaced Out	Hw	7	2		M/A 86	86
Liebler, Barbara	Stripe as a Design Module, The	Hw	4	2		M/A 83	52
Liebler, Barbara	Three English Tapestry Weavers	Hw	3	1		Ja 82	60
Liebler, Barbara	Using Light as a Design Element	Hw	5	3		Su 84	88
Liebler, Barbara	Variations on a Theme	Hw	8	5		N/D 87	26
Liebler, Barbara	Versatile Twill	Iw	6	1		Wi 80	26
Liebler, Barbara	Weaver's Bag of Tricks, A	Iw	1	3		Sp 76	30
Liebler, Barbara	Weaving Draft: Road Map to Success, The	Iw	1	2		Wi 76	26
Liebler, Barbara	Which Fiber?	Iw	4	1		Wi 78	48
Liebler, Barbara	Working Out Your Hangups	Iw	2	2		Wi 77	24
Liebler, Barbara	Yarn Shop Dilemma, The	Iw	1	1		Fa 75	16
Liggett, Brother Mark, OFM	Spinning in the Abbey	S-O	6	4		82	4
Lightbody, Donna M.	Easy Weaving	SS&D	6	2	22	Sp 75	63
Ligon, Linda	Albuquerque Group Proves: Co-Ops Can Work	Iw	1	1		Fa 75	8
Ligon, Linda	Ana Rossell: Weaving with Flair for C. A. R. E.	Iw	3	1		Fa 77	18
Ligon, Linda	Book That's Bound to Please, A	Hw	4	4		S/O 83	67
Ligon, Linda	Captured Shadows	Iw	1	2		Wi 76	12
Ligon, Linda	Colonel Ronin, Spinning Flyer	Iw	2	4		Su 77	25
Ligon, Linda	Conferences: Fiberworks Symposium	Iw	3	4		Su 78	26
Ligon, Linda	Confluence: A Gallery	Iw	2	3		Sp 77	10
Ligon, Linda	Connie LaLena: Colonial Textiles Today	Iw	3	1		Fa 77	15
Ligon, Linda	Deborah Christensen	Iw	2	2		Wi 77	16
Ligon, Linda	Dolly Curtis: Contrasts	Iw	3	4		Su 78	24
Ligon, Linda	Doubleweave Basketry of the Cherokees	Iw	4	1		Wi 78	28
Ligon, Linda	Dream—The Reality, The	Iw	3	4		Su 78	12

AUTHOR	TITLE	JOUR	VOL	NO	ISS	DATE	PAGE
Ligon, Linda	Ed Oppenheimer: Rugs	lw	5	1		Wi 79	31
Ligon, Linda	Even Beat, An	Hw	7	4		S/O 86	98
Ligon, Linda	First Lessons	Hw	7	5		N/D 86	106
Ligon, Linda	Floating Selvedges	Hw	7	3		M/J 86	92
Ligon, Linda	Gil Fernandez: Light and Color	lw	2	1		Fa 76	8
Ligon, Linda	Happy Endings	Hw	8	5		N/D 87	99
Ligon, Linda	Hemstitch in Time, A	Hw	8	2		M/A 87	98
Ligon, Linda	HGA Certificate of Excellence: A Report	lw	2	2		Wi 77	8
Ligon, Linda	Idea Notebook, An	lw	4	2		Sp 79	38
Ligon, Linda	Interface	Hw	4	3		M/J 83	76
Ligon, Linda	Jurying	lw	1	2		Wi 76	10
Ligon, Linda	Keeping Track	Hw	8	1		J/F 87	90
Ligon, Linda	Know Your Fibers: Karakul	lw	2	3		Sp 77	12
Ligon, Linda	Lacy Apron, My	Hw	4	1		J/F 83	40
Ligon, Linda	Leaf Printing	Hw	4	3		M/J 83	60
Ligon, Linda	Lee Carlin: Handweaving Entrepreneur	lw	3	1		Fa 77	26
Ligon, Linda	Lesley Shearer: Creation with Control	lw	2	4		Su 77	10
Ligon, Linda	Lifestyle: A Roundtable Discussion	lw	5	2		Sp 80	22
Ligon, Linda	Los Tejidos Nortenos	lw	1	4		Su 76	15
Ligon, Linda	Mary Woodard Davis Promotes Craft in Santa Fe	lw	1	1		Fa 75	6
Ligon, Linda	Matter of Style, A	Hw	2	4		Se 81	4
Ligon, Linda	Matter of Style, A	Hw	2	5		No 81	4
Ligon, Linda	Matter of Style, A	Hw	4	1		J/F 83	14
Ligon, Linda	Matter of Style, A	Hw	4	2		M/A 83	6
Ligon, Linda	Matter of Style, A	Hw	4	4		S/O 83	14
Ligon, Linda	Matter of Style, A	Hw	4	5		N/D 83	12
Ligon, Linda	Maurine Fair	lw	2	2		Wi 77	20
Ligon, Linda	Mending Warps	Hw	7	1		J/F 86	34
Ligon, Linda	Moorman Technique: Applications	lw	1	4		Su 76	12
Ligon, Linda	On Handwoven Upholstery	Hw	3	2		Mr 82	58
Ligon, Linda	On Spinning Cotton	lw	1	4		Su 76	6
Ligon, Linda	On the Double!	Hw	4	3		M/J 83	64
Ligon, Linda	On the Use of Borrowed Patterns and Designs	Hw	4	4		S/O 83	30
Ligon, Linda	One Hundred Sixty Years of Craftsmanship	lw	1	3		Sp 76	17
Ligon, Linda	Paper as Object	lw	2	3		Sp 77	19
Ligon, Linda	Photographic Processes for Textiles	lw	2	2		Wi 77	21
Ligon, Linda	Point of Departure	S-O	10	2		Su 86	53
Ligon, Linda	Production Weaving: From Nature-Inspired Warps to Linsey-Woolsey	lw	1	2		Wi 76	6
Ligon, Linda	Project Notebook, A	lw	3	1		Fa 77	31
Ligon, Linda	Raising a Spinner's Flock	lw	2	3		Sp 77	14
Ligon, Linda	Recycling—Ragtime	lw	3	4		Su 78	22
Ligon, Linda	Reflections on 7560 Weft Picks	Hw	8	3		M/J 87	98
Ligon, Linda	Sam Moya	lw	2	2		Wi 77	14
Ligon, Linda	Santa Fe Weaver Re-Creates Past	lw	1	1		Fa 75	4
Ligon, Linda	see Nell, Patti	lw	1	2		Wi 76	18
Ligon, Linda	Selvedge Notes	Hw	6	1		J/F 85	62
Ligon, Linda	Seminole Patchwork	lw	1	2		Wi 76	8
Ligon, Linda	Setting Up Shop	lw	2	4		Su 77	18
Ligon, Linda	Sheepskate Weaving	Hw	5	4		S/O 84	69
Ligon, Linda	Sherrie Smith	lw	2	1		Fa 76	10
Ligon, Linda	Slentre Briad	Hw	5	1		J/F 84	109
Ligon, Linda	Some Edgings	Hw	4	1		J/F 83	42

AUTHOR	TITLE	JOUR	VOL	NO	ISS	DATE	PAGE
Ligon, Linda	Things That Count	Hw	8	4		S/O 87	99
Ligon, Linda	Tim McIlrath	Iw	2	2		Wi 77	18
Ligon, Linda	Toys and Other Fun Stuff	Iw	2	1		Fa 76	13
Ligon, Linda	Vegetable Lamb of Tartary, The	Iw	1	4		Su 76	9
Ligon, Linda	Warren Seelig: A Conversation	Iw	3	2		Wi 78	20
Ligon, Linda	Way We Were...The Way We're Going, The	S-O	11	3		Fa 87	27
Ligon, Linda	Weaving a Fine Warp	Hw	2	5		No 81	58
Ligon, Linda	Weaving on a Dobby Loom	Iw	1	4		Su 76	10
Ligon, Linda C., ed.	Rug Weaver's Source Book, A	Fa	12	5		S/O 85	54
Ligon, Linda C., ed.	Rugweaver's Source Book: A Compilation of Rug Weaving Techniques, A	WJ	10	3	39	Wi 86	72
Ligon, Linda: with Barbara Gentry	Conferences: Convergence '78	Iw	3	4		Su 78	28
Liles, Dale	see Liles, James N.	SS&D	15	3	59	Su 84	76
Liles, James N.	Mineral Dyes 2, The	SS&D	13	4	52	Fa 82	60
Liles, James N.	Mineral Dyes, The	SS&D	13	3	51	Su 82	54
Liles, James N.; Dale Liles	Bancroft's Mordant: A Useful One-Pot Natural Dye Technique	SS&D	15	3	59	Su 84	76
Lilligren, Ingrid	"Carolyn Prince Batchelor: Vessels" (Exhibit)	Fa	12	3		M/J 85	77
Lilligren, Ingrid	Individual/Artistic Development: A Workshop by Francoise Grossen	Fa	11	3		M/J 84	45
Lind, Vibeke	Knitting in the Nordic Tradition	Kn	1	2	2	S-S 85	79
Lind, Vibeke	Knitting in the Nordic Tradition	Kn	3	1	5	F-W 86	70
Lind, Vibeke	Knitting in the Nordic Tradition	SS&D	18	1	69	Wi 86	38
Lindahl, Judy	Decorating with Fabric, Rev. Ed.	WJ	7	3	27	Wi 82	50
Lindahl, Judy	Decorating with Fabric/An Idea Book	WJ	7	3	27	Wi 82	50
Lindahl, Judy	Shade Book, The	WJ	7	3	27	Wi 82	50
Lindbergh, Susie	Marketable Weed Holders	SS&D	4	2	14	Sp 73	16
Lindenfeld, Lore	Contemporary Tapestry in Japan: Individuality After Centuries of Textile Conformity	Fa	10	3		M/J 83	44
Linder, Harry	Finishing Handspun Cotton	S-O	2			78	30
Linder, Harry	Man's Shirt in Peruvian Inlay	WJ	4	2	14	Oc 79	8
Linder, Harry	My African Shirt	Iw	1	4		Su 76	8
Linder, Harry	see Linder, Olive	SS&D	5	2	18	Sp 74	65
Linder, Harry	see Linder, Olive	SS&D	9	4	36	Fa 78	82
Linder, Harry	see Linder, Olive	Iw	3	2		Wi 78	42
Linder, Harry	see Linder, Olive	WJ	2	4	8	Ap 78	39
Linder, Harry	see Linder, Olive	Hw	5	1		J/F 84	66
Linder, Harry	see Linder, Olive	Hw	7	5		N/D 86	14
Linder, Harry	see Linder, Olive	S-O	3			79	10
Linder, Harry	see Linder, Olive	S-O	10	3		Fa 86	48
Linder, Harry	see Linder, Olive	WJ	11	2	42	Fa 86	14
Linder, Harry	see Linder, Olive	WJ	12	1	45	Su 87	70
Linder, Harry	Simply Natural	WJ	11	2	42	Fa 86	20
Linder, Harry; Olive Linder	Dyeing and Spinning Cotton Lint	SS&D	10	2	38	Sp 79	62
Linder, Harry; Olive Linder	Nahuala Spinning	S-O	2			78	23
Linder, Harry; Olive Linder	Suitcase Distaff, A	S-O	10	2		Fa 86	33
Linder, Harry P.	Crocheted Baby Bib, A	S-O	10	1		Sp 86	32
Linder, Harry P.	Spinning Fibers for Crochet	S-O	10	1		Sp 86	30
Linder, Harry P.	Techniques of Code Drafting	Hw	5	5		N/D 84	14
Linder, Olive	Contemporary Gown, Traditional Flavor	SS&D	6	3	23	Su 75	51
Linder, Olive	Cotton: What Should You Ask For?	S-O	8	3		Fa 84	36
Linder, Olive	Four State Conferences	SS&D	10	2	38	Sp 79	30
Linder, Olive	From Cotton Patch to Cotton Patches and Then Some	WJ	5	4	20	Sp 81	48

AUTHOR	TITLE	JOUR	VOL	NO	ISS	DATE	PAGE
Linder, Olive	Kathy Mincer: In Pursuit of Excellence	SS&D	13	2	50	Sp 82	31
Linder, Olive	Pushing the Limits with Rags	Hw	2	3		My 81	51
Linder, Olive	see Bowman, Susan	SS&D	10	3	39	Su 79	52
Linder, Olive	see Linder, Harry	SS&D	10	2	38	Sp 79	62
Linder, Olive	see Linder, Harry	S-O	2			78	23
Linder, Olive	see Linder, Harry	S-O	10	2		Fa 86	33
Linder, Olive	Seersucker	Hw	2	2		Mr 81	37
Linder, Olive	Sprang Time	SS&D	10	3	39	Su 79	88
Linder, Olive	Winter Elegance	S-O	9	4		Wi 85	38
Linder, Olive; Harry Linder	Evolution of an Idea: Olive and Harry Develop Some New Angles on Weaving a Stole, The	Hw	5	1		J/F 84	66
Linder, Olive; Harry Linder	Hand Spinning Cotton	SS&D	9	4	36	Fa 78	82
Linder, Olive; Harry Linder	Hand Spinning Cotton	Iw	3	2		Wi 78	42
Linder, Olive: Harry Linder	Handspinning Cotton	WJ	2	4	8	Ap 78	39
Linder, Olive; Harry Linder	Handspinning Cotton	S-O	3			79	10
Linder, Olive; Harry Linder	Handspinning Flax	Hw	7	5		N/D 86	14
Linder, Olive; Harry Linder	Handspinning Flax	S-O	10	3		Fa 86	48
Linder, Olive; Harry Linder	Handspinning Flax	WJ	12	1	45	Su 87	70
Linder, Olive; Harry Linder	King Cotton Is Back	SS&D	5	2	18	Sp 74	65
Linder, Olive; Harry Linder	Spinning Cotton with the Linders	WJ	11	2	42	Fa 86	14
Lindley, Susan	Annie Dempsey: Sculptural Crochet (Exhibit)	Fa	9	2		M/A 82	76
Ling, Lorraine	Salish Weaving, Then and Now	Iw	4	1		Wi 78	38
Lintault, M. Joan	Fabric Painting in India: The Kalamkaris of J. Gurappa Chetty	Fa	9	1		J/F 82	64
Linton, Dr. George E.	Twenty Years of Handweaving	H&C	20	2		Sp 69	11
Linton, George	Applied Textiles — Raw Materials to Finished Fabrics	H&C	13	3		Su 62	44
Linton, George	Modern Textile Dictionary, The	H&C	6	1		Wi 54	61
Linton, George E.	Applied Basic Textiles: Raw Materials, Construction, Color and Finish	H&C	18	2		Sp 67	43
Linton, George E.	Applied Textiles — Raw Materials to Finished Fabrics	H&C	13	1		Wi 62	44
Linton, George E.	Modern Textile Dictionary, The	H&C	15	1		Wi 64	43
Linton, George E.	Natural and Manmade Textile Fibers: Raw Material to Finished Fabric	H&C	18	2		Sp 67	43
Linton, George E., Ph.D. TexScD	Modern Textile & Apparel Dictionary, The	H&C	26	2		Ap 75	24
Lis, Mary Jane	Wool on the Hoof	SS&D	12	4	48	Fa 81	64
Lister, John A.	Tapestry Weavers of Edinburgh, The	H&C	12	1		Wi 61	22
Liv	Band	H&C	10	1		Wi 59	60
Livingston, Lois; Marion Rinehart	M.O.I.F.A.	SS&D	14	3	55	Su 83	46
Livingston, Marilyn	Warm Wool Sweater, A	S-O	10	4		Wi 86	40
Livingstone, Joan	"Gerhardt Knodel—Makes Places to Be" (Exhibit)	Fa	10	3		M/J 83	71
Livingstone, Joan	Keynote in Chicago: Knodel	SS&D	18	3	71	Su 87	37
Llewellyn, Charles; Deborah Llewellyn	Noble Tradition Preserved: An Ecuadorian Weaving Co-op, A	SS&D	11	3	43	Su 80	12
Llewellyn, Deborah	see Llewellyn, Charles	SS&D	11	3	43	Fa 80	12
Lloyd, Ann	Jacquard is Back	SS&D	18	4	72	Fa 87	10
Lloyd, Joyce	Dyes from Plants of Australia and New Zealand	SS&D	4	1	13	Wi 72	34
Lloyd, Joyce	Dyes from Plants of Australia and New Zealand	SS&D	8	2	30	Sp 77	38
Lloyd, Joyce	Dyes from Plants of Australia & New Zealand	SS&D	3	3	11	Su 72	13
Lo Presti, Louise	"Lace" (Exhibit)	Fa	9	6		N/D 82	79
Lock, Carolyn	"Dye-In" in Detail: For Novices in Nova Scotia, A	SS&D	7	2	26	Sp 76	36

AUTHOR	TITLE	JOUR	VOL	NO	ISS	DATE	PAGE
Lockwood, Diana W.	Symbolic or Sacred? A personal View	WJ	9	3	35	Wi 85	45
Lockwood, Sheri	From Sheep to Shawl in Four Hours	S-O	8	2		Su 84	43
Lodge, Jean	Satin Weave Evening Bag	WJ	10	1	37	Su 85	39
Loftis, Doris	Blood-Root in Your Own Back Yard	SS&D	1	3	3	Ju 70	22
Loftis, Doris	More Than Just Motor City	SS&D	3	1	9	Wi 71	37
Logiudice, JoEL	Mary Sue Kern: Embodied Dualities	Fa	13	5		S/O 86	26
Logsdon, Anne	Photoweavings of Woody Logsdon, The	Fa	14	4		S/O 87	26
Logsdon, Roslyn	see Kasper, Susan	SS&D	9	4	36	Fa 78	86
Lohmolder, Jo	Dyeing with Bark	SS&D	5	2	18	Sp 74	76
Lohse, Joyce	Desk Chair with Subtle Plaid Pattern	WJ	7	1	25	Su 82	24
Lommen, Sandy	Beautiful Fabric Is Not Enough	SS&D	15	2	58	Sp 84	40
London, Bill	Melody Oakroot-Cedar Weaver	S-O	10	3		Fa 86	45
London, Rhoda	Combining Weave Structures	TM			3	F/M 86	56
London, Rhoda	Pacific Basin School Closes	TM			7	O/N 86	10
London, Rhoda	Turkish Marbling on Cloth or Paper	TM			11	J/J 87	66
Lones, Darlene	see Lones, Steve	SS&D	6	4	24	Fa 75	31
Lones, Steve; Darlene Lones	Build Your Own Floor Loom	SS&D	6	4	24	Fa 75	31
Long, Doug	Photographing Your Fiber Work	Fa	4	5		S/O 77	45
Longbers, Ingeborg	Modern Norwegian Tapestries	H&C	5	1		Wi 53	12
Longbers, Ingeborg	Sätergläntan School in Sweden, Landmark in the History of Handweaving, The	H&C	1	3		Fa 50	4
Lonier, Terri	Altered Ego: An Interview with Pat Oleszko	Fa	10	1		J/F 83	26
Lonier, Terri	American Sojourn of African Textiles, An	Fa	11	1		J/F 84	66
Lonier, Terri	Artist's Collection: Claire Zeisler, An	Fa	12	6		N/D 85	29
Lonier, Terri	Conversation with Costumer Susan Nininger, A	Fa	10	6		N/D 83	63
Lonier, Terri	Debra Chase: Unwearable Wearables	Fa	12	3		M/J 85	12
Lonier, Terri	"Eyedazzlers!" (Exhibit)	Fa	11	3		M/J 84	77
Lonier, Terri	Historic Textiles for Contemporary Spaces	Fa	12	1		J/F 85	64
Lonier, Terri	Interview with Jhane Barnes: Designer, Weaver, Spinner, An	Fa	10	4		J/A 83	55
Lonier, Terri	Paper: Three Shows At the American Craft Museums (Exhibit)	Fa	9	5		S/O 82	84
Lonier, Terri	Textile Treasures At the Met's Costume Institute	Fa	11	5		S/O 84	37
Lonier, Terri	Textile Trends: Collecting in Chicago	Fa	12	6		N/D 85	26
Lonier, Terri	"Yves Saint Laurent: 25 Years of Design" (Exhibit)	Fa	12	1		J/F 85	76
Lønning, Kari	Art That Functions	Fa	8	3		M/J 81	40
Lønning, Kari	Kari Lønning: Exploring Color and Form in Rattan	Fa	11	1		J/F 84	12
Loper, Bobby Ann	Backstage at the Miss Universe Pageant	Fa	13	3		M/J 86	12
Lopez, Beatriz	Jaspe Process, The	SS&D	8	3	31	Su 77	54
Lorance, Marilyn	HGA Spinning Program	SS&D	11	2	42	Sp 80	67
Lorance, Marilyn	Nature's Colors, Naturally	SS&D	10	1	37	Wi 78	49
Lorance, Marilyn	Rainbow Fleece: A Happy Hazard Approach to Chemical Dyeing	Hw	2	4		Se 81	68
Lorance, Marilyn	Report on the HGA Handspinning Certificate of Excellence, A	S-O	4			80	6
Lorance, Marilyn	Woolworth: Experiments in Spinning	S-O	3			79	38
Lorant, Tessa	Knitted Lace Collars	Kn	4	1	9	Wi 87	60
Lorant, Tessa	Knitted Lace Doilies	Kn	4	1	9	Wi 87	60
Lorant, Tessa	Knitted Lace Edgings	Kn	1	2	2	S-S 85	79
Lorant, Tessa	Knitted Quilts & Flounces	Kn	1	2	2	S-S 85	79
Lorant, Tessa	Knitted Shawls & Wraps	Kn	4	1	9	Wi 87	60
Lorant, Tessa	Yarns for Textile Crafts	Hw	5	5		N/D 84	12
Lord, P. R.; M. H. Mohamed	Weaving: Conversion of Yarn to Fabric	WJ	8	2	30	Fa 83	64
Lord, P. S.; D. J. Foley	Folk Arts and Crafts of New England, The	H&C	22	1		Wi 71	41
Lorentz, H. A.	View of Chinese Rugs from the Seventeenth to the Twentieth Century, A	TMJ	3	4		De 73	47

AUTHOR	TITLE	JOUR	VOL	NO	ISS	DATE	PAGE
Lorenzo, Lauri	Haitian Voodoo Banners: Dazzling Invitations to the Spirits	Fa	13	6		N/D 86	11
Lorton, Henni	Contemporary Alpujarra Rugs	H&C	4	4		Fa 53	28
Lott, Gwynne	Our Time Has Come	WJ	2	3	7	Ja 78	3
Loud, Dana	From Rags to Riches: Artful Recycling	Fa	13	5		S/O 86	23
Lough, Ida	New Zealand Tapestry	H&C	19	3		Su 68	20
Lourie, Janice R.	Textile Designer of the Future, The	H&C	17	1		Wi 66	8
Loveland, Mary H.	Northern California Conference	H&C	17	3		Su 66	16
Lovell-Cooper, Sylvia	Think Big	SS&D	3	1	9	Wi 71	41
Lowell-LaRoque, Jane	"Coverlets: An American Tradition" (Exhibit)	Fa	7	1		J/F 80	71
Lowell-LaRoque, Jane	Seamstress...Sorceress...Artist	Fa	7	3		M/J 80	29
Lowell-LaRoque, Jane V.	Jane Rademacher: A Working Weaver in Rural Wisconsin	Fa	6	2		M/A 79	21
Lowell-LaRoque, Jane V.	"Wisconsin Fiber Miniatures" (Exhibit)	Fa	6	5		S/O 79	84
Lubell, Cecil, ed.	Textile Collections of the World	SS&D	8	2	30	Sp 77	37
Lubell, Cecil, ed.	Textile Collections of the World, Vol. 2 England	WJ	5	2	18	Fa 80	32
Lubell, Cecil, ed.	Textile Collections of the World, Vol. 3 France	WJ	5	2	18	Fa 80	33
Lubell, Cecil, ed.	Textile Collections of the World: Volume 3, France	SS&D	9	4	36	Fa 78	82
Lucas, Eleanor L.	Nantucket Lightship Baskets: A Sailor's Pastime Revisited	Fa	5	5		S/O 78	52
Lucas, Jane	Barbara Smith: Views from Within	Fa	10	5		S/O 83	18
Lucas, Jerie	Fur Fashions	SS&D	15	2	58	Sp 84	26
Lucas, Mary	Two Weeks in the South of France: At a Gobelins Tapestry Workshop	Fa	8	4		J/A 81	38
Lucey, Edmund A.	Commercial Dyes for Handweaving	H&C	1	3		Fa 50	54
Lucey, Edmund A.	Dyeing with the Direct or Substantive Colors	H&C	2	1		Wi 50	52
Lucey, Edmund A.	Finishing Handwoven Fabrics	H&C	1	2		Su 50	24
Lucey, Edmund A.	Mixing and Matching Colors in Dyeing	H&C	2	3		Su 51	26
Luddecke, Jane	"Headlines: A Hundred Years of Hats (1840–1940)" (Exhibit)	Fa	6	6		N/D 79	78
Luddecke, Jane	The Lushness of Nature: Jim Williams and His Needlepoint Art, The	Fa	6	4		J/A 79	50
Luddecke, Jane	Wearables	Fa	6	3		M/J 79	27
Luebbers, Karen	Summer Take-Along Project, A	Hw	6	2		M/A 85	92
Lukens, Petronel	Silk Culture Comments	H&C	22	2		Sp 71	15
Lumsden, Sharon Lappin	Tubular Double Weave	Hw	8	1		J/F 87	49
Lundahl, Gunilla	Memory of a Landscape	Fa	12	4		J/A 85	48
Lundback, Maja; Marta Rinde-Ramsback	Small Webs	H&C	10	4		Fa 59	60
Lundell, Laila	Rep Weaves	SS&D	19	1	73	Wi 87	51
Lundell, Laila	Rep Weaves	PWC	5	2	16		53
Lundell, Laila	Repweaves	WJ	12	2	46	Fa 87	65
Lundell, Laila	Stora Vävboken	WJ	6	2	22	Fa 81	39
Luniak, Bruno	Identification of Textile Fibres — Qualitative and Quantiative Analysis of Fibre Blends, The	H&C	5	3		Su 54	58
Lurçat, Jean	Designing Tapestry	H&C	4	2		Sp 53	61
Lurie, Amanda	Amanda Lurie: One Weaver's Path	Fa	10	4		J/A 83	16
Lusk, Jennie	"Kimono East/Kimono West" (Exhibit)	Fa	7	5		S/O 80	71
Lutz, Mrs. William C.	Weaving at Locust Grove	H&C	19	1		Wi 68	31
Lyman, Marie	Distant Mountains: The Influence of Funzo-e on the Tradition of Buddhist Clerical Robes in Japan	TMJ	23			84	25
Lyman, Susan	"Terminal": Drawing in Three Dimensions	Fa	11	4		J/A 84	60
Lynn, Harriett W.	Here Comes Christmas	SS&D	2	4	8	Fa 71	16
Lyon, David	Fabric of Movement, The	Fa	13	3		M/J 86	76
Lyon, David	Julie Green: The World of Fiber	Fa	14	1		J/F 87	40
Lyon, David	see Harris, Patricia	Fa	10	6		N/D 83	78
Lyon, David	see Harris, Patricia	Fa	12	2		M/A 85	27
Lyon, David	see Harris, Patricia	Fa	12	5		S/O 85	34
Lyon, David	see Harris, Patricia	Fa	13	2		M/A 86	18

AUTHOR	TITLE	JOUR	VOL	NO	ISS	DATE	PAGE
Lyon, David	see Harris, Patricia	Fa	14	1		J/F 87	10
Lyon, Linda	Christmas Miniatures, Part 1: Summer and Winter Coverlets	PWC			3	Oc 82	50
Lyon, Linda	Double Corduroy	PWC	3	1	7		51
Lyon, Linda	Leno Vest	PWC			6	Su 83	27
Lyon, Linda	Overshot Derived from 2/2 Twill: Apricot Accents	PWC	3	2	8		21
Lyon, Linda	Peculiar Piqué Pillow	PWC	4	2	12		30
Lyon, Linda	see Xenakis, Athanasios David	PWC	4	1	11		16
Lyon, Linda	Summer and Winter Revisited, Part 2: I. On Designing with Krokbragd, Krokbragd Mug Rugs	PWC			2	Ap 82	63
Lyon, Linda	Weaving Primer, Part 2	PWC	4	1	11		45
Lyon, Linda	Weaving the Night Fantastic	PWC			5	Sp 83	51
Lyon, Linda	White on White	PWC	3	3	9		60
Lyon, Linda; Athanasios David Xenakis	Rustic Roundel	PWC	3	1	7		36
Lyon, Linda; Connie Herring; Athanasios David Xenakis	Double Ecology Shawl	PWC	3	4	10		64
Lyon, Marge	Young Weavers in the Ozarks	H&C	8	2		Sp 57	15
Lyon, Mary, ed.	Crafts for the Aging — A Working Manual for Directors of Handcraft Programs for Older People	H&C	14	2		Sp 63	43
Lyon, Nancy	Crackle Weave, Part 1	SS&D	19	1	73	Wi 87	21
Lyon, Nicki	Help in Bridging the Gap	CW	8	1	22	Se 86	24
Lyric Books	Harmony Guide to Knitting Stitches, The	TM			9	F/M 87	74
Mabee-Zust, Mariah	Double Edge of Knitting, The	Fa	10	3		M/J 83	50
MacDonald, Claudia	Fiber At Artpark	Fa	10	6		N/D 83	47
Macdonald, Elizabeth	Weavers of Cyprus	H&C	5	4		Fa 54	24
MacDonald, Margaret	Double Woven House Boots	WJ	6	4	24	Sp 82	44
MacDougal, Marleah Drexler	Feltmaking in India: A Remnant of the Past	Fa	6	6		N/D 79	10
Macfarlan, A. & P.	Art of Knot Tying, The	H&C	18	3		Su 67	46
MacFarlane, Janet R.	Seminars on Early American Crafts	H&C	2	2		Sp 51	29
MacFarlane, Rosemary	Warping Adaptations for Fine Warps	SS&D	12	4	48	Fa 81	16
MacGregor, Olwen	Olwen's Buffalo	WJ	8	2	30	Fa 83	46
MacHenry, Rachel	Converting Images Into Sweaters	TM			10	A/M 87	72
MacInnes, Ginger	Complete Pleasure of Weaving, The	H&C	7	2		Sp 56	13
MacKenzie, Clinton D.	New Designs in Crochet	Fa	5	3		M/J 78	63
Mackie, Louise; Jon Thompson, eds.	Turkmen: Tribal Carpets and Traditions	Hw	3	5		N/D 82	14
Mackie, Louise W.	Turkish Carpet with Spots and Stripes, A	TMJ	4	3		76	4
Mackie, Louise W.	Two Remarkable Fifteenth Century Carpets from Spain	TMJ	4	4		77	15
Mackin, Jeanne	"Our Shining Heritage: Textile Arts of the Slavs and Their Neighbors" (Exhibit)	Fa	8	4		J/A 81	75
Mackin, Jeanne	"Skin Forms: Innovations in Leather" (Exhibit)	Fa	7	2		M/A 80	67
Mackley, M. Florence	Handweaving in Cape Berton	H&C	24	3		M/J 73	6
MacMillan, Susan L.	Greek Islands Embroideries	TMJ	4	2		75	80
MacNulty, Shirley W.	Knitted Yarn Over: This Simple Stitch Creates a Hole in the Fabric, The	TM			10	A/M 87	38
MacNutt, Dawn	Life and Times of Mary Black: A Visit with the Author of "The Key to Weaving", The	Fa	8	4		J/A 81	63
MacNutt, Dawn	Obsession with Trees, An	SS&D	9	4	36	Fa 78	88
MacNutt, Dawn	"Patricia McClelland: Woven Work" (Exhibit)	Fa	7	5		S/O 80	74
MacNutt, Dawn	Wear Your Best Apron	SS&D	8	4	32	Fa 77	65
Macomber, Dorothea	Five Crackle Weave Projects	H&C	9	3		Su 58	42
Macomber, Dorothea	Old & New Uses for Double Weave	H&C	8	4		Fa 57	16
Macomber, L. W.	Further Comments on Looms	H&C	5	3		Su 54	56
Madden, Gail	Braid on the Bias (error-corrected Kn f/w 86 v3 n1 i5 p11)	Kn	2	2	4	S-S 86	35
Madden, Linda	Cotton Lace	WJ	11	2	42	Fa 86	25

AUTHOR	TITLE	JOUR	VOL	NO	ISS	DATE	PAGE
Madison, Winifred	Jody House: Needlework Designer	Fa	5	6		N/D 78	25
Magee, Patricia L.	see Adams, Carol	SS&D	15	1	57	Wi 83	100
Maggs, Carol V.	see Neff, Ivan C.	Fa	7	6		N/D 80	34
Magoffin, Connie	Klara Johnson: A Weaver's Vision Realized	WJ	11	4	44	Sp 87	62
Magoffin, Connie	Planting a Dye Garden	WJ	10	2	38	Fa 85	36
Maidment, Margaret	Manual of Hand-Made Bobbin Lace Work, A	H&C	6	2		Sp 55	62
Maidment, Margaret	Manual of Hand-Made Bobbin Lace Work, A	SS&D	17	1	65	Wi 85	90
Mailand, Harold	Considerations for the Care of Textiles and Costumes — A Handbook for the Non-Specialist	SS&D	11	2	42	Sp 80	81
Mailand, Harold F.	Considerations for the Care of Textiles and Costumes, A Handbook for the Non-Specialist	SS&D	13	1	49	Wi 81	90
Mailand, Harold F.	Considerations for the Care of Textiles and Costumes: A Handbook for the Non-Specialist	Hw	3	5		N/D 82	12
Mailand, Harold F.	Considerations for the Care of Textiles and Costumes — A Handbook for the Non-Specialist	WJ	6	2	22	Fa 81	40
Maile, Anne	Tie-and-Dye Made Easy	H&C	23	3		M/J 72	34
Mailey, Jean	On Foreign Soil But Common Ground, Textile Assembly Meets in Spain	H&C	21	1		Wi 70	18
Mailey, Jean	see Dimand, M. S.	TMJ	4	1		De 74	85
Mailey, Jean E.	Mid-Twentieth Century Textures	H&C	8	3		Su 57	6
Maines, Rachel	Fiber Mandalas: Doilies As Spiritual Art	Fa	9	3		M/J 82	17
Maines, Rachel	Old Time Fancy Work: Examples of Lesser Known Needlework Techniques	Fa	8	3		M/J 81	16
Mairet, Ethel	Hand Weaving and Education	H&C	3	1		Wi 51	62
Mairet, Ethel	Handweaving Notes for Teachers	H&C	3	1		Wi 51	62
Major, Dana; John Major	Kazuko Nishigaki Creates in Ancient Tradition	SS&D	6	2	22	Sp 75	93
Major, John	see Major, Dana	SS&D	6	2	22	Sp 75	93
Major, Marjorie	Nova Scotia Weavers Arouse Interest in Wool	H&C	5	1		Wi 53	28
Malarcher, Pat	Evolution of An Artist: Michelle Lester	Fa	14	5		N/D 87	22
Malarcher, Pat	"Frank Lincoln Viner–Fantaisie: Constructions and Objects" (Exhibit)	Fa	7	1		J/F 80	73
Malarcher, Pat	"Jackie Winsor" (Exhibit)	Fa	6	4		J/A 79	68
Malarcher, Pat	"Lenore Tawney: A Personal World" (Exhibit)	Fa	5	6		N/D 78	63
Malarcher, Pat	Rapport with Fabric and Dye: Kiyomi Iwata, A	Fa	7	1		J/F 80	28
Malarcher, Pat	Sharon Hedges	Fa	5	3		M/J 78	56
Malarcher, Pat	Sheila Fox: Three-Dimensional Plaiting	Fa	6	5		S/O 79	22
Malarcher, Pat	"Sherri Smith: New Works" (Exhibit)	Fa	5	5		S/O 78	75
Malarcher, Pat	"Suellen Glashausser — Fences" (Exhibit)	Fa	6	3		M/J 79	77
Malarcher, Pat	Susanna Lewis	Fa	5	3		M/J 78	52
Malarcher, Patricia	"Akiko Kotani" (Exhibit)	Fa	8	4		J/A 81	73
Malarcher, Patricia	Applique Art of Nell Booker Sonnemann, The	Fa	7	3		M/J 80	24
Malarcher, Patricia	Architect-Weaver and His Workaday World: Bruce Bierman's Business is Good Design, An	Fa	7	6		N/D 80	60
Malarcher, Patricia	Basketmaker's Year "Down Under", A	Fa	8	4		J/A 81	47
Malarcher, Patricia	"Bernard Toale: Works in Fiber" (Exhibit)	Fa	7	2		M/A 80	65
Malarcher, Patricia	"Fashions of the Hapsburg Era: Austria-Hungary" (Exhibit)	Fa	7	3		M/J 80	75
Malarcher, Patricia	Fibre-Form-Fusion: Gathering Together in Canada	Fa	7	6		N/D 80	26
Malarcher, Patricia	Gathering for Enrichment: The New York Textile Study Group	Fa	12	5		S/O 85	48
Malarcher, Patricia	"In Praise of Heroes" (Exhibit)	Fa	10	1		J/F 83	78
Malarcher, Patricia	"Infrastructure" (Exhibit)	Fa	11	4		J/A 84	76
Malarcher, Patricia	Inspired by Fiber: Textile Sensibility in Other Media	Fa	10	6		N/D 83	33
Malarcher, Patricia	"James Bassler" (Exhibit)	Fa	8	6		N/D 81	71
Malarcher, Patricia	"Jan Wagstaff: Woven and Painted Canvas" (Exhibit)	Fa	8	6		N/D 81	64
Malarcher, Patricia	"Jayn Thomas" (Exhibit)	Fa	10	5		S/O 83	81
Malarcher, Patricia	"Joan Livingstone: Lamia Lemures" (Exhibit)	Fa	7	4		J/A 80	67
Malarcher, Patricia	JoAnn Giordano: A Modern Mythology	Fa	13	6		N/D 86	13

AUTHOR	TITLE	JOUR	VOL	NO	ISS	DATE	PAGE
Malarcher, Patricia	Joyce Crain: Walls of Light	Fa	12	5		S/O 85	55
Malarcher, Patricia	"Kiyomi Iwata: Works in Fiber" (Exhibit)	Fa	9	2		M/A 82	77
Malarcher, Patricia	"Leora Stewart: New Works—Deborah Warner: Four Corners Journal" (Exhibit)	Fa	6	6		N/D 79	71
Malarcher, Patricia	Liturgical Vestment: A Contemporary Overview, The	Fa	11	5		S/O 84	58
Malarcher, Patricia	Look At the Juried Show: Jurors and Artists Talk About What It Takes, A	Fa	9	5		S/O 82	53
Malarcher, Patricia	Miniatures in Fiber: Working Small—An Exciting Challenge for the Contemporary Fiber Artist	Fa	7	4		J/A 80	32
Malarcher, Patricia	Nets of Bernard Toale, The	Fa	9	3		M/J 82	26
Malarcher, Patricia	"New Elegance: Contemporary Wearable Art, The" (Exhibit)	Fa	12	4		J/A 85	44
Malarcher, Patricia	On the Edge: Maureen Connor — Shaping a Response to the Past	Fa	9	4		J/A 82	61
Malarcher, Patricia	"Patterns" (Exhibit)	Fa	10	2		M/A 83	76
Malarcher, Patricia	Plastics in Fiber: A Persistent Presence	Fa	12	1		J/F 85	56
Malarcher, Patricia	"Sculpture of Claire Zeisler" (Exhibit)	Fa	12	6		N/D 85	57
Malarcher, Patricia	Silk City: Paterson, New Jersey	Fa	13	1		J/F 86	31
Malarcher, Patricia	"Sirpa Yarmolinsky: Paper and Linen Constructions" (Exhibit)	Fa	9	1		J/F 82	84
Malarcher, Patricia	"Susan Goldin: Windows" (Exhibit)	Fa	9	3		M/J 82	76
Malarcher, Patricia	"Tapestries by Janet Taylor" (Exhibit)	Fa	9	5		S/O 82	81
Malarcher, Patricia	Textile Trends: The Museum Collection	Fa	12	6		N/D 85	23
Malarcher, Patricia	Virginia Davis	Fa	10	5		S/O 83	14
Malarcher, Patricia	"Voyage Continued" An Illuminating Experience (Exhibit)	Fa	8	2		M/A 81	16
Malarcher, Patricia	Web of India, The	SS&D	13	2	50	Sp 82	38
Malarcher, Patricia	What Makes a Basket a Basket?	Fa	11	1		J/F 84	34
Malarcher, Patricia	"Women Artists: Clay, Fiber, Metal" (Exhibit)	Fa	5	2		M/A 78	11
Malarcher, Patricia	"Works in Miniature" (Exhibit)	Fa	7	3		M/J 80	82
Malarcher, Patricia	"Woven and Graphic Art of Anni Albers, The" (Exhibit)	Fa	13	1		J/F 86	62
Malarcher, Patricia	"Young Americans: Fiber, Wood, Plastic, Leather" (Exhibit)	Fa	4	6		N/D 77	14
Malbin, Rosemary S.	Chained Weft for Surface Texture	SS&D	11	4	44	Fa 80	26
Malerich, Lee A.	Lee A. Malerich	Fa	14	1		J/F 87	27
Mallinckrodt, Casey	Missy Stevens: Connecting Art and Fabric	Fa	14	4		S/O 87	20
Malloy, Kim, OSB	Drawloom Special Harness for Double Weave	AT	1			De 83	77
Malloy, Kim, OSB	Eucharistic Vestments, The	WJ	6	1	21	Su 81	37
Malloy, Kim, OSB	Split-Harness Drawloom, The	CW	2	1	4	Oc 80	3
Malouff, Raye	Copyright Law and You, The	Fa	4	6		N/D 77	53
Mancini, Anne	Labor Banners of Australia	Fa	14	5		N/D 87	36
Mandell, Patricia	Giving New Life to Antique Wedding Gowns	Fa	14	3		M/J 87	18
Mangat, Terri	Creative Process: Terri Mangat, The	Fa	11	6		N/D 84	36
Mangum, Teresa	see Hyatt, Sharyn	Fa	9	4		J/A 82	66
Manker, Ernst	People of Eight Seasons — The Story of the Lapps	H&C	15	3		Su 64	44
Mann, Joyce P.	What to do with a Great Idea?	Hw	4	3		M/J 83	16
Manners, Karen	see Herring, Rluth	Kn	3	4	8	Fa 87	63
Manners, Karen	see Herring, Ruth	TM			14	D/J 87	76
Manno, Angela	Angela Manno	Fa	12	5		S/O 85	18
Mansfield, Susan	What's in a Name? Name Drafts Drawn by Hand or Computer	WJ	10	3	39	Wi 86	15
Many, Paul	Athens Tapestry Works	Fa	5	4		J/A 78	51
March, Heather	Homemade Felt	TM			2	D/J 85	60
Marcoux, Alice	"Ch'ing Dynasty Court Robes, A Splendorous Sampling" (Exhibit)	Fa	11	2		M/A 84	78
Marcoux, Alice	Jacquard Loom: Where It Comes from, How It Works, The	Fa	9	2		M/A 82	34
Marcoux, Alice	Jacquard Loomed: Turn-of-the-Century Fabrics	Fa	9	2		M/A 82	35
Marcus, Ruth-Claire	Auctioning Rugs Among the Navajos	TM			6	A/S 86	16
Marcus, Ruth-Claire	Convergence '86	TM			8	D/J 86	10
Marcus, Ruth-Claire	Precious Fibers Congress	TM			13	O/N 87	18
Marcus, Ruth-Claire	What's in a Bale of Used Kimonos?	TM			7	O/N 86	16

AUTHOR	TITLE	JOUR	VOL	NO	ISS	DATE	PAGE
Marcus, Sharon	Sharon Marcus	Fa	13	6		N/D 86	2
Marcus, Sharon	Sharon Marcus: Designing for Tapestry, One Approach to the Creative Process	Fa	11	6		N/D 84	26
Marein, Shirley	Off the Loom: Creating with Fibre	H&C	24	1		J/F 73	28
Marger, Mary Ann	Michele Tuegel's Paper Works	Fa	13	4		J/A 86	30
Margetts, Martina	Visit with Anni Albers, A	TM			2	D/J 85	24
Mariano, Linda	Encyclopedia of Knitting and Crochet Stitch Patterns, The	SS&D	8	4	32	Fa 77	72
Marinsky, Harry	see Brostrom, Ethel	H&C	2	3		Su 51	63
Mark, David	Sheep of the Lal Bagh, The	Iw	2	1		Fa 76	32
Markey, Barbara R.	Contemporary Vestments	H&C	9	3		Su 58	11
Markle, Marsha	"Entanglements" (Exhibit)	Fa	4	2		M/A 77	16
Markrich, Lilo	Darn That Hole	TM			5	J/J 86	38
Markrich, Lilo	History of Texture Stitches, A	TM			5	J/J 86	63
Markrich, Lilo	Japan's Masterful Embroideries	TM			12	A/S 87	68
Marks, Copeland	In Pursuit of the Elusive Huipil	H&C	24	4		Au 73	6
Marks, Copeland A.	Guatemala Weaver, The	H&C	26	5		Oc 75	2
Marks, Copeland H.	Weavings of the Guatemalan Highland Maya	SS&D	7	4	28	Fa 76	88
Marmoff, Kathryn Andrews	Handmade Rugs	H&C	9	2		Sp 58	60
Marquardt, Bertha	Tapestry Inlay for Fool-Proof Designing	SS&D	6	1	21	Wi 74	38
Marquess, Joyce	From Simple Twills to Dobby Fantasies...A Progression	Iw	4	4		Fa 79	38
Marquess, Joyce	Janet Higgins: Soft Sculpture in Motion	Fa	7	2		M/A 80	62
Marquess, Joyce	Navajo Saddleblanket, The	SS&D	8	3	31	Su 77	25
Marquess, Joyce	Weave a Mobius	SS&D	5	2	18	Sp 74	55
Marriage, Margaret S.	see Mincoff, Elizabeth	H&C	2	2		Sp 51	61
Marshall, Bertha	Fifth Grade Weavers in California	H&C	5	1		Wi 53	31
Marshall, Bertha	"The Robe," is Woven on a California Handloom	H&C	4	3		Su 53	14
Marston, Ena	Backed Weaves: Part 1	SS&D	8	3	31	Su 77	64
Marston, Ena	Backed Weaves, Part 2	SS&D	8	4	32	Fa 77	50
Marston, Ena	Backgrounds for Stitchery	SS&D	3	1	9	Wi 71	13
Marston, Ena	Balanced Integrated Weaves	SS&D	8	1	29	WI 76	10
Marston, Ena	Coat with Minimum Seams, The	SS&D	7	4	28	Fa 76	42
Marston, Ena	Cord Weaves, The	SS&D	5	4	20	Fa 74	34
Marston, Ena	Curves and Circles	SS&D	15	1	57	Wi 83	84
Marston, Ena	Designing with Loom-Woven Open Weaves	SS&D	13	1	49	Wi 81	22
Marston, Ena	Dr. Bateman and The Bateman Blend	SS&D	5	2	18	Sp 74	37
Marston, Ena	Fabric for Clothing	SS&D	13	3	51	Su 82	52
Marston, Ena	Four Seasons, Tapestries by Bernardi, The	H&C	20	2		Sp 69	8
Marston, Ena	Handweavers International Festival	H&C	21	1		Wi 70	10
Marston, Ena	Hatching	SS&D	10	3	39	Su 79	56
Marston, Ena	Layered Fabrics: Four-Harness, Two-Color Double Cloth, Part 1	SS&D	6	1	21	Wi 74	28
Marston, Ena	Layered Fabrics: Four-Harness, Two-Color Double Cloth, Part 2	SS&D	6	2	22	Sp 75	56
Marston, Ena	Layered Fabrics on Eight Harnesses	SS&D	6	4	24	Fa 75	50
Marston, Ena	Lines, Squares, Rectangles	SS&D	14	3	55	Su 83	72
Marston, Ena	More Cord Weaves	SS&D	6	3	23	Su 75	78
Marston, Ena	More Integrated Weaves	SS&D	8	2	30	Sp 77	20
Marston, Ena	New HGA Name Draft: Miniature Coverlet in Overshot, A	SS&D	12	3	47	Su 81	12
Marston, Ena	Northern California Weavers in Their Seventeenth Session	H&C	20	4		Fa 69	18
Marston, Ena	Openwork Weaves	SS&D	10	2	38	Sp 79	18
Marston, Ena	Overshot Overlay for Ethnic Clothing	SS&D	9	3	35	Su 78	88
Marston, Ena	Overshot Patterns	SS&D	4	2	14	Sp 73	20
Marston, Ena	Overshot Patterns: Emphasis on Miniatures	SS&D	11	1	41	Wi 79	40
Marston, Ena	Overshot: The Weave and the Designs	SS&D	11	2	42	Sp 80	74
Marston, Ena	Painted Warps	H&C	21	4		Fa 70	37

AUTHOR	TITLE	JOUR	VOL	NO	ISS	DATE	PAGE
Marston, Ena	Polly Yori (error-corrected H&C v21 n3 70 p45)	H&C	21	1		Wi 70	19
Marston, Ena	Polychrome Double Weave (error-corrected SS&D v7 n1 75 p64)	SS&D	7	1	25	Wi 75	52
Marston, Ena	Psychedelic Bookworm	SS&D	1	1	1	De 69	17
Marston, Ena	Selvages	SS&D	10	4	40	Fa 79	26
Marston, Ena	Shuttle	SS&D	2	3	7	Su 71	11
Marston, Ena	Shuttle	SS&D	2	4	8	Fa 71	14
Marston, Ena	Silk Production in Kohn Kaen	SS&D	7	3	27	Su 76	30
Marston, Ena	Silk Retrospective	SS&D	14	1	53	Wi 82	34
Marston, Ena	Some Loom-Woven Open Weaves (error-corrected SS&D v13 n1 81 p4)	SS&D	12	4	48	Fa 81	32
Marston, Ena	Southern California Conference	H&C	21	3		Su 70	30
Marston, Ena	Stars & Roses or Designing and Drafting Overshot	SS&D	4	3	15	Su 73	27
Marston, Ena	Summer and Winter, A Unit Weave	SS&D	4	4	16	Fa 73	25
Marston, Ena	Supplementary Weft Float Patterning	SS&D	9	4	36	Fa 78	63
Marston, Ena	Swaddling Clothes	SS&D	4	1	13	Wi 72	23
Marston, Ena	Theo Moorman, English Tapestry Weaver in San Francisco	H&C	20	1		Wi 69	12
Marston, Ena	To Weave a Tiny Tapestry	H&C	22	2		Sp 71	29
Marston, Ena	Variations on a Draft	SS&D	3	1	9	Wi 71	13
Marston, Ena	Variations on a Twill Theme: No. 1	SS&D	5	1	17	Wi 73	34
Marston, Ena	Variations on a Twill Theme, No. 2	SS&D	5	3	19	Su 74	34
Marston, Ena	Ways to Weave Overshot: Part 1	SS&D	11	3	43	Su 80	6
Marston, Ena	Ways to Weave Overshot: Part 2	SS&D	12	1	45	Wi 80	36
Marston, Ena	Ways to Weave Overshot: Part 3	SS&D	12	2	46	Sp 81	6
Marston, Ena	Weaving for Ethnic Clothing	SS&D	10	1	37	Wi 78	42
Marston, Ena	Weaving in Southeast Asia (addition SS&D v7 n4 76 p27)	SS&D	7	2	26	Sp 76	30
Marston, Ena	Woven Patchwork	SS&D	4	1	13	Wi 72	18
Marston, Ena; Shirley E. Held; Esther Dendel	8th International Biennial of Tapestry: Three Perspectives, The	SS&D	9	1	33	Wi 77	4
Marten, Eileen	Selecting Fleece for Spinning and Yarn Gauge	S-O	3			79	11
Marten, Michael, et al.	Worlds Within Worlds: A Journey Into the Unknown	Iw	4	2		Sp 79	64
Martin, Beryl	Batik for Beginners	SS&D	4	2	14	Sp 73	44
Martin, Catherine	Kumihimo, Japanese Silk Braiding Techniques	WJ	11	4	44	Sp 87	73
Martin, Catherine	Kumihimo: Japanese Silk Braiding Techniques	Fa	14	1		J/F 87	21
Martin, Edna; Beate Sydhoff	Swedish Textile Art	Fa	10	4		J/A 83	50
Martin, Elaine	Tradition and Change: Fiber '79	Iw	5	2		Sp 80	72
Martin, George	Spinning Wheels from the Busy Workshop of Anthony Cardarelle	H&C	17	3		Su 66	6
Martin, Gloria	see Scorgie, Jean	Hw	6	3		Su 85	38
Martin, Grace O.	Approaching Design Through Nature: The Quiet Joy	SS&D	9	2	34	Sp 78	50
Martin, Grace O.	Approaching Design Through Nature — The Quiet Joy	Fa	4	5		S/O 77	48
Martin, Jill	Apollo's Legacy or "A Dyer's Vision"	Hw	3	3		My 82	9
Martin, Jill	Hats, Hats, Hats	S-O	7	3		Fa 83	18
Martin, Jill	Tips on Mittens	S-O	7	2		Su 83	51
Martin, Jill	Using Your Mistakes	S-O	8	1		Sp 84	52
Martin, Jill	Vacation Dye Samples	Hw	4	3		M/J 83	58
Martin, Jude	see King, Bucky	SS&D	10	4	40	Fa 79	63
Martin, Karen Ericsson	Angel Threads: Creating Lovable Clothes for Little Ones	SS&D	18	2	70	Sp 87	38
Martin, Mary	Meet-and-Separate Technique	WJ	8	4	32	Sp 84	14
Martin, Richard	When Is Art Fashion and Fashion Art?	TM			11	J/J 87	12
Martin, Robert	Paper Works of Kathryn Maxwell, The	Fa	14	2		M/A 87	8
Martinson, Kate	Scandinavian Nålbinding: Needle Looped Fabric	WJ	12	2	46	Fa 87	12
Marvin, Grace	Novel Ski Poncho	H&C	14	4		Fa 63	34
Mary Meigs Atwater Weavers' Guild	Mary Meigs Atwater Recipe Book — Patterns for Handweavers	H&C	8	4		Fa 57	59

AUTHOR	TITLE	JOUR	VOL	NO	ISS	DATE	PAGE
Mason, Carole	Weaving and Sheepskin, Naturally	WJ	5	3	19	Wi 81	46
Mason, Lynn DeRose	Samplings	S-O	11	2		Su 87	30
Mason, Otis Tufton	Basketry Techniques: A Sampler (from 1902 Book)	Iw	4	1		Wi 78	26
Mastache de Escobar, Alba Guadelupe	"Technicas Prehaspánicas del Tejido", Investigaciones XX	TMJ	3	4		De 73	47
Masten, Ric	Caterpillar and the Butterfly, The	Iw	5	2		Sp 80	39
Mataraso, Ann	Basic Basketry	Hw	7	2		M/A 86	89
Matheison, Ian	Spinning Wheel, The	H&C	23	4		J/A 72	4
Matheson, Alice	see Starmore, Alice	Kn	2	1	3	F-W 85	79
Mathews, Cleve	"Issey Miyake: Fashion Without Taboos" (Exhibit)	Fa	12	3		M/J 85	70
Mathews, Kate	Embroidered Sambas of Madeleine Colaço, The	Fa	14	5		N/D 87	34
Mathews, Kate	Technicolor Tapestries of Teresa Graham Salt, The	Fa	14	1		J/F 87	11
Mathews, Rich	"Claire Zeisler" (Exhibit)	Fa	4	1		J/F 77	12
Mathews, Rich	Enduring Art of Jagoda Buic, The	Fa	11	4		J/A 84	64
Mathews, Rich	"Fiber in the Service of Art: The Work of Wilma King and Marilyn Grelle" (Exhibit)	Fa	4	2		M/A 77	18
Mathews, Rich	"Jagoda Buic" (Exhibit)	Fa	4	5		S/O 77	13
Mathews, Rich	Lausanne Notebook: Our Special Report on the 8th Lausanne Biennial of Tapestry, A	Fa	4	5		S/O 77	30
Mathews, Rich	"Ritzi and Peter Jacobi" (Exhibit)	Fa	4	5		S/O 77	12
Mathews, Rich	Washington Fiber	Fa	3	5		S/O 76	9
Mathews, Richard	"Patti Glazer, Woven Tapestry" (error-corrected Fa v3 n5 76 p2) (Exhibit)	Fa	3	4		J/A 76	6
Mathews, Richard; Joan Burton	"Mary Walker Phillips — Wall Hangings" (Exhibit)	Fa	3	4		J/A 76	8
Mathews, Sibyl	Needle-Made Rugs	H&C	12	2		Sp 61	59
Mathews, Tom	Personal History Involving the Spinning Wheel and One Man's Insatiable Curiosity, A	Fa	6	2		M/A 79	18
Mathews-Pulleyn, Kathryn	Dilys Stinson: Tapestry Maker	Fa	4	5		S/O 77	22
Mathews-Pulleyn, Kathryn	"Fiber Structures" Convergence '76 (Exhibit)	Fa	3	4		J/A 76	12
Mathieson, David	see Folts, Teressa	H&C	24	2		M/A 73	5
Mathieson, Ian	Spinning Wheel, The	H&C	23	1		J/F 72	10
Matlock, Ann	Personal Approach to Color, A	S-O	9	3		Fa 85	19
Matranga, Victoria	Anastazija Tamosaitis	SS&D	17	3	67	Su 86	54
Matsumoto, Kaneo	Jodai-Gire, 7th and 8th Century Textiles in Japan from the Shoso-in and Horyu-ji	Hw	8	1		J/F 87	18
Matsumoto, Kaneo	Jodai-gire: 7th and 8th Century Textiles in Japan from the Shosoin and Horyu-ji	Fa	13	1		J/F 86	45
Matteini, Cesare, ed.	Handicrafts in Italy	H&C	20	3		Su 69	42
Mattera, Joanna	Amazing Lace on Venetian Isle	TM			7	O/N 86	12
Mattera, Joanna	Conversation with Barbara Shawcroft: a Sculptor in Fiber, A	Fa	8	4		J/A 81	58
Mattera, Joanna	"Scandinavian Touch, The" A Traveling Exhibit (Exhibit)	Fa	10	1		J/F 83	82
Mattera, Joanne	80 Papers: Only a 9' by 30' Store, But a Veritable U.N. of Pulp	Fa	8	6		N/D 81	28
Mattera, Joanne	"Anne Flaten Pixley" (Exhibit)	Fa	6	6		N/D 79	68
Mattera, Joanne	Bringing Tapestry into the 20th Century	TM			1	O/N 85	48
Mattera, Joanne	By the Yard	TM			5	J/J 86	50
Mattera, Joanne	Contemporary Felting	SS&D	7	2	26	Sp 76	89
Mattera, Joanne	Cycle of Growth, A	Fa	7	2		M/A 80	24
Mattera, Joanne	Cynthia Pannucci: Relocating, Creating, Connecting	Fa	9	3		M/J 82	23
Mattera, Joanne	Deborah Ann Abbott: Power Loom Weaving on a New Hampshire Farm	Fa	9	1		J/F 82	35
Mattera, Joanne	Diary of a Collection	TM			13	O/N 87	36
Mattera, Joanne	Double Lives: Can You Love Your "Work" When It's Your "Job"?	TM			10	A/M 87	62
Mattera, Joanne	Exploring Wedge Weave	Iw	3	2		Wi 78	24
Mattera, Joanne	Fastening Alternative, A	SS&D	11	3	43	Su 80	27
Mattera, Joanne	Fiberarts Special: All About Yarn	Fa	7	1		J/F 80	Insert
Mattera, Joanne	Fran Mather: Handweaving in Asheville, North Carolina	Fa	9	1		J/F 82	38

AUTHOR	TITLE	JOUR	VOL	NO	ISS	DATE	PAGE
Mattera, Joanne	Garments from the Loom: Handweaver Randall Darwall Focuses on the Cloth	Fa	10	1		J/F 83	20
Mattera, Joanne	Great-Grandmother's Linens	TM			3	F/M 86	86
Mattera, Joanne	Here Today, Gone Tomorrow: The Transitory Sculpture of Virginia Gunter	Fa	8	2		M/A 81	18
Mattera, Joanne	History in Stitches, A	Fa	7	3		M/J 80	37
Mattera, Joanne	History of Bast Fibers, A	SS&D	8	4	32	Fa 77	27
Mattera, Joanne	History of Linen, A	SS&D	8	3	31	Su 77	16
Mattera, Joanne	History of Silk, A	SS&D	8	2	30	Sp 77	24
Mattera, Joanne	In and on the Surface: The Tapestries of Judy Branfman	Fa	10	3		M/J 83	22
Mattera, Joanne	Judy Chicago's Dinner Party: A Review	Fa	7	3		M/J 80	16
Mattera, Joanne	Linekin Bay Fabrics: Handweaving in a Maine Production Studio	Fa	9	1		J/F 82	39
Mattera, Joanne	Maridadi West: A Fort Collins, Colorado Fabric Design Studio with Its Roots in East Africa	Fa	9	2		M/A 82	24
Mattera, Joanne	"National Crafts '81: Works by the 1981 National Endowment for the Arts Craft Fellows" (Exhibit)	Fa	9	1		J/F 82	82
Mattera, Joanne	Navajo Techniques for Today's Weaver	SS&D	7	2	26	Sp 76	34
Mattera, Joanne	Navajo Techniques for Today's Weaver	Iw	1	2		Wi 76	28
Mattera, Joanne	"Patterns and Sources of Navajo Weaving" (Exhibit)	Fa	7	4		J/A 80	68
Mattera, Joanne	Pleating by Hand	Fa	9	1		J/F 82	60
Mattera, Joanne	Quiltmaker's Art, A	Fa	10	2		M/A 83	33
Mattera, Joanne	Quilts in Women's Lives	Fa	9	3		M/J 82	54
Mattera, Joanne	Right Out of History	Fa	9	3		M/J 82	55
Mattera, Joanne	Rugweaving: Teaching on Two Harnesses	Iw	5	1		Wi 79	27
Mattera, Joanne	Rugweaving Techniques for Two-Harness	SS&D	11	2	42	Sp 80	81
Mattera, Joanne	Rugweaving: Techniques for Two-Harness	Iw	5	1		Wi 79	62
Mattera, Joanne	Rugweaving: Techniques for Two-Harness	WJ	8	4	32	Sp 84	67
Mattera, Joanne	Rugweaving: Techniques for Two-Harness	Fa	8	3		M/J 81	51
Mattera, Joanne	see Howe, Katherine	Fa	9	4		J/A 82	26
Mattera, Joanne	"Silk as Ceremony: The Dress of China in the Late Ch'ing Dynasty Period (1759–1911)" (Exhibit)	Fa	8	3		M/J 81	75
Mattera, Joanne	Solving the Circle	SS&D	7	1	25	Wi 75	67
Mattera, Joanne	Stuff: Precedents and Alternatives to Polyester	Iw	5	3		Su 80	46
Mattera, Joanne	Succeeding with the Knitting Machine	T					
Mattera, Joanne	Surface Attraction	TM			7	O/N 86	20
Mattera, Joanne	Surface Design Association's Southeast Regional Conference	Fa	9	1		J/F 82	54
Mattera, Joanne	Synthetic Fibers, A Personal Assessment	Iw	4	2		Sp 79	48
Mattera, Joanne	Thread of Continuity: Paper as Fabric, Craft as Art, and Other Ambiguities, The	Fa	6	4		J/A 79	31
Mattera, Joanne	"Throbbing Needles II" (Exhibit)	Fa	7	2		M/A 80	71
Mattera, Joanne	Wendy Shah: Subtle Rhythms	Fa	7	5		S/O 80	21
Mattera, Joanne	Why Wool Felts	Fa	6	6		N/D 79	48
Mattera, Joanne, ed.	Quiltmaker's Art, Contemporary Quilts and Their Makers, The	PWC	4	2	12		52
Matthews, Marianne R.	Jerry Stefl: Fantasy, Beads, and Fiber	Fa	11	2		M/A 84	24
Mattie, Edward L.	Meaning in Crafts	H&C	10	3		Su 59	59
Matty, Norma P.	Rocky Mountain Weavers Display Fabrics for the Home	H&C	12	4		Fa 61	9
Mauersberger, Hubert R.	American Handbook of Synthetic Textiles	H&C	4	1		Wi 52	59
Mauldin, Barbara	Traditions in Transition: Contemporary Basket Weaving of the Southwestern Indians	Hw	7	1		J/F 86	18
Mauldin, Barbara	Traditions in Transition: Contemporary Basket Weaving of the Southwestern Indians	WJ	10	2	38	Fa 85	83
Mavigliano, George J.	Weaving Vehicle, The	SS&D	8	3	31	Su 77	79
Maxcy, Mabel	Nell Znamierowski At Texas	SS&D	3	4	12	Fa 72	24
Maxcy, Mabel E.	Mable Morrow–Appreciation for Indian Arts, Part 1	SS&D	5	1	17	Wi 73	29
Maxcy, Mabel E.	Mable Morrow—Collector, Scholar of Indian Arts, Part 2	SS&D	5	2	18	Sp 74	33
Maxcy, Mabel E.	Multi-Layered Tubular Hangings	SS&D	4	4	16	Fa 73	12

AUTHOR	TITLE	JOUR	VOL	NO	ISS	DATE	PAGE
Maxcy, Mabel E.	Weaving Again Offered at Texas Women's University	H&C	20	4		Fa 69	21
Maxson, Mary Lou	Japanese Country Weaving	WJ	3	3	11	Ja 79	43
Maxson, Mary Lou	Taking the Guesswork Out of Color Selection	Hw	2	4		Se 81	44
May, April	April May: Visions of Space	Fa	10	6		N/D 83	22
May, April	Visions of Space	SS&D	14	1	53	Wi 82	14
May, April D.	Inner Visions	SS&D	15	3	59	Su 84	57
May, C. J. Delabere	How to Identify Persian Rugs and Other Oriental Rugs	H&C	5	4		Fa 54	58
May, Florence	Silk Textiles of Spain — Eighth to Fifteenth Century	H&C	9	1		Wi 57	59
May, John	see Marten, Michael	Iw	4	2		Sp 79	64
Mayer, Alice W.	Clinch Valley: Each One Teach Others	SS&D	2	2	6	Sp 71	31
Mayer, Anita	Modular Clothing	Hw	7	3		M/J 86	58
Mayer, Anita	Small is Beautiful	Iw	6	1		Wi 80	18
Mayer, Anita	Wearing Handwovens with Style	WJ	10	3	39	Wi 86	22
Mayer, Anita Luvera	Clothing from the Hands That Weave	WJ	9	3	35	Wi 85	85
Mayer, Anita Luvera	Clothing from the Hands That Weave	TM			6	A/S 86	86
Mayer, Anita Luvera	Creative Clothing: Surface Embellishment	WJ	11	3	43	Wi 87	30
Mayer, Anita Luvera	Felted Fabric	SS&D	15	3	59	Su 84	46
Mayer, Anita Luvera	Sky Celebration	S-O	11	2		Su 87	36
Mayer, Anita Luvera	Tapestries to Wear	Hw	5	5		N/D 84	54
Mayer, Francis	Dyeing of Wool Blends	WJ	2	4	8	Ap 78	26
Mayer, Francis	Wool Dyeing and Mothproofing for the Handweaver	WJ	2	3	7	Ja 78	41
Mayer, Francis	Wool Finishing	WJ	3	1	9	Jy 78	31
Mayer-Thurman, Christa C.	see Davison, Mildred	TMJ	3	4		De 73	46
Mazur, Carole	"Textile Works: Lily Gilmore, Judith Moir, Sheila O'Hara" (Exhibit)	Fa	8	2		M/A 81	67
McCall's Needlework and Crafts Publications, eds.	McCall's Book of Quilts, The	Iw	1	1		Fa 75	20
McCandlish, Joan	Joan McCandlish	Fa	14	4		S/O 87	18
McCann, Kathleen	Architectural Imagery of Margery Freeman Appelbaum, The	Fa	13	1		J/F 86	12
McCann, Kathleen	"Costumes of Royal India, The" (Exhibit)	Fa	13	1		J/F 86	58
McCann, Kathleen	"Glorious Knits of Kaffe Fassett, The" (Exhibit)	Fa	13	2		M/A 86	53
McCann, Kathleen	Katagami: Japanese Stencil Cutting	Fa	13	2		M/A 86	36
McCarthy, Bridget Beattie	Architectural Crafts, A Handbook and Catalog	WJ	7	2	26	Fa 82	58
McCarthy, Bridget Beattie	Architectural Crafts: A Handbook and Catalog	Fa	10	4		J/A 83	49
McCarthy, Bridget Beatty	Chase Home	SS&D	16	4	64	Fa 85	44
McCarthy, Catherine L.	Kente on Four Harnesses	SS&D	16	3	63	Su 85	6
McCarthy, Judy; Sue Ferguson	Today's Conscious Aesthetic Philosophy 'Asks Us to Rationalize the Non-Rational'	SS&D	4	4	16	Fa 73	54
McCartney, Doris	Dye Session in the Park	SS&D	1	2	2	Mr 70	22
McCarty, Carole	Love-Spinning Farewell in Hawaii	SS&D	6	1	21	Wi 74	41
McCauley, Susan L.	Mudmee: The Ikat Tradition in Thailand	Fa	10	5		S/O 83	25
McCauley, Susan L.	Profile of a Thai Weaver	Fa	10	5		S/O 83	26
McCeary, Gay	Expanded Point Twill	Iw	4	3		Su 79	37
McClanathan, Barbara	Four-End Block Draft or Summer and Winter	WJ	8	4	32	Sp 84	22
McClellan, Alice	Intermountain Weavers: "Fiber Celebrated, 1985"	SS&D	17	4	68	Fa 86	42
McClelland, Elizabeth	Janice Lessman-Moss: Fiber Structures and Cultivated Contrasts	Fa	11	6		N/D 84	18
McClelland, Elizabeth	"Lilian Tyrrell: Tapestries" (Exhibit)	Fa	11	6		N/D 84	76
McClelland, Elizabeth	Material Matters: Textile Gifts to the Cleveland Museum of Art	Fa	12	3		M/J 85	50
McClelland, Elizabeth	"Microfibers" (Exhibit)	Fa	8	2		M/A 81	66
McClelland, Patricia Polett	Enlarged Patterns: A Fresh Look at Old Techniques	WJ	7	4	28	Sp 83	68
McClennen, Carol	Oedipus Jacket, The	S-O	7	4		Wi 83	31
McClinton, Katherine M.	Changing Church, Its Architecture, Art and Decoration, The	H&C	9	3		Su 58	62
McCloud, Nena	Yoga for Weavers	Fa	5	2		M/A 78	40
McComb, Richard	Where's the Sport in Sportswear?	TM			2	D/J 85	36

AUTHOR	TITLE	JOUR	VOL	NO	ISS	DATE	PAGE
McConnell, Kathleen	Andes Tradition, An	SS&D	18	2	70	Sp 87	29
McConnell, Kathleen	Herbs for a Healthy Angora	S-O	8	1		Sp 84	38
McCreary, Carol Fillips	Traditional Moroccan Loom, The	WJ	2	1	5	Jy 77	29
McCunn, Donald H.	How to Make Sewing Patterns	TM			3	F/M 86	76
McDaniel, Claribel	Contemporary Tapestries, A Midwest Designer's Approach	H&C	13	1		Wi 62	9
McDonald, Julie Jensen	"In the Garden of Strange Gods" (Exhibit)	Fa	14	4		S/O 87	41
McDonald, Pat	Planning Stripes	Hw	2	4		Se 81	30
McElroy, Jane	Soft Boxes: Ritual for Our Common Life	Fa	10	2		M/A 83	21
McFadden, George A.	see Mitchell, Peter J.	H&C	24	2		M/A 73	33
McFeely, Nancy W.	Casual Cushions	SS&D	3	1	9	Wi 71	9
McGalliard, Lorraine	Free and Casual Look Wool Jacket, The	WJ	6	3	23	Wi 81	8
McGeary, Gay	Fancy Coverlet Fringes	Hw	2	5		No 81	38
McGillveray, Brenda	Stones & Symbols	SS&D	18	1	69	Wi 86	71
McGoveran, Mary	Crocheting Wearable Fabric	TM			9	F/M 87	62
McGown, Pearl E.	Lore and Lure of Hooked Rugs, The	H&C	18	3		Su 67	45
McGrane, Jean-Ann	see Clark, Nancy	Hw	7	4		S/O 86	12
McGrath, Judy Waldner	Dyes from Lichens and Plants	SS&D	9	4	36	Fa 78	81
McGrath, Judy Waldner	Dyes from Lichens and Plants	Iw	3	2		Wi 78	41
McGrath, Judy Waldner	Dyes from Lichens and Plants	Fa	5	4		J/A 78	59
McGreevy, Susan Brown; Andrew Hunter Whiteford	Translating Tradition: Basketry Arts of the San Juan Paiutes	WJ	11	1	41	Su 86	14
McGregor, Sheila	Complete Book of Traditional Fair Isle Knitting, The	Kn	2	1	3	F-W 85	78
McGregor, Sheila	Complete Book of Traditional Fair Isle Knitting, The	TM			9	F/M 87	74
McGregor, Sheila	Complete Book of Traditional Scandinavian Knitting, The	Kn	3	1	5	F-W 86	70
McGregor, Sheila	Traditional Knitting	Kn	2	1	3	F-W 85	78
McGuire, E. Patrick; Lois Moran	Pricing & Promotion	Hw	6	2		M/A 85	71
McGuire, Patricia	"Art Couture/Haute Couture" (Exhibit)	Fa	9	1		J/F 82	86
McGuire, Patricia	Best Foot Forward: The Weavers Guild of Pittsburgh	SS&D	7	1	25	Wi 75	41
McGuire, Patricia	Fiber Ten	Fa	4	6		N/D 77	26
McGuire, Patricia	Joan Russell: Space Series	Fa	12	4		J/A 85	18
McGuire, Patricia	Louise Pierucci: A Triumph of Tenacity	SS&D	6	4	24	Fa 75	41
McGuire, Patricia	Recent Success of Carole Lubove-Klein: An Inspiring Yarn, The	Fa	9	5		S/O 82	20
McGuire, Patricia	"Stitcherhood Is Powerful" (Exhibit)	Fa	5	6		N/D 78	68
McGurk, Cecilia R.	see Gibson, Gordon D.	TMJ	4	4		77	71
McHugh, Maureen Collins	Wet-Cleaning Coverlets	SS&D	1	3	3	Ju 70	6
McIlvain, Myra Hargrave	Bawdry History of a Precious Commodity, The	Fa	13	3		M/J 86	14
McIlvain, Myra Hargrave	Bobbin Lace: An Exquisite Labor of Love	Fa	13	3		M/J 86	14
McIntee, Polly	Sweater of Many Colors, A	S-O	11	2		Su 87	15
McIntosh, Joan W.	Open-Weave Altar Hanging	SS&D	4	2	14	Sp 73	15
McIntyre, Walter	Time Warp on the Coldstream	SS&D	15	4	60	Fa 84	50
McIver, Lucy	Attu Basketry	H&C	24	1		J/F 73	35
McKay, David	McKay Modern English — German Dictionary	H&C	6	4		Fa 55	60
McKay, David	McKay Modern English — Swedish Dictionary	H&C	6	4		Fa 55	60
McKay, Isabel	Weaving Down Under	H&C	15	3		Su 64	20
McKay, Wendy	Weaving a Bedspread — A Case Study	Hw	8	4		S/O 87	89
McKay, Wendy: Ann Thiamann, Lynn Giles	Cabrillo College Stroke Center (error-corrected Hw v2 n4 81 p22)	Hw	2	3		My 81	12
McKee, Barbara; Edwin McKee; Joyce Herold	Havasupai Baskets and their Makers: 1930-1940	TMJ	4	2		75	80
McKee, Edwin	see McKee, Barbara	TMJ	4	2		75	80
McKee, Marguerite	Notes from a Beginning Complex Weaver	CW		25		Se 87	3
McKeown, Alice	Webschule Sindelfingen	SS&D	6	3	23	Su 75	8

AUTHOR	TITLE	JOUR	VOL	NO	ISS	DATE	PAGE
McKinley, Esther D.	Gravander Spinners, Raising Funds to Buy a Camel, The	H&C	18	2		Sp 67	12
McKinley, Sally	Weigle—Hubbell Exhibit	SS&D	3	1	9	Wi 71	36
McManus, Fran	Importance of Quality in the Art of Dyeing, The	S-O	7	2		Su 83	10
McManus, Fran	Stanley Bulbach	S-O	8	2		Su 84	55
McMillan, Sam	George Brett: Webs of a Mad Spider	Fa	8	6		N/D 81	32
McMillan, Sue	Baskets of Doug Elliot: Connecting with the Natural World, The	Fa	11	1		J/F 84	71
McMorris, Penny	Crazy Quilts	Fa	12	4		J/A 85	48
McMorris, Penny	"Emerging Quiltmakers" (Exhibit)	Fa	12	1		J/F 85	75
McMorris, Penny; Michael, Kile	"Art Quilt, The" (Exhibit)	TM			7	O/N 86	30
McMullan, Joseph V.; Donald O. Reichert	George Walter Vincent and Belle Townsley Smith Collection of Islamic Rugs	TMJ	3	2		De 71	43
McNair, Peg	Design Exercises for Inspitarion and Fun	Fa	14	1		J/F 87	47
McNair, Peg	Evolution of an Artist: Peg McNair	Fa	14	5		N/D 87	19
McNair, Peg	Exercises in Design	SS&D	11	2	42	Sp 80	55
McNair, Peg	Fibers Unlimited 1980: Whatcom Textile Guild	Hw	2	3		My 81	20
McNair, Peg	Personal Comment, A	Fa	3	4		J/A 76	32
McNeal, Dr. Lyle G.	Churro Sheep in the Navajo Tradition	WJ	10	2	38	Fa 85	31
McNeill, Mary	Weaving in Donegal (error-corrected H&C v23 n3 72 p11)	H&C	23	2		M/A 72	35
McNinch, Janet	Hops Strainers and Humouous Creatures	SS&D	3	1	9	Wi 71	26
McPherson, Maggie	Lacy Mohair Vest, A	S-O	10	2		Su 86	18
McRae, Annette	Raising Flax in Your Garden	S-O	3			79	4
McWilliams, Cheryl	see Jackson, Mary Lynn	SS&D	15	2	58	Sp 84	13
Mead, S. M.	Art of Taaniko Weaving, The	SS&D	4	1	13	Wi 72	34
Mead, S. M.	Traditional Maori Clothing—A Study of Technological Change	SS&D	8	1	29	WI 76	71
Meaney, Elaine	I Ching	SS&D	3	2	10	Sp 72	22
Meany, Janet	Profile of an HGA Rep	SS&D	17	1	65	Wi 85	89
Meany, Janet	Weaver's Commission Workshop	SS&D	10	3	39	Su 79	40
Meany, Janet K.	Log Cabin Rag Rugs	WJ	9	4	36	Sp 85	50
Meany, Janet K.	Rag Rug Traditions	WJ	9	4	36	Sp 85	56
Meany, Janet K.	Six Songs of Success	SS&D	18	3	71	Su 87	69
Meedam, Hanne	see Hamre, Ida	WJ	6	4	24	Sp 82	58
Meek, M. Kati	Lithuanian Pervarai: Producing a Twenty Shaft Pattern on a Twelve Shaft Loom	AT	1			De 83	159
Meek, M. Kati	Traditional Lithuanian Weaving in Chicago	SS&D	17	3	67	Su 86	50
Meigs, Margaret Wister	Weaving at Fort Hunter Museum	H&C	4	2		Sp 53	26
Meilach, Dona	Basketry...A New Approach to an Old Art Form	Fa	4	1		J/F 77	16
Meilach, Dona	Fiber Artists Find New Showcase in San Diego (Exhibit)	Fa	3	4		J/A 76	8
Meilach, Dona	Macramé: Creative Design in Knotting	H&C	22	2		Sp 71	43
Meilach, Dona	Modern Approach to Basketry with Fibers and Grasses, A	Fa	4	1		J/F 77	43
Meilach, Dona; Dee Menagh	Basketry Today with Materials from Nature	WJ	4	4	16	Ap 80	26
Meilach, Dona; Dee Menagh	Basketry Today, with Materials from Nature	Fa	7	2		M/A 80	22
Meilach, Dona; Lee E. Snow	Weaving Off-Loom	H&C	24	4		Au 73	5
Meilach, Dona Z.	Clamp and Discharge Demonstration (error-corrected Fa v5 n3 78 p3)	Fa	5	1		J/F 78	45
Meilach, Dona Z.	Creating Art from Fibers and Fabrics	SS&D	4	2	14	Sp 73	44
Meilach, Dona Z.	Creating Art from Fibers and Fabrics	H&C	24	2		M/A 73	5
Meilach, Dona Z.	Macrame Accessories	SS&D	4	3	15	Su 73	53
Meilach, Dona Z.	Manipulated Rope	Fa	5	1		J/F 78	46
Meilach, Dona Z.	Marian Clayden: Fabric Dyer	Fa	5	1		J/F 78	43
Meilach, Dona Z.	"Mingei — The Folk Arts of Japan" (Exhibit)	Fa	4	2		M/A 77	10
Meilach, Dona Z.	Serina Sherwin: Interview	Fa	4	6		N/D 77	49
Meilach, Dona Z.	"Toys and Games" (Exhibit)	Fa	4	1		J/F 77	7

AUTHOR	TITLE	JOUR	VOL	NO	ISS	DATE	PAGE
Meilach, Dona Z.; Jay Hinz; Bill Hinz	How to Create Your Own Designs	SS&D	6	4	24	Fa 75	31
Meilach, Dona Z.; Lee Erlin Snow	Weaving Off-Loom	SS&D	4	4	16	Fa 73	63
Meilach, Donna	Making Contemporary Rugs and Wall Hangings	H&C	21	3		Su 70	41
Meiling, Nancy	Bags	WJ	6	3	23	Wi 81	40
Meisch, Lynn A.	Fullus: Ikat Blankets of Tarabuco, Bolivia	WJ	10	1	37	Su 85	54
Meisch, Lynn A.	Spinning in Bolivia	S-O	10	1		Sp 86	25
Meisch, Lynn Ann	Costume and Weaving in Saraguro, Ecuador	TMJ	19 20			80,81	55
Meisch, Lynn Ann	Spinning in Ecuador	S-O	4			80	24
Melen	see Hoppe	H&C	26	3		M/J 75	30
Melen, L.	see Hoppe, E.	SS&D	6	3	23	Su 75	49
Mellen, Patricia	State Parks Feature Kentucky Crafts	H&C	26	3		M/J 75	9
Mellqvist-Johansson, Sylvia	see Johnson, Astrid	Hw	5	2		M/A 84	13
Meloy, Margaret	"Contemporary Directions in Fiber" (Exhibit)	Fa	14	4		S/O 87	42
Meloy, Margaret	"Jacque Parsley: Collage, A New Direction" (Exhibit)	Fa	11	6		N/D 84	76
Meloy, Margaret	Lida Gordon	Fa	13	5		S/O 86	19
Meloy, Margaret	"Lida Gordon: Recent Works" (Exhibit)	Fa	10	4		J/A 83	63
Meloy, Margaret	"Robin Becker and Joan Lintault: Visual Traces of the Past" (Exhibit)	Fa	11	1		J/F 84	80
Meloy, Margaret	"Web of Kentucky Thread, A" (Exhibit)	Fa	12	5		S/O 85	72
Meltzer, Bonnie	Alice's Apron	SS&D	5	2	18	Sp 74	29
Meltzer, Marilyn	But Is It Tapestry?	SS&D	5	3	19	Su 74	39
Meltzer, Marilyn	Weave It! 28 Projects for your Home	Hw	3	2		Mr 82	20
Meltzer, Marilyn	Weave It! 28 Projects for Your Home	WJ	8	4	32	Sp 84	66
Meltzer, Marilyn	Weave It! 28 Projects for Your Home (error-corrected WJ v6 n4 82 p61)	WJ	6	3	23	Wi 81	60
Meltzer, Steve	Photographing Your Craft Work	WJ	11	4	44	Sp 87	74
Meltzer, Steve	Photographing Your Craftwork; a Hands-On Guide for Craftspeople	Hw	7	3		M/J 86	12
Meltzer, Steve	Photographing Your Craftwork: A Hands-On Guide for Craftspeople	Fa	14	3		M/J 87	64
Meltzer, Steve	Photographing Your Fiber Art	Fa	10	4		J/A 83	35
Meltzer-Smith, Sandra Jo	Mushroom Dyes	SS&D	11	3	43	Su 80	53
Menagh, Dee	see Meilach, Dona	WJ	4	4	16	Ap 80	26
Menagh, Dee	see Meilach, Dona	Fa	7	2		M/A 80	22
Mendelson, Linda	Knitting Machine: A Creative Tool, The	Fa	5	3		M/J 78	32
Meneghini, Adelchi	see Reali, Glauco	Hw	7	1		J/F 86	18
Mercer, Linda	see Berent, Mary	S-O	11	1		Sp 87	21
Mercer, Paul	Tied Up in Knots	H&C	22	2		Sp 71	9
Mercer, Paul	Wool — Plants — Color	H&C	22	1		Wi 71	12
Merisalo, Viivi	see Pyysalo, Helvi	SS&D	2	2	6	Sp 71	34
Merrill, Ruth	Approaching the Workshop: A Teacher's Perspective	S-O	7	2		Su 83	52
Merrill, Ruth R.; Barbara M. Haight	Barbara 'n Me on Lichening and Learning	SS&D	7	2	26	Sp 76	34
Merrimack Valley Textile Museum	Homespun to Factory Made: Woolen Textiles in America, 1776–1876	SS&D	10	1	37	Wi 78	77
Merrit, Francis S.	Haystack Mountain School of Crafts, The	H&C	3	1		Wi 51	29
Merritt, Elveana	Figured Bead Leno Lace	WJ	6	1	21	Su 81	50
Merritt, Elveana	Four Harness Damask — A Pick-up Weave	WJ	5	1	17	Su 80	20
Mershon, Janis	Studies in Boundweave	SS&D	12	2	46	Sp 81	50
Metchette, Glenna	Spinning Fancy Yarns	SS&D	14	1	53	Wi 82	16
Metzler, Sandra	Family Album of Pomo Baskets, A	Fa	11	1		J/F 84	63
Metzler-Smith, Sandra J.	Documenting Your Textile Collection	Fa	9	5		S/O 82	55
Meyer, Florence	"Dione Christensen Fiberworks" (Exhibit)	Fa	6	2		M/A 79	63
Meyer, Peggy Frost	Yarn Design: The Fine Points in Black and White	WJ	12	2	46	Fa 87	38
Meyer, Zach	"Fibers" (Exhibit)	Fa	4	4		J/A 77	11

AUTHOR	TITLE	JOUR	VOL	NO	ISS	DATE	PAGE
Meyerowitz, Carol Orlove	Jews of Kurdistan, The	SS&D	14	2	54	Sp 83	23
Meyers, Judith Philipp	Pieces of History	Fa	14	5		N/D 87	54
Meyers, Ruth Nordquist, ed.	Notebook: Adapting Large Overshot Patterns	SS&D	14	4	56	Fa 83	16
Meyers, Ruth Nordquist, ed.	Notebook: Floats on the Surface (Betty Hagedorn)	SS&D	14	3	55	Su 83	90
Meyers, Ruth Nordquist, ed.	Notebook: Floats on the Surface (Diane Ruch)	SS&D	14	3	55	Su 83	90
Meyers, Ruth Nordquist, ed.	Notebook: Floats on the Surface (Esther Flory)	SS&D	14	3	55	Su 83	90
Meyers, Ruth Nordquist, ed.	Notebook: Floats on the Surface (Helen Cronk, Susan Orr)	SS&D	14	3	55	Su 83	90
Meyers, Ruth Nordquist, ed.	Notebook: Warmables (Alice Millette)	SS&D	15	1	57	Wi 83	80
Meyers, Ruth Nordquist, ed.	Notebook: Warmables (Judy Healey)	SS&D	15	1	57	Wi 83	80
Meyers, Ruth Nordquist, ed.	Notebook: Warmables (Nancy Britton)	SS&D	15	1	57	Wi 83	80
Michael, Kile	see McMorris, Penny	TM		7		O/N 86	30
Michaelis, Aimida	Rag Rugs	SS&D	2	4	8	Fa 71	25
+ Michaels-Paque, J.	Mathematical Design Concepts Relative to Aesthetic Concerns	AT	8			De 87	155
+ Michaels-Paque, Joan	Creative and Conceptual Analysis of Textiles, A	SS&D	12	2	46	Sp 81	74
+ Michaels-Paque, Joan	Cynthia Laymon: Pleated Interplay	Fa	12	5		S/O 85	12
+ Michaels-Paque, Joan	Syllabus for Success	SS&D	15	3	59	Su 84	11
Michels, Caroll	How to Survive & Prosper as an Artist	Hw	6	2		M/A 85	71
Mick, Catherine	From Elegance to Rag Weaving	WJ	7	3	27	Wi 82	64
Mickelson, Sylvia	Family Patterns	SS&D	2	4	8	Fa 71	17
Mies, Mary; Betty Bernstein	Some New Rules for Dyeing	SS&D	11	3	43	Su 80	9
Mikosch, Elisabeth	Catalogue of Kashmir Shawls in The Textile Museum	TMJ	24			85	23
Mikosch, Elisabeth	Scent of Flowers, Kishmir Shawls in the Collection of The Textile Museum, The	TMJ	24			85	7
Mikosch, Elizabeth	Kashmir East and West	TM		9		F/M 87	14
Milbank, Caroline Rennolds	Couture: The Great Designers	TM		8		D/J 86	72
Miles, Candice St. Jacques	Fabric of Creativity: Weaving Together Left– and Right–Brain Activites, The	Fa	11	6		N/D 84	44
Miles, Candice St. Jacques	Sally McKenna Walker's Sculpture: Tension Resolved Through Balance	Fa	11	4		J/A 84	14
Miles, Charles	Indian and Eskimo Artifacts of North America	H&C	14	3		Su 63	43
Miles, Miska	Annie and the Old One	Iw	2	1		Fa 76	33
Miles, Vera	Practical Four-Shaft Weaving	H&C	14	3		Su 63	43
Millard, Nancy	Handspun Crochet Book, The	S-O	8	4		Wi 84	11
Millen, Roger	Weave Your Own Tweeds	H&C	7	1		Wi 55	59
Miller, Bruce W.; Jim Widess	Caner's Handbook, The	Hw	6	5		N/D 85	20
Miller, Bruce W.; Jim Widess	Caner's Handbook, The	Fa	11	4		J/A 84	54
Miller, Carolyn A.	Contemporary Handweaving for the Home, Memphis Guild Exhibition	H&C	10	2		Sp 59	20
Miller, Dorothy	Banana, Ramie, and Hemp in Okinawa (error-corrected Fa v14 n3 87 p4)	Fa	14	2		M/A 87	46
Miller, Dorothy	From Seed to Dye	Iw	4	1		Wi 78	55
Miller, Dorothy	Hanaori: An Okinawan Brocaded Textile	AT	1			De 83	173
Miller, Dorothy	Indigo from Seed to Dye	Hw	3	4		Se 82	16
Miller, Dorothy	Indigo, From Seed to Dye	WJ	7	2	26	Fa 82	58
Miller, Dorothy	Indigo: From Seed to Dye	TM		2		D/J 85	76
Miller, Dorothy	Indigo: From Seed to Dye	PWC	3	3	9		68
Miller, Dorothy	Kumejima Dorozome: The Vegetable Dye and Mud Mordanting Process of Silk Tsugumi	AT	5			Ju 86	131
Miller, Dorothy	Miyako Jofu	AT	7			Ju 87	85
Miller, Dorothy	Personal Exploration of Indigo, A	Fa	13	5		S/O 86	32
Miller, Dorothy	Shifu: A Handwoven Paper Textile	Hw	6	3		Su 85	69
Miller, Dorothy	Shifu: A Handwoven Paper Textile of Japan	AT	4			De 85	43
Miller, Edward	Textiles: Properties & Behaviour	H&C	20	4		Fa 69	41
Miller, Ethel E.	Oscar Knopf's Ingenious Invention	H&C	10	2		Sp 59	24
Miller, Gammy	Gammy Miller: Coiled Poems	Fa	11	6		N/D 84	16

AUTHOR	TITLE	JOUR	VOL	NO	ISS	DATE	PAGE
Miller, Irene Preston	Possessed by Color	TM			3	F/M 86	71
Miller, Kristin	Medallion Quilting	TM			14	D/J 87	60
Miller, Lynn F.; Sally S. Swenson	Lives and Works, Talks with Women Artists	Fa	9	2		M/A 82	58
Miller, Mary Ann	The Longest Warp in the World or, The Double Two-Tie Unit Threading System	CW	3	3	9	Ap 82	2
Miller, Mary Jane	How I Design	TM			8	D/J 86	10
Miller, Suzanne	Flax	WJ	7	2	26	Fa 82	12
Millett, Sandra	Punch and Poke Quilting Without Thimbles	TM			7	ON 86	32
Milner, Ann	I Can Spin a Different Thread	Iw	5	3		Su 80	70
Mimoso, Sophie	Maralyce Ferree: Dual-Purpose Weavings	Fa	7	2		M/A 80	12
Minard, Juanita	Summer and Winter — A Stock of Options	SS&D	10	3	39	Su 79	42
Mincoff, Elizabeth; Margaret S. Marriage	Pillow Lace	H&C	2	2		Sp 51	61
Minichiello-Winters, Antoinette	see Goldberg, Barbara	Fa	9	3		M/J 82	25
Minkowitz, Norma	Norma Minkowitz	Fa	13	3		M/J 86	26
Minster, Marjorie	Bind Your Weaving Records with Weaving	SS&D	9	3	35	Su 78	66
Minton, Mary Cain	North California Conference	H&C	12	3		Su 61	30
Minton, Mary Cain	Northern California Conference	H&C	13	3		Su 62	16
Minton, Mary Cain	Northern California Conference	H&C	14	3		Su 63	20
Minton, Mary Cain	Northern California Conference	H&C	15	4		Fa 64	29
Mintzer, Arlene	Handspun: Inspiration from Commercial Sources	S-O	10	2		Su 86	33
Mitchell, Alison	Kumejima Kasuri: A Visit to a Remote Japanese Silk Center	WJ	10	1	37	Su 85	59
Mitchell, Alison	Preparing Silk in Kumejima	WJ	10	2	38	Fa 85	53
Mitchell, Lillias	Irish Spinning, Dyeing and Weaving: An Anthology	SS&D	18	3	71	Su 87	73
Mitchell, Lillias	Wonderful Work of the Weaver, The	SS&D	4	4	16	Fa 73	63
Mitchell, Peter	Name Drafting	Hw	3	2		Mr 82	34
Mitchell, Peter J.; George A. McFadden	Making a Bobbin Winder	H&C	24	2		M/A 73	22
Mitchell, Suzanne	Felting Knit Mohair	TM			13	O/N 87	66
Mitiguy, Harriet	New Hampshire Gives Dyeshop	SS&D	3	3	11	Su 72	21
Moes, Dini	Beating the Button(hole) Blues	SS&D	15	2	58	Sp 84	64
Moes, Dini	Coordinates	SS&D	15	4	60	Fa 84	46
Moes, Dini	Gala Raincoat	WJ	6	3	23	Wi 81	12
Moes, Dini	Horizontal Ribs & Vertical Cords	SS&D	17	4	68	Fa 86	84
Moes, Dini	Huck for Mary Black	SS&D	16	2	62	Sp 85	52
Moes, Dini	Lining the Overshot	SS&D	13	4	52	Fa 82	64
Moes, Dini	Monk's Belt	SS&D	18	4	72	Fa 87	52
Moes, Dini	One Fabric: 2 Faces	SS&D	14	2	54	Sp 83	16
Moes, Dini	Promise Kept, A	SS&D	16	3	63	Su 85	63
Moes, Dini	Reeds Too Fine? There is a Way	SS&D	14	4	56	Fa 83	27
Moes, Dini	Rugs for the Dream Auction	SS&D	17	2	66	Sp 86	58
Moes, Dini	Saint Severus: Parton Saint of Weavers	SS&D	16	2	62	Sp 85	58
Moes, Dini	Take Advantage of Turned Drafts	SS&D	13	2	50	Sp 82	58
Moes, Dini	Three in One	SS&D	18	2	70	Sp 87	74
Moes, Dini	Warping in Color	SS&D	14	4	56	Fa 83	24
Mohamed, M. H.	see Lord, P. R.	WJ	8	2	30	Fa 83	64
Moldovan, George	"Fabric/Nexus: New Connections" (Exhibit)	Fa	10	3		M/J 83	70
Molinari, Jean	Northwest Spinners: Success for Them, A Challenge for You	S-O	11	2		Su 87	50
Molnar, Gail	Give and Take of Apprenticeship: An Apprentice's Version, The	Fa	8	4		J/A 81	25
Moncrieff, R. W.	Wool Shrinkage and Its Prevention	H&C	6	2		Sp 55	61
Monico, Michele	Didier Legrand: Magic Afoot	Fa	12	4		J/A 85	12
Montgomery, Florence	Printed Textiles, English & American Cottons & Linens, 1700 — 1850	H&C	22	1		Wi 71	41
Montgomery, Larry	Piecing Cloth to Harness the Wind	TM			11	J/J 87	48

AUTHOR	TITLE	JOUR	VOL	NO	ISS	DATE	PAGE
Montgomery, Larry	Textile Apprenticeship in Northern California	TM			9	F/M 87	20
Montgomery, Larry	These Toes Won't Drown in Tears of Clown	TM			11	J/J 87	14
Montgomery, Pauline	Indiana Coverlet Weavers and Their Coverlets	SS&D	7	1	25	Wi 75	34
Montgomery, Pauline	Indiana Coverlet Weavers and their Coverlets	TMJ	4	2		75	81
Moody, Ella, ed.	Decorative Art in Modern Interiors 1963/64	H&C	15	1		Wi 64	43
Moon, Ellen	Creating Textures: V–, Ridge, and Post Stitches	TM			11	J/J 87	60
Moon, Ellen	Crochet Inspired by the Trees	TM			11	J/J 87	56
Mooney, David R.	Braiding Triaxial Weaves: Enhancements and Design for Artworks	AT	5			Ju 86	9
Mooney, David R.	Handweaving Triaxial Weaves with Braiding Techniques: Triaxial Braiding	AT	3			My 85	99
Mooney, David R.	Triaxial Weaves and Weaving: An Exploration for Hand Weavers	AT	2			De 84	9
Moore, Carla S.	Brushing Cotton	WJ	11	2	42	Fa 86	38
Moore, Gen	Twenty-Harness Madness	SS&D	12	4	48	Fa 81	46
Moore, Marcia	Reiko Mochinaga Brandon: Bridging Two Cultures	Fa	13	6		N/D 86	16
Moorman, Theo	Toward Abstraction and Simplicity	SS&D	3	1	9	Wi 71	30
Moorman, Theo	Weaving as an Art Form	H&C	26	5		Oc 75	12
Moorman, Theo	Weaving as an Art Form—A Personal Statement	SS&D	6	4	24	Fa 75	30
Moran, Lois	see McGuire, E. Patrick	Hw	6	2		M/A 85	71
Morgan, Gwen	Traditional Knitting	Kn	2	1	3	F-W 85	79
Morgenstern, Marvin M.	Thirty Twill Variations	H&C	22	3		Su 71	42
Morgenstern, Marvin M.	Whig Rose Study	WJ	7	2	26	Fa 82	40
Morgenstern, Marvin M.	Whig Rose Study (continued)	WJ	7	3	27	Wi 82	23
Morgret, Eugene D.	Handspun Yarns Made by the Blind	H&C	1	3		Fa 50	17
Moroney, Anne-Marie	Black Welsh Mountain Sheep	S-O	11	4		Wi 87	51
Morris, Barbara J.	William Morris, A Twentieth Century View of His Woven Textiles	H&C	12	2		Sp 61	6
Morris, Barbara J.	William Morris, His Designs for Carpets & Tapestries	H&C	12	4		Fa 61	18
Morris, Betty	see Hansen, Debby	H&C	24	3		M/J 73	43
Morris, Betty	Weaving in the Marketplace	H&C	24	3		M/J 73	42
Morris, Gitta	Making Clothes in Colonial Style	TM			6	A/S 86	20
Morris, Sandy	Block Sweater	Kn	2	1	3	F-W 85	56
Morris, Walter F. Jr.	Millenium of Weaving in Chiapas, A	WJ	10	1	37	Su 85	87
Morrison, Arline K.	Experimental Stitchery and Other Fiber Techniques	Fa	4	3		M/J 77	53
Morrison, Harriet B.	New Hampshire Weavers, The	H&C	1	2		Su 50	54
Morrison, Lois	Layered Trapunto	TM			12	A/S 87	50
Morrison, Phylis	Spiders' Games	Fa	8	4		J/A 81	41
Morrison, Phylis	Spider's Games, A Book for Beginner Weavers	WJ	7	2	26	Fa 82	60
Morrison, Phylis	Spider's Games: A Book for Beginning Weavers	SS&D	11	3	43	Su 80	74
Morrison, Ruth	Satin Piqué	PWC	4	3	13		34
Morrison, Ruth	see Glaves, Jeannine	S-O	9	4		Wi 85	16
Morrison, Ruth	Tablecloth in Bergman Weave	PWC	4	4	14		38
Morrison, Skye	Learning to See Pattern	TM			2	D/J 85	44
Morrison, Skye	Making a Square Kite with a Long Tail	Fa	5	4		J/A 78	40
Morrison, Skye	Skye Morrison: Yours on a Kite String	Fa	5	4		J/A 78	36
Morrow, Mable	Navajo: Textiles, Blankets, Rugs, Tapestries	SS&D	1	4	4	Se 70	3
Morrow, Mable	Navajo: Textiles, Blankets, Rugs, Tapestries	SS&D	2	1	5	De 70	5
Morse, Marcia	"Filaments of the Imagination" (Exhibit)	Fa	8	4		J/A 81	69
Morse, Marcia	Paper as Fiber	SS&D	15	3	59	Su 84	20
Morse, Martha	Mary E. Heickman, Texas Weaver and Teacher	H&C	17	3		Su 66	18
Mortensen, Diane	Microwave Dyeing	SS&D	10	4	40	Fa 79	12
Mortensen, Diane L.	Supplementary Warps: The One-Shuttle Solution (error-corrected SS&D v19 n1 87 p33)	SS&D	18	4	72	Fa 87	66
Moshimer, Joan	Rug Hooking: The Flourishing of a Time-Honored Technique	Fa	7	5		S/O 80	37
Moss, A. J. Ernest	Textiles and Fabrics — Their Care and Preservation	H&C	14	1		Wi 63	44
Moss, Gillian	Embroidered Samplers in the Collection of the Cooper-Hewitt Museum	WJ	9	1	33	Su 84	60

AUTHOR	TITLE	JOUR	VOL	NO	ISS	DATE	PAGE
Moss, Helen E.	Kumihimo: The Art of Japanese Braiding	Fa	14	1		J/F 87	20
Mudge, Christine	Damask	lw	6	1		Wi 80	46
Mudge, Christine S.	Finishing Wool and Linen	SS&D	9	3	35	Su 78	41
Mueller, Cynthia	Window Pane Delivery Blanket	PWC	3	1	7		8
Mühling, Ernst	Book of Batik, The	H&C	18	4		Fa 67	45
Muir, David	Binding and Repairing Books by Hand	Fa	6	4		J/A 79	16
Mulders, Lydia	Woven Murals	H&C	13	2		Sp 62	22
Mulkey, Philip O.	Handweaver's Jacquard Loom, A	H&C	7	4		Fa 56	46
Muller, Ann	Are You Buying a Loom? Some Points to Consider	H&C	2	1		Wi 50	25
Muller, Ann	Spinning Lesson, A	H&C	2	3		Su 51	17
Muller, Donna	Brighton Honeycomb	CW	5	3	15	My 84	12
Muller, Donna	Designing Four-Shaft Double Weaves	WJ	7	4	28	Sp 83	56
Muller, Magdalena	Computer Interacts: Programming the Pattern, The	SS&D	7	2	26	Sp 76	72
Muller, Marion	Containers of Human Experience: Fragments from the Life of Lois Polansky	Fa	14	5		N/D 87	32
Mumford, Lewis	"Art and Technics"	CW	2	1	4	Oc 80	4
Mundal, Maria	Aaklae Weaving	H&C	5	1		Wi 53	20
Mundal, Maria	Alphabet of Weaving, The	H&C	11	3		Su 60	59
Mundal, Maria	Rug Techniques	H&C	11	3		Su 60	59
Mundt, Ernest	Primer of Visual Art, A	H&C	4	1		Wi 52	62
Munro, Eleanor	Originals: American Women Artists	lw	5	4		Fa 80	76
Murphy, Mathilda C.	Church Paraments in Crackle Weave	SS&D	5	3	19	Su 74	54
Murray	Practical Modern Weaving	Fa	3	1		J/F 76	6
Murray, Bessie R.	see Black, Mary E.	SS&D	6	3	23	Su 75	50
Murray, Clare	Junque Quilts	Fa	14	4		S/O 87	6
Murray, Clare M.	Clare M. Murray	Fa	13	6		N/D 86	2
Murray, Gwen B.	Cotswold	S-O	11	1		Sp 87	47
Murray, Megan	"Art to Wear" (Exhibit)	Fa	11	1		J/F 84	76
Murray, Megan	"Fiber from the Marietta College Crafts National" (Exhibit)	Fa	11	2		M/A 84	76
Murray, Megan	Maskmaker Ralph Lee: Master Minding a Ghoulish Event	Fa	11	5		S/O 84	34
Murray, Megan	St. John's Cathedral Project	Fa	10	4		J/A 83	45
Murray, Megan	Textile Study Room: Metropolitan Museum, The	Fa	10	3		M/J 83	49
Murray, Rosemary	Essential Handbook of Weaving, The	Hw	3	1		Ja 82	20
Murray, Rosemary	Essential Handbook of Weaving, The	WJ	7	4	28	Sp 83	48
Murrow, Romedy	Dealing with Dog Hair	S-O	8	1		Sp 84	36
Murrow, Romedy	Learning the Flax of Life	S-O	9	3		Fa 85	49
Murtha, Judith Rush	Application of Computer Generated Weaves As Texture Maps, The	AT	3			My 85	75
Museum of International Folk Art	Spanish Textile Traditions of New Mexico and Colorado	Fa	6	6		N/D 79	51
Museum of New Mexico Press	Spanish Textile Tradition of New Mexico and Colorado	WJ	4	3	15	Ja 80	45
Museum of the Sinkiang-Uighur Antonomous Region	Silk Road: Fabrics from the Han to the T'ang Dynasty, The	TMJ	4	2		75	81
Musgrave, Belinda	Blouses, Shirts and Tops	Hw	8	2		M/A 87	14
Mustard, Frances E.	Easy Dyeing	lw	3	2		Wi 78	43
Myers, Diana K.	Temple, Household, Horseback: Rugs of the Tibetan Plateau	WJ	10	4	40	Sp 86	82
Myers, Diana K; Arthur Alden Lepper; Valrae Reynolds	Temple, Household, Horseback: Rugs of the Tibetan Plateau	Fa	13	2		M/A 86	41
Myers, Patricia Flaherty	see Cabrera, Roberto	TM			7	O/N 86	72
Myers, Ruth, ed.	Designer' Notebook	SS&D	12	2	46	Sp 81	29
Myers, Ruth, ed.	Early Fabrics	SS&D	12	3	47	Su 81	67
Myers, Ruth, ed.	Eight-Harness Check (Diane Fabeck)	SS&D	12	2	46	Sp 81	29
Myers, Ruth, ed.	Four-Harness Check (Eleanor Chase)	SS&D	12	2	46	Sp 81	29
Myers, Ruth, ed.	Notebook: Blouse Fabric (Avis Black) (error-corrected SS&D v17 n3 86 p5)	SS&D	12	3	47	Su 81	67

AUTHOR	TITLE	JOUR	VOL	NO	ISS	DATE	PAGE
Myers, Ruth, ed.	Notebook: Linsey-Woolsey (Ann Wedig)	SS&D	12	3	47	Su 81	67
Myers, Ruth, ed.	Notebook: Plain Weave on Spaced Warp (Alice Johnson)	SS&D	12	3	47	Su 81	67
Myers, Ruth, ed.	Notebook: Popcorn Weave (Sigrid Piroch)	SS&D	12	3	47	Su 81	66
Myers, Ruth, ed.	Notebook: Two- or Four-Harness Check (Marion Gaum)	SS&D	12	2	46	Sp 81	28
Myers, Ruth, ed.	Notebook: Two-Harness Log Cabin (Betty LaFara)	SS&D	12	2	46	Sp 81	28
Myers, Ruth Nordquist	Notebook: One Fabric — Two Faces	SS&D	13	2	50	Sp 82	16
Myers, Ruth Nordquist, ed.	Notebook: And the Threading is Easy	SS&D	13	4	52	Fa 82	12
Myers, Ruth Nordquist, ed.	Notebook: Baby Blankets and Afghans	SS&D	12	4	48	Fa 81	50
Myers, Ruth Nordquist, ed.	Notebook: Color Notes	SS&D	15	2	58	Sp 84	80
Myers, Ruth Nordquist, ed.	Notebook: Dusting Off the Inkle Loom	SS&D	14	1	53	Wi 82	44
Myers, Ruth Nordquist, ed.	Notebook: Some Light Behind the Weave	SS&D	13	3	51	Su 82	16
Myers, Ruth Nordquist, ed.	Notebook: Some Light Behind the Weave (Barbara Keller)	SS&D	13	3	51	Su 82	16
Myers, Ruth Nordquist, ed.	Notebook: Some Light Behind the Weave (Lucile Landis)	SS&D	13	3	51	Su 82	16
Myers, Ruth Nordquist, ed.	Notebook: Some Light Behind the Weave (Manasota Weavers)	SS&D	13	3	51	Su 82	16
Myers, Ruth Nordquist, ed.	Notebook:"Someday" File, The (Jeanean Middlebrooks)	SS&D	15	3	59	Su 84	66
Myers, Ruth Nordquist, ed.	Notebook:"Someday" File, The (Maggie Weyers)	SS&D	15	3	59	Su 84	66
Myers, Ruth Nordquist, ed.	Notebook:"Someday" File, The (Maxine Bickenstaff)	SS&D	15	3	59	Su 84	66
Myers, Ruth Nordquist,ed.	Notebook: "Someday" File, The (Wisconsin Fedeeration of Handweavers)	SS&D	15	3	59	Su 84	66
Myers, Ruth Nordquist, ed.	Notebook: Swivel, A Method of Treadling	SS&D	14	2	54	Sp 83	8
Myers, Ruth Nordquist, ed.	Notebook: Tartans	SS&D	13	1	49	Wi 81	24
Myers, Virginia D., ed.	Directions 1970	SS&D	2	3	7	Su 71	26
Myrinx, Elaine	Open Jurying in Pittsburg: Putting Your Work on the Line (Exhibit)	Fa	6	2		M/A 79	23
Nadeau, Elphege	I Say It's Easier Than It Sounds	H&C	4	4		Fa 53	44
Nagai-Berthrong, E.	see Vollmer, John E.	WJ	8	4	32	Sp 84	66
Nager, Sandra	Rapt with Ribbons	TM			12	A/S 87	14
Nakamura, Ann K.	Making Paper Cranes: A Hawaiian Wedding Ritual	Fa	13	6		N/D 86	9
Nakano, Eisha; Barbara B. Stephan	Japanese Stencil Dyeing: Paste Resist Techniques	Hw	6	3		Su 85	14
Nakano, Eisha; Barbara B. Stephan	Japanese Stencil Dyeing: Paste Resist Techniques	WJ	8	1	29	Su 83	51
Nakano, Eisha; Barbara B. Stephan	Japanese Stencil Dyeing: Paste-Resist Techniques	Fa	10	3		M/J 83	53
Nappen, Barbara	In the Web of Superstition: Myths and Folktales About Nets	Fa	9	3		M/J 82	30
Nash, Dominic	Warp Painting: A Manual for Weavers	WJ	6	3	23	Wi 81	59
Nash, Dominie	Warp Painting: A Manual for Weavers	Hw	3	5		N/D 82	12
Nash, Jeanne; Jeanne Schmelzer	Cristi — Sketch of a Guatemalan Weaver	Iw	5	4		Fa 80	28
Nass, Ulla	Complex "Harness Lace"	SS&D	9	3	35	Su 78	4
Nass, Ulla	Gifts from Ancient Peru	WJ	8	1	29	Su 83	32
Nass, Ulla	Harness Lace	SS&D	9	4	36	Fa 78	80
Nass, Ulla	Harness Lace	WJ	7	3	27	Wi 82	48
Nass, Ulla	"Harness Lace:" A New Leno Set-Up	SS&D	8	2	30	Sp 77	56
Nass, Ulla	Harness-Lace	Iw	3	3		Sp 78	50
Nass, Ulla	Weaves of the Incas	Hw	3	2		Mr 82	20
Nass, Ulla	Weaves of the Incas	WJ	6	4	24	Sp 82	58
Nathans, Barbara	Christening Blanket	S-O	4			80	60
National Woolcrafts Festival	National Woolcrafts Festival—Taranaki 1983 Pattern Book	WJ	8	2	30	Fa 83	62
Natural Colored Wool Growers Association	Fleece Directory	S-O	3			79	10
Naumann, Rose; Raymond Hull	Off-Loom Weaving Book, The	SS&D	4	4	16	Fa 73	63
Nava, Marinella	Book of Knitting, The	TM			9	F/M 87	76
Navajo School of Indian Basketry	Indian Basket Weaving	H&C	23	3		M/J 72	24
Navajo School of Indian Basketry	Indian Basket Weaving	Iw	4	2		Sp 79	63
Neal, Avon	see Parker, Ann	Iw	4	2		Sp 79	63
Neal, Avon	see Parker, Ann	Fa	5	2		M/A 78	58

AUTHOR	TITLE	JOUR	VOL	NO	ISS	DATE	PAGE
Neale, Mary Beth	Two Tubes in Double Weave (error-corrected SS&D v5 n4 74 p69)	SS&D	5	3	19	Su 74	8
Nebesar, Rebecca Lanxner	Drafter, The Draper, The Flat Patternmaker, The	TM		11		J/J 87	33
Nebesar, Rebecca Lanxner	Fitting the Fitted Sleeve	TM		9		F/M 87	28
Nebesar, Rebecca Lanxner	Poetry of Sleeves: Shaping and Sewing Cloth to Fit the Arm, The	TM		9		F/M 87	24
Nebesar, Rebecca Lanxner	Sewing a Set-In Sleeve	TM		9		F/M 87	27
Nechin, Sue	Art-to-Wear Markets, The	Fa	11	3		M/J 84	54
Needham, Bertha B.	Huckaback Lace, A Study of Fabric Structure	H&C	12	3		Su 61	26
Needle and Bobbin Club	Bulletin of the Needle and Bobbin Club, The	WJ	8	2	30	Fa 83	66
Neeland, Muriel M.	Michigan League of Handweavers	H&C	17	4		Fa 66	18
Neely, Cynthia H.	Double-Weave Pick-Up	TM		8		D/J 86	36
Neely, Cynthia H.	Three-Color, Weft-Faced Block Weave	SS&D	15	2	58	Sp 84	74
Neff, Ivan C,; Carol V. Maggs	Dictionary of Oriental Rugs	Fa	7	6		N/D 80	34
Neher, Evelyn	Four-Harness Huck	H&C	4	4		Fa 53	60
Neher, Evelyn	Freedom of Laid-in Design, The	H&C	3	3		Su 52	18
Neher, Evelyn	Woven Christmas Greetings	H&C	2	3		Su 51	33
Neher, Evelyn C.	Hemstitched Fringe on the Loom	H&C	2	2		Sp 51	8
Neidig, Dorothy A.	What Is a Synthetic?	SS&D	2	4	8	Fa 71	31
Neighbors, Jane F.	Reversible Two-Color Knitting	H&C	26	5		Oc 75	14
Nelipovitch, Kate; Susan Hick	Fashion Trends	WJ	6	3	23	Wi 81	6
Nell, Patti; Linda Ligon	Publish Your Own Craft Book	Iw	1	2		Wi 76	18
Nelson, Cornelia W.; William O. Nelson	Finishing Handwoven Fabrics	H&C	4	4		Fa 53	32
Nelson, Gladys	Ferne Cone — Knitting: The Stepchild of the Fiber Arts?	Fa	5	3		M/J 78	48
Nelson, Leslee Corpier	Critical Eye: Art Criticism and Fiber, The	Fa	14	1		J/F 87	13
Nelson, Lila	Card Woven Belt of East Telemark—An Adaptation of a Traditional Norwegian Technique	WJ	9	1	33	Su 84	30
Nelson, Lila	Finnweave in Norway: Yesterday and Today	PWC			2	Ap 82	14
Nelson, Lila	Nineteenth Century Tapestry in Billedvev, A	WJ	10	2	38	Fa 85	26
Nelson, Lila	Norwegian Tradition, The	SS&D	7	4	28	Fa 76	6
Nelson, Lila	Toothbrush Handle Rugs: Nålbinding with Rags	WJ	12	2	46	Fa 87	16
Nelson, Lila	Weaving in Rural Norway: A Living Tradition	Hw	8	3		M/J 87	52
Nelson, Lois	Song of the Bobbin	SS&D	4	3	15	Su 73	42
Nelson, Nanci Neher	Ridge (Twill) Weave of the Hopi	SS&D	14	2	54	Sp 83	52
Nelson, Ruthe	Utilitarian Hang-up	WJ	3	3	11	Ja 79	11
Nelson, Susan Venable; Valerie Bechtol	Grau-Garriga: An Interview	Fa	5	4		J/A 78	32
Nelson, William O.	see Nelson, Cornelia W.	H&C	4	4		Fa 53	32
Neruda, Pablo	Ode to My Socks	Fa	10	1		J/F 83	15
Nestel, Susan E.	Provocative Book List: A Student Comments, A	Fa	8	4		J/A 81	18
Nestor, Sarah, ed.	Spanish Textile Tradition of New Mexico and Colorado	SS&D	11	2	42	Sp 80	81
Neuner, Norma	Fabrications '75, San Diego	SS&D	6	3	23	Su 75	29
Newby, Alice Bartholomew	Carole Beadle: The Artist and Her Work	Fa	9	4		J/A 82	44
Newby, Alice Bartholomew	Felted Paper: A New Technique	Fa	9	4		J/A 82	42
Newman, Jay Hartley	see Newman, Thelma R.	Fa	4	5		S/O 77	48
Newman, Margaret	Five Block Diamond in Hand Weaving, Part V–Doubles, Eight Harness, The	SS&D	5	4	20	Fa 74	66
Newman, Margaret	Five Block Diamond in Handweaving	SS&D	3	1	9	Wi 71	38
Newman, Margaret	Miniature Musical Drafts	SS&D	4	4	16	Fa 73	70
Newman, Mattie E.; Helen C. Stuart	California Wonderland	SS&D	1	3	3	Ju 70	5
Newman, Rochelle	Boston Seven	SS&D	16	3	63	Su 85	71
Newman, Rochelle	"Carol Mecagni: Illuminated Tapestries" (Exhibit)	Fa	9	2		M/A 82	79

AUTHOR	TITLE	JOUR	VOL	NO	ISS	DATE	PAGE
Newman, Rochelle	"Current Directions: Conseie des Arts Textiles du Quebec" (Exhibit)	Fa	12	1		J/F 85	74
Newman, Rochelle	Harmony by Contrast	SS&D	14	3	55	Su 83	92
Newman, Rochelle	Victorian Tapestry Workshop: A New Tradition in Australia, The	Fa	10	3		M/J 83	38
Newman, Sandra Corrie	Indian Basket Weaving: How to Weave Pomo, Yurok, Pima and Navajo Baskets	Iw	1	1		Fa 75	20
Newman, Sandra Corrie	Indian Basket Weaving: How to Weave Pomo, Yurok, Pima and Navajo Baskets	Fa	4	1		J/F 77	40
Newman, Thelma R.	Contemporary African Arts and Crafts	H&C	26	1		J/F 75	30
Newman, Thelma R.	Contemporary African Arts and Crafts: On-Site Working with Art Forms and Processes	Fa	3	4		J/A 76	42
Newman, Thelma R.; Jay Hartley Newman	Container Book, The	Fa	4	5		S/O 77	48
Newsted, Jean	Handspun, Handwoven Saddle Blanket, A	WJ	8	2	30	Fa 83	22
Newton, Alan	see Ping, Gu	AT	2			De 84	185
Newton, Deborah	Alpaca Vest	Kn	3	4	8	Fa 87	21
Newton, Deborah	Designing with Ribs	Kn	2	2	4	S-S 86	62
Newton, Deborah	Double-breasted Jacket in Mosiac	Kn	2	1	3	F-W 85	45, 8B
Newton, Deborah	Fine Yarns: Special and Accessible	Kn	3	4	8	Fa 87	16
Newton, Deborah	Fulled Blazer	Kn	3	1	5	F-W 86	38
Newton, Deborah	Fulling Notes	Kn	3	1	5	F-W 86	37
Newton, Deborah	Great American Sweater, A	Kn	2	2	4	S-S 86	64
Newton, Deborah	Handknitting Gloves	TM			14	D/J 87	24
Newton, Deborah	Lace and Knots	Kn	3	4	8	Fa 87	20
Newton, Deborah	Lace Shawl	Kn	4	1	9	Wi 87	54
Newton, Deborah	On Designing: Brocade Blouse	Kn	1	1	1	F-W 84 CI	17 9
Newton, Deborah	On Designing in 2 Dimensions: Shawls and Scarves	Kn	4	1	9	Wi 87	30
Newton, Deborah	On Designing with Lace	Kn	1	2	2	S-S 85	21
Newton, Deborah	On Designing with Slip Stitch Bands	Kn	3	1	5	F-W 86	21
Newton, Deborah	Pleated Cardigan	Kn	3	2	6	Sp 87	20
Newton, Deborah	Pleats in Hand-Knit Fabrics	Kn	3	2	6	Sp 87	23
Newton, Deborah	Sampler of Knit Edgings and Applied Trims, A	TM			12	A/S 87	38
Ng, Mary	Backstrap Weaving in the Philippines	SS&D	9	1	33	Wi 77	18
Nichol, Meade	see Hansen, Helen	H&C	8	1		Wi 56	19
Nicholas, Kristin	Handmade Paper	WJ	6	2	22	Fa 81	12
Nicholas, Kristin	"How Much Is That Spinner in the Window?"	S-O	7	2		Su 83	42
Nicholas, Kristin	Wool Production from Small Flocks of Sheep	S-O	7	2		Su 83	39
Nicholls, Elgiva	Tatting	H&C	17	1		Wi 66	44
Nichols, Evelyn C.	Weft-Twined Weaving	SS&D	16	3	63	Su 85	82
Nicholson, Dick	see Nicholson, Suzanne	CW		24		My 87	11
Nicholson, Suzanne; Dick Nicholson	Glimåkra Adaptations	CW		24		My 87	11
Nickerson, Signe	Breeds of Sheep for Spinners: Corriedale	S-O	10	4		Wi 86	18
Nickolson, Anne McKenzie	Anne McKenzie Nickolson	Fa	12	6		N/D 85	20
Nicoli, Antony	Silk Reflections of C. J. Yao, The	Fa	13	1		J/F 86	47
Nicoll, Frances M.	Loom for the Handicapped, A	H&C	7	3		Su 56	22
Nicoll, Frances M., O.T.R.	Weaving in Therapy	H&C	11	3		Su 60	28
Niekrasz, Jennifer	Experimenting with Color and Two-Tie Weaving on the Rigid Heddle	PWC	4	4	14		21
Nielsen, Edith	Scandinavian Embroidery	Fa	5	6		N/D 78	75
Niemeier, Eileen	From Scraps to Wall Hangings	H&C	10	3		Su 59	19
Niles, Susan A.	see Paul, Anne	TMJ	23			84	5
Nixon, Elaine P.	Handwoven Tapestries Become Practical	WJ	6	1	21	Su 81	15
Noble, Carol Rasmussen	Indigenous Weft-Faced Garments of Peru	SS&D	13	3	51	Su 82	44
Noble, Carol Rasmussen	Peruvian Slings: Their Uses and Regional Variations	WJ	6	4	24	Sp 82	53
Noble, Carol Rasmussen	Treadle Loom in the Peruvian Andes, The	SS&D	8	3	31	Su 77	46

AUTHOR	TITLE	JOUR	VOL	NO	ISS	DATE	PAGE
Noble, Carol Rasmussen	Wedge Weave: A New Approach	WJ	5	2	18	Fa 80	49
Noble, Judith G.	Designing Yarn	S-O	2			78	53
Noble, Judy	Logistics Solved in Seattle	SS&D	6	3	23	Su 75	92
Noble, Judy	People on Exhibit At Henry Gallery	SS&D	6	1	21	Wi 74	84
Noble, Judy	Seattle Guild Garment Designs, Part 1	SS&D	10	3	39	Su 79	26
Noble, Judy	Seen Around the Country: Fibers Unlimited 1978	SS&D	10	2	38	Sp 79	101
Nodland, Marie	Minnesota Weavers Guild, The	H&C	22	3		Su 71	12
Noennig, Anita G.	see Shapiro, Stephen D.	Fa	11	2		M/A 84	46
Noma, Seiroku	Japanese Costume and Textile Arts	Hw	6	3		Su 85	14
Noma, Seiroku	Japanese Costume and Textile Arts	TMJ	4	2		75	81
Noordaa, Titia Vander	Linsey-Woolseys at the Sheburne Museum, The (error-corrected SS&D v16 n3 85 p90)	SS&D	16	2	62	Sp 85	59
Norbeck, Oscar E.	Indian Life Crafts	H&C	9	2		Sp 58	61
Norbury, James	Traditional Knitting Patterns	Kn	1	2	2	S-S 85	79
Nordin, Eva-Lisa	see Johnson, Astrid	Hw	5	2		M/A 84	13
Norman Lathrop Enterprises, publ	Index to How to Do It Information 1981	WJ	7	3	27	Wi 82	51
Norris, James E.	see Bair, Fred	Hw	8	4		S/O 87	12
North, Lois	Eighteenth Century Weaving Puzzle, An	H&C	10	3		Su 59	14
North, Lois	Sarah Fowler's Book of Drafts, Part 1	SS&D	6	1	21	Wi 74	8
North, Lois	Sarah Fowler's Book of Drafts, Part 3	SS&D	6	3	23	Su 75	74
North, Lois	Sarah Fowler's Book of Drafts, Part 4	SS&D	6	4	24	Fa 75	84
Northup, Wendy	Design Supermarket	TM			7	O/N 86	10
Northup, Wendy	Resisting Dyes: Three Ways to Put Color in Its Place	TM			1	O/N 85	30
Northup, Wendy	Surface Designers Meet in Nantucket	TM			9	F/M 87	16
Norton, Becky	Smart (Dumb)-Head Spinning	S-O	8	2		Su 84	44
Norton, Deborah	Junco Sato Pollack: Seashells of Silk	Fa	12	3		M/J 85	18
Norton, Mary K.	Spirit of St. Louis, The	SS&D	7	4	28	Fa 76	35
Norton, Mary K.	St. Louis Weavers' Guild	H&C	17	4		Fa 66	23
Nove, Eleanor	Primarily Weaving	SS&D	11	4	44	Fa 80	30
Nunn, Robin; Alan West	String Bags	SS&D	14	2	54	Sp 83	10
Nunneley, Faithe	Certificates of Excellence: What Goes On	SS&D	10	1	37	Wi 78	36
Nunneley, Faithe	Study Groups — A Personal View	SS&D	2	2	6	Sp 71	14
Nunneley, Faithe	Weavers Guild of Minnesota, Textile Workshop	H&C	22	1		Wi 71	13
Nunnelly, Gordon M., M. D.	Solving a Warping Problem	H&C	9	4		Fa 58	29
Nye, Thelma M., ed.	Swedish Weaving	SS&D	4	1	13	Wi 72	34
Nye, Thelma M., ed.	Swedish Weaving	H&C	24	1		J/F 73	28
Nygards-Kers, Ingrid	Greta Lein, Young Norweigan Designer-Weaver	H&C	14	1		Wi 63	15
Nyquist, Jan	Damask	CW	8	1	22	Se 86	3
Nyquist, Jan	Designing Damask	SS&D	10	4	40	Fa 79	16
Nyquist, Jan	Satin — The Designer Weave	CW	7	3	21	My 86	15
Nyquist, Janet	Christmas Card	CW	1	2	2	Fe 80	11
Nyquist, Janet	Drafting	SS&D	1	2	2	Mr 70	16
Nyquist, Janet	Drafting in Color	SS&D	1	1	1	De 69	5
Nyquist, Janet	Have You Tried Tricot?	SS&D	1	3	3	Ju 70	17
Nyquist, Janet	Method of Drafting	SS&D	1	1	1	De 69	4
Nyquist, Janet	Satin — The Designer Weave (error-corrected SS&D v10 n4 79 p66)	SS&D	10	3	39	Su 79	77
Nyquist, Janet	Speed Warping	SS&D	3	4	12	Fa 72	47
Nyquist, Janet	Terry Weave, or Turkish Towelling	SS&D	1	2	2	Mr 70	17
O'Sullivan, Sallie	Color and Weave Effects	SS&D	3	4	12	Fa 72	22
Oakes, Nancy	Simple and Striped	Kn	3	1	5	F-W 86	44
Oakland, Amy	On Lichen Dyeing	H&C	24	2		M/A 73	20
Oakley, Geraldine L.	Steps to a Tailored Jacket, An Illustrated Workbook	SS&D	13	3	51	Su 82	78

AUTHOR	TITLE	JOUR	VOL	NO	ISS	DATE	PAGE
Oakley, Helen	Cone of Aran Hats, A	TM		13		O/N 87	27
Oakley, Helen	Three Moods of Hooking Rugs, The	TM		2		D/J 85	10
Obbelohde-Doering, Heinrich	Art of Ancient Peru, The	H&C	3	4		Fa 52	62
Oberlink, Peter	Quilted Childhood Visions	Fa	14	1		J/F 87	6
Obeymeyer, Lindsay; Maria Katsaros	Teacher/Student Interface: Two Views of Education	Fa	14	1		J/F 87	34
Ocker, Emily	Lace Garland	Kn	4	1	9	Wi 87	38
Odegaard, Nancy; Dale Kronkright	Giving Your Baskets a Long, Healthy Life: A Basic Guide to Basketry Conservation	Fa	11	1		J/F 84	43
Oelsner, E. H.	Handbook of Weaves, A	Fa	3	1		J/F 76	4
Oelsner, G. H.	Handbook of Weaves, A	SS&D	7	1	25	Wi 75	34
Oelsner, G. H.	Handbook of Weaves, A	H&C	2	2		Sp 51	60
Oelsner, G. H.	Handbook of Weaves, A	H&C	13	3		Su 62	44
Oelsner, G. H.	Handbook of Weaves, A	Iw	2	4		Su 77	35
Ogden, Anne	"Paper and Felt Redefined" (Exhibit)	Fa	5	2		M/A 78	17
Ohle, Carolyn	Weaving Peace at Innisfree	Hw	4	1		J/F 83	22
Ohman, Polly	Cardweaving Patterns on a 4-Shaft Loom	WJ	6	4	24	Sp 82	36
Ojala, Liisa Kanning	Reinterpreting Rya: Irma Kukkasjärvi Energizes an Ancient Technique	WJ	9	4	36	Sp 85	26
Olendorf, Donna	Gerhardt Knodel	Fa	5	6		N/D 78	44
Oles, Jery	Mystery Sun Rug	WJ	8	4	32	Sp 84	10
Oliphant, Carrie	First Conference for Ontario Weavers' Guilds	H&C	6	3		Su 55	12
Oliver, Olga	Having an Inventor-Husband	SS&D	3	4	12	Fa 72	15
Olmsted, Anna W.	Rug Craftsmen	H&C	18	2		Sp 67	27
Olmsted, Rosemary R.	Rosemary R. Olmsted: Following Krokbragd's Crooked Path	Fa	11	3		M/J 84	28
Olson, Mabel C.	Ruth Clark, Tapestry Weaver	H&C	9	1		Wi 57	29
Olson, Pauline	Contracts: Olson	Iw	1	3		Sp 76	22
Omer, Martha	Designer Yarn — A Use for Acid Dyes	S-O	6	4		82	56
Ontario Handweavers and Spinners	Canadian Centennial Book 1967	H&C	19	1		Wi 68	46
Ontario Handweavers and Spinners Guild	Book of Giving, The	Iw	5	1		Wi 79	65
Opdahl, Martha	Martha Opdahl	Fa	13	4		J/A 86	27
Orel, Jaroslav	see Vaclavim, Antonin	Iw	5	1		Wi 79	61
Oren, Linda Lowe	Do It Yourself	SS&D	11	1	41	Wi 79	59
Orlowsky, Dzvinia	Michael Brennand-Wood	Fa	14	1		J/F 87	26
Orman, P.	Handloom Weaving	H&C	6	1		Wi 54	61
Ormond, Helen C.	Suggestions for Weavers of Liturgical Textiles	H&C	10	3		Su 59	29
Ormseth, Laurie	Merry Holoien: A Harmony of Color and Sound	Fa	13	2		M/A 86	6
Orr, Leah	Fiber World of Leah Orr, The	SS&D	9	3	35	Su 78	8
Osborne, Lily	Indian Crafts of Guatemala & El Salvador	H&C	17	2		Sp 66	43
Osburn, Dr. Burl	Constructive Design	H&C	1	3		Fa 50	64
Osterkamp, Peggy	Techniques for Better Weaving (error-corrected TM i9 D/J 86 p4)	TM			7	O/N 86	42
Ostlund	see Hoppe	H&C	26	3		M/J 75	30
Ostlund, E.	see Hoppe, E.	SS&D	6	3	23	Su 75	49
Osumi, Tamezo	Printed Cottons of Asia — The Romance of Trade Textiles	H&C	15	2		Sp 64	43
Oswald, Francis	Q & A on Vegetable Dyes	SS&D	1	1	1	De 69	11
Oswald, Francis	Q & A on Wool Dyeing	SS&D	1	1	1	De 69	11
Outram, Carol	see Humphries, Mary	CW	3	1	7	Se 81	4
Overcast, Roy	Appalachian Basketry	Fa	4	1		J/F 77	20
Overman, Ruth; Lula Smith	Contemporary Handweaving	H&C	7	1		Wi 55	59
Owens, Julie	Machine Knit Ribbing for Woven Goods	Hw	6	2		M/A 85	30
Owens, Julie	Sweater's Tale, A	Hw	6	4		S/O 85	82
Öz, Tahsin	Turkish Textiles and Velvets	TMJ	3	2		De 71	38
O'Callaghan, Kate	Contemporary Tapestry: On Looms, Warping, Setting Up Tapestry Study Course — Part 1	WJ	4	3	15	Ja 80	41

939

AUTHOR	TITLE	JOUR	VOL	NO	ISS	DATE	PAGE
O'Callaghan, Kate	Statement of My Ideas	WJ	5	4	20	Sp 81	35
O'Callaghan, Kate	Techniques of Tapestry Weaves Part 2: Making a Sampler	WJ	4	4	16	Ap 80	45
O'Callaghan, Kate	Techniques of Tapestry Weaves Part 3: Shading and Other Matters	WJ	5	1	17	Su 80	29
O'Callaghan, Kate	Techniques of Tapestry Weaves Part 4: Developing Design for Tapestry	WJ	5	2	18	Fa 80	15
O'Connor, Eileen	African Strip-Cloth Shirt Without Strips, An	WJ	6	3	23	Wi 81	33
O'Connor, Marcie Archer	Heathering	Kn	2	1	3	F-W 85	54
O'Connor, Marcie Archer	Knitting with Handspun	Kn	1	1	1	F-W 84 CI	55 46
O'Connor, Marcie Archer	Knitting with Handspun	Kn	1	2	2	S-S 85	54
O'Connor, Marcie Archer	Texture in Spinning	Kn	2	2	4	S-S 86	53
O'Connor, Marina	Summer Harvest, Winter Jacket	S-O	11	2		Su 87	13
O'Connor, Pat	Classic, The	Kn	2	1	3	F-W 85	58
O'Connor, Patricia	Papermaking	SS&D	14	3	55	Su 83	32
O'Connor, Paul	Twill Color and Weave Effects...From the Computer	Iw	6	1		Wi 80	28
O'Connor, Paul	Warp Color Changes in Double and Multilayer Weaves	WJ	12	2	46	Fa 87	55
O'Hara, Sheila	Sheila O'Hara	Fa	13	3		M/J 86	26
O'Hara, Sheila	You Are Now Weaving Oakland	AT	6			De 86	9
O'Shaughnessy, Marjorie	Verticals	SS&D	15	1	57	Wi 83	8
Paca, Al	Why Sew Those Lines? An Interview with Giorgio Furioso and Carolyn Thomas	Fa	7	4		J/A 80	25
Paca Al, ed.	Ritzi and Peter Jacobi: Conversation	Fa	8	4		J/A 81	50
Packard, Myles	Anne Swann	Fa	4	3		M/J 77	22
Packard, Myles	Emily Dubois	Fa	4	6		N/D 77	66
Packard, Rolfe	How to Buy a Floor Loom: A Primer (error-corrected Fa v6 n1 79 p60)	Fa	6	1		J/F 79	32
Pacque, Joan Michaels	Ten Commandments of Fiber Manipulators	SS&D	5	4	20	Fa 74	32
Padin, Carmen	"Structures in Fiber" (Exhibit)	Fa	5	6		N/D 78	70
Page, Judy	Texture with Handspun	WJ	6	2	22	Fa 81	20
Page, Marta	Planned Weaving for Your Wardrobe	H&C	2	4		Fa 51	30
Paine, Frank	Vera Grosowsky: Through the Surface	Fa	10	4		J/A 83	18
Painter, Hal	Weaving in the Woods	SS&D	5	2	18	Sp 74	73
Painter, Ingrid	Appeal from the American Sheep Farmers, An	S-O	9	2		Su 85	7
Painter, Ingrid	Polycerate Sheep	SS&D	13	3	51	Su 82	46
Painter, Ingrid	Spotting a Good Jacob	S-O	7	2		Su 83	18
Palmai, Clarissa	Textile Mounting	TMJ	18			79	55
Palmer, Jacqueline M.	Spiders: Masters of Natural Textiles	Fa	14	4		S/O 87	33
Palmer, Krissa Elaine	Handwoven Holloween, A	Hw	4	4		S/O 83	32
Pancake, Cherri; Karen Searle; Sue Baizerman	Stitched Finishes in the Guatemalan Tradition	Hw	2	5		No 81	29
Pancake, Cherri M.; Suzanne Baizerman	Guatemalan Gauze Weaves: A Description and Key to Identification	TMJ	19 20			80,81	1
Paoletti, Jo B.	see Anderson, Clarita	AT	3			My 85	173
Papa, Nancy	"Art Fabric '77: The Contemporary American Tapestry" (Exhibit)	Fa	4	4		J/A 77	12
Papa, Nancy	Doris Hoover: Quiltmaker and Folk Artist	Fa	6	1		J/F 79	16
Papa, Nancy	"Fiberworks 1976" (Exhibit)	Fa	4	1		J/F 77	9
Papa, Nancy	Gayle Luchessa	Fa	4	5		S/O 77	56
Papa, Nancy	"Joan Schulze" (Exhibit)	Fa	4	3		M/J 77	17
Papa, Nancy	Lia Cook, An Interview	Iw	4	4		Fa 79	24
Papa, Nancy	Organizing a Major Textile Show	SS&D	8	1	29	WI 76	28
Papa, Nancy	"Paper Sources" (Exhibit)	Fa	5	4		J/A 78	16
Papa, Nancy	"Power Garments" (Exhibit)	Fa	5	1		J/F 78	13
Papa, Nancy	San Francisco School of Fabric Arts, The	Fa	6	1		J/F 79	13
Papa, Nancy	"Tenth Annual Textile Exhibition" (Exhibit)	Fa	5	4		J/A 78	13
Papa, Nancy	Tenth Annual Textile Exhibition, Olive Hyde Art Gallery (Exhibit)	Fa	5	4		J/A 78	13

AUTHOR	TITLE	JOUR	VOL	NO	ISS	DATE	PAGE
Papa, Nancy	"Third Annual Fiber Show" (Exhibit)	Fa	5	6		N/D 78	65
Papa, Nancy	Weaving Through Portugal	SS&D	6	3	23	Su 75	89
Paqua, Al	Silken Gowns of Candiss Cole, The	Fa	6	3		M/J 79	41
+ Paque, Joan Michaels	Design Principles and Fiber Techniques	SS&D	5	1	17	Wi 73	77
+ Paque, Joan Michaels	Visual Instructional Macrame	SS&D	3	1	9	Wi 71	39
+ Paque, Joan Michaels	Why Macrame?	SS&D	3	3	11	Su 72	26
Paquin, Gerard A.	Iconography of Everyday Life in Nineteenth-Century Middle Eastern Rugs, The	TMJ	22			83	5
Pariseau, George E., M.D.	Design for a One-Treadle Loom	H&C	3	3		Su 52	15
Pariseau, George E., M.D.	Weaver Rose of Rhode Island 1839–1913	H&C	6	1		Wi 54	4
Park, Betty	"22 Polish Textile Artists" (Exhibit)	Fa	4	5		S/O 77	8
Park, Betty	"Amy Lipshie: Tapestries" (Exhibit)	Fa	12	3		M/J 85	76
Park, Betty	"Art of Basketry, The" (Exhibit)	Fa	4	2		M/A 77	9
Park, Betty	"Aurelia Muñoz" (Exhibit)	Fa	4	6		N/D 77	21
Park, Betty	"Baker/Rapoport/Wick" in New York (Exhibit)	Fa	4	5		S/O 77	15
Park, Betty	"Baltimore Album Quilts" (Exhibit)	Fa	8	6		N/D 81	69
Park, Betty	Carol Westfall: Adapting Dye Transfer Methods	Fa	5	1		J/F 78	64
Park, Betty	Conversation with Mildred Constantine	Fa	8	6		N/D 81	14
Park, Betty	Conversing with Gerhardt Knodel	Fa	12	1		J/F 85	27
Park, Betty	Cooper-Hewitt Museum, The	Fa	9	5		S/O 82	13
Park, Betty	"Cynthia Schira" (Exhibit)	Fa	5	3		M/J 78	13
Park, Betty	"Diane Itter: Recent Work" (Exhibit)	Fa	8	5		S/O 81	68
Park, Betty	"Dominic Di Mare" (Exhibit)	Fa	4	3		M/J 77	8
Park, Betty	Fabric Workshop: A Philadelphia Environment Where Experimentation Reigns, The	Fa	9	1		J/F 82	21
Park, Betty	"Felting" (Exhibit)	Fa	7	6		N/D 80	71
Park, Betty	"Ferne Jacobs: New Works" (Exhibit)	Fa	6	1		J/F 79	84
Park, Betty	"Fiber Art: An Uncommon Thread" (Exhibit)	Fa	9	2		M/A 82	78
Park, Betty	"Fiber Images" (Exhibit)	Fa	13	2		M/A 86	54
Park, Betty	"Fiberworks" (Exhibit)	Fa	4	6		N/D 77	10
Park, Betty	"From American Looms: Scheuer Tapestry Studio" (Exhibit) (error-corrected Fa v12 n6 85 p9)	Fa	12	5		S/O 85	76
Park, Betty	Helen Bitar	Fa	5	2		M/A 78	44
Park, Betty	"History of Knitting" (Exhibit)	Fa	5	3		M/J 78	10
Park, Betty	Influence from the East: Textiles and Textile Patterns in Western Art	Fa	12	2		M/A 85	22
Park, Betty	Interview with Mary Jane Jacob, An	Fa	9	6		N/D 82	13
Park, Betty	"Joan Livingstone/Recent Work: Felt/Wood" (Exhibit)	Fa	4	4		J/A 77	14
Park, Betty	"Joanne Brandford: Recent Nets" (Exhibit)	Fa	11	6		N/D 84	77
Park, Betty	"Joanne Segal Brandford — Nets" (Exhibit)	Fa	5	3		M/J 78	17
Park, Betty	John McQueen: An Interview	Fa	6	1		J/F 79	21
Park, Betty	"Joy Saville: Contemporary Quilting" (Exhibits)	Fa	9	4		J/A 82	72
Park, Betty	Kiyomi Iwata: A Singularity of Vision	Fa	13	1		J/F 86	10
Park, Betty	Lewis Knauss: New Work	Fa	9	3		M/J 82	11
Park, Betty	"Lia Cook" (Exhibit)	Fa	5	5		S/O 78	72
Park, Betty	"Macungie Notes — Lewis Knauss" (Exhibit)	Fa	5	2		M/A 78	15
Park, Betty	Magdalena Abakanowicz Speaks	Fa	10	2		M/A 83	11
Park, Betty	Marian Clayden's Clothing for Collectors	Fa	6	3		M/J 79	55
Park, Betty	"Mariyo Yagi" (Exhibit)	Fa	5	1		J/F 78	19
Park, Betty	"Michelle Lester: New Tapestries" (Exhibit)	Fa	6	1		J/F 79	85
Park, Betty	Neda Al Hilali: An Interview	Fa	6	4		J/A 79	40
Park, Betty	"Painted Weavings" Lia Cook and Neda Al-Hilali (Exhibit)	Fa	8	1		J/F 81	88
Park, Betty	Pat White: The "Small Things" Are Her Signature	SS&D	13	3	51	Su 82	58
Park, Betty	Pattern...Pattern...Pattern	Fa	9	1		J/F 82	11

AUTHOR	TITLE	JOUR	VOL	NO	ISS	DATE	PAGE
Park, Betty	Presence of Light, The	SS&D	15	4	60	Fa 84	36
Park, Betty	Rena Thompson: Echoes of Intuitive Truths	Fa	13	2		M/A 86	46
Park, Betty	Rites of Passage: Carol Shaw-Sutton's Twig and Thread Constructions	Fa	7	6		N/D 80	49
Park, Betty	Robert Pfannebecker: A Collector's Point of View	Fa	5	4		J/A 78	42
Park, Betty	Sheila O'Hara: Wry Humor and Virtuoso Weaving	Fa	10	1		J/F 83	64
Park, Betty	SS&D Interview: Cynthia Schira (error-corrected SS&D v10 n2 79 p56)	SS&D	10	1	37	Wi 78	4
Park, Betty	Success of Susan Kittredge, The	Fa	6	2		M/A 79	28
Park, Betty	Touch of the Poet: Wearables by Denise Welsh-May, A	Fa	6	6		N/D 79	52
Park, Betty	Transferring Feelings to Fabric: Jane Morias	Fa	5	1		J/F 78	52
Park, Betty	"Vanity Fair: A Treasure Trove from the Costume Institute" (Exhibit)	Fa	5	3		M/J 78	15
Park, Betty	Warren Seelig	Fa	7	5		S/O 80	59
Park, Betty	Whitney Museum of American Art, The (Exhibit)	Fa	9	2		M/A 82	11
Park, Betty	Woven Collages of Arturo Sandoval, The	Fa	6	5		S/O 79	70
Parker, Ann; Avon Neal	Molas: Folk Art of the Cuna Indians	Iw	4	2		Sp 79	63
Parker, Ann; Avon Neal	Molas — Folk Art of the Cuna Indians	Fa	5	2		M/A 78	58
Parker, Ella W.	Stripes in Summer and Winter Weave	H&C	4	3		Su 53	19
Parker, Ron	Fuzzy Politics of Wool, The	TM			13	O/N 87	20
Parker, Ron	Premium Wool—A Producer's Perspective	S-O	11	3		Fa 87	39
Parker, Ron	Sheep Book: A Handbook for the Modern Shepherd, The	S-O	8	1		Sp 84	10
Parker, Ron	Sheep Book: A Handbook for the Modern Shepherd, The	WJ	8	2	30	Fa 83	62
Parker, Ron	Sheep Book, The	Hw	4	5		N/D 83	14
Parker, Ron	Wool Forum: Growing and Working	S-O	11	2		Su 87	18
Parker, Ron; Teresa Parker	There's More Than One Way to Shear a Sheep	TM			13	O/N 87	61
Parker, Ron; Teresa Parker	Wool Forum: Producers and Consumers vs Bureaucracy	S-O	10	4		Si 86	7
Parker, Rozsika	Subversive Stitch, The	Fa	13	1		J/F 86	46
Parker, Teresa	see Parker, Ron	S-O	10	4		Si 86	7
Parker, Teresa	see Parker, Ron	TM			13	O/N 87	61
Parker, Xenia Ley	Creative Handweaving	SS&D	7	4	28	Fa 76	66
Parker, Xenia Ley	Hooked Rugs and Ryas	H&C	24	3		M/J 73	6
Parker, Zenia Ley	Hooked Rugs & Ryas	SS&D	4	3	15	Su 73	53
Parkinson, Alberta	Weaving the Girdle of Rameses on Nine Harnesses	CW	3	2	8	Ja 82	1
Parks, Betty	Collaboration: A Vision of Unknown Territory	Fa	12	5		S/O 85	20
Parks, Betty	Textiles and the Art of Kandinsky	Fa	9	4		J/A 82	11
Parks, Deborah	Parks' Bouquet	PWC	4	1	11		36
Parks, Deborah	Weaving Primer	PWC	3	3	9		4
Parks, Deborah	Weaving Primer	PWC	3	4	10		4
Parks, Deborah	Weaving Primer	PWC	4	2	12		36
Parks, Deborah	Weaving Primer, Part 1	PWC	4	1	11		44
Parr, Rowena	Through the "Almanack" Office Window	S-O	11	3		Fa 87	36
Parris, John	Revival of Cherokee Arts and Crafts, The	H&C	4	2		Sp 53	9
Parry, Nancy	Half Magic, Half Fiber	TM			12	A/S 87	16
Parshall, Priscilla	Costume for Dance: The Living Sculpture of Carleigh Hoff	Fa	8	1		J/F 81	28
Parslow, Virginia	Flax — From Seed to Yarn	H&C	3	2		Sp 52	30
Parslow, Virginia D.	Learning to Spin	H&C	8	1		Wi 56	10
Parslow, Virginia D.	Spinning Wheels	H&C	7	2		Sp 56	20
Parsons, Bernice	Lexington Fair in November	SS&D	3	4	12	Fa 72	6
Parsons, Jane	Words to the Wise	S-O	11	1		Sp 87	28
Parsons, L. E.; John K. Stearns	Textile Fibers	H&C	2	2		Sp 51	61
Partridge, Virginia	Made in New York State: Handwoven Coverlets 1820–1860	Hw	7	1		J/F 86	21

AUTHOR	TITLE	JOUR	VOL	NO	ISS	DATE	PAGE
Partridge, Virginia Parslow; Rita J. Adrosko	Made in New York State: Handwoven Coverlets 1820-1860	Fa	13	4		J/A 86	61
Partridge, William	Practical Treatise on Dying (sic) of Woollen, Cotton, and Skein Silk with the Manufacture of Broadcloth and Cassimere, A	WJ	7	2	26	Fa 82	59
Pasco, Henry H.	Handweaving for Pleasure and Profit	H&C	20	4		Fa 69	7
Pasquine, Ruth	"Barbara Heilmann-Levine: Tapestries and Paintings" (Exhibit)	Fa	10	2		M/A 83	69
Pasquini, Katie	Katie Pasquini: Mandala Quilts	Fa	10	4		J/A 83	20
Pasquini, Katie	Mandala	Fa	11	5		S/O 84	52
Pater, Stephen	Things to Know and Tell About Flame Retardants	WJ	8	2	30	Fa 83	50
Patera, Charlotte	Making Molas: Four Basic Techniques	Fa	8	5		S/O 81	38
Paternayan Brothers	Hand Knotted Rug Weaving	H&C	8	2		Sp 57	62
Paterson, Kathy	Overview, An	Fa	3	5		S/O 76	6
Patrick, Jane	Colonial Fabrics: A Glossary	Hw	3	5		N/D 82	25
Patrick, Jane	'Country' Overshot	Hw	6	4		S/O 85	48
Patrick, Jane	Fall '85 Fashion Scene	Hw	6	3		Su 85	18
Patrick, Jane	Finger Control: Or Getting the Most Out of Your Loom	Hw	4	2		M/A 83	70
Patrick, Jane	Getting Acquainted: A Survey Report	Hw	3	1		Ja 82	16
Patrick, Jane	Keep it Simple	Hw	6	3		Su 85	82
Patrick, Jane	Matter of Style, A	Hw	5	4		S/O 84	28
Patrick, Jane	Megablocks	Hw	4	1		J/F 83	60
Patrick, Jane	Twills of Charlotte Funk, The	Hw	6	5		N/D 85	36
Patrick, Jane	Warping: A Compleat Guide	Hw	3	3		My 82	64
Patrick, Jane; Ann Wittpenn	Weaving in the Fur Weft	Hw	4	1		J/F 83	33
Patterson, Joan	Weaving with Linen	H&C	9	3		Su 58	63
Patton, Ellen	"Fiber Forms '78" (Exhibit)	Fa	5	5		S/O 78	66
Patton, Patti	Betsy Benjamin-Murray	Fa	4	3		M/J 77	43
Paul, Anne	Re-Establishing Provenience of Two Paracas Mantles	TMJ	19 20			80,81	35
Paul, Anne; Susan A. Niles	Identifying Hands at Work on a Paracas Mantle	TMJ	23			84	5
Paul, Jan	Weaving Works for Worship	WJ	6	1	21	Su 81	40
Paul, Margot	see Stinchecum, Amanda Mayer	Hw	6	3		Su 85	14
Pauli, Karen	Will It Work? A Guide to Evaluating a Spinning Wheel	S-O	4			80	43
Pauly, Sarah Buie; Rebecca Wells Corrie	Kashmir Shawl, The	TMJ	4	2		75	80
Pauw, Alice Abbott	Georgia Dille Abbott	H&C	15	1		Wi 64	40
Payette, Lynn	Stitches for Silk-and-Metal Embroidery (error-corrected TM I4 A/M 86 p4)	TM			3	F/M 86	51
Payton, Curtis	see Payton, Dorothy A.	H&C	2	1		Wi 50	59
Payton, Dorothy A.; Curtis Payton	Terraspool Method of Warping, The	H&C	2	1		Wi 50	59
Paz, Octavio	In Praise of Hands	SS&D	6	4	24	Fa 75	31
Pearson, Katherine	American Crafts: A Source Book for the Home	Fa	11	4		J/A 84	54
Pearson, Michael	Fisher-Gansey Patterns of N. E. England	Kn	1	1	1	F-W 84	71
Pearson, Michael	Fisher-Gansey Patterns of Scotland and the Scottish Fleet	Kn	1	1	1	F-W 84	71
Pearson, Michael	Traditional Knitting	Kn	1	1	1	F-W 84	71
Pearson, Michael	Traditional Knitting	Kn	2	1	3	F-W 85	78
Pease, Marion D.	Weaving in a College Art Department	H&C	3	4		Fa 52	20
Peasley, Laura L.	see Snow, Edith Huntington	H&C	2	2		Sp 51	63
Peavy, Martin	Martin Peavy: An Improvisational Approach to Rugs	Fa	11	3		M/J 84	22
Peck, Nancy	Color-and-Weave Computer Program Review	CW	4	3	12	Ap 83	17
Peleg, Rina	Rina Peleg: Plaiting in Clay	Fa	10	6		N/D 83	16
Pellegrino, Mary C.	Quilted Gardens of Jean Carlson Masseau, The	Fa	13	2		M/A 86	9
Pellman, Kenneth	see Pellman, Rachel	TM			3	F/M 86	78
Pellman, Kenneth	see Pellman, Rachel	TM			11	J/J 87	73

AUTHOR	TITLE	JOUR	VOL	NO	ISS	DATE	PAGE
Pellman, Rachel; Kenneth Pellman	Amish Crib Quilts	TM		3		F/M 86	78
Pellman, Rachel; Kenneth Pellman	Amish Doll Quilts, Dolls, and Other Playthings	TM		11		J/J 87	73
Pemberton, Mildred	Round Rug Woven on a Hula Hoop, A	H&C	20	3		Su 69	12
Pencheff, Patricia	Kay Campbell: The Shifting Balance of Order	Fa	12	5		S/O 85	11
Pendergrass, Mary	Indigo Dyeing and the Problems of Crocking	WJ	4	3	15	Ja 80	30
Pendergrast, Mick	Maori Basketry for Beginners	SS&D	9	4	36	Fa 78	82
Pendleton, Mary	Navajo and Hopi Weaving Techniques	SS&D	5	4	20	Fa 74	64
Pendleton, Mary	Navajo and Hopi Weaving Techniques	H&C	26	2		Ap 75	21
Pendleton, Mary	Ohio Weaving Venture, An	H&C	4	4		Fa 53	23
Pendleton, Mary	Organizing a Weaving Workshop	H&C	5	2		Sp 54	44
Pennington, David A.; Michael B. Taylor	Pictorial Guide to American Spinning Wheels, A	SS&D	7	1	25	Wi 75	35
Pennington, David; Michael Taylor	Colonial Equipment	S-O	2			78	40
Pennington, David; Michael Taylor	Pictorial Guide to American Spinning Wheels, A	S-O	3			79	10
Pennington, Fred A.	Small Damask Designs	H&C	6	3		Su 55	54
Pentler, Fumiko	Raising Silkworms, The Glenna Harris Guild's Project	H&C	20	1		Wi 69	14
Pepin, Yvonne	Stalking the Wild Mushroom	SS&D	16	4	64	Fa 85	22
Pepin, Yvonne	Villa de Cordero Negro: "Country Home of the Black Lamb"	SS&D	17	3	67	Su 86	30
Perrault, Joe	Tie Your Own String Heddles	WJ	11	1	41	Su 86	65
Perry, Pamela	Fanfare: Fans from the Collection of The National Museum of American Art (Exhibit)	Fa	12	6		N/D 85	48
Perry, Pamela	Jody Klein: Quilted Constructions	Fa	12	2		M/A 85	18
Perry, Pamela	Working with Linen: Shirley Ruth Elgot	Fa	14	2		M/A 87	32
Pesch, Imelda	Macrané: Knotting, Braiding & Twisting	H&C	22	2		Sp 71	45
Peters, Rupert	Preparing a Warp	H&C	5	2		Sp 54	20
Petersen, Jill	"Peg McNair/Tapestries" (Exhibit)	Fa	4	3		M/J 77	12
Peterson, Edel J.	Yarns	Hw	6	1		J/F 85	4
Peterson, Jill	Handcrafted Clothing Construction: Some Considerations	Fa	3	5		S/O 76	32
Peterson, Lisa Lee	From Image to Woven Structure: A Video-Computer System for Textile Designers	AT	7			Ju 87	109
Petraitis, Ada	Dimai	CW	5	3	15	My 84	5
Petraitis, Ada	Dimai or Tied Lithuanian (Computer Drafts-Eleanor Best)	CW	4	2	11	Ja 83	16
Petrini, Marcy	Computers Don't Weave (error-corrected SS&D v14 n4 83 p4)	SS&D	14	3	55	Su 83	62
Petrini, Marcy	Learning from the Learning Exchange	SS&D	18	1	69	Wi 86	62
Petrini, Marcy	Nepal	SS&D	16	2	62	Sp 85	65
Pettersen, Carmen L.	Maya of Guatemala, Their Life and Dress, The	SS&D	8	4	32	Fa 77	72
Pettigrew, Dale	Anni Albers	Hw	6	4		S/O 85	76
Pettigrew, Dale	Bands and Beads	Hw	4	1		J/F 83	72
Pettigrew, Dale	Edward F. Worst: Craftsman and Educator	Hw	6	5		N/D 85	73
Pettigrew, Dale	From SOAR to Rendezvous	S-O	10	4		Wi 86	35
Pettigrew, Dale	Guide to Weaving Schools and Craft Schools, A	Hw	5	3		Su 84	33
Pettigrew, Dale	Interweave Forum: Fashion Fabrics 2	Hw	8	4		S/O 87	76
Pettigrew, Dale	Reflections: Spin-Off Rendezvous, September 13-20, 1987, YMCA of the Ozarks, Potosi, Missouri	S-O	11	4		Wi 87	55
Pettigrew, Dale	Ribbon: A Celebration of Life, The	Hw	6	5		N/D 85	70
Pettigrew, Dale	SOAR: A High Time	S-O	8	1		Sp 84	6
Pettigrew, Dale	Weaving with Tabby: An Introduction to Overshot	Hw	3	5		N/D 82	62
Pettit, Florence	America's Printed & Painted Fabrics	H&C	22	1		Wi 71	41
Pettit, Florence H.	America's Indigo Blues	SS&D	6	4	24	Fa 75	29
Pettit, Florence H.	America's Indigo Blues: Resist-printed and Dyed Textiles of the Eighteenth Century	TMJ	4	2		75	81
Pfeiffer, Judy	Shawls Without Seams	SS&D	18	2	70	Sp 87	43

AUTHOR	TITLE	JOUR	VOL	NO	ISS	DATE	PAGE
Phelps, Marie	Bedspreads	H&C	2	3		Su 51	46
Phelps, Marie	Handbags and a Hat	H&C	1	3		Fa 50	29
Phelps, Marie	On Selling Weaving	H&C	11	1		Wi 60	53
Philbin, Marianne, eds.	see Lark Book Staff	Hw	6	5		N/D 85	18
Philips, Mary Walker	Creative Knitting, A New Art Form	SS&D	3	2	10	Sp 72	38
Philips, Mary Walker	Step-by-Step Macrame	SS&D	3	1	9	Wi 71	39
Philips, Mary Walker	Step-by-Step Macramé: An Introduction to Creative Knotting	H&C	21	3		Su 70	40
Phillips, Constance	Black Cats and Green Stitches	TM			13	O/N 87	90
Phillips, Constance	Desperate Need for Chartreuse, The	TM			1	O/N 85	14
Phillips, Constance	Hot and Cold Running Fiber	TM			3	F/M 86	12
Phillips, Constance	Nose to the Grindstone	TM			7	O/N 86	90
Phillips, Janet	Weaver's Book of Fabric Design, The	Hw	5	3		Su 84	16
Phillips, Janet	Weaver's Book of Fabric Design, The	SS&D	15	3	59	Su 84	36
Phillips, Mary Walker	Creative Knitting	TM			9	F/M 87	76
Phillips, Mary Walker	Step-by-Step Knitting	SS&D	2	3	7	Su 71	26
Phillips, Mary Walker	Step-by-Step Macramé	SS&D	1	3	3	Ju 70	22
Pianzola, Maurice	see Coffinet, Julien	SS&D	5	4	20	Fa 74	64
Pianzola, Maurice	see Coffinet, Julien	H&C	23	5		S/O 72	34
Piazza, Virginia	"Kathryn Lipke/Fiber-Paper-Pulp: Works in Handmade Paper" (Exhibit)	Fa	4	4		J/A 77	13
Pickens, Nora	Mounting the Rio Grande Exhibit	SS&D	9	3	35	Su 78	58
Pickering, W. R.	see Landreau, Anthony	H&C	20	3		Su 69	43
Pickett, Alice	Alice Pickett: Rugmaker	Fa	7	5		S/O 80	55
Pickett, Alice	Construct a Simple Shaft-Switching Device	SS&D	16	3	63	Su 85	68
Pickett, Barbara Setsu	Approach to Teaching Design, An	Iw	3	2		Wi 78	16
Picton, John; John Mack Picton	African Textiles: Loom, Weaving and Design	WJ	8	3	31	Wi 83	64
Picton, John Mack	see Picton, John	WJ	8	3	31	Wi 83	64
Pierce, Judith	Costuming for Rock Music Videos	Fa	14	3		M/J 87	51
Pierce, Judith	Knitted Palette of Brenda French, The	Fa	13	2		M/A 86	43
Pierce, Judith	Quilted Autograph Collection, A	Fa	14	3		M/J 87	5
Pierce, Lynn	Lynn Pierce	Fa	14	4		S/O 87	18
Pierucci, Louise	Introduction to Tapestry, An (error-corrected SS&D v8 n2 77 p51)	SS&D	7	4	28	Fa 76	69
Pierucci, Louise	Introduction to Tapestry, Part 2, An	SS&D	8	1	29	WI 76	73
Pierucci, Louise	Papermaking: Where It's Going	SS&D	10	4	40	Fa 79	47
Pierucci, Louise	"Stitchery '77" (Exhibit)	Fa	4	3		M/J 77	11
Piette, Diane	see Safner, Isadora	WJ	5	4	20	Sp 81	45
Pilsk, Adele	Arrowcraft: Tennessee Cottage Industry	Fa	5	5		S/O 78	20
Pilsk, Adele	"Contemporary African American Crafts" (Exhibit)	Fa	6	6		N/D 79	74
Pilsk, Adele	Jimmie Benedict: Non-Stop Knotting	Fa	5	2		M/A 78	52
Pilsk, Adele	Kai Walters	Fa	4	6		N/D 77	42
Pilsk, Adele	Margaret and Tom Windeknecht: Computer Drafts	Fa	5	5		S/O 78	18
Pilsk, Adele	Mary Frances Davidson: A Tribute	Fa	5	1		J/F 78	58
Pinchin, Bryn	Conversation with Mary Andrews, A	Iw	5	4		Fa 80	24
Pinchin, Bryn	Mary Snyder	Iw	5	2		Sp 80	47
Pinchin, Bryn	Mo's Have It, The	S-O	7	3		Fa 83	23
Pinchin, C. B.	Jane Cox: Her Draft for Counterpins	Iw	4	3		Su 79	31
Pinchin, C. Bryn	More Than Four Can Double Your Fun	Hw	6	1		J/F 85	38
Ping, Gu; Alan Newton	Application of Computer-Aided Design Techniques to the Creation of Moss Crepe Weaves, The	AT	2			De 84	185
Piper, Aris	Hand Woven Garments	WJ	5	3	19	Wi 81	24
Piroch, Sigrid	Demystifying Complex Weaves: A Step-by-Step Exploration from Four to Sixteen Harnesses	WJ	10	3	39	Wi 86	8
Piroch, Sigrid	Evening Bags That Shine with Flash & Glitter	Hw	6	1		J/F 85	36

AUTHOR	TITLE	JOUR	VOL	NO	ISS	DATE	PAGE
Piroch, Sigrid	Is Complex Weaving for You?	WJ	10	2	38	Fa 85	10
Piroch, Sigrid	Miniature World, A	PWC	5	2	16		26
Piroch, Sigrid	Miniatures, Fine Threads, Complex Weaves	CW	7	2	20	Ja 86	3
Piroch, Sigrid	Notes on Using Metallic Yarn	Hw	6	1		J/F 85	I-9
Piroch, Sigrid	One Guild's Story: From Founding an Organization to Building Its Image	WJ	12	2	46	Fa 87	30
Piroch, Sigrid	Polychroma: Natural Dye Methods	SS&D	17	2	66	Sp 86	26
Piroch, Sigrid	Ropes for Every Use	Hw	7	4		S/O 86	14
Pissowotski, Inge	Farmer and His Wife, Figure Boundweave, A	WJ	5	4	20	Sp 81	8
Piucci, Joanna	Buyer's Guide to Sewing Machines, A	Fa	10	2		M/A 83	39
Piucci, Joanna	Sandra Holzman: Marbleized Fabrics	Fa	10	5		S/O 83	21
Piucci, Joanna A.	Tufted Rugs of Martha Opdahl, The	Fa	11	3		M/J 84	15
Place, Jennifer	Canadian Portfolio, A	Fa	9	6		N/D 82	29
Place, Jennifer	Exuberant Art of Elizabeth Browning Jackson, The	Fa	10	6		N/D 83	12
Place, Jennifer	Fantasy Figures: Shelly Fowler's Fabric Dolls	Fa	10	1		J/F 83	16
Place, Jennifer	"Focus on Handwoven Fabric: Ontario Handweavers and Spinners" (Exhibits)	Fa	9	4		J/A 82	74
Place, Jennifer	International Exposure Conference	Fa	10	5		S/O 83	51
Plath, Iona	Craft of Handweaving, The	SS&D	4	2	14	Sp 73	44
Plath, Iona	Decorative Arts of Sweden, The	H&C	17	3		Su 66	43
Plath, Iona	Handweaver's Pattern Book, The	WJ	8	1	29	Su 83	53
Plath, Iona	Handweaving	H&C	16	1		Wi 65	43
Plath, Iona	Practical Projects	H&C	15	4		Fa 64	17
Platus, Libby	Flameproofing Fibers	SS&D	8	2	30	Sp 77	29
Plevin, Ann	Teaching At a Men's Prison	Fa	14	1		J/F 87	36
Plowman, Judith	see Jackson, Constance	S-O	4			80	15
Plowman, Judith	see Jackson, Constance	S-O	6	4		82	10
Plowman, Judith	see Jackson, Constance	WJ	6	4	24	Sp 82	59
Plowman, Judith	Spinning a Fine Yarn	S-O	4			80	47
Plummer, Beverly	How Does Your Garden Grow? Plant Fibers and Handmade Paper	Fa	6	4		J/A 79	34
Poague, Susan	Computer-Aided Design Analysis	WJ	11	4	44	Sp 87	8
Pocock, Sylvia	Gold Arabesque Decorates New HGA Headquarters	SS&D	5	4	20	Fa 74	77
Pocock, Sylvia Domingo	Basic Approach to Designing and Drafting Original Overshot Patterns, A	SS&D	7	2	26	Sp 76	34
Pointing, K. G.; S. D. Chapman, eds.	Textile History, Vol 10, 1979; Vol 11, 1980	WJ	6	3	23	Wi 81	60
Pokornowski, Illa N.	see Eircher, Joanne B.	WJ	11	3	43	Wi 87	64
Polakoff, Claire	Into Indigo: African Textiles and Dyeing Techniques	WJ	5	1	17	Su 80	48
Polaski, Lois	European Craft Tour, A	H&C	23	1		J/F 72	16
Polaski, Lois	Handweaver & Craftsman Tour of Europe, 1972	H&C	23	2		M/A 72	13
Polster, Joanne	Brief Bibliography of Grant References, A	Fa	11	4		J/A 84	50
Polster, Nancy; Elsa Sreenivasam	Hi-Tech Banner Sculptures	Fa	12	3		M/J 85	42
Pompilio, Loretta	Soft People, The Art of Dollcrafting	Fa	7	2		M/A 80	43
Ponting, K. G.	Broadcloth and Doeskin	WJ	7	2	26	Fa 82	38
Ponting, K. G.	Discovering Textile History and Design	WJ	7	3	27	Wi 82	50
Ponting, Ken	Beginner's Guide to Weaving	WJ	8	4	32	Sp 84	67
Poon, Vivian	Contemporary California Costume	Fa	11	5		S/O 84	53
Poon, Vivian	Crossing Over—Fiber in Print	Fa	10	3		M/J 83	48
Poon, Vivian	"Deborah Warner's Visual Journal" (Exhibit)	Fa	10	6		N/D 83	76
Poon, Vivian	Jeff Glenn: Software for a High-Tech World	Fa	12	4		J/A 85	9
Poon, Vivian	"Julia Mitchell: Landscape Tapestries" (Exhibit)	Fa	10	6		N/D 83	80
Poon, Vivian	"Linda Maxwell and Caroline Dahl: Terror Sampler and Other Dogs" (Exhibit)	Fa	11	6		N/D 84	79
Poon, Vivian	Lisa Gardner: Cultural Perspectives	Fa	12	1		J/F 85	14
Poon, Vivian	"Michael Olszewski: Pleated and Stitched Silk" (Exhibit)	Fa	11	3		M/J 84	78

AUTHOR	TITLE	JOUR	VOL	NO	ISS	DATE	PAGE
Poon, Vivian	"Pin Rugs of Ellen Oltchick, The" (Exhibit)	Fa	10	6		N/D 83	74
Poore, Jenny	Thoughts from a New Zealander	SS&D	9	3	35	Su 78	65
Pope, F. Whipple	Methods of Dyeing — With Vegetable Dyes and Other Means	H&C	13	1		Wi 62	44
Porcella, Yvonne	Demonstration At Northern California	SS&D	3	4	12	Fa 72	19
Porcella, Yvonne	Needlepoint with Cardweaving	SS&D	4	2	14	Sp 73	13
Porcella, Yvonne	Pieced Clothing Variations	WJ	7	2	26	Fa 82	58
Porcella, Yvonne	Pin-Warp Collar	SS&D	4	3	15	Su 73	56
Porcella, Yvonne	San Francisco Invites HGA In '74	SS&D	4	1	13	Wi 72	19
Porcella, Yvonne	Weaver Who Wastes Not, A	SS&D	6	4	24	Fa 75	8
Porcella, Yvonne	Yvonne Porcella	Fa	13	6		N/D 86	3
Porcella, Yvonne	Yvonne Porcella: A Colorful Book	Fa	13	4		J/A 86	60
Portela, Carmo	Carmo Portela, Portuguese Tapestry Weaver	SS&D	17	4	68	Fa 86	35
Porter, John	Fiber Analysis: The Thread of Fate	Fa	9	4		J/A 82	49
Porter-Francis, Wendy	Flourishing Art: USA Hmong Women Show How to Stitch Pa ndau, Their Flowery Cloth, A	TM		9		F/M 87	33
Posner, Sally	Spinning in the Classroom	S-O	2			78	37
Posner, Sally	Teaching on a Shoe-String Budget	SS&D	5	1	17	Wi 73	9
Post, Margaret	Oriental Hem Stitch	SS&D	8	2	30	Sp 77	59
Post, Margaret	Traditional Ways with Dunkagäng	Hw	7	2		M/A 86	42
Potomac Craftsmen of Washington, D. C., ed.	Index to Handweaver & Craftsman: 1950 — 1965	H&C	18	2		Sp 67	44
Potter, Katie Forderhase	Up, Up and Away in my Handwoven Balloon	Hw	3	2		Mr 82	40
Poulin, Clarence	Tailoring Suits the Professional Way	TM		7		O/N 86	72
Poulsen, Grethe Poul	Danish Patterns for Handlooms	H&C	10	2		Sp 59	60
Poulton, Jim	Color and Weave Effects	WJ	5	3	19	Wi 81	14
Pourdeyhimi, B.	see Jackson, K. C.	AT	7			Ju 87	61
Pourdeyhimi, B.; K. C. Jackson	Note on the Diffusion of the Automatic Loom Within the British Cotton Industry, A	AT	6			De 86	101
Pourdeyhimi, B.; K. C. Jackson; K. Hepworth	Development of Weaving Using Automatic Looms, The	AT	4			De 85	107
Poussart, Anne	Woven Skirt and Its Development, The	WJ	8	3	31	Wi 83	39
Powell, Marian	One Thousand (+) Patterns	SS&D	8	3	31	Su 77	62
Powell, Marian	One Thousand (+) Patterns in 4, 6 and 8 Harness Shadow Weaves	WJ	1	3	3	Ja 77	32
Powell, Marian	Shadow Weave Offers an Opportunity for Many Variations	H&C	12	3		Su 61	20
Powell, Marian	Summer and Winter Study at Des Moines Weavers Guild	H&C	13	2		Sp 62	44
Powis-Turner, Margaret	New Images from the Loom: An Interview with Dick Sauer	SS&D	6	4	24	Fa 75	56
Pratt, Lenora	Experience with Native Materials	H&C	13	4		Fa 62	8
Preen, Maureen	Tale of Two Knitters, A	S-O	8	4		Wi 84	19
Presser, Fran	Closer Look at Cashgora, A	S-O	10	4		Wi 86	49
Preston, P. K.	Michelle Lester	Fa	5	2		M/A 78	48
Price, Susan	Convergence '82	Fa	9	6		N/D 82	54
Priest, Alice B.	Weaving on a Round Loom	H&C	19	2		Sp 68	35
Priest, Alice R.	Card Weaving, Patterns Translated to a Handloom	H&C	12	2		Sp 61	15
Prin, Monique	see Prin, Remy	WJ	5	3	19	Wi 81	52
Prin, Remy	see Thomas, Michel	WJ	8	4	32	Sp 84	67
Prin, Remy; Monique Prin	Pour Aborder....L'ikat	WJ	5	3	19	Wi 81	52
Prinzing, Debra	"Common Cord, The": Central Asian Textiles (Exhibit)	Fa	14	3		M/J 87	56
Pritchard, M. E.	Short Dictionary of Weaving — Concisely Arranged for Quick Reference, A	H&C	7	2		Sp 56	59
Pritchard, Mary J.	Siapo: Bark Cloth Art of Samoa	Fa	13	5		S/O 86	56
Proctor, Geri	Seaforms in Spokane	Hw	3	4		Se 82	14
Proctor, Richard	Principles of Pattern, The	H&C	21	2		Sp 70	41

AUTHOR	TITLE	JOUR	VOL	NO	ISS	DATE	PAGE
Proctor, Richard; Jennifer F. Lew	Surface Design for Fabric	Hw	7	1		J/F 86	18
Proctor, Richard M.	Principles of Pattern for Craftsmen and Designers, The	SS&D	3	1	9	Wi 71	38
Proctor, Richard M.; Jennifer F. Lew	Surface Design for Fabric	TM			2	D/J 85	78
Proctor, Richard M.; Jennifer F. Lew	Surface Design for Fabrics	WJ	10	2	38	Fa 85	82
Projansky, Ella	Sculptured Needlepoint Stitchery	Fa	5	6		N/D 78	76
Prosser, Evelyn Bingham	Weaving in San Francisco — Part 1	WJ	6	2	22	Fa 81	44
Prosser, Evelyn Bingham	Weaving in San Francisco — Part 2	WJ	6	3	23	Wi 81	50
Proud, Nora	Textile Dyeing and Printing Simplified	H&C	26	1		J/F 75	28
Proud, Nora	Textile Printing & Dyeing Simplified	SS&D	6	2	22	Sp 75	64
Proulx, Bibiane April	Corded Rep Weave and Velvet Rugs	SS&D	17	3	67	Su 86	80
Proulx, Bibiane April	Rep Weaves	WJ	7	4	28	Sp 83	10
Proulx, Bibiane April	Reps, Technique De Creation De Tissage Traditionnel Et Moderne	WJ	5	1	17	Su 80	48
Proulx, Bibiane April	Reps: Technique De Creation De Tissage Traditionnel Et Moderne	SS&D	17	2	66	Sp 86	85
Published in Scotland	Traditional Embroidery of Portugal	H&C	4	1		Wi 52	61
Pubols, Dorothy M.	Spinning and Use of Dog's Hair, The	WJ	4	1	13	Jy 79	36
Pulleyn, Rob	Conversation with Ed Oppenheimer, A	Fa	4	4		J/A 77	24
Pulleyn, Rob	"Ninth International Biennial of Tapestry" (Exhibit)	Fa	6	4		J/A 79	62
Pulleyn, Rob	Observations	Fa	3	3		M/J 76	38
Pulleyn, Rob, ed.	Basketmaker's Art: Contemporary Baskets and Their Makers, The	TM			11	J/J 87	72
Puryear, Marjorie Durko	Marjorie Durko Puryear	Fa	14	4		S/O 87	19
Putman, Greta	see Finch, Karen	Hw	7	3		M/J 86	14
Putman, Greta	see Finch, Karen, O.B.E.	SS&D	9	2	34	Sp 78	49
Pye, David	Nature and Art of Workmanship, The	H&C	19	4		Fa 68	42
Pye, David	Nature and Art of Workmanship, The	SS&D	6	1	21	Wi 74	32
Pyysalo, Helvi; Viivi Merisalo	Hand Weaving Patterns from Finland	SS&D	2	2	6	Sp 71	34
Quataert, Donald	Carpet-Makers of Western Anatolia, 1750–1914, The	TMJ	25			86	25
Quick, Betsy D.; Judith A. Stein	Ply-Split Camel Girths of West India	WJ	8	3	31	Wi 83	66
Quigley, Edward T.	Weaver of Scotland's Past	Hw	4	5		N/D 83	35
Quigley, Viola J.	Memphis Guild of Handloom Weavers, The	H&C	2	3		Su 51	50
Quigley, Viola Joyce	Liturgical Textiles	H&C	11	3		Su 60	53
Quinn, Cecelia	Quinn's Spinning Notes	S-O	5			81	55
Quinn, Celia	Basic Boot Socks	S-O	10	2		Su 86	13
Quinn, Celia	Elements of Yarn Structure	S-O	6	4		82	46
Quinn, Celia	Experimenting with Silk Crepe	S-O	10	4		Wi 86	36
Quinn, Celia	Fiber Foray: Color Exercises for the Beginner	S-O	9	3		Fa 85	36
Quinn, Celia	Fiber Foray: Getting Started with Line Flax	S-O	9	4		Wi 85	46
Quinn, Celia	Fiber Foray: Ginned Cotton	S-O	9	2		Su 85	26
Quinn, Celia	Fiber Foray: Spinning Combed Alpaca	S-O	9	1		Sp 85	26
Quinn, Celia	Fiber Foray: Spinning Silk Cap and Mawata	S-O	8	3		Fa 84	49
Quinn, Celia	Fiber Foray: Spinning Silk Cocoons	S-O	8	2		Su 84	27
Quinn, Celia	Fiber Foray: Working with Kid Mohair	S-O	10	1		Sp 86	44
Quinn, Celia	Fine Lace Shawl, A	S-O	8	4		Wi 84	14
Quinn, Celia	Frosted Pastel Cashmere Scarf, A	S-O	9	3		Fa 85	41
Quinn, Celia	Handspun Linen Towels	S-O	7	1		Sp 83	32
Quinn, Celia	Hooked Stick	S-O	9	2		Su 85	34
Quinn, Celia	Learning to Adjust the Bands That Govern the Flyer and Bobbin	S-O	11	2		Su 87	25
Quinn, Celia	Merino Scarf with Pastel Highlights	S-O	9	3		Fa 85	37
Quinn, Celia	Plying a Balanced Yarn for Knitting	S-O	11	4		Wi 87	30
Quinn, Celia	Ramie	S-O	8	4		Wi 84	50

AUTHOR	TITLE	JOUR	VOL	NO	ISS	DATE	PAGE
Quinn, Celia	Silk: A Fiber of Many Faces	S-O	8	3		Fa 84	30
Quinn, Celia	Yarn: A Resource Guide for Handweavers	Fa	13	3		M/J 86	60
Quinn, Celia	Yarn: A Resource Guide for Handweavers	TM		1		O/N 85	78
Quinn, Eva	How to Determine Tie-Up for Multi-Harness Huck Lace Patterns	SS&D	1	3	3	Ju 70	16
Quirke, Lillian Mary	Rug Book, The	SS&D	11	4	44	Fa 80	84
R. L. Shep, publ.	Textile Book List, The	WJ	5	3	19	Wi 81	52
Rabinowe, Victoria	Sprinkle, Dump And Dapple	SS&D	4	3	15	Su 73	55
Race, Mary E.	Weaving on a Diamond Grid: Bedouin Style	SS&D	12	1	45	Wi 80	20
Ragland, Marla	Penny Rupley	Fa	5	4		J/A 78	52
Raikos, Pam	Finishing Handwoven Garments: A Beginner's Guide	SS&D	12	4	48	Fa 81	40
Rainey, Sarita	Fiber Expressions: Knotting and Looping	WJ	4	2	14	Oc 79	39
Rainey, Sarita	Weaving Without a Loom	H&C	17	3		Su 66	43
Rainey, Sarita R.	Wall Hangings: Designing with Fabric and Thread	SS&D	3	1	9	Wi 71	39
Rainey, Sarita R.	Wall Hangings: Designing with Fabric and Thread	H&C	23	5		S/O 72	34
Rainey, Sarita R.	Weaving Without a Loom	H&C	22	3		Su 71	41
Ralph, William	Collecting Spinning Wheels	H&C	24	1		J/F 73	16
Ranill, Jane	Guide to Undertaking a Large Project, A	Hw	8	4		S/O 87	87
Ranne, Raija	see Haglich, Sr. Bianca	SS&D	8	3	31	Su 77	84
Rantanen, Kristi	Finnish Textile Art: From Byzantine to Bauhaus	Hw	8	3		M/J 87	68
Raphael, Chad	see Raphael, Jenifer	Fa	13	6		N/D 86	24
Raphael, Chad	see Raphael, Jenifer	Fa	13	6		N/D 86	25
Raphael, Jenifer; Chad Raphael	Tapa-Making in Tonga	Fa	13	6		N/D 86	24
Raphael, Jenifer; Chad Raphael	Tapa-Making Process, The	Fa	13	6		N/D 86	25
Raphaelian, H. M.	Hidden Language of Symbols in Oriental Rugs, The	H&C	5	1		Wi 53	61
Rapp, Sylvia	Temple Tapestry	SS&D	15	2	58	Sp 84	24
Rapport, Debra	Creative Process: Debra Rapport, The	Fa	11	6		N/D 84	34
Rasband, Judith	Color Crazed	Kn	2	1	3	F-W 85	73
Rasmussen, Peg	Man's Jacket: A Weaver's Challenge, A	SS&D	15	2	58	Sp 84	58
Rasmussen, Peg	Seat for All Seasons, A	WJ	6	2	22	Fa 81	21
Rasmussen, Peg	Taste of Honey(comb), A	SS&D	16	2	62	Sp 85	6
Rasmussen, Peg	Textured Cottons: Seamless, No-Sweat Shirt	WJ	6	3	23	Wi 81	25
Ratigan, Dorothy	Chanel Jacket	Kn	2	2	4	S-S 86	33
Rau, Joanne	Fiberworks and Interior Decorating	SS&D	13	1	49	Wi 81	45
Ravarra, Patricia	"Fifth Lodz Triennale, The" (Exhibit)	Fa	13	3		M/J 86	50
Raven, Lee	Another Look at Wool Scouring: Ingredients, Problems, and Techniques	S-O	9	4		Wi 85	25
Raven, Lee	Fiber Properties: Tenacity	S-O	7	1		Sp 83	38
Raven, Lee	Fine, Finer, Finest	S-O	9	4		Wi 85	24
Raven, Lee	Mabel Ross	S-O	9	2		Su 85	55
Raven, Lee	Problems with Your Flyer and Bobbin Wheel Spinning	S-O	11	4		Wi 87	23
Raven, Lee	Spinner's Knot, A	S-O	9	4		Wi 85	56
Raven, Lee	Spinning on the Charkha	S-O	7	1		Sp 83	24
Raven, Lee	Variations on a Midnight Rainbow	S-O	9	4		Wi 85	14
Rawlings, Marilyn; Jane Taylor	Picture Knits	Kn	2	2	4	S-S 86	78
Rawlings, Sandra	see Specht, Sally	SS&D	5	2	18	Sp 74	68
Rawson, Ruth	see Amon, Martha	H&C	12	3		Su 61	61
Raymond, Nish	Beiderwand Revisited	CW		24		My 87	20
Raymond, Nish	Cover It	Hw	6	1		J/F 85	64
Raymond, Nish	Little Bit of Bias, A (error-corrected Hw v4 n5 83 p94)	Hw	4	4		S/O 83	37
Read, Kay	Dyeing with Fiber Reactive Dyes on Cotton	WJ	4	2	14	Oc 79	42
Reade, Dorothy	Eugene Spinners, The	H&C	18	3		Su 67	20

AUTHOR	TITLE	JOUR	VOL	NO	ISS	DATE	PAGE
Reade, Dorothy	Twenty-five Original Knitting Designs	Kn	1	2	2	S-S 85	79
Reade, Dorothy	Twenty-five Original Knitting Designs	Kn	4	1	9	Wi 87	61
Reade, Dorothy	World Crafts Council, An American Spinner Meets Peruvian Craftsmen	H&C	20	1		Wi 69	8
Reader's Digest Association	Back to Basics: How to Learn and Enjoy Traditional American Skills	WJ	6	2	22	Fa 81	40
Reagan, Barbara M.	see Crews, Patricia Cox	AT	8			De 87	43
Reagan, Trudy	Dyeing Dangers	Fa	5	1		J/F 78	36
Reams, Dorothy E.	Martha Washington's Inaugural Gown	SS&D	7	3	27	Su 76	15
Redden, G. O.	Textile Repairing	H&C	11	3		Su 60	59
Redding, Debbie	Block Drafting, Profile Drafts, and a Few Other Related Things	Hw	4	3		M/J 83	19
Redding, Debbie	Choosing Yarns	Hw	1	1		F-W 79	48
Redding, Debbie	Convergence '84	Hw	5	4		S/O 84	17
Redding, Debbie	Don't Avoid the Draft, Learn to Read It!	Hw	2	1		F-W 80	12
Redding, Debbie	Drafting 101: Literacy in Weaving (error-corrected Hw v4 n1 83 p24)	Hw	3	5		N/D 82	73
Redding, Debbie	Drafting 101: Literacy in Weaving, Part 2	Hw	4	1		J/F 83	24
Redding, Debbie	How to Succeed at Teaching (By Really Trying)	Iw	4	4		Fa 79	48
Redding, Debbie	In Order to Weave You Must Be Warped!	Hw	1	2		S-S 80	6
Redding, Debbie	Incredible Color Copy Machine, The	Hw	2	4		Se 81	74
Redding, Debbie	It's Exactly the Same (sort of)	Hw	3	2		Mr 82	26
Redding, Debbie	It's Good to Be All Wet, Sometimes	Hw	2	3		My 81	22
Redding, Debbie	Learning Journey, A	Hw	4	4		S/O 83	16
Redding, Debbie	Learning Journey Starts at Home, The	Hw	4	2		M/A 83	18
Redding, Debbie	Learning to Weave	Fa	13	3		M/J 86	58
Redding, Debbie	Learning to Weave with Debbie Redding	WJ	9	4	36	Sp 85	78
Redding, Debbie	Learning to Weave with Debbie Redding	PWC	4	1	11		54
Redding, Debbie	Lord, Let My Words Be Pleasant Today for Tomorrow I May Have to Eat Them	Hw	5	5		N/D 84	26
Redding, Debbie	Motivation, Perspective, and Other Practical Philosophical Matters	Hw	3	3		My 82	24
Redding, Debbie	On Buying Your First Loom (and other torture)	Hw	4	5		N/D 83	18
Redding, Debbie	Planning a Project	Hw	3	1		Ja 82	23
Redding, Debbie	Second Week, The	Hw	5	3		Su 84	28
Redding, Debbie	see Green, Louise	Hw	2	1		F-W 80	21
Redding, Debbie	Understanding Yarns	Hw	5	1		J/F 84	18
Redding, Debbie	Unweaving Faulty Fabric	Hw	5	2		M/A 84	22
Redding, Debbie	Variety Is the Spice of Life, or Tabby Tricks	Hw	2	5		No 81	73
Redding, Debbie	Weaver's Wanderlust, A	Hw	3	4		Se 82	18
Redding, Debbie	What's in a Name? or: Sticks and Stones Can Break My Bones, But Names Can Sure Confuse Me	Hw	2	2		Mr 81	22
Redding, Deborah	see Green, Louise	Iw	2	4		Su 77	36
Redding, Eric	Do-It-Yourself Maintenance	Hw	2	3		My 81	32
Redding, Winogene	Why Not Tweeds?	H&C	1	3		Fa 50	30
Redding, Winogene B.	Do You Want to Sell Your Weaving?	H&C	5	1		Wi 53	30
Reddy, Mary	see Skowronski, Hella	SS&D	5	3	19	Su 74	62
Reddy, Mary	see Skowronski, Hella	SS&D	7	3	27	Su 76	79
Reddy, Mary; Hella Skowronski	Sprang a New Way	SS&D	6	2	22	Sp 75	22
Redfield, Gail	Manifold Twills—Unlimited Opportunity for Experimentation	SS&D	5	4	20	Fa 74	72
Redfield, Gail	Variations on an Algebraic Equation	H&C	10	3		Su 59	46
Redfield, Gail M.	Design for a Lunch Cloth in Three Techniques	H&C	19	3		Su 68	15
Redfield, Gail M.	Experiences with a Weaving Workshop	H&C	6	1		Wi 54	58
Redfield, Gail M.	Mitered Corners for Identical Warp and Weft Patterns	H&C	14	3		Su 63	21
Reding, Sgt. Lucy Frances	Weaving in Therapy, Your Patients Teach You the Best Methods	H&C	14	1		Wi 63	20
Redman, Jane	Certificate of Excellence, The	SS&D	8	1	29	WI 76	46
Redman, Jane	Certificate: Where Artist and Artisan Meet	SS&D	8	2	30	Sp 77	48

AUTHOR	TITLE	JOUR	VOL	NO	ISS	DATE	PAGE
Redman, Jane	Frame Loom Weaving	SS&D	8	1	29	WI 76	70
Redman, Jane	Frame Loom Weaving	Fa	3	5		S/O 76	39
Redman, Jane	Frame-Loom Weaving	Iw	2	1		Fa 76	33
Redman, Jane	Loom in My Tote-Bag, The	SS&D	5	4	20	Fa 74	83
Redmond, Cheryl	Camrose Ducote's Menagerie: An Empathy with Animals	Fa	10	3		M/J 83	27
Redmond, Cheryl A.	Sacred Places: Barbara Heller Weaves Landscapes Where Spirits Might Dwell, Places of Meditation (error-corrected Fa v7 n5 80 p5)	Fa	7	3		M/J 80	58
Redwood	Backstrap Weaving of Northern Ecuador	SS&D	5	3	19	Su 74	62
Redwood	Backstrap Weaving of Northern Ecuador	WJ	4	1	13	Jy 79	42
Reed, Brice	Kansans Learn There's More Than One Way to Skin a Sheep	Iw	1	1		Fa 75	18
Reed, Fran	Summary of Wool Bureau Report on Musk Ox Fiber	S-O	7	1		Sp 83	42
Reed, Irene C.	"Dolly Curtis Textile Graphics" (Exhibit)	Fa	6	2		M/A 79	70
Reed, J. H.	Weaving at La Villita, School and Shop in Restored Village	H&C	14	2		Sp 63	16
Reed, Kathy	Weaving Ecclesiastical Stoles and Chasubles	WJ	6	1	21	Su 81	46
Reed, Tim	Loom Book	SS&D	6	1	21	Wi 74	32
Reedy, Dorrie	Pennyroyal Pick-up	SS&D	15	1	57	Wi 83	79
Reekie, Stephanie	Child's Windcheater	S-O	6	4		82	58
Rees, Linda	Evolution of a Regional Juried Fiber Show: Fibers Unlimited, The	SS&D	17	3	67	Su 86	65
Rees, Linda	Journey in Thread, A	Hw	5	5		N/D 84	99
Rees, Linda	On Exhibiting: A Few Caveats	SS&D	7	1	25	Wi 75	60
Rees, Linda	Textiles on Display: The Installation of Fiber Exhibitions	SS&D	17	4	68	Fa 86	38
Rees, Linda	Tough Colors	Hw	2	4		Se 81	58
Rees, Linda E.	Handspinning Technique	H&C	24	3		M/J 73	32
Reese, Ralph Henry	"Karen Stoller: Fiber" (Exhibit)	Fa	8	1		J/F 81	96
Reese, Sharron	At Home with Flax	S-O	10	3		Fa 86	19
Reese, Sharron	Jigging...100% Hand Worsted	Hw	5	3		Su 84	18
Reese, Sharron	Jigging...100% Hand Worsted	S-O	8	2		Su 84	51
Reese, Sharron	Needlework Tool Case	S-O	10	3		Fa 86	21
Reesor, Tracy	Rubik Reworked	SS&D	14	3	55	Su 83	98
Reesor, Tracy	Spice Dyeing	WJ	6	4	24	Sp 82	47
Reeve, Beatrice	Weaving Courses at the Newark Museum	H&C	4	4		Fa 53	33
Reeve, Beatrice	Why Visit a Museum?	H&C	8	4		Fa 57	9
Regensteiner, Else	Art of Weaving, The	SS&D	2	1	5	De 70	30
Regensteiner, Else	Art of Weaving, The	H&C	21	4		Fa 70	43
Regensteiner, Else	Art of Weaving, The	SS&D	14	1	53	Wi 82	64
Regensteiner, Else	Art of Weaving, The, Second Edition	WJ	7	1	25	Su 82	64
Regensteiner, Else	Art of Weaving, The, Second Edition	Fa	9	4		J/A 82	53
Regensteiner, Else	Card Weaving, A New Approach by a Chicago Weaver	H&C	16	3		Su 65	19
Regensteiner, Else	Certificate of Excellence to be Offered	SS&D	5	4	20	Fa 74	52
Regensteiner, Else	Chicago Weaving: Development and Impact	SS&D	12	1	45	Wi 80	9
Regensteiner, Else	Color & Design in Decorative Fabrics	H&C	9	4		Fa 58	6
Regensteiner, Else	Excerpt from Geometric Design in Weaving, An	WJ	11	4	44	Sp 87	13
Regensteiner, Else	Geometric Design in Weaving	Hw	8	5		N/D 87	15
Regensteiner, Else	Geometric Design in Weaving	WJ	11	4	44	Sp 87	73
Regensteiner, Else	Geometric Design in Weaving	SS&D	18	4	72	Fa 87	55
Regensteiner, Else	Geometric Design in Weaving	PWC	4	4	14		53
Regensteiner, Else	Greek Craft Summer: The American Farm School	SS&D	7	3	27	Su 76	100
Regensteiner, Else	Handweaving 1969	H&C	20	2		Sp 69	4
Regensteiner, Else	Peruvian Journey	H&C	17	1		Wi 66	34
Regensteiner, Else	Program for a Study Group	SS&D	3	2	10	Sp 72	10
Regensteiner, Else	Program for a Study Group	SS&D	3	3	11	Su 72	43
Regensteiner, Else	Program for a Study Group	SS&D	3	4	12	Fa 72	42
Regensteiner, Else	Program for a Study Group, Part 4	SS&D	4	1	13	Wi 72	25

AUTHOR	TITLE	JOUR	VOL	NO	ISS	DATE	PAGE
Regensteiner, Else	Program for a Study Group, Part 5	SS&D	4	2	14	Sp 73	43
Regensteiner, Else	Program for a Study Group, Part 6	SS&D	4	3	15	Su 73	40
Regensteiner, Else	Program for a Study Group, Part 7	SS&D	4	4	16	Fa 73	43
Regensteiner, Else	Program for a Study Group, Part 8	SS&D	5	1	17	Wi 73	51
Regensteiner, Else	School of the Art Institute	SS&D	3	1	9	Wi 71	27
Regensteiner, Else	School of the Art Institute of Chicago Offers Weaving Classes	H&C	5	2		Sp 54	28
Regensteiner, Else	Tradition, Innovation — Identity	SS&D	1	2	2	Mr 70	3
Regensteiner, Else	Weaver's Study Course: Ideas and Techniques	SS&D	6	4	24	Fa 75	29
Regensteiner, Else	Weaver's Study Course: Ideas and Techniques	Fa	3	5		S/O 76	39
Regensteiner, Else	Weaving Sourcebook: Ideas and Techniques	WJ	8	4	32	Sp 84	65
Regensteiner, Else	Weaving Sourcebook: Ideas and Techniques	SS&D	15	2	58	Sp 84	90
Regensteiner, Else	Weaving Upholstery, The Qualities of a Sound Fabric	H&C	14	1		Wi 63	10
Reichard, Gladys A.	Navaho Religion, A Study of Symbolism	H&C	5	1		Wi 53	60
Reichard, Gladys A.	Navajo Shepherd and Weaver	SS&D	5	3	19	Su 74	62
Reichard, Gladys A.	Weaving a Navajo Blanket	SS&D	6	2	22	Sp 75	64
Reichardt, Jasia	see Jacob, Mary Jane	Fa	10	5		S/O 83	58
Reichert, Donald O.	see McMullan, Joseph V.	TMJ	3	2		De 71	43
Reid, Eve	"Space Sails" Soar (Exhibit)	Fa	13	4		J/A 86	51
Reid, Eve	"Women of Fiber: Six Michigan Artists" (Exhibit)	Fa	8	5		S/O 81	74
Reid, Mehry	Persian Carpet Designs to Color	WJ	8	3	31	Wi 83	67
Reinsel, Susan J.	"Needle Expressions '86" (Exhibit)	Fa	14	1		J/F 87	53
Reiser, Bertl	Post-War Influences in West German Weaving	H&C	4	3		Su 53	11
Reiss, Zenaide	Twining Variations	SS&D	4	1	13	Wi 72	43
Reiss, Zenaide	Warp Ikat	SS&D	12	4	48	Fa 81	4
Reiss, Zenaide	Warp Ikat: Part 2: Quick Design Effects	SS&D	13	1	49	Wi 81	16
Reith, Stephanie	Fraas—Slade: Painted Views	Fa	8	5		S/O 81	32
Reith, Stephanie J.	Las Artistas Del Valle: Images of Everyday Life in Colorado's San Luis Valley	Fa	10	3		M/J 83	24
Reith, Stephanie J.	Surface Design and the Garment Form	Fa	8	1		J/F 81	34
Reitz, Don	Boulder Designer-Craftsmen 1971	SS&D	2	4	8	Fa 71	8
Renee, Paula	Paula Renee	Fa	13	6		N/D 86	3
Renee, Paula	Tree of Life	SS&D	17	2	66	Sp 86	80
Renne, Elisha	Multiple Shaft Coverlet Drafts in the Allen-Stephenson Draft Book	AT	3			My 85	125
Renne, Elisha	Use of the Dobby Loom for Multi-Harness Weave Manipulation, The	WJ	9	3	35	Wi 85	9
Renne, Elisha	Woven Inspiration from West African Textiles	WJ	10	4	40	Sp 86	60
Renner, Paul	Color: Order and Harmony. A Color Theory for Artists and Craftsmen	H&C	17	1		Wi 66	43
Resen, Gail Johnson	Poetry in Fiber: Gail Johnson Resen Talks About Her Work	Fa	7	4		J/A 80	20
Reswick, Irmtraud	Traditional Textiles of Tunisia and Related North African Weavings	Hw	7	2		M/A 86	89
Reswick, Irmtraud	Traditional Textiles of Tunisia and Related North African Weaving	SS&D	17	3	67	Su 86	88
Reswick, Irmtraud H.	Traditional Handlooms and Weavings of Tunisia	SS&D	12	2	46	Sp 81	21
Reuter, Laurel	Elizabeth MacDonald: Finding the Ties That Bind Truth and Art	Fa	14	4		S/O 87	31
Revault, Jacques	Designs and Patterns from North African Carpets & Textiles	SS&D	6	4	24	Fa 75	30
Rex, Chris	Adinkra: Weft African Textile of Pride	Fa	9	6		N/D 82	36
Rex, Chris	Comfort Clothes	Hw	2	4		Se 81	79
Rex, Chris	Gobelins Royal Tapestry Works: Tradition and Change in France	Fa	10	3		M/J 83	58
Rex, Chris	Wailani Johansen, Quiltmaker: Sharing the Tradition of the Hawaiian Quilt	Fa	9	3		M/J 82	60
Rex, Stella Hay	Choice Hooked Rugs	H&C	5	4		Fa 54	57
Rex, Stella Hay	Choice Hooked Rugs	H&C	6	2		Sp 55	63
Reynders-Baas, Coby	Listening to Threads	WJ	11	4	44	Sp 87	21
Reynolds, Carol	see Wipplinger, Michelle	Hw	3	2		Mr 82	22
Reynolds, Donna	Classic Alpaca Sweater, A (error-corrected S-O v9 n2 85 p61)	S-O	9	1		Sp 85	24
Reynolds, Donna	Consideration of Professionalism, A	S-O	7	1		Sp 83	12
Reynolds, Donna	Handspun Knitwear That Lasts	S-O	7	2		Su 83	49

AUTHOR	TITLE	JOUR	VOL	NO	ISS	DATE	PAGE
Reynolds, Donna	Mohair Sweater	S-O	8	2		Su 84	46
Reynolds, Donna	Planning a Spinning Demonstration	S-O	9	2		Su 85	17
Reynolds, Donna	Practical Approach to the Great Wheel, A	S-O	8	4		Wi 84	39
Reynolds, Valrae	see Myers, Diana K.	Fa	13	2		M/A 86	41
Rhinehart, Jane	Making Men's Clothes	TM			7	O/N 86	72
Rhodes, Donna M.	How to Succeed At Failure	Fa	7	6		N/D 80	32
Rhodes, Elizabeth A.	Techniques of Haute Couture (error-corrected TM i7 O/N86 p5)	TM			6	A/S 86	52
Rhodes, Maribelle N.	Fiber Exhibition	H&C	23	1		J/F 72	35
Rhodes, Mary	Small Woven Tapestries	H&C	24	4		Au 73	5
Rhodes, Tonya Stalons; Harriet Tidball, ed.	Color Related Decorating Textiles — Rugs, Draperies, Upholstery; Shuttle Craft Monograph Fourteen, 1965	H&C	16	3		Su 65	44
Rhodes, Tonya Stalons; Harriet Tidball, ed.	Color Related Decorating Textiles: Rugs, Draperies, Upholstery	SCGM		14		65	1-35
Rial, Katherine	Weavers in Cleveland	H&C	6	3		Su 55	26
Riboud, Krishna	Newly Excavated Caftan from the Northern Caucasus, A	TMJ	4	3		76	21
Riccardi, Mary Elinor Steinbaugh	Warp Faced Patterning	SS&D	10	2	38	Sp 79	40
Rice, James W.	How to Match Colors When Dyeing Yarns or Fabrics for Textile Conservation Purposes	TMJ	2	4		De 69	27
Rice, James W.	Principles of Textile Conservation Science, No. 1. General Chemical and Physical Structural Features of the Natural Textile Fibers	TMJ	1	1		No 62	47
Rice, James W.	Principles of Textile Conservation Science, No. 10. An Investigation Into Cleaning and Conservation of Mixed Leather and Fiber Artifacts	TMJ	2	3		De 68	57
Rice, James W.	Principles of Textile Conservation Science, No. 11. Requirements for Bulk Storage Protection Against Insect Damage	TMJ	2	4		De 69	31
Rice, James W.	Principles of Textile Conservation Science, No. 12. Adhesives for Textile Conservation	TMJ	2	4		De 69	34
Rice, James W.	Principles of Textile Conservation Science, No.13. Acids and Acid Salts for Textile Conservation	TMJ	3	1		De 70	55
Rice, James W.	Principles of Textile Conservation Science, No.14. The Alkalies and Alkaline Salts	TMJ	3	1		De 70	55
Rice, James W.	Principles of Textile Conservation Science, No.15. The Control of Oxidation in Textile Conservation	TMJ	3	1		De 70	55
Rice, James W.	Principles of Textile Conservation Science, No.16. The Use and Control of Reducing Agents and "Strippers"	TMJ	3	1		De 70	55
Rice, James W.	Principles of Textile Conservation Science, No. 17. Solutions and Other Mixtures for Cleaning and Conservation of Textiles and Related Artifacts	TMJ	3	4		De 73	43
Rice, James W.	Principles of Textile Conservation Science, No. 2. Practical Control of Fungi and Bacteria in Fabric Specimens	TMJ	1	1		No 62	52
Rice, James W.	Principles of Textile Conservation Science, No. 3. Classification of Fibers Found in Ancient Textiles	TMJ	1	2		De 63	21
Rice, James W.	Principles of Textile Conservation Science, No. 4. The Conservation of Historical Textile Colorants	TMJ	1	2		De 63	55
Rice, James W.	Principles of Textile Conservation Science, No. 5. The Characteristics of Soils and Stains Encountered on Historic Textiles	TMJ	1	3		De 64	8
Rice, James W.	Principles of Textile Conservation Science, No. 6. The Wonders of Water in Wetcleaning	TMJ	2	1		De 66	15
Rice, James W.	Principles of Textile Conservation Science, No. 7. Characteristics of Detergents for Cleaning Historic Textiles	TMJ	2	1		De 66	23
Rice, James W.	Principles of Textile Conservation Science, No. 8. Drycleaning of Fine and Fragile Textiles	TMJ	2	2		De 67	21
Rice, James W.	Principles of Textile Conservation Science, No. 9. How Humidity May Affect Rug, Tapestry, and Other Textile Collections	TMJ	2	3		De 68	53
Rice, Mary Kellog	see Wada, Yoshiko	Hw	6	3		Su 85	14
Rice, Mary Kellogg	see Wada, Yoshiko	Fa	11	6		N/D 84	56
Rice, Mary Kellogg	see Wada, Yoshiko	Fa	12	2		M/A 85	55
Rice, Mary Kellogg	see Wada, Yoshiko	Fa	12	2		M/A 85	58
Rice, Miriam	Dyes from Mushrooms: A Spectrum of Extraordinary Color	TM			10	A/M 87	44
Rice, Miriam	see Sunström, Carla	SS&D	18	3	71	Su 87	73
Rice, Miriam C.	Let's Try Mushrooms for Color	SS&D	6	4	24	Fa 75	29

AUTHOR	TITLE	JOUR	VOL	NO	ISS	DATE	PAGE
Rice, Miriam; Dorothy Beebee	Mushrooms for Color	WJ	5	2	18	Fa 80	31
Rice, Miriam; Dorothy Beebee	Mushrooms for Color	Hw	2	3		My 81	70
Rice, Nancy Newman	"Fine Focus" (Exhibit)	Fa	12	2		M/A 85	74
Richards, H. Rex	Fibers — From Where to Where?	S-O	2			78	33
Richards, Iris	Christmas Project, A	WJ	1	2	2	Oc 76	12
Richards, Iris	Delight the Youngsters with Handwoven Puppets	WJ	7	2	26	Fa 82	72
Richards, Iris	Dog Fashions (error-corrected WJ v2 n1 77 insert for vol. 1)	WJ	1	3	3	Ja 77	33
Richards, Iris	Handwoven or Leather Flowers	WJ	4	1	13	Jy 79	34
Richards, Iris	Mood Lamp	WJ	3	2	10	Oc 78	44
Richards, Iris	Twice Woven Bolero	WJ	4	3	15	Ja 80	24
Richards, Iris	White Circular Wrap	WJ	4	3	15	Ja 80	7
Richardson, Pat	Fascination with Form, A	SS&D	12	3	47	Su 81	54
Richardt, Ericka	Queensland Inkle Loom	SS&D	4	3	15	Su 73	15
Richerson, Suzanne	"Claire Zeisler" (Exhibit)	Fa	6	4		J/A 79	69
Richerson, Suzanne	"Fiber Invitational" (Exhibit)	Fa	8	4		J/A 81	76
Richerson, Suzanne	Lucinda Sheets: A Quiltmaker's Mural is a Poem in Fabric	Fa	10	2		M/A 83	15
Richerson, Suzanne	Naomi Kark Schedl: A Concern with Empty Cradles	Fa	6	6		N/D 79	20
Richerson, Suzanne	"Naomi Kark Schedl: Coverings, Enclosures, and Pathways" (Exhibit)	Fa	11	4		J/A 84	73
Richerson, Suzanne	"Priscilla Sage: Small Paintings and Fiber Sculpture" (Exhibit)	Fa	8	3		M/J 81	69
Richerson, Suzanne	Rosalie Seeks: Cascading Dream Garden	Fa	12	1		J/F 85	21
Richerson, Suzanne	"Soft Art" (Exhibit)	Fa	4	4		J/A 77	16
Richter, Elizabeth Lee	Construction Details with Automatic Stitches	TM			11	J/J 87	64
Richter, Elizabeth Lee	So There Is a Use for Fancy Machine Stitches	TM			11	J/J 87	62
Ridgeway, Teresa	Fiber Reactive Dyes	SS&D	13	1	49	Wi 81	34
Ridgeway, Terese	Designing Rep Weave	SS&D	16	3	63	Su 85	28
Ridgeway, Terese	Holiday Greeting Cards	SS&D	15	4	60	Fa 84	61
Ridgeway, Terese	Master Weaver	SS&D	15	2	58	Sp 84	66
Ridgeway, Terese	Screen for All Seasons, A	SS&D	16	4	64	Fa 85	52
Ridgeway, Terese	Stepping Out	SS&D	18	1	69	Wi 86	82
Rigby, M. Edith	Natural Dyeing in Wisconsin	SS&D	12	2	46	Sp 81	8
Righetti, Maggie	In Stone They Are Not Writ	Kn	1	2	2	S-S 85	7
Righetti, Maggie	Knitting in Plain English	SS&D	18	4	72	Fa 87	55
Righetti, Maggie	Knitting in Plain English	TM			11	J/J 87	73
Righetti, Maggie	Methods for Multicolored Knitting	TM			6	A/S 86	40
Righetti, Maggie	Two Styles of Buttonholes	TM			3	F/M 86	32
Righetti, Maggie	Universal Yarn Finder, Vol. II	TM			1	O/N 85	76
Rinde-Ramsback, Marta	see Lundback, Maja	H&C	10	4		Fa 59	60
Rinehart, Marion	see Livingston, Lois	SS&D	14	3	55	Su 83	46
Rinehart, Marion	see Spillman, Trish	SS&D	9	3	35	Su 78	56
Ringler, Aina	Finnweave Can Be Fun	H&C	9	4		Fa 58	12
Ringler, Aina	Finnweave is Fun! The Way it is Woven in Finland	H&C	6	1		Wi 54	62
Ringler, Aina	Scandinavian Design, Contemporary Trend is Toward Simplicity	H&C	18	1		Wi 67	12
Rippy, Rachel	Fundamentals of Basketry	H&C	22	3		Su 71	25
Risseeuw, Mary	"Maximum Coverage: Wearables by Contemporary American Artists" (Exhibit)	Fa	8	1		J/F 81	93
Riswold, Margaret	Designs for Today from Great-Grandmother's Drafts	H&C	3	3		Su 52	20
Ritch, Diane; Yoshiko Iwamoto Wada	Making Fabric Flowers	TM			13	O/N 87	68
Ritch, Diane; Yoshiko Wada	Ikat: An Introduction Japanese Ikat—Warp—Weft—Figure	SS&D	7	1	25	Wi 75	34
Ritchey, Janet	Viditz-Ward Dyes in Evergreen; Students Still Blue	Iw	2	4		Su 77	13
Ritschard, Mlle. Claude	Lausanne Biennale: The Scene of an Adventure, The	Iw	4	2		Sp 79	19

AUTHOR	TITLE	JOUR	VOL	NO	ISS	DATE	PAGE
Rizner, Constance	Spinning Wheels	SS&D	14	3	55	Su 83	16
Rizner, Constance Bufkin	Seasonal Stoles	SS&D	18	2	70	Sp 87	22
Roach, Dianne Carol	Rugs for Interiors	SS&D	16	4	64	Fa 85	18
Robbins, Judy	Betty Williams: Colors of the Earth	SS&D	18	4	72	Fa 87	57
Roberts, Diane	Rag Prep	Hw	2	3		My 81	53
Roberts, Elizabeth	Go Adventuring with Your Pick-Up Stick (error-corrected H&C v2 n4 51 p64)	H&C	2	2		Sp 51	28
Roberts, Kaki	Belinda Raab: Exploring an Interior World	Fa	14	2		M/A 87	14
Roberts, Patricia	Patricia Roberts Knitting Book	Kn	2	2	4	S-S 86	79
Roberts, Patricia	Patricia Roberts Second Knitting Book	Kn	2	2	4	S-S 86	79
Roberts, Stephen	"Susan Lyman's Paper Structures" (Exhibit)	Fa	8	5		S/O 81	69
Robertson, R. B.	Of Sheep and Men	H&C	8	4		Fa 57	59
Robertson, Seonaid	Dyes from Plants	SS&D	5	3	19	Su 74	63
Robin and Russ Handweavers	Drafts and Designs, A Guide for 5-12 Harness Weaves	SS&D	3	3	11	Su 72	14
Robin and Russ Handweavers	Warp and Weft	SS&D	3	3	11	Su 72	13
Robinson, Bert	Basket Weavers of Arizona, The	H&C	6	2		Sp 55	61
Robinson, Charlotte, ed.	Artist & the Quilt, The	Fa	10	5		S/O 83	57
Robinson, Debby	Encyclopedia of Knitting Techniques, The	Kn	3	4	8	Fa 87	62
Robinson, Esther	Teneriffe Lace — Making Nanduti	SS&D	5	1	17	Wi 73	54
Robinson, Esther	Teneriffe Lace — Wooden Disc Loom	SS&D	5	1	17	Wi 73	52
Robinson, Harriet H.	Loom and Spindle: Life Among the Early Mill Girls	Fa	9	2		M/A 82	53
Robinson, Hester A.	Weaving in Hawaii	H&C	3	4		Fa 52	12
Robinson, Irma	Kasuri and I	SS&D	1	2	2	Mr 70	19
Robinson, Irma	Tablecloth in Double Weave, A	H&C	8	4		Fa 57	44
Robinson, Irma F.	Seattle Weavers' Guild, The	H&C	1	1		Ap 50	34
Robinson, John P., Jr.	Tyrian Purple	H&C	24	1		J/F 73	30
Robinson, Margaret	New Zealand Spinners	H&C	10	3		Su 59	23
Robinson, Sharon	Army of Softies: An Artist Talks About Her Delightfully Peculiar Obsession, An	Fa	8	6		N/D 81	25
Robinson, Sharon	Contemporary Basketry	SS&D	10	1	37	Wi 78	77
Robinson, Sharon	Contemporary Basketry	WJ	3	3	11	Ja 79	43
Robinson, Sharon	Contemporary Basketry	Hw	7	1		J/F 86	19
Robinson, Sharon	Contemporary Quilting	Fa	10	1		J/F 83	58
Robinson, Sharon	"Seven Sonoma County Fibre Artists" (Exhibit)	Fa	3	4		J/A 76	6
Robinson, Stuart	History of Dyed Textiles, A	H&C	21	3		Su 70	39
Robitaille, Annette	Blanket Weave, The	WJ	8	4	32	Sp 84	62
Robitaille, Annette	Four-Block Warp Rep (error-corrected WJ v8 n1 83 p50)	WJ	7	4	28	Sp 83	16
Robson, Deborah	Reading History in the Classifieds	S-O	11	3		Fa 87	20
Robson, Deborah	Weaving	Fa	10	4		J/A 83	43
Rocky Mountain Weavers Guild	Midwest Weavers Conference Workshops, 1973	SS&D	5	3	19	Su 74	62
Rodee, Marian E.	Southwestern Weaving	SS&D	9	3	35	Su 78	94
Rodee, Marian E.	Southwestern Weaving	SS&D	9	4	36	Fa 78	81
Rodee, Marian E.	Southwestern Weaving	Fa	5	2		M/A 78	58
Rodee, Marion E.	Old Navajo Rugs: Their Development from 1900 to 1940	Fa	8	6		N/D 81	73
Roe, Nancy	"Quilt National '83" (Exhibit)	Fa	10	5		S/O 83	82
Roe, Nancy	"Quilt National '85": A Proving Ground (Exhibit)	Fa	12	6		N/D 85	58
Roehr, Mary	Speed Tailoring	WJ	8	3	31	Wi 83	66
Rogers, Caroline S.	Merrimack Valley Textile Museum	SS&D	1	1	1	De 69	14
Rogers, Carrie	Loom to Build, A	lw	4	3		Su 79	66
Rogers, Carrie	Loom to Build, A	WJ	4	2	14	Oc 79	38
Rogers, Carrie M.	Loom to Build, A	SS&D	11	1	41	Wi 79	32
Rogers, Carrie M.	Story of My Dining Room Rug, The	WJ	6	4	24	Sp 82	24
Rogers, Fran	Dementia	S-O	9	4		Wi 85	51

AUTHOR	TITLE	JOUR	VOL	NO	ISS	DATE	PAGE
Rogers, Georgia M.	Greatest Sew on Earth, The	TM		11		J/J 87	38
Rogers, Georgia M.	Hobby of Queens, The	TM		3		F/M 86	12
Rogers, Grace L.	Peter Stauffer — Early 19th Century Weaver	H&C	7	1		Wi 55	12
Rogers, Nora	Cultures to Meet in California	Hw	6	1		J/F 85	18
Rogers, Nora	Spaced-Weft Twining of Ancient Peru: A Contemporary Interpretation	Iw	5	4		Fa 80	42
Rogers, Nora; Martha Stanley, eds.	In Celebration of the Curious Mind	Hw	4	3		M/J 83	13
Rogers, Nora; Martha Stanley, eds.	In Celebration of the Curious Mind—A Festschrift to Honor Anne Blinks on Her 80th Birthday	WJ	8	1	29	Su 83	52
Rogers, Phyllis, Joan Holborn	Mittens	S-O	4			80	61
Rohrer, Marge	History Lives on at Bishop Hill	Iw	4	3		Su 79	43
Rohrer, Marge	Weaving a Coverlet	S-O	6	4		82	28
Rolingson, Beth	American Tapestry Allicance, The	WJ	12	1	45	Su 87	32
Romey, Lucretia	Weaver Bird Nest—Ploceidae Family	SS&D	6	3	23	Su 75	7
Ronin, Col. James A.	Controlled Spinning	SS&D	3	3	11	Su 72	36
Ronin, Col. James A. ret.	Mechanization of the Bobbin-Flyer Spinning Wheel, The	S-O	2			78	44
Ronin, Col. James A. ret.	Two-Flyer Spinning Wheel, The	S-O	1			77	40
Ronin, Colonel James A.	Spinformation	S-O	10	3		Fa 86	48
Roosevelt, Lynn Nanney	Woven Traditions: The Liberty Textile Collection	Fa	14	2		M/A 87	6
Rose, Chris	Comfort Clothes	WJ	7	1	25	Su 82	64
Rose, Kathy	Alling Museum, The	Hw	3	5		N/D 82	33
Rose, Violet	Ruana for Beginners, A	Hw	8	4		S/O 87	48
Rosen, Norma	Making a Good Impression: A Guide to Rubber Stamp Printing	Fa	10	1		J/F 83	43
Rosen, Norma	Wearable Coils: Nigerian Hair Sculpture	Fa	12	4		J/A 85	33
Ross, Douglas	"Material/Culture" (Exhibit)	Fa	14	2		M/A 87	55
Ross, Ginny	see Schnitzler, Jeanne	Fa	5	4		J/A 78	63
Ross, Heather Colyer	Art of Arabian Costume: A Saudi Arabian Profile, The	WJ	8	3	31	Wi 83	64
Ross, Heather Colyer	Art of Arabian Costume: A Saudi Arabian Profile, The	Fa	10	1		J/F 83	57
Ross, Mabel	Essentials of Handspinning, The	S-O	8	2		Su 84	51
Ross, Mabel	Essentials of Handspinning, The	SS&D	15	3	59	Su 84	35
Ross, Mabel	Essentials of Yarn Design for Handspinners, The	SS&D	15	3	59	Su 84	35
Ross, Mabel	Essentials of Yarn Design for the Handspinners, The	S-O	8	2		Su 84	51
Ross, Mabel	Precise Control of Size and Quality in Handspun Yarn, Part 1, The	SS&D	16	3	63	Su 85	12
Ross, Mabel	Precise Control of Twist in Handspun Yarn, Part 2, The	SS&D	16	4	64	Fa 85	26
Ross, Mable	Essentials of Handspinning, The	Hw	2	3		My 81	73
Ross, Marjorie Ruth	Unusual Upholstery from Discarded Stockings	H&C	8	2		Sp 57	47
Ross, Nan	Those Musty Old Looms	SS&D	8	2	30	Sp 77	43
Ross, Ruth Custer	Values of Local Guilds	SS&D	4	2	14	Sp 73	7
Rossbach, Ed	Art of Paisley, The	Iw	6	1		Wi 80	72
Rossbach, Ed	Art of Paisley, The	WJ	6	3	23	Wi 81	59
Rossbach, Ed	Art of Paisley, The	Fa	8	4		J/A 81	34
Rossbach, Ed	Baskets as Textile Art	TMJ	4	2		75	81
Rossbach, Ed	Design in Handwoven Screens, Part 1	H&C	6	1		Wi 54	16
Rossbach, Ed	Design in Handwoven Screens, Part 2	H&C	6	3		Su 55	16
Rossbach, Ed	Ed Rossbach	Fa	11	6		N/D 84	60
Rossbach, Ed	New Basketry, The	SS&D	8	2	30	Sp 77	37
Rossbach, Ed	New Basketry, The	Fa	4	2		M/A 77	41
Rossbach, Ed	Thinking About Historical Baskets	Fa	11	1		J/F 84	32
Rossetter, Tabitha Wilson	L'Amour de Maman: The Acadian Textile Heritage	Fa	8	3		M/J 81	29
Rossi, Gail	Flourishing Art: China, Guizhou Women Continue to Embroider Their Legends, A	TM		9		F/M 87	30
Rossi, Gail	Guizhou Textiles	SS&D	18	1	69	Wi 86	39
Rossiter, Phyllis	Carol Clivio, Wizard of Spinning	S-O	8	4		Wi 84	53

AUTHOR	TITLE	JOUR	VOL	NO	ISS	DATE	PAGE
Rossiter, Phyllis	Christmas Tree Dye — A Natural!	S-O	9	4		Wi 85	22
Rossiter, Phyllis	Drum Carder, The	SS&D	15	4	60	Fa 84	71
Rossiter, Phyllis	Navajo Three-Ply Method, The	SS&D	16	1	61	Wi 84	10
Rossiter, Phyllis	Spinning: Where to Begin	SS&D	16	2	62	Sp 85	10
Rossiter, Phyllis	There's an Old Spinning Wheel in the Parlor	S-O	9	1		Sp 85	31
Rossiter, Phyllis J.	Singer Spinning Wheel, The	S-O	8	2		Su 84	34
Rossol, Monona	Hazards of Dyes By Class	Fa	12	6		N/D 85	43
Rossol, Monona	Hazards of Mordants and Dye-Assisting Chemicals	Fa	12	6		N/D 85	43
Rossol, Monona	Protecting Yourself: Fiber Art Hazards and Precautions	Fa	12	6		N/D 85	42
Rossol, Monona	Rules for Using Paints, Inks, and Dyes	Fa	12	6		N/D 85	42
Rotert, Bette	Essay: The Incredible, Flexible Rigid Heddle Loom	PWC			2	Ap 82	60
Roth, Bettie	Dress (size 14) Shaped on Loom (size 24")	SS&D	3	1	9	Wi 71	17
Roth, Bettie G.	Coat for Handwoven Yardage, A	WJ	7	3	27	Wi 82	6
Roth, Bettie G.	Creating a Public Textile Library	SS&D	9	3	35	Su 78	47
Roth, Bettie G.	Jacket for Hiking, A	WJ	8	3	31	Wi 83	69
Roth, Bettie G.	Liebes Legacy, The	SS&D	13	2	50	Sp 82	18
Roth, Bettie G.	Long Sweeping Evening Cape	WJ	6	3	23	Wi 81	26
Roth, Bettie G.	Sett and the Hand of the Fabric	SS&D	12	3	47	Su 81	16
Roth, Bettie G.	Textile Library Just for You, A	CW	6	2	17	Ja 85	24
Roth, Bettie G.; Chris Schulz	Handbook of Time Saving Tables for Weavers, Spinners, and Dyers	WJ	8	1	29	Su 83	51
Roth, Bettie G.; Chris Schulz	New Handbook of Timesaving Tables for Weavers, Spinners, and Dyers, The	WJ	10	3	39	Wi 86	72
Roth, Bettie G.; Chris Shulz	Handbook of Timesaving Tables for Weavers, Spinners, and Dyers	Hw	5	4		S/O 84	14
Roth, Mrs, Bettie G.	Fall Project: Loom Controlled Slacks (error-corrected H&C v26 n5 75 p45)	H&C	26	3		M/J 75	18
Rothacker, Chet	Projects Spark Interest	Hw	1	2		S-S 80	15
Rough, Joan Z.	Locker Hooking	SS&D	16	1	61	Wi 84	54
Rouse, Mary	Weaving at State University of Iowa	H&C	4	3		Su 53	24
Routh, Carol	Fun Approach to a Guild Show or Sale, The	Hw	8	2		M/A 87	32
Rowe, Ann P.; Elizabeth P. Benson; Anne-Louise Shaffer	Junius B. Bird Pre-Columbian Textile Conference, May 19 and 20, 1973, The	Iw	5	4		Fa 80	75
Rowe, Ann Pollard	After Emery: Further Considerations of Fabric Classification and Terminology	TMJ	23			84	53
Rowe, Ann Pollard	Century of Change in Guatemalan Textiles, A	WJ	7	2	26	Fa 82	57
Rowe, Ann Pollard	Interlocking Warp and Weft in the Nasca 2 Style	TMJ	3	3		De 72	67
Rowe, Ann Pollard	see Cahlander, Adele	WJ	5	4	20	Sp 81	45
Rowe, Ann Pollard	Technical Features of Inca Tapestry Tunics	TMJ	17			78	5
Rowe, Ann Pollard	Textile Evidence for Huari Music	TMJ	18			79	5
Rowe, Ann Pollard	Weaving Processes in the Cuzco Area of Peru	TMJ	4	2		75	30
Rowe, Ann Pollard	Woven Structures of European Shawls in The Textile Museum Collection, The	TMJ	24			85	55
Rowe, Ann Pollard, ed.	Junius B. Bird Conference on Andean Textiles, The	WJ	12	1	45	Su 87	70
Rowe, Ann Pollard; Junius B. Bird	Three Ancient Peruvian Gauze Looms	TMJ	19 20			80,81	27
Rowe, Anne Pollard	Warp-Patterned Weaves of the Andes	SS&D	8	4	32	Fa 77	72
Rowe, Anne Pollard; Elizabeth P. Benson; Anne-Louise Schaffer, eds.	Junius B. Bird Pre-Columbian Textile Conference, The	Fa	7	6		N/D 80	59
Rowe, Dilys	Wool from the Welsh Valleys	H&C	10	2		Sp 59	30
Rowe, Erica	Angora: Frivolous Fluff or Fantistic Fiber?	S-O	8	2		Su 84	13
Rowe, Erica	Angora: Producing Your Own Fibers	S-O	8	2		Su 84	17
Rowe, Erica	Guilds for Spinners	S-O	3			79	35
Rowe, Erica	Handspun Angora Mittens	S-O	8	1		Sp 84	51
Rowe, Erica	Rainbow Dyeing	WJ	8	2	30	Fa 83	31

AUTHOR	TITLE	JOUR	VOL	NO	ISS	DATE	PAGE
Rowe, Erica	Ruffles and Ridges: A Scanning Electron Microscopy Study of Vegetable Fibers	S-O	4			80	30
Rowe, Mary	Garden of Fair Isles, A	Kn	2	1	3	F-W 85	40, 8B
Rowe, Mary	Special Fitting	Kn	1	2	2	S-S 85	30
Rowland, Amy Zaffarano	Building on Experience: Virginia Jacobs' Fabric Constructions	Fa	7	4		J/A 80	39
Rowland, Amy Zaffarano	Muslin Ladies: Trapunto Drawings of Christine Meyers	Fa	10	3		M/J 83	19
Rowland, Amy Zaffarano	Songs in Fabric: Quiltmaker Nancy Herman Is An Unusual Musician	Fa	9	4		J/A 82	22
Rowlands-Tarbox, Jean L.	"Unsettled Images: Peggy Vanbianchi & Emily Standley" (Exhibit)	Fa	12	5		S/O 85	71
Rowley, Elaine	Alexis' Favorite	Kn	1	1	1	F-W 84 CI	46,56B 38
Rowley, Elaine	Beginnings...	Kn	4	1	9	Wi 87	25
Rowley, Elaine	Body in Question, The	Kn	3	2	6	Sp 87	54
Rowley, Elaine	Cast on in Pattern	Kn	3	3	7	Su 87	39
Rowley, Elaine	Consider Color	Kn	2	1	3	F-W 85	20
Rowley, Elaine	Contrasting Textures	Kn	2	2	4	S-S 86	67
Rowley, Elaine	Double Knitting	Kn	3	4	8	Fa 87	60
Rowley, Elaine	Guernsey Tradition, The	Kn	1	1	1	F-W 84 CI	24 16
Rowley, Elaine	Intarsia Technique	Kn	3	4	8	Fa 87	52
Rowley, Elaine	Knit and Purl	Kn	1	1	1	F-W 84 CI	40 32
Rowley, Elaine	Lace-Weave Tunic	PWC			5	Sp 83	18
Rowley, Elaine	Little Knowledge, A	Kn	3	1	5	F-W 86	41
Rowley, Elaine	Mossy Bog, A	PWC			3	Oc 82	43
Rowley, Elaine	Norse Kjøkken	PWC	3	1	7		16
Rowley, Elaine	Ornamental and Functional	Kn	1	2	2	S-S 85	36
Rowley, Elaine	Particular Guernsey, A	Kn	1	1	1	F-W 84 CI	25,56A 17
Rowley, Elaine	Perfect Pleats	Kn	3	2	6	Sp 87	24
Rowley, Elaine	Roomie Sweater	Kn	3	4	8	Fa 87	47
Rowley, Elaine	Sans Serif T	Kn	3	3	7	Su 87	22
Rowley, Elaine	see Xenakis, Alexis Yiorgos	Kn	1	2	2	S-S 85	74
Rowley, Elaine	see Xenakis, Alexis Yiorgos	PWC			6	Su 83	10
Rowley, Elaine	Sleeve Sweater	Kn	2	1	3	F-W 85	58
Rowley, Elaine	Slightly Left of Center Jacket	PWC			6	Su 83	44
Rowley, Elaine	T-Sweater	Kn	1	2	2	S-S 85	34, 72A
Rowley, Elaine	Undies Revealed: Petticoat	Kn	3	2	6	Sp 87	13
Rowley, Elaine; Alexis Yiorgos Xenakis	Turned Overshot	PWC	3	2	8		53
Rowley, Elaine D.	Crocheted and Knitted "Precious Littles"	PWC			3	Oc 82	58
Rowley, Elaine D.	Elaine's Knitted Top	PWC			2	Ap 82	89
Rowley, Elaine D.	Finns Can Knit Too or How to Knit a Finn	PWC			2	Ap 82	76
Rowley, Elaine D.	'Round and 'Round We Go, The Janet Sweater	PWC	1	1		No 81	50
Rowley, Elaine D.	Peruvian Hat	PWC			4	Ja 83	65
Rowley, Kathleen	Convergence '84	Fa	12	2		M/A 85	42
Rowley, Kathleen	Creative Cycle: Recharging, The	Fa	11	6		N/D 84	54
Rowley, Kathleen	"Glenn Brill: Recent Work" (Exhibit)	Fa	12	1		J/F 85	72
Rowley, Kathleen	Japanese Country Textiles (Exhibit)	Fa	13	5		S/O 86	49
Rowley, Kathleen	Jeannie Davidson: Costuming for Shakespearean Theater	Fa	11	5		S/O 84	66
Rowley, Kathleen	"Lia Cook: Shaped and Woven Constructions" (Exhibit)	Fa	12	4		J/A 85	66
Rowley, Kathleen	Linda Richards-Watson: Finding the Eclectic	Fa	10	4		J/A 83	12
Rowley, Kathleen	Making a Living: Eight Fiber Artists Tell How They Do It	Fa	9	5		S/O 82	38
Rowley, Kathleen	Marcia Morse: A Collaboration with Paper	Fa	11	2		M/A 84	20
Rowley, Kathleen	"Nance O'Banion: Painted Paper Skin Series" (Exhibits)	Fa	9	4		J/A 82	70
Rowley, Kathleen	"Quilts: A Tradition of Variations" (Exhibit)	Fa	10	2		M/A 83	68

AUTHOR	TITLE	JOUR	VOL	NO	ISS	DATE	PAGE
Rowley, Kathleen	San Francisco Tapestry Workshop: A European-Style Atelier in the United States, The	Fa	10	3		M/J 83	60
Rowley, Kathleen	"Tapestries of Trude Guermonprez: A Retrospective, The" (Exhibit)	Fa	10	3		M/J 83	68
Rowley, Kathleen	"Three Weavers: Thomasin Grim, Jane Lackey, Bhakti Ziek" (Exhibit)	Fa	9	6		N/D 82	82
Rowley, Kathleen	Vivian Poon: Exposing Facades	Fa	13	4		J/A 86	12
Rowley, Kathleen	Words in Fiber	Fa	11	2		M/A 84	66
Rowley, Kathleen M.	Sheila O'Hara's Geometrics	SS&D	12	4	48	Fa 81	20
Rowley, Kristen Carlsen	Tangential Textiles: From Quiltmaking to Points Beyond	Fa	9	2		M/A 82	22
Rowley, Kristin	Liza Lamb	Fa	13	5		S/O 86	18
Rowley, Kristin Carlsen	Kristin Carlsen Rowley: Rugmaker	Fa	7	5		S/O 80	52
Rowley, Kristin Carlsen	"With or Without a Loom" (Exhibit)	Fa	8	5		S/O 81	67
Royce, Beverly	Beverley Royce's "Recipe" for Merino	S-O	5			81	49
Royce, Beverly	Exotic Fiber Blends	S-O	9	4		Wi 85	43
Royce, Beverly	Merino Pullover	S-O	9	1		Sp 85	40
Royce, Beverly	Three Spun Threads	S-O	9	1		Sp 85	39
Royce, Beverly; Florence Van Kleek	Mohair Tam O'Shanter	S-O	8	1		Sp 84	49
Ruane, Joan	Have Spindle Will Travel	S-O	7	4		Wi 83	38
Rubbert, Toni	Silk Production of Lullingstone and Whitchurch, The	Hw	3	4		Se 82	27
Rubbert, Toni Condon	Mill Girls of 'Spindle City,' The	S-O	10	1		Sp 86	16
Rubbert, Toni Condon	Slater Mill Historic Site, The	S-O	8	2		Su 84	42
Rubbert, Toni Condon	There's a Lady Out Bantry Bay Way	S-O	7	4		Wi 83	32
Rubenstone, Jessie	Weaving for Beginners	SS&D	8	1	29	WI 76	70
Rubin, Deann Joy	Self-Portrait	SS&D	15	1	57	Wi 83	72
Rubin, Jean	Jann Rosen-Queralt: An Architecture of Indirection	Fa	12	2		M/A 85	47
Ruch, Theresa	see Sowles, Susan	SS&D	13	3	51	Su 82	30
Ruchti, Willie Jager	Karelian Red-Picking	WJ	5	2	18	Fa 80	34
Rucker, Karon	Double Weave for Fiber Art	SS&D	9	2	34	Sp 78	19
Rudich, Sally	Behind the Scenes: Your Own Studio	Fa	13	3		M/J 86	47
Rudich, Sally	Denim Production: The Making of an American Staple	Fa	13	5		S/O 86	11
Rudich, Sally	"Fiber R/Evolution" (Exhibit)	Fa	13	4		J/A 86	45
Rudich, Sally	Lee Company	Fa	13	5		S/O 86	13
Rudich, Sally	Limited Editions: The Wearable Books of Lois Morrison	Fa	12	3		M/J 85	91
Rudich, Sally	OshKosh B'Gosh	Fa	13	5		S/O 86	16
Rudich, Sally	Silken Dreams of Faraway Lands	Fa	12	4		J/A 85	80
Rudich, Sally	Wrangler	Fa	13	5		S/O 86	12
Rudick, Sally	David Johnson and Geary Jones	Fa	12	5		S/O 85	18
Rulli, Linda	Phan Nguyen Barker	Fa	13	5		S/O 86	18
Rummler, Ruth	Twice-Woven Rug	SS&D	4	2	14	Sp 73	19
Rupp, Michael	Juried Exhibit from Pattern to Free- Form	SS&D	6	1	21	Wi 74	42
Rupp, Michael E.	Why Explore Overshot?	SS&D	7	2	26	Sp 76	66
Rush, Beverly	Jean Wilson	Iw	5	2		Sp 80	43
Rush, Helene	Hollow Oak Vest	Kn	2	2	4	S-S 86	30
Rush, Helene	Overall and Underneath	Kn	3	1	5	F-W 86	42
Rush, Helene	Shirt for All Seasons, A	Kn	3	2	6	Sp 87	25
Rushfelt, Joy M.	Revival of Ikat	H&C	19	2		Sp 68	14
Rusoff, Beverly	Homage to Hats: Handmade Paper Drawing/Collages Honor a Women's Tradition	Fa	8	1		J/F 81	80
Russ, Stephen	Fabric Printing by Hand	H&C	16	2		Sp 65	43
Russell, Barbara	Angoras for the Spinner's Flock	S-O	7	3		Fa 83	45
Russell, Barbara	Dyeing Mohair and the Random Effect	S-O	6	4		82	54
Russell, Barbara	Preparing, Spinning and Dyeing Mohair	S-O	7	3		Fa 83	52
Russell, Elfleda	Imagery and Structure: The Tapestries of Marcel Marois	Fa	8	6		N/D 81	57

AUTHOR	TITLE	JOUR	VOL	NO	ISS	DATE	PAGE
Russell, Elfleda	Off-Loom Weaving	lw	1	4		Su 76	29
Russell, Harold W.	Basic Guide to Sett, Woolen Yarn (error-ccorrected H&C v18 n4 67 p45)	H&C	18	3		Su 67	32
Russell, Harold W.	New Craft Program at St. Benedict's Monastery	SS&D	2	3	7	Su 71	24
Russell, Harold W.; Fred J. Ahrens	Sectional Warp Beam	SS&D	5	2	18	Sp 74	25
Russell, Harold W.; Walter W. Ingenthron, Jr.	One-Spindle Twister	SS&D	3	1	9	Wi 71	10
Russell, Janet	Lace Index	Kn	1	2	2	S-S 85	79
Russell, Joan	Modular Weaves to Be Stuffed on the Loom	SS&D	5	4	20	Fa 74	97
Russell, Kate	Kate Russell: Weaving the Structure of Life	Fa	12	4		J/A 85	11
Rutherford, Karen Jenson	Design Concepts and Aesthetic Concerns of Corporate Art Collections	AT	8			De 87	193
Rutkovsky, Fran Cutrell	It Still Can Be Beautiful: Although Utilitarian	SS&D	7	3	27	Su 76	57
Rutovsky, Fran Cutrell	Fickle Feds Finger Fiber Felons	Fa	4	2		M/A 77	6
Rutt, Richard	Bishop of Leicester, The	Kn	4	1	9	Wi 87	10
Ryall, Pierre	Can a Weaver Earn a Living? Mais Certainement!	SS&D	7	3	27	Su 76	4
Ryall, Pierre	Weaving Techniques for the Multiple-Harness Loom	SS&D	11	2	42	Sp 80	83
Ryall, Pierre	Weaving Techniques for the Multiple-Harness Loom	WJ	5	1	17	Su 80	47
Ryan, Shirley	Paddle Warping — One Weaver Tells Why	Hw	3	3		My 82	68
Saarto	see Gustafsson	H&C	10	1		Wi 59	60
Sacks, Star M.	Embroidered Neckpieces of Theodora Elston, The	Fa	6	3		M/J 79	51
Saddler, Jane	see Hollen, Norma	H&C	19	4		Fa 68	44
Saddler, Jane	see Hollen, Norma	H&C	7	1		Wi 55	59
Saddler, Jane	see Hollen, Norma	H&C	16	4		Fa 65	44
Safanda, Elizabeth	see Bishop, Robert	Fa	7	1		J/F 80	15
Safford, Carleton L.; Robert Bishop	America's Quilts and Coverlets	TMJ	3	4		De 73	47
Safner, Isadora; Diane Piette	Weaving Book of Peace and Patience, The	WJ	5	4	20	Sp 81	45
Safner, Isadora M.	Weaving Roses of Rhode Island, The	WJ	11	1	41	Su 86	74
Safner, Isadora M.	Weaving Roses of Rhode Island, The	SS&D	17	3	67	Su 86	87
Safner, Isadora M.	Weaving Roses of Rhode Island, The	PWC	4	2	12		50
Sage, Jan	Teresa Nomura: Fabric and Fantasy	Fa	11	5		S/O 84	20
Sahlstrand, Margaret	Paper Clothing, East	Fa	11	2		M/A 84	36
Saito, Shirley	Mindy Alper: Sculpting in Papier Mache	Fa	11	4		J/A 84	18
Sakiestewa, Ramona	Pueblo Weaving: A Renaissance	lw	4	1		Wi 78	34
Salinger, Maude	Day in the Life of a Millgirl	SS&D	17	4	68	Fa 86	78
Salmon, Larry, ed.	see Carlano, Marianne, ed.	Hw	8	5		N/D 87	13
Salsbury, Nate	Alternative Summer and Winter Pickup Technique, An	lw	5	4		Fa 80	69
Salsbury, Nate	My Computer Designs a Bedspread	Hw	3	3		My 82	80
Salsbury, Nate	New Multi-Harness Drawdown Technique, A	lw	6	1		Wi 80	57
Salter, Deborah	Tapestries of Muriel Nezhnie Helfman	H&C	23	5		S/O 72	43
Saltzman, Ellen Lewis	Overshot Weaving	Hw	5	1		J/F 84	22
Saltzman, Ellen Lewis	Overshot Weaving	WJ	8	1	29	Su 83	51
Saltzman, Ellen Lewis	Overshot Weaving	Fa	10	4		J/A 83	50
Saltzman, Ellen Lewis	Overshot Weaving	PWC			6	Su 83	66
Salvador, Mari Lynn	Yer Dailege: Kuna Women's Art	Fa	9	1		J/F 82	58
Salzman, Myra	Feltmaking	SS&D	14	2	54	Sp 83	42
Samdahl, R.	Yarn Data Handbook	TM			1	O/N 85	76
Sampe-Hultberg, Astrid; Vera Diurson	Textil Bilderbok	H&C	3	3		Su 52	62
Sample, Joan	Thread Weaving	TM			8	D/J 86	64
Samuel, Alena	Chilkat Spinning	TM			1	O/N 85	55
Samuel, Cheryl	Breath of Our Grandmothers, The	WJ	8	1	29	Su 83	17
Samuel, Cheryl	Chilkat Dancing Blanket, The	SS&D	13	4	52	Fa 82	58

AUTHOR	TITLE	JOUR	VOL	NO	ISS	DATE	PAGE
Samuel, Cheryl	Chilkat Dancing Blanket, The	SS&D	13	4	52	Fa 82	66
Samuel, Cheryl	Chilkat Dancing Blanket, The	WJ	7	2	26	Fa 82	57
Samuel, Cheryl	Chilkat Dancing Blanket, The	PWC			3	Oc 82	63
Samuel, Cheryl	From Baskets to Blankets (error-corrected TM i7 O/N86 p5)	TM			5	J/J 86	30
Samuel, Cheryl	Temple of the Elelments, The	SS&D	17	3	67	Su 86	10
Sandoval, Arturo Alonzo	Arturo Alonzo Sandoval	Fa	11	6		N/D 84	58
Sarah Campbell Bluffer Gallery (Catalogue)	American Fiber Art: A New Definition	Hw	2	2		Mr 81	21
Sarchielli, Judith	Judith Sarchielli: Mukluk Maker	Fa	5	6		N/D 78	23
Sarginson, Peter	West Dean and the Tapestry Studio	Fa	11	2		M/A 84	65
Sass, Millie	Great Rip-Out, The	Kn	1	1	1	F-W 84 CI	5 3
Satterlee, Sarah	see Weills, Christopher	SS&D	14	1	53	Wi 82	64
Saulpaugh, Dassah	Coverlets and Bedspreads: Variety in Early American Design	H&C	17	4		Fa 66	8
Saulson, Sarah F.	California Rags	SS&D	18	1	69	Wi 86	44
Saulson, Sarah Fusfeld	Museum of American Textile History	SS&D	17	4	68	Fa 86	80
Sawyer, Alan R.	Mastercraftsmen of Ancient Peru	H&C	20	1		Wi 69	41
Sawyer, Alan R.	Tiahuanaco Tapestry Design	TMJ	1	2		De 63	27
Sayer, Chloe	Costumes of Mexico	WJ	10	3	39	Wi 86	72
Sayer, Chloe	Costumes of Mexico	TM			6	A/S 86	86
Sayer, Chloe	Crafts of Mexico	SS&D	9	4	36	Fa 78	82
Sayler, Mary	Peruvian Leno	SS&D	3	3	11	Su 72	45
Saylor, Mary C.	Reflection of the Past: Antique Looms, A	SS&D	7	3	27	Su 76	26
Sayward, Jessica Lee	Randall Darwall	SS&D	15	2	58	Sp 84	48
Scanlin, Tommye McClure	Big Bobbin Lace	Fa	13	2		M/A 86	32
Scanlin, Tommye McClure	Paper Weaving	Hw	7	4		S/O 86	28
Scarborough, Jessica	"American Hooked Rugs: 1850–1957" (Exhibit)	Fa	8	6		N/D 81	68
Scarborough, Jessica	Ana Lisa Hedstrom: The Intuitive Language of Shibori	Fa	13	1		J/F 86	26
Scarborough, Jessica	Art to Wear: Looking At the Movement	Fa	12	3		M/J 85	56
Scarborough, Jessica	Art/Culture/Future	Fa	13	5		S/O 86	52
Scarborough, Jessica	"Basketry: Tradition in New Form" (Exhibit)	Fa	9	3		M/J 82	83
Scarborough, Jessica	"Bella Tabak Feldman: Recent Sculpture" (Exhibit)	Fa	10	2		M/A 83	70
Scarborough, Jessica	Contemporary Archeology: The Baskets of Lissa Hunter	Fa	9	5		S/O 82	25
Scarborough, Jessica	Design by the Yard: Today's Fabric Innovators	Fa	12	5		S/O 85	30
Scarborough, Jessica	Earth Batik: Jessica Scarborough Buries Her Art in the Earth	Fa	7	6		N/D 80	41
Scarborough, Jessica	Ewa Kuryluk: Distillations in Fiber	Fa	12	2		M/A 85	14
Scarborough, Jessica	Fashioned from Paper: Rosina Yue's "Clothing" Constructions	Fa	8	1		J/F 81	76
Scarborough, Jessica	Fiber Lover's Guide to the San Francisco Bay Area, A	Fa	11	3		M/J 84	43
Scarborough, Jessica	"Fiber/Fabric '81" (Exhibit)	Fa	8	4		J/A 81	74
Scarborough, Jessica	"Fibers: From Function to Formalization" (Exhibit)	Fa	9	1		J/F 82	76
Scarborough, Jessica	"Five Artists: Quilts" (Exhibit)	Fa	13	5		S/O 86	47
Scarborough, Jessica	Fran Kraynek-Prince and Neil Prince	Fa	12	5		S/O 85	19
Scarborough, Jessica	Gyöngy Laky: Experimental Thinking in Textiles	Fa	11	1		J/F 84	21
Scarborough, Jessica	Hiroko Ogawa: Keeping Alive the Art of Sashiko	Fa	12	2		M/A 85	12
Scarborough, Jessica	Ice Tapestries: The Environmental Art of Phyllis Dukes	Fa	6	5		S/O 79	26
Scarborough, Jessica	Julie Silber: Exploring the Art and History of Quilts	Fa	12	6		N/D 85	14
Scarborough, Jessica	Levi Strauss & Co.	Fa	13	5		S/O 86	17
Scarborough, Jessica	Linted Palette of Slater Barron, The	Fa	12	4		J/A 85	42
Scarborough, Jessica	Olga de Amarol: Toward a Language of Freedom	Fa	12	4		J/A 85	51
Scarborough, Jessica	"Paper Clothing and More in San Francisco" (Exhibit)	Fa	11	2		M/A 84	75
Scarborough, Jessica	Patricia Bulitt: Gutsongs and Other Dances	Fa	11	5		S/O 84	50
Scarborough, Jessica	Sculptural Paper: Foundations and Directions	Fa	11	2		M/A 84	32
Scarborough, Jessica	Shady Ladies	Fa	11	3		M/J 84	12
Scarborough, Jessica	"Spindle City," Lowell, Massachusetts	Fa	9	2		M/A 82	53

AUTHOR	TITLE	JOUR	VOL	NO	ISS	DATE	PAGE
Scarborough, Jessica	Surface Design Conference 1985	Fa	12	5		S/O 85	46
Scarborough, Jessica	Textile Trends: Collecting in the San Francisco Area	Fa	12	6		N/D 85	28
Scarborough, Jessica	Therese May: Risking to Grow	Fa	12	4		J/A 85	15
Scarborough, Jessica	"Thomasin Grim: New Work" (Exhibit)	Fa	11	5		S/O 84	73
Scarborough, Jessica	Verina Warren	Fa	13	4		J/A 86	26
Scarborough, Jessica	Victoria Rivers: Sculpting in Fiber and Neon	Fa	12	1		J/F 85	22
Scarborough, Jessica	Visual Language of Bella Feldman, The	Fa	11	4		J/A 84	30
Scarborough, Jessica	Wall Hangings of Judith Content, The	Fa	13	2		M/A 86	10
Scarborough, Jessica	Way We Wore: San Francisco's Museum of Vintage Fashion, The	Fa	14	5		N/D 87	5
Scarborough, Jessica	Wefts of Light: Jayn Thomas' Fabric Hangings	Fa	9	1		J/F 82	23
Scarborough, Jessica	When Prison Is Home: Challenging the Creative Spirit	Fa	11	6		N/D 84	69
Scarlett, James D.	How to Weave Fine Cloth	SS&D	13	2	50	Sp 82	62
Scarlett, James D.	How to Weave Fine Cloth	Hw	2	3		My 81	72
Scarlett, James D.	How to Weave Fine Cloth	WJ	7	1	25	Su 82	63
Scarlett, James D.	How to Weave Fine Cloth	WJ	10	2	38	Fa 85	81
Schaffer, Anne-Louise	see Rowe, Ann P.	Iw	5	4		Fa 80	75
Schaffer, Anne-Louise, ed.	see Rowe, Anne Pollard, ed.	Fa	7	6		N/D 80	59
Schaffernicht, Elisabeth	Ontario Mohair Company, The	S-O	7	3		Fa 83	26
Schaller, Karin	Mary Crovatt Hambidge	Fa	11	5		S/O 84	24
Schedl, Naomi Kark	"Barbara MacCallum: Recent Work" (Exhibit)	Fa	12	4		J/A 85	68
Scheidig, Walter	Crafts of the Wiemar Bauhaus	H&C	18	3		Su 67	43
Scheinman, Pam	Casting Shadows: The Work of Pam Scheinman	Fa	5	1		J/F 78	60
Scheinman, Pam	Diane Itter	Fa	5	2		M/A 78	20
Scheinman, Pamela	"Anne Dushanko-Dobek: Silent Voices" (Exhibit)	Fa	11	4		J/A 84	77
Scheinman, Pamela	Carol Rosen: Paper Constructions	Fa	11	2		M/A 84	16
Scheinman, Pamela	"Patricia Malarcher: Pieced Reflections" (Exhibit)	Fa	11	2		M/A 84	77
Scheinman, Pamela	"Show Biz" (Exhibit)	Fa	7	4		J/A 80	69
Scheirman, Pam	Rags to Riches: Ragstrip Vest	WJ	6	3	23	Wi 81	30
Scheuer, Ruth Tannenbaum	Scheuer Tapestry Studio: Applying Old Techniques to New Ideas, The	Fa	10	3		M/J 83	39
Schevill, Margot	Art of Ixchel: Learning to Weave in Guatemala and Rhode Island, The	WJ	8	1	29	Su 83	57
Schevill, Margot	Sweetgrass, Cedar & Sage: Portrait of a Southwestern Weaver	WJ	10	1	37	Su 85	24
Schevill, Margot Blum	Evolution in Textile Design from the Highlands of Guatemala	WJ	12	2	46	Fa 87	66
Schevill, Margot Blum	Kate Peck Kent: An Anthropologist's Lifetime Involvement with Textiles	WJ	11	1	41	Su 86	11
Schevill, Margot Blum	Myth, Music, and Magic: The Needlework of Pilar Coover	TM			14	D/J 87	30
Schevill, Margot Blum	"Show of Complements, A" (Exhibit)	Fa	13	4		J/A 86	50
Schiess, Kate	Costume of a Plain People, The	TM			5	J/J 86	65
Schiller, Elaine Z.	Acadian Cotton Spinning	SS&D	5	3	19	Su 74	75
Schimmel, Heidrun	Traces of Time	Fa	9	3		M/J 82	70
Schira, Cynthia	Exciting Endeavor, An	SS&D	2	4	8	Fa 71	12
Schira, Cynthia	Notes for a Potential Tapestry Weaver	H&C	19	4		Fa 68	12
Schira, Cynthia	Notes on Ikat Weaving	H&C	24	2		M/A 73	6
Schira, Cynthia	Peruvian Multilayered Cloth	H&C	18	3		Su 67	11
Schira, Cynthia	Peruvian Weft Twining	H&C	17	3		Su 66	14
Schira, Cynthia	Plaiting, Possibilities for Use with Weaving	H&C	21	1		Wi 70	8
Schira, Cynthia	Weaving a Lifestyle: Cynthia Schira	Iw	5	2		Sp 80	27
Schira, Cynthia	West Indian Weaving, Nonloom Techniques of Interest	H&C	21	3		Su 70	17
Schleck, Robert J.	Wilcox Quilts in Hawaii, The	TM			13	O/N 87	78
Schlegel, Lee-lee	Arans: A Saga in Wool	S-O	4			80	15
Schlegel, Lee-lee	Arans: A Saga in Wool (error-corrected S-O V4 80 p4)	S-O	3			79	56
Schlegel, Lee-lee	Fireproofing	Fa	5	1		J/F 78	8
Schlegel, Lee-lee	This Thing Called Judging	SS&D	9	2	34	Sp 78	45
Schlegel, Mary	Philadelphia Guild Point System	SS&D	4	4	16	Fa 73	4

AUTHOR	TITLE	JOUR	VOL	NO	ISS	DATE	PAGE
Schlegel, Mary	Rainwindow: Watercolor Weaving	SS&D	5	2	18	Sp 74	8
Schlein, Alice	Observations on the Six-End Block Draft for Rug Weaving	WJ	6	4	24	Sp 82	30
Schlein, Alice	Weaver's Story of Two Prayer Shawls, Garments Used in Jewish Ritual, A	CW	3	3	9	Ap 82	6
Schlick, Donald	Modern Oriental Carpets: A Buyer's Guide	H&C	22	1		Wi 71	41
Schliske, Doreen	Weaving with the Past	Hw	3	5		N/D 82	15
Schluter, Lis	Handweaving	SS&D	4	4	16	Fa 73	63
Schmelzer, Jeanne	see Nash, Jeanne	Iw	5	4		Fa 80	28
Schmid, Claus-Peter	Photography for Artists and Craftsmen	SS&D	7	1	25	Wi 75	35
Schmidt, Heinrich J.	Alte Seidenstoffe	H&C	9	2		Sp 58	59
Schmidtke, Sheila	Margrit Schmidtke: An Evolving Artist	Fa	13	5		S/O 86	42
Schmoller, Irene Laughing Cloud	Cotton Glossary	WJ	11	2	42	Fa 86	13
Schmoller, Irene Laughing Cloud	Cotton: Legacy of Gods & Kings	WJ	11	2	42	Fa 86	11
Schmoller, Irene Laughing Cloud	see Ajeman, Norma	WJ	8	3	31	Wi 83	49
Schneider, Mary	Pique (A Brief Synopsis)	CW	7	22	20	Ja 86	22
Schneider, Paul	Grete Heikes: Weaver	Fa	6	1		J/F 79	14
Schnitzler, Jeanne; Ginny Ross	New Dimensions in Needlework	Fa	5	4		J/A 78	63
Schnur, Susan	Hopi Apocalypse	Fa	7	2		M/A 80	46
Schobinger, Helen J.	Associated Handweavers at Philadelphia	H&C	3	1		Wi 51	37
Schobinger, Helen J.	Peripatetic Weaver, The	H&C	1	1		Ap 50	12
Schobinger, Helen J.	Robert Harnden — Diplomat & Weaver	H&C	11	1		Wi 60	16
Schobinger, Helen J.	Summer Study in Sweden	H&C	9	3		Su 58	24
Schobinger, Helen J.	Summer with Finnish Weavers, A	H&C	3	2		Sp 52	12
Schoeberlein, Liz	"Midnight, May 30"	Fa	8	3		M/J 81	24
Schoenfeld, Klara	Craft Classes in London, Ontario	H&C	3	1		Wi 51	47
Schoenfeld, Klara	Kuvikas	H&C	12	2		Sp 61	20
Schofield, Eileen K.	see Zanoni, Thomas A.	Hw	6	5		N/D 85	20
Schofield, Maria, ed.	Decorative Art and Modern Interiors 1977, Vol. 66	SS&D	9	1	33	Wi 77	41
Schomp, Halcyon	see Jaeger, Hector	Hw	5	5		N/D 84	72
Schomp, Halcyon; Hector Jaeger	Changing Seasons, The	Hw	5	5		N/D 84	61
Schomp, Halcyon; Hector Jaeger	Notes from a Rugweaver's Journal	Hw	3	4		Se 82	35
Schorsch, Anita	Pastoral Dreams	Iw	3	2		Wi 78	41
Schreiber, LaVonne	Handwoven Silk Garments: Ikat Dress	WJ	3	2	10	Oc 78	30
Schreiber, LaVonne	Japanese Weaving Tools	WJ	9	2	34	Fa 84	47
Schreiber, Lavonne	Shinnosuke Seino: Innovator with Wool	WJ	12	2	46	Fa 87	34
Schrieber, La Vonne	Kasuri: The Japanese Ikat	SS&D	14	1	53	Wi 82	22
Schrieber, LaVonne	Learning to Weave in Japan	WJ	8	1	29	Su 83	79
Schrieber, Lavonne	Letter from Japan	WJ	12	1	45	Su 87	54
Schrum, Louaine M.	Revival of Double Weave in Scandinavia	H&C	8	1		Wi 56	22
Schuessler, Raymond	Mail Art: The Romance of Textiles on Stamps	Fa	12	4		J/A 85	26
Schultz, Kathleen	Create Your Own Natural Dyes	SS&D	7	2	26	Sp 76	34
Schulz, Chris	see Roth, Bettie G.	WJ	8	1	29	Su 83	51
Schulz, Chris	see Roth, Bettie G.	WJ	10	3	39	Wi 86	72
Schulz, Peter	Integrated Approach to Warping, An	Hw	3	3		My 82	30
Schwartz, Joyce B.	Timeless Stitches: Myrna Shiras' Stitched Drawings	Fa	8	3		M/J 81	65
Scorgie, Jean	California Poppy Tablecloth and Napkins	Hw	6	3		Su 85	60
Scorgie, Jean	Designing Your Handwoven Garments	Hw	7	5		N/D 86	40
Scorgie, Jean	"Design's on You" Contest Winners	Hw	8	4		S/O 87	31
Scorgie, Jean	Double Weave Jacket, A	Hw	4	4		S/O 83	48
Scorgie, Jean	Linbogarn Shirt	WJ	7	1	25	Su 82	53
Scorgie, Jean	Long Warps	Hw	6	2		M/A 85	43

AUTHOR	TITLE	JOUR	VOL	NO	ISS	DATE	PAGE
Scorgie, Jean	Tämä on Ihana!	Hw	7	1		J/F 86	45
Scorgie, Jean; Ann Sinclair	Posneg Program, The	SS&D	13	3	51	Su 82	26
Scorgie, Jean; Ann Sinclair	Using the Block Patterns Program	SS&D	13	4	52	Fa 82	16
Scorgie, Jean; Ann Sinclair	Using the Posneg Program	SS&D	13	3	51	Su 82	28
Scorgie, Jean, et al.	Kiton Acid Dye Sample Book of Wool Fibers, A	Hw	5	2		M/A 84	13
Scorgie, Jean; Gloria Martin	Four-Shaft Double Weave with Color and Weave Effects	Hw	6	3		Su 85	38
Scott, Chester M.	Carpets for a Historic Philadelphia House	H&C	16	3		Su 65	13
Scott, Gail R.	Tapestry: Technique and Tradition	H&C	22	3		Su 71	16
Scott, Gordon W.	Illustrated Guide to Making Oriental Rugs, An	Hw	8	1		J/F 87	16
Scott, Gordon W.	Illustrated Guide to Making Oriental Rugs, An	WJ	10	4	40	Sp 86	82
Scott, Gordon W.	Illustrated Guide to Making Oriental Rugs, An	Fa	12	6		N/D 85	46
Scott, Gordon W.	Illustrated Guide to Making Oriental Rugs, An	TM			2	D/J 85	78
Scott, Gordon W.	Illustrated Guide to Making Oriental Rugs, An	PWC	4	1	11		53
Scott, Michael	Crafts Business Encyclopedia, The	Iw	2	4		Su 77	34
Scott, Michael	Crafts Business Encylopedia, The	SS&D	9	1	33	Wi 77	40
Scott, Michael	Negotiating the Craft Fair Circuit: Important First Steps	Fa	12	2		M/A 85	50
Scott, Michael, ed.	see DuBoff, Leonard D.	Fa	12	2		M/A 85	54
Scott, Toni	Complete Book of Stuffed Work, The	Iw	3	4		Su 78	45
Scott, Toni	Complete Book of Stuffedwork, The	Fa	7	1		J/F 80	14
Scottish Arts Council	Master Weavers: Tapestry from the Dovecot Studios, 1912–1980	Fa	10	3		M/J 83	52
Seagroatt, Margaret	Basic Textile Book, A	SS&D	7	2	26	Sp 76	34
Seagroatt, Margaret	Coptic Weaves	H&C	19	4		Fa 68	42
Seagroatt, Margaret	Rug Weaving for Beginners	SS&D	4	1	13	Wi 72	34
Seagroatt, Margaret	Rug Weaving for Beginners: Woven Rugs, Tapestry Rugs, Knotted, Hooked and Braided Rugs	H&C	24	1		J/F 73	29
Seagroatt, Margaret	Wools of Britain, The	H&C	24	2		M/A 73	33
Searle, Karen	Card Woven Fringe: The ABCD's for the Beginner	WJ	10	2	38	Fa 85	21
Searle, Karen	Firfletting Fringe Treatment from Norway	WJ	9	4	36	Sp 85	40
Searle, Karen	Healing Historical Textiles	SS&D	10	4	40	Fa 79	60
Searle, Karen	Loom Shaped Top with Dukagång Inlay	WJ	11	3	43	Wi 87	8
Searle, Karen	Minneapolis Beehive Buzzes	SS&D	6	3	23	Su 75	48
Searle, Karen	Moorman Inlay Technique for Rigid Heddle Frame Looms	Hw	5	4		S/O 84	14
Searle, Karen	Moorman Inlay Technique for Rigid Heddle Frame Looms	PWC			6	Su 83	69
Searle, Karen	Moorman Inlay Technique, The	PWC	1	1		No 81	30
Searle, Karen	Scaffold Weaving: A Contemporary Garment Inspired by an Ancient Technique	WJ	10	2	38	Fa 85	65
Searle, Karen	see Baizerman, Suzanne	SS&D	8	2	30	Sp 77	37
Searle, Karen	see Baizerman, Suzanne	SS&D	10	2	38	Sp 79	74
Searle, Karen	see Baizerman, Suzanne	Iw	3	2		Wi 78	42
Searle, Karen	see Baizerman, Suzanne	Iw	3	4		Su 78	45
Searle, Karen	see Baizerman, Suzanne	Iw	5	4		Fa 80	38
Searle, Karen	see Baizerman, Suzanne	WJ	3	3	11	Ja 79	42
Searle, Karen	see Baizerman, Suzanne	WJ	6	4	24	Sp 82	57
Searle, Karen	see Baizerman, Suzanne	Fa	8	4		J/A 81	34
Searle, Karen	see Pancake, Cherri	Hw	2	5		No 81	29
Searle, Karen	Spinner's Specialty: Heathered Yarns, A	WJ	9	2	34	Fa 84	56
Searle, Karen	Sprang on the Loom	WJ	11	4	44	Sp 87	24
Searle, Nancy	Step on It: Nancy Searle's Technique for Patterned Double Weave	Hw	4	3		M/J 83	67
Searles, Nancy	Freeform Design Technique	PWC	3	4	10		18
Searles, Nancy	Freeform Twill & Freeform Searles Lace	CW		23		Ja 87	10
Searles, Nancy	Uneven-tied Overshot	PWC	3	4	10		14

AUTHOR	TITLE	JOUR	VOL	NO	ISS	DATE	PAGE
Searles, Nancy M.	Multiple Harness Weaving Course Part 4: Twill Derivatives (cont'd)	WJ	5	2	18	Fa 80	19
Searles, Nancy M.	Study Group Project, A	Hw	2	5		No 81	16
Searles, Nancy M.	Technique of Freeform Design, The	Hw	5	4		S/O 84	13
Searles, Nancy M.	Technique of Freeform Design, The	WJ	9	3	35	Wi 85	84
Searles, Nancy M.	Technique of Freeform Design, The	PWC	3	3	9		67
Sears, Victoria	American Quilt Study Group	Fa	9	3		M/J 82	53
Sebba, Anne	Samplers, Five Centuries of a Gentle Craft	Fa	8	4		J/A 81	34
Secretan, Hermine	Compact Sewing Kit Made from Thrums	SS&D	5	2	18	Sp 74	62
Secretan, Hermine A.	Circular Knitting	SS&D	3	2	10	Sp 72	28
Sector, Bob	Sheep Shearing Robots	S-O	8	1		Sp 84	16
Seeburger, Marze Marvin	Des Moines Weavers Learn to Spin	H&C	6	1		Wi 54	56
Seeley, Anne	How to Establish a Handweaving Businesss	H&C	2	4		Fa 51	32
Segermark, June	see Thorne, Sylvia	SS&D	3	1	9	Wi 71	18
Seifert, Walter	Spindlemuff is a Mythical Beast, The	H&C	24	2		M/A 73	36
Selander, Malin	Swedish Handweaving	H&C	11	1		Wi 60	59
Selander, Malin	Swedish Swatches—Blue Series	SS&D	3	3	11	Su 72	13
Selander, Malin	Swedish Swatches—Blue Series	H&C	21	1		Wi 70	41
Selander, Malin	Swedish Swatches—Green Series	SS&D	10	2	38	Sp 79	74
Selander, Malin	Swedish Swatches—Red Series	SS&D	6	1	21	Wi 74	32
Selander, Malin	Swedish Swatches—Yellow Series	H&C	14	2		Sp 63	43
Selander, Malin	Vavmonster	H&C	5	3		Su 54	58
Selander, Malin	Weave a Weave	Hw	7	5		N/D 86	10
Selander, Malin	Weave a Weave	WJ	11	3	43	Wi 87	64
Selander, Malin	Weave a Weave	Fa	13	5		S/O 86	60
Selander, Malin	Weave a Weave	SS&D	19	1	73	Wi 87	52
Selander, Malin	Weave a Weave	PWC	4	3	13		55
Selk, Karen	Kimono/Pants Ensemble, A	WJ	8	4	32	Sp 84	72
Selkurt, Claire	Harts and Flowers: Sweden's Märta Määs-Fjetterstrom's Designs Inspired a Textile Renaissance	WJ	9	4	36	Sp 85	30
Sellin, Helen	Chinese Drawloom: A Study in Weave Structure, The	WJ	9	2	34	Fa 84	6
Sellin, Helen	Damask and Weft Compound Weaves, Bibliography	CW	4	2	11	Ja 83	12
Sellin, Helen	Observations on a Chinese Drawloom	WJ	8	2	30	Fa 83	6
Sellin, Helen G.	Stitching Traditional Coverlet Weaves	AT	1			De 83	289
Sellin, Helen; Peggy Hoyt	Three-R's of Coverlets: Revival, Restoration, Research	PWC	5	2	16		33
Sellon, Patti	see Xenakis, Athanasios David	PWC	4	1	11		18
Sellon, Patti	see Xenakis, Athanasios David	PWC	4	2	12		20
Sellon, Patti; Athanasios David Xenakis	Library of Loom-controlled Patterns in Figured Piqué, A	PWC	4	2	12		18
Sellschopp, Dr. E. A.	General Patterson's Tapestry	TMJ	2	4		De 69	2
Selser, Christopher	see Kaufman, Alice	WJ	11	1	41	Su 86	14
Senders, Diane	Handspinning, Why Not Enjoy It	H&C	22	2		Sp 71	13
Serenyi, Peter	"Ten Boston Fiber Artists" (Exhibit)	Fa	5	5		S/O 78	67
Sermon, Margaret	Zoo Story	SS&D	2	4	8	Fa 71	10
Serpa, Geraldine	Pie in the Sky: The Irreverent Art of Geraldine Serpa	Fa	6	4		J/A 79	26
Serrure, Louis	Atlas de 4000 Armures de Tissage et Elements d'Ornementation Pour Articles d'Aille	WJ	6	4	24	Sp 82	59
Sethna, Nelly H.	Designer-Weaver in India, A	H&C	17	2		Sp 66	18
Seton, Julia M.	American Indian Arts	H&C	13	4		Fa 62	44
Sevensma, W. S.	Tapestries	H&C	17	2		Sp 66	43
Sewell, Suzy	Ribbon Wefts	WJ	10	3	39	Wi 86	40
Shaeffer, Claire	Sewing What You Weave	Hw	7	5		N/D 86	46
Shaeffer, Margaret W. M., ed.	Made in New York State: Handwoven Coverlets 1820-1860	WJ	10	2	38	Fa 85	81
Shaffer, Christine H.	Linen	H&C	12	2		Sp 61	29

AUTHOR	TITLE	JOUR	VOL	NO	ISS	DATE	PAGE
Shaffer, Frederick W.	Mola Design Coloring Book: 45 Authentic Indian Designs from Panama	Fa	11	1		J/F 84	58
Shaffer-Meyer, Rima	COE in Handspinning, The	SS&D	15	2	58	Sp 84	25
Shaffer-Meyer, Rima; Arlene M. Stein	Certificate of Excellence in Handspinning, The	SS&D	13	2	50	Sp 82	35
Shahzaman, Mahboob	Textile Arts of Multan, Pakistan	SS&D	4	3	15	Su 73	8
Shahzaman, Mahboob	Textile Arts of Multan, Pakistan: Part 2	SS&D	4	4	16	Fa 73	65
Shannon, Betty	see Glowacki, Dorothy	SS&D	8	2	30	Sp 77	89
Shannon, Betty	see Glowacki, Dorothy	SS&D	9	2	34	Sp 78	72
Shannon, Betty	see Glowacki, Dorothy	SS&D	10	2	38	Sp 79	91
Shannon, Betty	see Glowacki, Dorothy	SS&D	12	2	46	Sp 81	59
Shannon, Betty	see Glowacki, Dorothy	SS&D	13	2	50	Sp 82	50
Shannon, Betty	see Glowacki, Dorothy	SS&D	14	2	54	Sp 83	26
Shannon, Betty	see Glowacki, Dorothy	SS&D	15	2	58	Sp 84	69
Shannon, Betty	see Glowacki, Dorothy	SS&D	16	2	62	Sp 85	74
Shannon, Betty	see Glowacki, Dorothy	SS&D	18	2	70	Sp 87	35
Shannon, Betty	see Glowacki, Dorothy	SS&D	17	2	66	Sp 86	69
Shannon, Betty	see Weavers' Guild of Boston	SS&D	11	4	44	Fa 80	66
Shannon, Betty; Dorothy Glowacki	SS&D Index 1979, Issues 38-4I	SS&D	11	2	42	Sp 80	97
Shannon, Eileen	Smålands Weave on Eight Shafts	WJ	9	1	33	Su 84	47
Shapiro, Brenda	Spray Dyeing to Obtain Space-Dyed Yarns	SS&D	15	4	60	Fa 84	54
Shapiro, Stephen D.; Anita G. Noennig	How to Conserve Works of Art on Paper	Fa	11	2		M/A 84	46
Shapley, John	In Memoriam: Joseph V. McMullan, 1896–1973	TMJ	3	4		De 73	3
Shapley, John	In Memoriam: Leonard Carmichael, 1898-I973	TMJ	3	4		De 73	3
Shaver, Bee	Rags to Rugs (error-corrected H&C v14 n1 63 p46)	H&C	13	4		Fa 62	40
Shaw, Lynn C.	Lichens As Dyestuffs	SS&D	5	2	18	Sp 74	28
Shaw, Winifred	Start with a Square	SS&D	16	3	63	Su 85	50
Shawcroft, Barbara	Barbara Shawcroft	SS&D	3	1	9	Wi 71	25
Shawcroft, Barbara	"Tenth International Biennial of Tapestry: Four Views" (Exhibit)	Fa	8	6		N/D 81	52
Sheets, Lucinda	Summer Into Fall	Fa	10	2		M/A 83	15
Shep, R. L.	English Costume Society Symposium	TM			7	O/N 86	16
Shepard, Mark	More on....Charkha Techniques	S-O	8	2		Su 84	36
Sheppard, Margaret	Idea Notebook: A Workshop Necklace	Hw	7	5		N/D 86	25
Sheppard, Margaret	Variation on a Finnish Weave by a Texas Weaver (error-corrected H&C v17 n2 66 p48)	H&C	16	3		Su 65	20
Shepps, Vincent C.	Jurying by Point System	H&C	17	3		Su 66	7
Sherman, Vera	Wall Hangings of Today	H&C	23	4		J/A 72	27
Shermeta, Margo	Doublecloth Coverlets	Fa	13	5		S/O 86	6
Shermeta, Margo	"Karen Stahlecker" (Exhibit)	Fa	10	5		S/O 83	80
Shermeta, Margo	"Lynn Hall: Figure and Furniture" (Exhibit)	Fa	12	1		J/F 85	73
Shermeta, Margo	"New American Paperworks" (Exhibit) (error-corrected Fa v13 n3 86 p5)	Fa	13	1		J/F 86	64
Shermeta, Margo	Papermaking in Chicago	Fa	11	2		M/A 84	54
Shermeta, Margo	"Vibrant Structures" (Exhibit)	Fa	11	6		N/D 84	75
Sherrodd, Kristie	Fishperson's Earflap Hat	S-O	11	3		Fa 87	53
Sherwood, Thomas	"Fibers Unlimited" (Exhibit)	Fa	5	1		J/F 78	14
Sheward, Cynthia M.	Ossie Phillips: A Tradition of Mountain Weaving	Fa	14	2		M/A 87	25
Shillinglaw, Phyl	Introducing Weaving	SS&D	5	1	17	Wi 73	77
Shillinglaw, Phyl	Introducing Weaving	H&C	23	5		S/O 72	35
Shirley, Roz	Freeform Felt	SS&D	18	3	71	Su 87	81
Short, Melba Ellis	Handwoven Smocks	Hw	5	3		Su 84	66
Showalter, Pat	Felted Wool Landscapes	S-O	9	3		Fa 85	22
Shrauger, Carolyn	To Dress Your Room: Dress Your Loom	SS&D	7	3	27	Su 76	61
Shufro, Cathy	Here Are the Last of the Hatters	TM			2	D/J 85	14

AUTHOR	TITLE	JOUR	VOL	NO	ISS	DATE	PAGE
Shufro, Cathy	Quilting for World Peace	TM		10		A/M 87	14
Shufro, Cathy	see Stetson, G. Robert	TM		5		J/J 86	42
Shufro, Cathy	Tuxedo 100 Years Later, The	TM		7		O/N 86	54
Shull, Paula	Stained Glass Vest	S-O	11	4		Wi 87	29
Shulz, Chris	see Roth, Bettie G.	Hw	5	4		S/O 84	14
Shurtleff, Chris Ann	Handspinning for Needlework	S-O	7	2		Su 83	29
Shurtleff, Chris Ann	Organization Lets Creativity Flow	Hw	7	5		N/D 86	74
Sider, Sandra	Blueprinting on Fabric	Fa	13	5		S/O 86	36
Sider, Sandra	Blues in the Light: Cyanotype on Fabric	Fa	13	5		S/O 86	34
Sider, Sandra	Craft Today: The American Craft Museum (Exhibit)	Fa	14	2		M/A 87	54
Sider, Sandra	Esther Parkhurst	Fa	12	6		N/D 85	17
Sider, Sandra	"For the Floor" (Exhibit)	Fa	12	6		N/D 85	61
Sider, Sandra	Inspiration from the Past: Textile Treasures in the World of New York City Auctions	Fa	11	6		N/D 84	62
Sider, Sandra	"Master Dyers to the World" (Exhibit)	Fa	11	1		J/F 84	83
Sider, Sandra	"Ruth Kao: Silk Sense" (Exhibit)	Fa	12	1		J/F 85	72
Sider, Sandra	"Silk Roads/China Ships" (Exhibit)	Fa	11	4		J/A 84	74
Sider, Sandra	Textile Trends: Collecting in New York	Fa	12	6		N/D 85	24
Sieber, Roy	African Textiles	H&C	23	6		N/D 72	9
Sieber, Roy	African Textiles and Decorative Arts	SS&D	4	1	13	Wi 72	35
Sieber, Roy	African Textiles and Decorative Arts	TMJ	3	4		De 73	47
Siewert-Miller, Elisabet	From Paint to Fiber	SS&D	3	2	10	Sp 72	18
Sikes, Kraus	Guild: A Sourcebook of American Craft Artists, The	Hw	7	5		N/D 86	14
Silva, Arthur M.	California Indian Basketry: An Artistic Overview	Fa	4	1		J/F 77	40
Silver, Elizabeth	"Fibrations" (Exhibit)	Fa	6	5		S/O 79	85
Silverstein, Mira	International Needlework Designs	Fa	5	6		N/D 78	74
Siminoff	Back to the Gold Standard	H&C	1	3		Fa 50	24
Siminoff	Color and Dyeing	SS&D	2	1	5	De 70	24
Siminoff	Color and Dyeing	SS&D	2	2	6	Sp 71	30
Siminoff	Color and Dyeing	SS&D	2	3	7	Su 71	25
Siminoff	Color and Dyeing, Lesson 1	SS&D	1	4	4	Se 70	20
Siminoff	Color Control	SS&D	2	4	8	Fa 71	33
Siminoff	Use of Color and Dyeing, The	H&C	18	3		Su 67	45
Simmons, Max	Dyes and Dyeing	SS&D	10	4	40	Fa 79	65
Simmons, Max	Dyes and Dyeing	Iw	4	2		Sp 79	61
Simmons, Paula	Carding by Machine, Method of Fiber Preparation	H&C	20	3		Su 69	16
Simmons, Paula	Handspinners Guide to Selling, The	S-O	3			79	11
Simmons, Paula	Handspinner's Guide to Selling, The	SS&D	11	3	43	Su 80	74
Simmons, Paula	Handspun Yarns from Black Sheep Wool	H&C	14	3		Su 63	6
Simmons, Paula	How to Raise Sheep, Advice for Ambitious Spinners	H&C	22	2		Sp 71	24
Simmons, Paula	How to Raise Sheep: Advice for Ambitious Spinners, Part 2	H&C	22	3		Su 71	19
Simmons, Paula	Irregularity in Handspun	H&C	20	4		Fa 69	13
Simmons, Paula	Irregularity in Handspun Part 2	H&C	21	1		Wi 70	20
Simmons, Paula	Irregularity in Handspun Part 3	H&C	21	2		Sp 70	20
Simmons, Paula	Overtwist, A Spinner's Problem	H&C	19	1		Wi 68	37
Simmons, Paula	Production Spinning	Iw	4	4		Fa 79	61
Simmons, Paula	Spinning and Weaving with Wool	SS&D	9	2	34	Sp 78	47
Simmons, Paula	Spinning and Weaving with Wool	Iw	3	1		Fa 77	44
Simmons, Paula	Spinning and Weaving with Wool	WJ	2	2	6	Oc 77	35
Simmons, Paula	Spinning and Weaving with Wool	WJ	12	2	46	Fa 87	65
Simmons, Paula	Spinning and Weaving with Wool	Fa	5	2		M/A 78	58
Simmons, Paula	Spinning for Softness and Speed	SS&D	14	1	53	Wi 82	66
Simmons, Paula	Spinning for Softness and Speed	S-O	7	2		Su 83	14

AUTHOR	TITLE	JOUR	VOL	NO	ISS	DATE	PAGE
Simmons, Paula	Spinning for Softness and Speed	WJ	7	2	26	Fa 82	60
Simmons, Paula	Suggestions for Tailoring Material Woven of Handspun Yarns	H&C	18	4		Fa 67	17
Simmons, Paula	Weaving and Tailoring Handspun Yardage	S-O	2			78	48
Simmons, Paula	Weaving with Handspun Yarns: Suggestions for Beginning Spinners	H&C	17	4		Fa 66	4
Simmons, Paula	Weaving with Handspuns: A Shepherd Jacket	S-O	1			77	43
Simmons, Paula	When You Begin to Spin	H&C	17	3		Su 66	8
Simmons, Paula	Wool as a Cottage Industry	S-O	9	2		Su 85	42
Simons, Phid	Guatemalan Brocade Border, A	WJ	6	4	24	Sp 82	39
Simpson, Jeanne W.	St Louis Guild	H&C	9	1		Wi 57	44
Simpson, L. E.	Weaver's Craft, The	H&C	1	3		Fa 50	64
Simpson, L. E.; M. Weir	Weaver's Craft, The	H&C	8	4		Fa 57	59
Simpson, Marion	see Thilenius, Carol	Hw	3	4		Se 82	44
Sinclair, Ann	see Scorgie, Jean	SS&D	13	3	51	Su 82	26
Sinclair, Ann	see Scorgie, Jean	SS&D	13	3	51	Su 82	28
Sinclair, Ann	see Scorgie, Jean	SS&D	13	4	52	Fa 82	16
Singer, Charles, ed., et al.	History of Technology, A	H&C	8	2		Sp 57	59
Singletary, Suzanne	Underneath It All: A Brief History of Underwear and Fashion's Changing Silhouette	Fa	11	5		S/O 84	44
Singletary, Suzanne M.	Margot Strand Jensen: Soft Painting	Fa	11	1		J/F 84	18
Sitko, Jane Bradley	Good Hope Farm	SS&D	18	2	70	Sp 87	40
Sitko, Jane Bradley	Kathy Woell Original, A	SS&D	19	1	73	Wi 87	36
Sitko, Jane Bradley	Pueblo Deco	SS&D	18	4	72	Fa 87	40
Sitko, Jane Bradley	Winterthur Museum (error-corrected SS&D v13 n3 82 p4)	SS&D	13	2	50	Sp 82	24
Sizer, Theodore	Rug Hooking for Relaxation	H&C	17	2		Sp 66	8
Skelton, Maruta	see Lee-Whitman, Leanna	TMJ	22			83	33
Skinner, Milica Dimitrijevic	see Bird, Junius B.	TMJ	4	1		De 74	5
Skirm, Helen W.	New England Weavers Seminar	H&C	14	4		Fa 63	14
Skirm, Helen W.	New England Weavers' Seminar	H&C	16	4		Fa 65	33
Skirm, Helen W.	Weaving Neckties on a Twenty-Inch Loom	SS&D	1	4	4	Se 70	14
Skirm, Helen W.	Woolens from a 20-inch Loom	H&C	9	1		Wi 57	26
Skjöldebrand, Ingerlise	Treasure Chest of Swedish Weaving, The	Hw	4	2		M/A 83	15
Skjöldebrand, Ingerlise	Treasure Chest of Swedish Weaving, The	WJ	7	4	28	Sp 83	48
Skjöldebrand, Ingerlise	Treasure Chest of Swedish Weaving, The	PWC			5	Sp 83	68
Skjöldebrand, Ingerlise, ed.	Treasure Chest of Swedish Weaving, The	SS&D	14	3	55	Su 83	61
Skowronski, Hella	see Reddy, Mary	SS&D	6	2	22	Sp 75	22
Skowronski, Hella; Mary Reddy	Sprang and Weaving	SS&D	7	3	27	Su 76	79
Skowronski, Hella; Mary Reddy	Sprang Thread Twisting: A Creative Textile Technique	SS&D	5	3	19	Su 74	62
Skowronski, Hella; Sylvia Tacker	Doup Leno	TM			4	A/M 86	56
Skowronski, Hella; Sylvia Tacker	Doup Leno, A Quick and Simple System for Weaving Loom-Controlled Leno	Hw	2	3		My 81	72
Skowronski, Hella; Sylvia Tacker	Doup Leno, A Quick and Simple System for Weaving Loom-Controlled Leno	WJ	5	3	19	Wi 81	52
Skowronski, Hella; Sylvia Tacker	Doup Leno, A Quick and Simple System for Weaving Loom-Controlled Leno	SCGM		32		80	1-47
Skoy, Mary	Holiday Runners	WJ	12	2	46	Fa 87	22
Skoy, Mary Lonning	Beginner's Hat and Scarf	WJ	11	3	43	Wi 87	61
Skoy, Mary Lonning	Weaving on a Frame Loom: A First Project	WJ	6	4	24	Sp 82	58
Skreko, Margaret	Bedspread Fabric	CW	1	3	3	Ap 80	8
Skudera, Gail	"Cloth Forms" (Exhibits)	Fa	9	4		J/A 82	76
Skudera, Gail	"Fiber in Focus" (Exhibit)	Fa	10	6		N/D 83	82
Skudera, Gail	"Janet Markarian" (Exhibit)	Fa	13	4		J/A 86	53

AUTHOR	TITLE	JOUR	VOL	NO	ISS	DATE	PAGE
Skudera, Gail	"Nancy Hemenway: Aqua Lapis" (Exhibit)	Fa	11	5		S/O 84	72
Slade, Duncan	see Fraas, Gayle	Fa	10	1		J/F 83	99
Slason, Helen	Surface Interest Has Become a Favorite for Apparel Fabrics	H&C	18	3		Su 67	22
Slater, Deborah	Margareta Nettles — Weaver, Designer	H&C	23	1		J/F 72	22
Slater, Deborah	Norman Kennedy — Weaver at Williamsburg	H&C	23	1		J/F 72	23
Slater, Keith	see Goodfellow, Robin	S-O	10	4		Wi 86	46
Slaven, Pat	Confetti Sweater	S-O	11	4		Wi 87	26
Slivka, Rose, ed.	Crafts of the Modern World	H&C	19	4		Fa 68	45
Sloane, Eric	Museum of Early American Tools, A	H&C	15	3		Su 64	45
Small, Deborah	"Rose Kelly: Printed, Painted and Woven Textiles" (Exhibit)	Fa	9	6		N/D 82	84
Smart, Ellen S.	Preliminary Report on a Group of Important Mughal Textiles, A	TMJ	25			86	5
Smayda, Norma	HGA Education Directory, 1984	SS&D	15	4	60	Fa 84	6
Smayda, Norma	Rugs: An Exhibition of Contemporary Handwoven Floorcoverings	SS&D	17	4	68	Fa 86	83
Smayda, Norma	see Bliven, Jeanette	Hw	4	4		S/O 83	74
Smayda, Norma	Very Special Raddle, A	WJ	8	4	32	Sp 84	68
Smayda, Susan	Profile of an HGA Rep: Norma Smayda	SS&D	15	2	58	Sp 84	39
Smeltzer, Nancy	Color	SS&D	15	2	58	Sp 84	53
Smeltzer, Nancy	Costumes Through the Ages Stamp Collecting Kit	Fa	13	3		M/J 86	29
Smeltzer, Nancy	Everyday World of Fantasy, The	Fa	13	3		M/J 86	6
Smeltzer, Nancy	Mummery: Philadelphia's Happy New Year	Fa	14	3		M/J 87	39
Smeltzer, Nancy	Nancy Smeltzer	Fa	13	5		S/O 86	19
Smeltzer, Nancy	Quilting in France	Fa	13	2		M/A 86	49
Smeltzer, Nancy	Textile-Inspired Architecture	Fa	14	4		S/O 87	5
Smith, Anna Deavere	Weaver (A Poem for Martha Jones)	SS&D	16	3	63	Su 85	38
Smith, Barbara	On Designing and Creativity	Hw	5	5		N/D 84	96
Smith, Carolyn	Llama Wool	S-O	11	2		Su 87	32
Smith, Charles	Student Handbook of Color	H&C	18	1		Wi 67	43
Smith, Corless	"Quilt, The"	Fa	8	3		M/J 81	25
Smith, Dorothy N.	Different BUT Related	WJ	7	1	25	Su 82	32
Smith, Eunice	see Barrett, Clotilde	Hw	5	5		N/D 84	12
Smith, J. Weldon	Fiberworks' Tenth Anniversary	Fa	10	5		S/O 83	49
Smith, Jane Raven	Tailoring Handwoven Fabrics	H&C	8	1		Wi 56	48
Smith, John	Tapestries in Rope	H&C	17	1		Wi 66	10
Smith, Joyce	Decorative Techniques of the Sarakatsani	WJ	9	1	33	Su 84	14
Smith, Joyce Ronald	Taaniko	SS&D	7	2	26	Sp 76	34
Smith, Joyce Ronald	Weft Twining	TM		2		D/J 85	69
Smith, Kathleen B.	Linen Shift: Plain Sewing Makes the Most of Your Fabric, A	TM		9		F/M 87	46
Smith, Kenneth Loyal	Two Blankets: A Blanket for Baby Gregory	S-O	10	1		Sp 86	22
Smith, Lula	see Overman, Ruth	H&C	7	1		Wi 55	59
Smith, Mary	Boiled Wool	TM		13		O/N 87	63
Smith, Mary; Maggie Twatt	Shetland Pattern Book, A	Kn	2	1	3	F-W 85	78
Smith, Sue	Nature's Baskets	Iw	2	4		Su 77	26
Smith, Sue M.	Brookfield Basketry Institute, The	Fa	12	2		M/A 85	46
Smith, Sue M.	Natural Fiber Basketry	SS&D	15	3	59	Su 84	23
Smith, Sue M.	Natural Fiber Basketry	TM		10		A/M 87	76
Smith, William L.	Hobby or Business?	SS&D	18	4	72	Fa 87	44
Smith, William L.	Tax Tips-Education and Convention Expenses	SS&D	19	1	73	Wi 87	8
Snieckus, Mary Ann	Spinning Mohair in Lesotho	TM		8		D/J 86	66
Snodgrass, Cindy	Creative Process: Cindy Snodgrass, The	Fa	11	6		N/D 84	38
Snodgrass, Cindy	Dionysian Spirits: Dennis Valinski's Sculptures of Life	Fa	8	5		S/O 81	48
Snover, Susan	Fashion Focus: Sashes, Belts & Buckles	Hw	6	1		J/F 85	10
Snover, Susan	Rag Rugs on Overshot Threading	WJ	5	4	20	Sp 81	22

969

AUTHOR	TITLE	JOUR	VOL	NO	ISS	DATE	PAGE
Snover, Susan; Jean Sullivan	Wadmal — A Felted Fabric	SS&D	11	2	42	Sp 80	89
Snow, Edith Huntington	New Learns from the Old: Treasures in Museums for Today's Weavers, The	H&C	3	1		Wi 51	18
Snow, Edith Huntington; Laura L. Peasley	Weaving Lessons for Hand Looms	H&C	2	2		Sp 51	63
Snow, Jean Brooker	Creative Weave Drafting, Scandinavian Style	SS&D	17	4	68	Fa 86	61
Snow, Lee E.	see Meilach, Dona	H&C	24	4		Au 73	5
Snow, Lee Erlin	see Meilach, Dona Z.	SS&D	4	4	16	Fa 73	63
Snow, Marjorie; William Snow	Step-by-Step Tablet Weaving	SS&D	5	3	19	Su 74	62
Snow, William	see Snow, Marjorie	SS&D	5	3	19	Su 74	62
Snyder, Mary	Weave Three--Cocktail Skirt, Coating, Parka	SS&D	6	2	22	Sp 75	34
Snyder, Mary E.	Crackle Weave and Its Possible Variations	H&C	13	1		Wi 62	13
Snyder, Mary E.	Crackle Weave, The	SS&D	4	4	16	Fa 73	63
Snyder, Mary E.	Crackle Weave, The	Fa	3	1		J/F 76	4
Snyder, Mary E.	Lace and Lacey Weaves	SS&D	4	4	16	Fa 73	63
Snyder, Mary E.	Lace and Lacey Weaves	H&C	12	2		Sp 61	59
Snyder, Mary E.	Lace and Lacey Weaves	WJ	11	2	42	Fa 86	74
Snyder, Mary E.	Lace and Lacey Weaves	Fa	3	1		J/F 76	4
Snyder, Mary E.	Mexican Caprice	CW	2	2	5	Ja 81	7
Snyder, Mary E.	Patchwork	CW	2	2	5	Ja 81	2
Snyder, Mary E.	Planning Clothing Fabrics, Suggestions for Exploring Basic Weaves	H&C	15	1		Wi 64	9
Snyder, Mary E.	Projects At Chautauqua Summer School	H&C	23	3		M/J 72	14
Snyder, Mary E.	Scottish District Checks	H&C	16	2		Sp 65	9
Snyder, Mary E., ed.	Crackle Weave	H&C	13	2		Sp 62	43
Sober, Marion	Chain Link Braid Made of Leather Forms a Round, Open Trimming	SS&D	4	4	16	Fa 73	50
Sober, Marion B.	Splicing from Central America	H&C	22	4		Fa 71	18
Sober, Marion Burr	Chair Seat Weaving for Antique Chairs	SS&D	4	2	14	Sp 73	44
Sober, Marion Burr	Chair Seat Weaving for Antique Chairs	H&C	16	1		Wi 65	44
Sober, Marion Burr	Chair Seats Woven of Tape and Ash Splints	H&C	19	3		Su 68	13
Sober, Marion Burr	Decorative Braids Combine Well with Handwoven Material	H&C	19	4		Fa 68	18
Sober, Marion Burr, ORT	Therapy in Weaving	SS&D	1	1	1	De 69	3
Sobieszek, Robert A.	Sonja Flavin: Weaving for the Classics	Fa	11	3		M/J 84	70
Soby, James Thrall	Arp	H&C	10	1		Wi 59	59
Soderburg, Betty	Color from Plants	SS&D	4	4	16	Fa 73	63
Solberg, Jeanne Bingham	Weaver, The	Iw	5	1		Wi 79	11
Solmann, Vilhelm	Bizarre Designs in Silk — Trade and Traditions	H&C	5	3		Su 54	57
Solon, Marcia Goren	Pamela Studstill	Fa	12	2		M/A 85	32
Solyom, Bronwen	see Larsen, Jack Lenor	Fa	5	1		J/F 78	40
Solyom, Bronwyn	see Solyom, Garrett	TMJ	4	2		75	81
Solyom, Garrett	see Larsen, Jack Lenor	Fa	5	1		J/F 78	40
Solyom, Garrett; Bronwyn Solyom	Textiles of the Indonesian Archipelago	TMJ	4	2		75	81
Sommer, Elyse	Annotated Directory of Self-Published Textile Books	Iw	3	3		Sp 78	50
Sommer, Elyse	Career Opportunities in Crafts	Iw	2	4		Su 77	34
Sommer, Elyse	Career Opportunities in Crafts: The First Complete Guide for Success as a Crafts Professional	SS&D	9	1	33	Wi 77	41
Sommer, Elyse	Renie Breskin Adams: Artist...Teacher...Self-Seeker	Fa	5	3		M/J 78	36
Sommer, Elyse	Textile Collector's Guide	WJ	4	1	13	Jy 79	42
Sommer, Elyse, ed.	Annotated Directory of Self-Published Textile Books	WJ	3	1	9	Jy 78	36
Sommer, Elyse; Mike Sommer	New Look at Knitting...An Easier and More Creative Approach, A	Fa	5	3		M/J 78	59
Sommer, Elyse; Mike Sommer	Wearable Crafts	Iw	1	4		Su 76	29

AUTHOR	TITLE	JOUR	VOL	NO	ISS	DATE	PAGE
Sommer, Elyse; Renie Adams	Pillow Making as Art and Craft	Iw	3	4		Su 78	45
Sommer, Mike	see Sommer, Elyse	Iw	1	4		Su 76	29
Sommer, Mike	see Sommer, Elyse	Fa	5	3		M/J 78	59
Sonday, Milton	Counterchange & New Color	H&C	20	3		Su 69	23
Sonday, Milton; Nobuko Kajitani	Second Type of Mughal Sash, A	TMJ	3	2		De 71	6
Sonday, Milton; Nobuko Kajitani	Type of Mughal Sash, A	TMJ	3	1		De 70	45
Soroka, Joanne	Dovecot Studios	SS&D	12	4	48	Fa 81	36
Soroka, Joanne	Edinburgh Tapestry Company: A Thriving Anachronism in Scotland, The	Fa	10	3		M/J 83	59
Sortor, David	Return of the Magic Carpets	H&C	5	3		Su 54	16
Souchal, Geneviève	Masterpieces of Tapestry, from the Fourteenth to the Sixteenth Century	TMJ	4	2		75	81
Sousa, Jan	Mindspinning	Iw	5	4		Fa 80	10
Sousa, Jan	Paper and Fiber	Iw	5	3		Su 80	32
Southard, Doris	Bobbin Lace, A Simple Beginners' Pattern, Part 2	SS&D	5	4	20	Fa 74	81
Southard, Doris	Bobbin Lace — Just Twist, Cross, and Throw	SS&D	5	3	19	Su 74	77
Southard, Doris	Bobbin Lace: Part 3	SS&D	6	1	21	Wi 74	74
Southard, Doris	Bobbin Lace, Part 4: A Belt	SS&D	6	2	22	Sp 75	66
Southard, Doris	Bobbin Lace, Part 5: A Fringe	SS&D	6	3	23	Su 75	60
Southard, Doris	Bobbin Lace, Part 6: A Bookmark	SS&D	6	4	24	Fa 75	76
Southard, Doris	Bobbin Lace, Part 7: A Simple Edging & Corner Pattern	SS&D	7	1	25	Wi 75	79
Southard, Doris	Bobbin Lace, Part 8: Torchon in Technicolor	SS&D	7	2	26	Sp 76	80
Southard, Doris	Bobbin Lace: Part 9: Spiders	SS&D	7	3	27	Su 76	90
Southard, Doris	Bobbin Lacemaking	SS&D	9	3	35	Su 78	95
Sowles, Susan: Theresa Ruch	Weaving with Computers	SS&D	13	3	51	Su 82	30
Spark, Pat	Choosing the Fiber for Feltmaking	SS&D	17	4	68	Fa 86	20
Sparks, Kathy	see Hudson, Marjorie	S-O	11	3		Fa 87	47
Spaulding, K. B., Jr.	Kenneth Spaulding's Triumph: The Will to Weave	SS&D	7	1	25	Wi 75	18
Specht, Sally; Sandra Rawlings	Creating with Card Weaving	SS&D	5	2	18	Sp 74	68
Speckert, Gene K., OTR	Nylon Mats	SS&D	4	3	15	Su 73	29
Speckert, Gene K., OTR	Plastic Tote Bag	SS&D	4	2	14	Sp 73	57
Specktor, Denyse	Knitting Primer, The	Fa	11	4		J/A 84	54
Specktor, Denyse	Knitting Primer, The	TM			6	A/S 86	84
Speight, Jerry	Wear an Original Painting: Melody Weiler's Airbrushed Shirtscapes	Fa	8	1		J/F 81	13
Speirs, Gill	see Koenig, Marion	WJ	6	4	24	Sp 82	60
Speiser, Noémi	Kago-Uchi, The	AT	4			De 85	23
Speiser, Noémi	Manual of Braiding, The	Hw	4	4		S/O 83	24
Speiser, Noémi	Manual of Braiding, The	WJ	8	2	30	Fa 83	62
Speiser, Noémi	Manual of Braiding, The	PWC	3	1	7		60
Speiser, Noémi	Unusual Braids Produced by Loop Manipulation	WJ	10	1	37	Su 85	15
Spencer, Edith L.	New, Functional Inkle Loom, A	H&C	6	2		Sp 55	42
Spencer, Edith L.	Something Out of Nothing	H&C	8	3		Su 57	14
Spencer, Elsie	Handwoven Curtains for Headquarters	SS&D	6	1	21	Wi 74	22
Spencer, Elsie	Teneriffe Lace—with Variations	SS&D	4	4	16	Fa 73	31
Spencer, Elsie H.	Modern Twined Bags for Weaving Without a Loom	H&C	21	1		Wi 70	12
Spencer, Elsie H.	Woven Samplers	H&C	17	4		Fa 66	16
Spencer, Patricia	"Third International Exhibition of Miniature Textiles 1978" (Exhibit)	Fa	6	1		J/F 79	90
Sperlich, Elizabeth Katz	see Sperlich, Norbert	Iw	5	4		Fa 80	74
Sperlich, Norbert; Elizabeth Katz Sperlich	Guatemalan Backstrap Weaving	Iw	5	4		Fa 80	74
Sperry, Ellen	Draping a Blouse	TM			3	F/M 86	46
Speth, Lottie	Cushion Creations	SS&D	15	1	57	Wi 83	38

AUTHOR	TITLE	JOUR	VOL	NO	ISS	DATE	PAGE
Speth, Lottie	Designing for Industry	SS&D	2	4	8	Fa 71	21
Speth, Lottie	Tuck Tactics	SS&D	15	3	59	Su 84	80
Spiegel, Nancy	Guild Programs Within the Budget	H&C	8	2		Sp 57	46
Spillman, Trish; Marion Rinehart	Southwestern Spanish Textiles (error-corrected SS&D v9 n4 78 p34)	SS&D	9	3	35	Su 78	56
Spivak, Steven M.	see Anderson, Clarita	AT	8			De 87	67
Spivak, Steven M.	see Ulasewicz, Connie	AT	2			De 84	113
Spoering, Kathy	Primary Patterns	WJ	9	1	33	Su 84	53
Spooner, Brian	Afghan Carpets	SS&D	5	2	18	Sp 74	41
Spradley, J. L.	Spanish Colonial Spindle Whorls: The History and the Art	S-O	7	1		Sp 83	35
Sprague, Mary	"Jean Ray Laury: Quilted Work" (Exhibit)	Fa	9	1		J/F 82	84
Spray, Kathy	Eighteenth Century Mollie Costume	WJ	6	3	23	Wi 81	38
Sprenger, Elserine	Happy Dress	WJ	8	3	31	Wi 83	46
Sreenivasam, Elsa	see Polster, Nancy	Fa	12	3		M/J 85	42
St. Aubyn Hubbard, Geraldine	see Sutton, Ann	Hw	8	2		M/A 87	15
Stack, Lotus	Fiber in Minnesota: "Traditions/Transitions II" and "Art in Architecture" (Exhibit)	Fa	11	3		M/J 84	80
Stack, Lotus	see Butterfield, Mary Ann	WJ	9	2	34	Fa 84	39
Stack, Lotus	see Butterfield, Mary Ann	WJ	9	4	36	Sp 85	9
Stack, Lotus	see Butterfield, Mary Ann	WJ	10	1	37	Su 85	7
Stack, Lotus	Velvet Ikat	WJ	11	4	44	Sp 87	36
Stack, Lotus; Mary Ann Butterfield	Ounce of Prevention: Methods for Mounting, An	WJ	9	3	35	Wi 85	39
Stackel, I. M.	Conversing with Artist John Eric Broaddus	Fa	11	5		S/O 84	28
Staepelaere, Barbara	see Lambert, Patricia	WJ	12	1	45	Su 87	69
Staepelaere, Barbara	see Lambert, Patricia	TM			13	O/N 87	76
Staepelaere, Barbara	see Lambert, Patricia	PWC	4	4	14		53
Staff Members of the Tokyo National Museum	Textiles & Lacquer	H&C	10	1		Wi 59	59
Staff of Fiberarts Magazine	Fiberarts Design Book II, The	Hw	5	3		Su 84	18
Stahl, Sam	Berea College Fireside Industries Now Employ Sixty Weavers	H&C	19	2		Sp 68	5
Staines, Barbara	Betty Rodman, an Integrated Life	S-O	4			80	19
Staines, Barbara	Heirlooms Don't Just Happen	S-O	6	4		82	35
Stall, Edna Williamson	Story of Lauhala, The	WJ	8	2	30	Fa 83	63
Stamsta, Jean	Dorothy Meredith in Asia	H&C	16	3		Su 65	29
Stamsta, Jean	Jean Stamsta	SS&D	3	3	11	Su 72	15
Stanford, Shirley	Fiber and Architecture	Fa	3	3		M/J 76	14
Stanley, Martha	Cardwoven Selvedge for Weft-Faced Rugs, A	WJ	7	1	25	Su 82	48
Stanley, Martha	Perspective on Rug Design, A	WJ	7	2	26	Fa 82	66
Stanley, Martha	Rug Finishes: An Overview	Hw	2	5		No 81	32
Stanley, Martha	Rug Techniques: An Overview	WJ	6	4	24	Sp 82	34
Stanley, Martha	Rug Weaving: How to Avoid Drawing-in of the Warp	WJ	6	2	22	Fa 81	10
Stanley, Martha	Rug Weaving: Rug Yarns	WJ	6	3	23	Wi 81	44
Stanley, Martha Alice	Rug Weaving: Design Considerations	lw	5	1		Wi 79	20
Stanley, Martha, ed.	see Rogers, Nora, ed.	Hw	4	3		M/J 83	13
Stanley, Martha, ed.	see Rogers, Nora, ed.	WJ	8	1	29	Su 83	52
Stanley, Montse	Handknitter's Handbook, The	Kn	3	2	6	Sp 87	50
Stanley, Montse	Handknitter's Handbook, The	TM			14	D/J 87	76
Stanton, R. G.	Few Observations On "Remains", A	AT	4			De 85	9
Stanton, R. G.	On Mathematics and Treasures	AT	8			De 87	57
Stanton, R. G.	Work of L. H. C. Tippett, The	AT	7			Ju 87	179
Stanton, R. G., ed.	Ars Textrina	PWC	5	1	15		52
Stanton, R. G.; J. L. Allston	Comparison of Some Varied Themes	AT	2			De 84	217

AUTHOR	TITLE	JOUR	VOL	NO	ISS	DATE	PAGE
Stanton, R. G.; J. L. Allston	Some Remarks on the Work of Markham	AT	2			De 84	95
Stanton, Ralph, ed; Janet Hoskins, mg. ed.	Ars Textrina (Textile Journal)	Hw	7	5		N/D 86	11
Stanwood, Creighton	Boston Celebrates Its Fiftieth	SS&D	3	3	11	Su 72	10
Staples, Loretta	Culture & Costume in Edo Japan	SS&D	12	1	45	Wi 80	26
Stark, Ruthellen	Return to Basic Disciplines	SS&D	2	1	5	De 70	10
Starmore, Alice	Aran Knitting	TM		14		D/J 87	50
Starmore, Alice	Fair Isle Knitting	TM		8		D/J 86	44
Starmore, Alice; Alice Matheson	Knitting from the British Isles	Kn	2	1	3	F-W 85	79
Stavenow, Ake; Ake Huldt	Design in Sweden	H&C	14	1		Wi 63	44
Stearns, John K.	see Parsons, L. E.	H&C	2	2		Sp 51	61
Steedsman, Nell	Leamington Bags	SS&D	2	4	8	Fa 71	28
Steedsman, Nell	Patterns on a Plain Weave	H&C	12	1		Wi 61	61
Steele, Tommy	Hawaiian Shirt: Its Art and Its History, The	Fa	12	3		M/J 85	54
Steele, Zella	Five Harness Damask	H&C	18	1		Wi 67	20
Steele, Zella	Weaving Damask on a Damask Loom	H&C	21	4		Fa 70	4
Stein, Arlene M.	see Shaffer-Meyer, Rima	SS&D	13	2	50	Sp 82	35
Stein, Judith A.	see Quick, Betsy D.	WJ	8	3	31	Wi 83	66
Steinberg, Natali	Sheep to Shawl: A Wonderful Show	S-O	6	4		82	41
Steiner, Betty	Wintertime Warmer, A	SS&D	8	4	32	Fa 77	97
Steinhagen, Janice	Artisans from China Work Silken Magic	TM		5		J/J 86	14
Steinhagen, Janice	Thread City, Home for New Museum	TM		12		A/S 87	22
Stephan, Barbara B.	see Nakano, Eisha	Hw	6	3		Su 85	14
Stephan, Barbara B.	see Nakano, Eisha	WJ	8	1	29	Su 83	51
Stephan, Barbara B.	see Nakano, Eisha	Fa	10	3		M/J 83	53
Stephens, Cleo M.	Willow Spokes and Wicker Work	Iw	1	1		Fa 75	20
Stephenson, Sue H.	Basketry of the Appalachian Mountains	SS&D	9	3	35	Su 78	94
Stephenson, Sue H.	Basketry of the Applachian Mountains	Iw	2	4		Su 77	35
Sterk, Beatrijs; Dietmar Laue, eds.	Jahrbuch Textil 85/86	Hw	7	4		S/O 86	10
Stetson, G. Robert	Using Procion Dyes	Iw	3	3		Sp 78	31
Stetson, G. Robert; Cathy Shufro; Dennis Danaher	Imitating the Silkworm	TM		5		J/J 86	42
Stettner, Arianthé (see also Arianthé)	Arianthé: Notes from a Production Weaver	Fa	5	5		S/O 78	32
Stevens, Bernice A.	Tina McMorran	H&C	15	3		Su 64	14
Stevens, Bernice A.	Weavin' Woman, A	SS&D	3	2	10	Sp 72	38
Stevens, Connie	"Easy As Pie" Dye Method, An	S-O	9	1		Sp 85	22
Stevens, Rebecca A. T.	American Handcrafted Rug: Past and Present, The	TMJ	23			84	73
Stevens, Rebecca A. T.	Andrea V. Uravitch, "Wild and Domestic" (Exhibit)	Fa	10	2		M/A 83	71
Stevens, Rebeccah A. T.	Country of Origin, USA: A Decade of Contemporary Rugs	Fa	11	3		M/J 84	60
Stevens, Velma	Sad Songs of Spring	S-O	11	3		Fa 87	10
Stevenson, George B.	Weaving with Coconut Palm	WJ	8	2	30	Fa 83	65
Stewart, Donald C.	Setts of the Scottish Tartans, The	SS&D	6	3	23	Su 75	49
Stewart, Evelyn S.	Right Way to Knit: A Manual for Basic Knitting, The	TM		9		F/M 87	76
Stewart, Evelyn Stiles	Right Way to Macramé, The	H&C	22	3		Su 71	42
Stewart, Imogen	English Textiles Referred to by Celia Fiennes	AT	4			De 85	67
Stewart, Janice S.	Folk Arts of Norway, The	H&C	23	6		N/D 72	41
Stewart, Laura	Interweavings	Fa	11	3		M/J 84	47
Stewart-Pollack, Julie	Design for Interiors	Hw	5	2		M/A 84	52
Stickler, John C.	Chinese Brushwork Converted Into Classical Embroidery	H&C	22	2		Sp 71	11
Stiles, David	"Ann Trusty: Grid and Pattern" (Exhibit)	Fa	9	1		J/F 82	79

AUTHOR	TITLE	JOUR	VOL	NO	ISS	DATE	PAGE
Stillman, Yedida Kalfon	Palestinian Costume and Jewelry	Iw	4	3		Su 79	65
Stimmel, Arlene	see Edson, Nicki Hitz	Fa	5	3		M/J 78	59
Stimmel, Arlene	see Edson, Nicki Hitz	TM			4	A/M 86	74
Stinchecum, Amanda Mayer	Kosode: 16th–19th Century Textiles from the Nomura Collection	Fa	13	3		M/J 86	59
Stinchecum, Amanda Mayer; Monica Bethe; Margot Paul	Kosode, 16th and 19th Century Textiles from the Nomura Collection	Hw	6	3		Su 85	14
Stinson, Dilys	Weaving the Tapestries, A First-Person Account	Fa	11	2		M/A 84	64
Stirrup, Catherine A.	Mexican Pick-Up Weave	SS&D	3	1	9	Wi 71	38
Stockenstrom, Ann-Marie v.	Two Exhibitions in Sweden	H&C	18	1		Wi 67	22
Stocksdale, Joy	Limited-Edition Vests	TM			4	A/M 86	60
Stocksdale, Joy	Polychromatic Screen Printing	Fa	12	6		N/D 85	46
Stocksdale, Joy	Polychrome Screen Printing	Hw	6	5		N/D 85	20
Stockton, James	Designer's Guide to Color, and Designer's Guide to Color 2	Hw	6	5		N/D 85	18
Stoehr, Mary Kay	Crazy Quilt Wrap	Hw	5	5		N/D 84	71
Stoehr, Mary Kay	Finish Your Work	Hw	5	1		J/F 84	54
Stoehr, Mary Kay	Make It Fit	Hw	5	3		Su 84	64
Stoehr, Mary Kay	Unlocking the Secret of Space-Dyed Yarn for a Weft-Wise Design	Hw	7	3		M/J 86	52
Stofflet, Mary	Paper Vessels of Sylvia Seventy, The	Fa	11	2		M/A 84	70
Stoller, Irene	Convergence '78 Update: Visions and Revisions	SS&D	9	2	34	Sp 78	102
Stone, Peter	Oriental Rug Repair	WJ	6	4	24	Sp 82	57
Stone, Sarah Howard	French Hand Sewing	Hw	6	4		S/O 85	22
Storey, Isabelle B.	"Jody Klein's Paper Quilts" (Exhibit)	Fa	8	6		N/D 81	70
Storey, Joyce	Dyes and Fabrics	TM			8	D/J 86	72
Storey, Joyce	Textile Printing	TM			8	D/J 86	72
Storey, Joyce	Thames and Hudson Manual of Dyes and Fabrics, The	Iw	4	1		Wi 78	55
Storey, Walter Rendell	Adapting Handwoven Fabrics to Interior Design	H&C	4	3		Su 53	8
Storey, Walter Rendell	Decorator's Use of Handwoven Fabrics, A	H&C	4	4		Fa 53	4
Storey, Walter Rendell	Fabrics from Karen Bulow's Looms	H&C	5	1		Wi 53	14
Storey, Walter Rendell	Handwoven Fabrics: Accents of Distinction in Interior Design	H&C	4	1		Wi 52	4
Storey, Walter Rendell	Isabel Scott, Handweaver and Designer	H&C	4	2		Sp 53	14
Storey, Walter Rendell	Modern Tapestry on the New S. S. Andrea Doria	H&C	4	3		Su 53	35
Stothert, Karen E.	see Hagino, Jane Parker	TMJ	22			83	19
Stout, Carol	"Weavers of the Jade Needle" An Exhibition of Highland Guatemalan Textiles (Exhibit)	Fa	3	2		M/A 76	30
Stout, Pola	Education in Fashion and Fabric: Program at the Fashion Institute of Technology	H&C	16	3		Su 65	6
Stowell, Robert F.	To Wind Bobbins Use Your Spinning Wheel	H&C	7	4		Fa 56	17
Stoyer, Janet	Sewing with Silk	TM			4	A/M 86	35
Straight, Dixie	Shawl After Edgar Degas	Hw	5	5		N/D 84	64
Strand, Victoria	Christmas Greeting, A	H&C	12	4		Fa 61	17
Stratton, Charlotte Kimball	Rug Hooking Made Easy	H&C	7	1		Wi 55	61
Straub, Marianne	Handweaving and Cloth Design	SS&D	9	2	34	Sp 78	47
Straub, Marianne	Handweaving and Cloth Design	Iw	2	4		Su 77	36
Strauss, Lynn	Inspiration in Boundweave	Hw	7	2		M/A 86	38
Strauss, Lynn	Storytelling in Boundweave	Hw	7	2		M/A 86	35
Straw Into Gold	Hundred and One Questions for Spinners, A	WJ	3	2	10	Oc 78	46
Stribling, Mary Lou	Crafts from North American Indian Arts	Iw	1	2		Wi 76	28
Stribling, Mary Lou	Crafts from North American Indian Arts: Techniques, Designs and Contemporary Applications	SS&D	8	1	29	WI 76	70
Strickler, Carol	American Woven Coverlets	PWC	5	2	16		53
Strickler, Carol	Blended Drafts	Hw	6	2		M/A 85	37
Strickler, Carol	Block: An Exploration of Weaves, The	Hw	8	5		N/D 87	41
Strickler, Carol	Choosing Software for Soft-Wear Work	Hw	7	4		S/O 86	82

AUTHOR	TITLE	JOUR	VOL	NO	ISS	DATE	PAGE
Strickler, Carol	Color-Order Gamp	lw	2	4		Su 77	24
Strickler, Carol	Computer as a Design Tool, The	Hw	8	5		N/D 87	66
Strickler, Carol	Coverlet Care	Hw	6	4		S/O 85	61
Strickler, Carol	Coverlet Information Sheet	lw	6	1		Wi 80	55
Strickler, Carol	Coverlet Information Sheets, No. 3.1	lw	4	4		Fa 79	52
Strickler, Carol	Coverlet Information Sheets, Nos. 1–4	lw	3	1		Fa 77	38
Strickler, Carol	Coverlet Information Sheets, Nos. 2.1–2.2	lw	3	4		Su 78	41
Strickler, Carol	Coverlet Information Sheets, Nos. 2.3–2.4	lw	4	1		Wi 78	51
Strickler, Carol	Coverlet Information Sheets, Nos. 2.5–2.6	lw	4	2		Sp 79	57
Strickler, Carol	Coverlet Information Sheets, Nos. 5–6	lw	3	2		Wi 78	36
Strickler, Carol	Dearest Daughter	Hw	3	5		N/D 82	36
Strickler, Carol	Different Boundweave on Six Harnesses, A (error-corrected WJ v3 n1 insert for vol. 2)	WJ	2	4	8	Ap 78	36
Strickler, Carol	Drafting Plans for 4-Harness Rosepath Motifs	SS&D	5	1	17	Wi 73	58
Strickler, Carol	Eight-Shaft Twill Sampler, An	lw	6	1		Wi 80	52
Strickler, Carol	Fabric Analysis	Hw	6	5		N/D 85	83
Strickler, Carol	Granny's Coverlet (or how do you tell if your coverlet's real?)	S-O	6	4		82	26
Strickler, Carol	Huguenot Coverlets	WJ	1	2	2	Oc 76	8
Strickler, Carol	Inspiring Words	Hw	5	5		N/D 84	44
Strickler, Carol	Landes Hybrid	lw	1	3		Sp 76	11
Strickler, Carol	Overshot Gamp, An	lw	3	2		Wi 78	35
Strickler, Carol	Overshot Treadling Sampler	lw	3	3		Sp 78	45
Strickler, Carol	Pine Tree Borders, North and South	lw	5	3		Su 80	64
Strickler, Carol	Portfolio of American Coverlets, A	WJ	5	1	17	Su 80	47
Strickler, Carol	Portfolio of American Coverlets, A Vol. 4	SS&D	12	4	48	Fa 81	62
Strickler, Carol	Portfolio of American Coverlets, A Vol. 5	Hw	4	5		N/D 83	15
Strickler, Carol	Portfolio of American Coverlets, A Vol. 5	WJ	8	4	32	Sp 84	66
Strickler, Carol	Portfolio of American Coverlets, A Vol. 5	SS&D	15	2	58	Sp 84	90
Strickler, Carol	Portraits in Double Weave	WJ	1	3	3	Ja 77	30
Strickler, Carol	Rummaging for Treasures	SS&D	3	4	12	Fa 72	20
Strickler, Carol	Saga of My Draperies, The	Hw	5	2		M/A 84	71
Strickler, Carol	Sampling	lw	2	3		Sp 77	24
Strickler, Carol	Sampling	lw	3	1		Fa 77	43
Strickler, Carol	see Strickler, Stewart	Hw	6	4		S/O 85	88
Strickler, Carol	see Strickler, Stewart	Hw	7	2		M/A 86	80
Strickler, Carol	see Strickler, Stewart	Hw	7	3		M/J 86	30
Strickler, Carol	see Strickler, Stewart	Hw	8	4		S/O 87	60
Strickler, Carol	Software Programs for the Weaver and Textile Artist	Hw	6	3		Su 85	80
Strickler, Carol	Summer and Winter Treadling Gamp, A	lw	3	4		Su 78	43
Strickler, Carol	Thread That Runs So True — A Weaving Time Line	Hw	3	5		N/D 82	45
Strickler, Carol	Tips on Giving Programs and Workshops on "Computers in Weaving"	Hw	6	2		M/A 85	67
Strickler, Carol	Two Hundred Years of Textile Crafts	lw	1	3		Sp 76	26
Strickler, Carol; Barbara Taggart	Historical American Weaving in Miniature	lw	4	3		Su 79	48
Strickler, Carol; Barbara Taggart	Weaving in Miniature	lw	5	2		Sp 80	77
Strickler, Carol; Stewart Strickler	Coming to Terms	Hw	4	2		M/A 83	73
Strickler, Carol; Stewart Strickler	Computer Networking	Hw	8	3		M/J 87	89
Strickler, Carol; Stewart Strickler	Draft-Blender	Hw	8	2		M/A 87	68
Strickler, Carol; Stewart Strickler	Drawdown Programs for the Apple Computer	Hw	4	4		S/O 83	88

AUTHOR	TITLE	JOUR	VOL	NO	ISS	DATE	PAGE
Strickler, Carol; Stewart Strickler	Fabric Analysis Program, A	Hw	7	1		J/F 86	76
Strickler, Carol; Stewart Strickler	Faster than a Speeding Weaver	Hw	5	4		S/0 84	86
Strickler, Carol; Stewart Strickler	First Steps to Buying a Home Computer	Hw	5	2		M/A 84	90
Strickler, Carol; Stewart Strickler	Graphic Features on Home Computers	Hw	5	3		Su 84	89
Strickler, Carol; Stewart Strickler	In Defense of the Computer	Hw	5	5		N/D 84	87
Strickler, Carol; Stewart Strickler	Interface	Hw	3	5		N/D 82	71
Strickler, Carol; Stewart Strickler	Interface	Hw	4	1		J/F 83	69
Strickler, Carol; Stewart Strickler	Software Sourcelist Update	Hw	5	3		Su 84	90
Strickler, Carol; Stewart Strickler	Warp/Weft Calculator for the Apple II, The	Hw	5	1		J/F 84	84
Strickler, Stewart	How to Read a Basic Program	Hw	4	5		N/D 83	76
Strickler, Stewart	see Strickler, Carol	Hw	3	5		N/D 82	71
Strickler, Stewart	see Strickler, Carol	Hw	4	1		J/F 83	69
Strickler, Stewart	see Strickler, Carol	Hw	4	2		M/A 83	73
Strickler, Stewart	see Strickler, Carol	Hw	4	4		S/O 83	88
Strickler, Stewart	see Strickler, Carol	Hw	5	1		J/F 84	84
Strickler, Stewart	see Strickler, Carol	Hw	5	2		M/A 84	90
Strickler, Stewart	see Strickler, Carol	Hw	5	3		Su 84	90
Strickler, Stewart	see Strickler, Carol	Hw	5	3		Su 84	89
Strickler, Stewart	see Strickler, Carol	Hw	5	4		S/O 84	86
Strickler, Stewart	see Strickler, Carol	Hw	5	5		N/D 84	87
Strickler, Stewart	see Strickler, Carol	Hw	7	1		J/F 86	76
Strickler, Stewart	see Strickler, Carol	Hw	8	2		M/A 87	68
Strickler, Stewart	see Strickler, Carol	Hw	8	3		M/J 87	89
Strickler, Stewart	What Computer Should I Buy?	Hw	8	1		J/F 87	68
Strickler, Stewart; Carol Strickler	Five-Year Retrospective, A	Hw	8	4		S/O 87	60
Strickler, Stewart; Carol Strickler	Networking: Computer Enthusiasts Share Their Programs	Hw	6	4		S/O 85	88
Strickler, Stewart; Carol Strickler	Printers: Characteristics and Functions	Hw	7	3		M/J 86	30
Strickler, Stewart; Carol Strickler	Using Color Graphics: A Weaver's Experience	Hw	7	2		M/A 86	80
Strong, Gladys	I Am a Weaver	Hw	7	3		M/J 86	10
Strong, Ruth	Spirit Tracings of Barbara Heller, The	Fa	13	4		J/A 86	15
Strosnider, Ann	Bannerworks	Fa	10	5		S/O 83	66
Strosnider, Ann	If the Art Fits – Wear It! — Friends of the Rag	Fa	6	3		M/J 79	35
Strosnider, Ann	Joellen Benjamin-Fay: Public Artist, Private Businesswoman	Fa	6	5		S/O 79	64
Stuart, Donald	Convergence '86 Preview: Pangnirtung Weavers	SS&D	16	4	64	Fa 85	70
Stuart, Helen C.	Point Twill 125 Years Old	SS&D	3	4	12	Fa 72	41
Stuart, Helen C.	see Newman, Mattie E.	SS&D	1	3	3	Ju 70	5
Studley, Vance	Art and Craft of Handmade Paper, The	Fa	5	2		M/A 78	58
Studsgarth, Randi	" 'Genuine' Orientals from Denmark" (Exhibit)	Fa	8	2		M/A 81	64
Stumbough, Virginia	Absolutely Impossible Warp, The	Hw	5	1		J/F 84	16
Sullivan, Donna	Applicant 3-86	SS&D	18	4	72	Fa 87	32
Sullivan, Donna	Designing for Piqué (error-corrected PWC v4 n4 i14 p33)	PWC	4	3	13		28
Sullivan, Donna	Designing for Warp-face	SS&D	19	1	73	Wi 87	15
Sullivan, Donna	Designing with Modules	SS&D	16	4	64	Fa 85	54
Sullivan, Donna	Dimity Delight	PWC	5	1	15		17

AUTHOR	TITLE	JOUR	VOL	NO	ISS	DATE	PAGE
Sullivan, Donna	Eight-Shaft Primer: Lampas for Eight	PWC	5	2	16		34
Sullivan, Donna	Extra-Warp Woven-Pile	SS&D	17	1	65	Wi 85	19
Sullivan, Donna	Four Is Not Always Enough	PWC	4	3	13		18
Sullivan, Donna	Four-Shaft Primer: Tie Talk	PWC	4	4	14		14
Sullivan, Donna	Gauze Weave: Pick-up Versus Bead Gauze	SS&D	17	3	67	Su 86	14
Sullivan, Donna	Interface: A Wire Weaving	WJ	7	1	25	Su 82	20
Sullivan, Donna	Lampas for Eight	PWC	5	2	16		34
Sullivan, Donna	Lampas Library	PWC	5	2	16		38
Sullivan, Donna	Mitered Corners	SS&D	15	3	59	Su 84	82
Sullivan, Donna	Rainbow Blankets	PWC	4	4	14		27
Sullivan, Donna	Ribbed Piqué	SS&D	18	3	71	Su 87	30
Sullivan, Donna	S&W Wrapper	SS&D	15	1	57	Wi 83	24
Sullivan, Donna	"Santa" Stocking Stuffer	SS&D	15	4	60	Fa 84	64
Sullivan, Donna	Silk	SS&D	16	2	62	Sp 85	42
Sullivan, Donna	Spinning Silk	SS&D	16	2	62	Sp 85	39
Sullivan, Donna	Summer Blouse in Summer and Winter, A	PWC	4	4	14		18
Sullivan, Donna	Traditional Teddy: Overshot in Miniature	PWC	5	2	16		14
Sullivan, Donna; Madelyn van der Hoogt	Great Warping War, The	PWC	5	2	16		12
Sullivan, Jean	see Snover, Susan	SS&D	11	2	42	Sp 80	89
Sullivan, Jean H.	Variations on a Theme: A Seattle Weavers' Guild Study Group Project	Hw	8	2		M/A 87	64
Sullivan, Lia A.	Rural Program Helps Artists Reach Out	Fa	12	5		S/O 85	42
Sullivan, Mary Elizabeth	Thirty Interesting Years	H&C	8	1		Wi 56	16
Summa, Susan	Instant Gratification: Susan Summa Tells How and Why She Learned to Love the Knitting Machine	Fa	8	5		S/O 81	56
Summa, Susan	Preparing for a Show	Fa	10	4		J/A 83	44
Summar, Polly	Grace Kraft: Charting a Private World	Fa	14	3		M/J 87	16
Sumpter, Frances R.	Spinning Demonstrations	SS&D	3	4	12	Fa 72	31
Sunrise, Pearl	Pearl Sunrise: Weaving the "Old Way"	Fa	11	3		M/J 84	34
Sunset Books	Crochet: Techniques and Projects	TM			4	A/M 86	74
Sunshine, Joanna	"Karen Swanson" (Exhibit)	Fa	4	2		M/A 77	13
Sunström, Carla; Erik Sunström; Miriam Rice	Skapa Av Svampfärgat Garn	SS&D	18	3	71	Su 87	73
Sunström, Erik	see Sunström, Carla	SS&D	18	3	71	Su 87	73
Suntrader, Cid	Cid Suntrader: Weaving with Glass	Fa	14	4		S/O 87	5
Suter, Betty	Tatting	TM			6	A/S 86	64
Sutton, Ann	Color-and-Weave Design: A Practical Reference Book	Hw	8	4		S/O 87	13
Sutton, Ann	Colour-and-Weave Design: A Practical Reference Book	SS&D	18	1	69	Wi 86	38
Sutton, Ann	On Designing Fashion Fabrics	Hw	7	5		N/D 86	66
Sutton, Ann	Structure of Weaving, The	Hw	8	1		J/F 87	17
Sutton, Ann	Structure of Weaving, The	WJ	8	2	30	Fa 83	64
Sutton, Ann	Structure of Weaving, The	SS&D	15	1	57	Wi 83	102
Sutton, Ann	Structure of Weaving, The	PWC			6	Su 83	67
Sutton, Ann; Peter Collingwood; Geraldine St. Aubyn Hubbard	Craft of the Weaver, a Practical Guide to Spinning, Dyeing and Weaving, The	Hw	8	2		M/A 87	15
Sutton, Ann; Richard Carr	Tartans: Their Art and History	Hw	8	3		M/J 87	17
Sutton, Ann; Richard Carr	Tartans: Their Art and History	SS&D	16	3	63	Su 85	9
Suval, Judy	Qiviut: A Gift from the Musk Ox	SS&D	6	3	23	Su 75	15
Svenson, Mary Jane	Insulating Window Covering	WJ	6	1	21	Su 81	18
Svinicki, Eunice	Step by Step Spinning and Dyeing	SS&D	6	4	24	Fa 75	31
Svinicki, Eunice	Step by Step Spinning and Dyeing	Iw	2	3		Sp 77	32

AUTHOR	TITLE	JOUR	VOL	NO	ISS	DATE	PAGE
Swain, Margaret	Needlework of Mary Queen of Scotts, The	TMJ	3	4		De 73	47
Swales, Lois	Ups and Downs of the Long-Eyed Heddle	CW	5	2	14	Ja 84	8
Swan, Susan Burrows	Plain and Fancy, American Women and Their Needlework, 1700–1850	Fa	6	6		N/D 79	49
Swannie, Suzanne	Structure and Form in the Weaving of John Becker	AT	6			De 86	173
Swansen, Meg	4-Corner T-Shirt	Kn	3	3	7	Su 87	28
Swansen, Meg	Books on Guernseys	Kn	1	1	1	F-W 84 CI	71 54
Swansen, Meg	Confessions of a Backward Knitter	Kn	3	3	7	Su 87	27
Swansen, Meg	Faroese Shawls	Kn	4	1	9	Wi 87	26
Swansen, Meg	Square-rigged Vests	Kn	2	1	3	F-W 85	62
Swansen, Meg	Tools	Kn	1	1	1	F-W 84 CI	54
Swansen, Meg	Tools	Kn	1	2	2	S-S 85	10
Swanson, Janet	Janet Swanson	Fa	7	5		S/O 80	43
Swanson, Karen	Projects for a Six-Dent Rigid Heddle Backstrap Loom	H&C	21	4		Fa 70	9
Swanson, Karen	Rigid Heddle Weaving	Iw	1	2		Wi 76	28
Swanson, Karen	Rigid Heddle Weaving—New and Innovative Techniques on an Easy-to-Use Loom	SS&D	7	2	26	Sp 76	34
Swanson, Karen	Weaving with Rigid Heddle Backstrap Looms	H&C	21	2		Sp 70	13
Swantz, Sally J.	Weavcat I on the Apple	WJ	7	2	26	Fa 82	68
Swedish Homecraft Society	Swedish Patterns and Designs	H&C	2	4		Fa 51	61
Swendeman, Dorothy	Flat Tapestry Cartoon — Ready to Go, A	Hw	3	1		Ja 82	30
Swendeman, Dorothy	Weaving and Felt	Iw	5	3		Su 80	43
Swenson, Astrid	Russ-Knotting from Sweden	SS&D	4	3	15	Su 73	24
Swenson, Astrid	Short History of the Spinning Wheel, A	SS&D	7	3	27	Su 76	40
Swenson, Astrid	Weaver Looks at Sweden, A	SS&D	3	2	10	Sp 72	36
Swenson, Nancy	Rattle Your Dags	S-O	8	1		Sp 84	12
Swenson, Sally S.	see Miller, Lynn F.	Fa	9	2		M/A 82	58
Swingle, Daphne	Totems in Tapestry	H&C	22	2		Sp 71	5
Switzer, Chris	Llamas	S-O	5			81	31
Switzer, Chris	Scarf and Cap	S-O	4			80	58
Switzer, Chris	Travel Tidbits: Great Smoky Mountain National Park	Hw	7	4		S/O 86	38
Switzer, Chris	Travel Tidbits: Yellowstone Park Area	Hw	7	3		M/J 86	21
Swygert, Mrs. Luther M., ed.	Heirlooms from Old Looms — A Catalog of Coverlets Owned by the Colonial Coverlet Guild of America & Its Members	H&C	7	1		Wi 55	60
Sydhoff, Beate	see Martin, Edna	Fa	10	4		J/A 83	50
Sylvan, Katherine	Keep Warm! Large Rectangular Shawl	WJ	5	2	18	Fa 80	10
Sylvan, Katherine	Opera Elegance	SS&D	15	4	60	Fa 84	24
Sylvan, Katherine	Oval Cape	WJ	5	3	19	Wi 81	36
Sylvan, Katherine	Ruana	WJ	5	3	19	Wi 81	34
Sylvan, Katherine	Tale of a Talis, A	WJ	6	1	21	Su 81	42
Sylvan, Katherine	Three Color Progressions and Their Use in Sweater Jackets	WJ	5	4	20	Sp 81	38
Syverson, Gilda Morina	"Cynthia Laymon: Fiber/Paper Constructions" (Exhibits)	Fa	9	4		J/A 82	71
Szajman, Rena	"In the Presence of the Dragon Throne" (Exhibit)	Fa	4	3		M/J 77	13
Szajman, Rena	Jacqueline Enthoven: Portrait of a Stitchery Teacher	Fa	4	3		M/J 77	45
Szpakowski, Marceline	Raising the Silkworm in a Northern Climate	AT	2			De 84	157
Szumski, Norma J.	China: Fiber Arts in the People's Republic	SS&D	15	1	57	Wi 83	47
Szumski, Norma; Phyllis Clemmer; Clotilde Barrett	Handspuns for Tapestries	WJ	6	2	22	Fa 81	41
Tabard, Francois	see Verlet, Pierre	SS&D	10	2	38	Sp 79	73
Tabard, Francois	see Verlet, Pierre	Iw	4	4		Fa 79	72
Taber, Barbara; Marilyn Anderson	Backstrap Weaving	SS&D	7	1	25	Wi 75	34

AUTHOR	TITLE	JOUR	VOL	NO	ISS	DATE	PAGE
Taber, Barbara; Marilyn Anderson	Backstrap Weaving	WJ	8	1	29	Su 83	52
Tacker, Harold	see Tacker, Sylvia	SS&D	6	2	22	Sp 75	38
Tacker, Harold; Sylvia Tacker	Band Weaving	SS&D	6	2	22	Sp 75	64
Tacker, Harold; Sylvia Tacker	Band Weaving, The Techniques, Looms, and Uses for Woven Bands	H&C	26	3		M/J 75	31
Tacker, Sylvia	Alter Cloths and Shrines: The New Work of Janet Boguch	Fa	14	5		N/D 87	6
Tacker, Sylvia	Art Wear of Peggy Juve, The	Fa	14	1		J/F 87	25
Tacker, Sylvia	Cardweaving Without Cards	SS&D	13	2	50	Sp 82	42
Tacker, Sylvia	Coudre a Main: Costumes by Hand	Fa	12	2		M/A 85	49
Tacker, Sylvia	Dona Anderson: Edging Towards the Unknown	Fa	12	3		M/J 85	23
Tacker, Sylvia	D'Arcie Beytebiere: Windswept Designs in Pleated Silk	Fa	13	1		J/F 86	28
Tacker, Sylvia	Fibers Unlimited 1985	SS&D	17	3	67	Su 86	68
Tacker, Sylvia	Gail McDonnell	Fa	14	3		M/J 87	23
Tacker, Sylvia	Gridworks	SS&D	16	4	64	Fa 85	30
Tacker, Sylvia	Ikat-Woven Images	SS&D	18	1	69	Wi 86	68
Tacker, Sylvia	Peggy Conklin: Sculptured Paper	Fa	13	3		M/J 86	25
Tacker, Sylvia	see Harvey, Virginia I.	SS&D	8	4	32	Fa 77	4
Tacker, Sylvia	see Skowronski, Hella	Hw	2	3		My 81	72
Tacker, Sylvia	see Skowronski, Hella	WJ	5	3	19	Wi 81	52
Tacker, Sylvia	see Skowronski, Hella	TM			4	A/M 86	56
Tacker, Sylvia	see Skowronski, Hella	SCGM		32		80	1-47
Tacker, Sylvia	see Tacker, Harold	H&C	26	3		M/J 75	31
Tacker, Sylvia	see Tacker, Harold	SS&D	6	2	22	Sp 75	64
Tacker, Sylvia	Verkkonauhaa	SS&D	11	4	44	Fa 80	12
Tacker, Sylvia; Harold Tacker	Band Loom Offers New Approach to Weft Twining	SS&D	6	2	22	Sp 75	38
Taetzsch, Lyn	see Genfan, Herb	H&C	26	1		J/F 75	28
Taggart, Barbara	Control Dyeing with Indigo	SS&D	5	3	19	Su 74	53
Taggart, Barbara	Dyeing Natural Materials	SS&D	4	4	16	Fa 73	57
Taggart, Barbara	Dyepot	SS&D	2	4	8	Fa 71	29
Taggart, Barbara	Dyepot	SS&D	3	4	12	Fa 72	35
Taggart, Barbara	Dyepot	SS&D	3	3	11	Su 72	40
Taggart, Barbara	Dyepot in Australia	SS&D	5	4	20	Fa 74	56
Taggart, Barbara	Dyer's Library, A	SS&D	4	2	14	Sp 73	51
Taggart, Barbara	Reds and More Reds	SS&D	5	1	17	Wi 73	57
Taggart, Barbara	see Strickler, Carol	Iw	4	3		Su 79	48
Taggart, Barbara	see Strickler, Carol	Iw	5	2		Sp 80	77
Taggart, Barbara	Supermarket Dyeing	SS&D	3	2	10	Sp 72	34
Takami, Bruce	see Adelson, Laurie	Fa	6	4		J/A 79	22
Tallarovic, Joanne	Countermarche: Pure and Simple	WJ	8	3	31	Wi 83	85
Talley, Charles	Annikki Karvinen: Finnish Designer of Wovens	Fa	13	4		J/A 86	16
Talley, Charles	At Home in a Changing World	Hw	8	3		M/J 87	44
Talley, Charles	Charles Talley: A Candid Account of a Passionate Weaver and How He Got That Way	Fa	6	2		M/A 79	25
Talley, Charles	Dora Jung: The Artist and the Person	Fa	12	1		J/F 85	39
Talley, Charles	"Fabrications" (Exhibit)	Fa	6	4		J/A 79	76
Talley, Charles	"Fourth Nordic Textiltriennale" (Exhibit)	Fa	13	3		M/J 86	51
Talley, Charles	Handarbetets vanner: Artists and Craftsmakers Collaborate in Sweden	Fa	10	3		M/J 83	56
Talley, Charles	Hans Krondahl's "Homage to Garbo" (Exhibit)	Fa	11	4		J/A 84	79
Talley, Charles	In Memorium: Fiberworks Center for the Textile Arts 1973–1987	Fa	14	5		N/D 87	44
Talley, Charles	Kay Sekimachi: Successful on Her Own Terms	Fa	9	5		S/O 82	72
Talley, Charles	Maggie Sciaretta-Potter: The Virtuosity of a Miniaturist	Fa	6	6		N/D 79	16

AUTHOR	TITLE	JOUR	VOL	NO	ISS	DATE	PAGE
Talley, Charles	"Nance O'Banion: Rocks, Curtains, Windows, and Walls" (Exhibit)	Fa	12	5		S/O 85	69
Talley, Charles	Ongoing Feather: Jan Janeirós Search for a Personal Metaphor, The	Fa	6	4		J/A 79	46
Talley, Charles	Patchwork Re-Ordered	Fa	7	1		J/F 80	24
Talley, Charles	"Presence of Light, The" (Exhibit)	Fa	12	2		M/A 85	72
Talley, Charles	Sas Colby	Fa	8	5		S/O 81	29
Talley, Charles	Scandinavia: Contemporary Textile Art	Hw	7	5		N/D 86	14
Talley, Charles	Scandinavia Revisited: Reflections on the Weaver's Art	Hw	8	3		M/J 87	32
Talley, Charles	Textile Resource Guide to the Nordic Countries, A	Hw	8	3		M/J 87	77
Talley, Charles	Tiogruppen: When Working Together Works	Fa	11	6		N/D 84	41
Talley, Charles	Toronto's "unMuseum" for Textiles	Fa	12	4		J/A 85	43
Talley, Charles	"Weaver's Art: Selected Rug Traditions of the Middle East and China, A" (Exhibit)	Fa	6	5		S/O 79	76
Talley, Charles S.	Contemporary Textile Art in Scandinavia	Fa	9	6		N/D 82	43
Talley, Charles S.	Contemporary Textile Art: Scandinavia	SS&D	14	1	53	Wi 82	65
Talley, Charles S.	Contemporary Textile Art: Scandinavia	Hw	4	3		M/J 83	12
Talley, Charles S.	Contemporary Textile Art: Scandinavia	WJ	7	3	27	Wi 82	52
Talley, Charles S.	Contemporary Textile Art: Scandinavia	PWC			4	Ja 83	68
Talley, Charles S.	"Deborah Corsini: Tapestries" (Exhibit)	Fa	7	5		S/O 80	68
Talley, Charles S.	"Jan Janeiro: Recent Textiles" (Exhibit)	Fa	8	2		M/A 81	65
Talley, Charles S.	Kliots of Berkeley, The	Fa	7	4		J/A 80	44
Talley, Charles S.	Livin' and Workin' on the Land: Fiber Art Outside the Mainstream	Fa	8	6		N/D 81	38
Talley, Charles S.	"Miniature Textiles: 4th International Exhibition" (Exhibit)	Fa	8	3		M/J 81	72
Talley, Charles S.	Portraits of Three Weavers: Sandra Ikse-Bergman, Marja "Graset" Andersson, Elisabet Hasselberg-Olsson	Fa	8	2		M/A 81	46
Talley, Charles S.	Swedish Textiles Today: A Rich Tradition, A Supportive Society	Fa	8	2		M/A 81	42
Talley, Charles S.	"Swiss Tapestries" (Exhibit)	Fa	7	6		N/D 80	74
Talley, Charles S.	Well-Worn Path to Where? A View of Contemporary Swedish Textiles, The	Fa	8	2		M/A 81	44
Tanenbaum, Ruth	"Ellie Fidler — Tapestries" (Exhibit)	Fa	5	4		J/A 78	14
Tanenbaum, Ruth	French Tapestry Weaving in San Francisco	SS&D	8	3	31	Su 77	12
Tanenbaum, Ruth	"Modern Aubusson Tapestry, The" (Exhibit)	Fa	5	3		M/J 78	14
Tannenbaum, Ruth	Yael Lurie — Other Places, Other Visions	Fa	5	6		N/D 78	40
Tanner, Kersten	Finnish Techniques	SS&D	6	3	23	Su 75	45
Tanner, Virginia Leigh	Textured Weave—An Alternative	WJ	7	3	27	Wi 82	58
Tate, Blair	Warp: A Weaving Reference, The	Hw	6	3		Su 85	14
Tate, Blair	Warp: A Weaving Reference, The	WJ	10	1	37	Su 85	84
Tate, Blair	Warp: A Weaving Reference, The	Fa	12	3		M/J 85	54
Tate, Blair	Weaving, 'riting, and 'rithmetic	AT	6			De 86	57
Tatum, Phyllis	"Textiles New Mexico 1978" (Exhibit)	Fa	5	4		J/A 78	10
Tauntom Press, Inc.	Threads Magazine	WJ	10	3	39	Wi 86	73
Taylor, Carol	see Walker, Pauline	S-O	7	2		Su 83	16
Taylor, Dianne	Brief History of the International Biennial of Tapestry or "Watch Out for Women Who Knit", A	Fa	10	5		S/O 83	43
Taylor, Dianne	see Taylor, Elmer	Fa	10	5		S/O 83	33
Taylor, Dianne; Elmer Taylor	Biennale, The	SS&D	12	4	48	Fa 81	54
Taylor, Dianne; Elmer Taylor	Twelfth International Biennial of Tapestry	Fa	12	6		N/D 85	50
Taylor, Elmer	see Taylor, Dianne	SS&D	12	4	48	Fa 81	54
Taylor, Elmer	see Taylor, Dianne	Fa	12	6		N/D 85	50
Taylor, Elmer; Dianne Taylor	Eleventh International Biennial of Tapestry, The	Fa	10	5		S/O 83	33
Taylor, Jane	see Rawlings, Marilyn	Kn	2	2	4	S-S 86	78
Taylor, Michael	see Pennington, David	S-O	2			78	40
Taylor, Michael	see Pennington, David	S-O	3			79	10

AUTHOR	TITLE	JOUR	VOL	NO	ISS	DATE	PAGE
Taylor, Michael B.	see Pennington, David A.	SS&D	7	1	25	Wi 75	35
Taylor, Nathan	see Wetherbee, Martha	SS&D	17	4	68	Fa 86	88
Taylor, Nathan	see Wetherbee, Martha	TM		10		A/M 87	76
Taylor-Brown, Cameron	Cameron Taylor-Brown	Fa	14	2		M/A 87	24
Teal, Peter	Hand Woolcombing and Spinning: A Guide to Worsteds from the Spinning-Wheel	SS&D	10	2	38	Sp 79	72
Tedder, Lynn	Lynn's Pillows	PWC	4	3	13		25
Teilmann, Nina	Technique is Dukagang	SS&D	3	3	11	Su 72	22
Tejeda, Christina	Leanne Mahoney: Costuming for Ballet	Fa	11	5		S/O 84	64
Temple, Mary	Designed for Narrow Looms: A Summer Shirt Inspired by the Macedonian Chemise	WJ	10	1	37	Su 85	46
Temple, Mary	Three and Four Harness Krokbragd (error-corrected PWC i4 83 p76)	PWC		3		Oc 82	56
Temple, Nancy	"Micala Sidore: Sign Language" (Exhibit)	Fa	12	3		M/J 85	72
Templeton, Peg	Bouquet of Shawls, A	Hw	5	3		Su 84	75
Templeton, Peg	Geometric Proportions As a Design Tool	WJ	4	4	16	Ap 80	8
Templeton, Peg	Organize to Control Your Color	Hw	2	4		Se 81	48
TerBeest, Char	Char TerBeest: Basket Builder	Fa	9	4		J/A 82	17
TerBeest, Char	Wisconsin Willow: Adventures of a Basketmaker	Hw	7	3		M/J 86	13
TerBeest, Char	Wisconsin Willow...Adventures of a Basketmaker	TM		10		A/M 87	76
Tergis, Marilyn	I Was a Handweaver for the Textile Industry	H&C	23	5		S/O 72	36
Tergis, Marilyn	Using the Navajo Saddle-Blanket Weave	H&C	23	5		S/O 72	6
TerLouw, Betty	Making a Color Draw-Up	SS&D	13	2	50	Sp 82	37
TerLouw, Eliszabeth	Louise Todd: How Else Can This Be Woven?	SS&D	2	2	6	Sp 71	20
Termullo, Eileen	Weaving with Leather	Hw	5	1		J/F 84	52
Tewell, William H.	Damn That Barbara	SS&D	9	3	35	Su 78	54
Textile Museum	Textile Museum Journal, December 1965	H&C	17	2		Sp 66	45
Textile Museum	Textile Museum Journal, Vol.1, No.1	H&C	14	2		Sp 63	43
Thabet, Micheline	Tarascan Lace (error-corrected WJ v9 n1 84 p70)	WJ	8	4	32	Sp 84	48
Thabet, Micheline	Unique Finish from an Amazonian Bracelet, A	WJ	9	3	35	Wi 85	14
Theil, Linda	Color Xerography and the Fiber Artist	Fa	8	5		S/O 81	59
Theil, Linda	Hot-Air Balloons	TM		4		A/M 86	20
Theil, Linda	Tim Harding: Garments of Paradox	Fa	9	6		N/D 82	20
Thiamann, Ann	see McKay, Wendy	Hw	2	3		My 81	12
Thieme, Otto C.	see Eircher, Joanne B.	WJ	11	3	43	Wi 87	64
Thieme, Otto Charles	From Straw Mats to Hooked Rugs: Floor Coverings of the 19th Century	Fa	11	3		M/J 84	55
Thieme, Otto Charles	Pelete Bite: Kalabari Cut-Thread Cloth	Fa	10	5		S/O 83	46
Thieme, Otto Charles	Technological Change and the Textile Industry: The Impact of the Industrial Revolution and the Computer Revolution	Fa	11	1		J/F 84	54
Thieme, Otto Charles	Uncovering the Life and Weaving of John E. Schneider	SS&D	9	2	34	Sp 78	80
Thilenius, Carol	Finishing Handwoven Materials	lw	2	3		Sp 77	16
Thilenius, Carol	Five Harness Pattern on a Four Harness Loom, A	lw	4	3		Su 79	34
Thilenius, Carol	Reversible Two-Faced Knitting	S-O	7	1		Sp 83	40
Thilenius, Carol	Time Element, The	lw	4	4		Fa 79	56
Thilenius, Carol; Marion Simpson	Wooly Woolens	Hw	3	4		Se 82	44
Thimann, Ann	Yuki Tsumugi, Kasuri Weaving of Yuki Japan	SS&D	5	2	18	Sp 74	50
Thoeming, Bette; Kay Hulquist	Coverlet Homeconing '86	Hw	8	5		N/D 87	70
Thomas, Henry, Dr.	see Heintz, Dr. Kenneth	SS&D	5	4	20	Fa 74	60
Thomas, Kay	"Harmonist Needlework and Textiles" (Exhibit)	Fa	7	6		N/D 80	68
Thomas, Kay	"Stuffings" Exhibited At Pittsburgh	SS&D	5	1	17	Wi 73	83
Thomas, Mary	Mary Thomas's Book of Knitting Patterns	Kn	1	2	2	S-S 85	79
Thomas, Mary	Mary Thomas's Knitting Book	TM		9		F/M 87	76
Thomas, Michel; Remy Prin	Documents Sur Micro-Informatique Et Creation Textile	WJ	8	4	32	Sp 84	67

AUTHOR	TITLE	JOUR	VOL	NO	ISS	DATE	PAGE
Thomas, Mrs. Tollie	How to Tie on a New Warp	SS&D	2	2	6	Sp 71	30
Thomason, Roger	Designing Handwoven Clothing	SS&D	10	1	37	Wi 78	88
Thomason, Roger	Loom Designed Garments	SS&D	1	3	3	Ju 70	10
Thomason, Roger	Students Learn Creating with Fiber	SS&D	6	1	21	Wi 74	4, 10
Thomen, Lydia	Woven Banner: For the Class of '76, A	SS&D	7	2	26	Sp 76	7
Thompson, Chris	Seaming and Finishing	PWC		3		Oc 82	46
Thompson, Christine	Sililoquy: Commission Blues	PWC	4	1	11		9
Thompson, Gladys	Patterns for Guernseys, Jerseys and Arans, 3rd ed.	TM			9	F/M 87	74
Thompson, Gladys	Patterns for Guernseys, Jerseys & Arans	Kn	1	1	1	F-W 84	71
Thompson, Jon, ed.	see Mackie, Louise, ed.	Hw	3	5		N/D 82	14
Thompson, Kathleen; Alice Tipton	Martin's Creek Settlement: A Pictorial Weaving	S-O	9	3		Fa 85	39
Thompson, Nancy	Speed Spinning	Iw	4	1		Wi 78	46
Thompson, Paul	Work of William Morris, The	H&C	18	3		Su 67	45
Thomson, Francis Paul	Tapestry: Mirror of History	Fa	8	1		J/F 81	82
Thormahlen, Marian Oyen	Jacob Wool — A Handspinner's Delight	WJ	11	3	43	Wi 87	57
Thormahlen, Marian Oyen	My Wonderful Llamas and Their Wool	S-O	8	4		Wi 84	29
Thorne, Sylvia	From Sheep to Shawl	H&C	17	1		Wi 66	36
Thorne, Sylvia	It's Time to Rock	SS&D	3	1	9	Wi 71	28
Thorne, Sylvia	Sheep to Shawl	SS&D	3	2	10	Sp 72	33
Thorne, Sylvia; June Segermark	Bag, Hat and Quesquemitl	SS&D	3	1	9	Wi 71	18
Thornton, Sandra K.	Tapices of San Pedro de Cajas, Peru, The	WJ	12	1	45	Su 87	23
Thorpe, Azalea Stuart; Jack Lenor Larsen	Elements of Weaving	H&C	18	4		Fa 67	39
Thorpe, Azalea Stuart; Jack Lenor Larsen	Elements of Weaving (revised edition)	Iw	3	4		Su 78	44
Thorpe, Heather G.	Handweaver's Workbook	SS&D	6	2	22	Sp 75	63
Thorpe, Heather G.	Handweaver's Workbook, A	H&C	17	4		Fa 66	43
Thorpe, Heather G.	Handweaver's Workbook, A	H&C	7	3		Su 56	59
Thorpe, Heather G.	Have You Tried This?	H&C	8	1		Wi 56	29
Thorpe, Heather G.	It's in the Cards	H&C	3	4		Fa 52	17
Thorpe, Heather G.	Periodical Pool	H&C	6	3		Su 55	31
Thorpe, Heather G.	Practical Vertical File for Handweavers, A	H&C	6	2		Sp 55	54
Thostesen, Margaret	see Altpeter, Dorothy	H&C	2	1		Wi 50	62
Thresh, Christine	see Thresh, Robert	SS&D	4	3	15	Su 73	53
Thresh, Christine	Spinning with a Drop Spindle	SS&D	3	4	12	Fa 72	47
Thresh, Robert; Christine Thresh	Introduction to Natural Dyeing, An	SS&D	4	3	15	Su 73	53
Thurstan, Violetta	Use of Vegetable Dyes for Beginners, The	H&C	2	4		Fa 51	63
Thurstan, Violetta	Weaving Without Tears	H&C	7	4		Fa 56	60
Tidball, Harriet	Brocade	SCGM		22		67	1-50
Tidball, Harriet	Brocade, Shuttle Craft Guild Monograph Twenty-Two, 1968	H&C	19	3		Su 68	42
Tidball, Harriet	Build or Buy a Loom, Part 1 Patterns for Pick-Up, Part 2	SCGM		23		68	1-38
Tidball, Harriet	Build or Buy a Loom, Part 1; Patterns for Pick-Ups, Part 2. Shuttle Craft Guild Monograph Twenty-Three, 1968	H&C	19	3		Su 68	42
Tidball, Harriet	Color and Design, Shuttle Craft Guild Monograph Sixteen, 1965	H&C	17	2		Sp 66	47
Tidball, Harriet	Color and Dyeing	SCGM		16		65	1-54
Tidball, Harriet	Contemporary Costume: Strictly Handwoven	SCGM		24		68	1-44
Tidball, Harriet	Contemporary Costume: Strictly Handwoven, Shuttle Craft Guild Monograph Twenty-Four 1968	H&C	20	1		Wi 69	42
Tidball, Harriet	Contemporary Satins	SCGM		7		62	1-33
Tidball, Harriet	Contemporary Satins, Shuttle Craft Monograph Seven 1962	H&C	14	1		Wi 63	44
Tidball, Harriet	Contemporary Tapestry	H&C	15	3		Su 64	44

AUTHOR	TITLE	JOUR	VOL	NO	ISS	DATE	PAGE
Tidball, Harriet	Contemporary Tapestry	SCGM		12		64	1-46
Tidball, Harriet	Double Weave: Plain and Patterned	SCGM		1		60	1-34
Tidball, Harriet	Double Weave: Plain and Patterned, The	H&C	12	1		Wi 61	59
Tidball, Harriet	Foundations for Handweavers	H&C	6	4		Fa 55	60
Tidball, Harriet	Handloom Weaves	SCGM		33		57	1-38
Tidball, Harriet	Handloom Weaves, The	H&C	9	2		Sp 58	59
Tidball, Harriet	Handloom Weaves, The	Hw	6	3		Su 85	20
Tidball, Harriet	Handloom Weaves, The	WJ	9	4	36	Sp 85	78
Tidball, Harriet	Handwoven Specialties: 62 Articles for the Handweaver to Make	SCGM		11		64	1-38
Tidball, Harriet	Interior Decorating the Handloom Way	H&C	9	3		Su 58	59
Tidball, Harriet	Merry Christmas, Handweavers	SCGM		10		63	1-30
Tidball, Harriet	Mexican Motifs	H&C	13	3		Su 62	43
Tidball, Harriet	Mexican Motifs	SCGM		6		62	1-22
Tidball, Harriet	Peru: Textiles Unlimited	SCGM		25		68	1-36
Tidball, Harriet	Peru: Textiles Unlimited, Part 2	SCGM		26		69	1-46
Tidball, Harriet	Peru: Textiles Unlimited Shuttle Craft Guild Monographs Nos. 25 & 26, 1969	H&C	20	3		Su 69	43
Tidball, Harriet	Planning a Home Weaving Center	H&C	6	4		Fa 55	18
Tidball, Harriet	see Harvey, Virginia	H&C	21	1		Wi 70	42
Tidball, Harriet	see Harvey, Virginia I.	SCGM		28		69	1-39
Tidball, Harriet	Summer and Winter	Fa	3	1		J/F 76	4
Tidball, Harriet	Summer and Winter and Other Two-Tie Unit Weaves	H&C	18	2		Sp 67	45
Tidball, Harriet	Summer and Winter and Other Two-Tie Unit Weaves	SCGM		19		66	1-58
Tidball, Harriet	Supplementary Warp Patterning	SCGM		17		66	1-46
Tidball, Harriet	Supplementary Warp Patterning, Shuttle Craft Guild Monograph Seventeen, 1966	H&C	17	4		Fa 66	44
Tidball, Harriet	Surface Interest — Textiles of Today	H&C	12	2		Sp 61	59
Tidball, Harriet	Surface Interest — Textiles of Today	SCGM		2		61	1-22
Tidball, Harriet	Textile Structure and Analysis, A Home Study Course in Twelve Lessons	SCGM		18		66	1-31
Tidball, Harriet	Textile Structure and Analysis, Shuttle Craft Guild Monograph Eighteen, 1966	H&C	17	4		Fa 66	44
Tidball, Harriet	Thomas Jackson Weaver	Fa	3	1		J/F 76	4
Tidball, Harriet	Thomas Jackson, Weaver: 17th and 18th Century Records	SCGM		13		64	1-37
Tidball, Harriet	Thomas Jackson, Weaver, Shuttle Craft Monograph Thirteen, 1964	H&C	16	1		Wi 65	45
Tidball, Harriet	Two-Harness Textiles: The Loom-Controlled Weaves	SCGM		20		67	1-30
Tidball, Harriet	Two-Harness Textiles: The Loom-Controlled Weaves, Shuttle Craft Guild Monograph Twenty 1967	H&C	18	4		Fa 67	40
Tidball, Harriet	Two-Harness Textiles: The Open Work Weaves	SCGM		21		67	1-34
Tidball, Harriet	Two-Harness Textiles: The Open-Work Weaves, Shuttle Craft Guild Monograph Twenty-One, 1967	H&C	19	1		Wi 68	44
Tidball, Harriet	Undulating Weft Effects	SCGM		9		63	1-25
Tidball, Harriet	Undulating Weft Effects, Shuttle Craft Monograph Nine, 1963	H&C	14	3		Su 63	43
Tidball, Harriet	Warping with a Horizontal Reel	H&C	10	4		Fa 59	16
Tidball, Harriet	Weaver's Book — Fundamentals of Handweaving, The	H&C	12	3		Su 61	59
Tidball, Harriet	Weaver's Book of Scottish Tartans, The	H&C	13	2		Sp 62	43
Tidball, Harriet	Weaver's Book of Scottish Tartans, The	SCGM		5		62	1-46
Tidball, Harriet	Weaving Inkle Bands	SCGM		27		69	1-40
Tidball, Harriet	Weaving Inkle Bands, Shuttle Craft Guild Monograph Twenty-Seven 1969	H&C	21	1		Wi 70	42
Tidball, Harriet	Woolens and Tweeds	SCGM		4		61	1-46
Tidball, Harriet	Woolens and Tweeds, Shuttle Craft Monograph Four, 1961	H&C	13	1		Wi 62	43
Tidball, Harriet C. nee Douglas	Handweaver's Instruction Manual	SCGM		34		49	1-41
Tidball, Harriet Douglas	Handweavers' Instruction Manual	H&C	4	4		Fa 53	60
Tidball, Harriet Douglas	Mary Meigs Atwater: An Appreciation	H&C	4	1		Wi 52	18
Tidball, Harriet Douglas	Understanding Weaving Terms	H&C	2	2		Sp 51	20

AUTHOR	TITLE	JOUR	VOL	NO	ISS	DATE	PAGE
Tidball, Harriet, ed.	Peter Collingwood: His Weaves and Weaving	H&C	14	2		Sp 63	44
Tidball, Harriet, ed.	see Collingwood, Peter	SCGM		8		63	1-46
Tidball, Harriet, ed.	see Rhodes, Tonya Stalons	H&C	16	3		Su 65	44
Tidball, Harriet, ed.	see Rhodes, Tonya Stalons	SCGM		14		65	1-35
Tidball, Harriet; Virginia I. Harvey	Handloom Weaves, Enlarged Edition, The	PWC	4	1	11		54
Tidball, Harriett D.	Weaver's Word Finder	H&C	5	2		Sp 54	61
Tidwell, Elmyra	Elmyra Tidwell	Fa	14	3		M/J 87	22
Tidwell, Elmyra	Keeping the Glimakra Loom in Balance	CW	7	3	21	My 86	3
Tidwell, Elmyra	Wearable Fine Thread Tapestries	WJ	10	3	39	Wi 86	34
Tiffany Studios	Antique Chinese Rugs	H&C	21	2		Sp 70	43
Tillett, Leslie	Conferences: Where Do We Go from Here?	Iw	3	4		Su 78	32
Tillett, Leslie	Natural Dye Myth, The	Iw	4	2		Sp 79	55
Tillett, Leslie	Where Do We Go from Here?	SS&D	10	1	37	Wi 78	18
Tillman, Jean E.	In the Market Place	SS&D	2	2	6	Sp 71	5
Time-Life Books	Basic Tailoring: The Art of Sewing Series	TM		7		O/N 86	72
Timlin, Jean	Three Crafts in New Zealand, The	SS&D	1	2	2	Mr 70	18
Timlin, Jean, ed.	Spinning Survey	SS&D	2	3	7	Su 71	26
Timmons, Chris	Cows in Fiber	Fa	11	4		J/A 84	55
Timmons, Chris	Saving the Navajo Sheep	Fa	11	3		M/J 84	54
Timmons, Christine	Claudia Hopf: Drawing with Scissors	Fa	11	2		M/A 84	99
Tipton, Alice	see Thompson, Kathleen	S-O	9	3		Fa 85	39
Toale, Bernard	Art of Papermaking, The	Hw	7	3		M/J 86	12
Toale, Bernard	Art of Papermaking, The	Fa	11	2		M/A 84	58
Toale, Bernard	How to Make a Sheet of Paper	Fa	9	4		J/A 82	39
Toale, Bernard	"Paper" (Exhibit)	Fa	7	5		S/O 80	69
Toale, Bernard	Papermaking in the U.S.A.	Fa	9	4		J/A 82	34
Tod, Osma G.	Florida Spinner, Richard Butler, Chooses Flax	H&C	18	1		Wi 67	16
Tod, Osma Gallinger	Bobbin Lace	SS&D	2	1	5	De 70	28
Tod, Osma Gallinger	Brooks Lace and Weaving	H&C	20	1		Wi 69	29
Tod, Osma Gallinger	Joy of Hand Weaving, Second Edition, The	H&C	15	3		Su 64	43
Tod, Osma Gallinger	Weavers in Greece	H&C	19	2		Sp 68	21
Tod, Osma Gallinger; Oscar H. Benson	Weaving with Reeds and Fibers	SS&D	7	1	25	Wi 75	34
Tod, Osma; Joshphine Del Deo	Rug Weaving for Everyone	H&C	17	3		Su 66	43
Todd, Louise	Clothing	H&C	24	4		Au 73	28
Todd, Louise	Gauze At Moore College of Art	SS&D	3	3	11	Su 72	20
Todd-Cope, Louise	Linen Undergarments: A Proud Danish Heritage	Fa	14	2		M/A 87	51
Tomita, Jun; Noriko Tomita	Japanese Ikat Weaving	Hw	4	5		N/D 83	14
Tomita, Jun; Noriko Tomita	Japanese Ikat Weaving	Hw	6	3		Su 85	14
Tomita, Jun; Noriko Tomita	Japanese Ikat Weaving	WJ	8	2	30	Fa 83	64
Tomita, Jun; Noriko Tomita	Japanese Ikat Weaving	Fa	10	3		M/J 83	54
Tomita, Noriko	see Tomita, Jun	Hw	4	5		N/D 83	14
Tomita, Noriko	see Tomita, Jun	Hw	6	3		Su 85	14
Tomita, Noriko	see Tomita, Jun	WJ	8	2	30	Fa 83	64
Tomita, Noriko	see Tomita, Jun	Fa	10	3		M/J 83	54
Tomlonson, Judy Schroeder	Mennonite Quilts and Pieces	TM		3		F/M 86	78
Tompkins, Calvin	Merchants and Masterpieces: The Story of the Metropolitan Museum of Art	H&C	21	3		Su 70	41
Tonder, Meta	Thirty-three Tonder Laces	H&C	6	1		Wi 54	23

984

AUTHOR	TITLE	JOUR	VOL	NO	ISS	DATE	PAGE
Toneyama, Kojin	Popular Arts of Mexico, The	SS&D	6	4	24	Fa 75	31
Tooker, Dorothy	Tatting	SS&D	17	4	68	Fa 86	74
Tope, Carolyn	Braille Pattern Board Developed for Wasinger	SS&D	4	3	15	Su 73	18
Torbet, Laura, ed.	Encyclopedia of Crafts, The	SS&D	12	2	46	Sp 81	74
Torphy, Helen	Scotland	SS&D	15	4	60	Fa 84	10
Torry, Barbara	Tradition in Transition	SS&D	5	4	20	Fa 74	25
Tovey, John	Technique of Weaving, The	H&C	17	2		Sp 66	44
Tovey, John	Technique of Weaving, The	SS&D	7	2	26	Sp 76	34
Tovey, John	Technique of Weaving, The	WJ	8	3	31	Wi 83	65
Tovey, John	Weaves and Pattern Drafting	H&C	21	1		Wi 70	41
Tow, Dorathy	New Loom, A	H&C	17	1		Wi 66	16
Towne, Carroll A.	Macroweave Effect, The (error-corrected SS&D v12 n3 81 p6)	SS&D	12	2	46	Sp 81	16
Towne, Carroll A.	Making & Using the Loop Heddle Jig (error-corrected SS&D v13 n2 81 p4)	SS&D	13	1	49	Wi 81	10
Towner, George	Naomi Towner	SS&D	3	1	9	Wi 71	6
Towner, Naomi W.	How Much Yarn for the Job? Rya and Flossa	SS&D	8	4	32	Fa 77	14
Towner, Naomi W.	How Much Yarn for the Job? Tapestry	SS&D	9	1	33	Wi 77	73
Towner, Naomi Whiting	Build a Warp-Weighted Loom	SS&D	6	3	23	Su 75	36
Towner, Naomi Whiting	Conceptual Design in Weaving	Iw	3	2		Wi 78	14
Towner, Naomi Whiting	Gang: Technical and Conceptual Applications to Loom Controlled Weave Structures	AT	5			Ju 86	91
Towner, Naomi Whiting	How Much Yarn for the Job?	SS&D	6	4	24	Fa 75	36
Towner, Naomi Whiting	I Dust and Arrange My Tools	Fa	9	3		M/J 82	9
Towner, Naomi Whiting	"Karen Jenson Rutherford: Wall Hangings" (Exhibit)	Fa	7	6		N/D 80	72
Towner, Naomi Whiting	Memo to All Concerned Craftsmen (error-corrected SS&D v10 n4 79 p66)	SS&D	10	3	39	Su 79	10
Towner, Naomi Whiting	Provocative Book List: Recommended Reading for Fiber Students, A	Fa	8	4		J/A 81	16
Towner, Naomi Whiting	see Anderson, Clarita	SS&D	9	4	36	Fa 78	71
Towner, Naomi Whiting	Self-Stuffing Weft Cord Double Weave	AT	3			My 85	47
Towner, Naomi Whiting	SS&D Interview: Else Regensteiner	SS&D	10	2	38	Sp 79	4
Towner, Naomi Whiting; Helen Cushman	Anthrax Sterilization Methods and Their Effects on Fibers	SS&D	7	3	27	Su 76	94
Townsend, William D.	Weaving the Horror of the Holocaust	SS&D	15	3	59	Su 84	16
Tracht, Arthur	see Adelson, Laurie	WJ	10	1	37	Su 85	84
Tramba, Diane	Five Block Double Weave Using the Glimåkra Long Eyed Heddle Accessory	WJ	7	3	27	Wi 82	45
Tramutola, Buhnne	Adventures in Fleece	SS&D	18	2	70	Sp 87	38
Trayer, Blanche C.	Siminoff Textiles	H&C	9	1		Wi 57	18
Treganowan, D.	see Weeks, J. G.	H&C	21	2		Sp 70	41
Treimanis, Lilija	see Dzervitis, Aleksandra	SS&D	14	1	53	Wi 82	65
Treimanis, Lilija	see Dzervitis, Aleksandra	Hw	4	3		M/J 83	12
Treimanis, Lilija	see Dzevitis, Alexandra	WJ	7	3	27	Wi 82	49
Treimanis, Lilija	see Glauco, Reali	Hw	7	1		J/F 86	18
Trevisan, Mario							
Trilling, James	Appendix I: The Development of Interlace and Related Patterns	TMJ	21			82	104
Trilling, James	Appendix II: Remounting of the Tapestry Cat. No. 1, (Katrina De Carbonnel)	TMJ	21			82	109
Trilling, James	Bibliography: Late Roman, Early Byzantine Textile Art	TMJ	21			82	111
Trilling, James	Drawloom Textiles in Wool and Silk (with a Structural Analysis by Ann Pollard Rowe)	TMJ	21			82	96
Trilling, James	Resist-Dyed Textiles	TMJ	21			82	102
Trilling, James	Roman Heritage: Introduction, The	TMJ	21			82	11
Trilling, James	Table of Accession and Catalogue Numbers	TMJ	21			82	110
Trilling, James	Tapestries	TMJ	21			82	29
Trilling, James	Textiles with Patterns in Weft-Loop Pile	TMJ	21			82	93
Trotzig, Liv; Astrid Axelsson	Weaving Bands	SS&D	6	3	23	Su 75	49
Trujillo, Lisa Rockwood	Chimayó—A Town of Weavers	WJ	11	1	41	Su 86	60

AUTHOR	TITLE	JOUR	VOL	NO	ISS	DATE	PAGE
Trux, John	see Marten, Michael	Iw	4	2		Sp 79	64
Tschebull, Raoul	Kazak — Carpets of the Caucasus	H&C	23	1		J/F 72	31
Tschebull, Raoul	Kazak Rugs	TMJ	3	2		De 71	2
Tsunoyama, Yukihiro, ed.	Textile Art of the Andes—Catalogue of Amano Collection	WJ	7	2	26	Fa 82	59
Tsunoyama, Yukihiro, ed.	Textiles of the Andes: Catalog of Amano Collection	Hw	2	5		No 81	94
Tsunoyama, Yukihiro, ed.	Textiles of the Andes: Catalog of the Amano Collection	Fa	9	6		N/D 82	58
Tubbs, Gabi	Knitting Now	Kn	2	2	4	S-S 86	78
Tuer, Andrew W.	Japanese Stencil Designs	Fa	10	1		J/F 83	58
Tuinsma, Frieda Z.	Rocky Mountain Guild Observes Colorado Centennial	H&C	10	3		Su 59	16
Turczyn, Pam	Evolution of An Artist: Pam Turczyn	Fa	14	5		N/D 87	24
Turgeon, Lulu	Production Weaving in Quebec	Hw	3	3		My 82	54
Turnbaugh, Sarah P.	Common Sense Care of Baskets	SS&D	9	3	35	Su 78	90
Turnbaugh, Sarah Peabody	Ring Basket of the Anasazi, The	SS&D	9	1	33	Wi 77	101
Turnbaugh, Sarah Peabody	Technology of Basketry: North American Roots and Relations to Cloth, The	SS&D	8	1	29	WI 76	32
Turnbull, Krista Jensen	see Hacker, Katherine F.	Hw	7	4		S/O 86	11
Turnbull, Tom	How to Build a Loom	H&C	23	3		M/J 72	3
Turnbull, Tom	How to Build a Loom	H&C	23	4		J/A 72	12
Turner, Alta R.	Alice Stuart	H&C	12	1		Wi 61	16
Turner, Alta R.	Bound Weaving	H&C	15	3		Su 64	10
Turner, Alta R.	Bound Weaving	H&C	15	4		Fa 64	19
Turner, Alta R.	Finger Weaving: Indian Braiding	SS&D	4	4	16	Fa 73	63
Turner, Alta R.	Finger Weaving: Indian Braiding	H&C	24	3		M/J 73	6
Turner, Alta R.	Fingerweaving: Two Perspectives, The Historic View	SS&D	6	4	24	Fa 75	44
Turner, Alta R.	Fragment, Pre-Columbian Cloth Found in Utah	H&C	22	1		Wi 71	20
Turner, Alta R.	Montclair Museum Classes	H&C	11	4		Fa 60	25
Turner, Alta R.	Search for Handweaving in Greece, A (error-corrected H&C v21 n3 70 p42)	H&C	21	2		Sp 70	16
Turner, Kathryn	Portland Weavers Scholarship Show	SS&D	6	1	21	Wi 74	79
Turner, Kathryn M.	Suited to Silk	SS&D	18	2	70	Sp 87	68
Turner, Katy	Great Wheel, The	S-O	3			79	46
Turner, Katy	Legacy of the Great Wheel: Myths, History and Traditions with Practical Lessons, The	SS&D	15	1	57	Wi 83	103
Turner, Katy	Legacy of the Great Wheel, The	Hw	2	3		My 81	71
Turner, Katy	Legacy of the Great Wheel, The	WJ	5	4	20	Sp 81	44
Turner, Lew	Focus on Textiles	SS&D	13	3	51	Su 82	22
Twatt, Maggie	see Smith, Mary	Kn	2	1	3	F-W 85	78
Tyler, Mary	see De Peaux, Barbara	SS&D	8	1	29	WI 76	86
U. S. Department of Interior	Navajo Native Dyes	SS&D	1	4	4	Se 70	22
Uhlman, Ilse Etta	Marli-Weavers of Chicago, The	H&C	4	1		Wi 52	9
Uhlmann, Etta	Claire Zeisler	H&C	13	4		Fa 62	34
Uhlmann, Ilse Etta	Drapery for a Club	H&C	12	1		Wi 61	48
Uhlmann, Ilse Etta	Fabrics for a Glasshouse	H&C	9	2		Sp 58	49
Ulasewicz, Connie; Clarita Anderson; Steven M. Spivak	Analysis and Documentation of Coverlets (error-corrected AT v3 85 p269)	AT	2			De 84	113
Ulrich, George	Wealth of Fiber: Nigeria's Adire Cloth, A	Fa	13	5		S/O 86	39
Ulrich, Kenn	Seen Around the Country: Palestinian Costume Exhibit in New Mexico	SS&D	9	4	36	Fa 78	84
Underhill, Vera Bisbee; Arthur J. Burks	Creating Hooked Rugs	H&C	3	1		Wi 51	61
Unger, Mary	Four Place Mats (error-corrected WJ v6 n1 81 p28d)	WJ	5	2	18	Fa 80	52
University of Arkansas Cooperative Extension Service	Quilts	Fa	14	2		M/A 87	62
Upitis, Lizbeth	Ah, Shawls!	Kn	4	1	9	Wi 87	14
Upitis, Lizbeth	And a Necklace, Too	Kn	2	2	4	S-S 86	48

AUTHOR	TITLE	JOUR	VOL	NO	ISS	DATE	PAGE
Upitis, Lizbeth	Babushkas	Kn	4	1	9	Wi 87	48
Upitis, Lizbeth	Circular T	Kn	3	3	7	Su 87	15
Upitis, Lizbeth	Collections	Kn	1	1	1	F-W 84	68
						CI	7
Upitis, Lizbeth	Comfortable Cotton T's	Kn	3	3	7	Su 87	12
Upitis, Lizbeth	Florodora Bag	Kn	2	2	4	S-S 86	47
Upitis, Lizbeth	Fulled Knitting	Kn	3	1	5	F-W 86	34
Upitis, Lizbeth	Guernseys	Kn	1	1	1	F-W 84	48
						CI	40
Upitis, Lizbeth	If the Vest Fits...	Kn	3	2	6	Sp 87	40
Upitis, Lizbeth	Lace and Legs	Kn	1	2	2	S-S 85	64
Upitis, Lizbeth	Lapsang Souchong	Kn	3	3	7	Su 87	16
Upitis, Lizbeth	Latvia	Kn	1	2	2	S-S 85	62
Upitis, Lizbeth	Latvian Mittens	Kn	3	1	5	F-W 86	69
Upitis, Lizbeth	Latvian Mittens: Traditional Designs and Techniques	TM			6	A/S 86	84
Upitis, Lizbeth	Latvian Mittens: Traditional Designs and Techniques	PWC	1	1		No 81	58
Upitis, Lizbeth	Latvian Wedding Mittens	PWC			2	Ap 82	92
Upitis, Lizbeth	Mill End Mystery	Kn	3	4	8	Fa 87	36
Upitis, Lizbeth	Mitten Miniatures	Kn	4	1	9	Wi 87	50
Upitis, Lizbeth	Notes of a Textile Sleuth	Kn	2	1	3	F-W 85	22
Upitis, Lizbeth	Over the Shoulder T	Kn	3	3	7	Su 87	14
Upitis, Lizbeth	Rags to Riches	Kn	3	1	5	F-W 86	56
Upitis, Lizbeth	Return of the Reticule	Kn	2	2	4	S-S 86	44
Upitis, Lizbeth	Revivified Past, A	Kn	3	1	5	F-W 86	12
Upitis, Lizbeth	Soft Sleeveless Blouse	Kn	3	4	8	Fa 87	37
Upitis, Lizbeth	Standard T.	Kn	3	3	7	Su 87	14
Upitis, Lizbeth	Stocking Basics	Kn	1	2	2	S-S 85	66
Upitis, Lizbeth	Tempting and Tempestuous	Kn	3	2	6	Sp 87	8
Upitis, Lizbeth	Tons of T's	Kn	3	3	7	Su 87	8
Upitis, Lizbeth	Traditional Fair Isle Sweater	Kn	2	1	3	F-W 85	26, 8B
Upitis, Lizbeth	Travel Sweater	Kn	2	1	3	F-W 85	58
Upitis, Lizbeth	Undies Revealed: Camisole	Kn	3	2	6	Sp 87	12
Upitis, Lizbeth	V-Neck Jacket	Kn	3	4	8	Fa 87	37
Upitis, Lizbeth	Winter Birches: The Blouse	Kn	1	2	2	S-S 85	46, 72B
Upitis, Lizbeth	Winter Birches: The Jacket	Kn	1	2	2	S-S 85	44
Upson, Frieda	Summer and Winter Suiting	SS&D	12	1	45	Wi 80	62
Urbanek, Karen	Cashmere Challenge, The	S-O	10	1		Sp 86	37
Urbanek, Karen	Yuki Tsumugi	S-O	10	1		Sp 86	42
Utzinger, Karen	Handwoven Silk Garments: Ikat Shirt	WJ	3	2	10	Oc 78	29
Utzinger, Karen	Textile Equipment & Inventions Fair	SS&D	3	2	10	Sp 72	44
Utzinger, Karin	Finnish Transparent Weaving	WJ	5	1	17	Su 80	34
Ux, Katherine	On Teaching Weaving	H&C	11	3		Su 60	48
Vaclavim, Antonin; Jaroslav Orel	Textile Folk Art	Iw	5	1		Wi 79	61
Valk, Gene E.	It's a Frame-up	Hw	4	4		S/O 83	83
Van Artsdalen, Martha	MidAtlantic Fiber Association	SS&D	17	2	66	Sp 86	10
Van Artsdalen, Martha	New Elegance: Contemporary Art Wear, The	SS&D	16	1	61	Wi 84	50
Van Artsdalen, Martha	Tape Looms	SS&D	15	4	60	Fa 84	15
Van Artsdalen, Martha J.	High Tech—High Touch	SS&D	18	2	70	Sp 87	54
van Bode, Wilhelm; Ernst Kuhnel	Antique Rugs from the Near East	H&C	10	1		Wi 59	60
Van Cleve, Kate	Hand Loom Weaving for Amateurs	H&C	2	2		Sp 51	63
Van Cleve, Kate	Methods of Finishing Handwoven Fabrics: The Noel Stitch	H&C	8	4		Fa 57	27

AUTHOR	TITLE	JOUR	VOL	NO	ISS	DATE	PAGE
Van Cleve, Kate	Pioneer in a New Profession — The Boston School of Occupational Therapy	H&C	1	3		Fa 50	33
Van Cleve, Kate	Society of Arts and Crafts of Boston, Massachusetts, The	H&C	1	2		Su 50	5
Van Cleve, Kate	Two-Harness Rugs	H&C	4	2		Sp 53	53
Van Cleve, Kate	Weavers' Guild of Boston, The	H&C	3	1		Wi 51	55
Van Cleve, Kate	Weaving His Way Back	H&C	2	3		Su 51	11
van de Vrande, Let	Groot Plantaardig Verfboek	WJ	8	2	30	Fa 83	66
van der Hoogt, Madelyn	But What's the Tie-Up?	PWC	5	1	15		36
van der Hoogt, Madelyn	Countermarche Tie Up	CW	4	3	12	Ap 83	13
van der Hoogt, Madelyn	Coverlet from Start to Finish, A	PWC	5	1	15		20
van der Hoogt, Madelyn	Coverlet: Make Someday Today, Start a Coverlet, A	PWC	5	1	15		24
van der Hoogt, Madelyn	Coverlet: Weaving and Finishing Hints, A	PWC	5	1	15		34
van der Hoogt, Madelyn	Coverlet: Weaving and Finishing Hints, A	PWC	5	1	15		34
van der Hoogt, Madelyn	Double Piqué, Double Weave (error-corrected PWC v4 n4 i14 p33)	PWC	4	3	13		40
van der Hoogt, Madelyn	Drawloom Basics	Hw	7	2		M/A 86	61
van der Hoogt, Madelyn	Drawloom Magic	Hw	7	2		M/A 86	66
van der Hoogt, Madelyn	Looms We Use, The	CW	4	1	10	Se 82	6
van der Hoogt, Madelyn	Multishaft Overshot on Opposites	WJ	8	3	31	Wi 83	76
van der Hoogt, Madelyn	see Sullivan, Donna	PWC	5	2	16		12
van der Hoogt, Madelyn	see Xenakis, Athanasios David	PWC	4	3	13		36
van der Hoogt, Madelyn	see Xenakis, Athanasios David	PWC	4	3	13		42
van der Hoogt, Madelyn	Stitcher Designer Hints for Loom-Controlled Figured Piqué	PWC	4	3	13		48
van der Hoogt, Madelyn	Support System for Drawloom Weavers, A	CW	7	2	20	Ja 86	10
van der Hoogt, Madelyn	Turned Drafts in Double Two-Tie Unit Weave	WJ	9	2	34	Fa 84	13
van der Hoogt, Madelyn	Twills in Double Two-Tie Unit Weave	Hw	6	5		N/D 85	64
van der Hoogt, Madelyn	Weaving Places	PWC	4	1	11		8
van der Hoogt, Madelyn	What Is Piqué...And How Is It Like Beiderwand? (error-corrected PWC v4 n3 i13 p4)	PWC	4	2	12		7
van der Hoogt, Madelyn; Athanasios David Xenakis	Everything You've Always Wanted to Know About Tying Up a Countermarch Loom Without Really Trying...And with Perfect Success the First Time	PWC	4	2	12		44
van der Hoogt, Madelyn; Margaret Heller	Eight-Shaft Overshot on Opposites	PWC	4	4	14		34
van der Klift-Tellegen, Henriette	Knitting from the Netherlands, Traditional Dutch Fishermen's Sweaters	Kn	2	1	3	F-W 85	79
van der Klift-Tellegen, Henriette	Knitting from the Netherlands, Traditional Dutch Fishermen's Sweaters	Fa	12	4		J/A 85	45
van der Meulen-Nulle, L. W.	Lace	H&C	18	1		Wi 67	46
Van Dommelen, David	Decorative Wall Hangings — Art with Fabric	H&C	14	1		Wi 63	43
Van Gelder, Lydia	"Detailed Directions in Fiber" (Exhibit)	Fa	9	3		M/J 82	77
Van Gelder, Lydia	Ikat	SS&D	13	2	50	Sp 82	62
Van Gelder, Lydia	Ikat	Fa	8	3		M/J 81	50
Van Gelder, Lydia	In the Beginning	S-O	10	2		Su 86	43
Van Gelder, Lydia	Lace Weed	SS&D	2	2	6	Sp 71	27
Van Gelder, Lydia	Techniques for Designing and Weaving Warp, Weft Ikat — Double and Compound Ikat	WJ	5	3	19	Wi 81	51
Van Gelder, Lydia	Weft Ikat for Rugs	WJ	5	4	20	Sp 81	31
Van Kleek, Florence	see Royce, Beverly	S-O	8	1		Sp 84	49
Van Ord, Kay; Stewart Van Ord	From Sheep to Shawl	WJ	6	2	22	Fa 81	57
Van Ord, Stewart	see Van Ord, Kay	WJ	6	2	22	Fa 81	57
Van Sickle, Glanda	Fair Isle Vest	S-O	8	3		Fa 84	45
Van Sickle, Glenda	Dye Sampler Pullover, A	S-O	8	3		Fa 84	44
Van Steyvoort, Colette	Initiation a La Creation Dentelliere (French)	WJ	8	4	32	Sp 84	67
Van Stralen, Trudy	Production Dyeing with Natural Dyes	S-O	11	4		Wi 87	57
Van Til, Reinder	Folklore of Puppeteer Joan Mickelson, The	Fa	13	1		J/F 86	14
Van Til, Reinder	"German Wearable Textiles" (Exhibit)	Fa	12	6		N/D 85	59

AUTHOR	TITLE	JOUR	VOL	NO	ISS	DATE	PAGE
van Wagenen, Jared, Jr.	Golden Age of Homespun, The	H&C	4	4		Fa 53	61
Van Winckel, Nance	Who Can Figure It	Hw	8	5		N/D 87	30
Van Winckle, Nance	Privilege of Craft, The	Hw	8	5		N/D 87	30
Vanco, John	"Birth Symbol in Traditional Women's Art, The" (Exhibit)	Fa	13	3		M/J 86	52
VanDenburg, Niles	Weaving with Long-Eyed Heddles	SS&D	8	3	31	Su 77	63
Vander Lee, Jana	"Charms" (Exhibit)	Fa	3	3		M/J 76	6
Vander Lee, Jana	"Eleanor Merrill" (Exhibit)	Fa	4	1		J/F 77	8
Vander Lee, Jana	"Fiber" (Exhibit)	Fa	3	2		M/A 76	9
Vander Lee, Jana	"Flemish Tapestries of Willem De Kempeneer" (Exhibit)	Fa	3	5		S/O 76	7
Vander Lee, Jana	From Houston: Rochella Cooper, Anita Hickman	Fa	3	3		M/J 76	10
Vander Lee, Jana	"Glory of Russian Costumes, The" (Exhibit)	Fa	4	3		M/J 77	15
Vander Lee, Jana	"Houston Designer-Craftsmen 1976" (Exhibit)	Fa	3	4		J/A 76	9
Vander Lee, Jana	"K18–Stoffwechsel": A Report on the Exhibition and Symposium Held in Kassel, West Germany (Exhibit)	Fa	10	1		J/F 83	52
Vander Lee, Jana	Louise Robbins	Fa	3	2		M/A 76	26
Vander Lee, Jana	Mary Ruth Smith: Stitcher	Fa	3	1		J/F 76	6
Vander Lee, Jana	Stephanie Cole Kirsher	Fa	3	6		N/D 76	11
Vander Lee, Jana	"Weavers I: The Contemporary Handweavers of Houston" (Exhibit)	Fa	3	2		M/A 76	8
Vander Noordaa, Titia	Shelburne's Jacquard Loom: Is It a Computer? (error-corrected SS&D v17 n4 86 p10)	SS&D	17	3	67	Su 86	34
Vanderburg, Jan	"Miniature Fibers" (Exhibit)	Fa	7	1		J/F 80	65
VanGelder, Lydia	Lace Flower	SS&D	2	4	8	Fa 71	26
VanSlyke, Gail Rutter	Fabrics for Interiors	WJ	3	1	9	Jy 78	5
VanStan, Ina	Textiles from Beneath the Temple of Pachacamac, Peru	H&C	20	3		Su 69	42
Varadarajan, Lotika	Ajrakh: Traditions of Textile Printing in Kutch	TM			11	J/J 87	72
Varela, Osmund Leonard	Photographing Textiles for a Museum	TMJ	1	1		No 62	23
Vargo, Bessie Mae	Nativity Scene	WJ	6	2	22	Fa 81	8
Varney, Ethel B.	Weavers' Guild of St. Louis	H&C	6	2		Sp 55	50
Velderman, Pat	Computer Generated Overshot Variations	H&C	22	4		Fa 71	10
Veness, Tim	In Brief: Fiber Notes	Hw	7	5		N/D 86	53
Veness, Tim	Notes on Designing for Drape	Hw	7	5		N/D 86	76
Ventura, Carol	Sisal Production in Highland Guatemala	Fa	14	2		M/A 87	44
Verlet, Pierre, et al.	Book of Tapestry—History and Technique, The	SS&D	10	2	38	Sp 79	73
Verlet, Pierre, et al.	Book of Tapestry, The	Iw	4	4		Fa 79	72
Verlinden, Lieve	Double Woven Mailbag with Name Tags	WJ	7	1	25	Su 82	34
Vernon, Jeane	Drop Spindles	SS&D	4	4	16	Fa 73	45
Vernon, Jeanne	Basic Spindle Spinning	SS&D	4	3	15	Su 73	41
Vernon, Jeanne	Great Wool Wheel, The	SS&D	5	1	17	Wi 73	45
Viditz-Ward, Anton	Some Preliminary Chemistry for Dyers	Iw	3	3		Sp 78	29
Viemont, Bess M.	see Furry, Margaret S.	SS&D	5	2	18	Sp 74	68
Vierck, Charles	see French, Thomas	H&C	5	4		Fa 54	57
Vilsbøll, Anne	Show Your Work in Denmark	TM			14	D/J 87	16
Vinroot, Sally	Feeling for Color, A	Hw	2	4		Se 81	47
Vinroot, Sally; Jennie Crowder	New Dyer, The	Fa	9	4		J/A 82	53
Violante, Elizabeth	Hey, Sailor, Let Me Shorten Your Sleeve	TM			6	A/S 86	98
Vogel, Edna	Creating Textiles for Today's Interiors	H&C	3	1		Wi 51	5
Vogt, Cy	Naomi Julian: Weaver	Fa	5	6		N/D 78	28
Voiers, Leslie	Child's Play	SS&D	18	3	71	Su 87	22
Voiers, Leslie	Fall Foliage	Hw	5	5		N/D 84	69
Voiers, Leslie	Looking at Twills	Hw	4	4		S/O 83	27
Voiers, Leslie	Looking at Twills	Hw	4	5		N/D 83	14
Voiers, Leslie	Looking at Twills	Hw	7	1		J/F 86	21

AUTHOR	TITLE	JOUR	VOL	NO	ISS	DATE	PAGE
Voiers, Leslie	Looking at Twills	WJ	8	2	30	Fa 83	64
Voiers, Leslie	Looking at Twills	Fa	11	4		J/A 84	54
Voiers, Leslie	Looking at Twills	SS&D	15	1	57	Wi 83	102
Voiers, Leslie	Looking at Twills	PWC	3	1	7		63
Voiers, Leslie	Wrap Up Your Warp	SS&D	18	1	69	Wi 86	49
Vollmer, John E.	China and the Complexities of Weaving Technologies	AT	5			Ju 86	65
Vollmer, John E.; E. J. Keall; E. Nagai-Berthrong	Silk Roads, China Ships	WJ	8	4	32	Sp 84	66
von Ammon, Helen	Spinning with Down and Knitting with Feathers	S-O	10	4		Wi 86	15
von Kreisler-Bomben, Kristin	"Birth Project, The" First Showing of Judy Chicago's New Work (Exhibit)	Fa	10	1		J/F 83	81
Von Rosenstiel, Helene	American Rugs and Carpets from the Seventeenth Century to Modern Times	SS&D	10	4	40	Fa 79	65
Von Rosenstiel, Helene	American Rugs and Carpets: From the Seventeenth Century to Modern Times	Iw	4	2		Sp 79	65
Von Rosenstiel, Paul	see Hjert, Jeri	SS&D	10	2	38	Sp 79	74
Von Rosenstiel, Paul	see Hjert, Jeri	Iw	4	1		Wi 78	55
Von Rosenstiel, Paul	see Hjert, Jeri	WJ	3	3	11	Ja 79	42
Von Rosenstiel, Paul	see Hjert, Jeri	Fa	6	3		M/J 79	16
von Weise, Wenda	"Basketry Today: And Quilts from the Collection of Phyllis Haders" (Exhibits)	Fa	9	4		J/A 82	75
Voolich, Erica	Playing with Blocks: An Exploration of Multiharness Overshot	WJ	2	3	7	Ja 78	34
Voolich, Erica Dakin	see Lang, Elizabeth	PWC	5	1	15		52
Vozar, Linda	Grace Kraft: Not Just Another Piece of Cloth from the Factory	Fa	5	5		S/O 78	36
Vozar, Linda	Linda Nelson Bryan	Fa	4	6		N/D 77	58
V'Soske, Vesta S.	V'Soske Rugs Through the Years	H&C	5	4		Fa 54	8
Waagen, Alice K.	How to Teach Hands-On Skills: The Basics of Lesson Planning	SS&D	17	2	66	Sp 86	65
Waagen, Alice K.	One Hundred Years Ago in Handweaving: Handweaving as a Domestic Art	Hw	6	3		Su 85	8
Waagen, Alice K.	Weaving as an Occupational Therapy	Hw	5	5		N/D 84	18
Wachtel, Blanche	Ingenious Devices	H&C	22	2		Sp 71	25
Wada, Yoshiko	Kimono East/West	Fa	9	1		J/F 82	19
Wada, Yoshiko	see Ritch, Diane	SS&D	7	1	25	Wi 75	34
Wada, Yoshiko Iwamoto	Innovations in Indigo	Fa	13	5		S/O 86	29
Wada, Yoshiko Iwamoto	see Ritch, Diane	TM			13	O/N 87	68
Wada, Yoshiko Iwamoto; Shelley Karpilow	New Twist on Resist	TM			8	D/J 86	20
Wada, Yoshiko; Mary Kellog Rice; Jane Barton	Shibou, the Inventive Art of Japanese Shaped Resist Dyeing	Hw	6	3		Su 85	14
Wada, Yoshiko; Mary Kellogg Rice, Jane Barton	Art of Stitched Shibori, The (error-corrected Fa v12 n3 85 p8)	Fa	12	2		M/A 85	55
Wada, Yoshiko; Mary Kellogg Rice; Jane Barton	Shibori: The Inventive Art of Japanese Shaped Resist Dyeing	Fa	11	6		N/D 84	56
Wada, Yoshiko; Mary Kellogg Rice, Jane Barton	Stitched Shibori Techniques: A Sampling	Fa	12	2		M/A 85	58
Wadlington, Mary J.	Sewing No-No's and Know-How's—Make it Look Readymade not Homemake	WJ	9	1	33	Su 84	61
Waggoner, Phyllis	Boundweave: Learning from the Past	WJ	10	4	40	Sp 86	44
Waggoner, Phyllis	Colorful Scarves	WJ	12	2	46	Fa 87	48
Waggoner, Phyllis	Double Corduroy Rug (error-corrected WJ v11 n3 87 p78)	WJ	11	2	42	Fa 86	42
Waggoner, Phyllis	Figures in Boundweave	WJ	10	2	38	Fa 85	58
Waggoner, Phyllis	Twilled Cottolin Towels	WJ	11	1	41	Su 86	42
Waggoner, Phyllis	Two Block Rug in Boundweave	WJ	12	1	45	Su 87	26
Wagner, Liz	"Statements in Fibre" (Exhibit)	Fa	6	1		J/F 79	88

AUTHOR	TITLE	JOUR	VOL	NO	ISS	DATE	PAGE
Wahe, Matilda	Finnish Lace Weaves	H&C	10	2		Sp 59	56
Wakeland, Robin	Painted Muslin Ghost Dance Costumes of the Sioux, C–1890	Fa	8	1		J/F 81	15
Walbridge, T.	Dye Garden	SS&D	8	2	30	Sp 77	63
Wald, Pat Boutin	Color Theory for Handweavers Part 1: The Basics (Photo-corrections WJ v10 n3 86 p6)	WJ	10	2	38	Fa 85	40
Wald, Pat Boutin	Color Theory for Handweavers Part 3: Visual Illusions with Color	WJ	10	4	40	Sp 86	40
Wald, Pat Boutin	Color Theory for Handweavers Part 4: More Visual Illusions with Color	WJ	11	1	41	Su 86	37
Wald, Pat Boutin	Feltmaking	S-O	1			77	46
Walker, Barbara	Charted Knitting Designs	Kn	1	2	2	S-S 85	79
Walker, Barbara	Charted Knitting Designs: A Third Treasury of Knitting Patterns	TM			9	F/M 87	74
Walker, Barbara	Knitting from the Top	TM			9	F/M 87	76
Walker, Barbara	Second Treasury of Knitting Patterns	Kn	1	2	2	S-S 85	79
Walker, Barbara	Second Treasury of Knitting Patterns, A	TM			9	F/M 87	74
Walker, Barbara	Treasury of Knitting Patterns	Kn	1	2	2	S-S 85	79
Walker, Barbara	Treasury of Knitting Patterns, A	TM			9	F/M 87	74
Walker, Barbara G.	Easy Striped Knits	TM			4	A/M 86	54
Walker, Barbara G.	Second Treasury of Knitting Patterns, A	SS&D	2	1	5	De 70	31
Walker, Linda Berry	Border Cheviot	Hw	4	1		J/F 83	63
Walker, Linda Berry	Border Leicester	Hw	2	3		My 81	64
Walker, Linda Berry	Clun Forest	Iw	6	1		Wi 80	62
Walker, Linda Berry	Corriedale	Hw	3	1		Ja 82	73
Walker, Linda Berry	Cotswold	Hw	3	4		Se 82	71
Walker, Linda Berry	Handspinning as Art	S-O	2			78	56
Walker, Linda Berry	Jacob	Iw	5	4		Fa 80	64
Walker, Linda Berry	Karakul	Hw	3	2		Mr 82	60
Walker, Linda Berry	Lincoln	Iw	5	1		Wi 79	52
Walker, Linda Berry	Merino	Iw	5	3		Su 80	59
Walker, Linda Berry	North Country Cheviot	Hw	4	1		J/F 83	63
Walker, Linda Berry	Perendale	Hw	2	4		Se 81	69
Walker, Linda Berry	Rambouillet	Iw	4	3		Su 79	55
Walker, Linda Berry	Romney	Iw	5	2		Sp 80	63
Walker, Linda Berry	Scottish Blackface	Iw	4	4		Fa 79	60
Walker, Linda Berry	Wool: Choosing a Domestic Fleece	S-O	8	3		Fa 84	21
Walker, Louisa	Graded Lession in Macrame Knotting and Netting	H&C	23	3		M/J 72	24
Walker, Pauline; Carol Taylor	Ravensthorpe: A Festival of Wool	S-O	7	2		Su 83	16
Wallace, Anne	see Carpenter, Marie	Kn	3	4	8	Fa 87	63
Wallace, Anne	see Carpenter, Marie	TM			12	A/S 87	76
Wallace, Lysbeth	Midwest Tapestry Weaver	H&C	11	1		Wi 60	18
Wallace, Lysbeth	Piña	WJ	8	2	30	Fa 83	77
Wallace, Meg	Pick-Up Leno, A Two-harness Loom Technique	WJ	1	2	2	Oc 76	3
Wallace, Meg	Scouring a Fleece	WJ	1	2	2	Oc 76	18
Wallach, Nancy	Wearable Art at P. S. 152	Fa	7	6		N/D 80	25
Waller, Elsa	"Nancy Moore Bess: Baskets" (Exhibit)	Fa	7	5		S/O 80	74
Waller, Irene	Biennale, The	SS&D	14	4	56	Fa 83	20
Waller, Irene	"Conceptual Clothing" (Exhibit)	Fa	14	3		M/J 87	62
Waller, Irene	Craft of Weaving, The	SS&D	8	1	29	WI 76	70
Waller, Irene	Design Sources for the Fiber Artist	Iw	4	3		Su 79	65
Waller, Irene	Designing with Thread: From Fibre to Fabric	SS&D	5	1	17	Wi 73	77
Waller, Irene	Exploration of Materials, The	SS&D	8	4	32	Fa 77	55
Waller, Irene	"Fabric and Form: New Textile Art From Britain" (Exhibit)	Fa	9	6		N/D 82	80
Waller, Irene	Fine-Art Weaving	WJ	4	2	14	Oc 79	38
Waller, Irene	In Retrospect, Irene Waller	SS&D	12	4	48	Fa 81	10

AUTHOR	TITLE	JOUR	VOL	NO	ISS	DATE	PAGE
Waller, Irene	Katherine Virgils	Fa	10	5		S/O 83	12
Waller, Irene	Paper Abroad (Exhibit)	Fa	11	2		M/A 84	82
Waller, Irene	Sculpture Between Suggestion and Fact	Fa	9	3		M/J 82	100
Waller, Irene	Seen Around the Country: A Letter from England (error-corrected SS&D v10 n3 79 p75)	SS&D	10	2	38	Sp 79	103
Waller, Irene	Textile Sculpture	Fa	7	3		M/J 80	11
Waller, Irene	Theo Moorman	SS&D	17	4	68	Fa 86	60
Waller, Irene	Twelfth International Tapestry Biennale, The	SS&D	17	2	66	Sp 86	42
Waller, Irene	"Weaver's Life, Ethel Mairet, 1872–1952, A" (Exhibit)	Fa	11	4		J/A 84	78
Walrath, E. K.	Angel Sticks, An Aid to Warping	H&C	20	3		Su 69	15
Walrath, E. K.	Heddles, The Many Advantages of Using a Variety	H&C	17	4		Fa 66	20
Walsh, Joan Lea	Introduction to Silk Dyeing, An	WJ	3	2	10	Oc 78	14
Walsh, Joan Lea	Introduction to the Eucalypts: Substantive Dyes, An	WJ	3	2	10	Oc 78	47
Walsh, Joan Lee	Recipe for a Neutral Soap	WJ	3	3	11	Ja 79	17
Walters Art Gallery	Early Christian and Byzantine Art	H&C	4	1		Wi 52	62
Walters, James	Crochet Workshop	TM			4	A/M 86	74
Walters, Roberta	Kate Woolstenhulme: A Sense of Place	Fa	10	2		M/A 83	56
Waltner, Elma	see Waltner, Willard	Hw	4	4		S/O 83	75
Waltner, Willard; Elma Waltner	Wool Worker's Flock	Hw	4	4		S/O 83	75
Wanes, Betsy, ed.	see Lapin, Lynne, ed.	WJ	2	3	7	Ja 78	34
Warming, Wanda; Michael Gaworski	World of Indonesian Textiles, The	Fa	9	6		N/D 82	58
Warner, Lucy Ann	Overdyeing Your Yarns: A Way to Increase Your Palette	Fa	5	1		J/F 78	37
Warner, Lucy Ann	"Textiles New Mexico 1976" (Exhibit)	Fa	3	2		M/A 76	12
Warren, Anne	Machine Knitting with Handspun Cotton: First Experiments	S-O	11	2		Su 87	41
Warren, Barbara	see Cox, Doris	H&C	2	4		Fa 51	62
Warren, Hamilton	Arizona Arts Center at Sedona Offers Program Year Around	H&C	13	1		Wi 62	16
Warren, William L.; J. Herbert Callister	Bed Rugs 1722 — 1833	TMJ	3	4		De 73	47
Washington, Misti	Pine Needle Basketry	SS&D	16	4	64	Fa 85	46
Wasiqullah, Alexander	Textile Sleuth Extraordinaire	Fa	12	2		M/A 85	39
Wasiqullah, Alexandra	Marvelous Mezzaro, The	Fa	10	5		S/O 83	29
Wassef, Ramses Wissa	Woven by Hand	SS&D	6	3	23	Su 75	50
Wassef, Ramses Wissa; W. Forman; B. Forman	Tapestries from Egypt — Woven by the Children of Harrania	H&C	14	4		Fa 63	43
Wasserman, Andrea Stix	Polyester in Japan	TM			5	J/J 86	20
Wasserman, Tamara E.; Johathan Hill	Bolivian Indian Textiles: Traditional Designs and Costumes	WJ	6	3	23	Wi 81	60
Wasserman, Tamara E.; Jonathan S. Hill	Bolivian Indian Textiles: Traditional Designs and Contumes	Fa	9	6		N/D 82	58
Wasserman, Tamara E.; Jonathan S. Hill	Bolivian Indian Textiles: Traditional Designs and Costumes	Hw	3	2		Mr 82	22
Watkinson, Ray	William Morris as Designer	H&C	19	1		Wi 68	45
Watson, Aleta	E.E. Gilmore, Loom Builder and Weaver	H&C	23	5		S/O 72	24
Watson, William	Textile Design and Color	H&C	2	1		Wi 50	62
Watt, Ruth	French Weaving 1972	H&C	23	6		N/D 72	48
Waxler, Dorothy V.	National Standards Council of American Embroiderers	Fa	9	3		M/J 82	56
Wealington, Mary J.	Custon Touch, Creative Sewing Techniques, The	WJ	8	1	29	Su 83	51
Weaver, Ken	Ken Weaver on Rep Weaving	WJ	7	4	28	Sp 83	20
Weaver, Martin E.	Ardabil Puzzle, The	TMJ	23			84	43
Weavers Guild of Boston	Weavers' Wisdom: 250 Aids to Happier Weaving	WJ	10	3	39	Wi 86	72
Weavers' Guild of Boston Corey, Rosita; Betty Shannon, eds.	Weavers' Wisdom: 250 Aids to Happier Weaving	SS&D	11	4	44	Fa 80	66

AUTHOR	TITLE	JOUR	VOL	NO	ISS	DATE	PAGE
Weavers Guild of Boston, Monograph Three	Processing and Finishing Hand Woven Textiles	WJ	6	1	21	Su 81	54
Weaving Horizons	Spring and Summer Fashion Fabrics	Hw	6	3		Su 85	20
Webb, Mildred M.	Steps in Planning a Successful Sale	SS&D	5	3	19	Su 74	50
Weber, Jacobs & Field	Woven and Graphic Art of Anni Albers, The	WJ	11	1	41	Su 86	74
Wedd, J. A.	Sources of Design — Pattern & Texture	H&C	8	2		Sp 57	59
Weddle, Diane	String into Fuzz	S-O	5			81	12
Weeks, J. G.; D. Treganowan	Rugs and Carpets of Europe and the Western World	H&C	21	2		Sp 70	41
Weeks, Jeanne	see Larsen, Jack Lenor	SS&D	7	3	27	Su 76	34
Weeks, Jeanne	see Larsen, Jack Lenore	Fa	3	5		S/O 76	39
Wehrlin, Max	Raw Silk for the Handweaver	H&C	6	2		Sp 55	22
Weibel, Adele Coulin	Two Thousand Years of Textiles	H&C	4	1		Wi 52	59
Weigle, Palmy	Ancient Dyes for Modern Weavers	SS&D	6	2	22	Sp 75	63
Weigle, Palmy	Color Exercises for the Weaver	SS&D	8	2	30	Sp 77	37
Weigle, Palmy	Color Exercises for the Weaver	Iw	1	4		Su 76	29
Weigle, Palmy	Color Exercises for the Weaver	Fa	3	4		J/A 76	42
Weigle, Palmy	Double Weave	SS&D	10	3	39	Su 79	35
Weigle, Palmy	Double Weave	Iw	4	2		Sp 79	60
Weigle, Palmy	Double Weave	WJ	4	1	13	Jy 79	42
Weigle, Palmy	Indigo	SS&D	8	3	31	Su 77	67
Weigle, Palmy	Klara Cherepov's Diversified Plain Weave	SS&D	6	1	21	Wi 74	55
Weigle, Palmy	Siminoff	SS&D	1	3	3	Ju 70	20
Weigle, Palmy, guest ed.	see Brooklyn Botanic Garden	SS&D	5	3	19	Su 74	62
Weills, Christopher	Goodfellow Catalog of Wonderful Things, The	Iw	3	2		Wi 78	40
Weills, Christopher; Sarah Satterlee	Goodfellow Catalog of Wonderful Things No. 3, The	SS&D	14	1	53	Wi 82	64
Weiner, A. N.	Innovations in Looms	H&C	23	1		J/F 72	8
Weinstein, Ann	Liz Kregloe: A Collage of Interior Spaces	Fa	13	3		M/J 86	28
Weintraub, Fran	Tie-Dyed Warp	SS&D	4	1	13	Wi 72	38
Weir, Jean; Joyce Chown	Joyce Chown's "Fabricated Structure: Weir"	Fa	11	4		J/A 84	39
Weir, M.	see Simpson, L. E.	H&C	8	4		Fa 57	59
Weiss, Hedy	Mary Bero	Fa	12	2		M/A 85	36
Weissman, Julia	Bottom Line, The	Kn	3	4	8	Fa 87	11
Weissman, Julia	Buyer's Guide to Knitting Machines, A	Fa	9	2		M/A 82	43
Weissman, Julia	In This Corner, Knitting Machines	Kn	1	1	1	F-W 84 CI	64 50
Weissman, Julia	Manly Art of Knitting...What's Become of It, The	Kn	3	2	6	Sp 87	15
Weissman, Julia	Mary Walker Phillips	Kn	1	2	2	S-S 85	15
Weissman, Julia	Rag Trade: Picture Postcard, The (Susanna Lewis)	Kn	3	1	5	F-W 86	68
Weissman, Julia	Rag Trade, The	Kn	1	1	1	F-W 84 CI	70 53
Weissman, Julia	Rag Trade, The	Kn	1	2	2	S-S 85	53
Weissman, Julia	Rag Trade, The	Kn	2	1	3	F-W 85	76
Weissman, Julia	Rag Trade, The	Kn	2	2	4	S-S 86	59
Weissman, Julia	see Lewis, Susanna E.	Kn	3	1	5	F-W 86	71
Weissman, Julia	see Lewis, Susanna E.	TM			5	J/J 86	12
Weissman, Julia	see Lewis, Susanna E.	PWC	4	2	12		53
Welch, Nancy	see Hoover, Doris	WJ	7	1	25	Su 82	64
Welch, Nancy; Doris Hoover	Tassel Making	Fa	5	6		N/D 78	22
Weldon, Lynn L.	My Life	WJ	2	2	6	Oc 77	11
Wellman, Kathryn	Early American Craftsman's Holiday, An	H&C	2	2		Sp 51	30
Wellman, Kathryn, O.T.R.	Planning an Exhibition	H&C	3	4		Fa 52	26
Wells, Elizabeth	Exploring the Possibilities of Ancient Rose	H&C	11	1		Wi 60	22

AUTHOR	TITLE	JOUR	VOL	NO	ISS	DATE	PAGE
Wells, Oliver N.	Salish Weaving—Primitive and Modern	SS&D	3	2	10	Sp 72	38
Welters, Linda	Greek Chemises: Cut and Construction	WJ	10	1	37	Su 85	40
Weltge, Sigrid	Legacy of Color and Texture: Dorothy Liebes, 1899-1972, A	Iw	4	3		Su 79	25
Welty, Margaret	D. R. Wagner: 625 Stitches per Inch	Fa	10	6		N/D 83	24
Welty, Margaret	"Four x Four, A Collaboration: A Special Environment " (Exhibit)	Fa	7	1		J/F 80	69
Welty, Margaret	"Jennifer Gottdiener: Installation — Thread as Volume" (Exhibit)	Fa	7	5		S/O 80	70
Welty, Margaret	Shaping the World Through Design	Fa	9	4		J/A 82	48
Wendler, Maxine	Soft Cotton Baby Blanket	WJ	7	4	28	Sp 83	80
Wendler, Maxine	Upholstery	WJ	7	1	25	Su 82	22
Wennerstrom, Ann K.	Weaving a City Skyline	WJ	7	1	25	Su 82	30
Wentworth, Edward	America's Sheep Trails	H&C	20	3		Su 69	42
Werner Gustaf, publ.	Johanna Brunsson: Pionjär Inom Svensk Vävkonst	PWC	4	4	14		54
Wertenberger, Kathryn	Bead Leno	Hw	8	2		M/A 87	88
Wertenberger, Kathryn	Beyond the Fringe	Hw	2	5		No 81	27
Wertenberger, Kathryn	Christmas Is Coming: Woven Ornaments	SS&D	7	4	28	Fa 76	21
Wertenberger, Kathryn	Color Wheels and Color Blankets: Tools of the Designer	Hw	2	4		Se 81	50
Wertenberger, Kathryn	Color-and-Weave Effects	Hw	5	2		M/A 84	36
Wertenberger, Kathryn	Complementary Colors	Hw	6	5		N/D 85	90
Wertenberger, Kathryn	Counterchange	Hw	7	2		M/A 86	75
Wertenberger, Kathryn	Designing with Color	Hw	2	4		Se 81	32
Wertenberger, Kathryn	Diversified Plain Weave	Hw	8	5		N/D 87	62
Wertenberger, Kathryn	Double Weave	Hw	5	4		S/O 84	81
Wertenberger, Kathryn	Fabrics for Spring Ensembles	Hw	6	2		M/A 85	82
Wertenberger, Kathryn	Handwoven Trees	Hw	5	5		N/D 84	90
Wertenberger, Kathryn	Home Comfort	Hw	5	2		M/A 84	66
Wertenberger, Kathryn	Lesson in Cut and Sewn Handwoven Garments, A (error-corrected Hw v2 n2 81 p68)	Hw	2	1		F-W 80	36
Wertenberger, Kathryn	Metallic Yarns	Hw	6	1		J/F 85	89
Wertenberger, Kathryn	Mill End Yarns	Hw	5	4		S/O 84	77
Wertenberger, Kathryn	More Harnesses Make the Difference	Hw	2	3		My 81	40
Wertenberger, Kathryn	Notes on Uphlstering the Chair	Hw	5	2		M/A 84	110
Wertenberger, Kathryn	On Buying Used Looms	Hw	2	3		My 81	22
Wertenberger, Kathryn	On the Value of Making Samples	Hw	1	2		S-S 80	12
Wertenberger, Kathryn	Outrageous Colors	Hw	5	5		N/D 84	68
Wertenberger, Kathryn	Plaids (error-corrected Hw v5 n1 84 p7)	Hw	4	5		N/D 83	50
Wertenberger, Kathryn	Planning for Threading and Treadling	Hw	2	2		Mr 81	47
Wertenberger, Kathryn	see Alderman, Sharon D.	WJ	7	3	27	Wi 82	49
Wertenberger, Kathryn	see Alderman, Sharon D.	Fa	10	1		J/F 83	58
Wertenberger, Kathryn	Shadow Weave	Hw	8	1		J/F 87	76
Wertenberger, Kathryn	Supplementary Warp (Warp Brocade)	Hw	7	1		J/F 86	80
Wertenberger, Kathryn	Turned Drafts	Hw	6	3		Su 85	90
Wertenberger, Kathryn	Undulating Warps and Wefts	Hw	6	4		S/O 85	90
Wertenberger, Kathryn	Unusual Materials for Warp or Weft	Hw	7	4		S/O 86	78
Wertenberger, Kathryn	Waffle Weave	Hw	8	4		S/O 87	83
Wertenberger, Kathryn	Weaver's Challenge	Hw	5	1		J/F 84	27
Wertenberger, Kathryn; Nancy Kuwabara	Tucked Dresses	Hw	4	2		M/A 83	63
Wertheimer, Sheila	Applicant #029: Antonia Kormos	SS&D	10	2	38	Sp 79	68
Wertime, John T.	Flat-Woven Structures Found in Nomadic and Village Weavings from the Near East and Central Asia	TMJ	18			79	33
Wessel, Klaus	Coptic Art	H&C	17	1		Wi 66	44
West, Alan	see Nunn, Robin	SS&D	14	2	54	Sp 83	10
West, Virginia	Anne Brooke's Impeccable Woven Rugs	Fa	6	6		N/D 79	24

AUTHOR	TITLE	JOUR	VOL	NO	ISS	DATE	PAGE
West, Virginia	Batwings and Butterflies	Hw	6	2		M/A 85	41
West, Virginia	Coat Couture	SS&D	14	2	54	Sp 83	48
West, Virginia	Couturier Fashion Design	SS&D	13	4	52	Fa 82	34
West, Virginia	Couturier Fashions: Part 1, Couturier Fabric Design	SS&D	13	3	51	Su 82	8
West, Virginia	Designer Fabrics for Upholstery	Hw	5	2		M/A 84	72
West, Virginia	Ed Rossbach: Embracing the Fabric of Art	Fa	9	1		J/F 82	31
West, Virginia	From the Far West: Carpets and Textiles of Morocco	Hw	2	3		My 81	14
West, Virginia	Gary Trentham's Objets d'Art: An Interview	SS&D	11	3	43	Su 80	70
West, Virginia	Handwoven Clothing Today: The Couturier Touch	Fa	8	1		J/F 81	39
West, Virginia	Hemstitching	Hw	2	5		No 81	56
West, Virginia	Jappie King Black: The Siren and Other Tempting Crocheted Beings (error-corrected Fa v8 n2 81 p7)	Fa	7	6		N/D 80	14
West, Virginia	Magic of Matelassé, The	PWC	4	3	13		44
West, Virginia	Ninth International Biennial of Tapestry: A Prime Reflector, The	SS&D	11	1	41	Wi 79	96
West, Virginia	"Old Traditions/New Directions" (Exhibit)	Fa	8	6		N/D 81	66
West, Virginia	Sensuous Silk	Hw	7	1		J/F 86	52
West, Virginia	Symposium on Contemporary Textile Art	Fa	5	4		J/A 78	18
West, Virginia	Taking Charge of Your Design	Hw	8	5		N/D 87	46
West, Virginia	Variation of the Macedonian Shirt	WJ	7	2	26	Fa 82	50
West, Virginia	Virginia West Swatch Book, The	Hw	7	1		J/F 86	19
West, Virginia	Virginia West Swatch Book, The	WJ	11	3	43	Wi 87	63
West, Virginia	Virginia West Swatch Book, The	SS&D	17	2	66	Sp 86	85
West, Virginia	Virginia West Swatch Book, The	PWC	4	3	13		55
West, Virginia	Wear Your Wall Hanging	SS&D	4	2	14	Sp 73	11
West, Virginia	Weavers Bag — From Many Lands to Convergence '74, The	SS&D	5	1	17	Wi 73	38
West, Virginia	Weavers' Wearables	Hw	1	2		S-S 80	14
West, Virginia	Weaving a Lifestyle: Malin Selander	Iw	5	2		Sp 80	30
West, Virginia	Working with the Bias	WJ	12	1	45	Su 87	9
West, Virginia M.	Finishing Touches for the Handweaver	SS&D	1	3	3	Ju 70	22
West, Virginia M.	Star Spangled Banner, The	H&C	15	2		Sp 64	13
West, Virginia M.	Varied Hemstitching, Used for Finishing	H&C	18	2		Sp 67	19
West, Virginia W.	Finishing Touches: A Study of Finishing Details for Handwoven Articles	H&C	19	1		Wi 68	45
West, W. C.	Anyone Can Build a Spinning Wheel	SS&D	7	1	25	Wi 75	35
Westbrook, John R.,	Nelson Chang: Champion of Chinese Knotting	Fa	14	3		M/J 87	6
Westerink, Claire	Tapestry Weaving with Unspun Flax	WJ	11	2	42	Fa 86	49
Westerink, Claire; Erica Baker	Linen Knits	S-O	10	3		Fa 86	17
Westfall, Carol	Plaiting with Recycled Materials	SS&D	8	4	32	Fa 77	87
Westfall, Carol	see Glashausser, Suellen	SS&D	9	2	34	Sp 78	49
Westfall, Carol D.	Hexagonal Plaiting (error-corrected SS&D v10 n2 79 p56)	SS&D	9	4	36	Fa 78	40
Westfall, Carol D.; Dipti Desai	Bandhana (Tie Dye)	AT	8			De 87	19
Westfall, Carol D.; Dipti Desai	Gujarati Embroidery	AT	8			De 87	29
Westfall, Carol D.; Dipti Desai	Kantha	AT	7			Ju 87	161
Westfall, Carol D.; Dipti Desai	Phulkari	AT	6			De 86	85
Weston, Carol	Mexican Wedding	SS&D	2	4	8	Fa 71	30
Westphal, Katherine	Creative Process: Katherine Westphal, The	Fa	11	6		N/D 84	32
Westphal, Katherine	Sampler of Surface Design, A	Fa	10	5		S/O 83	39
Wetherbee, Martha	Shaker Baskets Today	SS&D	19	1	73	Wi 87	60
Wetherbee, Martha; Nathan Taylor	Legend of the Bushwhacker Basket	SS&D	17	4	68	Fa 86	88

AUTHOR	TITLE	JOUR	VOL	NO	ISS	DATE	PAGE
Wetherbee, Martha; Nathan Taylor	Legend of the Bushwhacker Basket	TM			10	A/M 87	76
Wetter, Cora M.	Old Wheel Spins Again, An	H&C	5	3		Su 54	31
Wettlaufer, George; Nancy Wettlaufer	Craftsman's Survival Manual	SS&D	6	2	22	Sp 75	63
Wettlaufer, Nancy	see Wettlaufer, George	SS&D	6	2	22	Sp 75	63
Wheater, Kathleen	Fabric of Sha Sha Higby's Imagination, The	Fa	14	3		M/J 87	35
Wheeler, Barbara R.	Wool: Mill-Prepared for Handspinners	S-O	8	3		Fa 84	23
Wheeler, Monroe, ed.	Textiles and Ornaments of India	H&C	7	3		Su 56	59
Whitaker, James H.	Iron and Steel Spinning Wheel: Reconstructed Treadle Sewing Machine, An	SS&D	8	4	32	Fa 77	60
Whitbourn, K.	Introducing Rushcraft	H&C	21	1		Wi 70	42
White, A. V.	Weaving is Fun	H&C	26	5		Oc 75	12
White, A. V.	Weaving is Fun	H&C	13	3		Su 62	43
White, Jamie Leigh	Cotton Jacket with Pleat	WJ	7	3	27	Wi 82	68
White, Jamie Leigh	Soft & Cozy: Cotton Receiving Blankets	WJ	11	2	42	Fa 86	34
White, John	Indian Fingerweaving, Traditional Use for Ceremonial Sashes	H&C	19	3		Su 68	4
White, John Kennardh	Twined Bags and Pouches of the Eastern Woodlands	H&C	20	3		Su 69	8
White, Marcia	African American Thread Fare	Fa	9	6		N/D 82	56
White, Pat	Certificate of Excellence in Handweaving: The Jurying, The	SS&D	14	1	53	Wi 82	48
White, Patrick E.	"Woven Works: Tradition and Innovation" (Exhibit)	Fa	12	6		N/D 85	60
White, Ruth	Rag Rugs with Overlapping Weft Ends	WJ	6	4	24	Sp 82	28
White, Ruth W.	Handweaver at the HemisFair, A	H&C	19	3		Su 68	12
White, Violet	Time Capsules	Hw	8	1		J/F 87	75
White, Virginia	Night Stories	TM			11	J/J 87	82
White, Virginia L.	Keeping Culture Alive with Needle and Thread	Fa	9	3		M/J 82	40
White-Hansen, Sue Ellen	Hawaiian Quilt, The	TM			13	O/N 87	22
Whiteford, Andrew; Herbert Zim	North American Indian Arts	SS&D	2	2	6	Sp 71	34
Whiteford, Andrew Hunter	see McGreevy, Susan Brown	WJ	11	1	41	Su 86	14
Whitelaw, Adrienne	Assomption Sash, A Long Tradition in French Canada	H&C	21	3		Su 70	12
Whitney, Gladys	Acadians Honor Tapestry Master	SS&D	6	4	24	Fa 75	7
Whitney, Marjorie	Workbook for Theory of Color	H&C	2	2		Sp 51	61
Whittaker, Lynn	Silks of Ed Lambert: In Pursuit of the Moving Image, The	Fa	9	5		S/O 82	60
Whittemore, A. P., Jr.	Farmcraft Story, The	H&C	7	4		Fa 56	27
Whonnock Spinners & Weavers	Fiber Heritage of the Salish	WJ	9	2	34	Fa 84	65
Wiberg, Birgit	see Fredlund, Jane	WJ	11	2	42	Fa 86	74
Wiberg, Birgit	see Fredlund, Jane	Fa	13	5		S/O 86	60
Wiberg, Birgit	see Fredlund, Jane	SS&D	18	2	70	Sp 87	38
Wick, Susan	Fifth International Tapestry Exhibit	H&C	22	4		Fa 71	16
Wickens, Hetty	Natural Dyes for Spinners and Weavers	SS&D	17	2	66	Sp 86	86
Wickins, Hetty	Natural Dyes for Spinners and Weavers	WJ	8	3	31	Wi 83	67
Wickins, Hetty	Natural Dyes for Spinners and Weavers	PWC	3	3	9		67
Wicks, Alice	Peter's Prickly Pants	SS&D	8	4	32	Fa 77	72
Wicks, Alice	Peter's Prickly Pants	Iw	2	1		Fa 76	33
Widess, Jim	see Miller, Bruce W.	Hw	6	5		N/D 85	20
Widess, Jim	see Miller, Bruce W.	Fa	11	4		J/A 84	54
Widman, Dag	Swedish Textile Art Today	H&C	24	1		J/F 73	32
Wight, James	Introduction for the Use of Procion Dyes	Fa	3	1		J/F 76	11
Wight, James	One Man's Loom	Iw	4	4		Fa 79	22
Wilcox, Don	Bark Papermakers of San Pablito, The	Fa	12	4		J/A 85	22
Wilcox, Don	Keeping Tradition Alive	Fa	14	1		J/F 87	44
Wilcox, Don	Painted Cloth Gardens on Wheels	TM			9	F/M 87	18
Wilcox, Don	Ritual Fiber: Weaving Hope for the Future Into the Fabric of Life	Fa	13	6		N/D 86	7

AUTHOR	TITLE	JOUR	VOL	NO	ISS	DATE	PAGE
Wilcox, Don	Woven Houses of Thailand, The	Fa	13	3		M/J 86	38
Wilcox, Leslie	Leslie Wilcox	Fa	12	5		S/O 85	19
Wilcox, R. Turner	Dictionary of Costume, The	H&C	21	2		Sp 70	42
Wild, J. P.	Textile Manufacture in the Northern Roman Provinces	H&C	21	4		Fa 70	44
Wild, John Peter	Classical Greek Textiles from Nymphaeum	TMJ	4	4		77	33
Wild, John Peter	Roman Textiles from Vindolanda, Hexham, England	TMJ	18			79	19
Wild, John-Peter	Some Early Silk Finds in Northwest Europe	TMJ	23			84	17
Wilde, Ruth C.	Why Not "Tromp as Writ" Commercially?	H&C	2	2		Sp 51	22
Wile, Leslie	New Carpet-Making School for Vragiana	SS&D	4	2	14	Sp 73	17
Wiley, Lois	Fiber Talks—Eloquently	SS&D	9	4	36	Fa 78	92
Wiley, Lois	Lynn Rothrock: Disturbing Creatures, Menacing Devil Dolls	Fa	6	1		J/F 79	75
Wilkinson, Dorothy	Logical Techniques of the Handloom Weaver Volume I, Warping and Beaming for a Treadle Loom	H&C	16	4		Fa 65	43
Wilkinson, Dorothy	Tribute to a Famous Weaver	H&C	17	4		Fa 66	32
Will, Christoph	International Basketry for Weavers and Collectors	TM			10	A/M 87	76
Will, Dorothy	Iowa Student Builds Her Loom	H&C	6	4		Fa 55	20
Willard, Janice	"Fiberous": Fiber as a Source of Inspiration (Exhibit)	Fa	10	1		J/F 83	80
Willard, Janice	On the Edge: Harmony Hammond — Collecting, Reclaiming, Connecting	Fa	9	4		J/A 82	58
Willcox, Donald	New Design in Weaving	H&C	22	2		Sp 71	43
Willcox, Donald	Techniques of Rya Knotting	H&C	23	3		M/J 72	27
Willcox, Donald A.	Techniques of Rya Knotting	SS&D	3	2	10	Sp 72	38
Willcox, Donald J.	New Design in Stitchery	SS&D	2	2	6	Sp 71	34
Willcox, Donald J.	New Design in Weaving	SS&D	2	3	7	Su 71	26
Williams, Ann	Coverlet Weaving	SS&D	14	4	56	Fa 83	32
Williams, Ann	Evening the Odds in Juried Competition	SS&D	17	3	67	Su 86	63
Williams, Betty	From Field and Garden	SS&D	2	3	7	Su 71	6
Williams, Dai	"Art of the Cuna, The" (Exhibit)	Fa	10	4		J/A 83	64
Williams, Gerry, ed.	Apprenticeship In Craft	SS&D	14	1	53	Wi 82	64
Williams, Gerry, ed.	Apprenticeship in Craft	Hw	3	3		My 82	19
Williams, Olive	Handwoven Cape on an Improvised Loom	H&C	22	3		Su 71	28
Williams, Sharon Flynn	Plant Pigments and Natural Dyeing	SS&D	14	2	54	Sp 83	32
Williams, Terry Tempest	Sources of Inspiration: Bear River Migratory Bird Refuge	Hw	5	5		N/D 84	59
Williams, Trevor I., ed.	see Singer, Charles, ed.	H&C	8	2		Sp 57	59
Willis, Elizabeth Bayley	Bhotiya Woolens from India	H&C	5	2		Sp 54	4
Willock, Jack	Colour, Texture, Ornament, Line: A Question for Managers—Do You Know How Your Designers Think?	AT	4			De 85	97
Wilson, Helen	Preparing a Columbia Fleece for Handweaving	WJ	2	2	6	Oc 77	22
Wilson, Jay	Patience and Planning	Fa	8	2		M/A 81	29
Wilson, Jean	Anita Mayer	Hw	2	2		Mr 81	28
Wilson, Jean	Challenge of One Technique	SS&D	3	4	12	Fa 72	36
Wilson, Jean	Edges, Joinings, Trims, Embellishments, Closures...and More	Hw	2	5		No 81	42
Wilson, Jean	Jean Wilson's Soumak Workbook	SS&D	14	1	53	Wi 82	65
Wilson, Jean	Joinings, Edges, and Trims	WJ	8	3	31	Wi 83	68
Wilson, Jean	Joinings, Edges, and Trims	Fa	11	3		M/J 84	58
Wilson, Jean	Joinings, Edges and Trims	SS&D	14	3	55	Su 83	50
Wilson, Jean	Joinings, Edges, and Trims	SS&D	15	1	57	Wi 83	103
Wilson, Jean	Joinings, Edges, and Trims	PWC	3	2	8		61
Wilson, Jean	Joinings, Edges and Trims: Finishing Details for Handcrafted Products	Hw	5	1		J/F 84	22
Wilson, Jean	Pile Weaves: Twenty-Six Techniques and How to Do Them, The	SS&D	5	4	20	Fa 74	64
Wilson, Jean	Soumak Workbook	WJ	7	3	27	Wi 82	50
Wilson, Jean	Stitches	SS&D	15	4	60	Fa 84	67
Wilson, Jean	Textiles Come Alive with Pile Weaves	SS&D	5	3	19	Su 74	93
Wilson, Jean	Weave with Style	WJ	4	4	16	Ap 80	26

AUTHOR	TITLE	JOUR	VOL	NO	ISS	DATE	PAGE
Wilson, Jean	Weaving is Creative	H&C	24	2		M/A 73	5
Wilson, Jean	Weaving Is Creative: The Weaver-Controlled Weaves	SS&D	5	3	19	Su 74	62
Wilson, Jean	Weaving Is for Anyone	H&C	18	3		Su 67	43
Wilson, Jean	Weaving Is Fun	SS&D	3	1	9	Wi 71	39
Wilson, Jean	Weaving Is Fun	H&C	22	4		Fa 71	26
Wilson, Jean	Weaving with Style	lw	5	1		Wi 79	58
Wilson, Jean	Weaving with Style	Hw	1	2		S-S 80	14
Wilson, Jean	Weaving You Can Use	SS&D	7	2	26	Sp 76	34
Wilson, Jean	Weaving Your Can Use	lw	1	2		Wi 76	28
Wilson, Jean; Jan Burhen	Weaving You Can Wear	SS&D	5	2	18	Sp 74	68
Wilson, Karen	Cindy Snodgrass: Wind Sculptures	Fa	6	5		S/O 79	56
Wilson, Kax	Corde du Roi	lw	5	3		Su 80	49
Wilson, Kax	Golden Brocades, The	lw	6	1		Wi 80	66
Wilson, Kax	Handweavers 1800—1840	lw	5	2		Sp 80	50
Wilson, Kax	History of Textiles, A	lw	5	1		Wi 79	64
Wilson, Kax	History of Textiles, A	WJ	4	4	16	Ap 80	26
Wilson, Kax	History of Textiles, A	Fa	8	6		N/D 81	73
Wilson, Kax	Jerga: A Twill in Harmony with its Heritage	Hw	6	5		N/D 85	60
Wilson, Kax	Kashmir or Paisley; Romance of the Shawl	lw	4	4		Fa 79	34
Wilson, Kax	Origins	lw	4	4		Fa 79	51
Wilson, Kax	Origins	lw	5	1		Wi 79	47
Wilson, Kax	Origins: Damask	Hw	2	3		My 81	68
Wilson, Kax	Tweed	lw	5	2		Sp 80	59
Wilson, Kax	Vignettes from Peru	lw	5	4		Fa 80	46
Wilson, Kay	Ko-Ssu	H&C	24	4		Au 73	42
Wilson, Linda	see Heyl, Maxine	WJ	7	2	26	Fa 82	20
Wilson, Particia	Sampling Draft	SS&D	2	2	6	Sp 71	12
Wilson, Patricia	Animal, Vegetable, Mineral: Grist for the Weaver's Loom	H&C	24	4		Au 73	23
Wilson, Patricia	Cedar Bark, A Versatile Natural Weaving Material	H&C	20	3		Su 69	7
Wilson, Patricia	Natural Materials: A Challenge to the Weaver	H&C	23	1		J/F 72	14
Wilson, Patricia	Twill Derivative and Unit Classes	SS&D	3	3	11	Su 72	38
Wilson, Patricia	Weaving Materials from the Sea	SS&D	2	1	5	De 70	3
Wilson, Sadye Tune	Fundraising Brings Kasuri Kimono Weaver to Nashville Workshop	SS&D	9	2	34	Sp 78	4
Wilson, Sadye Tune	Shaft Switching on a Jack Loom	SS&D	10	1	37	Wi 78	70
Wilson, Sadye Tune	SS&D Interview: Peter Collingwood	SS&D	10	4	40	Fa 79	4
Wilson, Sadye Tune; Doris Finch Kennedy	Coverlets	SS&D	14	4	56	Fa 83	34
Wilson, Sadye Tune; Doris Finch Kennedy	Of Coverlets: the Legacies, the Weavers	Hw	5	2		M/A 84	13
Wilson, Sadye Tune; Doris Finch Kennedy	Of Coverlets, The Legacies, The Weavers	WJ	8	4	32	Sp 84	65
Wilson, Sadye Tune; Doris Finch Kennedy	Of Coverlets, The Legacies, The Weavers	Fa	12	6		N/D 85	46
Wilson, Sadye Tune; Doris Finch Kennedy	Of Coverlets: The Legacies, The Weavers	SS&D	15	3	59	Su 84	36
Wilson, Sadye Tune; Doris Finch Kennedy	Of Coverlets—the legacies, the weavers	PWC	3	2	8		60
Wiltsie-Vaniea, Anne	Secret Treasures of Tibet	SS&D	18	3	71	Su 87	60
Wimmer, Gayle	Technique & History of the Polish Double-weave, The	H&C	24	3		M/J 73	8
Winchester, Nina	Cut and Sew Mittens	WJ	9	3	35	Wi 85	53
Windeknecht, Margaret	"Adding" Treadles for a Complex Weave	CW	3	3	9	Ap 82	4
Windeknecht, Margaret	Creative Overshot: Shuttle Craft Guild Monograph No. 31	lw	4	2		Sp 79	60
Windeknecht, Margaret	Two-Tie Unit for Rugs: Part 1, The Double-Faced Stuffer Weave and Summer-and-Winter, The	SS&D	16	1	61	Wi 84	82

AUTHOR	TITLE	JOUR	VOL	NO	ISS	DATE	PAGE
Windeknecht, Margaret	Two-Tie Unit for Rugs: Part 2 Warping and Weaving Methods, The	SS&D	16	2	62	Sp 85	34
Windeknecht, Margaret B.	Creative Monk's Belt	SS&D	9	1	33	Wi 77	28
Windeknecht, Margaret B.	Creative Monk's Belt	SS&D	9	1	33	Wi 77	40
Windeknecht, Margaret B.	Creative Monk's Belt	SS&D	9	1	33	Wi 77	28
Windeknecht, Margaret B.	Creative Monk's Belt	SCGM		30		76	1-40
Windeknecht, Margaret B.	Creative Overshot	SS&D	10	3	39	Su 79	35
Windeknecht, Margaret B.	Creative Overshot	WJ	3	4	12	Ap 79	46
Windeknecht, Margaret B.	Creative Overshot	SCGM		31		78	1-57
Windeknecht, Margaret B.	see D'Angelo, Anne A.	SS&D	4	3	15	Su 73	57
Windeknecht, Margaret B.	see D'Angelo, Anne A.	SS&D	4	2	14	Sp 73	44
Windeknecht, Margaret B.	Wool Dyed the Procion Way	SS&D	6	4	24	Fa 75	89
Windeknecht, Margaret B.; Thomas G. Windeknecht	Computer-Aided Design for Handweaving	CW	2	1	4	Oc 80	8
Windeknecht, Margaret; Thomas Windeknecht	Color and Weave	WJ	6	2	22	Fa 81	39
Windeknecht, Margaret; Thomas Windeknecht	Color-and-Weave	SS&D	12	4	48	Fa 81	62
Windeknecht, Margaret; Thomas Windeknecht	Color-and-Weave	Hw	2	4		Se 81	78
Windeknecht, Margaret; Thomas Windeknecht	Color-and-Weave	Fa	9	4		J/A 82	52
Windeknecht, Margaret; Thomas Windeknecht	Color-and-Weave	PWC	3	1	7		60
Windeknecht, Margaret; Thomas Windeknecht	Color-and-Weave on a Dark-Light Sequence	SS&D	12	4	48	Fa 81	24
Windeknecht, Margaret; Thomas Windeknecht	Color-and-Weave on Rosepath	SS&D	13	2	50	Sp 82	8
Windeknecht, Thomas	see Windeknecht, Margaret	SS&D	12	4	48	Fa 81	24
Windeknecht, Thomas	see Windeknecht, Margaret	SS&D	13	2	50	Sp 82	8
Windeknecht, Thomas	see Windeknecht, Margaret	SS&D	12	4	48	Fa 81	62
Windeknecht, Thomas	see Windeknecht, Margaret	Hw	2	4		Se 81	78
Windeknecht, Thomas	see Windeknecht, Margaret	WJ	6	2	22	Fa 81	39
Windeknecht, Thomas	see Windeknecht, Margaret	Fa	9	4		J/A 82	52
Windeknecht, Thomas	see Windeknecht, Margaret	PWC	3	1	7		60
Windeknecht, Thomas G.	see Windeknecht, Margaret B.	CW	2	1	4	Oc 80	8
Windt, Hal	Dyeing with Lichens	Hw	3	1		Ja 82	20
Winther, Doris Aino B.	Winter Warmer	SS&D	15	1	57	Wi 83	27
Wipplinger, Michele	Color Me Purple	Kn	2	1	3	F-W 85	70
Wipplinger, Michele	Dyes of Mexico	S-O	9	3		Fa 85	32
Wipplinger, Michele	Lichens	S-O	10	2		Su 86	34
Wipplinger, Michele	Personal Approach to Color, A	Fa	13	2		M/A 86	31
Wipplinger, Michele, ed.	Color Trends	WJ	10	1	37	Su 85	86
Wipplinger, Michele, ed.	Color Trends: A Color Service for Fiberists	SS&D	17	3	67	Su 86	86
Wipplinger, Michelle	Art of Silk Dyeing, The (Photo-corrections WJ v10 n3 86 p6)	WJ	10	2	38	Fa 85	46
Wipplinger, Michelle; Carol Reynolds; Elizabeth Black	Labrador Tea	Hw	3	2		Mr 82	22
Wiseman, Ann	Rug Hooking & Rug Tapestries	WJ	6	1	21	Su 81	54
Wiseman, Ann	Rug Tapestries and Wool Mosaics	H&C	21	3		Su 70	39
Wittenberg, Barbara	Or...Alternatives to the Fig Leaf	SS&D	9	3	35	Su 78	96
Wittpenn, Ann	Reversible Flamepoint Vest	WJ	5	3	19	Wi 81	9
Wittpenn, Ann	see Patrick, Jane	Hw	4	1		J/F 83	33
Woelfle, Gretchen	American Heritage: Three Rugmaking Traditions, An	Fa	7	5		S/O 80	31
Woelfle, Gretchen	April May: She Weaves Curtains with Images	Fa	7	6		N/D 80	28
Woelfle, Gretchen	"Artists' Quilts" (Exhibit)	Fa	8	4		J/A 81	70
Woelfle, Gretchen	Christo: Running Fence Remembered	Fa	7	5		S/O 80	24

AUTHOR	TITLE	JOUR	VOL	NO	ISS	DATE	PAGE
Woelfle, Gretchen	Floats of Fancy	Fa	8	2		M/A 81	52
Woelfle, Gretchen	"Nancy Youdelman: Shattered Glass" (Exhibit)	Fa	7	3		M/J 80	74
Woelfle, Gretchen	Rag Rugs: Helen Gushee Helps Keep a Tradition Alive	Fa	7	5		S/O 80	31
Woelfle, Gretchen Erskine	On the Edge: Betye Saar — Personal Time Travels	Fa	9	4		J/A 82	56
Woelfle, Gretchen Erskine	Unlimited Possibilities of Machine Knitting: Charlotte Cain's Patterns of Infinity, The	Fa	6	4		J/A 79	58
Woelfle, Gretchen Erskine	Warm Quilt — Look Again!, A	Fa	7	3		M/J 80	62
Wolf, Thomas	see Goldring, Marc	Hw	6	4		S/O 85	20
Wolfe, Gregory	Kitt Miller: Art Among Friends	Fa	14	3		M/J 87	10
Wolfe, Susan	Knits, Knuckles and Knots	Kn	2	2	4	S-S 86	4
Wolfe, Susan	Weaving a Web	PWC	4	3	13		5
Wolff, Colette	Cut, Paste, and Copy	TM			8	D/J 86	52
Wolff, Colette	Fashionable Quilts	TM			10	A/M 87	16
Wolff, Colette	For the Floor: An International Exhibit of Contemporary Artists' Rugs	Hw	6	2		M/A 85	20
Wolff, Colette	Making of an Exhibition: An Insider's Report, The	Fa	12	3		M/J 85	46
Wolff, Colette	Mastering the Art of Hand Appliqué	TM			4	A/M 86	49
Wolff, Colette	Quilters Flock to Houston Festival	TM			4	A/M 86	12
Wolff, Colette	Tons of Quilts at Liberty Festival	TM			6	A/S 86	22
Wollenberg, Jackie	Braiding with Bobbins	SS&D	7	1	25	Wi 75	90
Wollenberg, Jackie	Christmas Tree Tip Makes a Drop Spindle	SS&D	6	1	21	Wi 74	60
Wolter, Edith L.	Double Weave Pick-Up with Straight Diagonal Lines	WJ	7	4	28	Sp 83	61
Wonder, Danny	Jerri Finch-Hurley: Quilted Paintings	Fa	11	2		M/A 84	27
Wood, Geraldine	Musical Skirt, A	H&C	14	4		Fa 63	39
Wood, Gerry	Queen Anne's Pattern	H&C	10	4		Fa 59	15
Wood, Gerry	Weaving Skirts	H&C	9	4		Fa 58	18
Wood, Irene K.	Miniature Garments	SS&D	11	2	42	Sp 80	60
Woodsmall, Annabel Whitney	Contemporary Appliqued Beadwork	TIAM		2		79	1-40
Woodsmall, Annabel Withney	Contemporary Appliqued Beadwork	Iw	5	3		Su 80	71
Woodward, Carol H.	Silks from Siam	H&C	2	3		Su 51	23
Worsley, Marie	Nigerian Weavers	H&C	12	2		Sp 61	45
Worst, Edward F.	Dyes and Dyeing	SS&D	2	2	6	Sp 71	34
Worst, Edward F.	How to Weave Linens	H&C	4	2		Sp 53	61
Worst, Edward F.	Weaving with Foot Powered Looms	Fa	3	1		J/F 76	4
Worst, Edward F.	Weaving with Foot-Power Looms	SS&D	6	3	23	Su 75	49
Wright, Dorothy	Complete Book of Basketry, The	Iw	3	4		Su 78	45
Wright, Gilbert	Dyed Cotton Rug in Overshot	WJ	7	4	28	Sp 83	81
Wright, Helena, ed.	Merrimack Valley Textile Museum: A Guide to the Manuscript Collections, The	Hw	5	5		N/D 84	14
Wright, Jenny	Opinionated Knitter: Sheep to Shawl, The	Kn	4	1	9	Wi 87	20
Wright, Mary	Cornish Guernseys & Knit-frocks	Kn	1	1	1	F-W 84	71
Wright, Mary	Cornish Guernseys & Knitfrocks	Fa	11	1		J/F 84	58
Wright, Yolanda	Quilting by the Lake in Central New York	Fa	10	2		M/A 83	50
Writer's Digest Books	Craft Worker's Market, 1980	Iw	5	1		Wi 79	65
Wroten, Barbara	Glad Rags	SS&D	15	4	60	Fa 84	28
Wroten, Barbara	Hemming Ways	SS&D	18	3	71	Su 87	74
Wu, Han-Lien	New Technique for Pulled-Warp Ikat, A	Iw	5	3		Su 80	29
Wyndham, Lois	Convergence '86 Co-Hosts: The Ontario Crafts Council and The Ontario Handweavers and Spinners	SS&D	17	3	67	Su 86	38
Xenakis, Alexis Yiorgos	Afternoon with Elizabeth, An	Kn	1	1	1	F-W 84 / CI	10 / 4
Xenakis, Alexis Yiorgos	American Yarn Shops: On the Endangered Species List?	Kn	3	4	8	Fa 87	10
Xenakis, Alexis Yiorgos	Barbara Walker Mosaic, The	Kn	2	1	3	F-W 85	11
Xenakis, Alexis Yiorgos	Chenille Polo	PWC			6	Su 83	34
Xenakis, Alexis Yiorgos	Four Posts of Poverty, The	PWC	5	1	15		6

AUTHOR	TITLE	JOUR	VOL	NO	ISS	DATE	PAGE
Xenakis, Alexis Yiorgos	Glimakra Looms' N Yarns	PWC	4	1	11		48
Xenakis, Alexis Yiorgos	Greek Dower Sheet, A	Hw	1	2		S-S 80	36
Xenakis, Alexis Yiorgos	Jim "The Legend" Ahrens	PWC	4	4	14		6
Xenakis, Alexis Yiorgos	Knitted Trifle Bag	PWC	1	1		No 81	52
Xenakis, Alexis Yiorgos	Lee's Surrender — to Sachets	Hw	1	2		S-S 80	18
Xenakis, Alexis Yiorgos	Making Weaving History	PWC	4	3	13		6
Xenakis, Alexis Yiorgos	Meg Swansen: A Conversation with Alexis Xenakis	Kn	3	3	7	Su 87	26
Xenakis, Alexis Yiorgos	Men Who Knit	Kn	3	2	6	Sp 87	14
Xenakis, Alexis Yiorgos	Mistra	Kn	2	2	4	S-S 86	56
Xenakis, Alexis Yiorgos	One-Woman Publishing Show, A	PWC	5	2	16		6
Xenakis, Alexis Yiorgos	Ordinary Weaver and Her Extraordinary Rugs, An	PWC	4	2	12		4
Xenakis, Alexis Yiorgos	Overshot Part 2	PWC	3	3	9		6
Xenakis, Alexis, Yiorgos	Paired-Thread Finnweave Projects: The Gaza Dress, The	PWC			2	Ap 82	40
Xenakis, Alexis Yiorgos	Peruvian Mittens	PWC			4	Ja 83	62
Xenakis, Alexis Yiorgos	Scented Sachets	PWC	3	2	8		56
Xenakis, Alexis Yiorgos	see Kussube, Kay	PWC	4	2	12		27
Xenakis, Alexis Yiorgos	see Rowley, Elaine	PWC	3	2	8		53
Xenakis, Alexis Yiorgos	see Xenakis, Athanasios David	PWC			6	Su 83	39
Xenakis, Alexis Yiorgos	Time to Revitalize, A	PWC	4	1	11		10
Xenakis, Alexis Yiorgos	Timelessly Fashionable Turkish Coat, A	PWC	1	1		No 81	43
Xenakis, Alexis Yiorgos	Turkish Coat, A	Hw	2	2		Mr 81	39
Xenakis, Alexis Yiorgos	Ultimate T-Shirt, The	PWC			6	Su 83	29
Xenakis, Alexis Yiorgos	Weaving Places	PWC	4	2	12		28
Xenakis, Alexis Yiorgos	Windows: Kouverta	PWC	5	1	15		14
Xenakis, Alexis Yiorgos	Windows: Sendoni Curtains	PWC	4	1	11		4
Xenakis, Alexis Yiorgos; Elaine Rowley	Doupe Leno for the Harness Loom	PWC			6	Su 83	10
Xenakis, Alexis Yiorgos; Elaine Rowley	Knitting Video, The	Kn	1	2	2	S-S 85	74
Xenakis, Athanasios David	Afghans: Things to Consider and Finishes	PWC	3	1	7		10
Xenakis, Athanasios David	Bath Towel Set, A	PWC	1	1		No 81	24
Xenakis, Athanasios David	Blooming Leaf	PWC	3	3	9		51
Xenakis, Athanasios David	Bound Overshot	PWC	3	3	9		21
Xenakis, Athanasios David	Celtic Knot Box Cushion	PWC	3	4	10		60
Xenakis, Athanasios David	Celtic Knot (error-corrected PWC v4 n4 i14 '87 p33)	PWC	4	3	13		24
Xenakis, Athanasios David	Christmas Miniatures, Part 2: Krokbragd Bellpulls (error-corrected PWC i4 83 p76)	PWC			3	Oc 82	52
Xenakis, Athanasios David	Cotton Hanging — on a Chinese Folk Motif	PWC	1	1		No 81	39
Xenakis, Athanasios David	David's Back...And Picks Up Where He Left Off	PWC	5	2	16		42
Xenakis, Athanasios David	Designing for Finnweave	PWC			2	Ap 82	50
Xenakis, Athanasios David	Diagonal Corduroy	PWC	3	4	10		51
Xenakis, Athanasios David	Double Tartan	PWC	3	1	7		42
Xenakis, Athanasios David	Double Two-tie System Applied to Overshot	PWC	3	3	9		7
Xenakis, Athanasios David	Double Two-Tie Unit Weave: An Expansion of Options for Rigid Heddle Weaving, The	Iw	5	1		Wi 79	39
Xenakis, Athanasios David	Doupe Leno for the Rigid Heddle Loom	PWC			6	Su 83	14
Xenakis, Athanasios David	Egmont Sweater, The	PWC			2	Ap 82	82
Xenakis, Athanasios David	Even-Tied Overshot	PWC	3	3	9		40
Xenakis, Athanasios David	Even-Tied Overshot on a Rigid Heddle Loom	PWC	3	3	9		46
Xenakis, Athanasios David	Fabrics That Go Bump (error-corrected PWC i4 83 p76)	PWC			3	Oc 82	18
Xenakis, Athanasios David	Fantastic Finnweave, Part 1	PWC			2	Ap 82	18
Xenakis, Athanasios David	Fantastic Finnweave, Part 2	PWC			3	Oc 82	10
Xenakis, Athanasios David	Fantastic Finnweave, Part 2: Single-Thread Projects	PWC			3	Oc 82	14
Xenakis, Athanasios David	Fantastic Finnweave, Part 3	PWC			4	Ja 83	22

AUTHOR	TITLE	JOUR	VOL	NO	ISS	DATE	PAGE
Xenakis, Athanasios David	Fantastic Finnweave, Part 3	PWC			4	Ja 83	28
Xenakis, Athanasios David	Fiesta Plaid	PWC	3	1	7		39
Xenakis, Athanasios David	Figured Piqué	PWC	4	2	12		12
Xenakis, Athanasios David	Figured Piqué on a Ground of 2/2 Twill and 2/2 Hopsack	PWC	4	2	12		24
Xenakis, Athanasios David	Floor's the Limit, The	PWC	3	3	9		12
Xenakis, Athanasios David	Flower Curtain	PWC	4	1	11		32
Xenakis, Athanasios David	Four-Shaft Unbalanced Twill Braided Ribbon Inlay on Plain Weave Ground	PWC	4	1	11		27
Xenakis, Athanasios David	Halfghan	PWC	3	1	7		34
Xenakis, Athanasios David	Home Weaving: Linen'n Lace	Hw	1	1		F-W 79	44
Xenakis, Athanasios David	Incredible Five-Color, Two-Tie Afghan for a Super Kid, The	PWC	1	1		No 81	35
Xenakis, Athanasios David	Inlay Techniques	PWC	4	1	11		15
Xenakis, Athanasios David	Instructions: Pick-Up Figured Piqué (error-corrected PWC v4 n3 i13 p4)	PWC	4	2	12		39
Xenakis, Athanasios David	Isolated Overshot: Inlaid Runner	PWC	3	2	8		31
Xenakis, Athanasios David	Isolated Overshot: Linen and Cotton Teacloth	PWC	3	2	8		36
Xenakis, Athanasios David	Isolated Overshot: Razzle-dazzle Placemats	PWC	3	2	8		40
Xenakis, Athanasios David	Killarney	PWC	3	1	7		25
Xenakis, Athanasios David	Leno Fabrics	PWC			6	Su 83	18
Xenakis, Athanasios David	Macro Plaid, Macro Twill	PWC	3	1	7		55
Xenakis, Athanasios David	Multiple Rigid Heddle Adventure, Part 1, The	PWC	3	4	10		34
Xenakis, Athanasios David	One Heddle Two-Tie Weaving	PWC	1	1		No 81	24
Xenakis, Athanasios David	Orchid Shawl	PWC			5	Sp 83	38
Xenakis, Athanasios David	Other Finishes for Finnweave	PWC			2	Ap 82	49
Xenakis, Athanasios David	Overshot Derived from 2/2 Twill	PWC	3	2	8		7
Xenakis, Athanasios David	Overshot on Opposites	PWC	3	2	8		26
Xenakis, Athanasios David	Overshot on Opposites: Linen Hand Towels	PWC	3	2	8		29
Xenakis, Athanasios David	Paired-Thread Finnweave Projects: A Chessboard for the Nonfinn with Eight Harnesses, The	PWC			2	Ap 82	38
Xenakis, Athanasios David	Paired-Thread Finnweave Projects: Ben's Chessboard, The	PWC			2	Ap 82	38
Xenakis, Athanasios David	Paired-Thread Finnweave Projects: Five Placemats Based on a Chinese Lattice Design, The	PWC			2	Ap 82	34
Xenakis, Athanasios David	Paired-Thread Finnweave Projects: Lynn's Zebra, The	PWC			2	Ap 82	36
Xenakis, Athanasios David	Paired-Thread Finnweave Projects: Medusa, the Gorgeous Gorgon, The	PWC			2	Ap 82	43
Xenakis, Athanasios David	Pillow and Table Runner in Summer and Winter Weave	PWC	1	1		No 81	21
Xenakis, Athanasios David	Planning Figured Piqué Designs on Pre-Marked Graph Paper	PWC	4	2	12		16
Xenakis, Athanasios David	Preppy Look is in the Cards, The	PWC	1	1		No 81	6
Xenakis, Athanasios David	Quadruple Cloth on the Rigid Heddle Loom	PWC			2	Ap 82	74
Xenakis, Athanasios David	Quadruple Cloth on the Rigid Heddle Loom, Editor's Note	PWC			2	Ap 82	74
Xenakis, Athanasios David	Quatrefoil	PWC	3	3	9		53
Xenakis, Athanasios David	Red and Blue Canvas Weave Afghan	PWC	3	1	7		22
Xenakis, Athanasios David	see Herring, Connie	PWC	3	3	9		29
Xenakis, Athanasios David	see Herring, Connie	PWC	3	3	9		44
Xenakis, Athanasios David	see Lyon, Linda	PWC	3	1	7		36
Xenakis, Athanasios David	see Lyon, Linda	PWC	3	4	10		64
Xenakis, Athanasios David	see Sellon, Patti	PWC	4	2	12		18
Xenakis, Athanasios David	see van der Hoogt, Madelyn	PWC	4	2	12		44
Xenakis, Athanasios David	Simple Damask-Like Effects Using Element Diameter Differential and Element Tension Differential	AT	1			De 83	317
Xenakis, Athanasios David	Simple Methods for Deriving Satin Stitching Sequences and Damask Tie-Ups	CW	6	1	16	Se 84	19
Xenakis, Athanasios David	Star and Diamond	PWC	3	3	9		49
Xenakis, Athanasios David	Summer and Winter Revisited, Part 1: Two-Heddle Double Cloth	PWC			2	Ap 82	61
Xenakis, Athanasios David	Summer and Winter Revisited Part 4: Turned Pebble Weave	PWC			4	Ja 83	52
Xenakis, Athanasios David	Summer and Winter Unharnessed	PWC	1	1		No 81	10

AUTHOR	TITLE	JOUR	VOL	NO	ISS	DATE	PAGE
Xenakis, Athanasios David	Tablecloth in Summer and Winter	PWC	1	1		No 81	16
Xenakis, Athanasios David	Texture Possibilities of the Three-Tie Unit Weaves	PWC	4	4	14		49
Xenakis, Athanasios David	Tied Overshot Boundweave	PWC	3	4	10		9
Xenakis, Athanasios David	Tips on Weaving Linen on the Rigid Heddle Loom	PWC	1	1		No 81	20
Xenakis, Athanasios David	'Twill Skirt the Issue	PWC	1	1		No 81	49
Xenakis, Athanasios David	Two Alpaca and Wool Scarves	PWC	3	4	10		40
Xenakis, Athanasios David	Two Unusual Multishaft Curtains	PWC	4	1	11		40
Xenakis, Athanasios David	Two-tie Inlay	PWC	4	1	11		19
Xenakis, Athanasios David	Unharnessing the Summer and Winter Weave	Iw	4	4		Fa 79	42
Xenakis, Athanasios David	Victorian Garden (error-corrected PWC i8 p66)	PWC	3	1	7		31
Xenakis, Athanasios David	Weaving Figured Piqué on a Loom with One Warp Beam	PWC	4	2	12		14
Xenakis, Athanasios David	Weaving Primer, Part 3	PWC	4	1	11		46
Xenakis, Athanasios David	Why an Extra Beam?	PWC	1	1		No 81	34
Xenakis, Athanasios David	Woven Lace, Part 1: The Bronson Systems	PWC			5	Sp 83	10
Xenakis, Athanasios David	Woven Lace, Part 1: The Bronson Systems — 4-Thread and 8-Thread Atwater-Bronson	PWC			5	Sp 83	13
Xenakis, Athanasios David	Woven Lace, Part 1: The Bronson Systems — The Atwater-Bronson System	PWC			5	Sp 83	12
Xenakis, Athanasios David	Woven Lace, Part 1: The Bronson Systems — Tips on Weaving with Linen, Rigid Heddle Loom	PWC			5	Sp 83	14
Xenakis, Athanasios David	Xenakis Technique for the Construction of Four Harness Textiles, The	WJ	3	2	10	Oc 78	46
Xenakis, Athanasios David	Xenakis Technique, The	Iw	3	4		Su 78	46
Xenakis, Athanasios David; Alexis Yiorgos Xenakis	Shaped Silk Sheath	PWC			6	Su 83	39
Xenakis, Athanasios David; Linda Lyon	Simple Inlay on Sheer Plain Weave Ground	PWC	4	1	11		16
Xenakis, Athanasios David; Madelyn van der Hoogt	Bedford Cord Piqué	PWC	4	3	13		42
Xenakis, Athanasios David; Madelyn van der Hoogt	Twill Diaper Piqué (error-corrected PWC v4 n4 i14 p33)	PWC	4	3	13		36
Xenakis, Athanasios David; Patti Sellon	Figured Piqué Patterning with the Double Two-Tie System (error-corrected PWC v4 n3 i13 p4)	PWC	4	2	12		20
Xenakis, Athanasios David; Patti Sellon	Simple Inlay on a Leno Ground	PWC	4	1	11		18
Xenakis, Benjamin	Young Man in a T	Kn	3	3	7	Su 87	15
Yabsley, Suzanne	Texas Quilts, Texas Women	Fa	12	5		S/O 85	54
Yaksick, Karen	Grandma's Checkerboard Lace	Kn	4	1	9	Wi 87	52
Yaksick, Karen	Mr. Hunter's Lace	Kn	3	4	8	Fa 87	22
Yaksick, Karen	Now, That's a Cabled Sweater	Kn	3	1	5	F-W 86	30
Yamanaka, Norio	Book of Kimono: The Complete Guide to Style and Wear, The	Fa	10	3		M/J 83	53
Yamanobe, Tomoyuki	Arts & Crafts of Japan — Textiles	H&C	8	4		Fa 57	60
Yamanobe, Tomoyuki	Opulence, the Kimonos and Robes of Itchiku Kubota	Hw	6	3		Su 85	14
Yamanobe, Tomoyuki	see Barton, Jane	Hw	6	3		Su 85	14
Yanagi, Soetsu	The Unknown Craftsman (A Japanese Insight into Beauty)	Hw	5	5		N/D 84	12
Yannie, Barbara	Building Your Own Steam Cabinet	Fa	5	1		J/F 78	32
Yarnell, Grace	"Interweave '78" (Exhibit)	Fa	5	6		N/D 78	69
Yasinskaya, I.	Revolutionary Textile Design—Russia in the 1920's and 1930's	Fa	12	2		M/A 85	54
Yates, Margurite	see Yates, Raymond	H&C	5	4		Fa 54	59
Yates, Raymond F.	Hobby Book of Stenciling and Brush-Stroke Painting, The	H&C	3	1		Wi 51	63
Yates, Raymond F.	New Furniture from Old	H&C	2	4		Fa 51	63
Yates, Raymond; Margurite Yates	Early American Crafts & Hobbies	H&C	5	4		Fa 54	59
Yehling, Carol	Hair Dressing as a Fiber Art	Fa	7	1		J/F 80	20
Yolen, Jane	Girl Who Cried Flowers and Other Tales, The	Iw	2	1		Fa 76	33
Yoors, Jan	Gypsies, The	H&C	18	2		Sp 67	45
Yoors, Jan	Tapestries	H&C	5	1		Wi 53	18

AUTHOR	TITLE	JOUR	VOL	NO	ISS	DATE	PAGE
Young, Athalie Child	Contemporary Texas Natural Dye Workshop	SS&D	1	4	4	Se 70	18
Young, Dorothy M.	Workshop Tour to Sweden	SS&D	4	2	14	Sp 73	41
Young, Helen D	Heritage Linens with Modern Ideas	H&C	10	4		Fa 59	59
Young, Helen Daniels	Adventures with Guatemalan Weaving	H&C	4	1		Wi 52	26
Young, Helen Daniels	Guatemalan Looms	H&C	4	3		Su 53	16
Young, Helen Daniels	Jaspé Weaving	H&C	5	3		Su 54	30
Young, Jean	Woodstock Craftsmen's Manual	H&C	23	4		J/A 72	27
Youngmark, Lore	see Halsy, Mike	Fa	3	2		M/A 76	25
Yovovich, Noël	Mixed Media Vocabulary of Pamela Matiosian, The	Fa	13	6		N/D 86	6
Yue, Rosina	Creative Process: Rosina Yue, The	Fa	11	6		N/D 84	40
Zachofsky, Toni	Panel — A Statement of Unity, The	H&C	22	4		Fa 71	20
Zahle, Erik, ed.	Treasury of Scandinavian Design, A	H&C	15	1		Wi 64	43
Zanoni, Thomas A.; Eileen K. Schofield	Dyes from Plants: An Annotated List of References	Hw	6	5		N/D 85	20
Zausner, Judith	Industrial Fabric & the Woven Form	H&C	23	6		N/D 72	43
Zawistoski, Patsy	Make It Yourself with Handwoven Wool	S-O	9	1		Sp 85	12
Zechlin, Ruth	Complete Book of Handcrafts	H&C	19	2		Sp 68	44
Zechlin, Ruth	Complete Book of Handicrafts, The	H&C	10	3		Su 59	59
Zepeda, Susan G.	To the Walls: The 13th Lausanne Biennial (Exhibit)	Fa	14	4		S/O 87	41
Zerner, Amy	Fabric Collages (Exhibit)	Fa	14	3		M/J 87	64
Zethraus, Kamma	Textiles from an Ancient Danish Tomb	H&C	6	2		Sp 55	46
Ziebarth, Charlotte Molcar	Tapestry Effects in Boundweave Rugs	Iw	5	1		Wi 79	23
Ziegler, Luise	Changing Patterns in Midstream, Rethreading Made Unnecessary by New Device	H&C	13	2		Sp 62	12
Ziegler, Luise	New Approach to a Traditional Design	H&C	14	3		Su 63	11
Ziek, Bhakti	Bhakti Ziek	Fa	13	3		M/J 86	27
Ziek, Bhakti	Nek Chand's Fantasy Garden	TM			3	F/M 86	88
Ziek, Bhakti	Painting and Brocading on the Loom	TM			6	A/S 86	42
Ziek, Nona M.	see de Rodriguez, Judy Ziek	SS&D	10	3	39	Su 79	34
Zielinski, Miwa	Master Weaver: Stanislaw A. Zielinski, The	SS&D	10	3	39	Su 79	62
Zielinski, S. A.	Encyclopaedia of Hand-Weaving	H&C	10	4		Fa 59	59
Zielinski, S. A.	Encyclopedia of Hand-Weaving	H&C	1	3		Fa 50	63
Zielinski, S. A.	Master Weaver Library, Volume 1, A Treasury for Beginners and Volume 2, All About Looms	SS&D	11	3	43	Su 80	75
Zielinski, S. A.	On Teaching Weaving	H&C	19	1		Wi 68	38
Zielinski, S. A.; Robert Leclerc, ed.	All About Looms	MWL	2			'51–'73	
Zielinski, S. A.; Robert Leclerc, ed.	Composition and Designing	MWL	18			'51–'73	
Zielinski, S. A.; Robert Leclerc, ed.	Composition and Designing Part 2	MWL	19			'51–'73	
Zielinski, S. A.; Robert Leclerc, ed.	Contemporary Approach to Traditional Weaves: Crackle, M's & O's and others	MWL	8			'51–'73	
Zielinski, S. A.; Robert Leclerc, ed.	Contemporary Approach to Traditional Weaves: Overshot and Summer & Winter	MWL	7			'51–'73	
Zielinski, S. A.; Robert Leclerc, ed.	Creative Drafting and Analysis	MWL	3			'51–'73	
Zielinski, S. A.; Robert Leclerc, ed.	Double Weaves	MWL	15			'51–'73	
Zielinski, S. A.; Robert Leclerc, ed.	Everything a Weaver Should Know About Warps and Warping	MWL	5			'51–'73	
Zielinski, S. A.; Robert Leclerc, ed.	Fascination of Twills (Fourshafts)	MWL	9			'51–'73	
Zielinski, S. A.; Robert Leclerc, ed.	Fascination of Twills (Multishafts)	MWL	10			'51–'73	
Zielinski, S. A.; Robert Leclerc, ed.	Little Known Weaves Worth Knowing Better	MWL	16			'51–'73	

AUTHOR	TITLE	JOUR	VOL	NO	ISS	DATE	PAGE
Zielinski, S. A.; Robert Leclerc, ed.	More About Fabrics	MWL	20			'51–'73	
Zielinski, S. A.; Robert Leclerc, ed.	Pile Weaves, Rugs and Tapestry	MWL	14			'51–'73	
Zielinski, S. A.; Robert Leclerc, ed.	Resist Dyeing, Curiosities and Inventions	MWL	17			'51–'73	
Zielinski, S. A.; Robert Leclerc, ed.	Spot Weaves — Old and New	MWL	12			'51–'73	
Zielinski, S. A.; Robert Leclerc, ed.	Technology of Handweaving (equipment and its use)	MWL	6			'51–'73	
Zielinski, S. A.; Robert Leclerc, ed.	Traditional Texture Weaves and Exploring the Textures	MWL	11			'51–'73	
Zielinski, S. A.; Robert Leclerc, ed.	Treasury for Beginners	MWL	1			'51–'73	
Zielinski, S. A.; Robert Leclerc, ed.	Weaver Ponders His Craft Collection of Controversial Essays; Weaving In the Past, Complete Index with Reference, A	MWL	21 22			'51–'73	
Zielinski, S. A.; Robert Leclerc, ed.	Woven Lace and Lacey Weaves	MWL	13			'51–'73	
Zielinski, S. A.; Robert Leclerc, ed.	Yarns and Fibers	MWL	4			'51–'73	
Zielinski, Stanislaw A.	Encyclopedia of Hand-Weaving	WJ	2	1	5	Jy 77	29
Zielinski, Stanislaw A.	Encyclopedia of Handweaving	SS&D	8	3	31	Su 77	62
Ziemke, Dene	Consider Importing	SS&D	4	1	13	Wi 72	41
Ziemke, Dene	Constructing Front-Slung Treadles	SS&D	8	4	32	Fa 77	74
Ziemke, Dene	Ecclesiastical Weaving, Part 2	SS&D	9	4	36	Fa 78	42
Ziemke, Dene	Ecclesiastical Weaving, Part 3	SS&D	10	1	37	Wi 78	46
Ziemke, Dene	Ecclesiastical Weaving, Part 4	SS&D	10	2	38	Sp 79	65
Ziemke, Dene	Ecclesiastical Weaving, Part I	SS&D	9	3	35	Su 78	31
Ziemke, Dene	Loom Bench	SS&D	8	3	31	Su 77	49
Ziemke, Dene	Mini-Course—Maxi-Success	SS&D	6	2	22	Sp 75	88
Ziemke, Dene	Minimizing Water Damage	SS&D	9	2	34	Sp 78	56
Ziemke, Dene	Remodeling a Loom	SS&D	8	2	30	Sp 77	94
Ziemke, Dene	St. Louis Guild 50th Anniversary	SS&D	6	3	23	Su 75	93
Zim, Herbert	see Whiteford, Andrew	SS&D	2	2	6	Sp 71	34
Zimmer, Roni	Peruvian Straw Hat: Documenting a Declining Industry, The	Fa	12	3		M/J 85	39
Zimmermann, Arnold	Storytime...The Tale of Alain	Kn	1	2	2	S-S 85	26
Zimmermann, Arnold	Tale of Alain, The	Kn	1	2	2	S-S 85	26
Zimmermann, Elizabeth	Egmont Sweater, The	PWC			2	Ap 82	80
Zimmermann, Elizabeth	Exposition of the Epaulet Sweater	Hw	3	1		Ja 82	71
Zimmermann, Elizabeth	Gaffer's Gansey	Kn	1	1	1	F-W 84 CI	36,56B 28
Zimmermann, Elizabeth	Garter Stitch Ribwarmer	Kn	3	1	5	F-W 86	46
Zimmermann, Elizabeth	Knitter's Almanac	Kn	1	1	1	F-W 84	14
Zimmermann, Elizabeth	Knitter's Journey: New Zealand, A	Kn	4	1	9	Wi 87	18
Zimmermann, Elizabeth	Knitting a Seamless Sweater	TM			7	O/N 86	47
Zimmermann, Elizabeth	Knitting Without Tears	Kn	1	1	1	F-W 84	14
Zimmermann, Elizabeth	Knitting Without Tears	TM			9	F/M 87	76
Zimmermann, Elizabeth	Knitting Workshop	Kn	1	1	1	F-W 84	14
Zimmermann, Elizabeth	Michelin Man Sweater	Kn	2	2	4	S-S 86	72
Zimmermann, Elizabeth	Opinionated Knitter, The	Kn	1	2	2	S-S 85	12
Zimmermann, Elizabeth	Opinionated Knitter, The	Kn	2	1	3	F-W 85	8
Zimmermann, Elizabeth	Opinionated Knitter, The	Kn	3	4	8	Fa 87	45
Zimmermann, Elizabeth	Opinionated Knitter: Thoughts on Wool, The	Kn	1	1	1	F-W 84 CI	39 31
Zimmermann, Elizabeth	see Adams, Brucie	Hw	3	1		Ja 82	70
Zimmermann, Elizabeth	Shawl in the English Tradition, A	Kn	1	2	2	S-S 85	59
Zimmermann, Elizabeth	π Shawl, The	Kn	4	1	9	Wi 87	34

AUTHOR	TITLE	JOUR	VOL	NO	ISS	DATE	PAGE
Zimmermann, Elizabeth	Stonington Shawl	Kn	1	2	2	S-S 85	60, 72B
Zimmermann, Elizabeth	Traditional Shetland Shawl, A	Kn	1	2	2	S-S 85	59
Zimmermann, Elizabeth	Whither Pills?	S-O	8	4		Wi 84	38
Zimmermann, Elizabeth	Woolgatherings	Kn	1	1	1	F-W 84	14
Zinsmeister, Anna	Anna Zinsmeister	Fa	13	1		J/F 86	19
Zinsmeister, Anna	Blind Woman Is In My Weaving Class ... What Do I Do Now?, A	Fa	14	1		J/F 87	42
Znamierowski, Nell	Block Weaves as Color and Texture Effects	Hw	8	5		N/D 87	48
Znamierowski, Nell	Color Design for Garments	Hw	7	5		N/D 86	54
Znamierowski, Nell	Color Forecasting and the Weaver	Hw	7	3		M/J 86	33
Znamierowski, Nell	Jack Lenor Larsen	H&C	22	3		Su 71	6
Znamierowski, Nell	Journey Through Greece, Two Americans in Search of Native Weaving	H&C	14	2		Sp 63	8
Znamierowski, Nell	Nell Znamierowski, Weaver-Designer	SS&D	3	4	12	Fa 72	16
Znamierowski, Nell	Step-by-Step Rugmaking	SS&D	4	1	13	Wi 72	35
Znamierowski, Nell	Step-by-Step Rugmaking	H&C	23	5		S/O 72	34
Znamierowski, Nell	Step-by-Step Weaving	H&C	18	4		Fa 67	42
Znamierowski, Nell	Weaving in Crete	H&C	15	4		Fa 64	8
Zoller, Mary	Worsted Spinning	S-O	7	4		Wi 83	26
Zopetti, Patti	"Cynthia Schira" (Exhibit)	Fa	6	4		J/A 79	73
Zoppetti, Patti	"Jack Lenor Larsen: 30 Years of Creative Textiles" (Exhibit)	Fa	9	5		S/O 82	82
Zoppetti, Patti	"Tenth International Biennial of Tapestry: A Critic" (Exhibit)	Fa	8	6		N/D 81	54
Zorick, Jean	No Weavers Nearby? Form a Beginning Class—And a Guild	SS&D	5	4	20	Fa 74	87
Zorn, Elayne	see Cahlander, Adele	WJ	5	4	20	Sp 81	45
Zorn, Elayne	Sling Braiding in the Macusani Area of Peru	TMJ	19 20			80,81	41
Zorn, Elayne; Juan Cutipa Colque	Closer Look at Alpacas, A	S-O	9	2		Su 85	21